STANDARD
HANDBOOK
OF
PLANT
ENGINEERING

Other McGraw-Hill Handbooks of Interest

STANDARD
HANDBOOK
OF
PLANT
ENGINEERING

Robert C. Rosaler, P.E.   Editor-in-Chief

Second Edition

McGRAW-HILL, INC.

New York San Francisco Washington, D.C. Auckland Bogotá
Caracas Lisbon London Madrid Mexico City Milan
Montreal New Delhi San Juan Singapore
Sydney Tokyo Toronto

Library of Congress Cataloging-in-Publication Data

Standard handbook of plant engineering / Robert C. Rosaler, editor in
    chief.—2nd ed.
            p.   cm.
    Includes bibliographical references and index.
    ISBN 0-07-052164-6
    1. Plant engineering—Handbooks, manuals, etc.   I. Rosaler,
Robert C.
TS184.S7   1994
658.2—dc20   94-12951
                                                                    CIP

    2 3 4 5 6 7 8 9 0   DOH/DOH   9 0 9 8 7 6 5

ISBN 0-07-052164-6

*The sponsoring editor for this book was Robert W. Hauserman, the editing
supervisor was Stephen M. Smith, and the production supervisor was Pamela
A. Pelton. It was set in Times Roman by North Market Street Graphics.*

Printed and bound by R. R. Donnelley & Sons Company.

This book is printed on acid-free paper.

CONTENTS

BOARD OF ADVISORS

CONTRIBUTORS

Kenneth R. Albertson *Packing Division, Parker-Hannifin Corp., Irvine, California*

John C. Andreas *Consultant, MagneTek, St. Louis, Missouri*

George Arbocus *Elf Lubricants, Linden, New Jersey*

Association of Asbestos Cement Pipe Producers *Arlington, Virginia*

Robert H. Barbarin *Seal Group Staff, Parker-Hannifin Corp., Irvine, California*

Ron Barma *Communications Manager, Simpson Electric Co., Elgin, Illinois*

R. J. Batey *Furnas Electric Co., Batavia, Illinois*

Robert L. Bays *Technical Support Director, Huntington Laboratories, Inc., Huntington, Indiana*

Eric M. Bergtraun, CPE *Manager of Plant Maintenance and In-House Construction, National Semiconductor Corporation, Santa Clara, California*

William L. Byars *Packing Division, Parker-Hannifin Corp., Irvine, California*

Howard B. Cary *Senior Advisor, Welding Technology, Hobart Bros. Co., Troy, Ohio*

Arthur H. Cates *Packing Division, Parker-Hannifin Corp., Irvine, California*

R. B. Curry *Senior Engineer, Rexnord Corporation, Indianapolis, Indiana*

James L. Davis *Consulting Engineer, San Rafael, California*

JoAnn DeMarco *Senior Development Scientist, Loctite Corporation, Newington, Connecticut*

M. R. Dorfman *Senior Staff Engineer, Metco/Perkin Elmer, Westbury, New York*

B. W. Elliott Manufacturing Co. *Binghamton, New York*

Fafnir Bearings Division Engineering Staff *The Torrington Company, Torrington, Connecticut*

Anthony C. Fague *Director, Engineering, ADT Security Systems, Inc., Morris Plains, New Jersey*

Omar L. Feeler *Principal, Highways, Sverdrup Civil, Inc., St. Louis, Missouri*

Ricardo R. Gamboa *Manager, Engineering and Technical Services, Manville Mechanical Specialty Insulations, Schuller International, Inc., Denver, Colorado*

General Battery Corporation *Reading, Pennsylvania*

Raymond W. Giegerich *Director of Engineering (Ret.), Lovejoy, Inc., Downer's Grove, Illinois*

Casey C. Grant *Chief Systems and Applications Engineer, National Fire Protection Association, Quincy, Massachusetts*

Nils R. Grimm, P.E. *Section Manager, Mechanical, Sverdrup Corporation, New York, New York*

Michael R. Harrison *Vice President and General Manager, Manville Mechanical Specialty Insulations, Schuller International, Inc., Denver, Colorado*

S. D. Heden *EIMCO Process Equipment Company, Salt Lake City, Utah*

P. Richard Hergenrother *Miles Inc., Pittsburgh, Pennsylvania*

K. R. Horr *Furnas Electric Co., Batavia, Illinois*

D. K. Hubbard   *Furnas Electric Co., Batavia, Illinois*

William C. Hummel   *Manager, Structural Section, Sverdrup Facilities, Inc., St. Louis, Missouri*

Jim Iverson   *Manager, Technical Marketing, Industrial Business Group, Onan Corporation, Minneapolis, Minnesota*

William V. Jackson   *President, H. H. Felton & Associates, Dallas, Texas*

Charles Albert Johnson, Ph.D.   *Technical Director, National Solid Wastes Management Association, Washington, D.C.*

L. Johnson   *Furnas Electric Co., Batavia, Illinois*

R. Labak   *Furnas Electric Co., Batavia, Illinois*

Curt Lambdin   *Project Architect, Sverdrup Facilities, Inc., St. Louis, Missouri*

Paul F. Lienesch   *Philips Lighting Co., Somerset, New Jersey*

Chris S. Louskos   *Seal Group Staff, Parker-Hannifin Corp., Irvine, California*

Lawrence A. Loziuk, P.E.   *Principal Engineer, Vectra Technologies, Inc., Lincolnshire, Illinois*

John H. Marino   *President, Mining and Industrial Lubricants Consultants, Inc., Overland Park, Kansas*

Kenneth J. Moore, FCSI, CCS   *Specification Writer, Sverdrup Facilities, Inc., St. Louis, Missouri*

Russell N. Mosher   *Assistant Executive Director, American Boiler Manufacturers Association, Arlington, Virginia*

Lawrence G. Mrazek   *Senior Group Leader, Structural Section, Sverdrup Facilities, Inc., St. Louis, Missouri*

Stanley A. Mruk   *Executive Director, Plastics Pipe Institute, A Division of the Society of the Plastics Industry, Washington, D.C.*

James Murratti   *Director of Product Management, Loctite Corporation, Newington, Connecticut*

National Electrical Contractors Association, Inc.   *Washington, D.C.*

E. Novinski   *Senior Staff Engineer, Metco/Perkin Elmer, Westbury, New York*

Robert W. Okey   *University of Utah, Salt Lake City, Utah*

P. Eric Ralston   *Vice President and General Manager, Environmental Equipment Division, Babcock and Wilcox, Barberton, Ohio*

Richard G. Ramsdell   *Seal Group Staff, Parker-Hannifin Corp., Irvine, California*

Ranjit S. Randhawa   *The Foxboro Company, Foxboro, Massachusetts*

John E. Reinfurt   *Geotechnical Project Manager, Sverdrup Civil, Inc., St. Louis, Missouri*

Richard R. Roesler   *Miles Inc., Pittsburgh, Pennsylvania*

David E. Roos   *Manager, Applications Engineering, Product Application, Gates Rubber Company, Denver, Colorado*

Richard B. Ruch, Jr.   *Vice President, Roy F. Weston, Inc., West Chester, Pennsylvania*

Paul N. Salvucci   *Boston Gear Division of IMO Industries, Inc., Quincy, Massachusetts*

John B. Scannell   *Packing Division, Parker-Hannifin Corp., Irvine, California*

J. R. Shaffer   *Furnas Electric Co., Batavia, Illinois*

Navin H. Shah   *Deputy Manager, Structural Section, Sverdrup Facilities, Inc., St. Louis, Missouri*

Jaswant Singh   *Senior Vice President, Clayton Environmental Consultants, Inc., Cypress, California*

J. Stephen Slottee   *EIMCO Process Equipment Company, Salt Lake City, Utah*

Robert L. Smith, Jr.   *General Electric Company, Schenectady, New York*

Thomas Lee Smith, AIA, CRC   *Director of Technology and Research, National Roofing Contractors Association, Rosemont, Illinois*

William H. Snyder   *Director, Corporate Marketing Research, Johns-Manville Corp., Denver, Colorado*

Walter J. Sperko, P.E.   *President, Sperko Engineering Services, Inc., Greensboro, North Carolina*

R. Stone   *Furnas Electric Co., Batavia, Illinois*

Douglas H. Sturz   *Senior Acoustical Consultant, Acentech Incorporated, Cambridge, Massachusetts*

Richard J. Swanson   *Packing Division, Parker-Hannifin Corp., Irvine, California*

R. Lane Swensen   *Technical Writer, Bently Nevada Corporation, Minden, Nevada*

Donald C. Taylor   *EIMCO Process Equipment Company, Salt Lake City, Utah*

Clemens M. Thoennes   *Sales Programs Development, General Electric Company, Schenectady, New York*

William M. Throop, P.E.   *Envirex Inc., Waukesha, Wisconsin*

Tower Performance, Inc.   *Fairfield, New Jersey*

K. W. Tunnell Co., Inc.   *King of Prussia, Pennsylvania*

Eric E. Ungar   *Chief Consulting Engineer, BBN Systems & Technologies, Cambridge, Massachusetts*

Valve Manufacturers Association   *Washington, D.C.*

Jose L. Villalobos   *President, V & A Consulting Engineers, Oakland, California*

Ron Wacker   *Product Application Engineer, Gates Rubber Company, Denver, Colorado*

George W. Walsh   *General Electric Company, Schenectady, New York*

Robert C. Walther, P.E.   *President, Industrial Power Technology, Santa Rosa, California*

Waukesha Engine Division   *Dresser Industries, Inc., Waukesha, Wisconsin*

S. E. Winegardner   *Senior Engineer, Rexnord Corporation, Indianapolis, Indiana*

Eric W. Wood   *Director, Environmental and Industrial Acoustics, Acentech Incorporated, Cambridge, Massachusetts*

James R. Wright, P.E.   *Manager of Codes and Standards, Furnas Electric Co., Batavia, Illinois*

PREFACE TO
SECOND EDITION

In addition to updating all technical discussions, this Second Edition adds coverage of plant engineering management, with particular stress on maintenance and workplace safety. This reflects the increasing role of the plant engineer in corporate management.

The editor expresses appreciation for the excellent cooperation shown by the authors and their organizations in updating or entirely rewriting individual chapters as appropriate. Also, a thank you to the Board of Advisors of this edition, who helped redirect the emphasis of the work. Finally, a word of gratitude to Robert W. Hauserman and Stephen M. Smith of McGraw-Hill, who willingly provided wise editorial advice.

This Second Edition is dedicated to my dear departed brother George, who embodied all that is good in the world.

Robert C. Rosaler, P.E.

PREFACE TO
FIRST EDITION

Virtually every industrial activity has been affected, often in revolutionary ways, by the surge of technology. Because it is so central to virtually all manufacturing and service facilities, plant engineering is *uniquely* affected. It is "in the middle" in the sense that the plant engineer must, increasingly, have a broader knowledge of an ever-widening universe.

Events of the past decade have further served to accent the importance of the plant engineer's role in corporate operations, notably the demands for energy conservation and pollution control.

This Handbook is a response to these changing conditions and needs.

Arranging a logical structure and index to meet the needs of all engineers required considerable thought. The structure finally developed here is a reflection of the procedural sequences that occur in the plant facility itself: Planning and Construction, Plant Equipment Procurement and Operation, Maintenance. Individual equipment is covered broadly with descriptions of operational features, installation, and maintenance. Managerial aspects are included only where they interface closely with technical matter.

The objective of the book is to provide the reader with sufficient data on any specific equipment to permit judgment on choices and an insight into "how it works" and how to maintain it.

We want to express our appreciation to the authors and their organizations for their generous contributions and prompt execution of their tasks, and to the Board of Advisors for their guidance, particularly Leo Spector, Chairman of the Board and Editor of *Plant Engineering* magazine. For initial suggestions on the outline, we wish to thank Stewart Burkland. We also received excellent guidance and encouragement from Harold Crawford, Ruth Weine, and M. Joseph Dooher of McGraw-Hill. Our thanks go, too, to Dorothy Smith and Betsy Watson for helping to keep the project moving.

Saul Poliak, to whom this Handbook is dedicated, founded the National Plant Engineering Exposition and Conference which has been held both nationally and regionally since 1950. He has also pioneered similar expositions and conferences in the United Kingdom, Europe, Central America, and the Far East. It is widely recognized that he has been a major force in advancing the awareness of the critical plant engineering function in the industrial societies.

Robert C. Rosaler, P.E.
James O. Rice

P · A · R · T
A

ORGANIZATION OF THE PLANT ENGINEERING FUNCTION

SECTION 1

ORGANIZATION OF THE PLANT ENGINEERING FUNCTION

William V. Jackson
President
H. H. Felten & Associates
Dallas, Texas

THE PLANT ENGINEERING ORGANIZATION

In 1983, when the first edition of the *Standard Handbook of Plant Engineering* was published, a discussion of the structure of the plant engineering organization would have been straightforward. Organizational design parameters would have centered on the size of the plant, the relative size of the maintenance organization in relation to the other departments, and the complexity of the equipment and processes to be maintained. Alternative designs would have been limited to variations of a traditional, functionally oriented structure.

Today, however, it seems that all organizations, large and small, are replacing traditional organizations with multiskilled teams working together. *Self-directed* work teams are taking over the responsibilities formerly given to the first-line supervisors, who, by the way, have now become *team resources. Empowerment* has become the management buzzword of the nineties.

Plant engineering organizations are not immune to the changing roles of workers, first-line supervisors, and even upper management. Service organizations, like plant engineering, are frequently caught in the middle between the movement away from recognition of functional excellence (and the resulting organizational structure), and the functional expertise required to keep equipment and processes running at ever-increasing levels of quality and reliability.

Organizational Design Alternatives

Before discussing plant engineering organizations in detail, it is necessary to begin with an overview of organization design in a broader sense. The three basic ways to organize will be discussed, and the effect on each of these of the changing role of the first-line supervisor will be analyzed.

Three Types of Organizations.[1] Organizations can be structured by grouping together individuals with the same general work specialty (functional organization), collecting them by the output of the organization (product or project team organization), or a mixture of both types (the matrix organization). Each type of organization has its strengths and weaknesses.

Functional Organization. This is the traditional structure for plant and plant engineering organizations. All of the technical personnel (engineering and maintenance) are grouped together. Although within the plant engineering organization there may be some small project teams, for the most part the organization is structured functionally. Figure 1-1 shows an example of a plant functional organization.

Common characteristics of the functional organization are as follows:

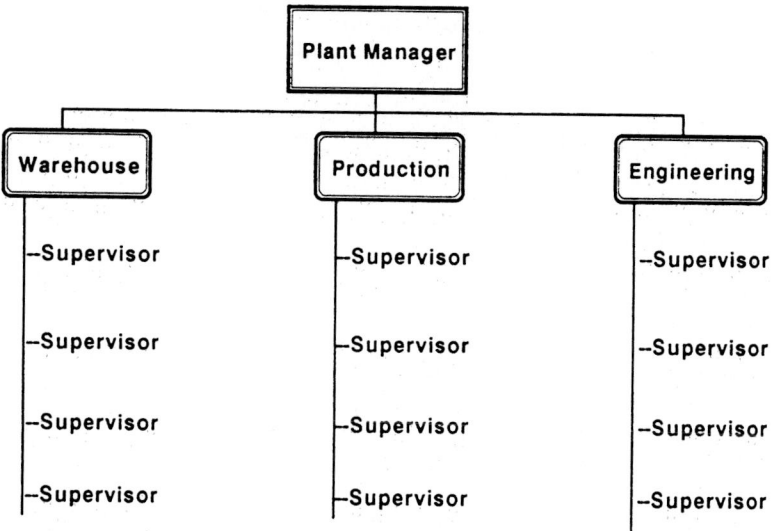

FIGURE 1-1   Functional plant organization.

- The division of labor, promotions and demotions, compensation system, and operating budgets are based on the functional competence of the organization and the individuals within the organization.
- Managers of the functional organizations have the most influence within the plant.
- Each function strives, and is rewarded for, maximizing its own goals; the goals of the organization as a whole are secondary.

  Strengths of the functional organization are as follows:

- There is organizational support for technical competence; members all "speak the same language."
- Organization members can specialize in their technical area of competence and let others be responsible for *the big picture.*
- Individuals are secure within the walls of their own stable environment.

  Weaknesses are as follows:

- Conflict between different functional organizations is unavoidable.
- The vertical hierarchy mandates decision making at the top; decisions are, therefore, slow in being made.
- Most of the organization members never see *the big picture.*
- Changing outputs of the organization take a long time to accomplish; bureaucracy is a frequent attribute of a functional organization.

  Product Organization.   This type organization is a popular one for companies wanting to move away from the inherent bureaucracy of a functional organization. This structure is well-suited to a rapidly changing environment. Under this form of organization, plant engineering personnel are combined into various product teams. Team members do several tasks to maximize the quality and quantity of the output of the team. Figure 1-2 shows an example of a product organization.

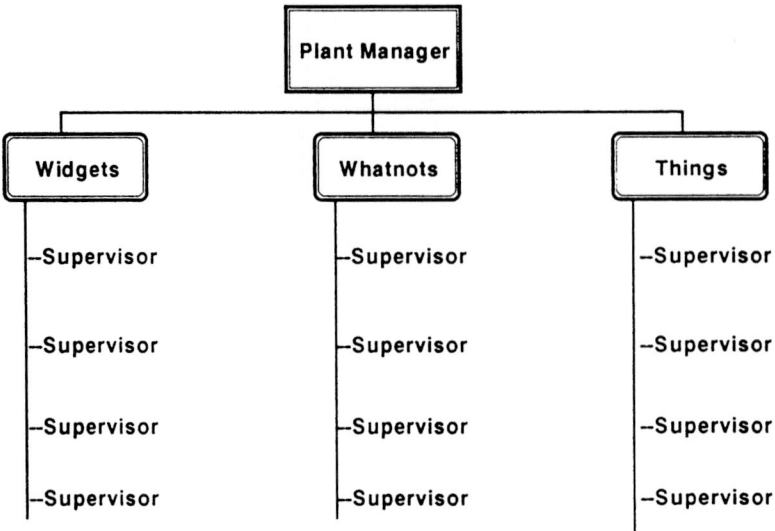

FIGURE 1-2   Product organization.

Common characteristics of the product organization are:

- There is a minimal need to coordinate with other teams.
- Promotions and demotions, monetary compensation, and influence depend on the members' ability to work together as a team to produce the desired output.
- Team leaders have the most influence in the organization.

Strengths of the product organization are:

- The organization is responsive to rapidly changing conditions.
- Conflicts with other teams are minimized.
- Team members all can easily see *the big picture.*
- Team members have an opportunity to develop additional skills and obtain more responsibility.

Weaknesses of this organization are:

- Technical competence of individual team members decreases as individuals attempt to learn additional skills. Generalists are rewarded; specialists are not.
- It can become difficult to attract technical specialists.
- Innovation is restricted to the specific product or products of the team.
- Teams compete for pooled staff resources.

Matrix Organization.   This organization is a combination of the functional and product organizations. The matrix organization attempts to combine the strengths of the other two types and eliminate, or at least minimize, the weaknesses of each. To some extent the matrix organization successfully accomplishes this, but not without some drawbacks of its own.

In a matrix organization, some parts of the plant are organized functionally and others by product. While plant engineering is typically one of the functional organizations, many members are assigned to the product teams. These people usually have dual reporting relationships; they are responsible to the product team leader for their normal day-to-day team activities, but are also responsible to the plant engineering organization for proper maintenance of their equipment and processes. Figure 1-3 shows a matrix organization.

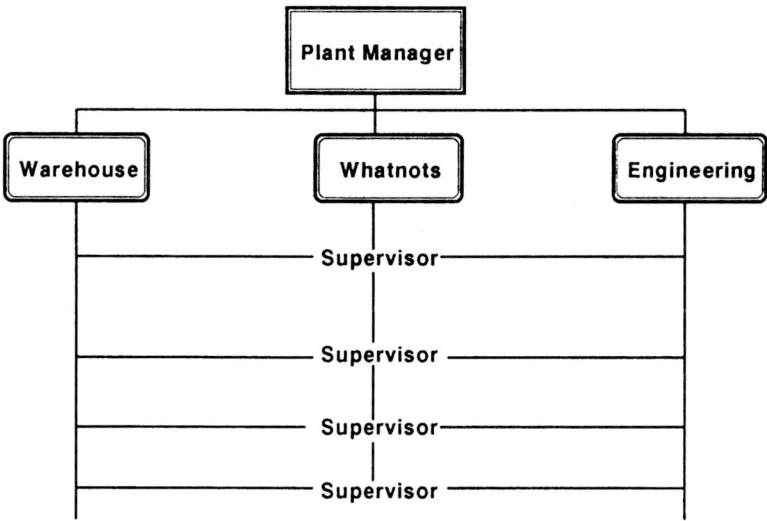

FIGURE 1-3   Matrix organization.

Strengths of the matrix organization are:

- This type of organization provides maximum flexibility.
- Multiple career paths are provided; both generalists and specialists are rewarded.

Weaknesses are as follows:

- Conflict management is difficult because two bosses must be dealt with.
- Dual compensation systems are necessary to reward both generalists and specialists.
- Few people have the experience and training to work within this type of complex environment.

The Role of the First-Line Supervisor

As organizations have changed from the traditional functional structure to the product or matrix structure, the role of the first-line supervisor is changing too. Since this position has the most impact on attempts to move toward participative management and empowerment of the workers, an understanding of the supervisor's role is necessary.

The relationship of the first-line supervisor to the workers in the organization undergoes a natural transition as the organization develops and workers obtain more and higher skill levels. Some roles to be discussed will occur naturally; others must be formally introduced to encourage the transition.

Factors Affecting the Supervisor's Role.   The factors that have had a major influence on the changing supervisor's role are as follows:

- The movement from specialized to generalized jobs
- The merging of line and staff positions with fewer levels of management
- Decision making being pushed to the lowest level possible
- Movement toward group instead of individual accountabilities
- Increased emphasis on team problem solving instead of individual problem solving

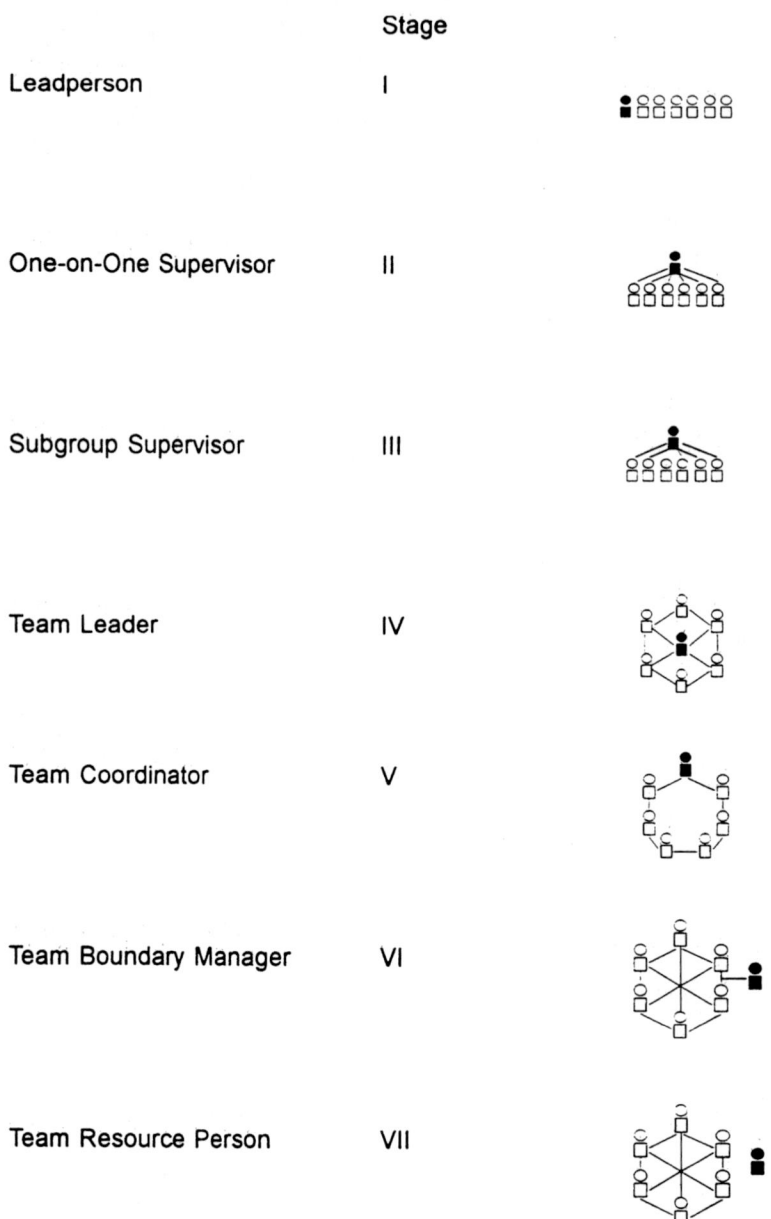

	Stage	
Leadperson	I	
One-on-One Supervisor	II	
Subgroup Supervisor	III	
Team Leader	IV	
Team Coordinator	V	
Team Boundary Manager	VI	
Team Resource Person	VII	

FIGURE 1-4   First-line supervisor's changing role.

A Developmental Model.   A developmental model of the first-line supervisor's changing role is shown in Fig. 1-4 and described as follows.[2]

The Leadperson.   The leadperson has a dual role of supervisor and worker. Typically, the individual chosen for the position is the highest qualified from a technical standpoint and serves as a role model for the group. As the individual workers develop higher skill levels, the leadperson can assign specific jobs and, if the organization permits, move to the role of a one-on-one supervisor.

One-on-One Supervisor. This is the traditional role of the first-line supervisor. The supervisor is responsible for directing and controlling a group of workers. He or she is totally responsible for the group's output, but gets others to do the work. The supervisor's interpersonal skills are more important in this role than technical skills.

As workers further develop their skills they require less direct supervision. Additionally, the workers tend to form their own informal subgroups. The supervisor then, often without realizing it, becomes a subgroup supervisor.

Subgroup Supervisor. In this role the supervisor manages by communicating with the subgroup leaders. The worker who does not become a part of a subgroup must still be managed individually. Some organizations tend to discourage the formation of informal subgroups, thinking that the authority of the supervisor will be challenged. This attempt to discourage subgroups usually fails and is a waste of time. More enlightened organizations recognize the process and attempt to use this role to their benefit.

As the subgroups develop, the supervisor may recognize the groups formally and create the position of group (or team) leader.

Team Leader. The team leader is responsible for the activities and output of a group of workers who share the same values, goals, and other common characteristics. The team leader manages the group by facilitating group interaction, problem solving, and decision making. Social skills of the team leader are much more important than technical skills. As team members develop production, troubleshooting, and problem-solving skills and become more adapt at leadership, the team leader becomes a team coordinator.

Team Coordinator. A team coordinator shares many leadership functions with other team members. Individual team members accept specific management-type activities. The team gradually develops the ability to manage its own responsibilities. When this happens, the team coordinator is free to become involved in other activities outside the team. As close contact with individual team members becomes less and less frequent, the supervisor assumes the role of team boundary manager.

Team Boundary Manager. The team boundary manager is removed from daily individual contact with team members. The manager still maintains responsibility for the team's activities and output, however, and must rejoin the team, as necessary, to ensure the quality and quantity of production. As the need to rejoin the team becomes infrequent, the boundary manager moves to the final supervisory role of team resource.

Team Resource. A team resource serves as a consultant to several work teams that are held accountable for their own work. At this point, the teams are truly *self-directed,* and the first-line supervisor's position no longer exists.

Design of the Plant Engineering Organization

The changing role of the first-line supervisor has many implications for the design of the plant engineering organization. No one type of organizational structure is ideal for all situations; each depends to a large extent on the role of the first-line supervisor or the organization's goal for what that role should become. Another primary factor influencing organization design is the relative maturity of the organization.

Plant Start-Ups. Plant start-ups are best managed by having the first-line supervisor function in the leadperson role. In these situations, the technical expertise of the workers is low. Supervisors should be selected, therefore, primarily for their technical abilities. Team training should be provided, however, to all workers and managers when possible to prepare them for an *eventual* transition into a team organization. Some organizations have attempted start-ups with self-directed work teams, usually with disastrous results. A *functional organization* works best for start-ups.

As the start-up is completed and workers gain in technical skills, the leadperson becomes a one-on-one supervisor. Many organizations remain at this stage of development for the duration of their existence. Since greater participation of workers usually leads to improvements in productivity and quality, however, further organization development is recommended. A one-on-one supervisor works best in a *functional organization*.

The subgroup supervisor usually functions in this role informally. As mentioned earlier, some organizations try to eliminate subgroups, usually without much success. Subgroups can exist in a functional organization and are typically the last stage of development before a formal transition into a team organization.

Transition to a Team Organization.   Organizations that want to move from an authoritative to a participative type of management frequently do so by changing their structure from a functional type to a *team organization*. Unfortunately, calling a group a team does not make it so. As discussed, a real team exists because of the changing role of the first-line supervisor. Calling a supervisor a *team leader* accomplishes nothing. Real teams can exist in a functional organization just as well as in a team organization.

Creating a Real Team Organization.   Creating effective work teams requires a high level of commitment by the organization. Both workers and managers need extensive training in team skills, social skills, technical skills, and problem-solving skills. Additionally, changes in attitudes are required for individuals to effectively work in the new environment. Lastly, management must be prepared to provide workers with the tools they will need to eventually become true self-directed teams.

Pseudo-Teams.   Plant engineering organizations are affected by the movement to pseudo-teams in two ways. First, the plant engineering organization is affected itself, just like any other organization. Second, since it is a service organization, plant engineering must function within the parameters set forth by the larger organization of which it is a part.

Plant Engineering in a Matrix Organization.   Plant engineering organizations work best as part of a matrix organizational structure. The weaknesses of a product team organization eventually lead to major issues with effective maintenance. This is due to two primary factors. First, maintenance must be managed by using tools not normally a part of the production-oriented manager's toolbox. Second, a significant portion of the maintenance effort is more efficiently performed by a core team of specialists. Examples are major repairs and overhauls, master preventive maintenance scheduling, planning and estimating of maintenance work, and operation of a computerized maintenance management system.

As organizations develop and mature, work teams become truly self-directed and supervisors are replaced by team resource persons. The key elements here are *develop* and *mature*. This type of organization is not created by outside influences. It is created from within with *support* from the outside.

Organizations that have reached this stage of development are candidates for a form of maintenance called total productive maintenance (TPM).

Total Productive Maintenance

The optimum form of maintenance in a manufacturing facility is the Japanese-developed technique of TPM. TPM, an enhancement of preventive maintenance (PM) consists of three principal concepts.[3] These are as follows:

- Maximizing equipment effectiveness
- Small group activities
- Autonomous maintenance by operators

Maximizing Equipment Effectiveness.   The aim of TPM is to utilize equipment at its maximum effectiveness. Elimination of all waste and losses caused by equipment is the goal. Zero downtime is viewed as an obtainable goal *because all failures can be prevented*.

Autonomous Maintenance by Operators.   Autonomous maintenance by operators means that *operators are responsible for maintenance.* Under TPM there is no division of labor between operators and maintenance. Although there is still a core maintenance group, more of the maintenance activities have been taken over by highly trained operators. Examples of operator-performed maintenance are equipment cleaning, lubrication, tightening loose hardware, and PM inspections.

Company-Led Small Group Activities.   Small group activities are led by management to ensure availability of autonomous workers who meet the requirements of new highly automated equipment and processes. The teams are still self-directed, but management is responsible for setting company goals, providing the necessary training, and providing teams the tools they need to accomplish the goals.

PRINCIPLES OF MAINTENANCE MANAGEMENT

Effective maintenance does not happen by accident. There are several basic principles of maintenance management that must be followed if an organization is to accomplish its mission.

The Maintenance Mission

The basic mission of maintenance is to provide optimum utilization of labor, materials, money, and equipment. This is accomplished by the following:

- Guaranteeing unlimited availability of facilities and equipment
- Preserving the capital investment
- Creating absolute reliability of facilities and equipment
- Ensuring the process operates within statistical control
- Repairing and restoring capacity that has deteriorated.
- Replacing or rebuilding expended capacity

Fundamental Functions of Maintenance Management

To accomplish the mission of the maintenance organization, these basic functions have been established:

- Organization
- Workload identification
- Work control
- Work planning
- Work scheduling
- Work performance
- Work assessment

Key Concepts

Several key management ideas provide the basis for effective maintenance management.[4] These are:

- A primary requirement for an effective maintenance function is the optimum utilization of funds.
- The key to the optimum use of funds is the application of a formal maintenance management system.
- The responsibility for maintenance rests with the plant engineer or maintenance manager.
- The management attitude and proficiency of plant engineers and maintenance managers are critical factors in total maintenance effectiveness.
- Action-oriented planning and controlling techniques are essential ingredients for daily management.
- Planning is the continuous process of matching the resources of labor, materials, money, and equipment with the needs of the facility.
- Maintenance requirements must continuously be evaluated against the complete mission of the facility.
- Effective management control requires the establishment of realistic performance goals, close attention to significant variances, and prompt corrective action.
- Accurate and timely management reports are essential for effective maintenance management.

Purpose of Maintenance Management

The purposes of maintenance management are as follows:

- Perform scheduled maintenance instead of waiting until the equipment fails.
- Provide effective control over use of maintenance resources.
- Provide the right level of maintenance.
- Initiate corrective action proactively instead of reactively.
- Relieve the maintenance supervisor from the daily administrative tasks that interfere with leadership of the work team.
- Correlate the resources of maintenance with the workload.
- Provide a method of assessing the difference between the actual cost of a job and what it should have cost.
- Provide the detailed information necessary to identify trouble areas that need specific attention.

Benefits of Maintenance Management

Benefits of successful maintenance management have been proven repeatedly. Most of the following benefits can be obtained within a short time; others will be realized eventually.[5]

- Economical attainment of anticipated life span of facilities and equipment.
- Improved reliability and availability of essential equipment, services, and utilities.
- Improved morale of maintenance personnel.
- Increased productivity of maintenance workers.
- Decreased need for capital investment by using existing facilities and equipment to their fullest life expectancy.
- Development of technical data to enable enhancement of facilities, equipment, and materials.
- Availability of data to support budget requirements.

CLASSIFICATION OF MAINTENANCE WORK

Work classification is a procedure that channels and prescribes the processing of each type of maintenance job. The factors that determine the appropriate work classification are the type of funds involved, the duration of the job, the urgency of the work, the repetitive nature of the work, the purpose of the work, and the type of customer. The six categories of work are:

- Emergency work
- Service work
- Routine work
- Preventive maintenance
- Project work
- Corrective work

Emergency Work

Work in this category involves critical safety work where life or limb is in danger. Additionally, emergency work is required when there is equipment or process failure that is causing product loss or poor quality. Emergency work can be initiated verbally; a written emergency work order is submitted, however, when time permits. Emergency work is limited to the same time frame as service work. All emergency work extending beyond that period should be classified as *corrective work* and subjected to the same controls.

Service Work

Service work is work to be done during operating periods. Service work is requested with a written work request and does not exceed the dollar limitation that the work control function is authorized to approve.

Routine Work

Routine work includes all work that is highly repetitive in nature and on which accumulated costs are needed for a given period. Examples of routine work are janitorial service, power plant watch standing, equipment checks, fire extinguisher checks, scheduled relamping, and routine housekeeping.

Preventive Maintenance

Preventive maintenance work is periodically scheduled inspections, lubrication, minor adjustment, and minor repair of dynamic equipment. To maintain the schedule, it does not include repair work beyond a predetermined scope, e.g., 20 min.

Project Work

Project work is work that consists primarily of modifying or upgrading facilities or equipment. This work, usually generated by functional or regulatory requirements, is differentiated from repair and maintenance (R&M) work.

Corrective Work

Corrective work is all maintenance work that does not fall into the above categories. To provide maximum control at minimum cost it is divided into two subcategories, *minor work* and *major work*. Determination of the cutoff points between majors, minors, and service work is accomplished by analyzing the workload. Decide the number of jobs and the worker-hours used, by worker-hour groups, and convert these figures into percentages by group (Table 1-1), and cumulative percentages (Table 1-2). All work except emergency work, routine work, and preventive maintenance inspections should be included in the analysis.

TABLE 1-1   Job Analysis—Percentages by Group

Worker-hour range	Percent of total jobs	Percent of worker-hours used
0–2	16	3
3–4	32	14
5–6	19	13
7–8	10	9
9–10	4	5
11–12	4	5
13–14	0	1
15–16	4	7
17–18	1	2
19–20	2	4
21–22	4	9
23–24	1	2
Over 24	5	27
Total	100	100

TABLE 1-2   Job Analysis—Cumulative Percentages

Worker-hours	Cumulative percentage of jobs	Cumulative percentage of worker-hours
Over 0	100	100
Over 2	84	97
Over 4	52	83
Over 6	33	70
Over 8	23	61
Over 10	19	56
Over 12	16	51
Over 14	15	50
Over 16	11	43
Over 18	10	41
Over 20	9	38
Over 22	6	29
Over 24	5	27

A histogram is then plotted for the number of jobs (Fig. 1-5) and for the worker-hours used (Fig. 1-6). Overlaying the two graphs (Fig. 1-7) shows the intersection of the two lines to be the most feasible point to issue major work orders. In the sample this point is close to 6 worker-hours. As indicated in the histogram, using 6 worker-hours means that 70 percent of

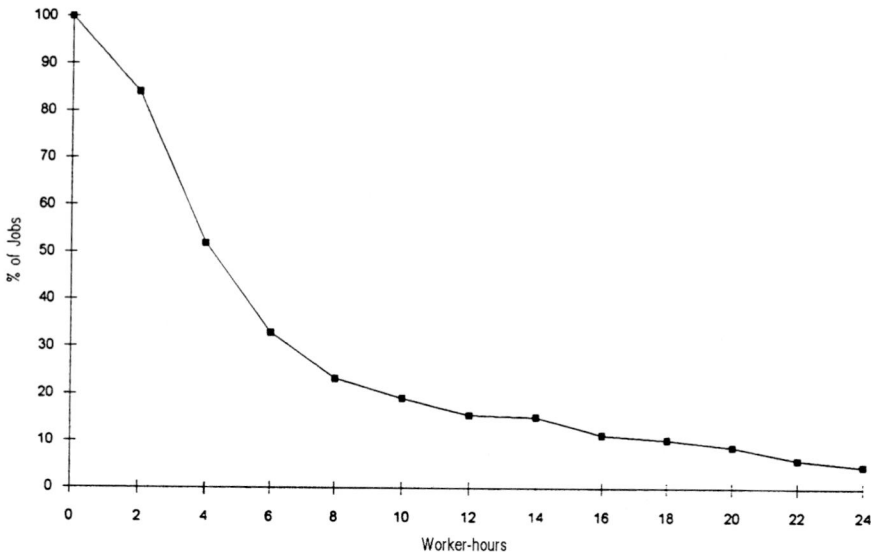

FIGURE 1-5 Cumulative percentage of jobs.

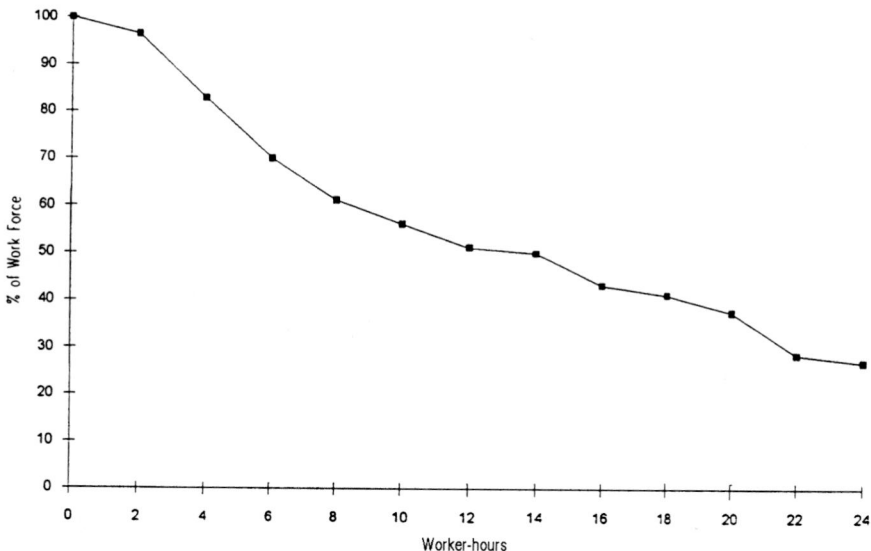

FIGURE 1-6 Cumulative percentage of worker-hours.

the work is controlled by only 30 percent of work orders. Further, using the histogram as a basis, the breakoff point between minor work and service work is designated as 4 worker-hours. Again, the objective is to provide maximum control at minimum cost.

Minor Work. Minor work is work that is more than that authorized as service work and less than that authorized as major work. Minor work is estimated by using historical records of previous similar jobs, or by consultation with skilled workers or supervisors.

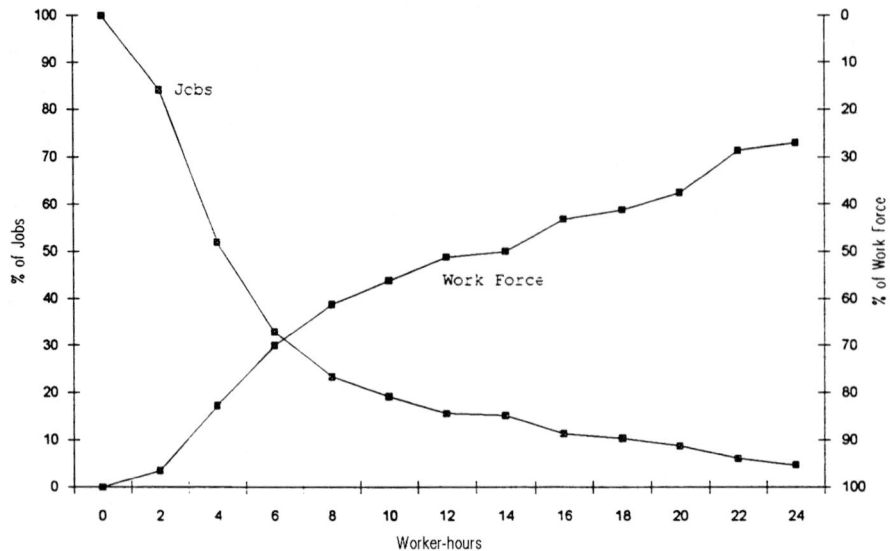

FIGURE 1-7   Job analysis.

Major Work.   Major work is all work more than that authorized as minor work. This work is carefully planned and formally estimated by using maintenance work standards. It is scheduled individually, and costs are tracked as needed for financial and performance evaluation.

WORK IDENTIFICATION

There are two methods of identifying maintenance work: planned formal inspections and work requests. Formal inspection is the primary method of work identification under maintenance management. These proactive inspections are planned, scheduled, and systematically performed by technically qualified personnel. Work requests are received by maintenance because of observations by personnel not performing a formal inspection. Personnel can be either part of the maintenance organization or part of another organization. A formal work request procedure is set up for this purpose.

Formal Inspection

Formal maintenance inspection is performed by personnel who are familiar with the facilities and equipment to be maintained, who know and understand maintenance standards, and who function according to a formal schedule. This schedule provides for complete coverage of the entire facility. The ideal benefits of maintenance management will be obtained when the maximum amount of work results from formal inspection.

There are three forms of formal inspection in maintenance. These are as follows:

- Preventive maintenance inspections
- Facility audits
- Operator inspections

Preventive Maintenance Inspections.   Preventive maintenance is the inspection, lubrication, minor adjustment, and minor repair of equipment. PM will help prevent and correct deficiencies in equipment and minimize breakdowns.

Responsibility.   It is the responsibility of the maintenance organization to plan, schedule, perform, and evaluate PM inspections. In some cases the actual performance of PM inspections may be performed by personnel outside the control of maintenance; the maintenance organization is, however, still responsible for ensuring their satisfactory and timely completion.

Equipment Inventory.   An accurate, current, and complete inventory of all equipment in the facility is the first step in setting up a PM program. Record basic data for each item of equipment, such as date of acquisition, book value, and the model and serial numbers of the equipment. Additionally, record detail data such as equipment classification, description, location, manufacturer information, size, and capacities.

Identify all equipment appropriate for PM. Consider factors such as the following[6]:

- Is its probability of failure such that it could cause injury or loss of life?
- Is standby equipment available if failure occurs?
- Will breakdowns seriously affect production schedules?
- Is the cost of making a PM inspection on the equipment greater than the probable cost of the breakdown repair?
- Is breakdown and/or serious damage to the equipment very unlikely, with or without PM?
- Will the equipment become obsolete before it is likely to break down?
- Is its probability of failure high enough to cause noncompliance with regulatory agencies?

Additionally, certain types of low-cost, low-priority equipment, such as small motors, water fountains, small refrigerators, and automatic door closers, may be replaced or repaired at time of breakdown more economically than being maintained by PM inspections. Ensure that, when these items are vital pieces of operating equipment, they are stocked to allow quick replacement at time of breakdown.

PM Checklists.   These are detailed step-by-step instructions for performing the PM inspection. The checklist will show all the important components of the equipment that require inspection, stating what is to be inspected and what to look for. Often the equipment manufacturer can provide a recommended inspection procedure and frequency. Figure 1-8 shows a typical PM checklist.

PM Schedules.   Once PM checklists have been developed, the next step is the development of a schedule that permits each item of equipment to be inspected at the planned frequency. First, however, the time required to perform each inspection must be estimated. This estimate should ideally be made by using formal work standards; an alternative, however, is to have initial estimates made by craftspeople familiar with the equipment and then adjust the estimates as experience is gained. The time allowed for servicing, including adjustments and minor repair, should be sufficient to allow the inspector to complete the service; however, there should be a definite time limit (20 min is usually adequate). Failure to establish specific guidelines will invariably result in missed PMs and poor schedule compliance.

Once the inspection checklists have received estimates, the master PM schedule can be developed. Divide the inspections by area and by the planned frequency, i.e., daily, weekly, biweekly, etc. Schedule the daily inspection first, then the weekly schedules, and so on. Continue until all PMs have been scheduled. Attempt to balance the work load by scheduling the less-frequent inspection at the most opportune times.

Facility Audits.   The facility audit (FA) can be considered as a PM inspection program for the facility. An FA is a planned and organized visual inspection performed by technically qualified and trained personnel. It will produce complete and quantitative reports of deficiencies, recommend maintenance priorities, and provide credible work planning and budget support data.

Facilities Inventory.   An accurate, current, and complete inventory of all facilities is the first step in setting up an FA program. Record general data for each facility's asset such as type of construction, square feet, age, and current replacement value. Record *detail* data such as a list of building components, type of material, size, and capacity. This type of information is necessary so that maintenance management can analyze the facility condition and make appropriate decisions regarding inspection schedules and procedures.

PREVENTIVE MAINTENANCE CHECKLIST			
Equipment: Ajax Motor/Pump Assembly Number: MP 274739	Frequency: Monthly		
PM Type: Static	OK	Adj	WO
1. Check main relief valve and adjust to maintain proper operating pressure.			
2. Check relief valve for sticking. Repair or replace as required.			
3. Check circulation by observing fluid in reservoir.			
4. Check temperature of oil for proper operation of heat exchanger.			
5. Check unit for excessive noise and vibration.			
6. Check pump volume control cylinder for freedom of operation.			
7. Check oil level in reservior and add oil if necessary. Use Mobil DTE.			
8. Check complete system for leaks. Repair or replace as required.			
9. Visually inspect all electrical equipment for deterioration, dust, and moisture.			
Comments:			

FIGURE 1-8   Preventive maintenance checklist.

Objectives.   The objectives of an FA program are as follows[7]:

- Assure a valid measure of total deferred maintenance backlog requirements
- Recommend priorities for maintenance and renewal needs
- Appraise the effectiveness of any preventive and corrective maintenance programs
- Provide cost estimates for the facility capital plan
- Enhance personnel safety by identifying potential hazards
- Increase the reliability of facility components by early identification of potential failures
- Reduce the total costs of maintenance by initiating early corrective action
- Obtain the full economical life of the facility through proper maintenance and reducing future capital investment

Inspection Schedule. The first step in preparing an FA inspection schedule is identifying the time requirements for the inspections. Department of the Navy procedures require FA inspections of all Navy facilities and establish time standards for various types of facilities. These standards are published in NAVFAC MO-322, Vol. 1, *Inspection of Shore Facilities.* There are standards for electrical, mechanical, structural, and special (e.g., elevators) inspections for different types of facilities based on the functional use of the buildings. Because of the wide variety of Naval facilities, most types of building are covered. The manual also provides recommended inspection frequencies for a variety of buildings and components. Table 1-3 shows a sample of the Navy Inspection Timetable.

Operator Inspections. Operator inspections should be used for equipment that has a full-time operator assigned. An example is forklift trucks. Recommended inspection work is machine cleaning, lubrication, and visual inspection of belts, bushings, and wiring. Use operator inspections to promote *ownership* of equipment by operators.

Responsibility. Operator inspections should be performed by the person assigned to operate the equipment. Instructions for the inspection should be posted on the equipment or written in a machine log book.

Schedules. These types of inspections are not formally scheduled but are usually performed either daily or weekly.

Work Requests

Work requests are often made by persons other than designated inspectors. A formal procedure that addresses this area must be developed and documented. Use standard forms that explain the parameters for generation and approval. The procedure should require that all work requests be received at a central work control point within the maintenance organization. Additionally, the procedure should establish control on the authority of personnel who approve the issue of work requests.

Also, establish and document a procedure for providing information to the requester such as notice of receipt, status, and estimated time of completion. This last step is important to the maintenance of good customer relations.

Predictive Maintenance

Predictive maintenance is a technique for figuring out the future point of failure for a machine component so that components can be replaced, on a planned basis, just before failure. Thus, equipment downtime is minimized and equipment component life is maximized.

TABLE 1-3   Navy Inspection Timetable (Partial)*

Line item description	Unit of measure	Time required, h			
		Electrical	Mechanical	Structural	Special
Buildings:					
Training	10,000 ft^2	1.0	1.3	1.5	
Storage	10,000 ft^2	1.2	1.2	1.7	
Medical	10,000 ft^2	1.5	2.0	2.3	
Administrative	10,000 ft^2	1.4	1.4	1.8	
Production	10,000 ft^2	1.9	2.1	2.4	
Maintenance	10,000 ft^2	1.9	2.1	2.4	
Buildings—roofs	10,000 ft^2	—	—	1.2	
Elevators:					
Hydraulic	Each				1.5
Cable	Each				2.5

* Use of the inspection timetable is not mandatory. The table is provided only as a guide for preparing inspection schedules.

The technique involves the measurement of various parameters that show a predictable relationship to component life span. Examples are as follows:

- Vibration of bearings
- Temperature of electrical connections
- Resistance of motor winding insulation

Using predictive maintenance consists of first establishing a historical perspective of the relationship of the chosen variable to component life. This is accomplished by taking readings (i.e., vibration of a bearing) at periodic intervals until the component fails. Figure 1-9 shows a typical curve that results from plotting the variable (vibration) against time. As the curve suggests, subsequent bearings should be replaced when vibration reaches 1.25 in/s (31.75 mm/s). Manufacturers of predictive maintenance instruments and software can provide recommended ranges and replacement values for most equipment components; this makes the historical analysis unnecessary in most applications.

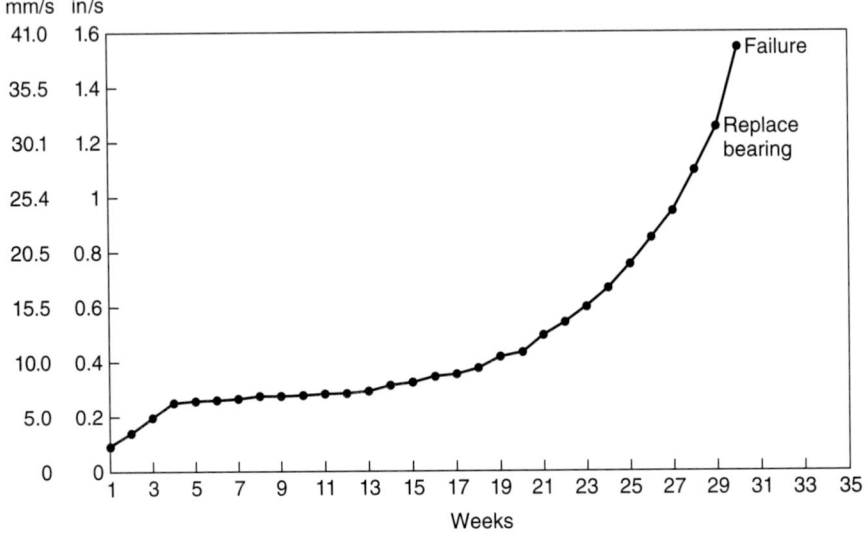

FIGURE 1-9   Vibration versus time for a bearing.

WORK CONTROL

An independent work control function is essential for the control of all maintenance work. An organization using a computerized maintenance management system (CMMS) usually incorporates the work control function into the operation of the computer system. The function should report either to the plant engineer or to the maintenance manager. This is essential to allow the function to make objective decisions concerning work priorities and schedules.

These basic control functions should be a part of work control[8]:

- Centralized work reception
- Planning and estimating
- Work order preparation and approval

- Shop scheduling and load planning
- Facility audits
- Technical support for long-range maintenance planning and budgeting
- Contract administration
- Root cause analysis

The number of people in the work control function depends on the maintenance workload. Small organizations can get by with only one person, provided that he or she is experienced and skilled. Some functions, if necessary, can be done by other staff personnel.

Work Reception

All maintenance work requests must go through work reception. The only exceptions should be emergency work requests. These may initially bypass work reception to avoid unnecessary delays; an emergency work request, however, must always be submitted when possible. This is necessary so that maintenance does not lose control of this important segment of its workload.

Work reception controls the step-by-step processing of all work requests, inspection reports from PM and FA inspections, and work orders.

Procedures

Work reception classifies each incoming work request into the various categories identified in the section "Classification of Maintenance Work." A work request log must be maintained that shows the request number, date received, originator, and class of work.

Work requests are then sent to the person designated to review and approve the work. Usually different individuals are delegated authority according to the work class.

After approval, the work requests are assigned priorities and then are planned and estimated according to the requirements of the particular class of work.

Prioritizing Maintenance Work

Maintenance must be managed under two constraints: limited funds and limited labor. These constraints decide the size of the *maintenance pie*. Unless the pie can be made bigger by additional money or workers, increasing the size of one slice decreases the size of the others.

Simple Priority Systems.   In order for maintenance to decide which customer or type of work gets its appropriate share of the resources, it is necessary to use some type of priority system. Frequently, this decision is left to the maintenance supervisor. A simple system of three priorities is often used. "A" work carries the highest priority, "B" the next highest, and "C" the lowest.

Unfortunately, this type of priority system is not usually a system at all, and "the wheel that squeaks the loudest often gets the most grease." Decisions are not made objectively, and maintenance suffers.

The RIME Priority System.   A priority system that overcomes these deficiencies was developed and copyrighted in 1964 by Albert Ramond and Associates, Inc., a Chicago consulting firm; it is called the RIME system. RIME stands for *ranking index for maintenance expenditures*. It is relatively complicated and cumbersome to use in all but very large organizations. Ramond modified the system, however, into a simplified version that is appropriate for even very small organizations.

The RIME system consists of two procedures: the ranking of each piece of equipment and the classification of each type of maintenance job. Each equipment type and job class is ranked on a scale of 1 to 10. Ten carries the highest priority. These decisions are made by maintenance and production management when the system is set up, and usually changed only when equipment or functional priorities of the facility are changed.

Establishing Equipment and Job Priorities.   Examples of equipment ranking and job classification indexes are shown in Tables 1-4 and 1-5.[9] These have been revised from the original Ramond version.

To decide work order priority, the equipment rank and job class is decided and these two factors multiplied together to give a priority number, with 100 being the highest available. Since the index will not always provide the correct priority, however, maintenance supervisors must have authority to change priority. Explanations for deviations must be required or the system will soon fail.

Some notes:

1. Any equipment with a safety hazard receives an equipment rank of 10.

2. Job class 10 is never used on a normal work order; this is reserved for critical safety items that warrant an emergency maintenance call.

3. Use a system that increases the RIME after a work order is a given age, e.g., 30 days. This will help ensure that low-priority work orders eventually get completed.

PLANNING AND ESTIMATING

The planning and estimating function is a key to effective maintenance management. This function plans jobs and estimates the number of hours that will be needed to accomplish the work. These estimates are the basis on which maintenance work is scheduled. It is also the foundation on which management evaluates maintenance labor and costs.

TABLE 1-4   Equipment Ranking

Rank		Description of equipment
10	Safety	Equipment with a safety hazard. Includes personnel and food safety.
9	Utilities	Utility equipment affecting several production lines. Includes boilers, compressors, etc.
8	Key production equipment	No standby equipment available; will shut down an entire line. Includes fryers, case packers, etc.
7	Multiple production equipment	Units for which standby equipment is available; shuts down part of a line. Includes extruders, packaging machines, etc.
6	Key material-handling equipment	No standby units available, no alternative method of moving product. Includes conveyers, etc.
5	Multiple material-handling equipment	Standby units available; alternative method for moving product exists. Includes forklifts, hand jacks, etc.
4	Support equipment	Includes all support units, such as shop equipment, office equipment, waste-handling equipment, etc.
3	Building and grounds	Includes cafeteria, offices, washrooms, parking lots, etc.

TABLE 1-5   Job Classifications

	Class	Description of work
10	Real safety, critical food safety	Critical safety work where life or limb is in danger. Actual product contamination. Work is an emergency. Call maintenance.
9	Breakdown, poor quality	Equipment, process failure. Items causing product loss, poor quality create emergency.
8	Preventive maintenance	Inspections, lubrication, and repairs to automatic lubricators or alarm systems. Work to prevent breakdowns or repair work.
7	Service work, food safety	Necessary work during operating periods. Potential for product contamination.
6	Spares, corrective maintenance	Work on spare parts or units, no additional spares. Corrective maintenance to reduce repetitive work.
5	Shutdown work	Necessary work, safety work not critical enough to require immediate shutdown.
4	Routine work, normal safety	Work on spare parts or units, normal maintenance, and routine safety work.
3	Production or quality improvement	Necessary work to improve quality or quantity of production or materials handling or quality of maintenance.
2	Cost reduction	Cost reduction work not falling into one of the higher classes.
1	Lavatories, painting, housekeeping	Keeping locker rooms and lavatory facilities operable. Protective painting to prevent rust.

Planning

Job plans prepared by the maintenance planner/estimator should specify the work to be done, material and equipment needed, how the work should be phased, and the various crafts needed.

Scope of Work.   The scope of work should correspond with the work request or the inspection report. Additionally, the scope of work should conform to the quality and quantity of maintenance expected. A scope of work must include the following:

- A complete description of the deficiency and desired results
- The exact location of the work
- Identification of special instructions or conditions

Material Coordination.   Identification of the materials necessary to accomplish the job is a key step in job planning. The following steps are necessary when planning all *major* corrective work. Step 5 is not applicable to *minor* corrective work.

1. Identify all materials and parts required for the job.
2. Check on the availability of parts in the stockroom.
3. Requisition necessary parts and materials.
4. Flag the work order as *awaiting parts* until the material is received.
5. Gather all parts and materials together in one bin identified with the work order number; put any special tools required with the parts and materials.

Critical Path Scheduling and Gantt Charts.   Planning of large maintenance projects often can benefit from the utilization of the critical path method (CPM) of scheduling and/or Gantt charts. Usually these two techniques are reserved for jobs over 1 week in duration or involving the coordination of many crafts or activities.

CPM Scheduling.   CPM scheduling is finding the shortest or most efficient time to do a job. The primary use of CPM is to provide all the information required to make decisions concerning time and cost of the project. The technique is not complicated once it becomes familiar to the planner. Additionally, several project management software programs are available to simplify the process of CPM scheduling. An example of a CPM schedule is shown in Fig. 1-10.

Gantt Charts.   Gantt charts are simply horizontal bar charts that show the relationship between various phases of a project. These charts are very helpful with tracking and controlling complicated projects. As with CPM scheduling, Gantt charts can be produced by project management software programs. An example of a Gantt chart is shown in Fig. 1-11.

Estimating

One important function of maintenance management is estimating. The main purposes of job estimating are as follows:

- Provide a cost estimate for management to use as a basis for approval of the work
- Provide information to aid in the preparation of a realistic work schedule
- Provide a basis for evaluating the effectiveness of the work control function.

Methods of Estimating.   There are three primary methods of estimating maintenance work. Each method has a use in maintenance management. The three methods are:

- Rough estimates
- Historically based estimates
- Work standards

Rough Estimates.   These are just intelligent *guesses* based on a broad idea of what similar jobs have taken in the past and on the planner's own experience. Often the planner supplements personal experience with that of a supervisor or worker.

Rough estimates are accomplished for all incoming work requests. These estimates are the basis on which the planner classifies the jobs into the various categories. Service work does not receive any additional estimates, but is ready to be scheduled as soon as the work requests are approved.

Historically Based Estimates.   These are estimates based on data gathered from accumulated experience. The data can be a file maintained by the planner. In an organization using a CMMS, the computer database is usually set up for quick access to historical data for estimating new work orders. Use historically based estimates for *minor* corrective work.

Work Standards.   Work standards are the average time necessary for a qualified worker, working at a normal pace and experiencing normal delays, to do a defined quantity of work, at a specified quality.[10] Although the adjectives *normal, qualified,* and *average* are vague terms, the consistent use of work standards does provide an effective means of workload planning and evaluation.

Although there are several forms of maintenance work standards, one of the best is the Naval *Engineered Performance Standards* (EPS). These standards use the "job slotting" technique that makes it possible to quickly arrive at a labor estimate. The Navy EPS handbooks are known as the NAVFAC P-700 series and cover all types of maintenance crafts. *Major* corrective work, routine work, and PM inspections should all be estimated by using formal work standards such as EPS, supplemented with historically based estimates when appropriate.

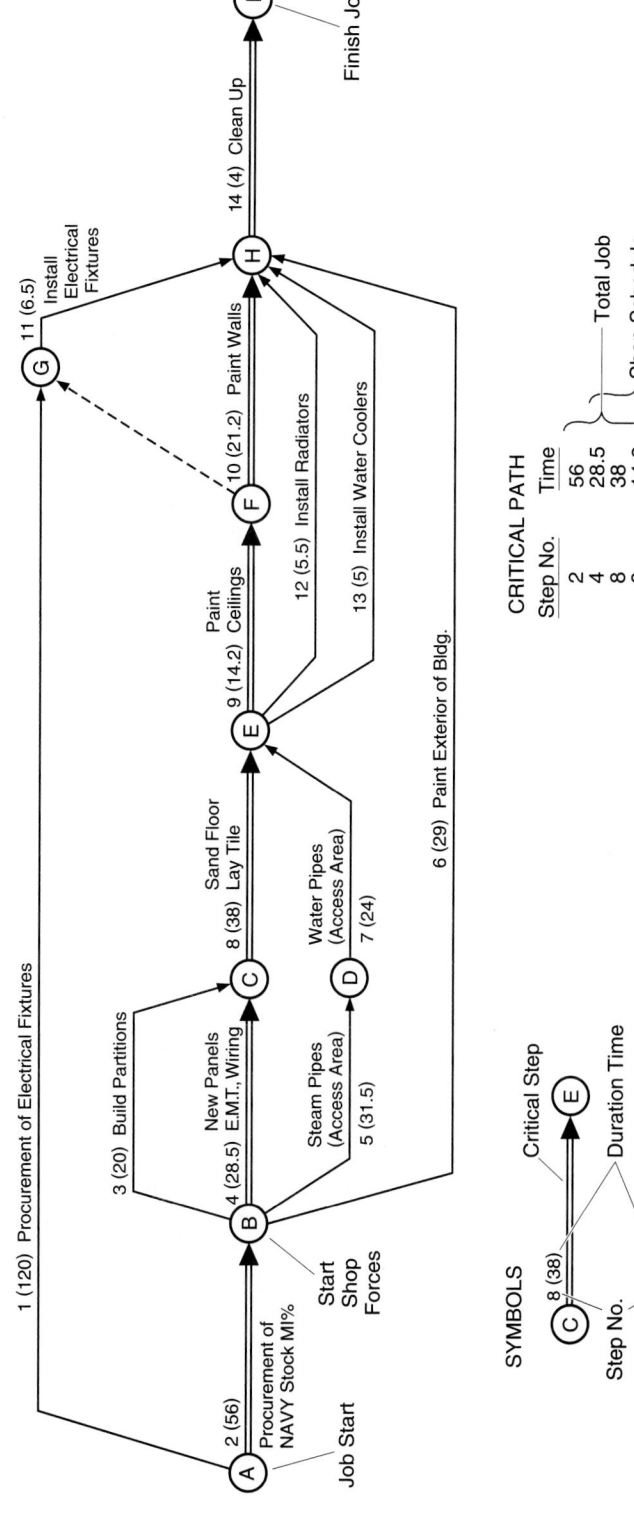

FIGURE 1-10 Sample CPM schedule.

1-25

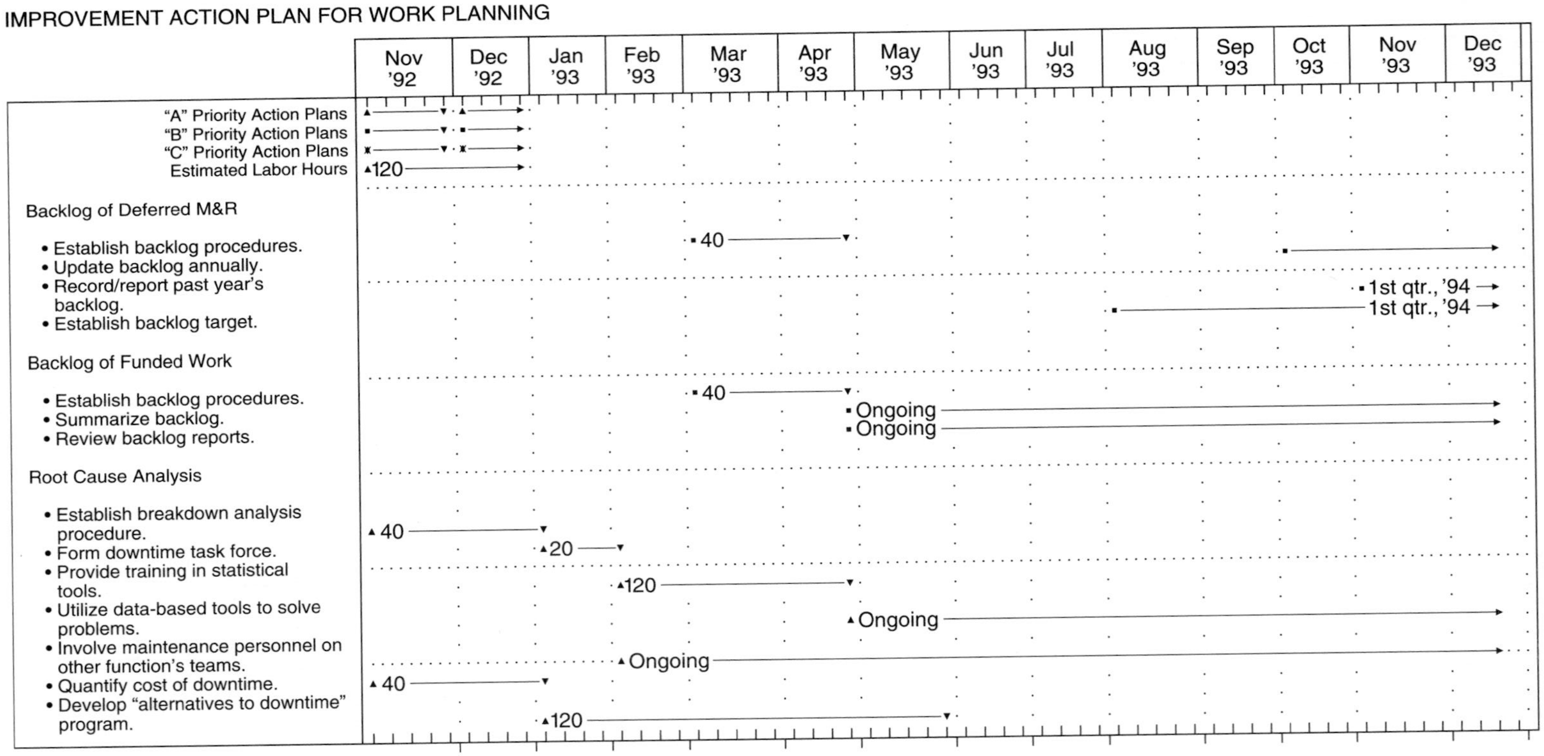

IMPROVEMENT ACTION PLAN FOR WORK PLANNING

FIGURE 1-11 Sample Gantt chart.

WORK SCHEDULING

Work scheduling commits maintenance personnel to specific work assignments sufficiently in advance to assure maximum coordination of labor, material, and equipment. The work schedule is a carefully prepared plan of action that has considered the availability of labor, material, and equipment and the relative priorities of the jobs.

Scheduling Principles

The major principles of effective maintenance work scheduling are as follows[11]:

- Schedules should be based on what is most likely to happen, not on what we would like to happen.
- Revision of the schedule should be expected.
- The schedule is a means to an end, not an end in itself.

Realistic Scheduling.   The first principle of effective scheduling requires that allowances be made for conditions as they actually exist in the plant. For example, if history suggests that 25 percent emergency time is the norm for a Monday start-up shift, then only 75 percent of the available time should be scheduled. Failure to plan for expected emergency time will invariably lead to missed schedules and unhappy customers.

Additionally, repeated instances of missed schedules will eventually cause customers to *pad* the needed-by dates so that they can be assured of having the work done on time. This is a *no-win* situation that can be corrected only by realistic schedules.

Expect Revisions.   There must be flexibility built into the system so that last minute disruptions can be addressed. Legitimate causes of revised schedules are emergencies at a higher rate than planned for, parts not arriving as expected, labor shortages due to illness, and jobs taking longer then estimated.

Means to an End.   It is easy for overzealous maintenance personnel to lose sight of the objective of a good work schedule, that is, to provide the customer with the highest quality service at the lowest cost. Planning for expected emergency time and allowing for flexibility in the schedule is the best method of ensuring that the objective is attained.

Scheduling Tools

The maintenance scheduler must have several items available before preparing the work schedule: the work order, the job plan (for major corrective work), the work order backlog, the labor availability report, the material availability report, the PM master schedule, and the production schedule.[12] In an organization using a CMMS, most or all these items are in the computer. Additionally, the scheduler must know the historical work order completion rates by day, shift, and department.

Work Order.   The scheduler must have a copy of the approved work order showing the scope of work, the job priority, labor and material estimates, and any special requirements of the work, such as specific availability dates or completion requirements.

Job Plan.   All major corrective work orders should have a detailed work plan developed by the planning function. The scheduler must know any requirements for nonstock parts, labor coordination requirements, special tools required, and the various project phases, if applicable.

Work Order Backlog.   The backlog consists of all uncompleted work orders compiled and maintained in a form that is readily available for review. Each work order is identified with its priority, the labor time estimates, a brief description of the work, status, submitted date, and required date. Organizations using a formal priority system will usually sort the backlog so that the highest-priority jobs are listed first.

A backlog report is the primary tool the scheduler uses to prepare the work schedule; its accuracy is critical, therefore, to an effective schedule. Take care to ensure that completed jobs are removed, partially completed jobs are identified, and that all known work requirements are in the backlog.

Besides using it as a scheduling tool, management uses the work order backlog as a tool to identify the projected work load for the department and the various work areas within the department. It is also an excellent early indicator of potential problems arising from variations in the maintenance work load or staffing. From a long-term standpoint, the backlog report is the best tool management has for identifying staffing requirements for the department.

Labor Availability Report.   This report shows the total number of hours available for work order scheduling. Identified on the report are reductions in labor due to vacations, other known absences, planned training, etc. Accuracy of this report is imperative.

Material Availability Report.   This report from the maintenance storeroom shows the status of any material ordered for a specific work order. Additionally, the scheduler should have quick access to the stores inventory report to check on the availability of stocked items. The scheduler should also be able to reserve stocked items for a specific work order, unless that is done on all jobs by the planner.

PM Master Schedule.   The scheduler uses the PM master schedule to place all PM work orders on the work schedule. Organizations using a CMMS will usually have the master schedule on the computer, and PM work orders will be automatically identified.

Production Schedule.   The maintenance scheduler should have a copy of the plant production schedule available. This will allow the scheduler to take advantage of opportunities to work on equipment during down days or shifts. It will also minimize revisions to the maintenance schedule.

Historical Completion Rates.   The scheduler must prepare a realistic work schedule to ensure long-term success of the scheduling procedure. To accomplish this, the scheduler should know what can be expected in the way of unplanned emergency work or other interruptions. This will usually be different depending on the department, shift, and day of the week. For example, start-up shifts on Mondays may have high instances of emergency calls, and on weekend shifts the emergency calls may be near zero. The schedule must be prepared accordingly.

Scheduling Procedure

Maintenance scheduling is both a weekly and a daily procedure. It begins each Friday with development of the weekly schedule starting with the following Monday. Each day during the week a daily schedule is prepared for the following day. The weekend schedule is prepared the preceding Thursday and Friday.

The scheduler starts with the highest priority available work from the backlog to build the weekly schedule; major corrective work available means work that has been completely estimated and for which a job plan has been developed. Work orders are pulled from the backlog and added to the schedule until all of the available time is used. If work order priorities dictate, then overtime is requested to accomplish the schedule.

Daily schedules differ from weeklies only in that they are revised as required to meet new requirements unknown when the weekly schedule was developed. This is usually due to identification of new work of higher priority than originally scheduled, variations between estimated and actual labor requirements, and changes to the production schedule. Whatever the reason, these items must be accommodated by a flexible maintenance work schedule.

ASSESSMENT OF MAINTENANCE WORK

A quick and accurate appraisal of work performed by maintenance is critical to effective maintenance management. The prompt identification of problems and the feedback of information for correction allows continuous improvement in the operation. The use of a CMMS as a management tool for maintenance simplifies this process.

Appraisal tools used in the assessment of maintenance work are a weekly control report, performance measurement, productivity measurement, variance reviews, and trend analysis.

Control Reports

A maintenance control report is a tabulation of specific variables identified by management as relevant to the performance of the maintenance function. The report, usually published weekly, shows the results of actual performance and relates these results to predetermined standards or goals. Control reports typically contain daily, weekly, and monthly data. Most CMMSs can produce control reports with a variety of information. An example of a portion of a maintenance control report is shown in Fig. 1-12.

Performance Measurement

Performance of maintenance workers is measured by the quantity and quality of work performed. Accountability for worker's performance cannot be provided without a system for providing this measurement.

Measurement of work quantity is provided by estimating labor and material for all corrective, routine, and PM work orders. Actual labor and materials used are compiled and variances reported to management on the weekly control report. In order to provide as accurate measurements as possible, use formal estimating methods, such as engineered performance standards or historical records of actual jobs, for major corrective jobs, routine work orders, and PM work orders.

Measuring the quality of work performed involves techniques other than simply comparing time and materials used to an estimate. A technique that works is the *work samples* program discussed in the section "Maintenance Training." The work samples program provides for a periodic review and evaluation of workers' completed jobs. The procedure also serves as a tool to calibrate workers on management's expectations of acceptable quality and quantity of work.

Productivity Measurement

Productivity is the percentage of the labor hours that is directly employed to accomplish a task. It does not include indirect activities or nonproductive time. Measurement of productivity can be made in various ways.

One method is to conduct a formal industrial engineering productivity study of the work force. If this method is used, ensure the productivity study includes a statistically valid work sampling of the work force.

Maintenance Control Report							
Week Ending:	Current Week			Month-To-Date			
Control Variable	Planned	Actual	Variance	Planned	Actual	Variance	%	Tgt.
Preventive Maintenance								
Emergency								
Corrective-Major								
Corrective-Minor								
Routine Work								
Service Work								
Project Work								
Total Productive Labor Hours								

FIGURE 1-12 Maintenance control report form.

Another method is to conduct a formal audit of the organization's maintenance management system.[13] A management audit provides a method to review, analyze, and recommend improvements in performance. By establishing a numerical rating system for the audit results, an effectiveness percentage can be derived. This effectiveness rating can then be correlated to an approximate productivity number.

Variance Reviews

Systematic management review of the variances between planned and actual process variables is a key step of effective control. In maintenance this activity is more important than normal because of the inherent variability of maintenance activities. A procedure should be developed and implemented to identify and review variances between planned and actual variables. Select specific data for variance review and report the information on the weekly control report.

Assign specific lead and support responsibilities for the variance review. Schedule a monthly meeting of maintenance staff for the specific purpose of reviewing variances.

Trend Analysis

A weekly control report gives results for a specific period, but a longer-range view is needed for planning. Trend charts show how various indexes are trending from one period to another.

Review of trends periodically is essential to timely management control. Many CMMSs can provide trend data from information in the database.

Management should develop trend data, including data by period, period to date, year, year to date, and previous year by period. Then analyze trend data at least monthly, including performance against targets for work order hours and costs, labor distribution, work scheduling compliance, priorities, production downtime, equipment breakdowns, and emergency time. Chart trend lines; report periodically; provide findings to management and all operational units.

INVENTORY CONTROL OF SPARE PARTS

Recent articles on the Japanese method of inventory control have caused increased awareness about the cost of excessive inventories. The just-in-time (JIT) method ensures that parts arrive as they are needed, but not before; the savings is significant because capital is not invested in unneeded parts and supplies.

In maintenance spare parts, using the JIT method in its entirety is probably not feasible; the idea, however, of keeping parts inventories at the lowest level possible *is* valid from an economic standpoint. A method that combines a systematic approach to setting inventory levels is recommended. Further, a technique for reducing existing inventory levels should be used.

Identification of Necessary Spares

Identifying the spare parts that should be kept in the maintenance stockroom is not a scientific technique. There are many variables that must be considered. The best method is to use all the resources available, including your own experience with the equipment and recommendations from manufacturers, vendors, and other organizations using the particular equipment. Another important factor is the priority that your process places on the reliability of the equipment.

Determining Stocking Levels

Once the necessary spare parts have been identified, the most difficult task is to decide the stocking levels for each part. Although this step can be very time-consuming, it is the most important part of controlling the inventory investment and ensuring that parts are always available when needed.

Economic Order Quantity Model.   A tool that speeds up this process is the *inventory control model* shown in Fig. 1-13. A spreadsheet program is used to make utilization of the model feasible for most parts. The model uses the standard accounting method of figuring out reorder points and economic order quantities (EOQ). Two variables that must be inserted in the equation are the company's *cost of capital* and the *administrative cost* of processing a purchase order. These values do not change quickly and usually can remain constant for a year at a time. In the model the cost of capital is 15 percent and the administrative cost is $10.

To use the model, the part name and number, the annual usage, the unit cost, and estimated delivery time are inserted. These values are either known or can be estimated accurately. The safety stock, the only information that requires a level of experience to decide, must then be entered. To help with this decision, the model shows five different alternatives and each one's effect on the average inventory value and inventory turn. The *model* column shows the value selected.

Reorder Points.   The model determines reorder points by calculating *minimum* and *maximum* values. The difference between the two is known as the EOQ. When the *minimum*

PART NAME:		Fuse		STOCK NO.:		E-346841	
	MODEL	ALT.1	ALT.2	ALT.3	ALT.4	ALT.5
ANNUAL USAGE	250	250	250	250	250	250
UNIT COST	$3.50	$3.50	$3.50	$3.50	$3.50	$3.50
SAFETY STOCK	10	19	10	5	3	2
DELIVERY TIME	4	4	4	4	4	4
USAGE RATE	4.81	4.81	4.81	4.81	4.81	4.81
MIN	19	19	19	19	19	19
REORDER POINT	29	38	29	24	22	21
CARRYING COST	0.525	0.525	0.525	0.525	0.525	0.525
EOQ	98	98	98	98	98	98
MAX	127	136	127	122	120	119
ORDERS PER YEAR	3	3	3	3	3	3
ANNUAL COST	$875	$875	$875	$875	$875	$875
AVERAGE INVENTORY	$207	$238	$207	$189	$182	$179
INVENTORY TURN	4	4	4	5	5	5
IOQ	59	68	59	54	52	51

P.O. COST = $10
COST OF CAPITAL = 15%
MIN = USAGE RATE (annual quan. used/52) X delivery time in weeks
REORDER POINT (RP) = MIN + SAFETY STOCK (SS)
MAX = RP + ECONOMIC ORDER QUANTITY (EOQ)
EOQ = Square root (2AP/S)
A = Annual quantity used
P = Cost of placing an order
S = Carrying cost of one unit (UNIT COST X COST OF CAPITAL)
AVERAGE INVENTORY VALUE (AIV) = ((EOQ/2) + SS) X UNIT COST
INVENTORY TURN (TURN) = ANNUAL COST / average inventory value
ANNUAL COST = UNIT COST X USAGE RATE X 52
IOQ = INITIAL ORDER QUAN. (used to establish immediate running rate for cost)

FIGURE 1-13 Inventory control model.

inventory level is reached, an order is placed to bring the inventory level back to the *maximum*. The formulas used are shown in Fig. 1-13.

Safety Stock. A *safety stock* value must usually be used to increase the *minimum* level. This is necessary because the factors used to determine the minimum values are averages and can change. For example, the actual usage in a given week or month will probably differ from the average. Delivery times are subject to many variables, such as inclement weather. The protection against these variables is a safety stock.

Inventory Turn. Inventory turn is an accepted basis of determining optimum inventory levels. It is the number of times the inventory turns over in a year. The objective of a good inventory control system is to maximize the inventory turn, minimize administrative costs in placing purchase orders, and eliminate unacceptable stock-out situations.

Initial Order Quantity. The *initial order quantity* (IOQ) is used when initially entering new items in stock. IOQ is especially useful when starting up an entire line or a plant. Initially ordering the EOQ will create an artificially high inventory level, cause a delay in establishing a running rate for budgeting purposes, and require an excessive investment in spare parts.

Inventory Reduction Techniques

A 10-step process is used to reduce inventory levels of maintenance spare parts and to keep these levels at the optimum size. This process has been used and does work. Reductions of 50 percent or more are possible in many situations without negatively affecting service levels of maintenance.

Determine Historical Usage Rates. The first step in the process is to find out the actual usage history for each part over the past 3 years. This period should be long enough to provide good data and yet be current enough to show recent deviations. Inventories that are maintained on computer databases make this step relatively simple.

Identify Zero-Usage Parts. The next step is to flag those parts showing zero usage during the 3-year period. Results from actual storerooms have shown 25 to 30 percent of parts carried in inventory have not turned in 3 years. Often the parts are no longer used in the plant.

Identify Exceptions. This is the most time-consuming step in the process. The objective is to eliminate all parts showing zero usage during the past 3 years. Exceptions should be made only for those items deemed to be *critical spares*. To this end the approach should be that all zero-usage parts will be removed unless *specifically justified*. Adequate time must be allowed for all concerned to review the list. It is recommended that maintenance workers be included in the review.

Remove Parts from Inventory. Physically removing identified parts from the stockroom is the next step. Four approaches should be used in this process:

1. Circulate a list of the parts to other facilities within the company. It is entirely possible that your junk is another organization's necessary spare parts. These can probably be sold to the other facility at some discount.

2. Contact vendors and return those parts that will be accepted. Restocking charges must usually be deducted from the price paid, but this is normally acceptable.

3. Solicit bids for bulk purchase of similar items, a good method for selling motors, gearboxes, etc.

4. Those parts that cannot be sold should be given away or junked. Under no conditions should these parts remain in the stockroom.

Remove Stock Codes. This step deletes the stock codes for canceled items from the plant parts catalog. This step is necessary to ensure that the parts will not be reordered inadvertently in the future. It also frees storage capacity in the computer database.

Adjust Min/Max Values. Those remaining parts in the stockroom should be reviewed to determine the optimum inventory levels; use the inventory control model to help in this process.

Identify Excess Inventory. Once the new min/max levels are decided for each item in stock, the excess quantities in inventory should be calculated. This is the *on-hand* quantity minus the new maximum level. Deciding those parts to be removed from inventory is accomplished by comparing the quantities on hand to the annual usage. Other variables to be considered are the value of the item to vendors and other locations and the replacement cost of the item (it may be obsolete and not replaceable at any price). The objective is to remove as many unnecessary parts from inventory as possible; exceptions must be justified.

Other Inventory Reduction Techniques.   Reduce the different type of motors, gearboxes, sprockets, variable-speed drives, motor starters, etc. The possibilities are almost unlimited. It is unnecessary to carry a spare for three dozen different gearboxes when one dozen different units will serve all applications in the plant. Set up standards and ensure that future installations comply.

Use vendors to carry spares. Many vendors, especially bearing suppliers, will agree to stock minimum quantities of what is needed to get your business. *A word of caution!* Be careful about special items that are difficult or impossible for the vendor to return if your needs change; one can be financially liable to purchase these items.

Procedures to prevent uncontrolled stockroom inventory must be carried out. Use the inventory control model to set min/max levels and IOQs for all new stock items. Beware of engineering projects from outside the plant engineering organization. Manufacturers' suggested spare parts lists are usually used by design engineers to provide initial spare parts. The quantities recommended on these lists are often excessive. *Require approval* before any parts can be ordered for stock.

Benefits of Controlling Parts Inventory

Benefits of reducing the inventory levels of maintenance spare parts are many. They include:

- Fewer storage cabinets and shelves are required.
- Less floor space is needed.
- Reduced labor is required to control the inventory.
- Retrieval of spare parts can be expedited because of less clutter in the stockroom.
- There is a one-time reduction in maintenance repair costs due to a reduction in min/max levels.
- The annual savings through better utilization of company money can be significant. Assuming a 15 percent return on capital, each $100,000 reduction in inventory value can yield $15,000 annually.

MAINTENANCE PROBLEM-SOLVING TOOLS

Effective maintenance frequently requires problem solving. A method of improving the efficiency of problem solving is the use of statistical tools. Although some of these techniques can be intimidating to maintenance workers, there are several simple tools that are very effective.

Simple Statistical Process Control Tools

The simple statistical process control tools are Pareto charts, fishbone charts, control diagrams, histograms, run charts, and scatter diagrams. These tools require a minimum amount of mathematics and can be used by all members of the maintenance team without extensive training.

Background.   Forty years ago, W. Edwards Deming and J. M. Juran began helping the Japanese improve the quality and productivity of their manufacturing systems. The well-documented successes of their efforts have resulted in a quality revolution affecting all aspects of business, both in the United States and abroad.

Methods of Improving Quality.   Continuous improvements in quality and productivity require a vast array of proven methods and techniques. Among these are statistical process control (SPC), statistical quality control (SQC), total quality control (TQC), just in time (JIT) inventory, and total productive maintenance (TPM).

Statistical Implications.   Inherent in the successful use of these methods and techniques is the ability to solve problems in a logical, systematic way, i.e., statistical problem solving. The use of statistical problem solving has become associated with the well-known control chart, a method of measuring the variation of a process and using this information to isolate special causes of process upsets from common causes. Although control charts are powerful statistical tools, their effective use requires a considerable amount of education and training, and, more important, other *simple* tools are more effective in solving problems encountered daily in a maintenance operation.

The Simple Tools

Pareto Chart.   This is a bar chart that ranks causes in descending order so that priorities can be assigned. Its use is the basis for the 80–20 rule (80 percent of the problems are due to 20 percent of the causes). An example of a Pareto chart is shown in Fig. 1-14.

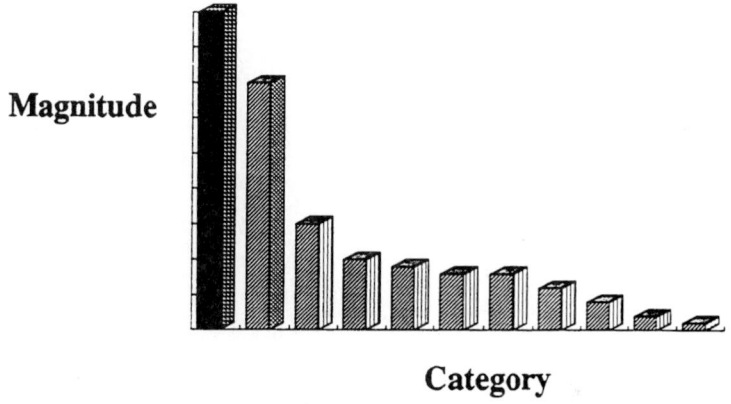

FIGURE 1-14   Pareto chart example.

Fishbone Chart.   This is also known as a *cause-and-effect* diagram or *Ishikawa* diagram after its originator. These charts show causes of a certain problem grouped by categories, usually *method, material, people, machines,* and *environment.* A fishbone chart is shown in Fig. 1-15.

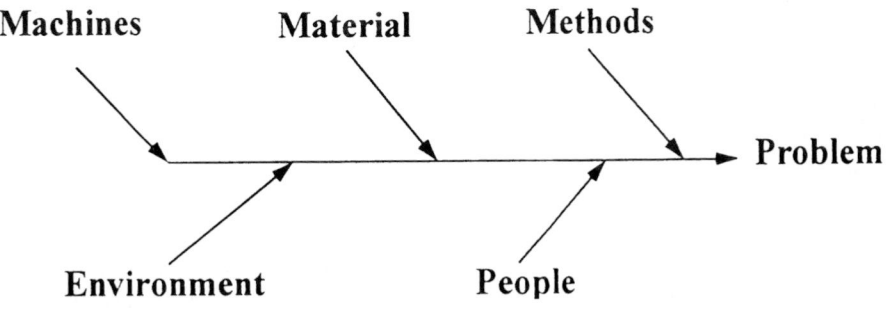

FIGURE 1-15   Fishbone chart.

Process-Flow Diagram. These diagrams are visual representations of the steps in a service or manufacturing process. These diagrams are useful during brainstorming sessions to help identify potential causes of a problem. A process-flow diagram is shown in Fig. 1-16.

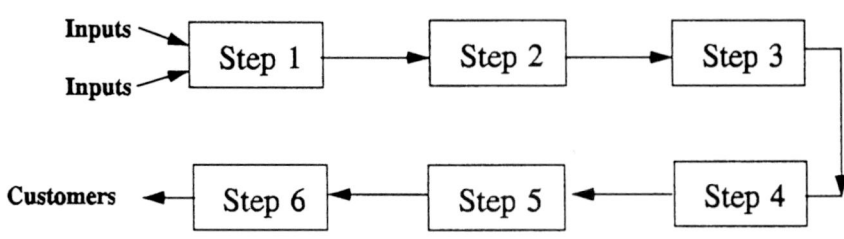

FIGURE 1-16 Process-flow diagram.

Histogram. Histograms are used to show the frequency that an incident occurs. These are often used with Pareto charts to help set priorities. Figure 1-17 shows a histogram.

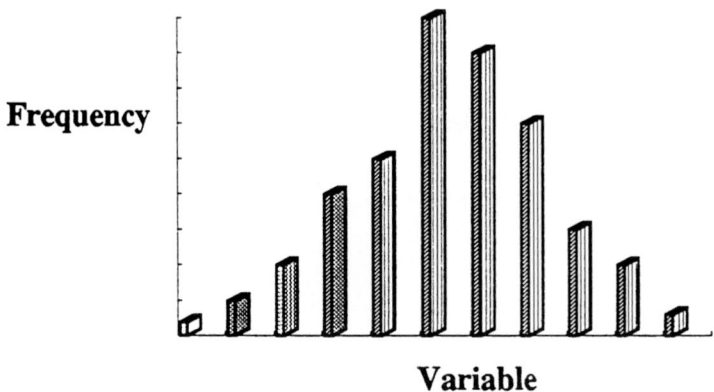

FIGURE 1-17 Histogram.

Scatter Diagram. These diagrams show the relationship between two variables. An example of a scatter diagram is shown in Fig. 1-18.

Run Chart. These charts show the relationship between a variable and a period. An example of a run chart is shown in Fig. 1-19.

MAINTENANCE TRAINING

Technical training of maintenance workers is becoming more important than ever. Equipment and processes are increasing in complexity, requiring that effective maintenance organizations devote additional resources to this area.

Compounding the problem is the changing organizational structures that mandate that all personnel receive ongoing training in working within the new environment. An example is the team training that is now a standard in many companies.

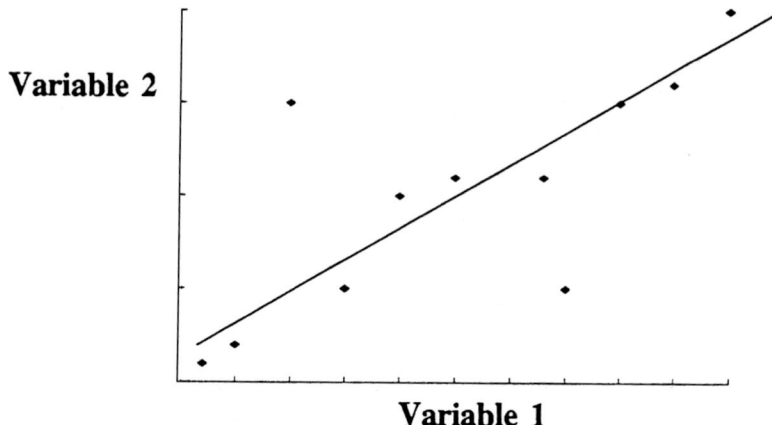

FIGURE 1-18   Scatter diagram.

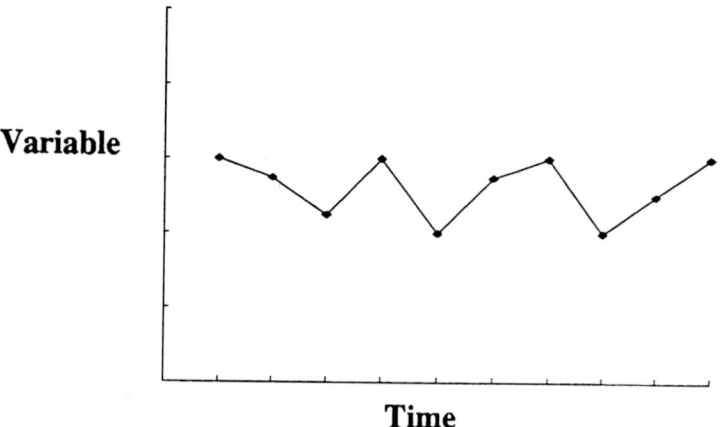

FIGURE 1-19   Run chart.

Many companies are having a serious problem with recruiting workers from outside the organization that have the technical and the social skills needed. One method of solving this problem is to provide the technical training to existing unskilled workers. The biggest advantage of this technique is that the trainees typically will have the social skills necessary. It is much easier to increase technical skills than it is to modify social skills.

Apprentice Training

An apprentice training program provides an opportunity for unskilled employees to qualify as skilled maintenance workers. The objectives of the program are as follows:

- To motivate employees to become highly skilled so that plants and equipment are professionally and efficiently maintained
- To develop flexibility, stability, and efficiency within the maintenance organization
- To create a foundation for employees on which future training, attitudes, and performance can be built

- To reward individual improvement with a pay increase based on successful completion of the training program and subsequent promotion

An employee selected for the training program is placed in the position of maintenance trainee. During the training program, candidates are instructed in basic craft skills and specific equipment skills required for progression to a maintenance worker position. Promotion is based on successful program completion and availability of a position within the maintenance organization. If a maintenance position is not available upon completion of the program, the candidate returns to the former job and pay grade until a position becomes available.

Academic Section.   The academic section of the apprentice training program consists of videotape or other type of preprogrammed instruction, one-on-one instruction, and hands-on instruction. The first few weeks of the program involve the academic section only. Later the instructional objectives section and on-the-job training section begin. The academic section should be completed within a fixed period to help ensure only qualified trainees graduate.

Contents of the academic section should be customized to the organization. Many companies offer generic training programs in a variety of formats. The possibilities are limited only by the organization's budget. Additionally, it is necessary to develop training courses for plant-specific equipment and processes. Local trade schools and junior colleges often can help set up courses and can also provide skilled trainers.

Instructional Objectives Section.   The instructional objectives section of the apprentice training program is self-paced within the program's period. This section begins approximately 10 percent of the way into the program.

Check Sheets.   Figure 1-20 shows an instructional objectives check sheet. This check sheet lists the required areas of training, objectives of each area, methods of training, and resources used in gathering data.

Additionally, the check sheet is used to record expected completion and review completion dates. Expected completion dates are filled in by the trainee, and review completion dates are filled in by the supervisor. To complete each area, the candidate must show knowledge of the area objectives and receive a pass grade. Grading is pass/fail and is decided by the supervisor. Failure to complete all areas within the program's period results in expulsion from the program. The reference key for the check sheets is as follows:

- Key to numbers used under *Objectives:*
    1 = Understand proper equipment operation
    2 = Know safety precautions
    3 = Locate and use manuals and prints
    4 = Troubleshoot mechanical malfunctions and make repairs
    5 = Troubleshoot electrical malfunctions and make repairs
    6 = Fully operate equipment
- Key to abbreviations under *Activities:*
    RE = Locate and review manuals
    OP = Learn operating skills
    OJT = On-the-job training

On-the-Job Training Section.   The on-the-job training (OJT) section of the apprentice training program consists of performing preventive maintenance and repairs on plant equipment. This section is self-paced within the program's period. To complete the section, the candidate must complete the OJT equipment PM and repair check sheets and pass the final performance test. The OJT section should begin simultaneously with the instructional objectives section.

AREA	OBJECTIVES	ACTIVITIES	RESOURCES	EXPECTED COMPLETION DATE	REVIEW COMPLETED DATE
1. Planning/ Scheduling System-2 days	1. Know elements of program and importance 2. Complete orientation	1. Schedule 3 shifts 2. Collect data 3. Fill out data card 4. Research files	S,M,PT,PS,MC		
2. Plant Maintenance Orientation - 1 day	1. Downtime 2. Accountabilities 3. Management 4. Identify all plant equipment and panels	1. Collect data 2. Meeting with Maintenance Manager 3. Tour 4. Flow diagram	M, S, PT, B		
3. Parts Purchasing - 2 days	1. System understanding 2. Parts room orientation	1. Recorder report 2. Budgeting 3. Buying	M, PA, GU		
4. Schematics- Component Electricity - 10 days	See Appendix, Instructional Objectives Area 4	1. Self-imposed print problems 2. Check out and testing of components	B, S, PT, M, C		
5. HVAC	1 through 6	RE - OP - OJT	E, B, S, PT, C		
6. Welding	1, 2 and 6	OP - OJT	E, B, S, PT, C - Vendor		
7. Sewer System	1 through 6	RE - OP - OJT	E, B, S, BT, C		
8. Conveyors	1 through 6	RE - OP - OJT	E. B, S, PT, C		
9. Roofing System	1 through 6	RE - OP - OJT	E, B, S, PT, C		
10. Floor System	1 through 6	RE - OP - OJT	E, B, S, PT, C		
11. Safety Checks	1 through 6	RE - OP - OJT	E, B, S, PT, C		
12. Fire Brigade	Know purpose and importance				
13. Conveyors	1 through 5	RE - OJT			
14. Presses	1 through 6	RE - OP - OJT			

FIGURE 1-20   Instructional check sheet.

Check Sheets.   Figure 1-21 shows the OJT equipment PM and repair check sheets. A trainee is required to obtain and perform PM and repairs on all equipment listed. To complete the check sheets, the candidate must do a significant PM or repair job on each piece of equipment listed. Each job must be verified by the supervisor as having been correctly performed. The supervisor then initials and dates the corresponding check sheet block.

Final Performance Test.   The final performance test is given after successful completion of the academic section, instructional objectives section, and OJT check sheets. This test

EQUIPMENT	WORK PERFORMED	DATE AND INITIALS
WIDGET PACKAGING		
Wrapping Machine		
WHATNOT PACKAGING		
Overwrap Machine		
Discharge Conveyor		
Transfer Conveyor		
THINGS PACKAGING		
Automatic Case Packer		
Case Sealer		
PROCESSING		
Widget Cleaning		
Drying		
Widget Baking		
Feed Conveyor		
Widget Wacker		
SHIPPING		
Conveyor Line - Trucks		
Conveyor Line - Rail Cars		
Overhead Door		
BUILDING AND GROUNDS		
Boiler		
Air Compressors		
Water Heater		

FIGURE 1-21 OJT equipment PM and repair check sheet.

requires the trainee to use most of the skills he/she learned during the program. Emergency work requests are filled out and given to the trainee. These work requests list 30 typical equipment maintenance problems. The candidate must troubleshoot and repair the problems within a given period. Failure to attain a passing grade results in program failure.

Maintenance Skills Inventory

The maintenance skills inventory system provides a method of learning a worker's skill levels. The system consists of a formal appraisal that is given to all workers every 12 months. The appraisal includes four evaluations. The results of these evaluations are assessed to identify areas in which a worker is proficient, and areas in which the worker requires training and development. The assessment can also be used to classify a worker for pay purposes.

Description. The program consists of four evaluations: technical skills, personal skills, team skills, and administration skills. Each evaluation has a rating system to assess a worker's skill level or professionalism. Assessments are made by both the worker being evaluated and the worker's supervisor. The supervisor's assessment is based on the worker's work samples and the supervisor's knowledge of the worker's work habits and ability. All assessments are reviewed by the maintenance manager, who also intervenes when a discrepancy exists between the worker's and the supervisor's assessments. When all evaluations are completed, the worker's skills ratio is calculated from appraisal scores. The skills ratio decides the worker's current skill level.

Technical Skills Evaluation. The technical skills evaluation assesses a worker's knowledge of and ability to do maintenance tasks. This evaluation consists of 10 categories.
   Scoring. Each category contains several evaluation areas that are scored on a five-point scale. Criterion for point scoring is as follows:

1 point   Worker cannot perform the task

2 points   Worker can perform the task if closely supervised

3 points   Worker can perform the task unsupervised but the completed job must be checked

4 points   Worker can perform task and no follow-up check is needed

5 points   Worker can perform the task and suggest changes to improve the operation

   Categories. The categories evaluated are welding, electrical, mechanical, hydraulics, pneumatics, plumbing, electronics, machining, carpentry, and operating. These can be modified to match specific plant requirements.
   Evaluation Sheets. Figure 1-22 shows part of an evaluation sheet used to record welding technical skill evaluation data. Similar evaluation sheets are developed for each category. The assessed score for each evaluation area is recorded by placing a check mark in the corresponding *Points* column. When all areas have been scored, each *Points* column is totaled by multiplying the number of check marks in that column by the column rating. The *Points* total is determined and divided by the number of evaluation areas to give the *Skills Ratio*.

Personal Skills Evaluation. The personal skills evaluation assesses a worker's performance in nontechnical individual areas. This evaluation consists of five categories.
   Scoring. Each category contains several evaluation areas that are scored on a 5-point scale. Criterion for point scoring is different for each category, but is similar to the following:

1 point   Performance is at goal minus 2

2 points   Performance is at goal minus 1

3 points   Performance is at goal

4 points   Performance is at goal plus 1

5 points   Performance is at goal plus 2

WELDING SKILLS EVALUATION FORM						
Evaluation Area	Points					Comments
	1	2	3	4	5	
1. Set up arc welder.						
2. Set up spot welder.						
3. Set up oxyacetylene unit.						
4. Set up plasma cutter.						
5. Set up wire welder.						
6. Choose appropriate weld and bead.						
7. Choose appropriate rod.						
8. Prepare surfaces to be welded.						
9. Demonstrate weld of various beads: butt, lap, and fillet.						
10. Weld with arc welder.						
11. Cut straight line in carbon steel with plasma cutter.						
12. Pierce holes in stainless steel with plasma cutter.						
13. Cut straight line in heavy gauge stainless with plasma cutter.						
14. Cut straight line in light gauge stainless with plasma cutter.						
Column Totals						
Total Points						
Skills Ratio						

FIGURE 1-22   Welding skills evaluation form.

Categories.   The categories evaluated are safety, attendance, performance, people skills, and method-improvement projects that have been initiated. These can be modified to match specific plant requirements.

Team Skills Evaluation.   The team skills evaluation assesses the performance of the worker's work team. This evaluation consists of four categories.

Scoring.   Each category contains several evaluation areas scored on a 5-point scale. Criteria for point scoring are different for each category, but are similar to:

1 point   Performance is at goal minus 2

2 points   Performance is at goal minus 1

3 points   Performance is at goal

4 points   Performance is at goal plus 1

5 points   Performance is at goal plus 2

Categories.   The categories evaluated are product quality, production downtime, maintenance emergency time, and preventive maintenance completion rates. These can be modified to match specific plant requirements.

Administration Skills Evaluation.   The administration skills evaluation assesses a worker's utilization of management procedures. This evaluation consists of four categories.

Scoring.   Each category contains several evaluation areas that are scored on a 5-point scale. Criteria for point scoring are different for each category, but are similar to:

1 point   Worker rarely follows procedures

2 points   Worker follows procedures over 50 percent of the time

3 points   Worker follows procedures 90 percent of the time

4 points   Worker always follows procedures

5 points   Worker always follows procedures and makes recommendations to improve procedures

Categories.   The categories evaluated are work order procedures, stockroom procedures, PM procedures, and statistical problem-solving skills. These can be modified to match specific plant requirements.

Work Samples

Work samples are used to ensure that the supervisor is periodically reviewing and evaluating the worker's completed jobs. Additionally, the work sample program helps to improve the worker's perception of management's expectations of job performance.

The work samples evaluation is an inspection of a worker's work. Work samples can be either PM work orders or corrective work orders. Each worker's work is sampled four times per month. Only one sampling per month can be a PM. Each PM can be used only once per calendar year as a work sample. An overall ratio of 20 percent PMs to 80 percent routinely scheduled work orders is required during each calendar year. Management is responsible for objectively performing work sample reviews and completing appropriate forms. The worker's supervisor is required to discuss each work sample evaluation with the worker and allow the worker to review the work sample form. Work samples are rated on a scale from 1 to 5. This rating system is included on each review form. A work sample review form is shown in Fig. 1-23. This form is used to record pertinent work sample evaluation data. The comments section must be completed to support the work sample rating.

The maintenance manager is responsible for operation of the work sample program. The manager maintains a file and work sample log on each worker. These files are available for review by respective workers and by management personnel. Twice per month the maintenance manager selects, for review, a completed work sample for each worker. The selection should be random to prevent the establishment of any predictable review cycle. Each sample (work order form) is submitted with a work sample review form and routed to the respective reviewer. A worker's work sample cannot be reviewed by his/her immediate supervisor. Each reviewer must return the completed form and work sample within two days. Additionally, twice per month the worker selects, for review, a completed sample of his/her work. The selection is entirely up to the worker. The sample is then reviewed according to the same criteria as that selected by the maintenance manager.

WORK SAMPLE REVIEW FORM

Date:	Rating:
Reviewer:	Worker:

Rating System:

1. It is apparent that work was either not done or performed so poorly it had to be redone to ensure reliability. Any job that requires redoing or causes downtime will be rated 1.

2. Work was performed, but craftsmanship was shoddy or haphazard. Job was not completed but was signed off as completed. In the case of a PM, too much time was spent writing work orders or no time was spent writing work orders. Required parts were handled incorrectly.

3. All work was completed to satisfactory requirements, but the job lacked 100% completion. Examples: failing to clean up work area, incomplete paperwork, or not running the equipment through a check run after completing the job.

4. Good job. No follow-up required and all paperwork was completed as necessary.

5. Superior job. Technician spent the extra effort required to not just do the job correctly, but to enhance and improve the equipment's performance or appearance. Examples: touch-up painting; straightening doors, brackets, hangers, etc.; replacing covers and missing hardware; timing and heat adjustments.

Description of Work Sample:

Work Order No.:	Est. Hrs.:	Actual Hrs.:

Description of Work:

Comments:

FIGURE 1-23   Work sample review form.

REFERENCES

1. Raab, A., "Three Ways to Organize," unpublished manuscript, 1986.
2. Bramlette, C. A., "Free to Change," *Training and Development Journal,* March 1984, pp. 32–39.
3. Nakajima, S., *Introduction to TPM,* Productivity Press, Cambridge, Mass., 1988, pp. 10–12.
4. NAVFAC MO-321, *Maintenance Management of Public Works and Public Utilities,* Department of the Navy, Washington, D.C., 1968, p. 7.

5. NAVFAC MO-321, *Maintenance Management of Public Works and Public Utilities*, Department of the Navy, 1968, p. 8.

6. Newbrough, E. T., *Effective Maintenance Management*, McGraw-Hill, New York, 1967, p. 64.

7. Rush, S. C., *Managing the Facilities Portfolio*, National Association of College and University Business Officers, Washington, D.C., 1991, pp. 8–9.

8. Applied Management Engineering, *Maintenance Management Audit*, R.S. Means Company, Kingston, Mass., 1991, p. 39.

9. Newbrough, E. T., *Effective Maintenance Management*, McGraw-Hill, New York, 1967, pp. 316–317.

10. NAVFAC P-700.2, *Planner and Estimator's Workbook*, Department of the Navy, Washington, D.C., 1980, p. 9.

11. Newbrough, E. T., *Effective Maintenance Management*, McGraw-Hill, New York, 1967, pp. 133–134.

12. Newbrough, E. T., *Effective Maintenance Management*, McGraw-Hill, New York, 1967, pp. 139–140.

13. Applied Management Engineering, *Maintenance Management Audit*, R.S. Means Company, Kingston, Mass., 1991, pp. 13–15.

THE BASIC PLANT FACILITY

SECTION 2

BUILDING CONSTRUCTION

CHAPTER 2-1
SOILS, ROCKS, AND DRAINAGE

John E. Reinfurt
Geotechnical Project Manager
Sverdrup Civil, Inc.
St. Louis, Missouri

INTRODUCTION

Soils and rocks are important materials to be considered in the design, construction, and performance of all facilities with which they interface or support. They also may be the sole construction material for dams, levees, and embankments. Soil and rock may be used in their natural state, or they may be remolded or chemically treated under controlled procedures to provide uniform design performance values and characteristics. When rock is found as a continuous consolidated layer, it is referred to as *bedrock*.

Since these materials have a great influence on the design and performance of any structure or utility, it is essential that a competent and experienced geotechnical engineer determine the design parameters and develop proper construction procedures and methods.

The geotechnical engineer will determine the nature and condition of the soil and rock to be encountered (or influenced) by the proposed facility by reviewing the stratigraphic column of the materials. This is done by taking borings, digging test pits, and performing other investigative procedures.

Borings are a basic and universal method used to penetrate and sample the soil and rock and to study water conditions below the ground surface. Samples are obtained according to established procedures as the borings advance. Standard penetration tests involve driving split spoon (split pipe), which results in a measurement of driving resistance in blow counts and provides a sample for viewing and possible testing. Thin-walled tubes also are pushed into the soil to obtain relatively undisturbed samples for laboratory testing or visual inspection. More sophisticated sampling and testing equipment and procedures may be used as dictated by the particular engineer and the materials and conditions encountered. Rock samples usually are obtained with core barrels, which cut a core of rock and retain it for withdrawal.

A boring log is a record of each boring that includes the date, location, elevations of the various soil strata, equipment used, personnel involved, and other pertinent general information. Detailed information derived from the boring is usually recorded beside a scaled vertical column to graphically represent the materials and conditions encountered. The geotechnical engineer prepares this record, which appropriately describes essential features at the correct location on the column. Standard penetration, pocket penetrometer, and other test determinations also will be recorded. These tests provide a measure of the strength and density parameters which may be used for preliminary evaluations.

For engineering purposes, soil is composed of mineral particles that can be separated by mechanical means. Air, water, or organic matter also may be present. The solid particles are materials derived from the physical and chemical weathering of rocks and the organic remains of plant and animal organisms. Rock is a natural aggregate of minerals bonded together by strong permanent cohesive forces that may require great force or power to disaggregate. However, irregularities and discontinuities appear in the rocks as erosion, weathering, and other forces deteriorate the rock mass, eventually creating soil.

Soils are described as residual or transported, according to the origin of their constituents. Residual soil is soil that has remained at its place of origin and may exhibit remanent rock structure. These soils are generally strong and stable, but may be surrounded by or contain blocks, pinnacles, or slabs of unweathered rock. Should the soil be compressible, the combination with relatively unweathered rocks may create foundation problems. Transported soils are the product of rock weathering and/or alteration: water, wind, or other means have carried them to a new location. Several deposits of transported soil, and most soils of organic origin, are soft or loose and unstable and may cause significant foundation problems.

SOIL PROPERTIES AND CLASSIFICATION

The distinction between different kinds of soil are based on the index properties, that is, the physical attributes of the soil particles and soil aggregates. Such properties can readily be determined by simple classification tests made according to the standard procedures of the American Society for Testing and Materials (ASTM). These can be correlated with more complex engineering properties such as compressibility, permeability, strength, and swelling.

For engineering purposes, classification may be in accordance with the Unified Classification System (Table 1-1). Boring logs should include descriptions of the basic soil group to which the materials belong (such as sand, silt, clay, organic soil, or gravel) and include adequate descriptions pertaining to relative density, consistency, color, odor, grain shape, stratification, interbedding, varied layering, and minor constituents. The method of deposition or origin should preferably be given.

TABLE 1-1 Soil Classification Chart

MAJOR DIVISIONS			GROUP SYMBOLS	TYPICAL NAMES
COARSE-GRAINED SOILS More than 50% retained on No. 200 sieve*	GRAVELS 50% or more of coarse fraction retained on No. 4 sieve	CLEAN GRAVELS	GW	Well-graded gravels and gravel-sand mixtures, little or no fines
			GP	Poorly graded gravels and gravel-sand mixtures, little or no fines
		GRAVELS WITH FINES	GM	Silty gravels, gravel-sand-silt mixtures
			GC	Clayey gravels, gravel-sand-clay mixtures
	SANDS More than 50% of coarse fraction passes No. 4 sieve	CLEAN SANDS	SW	Well-graded sands and gravelly sands, little or no fines
			SP	Poorly graded sands and gravelly sands, little or no fines
		SANDS WITH FINES	SM	Silty sands, sand-silt mixtures
			SC	Clayey sands, sand-clay mixtures
FINE-GRAINED SOILS 50% or more passes No. 200 sieve*	SILTS AND CLAYS Liquid limit 50% or less		ML	Inorganic silts, very fine sands, rock flour, silty or clayey fine sands
			CL	Inorganic clays of low to medium plasticity, gravelly clays, sandy clays, silty clays, lean clays
			OL	Organic silts and organic silty clays of low plasticity
	SILTS AND CLAYS Liquid limit greater than 50%		MH	Inorganic silts, micaceous or diatomaceous fine sands or silts, elastic silts
			CH	Inorganic clays of high plasticity, fat clays
			OH	Organic clays of medium to high plasticity
Highly Organic Soils			PT	Peat, muck, and other highly organic soils

*Based on the material passing the 3-in. (75-mm) sieve.

TABLE 1-1 Soil Classification Chart (*Continued*)

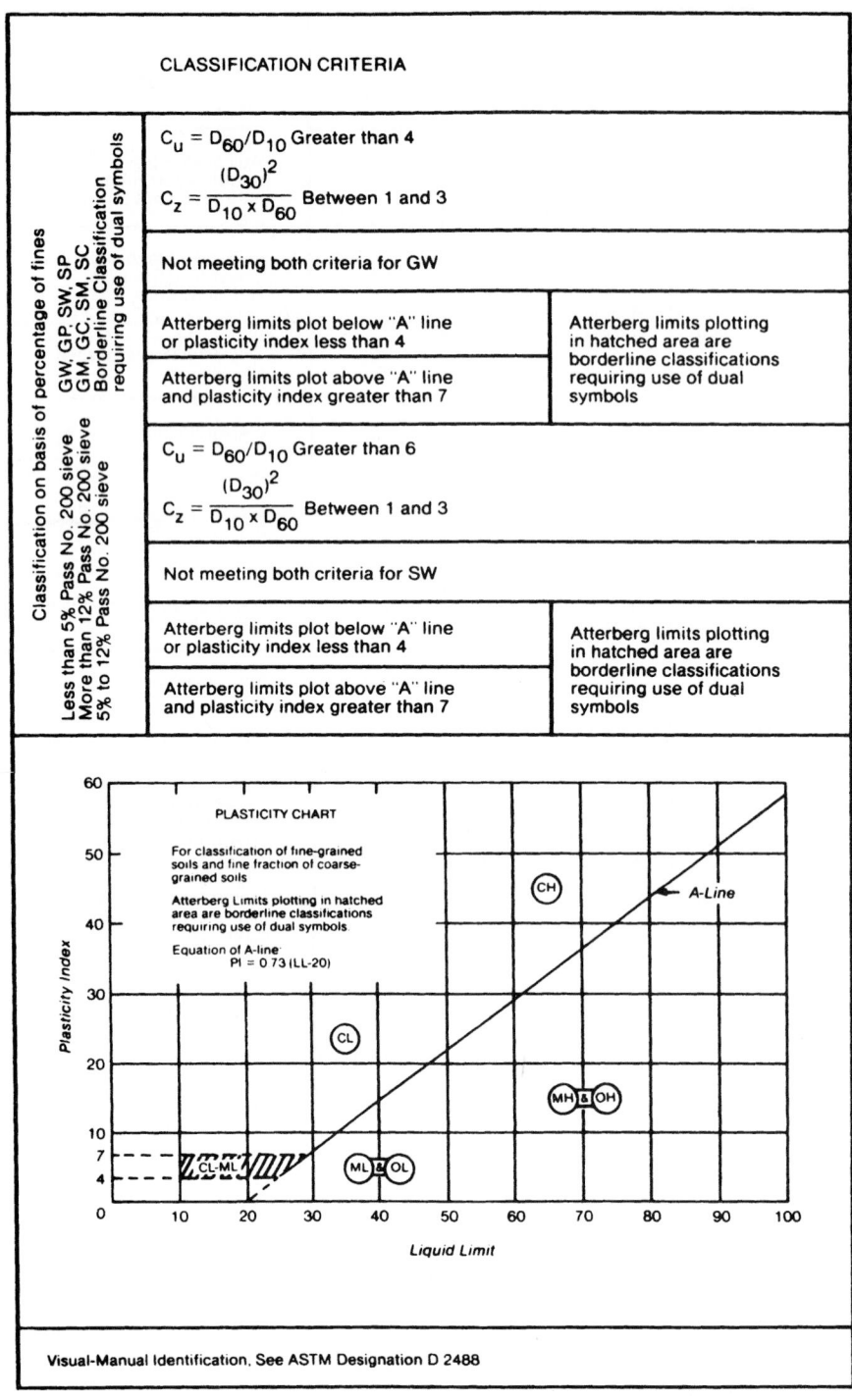

CLASSIFICATION CRITERIA

Classification on basis of percentage of fines

GW, GP, SW, SP — Less than 5% Pass No. 200 sieve
GM, GC, SM, SC — More than 12% Pass No. 200 sieve
Borderline Classification requiring use of dual symbols — 5% to 12% Pass No. 200 sieve

$C_u = D_{60}/D_{10}$ Greater than 4

$C_z = \dfrac{(D_{30})^2}{D_{10} \times D_{60}}$ Between 1 and 3

Not meeting both criteria for GW

Atterberg limits plot below "A" line or plasticity index less than 4	Atterberg limits plotting in hatched area are borderline classifications requiring use of dual symbols
Atterberg limits plot above "A" line and plasticity index greater than 7	

$C_u = D_{60}/D_{10}$ Greater than 6

$C_z = \dfrac{(D_{30})^2}{D_{10} \times D_{60}}$ Between 1 and 3

Not meeting both criteria for SW

Atterberg limits plot below "A" line or plasticity index less than 4	Atterberg limits plotting in hatched area are borderline classifications requiring use of dual symbols
Atterberg limits plot above "A" line and plasticity index greater than 7	

PLASTICITY CHART

For classification of fine-grained soils and fine fraction of coarse-grained soils

Atterberg Limits plotting in hatched area are borderline classifications requiring use of dual symbols.

Equation of A-line:
PI = 0.73 (LL-20)

Plasticity Index / Liquid Limit

CH   A-Line   CL   MH & OH   ML & OL   CL-ML

Visual-Manual Identification, See ASTM Designation D 2488

Source: 1980 Annual Book of ASTM Standards, Part 19, "Soil and Rock; Building Stones," Standard D 2487, pp. 377–388. Used by permission.

Particle Size and Shape

Particle size has the most influence on the physical characteristics; it is evaluated by determining the size and the distribution of sizes with sieve and/or hydrometer analyses. The results are conveniently presented on the semilogarithmic particle-size curve shown in Fig. 1-1, which provides information from which the permeability of the soil can be estimated and shows whether it is poorly or well graded. Particle shape depends to some extent upon its mineralogical constituents, origin, and geologic history. Silts, sands, and gravels composed of hard minerals like quartz may be less rounded than those derived from softer minerals under similar weathering conditions. These hard or soft particles may be angular or subangular and, if well worn by abrasion or attrition during transportation, rounded. Clay particles are flat and elongated, or *lamellar*.

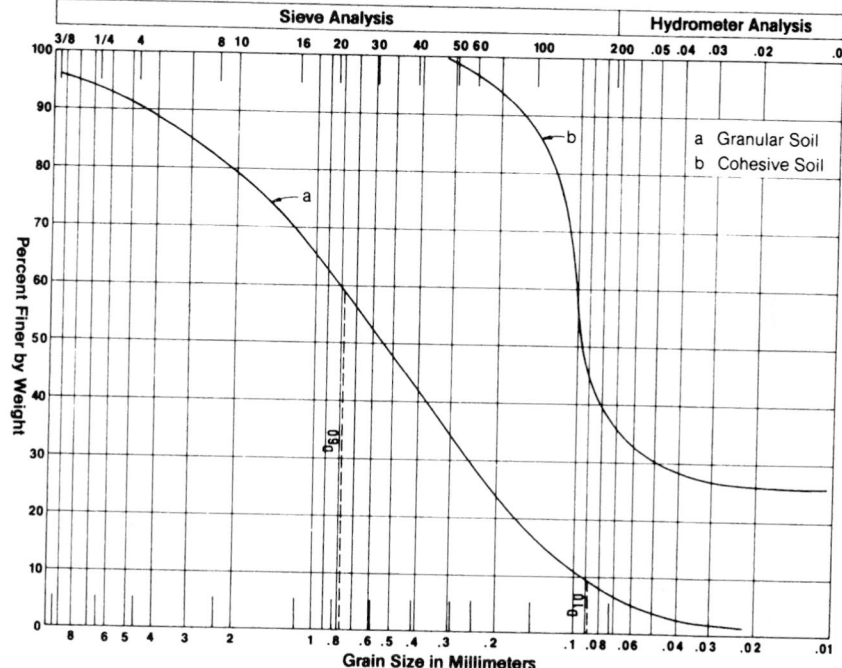

FIGURE 1-1   Grain-size distribution curve.

Soil Structure

Soil structure refers to the geometric arrangement of soil components. Clean sands, gravels, and silts have a single-grain structure that may be loose, honeycombed, or compact. Clay soils have dispersed or flocculent arrangements. A matrix binder which holds soil particles may create a framework of coarse grains either held in contact or held apart to form a "void-bound" structure with large empty spaces. The weight-volume relationship and other engineering properties described in the following paragraphs are used frequently to judge a soil structure.

Weight-Volume Relationships

In practice, the unit weight (v), moisture content (w), and specific gravity of solids (G_s), are readily determined, and from these the volume of air, water, and solids can be computed.

Some of these material characteristics not only are related to each other, but they can be correlated to many soil-engineering properties. For instance, the void ratio and the density are influenced by particle gradation as well as arrangement, and they are inversely related to each other. A soil having a high density is likely to reduce potential settlement, permeability, and the detrimental effects of water absorption, and increase both the bearing capacity and the shearing resistance.

Relative Density

The compactness or looseness of a granular soil, such as gravel, sand, inorganic silt, or a combination of these, can range from a minimum for that particular soil to a maximum to be compared to the existing void ratio. The relative density is expressed as a percentage between the loosest and densest. Thus, a soil would have a relative density of 0 in its loosest possible condition and 100 percent in its densest condition (Fig. 1-2).

Consistency

The consistency of undisturbed cohesive soil depends on its unconfined compressive strength and is described as very soft, soft, medium, stiff, very stiff, and hard (Table 1-2). The effect of

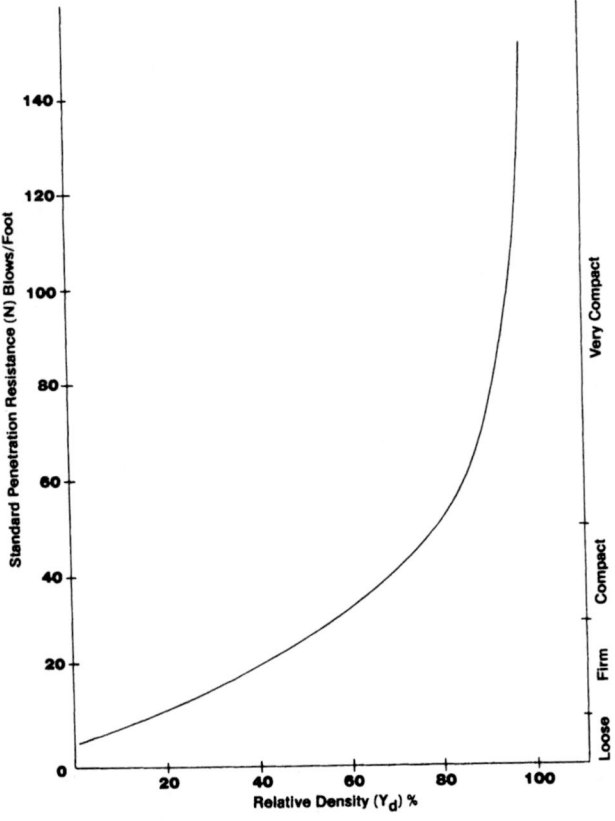

FIGURE 1-2 Standard penetration—relative density comparison.

TABLE 1-2   Consistency and Strength of Cohesive Soil

Consistency	Field identification	Unconfined compressive strength q_u, tons/ft²*
Very soft	Easily penetrated and deeply penetrated by fist or comparable blunt object	Less than 0.25
Soft	Easily and moderately penetrated a few inches by thumb or short blunt stick	0.25–0.5
Medium	Penetrated by thumb or stick, with effort up to 1½ in	0.5–1.0
Stiff	Can be indented by thumb and penetrated about ¼ in by ⅜-in-diam stick with much effort	1.0–2.0
Very stiff	Easily penetrated by fingernail; stick makes slight indentation	2.0–4.0
Hard	No penetration with stick; fingernail slightly penetrates	>4.0

*1 ton/ft² = 0.9765 kg/cm²; the units are therefore used interchangeably. Cohesive strength c and shear strength s are equal, and each is equal to one-half the unconfined compressive strength.

remolding on the consistency of a clay is the degree of sensitivity (S_t) expressed as a ratio of the unconfined compressive strength of the undisturbed soil to that of remolded soil at the same moisture content. The values of S_t vary between 2 and 4 for most clays, but for "quick" clays they may exceed 16.

The consistency of remolded soil changes with an increase or decrease in moisture content. With very high moisture content the soil may be fluid, and as the moisture decreases the soil will range down through a viscous fluid, a plastic solid, and a semisolid to a solid. Atterberg limits show the moisture content between the liquid, plastic, semisolid, and solid states of cohesive soil. These are known as the liquid (LL), plastic (PL), and the shrinkage (SL) limits. The numerical difference between the liquid and plastic limits is termed the plasticity index (PI or I_p). Liquid and plastic limits are both dependent on the amount and type of clay in a soil, but the plasticity index is ordinarily dependent only on the amount of clay present. With increasing LL, both the permeability and compressibility increase in soils having identical PI. Soils of equal LL show a decrease in permeability with an increase in PI, and the compressibility does not change.

Permeability

Permeability depends on the size of the voids between particles, which in turn depends on the size, shape, and the state of packing. Under identical voids and densities, the coarse-grained soils (sands and gravels) are more permeable than the fine-grained silts and clays. Where soils have similar textural characteristics, the permeability declines as the density rises. The permeability of the soil influences its drainage, compressibility, and susceptibility to frost action.

Capillarity

Water flows into unsaturated soils located above the groundwater table because of surface tension and attraction to the water at the phreatic surface. The height to which the water will rise depends on both the affinity of the soil for water and the size of the voids. For equal affinities, both the height and rate of rise are inversely related to the size of the voids. The height of capillary movement also is affected by evaporation and by changes in the groundwater level. For example, open gravel or rock roads that have given satisfactory performance for years may, when paved, develop problems from subgrade weakening due to capillary saturation.

Porewater Pressure and Effective Stress

The water in voids in saturated soil exerts a pressure (as it does in any vessel) that is called porewater pressure. The pressure is calculated by determining the height of the vertical unit column of water below the point of phreatic surface. The effective stress in any direction is the difference between all stresses (total stress) in that direction and the porewater pressure.

Both the deformability and the strength of a soil are dependent on effective stress. For a layer of fine-grained soil rapidly loaded locally, the viscous retardation of porewater flow builds up excess porewater pressure. This pressure is not only a function of the loading change, but also a function of soil properties. Excess porewater pressures can cause soil movements and failures.

Shear Strength

The shear strength s of a soil in any direction is the maximum shear stress that can be developed in the soil structure in that direction, c is a measure of cohesion, ϕ is the angle of internal friction, and, σ is the normal stress on the shear plane. The values of c and ϕ for any soil at a specified initial moisture content and unit weight depend on the conditions under which the loading is applied to the soil. Saturated clays tested under undrained conditions exhibit a constant shearing resistance. The angle of internal friction for the same clay tested under drained conditions may be as much as 30°. Clean sands and gravels, dry or saturated, do not display any cohesion. The angle of internal friction for dense sand varies between 33° and 46°, for loose sand between 28° and 34°, for dense inorganic silt between 25° and 35°, and for loose inorganic silt between 20° and 30°. For an extreme, dense, well-graded gravel, ϕ may be as high as 50°.

Shear-strength properties can be determined in the laboratory with triaxial compression (Fig. 1-3) or direct shear tests. In the field, standard penetration, pocket penetrometer, vane shear, or plate-loading tests are some that are used. In all cases, evaluation must be made with judgment. Factors affecting the results of soil strength tests are type of soil and test, size and shape of sample, dry density and moisture content, method and rate of loading, drainage conditions during test, permeability and structure, climatic conditions, sample disturbance, and time between sampling and testing.

Volume Change

Certain clay soils have large volume change with a change in moisture, that is, swelling with the addition of water and shrinking with dehydration. When swelling, they produce pressure that may seriously damage buildings and other facilities. These volume-change soils are difficult to recognize in borings; their potential for swelling and the pressures they will exert by swelling must be determined by testing.

Soil deformation may be defined as volume change attributed to rearrangement of solid particles, a change in shape of solid particles, and deformation by extrusion of pore water or

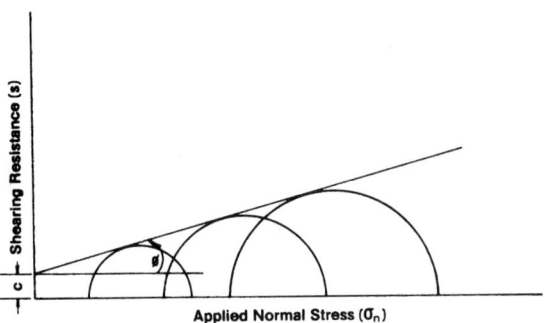

FIGURE 1-3 Strength envelope for soil.

air. In cohesionless soils, and to some degree in clays, the distortion of grains is mainly responsible for a volume change which is largely elastic and consequently reversible. Particle slipping and bending, and extrusion of porewater and air are major mechanisms in cohesive soils that exhibit slow time-dependent deformations, which may or may not be reversible depending on the interaction of many factors.

To determine time-dependent compressibility or swelling characteristics, tests are made on undisturbed or remolded specimens as a uniaxial test with restraint of lateral deformation. The results, the pressure-to-void ratio and time-to-compression ratio or swell, are graphically presented in Fig. 1-4.

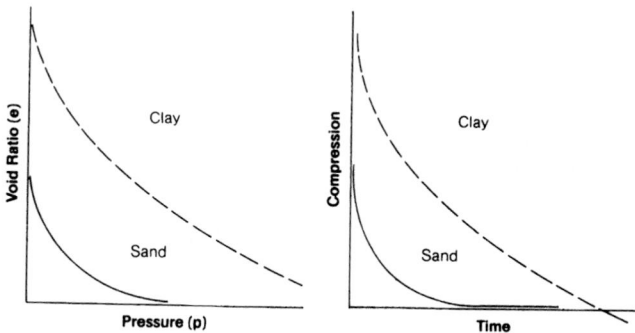

FIGURE 1-4   Diagrams of compressibility of soil.

Clays and sands undergo a reduction in void ratio as pressure increases. For sand, the rate of reduction decreases with load increases. The major part of the compression in sands under an increment of load takes place instantaneously. Clays require considerable time to attain final compression under a load increment.

Depending upon geologic history, soils are divided into normally consolidated or preconsolidated (overconsolidated) categories. The first never has been subjected to a pressure greater than the present overburden and, in the case of clay, has a liquidity index (I_L) of about 0.6 to 1.0. The second has had a pressure greater than the present overburden, and has an I_p varying from 0.0 to 0.6 for clay. Generally, normally consolidated rocks are more compressible than preconsolidated ones.

Unlike adding load, which causes settlement, removing the load can cause the soil to rise or heave. Heaving can occur in the bottom of an excavation because of stress release, excess hydrostatic pressure, and lateral displacement of soil from below.

CLASSIFICATION AND PROPERTIES OF ROCK

The behavior of a rock mass is governed by mechanical properties and also by the number and nature of discontinuities in the rock. Lithology, weathering, quality, structure, ground water, permeability, and engineering properties are significant factors to be considered during design and construction.

Lithology

Rock materials are classified by such lithologic terms as shale, granite, schist, and limestone; these reflect the mineralogy, texture, and fabric of the rock. Lithology suggests the mechanical properties and helps associate in situ features. For example, schists have foliated textures with directional differences in both strength and deformation moduli.

Weathering

Weathering is the action of altering the rock properties of color, texture, composition, or form. The effects extend below the earth's surface by groundwater movement through and around grains or along discontinuities or fissures. The variations in depth of weathering are often dictated by the differences in lithology. The strength of the rock is reduced by an increased degree of weathering. This condition usually will be described in boring logs in relative terms.

Rock Quality

Rock is characterized by its discontinuities and degree of weathering or alteration. Rock quality is used to define the approximate bounds of utility and to locate zones of poor quality. Rock quality designation (RQD) is a procedure based on modified core recovery that is most frequently used in estimating average rock quality. An RQD of less than 25 percent represents in situ rocks of poor quality, while over 90 percent is indicative of excellent quality. If applied, RQD should be noted in the boring logs.

Rock Structure

Discontinuities such as shears, shear-zones, foliations, and faults influence the behavior of rock through interactions between rock blocks and discontinuities. Several engineering properties of discontinuities including attitude, frequency, location, continuity, shape, roughness, tightness, and coating and/or filling materials play significant roles in assessing behaviors of both the rock mass and individual blocks of rock contained in them.

Permeability

In most rocks, the permeability is governed by the joints, fissures, or other openings present within the mass. High hydrostatic pressures can cause instability along planes of discontinuity, loss of strength, and excessive water discharge.

Strength

For intact rock, the uniaxial compressive strength and the modulus of elasticity at a stress level equal to one-half the ultimate strength of the intact rock are used to classify the rock materials and to verify the degree of weathering or alteration in the rock. The compressive strength also is used in ascertaining bearing capacities in certain jointed rocks.

The strength along discontinuities generally is derived from the basic shear strength and the resistance against dilation due to interlocking surface projections. Plane discontinuities may have a very low angle of inclination, whereas very irregular surfaces may display a high inclination.

Shearing resistance along the discontinuity depends also on the roughness and character of filling materials. A smooth, slick-sided joint may display low resistance, while the very rough surfaces will show much higher resistance. The shear strength of fill in discontinuities is largely dictated by the thickness and properties of the filling materials such as composition, grain size, moisture content, and plasticity. Highly plastic clayey fills of significant thickness generally have low frictional resistances. However, in discontinuities with very thin filling or coating materials, the initial strength properties may be dictated by the filling or coating, but the final strength may be controlled by the rock surface properties as the filling or coating is ruptured through.

Swelling

Free swell or excessive swelling pressure ordinarily is encountered in fill materials and in weathered or altered zones. The extent of these behaviors is dictated by the amount, composition, and properties of the material. Clay-mineral and particle-size determinations, Atterberg limit tests, and free-swell tests may be used in ascertaining the swelling index properties of rock minerals.

DRAINAGE

Surface and subsurface water must be considered as essential elements of design and construction. The subsurface investigation program includes obtaining information on subsurface water conditions and reliable location of the groundwater table at the time of the study. Any available historical data can be very useful to the designers.

Local, state, or national agencies may have requirements for the drainage design and may specify certain design procedures. These requirements will assist in determining runoff and sizing the drainage system.

Surface Drainage

All parts of the facility require good performance from the surface drainage system. The areal drainage pattern and surface topography will affect the site grading plan, which will include disposing or rearranging surface materials to eliminate surface water problems both during and after construction. The plan also must consider environmental protection regulations for the site. Topographic maps prepared by the U.S. Geological Survey are useful for analyzing both topography and drainage, and show elevation contours, bodies of water, streams, and other features from which the rates of water runoff can be established. Aerial photographs also can provide useful information for site evaluation. For final designs, however, an on-site survey is needed for more accurate detail.

Surface topography, precipitation, rate of runoff, and the nature of the soil must be considered in preparing a good drainage design. These parameters also should receive careful consideration when establishing both the floor elevations and grading plan elevations, since building distress often has been caused by inadequate drainage of the surface.

Ditches, swales, sewers, and earth slopes are the common ways of removing surface water to avoid ponding or water flowing into the excavation. Slope stability and erosivity should be analyzed to predict the possibility of slope failure and blocking of ditches and sewers. Silt fences or retention ponds may be required to retain eroded soil on the site. If space permits, ditches may be deepened to lower the ground water, but this is usually limited to a shallow depth.

Silty and fine sand soils require flat slopes, while soils with clay can be relatively steeper. Water seeping out of slopes exerts a seepage pressure which leaves the slopes less stable. To prevent erosion and scour, all slopes should have a protective covering compatible with both the soil type and the water velocities. During embankment construction and before each rain, embankments should be sloped for drainage and compacted to a smooth surface for quick runoff. Permanent slope protection should be installed as soon as a slope is finished.

Slope protection may be obtained from many different materials. For example, sodding or seeding works well on many slopes, while gravel or rock blankets may be selected for others. The availability of materials in an area may influence the type of material to be used. The higher water velocities in ditches may require using riprap, concrete, or asphaltic pavement for slope protection. Many specialty products provide good protection, and these may be economically feasible if local materials are limited. Wire baskets or "sausages" filled with smaller rocks than those required for riprap can contain a mass as effectively as riprap. Soil additives that serve as a cementing material to soil may increase the soil's erosion resistance sufficiently to withstand the design velocities.

Strength, workability, trafficability, and other soil characteristics will change with soil moisture changes. The best soil condition for most construction situations may be a dense soil at or very near its optimum moisture content. When a soil used for embankment construction becomes wet, the moisture content must be adjusted downward by either drying out the soil, blending it with other dryer material, or using additives (lime, cement, or silica grout) to gain stability.

Groundwater and Subsurface Drainage

Geotechnical investigation programs obtain information on groundwater; however, the design must consider the changes in groundwater depth that may come with seasonal change, amount of precipitation, and other natural phenomena. Water wells in the area, their effects on the groundwater level, and the effects of their retirement from service may be very important. Piezometers installed in bore holes will provide both short- and long-term information on groundwater elevations.

When the depth of excavation is greater than the distance to free water in a soil, drainage will be required during construction and may be required for the finished facility. In relatively impervious soils like clays and silty clays, the water inflow may be on the order of a seep, although pervious soils may provide an abundant flow. Drainage will permit construction in-the-dry and maintain the stability of the slopes and bottom.

A sump with ditches in the bottom of an excavation will collect water for pumping from the excavation, but well points, wells, or other extensive measures may be necessary for more severe water conditions. Berms and well points in stages on the berms may be the dewatering method for saturated slopes. Deep wells can withdraw large volumes of water to lower the ground water below the excavation depth in very pervious soils.

Drainage systems are used to keep water from contacting completed structures. An impervious blanket is placed at the surface to slope away from the building and carry surface water away. Perforated pipe sloped to drain in pervious material at or below the foundation level will remove moderate amounts of water. Such a system may be necessary under floor slabs to keep them dry and prevent uplift. Figure 1-5 shows a subsurface drainage system.

Drainage systems must be kept clean to function as intended, and an occasional clean-out opening should be considered for long runs of pipe. Most systems are closed, and the only infiltration may be from the particular soil being drained. A filter of graded sand and rock layers or filter fabric will prevent soil migration (see Fig. 1-6). The filter fabric is more easily installed and permits various arrangements.

An alternative to drainage is to waterproof building components that may be in contact with free water. Waterproofing must be carefully installed and may be expensive. Since waterproofing will not relieve water pressure against walls and slabs, this pressure must be included in the wall and slab design. Figure 1-7 shows a waterproofing design method.

COMPACTION AND STABILIZATION OF SOIL AND ROCK

When soil and rock are used in construction, they must be carefully considered and controlled to ensure a satisfactory product. Many aspects of construction procedures are not understood, especially compaction and stabilization processes. The design engineer of a plant facility must be cognizant of the behavior of materials and the operations necessary to obtain the desired results. If any portion of the earthwork operations is allowed to get out of control, future plant performance may be jeopardized.

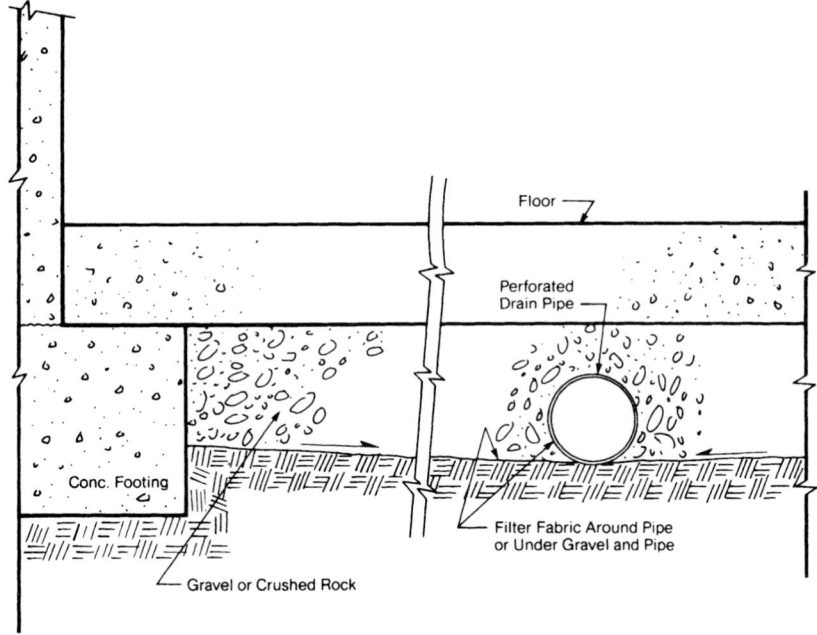

FIGURE 1-5   Subsurface drainage system.

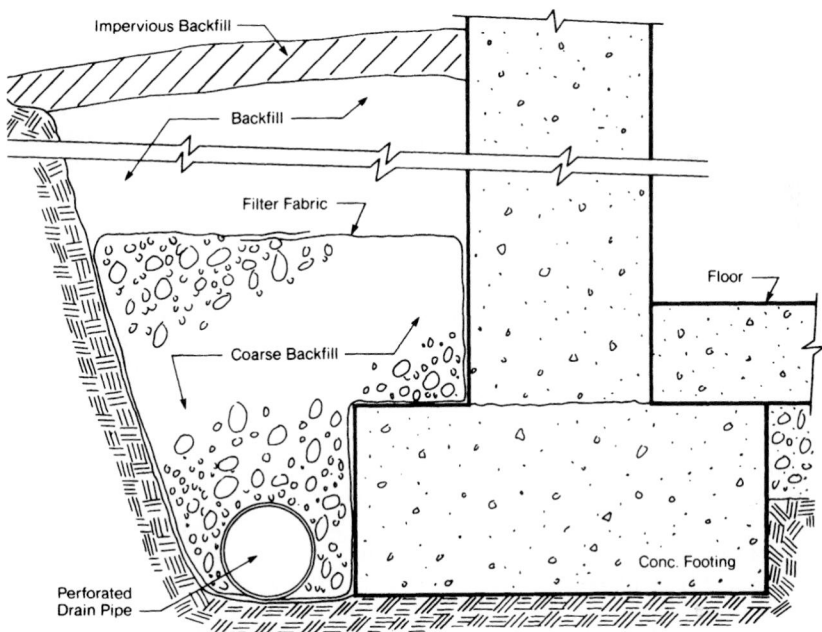

FIGURE 1-6   Method of preventing soil migration into drainage system.

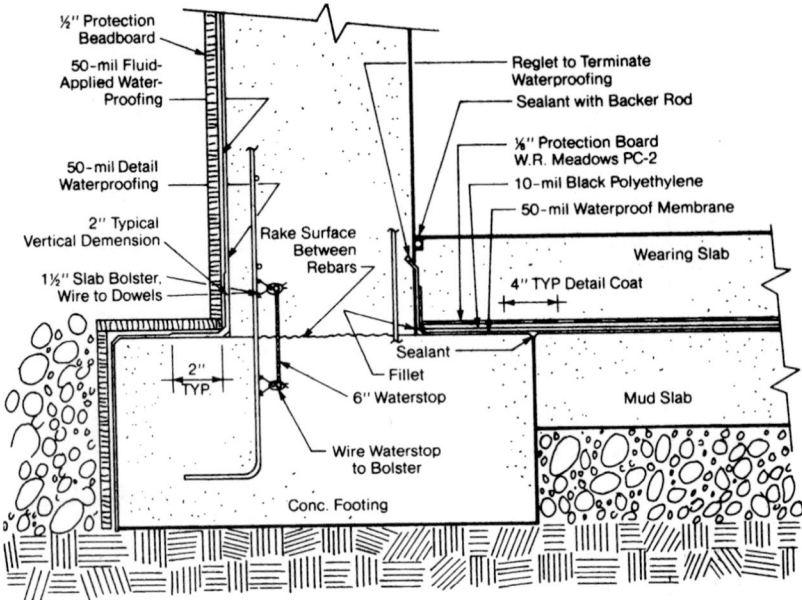

FIGURE 1-7 Waterproofing design method.

Soils and Rock as Construction Materials

In building construction, the most important use of soil and rock is in the construction of engineered fills. Fills are generally used to provide level building and plant sites. Engineered fills are fills that are properly designed, controlled, and constructed to support structures safely with acceptable settlements.

Control over soil and rock used as construction materials generally is limited to the materials available and the cost to excavate and haul the materials to the project site. In most areas, the materials are limited and the engineer must carefully choose the best available materials.

The greatest control of the soil and rock properties is through compaction. Sometimes the soil and rock materials must be altered by mixing or altering their composition to improve their behavior. A term for the processed soil and rock is stabilization.

Compaction

Compaction is a process to increase the density of a soil or fractured rock mass by rolling, tampering, or vibrating. Compaction procedures are familiar to design engineers and earthwork contractors. However, some aspects of compaction are not well understood. Three factors affect the process of increasing the density of a soil and fractured rock mass: moisture content, compaction effort, and material characteristics.

The geotechnical or design engineer usually establishes the compaction requirements of a project. For building sites, refer to the standard Proctor Test (ASTM D698) or the modified Proctor Test (ATM D1557). Generally, the maximum dry density by the modified method is 3 to 8 lb/ft^3 greater than the standard Proctor Test. For each soil with a given amount of compaction, there is an optimum moisture content at which the dry density is a maximum (Fig. 1-8).

In general, the engineer specifies that the earth fill material be compacted to 90, 95, or 100 percent of the standard or modified Proctor Test.

The use of rock fill beneath a plant site must be considered carefully. Rock fill must be compacted to minimize settlement. The design engineer should ensure that voids are minimized by specifying that all large rock fragments are surrounded by smaller rock and soil particles. Dumped rock fills tend to settle with time and could result in high maintenance cost during the life of the plant.

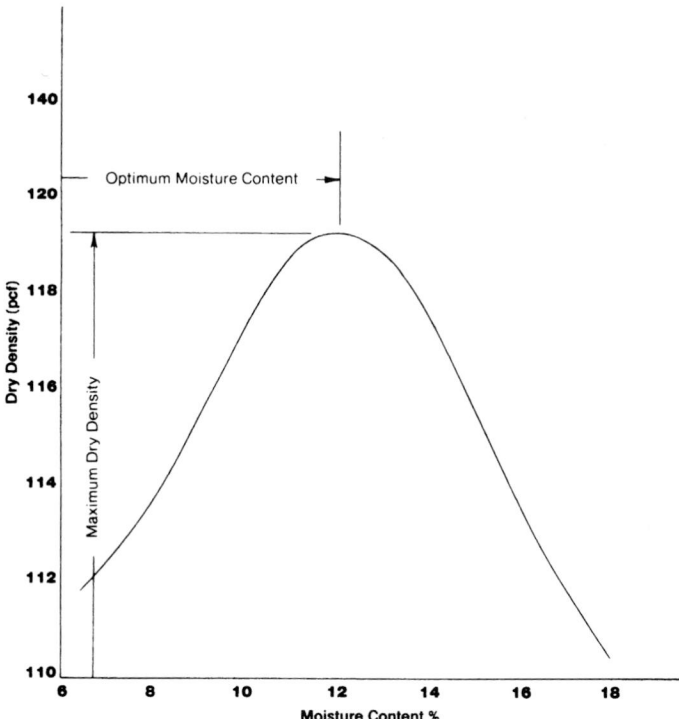

FIGURE 1-8 Relationship between dry density and moisture content for constant amount of compaction.

Stabilization

Sometimes the soils and rocks available cannot perform as required. To improve the properties of soil and rock, the earth materials are required to be stabilized. For improving earth materials at the site, in-place treatment can be used to decrease settlement, increase strength, and decrease seepage loss. Stabilization requires the expertise of qualified design professionals, as well as specialty contractors.

Surface treatments include soil cement lime stabilization and chemical stabilization. For stabilization of deep, loose sand deposits, vibrofloatation; dynamic compaction; and compaction, cement, and chemical grouting techniques are effective means. Where limestone sinkholes and old mine cavities are encountered below plant sites, grouting techniques have been used to fill the voids. Sometimes, foundation systems are designed to span the cavity. Other stabilization techniques are available, including soil freezing; however, their use is generally a last resort effort and usually very expensive.

CHAPTER 2-2
FOUNDATIONS

Navin H. Shah

Deputy Manager, Structural Section
Sverdrup Facilities, Inc.
St. Louis, Missouri

John E. Reinfurt

Geotechnical Project Manager
Sverdrup Civil, Inc.
St. Louis, Missouri

REVIEW

The foundation is the part of the structure that distributes the weight of the structure and superimposed loads, such as live, wind, and seismic loads, to the underlying earth or rock substrata. This distribution may occur by direct bearing of a footing on soil or rock or by transmitting the loads to a deeper strata through piles or drilled piers.

Many materials have been used for constructing shallow foundations, including timber and steel grillages, clay masonry, cut rock slabs, and cast-in-place concrete. Except for cast-in-place concrete, most of these systems generally are not used today. Cast-in-place concrete foundations usually are reinforced, especially where heavy concentrated loads are to be supported.

Piling and drilled piers are basically the same types and materials that have been in use for many years. However, their length and capacity have increased considerably.

GEOTECHNICAL INVESTIGATIONS REQUIRED

Knowledge of the subsurface materials and conditions that will interface with a structure is a critical requirement. Procedures and methods for obtaining this information are given in

Chap. 2-1, "Soils, Rocks, and Drainage." This information will indicate the best site location for a building, the possible need for dewatering, the data needed to establish the foundation support, the anticipated performance, and the need for bracing and shoring for foundations and pipe trenches. A geotechnical investigation will provide information and samples from which allowable bearing pressures, consolidation characteristics, shear strengths, swell potential, and other design parameters can be determined.

The investigative program must be extensive and go beyond the limits of vertical influence for both shallow or deep foundations. The cost of a geotechnical investigation program and selection of a foundation system is a very small percentage of the total cost of the project, but the overall performance of the structure depends upon the performance of the foundation and the materials beneath it. Where there is flexibility in locating the structure, or when the exact location, size, and shape of the building are not firm, the program must extend to the possible horizontal limits of the building footprint. An experienced geotechnical engineer can plan an effective program, but since earth materials vary in consistency and stratification, there must be flexibility in the program as the investigation progresses.

If the geotechnical program is planned after conceptual studies of the new facility have been made, the anticipated loading conditions, floor and grade elevations, and any special features should be given to the geotechnical engineer who will then emphasize and intensify the investigation in the critical areas.

The geotechnical investigative program includes determining the groundwater conditions at the time of the investigation. Piezometers may be installed to study porewater pressures in isolated soil zones or observation wells to observe static water levels for the period of the program or for extended periods of time. All possibilities of water and its influence must be considered in establishing floor and foundation elevations, the need for drainage, and the problems and additional cost inherent in constructing each type of foundation.

Unsatisfactory soil at a site may be removed and replaced under controlled compaction procedures, removed and replaced with other material, or altered by stabilization. Additional information on compaction and stabilization is given in Chap. 2-1, "Soils, Rocks and Drainage."

DESIGN CONSIDERATIONS IN SELECTING THE FOUNDATION

After the geotechnical investigation has been completed, a foundation type must be selected. The selection is based on many factors relating to the earth materials, groundwater, and the structure. Among these are magnitude of the load; type of load—dead, live, wind, seismic, or dynamic; application of load—vertical, lateral, and moments; depth to supporting strata; supporting capacity of the soil or rock; settlement anticipated under load; and the type of structure to be supported.

A foundation system should be designed and placed at a practical depth to prevent damage or undermining from frost, swelling soils, and future construction activities. In addition, the foundation must not sink into the ground or settle enough to damage the structure.

Types of Foundations

The three basic types of foundations used in building construction are footings directly bearing on soil or rock, piles, and drilled piers. The footings may be an individual column footing, combined footings supporting several columns, or a mat under the entire structure. Piles and drilled piers may be single or in groups. A concrete cap similar to the footings described previously is required to transmit the column loads to the piles and drilled piers. The decision on the foundation type and the interrelation of column supports must be based on the factors given in the preceding paragraph.

A column placed near a property line may require strapping a wall footing to an interior column footing. The imposition of large moments may require combining the footings in strips or mats.

Shallow Foundations.   Shallow foundations are located at the highest level below structure where adequate bearing material is available. The minimum depth of footing below grade is governed by either the normal frost penetration depth or the appreciable shrinkage and swelling of the soil due to changes in moisture content in the soil.

With rock-bearing footings the settlement under the structure is generally not a concern, but with soil-bearing footings the maintenance of equal settlement under dead loads is very critical. It may require proportioning the footings for reduced bearing pressures as the column load and the footing size increase.

Generally, the exact amount of settlement that can occur is not critical as long as the design bearing pressure is not exceeded. The differential amount of settlement between footings causes problems in a structure. More settlement, of course, increases the possibility of large differential amounts.

The amount of settlement (total or differential) can have different significance depending on the type and use of the structure. In a structure designed with continuous beams or frames, differential settlement between columns can induce large stresses. Unless these stresses are added to the design parameters, structural distress or failure may occur. Even when a structure is designed to provide simple span beams between columns, this settlement can cause problems in the function of the structure. Elevator guides may require realignment, doors may bind in the jambs, pressure may crack the glass in sashes, and the walls may crack, allowing moisture to penetrate and start corroding the supporting members.

When the strata that are relatively close to the surface are not adequate to support the anticipated loads, the loads must be carried to a more competent material at a greater depth by drilled piers or piles.

Drilled Piers.   Drilled piers are generally greater than 24 in (60 cm) in diameter and are excavated using large power augers. Piers may be cased or uncased, with a straight shaft or with belled bottoms. The choice depends on the material and the depth of the pier. A material with sandy seams or saturated soils may require casing to be lowered into the hole as drilling progresses. To be economical, this casing must be pulled as the concrete is placed. Because of the instability of the soil and casing required, these piers will not be belled. Piers drilled in stiff, firm clays can be belled to provide increased bearing area on the supporting soil layer. When the piers are relatively short, drilling larger-diameter shafts may be more economical than changing the auger to a belling device. When the pier is to be drilled to rock, a belling device is not generally usable, and the straight shaft must be used. Piers generally require light reinforcing unless they are in an area of high seismic activity or are subject to lateral or tensile forces. The drill pier rig normally is a large piece of equipment requiring overhead clearances of 60 feet (18.3 m). However, specially adapted rigs capable of working in low headroom areas of 12 feet (3.7 m) or less are available.

Concrete to be placed in the piers should have a slump of 4 to 10 in (10.2 to 25.4 cm) and have an unobstructed fall through the center of the reinforcement to prevent segregation of materials. Vibrating the upper 6 to 10 feet (1.8 to 3.0 m) of the pier will minimize honeycomb, or voids.

Pile Foundations.   Piles are another method of obtaining support from deep strata. Piles are normally driven into the ground, but some pile types are drilled into the ground. The most commonly used piles are steel H, concrete-filled pipe, cast-in-place concrete, steel thin-shell, prestressed-precast concrete, augered uncased, and timber piles.

Friction timber piles are generally used in lengths up to 60 feet (18.3 m) and with loads up to 40 tons (355.9 kN). Steel H piles are used for long, high-capacity piling bearing either on rock or into a hard soil layer. Tapered precast-concrete piling is generally used for conditions similar to those for which timber piles are used, but with longer lengths and higher capacity. Pipe, shell, and large uniform-diameter precast piling are used for displacement friction or for end-bearing piling. The common range of loads now carried on piling is from 20 to 200 tons (177.9 to 1779 kN) per pile.

Where existing foundations must have their capacity increased or where new deep foundations must be constructed within existing structures, specialized techniques may need to be employed. Recently, the use of small diameter piles, sometimes called pin or mini-piles, and Augercast piles are used because their installation equipment can be adapted to low overhead clearances. These types of piles are installed by specialized foundation contractors.

When driving high-displacement piling, some preboring may be required to prevent disturbing either adjacent structures or previously driven piles. All field-cast piles in a cluster should be driven before filling with concrete. Piles should not be driven closer than 16 feet (4.9 m) from concrete that is less than 24 h old.

The selection of the pile type depends on the capacity and length required, the earth material encountered and, of course, the cost of the piling. All these factors must be studied for each job since they will vary considerably with site, time, and availability of materials.

While the settlement of spread footings is usually recognized, piling settlement is often forgotten. The total movement at the pile butt will result from the tip movement caused by both loading the soil and elastic shortening of the pile, which may be considerable in long piling. In addition, concrete piling can experience long-term shortening due to creep in the concrete.

Generally, clusters of vertical piling will resist the amount of lateral force to be expected in a building, given the bending of piles and passive resistance of soil against the cap. Where large lateral forces are expected, the piling may have to be driven on a batter, or angle. A slope of 1 horizontal to 2 vertical is a practical limit for driving batter piles. A pile cluster with batter piles must be checked for stability for all loading conditions, which may include the condition that there is no lateral load.

Although the batter piles may be adequate for all lateral loads, the effects of pile settlement should also be considered. For instance, lateral movement of the pile caps from pile settlement, while limited, may cause distress in a rigid-frame structure.

Installation Problems and Construction Effects on Nearby Structures

Finally, in selecting the type of foundation, consideration must be given to installation problems and construction effects on nearby structures. The expertise of qualified geotechnical and structural engineers is needed to fully analyze and predict the effects of proposed plant facilities adjacent to existing structures.

GROUNDWATER EFFECTS ON FOUNDATION DESIGN AND CONSTRUCTION

Groundwater is discussed under "Groundwater and Subsurface Drainage" in Chap. 2-1, "Soils, Rocks, and Drainage." In many cases, the groundwater table is subject to variations throughout the year. The table is usually not a straight line, but will show undulations when profiled across the plant site. The geotechnical investigation program will show a reliable elevation for the table at the time of the study. The variations may be determined by installing piezometers or observation wells and monitoring them for a period of time. The rate of variation depends on soil permeability, while the amount of water is influenced by streams, tides, water wells, nearby impoundments, and precipitation. Rain or snow melt may saturate the soil as it filters down to the groundwater table.

Soil moisture content is a most important soil characteristic. Consistency, stability, strength, and sometimes the unit weight are functions of moisture content. Foundation design procedures allow for moisture changes, and these procedures usually include the worst moisture condition for the in situ soils. Maintaining the integrity of the foundation support material during construction is important.

Removing water and lowering the groundwater table are very common construction tasks, and may be necessary during construction both to improve the working conditions and to ensure construction that meets the design intent. The soil trafficability may be very poor in the presence of free water, for example, and the workers and equipment may disturb and remold the soil in undesirable ways.

Water should be removed as it enters an excavation. In relatively impervious soils, the groundwater may be a small amount that decreases as the slopes dry out. Small amounts may be diverted into sumps and pumped out. Where the excavation goes below the groundwater table in soil whose permeability may be on the order of 5×10^{-6} cm/s, special dewatering procedures are required with well points or wells. The designer may specify the method, or leave it to the contractor's discretion. Conditions at some sites may require special protection for foundations because of flowing water, while precautions may be required at others to prevent settlement due to loss of ground water. Seasonal fluctuations may be significant enough to schedule construction to eliminate the need for a dewatering system.

Free water exerts a hydrostatic force against foundations, floor slabs, and walls. The force, independent of the soil, is equal to the unit weight of the water times the height to which it can accumulate. For this condition, either the structure must be designed to resist the force, or the water must be removed with a permanent dewatering system. Other methods such as grouting the soil may be used to alleviate or remove the problem. All dewatering in the construction sequence must be continued until the facility has been completed to the point that raising the groundwater level will not cause damage to the structure or interfere with its use.

STRUCTURAL DESIGN

The structural design of all foundations involves two considerations: first, the function of the foundation as a supporting unit and second, the function of the materials themselves used in constructing the foundations.

The function of the foundation involves the stiffness of the unit and the balance of the loads against the supporting pressure. The service load condition should be used for establishing the stability of the foundation to applied loads.

The stiffness becomes critical when large footings, mats, or strapped foundations are considered. While lack of stiffness may not cause complete failure, it can lead to settlement or twisting of the superstructure. A foundation that is not designed to balance supporting pressures uniformly against gravity loads will create eccentricity, again resulting in settlement or twisting in the superstructure.

Particular care must be taken in the structural design of large footings or mats by the strength design (ultimate load) procedures to assure that enough stiffness is built into the footing. If concrete is the controlling material and requires large amounts of reinforcing, the design is probably too flexible.

As in all parts of the structure, the idea is to provide a design for the least cost that will adequately support the structure. However, it should be remembered that the results of a foundation failure are not only very serious, but repairs are difficult and costly.

Spread footings may be constructed in three basic ways: a uniform-thickness slab, sloped top, and stepped top. Because of the high cost of field labor involved in the last two, footings are generally limited to uniform-thickness slabs.

Shallow Foundations

Shallow foundation footings are designed as flat plates with a vertical and/or horizontal load and/or moment transmitted to the footing by the column, pedestal, or wall that it supports. Design of a square or rectangular footing should be according to the requirements of the chapter on footings in ACI 318, "Building Code Requirements for Reinforced Concrete," published by the American Concrete Institute. The footing depth must be adequate to provide anchorage of column anchor bolts or reinforcement in either tension or compression as the design conditions require.

Most concrete design textbooks follow through the design calculations for isolated soil-bearing footings. The Concrete Reinforcing Steel Institute (CRSI) *Handbook* and Portland Cement Association (PCA) *Notes on ACI 318* are readily available and provide sample calculations.

The bar size selected should always be checked to see that the distance from the critical section for moment to the edge of the footing at least equals the development length of the reinforcing plus 3 inches (7.7 cm).

If a footing is subjected to large external moments, reinforcing may be required in the top of the footing.

Although the code is not too clear on the requirement for minimum reinforcing, it is generally accepted that the requirement for $A_s = 0.0018bt$ (where b = breadth of slab and t = total thickness) be used each way. If the footing is rectangular with moment basically in one direction only, it may be prudent to provide $A_s = 200/f_y bd$ (where f_y = stress at yield point and d = effective depth to the reinforcing) in that direction to prevent sudden failure.

Pile Foundations

The design of a concrete cap, also called a pile cap, supported on piles, follows the same basic structural design as for spread footings on soil. The difference is in the distribution and application of load. Also, the load carried by a pile cap is generally much greater than that carried by a spread footing of similar size. As a result, shear is usually a controlling factor in establishing the thickness of the pile cap.

When one- or two-piles are used, the pile caps must be tied together with beams to prevent bending caused by eccentricity of the load when the pilings are driven off-center. It is generally considered adequate to design these beams for a moment of the column load times the radial tolerances specified for the pile group.

In addition to the requirements for shear at distances of d or $d/2$ (where d = effective depth to the reinforcing) from the face of the column as outlined in the ACI code, shear should be checked around the perimeter of an individual pile or across the corner of a cap. For pile caps over a two-pile foundation in which the piles are located inside the critical sections for shear, the code commentary recommends checking the footing for shear in deep flexural members. Some design handbooks also check for an extension of the Corbel shear provisions in this case. It is also important to ensure that adequate bond of the tension reinforcing is provided beyond the outside face of the pile.

When pile foundations are used in seismic zones, the pile caps must be tied together with tension-compression struts to prevent lateral moment and subsequent failure of the piles or structure caused by the eccentricity of the load on the piles.

Drilled Piers

Piers of 60 cm or greater diameter are called drilled piers. When smaller-diameter piles are drilled, they are usually considered drilled-in-place piles. A temporary steel casing must be lowered into the hole when access into the pier is required for inspection or cleaning.

While piers may be used as single units under column loadings, they can be clustered and tied together with a cap to provide more resistance in cases with large applied moments.

Some codes require the pier length to be limited to 30 times the diameter of the pier. In seismic zones, single drilled piers must be tied together with tension-compression struts for the reasons described previously in the "Pile Foundations" section.

Strap or Combined Footings

A column or other load source often will be located near an existing structure foundation or property line. An adequate isolated footing cannot be used without experiencing eccentricity. In this case, a common solution is to tie two foundations together to eliminate the eccentric moment. This can take the form of a combined foundation, or two foundations strapped together with a wall or grade beam (see Fig. 2-1). The figures show a few of the configurations that can be used.

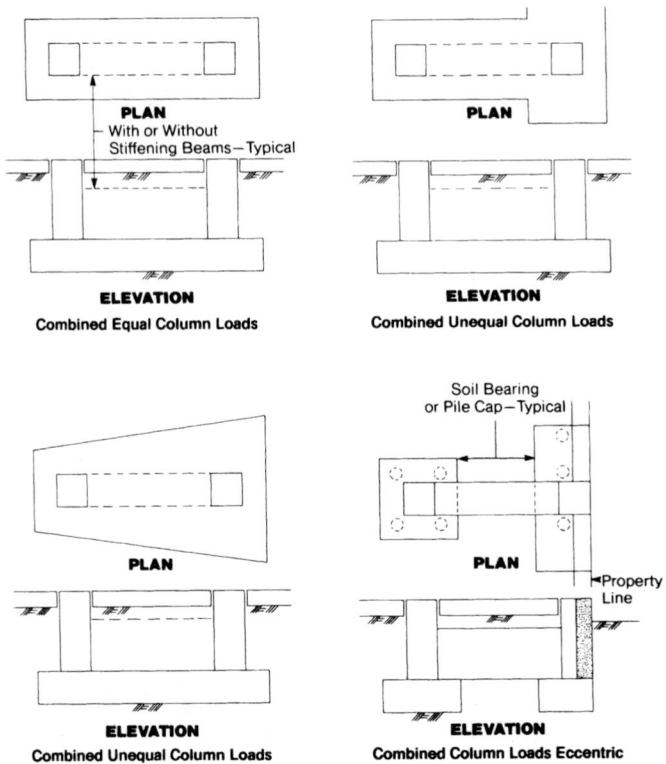

FIGURE 2-1 Strapped or combined footings.

Any solution that is stable and structurally sound is acceptable and can be used for soil-bearing, pile-supported, or drilled-pier foundations.

Mats

When loads are to be supported on a relatively weak soil, the footing sizes or pile spacing may result in the foundations almost overlapping. In this case, the best solution may be to provide a continuous mat foundation under the entire structure. Even when piles are used, a mat with a pattern of piles may be necessary to provide adequate support. An analysis based on the interaction between soil settlement and foundation deflections will indicate the best design. Care should be taken in selecting the thickness of the mat since one that is too flexible will not provide the necessary distribution of applied loads.

The mat should be extended beyond the perimeter columns if possible, again to provide better load distribution. Stiffening provided by a perimeter grade beam will aid in the distribution along an edge.

Post-Tensioning

The use of post-tensioning tendons in lieu of regular reinforcing may have some advantages in foundation design. While regular reinforced foundations will deflect under load and create some unequal soil pressure distribution, load-balancing post-tensioning may result in more uniform soil pressures with less materials. In addition, the post-tensioning tendons can be stressed in stages to increase the prestressing as continuing construction operations increase the load.

Normal prestressed concrete design concepts must be followed. These may require a review of the foundation for various load stages during construction, as well as the final service load combinations and final strength design (ultimate load) considerations. Because of the complexity in design and construction of post-tensioned foundations, they are very rarely used.

Equipment Foundations

Some equipment in a plant may produce vibrations. For the foundation design of such equipment, the knowledge of the dynamic analysis is sometimes necessary. Generally, the natural frequency of the equipment foundation system is kept significantly different from the equipment to minimize or avoid the resonance. Some equipment manufacturers recommend minimum foundation/equipment mass ratios. Often the equipment is isolated by vibration isolators, or the equipment foundation is isolated to minimize the transmission of vibration to other parts of the structure.

The foundation design for non-vibration-producing equipment is similar to the foundation design discussed earlier in this chapter.

RETAINING WALLS

When usage and site conditions require excavating the existing grade to provide two distinct levels, a retaining wall may be required to hold the earth without a long natural ground slope.

Retaining walls may be built using many different construction methods. Some of the more common methods are concrete, sheet piling, soil anchoring, reinforced earth, and slurry walls. At most plants, concrete walls are probably adjacent to, or are used as part of, the building foundations. Sheet piling often will be driven first to permit excavation, with a concrete wall-surfacing placed afterward to provide a more attractive surface. Figures 2-2 through 2-6 show typical retaining wall designs.

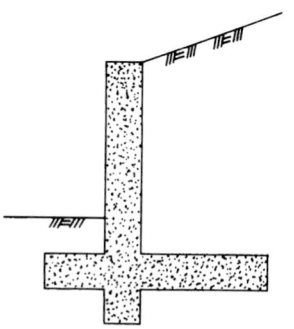

FIGURE 2-2 Concrete cantilever retaining wall.

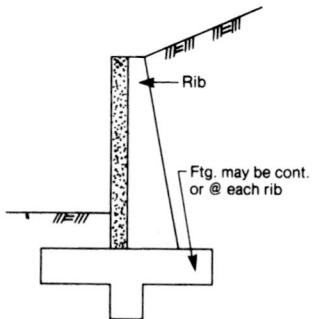

FIGURE 2-3 Concrete counterfort retaining wall.

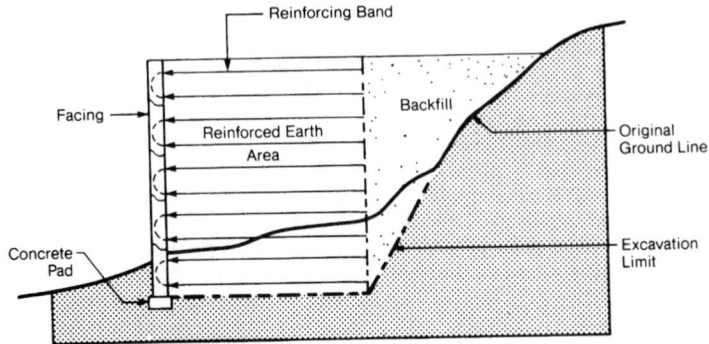

FIGURE 2-4   Reinforced earth structure.

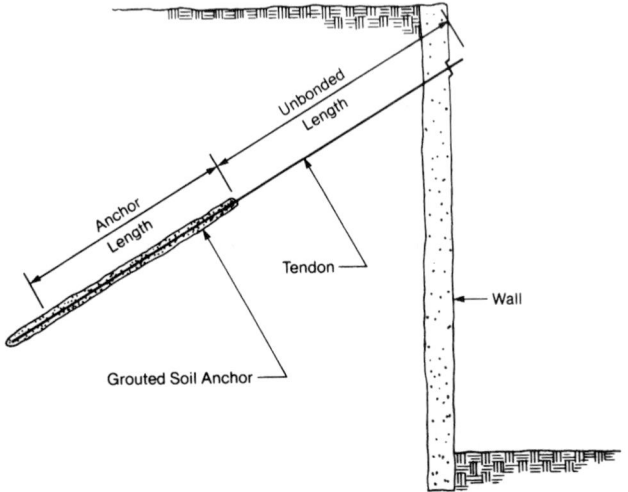

FIGURE 2-5   Soil-anchored wall.

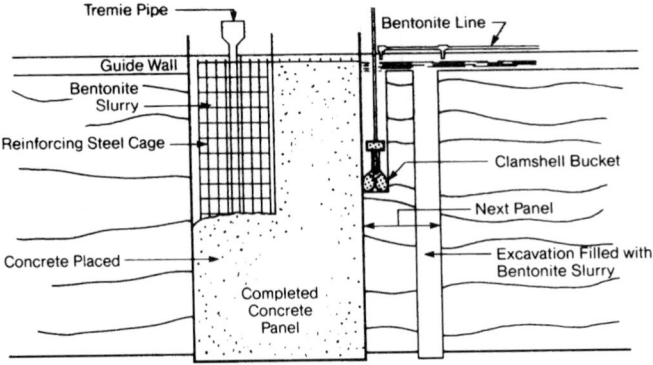

FIGURE 2-6   Slurry wall.

Concrete retaining walls may be designed to provide lateral stability and structural capability in various ways. The wall may be analyzed as a unit wall: each foot of wall is expected to retain a foot of earth behind the wall.

Another method is to span the wall horizontally between counterforts. This is usually more economical for very high walls, but the additional forming costs do not warrant its use for relatively low walls. Of course, the wall may be soil-bearing or pile-supported. The wall foundation is designed for gravity loads as well as overturning moment and sliding due to lateral earth pressure. For soil-bearing walls a shear key may be required to provide the necessary passive soil pressure to prevent sliding. When the wall is used as part of a building foundation, however, the floor slab may provide the necessary base restraint. The design should be checked for a temporary condition during construction, but with a reduced safety factor to assure stability during all phases. A reduced safety factor is warranted since sliding failures are usually gradual movements, and the short period during construction would not be long enough for a sliding failure to occur.

When the wall is pile-supported, the lateral resistance of the piles coupled with a shear key may provide adequate lateral restraint for low walls. Again, the floor slab may provide lateral support for the long-term condition. If the wall is high and pile-supported, the use of batter piles may be necessary.

When a wall has its face exposed to the atmosphere, a sand-gravel drainage area is commonly provided just behind the wall, with drain holes spaced through the wall to relieve the groundwater pressure that could otherwise be created. If local conditions indicate groundwater pressure could be a problem and the wall is part of a building foundation, a perforated drainpipe may have to be installed at the bottom of the sand-gravel area to divert the water into a storm-water drainage system.

As is the case for all walls, a retaining wall should be built with control joints spaced 20 to 30 feet (6.1 to 9.1 m) on-center to isolate the shrinkage cracking that will occur. This is even more critical for an exterior wall subject to extreme temperature changes.

Good practice dictates placing the control joints at the same location in both the continuous footing and the wall. Although the footing is not subject to much temperature change, shrinkage will occur and the footing will crack indiscriminately if there are no control joints, and these cracks will trace up through the wall at locations other than the wall joints. Drainhole pipes in the wall should be centered on the control joints, or wall cracking may also occur at the drain location.

When a retaining wall is also part of a building foundation, it must be designed for all conditions of loading that can occur. This can often result in the difficult design problem of establishing a footing that will provide the proper bearing and stability under varying loading conditions.

One solution is to separate the retaining wall from the building columns and footings. The effect of this solution on the support of the wall system must be studied, but no great problems will result if the support and connection details are studied and designed to agree with the anticipated movements.

CHAPTER 2-3
CONCRETE

William C. Hummel
Manager, Structural Section

Lawrence G. Mrazek
Senior Group Leader, Structural Section
Sverdrup Facilities, Inc.
St. Louis, Missouri

GLOSSARY

Many of the terms used to describe concrete, its use, and the materials from which it is made are found in reference materials printed and updated at intervals by the American Concrete Institute (ACI)[1] and the American Society for Testing and Materials (ASTM).[2] The reader is urged to become familiar with the latest issue at the time of use.

Structural concrete   Concrete used to form elements that are intended to support the loads generated by external forces and by its own weight. The term also identifies concrete of a quality specified for structural use. Materials most often used for structural concrete consist of a binder made of portland cement and water, and a variety of inert coarse and fine aggregate. Structural concrete may be plain or reinforced, but the most common type is reinforced.

Plain concrete   Concrete that is unreinforced or contains less reinforcement than the minimum amount specified for reinforced concrete in ACI Standard 318.[3] ACI 318.1/318.1R, "Building Code Requirements for Structural Plain Concrete and Commentary," covers the proper design and construction of plain concrete for structural purposes. Uses of plain concrete should be limited to structures having continuous contact with the ground or to structures capable of providing continuous vertical support. Arch-type structures in which the members are in compression under all loading conditions are an exception to this limitation. Footings, pedestals, walls, and slabs supported on the ground, or equipment pads supported by a structural system capable of providing continuous vertical support to the pad are common structural elements that meet the above requirements. In general, plain concrete is used only when the actual computed fiber stress in tension is less than 225 lb/in². Plain concrete used for structural purposes should have a minimum compressive strength of 2500 lb/in² (17.24 MPA) as required by ACI Standard 318.1/318.1R.

Reinforced concrete   Contains steel bars or wires that act together with the concrete to resist imposed forces. Reinforced concrete design in building construction is usually required to conform to ACI Standard 318, "Building Code Requirements for Reinforced Concrete."[3] Reinforcement is used to overcome the weak tensile strength of concrete, as well as add to its compressive load-carrying capacity. In members subject to bending or tension forces, the concrete is assumed to have no tensile strength; consequently, steel reinforcement is provided at locations subject to tensile stress. Concrete will often develop small cracks as it hardens, usually due to drying shrinkage, leaving no predictable capability to resist tension stress. Reinforced concrete is used for members supported above the ground on columns, walls, beams, or other isolated supports, in addition to foundations and slabs supported on the ground that are subject to large tension stresses caused by bending.

Normal-weight concrete Has a unit weight of about 150 lb/ft^3 (2400 kg/m^2) and is made with normal-weight aggregates commonly and naturally available in the construction locality. Natural rock, having the weight, strength, and durability properties similar to limestone, is most often used for normal-weight concrete. This concrete is frequently used because of the local availability of aggregates and its low cost.

Lightweight concrete Has a substantially lower unit weight than normal-weight concrete. The unit weight of structural lightweight concrete is between 90 and 120 lb/ft^3 (1440 and 1920 kg/m^3) in contrast with the 150 lb/ft^3 (2400 kg/m^3) unit weight of normal-weight concrete. This concrete is usually made with normal-weight fine aggregate (sand) and lightweight coarse aggregate [⅜ in (9.5 mm) or greater in size]. Concrete made with this combination usually weighs about 115 lb/ft^3 (1840 kg/m^3). When both the fine and coarse aggregates are lightweight material, the unit weight can be as low as 90 lb/ft^3 (1440 kg/m^3). The selection of structural lightweight concrete is usually based on the economic advantages inherent in supporting a lighter-weight structure. However, these advantages may not always exist due to the predicted higher cost of lightweight aggregates. Most lightweight aggregate is made by heat processes requiring a relatively high energy input and the price will accordingly escalate with energy costs. The availability of lightweight aggregate may significantly diminish because of reduced demand. Nonstructural insulating lightweight concrete, primarily used for thermal insulation, has a unit weight of 15 to 90 lb/ft^3 (240 to 1440 kg/m^3). Lightweight concrete has a lower thermal conductivity than normal-weight concrete and a greater potential for deflection with comparable strength.

Heavyweight concrete Is made with high-specific-gravity aggregates such as barite, ilmenite, iron, limonite, magnetite, or steel and often is used for radiation shielding. Its unit weight varies from 180 to 380 lb/ft^3 (2884 to 6088 kg/m^3).

Admixtures Admixtures are materials or substances other than cement, water, and aggregates which are added to the concrete immediately before or during mixing of the concrete. They are used to modify concrete properties while the concrete is plastic and after it has hardened to achieve a more economical mix and satisfy conditions during and after placement. Admixtures can be used to modify the properties before the concrete hardens by increasing workability, retarding or accelerating initial setting, and by improving pumpability. The effects of admixtures on concrete after hardening include increased strength without increasing the amount of cement; increased durability or resistance to freeze/thaw action; increased bond between old and new concrete; inhibited corrosion of embedded metals; the presence of fungicidal, germicidal, and insecticidal properties; and production of colored concrete. More information on admixtures can be found in "Chemical Admixtures for Concrete" (ACI212.3R) and also in the *ACI Manual of Concrete Practice,* MCP-1.[4]

Prestressed concrete Reinforced concrete in which internal compressive stresses have been introduced to reduce potential tensile stresses resulting from the application of internal or external loads. The internal stress is generally supplied by tensioned steel bars or wires, called tendons, that are anchored in the concrete before the load is applied. Steel tensioning done before the concrete is placed is called pretensioning; when done after placement, it is called post-tensioning. The advantages of prestressing include an almost zero-deflected structure when subjected to its own weight and nearly crack-free elements.

Pretensioning methods are normally performed at plants manufacturing precast concrete structural components such as slabs, beams, walls, and flanged members having a T or double-T (TT) configuration. Pretensioning requires anchoring and tensioning the tendons before the concrete is cast. The tendons are then released from their independent anchorage when the concrete is sufficiently hardened, compressing the concrete. This occurs when the force in the tendons is then transferred to each end of the member through the anchorage created by the bond between the tendons and the hardened surrounding concrete. Information on designing pretensioned structures can be obtained from the Precast, Prestressed Concrete Institute (PCI), *PCI Design Handbook,* 3rd edition, and other PCI materials.

Post-tensioning is most often performed at the construction site. Tendons are preplaced in ducts or tubes slightly larger than the tendons themselves and have the capability of being anchored at each end of the member to be stressed. Concrete is cast around the ducts complete with tendon anchorage devices. The tendons are tensioned with a portable jack when the concrete has reached about 75 percent of its specified design strength, and are anchored when the desired prestressing force is obtained. Two types of duct systems are available— bonded and unbonded. The bonded system is one in which a cement grout is injected into the duct after the tendon has been anchored. The grout fills the space between the tendon and the inside of the oversized duct, effectively bonds the tendon to the duct, and protects the tendon against corrosion. In the unbonded system (see Fig. 3-1), the tendons are pregreased with a corrosion-resistant material, and grout is not used. Information on designing post-tensioning structures and associated specifications and be obtained from the Post-Tensioning Institute's (PTI) *Post-Tensioning Manual* and other PTI and ACI technical data.

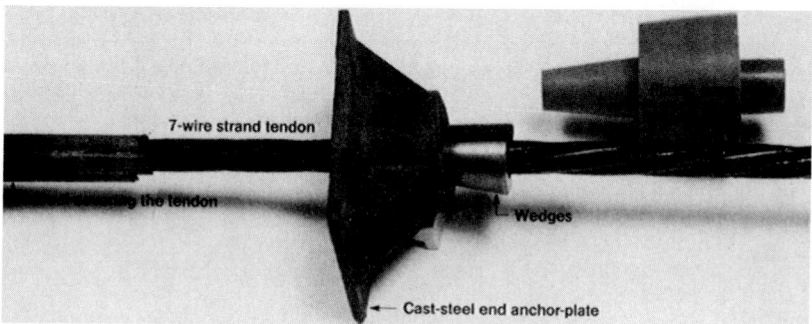

FIGURE 3-1   Unbonded post-tensioning system.

Precast concrete   Concrete members that are cast and cured in other than their final position, either in precast concrete manufacturing plants or at the construction site. Several advantages of these members include the elimination of the formwork and shoring required at the construction site, economies from mass production and reduced forming requirements, reduced concrete placing problems resulting from extreme weather conditions, and faster construction schedules since units can be made while or before foundations are installed. Products available from manufacturers generally include wall systems of solid or ribbed construction, hollow-core and solid- and ribbed-slab systems, as well as beams and girders in a variety of I and L shapes. Precast members are available in conventionally reinforced concrete and pretensioned, prestressed reinforced concrete. AASHTO Precast, Prestressed bridge girders are also available from precast plants.

Site-cast precast concrete is often used for tilt-up wall panels or lift-slab construction. In tilt-up construction, the wall slabs are usually cast against the building floor slabs and are tilted up into their final position (after they have hardened and cured) and then anchored to the structural frame. Lift-slab construction is a procedure in which the floor slabs of a multistory building are cast against the ground-floor slab and are jacked into final position on the building columns.

USE AS A BUILDING MATERIAL

Concrete is a composite material basically consisting of a binding medium within which are embedded various sizes of aggregate. The information in this chapter is mainly concerned with structural concrete in which the binding medium consists of hydraulic cement mixed with water. Portland cement and/or blends of portland cement are normally used for building construction. The cement and water combine chemically to harden to a rocklike material.

Concrete of this type can be used plain, but more often it is used in combination with steel reinforcing bars to form a variety of structural systems and building components.

The proper use of concrete requires an understanding of its constituent materials, structural properties, and behavior in concrete building systems. This chapter seeks to equip plant engineers with a broad knowledge of concrete terminology and its uses to permit them to deal intelligently with consultants they may engage to complete services of structural concrete design and related specifications. The chapter is also developed to help plant engineers assure themselves that design work performed by consultants conforms to generally accepted professional standards. Consequently, this chapter addresses the data required to specify the performance and properties of concrete and its components for use as a building material. The reader also is directed to various references for information concerning the analysis of structural properties and building systems, and to appropriate specifications and standards.

CONCRETE MATERIAL SPECIFICATIONS AND USAGE

Cements

Portland Cement. ASTM C150 is the governing specification for portland cement, which is available in five basic types. The normal color is light to medium gray, depending on the manufacturer, but white cements are available. White cement is often used for terrazzo-concrete floors, and when color admixtures are used to provide a colored concrete. Portland cement meets requirements for use in making structural concrete in accordance with ACI 318. The uses for the five types are:

Type I. For normal use when no special properties are required.

Type II. For general use, especially when moderate sulfate resistance or moderate heat of hydration is desired. It should be used for concrete either in direct contact with sewage or exposed to a moderate sulfate environment containing 150 to 1000 ppm (parts per million) of sulfate.

Type III. For use when high early strength is required. The normally specified 28-day strength can be obtained in 7 days. It is often used to speed form removal, or when service loads need to be applied sooner than 28 days.

Type IV. For use when low heat of hydration is desired. Heat is produced by the chemical reaction that occurs between the water and the cement. Very thick concrete sections lose the heat of hydration at a slow rate, allowing destructive temperatures to develop. The slower rate of temperature rise allows more time for the heat to dissipate, thus reducing the potential harm to the structure. This type of cement is rarely used and its availability is decreasing.

Type V. Used when high sulfate resistance is desired. Concrete exposed to substances with a sulfate content of over 1000 ppm should be made with this type of cement. Common uses include foundations in direct contact with high-sulfate soils, and structures associated with high-sulfate content wastewater.

Types IA, IIA, and IIIA. Air-entraining cements with the same uses as Types I, II, and III, respectively. These are used to provide greater workability of fresh concrete, but are more often used to provide greater capacity to resist the effects of freezing, thawing, and deicing chemicals after the concrete is cured.

Blended Hydraulic Cement. These are available in three basic types: portland blast-furnace slag cement, portland pozzolan cement, and slag cement. The governing specification is ASTM C575. Concretes made with these cements result in varieties of gray color and are usually darker than concrete made with portland cement. A tan-buff ("warmtone") cement also is available. Blended hydraulic cements, except for slag cements, may be used for making structural concrete according to ACI 318. These cements are not as available as portland cement; however, portland pozzolan cements may become more available with the increasing use of coal as a fuel, making more fly ash available as a pozzolan material. In general, blended hydraulic cements have a lower heat of hydration and gain strength at a slower rate than portland cement; they usually require a longer curing time, especially in cold weather.

ASTM designations for these types of cements are: Type 1S, portland blast-furnace slag cement; Types 1P and P, portland pozzolan cements; and Type S, slag cement. Types P and S are not recommended for structural concrete.

Calcium Aluminate Cement.   This is not covered by an ASTM specification, nor is it included in ACI 318 as an acceptable material for structural concrete. Its primary use is for concrete that is subjected to high temperatures [800 to 3000°F (427 to 1649°C)]. Lightweight aggregate is often used with calcium aluminate cement to provide greater heat resistance and insulation. Typical uses include lining steel chimneys and stacks, and other vessels and equipment for process industries; lining gas washers, ducts, sintering, or drying equipment; and insulating furnace walls. It also has been used in jet-engine testing structures. Manufacturers' literature often indicates using this cement as a structural material; before doing so, however, thorough investigation and testing are advisable to establish its properties, especially those related to long-term strength and durability under in-service moisture, heat, and weather conditions. This cement hardens very rapidly and has a high heat of hydration, making placing and curing procedures very critical. Information needed for using this cement is contained in a special 1978 ACI publication SP57, "Refractory Concrete," presently out of print; however, a xerographic copy may be purchased from ACI.

A summary of the state-of-the-art techniques of using refractory concrete including calcium aluminate cement has been reported by ACI Committee 547 in *Concrete International,* Vol. 1, No. 5, May 1979.

Expansive Cement.   This is a hydraulic cement that when mixed with water forms a paste and after setting tends to increase in volume to a significantly greater degree than portland cement paste.

It is used primarily to compensate for volume decrease due to shrinkage that normally occurs as concrete hardens. The governing specification is ASTM C845. The desirability of using these cements should be checked when sulfates are present in the environment. Three types of expansive cements, identified as K, M, and S, differ in the principal constituents and reactive aluminates which form the expansive qualities. These cements are often used to counteract the normal tendency for cement to shrink as it hardens. Common uses have been for grade floor slabs in an effort to reduce or eliminate joints placed in slabs to control shrinkage and to reduce or eliminate cracks that form because of drying shrinkage. This material has been extensively studied and continues to be investigated to determine its long-term results. ACI Standard 223, "Standard Practice for the Use of Shrinkage-Compensating Concrete," provides recommendations for using these cements. A high degree of quality control is needed in the proportioning, mixing, and placing to produce the desired shrinkage compensating and expansive effects.

Water

Water is required in combination with cement to form the binding substance in concrete. The water should be fresh (not salt water or ocean water), clean, and drinkable. Minerals and bacteria in the water are not usually harmful to the concrete if their concentration does not render the water unpotable. The Portland Cement Association (PCA) Booklet EB001.12T, "Design and Control of Concrete Mixtures," gives suggested limits for alkalis, chlorides, sulfates, and solids in mixing water. Water that is not drinkable may be used if it can produce mortar cubes having 7- and 28-day strengths equal to at least 90 percent of the strength of similar specimens made with drinkable water and if other properties such as durability are not affected. The test method for mortar cubes is established by ASTM C109, "Method of Test for Compressive Strength of Hydraulic Cement Mortars."

Aggregates

Aggregates are generally classified in terms of size (fine and coarse) and are identified as two separate ingredients. Fine aggregate material is either natural or manufactured sand (or both) graded and having a maximum size of ⅜ in (9.5 mm) and having only 2 to 10 percent passing a No. 100 sieve (150-μm mesh). Coarse aggregate is graded material normally having a maximum size not over 1½ in (38 mm), and with no more than 5 percent passing a No. 16 sieve (1.18 mm mesh). To permit concrete to completely surround the concrete reinforcement, coarse aggregate is usually specified to have maximum sizes of 1, ¾, ½, or ⅜ in (25.4, 19, 13, or 9.5 mm). The corresponding ASTM C33 grading designations for these coarse aggregate maximum sizes are 57, 67, 7, and 8, respectively. Aggregates are additionally classified in terms of weight—heavy, normal, and light—and apply to both fine and coarse materials. To provide uniformity, only one source of aggregate should be used. The aggregate comprises most of the concrete mix and has a significant influence on concrete properties and durability. Detailed information can be obtained from ACI 221R "Guide for the Use of Normal Weight Aggregates in Concrete" reported by ACI Committee 221 in the ACI *Manual of Concrete Practice,* Part 1.

Normal-Weight Aggregates. Normal-weight aggregates consisting of hard, stable, durable types of rock available in the construction area are most commonly used and should conform to ASTM Specification C33. Natural sand and manufactured sands, gravel, crushed gravel, crushed stone, or air-cooled blast furnace slag having a bulk dry unit weight of about 100 lb/ft^3 (1600 kg/m^3) are included in this classification.

It is most important to verify that the aggregates are sound and will not result in an alkali-aggregate reaction in the future "life" of the concrete structure. These reactions are internal and can lead to serious deterioration and even failure of the concrete after 15 to 20 years. A letter from the supplier and/or testing laboratory stating a history of the aggregate source with no apparent alkali-aggregate problems is recommended.

Lightweight Aggregates. Lightweight aggregates are covered by ASTM Specification C330. Lightweight aggregate is not as strong as normal-weight aggregate and has a bulk dry-unit weight between 30 and 70 lb/ft^3 (480 and 1120 kg/m^3). Additional cement may be needed to produce concrete having the same strength as normal-weight concrete due to the lower aggregate strength. The primary usefulness of lightweight aggregate is to produce concrete weighing about 35 lb/ft^3 (560 kg/m^3) less than normal-weight concrete, and to provide concrete with insulating properties greater than those of normal-weight aggregate. Most lightweight aggregate is manufactured from clay, shale, slate, industrial cinders, and fly ash. Natural lightweight aggregates consist of pumice, scoria, volcanic cinders, tuff, and diatomite; however, these materials are not widely available.

Reinforcement

Reinforcement may consist of deformed steel bars, welded wire fabric, and prestressing tendons, or combinations of each. Also, smooth undeformed wire may be used for the spiral reinforcement for concrete columns, and rolled structural steel sections may be used in composite, concrete-and-steel compression members. Nonmetallic materials such as fiberglass have been used, but are not widely accepted or tested at this time. Fiberglass bars can be obtained by special order.

Polypropolene and metal fibers have been injected into the concrete mix to effect better resistance to early shrinkage cracking.

Deformed Reinforcement.   Deformed bars should be specified to meet the following ASTM standards as well as standards in the ACI Standard 318, "Building Code Requirements for Reinforced Concrete."[3] These bars have deformations, or ridges, around their circumference. Bar diameters range from ⅜ to 1⅜ in. Bar size designations are related to the bar diameter given in multiples of ⅛ in. For example, a No. 4 bar has a diameter of 4/8 in. Grade 60 steel, having a yield point of 60,000 lb/in² (414 MPA), is commonly used. Smaller size bars, sizes 3 through 6 have been available in Grade 40 steel, having a yield point of 40,000 lb/in² (276 MPA). Steel with greater yield points may be used as prescribed by ACI 318. Welding of reinforcement is not generally recommended because of problems that may result from creating a brittle condition in the steel. Welding, if required, should be done in accordance with the "Reinforcing Steel Welding Code" (AWS D12.1) of the American Welding Society. Steel used for deformed bars includes billet steel conforming to ASTM A615 (the type of steel most often used); rail steel, axle steel, and low-alloy steel bars conforming to ASTM A616, A617, and A706, respectively, are all acceptable per ACI 318.

Welded Wire Fabric (WWF).   Welded wire fabric is available with either smooth or deformed wires. Smooth WWF and the wire material are covered by ASTM Specifications A185 and A82, respectively. Deformed WWF and its wire material are covered by ASTM Specifications A497 and ASTM A496, respectively. Additional WWF information is available in the *Manual of Standard Practice* and *Designing and Detailing Manual for Structural Concrete Slabs* published by the Wire Reinforcement Institute. Smooth WWF is most commonly used. WWF is commonly used to reinforce slabs on-grade; elevated slabs supported by columns, walls, etc.; and lightly reinforced walls. The precast concrete industry has used WWF to reinforce thin web members for shear.

Wire sizes vary in diameter from 0.135 to 0.628 in. The sizes were formerly given in U.S. steel wire gages, usually 4, 6, 8, or 10 gage. Present practice identifies the wire sizes by their cross-sectional area in hundredths of an inch; i.e., wire size 5.0 has a cross-sectional area of 0.05 in². "W" or "D" preceding the wire size number denotes smooth or deformed wire, respectively. The new wire-size designations of 4.0, 2.9, and 1.4 are the same as the commonly used old wire gage numbers of 4, 6, and 10.

The method used to designate WWF includes the spacing of the longitudinal and transverse wires. A typical designation is 6 × 8—W2.9 × W1.4, which means the longitudinal wires are spaced at 6 inches and the transverse wires at 8 inches, the longitudinal smooth wire size is 2.9, and the transverse smooth wire size is 1.4.

WWF is available in roll or sheet form. To permit handling, the sheet width is usually limited to 90 inches (2.3 m) or less. The maximum length is usually limited to 40 feet (12 m) for flat sheets and 200 feet (61 m) for rolls. WWF in rolls having longitudinal wire sizes of W2.9 or less will lie sufficiently flat to permit proper placement. Use of flat sheets is advisable where longitudinal wire sizes exceed W2.9 to allow satisfactory placement. Specification ASTM A884 covers the epoxy coating of plain and deformed welded wire fabric, for corrosion protection.

Prestressing and Post-Tensioning Tendons.   Three types of material are commonly used for prestressing tendons: uncoated stress-relieved wire, ASTM Specification A421; uncoated seven-wire stress-relieved strand, ASTM A416; and uncoated high-strength steel bar, ASTM A722. Although tendons used for post-tensioning can be obtained as a separate item, they more often are purchased as an integral part of a system complete with surrounding ducts or sheaths and end anchorages. Anchorages for post-tensioned-type systems should be required to develop the ultimate capacity of the tendon without exceeding the anticipated anchor set, and should be able to transmit the tendon force under both static and cyclic loading conditions. For more detailed descriptions of both bonded and unbonded post-tensioned materials refer to the Post-Tensioning Institute's "Guide Specifications for Post-Tensioning Materials," and Fig. 3-1, which illustrates an unbonded system.

Admixtures

Commonly used admixtures include air-entraining types conforming to ASTM C260 specifications; water-reducing types conforming to ASTM C494, Type A; set control types conforming to ASTM C494, Types B and D, which are retarders and a combination of water-reducing and retarder, respectively; and fly ash conforming to ASTM C618, Classes C or F. Air-entraining admixtures are used to provide better workability of fresh concrete in addition to increasing the durability of hardened concrete when subjected to freezing conditions and deicing chemicals. Fly ash is used to increase the workability and plasticity of fresh concrete and can be used to partially replace some of the cement in concrete without significantly affecting the strength of hardened concrete. Fly ash is also helpful in reducing the aggressive destructive action of seawater on hardened concrete. Type F fly ash has been used in combination with Type II cement to achieve greater than moderate sulphate resistance. The Bureau of Reclamation and other government agencies have recently initiated an *anti-washout admixture* to aid in placing concrete under water. Admixtures containing chlorides should be used only after a thorough investigation is made of the possible adverse effects they may have on embedded metallic materials, reinforcing, conduit, and the concrete itself. Follow ACI 318 regarding recommended maximum percentage of chlorides in concrete. Using admixtures in concrete is covered in depth by ACI Committee 212 report, entitled "Chemical Admixtures for Concrete" and also in the *ACI Manual of Concrete Practice,* Part 1.[4] Ensuring the compatibility of different admixtures in concrete is most important, preferably during the preparation of trial-mix designs.

PROPORTIONING CONCRETE MATERIALS

General Requirements and Procedures

Concrete materials are proportioned to provide necessary placability, strength, durability, and density. These are obtained by altering the quantities of the five major ingredients—cement, water, fine and coarse aggregates, and admixtures.

The basic objective in proportioning the ingredients is to produce, for the least possible cost, concrete with the specified physical, mechanical, and chemical properties needed in both its plastic and hardened states.

Selecting the proportions is basically a trial-and-error procedure. Each trial mixture is tested for its various plastic-state properties (such as slump, air content, and volume of concrete produced from the established amounts of each ingredient) and then placed in containers and allowed to harden into specimens suitable for testing the properties of the hardened concrete. The process is repeated until the specified properties are produced.

While the qualities and properties of each ingredient will vary, each has sufficient uniformity and identifiable properties to permit using pre-evaluated proportions and techniques to reduce the number of trials necessary to establish the desired results. Sufficient test data are usually available for a variety of concrete mixes that can be used to demonstrate the ability to satisfy the specified properties. ACI 318 recognizes this by providing procedures for establishing proportions on the basis of field experience. If this experience is not available, proportions must be established by making trial batches in a testing laboratory.

ACI Standards 211.1 and 211.2 are often used for establishing proportions for normal and lightweight concrete, respectively. Additional information and requirements concerning trial batches are provided in the PCA Bulletin EB001.13T, "Design and Control of Concrete Mixtures," and ACI 318. Methods for testing various properties of concrete are provided in Part 14 of the Book of ASTM Standards. Whether proportions are established by field experience methods or by trial batches, the services of a professional materials testing laboratory should be used wherever concrete is used for structural purposes.

Proportioning for Wet Concrete Properties

The properties of wet, or "plastic," concrete must be controlled to produce the required properties and appearances of hardened concrete. Most plastic concrete properties relate to the ease and homogeneity with which the materials can be mixed, the ability of the concrete to be properly placed in forms which establish its final hardened shape, and the ease of finishing the unformed surfaces. Concrete proportions should provide wet concrete having a plastic cohesive mass in which the aggregates are thoroughly coated with cement paste and are held in suspension in a well-distributed array. Mixes containing poorly graded coarse aggregates that lack the smaller size ranges or insufficient fine aggregates can produce a harsh texture that is difficult to consolidate, finish, or mold into smooth, formed surfaces. Such a mixture is considered to have poor workability. Mixes with excessively fine aggregates create a very smooth texture, but usually require greater amounts of cement paste and water to coat the aggregates and to provide an acceptable mortar matrix for the finished concrete product. This results in concrete that is more costly and which tends to have more cracks from drying shrinkage.

Concrete must be capable of both filling all corners in the forms and completely surrounding the reinforcing or other items embedded in the concrete without creating voids in the member being cast. The slump test, made in accordance with ASTM C143, establishes a measurement for evaluating the stiffness or consistency of fresh plastic concrete. This test is made by placing fresh concrete into a 12-inch high truncated cone mold in three layers and rodding each layer 25 times, removing the mold immediately after it is filled, and measuring the distance the concrete slumps [12 in (305 mm) minus the height of the concrete mound left after removing the cone form] (see Fig. 3-2). The commonly specified slumps range from 3 to 5 inches (76 and 127 mm). If a mechanical vibrator is used to consolidate the fresh concrete, a 4-inch (102-mm) slump is satisfactory for most work. Water-reducing and air-entraining

FIGURE 3-2   Slump test.

admixtures are often used to improve workability and consistency. High-range water reducers, superplasticizers, are used to temporarily increase the slump during concrete placement and to aid in placing concrete where there is reinforcing congestion.

Proportioning for Hardened Concrete Performance

Most of the properties of hardened concrete are controlled by the amount and quality of its constituent materials. The material quality, although not constant, is generally required to conform to governing ASTM standards, as discussed earlier in this chapter. Given a certain source of acceptable materials, the amounts of each material are established to meet certain desired properties of hardened concrete. Various types of strength (usually compressive strength), durability, and weight are the most commonly specified properties. Proportions selected for one property will usually affect the other properties, which are interrelated. Special surface finishes usually referred to as architectural concrete treatments, are also affected by the properties specified.

Compressive Strength. Compressive strength is usually specified relative to its age. Concrete gains strength with time when subjected to a moist environment. Building codes such as ACI 318 require the strength evaluation to be made after a 28-day time period in a specified moist environment. Compressive strength is determined by compressive tests made on samples of a specified size and shape. The most commonly used test methods are as follows:

ASTM C192, "Method of Making and Curing Concrete Test Specimens in the Laboratory"

ASTM C39, "Method of Test for Compressive Strength of Cylindrical Concrete Specimens"

ASTM C172, "Method of Sampling Fresh Concrete"

ASTM C31, "Method of Making and Curing Concrete Test Specimens in the Field"

For a mix to be acceptable according to ACI 318, test specimens cured and tested in the laboratory must always have a compressive strength that is 400 to 1200 lb/in^2 (2.76 to 8.27 MPA) greater than the specified design strength, depending upon the test history of strength for a particular concrete mix. A mix without a history of at least 30 tests made within the preceding 12 months is required to have a strength that is 1200 lb/in^2 (8.27 MPA) greater than the specified design strength. With a history of at least 30 consecutive tests, the additional strength required varies from 400 to 1200 lb/in^2 (2.76 to 8.27 MPA), according to the computed standard deviation. Refer to ACI 214, "Recommended Practice for Evaluation of Strength Test Results of Concrete," and to ACI 318.

With the aggregate in a mix being constant, strength is basically a function of the cement content and the water-cement ratio for a unit volume of concrete. Given a constant cement content, strength will decrease as the water-cement ratio increases. When strength data are not available from tests made on trial batches or from field experience, water-cement ratios and minimum cement contents can be used as the basis for selecting proportions to meet strength requirements (see ACI 318 and ACI 211.1). Such methods should be used only for normal-weight concrete with a specified strength of 4000 lb/in^2 (27.58 MPA) or less, and the concrete should contain no admixtures other than those provided for air entrainment. Although this method of proportioning without prior strength tests may be used, acceptance of concrete in place must be based on acceptable test results of the concrete placed in a structure (see "Concrete Quality Control" in this chapter).

Flexural Strength. Flexural strength is usually specified for concrete slabs on-grade, or roads or driveways subjected to high concentrated loads. When flexural strength is specified, it is usually required to be determined after a specimen has cured 28 days in a laboratory. The method for determining the flexural strength is specified by ASTM C78. A standard specimen is 6 in (152 mm) square in cross section and about 24 in (610 mm) long (refer to ASTM C31 and ASTM C192). Concrete used for slabs subjected to heavy concentrated wheel loads

[18,000 lb (3629 kg) or greater] should normally have a minimum flexural strength of 650 lb/in^2 (4.49 MPA) at 28 days. With a consistent source of aggregates, the cement content and the water-cement ratio have the greatest effects on this property. Strength decreases with decreasing amounts of cement and increasing amounts of water.

Splitting Tensile Strength.   Splitting tensile strength is usually specified in connection with lightweight aggregate concrete. Because lightweight is not usually as strong as normal-weight aggregate concrete and has potentially a greater variation in strength, this property is often specified where shearing forces are critical. Tests for this property are specified by ASTM C330, "Standard Specification for Lightweight Aggregates for Structural Concrete," and ASTM C496, "Test for Splitting Tensile Strength of Cylindrical Concrete Specimens." With a given source of aggregate, the cement content and the water-cement ratio have the greatest effect on this property. Strength decreases with decreasing amounts of cement and increasing amounts of water.

Proportioning for Durability

The satisfactory performance of hardened concrete can be threatened by chemical, climatic, abrasive, and erosive action. Resistance against such action can be achieved through material selections, as well as through varying proportions of materials. "Guide to Durable Concrete" (ACI 201.2R), "Standard Practice for Selecting Proportions for Normal, Heavyweight and Mass Concrete" (ACI 211.1), and "Erosion of Concrete in Hydraulic Structures" (ACI 210R), all included in Part I of the *ACI Manual of Concrete Practice,* provide practical information for producing concrete that resists these various types of deterioration. Durability against most forms of deterioration is improved as the water-cement ratio is decreased to about 0.45. The types of cement and aggregate used greatly influence resistance to various forms of chemical attack (see the section "Concrete Material Specification and Usage"). Aggregates should be selected on the basis of their inertness and reactance to the particular chemical environment where they are to be placed. Resistance to abrasion is enhanced by proportioning concrete for a strength of at least 4000 lb/in^2 (27.58 MPA) and using hard and sound, fine and coarse aggregates. Resistance to the climatic conditions of freezing and thawing is increased with the intentional entrainment of air in the cement paste and use of aggregates that do not absorb large amounts of water. Frost-resistant concrete should have 4½ to 6½ percent entrained air by volume, depending on the maximum size of the coarse aggregates. Air entrainment is usually achieved by using an air-entraining cement or admixture (see the section "Concrete Material Specifications and Usage").

Proportioning for Density

Concrete density is largely changed by the type of aggregate that is used. Heavyweight concrete is often used in connection with radiation shielding. A guide to proportioning for heavyweight concrete is provided in Appendix 4 of ACI 211, "Recommended Practice for Selecting Proportions for Normal Heavyweight and Mass Concrete." Unit weights from 180 to 350 lb/ft^3 (2880 to 5600 kg/m^3) can be obtained depending on the type of aggregate used. Iron and steel pellets are often used when attempting to achieve 350 lb/ft^3 (5600 kg/m^3) concrete.

Lightweight concrete is often used for its insulation and fire-protection qualities in addition to providing a lightweight structure. ACI 211.2, "Recommended Practice for Selecting Proportions for Structural Lightweight Concrete," provides data for this type of concrete. Unit weights from 90 to 115 lb/ft^3 (1440 to 1840 kg/m^3) can be obtained depending on the type of lightweight aggregate and the amount of natural sand that is used in the mix.

Minor changes in density can occur without changing the aggregate. These changes usually amount to about 15 lb/ft^3 (240 kg/m^3) and are related to both the amount of entrained and entrapped air, and the gradation and type of aggregate.

For certain applications, such as parking garages and structures containing liquids, crack control and impermeability of the concrete are second only to strength in importance. A dense, impermeable concrete with crack widths conforming to the recommendations of ACI 224R, "Control of Cracking in Concrete Structures," will inhibit the introduction of corrosive chemicals to reinforcing steel and prevent the leakage of stored contents. For structures containing liquids, follow ACI 350R, "Environmental Engineering Concrete Structures."

Proportioning Materials for Small Jobs

When concrete design strengths above 3000 lb/in^2 (20.7 MPA) are not required, and when only a small amount of concrete is required for a job (making field-mixed concrete possible), it may be impractical to determine the proportions in a testing laboratory in accordance with standard recommended procedures. Under such conditions, proportions established in accordance with Table 3.6.1, "Concrete Mixes for Small Jobs," in ACI 211.1-89, "Recommended Practice for Selecting Proportions for Normal, Heavyweight, and Mass Concrete," will usually provide concrete of satisfactory strength and durability provided the amount of water added will not produce a slump greater than 5 inches (127 mm). Concrete having a slump of 5 inches (127 mm) or less will tend to stick to the shovel and slide off as a unit, but not run off. If it runs off, it is too wet. Water should be added gradually and thoroughly mixed with the other materials to avoid excessive water. Material proportions for 1 ft^3 (0.02832 m^3) of concrete consisting of 23 lb (11 kg) cement, 47 lb (21 kg) sand, and 64 lb (29 kg) of coarse aggregate [stone or gravel of ¾ in (19 mm) maximum size] usually will result in a satisfactory mix for non-air-entrained concrete. Depending on the gradation of coarse aggregate, the sand and cement may have to be adjusted to produce the desired workability.

BATCHING AND MIXING CONCRETE

Batching consists of weighing, or volumetrically measuring, the ingredients for a batch or single quantity of concrete and placing them in a mixer. Mixing consists of combining the ingredients into a uniform plastic mass. The various ingredients need to be accurately measured and thoroughly mixed into a uniform mass within a specified time before placement. Mixing should be scheduled so that no more than 1½ hours elapse between the time cement is charged into the mixer and the time it is discharged for placement. If concrete is not satisfactorily measured and mixed, there can be adverse affects on placing ability, strength, durability, and permeability in addition to the creation of internal voids and surface defects. The temperature of mixed concrete should be controlled so that when delivered to the site for placement it is between 50 and 90°F (10 and 32°C). When fresh concrete is hotter, it may set too fast and is more susceptible to shrinkage and cracking. Special treatment is often necessary during extreme cold or hot weather (see the section "Environmental Effects on Concrete" in this chapter). A guide for batching and mixing concrete is provided in ACI Standard 304R, "Guide for Measuring, Mixing, Transporting, and Placing Concrete."

It is important that the total quantity of concrete required for any one element be batched, mixed, delivered, and placed before initial set occurs. It is equally important that the concrete be provided at such a rate that the element can be completely cast in a continuous operation without incurring cold joints between successively placed masses. A cold joint is a joint or discontinuity formed when a concrete surface hardens before the next concrete placement. It is characterized by poor bond to the hardened surface and usually is indicated by a defined line on vertical, formed surfaces. Concrete that has lost its flowability (determined by slump) as a result of partial initial set should never be retempered to the desired slump by adding water to the mix. Adding water under this condition will result in reduced strength and questionable durability. If it can be determined that the loss of slump is not the result of initial set caused by delays in delivery or placement, additional water can be added as long as the designed water-cement ratio or designed slump is not exceeded and recommended mixing is followed after the addition of water.

Mechanically Mixed Concrete

Concrete in amounts of 2 ft^3 (0.057 m^3) or more is most economically mixed in mechanically powered concrete mixers. Semiportable and stationary mixers are normally available in capacities ranging from about 2 ft^3 to 1 yd^3 (0.057 to 0.76 m^3). Truck-mounted mixers range in capacity between 3 and 15 yd^3 (2.29 and 11.47 m^3). Mixers with a rated capacity of 1 yd^3 (0.076 m^3) or larger should conform to the requirements of the Plant Mixer Manufacturers Division of the Concrete Plant Manufacturers Bureau. When mixers larger than 1 yd^3 (0.76 m^3) are used, some means of mechanical batching is usually required, especially when the element being cast requires a greater volume of material than can be mixed in a single batch. The requirements for batching and mixing equipment should meet the recommendations established by the Concrete Plant Manufacturers Bureau. In urban and neighboring areas, mechanically mixed concrete can usually be purchased from a ready-mix concrete plant.

Specifications governing batching, mixing, and transporting ready-mix concrete are established by ASTM C94, "Specification for Ready-Mixed Concrete." This specification includes a requirement for the purchaser to specify coarse aggregate size, slump, air content if air-entrained concrete is desired, the unit weight if lightweight concrete is used, and the 28-day design compressive strength. Two other alternatives for establishing material proportions can be used depending on the amount of responsibility the purchaser wishes to accept. Plant equipment and facilities should conform to the "Check List for Certification of Ready-Mixed Concrete Production Facilities" of the National Ready-Mixed Concrete Association. For reasons of quality control and economy, ready-mix concrete is used more often than site-batched and site-mixed concrete. When it becomes necessary to set up a site-batching and site-mixing plant, the plant equipment and operation should meet ASTM C94 Specifications and the recommended practice presented in ACI Standard 304. Materials should be placed in the mixers in a sequence to obtain preblending of cement, aggregate, and admixtures. About 5 to 10 percent of the water should enter the mixer initially and a like quantity should follow the introduction of other materials. The remainder of water should be added uniformly with the other materials. Admixtures that are liquid should enter with the water and those that are powdered should be ribboned into the mixer with the dry ingredients. After these starting procedures, the materials should be charged into the mixer simultaneously, and charging should be completed within the first 25 percent of the mixing time. Procedures for charging central mixing plants are less restrictive than for charging truck mixers. Mixing for batches of 1 yd^3 (0.076 m^3) or less should continue for not less than 1 min, and 15 s of mixing time should be added for each additional cubic yard (0.076 m^3) or fraction thereof being mixed.

Manually Mixed Concrete

When concrete is manually mixed, the aggregates and cement should be thoroughly mixed and blended before the water is added. Water should be gradually added to and mixed with the preblended dry materials. Mixing should be completed within 5 min.

PLACING CONCRETE

Concrete placement should be scheduled so that the discharge from the container that delivered the concrete and placement of the batch can be completed within about 1½ h after mixing or when the cement and water are mixed, depending on the particular concrete mix. Placing the concrete involves transporting the plastic concrete from the point of delivery to the location where it is required and consolidating it so it is free of voids and completely surrounds all embedded reinforcement and miscellaneous items.

Equipment used to place concrete should be clean and made of materials that will not cause adverse chemical reactions with fresh concrete. Aluminum pipe or equipment manufactured from aluminum should not be used to convey or place concrete. The reason is that concrete having hard aggregates causes adverse expansion of the aluminum piping that conveyed it on a large project. Apparently, the aggregates wore away aluminum filings from the inside of the pipe, thereby causing an expansive action, similar to that of nonshrink grout. Metallic equipment should be and normally is made of steel. Recommended practices for transporting and placing concrete are included in paper No. 68-33 reported by ACI 304, included in the *ACI Manual of Concrete Practice.*

Methods of Transporting Concrete

In many cases, when being placed at grade level, concrete may be dispensed directly from a truck-mounted mixer into the desired location by chutes which are normally carried on the truck. Other methods are often required, however, because of height restrictions or inaccessibility caused by formwork or reinforcement. Several such methods consist of crane-hoisted buckets, manual or motor-propelled buggies, conveyor belts, and pumps with hoses. Concrete that is to be pumped or carried on conveyors often requires special consideration when the mix design is being established. To prevent the dislocation of reinforcing or other embedded items, runways or other supports should be provided independent of reinforcement and embedded items. Transporting equipment should not travel directly over, or be supported on, reinforcement or other items embedded in the concrete.

Final Placement and Consolidation

The location for placing concrete and reinforcement should be clean of debris and free of ice and water. Concrete can be placed under water if special procedures described later in this paragraph are followed. Placement for a specific member should proceed at a rate such that fresh concrete is placed over underlying layers or adjacent to masses that are in a plastic state. This is required to prevent the formation of cold joints in a member. Concrete should be deposited in a manner to prevent segregation of the aggregates. Deep members such as walls should be placed in horizontal layers not exceeding 2 feet (0.61 m), and concrete should not be allowed to drop freely over reinforcing steel spacers, or other embedded materials. In walls or columns more than 6 feet (1.83 m) deep, concrete should be placed by using a tube, called an elephant trunk, sufficiently long such that the concrete will be placed near its final position. Each layer should be compacted by a mechanical vibrator in addition to rodding, to work out air pockets or voids and to drive the concrete into all corners and around reinforcement and embedded items. Each layer should be worked at least 6 in (152 mm) into a preceding layer. Additional information for consolidating concrete is included in ACI 309, "Guide for Consolidation of Concrete."

Shotcrete is a process by which concrete can be placed in varying thicknesses without using forms. The concrete is conveyed at high velocity through a hose and projected onto a surface. Special considerations for use of shotcrete are presented in ACI 506R, "Guide to Shotcrete."

Concrete can be placed under water if the water is not flowing at the time of placement. It should be deposited without allowing the concrete to drop freely through the water. An 8- to 12-in (254- to 305-mm) diameter pipe called a tremie is used to carry the concrete from a point above the water surface to its desired location beneath the water. The bottom of the tremie should remain in fresh concrete at all times during placement until the work is complete. Since the concrete cannot be rodded, vibrated, or otherwise disturbed for consolidating after it is deposited, a 6- to 9-in (152- to 229-mm) slump should be specified. The recommended water-cement ratio for tremie concrete is 0.44 by weight. More detailed information concerning the equipment, methods, and mixtures used for tremie concrete operations are included in ACI 304R, "Guide for Measuring, Mixing, Transporting, and Placing Concrete."

FORMWORK FOR CONCRETE

Fresh plastic concrete is made to conform to desired shapes by placing it in a mold. For structures supported on earth, the mold can be formed by shaping the earth. This method is usually restricted to members having a shallow depth, such as slabs, footings, and shallow beams. A temporary structure, commonly termed formwork, is normally used to form the required shape of the molds or to support prefabricated molds. The term formwork commonly includes the total system of support for freshly placed concrete, including all hardware and necessary bracing. ACI Standard 347R, "Guide to Formwork for Concrete," presents guidelines relative to types of forming systems as well as to formwork design.

Selection of Materials

Materials in contact with the concrete should be selected to produce the desired finishes and should not cause adverse reactions with fresh concrete. Common materials often used in contact with concrete are wood (plywood, or boards dressed on at least two edges and one face), wood products, steel, plastic, or fiberglass. Many manufactured forming systems are available for walls, columns, beams, joists (including two-way ribbed slabs), and necessary supports, scaffolding, and accessories. Form ties (which are rods used to hold opposite vertical form surfaces in position), should be factory-fabricated, adjustable in length, and capable of being removed such that no metal is closer than 1½ to 2 in (38 to 50 mm) to the concrete surfaces. Snap-off type ties are normally used and meet these requirements. Ties for below-grade construction should incorporate a water-seal washer. Wood or other porous materials used as forms should be coated with a material that will keep the forms from absorbing moisture from fresh concrete. Form-release agents should be used to prevent concrete bonding to the forms. Form-release agents should be types that will not impair or stain the concrete surface or prevent bonding of subsequent surface treatments. For concrete used in storing or containing potable water, form materials, including form release agents, should be nontoxic and meet federal and state regulatory requirements.

Design and Construction

Formwork should be designed to give adequate support to the lateral fluid pressures created by fresh concrete, as well as the weight of the fresh concrete, construction, and wind loads. Forms should be fabricated to be easily removed without damaging concrete surfaces and should be positioned and braced to produce concrete work conforming to the tolerances required by ACI 117, "Standard Tolerances for Concrete Construction and Materials and Commentary (ACI 117R)."

Form Removal

Formwork should not be removed until the concrete has sufficient strength to support both itself and the weights it will have to support during construction. Refer to the subsections "Curing Temperature" and "Duration of Curing" for information about the rate at which concrete gains strength and the procedures for determining concrete strength when terminating curing and removing forms.

CURING

The strength and durability of concrete is dependent upon its age and the temperature and moisture conditions to which it is subjected as it ages. Curing concrete relates to maintaining the moisture and temperature of freshly placed concrete during a definite period following placing or finishing to assure satisfactory hydration of the cementitious materials and proper hardening of the concrete. Detailed recommendations for concrete curing are given in ACI 308, "Standard Practice for Curing Concrete."

Curing Temperature

The temperature of the concrete during curing should be kept above freezing and below 180°F (82°C); however, the strength gain is very slow below 40°F (4.4°C). Reasonable curing periods can be obtained when the temperature of the concrete is kept above 50°F (10°C). Concrete temperatures over 110°F (43°C) are not usually reached except during steam curing. Refer to ACI 517.2R, "Accelerated Curing of Concrete at Atmospheric Pressure." Special provisions for hot- and cold-weather conditions should be followed, as described in the section in this chapter titled "Environmental Effects on Concrete." See Figs. 3-3 and 3-4 for the effects of low and high curing temperatures on concrete strength.

Moisture Retention

Due to loss of water required for the cement-water chemical action, accelerated drying of concrete will prevent adequate strength gain. To prevent rapid drying, one of the following procedures should be applied immediately after completing placing and finishing operations.

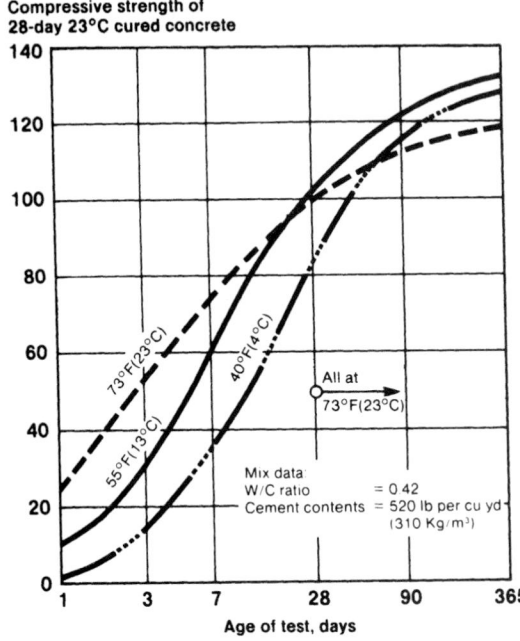

FIGURE 3-3 Effect of low temperatures on concrete compressive strength at various ages.

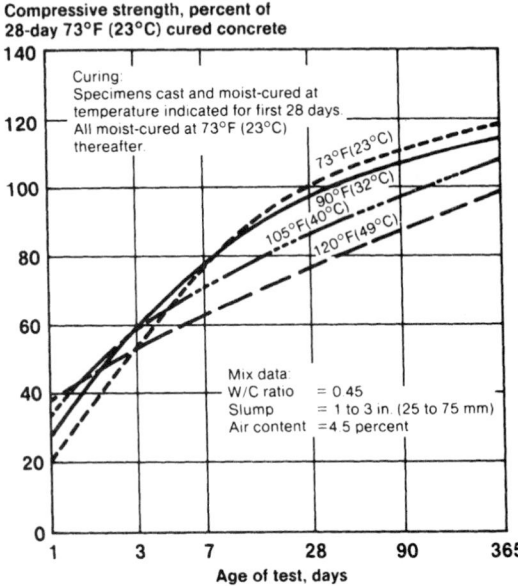

FIGURE 3-4 Effect of high temperatures on concrete compressive strength at various ages.

1. Keep absorptive mats or fabric continuously wet.
2. Use waterproof sheet materials conforming to ASTM C171, "Specifications for Waterproof Sheet Materials for Curing Concrete."
3. Use compounds conforming to ASTM C309 "Specifications for Liquid Membrane-Forming Compounds for Curing Concrete." Some of these compounds may prevent satisfactory bonding of the concrete to coatings, adhesives for floor coverings, or other materials that require bonding to the concrete surface. Curing compounds should be used in accordance with the specifications and the manufacturer's recommendations and should be applied immediately after the disappearance of any water sheen that may appear after finishing or after the use of other curing methods.
4. Keep nonabsorptive forms or absorptive forms moist and leave them in place.
5. Use a continuous steam or mist spray on the concrete surface.
6. Effect ponding or continuous sprinkling with water or application of sand kept continuously wet. However, these methods may adversely affect finished concrete surfaces.

Duration of Curing

Concrete should be cured for the period of time necessary to reach a compressive strength of at least 70 percent of the specified 28-day design strength. The length of time will vary depending upon the temperature and effectiveness of the moisture-retaining procedures used during the curing period. When the temperature during curing is above 50°F (10°C), a period of seven days is usually satisfactory and is generally considered to be the minimum desirable time, except three days is usually satisfactory when high-early strength cements are used, and as little as 18 to 24 h will suffice if steam curing is used. Test specimens used to establish strength criteria for terminating curing or removing forms should be cured under the same conditions as those used for the concrete work under consideration, and testing should conform to ASTM Standard Methods C31, C39, and C78. Forms used to support concrete elements should not be removed until the concrete has gained sufficient strength for the member to safely support its own weight and any additional superimposed loads to which it may be subjected. In some cases, strengths more than 70 percent of the specified 28-day design strength may be required.

QUALITY CONTROL

Concrete is made of many different materials produced by a variety of processes and trades of workers. Consequently, there is considerable opportunity for errors which can result in the production of an inferior product in which life safety could be in jeopardy. To provide a satisfactory concrete product, quality control is necessary in the areas of design and specification, and in the production, transportation, placement, finishing, and curing of concrete as well as in the maintenance of concrete structures.

For most projects, the first step in obtaining a quality project is to retain structural engineering consultants to produce designs and specifications, and to provide field observations during construction. These consultants should be selected on the basis of experience with the particular type and size of project and their quality control and checking procedures. The second step, similar to the first, involves the selection of contractors who are experienced in the type and size of the project and have the ability to provide a qualified construction superintendent. The contractor is basically responsible for carrying out the work described by the designs and specifications, including preparation of shop fabrication drawings and supplying and installing the proper materials. The third step involves the selection of a materials testing laboratory that is independent of the engineer or contractor, whose functions are to perform the specified inspection of batching and mixing equipment, test the concrete ingredients, and test the fresh and hardened concrete. This laboratory should be different from the laboratory used to develop the proportions for the types of concrete specified.

Concrete Specifications

Project specifications establish the basic quality of materials and construction, and the requirements for their testing. ACI Standard 301, "Specifications for Structural Concrete for Buildings,"[5] includes specifications that can be used by referral in the specific project specifications with the addition of supplemental requirements. Mandatory supplemental requirements include specifying the required 28-day design compressive strength of concrete used in each portion of the structure, and the various types and grades of reinforcing steel by ASTM Specification number and yield strength. Other supplemental requirements are also usually needed and are listed as options in these Specifications. In addition to ACI Specification 301, commercially produced guide specifications are available, some of which are adaptable to computerized reproduction and editing. Both publications need to be thoroughly reviewed and supplemented or edited for the specific project. Information about the availability of guide specifications can be obtained from the Construction Specifications Institute (CSI).

Shop Drawings

Shop drawings, catalog abstracts, and certificates of compliance are normally required to be submitted by the fabricator or manufacturer through the general contractor for review and acceptance by the owner or owner's representative to verify that the design drawings and specifications have been correctly interpreted. Having the consulting engineer who prepared the designs review such submittals is a recommended practice, since they relate to design considerations. Commonly required submittals are as follows:

1. Reinforcing steel shop drawings prepared in accordance with the Concrete Reinforcing Steel Institute's *Manual of Standard Practice* MSP-1; the ACI Committee 315 publication, *ACI Detailing Manual,* and the Wire Reinforcement Institute, Inc., publication, *Manual of Standard Practice—Welded Wire Fabric,* for welded wire fabric.

2. Manufacturer's specifications and installation instructions for proprietary reinforcing materials, including reinforcement accessories and bar couplings.

3. Mill certificates for reinforcing steel indicating the mill analysis and the tensile and bend tests.

4. Manufacturer's specifications and installation instructions for admixtures, bonding agents, waterstops, joint systems, sealants, chemical floor hardeners, and other proprietary materials.

5. Shop drawings of embedded steel items such as curb angles, connection plates, or other anchoring devices.

6. Material certificates for cement and aggregates signed by the contractor and manufacturer certifying that each material complies with or exceeds the specified requirements.

7. Laboratory reports on design mixes and results of concrete tests made during construction.

8. Architectural concrete submittals should include samples of concrete finishes, layouts of form work showing form-tie locations, types of form liners and construction joint locations. In addition, a full scale or half size mock-up sample should be built on the site to demonstrate the desired finishes for the project. Typical repairs should also be made to the mock-up to determine acceptable finishes after repair of damaged area.

Quality Control Tests during Construction

Fresh concrete should be sampled and tested to verify that it meets the requirements of the construction specifications and the approved preconstruction design mix, except in small jobs of little structural importance [50 yd^3 (38 m^3) or less]. Sampling should be accomplished in accordance with ASTM C172, "Standard Method of Sampling Freshly Mixed Concrete." ACI Standard 318 requires that "samples for strength tests of each class of concrete placed each day shall be taken not less than once a day, nor less than once for each 150 yd^3 (115 m^3) of concrete, nor less than once for each 5000 ft^2 (465 m^2) of surface area for slabs or walls." On a given project, if the total volume of concrete is such that the frequency of testing required by that previously stipulated "would provide less than five strength tests for a given class of concrete, tests shall be made from at least five randomly selected batches or from each batch if fewer than five batches are used." A variance to the preceding requirements involves a greater frequency of testing. Instead of "once for each 150 yd^3 (115 m^3)," once for 100 yd^3 or portion thereof (76.5 m^3) is specified. Additionally, three or four specimens are made for each test. One specimen is tested at seven days and two at 28 days. The fourth may be reserved for later testing if required. Refer also to ACI301.

Slump tests, in accordance with ASTM C143, should be made for at least one in every five concrete loads at the point of discharge; and one test should be made for each set of compressive-strength test specimens. (See Fig. 3-2.)

Air-content tests are usually made in accordance with ASTM C231, the pressure method, except where lightweight aggregate concrete is used. One test should be made for every five truck loads of concrete at the point of discharge when air entrainment is specified. For lightweight aggregate concrete, air-content tests should be made in accordance with ASTM C173, the volumetric method.

Concrete temperature should be tested hourly when the air temperature is 40°F (4.4°C) or below, when 80°F (27°C) and above, and each time a set of compression test specimens is made.

When concrete is pumped, sampling should be done on the concrete discharged at the effluent end of the hose as well as at the point of discharge from the container used for delivery.

Observation of Work during Construction

During construction, the work should be observed by an engineer familiar with the project plans, specifications, and construction techniques for the particular class of work being done. This observer should be someone other than the construction contractor's representative, preferably the engineer responsible for the design, or a qualified representative of the owner. The primary function of the observer is to see that the installation is proceeding in compliance with the general intent of the plans and specifications. A guide for observation or inspection of the work is provided by ACI Standard 311.4R, "Guide for Concrete Inspection," and the *ACI Manual of Concrete Inspection* (ACI SP-2). Although the contractor is basically responsible to perform the work in accordance with the plans and specifications, it is in the best interest of the owner to make provisions for independent observation and inspection, considering that once the work is in place, it is extremely expensive and time consuming to repair defective work and defend or prosecute liability claims. Some of the items that should be observed are as follows (this list is not exhaustive):

1. The basic layout of the building or structure.
2. Formwork conformance to the required shapes.
3. Conformance of the strength, size, spacing, location, support, and anchorage of reinforcing to information shown on the shop fabrication and design drawings and as described in the project specifications.
4. Removal of debris in forms where concrete is to be placed.

5. Conformance of fresh concrete to the specified properties; also, the performance of required sampling and testing.

6. The suitability of weather conditions and the implementation of protective measures for cold or hot weather.

7. Procedures for placement and consolidation.

8. Prompt implementation of curing methods and maintenance thereof for the required time periods.

9. Review of laboratory test results.

Conditions not fulfilling the intent of the design and specifications should be reported to the contractor immediately so that corrective measures can be initiated in a timely manner without a delay of the work. Defective work that remains uncorrected should be reported to the owner so corrective measures can be agreed upon with the contractor.

TESTING HARDENED CONCRETE MEMBERS

Testing hardened concrete by methods other than using concrete test specimens made at the time of placing concrete is accomplished when determining the in-place strength of questionable concrete that has not met the strength requirements of ACI318 and the specifications. These also are used to help evaluate the structural capacity of existing buildings. Test methods are basically two types, destructive and nondestructive. Detailed information on available testing methods can be obtained from a testing laboratory or from ACI. Testing should always be completed with the cooperation of, or under the direction of, a qualified engineering consultant.

Destructive Testing

Destructive testing is usually accomplished by removing a core of concrete from the structure and testing it in a laboratory. Diamond-tipped core bits are usually used to obtain undamaged specimens. Core samples are usually 3 to 4 in (76 to 102 mm) in diameter and have a length about twice the diameter. Such testing should be conducted in accordance with ASTM C823, "Standard Recommended Practice for examination and Sampling of Hardened Concrete in Constructions," ASTM C42, "Standard Method of Obtaining and Testing Drilled Cores and Sawed Beams of Concrete," and ACI 437R, "Strength Evaluation of Existing Concrete Building," reported by ACI Committee 437. The amount of destruction associated with this method is only at the point of core removal. Surrounding areas usually are not adversely affected. Metal-detecting devices should be used to locate reinforcement so that cores will not damage the reinforcement.

Load Tests. Load tests can also be destructive and are usually the "last resort" when attempting to determine if a structure meets design requirements. Load testing should be made in accordance with ACI 318, Chapter 20, and requirements of the local building official.

Nondestructive Testing

Nondestructive testing usually consists of one of the following methods:

1. Measuring the flow or travel of the pulse or train of waves on a measured path length through the concrete. Refer to ASTM C597, "Standard Test Method for Pulse Velocity Through Concrete."

2. Measuring the absorption or scatter of X-rays or gamma radiation, ASTM C104.

3. Measuring surface hardness by rebound or indentation-measuring devices, respectively, per ASTM C805, "Test Method for Rebound Number of Hardened Concrete," and ASTM C803, "Penetration Resistance of Hardened Concrete." (Windsor Probe)

4. The testing of embedded rods, called the pullout test, is also used to test strength. Follow ASTM C900.

New methods are constantly being developed, and information on recent developments can be obtained from ACI and testing laboratories. For any of the nondestructive methods, it is usually necessary to calibrate the equipment against compression tests of concrete core specimens representative of the concrete being tested.

The building owner, plant engineer and consulting engineer may have to make the following decision regarding a reoccurring problem: what to do when the specified 28-day compressive strength test results are low? The following is a step by step procedure that may be followed.

1. Test the spare set of test cylinders to obtain a comparison of results. These tests are then compared with the low test cylinders; also, determine if a certified concrete technician from a certified testing laboratory prepared the test cylinders. Were these cylinders protected and carefully handled?

2. If no apparent discrepancies are uncovered, require nondestructive tests be performed. At the same time, determine the effect of low strength on the particular structure by discussing the test results with the structural engineer of record. It is most important to know which area or part of the structure each set of test cylinders was taken. This information should be shown on the test report.

3. If questions still exist, cores should be taken from the structure and tested. ACI 318 considers concrete in an area represented by a set of core tests to be acceptable if the average of three core tests is equal to or greater than 85 percent of the specified concrete strength (f'_c) and if no single core test is less than 75 percent of f'_c. Additional cores may have to be extracted and tested if erratic strength tests result.

4. If the subject concrete strength remains questionable, remedial repair or strengthening measures should be considered, only with the consultation, agreement, and assistance of the structural engineer. Another option would be a load test in accordance with ACI 318.

5. If the load test fails, tear down and rebuild the structure in question.

ENVIRONMENTAL EFFECTS ON CONCRETE

The exposure of concrete to certain temperature extremes, wind, precipitation, and various chemicals can have detrimental effects on concrete during both its plastic and hardened states. In most cases, procedures can be adopted to minimize or eliminate detrimental effects if the adverse environment is known before the design and specifications are prepared. A description of commonly experienced adverse environmental conditions and recommended procedures to prevent or minimize their detrimental effects on concrete is presented in the following paragraphs. Information in addition to that presented can be obtained from ACI 201.1R, "Guide to Durable Concrete," reported by ACI Committee 201.

Temperature Extremes

Low Temperatures.   When concrete is placed during periods when the mean daily temperature falls below 40°F (4.4°C), the procedures described in ACI Committee 306R Report,

"Cold Weather Concreting," and ACI306.1, "Standard Specification for Cold Weather Concreting," should be followed to prevent fresh concrete from freezing and to provide proper curing conditions. These provisions make recommendations concerning the following: the temperature of fresh concrete delivered to the site, insulation on the forms, the use of insulating blankets to cover concrete during curing and heating the surrounding air, the curing interval and the interval before form removal (depending on maintaining the concrete temperature), and the requirements for maintaining above-freezing temperatures of forms or other surfaces against which concrete is placed. For the effects of low temperatures during curing on concrete compressive strength, see Fig. 3-3.

Hardened concrete exposed to freezing and thawing is subject to deterioration which is believed to be largely caused by hydraulic pressures created by an expanding ice-water system during freezing of the water that is absorbed in the concrete. To provide resistance against freezing and thawing, air entrainment (4.5 to 6.5 percent by volume depending on the aggregate size) is used, aggregates adequate for the exposure are selected, and a low water-cement ratio [about 5 gal (19 L) water per 94 lb (43 kg) of cement] is specified. Other methods that should be considered are providing sloped surfaces to prevent water puddles and providing joints in the work at close enough intervals to minimize development of tensile stresses and resulting cracking caused by thermal contraction and expansion. It is most important to follow ACI 306 with regard to exposing concrete to ambient air conditions, especially for thick, massive concrete placements. A shock effect due to a build-up of internal heat can cause detrimental surface cracking. An example is a bridge pier or large equipment pad.

High Temperatures. During hot weather, usually above 80°F (27°C), there is a potential for the quality of both fresh and hardened concrete to be impaired by premature set and by loss of the moisture needed for proper hydration of the cement. The potential is highest during dry and windy conditions. During these conditions, the recommendations in ACI Committee 305R, "Hot Weather Concreting," should be followed. The basic requirements consist of delivering and placing concrete at the lowest practical temperature, erecting wind shields and sunshades, cooling forms and dampening subgrades before concrete placement, completing finishing as rapidly as possible, and starting curing operations immediately after finishing. The use of set-retarding admixtures is helpful. A combination water-reducing and retarding admixture may be used to increase workability while maintaining the lowest possible water-cement ratio. Refer to Fig. 3-4 for the effects of high concrete temperatures on concrete compressive strength during curing.

Exposure to high temperatures after concrete has hardened can also have adverse effects. When members are subject to a temperature gradient between opposite faces, such as that which occurs when the top of a slab or beam receives greater exposure to heat from the sun in comparison to a bottom shaded surface, a bending stress is induced in the member that can cause cracking. To control such cracking, it may be necessary to provide additional reinforcement and/or to extend reinforcement beyond points at which bars are normally terminated. Concrete exposed to extremely high temperatures above 400°F (204°C) experiences a loss of compressive strength as the temperature continues to rise. Strength reduction will be in the range of 15 to 40 percent at 600°F (316°C).[6] The use of concrete in temperatures above 600°F (316°C) is not recommended without a detailed investigation as to the actual conditions of exposure and the types of cements and aggregates that are to be used. Instant exposure to temperatures between 200°F and 400°F could result in the evaporation of free moisture in the concrete and subsequent spalling due to the generation of high internal steam pressures.

Wind

Since it relates to premature loss of moisture in fresh concrete or the rate of cooling during cold weather, wind is detrimental only during placing and curing concrete. Placing concrete during windy periods may require provision of windshields, fog sprays, or enclosures to prevent detrimental effects such as plastic shrinkage cracking.

Precipitation

In the form of rain, precipitation can be detrimental during concrete placement. The greatest problem is caused by erosion of the cement paste before hardening occurs. Damage is usually limited to the exposed concrete surface finish and can often be repaired without having to demolish and replace the structure. If the concrete has not completely set after the rain ends, work can continue with additional concrete placement or filling in eroded areas. Puddles of water should be removed before placing additional concrete. When concrete has hardened and additional concrete cannot be worked into previous placements, patching can often be accomplished by using bonding agents before the concrete repairs. When erosion is deep and the concrete has hardened, repairs should be made only after consultation with and the approval of a professional structural engineer. See also Technical Bulletin 17, "Concrete Pavements Exposed to Rain during Construction," published by American Concrete Paving Association, 2625 Clearbrook Drive, Arlington Heights, IL 60005.

Chemical Attack

Chemical attack largely affects hardened concrete and is most often produced by chemicals in solution or by gases that react with moisture to form acids. Chemicals that attack concrete are inorganic and organic acids, alkaline solutions, salt solutions, bromine (vapor), sulfite liquor, chlorine (gas), and seawater. One of the most common corrosive agents is that of hydrogen sulfide gas found in domestic sewers, manholes, and the like. Sulfates often occur in soils and can cause serious deterioration when in contact with concrete, depending on the concentrations. Groundwater in earth fills that contain blast furnace slag or cinders is also likely to contain damaging amounts of sulfates. Inorganic acids may occur in peat soils as well as in process plants that use various types and concentrations of acids. Organic acids are often present from spillage in food processing plants or wood pulp mills.

Salts may be present in soils, and are often found in localities where ice removal is required. Salt and similar deicing chemicals are considerably more destructive if applied to concrete less than four months old. Aggressive chemicals should not be allowed to come in contact with concrete. Many of the chemicals that adversely affect the concrete also promote corrosion of steel reinforcement. The owner, plant engineer, and consultant are frequently faced with the task of determining whether the chemicals being used will damage concrete. Two excellent references are "Guide to Use of Waterproofing, Dampproofing, Protective and Decorative Barrier Systems for Concrete," ACI515.1R, and "Effect of Substances on Concrete and Guide to Protective Treatments," Portland Cement Association (PCA) IS001.07T. Protection of concrete against sulfate attack may be obtained by specifying a sulfate-resistant cement and a dense, high-quality concrete. Protection against high concentrations of acid is often provided by coatings or linings that prevent contact with the concrete. This method could be used to provide resistance for most types of chemical attack; however, the coatings or linings are usually very expensive and require frequent maintenance. For additional information concerning chemical attack refer to ACI 201.2R, "Guide to Durable Concrete."

REPAIRING CONCRETE

Repairs for concrete structures are usually of two basic types—cosmetic and structural. Materials and methods are related to the type of repairs being made. The selection of materials that will form strong bond-to-concrete surfaces with an equal or greater strength than the concrete itself is basic to either type of repair. Oil, dust, dirt, or other coatings that will prevent materials from bonding to concrete should be removed from the surface receiving the repair patch. Removing rust from reinforcing bars in the patch areas is equally important. The base concrete to receive the patches should be sound. Delaminated, spalled concrete should be removed before patching is started. In cases requiring the removal of deteriorated materials, the structural element may have to be temporarily shored before any materials are removed. Except for very minor defects, repairs should not be made without consultation with and direction from a professional structural engineer.

Repairing "Green" Concrete

"Green" concrete is concrete that has set but has not appreciably hardened. Minor defects less than about 1½ in (38 mm) deep that do not affect the structural capacity can often be patched by coating the defective surface with a neat cement grout and patching with a 2½:1 sand/cement mixture. For deeper defects, similar to those caused by rock pockets or honeycombing, all material should be removed down to sound concrete. A bonding agent should be applied to the sound surface before patching with a concrete mixture having a strength equal to that specified for the member being patched. Patching of new work should be accomplished within a day after form removal or discovery and before the concrete has dried. Patches should be moist-cured for at least three days. For additional information on repairing concrete surfaces, refer to Chapter VII on the *Concrete Manual* 7th ed., U.S. Department of the Interior, Bureau of Reclamation.

Repairing Hardened Concrete

Flowable pressure-injected epoxies are often used for repairing cracks for structural considerations. Holes and other such defects are often patched by using polymer modified cementitous mortar/concrete. Repair materials that can be applied to damp surfaces are often desirable, since creating or maintaining a dry surface is often difficult. It is most important to determine the properties of repair materials and to compare these properties with the concrete to be repaired. For example, there have been serious delamination problems with earlier epoxy overlays due to incompatible coefficients of thermal expansion. The owner/plant engineer should consult with a structural engineer familiar with repairs and also check the references listed in this manual before seeking advice from product manufacturers. The following references relate to concrete repairs. "A Guide to Repair of Concrete," *Concrete Construction* Volume 22, No. 3, March 1977; "Concrete Repair Basics," ACI SCM 24-91.CT92; "Repair and Rehabilitation of Concrete Structures," C-10.CT92 (An ACI Compilation); and "Use of Epoxy Compounds with Concrete," ACI 503R.

PHYSICAL AND MECHANICAL PROPERTIES OF HARDENED CONCRETE

The properties of hardened concrete vary with different types of aggregates, the water-cement ratio, the amount of entrained air, the 28-day compressive strength, curing methods, and the amount of moisture retained in the concrete. If accurate values of the various properties are desired, they should be established from laboratory tests made on specific design mixes. For most designs, however, approximate values are satisfactory, and approximate values are given for the properties described in the following text.

Compressive Strength

The values of compressive strength (f'_c) used in design are based on concrete specimens tested at 28 days; however, concrete will continue to gain strength after 28 days. See the section "Proportioning Concrete Materials" in this chapter. Strengths vary to the greatest extent with cement content and water-cement ratios and to a minimum extent with types of aggregate. Strength also is affected by the temperature of the concrete during curing (see Fig. 3-4). The strengths most often specified are 3000, 4000, and 5000 lb/in^2 (20.68, 27.58, and 34.47 MPA). Strengths as high as 8000 lb/in^2 can be obtained without great difficulty.

Common Uses of Concretes of Various Strengths

3000 lb/in^2 (20.68 MPA).   Grade beams; footings; slabs-on-grade not exposed to heavy traffic or metal wheels; beams; lightly loaded columns; and elevated slab systems consisting of two-way or one-way slabs supported on beams, joists, or waffle slabs.

4000 lb/in^2 (27.58 MPA).   Pile caps; drilled piers; spread footings on soils having a bearing capacity over 6000 lb/in^2 (287,000 Pa); slabs-on-grade for warehouses and light-to-medium industries; columns supporting heavy loads, flat slabs, flat plates, and elevated floor systems supporting live loads over 150 lb/ft^2 (7185 Pa); truck dock slabs; pavement for roads; prestressed and precast concrete construction; and liquid-containing structures (Ref. ACI350R, "Environmental Engineering Concrete Structures").

5000 lb/in^2 (34.47 MPA).   Pile caps for 100-t (900,000-N) or greater-capacity piles, heavy industrial floors, columns supporting heavy loads, precast concrete construction, and prestressed concrete supporting heavy loads or used on long spans.

6000 to 8000 lb/in^2 (41.34 to 55.12 MPA).   Post-tensioned parking garage decks and topping for industrial floors subject to steel wheels, columns, and precast, prestressed concrete.

Tensile and Flexural Strength

Concrete used in a structural member is not considered to have any ability to resist axial tension forces. Concrete actually does have some tensile strength, but it is very low (about 7 percent of the compressive strength) and is unpredictable. The only types of tensile stress resistance considered in the design of concrete structures is that associated with flexural strength and diagonal tension as it relates to shear strength. Both splitting tensile strength (used in evaluating the shear strength of lightweight concrete) and flexural strength should be determined by tests. Refer to the sections "Proportioning for Performance of Hardened Concrete," "Flexural Strength," and "Splitting Tensile Strength" in this chapter. The approximate values of flexural strength, often referred to as the modulus of rupture, are as follows:

$$9\sqrt{f'_c} \text{ lb/in}^2 \qquad (0.72\sqrt{f'_c} \text{ MPA})$$

as used in design of pavement[7] and

$$7.5\sqrt{f'_c} \text{ lb/in}^2 \qquad (0.62\sqrt{f'_c} \text{ MPA})$$

as used in determining stiffness of concrete members according to ACI 318 (f'_c is the compressive strength).

Shear Strength

There are basically two ways in which the shear capacity of concrete is evaluated. One is a measure of diagonal tension, and the other is a measure of interface shear friction. Shear friction is the resistance to relative displacement of a common point on each side of a common plane in a direction parallel to the direction of the applied load or torque. As a measure of diagonal tension resistance, shear strength varies with applied axial tension and compression, flexural stress, and torsional stress. A conservative estimate of ultimate shear strength as a measure of diagonal tension not subject to axial tension is $2\sqrt{f'_c}$ lb/in^2 ($0.17\sqrt{f'_c}$ MPA), where f'_c is the compressive strength. Interface shear friction resistance for unreinforced, uncracked concrete is approximately 12 percent of the compressive strength. Both interface shear friction resistance and shear as a measure of diagonal tension resistance are greatly increased by the use of steel reinforcement bars. For detailed evaluations of shear capacity, the requirements of ACI 318, "Building Code Requirements for Reinforced Concrete," should be followed. Additional information concerning concrete shear strength is available in ACI 426R, "Shear Strength of Reinforced Concrete Members," reported by ACI-ASCE Committee 426.

Modulus of Elasticity

Unlike steel, the stress/strain relationship of concrete is not exactly a direct proportion, but primarily varies with the weight and strength of concrete. For calculations involving the modulus of elasticity, E_c, a value equal to $W_c^{1.5} 33\sqrt{f'_c}$ lb/in^2 ($W_c^{1.5} 0.043 \sqrt{f'_c}$ MPA) has been widely accepted. Refer to ACI 318, "Building Code for Reinforced Concrete, Buildings" and its commentary[8]. W_c is unit weight of concrete in pounds per cubic foot and f'_c is the compressive strength of concrete in pounds per square inch. A standard test method for determining the modulus of elasticity is presented in ASTM C469.

Poisson's Ratio

The ratio of lateral strain to axial strain for concrete is variable. Values as low as 0.10 and as high as 0.30 have been observed[9]. Values between 0.15 and 0.20 are often used in analysis. A test method for determining Poisson's ratio is presented in ASTM C469, "Standard Test Method for Static Modulus of Elasticity and Poisson's Ratio of Concrete in Compression."

Unit Weight (Density)

The density of structural concrete primarily varies with the type of aggregate as follows:

Normal or regular weight: 150 lb/ft^3 (2400 kg/m^3)
All lightweight: 90 to 100 lb/ft^3 (1400 to 1600 kg/m^3)
Sand lightweight: 110 to 120 lb/ft^3 (1760 to 1920 kg/m^3)
Heavyweight: (See ACI Standard 211, Appendix 4.) 180 to 350 lb/ft^3 (2880 to 5600 kg/m^3)

Shrinkage

As concrete dries, it decreases in volume. This type of volumetric change is called concrete shrinkage. The amount of shrinkage increases with increasing amounts of cement and water used in the concrete mix and decreases with the addition of bonded reinforcement. Shrinkage is also affected by ambient relative humidity and its volume-to-surface ratio.

Creep

As defined by ASTM, creep is the time-dependent deformation that continues after the application of a load that is maintained on a solid material. Consideration of creep in concrete is important when evaluating deflections from bending (flexural) or axial compressive loads. The presence of deformed reinforcing steel in the direction and at the location of applied compressive stress reduces the amount of creep that would occur in unreinforced concrete. Creep is also related to concrete strength, the relative humidity of the surrounding air, volume-to-surface ratios, and the age of the concrete when the compressive load is applied.

Thermal Expansion Coefficient

The coefficient of thermal expansion varies primarily with the type of aggregate, but is about the same as steel. The approximate coefficient of thermal expansion for concrete commonly used in design is 0.00055 per unit of length per 100°F (0.00099 per 100°C).

Thermal Conductivity

The thermal conductivity of concrete varies primarily with the type of aggregate used. The conductivity in British thermal units per square foot per hour per degree Fahrenheit per inch thickness is about 12 for normal-weight and 4 for lightweight concrete.

Effects of Blasting, Jarring, and Shock Vibrations on Fresh Concrete

The plant engineer, owner, and consultant may be faced with a situation where fresh concrete is to be placed adjacent to a piece of vibratory equipment or where nearby blasting operations are taking place.

Several recent guidelines on this subject are suggested*:

Age of concrete	Particle velocity limit
Less than 10 h	0.1 in/s
10 to 24 h	4.0 in/s
More than 24 h	7.0 in/s

Another more recent test program at the Seabrook Power Station indicates more relaxed values for earlier ages as follows[†]:

Age of concrete	Peak particle velocity of ground vibrations
Up to 3 h	4.0 in/s
3 to 11 h	1.5 in/s
11 to 24 h	2.0 in/s
24 to 48 h	4.0 in/s
Over 48 h	7.0 in/s

Sound Transmission and Sound Absorption

Sound transmission values are proportional to the mass or density of the concrete media between the source of the sound and the receiver. Refer to "Lightweight Concrete Information Sheet No. 8," printed by the Expanded Shale, Clay, and Slate Institute.

Dense materials such as normal-weight concrete are not efficient in absorbing sound. However, porous materials, including lightweight concretes, have better sound absorbing

---

* See *Concrete Construction,* May 1983, article by Ralph Spears.
[†] See "Vibrations of Concrete Structures," ACI SP60.

qualities. Refer to "Sound Absorbing Value of Portland Cement Concrete," by F.R. Watson and K.C. Morrical, reprinted by the Portland Cement Association.

Also, refer to "Acoustics of Concrete in Buildings," Portland Cement Association, PCA IS159T.

Fire Resistance

Concrete is often used to protect steel against loss of strength when subjected to high temperatures. Structures made entirely of reinforced concrete have very good fire ratings. Lightweight concrete provides a better fire resistance rating than normal-weight concrete. An analytic procedure for determining the fire resistance of a concrete structure is presented in *Design for Fire Resistance of Precast Prestressed Concrete,* by Armand H. Gustaferro and Leslie D. Martin (published by the PCI). Thicknesses of concrete to be used as insulation to provide desired fire ratings for steel construction are provided by various insurance agencies and in Louis Przetak's *Standard Details for Fire-Resistive Building Construction,* McGraw-Hill, New York, 1977. Other references are "Guide for Determining the Fire Endurance of Concrete Elements," ACI 216R; "Reinforced Concrete Fire Resistance," Concrete Reinforcing Steel Institute (CRSI); and "Design for Fire Resistance of Precast, Prestressed Concrete," PCI.

ANALYSIS OF CONCRETE STRUCTURES

Analysis consists of determining the various types and maximum magnitudes of forces a member is required to support for prescribed loading conditions and of proportioning members to provide sufficient strength to resist the applied forces without exceeding prescribed factors of safety. Proportioning generally consists of selecting the reinforcement as well as the cross-section dimensions of the member. Loads consist of dead and live loads. Dead loads are static loads that include the mass of the members, the supported structure, and permanent attachments or accessories. Live loads may be static loads that can be moved from one part of the structure to another and/or moving or dynamic loads not permanently attached to the structure. Equipment or machinery can be considered a dead or live load depending on whether it is permanently a part of the building.

People, furnishings, traveling equipment, wind, snow, rain, the effects of earthquakes and temperature changes, moving water, ice pressure, debris, and lateral soil pressure are typical examples of live loads. Live loads are established by considering the actual loads associated with the use of the structure, environmental conditions to which the structure will be subjected, and various types and minimum magnitudes of loads established by local governing authorities for various types of structures. Local governing authorities often adopt basic building codes such as *The Uniform Building Code* (UBC), the *Building Officials and Code Administrators Code* (BOCA), the *American Insurance Association National Building Code,* or the *American National Standards Institute* "Building Code Requirements for Minimum Design Loads in Buildings and Other Structures," ANSI A58.1. These and other similar codes establish minimum loadings and requirements for designing and building structures.

The commonly referenced requirements for designing and constructing concrete are those established by the American Concrete Institute (ACI). The often-used ACI codes and standards are as follows:

1. ACI Standard 302.1R, "Guide for Concrete Floor and Slab Construction."

2. ACI Standard 313 and ACI 313R, "Standard Practice for Design and Construction of Concrete Silos and Stacking Tubes for Storing Granular Materials" and Commentary.

3. ACI Standard 318, "Building Code Requirements for Reinforced Concrete" and Commentary.

4. ACI Standard 318.1 and 318.1R, "Building Code Requirements for Structural Plain Concrete" and Commentary.

5. ACI Standard 350R, "Environmental Engineering Concrete Structures."

6. ACI Standard 343R, "Analysis and Design of Reinforced Concrete Bridge Structures."

Strength of Concrete Members[10]

Two basic methods for evaluating the strength of concrete members are widely accepted. One method [commonly called strength design method (SDM)] is based on analytic procedures that predict the maximum forces that can be sustained just before failure of concrete in compression or yielding of reinforcement in tension, or both simultaneously. The maximum forces predicted are compared to actual loads multiplied by a factor greater than 1. Assigning a larger factor to live loads than to dead loads has been customary. Recent practice has been to use load factors of 1.7 and 1.4, respectively, times the actual live and dead loads. Additionally, the strength provided by steel reinforcement is always made to be less than that which will allow sudden failure of the concrete in compression, so the yielding of steel and the associated large deflections will give a visual warning of excessive load without the threat of sudden collapse. This is the most widely used method at the time of this writing.

The second method, called the alternate design method, limits the applied loads to those established by a theory based on a straight-line relationship of stress to strain and by limiting internal member stresses to values well within the elastic range of the materials. Designs based on this method usually require greater amounts of concrete or reinforcement, or both, than is required when using the SDM.

The theories used for both design methods are described in the edition of ACI 318 current at the time of this writing. Design aids published at the time of this writing for both types of design are as follows:

1. *Design Handbook in Accordance with the Strength Design Method of ACI 318-89,* ACI SP-17.

2. *Design Handbook in Accordance with the Strength Design Method of ACI 318-89,* Vol. 2, "Columns," ACI Sp-17A.

3. *Reinforced Concrete Design Handbook—Working Stress Method,* ACI SP-3, is based on the Alternate Design Method.

4. "PCA Notes on ACI 318-89 Building Code Requirements for Reinforced Concrete with Design Applications," Portland Cement Association. In the past PCA has updated this reference to be consistent with revisions made in the ACI Standard 318.

5. Concrete Reinforcing Steel Institute's *CRSI Handbook.*

Considerations for Proportioning Concrete Members Based on the Strength Design Method (SDM)

Flexural Members.   Members proportioned by the SDM can be quite flexible if stressed to the maximum compressive capacity of the concrete and if the span-to-depth ratios are greater than 16 for members supported at both ends and greater than 8 for cantilever spans. Conditions that are especially sensitive to deflections are as follows:

1. First interior spans.

2. Members supporting masonry.

3. Members over and under windows and doors.

4. Long spans [30 ft (9.14 m) or greater] supporting drywall partitions or other materials susceptible to damage due to minor structure movements.

5. Members supporting equipment sensitive to vibration and deflection.

6. Heavily loaded spans [greater than 100 lb/ft^2 (4790 Pa)].

7. Locations where clearances are critical to the function of the structure.

8. Lightly loaded floors without dampening members such as walls.

9. Cantilevers.

Additional precautions when proportioning members are as follows:

1. Select member widths so the concrete can be easily consolidated around the reinforcement.

2. Use higher load factors when members are subject to cyclic loading that may fatigue concrete. Refer to *ACI Symposium* volume SP-41, "Fatigue of Concrete."

3. Maintain low tensile stress in the reinforcement to minimize cracking in concrete structures exposed to corrosive environments or liquid-containing structures.

Compression Members.   The size of columns should be proportioned so the concrete can be thoroughly compacted around the vertical and lateral reinforcement. This can usually be done by carefully selecting the size of reinforcement and sizing the column cross section to keep the required reinforcement percentage below 6 percent of the column cross-section area. Where columns are located in areas subject to damage from the impact of materials or mobile equipment, special consideration should be given to protect the column against loss of material. Also, in such cases, providing columns with sufficient stability to withstand such abuses is important.

REFERENCES

References to appropriate books, specifications, and standards also are included in the text discussions for the particular subjects.

1. ACI Publication 116R, "Cement and Concrete Terminology"; also, "Manual of Concrete Practice," MCP-1.2.

2. American Society for Testing and Materials: ASTM Standard C125, "Definition of Terms Relating to Concrete and Concrete Aggregates," Philadelphia, PA, latest edition.

3. ACI Standard 318, "Building Code Requirements for Reinforced Concrete."

4. American Concrete Institute, *ACI Manual of Concrete Practice,* Parts 1, 2, and 3, Detroit, MI, latest edition. This manual includes the four following references, along with many other ACI Standards and Reports relating to numerous phases of concrete technology.

5. ACI Standard 301, "Specifications for Structural Concrete for Buildings."

6. "Effect of High Temperature in Hardened Concrete," *Concrete Construction,* November 1971.

7. "Slab Thickness Design for Industrial Concrete Floors On-Grade," The Portland Cement Association, Philadelphia, PA, latest edition.

8. ACI Standard 318, Commentary on "Building Code Requirements for Reinforced Concrete."

9. Troxell, George E., Harmer E. Davis, and J. W. Kelley: *Composition and Properties of Concrete,* 2d ed., McGraw-Hill, New York, 1968.

10. Zia, Paul, H. Kent Preston, Norman L. Scott, and Edwin B. Workman: "Estimating Prestress Losses," *Concrete International,* June 1979.

CHAPTER 2-4

FLOORS

Kenneth J. Moore, FCSI, CCS

Specification Writer
Sverdrup Facilities, Inc.
St. Louis, Missouri

INTRODUCTION

Plant floors generally are subjected to extreme abuse, and receive minimum maintenance. Not only are they subjected to foot traffic, but also vehicles with hard rubber wheels, spilled chemicals, dropped products, and operating plant equipment. Combined with age, *floors of all kinds will deteriorate.* Floors must be considered as both working surfaces and traffic ways for moving people and products. Well-designed and well-maintained floor surfaces are safe and, in the long run, economical. The most expensive maintenance is usually replacement.

Floor product availability changes rapidly, with new developments almost weekly. Some products appear, fail, and disappear quickly. As a finished working surface, or with a wide variety of both integral and applied surface treatments, concrete continues to serve as the workhorse of floor construction. Some floors are considered special-purpose and require special treatments, for example, floors in food and beverage preparation areas must meet FDA or USDA requirements. Floors in clean rooms and some electronic production areas require dust-free and conductive type floors.

In the past, if a plant engineer wanted a floor to look clean and withstand abuse from production, it was painted and then repainted every year. Now floor finishes and treatments have improved greatly in both durability and appearance. Products are available for most types of service, but plant engineers must be aware of various product limitations and suitability for specific use. When using a floor finish, coating, or treatment, *suitability for the job must always be the concern.* The best source for this kind of information is the product manufacturer, who is usually expected to guarantee the product's performance.

In addition to suitability of use, safety considerations are also important. Restrictive fire and life safety regulations that are so prevalent affect not only structures, but finishes as well. The inappropriate application of a coating, for instance, may change a complying slip-resistant surface into a hazardous, slippery surface or into a surface that spreads fire, smoke, and toxic fumes. When a new plant is occupied, it is presumably in compliance with all applicable regulations and it should be maintained in the same way.

Whether installing a new floor or replacing an existing one, consideration should be given to:

1. Americans with Disabilities Act (ADA)
2. Slope for positive drainage
3. Tolerance limitations where automatic guidance system, conveying, and production equipment are in use
4. Temperature variations to which the floor will be subjected while in service

BASIC FLOOR MATERIALS

Concrete

Concrete, the basic material for most plant floors, has attributes of durability and strength. Without surface treatment it is absorbent, allowing soiling, buildup of grease and other chemicals, and surface dusting. Products and procedures are available to control these problems, making concrete an economical flooring material.

The basic concrete floor is an on- or above-grade monolithic slab that is placed and finished in continuous sequence after which it is allowed to cure. Finishing usually consists of troweling, possibly with special-purpose aggregates troweled into the uncured surface.

Finishes. Troweling the concrete surface consolidates (densifies) the surface and imparts either a smooth or textured surface. Since the durability of a concrete surface depends greatly on the aggregate (not the cement), care must be taken to prevent compressing the aggregate too far below the surface. If this happens, additional aggregate should be tamped into the surface and troweling continued.

Different surface characteristics are obtained by using trowels of various materials. Smooth surfaces are generally obtained with steel trowels, whereas various textures and slip resistant finishes are the result of using wood, magnesium, or aluminum trowels. Uncured surface also can be textured with burlap or stiff bristle brushes for rougher surfaces.

Special aggregates, other than mix aggregate, may be broadcast or tamped into the surface while the concrete is being finished. Metallic aggregates, such as processed iron filings, are frequently used to create highly durable surfaces in hard-use areas. By saturating the surface with well-compacted aggregate, the exposed cement can be reduced to as little as 5 percent of the exposed surface (normal concrete exposes 20 to 35 percent cement). Similarly, natural aggregates such as crushed granite, marble, trap rock, and hard river gravel are used to increase the surface durability; they can also be decorative.

Color is occasionally applied to concrete during the finishing process. This can be useful in identifying particular plant areas, especially hazardous areas. Color shakes (sprinkling the surface with dry color) should be kept to a minimum so as not to disturb the cement-to-aggregate balance. Color uniformity is difficult to control with this application method. Better uniformity can be obtained, at higher cost, by purchasing the concrete with the color premixed.

Texture of a concrete slab finish is an important part of a floor system. A smooth troweled finish is easy to clean, but when wet or similarly contaminated it can become slick and hazardous. A smooth steel trowel finish does not provide for good bond (tooth) for an applied finish. Concrete surfaces receiving an applied finish normally should have a light sandpaper finish; verify with the applied floor finish material manufacturer. A wood float or broom finish provides good slip resistance, but is difficult to keep clean; it can also be a problem for the application of a finish to be subsequently applied to the slab. Ridges resulting from a wood or broom finish that are nearly as high or higher than the thickness of the applied finish may allow concrete ridges to protrude through surface coating, or the surface coating may wear through prematurely to expose the concrete.

It is important to verify that the concrete finish is compatible with the applied finish, mortar setting bed, or adhesive material to be used in flooring system so a good bond is obtained for the system and adverse reaction does not occur within the system. Curing compounds normally should not be used because they prevent good bonding (adhesion) of the applied finish material; again it is necessary to verify the compatibility with finish material manufacturer.

Aggregates

Metallic Aggregates. Metallic aggregate toppings are usually iron particles mixed with binders and a cement matrix. Their purpose is usually to increase the surface durability. Occasionally, they are used to increase the conductivity of the floor, preventing buildup of static electricity. These toppings are most commonly mixed with a minimum amount of water, placed on the rough slab, tamped to a dense mass, and troweled to the desired finish. Surface rusting in little-used areas is not unusual. Emery, aluminum oxide, and ceramic granules may be similarly used in some systems.

Natural Aggregates. Natural aggregate toppings may be granite, marble, quartz, trap rock, or gravel. Maintenance and sealing are important if the aggregate's inherent durability is to be preserved.

Clay Products

Flooring products of a basic clay (earthen) composition are brick, quarry tile, and ceramic tile. These products are most frequently laid over a rough concrete slab, and are set in mortar or sand (for flexibility). Products vary in size from 1×1 in (25×25 mm) face to 12×12 in (300×300 mm) and larger, with thickness ranging from ¼ to 2¾ in (6 to 70 mm). This type of flooring is characterized by numerous mortar joints and a hard, nonresilient surface that is highly resistant to chemical attack. The joints are the most vulnerable part of the system and should be selected and installed with care.

Brick. Paving bricks were widely used as plant flooring, but they are not found frequently in modern construction. Improvements in concrete surfacing plus other product developments have reduced their use. Bricks are molded clays burned at high temperatures to form a dense, hard surface that can have various textures and glazes.

Chemical-resistant bricks are used for sanitary and industrial applications. Normally these units should comply with either ASTM C279 or C410. ASTM C279 has three types of units: Type I for use where low absorption and high acid resistance are not major factors, Type II for use where lower absorption and higher acid resistance are required, and Type III for use where minimum absorption and maximum acid resistance are required.

ASTM C410 has two types of units. Type T is normally used where superior resistance to thermal and mechanical shock is needed, but low absorption is not required. Type M is normally used where low absorption is required but thermal and mechanical shock is not required.

Areas subjected to washdown or chemical migration through joints should have a subfloor protected with an impervious membrane. The membrane should be selected relative to the service to which it will be subjected.

Resin mortars and grouts are normally used with chemical-resistant brick units. Resin mortars include furan, epoxy, phenolic, polyester, and vinyl ester based formulations. Resin grouts include epoxy and furan based formulations. Polyester mortars have a more limited resistance range than furan, and set shrinkage is greater than with other resin based products. Furan mortars are resistant to wide range of chemicals; they are not intended for application to concrete or metal. They can be used if an acid-resistant membrane waterproofing is applied over the concrete first. Epoxy mortars develop a good bond to concrete and exhibit very little shrinkage during their curing stage. They have excellent resistance to nonoxidizing acids and alkalies, but are only moderately resistant to many solvents.

Quarry and Ceramic Tile.   Quarry and ceramic tile are available in glazed or unglazed units. Unglazed tiles usually are used for flooring and may have abrasive units mixed with regular units for increased slip resistance—about 7 percent of abrasive tile is normal. Because of their higher cost, these products are usually confined to areas where sanitation or appearance is important. They also are used as decorative floor treatment.

Setting materials include mortars, adhesives, grouts, and waterproofing specifically designed for tile-setting applications.

Portland cement mortar, composed of portland cement, sand, and water or latex admixture, is mixed at the site. This mortar is suitable for most surfaces and ordinary types of installation. The thick bed, ¾ to 1 in (19.1 to 25 mm) on walls and nominally 1¼ in (32 mm) on floors, facilitates accurate slopes or planes in the finished tile work. This system is more expensive than the dry-set method, and may require recessing of the concrete subsurface.

Dry-set mortars are factory mixed formulations which require addition of water only at site. The dry-set mortar is suitable for use over a variety of surfaces. It is used in one layer, as thin as ³⁄₃₂ in (2.4 mm) after tiles are beat in, has excellent water and impact resistance, is water-cleanable, nonflammable, is good for exterior work, and does not require soaking of tile. Care should be exercised in pouring the concrete subsurface to provide a close tolerance on the levelness of the subfloor; this can be a problem especially if the floor is subjected to heavy wheel or concentrated loads. Because of its thin-setting bed this floor system affords little adjustment for uneven subsurfaces. Therefore, if voids develop because of this situation, the tile may break.

The advantage of latex mortar or admixture is to improve adhesion and provide greater resistance to frost damage, shock, and impact. Be sure to allow mortar to dry thoroughly before exposure to moisture from in-service conditions.

Epoxy and furan resin mortars are suitable for use where chemical resistance is required. Epoxy mortars provide high bond strength and high impact resistance. High-temperature-resistant epoxy formulas are available. Modified epoxy emulsion mortars are formulated for thin-set installations of ceramic tile on floors and walls, interior and exterior. Their features include high bond strength, ease of application, little or no shrinkage, and economical epoxy application. Epoxy adhesive is formulated for thin-setting tile where high bond strength is required.

Organic adhesives are solvent-release curing products that have limited serviceability for plant and commercial applications. They are applied in one thin layer and supply some flexibility to the tile facing. Their bond strengths vary greatly from manufacturer to manufacturer. Organic adhesives are not recommended for temperatures exceeding 140°F.

When using latex grout, grout film should be removed from exposed tile face as soon as possible as it is more difficult to remove than regular grout. This is especially true when trying to remove grout from tile with a porous surface.

Epoxy and furan resin grout afford the same benefits as their setting-bed counterparts. When using epoxy and furan resin grout, it is recommended the tile faces be waxed to prevent grout from permanently remaining on tile face. Provide expansion and control joints in accordance with Tile Council of America, Inc. (TCA), Handbook.

Wood

For finished plant areas such as showrooms, display areas, and lobbies, there are a number of prefinished and unfinished wood floor products. The products previously mentioned plus parquet and strip flooring of oak, pine, maple, and teak are all suitable for this use. These flooring materials require daily maintenance to preserve the exceptional finishes.

Metal

Metal is most frequently used for flooring in the form of gratings and plate, usually applied over a structural steel framework. Both stair and platform (or walkway) surfaces are made with these products. Strength, durability, low maintenance, and ease of cleaning are features of this type of metal flooring. Metal plate or grating systems can also be made portable for increased flexibility.

Metal plates may be steel, galvanized steel, or aluminum, with plain or "checkered" surfaces. Gratings can also be obtained in the same materials. The material size varies and should be engineered to support the loads imposed. Plate for walking surfaces is usually selected as checkered, with a raised-pattern slip-resistant surface. An epoxy or urethane coating with slip-resistant additives can be applied to a smooth surface plate to provide a slip-resistant surface. Care should be taken to select a coating with a low tabor abrasion rating to prevent having to recoat surface frequently.

Fiberglass and Plastic Grating

Fiberglass and acid-resistant plastic should be considered for grating, cover plates, and edge angles where high resistance to acid are required.

APPLIED FINISHES

Hardeners, Dustproofing, and Sealing

Surface treatments that harden and reduce dusting are basic to almost all concrete installations. Common examples are sodium silicate crystals and magnesium fluorosilicate crystals, which are both mixed with water. Liquid curing agents to promote uniform curing are similarly applied. Consideration should be given to the final floor finish intended in an area because curing agents can have an adverse effect on the bonding of resilient, resinous, coating, terrazzo, and clay types of flooring products.

Concrete Stains

A number of concrete stains are available, some of which both color and harden the surface. In addition, some wood-stain products can serve adequately as concrete stains.

Coatings

Coatings are applied in one to three applications, varying in thickness from 10 mil to 60-plus mils. They are applied by roller and spray, except for the self-leveling types which are squeegee applied.

Coatings are sometimes applied to prevent dusting, improve cleanability, provide identification of areas, and identify hazards. Coatings in the past traditionally were considered to be limited-life, high-maintenance finishes. Today, coatings offer more durability and cleanability than the old pigmented oils. They cure, rather than dry, to form a tough film that will withstand hard usage on light-duty, and medium-duty floors. Surface preparation is highly critical in accomplishing this durability, and the manufacturer's recommendations should be carefully followed in preparing new or old floors to preserve the product guarantees.

Terrazzo

There are three basic cast-in-place terrazzo types: sand cushion, bonded, and adhesive-bonded. Sand cushion consists of a ¹⁄₁₆-in (1.6-mm) sand cushion under an isolation membrane, followed by a 2-in (51 mm) reinforced concrete underbed and a ½-in (12.7-mm) terrazzo topping. This system provides the best insurance against cracking and general failures. A bonded terrazzo system has the underbed, which is normally 1½ to 1¾-in (38 to 44.4-mm) thick, bonded to the concrete slab. The topping is the same as the sand cushion system. This system, while more economical, affords less insurance against cracking and general failure. The concrete underbed should have a float finish. An adhesive-bonded terrazzo system is bonded directly to a smooth finished concrete underbed. A bonding agent is used in both the underbed and terrazzo topping mix. This system is more expensive than the bonded system, but less expensive than the sand cushion system. The adhesive-bonded system, because it is bonded to and made a part of the concrete subsurface, resists cracking better than the bonded system.

There are three resinous matrix terrazzo systems: polyacrylate-modified cement, epoxy resin, and polyester resin. Most polyacrylate-modified cement systems are free from objectionable odors, provide high bond strength, and are resistant to snow-melting salt, foodstuffs and urine. Epoxy resin terrazzo systems provide good resistance to impacts and indentations from point loading, and afford good resistance to most cleaning solutions (alkaline type) and mild acids (but not lactic, acetic, and other strong acids). Polyester resin terrazzo systems provide the highest compressive strength, abrasion resistance, and resistance to indentation. They have good chemical resistance, except to cleaning agents containing alkaline compounds. Odors given off during cure can be objectionable to building occupants and adversely affect some products produced in the plant.

The National Terrazzo and Mosaic Association Inc. recommends a resinous matrix terrazzo system when a conductive floor is required. They no longer recommend cementitious matrices. Cement matrix terrazzo systems should not be used in areas subjected to high levels of acids, alkalines, staining, or constant wetting.

Curing, sealing, and other compounds should not be used in areas where resinous terrazzo or bonded terrazzo will be applied.

RESINOUS FLOORING

Resinous coatings, such as epoxy, urethane, neoprene, acrylic, polyester, and vinyl esters, are normally trowel applied to a thickness between ⅛-in (3.2-mm) and ¼-in (6.4-mm) thick. There are resinous flooring systems that are chemical resistant, nonsparking, highly impact resistant, resilient, abrasion resistant, and conductive. Most of these systems are proprietary and vary in formulations and applications among the manufacturers; no single product contains all of these qualities, nor does a single manufacturer necessarily produce a line of products containing all these qualities.

Failure of these systems usually occurs as delamination from the base (a result of faulty preparation or moisture drive through slabs on-grade). Always verify the proposed application with the manufacturer. When resinous flooring is installed on below-grade or on-grade slabs, a good vapor retarder is required under the slab. The vapor retarder must prevent moisture migration from the subgrade through the concrete substrate. Moisture migration can cause delamination problems and possible deterioration of the floor system. For existing slabs, the selection of a primer that will also act as a vapor retarder will minimize this problem.

RESILIENT FLOORING

Resilient flooring, in the form of tile and sheet goods, is primarily for light- to medium-duty finished areas where a finished appearance is important. Tile is easy to install and repair, but has numerous joints. Sheet-goods flooring is more difficult to install and requires more fitting. However, it is not difficult to repair, and has fewer seams. Sheet goods are usually a minimum of 6-ft (1.83-m) wide and are made in long roll lengths.

Resilient tile flooring is usually $12 \times 12 \times \frac{1}{8}$ in ($305 \times 305 \times 312$ mm) thick and $36 \times 36 \times \frac{1}{8}$ in ($915 \times 915 \times 312$ mm) thick. Some manufacturers produce $\frac{1}{16}$-in (1.6 mm) (service gage) and $\frac{3}{32}$-in, $\frac{3}{16}$-in, and $\frac{1}{4}$-in (2.4-mm, 4.8-mm, and 6.4-mm) thick tiles. Some 9×9 in (228×228 mm) tile is still available, but in limited materials and colors. Vinyl composition tile is the most common. Vinyl, rubber, and cork tiles are also available.

When resilient flooring is installed on new below-grade or on-grade slabs, a good vapor retarder is required under the slab. The vapor retarder must prevent the moisture from migrating from the subgrade through the concrete substrate. Moisture migration can cause breakdown or softening of the floor adhesive. It can also cause bubbles in the flooring.

Resilient tile and sheet goods products, as well as accessories such as rubber and vinyl bases, all use adhesives applied to concrete or wood subfloors. Adhesive must be used as recommended by the tile manufacturer for a particular installation: above grade, below grade, wet area, alkali resistance, etc.

Sheet goods are available as homogenous, cushioned, noncushioned, slip resistant, chemical resistant, studded, welded seams (heat and chemical weld), static conductive, and static dissipative. Homogenous products are produced with the color throughout the depth of the product, not just in the wearing surface. When selecting a cushioned or noncushioned product select the proper wearing surface thickness for the service to which the floor will be subjected. Only a few manufacturers produce industrial grade products. No one product contains all the qualities mentioned above.

A static conductive or static dissipative floor is a system of tile or sheet goods and their adhesives, which when combined creates a pathway of moderate electrical conductivity that allows static charges to flow safely to the ground. A static conductive system should be used where an electrical resistance of 25,000 ohms to 1 megohm is required. A static dissipative system should be used where an electrical resistance of 1 megohm to 1000 megohms is required.

Studded tile and sheet goods are available in circles, squares, rectangles, dots, diamonds, and many more configurations.

CARPET

Very little carpet finds its way into the industrial plant. Carpet is usually confined to offices and showrooms, where it functions well and provides a degree of noise control. Special care must be taken in the selection of carpet to assure the selected carpet complies with ADA requirements.

MAINTENANCE

Floor maintenance is a continuing process, beginning immediately with first use. Floor surface deterioration is a direct result of debris accumulation. Where abrasive debris is present, sweeping one or more times a day will be necessary to prevent rapid damage. Daily sweeping is advisable for all floors, with more frequent attention to trouble spots. The decision to use a manual or a power sweeper is unimportant, with the choice often dependent upon the size of the area being maintained.

Continual attention to cleaning up spills and leaks of liquids of all kinds, from water to acids and alkalies, is essential to a long floor life. This is probably the most difficult type of cleaning to control, usually waiting until a walking hazard develops. Some types of spills can be controlled by dry absorbent floor granules, so a supply should be maintained in areas of frequent problems.

Floors of a more finished nature, such as resilient flooring, resinous flooring, and some clay tiles, require more than just sweeping. Mopping, anywhere from daily to weekly as the conditions dictate, is essential. Latent abrasive dust left after sweeping is very destructive to these surfaces and can be controlled only by mopping or power scrubbing. Water from this type of cleaning should be removed quickly to prevent deterioration of the adhesives.

Repairs

Repair work can be classified as emergency or permanent. Permanent repairs are those which restore a floor to its original state, usually requiring professional help. Too frequently, emergency repairs become accepted as permanent. Emergency repairs should not be forgotten or ignored. The plant engineer should proceed with permanent repairs as soon as feasible since delays usually result in an increasingly difficult repair job.

Emergency Repairs. Emergency repairs are necessary when floor damage results in a hazardous condition for walking or vehicular traffic, or structurally endangers the building. The emergency repair should relieve rather than accentuate the condition. Expedients such as placing boards or plywood over a hole, for instance, may constitute a hazard equal to that of the hole.

Most applied flooring materials do not require emergency repairs unless they are loose. When sheet goods, tile, or other film-like finishes come loose, temporary repairs can sometimes be made with a typical water-soluble white glue, with the area weighted for a few hours. When the permanent repair is made, the white glue should be removed.

Permanent Repairs. Ordinary concrete, wood block, and resilient tile repairs are frequently handled by plant maintenance personnel. Resilient sheet goods, seamless flooring, and other special concrete toppings and integral finishes require skillful repairs to restore the floor properly for its intended purpose. The use of a professional for this work is advisable.

Concrete. Repairing ordinary concrete floors can be routine, requiring few preparations. Materials needed include cement (portland cement type I or type III), clean sand, and coarse aggregate (clean rock or gravel ½ to 1 in (12.7 to 25 mm), approximating the aggregate used in the floor). If the patch is small or there is a concern that the patch will break loose of the original floor, a good latex concrete bonding agent will improve the bond. If floor is wet frequently, an epoxy bonding agent is advisable. All patching materials should be clean and the cement should be fresh.

Patching procedures should approximate the following:

1. Clean the area to be patched removing all loose material and dust, and wire-brush the reinforcing steel, if any (do not remove).
2. Repair vapor retarder, waterproofing, or insulation, if any.
3. Undercut edges of holes to about ½ in (1.27 cm); cut out cracks to about ½-in (1.27 cm) width and 1-in (2.54 cm) depth. Clean all surfaces.
4. Prepare the patching material in a clean mixer. For larger holes use a 1:2:4 or 1:2½:5 mix by volume of cement, sand, and coarse aggregate. Use a cement and sand mix only for small patches and cracks, about 1:2½. Mix with only enough clean, potable water to make a stiff

mix (should form a cohesive ball when squeezed, without excess water). A water supplement may be used to replace some mixing water to improve the bond to old concrete.

5. Dampen surfaces to be patched, particularly earth under slabs. Apply bonding agent to old concrete and reinforcing steel, or brush with a cream-like slurry of cement and water.

6. Place the patch-mix in the hole or the crack and compact it. Be sure the mixture fills undercuts and has good contact with reinforcing steel. Tamp in mixture until slightly higher than adjacent surface.

7. Trowel-finish, compacting flush with adjacent surfaces. Use the trowel to match the adjacent existing finish.

8. Apply a surface hardener and/or sealer, if appropriate.

Again, control of water is important. Excessive water contributes to shrinkage, which only weakens the patch. If a patch occurs at an expansion or control joint, the joint should be restored.

Where severe structural cracking occurs in a concrete floor, repairs must be engineered to restore the design strength of the slab. This is best left to professionals. Systems involving pressure-injected adhesives are also available for such restoration.

Resilient Tile and Wood Block.   Repairs to resilient tile and wood block are simpler if replacement units to match the original are available. Repair consists of removing and replacing the tile or block with a new unit. For removal of tile refer to "Recommended Work Practices for Removal of Resilient Floor Coverings." Color and pattern matching is always a problem with tile, so obtaining extra tile at the time of construction is advisable for future repairs.

SELECTION OF FLOORING SYSTEMS

When evaluating a product for use, review the manufacturer's data sheet for the compression strength, tabor abrasion resistance, and chemical resistance charts for resistances to products or cleaning materials to which the floor may be subjected. Remember to know what temperature each chemical will be at when it comes in contact with flooring system when reviewing chemical resistance charts. A product may excellently resist a chemical at normal temperature, but fail when subjected to the same chemical at a higher temperature.

Verify that vapors emitted into the air while curing will not affect the product produced at the plant or the production schedule (due to a personnel health hazard shut-down requirement), and that vapors will not cause harmful or dangerous conditions, such as an explosion if subjected to sparking. Always verify the suitability of a specific use with the manufacturer of the finish floor system. Compatibility must be checked when recoating or applying a different flooring over an existing applied finish floor system.

SURFACE PREPARATION

Surface preparation is as important as selecting the right product. Surface preparation is critical when repairing an existing floor system or applying a new floor finish system over a existing or new substrate. All traces of wax, oil, grease and other contaminants must be removed. This may be accomplished by one of the following methods, depending on severity of contamination.

1. Sprinkle an absorbing compound on contaminated areas. Allow the absorbing compound to absorb the contaminate, then sweep up.

2. Scrub the contaminated area with a detergent or commercial cleaner. If the contaminate has penetrated very deep into the subsurface, it may be necessary to seal the contaminated area after cleaning the area to prevent contaminate from coming to the surface again. Be sure to verify that all products used are compatible with floor finish material to be used. If an acid cleaning method is used, the surface must be checked to see that the pH factor and moisture content are within an acceptable range required by the floor finish material manufacturer.

3. Use an abrasive blast method, conforming to ASTM D4259. Abrasive air blasting is a cleaning method using pressurized equipment that meters abrasive particles into a stream of compressed air which then conveys them through a "blast hose" and, finally, a "blast nozzle" onto the surface to be cleaned. Abrasive blasting equipment is usually very portable and available at a reasonable cost.

   The main drawback to abrasive blasting is that it emits the blasting abrasive and the material it is removing into the air for a fair distance around the blast area. The dusting and fallout can be limited somewhat by using "wet blasting" equipment. Wet blasting equipment wets the abrasive flow with water to reduce dusting.

   There are a variety of abrasive materials available; care should be exercised in selecting the proper abrasive.

4. Use the blast track or scarifying method. In most cases this method will require the area be repaired with a self-leveling surfacing compound. If the patched area is to have a floor topping applied over it, verify that the surfacing compound is compatible with the applied floor finish system. If the area is to be left exposed, verify that the patching compound being used will be able to withstand the service to which it will be subjected. Blast track method employs a portable piece of equipment that propels steel shot, steel grit, or a mixture of both against the concrete surface. These units also are sealed to the surface by vacuum to recover and recycle the abrasive while removing dust and other particles. Scarifying is done with a portable piece of equipment that employs a wheel which rotates and impacts the concrete surface.

Verify that the tensile and compression strengths of the substrate are adequate to receive the resinous floor system being applied over it, and that it is adequate for the service to which the entire floor will be subjected. Also, verify that the finish surfacing will tolerate moisture if the floor is subjected to water cleaning or is frequently wet due to the manufacturing process.

Most floor finish system manufacturers require newly placed concrete to be cured minimum of 28 days before their floor finish product is applied. Verify requirements of the product being used with the manufacturer. Most field catalyzed (two or more components) systems have a minimum and maximum cure time (window) between coats. This window varies among manufacturers. If maximum recoat time is exceeded or patching of the cured surface is required, the surface should be roughened by lightly abrasive blasting, sanding, or a chemical softener (use only the chemical softener recommended by the flooring manufacturer). Feather the adjacent intact coating before applying the new coating to patched area.

If you have any doubts that the system will perform, do a sample test panel.

WORKMANSHIP STANDARDS

The ASTM standards listed in the Bibliography are standards for surface preparation of concrete. Before including them in a work description, read the reference standard and exclude any option not wanted. Knowledge of the standards also can be helpful in guidance of daily plant maintenance.

FIELD QUALITY CONTROL

To help ensure a durable flooring system, review the following during application of a flooring system.

1. Verify that the surface preparation has been properly completed and is acceptable for the product being applied.
2. Make sure that the air and surface temperatures do not exceed minimum or maximum limits specified in the manufacturer's product data sheet. Be sure that the air and surface temperatures are more than 5°F above dew point.
3. During mixing, observe that the thinners used are those required for the product and field conditions being encountered at the time of installation. Monitor that the amount of thinner being added is within limits stated in manufacturer's product data sheet. All these specifications should be listed on the manufacturer's product data sheet.
4. Be sure that the time elapsing between application of coats is within the time limits specified in manufacturer's product data sheet.

SUMMARY

Surface preparation is one of the most important factors in a durable floor system. Before starting an in-house plant floor finish project or allowing a contractor to start a floor finish project, the plant engineer should verify the following:

1. Concrete has been adequately cured. A minimum cure time of 28 days in normally required in most cases.
2. If curing, sealing, or hardening compound is to be used, verify that they are compatible with the floor finish system being applied.
3. The surfaces are free of dirt, grease, and other contamination immediately prior to start of application of the floor finish system.
4. The concrete surface and finish are acceptable to the floor finish material manufacturer and are capable of providing a good bond for the floor finish system being applied.

Acid etching to clean surfaces is not recommended by most flooring manufacturers, except when there is no other practical alternative.

Floor finish treatments, coatings, systems, and additives have multiplied to the point where it is impossible to categorize and comment on all. Even when restricted to those suitable for plant use, the number of products is overwhelming. This chapter has only briefly touched on some of the more commonplace floors. There is a floor for virtually every plant condition, with some form of concrete being the closest thing to an all-purpose floor. Obtaining and following the manufacturer's recommendations for maintaining and repairing the product and system are again stressed. Remember, neglect is the worst enemy of any floor.

BIBLIOGRAPHY

American Society for Testing and Materials (ASTM), 1916 Race Street, Philadelphia, PA 19103.

1. ASTM D4258, Surface Cleaning of Concrete.
2. ASTM D4259, Abrading Concrete.
3. ASTM D4260, Acid Etch of Concrete.

4. ASTM D4262, pH of Chemically Cleaned and Etched Concrete.

5. ASTM D4263, Indicating Moisture in Concrete by Plastic Sheet Method.

Construction Specification Institute (CSI), 601 Madison Street, Alexandria, VA 22314-9970. SpecGuides: A talk-you-through technical paper containing selection criteria, specification considerations, inspection reminders, references, and resources.

1. G09310, Ceramic Tile

2. G09636, Chemical Resistant Brick Flooring

3. G09650, Resilient Flooring

4. G09970, Fluid-Applied Resilient Flooring

5. G09680, Carpet

6. G09705, Resinous Flooring

Resilient Floor Covering Institute, 966 Hungerford Drive, Suite 12B, Rockville, MD 20850. *Recommended Work Practices for Removal of Resilient Floor Coverings.*

Tile Council of America, Inc., P.O. Box 326, Princeton, NJ 08542-0326. *Handbook for Ceramic Tile Installation.*

CHAPTER 2-5
WALLS, WINDOWS, AND ENTRANCES

Curt Lambdin
Project Architect
Sverdrup Facilities, Inc.
St. Louis, Missouri

INTRODUCTION

Walls, windows, and entrances are those parts of the plant that provide weather protection, visual and sound control, sanitary controls, access to spaces, and frequently, fire control. Most common building materials may be used as part of a system of walls, windows, and entrances. This chapter considers only those most prevalent in plant structures: wood, masonry, concrete, plastics and metals.*

It is important for the plant engineer to recognize that certain walls, windows, and entrances in modern plants are part of a fire-control system established by building codes and insurance requirements. In the case of doors and some windows, attached labels identify them as such. However, ceilings, walls, or floors are usually not so marked. Before modifying or repairing these components, establish whether they are fire rated and, if so, protect the integrity of the system. Refer to local code authorities or your professional consultant to determine whether a fire rating is required.

---

* A more detailed description of materials in Don A. Watson, *Construction Materials and Processes*, 2d ed., McGraw-Hill, New York, 1978, is recommended for reference.

WALLS

Masonry

Wall construction of brick, stone, and other earthen or cementitious building blocks is referred to as unit masonry. Units of various sizes are stacked, and the whole is unified with a cementitious jointing material, or mortar. Many types of units and their joints are water-absorptive. Masonry walls are constructed of one or more wythes (rows front to back), depending on the expected service. For exterior walls, the wythe exposed to the weather should be of durable quality with low absorption; the remaining wythes are basically for strength. Weathering ability is not important for interior walls and partitions; however, many plant situations demand high-performance masonry for chemical resistance, sanitation, or other special conditions.

Some of the traditional masonry products, such as gypsum block and structural clay tile (both glazed and unglazed), have limited availability. Glazed structural clay tile is still available from a very small number of manufacturers, but matching the color and size of older units may be expensive. A more economical finish to consider as a replacement for structural clay tile is ceramic tile.

Modern masonry construction frequently consists of brick and concrete masonry because the materials are readily available, durable, and relatively economical. Concrete masonry units (blocks and brick made of portland cement and aggregate) are a common backup material, and are used widely for interior and exterior wall facing. Glazed units are available, or various coatings may be applied to provide specific weathering or service characteristics. Coatings, of course, must occasionally be renewed. Where brick, a glazed unit, or stone is the exposed face, a coating is generally applied only to reduce absorption of water or soiling.

Standards. The quality of most masonry products is controlled by industrial and national standards too numerous to list here. The most definitive of these is the American Society for Testing and Materials (ASTM). Most of the material standards that will be needed by a plant engineer are included in the publication "ASTM Standards in Building Codes," available from ASTM. This publication also contains standards for many other building materials, as well as masonry.

Classifications. Modern masonry product lines have expanded to include a number of grades (quality) and finishes for the old, traditional materials—particularly brick, concrete masonry, and mortar. Although this complicates the selection process, it does permit selecting an economical product for a particular use.

Brick is classified by ASTM as SW (severe weather), MW (moderate or normal weather), or NW (nonweathering). This allows the plant engineer to select an exposed brick suitable for a particular climate or use, and yet select a less-expensive product when weathering is not critical.

Concrete masonry units are classified as load-bearing or non-load-bearing and are also controlled by ASTM by grade—Grade N (above- or below-grade, exposed to moisture), and Grade S (limited to above-grade use). Concrete masonry may also be standard or lightweight, depending on the type of aggregate used in the concrete mix.

Mortar, however, is graded by type according to its strength (see Table 5-1). Masonry mortar is frequently site-mixed from bulk ingredients, but the prepared masonry mortar mixes are convenient for maintenance and minor repairs. This eliminates stockpiling cement, sand, and lime. Such prepared mixes usually are available locally in 50-lb (2.3-kg) or 90-lb (4-kg) bags and, occasionally, in ready-to-use caulking-type cartridges. The cartridges can be very handy for resetting loose brick or stone, tuckpointing eroded joints, and resetting loosened quarry tile or brick flooring. It is possible to obtain masonry mortar from some ready-mix plants.

Loading Characteristics. Masonry walls can be designed to support heavy loads applied vertically, but are weak resisting lateral (horizontal) loads, as from high winds or vehicle

TABLE 5-1 Masonry Mortar*

Mortar type	Average compressive strength at 28 days, lb/in² (MPa)	Parts by volume of portland cement, cement, or portland blast-furnace slag cement	Parts by volume of masonry cement	Parts by volume of hydrated lime or lime putty	Aggregate, measured in a damp, loose condition
M	2500(17.2)	1	1	—	Not less than 2¼ and not more than 3 times the sum of the volumes of the cements and lime used
S	1800(12.4)	1		¼	
		½	1	—	
		1		over ¼ to ½	
N	750(5.2)		1	—	
		1		over ½ to 1¼	
O	350(2.4)		1	—	
		1		over 1¼ to 2½	
K	75(0.5)	1		over 2½ to 4	

* After ASTM C270.

impact. Masonry walls subject to lateral loads are usually reinforced with steel ladder-type or truss-type joint reinforcing and also are designed with deformed reinforcing steel rods vertically. Designing such structures is best left to professional consultants. However, it is important that the plant engineer, in restoring damaged walls, should replace reinforcing where affected by the patchwork.

Wood

A minimum amount of wood is used for modern plant construction. Although it is one of the least expensive construction products, fire codes prohibit such construction in larger plants, or require special fire treatment. Smaller new plants and older plants may still contain considerable amounts of wood. Fire-treated wood was once frequently used in roof construction, but over time it was found to deteriorate quickly and is now restricted by most code authorities.

Metal

Durability, strength, low maintenance costs, and reasonable first costs are factors that characterize metal products in plant construction. Walls, roof systems, doors, windows, and many other components are primarily metal, usually some form of steel or aluminum. The availability of many alloys, sizes, and shapes of both steel and aluminum contribute to their great versatility. The many forms of sheet and strip stock, bars, rods, tubes, and pipe, as well as structural shapes and custom-designed shapes, are evidence of this versatility.

A large consumer of metal products for construction is the building systems industry. Pre-engineered metal structures have steel supporting members, metal roofing, and metal wall panels.

Many of the building systems components, such as wall panels and roofing sheets, can be used for additions and alterations in other types of construction. Also, many products of a similar type are available in various strengths, configurations, and finishes. Insulated sandwich and plain metal panels for roofs and walls are frequently used with conventional steel and masonry construction, and have become a common form of large plant design. Some shapes, such as common corrugated panels, have become industry standards and do not change from year to year. These are good selections where the possibility of frequent replacement because of damage is expected and where future expansion is a consideration.

Many of the newer systems, including insulated metal panels, incorporate the use of the newer structural silicon sealants (see Chap. 2-8). In fact, one of the major responsibilities in the maintenance of walls, windows, and entrances is a good working knowledge of the state-of-the-art sealants.

Metals are used in plants in many other miscellaneous ways: as light framing members of wall and partition systems and window and entrance units (discussed further in this chapter), as floor components (Chap. 2-4), and for security and safety applications too numerous to list here.

Other Construction Materials

Cementitious Products. These are usually some form of cement mixed with an aggregate and water, with the most common products used in plants being concrete or some form of plaster. The structural aspects of concrete are discussed in other chapters.

Cementitious products have a major advantage in providing excellent fireproofing qualities. Usually applied or erected in a plastic state (precast or sitecast), cementitious products have great flexibility, which allows them to achieve special shapes and to conform to unique substrates. They can also be used very effectively in plants that must maintain sanitary standards for FDA or USDA criteria. The disadvantages are difficulty of repair and a lack of resiliency when cured. Because of its greater durability, concrete is the main cementitious product used in plant work.

Plaster is primarily a finish coating rather than a structural material. Most problems with plaster come from physical damage, and plaster use is therefore usually restricted to various fireproofing tasks and must be protected in contact areas. Some hard plasters, such as Keene's cement, are available for locations needing extra durability.

Plastics. Current use is limited to insulation, glazing, and a few wall-protective products. Advancements have been made in developing plastic windows, doors, and structural shapes, with the largest usage being impact doors for forklift truck areas and for windows and doors used in very wet or corrosive environments. As protective coatings and sheets, however, plastics find an increasing use in industrial applications. Tank linings, machinery finishes, wall and floor coatings, pipes, and food processing area finishes are a few of these uses. In the general area of coatings, finished fiberglass reinforced panels (FRP) have increased in usage since overcoming earlier problems with fire spread and smoke creation.

WINDOW AND ENTRANCE UNITS

Metal window and entrance units are common in modern plant construction. For many years, steel windows dominated the industry. Currently, there are fewer manufacturers of steel windows, but aluminum windows are plentiful. There is little difference in overall performance between the materials, but there is some variation in individual characteristics. For instance, steel is usually stronger, but aluminum is more weathertight because of better seals, and does not rust or require painting. In addition, because of the greater number of aluminum window manufacturers, there are more different window types available in aluminum. Any new or replacement exterior windows should have built into their system a thermal break. The major window problems are centered around glass breakage, hardware failure, and poor installation of perimeter sealants.

Steel entrance units continue their long-time popularity for plant installations. Many manufacturers produce units (doors and frames), and a wide selection of type and quality is available. Aluminum and stainless steel are most frequently used as major entrances to public and office areas, and at special locations where greater corrosion resistance is needed. For openings where fire ratings are necessary, steel frames with wood or steel doors are used. There are presently no fire-rated aluminum entrance assemblies. Glass is permitted in fire-rated doors but building codes do place severe restrictions on the size and type of glass permitted for various fire ratings.

MAINTENANCE AND REPAIRS

The materials previously discussed are combined in many ways with many other products to form wall, window, and entrance systems. *Systems* here is the key word, for all these elements must work together to provide a particular performance—for fire protection, for weatherability, or for service. In maintenance and repair work, the integrity of the system must be preserved.

Walls

Walls are most commonly built of masonry, concrete, or steel studs with a wall panel covering. Both masonry and concrete have general, widespread usage because of their durability and strength. Separately or in many combinations, the resulting walls and partitions offer the widest range of finished surfaces and a broad range of performance.

Plaster and Concrete Repairs

Routine wall and partition maintenance consists of cleaning and prompt patching of damage. Plaster and concrete repairs are not greatly different from concrete floor patching (see Chap. 2-4). It is essential to cut back damaged areas to solid, undamaged material; thoroughly clean the area; use a bonding agent or cement-water paste; and patch with a material matching the original. It is advisable to occasionally dampen the patch to promote curing and reduce shrinkage. Small breaks in concrete masonry can be patched in the same way. A piece of cardboard larger than the hole with a piece of string through the center can be used to keep patching materials from falling into the cells.

Masonry Repairs

Repairing masonry walls should be done with care to preserve the integrity of the original wall. When feasible, broken units should be replaced with whole units of the same type. This usually means cutting out the broken pieces with a chisel, including all of the old exposed mortar, to expose the adjacent units. A bonding additive can be combined with the mortar for improved bond. To insert the masonry unit, butter the edges of the unit and the sides of the hole with a fairly stiff mortar, insert and position the unit, and compress the mortar into the joint. Finish by tooling the joint to match the existing joints, adding mortar as needed. If the old units are very absorbent, dampening the new units before insertion is advisable.

Cracks in concrete, masonry, and plaster occur frequently; they require prompt attention. Static (nonmoving) cracks resulting from shrinkage or physical impact should be repaired with the same base material after cleaning the crack and cutting back to sound, tight material. It is helpful to lightly spray the crack with water to aid bonding of cementitious materials. Dynamic cracks resulting from expansion and contraction, or continuing building movement, should always be repaired with flexible sealants. This procedure prevents a buildup of rigid material in the crack, which will cause greater separation with the next movement (see Chap. 2-8).

Wall Panel Products

Wall panel products, such as drywall, hardboard, and metal panels are usually difficult to repair. Most frequently the quickest, most economical method is whole-panel replacement. Drywall repairs are possible, but are time consuming. A common repair procedure for drywall is to cut out the damaged area; screw furring strips around the perimeter of the hole allowing 1½ to 2 in (3.8 to 5.1 cm) exposure; then fill the hole with a piece of similar type and thickness of drywall, screwed to the furring strips; tape, sand, and paint. When repairing insulated metal panels, it is best to use a metal panel of the same material (steel or aluminum) to form the covering and then foam in place between the patches or cracks between patched-in panels and existing. This foam is a two-part polyurethane available in aerosol containers of various sizes.

Wood

The most important aspect of maintaining wood is maintaining the wood finish. Untreated wood must be finished to protect against early deterioration. Any disruption of the finish can lead to rotting and vermin infestation. Frequent inspection and touch-up of finishes are the best preventatives. Wood repairs usually involve replacing the damaged member, but occasionally minor damage can be repaired with wood fillers applied in thin layers to reduce shrinkage. If the structural integrity of the wood is reduced by damage, then replacement or "scabbing" (if not visually critical) is best to restore strength. Treated woods should always be replaced or repaired with like-treated woods.

Windows

Windows are usually identified or described by function, for example, single-hung, double-hung, center-pivoted, projected, fixed or picture, awning, hopper, or sliding. Windows that operate have a frame and sash, with the frame being the fixed portion that is built in or anchored to the wall. The sash is the fixed or operating frame containing the glazing, stops (or putty), and, occasionally, muntins (glass dividers). A fixed window has only the frame and glazing (maybe muntins) and is frequently referred to as a *fixed sash*.

Steel Windows. Plant buildings usually have windows of the steel pivoting or projected type, which are the simplest in operation and the easiest to install for remote operation. There is little that can go wrong with the functioning of these types of windows. Glass breakage is the major problem, and will be discussed under "Glazing." Rusted-out sills and hardware breakage (usually latches) are frequent problems with older windows. Although rusted-out sills can be repaired by removing the damaged part and welding in a new piece, it is sometimes difficult to find new sections to match the old. In this case replacement is advised. The cost difference between replacement and major repairs may be insignificant, depending on plant location. Replacement hardware may be unavailable locally for older windows, but companies such as Blain Window Hardware, Inc., stock many obsolete parts and can frequently supply replacement parts. It is advisable to send a sample for matching purposes.

Glazing. Replacing broken glass is a major maintenance cost for most plants. If breakage is in random locations, replacing with glass of the same kind is generally the most practical, especially if the glass is wire glass, laminated glass, or fire-rated glass. However, if breakage occurs frequently in one particular area, the plant engineer should consider using plastic glazing sheets for replacement, provided that a fire rating is not required.

Translucent fiberglass-reinforced plastic (FRP), acrylic, and polycarbonate sheets (clear, tinted, and opaque) make excellent replacements for glass in problem areas, but a few precautions are in order. If the existing sash has a glazing leg (recess) less than ½-in (1.27-cm) deep, only small panes of plastic glazing should be used since these products expand more than glass and require added leg space. Also, large pieces are flexible enough to blow out of frames with small glazing legs in high wind pressures or when accidently hit with a high-pressure steam hose; this feature may also be a security problem. The manufacturers can provide tables of recommended leg depths which can be used for pane selection or modifying the sash. In corrosive atmospheres, the plastic should be checked for chemical resistance to the agents present in the space.

Flat FRP panels are usually the most economical of the plastics, but are not available as clear sheets. Acrylic and polycarbonate sheets are closest to exact replacements for glass. Both have surfaces somewhat softer than glass and require care when cleaning to prevent scratching. In an area of blowing sand or other windblown abrasives, these products may become cloudy from the abrasion. The plant engineer must determine the problems this characteristic will cause in the specific locality.

Painting and Caulking.   The most important aspects of routine window maintenance are painting and caulking (see Chap. 2-8). Steel and wood windows must be kept painted to prevent deterioration. All rust, dirt, and loose paint should be removed before painting, and all bare steel or wood should be primed. A good-quality exterior enamel gives good performance. Some of the water-based paints are formulated for this use and can help reduce peeling paint on wood surfaces. Many metal window frames utilize weeps to drain water from internal gutter systems. They also use false trim caps over exterior frames to conceal internal components and enhance the window appearance. Sealant placed over weeps or sealed to these false trim caps will trap and divert water into the interior of the building rather than to the exterior as the manufacturer intended.

Entrances

Entrances include doors, door frames, hardware, and sometimes, glazing. Entrances are necessary for circulation of people and materials throughout spaces requiring fire, security, privacy, or environmental separation. Entrance units usually are described by the function and material of the door, such as single-swing wood, double-acting steel, and sliding aluminum. Steel doors of many functions are used widely in modern plants. Older buildings may have wood units. Aluminum and stainless steel are not usually used as decorative entrances, except in areas where their superior corrosion resistance is warranted.

Hardware.   Entrance units are second only to floors when it comes to abuse. Hardware failure is a major source of problems because the hardware is the working part of the entrance system. The door leaf and frame are subjected to impact damage and dents and punctures. Hardware, however, wears out, gets out of adjustment, is overstressed, and is otherwise abused. Thus, hardware maintenance is important to the service life of the entrance unit. For the larger plant, a stock of items that need frequent replacement or repair, such as closers and locksets, is recommended. Obtaining replacement parts for older door hardware is often difficult. Frequent tightening of bolts and screws helps reduce hardware breakage. Modern heavy-duty hardware is durable and reliable if reasonably maintained.

When considering hardware replacement, it is important that new hardware functions match the existing units as nearly as possible. Butts (hinges) may be plain or ball-bearing type. Ball-bearing butts are usually selected for heavy-duty service and should be replaced with the same type. Panic devices, if UL-rated, should be replaced with UL-rated devices. Avoid installing door-stop devices any closer than 18 in (45.7 cm) (preferably 24 in, or 61 cm) to the butt edge of the door to prevent overstressing the butts.

Hardware on fire doors is particularly important. Only the whole entrance assembly is fire-rated, and not the individual item, such as door, frame, or lockset. Therefore, fire-door hardware must be properly maintained if it is to function as originally rated and installed.

The new Americans with Disabilities Act (ADA) has made it necessary for each plant to consider whether its hardware complies with the act. A survey for ADA compliance should be done and hardware should be replaced as necessary to provide easy access for the disabled.

Unit Replacements.   When severe damage occurs at an entrance unit, doors and hardware are rather easily replaced. Frames, however, can be difficult. In plant construction, door frames are often steel, either rolled sheet-steel (hollow metal) or structural-steel channel sections with bar stops welded to the face. Both types of frames are often built-in, as walls are erected, and are almost impossible to remove without destroying the anchors (removing channel frames usually involves removing part of the wall). If the frames are clipped to the floor, the task is more difficult.

There is usually enough space at the jambs of hollow metal frames to slip in a hacksaw and cut the jamb anchors, generally three on each side of the opening. Frames are not usually anchored at the head in single or paired door openings. If there are no floor clips, the frames can then be removed and repaired. If there are floor clips, the frame is usually cut out and replaced with a new one. The plant engineer should consider the replacement costs of severely damaged steel doors and frames as opposed to repairs. For standard sizes and configurations, replacement may be less costly than major repairs.

Miscellaneous Doors.   Wood doors and frames are simpler than steel doors and frames to repair, but nevertheless are often replaced with steel for greater durability. More complex types of doors, such as rolling steel slat doors, rapid roll fabric doors, overhead acting doors, and most types of ornamental doors, are usually best repaired by service companies, particularly when such doors are equipped with power-actuated operators. Such operators may require sensitive adjustments for proper operation, and are easily damaged by improper maintenance. Problems related to these doors include malfunctioning relays, motor burnout, and broken springs.

Fire Doors.   Older types of fire doors are often equipped with closing devices controlled by fusible links, which permit the door to be held in the open position and still be self-closing in a fire. These fusible links should be replaced with magnetic contacts which are controlled by the fire alarm system. There are very few, if any, fire code officials who will still allow fusible links as part of a fire control system.

Summary.   The maintenance items listed previously are items that wear out or get damaged under normal usage of a building. This is not meant to imply that there is no other maintenance required for the individual systems. Every plant or building needs to have a regular maintenance schedule to take care of minor problems before they become major problems.

Regular maintenance should include cleaning, painting, inspecting, and repairing as necessary sealant joints, investigation of any new discoloration, cracking, or unusual wear patterns on an annual or biannual schedule. Discoloration, cracking, or unusual wear may be indications of larger problems that need attention.

It may be a cliche, but an ounce of prevention is still worth a pound of cure when it comes to plant maintenance.

BIBLIOGRAPHY

Architectural and Engineering Concrete Masonry Details for Building Construction, National Concrete Masonry Association, 6845 Elin St., McLean, VA 22101, 1967.

Blain Window Hardware, Inc., catalog, 1919 Blain Dr., Hagerstown, MD 21740.

Callender, John Hancock: *Time-Saver Standards for Architectural Design Data,* 6th ed., McGraw-Hill, New York, 1982.

Dalzell, J. Ralph: *Simplified Masonry Planning and Building,* McGraw-Hill, New York, 1972.

Dalzall, J. Ralph and G. Townsend: *Bricklaying Skill and Practice,* American Technical Society, Chicago, 1954.

Dalzell, J. Ralph and G. Townsend: *Masonry Simplified,* 2 vols., American Technical Society, 848 East 58th Street, Chicago, 1957.

Hornbostel, Caleb, and William J. Hornung: Materials and Methods for Contemporary Construction, 2d ad., Prentice-Hall, Englewood Cliffs, NJ, 1982.

Ramsey, C.G. and H. R. Sleeper: *Architectural Graphic Standards,* 8th ed., Wiley, New York, 1988.

Structural Clay Facing Tile Handbook, Facing Tile Institute, 333 North Michigan Avenue, Chicago, 1959.

Watson, Don A.: *Construction Materials and Processes,* 2d ed., McGraw-Hill, New York, 1978.

SPECIFICATIONS AND STANDARDS

"Abbreviations and Symbols Used in Builders' Hardware Schedules and Specifications," Builders' Hardware Manufacturers Association, 60 East 42nd Street, New York, NY 10017, 1961.

ANSI A42.1, "American Standard Specifications for Gypsum Plastering," American National Standards Institute, 1430 Broadway, New York, NY 10018, 1955.

ANSI A42.4, "American Standard Specifications for Interior Lathing and Furring," American National Standards Institute, New York, 1955.

ANSI A42.2 and A42.1, "American Standard Specifications for Portland Cement Stucco and Portland Cement Plastering," American National Standards Institute, New York, 1946.

"Guide to Portland Cement Plastering," Committee 524, American Concrete Institute, P.O. Box 4754, Bedford Station, Detroit, MI 48217.

ASTM Standards in Building Codes, latest ed., American Society for Testing and Materials, 1916 Race St., Philadelphia, PA 19103.

"Basic Builders' Hardware," Builders' Hardware Manufacturers Association, New York, 1969.

"Hardware for Hospitals," Builders' Hardware Manufacturers Association, New York, 1965.

"Hardware for Labeled Fire Doors," Builders' Hardware Manufacturers Association, New York, 1970.

"Hardware for Schools," Builders' Hardware Manufacturers Association, New York, 1966.

"Nomenclature for Steel Doors and Frames," A123.1, American National Standards Institute, New York, 1967.

"Recommended Practice for Portland Cement Plastering," Committee 624, American Concrete Institute, Detroit.

"Specifications for Aluminum Windows," Architectural Aluminum Manufacturers' Association, 35 East Wacker Drive, Chicago, IL 60601, 1970.

"Standardization of Terms and Nomenclature of Keying," Builders' Hardware Manufacturers Association, New York, 1969.

CHAPTER 2-6
ROOFING

Thomas Lee Smith, AIA, CRC

Director of Technology and Research
National Roofing Contractors Association
Rosemont, Illinois

INTRODUCTION

This chapter is intended to give the plant engineer an overview of the following: (1) materials for low-slope roofing (including deck, insulation, and roof coverings), (2) key design issues from the building owner's perspective, (3) application, from the building owner's perspective, (4) warranties, (5) maintenance, (6) installation of new penetrations and equipment, and (7) reroofing. Because of the importance of maintenance and the proper installation of new equipment or penetrations for an existing roof, and because these aspects of roofing are the ones that the plant engineer typically has the greatest opportunity to control or influence, *it is recommended that the plant engineer carefully review this chapter and Chaps. 2-5 and 2-7 on walls and thermal insulation.*

MATERIALS

The *roof system* is defined as an assembly of interacting roof components designed to weatherproof and, normally, to insulate a building's top surface. The roof assembly includes the *roof deck, vapor retarder,* and *roof insulation* (if they are present), and the *roof covering* (see Fig. 6-1).

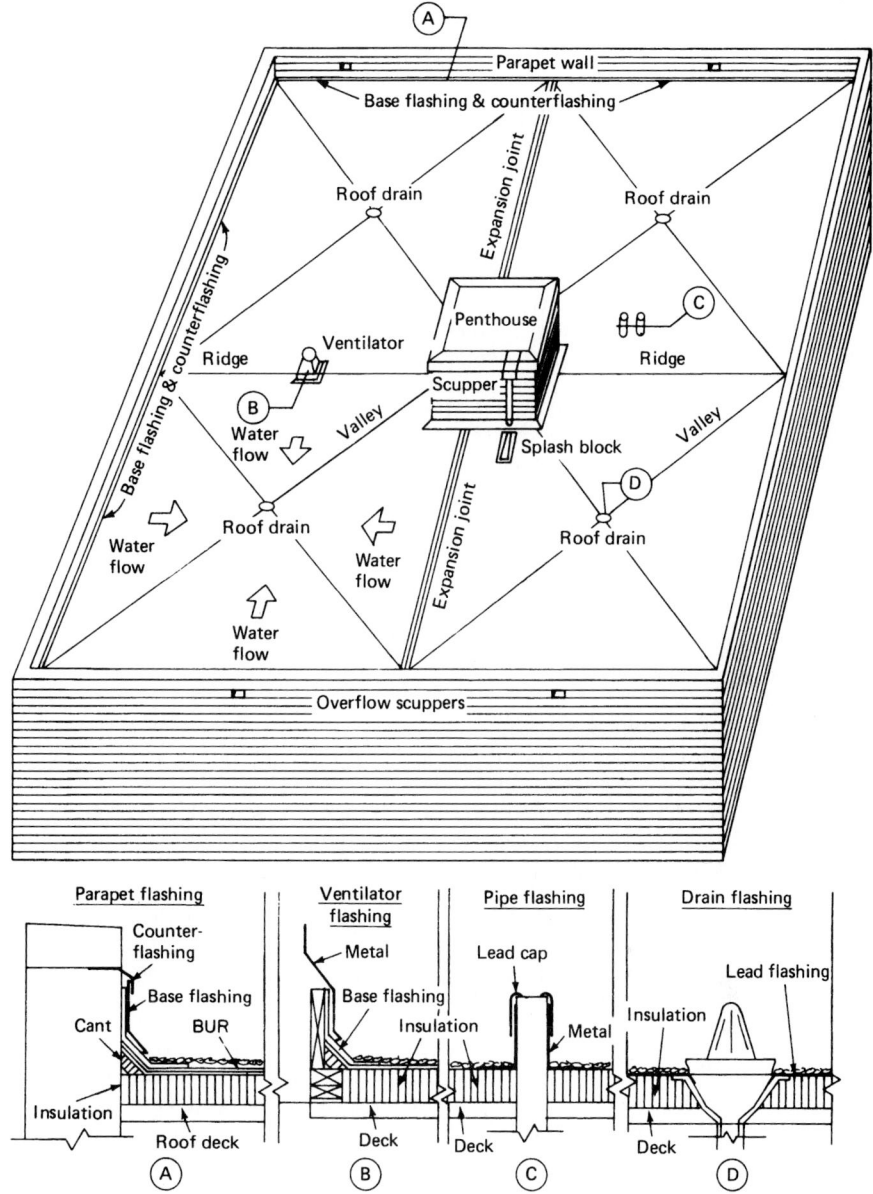

FIGURE 6-1 Typical roof arrangement (schematic).

The following section includes deck, vapor retarder, insulation, and low-slope roof covering materials. The discussion includes materials that are commonly used in the U.S. in the early 1990s. For further information, consult *The NRCA Roofing and Waterproofing Manual.*[1]

Decks

Cement-Wood Fiber Panels. These panels are composed of treated wood fibers that are bonded together with portland cement or any other binder and compressed or molded into flat panels.

Concrete Decks. Structural concrete decks can either be cast-in-place, post-tensioned, or precast (tees, double tees, channel slabs, flat slabs, or hollow-core slabs).

Lightweight Insulating Concrete Roof Decks and Fills. These are produced on the job site by combining insulating aggregates such as perlite or vermiculite, with portland cement and water. Another (and newer) variation of this type of deck is referred to as "cellular" lightweight insulating concrete. Rather than using aggregate, cellular concrete is produced with a foaming agent that creates small air cells within the matrix. The compressive strength and thermal resistance of lightweight insulating concrete decks depends upon the mix design and composition.

Lightweight insulating concrete may be cast over metal or over bulb-tee/formboard systems. Some types of lightweight insulating concrete may also be cast over concrete decks. For enhanced thermal resistance, molded expanded polystyrene (EPS) boards may be incorporated into the lightweight insulating concrete.

Poured Gypsum Concrete Decks. Although widely used many years ago, gypsum decks are now seldom used, except in a few locations in the U.S. This type of deck is produced on the job site by combining gypsum with wood fibers or mineral aggregates and water. The mixture is then cast on formboards.

Steel Decks. Steel deck panels are fabricated by roll-forming cold-rolled sheets. The panels are available in a paint (prime coat or prime and finish coat) or galvanized finish.

Steel decks can be fabricated with slots to allow downward-drying. These decks are often used with certain types of wet-fill toppings. Acoustical decks, which have numerous small perforations also are available. Batt insulation is usually installed in the flutes on the top side of the acoustical deck.

Thermosetting Insulating Fill. This fill is produced on the job site by mixing perlite aggregate with a hot asphalt binder. The mix is then placed over a structural deck. This fill provides some insulation, and it can be utilized to provide slope for drainage. Although more common many years ago, this type of system is still available.

Wood Planks or Panels. Wood decks can be composed of solid wood planks (usually tongue-and-groove) or sheathing panels. Sheathing was originally composed of all-veneer plywood, but more recently, oriented strand board (OSB) has been used. OSB is composed of compressed strand-like particles arranged in layers oriented at right angles to one another.

Vapor Retarders

A variety of materials are available for vapor retarders, including bituminous, kraft paper, polyethylene, and aluminum foil.

Insulation

Many of the insulation products described below are available in tapered configurations. (See also Chap. 2-7.)

Cellular Glass. This rigid insulation is composed of heat-fused closed glass cells.

Glass Fiber Batts. Batts or blankets (the only difference being the length of the product) are composed of glass fibers and a binding agent. The batts may be finished on one side with a kraft paper or aluminum foil facer, or they may be left unfaced.

Except in the case of metal roofing systems, glass fiber batts are typically not employed in low-slope roof systems.

Glass Fiber Board. This rigid insulation is composed of glass fibers and a binding agent, and faced on the top surface with kraft paper.

Mineral Wool Board. This rigid insulation is similar to glass fiber board, except that it is composed of mineral fibers (produced from molten rock). These boards are available faced or unfaced. This product was introduced into the U.S. roofing market around 1992.

Perlite. This rigid insulation is composed of expanded perlite, cellulose, and a binding agent.

Phenolic. This is a rigid plastic foam insulation. It was introduced into the U.S. marketplace in the early 1980s. In 1992, U.S. production of this product ceased.

Polyisocyanurate. This rigid plastic foam insulation resembles, and has essentially replaced, polyurethane board insulation due to improved fire resistance properties of the newer polyisocyanurate. These boards are also available as composites, which are factory produced by foaming the insulation to perlite, wood sheathing, or other types of substrates.

Polystyrene. Polystyrene is a rigid plastic foam. There are two distinctly different polystyrene products, molded expanded polystyrene (EPS), and extruded polystyrene.

Extruded polystyrene insulation is very resistant to water and water vapor, and is available in very high compressive strengths. Accordingly, it is the only type of insulation recommended for use in protected membrane roofs (PMRs). In PMRs, extruded polystyrene is placed above the roof membrane. The insulation is then covered with aggregate or concrete paver ballast.

Radiant Barrier System (RBS). RBS is an aluminum foil product with a low emittance (high reflectance) surface. An RBS is intended to reduce radiant heat transfer between a hot roof deck and cooler floor (or vice versa).

Reflective Insulation System (RIS). RIS is a double-sided aluminum foil product, used in combination with bulk insulation or in lieu of bulk insulation. The R-value is reportedly provided by the air space enclosed by the RIS.

Spray-Applied Polyurethane Foam (PUF). In addition to providing thermal insulation, this is a roofing system (when combined with other components). It is described in further detail later in this chapter.

Wood Fiberboard. This rigid insulation is manufactured from wood or cane fibers and binders.

Low-Slope Roof Coverings

Built-Up Roofs (BUR). This is the traditional low-slope roof covering. It is composed of bitumen (either asphalt or coal tar), felts (either organic, fiberglass, or polyester), and a surfacing (aggregate, coating, or cap sheet). The membrane is composed of between three and five plies of felt (as few as two plies are sometimes specified when polyester felt is used). The first ply is typically either set in a continuous layer of hot bitumen, or nailed to the deck. Subsequent layers of felt are set in a continuous layer of hot bitumen.

Cold-process (also known as cold-applied) is similar to hot-applied BUR, except that rather than using hot bitumen, asphalt-based cutbacks (a combination of asphalt and solvent), or emulsions (a combination of clay and asphalt particles dispersed in water) are typically used.

Liquid-Applied. Liquid-applied systems are supplied as either single or two-component elastomeric materials. Typically these systems are applied directly over concrete or plywood sheathing.

Metal. The metal roofing category includes a large variety of products. The type of metal used to form the products includes aluminum zinc alloy steel ("Galvalume"), aluminum, copper, and others. The steel and aluminum panels are available in several different types of paint finishes and colors. Many of the products are formed in a factory, while others are formed on the job site by the roofing contractor.

Metal panels include four primary types: Structural standing seam, architectural standing seam, exposed fastener, and traditional metal roofing. The standing seam panels are available with or without battens. The standing seam and exposed fastener panels are roll-formed, while traditional panels are typically press brake formed. The exposed fastener panels have largely been replaced by standing seam panels, except for very inexpensive construction.

Architectural and most traditional panels need to bear on a continuous structural substrate (deck) in order to carry live loads (e.g., snow), and they are typically used on relatively steep slopes, since they are water-shedding, rather than waterproofing elements. Structural panels have the capability of spanning between supports. Accordingly, they can be placed over purlins (as is the case with pre-engineered metal buildings), as well as over a continuous structural substrate. Some structural panels have the capability of being successfully used as low-slope coverings.

Modified Bitumen. Modified bitumen membrane systems are typically composed of prefabricated sheets of polymer modified asphalt, combined with polyester or fiberglass reinforcement (or a combination of each). The most widely used polymers for asphalt modification are atactic polypropylene (APP) or styrene-butadiene-styrene (SBS). These prefabricated sheets are commonly installed over one or more sheets (of the type used in built-up roofing). In the past, modified bitumen membranes were occasionally composed of a single layer. However, two or more layers are now predominantly used.

In addition to the common practice of using prefabricated modified bitumen sheets to construct the membrane, membranes can also be constructed with modified mopping asphalt and felts (of the type used for BUR construction). To modify asphalt for application by mopping or mechanical spreaders, styrene-ethylene-butylene-styrene (SEBS) polymers are utilized.

Single-Plies. The single-ply family of materials includes some distinctly different products. It should be noted that modified bitumen products are sometimes included in the single-ply category.

Before discussing the various single-ply materials, their attachment method will be reviewed. There are three primary methods for single-ply attachment: *ballasted, fully adhered,* and *mechanically attached.*

In the ballasted system, the membrane is laid loose over the substrate and then covered with ballast. The ballast can be either large aggregate or concrete pavers. In the second method of attachment, the membrane is fully adhered in a continuous layer of adhesive. In the third method of attachment, screws and plates (or continuous bars) are used to attach the membrane.

The single-plies can be classified as either being thermoset or thermoplastic materials. Thermoset materials normally cross-link (cure) during manufacturing. Once cured, these materials can only be bonded to themselves (e.g., at a seam) by the use of an adhesive or seam tape. Thermoplastic materials do not cross-link. Therefore, they should be capable of being welded together (typically with hot air) throughout their service life.

Chlorosulfonated Polyethylene (CSPE).   This synthetic rubber membrane is commonly known by the trade name "Hypalon." It is a thermoset product; however, it cures after it is installed on the roof. It is usually supplied in a white color.

Ethylene Propylene Diene Terpolymer (EPDM).   This is a synthetic rubber membrane. It is a thermoset product, available in a white color, but black is most common.

Polyisobutylene (PIB).   This is a thermoplastic product, available in black or white.

Polyvinyl Chloride (PVC).   This is a thermoplastic product, available in a variety of colors.

PVC Blends.   PVC blends (also known as *copolymer alloys*) are based upon PVC resin and are quite similar to PVC membranes.

Spray-Applied Polyurethane Foam (PUF).   Spray-applied polyurethane foam systems consist of polyurethane insulation, which is spray-applied to the substrate, followed by a surfacing. Traditionally, the foam was surfaced with a coating of latex (acrylic), polyurethane, or silicone. Mineral granules are sometimes applied to the wet coating for additional abrasion/impact resistance (either at traffic walkway areas or throughout the entire roof).

A more recent approach to surfacing is to utilize aggregate (similar to the type used for BUR) directly over the foam. In this system, coatings are used only on vertical surfaces (e.g., parapets or equipment curbs).

KEY DESIGN ISSUES

A complete discussion of design considerations for low-slope roof systems is beyond the scope of this book, for in most instances the plant engineer will not function as the roof designer. However, the plant engineer's input into the design process can play a key role in facilitating a good roof design. To the extent possible, it is recommended the plant engineer become familiar with the information in the following sections.

Familiarity with Roof Design

A common pitfall for designers (and hence the roof design) is *lack of familiarity with the principles of roof design.* This is manifested in selection of inappropriate materials or systems, inadequate details, or poorly prepared specifications. Thus, it is important for the building owner to retain a knowledgeable architect, engineer, roof consultant, or professional roofing contractor to execute the roof design work.

Building Owner's Requirements

The building owner should convey any special requirements to the roof designer. For example, if the building has unusually corrosive interior atmospheres or unusually high humidity, or exhausts contaminants (including grease and oil) onto the roof, these facts should be brought to the designer's attention so that appropriate materials and systems can be designed.

The building owner should also advise the designer of expectations regarding the roof's longevity, and the extent to which the owner is committed to maintenance. If the owner is unwilling to allocate adequate funds for maintenance, a more conservative durable system should be considered.

Similarly, advise the designer how detrimental leakage or a roof blow-off would be. For most buildings, these events are unpleasant, but generally manageable. But, if the roof is over very expensive electronic equipment or a critical facility such as a hospital, a more conservative roof design may very well be appropriate.

Also advise the roof designer if the owner's insurer has specific requirements related to the roof system. Failure to follow the requirements could result in higher insurance premiums.

Building Codes

The roof designer should be aware of building code requirements related to the design of the roof. All three U.S. model building codes now have provisions relating to roof systems (for new construction as well as reroofing).

Energy Efficiency

The building owner should advise the roof designer how energy efficient the roof is desired to be. Energy efficient roofs typically cost somewhat more, but can result in considerable savings over the life of the roof. (See Chap. 2-7.)

Also, the roof designer should be aware of code requirements related to thermal efficiency.

Roof Slope

Regardless of the type of materials or system specified, the plant engineer should verify that the roof designer has provided adequate slope for drainage. This simple task can greatly enhance performance and minimize problems.

For low-slope roofs, a designed slope of ¼ in/ft (6.4 mm/m) (¼:12) is typically sufficient [although with metal roofing, ½ in/ft (12.8 mm/m) (½:12) minimum is generally preferable].

Roof-Top Traffic

The plant engineer should advise the roof designer of anticipated roof-top traffic. If there will be periodic traffic (e.g., to maintain mechanical equipment), the designer should specify traffic walkway pads to protect the roof. Pads can also be beneficial around mechanical equipment, to protect against dropped tools. For aggregate ballasted systems, use of concrete pavers for walkways can be helpful in protecting the roof and provide a more comfortable surface to walk on.

For heavier roof-top loading, greater protective measures (e.g., the use of heavy concrete pavers) may be needed. For example, window washing equipment often causes damage to roof coverings, because the coverings do not have sufficient resistance to the high impact loads that can result as the equipment is moved around and dropped.

Contract Documents

A good roof design should be complemented with a good set of drawings and specifications, so that the design intent is clearly communicated to the contractor. At the outset of the design work, the building owner should request that the designer produce a good set of drawings and specifications (particularly when the roofing work is to be bid upon).

APPLICATION

Assuming that the roof has been adequately designed, and that quality materials have been specified and provided, the next step toward achieving a successful roof is to have the building owner contract with a professional roofing contractor for installation. After a professional contractor has been retained to perform the work, the following items are of importance:

- Convene a preroofing conference. This meeting is normally attended by the roofing contractor (including the job-site person who will be in charge of the work), the plant engineer (and perhaps other personnel representing the owner), the roof designer, and the general contractor. If the project has a lot of roof-top mechanical or electrical equipment, then these subcontractors should also attend the meeting.

  The purpose of the meeting is to review the salient features of the drawings and specifications to ensure that there is understanding by all parties. Special working hours, equipment shut-down procedures, contractor access points, and so on, should be reviewed.

  If there are problems with the design or other aspects of the project, the meeting should identify and resolve them prior to commencement of the field work. As part of this meeting, the roof deck should be reviewed to verify that it is ready for roofing.

- If the job is to have a full- or part-time inspector, an inspector should be retained who has knowledge of the type of roofing system being installed, and has the capability of working with the roofing crew in a cooperative spirit.

- Particularly for new construction, after completion of the work, care needs to be taken to avoid damage to the roof by other trades. This issue should be discussed during the preroofing conference.

By selecting a professional contractor, listening to his or her input of constructive suggestions, and educating other trades about avoiding abuse of the roof, a good roof can be delivered to the building owner.

WARRANTIES

Long-term roofing warranties are quite common. Accordingly, many building owners and designers have focused on specifying warranties, rather than focusing on other aspects that are more likely to result in a successful roof. In August 1992, the National Roofing Contractors Association (NRCA) issued a Consumer Advisory Bulletin on Roofing Warranties. The following excerpts are from that document:

> The length of a roofing warranty should not be the primary criterion in the selection of a roofing product or system because the warranty does not necessarily provide assurance of satisfactory roofing performance. The selection of a roofing system for a particular project application should be based upon the product's qualities and suitability for the prospective construction project. A long-term warranty may be of little value to a consumer if the roof does not perform satisfactorily and the owner is plagued by leaks. Conversely, if the roof system is well-designed, well-constructed, and well-manufactured, the expense of purchasing a warranty may not be necessary.
>
> Manufacturers who use long-term warranties as a marketing tool have encountered a highly competitive roofing market and have found themselves compelled to meet or exceed warranties of competitive manufacturers. It is suspected that in some cases the length of the warranty was established without appropriate technical research or documentation of in-place field performance.
>
> NRCA believes that the roofing consumer, with the assistance of a roofing professional, should focus his purchase decision primarily on an objective and comparative analysis of proven roofing system options that best serve his specific roofing requirements and not on warranty time frames.
>
> NRCA further advises that the roofing consumer consult the membrane warranty section of the *Roofing Materials Guide* for a comparative analysis of the specific provisions, remedies, limitations, and exclusions of the warranties of those roofing systems under consideration. All questions should be addressed to the respective roofing manufacturers for specific written clarification.

A complete copy of the bulletin is available from NRCA.

If the building owner does receive a warranty, it is recommended that the plant engineer be aware of its provisions so that the warranty is not inadvertently voided. Also, prior to the expiration date of the warranty, it is recommended the roof be inspected. If there are problems that are included in the warranty, these can then be brought to the attention of the company that issued the warranty.

MAINTENANCE

After a good roof has been delivered to the building owner, it is important for the owner to commit to a program of periodic roof inspections and follow-up maintenance or repairs as needed. While some systems require less maintenance than others, *no roof should be neglected after it is installed!*

The plant engineer's first task upon completion of a new roof is to set up a historical file. Historical files should also be established for existing roofs. Each separate roof should have its own file. For further information on setting up a file, see the *Manual of Roof Inspection, Maintenance, and Emergency Repair for Existing Single-Ply Roofing Systems* (published by NRCA and the Single-Ply Roofing Institute). Although this manual is for single-plies, the information regarding historical files is applicable to all roof systems.

If there are significant changes of the occupancy in the area below the roof (e.g., introduction of high humidity), or if contaminants are exhausted onto the roof, a roofing professional should be consulted, since these changes could be harmful to the roof unless corrective action is taken.

Semiannual inspections are recommended for all roofs. The purpose of these inspections is to determine if debris removal is needed (e.g., cleaning of roof drains) and to determine if the roof is showing signs of distress. In many instances, problems can be minimized if they are detected and corrected early. Without inspections, a small problem such as a puncture can go unnoticed until a large area of the roof is wet and in need of replacement.

In most instances, the plant engineer's staff does not have the roofing expertise to conduct thorough roof inspections, so they should be conducted by a roofing professional. However, if budget limitations prohibit hiring a professional to perform semiannual inspections, then as a compromise, the plant engineer's staff could conduct one inspection, and a professional could be retained to conduct the other one. The maintenance manual noted above provides useful information in this regard.

If the plant engineer suspects that the roof is overloaded by an unusually heavy snowfall, it is recommended that an engineer be consulted prior to commencement of snow removal. In the unlikely event that an engineer determines that removal is prudent, it is recommended that this work be performed by a professional roofing contractor to minimize roof damage. After the snow melts, the roof should be inspected and repairs made. A roof that has been shoveled should be rigorously inspected semiannually, since damage may not be apparent for many months or even a year or two.

If need for repair (e.g., at a split in the membrane) or routine maintenance (e.g., recoating) is identified, in most instances the plant engineer's staff does not have the expertise to perform the repair or maintenance. Unless the plant engineer is willing to commit to training personnel in roofing, repairs or maintenance of this nature should not be attempted, but rather, a professional roofing contractor should be retained.

In some unusual instances, the plant engineer's staff may be required to perform emergency repairs to minimize water infiltration until a roofing contractor arrives. The maintenance manual noted previously provides emergency repair information for single-ply membranes (including modified bitumen).

To assist in the care of the roof, many professional roofing contractors offer maintenance contracts to building owners.

By making a commitment to periodic inspections, with appropriate maintenance and repair, the roof's service life can be maximized and the building owner's roofing investment justified. In addition, the plant engineer should restrict rooftop access to authorized personnel in order to avoid roof damage and abuse.

INSTALLATION OF NEW PENETRATIONS AND EQUIPMENT

A common cause of roof leakage is improper installation of new penetrations (e.g., a communications conduit) or new equipment (e.g., an exhaust fan) through an existing roof. When new penetrations or equipment are installed, oftentimes the mechanic installing the equipment is the person who also flashes the new penetration. Unfortunately, in most instances the mechanic lacks sufficient roofing knowledge to perform the work successfully.

To avoid roofing problems, it is recommended that a roofing contractor perform the roofing-related work. Also, if the membrane is under warranty, the warrantor should be contacted in advance of the work. Otherwise, the work may void the warranty.

REROOFING

Reroofing is usually much more complicated than the roofing of a new building. Besides considering issues normally considered when designing a new roof, many additional issues arise when roof replacement is needed. For example, it is not uncommon to find existing building conditions that contributed to the demise of the existing roof. Unless these are adequately resolved in the new design (which may be difficult and expensive), they can be expected to adversely affect the new roof.

Accordingly, the selection of the roof designer for reroofing is typically of even greater importance than it is for new construction. A designer should be selected who is knowledgeable about reroofing design. Unlike most new construction, for reroofing many building owners retain a roofing contractor to perform both the design and the application.

As part of the design process, the deck integrity should be assessed by an engineer, if deck deterioration is suspected. And if the new roof system adds weight to the structure, the capacity of the structure should be evaluated by an engineer.

Another special aspect of reroofing design is the investigation for asbestos-containing materials. If the membrane (or other roof system components) is a type that may contain asbestos, samples should be taken and analyzed. In addition to investigating the membrane, other building components should also be evaluated. For example, if spray-on fireproofing materials are present on the deck's underside, samples should be taken. If insulated pipes are suspended from the roof structure and their jackets (including hanger support locations) are not capable of encapsulating fibers, samples should be taken. Under-deck sampling is recommended because of potential fiber release due to the reroofing work. Insulation around flues through the roof should also be sampled.

There are two primary approaches to reroofing. Either the existing system can be torn off down to the deck, or it may remain in place and a new roof covering installed over it. The tear-off option is the most conservative approach, as it allows a complete view of the top-side of the deck. If there are deteriorated areas, they will likely be found. Also, this approach eliminates entrapment of water in the existing roof. However, the tear-off option is often more expensive, and it exposes the interior to potential water damage during the reroofing process.

The recover option has the advantage of retaining the thermal value of the existing insulation, and the existing roof provides protection against sudden rainfall during the application process. In some parts of the U.S., this is not important, but in other areas, this advantage makes the recover option very desirable.

Prior to recovering, it is important to determine if there are areas of wet insulation. If so, it is recommended that those areas be removed. The utilization of nondestructive evaluation (NDE) can be very helpful in searching for wet insulation. There are three NDE methods: electrical capacitance meter, infrared thermography, and nuclear meter.

REFERENCE

1. *NRCA Roofing and Waterproofing Manual,* National Roofers Contractors Association, Rosemont, IL 60018-5607

CHAPTER 2-7

THERMAL BUILDING INSULATION

William H. Snyder
Director, Corporate Marketing Research
Johns-Manville Corp.
Denver, Colorado

GLOSSARY

Building insulation A product or system of products designed and installed in or at the building envelope to retard the flow of heat either out of the building (in winter) or into the building (in summer).

Thermal properties

k (thermal conductivity) Amount of heat in British thermal units (kilojoules) transmitted per hour through a square foot of material one inch thick when the temperature difference between the two surfaces of the material is maintained at 1°F. Units: (Btu)(in)/(h)(ft²)(°F) [W/(m)(K)].*

---

* SI conversions based on Standard for Metric Practice, ASTM E380-76 (also IEEE Standard 268-1976 and American National Standard Z210.1-1976).

C **(thermal conductance)** k/thickness Units: $(\text{Btu})/(\text{h})(\text{ft}^2)(°\text{F})$ $[\text{W}/(\text{m}^2)(\text{K})]$.

R **(thermal resistance)** $1/C$ Units: $(\text{h})(\text{ft}^2)(°\text{F})/\text{Btu}$ $[(\text{K})(\text{m}^2)/\text{W}]$.

U **(thermal transmittance)** The overall coefficient of heat transmission through a system of materials with possibly different cross sections (e.g., studs in walls) which considers the insulating value of air films at each surface:

$$U = 1/\Sigma R \qquad \text{Btu}/(\text{h})(\text{ft})^2(°\text{F}) \ [\text{W}/(\text{m}^2)(\text{K})]$$

where ΣR is the sum of the R values of each material, cavities, and air surfaces, through the cross section.*

INTRODUCTION

Basic Theory

Heat is transmitted from a heat source to a colder surface or area in three modes:

1. *Radiation.* This, the primary mode of heat transfer, operates via electromagnetic waves even in a vacuum (e.g., the sun heating the earth). The rate of heat flow is proportional to the fourth power of absolute temperature (R^4 or K^4) of the hot surface (K_H^4) minus K^4 for the cold surface (K_C^4); it is inversely proportional to the reflectivity of the surfaces and can be controlled by placing absorbing or reflective materials between the hot and cold surfaces.

2. *Conduction.* This mode operates as atomic or molecular activity: the more densely packed the molecules the higher the conductivity (e.g., steel conducts heat more readily than air). Conduction can be controlled by the use of less conductive materials and a discontinuous structure (e.g., plastic or glass instead of steel and foam or fiber instead of solids).

3. *Convection.* This mode operates by the natural flow of gases or liquids caused by the changes in density occurring with temperature differences (e.g., smoke and heated air from the fireplace are forced up the chimney by the denser cold air which displaces the lighter products). It can be controlled by limiting the size of spaces and hence the temperature differentials which would promote convection.

Therefore the total apparent conductivity k of a material as measured in tests is actually a complex function of the different forms of heat transmission described above. A graph of the components of thermal conductivity vs. density is shown in Fig. 7-1. Both the shape and position of the thermal conductivity curve will vary for different insulation materials, for different designs (e.g., fiber diameter, pore size, Freon, etc.) and for different mean test temperatures.

Amount of Insulation Required

The "right" amount of insulation can be defined as either the amount which meets standards and building codes or the economical amount. Since the oil embargo of 1973, the prices of energy have escalated rapidly, so the economical amount of insulation has become considerably more than previously accepted standards. Basically the right amount of insulation is that which minimizes the total costs over the life cycle on a present-value basis. Total costs are the sum of investment in insulation plus the energy cost to heat and cool the building.

---

* For systems of more than one type of cross section, weight each $1/\Sigma R$ by its proportion of the total area.

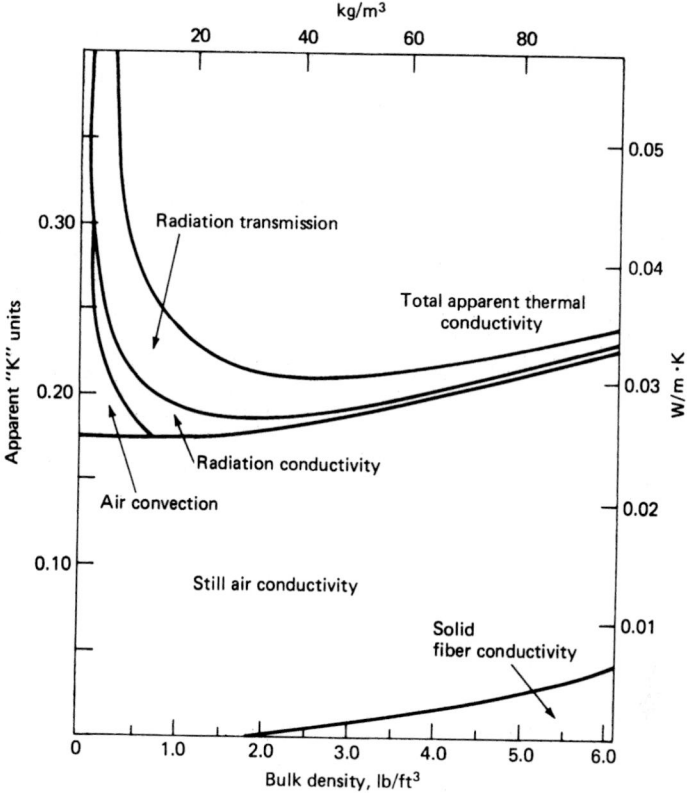

FIGURE 7-1   Graph of components of thermal conductivity vs. density for a typical glass fiber insulation. (*From C. M. Pelanne, "Heat Flow Principles in Thermal Insulation," Journal of Thermal Insulation, vol. 1, July 1971, Techonomic Publishing Co., Westport, Conn.*)

Since insulation can be added in discrete increments (e.g., R-11, R-19, R-22, R-30, etc.) the minimum total cost can be achieved by going to successively higher levels of insulation as long as the ratio of discounted life-cycle added savings to added cost, AS/AC, exceeds 1.0. AC is the added cost in dollars per square foot to go to the next higher level of insulation. *Note:* In some cases the HVAC system can be down-sized because of the additional insulation, and this reduces the added effective cost of the insulation.

PWF is the present-worth factor for annual energy savings over the life cycle (no units) as shown in Table 7-1. (Note that this variable has a wide range.)

In insulation calculations:

HES = heating energy savings for incremental insulation [dollars per square foot (square meter) per year]

EH = seasonal efficiency of heating system typically from 0.60 to 0.75 for gas and oil, approximately 1.0 for electric resistance and around 1.8 for heat pumps

CES = cooling energy savings for incremental insulation [dollars per square foot (square meter) per year]

EC = seasonal efficiency of cooling system (no units), typically around 2.0

TABLE 7-1   Present-Worth Factors*[†]

D (discount rate) minus EI (energy inflation rate)	Life cycle L, yr		
	15	30	50
0.10 (or 10%)	8.0	10.2	10.9
0.05 (or 5%)	10.7	16.2	19.6
0 (equal)	15.0	30.0	50.0

* PWF = [(1 + EI)/(D + EI)] {1 − [(1 + EI)/(1 + D)]^L}
[†] Table calculated based on EI = 0.10 (table accurate within 8 percent for EIs from 0.05 to 0.15).

Degree days = the sum of the daily average temperature differences from 65°F (60 or 55°F are sometimes used) (18.3°C, 15.6 or 12.8°C), counting only those days which are below the base, for an average year. These data are widely published.

$/Btu = local energy cost per unit per British thermal unit of content per unit (dollars per joule).

The HES, heating energy savings, can be fairly easily calculated by using the equation:

$$\text{HES} = \Delta U \times \frac{\text{degree days}}{\text{year}} \times 24\,\frac{\text{h}}{\text{day}} \times \frac{\$}{\text{Btu}} \qquad \text{(SI:J)}$$

where ΔU = the change in thermal transmittance from one level of insulation (or none) to the next higher level.*

The CES (cooling energy savings) is more complicated to calculate, and the reader is referred to more detailed references such as Ref. 2. Generally the cooling calculations do not contribute significantly to increased insulation unless the climatic conditions have low heating and high air-conditioning loads.

Example.   On a financial basis, what is the right amount of roof insulation for a metal roof deck without a ceiling (underside of roof exposed) considering heating only? (See Table 7-2.)

Solution[†].   Assumed for this example:

Degree days = 5500

$/Btu = $4.00/10⁶ Btu ($3.79/10⁹ J)

EH = 0.70

PWF = 16.2 (for discount rate = 15 percent, energy inflation = 10 percent and life = 30 years)

AC = $0.50 installation cost plus $0.05 per R of insulation per square foot ($5.38 + $3.05 per R per square meter)

Therefore the level of insulation which is the "best" from the financial standpoint is Case 6 from Table 7-2: C = 0.07 or R = 14.29 (SI: C = 0.40 or R = 2.52).

---

* Handbooks are available which list thermal design values for various building materials and describe methods for calculating U's. (See Ref. 1.)
[†] Conversion factors to SI units: C and U, watt per meter² per kelvin = 5.68 Btu/(h)(ft²)(°F); R, kelvin·meter per watt = 0.176 (h)(ft²)(°F)/Btu; savings, $/meter²·year = 10.76 $/(ft²)(year).

TABLE 7-2   Factors for Determining Amount of Roof Insulation

Calculating U's	Case							
	1	2	3	4	5	6	7	8
Amount of insulation $C = R$	None	0.15	0.13	0.10	0.08	0.07	0.06	0.05
R (resistance) values								
Outside air (15 mi/h)	0.17	0.17	0.17	0.17	0.17	0.17	0.17	0.17
Built-up roofing	0.33	0.33	0.33	0.33	0.33	0.33	0.33	0.33
Insulation	0	6.67	7.69	10.00	12.50	14.29	16.67	20.00
Metal deck	0	0	0	0	0	0	0	0
Structural beam	0	0	0	0	0	0	0	0
Inside surface (still air)	0.61	0.61	0.61	0.61	0.61	0.61	0.61	0.61
Total resistance (ΣR)	1.11	7.78	8.80	11.11	13.61	15.40	17.78	21.11
U Values								
Transmittance $U = 1/\Sigma R$	0.901	0.129	0.114	0.0900	0.0735	0.0649	0.0562	0.0474
ΔU	—	0.772	0.015	0.024	0.0165	0.0086	0.0087	0.0088
Calculating savings/cost ratio:								
HES = $\Delta U \times$ d.d. $\times 24 \times$ \$/Btu [\$/(ft^2)(yr)]	—	0.408	0.0079	0.0127	0.0087	0.0045	0.0046	0.0046
HES/EN, \$/(ft^2)(yr)	—	0.583	0.0113	0.0181	0.0124	0.0064	0.0066	0.0066
AS = PWF(HES/EN), \$/(ft^2)(yr)	—	9.45	0.183	0.293	0.201	0.104	0.107	0.107
AC, \$/ft^2	—	0.834	0.051	0.116	0.125	0.090	0.119	0.167
Ratio AS/AC	—	11.3	3.6	2.5	1.6	1.2*	0.9	0.6

INSULATING MATERIALS

Uses

Insulating materials commonly used for the building envelope of industrial and commercial buildings differ by area of application shown in Table 7-3.

TYPES OF INSULATING MATERIALS

Rock and Slag Wool

These are terms which denote a fibrous-type insulation produced by melting and fiberizing rock or the slag obtained as a by-product of the smelting of metallic ores. These products are available both in batt and loose-fill forms, which are principally used in residential applications.

Fiberglass

Fiberglass insulation wool is in many ways similar to rock and slag wool but utilizes a more refined process to produce glass, which is then fiberized. These products are available in batts, loose fill, and boards for both residential and industrial/commercial building envelopes.

Mineral Wool

This is a generic term which includes both fiberglass, rock, and slag wool.

TABLE 7-3   Insulation for Building Envelopes

Area	Products used	
	New buildings	Retrofit
Roof-ceiling	Cellular plastics	Cellular plastics
	Perlite boards	Perlite boards
	Fiberglass bds.	Fiberglass bds.
	Insulating concrete	Insulating concrete
	Cellulose (spray-on)	Cellulose (spray-on)
Walls	Cellular plastics	Cellular plastics
	Fiberglass batts	Fiberglass batts
	Rock wool batts	Rock wool batts
	Perlite	
	Vermiculite	
Floors		
Wood-framed	Fiberglass batts	Fiberglass batts
	Rock wool batts	Rock wool batts
Masonry	Cellular plastics	

Cellulose

Cellulose insulation is typically produced by converting used newsprint with the incorporation of flame-retardant chemicals to produce loose fill primarily for residential applications and spray-on forms for industrial and commercial applications.

Cellular Plastics

These are available in different compositions and forms. Polystyrene foam is used in the form of boards for industrial/commercial and residential applications. Polyurethane (and polyisocyanurate) foams are either boards or foamed-in-place primarily for industrial and commercial as well as some residential applications. Urea-formaldehyde foam is foamed in place and used almost entirely for residential applications.

Perlite

Perlite insulation is produced by expanding the naturally occurring perlite, a siliceous volcanic glass, into lightweight beads by rapid heating. The product is used to some extent as a loose fill but primarily manufactured with fibers to form roof insulation boards for industrial and commercial building.

Vermiculite

This type of insulation is produced by expanding the naturally occurring mica-like hydrated laminar mineral by heating it to a high temperature. It is used as loose fill, primarily in residential applications.

Insulating Concrete

This product is made by combining expanded perlite or expanded vermiculite with concrete or by adding a foaming agent to concrete. It is primarily used for industrial and commercial roof decks.

Comparative Properties

The properties of the various insulation products listed above are detailed in Table 7-4 (see also Ref. 2). Product information is available from individual manufacturers, and general information may be obtained from the following associations: Thermal Insulation Manufacturers Association, National Insulation Contractors Association, Mineral Insulation Manufacturers Association, National Cellulose Insulation Manufacturers Association, Perlite Institute, Vermiculite Association, Society of the Plastics Industry.

DESIGN AND INSTALLATION

Roof and Ceiling Insulation Assemblies

Insulation of roofs is normally the most cost-effective area of low-rise industrial/commercial buildings. (See also Chap. 2-6, "Roofing.")

Conventional Overdeck Insulation.   This uses a board-type insulation (fiberglass, perlite, foam, or a combination product) which is applied between the roof deck and the built-up roofing. To obtain hourly fire-resistance ratings, it is necessary to use perlite, gypsum board, or insulating concrete. Attaining Class A, B, or C burning brand ratings on the exterior surface depends on the exterior surfacing materials used.

Insulation above Roof Membrane.   This uses the same elements as the conventional system but with a moisture-resistant insulation (cellular plastic board) applied above the built-up roof and covered with a layer of crushed stone. Major advantages are improved membrane life through reduced temperature fluctuations and ability to add insulation to existing roofs of good condition (ability of roof to sustain added roof load must be checked).

Underdeck Insulation.   This type is applied below the roof deck. Mineral fiber batts or board insulation can be used. Care must be taken to avoid condensation problems at the deck (either a good vapor barrier on warm side or insulation above deck combined with the underdeck insulation will be needed). Spray-on foams or cellulose systems or mineral wool systems could also be used, depending on fire-code and vapor-barrier requirements.

Wall Insulation

Cavity Walls.   These consist of a structural masonry wall with rigid board insulation attached to the exterior before adding the face veneer (or brick, stone, block, stucco, etc.). Alternatively, the two masonry portions can be erected with a space for pourable insulation. Normally an air space is left between the board insulation and the face brick for passage of any wind-driven rain. Vapor barriers may or may not be necessary. Advantages of the cavity wall system are its high fire safety and thermal mass in the interior of the building. A disadvantage is the inability to add more insulation at a later time.

Interior Wall Insulation.   These systems involve attaching a layer of board-type insulation to the interior of the load-bearing masonry wall and then adding an interior finish such as gypsum board. Alternatively, studs and batt-type insulation with gypsum board can be used. Advantages of this system include ease of construction and ability to use as a retrofit method on existing buildings. A disadvantage is the loss of the thermal mass wall on the interior side.

TABLE 7-4   Properties of Insulating Materials*

Property	Fiberglass	Rock wool	Cellulose
Density, lb/ft³	0.6–1.0	1.5–2.5	2.2–3.0
Conductivity, k	Varies by density	0.27–0.34	0.27–0.31
Thermal resistance, R	3.16R/in (batts) 2.2R/in (loose)	3.7–3.2R/in (batts) 2.9R/in (loose)	3.7–3.2 R/in
Water vapor permeability	>100 perm-in	>100 perm-in	High 5–20% by wt
Water absorption	<1% by wt	2% by wt	Not known
Capillarity	None	None	
Fire resistance	Noncombustible	Noncombustible	Combustible
Flame spread	15–20	15	15–40
Fuel contributed	5–15	0	0–40
Smoke developed	0–20	0	0–45
Toxicity	Some	None	Develops CO when burned
Aging effect on			
Dimensional stability	None (batt)	None (batt)	Settles 0–20%
Thermal performance	Settling (loose)	Settling (loose)	Not known
Fire resistance	None	None	Inconsistent data
Degradation due to temperature	None below 180°F	None	None
Cycling	None	None	Not known
Animal activity	None	None	Not known
Moisture	None	Transient	Not severe
Fungal and bacterial action	Does not promote growth	Does not support growth	May support growth
Weathering	None	None	Not known
Corrosiveness	Noncorrosive	None	May corrode steel, aluminum, copper
Odor	None	None	None

* From Ref. 1.

SI conversion factors: density, kilogram per meter³ = 1.602 pounds per foot³; conductivity, watt per meter kelvin = 0.144 × k^2; thermal resistance, kelvin meter² per watt per meter = 6.94 × R/in; permeability, kilogram per pascal second meter = 1.46 E – 12 × perm-in; temperature, kelvin = (°F + 459.7)/1.8 = °C + 273.2.

Insulated Frame Wall Insulation.   Used on practically all residential buildings, it is also found on a significant portion of the small industrial and commercial buildings. Typically mineral-fiber batts are used to insulate the wall cavities. Alternatively, the cavities can be filled with foam-in-place polyurethane or a blown-in loose-fill fiber insulation. Additionally, cellular plastic foam boards can be added as exterior sheathing for added insulation. Advantages of this type of wall are its simple construction and ability to reach very low heat transmittance values (U's) with the combination of cavity and sheathing insulation. Disadvantages include limited fire resistance.

Sandwich Panels.   These are prefabricated building components used as walls with the insulation either foamed in place or laminated between the facings of the panel. Usually, panels are of steel and aluminum and are ½ to 6 in (0.025 to 0.15 m) thick. Advantages include high thermal performance per unit of wall thickness, high strength-to-weight ratio, and elimination of thermal short circuits through framing members. Disadvantages include poor acoustics and limited fire resistance unless cores include gypsum or other mineral boards.

Polystyrene foam	Polyurethane foam	Perlite (loose fill)	Vermiculite	Insulating cement
0.8–2.0	2.0	2–11	4–10	12–88
0.20 (extruded)	0.16–0.17 (unfaced & aged)	0.27–0.40	0.33–0.41	1.17 @ 40 lb/ft³
0.23–0.26 (molded)	0.13–0.14 (impermeable skin)			0.83 @ 25 lb/ft³
5 R/in (extruded)	5.8–6.2R/in (unfaced & aged)	2.5–3.7R/in	2.4–3.0R/in	0.85R/in @ 40 lb/ft³
3.85–4.35 R/in (molded)	7.1–7.7 (impermeable skin)			1.2R/in @ 25 lb/ft³
0.6 perm-in (extruded)	2–3 perm-in	High	High	Varies with density
1.2–3.0 perm-in (molded)				
0.02–4% by vol	Negligible	Low	None	NA
None	None	NA	None	None
Combustible	Combustible	Noncombustible	Noncombustible	Noncombustible
5–25	25–50	0	0	0
5–80	5–25	0	0	0
10–100	55–500	0	0	0
Develops CO when burned	Develops CO when burned	Not toxic	None	None
None	0–12% change	None	None	None
None	0.11 new to 0.17 aged	None	None	None
None	None	None	None	None
None below 165°F	None below 250°F	None below 1200°F	None below 1000°F	None below 1000°C
None	Not known	None	None	None
None	None	None	None	None
None	Limited data	None	None	None
Does not support growth	Does not promote growth	Does not promote growth	Does not promote growth	Does not support growth
Exposure to uv light causes degradation	None	None	None	Frost damage < 30 lb/ft³
None	None	None	None	None
None	None	None	None	None

Foundation and Floor Insulation

Most industrial and commercial buildings utilize a slab on or below grade. Insulation is accomplished with cellular plastic foam boards either on the interior or exterior of the foundation extending at least 2 ft below grade. Insulation beneath the slab is not used unless the slab is heated directly. Retrofit insulation is sometimes possible on the exterior foundation walls. The foam must be covered by the earth or a barrier coating to prevent degradation by ultraviolet light. Calculations of heat transmission through floors and foundations are quite involved. (See Ref. 2.)

Insulation for Metal Buildings

These represent a significant special case, at least for their walls and roofs. Because of their unique construction, many of the major insulation manufacturers have designed and marketed special insulation systems for metal buildings. Special computer analyses are generally available from manufacturers to compute energy savings and optimal levels of insulation for specific applications.

STANDARDS AND CODES

ASHRAE 90-75

American Society of Heating, Refrigeration, and Air Conditioning Engineers Standard 90-75 has provided the basis for energy conservation requirements in many building codes. This standard is a component performance-type specification for new buildings based on steady-state conditions with empirical adjustments for air infiltration, solar gains, and shading. At the time of this writing ASHRAE had a series of proposed standards in the 100.X series covering energy conservation in existing buildings.

Model Codes

The U.S. Department of Energy sponsored development of energy conservation codes through the National Conference of States on Building Codes and Standards (NCSBCS) for the three model codes:

1. The Uniform Building Code, administered by the International Conference of Building Officials in Whittier, California.
2. The Basic Building Code, administered by the Building Officials and Code Administrators International, Inc., in Chicago, Illinois.
3. The Standard Building Code published by the Southern Building Code Congress International, Inc., in Birmingham, Alabama. Most of the states have adopted one of the model code's energy conservation requirements and a few states have written their own requirements.

In addition to the energy conservation requirements, the building codes influence the use or manner of use of many insulation materials through their fire and smoke requirements.

REFERENCES

1. For technical information: *ASHRAE Handbook—1989 Fundamentals,* American Society of Heating, Refrigeration and Air-Conditioning Engineers, Inc., New York, 1989.
2. For information on insulation materials and applications: *An Assessment of Thermal Insulation Materials and Systems for Building Applications,* prepared by Brookhaven National Laboratory for the U.S. Department of Energy, June 1978 (available from the Superintendent of Documents, U.S. Government Printing Office, Washington, D.C. 20420, as stock number 061-000-00094-1).

CHAPTER 2-8
CONSTRUCTION SEALANTS

Kenneth J. Moore, FCSI, CCS
Specification Writer
Sverdrup Facilities, Inc.
St. Louis, Missouri

GLOSSARY

Adhesive (adhesion)   The ability of the material to remain adhered to the substrate.

Adhesion failure   Failure of a sealant to adhere to the surface to which it is applied.

Backer rod   A flexible, compressible strip of plastic foam inserted into a joint to limit the depth to which sealant can penetrate. Also causes sealant to exert pressure on, and form good contact against, the sides of the joint or opening.

Bond breaker   A tape used where there is insufficient depth of joint recess for application of backer rod.

Caulking (calking)   A puttylike material having little or no flexibility after drying, little adhesion to adjacent surfaces, and a low percentage of solids. For small, nonmoving joints (static) only.

Cohesive (cohesion)   The ability of the material to "hang together" without a splitting or tearing failure of the material itself.

Elongation   Amount of stretch exhibited by a sealant before rupture. Also, an increase in length expressed as a percentage of the ordinal length.

Caulking gun   A mechanical device, either manually or power operated, used to extrude construction sealant into a joint.

Joint filler   A class of materials used to fill space in joints not occupied by construction sealants.

Primer   A sealer for porous materials that is used before applying certain sealants, usually as recommended by the manufacturer.

Sealant   Commonly referred to as elastomeric, a medium to heavy-bodied material poured or extruded into a joint which cures to a flexible, tightly adhered seal, with a high percentage of solids and little, if any, shrinkage; for moving joints (dynamic).

INTRODUCTION

Construction sealant is a generic term describing materials and products having the primary function of sealing a joint within a building structure against weather intrusion. These materials are used wherever construction tolerances require a space to permit installing glazing, door frames, window frames, and at other miscellaneous penetrations through floors, walls, and roofs. Another use is at expansion and control joints.

The sealant industry has developed numerous products which vary widely in composition and performance. When selecting a sealant, one must consider the conditions the sealant will encounter when in service and the compatibility between the sealant being used and adjacent materials. Ignoring compatibility can lead to staining, splitting, and premature failure of joint sealant.

The successful use of an elastomeric sealant is dependent upon proper joint design and cleaning, joint priming (when required), proper adhesion of the sealant to the substrate, and effective cohesion of the sealant. Failure of any of the foregoing can result in joint failure.

Proper joint design varies with the type of sealant and should be verified with the sealant manufacturer. Good joint design usually includes a backer rod or bond breaker to provide proper joint configuration and proper depth of sealant and to restrict adhesion to sides of joint only. See Fig. 8-1 for recommended joint design for silicone sealants and Fig. 8-2 for most other types of sealant joint design.

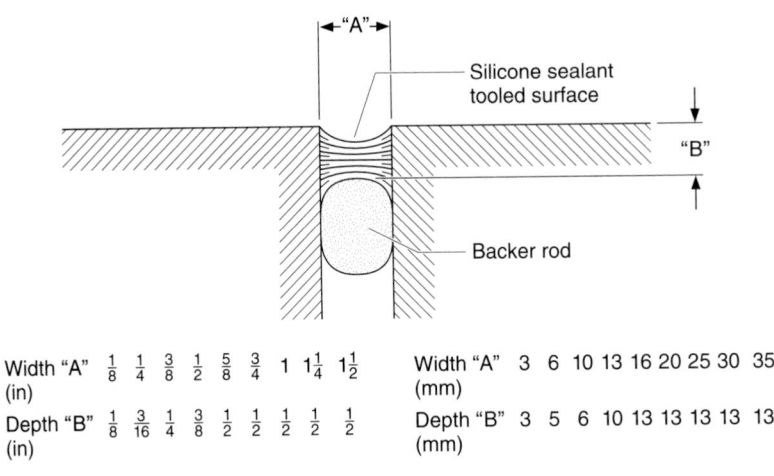

Width "A" (in)	$\frac{1}{8}$	$\frac{1}{4}$	$\frac{3}{8}$	$\frac{1}{2}$	$\frac{5}{8}$	$\frac{3}{4}$	1	$1\frac{1}{4}$	$1\frac{1}{2}$
Depth "B" (in)	$\frac{1}{8}$	$\frac{3}{16}$	$\frac{1}{4}$	$\frac{3}{8}$	$\frac{1}{2}$	$\frac{1}{2}$	$\frac{1}{2}$	$\frac{1}{2}$	$\frac{1}{2}$

Width "A" (mm)	3	6	10	13	16	20	25	30	35
Depth "B" (mm)	3	5	6	10	13	13	13	13	13

FIGURE 8-1   Joint design for silicone sealants.

BACKING MATERIAL

The purposes of sealant backup materials are:

1. To control sealant depth.
2. To help achieve a full-wetting of joint substrates when sealant is tooled.

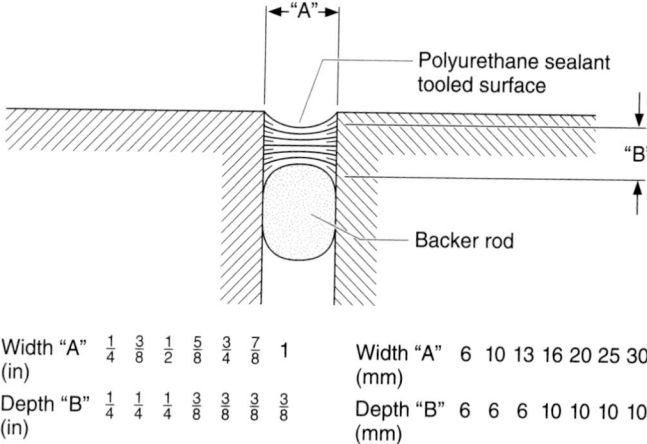

Width "A" (in)	$\frac{1}{4}$	$\frac{3}{8}$	$\frac{1}{2}$	$\frac{5}{8}$	$\frac{3}{4}$	$\frac{7}{8}$	1
Depth "B" (in)	$\frac{1}{4}$	$\frac{1}{4}$	$\frac{1}{4}$	$\frac{3}{8}$	$\frac{3}{8}$	$\frac{3}{8}$	$\frac{3}{8}$

Width "A" (mm)	6	10	13	16	20	25	30
Depth "B" (mm)	6	6	6	10	10	10	10

FIGURE 8-2   Joint design for most sealants other than silicone.

3. To control the shape of the sealant, which helps achieve good elongation without cohesion failure.

4. To prevent third-side adhesion, thus enabling sealant to work properly without being restricted by being fully adhered to full third side of joint.

SEALANT TYPES

Oil-Based Caulks

These are not recommended for marble and other natural stones that are susceptible to staining. In an exterior application they will last only one or two years; in a protected environment they may last as long as 10 years.

Butyl Caulks

These caulks are relatively soft, slow curing, high shrinkage products that will stain most porous substrates. They require no priming for most surfaces, show good adhesion to most materials, and have good water resistance.

Acrylic Latex Caulks

These caulks should be limited mostly to indoor use. They are fast skinning and can generally be painted in 30 to 60 min. Joint movement is generally ±7.5 percent to ±12.5 percent. Most also can be applied to damp substrates.

Solvent Release Acrylic Caulks

These have minimal surface preparation, nominally do not require priming, have good adhesion, and are ultraviolet and ozone resistant. They provide moderate movement capabilities of ±10 percent to ±12.5 percent. These caulks have relatively high shrinkage and poor low temperature elasticity, and they may give off noxious odors during the curing stage.

Polysulfide Sealants

These sealants offer movement capability of ±25 percent. They have good adhesion to steel, aluminum, and glass. Normally they do not require priming, except for porous surfaces such as concrete, concrete block, limestone brick, wood, and the like. Some manufacturers have special formulations that provide excellent resistance to some chemicals and petroleum products.

Urethane Sealants

Their movement range varies, most have a ±25 percent; some have a range of +100 percent and −50 percent. They have good resistance to abrasion, ultraviolet and ozone deterioration, are paintable, and provide long service life. They provide good adhesion to most substrates.

There are formulations that are well suited for traffic joints. They are available in one or two part products, in both gunable and self-leveling types.

Generally, urethane is sensitive to moisture in substrate during curing, and some stain porous substrates.

Silicones

Movement capability varies with the formulation. High modulus, structural sealants have as low as ±12.5 percent movement capability; medium modulus have ±50 percent capability, and low modulus have as much as 50 percent compression and 100 percent elongation capabilities. Silicones perform well and can be applied in cold environments. Once cured, silicones experience very little hardening. Most silicone sealants are not suitable for traffic joints nor submerged conditions.

MAINTENANCE

Successful maintenance and repair of sealed joints is a simple three-step procedure. Clean out the joint, correct the cause of failure, and reseal.

Replacement of or repair of an existing silicone sealed joint should be with a silicone sealant because it is difficult to adequately prepare a joint for proper adhesion by other types of sealants. This is due to the residue left by the silicone sealant, which remains on and in the surfaces of the existing joint.

Silicone sealant joints can be repaired as follows:

- If silicone is cured properly and performing in the application, but its appearance is poor (i.e., due to improper tooling), then cleaning the sealant surface with a solvent and surfacing the joint in the following manner should be sufficient.

  Clean sealant with a solvent (i.e. xylene, toluene) to remove dirt.

  Allow solvent to evaporate, mask the joint and apply a thin bead of fresh sealant over the cured sealant. Then tool the sealant and remove the masking material.

- If silicone sealant is cracked or a reapplication will not improve the joint appearance, then remove the old sealant and replace as follows:

  Cut away the old sealant. If excellent adhesion to the substrate is still maintained, then leave some sealant at the edges of the joint [up to ⅛-in (3-mm) thick]. If poor adhesion to the substrate is evident, remove sealant down to substrate and reclean the substrate and recondition as necessary (i.e., clean with xylene and reprime with appropriate primer).

Mask the joint, reapply the sealant. If resealing is not done shortly after cutting away the old sealant, the sealant may collect dirt and the joint will have to be recleaned using a solvent such as xylene or toluene before reapplying the fresh sealant. Then tool the joint and remove the masking material. Check adhesion after sealant has cured.

CHAPTER 2-9
ROADS AND PARKING LOTS

Omar L. Feeler
Principal, Highways
Sverdrup Civil, Inc.
St. Louis, Missouri

DESIGN

Design Coordination

Roads and parking areas are service facilities that should not in any way inhibit plant production or detract from or interfere with the surrounding community. Design coordination is therefore the key to successfully designing new plant roads and parking areas or expanding existing facilities.

Design Data Required

A broad range of data is needed to design roads and parking lots so they both serve their intended functions efficiently and require minimal maintenance to keep them in good condition.

Site and Plant Data. Table 9-1 shows the site and plant data that should be acquired and the appropriate information sources. Carefully check your sources to be certain the data are accurate since a small variation at this level can make a big difference in either the usefulness and efficiency of the resulting facilities or the schedule and costs to construct and maintain them.

Do not accept shortcut instructions that simply order you to place a road or parking lot in a given location. Table 9-1 is designed to provide information to confirm or deny the advisability of placing the facility on a given site, and may avoid considerable expense and inconvenience later. Carefully follow through on the items in Table 9-1 to assure yourself that the points have been considered and all instructions are valid.

TABLE 9-1   Site and Plant Data

Data required	Possible resources
Topographic surveys of site and surrounding roads or streets showing contours, all surface improvements, and property boundaries	Plant manager, developer, obtain by field surveys or aerial mapping.
Location of existing utilities	Utility companies
Location of springs or swamps	Site inspections
Location of rock outcrops	Site inspection
Present legal access to property	Deeds, plats, tax assessor's office
Condition and general capacity of existing roads and streets surrounding property	Site inspection; state, county, or municipal agency
Location and dimensions of plant building(s)	Plant layout, plant manager, plant designer
Location of shipping and receiving facilities. Rail? Truck? Number and type of trucks each day?	Plant manager, plant designer, corporate planner
Plant employment and hours by shifts	Plant manager, corporate planner
Location of employee entrances	Plant layout
Visitor requirements, plant tours? Will buses be involved?	Plant manager, corporate planner
Plant security requirements	Plant manager
Aesthetic requirements	Plant manager

Regulation and Permit Data.   Investigate federal, state, county, and municipal regulations to determine the requirements, what approvals and permits are required, and when submittals must be made. Agencies having jurisdiction might include (1) planning commissions, (2) local drainage districts, (3) environmental protection agencies, (4) departments of public works, (5) highway and street departments, (6) zoning commissions, and (7) corps of engineers.

Soils Data.   The amount and type of soils data required will vary widely between sites. An appropriate sampling and testing program is required to develop the data upon which the foundation designs can be based.

Running the sampling and testing program; analyzing the test data; making recommendations for slopes and special subdrainage; and designing the base, pavement, and surfacing are geotechnical functions that should be done by an experienced geotechnical engineer. The novice should never attempt to develop this important and critical information.

Traffic Data.   Traffic data are the determining factors in selecting road width, turning lane length, and total parking area, and in locating parking lot entrances and connections. The data given in Table 9-2 must be obtained or developed.

Road Geometry

Site Location.   The roadway location will be controlled by several factors, as follows:

1. Limits within which a permit can be obtained to connect existing roads
2. Preferred intersection location within above limits
3. Location of employee, truck, and bus parking
4. Location of existing facilities that are to remain
5. Location of future planned facilities

Review dock locations and truck routes for shipping and receiving to coordinate turning radii, maneuvering (apron) space, and other plant facilities and operations. Where possible, docks

TABLE 9-2   Traffic Data

Data required	Possible resources
Starting and quitting time for each shift at the plant	Plant manager, plant planner
Total employees each shift (maximum)	Plant manager, plant planner
Predicted employee traffic each shift	Plant manager, plant planner
Traffic counts on surrounding roads or streets and predicted future volumes	City, county, or state traffic agency, actual field count
Location of signals on surrounding roads and their probable capacity	City, county, or state traffic agency, field check and field count
Predicted truck traffic to the plant, expected peak hours, probable loads and probable configurations (single unit, semitrailer, double trailer, etc.)	Plant manager, plant planner
Are mass transit facilities available and convenient to the plant, or are they planned?	Local transit agency, field inspection
Does the plant have or plan to have special programs to reduce employee traffic (plant bus service, or incentives for van car pools) and, if so, how many employees are expected to use these programs?	Plant manager, plant planner
Do railroad lines cross the roadways and, if so, what is the anticipated train schedule?	The railroad, plant manager, plant planner

and loading areas should be free from general traffic areas, railroad crossings, and parked vehicles. Further examination should include the location of springs, swamps, sinkholes, ravines, steep hillsides, rock outcrops, areas difficult to drain, and refuse disposal areas. Although roads can be built in locations with features like these, they will certainly increase costs, and such areas should be avoided if possible.

Widths.   Total roadway width design is a function of traffic volume and interferences.

Traffic volume for design is generally expressed in terms of design hour volume (DHV). The peak volumes for most plant roads will be of short duration and will preferably occur for about 30 min for incoming and for about 15 min for outgoing flows.

Interferences have a direct bearing on the capacity and service level of any given roadway width, and in many instances become the controlling factor in establishing width. Interferences include road intersections, at-grade railroad crossings, security gates, parking lot entrances and exits, and pedestrian crossings. Each interference must be considered in establishing the roadway width. This may involve adding lanes near the interference such as intersections or security gates, without extending those lanes for the entire length of roadway.

For final design, the traffic analysis for roadway widths should be carefully completed, and an experienced traffic engineer should be used. The engineer will probably rely on procedures and analytical data contained in the *Highway Capacity Manual*[1] or the *Transportation and Traffic Engineering Handbook.*[2]

For preliminary approximations, the following rules of thumb may be appropriate, but they should never be used for final analyses:

1. On long stretches of road [more than 1000 ft (305 m)] without interferences, each lane can carry 1000 to 1200 passenger cars per hour. Minimum suggested lane width is 12 ft (3.66 m).
2. A single lane making an uninterrupted right-angle right turn will carry about 600 cars per h.
3. Through lanes operating with a signal system of approximately equal cross traffic will carry about 600 cars per lane per h.

Turning Lane Requirements.   At intersections, the roadway capacity often can be improved by adding lanes reserved solely for turning vehicles. The required lengths of these added lanes are completely dependent upon the amount of cross traffic, whether the intersection is signalized, and (in the case of left turns) the amount of opposing traffic. The *Highway Capacity Manual*[1] or the *Transportation and Traffic Engineering Handbook*[2] should be used to determine these requirements.

Horizontal Alignment.   The preferred horizontal alignment is, of course, a straight line; but when that is not possible, the radius used for any given curve is dependent upon superelevation (banking) and design speed. Normal road cross slope, for a straight section, is 0.02 ft/ft (2 cm/m), from the center of roadway. Maximum superelevation for a plant road will normally be 0.06 ft/ft (6 cm/m) where the minimum radius is also used, although 0.08 ft/ft (8 cm/m) might be appropriate on very long roads where icing conditions do not occur.

The minimum permissible radius can be calculated from the formula:

$$R = \frac{V^2}{15(e+f)}$$

where R is the minimum radius, V is the design speed, e is the maximum superelevation rate [normally 0.06 ft/ft (6 cm/m) for plant roads], and f is the friction factor (for paved roads use 0.17 for $V=20$, 0.16 for $V=30$, 0.15 for $V=40$, 0.14 for $V=50$, and 0.12 for $V=60$).

Using the previously established design controls discussed in the subsection "Site Location" and the above curve criteria, the designer can quickly establish a suitable horizontal alignment by trial and error.

Vertical Alignment.   The road should be designed with a smooth grade line, with gradual changes conforming to the existing terrain. A line with numerous breaks and short lengths of grade should be avoided. Grades over 6 percent should be avoided, and the flattest grades consistent with the terrain should be used.

Vertical curves should be used to connect tangent grade lines, and the curves should be long enough to provide minimum stopping sight distance, comfort, and appearance. The curve connecting two grades should not be shorter than

$$L = KA$$

where L is the length of vertical curve in feet, A is the algebraic difference of the intersecting grades in percent, and the values of K are listed as minimum or desirable minimum as follows:

Design speed, mph (km/h)	Minimum K value	
	Crest vertical curves	Sag vertical curves
30 (48)	30	40
40 (64)	60–80	60–70
50 (80)	110–160	90–110
60 (97)	190–310	120–160

Figure 9-1 illustrates both crest and sag vertical curves.

Where the roadway has curbs or curb and gutter, a minimum grade of 0.5 percent should be used to assure adequate drainage.

Parking Lot Geometry

Determining the Number of Lots and Location.   The number of parking lots to be constructed and their locations are a commonsense decision based on considering the following:

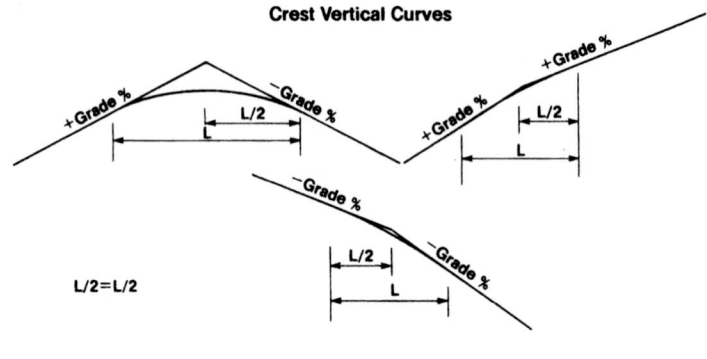

FIGURE 9-1 Typical vertical curves.

1. Available space
2. Proximity to facility served (employee entrance, truck dock, visitors' entrance)
3. Separation of cars, trucks, and buses if possible
4. Convenient entrances and exits

Parking lot geometry choices will be limited at most locations by the size and shape of the plant site, the location and layout of plant facilities, and the location of the plant road.

Efficient Layout. Each site must be considered on its own merits, and several preliminary layouts should be prepared to determine the most efficient mix of capacity and circulation, considering employees, visitors, trucks, and buses.
The following general rules will usually result in the most efficient use of space:

1. Make the lot rectangular if possible.
2. Make the long sides of the area parallel.
3. Avoid irregular shapes.
4. Align traffic aisles parallel to the longest side of the lot.
5. Use the perimeter of the lot for parking and not for traffic aisles.
6. Position each traffic aisle to serve parking stalls on both sides of the aisle.

Determining Spaces. The following terms are generally used in describing the dimensions of parking lot units:

1. Number of each type of vehicle to be parked
2. Good drainage
3. Easy snow removal

Geometric Limitations

1. Parking angle. The angle between the center line of the traffic aisle and the center line of the parking stall.
2. Stall width. The width at a right angle to the parking stall.
3. Curb length. The width of the stall parallel to the traffic aisle.
4. Stall depth. The stall dimension at right angles to the traffic aisle.

The selected parking angle will affect the capacity and circulation within the lot. Maximum capacity will result from a 90° parking angle, but reduced angles are easier to enter and exit and, therefore, generally result in better circulation. Parking angles of 45, 60, and 90° are the most commonly used, and the angle should be selected on the basis of the best mix of capacity and circulation, determined by evaluating trial layouts. A common stall width is 8.5 ft (2.59 m), and the other design dimensions for that width for the 45, 60, and 90° parking angles are as follows:

Parking angle	Curb length	Stall depth	Aisle width
45°	12′0″ (3.66 m)	19′5″ (5.92 m)	13′6″ (4.11 m)
60°	9′10″ (3 m)	20′9″ (6.32 m)	18′6″ (5.64 m)
90°	8′6″ (2.6 m)	19′0″ (5.79 m)	25′0″ (7.62 m)

Some agencies having jurisdiction over parking lot designs require wider stalls, or handicap stalls thus proportionately altering the previous numbers. Design work should not be started until these width requirements and number of required stalls are determined.

More detailed information on space design can be obtained from "Parking Principles, Special Report 125,"[3] or from the *Parking Design Manual.*[4]

The dimensions quoted and those in the suggested references are for passenger cars only and are still in common use, and some agencies may permit a percentage of stalls being smaller for compact cars. The same basic principles also apply for trucks and buses, but the dimensions for both stall and aisle widths must be adjusted to fit the equipment to be parked.

Entrances and Exits.   Entrances and exits should be designed for free traffic flow and, therefore, the number of entrances and exits will be determined by a study of the lot size and the amount of interference by street traffic. Entrances and exits should not be located close to other intersections, and separate entrances and exits should be considered if the maximum width of driveway opening cannot exceed 30 ft (9.1 m). In general, more entrances and exits will increase the circulation and permit rapid loading and unloading of the lot.

Base, Pavement, and Surfacing

Data Required.   Good soil sampling, testing, and analysis are essential in designing base, pavement, and surfacing; a geotechnical engineer should be retained for this work. Samples must be taken below the subgrade elevation to determine the soil-bearing capacity and water content.

In addition, data on the qualities of local aggregates, the projected traffic, and expected wheel loads are required.

Type and Design Selection.   There are many types of base materials and asphalt and concrete pavements, all of which are suitable if properly designed for the soil and load conditions.

Selection of type of base, pavement, and surfacing is therefore usually based on the availability and quality of local materials, the personal preference of the designer, cost, or, sometimes, upon the appearance desired.

The design begins at subgrade, and the analysis and design of the load-carrying surface should be made by an experienced geotechnical engineer.

If sufficient soil data are known, a preliminary "shotgun" design can be accomplished by the novice using design manuals published by the Asphalt Institute or the Portland Cement Association. These are available on request from local offices of either organization.

Asphalt pavements generally require seal coats, and it is important for parking lots to be sealed with materials that are resistant to gasoline and oil drippings. The Asphalt Institute manuals also cover seal coats.

Storm Drainage

Evaluating the Existing Drain System.   The existing drain system will ultimately dictate the required discharge points for road and parking lot drainage, and it is therefore essential that complete data on the existing system be obtained.

Where there is no storm sewer system, the following questions must be answered:

1. Are the location and direction of flow of all ditches, gulleys, or streams known?

2. Does the existing system pond or serve as a retention basin, and should it?

3. Do all parts of the existing system discharge from the plant property (are discharge points in some areas into sinkholes)?

Where there is an existing system, obtain the following data:

1. System location

2. The size and type of pipe in all segments of the system

3. Location, size, flow-line elevation, and top elevation of all manholes and inlets

4. The unused system capacity

Drainage Layout.   A system of properly designed ditches and culverts (open system) will be the least expensive if sufficient area is available and the roads and parking lots do not have curbs. At the edge of parking lots without curbs and at sidewalks adjoining a grassy area, begin the earth grading 1 in (2.5 cm) below the paved surface so that a water dam is not created by the grass. Sidewalks should have a cross slope so that water does not pond. Make sure that all runoff is uninterrupted, directed away from docks or loading areas and is picked up by a culvert or ditch.

If a closed pipe system is to be used, some areas may require minor ditches to direct the flow to planned gutters or inlets that discharge to a pipe system. Inlets should be located at all gutter low points and at any planned low points in parking areas. Additional inlets should be located along the roadway to prevent excessive width of spread in the gutter flow. This spacing depends on the inlet capacity, the gutter grade, and the roadway cross slope.

Determining Runoff and Sizing the System.   Almost every site is now under the jurisdiction of some local, state, or national agency with respect to drainage design, and these agencies specify the permits and procedures to be used in determining runoff, inlet spacing, and system sizing. The procedures vary from agency to agency, and it is imperative the designer contact the appropriate agency and follow its procedures. In the absence of any jurisdictional agency, the procedures of the county or state highway department are suggested for use so consistency is developed within the area. Where wetlands, ponds, or free-flowing streams involve fill material there is a high probability that a Corps of Engineers permit will also be required. For more information on wetlands contact the local Corps of Engineers or the EPA.

Signing

Signing on plant roads is often designed to be aesthetic as well as to deliver messages, and may be very individual in character. General guidelines for signing principles are contained in The Federal Highway Administration's *Manual on Uniform Traffic Control Devices.*[5]

Signals

Signals for plant roads usually occur at the intersections with existing roads and are therefore usually designed, constructed, and maintained by the local or state road agency. The agency should be contacted in the early phases of the project to confirm this and to furnish design data. Signal designs are based on the procedures described in the *Highway Capacity Manual.*[1]

Lighting

There are many light posts and standards of varying designs to achieve certain aesthetic requirements, and these can only be selected by searching supplier catalogs.

Certain lighting levels should be attained by spacing the selected light standards correctly. Rely on a competent lighting engineer to provide this design. Basic lighting information is found in Ref. 6 and is included in Chap. 3-5, "Lighting."

MAINTENANCE AND REPAIR

Many maintenance and repair procedures are weather-sensitive and should not be scheduled during adverse conditions. Cold and, particularly, freezing weather adversely affect the placing of asphalt and concrete, embankment construction, and beds for pipe laying. In emergencies, special measures will permit this construction without reducing quality, but the costs will be high. All work should be suspended when it rains or the work is saturated or flooded. Use the standard specifications of the state highway agency as a guide to permissible working conditions.

Maintenance

Roadway and parking lot maintenance consists of cleaning out the inlets on a regular schedule, sealing pavement cracks, sealing asphalt pavement, cleaning out ditches at regular intervals, removing snow, restriping, and replacing the luminaries in accordance with lighting standards.

Parking lot sizes and road length will dictate whether purchasing extensive maintenance equipment is warranted, whether the maintenance should be contracted, or whether parts of the maintenance will be done with hand equipment. Each maintenance phase should be evaluated to determine the most cost-effective procedure.

Repairs

Most pavement failures can be attributed to poor subgrade having wet or saturated soils or insufficient pavement design for the loads imposed. Freeze/thaw cycles and fatigue are also factors in pavement failures. Each repair should be evaluated separately to determine if it should be contracted out or if it can be handled by plant resources.

One of the most common causes of seal coat failure is the presence of dust on the cover pavement or aggregate, which prevents a good adhesion of materials. Cracks in asphalt pavements should be sealed to prevent water infiltration and loss of structural capacity. Joints should be routed and cleaned with air (hot air if available), and sealed with a joint sealing material, emulsified asphalt, cut back asphalt, or a proprietary material. It is suggested that joint sealing material comply with ASTM D-3405 and D-3406.

Concrete pavement patches should be made for the full lane width and full depth. Partial-lane-width patches should not be used. Patches should have a minimum length of 6 ft (1.83 m).

REFERENCES

1. *Highway Capacity Manual,* Spec. Rep. 209, Transportation Research Board of the National Academy of Sciences-National Research Council, 1985.

2. *Transportation and Traffic Engineering Handbook,* The Institute of Transportation Engineers, Prentice-Hall, Englewood Cliffs, NJ, 1982.

3. *Parking Principle,* Spec Rep. 125, Transportation Research Board of the National Academy of Sciences-National Academy of Engineering, 1971.

4. *Parking Design Manual,* Education Fund of the Parking and Highway Improvement Contractors Association, Inc.

5. *Manual on Uniform Traffic Control Devices for Streets and Highways,* U.S. Department of Transportation, Federal Highway Administration, 1988.

6. *Illuminating Engineering Society: IES Lighting Handbook,* IES, New York, 1987.

7. E.P.A. Headquarters
   Office of Wetland Protection (A-104F)
   Attention: Public Information Officer
   401 M Street S.W.
   Washington, D.C. 20460

SECTION 3

USING ELECTRIC POWER

CHAPTER 3-1
POWER DISTRIBUTION SYSTEMS*

National Electrical Contractors Association, Inc.
Washington, D.C.

---

* Updated for this Second Edition by Challenger Electrical Equipment Corp., Roseville, Calif., and by the Editor-in-Chief.

GLOSSARY

Frequently used terms are defined here. More complete definitions are available in the latest edition of the **National Electrical Code®**, published by the National Fire Protection Association.*

Ampacity   Current-carrying capacity of electric conductors, expressed in amperes.

Ampere   The unit of measure of electric current. Electric current is measured by the number of electrons that flow past a given point in a circuit in 1 s.

Branch circuit   The conductors between the final overcurrent device protecting the circuit and the outlets or utilization equipment.

Bus(es)   Metal conductors, usually copper or aluminum, of large size utilized to transmit large blocks of power.

Capacitor   A device capable of storing electric energy. It is basically constructed of two conductor materials separated by an insulator.

Circuit breaker   A device designed to open and close a circuit manually, and to open the circuit automatically (trip) on a predetermined overcurrent without injury to itself when properly applied within its rating.

Connected load   The sum of the continuous loads of the connected power-consuming apparatus.

Controller   A device, or group of devices, that serves to govern, in some predetermined manner, the electric power delivered to the apparatus to which it is connected.

Current   The movement of electrons through a conductor material.

Demand   The peak rate at which energy is consumed, specified usually in kilowatts.

Electromagnet   A magnet in which the magnetic field is produced by an electric current. A common form of electromagnet is a coil of wire wound on a laminated iron core, such as the potential element of a watthour meter.

Electromotive force (emf)   The force which tends to produce an electric current in a circuit. The common unit of electromotive force is the volt.

Electron   A negatively charged particle which revolves about the nucleus of an atom.

Equipment   A general term including material, fittings, devices, appliances, fixtures, apparatus, and the like used as a part of, or in connection with, an electric installation.

Fault   Any system problem, but usually a short between phase conductors or a short to ground.

Frequency   The number of cycles of an alternating current completed in a certain period of time, usually 1 s.

Fuse   A protective device made up of a conductor which melts and opens when the current through it is more than the ampere rating of the fuse.

Ground   A conducting connection, either intentional or accidental, permitting current to flow between an electric circuit or equipment and the earth.

Ground-fault circuit interrupter   A device whose function is to interrupt the electric circuit to the load when a fault current to ground exceeds some predetermined value that is less than that required to operate the overcurrent protective device of the supply circuit.

Impedance   The total vector sum of resistance and reactance opposing current flow in an ac system.

Inductance   The property of a coil or any part of a circuit which causes it to oppose any change in the value of the current flowing through it. The unit of measure of inductance is the henry (H).

---

* **National Electrical Code®** is a Registered Trademark of the National Fire Protection Association, Inc., Quincy, MA 02269.

Kilo A prefix meaning thousand, or 10^3.

Load The equipment or appliance which is operated by electric current. Also, the current drawn by such a device.

Load factor The ratio of average current to the maximum demanded.

Mega A prefix meaning million, or 10^6.

Ohm The unit of electric resistance. A circuit has a resistance of 1 Ω when 1 V applied to it produces a current of 1 A in the circuit (Ohm's law).

Outlet A point on the wiring system at which current is taken to supply utilization equipment.

Overcurrent Any current in excess of the ampacity of equipment or conductor. It may result from overload, short circuit, or ground fault.

Overload Operation of equipment in excess of normal, full-load rating or of a conductor in excess of rated ampacity.

Panelboard A single integral enclosed unit including cabinet buses and automatic overcurrent protective devices, with or without manual or automatic control devices, for the control of electric circuits; designed to be accessible only from the front.

Peak load The maximum demand on an electric system during any particular period. Units may be kilowatts or megawatts.

Power factor The relationship between the active power (watts) and the voltamperes in any particular ac circuit. It is defined as the ratio of the total active power to the total voltamperes. It is also numerically equal to the cosine of the angle of phase difference between the total circuit voltage and current.

Relay A switch operated by means of electromagnetism.

Resistance The tendency of a device or a circuit to oppose the movement of current through it. The unit of resistance is the ohm.

Switchboard An integrated, factory-coordinated combination of circuit protective devices, control devices, meters, relays, busbars, and wireways enclosed in a single, pre-planned unit designed to be a self-contained center. Protective devices may be individually compartment-mounted (switchgear) or group-mounted in barriered compartments. The entire structure is designed and built to operate as a coordinated unit.

Switching device A device designed to close and/or open electric circuits either manually or automatically.

Transformer A device which transfers electric energy from one coil to another by means of electromagnetic induction.

Utilization equipment Equipment which converts electric energy to mechanical work, chemical energy, heat, or light, or performs similar conversions.

VAR The term commonly used for voltamperes reactive.

Volt The practical unit of electromotive force, or potential difference. One volt will cause 1 A to flow when impressed across a 1-Ω resistance.

Voltampere Voltamperes are the product of volts and the total current which flows because of the voltage. In dc circuits and ac circuits with unity power factor, the voltamperes and the watts are equal. In ac circuits at other than unity power factor, the voltamperes equal the square root of (watts squared plus reactive voltamperes squared).

Voltage (of a circuit) The measured potential difference between any two circuit conductors or any conductor and ground.

Watt The practical unit of active power which is defined as the rate at which energy is delivered to a circuit. It is the power expended when a current of 1 A flows through a resistance of 1 Ω. $P_w = I^2 R$

Watthour The unit volume of electric energy which is expended in 1 h when the power is 1 W.

INTRODUCTION

Approximately 36 percent of all energy consumed in the United States each year is used by industry. About one-third of the energy is used in the form of electricity.

Some 80 percent of the electricity used by industry is applied for electric drives which are elements of electromechanical systems. These systems are used to *form* (extrude, roll, cast, press, and spin), *shape* (mill, ream, drill, hone, and tap), and *transport* (conveyors, elevators, brakes, fans, pumps, and compressors). The remaining 20 percent of industry's electrical use is applied for electrolytic processes, process heating, lighting, and comfort conditioning.

The larger a plant is, the more important is its electric distribution system. It must be capable of meeting the needs of all electric equipment, from the point of entrance of the power company's service (or the plant generating powerhouse) to the terminals of the utilization equipment. If electric power is not available when and where needed, the owner's investment in both plant and inventory becomes idled.

The electric distribution system which is best for a given plant depends on the value assigned to dependability and flexibility. For example, if electricity is needed to manufacture a product whose design is frequently changed, a flexible, easily changed system is best. When continuity of service is essential, as in some chemical processes when a batch could be ruined by a power failure, an extremely reliable system is best.

Flexibility and reliability are only two concerns affecting electric distribution systems. There are several others, not the least of which is cost, including initial cost and life-cycle cost.

The way in which an industrial power distribution system is designed, installed, and maintained has considerable influence on virtually all aspects of system performance. For optimum performance, those involved with operation of the electric distribution system require at least a basic understanding of the factors involved in the generation, transformation, distribution, and utilization of electricity.

Basics of Electricity

Direct Current. *Direct current* is current which flows through the circuit in the same direction at all times. A dc flow in which the level is always constant is often called a *continuous* current.

Direct current is used in some industrial electrolytic processes, in almost all vehicles, and for certain motors. However, most of the electric energy used in America is generated as alternating current.

Alternating Current. An *alternating current* is one which passes through a regular succession of changing positive and negative values by periodically reversing its direction of flow. Total positive and negative values of current are equal.

If a typical alternating voltage is plotted against time, it will resemble the curve shown in Fig. 1-1.

The curve is called a sine wave because it has the same shape as the curve described by the equation

$$e = E_{max} \sin \theta$$

where θ is an angle and e is the instantaneous voltage.

Figure 1-1 shows the variation in ac voltage through two cycles. Voltage is zero at the beginning of the cycle, rises to a maximum value, and then falls back to zero halfway through the cycle. In the second half of the cycle, the voltage achieves a maximum negative value and then returns to zero at the end of the cycle. The number of cycles which the voltage goes through in 1 s is called *frequency*. Frequency is expressed in *cycles per second,* also known as *hertz*. Most common ac power supplies in the United States have a frequency of 60 cycles per second (cps), or 60 hertz (Hz).

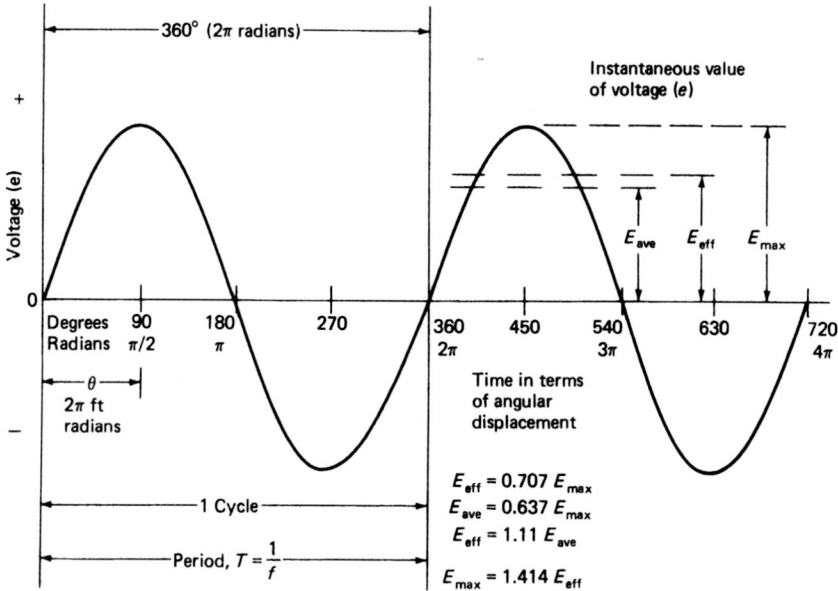

FIGURE 1-1 Sine-wave relationships.

Figure 1-1 shows that a cycle covers a definite period of time and is completed in 360° of the rotation of the armature of the generator. Accordingly, time may be expressed in terms of an angle of rotation:

$$\text{Period } T \text{ in seconds} = 360° \text{ or } 2\pi \text{ rad}$$

To express time, angle θ becomes

$$\theta = 2\pi ft \text{ rad}$$

where t is the time in seconds and f is frequency in hertz.

As such, the equation for the sine wave shown in Fig. 1-1 may be expressed as

$$e = E_{\max} \sin 2\pi ft$$

or

$$e = E_{\max} \sin \omega t$$

where $\omega = 2\pi f$ or

$$e = E_{\max} \sin \theta$$

A voltage sine wave can be expressed in three values by:

1. Maximum or peak value $E_{\max}$.
2. Average value E_{av}, which is equal to average value of e for the positive half or negative half of the cycle.
3. The root mean square (rms) or effective value (E_{eff}), a value of current which gives the same heating effect in a given resistor as the same value of direct current. Unless another description is specified, mention of alternating currents or voltages refers to the effective (rms) value.

Resistance is the only factor which opposes flow of current in a dc circuit.

Resistance also opposes flow in an ac circuit, but so do two other qualities: reactance from circuit *inductance* and *capacitance.*

As alternating voltage rises and falls, ac circuit amperage also rises and falls. If the circuit contains resistance only, voltage and current cycles are "in phase"; both voltage and current rise and fall at the same time, as shown in Fig. 1-2.

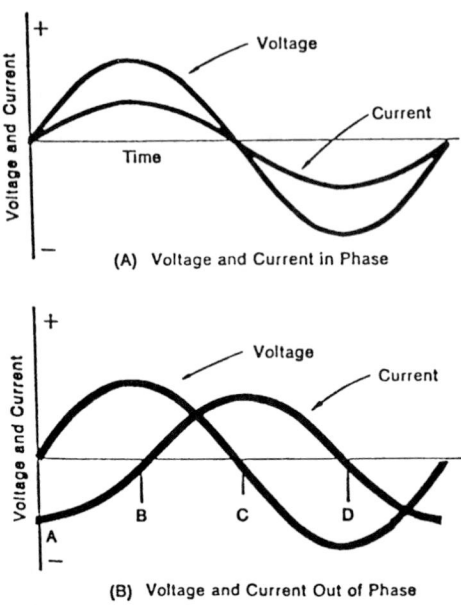

(A) Voltage and Current in Phase

(B) Voltage and Current Out of Phase

FIGURE 1-2 Voltage and current graphs.

Inductance is produced typically when a coil of wire is connected into an ac circuit. It opposes changes in current flow as voltage changes during a cycle, causing voltage and current to be out of phase, as shown in Fig. 1-2.

Capacitance typically is produced when a capacitor or condenser is inserted into an ac circuit. A capacitor or condenser also opposes voltage changes produced by a generator. As a result, voltage and current go out of phase, but in a direction which is opposite to that caused by inductance. In a purely inductive circuit, voltage leads current by 90°. In a purely capacitive circuit, voltage lags current by 90°.

Since all circuits contain resistance, total opposition to flow of ac current is dependent on the vector sum of the resistance, inductive reactance, and capacitive reactance in the circuit. This vector sum is called *impedance,* and is measured in ohms.

Ohm's law can be applied to ac circuits by substituting impedance for resistance:

$$I = \frac{E}{Z}$$

where I is the current, E is in volts, and Z is in impedance in ohms. In dc circuits, the power in watts is simply voltage times current, $P = EI$.

When ac current is used to operate a magnetic device, current lags applied voltage creating an out-of-phase relationship.

In Fig. 1-3 for example, the current wave is said to be θ degrees out of phase with the voltage wave, because it lags the voltage wave by the angle θ. It reaches its peak value θ degrees of angular displacement after the voltage wave reaches its peak. Thus, $P = EI \cos \theta$.

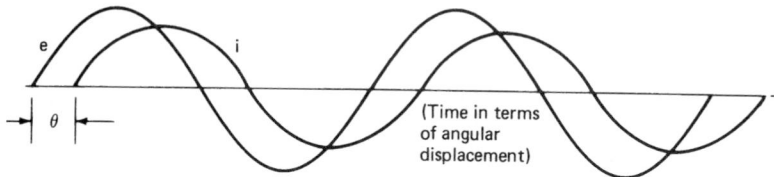

FIGURE 1-3   Current wave lagging voltage wave.

The cosine of the angle between the current and the voltage is known as the *power factor.* It is a measure of reactive power which produces additional heat in electric system components, *but performs no real work.* This relationship is illustrated mathematically in Fig. 1-4.

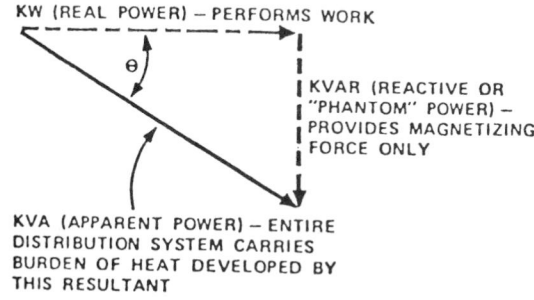

FIGURE 1-4   Power factor relationships.

Buying and Conserving Electric Energy

Purchased energy represents an increasing share of manufacturing costs. Most utilities use somewhat complicated methods to charge their customers for energy use. The basic charge is for actual kilowatthours used in a billing period. This charge is computed on a scale that recognizes blocks of energy use at different rates. The more energy used, the less is paid for each unit. This reflects the fact that overall utility company costs go down in proportion to the quantity of constant energy supplied by the system.

Most utilities also impose a charge for demand, expressed in kilowatts. This is a charge for maximum power requirements. It is determined by dividing energy consumed in a short (15- or 30-min) time period by the length of the time period. Thus, if 100 kWh is consumed in a 15-min demand interval, demand is 400 kW (100 kWh ÷ 0.25 h). Modern computer technology makes it possible to select the one demand interval of the billing period during which maximum wattage demand occurs.

A third charge sometimes imposed is a penalty for poor power factor. This charge is made to cover the cost of generating the unusable portion of electricity consumed in reactive power losses.

A fourth component of most utility bills, over which users have no control, is a *fuel adjustment charge.* This is added to cover the cost of fuel not included in the basic rate structure.

Careful examination of plant electric systems, utilizing a one-line diagram, can identify many steps to reduce energy consumption and electrical costs. Manual or automatic shutoff devices can be placed on short-term or rarely used equipment. Load-limiting and demand-limiting control devices can be installed. Power factor can be improved by the installation of capacitors or synchronous motors. Management can also investigate the feasibility of installing multifunction programmable controllers or centralized automated, computerized control to limit power and energy within the facility.

One-Line Diagram. There is no industrywide standard for the graphic description of electric systems, but most designers use a one-line diagram.

A one-line diagram of a plant's basic electric system should be developed and maintained. It can be used for system maintenance and as a management tool which can provide "instant" information on system loading and capacity.

Commonly used one-line diagram symbols are shown in Fig. 1-5; they are defined in IEEE Standard 315-1975, "Graphic Symbols for Electrical and Electronics Diagrams," ANSI Y32.2-1975.

The devices in switching equipment are referred to by numbers, according to the functions they perform. These numbers are based on a system which has been adopted as standard for automatic switchgear by IEEE. Numbers and their meanings are shown in Table 1-1.

A typical power-distribution diagram for an industrial facility is shown in Fig. 1-6. Note that the diagram is schematic. Locations shown refer to system relationships and not geography within the plant. One-line diagrams should be kept up to date as changes occur.

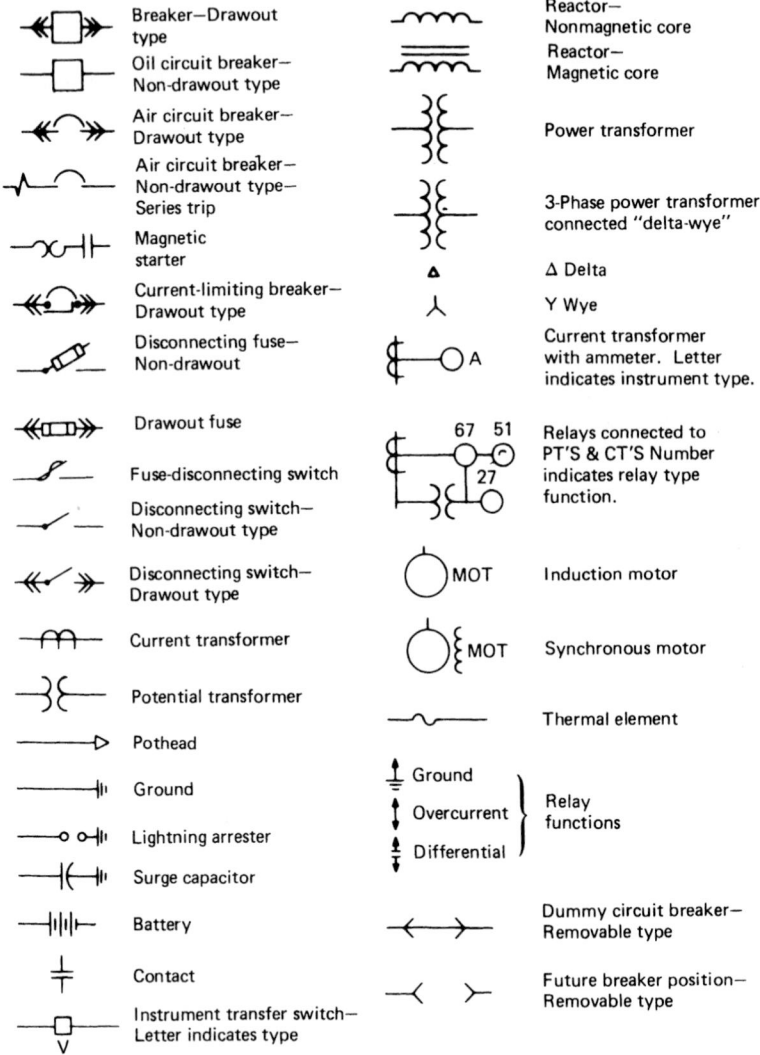

FIGURE 1-5 Commonly used symbols for one-line electrical diagrams.

TABLE 1-1   IEEE Device Numbers and Functions

Device no.	Function	Device no.	Function
1	Master element	51	AC time overcurrent relay
2	Time-delay starting or closing relay	52	AC circuit breaker
3	Checking or interlocking relay	53	Exciter or dc generator relay
4	Master contactor	54	High-speed dc circuit breaker
5	Stopping device	55	Power-factor relay
6	Starting circuit breaker	56	Field application relay
7	Anode circuit breaker	57	Short-circuiting or grounding device
8	Control power disconnecting device	58	Power rectifier misfire relay
9	Reversing device	59	Overvoltage relay
10	Unit sequence switch	60	Voltage balance relay
11	(Reserved for future application)	61	Current balance relay
12	Overspeed device	62	Time delay stopping or opening relay
13	Synchronous-speed device	63	Liquid or gas pressure level or flow relay
14	Underspeed device	64	Ground protective relay
15	Speed or frequency matching device	65	Governor
16	(Reserved for future application)	66	Notching or jogging device
17	Shunting or discharge switch	67	AC directional overcurrent relay
18	Accelerating to running transition contactor	68	Blocking relay
19	Starting to running transition contactor	69	Permissive control device
20	Electrically operated valve	70	Electrically operated rheostat
21	Distance relay	71	(Reserved for future application)
22	Equalizer circuit breaker	72	DC circuit breaker
23	Temperature control device	73	Load resistor contactor
24	(Reserved for future application)	74	Alarm relay
25	Synchronizing or synchronism check	75	Position-changing mechanism
26	Apparatus thermal device	76	DC overcurrent relay
27	Undervoltage relay	77	Pulse transmitter
28	(Reserved for future application)	78	Phase-angle measuring or out-of-step protective relay
29	Isolating contactor	79	AC reclosing relay
30	Annunciator relay	80	(Reserved for future application)
31	Separate excitation device	81	Frequency relay
32	Directional power relay	82	DC reclosing relay
33	Position switch	83	Automatic selective control or transfer relay
34	Motor-operated sequence switch	84	Operating mechanism
35	Brush-operating or slip-ring short-circuiting device	85	Carrier or pilot-wire receiver relay
36	Polarity device	86	Locking-out relay
37	Undercurrent or underpower relay	87	Differential protective relay
38	Bearing protective device	88	Auxiliary motor or motor generator
39	(Reserved for future application)	89	Line switch
40	Field relay	90	Regulating device
41	Field circuit breaker	91	Voltage directional relay
42	Running circuit breaker	92	Voltage and power directional relay
43	Manual transfer or selector device	93	Field-changing contactor
44	Unit sequence starting relay	94	Tripping or trip-free relay
45	(Reserved for future application)	95	
46	Reverse-phase-balance current relay	96	(Reserved for special applications)
47	Phase-sequence voltage relay	97	
48	Incomplete sequence relay	98	
49	Machine or transformer thermal relay	99	
50	Instantaneous overcurrent or rate-of-rise relay		

Source: ANSI C37.2-1970.

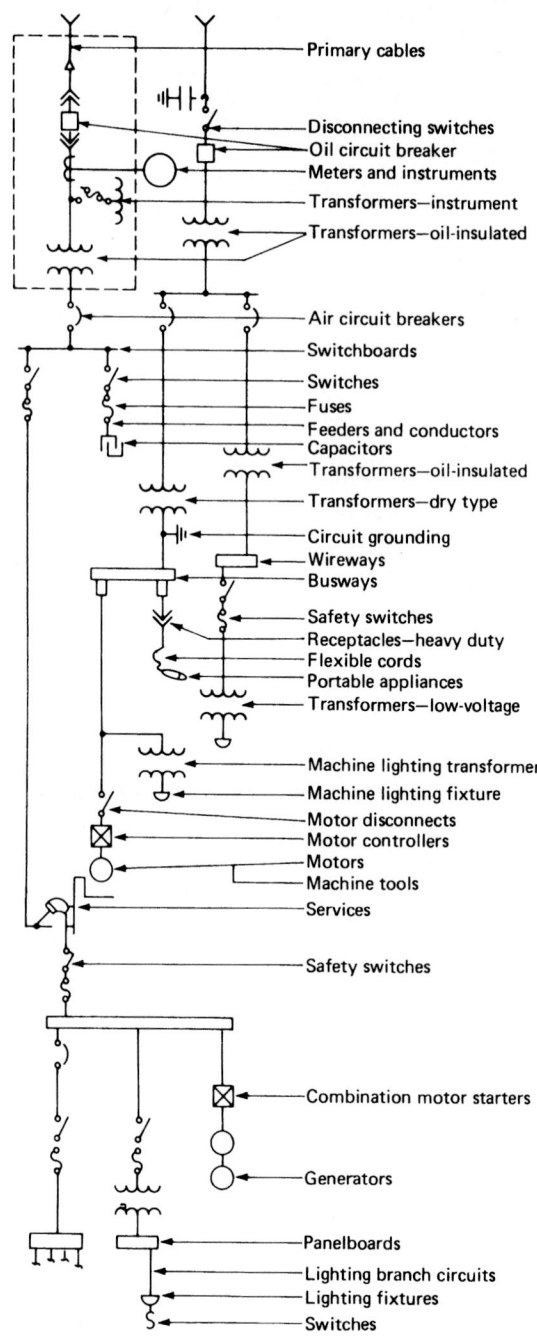

Primary cables

Disconnecting switches
Oil circuit breaker
Meters and instruments
Transformers—instrument
Transformers—oil-insulated

Air circuit breakers

Switchboards

Switches
Fuses
Feeders and conductors
Capacitors
Transformers—oil-insulated

Transformers—dry type

Circuit grounding
Wireways
Busways

Safety switches
Receptacles—heavy duty
Flexible cords
Portable appliances
Transformers—low-voltage

Machine lighting transformer
Machine lighting fixture
Motor disconnects
Motor controllers
Motors
Machine tools

Services

Safety switches

Combination motor starters

Generators

Panelboards
Lighting branch circuits
Lighting fixtures
Switches

FIGURE 1-6 Typical electrical distribution one-line diagram.

Standards

Standards relate to requirements, including agreed-upon definitions of terms, measurement and test procedures, and equipment dimensions and ratings. Some of the more commonly used standards relating to electric distribution systems follow.

National Electrical Manufacturers Association Standards. National Electrical Manufacturers Association (NEMA) standards establish dimensions, ratings, and performance requirements for electric equipment, regardless of manufacturer. NEMA standards are used widely in specifications.

National Fire Protection Association Standards Documents. National Fire Protection Association (NFPA) standards specify requirements for fire protection and safety.

NFPA's National Electrical Code®*. The NFPA's ***National Electrical Code®*** (NEC) is recognized as the minimum standard for the "practical safeguarding of persons and property from hazards arising from use of electricity." The **NEC®** may be supplemented by local requirements and ordinances pertaining to electric systems requiring more stringent safety measures. In general, the **NEC®** is nationally recognized. This Code is under constant review and is updated every 3 years. All plant engineers should have working knowledge of this Code.

Underwriters Laboratories, Inc. Standards. Underwriters Laboratories (UL), Inc., develops safety testing standards for electric equipment. Only equipment which complies with those requirements may be listed or labeled.

American National Standards Institute. The American National Standards Institute (ANSI) promotes, coordinates, and approves as American National Standards documents which have been prepared in accord with ANSI regulations. American National Standards carry the identification numbers both of ANSI and originating organizations. The sponsoring organization is responsible for keeping a standard up-to-date.

Occupational Safety and Health Act. The Occupational Safety and Health Act (OSHA) requires that employers provide a safe and healthful workplace for all employees.

Local Codes

Some large cities develop their own codes, but these generally are based on the ***National Electrical Code®***.

SYSTEM COMPONENTS

From point of service to point of use, electric power is directed, protected, and modified by segments of the system whose function, performance, and efficiency are vital to the utilizing equipment. To operate and maintain an industrial electric distribution system properly and to understand system planning fully, it is necessary to comprehend the function of each system component and its place in the overall system. Continued reference to Fig. 1-6, the one-line diagram, will aid in putting the various elements of the system into proper perspective.

---

* ***National Electrical Code®*** is a Registered Trademark of the National Fire Protection Association, Inc., Quincy, MA 02269.

Note that some system components have no normal operation and maintenance requirements. For such a device, it is necessary to have only a basic understanding of its appearance, construction, and function.

One such device is the *pothead,* used for connecting medium- and high-voltage cable systems to the internal distribution system. It is a terminator which permits termination of a complex cable at one end and attachment of cable lugs at the other. Its body usually is cast and can be filled with an insulating compound like petroleum jelly.

Outdoor high- and medium-voltage substations usually employ *oil-immersed circuit breakers* as a system protective device. These devices are equipped with direct-acting internal current transformers and trip coils enclosed in a jacket filled with a mineral oil. The oil jacket provides rapid cooling for contacts which become heated due to arcing action created by each switching operation. The oil-filled jacket is a better heat dissipator than air, so the device can be smaller than one which is air-cooled.

An oil-immersed circuit breaker must be located with care. The oil is flammable; a serious explosion or fire could result from a spark coming into contact with the cooling medium. In addition, in case of a leak a means for disposing oil, usually in the form of a gravel-filled drain, must be provided.

The oil must be examined periodically. Inspection ports are provided for this purpose. If the oil becomes contaminated, it must be replaced or drained and filtered.

Transformers

Transformers make possible the use of the high distribution and utilization voltages found in industrial electric systems. They are used to transform one primary voltage to a second primary level, to step from primary down to secondary voltage (not more than 600 V), and to step a secondary distribution voltage to a secondary utilization level.

The names used to categorize transformers relate to their applications:

General-purpose transformers.   Dry-type units rated 600 V or less. They are used for local step-down from a secondary distribution voltage to a utilization level, serving lighting and appliance loads. They also are called *general power* and *light* transformers or *lighting transformers.* Ceiling-suspended and floor-standing units are available.

Load-center transformers.   Either dry-type or liquid-filled units, primary rated from 2400 to 15,000 V. They are used for both indoor and outdoor applications to step down to a voltage of 600 V or less. Load-center transformer units may be used separately, in combination with separate protective and switching devices and secondary distribution switchboards, or in combination with primary and secondary switching and protection in a packaged unit called a substation or load-center substation. They are base-mounted, free-standing units.

Distribution transformers.   Single-phase and three-phase oil-immersed, pole-mounted, or platform-mounted units. They are primary rated from 480 to 15,000 V, with step-down to a secondary level (or to a lower high-voltage level for units over 10-kV primary). Distribution transformers in capacities up to 167 kVA are used for pole-line distribution. Other outdoor wiring systems use platform units rated up to 500 kVA.

Substation transformers.   Oil-immersed units which are primary rated from 2400 to 67,000 V, with secondary ratings ranging from less than 600 to 15,000 V. Substation transformers are used in utility distribution and industrial substations. Power transformers are available for over 67 kV.

A transformer's nameplate indicates its kVA rating.

Transformer Ratings

Insulation classifications include liquid and dry types. Liquid insulation can be subclassified by type of liquid. Dry-type transformers can be subclassified as ventilated or sealed gas-filled.

kVA rating includes both self-cooling and forced-draft (fan-cooled) ratings for a specified temperature rise. The self-cooled rating should not exceed the peak demand by more than 25 percent to achieve the most efficient operation. A significant increase in transformer capacity can be obtained by the application of proper fan cooling. This permits transformers to be applied to present load conditions with an optimum load factor while still being able to serve expanded loads.

Transformers are designed to withstand short-duration overloads without any damage except a shortening of the useful life. The permissible overload and its duration vary with ambient temperature, preloading condition, and duration.

Transformer voltage ratings include primary and secondary continuous duty levels at specified frequencies, along with each winding's basic impulse level (BIL). The primary winding's continuous rating is the nominal line voltage of the system. The secondary voltage rating is the value under no-load conditions. Secondary voltage change experienced under load is termed *regulation.* It is a function of the system including the transformer impedance and the load power factor. Good regulation can often be achieved by tap adjustments on the primary side.

The *basic impulse level* rating for a transformer winding identifies the transient overvoltage withstand capability of its insulation.

Voltage Taps.   Voltage taps are used either to compensate for small changes in primary supply to the transformer or to vary secondary voltage level with changed load requirements. A manually adjustable no-load tap changer is a common standard arrangement since tap changing under load is a highly complex problem.

Connections.   Delta primary and wye secondary connections such as those shown in Fig. 1-7 are the most common transformer connections utilized today. In older plants, such variations as the grounded wye secondary and delta-delta connections to provide power to three-phase equipment are frequently encountered.

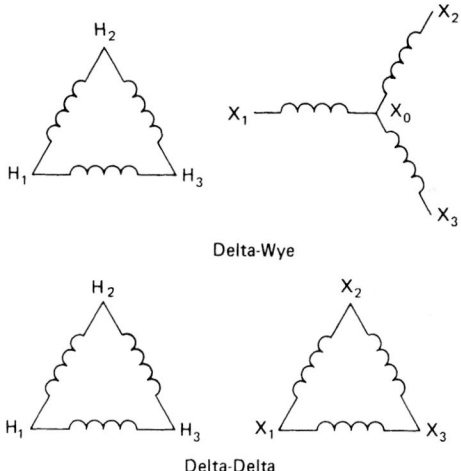

Delta-Wye

Delta-Delta

FIGURE 1-7   Three-phase transformer configurations.

Impedance.   A transformer's impedance is its opposition to current flowing through it with the secondary short-circuited. Impedance is expressed as the percentage of normal-rated primary voltage which must be applied to cause full-rated load current to flow in the short-circuited secondary. For example, when a 480- to 120-V transformer is impedance-rated at 5 percent, it means that 5 percent of 480 V, or 24 V, must be applied to the primary to cause rated load current to flow in the shorted secondary. When 5 percent of primary voltage causes such current, 100 percent of primary voltage will cause 20 times full-load-rated secondary current to flow through a solid short-circuit on the secondary terminals.

The lower a transformer's impedance, the higher the short-circuit current it can deliver. The impedance values of general-purpose transformers generally range between 3 and 6 percent.

Circuit Breakers (600 V and Below)

Two types of circuit breakers are commonly used for applications at 600 V and less: *power circuit breakers* and *molded-case circuit breakers.*

Power circuit breakers are open-construction assemblies on metal frames for service in switchgear compartments and similar enclosures. Molded-case circuit breakers also are used in switchgear. While their protective value is high, they offer few control options.

Circuit breakers can be subcategorized in a variety of ways, based on different characteristics, as follows:

Adjustable. Indicates that the overcurrent device of the circuit breaker can be set to trip at different values of current and/or time within a predetermined range.

Instantaneous trip. Indicates that no delay is purposely introduced in the tripping action of the circuit breaker. Automatic circuit breakers may have both time overcurrent and instantaneous tripping devices.

Inverse time. Indicates that a delay in the tripping action of the circuit breaker is purposely introduced. The delay decreases as the magnitude of the current increases.

Nonadjustable. Indicates that the circuit breaker does not have any adjustment to alter the value of current at which it will trip or the time required for its operation.

Generally speaking, circuit breakers are rated by a frame size which determines the maximum overcurrent trip setting and an interrupting capacity indicating the maximum short-circuit current which can be interrupted safely without damage to the circuit breaker.

Circuit breakers are sometimes used with integral current-limiting fuses to provide for interrupting current requirements up to 200,000 A, symmetrical rms.

New Developments in Circuit Breakers

Circuit Breakers with Internal Electronics. Maintenance and industrial electricians will find that many new circuit breakers now contain electronic circuits which allow for adjustability of trip characteristics to fit a broad range of protection requirements. This adjustability allows for the customizing of the circuit breaker trip curve to coordinate with other distribution equipment or to offer additional protection for individual circuits. Adjustment features are placed on the face of the breaker. Qualified design engineers or technicians can customize these trip settings to provide enhanced system protection. Also, ground fault capabilities can be installed in the circuit breaker and a level of adjustability to the ground fault protection can be included. Multiple circuit breakers with ground fault protection can be used sequentially or cascaded so that the smallest branch breaker in the sequence would clear the fault first, without tripping the main circuit breakers or other feeder breakers in the circuit. Manufacturer's instructions should always be followed when altering characteristics of the circuit breaker.

High-Fault-Current Circuit Breakers. In modern distribution facilities, very high levels of fault current are available, up to or exceeding 200,000 A. In the case of a fault (a short circuit), there may be in excess of 200,000 A passing through the distribution equipment and the circuit breaker to the fault. Circuit breakers which are not designed to interrupt these high levels of fault current may be damaged or destroyed as they try to open or clear the fault condition.

In the past, a fuse or a circuit breaker-fuse combination was required in order to offer fault current protection as high as 200,000 A. Many of today's circuit breakers are capable of opening at these very high fault levels without the assistance of fuses. Utility companies can advise users what the available fault current is. Facility engineers and service personnel should be aware of the fault current ratings of equipment within their facility and ensure that existing equipment is capable of safely clearing faults. When replacing existing equipment or adding new distribution equipment, care should be taken that new circuit breakers or distribution equipment meets or exceed the ratings required to safely clear an electrical fault.

Current-Limiting Circuit Breakers. There are also special types of circuit breakers which limit the amount of current that can flow through them during a short circuit condition. These are called *current-limiting circuit breakers.* In the case of very high levels of fault current being available from the power company, they restrict the amount of current that would pass through in the case of a fault and reduce the possibility of damage to downstream equipment.

SERIES (CASCADED) RATINGS.   Underwriters Laboratories recognized the short-circuit rating of a combination of devices, that is, two or more devices used in series. A combination of circuit breakers, where circuit breakers of a lower-fault-current capability could be used in conjunction with higher-fault-current circuit breakers on high-fault-current systems, or combinations of fuses and circuit breakers, are also recognized.

In the case of a system that has 200,000 A fault current available, a 200,000-A main circuit breaker might be used, and downstream from the 200,000-A main circuit breaker, there may be a 100,000-A feeder breaker, then a 65,000-A breaker, down to a 42,000-A breaker, protecting branch circuits, to the minimum circuit breaker available today, which is a 10,000-A interrupting capacity (AIC) breaker. All circuit breakers are labeled on the face with their AIC rating—the amount of fault current that can safely be interrupted by the breaker.

With the UL recognition of integrated or coordinated ratings, there is a requirement that distribution equipment be labeled with the coordination information of the circuit breakers installed in the distribution equipment. Service personnel must be mindful of the service rating of the equipment they are servicing and ensure that replacement or add-on equipment is rated equal to or higher than the markings on the distribution equipment call for. Circuit breakers should be rated higher than the available fault current. Or *use the series rating of equipment,* which is provided by the manufacturer and states what circuit breakers can be used in series. This will limit and prevent damage to equipment.

CRITICAL CIRCUITS.   In situations where series-rated equipment is used, caution should be taken that critical power circuits are not interrupted. In the case of a series-rated circuit breaker system and a high-fault-current situation, two circuit breakers would trip simultaneously and limit the amount of fault current passing to the lower rated breaker in the system. Thus two circuit breakers trip simultaneously; this terminates the power in the circuit in which the fault occurred as well the feeder circuit feeding the branch.

Care should be taken in the design of systems such that critical circuits are not used with series-rated systems. In the case of our 200,000-AIC main, if there were a high current fault at a downstream sight, the 100,000-AIC circuit breaker would interrupt and it would also cause the 200,000-AIC main circuit breaker to interrupt simultaneously, which would terminate power to the entire distribution system. If this were used in, say, a hospital, you would not want a short circuit in a panel board or a downstream distribution switchboard to also cause the main circuit breaker to trip, taking all power out of the hospital. In those types of critical situations, the minimum circuit breaker AIC rating should be no less than the available system fault current delivered by the utility.

SPECIAL CAUTIONARY NOTE: All circuit breaker manufacturers recommend that their circuit breakers be "exercised" annually via the "trip test" button. Exercising the circuit breaker actuates the trip mechanism. The trip mechanism of the circuit breaker is separate from the on-off handle mechanism, and annual operation of the trip mechanism ensures that the breaker will trip when called on to operate. This is also a test indication: if the breaker fails to trip, it has malfunctioned and should be replaced.

Switchboards and Switchgear

Switchboards and switchgear include buses, conductors, control devices, protective devices, circuit switching, interrupting devices, interconnecting wiring, accessories, supporting structures, and enclosures.

Switchgears can serve as main secondary service equipment, as main primary service equipment, and as load center equipment when located near load concentrations. The assembly and its devices provide for the control and distribution of electricity to utilization or sub-distribution equipment. Most switchgear manufactured since 1955 has been metal-enclosed, dead-front, free-standing type, with its circuit protective devices enclosed each in its own compartment. For certain types of load applications, the protective devices are group-mounted in separate cubicles instead of individual compartments.

Older switchboards may be live-front type with the devices wired and mounted to slate panels with the wiring exposed on the rear of these panels.

A preventive maintenance plan should be conducted for all plant switchgear. Normal maintenance includes checking and tightening cable connections, testing air circuit-breaker operations, and checking relay and meter calibrations.

Types and Functions of Switchgear.   The three most common types of switchgear used in industrial plants are:

1. Medium- and high-voltage metal-clad circuit breaker
2. Low-voltage power circuit breaker, either drawout or stationary (Molded-case breakers are being used more frequently for switchboard applications.)
3. Load interrupter switch and fused switchgear

Metal-Clad Switchgear.   This is metal-enclosed power switchgear characterized by removable circuit switching and interrupting devices. Major parts of the primary circuit are enclosed by grounded metal barriers. Instruments, secondary control devices, meters, relays, and their wiring also utilize grounded metal barriers to isolate them from primary circuit elements. All live parts are enclosed in grounded metal compartments, bus conductors are insulated, and mechanical interlocks are provided.

Low-Voltage Power Circuit Breaker Switchgear.   This is metal-enclosed and generally consists of: low-voltage power circuit breakers; bare or insulated bus and connections; control instruments, meters, and relays; and control wiring and accessories, together with cable and busway termination facilities. Circuit breakers may be drawout type, stationary air circuit breakers, or molded-case circuit breakers, usually of the solid-state, adjustable trip variety.

Metal-Enclosed Load Interrupter Switch and Fuse Switchgear.   This consists of fused load interrupter switches, bare or insulated bus and connections, power fuses, instruments for control, and control wiring and accessories. Both stationary and removable interrupter switches and power fuses are used.

Protective Relays.   Protective relays consist of an operating element and a set of movable contacts. In today's solid-state relays it is difficult to distinguish each of these elements visually. The operating element receives power from a control power source within the switchgear. It obtains input from a sensing element in the circuit. This input can be in the form of either a voltage or current variation. The relay measures the variation against its standard settings and, when a preset limit has been exceeded, it initiates an action by causing its contacts to assume a new configuration. This action is used to perform some other control function such as sounding an alarm or tripping a circuit breaker.

It is essential for all protective relays to be maintained in proper working order well within prescribed tolerances. Relay manufacturers provide complete maintenance and setting instructions including test procedures for all their relays. Such instructions should be kept in an overall operating manual in the plant engineer's office.

Directional Relays.   Directional relays are used to initiate an action when current flows in a direction other than normal. Such relays will initiate actions preventing the reverse flow of current through equipment.

Differential Relays.   Differential relays are so named due to their current-balance characteristic. If the current entering the protected section is not balanced by the current leaving it, the relay initiates an action. These relays are used most frequently for protection of transformers and substation buses where they permit or prevent casing of the breakers.

Voltage Relays.   Voltage relays are fundamentally similar to overcurrent relays, except voltage is used to activate the operating element. Some voltage relays are activated by overvoltage, others by overcurrent, and still others by a combination of the two conditions.

Ground Relays.   Ground relays are instantaneous relays that respond to unwanted ground current. As such, they are unaffected by load currents and so may be set to operate for single-phase-to-ground currents that are smaller than full-load currents.

Control power for relay use is supplied generally by the use of current and potential transformers. Low-voltage equipment operating at less than 1000 V to ground generally requires no potential transformers because relays and instruments are designed to function at normal low voltages.

Current Transformers.   Current transformers are transformers in which the switchgear bus usually forms the single turn of the primary winding while the secondary is a combination of many turns. As such, the ratio of the current flowing in the main bus to that which flows in the secondary of the transformer is directly proportional to the bus rating. All relays and instruments are calibrated to read directly based on this ratio. The full secondary current is usually 5 A. Maintenance personnel must be careful not to open-circuit the secondary side of a current transformer. The resulting voltage across the open terminals is the transformer turn ratio times the primary voltage and is very dangerous.

Safety Switches and Disconnecting Means

Each piece of utilization equipment located remote from its source of power or overcurrent protective device requires a disconnecting means. In most cases, a safety switch is provided for plant machinery which is not built with its own internal on-off switch designed to completely disconnect the device from the electrical system. A safety switch may be either fused or unfused. The disconnecting means is provided to permit equipment maintenance without the possibility of some remote-control device functioning to turn the machine on while the maintenance person is in contact with some dangerous part. Some of the commonly used switch types include safety switches and toggle, or snap, switches. A *safety switch* is a spring-loaded, quick-make, quick-break, device enclosed in a metal housing. Also known as service switches or disconnect switches, they are rated in amperes and/or horsepower. *Toggle,* or *snap, switches* are also used for disconnect purposes. They are designed for outlet box mounting and are rated by voltage and current. Another such device is the thermal motor switch or manual motor starter, intended as the overcurrent protective device for small motors. It is a combination of motor circuit protector circuit breaker and thermal overload device, built as an integrated unit designed for outlet box mounting.

Fuses

Many types of fuses are used in switches and other protective devices. The National Electrical Manufacturers Association lists standardized fuse types.

A fuse protects a circuit by means of a "link" or internal element which melts because of the heat caused by excessive current, thereby opening the circuit.

Fuses are selected on the basis of voltage, current-carrying capacity, and interrupting rating, in accordance with NEMA standards.

Spare part planning should include provisions to have the plant stock at least one complete set of each fuse in use in the plant.

Power Fuses (Over 600 V).   The NEMA E rating for power fuses requires that all fuses must carry their current rating continuously. Two types of power fuses are in common use: *current-limiting* and *expulsion-type.*

Current-Limiting Type.   These power fuses are designed in such a way that the melting introduces high arc resistance into the circuit during the first half-cycle's peak current, thus restricting short-circuit current.

Their current-forcing action produces transient overvoltages. Surge-protective apparatus may be needed to compensate.

Expulsion Type.   These fuses are generally used in distribution system cutouts or disconnect switches. An arc-confining tube with a deionizing fiber liner and fusible element provide fault current interruption. Production of pressurized gases inside the fuse tube extinguishes the arc by expelling it from the open end of the fuse.

Low-Voltage Fuses (600 V and below).   There are two styles of low-voltage fuse design, *plug* and *cartridge.*

Plug.   These fuses are of three basic types, all rated 125 V or less to ground and up to 30 A maximum. Although they have no interrupting rating, they are subjected to short-circuit test with an available current of 10,000 A. The three types are: Edison base without time delay and all ratings interchangeable, Edison base with time delay and interchangeable ratings, and type S base available in three noninterchangeable current ranges: 0 to 15, 16 to 20, and 21 to 30 A. These last two types normally have a time-delay characteristic.

Cartridge.   These fuses are either renewable or nonrenewable. Nonrenewable fuses are factory-assembled and must be replaced after operating. Renewable fuses can be disassembled and the fusible element replaced. Consult the NEMA standards and the code for fuse class definitions.

Wires and Cable

Wire and cable used for the distribution of electric power consists of a conducting medium usually enclosed within an insulating sheath and sometimes further protected by an outer jacket. The conducting medium is generally either copper or aluminum. The insulating medium can be made of any one of several materials depending on the ambient characteristics in which the wire is to be applied. Modern building wire is usually insulated with some form of plastic insulation. The various insulating materials are described in and defined by the ***National Electrical Code®,*** Tables 310 to 313.*

Outer cable jacket materials range from cross-linked polyethylene to copper armor. Each jacket type has its own unique set of rules for application.

The cable protection method, conduit, cable tray, or bare exposed, depends on many design considerations. Cables require no basic maintenance except to assure that they are not applied beyond their ampacity. Cable and wire ampacities are published in the ***National Electrical Code®*** and by the manufacturers who make cables. All cables used for normal electrical usage are sized in the United States in accordance with the American Wire Gauge (AWG) or circular mils.

Terminations of aluminum cables require periodic examination to ensure that "cold flow" has not loosened the connection. Lugs connecting aluminum cable must be tightened in exact

---

* ***National Electrical Code®*** is a Registered Trademark of the National Fire Protection Association, Inc., Quincy, MA 02269.

accordance with the recommendations of the equipment manufacturer. Maintenance personnel should possess a set of torque wrenches for aluminum cable maintenance. A program for terminal examination should be included in maintenance manuals.

Busways and Busbars

Busways and busbars perform the same functions as wires and cables, but their construction features and applications are far different.

Busbars can be cut, welded, bent, punched, drilled, plated, and insulated to meet specifications. They are most practical when configurations must be precise, terminal points inflexible, and installation locations confined.

Standard busway types, ampacities, components, and accessories are so numerous that almost any routing plan can be created. They can be enclosed or ventilated, installed indoors or out, and used either as point-to-point power feeders, as multipoint power sources, or as continuous power takeoff routes.

Motor Controllers and Motor Control Centers

All motor-operated devices require some form of motor controller to provide start-stop, reversing, and other functions. Sometimes these control elements are built into the machine and the controls are machine-mounted. More often than not the control of a building utility or process system motor is from a remote motor controller.

Motor controllers—commonly called *starters*—are usually magnetically operated devices with thermal overload protection built in through the application of melting alloy links. A preventive maintenance program is essential for motor starters if they are to continue to function properly. Remote controls with operating lights indicate only that the controls functioned. Therefore, it is necessary to make periodic inspections of these devices.

It is often more economical to group-mount motor controllers rather than individually mount them. A group of starters collected together into one integrated unit, is called a *motor control center*. NEMA has well-defined standards for type and class of wiring and the degree of interconnecting and interwiring present in any given center. This data can be obtained from the manufacturer and should be filed in the plant maintenance manuals together with complete detailed instructions for a periodic maintenance program. For further discussion, see Chap. 3-4.

Panelboards

Panelboards are assemblies of switching and overcurrent devices enclosed in a cabinet, usually wall-mounted, and protected by a cover or trim which can have a hinged door.

Panelboards provide for local protection and control of apparatus and lighting. They are usually composed of integrated groups of circuit breakers and fused switches providing protection for circuits terminating in their immediate area.

All of the maintenance and operating considerations previously discussed for circuit breakers and switches apply to panelboards. Unless the circuit breakers in a panelboard bear a *switching duty rating* and the panel nameplate or breaker is so marked, they are not designed for such service on a constant basis. Constant use for switching will shorten the life of a standard circuit breaker. Occasional use will not have a negative effect.

Panelboards serving lighting and appliance circuits which must be switched on at fixed times and off at other times can well be equipped with magnetic contactors. These devices operate in a manner similar to motor controllers except they contain no overload devices. They permit remote switching of panelboards without using the breakers as a switching device.

PRIMARY SERVICE METHODS

There are a number of different distribution methods used in modern industrial systems. In all of these, electric power is received from a public utility or in-house generating plant at some convenient primary voltage and passed through a control and distribution system to the point of utilization. There is no one standard system of industrial plant distribution. Each system is tailored to meet conditions specified at time of design. Prime factors in the type of system chosen are the required utilization voltage and the distances involved in the distribution. Because the number of plants in many areas has increased and moved further from the utility generators, utilities have been using higher voltages to transmit electricity to the plants. This technique also minimizes line losses and provides good voltage regulation. As a result, many utilities are distributing at up to 230 kV and some at 350 kV. In many cases the rates paid for power at higher voltages are low enough to generate savings which repay higher installation costs for a main substation within several years.

Systems utilizing primary power as their source require some point at which this power is received and transformed to a useful form. The point of connection is normally the plant substation. If the primary voltage is in the high voltage classification (34,500 V and above), chances are that the service is aerial. In these cases, service enters the substation from an overhead structure containing a series of disconnect switches and lightning arresters. The substation requires oil-filled circuit breakers on each feeder. Liquid-filled transformers change the incoming voltage to some more usable level and provide a method (either cable or bus) for distribution to the main secondary switchboard.

Main Substations

If the purchased power voltage can be used for the plant primary system without transformation, a plant main bus can serve the same purpose as a main substation.

The principal functions of a main substation are indicated in Fig. 1-8. This is a simple arrangement which meets the requirements of many smaller plants. More complex arrangements are needed when there is more than one incoming line, or more than one power transformer, or one of a number of other bus arrangements. For large plants with heavy loads in widely separated areas, substations may require transmission voltage feeders connected to the incoming-line bus.

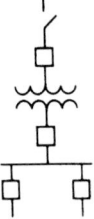

FIGURE 1-8 A typical main substation arrangement used by an industrial plant.

SECONDARY SERVICE METHODS

Many plants are switching to higher in-plant voltages to feed power over long distances throughout the plant without excessive line losses or loss of regulation. The most commonly used utilization voltages in new plants are 480 and 240 V, with 480 V becoming more popular. The best overall secondary utilization voltage is 480 V. It costs less and provides fewer line losses and less voltage drop.

Most new plants use load-center distribution, with unit substations being close to the loads and primary distribution being made at 2400, 4160, or 13,800 V. Primary-distribution voltage between master substation and load center should be selected based on size of the load and the distance to be covered. In general, 4160 V is used for loads under 10,000 VA and 13.8 kV for loads over 20,000 VA. For loads between 10,000 and 20,000 VA, 4160 V is used when plant layout is compact and 13.8 kV for long, rambling layouts.

The standard method of receiving and distributing secondary power is through use of radial systems.

Radial Systems

Conventional Simple Radial System.   A conventional simple radial system (Fig. 1-9) receives power at the utility supply voltage. Voltage is stepped down to the utilization level by a transformer.

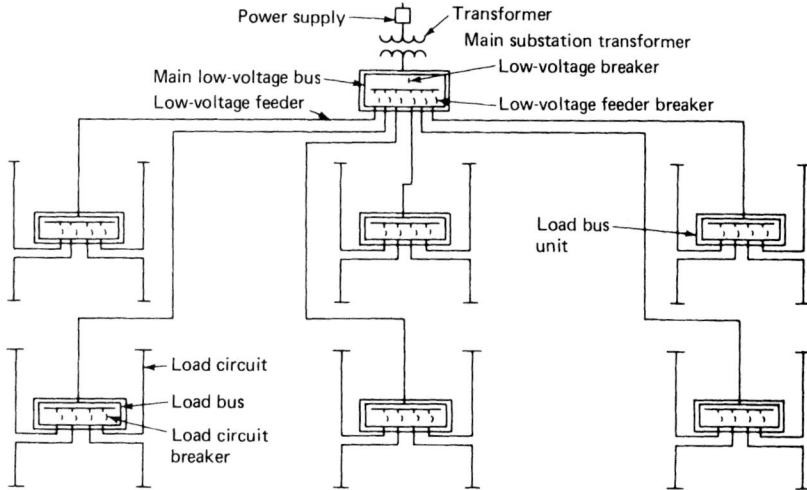

FIGURE 1-9   Conventional simple radial system.

Because the full building load is served from a single incoming substation, diversity among loads can be used to full advantage; installed transformer capacity can be minimized. The system's drawbacks include poor voltage regulation and poor service reliability.

Modern Load-Center Simple Radial System.   The modern load-center simple radial system (Fig. 1-10) distributes incoming power at the primary voltage to power-center transformers located in building load areas. These transformers step the voltage down to utilization levels.

Each transformer must have enough capacity to handle the peak load of its specific load area. Combined transformer capacity requirements, therefore, may exceed those of a conventional simple radial system. This approach results in reduced losses, improved voltage regulation, reduced cost of feeder circuits, and no need for large low-voltage feeder circuit breakers.

Unit Substations

A unit substation contains one or more sections of each of three main components.

A *primary section* provides for connection of incoming medium- or high-voltage circuits, usually with disconnecting and circuit protective devices such as switches and circuit breakers. A *transformer section* includes one or more transformers. A *secondary switchboard section* provides for connection of secondary distribution feeders, each with a circuit protective switching and interrupting device.

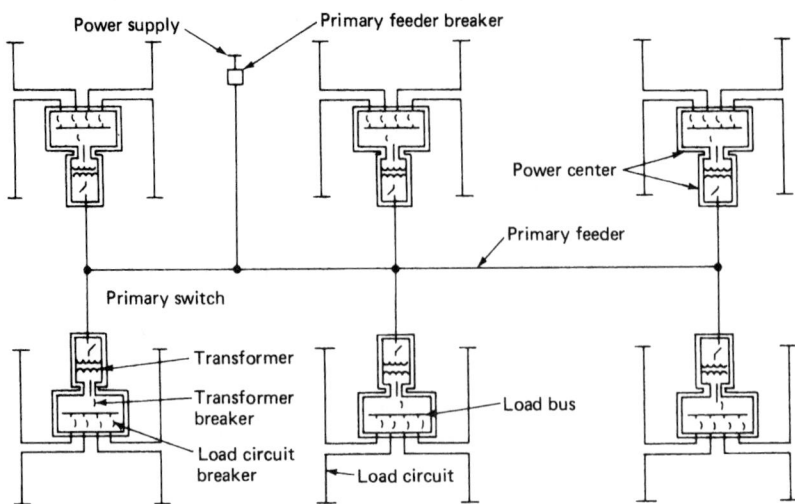

FIGURE 1-10 Modern simple radial system.

Unit substation sections usually are subassemblies designed for field connection into an integral single unit. Numerous types are available for both indoor and outdoor applications and are described fully in manufacturers' catalogs.

Unit substations can be either single-ended, fed by a single primary feed, or double-ended, fed from either end by a separate primary feed. Double-ended substations are usually designed so that either transformer can assume two thirds of the load in the event of a failure of one primary feeder. This is accomplished by the inclusion of a normally open tie circuit breaker in the switchgear lineup. The application of double-ended substations to industrial plants increases the reliability of the system and allows partial operation in the event of partial power failures. Plant operators must have a plan for immediate dumping of nonessential loads before closing the tie circuit breaker. This plan will keep essential processes functioning while power is down.

System Voltage.   The voltage class of both primary and secondary distributions is called *nominal system voltage.* This term identifies the basic voltage normally utilized, such as 120/208 or 277/480 V. The actual voltage of each nominal system may be a slight variation such as 125/216 or 265/460 V. Each utility company uses its own selected secondary system. When a plant buys or generates primary power, the secondary voltage can be set very close to the nominal system rating.

Ranges for standard nominal system voltages are covered in ANSI C84.1-1977. Nominal system voltages most often found in the United States are indicated below.

120 V.   A single-phase, two-wire system. Used for convenience outlets and incandescent lighting.

120/240 V.   A single-phase, three-wire system. Nominal voltage between the two-phase conductors is 240 V. Nominal voltage from each phase conductor to ground is 120 V; used for power equipment, power outlets, electric heating processes, and in some cases high-intensity discharge lighting.

240 V.   A three-phase, three-wire system, delta-connected, with 240 V between phase conductors and no ground or neutral conductor. Used for motor and three-phase power loads. This system is gradually being replaced by the more modern 120/208 V system with grounded neutral.

120/208 V. A three-phase, four-wire system, wye-connected with 208 V between phase wires and 120 V between phase and ground. This system permits single-phase, three-wire circuits to be taken from the system as well as 120 V single-phase circuits. The system is in general use for all types of loads. Recently, larger buildings have been designed to use a higher utilization voltage, but it often is converted to 120/480 V for convenience outlets and incandescent lighting.

277/480 V. A system similar in use and characteristics to 120/208 V for direct operation of motors, process equipment, and all forms of discharge lighting including fluorescent. Transformers are required to convert 277/480 to 120/208 V for uses described under that system.

4160 or 2400/4160 V. Sometimes used in large plants for internal distribution or for direct power operation on motors in excess of 250 hp.

Medium- and high-voltage systems are rarely used for distribution within plant buildings. In multibuilding sites higher distribution voltages may be found running between plant areas and between substations. A detailed discussion of medium- and high-voltage distribution or transmission systems is beyond the scope of this chapter.

Conductor Sizing and Load Growth

Wire and cables are usually sized exactly for the loads they serve. The sizes of feeders running to panelboards or switchboards usually allow for all spare circuits built into these devices, computed as if they were half-loaded.

Feeders serving grouped loads can usually have some additional load added to them because they are protected from overload by the natural diversity of equipment operation. Some study must be made of the actual use pattern of the equipment to determine the extent of the excess capacity available through this diversity.

All feeders serving either lighting, receptacle, or motor loads are sized to include a 25 percent factor to account for heating due to continuous loading. This factor must be maintained even when maximum loading is desired.

Most modern designers utilize only half a circuit's normal capacity during initial design; thus a 20-A receptacle circuit is loaded to only about 10 A initially. This approach permits addition of another 5 A of continuous load.

GROUNDING

The subject of electric system grounding is broad and complex, and is discussed here in brief overview.

Contemporary approaches hold that all power systems should have a grounded neutral included in the system. It is imperative for life safety that all metal elements of electric systems remain at ground potential at all times. Grounding should also take into account that buildings and equipment can build up a hazardous static charge of far greater magnitude than that encountered in winter when walking across a carpet and touching a doorknob. For tall structures or buildings located in isolated surroundings without other construction around, lightning can pose a potential hazard, which must be considered.

Ungrounded Systems

For many years industrial plants relied on an *ungrounded system,* essentially a delta-connected system without a grounded neutral. In this system, a single line-to-ground fault does not cause automatic circuit tripping. However, a second undetected ground on such a system can cause continuous nuisance tripping and even equipment burnout on devices not connected to the affected circuits. This is especially true on higher voltage systems. Ungrounded systems also pose the problem of transient overvoltages caused by grounded circuits. For all of these reasons there are now relatively few of these systems being installed, and existing ungrounded systems are being converted.

System Grounding

There are several types of grounded systems generally used in today's industrial plants. These are described briefly in the following paragraphs.

Resistance-Grounded Systems.   Resistance-grounded systems are characterized by a resistance connection between system neutral and ground. This system introduces impedance in the ground path which tends to limit the current flow to ground. This technique also limits overvoltages caused by an intermittent-contact line-to-ground short circuit. Resistance is used to provide a ground-fault current which can be used for protective relaying operation.

Solidly Grounded Systems.   Solidly grounded systems permit better control of overvoltages than any other scheme, but ground-fault currents can be higher.

These systems are used at operating voltages up to 600 V. The low line-to-neutral voltage reduces the risk of dangerous voltage gradients. A large magnitude ground-fault current helps attain optimum performance of phase-overcurrent protective devices.

Equipment Grounding

Equipment grounding is provided by a system of conductors utilized to maintain the metallic housings of electric system devices at ground potential. By grounding equipment in this manner, the system provides life safety and severely limits the fire hazard of short-circuit currents by providing a simple path to ground. This system should be periodically inspected and tested to maintain it in proper working order.

In general, it is an essential of a safe electric system that everything which might come into contact with a live system be maintained at ground potential. Further safety is gained by providing the system with a grounded neutral leg in the system.

System grounds can be derived from a ground attachment to a cold-water pipe ahead of the water meter or by a system of ground electrodes or some combination of these. A single ground point for the system should be established and periodically checked for continuity. Provision should be made to disconnect the system neutral during tests.

FAULT PROTECTION AND SYSTEM COORDINATION

Fault protection also is a complex subject. The principal types of faults which plague electric systems are three-phase short circuits, line-to-ground faults, and intermittent ground faults.

A three-phase bolted short circuit can be caused by any accident. The instant voltage fluctuations and the large overcurrent flowing in the system, coupled with the rapid decay of the system voltage, cause the circuit breaker to trip or the fuses to blow at the nearest point. The elapsed time for a circuit breaker to clear such a fault is from three to eight cycles depending on the size of the breaker. It is here that the design of the system is tested, because the circuit breaker is forced to open a circuit of far greater current than its trip rating. If breaker interrupting ratings are selected properly, clearing of three-phase bolted faults is simple. A fuse operates in the first one-half cycle. Fig. 1-11 illustrates a typical operating characteristic of current-limiting during a high-fault current interruption.

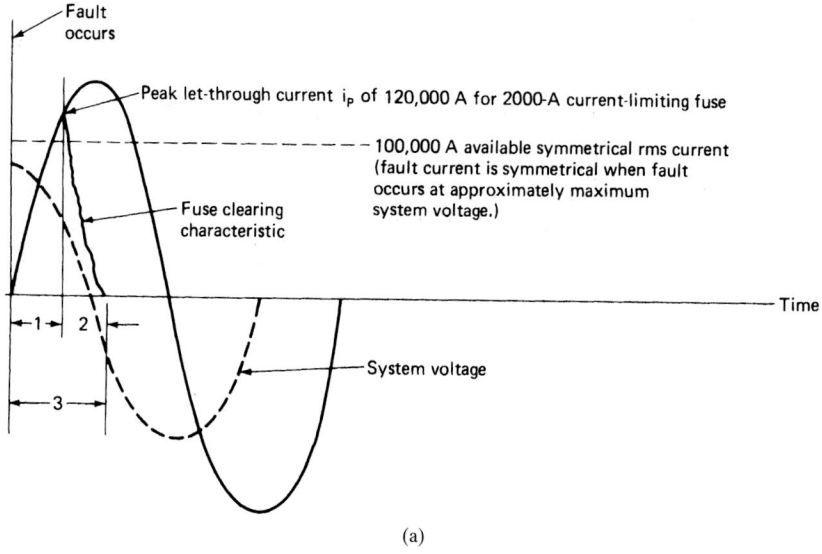

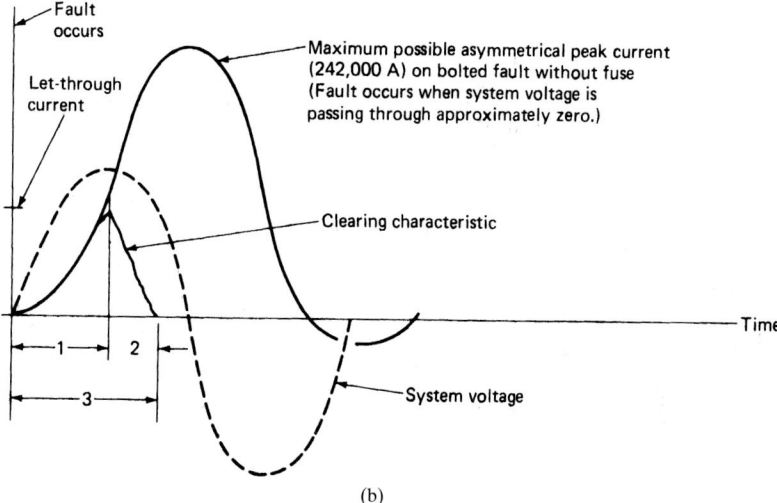

FIGURE 1-11 Typical current-limitation characteristics showing peak let-through and maximum prospective fault current as a function of the time of fault occurrence (100-kA available symmetrical rms current): (*a*) Fault occurring at peak voltage. (*b*) Fault occurring at zero voltage: 1 = melting time, 2 = arcing time, and 3 = total clearing time. *(Source: IEEE Standard 141-1976.)*

A solid line-to-ground fault causes system protective devices to react as they do for a three-phase short circuit.

The intermittent ground fault is the most difficult and therefore the most dangerous type of system fault. At no time does an overcurrent flow for a period long enough for the protective device to detect the problem and react. Intermittent ground faults are detected best by a *zero sequence* protection system. This system measures any current flow in the ground path and uses this current to operate a relay to cause the system protective device to operate and clear the fault.

Protective devices are usually coordinated so that the unit closest to the fault opens first. If the first unit in the system fails to clear the fault, the next one acts, and so on until the main opens, shutting the whole system down.

All circuit breakers, fuses, and most relays come with, or have available from the manufacturer, time-current operating curves. See Fig. 1-12 for comparative time-current curves of a typical induction overcurrent relay, plus instantaneous trip. By overlaying these curves and selecting services with coordinated operating times, it is possible to achieve the sequential operation needed.

Primary-system and even secondary-system protective relays are set to achieve this same system of sequential tripping.

It is incumbent on the operating personnel to never simply reclose a protective device that has opened on fault without first ascertaining the cause of the fault and either correcting it or removing the offending piece of equipment from the circuit.

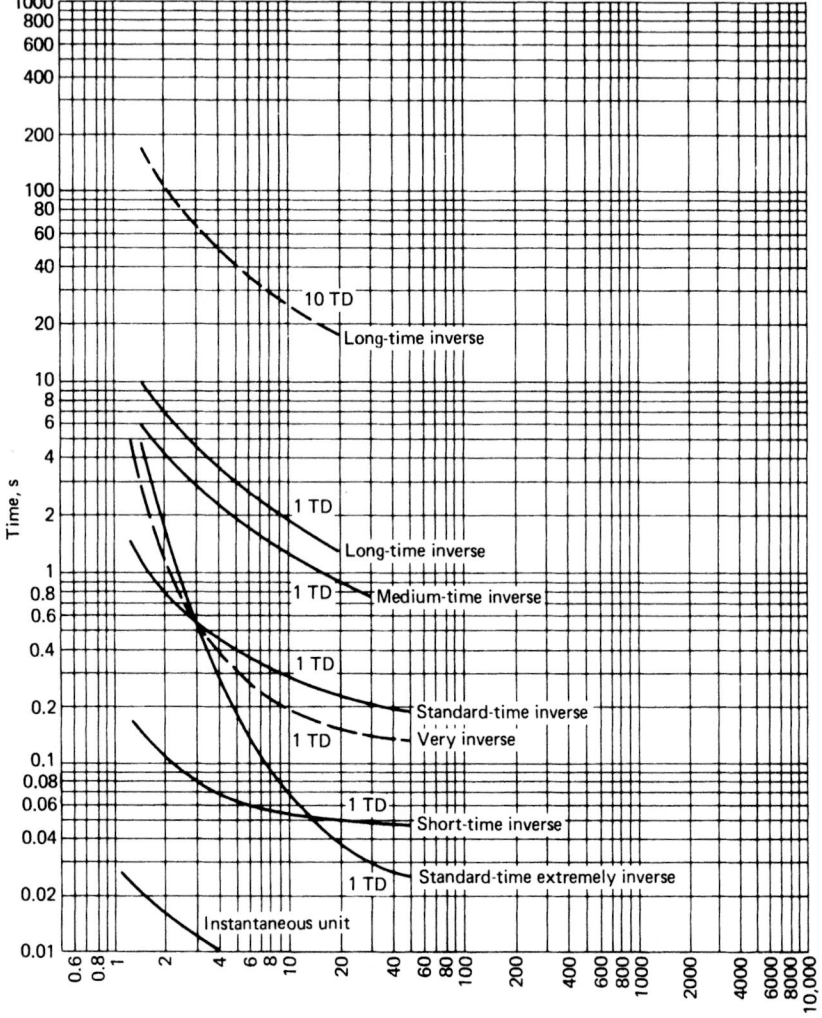

FIGURE 1-12   Comparative time-current curves of a typical induction overcurrent relay plus instantaneous trip.

SWITCHGEAR LOCATION AND WIRING

The best location for secondary switchboards is near the center of load. Frequently these are located on mezzanines above the plant floor, to isolate them from unauthorized personnel as well as to have them located near the load without taking valuable floor space.

In most industrial applications, a special enclosure is provided for a switchboard to isolate it from unauthorized personnel.

Wiring to equipment should be kept as short as possible, making load-center location of switchgear advantageous. Power switchboards are passive devices and require almost no operation. They are reset only if they trip under fault conditions.

Metering of utility company services can be done best at the single point of entry of service to the plant site. Metering of individual circuits for the purpose of monitoring energy use or some other function can be done anywhere in the plant. All such meters can be gathered in a single location with appropriate transmitters and telemetering equipment.

WIRING METHODS

Primary and Secondary Feeders

Two methods of running primary and secondary feeders in industrial plants are used: *overhead* and *underground.*

Overhead Distribution.   Overhead distribution is used to interconnect buildings of the same facility which are separate from one another, when plants are operating on a temporary basis, or when a plant is more or less in a state of continual change.

Underground Distribution.   Underground distribution is used for short distances, congested plant areas, or when the importance of high reliability justifies the extra expense.

A variety of raceways is available for distribution wiring. Rules governing the application and installation of raceways are discussed in various sections of the ***National Electrical Code®.*** * Adhering to these rules will help assure a safe, reliable installation.

Main feeders and *distribution feeders* for localized switchboards and panelboards usually are run in rigid metal conduit. Large power blocks are distributed in busways. Where plant floor use or equipment is changed frequently, it often is advantageous to distribute all main feeders in the form of interlocked armored cable run in cable trays.

The method of power distribution which is best for a given plant depends on characteristics of the plant itself. In some, workstations are fixed. In others, the production system is fluid and electrical demands change from product to product.

In the case of a fixed production system, electricity can be brought to the point of utilization in rigid conduit or by any of the other means already discussed. Plants which require more flexible power distribution often rely on a grid of busways which permits circuit-breaker-protected power takeoffs at any point.

Busways

Busway systems are widely used for feeders, plug-in subfeeders, and plug-in and trolley-type branch circuits.

They permit frequent changes in load layout, because they can be easily adapted to production-line rearrangement without seriously disrupting production.

---

* ***National Electrical Code®*** is a Registered Trademark of the National Fire Protection Association, Inc., Quincy, Massachusetts.

Busway systems also have the benefit of controlled voltage drop characteristics, permitting them to meet different voltage stability requirements.

The types of busway commonly employed for industrial applications follow.

Feeder Busway.   Low-impedance-type busway is frequently used for all types of high-capacity feeders and risers. Typical applications include transformer-vault-to-switchboard service runs, switchboard-to-load-center panel feeders, and welder feeders.

Plug-in Busway.   Plug-in distribution busway is extremely flexible because it has easily accessible plug-in openings along its length, permitting tap-ins. It can be run from a switchboard or tapped from a run of feeder busway to carry power to closely spaced machines and other loads. Branch circuits to motors also can be tapped in.

UTILIZATION EQUIPMENT CONTROLS

Small equipment and hand tools are run from plug-in-type receptacles. These receptacles should be grounded and, for safety, equipped with ground-fault interrupter devices. Locking-type receptacles should be used for tools or equipment which are subject to extensive movement during use.

All equipment and machinery should be supplied with a disconnect device within sight of the machine, preferably within easy reach of the operator. This is a code requirement because it is mandatory for maintenance of a safe work space.

Utilization equipment, such as fans, pumps, oil burners, and lighting fixtures on branch circuits, can be controlled by contactors such as push button switches, toggle or tumbler switches, and rotary snap-action switches.

Magnetic switches are widely used for motor control and where it is necessary to operate the switch contacts from remote pushbutton stations.

Small pieces of equipment and hand tools usually have controls built into them.

A variety of controls can be added to an existing plant to increase safety and/or reduce energy consumption and expense.

Microprocessor-based programmable controllers are available in different sizes, offering much diversity. Among the most popular is the so-called demand-based multifunction controller. Typically, this device provides demand control, remote start-stop, duty cycling, and optimal start-stop. The number of loads which can be controlled depends on the nature of the controller involved. In many cases they are modular, enabling addition of loads as needed. Devices such as these can be used for machinery, lighting, comfort cooling and heating, and other purposes. Each of the functions provided by a multifunction device generally can be performed by a smaller device which performs one function only, such as remote start-stop.

Timers and time-clock controls have been used for many years. Their function is generally to start and stop a certain operation at a predetermined time, for example, outdoor lighting.

Photocell controls are applied to lighting. As ambient lighting conditions fall to a certain predetermined point, the photocell activates lighting. When ambient lighting rises above that point, lighting is deactivated.

Dimming controls are available for fluorescent as well as mercury vapor lamps. They reduce light output to what is required for the tasks involved. The percentage of light reduction is close to the percentage of energy consumption reduction. In no case should lighting levels be reduced to less than what is required. Worker productivity will suffer; safety and security hazards may be created.

HAZARDOUS LOCATIONS

The dust and fumes put into the air by many industrial processes create an environment which is classified as electrically hazardous. Although the airborne substances may not be toxic, they can create an atmosphere which is subject to explosion and fire when heated by an electrical switching operation.

Electrical hazards are classified into three groups by the *National Electrical Code®,* in the chapter titled "Hazardous Locations."* Each group is further subdivided into divisions by degree of hazard and type of substance present.

The basic classifications are as follows:

Class I.   Air is contaminated by hazardous fumes or vapors including gases and airborne chemicals. This is subdivided into two divisions.

> *Division 1*   Locations where hazardous vapors and gases can or do exist under normal operations.
>
> *Division 2*   Areas where flammable vapors or gases are handled in proper containers but where hazardous concentrations are normally prevented by forced ventilation.

Class II.   Similar to class I except it includes atmospheres containing or likely to contain combustible dust. The divisions of this class resemble those of class I.

Class III.   This class of hazard deals with the presence of combustible materials in the manufacturing process and the presence of airborne particles created by the process. The divisions deal with the manufacturing site and the storage sites.

In addition to class and division of hazard, electrical hazards are further defined in each segment by group and designated by a letter such as "A," "B," etc.

The *National Electrical Code®* accurately defines each class, division, and type of hazard. The methods of wiring required are also defined in the same Code.

The plant operator must be able to identify those areas of the plant presenting identifiable hazards and must maintain wiring systems which conform to the probable hazard present. Great skill is needed to keep to a minimum the electric devices actually located in the highest hazard areas. Careful arrangement keeps control and switching devices in the area with the lowest classification. Explosion-proof wiring is expensive. It is often less expensive to remove or reduce the hazard than it is to provide the appropriate electric system.

It is essential for the plant engineer to become familiar with the rules of the Code and also with other publications of the National Fire Protection Association that further define the steps which can reduce the hazards.

BIBLIOGRAPHY

1. Beeman, D. L. (ed.): *Industrial Power Systems Handbook,* McGraw-Hill, New York, 1955.
2. "Constructing Electrical Systems" (Special Report), *Electrical Construction and Maintenance,* May 1979, pp. 59–90, 164–170.
3. G.E. *Specifier's Guide,* General Electric Co., Schenectady, New York.
4. Gonen, T.: *Electric Power Distribution System Engineering,* McGraw-Hill, New York, 1986.
5. *IEEE Recommended Practice for Electric Power Distribution for Industrial Plants,* The Institute of Electrical and Electronics Engineers, Inc., New York, 1976.
6. *Industrial and Commercial Power Distribution Course,* The Electrification Council, New York, 1975.
7. Kurtz, E. B., and Shoemaker, T. M.: *The Lineman's and Cableman's Handbook,* 7th ed., McGraw-Hill, 1986.
8. McPartland, Joseph F., and William J. Novak: *Electrical Equipment Manual,* 3d ed., McGraw-Hill, New York, 1965.
9. *National Electrical Code®*, National Fire Protection Association, Quincy, Massachusetts, 1981.

---

* *National Electrical Code®* is a Registered Trademark of the National Fire Protection Association, Inc., Quincy, MA 02269.

10. NECA Electrical Design Library: *Fault Detecting and Disconnecting Devices,* National Electrical Contractors Association, Washington, D.C., June 1977.

11. NECA Electrical Design Library: *Power Distribution Systems,* National Electrical Contractors Association, Washington, D.C., March 1977.

12. NECA Electrical Design Library: *Specifying Electrical Conductors,* National Electrical Contractors Association, Washington, D.C., June 1978.

13. *NECA Wiring Symbols Standard,* National Electrical Contractors Association, Washington, D.C., May 1976.

14. *Recommended Practice for Electrical Equipment Maintenance,* NFPA 70-B, National Fire Protection Association, Quincy, Massachusetts, 1977.

15. Smeaton, R. W.: *Switchgear Control Handbook,* 2d ed., McGraw-Hill, New York, 1987.

16. *System Neutral Grounding and Ground Fault Protection,* Westinghouse Relay Instrument Division, Westinghouse Electric Corporation, Coral Springs, Florida, January 1978.

17. Thumann, Albert: *Electrical Design, Safety, and Energy Conservation,* Fairmont Press, Atlanta, Georgia, 1976.

18. *Westinghouse Construction Specification,* 5th ed., Westinghouse Electric Corporation, Pittsburgh, Pennsylvania, 1978.

CHAPTER 3-2
ELECTRIC SYSTEMS MANAGEMENT

Robert C. Walther, P.E.
President
Industrial Power Technology
Santa Rosa, California

GLOSSARY

Demand   Level of power supplied from the electric system during a specific period of time.

Demand-side management (DSM)   Measures taken by a utility to influence the level or timing of a customer's energy demand. By optimizing the use of existing utility assets, DSM programs enable utilities to defer expenditures for adding new generating capacity.

Harmonic distortion   Continuous distortion of the normal sine wave, occurring at frequencies between 60 Hz and 3 kHz.

Linear load   A predictable nonprocess energy load that has a profile that changes with time and condition.

Noise   Continuous distortion of the normal sine wave occurring at frequencies above 5 kHz, usually of constant duration.

Nonlinear load   A load profile composed of process and cyclic loads that may have a broad swing in energy and demand requirements.

Off-peak   Hours during the day or night when utility system loading is low.

On-peak   Period during the day when the energy provider (utility) experiences the highest demand.

Power factor The fraction of power actually used by a customer's electric equipment, compared to the total apparent power supplied; usually expressed as a percentage. Applies only to ac circuits; dc circuits always exhibit a power factor of 100 percent.

Sag A decrease in voltage up to 20 percent below the normal voltage, lasting less than 2.5 s. Also called *undervoltage*. Can result in memory loss, data errors, flickering lights, and equipment shutdown.

Silicon-controlled rectifiers (SCRs) A control system utilized to control speed by modifying the sine wave profile of power to variable-speed ac motors.

Spike A sharp, sudden increase in voltage of up to several thousand volts lasting less than 0.001 s. Can cause catastrophic memory loss or equipment damage.

Surge An increase in voltage up to 20 percent above the normal voltage, lasting less than 2.5 s. Also called *overvoltage*. Can result in memory loss, data errors, flickering lights, and equipment shutdown.

Total harmonic distortion (THD) Term used to quantify distortion as a percentage of the fundamental (pure sine) of voltage and current waveforms.

Uninterruptible power supply (UPS) A system consisting of a rectifier/charger, a battery bank, a static inverter and a bypass switch, used to protect against short-term service interruptions and outside power disturbances.

INTRODUCTION

Electric system management is the process through which a facility management team ensures that a plant or building receives a sufficient, reliable supply of power at the level of quality required. This process also involves seeking to obtain that power at the lowest possible cost for the required class of service.

Until recently the main objective of electric system management was to guarantee uninterrupted operation of a facility's lighting, process, and environmental [heating, ventilating, and air conditioning (HVAC)] systems. This "lights on, motors turn" approach originated during the late nineteenth and early twentieth centuries, when energy consumption was dominated by linear loads. In recent years, however, nonlinear loads such as variable-speed motors, programmable logic controllers, and other electronic equipment have proliferated. Compared with linear loads, these nonlinear loads are much more sensitive to overvoltage, undervoltage, and other disturbances that have always existed on the utility power line. Such routine disturbances can cause problems ranging from minor equipment malfunctions to costly system shutdowns and damage to equipment. In addition, nonlinear devices can create their own power disturbances, which in turn cause problems in other parts of the facility and may feed back onto the utility distribution system.

The increased reliance on nonlinear loads has added new objectives to electric system management. While the guaranteed supply of power remains critical, issues of reliability and power quality are becoming paramount, and capacity requirements have increased. In addition, the need continues to control energy use and costs to remain competitive. In the face of these challenges, *plant managers must seek to identify their facility's risk of experiencing reliability and power quality problems and assess the economic impact of problems that might occur.* Then, working with a utility or consulting engineers, managers can design and implement a cost-effective risk management program.

This chapter gives an overview of the reliability and power quality issues involved in electric system management, and describes available remedies to power quality problems. In addition, it discusses utility rate structures, as well as demand-side management programs and other strategies for reducing or controlling energy use and/or demand.

RELIABILITY

A reliable power supply is one that delivers electricity sufficient to serve a facility's load at the grade of power quality desired, and one that provides for enough power during curtailment or other emergency conditions to ensure the safety of personnel and protection of critical processes and process equipment.

Quantity

To determine if a facility's electric service is sufficient for the load being supplied, it is necessary for plant managers to conduct a facility load profile. The profile will provide the management team with a thorough understanding of how a facility's electricity consumption varies hourly, daily, and seasonally.

One way to identify electricity consumption patterns is through analysis of a facility's demand chart. Electric utilities usually maintain records on kW (or kVA) demand in 15- or 30-min intervals to permit identification of and subsequent billing for the peak demand established during the billing period. Alternatively, the utility's metering system may incorporate electronic pulse recording that transmits and records similar information on magnetic tape. These data may be retrieved and used to compile a demand chart. If no utility records of customer demand are available, the utility should be asked to install demand recording instrumentation so load patterns can be analyzed.

Service voltages should also be examined to determine if voltage control measures are required. Table 2-1 shows national voltage standards set by the American National Standard Institute (ANSI) Guideline C84.1 for electrically operated equipment. In practice the voltage delivered to service entrances can vary, but most major utilities adhere to minimum and maximum voltage standards that are well within the ANSI standards.

TABLE 2-1   Customer Service Voltages

Nominal service voltage	ANSI C84.1 minimum utilization voltage*	PG&E's minimum service voltage	PG&E's maximum service voltage
120	108	114	126
208	187	197	218
240	216	228	252
277	249	263	291
480	432	456	504

* American National Standard Institute's C84.1 shown for customer information only. The utility has no control over voltage drop in customer wiring.

Quality

In terms of power quality, conventional utility service "to the fence" is not (nor has it ever been) 100 percent reliable. For some utility customers willing to pay a premium, the power supply may be made nearer to 100 percent reliable. Even at this higher level of service it may be necessary for some users to provide an in-house power conditioning system. (A more detailed discussion of power quality and power conditioning appears below.)

Performing routine maintenance procedures on process equipment on a regular basis will also help ensure improved reliability. See Sec. 16, "Maintenance and Repair Technology."

Despite the use of diagnostic and preventive measures by plant management, unexpected power outages and other failures do occur. In such instances, a well-managed plant electric system provides emergency power—enough to permit an orderly shutdown of equipment. Backup power may be supplied by diesel generators or a device known as an uninterruptible power supply (UPS), described below in "Correcting Power Quality Problems." In a growing number of facilities it may be economically feasible to provide on-site power generation through a cogeneration system. Cogeneration systems utilize waste or purchased fuels to generate power and recover waste heat, which then can be used to produce process heat in the form of steam, hot water, or hot air. Determining the potential benefits, both tangible and intangible, of a cogeneration system requires an in-depth analysis of all aspects of a facility's energy needs. (For further discussion of backup and emergency power, see Chap. 3-3, "Standby and Emergency Power.")

POWER QUALITY

Sources of Power Quality Problems

Even though today's utilities use advanced hardware and software at their substations and on their distribution systems, power disturbances occur. These irregularities can result from transmission or distribution system switching faults on the utility distribution system, lightning strikes, simultaneous operation of equipment (either within the plant or by customers nearby) or other causes. In many cases the disturbances can be traced to wiring and grounding problems within the plant itself. Common disturbances are outages, under- or overvoltages, spikes, sags or surges, or noise. (See Fig. 2-1.) These disturbances can range in duration from sustained outages lasting several hours to surges lasting only a few microseconds and undiscernible to plant operators.

The introduction of harmonic distortion to a system may take many forms. Determining acceptable levels of total harmonic distortion (THD) may require input from equipment manufacturers as well as engineering expertise. Inattention to THD in a sensitive circuit can lead to chasing phantoms.

Older electrical equipment such as motors, solenoids, and electromechanical controls are largely unaffected by disturbances of short duration. However, solid-state electronic equipment is far more susceptible to a wide range of disturbances. This vulnerability stems from the way an electronic device consumes the alternating-current (ac) power supplied to it—"chopping" it into the low-voltage, high-speed power it needs for digital processing. Problems arise when the alternating-current (ac) sine wave in the power supply deviates from its normal "clean" waveshape. When the sine wave becomes distorted, or "dirty," electronic devices are unable to convert ac power to direct-current (dc) power. As a result, they can experience interruption, data errors, memory loss, and even shutdown; in some cases the device may sustain damage.

Moreover, because of the way they draw current, *electronic devices can actually create their own power disturbances* (in the form of harmonic distortion, impulses, and voltage loss), and introduce these disturbances to the power distribution system—within a facility and on the utility line.

Monitoring Power Quality

When power quality problems are suspected, the plant manager should initiate a power quality survey of the plant to determine whether equipment troubles are attributable to utility operations or to conditions within the facility. The survey should include a thorough inspection, including an infrared scan, of the site's electric system, including wiring and connections, grounding, equipment closets and utility rooms, transformers and power conditioning equipment, and main and subbreaker panels. It is advisable to monitor at multiple locations, including the problem locations, such as transformers, service entrance, and any other suspect areas.

PROBLEM	DEFINITION	DURATION	CAUSE	EFFECT
OUTAGE 	Planned or accidental total loss of power in a localized area. A blackout is a wide-ranging outage.	Minutes to a few days	Catastrophic system failure, weather, small animals, human error (auto accidents, kites, etc.).	System shutdowns.
DROPOUT 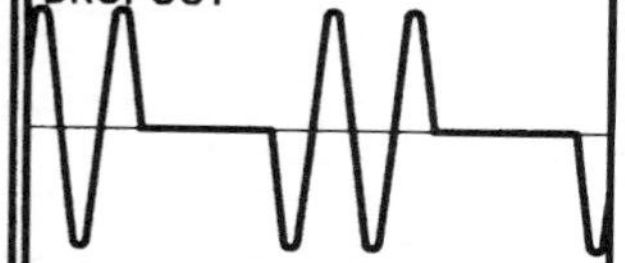	A very short planned or accidental power loss.	1 millisecond to 1 second	Utility switching operations attempting to maintain power to your area despite a failure somewhere on the system.	Equipment resets, data loss.
SAG/SURGE 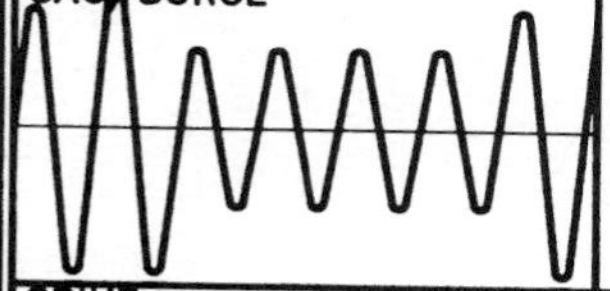	A decrease or increase in voltage that can be up to 20% above or below the normal voltage level (also called an over- or under-voltage).	Less than 2.5 seconds	Heavy load switching, air conditioning, disk drives, transformers, and other equipment drawing large amounts of power.	Memory loss, data errors, flickering or dimming lights, shrinking display screen, equipment shutdown.
SPIKE 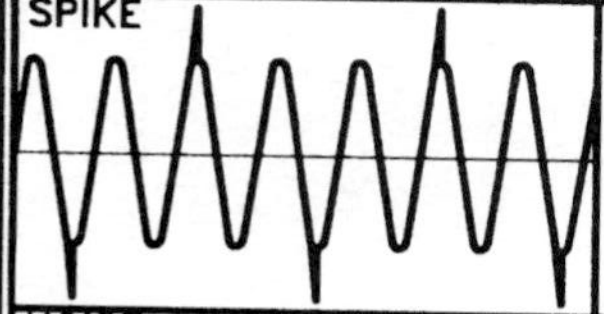	A sharp, sudden increase or decrease in voltage of up to several thousand volts. Also called an impulse, transient, or notch.	1 microsecond to 1 millisecond	Utility switching operations, on-and-off switching of heavy equipment or office machinery, SCR's firing, elevators, welding equipment, static discharges, and lightning.	Loss of data, burned circuit boards.
NOISE 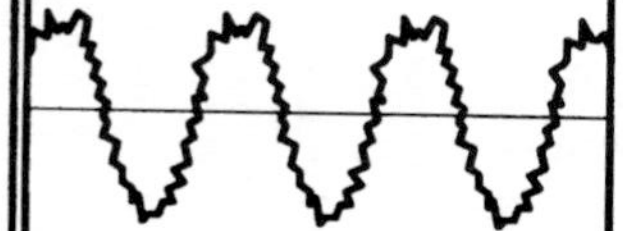	A high-frequency interference from 7,000 Hz to 50 MHz.	Usually of constant duration	Electromagnetic interference, micro-wave and radar transmissions, radio and TV broadcasts, arc welding, heaters, laser printers, thermostats, electric typewriters, loose wiring, improper grounding.	Although generally not destruc-tive, it can garble or wipe out stored data.

FIGURE 2-1 Power problem categories.

Monitoring can be conducted by either qualified in-house staff or with the assistance of utility personnel or consulting engineers.

Before monitoring begins, plant managers should establish acceptable limits for sensitive equipment. Some standard thresholds recommended by Basic Measuring Instruments of Foster City, Calif., are shown below. These may be modified according to the sensitivity of equipment at the site.

- Frequency tolerance: 0.1 Hz
- Swell voltage: 5 to 10 percent above nominal
- Sag voltage: 10 to 15 percent below nominal
- Impulse: two times nominal voltage
- Neutral-to-ground voltage: 2 to 5 V
- Neutral-to-ground impulse: one times nominal voltage
- High-frequency noise: 5 V
- Radio-frequency interference: 3 V/m
- Temperature: high and low temperatures depend on application; rate of change should not exceed 10°F (5°C) per hour.
- Humidity: high—70 percent relative humidity; low—30 to 40 percent relative humidity; rate of change should not exceed 20 percent relative humidity per hour

Figure 2-2 shows a checklist to follow in analyzing power quality problems.

Correcting Power Quality Problems

There are several types of remedies available to protect solid-state, power-sensitive equipment from power disturbances; most are simple and inexpensive.* In addition, disturbances can be prevented altogether by conditioning the power supply to smooth out the sine waveshape. Because power conditioning equipment is costly, it is best suited only for those applications requiring the highest grade of power.

Wiring and Grounding. According to the Electric Power Research Institute, approximately 80 percent of power quality problems at commercial and industrial facilities can be traced to problems within the facilities—improper grounding, inadequate wiring, loose connections, and the accumulation of dust and dirt from poor maintenance practices. The importance of a good, low-resistance ground cannot be overemphasized, especially since solid-state systems depend on the grounding for a reference to operate by and for dissipating stray power that could cause damage if left on the circuit. Adequate wiring and proper grounding are the lowest-cost prevention and cure for power quality problems.

In addition, care should be taken to ensure proper sizing of in-house transformers and conductors that supply power to silicon controlled rectifiers (SCRs). It is imperative that the circuit supplying an SCR be sized according to the manufacturer's recommendations and those of NEC and IEEE. SCRs have a potential to severely affect the total harmonic distortion of a power system. Utilization of isolation transformers may be necessary to prevent export of distortion throughout the facility.

Dedicated Circuits. Most power disturbances in the form of *noise* (distortions at frequencies above 5 kHz) are generated within the plant itself. As a result, an effective method of protecting critical or highly sensitive equipment is to locate the equipment on its own isolated circuit to protect it from power disturbances caused by other equipment in proximity. Dedicated circuits also prevent a circuit from being overloaded by tying it directly to the power source and by restricting access to it.

_____

* The following material is based on "Power Quality in Your Business," Pacific Gas & Electric Co., San Francisco.

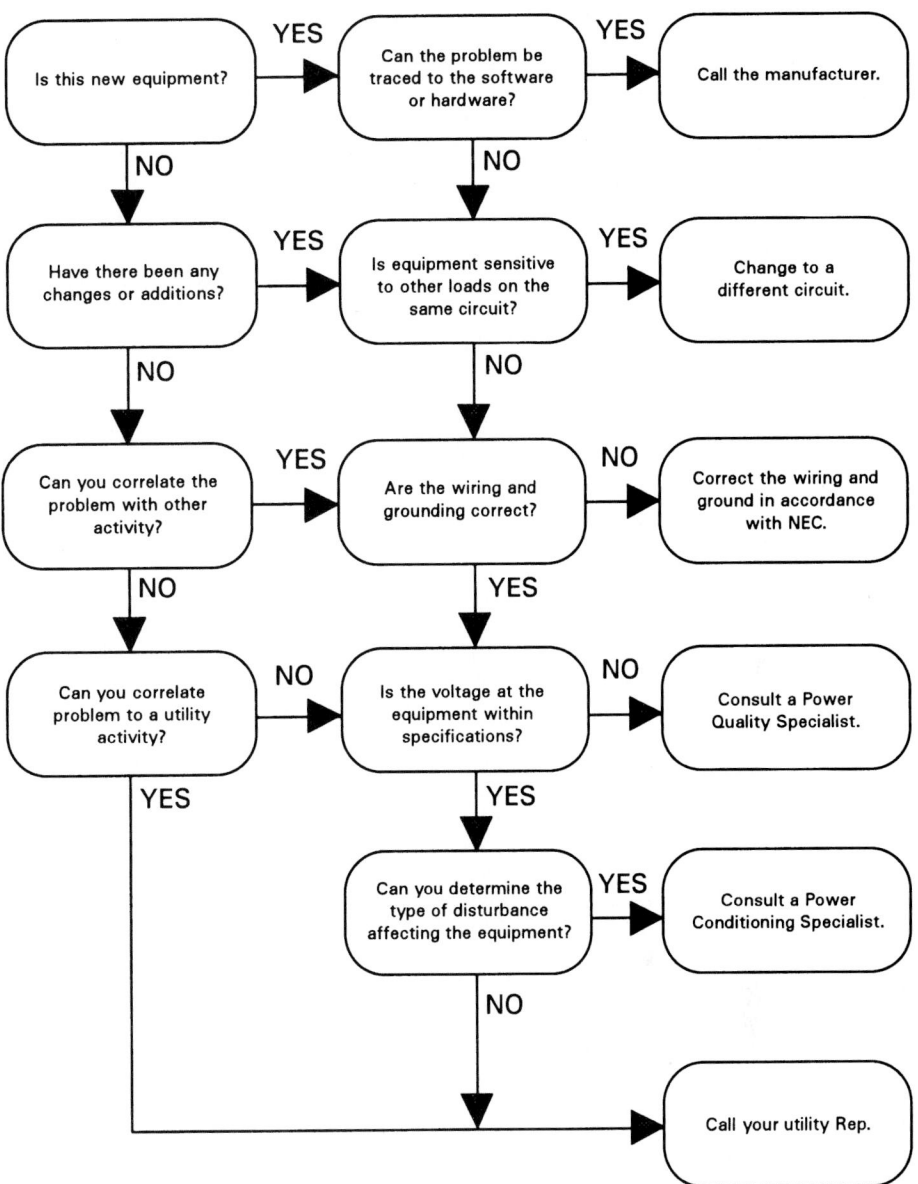

FIGURE 2-2   Power problem flowchart.

Spike Suppressors.   Spike suppressors reduce the amplitude of voltage spikes to safe levels and can eliminate many sudden changes in voltage. They are the simplest and least expensive protective devices; however, their capability depends on the quality of the suppressor purchased. Attention should be given to the specific nomenclature of a unit prior to installation. The attenuation ability of some units is minimal. Some suppressors feature a diagnostic light to indicate the device has been hit by a spike but is still working.

Isolation Transformers.   Isolation transformers filter out electrical noise and distortion from other on-site equipment or incoming power. They cannot, however, protect against other types of disturbances such as spikes and surges.

Voltage Regulators.   Voltage regulators maintain a relatively constant voltage by protecting against surges and sags through mechanical or electronic means. This option is more costly than those listed above, but is at the midpoint of the cost spectrum for power enhancement devices.

Uninterruptible Power Supply.   A UPS protects against short-term power interruptions and outside power disturbances. UPS systems typically consist of a rectifier/charger, a battery bank, a static inverter and an automatic or manual bypass switch. DC power is supplied to the inverter by the rectifier or batteries and converted to ac power, which is then fed to the protected equipment.

There are two types of UPS designs. An *on-line UPS* is continually fed the supply power and produces clean output. It offers protection against all power quality problems, including momentary outages. Protection against sustained outages is limited to the size of the battery bank. An on-line UPS typically has the capability to switch to the ac power source if some element of the UPS fails.

In an *off-line UPS,* electric supply power is connected directly to the load; the UPS is utilized only during ac power source interruptions. It alerts the user that supply power failure has occurred and that the load is now on battery power, which will last from about 5 to 15 min. The off-line UPS design does not protect against transients, sags, swells, or other abnormalities, though some models have integrated a few on-line power conditioning features that operate when the unit is engaged on-line. Off-line UPSs are best suited for small loads (up to 1.5 kVA) that can tolerate the milliseconds of switching time required when the power supply is interrupted.

Electric Motor-Generators (MG Set).   An MG set uses a motor driven by incoming utility power to spin an ac or dc generator that, in turn, produces electric power for the protected load. As a result, the protected load is electrically isolated from the incoming utility supply. An MG set has the capability to ride through momentaries; during sags it provides buffering to prevent transients from occurring on its output.

If equipped for both ac and dc generation, an MG set also can charge batteries for a UPS that supplies power during an outage for the duration of the battery charge—generally long enough to allow an orderly shutdown of a facility's computer or processing systems. MG sets are less energy-efficient and more expensive than voltage regulators, and require maintenance; however, they provide more complete protection.

UPS with Diesel Generator.   These systems combine an on-line UPS with backup generation to deliver a full, clean power supply during extended power outages. A battery bank keeps computers and processes in operation until the generator comes on-line.

Static Automatic Transfer Switches.   Static automatic transfer switches provide an alternative to full UPS protection if a facility is served by two synchronized utility power feeds. When the power supply to one feed is interrupted, the load is automatically transferred to the second power feed without affecting equipment.

Managing Risk

The majority of power quality problems can be corrected or avoided by implementing simple measures. Good risk management entails spending only as much as required to avoid catastrophic losses of data and/or equipment. In most instances, expensive power-conditioning equipment is unnecessary; basic mitigation measures (e.g., rewiring or reconfiguring grounding) will suffice.

As knowledge of power quality issues grows, educational opportunities for facility management teams are increasing. Many utilities, industry associations, and universities offer curricula designed to assist participants in diagnosing power problems and identifying practical, cost-effective solutions.

UTILITY RATE STRUCTURES

Utility rate structures form the basis for utility compensation for energy and demand capacity delivered. Knowledge of available options and their corresponding rate schedules is fundamental to developing a good managerial strategy. This section describes basic concepts and terms related to utility rate design and outlines some strategies for controlling consumption and reducing costs.

Utility rate structures are typically complex contracts individually tailored to each utility's load profile, power generating methods, fuel, and energy sources. Rates are also influenced by the distance between the utility's generating plants and the user, which affects power transmission costs. Because it is impossible to define a general rate schedule, the responsibility rests with the plant manager to become familiar with the rate structures of the electric utility serving each facility. Utility representatives will assist plant staff in interpreting rate schedules.

Energy and Demand Charges

Electric utility rates have two main components: energy charges and demand charges. Energy charges are based on the amount of energy consumed, measured in kilowatthours (kWh), during the billing period. Demand charges are based on the customer's maximum demand, measured in kilowatts (kW), during a specified period, usually monthly or during specific intervals when a utility experiences its highest demand (peak demand). Demand charges are designed to compensate a utility for capital and operating expenditures required to meet customer demand. The kW demand is defined as the average rate of energy draw from the utility system during a specified time segment—usually 15 or 30 min.

Demand charges also vary by season. Most utilities experience peak demand during the summer months, when air-conditioning use is highest. Other utilities experience peak demand in the winter months, when electric heating is the dominant load. In an effort to impose uniformity of loads throughout the year, utilities may also assess a demand penalty. For example, a summer-peaking utility may apply the demand charge established during the summer (period A) as a minimum demand charge during the winter (period B). This billing formula is commonly referred to as a *ratchet*.

Demand Reduction

Because energy costs affect a business's bottom line and its ability to remain competitive, every plant manager should develop a plan to control or reduce demand.

A facility's demand has two components: base load and variable load. The base load, which is fairly constant, represents the electric service required to maintain a facility's environment and comfort conditions (e.g., lighting and HVAC). The variable load, which is superimposed on the base load, depends on the business activity of the facility, weather, and other variables.

Base load reduction can be achieved by implementing programs to optimize the efficiency of lighting, motors, HVAC, process or other systems. (For further discussion of energy conservation options, see Sec. 15, "Energy Conservation Techniques.")

Variable load reduction can be obtained in several ways. In evaluating specific approaches, consideration should be given to the utility rate structure, the facility's electric system, and its relation to operations. Some potential strategies include:

- Inhibiting the simultaneous operation of large loads (e.g., large chillers or heat-treatment furnaces) during the period used by the utility to establish demand
- Rescheduling certain operations to other periods of the day or night to minimize their impact on peak demand
- Generating power on-site (using emergency equipment) to serve a particular load or group of loads during periods of high activity, thereby avoiding establishment of a new, higher peak demand
- Storing energy during inactive periods and retrieving it during high-demand periods (e.g., precooling; thermal storage, such as chilled water or ice storage; or preheating domestic water or other process fluids)

Rates

Utility rate schedules typically are designed to encourage use of electricity during off-peak hours when the utility's generating costs are lower. For example, a utility may offer off-peak rates that are considerably lower than on-peak rates, or it may provide incentives, such as reduced demand charges, to maximize load during nondaylight hours. This *time-of-day* billing strategy offers utility customers the potential to substantially reduce their energy costs by judiciously rescheduling certain plant operations to off-peak hours.

In recent years a few utilities have begun to experiment with another rate option known as *real-time pricing*. Under real-time pricing, the rate paid by customers can vary by the hour (or even smaller time intervals) to reflect the changes in the marginal cost to the utility of producing electricity throughout the day and night. Plant managers should evaluate real-time pricing carefully to determine its cost-effectiveness for particular applications; in some cases real-time pricing may actually raise energy costs.

Demand-Side Management

The term *demand-side management* (DSM) refers to measures taken by utilities to influence the level or timing of their customers' energy use in order to optimize the use of existing utility assets and defer the addition of new generating capacity. These measures take many forms, including:

- Financial incentives such as rebates and low-cost financing to encourage upgrading to higher-efficiency appliances or systems
- Informational services such as energy audits, publications, and seminars to alert customers to energy-saving opportunities
- Rate incentives such as real-time pricing or time-of-day rates to encourage customers to clip or shift loads during peak periods
- Fuel substitution programs to promote the use of one fuel over another

The main customer benefits derived from implementing DSM measures are increased efficiency and lower energy costs. It is important to note, however, that some DSM measures may also introduce power quality problems. For example, some electronic ballasts for fluorescent lighting can cause harmonic distortion. Similarly, variable-speed motors, though highly efficient, often have detrimental effects on the operation of nearby equipment requiring clean power because they introduce harmonics and/or noise to the system. For this reason, careful evaluation of the power quality characteristics of new, high-efficiency equipment is required before installation.

Power Factor Correction (Improvement)

Power factor indicates the degree to which a customer's electrical equipment causes the electric current delivered to the site to lag or lead with the voltage sine wave; in other words, it is a measure of how much reactive power the equipment requires to operate. Power factor is calculated by using metered measures of the amount of power used (in kilowatts) and the amount of reactive power used (in kilovolt-amperes—kVA). Lower power factors indicate the use of greater amounts of reactive power.

To recover the cost of supplying large amounts of reactive power, some utilities impose a financial penalty on customers with large electric loads. Even so, the economic incentive to improve power factor is minimal. When penalties are assessed, they may not be high enough to justify the cost of power factor correction.

If power factor improvement is desired, individual load correction procedures include:

- Applying high-power-factor utilization equipment such as high-power-factor lighting ballasts and distribution transformers
- Operating induction motors at near full load to improve the power factor of the motor
- Adding capacitors in stepped banks with automatic controls

Adding capacitors, however, can introduce system disturbances, including transient voltage, harmonic resonance and transient voltage magnification.

In general, it is best to avoid power factor problems altogether by purchasing or upgrading to equipment and systems that promote good power factor, and by correctly sizing all equipment, including conductors and transformers.

Customer-Owned Substations

In an effort to reduce energy costs, some industrial customers have opted to purchase distribution substations from their local utility. This option may reduce energy costs up to 10 percent or more, but it carries some risk because the utility is no longer responsible for repairing and maintaining the substation. In addition to the added repair and maintenance costs, plant staff may encounter difficulty in locating replacement transformers or other parts when problems occur. Service and maintenance expertise also may not be readily available.

BIBLIOGRAPHY

Basic Measuring Instruments, Foster City, Calif.:

Application Note 227: "How to Do a Power Quality Survey," undated.
Application Note 229: "How to Do IEEE Standard 519-1992 Compliance Testing," undated.
"8800 Powerscope: Performance, Productivity and Practicality for Power Disturbance Analysis," 1993.
"Electric Power Analyzers: Tools for Measuring Electric Power Quality, Power Flow, Disturbances, and Demand," 1993.
McEachern, Alexander: *Handbook of Power Signatures,* 1989.

Electric Power Research Institute, Palo Alto, Calif.:

"Wiring and Grounding for Power Quality," CU.2026.3.90, 1990.
"Power Quality Considerations for Adjustable Speed Drives," CU.3036.4.91, 1991.

PG&E Power Quality Enhancement, San Francisco:

"Power Notes on Power System Harmonics," January 1993.
"Power Notes on Surge Suppressors," July 1990.
"Power Notes on Uninterruptible Power Supply," January 1993.

CHAPTER 3-3
STANDBY AND EMERGENCY POWER

PART 1

ROTATING EQUIPMENT SYSTEMS

Jim Iverson

Manager, Technical Marketing
Industrial Business Group
Onan Corporation
Minneapolis, Minnesota

GLOSSARY

Automatic sequential paralleling system (ASPS) An emergency power supply system that operates multiple engine-generator sets in parallel. It allows the first set to reach acceptable speed after receiving the start command to be immediately connected to critical loads. It automatically synchronizes and connects remaining sets. It is often applied in health-care facilities with a 10-s transfer requirement.

Automatic transfer switch (ATS)   An electric switching device that alternately connects the load to the normal or emergency power source as required without operator involvement. It may also include controls that start and stop the engine-generator set, monitor voltage and frequency of both power sources, and perform other timing and logic functions. See also nonautomatic transfer switch.

Nonautomatic transfer switch   An electric switching device that alternately connects the load to the normal or emergency source as determined and initiated by an operator.

Prime mover   The engine that drives the generator through permanent coupling. It may be either spark-ignited, diesel cycle, or gas turbine.

Paralleling switchgear   Switchboard dedicated to control of engine-generators. Contains start sensor, synchronizer, reverse-power relay, and other controls. It closes generator output to the emergency bus through a fast-acting circuit breaker.

Paralleling load transfer equipment   Switchboard to transfer load from the utility to a single generator set and back again in a nonload break operation using fast-acting circuit breakers. Contains start sensor, synchronizer, protective relaying, load sharing, and other controls. Paralleling load transfer equipment is often applied in facilities to control a standby generator set used for load curtailment or in conjunction with interruptible rate utility programs.

INTRODUCTION

The emergency power supply system (EPSS) encompasses a wide variety of equipment. Equipment under the EPSS heading ranges from a simple, self-contained battery light to a complex, highly engineered, multiple engine-generator set system with a capacity of several megawatts. These two extreme examples suggest a division of these systems based on the source of emergency power. The first example uses a stored-energy device, a battery, as the power source while the second example uses rotating equipment, engine-generator sets, as the power source. Stored-energy systems and rotating-equipment systems are the two categories of emergency power supply systems. The subject of this part is rotating-equipment systems.

SYSTEM DESCRIPTION

When the normal power source fails, the EPSS functions to supply electric power to specific, select loads. The equipment that composes the system is largely determined by the characteristics and requirements of the loads being served. Two equipment groups, the emergency power source and the electric switching equipment, subdivide the system based on function. While the two equipment groups have independent functions, the groups are interrelated and both serve the common purpose of the complete system.

Emergency Power Source

The function of this equipment is to generate electric power. The engine-generator set is the principal part of the group. The generator is permanently coupled to and driven by a prime mover which may be a diesel, gasoline, or gaseous engine or a gas turbine. Figure 3-1 illustrates a typical diesel engine-generator set. Included in this group are an independent fuel supply with storage and the engine-generator set(s) with supporting equipment such as the governor, voltage regulator, exciter, cooling system, ventilation equipment, exhaust system, and engine control with meters and alarms.

FIGURE 3-1 Engine-generator set. (*Onan Corporation.*)

Electric Switching Equipment

The function of the electric switching equipment is to interconnect the generator power with the utilization equipment. Included in this group are transfer switches, illustrated in Fig. 3-2, either automatic or nonautomatic. The transfer switch is interlocked to prevent simultaneous closing to both the normal and emergency power source. Automatic transfer switches also monitor both sources and initiate starting of the system. Other electric switching equipment includes bypass-isolation switches if needed, paralleling load transfer equipment, and in the case of parallel operation of multiple engine-generators, paralleling and totalizing switchboards.

SYSTEM CLASSIFICATION

Recognizing the diversity of applications for emergency power supply systems, the National Fire Protection Association (NFPA) Committee on Emergency Power Supplies (NFPA Standard 110) has adopted the following system definitions based on type, class, category, and level.

Type

Response time is the criterion for determining the system type. Types range from uninterruptible power supply systems that "float" on-line to power systems with no response time requirement. Systems with response times of 60 s or shorter generally are automatic systems, while systems with no response time limit are often manual-starting or portable.

FIGURE 3-2   Transfer switch. (*Onan Corporation.*)

Class

Systems are placed in a class based on the length of full-load operation possible without refueling or recharging. The extremes of class are those of very short duration, 5 min, to those systems with indefinite duration based on the user's needs. Properly designed rotating-equipment systems have the capability of unlimited operation.

Category

The NFPA Committee on Emergency Power Supplies defined two categories. One category is stored-energy systems that receive energy from the normal power source. The requirements for stored-energy systems are contained in NFPA Standard 110A. The second category is rotating-equipment systems that use engine-generator sets as the power source, and is covered in NFPA Standard 110.

Level

The critical nature of the load being served by the EPSS determines the system level. For example, a system that supplies loads which support human life and safety is the most critical level. The lowest level defines a system that supplies loads which would result in economic loss when without power. The level of a legally required system greatly influences the requirements the equipment must meet.

SYSTEM JUSTIFICATION

Loss prevention, safety, and legal requirements are three common justifications for an EPSS. A fourth justification, energy economics, is becoming more common as the cost of energy rises. Many electric utilities offer interruptible or load curtailment rates, which can justify the cost of an engine-generator set and either a transfer switch or paralleling load transfer equipment. The significant savings on insurance also justifies the cost.

Loss Prevention

An EPSS in an industrial plant can prevent several kinds of measurable loss. Some examples are the loss of wages during production downtime, the loss of in-process product, the loss of data processing, and the loss of refrigerated storage. These examples, of course, are not exhaustive.

Safety

Loss of electric power can directly threaten personnel safety. Industrial processes that present a hazard when without power are one example. Emergency power is also needed to operate elevators, fire pumps, fire alarms, communication networks, and other safety-related equipment.

Legal Requirement

Most states and some major cities have adopted codes that require EPSSs in specific buildings. The classification of the required system is determined by the building occupancy. Because legal requirements change often and are different from state to state, check the current local regulations. A good source of additional information is the local inspector.

Energy Economics

Peak shaving, interruptible or load curtailment rate programs, cogeneration, and heat reclamation are methods for saving energy costs that are becoming feasible as the cost of energy rises. Peak shaving uses the emergency system to reduce utility demand charges by assuming loads during periods of peak demand. Cogeneration uses heat from the engines to make steam or hot water for industrial processes. Heat reclamation captures waste heat from the engine through heat exchangers for hot water or space heating or for cooling with absorption chillers. Many utilities offer interruptible rate programs which pay customers to either curtail load or switch to on-site generation to relieve demand on the utility.

SYSTEM CONSIDERATIONS

Most system considerations can be grouped under three headings: reliability, capacity, and quality.

Reliability

System reliability is the capability of the EPSS to fulfill its intended purpose predictably without problems. The degree of reliability necessary for an emergency system is closely related to the critical nature of the load being served. Many factors contribute to system reliability; those given here are preinstallation considerations. After installation, effective maintenance, exercise, and experienced operators contribute to reliability.

1. *Compatibility.*   Since all the equipment in the system is interrelated and must function toward a common purpose, it is important that each piece of equipment is coordinated with the rest of the system. A single design source for the complete system helps to ensure compatibility.
2. *Testing.*   Prototype testing during the development process of the engine-generator set ensures the fitness of the equipment for its intended purpose. Prototype testing helps to ensure performance under a variety of conditions such as overloads, surges, short circuits, and others that may occur in actual service. Testing of the complete system for compatibility and performance as specified before installation also increases reliability.

Capacity

One of the most important considerations for an EPSS is capacity, or the amount of power the system can generate. Determination of capacity requires careful study of the load equipment. List the voltage, current, and power requirements of each piece of load equipment. Include pertinent information about the load such as inertia, power factor, starting method, and other data which would affect capacity. Table 3-1 shows a load tabulation example.

Choose between full protection or selected protection. Full protection means a larger system, and selected protection means less capacity and special wiring costs. If needs increase in the future, consideration given to expansion can pay off.

Quality

The EPSS should generate power that is essentially equal in quality to the power of the normal source. Requirements such as frequency regulation, voltage regulation, waveform deviation, harmonic content, and noise interference define the quality of the emergency power.

REPRESENTATIVE SYSTEM

Illustrated in the simplified block diagram, Fig. 3-3, is a typical automatic sequential paralleling emergency system. This system, designed to meet NFPA-99 and 110 requirements consists of engine-generator sets, paralleling switchboards, totalizing board, and automatic transfer switches. In this system, three 400-kW engine generators furnish 1200 kW of power. The loads, 1200 kW total, are divided into three priorities of 400 kW each, matching the capacity of one engine-generator. If utility power is interrupted, an automatic transfer switch initiates starting of all three engine-generator sets simultaneously. When the first of the three engine-generators reaches operating voltage and frequency, the corresponding paralleling switchboard closes its circuit breaker connecting the generator power to the emergency bus. With one generator on-line, the priority control enables the first priority transfer switches and the most critical loads to receive power. The shaded line in Fig. 3-3 represents this power distribution. The second and third engine-generators are automatically synchronized with and closed to the emergency bus. As each successive generator is

TABLE 3-1 Emergency Electric Power Supplies—Load Tabulations for Example Location or Building (Onan-Fridley); Nominal Voltage 120/208, Frequency 60 Hz

Load (block) functional description	Load					Circuit no.	Phases used	Static loads			Running loads				Motor starting data						Notes
	Type	Class	Category	Level	Phase			kW	PF*	A	hp output	kW input	PF	A	NEMA motor code	Locked rotor			Starting sequence		
																kVA	PF	kW			
Incandescent lights exit—evacuation	10	2	A	1	1	5	A-N	2	1.0	–17									1		
Fluorescent lights, office—general	60	8	B	2	1	7	A-B-C	5.5	0.95	16									3		
Fire pump, 1	10	2	B	1	3	2	A-B-C				40	35	0.85	114	F	212	0.4	84.8	1		Across-line starting
Pump chiller, 1	60	8	B	3	3	7	A-B-C				40	35	0.85	114	F	212	0.4	84.8	3		Reduced-voltage starting, series reactor, 80%, closed transition
Elevators, 3 each	10	8	B	1	3	4	A-B-C				20	17.5	0.85	57	F	106	0.4	42.4	1		SCR controlled, one elevator at a time
Air compressor, 1	60	8	B	2	3	6	A-B-C				20	17.5	0.85	57	F	106	0.4	42.4	2		Compression relief during starting, low-inertia load

* PF = power factor

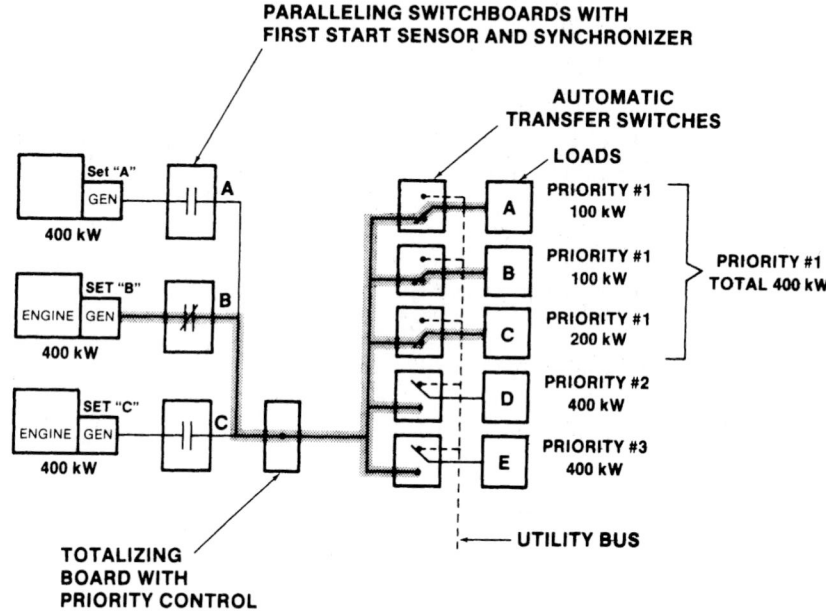

FIGURE 3-3   Automatic sequential paralleling system. (*Onan Corporation.*)

closed to the bus, the priority control enables the second- and third-priority transfer switches to operate.

COMPARISON OF PRIME MOVERS

Table 3-2 reviews the advantages and disadvantages of various types of systems.

Standard Units

Major components of an EPSS include a generator set, transfer switch control, and if applicable, paralleling switchgear. Units discussed are representative only of the sizes and features generally available from EPSS manufacturers.

Generator sets suitable for use in EPSSs include diesel units ranging from 12 to 1500 kW, and spark-ignited units from 5 to 100 kW; rated at 1800 r/min. Three-phase generators are available throughout the range, and single-phase generators are available up to 125 kW typically. Standard cooling systems are set-mounted radiators, with air-cooled models available at the low end of the range. For this type of service, a generator set should have at least a battery-charging alternator, battery-charge-rate ammeter, oil-pressure gauge, coolant-temperature gauge, and a run-stop switch on the engine control (Fig. 3-4). Desirable features, some of which may be required by codes, include an engine-cranking limiter, low-oil-pressure shutdown, high-coolant-temperature shutdown (water cooling), and running-time meter. Water-cooled engines will generally have available as options heat exchanger, city water, or remote radiator systems, and water-cooled exhaust manifolds.

Common sizes of transfer switch controls range from 40 to 3000 A. An automatic transfer switch offers completely automatic, unattended operation and can include time delays for engine starting, load transfer to the emergency power source, retransfer of load to the normal

TABLE 3-2 Advantages and Disadvantages of Various Types of Prime Movers

Advantages	Disadvantages
Gasoline reciprocating	
Lower initial cost than diesel	Fuel storage
Quick starting, especially in low ambients	Gasoline deteriorates over time
Lightweight	Lower thermal efficiency than diesel
Gaseous reciprocating	
Lower initial cost than diesel	Requires high Btu content (1100 Btu/ft^3) or derating
Fuel does not deteriorate over time	necessary
More efficient combustion than gasoline	May not be permitted in seismic risk areas without
Lower maintenance needs	backup fuel storage
Easy starting	
Diesel reciprocating	
Low maintenance requirements	Higher initial cost than gasoline or gaseous
Easy fuel storage	
Low operation costs	
Good thermal efficiency	
Availability in wide range of kW ratings	
Gas turbine	
Lightweight	Higher initial cost
Smaller than equivalent diesel	Longer start time
Low vibration, low noise	Poor partial load efficiency
No cooling water required	
Adaptable for cogeneration	
Multiple fuel capability	
Low maintenance	

power source, and stopping of the engine (Fig. 3-5). It often has voltage sensors for sensing either undervoltage or overvoltage conditions of the normal source voltage and usually for sensing undervoltage conditions of only the emergency source voltage. Operation indicator lamps and meters are also available, if not standard features. An exerciser which automatically test-starts the generator set on a regularly scheduled basis is a popular option.

Paralleling switchgear includes, for each generator set of the paralleling system, an ac ammeter, ac voltmeter, frequency meter, wattmeter, synchronizing lights, a circuit breaker for connecting generator output to the bus, and voltage and frequency adjustment controls. An ac ammeter, an ac voltmeter, and a wattmeter are also connected to the bus for readings of the total paralleling system output. While manual paralleling or automatic paralleling systems are available, the use of automatic systems is more prevalent. (Automatic paralleling switchgear has provisions for manual paralleling if necessary.)

SYSTEM PREPAREDNESS

Once an EPSS is correctly installed and correctly interconnected, system failure results usually from lack of maintenance support. Whether manual or automatic system start-up, preparedness depends on a maintenance program, system exercise, and competent maintenance personnel.

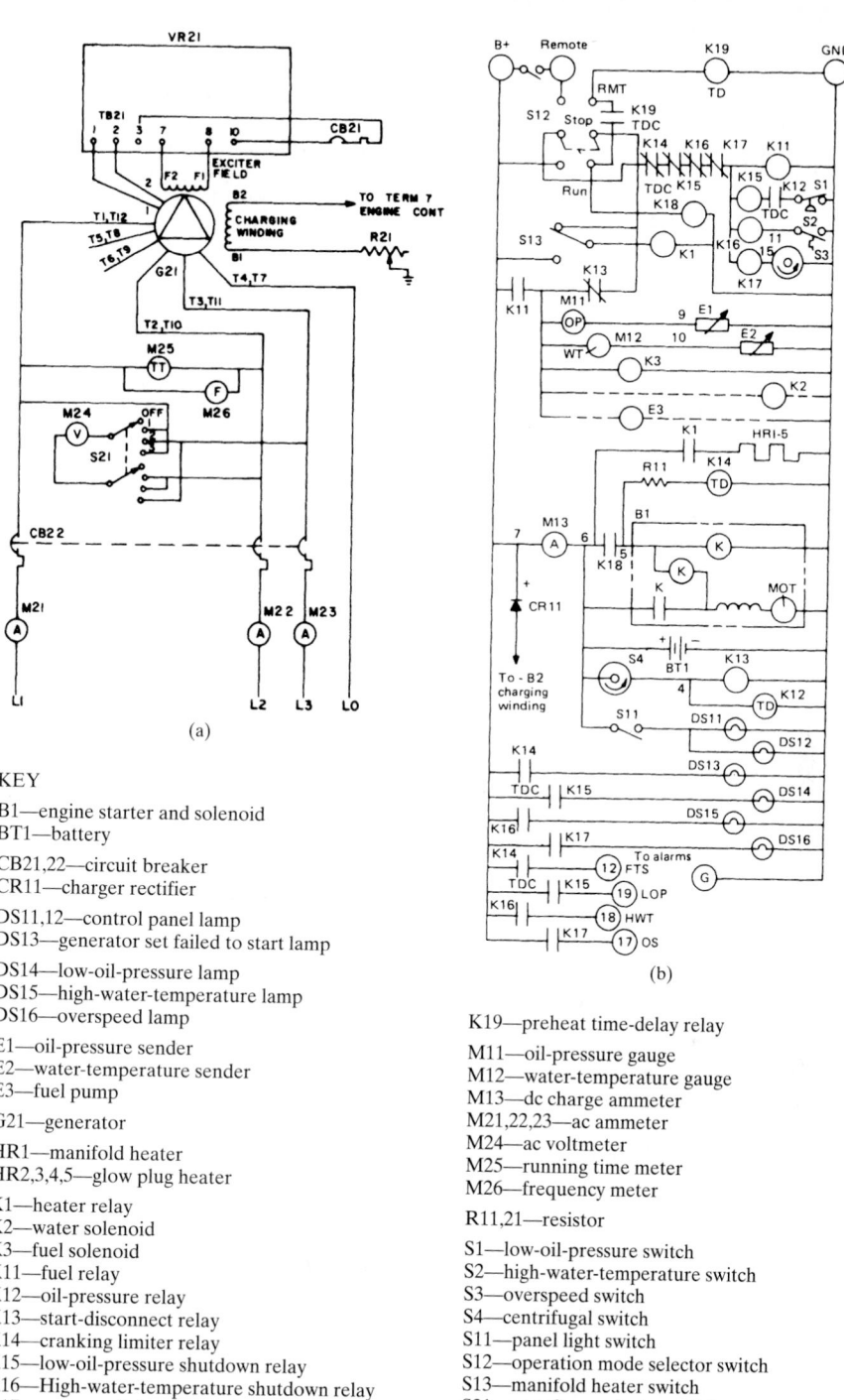

(a)

(b)

KEY

B1—engine starter and solenoid
BT1—battery

CB21,22—circuit breaker
CR11—charger rectifier

DS11,12—control panel lamp
DS13—generator set failed to start lamp

DS14—low-oil-pressure lamp
DS15—high-water-temperature lamp
DS16—overspeed lamp

E1—oil-pressure sender
E2—water-temperature sender
E3—fuel pump

G21—generator

HR1—manifold heater
HR2,3,4,5—glow plug heater

K1—heater relay
K2—water solenoid
K3—fuel solenoid
K11—fuel relay
K12—oil-pressure relay
K13—start-disconnect relay
K14—cranking limiter relay
K15—low-oil-pressure shutdown relay
K16—High-water-temperature shutdown relay
K17—overspeed shutdown relay
K18—starter pilot relay

K19—preheat time-delay relay

M11—oil-pressure gauge
M12—water-temperature gauge
M13—dc charge ammeter
M21,22,23—ac ammeter
M24—ac voltmeter
M25—running time meter
M26—frequency meter

R11,21—resistor

S1—low-oil-pressure switch
S2—high-water-temperature switch
S3—overspeed switch
S4—centrifugal switch
S11—panel light switch
S12—operation mode selector switch
S13—manifold heater switch
S21—ac voltage selector switch

VR21—voltage regulator

FIGURE 3-4 Schematic diagram of generator set. (*a*) AC generator set. (*b*) DC generator set control. All components are shown in the deenergized position. FTS—failed to start; LOP—low oil pressure; HWT—high water temperature; OS—overspeed. (*Onan Corporation.*)

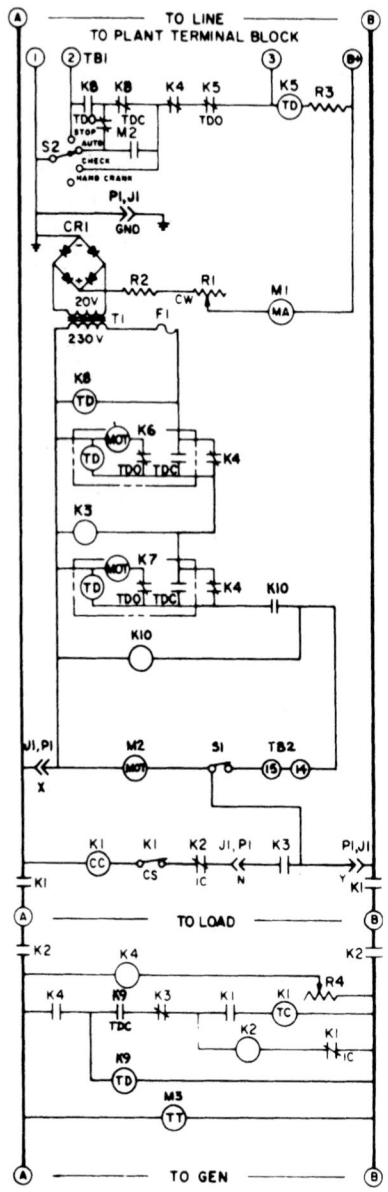

FIGURE 3-5   Schematic diagram of transfer switch. (*Onan Corporation.*)

Maintenance Program

Personnel establishing the maintenance program must prepare a maintenance performance schedule for the complete EPSS. Next, they must establish a means to document the system history of maintenance and service performed.

Although maintenance personnel prepare the maintenance schedule, they must include manufacturer's recommendations of maintenance items and schedules. Due to the infrequent nature of operation for these systems, some maintenance items require service intervals of operational hours while other items require time intervals of days, weeks, months, or years. Some items require both. (The EPSS should have a running time meter to indicate hours of operation).

The following gives a representative listing of maintenance items and maintenance intervals. Use only as a guideline for recognizing particular system maintenance needs and for establishing a schedule. A health-care facility, for example, might require additional items.

Every 8 Operational Hours

1. Check coolant level (water cooling).*
2. Check crankcase oil level.* Wait 15 min after shutdown for accuracy.
3. Check oil sump level (turbine).
4. Visually inspect generator set. Look for fuel, oil, or coolant leaks. Check exhaust if possible with generator set running. Note security of hardware and fittings.
5. Check fuel level.

Every 50 Operational Hours

1. Check air cleaner.* Perform more often in extremely dusty conditions. Replace if necessary.
2. Inspect governor and carburetor-injector-pump linkage. Clean if necessary. Perform more often in extremely dusty conditions.
3. Drain fuel filter sediment.

Every 100 Operational Hours

1. Clean and inspect crankcase breather.*
2. Change engine crankcase oil.* Change oil at least every 3 months, more often in extremely dusty conditions.

---

* Reciprocating engine only.

3. Replace engine oil filter element.* Coincide with engine oil changes.
4. Clean engine-cooling fins (air cooling).*

Every 250 Operational Hours

1. Replace fuel filter element.* For diesel fuel systems with two filters, the second filter from main fuel tank usually needs replacement after several thousand hours.
2. Inspect battery charging alternator.*
3. Replace the ignition points and spark plugs; time ignition (spark ignition).*
4. Check water filter (if equipped).*

Every 500 Operational Hours (Turbine Engine Only)

1. Replace fuel filter.
2. Clean and inspect fuel drain valve.
3. Replace oil filter element.
4. Clean and inspect combustion chamber liner assembly (liquid fuel).
5. Clean and inspect fuel nozzle assembly (liquid fuel).
6. Change oil. Turbine engine manufacturer may allow longer oil change periods if oil sample tests are performed and oil meets engine manufacturer's specifications.

Every 1000 Operational Hours

1. Check generator brushes (if applicable). Brushes must not stick in brush holders.
2. Clean generator. Blow out with low-pressure, filtered, compressed air.

Every 2500 Operational Hours

1. Clean and inspect combustion chamber liner assembly (gaseous fuel).
2. Clean and inspect fuel nozzle assembly (gaseous fuel).
3. Clean and inspect igniter plug.

In contrast to operational hours, the following items usually require inspection or maintenance on a regular basis. Time intervals are week, month, half-year, or year.

Every Week

1. Main fuel tank level—keep full as much as possible.
2. Day tank fuel level.
3. Coolant level (water cooling)—coolant should have rust inhibitor and antifreeze, if applicable.
4. Fan and alternator belts.
5. Hoses and connections.
6. Coolant heater operation (if applicable).
7. Oil heater operation (if applicable).
8. Batteries—check cleanliness, electrolyte level, and cable connections.
9. Battery charger—note charge rate.
10. Exhaust condensation trap—drain out water.
11. Emergency power supply area—note general cleanliness. Wipe down entire system. For an exceptionally clean area, longer intervals could be used.
12. Running tests. Start the generator set and note following (load is preferable):
    a. Fuel system—check operation of fuel solenoid auxiliary fuel pump (if applicable) and general fuel system operation.

_____

* Reciprocating engine only.

    b. Lubrication system—note engine oil pressure and record.

    c. Exhaust system—inspect for tight connections and leaks. Note condition of muffler, exhaust line, and exhaust support.

    d. Cooling system—note operating temperature and record (engine must run long enough to warm up).

    e. Battery charging—note charge rate of generator set.

    f. Meters—note general operation.

13. System documentation—check that operation manual, wiring diagram, maintenance schedule, and log are accessible to maintenance personnel.

Every Month

1. Cooling system (water cooling)—inspect for adequate water flow. Remove any material which interferes with radiator airflow, etc.

2. Ventilation—air inlets and outlets should have unrestricted airflow. Check security of duct work. Check operation of any motor-operated louvres.

3. Fuel system—drain water from main fuel tank and day tanks if applicable. Check fuel tank vents.

4. Battery—check specific gravity of electrolyte. Clean battery terminals.

5. System operation indicator lamps—test lamps with test switch, if equipped.

6. Transfer switch and paralleling switchgear (if applicable); inside cabinets should be clean and free of foreign objects. Check appearance of wiring insulation and color of terminals.

Every 6 Months

1. Cooling system (water cooling)—check for rust and scale. If necessary, flush out system and replace coolant.

2. Engine alarm shutdown devices.

3. Transfer switch control—inspect components and check settings of time delays, voltage sensors, and exerciser, if applicable. Clean cabinet with low-pressure, filtered, compressed air.

4. Generator set control—clean interior with low-pressure, filtered, compressed air.

5. Paralleling switchgear (if applicable)—inspect components, bus bars, and feeder connections. Clean cabinet with low-pressure, filtered, compressed air.

Every Year

1. Generator—measure insulation resistances of windings with a Megger®. Record readings.

2. Paralleling switchgear (if applicable)—perform insulation tests and record.

Maintenance Records

Records of maintenance and service performed on the emergency power supply system have two main benefits. They help to ensure that maintenance procedures were performed, and they provide an excellent system history. A maintenance record form should have entry provisions for the date, maintenance work performed, personnel involved, and general comments (form could also include provisions for labor and parts costs). It will show if schedules were met and if authorized personnel performed the maintenance.

Maintenance history can point out repeating problems or symptoms of a problem in the system. It can become a communication reference with a manufacturer for trouble-shooting, for repair, or for warranty purposes.

System Exercise

Most engines left idle for long periods of time will have difficulty starting. For this same reason, the EPSS needs a regularly scheduled exercise program to promote operation readiness. The program might utilize either an automatic exercise feature of a transfer switch control or manually initiated testing.

Frequent system use especially benefits the generator set. It evaporates water from the lubrication system and generator windings and coats internal moving parts with a film of oil.

Exercise, with load if possible, for at least 30 min should evaporate water in the lubrication system and minimize engine carbon buildup and exhaust-system fouling. System exercise should occur at least once a week.

An automatic exerciser can have settings for the length and number of unattended exercise periods. Manually initiated testing gives the same system benefits as automatic exercising, except that it does require the presence of maintenance personnel. However, personnel can use this time to increase their own system familiarity, to train other personnel, or to perform system inspection.

Competent Maintenance Personnel

One popular method to obtain competent maintenance personnel is through maintenance contracts. The manufacturer or manufacturer's representative usually offering the contract service ensures that personnel performing the maintenance are trained for the equipment and that maintenance procedures meet agreed schedules. If plant personnel perform maintenance procedures, they should receive prior equipment training. (Some manufacturers of emergency power supply systems offer such service schools or training sessions.)

REFERENCE STANDARDS

"Emergency and Standby Power Systems," NFPA 110.
"Electrical Power Distribution for Industrial Plants," IEEE Standard 141-1976.
"Recommended Practice for Emergency and Standby Power Systems," IEEE Standard 446-1987.
"Motors and Generators," ANSI/NEMA Standards Publication MG1-1978.
"Stationary Combustion Engines and Gas Turbines," NFPA 37.
"*National Electrical Code*®," NFPA 70.*
"Essential Electrical Systems for Health Care Facilities," NFPA 99.
"*Life Safety Code*®," NFPA 101.*

BIBLIOGRAPHY

Stromme, Georg: "Coordination Procedures for On-Site Power Generators," *Specifying Engineer,* May 1977, pp. 116–119.
Stromme, Georg: "Emergency and Standby Power Systems," *Building Operation Management,* July 1977.

---

* *National Electrical Code*® and *Life Safety Code*® are Registered Trademarks of the National Fire Protection Association, Inc., Quincy, MA 02269.

CHAPTER 3-3
STANDBY AND EMERGENCY POWER

PART 2

BATTERIES*

General Battery Corporation
Reading, Pennsylvania

GLOSSARY

Alkaline cell   Primary cell with excellent leakage protection capable of higher energy output than carbon-zinc cells.

Ampere-hour   A unit of electricity (symbol A·h) equal to the current flowing past any point in a circuit for 1 h at a constant A.

Ampere-hour capacity   The number of ampere-hours which a cell delivers under specified conditions of discharge rate, temperature, initial specific gravity, and final voltage.

Carbon-zinc cell   Low-cost primary cell with moderate leakage protection and low energy output.

---

* Updated for this Second Edition by the Editor-in-Chief.

Cycle   A discharge and its subsequent recharge.

Cycle service   A type of battery operation in which a battery is repeatedly discharged and recharged during the life of the battery.

Equalizing charge   An extended charge given to a cell or battery to ensure the complete restoration of the active materials within a cell to the fully charged condition.

Final voltage   A prescribed voltage at which a discharge is to be terminated, usually chosen to realize optimum useful capacity without overly discharging the battery.

Finish rate   The maximum value of current at which a charged or nearly charged cell or battery may be charged without causing excessive gassing or heating equal to 5 A per 100 A·h of 6- or 8-h rating.

Float service   A method of battery operation in which a battery is continuously connected to a bus whose voltage is set slightly higher than the open-circuit voltage of the battery. Under these conditions the battery will either charge or discharge into the load, according to the fluctuations in the bus voltage occasioned by varying load conditions. The bus voltage is set to maintain the battery during normal operation in a fully charged condition with a minimum of overcharging.

Gassing   The evolution of gases from either the positive or negative plate of a cell.

Level indicators   A float or visible reference mark used to indicate the electrolyte level within a cell.

Nickel-cadmium cell   A secondary cell commonly used in portable power applications.

Nominal voltage   The voltage rating of a cell or battery arbitrarily assigned to a cell type for the purpose of establishing the operating voltage range. For example, the nominal voltage of a lead-acid cell is 2 V and the nominal voltage of a nickel-cadmium cell is 1.2 V.

Specific gravity   The ratio of the density of the electrolyte to the density of water at standard conditions. The specific gravity (spgr) of battery electrolyte is usually measured with a hydrometer. Temperature, water loss, and state of charge will all effect the specific gravity of a cell.

INTRODUCTION

A *battery* is a device consisting of one or more cells that store chemical energy which can be converted into electric energy on demand. The unit of measure of this electric energy is the kilowatthour (kWh), but battery output is often rated in ampere-hour capacity (A·h) because it is an easily measured quantity used to indicate the work capability. A *cell* is the smallest unit a battery can consist of. The minimum components of a cell are two dissimilar electrodes, an electrolyte, a means of conducting the electric power from the cell, and a container. Other components such as separators, covers, and vents are added to improve performance, life, or usage of the cell. The capacity of a battery depends on the internal construction of the cells. The voltage of the battery is the sum of the voltage of each cell connected in series. Cell voltage is a function of the electrode and electrolyte material.

A *primary cell* is a cell that cannot be easily recharged because the electrochemical reaction is nonreversible. The major types of primary cells are carbon-zinc (CZn) and alkaline. These batteries are best used in applications where long shelf life, low current draw, infrequent use, and low initial cost are important. The disadvantages of these cells include low output current, high voltage drops at high current, and the inability to be recharged. The selection of the proper type will depend upon cost, energy output, current draw, frequency of use, and amount of leakage protection required. Primary cells can be found in flashlights, instrumentation, alarm systems, cameras, and many portable low-power devices.

Secondary cells are fully reversible. The chemical energy can readily be restored by supplying electric energy to the cell in a process called *recharging*. Cells can store only a limited amount of energy. No amount of overcharging will store additional energy. The lead-acid battery is the most common form of secondary cell; it provides most of the traction, stationary, and engine-starting requirements of industry. Advances in technology have resulted in sealed lead-acid batteries being used more frequently in portable power applications. The other type of secondary cell used in industrial plants is the nickel-cadmium (NiCd) battery. It is occasionally used in traction, stationary, and engine-starting applications when cost is not a major factor. The nickel-cadmium battery is frequently used in portable power applications because of its ability to provide lightweight, high-current output in repeated-cycle service for a reasonable cost.

BATTERY CLASSIFICATION BY USAGE

An industrial plant usually has many different types of batteries in a great variety of sizes and shapes. Batteries can range from a single cell weighing a few ounces to a large battery that fills a room and weighs many tons. The electric output of batteries can range from a few milliwatts to hundreds of kilowatts. Industrial plants frequently use batteries for portable power, motive power, engine cranking, and/or stationary applications.

Portable Power

These cells and batteries are designed to be easily carried and supply energy requirements for portable lighting, power tools, instrumentations, communications, and alarm signals. They are sealed to prevent leakage and can be either nonrechargeable (primary cell) or rechargeable (secondary cell) depending on load and usage. These batteries usually provide intermittent or steady low-current power for long periods of time. The life can range from a few hours to many years depending on load and cycle conditions. Table 3-3 lists typical ratings used in the selection of portable power cells.

TABLE 3-3 Typical Range of Ratings of Portable Power Cells

	Primary	Secondary
Weight, lb (kg)	0.1–5.0 (0.045–2.3)	0.1–5.0 (0.045–2.3)
Volume, in^3 (cm^3)	0.5–200 (6–2500)	1–200 (12–2500)
Voltage per cell	1.3–1.5	1.2–2.0
5-h capacity, A · h	0.1–6.0	0.1–10.0
No. of cycles	None	100–1000
Cost, dollars per cell*	1–20	2–40
General types	Carbon	Nickel-cadmium
	Mercury	Lead-acid (GEL)
	Alkaline	Lead-acid (sealed)

* 1993 dollars.

Motive Power

These batteries are designed for repeated-cycle service supplying the energy to propel and operate electrically powered industrial trucks, sweepers, scrubbers, personnel carriers, mine equipment, and over-the-road electric vehicles. Lead-acid industrial, golf cart, and automotive batteries are the most frequently used types for this service. These batteries usually provide intermittent moderate and high-current power for 3 to 10 h to and 80 percent depth of discharge between recharges. They are discharged 3 to 10 times a week with a life ranging from 1 to 7 years. Table 3-4 lists data on and ratings of typical motive power batteries. Figure 3-6 shows the internal construction of a typical motive power cell. This diagram points out some of the important design criteria used to achieve good performance and long life in motive power service.

TABLE 3-4 Typical Range of Ratings of Standard Motive Power Batteries

	Minimum	Maximum
Weight, lb (kg)	30 (14)	7,000 (3,200)
Length, in (cm)	10 (25)	60 (150)
Width, in (cm)	7 (0.8)	45 (120)
Height, in (cm)	9 (23)	36 (90)
Voltage per battery, V	6	96
No. cells	3	48
6-h capacity, A · h	50	2,000
Cycles	1,000	2,000
Life, years	1	7
Cost, dollars per battery*	100	15,000
General types:		
Industrial truck, mine, golf cart, automotive, electric vehicle		

* 1993 dollars.

Engine Cranking

These batteries are designed to furnish the electric energy requirements of internal combustion engines used in vehicular and stationary applications. These requirements include starting, lighting, and ignition (SLI). Some nickel-cadmium batteries are used in this type of service but most are either automotive or industrial lead-acid storage batteries. These batteries usually provide high-current power for a very short period of time during the engine-starting process. This results in a very shallow depth of discharge and very many cycles. Table 3-5 lists information and ratings of typical engine-starting batteries.

TABLE 3-5 Typical Range of Ratings of Standard Engine-Cranking Batteries

	Minimum	Maximum
Weight, lb (kg)	5 (2.3)	1,600 (700)
Length, in (cm)	4 (10)	45 (115)
Width, in (cm)	3 (7.5)	30 (76)
Height, in (cm)	3 (7.5)	20 (50)
Voltage per battery, V	6	64
No. cells	3	32
Cranking rate, A	50	3,500
Life, years	2	8
Cost, dollars per battery*	30	12,000
General types:		
Motorcycles, automotive, truck, marine, aircraft, diesel locomotive, and stationary diesel engine		

* 1993 dollars.

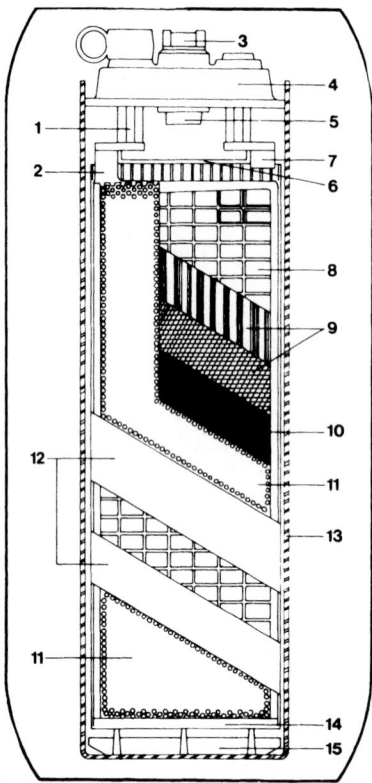

FIGURE 3-6 Internal construction of typical motive power cell. Key: 1, terminal post; 2, positive grid; 3, vent cap; 4, cover; 5, acid level indicator; 6, separator protector; 7, negative grid; 8, active material; 9, positive active material retention material; 10, positive active material retention material; 11, positive active material retention material; 12, separator; 13, container or jar; 14, positive active material retention material; 15, plate rest and sediment area.

Stationary

These batteries are designed to be permanently installed on supporting racks and operated in float service as the backup or emergency energy source for communication systems, switchgear and control equipment, emergency dc power for lighting and essential equipment, and uninterrupted power supplies (UPS). The most common types of stationary batteries are antimony and calcium lead-acid. A few nickel-cadmium and Edison batteries are also found in this service. The power requirements of stationary batteries vary depending on the service. Carefully selecting a battery to match the load and cycle requirements of a particular operation is very important in achieving the desired life. Stationary batteries are often custom-designed to match the usage requirements. Table 3-6 lists information about and ratings of typical stationary cells.

BATTERY CHARGING

There are many ways to charge a battery. Modern chargers are becoming more and more automated, reducing the maintenance needs and increasing the life of the battery. The charging methods used will depend on the type of service and battery. Battery recharge should always be conducted to return the correct amount of charge. Both *overcharging* and *undercharging* are detrimental to battery life.

Constant Current

This is a charge conducted at a constant rate. The rate is usually at or below the finish rate. A *trickle charge* is a low-rate constant-current charge given to maintain the battery at a fully charged condition. This should be used only when the charging rate is matched to the battery. Some portable power and a few small-size stationary batteries use the trickle-charge method.

Two-Step Charging

This is a motive power charge technique commonly used on motor generators. The type of charge consists of a high-rate charge followed by a lower finishing rate charge. The finish rate charge is often initiated by a temperature voltage relay (TVR) which detects the gassing voltage. A timer to limit the length of the finish rate charge is often started by the TVR in order to limit overcharging.

TABLE 3-6 Typical Range of Ratings of Standard
Stationary Cells

	Minimum	Maximum
Weight per cell, lb (kg)	10 (4.5)	1,800 (800)
Length per cell, in (cm)	3 (7.5)	19 (48)
Width per cell, in (cm)	3 (7.5)	18 (46)
Height per cell, in (cm)	6 (15)	60 (150)
No. cells	3	120
Voltage per battery, V	6	250
8-h capacity, A · h	10	8,000
Life, years	5	20
Cost, dollars per cell*	100	5,000
General types:		
Communication, utility,		
emergency lighting,		
uninterrupted power supplies		

* 1993 dollars.

Modified Constant Potential

This is a charging method frequently used in motive power service to automatically regulate the charging rate throughout a recharge. Ferromagnetic circuits are commonly used to control the initial rate, taper, and finishing rate of the recharge over a broad range of conditions.

Constant Voltage (Potential)

This is charging method frequently used with engine cranking and stationary batteries employing a charger with a voltage which is maintained at a constant value. The charging current is dependent on battery needs once the battery reaches the fixed potential. Stationary batteries frequently use a *float charge* which is a constant-voltage charge in which the voltage is set at a value slightly greater than the open-circuit potential to maintain all internal losses without overcharging the battery.

Charger Selection

Battery-charger selection is an important part of achieving good battery life and recharge efficiency. The following items should be considered when selecting a charger: automatic charging rate control; provisions for equalizing charge; fail-safe design (component failure will not harm battery); low electrolyte temperature rise during recharge; automatic over- and under-charge protection; automatic charger termination; charger protected from shorted and open-circuit output; charger protected from reverse polarity; polarity- and voltage-keyed connectors; high electrical efficiency and power factor; and low ac line draw.

BATTERY MAINTENANCE

It is a good practice to keep batteries clean and dry. Cleaning reduces losses due to contact resistance and prevents shorting or grounding through conductive dirt films. The heat dissipation is improved on clean batteries, which helps reduce operating temperature. Batteries are commonly operated between 40 and 120°F (6 and 71°C). Freezing should be avoided because it can permanently damage a battery. High-temperature storage or operation will effectively reduce life. For optimum performance and life, the manufacturer's recharge and maintenance instructions should be closely followed.

Portable power batteries require little maintenance beyond being kept clean, dry, and cool. Primary cell maintenance is limited to replacing when leaking or discharged. Secondary portable power cells require charging when discharged and replacement when leaking. Since most secondary portable power cells are nickel-cadmium, recharging should be conducted after a full discharge. Repeated charging after partial discharge will reduce the capacity.

Motive power, engine cranking, and stationary batteries require cleaning, watering, and charging. When cleaning, electrolyte on the cell covers or connectors should be neutralized and rinsed to prevent corrosion and shorting. Water that is approved for batteries or distilled water should be added as required to keep the electrolyte between the high and low level. The electrolyte level should always be above the plates. Gas bubbles created during charging displace volume causing the electrolyte level to increase. Therefore, water should be added when the battery is on charge and gassing. If water is added after the gas has dissipated from the electrolyte, room should be left for expansion.

Battery connections and charging equipment should be checked at least once a month. A loose or dirty connection can reduce performance or cause an explosion. Malfunctions in charging equipment can result in over- or undercharging which will reduce the life of the battery.

Maintenance records of batteries are useful in scheduling periodic maintenance functions such as checking charging equipment, keeping the battery clean, and maintaining levels. Records can also be used to locate problem areas.

BATTERY SAFETY

Caution should be used when storing, operating, or repairing a battery because of the chemical, explosive, and electrical safety hazards associated with all batteries.

Chemical

Batteries contain corrosive liquids which can be harmful on contact. Always wear protective clothing when exposed to corrosive liquids.

Explosive

Some batteries present an explosive safety hazard because of hydrogen gas released during charging. This hazard is controlled by ventilation and preventing ignition by sparks or open flame in charging areas.

Electrical

High-voltage batteries should be treated like any other high-voltage source for protection from shock hazards. Precaution should be taken to keep metal objects away from battery connectors and terminals to prevent shorting. A battery stores a large amount of energy which can be released rapidly when shorted.

Batteries are safe when proper safety practices are followed. All personnel working with batteries should be trained in the operation and safety practices provided by the battery manufacturer to prevent injury and damage to equipment.

SOURCES OF INFORMATION

Federal Specifications

Superintendent of Documents, U.S. Government Printing Office, Washington, DC 20402.

NEMA Standards

National Electrical Manufacturers Association, Suite 300, 2101 L Street, N.W., Washington, DC 20037.

BCI Standards

Battery Council International, 111 East Wacker Drive, Chicago, IL 60601.

IEEE Standards

Institute of Electrical and Electronic Engineers, 345 East 47th Street, New York, NY 10017.

BIBLIOGRAPHY

Fink, D.: *Standard Handbook for Electrical Engineers,* 13th ed., McGraw-Hill, New York, 1990.
Meurer, M.: *Sealed Battery Selection for Designers and Users,* McGraw-Hill, New York, 1990.

CHAPTER 3-4
MOTORS AND MOTOR CONTROLS

PART 1

ELECTRIC MOTORS

John C. Andreas
Consultant
MagneTek
St. Louis, Missouri

GLOSSARY OF COMMON MOTOR TERMS

Ambient temperature   The temperature of the surrounding cooling environment.

Amperes   The unit of intensity of electric current flowing in a conductor produced by the applied voltage.

Full-load amperes (FLA): The current drawn by the motor when the motor is delivering its rated horsepower at its rated speed (full-load speed) and with rated voltage and frequency applied to the motor.

Locked-rotor amperes (LRA) (starting current per ampere): The current drawn by the motor with the rotor locked (zero speed) and with rated voltage and frequency applied to the motor.

Service-factor amperes (SFA): The current drawn by the motor when the motor is delivering its service-factor horsepower with rated voltage and frequency applied to the motor.

Efficiency   How well a motor turns electric energy into mechanical energy, expressed as the ratio of mechanical power output (watts) to electric power input (watts).

$$\text{Efficiency \%} = \frac{\text{hp} \times 746}{\text{input watts}} \times 100$$

Alternatively, efficiency may be defined as

$$\text{Efficiency} = \frac{\text{mechanical energy out}}{\text{electrical energy in}}$$

But

$$\text{Mechanical energy out} = \text{electrical energy} - \text{motor losses}$$

Frequency   The number of complete cycles of current per second made by alternating current. While sometimes called cycles per second, the preferred terminology is hertz. The standard frequency in the United States is 60 Hz; however 50 and 25 Hz can be found in the United States as well as in other industrial nations.

NEMA   The National Electrical Manufacturers Association (NEMA), an organization which establishes voluntary standards and represents general practice in industry. NEMA has defined motor standards that include nomenclature, construction, dimensions, tolerances, operating characteristics, performance, quality, rating, and testing.

Phase   The number of circuits over which electric power is supplied. In a single-phase motor, power is supplied in a single circuit or winding. In a three-phase system, power is provided over three circuits, each circuit reaching corresponding cyclic values at 120° intervals. AC motors are typically qualified as single-phase or polyphase.

Poles   The number of magnetic poles in a motor, determined by the location and connection of the windings:

$$\text{Synchronous speed} = \frac{\text{frequency} \times 120}{\text{number of poles}}$$

Power   *Mechanical power* is the rate of doing work, usually expressed in terms of horsepower.

$$\text{Power (ft} \cdot \text{lb/min)} = \frac{\text{work (ft} \cdot \text{lb)}}{\text{time (min)}}$$

$$\text{Horsepower (hp)} = \frac{\text{ft} \cdot \text{lb/min}}{33{,}000} = \frac{\text{watts}}{745.7}$$

$$\text{Horsepower (metric)} = \frac{\text{m} \cdot \text{kg/min}}{4500} = \frac{\text{watts}}{735.5}$$

Electric power is measured and expressed in watts, kilowatts (1 kW = 1000 W), or megawatts (1 MW = 10^6 W).

In *dc circuits,*

$$P = VI$$

where P = power in watts, V = line voltage in volts, and I = line current in amperes.

In *single-phase ac circuits,*

$$P = VI \times \text{PF}$$

where PF is the power factor.

For *three-phase ac circuits,*

$$P = 3\ VI \times \text{PF}$$

If the voltage and current are not in phase (as in most magnetic circuits), the volt-amp product is not actual power but apparent power (voltage times total line current) measured in voltamperes (VA) or kilovoltamperes (kVA).

Power Factor   The cosine of the phase angle between line voltage and current in ac circuits. The phase angle is determined by the electrical characteristics of the load. See p. 3-94 for a detailed discussion of power factor.

Rotor   The rotating part of an electric motor.

Rated temperature rise   The NEMA allowable rise in temperature for a given insulation system above ambient, when operating under maximum allowable load (i.e., service-factor load).

Stator   The stationary part of an electric motor.

Service factor   A multiplier which indicates what percent higher than the nameplate horsepower can be accommodated continuously at rated voltage and frequency without injurious overheating (i.e., exceeding NEMA allowable temperature rise for given insulation systems).

Slip   The percentage reduction in speed from synchronous speed to full-load speed (known as *percent slip*). All ac induction squirrel-cage motors have slip.

$$\text{Percent slip} = \frac{(N_s - N_l) \times 100}{N_s}$$

where N_s = synchronous speed, r/min, and N_l = load speed, r/min.

Speed   The rotational velocity of the motor shaft, measured in terms of revolutions per minute (r/min).

Full-load speed: Motor speed at which rated horsepower is developed.

No-load speed: Motor speed when allowed to run freely with no load coupled.

Synchronous speed: The synchronous speed of an ac motor is that speed at which the motor would operate if the rotor turned at the exact speed of the rotating magnetic field. However, in ac induction motors, the rotor actually turns slightly slower. This difference is the slip and is expressed in percent of synchronous speed. Most induction motors normally have a slip of 1 to 3 percent.

Squirrel cage   A term used to describe the construction of one type of induction motor. The rotor is made of an iron core mounted on a concentric shaft. Copper, brass, or aluminum bars run the entire length of the core in slots on the core. These bars act as conductors and are fastened on each end of the rotor to end rings in order to form a complete short circuit within the rotor.

Torque   The turning effort of a motor, normally expressed in ounce-feet (for fractional horsepower motors) or pound-feet (for integral horsepower motors). A motor developing 15 lb·ft of torque develops a force of 15 lb at the end of a 1-ft-radius lever arm.

   Accelerating torque: The difference between the torque developed by the motor and torque required by the load at any given speed. This excess torque accelerates the motor and load.

   Breakdown torque: The maximum torque developed by the motor at rated voltage and frequency, without an abrupt drop in speed.

   Locked-rotor torque (also called *starting torque, static torque, breakaway torque*): The minimum torque developed at rest for all angular positions of the rotor with rated voltage applied at rated frequency.

   Pull-in torque: The torque of a *synchronous motor* that brings the driven load into synchronous speed. (There is no corresponding term for induction motors.)

   Pull-out torque: The maximum torque of a *synchronous motor* developed at synchronous speed with rated frequency and excitation.

   Pull-up torque: The minimum torque developed by the motor during the period of acceleration from zero speed (rest) to the speed at which breakdown occurs.

Voltage   A unit of electromotive force. One volt applied to a conductor offering 1 Ω of resistance will produce a current in that conductor of 1 A.

Wound-rotor induction motor   An induction motor in which the secondary circuit consists of a polyphase winding or coils whose terminals are either short-circuited or connected to an external circuit.

INTRODUCTION

Electric-motor application for the plant engineer is the common-sense matching of load requirements with motor characteristics. Motor types, styles, sizes, mountings, and enclosures vary greatly. So the first step in using electric motors correctly is to understand them and the terminology the motor industry uses to describe them.

   To help achieve such an understanding, the first part of this section presents a glossary of common motor terms essential to motor use and application. After that, motors and the many variables by which they are classified are discussed in terms of National Electrical Manufacturers Association (NEMA) standards, the unifying doctrine within the motor industry.

   There are many ways to classify motors. But whichever one might choose, a familiarity with NEMA classifications and standards will at some point be necessary. Thus NEMA standards are as good a basis as any on which to organize a discussion of motors for the plant engineer.

   NEMA is a nonprofit trade organization whose voluntary standards have been widely adopted by motor manufacturers and users alike. The NEMA standard "Motors and Generators" (MG1-1993) is designed to eliminate misunderstandings between manufacturer and purchaser and to assist the purchaser in selecting and obtaining the proper product for his or her particular needs.

   Motors are classified by size, application, electrical type, NEMA design letter, and environmental protection and cooling methods. They are rated for special standard environmental and operating service conditions by performance and mechanical configuration: voltage and frequency, locked-rotor kVA, service factor, horsepower, speed, torque, locked-rotor current, performance, temperature rise, duty cycle, and frame size.

Because of the large number of motor types and configurations, this section is limited to motors of most interest to plant engineers. Subfractional horsepower and special-use motors (such as small-instrument, small-fan, stepping, and timing motors, for example) are only rarely specified for plant-engineering applications.

Motor types and classifications are followed by a brief guide to motor selection, the essentials of picking the right motor for either a new or replacement application. Following this application guide are discussions of two of the more practical concerns that face the electric motor user: troubleshooting and energy efficiency.

The section ends with a list of references and sources of additional information for each of the areas discussed.

MOTOR CLASSIFICATION

NEMA standards for electric motors cover frame sizes and dimensions, horsepower ratings, service factors, temperature rises, and performance characteristics. Such standards provide greater availability, more convenience in use, a basis for accurate comparison, faster repair service, shorter delivery times, and maximum mechanical and electrical interchangeability from motor to motor.

Motors are classified by size, application, electrical type, design letter, environmental protection, and cooling methods.

Classifying by Size

Virtually all electric motors used by the plant engineer can be classified as either fractional or integral horsepower. Despite the obvious distinction of horsepower, frame size (discussed later in this section) actually determines to which category a motor belongs.

A fractional horsepower (FHP) motor is either a motor built in a frame which is designated by a two-digit frame number or in a three-digit frame smaller than the 140 series. An integral horsepower (IHP) motor is one built in a frame which has a three-digit frame number from 140 to 680.

Classifying by Application

NEMA also classifies electric motors by application as general-purpose, definite-purpose, or special-purpose. A general-purpose motor is an induction motor which has a continuous rating, service factor, and temperature rise in accordance with NEMA standards. General-purpose motors are built in quantity in standard ratings with standard operating characteristics and mechanical construction for a wide variety of common applications.

A definite-purpose motor, on the other hand, is designed for specific service conditions and applications. It differs from the general-purpose motor with respect to rating, service factor, and temperature rise, one or all of which have limits much narrower than those of general-purpose motors. Definite-purpose motors conform to established NEMA standards, are produced in high volume, and are often low in cost compared with general-purpose motors of the same ratings. However, use of a definite-purpose motor for a duty other than that for which it was intended must be carefully considered.

Special-purpose motors incorporate specialized operating characteristics and/or mechanical construction to serve one-of-a-kind applications not satisfied by general- and definite-purpose motors.

Because of both the limited scope of this discussion and the fact that the great majority of plant applications require general-purpose motors, only general-purpose motors are discussed here.

Classifying by Electrical Type

Figure 4-1 illustrates the family of ac and dc general-purpose motors which together can serve virtually all needs of the plant engineer. This family is organized according to the characteristics of the electric power driving the motor and the variations in motor winding and rotor configuration.

AC Motors

Single-Phase Induction Motors.   Alternating current motors fall into three major categories: single-phase, polyphase, and universal (ac-dc). Single-phase induction motors are inherently unable to start themselves. Thus these motors are classified by their means of starting as well as by their basic design, either induction or synchronous. Induction motors fall into two further categories: squirrel-cage and wound-rotor.

The squirrel-cage motor consists of a wound stator and laminated, cylindrical iron-cove rotor. Cast-aluminum conductors imbedded within the rotor and short-circuiting end rings form a "squirrel-cage" configuration.

Split-Phase Motors.   Split-phase motors use two windings—a main winding and a start winding (Fig. 4-2). The high resistance of the start winding creates a phase shift and induces a torque that causes initial motor rotation and acceleration. When a predetermined speed (the cutout point) is attained, a centrifugal mechanism opens the start-winding circuit. The motor then accelerates with only the main winding energized and runs as an induction motor. In some designs a current-sensing relay is used instead of a centrifugal switch.

Capacitor-Start Motors.   Capacitor-start motors are similar to split-phase motors except that a capacitor is placed in series with the start winding to produce greater starting and accelerating torque (Fig. 4-3). After the start winding is removed from the circuit by a centrifugal or electronic switch, performance is identical to that of split-phase motors.

Permanent Split-Capacitor Motors.   Permanent split-capacitor motors also have a start winding with a capacitor (Fig. 4-4). Because the capacitor and start windings are continuously energized, these motors operate at a higher power factor than other designs, although at the expense of a lower locked-rotor torque. Since no centrifugal switch is needed, the motor is usually shorter and often more reliable than other single-phase designs. These motors are usually used to drive fans or pumps with low starting torque requirements.

Two-Value-Capacitor Motors.   Two-value-capacitor motors have both a switched-start capacitor and a run capacitor to improve full-load current, starting torque, and power factor (Fig. 4-5). Both are connected in parallel to the start winding, with the start capacitor disconnecting as the motor accelerates. These motors provide good overall torque characteristics and are quiet-running.

Shaded-Pole Motors.   Instead of a start winding, shaded-pole motors have a continuous solid-copper loop around a small portion of each salient pole (Fig. 4-6). This shading coil causes the reaction necessary to start the motor, but produces rather low starting and accelerating torque. Because of their low starting torque, shaded-pole motors are best suited to light-duty applications such as direct-drive fans and blowers. Efficiency and power factor are also lower than that of other single-phase motors.

Wound-Rotor Motors.   Wound-rotor motors have a stator winding connected to the power source and a rotor winding connected to a commutator.

Unlike the squirrel-cage induction motor, the wound-rotor motor has controllable speed and torque. Their application is considerably different from squirrel-cage motors because of the accessibility of the rotor circuit. Various performance characteristics can be obtained by inserting different resistances in the rotor circuit.

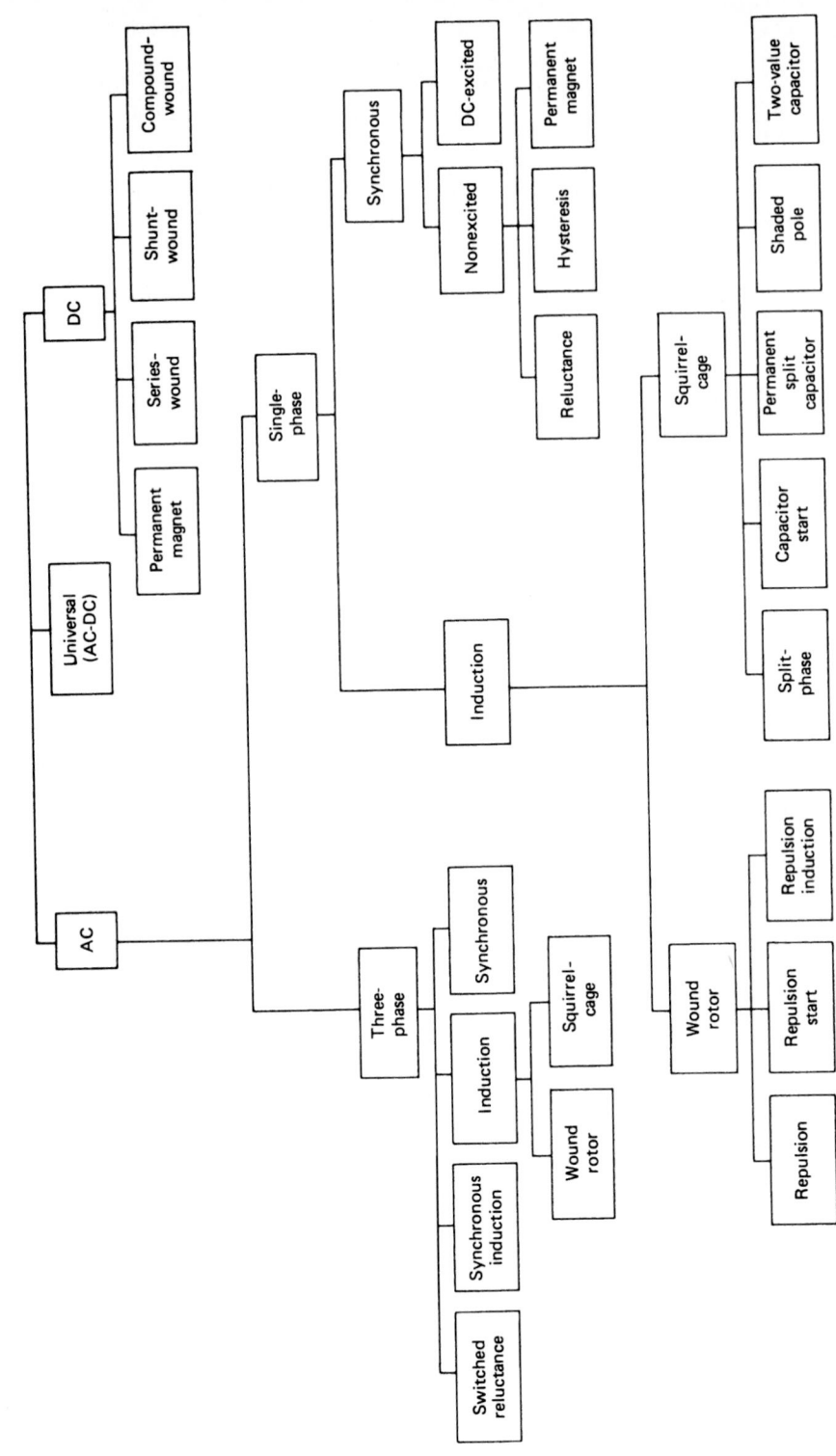

FIGURE 4-1 Electric motor family for plant engineers.

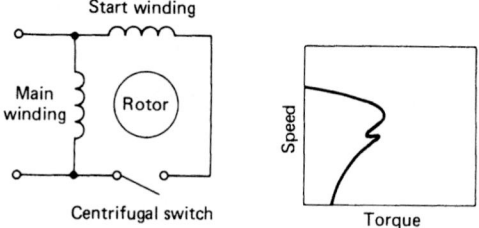

FIGURE 4-2 Schematic diagram and speed vs. torque diagram—ac split-phase motor.

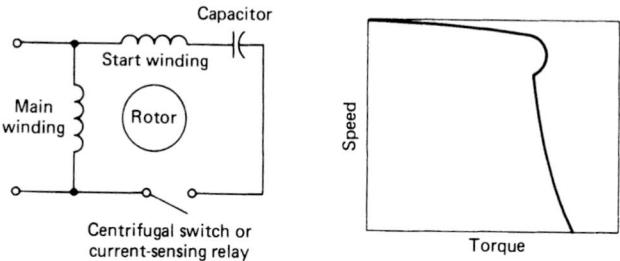

FIGURE 4-3 Schematic diagram and speed vs. torque diagram—ac capacitor-start motor.

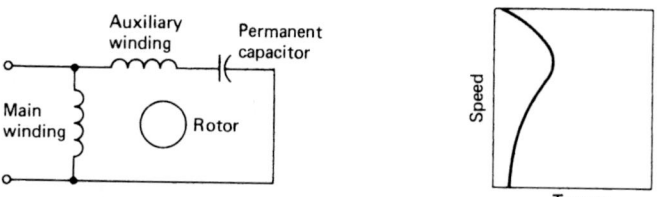

FIGURE 4-4 Schematic and speed vs. torque diagram—ac permanent split-capacitor motor.

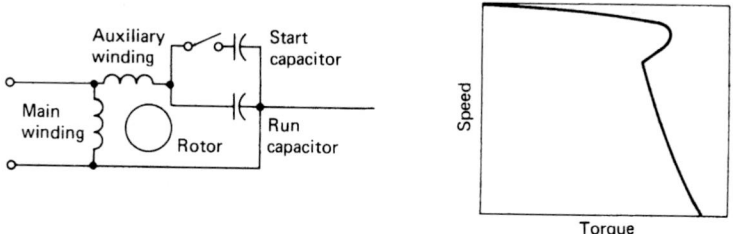

FIGURE 4-5 Schematic and speed vs. torque diagram—ac two-value-capacitor motor.

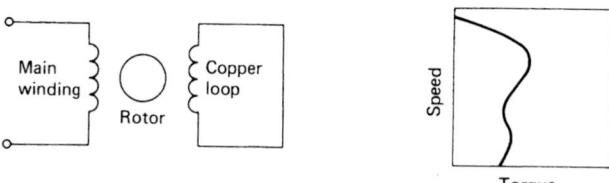

FIGURE 4-6 Schematic and speed vs. torque diagram—ac shaded-pole motor.

Wound-rotor motors may be used as constant-speed or as adjustable-speed motors. They are frequently used where high locked-rotor and accelerating torque with low starting current are required.

Repulsion Motors. Repulsion motors have an armature winding, commutator, and brushes (Fig. 4-7). Brushes are short-circuited and shifted to give the effect of two stator windings: a field winding at right angles to the brush axis and an induction winding along the brush axis. The induction winding induces current in the armature winding that reacts with the magnetic field set up by the field winding to produce starting torque. Repulsion motors feature good starting characteristics and are often used for heavy, hard-to-start loads.

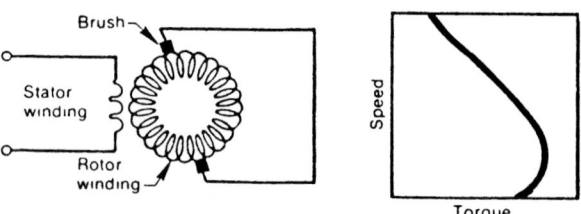

FIGURE 4-7 Schematic and speed vs. torque diagram—ac repulsion motor.

Repulsion-Start Motors. Repulsion-start motors are repulsion motors with a centrifugal switch (Fig. 4-8). At about 75 percent of synchronous speed, the switch short-circuits the commutator bars and the motor performs like a squirrel-cage motor. Repulsion-start motors are expensive and no longer widely used in industry.

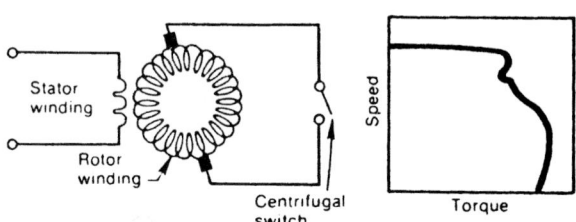

FIGURE 4-8 Schematic and speed vs. torque diagram—ac repulsion-start motor.

Repulsion-Start Induction-Run Motors. Repulsion-start induction-run motors are simply repulsion-start motors with the addition of a squirrel-cage rotor winding to improve speed regulation (Fig. 4-9). At a predetermined speed, a centrifugal switch shorts the commutator and the motor operates as a squirrel-cage induction motor. These motors are ideal for applications requiring high starting torque and low starting current.

Single-Phase Synchronous Motors. Single-phase synchronous motors are constant-speed motors that operate in synchronism with line frequency. As with squirrel-cage induction motors, speed is determined by the number of pairs of poles and is always a ratio of the line frequency.

Synchronous motors range from subfractional self-excited units to large horsepower, dc-excited motors for industrial drives. In the single-phase fractional horsepower range, synchronous motors are primarily used where precise constant speed is required.

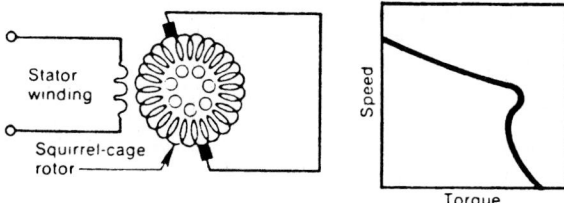

FIGURE 4-9 Schematic and speed vs. torque diagram—ac repulsion-induction motor.

Like single-phase induction motors, synchronous motors cannot start themselves. They employ self-starting circuits.

Nonexcited Reluctance Motors.   Reluctance synchronous motors have squirrel-cage construction with salient poles (Fig. 4-10). The rotor has one cutout for each pole, which together cause magnetic reluctance to be greater between poles than along the axis. The motor locks into synchronism in less than one cycle of applied voltage.

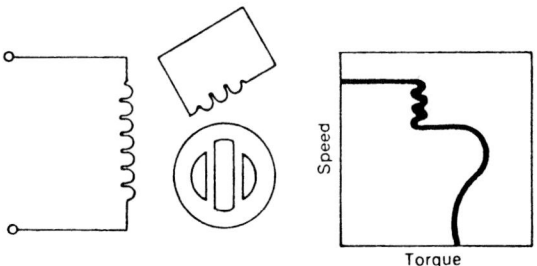

FIGURE 4-10 Schematic and speed vs. torque diagram—ac reluctance motor.

Efficiency and power factor are lower than for dc-excited synchronous or squirrel-cage induction motors. However, the motor is inexpensive, simple, and suitable for light loads.

Nonexcited Hysteresis.   Hysteresis motors have no physical pole arrangement on their rotors but develop fixed magnetic poles in some random angular position as they reach synchronous speed (Fig. 4-11).

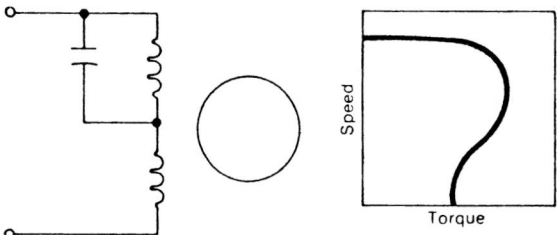

FIGURE 4-11 Schematic and speed vs. torque diagram—ac hysteresis motor.

Used as timing motors or for applications requiring precise constant speed, they are of secondary interest to plant engineers.

Nonexcited Permanent-Magnet Motors.   Permanent-magnet motors have permanent magnets embedded in a squirrel-cage-type rotor (Fig. 4-12a). They produce fixed poles that lock into step with the armature field. Because of its relatively high efficiency and power factor, this motor is popular in the fractional and lower integral horsepower range.

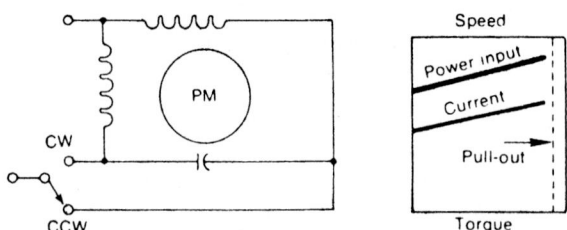

FIGURE 4-12a   Schematic and speed vs. torque diagram—ac permanent-magnet motor.

Three-Phase Motors.   The rotating magnetic field provided by three-phase ac power permits a simple and low-cost means of constructing an electric motor. In general-purpose use, three-phase motors require no start windings, switches, or starting or running capacitors, thereby eliminating some major sources of failures in single-phase motors.

The horsepower of three-phase motors ranges from ½ to 2500 or more. Starting current required is low to medium, about 5 to 7 times full-load current.

Three-phase motors can be easily reversed electrically, making them useful for applications involving control of direction of rotation or remote positioning. Different combinations of speed-torque characteristics are also available so that motor performance can be specifically matched to an application.

Three-Phase Induction Squirrel-Cage Motors.   Three-phase squirrel-cage motors are basically constant-speed machines, although operating characteristics can be varied to some degree by modifying the rotor design. These variations produce predictable changes in torque, current, and full-load speed.

Evolution and standardization within the motor industry have resulted in five fundamental types of three-phase induction motors known by NEMA design letters (discussed later in this section).

Three-Phase Synchronous Induction Motors.   The synchronous induction motor has a conventional three-phase stator winding. The rotor is modified to provide cutouts for a specific number of poles on the rotor face to match the polarity of the stator winding and flux guiding barriers are included to improve the pull-in and pull-out torques. Figure 4-12b shows a typical rotor configuration for a two-pole synchronous induction motor. Similar configurations are used for four-pole and six-pole synchronous induction motors. These motors start as an induction motor and at operating speed pull into synchronism and run at synchronous speed. The locked rotor current is considerably higher than the locked rotor current for the same horsepower induction motor. The power factor and efficiency are lower. However, they have the advantage of operating at synchronous speed. A typical speed-torque curve is shown in Fig. 4-12c. The pull-in torque is a function of the total mechanical inertia of the driven system. The motors have been built in ratings up to 100 hp. They are usually applied to multimotor drives, where all of the motors in the system must stay in synchronism.

Three-Phase Induction Wound-Rotor Motors.   Wound-rotor motors offer more speed and torque control than squirrel-cage induction motors, as well as the major advantage of accessibility of the rotor circuit. Performance characteristics can be varied merely by inserting different values of resistance in the rotor circuit.

FIGURE 4-12*b*   Synchronous induction motor rotor configuration.

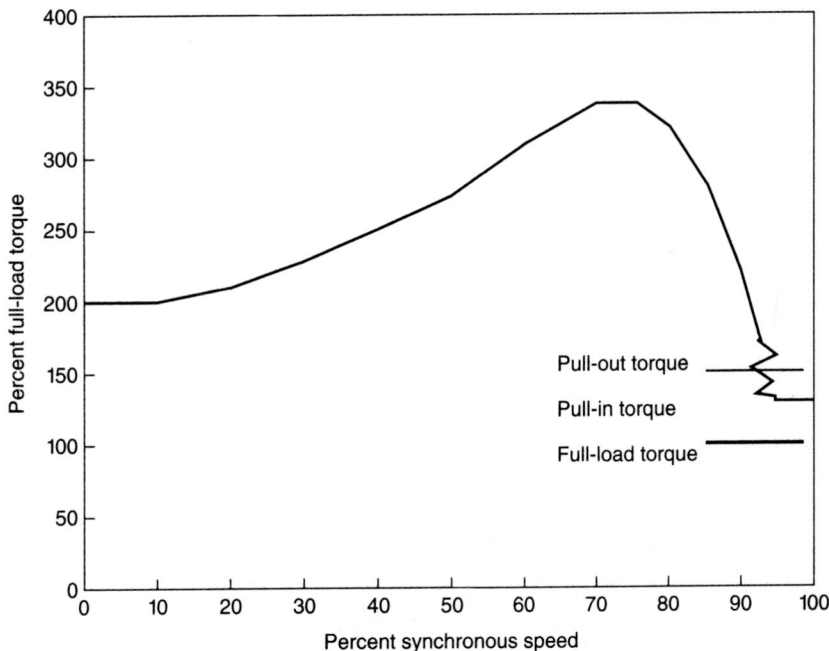

FIGURE 4-12*c*   Synchronous induction motor speed-torque curve.

Wound-rotor motors may be used as either constant-speed or adjustable-speed motors. With full load, the speed may be reduced by as much as 50 percent of synchronous speed for certain fixed loads such as fans or compressors. These motors are frequently used when high locked-rotor and accelerating torque with low starting current are required. They are also used where heavy or delicate loads must be accelerated gradually and smoothly, as in hoists and elevators. A variety of solid-state control systems are available for use in the rotor circuit of wound-rotor motors.

AC Three-Phase Synchronous Motors. Like single-phase motors, three-phase synchronous motors cannot start by themselves. One of two starting methods is used in most motors: dc excitation or reluctance.

Synchronous motors employing dc excitation, although offered in sizes as small as 20 hp, are primarily used in applications requiring 50 to several thousand horsepower. High-speed synchronous motors (from 514 to 1800 r/min) are normally used for the same applications as NEMA design A, B, or F squirrel-cage motors. Low-speed synchronous motors (below 450 r/min) are usually used as direct-connected drives for compressors and pumps, where they are more economical than induction motors with gear, chain, or belt drives.

These synchronous motors usually have pole-face squirrel-cage-type windings for both starting and damping. The motor is started as an induction motor with the dc field shorted, and at a predetermined speed the field is excited and the motor pulls into synchronism.

Switched Reluctance Motors. The switched reluctance motor (SRM) is a motor with double saliency with an unequal number of rotor and stator poles. The torque is produced by the tendency of the rotor poles to align with the poles of the excited stator phase and is independent of the direction of the phase current. The motor is singly excited from stator windings that are concentric coils wound in series on diagonally opposite stator poles. Figure 4-12*d* is a simplified diagram of an SRM drive. Shown in this figure is the phase winding and the switching circuit for one of the phases. Continuous rotation of the rotor is obtained by exciting the stator phases sequentially, the rotor stepping around in a direction opposite to that of the stator phase excitation. Output torque and speed depend on the control switching system including frequency, conduction angle, and ignition angle. Figure 4-12*e* illustrates the power output for different ignition angles and conduction angles. Because of their simple construction and relatively simple control system these motors are finding applications is adjustable speed drive systems.

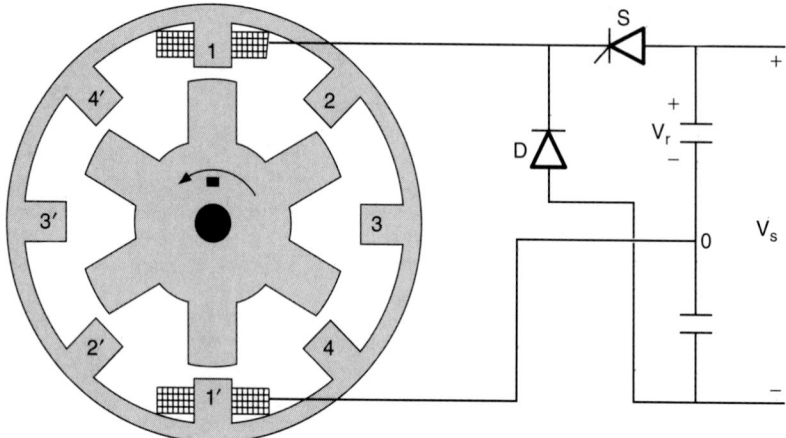

FIGURE 4-12*d* Simplified SRM motor drive system.

AVERAGE POWER VS. IGNITION ANGLE FOR DIFFERENT CONDUCTION ANGLES

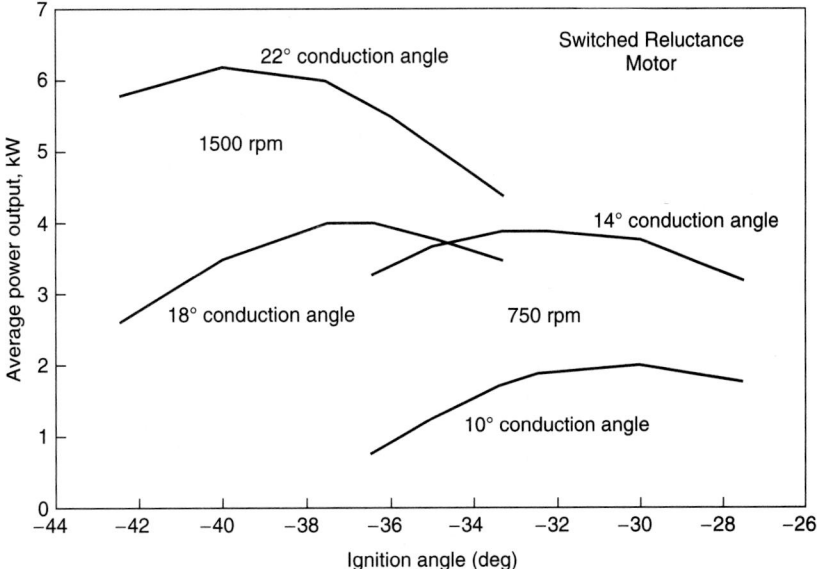

FIGURE 4-12*e*   Switched reluctance motor output power.

DC Motors.   DC motors see a wide variety of industrial applications because their speed-torque relationships can be varied to almost any useful form—for both motor and regeneration applications and in either direction of rotation. Many dc motors can be operated continuously over a speed range of 8:1. Speed control down to zero for short durations or for driving reduced loads is also common.

AC motors lose speed rapidly and sometimes stall at loads above twice their rated torque. DC motors, by contrast, are often applied where they momentarily deliver 3 or more times their rated torque. And in emergency situations, dc motors can supply over 5 times rated torque for a limited time without stalling if the required power is available.

DC motor speed can be regulated smoothly down to zero, immediately followed by acceleration in the opposite direction without power circuit switching. DC motors also respond quickly to changes in control signals due to their high torque-to-inertia ratio.

Wound-field dc motors are classified by the type of motor field: shunt-wound, series-wound, and compound-wound. Permanent magnet types are also popular, normally as fractional horsepower motors.

Shunt-Wound Motors.   Shunt-wound and stabilized shunt-wound dc motors can supply both constant speed at any control setting and a wide speed range that is field-controllable (Fig. 4-13). Most shunt motors are operated from adjustable voltage power supplies and, therefore, do not need auxiliary starting provisions.

A stabilizing winding helps prevent speed increases as the load increases at weak field settings. This winding has disadvantages in reversing applications, however, because it must be reversed with respect to the shunt winding when the armature voltage is reversed. Reversing contactors are normally used.

The shunt winding can either be connected to the same power supply as the armature (self-excited) or be separately excited. Care must be taken never to open the field of a shunt-wound motor that is running unloaded. The loss of field flux causes motor speed to increase to dangerously high levels.

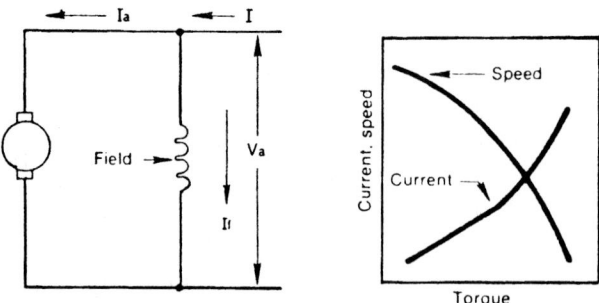

FIGURE 4-13 Schematic and speed vs. torque diagram—dc shunt-wound motor.

Series-Wound Motors.   In series-wound motors, the field flux is created by coils that are electrically in series with the armature (Fig. 4-14). When the motor starts, the current and, consequently, the magnetic field are at maximum values, producing a large starting torque. As the motor speeds up and the current is reduced, the field flux also becomes smaller. With no external load on the shaft, the field flux drops nearly to zero and motor speed becomes dangerously high. For this reason, series-wound motors should be used only where the load is directly connected or geared to the shaft.

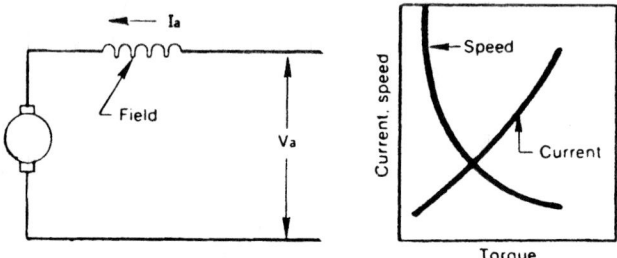

FIGURE 4-14 Schematic and speed vs. torque diagram—dc series-wound motor.

Compound-Wound Motors.   Compound-wound motors combine both series and shunt fields (Fig. 4-15). The disadvantage of series-motor overspeeding at light loads is avoided since there is so little current in the series field at no load that speed is determined by the shunt field alone. At higher loads, speed depends on the sum of the two fields, making speed reduction similar to that of a series motor.

Compound motors have high starting torques and fairly flat speed-torque characteristics at rated load. Because of the elaborate circuits needed to control compound motors, however, only large bidirectional types are built.

Permanent-Magnet Motors.   Permanent-magnet motors have fields supplied by permanent magnets (Fig. 4-16). Those fields create two or more poles in the armature by passing magnetic flux through it. The magnetic flux causes the current-carrying armature conductors to move, creating a torque. This flux remains basically constant at all motor speeds; speed-torque and current-torque curves are linear.

Permanent-magnet motors, available in fractional and low-integral horsepower sizes, have several advantages over field-wound types. Excitation power supplies and associated wiring are not required, and reliability is improved. Efficiency and cooling are also improved by elimination of the power loss associated with an excited field.

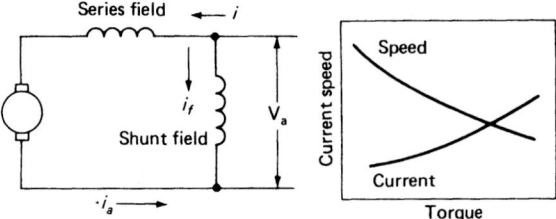

FIGURE 4-15 Schematic and speed vs. torque diagram—dc compound-wound motor.

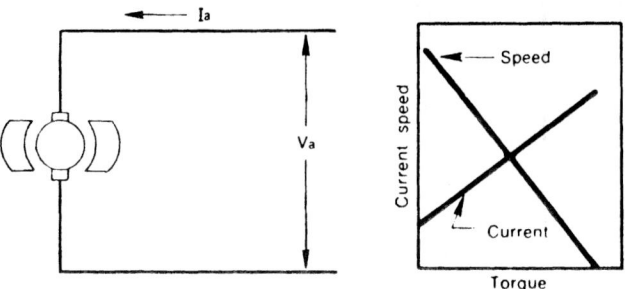

FIGURE 4-16 Schematic and speed vs. torque diagram—dc permanent-magnet motor.

Disadvantages are the absence of field control and special speed-torque characteristics. Overloads may also cause partial demagnetization that changes motor speed and torque characteristics until magnetization is fully restored.

Permanent-magnet motor performance is actually a compromise between compound-wound and series-wound motors. It has better starting torque but approximately half the no-load speed of a series-wound motor. In applications where compound motors are traditionally used, the permanent-magnet motor can offer slightly higher efficiency and greater overload capacity. In series-motor applications, permanent-magnet motors provide a cost advantage.

Brushless DC Motors.   The brushless dc motor consists of a rotor with permanent magnets mounted on it—usually permanently bonded to the rotor structure—and a stator with windings similar to an ac induction motor. In addition, an electronic controller is provided to control the switching of the stator winding. You might consider this as an electronic commutator. The advantage of this type of motor is the simplicity of the ac motor type of construction with the excellent performance of a dc drive system. This eliminates the mechanical commutator and its maintenance. The disadvantage, compared to a dc motor drive system, is the cost. The advantage is low maintenance and superior performance. This type of system, with proper ventilation, can provide precise full load torque down to zero speed.

Universal Motors.   Universal motors are essentially series motors that operate with nearly equivalent performance on direct current or alternating current up to 60 Hz. They differ from dc series motors in that they have different winding ratios and thinner iron laminations. A dc series motor runs on alternating current, but inefficiently. A universal motor, however, runs on direct current with essentially equivalent ac performance, but with poorer commutation and brush life than an equivalent dc series motor.

A universal motor has the highest horsepower per pound ratio of any ac motor because of its ability to operate at much greater speeds than any other 60-Hz motor. It is ideally suited for operation at a rated output, where an occasional overload or intermittent heavy load occurs. Stall torque may be as much as 10 times the continuous rated torque. The motor may even be operated in a stalled condition for short periods of time.

High starting torque, adjustable-speed characteristics, small size, and economy are all advantages of the universal motor. Universal motors are not more widely used, however, because their operating life is shorter, their size range is limited [to about 2 hp (1.5 kW)], and their very high speeds limit their applications.

Universal motors can be built to deliver speeds ranging from 4000 to 24,000 r/min and rated power from 0.1 to 1 hp (75 to 750 W). Efficiency varies from 30 percent for small sizes to 75 percent for large sizes.

Metric Motors.   There is an increasing trend to express electric motor output in kilowatts rather than horsepower. This is consistent with the International Electrotechnical Commission (IEC) standards for rotating electrical machines including induction motors.

Table 4-1 shows the comparison of the units of measure between the International System of Units (metric) and the Americal Customary System of units, as related to induction motor rating. This table also shows the induction motor kilowatt output equation for both systems of measurement and the conversion from one system to the other.

Table 4-2 shows the comparison between the IEC preferred kilowatt output rating converted to equivalent horsepower and the NEMA standard horsepower ratings.

TABLE 4-1   Comparison of the International System of Units (Metric) and American Customary System Units

Quantity	International System of Units (metric)	American customary units
Linear measure	Millimeter	Inch
Angular measure	Degree	Degree
Mass	Kilogram	Pound
Force	Newton	Pound-force
Torque	Newton meter	Pound-force foot
Power	Kilowatt	Horsepower

Output equation:

$$\text{kW output} = \frac{T \times n}{K \times 1000}$$

where
T = torque
n = speed, r/min
K = 9.549 if torque is in newton meters
= 7.043 if torque is in pound-force feet

Conversion of torque:
1. Pound-force feet to newton meters

$$\text{Newton meters} = 1.356 \times \text{pound-force feet}$$

2. Newton meters to pound-force feet

$$\text{Pound-force feet} = 0.7376 \times \text{newton meters}$$

Conversion to horsepower:
In American customary units

$$\text{Horsepower} = \frac{\text{kW}}{0.7457}$$

In metric units

$$\text{Horsepower} = \frac{\text{kW}}{0.7355}$$

TABLE 4-2   Comparison of IEC (Metric) Preferred Output
Ratings and NEMA Standard Horsepower Ratings

IEC preferred rating, kW	Equivalent horsepower, rounded	NEMA standard horsepower
0.06	0.080	¹⁄₁₂
0.09	0.121	⅛
0.12	0.161	⅙
0.18	0.241	¼
0.25	0.335	⅓
0.37	0.496	½
0.55	0.737	¾
0.75	1.005	1
1.1	1.475	1.5
		2
2.2	2.95	3
3	4.02	
3.7	4.96	5
4	5.36	
5.5	7.37	7.5
7.5	10	10
11	15	15
15	20	20
18.5	25	25
22	29	30
30	40	40
37	50	50
45	60	60
55	74	75
75	101	100
90	121	125
110	147	150
132	177	175
150	201	200
160	214	
185	248	250
200	268	
220	295	300

In order to compare the physical dimensions of the IEC and NEMA induction motors Table 4-3 shows the comparison of the IEC standard induction motor shaft heights H and the nearest NEMA standard shaft height D, for the T frame line of NEMA induction motors. The shaft height dimension H in millimeters for the IEC standard and the D dimension in inches for the NEMA standard motors are defined as the distance from the centerline of the shaft to the bottom of the mounting feet. For other mounting dimensions, the specific metric motor should be determined.

Classifying by Design Letter

Three-phase, squirrel-cage, IHP motors are the most widely used ac induction motors in industry. Classification of performance requirements has results in NEMA standardized designs that satisfy torque, horsepower, speed, and current requirements for a large number of applications. The classifications are distinguished by a NEMA design letter (A, B, C, and D).

TABLE 4-3 Comparison of IEC (Metric) Motor Shaft Heights and NEMA Shaft Heights for Induction Motors

	IEC standard dimensions		Nearest equivalent NEMA dimensions	
Frame number	H, shaft height, mm	Equivalent inches	NEMA frame	D, shaft height, in
56	56	2.20		
63	63	2.48		
			42	2.62
71	71	2.80		
			48	3.00
80	80	3.15		
60	60	2.36		
			56	3.50
100	100	3.94		
112	112	4.41		
			180T	4.50
132	132	5.20		
			210T	5.25
160	160	6.30	250T	6.25
180	180	7.09	280T	7.00
200	200	7.87		
			320T	8.00
225	225	8.86		
			360T	9.00
250	250	9.84		
			400T	10.00
280	280	11.02	440T	11.00
315	315	12.40		
			500	12.50
355	355	13.98		
			580	14.50
400	400	15.75		

Single-phase motors also have NEMA design letters, but they do not specify the performance characteristics to the same extent that the three-phase design letter does. The letters N and O are used for FHP motors and L and M for IHP motors.

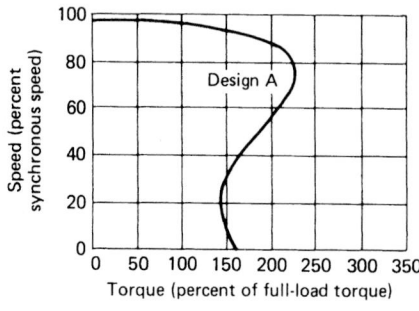

FIGURE 4-17 NEMA Design A.

Design A. NEMA design A motors are general-purpose motors with high starting (locked-rotor) currents and normal locked-rotor torques (Fig. 4-17). Slip is less than 5 percent, except for motors with 10 or more poles, which have a slightly greater slip. These motors are suitable in applications where load inertia is small and starts are infrequent. They are normally used where high breakdown torque (compared to NEMA design B motors) is required.

Design B. NEMA design B motors are general-purpose motors with normal starting torques and currents and relatively high breakdown torques (Fig. 4-18). Pull-up torque normally available allows rapid acceleration to full load speed. Slip is the same as design A. Design B motors are the most popular in industry. As

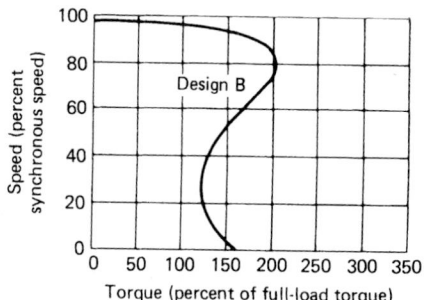

FIGURE 4-18   NEMA Design B.

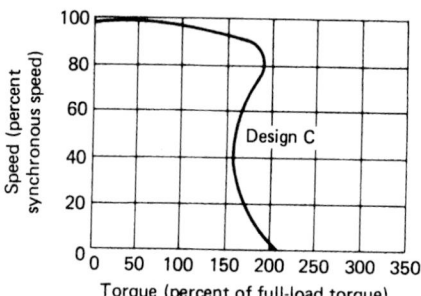

FIGURE 4-19   NEMA Design C.

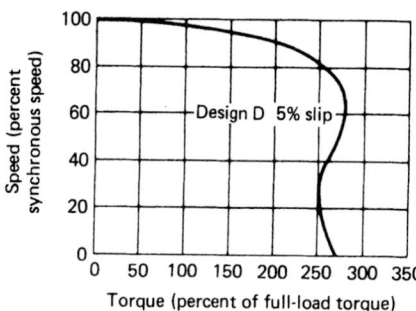

FIGURE 4-20   NEMA Design D.

the classification *general purpose* implies, the NEMA design B motors can be used to drive most loads such as pumps, fans, and conveyors.

Design C.   NEMA design C motors have high starting torques with normal starting currents (Fig. 4-19). Breakdown torques are normal, though slightly less than design B motors. Although slip is less than 5 percent, it is higher than the slip of a design B motor. These motors are typically used in applications where break-away loads are high and where starting torques higher than those available from design B motors are required. The motors have good running characteristics, although efficiency is somewhat poorer than that of design B motors.

Design D.   NEMA design D motors have very high starting torques, with moderate starting currents and high breakdown torques (Fig. 4-20). Slip is high, 5 percent or more at rated load. For design D motors with full-load slip in the 8 to 13 percent range, the maximum torque is usually at locked rotor and so does not exhibit a breakdown torque. Thus speed can fluctuate significantly with changing loads. For practicality these designs have been subdivided into several groups in terms of slip (5 to 8 percent, 8 to 13 percent, etc.). These motors are typically found in applications where heavy loads are suddenly applied or removed at frequent intervals.

Classifying by Environmental Protection and Cooling Methods

The two general NEMA classifications for motor enclosures are open (O) and totally enclosed (TE). An open machine is one having ventilating openings which permit passage of external cooling air over and around the windings of the motor. A totally enclosed machine is constructed so as to prevent the free exchange of air inside and outside the motor, but not sufficiently enclosed to be termed airtight. These enclosures are further designated by the degree of protection they provide (Table 4-4).

MOTOR RATINGS

The NEMA rating of a motor consists of the output of that machine along with any other characteristics assigned to it by the manufacturer. These characteristics include, but are not limited to speed, voltage, current, and service factor.

TABLE 4-4   Motor Enclosures

Types	Characteristics
	Open
Drip-proof (ODP)	Will not allow dripping liquids or solids to enter the motor when falling on the motor at an angle not greater than 15° from vertical.
Splash-proof	A splash-proof motor is similar to a drip-proof motor, except it is constructed to exclude liquids and solids falling on it any angle not more than 100° from the vertical.
Guarded	Motor openings are limited in size. Openings giving access to live or rotating parts do not permit the passage of a rod ¾ in (2 cm) in diameter and are at least 4 in (10 cm) away from those parts.
Semiguarded	Top half of the motor with limited-size openings as defined under Guarded type.
Externally ventilated	Motor cooled by air circulated by a separate motor-driven blower. Normally used on large low-speed motors where rotor fans cannot move sufficient air to properly cool the motor.
Pipe ventilated	Motor end shields are constructed to accept pipe or ducts to supply ventilating air. Air can be supplied from a source remote from the motor, if necessary, to supply clean air for cooling.
Weather protected, type 1	Ventilating passages minimize entrance of rain, snow, and airborne particles. Passages are less than ¾ in (2 cm) in diameter.
Weather protected, type 2	Motors have, in addition to type 1, passages to discharge high-velocity particles blown into the motor.
	Totally enclosed
Nonventilated (TENV)	Enclosed motor not equipped for cooling by external means.
Fan-cooled (TEFC)	Cooled by external integral fan mounted on the motor shaft.
Explosion-proof	Enclosed motor which withstands internal gas explosion and prevents ignition of external gas.
Dust-ignition-proof	Excludes ignitable amounts of dust and amounts of dust that would degrade performance.
Waterproof	Excludes liquids and airborne solids except around shaft.
Pipe-ventilated	Openings accept air inlet and/or exit ducts or pipe for air cooling.
Water-cooled	Cooled by circulating water.
Water–air-cooled	Cooled by water-cooled air.
Air-to-air cooled	Cooled by air-cooled air.
TEFC guarded	Fan cooled and guarded by limited-size openings.
There are two other classes of protection for both open and totally enclosed motors:	
Encapsulated windings	Machine having random windings filled with resin.
Sealed windings	Machine with form wound coils with windings and connections sealed against contaminants.

Voltage and Frequency

The standard voltages for FHP dc motors, universal motors, and 60-Hz, single-phase ac motors are 115 and 230 V. Three-phase ac motors at 60 Hz have standard voltages of 115 [15 hp (11 kW) and smaller], 230, 460, 575, 2300, 4000, 4600, and 6600 V.

Motors must operate successfully under running conditions within the limits specified for voltage and frequency variation by the NEMA operating-service conditions listed below. Successful operation within the variations specified, however, does not necessarily mean that the motor will be able to start and accelerate the load to which it is applied.

Service Conditions

Usual environmental service conditions are defined by NEMA as:

1. Ambient temperatures in the range of 32 to 105°F (0 to 40°C) or, when water cooling is used, in the range of 50 to 105°F (10 to 40°C).

2. Barometric pressure corresponding to an altitude not exceeding 3300 ft (1000 m)
3. Installation on a rigid mounting surface
4. Installation in areas or supplementary enclosures which do not seriously interfere with ventilation

Usual operating service conditions are:

1. Voltage variation up to 6 percent of rated voltage for universal motors and 10 percent of rated voltage for ac and dc motors.
2. Frequency variation not more than 5 percent above or below rated frequency.
3. Combined voltage and frequency variation not more than 10 percent above or below the rated voltage and frequency.
4. V-belt drive, flat-belt, chain, and gear drives, in accordance with NEMA standards.

Locked-Rotor kVA

Every ac motor (except three-phase wound-rotor types) rated $\frac{1}{20}$ hp and larger has a letter designation for locked-rotor kVA per horsepower (Table 4-5). It is calculated as follows:

TABLE 4-5   Locked-Rotor kVA/hp Code Designations

Code letter	Locked-rotor kVA/hp	Code letter	Locked-rotor kVA/hp
A	0–3.15	L	9.0–10.0
B	3.15–3.55	M	10.0–11.2
C	3.55–4.0	N	11.2–12.5
D	4.0 –4.5	P	12.5–14.0
E	4.5 –5.0	R	14.0–16.0
F	5.0 –5.6	S	16.0–18.0
G	5.6 –6.3	T	18.0–20.0
H	6.3 –7.1	U	20.0–22.4
J	7.1 –8.0	V	22.4 and up
K	8.0 –9.0		

$$\text{kVA/hp} = \frac{IE}{\text{hp} \times 1000} \quad \text{for single-phase motors}$$

$$\text{kVA/hp} = \frac{IE\sqrt{3}}{\text{hp} \times 1000} \quad \text{for three-phase motors}$$

where I is the locked-rotor amperage at rated voltage E.
For motors with dual ratings, the following rules determine the code letter to be used:

Motor type	Code letter corresponds to kVA/hp for
Multispeed	
Variable torque	Highest speed
Constant torque	Highest speed
Constant horsepower	Highest kVA/hp
Wye delta, starting on wye	Wye connection
Dual voltage	Highest kVA/hp
Dual frequency, 60/50 Hz	60-Hz kVA/hp
Part-winding start	Full-winding kVA/hp

TABLE 4-6 Service Factors

hp	3600	1800	1200	900	720	600	514	
			Synchronous speed, r/min					
1/20	1.4	1.4	1.4	1.4				
1/12	1.4	1.4	1.4	1.4				
1/8	1.4	1.4	1.4	1.4				
1/6	1.35	1.35	1.35	1.35				Fractional horsepower motors
1/4	1.35	1.35	1.35	1.35				
1/2	1.35	1.35	1.35	1.35				
1/2	1.25	1.25	1.25	1.15*				
3/4	1.25	1.25	1.15*	1.15*				
1	1.25	1.15*	1.15*	1.15*				
1/2–125	1.15*	1.15*	1.15*	1.15*	1.15*	1.15*	1.15*	Integral horsepower motors
150	1.15*	1.15*	1.15*	1.15*	1.15*	1.15*		
200	1.15*	1.15*	1.15*	1.15*	1.15*			

* In the case of three-phase squirrel-cage integral-horsepower motors, these service factors apply only to design A, B, and C motors.

Service Factor

NEMA service factor is a multiplier which indicates what percent higher than the nameplate horsepower can be accommodated continuously at rated voltage and frequency without injurious overheating (i.e., exceeding NEMA allowable temperature rise for given insulation systems). Service factors for general-purpose ac motors are shown in Table 4-6.

Level of Performance

NEMA also rates motors by level of performance, specifically horsepower, speed, torque, and locked-rotor current for each category of motor type and size. Tables specifying acceptable limits for each are too detailed to include here, but may be found in NEMA standard MG1-1993.

Temperature Rise

All standard motors unless otherwise stated are designed for use in a maximum ambient temperature of no greater than 104°F (40°C). The allowable temperature rise for the various enclosures and classes of insulation are shown in Table 4-7. For motors with a service factor of 1.15 or higher the temperature rise shall not exceed the values given in Table 4-7.

TABLE 4-7 Allowable Temperature Rise

Class of insulation	A	B	F	H
		Temperature, °C		
1. Windings—fractional horsepower motors				
a. Open motors other than those given in parts 1b and 1d	60	80	105	125
b. Open motors with 1.15 or higher service factor	70	90	115	
c. Totally enclosed nonventilated and fan-cooled motors, including variations	65	85	110	135
d. Any motor in a frame smaller than the 42 frame	65	85	110	135
2. Windings—integral horsepower motors				
a. Motors other than those given in parts 2b, 2c, 2d, and 2e	60	80	105	125
b. All motors with 1.15 or higher service factor	70	90	115	
c. Totally enclosed fan-cooled motors, including variations	60	80	105	125
d. Totally enclosed nonventilated motors, including variations	65	85	110	135
e. Encapsulated motors with 1.0 service factor, all enclosures	65	85	110	

Duty Rating

The duty or time rating of an electric motor is determined by the electrical design, the enclosure, the method of cooling, and the class of insulation system used. This rating is the length of time the motor may operate without causing overheating or reducing the normal life of the motor.

An intermittent duty motor is intended to operate for short periods of time totaling no more than 1 or 2 h/day. Motors with short-time ratings are designed to operate for no longer than the period shown on the nameplate. They must be shut off and allowed to cool to room temperature before being reactivated. Typical short-time duty ratings are 5, 15, 30, and/or 60 min. A motor with a continuous duty rating can be run indefinitely at rated load and voltage without injurious overheating or reduction in motor life.

Frame Designations and Assignments

The NEMA system for designating frame dimensions of motors consists of a series of numbers (frame number) in combination with letters. For convenience, manufacturers are allowed to use letters of the alphabet preceding the frame number for their own identification. However, such letters have no reference to the standards in Table 4-8 and vary in meaning from manufacturer to manufacturer.

The NEMA frame numbering system provides a useful relationship between motor horsepower and speed ratings and motor size. Although no such relationship currently exists for FHP motors, IHP motor horsepower and speed ratings and their assigned motor frames are supplied in MG13-1984 (Reaffirmed 1990).

APPLICATION AND SELECTION

Motor application begins by matching load requirements with motor characteristics. A correctly applied motor must be able to start the load, bring it up to operating speed, and run as long as necessary through all expected variations in the load.

The first step is determining the load characteristics to which the motor will be matched: power, torque, speed, and duty cycle. Starting torque, as well as running torque, must be considered. It may vary from a small percentage to a value several times the full-load torque. The greater the excess torque than that required to start the load, the more rapid the acceleration.

Power is the product of torque times speed. The term *load* usually refers to the horsepower required to drive a machine:

$$\text{Horsepower (hp)} = \frac{\text{torque} \times \text{r/min}}{5252}$$

Duty cycle (how much is asked from a motor how often and for how long) is the final parameter. The higher the duty cycle (i.e., horsepower load above rated and time of operation) at that load, the more care should be taken in the selecting the motor size.

Having established what load the motor must drive, the correct motor can be selected by considering the following factors. The speed-vs.-torque curve tells much about the performance characteristics of a motor (Fig. 4-21).

A standard general-purpose polyphase induction motor can be used when:

1. The momentary overload does not exceed 75 percent of the motor breakdown torque
2. The root-mean-square (rms) value of the motor losses over an extended period of time do not exceed the losses at the service factor rating of the motor
3. The duration of any overload does not raise the momentary peak temperature above a value safe for the motor's insulation system

TABLE 4-8   Frame Designations

FHP motors	

The following letters immediately follow the frame number and denote specific variations.

O	Face mounting
G	Gasoline-pump motors
H	A frame having an F dimension larger than that of the same frame without the suffix letter H
J	Jet-pump motors
K	Sump-pump motors
M	Oil-burner motors
N	Oil-burner motors
Y	Special mounting dimensions (consult manufacturer)
A	All mounting dimensions are standard except the shaft extension

IHP motors	

The following letters immediately follow the frame number and denote specific variations.

C	Face mounting on drive end (When the face mounting is at the end opposite the drive, the prefix F is used, making the suffix letters FC.)
CH	Face mounting dimensions different from those for the frame designation having the suffix letter C (The letters CH are considered to be one suffix and should not be separated.)
D	Flange mounting on drive end (When the flange mounting is at the end opposite the drive, the prefix F is used, making the suffix letters FD.)
E	Shaft extension dimensions for elevator motors in frames larger than the 326U frames
HP and HPH	Vertical solid-shaft motors having dimensions in accordance with MG1-18.625 (The letters HP and HPH are to be considered as one suffix and should not be separated.)
JM	Face-mounted close-coupled pump motor having antifriction bearings and dimensions in accordance with NEMA standards (The letters JM are to be considered as one suffix and should not be separated.)
JP	Face-mounted close-coupled pump motor having antifriction bearings and dimensions in accordance with NEMA standards (The letters JP are to be considered as one suffix and should not be separated.)
LP and LPH	Vertical solid-shaft motors having dimensions in accordance with NEMA standards (The letters LP and LPH are to be considered as one suffix and should not be separated.)
P and PH	Vertical solid-shaft motors having dimensions in accordance with NEMA standards
R	Drive-end tapered-shaft extension having dimensions in accordance with NEMA standards
S	Standard short shaft for direct connection
T	Included as part of a frame designation for which standard dimensions have been established
U	Previously used as part of a frame designation for which standard dimensions had been established
V	Vertical mounting only
VP	Vertical solid-shaft motors having dimensions in accordance with NEMA standards (The letters VP are to be considered as one suffix and should not be separated.)
X	Wound-rotor crane motors with double shaft extension.
Y	Special mounting dimensions (Consult manufacturer.)
Z	All mounting dimensions standard except the shaft extension(s) (Also used to designate machine with double shaft extension.)

Suffix letters are added to the frame number in the following sequence.

Suffix letters	Sequence
A	1
T, U, HP, HPH, JM, JP, LP, LPH, and VP	2
R and S	3
C, D, P, and PH	4
FC and FD	5
V	6
E, X, Y, and Z	7

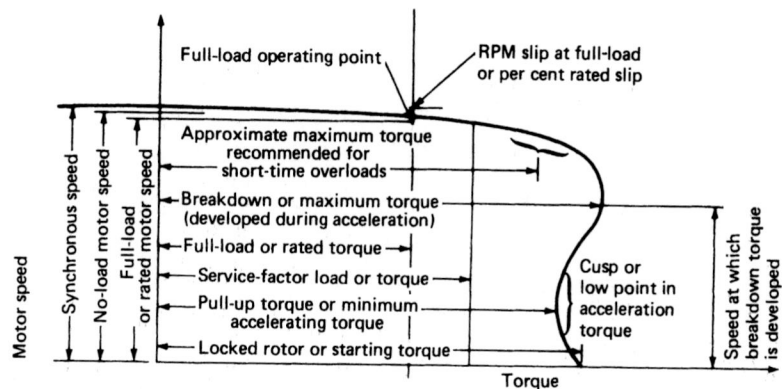

FIGURE 4-21 Speed-torque characteristics.

Power Supply

Power supply will be either single- or three-phase. A single-phase motor of the proper voltage can be used on a three-phase system if properly connected. But a three-phase motor cannot be used on single-phase supply. Three-phase motors generally cost less, perform better, and last longer than single-phase motors of the same size.

Voltage

Motor rating must match the nominal voltage and frequency of electricity supplied. Most motors are available in several standard voltages, but generally, the highest available voltage gives the lowest installation cost.

Horsepower

Mechanical power available at the motor shaft is the nominal horsepower rating at rated revolutions per minute. When installing a motor on new equipment, match the motor to the required horsepower computed when determining the load characteristics. When replacing a worn-out motor, review the application. Is the application overmotored? Could a lower horsepower rated motor be used? Many applications are overmotored as much as 50 percent. An energy efficient motor should be considered as the replacement if the horsepower load and operating hours justify it.

Type

Type of motor best suited to a particular application is a major question because of the wide variety of motor types available. Tables 4-9 and 4-10 provide some guidelines, the first one by motor characteristics, the second by application.

Coupling

If motor speed matches the input shaft speed, a simple mechanical coupling can be used. But if it turns at a speed different from that recommended or calculated for the equipment, a speed conversion drive is needed. It includes pulley and belt, gear, or chain and sprocket.

TABLE 4-9 Single-Phase Motors—Selection by Characteristics

Type	Horsepower ranges	Load-starting requirement	Starting current	Characteristics	Electrically reversible
Split-phase	$\frac{1}{20}$ to $\frac{1}{2}$	Easy	High	Small, inexpensive, simple construction; nearly constant speed	Yes
Capacitor-start	$\frac{1}{8}$ to 10	Hard	Medium	Simple construction, long service; nearly constant speed	Yes
Two-value capacitor	$\frac{1}{4}$ to 20	Hard	Medium	Simple construction, long service; nearly constant speed	Yes
Permanent-split capacitor	$\frac{1}{20}$ to 1	Easy	Low	Inexpensive, simple construction; speed reduced by lowering voltage	Yes
Shaded-pole	$\frac{1}{400}$ to $\frac{1}{2}$	Easy	Medium	Inexpensive for light duty	No
Wound-rotor (repulsion) types	$\frac{1}{8}$ to 10	Very hard	Low	Larger than other equivalent single-phase motors	No
Universal or series	$\frac{1}{150}$ to 2	Hard	High	High speed, small size; speed changes with load variations	Yes, some types
Synchronous	Very small fractional			Constant speed	

TABLE 4-10 Motor Selection by Application*

Application	Single-phase		Three-phase	
	Small, hp	Large, hp	Small, hp	Large, hp
Compressors				
Air	CS	CS,CP	B	B
Refrigeration	CS	CS,CP	B	C
Centrifugal	SP,CS	CS,CP	B	B
Reciprocating				
Loaded	CS	CS,CP	B	C
Unloaded	SP,CS	CS,CP	B	B
Conveyors and elevators				
Unloaded	CS,WR	CS,WR	B	B
Loaded	CS,WR	CS,WR	B	C
Cooling towers	CS	CS	B	B
Dryers	CS	CS,CP	B	B
Fans and blowers				
Centrifugal	SP,C	CS,CP	B	B
Propeller	SP,C,P	CS,CP	B	B
Unit heaters	SP,C,P	CS,CP	B	B
Machine tools				
Lathes	CS	CS	B	B
Milling machines	CS	CS	B	B
Drill presses	CS	CS	B	B
Grinders	CS	CS	B	B
Oil burners	SP	CS	B	B
Pumps				
Reciprocating	SP,CS	CS,CP,WR	B	B
Centrifugal	CP,CS	CS,CP,WR	B	B
Heavy oil	WR	CP,WR	B	D
Saws				
Metal, band saw	CS,U	CS	B	B
Wood, circular	CS,U	CS	B	B

* SP, split phase; CS, capacitor start; CP, two-value capacitor; C, permanent split capacitor; P, shaded pole; WR, wound rotor; U, universal; B, NEMA design B; C, NEMA design C; D, NEMA design D.

Enclosures

The drip-proof, general-purpose motor is suitable for dry, clean, and ventilated locations. Wet, dirty, or explosive conditions require other enclosures, such as totally enclosed fan-cooled or totally enclosed nonventilated motors in standard, severe duty, or explosion-proof construction. Table 4-11 matches enclosure to environment.

ADJUSTABLE SPEED SYSTEMS

The polyphase induction motor is basically a fixed-speed device, or at best a multiple-speed device with fixed speeds based on the stator winding configuration. The no-load or synchronous speed of the induction motor is

$$\text{Speed (synchronous)} = \frac{120 \times f}{p} \quad \text{r/min}$$

TABLE 4-11   Motor Enclosures

Condition or application	Drip-proof	Standard		Explosion-proof
		Totally enclosed	Severe-duty	
Atmospheric				
Dry	x	—	—	—
Humid	x*	—	—	—
Outdoor, mild	x*	—	—	—
Outdoor, severe	x*	x*	x	—
Chips				
Metal or plastic	—	x	x	—
Wood	x	x	x	—
Dust				
Abrasive, nonexplosive	—	x	x	—
Abrasive, explosive	—	—	—	x
Carbon, coal, or coke	—	—	—	x
Flour	—	—	—	x
Metal, nonexplosive	—	x	x	—
Metal, explosive	—	—	—	x
Sand	x	x	x	—
Sawdust	x	x	x	—
Textile fibers	—	x	—	—
Fumes				
Explosive	—	—	—	x
Nonexplosive	—	x	x	—
Corrosive	—	x*	x	—
Liquids				
Acid or alkali	—	x*	x	—
Dripping water	x*	—	—	—
Explosive	—	—	—	x
Nonexplosive	—	x	x	—
Paint	—	—	—	x
Petroleum, oil	—	—	—	x
Splashing water	x*	x*	x	—
Solvents				
Corrosive, nonexplosive	—	x*	x	—
Noncorrosive, nonexplosive	—	x	x	—
Noncorrosive, explosive	—	—	—	x

* Depending on concentration and/or severity, additional protection may be necessary.

where f = power input frequency, Hz, and p = number of magnetic poles in the motor stator winding.

The use of an adjustable frequency power supply (ac inverters) in conjuction with the induction motor results in an adjustable-speed drive system. The speed of the motor is adjusted by controlling the output frequency of the ac inverter. Thus the induction motor can be used on many adjustable-speed applications. The speed-torque motor performance at different input motor frequencies is illustrated by Fig. 4-22a. This permits the application of induction motor adjustable-speed systems to loads such as fans and pumps for flow control with considerable power savings over fixed-speed systems with dampers or valves for flow control. Figure 4-22b shows the performance of a 10-hp motor adjustable frequency system driving a fan load.

TROUBLESHOOTING

Table 4-12, a chart of motor problems and possible causes, can serve as a guide in identifying and correcting motor-system malfunctions.

ENERGY EFFICIENCY

Energy efficiency is a growing issue in the motor industry, and for good reasons. In addition to scarce energy resources, a great potential for energy conservation and reduced operating costs exists with the electric motor.

Today, energy efficient three-phase induction motors, both open and TEFC, are available in ratings from 1 to 500 hp (0.7 kW to 373 kW). In many locations the cost of electric power is high and energy-efficient motors can be justified on loads operating a high percentage of the time.

Factors to consider in the selection of energy efficient induction motors are:

1. Electric power cost savings and life-cycle cost comparison to standard motors
2. Improved ability to perform under adverse conditions such as abnormal voltage variations
3. Lower operating temperatures
4. Lower noise levels
5. Ability to accelerate higher inertia loads
6. Higher operating efficiencies at all load points

Efficiency and Power Factor

Motor efficiency is simply a measure of mechanical work output over electric power input. A motor's power factor is a measure of how well the motor uses the current it draws.

Total line current is made up of two components: real and reactive. Power factor is the ratio of *real power* to *apparent power,* or the cosine of the angle between the two. Technically, it is input kilowatts divided by the input kilovoltamperes.

Figure 4-23 shows efficiency and power factor as functions of loading for a typical small-integral horsepower polyphase motor. Efficiency is relatively stable over a wide range of loading conditions. But power factor drops off fast as the motor is unloaded—about a 15-percent spread between half- and full load. Proper application and sizing are thus important to maintain good power factor. A high power factor means that the motor requires less total

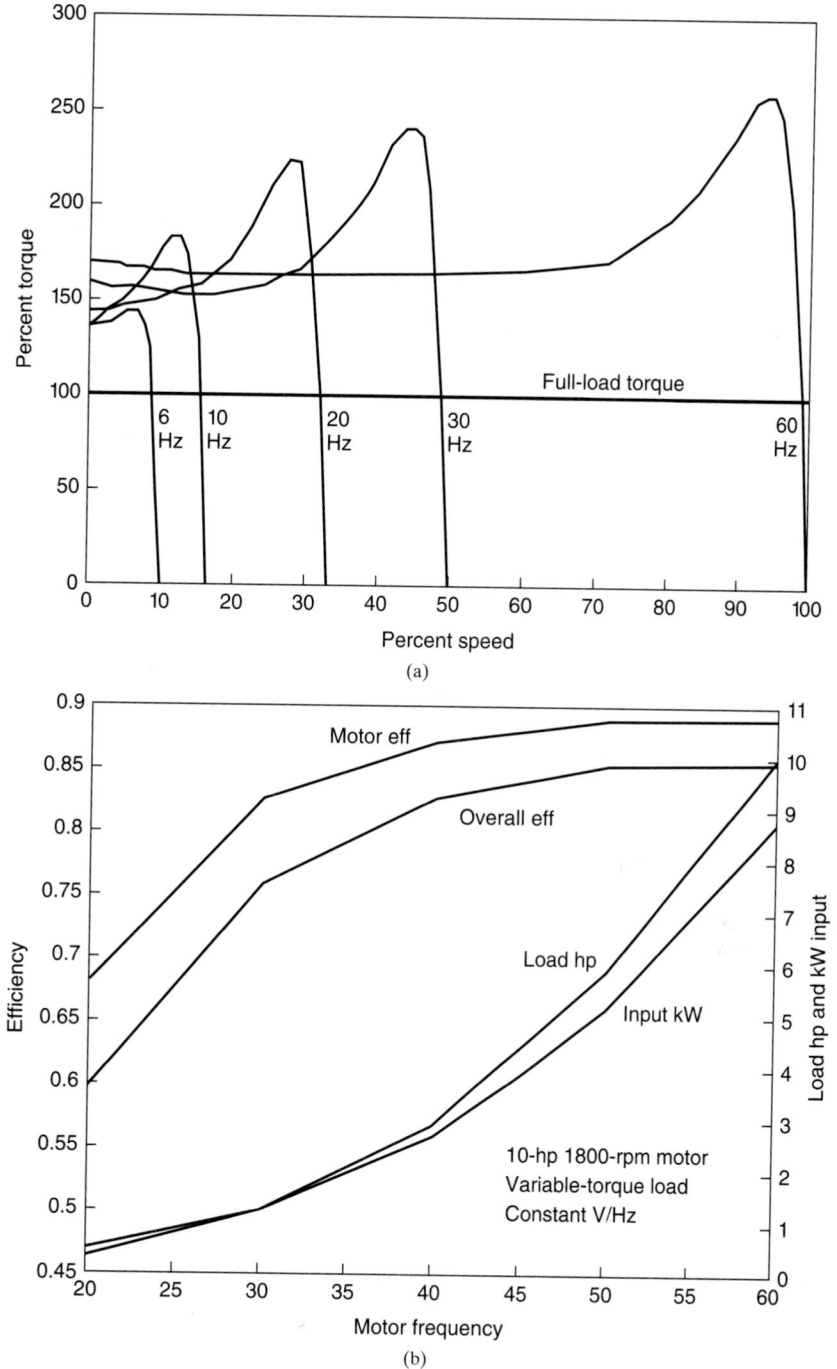

FIGURE 4-22   Induction motor adjustable frequency system. (*a*) Speed-torque curves. (*b*) Driving a fan load.

TABLE 4-12   Troubleshooting Guide

Trouble	Cause	What to do
Motor fails to start	Blown fuses	Replace with time-delay fuses matched to name-plate amperes. If motor has service factor greater than 1.0, use fuse size up to 12.5% of motor amperes. Check for grounded winding.
	Improper power supply	Check to see that power supplied (voltage-frequency phases) agrees with motor nameplate.
	Less than 208 V on a 208-V system	Use a 200-V motor.
	Low voltage	Inadequate wiring. Long or inadequate extension cords.
	Improper line connections	Check connections against diagram supplied with motor.
	Overload (thermal protector) tripped	Check and reset overload relay in starter. Check heater rating against motor nameplate current rating. Check motor load. If motor has a manual reset thermal protector, check whether tripped.
	Open circuit in winding or starting switch	Indicated by humming sound when switch is closed. Check for loose wiring connections, whether starting switch inside motor is closed, or if capacitor is defective.
	Mechanical failure	Check to see if motor and drive turn freely. Check belts, bearings, and lubrication.
	Short-circuited stator	Indicated by blown fuses and/or high no-load line current. Motor must be rewound or replaced.
	Poor stator coil connection	Repair or replace.
	Rotor defective	Look for broken bars or end rings.
	Motor may be overloaded	Reduce load; increase motor size.
	If three-phase, one phase may be open	Indicated by humming sound. Check lines for open phase. Check voltage with motor disconnected from line; one fuse may be blown.
	Defective capacitor	Check for short-circuited grounded, open or low value capacitor. Replace if necessary.
Motor stalls	Wrong application	Change type or size of motor. Consult motor service firm.
	Overloaded motor	Reduce load or increase motor size. Belt may be too tight.
	Low motor voltage	See that nameplate voltage is maintained.
Motor runs and then dies down	Power failure	Check for loose connections to line, to fuses, and to control. Check if thermal protector tripped, fuses blown, check overload relay, starter, and push-buttons.
Motor does not come up to speed	Not applied properly	Consult motor service firm for proper type and size of motor. Use larger motor.
	Voltage too low at motor terminals (because of line voltage drop or voltage drop in wiring to motor)	Use higher-voltage tap on transformer terminals; increase wire size.
	Starting load too high	Check load capability of motor.
	Shorted or weak capacitor	Replace capacitor.
	Low temperature (below 0°F)	Replace capacitor with one of higher value. Check ball bearing lubricant—use low-temperature grease.
	Broken rotor bars	Look for cracks near the end rings or broken rotor bars. A new rotor may be required as repairs are usually temporary.

TABLE 4-12   Troubleshooting Guide (*Continued*)

Trouble	Cause	What to do
Motor takes too long to accelerate	Excess loading; tight belts; high inertia load	Reduce load; increase motor size. Loosen belts.
	Inadequate wiring	Check for high resistance; increase wire size.
	Defective rotor	Replace with new rotor.
	Applied voltage too low	Check incoming voltage drop in wiring to motor. Power may have to supply higher voltage.
	Weak or shorted capacitor	Replace capacitor.
	Low starting torque	Replace with larger motor.
Motor overheats while running under load	Overload	Reduce load; increase motor size; belts may be too tight.
	Insufficient airflow over shell of "air-over" motor	Modify installation or change to a self-cooled motor.
	May be clogged with dirt to prevent proper ventilation of motor.	Good ventilation is apparent when a continuous stream of air leaves the motor. If it does not after cleaning, check with manufacturer.
	Motor may have one phase open (three-phase motors)	Check to make sure that all leads are well-connected and a fuse is now blown in one line.
	Grounded or shorted coil	Repair or replace the motor.
	Unbalanced terminal voltage (three-phase motors)	Check for faulty leads, connections, and transformers. Excessive single-phase loads on one circuit.
	Faulty connection	Clean, tighten, or replace.
	High or low voltage	Check voltage at motor with voltmeter; should not be more than 10% above or below rated.
	Rotor rubs stator bore	If not poor machining, replace worn bearings.
Motor vibrates after corrections have been made	Motor misaligned	Realign.
	Coupling out of balance	Balance coupling.
	Driven equipment unbalanced	Rebalance driven equipment.
	Defective ball bearing	Replace bearing.
	Balancing weights shifted	Rebalance rotor.
	Polyphase motor running single phase	Check for open circuit or blown fuses.
	Excessive end play	Adjust bearing or add shims to eliminate excess end play.
	High voltage	Correct.
Unbalanced line current on polyphase motors during normal operation	Unequal terminal volts	Check leads and connections. Check transformers.
	Single-phase operation	Check for open contacts, blown fuses.
	Unbalanced supply	Check line-to-line voltage.
Scraping noise	Fan rubbing air shield	Repair.
	Fan striking insulation	Repair.
	Bent shaft	Straighten shaft or replace rotor.
Noisy operation	Air gap not uniform	Check and correct end shield fits or bearing.
	Rotor unbalance	Rebalance.
	High voltage	Reduce line voltage by changing power taps.
Hot bearings, general	Loose on mounting surface	Tighten holding bolts.
	Bent shaft	Straighten or replace shaft or rotor.
	Excessive belt pull	Decrease belt tension.
	Pulleys too far away from bearing nose	Move pulley closer to motor bearing.
	Pulley diameter too small; slipping	Use larger pulleys (both motor and load). Check belt tension.
	Misalignment	Correct by realignment of drive.
Hot bearings, sleeve	Oil grooving in bearing obstructed by dirt	Remove end shield, clean bearing housing, and oil grooves; renew oil.

TABLE 4-12   Troubleshooting Guide (*Continued*)

Trouble	Cause	What to do
	Oil too heavy	Use recommended oil.
	Oil too light	Use recommended oil.
	Too much end thrust	Reduce thrust induced by drive, or supply external means to carry thrust.
	Dry bearing	Add oil.
	Badly worn bearing	Replace bearing.
	Feeder wick not touching shaft	Repair or replace wicking.
Hot bearings, ball	Insufficient grease	Maintain proper quality of grease in bearing. Replace sealed bearing.
	Deterioration of grease or lubricant	Remove old grease, wash bearings thoroughly in clean kerosene, and replace with new grease.
	Contaminated water in bearing	Replace bearing if sealed type. Eliminate source of moisture.
	Excess lubricant	Reduce quantity of grease. Bearing should not be more than ½ filled.
	Overloaded bearing	Check alignment, side, and end thrust.
	Broken ball or rough races	Replace bearing. First clean end shield housing thoroughly.

current, and the resulting lower line current means that less energy is wasted in all feeder circuits serving the motor.

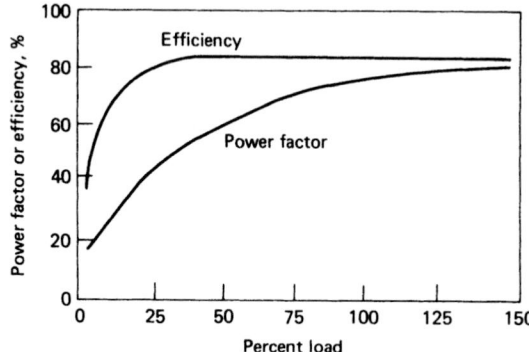

FIGURE 4-23   Efficiency and power factor vs. load.

Any inefficiency in the process of converting electric into mechanical energy occurs as heat, often referred to as watt losses, or simply losses.

To increase efficiency, it is necessary to minimize these losses. The rotors of energy-efficient motors are built with additional aluminum to reduce losses resulting from current flowing in the aluminum rotor bars. Additional copper is used in the stators to reduce losses in the motor. Most motors have 100 percent copper stator windings: few are aluminum-wire-wound. More steel, together with special processing, is also used in the motors to reduce the stator and rotor losses. This specially processed steel includes thinner laminations as well as silicon electric steels.

Windings in the most energy-efficient motors are designed for optimum winding distribution. The air gap is also optimized for the best power factor and efficiency performance. Stator and rotor slots are usually designed for optimum performance and are not compromised to serve other uses.

Table 4-13 compares the nominal full-load efficiencies of standard motors and energy-efficient motors for both open and TEFC 1800 r/min motors. Energy-efficient induction motors carry a premium price over standard motors. However, based on the cost of electric power and annual operating hours, this premium price is often paid back in a matter of months. The simplest payback formula for energy efficient motors is

$$\text{Payback (months)} = \frac{\text{price premium (dollars)}}{\text{kW saved} \times \text{cost per kWh} \times \text{annual running time (h)}} \times 12$$

There are other, more detailed, payback formulas available based on life cycle costing; however, the above formula is adequate when the payback is 2 years or less.

Table 4-14 has been developed to illustrate the energy cost savings for open 1800 r/min energy efficient motors. This table can be used as a guide by adjusting the electric power costs and operating hours to suit your installation.

BIBLIOGRAPHY

Alger, Philip L.: *Induction Machines,* 2d ed., Gordon Breach, New York, 1970.

Andreas, John C.: *Energy Efficient Electric Motors,* 2d ed., Marcel Dekker, New York, 1992.

Bodine, Clay: *Small Motor, Gearmotor and Control Handbook,* 4th ed., Bodine Electric Co., Chicago, 1978.

Bose, B. K.: *Adjustable Speed AC Drive Systems,* IEEE Press, Piscataway, N.J., 1981.

Cochran, Paul L.: *Polyphase Induction Motors,* Marcel Dekker, New York, 1989.

Fitzgerald, A. E., C. Kingsley, and S. D. Umans: *Electric Machinery,* 4th ed., McGraw-Hill, New York, 1983.

TABLE 4-13   Nominal Efficiency of Energy-Efficient Motors vs. Industry Average Standard Motors, 1800 r/min*

	Open motors		TEFC motors	
Motor hp	Standard motor	Energy-efficient motor	Standard motor	Energy-efficient motor
2	79.1	84.2	81.0	85.1
3	80.9	86.8	81.3	87.7
5	82.5	87.7	83.6	88.3
7.5	84.5	89.8	85.2	90.1
10	85.4	90.6	86.6	90.7
15	86.8	91.7	87.0	92.2
20	87.5	92.2	88.0	92.6
25	88.9	92.6	88.9	93.2
30	89.6	93.0	89.8	93.4
40	90.3	93.9	90.7	93.8
50	90.9	94.1	91.4	94.0
60	91.3	94.3	91.4	94.5
75	91.6	94.8	92.0	94.9
100	92.0	95.1	92.0	94.8
125	92.6	95.0	92.1	95.1
150	92.2	95.3	92.9	95.3
200	92.8	95.5	93.8	95.8
250	93.0	95.8	93.9	95.8
300	93.0	95.8		

* At full load.

TABLE 4-14   Annual Energy Savings in Dollars for Open, 1800-r/min Drip-Proof Motors*

hp	Standard motor efficiency, %	Energy-efficient motor efficiency, %	Annual kWh saving	Annual dollar saving
2	79.09	84.23	461	28
3	80.90	86.83	756	45
5	82.47	87.70	1,079	65
7.5	84.50	89.79	1,560	94
10	85.37	90.56	2,003	120
15	86.80	91.72	2,766	166
20	87.51	92.16	3,438	206
25	88.86	92.64	3,428	206
30	89.60	92.98	3,632	218
40	90.26	93.88	5,103	306
50	90.89	94.08	5,574	334
60	91.31	94.34	6,288	377
75	91.64	94.80	8,133	488
100	91.97	95.12	10,740	644
125	92.57	95.00	10,301	618
150	92.18	95.25	15,633	938
200	92.75	95.50	18,529	1,112
250	93.00	95.80	23,445	1,407
300	93.00	95.80	28,134	1,688

* Based on 6 cents/kWh power cost and 4000 h/year operation.

Lloyd, T. C.: *Electric Motors and Their Applications,* Wiley-Interscience, New York, 1969.

NEMA Standards Publication MG1-1993, *Motors and Generators,* National Electrical Manufacturers Association, Washington, D.C., 1993.

NEMA Standards Publication MG13-1984 (Reaffirmed 1990), *Frame Assignments for Alternating-Current Medium Induction Motors,* National Electrical Manufacturers Association, Washington, D.C., 1984.

Veinott, C. G.: *Theory and Design of Small Induction Motors,* McGraw-Hill, New York, 1959.

Wildi, Theodore: *Units and Conversion Charts,* IEEE Press, Piscataway, N.J., 1991.

ACKNOWLEDGMENTS

The following publications are acknowledged as partial sources for this section.

Form 5S1248, "Answers to Common Electric Motor Problems," Dayton Electric Manufacturing Company, Chicago.

Machine Design, Electrical and Electronics Reference Issue, sec. 7, "Motors," May 17, 1979, pp. 7–42.

NEMA Standards Publication MG1-1993, *Motors and Generators,* National Electrical Manufacturers Association. Washington, D.C., 1993.

NEMA Standards Publication MG13-1984 (Reaffirmed 1990), *Frame Assignments for Alternating-Current Medium Induction Motors,* National Electrical Manufacturers Association, Washington, D.C., 1984.

CHAPTER 3-4
MOTORS AND MOTOR CONTROLS

PART 2

MOTOR CONTROLS

James R. Wright, P.E.
Manager of Codes and Standards

R. J. Batey, K. R. Horr, D. K. Hubbard, L. Johnson, R. Labak, J. R. Shaffer, and R. Stone
Furnas Electric Co.
Batavia, Illinois

GLOSSARY

Definitions essential to an understanding of ac and dc motor control are provided. Most definitions are in accordance with National Electrical Manufacturers Association (NEMA) and American National Standards Institute (ANSI).

Accelerating relay   A relay used to aid in motor starting or accelerating from one speed to another. It may function by: current-limit (armature-current) acceleration; counter-emf (armature-voltage) acceleration; or definite-time acceleration.

Across-line starting   A method that connects the motor directly to the supply line on starting.

Actuator   The cam, arm, or similar mechanical piece used to actuate a device.

Ambient conditions   Conditions of the atmosphere adjacent to the electric apparatus. The specific reference may apply to temperature, contamination, humidity, etc.

Antiplugging protection   A control function that prevents application of counter-torque until the motor speed has been reduced to an acceptable value.

Brake   An electromechanical friction device employed to stop and hold a load. When the brake is set, a spring pulls the braking surface into contact with a braking wheel which is directly coupled to the motor shaft.

Branch circuit   The portion of a wiring system extending beyond the final overcurrent device protecting the circuit.

Blowout coil   Electromagnetic coil used in contactors and starters to deflect an arc when a circuit is interrupted.

Circuit breaker   A device designed to open and close a circuit by nonautomatic means and to open the circuit automatically at a predetermined overload of current without injury to itself when properly applied within its rating (ampere-, volt-, and horsepower-rated).

Closed-circuit transition (as applied to reduced-voltage controllers)   A method of motor starting in which power to the motor is not interrupted during the normal starting sequence.

Combination starter   A magnetic starter having a manually operated disconnecting means built into the same enclosure. The disconnect may be a motor-circuit switch (with or without fuses) or a circuit breaker.

Contactor   A device for repeatedly establishing and interrupting an electric power circuit. Definite-purpose contractors are those designed for specific applications such as air-conditioning, heating, and refrigeration equipment control.

Controller service   The specific application of the controller. General purpose: standard or usual service. Definite purpose: specific application other than usual.

Control, three-wire   Control function incorporating a momentary contact pilot device and a holding circuit contact to provide undervoltage protection.

Control, two-wire   Control function utilizing a maintained contact pilot device to provide undervoltage release.

Controller   A device, or group of devices, that governs in a predetermined manner the electric power delivered to the apparatus to which it is connected.

Controller function   To regulate, accelerate, decelerate, start, stop, reverse, or protect devices connected to an electric controller.

Controller, drum   A manual switching device having stationary contacts connected to a circuit by the rotation of a group of movable contacts.

Current-responsive protector   Devices that include time-lag fuses, magnetic relays, and thermal relays (normally located in the motor or between the motor and controller) that provide a degree of protection to the motor, motor control apparatus and branch-circuit conductors from overloads or failures to start.

Dash pot   Device employed to create a time delay. It consists of a piston moving inside a cylinder filled with a liquid or gas which is allowed to escape through a small orifice in the piston. Moving contacts actuated by the piston close the electric circuit.

Drop-out (voltage or current)   The voltage or current at which a device will return to its de-energized position.

Duty   Specific controller functions. Continuous: constant load, indefinitely long time period. Short time: constant load, short or specified time period. Intermittent: varying load, alternate intervals, specified time periods. Periodic: intermittent duty with recurring load conditions. Varying: varying loads, varying time intervals, wide variations.

Dynamic braking   The process of disconnecting the armature from the power source and either short-circuiting it or adding a current-limiting resistor across the armature terminals while the field coils remain energized.

Electromechanical   Term applied to any device which uses electric energy to magnetically cause mechanical movement.

Electronic control   Term applied to define electronic, static, precision, and associated electronic control equipment.

Electronic protector   A monitoring system in which current in the motor leads is sensed and the thermal characteristic of the motor reproduced during both heating and cooling cycles. Other circuits compensate for copper and iron losses and detect a lost phase.

Electropneumatic controller   An electric controller having its basic functions performed by air pressure.

Faceplate controller   Controller having multiple switching contacts mounted near a selector arm on the front of an insulated plate. Additional resistors are mounted on the rear to form a complete unit.

Feeder   The circuit conductors between the service equipment and the branch-circuit overcurrent device.

Float switch   A switch responsive to the level of liquid.

Foot switch   A switch designed for operation by an operator's foot.

Frequency   The number of complete variations made by an alternating current per second, expressed in hertz.

Fuse   An overcurrent protective device with a circuit-opening fusible member that is severed by the heat developed from the passage of overcurrent through it.

Field weakening   A method of increasing the speed of a wound field motor by reducing field current to reduce field strength.

Instantaneous   A qualified term applied to the closing of a circuit in which no delay is purposely introduced.

Interlock   An electric or mechanical device, actuated by an external source, and used to govern the operation of another device.

Interrupting capacity   The highest current at rated voltage that a device can interrupt.

Inverse time   A qualifying term indicating that a delayed action has been introduced. This delay decreases as the operating force increases.

Jogging (inching)   The intermittent operation of a motor at low speeds. Speed may be limited by armature series resistance or reduced armature voltage.

Latching relay   Relay that can be mechanically latched in a given position when operated by one element and released manually or by the operation of a second element.

Limit switch   A device that translates a mechanical motion or a physical position into an electric control signal.

Locked-rotor current   Steady-state current taken from the line with the rotor locked and with rated voltage (rated frequency in the case of ac motors) applied to the motor.

Locked-rotor torque   The minimum torque a motor will develop at rest for all angular positions of the rotor with rated voltage applied at the rated frequency.

Low-voltage protection (magnetic control only)   The opening of the motor circuit by the controller upon a reduction or loss of voltage. Manual restarting is required when the voltage is restored.

Low-voltage release (magnetic control only)   The effect of a device, operative on the reduction or failure of voltage, to cause the interruption of power supply to the equipment, but not preventing the re-establishment of the power supply on return of voltage.

Microprocessor controller   Motor controller that utilizes feedback control and a computer complete with processor, memory, I/O, keyboard, and display.

Motor circuit switch   A switch, rated in horsepower, capable of interrupting maximum operating overload current of a motor of the same horsepower rating at rated voltage.

Motor control circuit   The circuit that carries the electric signals directing controller performance but does not carry the main power current. Control circuits tapped from the load side of motor branch circuits' short-circuit protective devices are not considered to be branch circuits and are permitted to be protected by either supplementary or branch-circuit overcurrent protective devices.

Nonreversing   A control function that provides for motor operation in one direction only.

Normally open or closed   Terms used to signify the position of a device's contacts when the operating magnet is de-energized (applies only to nonlatching-type devices).

Off-delay timer   A device whose output is discontinued following a preset time delay after the input is de-energized.

Open-circuit transition   A method of reduced-voltage starting in which power to the motor is interrupted during normal starting sequence.

Operating overload   The overcurrent to which electric apparatus is subjected in the course of normal operating conditions that it may encounter. *Note:* Maximum operating overload is considered to be 6 times normal full-load current for ac industrial motors and control apparatus and 4 to 10 times normal full-load current, respectively, for dc industrial motors and control apparatus used for reduced- or full-voltage starting. It should be understood that these overloads are currents that may persist for a very short time only, usually a matter of seconds.

Operator's control (push button) station   A unitized assembly of one or more externally operable push button switches, sometimes including other pilot devices.

Overcurrent   Any current in excess of equipment or conductor rating. It may result from overload, short circuits, or ground faults.

Overload   Operation of equipment in excess of normal full-load rating. A fault such as a short circuit or ground fault is not an overload.

Phase-failure protection   Protection provided when power fails in one wire of a polyphase circuit to cause and maintain the interruption of power in all wires of the circuit.

Phase-lock servo   A digital control system in which the output of an optical tachometer is compared to a reference square wave to generate a system error signal proportional to both shaft velocity and position.

Phase-reversal protection   The prevention of motor energizing under conditions of phase sequence reversal in a polyphase circuit.

Pilot device   A low-current status indicating or initiating device such as a pilot light, push button, and limit or float switch.

Plugging   Motor braking by reversal of the line voltage or phase sequence in order to develop a counter-torque which exerts a retarding force.

Programmed control   A control system in which operations are directed by a predetermined input program consisting of cards, tape, plug boards, cams, etc.

Proximity switch   A device that reacts to the presence of an actuating means without physical contact or connection.

Pull-up torque (ac motors)   The minimum torque developed by the motor during the period of acceleration from rest to the speed at which breakdown occurs.

Push button   A master switch having a manually operable plunger or button for actuating the switch.

Rating, continuous   The substantially constant load that can be carried for an indefinite time.

Rating of a controller   Designation of operating limits based on power governed and the duty and service required.

Rating, eight-hour   The rating of a magnetic contactor based on its current-carrying capacity for 8 h without exceeding established limitations. Rating considerations include new, clean contact surfaces, free ventilation, and full-rated voltage on the operating coil.

Rating, make or break   The value of current for which a contact assembly is rated for closing or opening a circuit repeatedly under specified operating conditions.

Reactor, saturable   An inductor having the means to change the degree of magnetic saturation of its core(s) to control the magnitude of alternating current supplied to a load.

Regenerative braking   In ac motors, it results from the motor's inherent tendency (through a negative slip) to resist being driven above synchronous speed by an overhauling load. In shunt-wound dc motors, it occurs when driven by an overhauling load, when shunt field strength is increased, or when armature voltage is decreased (in adjustable-voltage drives).

Relay   A device operated by a variation in the conditions in one electric circuit to effect the operation of other devices in the same or other circuits. Examples include: current, latching, magnetic control, magnetic overload, open-phase, low or undervoltage, and overload.

Reset   A manual or automatic operation that restores a mechanism or device to its prescribed state.

Resistance starting   A form of reduced-voltage starting employing resistances that are short-circuited in one or more steps to complete the starting cycle.

Reversing   Changing the operation of a drive from one direction to the other.

Rod-and-tube (rate-of-rise) sensor   A thermostat consisting of an external metal tube and an internal metal rod that operates as a differential-expansion element. This element actuates a self-contained snap switch.

Service of a controller   The specific application in which the controller is to be used—either general-purpose or definite-purpose (crane and hoist, elevator, machine tool, etc.).

Starter   An electric controller for accelerating a motor from rest to normal speed. *Note:* A device designed for starting a motor in either direction includes the additional function of reversing and should be designated a reversing controller.

Starting, slow-speed A control function that provides for starting an electric drive only at the minimum speed setting.

Static control A system that may contain electronic components that do not depend on electronic conduction in a vacuum or gas. The electrical function is performed by semiconductors or the use of otherwise completely static components such as resistors, capacitors, etc.

Static controller A controller in which the major portion of all of the basic functions are performed through the control of electric or magnetic phenomena in solids such as transistors, etc.

Synchronous motor controller A controller consisting of a three-pole starter for the ac stator circuit, a contactor for the dc field circuit, an automatic synchronizing device to control the dc field contactor, and a cage-winding protective relay to open the ac circuit without synchronizing, in order to start a synchronous motor, accelerate it to synchronous speed, and synchronize it to supply frequency.

Switch A device for making, breaking, or changing the connections in an electric circuit. In controller practice, a switch is considered to be a device operated by other than magnetic means.

Switch selector A manually operated multiposition switch for selecting alternative control circuits.

Temperature-responsive protector A protective device for assembly as an integral part of a motor that provides a degree of protection to the motor against dangerous overheating due to overload and failure to start.

Test, dielectric The application of a voltage higher than the rated voltage for a specified time to determine the adequacy of insulating materials and spacings against breakdown under normal conditions.

Tests, application Tests performed by a manufacturer to determine those operating characteristics not necessarily established by standards but which have application interest.

Thermal cutout An overcurrent protective device that contains a heater element and renewable fusible member which open the motor circuit. It is not designed to interrupt short-circuit currents.

Thermistors Devices that sense temperature through changes in resistance. Signals from a thermistor may be amplified to interrupt the contactor holding coil to provide a degree of protection against motor locked-rotor conditions and running overloads.

Threading Signifies low-speed operation similar to jogging, but for longer periods with interlocked control.

Time, accelerating The time to change from one specified speed to a higher or lower speed while operating under specified conditions.

Time delay A time interval purposely introduced into the performance of a function.

Time response An output, expressed as a function of time, resulting from the application of a specified input under specified operating conditions.

Torque A turning or twisting force that tends to produce rotation.

CONTROL OF AC MOTORS

The control of an ac motor includes motor starting and stopping; governing the motor speed, torque, horsepower, and other characteristics; and protecting personnel and equipment.

Types of AC Motor Starters

Motor starters can be divided into three basic types (manual, magnetic, and electronic operation) and three categories (full voltage/across the line, reduced voltage, and multispeed).

Starters consist of a contactor to switch the electrical load and an overload relay which provides protection for the motor.

Control Selection Considerations

The selection of a specific motor control system also requires the consideration of a number of factors. Depending on the particular type, size, and application of the motor to be controlled and the particular characteristics of the driven load, motor control selection may be simple or complex.

Special Considerations.   Selection of the proper motor control system also involves several other key factors. These include: operator-vs.-automatic machine starting, expected starting requirements, continuous or intermittent machine operation, and special functions, if any, required during operation.

Separate from these special functions are requirements that specify the need to reverse direction or stop the motor, and the types and number of protective devices necessary to assure proper and continued operation.

Manual Motor Starters

Manual starters are typically used on small motors in applications requiring infrequent starting. In general, comments applying to magnetic controls also pertain to manual motor controls.

Full-Voltage Starting.   Full-voltage manual starters and contactors provide direct control for applications not requiring remote control and which permit automatic restarting.

Fractional-Horsepower Starting.   The simplest type of manual starting switch is the one- or two-pole fractional-horsepower toggle switch consisting of an ON-OFF snap-action mechanism. This method is generally applied to single-phase motors with ratings up to a maximum of 1 hp (0.75 kW) at 120 or 240 V, where only infrequent starting and stopping are required.

Magnetic Motor Starters

Three-Phase Magnetic Starting.   Three-phase magnetic starters are designed for full-voltage starting of squirrel-cage induction motors when full starting torque and current surge are permitted. They are also used for primary circuit control for wound-rotor (slip-ring) motors that have provision for manual starting and speed control in their secondary circuits.

Wound-Rotor Controls.   To control starting, accelerating, and regulation, a variable resistance is added to the rotor circuit. Full rotor resistance is used during motor starting. As the motor begins to accelerate, the resistance is reduced in steps. When the motor is connected to full line voltage (all resistance shorted out), it acts as a squirrel-cage motor.

The basic control circuit consists of a full-voltage starter and a balanced, adjustable three-phase resistor, wye-connected in the rotor circuit. Speed can be established for a given load by adjusting rotor resistance; once set, speed will vary with load conditions.

A static controller may be used to control the operating speeds of wound-rotor motors. In one method, a controlled saturable reactor is placed in the rotor circuit with the accelerating resistance. For fixed operating speeds, reactor saturation (which controls the motor speed) can be varied using a control resistor. Static controllers can also be used to reverse the direction of motor rotation by placing saturable reactors in the motor primary circuit rather than reversing contactors. Controlled reactor saturation directs the reversal of the motor rotation.

Synchronous Motor Starting.   This method is used for power-factor correction of heavy concentrations of induction motors. It is also used for constant-speed, slow-speed industrial drive applications and for maximum efficiency on continuous heavy loads in excess of 75 hp (55 kW). Three-phase ac power is connected to the stator and dc to the rotor (which has both a field and a squirrel-cage winding).

A full-voltage magnetic contactor connects the ac motor winding to the line, and the rotor winding is closed through a starting and discharge resistor. The motor starts and comes up to speed like a squirrel-cage motor. At the correct rotor speed, a polarized-field frequency relay and reactor automatically apply dc excitation to the field to synchronize the motor with maximum synchronizing torque, while drawing minimum line current.

Speed-Torque Characteristics.   Three-phase ac motors are designed to operate at speeds directly proportional to the frequency of the voltage applied to the stator field. However, while the motor's synchronous speed is directly proportional to the applied frequency, it is inversely proportional to the number of motor poles.

Since induction motors rely on rotor bars or windings to cut the flux of the rotating field to turn the rotor, they will operate at a speed slightly less than synchronous speed.

In constant-horsepower designs, output torque can vary inversely with motor speed. For applications requiring constant output torque, however, the air-gap flux must be held constant over the entire speed range of the motor.

Types of Motor Starters

Starters are rated or commonly described as being one of three types. These are traditional NEMA, definite purpose, and International Electrotechnical Commission (IEC) starters. Definite-purpose contactors and starters are an original equipment manufacturer (OEM) component found primarily in heating, ventilating, and air conditioning (HVAC), refrigeration, computer and power supply applications (Fig. 4-24). The plant engineer will ordinarily only come into contact with these devices on a repair or replacement basis. These contactors and starters are rated for motor loads in full-load and locked-rotor amperes and in amperes for resistive loads such as electric heating.

Some Basic Differences.   The primary difference between IEC and traditional NEMA starters is one of concept. A 10-hp (7.5-kW) NEMA starter can be used in virtually any 10-hp (7.5-kW) motor application. This is not the case for IEC control, which must be derated for difficult applications.

Not all applications require a heavy-duty industrial starter (NEMA type). In applications where space is limited and minimum maintenance required, IEC devices represent a very cost-effective solution.

IEC Starter Ratings.   Utilization categories are used with IEC devices to define the typical duty cycle for a starter or contactor. The IEC utilization categories are:

AC1   Noninductive or slightly inductive loads

AC2   Starting of slip-ring motors

AC3   Starting of squirrel-cage motors and switching off only after the motor is up to speed [make at load running amperes (LRA), break at full-load amperes (FLA)]

AC4   Starting of squirrel-cage motors with inching and plugging duty; rapid start/stop (make and break at LRA)

AC11   Auxiliary (control) circuits

NEMA Starter Ratings.   NEMA-type starters are rated for motor loads as shown on the NEMA ratings chart, Table 4-15. Some manufacturers also supply custom or motor-matched sizes which do not have standardized ratings, but may offer an economical alternative to the user.

(a)   (b)   (c)

FIGURE 4-24 (*a*) Typical definite-purpose starter. (*b*) Typical NEMA starter. (*c*) Typical IEC starter. (*Furnas Electric Co.*)

Maximum-Horsepower Plugging and Jogging. The starters must be derated for applications requiring repeated interruptions of stalled motor current or repeated closing of high transient currents encountered in rapid motor reversal, involving more than five openings or closings per minute and more than 10 in a 10-min period, such as plug stop, plug reverse, or jogging duty.

Ballast-Type, Tungsten, and Other Discharge-Type Lighting Loads. Contactors may also be used for controlling tungsten and other discharge-type lighting loads. Contactors are specifically designed for such loads and are applied at their full rating.

TABLE 4-15 Motor Starter Sizes

Single-phase horsepower		Three-phase horsepower			
115 V	230 V	200 V	230 V	460–575 V	Starter size*
⅓	1	1½	1½	2	00
1	2	3	3	5	0
2	3	7½	7½	10	1
3	5	10	10	15	1P, 1¾
3	7½	10	15	25	2
		15	20	30	2½
		25	30	50	3
		30	40	75	3½
		40	50	100	4
		50	75	150	4½
		75	100	200	5
		150	200	400	6

* NEMA Standard and custom sizes included.

Resistance Heating Loads.   Contactors may be employed to switch a load at the utilization voltage of a resistance heat-producing element with a duty which requires continuous operation of not more than five openings per minute.

Reduced-Voltage Starters (Electromechanical)

Unless prohibited by local utility restrictions, any size ac motor operating at any voltage can be started at full voltage. In actual application, however, when full voltage is applied to the motor terminals, its locked-rotor current may range anywhere from 6 to 10 times the value of normal running current. By design, this current may not harm the motor; however, it may damage the driven load because of the motor's high starting torque. Starters include overload relays which help provide protection to motor windings from harmful currents and resultant temperature rise that may be caused by overloading the motor, sustained low line voltage, or stalled rotor conditions.

Under these conditions, the application of a reduced-voltage starter could eliminate such potential problems.

Definition.   A reduced-voltage starter reduces inrush line current and/or starting torque to a polyphase squirrel-cage motor in one of three ways:

1. It reduces voltage applied to the motor during starting.
2. It uses only part of the motor windings during starting.
3. It changes motor winding connections.

Reduced-voltage starters are used when limitations exist for the amount of current that can be drawn from the electrical service.

The starting torque developed by the associated driven equipment is also reduced when a reduced-voltage starter is used. Each type has different charcteristics that determine where it may best be used.

Primary Resistor Starting.   Using this method, series resistance is added in each conductor to the motor. Control is used to gradually short out the resistance as the motor comes up to speed, until the motor is connected to the full line voltage.

Primary Reactor Starting.   This motor-starting method is similar to the primary resistor method except that reactors are substituted for the resistors.

Autotransformer Starting.   At starting, wye-connected autotransformer coils reduce motor terminal voltage in each conductor to 50, 65, or 80 percent of line voltage. After a timed interval, a manual switch or a contactor connects the motor across the line and bypasses the autotransformer coils, employing either an open or closed transition.

Part-Winding (Increment) Starting.   Though technically not reduced-voltage starting, part-winding controllers apply voltage through one starter to one motor winding followed by the second starter which connects voltage to the second winding. Three-step starters incorporate a series resistance with one motor winding to increase the motor terminal voltage gradually as the voltage drops across the resistor.

Wye-Delta Starting.   Although technically not reduced-voltage starting, a wye-delta starter energizes the motor windings through electric contacts that form a wye connection giving about 33 percent of full line voltage across each winding. After a set time delay, the motor windings are connected in a delta configuration. Wye-delta starting can be used in applications requiring a low starting torque when supplying full starting current would cause significant voltage drops.

Open vs. Closed Transition.   Two terms are used when discussing reduced-voltage starting: *open-transition* and *closed-transition* starters. These terms are used to describe circuit continuity during the starting sequence.

Any open-transition starter momentarily disconnects the motor from the line at the transition from one step to another. A closed-transition starter never disconnects the motor from the line during the starting sequence. Closed-transition starters provide a smoother start and a lower peak current flow than open-transition starters. An open-transition starter may have fewer contactors and is less expensive than its closed-transition equivalent.

SOLID-STATE MOTOR CONTROL FOR AC INDUCTION MOTORS

Solid-state reduced-voltage controllers and starters fall into a class of motor controllers known as *variable-voltage controllers*. These units do not change the frequency of the power applied to the motor, only the magnitude of the applied rms voltage. Solid-state starters provide an alternative method of reduced-voltage starting for various induction motors. Solid-state starters are able to give both a physical (mechanical) and an electrical "soft" start to the load.

Electromechanical vs. Solid-State Soft Starting

Electromechanical reduced-voltage starting is softer than across-the-line starting in both electrical and mechanical terms but it does not qualify as true soft starting. In Fig. 4-25, notice the abrupt changes in motor current and output torque that occur when a reduced voltage autotransformer starter makes the transition from reduced to full voltage. These discontinuous points cause shocks to the electrical and mechanical systems. Other drawbacks of this method of starting include a lack of adjustability, special motor requirements in some cases, complicated control schemes, large size, and uncertain starting characteristics under varying load conditions. In the case of a reduced-voltage autotransformer starter, the user is confined to the transformer tap settings to determine the amount of voltage first applied to the motor. Wye-delta starters will only work with wye-delta motors and part-winding starters require part-wind motors to give an effective reduced-voltage start.

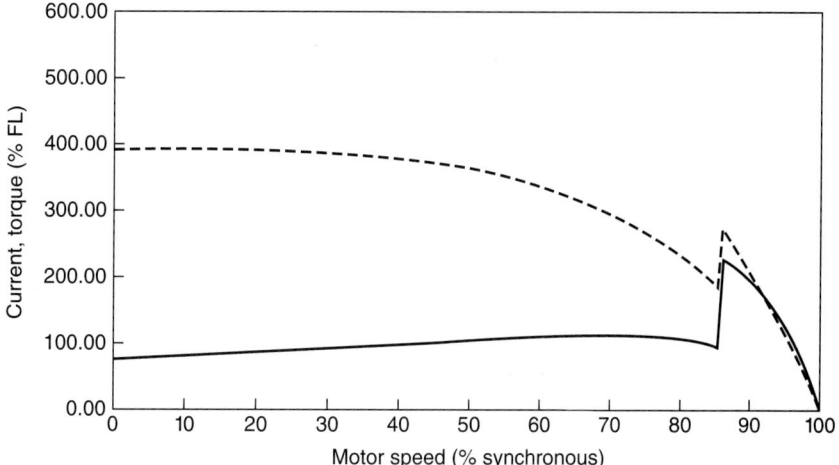

FIGURE 4-25   Starting current and torque, autotransformer starter.

Solid-state reduced-voltage starters (soft starts) apply an adjustable reduced voltage to the motor and then gradually increase the applied voltage until the motor is receiving full voltage (see Fig. 4-26). In this case there are no sudden changes in the voltage applied to the motor. As shown in Fig. 4-27, this prevents the sudden changes in current and torque that occur with reduced-voltage starting. Reducing the motor torque also reduces the accelerating torque and the mechanical stress on the system, and the load comes up to speed more slowly.

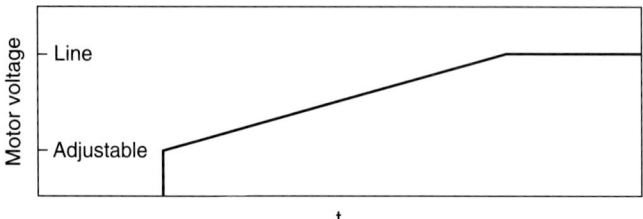

FIGURE 4-26 Solid-state soft start.

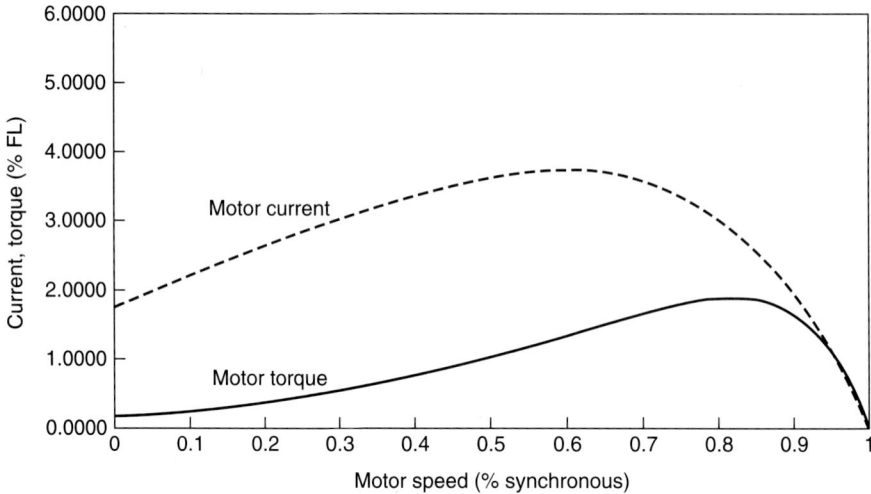

FIGURE 4-27 Starting current and torque for solid-state soft start.

Selection of Solid-State Motor Controls

Types of Solid-State Reduced-Voltage Motor Controls

Solid-State Motor Controller. A solid-state motor controller is a device consisting of an electronic control assembly and one or more solid-state power assemblies. It is used with an electromechanical motor starter. A controller can be used for single-speed, multispeed, and reversing applications when the proper electromechanical device is also used. A controller typically has no means of motor overload protection or ability to completely remove power from the motor.

For a single-speed nonreversing application, a motor controller is wired in series between a motor starter and motor. The motor starter provides the power isolation and overload protection while the controller switches the motor current ON and OFF.

Solid-State Motor Starter.   A solid-state motor starter is a device consisting of an electronic control assembly, one or more solid-state power assemblies, and motor overload protection. The main difference between a controller and starter is that the starter can be used without any other motor control device.

Solid-state starters usually incorporate additional features and functions providing additional motor control. These may include such things as overvoltage, overcurrent, phase-loss, phase-reversal, and overtemperature protection.

Starting Methods for Solid-State Motor Controls

Voltage Ramp Soft Start.   Voltage ramp soft-start units apply a reduced voltage to the motor on starting and then ramp the voltage up to line voltage in a more or less linear fashion (see Fig. 4-28). The *initial torque* or *initial voltage* adjustment determines the amount of voltage applied to the motor when the start signal is given. This voltage is usually adjusted so that the motor will develop just enough torque to overcome the mechanical friction in the system. On applications involving little friction (pumps, large inertial loads, fans) the initial voltage adjustment can be set relatively low. Applications involving much friction or demanding high locked-rotor torque (conveyors, positive displacement pumps) will require a higher torque setting. Ramping the voltage more quickly will cause the motor to accelerate more quickly and result in higher peak inrush currents.

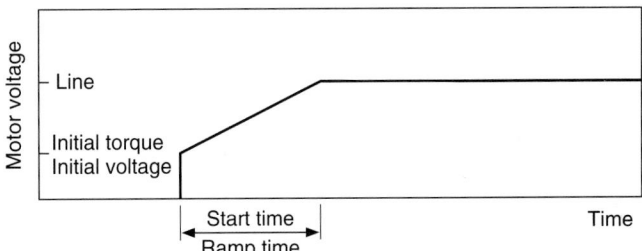

FIGURE 4-28   Voltage-ramp soft-start adjustments.

The key features of the voltage-ramp soft-start unit are that it can softly start varying loads, it does not limit motor torque, and it is easily adjusted. In general, it is desirable to bring the load up to speed as quickly as possible given the mechanical and electrical power distribution system constraints.

Applications for voltage-ramp-type soft-start controls generally fall into two categories: equipment protection and process protection. In terms of process protection, voltage ramp units are used to prevent spillage on conveying and packaging lines that results from the sudden acceleration of across-the-line starting. Electrical soft start is also a form of process protection, since power loss due to breaker tripping or generator shutdown would bring the process to a halt. Voltage-ramp units can be applied on variable-torque, constant-torque, high-inertia, and varying loads, and they give both physical and electrical soft start. As with any type of reduced voltage or soft starting means, it is necessary to evaluate some high-starting-torque applications to determine feasibility. Some loads demand such high torque at locked rotor that any kind of reduced voltage will not allow the motor to start.

Reduced-Voltage Current-Limit Soft Start.   Current-limit soft-start units limit the current drawn by the motor during starting. They allow the motor to draw as much current as it needs up to a user-defined limit and hold the motor to that amount of current until the motor comes up to speed or the unit either shuts down or removes the limit. The current is applied to the motor in one of two different fashions as shown in Fig. 4-29. The *current-limit amps* adjustment determines the maximum amount of current the motor will be allowed to draw during a normal start. The *ramp-time* adjustment determines how quickly the motor current ramps up to the limit amount. For units with a ramp-time adjustment, a shorter ramp time results in a harder physical start, higher starting currents (up to the limit amount) for a shorter time, and a shorter acceleration time.

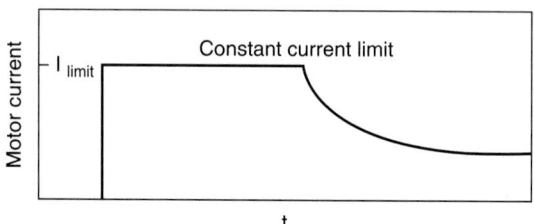

FIGURE 4-29   Current-limit units can apply the amount of current immediately or ramp up to the limit.

The key features of the current-ramp soft-start unit are that it limits the motor inrush current to a specific amount, it can provide physical soft start, and it limits motor torque. These units are used mainly for electrical soft start (reducing inrush current). The shutdown of production is a possibility with a current-ramp unit, since it limits the motor torque. Set the current-limit adjustment low enough to start the motor without light flicker, excessive voltage drop, or generator shutdown. If the unit has a ramp-time adjustment, it should be set to accelerate as quickly as possible given the mechanical system constraints.

Current-ramp units can be applied on variable-torque, some constant-torque, and high-inertia loads. They are not recommended for loads that vary considerably since they may not be able to start the load sometimes. As with any type of reduced-current or soft-starting means, it is necessary to evaluate high-starting-torque applications to determine feasibility. Some loads demand such high torque at locked rotor that any kind of reduced current will not allow the motor to start.

Environmental Conditions for Solid-State Motor Controls

Ambient Temperature.   When selecting a mounting location, *observe the specified ambient temperature range.* The ambient temperature is the temperature of the air surrounding the control. Operate the control at an ambient temperature as close to the recommended minimum temperature as possible, since some semiconductor devices may cease proper functioning temporarily if overheated, while others may be damaged permanently.

Avoid mounting locations near heat sources, such as: equipment that raises the ambient air temperature after a period of operation, e.g., power supplies, transformers, and starters; heat conducted into the control through the mounting surface; or radiated heat where a control is exposed by line of sight to the sun, extremely hot materials, or open flames.

When a mounting location with high ambient temperatures cannot be avoided, consider employing special cooling methods. Observe the following guidelines:

1. Position heat sinks such that air may move vertically between cooling fins across the heat sink surface. This allows ease of airflow for convection cooling.

2. In large systems, distribute components carrying large currents evenly throughout an enclosure to avoid localized hot spots.

3. Ventilated enclosures are effective, but take precautions to avoid air contamination by dust and conductive particles. Use air filters with fan cooling, since dust accumulation on heat sinks reduces their thermal efficiency.

4. Extreme situations may require heat exchangers or air conditioning of enclosures. Also, consider locating the entire control system in a separate room adjacent to the controlled machinery.

Humidity. During operation, heat is generated, and moisture seldom condenses on the equipment. A moisture problem is most likely to develop during inoperative periods or during storage. If necessary, apply humidity control measures during these periods.

Also, avoid dry conditions to prevent static electricity problems. Static electricity applied directly to module or circuit terminals can cause erratic control operation and, in some instances, can produce voltage breakdown failures in semiconductor devices.

Location. A vented Type 1 enclosure is acceptable in indoor locations where the location is dry and relatively dust-free. Type 1 enclosures allow air to enter the enclosure and cool the components inside. Any moisture present or an excessive amount of dust, dirt, or other airborne contaminants allowed to enter a Type 1 enclosure could cause damage to the motor control.

In situations where these conditions exist, a motor control must be mounted in a fully enclosed environmental enclosure. When installed in a sealed enclosure it is often necessary to add additional equipment to minimize or eliminate the heat generated by the motor control while it is operating. Consult the control manufacturer for recommendations.

Shock and Vibration. Shock and vibration can have a potentially damaging effect on solid-state motor controls. Special mounting provisions may be required to prevent such damage.

When determining the mounting location for a reduced voltage motor control, attempt at all costs to avoid mounting the device to a piece of equipment that constantly vibrates or has the tendency to shake during its normal operation. If this situation exists it may be necessary to mount the motor control off the machine, on a building support or other solid object.

Wiring Considerations for Solid-State Motor Controls

Low-Level-Signal Wiring. Coupled electrical noise can be viewed as an unwanted signal originating in other wiring. Solid-state control lines should be separated from noise sources by routing them through their own separate conduit.

When possible, ac lines or lines carrying high currents or inductive loads should not run close to and parallel to sensitive low-level-signal wiring. Besides being separated, they should intersect only at right angles.

Shielded Cable. Using twisted-pair shielded cable for low-level-signal wiring provides a very effective shield against electrostatic and magnetic coupling. The cable should have approximately 12 twists per foot.

The shield must be connected to control ground at only one point and shield continuity must be maintained over the entire length of the cable. Be certain the shield is insulated over its entire length to assure the one-point ground connection. When possible, route the cable around, rather than through, high-noise areas.

Note: For device grounding, attach the shield directly to a large grounded metal object such as a machine tool. Some devices achieve better noise immunity by grounding the shield at the input circuit rather than at the device. Also, in some cases, the shielding may be more effective by connecting the shield to signal common instead of ground.

Grounding. In solid-state control systems, the grounding practices employed have a significant effect on noise immunity. Each ground must be connected to its respective reference point by no more than one wire (one-point grounding). Two or more systems must never share a common single ground wire, either equipment ground or control common. For proper grounding practices, observe the following:

1. Minimum wire sizes, color coding, safety practices, etc., must comply with the ***National Electrical Code®*** and any local codes and regulations.*
2. Observe the recommendations specified on the data sheets for control system products.
3. For further information on grounding practices, refer to IEEE Standard 142-1972, "Recommended Practices for Grounding of Industrial and Commercial Power Systems."

Impedance coupling produced by ground sharing is a source of conducted noise that must be avoided. Guidelines for minimizing impedance coupling include:

1. Use individual signal return wires.
2. Where signal paths are shared, use conductors of large diameter, e.g., the conductor could be a heavy bus bar.

Use a separate dc power supply or separate ac branch circuit to power each control system. When a power source is shared, the line impedance (ac supply) or current capability (dc supply) must be sufficient to maintain rated voltage under all loading conditions.

Using Power-Factor-Correcting Capacitors.   The capacitive load of a power-factor-correcting capacitor has a very damaging effect on solid-state motor controls if used incorrectly. As shown in Fig. 4-30, when a capacitor is used it must be wired to some point on the line side of the motor control.

If the capacitor is wired to the output terminals of the solid-state motor control, damage will result to its silicon controlled rectifier (SCR) power devices.

Cost Considerations

The most significant cost to consider when purchasing a reduced-voltage soft-start motor control is the purchase price. But there are several other costs which must also be considered. In both new and existing installations, it is necessary to figure in the cost of installing the device. Depending on the location selected, the cost to install and wire the device could exceed the cost of the device itself.

Other factors to consider include product life and the elimination of potential downtime. Solid-state devices, when used properly, offer a much longer life than their electromechanical counterparts.

SPEED CONTROL OF ELECTRIC MOTORS

The term *speed control,* as applied to electric motors, covers a wide range of control functions including motor starting, control of motor speed during normal operation, and reversing and stopping of motors.

Operating requirements for specific motor applications must also be considered and generally include constant, variable, adjustable, and multispeed operation.

Constant Speed.   Motors of this type may be designed with speed ratings from 80 r/min and horsepower ratings ranging up to 5000 hp (3700 kW). A typical application is water pumps.

---

* ***National Electrical Code®*** is a Registered Trademark of the National Fire Protection Association, Inc., Quincy, MA 02269.

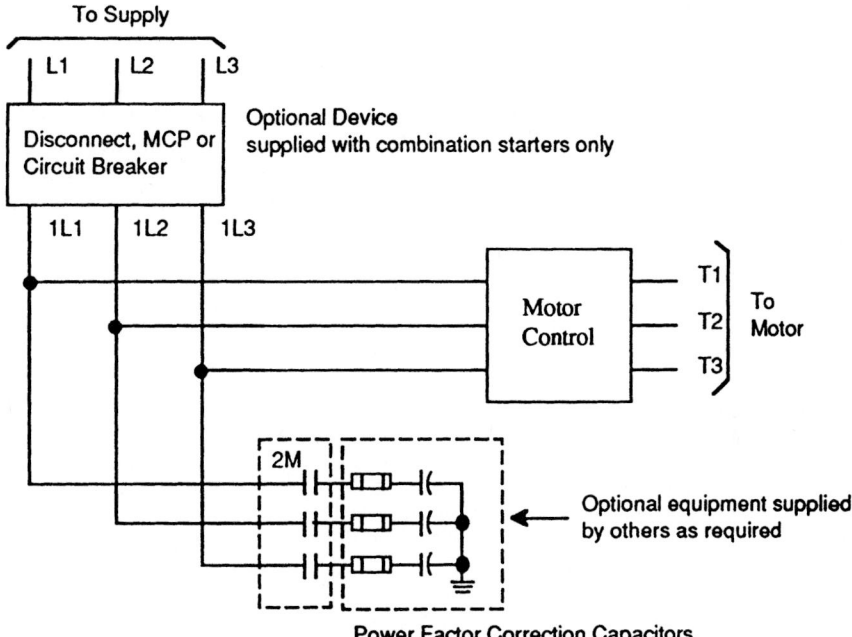

FIGURE 4-30   Wiring power-factor-correcting capacitors.

Variable Speed.   Variable-speed motors slow as the applied load is increased and speed up as the load is decreased. Applications include cranes and hoists.

Adjustable Speed.   Adjustable-speed motors can be varied over a wide speed range while the motor is running. Motor speed remains almost constant once set, even with load applied. A typical application is machine tools.

Multispeed.   Multispeed motors are designed to operate at two or more definite speeds. However, once adjusted to a particular speed, the motor speed remains nearly constant regardless of applied load changes. A typical application is turret lathes.

Multispeed Magnetic Starters

Applications.   Multispeed magnetic starters automatically reconnect multispeed motor windings for the desired speed in response to a signal received from push button stations or other pilot devices.

Consequent-pole multispeed motors having two speeds on a single winding (consequent pole) require a starter which reconnects the motor leads to half the number of effective motor poles at the high speed point. In this type of motor, the low speed is one-half the high speed.

Separate winding motors, having separate windings for each speed, provide more varied speed combinations in that the low speed need not be one-half the high speed. Starters for separate winding motors consist of a starter unit for each speed.

Multispeed motor starters are available for constant-torque, variable-torque, and constant-horsepower motors.

Constant Torque.   These motors maintain constant torque at all speeds. Horsepower varies directly with speed. This type of motor is applicable to conveyors, mills, and similar applications.

Variable Torque.   These motors produce a torque characteristic which varies as the square of the speed. This type of motor is applicable to fans, blowers, and centrifugal pumps.

Constant Horsepower.   This type of motor maintains constant horsepower at all speeds and therefore torque varies inversely with speed. This type of motor is applicable where the same horsepower is required at all speeds. The higher current required at low speed requires derating on starters for constant-horsepower applications. This type of motor is applicable to metalworking machines such as drills, lathes, mills, bending machines, punch presses, and power wrenches.

Operation.   Magnetic starters for multispeed applications select the desired speed in accordance with the pilot control.

The shock to machinery on the reduction of speed is greater than when the speed is increased. Therefore, the pilot control should be wired so that the stop button must be depressed before dropping to a lower speed. Time delays should be used for applications requiring full automatic operation.

These controls may be modified for compelling or acceleration pilot control.

Compelling control requires that the motor always be started at the lower speed and that the push buttons be operated in speed sequence to the next higher speed. To change to a lower speed, the stop button must be depressed and then the push buttons are pressed in speed sequence until the desired speed is reached.

Acceleration control provides that the motor be accelerated automatically with timers by progressively energizing the controls at the push button station from the lowest to the highest speed. To change to a lower speed, the stop button is depressed and then it is necessary to proceed as if starting from rest.

Deceleration control provides that the motor be decelerated automatically with a timer when going from high speed to low speed. The timer allows the motor to decelerate from high speed to a lower speed before automatically restarting the motor in low speed.

Motor Braking

Changing the speed of, or stopping, an electric motor can be accomplished using (1) electrically operated mechanical brakes or (2) dynamic or regenerative braking or plugging (either with an electromechanical starter or a solid-state starter), or by a combination of the two. Brakes are used for two purposes: (1) to provide the means of stopping a driven load quickly and accurately and (2) to hold the load in place after stopping is accomplished.

Dynamic Braking.   When very quick or accurate stopping is not a necessity, the motor may be used to stop itself. AC motors can be dynamically braked by removing the ac power source and reconnecting a dc power source (supplied either from batteries or rectified ac power). The motor then acts like a dc generator with a short-circuited armature. Energy is dissipated in the form of rotor heat.

Regenerative Braking.   In ac motors, regenerative braking is developed by the motor's natural tendency to resist being driven above synchronous speed by an overhauling load. As this situation occurs, a negative slip is developed. The energy absorbed in slowing down is put back into the power supply. Regenerative braking generally is not used with rectified power supplies because this process requires the reversal of armature current.

SOLID-STATE VARIABLE-SPEED AC MOTOR CONTROLS

One method of controlling the speed of ac motors is with a pulse-width-modulated (PWM) variable-frequency drive (VFD). In the simplest terms, the VFD converts ac line voltage into variable voltage and frequency, which is then used to control the speed of ac squirrel-cage motors. As a controller, start/stop, hand-off-auto, and various other control schemes may be applied.

This type of equipment is almost limitless in its use in very diverse applications such as conveyors, HVAC (air handlers), irrigation systems (pumps), machine tools, food processing, overhead cranes, textile mills, chemical processing, and automotive manufacturing.

The benefits derived by the use of a VFD are closer and more responsive control of motor speed; less mechanical wear on systems because of inherent soft start; substantial energy savings achieved on variable torque loads, e.g., fans and pumps; and elimination of noisy mechanical speed-control systems and their associated maintenance problems. Some of the main considerations in applying a drive are:

Environment.   This will determine the enclosure type. The open-chassis type is also available for installation in other enclosures.

Cooling.   If the ambient temperature is not within the manufacturer's rating, typically 104°F (40°C), steps must be taken so that the operational temperature is not exceeded.

Location.   The location should be convenient.

When sizing the VFD to match the connected mechanical load, the foremost consideration is *inertia,* which is a measure of an object's resistance to changes in speed, whether that object is at rest or moving at a constant speed. This speed can either be linear (feet per minute, ft/min) or rotational (revolutions per minute, r/min).

The term for inertia is WK^2, usually given as a numerical value, in units of lb · ft². (This is normally calculated by the mechanical engineer or a machine design company). This then directly affects the torque required.

Torque is the action of a force tending to produce or producing rotation. Torque may even exist when no movement or rotation occurs. Work, unlike torque, exists only when movement occurs.

Because most power transmission is based on rotating elements, torque is extremely important as a measurement of effort to produce work.

The amount of amperage required to produce a given starting torque may be higher than the output rating of the VFD; therefore, the drive must be sized to the calculated starting amperage for the given acceleration time.

Estimating Accelerating Torque (Rotational)

English

$$T = \frac{WK^2 \times dN}{308 \times t}$$

Metric

$$T = \frac{J \times 2dN}{60 \times t} = \frac{J \times dN}{9.55 \times t}$$

where T = acceleration torque, lb · ft (N · m)
WK^2 = total system inertia, in lb · ft² (i.e., the equivalent WK plus rotor inertia)
J = total system inertia in kg · m
dN = change in speed, r/min
t = time to accelerate, s

Note: In some cases inertia may be expressed by a metric value analogous to the English WK^2 whose dimension is N · m² = $J \times g$, where $g = 9.8$ m/s².

After torque has been calculated, the horsepower (or watts) can then be estimated:

English

$$hp = \frac{T \times N}{5250}$$

Metric

$$W = \frac{T \times 2N}{60} = \frac{T \times N}{9.55}$$

Estimate motor current if required:

English $\qquad$ Metric

$$I_m = \frac{\text{hp} \times 746}{1.73 \times E \times \text{Eff}_m \times \text{PF}_m} \qquad I_m = \frac{W}{1.73 \times E \times \text{Eff}_m \times \text{PF}_m}$$

Efficiency (Eff) and power factor (PF) of the motor are expressed as a decimal, typically 0.85 and 0.81, respectively.

These formulas are examples only. Gear and belt reductions, which can make great differences in the sizing of the drives, must also be taken into consideration. In the case of pumps and fans, full-load ampere nameplate ratings of the motors are usually all that is required.

In comparison with average across-the-line starters, initial cost can seem quite high. As compared to soft starters, the cost differential is reduced, but still higher. The previously mentioned advantages can offset the difference in price.

CONTROL OF DC MOTORS

The control of dc motors, as with ac motors, includes motor starting and stopping; governing motor speed, torque, horsepower, and other characteristics; and ensuring the safety of personnel and equipment. The methods of controlling dc motors, however, vary considerably.

DC Motor Starting and Braking

Starting Considerations.   Starting of dc motors rated 2 hp (1.5 kW) or less can generally be accomplished by manually operated, full-voltage starters. For dc motors rated above 2 hp (1.5 kW), reduced-voltage starting is usually recommended to avoid commutator damage. A common method of limiting starting current is by the addition of resistance (which is decreased in steps). The final step (larger motors or those with smooth starting requirements use several steps) is to connect the motor to full line voltage.

Braking.   Like ac motors, dc motors may be brought to a stop quickly by electromechanical brakes. Dynamic or regenerative braking schemes can also be used with dc motors.

Speed Control

DC motor speed is directly proportional to the applied armature voltage and inversely proportional to the field flux. Shunt field control and armature voltage control are, then, the two basic methods used to accomplish speed adjustment.

Shunt Field Control.   With the addition of a rheostat to the shunt field circuit, control is obtained by adjusting the rheostat to weaken the shunt field current. This, in turn, increases the motor speed and reduces the output torque.

The maximum standard speed range using field control is 3:1; specially designed motors can achieve speed ranges of 4:1 or more. For a specific motor, the nameplate rating should be checked or the manufacturer consulted if the allowable range of motor speed is not known.

Armature Voltage Control.   This method requires the application of a variable-voltage power supply with a capacity equal to that of the motor, while holding the shunt field current constant. The resulting speed is proportional to the motor counter emf. The torque remains constant at rated current, regardless of motor speed. In applications where a speed range of greater than 3:1 is required, armature voltage control should be used.

DC Drive Characteristics

Adjustable-Voltage Drive. DC motor armature voltage can be varied to obtain wider ranges of speed control than are available with standard dc motors. An ac-to-dc motor-generator set controls the dc motor speed by increasing the generator voltage while holding the motor field at full strength. When generator voltage reaches full value, the motor runs at base speed. If the speed control is increased further, the motor field is weakened while generator voltage is held constant, causing the motor speed to increase above its base.

Chopper Drives. The high-speed switch (chopper) characteristics of phase-controlled rectifiers (thyristors) can be used to create adjustable-speed dc drives. A constant-voltage rectifier or a dc bus is used as the incoming supply. When the first thyristor is turned on by a reference-level signal, the dc motor is connected to the constant-voltage bus. When motor speed rises above the reference level, a second thyristor is turned on, shutting off the first, and the motor is driven from power stored in an inductor. When the motor speed drops below the reference level, the first thyristor is turned on, turning off the second which again supplies power from the bus. Current transfer between thyristors is regulated by capacitor discharge through a transformer. Dynamic braking can be added by turning on a third thyristor that dissipates energy into a dynamic braking resistor. This type of drive is often used in applications such as adjustable-voltage hoists because power supplies can be subjected to wide voltage deviations.

PROTECTION OF MOTOR CONTROLLERS

Electrical Enclosure Types and Specifications

Electrical enclosures should be selected and specified according to NEMA Standard Publication No. 250. A brief description follows:

Type 1. Indoor use primarily to provide a degree of protection against contact with the enclosed equipment in locations where unusual service conditions do not exist.

Type 3. Outdoor use primarily to provide a degree of protection against windblown dust, rain, and sleet and to resist damage by the formation of ice on the enclosure.

Type 3R. Outdoor use primarily to provide a degree of protection against falling rain and to resist damage by the formation of ice on the enclosure.

Type 4. Indoor or outdoor use primarily to provide a degree of protection against windblown dust and rain, splashing water, and hose-directed water and to resist damage by the formation of ice on the enclosure.

Type 4X. Indoor or outdoor use primarily to provide a degree of protection against corrosion, windblown dust and rain, splashing water, and hose-directed water and to resist damage by the formation of ice on the enclosure.

Type 6. Indoor or outdoor use primarily to provide a degree of protection against the entry of water during occasional temporary submersion at a limited depth.

Type 6P. Indoor or outdoor use primarily to provide a degree of protection against the entry of water during prolonged submersion at a limited depth.

Type 7. Indoor use in locations classified as Class I, Groups A, B, C or D, as defined in the ***National Electrical Code®***.*

Type 9. Indoor use in locations classified as Class II, Groups E or G, as defined in the ***National Electrical Code®***.

---

* ***National Electrical Code®*** is a Registered Trademark of the National Fire Protection Association, Inc., Quincy, MA 02269.

Type 12.   Indoor use primarily to provide a degree of protection against dust, falling dirt, and dripping noncorrosive liquids.

Type 13.   Indoor use primarily to provide a degree of protection against dust, spraying of water, oil, and noncorrosive coolant.

Motor Overload (Running) Protection

Overload relays are intended to protect motors by "tripping" if heat generated in the motor windings is approaching damaging levels. This interrupts the control circuit and causes the contactor to open, disconnecting current to the motor.

Traditional NEMA designs use either melting alloy or bimetal strips, and have interchangeable heaters. NEMA has assigned classes in reference to the designed protection level provided by the individual overload relay. Class 10 overload relays are designed to protect artificially cooled motors such as submersible pump motors or other motors of low thermal capacity. Class 20 overload relays are designed to protect standard American T-frame industrial motors.

IEC designs use a bimetal-type triggering device with integral (nonreplaceable) heaters. IEC-type overload relays are set for trip speed equivalent to NEMA Class 10.

Melting-Alloy-Type Overload Relays.   The triggering mechanism in the melting-alloy type is a spring-loaded lever which is held in place by a solid plug of eutectic solder. When enough heat is generated, the solder melts, releasing the spring-loaded mechanism and opening the contact. Once the melting alloy cools enough to return to solid state, the spring-loaded triggering mechanism must be manually reset by turning it against a ratchet.

These overload relays are highly resistant to vibration. They can be adjusted only by changing heaters, cannot be modified for automatic reset, and are inherently sensitive to ambient temperatures.

Bimetal Overload Relays.   Traditional NEMA-style bimetal overload relays share the heater interchangeability of the melting-alloy type. They may also have the ability to adjust up or down the equivalent of one heater size, or about ±15 percent. IEC overloads are bimetal type, but have nonreplaceable integral heaters. To compensate for this, these units can typically be adjusted ±20 to 25 percent. Bimetal devices use the heat generated to cause deflection of one or more bimetal strips. Once this deflection is great enough, the trip mechanism is operated.

Bimetal overloads begin movement toward the trip point the moment current begins to pass through the heaters. Thus, as they near the trip point, they may be more sensitive to shock and vibration.

Both bimetal types may be provided with means of compensating for ambient temperature, which may be desirable if the motor and control are in dissimilar environments. For example, a motor in a deep well pump is in a constant ambient temperature, while its surface control is in a variable ambient. Where motor and heater are located in the same ambient, compensation may actually be harmful. The overload relay is supposed to track the thermal conditions in the motor windings, and a compensated overload would ignore the ambient portion of the total heat present.

Difficulties can arise when an IEC overload is used with a typical American industrial T-frame motor. There, the quick trip action may result in nuisance tripping under normal starting loads. To avoid this nuisance tripping, users often must set the built-in adjustment to increase the trip current level. While this does prevent nuisance tripping, it can be a misadjustment and may negate the overload relay's protection at running speed. In this situation, a heavily loaded motor could see excessive currents and a corresponding temperature rise (see Fig. 4-31). One engineering rule of thumb states that each 10°C increase in temperature reduces motor insulation life by 50 percent. Increasing the trip current setting to avoid nuisance trips may well lead to early motor failure.

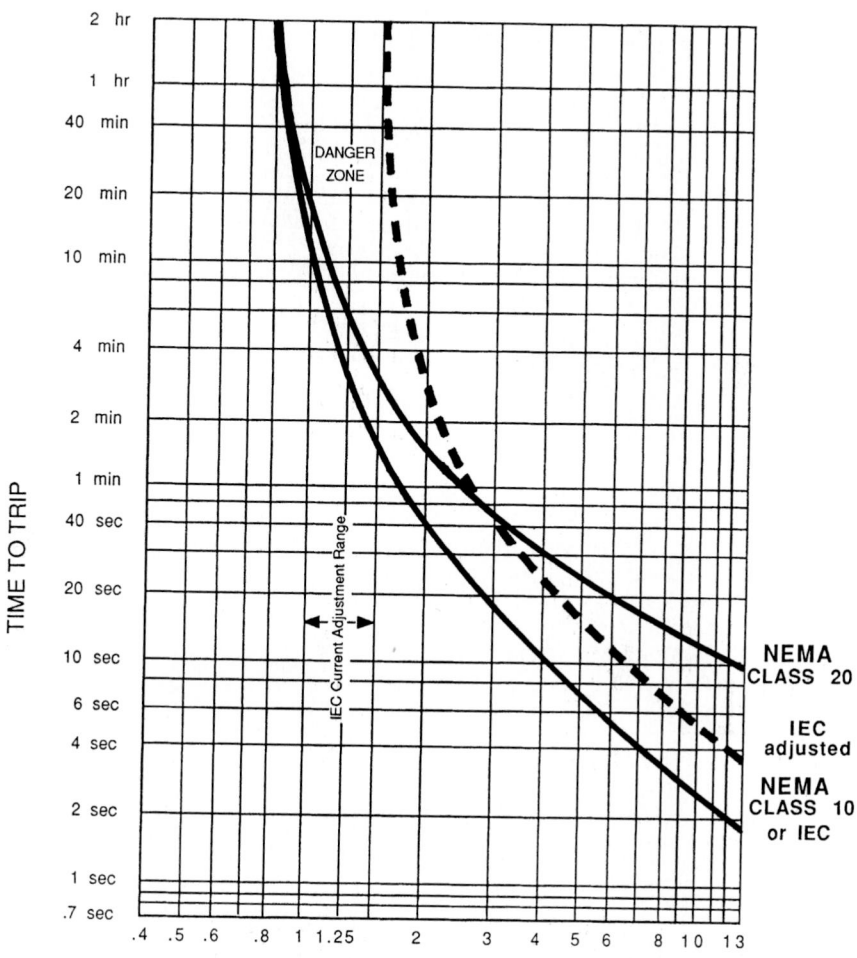

TIME-CURRENT CHARACTERISTICS AT 40°C
(Average trip curve)

FIGURE 4-31 Graph illustrating the dangers of adjusting an overload relay above the full-load current of the motor to prevent nuisance tripping on start-up.

Solid-State Overload Relays. These overload relays are of two types, self-powered and externally powered. The self-powered relay (Fig. 4-32) uses currents induced by the current flowing to the motor for power, while the externally powered units contain an electronic power supply and require a separate source of control power to operate. The advantage of the self-powered units is that they are simpler, require no extra wiring, and are self-protected from short circuits.

High-Accuracy Trip Curve Adjustments. Certain aspects of an overload relay's trip curves are critical for real motor protection. These include time-to-trip on locked rotor, motor overload conditions, and phase loss.

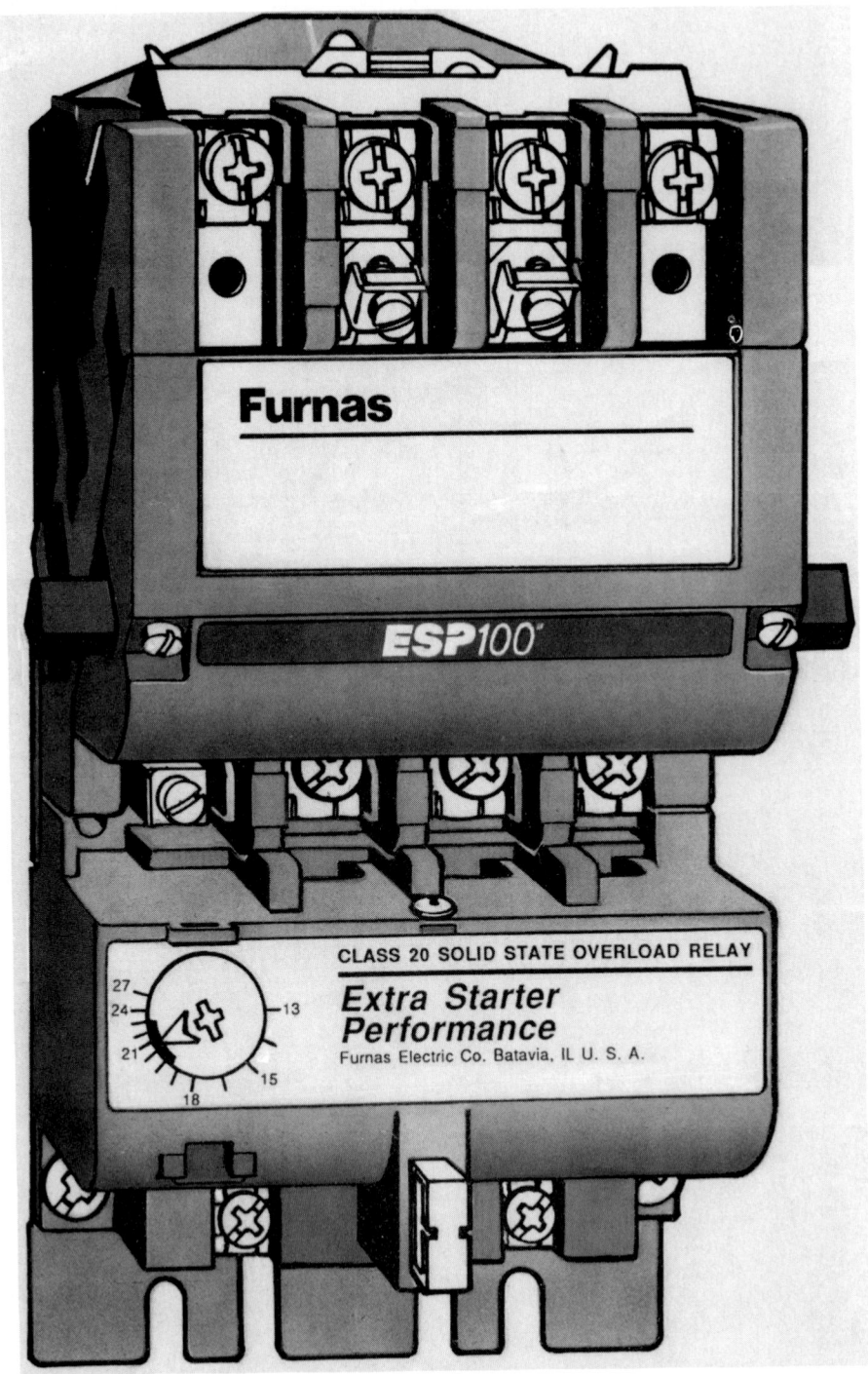

FIGURE 4-32 Starter with self-powered solid-state overload relay. (*Furnas Electric Co.*)

Thermal overloads are limited from approaching the ideal motor protection curves for these critical conditions. Because they do not directly measure current loading, but instead approximate it through use of heaters within the overload, they are subject to thermal overshoot (continued heat absorption after locked-rotor current is removed), residual heat remaining after reset, mechanical variables, and other difficulties in placing the various curves in optimum relationship with each other.

The solid-state overload has no such limitations. Optimum curves have been designed-in (see Fig. 4-33).

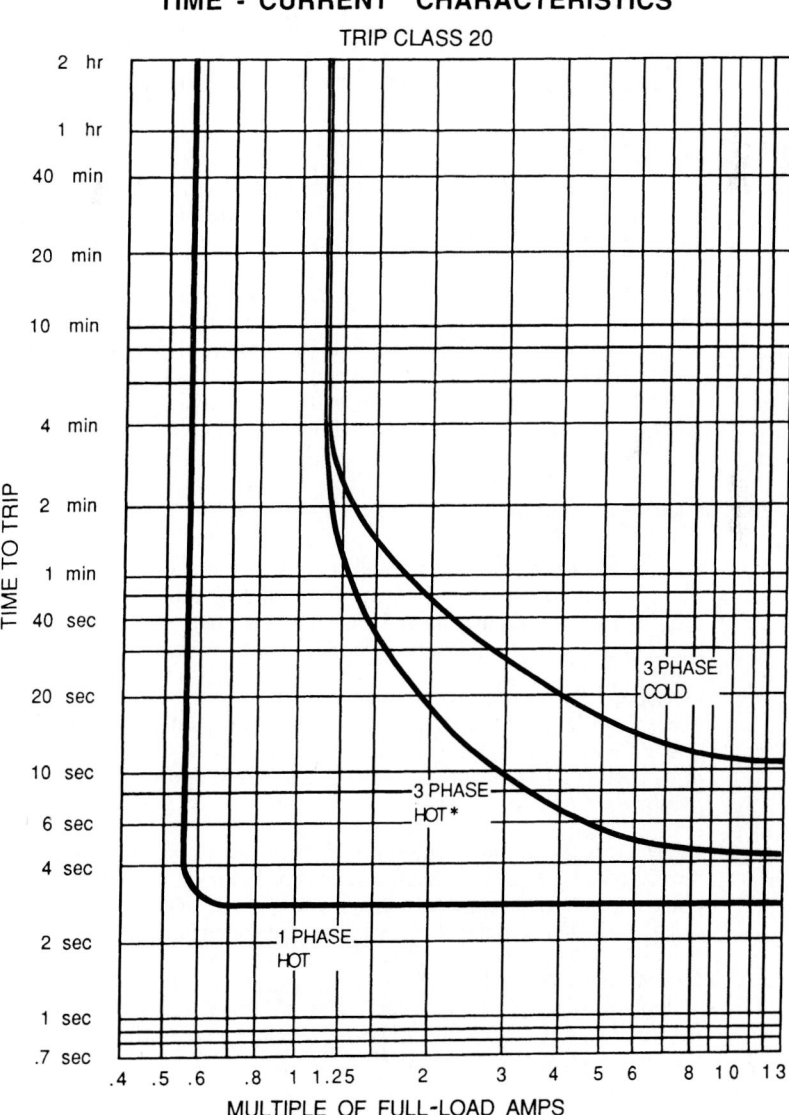

TIME - CURRENT CHARACTERISTICS

TRIP CLASS 20

* Typical. Hot trip times will vary depending on previous running condition and duration of off time.

FIGURE 4-33   Solid-state overload relay trip curve.

Short-Circuit Self-Protection. In the event of a short circuit, the thermal overload heaters often burn out and can consequently cause damage to the overload relay.

The self-powered solid-state overload is self-protecting in short-circuit conditions. Current sensors automatically saturate, and sensed current is well below the safe maximum limit of the electronics. This same protection isolates the electronics of the solid-state overload from damage due to spikes or transients in line current.

Open-Phase Protection. Phase failure may be caused by a blown fuse, an open connection, or a broken line. If phase failure occurs while the motor is stopped, stator current will rise to a very high value while the motor remains stationary, and excessive heating may damage the windings.

Thermal overload relays, to varying degrees, are or can be made sensitive to single phasing. Melting-alloy-type overload relays are somewhat sensitive to phase loss, in that sensing of current in all three phases is independent. Loss of one phase will increase current in the other two. If the motor is fully loaded, this increase may be enough to cause the overload to trip. On the other hand, phase loss with a lightly loaded motor may never cause tripping with this type of overload.

Many such overload relays are constructed with a differential trip mechanism, and are phase-loss sensitive. A phase-loss-sensitive overload relay, compensated for temperature variations, and with two poles energized at 115 percent of full-load amperage, shall trip in "less than 2 hours."

Neither this nor the sensitivity of the melting-alloy type to phase loss should be seen as true single-phasing protection. If single-phasing protection is a concern, complete protection may be provided by an electronic voltage monitor or solid-state overload relay.

The solid-state overload relay, by contrast, will trip within seconds under the same conditions. This provides enough of a delay to avoid nuisance tripping in momentary outages, but eliminates the potential for extended operation in phase loss condition under load.

Other Types of Motor Protection

Open-Field Protection. DC shunt and compound-wound motors can be protected against the loss of field excitation by installing field-loss relays in the shunt field circuit. Larger dc motors may race dangerously with the loss of field excitation, while other motors may not race because of friction and the fact that they are small.

Overspeed Protection. To prevent damage to a driven machine, materials in the industrial process, or the motor, overspeed protection is provided by controlling the power-supply frequency in ac motors and by limiting the maximum shunt field resistance or armature voltage in dc motors. Typical applications include paper and printing plants, steel mills, processing plants, and the textile industry.

Overtravel Protection. In applications where precise positioning is required, control devices (such as limit switches, cams, photoelectrics, etc.) are used to govern the starting, stopping, and reversal of electric motors. These devices can be used to control regular operation or as emergency switches to prevent the improper functioning of machinery.

Overvoltage Protection. Devices such as overvoltage relays provide a reduction in the level of applied voltage or a maintained interruption of power to the motor circuit when excessive voltage levels are experienced. High induced voltages may occur as a result of the interruption of inductive motor control circuits.

Reversed-Current Protection. Rectifiers are used to protect dc controllers in dc or three-phase ac systems that can be subject to damage when experiencing phase failures and phase reversals. It is also important to provide reversed-current protection for battery-charging equipment.

Reversed-Phase Protection.   Phase-failure and phase-reversal relays are used to prevent the operation of elevators and industrial machinery to protect motors, machines, and personnel from potential hazards when phase reversal or loss occurs. Interchanging two phases of the supply of a three-phase induction motor will reverse its direction of rotation.

Undervoltage Protection.   Undervoltage relays and three-wire control are employed to initiate the opening of a motor circuit and maintain it open on a reduction or failure of voltage. Undervoltage protection generally is applied where uncontrolled motor starting could result in potential hazards.

Undervoltage Release.   Undervoltage relays and two-wire control are employed to initate the temporary opening of a motor circuit on the reduction or failure of voltage. On restoration of full voltage, the motor is automatically restarted.

Short-Circuit Protection

For motors with greater than fractional horsepower ratings, devices such as fuses and circuit breakers must be installed ahead of the motor control apparatus to protect branch-circuit conductors, motor control apparatus, personnel, and the motor itself against fault conditions that may be the result of short circuits or grounds.

Definition.   Short-circuit current is the current that flows when a fault in the electrical system occurs—for example, when phase conductors are accidentally shorted out. Faults are commonly referred to as either *arcing* or *bolted* faults. The bolted fault does not involve an arc. Such a fault can result from incorrect wiring, conductors that make contact and are welded together during an arcing fault, or foreign objects such as a wrench or screwdriver inadvertently left across conductors during maintenance work. In an arcing fault, a complete connection is not made across the phases, and part of the voltage is consumed across the arc. The total fault current is, therefore, somewhat smaller than for a bolted fault.

When a fault occurs, the overcurrent device must safely open and interrupt the fault. Overcurrent devices such as fuses and circuit breakers, which interrupt fault currents, must have an *interrupting* rating equal to or greater than the available short-circuit current at their line-side terminals. Control devices, such as motor starters and overload relays, must have a *withstand* rating equal to or greater than the available short-circuit current. That is to say, they must be able to withstand the fault current for the time it takes the overcurrent device to interrupt the fault.

The available short-circuit current at any point in an electrical system is the worst-case or maximum short-circuit current that can flow under fault conditions. To safely apply overcurrent devices within their interrupting ratings, it is necessary to calculate the available short circuit currents at various points of application in an electrical distribution system. The procedure to calculate the magnitude of the fault current is described in various publications available from circuit protective device manufacturers.

Overcurrent devices and motor controls must be provided with marking which indicates their interrupting or withstand ratings, as appropriate. This enables the user to properly coordinate the protective device and motor controls with the available short-circuit current.

Circuit Protective Devices.   There are various types of short-circuit protective devices available for electrical circuits and equipment rated 600 V or less.

A disconnect switch or a nonautomatic circuit interrupter (breaker) can be used to provide an electrical circuit disconnect function. Overcurrent circuit protection is provided when fuses are added to the disconnect switch or thermal and/or magnetic trip units are added to the nonautomatic circuit interrupter.

Fuses.   Several types of fuses are in use: standard one-time, time-delay (or dual-element), and current-limiting. The standard one-time fuse has no time-delay feature. The time-delay dual-element fuses provide time delay where a heavy overload current might exist for a short time (normal motor starting). This type of fuse will not open the circuit during this brief time; however, if the overload continues, the fuse will cause the circuit to open. In a short-circuit condition, this type of fuse will open the circuit in an extremely short time.

Current-limiting-type fuses are used where extremely high short-circuit currents are available. They react to open the circuit in a fraction of a cycle, thereby limiting the actual current that can flow.

Circuit Breakers.   Types of circuit breakers now in use are thermal magnetic, magnetic only, and solid state.

A circuit breaker is opened thermally by a bimetal element in each breaker pole. The function and operation of the bimetal is the same as the overload relay on magnetic starters.

In a short-circuit condition, magnetic action, accomplished by an electromagnet in each breaker pole, causes the breaker to trip instantaneously. In a magnetic-only breaker, the thermal sensing bimetal is left out. Solid-state breakers utilize current transformers and solid-state circuitry in place of the thermal and magnetic trip units.

Sizing of the protective device should be in accordance with the ***National Electrical Code***®* (**NEC**), local code requirements, and equipment manufacturer specifications.

Protection of Solid-State Motor Controls

Solid-state reduced-voltage starters must be protected against faults and short circuits in the same manner as electromechanical reduced-voltage starters, in accordance with the **NEC.** Within this range there are two levels of protection—Type 1 and Type 2 protection. The **NEC** requirements normally afford Type 1 protection to solid-state reduced-voltage starters.

Type 1 protection. When Type 1 protected, the equipment is damaged (i.e., SCRs are shorted) and needs to be repaired, but the wiring and enclosure are intact. Type 1 protection is usually given by circuit breakers and class H, K, R, and RK-5 fuses.

Type 2 protection. When Type 2 protected, the equipment is not damaged during a fault/short circuit, and the equipment is protected by semiconductor, rectifier, and in some instances RK-1 fuses. Note that the semiconductor and rectifier fuses do not qualify as Underwriters Laboratories (UL) or **NEC** branch-circuit protection devices. However, occasionally a control manufacturer will use SCRs that can be protected by RK-1 fuses. Consult the manufacturer to be certain.

Solid-state reduced-voltage starters must also be protected against voltage transients. This is usually accomplished by installing metal oxide varistors (MOVs) line-to-line on line and load, or by connecting them from line-to-load across the SCRs. If MOVs are not provided, the SCRs will likely short-circuit due to voltage transients.

COMBINATION STARTERS

A combination starter (Fig. 4-34) combines a disconnect switch with or without fuses or a circuit breaker together with the starter and its accessories into one compact enclosed package.

The components are closely coordinated to work together, and the unit is rated for a particular value of short-circuit interrupting current. The unit may contain a thermal magnetic or magnetic-only circuit breaker and a starter, or a fusible or nonfusible switch and a starter. The suitability of the enclosure to its environment is an important consideration.

---

* ***National Electrical Code*®** is a Registered Trademark of the National Fire Protection Association, Inc., Quincy, MA 02269.

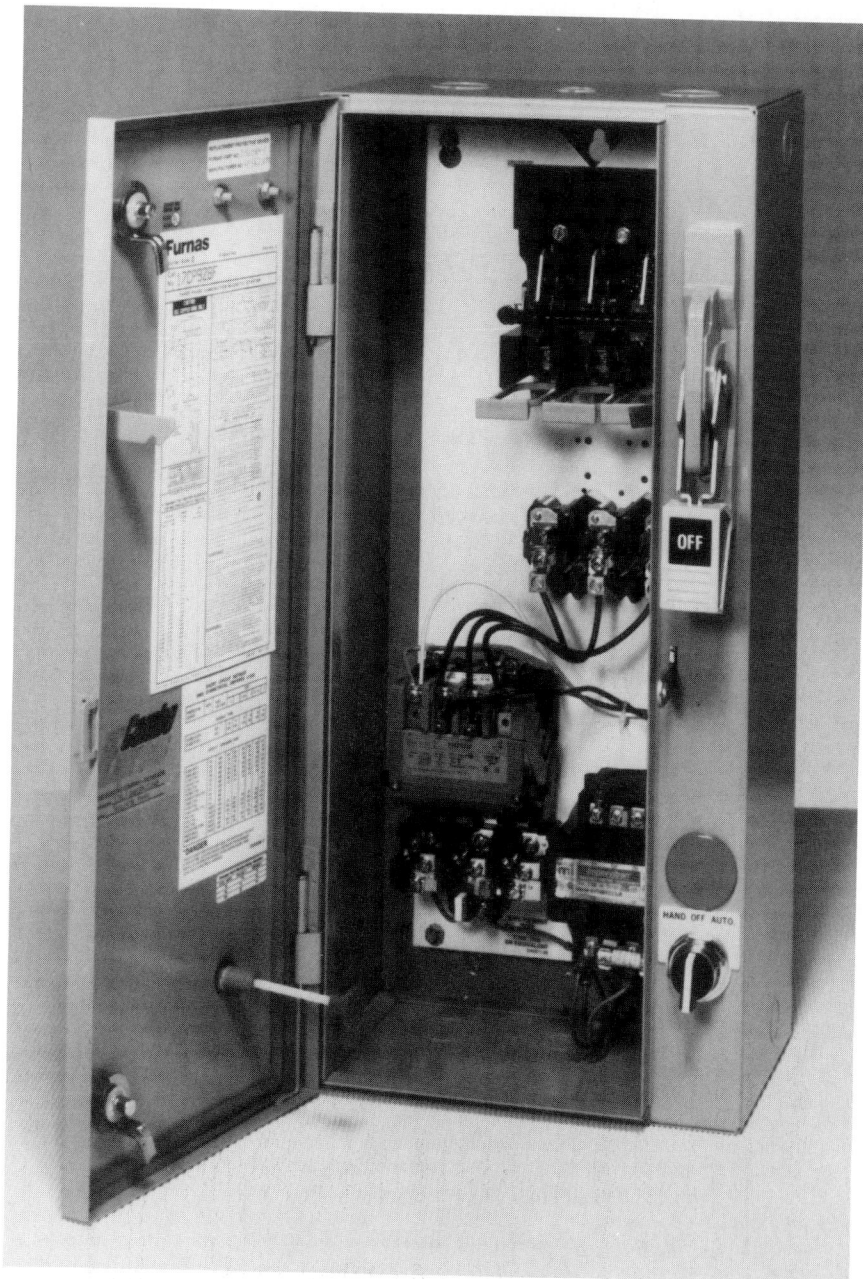

FIGURE 4-34   Combination starter. (*Furnas Electric Co.*)

Interrupting Rating

A combination starter must be capable of interrupting the total symmetrical available short-circuit current in amperes at the point of installation.

In a combination starter, the magnetic contactor or starter is coordinated with a circuit breaker or set of fuses so that the equipment will successfully complete a fault interruption up to its published rating.

TROUBLESHOOTING ELECTRIC MOTOR CONTROLS

Varying factors such as temperature, humidity, and atmospheric contamination may adversely affect the performance of motor controls. Misapplication of a control may also lead to serious trouble and is often regarded as the major cause of motor control problems. Visual inspection every 6 months or so, and less-frequent electrical checks with the proper instruments, will help to ensure that production will not be interrupted because of a starter failure that could have been prevented.

It is important to make a complete mechanical check of motor control equipment before and after installation. Damaged or broken parts can usually be found easily and quickly, and replaced if necessary. Visual checks should be made with the aid of a flashlight, air hose, and a small brush. Debris and dirt can be brushed from contacts and other areas of the switch; light rust and dirt on pole faces can be removed with compressed air and brush. Never use a file or abrasive of any kind on pole faces since this can upset the precise fit between core components. A simple tightening of terminal screws should be sufficient to correct many motor controller problems.

It is recommended that the following general procedures be observed by qualified personnel in the inspection and repair of motor controller involved in a fault. Manufacturer's service instructions should be consulted for additional details.

CAUTION—It must be understood that all inspections and tests are to be made on controllers and equipment which are de-energized, disconnected, and isolated so that accidental contact cannot be made with live parts and so that all plant-safety procedures will be observed.

Procedures

Enclosure. Substantial damage to the enclosure, such as deformation, displacement of parts, or burning, requires replacement of the entire controller.

Circuit Breakers. Examine the enclosure interior and the circuit breaker for evidence of possible damage. If evidence of damage is not present, the breaker may be reset and turned on. If it is suspected that the circuit breaker has opened several short-circuit faults or if signs of possible deterioration appear within the enclosure, the test described in paragraph AB 1-2.38 of the NEMA standards publication, "Molded Case Circuit Breakers," Publication AB 1, should be performed before restoring the breaker to service.

Disconnect Switch. The external operating handle must be capable of opening the switch. If it fails or if visual inspection after opening indicates deterioration beyond normal, such as overheating, contact blade or jaw pitting, insulation breakage, or charring, the switch must be replaced.

Fuse Holders. Deterioration of fuse holders or their insulating mounts requires their replacement.

Terminals and Internal Conductors. Indications of arcing damage and/or overheating, such as discoloration and melting of insulation, require the replacement of damaged parts.

Contactor.   Contacts showing heat damage, displacement of metal, or loss of adequate wear allowance require replacement of the contacts and, where applicable, the contact springs. If deterioration extends beyond the contacts, such as binding in the guides or evidence of insulation damage, the damaged parts of the entire contactor must be replaced.

Overload Relays.   If burnout of the current element of an overload relay has occured, the complete overload relay must be replaced. Any indication that an arc has struck and/or any indication of burning of the insulation of the overload relay also requires replacement of the overload relay. If there is no visual indication of damage, the relay must be electrically or mechanically tripped to verify proper functioning of the overload-relay contacts.

Final Check

Before returning the controller to service, checks must be made for the tightness of electric connections and for the absence of short circuits, grounds, and leakage. All equipment enclosures must be closed and secured before the branch circuit is energized.

For these and other complex problems, the manufacturer's wiring and schematic diagrams should be reviewed before attempting repairs. A listing of standard wiring diagram symbols is shown in Fig. 4-35. Also, to aid in troubleshooting, a listing of many of the possible motor control problems and their probable causes and solutions are presented in Table 4-16.

TROUBLESHOOTING OF SOLID-STATE MOTOR CONTROLS

Repairs and Service

The repair of solid-state devices is as varied as are the designs. Before attempting to service any solid-state device, caution should be exercised when removing any printed-circuit boards or solid-state power devices. While designed for use in an industrial environment, they often contain small components or circuits which could be damaged if improperly serviced. Consult the appropriate documentation supplied by the control manufacturer for specific information pertaining to the servicing of a solid-state motor control.

Tools Required for Troubleshooting

Typically, no special tools are required to troubleshoot solid-state reduced voltage motor controls. A digital multimeter or volt-ohmmeter and clamp-on ammeter are usually sufficient. The multimeter can be used to verify incoming and outgoing voltages or measure resistance or voltage drop across the SCRs, while the ammeter is used to measure motor current.

Preventive Maintenance

Solid-state reduced-voltage motor controls require very little preventive maintenance. About the only maintenance required is ensuring tight electrical connections, keeping filters and cooling fans clean and free to turn, and verifying that voltage transient protection is intact. The filter cleaning operation should be performed as often as the environment dictates.

Troubleshooting

Solid-state reduced-voltage starters and controllers typically comprise only two main sections, power and logic. Faults to the motor control will occur in one of these two places. When

ELECTRICAL SYMBOLS

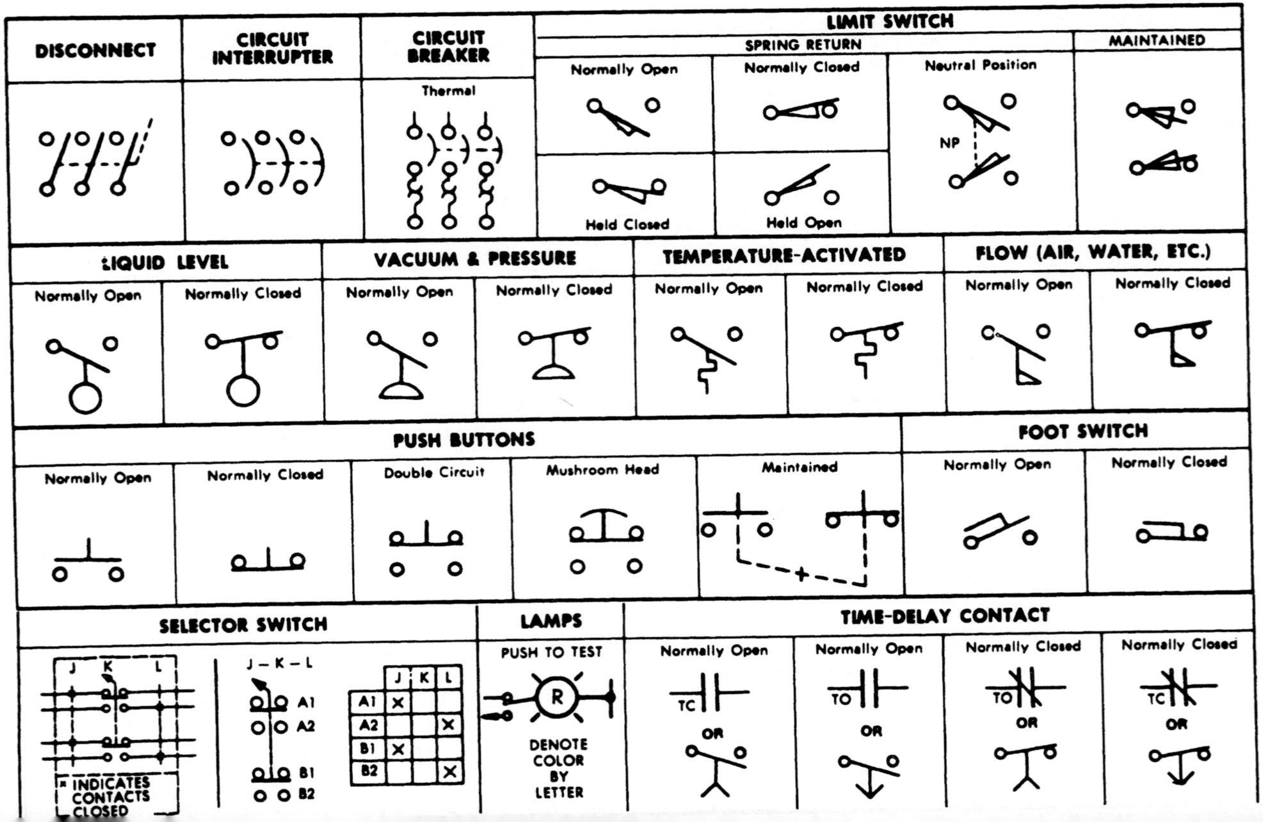
DISCONNECT
CIRCUIT INTERRUPTER
CIRCUIT BREAKER
Thermal
LIMIT SWITCH
SPRING RETURN
MAINTAINED
Normally Open
Normally Closed
Neutral Position
NP
Held Closed
Held Open
LIQUID LEVEL
Normally Open
Normally Closed
VACUUM & PRESSURE
Normally Open
Normally Closed
TEMPERATURE-ACTIVATED
Normally Open
Normally Closed
FLOW (AIR, WATER, ETC.)
Normally Open
Normally Closed
PUSH BUTTONS
Normally Open
Normally Closed
Double Circuit
Mushroom Head
Maintained
FOOT SWITCH
Normally Open
Normally Closed
SELECTOR SWITCH
J K L
* INDICATES CONTACTS CLOSED
J – K – L
A1
A2
B1
B2
LAMPS
PUSH TO TEST
R
DENOTE COLOR BY LETTER
TIME-DELAY CONTACT
Normally Open
Normally Open
Normally Closed
Normally Closed
TC
TO
OR

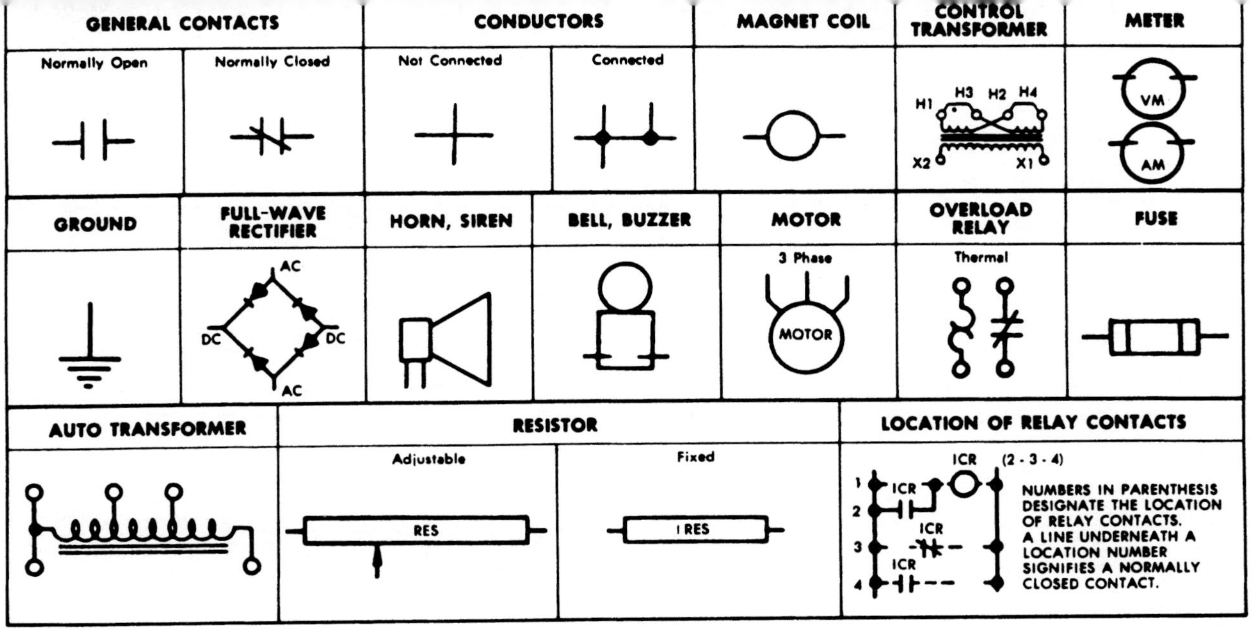

FIGURE 4-35 Wiring diagram symbols.

TABLE 4-16   Troubleshooting Motor Controls

Problem	Possible cause	Solution
I. Magnetic and mechanical parts		
Noisy magnet (humming)	1. Misalignment or mismating of magnet pole faces	1. Realign or replace magnet assembly.
	2. Foreign matter on pole face (dirt, lint, rust, etc.)	2. Clean (do not file) pole faces; realign if necessary.
	3. Low voltage applied to coil	3. Check system and coil voltage. Observe voltage variations during start-up time.
Noisy magnet (loud buzz)	4. Broken shading coil	4. Replace shading coil and/or magnet assembly.
Failure to pick up and seal in	1. Low voltage	1. Check system and coil voltage; watch for voltage variations during starting.
	2. Wrong magnet coil or wrong connection	2. Check wiring, coil nomenclature, etc.
	3. Coil open or shorted	3. Check with an ohmmeter, and when in doubt replace.
	4. Mechanical obstruction	4. Disconnect power and check for free movement of magnet and contact assembly.
Failure to drop out or slow dropout	1. "Gummy" substance on pole faces or magnet slides	1. Clean with nonvolatile solvent or degreasing fluid.
	2. Voltage to coil not removed	2. Shorted seal-in contact (exact cause found by checking coil circuit).
	3. Worn or rusted parts causing binding	3. Clean or replace worn parts.
	4. Residual magnetism due to lack of air gap in magnet path	4. Replace any worn magnet parts or accessories.
	5. Mechanical interlock binding (reversing starters)	5. Check interlocks for free pivoting. New bushing or light lubrication may be required.
II. Contacts		
Contact chatter (source probably from magnet assembly)	1. Broken shading coil	1. Replace assembly.
	2. Poor contact continuity in control circuit	2. Improve contact continuity or use three-wire control.
	3. Low voltage	3. Correct voltage condition. Check momentary voltage dip on starting.
Welding	1. Abnormal inrush of current	1. Use larger contactor; check for grounds, shorts, or excessive load current.
	2. Rapid jogging	2. Install larger jogging-rated device or caution operator.
	3. Insufficient tip pressure	3. Replace contact springs; check contact carrier for deformation or damage.
	4. Low voltage preventing magnet from sealing	4. Correct voltage condition. Check momentary voltage dip on starting.
	5. Foreign matter preventing contacts from closing	5. Clean contacts with nonvolatile solvent. Low-current or -voltage contactors, starters, and control accessories should be cleaned with solvent and acetone to remove solvent residue.

TABLE 4-16   Troubleshooting Motor Controls (*Continued*)

Problem	Possible cause	Solution
	6. Short circuit	6. Remove short fault and check for correct fuse or breaker size.
Short contact life or overheating	1. Filing or dressing	1. Do not file silver contacts. Rough spots or discoloration will not harm or impair their efficiency.
	2. Interrupting excessively high currents	2. Install larger device or check for grounds, shorts or excessive motor currents.
	3. Excessive jogging	3. Install larger device rated for jogging or caution operator.
	4. Weak contact pressure	4. Replace contact springs; check contact carrier for deformation or damage.
	5. Dirt or foreign matter on contact surface	5. Clean contacts with nonvolatile solvent.
	6. Short circuits	6. Remove short fault and check for correct fuse or breaker size.
	7. Loose connection	7. Clean and tighten.
	8. Sustained overload	8. Install larger device; check for excessive load current.
	9. Excessive wear	9. Higher than normal voltage may result in mechanical wear and bounce.
Contacts, supports, discoloring	1. Loose connections	1. Tighten hardware or replace.*
III. Coils		
Open circuit	1. Mechanical damage	1. Handle and store coils carefully.
Cooked coil (overheated)	1. Overvoltage or high ambient temperature	1. Check application and circuit. Coils will operate satisfactorily over a range of 85 to 110% of rated voltage.
	2. Incorrect coil	2. Check rating; replace with proper coil if incorrect.
	3. Shorted turns caused by mechanical damage or corrosion	3. Replace coil.
	4. Undervoltage, failure of magnet to seal in	4. Correct system voltage.
	5. Dirt or rust on pole faces increasing air gap	5. Clean pole faces.
	6. Sustained low voltage	6. Remedy according to local code requirements, low-voltage system protection, etc.
IV. Overload relays		
Nuisance tripping	1. Sustained overload	1. Check for equipment grounds and shorts and excessive motor currents due to overload. Check motor winding resistance to ground.
	2. Loose connections	2. Clean connections and tighten. This includes load wires and heater-element mounting screws.
	3. Incorrect heater	3. Check heater sizing and also check ambient temperature.
Failure to trip out (causing motor burnout)	1. Mechanical binding, dirt, corrosion, etc.	1. Clean or replace.
	2. Incorrect heater or jumper wires used or heaters omitted	2. Recheck ratings and heater size. Correct if necessary.

TABLE 4-16 Troubleshooting Motor Controls (*Continued*)

Problem	Possible cause	Solution
	3. Wrong calibration adjustment	3. Consult factory. Calibration adjustment is normally not recommended unless under factory supervision. It is customary to return units to factory for check and calibration.
V. Manual starters		
Failure to operate (mechanically)	1. Mechanical parts, including springs, worn or broken	1. Replace parts as needed.
	2. Welded contacts due to application or other abnormal cause	2. Replace contacts and recheck operation.
Trips out prematurely	1. Motor overload, incorrect heaters, or misapplication	1. Check conditions; replace or adjust as needed.
VI. Timers		
A. Pneumatic		
Erratic timing	1. Foreign matter in valve	1. Clean if at all possible, or replace timing head completely and exchange unit with factory.
Contacts do not operate	1. Adjustment incorrect on time-actuating screw	1. Follow service bulletin instructions for desired adjustment.
	2. Worn or broken parts in switch assembly	2. Replace defective parts.
B. Electronic relay		
Erratic timing	1. Loose connections	1. Check over unit visually.
	2. Timing relay worn out	2. Plug in new tested relay.
	3. Defective components	3. Check and replace if necessary.
Timer stops operating	1. Mechanical relay	1. Substitute good relay.
	2. Defective circuit components	2. Check over unit visually and with multimeters. Replacement of circuit board probably better than repair if relay normal.
C. Electronic (solid-state)		
Erratic timing	1. Loose connections	1. Visually inspect all connections.
	2. Check external connections	2. Check functions with multimeters in accordance with prescribed service instructions.
Timer will not time out	1. External connections	1. Systematically check system.
	2. Check power supply to timer	2. Fuses, etc.
	3. Initiation circuit open	3. See step 1.
	4. Contacts dirty	4. See step 1; clean if necessary.
VII. Limit switches		
Broken parts	1. Excessive overtravel of actuator	1. Use resilient actuator or operate within device tolerance.
Inoperative	1. Switch actuator out of position or broken	1. Inspect, repair, or replace.
	2. Lack of contact continuity	2. Clean contacts; replace contact block if necessary.
VIII. Drum controls		
Poor contact	1. Dirty rotor contacts and fingers	1. Inspect contacts; if copper, burnish with 4-0 sandpaper until clean; if silver, use a suitable solvent. Check for approximately $\frac{3}{64}$-in finger movement.
	2. Dirt or other foreign matter on horizontally mounted units	2. Clean systematically with contact cleaner and air.

TABLE 4-16   Troubleshooting Motor Controls (*Continued*)

	Problem	Possible cause	Solution
	Sluggish or hard operating switch	1. Dry bearings 2. Worn parts	1. Lubricate bearings sparingly. 2. Inspect carefully; replace worn parts.
IX.	Pressure switches Pressure switch inoperative	1. Foreign matter in pressure-sensing area 2. Contacts burned	1. Remove switch and clean opening. 2. Clean contacts; replace if necessary.
	Erratic operation	1. Worn parts 2. Diaphragm faulty	1. Inspect, adjust, or replace. 2. Replace diaphragm.
	Very frequent operation	1. Likely due to a waterlogged system	1. Drain part of water from pressure tank and, if possible, pump in about 4 lb air.
X.	Push buttons Button inoperative (mechanical) (electrical)	1. Shaft has dirt or residue binding 2. Contact board spring broken 3. Contaminated contacts and corrosion	1. Check, clean, and clear. 2. Replace contact board. 3. Clean.
XI.	Push button, pilot lamp No light	1. Bulb out or burned out 2. Broken parts, wire, or transformer 3. Short life of bulb due to excessive high voltage	1. Replace with proper unit. 2. Inspect, repair, or replace. 3. Replace with next higher voltage pilot lamp (brillance may be reduced slightly).

* Any contact replacement should include a complete set of replacement including the support springs, screws, etc.

a problem occurs in a motor control system, it is important to consider all aspects including the motor control, control wiring, sensing switches, programmable control equipment, etc.

Power Circuit, SCR.   Failures in the power section usually result in a shorted SCR. This failure may cause the motor to growl and rumble during starting or it may cause circuit breakers to trip during starting. Shorted SCRs can be determined by measuring the resistance across the motor control with an ohmmeter. (*CAUTION:* Disconnect the power prior to measuring the resistance.) A shorted SCR will read 0 Ω. Most controls have built-in shorted SCR detectors that will light an indicating light-emitting diode (LED) or open an alarm contact.

Power Circuit, Protective Devices.   A failed voltage-transient protective device must be checked visually unless an indicator is provided. The voltage transient protection should be inspected any time a shorted SCR occurs.

Logic Circuit.   Failures in the logic section usually prevent the motor control from doing anything or result in low voltage being applied to the motor (make certain this low voltage is not the result of an incomplete start sequence or some other adjustment). Logic failures usually require factory repair or replacement.

Control Circuits.   Should a controller fail to start, even though the logic and power sections are in working order, it may be that the proper control commands have not been received by the unit. Consult the unit's instruction manual to determine the required control inputs and check the control circuit for tripped overload relays, open circuits, open disconnects, etc.

Troubleshooting Solid-State Variable-Speed (AC) Drives

Repairs, if required, can be lengthy because with electronic equipment, training of employees to make repairs may be necessary. Repair costs may also be greater than for nonelectronic equipment. They will always be greater if factory personnel are required for on-site repairs. When there are a large number of units in place at one facility, training of the maintenance staff is most cost-effective.

Most controls have built-in diagnostics to expedite troubleshooting. For any other testing, a good analog multimeter is normally all that is required. The decision to repair a piece of equipment or replace it depends on the individual production schedules. For high-volume production lines, it may be best to keep spare drives on hand to swap out with a problem unit. Repairs can then be made under less stressful conditions.

In most cases, VFDs require very little maintenance. The only moving parts are relays and input/output contactors which may wear out mechanically. It is rare that contacts need to be replaced because arcing is normally nonexistent.

FIGURE 4-36   Motor control center. (*Furnas Electric Co.*)

MOTOR CONTROL CENTERS

Motor control centers are floor-mounted assemblies of one or more enclosed vertical sections having a horizontal common power bus and principally containing combination motor control units. The units are mounted one above the other in the vertical sections. These sections may incorporate vertical buses connected to the common power bus, thus extending the common power supply to the individual units. Units may also connect directly to the common power bus by suitable wiring (definition as stated by NEMA).

The common enclosure design (Fig. 4-36) and the use of combination starters offer both economy and ease of installation in multiple motor control installations. In addition, motor control centers (MCCs) provide proper coordination between short-circuit protective devices and the controller. Since MCCs are engineered systems, the components are closely coordinated to work together, and the unit is rated for a particular value of short-circuit interrupting duty at the point of its installation. MCCs may contain a molded-case circuit breaker and starter, or a fused switch and a starter.

MCCs centralize all the electric control apparatus for a given installation in housings which are convenient for easy field installation and maintenance. Use of MCCs can minimize the total amount of floor and wall space required by isolated motor control apparatus. The individual units generally are interchangeable and easily removable as well. With proper planning, MCCs can be designed with provisions to allow for future system expansion.

Vertical sections generally are 20 in (50.8 cm) wide by 90 in (228.6 cm) high, and most designs can accommodate up to six motor starter units per section.

Motor Control Center Specifications

Usually the following information is required to process an MCC order properly.

1. Service voltage
2. Configuration
3. Size of main horizontal bus
4. Bus bracing
5. Incoming service
6. Main protective device
7. Wiring NEMA class
8. Wiring NEMA type
9. Metering
10. Branch protective devices

1. Service Voltage.   Low-voltage ratings for industrial control apparatus are based on utilization voltage per NEMA ICSI-112.22 voltage rating and are as follows for 60-Hz alternating current, multiphase: 115, 200, 230, 460, and 575 V. Corresponding system voltages are 120, 208, 240, 480, and 600 V.

Enter the proper values for hertz, phase, and number of wires used in system.

2. Configuration.   The MCC should be of dead-front, indoor design and fabricated from code-gauge steel, with all sections joined to form a single assembly. All side, front, and rear cover plates should be field-removable.

The MCC enclosure should be (unless otherwise noted):

- NEMA 1 indoor construction
- Non-walk-in—front accessible

Main and branch units should be front-connected. The MCC should have space or provisions for future expansion, as noted on the plans.

The MCCs are to be constructed in accordance with the latest NEMA-ICS and UL 845 standards.

Individual sections are to be front-accessible, not less than 15 (38.1 cm) deep, and the rear of all sections should align. All bolts used to join current-carrying parts should be installed so as to permit servicing from the front only so that no rear access is required. An unobstructed conduit entry area is to be provided at the top and bottom of each standard control section.

3. Size of Main Horizontal Bus.   Mark as required. Busbar is to be UL rated for ____600 A ____800 A ____1200 A ____1600 A and ____2000 A.

4. Bus Bracing

Main Bus. The MCC should be bused with rectangular busbars made of ____tin ____silver plated copper, and braced for ____42,000 A ____65,000 A ____85,000 A ____100,000 A.

The through bus on the end section should be extended and predrilled to allow the addition of future sections with standard busbar splice plates.

Ground Bus. Specify amperage or size. Specify location if specific location is desired. Recommend always mounting in bottom front unless full length neutral bus is also required. Specify lug size required or ground cable size.

Neutral Bus. If required, shall be ____300 A ____600 A ____800 A, located in the ____incoming line section only ____full length, mounted in the bottom. Specify lug size required for neutral cable or actual neutral cable size.

5. *Incoming Cable Entry.* ____Lugs ____crimp-type connectors to terminate ____copper ____aluminum cable, should be furnished as detailed on plans for ____top ____bottom entry.

Bus Duct Entry. The MCC is to be fed by ____copper ____aluminum, ____A, ____bus duct, as detailed on plans, ____ and other sections of the specification. The MCC manufacturer is to be responsible for coordination, proper phasing, and internal busing to the incoming bus duct. Detailed plans of the incoming bus duct is to be supplied to the manufacturer of the MCC.

Unit Terminals. ____A (None) ____Bd (control terminals only) ____Bt (control and power terminals through Size 3)

Each protective device should have an individual door over the front, or common door for dual-mounted units, equipped with one or more voidable interlocks that prevent the door from being opened when the switches are in the ON position, unless the interlock is purposely defeated by activation of the defeater mechanisms. All breakers or fusible switches should be removable from the front of the MCC without disturbing adjacent units. The MCC should have space or provision for future units.

6. *Main Protective Device.* The main protective device, to be installed in the service section, is as indicated below.

Molded-case circuit breaker of the quick-make, quick-break, trip-free, ____ heavy duty, ____ extra heavy duty, ____ energy limiting, ____ solid-state type. It should be an ____ frame ____ two-pole ____ three-pole, 600-V breaker with a trip current rating of:

____400 A	____1000 A	____2000 A
____600 A	____1200 A	____2500 A
____800 A	____1600 A	____3000 A

and an interrupting capacity of not less than ____ A rms symmetrical at the system voltage.

The following accessory features are to be included: ____ shunt trip, ____ electrical operator, ____ ground-fault relaying, _____ (other).

Fusible switch of the quick-make, quick-break type. It should be a ____ two-pole ____ three-pole, ____ 240-V ____ 600-V unit with a continuous current rating of ____ 400 ____ 600 ____ 800 ____ 1200 A, and with ____ A class ____ fuses, suitable for application on a system with ____ A symmetrical available fault current.

Bolted pressure switch of the quick-make, quick-break type. It should be a ____ two-pole ____ three-pole ____ 240-V ____ 480-V unit with a continuous current rating of:

____800 A	____1600 A	____2500 A
____1200 A	____2000 A	____3000 A

and with ____ A class L fuses, suitable for application on a system with ____ A symmetrical available fault current.

The following accessory features are to be included: ____ shunt trip, ____ electrical operator, ____ ground-fault relaying, _____ (other).

Power circuit breaker with a ____ stationary ____ drawout frame, and a current rating of:

____600 A	____2000 A
____800 A	____3000 A
____1600 A	

It is to be ____ manually ____ electrically operated with a(n) ____ electromechanical ____ solid-state trip device, and an interrupting capacity of ____ A rms symmetrical at the system voltage.

The following accessory features are included: ____ short time delay, ____ ground-fault relay (trip), ____ shunt trip (M.O.C/B only), ____ control power transformer, _____ (other).

7. Wiring NEMA Class.   Indicate class I or class II as required. If class II, elementary or schematic drawings should be supplied with the order.

8. Wiring NEMA Type.   Mark as required. If C terminals are mounted in bottom wiring space section, additional unit space will be required for more than one row of terminals.
    Unit Terminals (B or C Wiring).   If B or C wiring, NEMA class is required indicate type of terminals desired.
    Pull-Apart Terminals.   Indicate where required.

9. Metering.   The following customer metering equipment should be furnished as shown on the plans.

Main Bus
____ Voltmeter, with ____-phase transfer switch
____ Ammeter with ____-phase transfer switch
____ Watthour meter(s) (two) (three)-element (with) (without) demand attachment
____ _____ Current transformer(s),
        _____ /5 or suitable rating
____ _____ Potential transformer(s), suitable rating
Branch Circuits
____ Ammeter(s), with ____-phase transfer switch
____ _____ Current transformer(s),
        _____ /5 or suitable rating

10. Branch Protective Devices.   All molded-case circuit breakers, fusible switches, and/or motor starter units used as a protective device in a branch circuit should meet the requirements of the appropriate paragraph below.
    Each protective device should have an individual door over the front, equipped with a voidable interlock that prevents the door from being opened when the switch is in the "on" position, unless the interlock is purposely defeated by activation of the defeater mechanism.
    Molded-case circuit breakers should be of the quick-make, quick-break, trip-free, ____ motor circuit protector (MCP), ____ thermal-magnetic type ____ solid-state, with frame, trip, and voltage ratings, either two-pole or three-pole, as indicated. All breakers should have an interrupting capacity of not less than ____ A rms symmetrical at the system voltage. All breakers should be removable from the front of the MCC without disturbing adjacent units. The MCC should have space or provision for future units.
    Fusible switches should be quick-make, quick-break units and conform to the ratings shown on the plans.
    All switches should have externally operated handles. Switches should be equipped with ____ fuse holders and class ____ fuses of ampere rating and type as indicated. Suitable for application on a system with ____ A symmetrical available fault current.
    NEMA or motor matched magnetic starters are to be furnished of the type and horsepower ratings as indicated. Thermal overload relays on starters should be ____noncompensated melting-alloy type ____bimetal ____bimetal ambient compensated ____self-powered solid-state type. Three overload elements should be furnished on each starter. The overload heater elements or solid-state overload should be sized from the actual motor nameplate data.
    The following accessory features should be furnished on each starter:

____Individual control power transformers

____Pilot light(s)

____Auxiliary contacts

____NO ____NC

Push buttons, selector switches, and other pilot devices shall be furnished as indicated.
    The checklist shown in Table 4-17 is provided to assist the plant engineer in installing and maintaining MCCs.

TABLE 4-17 Checklists for Installing and Maintaining Motor Control Centers

Installation quick checklist

Receiving
❏ Inspect package for damage.
❏ After unpacking, inspect equipment for damage in transit.
❏ If damaged or incomplete, substantiate claims against shipper with identification of parts, description of damage, and photographs.

Handling
❏ Simplify handling by leaving equipment on shipping skid.
❏ Use the lifting means provided for moving the equipment.
❏ Take care to use the proper method of moving a motor control center.

Storage
❏ Store in a clean, dry space at moderate temperature.
❏ Cover with a canvas or heavy-duty plastic cover.
❏ If storage area is cool or damp, cover equipment completely and heat to prevent condensation.

Location Selection
❏ Flat and level floor
❏ Overhead clearance
❏ Accessibility front and rear.
❏ Protection from splash and drip, dust, and heat.
❏ Space for future expansion.
❏ If bottom conduit entry is used, conduit should be in place and stubbed up before equipment is installed.

Installation Method
❏ Grout into the foundation.
❏ Weld channel sills to steel leveling plates.
❏ Embedded anchor bolts in floor.

Field Assembly
❏ Remove hardware and horizontal bus connecting links from shipping splits.
❏ Install first shipping split.
❏ Remove end cover plates of structures to be joined (if required).
❏ Carefully align second split with first. Bolt structure together per manufacturer's instructions.
❏ Remove horizontal wireway barrier or units to expose horizontal bus.
❏ Connect horizontal buses with bus links. Torque bolts to manufacturer's recommendations.
❏ Grommet top and bottom horizontal wireways.
❏ Install heater coils (check selection against motor nameplate data).
❏ Install fuses.

Conduit Entry at Top
❏ Remove top plates from structure.
❏ Cut conduit entry holes in top plates.
❏ Reinstall top plates.
❏ Install conduits

Incoming Line Connections
❏ Choose the shortest, most direct route from remote mains.

❏ If cables cannot be directly routed to terminals, provide adequate space for clamping the cables.
❏ Torque incoming lines to main lugs only per manufacturing recommendations.
❏ Torque all incoming connections to main circuit breakers and fusible disconnects as per the breaker or disconnect manufacturer's recommendations. The torque requirements will be found on a label located on the disconnecting device.

Outgoing Power and Control Wiring
❏ Disengage plug-in unit stabs from vertical bus. Connect control and power wiring to units.
❏ Use stranded wire.
❏ Leave enough slack to permit partial withdrawal of unit for test position maintenance.
❏ Pull wiring between units through vertical and horizontal wireway securing wires in the vertical wireway with wire ties provided.
❏ Route wiring between sections through the top or bottom horizontal wireways.
❏ Reinsert plug-in units to engage stabs.

Preoperation Checks
❏ Test insulation resistance of all circuits with the control center as ground.
❏ Remove restraining devices from contacts and shunts from current transformers. Make sure that all parts of magnetic devices operate freely.
❏ Check electrical interlocks for proper contact operation. Make sure that each motor is connected to its proper starter.
❏ Check all heater elements for proper installation.
❏ Check all timers for proper time interval setting and contact operation.
❏ Check fusible disconnect starters for proper fuse size. Clean the control center. Rid it of all extraneous material. Use a vacuum cleaner, not compressed air.
❏ Check all connections for mechanical and electrical tightness.
❏ Close all access plates and doors.

Energizing Motor Control Centers
❏ Make sure all unit disconnect handles and control center mains are turned to OFF.
❏ Turn on remote mains. Turn on motor control center main circuit breakers or fusible disconnects.
❏ Turn on unit disconnect handles one by one.
❏ Jog motors to check for proper rotation
❏ Adjust MCPs

Insulation Test (Megger)
❏ Measure phase to phase and phase to ground. Resistance measurements should be taken before a motor control center is placed into service and after installation or maintenance. When performing resistance measurements on motor control centers use an insulation tester (Megger) with a potential of 500–1000 V.

TABLE 4-17   Checklists for Installing and Maintaining Motor Control Centers (*Continued*)

WARNING: Before performing installation or maintenance, turn off electrical power to the control unit to avoid electrical shock.

WARNING: The main disconnect must be in the OFF position during all megger testing of the motor control center.

CAUTION: Devices such as solid-state components, capacitor units or any other devices which are not designed to withstand Megger voltage should be disconnected before testing the rest of the motor control center.

Take readings between each phase and from each phase to ground. This should be done with the branch disconnects OFF and again with the branch disconnects ON.

Branch Disconnects OFF:
Typically readings taken with all disconnects in the OFF position should be between 5–20 MΩ.

New equipment which was stored in a damp area may register lower on initial start-up. If readings are above 1 MΩ during start-up the following procedure may be observed to help dry the motor control center.

Energize several individual control units. If additional readings are above 1 MΩ, energize additional units.

After the equipment has been in operation for 48 h, the readings should be in the 5–20 MΩ range.

If at any time Megger readings are below 5 MΩ (1 MΩ during start-up) consult your local motor control center representative.

Branch Disconnects ON:
Before taking reading with the branch disconnects ON, disconnect all devices completing circuits between phases or between phases and neutral such as control transformers. Readings observed may be slightly lower than the OFF readings, but the start-up 1-MΩ lower limit still applies.

Record and keep a record of the Megger readings. Abrupt changes in resistive values may be an indication of potential failure. Even sudden changes within the 5–20-MΩ range may be an advance signal of insulation failure. The early detection of faulty insulation components can save costly repairs and downtime.

Maintenance quick checklist

Scheduling
❑ Schedule maintenance appropriate to the severity of service.
❑ Consider environment (dampness, heat, and dust), severity of operations, and the importance of the machinery being controlled.

❑ Control unit maintenance should coincide with inspection of the motor being controlled.
❑ Buswork inspection entails shutting down the entire control center.

Cleaning
❑ Use a vacuum cleaner, not compressed air.
❑ Excess deposits of foreign materials signify faulty gasketing.
❑ Pay particular attention to conductive deposits.

Loose Connections
❑ Periodic checking of tightness of connections promotes reliability and reduces heating.
❑ Overheating and discolorations signify loose connections.
❑ Torque horizontal bus bolts to manufacturer's recommendations.
❑ Torque incoming line connections to main lugs only to manufacturer's recommendations.
❑ Torque all incoming connections to main circuit breakers and fusible disconnects as per the breaker or disconnect manufacturer's recommendations.
❑ The torque requirements will be found on a label located on the disconnecting device.

Disconnect Operating Handle Adjustments
❑ Remove unit from center or place in test position.
❑ Adjust handles per manufacturer's recommendations.

Contacts
❑ Make sure that all contacts are free from extraneous materials, excess pitting or burning.
❑ Check for spring pressure.

Locking in Engaged Position
❑ To lock in ON, drill out the indentations on the disconnect operating handle and insert a padlock.
❑ To lock in OFF, as many as three padlocks may be inserted in the disconnect operating handle.

Field Additions of Sections
❑ For field additions of sections, follow the same procedure as for the field assembly of shipping splits.

Addition and Replacement of Control Units
❑ De-energize motor control center. Follow manufacturer's recommendations.

Adding to a Blank Unit Space
❑ Follow manufacturer's recommendations.

Installation Test (Megger)
❑ Same as previous

APPLICABLE CODES AND STANDARDS

American National Standards Institute (ANSI). Standards on a wide variety of electrical equipment, published by the American National Standards Institute.

Canadian Standards Association. Canadian standards on a wide variety of electrical equipment, published by the Canadian Standards Association, 178 Rexdale Boulevard, Rexdale, Ontario M9W1R3.

Machine Tool Electrical Standards. Standards of the National Machine Tool Builders Association, 7901 Westpark Drive, McLean, VA 22101.

National Electrical Code®. Standard of the National Fire Protection Association, Quincy, MA 02269.*

National Electrical Manufacturers' Association (NEMA). Standards on motors and control published by the National Electrical Manufacturers' Association, 2101 L Street N.W., Washington, D.C. 20037.

Underwriters Laboratories Inc. (UL). An independent organization that tests and makes recommendations based on safety and fire hazard conditions relating to the tested equipment. Standards are published by Underwriters Laboratories Inc., 333 Pfingsten Rd., Northbrook, IL 60062.

BIBLIOGRAPHY

Alerich, Walter N.: *Electric Motor Control,* Van Nostrand Reinhold, New York, 1975.

Chestnut, Harold: *Systems Engineering Tools,* Wiley, New York, 1965.

Chestnut, Harold, and Robert W. Mayer: *Servomechanism and Regulating System Design,* 2d ed., vol. I, and vol. II, Wiley, New York, 1959.

Cockrell, Wm. D.: *Industrial Electronics Handbook,* McGraw-Hill, New York, 1958.

DC Motors-Speed Controls-Servo Systems, Electro-Craft Corp., Hopkins, Minnesota, 1972.

Heumann, G. W.: *Magnetic Control of Industrial Motors,* Wiley, New York, 1961.

IEEE Standard 142-1972: *Recommended Practices for Grounding Industrial and Commercial Power Systems,* IEEE, New York.

Keucken, John A.: *Solid-State Motor Controls,* Tab Books, Blue Ridge Summit, Pennsylvania, 1978.

Kintner, Paul M.: *Electronic Control Systems in Industry,* McGraw-Hill, New York, 1968.

McPartland, J. F.: *Motor and Control Circuits,* McGraw-Hill, New York, 1975.

Millermaster, Ralph A.: *Harwood's Control of Electric Motors,* 4th ed., Wiley, New York, 1970.

American National Standards Institute: ANS/C2-1992, ***National Electrical Code,*** New York, 1992.

Siskind, Charles S.: *Electrical Control Systems in Industry,* McGraw-Hill, New York, 1963.

---

* ***National Electrical Code®*** is a Registered Trademark of the National Fire Protection Association, Inc., Quincy, MA 02269.

CHAPTER 3-5

LIGHTING

Paul F. Lienesch*
Philips Lighting Co.
Somerset, New Jersey

---

* Updated for this Second Edition by Paul F. Lienesch from chapter written for First Edition by Willard C. Allphin, GTE Sylvania Inc., Danvers, Massachusetts.

GLOSSARY

Adaptation   A lighting condition to which the eye is accustomed.

Angstrom   A unit of wavelength equal to one-ten billionth of a meter.

Arc discharge   An electric discharge characterized by high cathode current density and a low voltage drop at the cathodes.

Ballast   A device used with an electric discharge lamp to obtain the necessary circuit conditions (voltage, current, and waveform) for starting and operation.

Blackbody   The theoretical body which radiates the maximum at every wavelength.

Brightness   Perceived luminance.

Candlepower   In practical terms, the luminous intensity in all directions from an international standard candle.

Cavity ratio   A number depending upon the length, width, and height of a cavity.

Ceiling cavity   The cavity formed by the ceiling, the upper walls, and the plane of the fixtures.

Coefficient of utilization (CU)   Ratio of the lumens reaching the work plane to those leaving the lamps.

Color adaptation   The condition of the eyes when they are "used to" a particular color of illumination.

Color rendering index   The percentage by which color emitted by a lamp approaches that of a blackbody emitting light of the same correlated color temperature.

Color temperature (of a light source)   The temperature in kelvins at which a blackbody must operate to emit the same color of light as the light source.

Correlated color temperature (of a light source)   The temperature of a blackbody, the color of which most nearly matches that of the source.

Cosine law   The law that illumination on any surface varies as the cosine of the angle of incidence.

Cutoff angle (of a luminaire)   The angle between a horizontal line and the line of light at which a bare lamp first becomes visible.

Diffuse reflection   Light reflected at various angles from a matte (nonglossy)

Diffuse transmission   Light emitted in various directions after passing through a translucent material.

Disability glare   Light causing reduced visibility or visual performance.

Discomfort glare   Glare which produces discomfort. It is not necessarily associated with disability glare.

Efficacy   Lumens per watt of a light source (lm/W).

Electroluminescence   Light emitted by a phosphor excited by an electromagnetic field.

Electromagnetic spectrum   Electric and magnetic radiation including all wavelengths.

Equivalent sphere illumination (ESI)   The level of sphere illumination equivalent to the measured illumination on a task.

Fixture　The common term for a *luminaire* which is fixed in place.

Fluorescent lamp　A low-pressure mercury discharge lamp with fluorescent phosphors which shift the invisible shortwave radiation to longer, visible wavelengths.

Footcandle (fc)　The illumination on one square foot of surface with one lumen evenly distributed over it; or the illumination on one square foot of curved surface all points of which are at a distance of one foot from a standard candle.

Footlambert (fL)　The luminance of a uniformly transmitting or reflecting surface emitting one lumen per square foot (1 lm/ft^2).

Glare　Luminance in the visual field which produces discomfort or reduces the ability to see.

High-intensity discharge (HID) lamp　One of a group, including mercury, metal halide, and high-pressure sodium lamps.

High-pressure sodium lamp　Has a sodium vapor discharge in a ceramic tube surrounded by an outer bulb.

Illuminance　The amount of light per unit area falling on a surface.

Indirect lighting　Illumination from fixtures sending almost all of their light upward.

Lamp　A synthetic source of light. Unfortunately, the term is also used for a portable lamp bulb, housing, and shade plugged into an outlet.

Light-loss factor (LLF)　In aggregate, the illumination just before cleaning and relamping, divided by the initial (100 h for fluorescent) illumination.

Lumen　The amount of luminous flux on one square foot of surface, all points of which are one foot from a standard candle.

Lumen method　Method used to determine the number of lamps or fixtures needed to provide uniform illumination on a horizontal work surface.

Luminance　Number of lumens per square foot leaving a surface toward the eye or a measuring instrument.

Lux (lx)　The illumination on one square meter of surface with one lumen evenly distributed over it, or the illumination on one square meter of curved surface all parts of which are one meter from a standard candle.

Maintenance factor　Average illumination just before cleaning and relamping, divided by the initial (100 h for fluorescent) illumination. (Now called light-loss factor.)

Mercury lamp　A lamp whose light comes from a mercury arc in a tube surrounded by an outer bulb.

Metameric pair　Two colors which look alike under one color of light but different under another color.

Nanometer　Unit of wavelength equal to one-billionth of a meter (1×10^{-9} m).

Nit　The luminance of a uniformly transmitting or reflecting surface emitting one lumen per square meter.

Photopic vision　Vision when luminance of visual field is above about one footlambert.

Point-by-point method　Determining illumination at a point by adding the contributions of all light sources in the vicinity.

Polarized light　Light whose vibrations are confined to one plane.

Radiant energy　Energy traveling in the form of electromagnetic waves.

Scotopic vision　Vision where luminance of the visual field is below about 0.01 fL.

Shielding angle (of a luminaire)　Angle between a horizontal line and the line of sight at which a bare lamp first becomes visible.

Starter　A device used with fluorescent lamps other than rapid-start or instant-start, which first closes a circuit through the cathodes and then opens it, causing the arc to strike.

Troffer　A lighting unit, usually longer than it is wide, which is installed in the ceiling.

Tungsten-halogen lamp A gas-filled tungsten lamp containing certain halogens.

Ultraviolet radiation (uv) Radiation of shorter wavelengths than the visual range.

Veiling reflections Light reflected from a visual task which partially or entirely obscures the task.

Zonal cavity method Method for determining coefficients of utilization by taking into account the shapes and reflectances of three cavities for suspended fixtures and two cavities for ceiling-mounted fixtures.

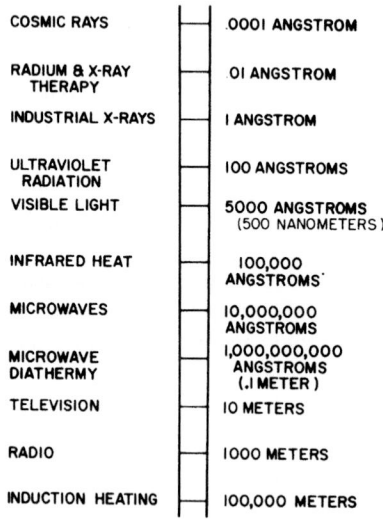

FIGURE 5-1 The electromagnetic spectrum, with a few types of radiation indicated. Each value actually represents a range.

LIGHT AND THE EYE

We are surrounded by radiation, most of it invisible: radio waves, microwaves, and a host of others, as indicated in Fig. 5-1. Only a small band of this enormous array of radiation is visible to the normal human eye, a band including from about 400 to 700 nm. (One nanometer equals ten angstroms.) As shown in Fig. 5-2, the band of visible radiation ranges through the colors of the spectrum from violet to red. Beyond the red is infrared (radiant heat) and beyond violet in the other direction is ultraviolet. We often say "ultraviolet light" but strictly speaking, it is not light since it is invisible.

As shown by the curve in Fig. 5-2, the eye is not equally sensitive to all parts of the visible spectrum, its peak of sensitivity being in the yellow-green. This is the *photopic* curve for luminance above about 1 fL. For night vision of luminances below 0.01 fL, the *scotopic* curve is

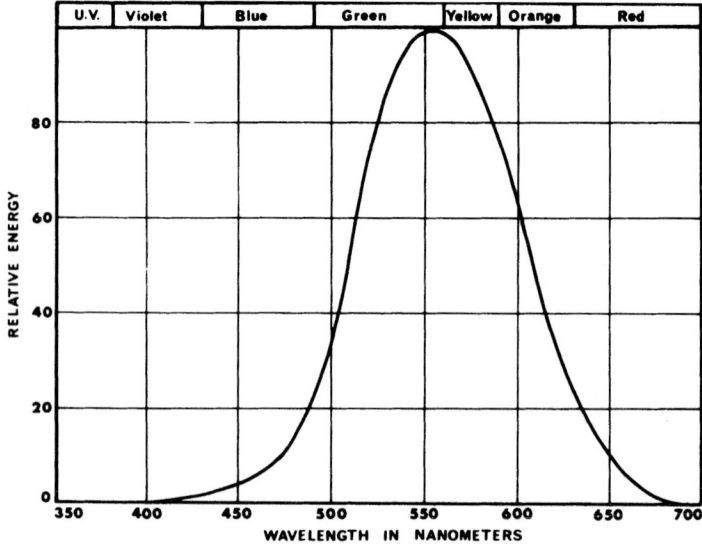

FIGURE 5-2 Photopic sensitivity curve of an average human eye.

displaced to the left by about 50 nm. Other curves fall between these two for luminances between 0.01 and 1 fL.

Near-ultraviolet from the sun is responsible for sunburn and tanning. Produced from electric sources, it is used to excite fluorescent paints and dyes, making them glow. Far uv has a sterilizing effect but can be very harmful to eyesight. As will be seen later, the inner tube of a mercury lamp produces harmful uv which is filtered out by the outer bulb.

"White" light usually includes all the colors in the visible spectrum, but the proportions can vary.

Illumination Levels

The eye adapts itself to an enormous range of illuminations from moonlight to sunlight, a range of almost a million to one, but neither condition would be desirable for close visual tasks. Working levels from electric lighting commonly range from 10 to 200 fc (108 to 2150 lx) but higher levels are used in special cases, particularly over small areas.

Speed and accuracy of seeing depend upon the size of the detail and its contrast with its background, as well as the illumination.

It should be noted that older eyes require more light than young eyes for the same visual performance.

Changes in adaptation take time, more in going from high to low than from low to high levels, as when one goes from daylight into a darkened movie theater. At first one can see scarcely anything, but as the eyes adapt, people and objects gradually become visible. Under industrial conditions, visual performance is reduced when a worker has to look back and forth between areas of widely different luminance.

Luminance

An important distinction must be made between brightness and luminance, since the two are often confused. Luminance has to do with an object and is a measure of the number of lumens per unit area going in a particular direction. *Brightness* concerns the effect on the eye and the brain produced by the luminance. For example, consider the headlights of an approaching car at night. If they are on high beam the brightness is so great as to be almost blinding, yet the same lighted headlamps seen in daylight are scarcely noticeable. The luminance toward the eye is the same in both cases, but the adaptation of the eye makes the headlights seem much less bright in daylight. Just as footcandles are lumens per square foot falling on a surface, footlamberts are lumens per square foot leaving a surface toward the eye or a measuring instrument.

Color Adaptation

The eye also adapts to colors. Consider, for example, adjacent rooms, one lighted by Cool White and the other by Warm White fluorescent lamps. Strictly speaking, the rendition of colors is not perfect in either case, but color adaptation of the eye makes both seem "normal." However, if someone who had been in the Cool White room for some time steps into the Warm White room, things will seem rather yellow at first. Soon this feeling disappears and things seem normal. In the same way, going into the Cool White room after being adapted to the Warm White room will make things seem bluish-green at first. Accurate matching of colors is not possible in either case, as will be seen in the "Inspection Lighting" section.

Glare

Glare is an important consideration in all lighting. There are two types: *discomfort glare* and *disability glare*. Discomfort glare is subjective, depending upon how the observer feels about it, and it varies greatly from one person to another in the same situation. *Disability glare* is objective and interferes, to a greater or lesser degree, with seeing the visual task. It is often assumed that discomfort glare and disability glare are merely different degrees of the same thing, but this is not the case. Either can be present without the other for a particular individual in a particular situation.

Veiling Reflections

Veiling reflections are a special case of disability glare. Often when looking at a glossy photograph or magazine page the reflection of a window or a lighting fixture prevents seeing details unless we tilt the material. What is seldom realized is that subtle reflections appear on most visual tasks in business and industry, and reduce ability to see detail easily and rapidly. Veiling reflections can usually be reduced by changing the relationship between the light sources and the work, but whatever veiling reflections remain must be compensated for by increasing the illumination.

Behavior of Light

When a ray of light strikes a smooth reflecting surface, most of it is reflected with the angle of reflection equal to the angle of incidence. This is *specular* reflection, as in Fig. 5-3. A ray striking an entirely matte surface is reflected equally in all directions. This is *diffuse* reflection, as in Fig. 5-4. Most surfaces give a combination of specular and diffuse reflection. See Fig. 5-5. No reflecting surface is perfect, so some of the light is absorbed by the material and goes off in heat.

Light passing through a translucent material leaves it as diffused light, as in Fig. 5-6.

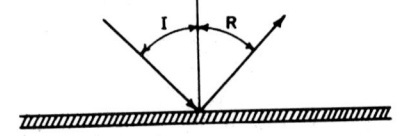

FIGURE 5-3   Specular reflection from a surface.

FIGURE 5-4   Diffuse reflection from a surface.

FIGURE 5-5   Combination of specular and diffuse reflection.

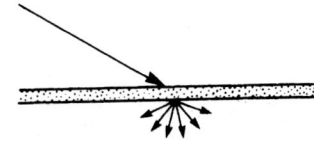

FIGURE 5-6   Transmission through a translucent substance.

A ray of light striking a transparent material is bent when entering the material and bent again when leaving it. See Fig. 5-7.

Light passing through a transparent object whose sides are not parallel is bent as in the prism of Fig. 5-8. This effect is used in some lighting fixtures, sometimes to reflect light and

FIGURE 5-7   Transmission through a transparent substance.

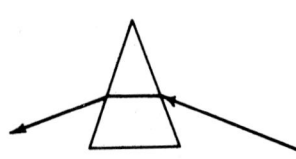

FIGURE 5-8   Path of light ray through a prism.

sometimes to refract it (change its direction). Transparent materials absorb some of the light just as reflecting surfaces do.

Polarized Light

Polarized light has been used to some extent in illumination and may become more widely used in the future. Polarizing materials can be used in lighting fixtures to reduce reflected glare spots and veiling reflections, but for each fixture there is only one angle from the vertical (Brewsters' angle) at which the greatest reduction occurs.

INCANDESCENT LAMPS

Incandescent lamps are too familiar to require any discussion of their operating principles, but certain characteristics are important to note. For example, Fig. 5-9 shows the effects of changes in the applied voltage on lumen output, wattage, and life. This chart offers an answer to claims for lamps with tremendously long life. For example, a lamp designed to last 3 times as long as normal would give only about 76 percent of the light. This may be desirable when small numbers of lamps are in difficult-to-reach locations, but is not economical for general lighting applications. The need for longer life in these cases is met by extended service lamps. See lamp manufacturers' catalogs.

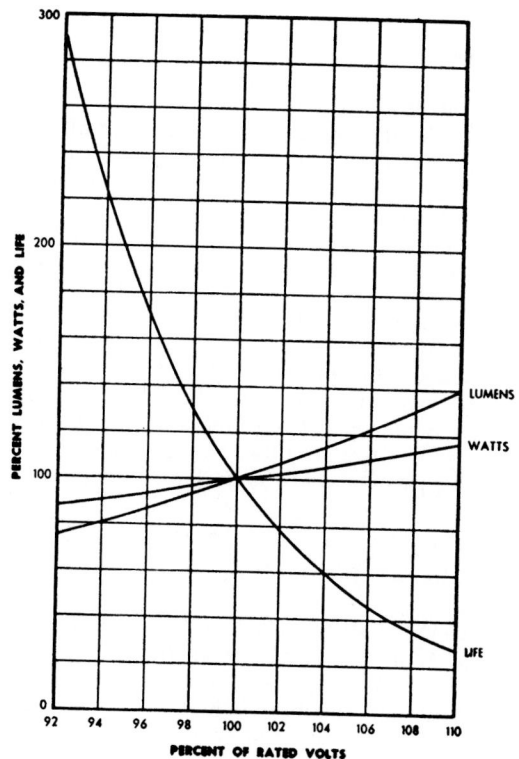

FIGURE 5-9   Incandescent lamp characteristics as affected by voltage.

There are also changes through life due to gradual wasting away of filament material and to interior bulb blackening.

The *rated average life* (not average rated life) of an incandescent lamp is the point at which 50 percent of a large batch will have failed under normal operating conditions. As seen in Fig. 5-10, some will fail early and some will last longer than average life. Operating lamps much beyond the rated point is not economical, however, because of the reduced output.

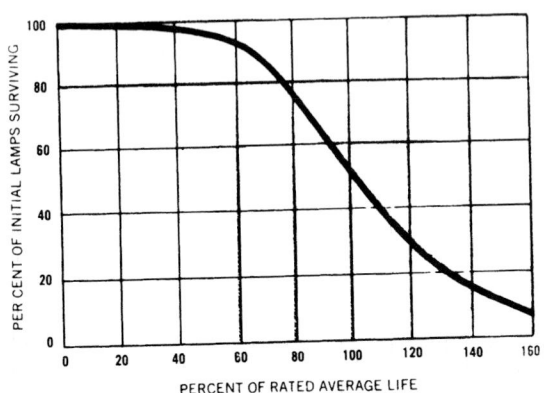

FIGURE 5-10 Typical life-expectancy curve for incandescent lamps.

Reflector Lamps

PAR-bulb and R-bulb lamps combine in one unit a light source and a highly efficient sealed-in reflector consisting of vaporized aluminum or silver applied to the inner surface of the bulb. PAR bulbs are made of hard or heat-resisting glass. PAR lamps up to 150 W in size, as well as a few special-service R lamps with heat-resistant-glass bulbs, can be used outdoors without danger of breakage from rain or snow. Larger PAR lamps and all other R lamps are not recommended for outdoor use unless protected from the elements. The 100-W PAR-38 and 150-W R-40 lamps are available in several colors.

In addition to flood and spotlight service, PAR-bulb lamps have found wide application in the automotive and aviation industries, and other applications where compact lighting units of precise beam control are necessary. Elliptical reflector (ER) type lamps provide a more concentrated spot of light than PAR or R type bulbs. ER lamps are also especially efficient when used in recessed-type fixtures since less light is trapped in the recess than with PAR lamps. Low-voltage PAR lamps, due to their low-voltage, compact-filament design, provide point-source optical control for maximum efficiency. They are less susceptible to breakage under conditions of mechanical shock or vibration due to their short, heavier low-voltage filaments.

High- and Low-Voltage Lamps

Lamps similar to those of the standard-voltage line are available for operation on 230 and 250 V. The low efficacy of these lamps as compared to like lamps of standard-voltage rating has already been mentioned. Other disadvantages resulting from the smaller filament wire diameter of high-voltage lamps are reduced mechanical strength, and larger overall light-source size which makes them less satisfactory for use in floodlight and projection equipment. The only gain achieved by the industrial use of these higher voltages is the reduction in ampere load which results from doubling the voltage, and the consequent saving in wiring cost. Lamps for operation on 30- and 60-V circuits are also available for use in train lighting and in country home service.

Tungsten Halogen Lamps

The improved characteristics of tungsten halogen lamps, such as longer life, higher efficacy, compact size, and greatly reduced bulb blackening during life, are a consequence of a tungsten halogen cycle. A simplified explanation of the cycle is that evaporated or sublimed tungsten from the filament combines with the halogen gas (iodine or bromine added to the fill gas) to form a tungsten halide. The bulb wall is hot enough so that the halide is in the gaseous phase at any point in the lamp. When the tungsten halide comes in contact with the very hot tungsten filament it disassociates into tungsten, which redeposits on the filament, and halogen gas. The gas is then available to react with more tungsten. Unfortunately, all the tungsten does not redeposit at the spots from which it vaporized. Hence this lamp also has a finite life.

Fused quartz or hard glass bulbs are used to withstand the high wall temperatures necessary to keep the tungsten halides vaporized.

Tungsten halogen lamps are both single- and double-ended. They may also be sealed into outer bulbs such as PAR types for good optical control. They are generally more expensive than conventional incandescent lamps. Because of their characteristics, tungsten halogen lamps find extensive application in floodlighting, aviation, photographic, photocopy, special effects, and special application lighting. They have found broad use in automobile headlighting.

ARC-DISCHARGE LAMPS

With the exception of exotic types such as luminescent panels and light-emitting diodes (LEDs), all electric light sources depend upon either an incandescent filament or an arc.

When a mercury arc, assisted by a small quantity of argon, is formed between two electrodes, it emits most of its energy in narrow bands or "lines" as shown in Fig. 5-11. The lines are drawn to the same height for general illustration, but in actual lamps the heights will vary depending upon gas pressure. Note that most of the lines lie in the invisible uv range. Only two of them are in the visible range, and these account for the bluish-green color of clear mercury lamps.

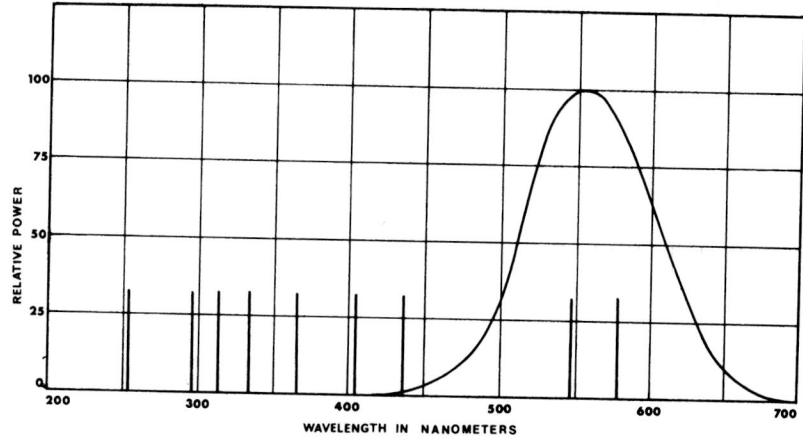

FIGURE 5-11   Energy-emission lines and the visibility curve for an average human eye. Mercury lines are shown with same length. Actual lamps produce different proportions of energy in different lines, the amount depending on the internal gas pressure.

Whereas incandescent lamps are self-limiting devices, a mercury arc would "run away with itself" if placed directly on the line. This is because the more current passing through an arc, the less its resistance. Thus a limiting device, usually a choke coil, is required. With all but the smallest sizes, more than line voltage is needed to start and operate the lamp, so a *ballast* both steps up the voltage and limits the current. See the section "High-Intensity Discharge Lamps" for more on mercury lamps.

Fluorescent Lamps

In a fluorescent lamp, a mercury arc, assisted by a small amount of argon, is formed between two coated-filament electrodes in a long tube. The arc emits most of its energy in invisible uv radiation which does not pass through the glass, but the coating of phosphors inside the tube converts this to visible light by shifting the short wavelengths to longer wavelengths.

The arc must be started either by applying a high voltage to ionize the gas, or by putting a current through each electrode, or *cathode*, to boil off electrons. Small lamps such as those used in desk lamps are sometimes started manually. With lamp and ballast in series across the line, a button is pressed momentarily to put a current through the cathodes. When the button is released, the arc strikes between the cathodes. Most of the early 40-W lamps had starters which performed this operation automatically, and some of these systems are still in use.

Instant-Start Lamps.   Instant-start lamps use a much higher voltage to start the lamps without preheating the electrodes; the ballasts are larger and more expensive, and lamp life is somewhat less. Long instant-start lamps are also called *slimlines*.

Rapid-Start Lamps.   Rapid-start circuits such as in Fig. 5-12 are used for nearly all 40-W fluorescent lamps and for high-output and very-high-output lamps. Current through the cathodes drops when the arc strikes.

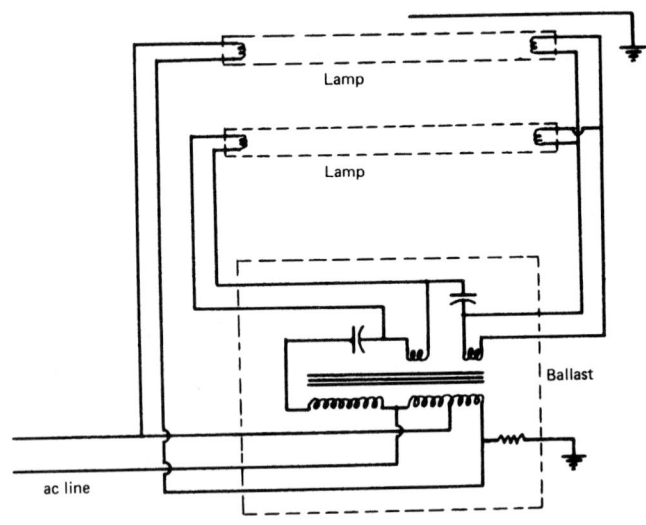

FIGURE 5-12   Series rapid-start circuit.

Ballasts are available for distribution systems from 120 to 277 V. This permits much smaller ballasts. Also, most ballasts for 40-W lamps and larger are power-factor-corrected.

The Electronic Circuit. The electronic circuit converts the normal 60-Hz circuit voltage to high frequency (approximately 25 kHz). The high frequency increases the overall system efficiency by increasing the lamp efficacy and by reducing the watts lost in the ballast. The circuit can be designed to operate the lamps in the rapid-start or instant-start mode (see Fig. 5-13).

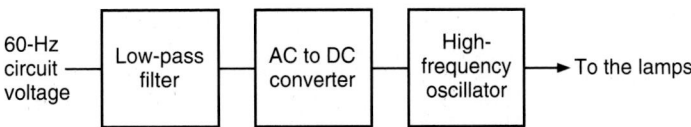

FIGURE 5-13   Block diagram of a high-frequency electronic ballast.

Fluorescent Lamp Colors. The use of differing phosphors permits a considerable range of colors to help produce a desired atmosphere ranging from cool to warm. The most popular fluorescent colors are known as Cool White and Warm White. Where a high degree of color rendition is required, lamps have been available but at the expense of lumen per watt efficacy. Premium color lamps, known as trichromatic phosphor lamps, are available today that combine high color rendering with lumen output that is often higher than the standard color lamps. Figure 5-14 shows spectral distributions of various fluorescent lamps.

Color Temperature. Physicists speak of a theoretical *blackbody* which absorbs all light falling on it. When heated to incandescence, such a body would give off a color of light depending upon its temperature in kelvins, K (Celsius temperature plus 273°). An incandescent lamp filament is close in behavior to a theoretical blackbody. Sunlight and daylight, since they originate from an incandescent body, are given color temperature ratings in kelvins.

Correlated Color Temperature. Fluorescent lamps and high-intensity discharge (HID) lamps, not having smooth spectrums, do not resemble a blackbody enough to have a true color temperature rating. However, for any such lamp there is a color temperature which it resembles. For example, a Cool White lamp having a correlated color temperature of 4100 K is closer to an incandescent lamp of that color temperature than it is to a lamp of any other color temperature.

Color Rendering Index. Color rendering index (CRI) is a measure, in percent, of how closely the correlated color temperature of a lamp approaches a true color temperature. In other words, the correlated color temperature of a lamp is the color the lamp is trying to produce. The CRI tells how well it is succeeding, with a value of 100 being the highest.

Voltage Variations. Voltage variations have less effect on fluorescent lamps than they do on incandescent lamps, but the voltage applied to a fluorescent lamp cannot be ignored. Standard ballasts are designed to operate at 118 V, but lamps on these ballasts will operate satisfactorily over a range from 110 to 125 V. When the voltage is too low, it may be difficult to start the lamp, particularly under humid conditions. When the voltage to a rapid-start lamp is too high, it may operate as an instant-start lamp, causing the cathode coating to be used up more rapidly.

Effect of Starts on Lamp Life. The number of starts does affect the life of a fluorescent lamp because a little of the cathode coating is lost at each start. Figure 5-15 shows mortality curves for 40-W rapid-start lamps for different operating periods. It used to be considered economical to leave lamps burning rather than shut them off for short periods. Now, with the emphasis on saving energy, and with the higher cost of electricity, the practice is to turn them off whenever not in use.

Lumen Maintenance. Lumen maintenance for fluorescent lamps is better than for incandescent lamps. Some manufacturers, in addition to giving initial lumens, give approximate lumens at 40 percent of rated average life. These run about 88 percent of initial for 40-W lamps, 87 percent for 48-in rapid start, and 75 percent for very-high-output lamps.

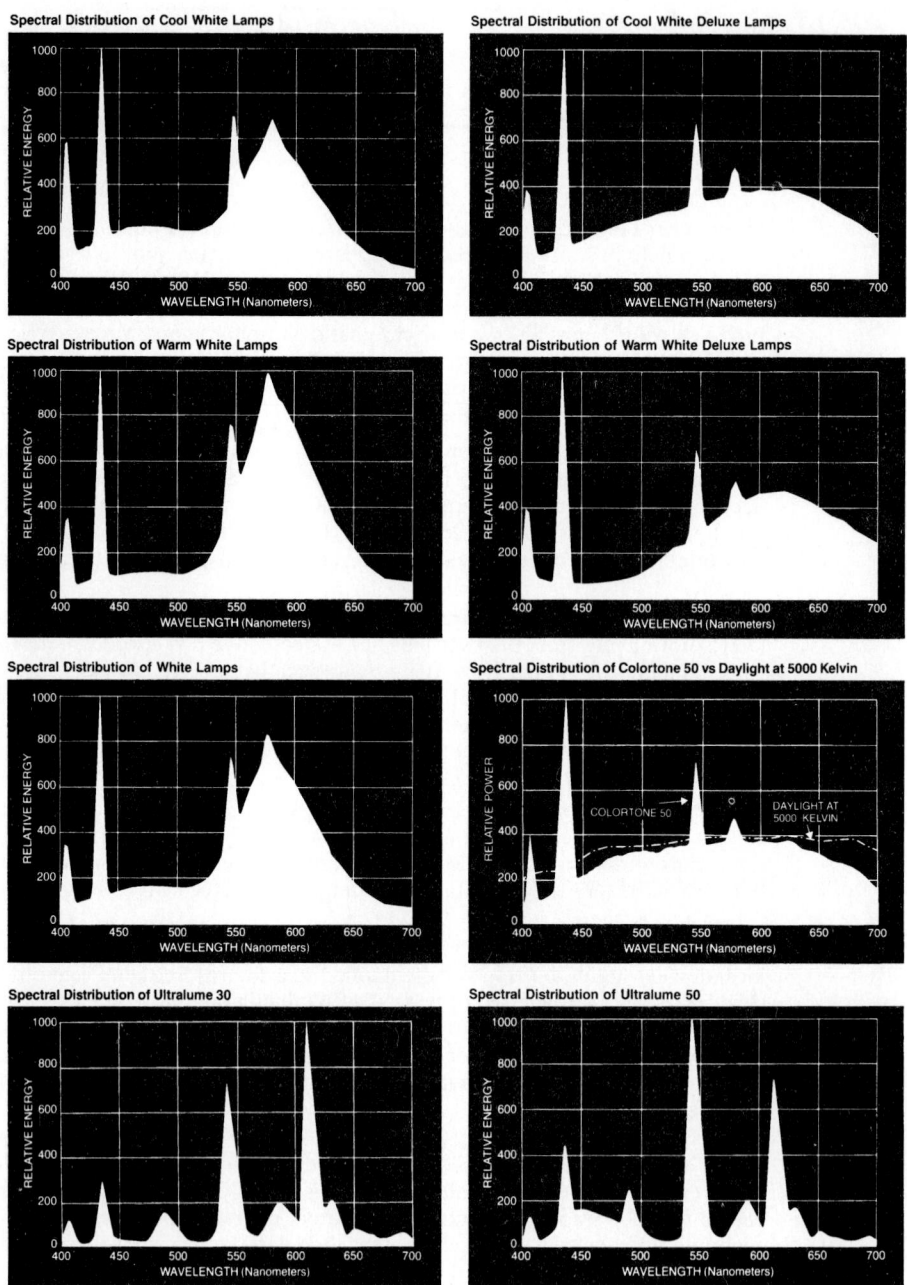

FIGURE 5-14 Spectral distributions of various fluorescent lamps.

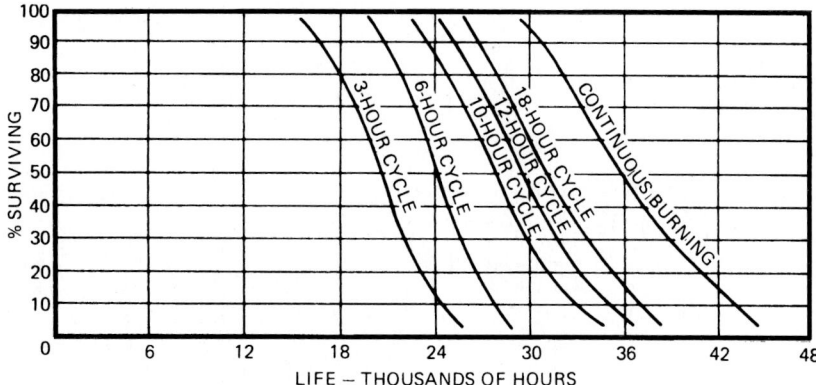

FIGURE 5-15 Typical mortality curves as a function of burning cycles for 40-W rapid-start lamps with a rated life of 20,000+ hours.

Low-Temperature Operation.   Low-temperature operation of standard lamps may not be satisfactory at ambient temperatures below 50°F (10°C). However, jacketed lamps are available and can be operated on low-temperature ballasts.

Compact Fluorescent Lamps.   Due to the continuing increase in energy costs, high-efficiency fluorescent retrofit lamps which can replace incandescent lamps become economically desirable. They are available as integral units where the entire lamp is replaced when it burns out. Other products are designed as adapter systems where the lamp plugs into a socket adapter and only the lamp requires replacement when it fails.

Most compact fluorescent lamps have a 10,000-h rated average life and outlast standard incandescent lamps by 10 to 13 times. The most significant benefit is energy savings. Available in wattages from 5 to 27 W, they replace 25- to 90-W incandescent lamps and can reduce energy consumption up to 76 percent with similar light output results.

Standard compact fluorescent lamps are made for luminaires specifically designed with socket and ballast to accept a specific wattage lamp. They are available in 5- to 40-W sizes and are suitable for a variety of applications where incandescent and standard fluorescent lamps were used previously.

High-Intensity Discharge Lamps

Mercury Vapor.   Mercury vapor, the basic (HID) lamp, is still used in some industrial and street-lighting installations. Construction details are shown in Fig. 5-16. When the lamp is turned on, full starting voltage is applied across the main electrodes and between the lower electrode and the probe near it, causing a glow discharge between the electrode and the probe. This discharge enables an arc to strike in the argon gas between the main electrodes. At first the arc gives off very little light, but its heat gradually vaporizes most of the mercury in the tube. This change builds up pressure and the arc becomes a true mercury-vapor arc. The quartz arc tube passes far uv, but the outer bulb absorbs this. Not shown in Fig. 5-16 is a mechanical-electric device for shutting off the arc if the outer bulb is broken. This is for the protection of eyesight. Mercury vapor lamps are available in wattages ranging from 40 to 1000. Their use for general lighting application has decreased due to their relatively poor efficacy compared to metal halide and high-pressure sodium.

Metal Halide Lamps.   Metal halide lamps are similar in general principles to mercury lamps but the arc tube is smaller and contains halides such as thorium iodide, sodium iodide, and

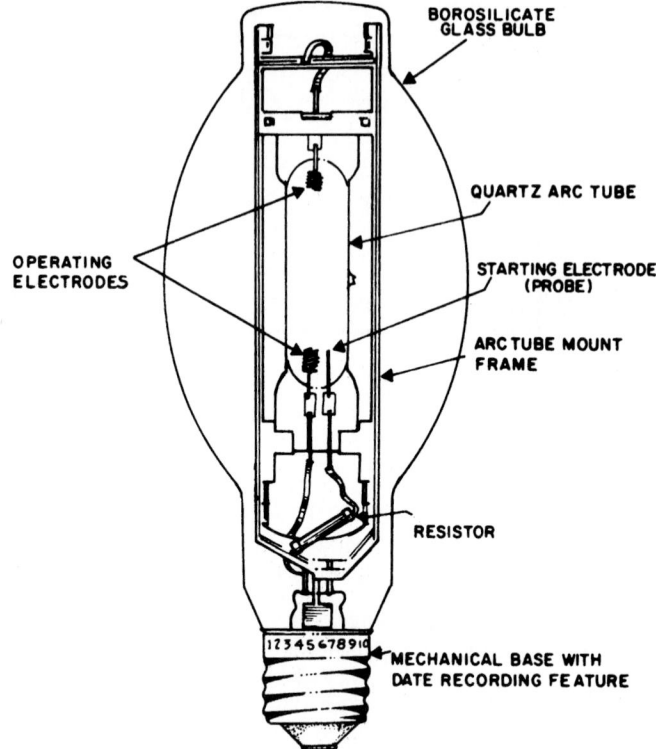

FIGURE 5-16 Typical mercury lamp.

scandium iodide in addition to the argon and mercury. These additives serve to improve the color appearance, color rendering properties, and luminous efficacy of the lamp in comparison to standard mercury lamps. See Fig. 5-17. Further color improvement can be achieved with phosphor coatings inside the bulb. Some metal halide lamps specify operation in a specific position, such as base up, base down, or horizontal.

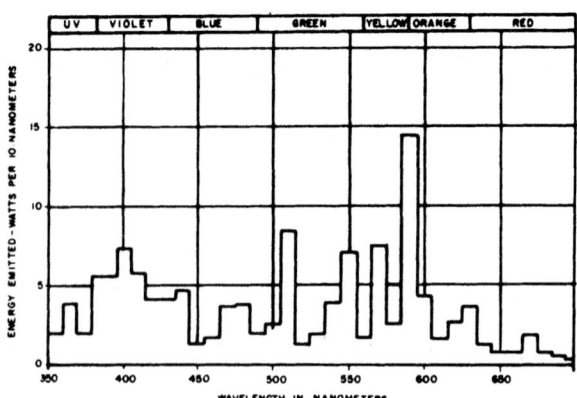

FIGURE 5-17 Spectral power curve of clear metal halide lamp.

Metal halide lamps are available in wattages ranging from 32 to 1500 W that make them suitable for industrial, commercial, and outdoor lighting applications. Standard metal halide lamps have color rendering properties similar to those of Cool White fluorescent lamps.

High-Pressure Sodium.   A high-pressure sodium lamp consists of a translucent ceramic arc tube enclosed in a clear or coated hard glass outer bulb. The clear bulb allows good optical control of the light, while the coated bulb has a light-diffusing effect. The arc discharge takes place between tungsten electrodes which are sealed with a ceramic sealing material in each end of the arc tube. High-pressure sodium lamps are used for industrial and outdoor lighting applications because of their relatively high efficacy compared to other light sources and therefore can reduce energy costs by 50 percent, for example, when replacing a mercury vapor system. The color appearance of high-pressure sodium is somewhat yellow and may not be suitable for applications where color analysis and comparisons are performed. However, color improvements have been made in newer high-pressure sodium versions, but they sacrifice efficacy. High-pressure sodium lamps are available in 35 through 1000 W sizes.

Low-Pressure Sodium Lamps.   Low-pressure sodium lamp technically do not belong to the group of high-intensity discharge sources but are generally put in this category because of their operating characteristics. The lamp consists of a U-shaped arc tube inside a clear outer bulb. There is a mixture of neon and argon gases which are used to start the lamp in the arc tube, together with pure sodium metal. Due to the high sodium content, the color is yellow, and, as a result, these lamps are recommended for applications only where color is not a consideration. They are highly efficient, with the 180-W lamp producing up to 200 lm/W consistently throughout lamp life.

Lumen Maintenance.   Lumen output depreciates at varying rates, depending on the lamp type. A lamp lumen depreciation chart (Fig. 5-18) can be used to predict light loss values over specific periods of time.

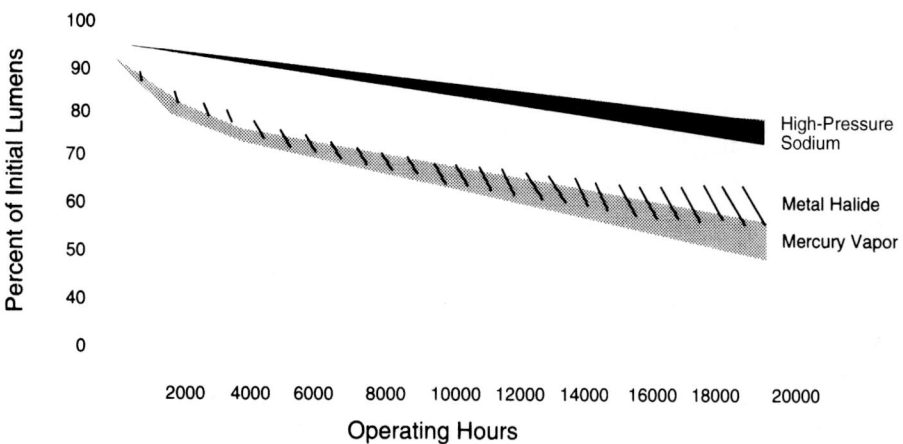

FIGURE 5-18   Approximate lumen maintenance for HID lamps.

Effect of Ambient Temperatures on Starting and Warm-Up.   All HID lamps can operate over a wide range of temperature, with high-pressure sodium lamp able to operate down to −40°F (−40°C) and the other sources down to −20°F (−29°C).

Warm-up and Restrike Characteristics.   All HID lamps must warm up for a specific period of time after being turned on before reaching 100 percent light output. If a momentary power outage occurs, the lamp must cool to a point at which the arc will restrike. Listed below are the warm-up and restrike characteristics.

Lamp type	Initial warm-up period, min	Restrike time, min
Mercury vapor	3–4	3–10
Metal halide	4–6	5–20
High-pressure sodium	4–6	2–4

ILLUMINATION

Illumination deals with both quantity and quality of light. Quantity is concerned with footcandles on the work plane and quality with such elements as color of light, glare, contrast, and shadows.

Quantity

For task lighting, enough light should be supplied to permit rapid and accurate seeing; and in nontask areas, enough for safety.

The Lighting Research Institute (LRI) sponsors research on light and vision and has provided the basis for footcandle recommendations in the *IES Lighting Handbook.* Some of these have been adopted by the American National Standards Institute (ANSI).

The high efficacy of modern light sources and the relatively low cost of electricity led to the general practice of providing uniform lighting over an entire area, based on the most difficult visual tasks performed there. Now, with higher electricity costs and demands to conserve energy, emphasis has turned to the treatment of individual work spaces. However, many areas must still be provided with general lighting, and this will be discussed further later in this chapter under "Lighting Layout."

To determine required illuminance values, review the illuminance values listed in the *IES Handbook Application Volume.* All tasks list an illuminance category which provides a range of illuminance values. These individual categories can be weighted for less or more illuminance depending on worker age, speed, and/or accuracy and reflectance of task background.

Equivalent Sphere Illumination.   Equivalent sphere illumination (ESI) is a concept which has been used by some people and challenged by others. It attempts to compensate for loss of visibility from veiling reflections. Considering a horizontal task, for example, the smallest loss from veiling reflections would occur if a direct light came over the shoulder of the subject. On the other hand, the loss would be nearly as small if the subject were inside a sphere with the light coming to the task uniformly from all directions. This situation can be approximated by measuring instruments which can be standardized. Using this method might show, for example, that where a footcandle meter placed on the work reads 100 fc (1076 lx), the ESI might be only 70 fc (753 lx).

Quality

Quality includes freedom from glare and excessive contrasts and light of suitable color quality.

Discomfort Glare.   Discomfort glare depends upon the average luminance of the lamp or fixture, or in cases of very uneven luminance, the brightest portion. It also depends upon the size and position in the field of view and the overall luminance to which the eye is adapted.

A subjective measure called *borderline between comfort and discomfort* (BCD) has been used in research to rate on a horizontal line of sight from a seated position near the rear wall of the room. Researches using BCD have led to the development of *visual comfort probability* (VCP). VCP means the percentage of a large group of people who would find a lighting installation comfortable.

For office work a value of 70 percent or higher is usually sought. Some fixture manufacturers publish VCP ratings for particular fixtures in various situations.

Color quality should be sufficient to meet the requirements of the work, and in offices lighting "environment" should be considered. This depends on color of finishes as well as on color of light.

Shadows

Shadows can be either bad or good, depending upon their degree. Sharp, black shadows of objects not only have an unpleasant appearance, they can cause accidents. At the other extreme, an installation without shadows has a "bland" appearance and objects lose their roundness or depth. There should be shadows which are illuminated, but to a lesser degree than the objects casting them.

LIGHTING CALCULATIONS

The two basic ways of designing for footcandles are the *lumen method,* sometimes called the flux method, and the *point-by-point method.*

Lumen Method

The lumen method is for uniformly distributed light on a horizontal work plane, usually 30 in (1 m) above the floor. The basic lumen formula is:

$$\text{footcandles} = \frac{\text{total lamp lumens} \times \text{CU} \times \text{LLF}}{\text{area of work plane in square feet}}$$

$$\text{lux} = \frac{\text{total lamp lumens} \times \text{CU} \times \text{LLF}}{\text{area of work plane in square meters}}$$

where CU is the coefficient of utilization and LLF is the light-loss factor (formerly called maintenance factor).

Coefficient of Utilization. The coefficient of utilization is obtained from a fixture catalog or data sheet for the fixture which has been chosen. The information which must be fed into the CU table includes ceiling reflectance, wall reflectances, and a factor depending on fixture mounting height and shape of room.

Zonal Cavity Method. In the zonal cavity method, this factor is broken down into three cavity ratios based on the volume between floor and work plane, that between work plane and fixtures, and that between fixtures and ceiling. Each cavity ratio depends upon the dimensions and reflectances of the cavity. Tables of cavity ratios can be found in the *IES Lighting Handbook.*

Determining Reflectances. A white ceiling in good condition can be assumed to have a reflectance of about 80 percent. For walls which are to be newly painted, some paint manufacturers furnish reflectances with their color chips. Existing walls can be measured with a footcandle meter and something of known reflectance. A convenient standard is the Kodak Neutral Test Card sold in photographic supply stores. One side has a reflectance of 18 percent and the other a reflectance of 90 percent. A clean piece of white blotting paper, if used as a standard, can be assumed to have a reflectance of about 85 percent.

Hold the standard against the wall and point the footcandle meter *toward* it from a distance of about 6 in, taking care not to cast a shadow on the card. Read the meter, then remove the card and take another reading where the card had been. The unknown reflectance will be:

$$\frac{\text{Reading from card}}{\text{Reading from wall}} \times \text{reflectance of card}$$

Light-Loss Factor.   Light-loss factor theoretically includes all of the following:

Light-loss factors not to be recovered:

    Fixture ambient temperature

    Voltage to fixture

    Ballast factor

    Fixture surface depreciation

    Room surface depreciation

Light-loss factors to be recovered:

    Room surface's dirt depreciation

    Lamp burnouts

    Lamp lumen depreciation

    Luminaire dirt depreciation

In practice, some of these are difficult to predict. Where a new area is to be lighted in an existing plant, the engineer can arrive at an overall LLF by taking footcandle readings in other areas just before fixtures are going to be cleaned and relamped and comparing them with the original values. It should be mentioned that initial ratings for fluorescent lamps are for lumens after 100 h operation, since there is a drop in the output of a new lamp in the first few hours. In calculations for lighting layouts, the lumen formula is rearranged to the form:

$$\text{Number of fixtures} = \frac{\text{designed fc} \times \text{floor area}}{\text{no. of lamps per fixture} \times \text{lumens per lamp} \times \text{CU} \times \text{LLF}}$$

where floor area is in square feet; if the lux is used in the calculation, floor area is in square meters.

Point-by-Point Method

When illumination is not to be uniform, the lumen method does not work. It is necessary to take a given point on the work plane and compute how much each fixture in the vicinity contributes to that point. For outdoor lighting, this gives a reliable value for the illumination at the point. For indoor lighting, the value will be a little low because the lumens reflected and re-reflected around the room are neglected. This is negligible in most cases because the fixtures are likely to be of the direct type.

The basic formula is:

$$\text{Illumination} = \frac{I \times \cos \theta}{d^2}$$

where illumination can be in either footcandles or lux and

    I = intensity in candlepower from the light source in the direction toward the measurement point

    θ = the angle between a line from the center of the fixture and the work plane at the point

    d = distance, ft (m), from center of light source to the point

The intensity is obtained from the candlepower distribution curve of the fixture. Figure 5-19 is an example of such a curve for an incandescent fixture. The values are plotted on a vertical plane passed through the center of the fixture. Since the fixture is symmetrical about its own vertical axis, the curve shows the intensity in all directions. For a rectangular fixture, curves are commonly shown for two vertical planes, one through the long axis of the fixture and the other at right angles to it as in Fig. 5-20. For more accurate results, a 45° plane can usually be obtained from the fixture manufacturer, and values between the planes can be estimated. Such work can be very laborious, and the method was seldom used until the advent of

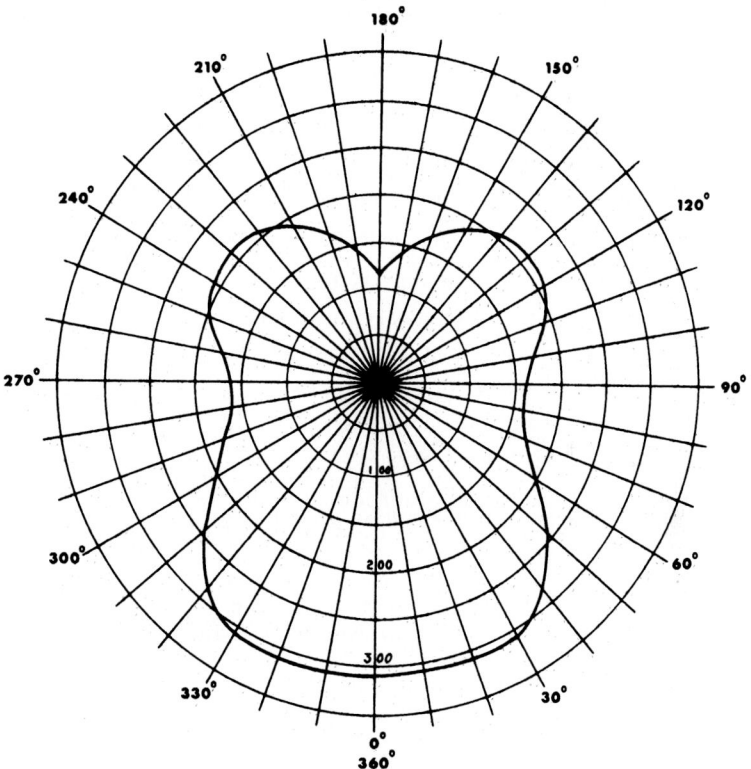

FIGURE 5-19   Candlepower distribution curve for an incandescent fixture with enclosing globe.

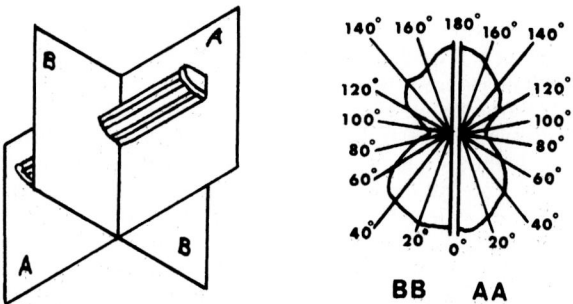

FIGURE 5-20   Candlepower distribution curves for a fluorescent fixture.

computers. Now there are computer programs which can make such computations very rapidly, once candlepower and positional data are fed in.

LIGHTING LAYOUTS

Steps in making a lighting layout can be summarized as follows:

1. Analyze lighting needs.
2. Establish illumination level.
3. Decide lamp type and size.
4. Choose lamp color.
5. Select fixture.
6. Decide mounting height.
7. Estimate maintenance conditions.

And, for uniform illumination by lumen method:

8. Measure or estimate reflectances.
9. Use method such as zonal cavity to find coefficient of utilization.
10. Determine or estimate light-loss factor.
11. Compute number of luminaires required.
12. Determine maximum spacing.
13. Make luminaire layout.

Some of the steps have already been discussed. Steps 3 and 4 involve the suitability of the lamp for the work. For example, a 400-W HID lamp would not be mounted 8 ft above the floor because its high luminance would cause direct glare. Again, a clear mercury lamp would not be used in an office on account of the color of its light.

Initial cost of lamp and equipment are important. Table 5-1 gives partial data for a few typical lamps used in industry. Others will be found in large lamp ordering guides or catalogs. With fluorescent and HID lamps, the actual efficacies are about 5 percent lower than those in Table 5-1, on account of ballast losses.

Fluorescent lamps have low luminance, so they can be mounted lower without excessive glare. They offer a choice of colors.

HID lamps give a large amount of light from a small package, so they can be mounted higher on wider spacings to reduce first costs.

In selecting an open-bottom fixture, cutoff angle is important. See Fig. 5-21. Its significance is illustrated in Fig. 5-22. Shielded fixtures have translucent plastic or prismatic enclosures which partially direct the light.

Indirect luminaires, which send 60 percent or more of their light upward, are often used in applications where the ceilings are not dropped. With dropped ceilings troffers are usually set in flush, each replacing an acoustic panel.

Another advantage of enclosed, flush-mounted troffers is that they can be connected to ducts for removing much of the heat given off by lamps and ballasts. In summer the heat can be discharged outdoors and in winter it can be used to help heat the building.

Downward distribution from luminaires varies from fairly narrow to wide, depending on the shape of their reflectors and the presence of control elements such as prisms. In a very-high-ceilinged industrial area, a narrow distribution may be used to avoid sending too much light to the walls. On the other hand, if there are tall machines with important details on vertical surfaces, low bay luminaires and luminaires with wide distribution patterns will help to illuminate the vertical surfaces.

TABLE 5-1   Lamp Applications for General Lighting

Category	Type and wattage range	Maximum lamp efficacy, lm/W	Average life, h	Characteristic features	Typical applications
Incandescent lamps	Incandescent lamps and reflector lamps, 3–1500	22	1,000	Easy to install, easy to use, many different versions, instant start, low price; reflector lamps allow concentrated light beams.	Task lighting—inspection areas, exit signs, rough surface areas, low- and high-voltage applications.
	Halogen, 50–1500	27	2,000	Compact, high light output, white light, easy to install, long life compared with normal incandescent lamps.	Accent lighting for inspection areas, quartz restrike systems, flood-lighting.
Fluorescent lamps	Tubular, 4–215	104	20,000	Wide choice of light colors, high lighting levels possible, economical in use.	4 ft and 8 ft widely used sizes in assembly, ware-house, and inspection areas where glare may be a problem.
Compact fluorescent lamps	Integral unit SL, 5–23	61	10,000	Energy-effective, direct replacement for incandescent lamps.	Most applications where incandescent lamps were used before.
	Standard compact PL, 5–40	80	10,000	Compact, long life, energy-effective.	Localized lighting, exit signs, stairwells.
High-intensity discharge lamps	Self-ballasted, 160–750	24	12,000; 16,000	Long life, good color rendering, easy to install, better efficacy than incandescent lamps.	Replacement for higher wattage incandescent lamps especially for high maintenance cost areas.
	Mercury vapor, 40–1000	63	24,000+	High efficacy, long life, reasonable color quality.	General assembly areas.
	Metal halide, 35–1500	125	15,000	Very high efficacy combined with excellent color rendering; long life.	Best suited for manufac-turing and warehouse areas where white light is desired.
	High-pressure sodium, 35–1000	140	24,000+	Very high efficacy, extremely long life, adequate color rendering to accommodate several luminaire types.	Most efficient source for production and ware-house areas; wide wattage selection.
	Low-pressure sodium, 18–180	200	18,000	Extremely high efficacy, very long life, high visual acuity, poor color rendering, monochromatic light	Warehouse and security areas.

In some general offices where people face up and down the room but not crosswise, fixtures with "bat-wing" distribution have been used. They emit most of their light sideways at high angles, so that light reaching a worker's desk comes from the sides. This minimizes veiling reflections.

Recommended spacing-to-mounting-height ratios or spacing criteria are given in fixture catalogs, and these are intended as maximums, not minimums. Illumination will be quite uniform if the ratios are not exceeded. It is customary to make the spacing from wall to first row half of that between rows.

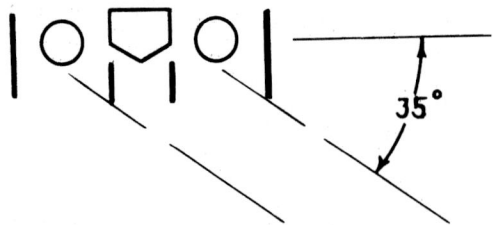

FIGURE 5-21   Meaning of cutoff angle.

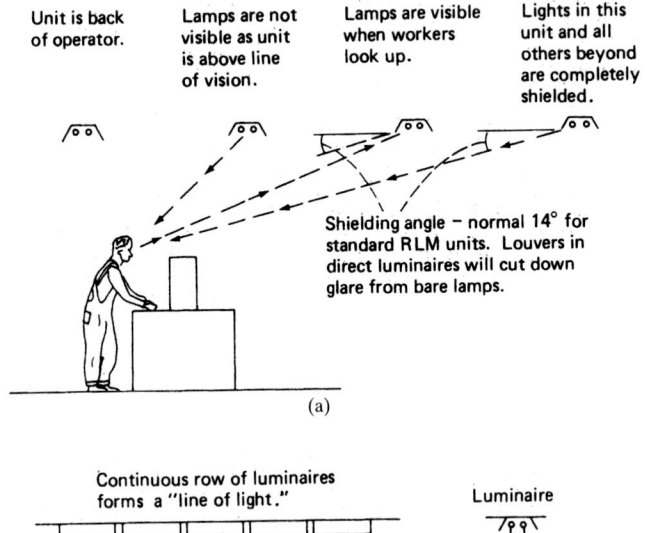

(a)

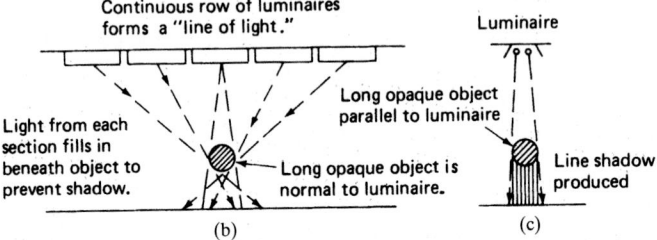

(b)   (c)

FIGURE 5-22   Shielding angles for direct luminaires. (*From W. Staniar, ed., Plant Engineering Handbook, 2d ed., McGraw-Hill, New York, 1959, p. 10-18. Copyright © McGraw-Hill Book Company, Inc. Reproduced by permission of McGraw-Hill Publishing Co.*)

For nonuniform lighting, luminaires are located with reference to the work spaces, bearing in mind that glare should not reach the worker's eyes from normal viewing angles and that light from shiny surfaces should not be reflected into the worker's eyes.

APPLICATIONS

Industrial Lighting

Luminaires (usually spaced symmetrically) that provide a reasonably uniform level of illumination throughout an area constitute a general lighting system. A good general lighting system makes it possible to change the location of machinery without rearranging the lighting, and also permits full utilization of floor space. Some manufacturing processes can be properly lighted by a good general lighting system alone, while others require supplementary lighting at individual machine or worker locations. Even if all the light for the immediate task is supplied locally, a general lighting system is also necessary for safety reasons and to maintain reasonable luminance ratios throughout the area. When work areas, such as workbenches, are close to walls a row of luminaires should be provided for them.

High-Ceiling Areas.   In high bay areas the work to be done commonly involves rather large three-dimensional objects that have diffuse reflecting characteristics. Under these circumstances the seeing task is not severe, and reflected glare presents no problem. For these applications a light source having a high lumen output, such as a high-wattage fluorescent or HID lamp, is desirable. Such sources in direct reflectors produce light with a directional component that causes slight shadows and mild highlights that aid in seeing. HID lamps are the most economical for high bay lighting.

In high bay areas where specular materials are fabricated, relatively large-area, low-brightness luminaires are recommended.

Low-Ceiling Areas.   Difficult seeing tasks are more common in low bay areas than in high bay areas. In some low bay areas the seeing task consists of diffuse three-dimensional objects which can be well-lighted with directional sources. Usually, however, some of the visual tasks involve specular or semispecular objects for which the optimum lighting might be an indirect system.

The provision of good visibility is an essential requirement for the lighting system, but it is also important that the lighting be comfortable visually. These two requirements are frequently, but not always, satisfied by the same characteristics of the system. For example, increasing the size and reducing the brightness of the luminaires will almost always improve visual comfort, and will usually improve the visibility of specular objects. It may not, however, improve the visibility of diffuse three-dimensional objects. Visual comfort is a function of the entire visual surround and can be controlled by proper painting of room surfaces and equipment and through careful luminaire selection.

Luminaires used for general lighting in low bay areas are nearly always of the direct or semidirect type, using either fluorescent or HID lamps. Lamps may be shielded by louvers, baffles, or other devices. All of these accessories improve visual comfort.

In areas where the ceiling is painted white or a light color, luminance ratios between the ceiling and the luminaires are considerably lower when semidirect luminaires are used rather than totally direct ones. The upward light in semidirect fluorescent units usually comes from slots or holes in the top of the reflector. The indirect component in HID luminaires comes from those designed with clear acrylic or glass reflector systems.

Inspection Lighting

Inspection lighting may involve color, direction, and amount of diffusion of the light. In many cases, color is not critical and the trichromatic types of fluorescent lamps will serve. When color is critical, particularly when colors must be matched to standards, special color-matching lamps may be required for good color rendition.

Metamerism is a phenomenon in which two colors match under one light source but fail to match under another. Such colors are called *metameric pairs*. The existence of the phenomenon explains the need for special care in inspecting colors.

Scratches are best revealed by sharp light as from a small, directional source, directed at a low angle perpendicular to the direction of the scratches. This also applies to small dents and "dings."

Transparent objects are often inspected on a table top of translucent glass or plastic lighted from below. Another example is the "perch" in a textile mill, where the cloth is pulled across a frame and seen against a window or a lighted panel.

Very small objects such as filaments or electronic grids can be inspected by silhouetting them on a translighted table.

Waves in shiny surfaces can be detected by viewing the reflected image of a fluorescent fixture having a diffusing panel on which narrow cross lines have been painted. Any waves will distort the reflected grid pattern.

Fine cracks in castings can be revealed by coating them with a fluorescent liquid and viewing them in a darkened room with uv produced by "black light" lamps. Any cracks will glow brightly.

One of the most subtle flaws to detect is the slight loss of sheen in a piece of plastic countertop material. An effective method is to suspend over the work a fluorescent fixture with a diffusing bottom, bordered on each side with a black panel as large as the fixture. Looking down at the material, the inspector sees a reflection of alternating dark and light areas. The important thing is the border between a light and dark area. When the product moves along, or when the inspector moves, and a reflected border enters a flawed area, it "leaps to view."

Warehouses

Luminaires can be mounted above the top shelf of a rack at a height equivalent to the distance between the aisles. HID lamps are the usual choice due to their high light output and energy efficiency. When aisles are long and narrow, luminaires with an asymmetric pattern of light distribution can be used to achieve optimal lighting efficiency.

Offices

Most offices today consist of a relatively large space or open plan with low partitions dividing individual work spaces. The work performed in these areas include a variety of tasks, such as reading, writing, typing, and working at computer stations. General illumination levels range from 30 to 70 fc with specific task areas having a minimum of 50 fc. Maximum illumination levels of 50 fc are usually recommended when video display terminals are present to minimize reflected glare from the terminal. Luminaires with parabolic louvers are a common choice to control glare and improve visual comfort.

New fluorescent systems, such as T8 lamps, electronic ballasts, and compact fluorescent lamps are growing in usage since they can reduce electricity costs up to 43 percent over the standard fluorescent systems that have been used for several years.

Painting. When decorating a new office or redecorating an old one, light colors should be used for large areas because of their higher reflectance and to give a psychological "lift" to the occupants. Three harmonizing colors, a slightly darker one for the lower walls, and a dark trim color for accents make a good arrangement.

OUTDOOR LIGHTING

The principal applications of outdoor lighting for industrial plants are building floodlighting and area lighting. Floodlighting is primarily for advertising purposes, but it does have a safety element if operated all night. It can be done from cornices, from units extending out on brackets, or from poles. Parking areas are lighted by clusters of floodlights on tall poles. HID lamps are indicated, and high-pressure sodium is often used on account of its high efficacy.

SAFETY LIGHTING

Both indoors and outdoors, lighting should be such that people will not trip over obstacles. Indoors this is not much of a problem because suitable general lighting will reveal any hazards. However, stairwells require particular attention. The edge of a step should not cast a shadow on the step below it, nor should a person cast a strong shadow across the steps. A continuous row of fluorescent strip fixtures, mounted overhead and shielded to prevent direct glare, is a good answer. Also, steps and risers can be given different colors.

Areas having inflammable or explosive vapors or dusts should be lighted with approved, enclosed luminaires.

Emergency Lighting

Emergency lighting requirements are defined by the **National Electrical Code**® and the **Life Safety Code**®, as well as by state codes.* Methods include generators which start automatically and serve emergency circuits when electric service fails, central battery systems, and individually battery-operated lights at strategic points.

Discussions of methods and equipment are found in the Codes.

MAINTENANCE

Cleaning

The long life of fluorescent and HID lamps necessitates cleaning between relampings if efficient delivery of light is to be maintained. A posted schedule on which the cleanings of different areas can be checked off is highly recommended.

Different reflecting and transmitting materials require different cleaning agents. Glass and porcelain enamel can be cleaned by most nonabrasive cleaners such as detergents or automobile glass cleaners. Synthetic enamels should be cleaned only with detergents. Plastics have a tendency to collect dust due to static charges. Detergents containing a destaticizing agent will prevent this, provided the plastic is merely rinsed after washing, and not wiped dry.

Relamping

In office areas, lamps are usually replaced as they burn out. With high-mounted industrial luminaires, however, scattered outages are sometimes allowed to accumulate until a noticeable reduction in light occurs at some area.

Large installations of fluorescent lamps where all lamps are turned on and off at the same time are sometimes handled by group replacement. At some point such as 80 percent of rated average life as predicted by the lamp mortality curve, a trained crew, using equipment designed for the job, replaces all lamps. Under this plan, when a lamp fails very early, its replacement is marked with a grease pencil so that when group replacement occurs, it can be saved and used to replace a future early failure.

Any HID lamp which fails early should be replaced at once because each lamp covers a wider area than does a fluorescent lamp.

Disposal of Burned-out Lamps

Both fluorescent and high-intensity discharge lamps contain small amounts of mercury. The arc tube of a mercury or metal halide lamp contains about 50 mg of mercury. While this

---

* **National Electrical Code**® and **Life Safety Code**® are Registered Trademarks of the National Fire Protection Association Inc., Quincy, Massachusetts.

amount is small, it many be enough to fall within regulatory guidelines. Disposal of lamps should be done in accordance with applicable local, state, and federal regulations.

TROUBLESHOOTING

Incandescent Lamps

Incandescent lamps present few problems in troubleshooting. The most common problem is short life, and this usually means that the socket voltage is higher than the rated lamp voltage. If some of the early failures do not show the normal blackening expected at full life, it may be that the lamps are subjected to shocks or blows, and rough-service lamps should be used. Or, if they are subjected to vibration, vibration lamps are recommended.

Sometimes small clearances, or venting arrangements in fixtures, cause the lamps to run hotter than they should. An indication of this is often a dark brown discoloration of the base. Another evidence is a loose base.

Fluorescent Lamps

A complete guide to troubleshooting fluorescent and HID lamps would take more space than is available here. Lamp manufacturers publish bulletins listing pages of troubles and remedies—not that the troubles are necessarily frequent. There are also testing instruments and test lamps for such things as checking the current delivered through the cathodes of a rapid-start lamp.

A few of the more obvious points for fluorescent lamps are:

Lamp improperly seated in lampholders

Corroded contacts in lampholders

Lamp at end of life, as evidenced by dense, black areas at ends

Ballast at end of life

HID Lamps

Similar points for HID lamps are:

Poor contact in socket

Voltage too high or low

Ballast not grounded

Lamp at end of life

Ballast at end of life

ENERGY CONSERVATION*

Because energy costs are high in many areas, the majority of manufacturing facilities give high priority to energy conservation. Although lighting represents only 4 percent of the total energy

---

* See also Sec. 15.

used in a typical facility, it gets a lot of attention because it is the most visible consumer of energy. Reducing lighting levels to substandard values to control energy consumption is counterproductive. Lighting technology has advanced to the point where significant energy savings can be achieved while optimum lighting levels are maintained. In fact, savings of as much as 50 percent in energy consumed by lighting are quite common with retrofits or new lighting systems.

The overall goal of an upgraded lighting system should be to reduce energy consumption and simultaneously improve the quality of the lighting. With the cost of energy continuing to rise, controlling the energy component in the total cost of lighting makes good economic sense.

Factors to be used in evaluating the savings possible through appropriate lighting include the cost of energy, light source efficacies, return on investment (ROI), and maximizing light.

Cost of Light

Electricity represents 86 percent of the total lighting cost, while the lamp itself represents a mere 3 percent. The cost of the energy consumed by a 100-W incandescent lamp during its life can be 10 times the original cost of the lamp, depending on lamp cost and electricity prices for a given region. Clearly, the substitution of more energy-efficient lamps suitable for the application will significantly reduce energy consumed by that lamp.

Regulations

The regulatory environment is rapidly changing. Some state as well as federal bodies have either passed or are considering legislation to set guidelines for wattage consumed by a lighting system in a specified area. Laws are also being considered that could make some standard lamps obsolete and illegal to use.

Methods of Conservation

Sections on lamps, switching, and use of daylight have already mentioned energy-saving aspects. For new installations, select the lamp of highest efficacy whose color is acceptable, even though fixed charges may be higher than for other types. For existing installations, the problem is to reduce the wattage somewhat without greatly reducing the quantity or quality of the illumination.

Merely removing some of the fluorescent lamps in an installation is not a good solution. Depending upon the type of circuit, removing one lamp from a two-lamp fixture may cause the other lamp to go out or to operate improperly. If both lamps are removed from a two-lamp fixture, a gap is left in the lighting pattern. If it is felt necessary to remove two lamps from a four-lamp fixture, be sure that both lamps are served from the same ballast. Some power will still be consumed unless the ballast is disconnected. A much better way is to substitute one of the new energy-saving lamps.

Energy-Saving Lamps

The energy shortage has prompted lamp manufacturers to design and produce lamps which have the same physical sizes as the lamps they replace and operate on the same ballasts but give somewhat less light and use less wattage. Thus, a plant can keep all fixtures properly lamped and save wattage without greatly reducing the illumination level.

Controls

Lighting system controls are an important component in reducing electricity costs and providing employees with the appropriate quantity of light. Devices such as photocells, dimmers, and motion sensors can be connected into a control system to regulate the amount of light depending on variables such as daylight, time of day, and presence of people.

Summary

Existing Systems

Consider energy-saving fluorescent systems and lamps.

Consider converting high-pressure sodium to mercury luminaires.

Add switches where circuits cover too much area.

Use daylight when available.

Turn off lights when not in use.

New Installations

Perform cost analysis to determine the most efficient lighting system.

Specify lamps with highest efficacy consistent with color requirements.

Lay out switching in rows parallel to windows and switch for small areas.

Plan to turn lights off when not in use.

Evaluate new lighting systems from both qualitative and quantitative perspectives.

BIBLIOGRAPHY

Allphin, Willard: *Primer of Lamps and Lighting,* 3d ed., Addison-Wesley, Reading, Massachusetts, 1973.

IES Lighting Handbook Reference Volume, Illuminating Engineering Society, New York, 1984.

IES Lighting Handbook Application Volume, Illuminating Engineering Society, New York, 1987.

IES RP-7, *Industrial Lighting,* Illuminating Engineering Society, New York, 1991.

Lighting Handbook, Philips Lighting Co., Somerset, N.J., 1984.

CHAPTER 3-6

ELECTRIC MEASURING INSTRUMENTS

Ron Barma
Communications Manager
Simpson Electric Co.
Elgin, Illinois

INTRODUCTION

Electrical measuring instruments are important to all aspects of plant maintenance and control. Some tasks require only simple yes or no checks, e.g., continuity, presence or absence of line power voltage, and current flow. Instruments for these tests may be rugged and inexpensive. Yet they must be safe, reliable, and accurate. Whether you are working on the production line, in the laboratory, or servicing equipment, measurements can yield cost savings proportional to instrument accuracy. Electrical measuring equipment is available in three basic configurations: hand-held, bench-mounted, and panel-mounted. The following paragraphs in this chapter provide: (1) overviews of uses for electric and electronic measuring instruments, (2) guides to the safe operation of these instruments, and (3) criteria for selecting particular instrument features.

THE MULTIMETER

There is a need for electrical measurement everywhere in the plant:

- Incoming component inspection
- Production line assembly
- Quality control
- Plant maintenance and repair

Popular with manufacturing and service professionals alike, the most versatile test instrument is the multimeter, combining measurement of ac and dc voltage, resistance (ohms), and current (amperes). Usually compact, battery-powered, and portable, two types of multimeter are widely available: the analog volt-ohm-milliammeter (VOM) and the digital multimeter (DMM).

VOLT-OHM-MILLIAMMETER

The analog volt-ohm-milliammeter (Fig. 6-1) is basically a test instrument, with several ranges for measuring volts, ohms, and amperes. The VOM consists of:

- An electromechanical meter movement and precision meter face
- Selection switches with resistors and rectifiers that allow the meter to measure various voltage, current, and resistance ranges

The analog display used by VOMs is well-suited to displaying quick trend information, nulling and peaking, ranges, and go/no-go readings. The dB scale can be used in conjunction with the ac voltage measurement to give an indication of the power gain of an amplifier. A zero (dB) power level must be chosen, typically 1 mW in 600Ω.

The power gain is defined as

$$dB = 10 \log_{10} \frac{P_2}{P_1}$$

Today's high-quality analog models feature taut-band construction which can operate for more than 20 million cycles with a repeatability error of less than ±0.02 percent. This corresponds to about 70 years of normal use. Taut-band construction also withstands moderate shock and vibration and operates on limited power of less than 5 μW.

The VOM is the best all-around electronic instrument for industrial plant maintenance. Various electrical tests can be made on rotating electrical equipment, such as motors and generators, to check all operating conditions. For example,

1. An ohmmeter can be used to check continuity of shunt field coils.
2. To test an armature for shorted coils, a voltmeter and milliammeter can be used together; they will indicate the presence of any shorted coils.

Measurement of rotating equipment depends, in part, on their operating characteristics. DC motors, for example, can be series, shunt, and combination series-shunt, or compound. In

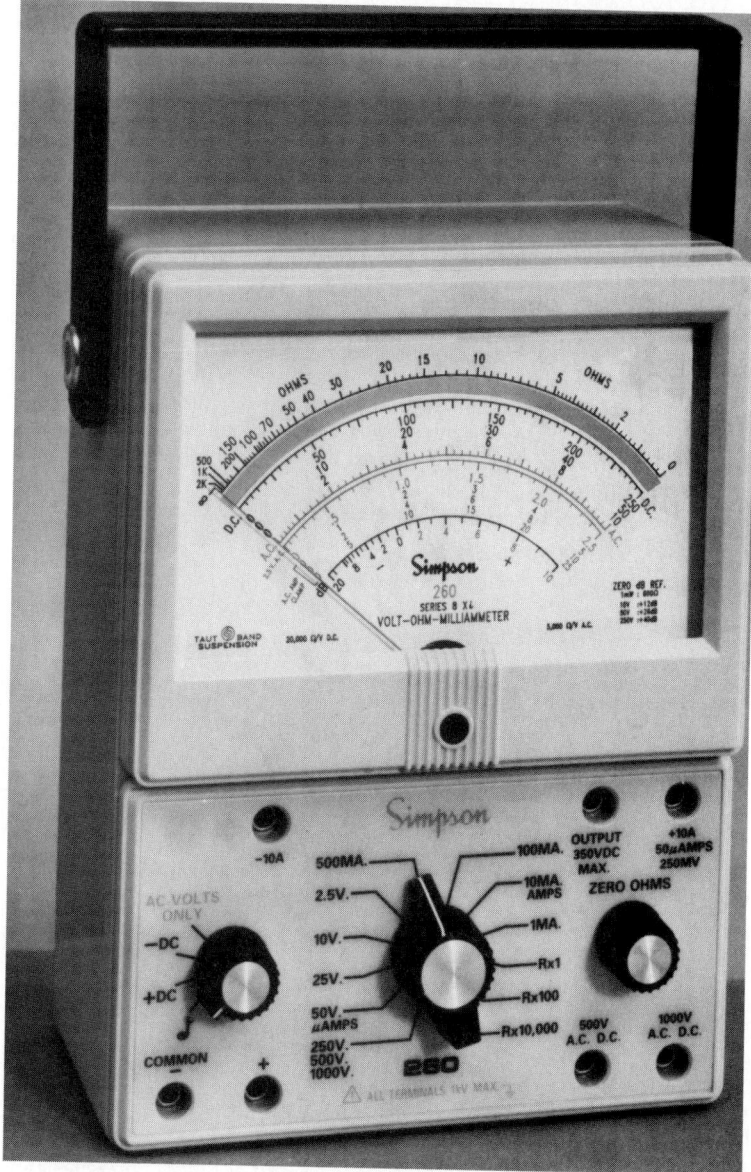

FIGURE 6-1   Analog volt-ohm-milliammeter (VOM).

the series type, where the field winding is in series with armature, the field strength changes with armature current and starting torque is high. An increased load reduces the speed and the torque increases. In the shunt type, the field winding is in parallel with the armature and the field strength does not vary with armature current. Starting torque is lower and speed varies little with load changes. In the compound type of motor, there are two sets of field windings, one set in parallel with the armature and the other set in series. Characteristics of the compound motor for both speed and load can be varied by adjusting relations of the two sets of windings. See Chap. 3-4, "Motors and Motor Controls."

A wide range of accessories such as high-voltage probes, temperature and high-frequency probes, and ac or ac/dc ampere clamp-ons have greatly increased the measurement capabilities of the analog multimeter, well beyond its VOM designation.

DIGITAL MULTIMETER

Digital multimeters (Fig. 6-2) have been evolving rapidly. The electronics of a present-day digital multimeter are extremely complex. In the simplest terms, it consists of an integrated analog-to-digital converter which measures voltage by comparing it to an internal reference voltage. In measurement of current, a resistance is placed in series with the load, and the DMM measures the voltage drop across the standardized resistance, converting it to a current measurement. Like its analog counterpart, the DMM measures voltage, current, and resistance, but displays measurements directly on a digital display. Digital multimeters today offer the kind of features that you would expect from integrated circuits (ICs) with recent advances in digital technology. Expanded capabilities include the following:

- Memory
- Frequency measurement sensing
- Peak hold and data hold
- Logic probes

FIGURE 6-2 Digital multimeter (DMM).

- Continuity beeper and diode test
- Capacitance measurement
- Analog bar graphs

Automatic range selection, and the features mentioned above, make the DMM more versatile and easy to use than ever before. Accessory adapters have also been developed to measure insulation resistance, watts, power factors, and ac line frequency. Some very recent designs in DMMs incorporate RS-232C interface capability. Here the multimeter is connected to a PC, ready to download stored readings for hard copy to document production test records or to build a database for future analysis or presentation via personal computer (PC) software.

METER SELECTION CRITERIA/FEATURES

When purchasing a panel, bench, or hand-held meter, the most important characteristics to select are:

- Root-mean-square (rms)
- Accuracy and resolution
- Range

RMS Sensing

Root-mean-square measures the power of an ac signal (i.e., of alternating currents and voltages, the effective current or voltage applied). It is that value of alternating current or voltage that produces the same heating effect as would be produced by an equal value of direct current or voltage. For a sine wave, it is equal to 0.707 times the peak value. For measuring perfect sine waves (Fig. 6-3), less expensive meters that average a rectified signal are sufficient. If your applications have varying wave intensity and frequency (Fig. 6-4), select "true rms" capability for voltmeters and clamp-on ammeters.

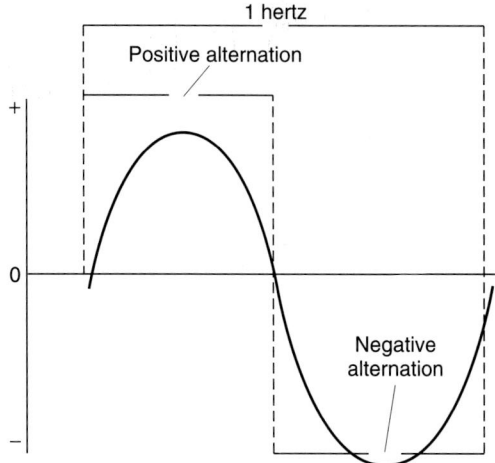

FIGURE 6-3 Sine wave.

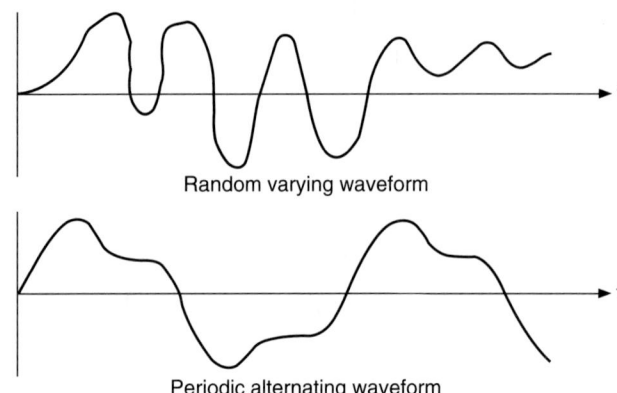

Random varying waveform

Periodic alternating waveform

FIGURE 6-4 Varying wave intensity and frequency.

Accuracy and Resolution

Accuracy and resolution indicate how fine and how reliable are the readings on the instrument. Accuracy is the maximum deviation to be expected between the meter reading and the actual value being measured. Accuracy is usually expressed as a percent of full scale for analog instruments and as a percent of reading for digital instruments. A high-accuracy analog voltmeter may have a specification of ±2 percent at full scale. This indicates that, when set to the 100-mA scale, for example, expect the reading to be within 2 percent of 100, or ±2 mA.

Resolution is the degree to which nearly equal values of a quantity can be discriminated. In analog meters, resolution is the difference between adjacent scale divisions. In digital meters, resolution is the value represented by a one-digit change in the least-significant digit.

Published accuracy and resolution data are useful in selecting a meter that meets your requirements economically.

Range

Range indicates the highest reading that can be safely measured with the meter. Several resistors internal to VOMs and DMMs allow readings over a very broad range.

Ammeters measure the entire current in the circuit. Attempting to measure current above the range of the meter can damage the movement or burn out internal components. Ammeters must be selected for the current range to be tested. Accessories such as shunts and amp-clamps extend the range of an ammeter.

VOLTMETERS

A voltmeter measures the electrical potential (voltage) between two points of a circuit. Depending on the application, voltmeters may be used to read fractions of a volt in a solid-state circuit one day and a 440-V power line the next. Applications such as cathode-ray tubes require measurements in the kilovolt range.

Voltmeter Selection Criteria/Features

Aside from having the required characteristics of rms sensing, accuracy, resolution, and range, a voltmeter must also have the correct resistance for the application.

Many solid-state and logic circuits operate on very low current. Putting a low-resistance meter in parallel with a solid-state circuit may increase current enough to damage sensitive components. In addition, the current change may be sufficient to bias the PN junction in solid-state devices, altering the circuit current paths. Generally, a meter is considered high resistance when the input resistance is 10 MΩ or higher.

Sensitivity and Meter Loading

Sensitivity is a ratio of the response of a measuring device (meter) to the magnitude of the measured quantity (volts, ohms, amperes, etc.). Voltage-measuring devices are rated in ohms per volt (Ω/V). On any particular range, it is obtained by dividing the resistance of the instrument (in ohms) by the full-scale voltage value of that range. A meter with a 100-kΩ resistance on the 0–100-V range has a 1000-Ω/V rating. A meter with a 2-MΩ resistance on the 0–100-V range has a 20-kΩ/V rating.

The loading effect of a voltmeter can be demonstrated by using these two meters (Fig. 6-5). First the 1000-Ω/V meter is used to measure the voltage across the 100-kΩ resistor in the circuit of Fig. 6-5a. As soon as the meter is placed across R2, a parallel combination of resistance (R2 and the 100-kΩ internal resistance of the meter) is formed. This forms a total resistance of 50 kΩ. By Ohm's law ($V = IR$) the voltage drop across R2 should be 40 V, the circuit current (0.4 mA) times the 100-kΩ resistance. However, multiplying the 50-kΩ parallel bank by the circuit current of 0.4 mA gives 20 V, an error of 50 percent.

In Fig. 5b, the 2-MΩ resistance meter measures the same voltage drop, only this time the parallel resistance of R2 and the meter (100 kΩ//2 MΩ) equals 95,239 Ω. Now the circuit current of 0.4 mA times the parallel bank of 95,239 Ω equals approximately 38 V. It is obvious that meter 1 is loading down the circuit. For circuits with very high impedance, another form of meter is necessary, such as the DMM.

Voltmeter Operation

When operating a voltmeter, take precautions to prevent damage to the meter and the circuit under test:

- Always connect the meter in parallel to the circuit (Fig. 6-6).
- Select a voltage range that provides a midscale reading. When testing a 5-V circuit, select the 10-V scale. If circuit voltage is unknown, select the highest scale and work downward.
- Observe the correct polarity, particularly with analog meters. A reversed-polarity signal can bend the meter needle, damage the movement, or burn calibration inside the instrument.
- Select a meter with the proper resistance for the circuit being tested.

Voltmeter Accessories

Accessories can expand the range and versatility of the voltmeter. Some common accessories are:

- High-voltage probe allows a voltmeter to read voltages above 1 kV, which are common to cathode-ray tubes.
- Temperature probe uses a voltmeter scale to display temperature. Use for heating, ventilating, and air conditioning (HVAC), refrigeration, or machine operating temperatures. Infrared-sensitive noncontact temperature probes are available for fragile or moving objects.

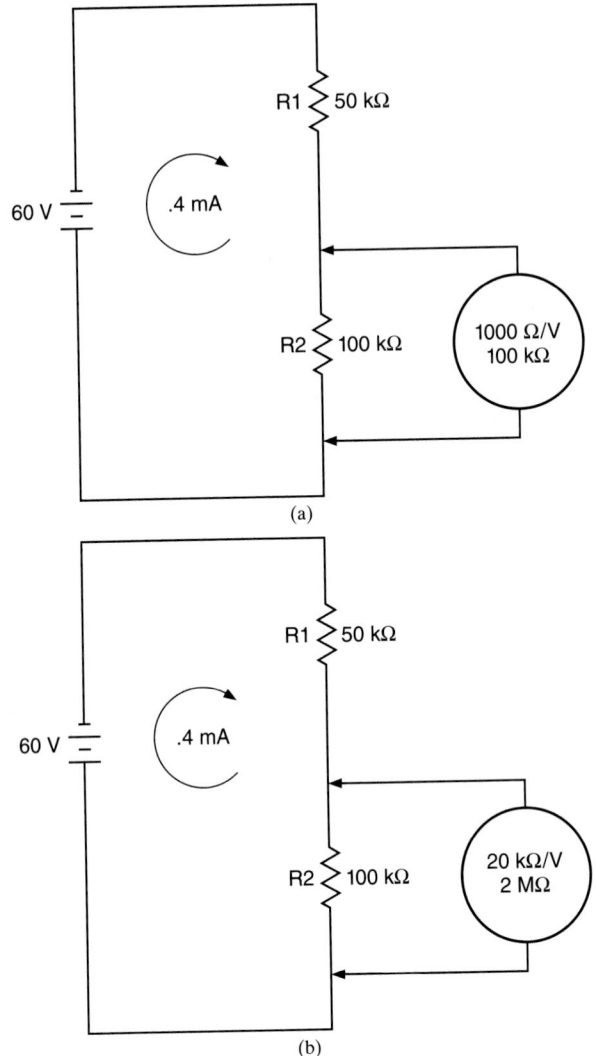

FIGURE 6-5 (*a*) Loading effect of a voltmeter. (*b*) Correct reading with a 2-MΩ meter.

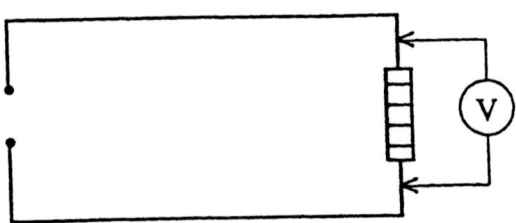

FIGURE 6-6 Connect the voltmeter in parallel to the circuit.

AMMETERS

An ammeter measures the current flowing past a single point in a circuit. Ammeters may be required to read microamperes (μA) through more than 1000 A in welding and manufacturing equipment. Ammeters measure the power demanded in a circuit. Therefore, an ammeter is useful in determining varying loads on motors and other machinery. There are two major types of ammeter. The *direct-wire* type connects to the circuit with wires. *Clamp-on* types have jaws that close over the conductor, taking a reading without interrupting the circuit. Clamp-on ammeters have a higher current range than direct-wire.

Ammeter Selection Criteria/Features

The most important characteristics to select from are:

- Range
- Direct wire or clamp-on

Range

Range is the highest amperage the meter can safely read without being damaged. Typical hand-held instruments may have a maximum capacity of 2 A. Some bench models range up to 10 A. Accessories such as shunts (for dc) and amp-clamps (for ac) allow meters to handle much higher current ranges.

Direct Wire or Clamp-on

Multimeters are wired in series with a circuit when measuring current. This requires that the circuit be turned off and disconnected, and the meter probes connected to complete the circuit again. This is practical for small circuits and bench operations, but may not be acceptable for high-current or continuous-usage machinery.

AC above 1 A may be measured by a clamp-on meter. The complete ammeter measurement and display function is contained in the handle of the meter (Fig. 6-7). Clamp the jaws of the meter over the current-carrying conductor, and internal circuitry selects the proper range and displays the reading. Clamp-on meters are most useful in:

- High-current applications
- Circuits where current cannot be interrupted

Ammeter Operation

When operating an ammeter, take precautions to prevent damage to the meter and the circuit.

Direct-Wire Ammeter

- Always connect the ammeter in series with the circuit under test, Fig. 6-8.
- Before reapplying power to the circuit, select a current range that provides a midscale reading. When testing a 2-A circuit, select the 5-A scale. If circuit voltage is unknown, select the highest scale of the meter and work downward.
- If the current is above the range of the meter, select a current shunt or amp-clamp.

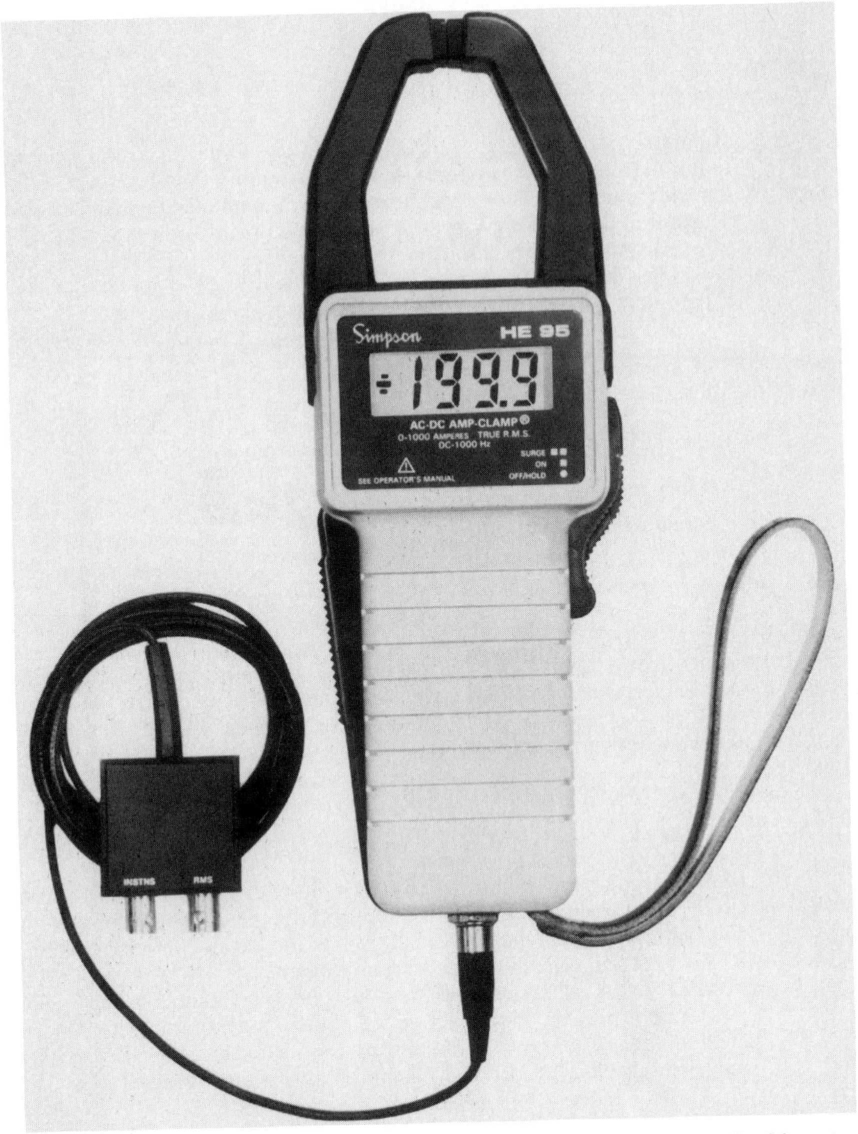

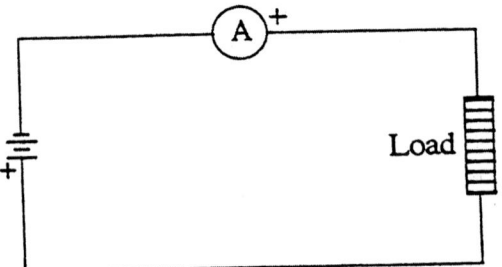

FIGURE 6-7 The ammeter measurement and display function is contained in the handle of the meter.

FIGURE 6-8 Connect the ammeter in series with the circuit under test and observe polarity.

Clamp-on Ammeter.   The ac clamp-on ammeter is actually a special application of a current transformer. Clamp-on ammeters can be used to determine the current loading and to check that current densities are not being exceeded for the cables and wiring involved. Even though circuits are initially in balance, they tend to get out of balance as a result of machines being added to the system.

Depending on the size of the instrument, ranges covered may be as high as 2000 A. More common ranges are 500, 250, 100, 50, and 10 A ac. Some clamp-on meters also provide ac voltage measurement capability through use of separate plug-in leads. Others include analog outputs so that measurements can be sent to chart recorders and displayed on oscilloscopes. DC clamp-on meters are also available, but they utilize a different operating principle.

- Select an instrument appropriate for the frequency in the circuit being tested.
- Use as far away from transformers and other conductors as possible.
- Make sure only the conductor from the circuit under test is within the jaws of the clamp.

Ammeter Accessories

Accessories can expand the range and versatility of an ammeter. Some common accessories are:

- *A current multiplier* is used only with clamp-on ammeters to multiply the amps reading of extremely low current ac circuits. Current multipliers typically multiply the current reading by a factor of 10.
- *An amp-clamp* extends the range of direct wire ammeters by permitting clamp-on operation. The amp-clamp replaces the direct-wire ammeter leads, then clamps over the conductor.
- *A shunt* extends the range of the ammeter by bypassing some of the current around the meter.

OHMMETERS

An ohmmeter measures electrical resistance of any component or circuit between the test probes. Ohmmeters may read a very low resistance in conductors, or, using a special instrument, test the very high resistance of insulators.

An ohmmeter operates by applying power to the circuit, then measuring the circuit current.

Ohmmeter Selection Criteria/Features

Select an ohmmeter with the best features for your application, such as:

- Audible continuity checking
- Testing voltage
- Diode testing

Audible Continuity Checking.   To simplify testing, some meters produce an audible tone when the instrument detects circuit continuity. This feature is most useful for testing circuits that are difficult to reach or the technician is unable to watch the display while making the connection.

Testing Voltage.   The voltage applied by the ohmmeter to the circuit affects how the circuit operates. Most general-use ohmmeters apply 1.5 V to the circuit. Meters designed for use with solid-state circuits may apply just a few microvolts. Voltage at this level can detect even the small resistance caused by corroded terminals that can disrupt circuit operation.

High-voltage testers, with either a battery or a hand-cranked generator, are used in testing insulation. Testing voltage may exceed 5000 V.

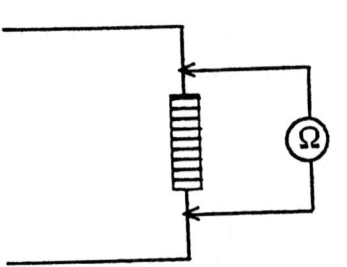

FIGURE 6-9 Connect the ohmmeter in parallel with the item under test with power OFF.

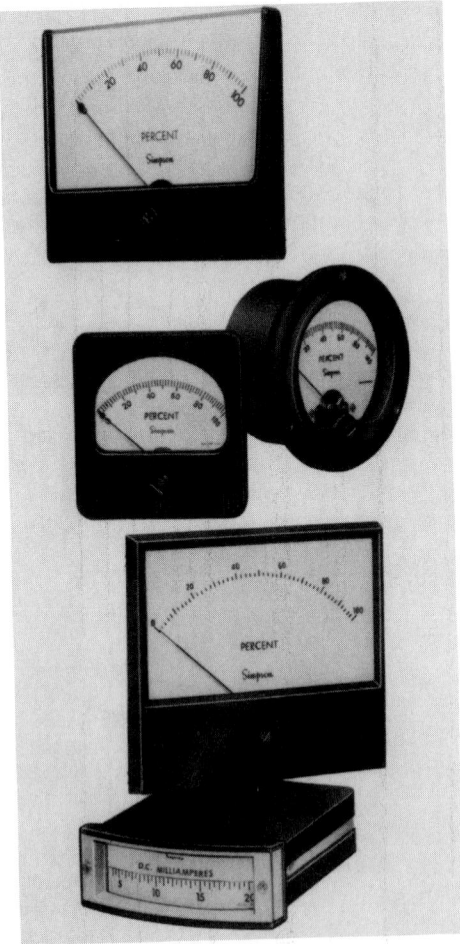

FIGURE 6-10 Panel meter styles.

Diode Testing. A diode testing function measures the forward bias voltage of a diode or semiconductor. Instead of displaying ohms, the meter displays the voltage required to bias (turn on) the PN junction of a solid-state device.

Ohmmeter Operation

- Connect the ohmmeter only to an unpowered circuit.
- Always zero the meter before each use to compensate for battery condition.
- Connect the leads in parallel with the item under test (Fig. 6-9).
- Select a resistance range that will provide a midscale reading. If you are using an 11-kΩ circuit, select the 20-kΩ scale.

PANEL METERS

Analog

Analog panel meters come in many standard models and ranges as well as in custom versions. The two classic meter styles are round and rectangular. The rectangular type provides maximum space for the scale arc. For minimum use of panel space, edgewise reading meters are available, but they often introduce parallax problems and are limited to short angular pointer swings (see Fig. 6-10).

With proper calibration, panel meters can be mounted horizontally or vertically. This subjects them to environmental factors which must be considered, such as ambient temperature, magnetic panels and stray fields, shock and vibration, and moisture and dirt. Ruggedized construction, case sealants, and self-shielding movements are available in certain models to withstand extreme environmental conditions.

Analog panel meters are available that measure dc voltage and current, ac voltage and current, temperature, motor load, elapsed time, and frequency. Analog meters are preferred where readings are constantly changing or fluctuating.

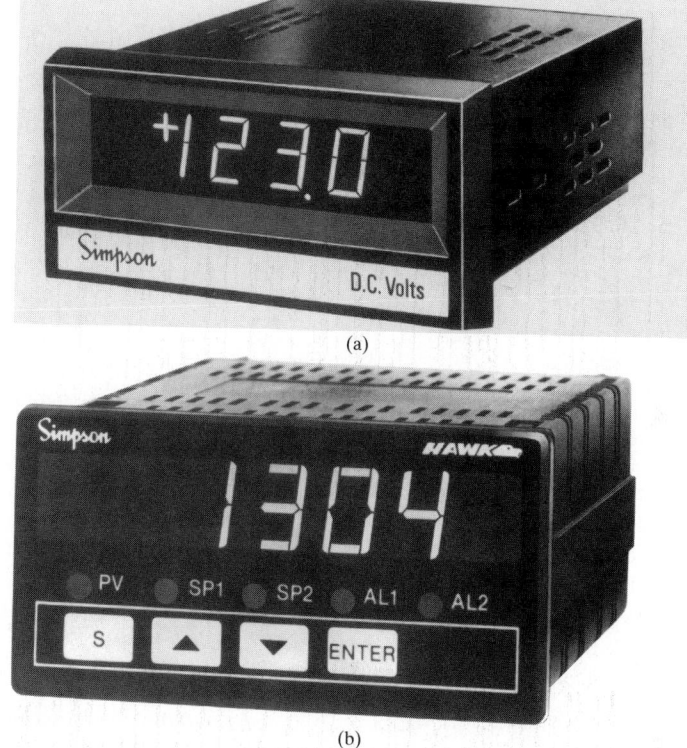

FIGURE 6-11 (*a*) Digital dc measuring meter; (*b*) microprocessor-based controller/indicator.

Digital

A digital panel meter (DPM) can be as simple as a dc measuring unit or as complex as a microprocessor-based controller (Fig. 6-11). DPMs differ from analog in that they have their own power supply and are generally more accurate. Controller/indicators are available for monitoring a variety of process variables: ac/dc voltage and current, TRMS ac voltage and current, 4 to 20 mA dc, 1 to 5 V dc, resistance, three-wire potentiometer, frequency, tachometer, resistance-temperature detector (RTD), and thermocouples.

Built-in displays are available as liquid-crystal displays (LCDs), light-emitting diodes (LEDs), or planar gas-discharge units. Accuracies are generally from 0.1 to 1.0 percent. Analog-to-digital circuitry is kept to a minimum to reduce cost but not reliability.

Digital panel meters overcome the problems of parallax, polarity, and reading error often encountered with analog meters.

Both analog and digital meters have their place in the field of test and measurement.

OTHER METERS

Other meters and measuring devices can be useful in the plant. Although not all of these meters are electrical measuring devices, they are often used by the same assembly or maintenance personnel who use multimeters. These devices are often manufactured by the same companies that make multimeters. They include:

- Microwave leakage detectors
- Frequency counters
- Sound/noise measuring instruments

Microwave Leakage Detectors

More and more processes use microwaves for heating and drying. Maintenance personnel need a hand-held microwave leakage detector to test seams, joints, and door seals to locate microwave leakage. The unit of measurement of microwave radiation is milliwatts per square centimeter (mW/cm^2).

Frequency Counters

A frequency counter measures the frequency of electrical signals. The frequency counter is often used during troubleshooting and assembly procedures for computers and other electronic devices as well as any device using oscillators. A frequency counter with a lowpass filter eliminates incorrect signals from high-frequency noise.

Sound/Noise Measurements

Occupational Safety and Health Administration (OSHA), Walsh-Healy, and other applicable regulations require documentation of dosage levels of workplace noise. Select a sound/noise meter that is compatible with a sound dosimeter or strip chart if you require a permanent record.

Sound/noise meters also require a specialized tool for calibration. Calibrators may provide a single output or several ranges for calibrating instruments.

CONCLUSION

Electrical test equipment comes in a wide variety of configurations to meet the needs of plant maintenance, assembly, and other operations. Selecting meters to economically meet your exact needs can be done by studying instrument specification sheets. Proper maintenance and handling ensures long life of the instrument. Keep in contact with leading manufacturers to stay up to date in this rapidly changing field.

SECTION 4

IN-PLANT PRIME POWER GENERATION AND COGENERATION

CHAPTER 4-1
BOILERS

Russell N. Mosher
Assistant Executive Director
American Boiler Manufacturers Association
Arlington, Virginia

TERMINOLOGY

Since the term *boiler* alone does not adequately describe the complete system for providing the motive force or energy, it is necessary to know and understand the component functions that go into making the boiler a complete unit. Comprehending the definitions in the terminology used by the industry is the first step in sorting out the perceived mysteries of understanding.

A *boiler* is a closed vessel in which water is heated, steam is generated, or steam is super-heated (or any combination of these) under pressure or vacuum by the application of heat from combustible fuels, electricity, or nuclear energy. Boilers are generally subdivided into four classic types—residential, commercial, industrial, and utility.

Residential boilers produce low-pressure steam or hot water primarily for heating applications in private residences.

Commercial boilers produce steam or hot water primarily for heating applications in commercial use, with incidental use in process operations.

Industrial boilers produce steam or hot water primarily for process applications, with incidental use as heating.

Utility boilers produce steam primarily for the production of electricity.

Within these four generic types of boilers, specific types of boilers emerge, with their classification based on their use. An example would be a *heat-recovery boiler* (Fig. 1-1) which recovers normally unused energy and converts it into usable heat. Likewise, a *fluidized-bed boiler* is one which utilizes a fluidized-bed combustion process. In this type of process, fuel is burned in a bed of granulated particles which are maintained in a mobile suspension by an upward flow of air and combustion products. This technology, in use for over 40 years, is currently being adapted as a combustion process to be installed within a boiler.

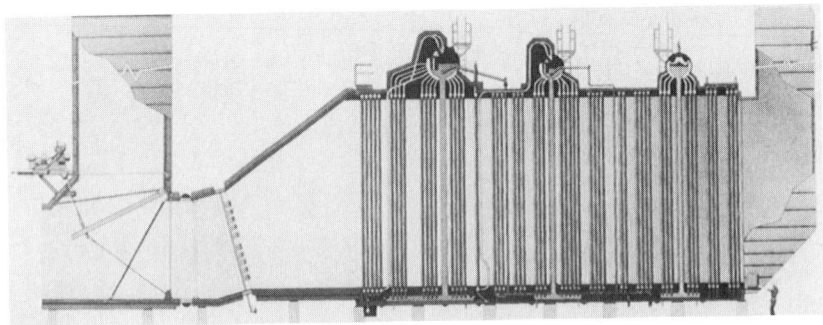

FIGURE 1-1   Heat-recovery boiler.

Generally, boilers are furnished either *packaged* or *field-erected*. A *packaged boiler* is one which is equipped and shipped complete with fuel-burning equipment, mechanical-draft equipment, automatic controls, and accessories. It is usually shipped in one or more major sections. *Field-erected boilers* are those that are shipped from the factory as tubes, casings, drums, fittings, etc., and completely assembled in the field.

The generally accepted reference for the *capacity* of a boiler is the manufacturer's stated output rate for which the boiler is designed to operate over a period of time. The *maximum continuous rating* is the maximum load in pounds (kilograms) of steam per hour for a specific period of time for which the boiler is designed. Likewise, then, the *capacity factor* is the total output over a period of time divided by the product of the boiler capacity and the time period.

INTRODUCTION

Modern boilers provide most of the motive force in the world and are probably the least understood of all mechanical pieces of equipment. They are subjects for engineering, congressional legislation, agency legislation, and physical laws, all of which shape their destiny. Despite all this attention this age-old energy source is still shrouded in mystery.

This chapter explains the theoretical and practical aspects of modern boiler equipment. The objective is to enlighten the reader on the principles of boiler design, to characterize the available equipment, and to explain the need to achieve maintenance for maximum and sustained utilization of equipment.

BOILER APPLICATION

Modern boilers range in size from those required to provide steam or hot water to heat homes, through mid-size units which provide energy to drive presses, to very large units used as the primary motive force in producing electric power. Boilers can be arranged for firing almost any type of fuel available, provided the designer is cognizant of the fuel to be employed prior to making the initial calculations for sizing.

The primary purpose of a boiler is to generate steam or hot water at pressures and/or temperatures above that of the atmosphere. Steam or hot water is produced by the transfer of heat from the combustion process taking place within the boiler, thereby elevating its pressure and temperature.

With this higher pressure and temperature, it follows that the containment vessel or pressure vessel must be designed in such a way as to encompass the desired design limits with a reasonable factor of safety. For the sake of economy, the capacity of the unit must be generated and delivered with minimum losses.

In smaller boilers used in home heating applications, the maximum operating pressure for steam is usually 15 psig (104,000 N/m^2). In the case of hot water, this is equal to 450°F (232°C).

Larger boilers are designed for various pressures and temperatures, depending upon the application within the heat cycle for which the unit is being designed. A boiler designed to heat a large college campus may require a certain capacity at an elevated pressure and a superheated temperature which provides the force to transmit the steam to its final use point. In other cases, very high pressures and temperatures are required in order to implement chemical reactions, to provide drying steam in a paper cycle, or to provide the needed energy to drive a large piece of mechanical equipment.

The dependability and safety record displayed by today's modern boilers is the product of almost 100 years of design experience, control fabrication, and monitored operation of boilers. The properties of steam and water have been accurately graphed for use by the engineer.

With the use of computers, the boiler design engineer has gained a new understanding of boiler thermal dynamics and heat transfer and has expanded the understanding of the burnability of fuels in a safe and efficient manner, thus developing units to produce the large amounts of steam required today. Advances in metallurgical fields have yielded better-quality steels and alloys, which allow use of the high pressures and temperatures required.

A large central-station boiler is designed on the basis of the output cost of electricity produced. Its operation is under close control, and the load cycle follows a very well defined and predictable pattern based on area power requirements.

The industrial boiler, however, is usually a single unit installed primarily as an important step in the production of a product. Its use is merely a means whereby the product can be fabricated in the shortest amount of time, with the lowest materials cost, and shipped. Hence, it is frequently called upon to perform a difficult task, often under unfavorable conditions of steam load, water, and fuel. Plant load cycles are usually highly unpredictable, and the boiler must be ready at any time to achieve the required capacity in the shortest amount of time without hesitation.

Many factors must be taken into consideration when one is designing a boiler. After the decision has been made as to what fuel must be burned, it is necessary to determine how much input steam is necessary to satisfy the requirements or demands upon the boiler. Operating parameters include minimum, maximum, and normal load range; length of time in a cycle; and type of load, whether constant or fluctuating. All of these parameters must be analyzed for proper size selection.

The basic components of a boiler are the *furnace* and the *convection* sections. In the *furnace* section (Fig. 1-2), the products of combustion are consumed and heat is released and transferred into the water, thereby producing steam or heating the water. This space must be designed for the three "T's" of combustion—time, turbulence, and temperature. *For complete combustion, it is necessary for the fuel to have sufficient time to be completely consumed;* there must be sufficient turbulence for complete mixing of fuel and air for efficient burning; and there must be a high enough temperature to allow the products to be ignited.

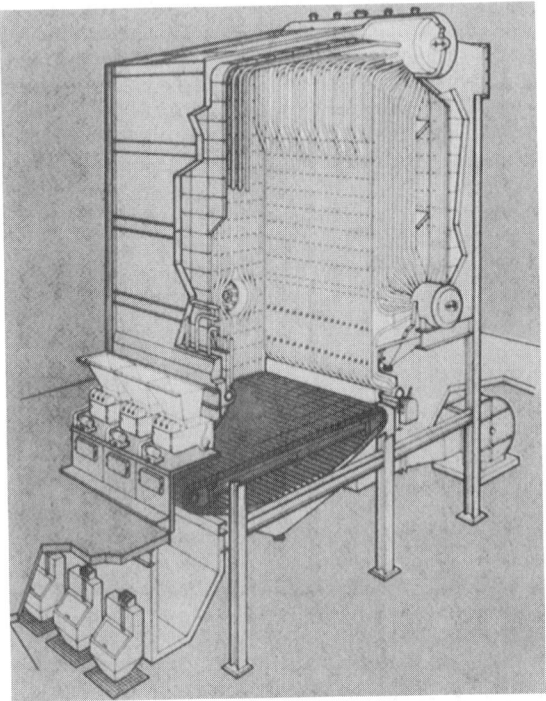

FIGURE 1-2   Furnace section. (*Babcock & Wilcox Company.*)

The shape of the furnace is controlled by the type of fuel and burning method. Adequate provisions must be made for instituting and maintaining ignition and combustion of the fuel. For those units with solid-fuel firing, adequate provision must be made to allow for the removal of unburned combustibles and/or ash.

The *convection* section (Fig. 1-3) of a boiler is that portion in which heat contained in the combustion gases is transferred to the water for the production of steam. The selection of heating surface and tube spacing depends completely upon the type of fuel producing the flue gas with its entrained particles. Adequate provision must be made in this section to allow any unburned particles to pass through and be collected in downstream separators. Pressure drop and volumetric flow are influencing factors which dictate the overall design of the convection section. Generally, a higher gas volume through a fixed flow area produces a greater pressure drop. A greater pressure drop enhances the transfer to a point where economic decisions must be made on inputs of auxiliary equipment to produce the necessary flow of these gases.

The steam and water circulation rate within the pressure vessel decides the effectiveness of the heat-transfer surface. When new feedwater is added to the system, precipitates fall out which might be removed as blowoff. Provisions are usually made in the lower portion of the convection section whereby a boiler operator may remove these particular precipitates by opening boiler blowoff valves.

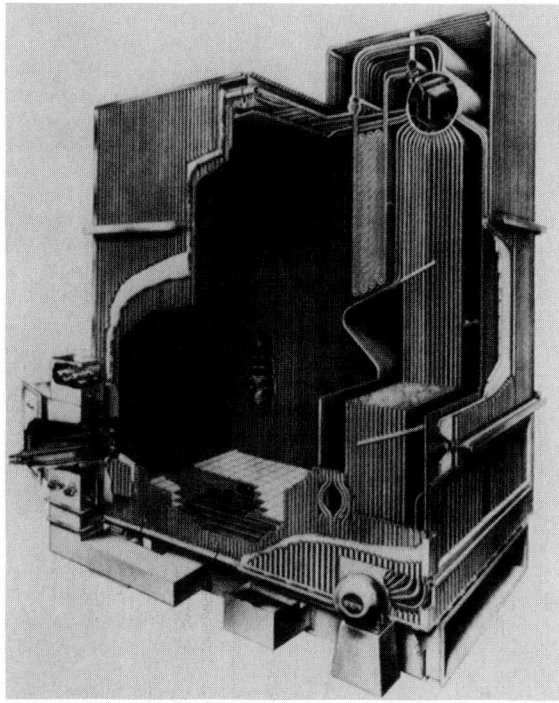

FIGURE 1-3   Convection section. (*Combustion Engineering, Inc.*)

Many applications utilizing boiler equipment require steam at a very high rate of purity. Boiler designers therefore install steam-separating equipment in the boiler drum to remove entrained moisture and solids before the steam is taken from the boiler to the system. These steam separators come in a variety of types including cyclones, mist deflectors, and baffle plates.

In some applications, the heating surface or tubes are of the bare-tube type. In other cases, the heating surface will be of the extended surface or fin-tube type. Utilizing fin tubes allows greater tube surface within the convection section. Greater heat-transfer levels can be achieved with the use of this type of tubing.

BOILER CLASSIFICATIONS

Characteristically, boiler types are generally classified as either *firetube* or *watertube*.

Firetube Boilers

In the *firetube* boiler (Fig. 1-4), the flame and products of combustion pass through the tubes. The heated water or other medium surrounds the internal furnace and the tube bundles.

Various types of furnaces are used in conjunction with firetube boilers. Some are long, cylindrical tubes while others are firebox (Fig. 1-5) arrangements allowing the burning of solid fuels. In most cases, the firetube boiler includes a shell to contain the water and steam space. Within the shell will be tube sheets and tubes which are portions of the pressure vessel containment. The furnace or firebox provides space for the combustion process from the heat source.

FIGURE 1-4 Firetube boiler. (*Cleaver-Brooks Division.*)

FIGURE 1-5 Firebox boiler. (*Kewanee Boiler Corporation*)

Many types of firetube boilers are being supplied to industry. One type is the *horizontal return tubular boiler* (Fig. 1-6). In this unit, the products of combustion travel across the shell and back through the tubes within the pressure vessel. These units are usually horizontally brick-set.

FIGURE 1-6   Horizontal-return tubular boiler (*Zurn Industries, Inc.*)

Another type of firetube unit is the *Scotch marine boiler.* This design was developed originally for shipboard installation. This type of boiler can be fired with either solid, liquid, or gaseous fuels.

Because the Scotch marine boiler is a very compact type of unit, it has become readily adaptable for stationary service. When modifications to the basic type are made in adapting it to process and heating use, it is called a *modified Scotch marine boiler.*

Another type of firetube unit currently being marketed is the *vertical-type boiler.* In this particular unit the fuel or heat source is in the bottom, and the products of combustion rise up through tubes and are emitted from the top of the unit.

Watertube Boilers

Watertube boilers come in a variety of arrangements and designs. In this type of unit, the products of combustion usually surround the tubes (Fig. 1-7), and the water is inside the tubes which are inclined upward toward a vessel or drum at the highest point of the boiler. The configuration of these tubes generally describes the type of boiler. Some manufacturers offer straight-tube units while others offer units with bent tubes (Fig. 1-8). Other configurations of watertube boilers describe the various types in terms of the variations of pressure vessel arrangement.

In a *box-header watertube* boiler, the watertubes are connected to rectangular headers which are arranged so that the circulating water and steam mixture will rise toward a collection drum. The box headers are usually on either end of the tube bundles, and the products of combustion pass between the headers and around tube bundles.

FIGURE 1-7   Commerical watertube boiler. (*Bryan Steam Boiler Company.*)

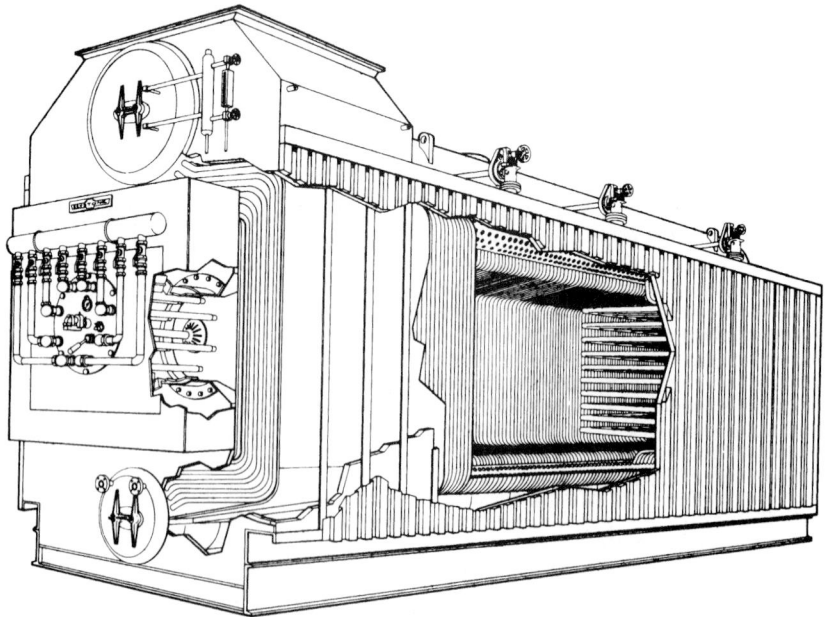

FIGURE 1-8   Bent-tube boiler.

Some boilers are of the *long-drum* type; that is, when viewed from the front of the boiler (Fig. 1-9), the drum is the length of the boiler. Its corollary is the *cross-drum* boiler. When viewed from the front of the unit, the drums are installed perpendicular to the long centerline or across the boiler.

FIGURE 1-9   Long-drum boiler. (*Zurn Industries, Inc.*)

Firetube units are generally furnished in applications up to approximately 30,000 lb (13,500 kg) of steam per hour. They are furnished for low-pressure operation [15 psig (104 kN/m^2) and under] and as power boilers [up to approximately 300 psig (2100 kN/m^2) of steam pressure]. Watertube boilers for use in industrial applications are furnished in capacities up to almost 1 million lb (450,000 kg) of steam per hour. Design pressures vary from 100 psig (700 kN/m^2) up through 1200 or 1400 psig (8.3 or 9.6 MN/m^2) with steam temperatures ranging from saturated to 1000°F (540°C).

Packaged Boilers

Many manufacturers supply both watertube and firetube units already packaged, or shop-assembled. A *packaged* steam or hot-water boiler is one which is generally shop assembled and includes all major components: burner, draft equipment, pressure vessel, trim, and controls. The main limitation to packaging boilers is the capability of their being handled by trucking or railroad equipment. Most manufacturers have designed complete lines of firetube and watertube boilers which can be shipped by either truck or railroad. Some manufacturers have utilized shop-assembling procedures to fabricate a boiler which can be assembled easily in the field. These components may be a single portion of the vessel or multiple major parts which can be brought together in the field.

BOILER COMPONENTS

To understand the operation of a boiler, it is necessary to observe what happens from input to output of the unit. Several cycles are involved in the complete operation of the unit. The heat cycle, the water and steam cycle, and the boiler-water circulation cycle all interact to produce the output of the boiler. Fuel and water are brought to the unit; water is heated to its final pre-designated condition (water and/or steam) and transported to the point of its end use. When the heat has been taken out of the water, the remaining steam and water mixture (or condensate), if usable, is returned to the unit and recycled.

Furnace*

In the fuel cycle, the solid, liquid, or gaseous fuel is delivered to the boiler where it is mixed with air and burned. This liberation of heat is usually achieved in the *furnace* portion of the boiler (Fig. 1-1). Furnaces can be of either the *refractory* or the *water-cooled* type.

In the *refractory-type* furnace, refractory brick forms the envelope of the furnace. These refractory furnaces are usually backed with insulation and a casing material. For the *water-cooled* wall-type furnace, the envelope consists of tubes placed close to each other, which thereby absorb heat and help in the production of steam. These water-cooled furnaces can have either tube and tile, tangent-tube, or welded-membrane walls.

The basic function of the furnace is to allow for the combustion of the fuel. It is necessary that the furnace size be sufficient to allow for adequate combustion of the fuel, time for its combustion, and for enough turbulence to permit efficient combustion.

Boiler Section

This is usually referred to as the boiler or convection section of the unit. Closely spaced tubes are arranged to allow passing of the products of combustion around the tubes or through the tubes, depending on the type of unit. Most of the steam is generated in the boiler portion of the unit. In watertube units, if additional steam temperature is required by the process, the steam is then routed to a superheater.

Superheater

In a superheater unit (Fig. 1-10), the steam is directed back through the products of combustion to take on additional heat. This additional heat results in considerable energy gain by the steam which will be liberated in end use. This end use can be a steam turbine or other type of equipment requiring considerable energy release for its operation.

Superheaters are either of the radiant or convection type. In a radiant superheater, the tubes are usually located in the furnace section of the boiler. Convection-type superheaters are usually located behind the screenwall of the convection section. Radiant-type superheaters receive their heat by direct radiation from the flame, while convection superheaters receive their heat primarily from the passage of the products of combustion around the tubes.

---

* See also Chap. 4-3.

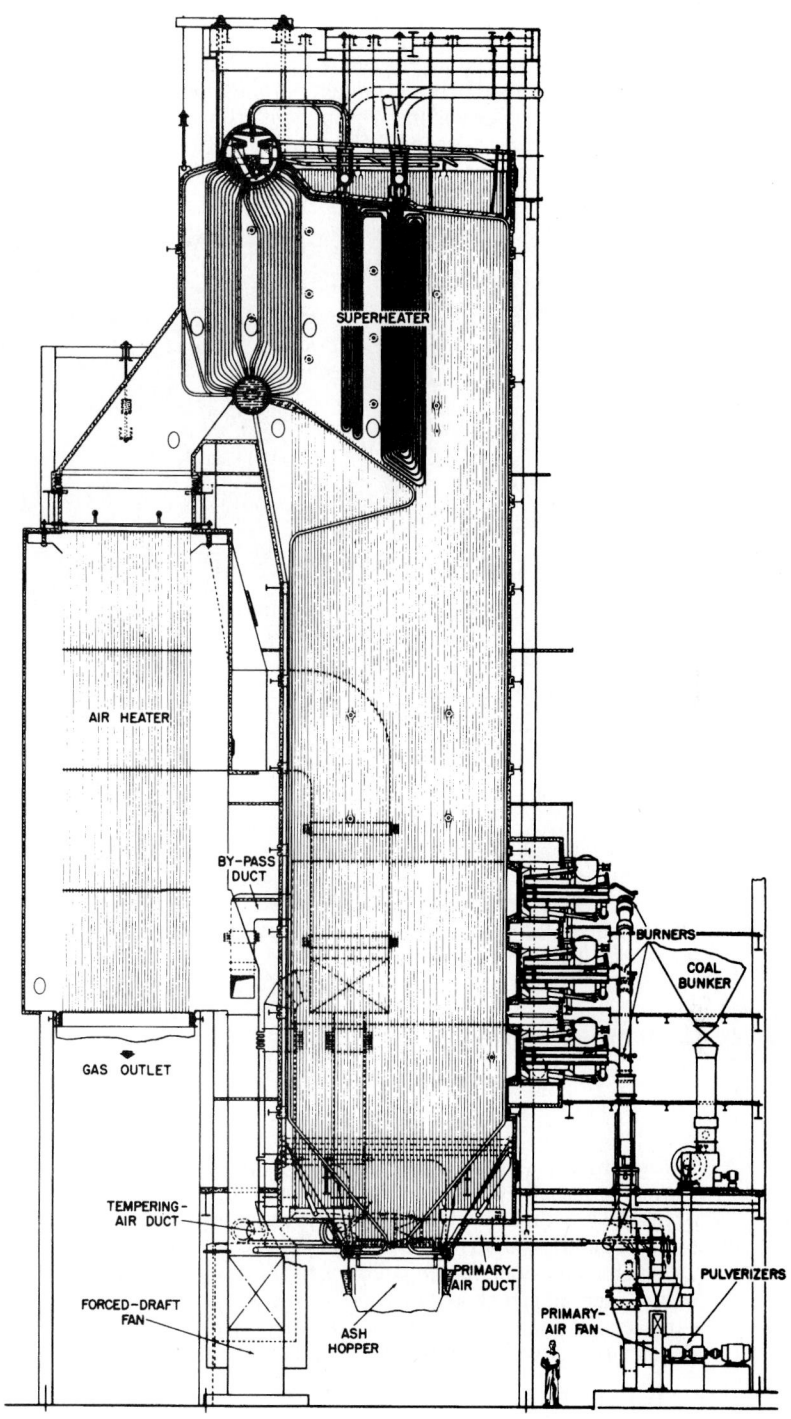

FIGURE 1-10 Boiler with superheater unit. (*Riley Stoker Corporation.*)

Air Heaters

It is often desirable to preheat the air for combustion prior to bringing it in contact with the fuel (Fig. 1-11). This is necessary when burning fuels of very high moisture content. In an air heater, the ambient air volume is brought in and preheated by utilizing sensible heat from the boiler flue gas being discharged from the unit. This increases overall efficiency, eliminating the use of extra fuel for this purpose. This is one type of *heat recovery unit.*

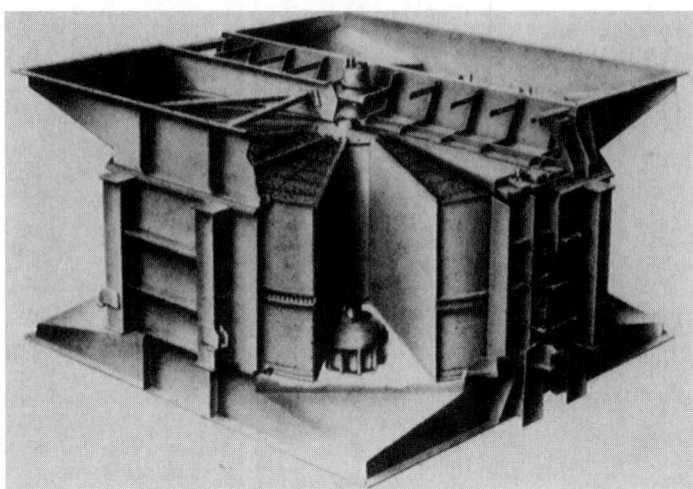

FIGURE 1-11   Air heater. (*C-E Air Preheater.*)

Economizers

An economizer (another type of heat recovery unit) is a boiler component which preheats incoming feedwater from its supplied temperature, utilizing sensible heat from the boiler outlet flue gas being exhausted from the unit. As in the air-heater principle, raising this inlet feedwater temperature (Fig. 1-12) increases the efficiency of the unit by eliminating the use of additional fuel for this operation.

OPERATION AND MAINTENANCE

Start-Up

Before any preparation can be made to start up a boiler, new or otherwise, the operator's manual furnished by the boiler manufacturer for the particular make and model unit must be available. It is important that operating personnel carefully follow the procedures in the manual, particularly the safety precautions, before attempting to activate the equipment.

When a new boiler is prepared for its initial operation, procedures should be followed to ensure high efficiency at which the unit can operate a long life, and the economies to be expected from an engineered piece of equipment. Even though the unit has been checked by the manufacturer, the following precautions should be observed:

1. The unit should be thoroughly examined on both the water side and the fire side to make sure that no foreign material is present.

2. All piping such as blowdown piping, steam piping, and feedwater piping should be checked to ensure that the piping has been properly installed so that there will be no dan-

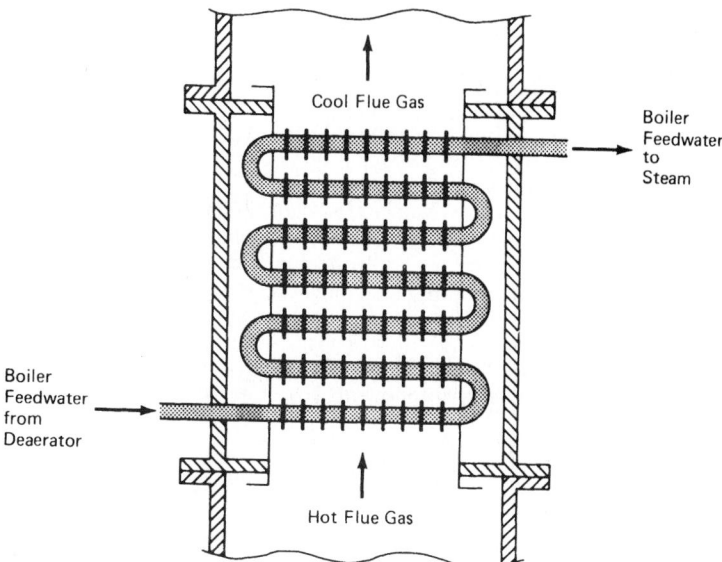

FIGURE 1-12   Principle of economizer. (*Enerex, Inc.*)

ger to any individuals. Items such as the gauge, gauge glasses, and controls should be checked for any evidence of damage or breakage either incurred during transportation or caused by installation personnel working around the equipment after it was placed.

3. Electrical equipment such as motors, pumps, blowers, and compressors should be operated whenever possible to assure proper rotation. Items such as control valves, interlocks, motorized valves, and limit switches should be checked wherever possible to ensure their proper operation.

4. All fuel lines should be checked per the installation instructions in the manual.

After a thorough inspection of the unit has been completed, the next steps to start-up follow.
    Caution: All manufacturers of boilers usually supply operating instruction manuals with their equipment. Before starting the unit, be sure that the manual of instructions has been thoroughly read and understood.

Drying Out and Boiling Out

Since the refractories and insulation of the unit may contain absorbed moisture and since (at initial start-up) the boiler is filled with water that is at the supplied temperature (which is colder than normal), the initial firing of the unit should be maintained at as low a level as possible. The boiling-out period should be continued at approximately 50 percent of the unit operating pressure for a long enough time to ensure that all oils and materials to be removed by the boiling-out process have been dislodged. Experience has indicated that a 12-h minimum boil-out period is generally sufficient to complete the cleaning. However, factors such as chemical concentration, amount of material to be removed, and pressure may modify boil-out time.

Cleaning

The system must be carefully cleaned before the boiler is connected into the system. Many clean boilers have been ruined with system contaminants such as pipe dope, cutting oil, and metal shavings or chips. Many contractors will use a new boiler for heating and curing a building under construction. Special care must be taken to assure that *adequate water treatment is provided by the contractor during this initial use of the boiler.* Succeeding owners can receive a badly scaled or damaged boiler through contractor misuse. Moreover, as new zones are cut into a system, *cleaning of these zones is required to prevent damage to the boiler. Only one boiler should be used to boil out a system.*

Cleaning Improves a Steam or Hot-Water Heating System. One important phase in completing boiler installation is too often neglected in the specifications. *No provision usually has been made for cleaning the system.* It is sometimes drained for changes and adjustments but never actually cleaned. The architect, engineer, or contractor selects boilers for applicable installations. The selection may represent the best system; but it will be better if it is a clean system.

How to Tell If a System Needs Cleaning. There are definite symptoms of an unclean system. A typical checklist follows. If any of the items are positive, the system needs cleaning.

1. Obviously discolored, murky, dirty water
2. Gases vented at high points in the heating area that ignite and burn with an almost invisible bluish flame
3. A pH alkalinity test that gives a pH test reading below 7 (A pH lower than 7 indicates the water in the system is acid.)

No matter how carefully a system is installed, certain extraneous materials do find their way accidentally into the system during construction. Pipe dope, thread-cutting oil, soldering flux, rust preventives or slushing compounds, coarse sand, welding slag, and dirt, sand, or clays from the jobsite are usually found. Fortunately the amounts of these are usually small and do not cause trouble. However, in some instances there may be sufficient quantities to break down chemically during the operation of the system, causing gas formation and acid in the water system. Hot-water systems, in most cases, naturally operate with a pH of 7 or higher. The condition of the water can be quickly tested with Hydrion paper, which is used in the same manner as litmus paper except that it gives specific pH readings. A color chart on the side of the small Hydrion dispenser gives the readings in pH units. Hydrion paper is inexpensive and readily obtainable through appropriate wholesale and retail channels.

A system that tests acid (below 7 on the scale, sometimes as low as 4) will usually have the following symptoms:

1. Gas formation (air trouble)
2. Pump seal and gland problems
3. Air vent sticking and leaking
4. Frequent operation of relief valves
5. Piping leaks at joints

Once this condition exists, the symptoms continue until the situation is corrected by cleaning the system. Many times, because of gas formation, automatic air vents are added throughout the system to attempt a cure. The excessive use of automatic air vents can defeat the function of the air-elimination system since the small quantities of entering air must be returned to the expansion tank to maintain the balance between the air cushion and the water volume.

If a system is permitted to deteriorate with resultant leaks and increased water losses, serious boiler damage can occur. Therefore, the chief consideration is to maintain a closed system that is clean, neutral, and watertight.

How to Clean a Heating System. Cleaning a system (either steel or copper piping) is neither difficult nor expensive. The materials for cleaning are readily available. Trisodium phosphate, sodium carbonate, and sodium hydroxide (lye) are the materials most commonly used for cleaning. They are available at paint and hardware stores.

The preference is in the order named, and the substances should be used in the following proportions; use a solution of *only one type* in the system.

Trisodium phosphate, 1 lb for each 50 gal (1 kg for 420 L) in the system

Sodium carbonate, 1 lb for each 30 gal (1 kg for 240 L) in the system

Sodium hydroxide (lye), 1 lb for each 50 gal (1 kg for 420 L) in the system

Fill and vent the system and circulate the cleaning solution throughout, allowing the system to reach design or operating temperatures if possible. After the solution has been circulated for a few hours, the system should be drained completely and refilled with fresh water. Usually, enough of the cleaner will adhere to the piping to give an alkaline solution satisfactory for operation. A pH reading between 7 and 8 is preferred, and a small amount of cleaner can be added if necessary.

A clean, neutral system should *never* be drained except for an emergency or for such servicing of equipment as may be necessary after years of operation. Antifreeze solution in the system should be tested from year to year as recommended by the manufacturers of the antifreeze used. Without a doubt, the clean system is the better system.

Arrangements for Cleaning Heating Systems.   Much of the dirt and contamination in a new system can be flushed out prior to boil-out of the system. This is accomplished by first flushing the system to waste with clear water and then using a chemical wash.

The boiler and circulating pump are isolated with valves, and city water is flushed through the successive zones of the system, carrying chips, dirt, pipe joint compound, etc., to waste with it. This is followed by a chemical flush. Removal of pipe chips and other debris before operating the isolation valves of the boiler and pump will help to protect this equipment from damage by such debris. After this flushing process is complete, the usual boil-out procedure is accomplished.

Caution: *If one zone is flushed and boiled out before other zones are completed or connected, this flushing process should be repeated on completion of additional zones, loops, or sections of the piping.*

When a boiler is fired for the first time (or started again after repairs or inspection), vapor and water may be observed as a white plume in stack discharge or as condensate on the boiler fire sides and services. Generally, this condition is temporary and it will disappear after the unit reaches operating temperature. This condensation should not be confused with the stack plume that occurs when the boiler is operating during extremely cold weather.

When cool-down of a boiler is required, the unit should be permitted to cool over a period of 12 h, losing its heat to the atmosphere. Forced cooling is not recommended; it will possibly loosen tubes in the tube sheets or cause other damage to the pressure parts.

Water Treatment*

Water treatment is required for satisfactory operation of a boiler at the initial start-up to prevent any deposition of scale and to prevent any corrosion from acids, oxygen, and other harmful substances that may be in the water supply. A qualified water-treatment specialist should be consulted and the water should be appropriately treated.

The basic aims and objectives of boiler-water conditioning are to:

1. Prevent the accumulation of scale and deposits in the boiler
2. Remove dissolved gases from the water
3. Protect the boiler against corrosion

---

* Also see Chap. 6-1.

4. Eliminate carryover and/or timing (steam)
5. Maintain the highest possible boiler efficiency
6. Decrease the amount of boiler downtime for cleaning

Water treatment should be checked and maintained whenever the boiler is fired.

Caution: The purchaser should be sure that the boiler is not operating for approval tests or any other operation of firing without water treatment.

It should also be noted that water boilers may well need chemical treatment for the first filling of water as well as additional periodic chemical treatment depending on the system's losses and the make-up requirements. Water treatment may vary from season to season or over a period of time and, therefore, there should be a requirement that the water-treatment procedure be checked no fewer than four times a year and possibly more frequently if the local water conditions require it. When the system is drained and then refilled, chemical treatment is required inasmuch as raw water has been put into the boiler system.

There are two major methods of boiler feedwater treatment, external and internal.

External Feedwater Treatment.   This type of treatment is performed in separate tanks, containers, or other necessary devices for the removal of oxygen and other detrimental gases, and the removal of magnesium carbonate, calcium carbonate, silica, iron, etc. There are also filters available for the removal of foreign matter. A common method of removing gas from the boiler water is to use deaerating feedwater heaters. One method of removing the magnesium and calcium carbonates is to use sodium zeolite softeners. There are filters and other equipment presently manufactured that will cover virtually every requirement for water treatment.

Internal Feedwater Treatment.   Internal feedwater treatment is generally nothing more than the addition of the proper chemicals to prevent the deposition of scaling materials on the hot surfaces of the boiler. A sludge formed by the chemicals with calcium and/or magnesium carbonates drops to the bottom of the boiler or remains in suspension. In steam boilers, this sludge can be removed by proper blowdown procedures. The chemicals that are to be added to the boiler water, the blowdown procedure, and the analysis and maintenance of the feedwater conditioning should be handled by a water-treatment consultant.

Care of Idle Boilers

Boilers that are used on a seasonal basis and will be idle for a long period of time (more than 30 days) should be laid up by using either a dry or a wet method of protection during the periods of inactivity.

Boilers Laid Up Dry.   If a boiler is subject to freezing temperatures or if it is to be idle for an excessive period of time, the following procedures should be carried out so that the boiler is not damaged during its period of inactivity:

1. Drain and clean the boiler thoroughly (both fire and water sides) and dry the boiler out.
2. Place lime or another water-absorbing substance in open trays inside the boiler and close the unit tightly to exclude all moisture and air.
3. All allied equipment such as tanks, pumps, etc., should be thoroughly drained.

Boilers Laid Up Wet.   In order to protect the boiler during short periods of idleness, it should be laid up wet and in the following manner:

1. Fill the boiler to overflowing with hot water. The water should be at approximately 120°F (45°C) to help drive out the free oxygen. Add enough caustic soda to the hot water to maintain approximately 350 parts per million (ppm) of alkalinity and also add enough sodium sulfite to produce a residue of 50 to 60 ppm of this chemical.
2. Check all boiler connections for leaks and take a weekly water sample to make sure that alkalinity and sulfite content are stable.

Restarting Boilers.   Upon restarting a boiler that has been laid up dry, laid up wet, or has been cooled down for repairs, be sure to follow the recommended start-up procedure as defined in the operating manual provided by the manufacturer.

Preparation for Lay-Up.   When a boiler is being cleaned in preparation for lay-up, the water side of the unit should be cleaned and then the unit should be fired to drive off gases. The fire side should then be cleaned. An oil coating on the fire-side metal surfaces is beneficial when the boiler is not used for extended periods of time. Another helpful treatment would consist of completely filling the boiler with an inert gas and sealing it tightly to prevent any leakage of the inert gas. This will help prevent oxidation of the metal. Fuel-oil lines should be drained and flushed of residual oil and refilled with distillate fuel. If all boilers are to be laid up, care of oil tanks, lines, pumps, and heaters is similarly required.

Burner Care

A planned preventive maintenance program is a direct route to safe, dependable boiler unit operation. Boilers are supplied with engineering fuel-burning equipment that must be maintained through a regular, conscientious maintenance program to keep it in satisfactory operating condition. Oil nozzles, igniters, electrodes, and internal burner parts should be checked as part of a regular monthly maintenance program. The settings of spark gaps and nozzle openings as well as their general dimensions should be checked for both wear and cleanliness. Specific instructions as to the method of cleaning, methods of adjustment, and particular dimensions are contained in the instruction manual furnished by the boiler manufacturer.

The best method of keeping a planned preventive maintenance program in effect is to keep a daily log of pressure, temperature, and other gauge data as well as of water-treatment data. In the event that a variation appears from the normal readings, the trouble can be quickly analyzed and corrected to avoid serious problems. For example, an oil-fired unit showing a drop in oil pressure can indicate a faulty regulating valve, a plug strainer, an air leak in the suction line, or a change in the operation of some other piece of equipment in the oil line. A decrease in oil temperature can indicate malfunction of the temperature controls or a malfunction or fouling of the heating element.

For example, in a gas-fired unit, a decrease in the gas pressure can indicate a malfunction of the regulator, a drop in the gas supply pressure, or some restriction in the gas flow possibly caused by one or more controls or valves not operating properly.

Items to Be Checked Periodically.   Such items as linkages and other mechanical fastenings and stops should be periodically checked for tightness and visually checked for any movements or vibration. Any items that are loose or that have changed in position should be thoroughly checked and readjusted as necessary.

Stacks should be checked daily for haze or smoke conditions. A cloudy, hazy, or smoky stack indicates a possible need for burner adjustment. The fire may not be receiving enough air; there may be improper control of air/fuel ratios; there could be a change of fuel delivered, etc.

Stack temperatures should be checked and noted on the log; however, one must bear in mind that a rise in stack temperature does not always mean poor combustion or a fouled water site or fire site. Stack temperatures will vary proportionally as the low point changes. Stack temperatures should be observed in relation to the firing rate and a comparison should be made with previous records of the same firing rates. Stack temperatures can vary as much as 100°F (55°C) from high fire levels to low fire levels, and therefore caution must be exercised before interpreting the stack temperature reading.

Fire-Side Maintenance.   Periodic inspection and fire-side cleaning should be performed when the exit fuel gas temperature is more than 100 to 175°F (55 to 97°C) above normal operating temperature. Cleaning should be performed immediately upon shutdown. The boiler manufacturer's recommended procedures for all fire-side maintenance should be followed.

Burner, access, or head gaskets should be inspected and replaced as required. All refractories should be inspected for excessive cracking, chipping, erosion, or loose sections. This inspection should be carried out when the boiler is open for cleaning, or at least once a year.

Fuel solenoid valves and motorized valves should be visually checked by observing the fire when the unit shuts down. If the fire does not cut off immediately, the valve could be fouling or showing wear. If this occurs, the valve should be repaired or replaced immediately to avoid any serious problems.

All switches, controls, safety devices, and other equipment associated with the boiler should be periodically checked. Do not assume that all safety devices, switches, controls, etc., are operating properly. They should all be checked periodically on a planned maintenance schedule and any malfunctions noted and repaired.

Spare Parts

Be sure spare parts for your equipment are readily available. Consult the boiler manufacturer for a suggested parts list.

Manual

The operator's manual supplied with your boiler is an excellent guide to the control functions, control care, and control adjustments. It is important to know and use the instruction manual. The manual should be kept in a place where it will be readily available for the operator's use.

Water-Level Controls

The purpose of water-level controls is to maintain the water inside the boiler at the proper operating level. All water-level controls have a range of operations—not one set point. Water-level controls with gauge glasses should be so set that the water level is never out of sight, either low or high.

Water columns, gauge glasses, and low-water cutoffs on a steam boiler should be flushed at least once every shift. The purpose of this flushing is to prevent any accumulation of sludge or dirt that could possibly cause a control failure. When flushing the water column, it is advisable to test the operation of the low-water cutoff.

The water-level control that is most frequently found on boilers is a combination level indicator and low-water cutoff that is often incorporated in a water-column arrangement. This combination control allows for visual inspection of the water level, and in addition it functions to interrupt the electric current to a burner circuit in the event that an unsafe water level should develop.

Local water conditions and the introduction of treatment chemicals to a boiler will vary the amount of sediment accumulation in a control float bowl or a water column. For heating boilers and power boilers it is recommended that the boiler safety control be blown down regularly at least once a week when the boiler is in operation; however, power boilers may require a more frequent blowdown depending on operating and water conditions. When blowing down a control, it is advisable to check the operation of the low-water cutoff at a low-fire burner setting.

Monthly, the low-water cutoff should be tested under actual operating conditions. With the burner operating and the boiler steaming at the proper water level, close all the valves in the feedwater and condensate return lines for the duration of the test and shut off the feedwater pump, if required, so that the boiler will not receive any placement water. Then carefully observe the waterline to determine where the cutoff switch stops the burner in relation to the lowest permissible waterline established by the boiler manufacturers. The boiler water level should never be allowed to drop below the lowest visible part of the water-gauge glass. If the cutoff does not function during this test, immediately stop the operation of the burner. Then determine the cause of the failure and remedy it. The slow steaming evaporation test should then be repeated to verify that the control does function correctly.

If the burner cutoff level is not at, or slightly above, the lowest permissible water level, the low-water cutoff should be moved to the proper elevation, or should be serviced, repaired, or even replaced if necessary.

The low-water cutoff should be dismantled and checked at yearly intervals by a qualified technician to the extent necessary to ensure freedom from obstructions and proper functioning of the working parts. Inspect connecting lines to the boiler for any accumulation of sediment or scale, and clean as required. Examine all visible wiring for brittle or worn insulation, make sure electric contacts are clean, and where applicable, check mercury switches for any discoloration or mercury separation. Normally, operating mechanisms should not be repaired in the field. Replacement parts and complete replacement mechanisms, including necessary gaskets and installation instructions, are available from the manufacturer.

On boilers, the low-water cutoff may be checked periodically by manually tripping the control. Instructions on the method of tripping the specific control are found in the operator's manual supplied by the manufacturer.

Allied Boiler Equipment

It is recommended that a thorough check be made of all grease fittings, oil fittings, and other lubrication points and that a maintenance program be instituted to assure proper lubrication of all moving parts as required by the manufacturer. Such items as air compressors, blower bearings, motors, and other mechanically operated equipment do require lubrication from time to time. Consult the instruction manual for the detailed points and instructions; do not fail to establish a continuing maintenance program.

Depending upon the particular conditions of installation, such items as oil strainers, air filters, screens, etc., will accumulate foreign matter. All filters, screens, and strainers should be periodically cleaned to avoid any obstruction or malfunction. A smoke condition in the burner can be caused by an obstructed air inlet to the blower or by an obstructed compressor air filter just as well as by excess fuel input. A reduction in oil flow can be caused by a dirty oil strainer. A regular maintenance program should be set up according to the particular installation conditions to prevent any accumulation of foreign material.

Fuel-Oil System

Tanks should be checked annually for the presence of water and sludge. Fill should be checked for tightness of covers and proper gaskets after each delivery. Make certain the fill box is above grade to prevent water seepage into the tanks. Check vent pipes for obstructions.

Heaters

Heaters should be checked annually for the presence of water or sludge and for "coking" of heat-exchanger surfaces.

Pumps

Pumps should be checked at least monthly for leaky shaft sills and worn or loose drive mechanisms.

Piping

Oil lines should be checked at least monthly for external leaks and damage.

General Precautions.   The oil-line vacuum gauge should be checked daily. Gauge readings that increase or are erratic indicate potential trouble. In this case, strainers should be checked and cleaned, and oil lines checked for obstructions or internal sludge buildup.

When taking an oil circulation and heating system out of service, precautions should be taken so that start-up will not be obstructed by congealed fuel oil. This may require flushing the lines with a lighter-grade oil and/or shutting down the system on the lighter-grade fuel.

Electric Contacts

Electric contacts on such items as starters, contactors, and controls should be periodically checked for cleanliness and arc burns. Dust should not be permitted to accumulate on any contact. Covers on controls must be in place and control cabinet doors should be closed except during the period when access is actually required for service.

Caution: Power must be shut off before any control cover or cabinet is opened.

Steam Systems

It is recommended that a periodic check of the steam system be conducted to prevent boiler malfunction due to external problems.

- Check to assure that cold makeup water is not being fed into a hot boiler.
- Check the feedwater-treatment equipment to make sure that it is operating properly.
- Check items such as feed pumps, valves, and other equipment to assure proper performance.
- Check safety valves in accordance with instructions by ASME Boiler & Pressure Vessel Code, Sec. VI, "Recommended Rules for Care and Operation of Heating Boilers."

Hot-Water Systems

The following checks should be made periodically to prevent boiler problems:

- Expansion tanks should be checked to ensure proper performance.
- Water circulators should be checked to make sure that circulation is maintained in all operating conditions.
- Extreme fluctuations of pressure gauges can be indicators of system problems. Check the system for a possible lock in the expansion tank. The air-removal device or connection on top of the boiler should be checked to ensure that it is functioning properly.
- Piping should be checked to make sure that there are no stoppages due to the piping being air-bound.
- Air vents at the high points of the systems should be checked to ensure that they are not bleeding air into the system during pump starts.
- Weeping safety valves not only cause undesirable watermarks and steam losses but may indicate valve malfunction. A check for excessive amounts of system makeup water should be made by means of a water meter on the inlet line.
- A check should be maintained whenever the equipment is switching from a cooling to a heating cycle to ensure that the boiler is not shocked by extreme system changes. When a boiler is used with a cooling/heating system, switching to the chilling cycle should be handled with care. Proper controls should be installed in the system to prevent chilled water from entering the boiler.

When a hot-water system is in use, it is recommended that circulation be maintained. If it is necessary to shut down the circulators, the system will cool down to ambient temperature and can then cause damage at start-up. This is referred to as *thermal shock.* Particular instructions and recommendations made in the instruction manual should be observed to assure the long life of the boiler.

When a boiler is being drained for inspection, it is recommended that a flow of water be maintained in the boiler with a high-pressure hose to keep any sediment thoroughly agitated and in suspension to prevent caking of the sludge that can be extremely difficult to remove at a later date.

TABLE 1-1 Recommended Periodic Testing and Verification Checklist

Item	Frequency	Accomplished by	Remarks
Gauges, monitors, & indicators	Daily	Operator	Make visual inspection and record readings in log
Instrument & equipment settings	Daily	Operator	Make visual check against factory-recommended specifications
Firing rate control	Weekly	Operator	Visual inspection
	Semi-annually	Service technician	Verify factory settings; check with combustion test instruments
Fuel valves			
Pilot valves	Weekly	Operator	Open limit switch; make audible and visual check; check valve position indicators; check fuel meters
Main gas valves	Annually		
Main oil valves		Service technician	Perform leakage tests; refer to manufacturer's instructions
Combustion safety controls			
Flame failure	Weekly	Operator	Close manual fuel supply for (1) pilot, (2) main fuel cock and/or valve(s); check safety shutdown timing; log
Flame signal strength	Weekly	Operator	If flame signal meter has been installed, read and log; for both pilot and main flames, notify service organization if readings are very high, very low, or fluctuating. Refer to manufacturer's instructions
Pilot turn down tests	As required/ annually	Service technician	Required after any adjustments to flame scanner mount or pilot burner; verify annually
Refractory hold in	As required/ annually	Service technician	See pilot turn down test
Low-water cutoff	Monthly	Operator	
High limit safety control	Annually	Service technician	Refer to manufacturer's instructions
Operating control	Annually	Service technician	Refer to manufacturer's instructions
Low draft interlock	Annually	Service technician	Refer to manufacturer's instructions
Atomizing air steam interlock	Annually	Service technician	Refer to manufacturer's instructions
High- & low-gas-pressure interlock	Annually	Service technician	Refer to manufacturer's instructions
High- & low-oil-pressure interlock	Annually	Service technician	Refer to manufacturer's instructions
High- & low-oil-temperature interlock	Annually	Service technician	Refer to manufacturer's instructions
Fuel valve interlock switch	Annually	Service technician	Refer to manufacturer's instructions
Purge switch	Annually	Service technician	Refer to manufacturer's instructions
Burner position interlock	Annually	Service technician	Refer to manufacturer's instructions
Rotary cup interlock	Annually	Service technician	Refer to manufacturer's instructions
Low fire start interlock	Annually	Service technician	Refer to manufacturer's instructions
Automatic changeover control (dual fuel)	At least annually	Service technician	Under supervision of gas utility
Safety valves	As required	Operator	In accordance with procedure in ASME boiler code

Recommended Periodic Testing and Verification

Once equipment has been placed in service, it becomes the owner's responsibility to maintain it. Maintenance should include periodic testing and verification of controls and safety devices. Records or logs of such maintenance should be kept by the owner and/or boiler operator.

The maintenance and testing is in addition to those inspections required by the various governmental agencies or insurance companies. A list showing the recommended frequency of periodic testing and verification is found in Table 1-1.

BIBLIOGRAPHY

Boiler & Pressure Vessel Code, American Society of Mechanical Engineers (ASME), New York, 1980.

"Combustion Engineering," Combustion Engineering, Inc., Stamford, Conn., 1967.

D. Gunn and R. Horton: *Industrial Boilers,* John Wiley & Sons, New York, 1989.

A. Kohan: *Boiler Operator's Guide,* 3d ed., McGraw-Hill, New York, 1993.

D. Lindsley: *Boiler Control Systems,* McGraw-Hill, New York, 1991.

Packaged Firetube Engineering Manual, American Boiler Manufacturers Association, 1971.

Carl D. Shields: *Boilers,* McGraw-Hill, New York, 1961.

"Steam/Its Generation and Use," Babcock & Wilcox Co., Wilmington, N.C., 1980.

CHAPTER 4-2

FUELS AND COMBUSTION EQUIPMENT*

P. Eric Ralston
Vice President and General Manager
Environmental Equipment Division
Babcock and Wilcox
Barberton, Ohio

GLOSSARY

Grindability   A term used to measure the ease of pulverizing a coal in comparison with a standard coal chosen as 100 grindability.

Gross (higher) heating value   The heat released from the combustion of a unit of fuel quantity (mass) with the products in the form of ash, gaseous CO_2 (carbon dioxide), SO_2 (sulfur dioxide), N_2 (nitrogen), and liquid water exclusive of any water added directly as vapor.

Net (lower) heating value   Calculated from the gross heating value as the heat produced by a unit quantity of fuel when all water in the products remains as vapor. This calculation (ASTM Standard D 407) is made by deducting 1030 lb (470 kg) of water derived from the fuel, including both the water originally present as moisture and that formed by combustion.

---

* A portion of this material was adapted by permission from *Steam: Its Generation and Use*, published by Babcock & Wilcox Co. in 1992.

Proximate analysis   The determination of moisture, volatile matter, and ash and the calculation of fixed carbon by difference.

Ultimate analysis   The determination (using a dried sample) of carbon, hydrogen, sulfur, nitrogen, and ash and the estimation of oxygen by difference.

SOLID FUELS

Characteristics

Coal

Coal Analysis.   Customary practice in reporting the components of a coal is to use proximate and ultimate analyses (see Glossary).

The scope of each is indicated in the analyses of a West Virginia coal (Table 2-1) in which the ultimate analysis has been converted to the as-received basis. The analysis on the as-received basis includes the total moisture content of the coal received at the plant. Similarly, the as-fired basis includes the total moisture content of the coal as it enters the boiler furnace or pulverizer. Standard laboratory procedures for making these analyses appear in ASTM D 271, "Sampling & Analysis, Laboratory, Coal & Coke."

TABLE 2-1   Coal Analyses on As-Received Basis (Pittsburgh Seam Coal, West Virginia)

Proximate analysis		Ultimate analysis	
Component	% by wt	Component	% by wt
Moisture	2.5	Moisture	2.5
Volatile matter	37.6	Carbon	75.0
Fixed carbon	52.9	Hydrogen	5.0
Ash	7.0	Sulfur	2.3
Total	100.0	Nitrogen	1.5
		Oxygen	6.7
Heating value,		Ash	7.0
Btu/lb	13,000	Total	100.0
(kJ/kg)	(30,238)		

A list of other testing standards is given in Table 2-2.

ASTM Classification by Rank.   Coals are classified in order to identify their end use and also to provide data useful in specifying and selecting burning and handling equipment and in the design and arrangement of heat-transfer surfaces.

One classification of coal is by rank, i.e., according to the degree of metamorphism, or progressive alteration, in the natural series from lignite to anthracite. In the ASTM classification, the basic criteria are the fixed-carbon content and the calorific values (in British thermal units) calculated on a mineral-matter-free basis.

In establishing the rank of coals, it is necessary to use information showing an appreciable and systematic variation with age. For the older coals, a good criterion is the "dry, mineral-matter-free fixed carbon or volatile [matter]." However, this value is not suitable for designating the rank of the younger coals. A dependable means of classifying the latter is the "moist, mineral-matter-free Btu," or calorific value, which varies little for the older coals but appreciably and systematically for younger coals. Table 2-3, ASTM D 388, is used for classification according to rank or age.

TABLE 2-2   ASTM Standards for Testing Coal, Specifications, and Definitions of Terms

ASTM Standards for Testing Coal

*D 1756	Carbon Dioxide in Coal
*D 2361	Chlorine in Coal
*D 291	Cubic Foot Weight of Crushed Bituminous Coal
*D 440	Drop Shatter Test for Coal
*D 547	Dustiness, Index of, of Coal and Coke
*D 1857	Fusibility of Coal Ash
*D 1412	Equilibrium Moisture of Coal at 96 to 97% Relative Humidity and 30°C
*D 2014	Expansion or Contraction of Coal by the Sole-Heated Oven
*D 720	Free-Swelling Index of Coal
D 409	Grindability of Coal by the Hardgrove-Machine Method
*D 2015	Gross Calorific Value of Solid Fuel by the Adiabatic Bomb Calorimeter
D 1812	Plastic Properties of Coal by the Gieseler Plastometer
D 2639	Plastic Properties of Coal by the Automatic Gieseler Plastometer
D 197	Sampling and Fineness Test of Powdered Coal
*D 271	Sampling and Analysis, Laboratory, of Coal and Coke
D 492	Sampling Coals Classified According to Ash Content
*D 2234	Sampling, Mechanical, of Coal
*D 2013	Samples, Coal, Preparing of Analysis
*D 410	Screen, Analysis of Coal
D 311	Sieve Analysis of Crushed Bituminous Coal
D 310	Size of Anthracite
*D 431	Size of Coal, Designating from its Screen Analysis
*D 1757	Sulfur in Coal Ash
*D 2492	Sulfur, Forms of, in Coal
*D 441	Tumbler Test for Coal

Specifications

*D 388	Classification of Coals by Rank
*E 11	Wire-Cloth Sieves for Testing Purposes
E 323	Perforated-Plate Sieves for Testing Purposes

Definitions of Terms

*D 121	Coal and Coke
D 2796	Lithological Classes and Physical Components of Coal
*D 407	Gross Calorific Value and Net Calorific Value of Solid and Liquid Fuels

* Approved as American National Standard by the American National Standards Institute.

The basis for the two ASTM criteria (the fixed-carbon content and the calorific value calculated on a moist, mineral-matter-free basis) are shown in Fig. 2-1 for over 300 typical coals of the United States. The classes and groups of Table 2-3 are indicated in Fig. 2-1. For the anthracitic and low- and medium-volatile bituminous coals, the moist, mineral-matter-free calorific value changes very little; hence the fixed-carbon criterion is used. Conversely, in the case of the high-volatile bituminous, subbituminous, and lignitic coals, the moist, mineral-matter-free calorific value is used, since the fixed-carbon value is almost the same for all classifications.

Other Classifications of Coal by Rank.   There are other classifications of coal by rank (or type) which are currently in limited use on the European continent. These are the International Classification of Hard Coals by Type, and the International Classification of Brown Coals. Other criteria for the classification of coal by rank have been proposed by various authorities.

Volatile Matter and Heating Value.   The composition of the fixed carbon in all types of coal is substantially the same. The variable constituents of coals can, therefore, be considered as concentrated in the volatile matter. One index of the quality of the volatile matter, its heating

TABLE 2-3   Classification of Coals by Rank[a] (ASTM D 388)

Class	Group	Fixed carbon limits, % (dry, mineral-matter-free basis)		Volatile matter limits, & (dry, mineral-matter-free basis)		Calorific value limits, Btu/lb (moist,[b] mineral-matter-free basis)		Agglomerating character
		Equal or greater than	Less than	Greater than	Equal or less than	Equal or greater than	Less than	
I. Anthracitic	1. Meta-anthracite	98	—	—	2	—	—	⎫
	2. Anthracite	92	98	2	8	—	—	⎬ Nonagglomerating
	3. Semianthracite[c]	86	92	8	14	—	—	⎭
II. Bituminous	1. Low volatile bituminous coal	78	86	14	22	—	—	⎫
	2. Medium volatile bituminous coal	69	78	22	31	—	—	⎬ Commonly agglomerating[e]
	3. High volatile A bituminous coal	—	69	31	—	14,000[d]	—	
	4. High volatile B bituminous coal	—	—	—	—	13,000[d]	14,000	⎭
	5. High volatile C bituminous coal	—	—	—	—	⎰11,500	13,000	
						⎱10,500[e]	11,500	Agglomerating
III. Subbituminous	1. Subbituminous A coal	—	—	—	—	10,500	11,500	⎫
	2. Subbituminous B coal	—	—	—	—	9,500	10,500	⎬
	3. Subbituminous C coal	—	—	—	—	8,300	9,500	Nonagglomerating
IV. Lignitic	1. Lignite A	—	—	—	—	6,300	8,300	⎭
	2. Lignite B	—	—	—	—	—	6,300	

[a] This classification does not include a few coals, principally nonbanded varieties, which have unusual physical and chemical properties and which come within the limits of fixed carbon or calorific value of the high volatile bituminous and subbituminous ranks. All of these coals either contain less than 48% dry, mineral-matter-free fixed carbon or have more than 15,500 moist, mineral-matter-free British thermal units per pound.

[b] Moist refers to coal containing its natural inherent moisture but not including visible water on the surface of the coal.

[c] If agglomerating, classify in low volatile group of the bituminous class.

[d] Coals having 69% or more fixed carbon on the dry, mineral-matter-free basis shall be classified according to fixed carbon, regardless of calorific value.

[e] It is recognized that there may be nonagglomerating varieties in these groups of the bituminous class, and there are notable exceptions in high volatile C bituminous group.

value, is perhaps the most important property as far as combustion is concerned, and this bears a direct relation to the properties of the pure coals (dry, mineral-matter-free). The volatile matter in coals of lower rank is relatively high in water and CO_2 and consequently low in heating value. The volatile matter in coals of higher rank is relatively high in hydrocarbons, such as methane (CH_4), and consequently is relatively high in heating value.

The relationship of the heating value of the volatile matter to the heating value of the pure coal is shown in Fig. 2-2 for a large number of coals.

Commercial Sizes of Coal

BITUMINOUS.   Sizes of bituminous coal are not well standardized, but the following sizings are common:

Run of Mine. This is coal shipped as it comes from the mine without screening.

Run of Mine (8 in [20 cm]). This is run of mine with oversized lumps broken up.

Lump (5 in [12.5 cm]). This size will not go through a 5-in (12.5 cm) round hole.

Egg (5 × 2 in [12.5 × 5.1 cm]). This size goes through 5-in (12.5 cm) holes and is retained on 2-in (5.1 cm) round-hole screens.

Nut (2 × 1¼ in [5.1 × 3.2]). This size is used for small industrial stokers and for hand firing.

Stoker Coal (1¼ × ¾ in [3.2 × 1.9 cm]). This is used largely for small industrial stokers and for domestic firing.

Slack (¾ in [1.9 cm] and under). This is used for pulverizers and industrial stokers.

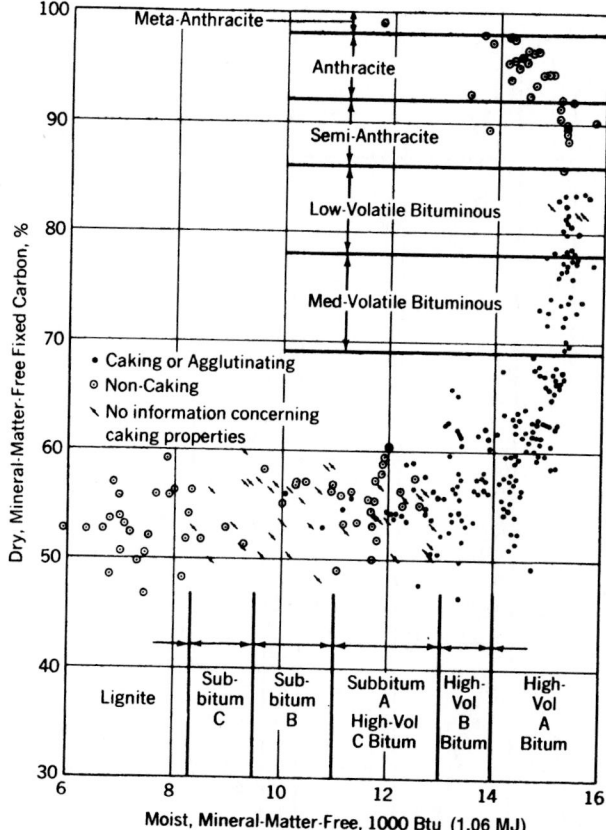

FIGURE 2-1 Distribution plot for over 300 coals of the United States, illustrating ASTM classification by rank as defined in Table 2-3.

ANTHRACITE.   Definite sizes of anthracite are standardized in Table 2-4.

Moisture Determination.   Moisture in coal is determined quantitatively by definite prescribed methods. It is preferable to determine the moisture in two steps: (1) prescribed air drying to equilibrium at 10 to 15°C above room temperature, and (2) prescribed oven drying for 1 h at 104 to 110°C, after pulverizing (see ASTM Standard D 271).

Since it is the surface moisture that must be evaporated prior to efficient pulverizing of coal, the air-dried component of the total moisture value should be reported separately.

ASTM Standard D 1412 provides a means of estimating the bed moisture of either wet coal showing visible surface moisture or coal that may have lost some moisture. It may be used for estimating the surface moisture of wet coal, i.e., the difference between total moisture, as determined by ASTM Standard D 271, and equilibrium moisture.

Grindability Index.   A coal is harder or easier to grind if its grindability index is less or greater, respectively, than 100. The capacity of a pulverizer is related to the grindability index of the coal.

Coal Ash.   The presence of ash is accounted for by minerals associated with initial vegetal growth or by those which entered the coal seam from external sources during or after the period of coal formation.

The composition of the coal ash is customarily determined by chemical analysis of the residue produced by burning a sample of coal at a slow rate and at moderate temperature (1350°F) under oxidizing conditions in a laboratory furnace. It is thus found to be composed

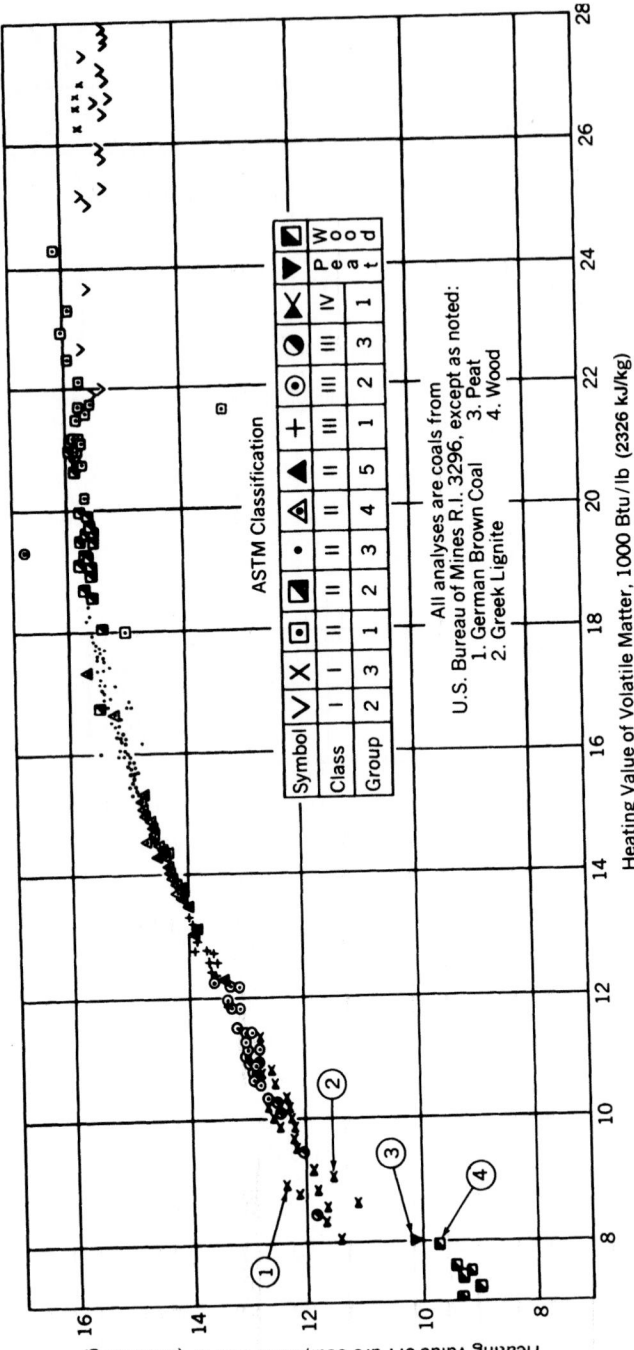

FIGURE 2-2 To illustrate a suggested coal classification using the relationship of the respective heating values of "pure coal" and the volatile matter.

TABLE 2-4   Commercial Sizes of Anthracite
(ASTM D 310)
(Graded on round-hole screens)

	Diameter of holes, in*	
Trade name	Through	Retained on
Broken	4⅛	3¼ to 3
Egg	3¼ to 3	2⁷⁄₁₆
Stove	2⁷⁄₁₆	1⅝
Nut	1⅝	¹³⁄₁₆
Pea	¹³⁄₁₆	⁹⁄₁₆
Buckwheat	⁹⁄₁₆	⅜₁₆
Rice	⅜₁₆	⅛₁₆

* Metric standards will vary in names and sizes.

chiefly of compounds of silicon, aluminum, iron, and calcium, with smaller amounts of magnesium, titanium, sodium, and potassium. The analyses of coal ash in Table 2-5 indicate what may be expected of selected coals from various areas of the United States.

Coals may be classified into two groups on the basis of the nature of their ash constituents. One is the bituminous-type ash and the other is the lignite-type ash. *Lignite-type ash* is ash having more CaO plus MgO than Fe_2O_3. By contrast, *bituminous-type ash* has more Fe_2O_3 than CaO plus MgO.

FREE-SWELLING INDEX.   The ASTM Standard method D 720 is used for obtaining information regarding the free-swelling property of a coal. Since it is a measure of the behavior of rapidly heated coal, it may be used as an indication of the caking characteristics of coal burned as a fuel.

ASH FUSIBILITY.   The determination of ash fusion temperatures (initial deformation, softening, hemispherical, and fluid) is a laboratory procedure, developed in standardized form (ASTM Standard D 1857).

Ash melts when heated to a sufficiently high temperature. If insufficiently cooled, the ash particles remain molten or sticky and tend to coalesce into large masses in the boiler furnace or other heat-absorption surfaces. This problem is dealt with by adequate design of burners and furnace arrangement, knowing the ash fusion temperatures for the fuels to be burned.

VISCOSITY OF COAL-ASH SLAG.   Measurement of viscosity of coal-ash slags provides reliable data that can be used for determining suitability of coals for use in slag-tap-type boilers.

Other Solid Fuels

Coke.   When coal is heated with a large deficiency of air, the lighter constituents are volatilized and the heavier hydrocarbons crack, liberating hydrogen and leaving a residue of carbon. The carbonaceous residue containing the ash and a part of the sulfur of the original coal is called *coke.*

Undersized coke, called *coke breeze,* usually passing a ⅝-in (17-mm) screen, is unsuited for charging blast furnaces and is available for steam generation. A typical analysis of coke breeze appears in Table 2-6.

Coke from Petroleum.   The heavy residuals from the various petroleum cracking processes are presently utilized to produce a higher yield of lighter hydrocarbons and a solid residue suitable for fuel. Solid fuels from oil include delayed coke, fluid coke, and petroleum pitch. Some selected analyses are given in Table 2-7.

Some of these cokes are easy to pulverize and burn, while others are quite difficult. The low-melting-point pitches may be heated and burned like heavy oil, while those with higher melting points may be pulverized and burned.

TABLE 2-5 Ash Content and Ash Fusion Temperatures of Some U.S. Coals and Lignite

	Low-volatile bituminous	High-volatile bituminous				Subbituminous	Lignite
	Pocahontas No. 3	No. 9 Ohio	Pittsburgh	No. 6 Illinois	Utah	Wyoming	Texas
Seam location	West Virginia		West Virginia				
Ash, dry basis, %	12.3	14.10	10.87	17.36	6.6	6.6	12.8
Sulfur, dry basis, %	0.7	3.30	3.53	4.17	0.5	1.0	1.1
Analysis of ash, % by wt							
SiO_2	60.0	47.27	37.64	47.52	48.0	24.0	41.8
Al_2O_3	30.0	22.96	20.11	17.87	11.5	20.0	13.6
TiO_2	1.6	1.00	0.81	0.78	0.6	0.7	1.5
Fe_2O_3	4.0	22.81	29.28	20.13	7.0	11.0	6.6
CaO	0.6	1.30	4.25	5.75	25.0	26.0	17.6
MgO	0.6	0.85	1.25	1.02	4.0	4.0	2.5
Na_2O	0.5	0.28	0.80	0.36	1.2	0.2	0.6
K_2O	1.5	1.97	1.60	1.77	0.2	0.5	0.1
Total	98.8	98.44	95.74	95.20	97.5	86.4	84.3
Ash fusibility							
Initial deformation temperature, °F*							
Reducing	2900+	2030	2030	2000	2060	1990	1975
Oxidizing	2900+	2420	2265	2300	2120	2190	2070
Softening temperature, °F*							
Reducing		2450	2175	2160		2180	2130
Oxidizing		2605	2385	2430		2220	2190
Hemispherical temperature, °F*							
Reducing		2480	2225	2180	2140	2250	2150
Oxidizing		2620	2450	2450	2220	2240	2210
Fluid temperature, °F*							
Reducing		2620	2370	2310	2250	2290	2240
Oxidizing		2670	2540	2610	2460	2300	2290

* °C = (°F − 32) × ⁵⁄₉.

TABLE 2-6 Analyses—Bagasse and Coke Breeze

Analyses (as-fired), % by wt	Bagasse	Coke breeze
Proximate		
Moisture	52.0	7.3
Volatile matter	40.2	2.3
Fixed carbon	6.1	79.4
Ash	1.7	11.0
Ultimate		
Hydrogen, H_2	2.8	0.3
Carbon, C	23.4	80.0
Sulfur, S	Trace	0.6
Nitrogen, N_2	0.1	0.3
Oxygen, O_2	20.0	0.5
Moisture, H_2O	52.0	7.3
Ash, A	1.7	11.0
Heating value, Btu/lb	4000	11,670
(kJ/kg)	(9304)	(27,144)

TABLE 2-7 Selected Analyses of Solid Fuels Derived from Oil

Analyses (dry basis), % by wt	Delayed coke		Fluid coke	
Proximate:				
VM	10.8	9.0	6.0	6.7
FC	88.5	90.0	93.7	93.2
Ash	0.7	0.1	0.3	0.1
Ultimate:				
Sulfur	9.9	1.5	4.7	5.7
Heating value,				
Btu/lb	14,700	15,700	14,160	14,290
(kJ/kg)	(34,192)	(36,518)	(32,936)	(33,239)

Wood.   Analyses of wood ash and selected analyses and heating values of several types of wood are given in Table 2-8.

Wood or bark with a moisture content of 50 percent or less burns quite well; however, as the moisture content increases above this level, combustion becomes more difficult. With moisture content above 65 percent, a large part of the heat in the wood is required to evaporate the moisture, and little remains for steam generation.

Bagasse.   Bagasse is the refuse from the milling of sugar cane. It consists of matted cellulose fibers and fine particles. Mills grinding sugar cane commonly use bagasse for steam production. A selected analysis of bagasse is given in Table 2-6.

Other Vegetable Wastes.   Food and related industries produce numerous vegetable wastes that are usable as fuels. They include such materials as grain hulls, the residue from the production of furfural from corncobs and grain hulls, coffee grounds from the production of instant coffee, and tobacco stems.

Solvent-Refined Coal.   Solvent-refined coal is made by dissolving the organic material in coal in a coal-derived solvent. The finished product is a solid with a melting point of 284 to 293°F (140 to 145°C). It can be burned as an oil or a solid.

Municipal Solid Waste.   Municipal solid waste (MSW) can be burned as received or by preparing a refuse-derived fuel (RDF) by shredding the MSW and removing ferrous and nonferrous inorganic materials. The heating value of MSW can range from 3500 to 6500 Btu/lb (8.1 to 15.2 MJ/kg), and the moisture and ash can vary just as widely in similar or opposite directions.

TABLE 2-8   Analyses of Wood and Wood Ash

Wood analyses (dry basis), % by wt	Pine bark	Oak bark	Spruce bark*	Redwood bark*
Proximate analysis, %				
Volatile matter	72.9	76.0	69.6	72.6
Fixed carbon	24.2	18.7	26.6	27.0
Ash	2.9	5.3	3.8	0.4
Ultimate analysis, %				
Hydrogen	5.6	5.4	5.7	5.1
Carbon	53.4	49.7	51.8	51.9
Sulfur	0.1	0.1	0.1	0.1
Nitrogen	0.1	0.2	0.2	0.1
Oxygen	37.9	39.3	38.4	42.4
Ash	2.9	5.3	3.8	0.4
Heating value, Btu/lb	9030	8370	8740	8350
(kJ/kg)	(21,004)	(19,469)	(20,329)	(19,442)
Ash analysis, % by wt				
SiO_2	39.0	11.1	32.0	14.3
Fe_2O_3	3.0	3.3	6.4	3.5
TiO_2	0.2	0.1	0.8	0.3
Al_2O_3	14.0	0.1	11.0	4.0
Mn_3O_4	Trace	Trace	1.5	0.1
CaO	25.5	64.5	25.3	6.0
MgO	6.5	1.2	4.1	6.6
Na_2O	1.3	8.9	8.0	18.0
K_2O	6.0	0.2	2.4	10.6
SO_3	0.3	2.0	2.1	7.4
Cl	Trace	Trace	Trace	18.4
Ash fusibility temp, °F				
Reducing				
Initial deformation	2180	2690		
Softening	2240	2720		
Fluid	2310	2740		
Oxidizing				
Initial deformation	2210	2680		
Softening	2280	2730		
Fluid	2350	2750		

* Salt water stored.

Coal Processing and Transporting

The purpose of coal preparation is to improve the quality of the coal or to make it suitable for a specific purpose by (1) cleaning to remove inorganic impurities, (2) special treatment (such as dedusting), or (3) sizing by crushing and screening.

Economic Factors.   All coals have certain properties which place limitations on their most advantageous use.

To define the limitations of various types of coal-burning equipment in service, specifications covering several important properties of coal are necessary. For certain types of stokers, for instance, a minimum ash-softening temperature, maximum ash content, and maximum sulfur content of the coal are specified to prevent excessive clinkering. For pulverized-coal firing, it is necessary to specify ash-slagging and ash-fouling parameters for a dry-ash installation. Within these and other equipment limitations there is usually a wide range of coals that can be satisfactorily burned in a specific steam boiler, and the choice depends primarily on economics—which coal will produce steam at the lowest overall cost, including cost at the mine, shipment, storage, handling, operating, and maintenance costs. To burn a wide range of coals often requires a larger initial investment than would otherwise be necessary. However, since fuel cost represents a large part of the overall operating cost the investment may be more than offset by fuel savings.

Nature of Impurities in Coal.   Impurities can be divided into two general classifications—inherent and removable. The inherent impurities are inseparably combined with the coal. The removable impurities are segregated and can be eliminated, by available cleaning methods, to the extent that is economically justified.

Mineral matter is always present in raw coal and forms ash when the coal is burned. The ash-forming mineral matter is usually classified as either inherent or extraneous. Ash-forming material organically combined with the coal is considered as inherent mineral matter. Generally the inherent mineral matter contained in coal is about 2 percent or less of the total ash. Extraneous mineral matter is ash-forming material that is foreign to the plant material from which the coal was formed. It consists usually of slate, shale, sandstone, or limestone.

Sulfur is always present in raw coal in amounts ranging from traces to as high as 8 percent or more. This results in the emission of sulfur oxides in the stack gases when the coal is burned.

Moisture, which is inherent in coal, may be considered to be an impurity. It varies with different ranks of coal, increasing for lower-rank coals from 1 to 2 percent in anthracite to 50 percent or more in lignite and brown coals. Moisture that collects on the exposed surfaces of coal is commonly called *surface moisture* and is removable.

Cleaning Methods.   The principal benefit of cleaning is the reduction in ash content. With ash content reduced, shipping costs and the requirements for storage and handling decrease because of the smaller quantity of coal necessary per unit of heating value.

Cleaning at Mine Face.   Efforts to reduce the impurities loaded in the mine usually result in increased mining cost; hence economics plays an important part in determining the amount of cleaning done.

Mechanical Picking.   Many mechanical picking devices employ differences in physical picking dimensions of coal and impurities as a means of separation. Bituminous coal fractures into rough cubes, whereas slate and shale normally fracture as thin slabs. A slot-type flat picker can be installed on shaker screens, shaking conveyors, and chutes.

Froth Flotation.   The incoming coal feed may be agitated in a controlled amount of water, air, and reagents that cause a surface froth to form, the bubbles of which selectively attach themselves to coal particles and keep them buoyant while the heavier particles of pyrite, slate, and shale remain dispersed in the water. This method can be used in cleaning smaller particles, 1/10 in by 0 (no minimum), particularly particles smaller than 48 mesh.

Gravity Concentration.   Removal of segregated impurities in coal by gravity concentration is based on the principle that heavier particles separate from the lighter ones when settling in a fluid. This principle is applicable because most common solid impurities are heavier than coal (Table 2-9).

The commercial processes used in gravity concentration can be divided into two main classifications—wet and dry (or pneumatic).

Cleaning by Gravity Concentration

Wet Processes.   Most cleaning of bituminous coal and lignite is accomplished by wet processes. Table 2-10 lists the methods and types of equipment generally used and the extent of application of each method, expressed in percent.

Dry Processes.   The principal pneumatic cleaning process uses tables equipped with riffles, with air as the separating medium. Admitted through holes in the tables, the air is blown up through the bed of coal. The motion of the tables plus the airflow segregates the coal and impurities.

TABLE 2-9   Typical Specific Gravities
of Coal and Related Impurities

Material	Specific gravity
Bituminous coal	1.10–1.35
Bone coal	1.35–1.70
Carbonaceous shale	1.60–2.20
Shale	2.00–2.60
Clay	1.80–2.20
Pyrite	4.80–5.20

TABLE 3-10   Types of Wet Processes Used
for Cleaning of Bituminous Coals and Lignite

Equipment or method used	Percent of cleaning done by wet processes
Jigs	46.7
Dense-media method	29.2
Concentrating tables	13.9
Flotation method	2.6
Classifiers	1.4
Launderers	1.3
Total	95.1

Washability Characteristics of Coal.   There is a general correlation between specific gravity and ash content, although the relation differs for various coals. Ash contents corresponding to various specific gravities for bituminous coal are shown in Table 2-11.

TABLE 2-11   Typical Ash Contents of Various
Bituminous Coal Specific Gravity Fractions

Specific gravity fraction	Ash content, % by wt
1.3–1.4	1–5
1.4–1.5	5–10
1.5–1.6	10–35
1.6–1.8	35–60
1.8–1.9	60–75
Above 1.9	75–90

Float-and-sink tests run in a laboratory provide data useful for rating and controlling cleaning equipment and evaluating efficiencies obtained, both quantitative and qualitative.

Special Treatment

Dedusting.   Dedusting is a type of air separation with classification according to size. Air passed through the coal entrains a large percentage of the "fines." The fine coal is recovered from the air with cyclone separators and bag filters. This process is often employed to remove fines prior to wet cleaning.

Mechanical Dewatering and Heat Drying.   The larger sizes of coal can be easily dewatered, and natural drainage is sometimes provided by special hoppers (or bins), screen conveyors, perforated-bucket elevators, and fixed screens. However, when the fine sizes must be dried or when lower moisture content is required for the large coal, mechanical dewatering or thermal drying is necessary.

Mechanical dewatering devices may be shaker screens, vibrating screens, filters, centrifuges, and thickening or desliming equipment. Thermal drying is used to obtain low-moisture-content coal, especially for the finer sizes. Various types of thermal dryers are rotary, cascade, reciprocating-screen, conveyor, suspension (including flash and venturi dryers), and fluidized-bed.

Dustproofing. Oil is commonly used for dustproofing coal. When coal is sprayed with oil, the film causes some dust particles to adhere to the larger pieces of coal and others to agglomerate into larger lumps not easily airborne. Calcium chloride absorbs moisture from the air, providing a wet surface to which the dust adheres.

Freezeproofing. To prevent freezing of coal during transit or storage, spray oil may be used, and it is applied to the coal in the same manner as dustproofing. As an alternative and less costly method, the car hoppers may be heavily sprayed with oil. Another freezeproofing method is thermal drying of the fine coal.

Sizing by Crushing and Screening

Sizing Requirements. Generally acceptable coal sizings for various types of fuel-burning equipment are given in the section covering the equipment. The degradation in coal sizing resulting from handling is an important consideration in establishing sizing specifications for steam plants, where the maximum permissible quantity of fines in the coal is set by firing-equipment limitations.

Crushers and Breakers. Many types of crushing and screening equipment are used commercially. Representative types are the Bradford breaker, single-roll crusher, double-roll crusher, and hammer mill.

Screens. Many types of screens are used for sizing, including the gravity bar screen or grizzly, revolving screen, shaker screen, and vibrating screen.

Transportation of Coal. Transportation costs may represent a large portion of the delivered cost of coal. Transportation may affect the condition of the received coal if freezing occurs in transit or if there is a change in moisture content or a degradation of size.

When freezing in transit is anticipated, its effect may be ameliorated by special treatment of the coal at the point of loading.

The moisture content of the coal will depend on sizing, condition at time of loading, and weather conditions during transit.

Size degradation depends in a large measure on the friability of the coal but it is also affected by the amount of handling and shaking in transit.

Handling and Storage at Consumer's Plant

Unloading. When coal is received by rail, if the surface moisture of the coal is high, it may be necessary to rap the car sides with a sledge or to use a slice bar from above in order to start the coal flowing. If this high-moisture coal has been in transit several days at freezing temperatures, it may be frozen into a solid mass, and unloading is a serious problem. In hot, dry weather the coal, on arrival, may be so dry that a high wind can blow the fines away as dust.

Frozen Coal. Successful equipment for unloading frozen coal includes steam-heated thawing sheds, oil-fired thawing pits, and the radiant-electric railroad-car thawing system. Another device is a car shakeout, in which a motor-driven eccentric shaker clamped to the top flanges of the car transmits a vibratory motion to the car body.

When expensive equipment is not economically justified, the methods used depend primarily on manual labor and slice bars, sledges, portable oil torches, and steam or hot water.

Mechanical Handling. Extensive equipment, covering the range of plant requirements from a few tons per day to the largest, is available for transferring coal from the railroad cars either to outside storage or to inside bunkers or hoppers. When pulverizers are used, it is desirable to include a magnetic separator somewhere in the system. Frequently a coal crusher will make it economically possible to use coal that is not screened or sized.

Outside Storage at or near Plant. Outside storage of coal at or near the plant site is often necessary, and in some cases required, to assure continuous plant operation.

The changes that may affect the value of stored coal are loss in heating value, reduction of coking power, reduction of average particle size (weathering or slacking), and, most important, losses from self-ignition or spontaneous combustion. Direct loss of stored coal by wind or water erosion is possible and may become a serious nuisance.

Oxidation of Coal. Many constituents of pure coal begin to oxidize when exposed to air. Oxidation of coal is affected by length of time exposed to air, coal rank, size or surface area, temperature, amount and size of pyrites particles, moisture, and amount of mineral matter or ash.

All coals may be safely stored, provided proper procedures are used. Coal can be successfully stored by the following methods outlined by the Bureau of Mines.

Selection of Storage Site. The site should be level solid ground, free of loose fill, properly graded for drainage, and compacted by a bulldozer. Consideration should be given to access and provision for coal delivery as well as to protection from prevailing winds, tides, flooded rivers, and spray from salt water.

Storage in Small Amounts. No special precautions are required for anthracite. Sized (double-screened) bituminous coals may be stored in small conical piles from 5 to 15 ft (1.5 to 4.6 m) high. Slack sizes of bituminous coal may be compacted with a bulldozer. Subbituminous coal and lignite should be stored in small piles and thoroughly packed.

Storage in Large Amounts. Anthracite coal is very safe to store in large high piles that permit drainage.

Bituminous coal should be stockpiled in multiple horizontal layers. Each layer should be spread out to vary from 1 to 2 ft (22 to 44 cm) in thickness and thoroughly packed to eliminate air spaces. The top should be slightly crowned and symmetrical to permit even runoff of water. All sides and the top should be covered with a 1-ft (22-cm) compacted layer of fines and then capped with a 1-ft (22-cm) layer of sized lump coal.

Subbituminous coal and lignite should be stockpiled by using the same system of layering and compacting, but the coal layers should be thinner, not more than 1 ft (22 cm) thick, to ensure good compaction.

Inside Storage and Handling. Dry anthracite coal flows easily; however, other fine, wet coals feeding from a bottom-outlet bunker may have a tendency to "rat-hole" or "pipe" all the way to the top surface. When this occurs, coal flow to the feeders is intermittent and spasmodic. From studies of actual plant operations it has been found that hang-ups of coal may begin when there is a surface-moisture level of 5 to 6 percent.

Bunker Design. The purpose of the bunker is not only to store a given capacity of coal but also to function efficiently as part of the system in maintaining a continuous supply of fuel to the pulverizer or stoker. In the design of bunkers, careful consideration should be given to capacity, shape, material, and location.

Bunker Fires. A fire in the coal bunker should be recognized at once as a serious danger to personnel and equipment. Steam or carbon dioxide may be piped in directly to covered bunkers and to the affected areas in open-top bunkers. If the hot coal is run through the fuel-burning equipment, special care should be taken to feed uniformly, without interruption.

Stokers

Mechanical stokers are designed to feed fuel onto a grate within the furnace and to remove the ash residue. The grate area required for a stoker of given type and capacity is determined from allowable rates established by experience. Table 2-12 lists typical fuel-burning rates for various types of stokers, based on using coals suited to the stoker type in each case. The prac-

TABLE 2-12   Stoker/Grate System Overview

Stoker type	Grate type	Fuel	Typical release rate, 1000 Btu/h ft² (MW/m²)		Steam capacity, 1000 lb/h (kg/s)	
Underfeed:						
Single retort	—	Coal	425	(1.34)	25	(3.15)
Double retort	—	Coal	425	(1.34)	30	(3.78)
Multiple retort	—	Coal	600	(1.89)	500	(63.0)
Overfeed:						
Mass	Vibrating: water-cooled	Coal	400	(1.26)	125	(15.8)
	Traveling chain	Coal	500	(1.58)	80	(10.1)
	Reciprocating	Refuse	300	(0.95)	350	(44.1)
Spreader	Vibrating:					
	air-cooled	Coal	650	(2.05)	150	(18.9)
		Wood	1100	(3.47)	700	(88.2)
	water-cooled	Wood	1100	(3.47)	700	(88.2)
	Traveling	Coal	750	(2.37)	390	(49.1)
		Wood	1100	(3.47)	550	(69.3)
		RDF*	750	(2.37)	400	(50.4)

* Refuse-derived fuel.

tical steam-output limit of boilers equipped with mechanical stokers is about 500,000 lb/h (63 kg/s).

Almost any coal can be burned successfully on some type of stoker. In addition, many by-products and waste fuels, such as coke breeze, wood wastes, pulpwood bark, and bagasse, can be used either as a base or auxiliary fuel.

Mechanical stokers can be classified into four main groups, based on the method of introducing the fuel to the furnace:

1. Spreader stokers

2. Underfeed stokers

3. Water-cooled vibrating-grate stokers

4. Chain-grate and traveling-grate stokers

Spreader Stokers.   The spreader stoker is the one most commonly used in the capacity range up to 500,000 lb/h (63 kg/s) because it responds rapidly to load swings and can burn a variety of fuels. The spreader stoker is capable of burning a wide range of coals, from high-rank Eastern bituminous to lignite or brown coal, as well as a variety of by-product waste fuels.

As the name implies, the spreader stoker projects fuel into the furnace over the fire with a uniform spreading action, permitting suspension burning of the fine fuel particles (Fig. 2-3). The heavier pieces, which cannot be supported in the gas flow, fall to the grate for combustion in a thin, fast-burning bed.

Grates for Spreader Stokers.   Spreader-stoker firing is old in principle, and the first grate design was a stationary type, with the ash removed manually through the front doors.

Stationary grates were soon followed by dumping-grate designs, in which grate sections are provided for each feeder and the undergrate air plenum chambers are correspondingly divided. This permits the temporary discontinuance of the fuel and air supply to a grate section for ash removal without affecting other sections of the stoker.

The continuous-ash-discharge traveling grate has no interruptions for removing ashes and because of the thin, fast-burning fuel bed, this design increased average burning rates approximately 70 percent over the stationary and dumping-grate types. Continuous-cleaning grates of reciprocating and vibrating designs have also been developed.

The normal practice of all continuous-ash-discharge spreader stokers is to remove the ashes at the front or feeding end of the stoker. This permits the most satisfactory fuel-

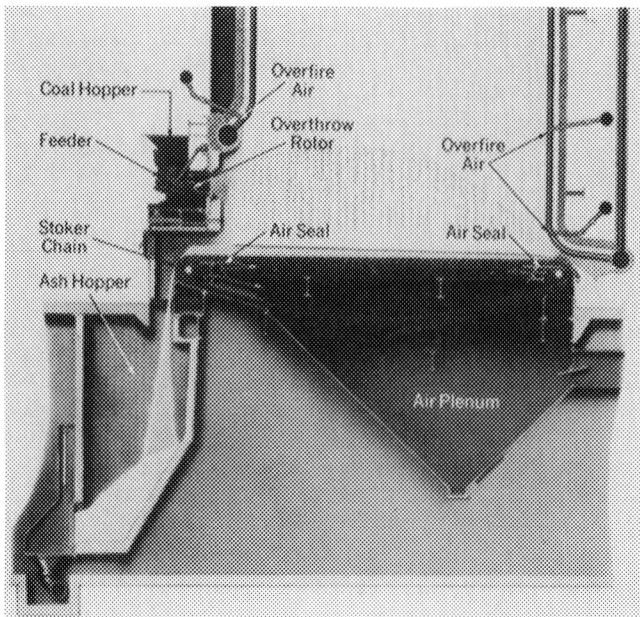

FIGURE 2-3   Traveling-grate spreader stoker with front-ash discharge.

distribution pattern and provides maximum residence time on the grates for complete combustion of the fuel.

Overfire Air.   An overfire air system, with pressures from 15 to 30 in (3.7 to 7.5 kPa) of water, is essential to successful suspension burning. It is customary to provide at least two rows of evenly spaced high-pressure-air jets in the rear wall of the furnace and one in the front wall. This air mixes with the furnace gases and creates the turbulence required for complete combustion.

Carbon Reinjection.   Partial suspension burning results in a greater carryover of particulate matter in the flue gas than occurs with other types of stokers. In general the arrangement of the collection equipment is such that the coarse carbon-bearing particles can be returned to the furnace for further burning and the fine material discharged to the ash removal system.

Reintroducing the fly carbon into the furnace results in an increase in boiler efficiency of 2 to 3 percent.

Fuels and Fuel Bed.   All spreader stokers, and in particular the traveling-grate spreader type, have an extraordinary ability to burn fuels with a wide range of burning characteristics, including coals with caking tendencies. High-moisture, free-burning bituminous and lignite coals are commonly used, and some low-volatile fuels, such as coke breeze, have been burned in a mixture with higher-volatile coal. Anthracite coal, however, is not a satisfactory fuel for spreader-stoker firing.

Coal size segregation is a problem with any type of stoker, but the spreader stoker can tolerate a small amount of segregation because the feeding rate of the individual feeder-distributors can be varied. Size segregation, where fine and coarse coal are not distributed evenly over the grate, produces a ragged fire and poor efficiency.

Firing of By-Product Waste Fuels.   By-product wastes having considerable calorific value can be used as a base fuel or as a supplementary fuel in the generation of steam for power, heating, or industrial processes. Bark from wood-pulping operations and bagasse from sugar refineries are good examples. Others include coffee-ground residue from instant-coffee manufacture, corncobs, coconut and peanut hulls from furfural manufacture, bark and sawdust from woodworking plants, and municipal solid waste. Spreader-stoker firing provides an excellent way to burn these wastes.

Waste fuels with high moisture content may present problems in maintaining combustion unless there is enough auxiliary fuel to maintain the average moisture of the total fuel input at a maximum of about 50 percent. Preheated air, at temperatures dependent upon the fuel moisture content, aids in drying and igniting the fuel as it is fed into the furnace. Air temperatures up to 450°F (240°C) are common in bark-fired units. High air temperatures may require the use of alloy grate materials in order to reduce maintenance.

Underfeed Stokers.   Underfeed stokers are used principally for heating and for small industrial units with a capacity of less than 30,000 lb/h (3780 kg/s). Underfeed stokers are generally of two types: the horizontal-feed, side-ash-discharge type, Fig. 2-4; and the gravity-feed, rear-ash-discharge type, Fig. 2-5.

In the side-ash-discharge underfeed stoker (Fig. 2-4), fuel is fed from the hopper by means of a reciprocating ram to a central trough called the retort. On very small heating stokers, a screw conveys the coal from the hopper to the retort. A series of small auxiliary pushers in the bottom of the retort assist in moving the fuel rearward, and as the retort is filled, the fuel is moved upward to spread to each side over the air-admitting tuyères and side grates. The fuel rises in the retort and burns, and the ash is intermittently discharged to shallow pits, quenched, and removed through doors at the front of the stoker.

The single-retort and double-retort, horizontal-type stokers are generally limited to 25,000 to 30,000 lb of steam per hour with burning rates of 425,000 Btu/(ft^2)(h) (1.34 MW$_T$/m^2) in furnaces with water-cooled walls. The multiple-retort, rear-end-cleaning type (Fig. 2-5), has a retort and grate inclination of 20 to 25°. This type of stoker can be designed for boiler units generating up to 500,000 lb/h (63,000 kg/s). Burning rates up to 600,000 Btu/(ft^2)(h) (1.89 MW$_T$/m^2) are practicable.

The burning rates for underfeed stokers are directly related to the ash-softening temperature. For coals with ash-softening temperature below 2400°F, the burning rates are progressively reduced.

With multiple-retort stokers, overfire-air systems are also frequently provided.

The size of the coal has a marked effect on the relative capacity and efficiency of an underfeed stoker. The most desirable size consists of 1 in (25.4 mm) top size × 0.25 in (6.4 mm) with a maximum 20 percent through 0.25 in (6.4 mm) round screen. A reduction in the percentage of fines helps to keep the fuel bed more porous and extends the range of coals with a high coking index.

In general, underfeed stokers are able to burn caking coals. The range of agitation imparted to the fuel bed in different stoker designs permits the use of coals with varying degrees of caking properties. The ash-fusion temperature is an important factor in the selection of the coals. Usually, the lower the ash-fusion temperature, the greater the possibility of clinker trouble.

Water-Cooled Vibrating-Grate Stokers.   An entirely different design of stoker is the water-cooled vibrating-grate hopper-feed type, Fig. 2-6. This stoker consists of a tuyère grate surface mounted on, and in intimate contact with, a grid of water tubes interconnected with the boiler circulation system for positive cooling. The entire structure is supported by a number of flexing plates allowing the grid and its grate to move freely in a vibrating action that conveys coal from the feeding hopper onto the grate and gradually to the rear of the stoker. Ashes are automatically discharged to an ash pit.

Vibration of the grates is intermittent, and the frequency of the vibration periods is regulated by a timing device to conform to load variations, synchronizing the fuel feeding rate with the air supply.

Water cooling of the grates makes this stoker especially adaptable to multiple-fuel firing since a shift to oil or gas does not require special provision for protection of the grates. A normal bed of ash left as a cover gives adequate protection from furnace radiation.

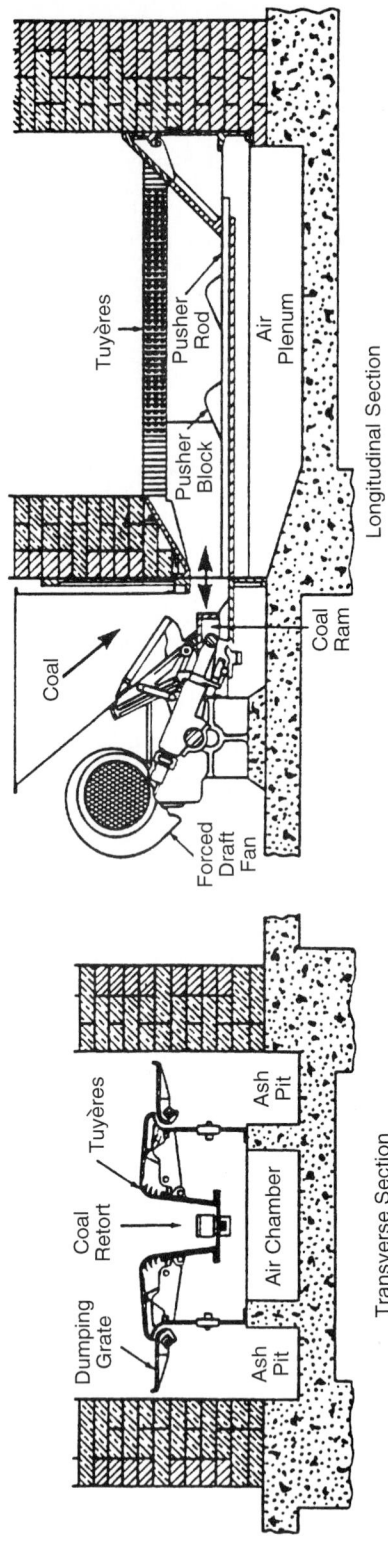

FIGURE 2-4 Single-retort underfire stoker with horizontal feed, side ash discharge.

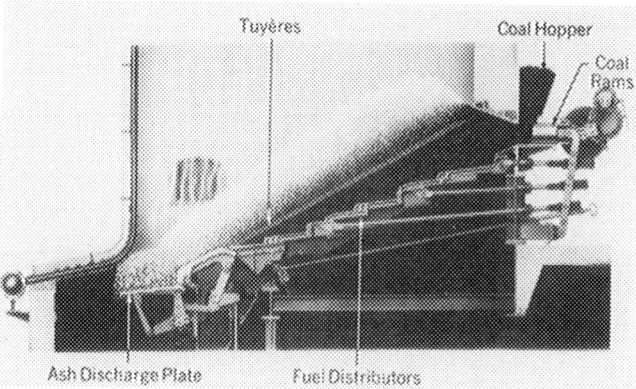

FIGURE 2-5   Multiple-retort gravity-feed type, rear-ash-discharge under-feed stoker.

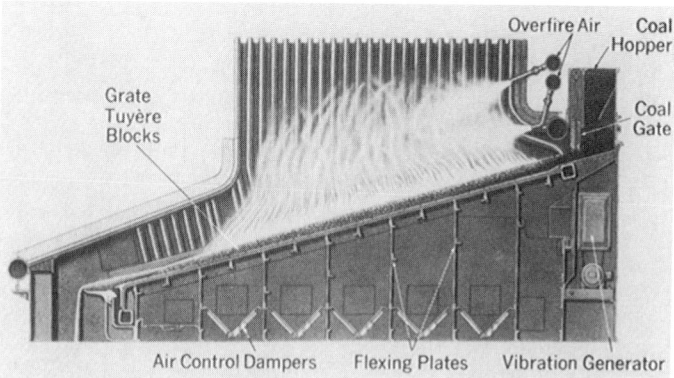

FIGURE 2-6   Water-cooled vibrating-grate stoker.

Chain-Grate and Traveling-Grate Stokers.   Traveling-grate stokers, including the specific type known as the chain-grate stoker (Fig. 2-7), have assembled links, grates, or keys joined together in endless belt arrangements that pass over the sprockets or return bends located at the front and the rear of the furnace. Coal enters the furnace after passing under an adjustable gate to regulate the thickness of the fuel bed, is heated by radiation from the furnace gases, and is ignited. The fuel bed continues to burn as it moves along, and ash is discharged from the end of the grate into the ash pit. Generally these stokers use furnace arches (front and/or rear) to improve combustion by reflecting heat into the fuel bed.

Chain-and traveling-grate stokers can burn a wide variety of fuels.

Preparation and Utilization of Pulverized Coal

The capacity limitations imposed by stokers are overcome by the pulverized-coal system. This method of burning coal also provides:

1. Ability to use coal from fines up to 2-in (5-cm) maximum size

2. Improved response to load changes

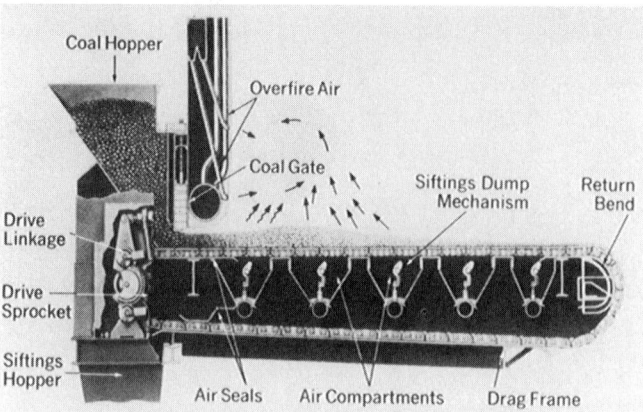

FIGURE 2-7 Chain-grate stoker. (*Courtesy of Detroit Stoker Company.*)

3. An increase in thermal efficiency because of lower excess air used for combustion and lower carbon loss than with stoker firing

4. Improved ability to efficiently burn coal in combination with oil and gas

Pulverized-Coal Systems. The function of a pulverized-coal system is to pulverize the coal, deliver it to the fuel-burning equipment, and accomplish complete combustion in the furnace with a minimum of excess air.

A small portion of the air required for combustion (15 to 20 percent) is used to transport the coal to the burner. This is known as primary air and is also used to dry the coal in the pulverizer. The remainder of the combustion air (80 to 85 percent) is introduced at the burner and is known as secondary air.

Two principal systems—the bin system and the direct-firing system—have been used for processing, distributing, and burning pulverized coal. The direct-firing system is almost exclusively the one being installed today.

Bin System. The bin system is primarily of historical interest. In this system the coal is processed at a location apart from the furnace, and the end product is pneumatically conveyed to cyclone collectors which recover the fines and clean the moisture laden air before returning it to the atmosphere. The pulverized coal is discharged into storage bins and later conveyed by pneumatic transport through pipelines to utilization bins and from there to the furnace.

Direct-Firing System. The pulverizing equipment developed for the direct-firing system permits continuous utilization of raw coal directly from the bunkers. This is accomplished by feeding coal of a maximum top size directly into the pulverizer, where it is dried as well as pulverized, and then delivering it to the burners in a single continuous operation. Components of the direct-firing system are illustrated in Fig. 2-8.

There are two direct-firing methods in use—the pressure type and the suction type.

PRESSURE FIRING. In the pressure method, the primary-air fan, located on the inlet side of the pulverizer, forces the hot primary air through the pulverizer where it picks up the pulverized coal and delivers the proper coal-air mixture to the burners. On large installations, primary-air fans operating on cold air force the air through the air heater first and then through the pulverizer.

SUCTION FIRING. In the suction method, the air and entrained coal are drawn through the pulverizer under negative pressure by an exhauster located on the outlet side of the pulverizer. With this arrangement the fan handles a mixture of coal and air, and distribution of the mixture to more than one burner is attained by a distributor beyond the fan discharge.

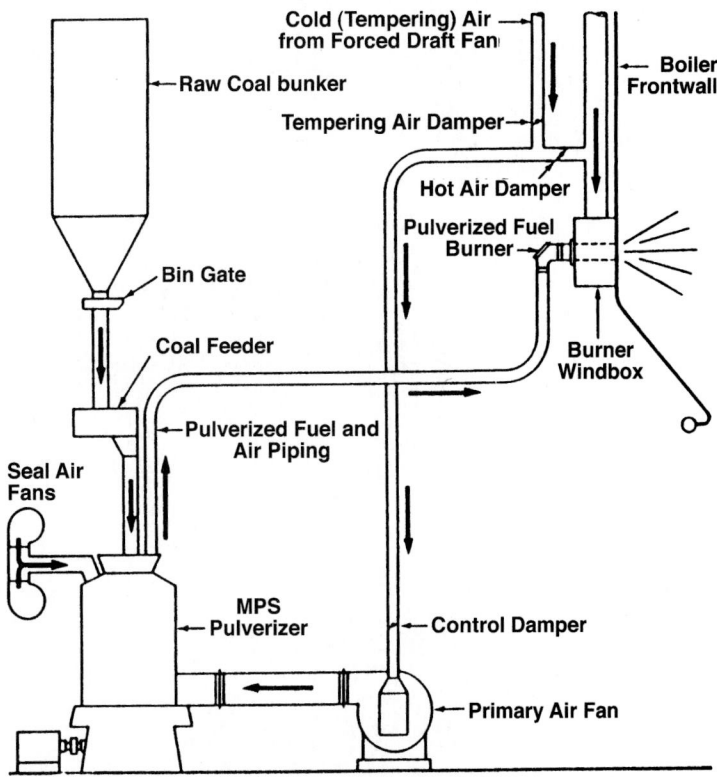

FIGURE 2-8   Direct-fired, hot fan system for pulverized coal.

In the direct-firing system the operating range of a pulverizer is usually not more than 3 to 1 (without change in the number of burners in service) because the air velocities in lines and other parts of the system must be maintained above the minimum levels to keep the coals in suspension. Most boiler units are provided with more than one pulverizer, each feeding multiple burners. Load variations beyond 3 to 1 are accommodated by shutting down (or starting up) a pulverizer and the burners it supplies.

Types of Pulverizers.   All pulverizing machinery operates to grind by impact, attrition, compression, or a combination of two or more of these.

Medium-Speed Pulverizers.   There are two groups of medium-speed (75 to 225 r/min) pulverizers, classified as the ball-and-race and roller types. The principle of pulverizing by a combination of crushing under pressure, impact, and attrition between grinding surfaces and material is used in each group, but the method is different.

MEDIUM-SPEED BALL-AND-RACE PULVERIZERS.   The ball-and-race pulverizer works on the ball-bearing principle. The Type EL pulverizer, illustrated in Fig. 2-9, has one stationary top ring, one rotating bottom ring, and one set of balls that make up the grinding elements. The pressure required for efficient grinding is obtained from externally adjustable dual-purpose springs. The bottom ring is driven by a yoke which is attached to the vertical main shaft of the pulverizer. The top ring is held stationary by the dual-purpose springs.

MEDIUM-SPEED ROLLER-TYPE PULVERIZERS.   This type of pulverizer can be of a design in which the ring is stationary and the rolls rotate or one in which the rolls are mounted off the mill housing and the ring rotates. In the first type, grinding elements consisting of three or more cylindrical rolls, suspended from driving arms, revolve in a horizontally positioned

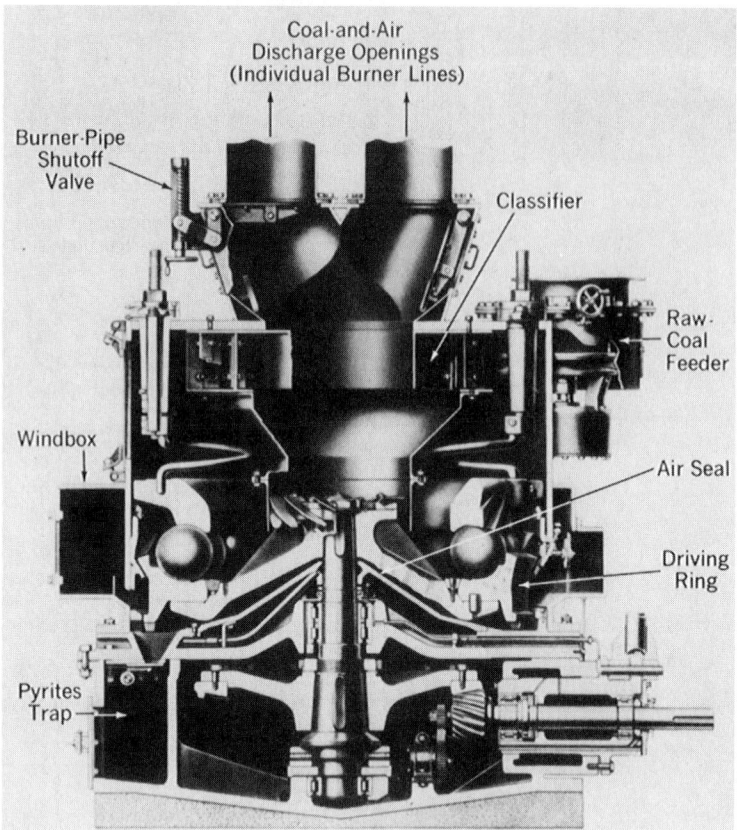

FIGURE 2-9 Babcock & Wilcox Type EL single-row ball-and-race pulverizer.

replaceable race. The principal components of the second type, the bowl mill, are a rotating bowl equipped with a replaceable grinding ring, two or more tapered rolls in stationary journals, a classifier, and a main drive.

TUBE MILL. One of the oldest practical pulverizers is the tube mill, in which a charge of mixed-size forged-steel balls in a horizontally supported grinding cylinder is activated by gravity as the cylinder is rotated. The coal is pulverized by attrition and impact as the ball charge ascends and falls within the coal.

High-Speed Pulverizers. High-speed pulverizers use impact as a primary means of grinding through the use of hammerlike beaters, wear-resistant pegs rotating within a cage, and fan blades integral with the pulverizer shaft.

Selecting Pulverizer Equipment. A number of factors must be considered in the selection of pulverizer equipment. If selection anticipates the use of a variety of coals, the pulverizer should be sized for the coal that gives the highest base capacity. *Base capacity* is the desired capacity divided by the capacity factor. The latter is a function of the grindability of the coal and the fineness required (see Fig. 2-10).

The percentage of volatile matter in the fuel has a direct bearing on the recommended temperature for combustion of the mixture of primary air and fuel. The generally accepted safe values for pulverizer exit temperatures for fuel-air mixtures are given in Table 2-13. The temperature of the primary air entering the pulverizer may run 650°F (345°C) or higher, depending on the amount of moisture in the coal.

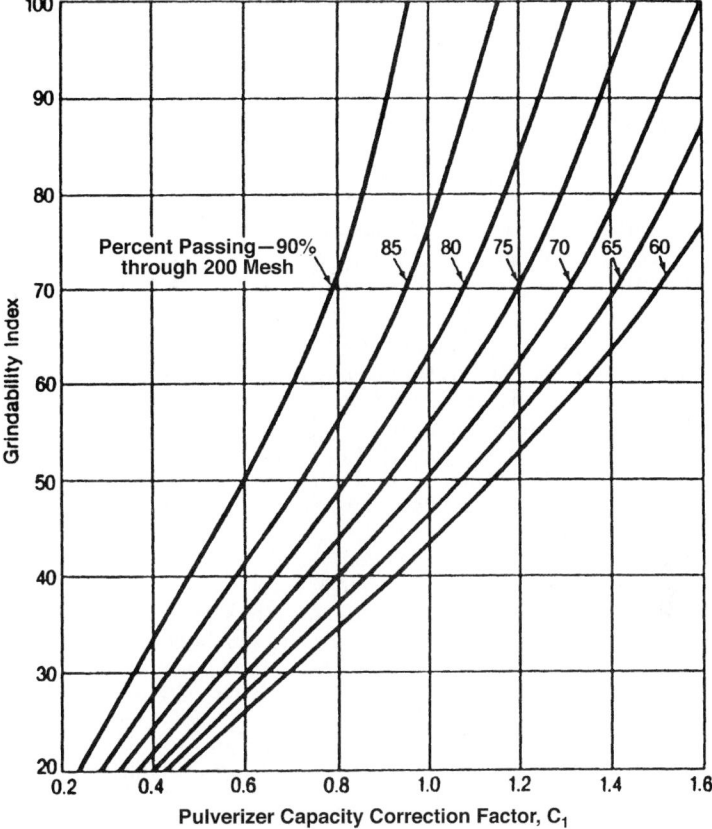

FIGURE 2-10 Capacity correction factor.

Fine grinding of coal is necessary to assure complete combustion of the carbon for maximum efficiency. The required pulverized fuel fineness is expressed as the percentage of the product passing through various sizes of sieves. Coal classification by rank and end use of product determine the fineness to which coal should be ground (Table 2-14).

Burning Equipment for Pulverized Coal. The burner is the principal component of equipment for firing pulverized coal. Coal must be pulverized to the point where particles are small enough to assure proper combustion (Table 2-14). In the direct-firing system the coal is dried

TABLE 2-13 Typical Pulverizer Outlet Temperature

Fuel type	Volatile content, %*	Exit temperature, °F (°C)†	
Lignite and subbituminous	—	125–140	(52–60)
High volatile bituminous	30	150	(66)
Low volatile bituminous	14–22	150–180	(66–82)
Anthracite, coal waste	14	200–210	(93–99)
Petroleum coke	0–8	200–250	(93–121)

* Volatile content is on a dry, mineral-matter-free basis.
† The capacity of pulverizers is adversely affected with exit temperatures below 125°F (52°C) when grinding high moisture lignites.

TABLE 2-14 Typical Pulverized Coal Fineness Requirements—Percent Passing 200 U.S. Standard Sieve

	High rank* fixed carbon, %			Low rank (fixed carbon <69%) heating value, Btu/lb[†]		
Furnace or process:	97.9 to 86.0	85.9 to 78.0	77.9 to 69.0	Above 13,000	13,000 to 11,000	Below 11,000
Marine boiler	—	85	80	80	75	—
Water-cooled	80	75	70	70	65	60
Cement kiln	90	85	80	80	80	—
Blast furnace	N/A	N/A	N/A	80	80	N/A

* ASTM classification.
[†] Btu/lb × 2.326 = kJ/kg.

and delivered to the burner in suspension in the primary air, and this mixture must be adequately mixed with the secondary air at the burner.

Piping and Nozzle Sizing Requirements.   Size selection of nozzles for pulverized-coal piping and burners requires flow velocities that are high enough to keep the coal particles in suspension in the primary air stream. This generally requires 40 to 70 percent of the pulverizer's full-load airflow requirement at zero output. Horizontally arranged burner nozzles should be sized for no less than 3000 ft/min at the minimum pulverizer capacity.

Standards of Burner Performance.   Operators of pulverized-coal equipment should expect ignition of the pulverized coal to be stable, without the use of supporting fuel, over a load range of approximately 3 to 1. Most boilers are equipped with many burners so that a wider capacity range is readily obtained by varying the number of burners and pulverizers in use. The loss of unburned combustibles should be less than 2 percent with excess air in the range of 15 to 22 percent, measured at the furnace outlet. The design should avoid the formation of deposits that may interfere with the continued efficient and reliable performance of the burner.

BURNERS.   The most frequently used burners are of the circular single-register type designed for firing pulverized coal only (Fig. 2-11). This type can be equipped to fire any com-

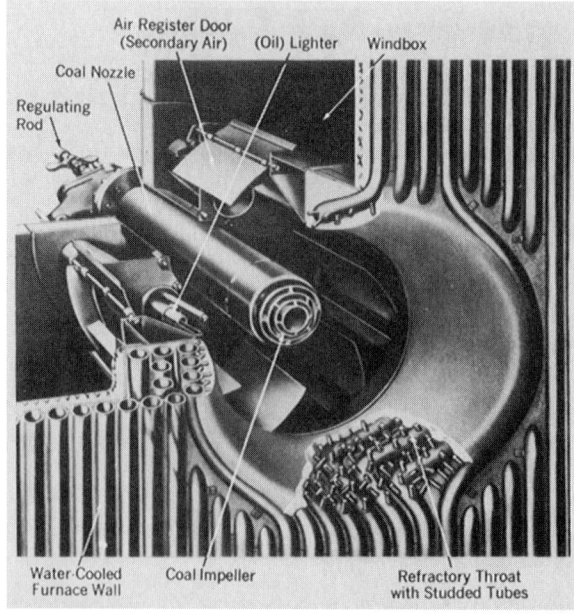

FIGURE 2-11   Circular register burner for pulverized-coal firing.

bination of the three principal fuels. However, combination firing of pulverized-coal with oil in the same burner should be restricted to short emergency periods because of the possibility of coke formation on the pulverized-coal element.

LIGHTERS (IGNITERS) AND PILOTS.   In starting up the burner on pulverized coal, it is necessary to keep the igniters in operation until the temperature in the combustion zone becomes high enough to assure self-sustaining ignition of the main fuel. The self-igniting characteristics of pulverized coal vary from one fuel to another. In some instances completely reliable ignition is obtained down to a quarter load. When firing pulverized coal with a volatile matter content less than 25 percent, it may be necessary to activate the igniters even at high loads.

Excess Air   Pulverized coal requires more excess air for satisfactory combustion than either oil or natural gas. An acceptable quantity of unburned combustible coal is usually obtained with 15 percent excess air at high loads. This allows for the normal maldistribution of primary-air, coal, and secondary air.

LIQUID FUELS

Characteristics

Fuel Oil.   It is common practice in refining petroleum to produce fuel oils complying with several specifications prepared by the ASTM and adopted as a commercial standard by the National Bureau of Standards (Table 2-15).

Fuel oils are graded according to gravity and viscosity, the lightest being No. 1 and the heaviest No. 6. Grades 5 and 6 generally require heating for satisfactory pumping and burning. The range of analyses and heating values of the several grades of fuel oils are given in Table 2-16.

The gross heating value, density, and specific gravity of various fuel oils for a range of API gravities are shown in Fig. 2-12. The abscissa on this figure is the API (American Petroleum Institute) gravity and sp gr at 60–60°F (15°C) represents the ratio of oil density at 60°F (15°C) to water density also at 60°F (15°C).

Fuel oils are generally sold on a volume basis, with 60°F as the base temperature. Correction factors are given in Fig. 2-13 for converting known volumes at other temperatures to the 60°F (15°C) standard base. This correction is also dependent on the API gravity range as illustrated by the three parametric curves of Fig. 2-12.

Since equipment for handling and, especially, burning of fuel oil is usually designed for a maximum oil viscosity, it is necessary to know the viscosity characteristics of the fuel oil to be used. If the viscosities of heavy oils are known at two temperatures, viscosities at other temperatures can be closely predicted by a linear interpolation between these two values located on the standard ASTM chart of Fig. 2-14. Viscosities of light oils at various temperatures within the region designated as No. 2 fuel oil can be found by drawing a line parallel to the No. 2 boundary lines through the point of only one known viscosity and temperature.

Shale Oil   Oil shale is not actually a shale nor does it contain oil. It is generally defined as a fine-grained, compact, sedimentary rock containing an organic material called kerogen. Heating the oil shale to about 875°F (468°C) decomposes this material to produce shale oil.

Pitch and Tar   The liquid and semiliquid residues from the distillation of petroleum and coal are known as pitch and tar. Most of these residues are suitable for use as boiler fuels. Some handle as easily and burn as readily as does kerosene, whereas others give considerable trouble.

Coal Oil Mixture (COM)   Pulverized coal can be mixed with oil and kept in suspension by agitation, recirculation, or by use of additives. Transportation by pipeline is possible, but truck, train, or barge shipment may be more economical. COM is burned with equipment similar to that used for oil firing.

TABLE 2-15 ASTM Standard Specifications for Fuel Oils[a]

Grade of fuel oil[b]	Flash point, °F (°C) Min	Pour point, °F (°C) Max	Water and sediment, % by vol Max	Carbon residue on 10% bottoms, % Max	Ash, % by wt Max	Distillation temperatures, °F (°C) 10% point Max	90% point Min	90% point Max	Saybolt viscosity, s Universal at 100°F (38°C) Min	Universal at 100°F (38°C) Max	Furol at 122°F (50°C) Min	Furol at 122°F (50°C) Max	Kinematic viscosity, centistokes At 100°F (38°C) Min	At 100°F (38°C) Max	At 122°F (50°C) Min	At 122°F (50°C) Max	Gravity, deg API Min	Copper strip corrosion Max
No. 1	100 or legal (38)	0	trace	0.15	—	420 (215)	—	550 (288)	—	—	—	—	1.4	2.2	—	—	35	No. 3
No. 2	100 or legal (38)	20[f] (−7)	0.10	0.35	—	[d]	540 (282)	640 (338)	(32.6)[f]	(37.93)	—	—	2.0[e]	3.6	—	—	30	—
No. 4	130 or legal (55)	20 (−7)	0.50	—	0.10	—	—	—	45	125	—	—	(5.8)	(26.4)	—	—	—	—
No. 5 (Light)	130 or legal (55)	—	1.00	—	0.10	—	—	—	150	300	—	—	(32)	(65)	—	—	—	—
No. 5 (Heavy)	130 or legal (55)	—	1.00	—	0.10	—	—	—	350	750	(23)	(40)	(75)	(162)	(42)	(81)	—	—
No. 6	150 (65)	—	2.00[g]	—	—	—	—	—	(900)	(9,000)	45	300	—	—	(92)	(638)	—	—

No. 1: A distillate oil intended for vaporizing pot-type burners and other burners requiring this grade of fuel.

No. 2: A distillate oil for general purpose domestic heating for use in burners not requiring No. 1 fuel oil.

No. 4: Preheating not usually required for handling or burning.

No. 5 (Light): Preheating may be required depending on climate and equipment.

No. 5 (Heavy): Preheating may be required for burning and, in cold climates, may be required for handling.

No. 6: Preheating required for burning and handling.

[a] Recognizing the necessity for low sulfur fuel oils used in connection with heat treatment, nonferrous metal, glass, and ceramic furnaces and other special uses, a sulfur requirement may be specified in accordance with the following table:

Grade of Fuel Oil	Sulfur, Max, %
No. 1	0.5
No. 2	0.7
No. 4	no limit
No. 5	no limit
No. 6	no limit

Other sulfur limits may be specified only by mutual agreement between the purchaser and the seller.

[b] It is the intent of these classifications that failure to meet any requirement of a given grade does not automatically place an oil in the next lower grade unless in fact it meets all requirements of the lower grade.

[c] Lower or higher pour points may be specified whenever required by conditions of storage or use.

[d] The 10% distillation temperature point may be specified at 440°F (226°C) maximum for use in other than atomizing burners.

[e] When pour point less than 0°F is specified, the minimum viscosity shall be 1.8 cs (32.0 s, Saybolt Universal) and the minimum 90% point shall be waived.

[f] Viscosity values in parentheses are for information only and not necessarily limiting.

[g] The amount of water by distillation plus the sediment by extraction shall not exceed 2.00%. The amount of sediment by extraction shall not exceed 0.50%. A deduction in quantity shall be made for all water and sediment in excess of 1.0%.

Source: ASTM D 396.

TABLE 2-16   Range of Analyses of Fuel Oils

Characteristic	Grade of fuel oil				
	No. 1	No. 2	No. 4	No. 5	No. 6
Weight, %					
Sulfur	0.01–0.5	0.05–1.0	0.2–2.0	0.5–3.0	0.7–3.5
Hydrogen	13.3–14.1	11.8–13.9	(10.6–13.0)*	(10.5–12.0)*	(9.5–12.0)*
Carbon	85.9–86.7	86.1–88.2	(86.5–89.2)*	(86.5–89.2)*	(86.5–90.2)*
Nitrogen	Nil–0.1	Nil–0.1	—	—	—
Oxygen	—	—	—	—	—
Ash	—	—	0–0.1	0–0.1	0.01–0.05
Gravity					
Deg API	40–44	28–40	15–30	14–22	7–22
Specific,	0.825–0.806	0.887–0.825	0.966–0.876	0.972–0.922	1.022–0.922
lb/gal	6.87–6.71	7.39–6.87	8.04–7.30	8.10–7.68	8.51–7.68
Pour point, °F	0 to −50	0 to −40	−10 to +50	−10 to +80	+15 to +85
Viscosity					
Centistokes @ 100°F	1.4–2.2	1.9–3.0	10.5–65	65–200	260–750
SSU @ 100°F	—	32–38	60–300	—	—
SSF @ 122°F	—	—	—	20–40	45–300
Water & sediment, vol %	—	0–0.1	Tr to 1.0	0.05–1.0	0.05–2.0
Heating value, Btu/lb, gross (calculated)	19,670–19,860	19,170–19,750	18,280–19,400	18,100–19,020	17,410–18,990

* Estimated.

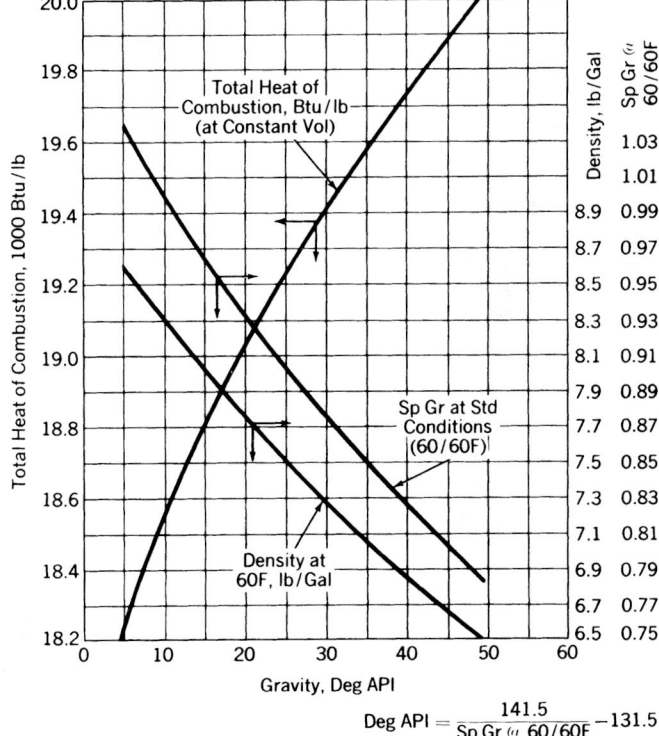

$$\text{Deg API} = \frac{141.5}{\text{Sp Gr } @ \text{ 60/60F}} - 131.5$$

FIGURE 2-12   Heating value, weight (pounds per gallon), and specific gravity of fuel oil for a range of API gravities.

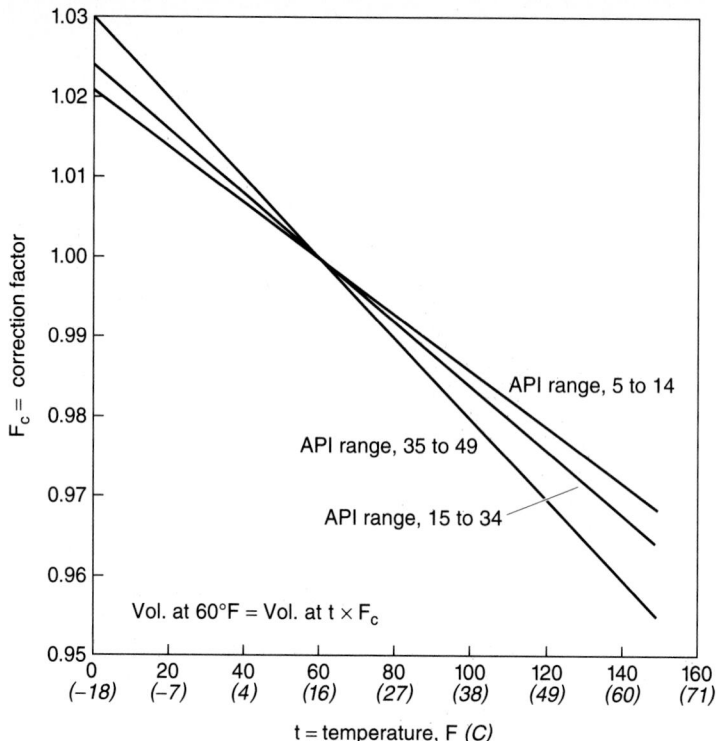

FIGURE 2-13   Oil volume-temperature correction factors.

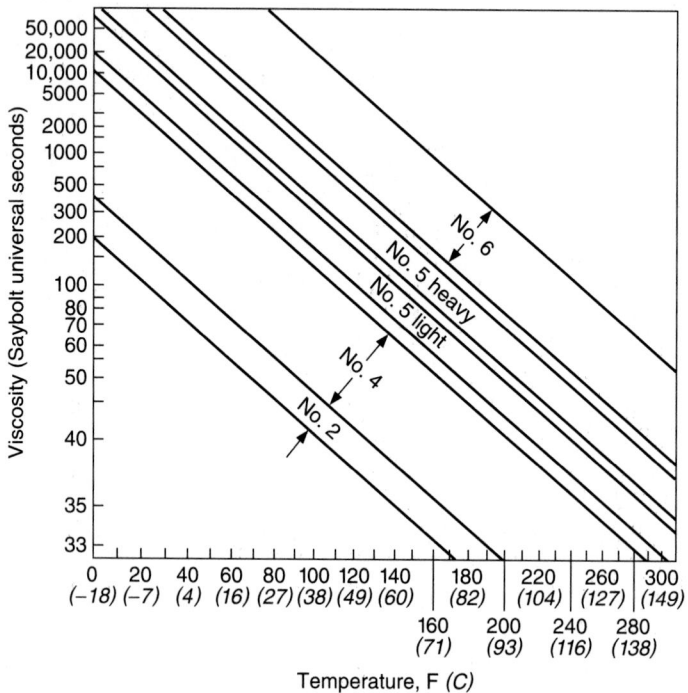

FIGURE 2-14   Approximate viscosity of fuel oil at various temperatures.

Preparation and Utilization of Oil

Preparation.   Most petroleum is refined to some extent before use, although small amounts are burned without processing. The refining of crude oil yields a number of products having many different applications. Those used as fuel include gasoline, distillate fuel, residual fuel, jet fuels, still gas, liquefied gases, kerosene, and petroleum coke.

Transportation, Handling, and Storage.   A worldwide system for distributing petroleum (and its products) has been developed because petroleum has a high calorific value per unit volume, is in easily handled liquid form, and has varied applications.

The serious hazard inherent in possible oil-storage-tank failure is overcome by storing oil in underground tanks or by protecting surface tanks by surrounding them with cofferdams of sufficient capacity to hold the entire contents of any tank so protected. The National Fire Protection Association has prepared a standard set of rules for the storage and handling of oils.

To facilitate pumping heavy fuel oil, heating equipment is usually provided in storage and transportation facilities. Storage tanks, piping, and heaters for heavy oils must be cleaned at intervals because of fouling or sludge formation. Various commercial compounds are helpful in reducing sludge.

Oil-Burning Equipment

The burner is the principal component of equipment for firing oil. Burners are normally located in the vertical walls of the furnaces.

Oil Burners.   The most frequently used burners are the circular type. Figure 2-15 shows a single circular-register burner for gas and oil firing.

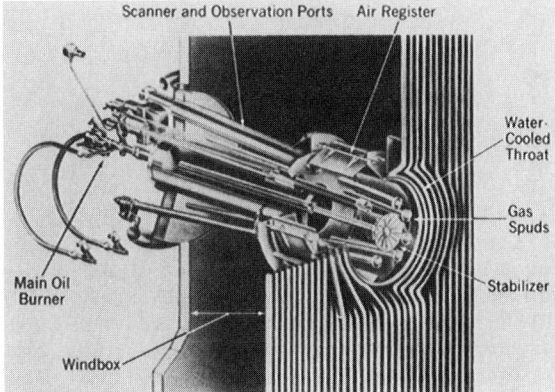

FIGURE 2-15   Circular register burner with water-cooled throat for oil and gas firing.

The maximum capacity of the individual circular burner ranges up to 300×10^6 Btu/h (316×10^4 kJ/h). In circular burners the tangential "doors" built into the air register provide the turbulence necessary to mix the fuel and air and control flame shape. Although the fuel mixture as introduced to the burner is fairly dense in the center, the direction and velocity of the air, plus dispersion of the fuel, completely and thoroughly mix it with the combustion air.

In order to burn fuel oil at the high rates demanded of modern boiler units it is necessary that the oil be *atomized,* i.e., dispersed into the furnace as a fine mist, to expose a large amount of oil particle surface to the air and assure prompt ignition and rapid combustion.

For proper atomization, oil of grades heavier than No. 2 must be heated to reduce viscosity to 135 to 150 SSU (Saybolt seconds universal). Steam or electric heaters are required to raise the oil temperature to the required level, i.e., approximately 135°F (57°C) for No. 4 oil, 185°F (74°C) for No. 5 oil, and 200 to 220°F (93 to 104°C) for No. 6 oil.

Steam or Air Atomizers.   Steam atomizers are the most widely used. In general they operate on the principle of producing a steam-fuel emulsion which, when released into the furnace, atomizes the oil through the rapid expansion of the steam. The atomizing steam must be dry because entrained moisture causes pulsations which can lead to loss of ignition. Where steam is not available, moisture-free compressed air can be substituted.

Steam atomizers are available in sizes up to 300×10^6 Btu/h input—about 16,500 lb (7500 kg) of oil per hour. Oil pressure is much lower than that required for mechanical atomizers. Maximum oil pressure can be as much as 300 lb/in^2 (2040 kPa) and maximum steam pressure 150 lb/in^2 (1020 kPa). The steam atomizer performs more efficiently over a wider load range than other types. It normally atomizes the fuel properly down to 20 percent of rated capacity.

A disadvantage of the steam atomizer is its consumption of steam. A good steam atomizer can operate with a steam consumption as low as 0.02 lb of steam per pound of fuel oil at maximum atomizer capacity.

Mechanical Atomizers.   In mechanical atomizers the pressure of the fuel itself is used as the means for atomization.

The return-flow atomizer is used in many units where the use of atomizing steam is objectionable or impractical. The oil pressure required at the atomizer for maximum capacity ranges from 600 to 1000 lb/in^2 (4080 to 6700 kPa), depending on capacity, load range, and fuel. Mechanical atomizers are available in sizes up to 180×10^6 Btu/h (190×10^6 kJ) input—about 10,000 lb (4500 kg) of oil per hour.

Excess Air.   It is necessary to supply more than the theoretical quantity of air to assure complete combustion of the fuel in the furnace. The amount of excess air provided should be just enough to burn the fuel completely in order to minimize the sensible heat loss in the stack gases. The excess air normally required for oil firing, expressed as percent of theoretical air, is generally between 5 and 7 percent.

GASEOUS FUELS

Characteristics

Natural Gas.   Of all chemical fuels, natural gas is considered the least troublesome for steam generation. It is piped directly to the consumer, eliminating the need for storage at the consumer's plant. It is substantially free of ash and mixes intimately with air to provide complete combustion at low excess air without smoke.

The high hydrogen content of natural gas compared with that of oil or coal results in the production of more water vapor in the combustion gases, thus causing a correspondingly lower efficiency of the steam-generating equipment. This can be taken into account in the design of the equipment and evaluated in comparing the cost of gas with other fuels.

Analyses of natural gas from several United States fields are given in Table 2-17.

Gaseous Fuels from Coal.   A number of gaseous fuels are derived from coal either as by-products or from coal gasification processes. Table 2-18 lists selected analyses of these gases according to the various types described in the following paragraphs.

Coke-Oven Gas.   A considerable portion of coal is converted to gases or vapors in the production of coke. The noncondensable portion is called *coke-oven gas.* Constituents depend on the nature of the coal and coking process used (Table 2-18).

Blast-Furnace Gas.   The gas discharged from steel-mill blast furnaces is used at the mills in heating furnaces, in gas engines, and for steam generation. This gas is quite variable in quality but generally has a high carbon monoxide content and low heating value (Table 2-18).

TABLE 2-17   Selected Samples of Natural Gas from U.S. Fields

Sample no. Source:	1 Pa.	2 S.C.	3 Ohio	4 La.	5 Ok.
Analyses:					
Constituents, % by vol					
H_2, Hydrogen	—	—	1.82	—	—
CH_4, Methane	83.40	84.00	93.33	90.00	84.10
C_2H_4, Ethylene	—	0.25	—	—	—
C_2H_6, Ethane	15.80	14.80	—	5.00	6.70
CO, Carbon monoxide	—	—	0.45	—	—
CO_2, Carbon dioxide	—	0.70	0.22	—	0.80
N_2, Nitrogen	0.80	0.50	3.40	5.00	8.40
O_2, Oxygen	—	—	0.35	—	—
H_2S, Hydrogen sulfide	—	—	0.18	—	—
Ultimate, % by wt					
S, Sulfur	—	—	0.34	—	—
H_2, Hydrogen	23.53	23.30	23.20	22.68	20.85
C, Carbon	75.25	74.72	69.12	69.26	64.84
N_2, Nitrogen	1.22	0.76	5.76	8.06	12.90
O_2, Oxygen	—	1.22	1.58	—	1.41
Specific gravity (rel to air)	0.636	0.636	0.567	0.600	0.630
HHV					
Btu/ft³ at 60°F and 30 in. Hg	1,129	1,116	964	1,022	974
(kJ/m³ at 16°C and 102 kPa)	(42,065)	(41,581)	(35,918)	(38,079)	(36,290)
Btu/lb (kJ/kg) of fuel	23,170	22,904	22,077	21,824	20,160
	(53,893)	(53,275)	(51,351)	(50,763)	(46,892)

TABLE 2-18   Selected Analyses of Gaseous Fuels Derived from Coal

Analysis no.	Coke oven gas 1	Blast furnace gas 2	Carbureted water gas 3	Producer gas 4
Analyses, % by volume				
Hydrogen, H_2	47.9	2.4	34.0	14.0
Methane, CH_4	33.9	0.1	15.5	3.0
Ethylene, C_2H_4	5.2	—	4.7	—
Carbon monoxide, CO	6.1	23.3	32.0	27.0
Carbon dioxide, CO_2	2.6	14.4	4.3	4.5
Nitrogen, N_2	3.7	56.4	6.5	50.9
Oxygen, O_2	0.6	—	0.7	0.6
Benzene, C_6H_6	—	—	2.3	—
Water, H_2O	—	3.4	—	—
Specific gravity (relative to air)	0.413	1.015	0.666	0.857
HHV—Btu/ft³ (kJ/m³)				
at 60°F (16°C) and	590	—	534	163
30 in. Hg (102 kPa)	(21,983)	—	(19,896)	(6,073)
at 80°F (27°C) and	—	83.8	—	—
30 in. Hg (102 kPa)	(3,122)	(3,122)		

Water Gas.   The gas produced by passing steam through a bed of hot coke is known as water gas. Carbon in the coke combines with the steam to form hydrogen and carbon monoxide.

Water gas is often enriched by passing the gas through a checkerwork of hot bricks sprayed with oil, which in turn is cracked to a gas by the heat. Such enriched water gas is called *carburetted water gas* (Table 2-18).

Producer Gas.   When coal or coke is burned with a deficiency of air and a controlled amount of moisture (steam), a product known as *producer gas* is obtained. This gas, after removal of entrained ash and sulfur compounds, is used near its source because of its low heating value (Table 2-18).

"Synthetic Natural Gas."   "Synthetic natural gas" is made from coal by one of the many gasification processes resulting in a low-Btu gas which is then methanated.

Carbon Monoxide.   In the petroleum industry, the efficient operation of a fluid-catalytic-cracking unit produces gases rich in carbon monoxide. To reclaim the thermal energy represented by these gases, the fluid-catalytic-cracking unit can be designed to include a CO boiler that uses the CO as fuel to generate steam for use in the process.

Processing and Utilization of Natural Gas

Processing.   Propane and butane are often separated from the lighter gases and are widely used as bottled gas. They are distributed and stored liquefied under pressure. Natural gas containing excessive amounts of hydrogen sulfide is commonly known as "sour" gas. The sulfur is removed before distribution.

Transportation, Handling, and Storage.   A pipeline is an economical means for transporting natural gas overland. Tankers are employed for overseas transportation of natural gas. The gas is liquefied under pressure (liquefied natural gas, LNG) for ease of transportation.

Gas-Burning Equipment

Natural-Gas Burners.   An example is the variable-mix multispud gas element (Fig. 2-15) for use with circular-type burners. Simultaneous firing of natural gas and oil in the same burner is possible.

To provide safe operation, ignition of a gas burner should remain close to the burner wall throughout the full range of allowable gas pressures, not only with normal airflows, but also with much more airflow through the burner than is theoretically required.

Burners for Other Gases.   Many industrial applications utilize coke-oven gas, blast-furnace gas, refinery gas, or other industrial by-product gases. With these gases, the heat release per unit volume of fuel gas may be very different from that of natural gas. Hence, gas elements must be designed to accommodate the particular characteristics of the gas to be burned. Other special problems may be introduced by the presence of impurities in industrial gases, such as sulfur in coke-oven gas and entrained dust in blast-furnace gas.

Lighters (Igniters) and Pilots.   Usually the ignition device is a spark device energized only long enough to assure that the main flame is self-sustaining. Although ignition should be self-sustaining within 1 or 2 s after the fuel reaches the combustion air, in a fully automated burner it is customary to allow 10 to 15 s "trial for ignition" so that the fuel can reach the burner after the fuel shutoff valve on the burner is opened. There are applications where a continuously burning lighter or pilot is needed. This is particularly true in the use of a by-product fuel, such as gas from a chemical process.

Excess Air.   It is possible to operate most units with as little as 5 to 7 percent excess air at the furnace outlet at full load, and some boilers have operated with less than 2.5 percent excess air without excessive loss of unburned combustibles.

At partial loads on all units, regardless of the fuel fired, it is necessary to increase the excess air as the load is reduced. Burner dampers are designed not to close tightly in order to permit the air to protect the idle burner(s) from overheating by radiant heat from nearby operating burners.

EFFECT OF COAL AND MULTIFUEL FIRING ON INDUSTRIAL BOILER DESIGN*

Coal is a complex fuel, and it is necessary to establish its source as well as its physical and chemical characteristics before considering boiler size or selecting equipment. Adding wood, oil, or gas to obtain combined fuel firing further affects the design criteria employed to properly design the boiler furnace.

A properly designed furnace performs two functions: (1) burning the fuel completely and (2) cooling the products of combustion sufficiently so that the convection passes of the boiler unit are maintained in a satisfactory condition of cleanliness with a reasonable amount of soot blowing. When the average temperature of gas leaving a coal-fired furnace is too high, the ash particles are molten or sticky, a condition which leads to an excessive need for cleaning the ash deposits from the upper furnace and the high-temperature zones of the convection passes.

The fouling and slagging classification of the coal, as characterized by the ash analysis, establishes furnace sizing, spacing and arrangement of tubes in convection passes, and placement of soot blowers for the furnace walls and convection passes. The slagging characteristic governs burner clearances, heat input per unit of furnace cross-sectional area, and the number of furnace-wall soot blowers provided to control buildup of slag on the furnace walls. The fouling characteristic sets a relationship of gas temperature entering the tube bank for a given side spacing of tubes and tube bank depth according to soot-blower cleaning radius.

Effect of Design Parameters on Boiler Sizing

The substantial effect on boiler sizing of the coal-ash classification is made clear by comparison of units sized for three types of coal. In general, an increased fouling tendency requires an increase in the furnace surface to lower the gas temperature entering the superheater, and an increased slagging potential of a coal causes furnaces designed for Western coals to be substantially more conservative than those designed to fire Eastern bituminous coals.

Figure 2-16 shows three boiler sizes. Boiler A is designed to fire a West Virginia bituminous coal classified as having a low slagging and low fouling potential. The slightly larger boiler B is designed to fire an Alabama bituminous coal classified as having a medium slagging and a medium fouling potential. Boiler C is the largest, designed to fire a Wyoming subbituminous lignitic ash coal classified as having a severe slagging and medium fouling potential.

The difference in the size of the unit for the West Virginia coal and the unit for the Alabama coal can be attributed primarily to the difference in fouling potential. The furnace height has been increased substantially to reduce the temperature of the gas entering the superheater, thereby reducing the fouling problem. The increased furnace depth and height of the Wyoming coal unit over the dimensions of the unit sized for the Alabama coal are primarily attributed to the difference in the slagging potential of the ash. The lignitic ash results in considerably more slag buildups on the furnace walls, thereby decreasing heat transfer and

---

* A portion of the material in this section has been adapted with permission from the paper of the same title by J. D. Blue, J. L. Clement, and V. L. Smith that was presented at the TAPPI Engineering Meeting, October, 1974.

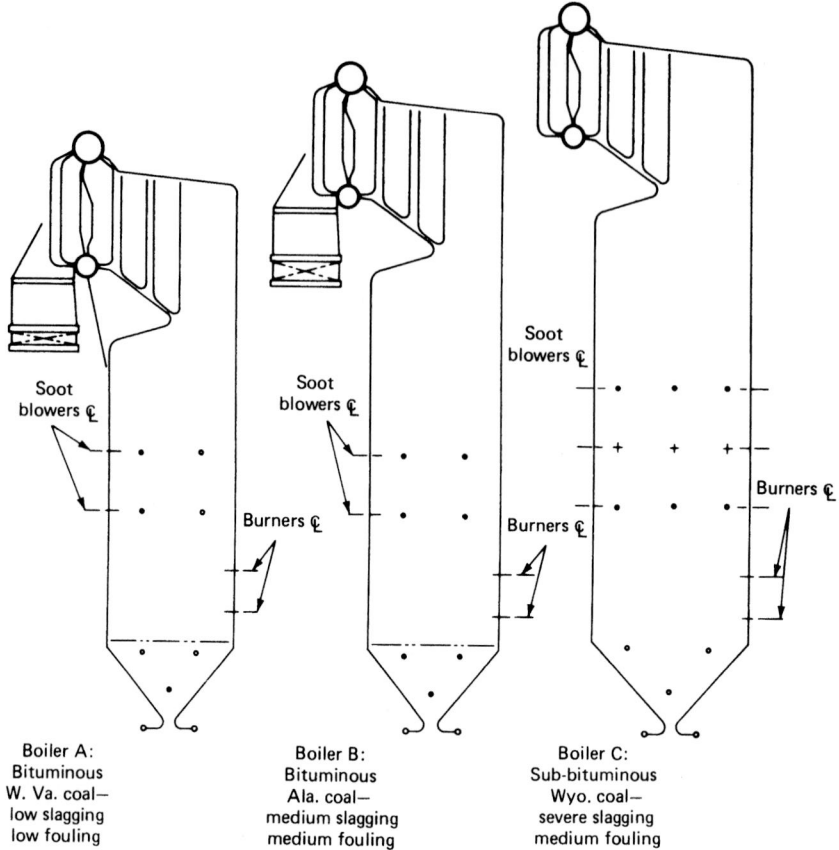

Boiler A:
Bituminous
W. Va. coal—
low slagging
low fouling

Boiler B:
Bituminous
Ala. coal—
medium slagging
medium fouling

Boiler C:
Sub-bituminous
Wyo. coal—
severe slagging
medium fouling

FIGURE 2-16   Influence of ash characteristics on furnace size.

requiring considerably more furnace surface. The furnace depth has been increased to control slagging by reducing the input per plan area.

Oil/Gas Capability

A boiler designed to use coal and/or wood as the primary fuel is frequently required to provide steam-generating capability when fired with oil and/or natural gas.

The design of a boiler for alternative fuels generally requires a compromise. For example, the steam temperature resulting from the effects of a fixed furnace and superheater surface on various fuels is illustrated in Fig. 2-17. The superheater surface in this illustration is designed to provide full-rated steam temperature on oil. The operation with gas or bark as a fuel produces the desired steam temperature at 45 and 55 percent of full load rating, respectively. The steam temperatures on these fuels would have to be moderated at higher loads to control the terminal temperature. The extent of alloy tubing used in fabrication of the superheater is governed by gas firing where the highest potential steam temperatures exist.

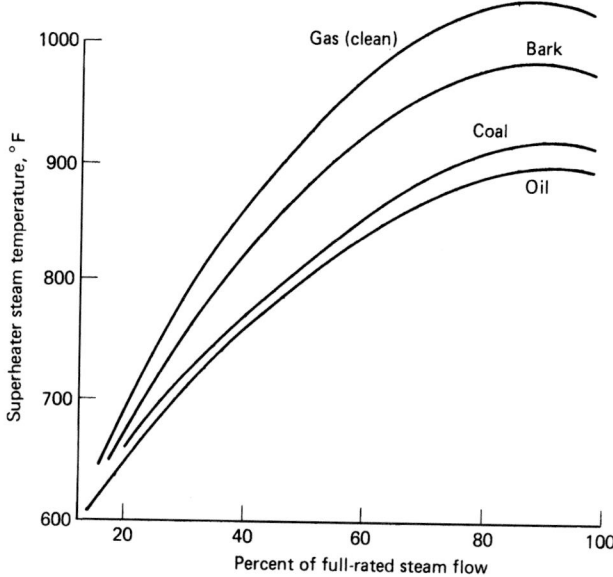

FIGURE 2-17   Effect of fuel on uncontrolled superheater steam temperature.

Stoker or Pulverized Coal

A decision to design for stoker or pulverized-coal firing is generally one of economics. A comparison of boilers designed to generate equal steam rates is characterized as follows:

1. The furnace volume is less for stoker firing because burning lower in the furnace gives more effective use of total furnace surface.
2. The furnace width is less for pulverized-coal firing.
3. Pulverized-coal-fired boilers are more responsive to load change.
4. Stoker firing requires a lower operating horsepower.
5. Thermal efficiency is higher for pulverized coal (PC) by virtue of the lower unburned-carbon loss (UCL).

Furnace Maintenance

Preventive maintenance includes a policy of operating equipment properly and within its range of capability and keeping the equipment clean and in prime operating condition. This is verified by instrumentation and in-service observations. Preventive maintenance also includes regularly scheduled outages to make those inspections which cannot be made during operation and to perform necessary repairs.

In-Service Maintenance

Safety.   Primary emphasis should be on safe operation, the avoidance of conditions that could result in explosive mixtures of fuel in the furnace or other parts of the setting, and the protection of furnace pressure parts to prevent excessive thermal stresses or overheating that would result in failure.

Furnace and Setting.   The prevention of furnace explosions deserves top priority because of potential personnel injury, the high cost of repairs, and the effect of outage time on the industrial processes. Four items are of major importance in the prevention of furnace explosions:

1. Optimum operating procedures and operator training
2. Optimum burner observation with prompt detection of flame failure
3. Detection of unburned combustibles in the flue gas
4. Positive, immediate indication of fuel-air relation at the burners

The majority of furnace explosions result from failure to detect a loss of ignition, even though other indications such as dropping boiler pressure, steam temperature, and exit-gas temperature show that fuel is either not being burned or is being burned incompletely. This emphasizes the fact that *nothing takes the place of seeing the fire.* Therefore, a reliable remote indication of positive ignition on all burners must be relayed to the operator at the central control point. A *combustibles alarm* to indicate the presence of unburned combustibles in the flue gas is considered a good backup for flame observation.

The measurement of furnace pressure on both pressurized and suction-type units is required to assure that design pressures of the casing or containment are not exceeded. Some form of differential gas- or air-pressure measurement, in conjunction with time lapse, is required as an indication that the setting has been adequately purged prior to firing. This is a necessary operating guide to assure a proper fuel-air ratio at the burners.

Variables in Efficiency Losses.   There are two variables in dry gas loss: stack temperature of the gas and weight of the gas leaving the unit. Stack temperature varies with the degree of deposit on the heat-absorbing surfaces throughout the unit, and it varies with the amount of excess combustion air. The effect of excess air is twofold: (1) It increases the gas weight, and (2) it raises the exit-gas temperature. Both effects increase dry gas loss and thereby reduce efficiency. A rough rule of thumb gives an approximate 1 percent reduction in efficiency for about a 40°F (22°C) increase in stack-gas temperature on coal-fired installations.

In coal-fired units, unburned-combustible loss includes the unburned constituents in the ash-pit refuse and in the flue dust.

Monitoring Efficiency.   Continuous monitoring of flue-gas temperatures and flue-gas oxygen content by a regularly calibrated recorder or indicator and by periodic checks on combustibles in the refuse will indicate if original efficiencies are being maintained. If conditions vary from the established performance base, corrective adjustments or maintenance steps should be taken.

High exit-gas temperatures and high draft losses with normal excess air indicate dirty heat-absorbing surfaces and the need for soot blowing.

High excess air normally increases exit-gas temperatures and draft losses and indicates the need for an adjustment to the fuel/air ratio. The high excess air may, however, be caused by excessive casing leaks or by cooling air, sealing air, or air-heater leaks.

High combustibles in the refuse indicates a need for adjustments or maintenance of fuel-preparation and -burning equipment.

Water-Side Cleanliness.   One of the best preventive steps that can be taken to assure safe, dependable operation is the maintenance of boiler-water conditions that will ensure against any internal tube deposits that could cause overheating and failure of furnace tubes.

Outage Maintenance.   Outages for preventive maintenance should be scheduled as required to prevent equipment failures.

Water-Side Cleaning.   Chemical or acid cleaning is the quickest and most satisfactory method for the removal of water-side deposits. It is, however, extremely important to use a procedure of known reliability under careful control.

Gas-Side Inspection.   During outage periods, the furnace should be thoroughly inspected; the objectives should be:

1. To detect any possible signs of overheating of tubes; furnace wall tubes should be examined for swelling, blistering, or warping
2. To discover any possible signs of erosion or corrosion
3. To detect any misalignment of tubes from warpage
4. To locate any deposits of ash or slag, not removed by sootblowing, that interfere with heat transfer or free gas flow in the furnace
5. To determine the condition of fuel-preparation and -burning equipment, particularly if routine sampling of ash has indicated the presence of increasing amounts of unburned combustible material
6. To determine the condition of any refractory exposed to furnace gases, such as burner throats or furnace walls

Gas-Side Cleaning.   When ash deposits contain an appreciable amount of sulfur, they should be removed prior to any extended outage, since these deposits can absorb ambient moisture to form sulfuric acid that will corrode furnace pressure parts.

CHAPTER 4-3
ELECTRIC GENERATORS

Clemens M. Thoennes
Sales Programs Development
General Electric Company
Schenectady, New York

GLOSSARY

Armature　The member of a rotating electric machine in which an alternating voltage is generated by virtue of relative motion with respect to a magnetic-flux field.

Class F　ANSI and IEC temperature standard of 155°C.

Core　An element of magnetic material, serving as part of a path for magnetic flux. In rotating machines, this is frequently part of the stator, a hollow cylinder of laminated magnetic steel, slotted on the inner surface for the purpose of containing the armature windings.

Exciter　The source of all or part of the dc field current for the excitation of an electric machine.

Field　An insulated winding in rotating synchronous electric machinery whose purpose is the production of the main electromagnetic field of the machine.

Permeability　A property of materials which expresses the relationship between magnetic induction and magnetizing force. An indication of the relative ability to conduct magnetic flux.

Power factor　The ratio of the active power in watts to the apparent power in voltamperes. It is also the cosine of the phase angle between the voltage and current.

Reactance　The imaginary part of impedance.

Reactive power　The imaginary power required to magnetize the air gaps in motors and transformers in ac electric circuits.

Short-circuit ratio　In synchronous electric machines, the ratio of the field current for rated open-circuit armature voltage and rated frequency to the field current for rated armature current on a sustained symmetrical short circuit at rated frequency.

Slip　Difference between synchronous and actual speed, usually expressed as a percentage of synchronous speed.

Synchronous speed　Speed in rpm (revolutions per minute) relating to ac frequency. It equals 120 times the frequency in hertz per number of poles.

INTRODUCTION

There are three basic types of rotating electric generators: synchronous ac, induction ac, and rotating dc.

Virtually all of the power generated by electric utilities and industrial turbine generators is supplied by synchronous ac generators. This type of generator includes an excitation system which is used to regulate the output voltage and power factor. The emphasis in this chapter will therefore be on synchronous ac generators.

Induction generators are squirrel-cage induction motors which are driven above synchronous speed. They do not have an excitation system and hence cannot control voltage or power factor. The system must supply the excitation. Induction generators are generally applied where relatively small waste energy or hydro potential exists; they are driven by a steam turbine, a gas expander, or a hydraulic turbine to recover the power in the energy stream. In these cases it is economical to adjust power factor and voltage on other larger synchronous generators in the system.

Rotating dc generators have been replaced almost entirely by static silicon rectifiers. The demand for rotating dc generators is limited to a few very special applications such as elevators and large excavators. No practical method has been developed for reducing the high maintenance associated with the commutators and brushes of dc generators.

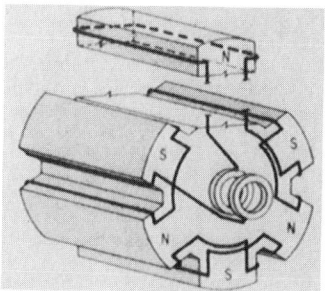

FIGURE 3-1   Simplified six-pole generator field.

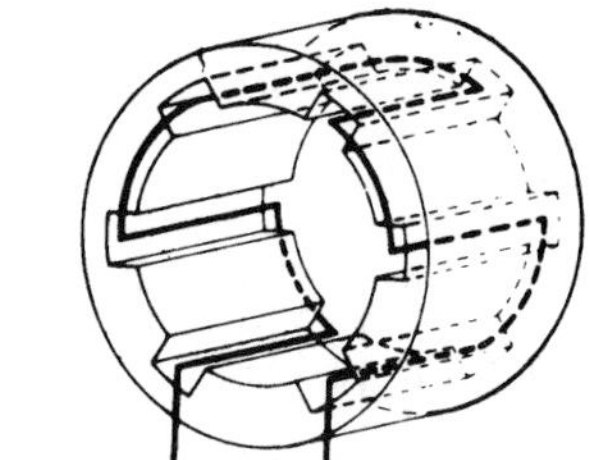

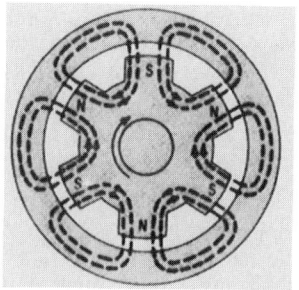

FIGURE 3-2   Simplified generator armature.

FIGURE 3-3   Generator magnetic circuit.

SYNCHRONOUS GENERATORS

The fundamental principle of operation of synchronous ac generators is that relative motion between a conductor and a magnetic field induces a voltage in the conductor. The magnitude of the voltage is proportional to the rate at which the conductor cuts lines of flux. The most common arrangement is with a cylindrical electromagnet rotating inside a stationary conductor assembly. The electromagnet is called the *field* and it is shown in simplified schematic form in Fig. 3-1. The conductors constitute the *armature* and are illustrated in Fig. 3-2. An external source of dc power is applied through the collector rings on the rotor. The flux strength and hence the induced voltage in the armature are regulated by the dc current and voltage supplied to the field. Alternating current is produced in the armature by the reversal of the magnetic field as north and south poles pass the individual conductors.

Lines of magnetic flux always form a closed circuit as shown in Fig. 3-3. Confining the flux field in materials with high permeability (low resistance to magnetic flux) intensifies the flux density. The permeability of certain steels is thousands of times greater than air. The flux density at the pole faces is proportional to the ampere turns on the poles and the combined permeability of all the materials in the circuit including the rotor core, the stator core, and the air gap.

The stator core is built up with steel laminations to provide both the high-permeability magnetic path and a high-resistance electric path to minimize induced voltage and inherent heat generation.

The simplified drawing of an armature winding in Fig. 3-2 shows a single phase only. All generators except those with very small ratings have three phases, each phase consisting of several conductors.

There are two parameters that limit the output of a generator:

1. *Flux density saturation.* As field-exciting current is increased, a point is reached where the flux density no longer increases because of iron saturation in the core. Normally the generator rating in kilovoltamperes (kVA) is near this flux saturation point.

2. *Temperature rise in the windings and insulation due to losses.* This includes losses due to excitation current in the field windings, ac current in the armature windings, the magnetic circuit, and any stray currents or magnetic fields that are generated.

Synchronous ac generators are classified by their method of cooling and excitation system. The design chosen is determined by the type of prime mover driving the generator, the power required, and the operating duty (e.g., continuous versus intermittent operation, clean versus dirty environment).

AIR-COOLED GENERATORS

Air-cooled generators are produced in two basic configurations: open ventilated (OV) and totally enclosed water-to-air-cooled (TEWAC). In the OV design, outside air is drawn directly from outside the unit through filters, passes through the generator, and is discharged outside the generator. In the TEWAC design, air is circulated within the generator and passes through frame-mounted, air-to-water heat exchangers.

The stator frame for an air-cooled generator is divided into an inner and an outer section, both of which mount on a single-base fabrication. The inner frame is a very simple structure, designed to support the stator core and winding, while providing some guidance to the air flow in the machine. The stator core, made from grain-oriented silicon steel for low loss and high permeability, is mounted rigidly in the inner frame. Isolation of the core vibration from the remainder of the structure is accomplished through the use of flexible pads between the feet on the inner frame and the base structure.

The outer frame is a simple fabricated enclosure that supports either the air inlets and silencers if the unit is open-ventilated (Fig. 3-4) or the roof and cooler enclosure if the unit is totally enclosed water-to-air-cooled. The outer frame further acts as an air guide to complete the ventilation paths, and as a soundproof enclosure to keep noise levels low. Since the rotor is pedestal mounted, the end shields are very simple structures. As with the inner frame, the outer frame is designed to be free of resonances in the range of operating frequencies.

The entire generator is mounted on a single fabricated base that supports the pedestals, the inner and outer frames, and the brush rigging or the exciter. The base contains piping for oil supplies, conduit for wiring, and a number of components associated with the main leads, such as lightning arresters and surge capacitors. The structural vibration of the base must be well away from any frequency of concern.

The stator winding is a conventional lap-wound design. The materials of modern generators are all designed and tested to provide reliable performance at Class F temperatures for the life of the machine. The stator bar copper is stranded and insulated with Class F materials and is Roebelled for minimum losses. The exterior of the bar is taped with a conducting armor in the slot section, and a semiconducting grading system is applied to the end arms. In this way the bar is fully protected from the effects of high electrical voltage gradients.

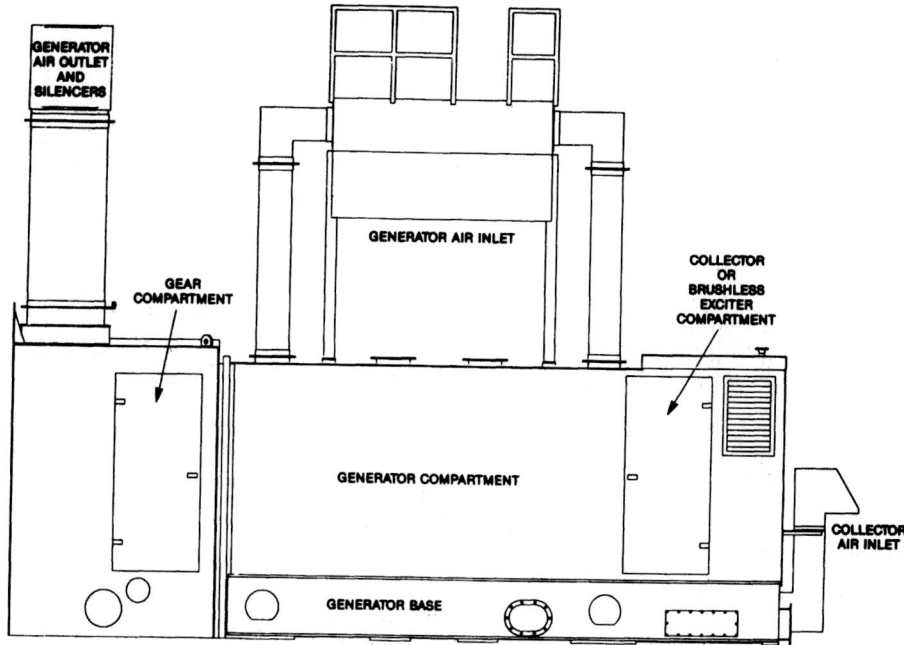

FIGURE 3-4 Generator packaging.

The bars are secured in the slots with fillers and top-ripple springs to restrain the bars radially and with side-ripple springs to increase friction between the bar and the slot wall. The side-ripple springs are also conducting to ensure proper grounding of the bar surface.

The end-winding support system utilizes resin-impregnated glass roving ties (Fig. 3-5). All the strands are brazed together in a solid block and then the top and bottom bars are brazed together with solid copper plates. This provides a solid electrical connection and a rugged mechanical joint.

The rotor (Fig. 3-6) is a simple single-piece forging, pedestal mounted, with tilting-pad bearings for smooth operation. On smaller units, the rotor is sufficiently short so that the second critical speed is above running speed, thus simplifying balance. The retaining ring is non-magnetic stainless steel with low losses and good stress-corrosion resistance. The rings are shrunk onto the rotor body, thus eliminating any risk of top burn breakage. The retaining ring is secured to the rotor body with a snap ring, a design that minimizes the stresses in the tip of the retaining ring.

High-efficiency, radial-flow fans are mounted on the centering ring at each end of the rotor. The fans provide cooling air for the stator winding and core. The rotor winding, which is a directly cooled radial flow design, is self-pumping and does not rely on the fan for air flow. The overall ventilation pattern is shown in Fig. 3-7.

The rotor winding fits in a rectangular slot and is retained by a full-length wedge on the shorter machines. When cross slots are required on longer rotors, several wedges are used in each slot. The rotor slot insulation, turn insulation, and other materials in contact with the winding are full Class F materials.

HYDROGEN-COOLED GENERATORS

To keep the size, weight, ability to ship, and cost of a larger generator within reason, a more optimal cooling medium needs to be used. Hence the development of hydrogen cooling.

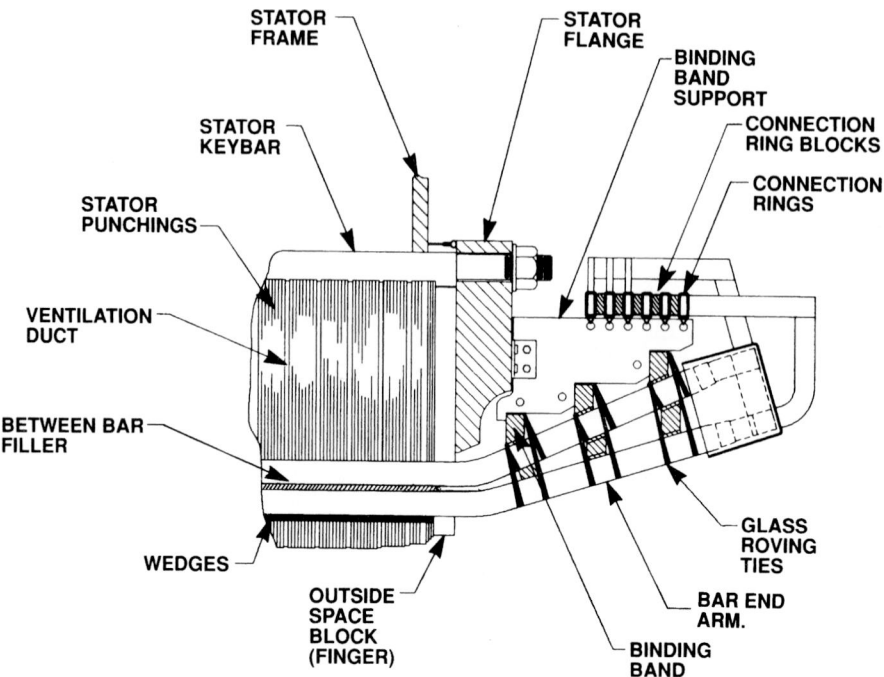

FIGURE 3-5   Stator end-winding section.

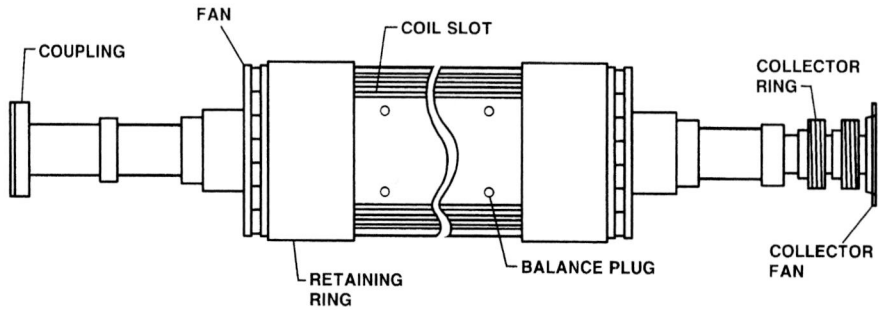

FIGURE 3-6   Generator field.

How well the armature winding of a generator is cooled has a significant influence on the overall size of a synchronous generator. The cooling of the armature winding is dependent on a number of factors: cooling medium (air, hydrogen, water), insulation thickness, and overall electrical losses (I^2R + load loss). As Table 3-1 shows, relative heat removal capability improves from air to hydrogen, with increased hydrogen pressure, and even more significantly with the use of water cooling. Conventional hydrogen cooling can be utilized on generators rated approximately 300 MVA and below, while direct water cooling of armature windings is applied to units above 250 MVA. This division results from design optimization. While it is possible to apply water cooling on machines rated below 250 MVA, the cost/performance benefit suffers. Water cooling adds manufacturing complexity, as well as requires the need for an auxiliary water cooling and deionizing skid, plus associated piping, control,

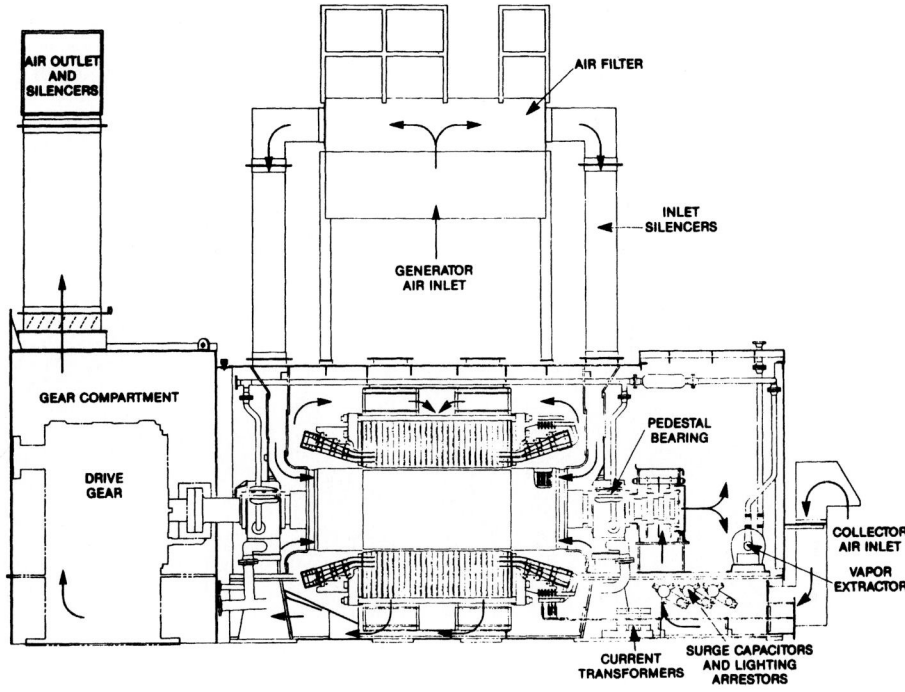

FIGURE 3-7   Generator cross section and ventilation paths.

and protection features. At higher ratings, the cost of this complexity is offset by the advantage of producing a generator of significantly smaller size than a comparable conventionally cooled generator.

TABLE 3-1   Air, Hydrogen, Water Heat Removal Comparison

Fluid	Relative specific heat	Relative density	Relative practical vol. flow	Approx. rel. heat removal ability
Air	1.0	1.0	1.0	1.0
Hydrogen, 30 lb	14.36	0.21	1.0	3.0
Hydrogen, 45 lb	14.36	0.26	1.0	4.0
Water	4.16	1000.0	0.012	50.0

Hydrogen-cooled generator construction (Fig. 3-8), except for the frame, is very similar to that of air-cooled generators. Because of the need to contain 30 to 45 psig (210–310 bars) hydrogen, the stator frame uses thick plate cylindrical construction. End shields are appropriately more rugged, and contain a hydrogen seal system to minimize leakage. Conventional hydrogen cooling, while available for generators rated below 100 MVA, is most often applied to steam-turbine-driven units above 100 MVA, as well as gas turbines above 100 MVA.

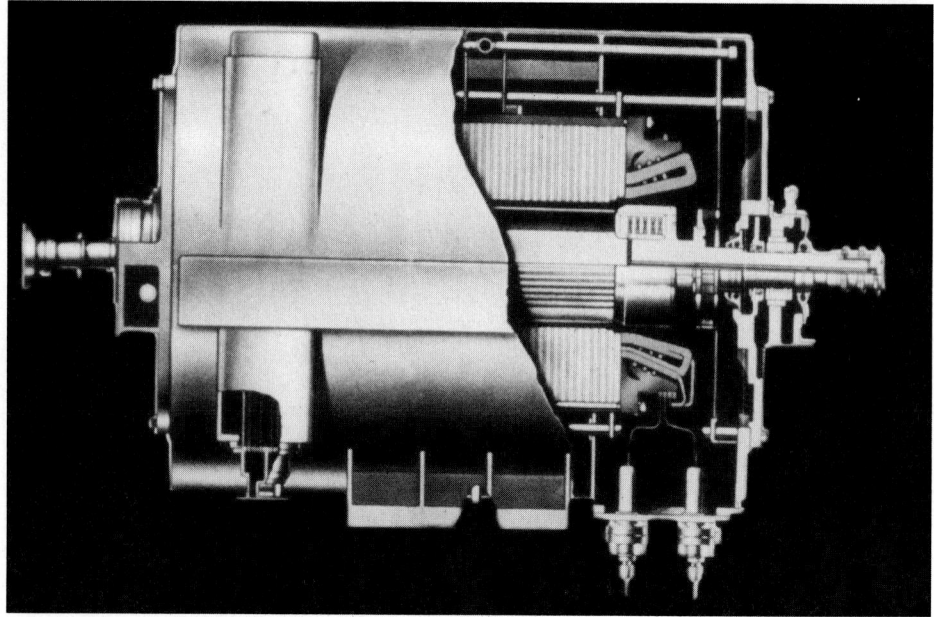

FIGURE 3-8 Hydrogen-cooled generator.

HYDROGEN/WATER-COOLED GENERATORS

Even more compact generator designs can be achieved through the use of direct water cooling of the generator armature winding (Fig. 3-9). These designs employ hollow copper strands (Fig. 3-10) through which deionized water flows. The cooling water is supplied via a closed-loop auxiliary-base-mounted skid. The cool water enters the winding through a distribution header on the connection end of the generator and the warm water is discharged in a similar manner on the turbine end of the generator (Fig. 3-11).

The armature voltage and current of hydrogen/water-cooled generators are significantly higher than those of air- or hydrogen-cooled units. As a result, the insulation voltage stress and forces on the armature windings can be several orders of magnitude larger than those experienced on lower-rated units. These present unique design requirements which must be addressed with specially configured epoxy-mica-based material systems.

Excitation System

The excitation system provides magnetizing power (about 1 percent of generator output power) for the rotating field winding and accurately controls the amount of magnetizing power to maintain close regulation of the generator output voltage and power factor.

Several excitation systems presently exist; these are classified according to the exciter power source:

- DC generator with commutator
- AC generator and stationary rectifiers
- AC generator and rotating rectifiers (brushless)
- Transformers on the main generator and rectifiers (static excitation)

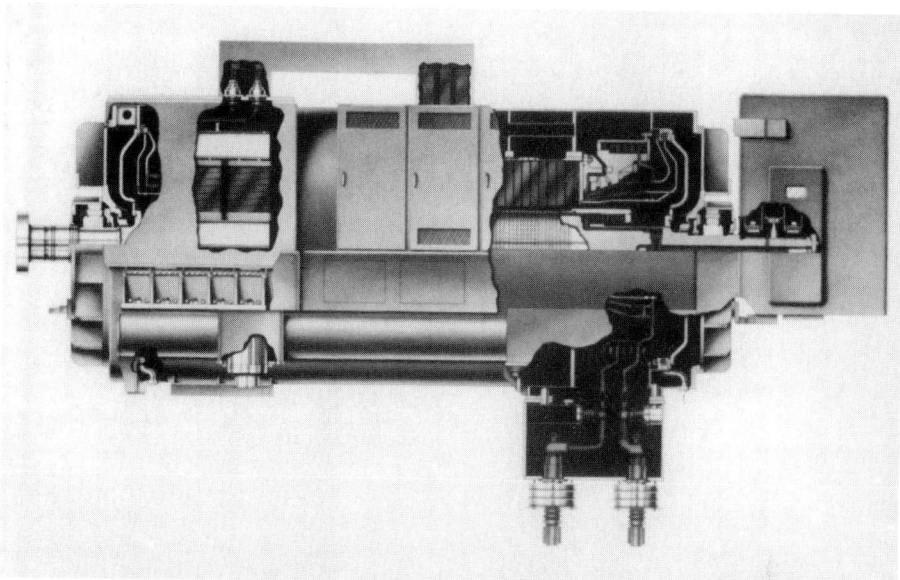

FIGURE 3-9   Water-cooled generator.

FIGURE 3-10   Hollow copper strand construction.

A schematic diagram of the dc generator with commutator connected to the main shaft is shown in Fig. 3-12. (They can be driven by separate motors or steam turbines.) The excitation power is taken from the commutator on the dc-generator rotor and applied to the main-generator rotating field through collector rings. The main-generator output voltage is controlled by using a voltage regulator to vary the excitation of the dc-generator stator.

Since commutator-type dc-generator excitation systems are inherently high in maintenance due to the commutator and brushes, the invention of solid-state rectifiers has reduced the use of this equipment in favor of ac generators rectified to dc using silicon diode rectifiers. The two methods of implementing these systems are based on either stationary rectifiers or rotating rectifiers.

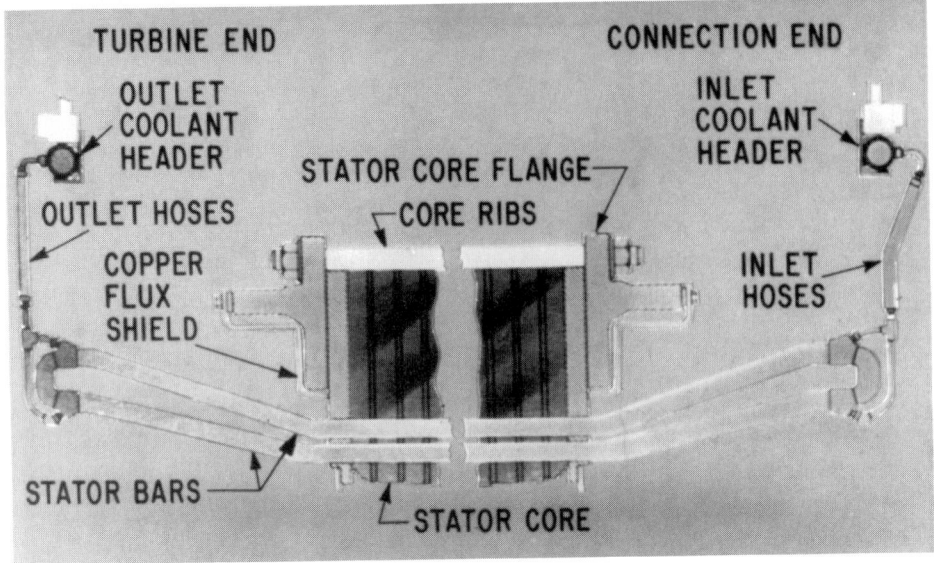

FIGURE 3-11 Water-cooled stator winding.

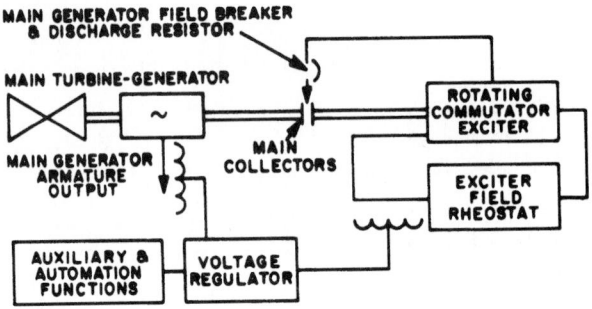

FIGURE 3-12 DC commutator excitation system.

The stationary rectifier system is shown schematically in Fig. 3-13. The ac exciter has a rotating field, as does the main generator. The exciter output is taken from its stationary armature windings, converted to dc by silicon diode rectifiers, and applied to the main-generator rotating field through collector rings. The control system is similar to the dc-generator system, except that the excitation to the exciter rotating field is transferred by collector rings. This type of system is used for generators larger than 400,000 kVA where the excitation power can be as high as 7000 kW.

An alternative ac exciter system known as the *brushless* or *rotating rectifier* is shown in Fig. 3-14. It reverses the exciter field and armature and thereby eliminates both sets of collector rings. The main generator output voltage is controlled through the exciter field in the stator. The exciter armature and silicon diode rectifiers are on the main shaft, directly connected to the main-generator field, and generator control is effected through the air gap of the exciter by varying the stationary exciter field current. This system eliminates all collector rings, hence the name *brushless exciter.*

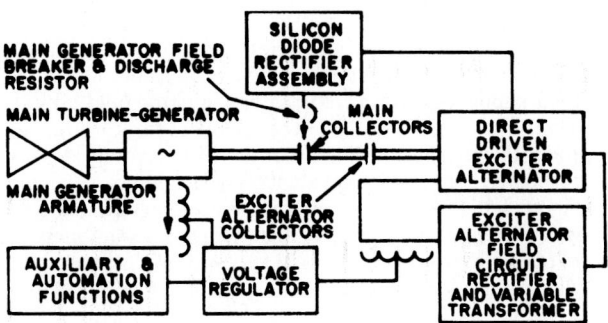

FIGURE 3-13   AC generator with stationary rectifier excitation system.

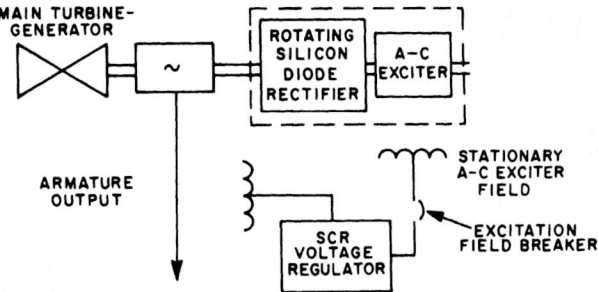

FIGURE 3-14   AC generator with rotating rectifier (brushless) excitation system.

A static excitation system (see Fig. 3-15) eliminates the need for a separate generator for excitation. The excitation power is provided by the main-generator terminals through excitation transformers. The controlled ac output of the transformers is converted to dc by silicon diode rectifers and applied to the main-generator field through collector rings.

When comparing excitation systems, each has its advantages: While the brushless system eliminates collector rings, a failure of the rotating rectifier can cause a shutdown. In contrast, the static excitation system normally provides parallel sets of stationary rectifiers, so a full load can be carried with one bank out of service. However, this system requires periodic brush maintenance, which can be done while operating.

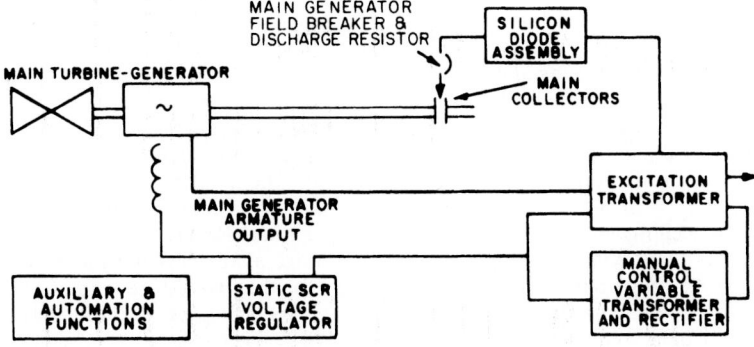

FIGURE 3-15   Static excitation system.

For applications where more than a base-level excitation system performance is required, static compound power source exciters can be utilized.

In a compound system, excitation power is derived from both a voltage source and a current source. The voltage source supports operation during no-load conditions, when the generator is supplying load current, a portion of the field excitation is derived from the generator load current. Combining the potential and current sources enables full excitation power to be supplied through system disturbances with severely depressed generator line voltage. This performance feature can be valuable in certain power system applications.

Figure 3-16 illustrates a simplified block diagram of a typical system. The rectifier bridge is a shunt-thyristor type, meaning that the bridge component arrangement is such that the firing point of the thyristors can be used to control or "shunt" the amount of excitation current that reaches the generator field.

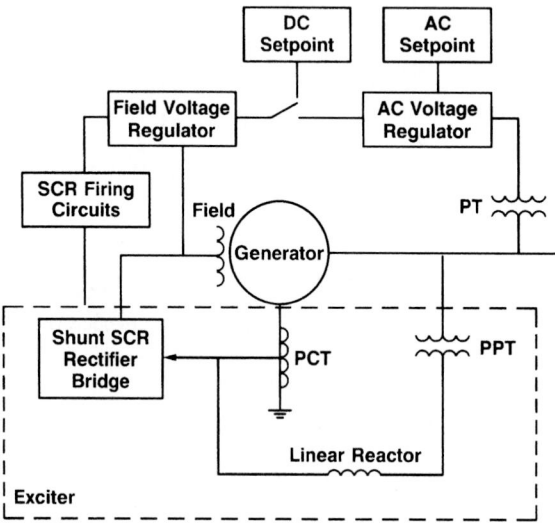

FIGURE 3-16   Shunt-SCR simplified block diagram.

The principal function of the excitation system is to furnish power in the form of direct current and voltage to the generator field, creating the magnetic field. The excitation system also comprises control and protective equipment which regulates the generator electrical output. In today's complex power system transmission design, the performance and protection features of an excitation system should be evaluated just as carefully as hardware design characteristics.

Excitation voltage is a key factor in controlling generator output. One desirable characteristic of an excitation system is its ability to produce high levels of excitation voltage (ceiling) very rapidly following a change in terminal voltage. A *high initial response* (HIR) excitation system is defined by IEEE as one that reaches 95 percent of the specified ceiling voltage in 0.1 second or less. For units tied into a power system grid, such quick action to restore power system conditions reduces the tendency for loss of synchronization.

A second desirable performance feature of an excitation system is the level or amount of ceiling voltage it can achieve. *Response ratio* (RR) (or *nominal response*) is a useful term for quantifying the forcing or ceiling voltage available from the exciter. Response ratio is the average rate of rise in exciter voltage for the first half second after change initiation divided by the rated generator field voltage. Thus, it is expressed in terms of per unit (pu) of rated field voltage.

In general, conventional rotating exciters, such as rotating rectifiers, have slower response time due to the time constants of the rotating magnetic components. In fast-acting static exciters, maximum exciter output is available almost instantaneously by signaling the controlling thyristors to provide full forcing. Figure 3-17 illustrates an important distinction between HIR exciters and conventional exciters. Since RR is proportional to the area under each curve, the HIR exciter, having achieved the specified 150 percent ceiling almost instantaneously, will exhibit a higher RR. Following this reasoning, the compound exciters can provide the highest overall performance levels since they employ an HIR thyristor-controlled rectifier bridge and, in addition, can capitalize on the fault current itself to drive the magnetic components of the exciter to high ceiling output voltages.

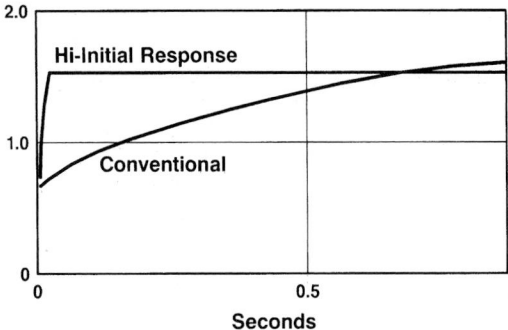

FIGURE 3-17 Excitation system performance from unity power factor.

Operation

When a generator is operating alone with an isolated load, the power factor and reactive power are determined by the load. When it operates as part of a system of generators and loads (i.e., power grid), however, the reactive power supplied by each generator can vary depending on the level of excitation of each machine. Therefore, changing the excitation of one generator in a system will change the power factor of that unit, while the voltage and frequency of the power grid will remain constant by the collective action of the other generators.

The effect of varying excitation or field current on generator performance is typically shown in excitation V curves and reactive capability curves. Typical curves of this type are shown as Figs. 3-18 and 3-19, respectively, for a hydrogen-cooled generator. The excitation V curve shows the amount of excitation required to produce a desired power factor at any power output of the generator, while the reactive capability curve defines the limits of operation. Using these curves, an operator can cause a generator to produce reactive power by increasing the field current (excitation) or absorb reactive power by decreasing the field current. This would correspond to moving along the vertical axis on the reactive capability curve. To move horizontally along this curve, the power supplied to the generator by the driving machinery would have to be increased. This highlights two important facts of generator operation in a power system:

1. The reactive power (power factor) of the power delivered by the generator is controlled by the generator field current (excitation).

2. The amount of power delivered by the generator is controlled by the machinery driving the generator.

The stability of a generator is a function of its short-circuit ratio and the response time of its excitation system. The short-circuit ratio is the ratio of field current for open-circuited

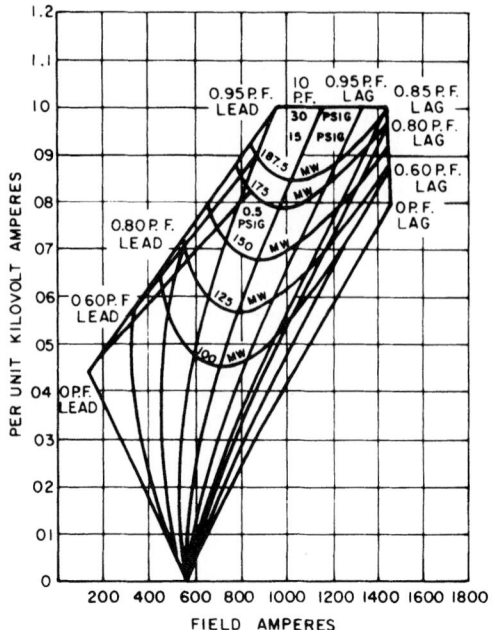

FIGURE 3-18   Generator excitation *V* curves.

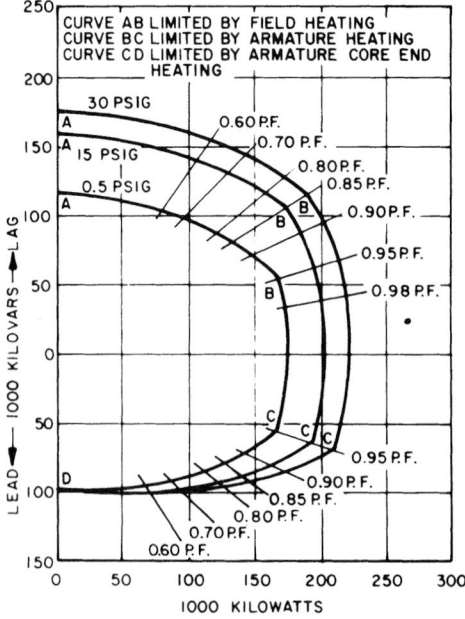

FIGURE 3-19   Reactive capability curve.

armature voltage at rated frequency to the field current for rated armature current on a sustained symmetrical short circuit at rated frequency. The higher the short-circuit ratio of a generator, the more stable the design.

A typical type of upset condition examined when determining generator stability is a short circuit. In examining the transient conditions during upsets, the term *reactance* is used. It is defined here as the ratio of open-circuit armature voltage at some field current to the short-circuit armature current at the same field current and is expressed in ohms (Ω). Reactances are usually given as a ratio to a base reactance in either percent or per unit. The base is generally taken as the ratio of phase voltage to phase current. Following a short circuit, the reactance can decrease to about 0.15 per unit and the armature current can increase to 10 or 15 times rated value. This condition will occur for a few cycles and is called the subtransient reactance (X''_d). The reactance increases after a few cycles to the transient reactance (X'_d) and continues to increase to a steady-state value known as the synchronous reactance (X_d). The synchronous reactance is typically 1.5 per unit, and the armature current will be about twice the rated current, assuming a three-phase short circuit. Since the synchronous reactance is inversely proportional to the short-circuit ratio when the saturation effects of the magnetic circuit are neglected, and since it is desirable to minimize the changes in generator operation (changes in armature current) due to upset conditions, a short-circuit ratio is a good measure of generator stability.

When a generator is started, it is first brought to rated speed by the driving equipment, and the field current is adjusted to produce rated generator voltage on an open circuit. The value of field current is shown as the extreme lower end of the excitation V curve. The frequency, voltage, and phase angle of the generator output are checked to ensure they are consistent with the power system, and the circuit breakers are closed to connect the generator to the system.

During operation, a number of protective devices are used to detect abnormal conditions and promptly isolate the troubled area to prevent damage to the generator. Relays can be provided to trip the generator upon the occurrence of any of the following conditions: unbalanced differential phase currents, phase-to-phase or ground faults, external phase-to-phase or ground faults, loss of excitation, out-of-step reverse power flow, unbalanced loading, lightning, and overvoltage. Alarms also indicate a field ground fault or excessive stator winding temperatures, which are measured by resistance temperature detectors (RTDs). The latter two conditions may not require an instantaneous trip, so the operator can plan the maintenance shutdown.

INDUCTION GENERATORS

The stator of an induction generator is similar to a synchronous generator. The rotor differs from the synchronous generator rotor in that there is no excitation and the conductors are shorted together at the rotor ends by an annular ring. This arrangement resembles a squirrel cage, which lends its name to the type of winding.

The induction generator supplies real power in *kilowatts*, which displace high-cost energy from the system. The imaginary power, *kilovars*, is drawn by the induction generator; it requires installed capability by some other device on the system, but consumes only a negligible amount of energy.

An induction machine operates at synchronous speed at zero load. The rotor turns at the same speed as the rotating flux field in the stator, and no lines of flux are cut. When a load torque is applied, the rotor speed drops off or "slips" until full torque is reached at 2 to 5 percent slip. As a generator, the driver must overspeed the generator by 2 to 5 percent to achieve full electric output.

Induction generators cannot operate independently in an isolated system. They can only function in parallel with synchronous generators that regulate voltage and supply the kilovars necessary to overcome the lagging power of the induction generation.

Induction generators are simpler and lower in initial cost than synchronous generators. They have been applied to recover power by expanding waste-gas streams and low-pressure steam. In some applications an energy-recovery turbine or expander drives an induction generator-motor and another pump or compressor on the same shaft. The generator-motor can either supply or absorb torque when the power of the other two devices is out of balance.

DC GENERATORS

The operating principle of the dc generator is very similar to that of the ac generator. In the dc generator the field is located in the stator while the armature rotates, generating alternating current in the armature windings. The commutator and brushes provide a means of transferring the output from the rotor to the stator, as well as of mechanically rectifying the alternating current. Figure 3-20 illustrates a dc-generator brush rigging and commutator. The commutator is a wearing surface for the brushes. It consists of individual copper segments insulated from each other by mica and connected to the armature windings. The armature-winding connections to the commutator and the brush spacing have to be carefully arranged so that brushes of opposite polarity contact windings which are 180 electrical degrees out of phase.

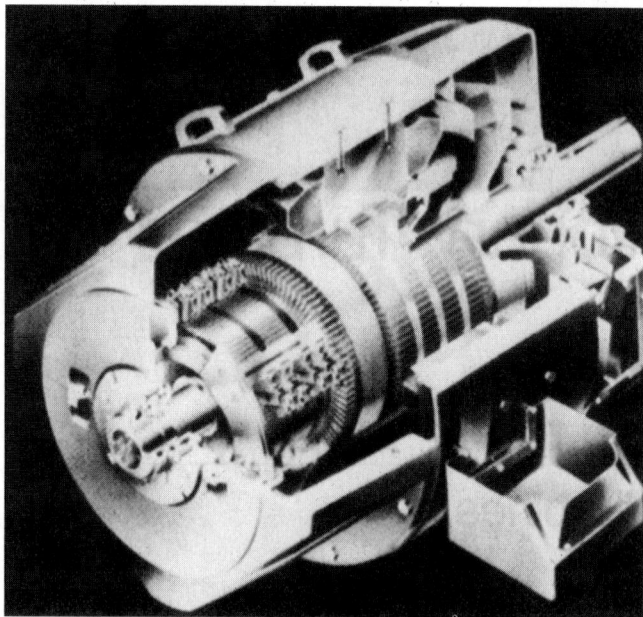

FIGURE 3-20   DC generator (General Electric Co.).

Many dc generators driven by motors have been installed in industrial plants, such as steel mills, to provide power for variable-speed drives. However, the advances in static silicon-rectifier dc power sources have reduced the market for dc generators primarily to replacement and repair parts, with very few new installations.

ACKNOWLEDGMENT

The author acknowledges the support and contribution provided by the Engineering Staff of GE's Power Generation Business.

BIBLIOGRAPHY

"American Standard Requirements for Cylindrical Rotor Synchronous Generators," C50.13-1965, American Standards Association (now ANSI) New York, 1965.

"Electric Generators," special report, *Power,* McGraw-Hill, New York, March 1966.

Fenton, R. E. and J. J. Gibney: *GE Generators–An Overview,* Turbine State-of-the-Art Conference, GER-3688, Asheville, North Carolina, August 1991.

Fink, Donald G. (ed.): *Standard Handbook for Electrical Engineers,* 11th ed., McGraw-Hill, New York, 1978.

"Guide for Operation and Maintenance of Turbine-Generators," IEEE Standard 67-1972 (ANSI C50.30-1972), The Institute of Electrical and Electronics Engineers, Inc., New York, 1972.

Jay, Frank (ed.): *IEEE Standard Dictionary of Electrical and Electronics Terms,* 2d ed., The Institute of Electrical and Electronics Engineers, Inc., New York, 1977. Distributed in cooperation with Wiley-Interscience, New York.

O'Brien, K. G., et al.: *Generator Excitation Systems,* Turbine State-of-the-Art Conference, GER-3581B, Asheville, North Carolina, August 1991.

CHAPTER 4-4
STATIONARY TURBINES

PART 1

GAS TURBINES

Clemens M. Thoennes
Sales Programs Development
General Electric Company
Schenectady, New York

GLOSSARY

Aircraft derivative gas turbine   An aircraft jet engine modified for ground applications to produce shaft power instead of thrust.

Base rating   The designed rating point of a gas turbine at which it is suitable for continuous operation. Referenced to standard ISO conditions. (See "ISO rating.")

Cogeneration   The sequential production of heat and power or recovery of low level energy for power production.

Combined cycle   A combined steam and gas turbine arrangement in which the gas turbine exhaust is ducted to a heat-recovery steam generator which supplies steam to the steam turbine.

Compression ratio   The ratio of the compressor discharge pressure to the suction pressure.

Firing temperature   The mass-flow mean total temperature of the working fluid measured in a plane immediately upstream of the first-stage turbine buckets.

Fuel consumption   The input fuel heating value per unit of time to a gas turbine, generally measured in Btu/h (kJ/h), also called heat consumption. It is generally stated in terms of the lower heating value (LHV) of the fuel by gas turbine manufacturers, but can also be in terms of pounds per hour, where typical heating values are 18,500 Btu/lb (42,940 kj/kg) for liquid fuels and 21,500 Btu/lb (49,902 kj/kg) LHV for natural gas. (Also see "Specific Fuel Consumption.")

Heat rate   The fuel consumption of a gas turbine divided by the output. For mechanical drive gas turbines this is the net output including the on-base auxiliary power losses. For generator-drive gas turbines this includes these auxiliaries plus the generator losses. It does not include the power requirements for off-base lubrication oil cooling or heavy fuel treatment, unless specified as in certain totally packaged designs. Expressed as British thermal units or kilojoules per kilowatthour or horsepower hour. It is usually expressed in terms of the LHV of the fuel.

Heavy-duty industrial gas turbine   A type of gas turbine designed specifically for ground applications using a design philosophy similar to that of the steam-turbine industry. Casings are split on the horizontal centerline, with on-site maintenance planned after long periods of operation.

Heavy fuel   Liquid petroleum fuels that are ash bearing and not true distillates. These can be crude oil or residuals (No. 5 or 6), or a blend of a distillate and residuals.

High heating value   The gross heating value of the fuel. This includes the latent heat required to vaporize the water in the products of combustion, which is not truly available to a combustion device having an exhaust temperature higher than 212°F (100°C).

Hot gas path   The path of the working fluid of a gas turbine during and after combustion. It includes the fuel nozzles, combustion chamber and liner (if required), transition pieces to the turbine, stationary and rotating airfoils (nozzles and buckets), and exhaust plenum and ducting.

ISO rating   The rated output of a gas turbine at standard site conditions as specified by the International Standards Organization: sea-level altitude, standard atmospheric pressure of 14.7 psia (101.4 kPa) at the turbine inlet and exhaust, 59°F (15°C) ambient temperature, and 60 percent relative humidity.

NO_2   Oxides of nitrogen include both NO and NO_2. Emission limits are generally based on parts per million by volume (ppmv) of the total of NO and NO_2 emitted by combustion devices.

Peak rating   The designed rating point for gas turbines for peak-load service generally operated at less than 1000/yr. Not generally used for industrial applications which are base-loaded.

Regenerative cycle   A gas turbine that includes a gas-to-gas heat exchanger which transfers heat from the exhaust to the compressor discharge air to reduce fuel consumption.

Simple cycle   A gas turbine that exhausts to the atmosphere without heat recovery.

Specific fuel consumption (SFC)   The gas turbine fuel consumption per unit of output. SFC is usually stated in terms of pounds per kilowatthour or pounds per horsepower hour using LHV.

Specific work   The output of a gas turbine per unit of air flow. It can be horsepower seconds per pound or British thermal units per pound (kilojoules per kilogram).

Thermodynamic efficiency   The net output of a gas turbine divided by the input. It is the reciprocal of heat rate after normalizing units. For example:

$$\text{Thermal efficiency} = \frac{1}{\text{heat rate (Btu/kWh)} \times 3412 \text{ Btu/kWh}}$$

PRINCIPLES

Thermodynamic Fundamentals

A schematic diagram for a simple-cycle, single-shaft gas turbine is shown in Fig. 4-1. Air enters the axial flow compressor at point 1 of the schematic at ambient conditions. Since these

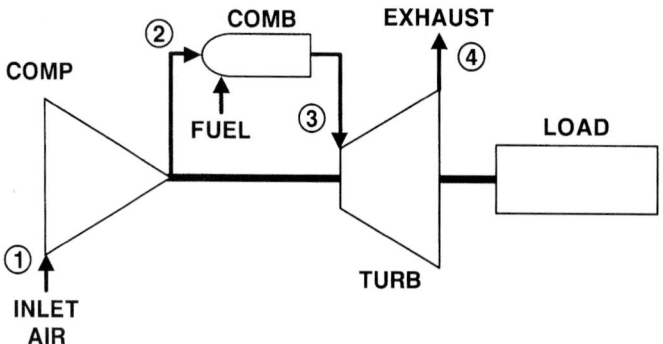

FIGURE 4-1   Simple-cycle, single-shaft gas turbine.

conditions vary from day to day and from location to location, it is convenient to consider some standard conditions for comparative purposes. The standard conditions used by the gas turbine industry are 59°F (15°C), 14.7 psia (1.013 bar), and 60 percent relative humidity, which were established by the International Standards Organization (ISO). These conditions are frequently referred to as ISO conditions.

Air entering the compressor at point 1 is compressed to some higher pressure. No heat is added; however, the temperature of the air rises due to compression, so that the air at the discharge of the compressor is at a higher temperature and pressure.

Upon leaving the compressor, air enters the combustion system at point 2, where fuel is injected and combustion takes place. The combustion process occurs at essentially constant pressure. Although very high local temperatures are reached within the primary combustion zone (approaching stoichiometric conditions), the combustion system is designed to provide mixing, dilution, and cooling. Thus, by the time the combustion mixture leaves the combustion system and enters the turbine at point 3, it is at a mixed average temperature.

In the turbine section of the gas turbine, the energy of the hot gases is converted into work. This conversion actually takes place in two steps. In the nozzle section of the turbine, the hot gases are expanded and a portion of the thermal energy is converted into kinetic energy. In the subsequent bucket section of the turbine, a portion of the kinetic energy is transferred to the rotating buckets and converted to work.

Some of the work developed by the turbine is used to drive the compressor, and the remainder is available for useful work at the output flange of the gas turbine. Typically, more than 50 percent of the work developed by the turbine sections is used to power the axial flow compressor.

The thermodynamic cycle upon which all gas turbines operate is called the *Brayton cycle*. Figure 4-2 shows the classical pressure-volume (PV) and temperature-entropy (TS) diagrams for this cycle. The numbers on this diagram correspond to the numbers also used in Fig. 4-1. Every Brayton cycle can be characterized by two significant parameters: pressure ratio and firing temperature. The pressure ratio of the cycle is the pressure at point 2 (compressor discharge pressure) divided by the pressure at point 1 (compressor inlet pressure). In an ideal cycle, this pressure ratio is also equal to the pressure at point 3 divided by the pressure at point 4. However, in an actual cycle, there is some slight pressure loss in the combustion system and, hence, the pressure at point 3 is slightly less than at point 2. The other significant parameter is the *firing temperature*, which is the highest temperature reached in the cycle. The most accepted definition of firing temperature is the mass-flow mean total temperature at the first-stage nozzle trailing edge plane. In a gas turbine without first-stage turbine nozzle cooling (in which air enters the hot gas stream after cooling down the nozzle), the total temperature immediately downstream of the nozzle is equal to the temperature immediately upstream of the nozzle. With turbine nozzle cooling, this cooling air mixes with the hot gases expanding through the nozzle. This definition utilizes a temperature that is indicative of the cycle temperature represented by point 3 of Fig. 4.2.

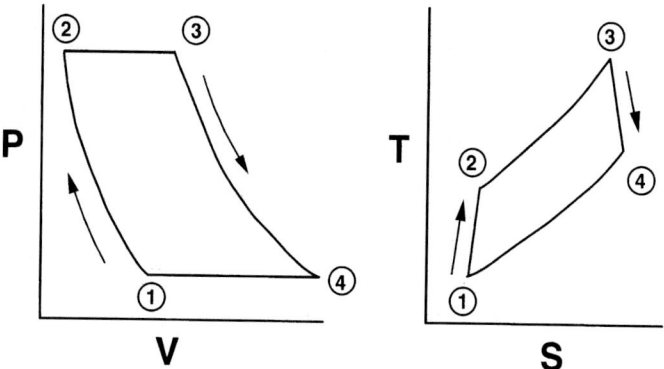

FIGURE 4-2   Brayton cycle.

An alternate method of determining firing temperature is defined in ISO document 2314, "Gas Turbines-Acceptance Tests." The firing temperature here is really a reference turbine inlet temperature, and is not generally a temperature that exists in a gas turbine cycle. It is calculated from a heat balance on the combustion system, using parameters obtained in a field test. This ISO reference temperature will always be less than the true firing temperature, in many cases by 100°F (37°C) or more for machines using air extracted from the compressor for internal cooling. Figure 4-3 shows how these various temperatures are defined.

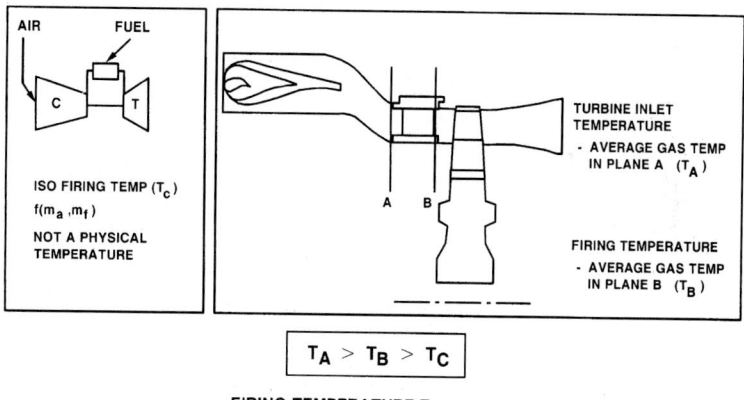

FIGURE 4-3   Definition of firing temperature.

The thermal efficiency of the Brayton cycle can be calculated using classical thermodynamic analysis. The compression ratio of the working fluid and the temperatures of heat addition and heat rejection are very important parameters. The results of such an analysis are shown in Fig. 4-4. These calculations are based on an ambient temperature of 59°F (15°C), actual component efficiencies, and real gas relationships. The results are plotted as thermal efficiency vs specific work for two different firing temperatures.

The observations that can be made from these curves are:

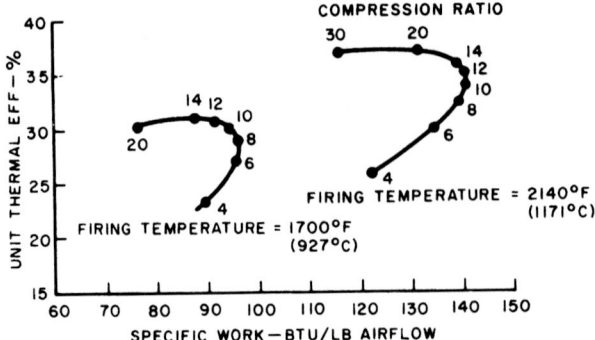

FIGURE 4-4   Efficiency vs. specific work of gas turbine cycles.

- Thermal efficiency increases as heat is added.
- For a given firing temperature there is an optimum pressure ratio for achieving maximum thermal efficiency.
- For a given firing temperature there is an optimum pressure ratio for achieving the maximum specific work which is different from the optimum thermal-efficiency pressure ratio.

Design Features

There are many different design features among the gas turbines available for industrial plant applications. Some of the more important characteristics are:

- One or more shafts
- Heavy-duty industrial type or aircraft derivative
- Combustion-chamber design

As shown in Fig. 4-1, single-shaft gas turbines are configured in one continuous shaft and, therefore, all stages operate at the same speed. These units are typically used for generator-drive applications where significant speed variation is not required.

A schematic diagram for a simple-cycle, two-shaft gas turbine is shown in Fig. 4-5. The low-pressure or power turbine rotor is mechanically separate from the high-pressure turbine and

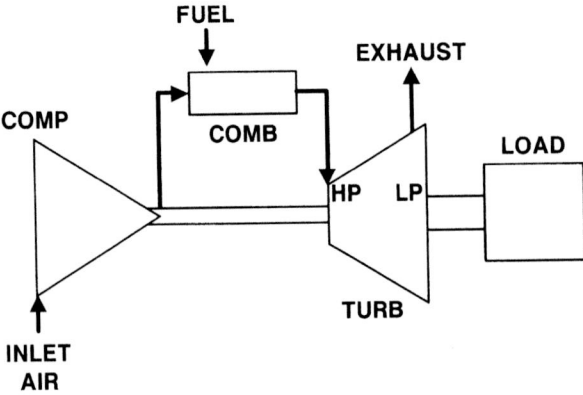

FIGURE 4-5   Simple-cycle, two-shaft gas turbine.

compressor rotor. This unique feature allows the power turbine to be operated at a wide range of speeds, and makes two-shaft gas turbines ideally suited for variable-speed applications.

All of the work developed by the power turbine is available to drive the load equipment since the work developed by the high-pressure turbine supplies all the necessary energy to drive the compressor. Further, the starting requirements for the gas turbine load train are reduced since the load equipment is mechanically separate from the high-pressure turbine.

The designs of gas turbines have evolved from two distinct philosophies. Industrial-type units have been based on the technology developed in the steam-turbine industry for large central stations. Of robust construction, with casings split along the horizontal centerline, these units are designed for long periods of continuous operation, generally have the capability to burn a variety of fuels, and are maintained on site. Aircraft-derivative gas turbines are jet engines modified to produce shaft power instead of thrust. Of lightweight construction, aircraft-derivative gas turbines are generally derated from flight-takeoff firing temperatures to allow long periods of continuous operation; they can usually be maintained on site, or are suitable for quick change-out and replacement with a spare engine. Aircraft-derivative units generally do not have the fuel flexibility of heavy-duty units.

Another distinguishing characteristic of gas turbine designs is the type of combustion section. There are three general types: a series of small cylindrical chambers or cans, an annular chamber surrounding the shaft, and large single off-base combustors. The series of small cylindrical combustors is best suited to full-scale combustion development testing, a key factor in success-

FIGURE 4-6   Cross section of an MS7001FA single-shaft gas turbine. (*General Electric Co.*)

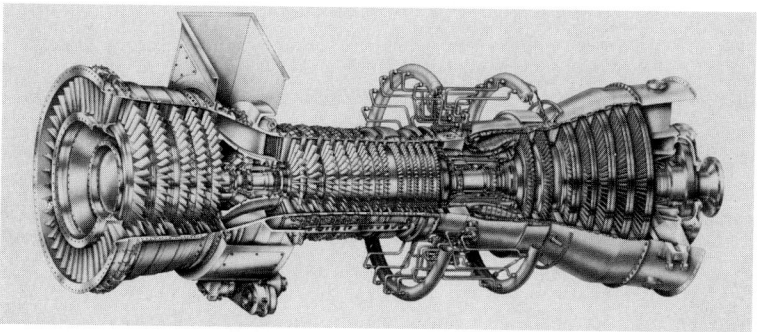

FIGURE 4-7   Cross section of an LM6000 two-shaft gas turbine. (*General Electric Co.*)

fully introducing a new model. New materials and designs can be developed without going to the expense of prototype testing. Also, investigations of unusual fuels and methods of reducing objectionable emissions such as NO_x can be easily made. The annular combustion chamber has minimum ducting, weight, and length and is therefore best suited to aircraft-type units.

Figures 4-6 and 4-7 illustrate many of the characteristics of the different gas turbine designs mentioned previously. Figure 4-6 is the General Electric Model Series 7001FA single-shaft heavy-duty gas turbine, and Fig. 4-7 is the General Electric LM6000 aircraft-derivative unit.

The compressor for the MS7001FA is an axial-flow, 18-stage compressor with extraction provisions at stages 9 and 13. Stages 0 and 1 have been designed for operation in transonic flow using design practices applied by aircraft gas turbine designers for high bypass ratio aircraft engines. Compressor surge control is accomplished through variable inlet guide vanes (VIGV) and selective bleed. At 100 percent speed, the VIGV are fully open for simple-cycle applications. For combined-cycle applications the VIGV are positioned at an intermediate setting and opened as a function of load and exhaust temperature to maintain maximum thermal efficiency. The 9th and 13th stage bleed valves close during start-up when the generator breaker closes.

The low stage loading has resulted in a very rugged compressor with a high level of compressor efficiency.

The MS7001FA combustion system consists of 14 combustion chambers with 14-in (36-cm) nominal-diameter combustion liners. Transition pieces conduct the combustion gases to the first-stage nozzle.

The MS7001FA turbine is a three-stage design, with the first-stage blade unshrouded and the second- and third-stage blades equipped with integral Z form tip shrouds.

Each of the three rotor stages consists of 92 investment-cast blades. The first- and second-stage blades and all three nozzle stages are air cooled. The first-stage blade is made of directionally solidified construction and is convectively cooled via serpentine passages, with turbulence promoters formed by coring techniques during the casting process (Fig. 4-8). The cooling air leaves the blade through holes in the tip as well as in the trailing edge.

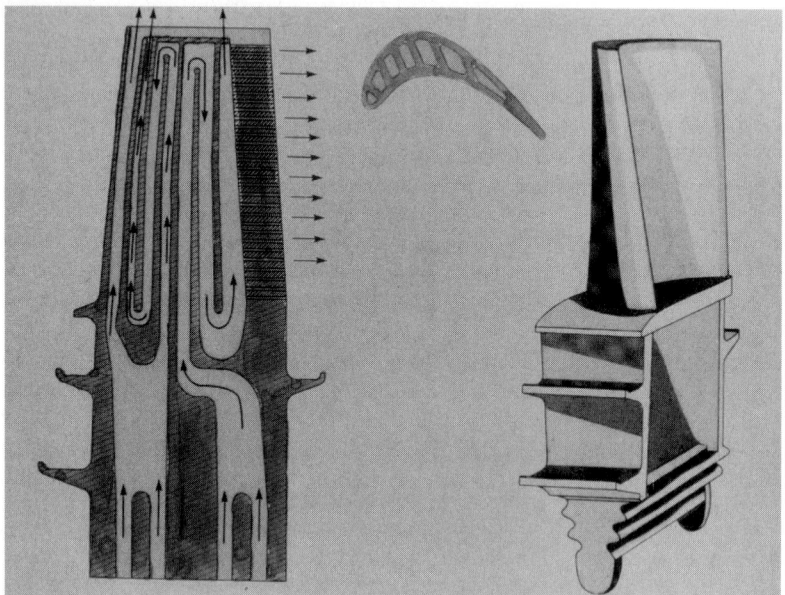

FIGURE 4-8   First-stage bucket cooling passages.

The second-stage blade is cooled by convective heat transfer using STEM (shaped tube electrode machining)–drilled radial holes, with all cooling air exiting through the tip.

The first-stage nozzle contains a forward and aft cavity in the vane, and is cooled by a combination of film, impingement, and convection techniques in both the vane and sidewall regions. There are a total of 575 holes in each of the 24 segments.

The second-stage nozzle is cooled by a combination of impingement and convection techniques, while the third-stage nozzle is cooled by convection only.

The efficient use of cooling air made possible by these advanced cooling methods is further enhanced by the reduced vane surface area of the first-stage nozzle, which is achieved by low solidity.

The LM6000 is a dual-rotor "direct drive" gas turbine. The LM6000 takes advantage of the fact that the low-pressure rotor normal operating speed of its parent turbofan aircraft engine is approximately 3600 rpm. The LM6000 gas turbine concept provides for direct coupling of the gas turbine low-pressure system to the load and maintains an extraordinarily high degree of commonality with the aircraft engine, as illustrated in Fig. 4-9. This is unlike the traditional aeroderivative approach, also shown in Fig. 4-9, which maintains a high degree of commonality with the aircraft engine in the gas generator only, and adds a unique power turbine. By maintaining high commonality, the LM6000 offers reduced parts cost benefits and demonstrated reliability.

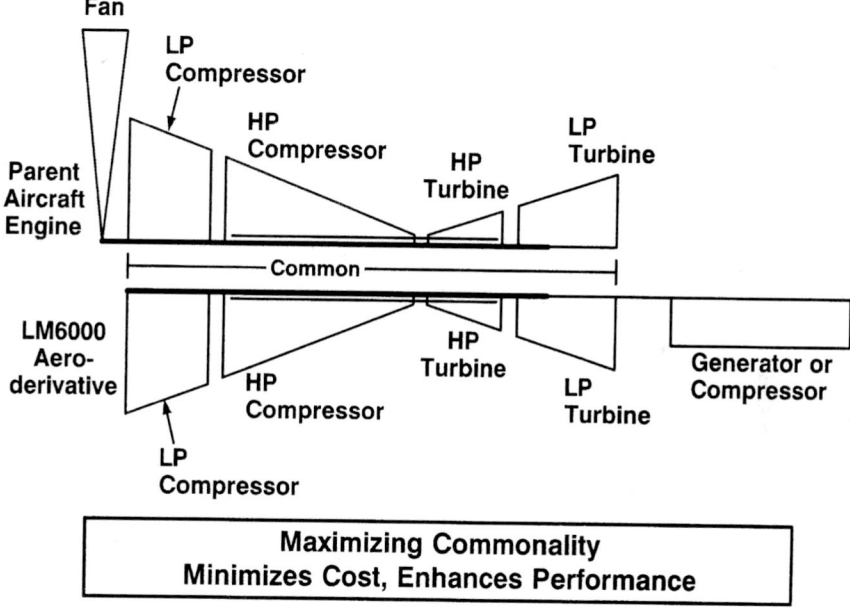

FIGURE 4-9 LM6000 concept.

The LM6000 consists of a low-pressure rotor made up of a five-stage low-pressure compressor (LPC) with variable inlet guide vanes, driven by a five-stage low-pressure turbine via a concentric shaft through the high-pressure rotor. This low-pressure rotor is also the driven equipment driver, providing the option for either cold-end or hot-end drive arrangements. The high-pressure rotor consists of a 14-stage high-pressure compressor with six stages of variable guide vanes driven by a two-stage air-cooled high-pressure turbine. The overall compression ratio is 29:1.

The LM6000 utilizes an annular combustor with 30 individually replaceable fuel nozzles, and is equipped with an engine-mounted accessory drive gearbox for starting the unit and driving critical accessories.

PERFORMANCE CHARACTERISTICS

Gas Turbine Ratings

Since the introduction of the first industrial gas turbines in the 1950s there has been a continuous growth in performance. During this period there have been significant developments in the metallurgy of hot-gas path parts and in coatings, cooling techniques, instruments, control systems, and component efficiencies. Ratings for specific frame sizes have grown threefold. Indications are that ratings and efficiency values will continue to increase as new techniques are developed for increased air and water cooling of hot-gas parts.

Therefore, any table of specifications for gas turbines can only represent a "snapshot" in time of what is a dynamic, ever-changing picture. Nevertheless, Tables 4-1 and 4-2 are offered to represent the state of the art of gas turbine technology in the early 1990s.

TABLE 4-1   GE Gas Turbine Performance Characteristics: Generator Drive Gas Turbine Ratings

Model no.	Fuel gas/ distillate	Output, kW	Heat rate, Btu/kWh (LHV)	Exhaust flow, lb/h	Exhaust temp., deg. F	Freq., Hz
PG5271(RA)	G	20,260	12,820	781,000	969	50 and 60
	D	19,940	12,920	783,000	970	
PG5371(PA)	G	26,300	11,990	985,000	909	50 and 60
	D	25,800	12,070	988,000	910	
PG6541(B)	G	38,340	10,860	1,104,000	1,002	50 and 60
	D	37,520	10,970	1,107,000	1,003	
PG7111(EA)	G	83,500	10,480	2,351,000	986	60
	D	82,100	10,560	2,358,000	986	
PG7171(E/F)	G	125,000	10,030	3,309,000	991	60
	D	122,410	10,130	3,318,000	992	
PG7221(FA)	G	159,000	9,500	3,387,000	1,093	60
	D	144,800	9,580	3,397,000	1,095	
PG9171(E)	G	123,400	10,100	3,256,000	1,001	50
	D	121,300	10,170	3,265,000	1,002	
PG9301(F)	G	212,200	9,995	4,860,000	1,081	50
	D	208,000	10,080	4,875,000	1,082	
PG9311(FA)	G	226,500	9,570	4,877,000	1,093	50
	D	222,000	9,650	4,892,000	1,095	
LM6000(PA)	G	39,970	8,790	982,300	840	60
	D	39,920	8,850	982,100	856	
LM6000(PA)	G	39,170	8,960	982,300	840	50
	D	39,120	9,030	982,100	856	

TABLE 4-2   Mechanical Drive Gas Turbine Ratings

Model no.	Cycle (SC-simple) (RC-regenerative)	Fuel (G-gas) (D-dist.)	Output, hp	Heat rate, Btu/hph (LHV)	Output shaft speed, rpm	Exhaust temp., F	Exhaust flow, lb/hr
M3142(J)	SC	G	14,600	9,530	6,500	979	415.0
		D	14,250	9,680	6,500	979	415.0
M3142R(J)	RC	G	14,000	7,410	6,500	668	415.0
		D	13,650	7,500	6,500	668	415.0
M5261(RA)	SC	G	26,400	9,380	4,860	988	740.4
M5352(B)	SC	G	35,000	8,830	4,670	915	977.9
M5382(C)	SC	G	38,000	8,700	4,670	960	993.4
M5352R(C)	RC	G	35,600	6,990	4,670	970/693	956.2
M6501(B)	SC	G	50,010	7,930	4,860	1,022	1,039.6
M7111(EA)	SC	G	108,200	7,790	3,460	1,001	2,224.7
LM6000(PA)	SC	G	56,130	6,370	3,600	836	999.5

In Table 4-1 the models are heavy-duty gas turbine-generator sets. The PG7221(FA) incorporates the MS7001FA gas turbine, the technological state of the art in the early 1990s. Aircraft-derivative state of the art is embodied in the LM6000(PA) unit.

Factors Affecting Gas Turbine Performance

Since the gas turbine is an ambient-air-breathing engine, its performance will be changed by anything affecting the mass flow of the air intake to the compressor, most obviously changes from the reference conditions of 59°F (15°C) and 14.7 psia (101.4 kPa). Figure 4-10 shows how ambient temperature affects output, heat rate, heat consumption and exhaust flow for a single-shaft MS7001EA. Each turbine model has its own temperature-effect curve, since it depends on the cycle parameters and component efficiencies as well as air mass flow.

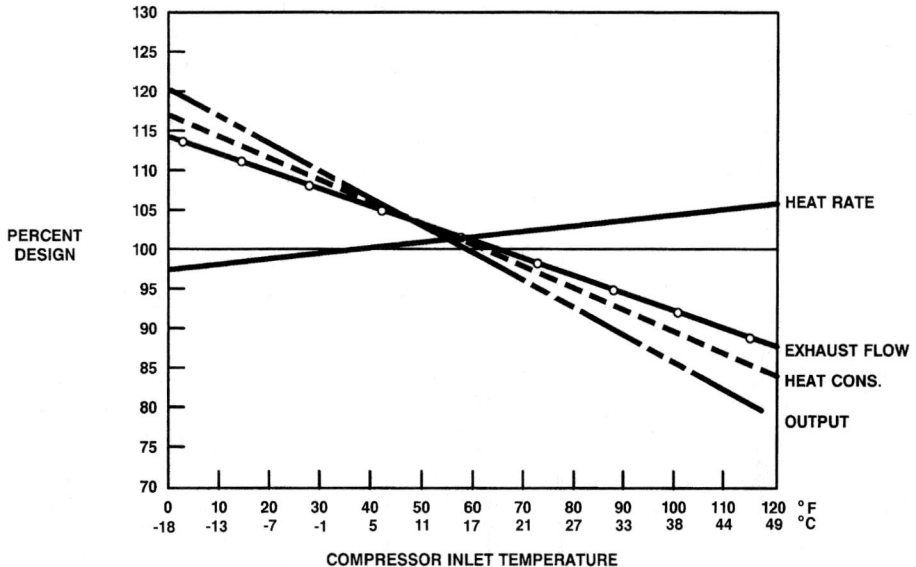

FIGURE 4-10   Effect of ambient temperature on MS7001EA.

Correction for altitude or barometric pressure is simpler. The less-dense air reduces the airflow and output proportionately; heat rate and other cycle parameters are not affected. A standard altitude correction curve is presented in Fig. 4-11.

Similarly, humid air, being less dense than dry air, will also have an effect on output and heat rate as shown in Fig. 4-12. In the past, this effect was thought to be too small to be considered. However, with the increasing size of gas turbines and the utilization of humidity to bias water and steam injection for NO_x control, this effect has greater significance.

Inserting air filtration, silencing, evaporative coolers, chillers, and exhaust heat recovery devices in the inlet and exhaust systems causes pressure drops in the system. The effects of these pressure drops are unique to each design. Shown in Fig. 4-13 are the effects on the MS7001EA.

Fuel type will also impact performance. Tables 4-1 and 4-2 show that natural gas produces nearly 2 percent more output than does distillate oil. This is due to the higher specific heat in the combustion products of natural gas, resulting from the higher water vapor content produced by the higher hydrogen/carbon ratio of methane.

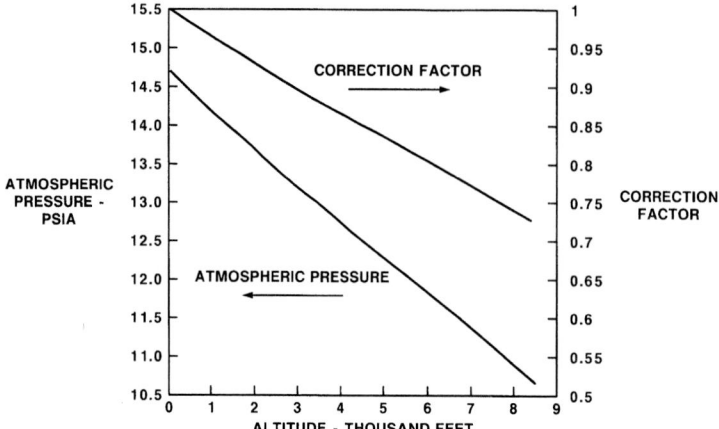

FIGURE 4-11 Altitude correction curve.

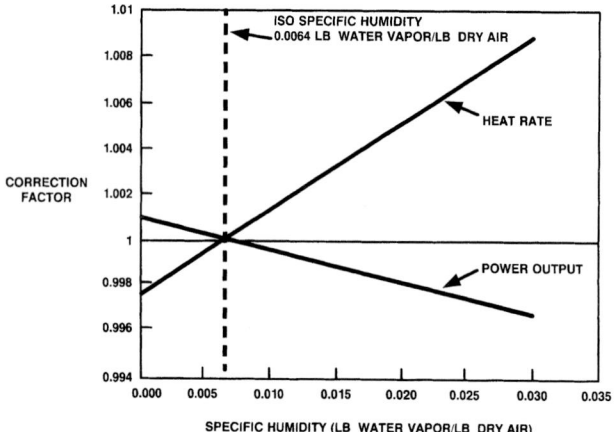

FIGURE 4-12 Humidity effect curve.

4 INCHES H₂O INLET DROP PRODUCES:

1.42% POWER OUTPUT LOSS
0.45% HEAT RATE INCREASE
1.9°F EXHAUST TEMPERATURE INCREASE

4 INCHES H₂O EXHAUST DROP PRODUCES:

0.42% POWER OUTPUT LOSS
0.42% HEAT RATE INCREASE
1.9°F EXHAUST TEMPERATURE INCREASE

FIGURE 4-13 MS7001EA pressure drop effects.

OPERATION AND MAINTENANCE

Starting Procedures

In order to start up a gas turbine, another small prime mover is required to accelerate the unit to a preselected speed until firing occurs and the unit becomes self-sustaining. The starting device is then uncoupled from the gas turbine by a clutch. Starting devices can be:

- Motors
- Diesel engines
- Expansion turbines
- Steam turbines
- Generators (via frequency conversion)

Normal Operation

Most gas turbine-generators normally operate at synchronous speed at full capability. Fuel flow is governed to maintain the firing temperature at its design limit. Therefore, the output of the unit will vary with ambient temperature. Units that are synchronized in a grid can also operate at part load using a droop or speed/load control characteristic. This is illustrated in Fig. 4-14. Because the unit is synchronized to the system, the speed is essentially constant. Therefore, varying the speed set point effectively varies the load. The family of diagonal lines represents different settings of the speed/load control knob. Isolated gas turbine-generators can be furnished with an isochronous control mode. Load changes result in transient speed excursions which are instantaneously corrected by modulating fuel flow. Whether a gas turbine is on droop or isochronous control, the maximum firing temperature control will always provide an upper limit to prevent overfiring. Many other backup and protective controls and alarms are also provided.

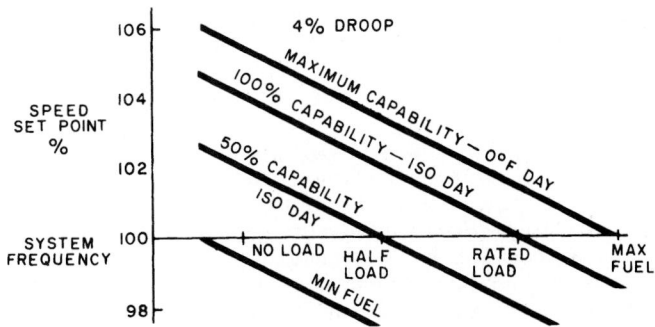

FIGURE 4-14 Typical droop speed control characteristics.

Mechanical-drive gas turbines normally operate on speed/load control with the set point provided by the process control system. Figure 4-15 depicts a typical performance curve for a two-shaft mechanical-drive gas turbine, with the load characteristic of a process compressor system superimposed. A process controller might receive the suction or discharge pressure signal of the driven compressor and generate the appropriate speed/load set point of the gas turbine. Again the fuel flow is still limited by the maximum-firing-temperature control.

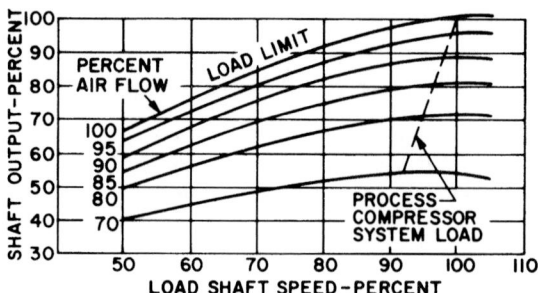

FIGURE 4-15   Two-shaft mechanical drive gas turbine performance curve with a process compressor system load curve.

Gas Turbine Emissions

The gas turbine is one of many types of combustion devices that have been subject to strict environmental codes in recent years. Limits have been placed on the following types of objectionable emissions:

- Oxides of nitrogen, NO_x
- Oxides of sulfur, SO_x
- Particulates
- Unburned hydrocarbons
- Carbon monoxide, CO

The development of combustion systems has progressed to the point where typical gas turbine emissions of particulates, unburned hydrocarbons, and carbon monoxide fall well below the environmental limits. Figure 4-16 shows the reverse-flow cannular combustion system that has been the object of some of the most intensive development programs. Liquid fuels are atomized by high-pressure air as they are injected through the fuel nozzle. This has been very effective in reducing emissions of unburned hydrocarbons and particulates. Most of the compressor discharge air flows through the combustion liner downstream of the reaction zone. This cools the products of combustion and reduces the formation of NO_x. Injection of water or steam into the reaction zone further reduces NO_x formation. In response to continuing reduction of allowable NO_x emissions, water or steam injection is being supplanted by dry low NO_x technology.

There are two sources of NO_x emissions in the exhaust of a gas turbine. Most of the NO_x is generated by the fixation of atmospheric nitrogen in the flame. This is called *thermal NO_x*. NO_x is also generated by the conversion of a fraction of any nitrogen chemically bound in the fuel (called *fuel-bound nitrogen* or FBN). Lower quality distillates and low-Btu coal gases from gasifiers with hot gas cleanup carry varying amounts of bound-nitrogen, which must be taken into account when emissions calculations are made. The methods described below to control thermal emissions are ineffective in controlling the conversion of FBN to NO_x. In fact, these methods result in the conversion of a greater fraction of FBN to NO_x. If fuels with high bound nitrogen levels become common, other control techniques will have to be used.

Thermal NO_x is generally regarded as being generated by a chemical reaction sequence called the *Zeldovich Mechanism*. This set of well-verified chemical reactions postulates that the rate of generation of thermal NO_x is an exponential function of the temperature of the flame. It, therefore, follows that the amount of NO_x generated is a function not only of the temperature but also of the time the hot gas mixture is at flame temperature. It turns out to be a linear function of time. Thus, temperature and residence time determine NO_x emission levels and are the principle variables that a gas turbine designer can alter to control emission levels.

Since flame temperature of a given fuel is a unique function of the equivalence ratio, the rate of NO_x generation in a flame can be cast as a function of the equivalence ratio. This is illustrated

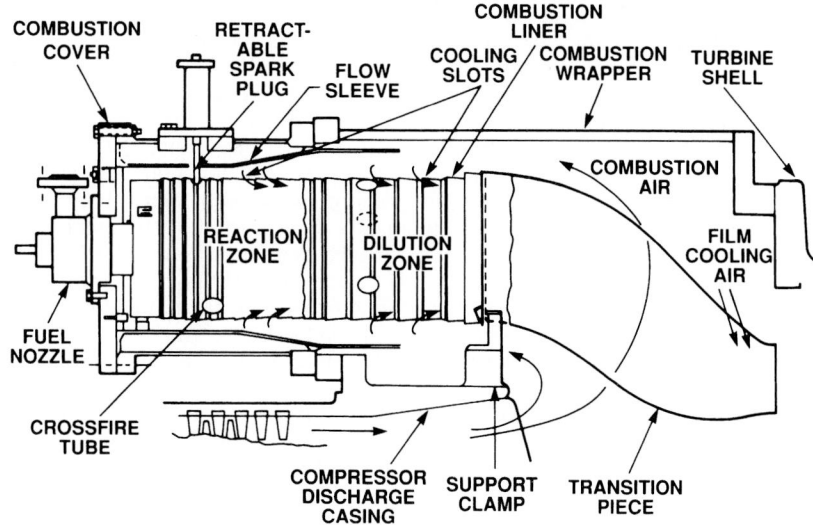

FIGURE 4-16   Reverse-flow combustion system.

in Fig. 4-17, which shows that the highest rate of NO_x production occurs at an equivalence ratio of 1 when the temperature is equal to the stoichiometric, adiabatic flame temperature.

To the left of the maximum temperature point, there is more oxygen available than there is fuel and the flame temperature is lower. This is called *fuel lean operation.* In this case, the equivalence ratio is less than unity.

Since the rate of NO_x formation is a function of temperature and time, it follows that some difference in NO_x emissions can be expected when different fuels are burned in a given combustion system. Since distillate oil and natural gas have approximately a 100°F (37°C) flame

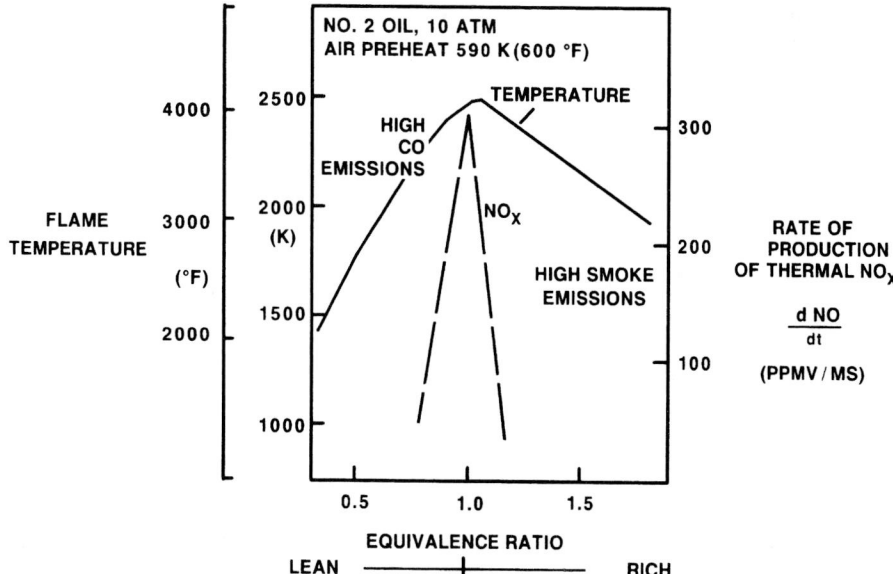

FIGURE 4-17   Rate of NO_x production.

temperature difference, a significant difference in NO_x emissions can be expected, all other things (reaction zone equivalence ratio, water injection rate, etc.) being equal.

As can be seen from Fig. 4-17, the rate of NO_x production falls drastically as temperature decreases (i.e., the flame becomes fuel lean). This is because of the exponential effect of temperature in the Zeldovich Mechanism and is the reason why diluent injection (usually water or steam) into a gas turbine combustor flame zone reduces NO_x emissions. For the same reason, very lean combustors can be used to control emissions. This is desirable for reaching the lower NO_x levels now being required in many applications. There are, however, two design challenges with very lean combustors: First, care must be taken to assure stability at the design operating point; second, it is necessary to have turndown capability, as a gas turbine must ignite, accelerate, and operate over the load range. At lower loads, the flame could be fuel lean and not burn well or it could become unstable and blow out.

In response, designers use staged combustors so that only a portion of the flame zone air is brought into contact with the fuel at lower load or during startup. Staged combustors can be of two basic types: *fuel staged* or *air staged*. In the simplest and most common configuration, a fuel-staged combustor has two flame zones, each receiving a constant fraction of the combustor air flow. Fuel flow is divided between the two zones so that at each machine the amount of fuel fed to a stage is matched to the amount of air available. An air-staged combustor has a mechanism for diverting a fraction of the air flow from the flame zone to the dilution zone at low load to increase turndown. These methods can be combined.

Maintenance

Periodic inspection, repair, and replacement of parts are required to maintain gas turbines. The frequency of maintenance is heavily dependent on the type of fuel, the start-up frequency, and the environment. Although control systems carefully sequence start-up, there is an inherent thermal cycle which reduces parts life if frequently repeated. The parts life of peaking gas turbines that run for 4 h/day is lower than that of continuous-duty units. However, most industrial plants operate for many more than 100 fired hours per start and therefore do not have this problem.

The general environment can also affect the parts life of gas turbines. Many plants are located in areas with corrosive or abrasive matter in the atmosphere. Desert sandstorms, saltwater mist, chemical fumes, and airborne fertilizers are examples. However, the effects of these types of environments can be minimized by multistage high-efficiency inlet-air filters and mist eliminators as well as the presence of correct materials and protective coatings in the compressor and turbine.

The most important factor in gas turbine maintenance is the type of fuel burned. Natural gas is the cleanest fuel and incurs minimum maintenance costs and downtime. It is common for gas turbines in base-load industrial service to operate at full load on maximum-exhaust-temperature control continuously for three years. Not many industrial plants or processes can operate for such long periods, hence gas turbines are generally maintained at shorter intervals during process outages.

Normally, No. 2 distillate oil contains very little contamination, but it does burn with greater radiation, or luminosity, than natural gas. This decreases the life of hot-gas-path parts. The low lubricity of distillate oil decreases the life of parts of fuel forwarding and metering systems as well. Heavy fuel oils, both crude and residual, generally burn with additional radiation and have contaminants which accelerate corrosion and deposition of the hot-gas-path parts. Sodium and potassium must be removed from these fuels to prevent hot corrosion, and vanadium must be inhibited by the use of magnesium additives.

Preventive maintenance practices generally consist of several different types of maintenance procedures:

- Running inspection
- Combustion inspection
- Hot-gas-path inspection
- Major inspection

Running inspections include load vs exhaust temperature measurements, vibration monitoring, and fuel-flow and fuel-pressure measurements. Sophisticated electronic equipment is planned to enhance trend monitoring and on-line diagnostics.

In a combustion inspection the unit is shut down and some disassembly is required to repair or replace combustion parts such as fuel nozzles and liners. Visual or boroscope inspections can also be made of turbine nozzles and buckets during these inspections.

A hot-gas-path inspection includes disassembly of the turbine casing. A major inspection includes a disassembly of the compressor casing as well as the turbine casing. A major inspection essentially returns the gas turbine to its new, or *zero time,* condition. For an MS7000 operating on natural gas or distillate, combustion, hot-gas-path, and major inspections occur at 8, 24, and 48 thousand fired hour intervals, respectively.

Many gas turbine parts are fabricated from expensive superalloys. Minimum maintenance costs can be achieved by repairing these parts during an inspection to extend their life. Spare sets of parts can be used as replacements to minimize downtime. In some critical continuous-process plants, it is more economical to maintain production without outages rather than extend parts life by repairs.

Typical crew sizes and trade skills needed to perform combustion, hot-gas-path, and major inspections on an MS7001E unit are shown in Table 4-3. Furthermore, as an indication of typical maintenance worker-hour requirements which may be used in initial planning phases, Table 4-3 also presents average worker-hours per downtime (calendar) hour for some of the more prevalent types of inspection activity that occur during the life of a gas turbine.

TABLE 4-3 Typical Achieved Crew Size and Skills—Combustion, Hot-Gas-Path, and Major Inspection
Baseload duty (gas fuel) MS7001E gas turbine

	Worker-hours		
Trade skill	Combustion	Hot-gas-path	Major
Millwright	136	2340	4730
Crane Operator	3	68	112
Instr/Elec/NDT Tech	13	36	78
Carpenter	0	48	60
Welder	0	4	12
Pickup/Driver	0	200	300
	152	2696	5292
Elapsed times	$(3 \times 10$ h shifts$)$	17 days $(2 \times 10$ h shift/day$)$	22 days $(2 \times 10$ h shift/day$)$

APPLICATIONS IN PLANTS

General Discussion

There are several different application categories for stationary gas turbines. These include:

- Pipeline pumping stations
- Offshore platforms
- Electric utility stations, including:
  Base-load
  Midrange (1500 to 3000 h/yr)
  Peaking duty
- Industrial plants

Pipeline pumping stations are generally base-loaded around the year, or through all except the summer months. There are many applications of simple-cycle gas turbines in remote areas. There have also been a very small number of combined steam and gas turbine cycles in this category.

Most offshore-platform applications have been simple cycles due to weight and "footprint" constraints, with wide application of aeroderivative units.

In electric utility service, thousands of gas turbines around the world have been applied to serve peak loads (up to 1500 h/yr) in the simple-cycle mode. Because of limited operation, fuel consumption is not as significant a factor as are capital costs, operating labor, and maintenance. Most gas turbines that are applied in midrange or base-load electric utility service combine steam and gas turbine cycles, but a small number also have used regenerative cycles.

Many of the gas turbines applied in electric utility combined-cycle service are supplied as part of a complete package by the gas turbine manufacturer. The manufacturer supplies or specifies all the major equipment, such as heat-recovery steam generators (HRSGs), steam turbines, and plant controls, to optimize plant performance through an integrated approach. Table 4-4 lists typical performance specifications for three versions of combined cycles based on the MS7001E gas turbine.

TABLE 4-4 Typical Performance of a Combined Cycle, Based on 59°F (15°C) Sea-Level Site, with Natural Gas Fuel

Plant designation	Output, kW	Heat rate (LHV), Btu/kWh (kJ/kWh)	Gas turbine configuration
STAG* 107EA	124,100	7055 (7440)	One MS7001EA
STAG* 207EA	249,400	7020 (7410)	Two MS7001EA

* Registered trademark of General Electric Co.

Most gas turbines applied in industrial plants are in base-load service. There are many simple-cycle gas turbines applied throughout the world in industrial plants where fuel supplies are abundant. However, generally all gas turbines applied in industrial plants are equipped with some type of heat recovery to improve overall energy efficiency. Figure 4-18 illustrates some of the ways in which the high-temperature exhaust of gas turbines has been recovered in industrial plants. In Fig. 4-18 the exhaust gases are used to generate low-pressure process steam. The HRSGs can be unfired or have supplementary firing to increase steam output. In Fig. 4-18 higher-pressure steam is generated for a steam turbine. Typical upper limits for steam conditions of unfired HRSGs are 850 psig, 825°F (5964 kPa, 441°C). Fired HRSGs have been applied with steam conditions as high as 1450 psig, 950°F (10,100 kPa, 510°C). In Fig. 4-18 a two-pressure HRSG is shown. When high-pressure turbine inlet steam is generated in an unfired HRSG, typical stack temperatures are a relatively high 400 to 450°F (204 to 232°C). Additional heat can be recovered when a 25- to 150-psig (276- to 1138-kPa) saturated steam generation section is included.

In Fig. 4-18 a regenerative-cycle gas turbine is followed by a low-pressure process steam generator. One of the consequences of the low fuel consumption of the regenerative-cycle gas turbine is a reduction of the regenerator exhaust gas temperature to approximately 600°F (316°C). This arrangement should be selected when only a relatively small amount of process steam is required.

Finally, in Fig. 4-18, the heat in the exhaust gas is used directly in the process or as preheated combustion air for a fired process heater.

In all these cycles the process is known as *cogeneration,* and the fuel utilization effectiveness is improved by recovering heat from the gas turbine exhaust. A parameter used to define the thermal performance of a cogeneration system is *fuel-chargeable-to-power* (FCP). The FCP is the incremental fuel-power ratio for the cogeneration system relative to the case with which it is being compared (usually a non-cogeneration alternative). For a plant generating electric power only (an industrial or a utility), the fuel-chargeable-to-power and net plant heat rate are interchangeable terms. Net plant heat rate in Btu/kWh is the more commonly used term for plants generating electric power only.

The FCP concept is illustrated in Fig. 4-19. Stated in simple terms, the FCP is the total fuel burned in the cogeneration system minus the fuel which would have been required if all

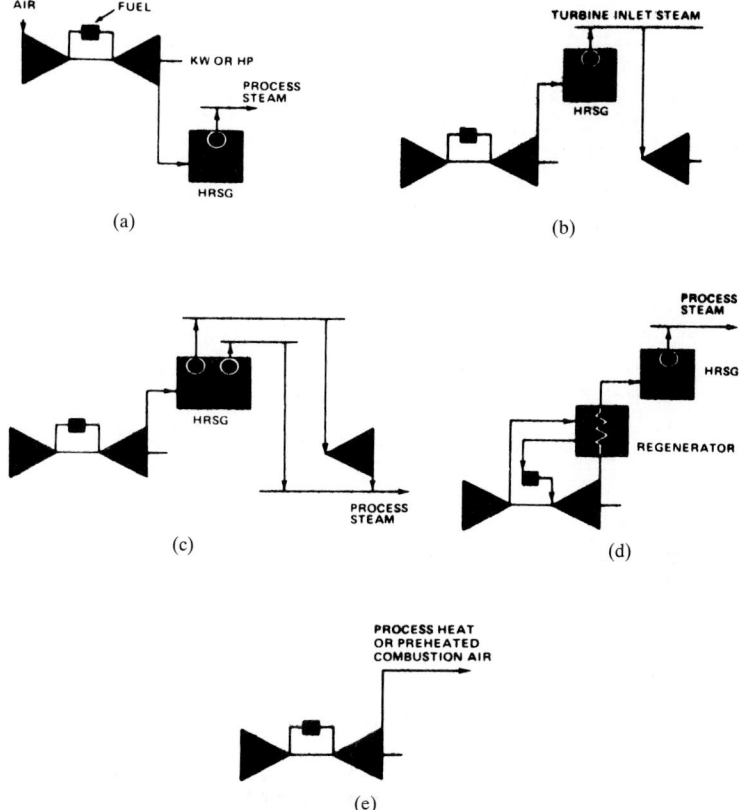

FIGURE 4-18   Industrial gas turbine heat recovery cycles.

power were purchased (process fuel credit) divided by the gross power generated minus the difference in powerhouse auxiliaries.

The heat recovery capability and fuel chargeable-to-power for typical gas turbines is shown in Table 4-5.

Steam turbines are often used in cogeneration systems that produce heat for industrial processes as well as power. A typical application is shown in Fig. 4-20. In this case an auto-

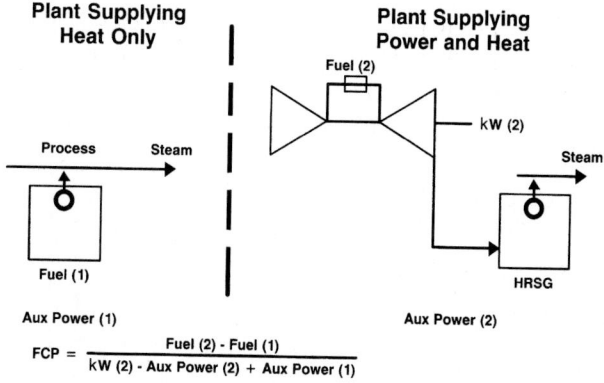

$$FCP = \frac{Fuel\ (2) - Fuel\ (1)}{kW\ (2) - Aux\ Power\ (2) + Aux\ Power\ (1)}$$

FIGURE 4-19   Fuel chargeable to power.

TABLE 4-5 Steam Generation and Fuel Chargeable-to-Power with Gas Turbine and Exhaust Heat Boilers

	Generator drives—natural gas fuel						
Gas turbine type	MS5001 (PA)	MS6001 (B)	MS7001 (EA)	MS7001 (F)	LM2500-PE	LM5000-PC	LM6000-PA
Gas turbine model	PG5371 (PA)	PG6541 (B)	PG7111 (EA)	PG7221 (F)	PGLM2500-PE	PGLM5000-PC	PGLM6000-PA
ISO base rating (kW)	26300	38340	83500	159000	21790	33630	39970
Performance at 59°F, sea level, natural gas fuel output (kW)							
Unfired	25890	38000	82680	156500	21540	33190	39700
Supp fired	25710	37820	82330	155700	21400	32970	39550
Fully fired	25430	37530	81780	154400	21220	32620	39320
Speed (rpm)	5100	5100	3600	3600	3600	3600	3600
Fuel [MBtu/h (HHV)]	344.6	462.3	967.8	1678.1	236.5	355.4	390.0
Exhaust flow (lb/h)	971,400	1,083,000	2,343,000	3,387,000	535,000	950,800	982,300
Exhaust temp. (°F)							
Unfired	906	1007	968	1103	993	823	844
Supp fired	909	1010	990	1106	996	826	846
Fully fired	913	1014	993	1111	1001	830	849
HRSG performance fuel [MBtu/h (HHV)]							
Supp fired	221.5	214.2	475.7	564.5	107.9	242.1	244.4
Fully fired	878.7	904.4	1989.6	2592.3	438.4	845.5	850.0

Steam conditions (psig/°F)	Steam K lb/h	GT Btu/kWh	Steam K lb/h	GT Btu/kWh	Steam K lb/h	GT Btu/kWh	Steam K lb/h	GT Btu/kWh	Steam K lb/h	GT Btu/kWh	Steam K lb/h	GT Btu/kWh	Steam K lb/h	GT Btu/kWh
Unfired														
160/371	143.4	6650	193.2	6060	403.5	5840	704.0	5320	93.4	5770	117.8	6440	127.8	5960
420/655	114.4	7240	159.0	6420	331.5	6200	592.9	5530	76.5	6110	90.9	6950	99.8	6370
630/755	104.4	7560	148.0	6610	307.0	6410	559.2	5630	71.0	6280	81.0	7230	89.5	6610
895/830	96.2	7870	139.4	6800	288.5	6600	533.0	5740	66.8	6440	—	—	—	—
895/830	96.2	6360	139.4	5920	288.5	5680	533.0	5270	66.8	5640	—	—	—	—
160/371	32.3	—	27.6	—	63.0	—	61.4	—	14.3	—	—	—	—	—
1315/905	—	—	130.8	5920	269.5	5680	510.0	5270	—	—	—	—	—	—
160/371	—	—	34.3	—	78.7	—	74.9	—	—	—	—	—	—	—
1525/955	—	—	125.8	5920	258.5	5870	495.0	5270	—	—	—	—	—	—
160/371	—	—	37.8	—	86.9	—	82.0	—	—	—	—	—	—	—
Supp fired														
420/655	301.0	5960	338.0	5630	730.0	5380	1059.0	5080	167.2	5380	297.5	5750	307.5	5380
630/755	289.5	5980	324.5	5670	701.0	5410	1017.0	5100	160.6	5410	285.5	5790	295.5	5400
895/830	281.0	6030	315.0	5710	681.0	5440	988.0	5130	156.8	5380	277.5	5810	287.0	5430
1315/905	273.5	6100	306.5	5770	663.0	5490	962.0	5170	151.8	5490	270.0	5870	279.5	5470
1525/955	269.0	6080	301.5	5740	652.0	5470	946.0	5150	149.4	5460	265.5	5860	274.5	5470
Fully fired														
630/755	777.0	4610	836.0	4710	1826.0	4390	2526.0	4370	406.5	4540	734.0	4780	745.0	4570
895/830	757.0	4610	815.0	4690	1779.0	4390	2460.0	4380	396.0	4540	715.0	4790	726.0	4560
1315/905	740.0	4610	796.0	4710	1739.0	4390	2405.0	4380	387.0	4550	699.0	4780	710.0	4550
1525/955	726.0	4650	782.0	4700	1708.0	4380	2362.0	4380	380.0	4550	686.0	4800	697.0	4560

* Gas turbines and boilers fueled with natural gas and all fuel data based on higher heating value (HHV).
Unfired single-pressure boilers 92% effectiveness for SH and evaporator; supplementary fired to 1600°F, 86.8% to 90.5% effectiveness; fully fired to 10% excess air with 300°F stack temperature.
For two-pressure boilers, criterion of minimum 300°F stack temperature may require less than 92% low-pressure boiler effectiveness.
Assumes 0% exhaust bypass stack damper leakage, 3% blowdown, 1½% radiation and unaccounted losses, and 228°F feedwater for all cases.
Standard gas turbine inlet losses; exhaust 10° H_2O for unfired, 14° H_2O for supplementary fired, and 20° H_2O for fully fired.
LM2500, LM5000, and LM6000 values based on guarantee, not average engine performance.
Fuel chargeable to gas turbine power assumes GT credit with PH auxiliaries and equivalent 84% boiler fuel required to generate steam.
Lower heating value (LHV)—21515 Btu/lb; HHV = LHV × 1.11.

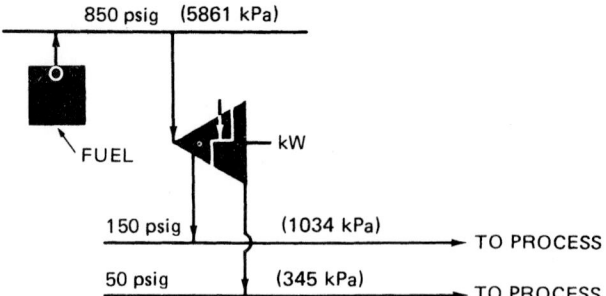

FIGURE 4-20   Typical noncondensing steam turbine application.

matic-extraction noncondensing unit supplies steam at two different pressure levels to the process. A typical value of fuel chargeable to power for noncondensing steam turbine cycles is 4200 Btu/kWh (4431 kJ/kWh) HHV. This is an equivalent thermal efficiency of 80 percent, which is far higher than that of most other types of prime movers. The high efficiency of the noncondensing steam turbine cycle is due to the fact that heat losses to the surroundings are minimized. The only losses are the boiler inefficiency (stack losses), generator, seals, bearing friction, radiation, and additional auxiliary power requirements.

One method of displaying the many options available by using a gas turbine in a cogeneration application is shown in Fig. 4-21. This diagram has been developed for the GE MS7001EA gas turbine-generator.

Point A represents the MS7001EA gas turbine-generator exhausting into an unfired low-pressure HRSG. Point C is a combined-cycle configuration based on use of a two-pressure-level unfired HRSG. The steam turbine in the C cycle is a noncondensing unit expanding the HP HRSG steam to the 150 psig (1034 kPa) process steam header.

Points B and D in Fig. 4-21 represent operation of the HRSG with supplementary firing to a 1600°F (878°C) average exhaust gas temperature entering the heat transfer surface. The temperature used for the HRSG firing in Fig. 4-21 has been arbitrarily limited to 1600°F (878°C) even though higher firing temperatures (and thus steam production rates) are possible in the exhaust of this unit.

The envelope defined by A, B, C, and D in Fig. 4-21 represents the most thermally optimized use of a gas turbine in a cogeneration application (i.e., provides the lowest FCP). Oper-

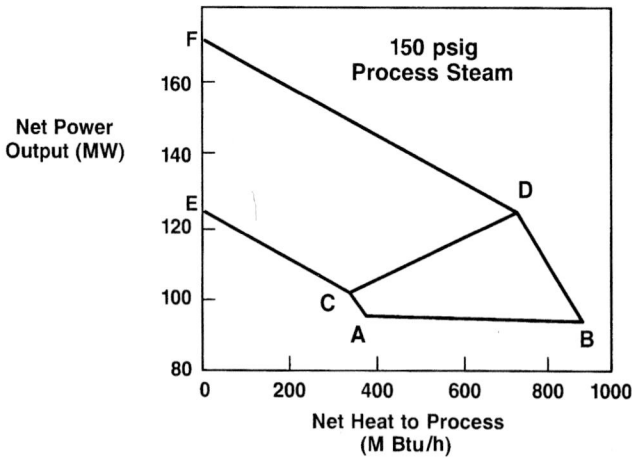

FIGURE 4-21   Performance envelope for gas turbine cogeneration system.

ation along the line CE, DF, or any intermediate point to the left of line CD represents the use of condensing steam turbine power generation with the E and F points applicable for combined-cycle operation without any heat supplied to process. Thus, the cycles along line EF are combined cycles providing power alone.

Performance envelopes for many of the gas turbines included in Table 4-5 are presented in Figs. 4-22 and 4-23. These data are on the same basis as Fig. 4-21 except for point C. Point C for all units except the various MS7001 models is based on 850 psig (5464 kPa), 825°F (441°C) initial steam temperature to the noncondensing steam turbine. Furthermore, the only condensing power illustrated is based on unfired, two-pressure-level HRSG designs.

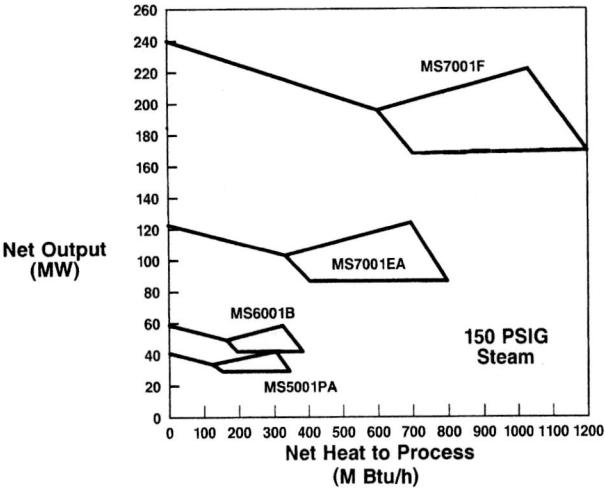

FIGURE 4-22   Gas turbine cogeneration systems MS options, 60 Hz.

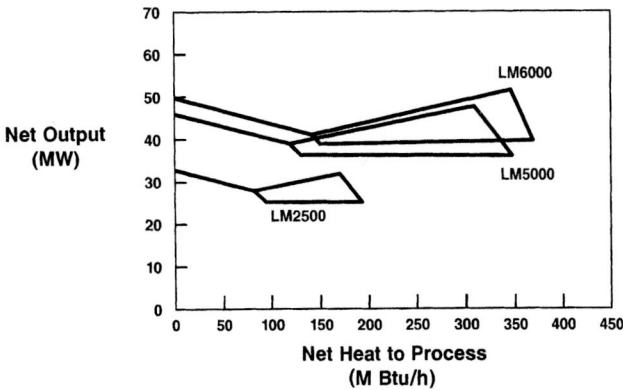

FIGURE 4-23   Gas turbine cogeneration systems LM options, 60 Hz.

ACKNOWLEDGMENT

The author acknowledges the support and contribution provided by the Engineering Staff of GE's Power Generation Business.

BIBLIOGRAPHY

1. "Performance Specifications 1980," *Gas Turbine World*, December 1979.

2. In *Power Engineering,* a series of seven articles:

    (a) Carlstrom, L. A., H. F. Heissenbuttel, and A. H. Perugi: "Gas Turbine Combustion System: Key to Improved Availability," May 1978.

    (b) Patterson, J. R., and C. M. Grant "Operating Gas Turbines for Extended Component Life," June 1978.

    (c) DuBois, M. R., and R. J. Fresneda: "Inspection and Maintenance of Gas Turbine Nozzles, Buckets and Rotors," July 1978.

    (d) Scheper, G. W., A. J. Mayoral, and E. J. Hipp: "Maintaining Gas Turbine Compressors for High Efficiency," August 1978.

    (e) Bingham, P. J., P. H. Huhtanen, and H. G. Starnes: "Maintenance of Gas Turbine Accessory Equipment," Sept. 1978.

    (f) Kiernan, J. G., A. D. Foster, and D. T. Harden: "Gas Turbine Fuels and Fuel Systems," October 1978.

    (g) Stretch, R. H., J. N. Shinn, and D. B. Brudos: "Calibration and Troubleshooting of Gas Turbine Control," November 1978.

3. Doherty, M. C., and D. R. Wright: "Application of Aircraft Derivative and Heavy Duty Gas Turbines in the Process Industries," ASME Paper 79-GT-12, *ASME Gas Turbine Conference,* San Diego, CA, March 1979.

4. Hilt, M. B., and R. H. Johnson: "Nitric Oxide Abatement in Heavy-Duty Gas Turbine Combustors by Means of Aerodynamics and Water Injection," ASME Paper No. 72-GT-53, March 1972.

5. Hilt, M. B., and J. Waslo: "Evolution of NO_x Abatement Techniques Through Combustor Design for Heavy-Duty Gas Turbines," *Journal of Engineering for Gas Turbines and Power,* Vol. 106, October 1984, pp 825–83.

6. Dibelius, N. R., M. B. Hilt, and R. H. Johnson: "Reduction of Nitrogen Oxides from Gas Turbines by Steam Injection," ASME Paper No. 71-GT-58, December 1970.

7. Miller, H. E.: "Development of the Quiet Combustor and Other Design Changes to Benefit Air Quality," American Cogeneration Association, San Francisco, March 1988.

8. Cutrone, M. B., M. B. Hilt, A. Goyal, E. E. Ekstedt, and J. Notardonato: "Evaluation of Advanced Combustor for Dry NO_x Suppression with Nitrogen Bearing Fuels in Utility and Industrial Gas Turbines," ASME Paper 81-GT-125, March 1981.

9. Zeldovich, J.: "The Oxidation of Nitrogen in Combustion and Explosions," *Acta Physicochimica USSR,* Vol. 21, No. 4, 1946, pp 577–628.

10. Washam, R. M.: "Dry Low NO_x Combustion System for Utility Gas Turbine," ASME Paper No. 83-JPGC-GT-13, September 1983.

11. Davis, L. B., and R. M. Washam: "Development of a Dry Low NO_x Combustor," ASME Paper No. 89-GT-255, June 1989.

12. Wilson, D. G.: *The Design of High Efficiency Turbomachinery and Gas Turbines,* M.I.T. Press, 1988.

13. Brandt, D. E.: "Gas Turbine Design Philosophy," 1991 Turbine State of the Art Conference: GER-3434A: Asheville, NC: August, 1991.

14. Fogg, H. E.: "Aeroderivative Gas Turbines," 1991 Turbine State of the Art Conference, GER-3695, Asheville, NC, August 1991.

15. Hopkins, J. E.: "Gas Turbine Performance Characteristics," 1991 Turbine State of the Art Conference, GER-3567B, Asheville, NC, August 1991.

16. Walsh, E. J., and M. A. Freeman: "Gas Turbine Operation and Maintenance Considerations," 1991 Turbine State of the Art Conference, GER-3620A: Asheville, NC, August 1991.

17. Kovacik, J. M.: "Cogeneration Application Considerations," 1991 Turbine State of the Art Conference, GER-3430B, Asheville, NC, August 1991.

18. Davis, L. B.: "Low NO_x Combustion for Gas Turbines," 1991 Turbine State of the Art Conference, GER-3568B, Asheville, NC, August 1991.

CHAPTER 4-4
STATIONARY TURBINES

PART 2
STEAM TURBINES

Clemens M. Thoennes
Sales Programs Development
General Electric Company
Schenectady, New York

GLOSSARY

Automatic-admission turbine A steam turbine with the capacity to admit steam at two or more pressures. Valve gear at the low-pressure opening can automatically control the pressure in that header by internally varying the downstream turbine flow-passing capability.

Automatic-extraction turbine A steam turbine with the capacity to extract steam. The pressure of the extracted steam is controlled by a valve gear at that opening, as with an automatic-admission turbine. *Note:* Steam turbines can be furnished with automatic extraction and admission capability at the same opening.

Available energy The difference in enthalpy between an inlet steam condition (a specific pressure and temperature) and an exhaust pressure along a path of constant entropy.

Back-pressure turbine A steam turbine that exhausts at a pressure equal to or greater than atmospheric pressure. It is also referred to as a *noncondensing* turbine.

Bottoming cycle An energy recovery cycle that uses waste heat from another source to generate power. A steam turbine bottoming cycle uses steam generated by a waste-heat exhaust stream.

Bucket   A blade located on the rotor of a steam turbine which transfers energy from the steam to the rotating shaft.

By-product power   Power generated coincidentally when supplying useful heat. (See also "Noncondensing power" and "Cogeneration.")

Cogeneration   The simultaneous production of power and other forms of useful energy—such as heat or process steam. U.S. government agencies restrict the definition of cogeneration to electric power generation only, while various industrial associations extend it to include mechanical-drive power.

Feedwater heater   A steam-to-water heat exchanger that heats the boiler feedwater, generally with steam extracted from a steam turbine. In a closed feedwater heater the two fluids are separated by the use of shell and tube construction. In an open feedwater heater the fluids are mixed. A *deaerator* is an open feedwater heater that separates entrained gases from the feedwater by vigorous agitation with steam.

Fuel chargeable to power (FCP)   See Part 1 of this Chapter.

Impulse design   A stage design approach characterized by a large pressure drop occurring in the nozzles and relatively little pressure drop across the buckets.

Mechanical-drive steam turbine   A turbine used to drive devices other than electric generators, such as pumps or compressors. It is generally designed to operate over a wide speed range.

Mollier diagram   A plot of enthalpy vs. entropy of a fluid, which includes lines of constant pressure and temperature.

Noncondensing power   Power generated by steam that is expanded through a turbine and either exhausts or extracts at a pressure equal to or greater than atmospheric pressure.

Nozzle   Stationary blade in steam path generally utilized to turn, accelerate, and direct steam flow for efficient energy transfer to the rotating blades, or *buckets*.

Pressure control   The ability of steam turbine governor systems to maintain constant pressure in a steam line by the action of a valve gear, as the turbine supplies steam to the header or draws steam from it.

Pressure rise point   In an automatic-extraction steam turbine the maximum exhaust flow with zero extraction flow.

Reaction design   A stage design approach characterized by an approximately equal pressure drop in the nozzle and associated bucket.

Steam rate   The mass flow rate of steam required to produce a unit of output, in pounds per kilowatthour (kilograms per kilowatthour) or pounds per horsepower hour. The *theoretical steam rate* (TSR) assumes a perfect expansion process between two conditions. An *actual steam rate* is based on the actual expansion, including the inefficiency of the turbine and generator.

Uncontrolled extraction   An opening in a steam turbine casing between two stages. The pressure of the extraction steam available is uncontrolled and is a function of the steam flow to the following stage.

TYPES OF TURBINES

There are many different types of steam turbines in industrial-plant service. These can be broadly classified as either *condensing* or *noncondensing*. Condensing steam turbines have a subatmospheric exhaust pressure, while noncondensing units exhaust at atmospheric or higher pressure. When steam is expanded to subatmospheric pressure in a condensing steam turbine, its temperature is generally reduced to less than 130°F (54°C). This low-temperature energy is usually not useful and is generally classified as waste heat. On the other hand, steam exhausted from noncondensing steam turbines is much higher in temperature and pressure and is useful in many industrial processes or heating applications.

Figure 4-24 shows schematic diagrams of three different configurations of noncondensing steam turbines. All three exhaust into a low-pressure header. The single automatic-extraction noncondensing (SAXNC) unit also extracts steam at another higher-pressure header. The double automatic-extraction noncondensing (DAXNC) unit extracts steam at two additional pressure levels. The term *automatic extraction* implies that the steam flow is automatically controlled (governed) internally to maintain constant pressure in the header independent of the extraction flow. Figure 4-25 is a cross-sectional view of a typical single automatic-extraction noncondensing steam turbine. The high-pressure section consists of the turbine inlet valve gear, a high-pressure turbine control stage, five additional turbine stages, and the extraction opening. The exhaust section includes the extraction valve gear, three additional turbine stages, and the exhaust opening. The turbine governor operates both sets of valve gears in concert to control the pressure in the extraction steam line and one other variable,

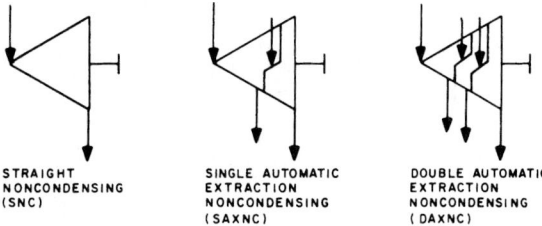

STRAIGHT
NONCONDENSING
(SNC)

SINGLE AUTOMATIC
EXTRACTION
NONCONDENSING
(SAXNC)

DOUBLE AUTOMATIC
EXTRACTION
NONCONDENSING
(DAXNC)

FIGURE 4-24 Schematic diagram of types of noncondensing steam turbines.

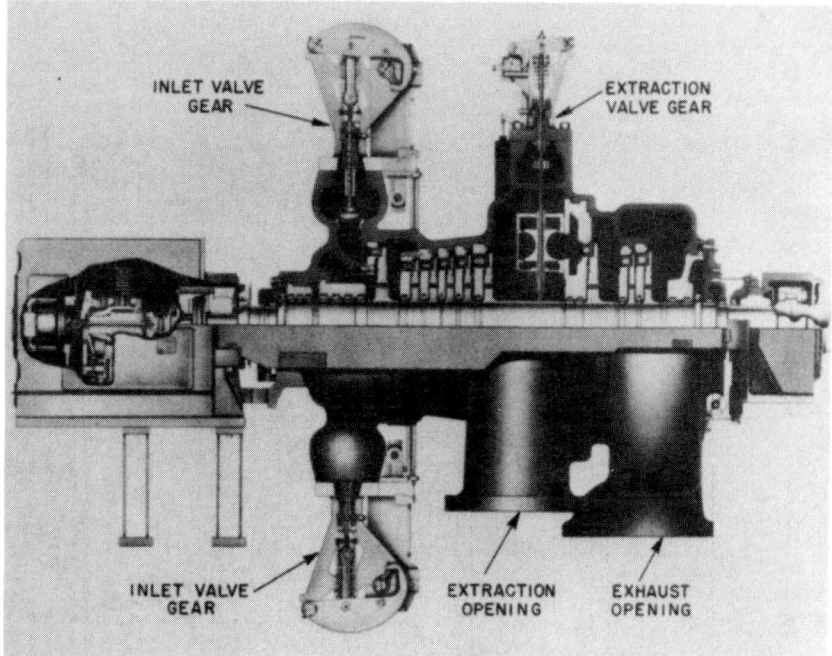

FIGURE 4-25 Cross-sectional view of a single automatic-extraction noncondensing steam turbine. (*General Electric Co.*)

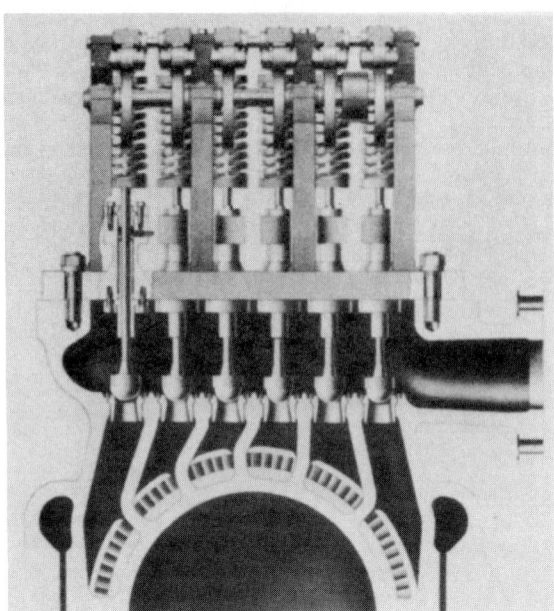

FIGURE 4-26   Axial cross-sectional view of a steam turbine inlet valve gear. (*General Electric Co.*)

FIGURE 4-27   Axial cross-sectional view of a spool-type extraction valve. (*General Electric Co.*)

such as exhaust pressure or the power output. Figure 4-26 is an axial cross-sectional view of the upper-inlet valve gear. It consists of six poppets which are individually operated through cam action lifts. This arrangement minimizes throttling losses for high-efficiency operation over a wide range of steam flow. Units can be furnished with the upper-inlet gear only or an upper- and lower-inlet valve gear for increased flow capacity. Figure 4-27 is an axial cross-sectional view of a spool-type extraction. It is a variable restriction which is mounted downstream of the extraction opening. Notice that it is the steam flow to the exhaust, and not the extracted steam, which actually passes through the extraction valve.

Condensing steam turbines in industrial plants can also include automatic-extraction capability. Figure 4-28 is a schematic illustration of condensing steam turbine types; straight condensing, single automatic-extraction condensing (SAXC), and double automatic-extraction condensing (DAXC). A cross-sectional view of a typical DAXC steam turbine is shown in Fig. 4-29. Notice the relatively large exhaust casing required to pass the low-density subatmospheric exhaust steam flow. A DAXC steam turbine has the capability to control two extraction-pressure levels and also independently control the amount of power produced by varying steam flow to the condensing exhaust.

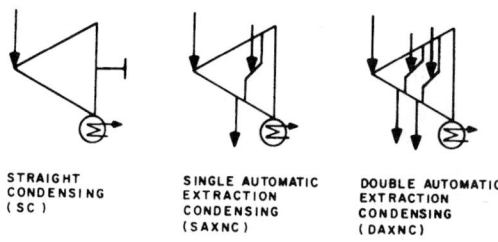

STRAIGHT
CONDENSING
(SC)

SINGLE AUTOMATIC
EXTRACTION
CONDENSING
(SAXNC)

DOUBLE AUTOMATIC
EXTRACTION
CONDENSING
(DAXNC)

FIGURE 4-28 Schematic diagram of types of condensing steam turbines.

FIGURE 4-29 Cross-sectional view of a double automatic-extraction condensing steam turbine. (*General Electric Co.*)

Automatic admission capability is another feature that can be specified for industrial steam turbines. Some industrial plants have an excess of low-pressure steam which can be admitted through an extraction/admission opening and then expanded through the low-pressure section. In some cases, the turbines extract steam during normal operation and only admit steam during process upsets or outages.

The control stage and additional stages between each of the turbine pressure levels constitute a turbine section. For example, on a DAXC or DAXNC unit, there are three such sections, referred to as HP, IP and LP for high, intermediate, and low pressure. Each section is designed to pass a specified maximum flow. Turbine section efficiency falls off as the actual section flow (as a fraction of design flow) is reduced. The proper sizing of each turbine section is a key part of turbine design optimization and should take into account the expected duration of operation at different flows. Large, but infrequent or upset condition flows are often handled better by the use of external pressure-reducing stations to bypass one or more turbine sections.

Steam turbines can also be furnished with uncontrolled extraction openings. However, the pressure at an uncontrolled extraction varies with steam flow. The variation from normal conditions in absolute pressure is approximately proportional to the variation in flow through the following stage. Therefore, uncontrolled extractions are not generally suitable to supply process steam headers. On the other hand, uncontrolled extractions are suitable to provide feedwater heating in many cases. When steam is extracted from a turbine to heat only the feedwater for that turbine, then the requirements for extraction steam will also be proportional to steam flow. Large steam turbines in central stations can have as many as six uncontrolled extractions to supply different stages of feedwater heaters.

The steam turbines illustrated in Figs. 4-25 to 4-29 are of multivalve, multistage construction. Smaller steam turbines are available with a single throttling valve on the inlet and with one (or more) turbine stage(s). These units are classified as single-valve/multistage or single-valve/single-stage. This type of construction reduces the initial cost of the steam turbine, but at a penalty in efficiency, which can be less than half that of the multistage/multivalve type. Single-valve/single-stage units are generally applied in small (fewer than 1000 hp [746 W]), mechanical-drive service.

TURBINE DESIGN CHARACTERISTICS

Turbine Stage Design and Construction

Steam turbine stage designs are generally either of an *impulse* or *reaction* type.

In the impulse design, most of the stage pressure drop occurs in the stationary nozzles, with relatively little pressure drop in the buckets (or moving blades). Because there is little pressure drop across the buckets, it is possible to mount them on the periphery of a wheel without generating a large axial thrust on the rotor. This *wheel and diaphragm* construction, typical of the impulse design, is shown in Fig. 4-30.

In the reaction design, approximately equal pressure drop occurs in the nozzles and buckets. To reduce the associated axial thrust on the rotor, a *drum* construction is used with the reaction design, as shown in Fig. 4-31. Even with a drum rotor, it is usually necessary to build a *balance piston* into the rotor to balance the stage thrust, unless the turbine section is double-flowed.

Peak efficiency is obtained in an impulse stage with more work per stage than in a reaction stage for a given stage diameter. It is normal, therefore, for an impulse turbine section to require either fewer stages on the same diameter or the same number of stages on a smaller diameter.

With less pressure drop across the bucket, the bucket tip leakage of an impulse design is much less than that of a reaction design. There is more pressure drop across the diaphragm of an impulse design than that of a reaction design; however, the leakage diameter is considerably less. In addition, there is sufficient room in the inner web of the diaphragm to mount spring-backed packings with a generous amount of radial movement and a large number of labyrinth packing teeth. In total, then, the shaft leakage around the nozzles is lower for an

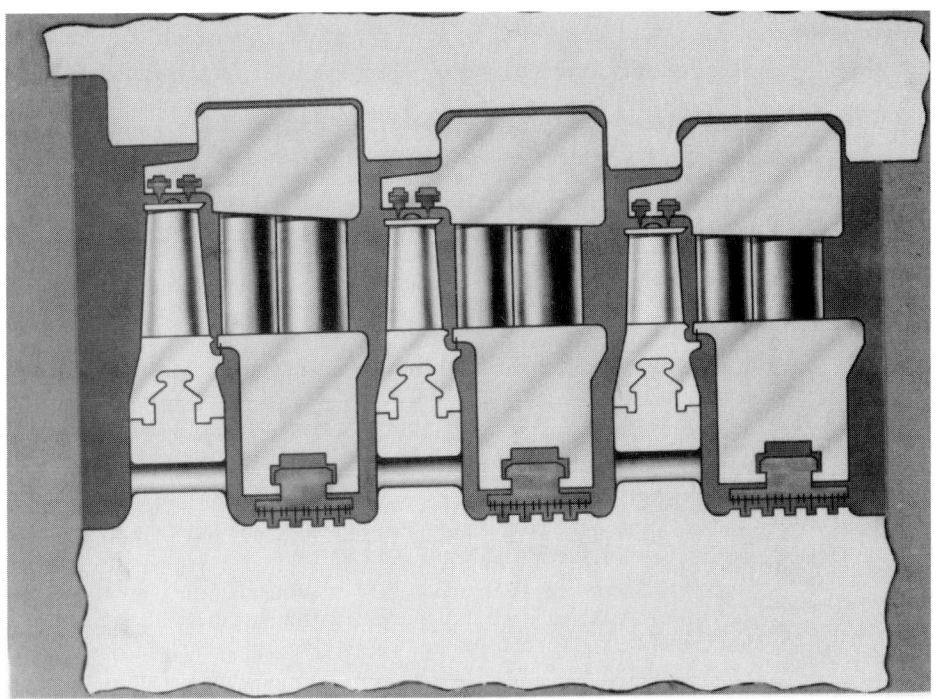

FIGURE 4-30   Typical impulse stages, wheel and diaphragm construction.

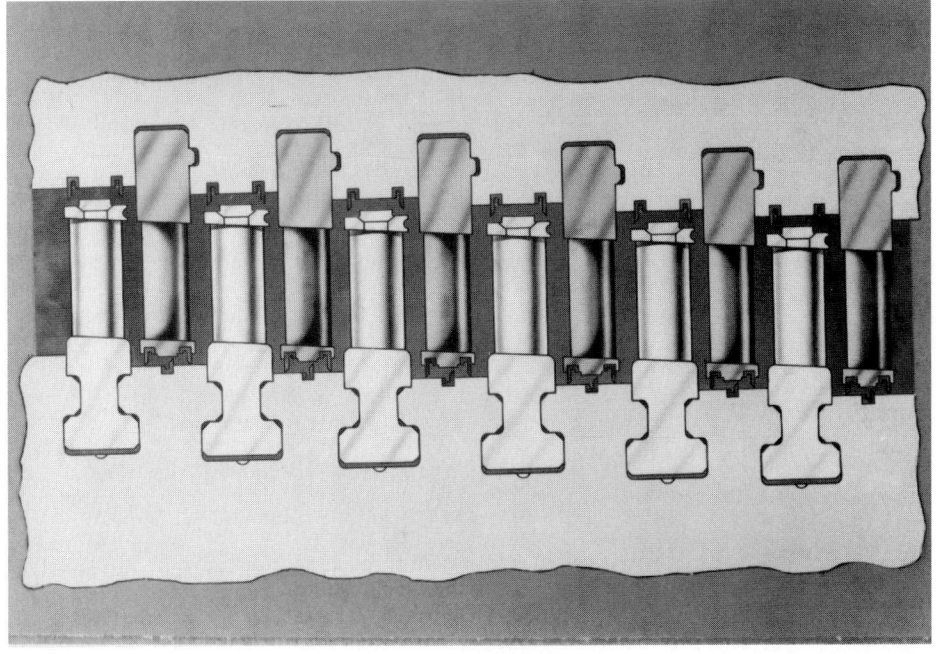

FIGURE 4-31   Typical reaction stages, drum rotor construction.

impulse stage than for a reaction stage. With the impulse stage, this leakage is diverted through wheel holes. However, with the reaction stage, this leakage re-enters the steam path between the nozzles and buckets, resulting in an additional loss, due to the disturbance of the main steam flow.

Leakage flows in a turbine stage can easily be calculated and the results show that for stages typical of today's industrial steam turbines tip leakage flows are 2 to 4 times greater for a reaction design than for an impulse design, and shaft packing flows are 1.2 to 2.4 times greater for a reaction design. The importance of these leakages becomes greater with the smaller volume flows typical of industrial applications.

In addition to lower leakage flows, the impulse wheel-and-diaphragm construction has significant advantages in the areas of thermal stress and, therefore, low-cycle fatigue resistance. Specific characteristics impacting these areas include:

- Rotor body diameters are small, thereby significantly reducing thermal stress.
- Bucket dovetails are located on the wheel peripheries away from the rotor surface, separating centrifugal from rotor thermal stress.
- Fewer stages and smaller stage diameters permit more compact designs with smaller components, especially shells.
- Wheel shapes on the periphery of the rotor act as fins and improve heat transfer to the interior of the rotor, thereby reducing thermal stress.
- Centerline-supported diaphragms allow movement of the diaphragms with respect to the shell without rubbing; if the stationary blading is held in a blade carrier (as in reaction/drum designs), thermal distortion of the blade carrier can cause rubbing.
- Ample room between wheels permits the use of large wheel fillets to minimize thermal stress.

Thermodynamic Considerations

The properties of steam are well documented in steam tables.[1] These tables, or associated numerical formulations, are useful in the calculation of detailed steam turbine cycle performance. A familiar graphical representation of steam properties is the *Mollier diagram,* which is a plot of enthalpy (h) versus entropy (s). An ideal turbine expansion is represented by a vertical path on the Mollier diagram.

Several terms and concepts are commonly used in the discussion of actual steam turbine thermodynamic performance characteristics.

Available Energy.   The available energy is the difference in enthalpy between an initial thermodynamic state (pressure, temperature) and a final thermodynamic state at a lower pressure and at constant entropy, associated with an ideal turbine expansion.

Theoretical Steam Rate.   The theoretical steam rate is the ratio between mass flow and work output for an ideal turbine expansion, in lb/kWh or kg/kWh. The work output is the product of the mass flow and the available energy. Therefore,

$$\text{TSR (lb/kWh)} = 3412.14 \ (\text{Btu/kWh})/\text{AE (Btu/lb)}$$

$$\text{TSR (kg/kWh)} = 3600.00 \ (\text{kJ/kWh})/\text{AE (kJ/kg)}$$

The performance of actual steam turbines includes several different types of losses and irreversibilities. The efficiency of a steam turbine-generator (TG) is defined as the output at the generator terminals divided by the available energy. Typical industrial steam turbine efficiencies are 70 to 80 percent. The *actual steam rate (ASR)* is defined as the TSR divided by the turbine-generator efficiency.

Example. Consider a turbine operating with inlet steam conditions of 1250 psig, 900°F (8720 kPa, 482°C). For an isentropic expansion to 4.0 in HgA (inches of mercury absolute) (13.55 kPa), the available energy determined from the steam tables is:

$$AE = 521 \text{ Btu/lb (1212 kJ/kg)}$$

The theoretical steam rate is:

$$TSR = 3412.14/521 = 6.541 \text{ lb/kWh}$$

$$= 3600.00/1212 = 2.97 \text{ kg/kWh}$$

For a steam turbine efficiency of 0.75, the actual steam rate would be:

$$ASR = 6.541/0.75 = 8.72 \text{ lb/kWh}$$

$$= 2.97/0.75 = 3.96 \text{ kg/kWh}$$

The actual steam rate can be used to determine the required steam flow to produce a given output. To produce 20,000 kW, the required steam flow would be:

$$\text{Steam flow} = ASR \times \text{output} = 8.72 \times 20,000 = 174,400 \text{ lb/h}$$

$$= 3.96 \times 20,000 = 79,200 \text{ kg/h}$$

When steam turbines exhaust or extract into a process header, the value of enthalpy at that point is also of interest. In order to determine exhaust or extraction enthalpy, actual steam rates or turbine efficiencies are commonly defined for the various sections of the turbine.

Performance characteristics of industrial steam turbine-generators are generally plotted as curves relating throttle (and extraction) flows to generator output. Figure 4-32 shows a typical performance curve of a straight condensing or noncondensing steam turbine. The plot of throttle flow versus generator output approximates a straight line. The plot is known as the *Willans line.* The intercept of this line at zero load represents the steam flow required to supply the no-load losses of the set.

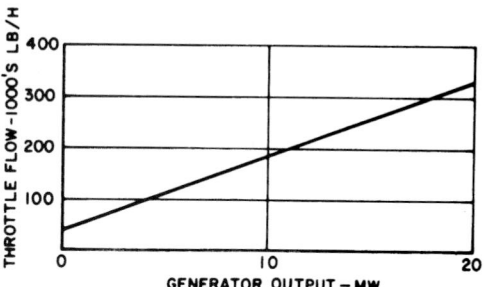

FIGURE 4-32 Performance curve of a straight condensing or straight noncondensing steam turbine.

The performance curve of a typical single automatic-extraction turbine is shown in Fig. 4-33. The zero extraction line is similar to the performance of a straight condensing or noncondensing unit. The family of parallel lines indicates the performance for various values of extraction flow. A certain minimum amount of flow is required at the exhaust end to cool the turbine buckets. This limit is indicated on the left-hand side of the plot. Also, the geometry of

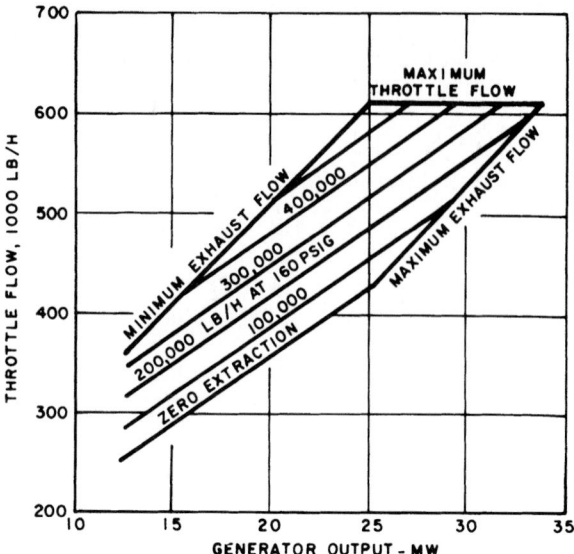

FIGURE 4-33 Performance curve of a single automatic-extraction steam turbine.

the section will limit it to a maximum flow capability, which is shown on the right-hand side. The intercept of the maximum exhaust flow line and the zero extraction line is called the *pressure rise* point. Additional flow can be put through the exhaust end, but only if the pressure ahead of the extraction valve gear increases. This also causes an increase in the extraction pressure. This is not a normal mode of operation.

Performance of Mechanical-Drive Steam Turbines

Steam turbines are also selected as drivers for pumps and compressors that generally require variable speed. Process compressors as large as 60,000 hp (44,800 kW) are in service with variable-speed steam turbine drives. Special robust buckets are required for these turbines to withstand the vibratory stresses inherent with continuous operation over a wide speed range. In other respects, large multistage/multivalve mechanical-drive steam turbines are similar to corresponding turbine-generator sets.

Single-valve/single-stage mechanical-drive steam turbines are very common in small sizes [less than 1000 hp (746 kW)] in industrial plants. This type of construction has a low cost, but efficiency drops to a range of 40 to 50 percent. These small units are often used in parallel or as a backup to motor drives to provide added reliability against a loss of either electric power or steam supply. Small mechanical-drive steam turbines also can be selected as drives for hazardous locations. However, the low efficiency of these types of turbines is an increasingly important disadvantage with high energy costs.

Control Systems

The philosophy applied to steam turbine control systems has developed over time, and is summarized in Table 4-6.

TABLE 4-6 Steam Turbine Control Philosophy

---

1. Clear separation between control and protection shall be provided.
2. Controls use two out of three (3) redundancy from sensor to actuator for all vital and important functions.
3. A single failure in the controls will not cause a shutdown. It will cause a diagnostic alarm, and it is repairable on-line.
4. Controls comply with IEEE 122 std. (e.g., can reject rated load without causing a turbine trip).
5. A protection system backup is provided for all control functions.
6. A double set of steam valves is provided for all major admissions. One set for controls and one set for protection.
7. Protection (trips) are classified according to criticality: vital have conceptual redundancy.

The main functions of a modern steam turbine control system are:

- Speed and acceleration control during start-up
- Initialization of generator excitation
- Synchronization and application of load in response to local or area generation dispatch commands
- Pressure control of various forms: inlet, extraction, back pressure, etc.
- Unloading and securing of the turbine
- Sequencing of the above functions under constraint of thermal stress
- Overspeed protection during load rejection and emergencies
- Protection against serious hazards, e.g., loss of lubrication oil pressure, high exhaust temperature, high bearing vibration
- Testing of steam valves and other important protective functions

Additional control and monitoring functions are also required in most applications, such as:

- Monitoring and supervision of a large number of pressures, temperatures, etc., to provide guidance and alarms for operators
- Start-up and monitoring of turbine-generator auxiliaries such as lubrication oil, hydraulic, and steam seal systems
- Display, alarm, and recording of the above functions and data
- Diagnosis of turbine or generator problems
- Health check and diagnostics of the electronic system itself

The first group of functions must be performed with high control bandwidth or very high reliability, or both, to ensure long-term reliable operation and service of the turbine. It is for these reasons that turbine controls and protection are closely coupled with the turbine detailed design. The first group of functions, together with the input and output (I/O) devices required, are included in the turbine unit control system, which is an integral part of the steam turbine hardware.

Steam turbine unit control systems have many capabilities to control steam pressures. The most common feature is steam pressure control of straight noncondensing or automatic-extraction noncondensing units. The synchronized generator is "locked into" the grid frequency, and the turbine inlet and extraction control valves maintain flow through the sections of the turbine in response to extraction and exhaust steam pressure signals. This type of system follows heat demands. The electricity that is generated in this manner is called *by-product power.*

When automatic-extraction steam turbines have a condensing exhaust, the control system can control pressure as well as power generation by varying flow to the condenser. The amount of power called for by the steam turbine unit control system can be continuously modulated by the plant control system.

Another control mode is initial pressure control. When a steam turbine is supplied by a heat recovery boiler or a by-product fuel boiler, the amount of steam generated can vary independently. Initial pressure control allows the steam turbine to draw all the available steam out of the header while maintaining constant pressure.

A characteristic of the unit control system is that all essential turbine control and protection functions are included to allow a unit to operate safely even if other supporting systems should fail. Another characteristic is that the control point interface (i.e., the interface between the turbine and the control system) remains in the turbine supplier's scope, while interface to plant controls can be made at data point level, which does not include critical and rapidly varying commands and feedback signals and, therefore, is a more suitable point of interface to plant controls. Yet another characteristic of unit control functions is that they must be performed either continuously or very frequently to provide satisfactory control.

The second group of functions can be performed less frequently (i.e., every few seconds or more), and turbine operation may be continued in most cases during short-term interruptions in the monitoring functions as long as the unit control is performing correctly.

The second group of functions is called TGM, for turbine generator monitoring. The TGM functions can be included in the unit control system or in the plant control system.

OPERATION AND MAINTENANCE

Starting Procedures

Before a steam turbine-generator can be started, proper operation of a number of auxiliary systems must be assured, including:

- Bearing oil pump and seal oil pump, where applicable
- Hydraulic control fluid pump
- Condenser vacuum pump, where applicable
- Generator cooling system (air or hydrogen pressure and circulating water)
- Emergency trip system

Drains in all steam lines must be opened to prevent slugs of water from entering the turbine. Units of 10 MW or larger are generally furnished by a turning gear. This is then engaged to rotate the unit slowly. The steam lines are preheated and the gland seal exhaust system is put into operation. Steam is very gradually admitted to the turbine, and the turbine rolls off the turning gear and is gradually accelerated. The rate of acceleration selected will depend on the casing metal temperature, which depends on the duration of the previous outage. Acceleration time can vary from 10 to 30 min. During this period vibration and turbine shell temperature are monitored.

As the unit approaches synchronous speed, the generator breaker is in the open position and the excitation system regulates voltage to match the bus voltage. The operator then matches the frequency and phase angle before the generator breaker is closed. The unit then picks up load at a rate again depending on the temperature of the unit before start-up. Typical loading times are 30 to 60 min, depending on whether the unit was hot or cold before starting. Many of these starting functions can be handled automatically by modern turbine unit control systems, as discussed previously.

Normal Operation

During periods of normal operation several parameters are monitored, including turbine shell temperature and pressure, exhaust hood temperature, bearing oil temperature and pressure, condenser vacuum, shaft vibration, hydraulic oil pressure, and generator gas and winding temperatures.

Control systems generally contain many automatic protection and alarm systems. A typical protection system includes a main stop valve which is spring-loaded to close and is mounted ahead of the turbine inlet valve. Hydraulic oil keeps this valve open if several protection devices all indicate safe operation. These include an overspeed governor, bearing oil pressure relay, a manual trip relay, and where applicable, a low-vacuum relay and nonreturn valve relays.

Maintenance

A limited amount of running maintenance is required in addition to data logging. This includes periodic lubrication of valve gear (monthly or quarterly) and H_2 replenishment for hydrogen-cooled generators (three times a month).

The turbine shell is generally removed for a warranty inspection after the first year's operation. Shutdowns thereafter can be at intervals of 3, 4, or 5 yrs. Long periods of operation with minimal maintenance require steam of high purity. Carryover of certain contaminants in the steam can cause deposits, erosion, and stress cracking. A list of common deposit- and corrosion-causing contaminants is given in Table 4-7.

TABLE 4-7   Common Water Contaminants

Deposit-forming	Corrosion-causing
Calcium salts	Ammonia
Magnesium salts	Oxygen
Silica	Chlorides
Iron salts	Sulfides
Organic matter	Carbonates
Copper salts	Bicarbonates
Sulfates	
Nitrates	

These contaminants can enter the steam supply system with the makeup water or in process heat exchange equipment. They can exist in the boiler drum in relatively high concentrations without causing problems. It is only when they are carried over into the exiting steam that they enter the turbine. Efficient boiler drum separators can limit total dissolved solids to as little as 0.5 to 1.0 ppm. Silica is difficult to separate from the steam and must be controlled in the boiler feedwater. Care must also be taken with the fluid used to attemperate the steam exiting the superheater. Contaminated process returns can bypass the steam separation in the drum as attemperator fluid. This should be maintained at less than 1.0 ppm total dissolved solids.

Primary water treatment conditions the makeup water before it enters the cycle. Secondary water treatment is the addition of chemicals to the cycle to "polish" the feedwater. Boiler blowdown is the removal of solids from the cycle to prevent high concentrations in the drum. Monitoring purity is a very important part of steam turbine maintenance.

The effect of steam impurity may be observed by visually inspecting steam path components (turbine buckets and nozzle partitions) for damage or deposits. These conditions can significantly affect availability if they are not identified until the unit is opened for a regularly scheduled outage. This is particularly true if new parts are needed but have not been ordered. One feature available to help in planning for maintenance outages is the borescope-access port. These ports permit the insertion of optical devices (i.e., borescopes) for the visual inspection of buckets and nozzle partitions without having to disassemble the major turbine components.

Many types of deposits can be removed by washing the turbine at reduced speed with wet steam. Persistent deposits are removed by opening the turbine. Water washing and rinsing remove most soluble deposits. Steam cleaning and/or blasting with a fine-grade abrasive may be required for hard deposits like silica or iron oxide.

APPLICATIONS IN PLANTS

Cogeneration

Cogeneration is the simultaneous generation of power and useful heat. Steam turbines are the most common prime movers used in cogeneration.

In *thermally optimized* steam turbine cogeneration cycles, steam is expanded in noncondensing or automatic-extraction noncondensing steam turbine-generators which extract and/or exhaust into the process steam header(s). The fuel chargeable to power (FCP) for these systems is typically in the 4000 to 4500 Btu/kWh HHV range. The influence of initial steam conditions and process steam pressure on the amount of cogenerated power per 100 million Btu/h net-heat-to-process (NHP) is shown in Fig. 4-34. The increase in cogenerated power through the use of higher initial steam conditions, as well as lower process pressures, is readily apparent.

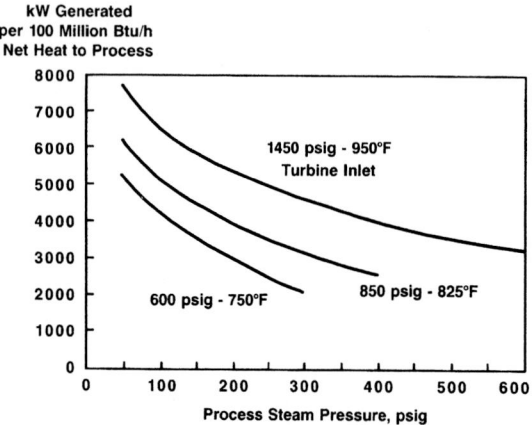

FIGURE 4-34   Cogeneration power with steam turbines.

Studies have shown that the higher steam conditions can be economically justified more easily in industrial plants having relatively large process steam demands. Data given in Fig. 4-35 provide guidance with regard to the initial steam conditions normally considered for industrial cogeneration applications. Higher energy costs experienced since the mid-1970s are favoring the upper portion of the bands shown in Fig. 4-35. However, particularly above 1800 psig (12,411 kPa), the capital costs should be carefully understood. Material changes in the turbine and steam generator can significantly increase first cost.

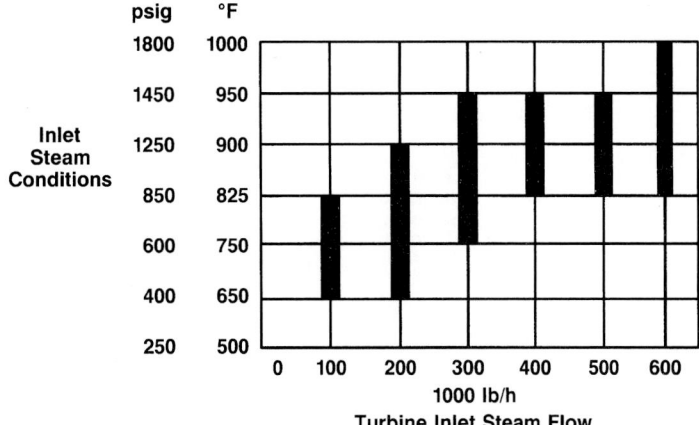

FIGURE 4-35   Range of initial steam conditions normally selected for industrial steam turbines.

Even through the use of most effective steam turbine cogeneration systems, the amount of power that can be cogenerated per unit of heat energy delivered to process will usually not exceed about 85 kW per million Btu net heat supplied. This is generally less power than is required to satisfy most industrial plant electrical energy needs. Thus, with thermally optimized steam turbine cogeneration systems, a purchased power tie or condensing power generation is necessary to provide the balance of the plant power needs.

Condensing steam turbine power generation, although not necessarily energy-efficient, has proven economic in many industrial applications. Favorable economics are often associated with systems where:

- Condensing power is used to control purchased power demand.
- Low-cost fuels or process by-product fuels are available.
- Adequate low-level process energy is available for a bottoming cogeneration system.
- Condensing provides the continuity of service in critical plant operations where loss of the electric power can cause a major disruption in process operations and/or plant safety.
- Utility-specific situations favor power sales, particularly if low-cost fuels are available.

Steam turbine efficiency is another important parameter in cogeneration plants. In noncondensing steam turbine applications, the turbine efficiency has only a minor effect on FCP. However, the amount of high-efficiency by-product power generated is directly proportional to the turbine efficiency. Converting fuel energy into low-temperature heat is a simple process, and high efficiencies of 85 to 90 percent can be achieved. However, converting fuel energy into power is much more difficult, and efficiencies are only 33 to 35 percent in the largest, most modern central stations. Therefore, high-efficiency multistage/multivalve noncondensing steam turbines should be preferred over inefficient single-valve/single-stage designs because more of the fuel energy is converted to a more valuable quantity—power.

Feedwater Heating

Feedwater heating is another method of enhancing the amount of by-product power generated for a given process heat load. Figure 4-36 illustrates a single automatic-extraction noncondensing steam turbine with a single heater and a second higher-pressure feedwater heater. The second heater increases the amount of by-product power by 2550 kW.

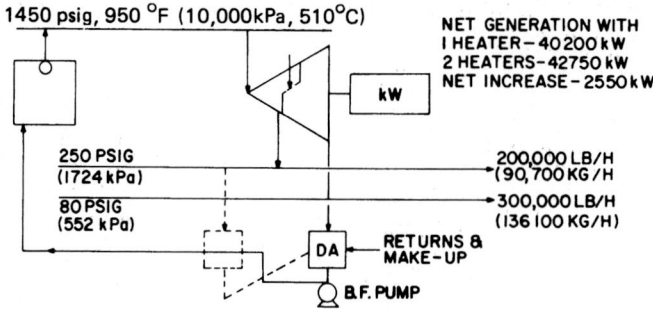

FIGURE 4-36   Effects of feedwater heating on by-product power generation.

As was the case with gas turbines, or any other type of heat engine applied to a cogeneration system, FCP or the quantity of by-product power is not the only factor to be considered. The investment in this equipment must be justified in terms of rate of return or a similar criterion.

In the case of large variable-speed drivers, mechanical-drive steam turbines often are the only viable solution. For example, a schematic diagram of a large ethylene plant driver is shown in Fig. 4-37. The charge gas compressor has a speed and power beyond that of suitable gas turbines or direct-drive motors. Process heat recovery produces steam at 1500 psig, 950°F (10,446 kPa, 510°C) and there is a large process heat demand at 300 psig (2070 kPa). A single automatic-extraction condensing steam turbine is ideally suited as a driver in these types of plants.

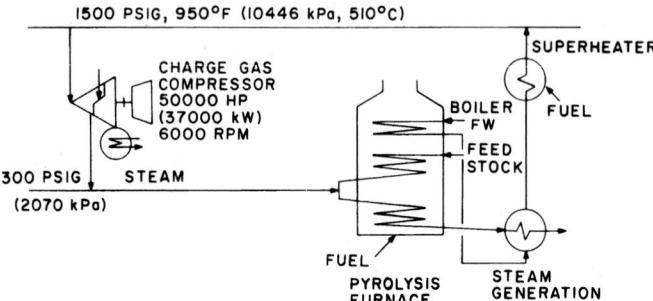

FIGURE 4-37   Schematic diagram of a large mechanical-drive steam turbine in an ethylene plant.

ACKNOWLEDGMENT

The author acknowledges the support and contribution provided by the Engineering Staff of GE's Power Generation Business.

REFERENCES

1. *ASME Steam Tables,* The American Society of Mechanical Engineers, New York, 1967.

2. *Theoretical Steam Rate Tables,* The American Society of Mechanical Engineers, New York, 1969.

3. Salisbury, J. K.: *Steam Turbines and Their Cycles,* Wiley, New York, 1950.

4. Newman, L. E.: *Modern Turbines,* Wiley, New York, 1944.

5. Kovacik, J. M., and W. B. Wilson: "Turbine Systems to Reduce Petroleum Refining and Petrochemical Plant Energy Costs," *Petroleum Division Conference,* ASME Paper 76-PET-62, Mexico City, Mexico, September 1976.

6. Kovacik, J.: "Cogeneration Application Considerations," 1991 Turbine State of the Art Conference, GER-3430B, Asheville, NC, August 1991.

7. Couchman, R. S., et al.: "Steam Turbine Design Philosophy and Technology Programs," 1991 Turbine State of the Art Conference, GER-3705, Asheville, NC, August 1991.

8. Kure-Jensen, J., et al.: "Steam Turbine Control System," 1991 Turbine State of the Art Conference, GER-3687, Asheville, NC, August 1991.

CHAPTER 4-5

DIESEL AND NATURAL GAS ENGINES

Waukesha Engine Division

Dresser Industries, Inc.
Waukesha, Wisconsin

GLOSSARY

Brake horsepower (bhp)   The horsepower delivered by the engine shaft at the output end.[1] The name is derived from the fact that it originally was determined by a braking device on the engine flywheel.

Brake mean effective pressure (BMEP)   The average cylinder pressure to give a resultant torque at the flywheel.[2]

$$\text{BMEP (lb/in}^2) = \frac{792,000 \times \text{bhp}}{(\text{r/min}) \times \text{displacement (CID)}} \text{ (four-stroke cycle)}$$

$$\text{BMEP (lb/in}^2) = \frac{396,000 \times \text{bhp}}{(\text{r/min}) \times \text{displacement (CID)}} \text{ (two-stroke cycle)}$$

$$\text{BMEP (kPa)} = \frac{600,000 \times \text{kW}}{(\text{r/min}) \times \text{displacement (L)}} \text{ (two-stroke cycle)}$$

$$\text{BMEP (kPa)} = \frac{1,200,000 \times \text{kW}}{(\text{r/min}) \times \text{displacement (L)}} \text{ (four-stroke cycle)}$$

Compression ratio   The ratio of the volume of cylinder space above the top piston ring with the piston at *bottom* dead center to the volume in the cylinder above the top ring when the piston is at *top* dead center.

Cycle   The complete series of events in each cylinder, including introduction and compression of air, burning of fuel, expansion and expulsion of the working medium in the engine.[1]

Diesel engine   An engine in which the fuel is ignited entirely by the heat resulting from the compression of the air supplied for combustion.[1]

Displacement   The volume of an engine's cylinder swept by the piston. It is equal to the area of each piston multiplied by the stroke multiplied by the number of cylinders and is expressed in cubic inches displacement (CID) or liters.

Duty cycle   A term used to describe the load pattern imposed on the engine. Continuous, or heavy-duty, service is generally considered to be 24 h/day with little variation in load or speed.[2] Intermittent, or standby, service is classed as duty where an engine is called upon to operate only in emergencies or at infrequent intervals.

Four-stroke cycle engine   An engine completing one cycle in four strokes of the piston or two shaft revolutions. The cyclic events are designated by the following strokes: (1) induction or suction stroke, (2) compression stroke, (3) power or expansion stroke, (4) exhaust stroke.[1]

Gas engine   An engine in which the fuel in its natural state is a gas and the air-fuel mixture is ignited by a spark within the combustion chamber or the prechamber.

Intercooler   A device used to cool the intake air after it leaves the turbocharger compressor but before it enters the engine cylinders. This device is sometimes called an *aftercooler* or *charge air cooler.*

Naturally aspirated   A term used to describe an engine which does not use a device to increase the pressure on the intake air of the engine before it enters the cylinder.

Opposed piston engine   One that uses the working medium simultaneously between two pistons in the same cylinder.[1]

Power   The rate of doing work. Engine power output is expressed in units of horsepower, equivalent to 550 ft·lb/s, or kilowatts, equivalent to 1000 J/s. Here are some conversion formulas:

Useful Equivalents

$$1 \text{ hp (U.S.)} = 550 \text{ ft} \cdot \text{lb/s}$$

$$1 \text{ hp (metric)} = 0.9864 \text{ hp (U.S.)}$$

$$1 \text{ hp (U.S.)} = 1.0138 \text{ hp (metric)}$$

$$1 \text{ kW} = 1000 \text{ J/s}$$

$$= 1000 \text{ N} \cdot \text{m/s}$$

$$1 \text{ kW} = 1.341 \text{ hp (U.S.)}$$

Engine power expressed by various engine manufacturers throughout the world should be specified as to the conditions under which the engine was run or the conditions to which the horsepower is corrected. Rating societies such as the Diesel Engine Manufacturers Association (DEMA), the Society of Automotive Engineers (SAE), German Industry Standards (DIN), British Standards (BS), and International Standards Association (ISO) all have their ratings for temperature and barometric conditions to which engine manufacturers relate their data. Manufacturers usually specify their engine performance and rating standards as well as methods of correcting the power available to expected site conditions of temperature and barometric pressure.

Speed regulation   The incremental difference between no-load (NL) speed and full-load (FL) speed divided by the full-load speed. This is sometimes referred to as speed droop.

$$\frac{(\text{NL speed}) - (\text{FL speed})}{(\text{FL speed})} \times 100 = \text{percent speed regulation}$$

Torque   Twisting effort of an engine described in pound · feet (Ref. 2):

$$T \text{ (U.S.)} = 5252 \times \frac{\text{bhp}}{\text{r/min}}$$

Turbocharger   A rotary air compressor driven by a turbine using exhaust gas as the driving fluid and compressing intake air into the engine.

Two-stroke cycle engine   An engine completing one cycle in two strokes of the piston or one shaft revolution. The cyclic events are designated by the following strokes: (1) induction and compression stroke, (2) expansion and exhaust stroke.[1]

INTRODUCTION

Stationary internal combustion engines are employed in plant applications primarily for emergency and prime electric power generation as well as for compressors, blowers, chillers for air conditioning and refrigerating and pumping equipment. Diesel engines are widely used for emergency fire and flood pumps as well as for in plant engine-generator sets and they have found acceptance in some areas as prime movers for compressor equipment used for air conditioning or refrigeration. In sewage treatment plants, where gas is produced as a by-product and captured for use as engine fuel, gas engines have become popular for driving blowers required for the aeration process, pumping effluent, and for prime power generation. Landfill gas, a by-product of the urban sanitary landfill, is one of the latest alternative gaseous fuels used to generate electricity for sale to the utility power grid.

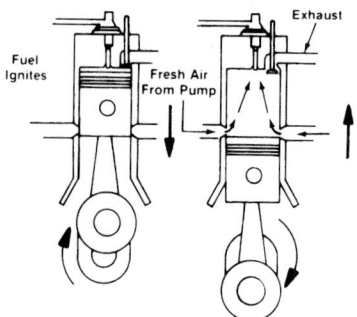

TWO-STROKE DIESEL ENGINE

FIGURE 5-1 Two-stroke diesel engine. (*Waukesha Engine Division, Dresser Industries, Inc.*)

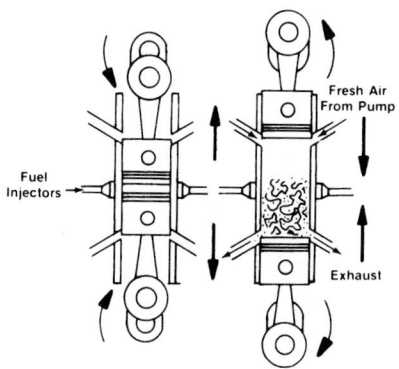

OPPOSED-PISTON DIESEL ENGINE

FIGURE 5-2 Opposed-piston diesel engine. (*Waukesha Engine Division, Dresser Industries, Inc.*)

DIESEL ENGINES

Principles

The diesel engine is an engine in which the cylinder is charged with air which is then compressed until it is hot enough to ignite fuel injected into the combustion space. The fuel is ignited by the hot air, and the expanding gases drive the piston down on the power stroke. The compression ratios of diesel engines cover an approximate range from 12:1 to as high as 23:1.

Engine types fall into two categories: two-stroke cycle and four-stroke cycle. Typical two-stroke-cycle engine arrangements are shown in Figs. 5-1 and 5-2. A typical four-stroke-cycle engine arrangement is shown in Fig. 5-3.

There are many types of combustion chamber designs which manufacturers use to mix fuel and air. There are claimed advantages for each type. These may be fuel economy, ability to make use of simpler fuel systems, wide speed range coverage, or firing pressure minimization. These systems generally fall into an *open-chamber* (Fig. 5-4) or *divided-chamber* (Fig. 5-5) category.

The open chamber design has the advantage of easier starting and has less heat rejected to the cooling system, but has greater demands on the injection system. The divided-chamber engines can operate with less sophisticated injection equipment

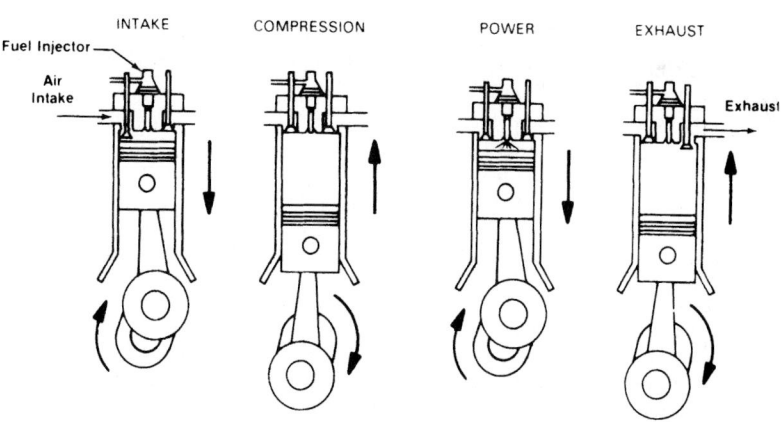

FOUR-STROKE DIESEL ENGINE

FIGURE 5-3 Four-stroke diesel engine. (*Waukesha Engine Division, Dresser Industries, Inc.*)

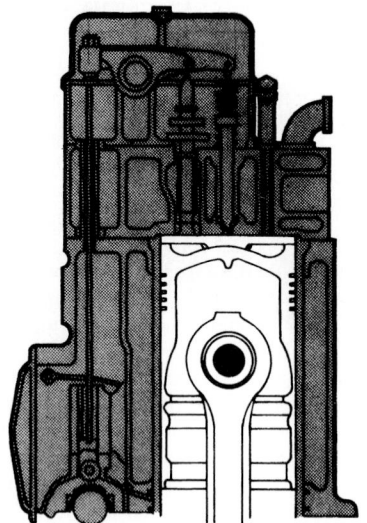

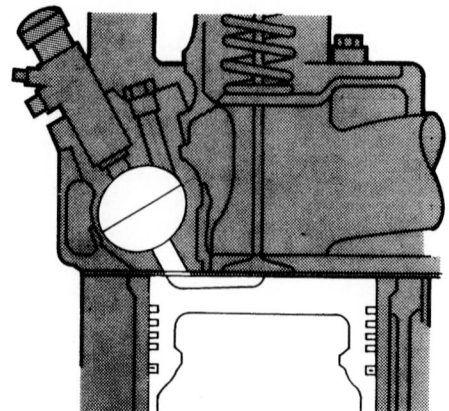

FIGURE 5-4 Open combustion chamber. (*Wauke-sha Engine Division, Dresser Industries, Inc.*)

FIGURE 5-5 Divided combustion chamber. (*Wau-kesha Engine Division, Dresser Industries, Inc.*)

since the air and fuel mixing is aided by more rapid air motion. Better fuel economy can be attained with an open-chamber design, while a divided chamber permits lower emissions.

Engines are frequently *turbocharged* to increase the horsepower taken from a given displacement engine. Turbocharging utilizes some of the waste heat energy and velocity of engine exhaust gas to drive a turbine connected to a high-speed centrifugal compressor. The power from a given package size can be more than doubled provided the engine components are strong enough to withstand the higher cylinder pressures. The highly turbocharged engines usually have a means of reducing the air temperature after the air leaves the compressor by means of an air-to-air cooler or an air-to-water cooler. These devices are known as charge air coolers, aftercoolers, or intercoolers.

Performance Characteristics

The performance of a diesel engine is affected by air temperature, air pressure, and humidity. Correction factors are employed to assure that the power specified takes into account the losses that are expected with altitude or temperature conditions at the site. These correction factors are usually specified by the Society of Automotive Engineers (SAE), German Industry Standards (DIN), British Standards (BS), or the International Standards Organization (ISO).

Fuels

Introduction.   Diesel engines can be designed to use a wide variety of fuels; however, if fuel other than diesel grade 1 or 2 is used, the manufacturer should be consulted. Jet A fuel can be used in diesel engines if it has a 40 octane minimum.

Fuel consumption rates on diesel engines are generally specified as brake specific fuel consumption and its units are in pounds per brake horsepower hour, grams per brake horsepower hour, or grams per kilowatthour. (See Fig. 5-6.)

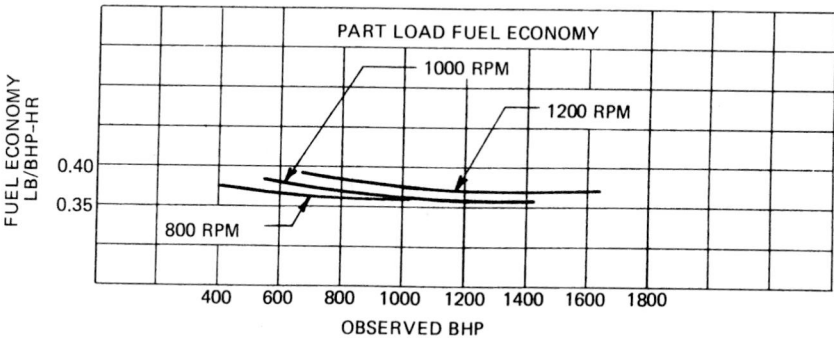

FIGURE 5-6 Fuel consumption rates for the diesel engine. (*Waukesha Engine Division, Dresser Industries, Inc.*)

Diesel Fuel Oil Specifications. It is important that the fuel oil purchased for use in an engine be as clean and water-free as possible. Dirt in the fuel can clog injector nozzles and ruin the finely machined precision parts in the system. Water in the fuel will accelerate corrosion of these parts. Reputable fuel suppliers deliver clean, moisture-free fuel. Most of the dirt and water in the fuel is introduced through careless handling, inadequate filtration, dirty storage tanks or lines, and poorly fitted tank covers.

There are fuel composition requirements that must be met when purchasing diesel fuel. Table 5-1 lists fuel properties for No. 2 diesel fuel and their limits. Definitions of the more critical properties follow.

TABLE 5-1 Fuel Oil Recommendations Chart

Fuel oil physical properties	Limits	ASTM test method
Fuel grade	Diesel no. 2	
API gravity	30 min	D 287
Cetane number	40 min*	D 613
Sulfur, %	0.7 max	D 129
SSU viscosity, at 100°F (37.7°C)	30–50	D 88
Water and sediment, %	0.1	D 96
Pour point, min	10°F	D 97
	(5.5°C)	
	below ambient air	
Carbon residue	0.25%	D 189
Ash, % max.	0.02	D 482
Aklali or mineral acid	Neutral (pH 7)	D 974
Distillation point		D 158
10% min	450°F	
	(232°C)	
50%	475–550°F	
	(246–288°C)	
90% max	675°F	
	(357°C)	
End point max	725°F	
	(385°C)	
Cloud point	†	D 97

* For automatic starting units, a fuel with 50 cetane minimum is recommended.
† Cloud point should not be more than 10°F (5.5°C) above pour point.
Source: Waukesha Engine Division installation manual.

Diesel Fuel Properties

API Gravity.   The specific gravity, or density in pounds per gallon.

Ash.   The mineral residue in fuel. High ash content leads to excessive oxide buildup in the cylinder and/or injector.

Cetane Number.   Ignitability of the fuel. The lower the cetane number, the harder it is to start and run the engine. Low-cetane fuels ignite later and burn more slowly. Explosive detonation could be caused by having excessive fuel in the chamber at the time of ignition.

Cloud and Pour Points.   The pour point is the temperature at which the fuel will not flow. The cloud point is the temperature at which the wax crystals separate from the fuel. The cloud point must be no more than 10°F (5.5°C) above the pour point so the wax crystals will not settle out of the fuel and plug the filtration system. The cloud point should also be at least 10°F (5.5°C) below the ambient temperature to allow the fuel to move through the lines.

Distillation Point.   Temperature at which certain portions of the fuel will evaporate. The distillation point will vary with the grade of fuel used.

Sulfur.   Amount of sulfur residue in the fuel. The sulfur combines both with any moisture in the fuel and the water vapor formed during combustion to form sulfuric acid. This acid can quickly corrode engine parts. The lower the sulfur content of the fuel, the better.

Viscosity.   Influences the size of the atomized droplets during injection. Improper viscosity will lead to detonation, power loss, excessive smoke, and unnecessary wear on the injector system.

Fuel Systems

Installation of a diesel engine requires special planning to handle fuel delivery, storage, and piping (Fig. 5-7).

Fuel Tanks.   Most diesel engine installations utilize a two-tank system, with both a main storage tank and a day tank.

Day Tanks.   A day tank is designed to keep a clean supply of fuel oil close to the engine and to provide an immediate supply of fuel when the engine is started. By locating the day tank close to the engine, the fuel-transfer pump will be able to draw fuel more easily, without having to develop high suction pressures.

The day tank is generally sized to hold enough fuel for several hours of operation or whatever local fire codes allow. It is often a 275-gal (1000-L) standard commercial tank installed at or above floor level.

If the day tank is positioned above the level of the engine fuel-transfer pump, the flow of the fuel will maintain a constant pressure at the fuel-transfer pump inlet.

A positive shutoff should be added just beyond the day tank whenever the tank is above the level of the fuel-injection pump. If the day tank is mounted on a structure that is subject to vibration, a flexible connector should be added between the tank and the fuel piping. (Actually, flexible connections are recommended between an engine and any support system, whether it involves fuel, air, water, or oil.) The weight of both the tank and the fuel must be considered when designing and mounting the tank.

Main Storage Tanks.   Spherical or cylindrical tanks should be used for added strength. Avoid square tanks. Main storage tanks are generally large enough to hold a 10-day fuel supply. (Local codes may dictate tank sizes.) If fuel delivery is uncertain due to weather, traffic, or any other reason, the tank size should be increased.

The location of the main storage tank is influenced by the method of delivery. If the fuel oil will be delivered by railroad tank cars, the tank and filler opening should be near the railroad siding. If a truck will be delivering the fuel, the tank and filler opening should be close to the road. Tanks should always be located so as to minimize the length of the fuel lines.

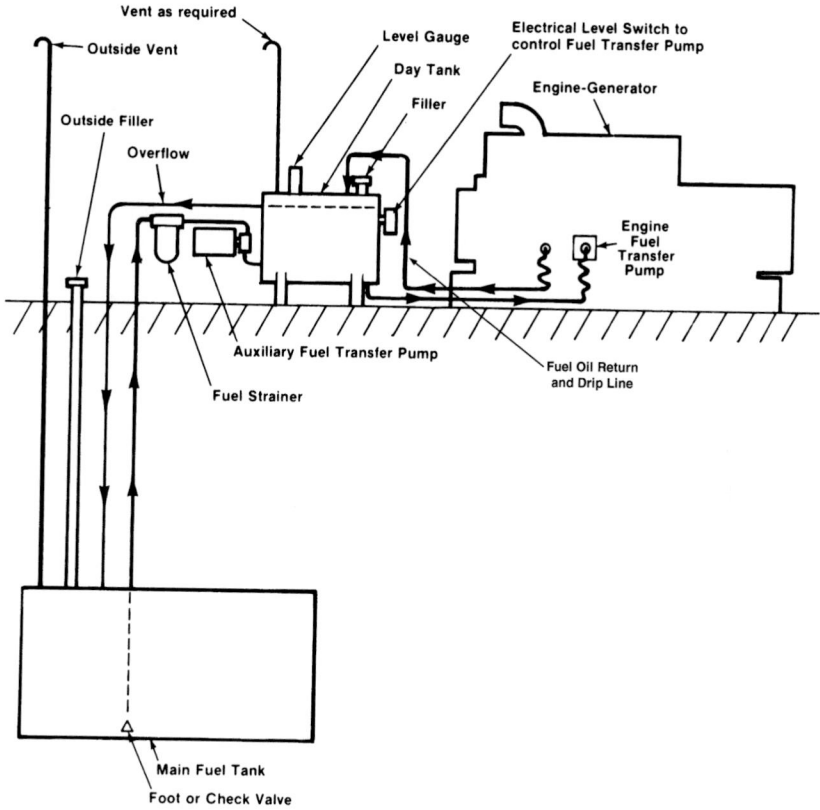

FIGURE 5-7   Typical diesel fuel-oil system. (*Waukesha Engine Division, Dresser Industries, Inc.*)

Underground fuel oil tank storage is no longer permitted. Above-ground storage does require containment around the tank, and heating may be required in cold climates. As with day tanks, the fuel pickup should never draw from the bottom of the main storage tank. The tank should be installed lower at one end to allow the dirt and water that settle out of the fuel to be drained off or pumped out. Underground tanks should be bottom pumped at least twice each year to remove all accumulated water and sludge. Above-ground tanks are more subject to condensation, so they should be bottom pumped more frequently.

Caution: Diesel fuel tanks, fittings, and lines should never be made of galvanized steel nor should they be of a zinc alloy material. The sulfur in the fuel will corrode these metals, gumming up the injection pump and injectors.

Heating lines can be added to warm the fuel and keep it at a temperature at which it can be easily pumped to the engines. The manufacturers of such components should be consulted for further information.

The vent pipe to the outside must have at least a 1-in (2.5-cm) diameter, and an approved flame arrester must be incorporated into the vent.

Strainers and Filters.   Strainers and filters are an important part of any diesel fuel system. Without the cleaning action of these components, the dirt and grime in the fuel would destroy the finely machined parts in the injectors and the injection pump.

A filter should be placed just before each meter and each pump. To assure proper maintenance, it should be located in an easy-to-reach position. Also, try to leave enough room under each filter for a catch basin to avoid messy, dangerous fuel oil spills.

Separators should be added to a system, particularly at the main storage tank outlet, to remove sediment.

Shutoff Valves. A shutoff valve should be incorporated in the fuel system at the fuel tank outlet and at the point where the fuel line enters the building or engine room and wherever applicable local codes so dictate.

Fuel-Transfer Pumps. Transfer pumps are used to supply fuel to the injection pump, or to raise fuel to a tank or engine at a higher level. Centrifugal pumps cannot be used as transfer pumps because they are not self-priming. Positive-displacement pumps must be used.

Fuel Return Lines. Fuel return lines take the hot excess fuel not used in the engine cycle away from the injector and back to either the fuel storage tank or the day tank. The heat from the excess fuel is dissipated in the tank. ***CAUTION:*** *Never run a fuel return line directly back to the engine fuel supply lines. The fuel will overheat and break down.*

The fuel return lines should always enter the storage or day tank above the highest fuel level expected. This will prevent fuel in the storage tank from running back into the fuel return line.

NATURAL GAS ENGINES

Principles

Gas engines can be two-cycle or four-cycle and either naturally aspirated, turbocharged or intercooled (aftercooled). Gas engines may be stoichiometric (air fuel ratio of approximately 16:1, or rich burning) or lean combustion (air fuel ratio of approximately 30:1, or lean burning). The fuel can be introduced into the intake air by a carburetor or injected into the intake port just ahead of the inlet valve or directly into the combustion chamber.

The combustion chamber can be either open type or divided type (see section on diesel engines).

Performance Characteristics

Like diesel performance, the performance of a gas engine is affected by air temperature, air pressure, and humidity. Correction factors are used to ensure that the power specified will take into account the losses expected with the altitude and temperature conditions anticipated at the site. The rating societies mentioned previously, in the discussion of diesel engine performance, supply methods of correcting power on spark-ignited engines.

The fuel consumption of a gas engine usually is expressed in British thermal units per brake horsepower (kilocalories per metric horsepower) (see Fig. 5-8).

Fuels

A gas engine can be adjusted to accept a wide variety of fuels. Among these are:

1. Pipeline quality natural gas
2. Digester gas from sewage treatment plants
3. Methane from sanitary landfills (landfill gas)

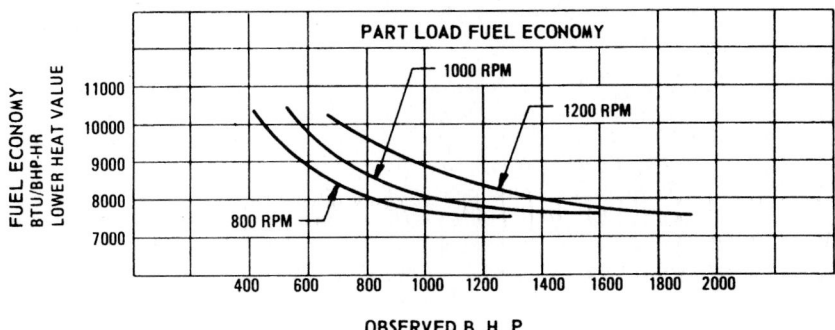

FIGURE 5-8 Fuel consumption rates for the natural gas engine. (*Waukesha Engine Division, Dresser Industries, Inc.*)

4. HD-5 Propane and LP gas
5. Pyrolytic gas from hydrocarbon sources
6. Field gas (wellhead gas)

The octane number for various gaseous fuels available for gas engines can be calculated from their known constituents. The heating value of engine fuel can also be obtained with a calorimeter and is nearly always expressed as lower heating value (LHV).

Fuel System.   The gas engine can be *naturally aspirated* or *turbocharged*. Since the manifold pressure of the turbocharged engine can be as high as 23 psig (160 kPa), the pressure of the natural gas supply should be in the 30- to 50-psig (200- to 350-kPa) range in order to have the engine operate properly. Conversely, the gas supply to the naturally aspirated engine can be at a pressure as low as 0.5 (3.5 kPa) psig (but is normally preferred at a 5- to 10-psig [3.5- to 7-kPa] span.) since the engine manifold operates at atmospheric pressure or less. Turbocharged engines of the draw-through carburetor type are now available for operation on gas pressures as low as 0.5 psig (3.5 kPa). They are designed with special carburetors located on the inlet side of the turbocharger compressor.

The gas pressure regulators to reduce the supply pressures to the required engine carburetor inlet pressures are usually mounted on the engine. Experience has proved that it is best to supply one regulator per carburetor (on dual-carburetor engines), mounted as close to the carburetor as possible. This minimizes line drops and governing instability.

The type and number of gas shutoff devices and pressure-sensing switches are determined by applicable safety codes and control circuit requirements. A low gas pressure switch is commonly specified.

SYSTEMS COMMON TO BOTH DIESEL AND NATURAL GAS ENGINES

Lubrication System

Although the lubrication system is one of the simplest systems of the engine, its importance should not be underestimated. It is the most important support system of the engine and cannot be neglected except at the expense of premature engine failure.

The lubrication system of an industrial engine is almost completely assembled before it leaves the factory. On large-displacement engines, the free-standing lube oil filter (and in some cases the oil cooler) is the only major lubrication component usually shipped free of the engine. (Smaller engines have the oil filter mounted directly on the engine.)

Lubricating Oil Filter Installation.   Position the lube oil filter as close to the engine as possible.

   Caution: Do not put the filter near the exhaust outlet or other places where the temperature could become excessively warm. Excessive heat will speed oil deterioration and will also create a fire hazard in the event of an oil spill or line rupture.

   It is important to use pipe of adequate size between the engine and lube oil filter in order to maintain the proper oil pressure to the engine. Consult the engine supplier for recommendations. If they are not galvanized or zinc-plated, black iron or steel pipes should be used to carry oil. *Caution: After welding, flush pipes with muriatic acid to remove all welding scale, and rinse thoroughly to neutralize the acid and ensure clean piping.*

Flexible Connections.   Flexible connections designed to handle hot lubricating oil at pressures up to 100 lb/in^2 (690 kPa) should be used between the engine and the free-standing oil filter. Position the connections as close to the engine as possible. Supports should be added under the oil filter lines to minimize vibration and prevent breakage.

Lubricating Oil Recommendations.   Lube oil selection is the responsibility of the engine operator and the oil supplier. The refiner is responsible for the performance of the lubricant.

   Most engine warranties are limited to the repair or replacement of parts that fail due to defective material or workmanship during the warranty period. These warranties do not include satisfactory performance of lube oil. That is considered the responsibility of the oil supplier.

   Assistance in lubricant selection can be obtained from a publication of the Engine Manufacturer's Association, One Illinois Center, 111 E. Wacker Drive, Chicago, IL 60601. This book, *EMA Lubrication Oils Data Book for Heavy-Duty Automotive and Industrial Engines,* has a table of lubricants and their performance grades. Consult the engine manufacturers concerning oil recommendations for their various engines. It is common to find that different oils are used for gas and diesel engines, as well as for different models of each type.

   Accessories available for lube oil systems are such items as flowmeters and oil-level regulators. These can be unit-mounted and automatically add oil as it is consumed as well as measure and record the quantity of oil consumed. It is also possible to obtain engine-mounted switches for low and high engine lube oil levels to signal a warning and/or cause engine shutdown.

   On larger engines, use an air-motor- or electric-motor-driven prelube pump to fill and pressurize the lube oil system before cranking and operating the engine. In addition, use a lube oil heater to keep the oil warm and in condition for positive lubrication of vital areas on start-up wherever low ambient temperature may be encountered.

Cooling Systems

Cooling systems in liquid-cooled engines are affected by the mineral content and corrosiveness of water put into the system—be it cooled by radiator, heat exchanger, or standpipe. In all cases, recommended practice is to use treated water so as to minimize long-term effects on the engine.

Radiator Cooling.   The most common cooling arrangement is that of the stationary engine with a unit-mounted radiator. In this case, the cooling fan is belt-driven from the front of the engine. Usually a pusher fan is used to prevent hot air from being drawn over the set and its operator. The radiator has to be sized for the maximum expected ambient operating temperature (including room heat sources such as generator losses), the maximum rated engine horsepower or kilowatt load, and the type of coolant used (ethylene glycol). The radiator has to cool the heat rejected to the engine-jacket water, the heat rejected from the engine lube oil, and (if applicable) the heat rejected from the intercooler circuit. Some radiators are dual-core units, with one core for the jacket-water circuit and a second core for the intercooler oil-cooler circuit. This is required on natural gas engines to keep the water entering the inter-cooler at 130°F (54°C) maximum.

A radiator-cooled unit (Fig. 5-9) is self-contained and, therefore, adaptable to mobile installations and/or relocation. Since the radiator is sealed, it does not waste water and does not contaminate drain water. However, the horsepower required to drive the fan is lost for other uses, and the relatively large radiator airflow both in and out of the engine room has to be handled judiciously. Other installation items are louvers (fixed or variable), vertical dis-charge air scoops, and air discharge duct adaptors.

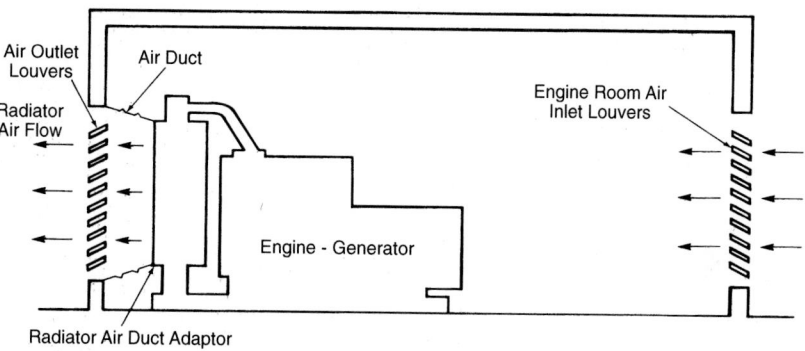

FIGURE 5-9   Radiator cooling. (*Waukesha Engine Division, Dresser Industries, Inc.*)

Cooling by use of a remote-mounted radiator is also common. This system is quite flexible since the radiator can be mounted outside, which reduces engine-room airflow. Also, the core can be horizontal, which makes the radiator insensitive to wind direction. Roof mounting of the radiator is quite common; if the roof height causes an increase over the recommended jacket-water pressure, a hot well (Fig. 5-10) and auxiliary pump can be added. Other installa-tion considerations are automatic louvers, vertical vs. horizontal core, remote surge tank, pip-ing sizes to control line-pressure drops, and sound-limit requirements.

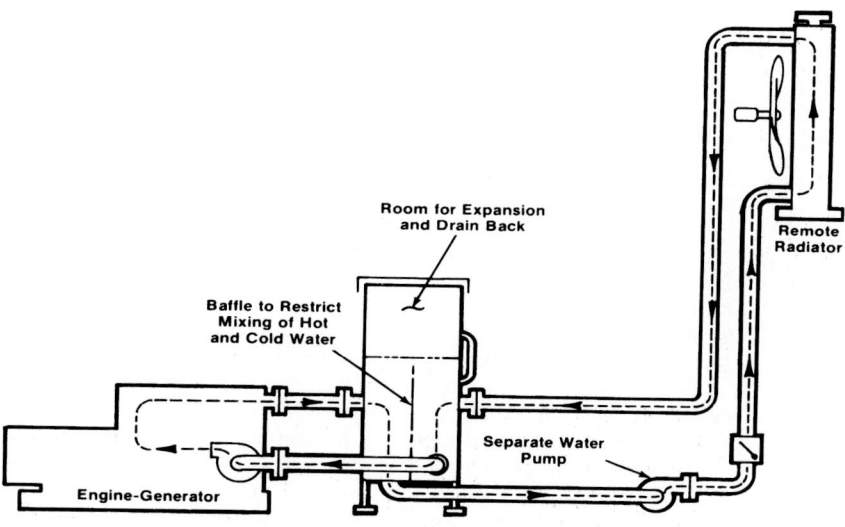

FIGURE 5-10   Hot well cooling. (*Waukesha Engine Division, Dresser Industries, Inc.*)

Heat-Exchanger Cooling. In applications where cool water is plentiful, or where it is desirable to preheat a water supply for other processes, engines using heat-exchanger (Fig. 5-11) cooling are used. If conservation of raw water is important, raw water can be controlled thermostatically to limit its flow to the minimum required.

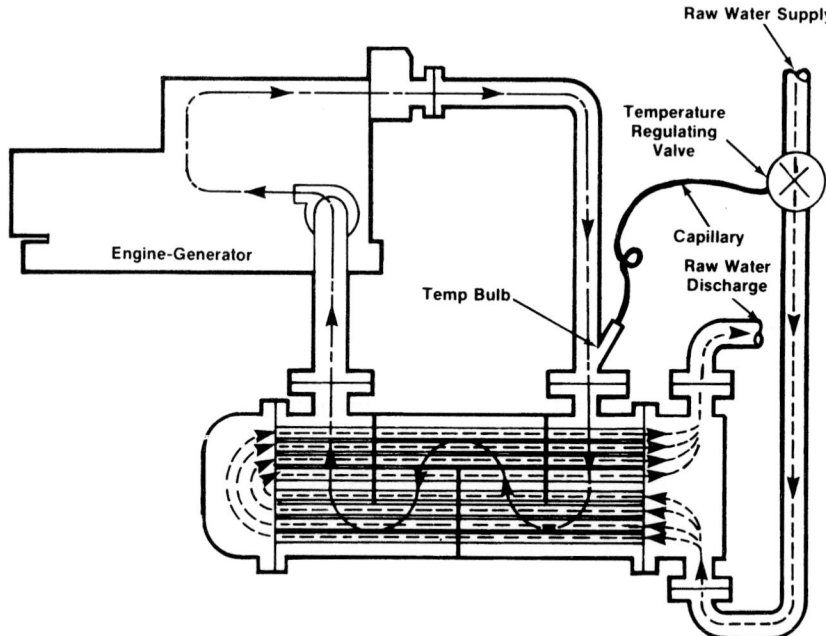

FIGURE 5-11 Heat-exchanger cooling. (*Waukesha Engine Division, Dresser Industries, Inc.*)

The raw-water pressures are not imposed on the engine jacket; engine cooling is not greatly affected by ambient temperatures; engine-room airflow requirements are much lower than unit-mounted radiator applications; and engine-jacket-water heat can be used constructively.

City-Water Cooling or Standpipe Cooling. Occasionally used with standby-service engine-generator systems, city-water cooling is simply the blending of cold raw water into the jacket water during operation through the use of water-pressure-regulating and thermostatic-control valves and diverting the excess to waste (Fig. 5-12). *Caution: Although inexpensive to install, this method introduces minerals and corrosive elements into the engine water jacket and is dependent on a municipal water supply which could become inoperative in time of disaster.)*

Ebullition (Ebullient) Cooling. Engines and engine-generator systems, intended for applications where recovery of the heat in jacket water (for utility heating, air conditioning through absorption chillers, or processing needs) may be of genuine economic value, are sometimes equipped with ebullition cooling (Fig. 5-13).

Ebullient cooling is a process whereby jacket water is circulated through the engine at near-boiling temperature, vaporized at the top of the engine, and then condensed and recirculated. Cooling is accomplished by capturing the heat of vaporization for process or other uses.

By omitting the jacket-water pump and taking advantage of the natural circulation of water with temperature differences, the engine may be operated at jacket-water temperatures well into the boiling range [15 psig, 250°F max (103 kPag, 127°C)]. A considerable amount of heat in the form of low-pressure steam may be recovered. When ebullition cooling is being

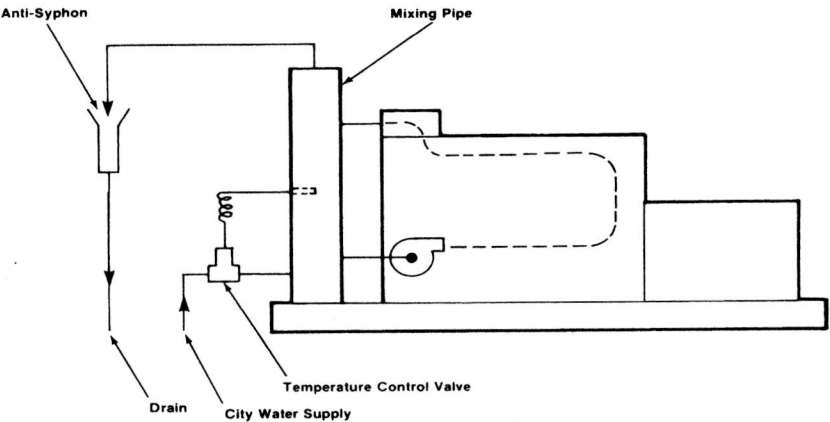

FIGURE 5-12   City-water cooling. (*Waukesha Engine Division, Dresser Industries, Inc.*)

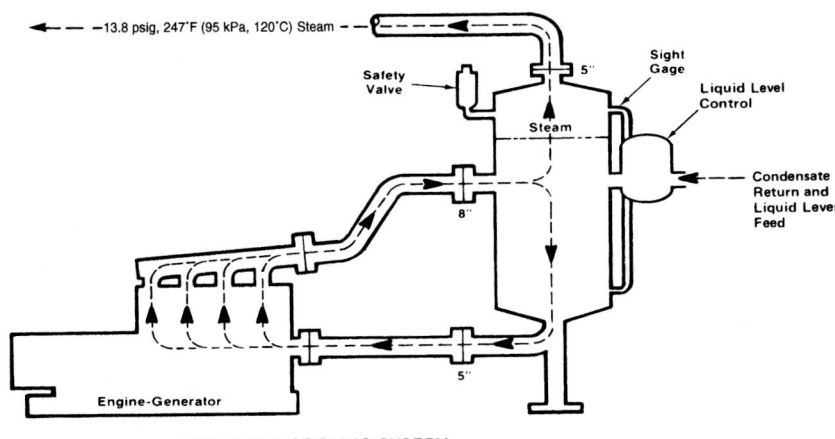

FIGURE 5-13   Ebullition cooling. (*Waukesha Engine Division, Dresser Industries, Inc.*)

considered, however, the engine manufacturer should be consulted since some engine designs are not offered with this option. In general, the two big advantages of ebullient cooling are the recovery of normally wasted heat energy and optimum use of water.

Waste-Heat Recovery Systems

Where the waste heat of an engine can be used, electric power generation with waste-heat recovery has pronounced advantages. With a conventional engine generator, something on the order of 32 percent of the fuel energy is converted to useful electric power, while the remaining 68 percent is wasted to the atmosphere. With an engine jacket-water and exhaust-heat recovery system, the recovered heat energy is about 50 percent of the fuel burned, reducing waste heat by about 18 percent.

A typical heat balance on engines of identical size for both gas and diesel engine-generators, is shown in Table 5-2.

TABLE 5-2   Typical Heat Balance

	Conventional cooling system	Cooling system with engine jacket and exhaust heat recovery
500-kW natural gas engine generator*		
Electric power	30%	30%
Jacket water heat	38% ⎫	38% ⎫ 54% recoverable
Exhaust heat	24% ⎬ 70% wasted	Exh recoverable 16% ⎭
		Exh lost 8% ⎫ 16% wasted
Radiated heat lost to atmosphere	8% ⎭	8% ⎭
	100%	100%
500-kW diesel engine generator†		
Electric power	35%	35%
Jacket water	32% ⎫	32% ⎫ 48% recoverable
Exhaust heat	24% ⎬ 65% wasted	Exh recoverable 16% ⎭
		Exh lost 8% ⎫ 17% wasted
Radiated heat lost to atmosphere	9% ⎭	9% ⎭
	100%	100%

* Based on 7900 Btu (bhp)(h) at rated load (LHV) and 95 percent generator efficiency.
† Based on 0.380 lb/(bhp)(h) at rated load [18,200 Btu/(lb)(LHV)] and 95 percent generator efficiency.

Figure 5-14 shows a simple representative arrangement for engine heat recovery. Engine jacket water and exhaust are passed through a first heat exchanger where the water temperature is increased as the exhaust gas is cooled. It then passes through a second heat exchanger where the building or process water is heated and the jacket water is returned to the engine for cooling.

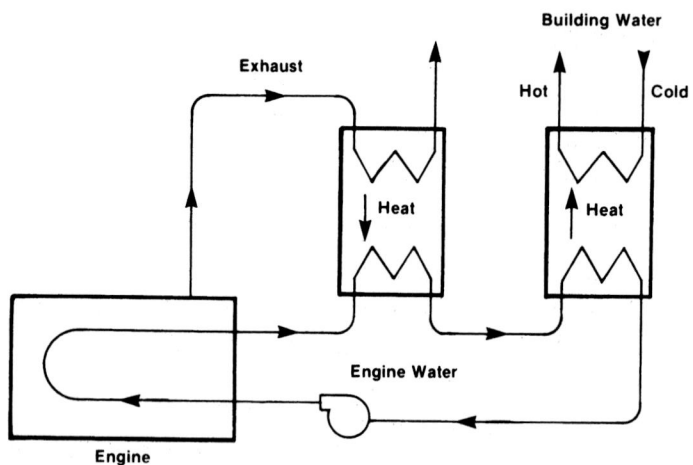

FIGURE 5-14   Representative heat-recovery arrangement. (*Waukesha Engine Division, Dresser Industries, Inc.*)

The amount of waste heat readily recoverable in a representative system of this kind is approximately 71 Btu/(bhp)(min) for a gas engine and 56 Btu/(bhp)(min) for a diesel engine.

Exhaust System

Every engine manufacturer specifies a maximum exhaust back pressure limit at the exhaust outlet of the engine (Fig. 5-15). Typical values can range from 12 to 20 in (30 to 52 cm) H_2O depending on the engine models. To exceed these values could result in engine damage, interfere with good long-life engine operation, or detract from good performance.

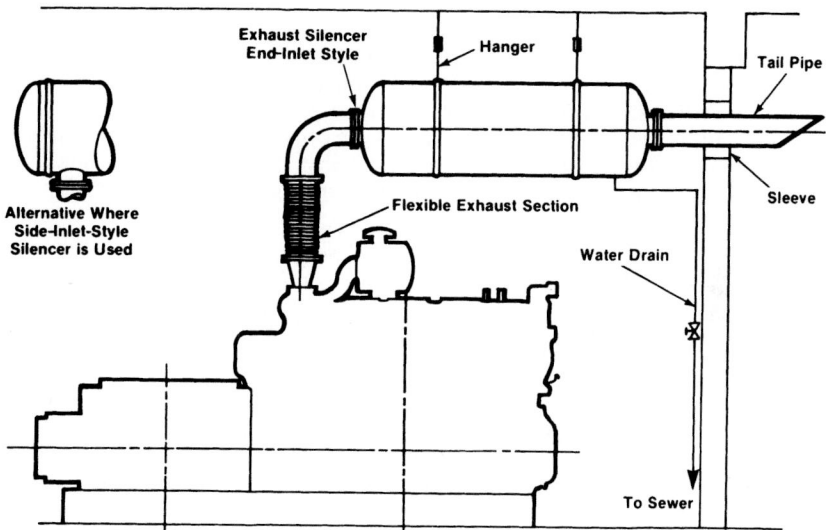

FIGURE 5-15   Horizontal exhaust schematic. (*Waukesha Engine Division, Dresser Industries, Inc.*)

Since sound levels are becoming more critical daily, silencers are selected to give adequate noise attenuation. Unfortunately, this usually increases the exhaust flow pressure or drop through the silencer.

Silencers and exhaust pipes in engine rooms are usually insulated to reduce heat radiation and noise. A flexible exhaust connection is mounted at the engine to isolate engine vibration; also, the exhaust line is sloped away from the engine with a drain to avoid the accumulation of condensation. Additional flexible connectors are necessary to compensate for thermal growth.

Emissions

Exhaust products of either diesel or natural gas engines contain oxides of nitrogen (NO and NO_2), carbon monoxide (CO), hydrocarbons (HC), and sulfur oxides (SO_2 and SO_3) if the fuel contains sulfur.

Emissions of these products are subject to regulation under federal, state, and local laws. The plant engineer should be aware of the regulations covering a specific site and, if necessary, consult the engine manufacturer for emission information.

Starting Systems

The most frequently used starter systems are electric motors and air starters. The electric starters are usually 12- or 24-V dc cranking motors. The higher voltage is preferred on larger engines because of the high power required for annunciator controls and/or power circuit-breaker tripping. Adequately sized and maintained lead-acid batteries are the most practical and economical solution for the battery source today. However, nickel-cadmium and other types of battery requiring less maintenance are often specified.

All the batteries require an adequately sized battery charger to keep the battery fully charged both with the engine operating and when down. In low ambient temperatures, both batteries and engines must be kept warm to ensure good starting and operation.

Many starting systems use one or more air starters per engine. The common air motor will crank an engine with an applied air pressure of between 90 and 150 psig. Starters can be controlled through a hand or a solenoid valve both manually or automatically. They also have an inline oiling system to ensure motor life.

The air starting system usually includes a remote high-pressure air receiver (approximately 250 psig [1.7 mPa]) with an air regulator to drop pressure to the cranking motor. Again the pipe losses and line sizes have to be considered to ensure good cranking. The compressors to pressurize the receivers are normally driven by electric motors and are automatically started and stopped by a pressure-switch sensor at the air receiver.

Engine-Speed Governing System

The engine governor is the most important device with respect to engine performance. On smaller units, engine-mounted mechanical governors provide adequate speed and frequency control with approximately 3 to 10 percent steady-state speed regulation from no load to full load.

Hydraulic isochronous governors are also available for medium to large engines, and these provide excellent speed control with adjustable speed regulation of 0 to 5 percent. In engine-generator applications, this permits running isochronously as a single unit or with adjustable regulation for multiunit manual parallel operation and load sharing.

More precise governing is available on both small and large engines with electric governors. This type depends on engine speed with a magnetic pulse pickup on the flywheel ring gear teeth, and provides speed and load control with an electric or electrohydraulic actuator connected to the engine throttle or fuel injection pump.

The electronic control of the governor is solid-state and is usually mounted in the control panel or generator switch gear.

Electric governing permits operation of multiengine generator units in parallel isochronously, that is, at constant frequency under steady-state operation regardless of load, with each engine taking an equal share of the overall load.

Additionally, the electric governor is extremely fast with respect to transient load response and will handle up to 50 percent sudden load changes with a speed deviation of approximately 3 percent and recovery within approximately 2 s for diesel engines, and with a speed deviation of approximately 4 to 5 percent and recovery within approximately 3 s for carburetted gas engines. Response varies by engine type: naturally aspirated, turbocharged-intercooled stoichiometric, or lean combustion.

Where automatic operation includes coming on-line in parallel with other engine generators or the utility, the electric governor with isochronous load-sharing control is desirable. In conjunction with the proper switchboard relaying, units can be added or removed on a load-sharing basis or on load control basis as the situation may demand. A good 24-V dc battery system is required as a power supply to the electric governor.

INSTALLATION AND MAINTENANCE OF DIESEL AND NATURAL GAS ENGINES

The engine installation should be designed with maintenance requirements in mind. Serviceable components such as filters, fittings, and connections should be readily accessible to the engine operator. Routine engine maintenance will not be neglected if the operator has easy access to the engine.

Sufficient service space must be present on all sides of the engine to allow for removal of even the largest engine components. An overhead crane should be incorporated into the engine-room design to assist the mechanic-operator in removing heavy assemblies. Air line connections will be necessary for air power tools, as will scaffolding for servicing the engine.

Ventilation

In engine-generator installations sufficient airflow must be provided into the engine room for ventilation and combustion air. It is also good practice to calculate the amount of heat transferred to the room air (i.e., engine and generator radiator heat, plus any other heat sources) to determine the temperature rise of the engine-room air. In many cases it is necessary to increase the engine-room airflow to maintain reasonable operating temperatures.

The following are *general rule of thumb values* that assume the only radiating heat source in the engine room is the engine-generator set. For greater accuracy, an independent engineering study should be made covering the following points:

Cubic feet per minute of air required to limit air room temperature rise to 18°F (10°C), over normal ambient = 45 × kilowatt rating

Cubic feet per minute of combustion air required = 3.5 × kilowatt rating for diesel engines

Cubic feet per minute of combustion air required = 2.4 × kilowatt rating for gas engines

The total air requirement equals the sum of the cubic feet per minute of combustion air plus the cubic feet per minute required to limit the room temperature rise.

Other ventilation considerations are filters for sandy or dusty areas and louvered openings at both inlet and outlet air openings. The louvers can be motor-operated and temperature-controlled.

Cooling System

Potential problems with the engine cooling system can be avoided if the following considerations are incorporated into the design and installation of the cooling system.

Excessive fittings, elbows, and connectors in the system piping will impede coolant flow. Use of fittings should be kept to a minimum.

An expansion-tank balance line should be incorporated into the cooling system, running to the suction side of the water pump. This balance line will maintain a net positive suction at the inlet of the pump and reduce the possibility of air locks and cavitational erosion.

All filters, fill points, and bleed cocks should be installed in an easy-to-reach location.

Place the radiator away from a wall or any other obstruction that causes air recirculation or restricts airflow. These obstructions would also include any dirt source, vehicle travel path, air-conditioning units, or exhaust stacks and chimneys. Remember that the radiator must be in a location where it can be cleaned and serviced.

In installations where gaseous or LP fuels are used, keep all floor drains and service trenches out of the engine enclosure. LP and some constituents of natural gas can be heavier than air and will quickly flow into such low spots, creating a fire hazard.

Exhaust System

Plan the exhaust system so that the gases are expelled to a safe outside area, consistent with all local building and environmental codes. Do not discharge gases near windows, ventilation shafts, or air inlets. The exhaust outlet must be designed to keep out water, dust, and dirt.

To avoid metal stress and turbocharger damage, support the exhaust system independently, keeping the weight of the piping off the engine. Roller-type supports and flexible exhaust connections should be used to absorb thermal expansion. (If overhead cranes and hoists are used in the engine room, the exhaust-system piping may have to be supported from below.)

A condensate trap and drain should be designed into the exhaust system. The drain should be in an easy-to-reach location.

If the exhaust systems of more than one engine are to be connected to a common exhaust, the engine manufacturer should be consulted beforehand. Exhaust-system back flow (common in such connections) could result in an engine that is not running.

Exhaust-system back pressure should be checked periodically. The back pressure must fall within the limits established by the engine manufacturer.

Air Induction

As with other engine systems, accessibility is the key to air-induction system maintenance. The filter element should be positioned so that it can be easily removed and replaced. The filter should always be positioned at the entrance to the air induction system; when combustion air is ducted in from outside the engine room, the filter should be at the opening to the piping. All systems should be equipped with a restriction indicator to show excess pressure drop due to filter-element plugging.

Always locate the air inlet away from concentrations of dirt, exhaust stacks, fuel tanks, tank vents, and stockpiles of chemicals and industrial wastes. Try to duct air to the engine from a cool, dry, dirt-free area. The ambient temperature at the air inlet location should ideally be 60 to 90°F (15 to 32°C).

Run all air ducts away from engine exhaust pipes, heating lines, or other hot areas. Remember to allow clearance for overhead lifts and cranes when air ducts run through the engine room.

Air ducts should be thoroughly sealed to avoid drawing dirty air in behind the filter. The ducting must be checked periodically for leaks.

Air-system ducting should be seamless, welded-seam, or PVC piping. Flanged fittings with gaskets, not threaded connections, should be used between pipe sections to avoid restrictions in the system. The best ducting system is as short and straight as possible, using long-radius bends and low-restriction fittings. Never allow air-duct restriction to exceed 2 in (50.8 mm) of water column. Air ducting systems must be leak-free under vacuum conditions.

Engine Alignment

The alignment of the engine mount and the alignment between the engine and the driven equipment is critical to long engine life. Alignment should be checked periodically according to the manufacturer's recommendations.

SELECTION OF ENGINES

There are several factors to consider in the selection of an engine.

Type of Fuel

The type of fuel chosen will depend to a large degree on availability, price, local building codes, and pollution restrictions. For instance, in some communities, natural gas is not available for industrial use, while in others, local building codes will prohibit storage of diesel fuel.

The price of one fuel may preclude its use in comparison with another type of fuel. Moreover, emissions restrictions may have a bearing on what type of fuel may be used. All of these are factors in choosing an engine.

Horsepower Load and Speed

The load and speed of the equipment to which the engine will be coupled are key considerations in engine selection. The aim is to match the prime mover to the power required at a speed which will be compatible with the equipment to be driven, while maintaining optimum efficiency.

Duty Cycle

The duty cycle should be examined to determine whether continuous or intermittent operation of the equipment is required, because this affects engine selection.

Brake Mean Effective Pressure (BMEP)

This is important because the higher the figure, the greater the chance for higher stress on working parts of the engine. This could mean higher maintenance costs and earlier need for rebuilding.

Fuel and Oil Consumption

With the cost of petroleum or fossil-based fuels tending to rise over time, this is becoming an increasingly significant factor in the selection of an engine.

Torsional Compatibility

A torsional analysis should be conducted to determine whether the engine and driven equipment are compatible with respect to operating stress in the shaft system.

SELECTION OF ENGINE GENERATORS

Both diesel and gas engines perform very satisfactorily for in-plant power generation when properly applied and installed. The varied nature of these applications depends on factors such as:

1. The specific characteristics of the plant's product and its production process as well as its sensitivity to power failure
2. The plant power needs in terms of availability of purchased power and the reliability of normal power sources
3. Economic considerations in terms of location, cost of purchased power, demand charges, and equipment
4. Economic considerations of in-plant generated power in terms of capital outlay, operation, maintenance, and fuel cost

Once the decision has been made that in-plant engine-driven power generation will be used to provide electric power, whether on the basis of prime, cogeneration, peaking service, emergency standby, or a combination of any of these, there are a number of considerations to be investigated.

Purpose

The purpose of the installation should be stated and careful thought given to definition of the electrical load requirements.

- Will the power generators supply all of the plant load or only a part of the total?
- What is the power factor characteristic of the load? (Engine generators are normally rated at 0.8 power factor lagging.)
- Will there be any attempt to control or improve power factor?
- What is the largest block kilowatt loading anticipated and what large motors are to be started and on what basis—across the line, reduced voltage?
- Are computer loads, SCRs, inverters, x-ray, or heavy welding equipment involved?
- What are the code requirements? NFDA? CSA? Others?

Amount of Equipment

Selection of the size and number of units to handle the load demands thoughtful consideration.

Emergency standby protection (see also Chapter 3-3) may be provided by a single unit rated to protect a known segment of load that can be isolated with a two-way transfer (normal emergency) switch (Fig. 5-16). The size of this type of unit may range from 50 kW or under to approximately 1500 kW (Fig. 5-17).

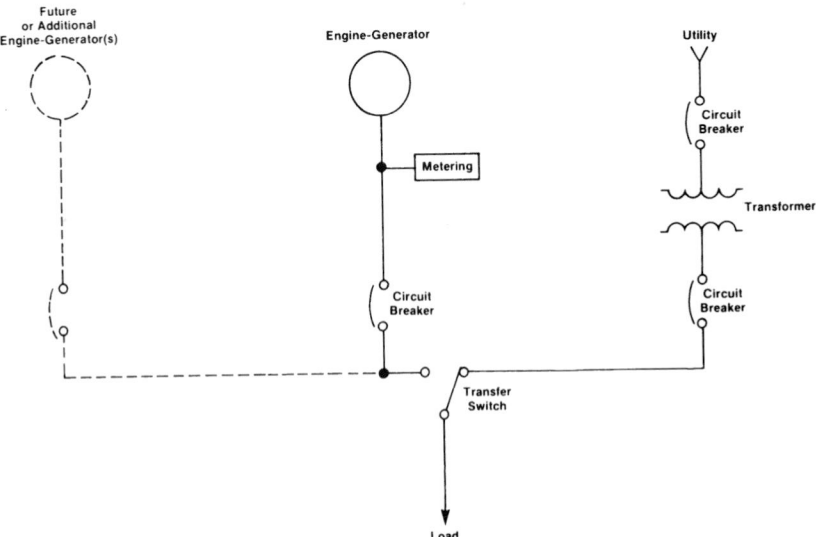

FIGURE 5-16   Normal emergency standby without utility parallel. (*Waukesha Engine Division, Dresser Industries, Inc.*)

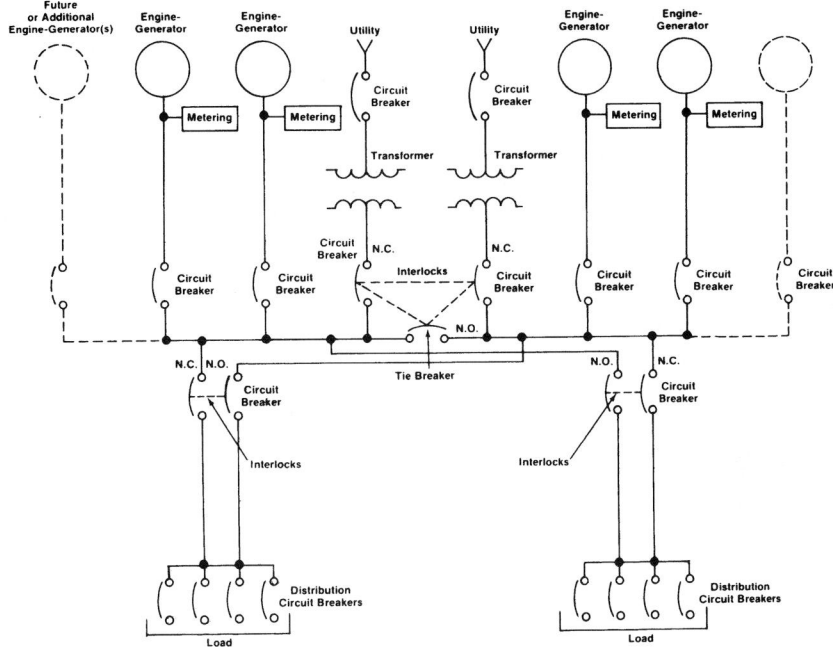

FIGURE 5-17   Normal emergency standby with peaking capability or selection of critical loads for limited kilowatt generation (without utility parallel). (*Waukesha Engine Division, Dresser Industries, Inc.*)

For loads well over the 1000-kW range, it is customary to provide multiple engine-generator units, sometimes as many as eight units operating in parallel on a common or split bus for total load capability to 10,000 kW and beyond.

Generally available emergency standby units are rated at 1800 r/min synchronous speed for 60-Hz service up to approximately 1000 kW and at 1200 r/min up to 2000 kW, while prime power units are available in both 1200 and 900 r/min synchronous speed for 60-Hz service up to 3000 kW rating per unit.

The same ratings are available for 50-Hz service at synchronous speeds of 1500, 1000, and 750 r/min. Much larger units and units with slower speeds are also available.

When selecting size and number of units, it is most helpful to study the plant electrical load profile over the course of a year. If this is not available, a profile based on connected loads with anticipated load and diversity factors can be developed. Single-unit emergency standby generators are often applied with load factors of only 50 to 75 percent of rating. Multiunit prime power installations favor load factors in the 75 to 90 percent range, as this selection results in optimum fuel economy and overall operating efficiencies. Future growth of plant electrical loads must be anticipated.

Fuel Selection

As with engines in direct-drive applications, this may be determined by availability and cost.

Natural Gas.   This is an excellent engine fuel and is often available on an uninterrupted basis. Where necessary, LPG or propane can be stored as backup or secondary fuel supply.

Sewage treatment plants are increasingly turning to power generation, utilizing the process-waste gas from digesters to fuel the engine. Coal gasification, wood-chip processing, and numerous other process-waste gases may be suitable for burning in a gas engine but should never be used without consulting the engine manufacturer for specific approval.

No. 2D Diesel Fuel Oil.   This is commonly used in small and medium-size engines. Large diesel engines have the capability of burning heavier fuels such as No. 4D and heavier residual fuels; these may require special handling, heating, centrifuging, and filtering. Diesel fuel has the advantage of large-volume onsite storage capability.

Location of Equipment

Locating the engine generator(s) in the plant may involve many practical considerations. Often it is advantageous to locate them near other heavy plant equipment such as boilers, large air conditioners, or compressors. Standby power generation equipment is normally automatically controlled and, by locating it close to other equipment requiring periodic operator attention, it may also get the attention it deserves.

Figure 5-18 shows typical envelope dimensions for both gas and diesel generator sets. Minimum clearance on all sides is also charted and can be used for preliminary space estimates.

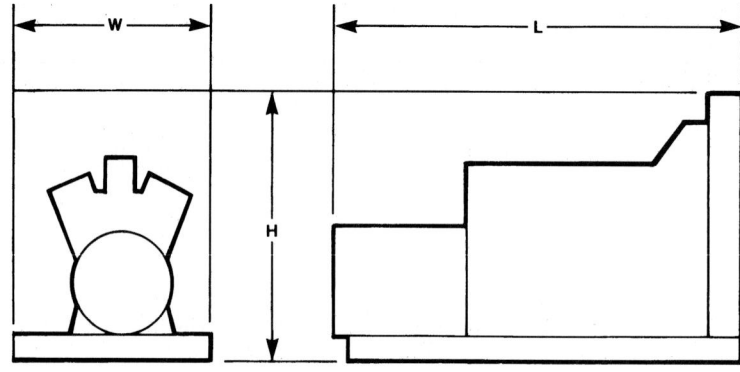

(Length, Width, and Height Are In Inches)

kW	RPM	L	W	H	WT, LB
50	1800	88	30	50	2,300
100	1800	110	36	55	4,200
150	1800	114	36	60	4,500
200	1800	114	42	60	6,000
250	1800	114	42	60	7,000
300	1800	140	56	90	13,000
400	1800	160	69	90	16,000
500	1800	180	72	90	19,000
600	1200	210	74	121	32,000
700	1200	216	84	124	32,500
800	1200	222	84	124	33,000
900	1200	222	96	124	35,000
1000	1200	222	96	127	36,000
*1200	1200	186	80	98	38,000
*1500	1200	262	78	113	42,000
*2000	900	330	72	139	45,000
*2500	900	363	72	139	52,000
*3000	900	363	72	139	52,000

* - Indicates less cooling radiator

FIGURE 5-18 Approximate space envelope for gas and diesel engine generators. (*Waukesha Engine Division, Dresser Industries, Inc.*)

For final determinations, always work from the equipment manufacturer's specific space requirements for optimum clearances both around the unit and overhead for efficient maintenance, major overhaul, and repair.

Cooling

Adequate cooling of both gas and diesel engines is essential to good performance and equipment life.

On emergency standby units, it is common to waste the recoverable heat. On prime power applications, there is increasing attention given to heat recovery from the engine jacket water and exhaust for process use in the plant.

The Electric Control System

This system, together with its attendant complexities, requires determination of the power-generation voltage and control voltages.

Decisions as to the mode of operation, such as manual, semiautomatic, automatic, or unattended operation, must be made. Adequate metering, monitoring, readout, and display decisions must be made. Independent engine generation on isolated plant loads or multiunit engine generation in parallel operation against plant loads must be determined. Will the engine generators always operate isolated from the utility or will there be occasions to parallel with the utility's power?

Both peaking service and cogeneration may call for parallel operation with the utility, and this requires review with the power company at the planning stage.

Electric Controls.   After the kilowatt size of unit(s) is selected, the generated output voltage should be considered.

1. Voltages of 208/120 wye or 240/139 wye can be economically utilized in the lower kilowatt ranges since no transformers should be required in plants (facilities) using only these voltages.
2. Voltage of 480/277 wye is the most commonly generated voltage with minimum capital cost in both generator and switchgear.
3. Voltage of 4160/2400 wye is the common generated voltage for larger plants and more extensive power distribution systems. This voltage level increases the cost of the engine-generator unit and its associated generator switchgear, but may effect savings in the plant distribution system.

A further consideration is the engine generator and panel control voltage. Generally, this is supplied from a dc battery source which allows control and operation of the engine and breakers without ac voltage from either utility or generators. Engine-generator sets in the 150- to 1500-kW range require a 24-V dc battery source to start and run. An alternate is 100 to 150 psig air pressure to start and 24, 48, or 125 V dc to run and control. For large, multiunit engine-generator sets and their associated switchgear, 48 or 125 V dc is recommended for the most reliable circuit-breaker operations.

Metering.   When 24-V dc engine starting batteries are used for control purposes, the control should be run from the set of batteries with the highest voltage to minimize the effects of voltage dip when starting engines or tripping circuit breakers.

Single-unit metering would include at least a frequency meter, voltmeter, ammeter, and wattmeter; for emergency service, 3½-in (9-cm) ± 2 percent accuracy panel meters are both generally adequate. Prime power service with long-term continuous operation, often with multiple units in parallel, demands 4½-in (11.5-cm) switchboard meters of 1 percent accuracy. These sets should also include an indicating wattmeter for each engine generator. Additional meters that may be considered are: those reading kilowatthours, kilovoltamperes reactive (kvar), and power factor. Of increasing interest on prime power multiunit applications are recording meters on the output bus for voltage, frequency, and kilowatts and/or kilowatthours. More recently available are digital readout meters providing greater accuracy, but with limitations with respect to indication of transients, which is an important characteristic of engine-generator sets.

Protection. The electrical protection of the generator system can vary from simple molded-case circuit breakers to insulated-case breakers and to metal-frame air circuit breakers. Both insulated-case and air breakers are available with either fixed mounting or drawout provisions. For optimum flexibility in long-term use, the drawout breaker is superior and recommended. Since engine generators have a limited short-circuit capability, care should be taken in breaker selection for both generator and distribution to achieve proper selective trip coordination. Where selective trip coordination is required, the generator must be supplied with three per unit short-circuit sustain capability for 10 s.

Additional protection to consider is generator differential and ground fault. Usually, generator-differential protection is used on 4160-V systems where generator internal damage requires early detection to protect capital investment.

Ground-fault protection also protects equipment and personnel and is less expensive to install. Most circuit-breaker manufacturers provide optional ground-fault tripping integral with the breaker. Many different types of ground-fault protection are available, and consideration must be given to select and specify protection consistent with the existing plant grounding system and specific application. More sophisticated methods of fault detection are available, but are usually associated with megawatt generator sizes since protection cost is very high.

When engine generators are operated in parallel with the utility, certain cautions must be observed. The utility, being an "infinite" source, can cause severe damage to the engine generator should the utility's protection system open and then reclose (out of phase). Conversely, should the upstream utility protection system open and then not reclose, the generators can feed a fault from the reverse direction, which can be hazardous to both personnel and equipment. Whenever parallel operation with the utility is being considered, review the relaying used to protect against the occurrences mentioned with the local utility company.

Many breaker and/or transfer switch configurations are possible, each with its own advantages and disadvantages dependent upon application (Figs. 5-19 to 5-21).

Engine Control. After the power distribution format is known, the engine-control (starting and stopping) mode(s) must be considered. For single emergency standby units the unit should start, come up to rated frequency and voltage, and provide power whenever the utility source fails. Normal engine protection would include shutdown on engine low oil pressure, high water temperature, overspeed, and failure to start. Additional features available and actually included for hospital duty are warnings before shutdown on low oil pressure and high water temperature. On prime power units, additional considerations are warning and/or shutdown on high oil temperature, low oil level, high vibration, and engine overload.

Some extremely critical applications may call for the generator set not to stop for any reason, as nuisance shutdown cannot be tolerated and the possibility of generator set failure or destruction may be less costly than the process it controls.

Engine control is only a part of the overall system control. System control is offered in varying degrees of complexity. Single standby units have very simple system controls, while prime power multiunit applications must determine the quantity of units required to satisfy power demand while also controlling plant loads to prevent high peak loading or overloading. When operating in parallel with the utility, controls can be programmed to accept: (1) fixed utility supply with load variations picked up by the engine-generator sets, (2) variable utility supply with peak demands picked up by the generator sets, or (3) fixed generator set output with load variations being picked up by the utility (this mode includes capability of supplying power to the utility over low plant load conditions).

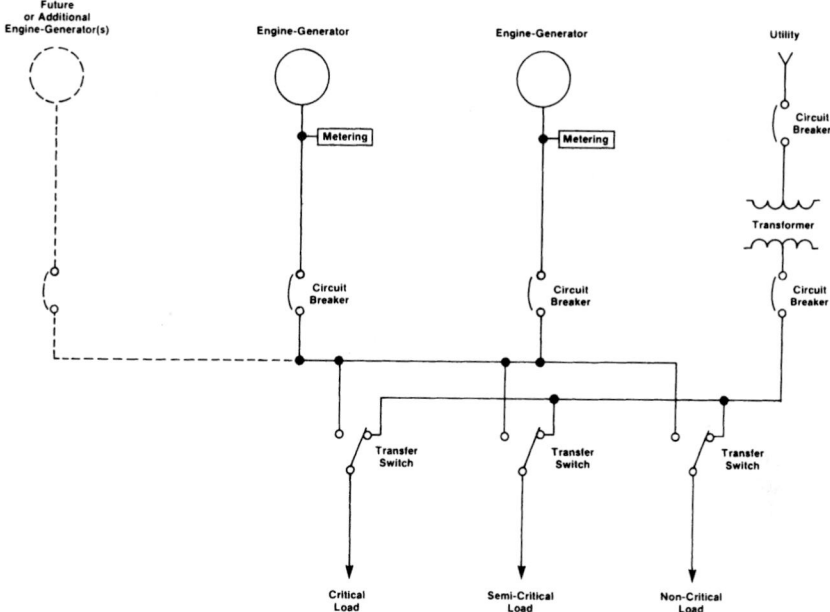

FIGURE 5-19   Multiunit standby or cogeneration in parallel with utility or in independent operation. (*Waukesha Engine Division, Dresser Industries, Inc.*)

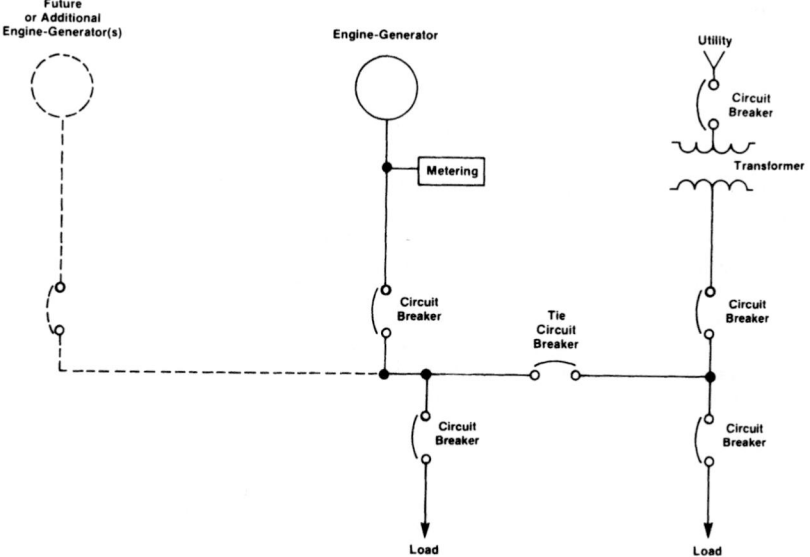

FIGURE 5-20   Isolated loading for peak shaving without parallel utility (breakers interlocked) or peak shaving and parallel operation with utility. (*Waukesha Engine Division, Dresser Industries, Inc.*)

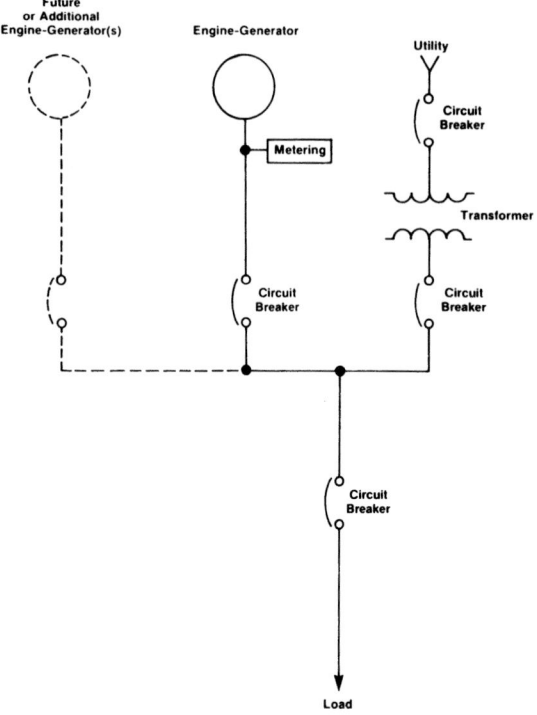

FIGURE 5-21 Isolated loading for standby (breakers interlocked) or peak shaving and cogeneration with parallel operation
with utility. (*Waukesha Engine Division, Dresser Industries, Inc.*)

Generally speaking, the control logic can do almost anything the engineer may require in
a given situation; however, simplicity is the key to both cost and long-term performance. Simpler systems are easier to maintain, whereas complex systems may require a wider variety of
engineering skills to maintain and troubleshoot problems.

The system control can start and stop generator sets on the basis of actual kilowatt
demand; an alternative simple approach would be to know the load profile and manually
operate or utilize real-time devices to start and stop units.

Today solid-state programmable controllers, which can be used in place of the more conventional relay logic in control circuits, are available. Some of these controllers are versatile
and allow control logic to be changed simply. Many allow computer input-output links for
record-keeping purposes.

These versatile programmable controllers provide flexibility and a ready means of tailor-
ing sequence, time, and load functions to a particular plant's needs. Selected performance
indicators can be linked to provide readouts and printouts as may be required for efficient
operation and recording purposes.

REFERENCES

1. *Standard Practices for Law and Medium Speed Stationary Diesel and Gas Engines,* Diesel Engine
   Manufacturers Association, Cleveland, Ohio, 1972.

2. Gunther, F. J.: "Engines," in *Pump Handbook,* Igor J., Karassik, William C. Krutzsch, Warren H.
   Fraser, and Joseph P. Messina (eds.), sec. 6.1.3, McGraw-Hill, New York, 1986.

SECTION 5

HEATING, VENTILATING, AND AIR CONDITIONING

CHAPTER 5-1
HEATING AND VENTILATING*

Nils R. Grimm, P.E.

Section Manager, Mechanical
Sverdrup Corporation
New York, New York

---

* The material presented in this chapter is based on the author's notes, technical experience, and data from: The American Society of Heating, Refrigerating and Air Conditioning Engineers (ASHRAE): *Industrial Ventilation;*[1] the American Conference of Industrial Ventilation Design Manual: *Mechanical Engineering;* NAVDUCKS DM-3; Buffalo Forge: *Fan Engineering;* Carrier Corporation's *System Design Manual,*[2] and *Woods Practical Guide to Fan Engineering.*[3]

INTRODUCTION

The purpose of this chapter is to provide the plant engineer with a ready reference to practical solutions of day-to-day heating and ventilating problems.

One of the cardinal rules of a good, economical, energy-efficient design is to avoid designing a system (be it heating, ventilating, exhaust, humidification, dehumidification, etc.,) to meet only the stringent (critical) requirements of a small or minor portion of the total area served. If possible, the critical area should be isolated and treated separately.

The formulas and data presented in this chapter are for sea-level locations. Correction factors are discussed in the section of this chapter entitled "Altitude Corrections for Heating and Ventilating Systems."

CLIMATIC CONDITIONS

When possible, the outdoor design conditions should be obtained from official weather stations such as those of the U.S. Weather Service, U.S. Air Force, U.S. Navy, Canadian Atmospheric Environment Service, etc., or from the latest edition of ASHRAE's *Handbook of Fundamentals* in the chapter "Weather Data and Design Conditions."

Data from many weather stations at specific locations and elevations furnish a network from which, by interpolation, good estimates can be made of the expected conditions at locations without weather stations.

Adjustments for Climate

When design requirements are extremely important, it may be advisable to retain a competent applied meteorologist to develop data that can show a comparative relationship with the nearest official station having a record for a long period. If this is not feasible, the following general rules will apply in adjusting the design data supplied for the weather stations listed to fit some other location.

Adjustment for Elevation. For a lower elevation, the design values should be increased, while for a higher elevation, the values should be decreased. The increments used in these adjustments are generally

Dry-bulb (db) temperature   1°F per 200 ft (1°C per 100 m)
Wet-bulb (wb) temperature   1°F per 500 ft (1°C per 300 m)

In the winter, where cold-air drainage (principally in hilly or mountainous areas) or considerable radiation cooling occurs at a site, these adjustments do not apply.

Adjustment for Mass Modification. Short-distance variations are most extreme near large bodies of water where air moves from the water over the land in summer. Along the west coast of the United States, both dry-bulb and wet-bulb temperatures increase with distance from the ocean. In the region north of the Gulf of Mexico, dry-bulb temperatures increase for the first 200 to 300 mi (322 to 482 km) with a slight decrease in wet-bulb temperatures caused by mixing with drier air inland. Beyond this 200- to 300-mi (322- to 482-km) belt, both dry-bulb and wet-bulb values tend to decrease at a somewhat regular rate.

Adjustment for Vegetation. The difference between large areas of dry surfaces and large areas of dense foliage upwind from the site can account for variations of up to 2°F (1.1°C) wb and 5°F (2.8°C) db. The warmer temperatures are associated with the dry surfaces. Adjustments for vegetation require the assistance of a consulting applied meteorologist.

Seasonal Considerations

Preferably the winter outdoor design temperature should be based on a temperature minimum that will exist 99 percent of the time. The 99 percent value represents a specific temperature that will be equaled or exceeded in a negative direction by 1 percent of the approximately 2200 h of total annual heating. Then, in a normal winter, the outdoor design temperature will be equal to or below this temperature for approximately 22 h.

It is recommended that, if economically possible, the summer outdoor design (dry-bulb and wet-bulb temperatures) conditions for ventilation systems be based on conditions not exceeded more than 5 percent of the time. The 5 percent value represents specific dry-bulb and wet-bulb temperatures that will not be equaled or exceeded more than 5 percent of the approximately 2900 h of total annual cooling. Thus, in a normal summer, the outdoor design conditions will be equal to or above these conditions a total of approximately 145 h.

HEATING

General

In general there are three types of heating systems: steam, hot-water, and hot-air. These, in turn, are further categorized below.

Steam

Low-Pressure Steam.   Less than 15 psig (1 bar) operating pressure. This is the most common steam system for comfort heating.

High-Pressure Steam.   Greater than 15 psig (1 bar) operating pressure. This system is used mainly in process heating and in distribution systems.

Vacuum Steam.   This system operates below atmospheric pressure. Less than 1 psig (0.07 bar) operating pressure. It is rarely used today for comfort heating.

Hot-Water.   Though there are no standards on the precise values that define "low," "medium," and "high" temperatures, the following are typical.

Low-Temperature, ≤200°F (93°C).   This is one of the most common heating systems.

Medium-Temperature, >200°F (93°C) but <260°F (127°C).   The application of this system is the same as high-temperature water systems.

High-Temperature, 260 to 450°F (127 to 232°C).   This system is rarely if ever used for space heating because of the potential for scalding personnel as a result of a leak. It is mainly used for heat-distribution systems and, in some processes, heating where water is preferred to steam in the same temperature range.

Hot-Air

Comfort Heating.   The temperature of the discharge supply air emanating from the heating device is generally not greater than 200°F (93°C).

Process Heating.   The temperature of the discharge supply air of the heating device can be considerably higher than 200°F (93°C), depending on the process requirements.

Infrared.   Infrared heating systems are used primarily for industrial heating requirements where (1) it is impractical to heat the total volume of space, (2) it is required to bring the total area only to minimum standards, or (3) it is necessary to heat a small area or areas (such as a workstation) to an acceptable level. It is also used in some dyeing and baking ovens.

In designing heating systems using infrared heaters for industrial spaces (especially with high ceilings and cold climates), the relative humidity at the roof level must be maintained below the point where condensation will occur. Figure 1-3 in the section, "Humidity Control," later in this chapter, shows maximum relative humidity values that can be maintained without condensation occurring.

Energy Sources

The following table lists common energy sources for the heating systems listed above:

Energy source	Comment
Coal	Various grades of hard and soft coal.
Oil	No. 2, 4, 5, or 6.
Gas	Natural, liquid natural, propane or butane.
Electricity	60-Hz, 120-V, single-phase; 240-V, three-phase. Industrial process heaters frequently operate at higher voltages.
Wood	Depending on the moisture content and type, the heating value can generally range from 4000 to 7500 Btu/lb (9 to 17 kJ/kg).
Solar	Applicable with low-temperature water and steam systems. The capability of generating medium-temperature water and high-pressure steam [125 psig (8.6 bars)] has still not been developed for commercial purposes.

System Components

Steam-Heating System.   The principal components are: boilers or generators; the boiler feed system; the deaerator; makeup water; chemical treatment; the fuel system; distribution supply and return (condensate), piping, supports, expansion, and insulation; end-use distributors such as radiators, coils, and radiation panels (radiant heat); process equipment; valves, vents, traps, and drains; condensate pumps and receivers; controls and safety devices.

Vacuum System.   In general this system has the same components as a steam system except for the following: the condensate pump is replaced by a vacuum pump; all air is vented from the system by the vacuum pump and there are no other automatic air vents; the traps used are specifically designed for vacuum service.

Hot-Water System.   The basic components here are: generator (boiler); feedwater, fuel, and makeup water systems; chemical treatment; expansion or compression system; pumping system; supply and return piping systems and their supports, expansion, and insulation; end-use distributors such as convectors (radiators), coils, radiation panels (radiant heat); process equipment; valves, vents, and drains; controls and safety devices.

Equipment Selection

In this chapter we are concerned more with the end use than with the distribution and pumping systems. The reader is referred to Sec. 9 of this book for a discussion of distribution and pumping systems.

Suggested Procedure

Environmental Conditions

OUTDOOR DESIGN CONSIDERATIONS.   The procedure to determine the impact of outdoor design conditions was discussed previously in this chapter, under "Climatic Conditions."

INDOOR DESIGN SELECTION.   In order to avoid overdesigning the heating system so as to conserve energy and to minimize construction costs, each space or area should be analyzed separately to determine the minimum temperature that can be maintained and whether humidity control is required or desirable. For a discussion on humidity control see "Humidity Control" later in this chapter.

The U.S. government has set 68°F (20°C) as the maximum design indoor temperature for personnel comfort during the heating season in areas where *employees* work. In *manufacturing areas* the process requirements govern the actual temperature. From an energy-conservation point of view, if a process requires a space temperature greater than 5°F (2.8°C) above or below 68°F (20°C), it should, if possible, be treated separately and operate independently from the general personnel comfort areas. The staff members working in such areas should be provided with supplementary spot (localized) heating and/or ventilating systems as the conditions require in order to maintain personnel comfort.

If the stored products permit, garages and warehouses should be designed for the lowest temperature that is needed to prevent freeze-ups. In such buildings, locations to which personnel are assigned could have supplemental electric heaters, or hot-air or infrared heating systems. The process engineering department or quality control group should determine the manufacturing process space temperature. The manufacturer of the particular process equipment can be an alternative source for the recommended space temperature. The air temperature at the ceiling may vary beyond the comfort range and should be considered in calculating the overall heat transmission to the outdoors. A normal 0.75°F (0.42°C) increase in air temperature per foot (0.3 m) of elevation above the breathing level [5 ft (1.5 m) above finish floor] would be expected in normal applications, with an approximately 75°F (42°C) temperature difference between indoors and outdoors.

Determining the Design Heating Load

General.   From a physiological point of view, the ideal heating system would minimize the radiation and convection losses from the worker's body to the surrounding surfaces (to the point where the body will not detect a cooling sensation), while maintaining warm feet and a cool head for the workers. From an industrial or process point of view, the ideal heating system is one that satisfies the equipment and product's requirements at minimum energy expenditure and cost. Most heating systems must be designed as a compromise between these ideal goals and minimizing the life-cycle (sum of capital, energy, and maintenance) costs.

In colder climates, having floors (above unheated areas or on grade) and exterior walls well insulated is no guarantee that downdrafts from windows or exposed walls will not create a pool or pools of chilly air over large areas of the floor. When the floor slabs are on grade or above unheated spaces, it is especially important to provide a heating system that will deliver sufficient heat near the floor to counteract the downdrafts at the exterior walls and windows and the heat loss through the floor slabs.

It is reasonable to expect a normal commercial space-heating control system to maintain a specified space temperature within ±2°F (±1°C) of the thermostat set point. This is within the tolerance of personnel comfort heating. However, some industrial processes may be adversely affected if the ambient temperature varies more than ±0.5°F (±0.3°C) from the set point. If closer temperature control is required, that is, less than ±1°F (±0.6°C) from the set point, more sophisticated (and expensive) industrial controls must be considered.

Design.   One of the cardinal rules for a good, economical, energy-efficient design is *not* to design the total system (be it heating, ventilating, air conditioning, exhaust, humidification, dehumidification, etc.) to meet the most critical requirements of just a small (or minor) portion of the total area served. That critical area should be isolated and treated separately.

The designer today has the option of using either a manual method or a computer program to calculate heating and cooling loads, select equipment, and size piping and ductwork. For large or complex projects, computer programs are generally the most cost-effective and *should be used.* On projects where life cycle costs and/or annual energy budgets are required, *computer programs should be used.*

Where one or more of the following items will probably be modified during the design phase of a project, *computer programs should be used:*

- Building orientation
- Wall or roof construction (overall U value)
- Percentage of glazing
- Building or room sizes

However, for small projects, a manual method should be seriously considered before one assumes automatically that computer design is the most cost-effective for all projects.

Regardless of the computer program used, its specific input and operating instructions must be strictly followed. It is common to trace erroneous or misleading computer output data to mistakes in inputting the design data into the computer. *It cannot be overstressed that to get meaningful output results, the input data must be correctly entered and checked after entry before the program is run.* It is also a good policy, if not a mandatory one, to independently check the computer results the first time you run a new or modified computer program, to ensure the results are valid.

With the outdoor and inside design temperatures for each space determined, the heating load for each space can be calculated. The method for calculating heating loads as found in standard references such as the latest edition of ASHRAE's *Handbook of Fundamentals,*[4] Carrier Air Conditioning Company's *System Design Manual,*[2] and Buffalo Forge Company's *Fan Engineering*[8] should be used: The heating load from each space consists of the heat loss through the walls, floors, roof, and glass by conduction and convection plus the infiltration and ventilation losses. Radiation losses from the space to the outside are generally neglected.

Infiltration

The *infiltration heating load* is the amount of heat that must be provided to raise the temperature of the outside air leaking into the heated space through cracks and/or spaces in and around doors, windows, skylights, floors, walls, shafts, stairwells, etc., to the inside design air temperature.

Outside air infiltrates the building structure as a result of the pressure difference between inside and outside of the structure (inside is negative with respect to outside). The pressure difference may be due to wind or to the density difference of outside and inside air, often called the "chimney" or "stack" effect. It also can be caused mechanically by exhausting more air from the structure than is supplied to the structure.

Outside air infiltration is usually a significant portion of the heating load, especially in the colder climates. It is also important in determining the humidification requirements if the relative humidity of the space must be maintained above 10 percent during the heating season in the colder climates.

In buildings that have inadequate makeup air, the cracks around windows and doors are usually the major source of air leaking into the structures.

For a detailed discussion of infiltration, wind effect on structures, air density difference, and methods of calculating the quantity of air infiltrating a building, the reader is referred to the chapter "Infiltration and Ventilation" in the latest ASHRAE *Handbook of Fundamentals.*[4]

Methods for Determining Heating Load

Air-Change Method.   A quick method of determining the infiltration heating load is the *air-change method.* Though this method is not as accurate as the crack method, if used properly it will produce acceptable results.

The air-change method assumes the total air volume within a space will be completely exchanged with (displaced by) outside air a certain number of times each hour. In using this method it is difficult to define the proper space volume, particularly for high-ceiling areas. There is a tendency to assume a high rate of change per hour, especially in high-volume areas. This will result in overestimation of the heating load. As a result, in order to obtain a good estimate of the infiltration load, a greater amount of experience and judgment is required with this method than with the crack method. Nevertheless, the author has obtained satisfactory results with this method, using Table 1-1 in conjunction with Table 1-2, when time and/or the degree of accuracy does not permit or warrant the use of the crack method.

TABLE 1-1   Air Changes Occurring under Average Conditions Exclusive of Air Provided for Ventilation*

Kind of room	Number of air changes per hour
Spaces with no windows or exterior doors	0.5
Spaces with windows or exterior doors on one side	1
Spaces with windows or exterior doors on two sides	1.5
Spaces with windows or exterior doors on three sides	2

* Spaces with weatherstripped windows, or with storm sash, use two-thirds these values.

TABLE 1-2   Infiltration through Doors in Winter with a 15-mi/h Wind Velocity and Doors on One or Adjacent Windward Sides

Description	ft^3/(min) per (ft^2) area	
	Infrequent use	Average use 1 and 2 story building
Revolving door	1.6	10.5
Glass door, $\frac{3}{16}''$ crack	9.0	30.0
Wood door, $3' \times 7'$	2.0	13.0
Small factory door	1.5	13.0
Garage and shipping room door	4.0	9.0
Ramp garage door	4.0	13.5

The air-change-per-hour infiltration-load formula is

$$g = \frac{CH}{h} \times (\text{space volume}) \, 0.018(t_o - t_i) \qquad (1)$$

where
g = space-infiltration load, Btu/h (metric conversion: Btu/h $\times$ 0.293 = W)
CH/h = the number of air changes per hour selected from Table 1-1 or as specified by the engineer
space volume = the volume of the space corresponding to the selected CH/h, ft^3
0.018 = a constant equal to the specific heat of moist air at 70°F db and 50 percent relative humidity (RH) (0.244 Btu/(lb)(°F) divided by the specific volume of moist air at 70°F db and 50 percent RH (13.5 ft^3/lb)

$$\frac{0.244 \text{ Btu/(lb)(°F)}}{13.5 \text{ ft}^3\text{/lb}} = 0.018 \text{ Btu/(ft)}^3\text{(°F)}$$

t_o = outside design air temperature, °F
t_i = inside (space) design air temperature, °F

Door Infiltration Method.   The door infiltration-load formula is

$$g = \text{outside airflow} \ (1.08)(t_o - t_i) \tag{2}$$

where
g = door infiltration load, Btu/h (metric conversion: Btu/h × 0.293 = W)

outside airflow = cubic feet of air per minute selected from Table 1-2 times the number of square feet of door openings, ft³/min

1.08 = a constant equal to the specific heat of moist air at 70°F db and 50 percent RH [0.244 Btu/(lb)(°F)], divided by the specific volume of moist air at 70°F db and 50 percent RH (13.5 ft³/lb) multiplied by 60 to convert minutes into hours, Btu/(ft³/min)(h)(°F)

t_o = outside air temperature, °F

t_i = inside (space) air temperature, °F

To obtain the total building-infiltration heating load in Btu/h, one must add all the individual space-infiltration loads calculated by the air-change method [Eq. (1)] to the door-infiltration loads calculated with Eq. (2).

Though Table 1-1 was originally developed for residential buildings, here it is used in conjunction with Table 1-2 to estimate the infiltration loads of industrial office and manufacturing spaces with the following guidelines:

1. Table 1-1 can be used as shown for offices, laboratories, cafeterias, and other spaces having hung ceilings no higher than 10 ft (3 m).

2. For manufacturing plants, warehouses, and other areas with operable windows that occupy almost the entire exterior wall area, the number of changes per hour shown in this table should be increased by approximately 50 percent.

3. For manufacturing plants, warehouses, and other areas that have no exterior windows or a moderate number of them, with a height from the floor to the underside of the floor or roof above of 15 to 25 ft (4.6 to 7.6 m), the number of changes per hour shown in this table should be decreased by approximately 50 percent.

All values in Table 1-2 are based on the wind blowing directly at the door. When the prevailing wind direction is oblique to the doors, multiply the above values by 0.60 and use the total door area on the windward side(s). Table 1-2 is based on a wind velocity of 15 mi/h. For design wind velocities different from the base, multiply the table values by the ratio of velocities. Multiply the table values by $(V_e - V/15)$ for doors on the leeward side of the building. V_e is the equivalent velocity in miles per hour. V is the design or actual velocity in miles per hour.

Doors on opposite sides increase the above values 25 percent. Vestibules may decrease the infiltration as much as 30 percent when door usage is light. If door usage is heavy, the vestibule is of little value in reducing infiltration. Heat added to the vestibule will help maintain room temperature near the door.

Air curtains can, if properly sized and installed, reduce the infiltration on heavily used doors from 60 to 80 percent. However, installation of air curtains will not significantly reduce the heating energy cost; in fact, it may increase that cost. Therefore, the use of air curtains should be evaluated from a comfort, hygienic (if food and drugs are manufactured or processed), and life-cycle-cost standpoint.

VENTILATION

General

The optimum design goals of a general ventilation system for any space are to promote the health, comfort, and well-being of the occupants and the quality of the manufacturing process therein at minimum life-cycle and energy costs. These objectives can be accomplished by controlling the thermal conditions or the amounts of contaminants, or both, in the space environment.

Due to the high ambient dry- and wet-bulb temperatures prevalent during the summer months in many parts of the world, it is virtually impossible to achieve comfortable indoor environmental conditions with ventilation air only. Where ventilation systems are designed, it is recommended that they be designed for the greatest change of air that can be economically provided and that, where possible, the discharge distribution be designed to increase the evaporation rate from the bodies of personnel occupying the area.

The ventilation requirements for providing a safe working environment for personnel exposed to toxic, noxious, or hazardous gases or liquids are beyond the scope of this chapter. The reader is referred to Chap. 5-3 and to standard references such as: *Industrial Ventilation, A Manual of Recommended Practice;*[1] *Handbook of Ventilation for Contaminant Control,*[5] *Plant and Process Ventilation;*[6] and OSHA's requirements.

Likewise, determining the ventilation needed to maintain the thermal equilibrium of the body is beyond the scope of this chapter. The reader is referred to standard references such as the latest editions of *Industrial Ventilation, A Manual of Recommended Practice*[1] and ASHRAE's *Handbook of Fundamentals.*[4]

The two basic types of ventilation systems are *natural* and *mechanical.*

Natural Ventilation

Natural, or gravity, ventilation has a limited application since its effectiveness is directly dependent on prevailing winds outside the building and temperatures (stack effect) inside the building. It should be considered only for locations that have a reliable prevailing wind and where the personnel, manufacturing process, or product stored can tolerate temperature and/or humidity conditions above or below the design space values for prolonged periods.

In considering the feasibility of designing a natural ventilating system, the following guidelines are suggested:

1. Systems should be designed for wind velocities of half the average seasonal prevailing velocity.
2. In order to take maximum advantage of the stack effect (density difference), the supply air should enter through openings at or near the floor level of the space to be ventilated and leave through openings high in the wall and/or through gravity roof ventilators.
3. Locate air inlet openings on the side of the building facing directly into the prevailing wind.
4. Locate air outlets where prevailing wind movements will create low-pressure areas, i.e., on the side directly opposite the direction of the prevailing wind. Outlets may be placed on a roof in the form of individual gravity ventilators, continuous monitors, or ridge ventilators.
5. Inlet openings should not be obstructed by buildings, trees, signboards, indoor partitions, etc.
6. Greatest flow per unit area of total opening is obtained by using inlet and outlet openings of nearly equal areas.
7. Direct short circuits between openings on two sides at a high level may clear the air at that level without producing any appreciable ventilation at the lower level of occupancy.
8. The vertical distance between the inlets and outlets should be as great as possible in order to develop the greatest ventilation benefit from the temperature difference.
9. In multistory structures, openings in the neutral pressure zone are least effective for ventilation.

In general, natural ventilation for spaces is inadequate for the following cases:

1. Offices having an open window area that is less than 5 percent of the floor area
2. Offices more than 24 ft (7.3 m) deep and lacking cross ventilation

3. Offices with cross ventilation but having occupied space that is more than 35 ft (10.7 m) from a window or air inlet

4. Toilet rooms having window area that is less than 9 ft^2 (0.8 m^2) or less than 0.2 ft^2 (0.02 m^2) for each foot (0.3 m) of height or 5 percent of the floor area.

5. Cafeteria or assembly areas having a window area that is less than 6 percent of the floor area.

An estimate of the quantity of ventilation air required for natural ventilation can be obtained by applying the following rule of thumb (originally derived for residences, it can be applied to offices and other light-work areas): The ventilation air quantity should be based on changing the air within the space (with outside air) at least 30 times per hour in locations above latitude 37°N or below 37°S and 60 times per hour in locations between those latitudes and the equator.

For a detailed discussion of wind velocity and stack effect on buildings, the reader is referred to the latest edition of ASHRAE's *Handbook of Fundamentals.*[4]

Calculations for Natural Ventilation.   The minimum airflow quantities for ventilation can be calculated from:

$$Q = \frac{H}{60C_p \rho(t_i - t_o)} \tag{3}$$

where Q = ventilation airflow required, ft^3/min (metric conversion: ft^3/min × 0.000472 = m^3/s)

H = quantity of heat required to be removed, Btu/h; see discussion under "Mechanical Ventilation"

1/60 = constant to convert hours to minutes

C_p = specific heat of air at constant pressure at 70°F db and 50 percent RH = 0.244 Btu/(lb)(°F)

ρ = density of standard air (at 70°F db and 50 percent RH) = 0.0741 lb/ft^3

t_i = inside (space) design air temperature, °F db

t_o = outside design air temperature °F db (see discussion under "Climatic Conditions" to select values for t_o and t_i)

Note that the constant 1.1 can generally be substituted for the factor $60C_p\rho$ since it equals $60(0.244) \times 0.0741$ which closely approximates 1.1.

The minimum size required for the inlet air openings to provide the design airflow rates at the prevailing wind velocity can be calculated from:

$$A = \frac{Q_a}{EV} \tag{4}$$

where A = free area of inlet opening, ft^2 (metric conversion: ft^2 × 0.0929 = m^2)

Q_a = required ventilation airflow, ft^3/min, through the opening of area A. The number of openings should, where feasible, be selected to obtain a velocity as uniform as possible from the ventilation air across the space. Therefore, Q_a is equal to Q from Eq. (3) divided by the number of openings; i.e., $Q_a = Q/$(no. of openings).

E = effectiveness of opening (E should be taken as 0.50 to 0.60 for perpendicular winds, and 0.25 to 0.35 for diagonal winds.)

V = wind velocity, ft/min (mi/h × 88 = ft/min)

It is recommended that one-half the average velocity of the seasonal prevailing wind be used.

The flow of air due to the thermal forces within a building or space that has minimum internal resistance (to airflow) can be calculated using the following formula:

$$Q_t = 9.4A\sqrt{h(t_i - t_o)} \tag{5}$$

where Q_t = air flow, ft³/min, due to thermal forces only (metric conversion: ft³/min × 0.000472 = m³/s)

A = free area, ft², of inlets or outlets if they are equal. If they are not equal use the smaller value.

h = vertical height, ft, between inlet and outlet

t_i = average temperature of indoor air, °F db, at height h above the floor

t_o = outdoor temperature, °F db. For this formula it is assumed that both the indoor temperature at the floor and the outdoor temperature are close to 80°F.

9.4 = constant of proportionality, including a value of 65 percent for effectiveness of openings. This should be reduced to 50 percent (constant = 7.2) if conditions are not favorable.

The increase in airflow from unequal inlet and outlet areas can be approximated from Fig. 1-1. The value C_t obtained from Eq. (5) can be increased by increasing the percent obtained from Fig. 1-1.

Ratio of Outlet to Inlet or Vice Versa.   The combined flow due to wind and thermal forces (stack effect) is not equal to the flows estimated separately [Q_a from Eq. (4) and Q_t from Eq. (5)]. The flow can be approximated from Fig. 1-2 by entering at the bottom the ratio $Q_t/(Q_a + Q_t)$ and reading the factor that must be multiplied by the flow due to thermal effect Q_t to obtain the combined total flow. The combined flow is Q_t (factor from Fig. 1-2).

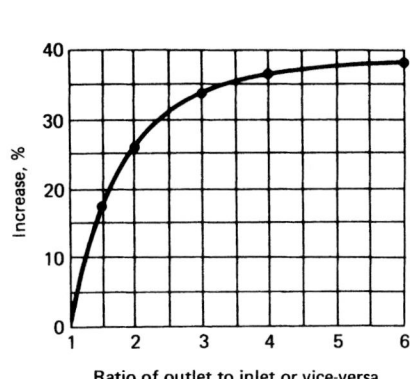

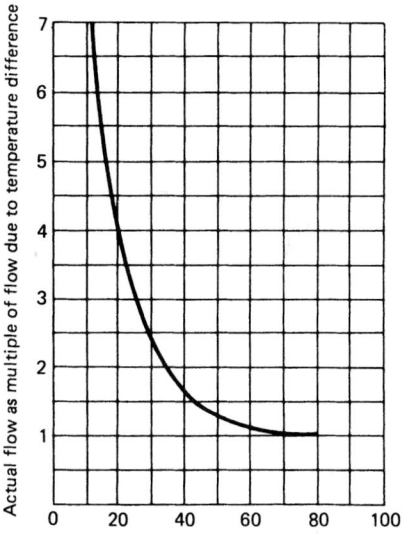

FIGURE 1-1   Increase in flow caused by excess of one opening over another.

FIGURE 1-2   Determination of flow caused by combined forces of wind and temperature difference.

When the flows Q_a and Q_t are equal, the actual combined flow will be about 30 percent greater than either Q_a or Q_t.

Selection of Natural Ventilation Equipment.   Once the number of cubic feet per minute of air required for natural ventilation and the inlet and outlet areas have been determined, the following items of equipment can be selected:

1. Operable windows

2. Weatherproof louvers

3. Doors

4. Operable skylights

5. Roof ventilators (gravity type)

6. Specially designed inlets and outlets

The location and size of the equipment (inlets and outlets), as previously discussed, are critical. The possible requirement that all or part of the ventilating equipment may have to be operating during severe precipitation storms, without incurring water and wind damage to the space, must not be overlooked when selecting equipment.

Gravity Roof Ventilator.   In general, all equipment should be selected for high flow-coefficient values. One of the most efficient units is the gravity roof ventilator. A roof ventilator should be selected for its:

1. Ability to utilize wind energy to induce flow by centrifugal or ejector action and the chimney effect.

2. Ruggedness.

3. Corrosion resistance.

4. Stormproof features (weatherproof inlets and outlet). Ventilators can be stationary, pivoting, oscillating, or rotating. They may also have manual dampers or dampers controlled automatically by a space thermostat or the wind velocity.

Mechanical Ventilation

General mechanical ventilation is required:

1. When the design quantities of outside ventilation and exhaust air cannot be supplied continuously by natural forces

2. When it is mandatory to have a positive supply and/or exhaust ventilating system

3. When it is required to pressurize an area by supplying substantially more ventilation supply air (outside air) than the exhaust or return air from the space

4. When a process requires a specified quantity of supply or exhaust air

5. For spaces containing fumes and vapor with specific gravity greater than that of air (in which case the exhaust intakes must be located at the floor level)

Mechanical ventilation systems range from the simplest type (consisting of through-the-wall propeller fans with roof-type exhaust fans and manual controls) to complex systems that have multiple supply and exhaust fans, distribution ducts, registers and/or grilles, filters, duct insulation, and automatic controls.

Calculations for Mechanical Ventilation.   Ventilation systems are designed to perform one or both of the following functions:

1. To control odors, maintain acceptable O_2 and CO levels, and to provide the quantities of supply and exhaust air required by the processes within an area

2. To maintain space temperatures (as far as possible without air conditioning) at a specified design temperature

Pressure Requirements.   The ventilation-air quantity calculated from the appropriate factors listed in "Table of Outdoor Air Requirements for Ventilation," ASHRAE Standard ANSI/ASHRAE 62-1989,[7] should be considered the exhaust-air quantity. Therefore, in order to determine the quantity of ventilation supply air, the designer has to determine whether the space in question should be under a negative, neutral, or positive pressure.

POSITIVE PRESSURE.   When there is no code or process requirement, it is suggested that the ventilated space be under a positive pressure. That is, the supply air quantity to the space is greater than the exhaust air quantity from the space. Under these conditions the quantity of supply air can be up to 10 percent greater than the quantity of exhaust air.

NEUTRAL PRESSURE.   The supply air quantity equals the exhaust air quantity.

NEGATIVE PRESSURE.   The supply air quantity is less than the exhaust air quantity. If no specific value is stipulated, then the quantity of supply air should not be less than 90 percent of the quantity of exhaust air.

Controlling Odors.   The quantity of ventilation exhaust air required to control odors and maintain acceptable O_2 and CO levels within a space can be calculated with the following formula:

$$Q_p = f_{vp}N_p \tag{6}$$

where Q_p = ventilation exhaust air required, ft³/min, because of number of workers within the space (metric conversion: ft³/min $\times$ 0.000472 = m³/s)

f_{vp} = ventilation airflow, ft³/min, per person based on activity level of those working. This value can be obtained from "Table of Outdoor Air Requirements for Ventilation," ASHRAE Standard ANSI/ASHRAE 62-1989.[7]

N_p = number of people working in or assigned to the space

Note: If the physical activity levels differ markedly among the workers within a space, it is a matter of engineering judgment whether the ventilation rates should be calculated separately to determine the total airflow or whether one activity level can be selected to determine the required rate.

The quantity of ventilation exhaust air from spaces where people are not permanently assigned (transient), or from spaces where the number of people assigned per square foot of floor area is so small that another factor (e.g., area, number of workers) will govern, can be calculated with the following formula:

$$Q_s = f_s N_u \tag{7}$$

where Q_s = ventilation exhaust air required, ft³/min, to flow from the space (metric conversion: ft³/min $\times$ 0.000472 m³/s)

f_s = ventilation airflow per unit, such as ft³/(min)(ft²) of floor area or ft³/min per locker. This value is obtained from "Table of Outdoor Air Requirements for Ventilation," ASHRAE Standard ANSI/ASHRAE 62-1989.[7]

N_u = number of units corresponding to the space and f_s

Process Requirements.   The process exhaust requirements should be obtained from the process engineering department. As a second choice, the manufacturer of the process equipment should be consulted.

The quantity of ventilation air calculated by Eq. (6) or (7) for the same space must be compared with the process supply and exhaust rates. If it is greater than the required process exhaust, then the quantity of ventilation exhaust air calculated by Eq. (6) or (7) will govern and be used to determine the quantity of space supply air. If, however, the process exhaust air requirements are greater than the ventilation exhaust calculated by Eq. (6) or (7), then the quantity of process exhaust air will govern and will be used to determine the quantity of ventilation supply air.

The ventilation supply and exhaust rates that satisfy the space odor, O_2, CO, and process requirements must be checked to see if they have sufficient cooling capacity to remove the internal space heating load during the summer season.

Internal Space Heat Gain.   The internal space heat gain is the sum total of the sensible heat from people, lights, process, and solar radiation. For our ventilation-load calculations only, the space heat loss through the exterior walls, doors, windows, and roof can be neglected. Note that since we are not considering air conditioning, the space design temperature must be higher than the outdoor design temperature.

PERSONNEL.   The heat gain from the personnel working within the space can be calculated from

$$g_p = f_{shp}N_p \tag{8}$$

where g_p = heat gain from the people within the space, Btu/h (metric conversion: Btu/h ×
0.0293 = W)

f_{shp} = sensible heat rate per person, Btu/h. This value depends on the activity level of
the workers. It is obtained from "Table of Rates of Heat Gain from Occupants
of Conditioned Spaces," ASHRAE *Handbook of Fundamentals*[4]

N_p = number of people working or assigned to the space

LIGHTS.   The heat gain from the lights is equal to the total wattage installed in the space
multiplied by 3.4.

$$g_l = 3.4t_l \tag{9}$$

where g_l = heat gain from electric lights, Btu/h (metric conversion: Btu/h × 0.0293 = W)

t_l = total number of watts from the lights that are energized during the time the
design outdoor air temperature is anticipated. When fluorescent lights are used,
the heat generated in the ballast must be added to the tube wattage to obtain the
total lamp wattage. It is usually satisfactory to increase the tube wattage by 25
percent to include the ballast wattage.

PROCESS LOAD.   Information concerning the amount of heat from the process should
come from the process engineering department and the quantity should be expressed in
British thermal units per hour. This load, like the lighting load, must coincide in the time with
the maximum design outdoor air temperature.

If process-load data cannot be obtained from the process engineering department, then an
estimate can be made by the following methods:

1. If the process is electrically powered with all the process heaters, motors, etc., located within
   the space, and if it is possible to measure the average power demand in watts or watthours
   for 1 h coincident with the time of the design outdoor temperature, then the process internal load will equal this value converted directly into British thermal units per hour.

2. If this is not possible, list the total nameplate horsepower and heater loads of all the process equipment that will be energized during the time of the design outdoor temperature.
   The values in this list should all be converted to one set of units, then multiplied by a diversity factor to obtain the simultaneous demand. Generally, multiplying the total connected
   nameplate load by 50 percent will give a reasonable approximation.

3. If the process equipment is supplied with other energy sources, such as steam, hot water,
   gas, and oil, then the manufacturer of the equipment should be contacted for the internal
   heat load to the space.

4. The internal power load is generally constant throughout the year. If this is the case, then
   the internal load may be measured at any season of the year.

TOTAL INTERNAL SPACE HEAT LOAD.   The total internal space heat load is equal to the heat
gain from personnel plus heat gain from lighting plus the total process load:

$$g_{ti} = g_p + g_l + g_{process} \tag{10}$$

where g_{ti} = total internal heat gain to the space (people + lights + process), Btu/h (metric
conversion: Btu/h × 0.293 = W).

To check whether the ventilation flow, in cubic feet per minute (to control odor, CO, and
O_2), is adequate to maintain the design space temperature in the summer, the following formula should be used:

$$t_i = t_o + \frac{g_{ti}}{1.08Q_v} \tag{11}$$

where t_i = inside space dry-bulb temperature, °F [metric conversion: (°F − 32)5/9 = °C]

t_o = outside design dry-bulb temperature in summer, °F (see "Climatic Conditions")

Q_v = ventilation airflow determined in this section, ft³/min (metric conversion:
ft³/min × 0.000472 = m³/s)

If t_i from Eq. (11) is less than the inside design space dry-bulb temperature, then the ventilation air Q_v is adequate to maintain space dry-bulb temperatures in the summer. The space humidification should be checked at this point (see the discussion on dehumidification under "Humidity Control"). If t_i from Eq. (11) is greater than the inside design space temperature, then the ventilation air Q_v is inadequate and must be increased or a higher design temperature must be accepted.

Ventilation Air Quantity.   To calculate the quantity of ventilation air required to maintain the original space design dry-bulb temperature, the following formula should be used:

$$Q = \frac{g_{ti}}{1.08(t_i - t_o)} \tag{12}$$

where Q = summer ventilation air quantity, ft³/min (metric conversion: ft³/min × 0.000472 = m³/s)
g_{ti} = total internal heat gain to the space, Btu/h (people + lights + process)
t_i = inside dry-bulb design air temperature, °F
t_o = outside dry-bulb design air temperature, °F

The preceding procedure is repeated for each space within the structure.

For energy conservation the additional ventilation required during the summer months should be provided by two-speed fans or additional exhaust fans that will be used only during warm weather. The reader is referred to Sec. 15 of this book for a comprehensive discussion of energy conservation technology.

As the temperature differential between the inside space and outside design diminishes, the required ventilation airflow increases rapidly. There is a point where it will be more economical to air-condition the space, rather than to try to ventilate it. To determine whether it is more economical to air-condition or to ventilate, a detailed study should be performed. Although such a study is beyond the scope of this chapter, the following guidelines are suggested:

1. If the design space temperature is no more than 5°F (2.8°C) higher than the outdoor design temperature, air conditioning is usually more economical than ventilation to maintain the space temperature.

2. If the design space temperature is between 5 and 10°F (2.8 and 5.6°C) higher than the outside design temperature, a ventilation system may be more economical than an air-conditioning system to maintain space dry-bulb temperature.

3. When the space temperature is more than 10°F (5.6°C) higher than the outdoor design temperature, a properly designed ventilating system will usually be capable of maintaining the space dry-bulb conditions. However, space dehumidification may be required to control the humidity.

Selection of System Size.   After determining the ventilation supply and exhaust quantities for each space within the structure, the designer must decide on the type and size of mechanical ventilating system that will most effectively meet the project's needs.

Some of the factors to be considered are:

1. Should the total building be ventilated with one system or with more than one independent system?

2. Is a supply fan system required to provide the makeup air for the exhaust system?

3. Although we are only considering ventilation in this section, space for heating equipment, depending upon the geographic location, may also be required.

4. The fewer the number of pieces of mechanical equipment installed, the less maintenance is required.

If the structure is one-story, with spaces having at least one external wall, it may be more economical to install rooftop exhaust fans with through-the-wall supply fans, thereby keeping the ductwork and automatic controls to a minimum.

On the other hand, in multistory structures or single-story structures with numerous spaces per floor, a ducted supply and exhaust system is more common. The designer should combine compatible respective supply and exhaust systems where governing codes or process requirements permit. This will usually require more sophisticated automatic controls, especially if the process equipment in all the spaces is not operated at the same time.

Good engineering practice as well as energy conservation considerations mandate that all spaces operating at the same time be served by the same system. This does not preclude the use of many fans or systems. It does mean that areas that operate at different times or processes that are operated intermittently should be on separate systems, so that they can be shut off when not required. Although duct design is beyond the scope of this chapter, the reader is referred to standard references such as the latest edition of *Industrial Ventilation, A Manual of Recommended Practice*[1] and ASHRAE's *Handbook of Fundamentals.*[4] As a guide, Table 1-3 lists representative velocities in ducted systems.

The reader is referred to the following sections of this book for additional related information:

- Section 11 for instrumentation and automatic controls
- Section 12 for noise and vibration control
- Section 15 for energy conservation techniques

In order to achieve the maximum cooling effect (air motion in the occupied zone), registers or grilles are preferred to diffusers for distributing the ventilation supply air.

Depending on the geographic location, different quantities of supply air may be highly desirable to maximize the cooling effect during the warmer months and minimize the energy cost during the heating season. The capacity of the exhaust fan system need not be increased during the summer ventilation season, if additional, strategically located relief air capability is provided. Methods of providing increased supply air (depending on the building interior space arrangement, construction, and proposed ventilating system) can vary from opening

TABLE 1-3   Suggested and Maximum Duct Velocities

Designation	Recommended velocities, ft/min (m/s)		Maximum velocities, ft/min (m/s)	
	Schools, theaters, public buildings	Industrial buildings	Schools, theaters, public buildings	Industrial buildings
Outside air intakes	500	500	900	1200
	(2.5)	(2.5)	(4.6)	(6.1)
Filters*	300	350	350	350
	(1.5)	(1.8)	(1.8)	(1.8)
Heating coils	500	600	600	700
	(2.5)	(3)	(3)	(3.6)
Air washers	500	500	500	500
	(2.5)	(2.5)	(2.5)	(2.5)
Suction connections	800	1000	1000	1400
	(4.1)	(5.1)	(5.1)	(7.1)
Fan outlets	1300–2000	1600–2400	1500–2200	1700–2800
	(6.6–10.2)	(8.1–12.2)	(7.6–11.2)	(8.6–11.2)
Main duct	1000–1300	1200–1800	1100–1600	1300–2200
	(5.1–6.5)	(6.1–9.1)	(5.6–8.1)	(6.6–14.2)
Branch ducts	600–900	800–1000	800–1300	1000–1800
	(3–4.6)	(4.1–5.1)	(4.1–6.6)	(5.1–9.1)
Branch risers	600–700	800	800–1200	1000–1600
	(3–3.6)	(4.1)	(4.1–6.1)	(5.1–8.1)

* These velocities are for total face area, not the net free area; other velocities in this table are for net free area.

windows to installing manual or automatic relief dampers (connected to exterior relief louvers), to increasing the proposed exhaust system's capacity proportionally.

The supply registers or grilles should be selected so that they will deliver the required air quantities in cubic feet per minute, have terminal velocities comparable to those shown in Table 1-4, and have a maximum resistance to airflow of 0.25 in H_2O (62.25 Pa).

TABLE 1-4 Suggested Terminal Velocity for Supply Registers and Grilles

Area	Terminal velocity	
	ft/min	m/s
Private office	50–100	0.25–0.50
General office	100–150	0.50–0.75
Industrial plants and process areas	150–200	0.75–1
Corridors	300	1.5

If, during the summer, the cooling effect from the ventilation system is to be maximized, higher terminal velocities should be considered (see Table 1-4). During the heating season the lower velocities will result in a more comfortable environment for the staff.

Supply registers and grilles should be the double-deflecting type. Greater care is required for the selection of systems using supply grilles than for registers to assure proper air-conditioning capability. In lieu of air conditioning, the degree of cooling comfort can be maximized if the supply air is capable of absorbing heat. If the dry-bulb temperature of the air is reasonably lower than human body temperature, or if its humidity is low enough to allow evaporation of sweat, a blast of air with a velocity up to 400 or 500 ft/min (2 or 2.5 m/s) directed at the workers will be effective. Velocities higher than 500 ft/min (2.5 m/s) should not be used. If the air is at or above body temperature, or nearly saturated, this method of blast or velocity cooling should not be considered since its use will actually decrease the workers' comfort level.

Table 1-5 can be used as a guide to the maximum environmental dry- and wet-bulb temperatures that healthy workers can tolerate in an 8-h day.

In general, in office space or equivalent, return registers or grilles, when located at or adjacent to the floor, should be sized for low air volumes per grilles or register, and the velocities should be between 300 and 500 ft/min (1.5 and 2.5 m/s). If return registers and grilles are mounted high on the sidewall or in the ceiling, they may be selected to carry air at 600 to 1200 ft/min (3 to 6 m/s) with no objectionable noise generated. The return registers or grilles should be selected so that they will deliver the required air quantities, have velocities over the gross area as shown in Table 1-6, and have a maximum resistance to airflow of 0.2 in of water (50 Pa).

Exterior intake (supply) storm louvers should be designed to minimize the entrance of rain and/or snow. A plenum should be provided immediately behind the louver, with its bottom pitched so that any moisture entering the louver will drain out the bottom portion of the louver. All joints in the lower portion of this plenum must be waterproof. Louvers should be provided with bird screen [0.25 in (0.006 m) grid minimum]. In cold climates there should be a means to stop the airflow so as to minimize heat loss when the system is not operating. Dampers are commonly used for this purpose; they can be manual or automatic depending on the complexity of the system.

HUMIDITY CONTROL

General

Depending on the activity or functions taking place within a space, humidity control may or may not be required.

TABLE 1-5   High Environmental Dry- and Wet-Bulb Temperatures* That Can Be Tolerated in Daily Work by Healthy, Acclimatized Employees Wearing Warm-Weather Clothing

Activity	Relative humidity, %	Air velocity					
		15–25 ft/min (0.08–0.13 m/s)		100 ft/min (0.5 m/s)		300 ft/min (1.5 m/s)	
		Dry-bulb, °F(°C)	Wet-bulb, °F(°C)	Dry-bulb, °F(°C)	Wet-bulb, °F(°C)	Dry-bulb, °F(°C)	Wet-bulb, °F(°C)
Summer season, light sedentary activities	80	89 (31.7)	84 (28.9)	91 (32.8)	85 (29.4)	93 (33.9)	87 (30.6)
	60	94 (34.4)	82 (27.8)	96 (35.6)	84 (28.9)	98 (36.7)	85 (29.4)
	40	100 (37.8)	79 (26.1)	101 (38.3)	81 (27.2)	103 (39.4)	82 (27.8)
	20	109 (42.8)	75 (23.9)	110 (43.3)	75 (23.9)	110 (43.3)	75 (23.9)
	5	119 (48.3)	69 (20.6)	118 (47.8)	69 (20.6)	117 (47.2)	68 (20.0)
Summer season, heavy work	80	83 (28.3)	78 (25.6)	86 (30.0)	81 (27.2)	89 (31.7)	83 (28.3)
	60	88 (31.1)	76 (24.4)	90 (32.2)	78 (25.6)	93 (33.9)	80 (26.7)
	40	93 (33.9)	73 (22.8)	95 (35)	75 (23.9)	97 (36.1)	76 (24.4)
	20	100 (37.8)	69 (20.6)	101 (38.3)	70 (21.1)	102 (38.9)	70 (21.1)
	5	107 (41.7)	64 (17.8)	107 (41.7)	54 (17.8)	106 (41.1)	63 (17.2)
Winter season, light or heavy	80	78 (25.6)	73 (22.8)	81 (27.2)	77 (25.0)	85 (29.4)	79 (26.1)
	60	81 (27.2)	71 (21.7)	85 (29.4)	74 (23.3)	88 (31.1)	76 (24.4)
	40	86 (30.0)	68 (20.0)	89 (31.7)	70 (21.1)	91 (32.8)	72 (22.2)
(75 ET)	20	91 (32.8)	63 (17.2)	93 (33.9)	65 (18.3)	94 (34.4)	66 (18.9)
	5	97 (36.1)	58 (14.4)	97 (36.1)	58 (14.4)	97 (36.1)	59 (15)

* Including radiation effect.

For comfort and prevention of material deterioration, the relative humidity generally should not exceed 60 percent at any point in occupied spaces. A notable exception is in textile mills. Normally the relative humidity should not fall below 20 percent to prevent human throats and nostrils from becoming dry and furniture from drying excessively.

Comfort

During the heating season it is beneficial to the health and comfort of the people within a space to maintain the relative humidity above 25 to 30 percent. In colder climates the possibility of excessive condensation on cold surfaces such as exterior glass windows must be avoided. See Fig. 1-3 for maximum space relative humidity without condensation on surfaces.

For a comfort heating application it is possible to supply an acceptable degree of comfort to the average person with a relatively low space dry-bulb temperature and a higher relative

TABLE 1-6   Suggested Gross Velocities for Return Air Registers or Grilles

	Gross velocity access face, ft/min (m/s)
Office area (location of returns)	
Above occupied zone	800–1250
	(4.1–6.4)
Within occupied zone not near personnel	600–800
	(3–4.1)
Within occupied zone near personnel	300–600
	(1.5–3)
Door or wall louvers	500–1000
	(2.5–5)
Industrial plants	800–1200
Process areas—Corridors	(4.1–6)

humidity in lieu of a relatively high dry-bulb temperature and lower relative humidity. *Under certain conditions this can result in lower total energy costs.*

Humidity control during the summer months may be justified from both a personal comfort and productivity point of view. The locations in the world where it is more economical (or for that matter, physically possible) to control the humidity (dehumidify) for personnel comfort (space design conditions around 80°F db and 50 percent RH) without air conditioning are extremely few.

Table 1-7 is to be used with Fig. 1-3 to correct relative humidities where condensation will occur for space or room temperatures of 60 and 80°F (15.6 and 26.7°C).

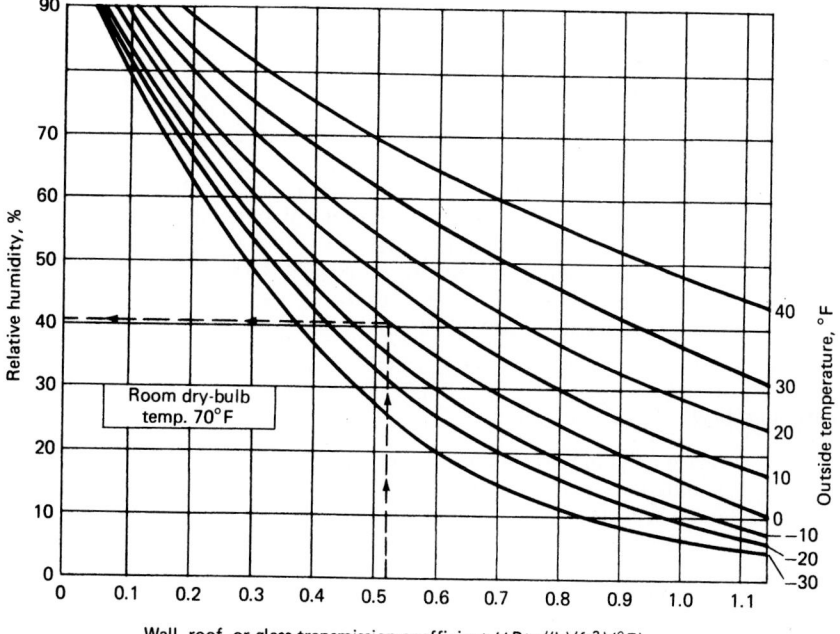

FIGURE 1-3   Maximum room RH without condensation.

TABLE 1-7   Correction in Room RH, Percent, for Wall, Roof, or Glass Transmission Coefficient U

Outdoor temp, °F db	Transmission coefficient, Btu/h(ft²)(°F)					
	$U = 1.1$		$U = 0.65$		$U = 0.35$	
	Room temp, °F db					
	60	80	60	80	60	80
−30	+1.0	−1.0	+1.5	−2.0	+2.5	−2.0
−20	+1.0	−1.5	+2.5	−2.5	+3.0	−2.0
−10	+2.0	−2.0	+3.5	−3.0	+3.0	−2.0
0	+3.5	−2.5	+4.0	−4.0	+3.5	−2.5
10	+5.0	−3.5	+5.0	−4.5	+4.0	−3.0
20	+7.0	−4.0	+6.5	−5.0	+4.5	−3.5
30	+9.0	−7.5	+8.5	−6.0	+5.0	−4.0
40	+12.0	−9.5	+9.5	−7.5	+6.0	−4.5

Process

It is not uncommon for a particular manufacturing process or product storage area to require that the space humidity and temperature be controlled year-round within a specified range. Whenever possible the manufacturer's required relative humidity and room temperature should be maintained. When the manufacturer's or process humidity range is not available, Table 1-8 can be used as a guide.

The industries and products in Table 1-8 will derive great benefit when protected against humidities lower than the levels shown. Humidifiers, with the capacity to maintain at least the relative humidities indicated, should be provided where required.

Static Electricity Control

In explosive environments, humidity control that maintains the space relative humidity at or above 50 percent is strongly recommended to minimize the possibility of static electricity causing an explosion. Some codes and insurance carriers specify minimum space humidity levels in explosive environments.

In situations where a person receiving a static electricity shock could sustain an injury or where a product could be damaged during manufacturing or processing, the economic merits of humidity control should be evaluated. There are other processes, such as computer applications, where humidity control is required not only to minimize the static electricity problem but also to stabilize the physical size of the computer key punch cards. Computer manufacturers' specifications should be carefully followed.

Dehumidification

Space dehumidification is generally accomplished by supplying air to the space to be dehumidified at a sufficiently lower moisture content that the supply (ventilating) air can absorb the space latent load without exceeding the design condition. The three most common methods used to dehumidify a space are:

1. Passing the total supply (ventilation) air through a dehumidifier prior to discharging it within the space

2. Passing part of the supply (ventilation) air through a dehumidifier, then mixing the dehumidified airstream with the mainstream prior to discharging the total supply (ventilation) air within the space

TABLE 1-8   Recommended Relative Humidities

Industries or products	RH, %	Industries or products	RH, %	Industries or products	RH, %
Abrasives	50–60	Cordage	60–70	Labels	40–50
Agronomy	60–70	Cotton	60–70	Laboratories	50–*
Air conditioning	30–40	Decals	50–60	Lace	50–60
Animal rearing	50–60	Egg storage	70–80	Leather	45–55
Antiques	30–40	Elastic yarns	50–60	Letterpress printing	40–50
Apple storage	70–80	Electronic computers	40–50	Lithography	45–55
Art galleries	30–40	Environmental chambers	*	Meats	75–85
Bag making	40–50	Film processing	50–60	Mullers	80–90
Bag storage	50–60	Film storage	40–50	Museums	40–50
Bakeries	60–70	Florists	50–60	Pharmaceuticals	*
Belting	50–60	Food storage	60–70	Photography	40–50
Bowling alleys	30–40	Fruit storage	70–80	Pipe organs	40–50
Braiding	45–55	Furniture	40–50	Printing	40–50
Breweries	65–75	Glass (lenses)	50–60	Radium	40–50
Cabinet making	30–40	Gloves	50–60	Rayon	45–50
Candy	40–50	Gluing	50–60	Silks	50–60
Carpet	50–60	Greenhouses	*	Synthetics	45–55
Cartons	40–50	Hatcheries	60–70	Tapes	40–50
Cellophane	40–50	Hats (fur felt)	50–60	Textiles	45–55
Ceramics	40–50	Horticulture	40–50	Tobacco	50–60
Cereals	35–45	Hosiery	50–60	Wood	40–50
Cigarettes	50–60	Hospitals	40–50	Wool	50–60
Cigars	60–70	Incubators	60–70	X-ray	45–55
Containers, paper	40–50	Knitting	50–60	Yarn	50–60

* For these applications the range can be so great that consultation with specialists in these areas is recommended.

3. Recirculating space air through one or more dehumidifiers located within or adjacent to the space to be dehumidified

Moisture can be removed from an airstream by passing it through a *mechanical* or *chemical* dehumidifier.

Mechanical.   With *mechanical dehumidification* the airstream to be dehumidified is passed over the fins of a cooling coil where it is cooled below its dew point, thereby condensing moisture out of the incoming airstream. The amount of moisture condensed depends on how much lower the average coil temperature is than the dew point of the entering airstream. The greater the differential, the more water is condensed, and the drier the outgoing air. The desired cooling-coil temperature is usually controlled by circulating either a refrigerant (e.g., one of the fluorocarbons such as R123 or R22) or chilled water through the coils.

Chemical.   With *chemical dehumidifiers* the airstream is brought in contact with a substance which absorbs moisture out of the airstream that is passed over it. The amount of moisture absorbed depends on various factors such as dew point of the entering air, strength of the sorbent, surface area of sorbent, efficiency of contact of air molecules with the sorbent, duration of contact with sorbent, etc. Since the sorbent becomes saturated with moisture and must be replaced or regenerated (usually heat-dried) to enable it to again absorb moisture, a duplex system is desirable. This will assure continuous operation with one of the units in operation while the other is in a regeneration cycle.

    Sorbents.   Sorbents are solid or liquid materials which have the property of extracting and holding other substances (usually gases or vapors, e.g., water vapor) brought into contact with them. The sorption process always generates heat, the major part of which is the result of the condensation of water vapor. For commercial dehumidifying systems and equipment, a sorbent should have the following characteristics:

1. Suitable vapor-pressure characteristics, including high absorptive capacity.
2. Stability, i.e., it should not break down structurally or chemically in its operation and application, and should resist contamination by impurities.
3. Relative chemical inertness, i.e., it should be noncorrosive, odorless, nontoxic, and nonflammable.
4. Low viscosity and good heat transfer characteristics (liquids); relatively high density to avoid excessive bulk (solids)
5. Capability of regeneration or reactivation with methods and temperatures generally available.
6. Ready availability at moderate cost.

Common absorbents are lithium chloride, calcium chloride, lithium bromide, silica gel, and alumina gel.

Load Calculations

General. The actual net internal moisture (latent) load of a space is the algebraic summation of the following loads:

1. Gain in latent load from the occupants (see ASHRAE *Handbook of Fundamentals,*[4] "Table of Rates of Heat Gain from Occupants of Conditioned Spaces")
2. Net gain or loss in latent load from the process or products (gain if process or products give up moisture, loss if they absorb moisture)
3. Gain in latent load from aqueous (water) surfaces within the space
4. Gain in latent load from open flames within the space
5. Net gain or loss from water vapor migration through cracks, around doors, windows, and other openings*
6. Net gain or loss from water vapor transmitted through the building surfaces*
7. Net gain or loss from the moisture load of the ventilation (outside) air*

Generally, in a reasonably constructed building the internal space moisture load due to moisture migration through cracks and openings and its transmission through the building surfaces can be neglected.

Latent Loads

LATENT LOAD FROM PERSONNEL. The space latent load due to the personnel working within the space can generally be neglected if there is an average >300 ft^2 (27.9 m^2) of floor area per person. If necessary, however, it can be calculated using the following formula.

$$PLL = LL \times NP \times \frac{1}{h_{fg}} \qquad (13)$$

where   PLL = personnel latent load per hour, lb/h (metric conversion: lb/h × 0.4536 = kg/h)
         LL = latent load per hour, Btu/h per person. This value is obtained from ASHRAE *Handbook of Fundamentals,*[4] "Table of Rates of Heat Gain from Occupants of Conditioned Spaces." Enter at appropriate degree of activity of the personnel within the space.
         NP = average number of personnel working, or in the space, for more than 1 h
         h_{fg} = difference in enthalpy, Btu/lb between saturated vapor and liquid. This value is obtained from a saturated steam table such as the one in ASHRAE *Handbook of Fundamentals,*[4] in the chapter on psychometric tables, entitled "Thermody-

---

* The load will be a gain in space latent load if the design space moisture content in grains of moisture per pound of dry air is less than the moisture content at the adjacent area or of the outside air, in grains of moisture per pound of dry air.

namic Properties of Water at Saturation." Enter the space dry-bulb temperature in degrees Fahrenheit.

LATENT LOAD FROM PROCESS OR PRODUCT.   This value must be obtained from the process engineering department or its equivalent. It should be given in units of pounds (or kilograms) of moisture dissipated into the space or absorbed from the space per hour of production. Average hourly values are generally adequate.

Evaporation Load from Open Tanks.   If this load is not available from the process engineering department and it can reasonably be assumed that the fluid within the tank or tanks is similar to water as far as evaporation is concerned, the following formulas can be used to estimate this load:

$$w_v = S\left(\frac{95 + 0.425V}{\lambda_v}\right)(e_w - e_a) \qquad \text{For air flow parallel to the long axis of the tank} \tag{14}$$

$$w_v = S\left(\frac{201 + 0.88V}{\lambda_v}\right)(e_w - e_a) \qquad \text{For air flow transverse to the long axis of the tank} \tag{15}$$

where w_v = pounds of water evaporated into the airstream (space), lb/h (metric conversion: lb/h × 0.4536 = kg/h)

S = area of exposed water surface, ft^2

V = velocity of air flowing across the tank, ft/min. This velocity can be the design velocity across the tank, or it can be movement across the tank. In existing systems it may be possible to measure the actual velocity across tanks.

λ_v = latent heat of evaporation, Btu/lb. This value is obtained from Fig. 1-4 by entering the graph with the temperature of the fluid in the tank.

e_w = vapor pressure of the liquid in the tank, inHg. This value is obtained from Table 1-9 by entering the table with the temperature of the fluid in the tank.

e_a = vapor pressure of the air (for our purposes) within the space, inHg $e_a = e_w h$, where h is space relative humidity. This is the design space relative humidity.

Open Flames.   Generally, the amount of moisture added to a space as a result of burning a hydrocarbon or hydrogen fuel in an open flame within the space can be neglected.*

LATENT LOAD FROM MIGRATION THROUGH CRACKS AND OPENINGS.   The infiltration latent load will increase the space design dehumidification load when the moisture content of the design outside air conditions exceeds the space design conditions and reduce the load when it is less. From a psychrometric chart (such as the one in ASHRAE *Handbook of Fundamentals*[4] in the chapter on psychometrics), one can compare the design outside air moisture content with the space design conditions to determine if this load will increase or decrease the space dehumidification load.

When the outside air has less moisture than the space (which is usually the case during the heating season), this load can be omitted, since it will result in a conservative design. There are three general categories of this load:

Category One.   The space is mechanically ventilated. Furthermore, the space is not under a negative pressure (that is exhausted and/or returned from it or does not exceed the air supplied to it). Under these conditions, the latent load due to infiltration for all practical reasons will be zero and therefore can be omitted.

Category Two.   The space is mechanically ventilated. Furthermore, the space is under a negative pressure. Under these conditions the latent load from the infiltration must be accounted for. Assuming that the difference between the total air quantity exhausted from

---

* If there is a need to calculate this value, refer to one of the many references on the combustion reactions of common fuels.

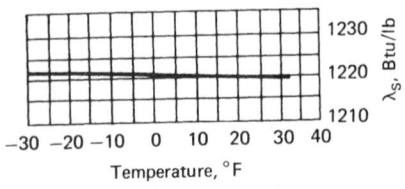

Latent heat of sublimation of ice

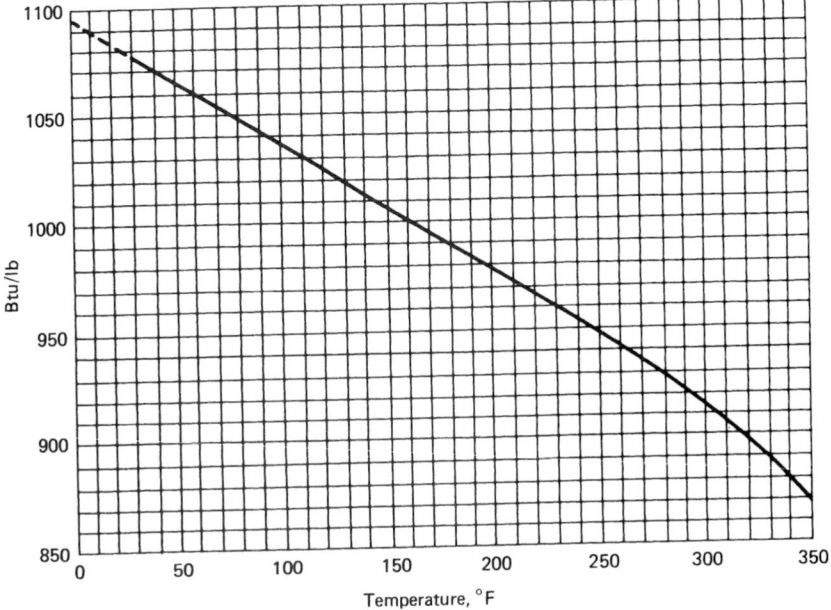

FIGURE 1-4 Latent heats of water and ice.

the space and that supplied to it will come from the outside air infiltrating the building, one can reasonably estimate this load by using the following formula.

$$\text{ILL} = \frac{\text{exhaust} - \text{supply}}{100{,}000} \times 60 \frac{\text{min}}{\text{h}} \ (f) \tag{16}$$

where   ILL = infiltration latent load through cracks and openings, lb/h (metric conversion: lb/h × 0.4536 = kg/h)

exhaust = total exhaust plus return air from the space, ft³/min

supply = total supply to the space, ft³/min

f = factor taken directly from Table 1-10 when the number of grains of moisture per pound of outside air of the space design is greater than that of the outside air. (This can be verified by comparing the design space conditions with the design outside air conditions on the appropriate psychromatic chart. If the number of grains of moisture per pound of air at the design outside conditions is greater than that of the design space (inside) conditions, then the factor f must be obtained from a psychrometic chart. Enter a psychrometric chart with the design outside dry-bulb and wet-bulb temperatures or the relative humidity and read the corresponding grains of moisture per pound of air. Repeat the same procedure with the space design conditions. Factor f is the difference between the outside and the inside grains per pound of air.

TABLE 1-9 Vapor Pressures e_w of Ice* and Water,† inHg

$t,{}^\circ F$	0	1	2	3	4	5	6	7	8	9
−20	.0126	.0119	.0112	.0106	.0100	.0095	.0089	.0084	.0080	.0075
−10	.0222	.0209	.0199	.0187	.0176	.0168	.0158	.0150	.0142	.0134
−0	.0376	.0359	.0339	.0324	.0306	.0289	.0275	.0259	.0247	.0233
+0	.0376	.0398	.0417	.0441	.0463	.0489	.0517	.0541	.0571	.0598
10	.0631	.0660	.0696	.0728	.0768	.0810	.0846	.0892	.0932	.0982
20	.1025	.1080	.1127	.1186	.1248	.1302	.1370	.1429	.1502	.1567
30	.1647	.1716	.1803	.1878	.1955	.2035	.2118	.2203	.2292	.2383
40	.2478	.2576	.2677	.2782	.2891	.3004	.3120	.3240	.3364	.3493
50	.3626	.3764	.3906	.4052	.4203	.4359	.4520	.4686	.4858	.5035
60	.5218	.5407	.5601	.5802	.6009	.6222	.6442	.6669	.6903	.7144
70	.7392	.7648	.7912	.8183	.8462	.8750	.9046	.9352	.9666	.9989
80	1.032	1.066	1.102	1.138	1.175	1.213	1.253	1.293	1.335	1.378
90	1.422	1.467	1.513	1.561	1.610	1.660	1.712	1.765	1.819	1.875
100	1.932	1.992	2.052	2.114	2.178	2.243	2.310	2.379	2.449	2.521
110	2.596	2.672	2.749	2.829	2.911	2.995	3.081	3.169	3.259	3.351
120	3.446	3.543	3.642	3.744	3.848	3.954	4.063	4.174	4.289	4.406
130	4.525	4.647	4.772	4.900	5.031	5.165	5.302	5.442	5.585	5.732
140	5.881	6.034	6.190	6.350	6.513	6.680	6.850	7.024	7.202	7.384
150	7.569	7.759	7.952	8.150	8.351	8.557	8.767	8.981	9.200	9.424
160	9.652	9.885	10.12	10.36	10.61	10.86	11.12	11.38	11.65	11.92
170	12.20	12.48	12.77	13.07	13.37	13.67	13.98	14.30	14.62	14.96
180	15.29	15.63	15.98	16.34	16.70	17.07	17.44	17.82	18.21	18.61
190	19.01	19.42	19.84	20.27	20.70	21.14	21.59	22.05	22.52	22.99
200	23.47	23.96	24.46	24.97	25.48	26.00	26.53	27.07	27.62	28.18
210	28.75	29.33	29.92	30.52	31.13	31.75	32.38	33.02	33.67	34.33
220	35.00	35.68	36.37	37.07	37.78	38.50	39.24	39.99	40.75	41.52
230	42.31	43.11	43.92	44.74	45.57	46.41	47.27	48.14	49.03	49.93
240	50.84	51.76	52.70	53.65	54.62	55.60	56.60	57.61	58.63	59.67
250	60.72	61.79	62.88	63.98	65.10	66.23	67.38	68.54	69.72	70.92
260	72.13	74.36	74.61	75.88	77.16	78.46	79.78	81.11	82.46	83.83
270	85.22	86.63	88.06	89.51	90.97	92.45	93.96	95.49	97.03	98.61
280	100.2	101.8	103.4	105.0	106.7	108.4	110.1	111.8	113.6	115.4
290	117.2	119.0	120.8	122.7	124.6	126.5	128.4	130.4	132.4	134.4
300	136.4	138.5	140.6	142.7	144.8	147.0	149.2	151.4	153.6	155.9
310	158.2	160.5	162.8	165.2	167.6	170.0	172.5	175.0	177.5	180.0
320	182.6	185.2	187.8	190.4	193.1	195.8	198.5	201.3	204.1	206.9
330	209.8	212.7	215.6	218.6	221.6	224.6	227.7	230.8	233.9	237.1
340	240.3	243.5	246.8	250.1	253.4	256.7	260.1	263.6	267.1	270.6
350	274.1	277.7	281.3	284.9	288.6	292.3	296.1	299.9	303.8	307.7
360	311.6	315.5	319.5	323.5	327.6	331.7	335.9	340.1	344.4	348.7
370	353.0	357.4	361.8	366.2	370.7	375.2	379.8	384.4	389.1	393.8
380	398.6	403.4	408.2	413.1	418.1	423.1	428.1	433.1	438.2	443.4
390	448.6	453.9	459.2	464.6	470.0	475.5	481.0	486.6	492.2	497.9
400	503.6	509.3	515.1	521.0	526.9	532.9	538.9	545.0	551.1	557.3

* Adapted from data of *International Critical Tables*, vol. 3, National Research Council, by McGraw-Hill, New York, 1928, p. 210.

† Adapted from data of J. H. Keenan and F. G. Keyes, *Thermodynamic Properties of Steam*, Wiley, New York, 1936. These data differ but slightly from the data of J. A. Goff and S. Gratch, "Thermodynamic Properties of Moist Air," *Trans. ASHVE*, vol. 51, pp. 125–164, 1945, and corrections thereto by J. A. Goff, "Saturation Pressure of Water on the New Kelvin Temperature Scale," *Trans. ASHVE*, vol. 63, pp. 347–354, 1957.

Source: This table was reproduced with permission from R. Jorgensen (ed.): *Fan Engineering,* 7th ed., Chap. 1, p. 8, copyright © 1970 by Buffalo Forge Company.

TABLE 1-10 Space Temperature, °F db*

RH, %	50	55	60	65	70	72	75	80	85	90
30	0	4	8	12	17	19	24	31	39	48
35	4	7	12	17	21	25	30	37	47	59
40	7	11	16	22	29	30	37	48	59	72
45	9	14	20	27	35	36	44	55	68	83
50	12	16	24	32	40	42	50	63	78	95
55	15	19	28	36	45	47	57	69	87	105
60	17	22	32	41	51	53	64	79	96	116
65	20	26	36	45	57	59	70	87	106	128
70	23	30	40	50	62	65	77	95	115	140
75	25	33	43	54	67	70	83	100	121	152
80	28	36	47	59	73	76	89	108	130	164

* Figures in this table are grains of moisture per pound of dry air. This table assumes that entering air will always provide 15 gr.

Category Three. The space is ventilated with a natural (gravity) ventilation system. Under this condition, the latent load due to infiltration must be accounted for. This load can be estimated by using the air-change method (described under "Infiltration" previously in this chapter) in conjunction with the following formula:

$$\text{ILL} = \left(\frac{\text{NCH} \times S}{100,000} \frac{1}{60} \right) f \tag{17}$$

where ILL = infiltration latent load through cracks and openings, lb/h (metric conversion: lb/h × 0.45359 = kg/h)

NCH = number of changes of air within the space per hour. See "Infiltration" to determine this value.

S = space volume, ft^3

f = factor. See notes under Eq. (16).

LATENT LOAD FROM OUTSIDE AIR. The discussion in the first paragraph of "Latent Loads from Migration through Cracks and Openings" is equally applicable to this load. In this case we are concerned only with the latent load that results in the introduction of outside air (via the mechanical ventilation system) into the space. Therefore, this load can be calculated using the following formula:

$$\text{OLL} = \frac{(\text{OA} \times 60/1)f}{100,000} \tag{18}$$

where OLL = outside air latent load, lb/h (metric conversion: lb/h × 0.45359 = kg/h)

OA = outside air (quantity), ft^3/min

f = factor. See notes under Eq. (16).

Total Space Dehumidification—Design Latent Load. The total dehumidification latent load (TDLL) for a space is equal to the algebraic summation of the personnel latent load (PLL), process latent load, evaporation open tank load, latent load from open flame(s), infiltration latent load from moisture migration through cracks and openings (ILL), and the outside air latent load (OLL):

$$\text{TDLL} = \text{PLL} \pm \text{process load } w_v + \text{open flame load} \pm \text{ILL} \pm \text{OLL} \tag{19}$$

Units for this load are pounds per hour (metric conversion: lb/h × 0.45359 = kg/h).

Selection of Dehumidifying Unit. The decision to use a mechanical or chemical dehumidifier depends on the designer's experience and the application, availability, and serviceability of the manufacturer's units. Generally, mechanical dehumidifiers are used when the design space relative humidity is 45 percent or higher and the dry-bulb temperature is approximately 75°F (23.9°C). Chemical dehumidifiers are used when lower space moisture values are required.

After calculating the design space dehumidification load, the designer should review the manufacturer's catalog selection data and determine which types and capacities of units are most appropriate.

Humidification

Space humidification is generally accomplished by either adding moisture to the supply (ventilation) air prior to its discharge into the space or adding moisture directly to the space. Sufficient moisture must be added to the normal (nonhumidified) space moisture content to satisfy the design (space) relative humidity at the design dry-bulb temperature.

Table 1-11 lists the various types of humidifiers commercially available in order of increasing maintenance requirements.

The five types of humidifiers are available in both the duct type (adds moisture to the supply airstream) and the space recirculating type (adds moisture directly to the space).

TABLE 1-11 Humidifier Types

1. Steam
2. Water spray (atomizing)
3. Centrifugal (atomizing)
4. Pan evaporation
5. Wick evaporation

Load Calculations.   The procedure for calculating the design humidification load is as outlined in the dehumidification "Load Calculations," except for the following modifications:

Evaporation Load from Open Tanks.   Since the evaporation from open tanks located within the space will always add moisture to the surrounding area, this load may safely be omitted if the exposed tank surface area is a small fraction of the space area. On the other hand, if the tank surface area is large in comparison with the space, omitting this load can result in seriously overdesigning the humidification system.

Latent Load from Migration through Cracks and Openings.   The moisture migrating through cracks and openings will increase the space design humidification load whenever the outside or adjacent area's moisture content is greater than the space moisture content and decrease it when it is less. This load calculation generally can be omitted when time or the degree of accuracy of the humidification design load does not warrant it. It can also be safely omitted when the outside air moisture content is greater than the space moisture content (which is not the usual case during the heating season), since it will result in a conservative design load.

Latent Load from Outside Air.   This load must be accounted for since it is generally the major portion of the space humidification design load.

Total Space Humidification—Design Latent Load.   The total humidification latent load (THLL) for a space is equal to the algebraic summation of the personnel latent load (PLL), process latent load, evaporation open tank load, latent load from open flame(s), infiltration latent load from moisture migration through cracks and openings (ILL), and the outside air latent load (OLL).

$$\text{THLL} = -\text{PLL} \pm \text{process load} - w_v - \text{open-flame load} \pm \text{ILL} \pm \text{OLL} \qquad (20)$$

THLL is expressed in pounds per hour (metric conversion: lb/h $\times$ 0.45359 = kg/h).

Selection of Humidifying Unit. The decision as to which type of humidifying unit should be selected depends on the application, availability, and serviceability as well as the designer's experience. After calculating the design space dehumidification load, the designer should review the manufacturer's catalog selection data and determine which types and capacities of units are the most appropriate.

The manufacturer's sizing and installation requirements should be adhered to in order to avoid the annoying problems of condensation of water, caused by impingement of the discharge from the humidifier on adjacent surfaces (especially on colder surfaces), and of supersaturation of the air in the vicinity of the humidifier discharge to the point where condensation commences.

ALTITUDE CORRECTIONS FOR HEATING AND VENTILATING SYSTEMS

General

The following material is a simplified discussion of the general altitude corrections required for heating and ventilating systems. The formulas and data presented in this chapter are for sea-level locations and generally can be used without correction for elevations up to 1500 ft (460 m). The effect of altitude at elevations up to 10,000 ft (3050 m) on the thermal properties of air (such as viscosity, thermal conductivity, and specific heat) is very small and can be neglected.

Corrections

When designing heating and ventilating systems for higher elevations [above 1500 ft (460 m)], corrections for air density, airflow (in cubic feet per minute or cubic meters per second), duct air friction, specific humidity, steam gauge pressure, and boiling temperature should be made. The correction factors should be obtained from the manufacturer of the equipment to be selected. The procedure presented here is to design a system as if it were at sea level, then (before selecting the equipment) to adjust the manufacturer's sea-level capacities by using the appropriate correction factor corresponding to the altitude of installation. In the event manufacturer's elevation (altitude) correction factors are not available, the factors from Tables 1-12 to 1-16 can be used.

Airflow Correction. Multiply the airflow at sea level by the appropriate correction factor to maintain the same mass flow rate (heating or cooling capability) at the actual altitude as exists at sea level.

Air Friction Correction. The duct air friction (standard air) is obtained from a standard duct friction chart, with the corrected airflow (in cubic feet per minute or cubic meters per second) for altitude from Table 1-13 and the duct sizes.

Heating Medium Corrections

Hot Water. No correction is needed.

Steam. Although altitude causes no change in the saturated temperature-pressure relationship, there is a change in the temperature corresponding to a certain gauge pressure (Tables 1-14 and 1-15).

Gas. The recommendation of the American Gas Institute for operating gas-fired heating units for altitude operation is as follows: Ratings need not be corrected for elevations up to 2000 ft (610 m). For elevations above 2000 ft (610 m), ratings should be reduced 4 percent for each 1000 ft (305 m) above sea level.

TABLE 1-12   Airflow Correction Factor, ft³/min (m³/s)

Elevation, ft (m)	Correction factor at 70°F (21.1°C)
2,500 (760)	1.1
5,000 (1,500)	1.2
7,500 (2,290)	1.33
10,000 (3,050)	1.46

TABLE 1-13   Duct Air Friction Correction Factors*

Elevation, ft (m)	Temp corr. factor F_1	Temp., °F (°C)	Temp. corr. factor F_2
2,000 (610)	0.944	0 (18)	1.120
4,000 (1,220)	0.890	50 (10)	1.031
6,000 (1,830)	0.838	100 (38)	0.957
8,000 (2,440)	0.788	150 (66)	0.894
10,000 (3,050)	0.742	200 (93)	0.840
		250 (121)	0.792
		300 (149)	0.749

* Duct air friction (at altitude and temperature) = duct air friction (standard air) $\times F_1 \times F_2$.

TABLE 1-14   Steam Gauge Pressure Reductions from Sea Level*

Elevation, ft (m)	Gauge pressure correction, psig (bars)
2,500 (760)	−1.3 (− 0.09)
5,000 (1,500)	−2.6 (−0.182)
7,500 (2,290)	−3.6 (−0.252)
10,000 (3,050)	−4.6 (−0.323)

* Altitude gauge pressure = sea-level gauge pressure − gauge pressure correction.

TABLE 1-15   Corresponding Saturated Steam Temperature at Various Altitudes and Gauge Pressures*

Elevation, ft (m)	Barometric pressure, psia (bars)	Saturared temperature at barometric pressure,°F (°C)	Saturated temperatures, °F (°C) Steam pressure, psig (bars) 2 (0.14)	10 (0.69)	50 (3.45)	100 (6.9)
0 (0)	14.7 (1.01)	212 (100)	218.5 (103.6)	239.4 (115.2)	253.6 (123.1)	288.6 (142.6)
2,500 (760)	13.41 (0.92)	207.3 (97.4)	214.4 (101.3)	236.4 (113.6)	296.3 (146.8)	287.9 (142.2)
5,000 (1,500)	12.23 (0.84)	202.9 (94.9)	210.4 (99.1)	233.6 (112)	251.4 (121.9)	287.2 (141.8)
7,500 (2,290)	11.12 (0.77)	198.3 (92.4)	206.3 (96.8)	230.9 (110.5)	293.9 (145.5)	286.6 (141.4)
10,000 (3,050)	10.10 (0.7)	193.7 (89.8)	202.4 (94.7)	228.2 (109)	292.8 (144.9)	285 (141.1)

* The heating equipment must be selected at the reduced temperatures.

TABLE 1-16   Minimum Required Primary Air (ft³/min and m³/s) for Electric Resistance Heaters at High Altitudes

Heater wattage	Elevation							
	2500 ft	760 m	5000 ft	1500 m	7500 ft	2290 m	10,000 ft	3050 m
500	39	0.018	43	0.020	47	0.022	51	0.024
1000	77	0.036	85	0.040	93	0.043	102	0.048
1500	110	0.052	121	0.057	132	0.062	146	0.069
2000	148	0.070	162	0.076	178	0.084	197	0.093
2500	181	0.085	198	0.093	218	0.102	240	0.113
3000	219	0.103	241	0.114	264	0.125	291	0.137
3500	252	0.119	277	0.131	304	0.143	335	0.158
4000	290	0.137	319	0.151	350	0.165	385	0.182
4500	323	0.152	354	0.167	382	0.180	429	0.202
5000	362	0.171	396	0.187	437	0.206	480	0.227

Electricity.   Altitude does not affect the capacity output of electric resistance heaters. However, it is necessary to increase the minimum required actual primary air volume over that published in order to maintain the same minimum air weight flow (Table 1-16). Failure to compensate for the reduction in air weight flow may trip the heater element's thermal overload.

Pump Correction.   Altitude affects the operation of pumps installed in open systems because it reduces the available net positive suction head (NPSH). The available NPSH must always be equal to or greater than the required NPSH in order to produce flow through the pump.

Motor Correction.   Since the effectiveness of cooling air depends on its density, motor cooling decreases with altitude. To compensate for this decrease, it is necessary to provide additional margin for the increase in motor temperature. Contact the motor manufacturer for recommendations and requirements.

Relative Humidity Correction.   The following adjustments are required to calculate loads at high altitude:

1. The design outside and room air moisture content must be adjusted to the new elevation by one of the following methods:
    a. If the dry-bulb temperature and percent relative humidity are given, divide the specific humidity at sea level by the air-density ratio.
    b. If the dry-bulb and wet-bulb temperatures are given, obtain the specific humidity at the altitude by using the following formula:

$$W_1 = W_0 + \frac{P_0 - P_1}{P_1} \times W_s \tag{21}$$

where W_1 = specific humidity
   W_0 = specific humidity at altitude for specified db and wb, lb/lb (kg/kg) of dry air
   W_s = specific humidity at sea level and saturated wb temperature, lb/lb (kg/kg) of dry air
   P_0 = barometric pressure, psia (bars)
   P_1 = altitude pressure, psia (bars)

2. The values of specific humidity can be obtained from the National Weather Service or from standard design references, such as ASHRAE's *Handbook of Fundamentals.*[4]

EQUIPMENT SELECTION

General

When selecting equipment, check with the equipment manufacturer to be sure that the catalog used to select the equipment is current; also be sure to follow recommended selection procedures. If there is any doubt, consult the manufacturer's representative to confirm that the unit and/or equipment selection is appropriate. Guidelines in the selection of dehumidification and humidification units are discussed under "Humidity Control."

Generally systems with the lowest installed cost are less efficient and may have the highest operating costs. *The total life-cycle cost should be determined,* since only with proper evaluation of initial, operating, and maintenance costs over the expected life of alternative equipment selections, can the most energy- and cost-efficient unit be selected.

Variable-Airflow Units

From an energy-conservation standpoint, when requirements permit the supply and/or return air quantities to be varied, variable-airflow units should be evaluated. There are four principal ways to achieve variable airflow. They are listed below in order of electric power saved:

1. Variable-pitch axial-flow fans
2. Fan-speed control
3. Inlet-vane (vortex dampers) control
4. Discharge-damper control

Variable-pitch axial-flow fans are not generally available in commercial heating and ventilating units. However, where large-capacity [above 75,000 ft^3/min (35.4 m^3/s) supply and exhaust volumes are required, this method of varying the fan's capacity should be evaluated.

Fan speed control is commercially available in two forms:

1. Electric control of speed of induction motors by one of the following methods:
   a. Voltage control
   b. Frequency control
   c. Multiple-speed (winding) motors
   d. Wound rotor motors
2. Mechanical control of speed of fans by one of the following methods:
   a. Fluid couplings
   b. Eddy current couplings
   c. Torque converters

Control of fans' speed is usually economical when large fans are required.

When variable-air-volume systems for energy conservation are evaluated, serious consideration should be given to evaluating ac adjustable-frequency-drive controls and motors on the bases of reliability, performance, and economy.

Outdoor Installation

If units are to be installed outdoors, it is recommended that they be specifically designed by the manufacturer and factory-assembled for outdoor installation. If such units are not available, then the following minimum weatherproofing should be provided.

1. Gaskets for all access doors and panels
2. Sealing washers under all removable panel screws
3. Two coats of epoxy paint, minimum total thickness 10 mils (0.000254 m)
4. Cadmium-plated or stainless-steel damper shafts

5. Stainless-steel or nonferrous-metal damper linkages
6. Stainless-steel or anodized aluminum dampers
7. Stainless-steel panel fasteners
8. Totally enclosed removable belt guards, if the fan drive is external to the unit
9. Totally enclosed motors

Heating and ventilating air-handling units generally are not designed as roof-mounted units (that is, for mounting directly on roof curbs). They should be mounted on a steel dunnage, fabricated to the particular unit's dimensions with appropriate pitch pockets at all roof penetrations. If ductwork and piping installation does not require more height, a minimum of 18 in (0.457 m) clearance under the dunnage beams should be provided for inspection and painting of the unit and the steel.

Unit Selection Criteria

The engineer must determine whether a single-zone heating and ventilating unit or a multizone heating and ventilating unit is more appropriate. See Figs. 1-5 and 1-6. Though the capacity and types of fans commercially available in heating and ventilating units vary with each manufacturer, the following are fairly typical.

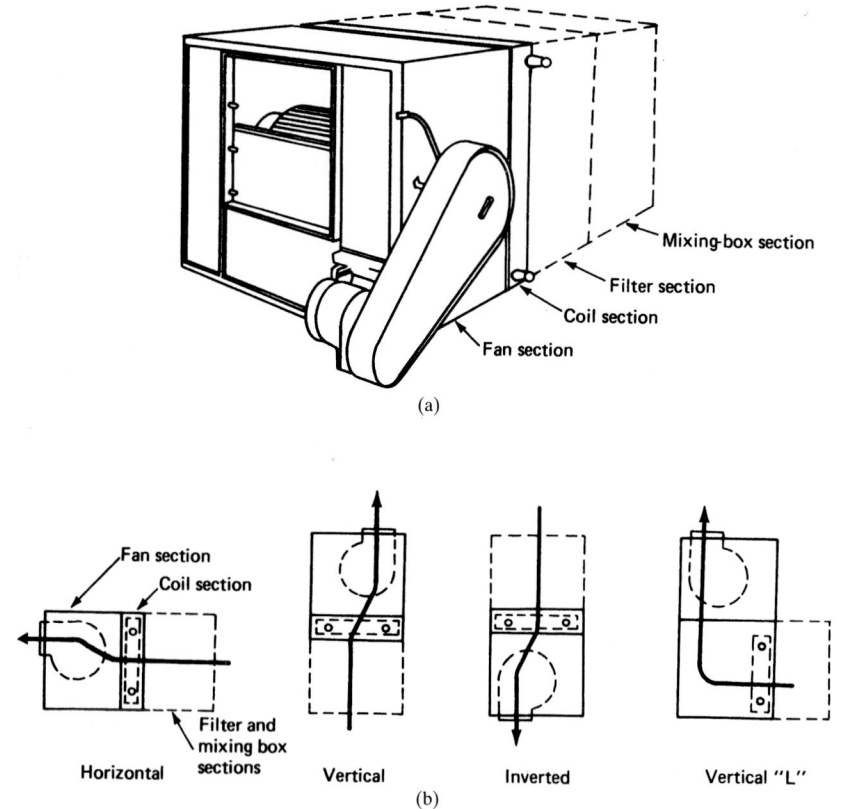

FIGURE 1-5 (*a*) Typical single-zone draw-through heating and ventilating unit. (*b*) Typical arrangements for a single-zone draw-through heating and ventilating unit; the dotted line indicates an accessory section. *Note:* Blow-through units are available from some manufacturers. (*American Air Filter Co., Inc.*)

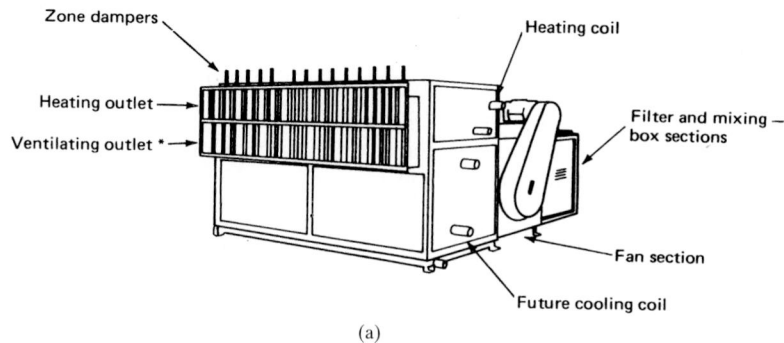

(a)

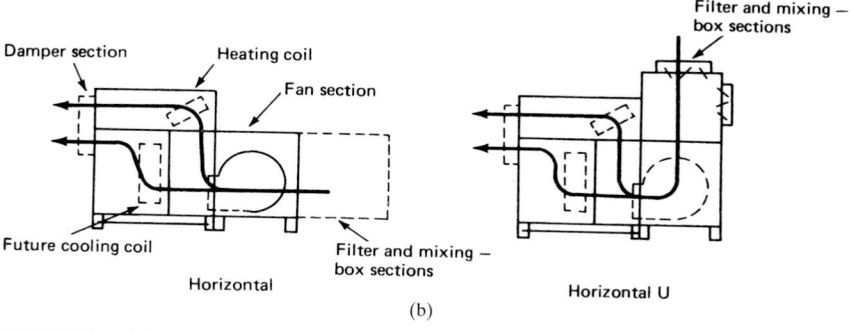

(b)

FIGURE 1-6 (*a*) Typical multizone heating and ventilating unit. Such units have the ability to simultaneously heat and ventilate with provision for future cooling. For heating and ventilating service, a cooling coil would not be provided; a balancing plate would be provided instead of the cooling coil. *If a cooling coil is installed, this will be the cold air outlet. (*b*) Typical arrangements for a multizone unit; dotted lines indicate the accessory section. (*American Air Filter Co., Inc.*)

1. *Single-zone draw-through units.*   These are nominally available in the following capacity ranges:

   With forward-curved low- and medium-pressure fans (see discussion, "Fan Selection Procedures," for pressure ranges): 800 to 60,000 ft³/min (0.378 to 28.32 m³/s).
   With low-pressure fans, capacities up to 75,000 ft³/min (35.4 m³/s) are available.
   With backward-inclined or airfoil low- and medium-pressure fans: 1500 to 50,000 ft³/min (0.708 to 28.32 m³/s).
   With low-pressure fans, capacities up to 75,000 ft³/min (35.4 m³/s) are available.
   With airfoil high-pressure fans: 2500 to 50,000 ft³/min (1.18 to 23.6 m³/s).

2. *Multizone blow-through units.*   These are nominally available in the following capacity ranges:

   With forward-curved low- and medium-pressure fans: 1200 to 40,000 ft³/min (0.556 to 18.88 m³/s).
   With backward-inclined or airfoil low- and medium-pressure fans: 1500 to 40,000 ft³/min (0.708 to 18.88 m³/s).
   With airfoil high-pressure fans: 2500 to 35,000 ft³/min (1.18 to 16.52 m³/s).

If the unit is required to serve areas that will be satisfied with the same supply-air temperature, then a single-zone heating and ventilating unit should be selected. If various supply-air temperatures are required for the areas to be served, then the engineer must choose between a multizone unit and a single-zone unit with reheat coils in the zone ducts. This decision should be based on evaluating initial, operating, and maintenance costs. It may be stated that:

1. Long duct runs and a readily available heating medium in the areas to be served favor a single zone with reheats.

2. From a maintenance and operating standpoint, it is desirable to serve all equipment from one area. This favors a multizone unit.

3. If there is a potential for air conditioning in some or all of the areas to be served, a multizone unit would probably be a wise choice.

With the required airflow (previously calculated) and the design engineer's decision on the type of unit to be installed (single-zone or multizone), one can determine the unit size (unit number) by entering the equipment manufacturer's catalog selection tables for the selected type of unit (single-zone or multizone) with the required airflow and reading off the unit size.

If the unit being selected has no future air-conditioning requirement, it should be selected at a higher coil velocity, 800 to 1000 ft/min (4.06 to 5.08 m/s). If the unit being selected has a future air-conditioning requirement, it should be selected at a coil velocity of about 550 ft/min (2.79 m/s), not at 800 to 1000 ft/min (4.06 to 5.08 m/s).

Once the unit size has been chosen, the following items can be read from the catalog:

1. Number and size of fans that will fit within the unit

2. Areas of coils that will fit within the unit

3. Size of the unit

4. Type and size of coils

5. Type and size of fans and maximum horsepower

6. Type and size of filters

7. The outlet velocity, fan speed (revolutions per minute), and brake horsepower at the corresponding static pressure (across the fan).

To determine the required fan speed and the minimum brake horsepower to deliver the design airflow, one must first calculate the total system static pressure against which the fan must operate. The total system static pressure is the summation of the following losses: duct, diffusers and/or registers, unit casing, coils, filters, etc.

Coil Selection Parameters

General.   Heating and ventilating units in general can be supplied with *steam, hot-water,* or *electric heating coils* (see Fig. 1-7).

Steam Coils.   Steam coils are available in two basic types, standard and distributing (nonfreeze). *Standard* coils are less expensive than distributing coils and should be used whenever the supply-air temperature to the coil is above the freezing temperature. *Distributing* coils are designed to prevent, or at least to minimize, the possibility of freezing the steam condensate within the coil, when the supply-air temperature is below freezing. Therefore, distributing (nonfreeze) coils should be used when the air to the coil could be below freezing temperature.

Hot-Water Coils.   Hot-water coils are available in two basic types, standard and cleanable. *Standard* coils are less expensive and should be used whenever the heating water is clean. That is, the hot water will not form scale or precipitate sludge deposits (within the tubes) that will cause a measurable loss in the coil's ability to transfer heat from the water to the coil fins.

Cleanable coils are designed to be used when the heating water has the tendency to form scale on, or to precipitate sludge deposits within, the tubes. With cleanable coils, the cleaning or cleanability referred to deals with the *inside* of the tubes. There is no difference between the air-side design of cleanable coils and that of standard coils having the same number of fins per inch. When cleanable coils are specified, removable plugs on both ends of every tube in the coil should be specified so that each tube can be thoroughly cleaned (punched through).

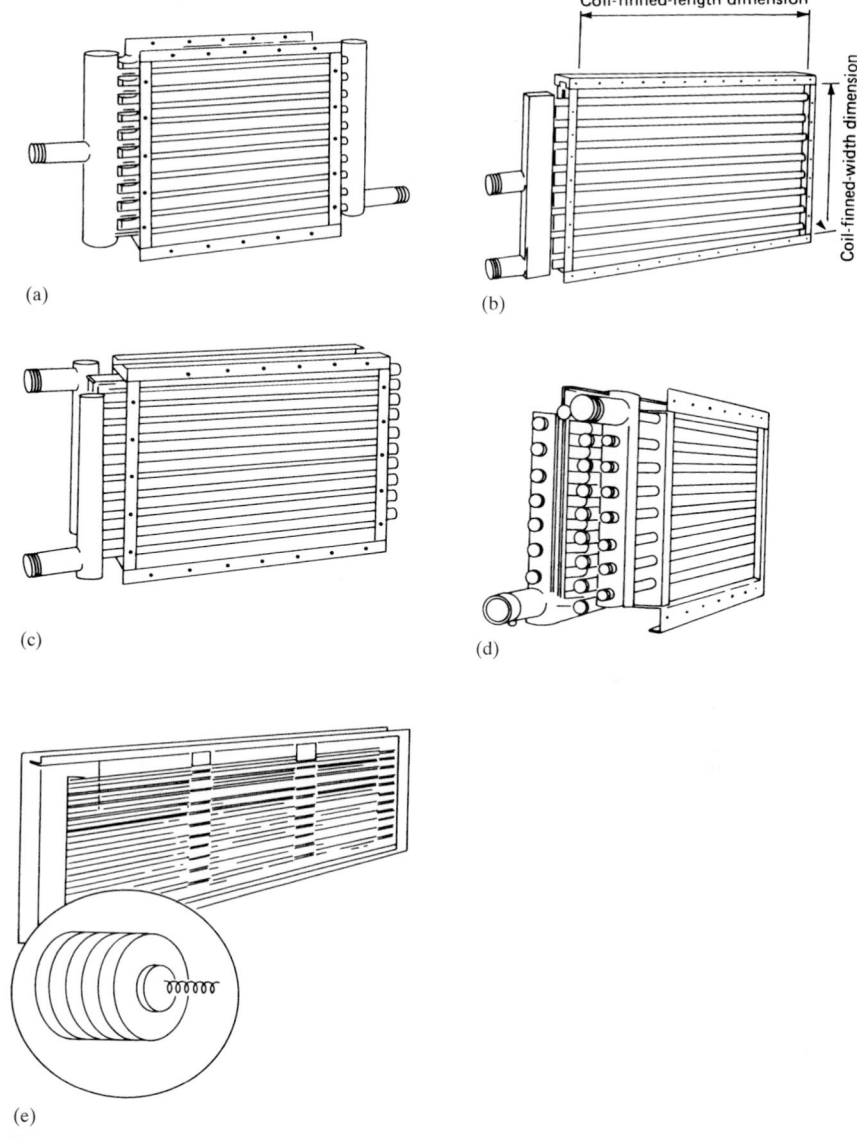

FIGURE 1-7 Typical heating coils: (*a*) Standard steam coil. (*b*) Distribution coil. (*c*) Standard water coil. (*d*) Cleanable-tube water coil. (*e*) Electric resistance coil.

Electric Coils. Electric resistance coils are best employed where the electric energy rates are lower than the prevailing fossil fuel rates for the same amount of heat (British thermal units per hour or watts) transferred from the coil to the airstream, or where the required service life of the heating system in question is so short (such as a temporary installation) that the higher capital and operating costs of a heating plant cannot be economically justified.

Coil Construction. The coil frames (casings) are generally of galvanized steel. If a hygienic environment is necessary or a corrosive environment is encountered, special frames of aluminum, stainless steel, etc., can be furnished. Heating coils are usually one- or two-row coils. Four- and six-row coils can be provided on special order. Water and steam coils are normally furnished with copper tubes.

Fins. Aluminum or copper coil fins are standard on water and steam coils. Since the copper fins are of significantly greater cost than aluminum, one should evaluate the corrosiveness of the airstream with respect to the application of aluminum fins on a life-cycle cost basis, before selecting the fin material. Water and steam coils are available with fin spacings of 6, 8, 11, and 14 fins per inch (2, 3, 4, and 6 fins per centimeter). In general, the more fins per inch, the greater the ability to transfer heat from the heating medium to the airstream for the same coil velocity, material, number of rows, and mean effective temperature difference. From the manufacturer's point of view, for the same heating requirement and coil velocity, it is cheaper to produce coils with more fins per inch and fewer rows. However, from the operation performance and maintenance standpoint (though there may be little difference between the air resistance of coils with more fins per inch—and fewer rows—and coils with fewer fins per inch—and more rows), if the airstream is dirty, the installation with more fins per inch will have a greater potential for plugging (filling the space between the fins). This not only will significantly increase the coil's air resistance but can create a fire hazard if the particles retained undergo spontaneous combustion due to the heat they will absorb from the hot coil. Furthermore, both the time required for cleaning and the frequency of cleaning will increase as the space between adjacent fins is decreased.

The following is a guide to determine the optimum number of fins per inch:

1. Select no more than 8 fins per inch (3 fins per centimeter), provided that the heating load can be met with no more than two rows.

2. If the air is dirty (has a tendency to plug the coil), select fewer than 8 fins per inch (3 fins per centimeter) and no more than 2 rows. This may require increasing the coil area or temperature or both.

3. If the air is clean (does not have a tendency to plug the coil) and increasing the number of fins per inch will result in reducing the number of rows, then the greater fin spacing may be desirable.

Though heating coils can be selected with velocities ranging from as low as 200 ft/min (1.02 m/s) to as high as 1500 ft/min (7.62 m/s), the optimum range for overall economy and performance is 800 to 1000 ft/min (4.06 to 5.08 m/s). Exceptions to this are:

1. If the air is dirty, it may be desirable to decrease the coil velocity in order to satisfy the heating load with no more than 8 fins per inch and 2 rows (greater coil area).

2. If there is a requirement for future air conditioning, the air velocity of the coil selected should be 500 to 550 ft/min (2.54 to 2.79 m/s).

Hot-water coil ratings are based on counterflow of air and water, i.e., the hot-water supply to the coils must enter the coil tubes on the leaving-air side and the water must leave the coil tubes on the entering-air side. The optimum water velocity for economical heat-transfer rate and water head loss will normally be in the range of 2.5 to 4 ft/s (0.0127 to 0.0203 m/s). Water velocities above 8 ft/s (0.041 m/s) or below 0.5 ft/s (0.0025 m/s) should not be used. The water velocity within the tubes is a function of the number of coil circuits for coils of the same tube diameter.

Most manufacturers provide three standard circuiting arrangements to produce the optimum velocity for each application: single serpentine, half-serpentine, double serpentine. Single serpentine has the greatest applicability and is the most commonly used. Half-serpentine increases water velocity; double serpentine decreases water velocity.

The availability of the heating medium (steam or hot water) usually determines whether a steam- or water-heated coil will be selected. Likewise, the choice between standard and steam distribution type (if steam coils are selected) or standard and cleanable type (if water coils are selected) depends on the installation in question (see under "Coil Selection Parameters").

The plant engineer should determine the preferable coil fin spacing on the basis of previous discussion and past experiences. This data of the discussion may have to be modified, depending on actual fin spacing available from coil manufacturers.

Since the actual procedure in selecting a heating coil varies with each manufacturer and there are many parameters in the selection procedure, the coil manufacturer's procedure must be strictly followed in order to select a coil with a capacity equal to or slightly greater than the required heating load.

Filter Selection

General. The selection of the type of filter should be based on the following parameters:

1. *Efficiency.* This parameter is defined as the ability to retain airborne particles. What degree of air cleanliness is required? *The greater the particle retention* (which could be viewed technically as obstructions in the airstream), *the higher the operating and maintenance costs.*

2. *Air volume.* How critical are fluctuations in air volume to the performance of the heating and ventilation system as a result of increasing system resistance (static pressure) caused by dust and/or the retention of dust on the filter medium? The Roll-O-Matic® (American Air Filter Co., Inc.) and electrostatic filters maintain a relatively constant static pressure drop across the filter medium for the life of the filter. In contrast, as cartridge-type filters go from the clean to dirty state, the static pressure across them undergoes the greatest increase.

Replacement. As a rule of thumb, filters should be replaced or cleaned when the initial air resistance has doubled. However, if the system's fans can deliver the required air quantities against the higher system static pressure, then the point at which the filters should be replaced or cleaned can be determined by economics. That is, filters should be changed when the replacement or cleaning costs are equal to the cost of the additional energy (due to the increase in air resistance above the initial resistance) in the time span it takes to go from clean to dirty filters.

The types of filters and filter boxes commercially available are shown in Fig. 1-8. Typical data on filter media, efficiency, maximum air volumes, air velocity, and air resistance are shown in Fig. 1-9 for different types of filters commercially available.

Fan Selection

General. Heating and ventilating fans are available in three pressure classes. These are determined by the total static pressure the unit's fan (or fans) is designed to develop. The pressure classes are:

1. Low-pressure (class 1) total static pressure up to 3 inH$_2$O (747 Pa)
2. Medium-pressure (class 2) total static pressure 3 to 5 inH$_2$O (747 to 1245 Pa)
3. High-pressure (class 3) total static pressure 5 to 10 inH$_2$O (1245 to 2490 Pa)

Heating and ventilating unit fans are typically centrifugal. They are, depending on the unit's capacity, available in forward-curved, backward-inclined, and airfoil wheel designs (see Fig. 1-10). *Forward-curved* fans are most common in heating and ventilating, especially in the smaller units. *Backward-inclined* fans are used in the larger units where their nonoverloading characteristics and greater stable operating range (compared to forward-curved fans) are desired. Because of their greater efficiency, nonoverloading characteristics, and quieter operation, *airfoil* fans are frequently used in high-pressure applications where greater motor horsepower is required.

Fan noise is a function of the fan design, air-volume flow rate, total pressure, and efficiency. The quietest fan operation will be obtained when a fan is selected at its most efficient operat-

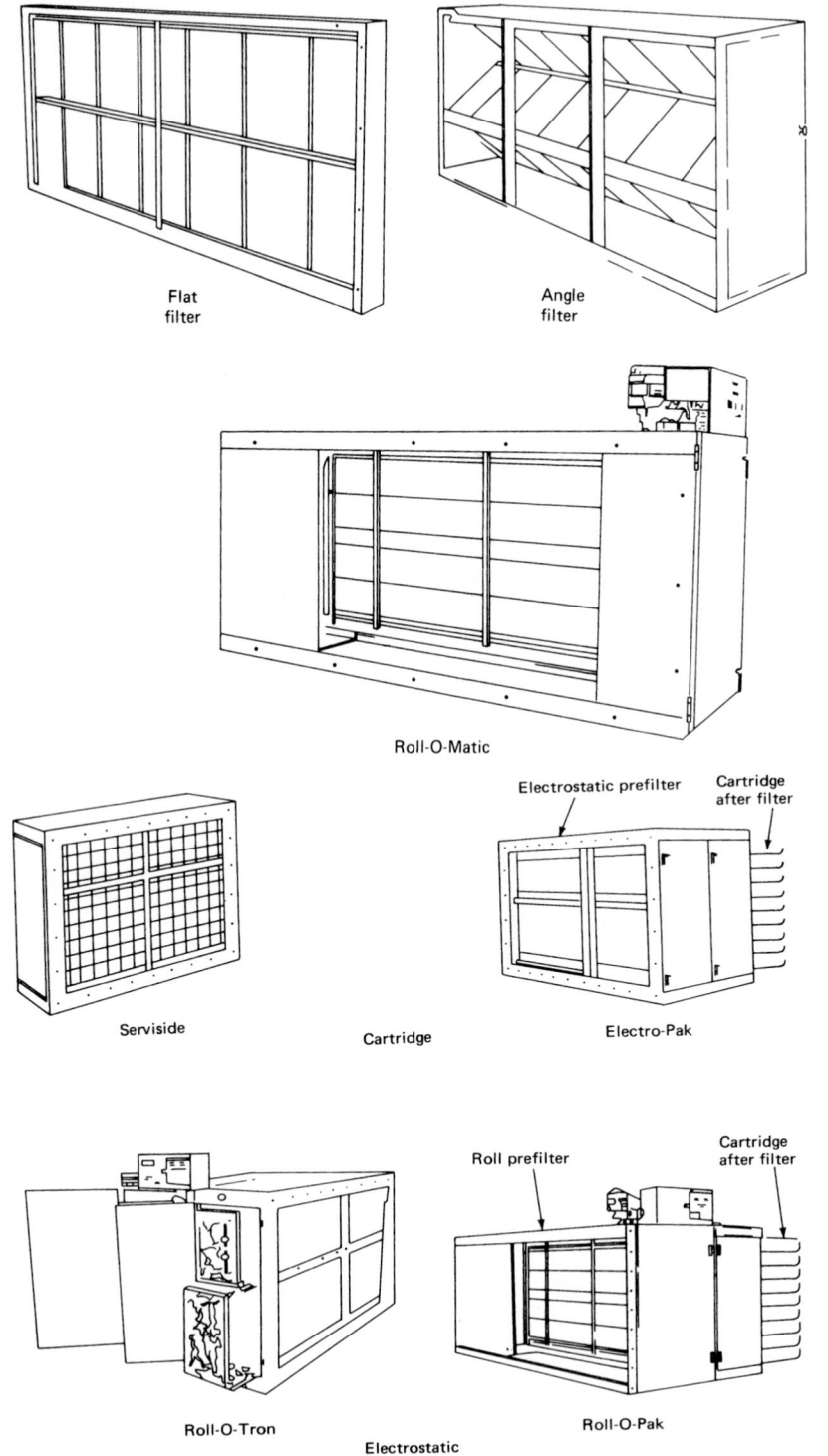

Flat
filter

Angle
filter

Roll-O-Matic

Serviside

Cartridge

Electrostatic prefilter

Cartridge
after filter

Electro-Pak

Roll-O-Tron

Electrostatic

Roll prefilter

Cartridge
after filter

Roll-O-Pak

FIGURE 1-8 Typical filters and filter boxes. Generally throwaway, renewable, or cleanable filter types are available in flat or angle-unit filter boxes (*American Air Filter Co., Inc.*)

(a) Typical Comparative Filter Performance

Type	Maintenance cost	Maintenance required	Constant air volume	Media number	AFI (weight)	NBS dust spot (discoloration)	ServiSide® housing extension required & size	Maximum face volume, ft/min	Recommended face volume, ft/min
5700 [Throwaway]	High	Replace filters every 4–10 weeks	No	—	70–75%	—	—	500	300
Amer-Frame [Renewable] Glass	Low	Change media every 6–12 weeks	No	—	75–80%	—	—	500	300
Polyurethane	Moderate	Clean filters every 6–12 weeks	No	—	65–75%	—	—	450	350
HV-2 [Cleanable]	Moderate	Clean filters every 6–12 weeks	No	—	70–80%	—	—	625	500
Roll-O-Matic®	Low	Change media once a year	Yes	—	75–80%	—	—	600	500
Dri-Pak®	Low	Change media once a year	No	30 40 60 90 100 or 10	— — — — —	30% 38–40% 50–55% 80–85% 93–97%	No Yes—10" Yes—26" Yes—26" Yes—26"	625 625 500 or 625 500 or 625 500 or 625	625 625 500 or 625 500 or 625 500 or 625
ServiSide® [Cartridge] Varicel®	Low	Change every 6–12 months	No	6 9 10	— — —	55–60% 85–90% 90–95%	No No No	625 500 500	625 500 500

Approx. efficiency columns: AFI (weight) and NBS dust spot (discoloration)

*2000 Series rated at 500 ft/min, 2500 Series rated at 625 ft/min.

FIGURE 1-9 Typical filter performance data. (*American Air Filter Co. Inc.*)

(*b*) **Typical Filter Air Resistance**

Reference velocity, ft/ min	Flat bank		Standard angle		Servi-Side®	Roll-O-Matic®	Roll-O-Pak®	Electronic	Electro-Pak®
	TA ren. poly	HV-2	TA ren. poly.	HV-2					
300	0.12	0.06	0.09	0.04	——	0.40	——	——	——
400	0.16	0.11	0.12	0.07	——	0.40	——	——	——
500	0.21	0.16	0.14	0.09	0.5	0.40	0.6	0.15	0.55
600	0.28	0.24	0.18	0.13	——	0.40	——	——	——
700	——	0.32	0.23	0.17	——	0.40	——	——	——

Filters* (Inches of water)

*Resistance shown based on clean filters.

FIGURE 1-9 (*Continued*)

ing point. Since it is not realistic to assume the system air volume and resistance will be constant or will match the fan's performance at maximum efficiency, fans should be selected, if possible, in the range from maximum efficiency to 90 percent maximum efficiency. Sound power level specifications for the fans being selected are not always available. Since low outlet velocities do not necessarily assure quiet operation, Fig. 1-11 can be used to determine the appropriate fan outlet velocity range. By entering Fig. 1-11 with the total static pressure, one can read the outlet velocity range corresponding to the maximum efficiency and 90 percent maximum efficiency curves.

Adjustable motor-drive sheaves should be used on V-belt-driven fans to provide the capability for minor adjustment of airflow and static pressure in the field.

The types and capacity ranges of typical commercially available ventilation fans are shown in Fig. 1-12. The fan section of a heating and ventilating unit (see Fig. 1-5) can also be used as a ventilation fan with or without ductwork.

Selecting Unit Heaters

General.   The revolving unit heater is ideally suited for large industrial spaces. Some of the advantages are:

1. More heat coverage: up to 145×145 ft (44.2×42.2 m) with a standard heater
2. Uniform heat: minimizes hot and cold spots, no steady hot blasts
3. Low floor-to-ceiling temperature differentials

Forward curved—FC

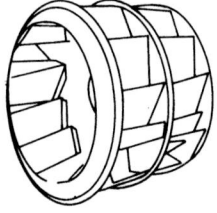

Backward inclined—BI

Airfoil—AF

FIGURE 1-10   Typical fan wheels.

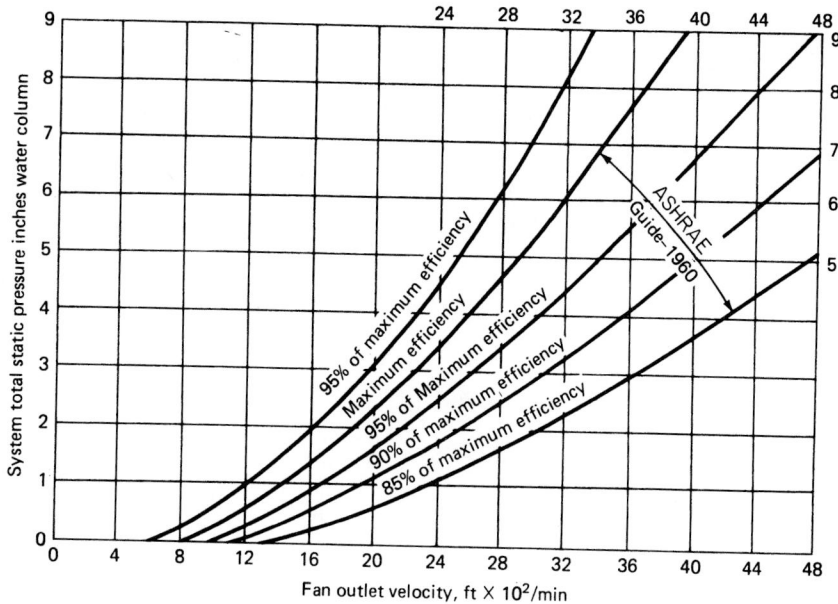

FIGURE 1-11 Typical fan performance. The suggested range of outlet velocity approximates the curves plotted for maximum efficiency and 85 percent of maximum efficiency as indicated by arrows.

4. Steam, hot water, high-temperature hot water, and gas can be used as heating media

5. Discharge designs to 65-ft (19.81-m) mounting heights

6. Effective summer air circulation

7. Low installed and operating costs

Unit heaters can be powered by gas, propane, or electricity. Data on them can be obtained from manufacturers.

When selecting electric unit heaters care must be taken to ensure electrical compatibility with other electric systems of the unit. Adequate power and wiring should also be available.

Controls. Summer ventilation can be provided, with fixed or revolving units mounted within the roof truss spaces or adjacent to the exterior walls, by installing a fresh-air intake duct from the roof or exterior wall. This provides a source of fresh outside air for some cooling and maintains positive pressure within the building, thus increasing the efficiency of the exhaust system.

A damper box mounted above the motor and fan provides for admission of air from above the roof for summer ventilation or from the truss area for winter heating. This is controlled within the box by the functioning of the two sets of dampers which are manually or automatically operated, as desired. Fresh-air roof intakes and damper boxes are available from manufacturers.

Automatic temperature controls should be provided to cycle the units on and off in order to maintain space temperatures during the heating season and provide outside ventilation air during the summer.

Selection Procedure. To minimize installation, maintenance, and energy costs, it is desirable to select the minimum number of units that will provide a uniform distribution of heat (minimum temperature differential) throughout the space. For exterior areas, unit heaters should be positioned so that their discharge "wipes" the exterior walls and windows. It is more prac-

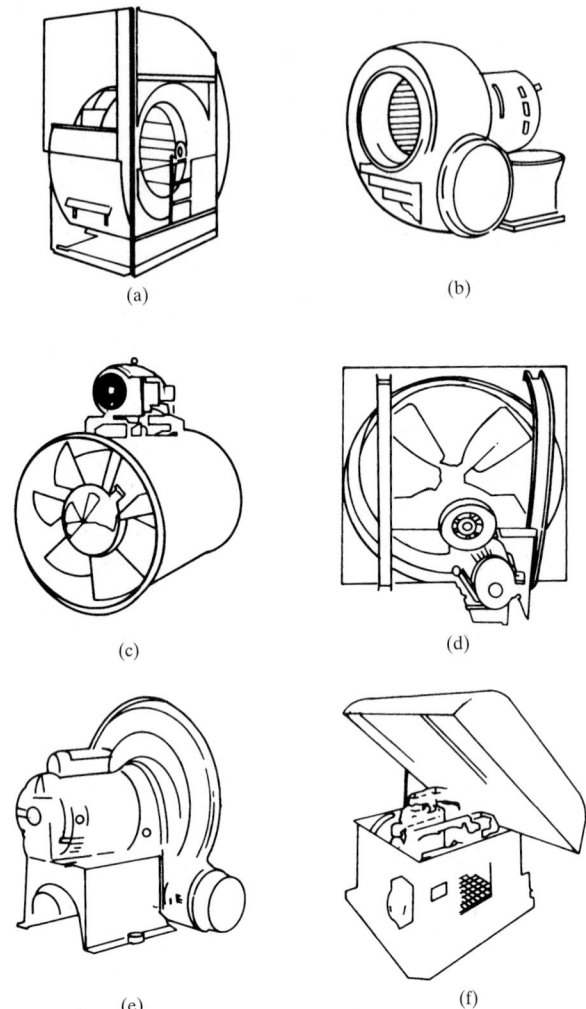

(a)   (b)

(c)   (d)

(e)   (f)

FIGURE 1-12 Typical ventilating fans. (*a*) Aerofoil®, a high-efficiency, low-noise-level fan for quality, optimum design air-conditioning and ventilation systems. Construction features include wheel blades that combine the best of backward-curved and airfoil designs. Capacities vary from 687 to 661,000 ft³/min and pressures up to 12 inHg. (*b*) Baby vent sets—a quiet, reliable fan with a sturdy corrosion-resistant cast-iron housing that is rotatable to obtain any 45° angular discharge. Widely used as a component on many industrial products. Features include all-weather cover, drain, nonspark aluminum wheel, heat slinger, antivibration pads, special corrosion-resistant materials and/or protective coatings. Capacities range from 47 to 1765 ft³/min with pressures to 1 inHg. (*c*) Axial-flow fan. These efficient, low-noise vane-axial fans with limited load horsepower characteristics are available with either fixed-pitch steel or aluminum, or adjustable-pitch aluminum wheels, enabling the user to match pressure/volume requirements exactly. Capacities greater than 300,000 in³/min are available. (*d*) Propeller fan. Such fans may include belt or direct drive, penthouses, wall or ceiling shutters, wall boxes, filters, wire guards, and spark-resistant construction. Wheel sizes from 8 to 120 in. Capacities from 500 to 240,000 ft³/min and up to 1 in static pressure (SP) or higher. (*e*) Electric blower/exhauster. Small package units like this are used for small furnace draft, handling particles of wood, metal, and abrasives in collecting systems, and many more jobs requiring moderate volume against low pressures. Their capacities range from 30 to 700 ft³/min. (*f*) Power roof ventilators are engineered and built to meet the demand for high-capacity exhaust and supply air. Will withstand hurricane-force winds, heavy snow loads, and corrosive atmospheres. Filters, dampers, screens, heating coils available. Capacities from 1000 to 250,000 ft/in. Pressures from free delivery to over 1 in SP. (*Buffalo Forge Co.*)

tical to treat exterior door heating requirements separately, especially loading-dock areas. For interior areas, the unit heaters should be positioned so that their discharge provides uniform air motion (heat distribution).

The major exception to these guidelines occurs when spot heating is the primary requirement. In this case, the units should be positioned to provide a uniform distribution over the area where localized heating is required and to position units in the remaining area so as to maintain a specified minimum temperature determined by the process or product stored or to prevent freeze-ups.

Since there are various combinations of unit heater capacities and distribution patterns, the selection is a trial-and-error procedure. It is recommended that the units be selected from manufacturers' data, and that the selection be based on appropriate distribution patterns and the available mounting height for the layout of the space to be heated before checking for adequate capacity. This is preferable to selecting the units on the basis of capacity and *then* checking for adequate distribution.

If the total capacity of the unit heaters tentatively selected is less than the required design space heating load, proceed as follows.

1. If unit heaters with greater capacity and approximately the same distribution pattern are available, they should be selected, and the new total heating capacity should then be checked against the required design load.

2. If units of larger capacity are not available, more unit heaters must be added. Care must be exercised to add the required units where the greatest heat loss occurs so as to minimize the possibility of overheating some areas.

3. In some cases it may be required to combine steps 1 and 2 to obtain the best solution.

If the total capacity of the selected units is greater than the space heating load, proceed as follows.

1. If possible, select units with less capacity but with approximately the same distribution pattern.

2. Select automatic controls that will cycle the unit heaters without causing excessive temperature variation.

3. Combining steps 1 and 2 may be the most practical solution.

The final selection should result in the installed heating capacity of the units being equal to or slightly more than the design heating load.

Figure 1-13 illustrates typical revolving and fixed vertical-discharge steam or hot-water unit heaters. These units are available in increment sizes and typically have a capacity of 30,000 to 60,000 Btu/h (879 to 1758 W) in the smaller sizes and 750,000 to 1,200,000 Btu/h (21,975 to 35,160 W) in the large sizes, depending on whether the heating medium used is steam or hot water. Steam units are generally rated at 5 lb/in^2 (0.345 bar) steam pressure and 60°F (15.6°C) entering air to the heating coil. Hot-water units are generally rated at 200°F (93.3°C) entering water and 60°F (15.6°C) entering air to the heating coil.

Whenever the steam pressure, entering hot-water temperature, or entering air temperature is greater or less than the values that the manufacturer's published capacities were based upon, the published capacities must be corrected in order to obtain the heating capacity of the unit selected under the actual operating conditions: the temperature of the entering heating medium (steam or hot water) and the entering-air.

The physical sizes of the basic fixed- and revolving-discharge unit heaters are the same. Typically the smaller sets are about 16 × 16 in by 18 in high (0.406 × 0.406 m by 0.457 m), with the larger sizes about 50 × 60 in by 50 in high (1.27 × 1.52 by 1.27 m). The fixed discharge models will add about 6 in (0.152 m) to the height of the smaller units and as much as about 10 in (0.254 m) to the larger units. The revolving discharge models will add about 12 to 24 in (0.301 to 0.610 m) to the height of the smaller units and as much as 24 to 50 in (0.610 to 1.27 m) to the height of the larger units, depending on the type of discharge selected.

In general, the larger the unit, the higher the (maximum) mounting height and the greater the area covered per unit. Also revolving discharge unit heaters (especially in the larger sizes)

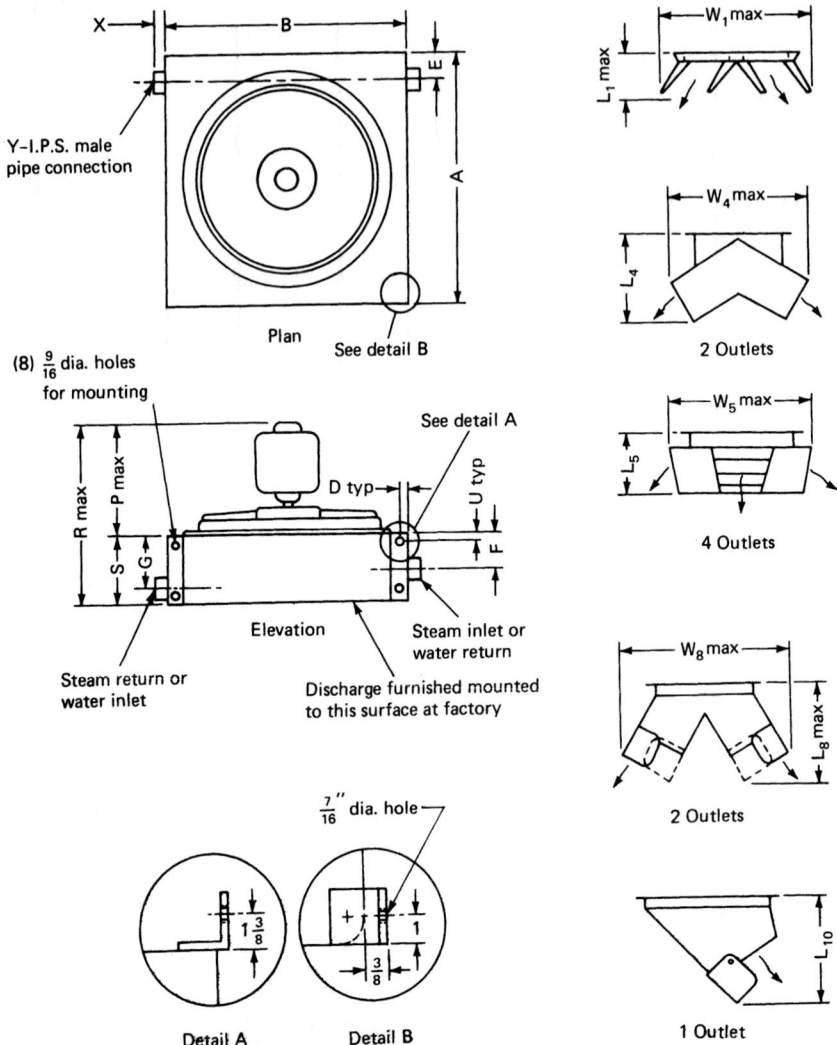

FIGURE 1-13 Typical revolving and fixed vertical-discharge steam or hot-water heaters. (*Wing Industries Inc.*)

can cover greater areas than fixed discharge units. Typically, fixed and revolving discharge heaters have a maximum mounting height in the smaller sizes of 8 to 12 ft (2.44 to 3.66 m), depending on the model selected. The larger sizes have a maximum mounting height of 25 to 50 ft (7.62 to 15.24 m), depending on the model selected for fixed and revolving discharge heaters. However, the largest revolving unit heater has a minimum mounting height of about 25 ft (7.62 m) and covers an area of about 90 × 90 ft (27.4 × 27.4 m) to a maximum mounting height of about 65 ft (19.81 m) and covers an area of about 140 × 140 ft (42.67 × 42.67 m).

Figure 1-14 illustrates a typical horizontal discharge steam or hot-water unit heater. Such units are used when it is desirable to obtain heat distribution by using a number of small heaters, in areas such as offices, showers, stockrooms, etc., where it is neither economically nor physically practical to use large heaters. These units are available in increment sizes and typically have a capacity of about 15,000 Btu/h (439.5 W) in the smallest size to about 10^6 Btu/h (29,300 W) in the largest size.

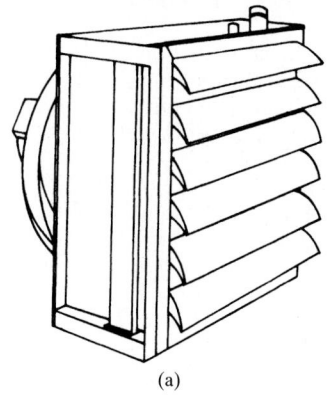

(a)

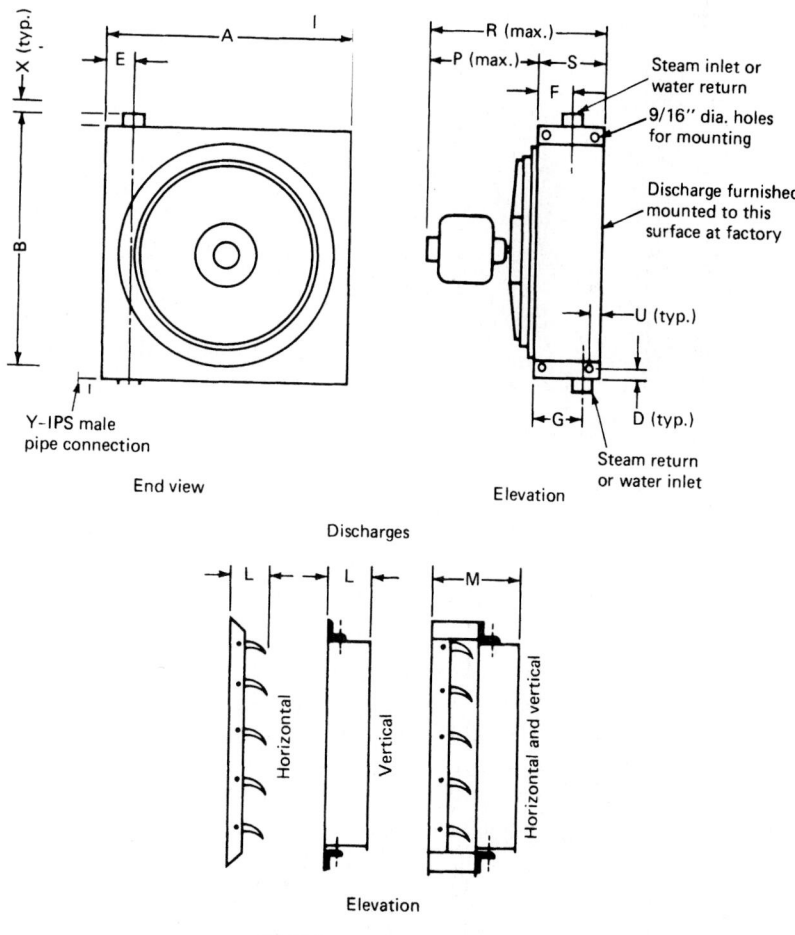

(b)

FIGURE 1-14 Typical horizontal steam or hot-water unit heater. (*a*) Sketch; (*b*) end and elevation views. (*Wing Industries Inc.*)

Whenever the steam pressure, entering hot-water temperature, or entering air temperature is greater or less than the values that the manufacturer's published capacities were based upon, the published capacities must be corrected in order to obtain the heating capacity of the unit selected under the actual conditions: entering heating medium (steam or hot water) and entering air temperature.

The smaller units are typically 12 in (0.305 m) wide by 12 in (0.305 m) high by 12 in (0.305 m) deep (face of coil to back of motor). The smallest unit has a maximum mounting height of about 8 ft (2.44 m) and a horizontal effective heating throw of about 20 ft (6.10 m). The largest unit has a maximum mounting height of about 20 ft (6.10 m) and a horizontal effective heating throw of about 100 ft (30.5 m).

Figure 1-15 illustrates a typical electric horizontal-discharge unit heater. These units have the same application as horizontal steam or hot-water unit heaters. They are available in increment sizes and typically have a capacity of about 4 kW in the smallest size to about 45 kW in the largest. The electrical characteristics of the units are typically 208 and 240 V, single- or three-phase; 277 V single-phase; and 480 V three-phase up to about 10-kW capacity. Above 10-kW capacity, only three-phase is available at 208, 240, and 480 V, depending on the size. The smallest unit has a maximum mounting height of about 8 ft (2.44 m) and a horizontal effective heating throw of about 12 ft (3.66 m). The largest unit has a maximum mounting height of about 18 ft (5.49 m) and a horizontal effective heating throw of about 40 ft (12.19 m).

Whenever the entering air temperature to the heater is greater or less than the value that the manufacturer's published capacities were based upon, the published capacities must be corrected in order to obtain the heating capacity of the unit selected under the actual entering air temperatures.

FIGURE 1-15 Typical electric horizontal unit heater. (*Emerson Electric Co.*)

Selection of Infrared Radiant Heaters

Since infrared radiant energy produces heat only when it is absorbed by a body whose temperature then rises (thereby producing heat), the manufacturer's selection procedures should be strictly followed. Following is a list of general limitations on the application of infrared heaters:

1. Do not mount in an explosive environment.
2. Observe minimum spacing to combustible materials [approximately 24 in (0.61 m) minimum, end or side spacing from fixture to combustible materials and at least 5 ft above them].
3. Do not mount in a recessed position, unless approved by the manufacturer.
4. For efficient operation, do not direct radiation onto window glass.
5. Do not use in high humidity or in corrosive environments.
6. Do not mount closer to personnel than 4 ft (1.22 m).

From the point of view of both energy conservation and personnel comfort it is desirable not only to cycle the panels on and off automatically from a space thermostat, but also to de-energize selective panels as the heating load decreases. In determining the panels that are to be de-energized in milder weather, care must be taken so that the remaining active panels will uniformly heat the space without overheating the area directly below the (active) panels.

Electric and gas-fired infrared unit heaters are commercially available, generally with three distribution patterns:

1. Narrow distribution pattern (45°)
2. Medium distribution pattern (60°)
3. Broad distribution pattern (90°)

One of the significant parameters in determining the distribution pattern (narrow, medium, or broad) is the required mounting height of any unit. In general:

Narrow (beam) distribution pattern is suitable at mounting heights of 40 to 45 ft (12.2 to 13.7 m).

Medium (beam) distribution pattern is suitable at mounting heights up to 35 ft (10.7 m).

Broad (beam) distribution pattern is suitable at mounting heights up to 25 ft (7.6 m).

Figure 1-16 illustrates a typical electric narrow-beam infrared heater. Such a heater has the following characteristics:

1. This type is typically a deep-well reflector with precise optical design that confines energy within a 45° beam angle with little spill or scatter. It is a good choice for high mounting, since it generally does not require heaters with 5 percent additional wattage for each foot (0.33 m) above a 10 ft (3.1 m) mounting height.
2. The housing on some models can be swiveled up to 45° in either direction from the vertical.
3. They are available for indoor or outdoor exposed applications.

Three different heating elements are available: metal sheath, quartz tube, and quartz lamp. When used outdoors, the *metal sheath* must be shielded from the wind for maximum heating efficiency. Units with metal-sheath elements are available in increments from 600 to 2000 W, with electrical characteristics of 120, 208, and 240 V single-phase for the smaller units and 208, 240, 277, and 480 V single-phase for the larger ones. Units with *quartz-tube* elements are available, in increments, from 550 W to 15.4 kW, with electrical characteristics of 120, 208, and

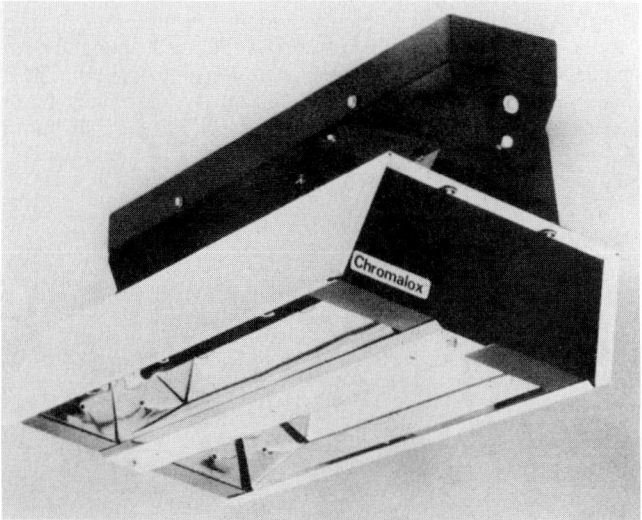

FIGURE 1-16 Typical electric narrow-beam infrared heater. (*Chroma-lox*®—*E. L. Wiegand Div., Emerson Electric Co.*)

240 V single-phase for the smaller units and 208, 240, and 277 V single-phase for the larger ones. Units with *quartz-lamp* elements are available, in increments, from 800 to 3800 W, with electrical characteristics of 120, 208, and 240 V single-phase for the smaller units and 480 and 600 V single-phase for the larger ones.

Figure 1-17 illustrates a typical electric medium- or broad-beam infrared heater. Double-element fixtures are available which provide double heating capacity in a single infrared radiant heater. They are applicable to indoor and outdoor protected use. They can be mounted directly to a ceiling or hung from chains. *Broad-beam* units have a 90° distribution pattern, with a symmetrical reflector for low to medium mounting height. *Medium-beam* units have a 60° symmetrical distribution pattern for medium mounting height. Units are available for medium mounting height; these have a 60° asymmetrical perimeter distribution pattern. Units are available with metal-sheath, quartz-tube, or quartz-lamp elements. Nominal capacities range from 1100 to 7600 W. Though all units require single-phase voltage, their voltage requirements vary, depending on the model and type of element. In general, the smaller units are available in 120, 208, and 240 V, though some units are also available in 277 and 480 V. The medium-size units generally are available in 208 and 240 V, though some units are also available in 277 and 480 V. The larger units generally are available in 480 and 600 V, except for the largest unit which may be restricted to 600 V.

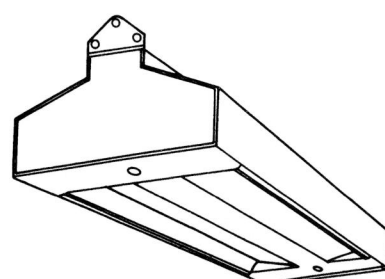

FIGURE 1-17 Typical electric medium- or broad-beam infrared heater.

Figure 1-18 illustrates a typical gas infrared heater. Code requirements may restrict the use of, or require special installation procedures for, gas heaters. These heaters are available with natural gas or liquid propane (LP) gas fuels. In general, units are available in increments from 30,000 to 160,000 Btu/h (879 to 4588 W).

Selection of Radiant Ceiling Panels

The type of radiant ceiling panel shown in Fig. 1-19 is most effective for spot or local heating of finished or semifinished areas with moderate mounting heights. The usual mounting height is about 9 to 10 ft. The number of panels required is obtained by dividing the heating capacity per panel into the required heating load for the area or space. The electric service must be checked to ensure that there is adequate capacity for these heaters. From the point of view of both energy conservation and personnel comfort, it is desirable not only to cycle the panels on and off automatically from a space thermostat, but also to de-energize selective panels as the heating load decreases. In determining the panels that are to be de-energized in milder weather, care

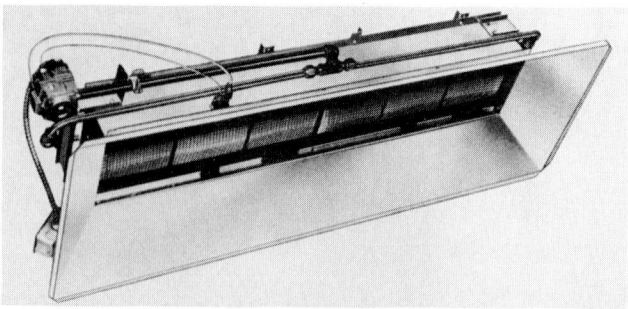

FIGURE 1-18 Typical gas infrared heater. (*Chromalox®—E. L. Wiegand Div., Emerson Electric Co.*)

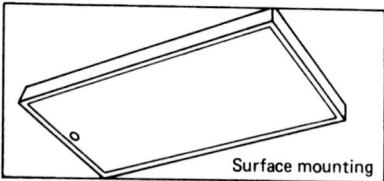 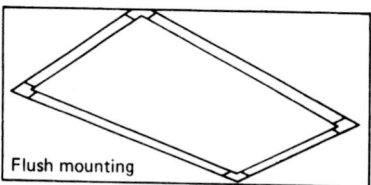

FIGURE 1-19 Typical radiant ceiling panels.

must be taken so that the remaining active panels will uniformly heat the space without overheating the area directly below the (active) panels.

Figure 1-19 illustrates a typical electric surface- and flush-mounted radiant ceiling panel. Such units are prewired with 40-in (1.02-m) flexible cable [standard 2 × 4 ft (0.61 × 1.22 m) module] and are designed to produce uniform heat over the entire panel surface. They are available in capacities of 500 and 750 W at 120/240, 208, and 277 V single-phase. The units can be controlled by line or low-voltage thermostats, manual switches, or automatic time control switches.

Operating and Maintenance Guide

In the absence of operating and maintenance instruction from the equipment manufacturer, the following should be considered:

Fans. Before initial startup or after servicing, perform this checklist:

1. Carefully review all work done on the fan.
2. All foundation bolts, wheel hub set screws, and bearing collars must be tight.
3. Access doors should be tightly sealed.
4. All safety devices should be in place.
5. Check bearings alignment and lubrication.
6. Couplings must be in alignment and lubricated.
7. Turn over the fan wheel by hand to check that it runs freely and does not bind or strike fan housing.
8. Check electrical wiring to the drive motor.
9. V-belt drive must be in alignment with belts properly tensioned. Use of a belt tension checker is recommended.
10. Duct connections from fan to ductwork must not be distorted. Expansion joints between duct connections should be used where expansion is likely to occur or when the fan is mounted on vibration isolators. All duct joints should be sealed to prevent air leaks. All debris must be removed from ductwork and fan.
11. Dampers and variable inlet vanes (VIVs) should operate freely and the blades close tightly. Adjust linkage to close any open blades. Close all dampers and VIVs during starting periods to reduce power use.

After performing prestart checklist, follow this procedure:

1. "Bump" motor to see if fan turns free and check for proper wheel rotation.
2. Bring fan up to speed. If fan does not come to speed in 20 s, stop fan and investigate cause.
3. At first indication of trouble or vibration, stop the fan and check for the problem.
4. Do not operate in stall range.
5. After a run-in period, usually about 8 h, recheck all alignments and inspect the bearings. Check the lubricant. Check that all bolts and set screws are tight.
6. After 30 days of operation, all foundations, structures, and supports should have stabilized their position, and another check is indicated.

All fans should be checked for balance at initial start-up, after repair, and at regular intervals.

1. Before any attempt is made at balancing, check other causes of vibration or unbalance under "Vibration and noise" as in the table of frequently experienced fan troubles below.
2. Portable instruments are available that will indicate vibration displacement in mils (mm) and velocity in in/s (mm/s). The equipment manufacturer should be contacted to obtain the normal operation, alarm, and shutdown displacement and velocity for their rotating equipment.

Maintenance

1. A definite time schedule for inspecting all rotating parts should be established. The frequency of inspection depends on the severity of operation, but is typically every 30 days of operation and at normal outages.
2. Fan bearing and flexible coupling alignment should be checked at regular intervals. Misalignment can cause overheating, wear of bearing dust seals, bearing failure, and unbalance.
3. Fan bearings should be lubricated at regular intervals and inspected periodically in accordance with the bearing manufacturer's recommendations. Use the same product when relubricating, because all greases are not chemically compatible. When changing to another lubricant, flush out all of the old thoroughly before adding new lubricant.
4. Bearings on high-speed fans tend to run hot, 50° to 100°F (10° to 38°C) above ambient. Do not replace a bearing because it feels hot to the touch. Place a contact thermometer against the bearing pillow block and check the temperature.
5. All metal couplings and all gear-type couplings require periodic lubrication inspections. Other flexible couplings such as disk-ring type or rubber insert type should be inspected for wear.
6. Foundation bolts and all set screws should be inspected for tightness, at least annually.
7. Fans should be inspected for wear and dirt periodically (at least annually). The wheel might have to be cleaned. A washdown with steam or water jet is usually sufficient. Cover the bearings so water will not enter the pillow block. Dirt piled in the housing should be removed. Fan wheels having badly worn blades should be replaced or rebuilt. Rebuilt or repaired wheels require careful balancing before being returned to service.
8. On V-belt drives check belt wear, alignment, and belt tension.
9. If excessive vibration or bearing temperature occurs, it might be due to unbalance, misalignment, loose belts, poor lubrication, dirt buildup on the wheel, etc.
10. Repainting of exterior and interior parts of fans and ducts will extend the service life of the installation. Competent advice should be secured when corrosive fumes are present.
11. Never run the fan at a higher speed than it was designed.
12. Heating coil: Clean fin tube heating element at least once a year; more often under unfavorable conditions. Unless heating element is kept reasonably free of dirt, lint, and grease, its original heating capacity will be reduced, possibly to a serious degree, and motor damage may result. Three commonly used cleaning methods are:
    a. Loosen dirt by brushing fins on side where air enters heating element and then turn on fan to blow dirt from unit.
    b. Use high-pressure air hose to loosen dirt by blowing from side where air leaves heating element.
    c. Vacuum cleaning: Thoroughly vacuum intake side of fan with vacuum cleaner. For thorough cleaning of heating element, remove motor and fan and spray a mild alkaline cleaning solution over the heating element. After a few minutes, follow by a hot water rinse. (A steam gun can be used for spraying cleaning solution and hot water.)
13. Dampers and linkage:
    a. Inspect crank arm pivots and damper rods for wear. Replace worn parts.
    b. Lubricate damper pivot rod bearings every 3 months with silicone spray, graphite, or equivalent.

c. Face and bypass heating coils should be periodically inspected for continuous satisfactory operation. Loose nuts, bolts, and screws should be tightened. Crank arm pivots and damper rods should be checked for wear and replaced if worn.

14. Filters:

a. As far as possible, have uniform airflow across the filter face.

b. Provide prefilters with high-efficiency filters for longer service life.

c. Prevent water and solid particles from impinging on the filter media.

d. Provide draft gauges across the filter media to determine when the filter should be changed and/or serviced. Note with variable volume, system draft gauges should be checked at design maximum air volume to determine whether the filters should be changed.

e. Provide ample direct access to each filter bank for servicing.

f. Air volumes less than 25 percent or more than 125 percent of normal rating require careful selection of filters for optimum performance.

g. Always maintain airflows across filter media within the manufacturer's recommendations.

h. Do not exceed the manufacturer's recommended final resistance values for the particular filter media.

i. Do not install electrostatic air cleaners where sensible moisture—that is, free moisture (water droplets)—is present in the air stream.

j. Remember lint in atmospheric dust is difficult to remove from viscous impingement filters and may cause electrical short circuit in electrostatic filters.

k. Select filters based on *life cycle costs,* not first costs. Filter manufacturers such as American Air Filter have programs that select filter type and medium based on life cycle costs.

15. Bearings: It is standard for bearing manufacturers to base the service life of their bearings on millions of revolutions and for the plant design/operating engineer to base the required bearing service life on the hours between failure. It is the authors position that the plant design/operating engineer should specify the required hours between failure and the environment the bearing will operate in and make the bearing manufacturer responsible to design and calculate the required L_{10} etc., to obtain the specified hours of operation between bearing failure. To determine the hours of operation between bearing failure, the author has found the following table helpful:

Description of service	Hours of service
For equipment that operates only a few hours a week, or when first costs are more important than service life	10,000
Equipment operates 8 h a day, 5 days a week	20,000
Equipment operates 24 h a day, 365 days a year	50,000

In order to obtain the design bearing life, one must lubricate and service the bearings in strict accordance with the manufacturer's recommendations.

16. The most frequently experienced fan troubles are listed below:

Complaint/symptoms	Possible cause
Capacity or pressure below rating	1. Total resistance of system higher than anticipated
	2. Speed too low
	3. Dampers to VIVs not properly adjusted
	4. Poor fan inlet or outlet conditions
	5. Air leaks in system
	6. Damaged wheel
	7. Incorrect direction of rotation
	8. Wheel mounted backwards on shaft
Vibration and noise	1. Bearings, couplings, wheel, or V-belt drive misaligned
	2. Unstable foundation or mounting

Complaint/symptoms	Possible cause
	3. Foreign material in fan or material buildup on the wheel causing unbalance
	4. Worn bearings
	5. Damaged wheel or motor
	6. Broken or loose bolts and set screws
	7. Bent shaft
	8. Worn coupling
	9. Fan wheel or driver unbalanced
	10. 120-Hz magnetic hum due to electrical input
	11. Fan delivering more than rated capacity
	12. Loose dampers or variable inlet vains
	13. Speed too high or fan rotating in wrong direction
	14. Vibration transmitted to fan from some other source
Overheated bearings	1. Too much grease in bearings
	2. Poor alignment
	3. Damaged wheel or drive
	4. Abnormal end thrust
	5. Dirt in bearing
	6. Excessive belt tension
Overload driver	1. Speed too high
	2. Discharging over capacity because existing system resistance is lower than original rating
	3. Specific gravity or density of gas above design value
	4. Packing too tight or defective (fans with stuffing box)
	5. Wrong direction of rotation
	6. Poor alignment
	7. Wheel wedging or binding on inlet bell
	8. Motor improperly wired
Unit fails to maintain temperature	1. Undersized heater, boiler, pump, or piping
	2. Excessive exhaust air (exhaust fans may have been added since heating was installed)
	3. Unit heater mounted too high—heater air not delivered to floor level
	4. Thermostat—improper location or setting, or not functioning
	5. Dirty or clogged fin tube heating element
Unit blows cold air	1. Manual shutoff valve closed
	2. Insufficient steam pressure or lack of hot water
	3. Aquastat not functioning
	4. Improper venting
	5. Steam trap not functioning
	6. Drip leg too short (steam system)
	7. Return line plugged (steam system)
	8. Pump undersized or not operating (hot-water system)
Unit does not operate when heat is required	1. Defective motor or electrical connections
	2. Thermostat, aquastat, or pressure limit control not functioning
Unit heater fails to deliver heat to floor	1. Unit mounted too high
	2. Final temperature too high
	3. Louvers not adjusted properly
	4. Undersized unit heater (insufficient air delivery)
	5. Cross ventilation or drafts
	6. Obstructions to airflow

Complaint/symptoms	Possible cause
Unit leaks	1. Nut and ferrule connection loose 2. Internal corrosion 3. Crack in brazed connection
Employees complain of hot blast	1. Air stream aimed directly at employees 2. Louvers not adjusted properly 3. Excessive final air temperature 4. Revolving discharge unit not revolving
Unit operates too long	1. Thermostat installed on cold wall or otherwise improperly located 2. Heavy exhaust fan load may have been increased since heating system was installed 3. Aquastat or pressure limit control not functioning properly 4. Unit is undersized
Frequent motor failure	1. Voltage fluctuations too high or too low 2. Excessive or insufficient lubrication 3. Wiring to motor undersized 4. Improper electrical connections 5. Motor operating in too high air temperature 6. Restricted airflow through unit due to clogged fin tube heater elements, closed louvers, too much duct work connected to unit 7. Fan out of balance 8. Unbalanced voltage on 3-phase power
Heating coil tube element failure	1. Severe internal corrosion from feedwater 2. Type of boiler treatment 3. Entrained air causing water hammer

REFERENCES AND BIBLIOGRAPHY

1. *Industrial Ventilation, A Manual of Recommended Practice,* latest ed., American Conference of Industrial Ventilation (Committee on Industrial Ventilation), Lansing, Michigan, 1980.

2. Carrier Air Conditioning Company: *System Design Manual,* part 1, "System Load Estimating," Syracuse, N.Y., 1960.

3. Daly, B. B. (ed.): *Woods Practical Guide to Fan Engineering,* 3d ed., International Publications Service, New York, 1978.

4. ASHRAE: *Handbook of Fundamentals,* latest ed., American Society of Heating, Refrigeration and Air Conditioning Engineers, New York.

5. McDermott, Henry J.: *Handbook of Ventilation for Contaminant Control,* Ann Arbor Science, Ann Arbor, Michigan, 1976.

6. Hemeon, W. C. L.: *Plant and Process Ventilation,* Industrial Press, New York, 1963.

7. ASHRAE Standard ANSI/ASHRAE 62-1989, *Ventilation for Acceptable Indoor Air Quality,* latest ed., American Society of Heating, Refrigeration and Air Conditioning Engineers, Atlanta.

8. *Fan Engineering,* latest ed., Buffalo Forge Company, Buffalo, N.Y.

9. ASHRAE, *Handbook of HVAC Systems and Applications,* latest ed., American Society of Heating, Refrigeration and Air Conditioning Engineers, Atlanta.

10. ASHRAE, *Handbook of Equipment,* latest ed., American Society of Heating, Refrigeration and Air Conditioning Engineers, Atlanta.

11. *Cameron Hydraulic Data,* latest ed., Ingersoll Rand Company, Woodcliff Lake, N.J.

CHAPTER 5-2

AIR CONDITIONING

James L. Davis
Consulting Engineer
San Rafael, California

Modern air conditioning represents one of man's most successful efforts to control the environment, yet it has come into full bloom almost unnoticed, bringing comfort, well-being, and the fruits of greater productivity to millions. That is what air conditioning is intended for: creating a comfortable climate in a manner that is not noticeably contrived.

Not many years ago, even crude air conditioning was a luxury. Today, good air conditioning is a necessity. No one would consider building a modern shopping center, office building, or theater without it. People take for granted that it will be provided, and various types of systems and combinations of systems have been developed to accomplish this.

OBJECTIVES

The principal objective of any air conditioning system is to provide for occupant comfort and, hence, improved worker productivity. The parameters of occupant comfort have been studied in depth by the American Society of Heating, Refrigeration, and Air Conditioning Engineers (ASHRAE) and were found to define a relatively small band of temperature and humidity conditions which have some seasonal variations. Design conditions for any air-conditioning system should fall within this band. See Fig. 2-1.

Indoor air quality became an important issue in the early 1990s, and the air-conditioning system has had a major impact on it. Care must be taken in the design of the system to provide adequate ventilation air of good quality to dilute contamination which is generated in the conditioned space and not captured at the source. The quality of both ambient outside air and recirculated air must be monitored and corrected as necessary before either is allowed to enter the conditioned space. Additionally, the equipment must be designed so that it does not allow standing water or dirt accumulation within air handlers or ducting. While occupant comfort is the primary objective of air conditioning, it is not the only one. Another consideration which has a strong impact on design decisions is energy efficiency. Minimum levels of

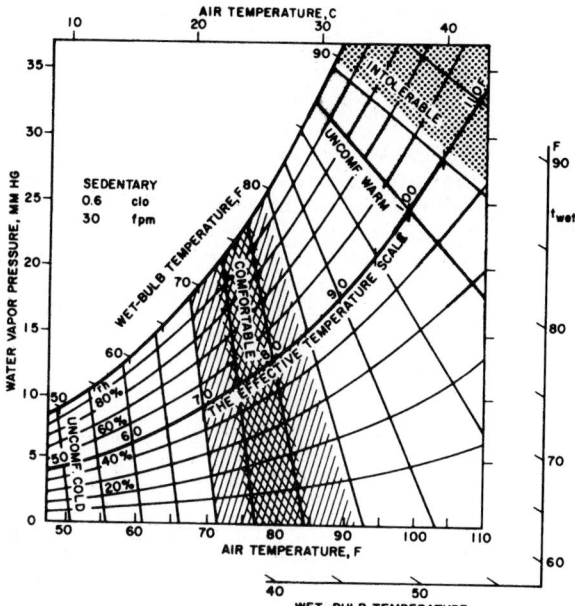

FIGURE 2-1 Comfort zone temperatures and humidity. (*Reproduced with permission from ASHRAE:* Handbook of Fundamentals,© 1981, ASHRAE, New York.)

efficiency for equipment and systems are mandated by governmental regulations which vary regionally, but in some cases higher levels of efficiency are made desirable by considerations such as operating costs.

DESIGN CONSIDERATIONS

There are many issues which must be considered in the design of an air-conditioning system that are subjective in nature but critical to the success of the project. One of the most important of these is the owner's objective for the building. For example, if the building is being built for sale, the air-conditioning design will likely be governed by first cost. Conversely, if it is to be the owner's home office, performance and operating cost will more likely control the design. The owner's objectives and intended use of the facility will also affect the precision of temperature and humidity control provided and will define acceptable sound levels and other aesthetic issues.

The architectural design of the building and the design of the air-conditioning system are integrally linked and must be symbiotic. For example, while the architectural design can have a major effect on the thermal load on the building, the system design may dictate the need for mechanical rooms and duct spaces which alter the floor plan and planned space utilization.

In addition to energy regulations, there are many other codes which must be considered in design of an air-conditioning system. Probably the most important is the *Life Safety Code*® which sets requirements for the system to assist with smoke removal in the event of a fire.* The duct work must comply with fire regulations such as installation of fire dampers when it penetrates fire break zones within the building. All the equipment including the ducting must be supported and restrained in accordance with building and seismic codes.

* *Life Safety Code* is a Registered Trademark of the National Fire Protection Association, Inc., Quincy, MA 02269.

Once the building shell is defined and we have given consideration to the items listed above, the next step in the design of a system is to perform a *thermal load study*. We begin by setting the indoor and outdoor design conditions for heating and cooling. In some areas, these conditions are set by regulation. In the absence of regulation, design conditions can be obtained from the *ASHRAE Load Calculation Manual*. Next, we examine the floor plan for the building and try to identify areas of the building which are physically close together and have similar heat load characteristics. We group these areas into control zones for the system, since the similarity of load will allow the simplest control and the physical proximity will limit the piping required to connect the areas within the control zone. The actual load calculations are usually done by a computer program into which we enter data on the physical description of the space and its internal loads such as people, lighting, equipment, and processes. The programs take into account the movement of the sun and time variation of the internal loads as well as the effects of ventilation and infiltration of outside air. The output of the program is an analysis of the thermal load for each zone and for the building as a whole, identifying the date, time, and magnitude of the peak heating and cooling loads.

Capacity Determination

Once we determine the thermal load characteristics of the building, the next step is to select appropriate types and sizes for the equipment to be installed. It is usual to study the application of more than one type of system and various types of hardware to the building so that we can determine which will best meet the owner's requirements for first cost, energy efficiency, operating effectiveness, aesthetics, etc. On the basis of these studies, we make decisions that identify the basic operation of the system and the kinds of equipment to be installed. Many, if not most, of the decisions as to type, size, and capacity of equipment are made at this stage. Government regulations affect these decisions, for example, by limiting the use of some types of systems and equipment and mandating maximum reserve capacities which can be provided. Heating and cooling capacities must not only be adequate to meet the peak loads imposed, they must also provide for such events as building warm-up or cool-down after a weekend or holiday. We must also provide an allowance for control of relative humidity which can require substantial heating or cooling capacity. We must size piping, duct work, pumps, and fans to provide adequate flows of heated or cooled media to the terminal devices which deliver heating or cooling to the space. This design work is a specialty in itself.

EQUIPMENT AND SYSTEMS

Cold Sources

Vapor-Compression Refrigeration.   One of the most common sources of cooling in use today is *vapor-compression refrigeration*. In this system, a refrigerant is passed through a metering device (expansion valve or capillary tube) into the coils of a heat exchanger. The refrigerant absorbs heat from the medium on the other side of the exchanger and evaporates, lowering the temperature of the medium. The refrigerant vapor moves to a compressor which raises its pressure and temperature and then to a condenser where heat is removed from the vapor, allowing it to condense and become liquid. The liquid returns to the metering device to begin the cycle again. See Fig. 2-2.

The refrigerant can be any of a wide variety of materials, commonly CFCs (Freon®) or ammonia, and the transfer medium can be air, water, glycol solution, or others. The basic cycle operation is the same.

If the evaporator transfer medium is air which will be delivered to the conditioned space, the system is referred to as a *direct-expansion system*. Generally, if the evaporator medium is liquid, e.g., water or glycol solution, the refrigeration system is called *indirect* and the refrig-

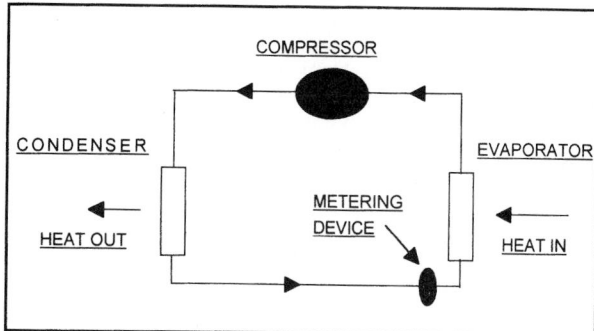

FIGURE 2-2   Basic vapor-compression refrigeration cycle.

eration source is called a *chiller. Vapor-compression refrigeration systems are* frequently classified by the type of compressor device used. Some common types are reciprocating (piston), kinetic (centrifugal), and rotary (screw, scroll, vane, gear). While each type has its unique operating characteristics, they all make the same contribution; they raise the pressure and temperature of the refrigerant vapor.

A matter of some concern in the modern world is the environmental impact of many of the refrigerants in common use, specifically, chlorofluorocarbons (CFCs) which have been shown to damage the earth's ozone layer. CFCs are being eliminated, their manufacture is being discontinued, and manufacturers are developing substitutes. Care must be taken to avoid venting CFCs to the atmosphere, and replacement equipment should be specified which does *not* use CFC refrigerants. One refrigerant which has been reexamined and is experiencing a surge in popularity is ammonia. Properly handled, it can be an economical, efficient, and safe alternative.

Absorption Chillers.   In the early 1990s an old technology, *absorption cooling,* was reborn and has been developed to provide a refrigeration source without CFC or ammonia. The *absorption chiller* uses a secondary fluid to absorb the vaporized refrigerant from the evaporator. Heat is released in the absorption process which is discharged through the condenser. The mixture of refrigerant and absorber fluid goes to the generator where heat is added which causes the refrigerant to distill. The liquid refrigerant flows to the metering device and the absorbent returns to the absorbent reservoir. Common refrigerant-absorbent combinations are water-ammonia and water–lithium bromide. There have been many variations of the process used over the years, but these are the most common today. Until recently, these systems had the reputation of being bulky and difficult to operate efficiently. New technological developments have eliminated most of these objections. Absorption chillers have the additional advantage that they can make use of heat that would otherwise be waste, such as residual heat from steam processes or hot process fluids which need cooling. The absorption chiller can even use its own rejected heat as part of the heat required by the generator, thus increasing further the efficiency of the system.

Evaporative Cooling.   In areas where the relative humidity is generally below 50 percent, evaporative coolers of various types can be effective and economical as a source of cooled air for air conditioning. *Direct evaporative coolers* convey air that is to be delivered to the conditioned space through a zone of contact with water, either a pad or a spray. Each pound of water evaporated absorbs approximately 1000 Btu/lb (2321 kJ/kg) and lowers the air temperature. This process cannot cool air below the dew point of the outside air. In fact, it cannot reach dew point. The other drawback to direct evaporative cooling is that all of the water evaporated from the cooler is carried into the conditioned space. This means that a high volume of ventilation is required to prevent the conditioned space from becoming excessively humid.

A system that eliminates the humidity problems related to direct evaporative coolers first cools outside air by evaporation and then uses an air-to-air heat exchanger to transfer the cooling to the circulating airstream. This indirect system does not produce as much cooling effect as a direct system, but it adds no moisture to the circulating air.

The ultimate in evaporative cooling is the *two-stage evaporative cooler,* in which circulating air is first cooled by passing through an indirect evaporative cooler and then is sent through a *direct evaporative cooling stage.* With this scheme, the air can be cooled below the outdoor dew point and the amount of humidity carried into the space is reduced. Even in areas where the temperature and humidity are not always favorable, this system can be used to supplement a refrigeration system and reduce overall operating cost and energy consumption.

Thermal Storage.   One problem with refrigerated air conditioning is that the peak cooling demand generally falls during the heat of the day, which means that the refrigerator needs to work harder to reject its heat at the higher temperature, and the cost per kilowatthour for electricity as well as utility demand charges are the highest. Thermal storage systems allow us to generate cold when the outside temperature is low and when the kilowatthour and demand rates are also minimum. This cold is commonly stored in the form of ice, cold water, or eutectic salts and used the next day as needed. In one case, a company generated enough "snow" in the basement of its building during the winter to provide cooling for several months at no cost.

Free Cooling.   From an economic standpoint, the best way to provide cooling is at no cost. Obviously, using waste heat to run an absorption chiller is one way to achieve this, but there are others as well. For example, the outside air intake system can be configured so that it will use 100 percent outside air if it is cooler than return air and the demand is for cooling, which is a fairly common situation. This is the basic operation of an *economizer.*

Or, if outside temperature and humidity conditions permit, the cooling tower piping can be modified so that the tower's evaporative cooling can be used to cool system circulating water when the chiller is not operating. This process is referred to as *tower free cooling.*

We should always be alert to process waste such as chilled fluids or airstreams which might be recovered economically to improve the overall energy efficiency of our facilities.

Heat Sources

Just as we must be able to cool the air entering our conditioned space, we must also sometimes be able to heat it. The source of the heat and the way it is transmitted to the conditioned space will have a large effect on the system's operating characteristics.

*Furnaces.**   Probably the most common heat source is the *direct-heating furnace* in which circulating air is heated by contact with an electric heat element or with the surface of a heat exchanger which is heated by combustion gases from burning gas or liquid fuel. A direct-heating furnace can be built into the ducting of an air-conditioning system and become integral to the system. Similar, but somewhat less common, are radiant heaters which transmit infrared heat waves generated from an electric heating element or other heated surface. Infrared waves are absorbed by surfaces within the space to generate heat. In situations where it is difficult to control airflow through the space, this type of heater is most effective and energy-efficient.

Boilers.†   In larger installations, it is frequently more practical to generate a heated fluid at some central location and to pipe it to points of use throughout the space. The devices used to do the heating are generically called *boilers* even if they do not actually boil the fluid.

---

* Also see Chap. 4-3.
† Also see Chap. 4-2.

Common boilers are fired with natural gas, liquefied petroleum gases, liquid fuels, coal, wood, or electricity, depending on what is most readily available. Considerations in the choice of a boiler would certainly include economy, efficiency, and ease of operation. Today, we are seeing the growth of emission control regulations for boilers, which will need to be considered in future selections of equipment.

Boilers are generally designed to operate in one of three pressure ranges: hot water, which operates around 180°F (83°C); low-pressure steam, up to 15 psig (103 kPa); and high-pressure steam, up to 100 psig (689 kPa). Hot-water boilers are the least trouble to operate, but they require the highest volume of circulation to deliver a given amount of heat. The main advantage of low-pressure steam is that, while the boiler is still simple to operate and maintain, a given amount of steam will deliver many times more heat because of the release of latent heat of vaporization, which for water is about 1000 Btu/lb (2321 kJ/kg) compared to 20 to 50 Btu/lb (116 to 290 kJ/kg) delivered by hot water. This means that smaller piping and pumps are required to supply a given amount of heat. High-pressure steam boilers offer the most efficient delivery of heat available, but present substantial operating difficulties. They usually require constant supervision by a qualified stationary engineer and have heavy maintenance and inspection requirements.

Heat Reclaim.   Waste heat from processes, such as rejected heat from refrigeration equipment, hot exhaust airstreams, steam condensate, and cooling water outflows, represents a good potential for reclamation and its resulting energy savings. Heat, in the form of hot water or steam, is a common by-product of electrical generation. The capture and constructive use of this heat is a key factor in the viability of most cogeneration projects.

Solar Heating.   A source of low-cost heat energy in many areas is capture of the sun's rays to generate hot water in solar cells. The technology for this capture is well-proven, and there is a wide variety of equipment available to meet the needs of the project. One problem with solar heating is that the time when the heat is most available is also the time when it is least needed, unless you are using the heat to generate an absorption chiller or have some way to store it.

Heat Pumps.   *Heat pumps* are really specialized refrigeration units which move heat from one place (the evaporator) to another (the condenser). Some units are configured to be reversible so that the same machine can be a heater or cooler, depending on control settings.

If the unit is to be a heat supply, the evaporator is installed outdoors, in the ground, or in a water stream which can be cooled. If the evaporator side temperature falls to 45°F (11°C), the system will generally cease to function, so a supplemental heat source should be provided if that is anticipated. Heat pumps can deliver heat for about 25 percent of the cost of generating it with electric heaters.

As a cooler, the evaporator is installed in the conditioned space and the condenser is installed outdoors. In this configuration, the heat pump is no different from any other direct-expansion air conditioner.

Heat Rejection

Refrigeration systems cannot "manufacture" cold. They gather heat energy through the evaporator, concentrate it (raise its temperature) and move it to another place (the condenser), where it is discharged. The place where heat is removed is cooled. When we use refrigeration equipment to cool air or other fluid, we must provide a means to exhaust that heat.

Condensers.   Probably the most common heat-rejection device is a *condenser,* which is really just a simple heat exchanger in which the refrigerant transfers heat energy to the cooling fluid, usually air or water. The relative flow rates of refrigerant and cooling fluid are controlled to compensate for variations in load or cooling fluid temperature. Air-cooled condensers are usually provided with blade-type fans to move cooling air through the heat exchanger. Condensers must be inspected and cleaned regularly to maintain their heat-transfer efficiency. Controls and fans must be maintained regularly to assure continued performance.

Cooling Towers.*   A more effective method of removing heat from the refrigerant is to use evaporative cooling in a *cooling tower.* There are two types of cooling towers in use for air conditioning: closed and open types.

In the *closed type,* the refrigerant is circulated through pipes inside the tower while water from the tower reservoir is sprayed on the outside of the tubes; heat is transferred to the water, causing evaporation and cooling. Closed-type towers generally are more expensive to buy and install because of the higher plumbing requirements mentioned earlier. They do, however, eliminate the need for one heat exchanger. While there is the risk of release of a large amount of refrigerant in the case of a plumbing failure, the system is better protected if the reservoir should become contaminated because the reservoir fluid has no direct contact with the chiller.

In an *open-type* cooling tower, heat is transferred from the refrigerant to water outside of the tower, and the warm water is sprayed directly into the tower, where part of it evaporates, cooling the remainder. The cool water flows to the tower reservoir from which it is pumped back to the heat exchanger. Open-type cooling towers have the lowest initial cost, and their plumbing requirements are not as stringent, since the plumbing is carrying water instead of refrigerant. If the water in the tower becomes contaminated, the contamination will be circulated to the heat exchanger and can cause damage to the chiller. Either type of tower can have a fan installed to increase its cooling effectiveness, but some rely on the convective air movement induced by the heated air.

Cooling Tower Water.   Makeup water for the tower reservoir can be a major operating cost of the system. There are three main ways in which we lose water from the reservoir: First, water is evaporated to generate cooling effect; this requires about 1 lb (1 pint) [2.2 kg (0.47 L)] of water for each 1000 Btu (1055 kJ) of cooling effect and can represent a substantial amount; second, a relatively small amount of water is carried off as mist by the circulating air in the tower; and third, we must send a certain amount of tower water to waste and replace it with fresh to prevent build up of minerals in the reservoir (this is called *blowdown*). The amount of blowdown required depends on the purity of water available and the rate of evaporation from the tower, but is generally in the area of 10 percent of the volume circulated.

Control of tower water chemistry can become quite involved and is probably best left to a specialty contractor. Water must be carefully tested to prevent corrosion, scaling, and growth of organisms such as algae and bacteria which can cause sicknesses such as Legionnaires' disease.

In areas where water is scarce, expensive, or of low quality, consideration should be given to using other means of handling rejected heat. This is also true of areas where the ambient air is unusually dirty, as this will cause fouling of the tower. In addition to careful maintenance of water chemistry, the evaporation surfaces and the reservoir of all cooling towers should be cleaned regularly to maintain efficient operation. If a fan is used, both the fan and its controls should be maintained regularly.

Distribution

Fans.[†]   Fans for supplying air to the space through the ductwork can be placed in one of two general classifications: (1) centrifugal fans or (2) axial fans. Centrifugal fans induce airflow within the fan wheel that is substantially radial to the shaft, while axial fans induce flow within the wheel that is substantially parallel to the shaft. Centrifugal fans operate in a scroll-type housing. Axial fans, on the other hand, operate within a cylindrical or ring-type housing.

---

* See also Chap. 6-2.
† See also Chap. 5-1.

Fans in air-conditioning systems are used for three general purposes:

1. To move the conditioned air from the conditioning apparatus to the conditioned space
2. To return the air from the conditioned space to the conditioning apparatus
3. To exhaust air from the conditioned space or to supply outside air to the conditioning apparatus

Centrifugal Fans. Centrifugal fans may be further classified as (1) backward-inclined (BI), (2) forward-curved (FC), and (3) airfoil. In the BI fan, the tip of the blade is sloped backward, opposite to the direction of rotation. In the FC fan, the blade is sloped in the direction of rotation. As with the BI fan, the blade of the airfoil fan is sloped opposite to the direction of rotation. However, the airfoil shape of the blade results in higher efficiency and a lower noise level.

With the forward-curved blade wheel, a forward movement is imparted to the air by the blade. This motion causes the air to leave at a higher velocity than that produced by either the BI or airfoil blade.

Because the pressure produced by a fan is related to the forward motion of the air at the tip of the blade, a fan with FC blades can operate at a lower rotating speed for a given volume requirement than a fan with backward-inclined blades. In other words, where a large volume of air is needed at low rotational speed, the FC fan wheel is usually selected.

Generally, for a given application, the BI or airfoil fan will require less power than the FC fan. In spite of the higher rotational speed required by BC and airfoil fans, they are, when properly selected, as quiet or quieter than the FC. In small-size fans [generally less than 24-in (62-cm) diameter], the high rotational speed requirement can result in excessive belt speeds. Here, the low-speed characteristics of the FC fan are desirable. Where high static pressures and medium air volumes are specified, the airfoil fan is usually selected. Figure 2-3 illustrates the general configurations of these fans.

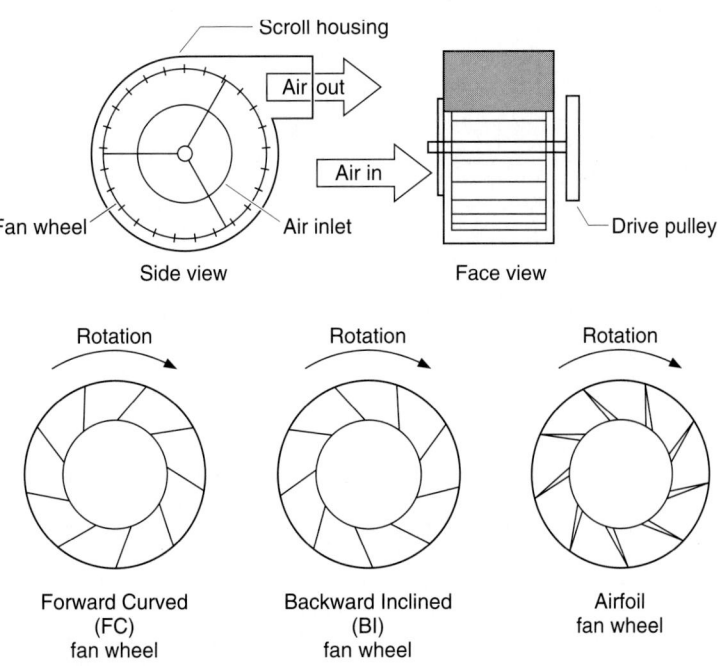

FIGURE 2-3   Centrifugal fans.

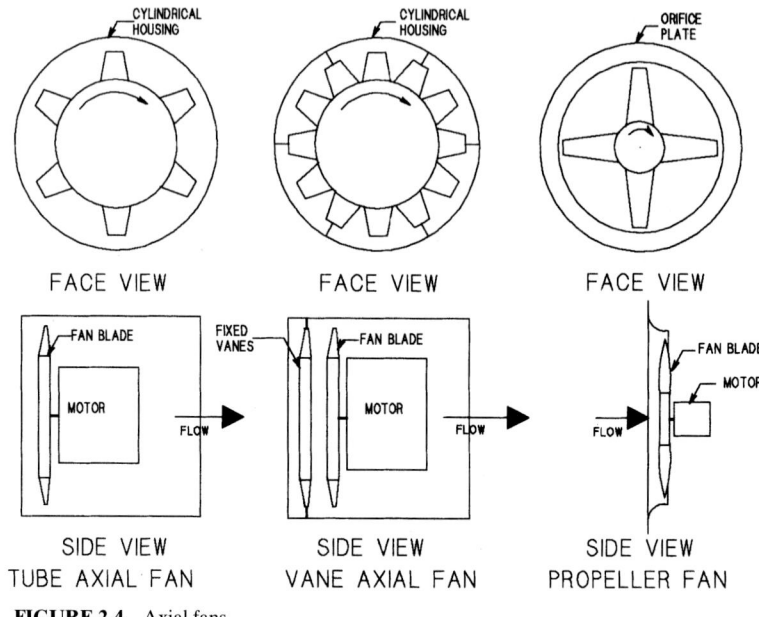

FIGURE 2-4   Axial fans.

Axial-Flow Fans.   There are three general types of axial-flow fans: *tube axial, vane axial,* and *propeller.* These are shown schematically in Fig. 2-4.

TUBE AXIAL FANS.   Tube axial fans may be considered to be heavy-duty propeller fans. They are generally arranged for duct connection, while propeller fans are usually arranged for wall mounting. Tube axial fans are built for pressures up to 3 in (7.7 cm) water column. Generally, their application is limited to industrial duties where noise is not important.

VANE AXIAL FANS.   Vane axial fans are similar to tube axial fans except for the addition of stationary vanes downstream from the fan wheel. The vanes straighten the flow, increase the static efficiency, and permit more diversified duct applications.

Vane axial and tube axial fans are often used where space is limited. For this reason, they are often the logical choice in transportation and marine applications. Improved vane axial fans can be both as quiet and as efficient as centrifugal fans.

PROPELLER FANS.   Propeller fans are low-pressure, high-volume fans which are seldom used in applications that require more than 0.75 in (19 mm) water static pressure. They consist of a stamped or cast fan wheel in an orifice ring and may be directly or belt driven. The power required by a propeller fan is lowest at maximum air volume and minimum static pressure.

Ducts.   To deliver air to the conditioned space, to return it to the conditioning apparatus, and to provide outside air, conduits are needed; they are called *ducts.* Ducts work on the principle of air pressure difference. If a pressure difference exists, air will move from the higher pressure to the lower. The greater the pressure difference, the faster the air will flow.

Ducts can be made of any of a variety of materials as long as it is not combustible. Pressure in the ducts is small, so materials with a great deal of strength are not needed. Originally, hot-air ducts were thin, tinned sheet steel. Later, galvanized sheet metal and aluminum sheet, and finally insulated ducts of fiberglass etc. were developed. Passageways formed by studs or joists and false ceilings are sometimes used for return air if no fire hazard exists.

When ducts pass through unconditioned spaces, they must be insulated to prevent heat exchange with the environment and the resulting thermal losses. If they pass through building fire breaks or from one floor to the next, ducts must be fitted with fire dampers to prevent spread of fire through the duct system. Ducts commonly used for carrying air are round, square, and rectangular. Round ducts are more efficient in terms of the volume of air handled for a given perimeter; that is, less material is required for the same capacity as a square or rectangular duct. Friction losses are also less in a circular duct with the same flow velocity.

The duct system should, by design, deliver balanced amounts of air to all parts of the conditioned space. It is still necessary to provide flow-balancing dampers throughout the system. This allows for precise flow adjustments to meet requirements but balancing is much easier if the system is properly designed. The system losses due to friction and fittings should be minimized since these losses represent fan energy which must be provided continuously throughout the life of the building. Another consideration in the design of a ducting system is noise generation. The main source of noise in ducts is high-velocity air; the higher the velocity, the more noise is generated. Some types of duct fittings inherently generate noise when air flows past them and others respond to particular air velocities and become noisy. In some environments, duct noise is acceptable, but in typical office settings, it must be held to low levels to avoid occupant complaints.

Care should be taken in duct design and installation to eliminate collection points for moisture and dirt. Ducts must be inspected regularly and repaired, if needed, to maintain system performance. Damaged and leaking ductwork can reduce operating efficiency substantially. Ducts require periodic internal inspection and cleaning if necessary; failure to do so can lead directly to serious indoor air quality problems.

Piping. In many installations, particularly large ones, it is most efficient to generate heat and cold at a central location and to deliver it to air-conditioning apparatus located near the conditioned space. Cold is usually carried by water or glycol solution and heat is usually moved in the form of hot water or steam. Proper insulation of all system piping is mandatory to prevent unacceptable levels of thermal loss which require the central plant to work harder and to consume more energy.

Water Piping. Water piping arrangements for air conditioning can be divided into three general classifications: *one-pipe, two-pipe,* and *four-pipe.* The first two are arranged so that either hot or cold water can be circulated through the piping. However, when hot water is being circulated in a one-pipe or two-pipe system, only hot water is available to each heat exchange coil connected to that circuit. Conversely, when cold water is being circulated, only cold water is available to each coil. The four-pipe configuration is actually two two-pipe systems, one for hot water, the other for cold water. The hot water and cold water do not mix or use common piping.

ONE-PIPE DESIGN.   In the *one-pipe* design, a single pipe loops the building and constitutes both the supply and return main. The same pipe size is maintained throughout its length because all of the water that is circulated passes through the one main.

At each branch takeoff to a unit, a flow fitting is installed which causes some of the water from the main to flow through the coil of the unit. The water returning to the main is at a different temperature from the water flowing in the main. The mixing of the water from the unit with the water in the main changes the temperature in the main; a cold main gets warmer, and a hot main gets cooler. This represents one limitation of this design; if too many units are connected to a circuit, the units downstream will receive water whose temperature has been changed so much that the unit cannot function.

The coils in the units must be selected for a low pressure drop since the flow fittings are designed to limit pressure drops so that overall pump head can be kept within a reasonable range. One-pipe configurations are more commonly used for heating applications than for cooling or heating/cooling. Properly designed and installed, a one-pipe system can provide considerable savings in first cost. Figure 2-5 shows a schematic layout for this design.

TWO-PIPE DESIGN.   There are two general methods of arranging piping for two-pipe circulation:

In the *direct-return* arrangement, the length of travel of the water is different for each unit. The water flowing through the first unit has a much shorter distance to travel than the last unit. Balancing flow in this arrangement is difficult, since each unit sees a different pressure drop. This design is represented in Fig. 2-6.

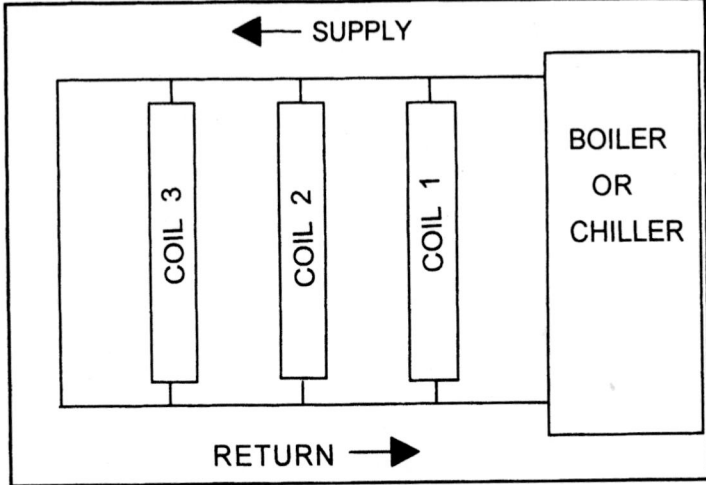

FIGURE 2-5   One-pipe water piping.

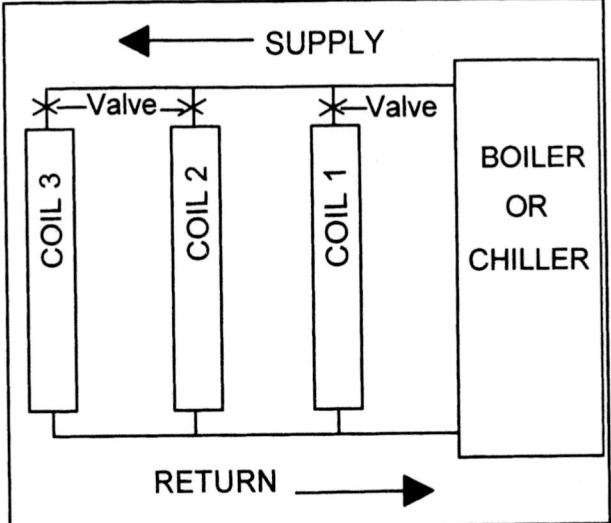

FIGURE 2-6   Two-pipe direct-return water piping.

In the *reverse-return* design, the length of travel of the water from the chiller or boiler through any of the units and back is essentially the same. This is accomplished by making the unit nearest the source on the supply main the farthest away on the return main. In other words, the water flowing from the supply main to the first unit must flow through the entire length of the return main before it returns to the chiller or boiler. From this description, it would appear that this arrangement is self-balancing. In practice, it is necessary to install balancing valves or orifices in the piping to each unit to provide the exact flow required. Obviously, this design is more costly to install than the previous two, but its flexibility and simplicity of operation make it more widely used. See Fig. 2-7 for typical layout of this system.

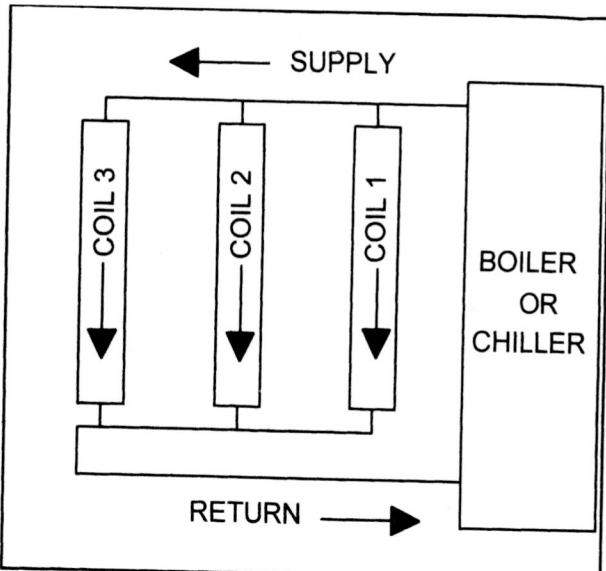

FIGURE 2-7   Two-pipe reverse-return water piping.

FOUR-PIPE SYSTEM.   As stated before, a *four-pipe system* is essentially two two-pipe systems, one for hot water, one for cold. This is the only system that can provide heating and cooling to all the units simultaneously. The most common configuration of the four-pipe system uses separate coils for heating and for cooling; however, this is not necessary. It is possible to arrange the plumbing so that one coil can be used. There is a loss of flexibility and control, but the installation costs are substantially reduced. The four-pipe arrangement gives the ultimate in simplicity of design, room control, and economy of operation even though it has a higher first cost. A typical flow diagram is shown in Fig. 2-8.

Steam Piping*   Steam used in air conditioning is usually low pressure (15 psig or less). Because of the higher heat content of steam, the size of piping required for a given heat load is much smaller than that for hot water. The surface temperature of the pipe is sufficiently

---

* See also Chap. 5-1.

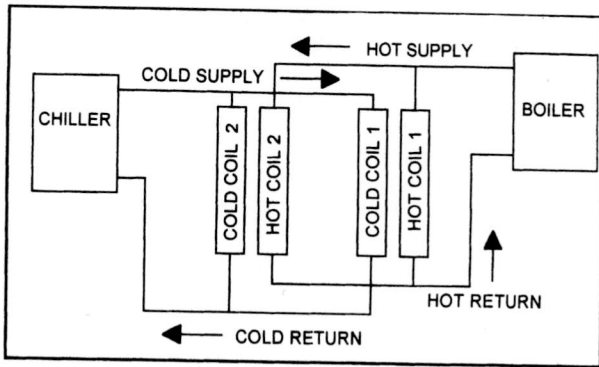

FIGURE 2-8   Four-pipe water piping configuration.

high to present a hazard to personnel, and protection must be provided. Also, because of the higher surface temperature, proper insulation is even more important than with hot water pipes to prevent thermal loss.

Since the heat release from steam is accompanied by condensation, care must be taken in the design to provide means to return the condensate to the boiler. Regular inspection and maintenance of steam system components is critical to efficient operation of the system.

Terminal Devices. Terminal devices are the pieces of hardware that actually deliver heat or cooling generated in a central plant to the conditioned space. There is a wide variety of such devices to meet the requirements of different operating systems and facilities.

Hydronic Heaters and Steam Radiators. Hydronic heaters and steam radiators are located within the conditioned space and transfer heat from steam or hot water to room air; they are not widely used for cooling. Units of this type generally use convective flow and radiation to distribute the heat throughout the area.

Unit Heater/Coolers. Unit heater/coolers are also mounted within the conditioned space and consist of one or two heat exchangers, usually fin-and-tube coils which are connected to hot- and/or cold-water sources and a fan which moves air through the coils and distributes it around the area.

It is more common to use the output of the central plant in an air handler which serves a relatively large area of the facility. In the air handler, hot water (or steam) and chilled water are used to adjust the temperature of the air to be supplied to the space. The air handler also usually introduces a controlled amount of fresh air, filters the air stream, and adjusts humidity as needed. The output of an air handler is then delivered through the duct system to a terminal device and into an individual conditioned space.

Air Registers. The simplest terminal devices are *air registers,* which are boxes with louvers on the downstream side that direct the airstream to optimize distribution within the space. Air registers can be round, square, rectangular, or any of various specialized shapes such as linear. All registers have the same general design considerations: air distribution, mixing, noise, and perceived air movement. The higher the air velocity through the register, the better it will distribute the conditioned air and, generally, the better the conditioned air will mix with room air. Higher air velocity, however, causes noise and the increased air movement is perceived as drafts by the occupants. Selection of air registers must provide the best possible balance of conflicting needs. Air registers can be fitted with a number of accessory devices such as flow-control dampers which can be operated manually or mechanically to meet specific needs of the occupants of the space.

Variable Air Volume (VAV) Boxes. When we study the thermal loads on a building, we find that all the spaces do not behave the same. Some spaces may need heating while others need cooling and still others may only need ventilation. Several schemes have been devised to accommodate all these needs at once, but most of them involve, for example, cooling a fixed volume of air and then reheating it for some spaces. This is wasteful of energy and not generally acceptable in modern practice. In order to overcome these problems, the *variable air volume* (VAV) system was developed. In this system, air is cooled enough to be suitable for cooling use in a cooling-only air handler and delivered to a zone control VAV box. If the space needs cooling, the VAV box damper opens and allows the cool air to flow into the space until it is satisfied, at which time it goes to a minimum flow setting which provides for ventilation. If the space needs heating, a reheat coil is activated, but the airflow volume is not allowed to increase from minimum. Thus, while there is reheating of a cooled airstream, the volume and consequently the wasted energy are minimized. Since, at any time, some boxes will be open and others closed, the overall fan volume requirement will change. In order to accommodate the changing air demand, variable-volume fans are used. These are either variable-speed fans or they are fitted with mechanical devices to reduce their output. It should be apparent that all the spaces to be served by a VAV box must have similar requirements for heating and cooling.

There are a large number of variations on the basic idea of the VAV system and each has its unique applications. If appropriate adjustments are made to the operating set points of the system in response to changing conditions, a VAV system can provide energy-efficient operation and excellent control of the space conditions.

A particular limitation of VAV systems is their inability to handle high heating demand such as recovery from a shutdown or in spaces which have high thermal losses. In general, VAV systems should not be shut down but instead have their operating temperature lowered, and recovery should be started early enough to allow for slow heating. In areas of high heat loss, the best solution usually is to provide auxiliary local heating.

Air Cleaning and Filtration

Air pollution is a growing problem as urban areas increase in population and industries expand. Contaminants should be controlled at their source whenever possible. When we fail to do this, the contamination is spread throughout the area and into neighboring spaces. Because of these failures, cleaning the air has become an important part of air conditioning. Air contaminants, as all foreign matter in the air is called, include solids, liquids, gases, and vapors. Efficient air-conditioning systems will remove 75 to 95 percent of these contaminants.

Types of Contaminants*

Solids. Solid particles, kept in suspension by the air movement, fall into three general groups:

1. *Dust* can have its origin in animal, vegetable, or mineral material. Representative particle sizes are atmospheric dust, 0.001 to 30 μm; coal dust, 1 to 100 μm; and other dust, 600 μm and up.
2. *Fumes* are formed from materials which are normally solids but have been put into a gaseous state usually by an industrial process. Particle sizes are about 1 μm.
3. *Smoke* is caused by incomplete combustion. It consists of solid particles carried in the air by products of combustion. Particle size range is 0.01 to 13 μm. Oil and tobacco smoke particles range from 0.01 to 1 μm.

Gases. Gases are on the increase as air contaminants. They include: carbon monoxide, sulfur oxides, nitrogen oxides, and hydrocarbons.

Vapors. Vapors are gases that have condensing temperatures and pressures close to normal ambient.

Liquids. There are also liquid impurities in the air. Two of the most common are:

Mists: Small liquid particles ejected into the air by splashing, mixing, or atomizing.

Fogs: Small liquid particles formed by condensation. Fogs indicate that the air has reached saturation for that chemical.

Pollen, Molds, and Bacteria. Special air cleaning processes may be provided for pollen (10 to 1000 μm), mold spores (10 to 30 μm), and bacteria.

Air Cleaning Techniques.
The air cleaning technique to be used depends on the contaminants to be removed.

Solid particles can be removed by:

1. Centrifugal force for large particles
2. Washing for wettable particles
3. Screens to block larger particles
4. Adhesives: the air is blown against a sticky surface and the dirt particles stick to the adhesive
5. Electrostatic charge: the particles are electrically charged and attracted to a surface with an opposite charge

---

* See also Chap. 5-3.

Liquids can be removed by:

1. Absorbents: chemicals to absorb or react with the liquid
2. Deflector plates: the air impinges on a plate and is forced to change direction; the liquid sticks to the surface
3. Settlement chambers: air velocity is reduced and droplets fall to the bottom

Processes to remove gases and vapors include:

1. Condensation: cool the contaminant to its dew point and remove it as a liquid
2. Chemical reaction: expose air to chemical solution such as potassium permanganate
3. Adsorption: pass airstream through activated charcoal

Filter Efficiency. It is possible to remove almost 100 percent of the contaminants in air, but to do so is expensive. Removal of 90 to 95 percent is much more practical.

Filter efficiency is measured by:

1. *Arrestance:* the weight fraction of a sample of standard synthetic dust which is captured by the filter.
2. *Dust spot test:* air which has been filtered through a test filter is filtered again with a very fine filter paper. The amount of discoloration of the filter paper is used as a measure of the amount of contamination the test filter left in the airstream.
3. *Particle size efficiency:* the relation between filter effectiveness and particle size.

Filter Types. Filters can be divided into three classifications: (1) adhesive, (2) dry, and (3) electrostatic.

Adhesive filters usually consist of a frame filled with fibrous material which has been treated with a sticky material. As air passes through the filter, it is slowed, and dirt particles stick to the adhesive. When the filter has trapped as much dirt as it can hold, it is either cleaned or thrown away, depending on its construction. There are also self-cleaning versions of the adhesive filter.

Dry filters are really very fine screens which will not allow dirt particles to pass. When they are loaded, they are usually thrown away.

These two types of filters must be inspected regularly and replaced promptly when needed to maintain efficient performance of the whole air-conditioning system. Filters should be visually inspected for mechanical damage or other indications of failure and the pressure drop across the filter should be measured with a manometer. If the pressure drop is 25 percent of the overall fan static pressure, the filter should be replaced or cleaned.

The *electrostatic filter* puts a static electrical charge on all particles which pass through it. The charged particles are then attracted to collector plates with an opposite charge. Usually, the air is first passed through a throwaway adhesive-type air filter to remove most of the larger particles of dirt. The air is then fed through a highly ionized field generated by a high-voltage wire suspended between ground wires. The electrical field puts a positive charge on any particles which pass through it, and they are drawn to the grounded collector plates (negative potential). Voltages as high as 12 kV are commonly used. Because of its high voltage, the electrostatic filter can be dangerous. Units should be designed to shut off the high voltage if the service doors are opened. The electronic cells and protective screens must be cleaned every 2 to 3 months. Some electronic air cleaners come equipped with self-cleaning systems which minimize the maintenance required.

Humidity Control

As we discussed earlier, occupant comfort depends on maintaining an acceptable combination of temperature and humidity. Insufficient humidity causes dry skin, breathing discomforts, and drying of hygroscopic materials such as wood and natural fibers. Dry air promotes the generation of static electricity. Excess humidity can cause swelling of hygroscopic materials and condensation on cold surfaces such as windows and outside wall. Relative humidity above 70 percent promotes mildew, mold, and rot.

In order to quantify the concept, we must define *humidity*. We can speak of humidity in two ways:

- *Absolute humidity* refers to the actual amount of water vapor contained in a given amount of air. Absolute humidity is measured in units such as grains moisture per pound (kilogram) of air.

- *Relative humidity* relates the amount of moisture in the air to the maximum amount it could hold under the current conditions of temperature and pressure. Relative humidity is expressed as a percentage.

The ability of air to hold moisture increases with temperature, and decreases with pressure. In air-conditioning situations, the pressure changes encountered are usually small, so it is permissible to ignore the effect of pressure.

From the above, we can see that, for a sample of air with a fixed absolute humidity, the relative humidity will decrease with increasing temperature. The relationships between relative humidity, absolute humidity, temperature, and pressure are shown graphically in a psychrometric chart which can be used for analysis of a given situation. A simplified version is shown in Fig. 2-1. Experience has shown that, for normal temperatures in office environments, a relative humidity of about 50 percent is desirable for comfort. For example, if we import some outside air and the outside conditions are 30°F (−1°C) and 90 percent relative humidity (RH), by the time it is heated to 72°F (22°C), its RH will be 18 percent. We would need to add moisture to the heated air to maintain comfort level. Conversely, if we are cooling the building, and we bring in outside air at 90°F (33°C) and 40 percent RH, by the time it is cooled to 72°F (22°C), its relative humidity will be nearly 70 percent, so we will need to remove moisture.

Humidity Control Equipment   Equipment to control the humidity of air delivered to the conditioned space is generally simple, readily available, and dependable. Devices to add moisture are called *humidifiers*. One common type injects a water mist or low-pressure steam into the warm airstream; another uses a plate, disk, or belt which is wetted and placed in the warm airstream. If there is no airstream into the space, as in the case of hydronic heating, a cabinet-type humidifier, which circulates room air and adds moisture to it, is used.

There are two common methods of removing moisture from (dehumidifying) the conditioned air:

1. First, we can cool the air until its relative humidity exceeds 100 percent, and moisture will condense, lowering the absolute humidity. When we reheat the air to delivery temperature, its relative humidity will be lower. Cooling and then reheating the air is not energy-efficient and in some cases is forbidden by code.

2. Alternatively, we can pass the air through a desiccant material such as silica gel, which will absorb moisture out of the air, lowering its relative humidity, since the temperature is constant. The silica gel is then removed from the airstream and heated to drive off the moisture; the gel can then be recycled. As with humidifiers, dehumidifiers can be mounted in air handlers or ducts, or they can be installed in cabinets in the conditioned spaces.

CONTROLS AND INSTRUMENTATION

A critical component of the effectiveness and efficiency of any air-conditioning system is its control system. The basic requirement of any control is that it measure something which is affected by the system (e.g., room temperature), compare it to a desired level (the set point), and generate a signal which is related to the difference between measured level and set point.

The simplest example would be a room thermostat which measures room temperature, compares it to a set point, and generates an on-off signal depending on the relation of room temperature to the set point. There are many variations on this simple device, with increasing levels of complexity, that are used to control air-conditioning equipment. In order to provide more precise control, it is necessary to have a controller which will generate a signal proportional to the error and actuators which will respond proportionally. An easy way to get these control characteristics is to use pneumatic devices and compressed air for control. Pneumatic devices are mechanically simple and well-proven to be dependable. They are widely used in larger installations.

The trend today is to use control systems which are based on digital computers. Until recently, this meant providing a means to convert digital control signals to analog signals that could be interpreted by "analog" (human) operators. These converters are expensive, difficult to operate, and undependable. Now, with direct digital control (DDC), the computer can interact directly with its operators, giving precise and dependable control. Another technology that has become practical recently is the use of computer systems to control whole buildings, including lighting, air conditioning, life safety, and security systems, to make facilities more responsive to the needs of their occupants and more energy-efficient.

COMMISSIONING

In order to assure that the new system functions as intended and delivers the levels of comfort and energy efficiency we expect, it is necessary that some care be taken at the start-up of the system, a process known as *commissioning*.

The commissioning process begins during the design phases of the system and is usually handled by a separate contractor hired by the owner or architect. During the design phase, the commissioning contractor reviews the plan for operability and maintenance issues. During construction, the commissioning contractor verifies that the proper equipment has been installed and that it has been installed according to the specifications. When the system is installed, the commissioning contractor oversees performance of an air and water balance study, verifies the results, and specifies necessary corrective actions. The commissioning contractor tests all controls for correct operation and confirms that all spaces are maintained at appropriate temperatures. The commissioning contractor uses the operating and maintenance materials delivered by the installation contractor to develop operating manuals and a maintenance program for the system and reviews the design drawings for accuracy.

The use of a separate commissioning contractor hired by the owner is a relatively new practice, but its use is growing because it offers the owner superior system performance with less effort than would be obtained with separate groups responsible for the various functions.

SYSTEM MAINTENANCE AND OPERATION

While mechanical maintenance was once the responsibility of trained technical personnel, increasingly sophisticated systems and equipment require overall management programs to handle organization, staffing, planning, and control. These programs should meet present and future energy management requirements, upgrade management skills, and increase communication among the beneficiaries of cost-effective maintenance.

Maintenance programs should include:

1. Management maintenance policy, which defines the objectives and type of program, provides for organizing and staffing, and directs and controls its effectiveness, performance, and cost.
2. Inventories and records of the systems, system components, equipment, and controls.

3. Procedures and schedules
   a. Operating instructions
   b. Inspection procedures and schedules
   c. Service and repair procedures and schedules
4. Monitoring of data
   a. Quality control
   b. Tracking
   c. Reporting
5. Operating and maintenance manuals

CHAPTER 5-3
INDUSTRIAL VENTILATION

James L. Davis
Consulting Engineer
San Rafael, California

INTRODUCTION

Modern industrial facilities have a legal and moral obligation to protect their workers from the increasing number of toxic chemical compounds and substances used or produced in their operations and from excessive heat by providing well-designed ventilation systems (which can also prevent release of toxic materials outside the work area).

Evaluation of work place exposures to hazardous materials is the work of industrial hygienists, who can evaluate the hazard in collaboration with an engineer who can design a proper protective system. (See Chap. 14-5, "Toxic Substances and Radiation Hazards.")

In general, it is advisable to separate the equipment used for ventilation of industrial work areas from that which serves office/commercial areas. This is because the industrial areas usually have substantially larger heat loads and the air is frequently contaminated. In addition, the hours of operation and load variation for the industrial facility are not compatible with the office operation, so a combined system cannot operate efficiently.

KINDS OF CONTAMINANTS

Heat

One of the most common and potentially most harmful forms of contamination from industrial operations is heat. Excessive heat results in elevated skin temperature for workers, causing discomfort and reduced productivity, and which, if not relieved, can cause heat stress or heat stroke. The principal method of heat dissipation for humans is by evaporation of perspiration from the skin. An alternative method is exposure to cool ambient air, if that is available. From the standpoint of the worker, there are two sources of heat: environmental heat and body heat generated as a result of doing work. Heat from both sources must be removed from the body or the body's temperature will rise until a harmful level is reached.

Heat from the environment is transferred to the worker in various ways: (1) it can be *conducted* from a hot item with which the worker has contact, e.g., by sitting on a warm bench or leaning against a warm wall; (2) it can be *convected* to the skin by contact with warm ambient air; and (3) it can be *radiated* as infrared waves from a hot surface in the area. Infrared waves do not heat air they pass through, but they heat any surface they strike, including the worker. Obviously, the higher the temperature of the ambient air, the more difficult it is for the worker to rid excess heat, and the higher the risk of heat stress.

Humidity retards evaporation of perspiration and, consequently, the release of heat by this means. Humidity must be controlled at reasonable levels to promote cooling and assure a healthy working environment.

Toxic Substances

The health hazard potential of any airborne substance is characterized in terms of the maximum concentration to which workers can be exposed without showing adverse health effects, e.g., parts per million of air, or milligrams of contaminant per cubic meter of air. The numbers used by the American Congress of Industrial Hygienists are called *threshold limit values* (TLVs) for each substance. The Occupational Safety and Health Administration (OSHA) has also developed a set of values which are legally binding standards. These are called *permissible exposure limits* (PELs).

FORMS OF CONTAMINANTS

Solids

Dust.   Dust can have its origin in almost any material which has been divided into small particles, usually as a result of some mechanical process.

Fumes.   Fumes are formed from materials which are normally solids but have been put into a gaseous state by some industrial process.

Smoke.   Smoke is caused by incomplete combustion. It consists of solid particles carried in the air by products of combustion.

Gases

Gases are chemical substances which are normally in a gaseous state. They are on the increase as air contaminants. The group includes carbon monoxide, sulfur oxides, nitrogen oxides, and hydrocarbons.

Vapors

Vapors are gases which have condensing temperatures and pressures close to normal ambient.

Liquids

Mists are small liquid particles ejected into the air by splashing, mixing, or atomizing. Fogs are small liquid particles formed by condensation. Fog indicates that the air is saturated with that chemical.

SOURCES OF CONTAMINATION

Processes

Steam Cleaning.   Areas where steam is used for cleaning purposes or where steam is escaping usually require special attention because condensing steam adds substantial amounts of heat and humidity to the air. Design consideration should always be given to isolating these areas from other parts of the facility.

Hot Tanks and Chemical Baths.   These tanks are usually open to the air and permit high levels of release of chemicals into the air both by evaporation and mist formation. The chemicals released may be toxic or explosive and therefore must be controlled. The heat released from these tanks can raise the environment temperature considerably. These operations should also be isolated from the rest of the facility.

Open Flames.   Equipment which involves the use of open flames, such as tank heaters, releases the products of combustion into its environment. Some of the principal products of combustion which must be dealt with are water vapor, which adds to humidity, and heat, which raises the temperature. An additional consideration is the need to supply adequate fresh air for combustion.

Atomizing Operations.   Operations which involve creating a mist of some material, such as paint spraying, put chemical substances which are frequently toxic and/or flammable into the work space.

Welding.   Welding operations add heat equivalent to the power capacity of the welding machine and, generally, toxic fumes (depending on the process) to the work space.

Processed Materials.   Materials which have been processed and are brought into the space at a temperature higher than room temperature add heat to the room. The amount of heat depends on the nature of the material, its temperature, and how long it is in the space.

Process Piping.   Process piping running through the conditioned space can add substantial amounts of heat to the space, particularly if it is not well-insulated. It should be apparent that the heat lost from these pipes is both an additional load on the process they serve and an extra load on the ventilation system for the conditioned space. The installation of adequate insulation on process piping is crucial in controlling the working environment.

Equipment and Machinery

Motors and Transformers.   Motors and transformers generate heat in the course of their operation for a variety of reasons. The amount of the input energy which is converted directly to heat is represented by the unit's electrical efficiency; if 10 percent of the input energy is converted directly to heat, the efficiency would be 90 percent. The efficiencies of motors and transformers are generally related to their size, smaller units being less efficient. Motor efficiencies can go as low as 50 percent, so their heat contribution to the conditioned space can be substantial. The heat from these units is mostly delivered in the form of heated air from the unit's cooling system, and is, therefore, convective. If the unit is allowed to operate at a high enough temperature, it can generate a significant radiant heating effect.

In addition to the heating effects due to inefficiency, the energy expended as work by motors is eventually converted to heat. If the work is done within the conditioned space, it must be considered as part of the overall heat load.

Ovens, Furnaces, Forges.   These devices use relatively high temperatures to perform their functions. If the device is heated by combustion, the products of combustion are generally exhausted outside the work space, but the heat remains. Because of the high temperatures involved, most of the heat transfer from these systems is by radiation to the surrounding area, although there is a significant convective component.

Another factor related to this kind of equipment is that when material is heated, it frequently gives off chemical vapors which can be hazardous to workers in the area.

Dryers.   Dryers may be of various types: open, closed, vented, or unvented, and with heat provided by various sources. In order to determine the amount of heat and moisture added to the work space, each installation must be analyzed individually.

Internal Combustion Engines.   Internal combustion engines are common in the industrial environment in such forms as forklifts, trucks, generators, and various small maintenance machines. The products of combustion of these machines are frequently vented within the conditioned space and can present a serious personnel hazard. Heat generated both from the combustion of fuel and work expended are released into the space and become part of the heat load which must be removed.

TREATMENT TECHNIQUES

Minimization

The most economical and most effective method to protect workers from work space contamination is to minimize it at its source. This is accomplished by designing the process to reduce the amount of contamination generated and by providing means to prevent contaminants from being released into the work space.

Shielding

Once a contaminant is released into the workspace, it becomes important that workers be protected from its effects. This can be done by, for example, providing shields which block the passage of radiated heat from a source to the workers. Similarly, protective clothing and respiratory protection devices can be used to prevent harmful effects.

Ventilation

There are two principal parts to any industrial ventilation system: the supply system, which delivers air to the work space, and the exhaust system, which removes contaminated air from the work space to maintain a healthy environment. The balance between the two parts is critical to the successful operation of the overall system. If, for example, there is an excess of supply air, contaminated air will be forced out of the work area into surrounding areas such as offices. Conversely, insufficient supply air will cause a pressure reduction in the work area and unconditioned outside air will be drawn into the space. This can markedly increase the load on the temperature and humidity control systems and adversely impact worker comfort. Further, the reduced space pressure increases the pressure differential of exhaust fans and can degrade their performance to the point that they no longer control contamination.

It is generally desirable to separate the ventilation system which serves the industrial facility from that for the other areas. One reason for this is that the industrial facility usually has a higher heat and humidity load. If the equipment for the whole plant is sized on the basis of these loads, it will be unnecessarily large and both first cost and operating cost will be increased. Other reasons include: possibility of contamination of other areas from the industrial facility, and difficulty of efficiently accommodating different schedules in industrial and other areas.

Supply Systems.   A well-designed supply system will consist of an air inlet section, air filters, heating and/or cooling equipment, a fan, and distribution system for delivering the air to the work space.

A recirculating air system is a supply system with the addition of return ducting to bring air back to the fan and provision to remove contaminants from the return air before it is recirculated.

Some generic types of supply air systems include:

The heating, ventilating, and air conditioning (HVAC) system, which provides a general supply of conditioned air to the space to create a comfortable environment in the work place.

The makeup air system which is designed to replace air removed by exhaust systems. Makeup air is usually cleaned and adjusted to an appropriate temperature (tempered) before delivery to the space.

Dilution air is delivered to the space in sufficient quantity to dilute a contaminant which has been released into the air. It is usually cleaned and tempered before entering the space. Spot supply is provided to give local dilution of contaminants and to provide localized cooling for workers in hot working environments.

Exhaust Systems

General Exhaust Systems.   General exhaust systems remove substantial quantities of air from the conditioned space without any specific location; for example, roof vents fit this classification. These systems are useful for heat removal and they are frequently coupled with dilution supply systems for removal of contaminants which could not be controlled at their source. Since the general exhaust system is removing a large amount of air from the space, if dilution supply is not used, a makeup air supply system must be used to replace the air removed to prevent reduced pressure in the space.

Local Exhaust.   The purpose of a local exhaust system is to capture contaminants at their source, before they can spread through the area. This is the most effective and economical approach to removal of contaminants because the result is achieved by moving a much smaller quantity of air, which makes the equipment required proportionally smaller and less expensive to install and to operate. Since less air is being removed from the conditioned space, there is less need for makeup air. The makeup air system can be smaller and the cost to condition makeup air is reduced.

Design of Local Exhaust Systems.   A typical local exhaust system consists of one or more intake devices (hoods), a duct system (including an exhaust stack), a fan, and an air-processing system.

The intake devices must be carefully designed to provide adequate air velocity at their face to assure capture of contaminants, but the velocity must not be so high as to generate unacceptable noise or drafts. They must be placed to pull the contaminants away from workers in the area, particularly process operators, and so that they contain any release effectively. The intake devices must not be damaged by the environment and must be designed so that they will not plug easily if there are solids in the airstream.

The duct system is the piping which carries the contaminated air from the intake devices to the air cleaner, to the fan, and finally to the exhaust. Consideration must be given in the design of the ducting system to the velocity of airflow at all points in the ducts. Air velocity must be adequate to keep any solids suspended in the airstream, but excessive air velocity can generate noise and increase system operating costs. Also, the large pressure differentials needed to create high air velocities can require heavy-duty ducting which raises first cost. The fluid dynamics of the system should be studied to assure that the system offers a minimum of resistance to airflow and that flows in all parts of the system are inherently balanced. Balancing devices require maintenance and cause system losses which increase operating costs. The exhaust stack deserves as much design attention as any other component of the system. In addition to minimizing friction losses, the stack must be tall enough to ensure adequate dilution of the exhaust stream before it falls to earth, and that exhaust air is not entrained into any of the building's air intakes.

The system fan must be designed to have adequate capacity in terms of volume flow and operating pressures, but we should avoid oversizing, since that increases first cost and operating cost. It should be appropriate for the materials which will be passing through it. For example, if the airstream contains solid particles, we might choose a radial-blade fan because it will resist plugging, or if the airstream contains corrosive material, we might use a stainless steel or fiberglass fan.

The present emphasis on low air pollution and high energy efficiency requires that air be processed before it is released to the environment. Since the air to be exhausted is at room temperature or higher, we can increase our energy efficiency if we pass it through a heat exchanger to preheat makeup air. Air that contains contaminants must be given appropriate treatment so that it is acceptably clean when it is released. Some treatment systems in common use are particle filters, which trap solid particles or liquid droplets; scrubbers, which use liquid spray to capture particles and, in some cases, to remove substances by chemical reaction; absorbers and adsorbers, which attract and capture specific substances; and oxidizers, which remove specific substances by chemical reaction and give off a product which is harmless.

CONCLUSION

Although the lists of load sources and treatments are not exhaustive, areas are discussed that are the most frequently encountered. From the examples, it should be apparent that loads differ widely, as do the methods of handling them. The following seem to hold true in nearly all situations:

- It is more efficient and effective to handle process contamination, including heat and humidity, separately from the regular air-conditioning system.
- It is most effective to minimize the release of contaminants at their source either by reducing generation or by containment.

SECTION 6

WATER: USE AND DISPOSITION

CHAPTER 6-1

PURIFICATION AND TREATMENT

S. D. Heden
J. Stephen Slottee
Donald C. Taylor
EIMCO Process Equipment Company
Salt Lake City, Utah

Robert W. Okey
University of Utah
Salt Lake City, Utah

GLOSSARY

Activated carbon A highly adsorptive material used to remove organic substances from water.

Aeration The process of bringing water and air into close contact to remove or modify constituents in the water.

Chemical coagulation Destabilization of colloidal and suspended matter by the reduction of electrostatic repulsive forces between particles with chemicals.

Disinfection The water treatment process that kills disease-causing organisms in water, usually by adding an oxidizing agent.

Filtration The water treatment process involving the removal of suspended matter by passing the water through a porous medium.

Flocculation The water treatment process following coagulation, which uses gentle stirring to bring suspended particles together so they will form larger, more settleable particles called *floc*.

Hardness A characteristic of water, caused primarily by the salts of calcium and magnesium.

Ion exchange A reversible process where ions of a given species are exchanged between a solid (ion-exchange resins) and a liquid for an ion of another species.

Precipitation An aqueous chemical reaction that forms an insoluble compound which is commonly removed by sedimentation or filtration.

Reactivate To remove the adsorbed materials from spent activated carbon and restore the carbon's porous structure so it can be used again.

Sedimentation The water treatment process that involves reducing the velocity of water in basins so the suspended material can settle out by gravity.

Sludge dewatering A process to remove a portion of water from sludge.

Softening The water treatment process that removes the hardness-causing constituents in water—calcium and magnesium—by precipitation.

Solids contact A process where coagulation, flocculation, and sedimentation are enhanced by previously formed solids.

INTRODUCTION

The unit operations for water purification and treatment include:

Sedimentation	Crystallization
Disinfection	Evaporation
Ion exchange	Activated-carbon treatment
Precipitation	Reverse osmosis
Filtration	

The industries that are major users of water are:

Power generation	Petroleum
Beverage	Pulp and paper
Aluminum	Chemical
Iron and steel	Food
Textile	

Figure 1-1 illustrates the unit operations most commonly used for treating water. Water is used primarily for boiler feed, industrial processes, cooling tower makeup, and potable supply.

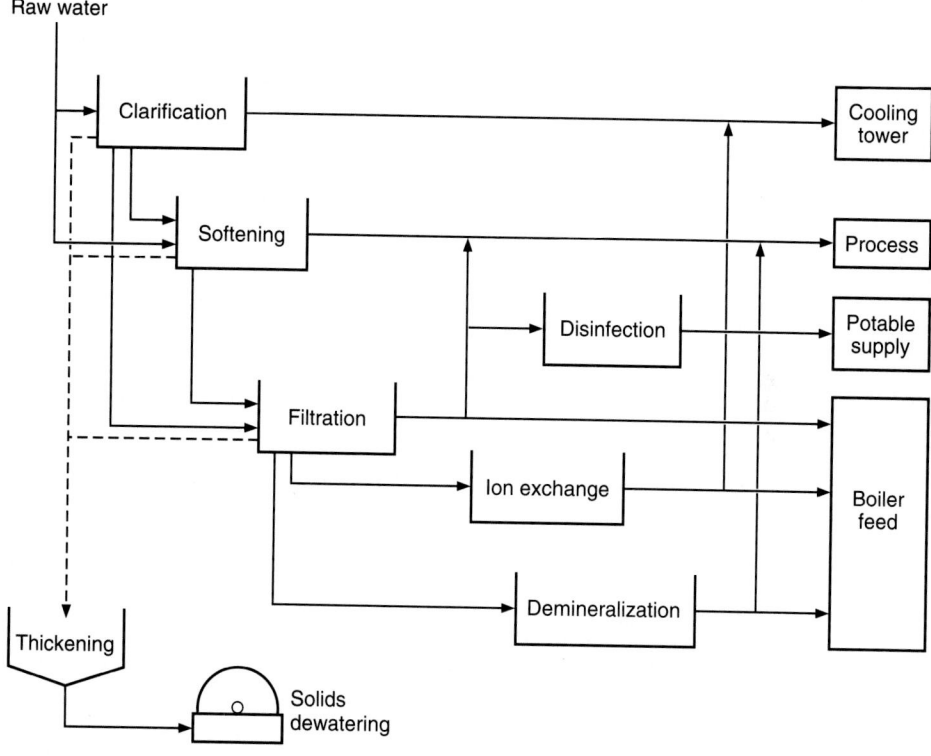

Raw water

FIGURE 1-1 Water-treatment diagram.

IMPURITIES IN WATER

All natural waters contain suspended or dissolved inorganic or organic chemicals to some degree. Whether they are present in high enough concentrations to be considered as impurities depends on the water use(s).

The impurities can be classified as:

Inorganic	Organic	Biologically active
Suspended	Suspended	Bacteria
Colloidal	Immiscible	Viruses
Dissolved	Miscible	Algae
	Soluble	Protozoa

In turbulent streams, suspended solids range from small pebbles down to colloidal clay particles 0.1 to 0.001 μm in diameter. The water may also contain organic solids, algae, and bacteria. Dissolved inorganic solids are usually bicarbonates, sulfates, and chlorides of calcium, magnesium, and sodium as well as compounds of silica, iron, and manganese. Nonferrous metals and organic compounds may be present in low concentrations which nevertheless exceed the EPA's proposed limits.

The biggest problem caused by dissolved solids in water is *hardness*, i.e., the presence of calcium and magnesium compounds. Other dissolved solids may be considered as impurities, depending upon their concentrations and the intended water use.

SEDIMENTATION PROCESSES

Sedimentation processes are used to clarify turbid and/or colored waters and to remove dissolved impurities such as iron, manganese, calcium, and magnesium compounds as well as silica and fluorides.

Removal of Suspended Solids

On a few occasions unaided sedimentation will be employed to remove suspended solids, but usually the process will include the addition of chemicals to improve removal of solids. The particles suspended in water result in a turbid, or colored, appearance that is objectionable, and they have a static charge (usually negative) that causes the particles to repel each other and remain suspended. By adding certain chemicals it is possible to neutralize these charges, permitting the particles to agglomerate and settle from the liquid more effectively. The current practice is to refer to this neutralization or destabilization step as *coagulation* and the subsequent gathering together of the particles into larger, more settleable "flocs" as *flocculation*. Inorganic chemicals such as aluminum sulfate (alum), ferrous sulfate (copperas), ferric chloride, and sodium aluminate, as well as a long list of organic polymers, are used for coagulating and flocculating suspended matter from water. Coagulation takes place very quickly— a few seconds to one minute—and the chemicals should be added with intense mixing in order to obtain maximum efficiency. Flocculation, on the other hand, normally requires detention periods of 20 to 45 min, and, once the chemicals have been added, should be accomplished by relatively gentle mixing. The mixing is carried out in a flocculation basin, and its purpose is to bring about the maximum collisions between the suspended particles without shearing or breaking apart the particles that have already been formed.

This will limit the particle velocities to the range of 1 to 6 ft/s (0.305 to 1.83 m/s), depending upon the "toughness" of the floc that is produced. Equipment should be provided for varying the intensity of the mixing so that the optimum velocities can be achieved.

Organic polymers (polyelectrolytes) are frequently used as flocculant aids. They facilitate the gathering of the already coagulated or destabilized particles into larger and less fragile floc particles that have better settling characteristics. The type and amount of chemicals required to treat a given supply of water are best determined by laboratory jar tests. These tests should be made on fresh samples at the same temperatures and other conditions that will be present in the full-scale plant. No other reliable method has been found for predicting the best chemicals and optimum dosages for clarifying a water. Typically, inorganic coagulants (alum, ferric chloride, etc.) might range from 10 to 100 mg/L, cationic organic coagulants from 1 to 5 mg/L, and anionic organic flocculants from 0.1 to 1.0 mg/L. Many suppliers of chemicals and equipment manufacturers will perform jar-test studies at reasonable fees and make recommendations as to the best chemicals, equipment, and sizing for treating a water supply.

Sedimentation, with or without chemical treatment, is usually carried out in continuous, flow-through settling units with horizontal flow patterns (Fig. 1-2). Important exceptions to this are the solids contact clarifiers and reactors which are discussed later. Settling units are normally rectangular, with the flow along the length of the basin, or circular, with the flow radially outward from a central inlet compartment. Mechanical scraping mechanisms are employed to move the settled sludge along the bottom to hoppers or sumps from which it is discharged. The mechanical design of the scraper mechanism should be carefully evaluated when considering such equipment, as should the inlet distribution and effluent collection system. The settling zone of the unit must provide sufficient area and volume so the bulk of the solids will settle before reaching the effluent collector. Proper design of the inlet distributor and effluent collector will result in the most effective operation of the settling zone. Typical settling-area designs would allow liquid flow to range from 0.35 to 0.75 gal/min · ft^2 (0.85 to 1.80 m^3/h · m^2) and settling-unit detention times from 2.5 to 4.0 h.

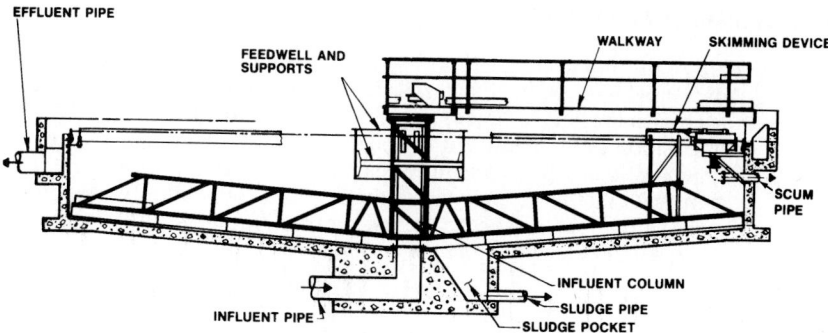

FIGURE 1-2   Illustrative section of settling unit.

Temperature and changes in temperature of the liquid being treated are extremely important considerations in the design and operation of sedimentation units. The rate at which a particle settles in water is inversely proportional to the kinematic viscosity, a property that varies with the temperature. Thus, the settling rate of a given particle at 40°F (4.4°C) is only 63 percent of what it would be at 70°F (21.1°C). Rapid changes in inlet water temperatures to settling units will cause thermal currents, which at best are disruptive to the settling of particles and at worst are totally upsetting. Manufacturers typically limit changes to 2°F (1°C) per hour in their performance warranties. The rate at which chemical reactions proceed in water is higher at higher water temperatures. A common rule of thumb is a doubling of the rate for each 18°F (10°C) increase in temperature. In general, warm but constant water temperature is desirable in treating water.

Solids contact units combine, within the settling unit, the coagulation and flocculation function with the ability to internally recirculate solids that have been formed by earlier reactions (Fig. 1-3). Besides the economies attainable by combining these functions within a single unit, improvements in settling characteristics and reaction rates permit higher design rates for this type of unit. Most industrial water-treatment applications now use some form of solids contact or combination treatment equipment. A variety of units are available from manufacturers of such equipment, and a careful comparison of the process and the mechanical features of each is advisable.

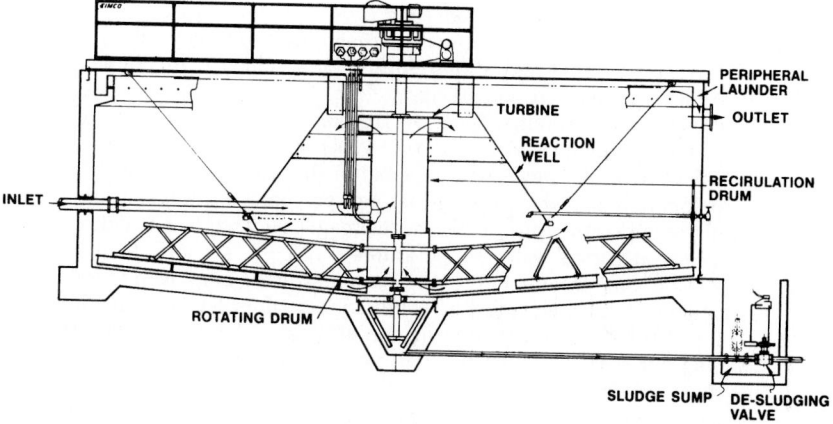

FIGURE 1-3   Illustrative section of solids contact unit. (*EIMCO.*)

Removal of Dissolved Impurities

Up to this point we have discussed sedimentation processes primarily from the standpoint of removing suspended materials from water. The removal of dissolved mineral impurities such as in the lime or lime–soda ash softening process is an equally important aspect of sedimentation in the treatment of water. In the softening process, hydrated lime or hydrated lime and soda ash are added to react with the dissolved CO_2 and the calcium and magnesium salts that commonly cause the hardness of water. The following equations describe some of the reactions that take place in the formation of the calcium carbonate and magnesium hydroxide precipitates:

$$CO_2 + Ca(OH)_2 \rightarrow CaCO_3 + H_2O$$
$$Ca(HCO_3)_2 + Ca(OH)_2 \rightarrow 2CaCO_3 + 2H_2O$$
$$Mg(HCO_3)_2 + 2Ca(OH)_2 \rightarrow 2CaCO_3 + Mg(OH)_2 + 2H_2O$$
$$CaSO_4 + Na_2CO_3 \rightarrow CaCO_3 + Na_2SO_4$$

A coagulant is normally added along with the lime and soda ash to improve clarity of the product water. When the lime requirements are high, economies can usually be realized by using quicklime (CaO) in a lime slaker to convert it to the hydrated lime [$Ca(OH)_2$]. When requirements reach approximately 200 lb/h (90 kg/h), the economies of quicklime should be investigated.

Neither calcium carbonate nor magnesium hydroxide is completely insoluble, so some amount, depending upon the type of treatment, temperature, and other conditions, will remain in solution. Unlike most compounds, $Mg(OH)_2$ and $CaCO_3$ are less soluble at higher temperatures, rather than more soluble. In addition to the viscosity and reaction rates mentioned earlier, this is a further advantage to treating warm water. The hot-process softener, sometimes used for treating boiler feedwater, uses steam to heat the water to more than 200°F (93°C) and takes advantage of these factors to produce a water of lower hardness in smaller-sized units than could be used in a cold process. These high-temperature units also accomplish silica (SiO_2) removal, which is often necessary when treating boiler feedwater. This is described in further detail later.

As already mentioned, solids contact units are particularly well-suited to lime-soda softening applications. Calcium carbonate and, to some degree, magnesium hydroxide have a tendency to supersaturate (remain in solution at considerably higher than theoretical concentrations), and solids contact operation reduces this tendency. By mixing the chemicals and the untreated water in the presence of recycled solids, a large surface area is provided on which the precipitate will form. This "seeding" not only reduces the supersaturation, but also results in the growth of larger particles that settle more rapidly. Overall, chemical usage efficiency is improved because the lower calcium and magnesium values attained through solids contact require no additional chemicals.

Hot-process lime treatment has been used to remove silica from boiler feedwater where extremely low concentrations requiring ion exchange are not necessary. The silica is removed by adsorption on freshly precipitated magnesium hydroxide. The removal is therefore dependent upon the amount of $Mg(OH)_2$ precipitated. The effectiveness of the process is enhanced by the high temperatures and can be further improved by solids contact. Often there is insufficient natural magnesium available in the water, so it is supplemented by the addition of dolomitic lime, which contains a high percentage of magnesium oxide. This is feasible in a high-temperature process where the magnesium oxide will hydrate, something it will not usually do at normal water temperatures.

Cold lime-treatment processes are now being employed to reduce silica for cooling-water systems in specially designed solids contact units. By providing intense mixing and pumpage for high solids contact concentration and long detention times, the silica can be reduced at cold-water temperatures to levels formerly attainable only in hot-process treatment. Some of these systems use a two-stage sedimentation process where lime treatment at a high pH is used in the first stage. Soda ash and CO_2 (carbonic acid) are added in the final stage for stabilization.

Tube and Plate Settlers

Tube and plate settlers have been used for many years as sedimentation units. There are a variety of designs, but basically all of them use inclined surfaces with relatively close spacing (Fig. 1-4). The water to be treated is passed between the surfaces at velocities which permit suspended solids to settle and to coalesce on the lower tube or plate surface. The angle of inclination (45° or more) enables the settled solids to slide downward into a sludge-concentration compartment located at the bottom of the treatment unit.

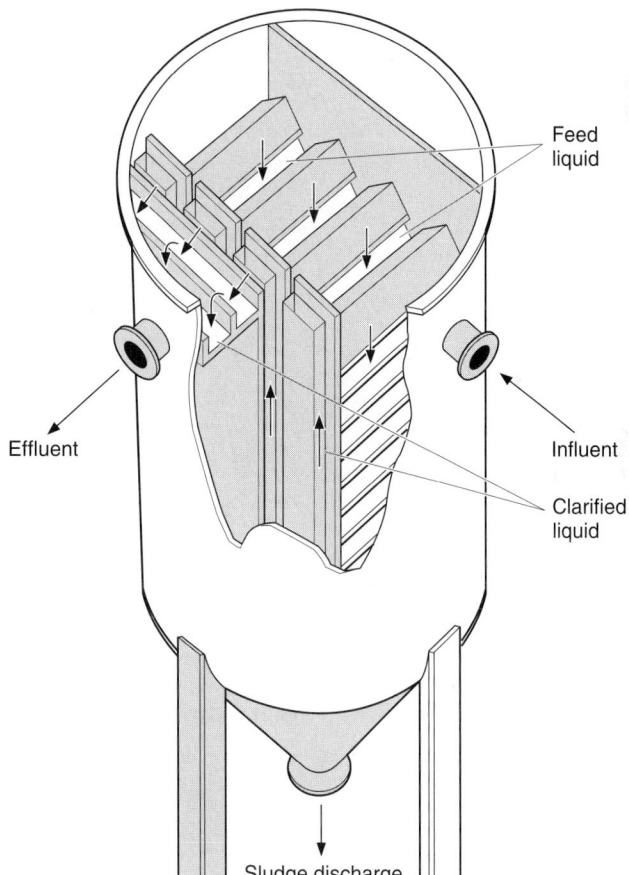

FIGURE 1-4 Stacked chevron clarifier (Delta-Stak™ clarifier). (*EIMCO.*)

These units permit efficient clarification at detention times substantially less than those used in conventional clarifiers. Total settling detention times may be as low as 10 min, greatly reducing the plant size.

The units are cost-effective for many applications, even though the inclined tubes or plates add appreciably to the equipment cost. These settling units are best for discrete solids settling where detention time is not a significant factor.

GRANULAR-MEDIA FILTRATION

Granular-media filters are used in water treatment to remove relatively small amounts of suspended matter when a high clarity is needed. They are constructed in a variety of materials [concrete, steel, glass-fiber–reinforced plastic (FRP), etc.], of either open-gravity or enclosed pressure type, and for downflow or upflow filtering.

The traditional filter is a batch operation where solids are collected in the filter media until the pressure drop becomes excessive or there is *breakthrough* and solids begin to pass with the effluent. The unit is then taken off line, backwashed to remove the solids, and returned to service. The wash water volume is normally less than 5 percent of the filtered water produced. Many filters employ an air scour prior to or simultaneously with the water wash. If air is not used, a rotary surface wash using high-pressure water jets should be included. A popular style filter used in many industrial applications incorporates a backwash water storage compartment above the filtering compartment (Fig. 1-5).

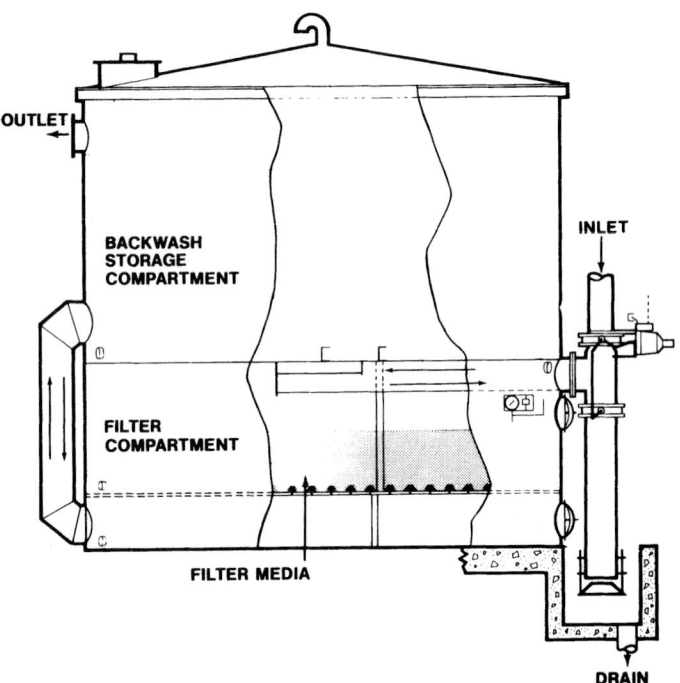

FIGURE 1-5   Granular-media filter.

Filters are available in many different designs and configurations, most of which work well for their particular application. In installing new equipment, care should be taken in selecting equipment from a reputable supplier who has had experience with similar applications.

More recently, continuous-flow filters have received acceptance for many applications. They have the advantage of not requiring interruption of service for backwashing. Dirty media are continually removed from the bottom of the filter, cleaned in a separate media washer, and returned to the top of the media bed. The small amount (less than 5 percent) of dirty backwash water flows continually and can be more easily recycled to an upstream clarifier or otherwise disposed of than can the intermittent, high-volume backwash flows from traditional filters (Fig. 1-6).

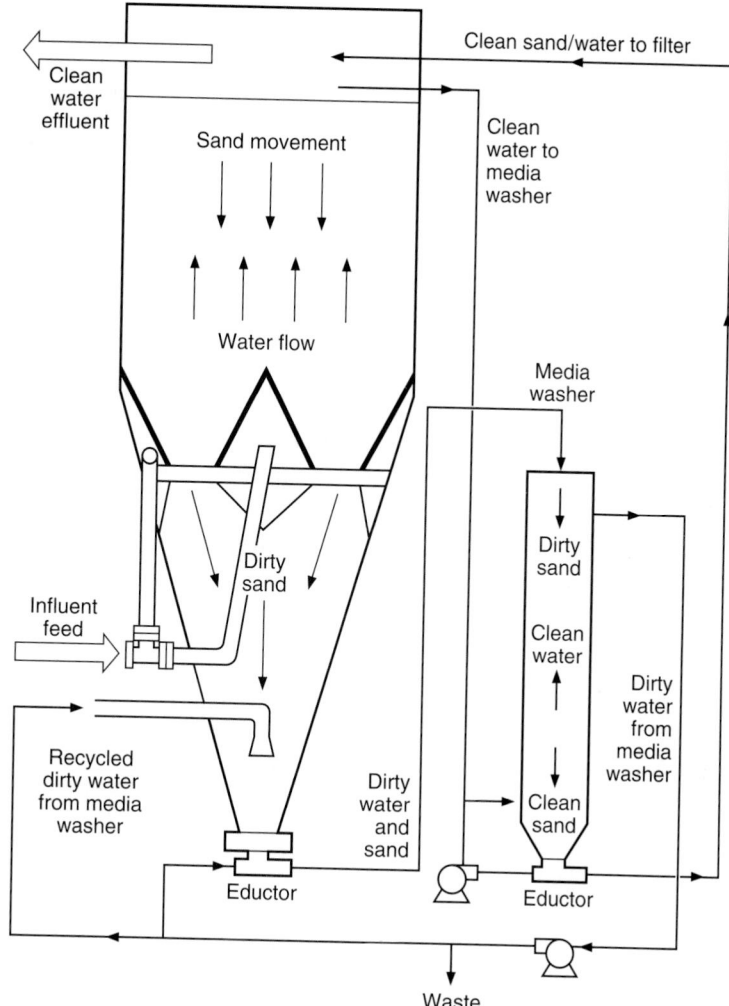

FIGURE 1-6   Continuous-flow granular-media filter (Rotoco™ filter). (*EIMCO.*)

CARTRIDGE FILTERS

Cartridge filters are broadly used in industry for filtering water and many other liquids. In water applications they are generally the final polishing unit where high clarity is needed for the product or to protect downstream equipment or processes. Since the cost of replacing disposable cartridges can be significant, sizing the equipment and selecting the filtering material should be done carefully to optimize overall costs.

ION EXCHANGE

Applications of ion exchange for softening, dealkalizing, or demineralizing water include municipal water supply, boiler feedwater, and industrial process water as well as treatment of industrial process water and boiler feedwater.

Ion exchange is a process where ions of a given species are exchanged with another species. The most common form of ion exchange is found in domestic water softening. When water containing salts of calcium and magnesium is passed through a sodium exchanger, the sodium ions of the bed replace the calcium and magnesium to produce an effluent of close to zero hardness.

In addition to sodium ion exchange, other cation and anion exchangers are used for more specialized applications. The terms *demineralization* and *deionization* refer to the removal of cations and anions from water, by cation-anion exchange. A cationic exchanger replaces hydrogen for cations such as calcium, magnesium, and sodium. An anion exchanger replaces the unwanted anions, such as chloride, with hydroxide. If the waste stream is passed through a cationic exchanger followed by an anionic exchanger, the resulting hydrogen and hydroxide react to form water, producing a stream lower in total dissolved solids.

When an ion exchange resin is exhausted, the resin is regenerated. For the sodium ion exchanger, a salt solution is used for regeneration. The theoretical salt requirement is about 0.17 lb (0.08 kg) per 1000 grains of hardness removed. The actual efficiency is 40 to 60 percent. It is possible to obtain higher exchange capacities by increasing the amount of salt used per regeneration; however, for average industrial applications, the amount of salt used with the high-capacity resin cation exchanger is usually 0.4 lb/1000 grains (0.18 kg/1000 grains).

For cationic exchangers, either sulfuric or hydrochloric acid is used. Sulfuric acid is generally used because of its low cost, but hydrochloric acid can be used when high-calcium water would result in poor efficiency from the precipitation of calcium sulfate in the exchanger bed. Anion-exchange resins are commonly regenerated with sodium hydroxide.

Cation- and anion-exchange resins may be weak or strong. Weak-acid resins are capable of removing metals that are associated with carbonate and bicarbonate alkalinity. Strong-acid resins are not as selective; they can exchange a wide range of cations. The weakly basic resins remove the strongly ionized acids but not the weakly ionized ones. The effluent contains the same amount of silica as the influent water plus carbon dioxide equivalent to the bicarbonate alkalinity and free carbon dioxide. The concentration of carbon dioxide can be reduced to 5 to 10 mg/L in a degasifier or a vacuum deaerator. Strongly basic resins remove both strongly ionized and weakly ionized acids. At the end of each operating run, the weakly basic anion exchanger is backwashed, regenerated with a solution of sodium carbonate or caustic soda, rinsed, and returned to service. Caustic soda is used to regenerate the strongly basic resins.

Where a minimum amount of dissolved solids is required in the treated water, mixed cation-anion beds are used. Regeneration of the mixed bed consists of separating the anion resin from the cation resin and regenerating each separately.

Figure 1-7 illustrates the operating options for demineralizing systems. Selection of ion-exchange processes is based upon:

- Raw-water characteristics
- Treated-water characteristics required
- Operating costs: chemicals, energy, waste disposal, qualified operating labor, and maintenance
- Capital costs
- Available space

In most cases, the services of a qualified consulting engineer should be used to evaluate alternatives and recommend the optimum method of treatment.

It is essential that the influent water to ion exchangers be free of suspended solids. Silt and organic matter are particularly objectionable, since these materials can deposit in the exchanger beds and reduce the capacity of the units by coating the exchanger resins with films which either prevent or retard the movement of anions and cations through the resins. The influent water may require a preliminary treatment of sedimentation and/or filtration.

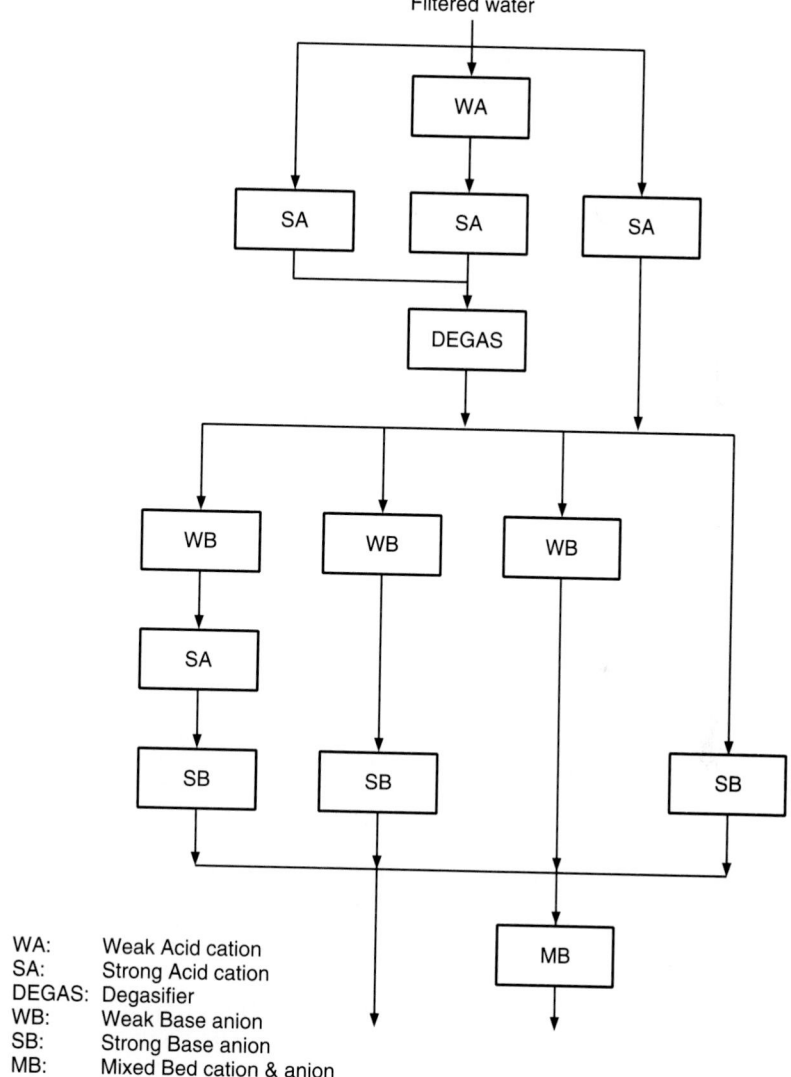

WA: Weak Acid cation
SA: Strong Acid cation
DEGAS: Degasifier
WB: Weak Base anion
SB: Strong Base anion
MB: Mixed Bed cation & anion

FIGURE 1-7 Alternatives for a demineralization system.

PRESSURE-DRIVEN MEMBRANE SEPARATION

Membrane separation processes are characterized by a thin film, a membrane, which acts as a selective barrier between two solutions. The membrane allows the passage of certain components while restricting the passage of others to accomplish a separation. The driving force may be electrical (electrodialysis); concentration (dialysis, pervaporation); or pressure (reverse osmosis).

Pressure membrane separation is increasingly used for potable water treatment and in water reuse processes. Applications include softening, organic removal, and desalination of brackish well water, surface water, and seawater. For some applications membrane processes offer the advantages of superior water quality, reduced chemical usage, less chemical waste production, and lower energy consumption.

Pressure-driven membrane processes include the following:

1. *Reverse osmosis* separates dissolved solids from water; also called hyperfiltration.

2. *Nanofiltration* separates dissolved solids in the nanometer (0.001 μm) size range from water including large molecular weight dissolved inorganic compounds such as hydrated divalent ions and organic compounds with a molecular weight greater than about 400.

3. *Ultrafiltration* separates macromolecules or particles larger than about 0.2 to 2 μm from water.

4. *Microfiltration* separates fine suspended solids and colloidal suspensions from water.

Reverse osmosis, nanofiltration, and ultrafiltration are typically used in the *cross-flow* configuration, where the feed stream flows across or tangential to the membrane surface. The constant flow across the surface of the membrane minimizes the buildup of cake. A recycle stream may be required. The *permeate* passes through the membrane, and the *concentrate* or *retentate* retains the dissolved and suspended solids rejected by the membrane.

REVERSE OSMOSIS

Systems

A reverse-osmosis (RO) system consists of the following essential parts:

1. A pretreatment section usually includes chemical feed systems for the injection of a coagulant, acid for the control of pH and hence calcium carbonate precipitation, a sequestering agent (often polyphosphate compounds) for the control of iron and calcium sulfate precipitation, and a granular-media filter for the removal of coagulated solids. When the suspended solids level is consistently high (>50 mg/L), the overall system may be best served by including a clarifier in the flowsheet. Also, in many cases, it will be necessary to remove chemically some hardness and perhaps silica from the system in a presoftening step. Raw-water silica values which will concentrate to 150 mg/L will require SiO_2 control; but the economics of pH adjustment, the danger of membrane damage, and possible precipitation of silica should also be considered.

2. The reverse-osmosis system itself consists of the high-pressure pump or pumps, the pressure vessels, the membranes themselves, and necessary interconnecting piping, valves, and fittings.

3. A posttreatment system which consists of chemical feed systems for the feeding of corrosion control chemicals and chlorine for control of biological growth in the distribution system.

Any RO system that does not receive water from a highly controlled source will require pretreatment for the removal of suspended solids and colloids.

In general, some provision should be made for cleaning the membranes even though the pretreatment system is nominally satisfactory for the reduction of solids and colloidal material in the raw water.

Reverse-osmosis membranes make a separation between the dissolved solids phase and the liquid phase by reversing the flow that normally occurs through a semipermeable membrane when the concentration of a given salt is different on the two sides of the membrane. Normally, the flow will proceed in such a fashion as to equalize the concentration, and hence pressure equal to the osmotic pressure plus an additional driving force is provided to permit flow from the more concentrated to the less concentrated side—thus the term *reverse osmosis*.

The flow proceeds through the membrane, passing between the atoms in the polymer lattice. Flow is accompanied by a loose association between the transported species and the membrane driven by the pressure differential. Typically, brackish water systems operate at 200 to 600 psig (1379 to 4137 kPa) and seawater systems at 800 to 1000 psig (5516 to 6895 kPa).

A key feature of the RO process is cross-flow filtration. While some water is passing through the membranes there is a constant flow of water flushing the rejected salts away from the membrane surface. The ratio of these two flows is determined by the design recovery rate, the product flow divided by the feed flow. This is an important design factor that should be determined by the membrane manufacturer. Most manufacturers have special computer programs to calculate the maximum recovery rate based on a feedwater analysis.

In general, the flow per square foot of membrane surface is quite low. The range is 8 to 20 gal/ft^2 · day depending on the level of suspended solids in the feedwater.

Figure 1-8 is a schematic drawing of a typical RO system. The illustration shows all the essential components identified in the preceding discussion together with a cleaning system. The cleaning system is employed simply by opening the brine valve and reducing the pressure to zero in the membranes themselves and flushing detergent-carrying water through the membranes at relatively high velocity. After the membranes have been scrubbed this way for 15 to 30 min, the treatment rate will be restored to normal or near normal values unless the fouling is extraordinary.

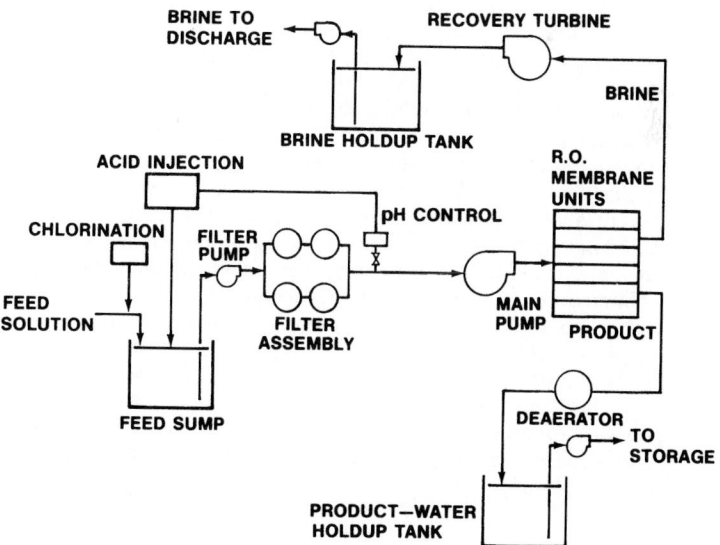

FIGURE 1-8   Basic flow diagram for a single-stage reverse-osmosis plant.

There are several methods to measure the fouling tendency of the feedwater. Most are approximations and cannot be used as a guarantee of fouling control. The only way to positively determine the fouling nature of a given feed is to perform a pilot test.

The quality of the water with respect to its suitability for introduction into a reverse-osmosis system may be measured in a crude fashion through the use of a test yielding what is called the silt density index (SDI).

The SDI test is performed by measuring the time T_1 to collect 500 mL of filtrate through a 0.45-μm filter at exactly 30 psi. The filter is allowed to flow for 15 min, then the time T_2 for another 500 mL is measured. These times are compared in the formula given below. If the filter plugs before 15 min, the feedwater needs additional treatment before going to the RO.

$$\mathrm{SDI} = \left(1 - \frac{T_1}{T_2}\right) \frac{100}{15}$$

In general, SDI readings should be less than 5.0. Less than 3.0 is considered ideal.

Applications

Reverse-osmosis systems find their application in a number of areas. However, the most significant are:

1. Inclusion in systems for providing low-conductivity water for boiler makeup and related purposes
2. The production of potable water where such supplies are not conveniently available
3. Industrial waste treatment and water recovery

Of the preceding, perhaps the most significant application of reverse osmosis is in the deionization systems for the production of low-conductivity boiler feedwater.

In most instances where the raw-water supply contains more than 300 to 400 mg/L total dissolved solids (TDS), an overall system economy may be shown by utilizing reverse osmosis for removing the bulk of the dissolved solids at a high recovery rate prior to discharge of the product to the ion-exchange polishing system. The approach is to replace the cationic-exchange, degasification, and anionic-exchange subsystems with the reverse-osmosis system and to employ the mixed-bed polishing subsystem for the removal of residual solids. In some instances, it can be shown that this puts a somewhat higher load on the mixed-bed polisher. However, if this load is less than 50 mg/L TDS, it does not constitute an improper or unreasonable burden in terms of cycle time or regeneration frequency. This type of system usually produces a less expensive water at roughly the same recoveries as would be experienced with the full deionizing (DI) system and often does not produce the quantity of solids in the backwash and regenerating stream that the DI system will produce. The preceding is a generalization only, and a careful cost comparison should be made in any specific situation.

Sometimes only high-salinity waters are available for process and other purposes, and the supply of potable water is either limited or nonexistent. In these cases, a reverse-osmosis facility can be installed to produce water for the plant at comparatively low cost.

Many industrial wastes are highly amenable to treatment by reverse-osmosis systems. The most commonly encountered RO application is in the area of metal contamination or the presence of excessive dissolved materials in the effluent. Often when RO systems are employed for treatment, the water is suitable or can easily be made suitable for reuse and can constitute a supply for processes or sometimes even boiler feedwater.

Cost of RO Systems

Table 1-1 contains a brief summary of capital and operating costs of RO systems as a function of salinity. The actual cost will vary as a function of the overall recovery employed in the system.

NANOFILTRATION

Nanofiltration, also referred to as *ultra-low-pressure reverse osmosis,* was developed to fill the gap between reverse osmosis and ultrafiltration. In water purification, nanofiltration has been

TABLE 1-1   RO System Costs, 1992 Dollars

Capacity, gal/day	Pressure, psi	Feed salinity, mg/L NaCl	Capital cost, $	O&M cost, $/1000 gal
50,000	250	1,000	55,000	0.90
150,000	250	1,000	160,000	0.80
500,000	250	1,000	475,000	0.75
1,000,000	250	1,000	850,000	0.65
2,500,000	250	1,000	2,000,000	0.60
10,000	850	35,000	60,000	4.30
50,000	850	35,000	200,000	3.50
100,000	850	35,000	380,000	3.20
500,000	850	35,000	1,500,000	3.00

Data supplied by Fluid Systems Corporation, San Diego, California. To convert gallons to cubic meters divide by 264 gal/m³. Based on power at $0.10/kWh; element replacement $0.17/1000 gal brackish, $0.30/1000 gal seawater; chemicals $.04/1000 gal brackish, $0.05/1000 gal seawater; operator $0.15 to $0.50/1000 gal; maintenance $0.06/1000 gal. RO recovery rate: 75% for brackish, 25 to 40% for seawater.

found to effectively remove selected salts to reduce total hardness at lower pressures than RO systems. The nanofiltration membrane employed for this application has been referred to as a "softening membrane." The softening membrane also effectively removes color and THM (tri-halo methane) precursors.

Softening membranes operate at pressures of 75 to 250 psi (517 to 1724 kPa) as compared to 200 to 600 psi (1379 to 4137 kPa) for RO and 50 to 150 psi (345 to 1034 kPa) for ultrafiltration membranes. The process flow scheme, including pretreatment, is similiar to a typical brackish water reverse-osmosis plant.

Nanofiltration softening membranes may be an economic alternative to conventional softening. Possible advantages of membrane filtration for softening include smaller space requirements, no lime requirement, superior quality water, and less operator attendance. As for all membrane separation processes, suitability of softening membranes for a given application must be made on a case-by-case analysis.

ULTRAFILTRATION SYSTEMS

Ultrafiltration (UF) is a pressure-driven membrane process similar in some ways to reverse osmosis. However, in this case, as opposed to the situation encountered in RO systems, the flow of water through the membrane is generally through pores and not through the space between the lattices in the polymer, so osmotic pressure is not a factor. Furthermore, there is little or no chemical interaction between the transported species and the membrane itself. UF membranes may be tailor-made to meet virtually any type of removal specification.

UF systems are often used to remove very fine particles from water streams, e.g., in preconditioning water prior to RO treatment and sometimes for the removal of large organic molecules. UF systems have been used in this regard to remove colored colloids, bacteria, and viruses as well as fine suspended solids. In water-reuse applications, UF has been employed to remove submicron-size particles of activated carbon from the treated waste stream. UF membranes do not reject dissolved salts.

UF systems have been used in the removal of tramp oils from various wastewater streams. In some instances it has been possible to concentrate the oil in the UF system up to as much as 50 percent, thereby making the recovery of that material comparatively easy.

A schematic diagram of a typical UF system is shown in Fig. 1-9. As can be seen, UF systems usually employ a fairly high volume of recycle. The quantity of permeate on each pass is small relative to the material which is passed by the membrane.

Operating pressure is in the range of 10 psig (69 kPa) to 200 psig (1379 kPa). Daily cleaning is common, particularly in highly fouling waste streams.

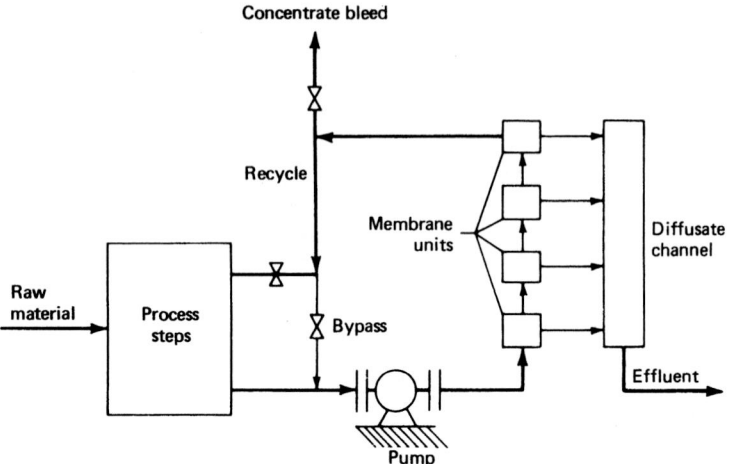

FIGURE 1-9   Typical flowsheet for an ultrafiltration system.

MICROFILTRATION

Microfiltration uses membranes to remove colloidal and very small suspended particles, including most bacteria, in the size range of 0.05 to 2.0 μm. Dissolved species are not removed. In water treatment, microfiltration may be found as a pretreatment step for ultrafiltration, nanofiltration, or reverse osmosis.

EVAPORATIVE SYSTEMS

Evaporative systems are used in some applications for the production of very high quality water from saline waters or wastewater. With high energy costs, evaporative systems (except under very special circumstances) appear to offer a less satisfactory solution than alternative systems such as membrane filtration to many desalination problems. Nevertheless, the need for ultrapure water in process applications such as electronics and pharmaceutical manufacture, production of high-pressure steam for electrical power generation, and increasingly stringent discharge regulations provide applications for evaporative systems. Where waste energy is available, evaporation procedures should be considered as a possible candidate in any water recovery system analysis.

Evaporator system types such as multistage flash (MSF), multiple-effect distillation (MED), and vapor recompression, both thermal and mechanical, are applied to water recovery situations. Evaporator configurations such as horizontal tube, falling film, rising film, and forced circulation are utilized, depending on the requirements for the application. Generally speaking, economy ratios of 5 to 12 lb of water per 1000 Btu (2 to 5 kg H_2O per 10^6 J) are possible. Maintenance requirements such as cleaning of heat-transfer surfaces and pump and compressor maintenance will vary with type of evaporator system and should be examined closely along with capital and energy costs. The substantial advantage that an evaporator offers is that, even if the source has variable salinity or extremely high salinity, the quality of the product will be essentially unchanged. Furthermore, the amount of energy required to run the system is independent of the salinity.

System costs for some evaporator systems are shown in Table 1-2.

TABLE 1-2   Evaporator Capital and Operating Costs, 1992 Dollars

Evaporation capacity, gal/day	Capital costs, $	Operating costs, $/1000 gal	Principal energy source
13,000	450,000	47.85	Low-pressure steam
283,000	1,200,000	14.21	Low-pressure steam
346,000	1,800,000	10.81	Electric power

The data are based on the following assumptions:
1. Materials of construction for process contact parts are type 316 stainless steel.
2. Steam costs are $5/1000 lb.
3. Electric power cost is $0.035/kWh.
4. Operating labor cost is $25/h.
5. The annual cost of maintenance and depreciation is 10% of capital costs.
6. Capital costs are inclusive of installation and structural supports, but do not include foundations or buildings.

Prices supplied by Dedert Corporation, Olympia Fields, Illinois. To convert 1000 gal to cubic meters, multiply by 3.8 m³/1000 gal.

CHLORINATION

Chlorine compounds (sodium hypochlorite, calcium hypochlorite, and chlorine gas) are strong oxidizing agents commonly used for disinfection, and taste and odor control. Chlorine will oxidize ferrous iron, manganese, and sulfide ions, as well as react with ammonia or amines to form chloramines. Chloramines are weaker disinfectants than chlorine, but are useful for maintaining a residual chlorine content in water mains. The advantage of chlorine is that it is an inexpensive method of disinfection. The disadvantage of chlorination is its reaction with organic material to form chloroorganic compounds, of which trihalomethanes are included. The maximum contaminant level (MCL) for trihalomethanes for drinking water is set at 0.10 mg/L.

Chlorine dioxide is also used as an oxidant and disinfectant to a limited extent. When it is used for the treatment of potable water, trihalomethanes are not produced.

OZONIZATION

Ozone (O_3) is a powerful oxidizing agent used for color, taste, and odor removal and for organic oxidation, bacterial disinfection, and virus inactivation. Ozonization followed by activated carbon treatment appears to be effective in meeting proposed drinking water standards. The advantage of ozone is that it reacts quickly, leaving no residual or trihalomethanes. The disadvantage is high capital and energy costs and the inherent danger of using a toxic substance.

ACTIVATED CARBON TREATMENT

Activated carbon is an adsorbent used for removing taste- and odor-causing material and chlorinated compounds (e.g., trihalomethanes). It is available in powered (PAC) and granular (GAC) forms. High surface area and pore size distribution and particle surface chemistry give activated carbon its adsorbent nature. A variety of materials, including bituminous coal, lignite, petroleum coke, wood, and nutshells, are used to make activated carbon. The pore size distribution and surface chemistry of the activated carbon is dependent on the original material.

When the efficiency of the activated carbon is diminished by coating the surface of the activated carbon with adsorbed material, reactivation is required. This is accomplished by oxidizing the adsorbed material in regeneration furnaces at temperatures around 800°C, or chemical treatment with phosphoric acid, potassium hydroxide, or zinc chloride.

APPLICATIONS (FLOWSHEETS)

Figure 1-10 depicts many treatment systems that can be developed by applying the various treatment methods that have been discussed. Many options are shown, and the most suitable can be selected on the basis of raw-water characteristics and the treated-water requirements. The diagram is by no means complete; it does, however, illustrate some common treatment scenarios.

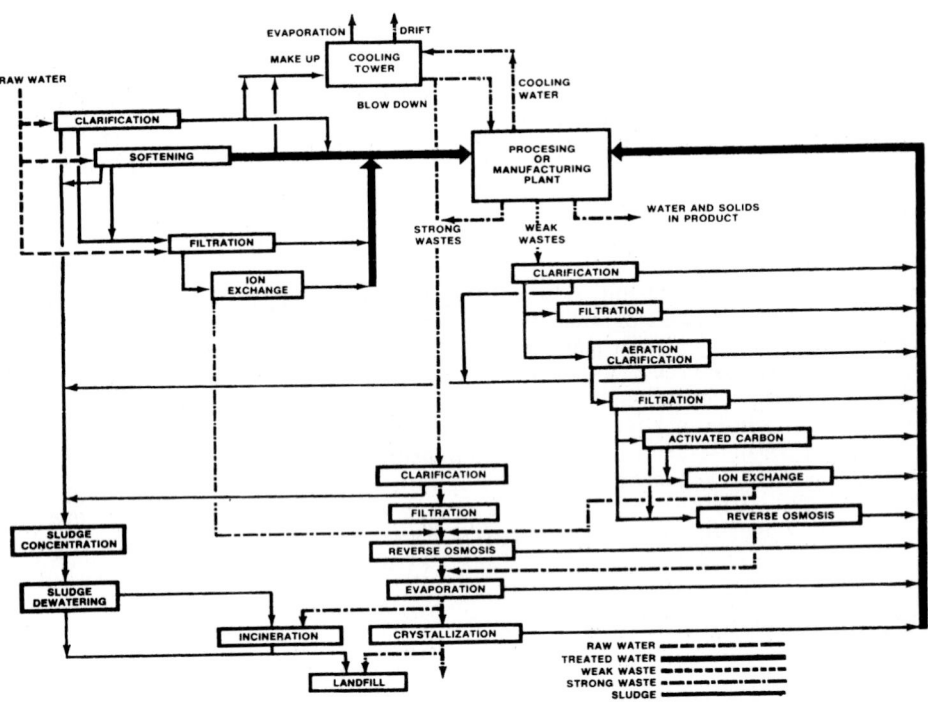

FIGURE 1-10 Diagram of water and waste treatment.

Obviously, raw-water supplies vary widely in quality and, although not indicated on the diagram, can be used without any treatment in some cases. Potable supplies will all require disinfection. When selecting any system to be used for potable purposes, the local governing health departments should be consulted so all their requirements are met.

The minimum water quality required at each point of use must be established and the method or series of treatments that can conservatively meet these requirements under any and all raw-water conditions must be selected. Consideration must be given to the degree of automation and the quality and training of operators and maintenance personnel.

Chemical feeders, controllers, and instrumentation are an important part of water-treatment installations. These accessories are probably the source of most of the operational and maintenance problems, and the same care should be given to their selection as to the major equipment.

Water treatment is a continuous operation that must be monitored by testing. The complexity depends on the process. Qualified personnel, familiar with the laboratory techniques, must be assigned to this task.

WATER RECYCLING AND REUSE

A reuse-treatment plant is usually nothing more than a water-treatment plant using as a source of supply the discharge from either a domestic or an industrial wastewater treatment plant. Figure 1-11 is a flow diagram of such a plant using treated domestic sewage as a source and treating it further for use in an electrical generating station. Except for the nitrification towers which are included because of a considerable savings in operating chemicals, the balance of the plant is a typical water-treatment plant.

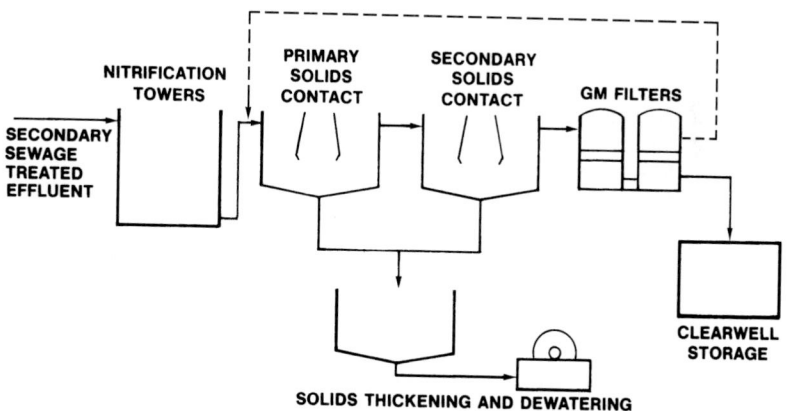

FIGURE 1-11   Flow diagram for reuse treatment.

Waste-treatment plants, particularly those using biological treatment, are subject to upsets on occasion, and this can be troublesome to the operation of the reuse-treatment plant. The design of a reuse treatment plant should include adequate storage, recycle, or bypass facilities needed for the inevitable upsets that will occur upstream.

RECOMMENDED REFERENCES

The Betz Handbook of Industrial Water Conditioning, 9th ed., Betz Laboratories, Trevose, Pa., 1991.

Drew Principles of Industrial Water and Other Uses, 11th ed., Ashland Chemical Inc., Boonton, N.J., 1992.

The Nalco Water Handbook, 2d ed., Nalco Chemical Co., Naperville, Ill., 1988.

Principles and Practices of Water Supply Operations, Vol. 2: Introduction to Water Treatment, American Water Works Association, 1984.

Standard Methods for the Examination of Water and Waste Water, 17th ed., American Public Health Association, Washington, D.C., 1989.

Water Treatment Plant Design, 2d ed., American Society of Civil Engineers, Denver, Colo., 1990.

Water Treatment Principles and Design, James M. Montgomery Consulting Engineers, John Wiley & Sons, New York, 1985.

Practical Principles of Ion Exchange, Dean L. Owens, Tall Oaks Publishing, Inc., Voorhees, N.J., 1985.

Solid-Liquid Separation, Ladislar Svarovsky, ed., Butterworth Heinemann, Boston, 1990.

CHAPTER 6-2
WATER COOLING SYSTEMS

Tower Performance, Inc.
Fairfield, New Jersey

GLOSSARY

Approach   The difference between the cold-water temperature and the ambient or inlet wet-bulb temperature. Units: °F (°C).

Blowdown   Water discharged from the system to control concentration of salts or other impurities in the circulating water.

Cell   The smallest tower subdivision which can function as an independent unit with regard to air and water flow; it is bounded on exterior walls or partitions. Each cell may have one or more fans or stacks and one or more distribution systems.

Cold-water temperature (CWT)   Temperature of the water entering the cold-water basin before addition of makeup or removal of blowdown. Units: °F (°C).

Counterflow tower   One in which air, drawn in through the air intakes (induced draft) or forced in at the base by the fan (forced draft), flows upward through the fill material and interfaces countercurrently with the falling hot water.

Crossflow tower   One in which air, drawn or forced in through the air intakes by the fan, flows horizontally across the fill section and interfaces perpendicularly with the falling hot water.

Design conditions   Defined as the hot-water temperature (HWT), cold-water temperature (CWT), gallons (liters) per minute, and wet-bulb temperature (WBT) in mechanical-draft towers. In natural-draft towers, design conditions are HWT, CWT, GPM, and WBT plus either dry-bulb temperature (DBT) or relative humidity (RH).

Distribution system   Those parts of a tower, beginning with the inlet connection, which distribute the hot circulating water within the tower to the points where it contacts the air. In a *coun-*

terflow tower, this includes the header, laterals, and distribution nozzles. In a *crossflow* tower, the system includes the header or manifold, valves, distribution box, basin pan, and nozzles.

Drift   Water lost from the tower as liquid droplets entrained in the exhaust air. It is independent of water lost by evaporation. Units may be in pounds (kilograms) per hour or percentage of circulating water flow. Drift eliminators control this loss from the tower.

Drift eliminators   An assembly constructed of wood, plastic, cement asbestos board, steel, or other material which serves to minimize entrained droplets from the discharged air.

Fan stack   Cylindrical or modified cylindrical structure in which the fan operates. Fan stacks are used on both induced-draft and forced-draft axial-flow propeller fans. Also known as *cylinder.*

Hot-water temperature (HWT)   Temperature of circulating water entering the distribution system. Units: °F (°C).

Makeup   Water added to the circulating water system to replace water lost from the system by evaporation, drift, blowdown, and leakage.

Plenum   The enclosed space between the eliminators and the fan stack in induced-draft towers or the enclosed space between the fan and the filling in forced-draft towers.

Pumping head   Minimum pressure required to lift the water from basin curb to the top of the system. Pumping head is equal to static head plus friction loss through the distribution system. Units: ft (m).

Range   Difference between the hot-water temperature and the cold-water temperature. Units: °F (°C). Also known as *cooling range.*

Recirculation   This term describes a condition in which a portion of the discharge air enters the tower along with the fresh air. The amount of recirculation is determined by tower design, tower placement, and atmospheric conditions. The effect is generally evaluated on the basis of the increase in the entering wet-bulb temperature compared to the ambient.

Water loading   Circulating water flow of effective horizontal wetted area of the tower. Units: gal/min · ft^2 (m^3/h · m^2).

Wet-bulb temperature (WBT)   Temperature indicated by a psychrometer. Also known as the *thermodynamic wet-bulb temperature* or the *temperature of adiabatic saturation.* Units: °F (°C).

INTRODUCTION

With the growth in the number and sizes of manufacturing plants of all types and the attendant high heat-rejection rates, cooling-tower requirements have increased dramatically. These trends are coupled with environmental aspects, including water conservation and limitations on thermal and chemical discharges. As a result, the plant engineer has witnessed an upsurge in the specification and use of cooling towers.

COOLING SYSTEM OPTIONS

Once-Through Cooling Systems

Many plants operating today are once-through cooling systems, as shown in Fig. 2-1, utilizing water from a lake or river to supply cooling water to the heat exchangers. The heated water is then returned to the body of water.

As a result of all the heat being discharged to rivers, lakes, etc. by plants operating with once-through cooling systems, the term *thermal pollution* has assumed greater significance and has resulted in the enactment of environment-related legislation. Consequently, once-through cooling is not available as an option in many cases.

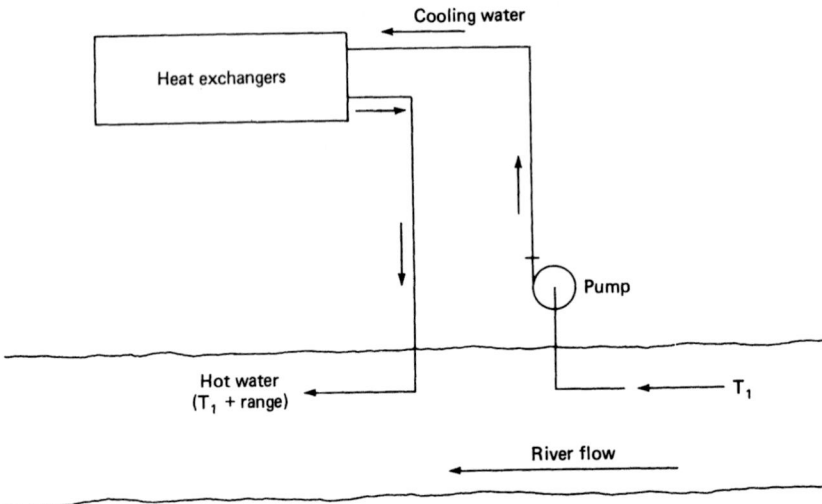

FIGURE 2-1 Once-through cooling.

Closed-Cycle Cooling Systems

Closed-cycle cooling refers to the water side of the system and generally takes the form of a cooling tower. Figure 2-2 shows the relationship of the cooling tower to the cooling system. The cooling water is continuously recirculated through the plant. The cooling tower is used to remove the heat added to the circulating cooling water by the heat exchangers. Water withdrawn from the natural source would be used only for makeup of losses.

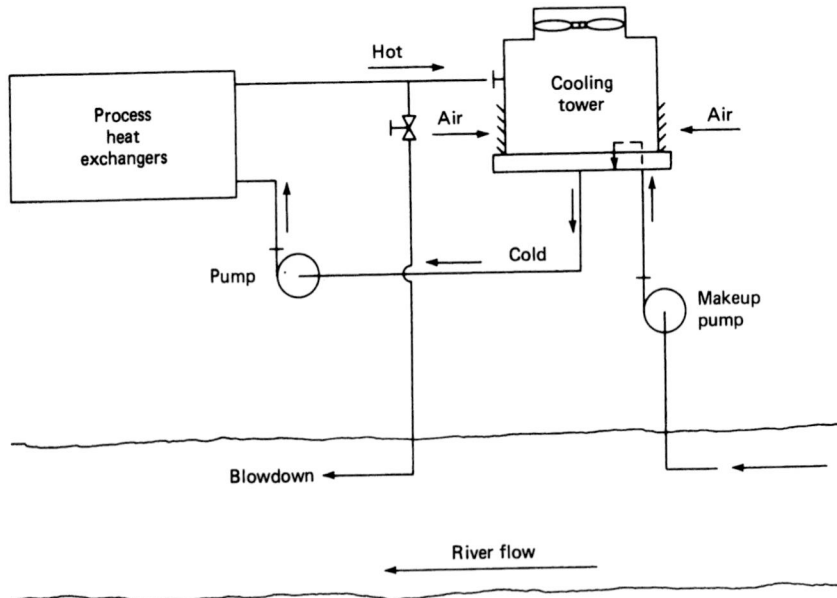

FIGURE 2-2 Closed-cycle cooling-tower system.

Cooling Towers. Cooling tower designs currently available to plant designers fall into *natural-draft* and *mechanical-draft* designs. The natural-draft design utilizes large-dimension concrete chimneys to induce air through the cooling media. In the mechanical-draft design, large-diameter fans driven by electric motors induce or force the air through the circulated water which flows over the fill surface provided to interrupt the flow of water and increase the time of contact between air and water, thereby permitting the efficient transfer of heat from the water to air.

Spray Ponds. An alternative to cooling towers in closed-cycle cooling systems is a spray pond, where warm water is pumped through pipes from the heat exchangers and then out of the spray nozzles. The nozzles atomize the warm water into fine droplets. The basic arrangement of a spray pond is shown in Fig. 2-3. The spray nozzles are usually located about 5 ft (1.52 m) above the pond surface. Height of the sprays is about 6 ft (2 m). A nominal water loading rate of 1 gal/min · ft^2 (2.44 m^3/h · m^2) of pond area and wind speed of 5 mi/h (8.05 km/h) would be typical design parameters for such a pond. Performance is strongly dependent on wind speed and direction, and is limited by the relatively short contact time between the air and water spray.

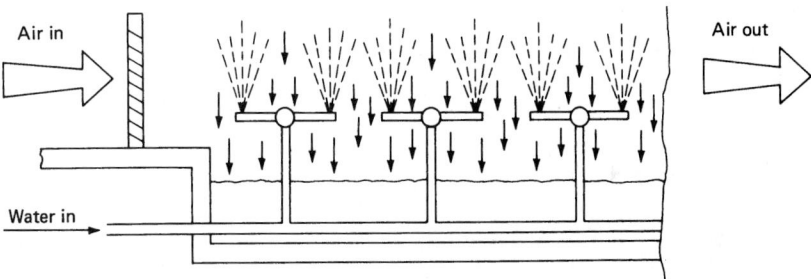

FIGURE 2-3   Spray pond.

Objections to spray ponds include excessive water losses due to drift, which may cause localized icing and fogging, and relatively high pumping costs. The land area required for a spray pond system compared to a cooling tower installation is about 8 to 1.

Atmospheric Cooling Towers. When there is a need for larger cooling ranges and closer approaches, the natural-draft or atmospheric spray and deck-filled towers might be considered. Wooden or plastic fill decks are installed on spray coolers to increase the time of contact between water and air. Various types of fill packing and spacing are utilized, and heights of towers vary in relation to the extent of cooling to be accomplished. The cooling is dependent on the efficiency of the fill decking and the wind velocity passing through the tower, as the water descends through the decking.

The advantages are (1) no electric power is required except for pumping head and (2) no mechanical equipment is necessary, reducing maintenance requirements. The disadvantages are (1) atmospheric towers have limited capacities, since they are solely dependent on ambient atmospheric conditions, (2) at low- or no-wind conditions they are inefficient, (3) water loss as a result of high wind velocities can be appreciable, and (4) a rather high pumping head is required to allow for maximum air-water contact time.

The large natural-draft hyperbolic cooling towers are found only in utility power station service in the United States. The economics of plant designs will favor the mechanical-draft type because of the rather short amortization period. Natural-draft towers work better when wet-bulb temperatures are low and relative humidity is high or if heavier demand is in the winter. A combination of low design wet-bulb and high inlet and exit water temperatures would enhance the operation of a hyperbolic tower. Because of the tremendous size of these units, 500 ft (155 m) high and 400 ft (122 m) in diameter at the base, they are more practical when the circulating cooling water flow rate is about 200,000 gal/min and higher.

Mechanical-draft towers have a positive control of the air delivery through the packing by the use of large-diameter fans. Therefore, they can be designed for close control of cold-water temperature. Counterflow and crossflow designs are indicated in Figs. 2-4 and 2-5.

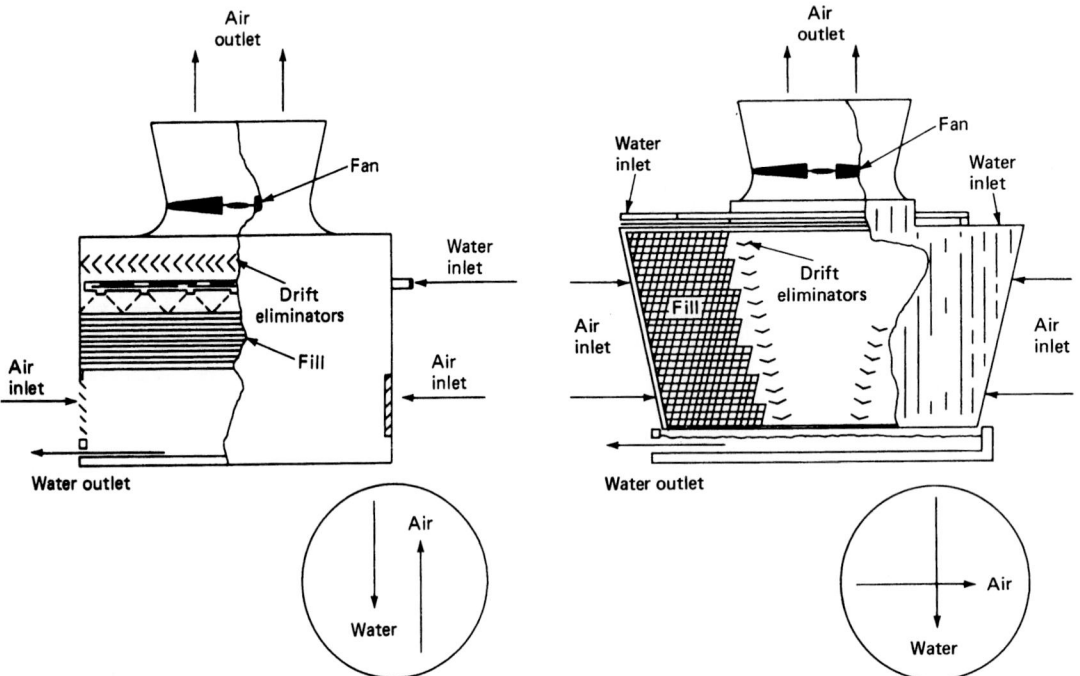

FIGURE 2-4   Mechanical-draft counterflow tower.   **FIGURE 2-5**   Mechanical-draft crossflow tower.

COOLING-TOWER OPERATION

Theoretical Concepts

The basic equations covering combined mass- and heat-transfer phenomena have been covered in the literature.[1] The analysis combines the sensible and latent heat transfer into an overall process based on enthalpy potential as the driving force.

The process is shown schematically in Fig. 2-6, where each particle of bulk water in the tower is assumed to be surrounded by an interfacial film to which heat is transferred from the water. This heat is then transferred from the interface to the main air mass by (1) a transfer of sensible heat and (2) mass heat transfer (latent) resulting from the evaporation of a portion of the bulk water. This can be represented by the equation

$$\frac{KaV}{L} = \frac{T_1}{T_2} \frac{dT}{h_w - h_a}$$

(1)

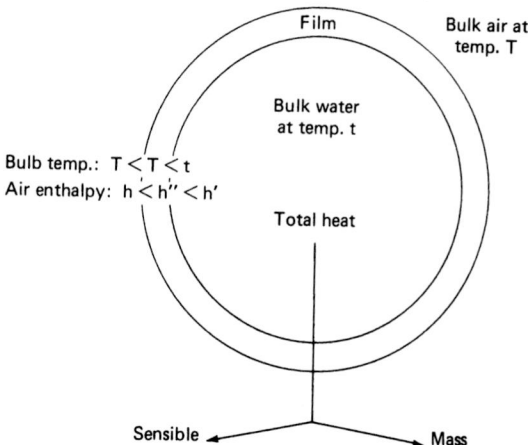

FIGURE 2-6   Schematic of a water droplet with interface film.

where KaV/L = tower characteristic
T_1 = hot-water temperature, °F (°C)
T_2 = cold-water temperature, °F (°C)
T = bulk water temperature, °F (°C)
h_w = enthalphy of air-water vapor mixture at bulk water temperature, Btu/lb dry air (J/kg)
h_a = enthalphy of air-water vapor mixture at wet-bulb temperature, Btu/lb dry air (J/kg)

This equation is commonly referred to as the Merkel equation. The derivation can be found in Ref. 2.

The left side of the equation is called the *tower characteristic*. The laws of thermodynamics demand that the heat discharged by the water descending down through the cooling tower must equal the heat absorbed by the air rising upward through the tower, or:

$$L\,(T_1 - T_2) = G(h_2 - h_1)$$

$$\frac{L}{G} = \frac{h_2 - h_1}{T_1 - T_2} \tag{2}$$

where L = mass water flow, lb/h · ft² (kg/h · m² plan area
T_1 = hot-water temperature, °F (°C)
T_2 = cold-water temperature, °F (°C)
G = mass airflow, lb dry air/h · ft² (kg/h · m²)
h_2 = enthalphy of air-water vapor mixture at exhaust wet-bulb temperature, Btu/lb (J/kg) dry air
h_1 = enthalphy of air-water vapor mixture at inlet wet-bulb temperature, Btu/lb (J/kg) dry air
L/G = liquid-to-gas ratio, lb water/lb dry air (kg/kg)

Equations (1) and (2) or the tower characteristic can be represented graphically by the diagram in Fig. 2-7. The interfacial film is assumed to be saturated with water vapor at the bulk water temperature T_1 (A in Fig. 2-7). As the water is cooled to temperature T_2, the film enthalpy follows the saturation curve to B.

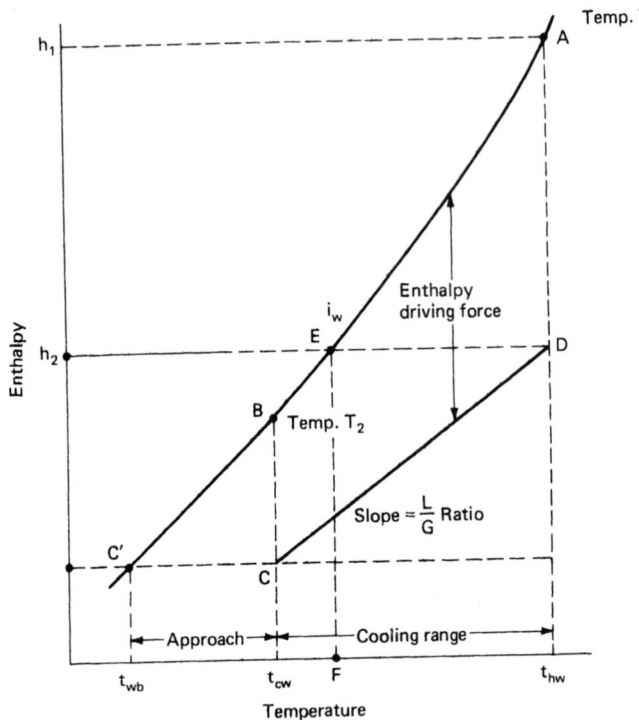

FIGURE 2-7   Graphical representation of tower characteristic.

Air entering the tower at wet-bulb temperature T_{wb} has an enthalpy C'. The origin of the air operating line, point C, is vertically below B and is positioned to have an enthalpy corresponding to that of the entering wet-bulb temperature. The heat removed from the water is added to the air so its enthalpy increases along line CD, having a slope equaling the L/G ratio. The vertical distance BC represents the initial driving force.

Point D represents the air leaving the cooling tower. It is the point on the air operating line vertically below A. The projected length CD (or AB) is the cooling range.

The coordinates refer directly to the temperatures and enthalpy of the water operating line AB, but refer directly only to the enthalpy of a point on the air operating line CD. The corresponding wet-bulb temperature of any point on CD is found by projecting the point horizontally to the saturation curve, then vertically down to the temperature coordinate. DEF shows this projection for the outlet air wet-bulb temperature of point D. Point F is the outlet air wet-bulb temperature.

The following integral is represented by the area $ABCD$:

$$\int_{T_2}^{T_1} \frac{dT}{h_w - h_a}$$

where T_1 = hot-water temperature, °F (°C)
$\quad\quad\quad T_2$ = cold-water temperature, °F (°C)
$\quad\quad\quad T$ = bulk water temperature, °F (°C)
$\quad\quad\quad h_w$ = enthalphy of air-water vapor mixture at bulk water temperature, Btu/lb dry air (J/kg)
$\quad\quad\quad h_a$ = enthalphy of air-water vapor mixture at wet-bulb temperature, Btu/lb dry air (J/kg)

This value is characteristic of the tower, varying with the rates of water and airflow. An increase in the entering air wet-bulb temperature moves the origin *C* upward and the line *CD* shifts to the right to establish equilibrium. Both the inlet and outlet water temperatures increase, while the approach decreases. The curvature of the saturation line is such that the approach decreases at a progressively slower rate as the wet-bulb temperature increases.

An increase in the heat load increases the cooling range and increases the length of line *CD*. To maintain equilibrium, the line shifts to the right, increasing hot- and cold-water temperatures and the approach.

The increase causes the hot-water temperature to increase considerably faster than does the cold-water temperature.

In both these cases, the area *ABCD* should remain constant—actually it decreases about 2 percent for every 10°F (5.6°C) increase in hot-water temperature. The cooling tower designers take this into consideration in their initial design by applying a hot-water temperature correction to design figures when the design hot-water temperature exceeds 110°F (43.5°C). See Fig. 2-8.

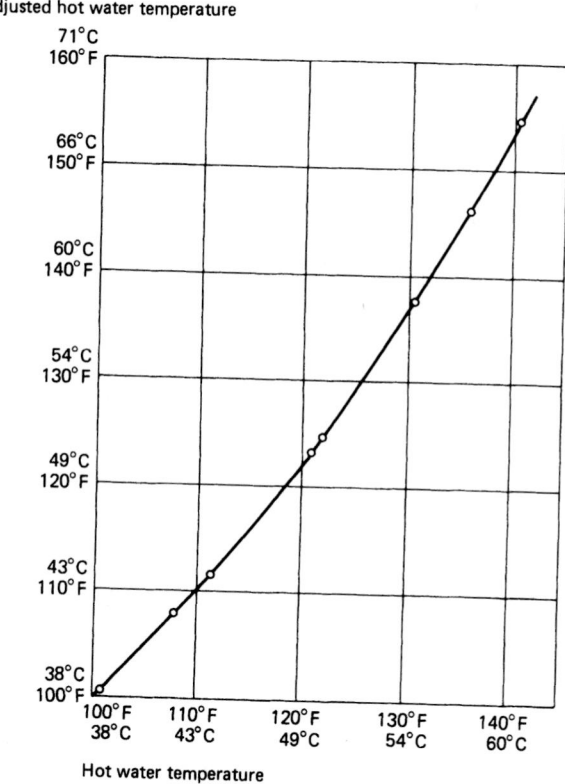

FIGURE 2-8   Plot of hot-water temperature adjustment.

However, a change in *L/G* will change this area. It has been found that a logarithmic plot of *L/G* vs. *KaV/L* at a constant airflow results in a straight line. This line, when plotted on the demand curve for the design conditions, is the tower characteristic curve. The slope of the curve depends on the tower packing. In the absence of more specific data, splash-type packing will have a slope of −0.6.

Knowing the wet-bulb temperature, the range, the approach, and the L/G ratio, we can determine KaV/L by referring to the charts in the Cooling Tower Institute *Blue Book*.[3] A typical tower characteristic curve which would be submitted by a manufacturer is shown in Fig. 2-9. The complete set of cooling tower performance curves in the CTI *Blue Book* is to the cooling tower engineer what the steam tables are to the turbine engineer. The set of curves can be used to predict the performance of a given cooling tower under widely varying conditions of service.

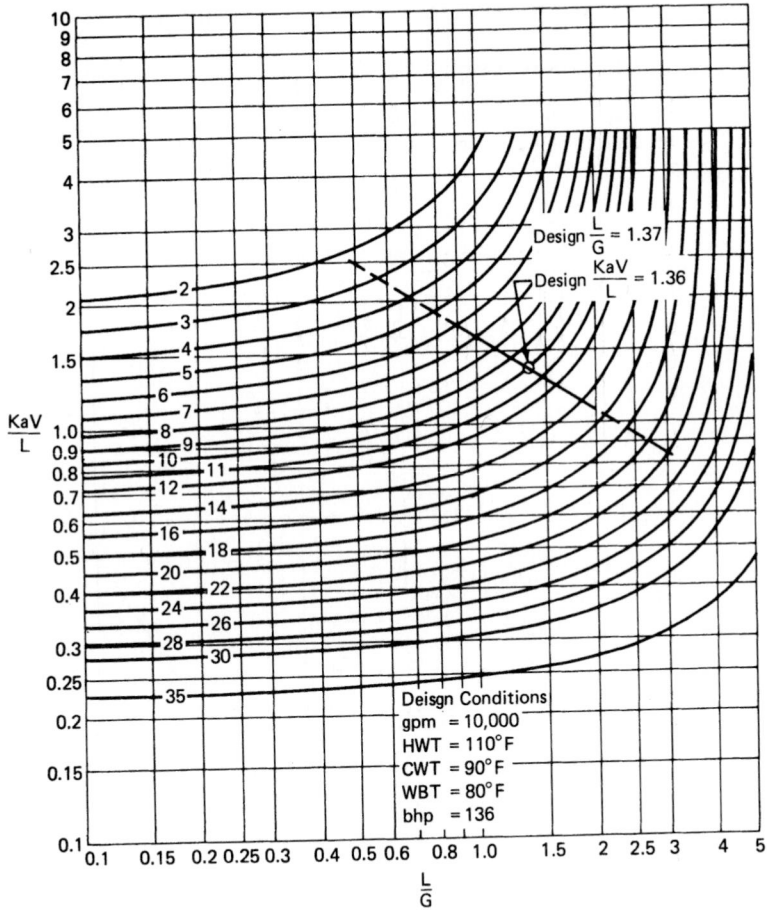

FIGURE 2-9   Tower characteristic curves.

The most important design characteristic is L/G. The plant engineer should have on file the design L/G ratio for each tower in the plant. When bids are solicited for a new cooling tower, the specifications should call for the characteristic curve for the tower proposed to be submitted with the bid package.

Design Parameters

Cooling towers are designed to meet a condition of operation specified by the plant engineer. This condition requires the removal of a heat load of a specified magnitude. When the cooling-water flow rate is selected, the specification can be set. The cooling tower is specified to cool a water quantity [gal/min (m³/h)] through a definite temperature gradient (range) to a final temperature which is a certain number of degrees above the design wet-bulb temperature (approach). Only infrequently will the tower operate at this point, since the plant will normally level out at a slightly different requirement and/or the wet-bulb temperature will be other than the design value. For this reason the tower characteristic curve should be supplied by the manufacturer.

The design wet-bulb temperature is usually based on National Weather Service records and is chosen as the temperature which will not be experienced more than, say 1, 2½, or 5 percent of the time during the summer months of June, July, August, and September. The design wet-bulb temperature should be selected only after some reference has been made to the economics of the plant being served, the seasonal requirements of cooling, and the tabulated Weather Service record for the locality. Choosing the 1 percent frequency level would be judicious when the cooling tower is serving a temperature-sensitive process, or in production of a high-profit product.

The three design levels shown in Table 2-1 are 1, 2½, and 5 percent of the 2928 summer hours, June through September, rounded off to the nearest whole degree. For selecting design temperatures at locations between the cities shown in the table, use data from the city or town nearest the locality of the plant installation. For major installations involving large expenditures or critical temperature balance, make further detailed studies with the assistance of a meteorologist.

STANDARDS AND SPECIFICATIONS

The Cooling Tower Institute has developed over the years several standards which are important to industrial cooling-tower design. When writing a specification for a new tower, if you state, "This is to be a CTI Code tower," the CTI standards immediately become a part of your specifications and your contract with the manufacturer. Applicable standards include:

1. "Redwood Lumber Specification," Standard 103
2. "Gear Speed Reducers," Standard 111
3. "Pressure Preservative Treatment of Lumber," Standard WMS-112
4. "Douglas Fir Lumber Specifications," Standard 114
5. "Timber Fastener Specification," Standard 119
6. "Asbestos Cement Materials," Standard 127
7. "Acceptance Test Code," Bulletin ATC-105

When standards are specified, manufacturers are protected since all bidding will be on the same basis; the buyer is protected with the assurance of getting a quality product.

Suggested Cooling-Tower Specifications

I. General

This specification covers the construction of an induced-draft, counterflow water cooling tower at (location) for (company) (hereafter referred to as Owner).

Each cell of the cooling tower is to be capable of individual operation with its own water supply and mechanical equipment. The design and construction of the cooling tower shall conform to the latest applicable provisions of the Cooling Tower Institute standards and shall be a CTI Code Tower.

Bids are to be submitted on CTI bid forms with all items completed.

TABLE 2-1 Summer, June–September, Design Wet-Bulb Temperature

	1%	2½%	5%		1%	2½%	5%
Alabama				**Indiana**			
Birmingham	79	78	77	Evansville	79	78	77
Huntsville	78	79	76	Indianapolis	78	77	76
Mobile	80	79	79	South Bend	77	76	74
Alaska				**Iowa**			
Anchorage	61	61	59	Des Moines	79	77	76
Fairbanks	64	63	61	Mason City	77	75	74
Arizona				Sioux City	79	77	76
Flagstaff	61	60	59	**Kansas**			
Phoenix	77	76	75	Dodge City	74	73	72
Tucson	74	73	72	Goodland	71	70	69
Arkansas				Topeka	79	78	77
El Dorado	81	80	79	Wichita	77	76	74
Fayetteville	77	76	75	**Kentucky**			
Little Rock	80	79	78	Lexington	78	77	76
California				Louisville	79	78	77
Arcata/Eureka	60	59	58	Peducah	80	79	78
Bakersfield	72	71	70	**Louisiana**			
Fresno	73	72	71	Baton Rouge	81	80	79
Los Angeles	69	68	67	New Orleans	81	80	79
Sacramento	72	70	69	Shreveport	81	80	79
San Diego	71	70	68	**Maine**			
San Francisco	65	63	62	Augusta	74	73	71
Colorado				Portland	75	73	71
Denver	65	64	63	**Maryland**			
Grand Junction	64	63	62	Baltimore	79	78	77
Pueblo	68	67	66	**Massachusetts**			
Connecticut				Boston	76	74	73
Hartford	77	76	74	Worcester	75	73	71
New Haven	77	76	75	**Michigan**			
Delaware				Battle Creek	76	74	73
Wilmington	79	77	76	Detroit	76	75	74
District of Columbia				Saginaw	76	75	73
Washington	78	77	76	**Minnesota**			
Florida				Alexandria	76	74	72
Jacksonville	80	79	79	Duluth	73	71	69
Miami	80	79	79	Minneapolis/St. Paul	77	75	74
Orlando	80	79	78	Rochester	77	75	74
Pensacola	82	81	80	**Mississippi**			
Tampa	81	80	79	Greenwood	81	80	79
Georgia				Meridian	80	79	78
Atlanta	78	77	76	McComb	80	79	79
Macon	80	79	78	**Missouri**			
Valdosta	80	79	78	Joplin	79	78	77
Hawaii				Kansas City	79	77	76
Honolulu	75	74	73	Springfield	78	77	76
Idaho				**Montana**			
Boise	68	66	65	Billings	68	66	65
Idaho Falls	65	64	62	Butte	60	59	57
Pocatello	65	63	62	Great Falls	64	63	61
Illinois				**Nebraska**			
Chicago	78	76	75	Grand Island	76	75	74
Peoria	78	77	76	North Platte	74	73	72
Springfield	79	78	77	Omaha	79	78	76
				Scotts Bluff	70	69	67

TABLE 2-1   Summer, June–September, Design Wet-Bulb Temperature (*Continued*)

	1%	2½%	5%		1%	2½%	5%
Nevada				Columbia	79	79	78
Elko	64	62	61	Spartanburg	77	76	75
Las Vegas	72	71	70	South Dakota			
Reno	64	62	61	Pierre	76	74	73
New Hampshire				Rapid City	72	71	69
Concord	75	73	72	Sioux Falls	77	75	74
Manchester	76	74	73	Tennessee			
New Jersey				Chattanooga	78	78	77
Newark	77	76	75	Knoxville	77	76	75
Trenton	78	77	76	Memphis	80	79	78
New Mexico				Nashville	79	78	77
Albuquerque	66	65	64	Texas			
Carlsbad	72	71	70	Abilene	76	75	74
Roswell	71	70	69	Amarillo	72	71	70
New York				Austin	79	78	77
Albany	76	74	73	Big Spring	75	73	72
Binghamton	74	72	71	Corpus Christi	81	80	80
Buffalo	75	73	72	Dallas	79	78	78
New York	77	76	75	El Paso	70	69	68
North Carolina				Houston	80	80	79
Asheville	75	74	73	Utah			
Charlotte	78	77	76	Richfield	66	65	64
Raleigh	79	78	77	St. George	71	70	69
North Dakota				Salt Lake City	67	66	65
Bismarck	74	72	70	Vermont			
Fargo	76	74	72	Burlington	74	73	71
Minot	72	70	68	Virginia			
Ohio				Norfolk	79	78	78
Cincinnati	78	77	76	Richmond	79	78	77
Cleveland	76	75	74	Roanoke	76	75	74
Columbus	77	76	75	Washington			
Oklahoma				Ellensburg	67	65	63
Ponca City	78	77	76	Seattle/Tacoma	66	64	63
Oklahoma City	78	77	76	Spokane	66	64	63
Tulsa	79	78	77	West Virginia			
Oregon				Charleston	76	75	74
Medford	70	68	66	Morgantown	76	74	73
Pendleton	66	65	63	Parkersburg	77	76	75
Portland	69	67	66	Wisconsin			
Pennsylvania				Green Bay	75	73	72
Altoona	74	73	72	Madison	77	75	73
Harrisburg	76	75	74	Milwaukee	77	75	73
Philadelphia	78	77	76	Wyoming			
Pittsburgh	75	74	73	Casper	63	62	60
Rhode Island				Cheyenne	63	62	61
Providence	76	75	74	Rock Springs	58	57	56
South Carolina							
Charleston	81	80	79				

Attached Plant Safety Requirements are a part of this specification and will become a part of the issued contract.

II. Facilities Furnished by Others

A. Power wiring, motor controls, and all electrical labor.
B. Materials and installation labor for external piping to and from the tower, including valves.
C. Necessary concrete cold-water basin.
D. 110-V, 60-Hz, _____ kW, single-phase power to contractor at one location at the tower site. (Additional facilities which others are willing to supply to contractor.)

III. Design Data

Circulation rate _____ gal/min (m³/h)

Water temp. to tower _____ °F (°C)

Water temp. from tower _____ °F (°C)

Inlet wet-bulb temperature _____ °F (°C)

Range _____ °F (°C)

Approach _____ °F (°C)

Wind velocity max. _____ mi/h (m/s)

Wind loading max. _____ lb/ft² (kg/m²)

Basin depth _____ ft (m)

Tower location _____ ft (m)

Drift loss _____ percent

Bidder to include tower characteristic curve with bid and state design L/G ratio.

IV. Evaluation

A. Fan horsepower evaluation will be added to the base price of the tower at $_____ per horsepower. (or $_____ per horsepower per year for _____ years).
B. Pumping head evaluation will be added to the base price of the tower at $_____ per foot (meter) of head.
C. Concrete cold water basin evaluation will be added to the base price of the tower at $_____ per square foot (meter) of plan area at the base of the tower.

V. Materials

A. General
   1. *Lumber.* All lumber used shall be heart redwood as graded and specified in CTI Standard 103, Grades II and III. No plywood is allowed in any portion of the tower. (Alternative: Douglas fir.)
   2. *Preservative treatment.* All lumber shall be treated. Lumber shall be cut to dimensions, notched, and drilled prior to preservative treatment. Treatment to be with chromated copper arsenate, Type B (CCA-b), and in accordance with CTI Standard WMS-112.
   3. *Hardware.* (See CTI Standard TPR-126 for Charting of Materials.) All bolts, nuts, and washers shall be _____. All nails shall be _____. Other hardware, such as connectors and base anchors, shall be galvanized or cast iron.

B. Component Parts
  1. *Framework*
    a. All tower columns shall not be less than 4×4 in $(10 \times 10$ cm) nominal.
    b. All connections and joints are to be carefully fitted and bolted. Nailing or notching of structural members will not be permitted. Nonframework members such as fill, sheathing, and louvers shall not be called on to furnish part of the structural strength of the tower.
  2. *Fan deck*
    a. Fan deck shall be designed for a live load of 60 lb/ft² and shall be reinforced for any concentrated or distributed dead loads. Fan decking shall be tongue and groove with nominal 2-in (5-cm) thickness.
    b. On counterflow selections one access door per fan cell shall be furnished through the fan deck. A ladder is to be supplied for access from the fan deck to the drift eliminators.
  3. *Fill.*   Tower fill shall be pressure-treated, clear heart redwood, treated Douglas fir, cement asbestos, or PVC. On crossflow selections, fill supports to be PVC-coated steel hangers. Bidder to specify vertical and horizontal spacing of fill bar, fill bar size and fill depth.
  4. *Drift eliminators.*   Shall be treated redwood, treated Douglas fir, PVC, or cement asbestos.
  5. *Hot-water distribution system*
    a. *Counterflow.*   The tower shall be provided with a complete water distribution system fabricated from PVC pipe. The header and laterals shall have self-draining, nonclogging, full-pattern spray nozzles. Piping shall terminate with one flanged connection for each cell approximately 1 ft (0.3 m) outside the tower casing to permit shutdown of any cell without affecting operation of other cells.
    b. *Crossflow.*   The hot-water distribution basin floor shall be constructed of tongue-and-groove redwood (or Douglas fir) with downtake orifice nozzles constructed of polypropylene with integral splash surface diffusers. Each basin shall have a flow-control valve capable of full shutoff.
  6. *Fans and drives*
    a. Fan shall be propeller type with at least six adjustable-pitch blades of reinforced epoxy, AMCA (Air Moving and Conditioning Association) rated, and statically and dynamically balanced prior to shipment.
    b. All motors shall be suitable for across-the-line starting and shall be designed for cooling-tower service. Motors shall be installed outside the exit airstream and nameplate rating shall not be exceeded when tower is operating within the limits of design conditions specified. Motors shall be wired for 3-phase, 60-Hz, _____-V power.
    c. The fans shall be driven through right-angle, heavy-duty, cooling-tower reduction-gear assemblies having a minimum service factor of 2.0. Reduction gears shall be provided with vent line and oil fill line extending to outside of fan stack. Oil fill line shall include oil level sight gauge. Reducers shall conform to CTI Standard 111.
    d. The drive-shaft assembly connecting the motor and gear reducer shall be the nonlubricated design. Two drive-shaft guards shall be supplied, with one at each end of each shaft.
    e. Supports for motor and reducer assembly shall be of unitized steel construction. Minimum thickness of steel employed shall be ¼ in (6.4 mm).
    f. One vibration cutout switch shall be provided with each fan.
  7. *Fan stack.*   Fan stacks shall be venturi entrance type, not less than 6 ft (1.33 m) high, constructed of glass-reinforced polyester.
  8. *Partitions.*   Towers consisting of two or more cells shall have a solid transverse partition wall between all cells which extends from louver face to louver face and from basin-curb level to fan-deck and distribution-deck levels. All partition walls will be

constructed of treated redwood, Douglas fir, or corrugated fiberglass-reinforced polyester plastic.

9. *Casing.* Tower casing shall be single-wall 8-oz 4.2 or 5.33 corrugated fiberglass-reinforced polyester plastic. Casing sheets shall have a minimum of one corrugation overlap at all seams and shall be of watertight design.

10. *Air-inlet louvers.* Louvers shall be of treated redwood, Douglas fir or fiberglass-reinforced polyester plastic supported on spans of 4 ft (1.22 m) or less.

11. *Access*
    a. At least one ladder and one stairway at opposite ends of the tower shall be provided extending from the ground level to the top of the fan deck.
    b. Stairways and ladders shall be in accordance with OSHA requirements.
    c. Handrails around the top of the tower shall be provided in accordance with OSHA requirements.
    d. Access to plenum chamber on crossflow towers shall be through the end-wall casing at basin curb elevation. Access doors will be provided through each partition wall. A walkway shall be provided at basin-curb level from end wall to end wall.

VI. Drawings

The cooling-tower manufacturer shall submit three copies of complete drawings for approval. Catalog drawings will not be considered acceptable as approval drawings. Approval drawings shall clearly show exact dimensions and all construction details.

VII. Testing

ACCEPTANCE TEST. The cooling-tower manufacturer shall conduct an acceptance test in accordance with the Cooling Tower Institute "Acceptance Test Procedure for Industrial Water Cooling Towers," CTI Bulletin ATC-105, Latest Revision. The cooling-tower manufacturer shall quote a separate price for conducting the acceptance test.

VIII. Guarantee

The cooling tower shall be guaranteed for a period of 1 year after structural completion or 18 months after shipment, whichever occurs first. Any defective parts or workmanship shall be repaired at the cooling-tower manufacturer's expense.

OPERATION AND MAINTENANCE

Evaporation Loss

In the usual cooling-tower operation, the water evaporation rate is essentially fixed by the rate of removal of sensible heat from the water, and the evaporation loss can be roughly estimated as 0.1 percent of the circulating water flow for each Fahrenheit degree of cooling range.

Drift Loss

Cooling-tower drift loss is the entrained liquid water droplets discharged with the exit air. The function of drift eliminators is to limit the number of escaping droplets to an acceptable level. Most design specifications state the permissible drift loss as a percentage of the circulating water flow. Most modern cooling towers are designed with drift eliminator face velocities below 650 ft/min (198.1 m/min), and entrainment losses less than 0.008 percent of the water circulation rate.

Blowdown. Cooling-tower blowdown is a portion of the circulating water that is discharged from the system to prevent excessive buildup of solids. The maximum concentration of solids that can be tolerated is usually determined by the effects on the various components of the cooling system, such as piping, pumps, heat exchangers, and the cooling tower itself. The required blowdown rate is determined from a material balance, yielding the equation:

$$b = \frac{e}{r - l} - d$$

where b = blowdown rate, gal/min (m³/h)
e = evaporation loss, gal/min (m³/h)
r = ratio of solids in blowdown to solids in makeup, cycles of concentration
d = drift loss, gal/min (m³/h)

Makeup Water Rate. To hold a given solids concentration ratio, sufficient water must be added to the recirculating water system to make up for evaporation, blowdown, drift, and other losses. The required makeup rate may be computed by either of the equations:

$$M = b + e + d$$

or

$$M = \frac{r}{r - 1} e$$

where M = makeup rate, gal/min (m³/h)
b = blowdown rate, gal/min (m³/h)
e = evaporation loss, gal/min (m³h)
r = ratio of solids in blowdown to solids in makeup, cycles of concentration
d = drift loss, gal/min (m³/h)

Proper maintenance of the mechanical equipment and distribution system will ensure optimum operation from the cooling tower over a long period of time. Motors must remain properly lubricated, gearbox oil should be maintained at the proper level, and drive-shaft alignment should be checked on a regular basis. Uniform distribution of hot water within the tower is essential in order to maintain optimum tower performance. Refer to Table 2-2 for a suggested preventive maintenance schedule for key tower components.

COLD-WEATHER OPERATION

General

The successful operation of induced-draft cooling towers during extremely cold weather very often presents a problem to the plant operators. Ice tends to form on the air-intake louvers and filling immediately adjacent to the louvers. This is because the water in contact with the airstream will intermittently splash on the louver boards, where it freezes, and will eventually build up to the point where the flow of air is restricted. Also, subcooling will be obtained in the area of the filling immediately adjacent to the louvers, where ice will build up during periods of light load or high air velocity. Particular care must be taken in starting up fans that have been shut down for an appreciable length of time because of the possibility of unequal ice loading on the blades. If a fan is started up in an unbalanced condition, the gear unit could be torn from its mounting, causing permanent damage to the mechanical equipment and surrounding tower structure.

Control of Ice on Air-Intake Louvers and Filling

Every effort should be made to maintain the design water quantity and heat load per cell. In the event of a reduction in the plant heat load, it is extremely important that the water quan-

TABLE 2-2   Master Periodic Inspection Chart

Weekly	What to look for	What to do
Fan	Noise, vibration, tower sway	Visually check for damage, check weep holes water in fan blades.
Speed reducer	Noise, rapid vibration, oil leaks	Check oil level, check oil for water or other contamination; check breather pipe for clogging; shaft for misalignment. Run idle units for 10 minutes.
Drive shaft	Vibration, broken disks	Replace broken disks. Tighten bolts.
Suction pit screen	Debris	Remove debris.

Monthly	What to look for	What to do
Speed reducers	Routine check	Check oil level and contamination. Inspect oil on high and low speed shaft for lubrication.
Drive shaft	Routine check	Check alignment.
Nozzles	Scale, corrosion, debris	Clean; replace if damaged.
Headers and laterals	Scale or clogging	Spot-check nozzles on side of tower opposite from risers. Clean.
Distribution decks	Algae, debris, channeling deposits of lime, scales, etc.	Clean with steam, high-pressure hose, or stiff brush.

Yearly	What to look for	What to do
Tower	Routine check	Shut down; clean thoroughly from top to bottom including basin.
Grid decks	Warping, water channeling	Replace individual bar as needed.
Structure	Decay, excessive delignification	Use ice pick. Replace structural members if necessary.
Bolts	Looseness, corrosion	Tighten all bolts; replace those corroded.
Wall sheathing	Leaks	Caulk as necessary. Keep tower wet.
Mechanical equipment	Fan blade damage, unbalance, pitch, fan shaft looseness, speed reducer wear, shaft alignment	Make checks and corrections as necessary.
Basin	Dirt, debris, signs of oil	Clean thoroughly.

tity be reduced proportionately and that cells be shut down to maintain the design quantity per cell; that is, riser valves should be shut on idle cells. In addition, the water temperature in the basin should be maintained at a reasonable value, such as 60 to 70°F (15.6 to 21.1°C), by reducing the volume of air entering the tower.

The greater the air volume moved by the fans, the greater the amount of ice formation. It is our recommendation that the fan motors on a multicell cooling tower be reduced from full speed to half speed as required to maintain the temperature of the water in the basin at 60 to 70°F (15.6° to 21.1°C). In the event that all fans are running at half speed and the basin temperature falls below 60°F (15.6°C), it will then be necessary to shut down the fans as required to maintain this temperature.

Usually the water concentration in gallons per square foot (liters per square meter) of cell area is sufficient to cause a reverse of airflow when the fans are not operating. This will tend to melt any ice that is formed on the filling and the louvers. In a multicell tower, the fans should remain turned off for approximately 12 h and then turned back to low speed. The adjoining cell should then have its fan turned off for the same period of time, and this operation should be repeated on the other cells during cold weather.

Should this procedure prove ineffective in controlling the ice formation, one of the following recommendations should be followed:

1. Remove ice from the louvers with a steam hose. Be careful not to allow the ice load on the fill to exceed its design value, causing the filling to collapse during thawing.
2. Remove louver boards. Some counterflow and straight-sided crossflow towers have the top louver board and every fifth louver beneath of double width. The intermediate louver boards may be removed, thereby reducing the amount of ice forming between these louver blades and choking off the air supply.
3. Install reversing switches on low-speed fan motor terminals. This will reverse the flow of air through the tower, which will quickly melt any ice that is formed on the louvers and filling. The fan motors should not be operated in reverse for more than about 30 min at a time. During extreme cold weather, each of the fans operating at half speed should be reversed once a day to remove ice from the air-intake louvers.

NOMENCLATURE

a = area of transfer surface per unit of tower volume, ft^2/ft^3
b = blowdown rate, gal/min
d = drift loss, gal/min
e = evaporation loss rate, gal/min
g = mass airflow, lb dry air/h · ft^2
h = enthalpy of air-water vapor mixture, Btu/lb dry air.
h_a = enthalpy of air-water vapor mixture at wet-bulb temperature, Btu/lb dry air.
h_w = enthalpy of air-water vapor mixture at bulk water temperature, Btu/lb dry air.
h_1 = enthalpy of air-water vapor mixture at inlet wet-bulb temperature, Btu/lb dry air.
h_2 = enthalpy of air-water vapor mixture at exhaust wet-bulb temperature, Btu/lb dry air.
k = overall enthalpy transfer coefficient, lb/h · ft^2 per lb water/lb dry air
l = mass water flow, lb/h · ft^2 plan area.
m = makeup rate, gal/min
r = ratio of solids in blowdown to solids in makeup (cycles of concentration).
t = bulk water temperature, °F
t_1 = hot-water temperature, °F
t_2 = cold-water temperature, °F
v = effective cooling-tower volume, ft^3/ft^2 plan area
KaV/L = tower characteristic
L/G = liquid-to-gas ratio, lb water/lb dry air

REFERENCES

1. Sherwood, T. K., and R. L. Pigford: *Absorption and Extraction*, 2d ed., McGraw-Hill, New York, 1952, pp. 102–104.
2. Kern, D. Q.: *Process Heat Transfer*, McGraw-Hill, New York, 1950.
3. "Cooling Tower Performance Curves," *Blue Book*, Cooling Tower Institute, Houston.

PLANT OPERATION EQUIPMENT: SELECTION AND MAINTENANCE

SECTION 7

MECHANICAL POWER TRANSMISSION

CHAPTER 7-1

GEARING AND ENCLOSED GEAR DRIVES

Paul N. Salvucci

Boston Gear Division of IMO Industries, Inc.
Quincy, Massachusetts

GEARING

Functions of Gear Drives

The major functions of gears and gear drives are: reduction of speed, multiplication of torque, and positioning of shafts. Gears are used to transmit rotary motion and power, in a uniform manner, from one shaft to another.

Speed Reducer Economically, it is normally better to use a small, high-speed prime mover and gear-reducer combination than a larger, low-speed power source.

Speed Increaser In some instances, it is impractical to operate a prime mover at a speed high enough to suit requirements of the driven equipment. For such applications, gears may be used as a speed increaser.

Shaft Orientation Gears may provide desired orientation and relative rotation of shafts. Some common arrangements available are: in-line, parallel shaft, and right angle. Miter gears (1:1 ratio bevel gears), for example, serve the specific purpose of providing a 90° shaft orientation. Other angles can be supplied by specially designed gears of several types.

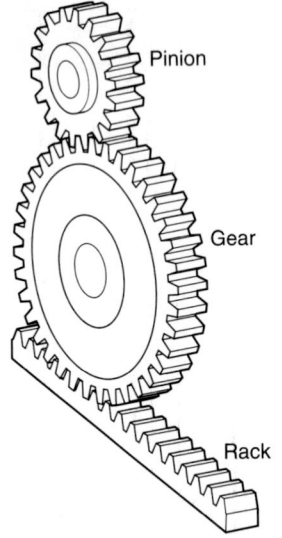

FIGURE 1-1 Spur gears and spur rack. (*Extracted from Ref. 2.*)

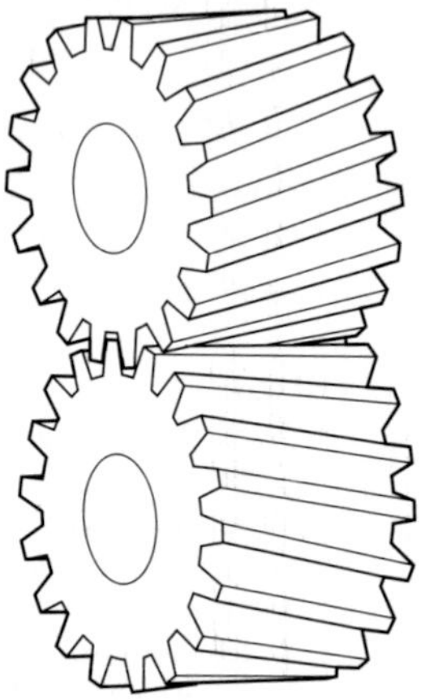

FIGURE 1-2 Parallel helical gears. (*Extracted from Ref. 2.*)

Gear Types

The most common types of gears are illustrated in Figs. 1-1 to 1-13. Other available types are generally modifications of the basic gears shown.

Spur gears   A spur gear has a cylindrical pitch surface and teeth that are parallel to the axis. Spur gears operate on parallel axes (Fig. 1-1).

Spur rack   A spur rack has a plane pitch surface and straight teeth that are at right angles to the direction of motion (Fig. 1-1).

Helical gears   A helical gear has a cylindrical pitch surface and teeth that are helical. Parallel helical gears operate on parallel axes. External helical gears on parallel axes have helices of opposite hands. If one of the members is an internal gear, the helices are of the same hand (Fig. 1-2.)

Single-helical gears   Gears have teeth of only one hand on each gear (Fig. 1-3).

Double-helical gears   Gears have both right-hand and left-hand teeth on each gear. The teeth are separated by a gap between the helices (Fig. 1-4). Where there is no gap, they are known as *herringbone gears* (Fig. 1-5).

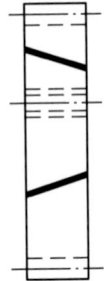

FIGURE 1-3 Single helical gears. (*Extracted from Ref. 2.*)

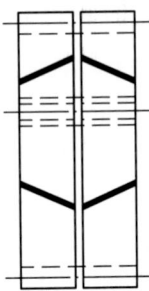

FIGURE 1-4 Double helical gears. (*Extracted from Ref. 2.*)

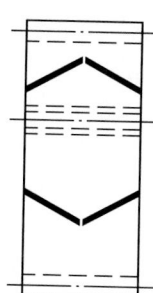

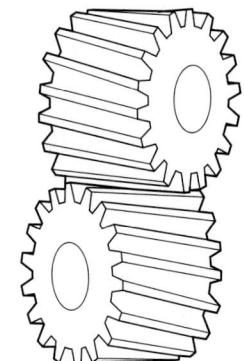

FIGURE 1-5 Herringbone gears (*Extracted from Ref. 2.*)

FIGURE 1-6 Crossed helical gears. (*Extracted from Ref. 2.*)

Crossed helical gears   These gears operate on crossed axes. The term *crossed helical gears* has superseded the old term *spiral gears.* There is, theoretically, point contact between the teeth at any instant. These gears have teeth of the same or different helix angles, of the same or opposite hand, or a combination of spur and helical or other types that can operate on crossed axes (Fig. 1-6).

Wormgearing   Wormgearing includes worms and their mating gears. The axes are usually at right angles (Fig. 1-7).

Wormgear (wormwheel)   This gear is the mate to a worm. A wormgear that is completely conjugate to its worm has a line contact and is said to be *enveloping.* An involute spur gear or helical gear used with a cylindrical worm has point contact only and is said to be *nonenveloping* (Fig. 1-7).

Cylindrical worm   This has one or more teeth in the form of screw threads on a cylinder.

Enveloping worm (hourglass)   This has one or more teeth and increases in diameter from its middle portion toward both ends, conforming to the curvature of the gear (Fig. 1-7).

Double-enveloping wormgearing   This comprises enveloping (hourglass) worms mated with fully enveloping wormgears (Fig. 1-8).

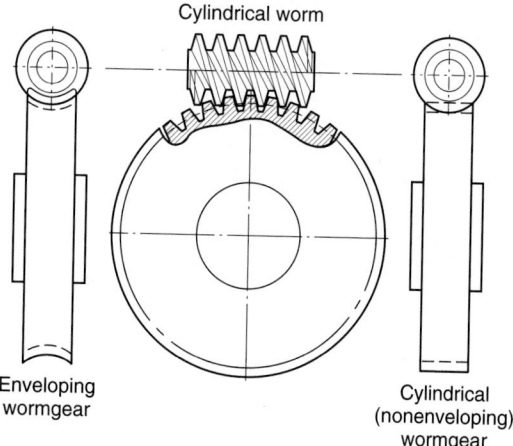

Cylindrical worm

Enveloping wormgear

Cylindrical (nonenveloping) wormgear

FIGURE 1-7 Cylindrical, single-enveloping wormgearing. (*Extracted from Ref. 2.*)

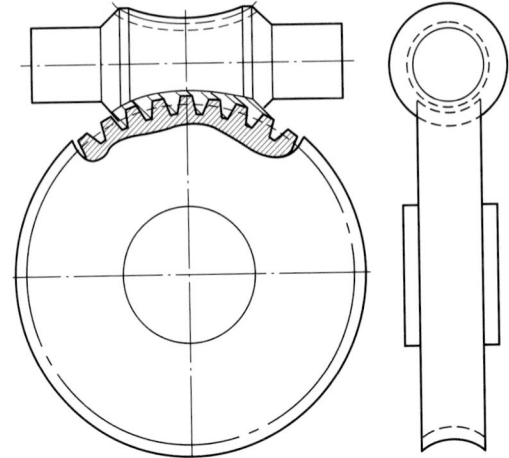

FIGURE 1-8 Double-enveloping wormgearing. (*Extracted from Ref. 2.*)

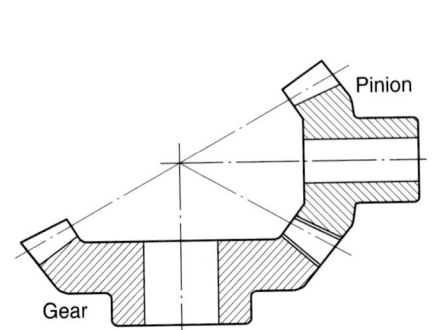

FIGURE 1-9 Bevel gears. (*Extracted from Ref. 2.*)

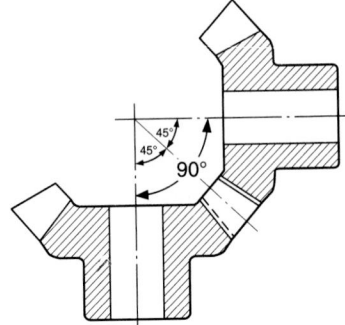

FIGURE 1-10 Miter gears. (*Extracted from Ref. 2.*)

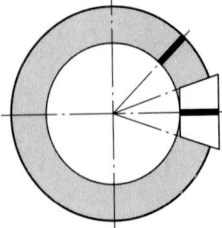

FIGURE 1-11 Straight bevel gears. (*Extracted from Ref. 2.*)

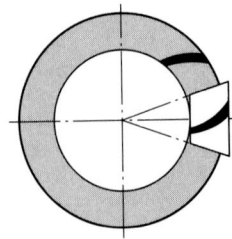

FIGURE 1-12 Spiral bevel gears. (*Extracted from Ref. 2.*)

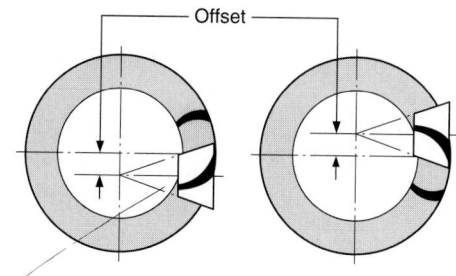

Offset

FIGURE 1-13   Hypoid gears. (*Extracted from Ref. 2.*)

Bevel gears   These gears have conical pitch surfaces and operate on intersecting axes that are usually at right angles (Fig. 1-9).

Miter gears   These are mating bevel gears with equal numbers of teeth and with axes at right angles (Fig. 1-10).

Straight bevel gears   These have straight tooth elements which, if extended, would pass through the point of intersection of their axes (Fig. 1-11).

Spiral bevel gears   These gears have teeth that are curved and oblique (Fig. 1-12).

Hypoid gears   Similar in general form to bevel gears, hypoid gears operate on nonintersecting axes (Fig. 1-13).

Gear Geometry

Gear-Tooth Action   Gears of all types have the common characteristic of theoretically smooth transmission of motion through engagement of successive teeth. Certain design parameters must be met to ensure that one pair of teeth starts engagement before the preceding pair leaves off.

Standard Tooth Forms   The involute form is almost universally used for spur and helical gears and has some application for worm and bevel gears. The involute provides for accuracy of motion transmission, even when there is some change in center distance between gears. It also offers a number of manufacturing advantages. In worm and bevel gearing, conjugate forms are used to suit the manufacturing processes employed.

Modified and Special Tooth Forms   Common modifications to involute gear teeth are: long and short addenda, stub teeth, tip and root relief, and crowning. Special tooth forms are sometimes used to provide higher capacity. Normally, accurate mounting of the gears must be maintained to realize this advantage.

Gear Materials and Heat Treatment

Common Materials   Gears may be made up of a wide range of materials that may be ferrous, nonferrous, and nonmetallic. For industrial applications, steel and iron are most commonly used for spur, helical, and bevel gears. Wormgear pairs generally are made up of bronze or iron for the gear and steel for the worm. Use of plastics is generally limited to light applications, particularly those in which minimal lubrication is available.

Hardened vs Unhardened Material   Since the gear set rating is governed to a great extent by hardness of the teeth, heat treating often is used to provide higher capacity in the same space. Pinions, which endure more load cycles, generally are made slightly harder than their mating gears. Hardening adds to the cost, particularly where an additional finishing operation is required to correct distortion. For some applications, untreated gears may prove more economical. Obviously, this will be true when the equipment arrangement will not permit use of smaller hardened gears.

Material Selection   Information regarding material selection and properties is contained in the "Gear Handbook" AGMA 390.03 and/or "Gear Classification and Inspection Handbook" ANSI/AGMA 2000-A88 (Ref. 1).

Many factors influence the selection of gear materials, and their relative importance will vary. These factors include:

- Mechanical properties
- Grade and heat treatments
- Cleanliness
- Dimensional stability
- Availability and cost
- Hardenability and size effects
- Machinability and other manufacturing characteristics

Specific material and heat treatment combinations should be based on an analysis of the overall application requirements and conditions.

The following factors should be considered when making a material or heat treatment selection:

- Safety factor, loading, duty cycle, mounting, gearing enclosure, lubrication, and ambient atmospheric conditions.
- For replacement gearing, the life obtained from the previous gearing should be evaluated. If satisfactory, replace with similar material. If longer life is required, selection of a heat-treatment specification yielding a higher hardness and, if necessary, a better material, may provide the desired improvement.
- Annealed carbon steels, bar stock, forgings, or castings, are usually satisfactory for pinions and gears for uniform or moderate shock loads when the size of the gearing is not an important factor.
- Annealed carbon-steel pinions with cast-iron gears are sometimes used for the same reason mentioned above for annealed carbon steels.
- Alloy-steel pinions are used when there are increased loads or greater life is desired. They may be used with cast iron or annealed (forged or cast) steel gears, usually when the ratio is about 6:1 or higher.
- Alloy-steel pinions and gears, heat-treated, should be used with the higher hardness ranges when space limitation is a factor, i.e., where smaller center distances and face widths may be necessary.
- Steel pinions and gears which are to be machined and cut after heat treatment should have the pinion hardness specified as follows:
  Ratios up to 2:1; pinion and gear to be same minimum hardness
  Ratios from 2:1 to 8:1; minimum hardness of pinion to be 40 Bhn (Brinell hardness number) higher than minimum gear hardness
  Ratios of 8:1 and higher; pinion to be more than 40 Bhn harder at minimum than gear
- Steel pinions and gears hardened to 400 Bhn or higher after cutting are generally specified with the same hardness, unless extremely high hardness is desired for the pinion.
- A range of 40 Bhn should be specified for minimum hardnesses up to 285 Bhn. A range of 50 Bhn should be specified for minimum hardnesses over 302 Bhn.[1] For example, a pinion might be specified with a range from 285 to 321 Bhn and the mating gear from 223 to 262 Bhn.
- When core hardness is a requirement, consideration should be given to the size and shape of the cross sections involved.
- Where impact loads exist, the use of alloys and the lowering of hardness are recommended for carburized gears and pinions.
- When accelerated wear is encountered in service, heat-treated gearing providing greater hardness will, in most cases, help to alleviate this condition. Consult with an AGMA company member for appropriate recommendations.

Manufacturing Processes

Generating   Most gear teeth are produced by a generating process that takes into account the shape of the tool and relative motions between the tool and workpiece. Examples are: hobbing, shaping, rolling, grinding, and shaving.

Forming   The forming process produces gear teeth by a direct replication method. Examples are: casting, molding, and broaching.

Finishing   Finishing operations remove a relatively small amount of material from gear teeth. These may be used to improve accuracy and finish. Shaving is used to improve profile and finish on relatively soft gears. Grinding and honing are employed for harder gears.

Size Limitations   General limitations on gear diameters are listed below (Table 1-1). A specific company may have the capability of producing larger gears of a particular type. Spur gears of very large diameter for low-speed application have been cut in arc sections and also fabricated from rack sections, bent to the proper radius of curvature.

TABLE 1-1

Gear type	Approximate maximum diameter	
	in	m
Spur	400	10
Helical	400	10
Straight bevel	100	2.5
Spiral bevel	90	2.3
Wormgear	150	4

Accuracy Requirements

Requirements for gear accuracy may be governed by several factors. Operating speed and gear size are probably the most important. From an application standpoint, specifications on sound level and smoothness of motion transmission are often controlling.

AGMA 390, "Gear Handbook," contains a classification system covering tolerances for common types of gears. In this system tolerances are tabulated for a series of *quality numbers* that range from Q3 to Q15. The higher the quality number the more precise are the tolerances. The handbook covers the gears themselves and does not apply to gears in enclosed drives.

By far the majority of applications can be satisfied by gears in the range of Q5 to Q8. Rarely does an application require a gear more precise than class Q14. AGMA 390 tabulates a range of suggested quality numbers for various applications. This is only a guide. Judgment should be used in making a final selection to meet the specific conditions involved.

Precise Motion Transmission   Many applications use gears as a means for precise transmission of motion. Usually, high AGMA quality numbers (Q12 to Q14) are required for these gears. Examples of such applications are: navigational tracking, telescopes, and index devices for machine tools.

High-Speed Considerations   Gear inaccuracies become more critical as operating speed increases. The most obvious problem may be a high noise level. In addition, the dynamic loads on the teeth caused by these errors may be a substantial part of the total transmitted load.

Pitch line velocity, which takes into account size as well as rotational speed, is the usual measure of gear speed. The unit normally used to measure this velocity at tooth mesh is feet per minute.

AGMA 390 suggests the following quality numbers for power drives in the machine tool industry.

Gear pitch line velocity, ft/min (m/min)	Quality number
0–800 (0–245)	Q6–Q8
800–2000 (245–610)	Q8–Q10
2000–4000 (610–1220)	Q10–Q12
Over 4000 (1220)	Q12 and up

Accuracy vs Cost   Cost of manufacturing and inspection escalates rapidly with increasing quality number. Therefore, the user should use care to avoid specifying higher classes than required for the application.

Cost.   Table 1-2 compares relative first cost vs gear type.

TABLE 1-2

Gear type	First cost*
Spur	Very low
Wormgear	Low
Helical	Moderate
Herringbone & bevels	High

* Cost per unit hp (kW) or torque.

Mounting of Gears   Close attention must be given to the mounting of gears and the maintenance of alignment under operating conditions. Obviously, precision of mounting must match that of the gears.

Additional Considerations   When specifying the quality of a given gear, there are additional or special considerations that should be reviewed.

- Backlash allowances in tooth thickness
- Matching gears as sets
- Replacement gearing

Enclosed Gear Drives

Advantages   Enclosed gear drives marketed by gear manufacturers offer several advantages over open power-transmission devices.

- Safety—protection from moving parts
- Retention of lubricant
- Protection from environment
- Economics of quantity manufacture
- Availability

TABLE 1-3 Enclosed Gear-Drive Units—Features (Refer to Figs. 1-14 to 1-17.)

Type of unit	Ratio range*	Horsepower range*	(kW)	Efficiency, %[†]	Fig. no.
Helical & double helical					
Single reduction	to 7:1	to 20,000	(14,920)	96–98	1-14
Double reduction	5:1–40:1	10,000	(7,460)	95–97	1-15
Triple reduction	20:1–300:1	3,000	(2,238)	93–95	—
Quadruple reduction	150:1–1000:1	1,000	(746)	91–93	—
Bevel, helical	5:1–40:1	3,000	(2,238)	95–97	—
Bevel helical, helical	20:1–300:1	2,000	(1,492)	93–95	—
Bevel					
Single bevel	to 9:1	2,000	(1,492)	96–98	
Wormgear					
Single reduction	5:1–70:1	300	(224)	50–96	1-17
Double reduction	25:1–4900:1	100	(74)	20–92	1-16
Helical, worm	20:1–300:1	150	(112)	50–94	—

* The information on ratio and horsepower ranges is approximate and is for the product usually offered.
[†] Efficiency is based on transmission of full rated power.

Types and Features Enclosed gear drives generally are classified by the principal type of gearing used. They may have a single set of gears or additional gears of either the same or different types to form multiple reductions. Figures 1-14 to 1-19 provide illustrations of common types. Table 1-3 covers important features of each.

Mounting Gear drives may be designed for base, flange, or shaft mounting. The last type makes use of a hollow output shaft for direct mounting on the driven shaft (refer to Fig. 1-20). A reaction arm or similar device is required to secure the unit against rotation.

Gear Motors A gear motor is an integral drive unit incorporating an electric motor and gear reducer, with the frame of one supporting the other. Some designs use motors with special shaft ends and/or mountings, while others adapt standard motors (refer to Fig. 1-21).

FIGURE 1-14 High-speed single-reduction helical gear drive. (*Philadelphia Gear Corporation.*)

FIGURE 1-15 Double-reduction helical gear drive. (*Philadelphia Gear Corporation.*)

FIGURE 1-16 Double-reduction wormgear drive. (*Boston Gear Division of IMO Industries, Inc.*)

FIGURE 1-17 Single-reduction wormgear drive. (*Boston Gear Division of IMO Industries, Inc.*)

FIGURE 1-18 Single-reduction spiral bevel gear drive. (*The Falk Corporation.*)

Normal Speed vs. High Speed AGMA standards for enclosed gear drives, used in general industrial service, limit input speed to 3600 r/min. An additional limitation is imposed: 5000 ft/min (1500 m/min) pitch line velocity for helical and bevel units and 6000 ft/min (1800 m/min) sliding velocity for cylindrical wormgears. Above these limits, special consideration should be given to such items as gear quality, lubrication, cooling, bearings, etc. See Refs. 3 and 4.

INSTALLATION AND MAINTENANCE

The variety of types and sizes of gears and enclosed gear drives makes it impractical to cover installation and maintenance in specific detail. The user should refer to the manufacturer's literature, nameplate data, and warning tags. Such information should take precedence over the generalized comments that follow.

FIGURE 1-19 Double-reduction spiral bevel-helical gear drive. (*The Falk Corporation.*)

FIGURE 1-20 Shaft-mounted double-reduction helical gear drive. (*The Falk Corporation.*)

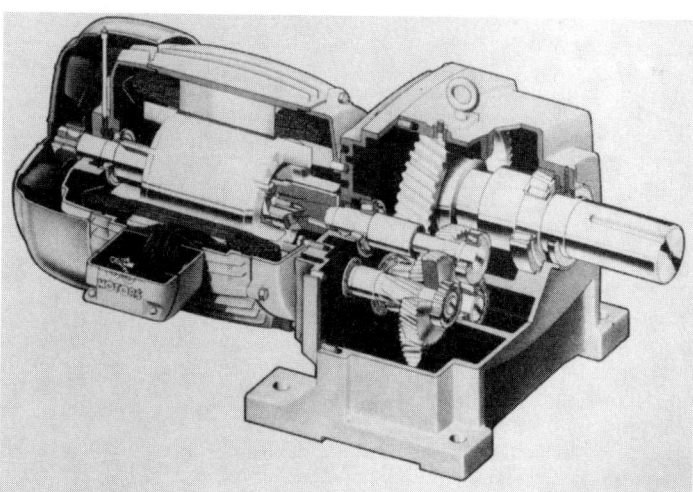

FIGURE 1-21 Triple-reduction helical gear motor. (*U.S. Electrical Motors.*)

Mounting and Installation of Gears

Accuracy of mounting must be commensurate with the quality of the gears themselves to obtain optimum results. Some types of gears require close endwise positioning of either or both members of a pair to obtain proper operation. Examples are bevel gears (both), cylindrical wormgears (gear only), double-enveloping wormgears (both). This positioning must be provided by bearings of suitable capacity to accommodate the thrust loads involved.

Provision must be made for adequate lubrication of open or semi-enclosed gears and guarding for safety. See Chap. 17-1, "Lubricants," for information on gear lubrication. Reference 5 also provides information on lubricant types and methods of lubrication.

Installation and Start-Up of Enclosed Gear Drives

The handling, installation, and servicing of a new enclosed gear drive deserves close attention to avoid damage and to assure proper operation. A checklist of important items is provided in Table 1-4.

TABLE 1-4 Installation and Start-Up Checklist

Step	Instruction
Storage	If necessary to store or maintain the gear unit in an inactive condition for more than a month, contact the manufacturer to determine need for protective action.
Handling	Observe manufacturer's instructions for unpacking and handling of gear drive.
Foundation	Provide adequate foundation commensurate with size and type of unit. Surface is to be level unless drive has been specifically designed for other positioning.
Accessibility	Provide adequate space to permit future maintenance.
Auxiliary parts	Assemble components, such as coupling hubs, sprockets, etc., to shafts with shrink or slip fits in accordance with instructions. Do not force fit.
Alignment	Align shafts and auxiliary drives accurately. Most couplings are designed to accommodate only minor misalignment.
Guards	Install suitable guards for safety in accordance with OSHA standards.
Lubrication	Observe manufacturer's instructions, using the specified lubricants. *Note: Most gear drives are shipped without lubricant.*
Rotation	Check for proper rotation and freedom from obstructions before start of full operation. For pressure lube systems, make certain pump is delivering oil.
Operation	Inspect for oil leaks and unusual noise or vibration immediately after start-up. Check oil temperature after several hours. A temperature of 180 to 200°F (82 to 94°C) is not unusual for most gear drives. After first week, recheck alignment and tightness of all fasteners, fittings, and pipe plugs.

Lubrication of Enclosed Gear Drives Improper lubrication is one of the major causes of failure of gear drives. The gear manufacturer's instructions must be followed to assure proper operation.

Reference 6 provides detailed information on recommended lubricants and maintenance procedures. Gear type, size, and speed, along with ambient temperature range, are major influencing factors on lubricant selection.

The gear unit should be drained and cleaned with a flushing oil after 4 weeks of initial operation. For refilling, either the filtered original lubricant or new lubricant may be used. For normal operation, oil changes should be made after every 2500 h of service.

Periodic checks must be made on oil levels, oil cups, and grease fittings. When pressure lubrication is used, proper functioning of pump, filter, and cooler should be frequently audited.

Seals and Breathers It is recognized that gear drives applied in certain industries and atmospheric conditions should be equipped with special oil seals and breathers. Extremely dusty or corrosive environments as well as severe moisture and vapor-laden atmospheres have special requirements. Applications subject to direct or indirect washdown, such as paper, food, and drug industries may preclude use of breathers. In these cases, expansion chambers may be used.

Troubleshooting

Alertness to changes in operating characteristics, such as increased temperature rise over ambient noise and vibration and oil leakage, can prevent costly shutdowns. Table 1-5, "Trouble Chart," provides a checklist to diagnose various problems in operation.

TABLE 1-5   Trouble Chart

Trouble	What to inspect
Heating	Is unit and fan assembly covered with dirt?
	Is unit overloaded?
	Has recommended oil level been exceeded or is level too low?
	Are couplings in alignment?
	Have bearings been properly adjusted?
	Are oil seals or stuffing boxes the cause?
	Is oil clean or is sludge content high?
	Has oil filter been cleaned?
	Is oil pump functioning?
Shaft failure	Check alignment; most shafts fail owing to misalignment. Some troubles are caused by use of rigid couplings. Is overhung load beyond capacity of unit?
	Is unit subject to high energy loads or extreme repetitive shocks not previously considered?
Bearing Failure	Rust formation caused by high humidity or the entrance of water.
	Unsuitable lubricant.
	Abnormal loading causing excessive deflection results in flaking, cracks, and fractures. Improper adjustment causes abnormal loading if bearings are pinched or abnormal gear wear if bearings are too free. This is dependent upon type of bearing and the possible lack of lubrication.
Oil leakage	Check oil seals and replace if worn.
	Check stuffing boxes and adjust or replace packing.
	Check tightness of drain, level, and other plugs or fittings.
Wear	Backlash may be insufficient.
	Misalignment due to worn bearing.
	Incorrect lubrication.
	Insufficient lubrication.
	Lubricant carrying foreign matter, viz., abrasive dirt or particles of worn metal teeth.[7]
	Excessive temperature.
	Excessive speeds.
	Excessive loads.
Noise or vibration	Bad alignment.
	Loose or worn bearings.
	Insufficient lubrication.
	Excessive lubrication.

APPLICATION OF GEARING AND ENCLOSED GEAR DRIVES

Gear Ratings

AGMA has developed rating formulas for most types of gearing and enclosed gear drives. The ratings determined from these formulas are intended for applications where loads of a uniform nature are applied for no more than 10 h/day. It is these ratings that normally are tabulated in manufacturers' catalogs.

Service Factors

In selecting gearing or an enclosed gear drive for an application, the horsepower to be transmitted is multiplied by a service factor to determine an *equivalent horsepower*. Service factors have been developed from the experience of manufacturers and users to allow for the nature and duration of the transmitted load. Table 1-6 provides a tabulation of service factors extracted

TABLE 1-6 AGMA Standard Practice for Enclosed Speed Reducers or Increasers Using Spur, Helical, Herringbone, and Spiral Bevel Gears

Prime mover	Duration of service, h/day	Driven machine load classifications		
		Uniform	Moderate shock	Heavy shock
Electric motor, steam turbine, or hydraulic motor	Occasional, ½	0.50	0.80	1.25
	Intermittent, 3	0.80	1.00	1.50
	Over 3 up to and incl. 10	1.00	1.25	1.75
	Over 10	1.25	1.50	2.00
Multicylinder internal combustion engine	Occasional, ½	0.80	1.00	1.50
	Intermittent, 3	1.00	1.25	1.75
	Over 3 up to and incl. 10	1.25	1.50	2.00
	Over 10	1.50	1.75	2.25
Single-cylinder internal combustion engine	Occasional, ½	1.00	1.25	1.75
	Intermittent, 3	1.25	1.50	2.00
	Over 3 incl. 10	1.50	1.75	2.25
	Over 10	1.75	2.00	2.50

from Ref. 3 for enclosed speed reducers or increasers using spur, helical, herringbone, and spiral bevel gears. The factors for other types of gears vary slightly from those shown.

Application Classification

Most AGMA standards for enclosed gear drives provides tables for various applications as a guide for selecting service factors. This information is usually also contained in manufacturers' catalogs.

Product Selection

After the equivalent horsepower has been determined, selection of gearing or enclosed gear drives can be made by comparing this figure with the basic rating. It is necessary that the product selected have a rated load capacity equal to or in excess of the equivalent horsepower. An enclosed gear drive usually must also be checked for thermal rating. This is the horsepower that can be transmitted continuously for 3 h or more without causing a temperature of more than 100°F (38°C) above ambient temperature. Should this limitation prevail, several alternatives are available, such as auxiliary cooling systems, oil pans to reduce churning, or selection of a larger unit.

Systems Considerations

An essential phase in the design of a system of rotating machinery is the analysis of the dynamic (vibration) response of a system to excitation forces.

The dynamic response of a system results in additional loads imposed on the system and relative motion between adjacent elements in the system. The vibratory loads are superimposed upon the mean running load in the system and, depending upon the dynamic behavior of the system, could lead to failure of the system components.

In a gear unit, these failures could occur as tooth breakage or pitting of the gear element, shaft breakage, or bearing failure.

Any vibration analysis must consider the complete system, including prime mover, gear unit, driven equipment, couplings, and foundations. The dynamic loads imposed upon a gear unit are the result of the dynamic behavior of the total system and not of the gear unit alone. For further information, see Ref. 8.

Sound and Vibration

The greatest concern regarding sound and vibration of gear drives is the contribution to the industrial noise level. A second concern is that these may be symptomatic of abnormal wear and impending failure.[9-12] Refer to Sec. 12 of this Handbook, "Noise and Vibration Control," for additional information.

REFERENCES: AGMA STANDARDS APPLICABLE TO ENCLOSED GEAR DRIVES

1. "Gear Materials and Heat Treatment Manual," ANSI/AGMA 2004-B89 and AGMA 390.03, 1973.
2. "Gear Nomenclature, Definitions of Terms with Symbols," ANSI/AGMA 1012-F90.
3. "Standards for Spur, Helical, Herringbone, and Bevel Enclosed Drives," ANSI/AGMA 6010-E88.
4. "Practice for High Speed Helical and Herringbone Gear Units," AGMA 421.06, 1969.
5. "Lubrication of Industrial Open Gearing," AGMA Specification 251.02, 1974.
6. "Lubrication of Industrial Enclosed Gear Drives," AGMA Specification 250.04, 1981.
7. "Nomenclature of Gear Tooth Failure Modes," ANSI/AGMA 110.04, 1989.
8. "Systems Considerations for Critical Service Gear Drives," AGMA Information Sheet 427.01, 1976.
9. "Sound for Enclosed Helical Herringbone and Spiral Bevel Gear Drives," ANSI/AGMA 6025-C90.
10. *Gear Sound Manual:* "Fundamentals of Sound as Related to Gears," AGMA 299.01, Sec. 1, 1978.
11. "Assembling Bevel Gears," ANSI/AGMA 2008-B90.
12. "Gear Classification and Inspection Handbook," ANSI/AGMA 2000-A88.
13. "Practice for Enclosed Cylindrical Wormgear Speed Reducers and Gearmotors," ANSI/AGMA 6034-A87.
14. "Standards for Gearmotors using Spur, Helical Herringbone, Straight Bevel or Spiral Bevel Gears," ANSI/AGMA 6019-E89.
15. "Practice for Spur, Helical and Herringbone Gear Shaft Mounted Speed Reducers," AGMA 480.06, 1977.

CHAPTER 7-2
BEARINGS

PART 1

ROLLING ELEMENT BEARINGS
Fafnir Bearings Division Engineering Staff
The Torrington Company
Torrington, Connecticut

GLOSSARY*

Aligning bearing A bearing which, by virtue of its shape, is capable of considerable misalignment.

Antifriction bearing A term given to ball and roller bearings to distinguish them from non-rolling-element bearings, i.e., sliding bearings.

Average life See median life.

Axial internal clearance The measured maximum possible movement parallel to the bearing axis of the inner ring in relation to the outer ring.

Axial load See thrust load.

Ball bearing An antifriction bearing with balls as rolling elements.

---

* Based upon ANSI/ABMA Standard 1—1990.

Basic dynamic radial (axial) load rating   The constant stationary radial load (constant centric axial load) that a rolling bearing can theoretically endure for a basic rating life of 1 million (10^6) revolutions.

Basic static-load rating   The static load that corresponds to a total permanent deformation of ball and race, or roller and race, at the most heavily stressed contact of 0.0001 in (0.00254 mm) of the ball or roller diameter.

Bearing runout   Displacement of the surface of a bearing relative to a fixed point when one raceway is rotated with respect to the other raceway.

Bearing series   A graduated dimensional listing of a specific type of bearing.

Bore   The area of the bearing making contact with the bearing seat on the shaft.

Boundary dimensions   Dimensions for bore, outside diameter, width, and corners.

Cage   A bearing part which partly surrounds all or several of the rolling elements and moves with them. Its purpose is to space the rolling elements and generally also to guide and/or retain them in the bearing.

Cage pocket   An aperture or gap in a rolling bearing cage to accommodate one or more rolling elements.

Combined load   A combination of all radial and axial forces on a bearing.

Cone   An inner ring of a tapered roller bearing.

Conrad ball bearing   A deep-groove, radial non-filling-slot type ball bearing in which each ring has uninterrupted raceway grooves.

Cup   An outer ring of a tapered roller bearing.

Diametral clearance   See radial internal clearance.

Double-row bearing   A rolling bearing with two rows of rolling elements.

End play   See axial internal clearance.

Equivalent load   The calculated, constant, stationary load which, if applied to a bearing, would give the same life as attained under actual conditions of load and rotation.

Filling slot bearing   A deep-groove, radial ball bearing having a loading slot in one shoulder of each ring to permit the insertion of a larger number of balls.

Fixed bearing   A bearing that positions a shaft against axial movement in both directions.

Flanged housing   A bearing housing with a radial flange with bolt holes for mounting on a support perpendicular to the bearing shaft.

Floating bearing   A bearing so designed or mounted as to permit axial displacement between shaft and housing.

Full-complement bearing   A rolling bearing without a cage in which the sum of the clearances between the rolling elements in each row is less than the diameter of the rolling elements and small enough to give satisfactory function of the bearing.

Housing bearing seat   The part of the housing bore which contacts the outside diameter of the bearing.

Housing fit   The amount of interference or clearance between the bearing outside surface and the housing bearing seat.

Inch series bearing   A rolling bearing that conforms to an inch series of a standardized dimension plan.

Internal clearance   See radial and axial internal clearance.

Lateral travel   See end play.

Life   For an individual rolling bearing, the number of revolutions (or hours at some given constant speed) that the bearing runs before the first evidence of fatigue develops in the material of either the rings (or washer) or any of the rolling elements.

Load rating   See basic dynamic radial (axial) load rating.

Lubrication groove   A continuous recess in a bearing or housing to permit relubrication.

Lubrication hole   A hole in the bearing rings to provide lubricant to the rolling elements.

Median life   The life attained or exceeded by 50 percent of a group of apparently identical rolling bearings operating under the same conditions (L_{50}).

Metric series bearing   A rolling bearing that conforms to a metric series of a standardized dimension plan.

Minimum life   See rating life.

Multirow bearing   A rolling bearing with more than two rows of rolling elements supporting load in the same direction. It is preferable to specify the number of rows and type of bearing, for example "four row cylindrical roller radial bearing."

Needle roller   A cylindrical roller of small diameter with a large ratio of length to diameter. It is generally accepted that the length is between 3 and 10 times the diameter, which does not usually exceed 5 mm. The ends of a needle roller may be any one of several shapes.

Needle roller bearing   An antifriction bearing with needle rollers as rolling elements.

Nonseparable bearing   A rolling bearing in which neither bearing ring can be freely separated.

Outside diameter   The outer ring outside diameter (OD) of a radial bearing or the housing washer outside diameter of a thrust bearing.

Pillow block   An assembly comprising a radial-type bearing and a bearing housing which has a base with bolt holes for mounting on a support parallel with the bearing shaft.

Pitch diameter, rolling elements   The diameter of the pitch circle generated by the center of a rolling element as it traverses the bearing's axis of rotation.

Pocket   See cage pocket.

Preload   Force applied on a bearing, for example, by axial adjustment against another bearing, before the "useful" load is applied (external preload), or force induced in a bearing by raceway and rolling element dimensions resulting in "negative clearance" (internal preload).

Raceway   The surface of a load-supporting part of a rolling bearing, suitably prepared as a rolling track for the rolling elements.

Radial bearing   A rolling bearing designed to support primarily radial load, having a nominal contact angle between 0 and 45° inclusive. Principal parts are inner ring, outer ring, and rolling elements with or without a cage.

Radial internal clearance   For a single-row, radial contact bearing, this is the average outer ring raceway diameter, minus the average inner ring raceway diameter, minus twice the rolling element diameter.

Radial load   A load acting in a direction perpendicular to the bearing axis.

Radial play   See radial internal clearance.

Rating life   The rating life of a group of apparently identical bearings is the life in millions of revolutions that 90 percent of the group will complete or exceed (L_{10}).

Retainer   See cage.

Ring   An annular part of a radial rolling bearing incorporating one or more raceways.

Roller bearing   An antifriction bearing with rollers as rolling elements.

Sealed bearing   A rolling bearing that is fitted with a seal on one or both sides of the bearing.

Self-aligning bearing   A bearing with built-in compensation for shaft or housing deflection or misalignment.

Self-contained bearing   See nonseparable bearing.

Separable bearing   A bearing assembly that may be separated completely or partially into its component parts.

Separator   See cage.

Shaft bearing seat   The portion of the shaft on which the bearing is mounted.

Shaft fit   The amount of interference or clearance between the bearing inside diameter and the shaft bearing seat diameter.

Shield   A circular part fixed to one bearing ring to cover the interspace, but not in contact with the other ring.

Single-row bearing   A bearing having only one row of rolling elements.

Special bearing   A bearing not meeting the requirements of standard or established line bearings.

Spherical (radial) roller bearing   An internally self-aligning, radial rolling bearing with convex or concave rolling elements to accommodate misalignment.

Spherical roller thrust bearing   An antifriction thrust bearing using spherical rollers as rolling elements.

Standard bearing   An antifriction bearing conforming to ABMA (American Bearing Manufacturers Association), "General Boundary Plans of Metric and Inch Dimensions."

Static equivalent radial (axial) load   The calculated static radial or static centric thrust load that, if applied to a bearing, would cause the same total permanent deformation at the most heavily stressed rolling element and raceway contact as that which occurs under an actual condition of loading.

Static load   A load acting on a nonrotating bearing.

Tapered roller   A roller with one end smaller than the other. The general shape is that of a truncated cone.

Thrust bearing   A rolling bearing designed to support primarily axial load, having a nominal contact angle of greater than 45° up to and including 90°. Principal parts are shaft washer, housing washer, and rolling elements with or without cage.

Thrust load   A load acting in a direction parallel with the bearing axis.

Washer (thrust bearing)   An annular part of a thrust rolling bearing incorporating one or more raceways.

INTRODUCTION

Antifriction (rolling-element) bearings are used wherever the reduction of friction is required at the interface of dynamic and static components in machinery. A principal advantage of these bearings is their ability to operate at friction levels considerably lower than those of plain or oil-film bearings, while maintaining coefficients of friction at start-up that are close to those in normal operation. Favorable operating characteristics resulting from these lower friction levels are higher operational speeds, lower operational temperatures, and reduced operational torque (thus reduced power consumption).

The complement of rolling elements in antifriction bearings comprises balls or rollers (or even a combination of both in some special designs). In concept, the balls or rollers are arranged within a bearing primarily to support either pure radial or pure thrust loading, but they sometimes have the capability to accomplish both.

Bearings usually consist of four essential components: the inner ring and outer ring with their raceways; a complement of rolling elements (balls or rollers); and a cage, retainer, or separator. In operation, the hardened and ground surfaces of the raceways form the track for the rolling elements (load-supporting members) to follow while transmitting load from the dynamic members of an assembly to the stationary members. Many bearings are also designed with integral shields or seals to allow the bearings to be prelubricated and to protect the rolling elements from contamination. Bearings are often supplied in housed units for simplified mounting.

APPLICATION INFORMATION

Bearing Life

The life of a bearing is expressed as the number of revolutions or the number of hours at a given speed for which the bearing will operate before any evidence of fatigue develops on the rolling elements or the raceways. Life may vary from one bearing to another, but stabilizes into a predictable pattern when considering a large group of the same size and type of bearings. The *rating life* of a group of such bearings is the number of hours or revolutions (at a given constant speed and load) that 90 percent of the tested bearings will exceed before the first evidence of fatigue develops. This is called L_{10} life or *minimum life.*

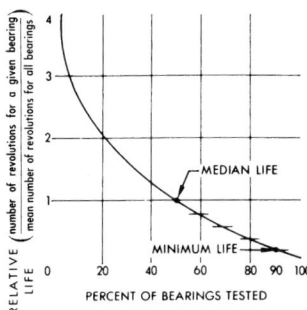

FIGURE 2-1   Median life curve.

Median Life.   The results of testing a large group of ball or roller bearings may be graphically illustrated. The distribution curve shown is obtained by plotting relative life vs percent of bearings tested (see Fig. 2-1). From the curve in Fig. 2-1 it is apparent that the median L_{50} life is approximately five times the minimum life. About 50 percent of the bearings will exceed the median life. Since it is not possible to predict the exact life of a single bearing, a safety factor must be allowed to minimize the chances of early failure.

The cost of replacing a bearing plus the expense of machine downtime may greatly exceed the relatively low cost of the bearing. Therefore, most designers prefer to use the L_{10} minimum life as a basis for design. In some applications where safety or maintenance economy is not critical and low initial bearing cost is desirable, the median-life value may be used.

Life-and-Load Relationship.   Empirical calculations and experimental data point to a predictable relationship between bearing load and life. This relationship may be expressed by formulas. In these empirical formulas the bearing life is found to vary inversely as the applied load to an exponential power. The assigned value of the exponent depends upon the basic type of rolling element. For all types of roller bearings the formula is

$$\text{Life} = \left(\frac{\text{basic dynamic capacity}}{\text{load}} \right)^{3.33} 10^6 \text{ revolutions}$$

For all types of ball bearings the formula is

$$\text{Life} = \left(\frac{\text{basic dynamic capacity}}{\text{load}} \right)^3 10^6 \text{ revolutions}$$

Ring Rotation Factors (RF).   The basic dynamic load rating, often referred to as *dynamic capacity,* of a radial bearing is based on the inner ring rotating with respect to the applied load. The bearing dynamic capacity does not have to be downgraded when the outer ring rotates. If the inner ring or outer ring rotates with respect to load, the rotation factor is 1.0.

Effect of Load.   It is also evident from the exponential character of the basic life-load relationships, that for any given speed, a change in load may have a substantial effect on the life. For a roller bearing, if the load is doubled, the life is reduced to one-tenth its former calculated duration. Similarly, if the load is halved, the life is increased tenfold. For a ball bearing, if the load is doubled, the life is reduced to one-eighth its former value. Likewise, if the load is reduced one-half, the life is increased eightfold.

Effect of Speed.   The preceding expressions are independent of the speed of the bearing. If bearing life is measured in hours, an increase in speed results in a decrease in hours of life. The number of revolutions per unit time determines the hours of life available before the fatigue limit of the bearing is reached. If the speed is doubled, the hours of life are halved. Conversely, if the speed is reduced by 50 percent, the hours of life will be doubled.

The limiting speed of a bearing is dependent on factors such as bearing type, application loads, mounting arrangement, and lubrication conditions. This will be discussed in a later section.

Selection of Bearing Type

Selection of bearing type is made after the general design concept of the machine has been established and the magnitude of the loads and speeds estimated. Special conditions can directly affect bearing operation and must be considered. These include ambient or localized temperatures, shock or vibration, dirt or abrasive contamination, difficulty in obtaining accurate alignment, space limitations, need for shaft rigidity, and reliability of lubrication.

Selection of the proper type of bearing is not an exact science. The fields of application for many types of bearings overlap, and the value of experience in bearing applications cannot be overemphasized. Each type of bearing, however, has inherent features, which determine its relative suitability for a specific application. Careful analysis of these features and familiarization with the fundamental characteristics of each type of bearing will help in selecting the proper bearing.

As an aid to experienced designers and inexperienced bearing users alike, the similarities and differences of ball and roller bearings are outlined. Table 2-1 shows the relative operating characteristics of each cataloged bearing type.

Ball Bearings vs. Roller Bearings.   Using balls as the rolling elements in bearings offers certain performance advantages. Most of the advantages of ball bearings are derived from the small areas of contact between the ball and raceways.

Ball bearings may be operated at higher speeds, with less internal friction and less heat generation. They have a greater inherent ability to accommodate slight misalignment. Under certain conditions of combined loading, ball bearings occupy less space than required for roller bearings of the same bore size.

Rollers are not limited to a single geometric shape. There are several types, such as tapered rollers, spherical rollers, and cylindrical rollers. For a given load and diameter of rolling element, rollers transmit load through a larger contact area than do balls. This allows roller bearings to support greater loads and accommodate far more shock than ball bearings of equivalent size. For a given applied load, contact area stresses for roller bearings are lower than for ball bearings, and, therefore, they produce lower elastic deformation. Since the larger contact areas create more friction, permissible operating speeds for roller bearings are lower than those for ball bearings.

Selection of Bearing Size

Once the designer selects a suitable type of bearing for a set of specific conditions, the size of the bearing is determined. In many cases more than one bearing type will satisfy the operating conditions. In these instances the designer should determine the most suitable size of each type considered and make the final selection on the basis of mounting simplicity, space considerations, and overall economy.

The basic parameters affecting the choice of bearing size are radial load, thrust load, speed, required life, ring rotation, and shock or vibration conditions. Other factors such as misalignment, abnormal temperature, contamination, and poor lubrication will seriously reduce service life, but their exact effect cannot be determined. These factors should be eliminated by proper mounting design rather than by attempting to estimate their effect on bearing life.

TABLE 2-1 Relative Operating Characteristics

Bearing type/style		Radial capacity	Thrust capacity	Limiting speed	Resistance to deflection	
					Radial	Axial
Ball radial						
Conrad		M	M2	H	M	L
Maximum-capacity		M+	M1, L1	M	M+	L+
Angular-contact		M	M1+	H	M	M
Roller radial						
Cylindrical	2 flanges	H	N	M+	H	N
	3 flanges	H	L2	M+	H	NR
	4 flanges	H	L2	M+	H	NR
Journal	No flange	H+	N	L	H+	N
Spherical		H	M2	M	H−	M
Tapered roller						
Single-row		H−	M1+	M	M−	M
Single-row, steep angle		M+	H1	M−	M	H
Double-row		H	M2+	M	H	M
Double-row, steep angle		M+	H2	M−	M	H
Four-row		H+	H2	M−	H+	H
Thrust						
Angular-contact ball		L+	H1−	M	L	H−
Ball		N	H1	M−	N	H
Cylindrical roller		N	H1+	L	N	H+
Spherical roller		N	H1+	L	N	H+
Tapered roller		N	H1+	L	N	H+

NR   Not Recommended
N   None
L   Low
M   Moderate
H   High
1   One Direction
2   Both Directions

Limiting Speeds. The ability of a bearing to operate at high speeds is dependent upon the rate at which generated heat is dissipated. Maximum speed is governed by bearing type, size, and load; ambient temperature; and type of lubricant.

The geometric design of a bearing and the method of positioning the rolling elements basically determine the coefficient of friction. Since frictional losses are proportional to the peripheral speed, it follows that the smaller the bearing the greater the speed at which it may operate. A common presentation of limiting speeds used by many bearing manufacturers is either the $P_d N$ value, where P_d is the bearing design pitch diameter in mm and N is the operating speed in revolutions per minute, or a dN value, where d is the bearing bore in mm and N is the speed in rpm. Typical values are shown in Table 2-2.

Elastic deformation of the raceways and rolling elements is increased by heavy loads, and this creates additional heat, thereby limiting the allowable speed.

Ambient temperature may affect the rate of heat dissipation. Applications having a high ambient temperature require careful selection of the method of lubrication.

The type of lubricant is a basic criterion for establishing limiting speeds. Lubricants with high viscosity offer more frictional resistance; therefore, oil is preferable to grease for higher speeds. Modern grease formulations, however, are allowing operational speeds in the 1 to 2 million $P_d N$ range in selected applications, notably high precision spindles. The use of circulating oil or oil mist can allow higher speed limits than oil-bath or grease lubrication. The bearing manufacturer should be consulted for limiting speeds of bearings in specific applications.

Fits and Shaft and Housing.   To ensure the full utilization of bearing capacity under operating conditions, it is important to have the proper fit between inner ring and shaft, and outer ring and housing. The tolerances to which the bearing is made are standardized, so desired fits may be obtained by controlling the dimensions and tolerances for the shaft and housing.

Normally, the problem in fit determination is to make the rotating ring of the bearing and its associated shaft or housing rotate as a single unit by using an interference fit. The fit of the nonrotating ring should be loose, with minimum clearance, for ease of assembly and axial movement in the housing.

The amount of interference fit employed should not create in the bearing rings excessive stress that might result in early fatigue failure. Under conditions of light load, the interference fit can be small. As the loads increase or shock loading is introduced, the interference must be increased so that no clearance exists and none can be induced by the load. This is the only effective means of preventing "creep." As a rule, axial clamping cannot be relied on to prevent creep since the clamping force must be excessively high. Thus, the heavier the load, the tighter the fit.

The degree of fit is designated in the American Bearing Manufacturers Association (ABMA) tolerance system. This tolerance system is also in accordance with that adopted by the American National Standards Institute (ANSI). These various fits apply to all ball thrust bearings and radial bearings except tapered roller bearings. (For tapered roller bearings, an adaptation of the recommended ABMA fitting practice has been made for the convenience of designers.)

Special Materials for Bearings.   The standard materials for ball and roller bearings are usually ANSI 52100 or equivalent "ball bearing steel" or case carburized steels. Industrial demands for special bearings to meet abnormal service requirements spur the continual search for new and improved bearing materials. High temperatures, corrosive atmospheres, massive size, marginal lubrication, complex design, and space and weight limitations are typical abnormal requirements.

Conventional bearing steels are often inadequate when these problems are present. Sustained high operating temperatures reduce hardness, wear resistance, yield strength and, therefore, bearing life. Conventional bearing steels also lack resistance to the oxidation that takes place at elevated temperatures.

Materials such as 440-C stainless or corrosion-resistant coated steels may be required for severely adverse environments. For extremely high speeds and high temperatures, special alloy steels and materials such as metallic carbides and ceramics are used.

The combination of bearing size, complexity of design, and space and weight limitations can be a governing factor in the selection of bearing material. For example, a large-diameter, thin-section bearing with integral gear teeth and bolt holes would require a material that could be selectively hardened.

Monel and beryllium copper are not as hardenable as bearing steels and are nonmagnetic and resist saltwater corrosion. These qualities make them excellent materials for marine applications.

Although low-carbon steels are the most popular, a variety of other materials is also used for bearing cages. Molded nylon, synthetic resin-impregnated fabrics, and bronze/brass are popular in the normal temperature ranges. High-performance polymers, carbon steel, certain stainless steels, and iron-silicon bronze are used for higher temperatures.

Mounting Design

Mounting design varies widely, depending upon the type of bearing used and the requirements of the application. Selection of bearing type and mounting design are closely related since many cases exist where selection of bearing type is influenced by mounting design considerations.

TABLE 2-2 Limiting Speeds

Radial ball and roller bearings P.D. × N values (PD* in millimeters × R.P.M.)

Bearing type series	Cage type	ABEC-1 RBEC-1 Grease	ABEC-1 RBEC-1 Oil†	AFBMA Class 2,4 Grease	AFBMA Class 2,4 Oil	ABEC-3 Grease	ABEC-3 Oil†	ABEC-3 Oil mist	ABEC 5 and 7 Grease	ABEC 5 and 7 Circulating oil	ABEC 5 and 7 Oil mist
		Ball bearings									
Single row											
Nonfilling slot 9300K, 9100K, 200K	Ball piloted molded nylon (PRB)	250,000	300,000	—	—	250,000	300,000	—	300,000	300,000	300,000
	Pressed steel, bronze	300,000	350,000	—	—	300,000	350,000	—	350,000	400,000	450,000
300K	Ring piloted molded reinforced nylon (PRC)	350,000	400,000	—	—	350,000	450,000	—	400,000	550,000	650,000
XLS and variations	Composition (CR)										
Filling slot 200W and variations, 300W and variations	Ball piloted molded nylon (PRB)	250,000	250,000	—	—	250,000	—	—	—	—	—
	Pressed steel	250,000	300,000	—	—	300,000	—	—	—	—	—
Angular contact	Ball piloted pressed steel, molded nylon (PRB)	250,000	300,000	—	—	300,000	350,000	—	—	—	—
7200WN	Ring piloted bronze (MBR), ball piloted bronze (MBR)	300,000	400,000	—	—	—	—	—	—	—	—
7300WN	Ring piloted molded reinforced nylon (PRC)	350,000	400,000	—	—	350,000	400,000	—	—	—	—
Angular contact—extra precision 2M9300WI, WO, 2M200WI, 2M300WI, 2M9100WI 2MM9300WI, WO, 2MM9100WI 2MM200WI, 2MM300WI	Ring piloted composition (CR or PRC)	350,000	400,000	—	—	750,000	1,000,000	1,200,000	1,000,000	1,400,000	1,700,000
Double row 5200	Ball piloted molded nylon (PRB), pressed steel	250,000	300,000	—	—	—	—	—	—	—	—
5300	Ball piloted bronze (BR)										

Cylindrical roller bearings

RU, RIU RN, RIN RJ, RIJ RF, RIF RT, RIT RP, RIP 5200WS	Bronze	150,000	300,000	—	—	—	—	—	—
	Roller piloted pressed steel	150,000	300,000	—	—	—	—	—	—

Spherical roller bearings

239, 230, 240	Pressed steel	150,000	300,000	—	—	—	—	—	—
231, 241, 222	Bronze								
232, 213, 223	Molded reinforced nylon								
233									

Tapered roller bearings

TS, TSS	Pressed steel	—	—	150,000	300,000	—	—	—	—
TDI,	Bronze								
TDO, TDOC, TDOD									

* $\dfrac{\text{Bore} + \text{O.D.}}{2}$

† For oil bath lubrication, oil level should be maintained between ⅓ and ½ from the bottom of the lowest ball.

Note: Single or double normal contact (P or PP) sealed bearings should not exceed 350,000 PN.

Most applications require the use of more than one bearing on a shaft. Two identical bearings or a combination of different types and sizes may be used on a common shaft. The advantages of each combination should be evaluated by the designer in selecting bearings.

A *fixed*-bearing mounting locates the shaft and carries any thrust loads that exist in the application. A *float*-bearing mounting accommodates relative axial movement between the shaft and housing. Various combinations of these two basic mountings are used:

1. Fixed-float mounting
2. Fixed-fixed (or opposed) mounting
3. Float-float mounting

The fixed and float arrangement may be necessary: (1) when thermal expansion or contraction of the shaft with respect to the housing occurs, (2) when separate housings are required for two or more bearings on a common shaft, or (3) to optimize bearing loading.

The fixed and float combination offers many desirable features for heavy industrial equipment. The upper half of Fig. 2-2 shows a typical arrangement. The axial location is accomplished through the fixed bearing since it is clamped rigidly to the shaft and the housing. A two-row tapered roller bearing is shown in the fixed position. However, other radial bearings capable of taking thrust loads in both directions and applied radial loads may be used. For the float position the cylindrical roller bearing shown supports relatively heavy loads and permits free axial displacement. A type TDO or TNA tapered roller bearing or a spherical roller bearing may be used if the sliding pressures between the outer ring and the housing bore are not excessive.

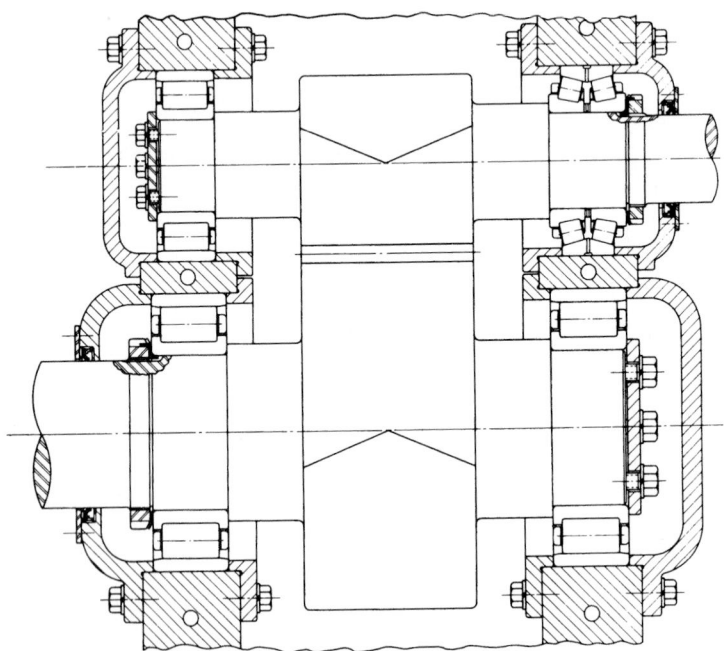

FIGURE 2-2   Typical fixed- and float-bearing arrangements.

The lower half of Fig. 2-2 demonstrates the float-float mounting. A pair of cylindrical roller bearings permits the entire shaft to float. A herringbone gear is used and the floating shaft allows the gears to mesh properly. The arrangement shown permits manufacturing economies since gear axial alignment is assured without very accurate machining or shimming of the bottom housing cover and end plate. A pair of type TDO or TNA tapered roller bearings or a pair of spherical roller bearings, not fixed axially in their housings, may be used if the sliding pressures are not excessive.

Figure 2-3 illustrates a typical mounting arrangement for a rotating housing where the bearings will be subjected to a radial load with a requirement for axial rigidity. A gap is left between the clamping ring and the face of the inner ring to provide for tolerance accumulation. Use of a spacer between the faces of the outer rings allows through-boring of the housing. Although maximum-capacity (types BH or BIH) ball bearings are shown, Conrad (types BC or BIC) ball radial bearings could also be used when there are moderate loads. Applications such as flywheels or spur gear hubs require a tight fit of the outer ring in the housing with a loose fit of the inner ring on the shaft.

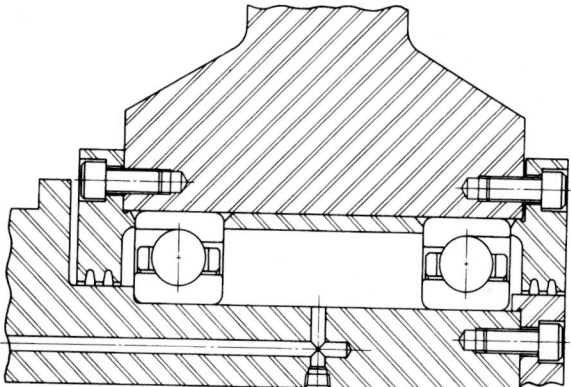

FIGURE 2-3   Typical fixed-fixed bearing arrangement.

Seals and Closures.   Seals are used to protect the bearing from contamination as well as to retain the lubricant. There are three basic types of seals:

1. *Contact seals.*   The most common types for prelubricated bearings are integral rubber lip or felt contact seals. For open-type bearings, external commercial cartridge seals or packings are mounted outboard of the bearings. These are usually standard components made by several manufacturers.

2. *Shields* and *labyrinth seals.*   These are noncontact seals with slight clearance between stationary and rotating members depending on the lubricant to effect a frictionless closure.

3. *Slinger seals.*   External types depend on centrifugal force to fling foreign matter away from the shaft. Internal slinger-type seals are used to distribute lubricant within the housing.

The basic types of integral bearing seals and end closure arrangements are shown in Figs. 2-4*a* and 2-4*b*, respectively.

Types DD and LL   Integral shields and labyrinth seals. These constructions are usually pressed steel members, which are designed with close clearances between the fixed and rotating parts of the bearing. Both designs provide lower bearing torques than contact seals and are usable for high-speed and high-temperature applications.

Type PP   Integral contact seals. These constructions usually consist of a synthetic rubber lip seal or a felt seal held by a pressed steel member that is fixed in the bearing outer ring. The rubber lip seal is a popular design for prelubricated standard width ball bearings.

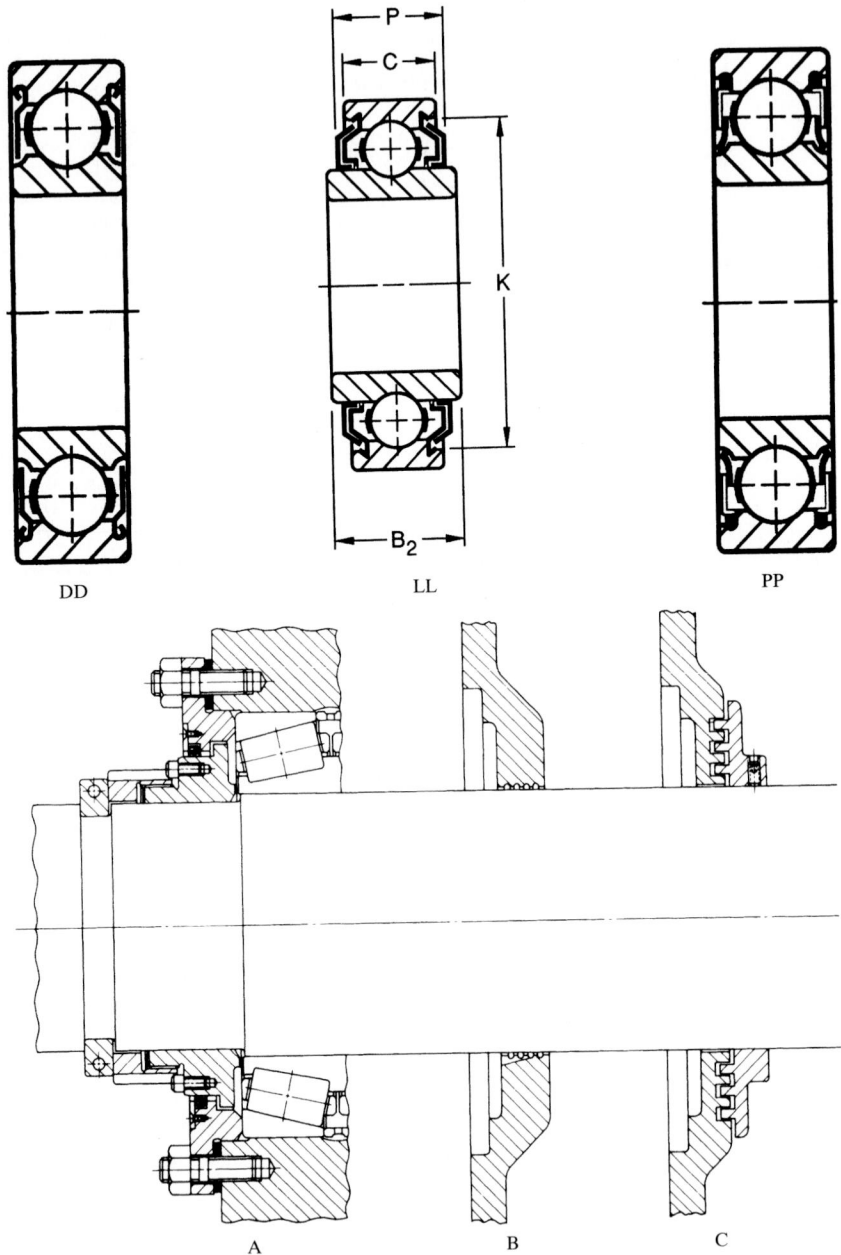

FIGURE 2-4a Integral seals and shields.

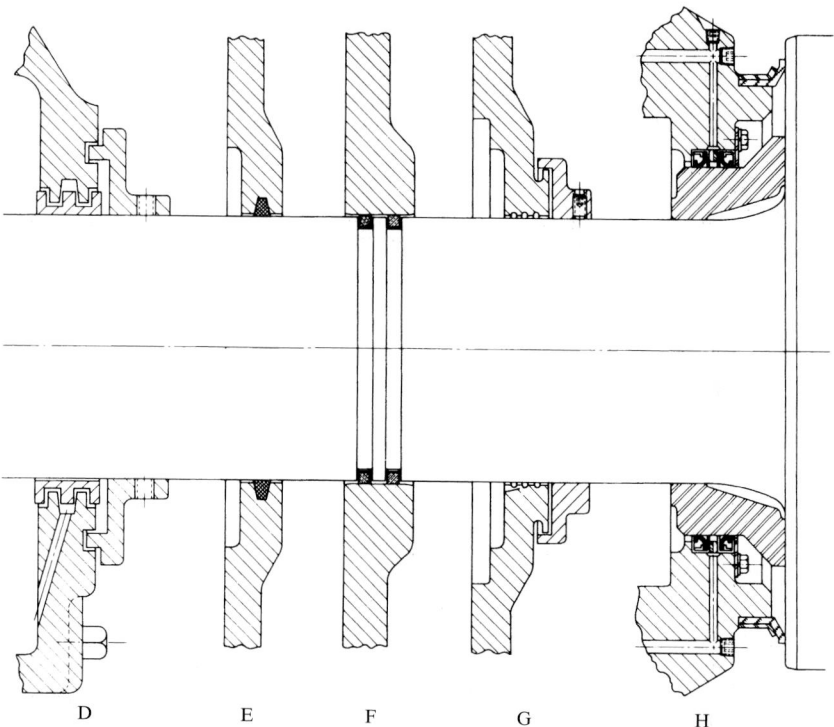

D   E   F   G   H

FIGURE 2-4b   Basic sealing arrangements.

Type A   Commercial seals. The contact lip may be synthetic rubber or leather, spring-backed for more positive sealing. Consult manufacturers' literature for shaft finish and limiting speeds. May be used for either grease or oil.

Type B   Annular grooves. Shown here with drain slot at bottom, these may be in either the shaft or the housing, or in both. The effectiveness is increased by keeping the running clearance small and by using multiple grooves. Used for oil grease lubrication.

Type C   Axial labyrinth seals. Do not require a split housing. Clearance must be allowed for axial movement. Effective for abrasive environment. Use for oil or grease.

Type D   Radial labyrinth seals. Used with a split housing or end cap. Bore of grooved sealing ring is slightly larger than shaft, allowing it to float axially. Angular surface of housing groove reduces pumping action. Suitable for oil or grease.

Type E   Felt seals. Provide medium effectiveness at low speeds but lose their effectiveness at high speeds and high temperatures. In most cases, it functions as a contact seal, but after "wearing in" often functions as a simple close-clearance annulus seal. Not suitable for an abrasive environment. Use for grease lubrication.

Type F   Piston ring seals. Modification of the labyrinth seal. The piston rings are stationary and are mounted under radial compression in the housing. The split rings have rabbeted joints. Clearances between the rings and grooves are slight. This seal accommodates axial displacement. It is easy to install or remove, and can be used with a spacer or in shaft grooves as shown. Accepting deflection and misalignment, it offers a relatively positive closure augmented by a grease annulus. A particularly effective seal for an abrasive environment, it is suitable for grease and oil.

Type G Combination annular groove-axial labyrinth seals. Annular grooves retain lubricant in the housing. The external flinger serves as a shield and flings contaminants away from the seal. It is suitable for grease and oil.

Type H Triple combination of lip contact seals. Two commercial seals are mounted and opposed with a spacer in between to allow relubrication of the contact surfaces. A face contact seal is also used to prevent the entrance of contaminants. It is used primarily for grease.

PHYSICAL DESCRIPTION

Ball Bearings

Radial Ball Bearings. There are three major types of radial ball bearings with a metric bore range of 10 to 320 mm and an inch bore range of ⁵⁄₃₂ in to 40 in normally listed in bearing catalogs.

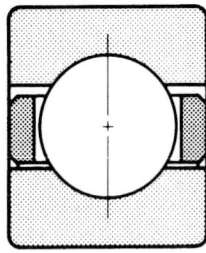

FIGURE 2-5 Conrad-type ball bearing.

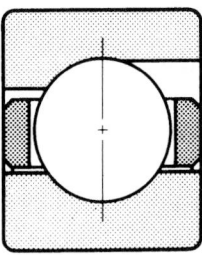

FIGURE 2-6 Maximum-capacity-type ball bearing.

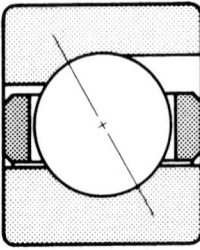

FIGURE 2-7 Angular-contact-type ball bearing.

Radial

    Conrad (see Fig. 2-5)

    Maximum capacity (loading groove) (see Fig. 2-6)

Angular contact

    Single row (see Fig. 2-7)

Wide inner

    Locking collar (see Fig. 2-8*a* and *b*)

    Setscrew (see Fig. 2-8*c*)

Selection of the proper type of ball bearing is determined by consideration of the direction and magnitude of the bearing load. Ball bearings are particularly suited to high-speed operation because they have a lower coefficient of friction than roller bearings.

Figure 2-5 shows the Conrad, or deep-groove radial, ball-bearing type. Although it is primarily a radial bearing, it is capable of handling moderately high thrust loads from either direction and operating at relatively high speeds. The bearing rings have symmetrical, deep-grooved raceways without ball-loading grooves or a counterbore. The raceways are precision-ground to conform closely to ball curvature, consistent with minimum friction, maximum capacity, and practical manufacturing techniques. Balls are selected for uniformity to ensure optimum internal load distribution. The bearing utilizes the maximum number of balls which can be inserted between the raceways by eccentrically displacing the inner and outer rings. Balls are spaced by a cage (a ball-piloted cold rolled steel design is shown here). For higher speeds, and when other

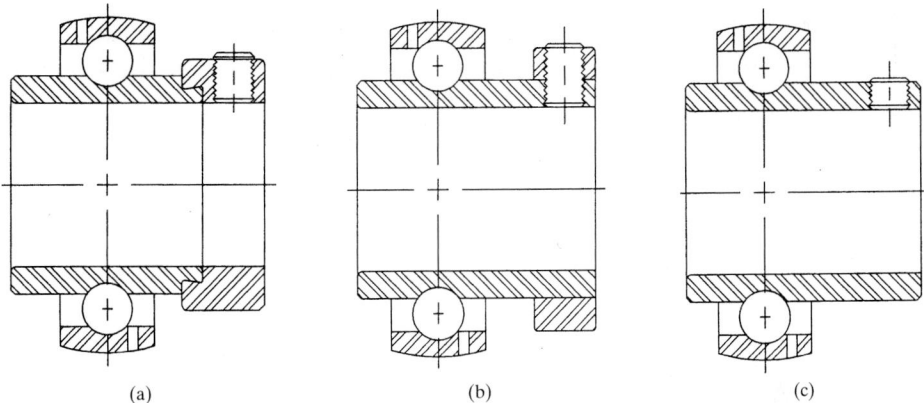

FIGURE 2-8   Bearing with (*a*) eccentric locking collar, (*b*) concentric locking collar, (*c*) set-screws in the inner ring.

operating conditions warrant, the cage may be ring-piloted and made of other materials such as bronze or polymers. The nonseparable bearing construction facilitates handling.

The maximum-capacity ball bearing shown in Fig. 2-6 has the greatest radial capacity obtainable in a single-row ball bearing with cage, but because of the ball-loading grooves in the inner and outer rings, it has limited thrust loading in both directions. This type of bearing may be identical to a deep-groove radial (Conrad) bearing, but the ball-loading grooves allow an increased number of balls to be inserted into the bearing. This increased number of balls results in a higher theoretical radial load rating compared to a comparably sized Conrad bearing, thus leading to the term "maximum capacity."

The design of angular-contact ball bearings, as shown in Fig. 2-7, is similar to the maximum-capacity type, but the outer ring is counterbored; this substantially reduces the raceway shoulder on one side. The counterbore allows a maximum complement of balls in a one-piece, machined-bronze cage to be assembled in the bearing. The outer ring is thermally expanded and slipped over the cage, ball, and inner-ring assembly. After cooling, the bearing is nonseparable. This design allows the bearing to resist heavier thrust loads and minimizes axial deflection under load in one direction only against the full shoulder side of the bearing.

Angular-contact bearings can be furnished in matched pairs for duplex mounting (Fig. 2-9). When the bearings supplied for opposed mounting are placed together, there will be a small gap between the inner rings (type DB) or outer rings (type DF) before clamping. After clamping together, an internal preload is introduced in the set which increases the axial and radial rigidity of the duplexed pair. When supplied for tandem mounting (type DT), very heavy unidirectional thrust loads may be almost equally distributed among the bearings of the set. Details of application for DB and DF pairs should be submitted to the engineering department of the bearing manufacturer for preload recommendations.

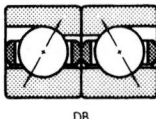
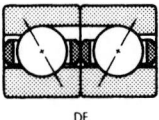
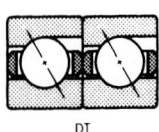

DB   DF   DT

FIGURE 2-9   Duplex mounting of matched-pair angular-contact ball bearings.

Radial Ball Bearings with Locking Devices. The internal constructions of these bearings are basically the same as deep-race, single-row radial types with ability to carry radial, thrust, and combined loads. However, the bearings have a wide inner ring design that allows them to be slip-fitted and locked on straight shafts without shoulders, lockouts, or adapters. The most widely used locking devices are the cam (eccentric) locking collar, the concentric setscrew locking collar and setscrews in an extended end of the bearing inner ring (see Fig. 2-8).

These bearings are made with either straight or spherical OD outer rings, are usually pre-lubricated with grease and have double integral contact or labyrinth seals or shields.

Radial Ball Bearing Housing Units. Many types of housing units with wide inner ring bearings are available. The four most common basic housing constructions are pillow blocks, flanged cartridges, cylindrical cartridges, and take-up units (see Fig. 2-10). These units are

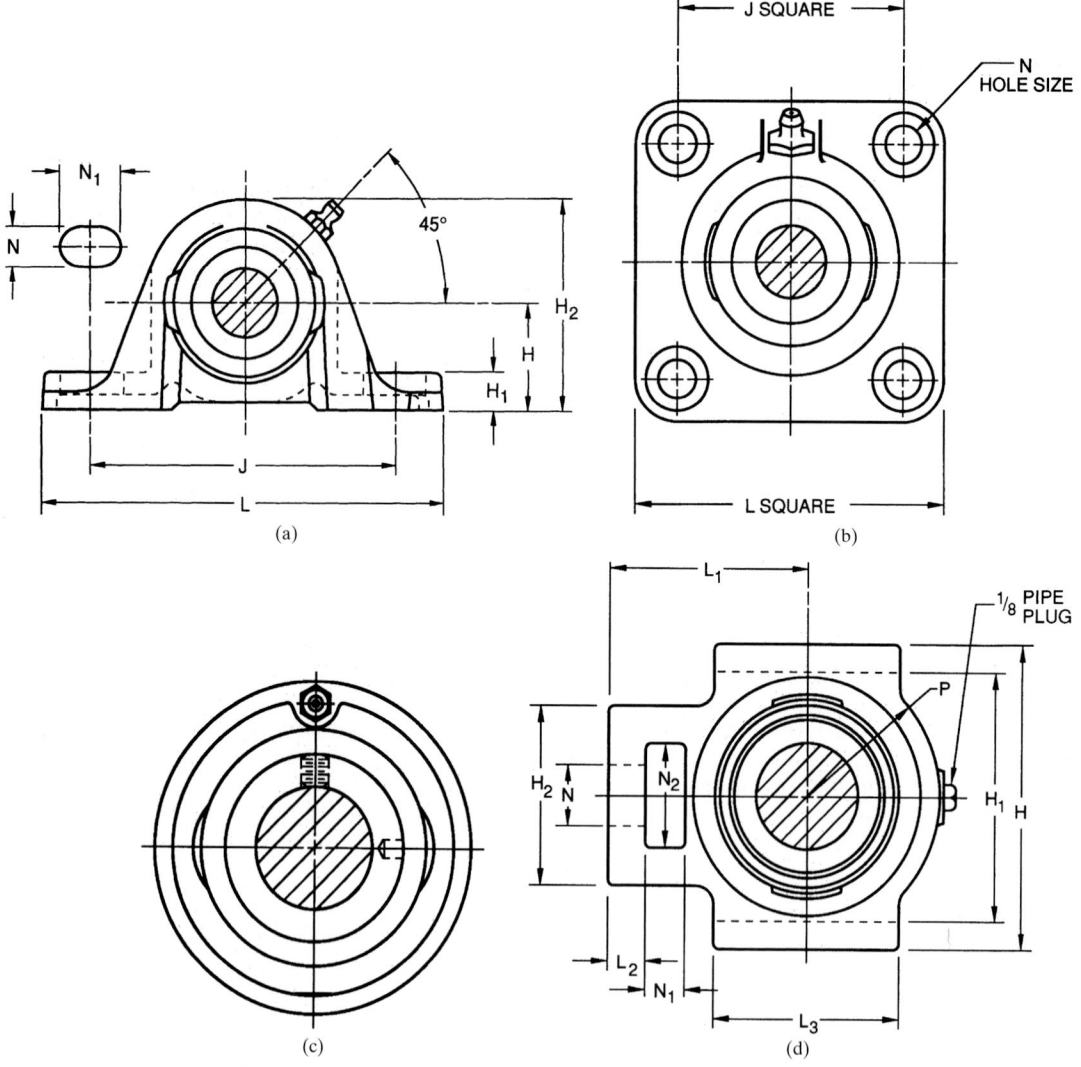

FIGURE 2-10 Ball bearing housing units. (*a*) Pillow block; (*b*) flange cartridge; (*c*) cylindrical cartridge; (*d*) take-up unit.

usually assembled with prelubricated, double-sealed wide inner bearings that incorporate a self-aligning feature to allow the bearing to be aligned at mounting. The housings are generally made of cast gray or malleable iron, pressed steel, rubber or other materials and are usually designed to permit bearing relubrication.

Ball Thrust Bearings.   Ball thrust bearings are used for lighter loads and higher speeds than roller thrust bearings.

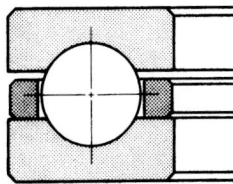

FIGURE 2-11   Ball thrust bearing.

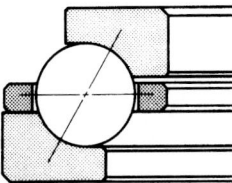

FIGURE 2-12   Angular contact ball thrust bearing.

Type TVB ball thrust bearings (Fig. 2-11) are separable, and consist of two hardened and ground steel washers with grooved raceways and a cage that separates and retains precision-ground and -lapped balls. The standard cage material is bronze, but this may vary according to the requirements of the application. Type TVB bearings provide axial rigidity in one direction, so using them to support radial loads is not recommended. They are very easily mounted. Usually the rotating washer is shaft mounted. The stationary washer should be housed with sufficient outside diameter clearance to allow the bearing to assume its proper operating position. In most sizes both washers have the same bore and outside diameter. The housing must be designed to clear the outside diameter of the rotating washer, and it is necessary to step the shaft diameter to clear the bore of the stationary washer.

Type TVL (Fig. 2-12) bearings are separable angular-contact ball bearings designed primarily for unidirectional thrust loads The angular-contact design, however, will accommodate combined radial and thrust loads since the loads are transmitted angularly through the balls. The bearing has two hardened and ground steel rings with ball grooves and a one-piece bronze cage that spaces the ball complement. Although not strictly an annular ball bearing, the larger ring is called the outer ring, and the smaller the inner ring. Usually, the inner ring is the rotating member and is shaft mounted. The outer ring is normally stationary and should be mounted with outside diameter clearance to allow the bearing to assume its proper operating position. If combined loads exist, the outer ring must be radially located in the housing.

A type TVL bearing should always be operated under thrust load. Normally, this presents no problem as the bearing is usually applied on vertical shafts in oilfield rotary tables and machine-tool indexing tables. If a constant thrust load is not present, it should be imposed by springs or other built-in devices.

Low friction, cool running, and quiet operation are advantages of the type TVL bearing, which may therefore be operated at relatively high speeds. The bearing is also less sensitive to misalignment than other types of rigid thrust bearings.

Roller Bearings

Tapered Roller Bearings.   Tapered roller bearings are generally considered to offer the best support for combinations of heavy radial and thrust loads at moderate speeds.

A single-row tapered roller bearing consists of an inner ring called a *cone,* an outer ring called a *cup,* a bronze or steel cage, and a complement of controlled-contour rollers. In multiple-row tapered roller bearings one or more cones, cups, and cage assemblies may be used.

Tapered rollers and raceways are designed on the geometric principle of a cone (Fig. 2-13). Extensions of the lines of contact between the rollers and the raceways all meet at a common point on the axis of the bearing. The design assures true geometric rolling. The large ends of the tapered rollers are spherically ground to match the spherically ground face on the guiding cone rib. Under load, the nominal pressure exerted between these two ground surfaces accurately positions the rollers within the load zone.

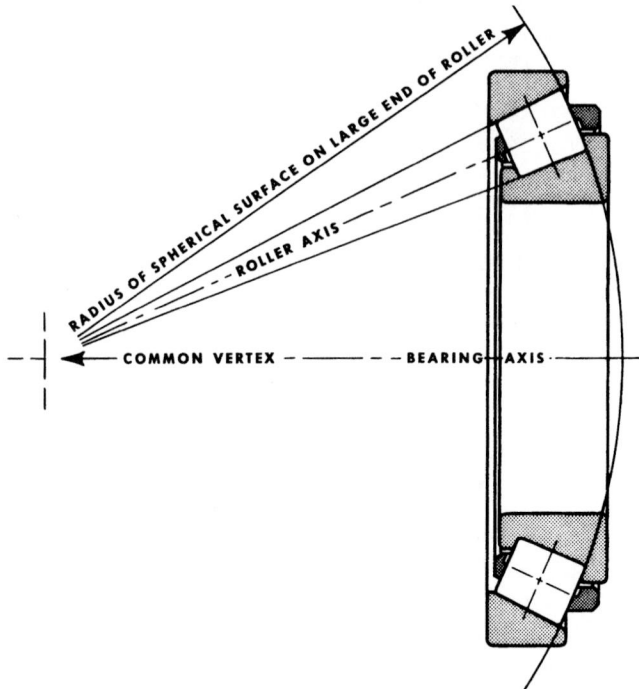

FIGURE 2-13 Geometric principle of tapered roller bearing.

Single-Row Tapered Roller Bearings. There are three types of single-row tapered roller bearings: TS, TSF, and TSS (Fig. 2-14). Each has a cup and a cone with a cage and roller assembly. Type TS serves as the basic design for the others.

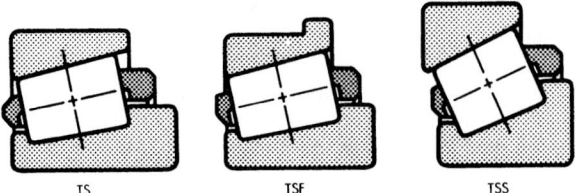

FIGURE 2-14 Single-row tapered bearings.

Since a single-row tapered roller bearing supports thrust loads from one direction only, the preferred mounting is in opposed pairs. The proper internal clearance for the two bearings may be obtained by axial adjustment at the time of assembly.

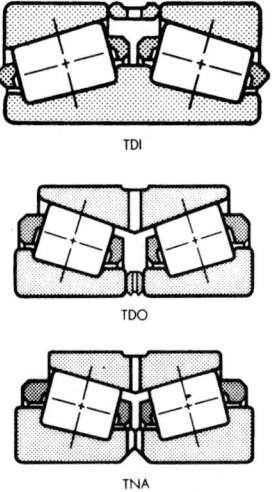

TDI

TDO

TNA

FIGURE 2-15   Two-row tapered roller bearings.

Type TSF bearings are identical with type TS except that the cup of the TSF type incorporates an external flange which, in some mountings, facilitates location and permits economies in design. When through-boring of the housing is advantageous, the use of the type TSF bearing is suggested.

Type TSS bearings are similar to type TS, but have a steeper angle of contact. These bearings are recommended for applications where the thrust load is predominant.

Two-Row Tapered Roller Bearings.   Three basic types of two-row tapered roller bearings are available: TDI, TDO, and TNA (Fig. 2-15). Two-row tapered roller bearings have twice the radial capacity of single-row bearings of the same series and are used in positions where radial loading is too severe for single-row bearings. They have the further advantage that a two-row bearing can take thrust loads in both directions, thus allowing all applied thrust and shaft location to be taken at one position. This often simplifies design and reduces the danger of bearing clearance changes due to axial shaft expansion.

Similar to single-row tapers, steep-angle versions offer greater thrust capacity with reduced radial capacity. These are widely used as backup thrust bearings in rolling mills and other applications where heavy thrust loads are encountered.

The TDI design is such that the contact angles converge as they approach the axis of rotation (see Fig. 2-15). Consequently, use of these bearings will not appreciably increase the rigidity of the shaft mounting, and they should not be used singly on a shaft since they will not resist overturning moments.

In the TDO and TNA, the contact angle lines diverge as they approach the axis of rotation, thus increasing the rigidity of the shaft mounting (see Fig. 2-15). Therefore, these bearings are suited for resisting overturning moments. Due to the increased bearing rigidity, housing bore alignment is somewhat more critical than with TDI styles.

Cylindrical Roller Bearings.   Six standard types of cylindrical roller bearings are shown in Fig. 2-16. All six types have the same roller complements and, consequently, the same capacity for a given size. All types can be mounted with interference fits on either the inner or outer ring, or both. In the latter case, a bearing with increased internal clearance must be specified to provide proper running clearance.

For convenience, bearings are listed according to bore, with both metric and inch bearings in the same figure. Inch bearings are identified by the letter "I" in the type code of the bearing number; thus where RN denotes a particular type of metric bearing, RIN denotes an inch bearing of the same type.

Types RU and RIU have double-ribbed outer and straight inner rings. Types RN and RIN have double-ribbed inner and straight outer rings. The use of either type at one position on a shaft is ideal for accommodating nominal expansion or contraction. The relative axial displacement of one ring to the other occurs with minimum friction while the bearing is rotating. These bearings may be used in two positions for shaft support if other means of axial location are provided.

Types RJ and RIJ have double-ribbed outer and single-ribbed inner rings. Types RF and RIF have double-ribbed inner and single-ribbed outer rings. Both types can support heavy radial loads, as well as light unidirectional thrust loads up to 10 percent of the radial load. The thrust

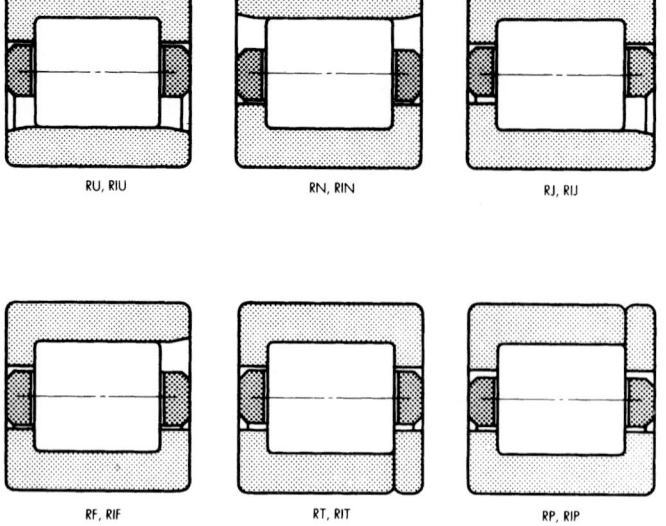

FIGURE 2-16 Standard types of cylindrical roller bearings.

load is transmitted between the diagonally opposed rib faces in a sliding action rather than a rolling action. Thus, when limiting thrust conditions are approached, lubrication can become critical. When thrust loads are very light, these bearings may be used in an opposed mounting to locate the shaft. In such cases, shaft end play should be adjusted at time of assembly.

Types RT and RIT have a double-ribbed outer ring and a single-ribbed inner ring with a loose rib, which allows the bearing to provide axial location in both directions. Types RP and RIP have a double-ribbed inner ring and a single-ribbed outer ring with a loose rib.

Types RT and RP (RIT and RIP) provide heavy radial capacity and light thrust capacity in both directions. Factors governing the thrust capacity are the same as for RF and RJ (RIF and RIJ) bearings.

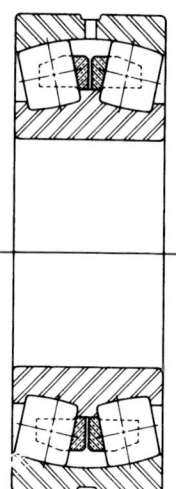

FIGURE 2-17 Self-aligning spherical roller bearing.

A type RT or RP (RIT or RIP) bearing may be used in conjunction with a type RN or RU (RIN or RIU) bearing for applications where axial shaft expansion is anticipated. In such cases the fixed bearing is usually placed nearest the drive end of the shaft to minimize alignment variations in the drive. Shaft end play (or float) is determined by the axial clearance in the bearing.

Spherical Roller Bearings. The self-aligning spherical roller bearing (Fig. 2-17) is a combination radial and thrust bearing designed for taking misalignment under load. When loads are heavy, alignment of housings difficult, and shaft deflections excessive, the use of spherical roller bearings assures best service life results.

With the spherical rollers operating on the spherically shaped outer race, the assembly of the inner ring, retainers, and rollers may take up to ±1½° of misalignment and continue to function with full capacity. High radial load capacity is secured by a large area of roller-to-race contact. Double-direction thrust capacity results from angular location of rollers relative to bearing axis.

Shaft deflections and housing distortions caused by shock loads are compensated for by the internal self-alignment of the free-rolling bearing elements. The binding stresses that limit service life of non-self-aligning bearings cannot develop in spherical roller bearings. The retainers ride on the center flange of the inner ring rather than on the rollers. Unit design and construction make the spherical roller bearing simple to handle at assembly point or during removal for maintenance.

A disassembled view of a spherical roller bearing pillow block is shown in Fig. 2-18. This consists of the pillow block, bearing, adapter, locknut, lockwasher, stabilizing ring, and triple labyrinth seals. The split design allows for ease of inspection and installation. Housings are designed to accommodate either grease or oil lubrication and are easily adapted to circulating oil lubrication systems.

FIGURE 2-18 Spherical roller bearing pillow block.

Because the bearings are self-aligning, shaft misalignment is not considered critical. Standard split pillow blocks are designed to provide static and dynamic alignment. A variety of sealing arrangements are available in addition to the labyrinth seals for more demanding requirements.

Roller Thrust Bearings.   Cylindrical roller thrust bearings withstand heavy loads at relatively moderate speeds. Special design features can be incorporated into the bearing and mounting to attain higher operating speeds. Because loads are usually high, extreme pressure lubricants should be used with roller thrust bearings. Preferably, the lubricant should be introduced at the bearing bore and distributed by centrifugal force.

Type TP cylindrical roller thrust bearing (Fig. 2-19) has two hardened and ground steel washers, with a cage retaining one or more rollers in each pocket. When two or more rollers are used in a pocket they must be of different lengths and placed in staggered positions in adjacent cage pockets to create overlapping roller paths. This prevents wearing grooves in the raceways and prolongs bearing life.

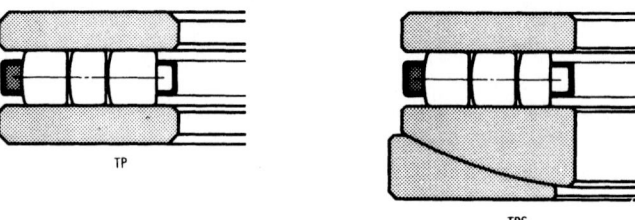

FIGURE 2-19 Cylindrical roller thrust bearings.

Because of the simplicity of their design, TP bearings are economical. Since minor radial displacement of the raceways does not affect the operation of the bearing, its application is relatively simple and often results in manufacturing economies for the user. Shaft and housing seats, however, must be square to the axis of rotation to prevent initial misalignment problems.

Type TPS bearing (Fig. 2-19) is the same as type TP, except one washer is spherically ground to seat against an aligning washer, thus making the bearing adaptable to initial misalignment. Its use is not recommended for operating conditions where alignment is continuously changing (dynamic misalignment).

Type TTHD tapered roller thrust bearing (Fig. 2-20) has an identical pair of hardened and ground steel washers with conical raceways, and a complement of tapered rollers equally spaced by a cage.

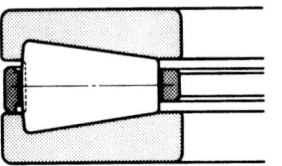

FIGURE 2-20 Tapered roller thrust bearing.

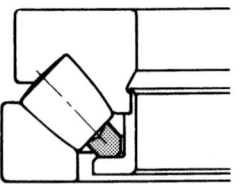

FIGURE 2-21 Spherical roller thrust bearing.

TTHD bearings are well suited for applications such as crane hooks where extremely high thrust loads and heavy shock must be resisted and some measure of radial location obtained. For very low speed, extremely heavily loaded applications, these bearings are supplied with a full complement of rollers for maximum capacity.

The TSR spherical roller thrust bearing design (Fig. 2-21) achieves a high thrust capacity with low friction and continuous roller alignment. The bearings can accommodate pure thrust loads as well as combined radial and thrust loads. This design allows higher speeds than do any of the other roller thrust bearing designs. Typical applications are air regenerators, centrifugal pumps, and deep-well pumps.

Because the spherical roller thrust bearing must always carry some thrust load, it cannot be used as a float bearing. Most applications require the use of two or more bearings on a shaft: a fixed bearing and a float bearing.

Needle Roller Bearings. Size for size, needle bearings (Fig. 2-22) have more rollers and more lines of contact, and thus generally have higher capacities than other roller bearings. This is particularly true under static, slow-rotating, or oscillating conditions. Both types have a far higher capacity in less radial space than other antifriction bearings.

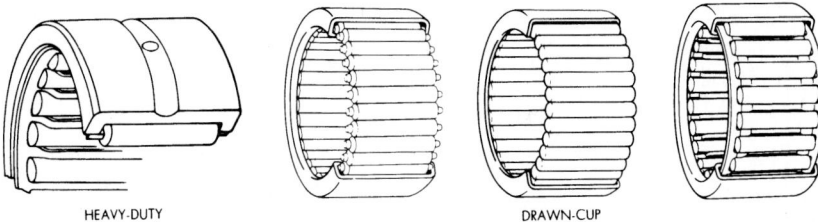

FIGURE 2-22   Needle roller bearings.

The heavy-duty bearing has an outer race that is deeply hardened, while the race of the drawn-cup bearing has a thin, hardened case over a relatively ductile core. Thus, the heavy-duty bearing can withstand heavier shock or more continuous loads than the drawn-cup bearing, which should never be dynamically loaded, even momentarily, beyond the load limit given in the manufacturer's tabular data. The smaller, more compact cross section is provided by the drawn-cup bearing with its smaller roller diameter and thin-steel outer race, as opposed to the larger roller diameter and thick outer race of the heavy-duty bearing.

For moderate speeds, both types are satisfactory. However, the cage in the roller bearing allows higher speeds for a given shaft size.

MOUNTING AND MAINTENANCE

General Installation Rules

Depending on the size of bearing and the application, there are different methods for mounting bearings. In all methods, however, certain basic rules must be observed.

Maintain Cleanliness.   Choose a clean environment. Work in an atmosphere free from dust or moisture. If this is not possible (and sometimes in the field it isn't), the installer should make every effort to ensure cleanliness by the use of protective screens, clean cloths, and the like.

Plan the Work.   Know in advance what you are going to do and have all necessary tools at hand. This reduces the amount of time for the job and lessens the chance for dirt to get into the bearing.

Preparation and Inspection.   All component parts of the machine should be on hand and thoroughly cleaned before proceeding. Housings should be cleaned, even to blowing out the oil holes. *Do not use an air hose on bearings*. If blind holes are used, insert a magnetic rod to remove metal chips that might have become lodged during fabrication.

Shaft shoulders and spacer rings contacting the bearing should be square with the shaft axis. The shaft fillet must be small enough to clear the radius of the bearing.

On original installations, all component parts should be checked against the detailed specification prints for dimensional accuracy. Shaft and housing should be carefully checked for size and roundness.

Mounting Straight-Bore Bearings

Heat-Expansion Method.   Most applications require a tight interference fit on the shaft. Mounting is simplified by heating the bearing to expand it sufficiently to slide easily onto the shaft. Two methods of heating are in common use:

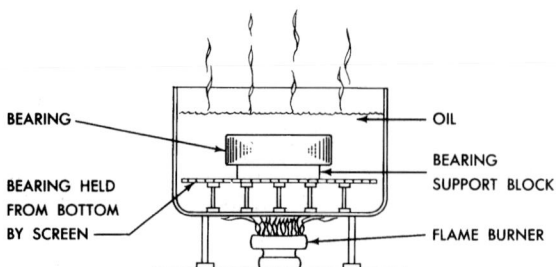

FIGURE 2-23 Typical arrangement for heat expansion method.

1. Immersion in a tank of heated oil (Fig. 2-23)

2. Induction heating

The first is accomplished by heating the bearing in a tank of oil having a high flash point. The oil temperature should not exceed 250°F (120°C). A temperature of 200°F (93°C) is sufficient for most applications. The bearing should be heated at this temperature, generally for 20 or 30 min, until it is expanded sufficiently to slide onto the shaft very easily.

The induction-heating method is particularly suited for mounting small bearings in production-line assembly. Induction heating is rapid, and care must be taken to prevent bearing temperature from exceeding 200°F (93°C). Trial runs with the unit are usually necessary to obtain the proper timing. Thermal crayons which melt at predetermined temperatures can be used to check the bearing temperature.

While the bearing is still hot, it should be positioned squarely against the shoulder. Lockwashers and locknuts or clamping plates are then installed to hold the bearing against the shoulder of the shaft. As the bearing cools, the locknut or clamping plate should be tightened.

The oil bath is shown in Fig. 2-23. The bearing should not be in direct contact with the heat source. The usual arrangement is to have a screen several inches off the bottom of the tank. Small support blocks separate the bearing from the screen. It is important to keep the bearing away from any localized high-heat source that may raise its temperature excessively, resulting in race hardness reduction.

Flame-type burners are commonly used, but may have to be replaced with some other heat source to comply with local safety regulations. An automatic device for temperature control is desirable. If safety regulations prevent the use of an open heated-oil bath, a mixture of 15 percent soluble oil in water may be used. This mixture may be heated to a maximum temperature of about 200°F (93°C) without being flammable. The bath should be checked from time to time to ensure its proper composition as the water evaporates. The bath leaves a thin film of oil on the bearing sufficient for temporary rust prevention, but normal lubrication should be supplied to the bearing as soon as possible after installation. Be sure all of the oil-in-water solution has been drained away from the bearing.

Arbor Press Method. The alternative method of mounting, generally used only on smaller sizes (Fig. 2-24), is to press the bearing onto the shaft or into the housing. This can be done by using an arbor press and a mounting tube. The tube can be of soft steel.

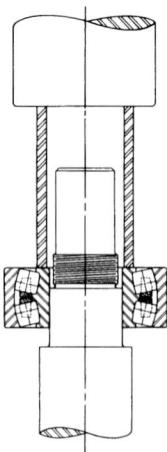

FIGURE 2-24 Arrangement for typical arbor press mounting.

To press-fit the bearing on its shaft seat, the inside diameter of the tube should be slightly larger than the shaft. The outside diameter of the tube should not exceed the maximum shoulder height given in the tables of dimensions. The tube should be faced square at both ends, thoroughly clean inside and out, and long enough to clear the end of the shaft after the bearing is mounted.

If the outer ring is being pressed into the housing, the outside diameter of the mounting tube should be slightly smaller than the housing bore, and the inside diameter should not be less than the recommended housing-shoulder diameter in the tables of dimensions.

Coat the shaft or housing bore with light machine oil to reduce the force needed for the press fit. Carefully place the bearing on the shaft, with a smooth blended OD corner, making sure it is square with the shaft axis. Apply steady pressure from the arbor ram to drive the bearing firmly against the shoulder. Never attempt to make a press fit on a shaft by applying pressure to the outer ring, or to make a press fit in a housing by applying pressure to the inner ring, as internal bearing damage (race brinelling) may result.

Straight-Bore-Bearing Removal

Bearing pullers of various types and designs are available from several manufacturers. These pullers are useful in removing bearings up to about 10-in (25-cm) bore. The preferred method utilizes a split ring which is placed behind the inner ring. The pulling device is assembled so as to cause the split ring to push the bearing off the shaft. If machine elements interfere with this method, a prong-type puller may be used with a roller bearing that has side flanges on the inner ring. Insert the prongs of the puller behind the flange and pull the bearing off the shaft.

Hydraulic Method.   Remove lockplate or locknut. Provide a means for pulling the bearing off the shaft. A bearing puller applied to the outer ring may be used without fear of brinelling the races since only a nominal force is required for removal by this system. Or, the shaft may be placed in a vertical position, simply allowing gravity and slight manual force to remove the bearing. Pull the bearing all the way off the shaft quickly to prevent freezing after the loss of oil pressure as the bearing clears the oil groove.

Mounting Bearings in Housings

To facilitate installing the bearing in the housing and to minimize fretting corrosion during operation, coat the housing with a light-grade machine oil. Make sure the outer ring is square with the housing bore before inserting it. If the outer ring becomes misaligned and sticks, do not attempt to force it farther into the housing. Use a soft brass or steel bar and tap the outer ring until it becomes free and is realigned. An assembly plate for holding the outer ring in alignment with the inner ring is often useful for applications in which conditions tend to result in misalignment.

In case of outer-ring rotation, where the outer ring is a tight fit in the housing, the housing member can be expanded by heating. Split housings present no alignment problems during installation, but the housings should be checked carefully for size and roundness.

Internal Clearance

Internal clearance is the amount of radial play within a bearing. This clearance accommodates the effects of tight shaft and housing fits, radial thermal expansion, speed, and other operating conditions.

The internal clearance in radial bearings other than tapered roller bearings is defined as *diametral clearance*. The diametral clearance is the amount of radial play built into the bearings (see Figs. 2-25 and 2-26).

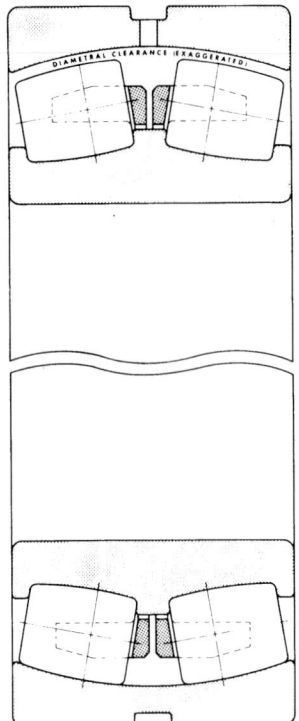

FIGURE 2-25 Internal clearance of a spherical ball bearing.

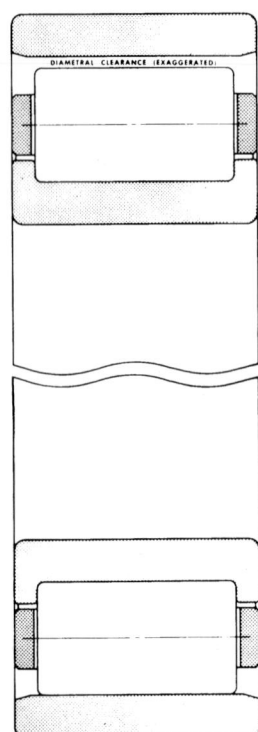

FIGURE 2-26 Internal clearance of a cylindrical ball bearing.

Straight-bore or tapered-bore bearings installed with interference fits will result in a reduction of internal or diametral clearance. Several factors influence the reduction of internal clearance. When the bearing inner ring is pressed onto a solid steel shaft, reduction of internal clearance is approximately 80 percent of the shaft interference fit for a standard series radial bearing. For an outer ring pressed into a heavy-section steel or cast-iron housing, the reduction of internal clearance is about 60 percent of the housing-interference fit. If the shaft is hollow, the housing walls are thin, or materials other than steel are used, clearance reduction may vary considerably from the above percentages.

Tapered-bore spherical roller bearings require a slightly greater interference fit with the shaft than straight-bore bearings of corresponding size. The resultant fit cannot conveniently be determined by direct shaft measurement. It can be checked by the distance the bearing is pressed onto a carefully gauged tapered shaft, or more easily by the effects of radial expansion of the inner ring as it is pushed onto the taper.

Lubrication

Since the lubricant affects bearing life and operation, selecting the proper lubricant is an important design function. The purpose of lubrication in bearing applications is to:

1. Minimize friction at points of contact within the bearings
2. Protect the highly finished bearing surfaces from corrosion
3. Dissipate heat generated within the bearings
4. Remove foreign matter or prevent its entry into the bearings

Two basic types of lubricants used with antifriction bearings are oils and greases. Each has its advantages and limitations.

Since oil is a liquid, it lubricates all surfaces and is able to dissipate heat from these surfaces more readily. Because oil retains its physical characteristics over a wider range of temperatures, it may be used for high-speed and high-temperature applications. The quantity of oil supplied to the bearing may be accurately controlled. Oil lubricants can be circulated, cleaned, and cooled for more effective lubrication.

Grease, which is easier to retain in the bearing housing, aids as a sealant against foreign matter and corrosive fumes.

Oil Lubrication

1. Oil is a better lubricant for high speeds or high temperatures. It can be cooled to help reduce bearing temperature.
2. Oil is easier to handle, and with oil it is easier to control the amount of lubricant reaching the bearing. It is harder to retain in the bearing. Lubricant losses may be higher than with grease.
3. As a liquid, oil can be introduced into the bearing in many ways, such as drip feed, wick feed, pressurized circulating systems, oil bath, or air-oil mist. Each is suited to certain types of applications.
4. Oil is easier to keep clean for recirculating systems.

Grease Lubrication

1. This type of lubrication is restricted to lower-speed applications within the operating-temperature limits of the grease.
2. Grease is easily confined in the housing. This is important in the food, textile, and chemical industries.
3. Bearing enclosure and seal design is simplified.
4. Grease improves the efficiency of mechanical seals to give better protection to the bearing.

For all new applications, a competent bearing or lubrication engineer should be consulted to recommend the specific lubricant and method of lubrication for the specific bearing's operating and ambient conditions.

BIBLIOGRAPHY

For additional or more detailed information on a specific bearing type or application, refer to the bearing manufacturers' catalogs and or one of the following:

ABMA Standards, The American Bearing Manufacturers Association, Inc.*
SKF Industries, Inc., Front Street and Erie Avenue, P.O. Box 6731, Philadelphia, PA 19132.
The Timken Company, 1835 Dueber Avenue S.W., Canton, OH 44706.
The Torrington Company, 59 Field Street, Torrington, CT 06790.

* Recently changed to the Anti-Friction Bearing Manufacturers Association (AFBMA).

CHAPTER 7-2
BEARINGS

PART 2

PLAIN BEARINGS*

INTRODUCTION

A *plain bearing* is any bearing that works by sliding action (with or without lubricant). This group encompasses essentially all types other than rolling-element bearings. Many of the basic principles dealing with plain-bearing loading and lubrication are explained in the prior section, and the reader is advised to review these basics before continuing with the more specific and detailed treatment here.

Plain bearings are often referred to as *sleeve bearings* or *thrust bearings,* terms that designate whether the bearing is loaded axially or radially.

Lubrication is critical to the operation of plain bearings, so their application and function is also often referred to according to the type of lubrication principle used. Thus, terms such as hydrodynamic, fluid-film, hydrostatic, boundary-lubricated, and self-lubricated are designations for particular plain bearings.

---

* Updated for this Second Edition by the Editor-in-Chief.

BEARING TYPES

Journal or Sleeve Bearings

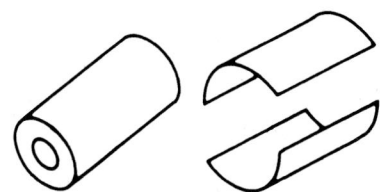

FIGURE 2-27   Sleeve or journal bearings.

These bearings (Fig. 2-27) are cylindrical or ring-shaped bearings designed to carry radial loads. The terms *sleeve* and *journal* are used more or less synonymously since sleeve refers to the general configuration while journal pertains to any portion of a shaft supported by a bearing. In another sense, however, the term journal may be reserved for two-piece bearings used to support the journals of an engine crankshaft. Sleeve bearings may be lubricated by either hydrostatic, hydrodynamic, or boundary means. In practice, most of them are designed to operate hydrodynamically, and hydrodynamic lubrication is normally implied when the terms sleeve or journal bearing are used.

The simplest and most widely used types of sleeve bearings are cast-bronze and porous-bronze (powdered-metal) cylindrical bearings. Cast-bronze bearings are oil- or grease-lubricated. Porous bearings are impregnated with oil and often have an oil reservoir in the housing.

Cast bearing bores are held within a few thousandths of an inch and are often finish-machined after installation to provide extreme accuracy of shaft position. Porous bearings are sized more accurately and are mounted with a special sizing tool so that no finish machining is needed. Machining poses the danger of smearing or closing the all-important pores.

Oscillating or slow-moving sleeve bearings cannot develop hydrodynamic lubrication, so their design criteria are different from those of other sleeve bearings. Oscillating bearings are generally designed on the basis of allowable wear or upon the load that produces "pounding out."

Engine bearings are designed to operate under hydrodynamic conditions. Their surfaces are smooth, and clearances are optimized to maximize load capacity while allowing enough oil flow to aid cooling.

Plastic and carbon graphite bearings are being used increasingly in place of metal. Originally, plastic was used only in small, lightly loaded bearings where cost saving was the primary objective. More recently plastics with high load-carrying capacities have been developed for direct replacement of metals. Also, plastics are used because of functional advantages, including resistance to abrasion, and are being made in large sizes.

Thrust Bearings

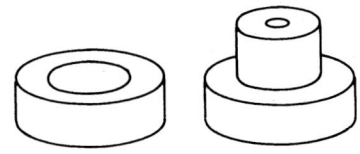

FIGURE 2-28   Thrust bearings.

This type of bearing (Fig. 2-28) differs from a sleeve bearing in that loads are supported axially rather than radially. Thin, disklike thrust bearings are called thrust washers.

Hydrodynamic action in a thrust bearing can be improved by putting grooves in the surface, rather than having it flat. Small surface irregularities—either etched-in deliberately or resulting as a normal consequence of manufacturing—aid hydrodynamic action. Even assembly misalignment can help produce hydrodynamic behavior. Geometry of the grooves can be optimized for particular loads, speeds, and oil viscosities. For full hydrodynamic action, a thrust bearing must have tapered lands on tilting pads.

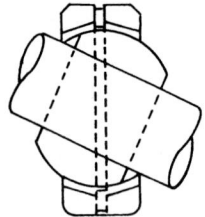

FIGURE 2-29   Spherical bearings.

Spherical Bearings

The outside diameter of this type of bearing is spherical (or at least curved) to permit "wobble" of the bearing axis. This ball-and-socket action compensates for shaft and mount misalignment; thus these bearings (Fig. 2-29) are called *self-aligning.* Once the spherical tilt accommodates misalignment, subsequent bearing relative motion is normally between the shaft and the cylindrical bore in the ball.

When the ball is enclosed at the end of a link, the bearing is called a *rod-end bearing.* These bearings are normally used in oscillating linkages, and most of the relative motion is between the ball and the socket.

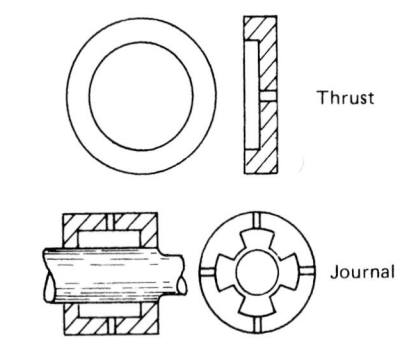

FIGURE 2-30   Hydrostatic bearings.

Hydrostatic Bearings

Hydrostatic bearings (Fig. 2-30) can be either of the thrust or sleeve (journal) type. Bearing characteristics are highly predictable, including such characteristics as stiffness, friction, and oil flow. Advantages include nearly zero starting friction, the ability to carry heavy loads at low speeds, and negligible wear. But hydrostatic bearings are expensive and require bulky equipment to provide pressurized oil. However, machines with hydrostatic bearings maintain their accuracy, so savings in depreciation can be significant. This type of lubrication is used most frequently in machine tools, but it is also employed in gyroscopes and other precision instruments where low friction is important.

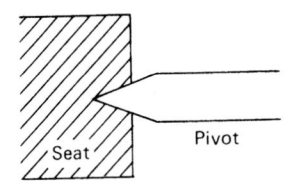

FIGURE 2-31   Pivot bearing.

Jewel and Pivot Bearings

These bearings (Fig. 2-31) are suitable for tiny, lightly loaded shafts in such applications as watches, meters, and instruments. The shaft does not pass through the bearing but rests in a cone or cup on each end. The pivots (pointed shaft ends) are usually hardened steel, and seats are usually sapphire, glass, beryllium copper, carbide, or carbon. The bearing normally is lubricated with a light nongumming oil.

These bearings operate in the boundary regime, but because of the small radius of contact, they have lower friction than rolling-element bearings. Jewel bearings come in a variety of standard designs.

Gas Bearings

Gas bearings are lubricated with a gas (usually air) instead of with an oil. They can either be externally pressurized (hydrostatic) or self-acting (hydrodynamic). A special type of self-acting gas bearing uses metal-foil interleaved to form a raceway and is thus called a *foil bearing.*

The operating principles and relative merits of hydrodynamic and hydrostatic gas bearings are similar to those of their oil-lubricated counterparts. The hydrostatic type can support loads at rest or low speed but requires an expensive and complex pumping system. The hydrodynamic type is simpler but must have significant relative motion to function and must be built to very close tolerances.

Gas bearings are used mainly for applications demanding extremely high rotational speeds or uniformly low frictional drag. Ambient atmospheres can be used as the working lubricant, so gas bearings also are used where possible contamination from oil lubricants must be avoided. The design of gas bearings is usually complex and requires sophisticated engineering. They usually are an integral part of the equipment in which they are used. However, some gas bearings are available as off-the-shelf components.

Most gas bearings demand small operating clearances, so they require precision manufacturing methods. They also are susceptible to overload, vibration, and dust contamination. Another problem is that they are subject to instabilities caused by the dynamics of a gas film or by unbalanced rotating masses.

HOW BEARINGS FAIL

The failure mode anticipated in a bearing influences decisions on the selection of a bearing type, bearing material, lubricant, and bearing surface finish. Typical failure modes include:

- Loss of shaft positioning from wear; seizure by overheating and loss of clearance
- Seizure by failure of lubricant and galling of contacting surfaces
- Destruction of journal by hard particles imbedded in the bearing surface
- Edge loading caused by dimensional instability of bearings and housings, or by shaft deflection
- Fatigue of bearing surface; high friction

Friction

The frictional properties of any plain bearing depend on the lubrication system. Either hydrodynamic or hydrostatic lubrication can provide low friction. The lowest friction levels are attained in gas bearings or with magnetically supported bearings.

Friction in hydrodynamic and hydrostatic bearings is a function of lubricant viscosity and shear rate. Shear rate increases with increasing rotational speed and decreasing film thickness. The friction coefficient is generally below 0.001.

The friction in boundary and self-lubricated bearings varies widely and is difficult to predict for a given bearing-lubricant system. The range of coefficients of friction is 0.01 to 0.10 for boundary lubrication and 0.01 to 0.3 for self-lubrication.

Caution must be used when applying friction-coefficient handbook data. Conditions under which the values were measured should be known, and these conditions should be duplicated in the application. Coefficient of friction tends to increase with increasing surface roughness with dryness and cleanliness of surfaces, and with decreasing temperature.

Wear

Wear of plain bearings is strongly influenced by the state of lubrication and, conversely, wear characteristics influence the various lubrication states.

Hydrostatic bearings do not wear if operating properly because the bearing surfaces are separated by a film of oil, even when the bearing is stationary. Erosion of flow restrictors in hydrostatic bearings with high flow rates can and eventually does cause failure. Plugging of flow restrictors by wear debris can cause catastrophic failure. In gas-lubricated, externally pressurized bearings, occasional rubs and resulting wear can occur under impact and vibration loads.

Hydrodynamic bearings wear very slowly. Wear occurs during start-up and slowdown when the speed is too low to produce sufficient fluid pressure to support the bearing surfaces on a lubricant film. If hard debris (harder than the journal surface) imbeds in a babbitt or plastic bearing and protrudes above the bearing surface, the journal can wear seriously during start-up.

In a severe and catastrophic type of journal wear—known as *wire wooling*—the journal surface is machined by hard scabs of wear debris that pack into the babbit surface. In this failure the journals are deeply grooved and can no longer generate a hydrodynamic film.

Boundary-lubricated and self-lubricating bearings wear much faster than fluid-film bearings. Self-lubricating plastic bearings wear at higher rates than boundary-lubricated, metal-alloy bearings.

Babbitts are subject to fatigue damage in which pieces of the babbitt metal spall out of the surface. This might be considered as a catastrophic type of failure after a prolonged (but undetectable) period of wear buildup. Babbitt fatigue is most likely in bearings subjected to reciprocating or vibrating loads.

Babbitts and leaded bronzes are also susceptible to cavitation erosion. This is a form of wear in which shock waves, from gas bubbles collapsing in the lubricant, produce surface pits. Eventually, the removal of surface material impairs performance. Cavitation erosion has a characteristic lacy appearance and often is found around lubrication feed holes and slots in bearings subjected to vibratory or impact loading—such as in internal combustion engines.

Heat

Heat is generated either by shearing of the oil film or by rubbing contact. In hydrostatic and hydrodynamic bearings, heat generation at running speeds is the result of oil shear, and the amount of temperature rise can be estimated if oil viscosity and shear rates are known. Temperature can be regulated by controlling the oil flow through the bearing or by using external cooling.

High-speed and close-clearance fluid-film bearings are difficult to keep cool. The flow rate through a journal varies with the cube of oil-film thickness and linearly with supply pressure.

Boundary-lubricated and self-lubricating bearings are more sensitive to sliding velocity than fluid-film types because the coefficient of friction is as much as 10 times greater in the first two. Frictional heating is a function of bearing pressure, sliding velocity, and coefficient of friction. Therefore, if the coefficient of friction remains constant for a range of loads and speeds, a rough indication of heat load is provided by the *pressure-velocity* (PV) factor.

Plastic bearing materials are sensitive to PV because of their low thermal conductivities and high thermal-expansion rates.

Lubrication

Although some materials have an inherent lubricity or can be lubricated by virtue of a film of slippery solid, most bearings operate with a fluid film—generally oil but sometimes a gas.

By far the largest number of bearings are oil-lubricated. The oil film can be maintained through pumping by a pressurization system—in which case the lubrication is termed *hydrostatic*. Or it can be maintained by a squeezing or wedging of lubricant produced by the rolling action of the bearing itself—termed *hydrodynamic* lubrication. If loads are too high or speeds too slow, the hydrodynamic action begins to break down (allowing, in some cases, metal-to-metal contact), a condition referred to as *boundary* lubrication.

Hydrostatic Lubrication The main virtue of hydrostatic lubrication is that it can accommodate heavy loads at low speeds because it does not depend upon relative motion to maintain the lubrication film. Instead, lubricant is supplied from a special pump and feed lines to the bearing or bearings. The oil is fed through flow restrictors, which generally are in the stationary part of the bearing. The flow restrictors automatically adjust the oil flow for the applied load. Another advantage of this lubrication system is low deflection in certain load ranges, making it preferred for many high-precision machine tools. The disadvantage of hydrostatic lubrication is its high cost and complexity.

Hydrodynamic Lubrication   This form of lubrication occurs more or less naturally in properly finished, sized, and lubricated holes and shafts. Essentially, rotation of the journal causes it to "roll up" one side of the bearing, thus creating a wedge-shaped channel into which lubricant is forced. The forcing of the lubricant into this wedge creates sufficient pressure to keep the journal riding on the oil film. This form of the lubricant is generally preferred because it is simple and dependable. Also, the lubrication action improves as speed increases, which in most applications goes hand-in-hand with an increase in loads experienced as speed increases. Its main drawbacks are an inability to carry heavy loads at low speed and appreciable wear under frequent stops or starts, or motion reversals.

The oil for hydrodynamic lubrication can be fed from an oil reservoir, or the bearing can be made of a porous metal that is impregnated with oil that "bleeds" to the bearing surface as the shaft rotates. (Most porous-metal bearings, however, operate under boundary or mixed-film conditions.)

Boundary Lubrication   This form of lubrication is essentially a breakdown of hydrodynamic action. At high loads or low speeds, the pressure of the hydrodynamic film cannot prevent metal-to-metal contact. So the opposing surfaces partially ride on an oil film and partially rub together as surface high points contact.

Lubrication is provided by lubricant decomposition products or surface-active additives which form a thin, soft, solid film on the metal surfaces and prevent metal-junction adhesion.

Boundary lubrication is not the most desirable operating mode, yet at times it is completely unavoidable. It is found mainly with slow-moving loads where the cost and expense of a hydrostatic system is not warranted. Hinge bearings in aircraft landing gears, for example, do not move fast enough to develop hydrodynamic films, yet hydrostatic systems would be too heavy, costly, and cumbersome.

Boundary-lubricated bearings using grease require special consideration to ensure adequate distribution of the lubricant. Grease travels only where is is carried on a moving surface, so the moving shaft carries a gob of grease at the center of the bearing, in a band only somewhat wider than the original gob. For this reason, sleeve bearings are grooved to distribute the grease over the entire load-bearing area, ensuring an adequate grease supply for boundary-film maintenance. In addition, the grooves collect wear debris, preventing it from damaging the bearing surface.

Many different groove designs are used (see Fig. 2-32). Some were developed for special applications; however, all are designed for easy manufacture. Basic principles to follow when selecting a groove design are:

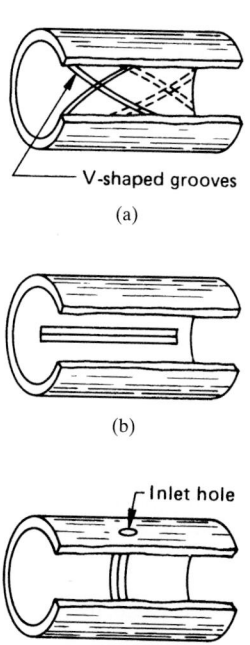

V-shaped grooves

(a)

(b)

Inlet hole

(c)

FIGURE 2-32   Adding grooves to distribute grease.

- Grooves must carry the grease over the entire bearing width.
- Grooves must be placed so that the shaft contacts the grease within them. (A simple axial slot opposite the point of maximum load does not feed to the load zone because of internal clearances.)
- Groove edges should be rounded so that they do not act as scrapers that clean grease from the shaft.

Groove cross section is usually V-shaped, but it can be rectangular or semicircular. A flat-bottom V groove provides ample reservoir capacity and reduces edge scraping. Groove width and depth are not critical as long as they do not weaken the bearing structurally or carve up too much of the bearing area. As a rule, groove depth should not exceed one-third the bearing wall thickness.

The 00 design is appropriate for continuous rotation under heavy loads. Conventional design calls for the grooves to be machined within about 0.125 in (3 mm) of the ends to retain the lubricant within the bearing area. However, under heavy loads where bearing temperature is high and debris becomes a problem, the grooves should exit through the ends, so that periodic flushing with fresh grease removes debris and lubricant decomposition products. Experiments with these *nonrecirculating* grooves indicate lower wear than with recirculating grooves.

The *straight axial* groove is a simple arrangement for moderate, unidirectional loads and continuous rotation. The axial slot should be located about 20° from the load line, counter to the direction of shaft rotation. This design spreads grease over the bearing width and still provides maximum bearing area. However, its lubricating effectiveness is not as good as that of the 00 design.

A circumferential slot in the center of the bearing is effective for oscillating bearings, especially in applications where load direction varies.

COMPARING PLAIN BEARINGS AND ROLLER-ELEMENT BEARINGS

Friction

The torque required to put a bearing into motion from rest is usually higher than the torque required to keep it running once it is in motion. *Starting friction* thus has an important influence on the power required in a drive system.

Externally pressurized bearings have very low starting torque. Roller bearings have a low starting torque. Unpressurized sleeve (fluid-film) bearings have substantially higher starting torque. The coefficient of friction at start-up for self-lubricated bearings is highly variable. It may range from 0.04 to 0.16.

The fluid-film bearing has a high starting torque because it must pass through boundary lubrication stages as it comes up to speed. Once running under a hydrodynamic film, the fluid-film bearing exhibits friction characteristics comparable to a rolling-element bearing.

At running speed, the friction characteristics of various bearing types cannot be summarized in a few words. The externally pressurized bearing runs with low friction. Friction in a self-lubricating sleeve bearing is quite variable, depending upon the application.

Running friction for a rolling-element bearing is lower than starting friction. If torque characteristics are critical to a design, recommended practice is to measure starting and running frictional characteristics experimentally.

If a bearing must be started repeatedly under heavy load, rolling-element bearings are a better choice than sleeve bearings. If the increased complexity is acceptable, externally pressurized (hydrostatic) bearings are the best choice of all. If starting load is light and load increases gradually with speed, the conventional hydrodynamic sleeve bearing usually is preferred.

Noise

Whenever a machine is subject to a noise-reduction program, bearings are normally involved in one way or another. Even if bearings are not generating noise, they often have much to do with noise transfer.

Generally, rolling-element bearings are noisier than fluid-film bearings. Minor inaccuracies in rollers or raceways can generate sounds that are amplified by the machine structure. Improving bearing quality can reduce this effect.

Fluid-film bearings under steady radial load generally do not produce any noise whatsoever. However, if this type of bearing is reversed frequently, it can generate considerable noise if it doesn't have enough lubricant to fill the bearing. Fluid-film bearings running unstable in a whirling mode can also produce noise.

Size

A bearing requiring a separate pressurized lubrication system requires more total space than a self-lubricating type. The relative space required at the actual load-support point is not a clear-cut matter. A pressurized bearing can conceivably be more compact than self-contained bearings at the load-support point.

For self-contained bearings, the sleeve bearing requires less radial space than a rolling-element bearing; however, the sleeve bearing requires slightly more axial space. Needle bearings require about as much space as journal bearings.

Cost

Hardware Costs   In high-volume lots, sleeve bearings and bushings are considerably less costly than rolling-element bearings. In mid-range volumes, prices for the two types are comparable. For special designs in small quantities, sliding bearings are usually more costly than rolling-element bearings. Dry-film and boundary-lubricated bearings usually employ proprietary materials that are expensive. Powdered-metal bearings, however, are inexpensive.

Design Costs   Rolling-element and dry-lubricated bearings normally require the least engineering cost to the end user. Manufacturers of rolling-element bearings, in particular, can provide considerable cost-saving assistance by virtue of well-documented design manuals.

Self-acting sleeve bearings, in contrast, may require considerable end-user design effort except for light-duty applications or where there is considerable application experience.

The behavior of externally pressurized bearings usually can be predicted easily by simple calculations, but considerable design effort may be required to verify the design completely.

Shop Costs   Rolling-element bearings normally require precise housings and shafts and thus require fairly costly machining for products in which they are used. Sleeve-bearings, in contrast, generally operate well with less finely prepared machine finishes. Many plain bearings operate satisfactorily with lathe-turned journals.

Maintenance Costs   If the bearing lubrication is self-contained, maintenance costs are normally determined by sealing requirements. If there is full-pressure lubrication, costs may be determined by the amount of filtration needed to keep out contaminants. Generally, rolling-element bearings have the lowest maintenance costs because of the lower lubrication requirements. The very minimum maintenance cost is associated with self-lubricating bearings—provided that they deliver sufficient service life.

Replacement Costs These costs depend more on the specific design than on the type of bearing used. In general, however, sliding bearings normally are replaced more easily than rolling-element types. Both types can be damaged during installation if not handled properly. Sliding bearings can often be replaced quickly by machining from bar stock or by altering available stock sizes.

Cost of Failure Rolling-element bearings usually give ample warning that they are approaching failure (by virtue of increasingly noisy operation). They usually fail from fatigue. Sliding bearings, on the other hand, usually perform well until just moments before violent failure.

If a rolling-element bearing fails at high speed, the failure is usually total and catastrophic. With a journal bearing, the effect is normally less drastic. Often, only a bit of polishing can put it back into service. However, sliding bearings are capable of total catastrophic failure.

BIBLIOGRAPHY

Basics of Design Engineering, 1993 volume, published annually by Penton Publishing Company, Cleveland, Ohio.

CHAPTER 7-3
SHAFT DRIVES AND COUPLINGS

PART 1
BELT DRIVES

David E. Roos
Manager, Applications Engineering
Product Application
Gates Rubber Company
Denver, Colorado

BELT DRIVES

Belt drives are the most widely used method of flexible power transmission. Improvements in materials and method of manufacture have allowed the introduction of new belts with much broader application capabilities.

Belt drives basically fit into four types; flat, V, V-ribbed, and synchronous. Although each of these basic belt types are more suitable in specific application areas, most applications can be successfully designed with more than one type of belt.

Flat belts, one of the earliest forms of flexible power transmission, are generally more suited to high-speed, low-horsepower applications. At low speeds and high loads flat-belt drives usually become too large to be cost effective.

V belts are the most commonly used today and they are the only belts that can be used on variable pitch and wide range variable speed drives.

V-ribbed belts are described by some as guided flat belts. Their thinner cross section make them suitable for operation on smaller diameters at higher speeds.

Synchronous (timing) belts are specifically designed as alternatives to roller chains and gears on drives, which require exact speed ratios and synchronization between the driver and driven machines. They are also widely used today in low-maintenance, energy-efficient applications.

FLAT BELTS

Flat belts are still widely used for power transmission. Their thin, flexible cross section allows them to operate over small diameters and, in some cases, at very high speeds. Many different sizes and constructions are available for a wide variety of uses. Flat belts are either of fully molded or woven construction and may or may not have a tensile member.

One significant disadvantage of flat belts is that they depend entirely on friction in order to transmit power. Thus they require higher belt tension to do the same work, which results in higher shaft and bearing loads. The need for higher tension may cause more belt stretch, causing the belt to slip more easily than V belts.

V BELTS

The problems of high tension with flat belts led to the development of V belts. Unlike flat belts, which depend only on friction, V belts have deep V-shaped cross sections that wedge into the sheave groove to provide added capacity. Because of the wedging action, V belts are highly stable and can operate at tensions considerably lower than those needed by flat belts. Thus, V-belt drives can be more compact and allow for smaller shafts and bearings.

The load on a banded or covered V belt is carried by a tensile section located near the top of the belt. This section can contain one or more layers of cord, depending on the method of manufacture (Fig. 3-1). Generally, most V belts today use lower modulus polyester tensile cords, which provide significantly improved capacity compared to older tensile types for V belts.

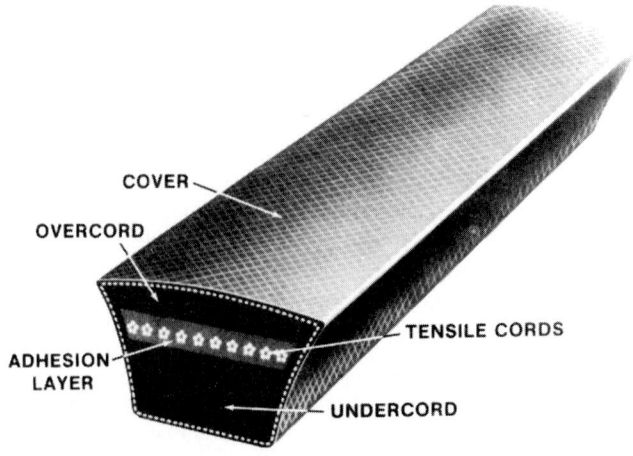

FIGURE 3-1 Typical V-belt construction.

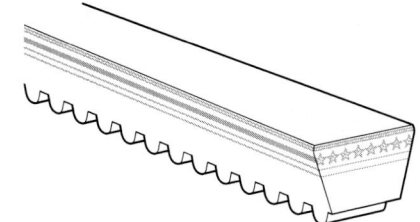

FIGURE 3-2   Molded-notch V belt.

A very widely used variation of the banded V belt is the bandless molded notch or molded cog belt (Fig. 3-2).

The molded notches in these belts provide greater flexibility allowing the belt to operate on smaller diameter sheaves. This provides for even more compact drives where space is limited.

V belts operate over a wide range of speed and provide a broad choice of center distance. While V belts can operate at very high speeds, standard sheaves are normally limited to a 6500 ft/min (33 m/s) maximum for safety purposes. Beyond this speed, special materials and balancing may be required.

There are four basic types of V belts: heavy duty industrial, light duty industrial, agricultural, and automotive. The first two are described in the paragraphs following; the last two are outside of the scope of this book.

HEAVY-DUTY V BELTS

Classical

This line of belts includes four standard cross sections—A, B, C, D (13C, 16C, 22C, 32C). These range in width from ½ in (13 mm) for an A section to 1½ in (32 mm) for a D section (Fig. 3-3). Also available are the molded notch cross sections—AX, BX, CX (13CX, 16CX, 22CX). Classical belts can be used in single or multiple belt drives and can transmit hundreds of horsepower continuously and absorb reasonable intermittent shock loads. Operating temperature limits range from −30 to +140°F (−34 to +60°C). These belts also provide excellent oil resistance.

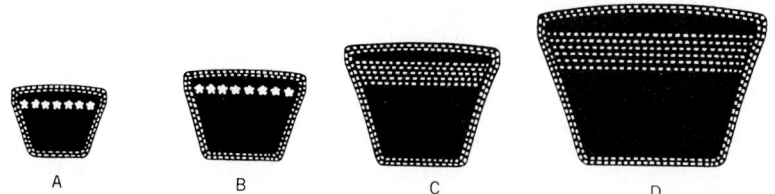

FIGURE 3-3   Classical V-belt cross sections.

Classical banded and bandless molded notch belts are also available in a joined configuration, where two or more belt strands are connected across the top by a tie band (Fig. 3-4). The joined belt improves lateral stability making it almost impossible for individual belts to turn over in the groove or jump out of the sheave. The tie band rides above the sheave outside diameter and does not interfere with the normal wedging action of the individual belts. Joined belts do not carry any higher horsepower rating, but should be designed using published single belt horsepower ratings.

Another variation of the classical belt is the double-V or hexagonal-V belt (Fig. 3-5). Double-V belts are used when power input or power takeoff is required on both sides of the belt. This is necessary when the driver and driven sheaves must rotate in opposite directions. (Drives with several counter-rotating shafts are called *serpentine* drives.) Double-V belts are available in AA, BB, CC, DD (13D, 16D, 22D) cross sections.

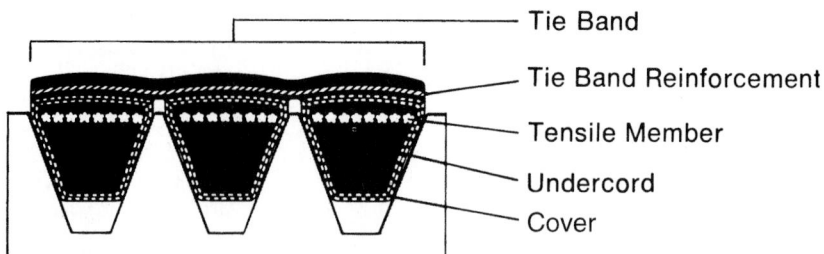

FIGURE 3-4   Joined V-belt tie band configuration.

Narrow

These belts can be used on the same applications as the classical belts, but allow for a lighter, more compact drive. Three cross sections—3V, 5V 8V (9N, 15N, 25N)—replace the four classical cross sections (Fig. 3-6). Also available are the bandless molded notch cross sections—3VX, 5VX (9NX, 15NX). These belts range in width from ⅜ in (9 mm) for the 3V to 1 in (25 mm) for the 8V.

Narrow belts, because of their relatively higher horsepower capacity, usually provide substantial space and weight savings compared to classical belts. For instance, narrow belts can transmit the same horsepower loads in ½ to ⅔ the space of a classical belt drive. Narrow belts often allow the use of greater speed ratio between driver and driven machine.

In addition to exhibiting excellent oil and heat resistance, most classical and narrow industrial V belts meet industry standards for static conductivity. This allows for safe operation in potentially hazardous environments.

Variable Speed

Within certain limits, V belts are well suited to drives that must run at varying input or output speeds. These are common in the air-moving industry and are referred to as *variable-pitch* drives. These drives must incorporate special sheaves. Speed ratio on these drives is controlled by moving one sheave sidewall relative to the fixed sidewall so that the belt can ride at different pitch diameters. Variable-pitch drives using a single variable-pitch sheave and classical cross section belts will yield only about 1.4:1 overall speed variation.

Wide range *variable-speed* drives can easily allow for overall speed variations of up to 10:1 and transmit up to 100 horsepower (75 kW). Generally the higher the horsepower load, the lower the speed ratio. Variable-speed belts have a wide, thin cross section in comparison to other V belts (Fig. 3-7).

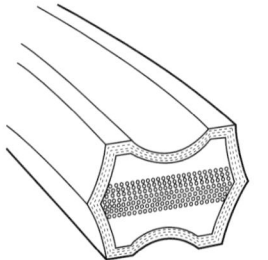

FIGURE 3-5   Double-V belt.

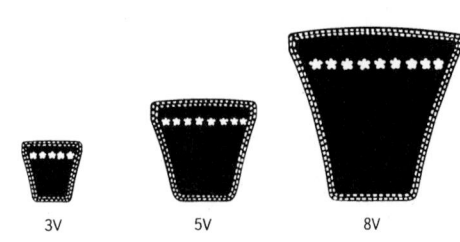

FIGURE 3-6   Narrow V-belt cross section.

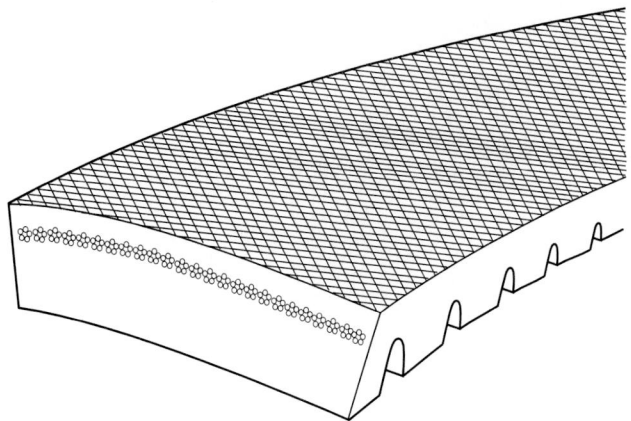

FIGURE 3-7   Variable-speed belts.

Unlike a gear transmission where speed variation is limited to finite discrete steps, variable-speed belt drives offer an infinite selection of speed ratios within the design range. In simple applications, speed is varied manually by moving the sliding motor base in and out or by adjusting an idler. On other drives, the adjustable or movable sheave sidewall is controlled through a mechanical linkage while the center distance is fixed. The driven sheave is generally spring loaded to provide adequate belt tension. In applications such as recreational vehicles, e.g., snowmobiles, the speed ratio is controlled by sensing speed and/or torque requirements of the drive, which in turn control the shifting mechanism.

The variable-speed operation can generate high frictional heat buildup and sidewall stresses. The wide, thin section is more easily subject to collapsing under high loads. In the past few years, manufacturers have developed improved materials and constructions to withstand the heat and high belt sidewall stresses. As a result, variable-speed belts are moving into more demanding applications.

These belts are used in many industrial, agricultural, automotive, and recreational vehicle applications where speed variation is a requirement.

LIGHT-DUTY V BELTS

These belts are similar to classical belts, except they have a slightly thinner cross section. This makes them ideally suited for the smaller sheaves typically found on many fractional-horsepower drives. Since they are generally intended to be used in single, not multiple, sets and on drives with less than one horsepower, they are often referred to as fractional-horsepower belts. Standard cross sections are 2L, 3L, 4L, and 5L and range in width from ¼ to ⅝ in (6 to 16 mm).

Usually, light-duty belt drives operate on an intermittent basis. Service requirements may vary from 1–3 h/week for a power lawn mower to 40 or more h/week for office machines or commercial power tools.

V-RIBBED BELTS

Ribs on the bottom side of V-ribbed belts (Fig. 3-8) mate with corresponding grooves in the sheave. This tracking guides the belt and makes it more stable than a flat belt. Like V belts, V-ribbed belts operate in grooved sheaves, but they do not have the full wedging capability of V

FIGURE 3-8 V-ribbed belt.

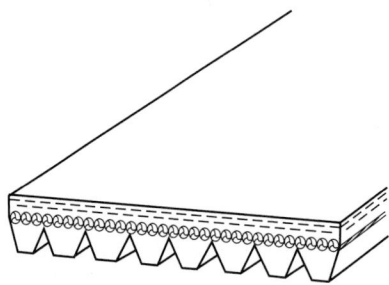

FIGURE 3-9 Truncated-rib V belt.

belts. As a result, they must operate at tensions slightly higher than V belts, but significantly lower than flat belts. A variation used more often today uses a truncated rib (Fig. 3-9) which provides a little more wedging action.

Because of their lightweight and thin construction, V-ribbed belts develop less centrifugal and bending tension as they are bent around small diameter sheaves. Compared to a V belt, V-ribbed belts have a continuous tensile section across the entire belt width providing additional load capacity.

V-ribbed belts are used in applications requiring a high-speed ratio such as clothes dryers or on drives such as small power tools that require very small drives. V-ribbed belts are also more common on automotive front-end engine applications such as serpentine drives. V-ribbed belts require closer alignment than V belts to minimize stress on the ribs.

ROUND BELTS

The use of round belts is diminishing in power transmission today in favor of today's improved V belts. Because of their round design, they are still used often in drives where the shafts are in different planes. Consequently, they are still used in roller conveyors that must run around curved corners. Although different sizes and constructions may be available, the most common are ½-in (12.5-mm) and ⁹⁄₁₆-in (14-mm) diameters.

SYNCHRONOUS BELTS

Synchronous belts, sometimes referred to as *timing* or *positive drive* belts, are especially suited to applications requiring a synchronized input and output speed (Fig. 3-10). Synchronous belts are designed to overcome the "creep" or slip of V-belt and flat belt drives. These belts eliminate slip by transmitting power through the positive engagement of the belt teeth against the pulley or sprocket teeth. Thus, precise speed ratios and synchronization are possible in such applications as automotive camshafts, machine tool indexing heads, computer printers, and robotics.

Synchronous drives have an advantage over gears and chains in that they can transmit high loads over a wide range of speeds with very low noise and no lubrication. The limited shock absorbing characteristics of the teeth against the sprocket can be helpful on some applications. Synchronous belts, like V-ribbed belts, require closer alignment tolerances in order to avoid premature wear or failure.

There are several situations (where synchronization is not important) in which synchronous belts have an advantage over V belts. These belts use an extremely high modulus, low stretch tensile cord such as fiberglass or Aramid to maintain uniform spacing between the belt teeth. This low growth under load results in minimal need for center distance adjustment. Therefore, in addition to being low maintenance items, synchronous belts are often used on drives with limited space for center distance adjustment. Since they do not slip, they exhibit a consistently high level of drive efficiency—generally about 98 percent in power transmission.

FIGURE 3-10   Synchronous belt.

There are three basic tooth configurations associated with synchronous belts. The standard trapezoidal shape was introduced in the 1940s. In the 1970s the *high torque drive* (HTD) belt was introduced with a round-shaped tooth. In more recent years a number of modified curvilinear tooth belts have been introduced with a tooth shape similar to gear teeth (Fig. 3-11). It is very important that each belt type be run in compatible pulleys or sprockets.

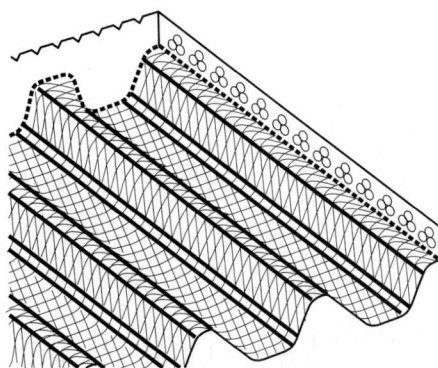

FIGURE 3-11   High torque drive belt.

BELT SELECTION

To aid in the selection of the proper belt for each application, manufacturers provide technical and performance data on their belts. In addition, the Rubber Manufacturers' Association (RMA) and the Mechanical Power Transmission Association (MPTA) have worked together to publish engineering standards and bulletins for most types of belts and drive hardware (see references at the end of the chapter). These publications contain information that supplements design catalogs.

There are four basic questions that need to be answered in the drive design:

1. What horsepower is required of the drive?
2. What is the speed (rpm) of the driver shaft?
3. What is the speed (rpm) of the driven shaft?
4. What is the approximate desired center distance?

In addition to the basic elements, there are a number of special drive characteristics that may require consideration. These might include:

- Special environmental conditions such as abrasives, chemicals, etc.
- Overhung load (OHL) considerations for gear motors and reducers
- Driven pulley inertia (WR^2) requirements for equipment such as piston compressors, crushers, etc.
- Special drive characteristics such as shock loads, inherent misalignment, clutching requirements, etc.

Also, while selecting and evaluating the drive, consider the following points:

- Selecting larger diameter pulleys will keep drive face width to a minimum.
- Selecting larger diameter pulleys will keep drive tensions and shaft load at a minimum.
- Larger diameter pulleys will often give a more economical drive, but should not be so large that multiple V-belt capability is sacrificed.
- If space is limited, consider using the smallest diameter drive. However, pulleys on electric motors must be at least as large as the National Electric Manufacturers Association (NEMA) minimum recommended standards.
- When the drive is between two belt cross-section sizes, the larger section will usually be more economical. However, it is always recommended to check drives in both cross sections.

Selecting an optimum belt drive involves many factors, but drive selection can be readily accomplished using manufacturers' design literature. *Many manufacturers also offer computer programs for drive design selection.*

MAINTENANCE AND SAFETY

Once a belt drive has been selected it requires a minimum of maintenance, but certain procedures can help reduce equipment downtime, extend service life, and increase safety.

Installing Belts

When installing belts on any multiple-belt drive, *always replace all the belts* because older belts naturally become worn and stretched from use. If old belts are mixed with new belts, the new belts will be tighter, carry more than their share of the load, and probably fail before their time.

Be sure to use a set of belts from a single manufacturer. If brands are mixed, the belts may have different characteristics and could work against each other. This could result in unusual strain and reduce the life of the belts.

There are two ways to assure a well-matched drive system depending on the method of matching used by the belt manufacturer.

Most manufacturers today use a no-match or single match system. Because of improved manufacturing systems and inspection procedures, manufacturers like Gates Rubber Co. can build belts to overall length tolerances that are within the RMA matching tolerances specified in the appropriate standard.

Some belt manufacturers, and some specialty belts, may still use the older, conventional matching system. Each belt is measured under industry standard tension in V sheaves and marked with a "punch" or match number designating the small increment of length within the overall belt length tolerance. With 50 as ideal, these match numbers generally run from 47 to 53. Belts using match numbers are grouped in sets within the limits given in Table 3-1.

TABLE 3-1   Belt Matching Limits

Belt length		
Inches	Millimeters	
Up to 63	Up to 1,600	Use only one number
63–150	1,600–3,810	Within two consecutive match numbers only
150–250	3,810–6,350	Within three consecutive match numbers only
250–375	6,350–9,525	Within four consecutive match numbers only
375–500	9,525–12,700	Within five consecutive match numbers only
Over 500	Over 12,700	Within six consecutive match numbers only

Belts intended to be run as single belts, such as light-duty, V-ribbed, and synchronous belts do not require a matching system.

After the belts have been properly selected, it is time to put them on the drive. The most important rule is *never to pry or roll the belts onto the pulley.* Prying the belt may cause invisible damage to the tensile cords, shortening the belt's life. The proper way to install the belt is to use the drive adjustment, generally the motor base, to move the pulleys closer together allowing the belt to be easily placed onto the pulleys. A sturdy pry bar will help move the motor. Keep the rails free of dirt, grit, and rust; lubricate them frequently. This will make the belt change easier and safer.

Be sure to properly align the motor and driven pulleys. V-belt drives should be aligned to within $\frac{1}{2}°$ or $\frac{1}{16}$ in/ft (4.8 mm/m) of center distance. V-ribbed and synchronous belt drives should be installed and aligned to within $\frac{1}{3}°$ or $\frac{1}{10}$ in/ft (7.7 mm/m) of center distance. Misaligned drives can result in V-belt turnover and premature and unusual belt wear leading to shorter belt life.

The final installation procedure involves properly tensioning the belt or belts for long, trouble-free service. Here are three helpful tensioning tips:

• The best tension for the belt is the lowest tension at which the V belt will not slip, or synchronous belts will not ratchet (jump grooves). Too much tension shortens belt life and may also overload shafts and bearings.

• Tension the drive and allow it to run-in for at least 15 min. The more lightly loaded the drive, the longer the run-in period. Check and retension the drive to the recommended tension.

• Check the V-belt tension periodically and retension as necessary. Synchronous belts generally should not be retensioned after the initial run-in period. Most belt manufacturers publish tensioning procedures in their design catalogs. Some manufacturers, such as Gates, also make available computer aided design and tensioning programs.

Belt Safety

Safety is a critical factor in the efficient operation of belt drives. The maintenance personnel can take several positive steps to help ensure drives run smoothly and safely:

1. Keep belt drives properly guarded. Regulatory agencies (particularly the Occupational Safety and Health Administration [OSHA]), insurance companies, and other safety authorities require that drives be completely guarded. The guard should allow proper ventilation but should not have gaps that allow workers to reach inside and become caught in the drive. The guard also prevents debris from entering into and damaging the belt drive.

2. Always turn the equipment off before working on the drive. Lock and tag the control box to indicate maintenance personnel are working on the drive.

3. Check position of all components. Make sure machine components such as flywheels are in a safe position and that clutches are in neutral position so as to avoid accidental movement or start-up.

4. Wear proper clothing. Loose or bulky clothing, such as neck ties, loose sleeves, or lab coats may become entangled in the drive. Wear gloves when inspecting pulleys to avoid being cut by nicks or burrs in the metal.

5. Keep the area clean. Debris and loose tools or other obstructions near the drive may result in tripping or falling. Keep floors clean.

6. Use proper tools and procedures. Never attempt to roll or pry belts onto the pulleys. In addition to causing unseen damage to the belt tensile cords (leading to early failure), you may painfully injure fingers or hands. Follow recommended installation procedures as discussed previously.

Belt Inspection

If proper belt inspection procedures are followed, 90 percent of all maintenance problems can be eliminated. A properly installed belt drive is a remarkably trouble-free piece of equipment. But, to assure continued trouble-free service, quick, periodic inspections of the belt drive should be made a part of the routine preventative maintenance schedule.

The inspection period may be influenced by a number of factors. These include, but are not limited to, drive operating conditions, critical nature of the equipment, temperature extremes in the drive vicinity, other environmental factors, and accessibility of the equipment.

Look, listen, feel, and smell. Watch the drive operate. Remove the guard *temporarily* if necessary. Look for excessive or unusual belt vibration. Listen for unusual noise. Feel the driver and driven machine for excessive vibration. Unusual odors may suggest badly slipping belts or worn or damaged bearings. Stop the drive, tag the control box for safety, and carefully inspect the drive components.

Belts   Immediately, but carefully, grasp or touch the belt. Your hand can safely tolerate up to about 140°F (60°C) surface temperature. If the V belt is uncomfortably hot, it may be slipping excessively due to inadequate tension. Check belt tension and retension as necessary. Never use a belt dressing to quiet a slipping V belt. It causes the belt to collect dirt and grit and damages the belt. Inspect the belt for any damage or unusual wear. Cracking, fraying, excessive wear, or loss of teeth (on a synchronous belt) might require belt replacement. Replace all the V belts in the set with a matched set of new belts from one manufacturer.

Pulleys   Inspect the pulleys for unusual damage or excessive wear on V-belt sheaves. Small nicks or burrs may be smoothed over with a file or emery cloth. Manufacturers' groove gages may be used to check for excessive wear on V-belt sheaves. If more than $\frac{1}{32}$ in (0.8 mm) of wear can be seen, the sheaves should be replaced. Visible wear on synchronous sprockets always suggests replacement.

Guards and Other Components   Check guards for damage and repair or replace as necessary. Check shafts, brackets, and bearings for damage and correct as necessary.

Reassemble the drive, turn it on, and again look and listen for unusual signs to ensure the equipment is operating properly.

TROUBLESHOOTING

Occasionally belts may fail prematurely or in an unusual manner. Troubleshooting a belt drive problem requires that you identify the causes. Proper procedures can make the investigative process easier for you and your belt supplier.

1. Describe the problem.
   - What is wrong?
   - When did it happen?
   - How often does it happen?
   - What is the drive application?
   - Have the machine operations or output changed?
   - What kind of belt(s) are you using?
   - What are your expectations for belt performance in this application?

2. Identify symptoms and record any unusual observations. These might include any of the following.
   - Premature belt failure.
   - Severe or abnormal belt wear.
   - Banded (joined) belt problems.
   - V belt turns over or jumps off sheave
   - Belt stretches beyond take-up
   - Belt noise
   - Unusual vibration
   - Problem with pulleys
   - Problems with drive components
   - Hot bearings
   - Performance problems

Belt Failure

The most common symptoms, causes, and corrections of V-belt and synchronous-belt failures are shown in Tables 3-2 and 3-3.

TABLE 3-2   Why V Belts Fail

Trouble area and observation	Probable cause	Corrective action
Worn side patterns	Constant slip	Re-tension drive until belt stops slipping
	Misaligned sheaves	Align drive
	Worn sheave	Replace sheave
	Incorrect belt	Replace belts
Bottom of belt cracking	Belt slipping, causing heat buildup and gradual hardening of undercord	Install new belt, tension to prevent slip
	Idler installed on wrong side of belt	Refer to a V-belt installation manual
	Improper storage	Follow proper storage procedures
Bottom and sides burned	Belt slipping under starting or stalling load	Replace belt and tighten drive until slippage stops
	Worn sheave	Replace sheave
Belt turnover	Foreign material in grooves	Remove material, shield drive
	Misaligned sheaves	Align drive
	Worn sheave	Replace sheave
	Tensile member broken through improper installation	Replace with new belt(s) and follow proper installation procedure
	Incorrectly aligned idler pulley	Carefully align idler, checking alignment with drive loaded and unloaded
Belt pulled apart	Extreme shock load	Remove cause of shock load or redesign drive for increased capacity
	Belt came off drive	Check drive alignment, foreign material in drive; ensure proper tension and drive alignment

TABLE 3-3 Why Synchronous Belts Fail

Trouble area and observation	Probable cause	Corrective action
Excessive belt edge wear or cracking	Flange damage	Repair flange or replace sprocket
	Belt too wide	Use proper width belt and sprocket
	Misaligned drive	Align drive
	Rough flange surface	Repair flange
	Improper tracking	Correct alignment
	Belt hitting drive guard or bracketry	Remove obstruction or use inside idler
Tensile break	Excessive shock loads	Redesign drive for increased capacity
	Subminimal diameter	Redesign drive using larger diameters
	Improper handling or storage prior to to installation	Follow proper handling and storage procedures
	Extreme sprocket run-out	Replace sprocket
	Misaligned drive	Align drive
Belt cracking	Subminimal diameter	Redesign drive using larger diameters
	Backside idler	Use inside idler or larger diameter backside idler
	Extreme low temperature at start-up	Pre-heat drive environment
	Extended chemical exposure	Protect drive
Premature tooth wear	Too low or high belt tension	Correct belt tension
	Belt running off unflanged sprocket	Align drive
	Incorrect belt profile for sprocket (i.e. HTD, GT, etc.)	Use proper belt/sprocket combination
	Worn sprocket	Replace sprocket
Tooth shear	Excessive shock loads	Redesign drive for increased capacity
	Less than 6 teeth-in-mesh	Redesign drive
	Worn sprocket	Replace sprocket
	Incorrect belt profile for sprocket	Use proper belt/sprocket combination
	Misaligned drive	Align drive
	Belt under tensioned	Correct belt tension

BIBLIOGRAPHY

The following are publications of the Rubber Manufacturers Association, Washington, D.C.:

IP-3   *Power Transmission Belt Technical Bulletin* The complete set of IP-3-1 through 3-13 is listed below (also available separately).

IP-3-1   *Heat Resistance of Power Transmission Belts (1987).*

IP-3-2   *Oil & Chemical Resistance of Power Transmission Belts (1987).*

IP-3-3   *Static Conductive V Belts (1985).*

IP-3-4   *Storage of Power Transmission Belts (1987).*

IP-3-6   *Use of Idlers with Power Transmission Belt Drives (1987).*

IP-3-7   *V-Flat Drives (1972).*

IP-3-8   *High Modulus Belts (1987).*

IP-3-9   *Joined V Belts (1987).*

IP-3-10   *V Belt Drives with Twist & Nonalignment (1987).*

IP-3-13   *Mechanical Efficiency of Power Transmission Belt Drives (1987).*

IP-3-14   *Drive Design Procedure for Variable Pitch Drives (1987).*

IP-20   *Specification: Joint MPTA/RMA/RAC Classical V Belts (1988).* A, B, C, and D Cross Sections.

IP-21   *Specifications: Joint RMA/MPTA Double V Belts (1984).* AA, BB, CC, DD Cross Sections.

IP-22   *Specification: Joint MPTA/RMA/RAC Narrow Multiple V Belts (1983).* 3V, 5V, and 8V Cross Sections.

IP-23   *Specification: Joint RMA/MPTA Single V Belts (1991).* 2L, 3L, 4L, and 5L Cross Sections.

IP-24   *Specification: Joint MPTA/RMA/RAC Synchronous Belts (1983).* MXL, XL, L, H, XH, and XXH Belt Sections.

IP-25   *Specification: Joint MPTA/RMA/RAC Variable Speed Belts (1991).* Twelve Cross Sections.

IP-26   *Specification: Joint MPTA/RMA/RAC V-Ribbed Belts (1977).* H, J, K, L, and M Cross Sections.

CHAPTER 7-3
SHAFT DRIVES AND COUPLINGS

PART 2

FLEXIBLE COUPLINGS

Raymond W. Giegerich
Director of Engineering (Ret.)
Lovejoy, Inc.
Downer's Grove, Illinois

INTRODUCTION

A *flexible coupling* may be defined simply as a device that transmits power from one shaft to another, while permitting some degree of misalignment between the shafts.

If two shafts could be perfectly aligned, they could be connected with a sleeve or two flanges bolted together. In reality, some misalignment between the shafts is always present and that is why a flexible coupling *must* be used. Flexible couplings are perhaps the most mistreated parts of any machinery, both at the time of selection and during installation. But high maintenance costs and lost production time can be avoided with proper selection and installation.

Flexible couplings differ from many other types of power transmission equipment in that there are so many from which to choose. In contrast with V belts, chain drives, ball bearings, and so on, where there is extensive interchangeability from one brand to the next, complete interchangeability among coupling brands is rare because there are so many types of couplings. Numerous "specialty" types also exist.

Each type of coupling has its advantages and its limitations in performance and application. Before a brand or size of coupling can be chosen it is essential that the right type of coupling for the application be determined.

A flexible coupling will free up the system, providing some motion relief between the driving and driven equipment shafts. But no one coupling type is the answer to all of the problems that can exist in a drive system. When choosing a coupling try to find the best coupling for the application. Among the factors affecting the type of coupling that will work best are:

Power capacity required

Space available

Ambient temperature

Environment (chemical exposure, weather conditions, etc.)

Torque overloads, reversing, start/stop frequency

Alignment problems

Ease of installation

Maintenance required

Torsional stiffness and backlash tolerance

Damping capacity

Axial freedom

High speed capacity

Type of driver and driven equipment

SHAFT ALIGNMENT

Coupling catalogs list the maximum tolerable misalignment for the coupling in terms of angular, parallel, and (sometimes) axial capacity. The initial alignment can change for a number of reasons, such as foundation settling, bearing wear, loosened mounting bolts, temperature changes, vibration, and movement of the connected machines from external forces induced by piping, belts, and chain drives. At installation, always strive for the best possible initial alignment of the shafts, so that the coupling has enough reserve misalignment capacity to accommodate future shifting of the connected equipment.

Parallel Misalignment

This type of misalignment is the easiest to measure and correct (see Fig. 3-12). It can be corrected by shimming the lower machine part or shifting one or the other from side to side. The amount of offset, E, is found from the equation

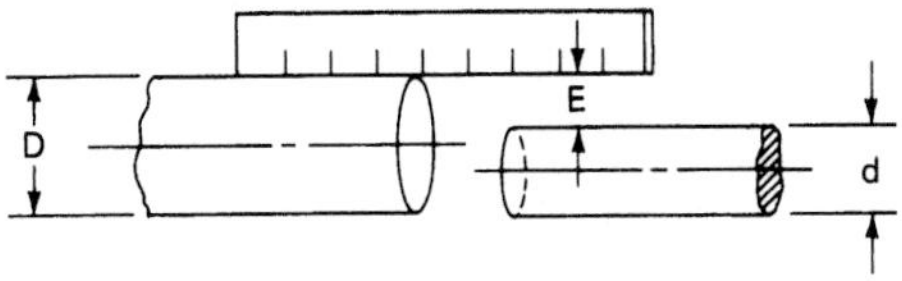

FIGURE 3-12   Parallel misalignment.

$$\text{Offset} = E - \frac{D-d}{2}$$

This is the amount that one machine or the other must be shifted. If the two shafts have the same diameter, then the offset is simply equal to E.

Angular and Combination Misalignment

This is more difficult to measure and correct (see Fig. 3-13). In most cases correction will be by trial and error in order to get the equipment aligned to the point where only parallel mis-

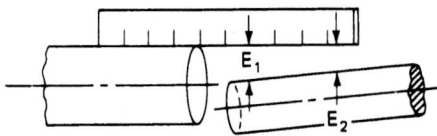

FIGURE 3-13 Combination misalignment.

alignment exists, and then correcting as described in the preceding paragraph. Combinations of angular and parallel are common. The most frequently used tools for correcting misalignment are a straight edge, feeler gages, and dial indicators. The references at the end of the chapter list some articles on alignment. Coupling manufacturers can help to guide the installation of their particular types of coupling.

TYPES OF FLEXIBLE COUPLINGS

Flexible couplings may be categorized in various ways, and there is no industry standard of reference. Terminology varies somewhat among manufacturers. There is general agreement, though, that there are two major categories of couplings: *elastomeric* and *all metal*. Within each major category there are subcategories as follows:

Elastomeric Type

Jaw type (elastomer in compression)

Sleeve type (elastomer in shear)

Doughnut, free mounted (compression)

Pin and bushing (compression)

Tire (shear)

Molded or vulcanized (shear)

All-Metal Type

Metallic membrane type

- Laminated disc
- Flexible link
- Diaphram
- Servo disc

Metallic gear

Metallic miscellaneous type

- Grid
- Wrapped spring
- Offset
- Helically formed beam and bellows
- Chain

These are the principal types of couplings made. There are some variations and combinations in specialty types that are not mass produced.

TERMINOLOGY

Some terms used in the industry are:

1. *Torsional stiffness.*   A measure of the amount that one half of a coupling will "twist" with relation to the other half when torque is applied. If one half of the coupling is locked down, and torque is applied to the other half, there will be some amount of twist. In elastomeric couplings this will be a larger amount than in an all-metal couplings. Torsional stiffness is usually expressed in pounds inch per radian.

2. *Backlash.*   The amount of free movement between two rotating parts. This occurs because of the clearance between connecting parts of a coupling. A disc coupling has no backlash; a jaw coupling, depending on the fit of the spider, will have some backlash.

3. *Spacer.*   The portion of the coupling which spans the gap between the ends of the shafts when the shafts are an extended distance apart. Sometimes called a *dropout,* this type of coupling is common on pump and fan drives.

4. *Reactionary loads.*   All couplings have some degree of radial stiffness, that is, they resist parallel misalignment. When the two shafts are offset, the coupling resists that offset by creating a side load. The side load causes the shaft to bend slightly and that creates a radial load on the bearings, called a reactionary load. This can be a very harmful bearing load and is a crucial factor in coupling selection and installation.

In the following text, when the term *high reactionary load* is used it means that the coupling will exhibit this condition when the shafts are misaligned beyond the manufacturer's recommended limits.

5. *Damping.*   The ability of a coupling to reduce the vibration level from one shaft to the next. Depending on the flexing element between the coupling halves, vibration may be reduced significantly or not at all. Most types of all-metal couplings cannot reduce vibration levels, while elastomeric couplings can significantly reduce them, depending on the elastomeric material.

6. *Engagement.*   A single engagement means that the coupling halves are engaged in just one plane (e.g., a jaw type coupling). Double engagement couplings, which are engaged in two planes, are all separated by a spacer of some type, such as an elastomeric sleeve or a gear sleeve. Double engagement is required in order for all-metal couplings to have parallel misalignment capability.

ELASTOMERIC COUPLINGS

The characteristics of elastomeric couplings are as follows:

- Torsionally soft
- Good damping
- No lubrication or maintenance
- Can be visually inspected for wear or damage
- Elements usually field replaceable
- Usually have lower reactionary loads on bearings
- Usually less expensive than all-metal couplings for comparable torque ratings

Their limitations are:

- Operating temperature limited to about 200°F (93°C)
- More sensitive to chemical exposure than all-metal types
- Not torsionally stiff
- Usually require more space for comparable torque than all-metal types

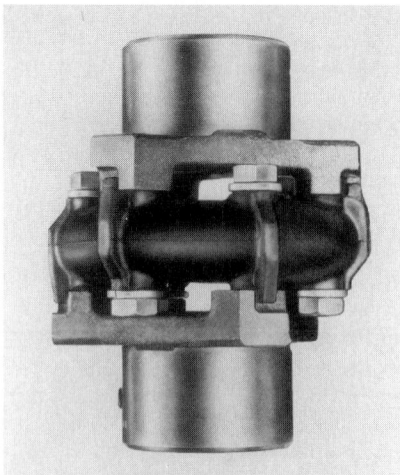

FIGURE 3-14 Rubber-doughnut coupling.

FIGURE 3-15 Rubber-tire coupling. (*Reproduced by permission of Reliance Electric Co.*)

- Torsionally stiff
- Good temperature and chemical resistance
- High torque in a small space
- Available in stainless steel

    Their limitations are:

- Fatigue plays a major role in failure
- May need lubrication
- Most cannot damp out vibration
- Require very careful installation

Types of Elastomeric Flexible Couplings

- *Jaw type*   A single engagement coupling with interlocking jaws.
- *Sleeve type*   A double engagement coupling.
- *Doughnut type*   Doughnut type couplings are single engagement with a set of driving bolts alternately engaging the doughnut from the driving to the driven hub (see Fig. 3-14).
- *Pin and bushing type*   This type of coupling transmits torque thru pins that project out from the two hubs and engage elastomeric bushings.
- *Tire type*   Three different types of couplings fall into this category.

    1. External, axially clamped type   This type of coupling is distinguished by the obvious tire form (see Fig. 3-15). The tire is clamped by plates, using axially positioned bolts.

    2. Inverted tire type   This design confines the tire inside a housing, preventing the problem with centrifugal force which causes the bearings to be thrust loaded.

    3. Molded urethane tire type   This "tire" is molded to a sleeve, called a shoe.

- *Molded rubber*   This category of couplings is usually associated with designs that have an elastomer that is bonded, molded to, or compressed within one or more of the coupling components.

ALL-METAL COUPLINGS

The characteristics of all-metal couplings are as follows:

Types of All-Metal Couplings

- *Laminated disc type*   These are among the oldest type of mass-produced flexible couplings (see Fig. 3-16). They consist of two hubs that are connected by a laminated disc pack or, in most cases, by two sets of disc packs with a spacer between them.
- *Flexlink type*   Constructed of two flanges onto which hubs are mounted, power is transmitted across flexlinks rather than discs.
- *Diaphragm type*   This type of coupling is considered for high performance applications, such as in areas where reliability is very important and accessibility is very limited.
- *Servo disc type*   This classification is for small disc type couplings used for servo-motion applications.
- *Gear type*   Gear couplings consist of two hubs with external gear teeth and a connecting sleeve with internal gear teeth (see Fig. 3-17).
- *Grid type*   In this design a steel grid, which looks like a lacing, intertwines between serrations that project outwardly from two hubs (see Fig. 3-18).
- *Wrapped spring type*   This coupling consists of three separately wound square wire springs, tightly wrapped.
- *Offset type*   This type of coupling is unique in its ability to handle very large parallel offsets.
- *Beam and bellows type*   Both of these types of couplings are essentially of curved beam construction for light duty applications.
- *Chain type*   The chain type coupling consists of two sprockets with bored hubs connected by a standard, double roller chain (see Fig. 3-19). Also available from some manufacturers with silent chain or plastic chain.

SELECTION

Usually, couplings are supplied as part of any new piece of equipment. There are cases, however, when either the coupling does not meet its expectations or the machinery was supplied

FIGURE 3-16   Disc-pack coupling. (*Reproduced by permission of Rexnord Corp.*)

FIGURE 3-17   Gear-type coupling.

FIGURE 3-18   Steel-grid coupling. (*Reproduced by permission of The Falk Corporation.*)

FIGURE 3-19   Chain coupling. (*Reproduced by permission of FMC Corporation.*)

without a coupling. Then a new coupling must be selected and *selecting the right type of coupling is crucial to success.* No one coupling will suit all of the many conditions that affect coupling selection. Table 3-4 has been prepared to help sort out the factors that should receive primary consideration in selecting a type of coupling.

Table 3-4 is intended only to be a guideline. Check with the coupling manufacturer of your choice before eliminating its coupling from contention because the coupling may have a hidden feature which can overcome the problem.

Where numerical values are not assigned the couplings are rated good, fair, or poor. *Good* means the coupling is recommended for that application and *poor* means the coupling is probably not suitable.

In addition to rating couplings in terms of horsepower and torque at various rpm's, most manufacturers provide the coupling rating in horsepower per hundred rpm. For example, if a pump requires 50 hp (37.3 kW) at 1750 rpm, it needs a coupling that can handle 2.86 hp (2.13 kW) at 100 rpm. Service factors must be added if necessary.

The equation is:

$$\text{hp (coupling rating)} = \frac{\text{hp}}{N} \times 100$$

where hp is the required horsepower at N, the operating rpm.

In the process of selecting the right type of coupling several factors have to be considered. Primary information for selection:

1. Horsepower and/or torque
2. RPM
3. Shaft sizes and keyways
4. Prime mover (e.g., electric motor, internal combustion engine)
5. Description of the driven equipment

   Secondary (but maybe essential) information:

1. Environmental conditions
2. Start/stop/reverse requirements

TABLE 3-4   Coupling Selection Factors

Type of coupling	Torque range[1] (lb-in)	Angular misalignment[2]	Parallel misalignment (in)	Damping capacity	Reactionary loading when misaligned	Torsional stiffness	Torque capacity to diam. ratio	Maintenance req'd
Jaw	170,000	1.5	.015	F	F	F	G	G
Sleeve	72,000	1.5	.020	G	G	P	F	G
Doughnut	22,000	3.0	.080	G	F	P	F	G
Pin and bushing	13,000	5.0	.050	G	G	F	F	G
Tire external	453,000	4.0	.12	G	F	F	F	G
Tire internal	142,000	.2	.042	G	F	F	F	G
Tire bonded	170,000	4.0	.18	F	F	F	F	G
Molded	177,000	.5	.02	G	F	P	F	G
Metallic-disc	1,700,000	.12	.01	P	P	G	G	G
Flexible link	88,000	2	.25	P	G	G	F	G
Diaphragm	6,000,000	Note 3		P	P	G	G	G
Servo disc	15	3	.02	F	G	G	P	G
Gear	60,000,000	.5	.15	P	P	G	G	F
Grid	7,500,000	.10	.05	F	P	F	G	F
Wrapped spring	2,000	4.5	.04	F	G	F	G	G
Offset	460,000	.5	17	P	G	F	F	F
Beam	230	5	.01	F	G	F	F	G
Bellows	250	17	.07	F	G	G	F	G
Chain	1,300,000	1.5	.03	P	P	F	G	F

G=good, F=fair, P=poor.
Note: Combinations of torque and misalignment values shown are not for any one size of coupling.
1. Approximate torque range with a service factor of 1.0. Some manufacturers may offer higher torque couplings, some may not be as high.
2. Initial installation should be well within these values unless otherwise specified by a manufacturer. For most couplings, both the maximum angular and parallel misalignment values cannot exist at the same time. RPM is also a factor affecting misalignment.
3. Contact manufacturers for misalignment information.

3. Space limitations
4. Shaft fits, special bores
5. Is this a retrofit? If so, what is the application history?
6. Probable alignment conditions
7. Axial movement
8. Special balancing
9. Conditions or requirements peculiar to certain industries
10. For internal combustion engine driven applications there is a need for considerable data about the engine and usually about the driven side. Data needed includes:
    Engine manufacturer
    Engine power data
    SAE flywheel and flywheel housing data
    Driven equipment data, including inertia
    Operating speed range
    Temperature range
    Pump mounting bracket data if applicable
    Alignment conditions

TRADEOFFS

When selecting the right *type* of coupling, frequently tradeoffs must be made between one desirable feature and another. For example, a coupling cannot be both torsionally very stiff and at the same time have good damping characteristics. In this case a desired attribute has to be sacrificed. You may opt for torsional stiffness in the coupling then add damping somewhere else in the power train.

In retrofit applications, where several coupling failures have occurred, beware of simply changing brands of the same type of coupling. The wrong type of coupling may have been used in the first place and another type of coupling, not another brand, should be considered in order to prevent perpetuating the problem.

SERVICE FACTORS

Always refer to the "Service Factors" page of the coupling catalogue. Service factors are applied for two reasons. One is to provide good coupling life for those couplings that have parts that wear out. The other is to prevent coupling failure due to fatigue or sudden rupture of the torque transmitting element.

Do not "over-service-factor" an application. If enough service factor is applied to a flexible coupling, or any power transmission component, the component will outlast the machine by far. But, an oversized coupling can cause damage to shafts and bearings in addition to taking up more space and adding unnecessary weight and cost to the system. No amount of "over-service-factoring" will compensate for not selecting the right coupling. When sizing, always try to determine the amount of torque required at the point of operation, rather than just making selections based on the motor hp and rpm.

INSTALLATION

In reality, the alignment of the equipment can be quite complicated because, in most instances, once the equipment is aligned the couplings cannot be installed without moving the machines again. It is therefore essential to plan ahead . . . and this is where the right type of coupling can save time during installation.

If a coupling has a driving and driven hub with machined outside surfaces that are concentric to the bore, these hubs can be premounted on the shafts. The machined diameters rather than the shafts are then used as reference points. The flexible element may have to be installed after the machine parts are aligned. With many coupling designs the whole pre-assembled coupling can be installed with the machined surfaces used as a point of reference.

Some coupling designs force the installer toward good alignment or the coupling cannot even be assembled. The gear coupling is a good example. The flanges cannot be bolted together if alignment isn't very close because of the very small clearance between the external and internal gear teeth.

A good rule of thumb is: If you have to force any of the connecting parts of the coupling together in order to get the coupling assembled, you have probably exceeded the misalignment capacity of the coupling. For example, if the bolts that couple the flanges together in the gear coupling don't "drop" into place so that the flanges slide easily over the hubs, the shafts are out of alignment.

Types of couplings that are difficult to assemble if misaligned are: gear, jaw, some doughnut types, pin and bushing, laminated disc, flexible link, diaphragm, servo disc, grid, and possibly chain.

Axial misalignment is often overlooked and yet it can be very critical in the installation of some types of couplings. A coupling may seem to have a good deal of axial freedom but that "softness" can lead to early failure of the coupling. Consider the laminated disc type. It gets its misalignment ability from the flexing of the discs, but only within 1° at the most per disc set. If the machine parts are pulled apart or pushed together after angular and offset alignment are corrected, the coupling will be axially misaligned. This causes the discs to bend beyond their 1° limit and can lead to early disc failure due to fatigue of the laminates. Great care must be taken at the final step in the installation. Other types that are sensitive to axial compression or expansion are flexible link, diaphragm, servo disc, beam, bellows, wrapped spring, offset, some doughnut types, and possibly tire.

Always use care in torquing down setscrews and cap screws. Interference fits between the hub and shafts, as opposed to slide fits, are a matter of judgment and plant rules. Interference fits are recommended for installations where vibration is high or it is essential that the coupling movement on the shaft be zero at all times. Clamped hubs, or tapered bores are also a solution for good tight fits.

MAINTENANCE

The type and frequency of maintenance of a coupling is often more a matter of the severity of the application than of the coupling design. Maintenance must be based on the manufacturer's recommendations and the level of reliability required in the application.

Except for those couplings requiring lubrication, no definite schedule can be accurately prescribed by the manufacturers. One rule, though, would be that for those types requiring careful bolt tightening and/or accurate alignment, the coupling should be checked a short period of time after installation—perhaps at about 100 h. This will ensure that no major changes have occurred during the break in period.

If vibration or noise exists within or nearby the coupling, it may be a sign that the alignment is off or coupling failure is imminent.

Elastomeric couplings are usually easily examined. Look for permanent compression in the spider or cushions in jaw type couplings. In any elastomer look for tears or cracks, unusual bulges, elastomeric residue below the coupling, extremely hot surfaces, or looseness between the connecting parts beyond the coupling's original condition. A history of replacement of elastomers should be kept and scheduled replacements made.

All-metal couplings, in addition to scheduled lubrication (if required) may require periodic inspection of the torque transmitting parts. The type of coupling will determine the kind and frequency of inspection. For example, disc couplings may be inspected for loose bolts and small surface cracks at the outer laminates without disassembly. Grid, gear, and chain types will require some disassembly to check for wear, and this should be done at the time of lubrication.

REFERENCES

1. Dreymala, J.: "Try Dial Indicators for Close Alignment of Coupling Connected Machinery," *Power,* June 1971, pp. 96–98.

2. Jackson, C.: "Techniques for Alignment of Rotating Equipment," *Hydrocarbon Processing,* January 1976, pp. 81–85.

3. Campbell, A. J.: "Optical Alignment Saves Equipment Downtime," *Oil and Gas Journal,* November 1975, pp. 54–56.

4. Murray, M. G.: "Minimum Movement Machinery Alignment," *Hydrocarbon Processing,* January 1979, pp. 112–114.

5. "Reverse Indicator Method of Alignment," Hughes & Associates, Houston, Texas, 1974.

6. Calistrat, M. M.: "Flexible Coupling Installation," *Proceedings of the National Conference on Power Transmission, 1981,* Illinois Institute of Technology, Chicago.

Note: *Always keep latest catalogs and application notes of leading manufacturers.*

CHAPTER 7-3

SHAFT DRIVES
AND COUPLINGS

PART 3

CHAIN DRIVES

R. B. Curry
S. E. Winegardner
Senior Engineers
Rexnord Corporation
Indianapolis, Indiana

INTRODUCTION

Chain drives are one of the most efficient methods used to transmit mechanical power between two or more parallel rotating shafts that cannot be directly coupled. A typical chain drive consists of a series of assembled links (commonly referred to as the chain) and two or more sprockets (Fig. 3-20). Power is transmitted through the chain by positive engagement with a driven sprocket to one or more drive sprockets that are keyed to rotating shafts. Roller chain, engineered chain, and silent (inverted tooth) chain are the three principal types of chain used in industrial drive applications.

FIGURE 3-20   A roller chain drive operates multiple rolls in a heat-treating furnace.

Some benefits of a chain drive, compared to a belt drive, are:

1. Shaft center distances are relatively unrestricted.
2. Chains are easily installed and maintained.
3. Chain drives provide a highly efficient, positive drive and a fixed ratio means of providing power.
4. Chain drives operate in adverse environmental conditions such as high temperatures and corrosive, dusty, and generally dirty surroundings.
5. Chain drives do not require pre-tension between shafts for power transmission, thereby reducing bearing loads.

Some benefits of a chain drive, compared to a gear drive, are:

1. The load in a chain drive is distributed over a number of sprocket teeth simultaneously.
2. Chain drives are generally more compact.
3. All components rotate in the same direction, eliminating the need for additional components to maintain that feature.

This chapter encompasses basic design, application, use, and maintenance of roller chain. Additional information on this subject and other chain applications, along with sprocket selection procedures, can be obtained from manufacturers' catalogs. *The reader is cautioned that all calculations are only examples to aid in understanding concepts.* All design work should be done by those versed in this subject and/or with the cooperation of the manufacturer.

ROLLER CHAIN DESIGN

Roller chain drives are used in a wide range of power transmission applications for all basic industries such as food processing, materials handling, oil field equipment, construction, agricultural equipment, and machine tools.

Fourteen standard sizes of single- and multiple-width roller chain are listed in ANSI B29.1[1] (Figs. 3-21 and 3-22). Table 3-5 shows the chain number, corresponding pitch size, and the ANSI minimum ultimate tensile strength for single-width chain. This standard includes those roller chains that are intended for use in power transmission and conveying applications. These chains *are not intended* for use in overhead hoists or lifting applications. For specific information on hoist and leaf type chains, see ANSI B29.24 and B29.8, respectively.

FIGURE 3-21   Single-width roller chain.

FIGURE 3-22   Multiple-width roller chain.

The chain number can be broken down to determine the pitch and general type of roller chain. The rightmost digits indicate the type, "1" indicates a lightweight chain, "5" indicates a bushing only (with no rotating roller), and "0" designates a standard roller chain. The remaining digit(s) are multiplied by ⅛ in (3.2 mm) to obtain the pitch in in (mm). Thus, a #35 roller chain is a 0.375-in (9.6-mm) pitch roller chain with an integral roller/bushing design.

TABLE 3-5   Standard Single-Width Roller Chain Size and Strength

	Chain pitch		Minimum ultimate strength	
Chain number	in	mm	lb	N
25	0.250	6.35	780	3,470
35	0.375	9.52	1,760	7,825
41	0.500	12.70	1,500	6,672
40	0.500	12.70	3,125	13,900
50	0.625	15.88	4,880	21,710
60	0.750	19.05	7,030	31,720
80	1.000	25.40	12,500	55,600
100	1.250	31.75	19,530	86,870
120	1.500	38.10	28,125	125,100
140	1.750	44.45	38,280	170,270
160	2.000	50.80	50,000	222,400
180	2.250	57.15	63,280	281,470
200	2.500	63.50	78,125	347,500
240	3.000	76.20	112,500	520,400

The minimum ultimate tensile strength refers to the minimum allowable tensile strength that the American Chain Association and ANSI have determined that manufacturers of roller chain must meet. Reputable manufacturers can easily meet or exceed this value. The minimum ultimate tensile strength for multiple-width roller chain is equal to the minimum ultimate tensile strength of single-width roller chain times the number of strands in the multiple-width roller chain.

ANSI standard roller chain generally can be identified by three critical dimensions (Fig. 3-23). The first is pitch, which is the distance between the centers of adjacent pins. The second is the roller diameter, which is the outside diameter of the roller. The third is the chain width, which is the minimum distance between roller link plates. Note that the chain width is not the overall width. Both the chain width and roller diameter are approximately ⅝ of the pitch.

Basic component part nomenclature, as recognized by the American Chain Association, is shown in Fig. 3-24.

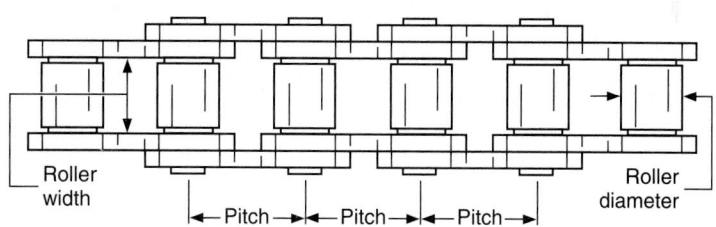

FIGURE 3-23   The three critical dimensions.

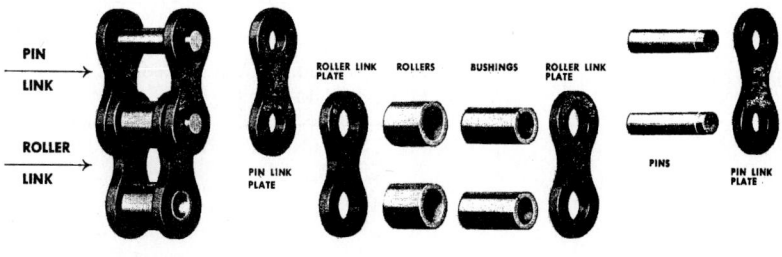

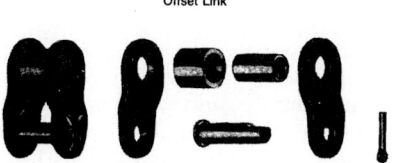

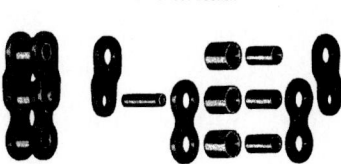

FIGURE 3-24   Basic part nomenclature.

Interchangability between manufacturers is achieved by conformance to ANSI B29.1M. While standard roller chains from different manufacturers will intercouple and fit over the same sprockets, it is not a recommended practice. Small differences in material, heat treatment, and manufacturing specifications can contribute to premature failure of the drive.

Standard roller chain strength and life is very dependent on the quality of materials and heat treatment of component parts and press fits. Standard roller chain utilizes press fits at the bushing-to-roller link plate joints and the pin-to-pin link plate joints. These press fits are what hold the chain together during operation. Proper press fits (generally 0.003 to 0.006 in [0.08–0.16 mm]) contribute significantly to enhancement of fatigue life.

Some manufacturers go beyond a simple press fit by cold working the roller link plate and pin link plate pitch holes before assembly. This imparts residual compressive stresses around the hole and improves the geometry of the hole. Cold working can be done before or after heat treatment. Post-heat treatment yields the greatest return because the residual stresses are retained. This results in improved pin plate and bushing plate fatigue life. This is a particularly important feature to look for when the chain drive is subjected to a combination of low speed and high loading.

Speed and horsepower ratings are the prime considerations in engineering a chain drive. The ratings are normally listed for the smaller sprocket, regardless of whether it is the drive or driven member. Chain manufacturers should be consulted when special conditions such as composite duty cycles, idlers, or more than two sprockets are involved in the drive cycle.

The speed and horsepower ratings are based on approximately 15,000 h of service life at full-load operation and a service factor of 1.0. Operating conditions that establish the service factor are shown in Table 3-6. Strand factors for multiple-width chains are given in Table 3-7. Note that the strand factors are not equal to the number of widths in a multiple-width chain.

TABLE 3-6   Service Factors

	IC engine w/hydraulic drive	Electric motor or turbine	IC engine w/mechanical drive
Uniform load	1.0	1.0	1.2
Moderate shock load	1.2	1.3	1.4
Heavy shock load	1.4	1.5	1.7

TABLE 3-7   Multiple-Strand Factors for Multiple-Width Chains

Number of strands	Multiple-strand factor
2	1.7
3	2.5
4	3.3
5	4.1
6	5.0
7 or more	Consult manufacturer

Specialty roller chains have been developed for particular applications. For example, double pitch chain is an economical choice for slower speed drives on relatively long centers. Heavy series roller chain is used when conditions demand additional capacity to withstand the shortened sideplate fatigue life imposed by low-speed/high-load applications. Flexible joint type chain has been designed for smaller horsepower drives where the chain follows a guided serpentine path. Lubricated joint chains have oil-impregnated bushings to provide cleaner and longer operating life where either lubrication is restricted or external lubrication is absent.

Standard roller chain made of stainless steel is recommended for applications where high resistance to corrosive attack is required. When stainless is considered, specific attention must be paid to the corrosive environment and compatibility with manufacturers' offerings. It should be noted that most stainless chains have ⅓ to ¼ the horsepower capacity of conventional carbon steel roller chains.

SILENT CHAIN DRIVES

Silent (inverted tooth) chain is a drive chain constructed of sidebars (links), joint components, pins, and bushings that are unique to each manufacturer (Fig. 3-25). These chains do not have rollers, and the joint design of each manufacturer will prevent sections of chains of different manufacturers from being coupled together. The sidebars are designed to mesh with sprocket teeth in a gear-type engagement. Generally a silent chain drive is selected for high-speed/high-load applications and for smooth, quiet operations in industrial services such as electric generating plants, automotive test stands, machine tools, and ventilating systems.

FIGURE 3-25   Silent chain drive.

There is a wide range of silent chain-link configurations available from various manufacturers.[2] Most silent chain manufacturers produce chains of their own design that will transmit more horsepower at higher speeds than ANSI-standard chains. For this reason, silent chains cannot be interchanged on different manufacturers' sprockets. However, the SC series of silent chains shown in ANSI Standard B29.2 is interchangeable on sprockets among manufacturers.

ENGINEERING STEEL CHAIN DRIVES

Engineering steel chain drives are especially suited for heavy-duty applications. The normally offset sidebar chain (Fig. 3-26) can handle speeds up to 1000 ft/min (305 m/min) and power requirements as high as 500 hp (370 kW). These chains are commonly used in elevator drives, large conveyor drives, drum drives, and applications with poor operating conditions.

The eight sizes of engineering steel chain available are listed in ANSI Standard B29.10. Table 3-8 shows the chain number, the pitch

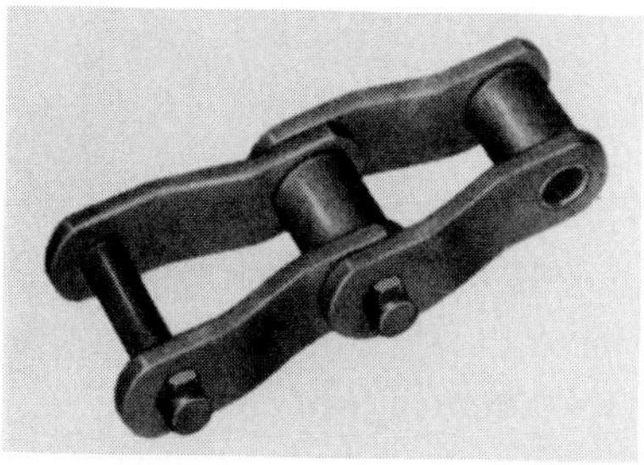

FIGURE 3-26   Engineering steel drive chain.

size, and the minimum ultimate strength for each of the eight chains. As is the case with roller chain, speed and horsepower ratings are the prime considerations in selecting a chain drive. Normally, the ratings are listed for the smaller sprocket, regardless of whether or not it is the driver or driven member. Chain manufacturers should be consulted for proper drive selections when special conditions are encountered.

TABLE 3-8 Engineering Steel-Chain Size and Strength

Chain number	Chain pitch		Minimum ultimate strength	
	in	mm	lb	kn
2010	2.500	63.5	57,000	254
2512	3.067	77.9	77,000	342
2814	3.500	88.9	106,000	471
3315	4.073	103.4	124,000	552
3618	4.500	114.3	171,000	701
4020	5.000	127.0	222,000	987
4824	6.000	152.4	315,000	1401
5628	7.000	117.8	425,000	1890

DESIGN SUGGESTIONS FOR ENGINEERING A DRIVE

This section is intended to provide general suggestions or guidelines for evaluating and determining some of the mechanical design details in the drive design process.

Center Distance

Adjustable centers should be included in the initial design to allow compensation for wear. Adjustment range should be at least 1½ pitches. A center distance of 30 to 50 pitches is preferred. Minimum center distance should equal the diameter of the large sprocket plus half the diameter of the small sprocket. These proportions assure the suggested minimum chain wrap of 120° on the small sprocket. Absolute miminum center distance must be enough to provide clearance between sprocket teeth. Maximum center distance should be limited to 80 pitches. If maximum center distance exceeds 80 pitches, the catenary should be supported by one or more idlers or guides.

When sprocket centers cannot be adjusted, make a conservative drive selection by using a larger service factor than indicated. Providing good lubrication will have a positive impact on drive life, particularly drives with fixed centers. Fixed centers should have an automatically or manually adjustable idler as a method for taking up chain slack.

Chain Tightener

The purpose of a chain tightener is to remove control slack without creating excess tension. Chain tightening devices are often used for the following purposes:

1. To control chain slack when drives are on fixed centers.

2. To control chain slack and pulsations on drives with vertical centers.

3. To eliminate the whipping action sometimes found in drives with long centers.

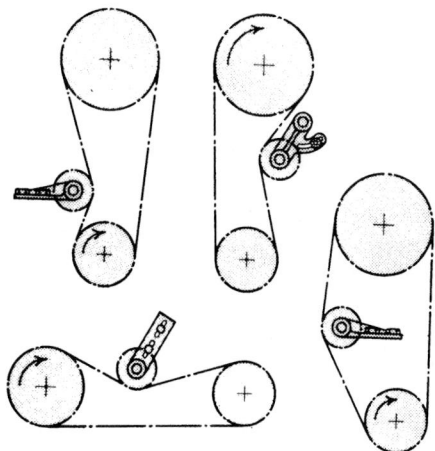

The most common type of chain tightener is an idler sprocket mounted on an adjustable bracket, either manually adjusted or spring loaded. Rollers, shoes, and vibration dampeners are also used for regulating chain excess tension. The idler design and installation should be capable of providing enough adjustment to remove two full pitches of chain. This avoids the need for a less desirable offset link.

An idler sprocket should have a minimum of 17 teeth and should be located adjacent to the driver sprocket on the non-load-carrying span of chain. At least three teeth of the idler should be in full engagement. The tightener sprocket can contact the chain on either the inside or the outside. Some typical arrangements of chain tighteners are shown in Fig. 3-27.

FIGURE 3-27   Chain tighteners used to control tension.

Low-Speed Drives

Ratings are not shown in the horsepower tables for extremely low speeds. For operation at these speeds, select chain on a chain strength basis. The ratio of ultimate tensile strength to working load should be at least 6:1.

Drive Ratio

The drive ratio is determined by the speeds of the driving and driven shafts. Normally, the speed ratio should be limited to approximately 7:1. Properly engineered, drives with ratios up to 10:1 will perform satisfactorily. However, double-reduction drives with smaller ratios have better operating characteristics and are often more economical than large ratio, single-reduction drives. Minimum chain wrap on the small sprocket always should be at least 120°.

Relatively large diameter sprockets should be selected for 1:1 and 2:1 ratio drives, especially if the drives required to operate on long fixed horizontal centers with the slack strand on top. This assures adequate distance between the two spans of chain and prevents them from striking as as wear accumulates.

Chain Pitch

Use the smallest pitch chain that will handle the horsepower and load requirements. Single-strand chains satisfy most requirements and are usually more economical. Use small pitch, multiple-strand chains for high speed drives or when noise reduction is required. This allows a larger number of teeth in the driver sprocket (otherwise, typically small) and results in smoother operation. When the lowest possible noise generation is required, choose a smaller pitch, a wider chain, and a driver sprocket with at least 25 teeth.

Chordal Action

The rise and fall of each pitch of chain as it engages a sprocket is termed *chordal action* and causes repeated chain speed variations. As illustrated by Fig. 3-28, chordal action and speed variation decrease as the number of teeth in the small sprocket are increased.

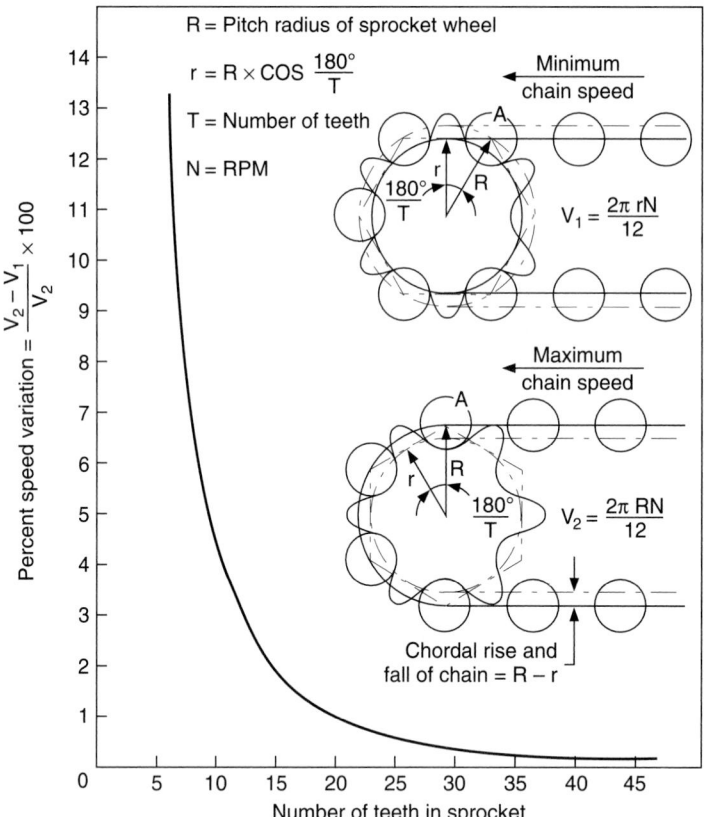

FIGURE 3-28 Variations in chain speed due to chordal action.

Number of Teeth for Small Sprockets

The minimum number of teeth recommended for the small sprocket used with roller chain varies with operating conditions. The following are general guidelines:

- 50 to 100 ft/min (15–30 m/min), 15 teeth
- 100 to 300 ft/min (30–90 m/min), 17 teeth
- 300 to 500 ft/min (90–140 m/min), 19 teeth
- Over 500 ft/min (140 m/min), 23 teeth

Whenever possible, an odd number of teeth should be selected for the small sprocket. This causes the chain to continually seat on different sprocket teeth on each revolution, thereby creating a more even wear pattern on the sprocket and roller chain.

Number of Teeth for Large Sprockets

The number of teeth in the large sprocket has an appreciable effect on the amount of joint wear (or pitch elongation) that can be accommodated by the chain before it tends to jump or ride over the teeth. This is shown in Fig. 3-29. Generally, a roller chain has reached the end of its useful wear life when the elongation per pitch is in the range of 2 to 3 percent of pitch.

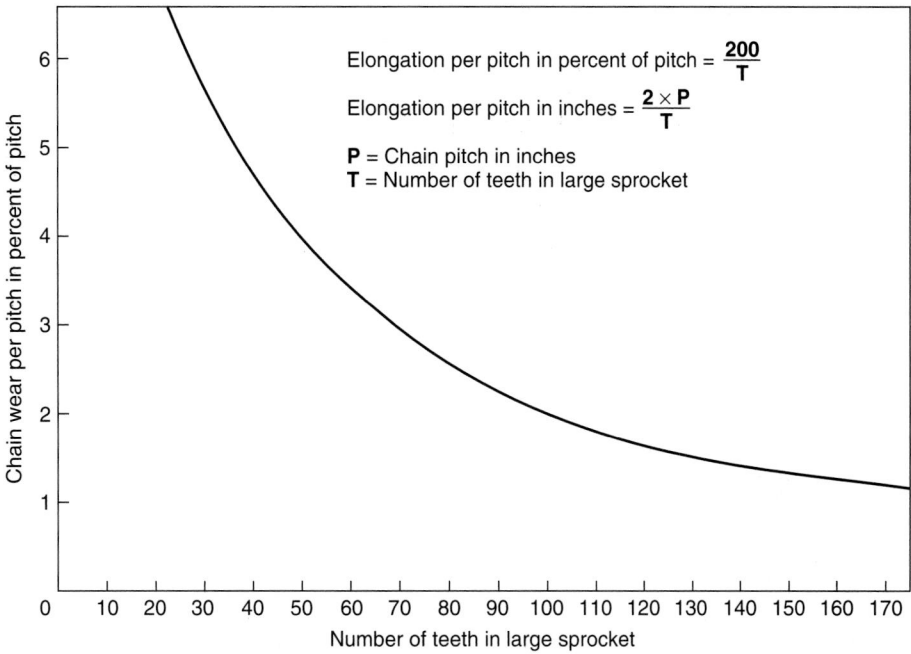

FIGURE 3-29 Variations in useful chain life based on pitch elongation and number of teeth in large sprocket.

Drive Arrangements

Illustrated in Fig. 3-30 are the drive arrangements recommended for optimum drive life. The preferred direction of rotation is indicated, although arrangements *A, B,* and *C* will operate satisfactorily in either direction. Consult the chain manufacturer for approval on other drive arrangements.[3]

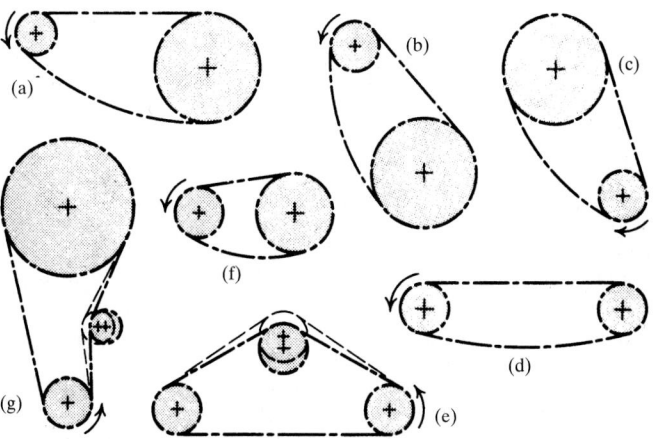

FIGURE 3-30 Preferred drive arrangements.

DRIVE SELECTION PROCEDURE

The proper steps for selecting a chain drive are listed below:

1. Although horsepower and speed are the prime considerations for selecting a drive, the following information is also necessary:
   - Source of power
   - Horsepower to be transmitted
   - Size and speed of driving shaft
   - Size and speed of driven shaft
   - Approximate center distance
   - Relative positions of shafts
   - Type of driven equipment
   - Operating conditions
   - Space limitations

2. Establish the service factor from the actual operating conditions. The service factor is a factor by which the transmitted horsepower is multiplied to compensate for drive conditions. The composite or final service factor is the product of the separate service factors (see Table 3-6).

3. Calculate the factored horsepower value by multiplying the horsepower to be transmitted by the final service factor.

4. Make a trial chain selection based on the design horsepower and revolutions per minute of the small sprocket (Fig. 3-31).

5. Determine the number of teeth in the small sprocket from the speed-horsepower charts.

6. Check the small sprocket for bore capacity, number of teeth, and availability.

7. Divide the speed of the faster-turning shaft by the speed of the slower shaft to determine the drive ratio.

8. Calculate the chain length and exact sprocket centers.

9. Determine the chain sag. The chain sag should be approximately 2 percent of the distance between shaft centers at the initial installation.

10. Determine the method of lubrication.

DRIVE SELECTION EXAMPLE

Application

Select a roller chain drive for the following conditions:

Source of power	Gearmotor
Horsepower to be transmitted	10 hp (7.5 kW)
Size of driving shaft	2.438 in (62 mm) diameter
Speed of driving shaft	100 r/min
Driven equipment	Uniformly fed coal elevator for power plant
Size of driven shaft	2.938 in (75 mm) diameter
Speed of driven shaft	42 r/min
Approximate center distance	24 in (610 mm)
Relative position of shafts	On same horizontal plane
Space limitations	None

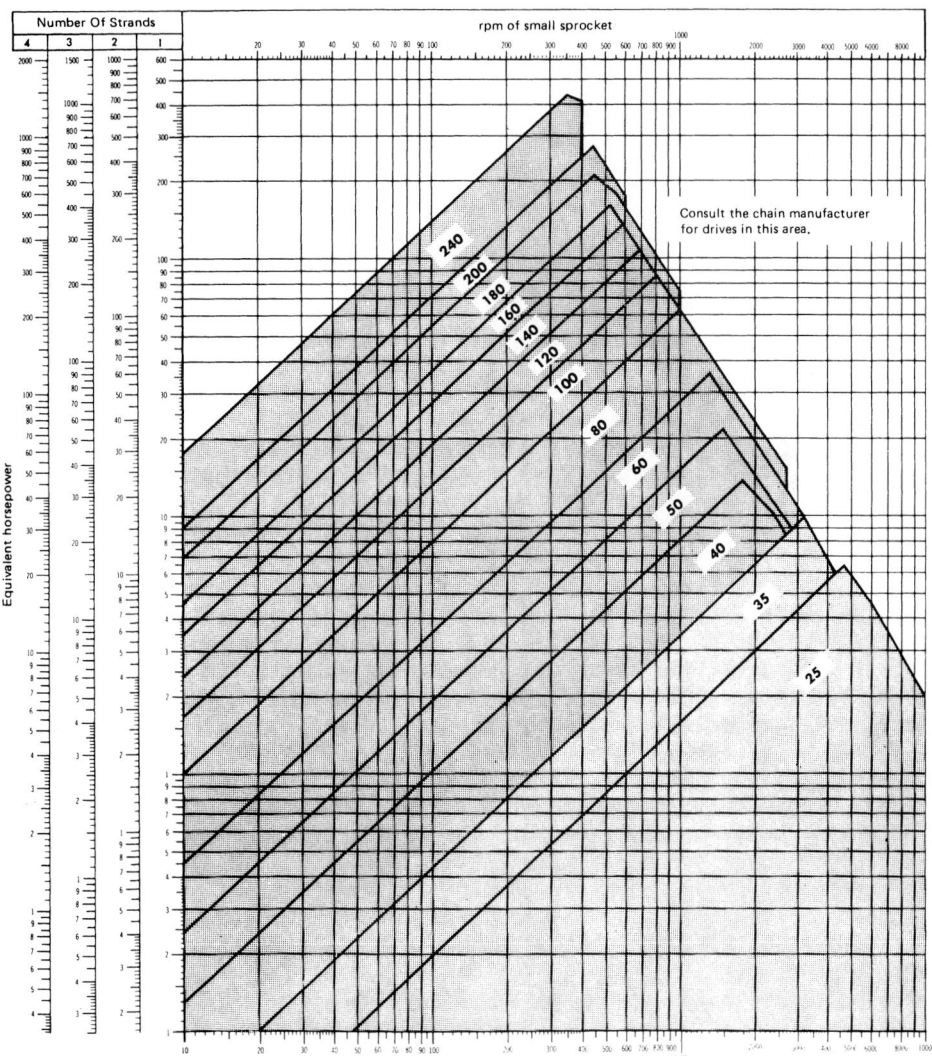

FIGURE 3-31   Trial selection chart for ANSI standard roller chains.[1]

Solution

Service Factor.   The service factor listed in Table 3-6 for a uniformly fed elevator driven by a gear motor is 1.0.

Equivalent Horsepower.   The equivalent horsepower is $10 \times 1.0 = 10$ hp.

Trial Chain.   In Fig. 3-31 note that the intersection of the 100 r/min vertical line and the 10 hp (7.5 kW) single-strand horizontal line falls in the area for No. 100 chain. Thus, the trial chain is No. 100 single strand.

Small Sprocket.   In Table 3-9 for No. 100 roller chain, the 100 r/min column lists 10.3 hp (7.68 kW), which corresponds closely to the equivalent horsepower of 10 required for this application. This rating is for single-strand chain when used with a 17-tooth sprocket.

TABLE 3-9 Speed-Horsepower Ratings for No. 100 Roller Chain

Horsepower for single strand chain ▲

Number of teeth in small sprocket	Maximum bore, inches	rpm of small sprocket																		
		25	50	100	200	300	400	500	600	700	800	900	1000	1200	1400	1600	1800	2000	2200	2400	2600
11	2.000	1.85	3.45	6.44	12.0	17.3	22.4	27.4	32.3	37.1	32.8	27.5	23.4	17.8	14.2	11.6	9.71	8.29	7.19	6.31	1.29
12	2.250	2.03	3.79	7.08	13.2	19.0	24.6	30.1	35.5	40.8	37.3	31.3	26.7	20.3	16.1	13.2	11.1	9.45	8.19	7.19	0
13	2.500	2.22	4.13	7.72	14.4	20.7	26.9	32.8	38.7	44.5	42.1	35.3	30.1	22.9	18.2	14.9	12.5	10.6	9.23	8.10	0
14	2.813	2.40	4.48	8.36	15.6	22.5	29.1	35.6	41.9	48.2	47.0	39.4	33.7	25.6	20.3	16.6	13.9	11.9	10.3	9.05	0
15	3.250	2.59	4.83	9.01	16.8	24.2	31.4	38.3	45.2	51.9	52.2	43.7	37.3	28.4	22.5	18.4	15.5	13.2	11.4	10.0	0
16	3.500	2.77	5.17	9.66	18.0	26.0	33.6	41.1	48.4	55.6	57.5	48.2	41.1	31.3	24.8	20.3	17.0	14.5	12.6	11.1	0
17	3.813	2.96	5.52	10.3	19.2	27.7	35.9	43.9	51.7	59.4	63.0	52.8	45.0	34.3	27.2	22.3	18.7	15.9	13.8	0.79	0
18	4.188	3.15	5.88	11.0	20.5	29.5	38.2	46.7	55.0	62.3	68.6	57.5	49.1	37.3	29.6	24.2	20.3	17.4	15.0	0	
19	4.563	3.34	6.23	11.6	21.7	31.2	40.5	49.5	58.3	67.0	74.4	62.3	53.2	40.5	32.1	26.3	22.0	18.8	16.3	0	
20	4.875	3.53	6.58	12.3	22.9	33.0	42.8	52.3	61.6	70.8	79.8	67.3	57.5	43.7	34.7	28.4	23.8	20.3	17.6	0	
21	5.250	3.72	6.94	13.0	24.2	34.8	45.1	55.1	65.0	74.6	84.2	72.4	61.8	47.0	37.3	30.6	25.6	21.9	19.0	0	
22	5.625	3.91	7.30	13.6	25.4	36.6	47.4	58.0	68.3	78.5	88.5	77.7	66.3	50.4	40.0	32.8	27.5	23.4	20.3	0	
23	5.813	4.10	7.66	14.3	26.7	38.4	49.8	60.8	71.7	82.3	92.8	83.0	70.9	53.9	42.8	35.0	29.4	25.1	7.74	0	
24	6.000	4.30	8.02	15.0	27.9	40.2	52.1	63.7	75.0	86.2	97.2	88.5	75.6	57.5	45.6	37.3	31.3	26.7	0		
25	6.125	4.49	8.38	15.6	29.2	42.0	54.4	66.6	78.4	90.1	102	94.1	80.3	61.1	48.5	39.7	33.3	28.4	0		
28	7.000	5.07	9.47	17.7	33.0	47.5	61.5	75.2	88.6	102	115	112	95.2	72.4	57.5	47.0	39.4	33.7	0		
30	7.625	5.47	10.2	19.0	35.5	51.2	66.3	81.0	95.5	110	124	124	106	80.3	63.7	52.2	43.7	10.0	0		
32	8.250	5.86	10.9	20.4	38.1	54.9	71.1	86.9	102	118	133	136	116	88.5	70.2	57.5	45.2	0			
35	9.125	6.46	12.0	22.5	42.0	60.4	78.3	95.7	113	130	146	156	133	101	80.3	65.8	55.1				
40		7.46	13.9	26.0	48.5	69.8	90.4	111	130	150	169	188	163	124	98.1	80.3	0				
Lubrication type ■		A		B											C						

▲ Ratings are based on a service factor of 1. For a complete list of service factors, refer to Table 3-2.
The ratings tabled above apply directly to lubricated, single strand, standard roller chains.
■ Type A: Manual or drip (maximum chain speed 500 fpm)
Type B: Bath or disk (maximum chain speed 3500 fpm)
Type C: Forced (pump)

Check the Small Sprocket.   As shown in the rating table, the maximum bore of a 17-tooth No. 100 sprocket is larger than the 2.438-in (62-mm) bore required; therefore, the selection is satisfactory.

Drive Ratio.   The drive ratio equals:

$$\frac{100 \text{ r/min}}{42 \text{ r/min}} = 2.38 : 1$$

Number of Teeth in Large Sprocket.   The number of teeth in the large sprocket equals 2.38 × 17 = 40.5 teeth. Use a 40-tooth sprocket.

Center Distance and Chain-Length Computations.   The chain length is a function of the number of teeth in each sprocket and the center distance between shaft centerlines. In addition, the chain must consist of an integral number of pitches, with an even number preferred in order to avoid the use of an offset assembly.

The most convenient method to obtain this information is by using center distance tables. If these tables are not available, then the values must be calculated.

A pitch diameter PD for any sprocket can be calculated when the chain pitch P and the number of teeth n or N are known.

$$PD = \frac{P}{\sin\left(\dfrac{180}{n \text{ or } N}\right)}$$

$$P = 1.250 \qquad n = 17 \qquad N = 40$$

$$PD_{17} = \frac{1.250}{\sin\left(\dfrac{180}{17}\right)} \qquad\qquad PD_{40} = \frac{1.250}{\sin\left(\dfrac{180}{40}\right)}$$

$$PD_{17} = \frac{1.250}{.18375} \qquad\qquad PD_{40} = \frac{1.250}{.07846}$$

$$PD_{17} = 6.803 \qquad\qquad PD_{40} = 15.932$$

The center distance (CD = 24.00 in) has to be converted to chain pitches for the remaining calculations.

$$C = \frac{CD}{P}$$

$$C = \frac{24.00}{1.250}$$

$$C = 19.2$$

Referring to Fig. 3-32, another calculation needed to determine the chain length required for this application is angle a, in degrees.

$$C = 19.2 \qquad n = 17 \qquad N = 40$$

$$a = \sin^{-1}\left(\frac{\dfrac{1}{\sin\dfrac{180}{N}} - \dfrac{1}{\sin\dfrac{180}{n}}}{2 \times C}\right)$$

$$a = \sin^{-1}\left(\frac{\dfrac{1}{\sin\dfrac{180}{40}} - \dfrac{1}{\sin\dfrac{180}{17}}}{2 \times 19.2}\right)$$

$$a = 10.964°$$

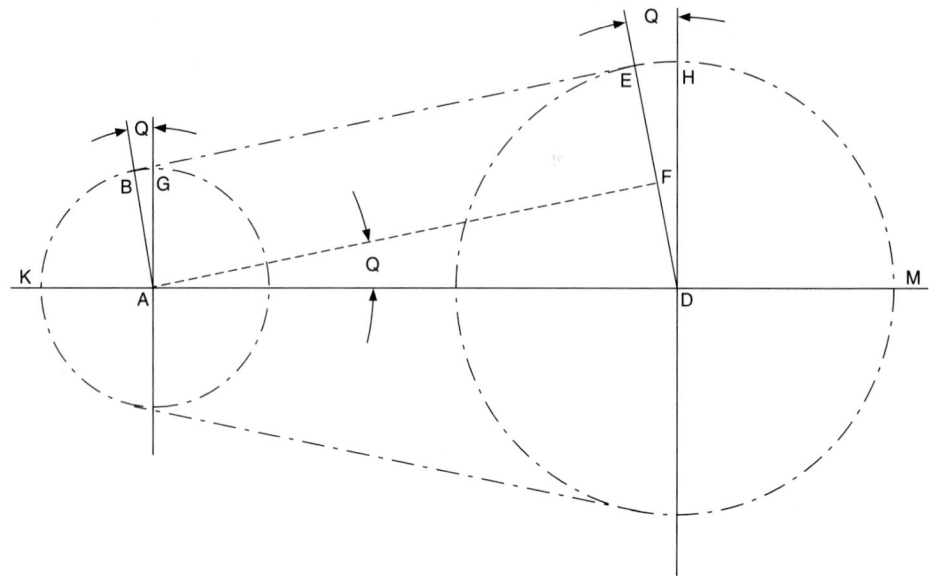

FIGURE 3-32 Calculation for chain length.

The entire length of chain in pitches L becomes

$$L = 2 \ (BE + ME + KB)$$

and can be calculated by

$$L = 2 \left[C \cos a + \frac{N+n}{4} + \frac{a}{360} \ (N-n) \right]$$

$$L = 2 \ [(19.2 \times .982) + 14.25 + .700]$$

$$L = 67.61 \text{ pitches (round up, 68)}$$

As stated in the opening paragraph, chain length must be a whole number with an even number preferred, so this calculation was rounded to 68 pitches.

An approximation of chain length can be calculated by the formula:

$$L = 2C + \frac{N+n}{2} + \frac{(N-n)^2}{4\pi^2 C}$$

$$L = 38.4 + 28.5 + .698$$

$$L = 67.598$$

When the calculated chain length is rounded to the next even number of pitches, the center distance must be revised to reflect the longer or shorter chain length. By solving the following formula a corrected center distance can be calculated.

$$C = \frac{L - n\dfrac{90-a}{180} - N\dfrac{90+a}{180}}{2 \cos a}$$

$$C = \frac{68 - 7.465 - 22.436}{1.963}$$

$$C = 19.404 \text{ pitches of chain}$$

Remember this value has to be converted from pitches of chain to a center distance in inches.

$$AD = C \times 1.250 \text{ (RC 100 pitch)}$$

$$AD = 19.404 \times 1.250$$

$$AD = 24.255 \text{ in}$$

In designing a chain drive, it is important that the theoretical center distance (as obtained from center distance tables or calculations) should not be exceeded. This means that center distances based on table or calculated dimensions require negative tolerances. When a plus tolerance is permitted, there is risk of the new chain being too tight around the sprockets, which could result in chain damage either in installation or during the break-in period.

If chain drive centers are not adjustable and chain length has to rounded to the next larger even number, the amount of sag in the chain can be calculated by the following formula:

$$Z = \sqrt{.375UE}$$

where Z = sag, in
   U = unsupported horizontal length of catenary, in
   E = excess chain, in

When extreme accuracy of chain length or center distance is required, consult a chain manufacturer.

Lubrication.   The No. 100 rating table specifies type A manual or drip lubrication for a drive operating under these conditions. However, it is suggested that a casing with bath or disk lubrication be considered to extend the life of the chain and sprockets.

The drive selected for this application consists of:

17-tooth RC 100 driving sprocket

40-tooth RC 100 driven sprocket

68 pitches of RC 100 chain

LUBRICATION

Lubrication is the most important factor in maintaining high chain efficiency and providing a long service life.

The primary purpose of chain lubrication is to provide a clean film of oil at all load-carrying points where relative motion occurs. The lubrication method recommended in the speed-horsepower selection charts should be used to ensure proper lubrication at all times for a drive chain selection.

Several methods of lubrication have been developed to fit a particular range of horsepower, chain speed, and relative position of shafts. Manual or drip lubrication is used for open running drives which operate in a nonabrasive atmosphere. These methods should be confined to low-horsepower drives with a chain speed under 600 ft/min (183 m/min). Bath lubrication is the simplest automatic method of lubricating encased chain drives and is highly satisfactory for low or moderate speeds. Disk lubrication is used for moderately high-speed drive arrangements unsuitable for oil-bath lubrication. Forced lubrication or oil-pump lubrication is recommended for large-horsepower drives, heavily loaded drives, high-speed drives, or where oil-bath or oil-disk lubrication cannot be used (Fig. 3-33).

Chains can be lubricated with any neutral grade of straight mineral oil in the 20 to 50 viscosity range, depending on the temperature. For difficult operating conditions, such as high temperature or an abrasive atmosphere, consult a lubricant manufacturer for proper lubricant selection.

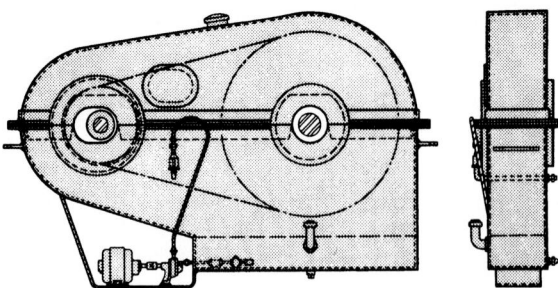

FIGURE 3-33 Forced lubrication. An oil pump is used to provide a continuous spray of oil to the inside of the lower span of chain.

CASINGS

Casings are important considerations in providing adequate lubrication to prolong the efficiency and service life of a chain drive. Casings contain the lubricant, exclude foreign materials from the lubricant, and function as a safety guard. There are four basic types of casings used with chain drives.

The oil-bath or oil-disk casing is used with the bath and disk methods of lubrication, with variations from the standard casing available depending on the chain speed and shaft center distances (Fig. 3-34). The second type of casing is used in outdoor applications when water, dust, and other contaminants are present, when extra protection against oil leakage is needed, or when forced lubrication is used (Fig. 3-35). The weather-resistant casing is the third type of construction, and it is used when additional precaution against contamination is desired. Guard-type casings are used primarily as a safety device rather than a lubrication accessory and are employed when other types of casings are not compulsory.

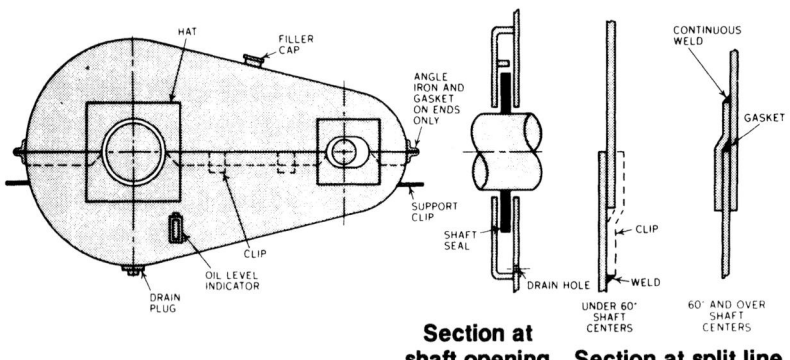

FIGURE 3-34 Oil-bath or oil-disk casing.

MAINTENANCE

Proper care of chain drives includes establishing regular periods of inspection. All drives should have an initial inspection after the first 100 h of operation, a second inspection after the next 500 h, and periodically thereafter. The periodic inspections of vertical center drives and drives sub-

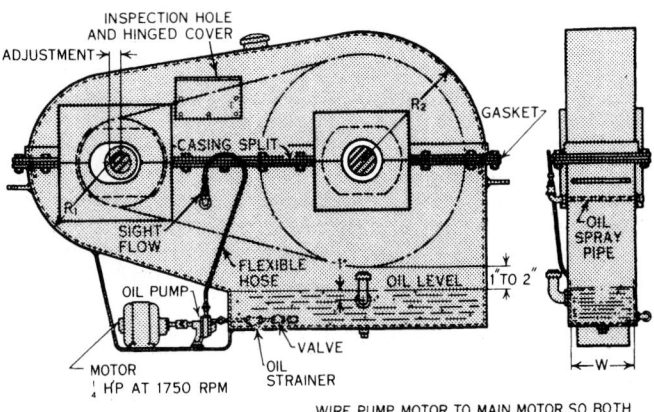

FIGURE 3-35 Casing for forced lubrication.

ject to shock loading, reversal of rotation, or dynamic braking should be made at more frequent intervals. During the inspection, the chain tension should be carefully tightened.

Inspection of chain drives should include the following review.

Check the Drive Components

The chain and sprockets should be checked for accumulation of dirt or foreign materials. Foreign materials packed into the chain or sprockets may cause premature drive failure. A thorough visual inspection for cracked, broken, deformed, or corroded components should be completed. If any are found, the entire chain and sprocket assemblies should be replaced since other sections of the chain may be near failure as well. If an old section of chain is connected to a new section of chain, the drive will run rough and noisy and may ultimately damage the drive.

Inadequate lubrication is the most common cause of drive failure. Inadequate lubrication can be identified by one or more of the following:

1. Chain joints with brown or rusty color indicate fretting or corrosive attack.
2. Stiff or frozen chain joints indicate either broken components and/or significant lack of lubrication.
3. Grooving or galling of pins.
4. Blue or purple tint to pins indicates frictional heating. Properly lubricated chain will not show brownish color at the joints and pins will be highly polished and smooth.

Check Sprocket Alignment

If wear is apparent on the inner surface of the roller link sidebars and on the sides of the sprocket teeth, then sprockets and/or shafts are misaligned. This condition should be corrected immediately to prevent undue wear of chain and sprocket teeth. ***Caution***: Tighten setscrew in sprocket hub after adjustment has been made. If sprockets are well aligned, check setscrews in sprocket hubs and retighten if necessary.

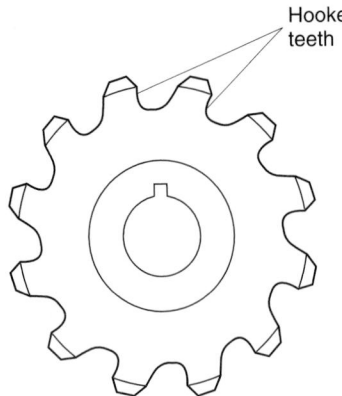

Hooked teeth

FIGURE 3-36 Worn sprocket.

Check Sprocket Tooth Wear

Excessive tooth wear will result in hook-shaped teeth (Fig. 3-36). When sprockets are found in this condition, they should be replaced. If new sprockets are not immediately available, then reverse the sprocket if physically possible. This will present the unworn tooth faces to the chain. If the worn sprocket is in a reversing drive, the sprockets must be replaced.

New chain should not be installed on worn sprockets as the unworn chain pitch will not match the worn pitch pattern of the sprockets. If new chain is installed on worn sprockets, the results will be excessive break-in wear, followed by reduced wear life and/or tensile failure of the chain due to uneven load distribution on the sprockets.

Check Chain Tension

Adjust sprocket centers to take up excess slack and provide proper chain tension. This is particularly important at the initial 100-h check since some slack will be apparent as a result of the initial seating of chain joint components. A sudden increase in slack indicates permanent yielding of components and would be the result of excessive overloading or shocks. See "Drive Installation" at end of this chapter.

Chain elongation up to 3 percent over original chain length indicates that the chain has reached the end of its useful wear life and is riding near its limit of allowable height on the sprocket teeth. Another factor to be considered when determining allowable chain wear is the number of teeth in the large sprocket. If there are more than 67 teeth, the percentage of allowable wear then becomes less than 3 percent, or 200 divided by the number of teeth.

If the chain centers are vertical or fixed and nonadjustable, it is especially important to control the excess chain to prevent the chain from sagging away from the lower sprocket and jumping sprocket teeth. This can happen when the chain elongates approximately ½ chain pitch. If these values are exceeded, the chain *and* sprockets should be replaced.

Check Oil Level

If manual lubrication is being used, make sure that the maintenance schedule is being followed and that the oil is being properly applied. Proper application includes using the thickest oil that will still penetrate through the side plates and reach the pin and bushing bearing surface. Application of oil to the roller only is not sufficient. Grease or heavy gear oils are specifically not recommended, as they will not penetrate to the pin and bushing bearing surface.

The oil level should be checked when the drive is not operating, allowing enough time for the lubricant to accumulate in the casing sump. Also check to be sure there is no sludge accumulation. Any oil addition should be made when the drive is not operating.

Check Oil Flow

If the oil system includes a pump, the function of the pump should be checked by viewing oil flow through a site tube or flow meter. If this is not possible, the lubrication system should be operated with the drive OFF and checked by looking through an inspection door to make sure that adequate oil is discharging from the nozzle(s) and the discharge is striking the chain.

It is the preferred practice to start the oil system before the drive is operational to assure oil delivery to contact surfaces before loading occurs. This will further improve the wear life of drive components.

Change Oil

After the first 500 h of operation, drain the lubricant and refill the casing with fresh oil. If the system includes a filter, it should be removed and cleaned or changed if a disposable filter is used. The lubricant should be changed after each 2500 h of operation if operating conditions do not cause contamination. If at any time the lubricant is found to be contaminated, the casing and pump system should be flushed and the chain carefully recleaned. If the chain is found thoroughly dry, remove the chain and immerse in oil and reinstall.

DRIVE INSTALLATION

Accurate alignment, proper chain tension, good lubrication, and periodic inspection are required to obtain maximum chain and sprocket life. To assist you in safely installing the chain and sprockets, careful attention should be given to the following instructions.

Caution: Shut off and lock out all power to the equipment so that it cannot be started accidentally during these installation steps. Failure to do so can result in serious personal injury.

- *Shaft alignment.*   Mount the sprockets on their respective shafts. As illustrated in Fig. 3-37, align the shafts horizontally with a machinist's level, and adjust the shafts for parallel alignment with a vernier, caliper, or feeler bar. The distance between shafts on both sides of the sprockets must be equal. When shafts have been accurately aligned, the motor, bearings, and the like should be bolted securely in place so that alignment will be maintained during operation.

- *Sprocket alignment.*   Sprockets must be in axial alignment for correct chain and sprocket tooth engagement. Apply a straight edge, or heavy cord to the machined sprocket surfaces as shown in Fig. 3-38. When a shaft is subject to end float, the sprocket should be aligned for the normal running position. Tighten setscrews in sprocket hubs to guard against lateral movement and to hold key in position.

FIGURE 3-37 Aligning shafts.   **FIGURE 3-38** Aligning sprockets.

FIGURE 3-39 Inserting connecting link.

FIGURE 3-40 Determining chain sag.

TABLE 3-10 Sag Based on 2% of Sprocket Centers

Shaft	in	20	30	40	50	60	70	80	90	100	125	150
centers	mm	508	762	1016	1270	1524	1778	2032	2286	2540	3175	3810
Sag	in	.50	.63	.88	1.00	1.25	1.50	1.63	1.88	2.00	2.50	3.00
	mm	12.7	16.0	22.4	25.4	31.8	38.1	41.4	47.8	50.8	63.5	76.2

- *Chain installation.* Inspect chain to make sure it is free from dirt or grit before it is installed. Fit the chain around both sprockets bringing the free ends together on one sprocket as shown in Fig. 3-39. Insert connecting link and secure in place.

  Caution: Due to their flexibility, chains can be somewhat difficult to handle. When installing the chain, pick it up by the end links to avoid the possibility of pinching fingers or hands. Failure to do so may result in personal injury.

- *Chain tension.* Adjust drive centers for proper chain tension, as outlined below.

  Normally, horizontal and inclined drives should be installed with an initial sag equal to approximately 2 percent of sprocket centers. Vertical center drives, and those subject to shock loading, reversal of rotation, or dynamic braking, should be operated with both spans of chain almost taut. Periodic inspection of such drives should be made to avoid operation with excessive slack and to maintain proper chain tension.

  To determine the amount of sag, pull one side of the chain taut allowing all the excess chain to accumulate in the opposite span. As illustrated in Fig. 3-40, place a straight edge over the slack span and, pulling the chain down at the center, measure the amount of sag. If necessary, adjust drive centers for proper sag that will result in correct chain tension. (See Table 3-10.)

Warning: The drive should be enclosed in an oil retaining casing or safety guard. Failure to enclose a drive could result in serious personal injury.

CHAPTER 7-3
SHAFT DRIVES AND COUPLINGS

PART 4

FLEXIBLE SHAFTS FOR THE TRANSMISSION OF ROTARY MOTION

B. W. Elliott Manufacturing Co.
Binghamton, New York

INTRODUCTION

Flexible shafting is a direct, mechanical method for transmitting rotary power or motion between two points through a simple or complex path. In its many applications, flexible shafting has simplified and/or replaced conventional methods of power or motion transmittal such as gears, belts, pulleys, and universal joints.

The benefits of using (Fig. 3-41) flexible shafting are becoming increasingly apparent to design engineers familiar with its capabilities. Flexible shafting provides a high degree of freedom in locating transmission system components and dramatically reduces or eliminates the need for precise alignment between driving and driven shafts. It is relatively unaffected by vibration, highly efficient (80 to 95 percent) and, being intrinsically safe, does not require expensive safety guards. It solves space- and weight-related problems and operates where temperatures, chemical and biological contaminants, or nuclear radiation are primary design considerations.

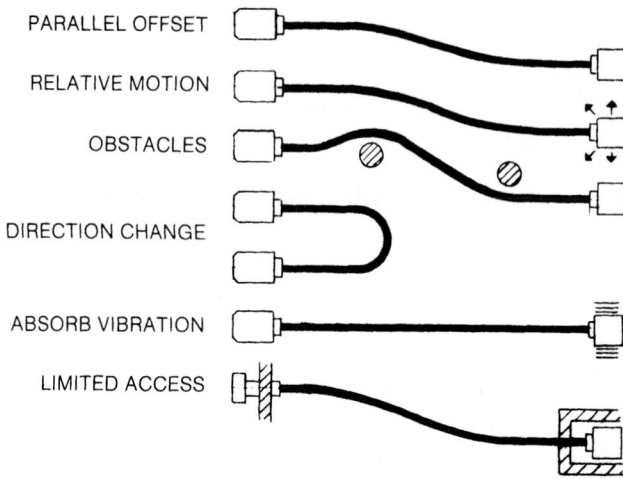

PARALLEL OFFSET

RELATIVE MOTION

OBSTACLES

DIRECTION CHANGE

ABSORB VIBRATION

LIMITED ACCESS

FIGURE 3-41 Typical benefits of flexible shafts.

SHAFT ALIGNMENT

When mounting a motor to drive a pump, a gearbox, or any device with self-contained bearings, a conventional coupling can absorb only small amounts of misalignment [typically less than 2° in angularity and 0.005 in (0.13 mm) in parallel misalignment]. The large tolerance for misalignment inherent in the flexible shaft allows the production engineer to do away with time-consuming and expensive realignment requiring dial indicators every time a motor is removed and replaced.

RELATIVE MOTION BETWEEN SHAFTS

Use in printing machinery and paper-coating equipment, or whenever power must be transmitted from a stationary motor to a moving carriage, are natural applications for flexible shafting. The shafting will absorb the relative motion between the driving and the driven member without resorting to constant-velocity universal joints.

MORE THAN ONE ANGLE IN POWER-TRANSMISSION PATH

When the power must be transmitted through several angles or a complex path to the driven member, a flexible shaft is much easier to apply than a series of universal gearboxes. When using gears, an angle other than 90° will require two gearboxes with their attendant alignment and expense problems.

POWER TRANSMISSION AT ANGLES OTHER THAN 90°

Flexible shafting can be used for small angles and angles other than the standard 90° available with gearboxes. As a side benefit, the flexible shafting does not have to be mounted as a gearbox needs to be.

SHOCK AND VIBRATION ABSORPTION

The flexible shaft will act as a heavily damped spring in the system to absorb the shock of sudden machinery stops and starts. It will also tend to smooth out vibration in the drive system. This heavy internal damping can cause a temperature rise in the shaft if it is used with a continuously pulsating driver, such as a single-cylinder engine. To reduce the heating, the shaft should be oversized in applications like this.

The engineer can apply flexible shafting in many applications where solid shafting and/or gearboxes would provide an expensive system that is difficult to align and maintain. *The shafting manufacturer should be consulted as early as possible in the design process to allow use of predesigned shafting whenever possible.* Consultation in the early design stage will eliminate use of nonstandard sizes, which, in turn, will result in lower final cost and shorter delivery cycles.

WHAT IS A ROTARY-MOTION FLEXIBLE SHAFT?

The flexible shaft is made of a flexible core in casing. The core is made up of layers of wire wound helically over one center wire (which acts as a mandrel) with each layer being wound in the opposite direction. The core is then covered by a flexible casing, which acts as a bearing surface for the core and at the same time acts as a support for the core. The casing also acts as a cover to hold in lubricant, keep out dirt, and provide safety for anyone in the immediate area.

Flexible shafting can be supplied in a large variety of design configurations and materials in response to customer needs. There are two primary types of flexible shafting: *power drive* and *remote control.*

POWER DRIVE

Flexible shafting for power drive applications is primarily designed for continuous operation at speeds exceeding 100 revolutions per minute where torque must be carried in one direction of rotation. However, it also may be used where intermittent operation is an application requirement. For core selection, see Table 3-11.

REMOTE CONTROL

Flexible shafting for remote control applications is designed for intermittent operation at speeds of 100 revolutions per minute or less. Remote control shafting has a higher torque handling capacity than power drive shafting, for a given shaft diameter, and is also designed to rotate either clockwise or counterclockwise without adversely affecting its torque/deflection characteristic. For remote control core selection, Table 3-12.

TABLE 3-11   Power Drive Core Selection

| Reference core size | Rated speed (rpm)[a] | Maximum dynamic torque capacity (lb·in) (windup direction) straight and curved shafts | | | | | | | | | | | Wgt., lb/100 ft | Min. oper. rad., in (cm) |
| | | Radius of curvature (in) | | | | | | | | | | | | |
		50 to str.	25	20	15	12	10	8	6	5	4	3		
13[b]	9000	2.4	2.2	2.0	2.0	1.92	1.90	1.70	1.50	1.25	1.00	.50	3.32	2 (5)
15[b]	7600	7.0	6.4	6.0	5.8	5.4	5.0	4.6	3.6	2.0	1.5		4.69	2.5 (6.2)
19	6000	9.4	8.6	8.0	7.6	7.0	6.6	6.0	4.8	3.4	2.0		7.44	3.4 (8.7)
25[c]	5000	22.0	20.0	18.8	17.6	16.0	15.0	12.6	10.8	9.0			12.92	4.5 (11.5)
25[d]	5000	25.0	23.0	21.8	19.6	18.0	17.0	14.6	12.4	10.0	7.6		13.12	4 (10)
31[c]	3600	30.0	28.0	26.4	25.0	23.0	21.0	18.0	14.0				20.19	5.5 (14)
31[d]	3600	36.0	33.0	31.6	30.0	28.0	26.0	22.0	18.0	11.0			19.43	5 (12.6)
40[c]	3000	60.0	54.0	50.0	46.0	42.0	38.0	30.0	24.0				27.93	6.6 (17)
40[d]	3000	80.0	66.0	63.0	58.0	51.0	46.0	37.0	22.0				29.36	6 (15)
50[c]	2300	148	124	110	92	72	56						52.03	8.8 (22.5)
50[d]	2300	136	110	104	94	80	72	56					57.03	8 (21)
63[c]	1800	248	200	176	124	84							79.15	11 (28)
63[d]	1800	220	204	192	180	152	130						84.22	10 (25)
75	1500	340	224	156	76								116	13 (33)
100	1200	760	520	420									206	17.5 (45)
125	900	1500	720										347	22 (56)

[a] Above the rated speed torque capacity decreases directly as the speed increases. Below rated speed, torque capacity does *not* increase. For low-speed applications, consider the use of remote control core.
[b] Not available as standard power drive flexible shaft assembly.
[c] Standard power drive core.
[d] High-efficiency power drive core.

Note: The ratings above apply under the following conditions. (1) The flexible shaft is adequately supported at points along its length. For an unsupported shaft, multiply the calculated torque by 1.6. (2) The flexible shaft is in continuous operation. (3) These ratings are based on temperature rise. With intermittent operation, the shaft may not heat up and the ratings may be exceeded.

TABLE 3-12   Remote Control Core Selection

| Nominal diameter, in | Actual diameter, in | Weight per 100 ft-lb | Yield torque,* lb-in | Torsional deflection, degrees/foot | | | Minimum operator radius, in |
				Torque, lb-in	Wind	Unwind	
0.13	0.125 to 0.127	3.32	9	1	41°	41°	3.0
0.15	0.146 to 0.147	4.78	20	1	7°	10°	3.5
0.19	0.182 to 0.186	7.40	30	1	4°	5°	4.0
0.19 HT	0.182 to 0.186	7.40	50	1	2.5°	4°	4.5
0.25	0.243 to 0.247	12.87	70	5	5.5°	6°	5.0
0.25 HT	0.240 to 0.243	12.07	80	5	6°	6°	6.0
0.31	0.303 to 0.307	19.59	120	10	6°	6°	6.0
0.31 HT	0.303 to 0.307	19.59	190	10	5.5°	5.5°	7.5
0.40	0.374 to 0.378	29.55	200	10	3°	3.5°	7.0
0.40 HT	0.370 to 0.376	28.92	200	10	1.5°	2°	9.0
50	0.494 to 0.500	51.40	340	100	10°	10°	9.0
63	0.617 to 0.626	80.67	900	100	3°	5.5°	11.0
75	0.740 to 0.747	116.14	900	100	4°	4°	15.0
100	0.990 to 0.997	206.44	1600	800	5°	7°	18.0
125	1.292 to 1.299	347.17	1900	800	3°	3°	21.0
162	1.611 to 1.618	547.61	3500	800	2°	2°	24.0

HT = high torque.
* Each core will sustain damage over this load. Short term overloads should not exceed 75% of this value.

FLEXIBLE COUPLINGS

These are short lengths of core that are supplied with couplings that interconnect the driving and driven elements and are available for both power drive (continuous speed—over 100 revolutions per minute) and remote control (intermittent speed—less than 100 revolutions per minute) operation. Flexible couplings under 16 in (40 cm) long do not require casings. (See Fig. 3-42.)

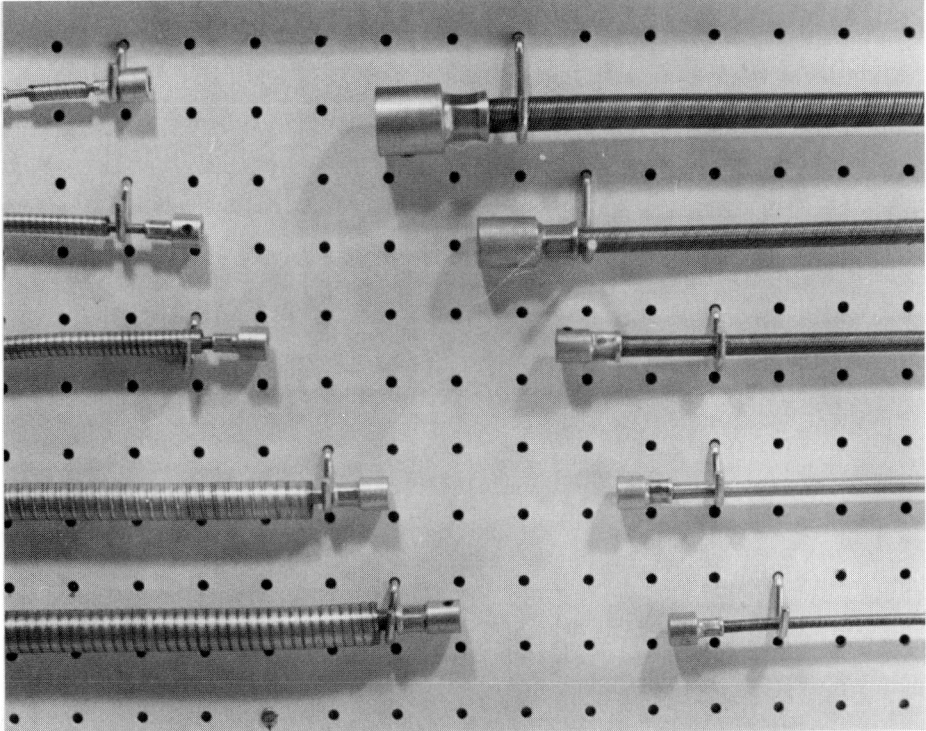

FIGURE 3-42 Typical flexible shaft flexible couplings with setscrews used to hold them in place.

Since flexible shafting is relatively stiff in torsion and compliant in bending, flexible couplings inherently possess a unique combination of characteristics that permit them to accommodate both lateral and angular misalignment while being subjected to torsional loading.

Available flexible shaft diameters range from 0.050 to 1.625 in (1.3 to 41 mm) and power drive shafts are capable of transmitting up to 20 hp (15 kW) (Fig. 3-43). For manual remote control, torques as high as 3500 in-lb (4040 cm-kg) can be transmitted.

CRITICAL PROPERTIES

Typically, the plant engineer is not expected to design a flexible shaft; that can be left to the engineering department of the flexible-shaft manufacturer. However, the engineer must know what is expected of the flexible shaft and must provide the manufacturer with

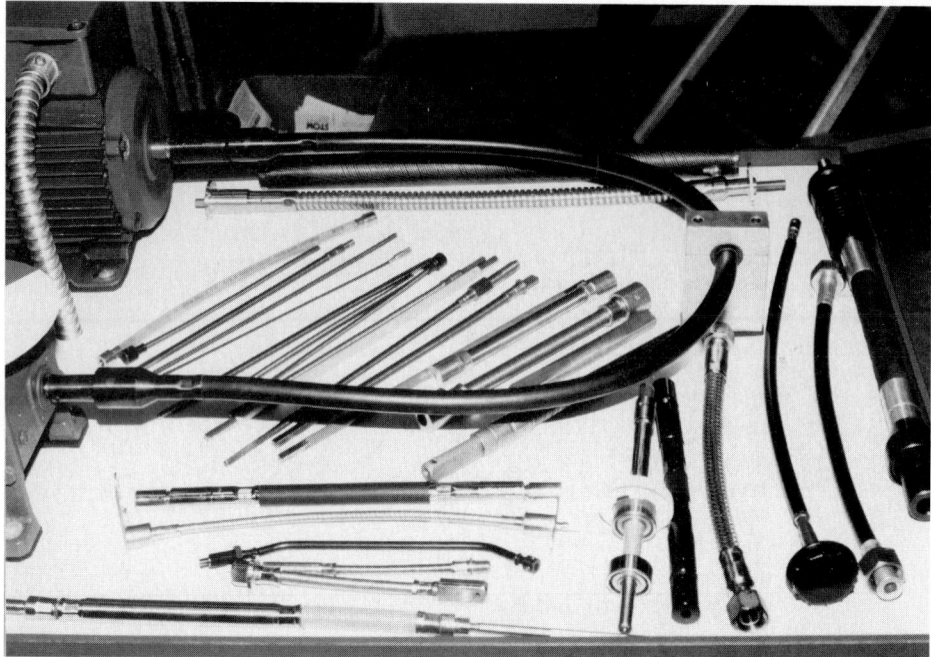

FIGURE 3-43 Wide range of sizes and types of flexible shafts with a variety of end fittings, some of which are shown here.

certain basic data so that a suitable selection or design can be provided. Some of the critical factors are:

1. Type of shaft, i.e., remote control or power
2. Manual or dynamic operation
3. Maximum torque to be transmitted
4. Horsepower of driving unit
5. Peak allowable rpm
6. Direction(s) of rotation
7. Total permissible angular deflection
8. Cycling time or duty-cycle rest periods available
9. Minimum bend radius
10. Length of shaft
11. Ambient temperature
12. Unusual service conditions

Note that not all these data will apply in all instances, but the more background the manufacturer can be given, the more suitable and economical the flexible-shaft design will be.

In many instances, a predesigned shaft or a flexible shaft/flexible coupling will solve the plant engineer's power transmission problem. However, if the requirements are unusual, a special shaft may have to be designed. Obviously, whenever possible predesigned shafts should be selected because they are the less costly solution.

STANDARD POWER DRIVE FLEXIBLE SHAFTS

Standard power drive shafts are available with built-in bearings and couplings on the end that can be bored out and held in place with setscrews to suit the particular application (see Fig. 3-44).

FIGURE 3-44   Standard power drive flexible shaft with built-in bearings and couplings; this offers a very simple hook-up.

CASINGS AND FITTINGS

In many applications, a bare flexible shaft equipped with suitable fittings, as described above, is perfectly adequate for the task at hand. In other cases, however, a flexible shaft should be used with special fittings and a casing.

End fittings are installed on both the casing and the shaft core itself. The casing fittings keep the shaft assembly fixed in place; neither these fittings nor the casing rotate. Casing fittings may be of several types, for example, a loose male (or female) threaded coupling nut or a quick disconnect. With shaft-end fittings, even more choices are available: integrally formed drive square, tang fitting, male or female spline, hollow square, panel mounting, or setscrew. The choice of fittings depends to a large extent on the application, how accessible the shaft is, and how often it is expected to be serviced. If a shaft is to rotate at high speeds for prolonged periods and has to be lubricated regularly to compensate for this severe service, it is recommended that the assembly be designed for easy withdrawal of the shaft from the casing. In that event, one end of the shaft is usually swaged square so that the drive that does not permanently lock the shaft into the casing at both ends.

A casing provides the following benefits:

1. It keeps the flexible shaft properly lubricated for longer periods of time.
2. It offers intermediate points of attachment when shaft length exceeds 18 in (46 cm).
3. It keeps plant personnel from coming into contact with a high-speed rotating member.
4. It protects the flexible shaft against hostile environments.

Casings can be classified into two types: metallic and covered. *Metallic* casings are neat, strong, durable, and bendable. Although they will retain grease, they are not oil- or watertight.

Covered casings are more expensive because their construction is more elaborate. Following an inner liner that may be either metallic or plastic, the casing is reinforced with layers of steel braid, and finished off with a final outer sheath of rubber or plastic. This type of casing permits the flexible shaft to operate under water, hydraulic fluid, or other liquid, so long as the fluid does not attack the elastomeric outer covering.

SHAFTS THRIVE ON SPEED

Power shafts function most efficiently when operated at high speed. The reason stems from basic engineering principles: Transmitted horsepower is directly proportional to speed.

$$hp = KTN$$

where T is torque, N is speed, and K is a constant to reconcile the units of torque and peripheral speed being used in the equation.

Typically, if torque is expressed in foot pounds and speed in revolutions per minute, hp = $0.00019 \times$ ft-lb $\times$ rpm. For torque expressed in inch pounds, hp = $0.000016 \times$ in-lb $\times$ rpm. Therefore, for a given horsepower requirement, the higher the shaft speed, the less the torque on the shaft and therefore, the smaller the shaft needed to accomplish the task. This factor should be kept in mind during the early stages of design, because quite often the insertion of a suitable speed-reduction device at the correct location in the drive train may serve to reduce the overall cost of the assembly.

A power shaft is meant to rotate at the highest permissible speed; it is, therefore, important to consider this factor in the design. If a speed reducer is necessary, insert it at the correct end of the shaft. Thus, if motor speed is 5000 rpm and final operating speed is to be 500 rpm, the speed reducer should be inserted at the output, not at the motor end. Conversely, if a speed-up is desired, the speed increaser should be inserted at the motor end.

SHAFT RADIUS OF CURVATURE

Although rotary-motion flexible shafts are almost snakelike in their ability to reach into inaccessible areas, there is a limit to how much they may be bent without damaging them. This is the minimum operation radius (MOR). Each shaft construction (diameter, number of wires per layer, and number of layers) leads to a different MOR, which is always available from the manufacturer. The MOR is established by calculations based on the diameter and material of the mandrel wire.

It should come as no surprise that the amount of torque load a flexible shaft can comfortably manage is in inverse proportion to the MOR. The more a flexible shaft is curved, the higher the internal friction, the greater the heat generated, and the smaller the permissible continuous load. Here again, these figures are known for each construction and should be rigidly adhered to if overload or early failure of the shaft is to be avoided. Table 3-11 shows typical values for a range of high-tensile-steel power shafts, including such basic parameters as diameter, radius of curvature vs torque capacity, torsional breaking load, and weight per foot.

In using Table 3-11, remember that the torque-carrying capacities are shown for shafts rotating in the direction that tightens up the outer layer. If the same shaft is rotated so as to unwind the outer layer—clockwise for a left-hand flexible shaft or counterclockwise for a right-hand shaft—its torque capability is reduced by up to 50 percent. See Fig. 3-45 for an example of right- and left-hand shaft application.

SHAFT LIFE

As a rule of thumb, a power shaft running under no load at the MOR can be expected to have a useful life in excess of 10^8 revolutions. Such factors as service temperature, number of shaft bends, torque output, speed, shock loading, and operating radius can reduce shaft life.

A remote-control shaft, under manual operation, will last many years, When remote-control shafts are used for dynamic operations, it is very important that the duty cycle not exceed 5 min ON and 2 min OFF.

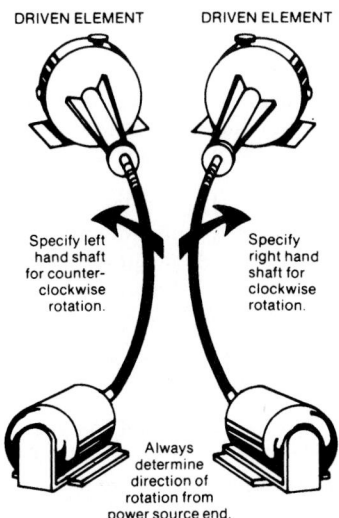

DRIVEN ELEMENT   DRIVEN ELEMENT

Specify left hand shaft for counter-clockwise rotation.

Specify right hand shaft for clockwise rotation.

Always determine direction of rotation from power source end.

FIGURE 3-45   Direction of rotation.

SHAFT SELECTION

To select the proper shaft, determine the following items:

1. Torque requirement
2. Shaft radius of curvature
3. Length of path between driving and driven systems
4. Operating speed
5. Acceptable torsional deflection or backlash

Determining the torque requirement on a shaft may not be easy. Remote-control shaft requirements can be determined by attaching a lever of known length to the device to be turned and pulling the end of the lever with a spring scale. Use the highest torque as the required torque. Measuring torque on a power shaft is more difficult because the requirement is dynamic. The best way is to instrument-load with a torque cell and measure the torque under operating conditions. Component manufacturers usually have these data available. A shaft efficiency of about 90 percent should be attainable for most applications; therefore, increasing the output torque by about 10 percent leads to the input torque.

The shaft path should then be examined. A drawing should be made that shows the path in a true view. The MOR should be determined from this drawing. A full-scale prototype can be used. The length of the shaft can also be determined at this time. For power shafts, the operating speed is generally given. For remote-control shafts, in which the speed is essentially zero, the amount of torsional deflection acceptable between the turning device and the turned device is the important consideration.

DOS AND DON'TS

Used intelligently, flexible shafts are the product designer's allies. They are more flexible than universal joints; they are more versatile than gear systems because they are totally unaffected by the exact angle or offset necessary; finally, flexible shafts offer an inherent shock-absorption capability, ease of installation, and maintenance unmatched by other forms of rotary-motion transmission.

However, flexible shafts do have to be treated carefully if they are to provide the service life built into them. They cannot be bent completely out of shape and must be used at radii equal to or greater than the MOR specified by the manufacturer. They should be secured approximately every 18 in (46 cm) to prevent the possibility of helixing. They must be lightly lubricated as preventive maintenance at regular intervals. Replacement must match the original design because a remote-control shaft is not interchangeable with a power shaft. The type of service expected must be clearly specified. Two differently built shafts, even of the same diameter and length, are not interchangeable. A remote-control shaft is intended for low-speed continuous or high-speed intermittent operation in either direction with minimum backlash. On the other hand, a power shaft is intended for high-speed continuous operation, but in one direction only. Above all, flexible shafts must be designed for the task they are to perform. For this reason, early consultation between the user's engineering department and the shaft manufacturer is highly recommended.

Follow these simple, basic suggestions, and the design flexibility of a rotary-motion flexible shaft will be applied to utmost advantage.

TYPICAL APPLICATIONS

Flexible-shaft flexible couplings in lengths of 6 in (15 cm) or less are ideal for connecting a driven member to its power source when a small amount of angular, parallel, or combined misalignment must be accommodated. Not only does a motor-type coupling readily compensate for the misalignment, but it will also handle a certain amount of shock loading and attenuate vibration.

Longer segments of flexible shaft, from 1 to 100 ft (0.3 to 30.5 m), are ideal for transmitting rotary motion to very distant locations, either for remote control or for power transmission.

Flexible-shaft applications in industry are wide ranging, so it would be quite a task to list them all. However, a few typical cases may help to demonstrate how rotary-motion problems have been avoided or solved with a flexible shaft:

An operating device on a swinging oven door has to rotate freely, no matter how much the angle changes as the door opens and closes.

Two rotating devices have to be synchronized through a central gearbox, even though one of the devices moves laterally while the other stays fixed in place.

A crane operator has to know which way the cable is unreeling, even though neither reel nor load is visible from the cab.

Condenser or other heat-exchange tubing 35 ft (10.7 m) from the header end has to be cleaned out.

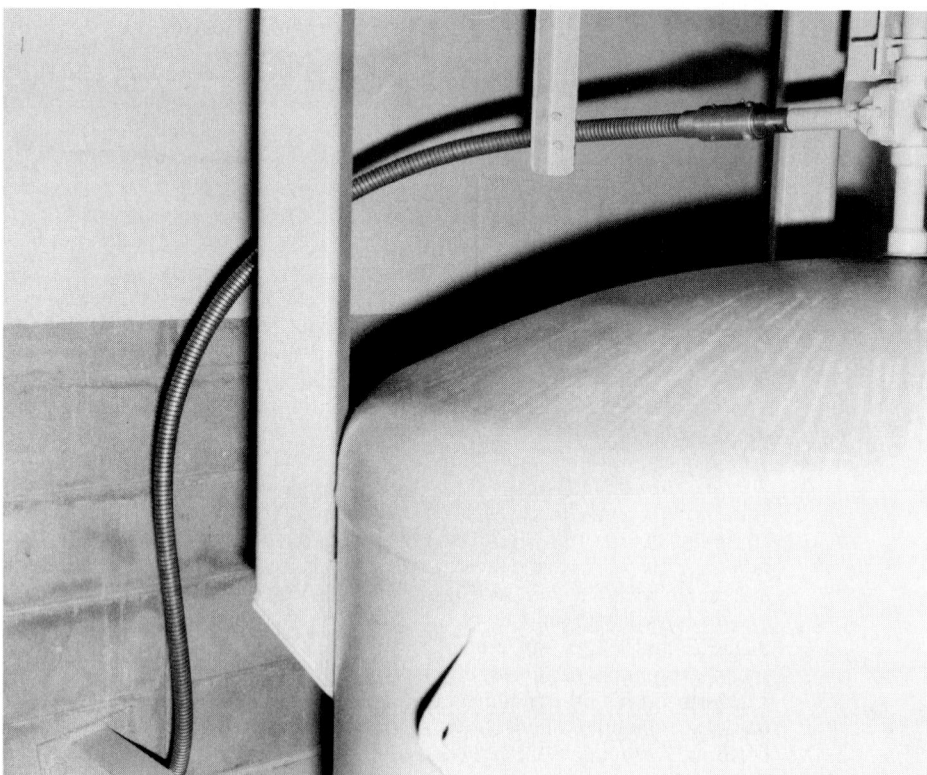

FIGURE 3-46   Flexible shaft operating valve in remote location underneath a tank.

FIGURE 3-47 ⅜-in (9.5-mm) size flexible shaft drives eccentric inside of steel shell to vibrate concrete; operation speed up to 13,000 rpm.

Several door-actuating devices have to be moved simultaneously, all by one driving motor and each one at a different angle to it.

A small, buried control has to be readily turnable from "outside;" a valve has to be closed from a remote location (Fig. 3-46); a potentiometer has to be adjusted in an "unreachable" spot; a switch has to be operated from far away; and a rotating vibrator head has to be driven while in concrete (Fig. 3-47).

The above examples serve to illustrate the wide variety of problems that flexible shafts can solve. This type of drive should always be investigated by the plant engineer as a possible alternative to other conventional drives.

CHAPTER 7-4
FLUID SEALS

Kenneth R. Albertson
Packing Division

Robert H. Barbarin
Seal Group Staff

William L. Byars
Packing Division

Arthur H. Cates
Packing Division

Chris S. Louskos
Seal Group Staff

Richard G. Ramsdell
Seal Group Staff

John B. Scannell
Packing Division

Richard J. Swanson
Packing Division
Parker-Hannifin Corp.
Irvine, California

INTRODUCTION

Packings and *seals* are devices or materials designed to create and/or maintain a fluid-pressure differential across the interface or gap between two relatively movable and/or separable components of a fluid system. (*Fluids,* in this context, include liquids and gases, with or without entrained solids.)

Included within this category of packings and gaskets are static seals, reciprocating dynamic seals, rotary dynamic seals, and flexural sealing devices, involving an almost unlimited variety of sizes and configurations and a broad range of common and exotic materials and material combinations.

Because of the complexity of the subject, only a brief overview is possible in this handbook. Although the information provided may help in solving relatively simple problems, a competent supplier should be consulted for assistance with most sealing applications.

MATERIALS

Tables 4-1 and 4-2 list the most commonly used seal and packing materials and give a few pertinent facts about each. All of the facts given for any material do not necessarily apply to all members of the group. They merely suggest the range of uses of materials within that group. For instance, elastomers are represented as having a temperature range of -178 to $+500°F$ (-115 to $260°C$), but only a few specific compounds will serve very long at either of these extremes and no compound will function at both.

STATIC SEALS

Gaskets

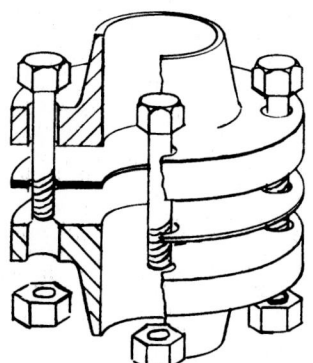

FIGURE 4-1 Flat gasket between two flanges.

Gaskets are seals placed between two static faces (Fig. 4-1). They are made of deformable materials which, when clamped, will flow into surface imperfections of the mating surfaces to prevent fluids from escaping through the joint. For relatively low pressures and temperatures, nonmetallic gaskets may be used. For more severe applications, metallic gaskets are required.

As a rough guide to this selection, it is common practice to multiply the operating pressure, in pounds per square inch, by the operating temperature, in degrees Fahrenheit. If this value exceeds 250,000, the use of metallics is indicated.* In any case, however, nonmetallic gaskets should not be used at temperatures above 850°F (450°C) or at pressures above 1200 lb/in²

---

* In SI units, find the value of $[P(1.8C + 32)]$, where P is the pressure in megapascals and C is temperature in degrees Celsius. If the result exceeds 1720, the use of metallics is indicated.

TABLE 4-1   Materials Commonly Used in Seals

Materials and notes	Temperature range, °F (°C)	Commonly sealed fluids	Types of seals in which the material is commonly used
Aluminum	−300 to +800 (−185 to +430)	Water, weak acids except acetic, steam, air, oxygen, dry bromine and chlorine, aliphatic and aromatic fluids, acetone, alcohols, petroleum oils, hot sulfur-bearing gases	Compression packing (as foil), gaskets (solid or as jacketing over asbestos, rubber, or other filler)
Asbestos, white (chrysotile) and blue (crocidolite); fire-resistant fibrous minerals; formerly used in sealing industry, but now obsolete due to regulatory restrictions by governmental agencies	−300 to +1000 (−185 to +540)	Water, strong acids and bases, steam, air, chlorine, alcohols, petroleum fluids	
Brass	−300 to +500 (−185 to +260)	Water, mild acids and bases, oxygen, steam, dry bromine and chlorine, aliphatic and aromatic fluids, acetone, alcohols, petroleum oils except sulfur-containing oils	Diaphragms, gaskets (as sheet, corrugated, or spiral-wound types)
Bronze	−300 to +500 (−185 to +260)	Similar to brass	Gaskets (with asbestos or TFE in spiral-wound types)
Cast iron	−50 to +1000 (−45 to +540)	Similar to iron	Mechanical seals, piston rings; not usually a gasket material
Ceramics: Excellent resistance to oxidation at elevated temperatures, but quite abrasive unless given a very smooth finish	−300 to >1500 (−185 to >815)	Water, strong acids and bases, steam, air, chlorine, alcohols, petroleum fluids; chemical resistance similar to glass	Mechanical seals, filler material for metallic types of gaskets
Copper	−300 to +600 (−185 to +315)	Water, mild acids and bases, oxygen, steam, dry bromine and chlorine, aliphatic and aromatic fluids, acetone, alcohols, petroleum oils except sulfur-containing oils; not recommended for use above 600°F (315°C) unless oxygen-free	Compression packing (foil), gaskets (solid, as jacketing over filler or with filler in spiral-wound type)
Cork: Cork particles bonded together in sheet form with resin or an elastomer	−22 to +300 (−30 to +150)	Mild acids and bases, water, coolants, petroleum oils	Gaskets
Elastomers: See Table 4-2 for details	−178 to +500 (−115 to +260)	Wide range of fluids; see Table 4-2	Cup and flange packings, diaphragms, gaskets, O-rings, oil seals, PolyPak®, T-seals, U-cups, V-packings, backup rings, wipers; reinforced with fabric in some of these products
Glass fibers	—	Added to nylon, TFE, etc., to improve resistance to wear, extrusion, creep, etc.	—
Graphite: Excellent chemical resistance, but oxidizes at elevated temperatures; good lubricant; porosity and oxidation effect can be modified by impregnating	−450 to +1500 (−270 to +815)	Water, all concentrations of acids and bases if not strongly oxidizing, nitric acid to only 100°F if concentration over 25%, steam, air to 960°F, aliphatic and aromatic fluids, acetone, alcohols, petroleum oils	Compression packing (in fiber form), gaskets, mechanical seals; in powdered form, added to elastomers and plastics to reduce friction
Hastelloy®: Union Carbide trademark for a series of high-strength nickel-base corrosion-resistant alloys	−300 to +2000 (−185 to +1100)	Noted for their superior corrosion resistance; individual applications should be investigated; boiling acids and bases, salts, chlorine, hypochlorites, and seawater	Gaskets (solid, as jacketing over filler or with filler in spiral-wound type), mechanical seals

TABLE 4-1 Materials Commonly Used in Seals (*Continued*)

Materials and notes	Temperature range, °F (°C)	Commonly sealed fluids	Types of seals in which the material is commonly used
Inconel®: International Nickel trademark for nickel-chromium alloys	−300 to +2000 (−185 to +1100)	Noted for high-temperature strength and corrosion resistance; individual applications should be investigated; resists chloride ion stress corrosion cracking, organic acids in food products, alkaline sulfur compounds, ammonia, dry gases, steam, air, carbon dioxide; resists progressive oxidation to 2000°F (1100°C), sulfur atmospheres	Gaskets (solid, as jacketing over filler or with filler in spiral-wound type), mechanical seals
Iron: Soft and low-carbon steel	−50 to +1000 (−45 to +540)	Widely used on an economical heavy-cross-section gasket; sulfuric acid at high concentrations, hydrochloric not satisfactory at any concentration, most alkalies, air, water, steam, oxygen, acetone, acetylene	Gaskets (solid, as jacketing over filler or with filler in spiral-wound type), mechanical seals
Lead: Soft metal, melts above 500°F (260°C)	−300 to +212 (−185 to +100)	Water, dry bromine and chlorine, aliphatic and aromatic fluids, acetone, alcohols, petroleum oils	Compression packing (as foil or insert in channel-type packing); gaskets (solid or jacketing over filler)
Leather: Porosity can be controlled or virtually eliminated with waxes, oils, etc., that also extend its temperature range and the types of fluids it can withstand	−70 to +212 (−55 to +100)	Water, weak acids and bases, air, aliphatic and aromatic fluids, alcohols, petroleum oils	Cup and flange packings, gaskets, oil seals, U-cups, V-packings
Molybdenum disulfide (MoS₂) in a silvery powder form	—	—	May be mixed with most seal materials to reduce friction without causing corrosion
Monel®: International Nickel trademark for group of alloys primarily of nickel and copper plus small amounts of other ingredients	−300 to +1500 (−185 to +815)	Noted for high-temperature properties and corrosion resistance; resists chloride ion stress corrosion cracking; most acids (including hydrofluoric) and alkalies; not satisfactory with strong oxidizing acids; fresh and seawater, air, dry gases, neutral and alkaline salts	Gaskets, mechanical seals
Nickel	−300 to +1400 (−185 to +760)	Not as all-around-resistant as Monel; resists chloride ion stress corrosion cracking; fresh and seawater, alkalies, natural and alkaline salts; not satisfactory with strong, hot, sulfurous and oxidizing acids	Gaskets, as jacketing over graphite or glass fiber
Nylon (polyamide)	−65 to +300 (−55 to +150)	Air, hydraulic fluids	Fabric, as reinforcement for U-cups, V-rings, diaphragms; solid, for backup rings
Paper: Due to porosity it is impregnated except where needed merely to exclude dust and dirt	to +300 (to +150)	Aliphatic and aromatic fluids, petroleum oils	Gaskets
Plastics: See nylon, polyurethane, TFE			
Polyamides: See nylon			
Polyurethane: A very tough wear-, extrusion-, and abrasion-resistant group of materials spanning the range from elastomers to plastics; good resistance to petroleum fluids, air, and aging	−65 to +200 (−54 to +130)	Petroleum-base hydraulic fluids, especially in high-pressure heavy-duty systems; not satisfactory with hot water	Cup and flange packings, O-rings, PolyPak®, U-cups, V-packings, adapters, backup rings, scrapers

TABLE 4-1   Materials Commonly Used in Seals (*Continued*)

Materials and notes	Temperature range, °F (°C)	Commonly sealed fluids	Types of seals in which the material is commonly used
Rubber: See elastomers (Table 4-2)			
Silver	−300 to +1200 (−185 to +650)	Food and drug industry; acetic acid and acetic anhydride, carbon tetrachloride, wet chlorine, formaldehyde, formic acid, hydrofluoric acid over 65%, magnesium chloride, oxalic acid	Gaskets, plating for spring-type metal seals
Stainless steel	−300 to +1600 (−185 to +870)	Resistant to multitude of corrosive media depending on operating conditions and alloy selection; water, air, acids, bases, gases, alcohols, petroleum fluids	Mechanical seals, gaskets (solid, as jacketing over asbestos in spiral-wound type)
Steel: Low-carbon	−50 to +1000 (−45 to +540)	Same as iron	Gaskets, mechanical seals
TFE (also PTFE): (poly) tetrafluoroethylene or Teflon® Du Pont; a plastic having excellent chemical resistance and low friction; softens above 500°F (260°C); creeps under stress	−300 to +500 (−185 to +260)	Water, all concentrations of acids and bases, steam, air, oxygen, bromine, chlorine, aliphatic and aromatic fluids, acetone, alcohols, petroleum oils	Compression packing, cup and flange packings, diaphragms, O-rings, piston rings, spring-actuated U-cups, tape, backup rings, cap strips, coating for spring-type metal seals, rubber, etc., mechanical seals
Titanium	−300 to +2000 (−185 to +1100)	Nitric acid, except fuming, other oxidizing acids, mixed acids, wet chlorine, phosphoric acid to 30%, chlorine compounds, hydrogen sulfide, fresh and seawater, salt solutions, alkaline solutions, organic acids	Gaskets
Vegetable fibers, such as cotton, flax, hemp, jute, and ramie: Usually impregnated with neoprene or other rubber to reduce porosity, while the fibers reinforce the rubber and reduce swelling in some fluids; exposed fibers hold fluid, aiding lubrication	−20 to +200 (−30 to +95)	Water, ammonia, aliphatic and aromatic fluids, petroleum oils	Compression packing, gaskets
Wool felt	−100 to +160 (−75 to +70)	Water, ammonia, aliphatic and aromatic fluids, petroleum oils	Gaskets, impregnated with an elastomer or plain, for dust seals

TABLE 4-2   Elastomers Commonly Used for Seals

No. and designations*	Temperature range, °F (°C)	Properties and uses
1. Butyl (P) isobutene-isobutene-isoprene (C) IIR (A)	−75 to +225 (−60 to +110)	Used for vacuum and gases because of its low permeability rate; in other sealing applications, generally superseded by ethylene propylene because of the superior heat resistance and recovery of ethylene propylene; types of seal: diaphragms, gaskets, O-rings
2. Epichlorohydrin (P) Hydrin® (Goodrich) 2a. Polychloromethyl Oxirane (C) CO (A) 2b. Ethylene oxide (oxirane) + chloromethyl oxirane (C) ECO (A)	−40 to +325 (−40 to +163) −50 to +325 (−45 to +163)	Low permeability rate, good resistance to weathering and to oils and other hydrocarbons; usefulness limited because it tends to corrode metals and has poor recovery; types of seal: diaphragms, gaskets
3. Ethylene propylene (P) 3a. Ethylene propylene copolymer (C) EPM (A) 3b. Ethylene propylene terpolymer (C) EPDM (A)	−70/60 to +250/400 (−57/−50 to +120/205)	Very good resistance to water, steam, weak acids and bases, Skydrols® (Monsanto), and other phosphate esters; swells severely in petroleum products and other hydrocarbons; types of seal: diaphragms, gaskets, O-rings, oil seals, T-seals, U-cups, V-packings
4. Fluorocarbon elastomer (P, C) Fluorel® (3M) (P) Viton® (Du Pont) (P) Technoflon® (Ausimont) FKM (A) formerly FPM (A)	−40/0 to +400 (−40/−20 to +200)	Good resistance to wide range of fluids including hydrocarbons and air; hardens in high-temperature water; special, very expensive type (Du Pont Viton GLT) good down to −40°F, otherwise low-temperature limit for seals is 0 to −15°F; excellent high-temperature resistance; types of seal: diaphragms, gaskets, O-rings, oil seals, T-seals, U-cups
5. Fluorosilicone (P, C) FVMQ (A)	−100 to +350/400 (−73 to +175/205)	Has resistance to a wide range of fluids, including hydrocarbons; an expensive elastomer generally restricted to static seals owing to lack of toughness; types of seal: gaskets, O-rings
6. Natural Rubber (P) natural polyisoprene (C) NR (A)	−30 to +225 (−34 to +110)	Has excellent recovery, but seldom used for seals because of poor resistance to aging and to most fluids
7. Neoprene (P) chloroprene (P, C) CR (A)	−70/−40 to +250/300 (−55/40 to +120/150)	An "in-between" elastomer, having fair resistance to both hydrocarbons and to oxidation and aging; one of the earliest synthetics; primary seal usage is in refrigerants and silicate esters; types of seal: braided packing, diaphragms, gaskets, O-rings, U-cups
8. Nitrile (P) Buna-N (P) Acrylonitrile NBR (A)	−70/−20 to +180/275 (−55/−30 to +80/135)	The most commonly used elastomer for seals owing to its resistance to petroleum fluids (fuels, hydraulic and lubricating oils), its useful temperature range, and its low cost; types of seal: braided packing, cup and flange packings, diaphragms, gaskets, O-rings, oil seals, sealants, T-seals, U-cups, V-packings
9. Perfluoroelastomer (P, C) Kalrez® (Du Pont) (P)	−30 to +500 (−34 to +260)	Resists a very wide range of fluids and extra-high temperatures; use limited owing to extremely high cost

TABLE 4-2 Elastomers Commonly Used for Seals (*Continued*)

No. and designations*	Temperature range, °F (°C)	Properties and uses
10. Phosphazene (P) EYPEL-F® (Ethyl Corp) (T) Phosphonitrilic fluoroelastomer (C)	−85 to +350 (−65 to +177)	Similar to fluorosilicone in its fluid resistance and temperature range but tougher, making it more suitable for dynamic applications; excellent vibration damping characteristics, liquid oxygen compatible, high performance commercial and military applications; relatively expensive resulting in limited use (now obsolete)
11. Polyacrylate (P, C) ACM (A)	0 to +350 (−18 to +177)	Resists hydrocarbons, ozone, sunlight, but water resistance, mechanical properties, and recovery are poor; often used to seal automatic transmission and power-steering fluids; types of seal: gaskets, O-rings
12. Polysulfide (P, C) Thiokol (P) EOT (A)	−75 to +225 (−60 to +107)	Resists many solvents that no other elastomer can handle; has good resistance to oxygen and ozone and good low-temperature flexibility; heat resistance, strength, and recovery poor; types of seal: cup and flange packing, diaphragms, gaskets, O-rings
13. Polyurethane (P) 13a. Polyester polyurethane (C) AU (A) 13b. Polyether polyurethane (C) EU (A)	−65 to +200 (−54 to +93)	Very tough, high-tensile-strength elastomer with excellent resistance to abrasion and wear; good resistance to petroleum-type hydraulic fluids and other hydrocarbons and to ozone and aging; poor resistance to water, acids, high temperatures; poor recovery; types of seal: cup and flange packings, O-rings, U-cups, V-seals; also used for backup rings and wipers
14. Saturated Nitrile (P) Hydrogenated Nitrile (P) Hydrogenated polybutadiene acrylonitrile (C) polymethylene cyano polybutadiene (C) HNBR (A) Therban® (Bayer Corp.) (T) Zetpol® (Zeon Chemical Co.) (T)	−40 to +325°F (−40 to +165)	Enhanced derivative of the nitrile class of polymer with substantially improved heat and oil resistance due to its saturated backbone; increased mechanical strength, permeation and dynamic properties; improved resistance to a variety of aggressive fluids in automotive and oil well industries; relatively expensive
15. SBR (P, A) GR-S (P) Buna-S (P) styrene butadiene (C)	−70 to +225 (−57 to +107)	Most commonly used elastomer today because most automobile tires are made from it; very limited use in seals owing to its poor resistance to hydrocarbons, ozone, sunlight, and aging
16. Silicone (P) Silastic® (Dow Corning) (P) 16a. Phenyl vinyl methyl silicone (C) PVMQ (A) 16b. Vinyl methyl silicone (C) VMQ (A)	−75/60 to +400/500 (−60/−50 to +205/260) −175 to +400 (−115 to +205)	Has wide temperature range with good resistance to oxygen, ozone, high-temperature-air aging; excellent recovery, but is not very tough; has poor resistance to most fluids, and is quite permeable to gases; in seal use, is confined almost entirely to static applications; types of seal: diaphragms, gaskets, O-rings, sealants
17. Tetrafluoroethylene propylene copolymer (C) Aflas® (3M) (P) Aflas® TFE (3M) (P)	−40/+28 to +400°F (−40/−3 to +200)	Broad chemical resistance including areas where standard fluorocarbon is deficient, such as caustics, acids, amines, steam, brine, pulp and paper liquors and alcohols. Still good resistance to oils, lubricants and various automotive fluids; excellent electrical resistance; broad range between stiffening point (TR-10) and brittle point. Useful for various types of seals, diaphragms, gaskets, hoses, and electrical connectors

*P = popular term, T = trade name, C = chemical name, A = designation per ASTM D1418.

(8.3 MPa). Generally pressure, temperature, and fluid determine the gasket material, while dimensional and mechanical features of the joint determine the gasket type.

Nonmetallic Gaskets.   Nonmetallic gaskets in general are more economical than metallic. They are also softer, thereby sealing at a lower seating stress. These gaskets include rubber, both synthetic and natural, paper, plant fibers, cork, cork combined with rubber, inorganic composites, PTFE (polytetrafluoroethylene or Teflon®), and carbon sheet.

An almost limitless variety of nonmetallic gasket materials is produced by combinations of the above materials. This allows the designer to select the most economical combination to provide the sealing capability, strength, and durability required to fit the operating conditions of a given system.

Metallic and Combination Gaskets

FIGURE 4-2 Corrugated gasket with filler. (*Reproduced by permission of Parker Seal Co.*)

Corrugated Gaskets. Corrugated gaskets are made from thin metal which is corrugated with concentric waves (Fig. 4-2). These are essentially line-contact seals with multiple corrugations providing a labyrinth effect. They are used in special shapes, with complicated hole and corrugation patterns, as engine head and manifold gaskets, and also used in lightweight fuel and hydraulic systems. This type of gasket, with fillers, is used extensively in large, bolted hot-gas duct systems. With this construction, large, oddly shaped gaskets can be fabricated in pieces and assembled on the flange.

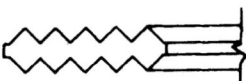

FIGURE 4-3 Flat-metal gasket with grooves. (*Reproduced by permission of Parker Seal Co.*)

Flat Metal Gaskets. Flat metal gaskets are washer-shaped and are relatively thin. The face width is at least 1.5 times the thickness (Fig. 4-3). They can be used with flat surfaces as cut, or grooves may be machined in the surfaces to reduce the contact area. These reduced-area types have less friction, and are therefore useful in screwed attrition joints.

All types seal by brute compressive force flowing the gasket into the flange contact surfaces, and finishes are therefore important. Nevertheless, this can be an economical gasket. Some uses include valve bonnets, ammonia fittings, heat exchangers, and tongue-and-groove joints.

FIGURE 4-4 Spiral-wound gasket with asbestos filler. (*Reproduced by permission of Parker Seal Co.*)

Spiral-Wound Gaskets. Spiral-wound gaskets are made by spirally winding a V-shaped metal strip with a soft filler (Fig. 4-4). These gaskets have good resilience and sealability. This type is suited to assemblies subject to extremes in joint relaxation, temperature or pressure cycling, and shock or vibration. They are available in a wide variety of metals and filler materials and are produced in circular or moderately noncircular shapes. The inner and outer metal plies of the gasket must be under compression. Preferred flange surface finish is 125 to 250 rms.

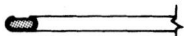

FIGURE 4-5 Metal-jacketed gasket with filler partially enclosed. (*Reproduced by permission of Parker Seal Co.*)

Metal-Jacketed Gaskets. Metal-jacketed gaskets are made with a soft compressible filler partially or wholly enclosed in a metal jacket (Fig. 4-5). The entire inner lap must be under compression since this is the primary seal. They are used for circular and noncircular applications including heat exchangers, valves, pumps, compressors, and boilers. In some instances the double-jacketed type is used as rib work in a spirally wound outer gasket for heat exchangers. They require 20 to 30 percent compression

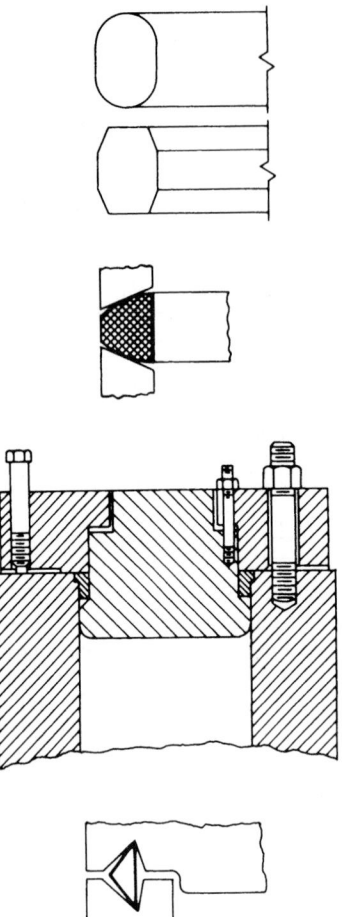

FIGURE 4-6 Heavy-cross-section gaskets; from the top down: oval gasket (*Reproduced by permission of Parker Seal Co.*) octagonal gasket (*Reproduced by permission of Parker Seal Co.*) lens gasket (*Reproduced by permission from Machine Design, September 13, 1973*); Bridgeman joint (*Reproduced by permission from Petroleum Refinery, May 1956*); delta gasket (*Reproduced by permission from Machine Design, September 13, 1973.*)

FIGURE 4-7 Round-cross section metal gasket. (*Reproduced by permission of Parker Seal Co.*)

and are not normally used for joints requiring close maintenance of compressed thickness. When temperatures exceed 900°F (480°C), metallic fillers can be used.

Heavy-Cross-Section Gaskets. The heavy-cross-section gaskets are widely used in the petroleum and processing industries. These gaskets are designed for use in flanges that are specially machined to accept them. Among this group are specialized cross sections including oval, octagonal, lens, Bridgeman, and delta (Fig. 4-6). They are used in high-pressure and high-temperature services including oil-field drilling and production equipment, pressure vessels, valve bonnets, and piping systems. Some of these gaskets are pressure-actuated.

Round-Cross-Section Solid-Metal Gaskets. These gaskets are usually made from wire formed to size and welded (Fig. 4-7). They seal by line contact with high local gasket stresses at low flange loadings. Flange faces are usually grooved or otherwise faced to accurately locate the gasket during assembly. This type is useful in vacuum or other bolted flange systems where efficient seals are needed.

Light-Cross-Section Gaskets. This type can be used in elastomeric O-ring-type installations sealing extremes in vacuum, high-temperature or -pressure, cryogenic, or nuclear applications (Fig. 4-8). They require very little load for initial sealing. Pressure of the system acts on the specially designed seal bellows area, increasing tightness. Flange finish can be 32 to 100 rms for coated seals and 4 to 32 for uncoated.

Installation. Installation of any gasket is a very important factor in achieving a sealed joint. Flange surfaces must be clean and free from nicks, scratches, weld splatter, and any other foreign material. They must be flat and free from warpage. The clamping force or bolt load must be applied in an even stepwise manner to assure uncocked flanges and a uniformly applied load. *It is the joint that leaks. It is the gasket that seals.*

O-Rings

The O-ring is a versatile, compact, inexpensive sealing device (Fig. 4-9). It is made in a variety of elastomers and may be used as a face seal, a radial squeeze seal, a tube-fitting seal, or occasionally in other configurations.

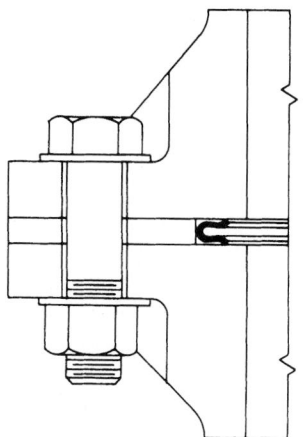

FIGURE 4-8 Light-cross-section metal gasket. (*Reproduced by permission of Parker O-Seal Division, Culver City, California.*)

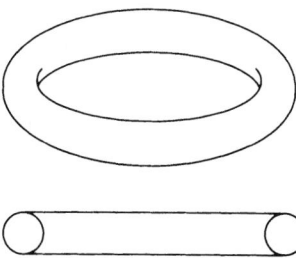

FIGURE 4-9 O-ring. (*Reproduced by permission from Parker O-Ring Handbook No. ORD5700, page A1-1. Parker O-Ring Division, Lexington, Kentucky.*)

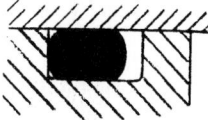

FIGURE 4-10 Assembled O-ring showing squeezed section and extra void.

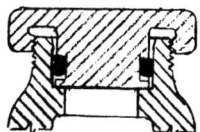

FIGURE 4-11 Static O-ring seal—male gland. (*Modified with permission from Parker O-Ring Handbook ORD5700, Figure A5-1, Parker O-Ring Division, Lexington, Kentucky.*)

Materials. O-ring elastomers are selected for their ability to withstand the conditions of particular sealing applications. The most commonly used O-ring-seal elastomers, together with some other elastomers that are occasionally discussed, are described in Table 4-2.

Applications. O-rings in use are confined in a cavity, or "gland," in which the cross section is squeezed in one direction to provide the lines of contact with mating surfaces that create the sealing function. The combination of an O-ring and its gland makes up the O-ring seal.

When using an O-ring as a seal, the amount of squeeze on the cross section is usually critical. With too much squeeze, there can be assembly problems due to the force required to close the assembly, or even internal rupture of the O-ring. With too little, the O-ring is likely to leak at low temperatures and to suffer from premature failure due to high compression set. A normal squeeze is in the region of 25 percent. It should be no less than 0.007 in (0.18 mm) and no greater than 40 percent.

The material in an O-ring behaves as an incompressible fluid. Therefore, although the O-ring is squeezed in one direction only, it must be free to bulge out at right angles to the direction of the squeeze, and to have extra space within the gland to allow for thermal expansion and normal volume swell when in contact with the system fluid (Fig. 4-10). Standard gland dimensions established by O-ring manufacturers generally allow for 5 percent thermal expansion and about 20 percent volume swell. Allowing for thermal expansion is a necessity, or else the incompressible seal will extrude at high temperatures. Volume swell caused by fluids can be resisted in a number of cases by rugged gland structure or restricted access.

1. Radial squeeze static O-ring seals, whether of the rod (male gland, Fig. 4-11) or piston (female gland, Fig. 4-12) type, usually have a moderate amount of squeeze that is sufficient to assure good low-temperature performance but not enough to cause undue assembly problems.

2. Face-type rectangular grooves for O-ring seals may provide a heavier squeeze, which makes for a more reliable sealing function (Fig. 4-13). The extra squeeze is acceptable in this design because the cross section is

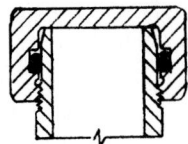

FIGURE 4-12 Static O-ring seal—female gland. (*Modified with permission from Parker O-Ring Handbook ORD5700, Figure A5-1, Parker O-Ring Division, Lexington, Kentucky.*)

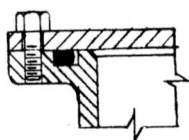

FIGURE 4-13 Static-face-type O-ring seal.

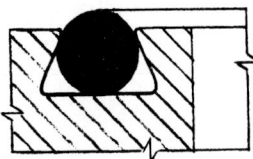

FIGURE 4-14 O-ring in a dovetail groove. (*Modified with permission from Parker O-Ring Handbook ORD5700, Parker O-Ring Division, Lexington, Kentucky.*)

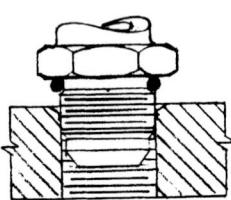

FIGURE 4-15 MS33656-tube-fitting end with O-ring and MS33649 boss.

FIGURE 4-16 Improved tube-fitting boss, SAE J514 and MS16142.

generally deformed by a straight axial pull exerted by flange or cover bolts, so that assembly is not a problem. A variation is the dovetail groove, designed to capture the O-ring in a face-type assembly so that the ring cannot drop out when the cover is removed (Fig. 4-14). These are particularly vulnerable to modification. If deviation from the standard is desired, it must be studied carefully to assure that a maximum-tolerance O-ring will not overfill it and a minimum-tolerance ring will still be retained.

3. Tube fittings are sealed with a separate series of O-ring sizes established for the purpose. In this type of application, the gland is essentially triangular. There are two standards in the United States for the O-ring cavity, or boss. The older is described in Military Standard MS33649 (Fig. 4-15). The new improved style is per MS16142 (Fig. 4-16).

Sealants and Tapes

Sealants are liquids or pastes that are applied between mating surfaces to prevent leakage. Some are formulated to harden after being applied to a joint so that they can contain high pressures. Others remain semiliquid for long periods of time so that joints can be opened easily after prolonged use. Sealants of this latter type are well known for threaded pipe joints. Tapes are also used for this and similar applications. In selecting a sealant, as for seals of other types, a material must be found that will function through the full anticipated temperature range and will not be adversely affected by the fluids and pressures that will be encountered.

RECIPROCATING SEALS

Introduction

The effectiveness of a reciprocating piston or rod seal made of an elastomer or a deformable thermoplastic material depends on the three variables of seal design and the effect of many factors on these variables. The primary factors influencing reciprocating seal design are the fluid to be sealed, the temperatures and pressures to be encountered, the length and speed of stroke, the surface finishes, the amount of clearance, the type of bearings, the space available for the seal, and the desired performance.

Seal Design

The three variables of seal design are the overall shape, the lip configuration, and the properties of the material.

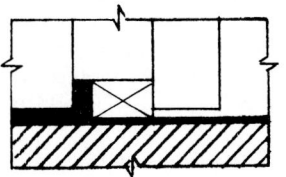

FIGURE 4-17   Seal riding on thin film of fluid.

Seal Shape.   If permeability is disregarded, the only requirement for an effective seal is an unbroken line of contact between the sealing element and the mating surfaces. In a dynamic seal, this ideal situation can only be approached. Preferably, the seal surface rides on a thin film of the system fluid that provides lubrication and retards wear (Fig. 4-17).

Figure 4-18 shows a number of typical seal shapes ranging from pure lip seals on the left to pure compression or pure squeeze types on the right.

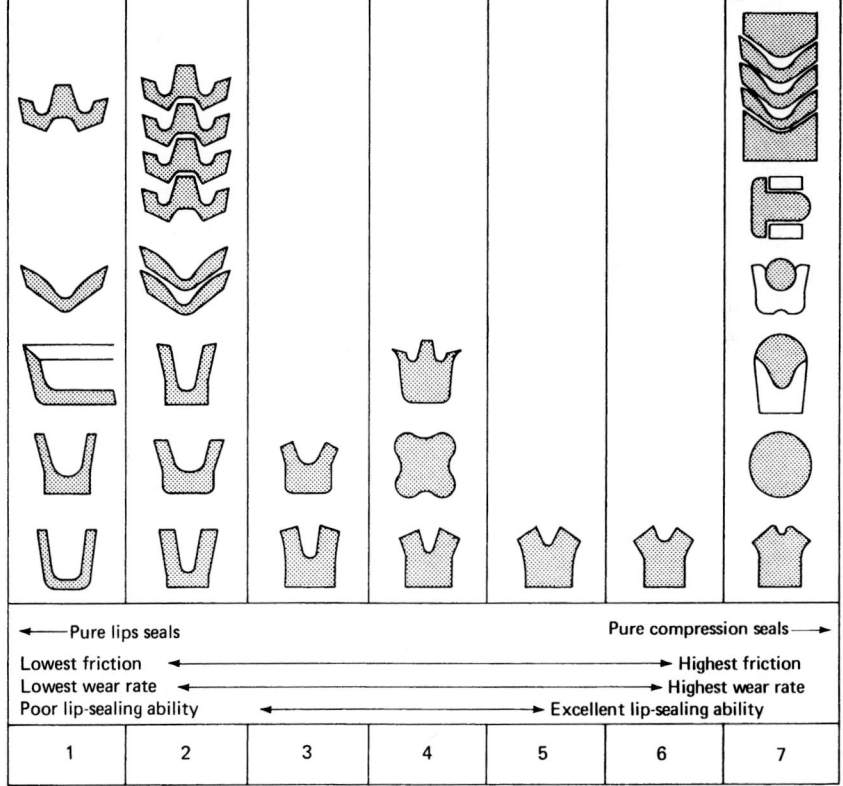

FIGURE 4-18   Basic shape chart. (*Reproduced by permission of Parker Packing Division, Salt Lake City.*)

When there is little or no system pressure, and assuming that all the seal designs are made of the same material, the only force available to cause a pure lip-type seal to conform with the mating surface is the light load required to bend the lip. A pure compression type, however, generates a much higher wiping or sealing load because a relatively incompressible material must be deformed.

Examining these seal shapes, it will be seen that with low fluid pressure, a pure lip-type seal should have little friction and wear, but also it cannot be expected to seal as positively as the pure compression types. The pure compression types, however, will produce more friction and will wear more rapidly. Similarly, the intermediate shapes can be expected to produce intermediate results.

Stability.   Long strokes, too slow or too rapid speed, poor lubrication, eccentricity due to inaccurate machining or eccentric loads, and a number of other factors tend to cause a seal to twist in its gland, resulting in premature seal failure. The ability of a seal to resist this twisting action is called *stability*.

Seal stability generally depends on two factors: the basic shape of the seal and the amount of gland fill (Fig. 4-19). A square seal is more stable than a round seal, and a rectangular seal is more stable than a square seal. Usually, the more completely a seal fills the gland, the greater its stability will be. For most seals, however, it is important that the gland not become overfilled since this will cause excessive friction, wear, and extrusion of the seal. When a seal becomes unstable, leakage usually results and the seal is often damaged as well.

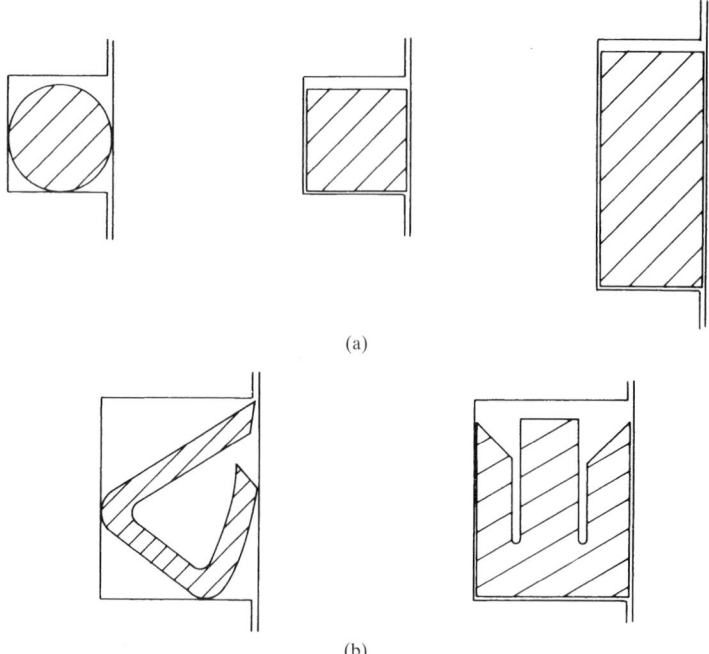

(a)

(b)

FIGURE 4-19   Stability guide: (*a*) basic shape; (*b*) gland fill. The square shape is better than the round and the rectangular is better than the square. The higher the gland fill, the more stable the seal. Overfill can cause high friction and heat, and subsequent seal damage. Stiffer seal materials also improve sealability. (*Reproduced by permission of Parker Packing Division, Salt Lake City.*)

In addition to the shape factors mentioned above, a stiffer, higher-modulus material will resist twisting much better than a softer, more flexible material.

Lip Configuration.   A refinement of the basic seal shape analysis takes into account the shape of the sealing lip. Figure 4-20 shows the five common lip shapes as they appear in the

Contact type number	Free shape of contact	Low-pressure sealing ability	Ability to clean surface without trapping particles	Hydroplaning tendency	Deformed lip shape and force vector distribution
1		High	Low	Medium	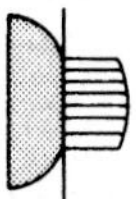
2		Low	Very high	High	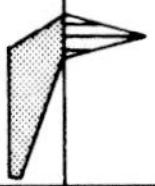
3		High	High	Medium	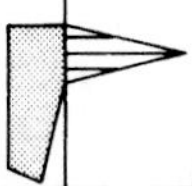
4		Very high	Low	Low	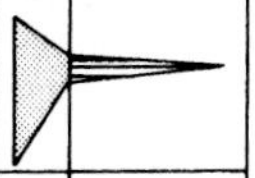
5		Medium/ high	High	Medium/ high	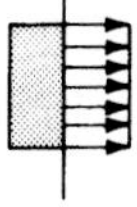

Notes:

(a) Highest unit loading will give highest sealability.
(b) Concentration of vector forces best for wiping.
(c) Lubrication will pass low unit loading patterns.

FIGURE 4-20   Lip shapes and unit loading chart. (*Reproduced by permission of Parker Packing Division, Salt Lake City.*)

free state and as they appear in the installed state. Also shown is a force vector distribution curve associated with each lip shape. High unit loading improves sealability and film breaking. Therefore seals, especially squeeze seals with the lip shape shown in No. 4 (a back-beveled lip), would be extremely dry and, therefore, excellent for wiping oil film. If lower friction (and lower sealability) is desired, a lip shape such as No. 2 would be selected because of the low force vectors associated with this particular shape.

Properties of Seal Material

Fluid Compatibility.   When the basic seal shape has been determined and the lip shape has been established, the seal material must be selected. One of the first considerations should be fluid compatibility. A fluid is considered incompatible with a compound if it causes enough physical-property changes to reduce the sealing function or shorten the working life of the compound. Many fluids will cause seals to swell enough to produce excessive friction and wear. Other fluids may cause physical breakdown of the basic polymer used in the seal, whereas another class of fluids may harden the material so that it no longer has sufficient resilience to conform and establish a sealing line.

Temperature Range.   Closely associated with fluid compatibility is the heat resistance of seal compounds. Heat resistance is a time-temperature function. The higher the temperature experienced by a seal, the shorter its life will be. Some problems stem from the fact that most seal materials expand about 10 times as much as do the metallic materials that contain them. The more serious problems, however, are related to resilience and hardness. High temperatures tend to reduce the resilience and the hardness of seal materials, though many of these materials will eventually harden if the high temperature persists for an extended time. The loss of memory at elevated temperatures, however, means that the seal will assume the shape of the gland. As the temperature falls, the deformed seal shrinks more than its surroundings and pulls away from the mating surfaces, resulting in leakage.

Seal materials also lose resilience at low temperature, although the resilience is regained on warming. The loss of resilience means that the seal is slower to respond to dynamic change such as vibration or wobbling at low temperatures, becoming another cause of leakage until the system warms to normal operating conditions.

The temperature at which these two effects—thermal contraction and loss of resilience—becomes a problem varies with the seal material, but in many cases the fluid being sealed poses more restrictive limits on the temperature range than does the sealing element. This is true due to changes in fluid viscosity characteristics at low temperatures and to thermal degradation of the fluid at high temperatures, resulting in aggressive decomposition by-products that damage the seal.

Memory and Resilience.   The "memory" of a seal material is another important property. It is defined as the ability to return to the original shape on removal of a deforming force, and it is measured by use of the compression set test. Resilience is similar, but implies quick recovery, enabling the seal material to follow rapid variation in the surface passing under the sealing line. With rapid response, very little fluid will be lost on each cycle. The resilience of elastomers is determined with a Bashore resiliometer.

Abrasion Resistance.   The life of a seal can be directly related to its abrasion resistance. This property can be measured by various types of abrader wheels or pads. However, these tests generally give only relative abrasion resistance between polymers and do not give good results for predicting seal life in a particular application. Polyurethane and carboxylated nitrile are known for their excellent abrasion resistance, with polyurethanes being the leader.

Extrusion Resistance.   Extrusion resistance is another property that must be considered in maximizing seal life. Extrusion resistance is a function of the seal compound and the size of the extrusion gap between the piston bore and the piston, or between the rod and the rod throat. It is also inversely proportional to temperature, pressure, and the frictional drag on the seal.

Extrusion of the seal is one primary cause of seal leakage. This type of leakage can be massive in that a seal can be progressively torn away until a major gap develops at the lip.

Extrusion can be controlled by following one or more of the directions listed below.

1. Use a backup ring. A backup ring is an auxiliary device made of an extrusion-resistant compound that is placed behind the seal to protect it from extruding under pressure (Fig. 4-21).
2. Select an extrusion-resistant compound for the seal itself. (High-tensile-strength modulus and, sometimes, hardness will correlate with increased extrusion resistance.)
3. Reduce the clearance gap between the two dynamic surfaces.
4. Maintain concentricity between the cylinder and bore and between the rod and its housing. (This requires the use of bearings within the cylinder or nonmetallic wear bands on the piston or rod to avoid side loading the seals. Seals are not designed to carry side loads.)

Exclusion Devices (Wipers and Scrapers).   Although exclusion devices are not seals, they play an important part in extending seal life and minimizing leakage. Whenever a reciprocating rod is exposed to dust, ice, snow, mud, or other abrasive materials, it is important that a wiper be included in the system to clean the rod before it can carry these foreign materials in through the seal, abrading it and contaminating the system.

There are many types and styles of exclusion devices available, and one can be found that is appropriate for almost any environment.

Common Reciprocal Seal Configurations.   Based on the three factors of seal design (seal shape, lip shape, and material), a wide variety of seal designs are possible. Given the perfor-

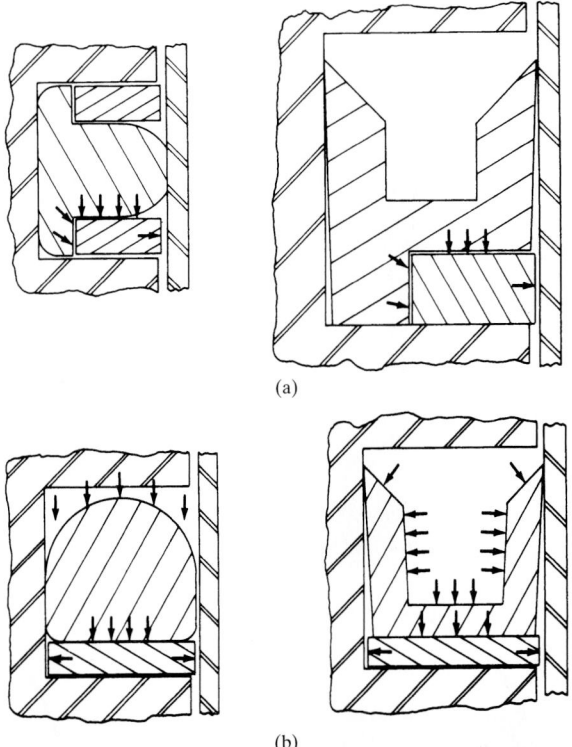

(a)

(b)

FIGURE 4-21   Extrusion resistance: (*a*) Positively actuated back-ups. (*b*) non-positively actuated backups. (*Reproduced by permission of Parker Packing Division, Salt Lake City.*)

mance criteria of a given seal application, this variety is beneficial in the selection of the optimal seal design. The following is a list of some of the common seal configurations used in hydraulic and pneumatic cylinders. A short description of each seal follows as a guide to assist in the seal selection process.

Loaded Lip Seals.   Loaded lip seals are multi-purpose seals that combine an O-ring type synthetic O-spring or a stainless steel coil spring, with a conventional lip-type seal to produce a unique sealing device capable of sealing both vacuum and high or low pressure. Various combinations of O-spring and shell materials ensure the proper combination of abrasion, extrusion, temperature resistance and fluid compatibility.

As shown in Fig. 4-22*a*, the loaded lip seal is available in three different styles. The square and rectangular styles with the scraper lip design are suitable for a wide variety of rod and piston applications. The rectangular style with the beveled lip design provides additional squeeze and is suitable for sealing both high-pressure rod seal applications and unidirectional piston seal applications.

Cap Seals.   Cap seals (Fig. 4-22*b*) are bidirectional squeeze-type seals ideal for use as piston seals in fluid power cylinders. This seal is suitable for direct substitution with O-rings and T seals in industrial no-backup O-ring grooves. This seal design combines the strength of a thermoplastic lip with the resilience of a rubber energizer to provide no-drift sealing over a wide range of pressures in a variety of cylinder piston applications.

T-Seals.   T-seals (Fig. 4-22*c*) are designed for direct replacement of O-rings in long stroke hydraulic applications where spiral failure due to rolling of the O-ring in the seal groove has occurred. T-seals are also useful where extrusion of the seal element is probable as the backup

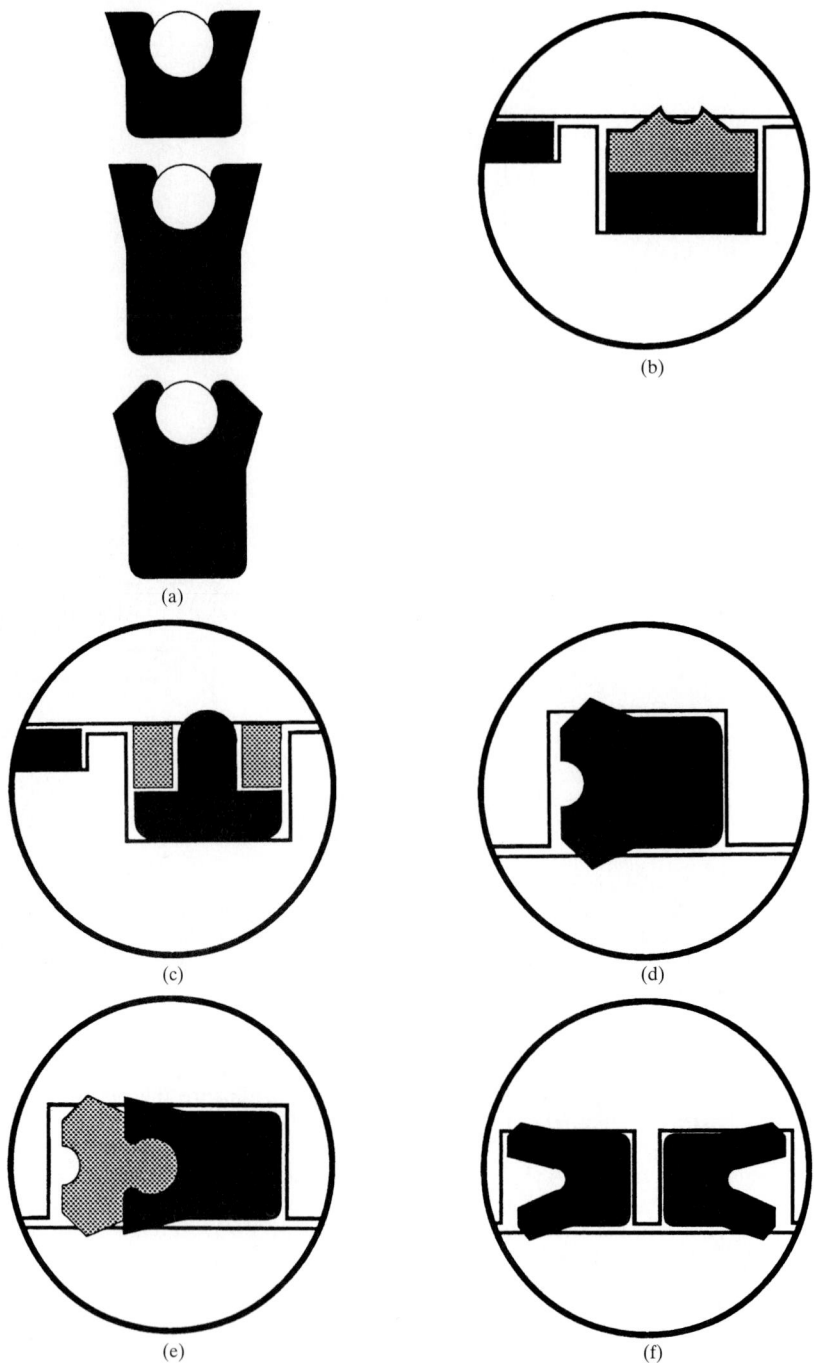

FIGURE 4-22 Common reciprocating seal configurations. (*a*) Loaded lip seals; (*b*) cap seals; (*c*) T-seals; (*d*) chamfer lip seals; (*e*) multiple lip seals; (*f*) U-cups. (*Reproduced by permission of Parker Packing Division, Salt Lake City.*)

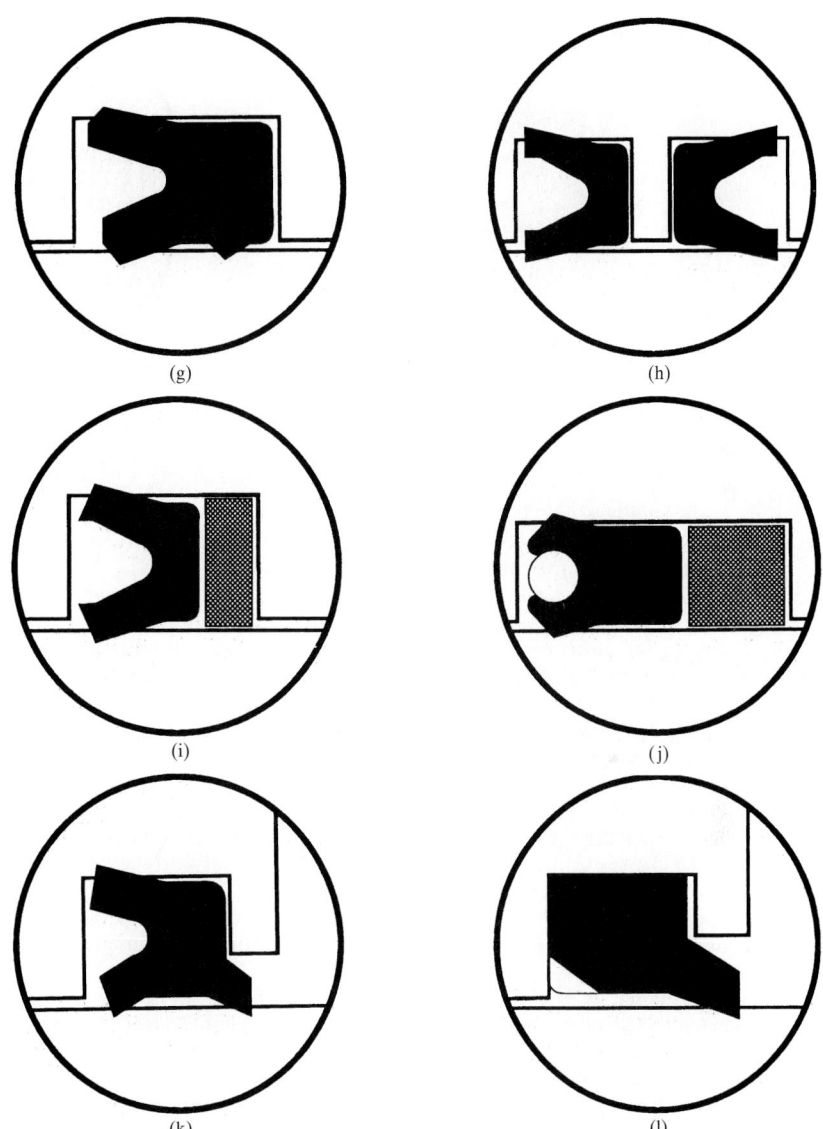

FIGURE 4-22   Common reciprocating seal configurations. (*g*) Double lip U-cups; (*h*) U-packings; (*i*) backup ring; (*j*) modular backup; (*k*) double lip wiper/seal; (*l*) snap-in wiper. (*Reproduced by permission of Parker Packing Division, Salt Lake City.*)

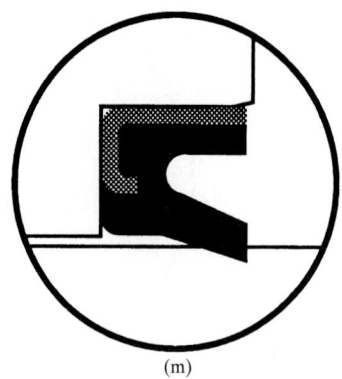
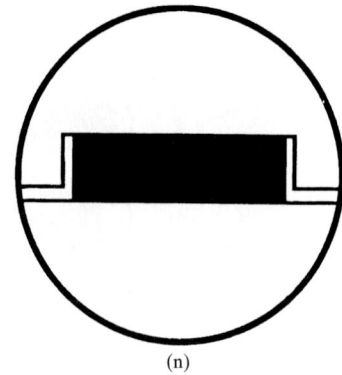

(m)   (n)

FIGURE 4-22   Common reciprocating seal configurations. (*m*) Metal can wiper; (*n*) wear band. (*Reproduced by permission of Parker Packing Division, Salt Lake City.*)

components of the T-seal function as antiextrusion devices. Because of the extrusion resistance of the T-seal geometry, higher system pressures may be employed. T-seals are used in both piston and rod applications.

Chamfer Lip Seals.   Chamfer lip seals (Fig. 4-22*d*) are unidirectional seals designed for use in reciprocating devices such as cylinders and spool valves. Cut lip seals are directly interchangeable with O-rings and T-seals in MIL-G-5514F grooves and provide better low-pressure sealing, improved stability, and extrusion resistance and offer a balance between wear resistance and low friction.

Multiple Lip Seals.   Multiple lip seals (Fig. 4-22*e*) are a combination of a rubber sealing element snapped into a thermoplastic shell. The shell provides an additional sealing lip and protects the softer rubber lip from extruding. This seal design requires a greater groove length than customary loaded lip seal designs. Multiple lip seals minimize seal leakage where excessive tolerances must be used or where worn or older equipment must be replaced.

U-Cups.   U-cups (Fig. 4-22*f*) are unidirectional lip-type seals that are used mainly for heavy-duty applications in mobile and industrial hydraulic cylinders. They are available in three styles: the symmetrical U-cup design for both rod or piston applications, the nonsymmetrical rod design for rod applications, and the nonsymmetrical piston design for piston applications.

Double Lip U-Cups.   Double lip U-cups (Fig. 4-22*g*) use a secondary lip to stabilize the seal in its groove. This U-cup design is highly resistant to side loading and insensitive to pressure spikes. This design helps to reduce leakage under severe operating conditions. The secondary sealing lip helps to reduce fluid pressure buildup between the rod seal and wiper.

U-Packings.   U-packings (Fig. 4-22*h*) are especially adapted to low-speed, low-pressure applications. The compact configuration of these seals and their inherent low friction make them suitable pneumatic seals. U-packings are typically symmetrical lip-type seals. The lip designs vary depending on the application (scraper lips for piston seal applications and beveled lips for rod applications). Nonsymmetrical designs with rounded lips are also available for nonlubricated pneumatic applications.

Backup Rings.   Backup rings (Fig. 4-22*i*) are designed as antiextrusion devices. Excess pressure can cause soft seal materials to extrude into gaps between metal surfaces. The harder backup ring material supports the seal. Backup rings are placed behind the seal or can be designed into the seal configuration.

Modular Backups.   Modular backups (Fig. 4-22*j*) are devices designed to prevent extrusion. Modular backups are generally installed to absorb shock loads and to prevent extrusion of seals in high-pressure applications.

Double Lip Wiper/Seals.   Double lip wiper/seal rings (Fig. 4-22*k*) are one-piece snap-in rod wipers. With their one-component design, these wipers can provide both sealing and wiping action in low-pressure systems. As the external lip scrapes foreign matter from the rod, the other lips act as an effective pressure seal in low-pressure pneumatic applications or as a secondary seal to trap slight leakage in high-pressure hydraulic systems.

Snap-in Wipers.   Snap-in wipers (Fig. 4-22*l*) are designed to provide rod wiping action and protect the cylinder from contamination. They are generally available in two designs. One is designed to fit MS28776 wiper ring grooves and the other is designed with a heavier cross section for use in heavy-duty applications.

Metal Can Wipers.   Metal can wipers (Fig. 4-22*m*) are designed for press-fit in open face rod wiper glands and do not require additional retention devices such as snap-rings or face plates. Metal can wipers are generally chosen for use in severe rod wiper environments such as frozen or dried mud and even light weld splatter.

Wear Bands.   Wear bands (Fig. 4-22*n*) are bearings especially compounded of high strength/reinforced material to prevent metal-to-metal contact of moving parts in reciprocating piston and rod applications. Use of wear bands may allow the use of lighter weight components such as aluminum pistons and heads, and in addition, act to maintain centering on pistons and rods, thus avoiding scoring and over-stressed conditions caused by side loading.

Installation.   The elongation of a seal compound is important if stretch-in applications are being considered. The forces required to install a seal should also be taken into account if large cross sections are being considered, even in rod applications, where the seal is folded rather than stretched in assembly. The 100 percent modulus of a seal compound is a good guide to ease of installation. Table 4-3 is also helpful.

TABLE 4-3   Seal Installation Guide

For thermoplastic materials only: Rigid materials require split seals or separable gland

	Minimum I.D rod seal		Minimum O.D. piston seal	
	Thermoplastic seal material hardness		Thermoplastic seal material hardness	
Cross section	90A	55D	90A	55D
⅛″	¾″	1″	1¼″	1¾″
³⁄₁₆″	1″	1¾″	1¾″	2¾″
¼″	1¾″	2¾″	3″	4½″
⅜″	3″	5″	6″	8″
½″	6″	8″	10″	12″
¾″	8″	9″	15″	17″
1″	10″	10″	20″	25″

The sealing process consists of many compromises. An extremely important compromise is in the choices made between the level of sealability desired versus the seal/metal interface and life desired by the seal application.

The surface finish of the metal and texture of the metal's surface are important in determining the amount of seepage or leakage that will occur. In the most simplistic terms, most seal manufacturers publish a surface finish requirement of 8 to 16 rms for dynamic surfaces and 16 to 32 rms for static sides of the seal housing or gland.

In the future, environmental concerns about fluid leakage and increased customer demands for leak-free equipment will require different specifications on seals and metal conditions. Thus, two schools of thought exist concerning surface finishes versus the acceptable amount of seal seepage allowed and resulting seal life.

At 8 to 16 rms on a dynamic surface good sealability can be achieved. Many people use a chrome-plated and polished surface at this finish. Minute amounts of fluid can be carried in the small irregularities of the metal, which will lubricate the seal adding to seal life. The amount of fluid film that goes out of the system can now collect at the wiper and appears in the form of seepage over time. In many industrial applications some seepage is acceptable as a compromise.

In showroom or food-processing environments this same seepage is unacceptable. More specific requirements are needed to prevent seal seepage. In these circles, 8 to 16 rms is not sufficient. Finishes as low as 4 to 8 rms are now required with special seal combinations with highly polished rods. The tradeoff here is lubrication for the seal system. Since the small peaks and valleys in the metal are very small, little or no lubrication is carried to lubricate seals. It is important to evaluate the costs associated to achieve these finishes. Figure 4-23 shows how lubrication properties diminish as the seal surface becomes very smooth.

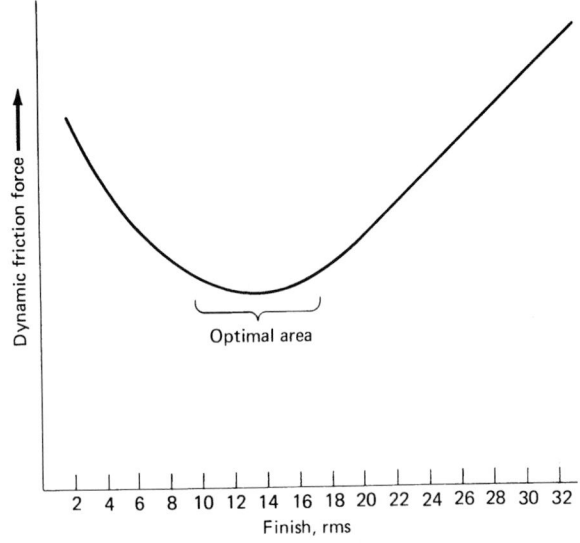

FIGURE 4-23   Friction-vs-surface-roughness curve. (*Reproduced by permission of Parker Packing Division, Salt Lake City.*)

Since the need for better surface finishes is growing, a new method to describe finishes is required. There is a system that describes finishes in more detail. The values frequently used to define surface roughness are the R_t, R_{max}, R_a, and R_p.

R_t is the vertical distance between the highest and the lowest point of the roughness profile over a measured length.

R_{max} may replace R_t. R_{max} is the maximum peak-to-valley difference over a measured distance, representing the highest value measured in one of five consecutive sample lengths.

R_p is the vertical difference between the highest point and the medium line of a roughness profile.

The average peak-to-valley height R_a is the arithmetical mean of the absolute values of all peak-to-valley relationships over the measured length. R_z is the mean of five consecutive measurements of R_a.

The above measurements only define the peak-to-valley relationship of the metal surface. The shape of the peak is also important. Is the peak round, sharp, flat, or square? Different machining techniques will produce different results. A magnified surface that resembles the texture of the surface of an orange produces good sealing results at an acceptable life level.

Investigate the available measuring instruments to produce the surface finish that will achieve the desirable compromise.

Notes

1. When in doubt contact the seal supplier for guidance.

2. Test all new seal designs under conditions as close as possible to the conditions of use. (The vendor can provide guidance but cannot actually test all seals under all the conditions encountered in the field.)

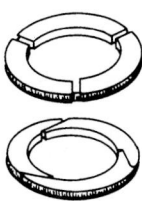

FIGURE 4-24 Segmental metal rings. (*From W. Staniar, "Plant Engineering Handbook," 2d ed., Fig. 27-23d, p. 27–22. Copyright © 1959, McGraw-Hill Book Co., Inc. Reproduced by permission of the publisher.*)

3. If a premature failure occurs, save the failed seal and the mating parts to assist in a failure analysis.

Rigid Packings. Rigid packings, generally of cast iron or reinforced TFE (tetrafluoroethylene), are most commonly used on gas compressors. These range in form from the simple bevel or step-joint piston ring to rather complex spring-assisted segmental styles (Fig. 4-24). The need for "clear" (unlubricated) compressed gas or air systems has accentuated the use of the reinforced TFE style.

ROTARY SEALS

Introduction

Rotary sealing devices may be subdivided into four categories:

1. Clearance seals (controlled clearance, labyrinth, wind-back)
2. Mechanical face seals (mechanical seals, face seals)
3. Compression packings
4. Lip seals (oil seals)

Although most types are commonly used alone, severe conditions often require two or more types in a single application.

Rotary packings and seals present a specific group of problems to the seal designer. Typically rubbing speeds are high, and the seal-rubbing interface is confined to a very limited area. The problem of dissipating the resultant heat differentiates rotary applications from reciprocating applications where the heat is incurred over a relatively large area of a rod or a cylinder bore.

Factors such as fluid, temperature, pressure, interface velocity, allowable leakage, necessary life, space, and cost will determine which type of rotary seal is best suited for any individual application. No attempt can be made in this limited discussion to provide all the information needed to make such a selection. Rather, the following section is intended to acquaint the reader with the basic types, principles, and terminology.

Clearance Seals

Clearance seals, as a group, are intended to reduce leakage while avoiding actual contact between the moving parts.

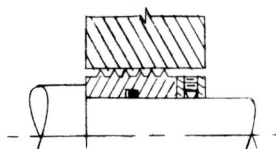

FIGURE 4-25 Labyrinth seal.

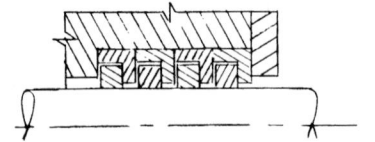

FIGURE 4-26 Multiple-unit floating bushing seal.

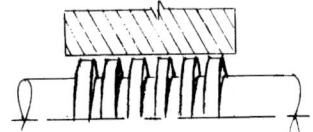

FIGURE 4-27 Wind-back seal.

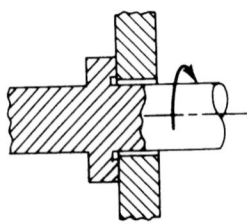

FIGURE 4-28 Simplified face seal. (*Reproduced by permission from "Sealing Is Our Business," Fig. 5-15. Copyright © January 1975, Parker Seal Group, Lexington, Kentucky.*)

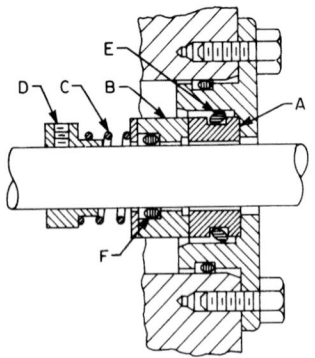

FIGURE 4-29 Typical mechanical face seal. (*Reproduced by permission from "Sealing Is Our Business," Fig. 5-18. Copyright © January 1975, Parker Seal Group, Lexington, Kentucky.*)

Labyrinth Seals. A simple labyrinth is shown in Fig. 4-25. Numerous variations of this type are feasible, involving stepped diameters, barrier fluid areas, drains, etc. Since clearances must be kept small and contact generally avoided, substantial design problems result when wobble, end play, and thermal expansion are taken into account.

Labyrinths have, essentially, no pressure or speed limitations because of their noncontacting nature. Similarly, no temperature limits are imposed other than those of the materials of construction. Since these materials are not required to be deformable, and no rubbing contact is involved, material choices for high temperatures normally present no problem.

Bushing Seals. Bushings, most simply, are sleeves with a small clearance around a shaft, leakage being limited by laminar- and turbulent-flow considerations in the small annulus thus created. A noncontact situation is desired, and the need for small clearance, when viewed in the light of shaft runout, angularity, vibration, thermal expansion, etc., generally results in a floating-sleeve design. Figure 4-26 represents a multiple-unit floating-sleeve or bushing design, each bushing being free to center itself diametrally with reference to the shaft. As in other rotary-seal types, designs will often allow for drains, buffer or barrier fluids, etc.

Wind-Back Seals. The tendency of fluid in close proximity to a moving surface (as in a small annulus) to move with the surface is made use of in a variety of self-pumping or *wind-back* applications. Figure 4-27 shows a sample representational wind-back, where the tendency of the fluid to flow to the left is balanced by the pumping force of the helical land.

Mechanical Face Seals

A face seal in its simplest conceptual form would be as illustrated in Fig. 4-28. As may be observed, the sealing interface is on a plane at right angles to the rotational axis. Thus a certain amount of shaft runout could be accommodated without distorting the relationship between the two parts at the sealing interface.

This conceptual design, however, could not compensate for wear at the seal interface, nor could it accommodate axial motion.

In Fig. 4-29 the design is modified to provide replaceable rubbing portions, and to provide

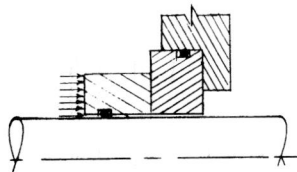

FIGURE 4-30   Unbalanced face-seal head.

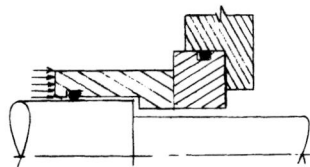

FIGURE 4-31   Balanced face-seal head.

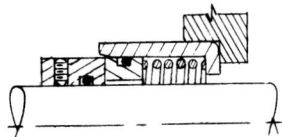

FIGURE 4-32   Mechanical seal with rotating seat.

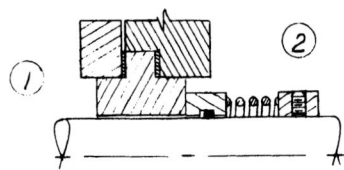

FIGURE 4-33   Seal head on outside of seat: (1) fluid; (2) atmosphere.

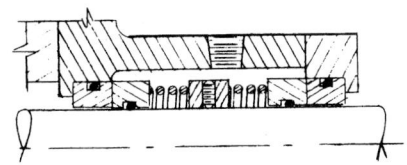

FIGURE 4-34   Double mechanical seal.

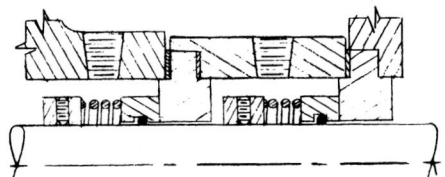

FIGURE 4-35   Tandem-type mechanical seal.

axial spring force to accommodate wear and small amounts of axial motion. A replaceable seat *A* has been inserted in the housing, a replaceable head *B* replaces the rotating shoulder, a spring *C* bearing against a collar *D* keeps the seal interface in contact, while secondary seals *E* and *F* seal the leak paths thus created. Secondary seal *E* is essentially static, whereas *F* will experience motion as end play and wear are accommodated. Figure 4-29 is thus a simple mechanical face seal. Seal types discussed here may be considered to be modifications or expansions of this basic configuration.

Balance Seals.   Figure 4-29 shows the contained fluid pressure against the left radial surface of the head *B* as it tends to force the head to the right, thus increasing the interface pressure established by the spring in proportion to the fluid pressure contained. This is shown in simplified form in Fig. 4-30. If the design is modified by use of a stepped shaft, as in Fig. 4-31, one will observe that the annular area on the left end of the head is reduced, proportionately reducing the fluid-pressure induced component of the interface pressure. In industry terminology, Fig. 4-31 is referred to as "balanced" and Fig. 4-30 as "unbalanced." Balanced seals are normally specified for higher pressures or for the sealing of "light" liquids.

Rotating Seat.   Seals may be designed and installed with the seat stationary (as in the preceding examples) or rotating (Fig. 4-32).

Outside Installation.   A further variation is shown later in Fig. 4-34. Figures 4-29 and 4-32 show the seal head on the fluid side of the seat (an inside installation), and Fig. 4-33 shows an outside installation.

Clamped Seat.   Figure 4-33 shows a further variation with the seat clamped, as opposed to the relatively free O-ring mounting shown in the preceding sketches. The secondary seal at the seat is a flat gasket.

Double Seals.   It is often necessary or desirable to circulate a secondary fluid in a chamber formed by a double (Fig. 4-34) or tandem (Fig. 4-35) seal arrangement. This secondary fluid could be at a higher or lower pressure than the primary fluid. Such an arrangement may be used for a wide variety of purposes, ranging from safety (in the case of a toxic or flammable primary fluid) to simple redundancy. Problems with fluids containing abrasives, or those which tend to crystallize on cooling or on contact with the atmosphere, are commonly handled in this fashion. This method may also be utilized to provide interface lubrication when sealing gases.

An alternative form of rotary seal (a throttle bushing, rings of soft packing, an oil seal, etc.) may be employed either inboard or outboard of the primary mechanical face seal for similar purposes.

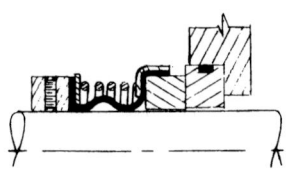

FIGURE 4-36 Mechanical seal with elastomeric or TFE bellows.

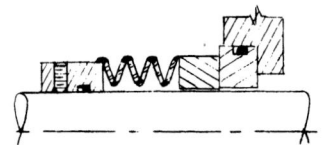

FIGURE 4-37 Mechanical seal with metal bellows.

For simplicity all of the examples shown depict a single spring. However, a number of small, evenly spaced springs are often employed to provide a more uniform load around the circumference of the head.

Seals with Bellows. The motion of the secondary seal associated with the head tends, in most designs, to "fret" or wear the adjacent sealed surface. In order to avoid this, recourse is often had to bellows designs, of elastomer or TFE, in which the motion in question is absorbed by deformation of the bellows (Fig. 4-36).

A further modification (Fig. 4-37) uses a welded metal bellows which performs a dual function as a motion-absorbing seal and as the actuating spring.

The Secondary Seal. In the preceding paragraphs, O-rings, gaskets, and bellows have been mentioned as secondary seals. Actually, a wide variety of secondary seals are used in mechanical face-seal assemblies. The secondary seal at the seat is generally static, leading most often to use of a simple O-ring gasket. The secondary seal associated with the head, however, is subjected to various degrees of small-magnitude motion as the head moves in response to axial shaft motion and face wear. Thus, a wider variety of wedges, X-rings, V-rings, coated O-rings, and other, more sophisticated, seal forms will be noted.

Compression Packings

Compression packings, also called soft packings, braided packings, and rope packings, are among the oldest packings known to industry. Such packings characteristically depend on axial pressure provided mechanically by a gland follower to radially distort the rings into intimate contact with the sealed surfaces. A broad range of materials and combinations of materials and impregnants or saturants, ranging from flax, cotton, and synthetics to the latest exotics, are used in compression-packing manufacture.

Types of Construction

Cross Briad. Strands of yarn cross the surface diagonally, interlocking to form a dense, yet flexible, structure that cannot unravel in service. Lubrication of individual strands in the braiding process provides a more uniform distribution of antifriction materials and yarn density for increased life of the packing.

Square Braid. Strands of yarn cross over and under other strands in the same running direction and produce square cross sections. Other names for this construction are square, plaited, or flax braid. This type of construction is normally specified for high-speed rotary service at low pressure.

Braid over Braid. This type is formed by one or more layers of braided yarns covering a core of braided, twisted, or homogeneous materials and producing an initially round construction. It may be calendered square or rectangular into a dense, highly lubricated packing for low-speed and high-pressure applications.

Twisted.   Strands of yarn are twisted in the same running direction to the required round size. This type is recommended only for low-speed, low-pressure utility use when the packing space is small or when the available cross section is larger than the required packing space. The individual strands are easily removed to fit emergency requirements.

Laminated.   Coils, spirals, or rings are cut from molded slabs of fabric and rubber materials. This construction is normally used for the liquid end of reciprocating rams or pump pistons.

Wrapped.   Rubber-impregnated fabric materials are rolled or calendered into a square or rectangular cross section alone or over a homogeneous core for high resilience. Typical use is in applications with high lateral movement in the equipment.

Plastic.   Lubricated plastic packings contain oil, fiber materials, graphite, grease, or mica. They are usually square and within a cotton jacket for handling or within an asbestos jacket to prevent extrusion. They are normally used to seal gases or in applications in which the packing must supply part or all of the lubrication.

Metallic.   Metal packings of lead, copper, aluminum foil, or ribbon are spirally wrapped, folded, or twisted into a square or rectangular cross section. Normal use is in high-pressure, high-temperature service and corrosive fluids.

Cutting and Installing Packing Rings

Pumps and Agitators

1. Remove old packing from the stuffing box. Clean the box and shaft thoroughly and examine the shaft for wear or scoring. Replace the shaft or sleeve if wear is excessive. Check the bearing by moving the shaft up and down.

2. Use the right size of coil packing to be sure the packing will fit and can compensate for shaft wear, if any. To determine the correct packing size, measure the diameter of the shaft and then the inside diameter of the stuffing box. Subtract the shaft diameter from the inside-diameter measurement and divide by 2 for the required size.

FIGURE 4-38   Butt joint. (*Reproduced by permission of Parker Packing Division, Salt Lake City, Utah.*)

3. Cut the packing into individual rings. *Never wind packing in a continuous length into a stuffing box.* For pumps and agitators cut rings with a butt (square) joint (Fig. 4-38). The best way to cut packing rings is to cut them on a mandrel of the same diameter as the shaft in the stuffing-box area. Hold the coiled packing tightly and firmly on the mandrel but do not stretch it excessively. Cut the ring and try it in the stuffing box to make certain that it fills the packing space properly, with no gap in the joint at the outside diameter of the ring.

4. Install one ring at a time. Make sure it is clean and has not picked up any dirt in handling before installing it. If clean oil is available, lubricate each ring thoroughly; the shaft and the inside of the stuffing box would also benefit from lubrication. Joints of successive rings should be staggered and be kept at least 90° apart. Each ring should be firmly seated with a tamping tool. When enough rings have been individually seated to allow the nose of the follower to reach them, the individual tamping should be supplemented by the follower. Never depend entirely on the follower to seat a set of rings properly; this practice will jam the last rings installed but leave the front rings loose in the box. The result is excessive and rapid wear of rear rings, erratic packing performance, or sometimes, twisting and tearing of the front rings which are loose in the stuffing box.

5. After last ring is installed, take up bolts finger tight. Start the pump, and take up bolts until leakage is decreased to no more than 10 drops per minute. Stopping leakage entirely at this point will cause the packing to burn up.

6. Allow the packing to leak freely when starting up a newly packed pump. It will take about one working day to break in a set of packing to a point where the leakage is stabilized at a uniform acceptable rate.

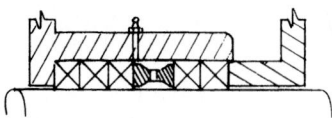

FIGURE 4-39 Packing set with lantern ring in a stuffing box. (*Modified from Parker Compression Packing Catalog, No. PPD3901-A, by permission of Parker Packing Division, Salt Lake City, Utah.*)

FIGURE 4-40 Skive joint. (*Reproduced by permission of Parker Packing Division, Salt Lake City, Utah.*)

7. If at all possible, provide, through a lantern ring (Fig. 4-39), means of lubricating the shaft and packing by supplying grease, oil, water, or the liquid handled in the pump. Make sure the lantern ring, as installed, is slightly behind the lubricant fitting so it will move under the fitting as follower pressure is applied.

Valves and Expansion Joints

1. Carefully perform all the operations outlined under steps 1, 2, 3, and 4 as given for pumps and agitators. Rings used on valves and expansion joints should be cut with a skive joint (45°). See Fig. 4-40.

2. Bring the follower down on the packing to the point where heavy resistance to wrenching is felt. During this time turn the valve stem back and forth to determine ease of turning. Do not wrench to the point at which the stem will not turn.

3. After the valve has been on the line a day or so, even if no leakage exists, the follower should be tightened slightly. If it is leaking at all, tighten the follower until there is no leakage.

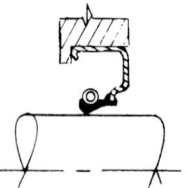

FIGURE 4-41 Typical oil seal with garter spring.

Lip-Type Rotary Seals

Lip-type rotary seals are often called *oil seals,* though they are by no means restricted to sealing oils, or *rotary-shaft seals*. Elements common to this class of seals are a flexible sealing lip that rides on the surface of the rotating shaft and a formed metal cup that holds the sealing element and is pressed into the seal housing. Generally there is also a garter spring that helps maintain contact of the lip (Fig. 4-41). The sealing element may be elastomeric, leather, or plastic.

The primary use of oil seals is in low-pressure applications, generally below 8 lb/in^2 (55 kPa). Surface speeds may be quite high, ranging up to 4000 ft/min (20.5 m/sec). Occasionally there are special designs that can tolerate much higher pressures, but at high pressure the surface speed must be slow.

Oil seals are well suited to low-pressure applications because the narrow contact band of the sealing lip keeps friction and its associated heat low while permitting ready dissipation of the heat that is generated. The sealing-element material may be varied to resist special fluids and unusual temperature extremes.

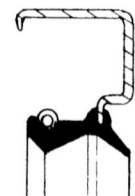

FIGURE 4-42 Oil seal with dirt lip. (*Reproduced by permission of Parker O-Seal Division, Culver City, California.*)

Dirt-Lip Design. One of the most common variations on the basic design is a second lip pointing outward for use where abrasive dust could damage the primary sealing lip or where external fluid splash could enter and contaminate the internal medium (Fig. 4-42). The secondary or *dirt lip* is not spring-loaded, but relies on the resilience of the material to maintain contact with the shaft.

FIGURE 4-43   Oil seal with nose-seal gasket. (*Modified with permission from "Sealing Is Our Business," Copyright © 1975, Parker Seal Group, Lexington, Kentucky.*)

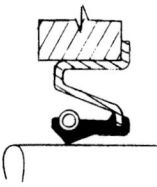

FIGURE 4-44   Oil seal with pry-out flange. (*Modified with permission from "Sealing Is Our Business," Copyright © 1975, Parker Seal Group, Lexington, Kentucky.*)

FIGURE 4-45   Oil seal with inner case. (*Modified with permission from "Sealing Is Our Business," Copyright © 1975, Parker Seal Group, Lexington, Kentucky.*)

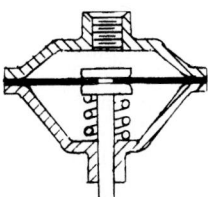

FIGURE 4-46   Flat diaphragm. (*From sketch by J. B. Scannell.*)

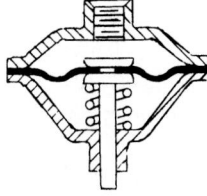

FIGURE 4-47   Diaphragm with convolution. (*From sketch by J. B. Scannell.*)

Nose-Seal Gasket.   Another modification includes a nose-seal gasket to prevent static leakage around the drawn cup (Fig. 4-43).

Cup Designs.   Besides variations in the sealing element, the metal cup may be made in any number of styles. For instance, a pry-out flange may be incorporated to make the seal accessible from either the outside (Fig. 4-44) or from the fluid side. Often an inner case, which protects the spring and the sealing lip and makes the assembly more rigid, is provided (Fig. 4-45).

FLEXURAL SEALING DEVICES

Diaphragms, bellows, and expansion joints are variations of a class of sealing devices that are attached to one or more components of a system, absorbing the relative motion between such components or absorbing fluid displacement by deformation of the sealing device itself.

The simplest of these devices is the flat diaphragm (Fig. 4-46). These are generally cut from reinforced or unreinforced elastomeric sheet, although metal, leather, and plastics find use in some situations. The range of motion which can be accommodated by the flat diaphragm is limited, and a molded or formed convolution is often added to accommodate additional travel (Fig. 4-47).

The *tubular diaphragm*, or bellows, accommodates large axial motion for a given diameter (Fig. 4-48), as does the rolling diaphragm (Fig. 4-49).

A heavy-duty form of bellows is the *expansion joint* (Fig. 4-50), most commonly fabricated of rubber with fabric and metal reinforcement, but also of TFE or with a TFE liner. These devices absorb vibration and relative movement between sections of piping or duct systems.

Although a degree of standardization exists among these products, most are produced to order for specific applications, and competent suppliers should be consulted for detailed information.

INFORMATION REQUIRED FOR TECHNICAL ASSISTANCE

When assistance is needed in seal design, the consultant will need specific details about the

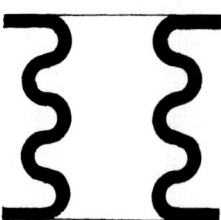

FIGURE 4-48 Bellows. (*From sketch by J. B. Scannell.*)

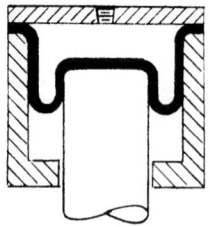

FIGURE 4-49 Rolling diaphragm. (*From sketch by J. B. Scannell.*)

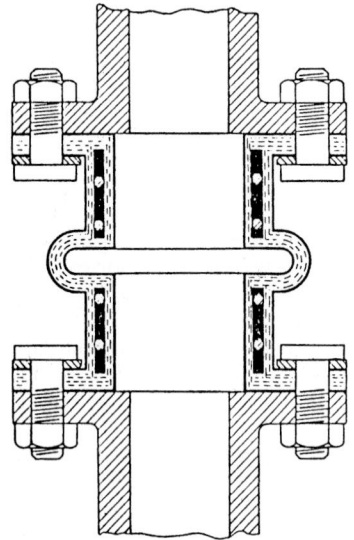

FIGURE 4-50 Expansion joint. (*From W. Staniar, "Plant Engineering Handbook," 2d ed., Fig. 27-43, p. 27–52. Copyright © 1959, McGraw-Hill Book Co., Inc. Reproduced by permission of the publisher.*)

application. The following comments may be helpful in collecting the necessary pieces of information.

Data Needed for All Seal Designs

1. Temperature
    a. Maximum operating temperature
    b. Time at maximum temperature. The time at maximum temperature is particularly important when the maximum is too high for normal seal materials. If the time is sufficiently short and will be experienced once or only a few times, an inexpensive material may be suitable since degradation due to high temperature, though generally irreversible, is time-dependent.
    c. Minimum operating temperature. If the minimum operating temperature is very low, it will have a great influence on the selection of a seal material. In general, however, low-temperature effects are reversible. If a seal does not operate at low temperature, it will generally function normally when warmed up. A seal is considered to be operating, in this sense, if it must contain a fluid, even though the device in which it is installed may not operate at the low temperature.
    d. Normal operating temperature
2. Pressure
    a. Maximum pressure
    b. Operating pressure
    c. Minimum pressure (or vacuum level for vacuum seals)
3. Medium (to be sealed). Length of time of seal contact with the medium.
4. Configuration. The seal consultant needs to know the arrangement, materials, and sizes of surfaces in the vicinity of the seal. In some cases, a few dimensions will suffice. Often it is necessary to provide dimensional drawings or sketches of the pertinent parts. Surface roughness values of mating parts are also important to seal design.

Additional Data for Reciprocating Seals

1. Length of stroke
2. Stroke rate
3. Mode of operation (i.e., actuator, operated by the fluid pressure, or pump, generating fluid pressure).
4. Duty cycle
5. Eccentricity (There should be bearings to minimize the effects of side loading. How much eccentricity do they permit?)

Troubleshooting for Reciprocating Seals

Any discussion of sealing technology would not be complete without a brief review of service problems. All the possible environmental and operating considerations are seldom available when initial seal selection is undertaken and, as a result, it is sometimes necessary to reevaluate the seal selection in light of actual field performance.

When seal problems do occur, a visual examination of the worn or damaged seal is generally sufficient to allow the necessary corrective action to be initiated. Following are some of the more common types of problems which may be the cause of seal failure:

1. Slow, uniform leakage
   a. Poor low-pressure sealability (especially in a lip seal).
   b. Too little initial interference (squeeze-type seal).
   c. Loss of interference or squeeze due to wear or compression set.
   d. Seal shrinkage after installation (possibly chemically induced, or by leaching of plasticizers by solvent action).
   e. Possible omission or failure of static seal(s).
   f. Microscopic debris lodged under seal lip (lint, fiber, etc.).
   g. Scored lip due to passage of sharp particle under seal, leaving cut or nick.
   h. Seal lip nicked or cut during installation (note whether leak starts immediately after seal installation).
   i. Nonrepetitive overheating hardens compound (which loses its ability to conform to dynamic surface deviations).
   j. Off-center alignment puts all clearance on one side, all compression on the other (due to bearing wear, excessive side loads, etc.).
   k. Check *static* surfaces of dynamic seal (groove surfaces). They may have problems f, g, or h hidden from view, and without self-cleaning tendency.
2. Gradually increasing leakage
   a. Progressive wear.
   b. Increasing compression set.
   c. Progressive tear or erosion from initial nick.
   d. Fine score mark on dynamic surface abrades seal lip progressively.
3. Sudden, copious leakage
   a. Extruded seal.
   b. Torn seal lip (see 1d, e, f, g, h, and i; and 2d).
   c. Twisted seal.
   d. Dramatic bearing failure due to excessive side load, shock, etc.
   e. Spiral failure.
   f. Massive infusion of contamination (due to incorrect fluid added to system, or to upstream introduction of dirt or wear debris).

> *g.* Slow rod seal leakage builds up behind tight wiper, then dumps, giving *appearance* of catastrophic seal failure. If leak rate then diminishes, look for slow leak or erratic leak causes. If high leak rate continues, look for true catastrophic leak origin.
>
> *h.* Reverse-pressure blowout of piston seal due to pressure trap or failure of opposed seal.

4. Erratic (start-stop) leakage
  - *a.* Cold start-up shrinks seal; friction/fluid heating restores size.
  - *b.* Intermittent eccentric loading.
  - *c.* Fibrous contamination working its way past seal lips.
  - *d.* Unstable seal (twists and returns, cocks, etc.) usually caused by shock loading.
  - *e.* Rod seal leaks slowly, tight wiper periodically dumps accumulated leakage (see 3*g*).
  - *f.* Fluid viscosity changes as temperature cycles (e.g., fork lift truck alternately entering and leaving cold storage area).

5. Stick-slip operation
  - *a.* Worn-away low-friction surface treatment.
  - *b.* Breakdown of fluid lubricity due to contamination or deterioration of fluid.
  - *c.* Viscosity change due to temperature.
  - *d.* Excessive burnishing of dynamic surface to finer finish destroys ability of surface to maintain lube film (e.g., may go from 12 rms to 4 rms).

6. Seizing
  - *a.* Seal and bearing swell due to incompatible fluid and compound (possibly running hotter than temperature at which fluid *is* compatible).
  - *b.* Thermal expansion of compound.
  - *c.* Pressure trap between dual squeeze seals or incorrectly installed lip seals.
  - *d.* Wedging of seal or back-up device into extrusion gap (if used, it is usually the backup device that extrudes).
  - *e.* In low-pressure systems, shock or other factors cock, cant, or misorient the seals in grooves. This may become more common as OSHA rulings force reduction of pneumatic pressures.
  - *f.* Bent rod, cocked head, etc., often due to unreported accident.

7. Scored rod or ram
  - *a.* Internally generated contamination.
  - *b.* Externally introduced rod dirt, dirty make-up, or disassembly/re-assembly dirt.
  - *c.* Misoriented exclusion devices (wiper/scraper); eccentric installation.
  - *d.* Misaligned (eccentric) loads cock ram into metal-to-metal contact with head.
  - *e.* Wiper in vertical ram forms catch-all pocket.

8. Drift
  - *a.* Inspect valve for leakage and full closure *before* disassembly. (Disconnect return line on valve and inspect visually for leakage.)
  - *b.* See problems 1 and 2, as applied to piston seals.
  - *c.* Misapplied cast iron rings in a "hold" cylinder (right ring in the wrong job).
  - *d.* In "retract-mode" creep, check rod seal as well as piston seal.
  - *e.* Static internal seals may provide leakage path past piston.

9. Increasing cylinder drag
  - *a.* Seal swell caused by improper (incompatible) *installation* lubricant (e.g., EPR seal lubed with petro-based grease or oil).
  - *b.* Packing of contaminants into wiper groove of vertical ram.
  - *c.* Thermal expansion of bearings and/or seals.
  - *d.* *Apparent* drag increase due to undetected flow restriction in supply or return line, by-passing of pressure through improperly closing valve, or obstructed check valve, etc.
  - *e.* Cocked or twisted seal by-passing fluid and wedging into extrusion gap.

10. Increasing cylinder/rod temperature
  - *a.* See causes for problem 9. In their earlier stages, these problems may appear as hotter-running cylinders.

b. Internal leakage "throttling" past seals can cause rapid heating.

c. Decreased lubricity of fluid can boost friction and heating (hotter fluid has lower viscosity = lower lubricity = higher friction = hotter fluid = lower viscosity, etc.). Contaminated or deteriorated fluid can cause same cycle.

d. Diluted fluid can boost friction, etc.

e. Condensation in reservoirs can emulsify or hit cylinder as slugs of fluid with near-zero lubricity. Also, hot water can *swell* compounds such as urethanes, increasing friction.

SECTION 8

MATERIALS HANDLING

CHAPTER 8-1
PLANNING MATERIALS HANDLING

K. W. Tunnell Co., Inc.
King of Prussia, Pennsylvania

MATERIALS-HANDLING DEFINITIONS

Materials-handling technology includes hardware and systems which can be categorized as follows:

- Containerization
- Fixed-path handling
- Mobile handling
- Warehousing

Containerization. This classification covers the broad spectrum of confinement methods that are used for storage through all phases of the manufacturing, or process, cycle. The materials-handling engineer employs the unit-size principle to optimize the quantity, size, and weight of the load to be handled or moved and is able to specify the best container after considering material and other production-system parameters. Pallets, skids, tote boxes, wire-mesh containers, covering a wide range of sizes and materials, are included within the category.

Fixed-Path Handling. This classification applies to movement and storage of unit loads of material with an intermittent or a continuous flow over a fixed path from one point to another. Fixed-path-handling equipment is secured to, and is considered part of, the facility. Once installed it is more difficult to modify or replace; therefore a considerable amount of planning and interfacing with other functions has to be considered. This equipment, if installed above the floor surface, can effectively utilize what would otherwise be dead space. Chutes, conveyors, elevators, bridge cranes, palletizing equipment, and robots are examples of fixed-path-handling equipment.

Mobile Handling. This classification includes all handling systems that move material over various paths within a manufacturing or processing cycle. Handling equipment allows a considerable degree of flexibility in moving material in an intermittent flow but requires special facility requirements, such as aisle sizes, clearances, door openings, and running and maneuvering surfaces. Equipment in this category consumes more energy per unit load moved than most other systems and generally requires trained personnel for operation. Equipment in this category ranges from simple two-wheeled hand trucks to specially designed over-the-road vehicles and also includes skid trucks, floor trucks, powered walkie lift trucks, powered lift trucks, and mobile hydraulic cranes.

Warehousing.   This classification of materials handling considers the systems, equipment practices, and requirements dedicated to the following operations within the manufacturing, processing, or distribution cycle:

- Receiving
- Storage of raw, in-process, and finished materials
- Movement in and out of storage
- Order picking and accumulation
- Containerization for shipping
- Loading and shipping

This area of materials handling involves a wider range of planning and analysis. Consider some of the following factors:

1. Location of activity
2. Sizing and physical characteristics relating to product size, type, and volume
3. Number of stockkeeping units
4. Storage equipment
5. Selection of materials-movement methods
6. Packaging methods for shipping

The range of solutions covers the full spectrum, from a single warehouse that shares movement equipment with other parts of the operation to a self-contained, specially equipped, fully automated warehouse.

INTRODUCTION

Materials handling deals with the movement of materials from receiving, through fabrication, to the shipment of the finished product. More broadly, handling and distribution are considered to be one overall system. This viewpoint gives consideration to all handling activities involved in movement of materials from all sources of supply through the various plant and central warehouse operations to the customer distribution network.

The activities related to the flow of the materials are either viewed as separate activities or treated as one element in an integrated handling system. Not everyone agrees that materials-handling activities should be viewed as an overall system. Progressive plant engineering personnel, however, recognize that materials handling represents the efficient integration of workers, materials-control systems, and equipment, as well as the movement of materials. Materials-handling applications must take into account operating costs and time-phased material flow.

Inefficient materials handling and storage increase product cost, delay product delivery, and consume excessive square feet of plant and warehouse space. Studies have indicated that actual materials-handling cost runs between 20 and 50 percent of the total product cost *even though it does not add any value to the finished product.* In addition, from 80 to 95 percent of the total overall time devoted to processing a customer order from fabrication to shipment is devoted to materials handling and storage. Product manufacturing time, therefore, is only a small percentage of the overall process time.

A properly designed and integrated materials-handling system provides tremendous cost-saving opportunities and customer-service improvement potential. The correct selection of a handling method can reduce handling costs per unit by as much as 200 percent. Improvement in storage, such as high-rise storage applications, can reduce unit storage space cost by 20 to 40 percent. Work-in-process inventory can be reduced 30 to 50 percent through compressed cycle times. The reduced cycle times will also result in shorter customer delivery cycles.

The significant impact of materials-handling costs on total product cost has resulted in a great deal of attention and substantial resources being directed toward discovering more efficient methods to reduce handling costs. This effort is expected to receive even greater concentration in the future. The following trends are beginning:

- Most manufacturing managers now recognize that materials handling is a prime area of cost-reduction opportunities.
- Many manufacturers have become environmentally aware, which is reflected in products such as lift trucks with reduced emissions and recyclable plastic and corrugated pallets.
- Pre-engineered storage and handling systems with proven success records are being offered to help reduce installation and start-up times.
- Computer systems are being designed to enable the manager to electronically track materials from the point of entry to exit.
- Computer-based technology will employ more powerful and sophisticated techniques such as queueing theory, simulation facilities, and flow-planning techniques to consider and select optimum solutions from a wide range of variables and materials-handling options.
- Handling systems will become more automated by employing computer-controlled systems, robot loading and unloading, driverless vehicles, and automatic storage and retrieval systems. These automation principles will be applied in receiving, manufacturing operations, warehousing, and shipping.

It should be recognized that materials handling is an extremely broad-based subject which more often deals with the application of equipment and mechanical devices than fundamental engineering principles or basic physical laws. At least in part, it requires the application of subjective and experienced judgment and has even been described (with some justification) as more of an art than a science. Based on this fact and the trends in materials handling already discussed, this chapter outlines the methodology for solving materials-handling problems as well as the classification of hardware.

However, it is suggested that plant engineers involved continually with materials-handling projects should be familiar with additional sources of current information not only from reference books but also from specialized trade periodicals, professional societies, and trade associations. (See the reference section at the end of this chapter.)

SOLVING MATERIALS-HANDLING PROBLEMS

Materials-handling activities and installations vary in complexity from operation to operation. The plant engineer can solve most materials-handling problems by keeping two points in mind: one is to thoroughly understand the materials-handling principles; the other is to recognize that a materials-handling system is composed of a series of interrelated handling activities. The plant engineer should therefore apply materials-handling principles to improve each separate materials-handling activity and then interrelate the handling activities by applying flow-planning principles.

Principles of Materials Handling

The collective experience and knowledge of many materials-handling experts has been organized into a framework of generalized principles. The principles are basic and can be used universally. They include:

1. Integrate as many handling activities, such as receiving, storage, production, and inspection, as is practical into a coordinated system.
2. Arrange operation sequence and equipment layout so as to optimize materials flow.
3. Simplify handling by reducing, eliminating, or combining unnecessary movement and/or equipment.
4. Use gravity to move material wherever practical.
5. Make optimum use of the building cube.
6. Increase the quantity, size, and weight of the load handled.
7. Use mechanized or automated handling equipment whenever it can be economically or safely justified.
8. Select handling equipment on the basis of lowest overall cost when considering the material to be handled, the move to be made, and the methods to be utilized.
9. Standardize methods as well as types and sizes of handling equipment.
10. Use methods and equipment that perform a variety of tasks and applications.
11. Plan preventive maintenance, and schedule regular repairs on all handling equipment.
12. Determine the effectiveness of handling performance in terms of expense per unit handled.
13. Move materials in as direct a path as possible, minimizing backtracking.
14. Deliver materials directly to work areas whenever practical, and plan the minimum of material in the area.
15. Move the greatest weight or bulk the shortest distance.
16. Provide alternative plans in case of a breakdown.

Steps in Solving Handling Problems

The general methods that are used for solving other operational problems are applicable in the materials-handling area. The factors that must be considered relate to how to most efficiently move certain volumes and types of materials by a particular method. The steps involved in systematically solving these problems consist of:

- Problem identification
- Problem analysis and quantification
- Selection and evaluation of alternatives
- Project justification

Problem Identification. Identification of materials-handling problems includes determining the impact of interfacing activities such as production control, manufacturing, vendors, shipping, and receiving. The buildup of material in front of a machine or a truck dock may not be a problem of too little storage but rather one of lot sizing or inefficient truck-loading systems. Most importantly, a costly handling route between two distant machines may not be caused by the handling mechanism but by the location of the equipment itself.

Problem Analysis and Quantification. Qualitative and quantitative answers are obtained through use of industrial engineering techniques such as flow diagrams, flowcharts, from-to charts, and activity-relationship charts. For the detailed application of these manual techniques see Refs. 1 to 4.

Computer-aided techniques are useful when large amounts of data are involved.[5]

Selection and Evaluation of Alternatives In the selection of alternatives three general types of criteria are involved.

Movement.   Movement involves the study of routes in terms of the combination of handling equipment and containers jointly rather than on an individual product basis. Under this criterion, distances from and to locations, outside travel, and frequencies would be minimized.

Criteria Which Cannot Be Directly Costed.   These involve criteria such as:

1. *Performance.*   The potentials for relocation of equipment at future time periods, as related to the handling equipment, and for material design changes, as they relate to the containers themselves.
2. *Delicacy.*   The nature of the part and its requirements for special handling, dunnage, or containers—particularly to avoid damage.
3. *Interfaces.*   Production control and manufacturing departments, vendors, shipping, receiving, and intersite movement requirements.
4. *Uniformity.*   The need to standardize or at least unitize containers to provide uniform handling characteristics. This provides for the use of idealized container sizing and packing techniques, including proper dunnage for irregular loads. On the other hand, it requires the special handling and designs for special irregular-sized parts.

Cost-Effectiveness.   This involves the analysis in concept of all standard operating costs, equipment life, maintenance and spare usage for equipment, and intermediate storage.

Generally, the analysis will be dominated by the cost-effectiveness of the alternatives involving cost components as follows.

- *Capital Investment Costs.*   One-time charges incurred at the time of equipment procurement that include:
  1. Equipment cost, including freight
  2. Installation costs
  3. Special maintenance requirements
  4. Special power and fuel facilities
  5. Rearrangement and alteration of facilities to accommodate equipment
  6. Engineering support
  7. Supplies

- *Fixed Costs.*   Determined or assigned to a system, a piece of equipment, or an activity on a time-period basis; include:
  1. Depreciation
  2. Taxes
  3. Insurance
  4. Supervision

- *Variable Costs.*   Can be considered the cost of performing an operation or activity. In the case of equipment, it is the cost of using the equipment. The following items are included within this component.
  1. Equipment-operating personnel or personnel manually performing a materials-handling task
  2. Power and fuel costs
  3. Lubricants
  4. Maintenance labor supplies

- *Indirect Costs.*   Affected in other areas of company operation as a result of changing a method, adding new equipment, or changing the materials-handling system, and may consist of:
  1. Space occupied
  2. Effect on taxes
  3. Values of repair parts
  4. Changes in production rate and quality of product
  5. Downtime

A summary of such an analysis is contained in Table 1-1.

TABLE 1-1 Annual Operating Cost

Cost component	Present manual method, $	Proposed method, $		
		Conveyor	Fork lift, electric	Fork lift, propane
1. Capital equip. investment				
Equipment cost		6,000	25,000	27,000
Freight		500	800	800
Installation		8,000		
Fuel-power facilities			4,000	
Alterations to facility		10,000		
Engineering support		1,000		
Supplies				
Total capital investment		25,500	29,800	27,800
2. Fixed cost				
Depreciation		5,100	6,560	6,160
Taxes		750	3,500	4,000
Insurance		200	1,000	1,000
Supervision			1,400	1,400
Total fixed cost		6,050	12,460	12,560
3. Variable cost				
Operators-loaders	(5)* 50,000	(2)* 20,000	(1)* 12,000	(1)* 12,000
Power-fuel		1,200	2,300	800
Lubrication		20	150	150
Maintenance			1,500	2,000
Total variable cost	50,000	21,220	15,950	14,950
4. Indirect cost				
Space occupied		1,500		
Effect on taxes		1,000		
Changes in prod. rate				
Downtime		200		
Total indirect		2,700		
Total operating cost (2 + 3 + 4)	50,000	29,970	28,410	27,510
Annual cost savings		20,030	21,590	22,490

* Number of units employed.

JUSTIFICATION OF MATERIALS-HANDLING PROJECTS

The most common methods of determining the profitability of materials-handling investment are payoff period, return on investment (ROI), and discounted cash flow.

The *payoff-period* method indicates the amount of time that new equipment or a system will take to produce the savings to recover the capital investment. The investment is divided by the annual savings to give the time (in years) needed to break even. In Table 1-1:

$$\text{Payoff period} = \frac{\text{total capital investment}}{\text{annual cost savings}}$$

This method is a good risk indicator and measure which can be useful to indicate the projects that would be worth considering for closer study, but the actual profitability of new equipment depends on how much useful life is left after the payoff period. Some caution is therefore advised if the payoff period is to be the sole determinant for equipment justification, because cheaper equipment having a low useful life will always appear to be the best investment opportunity.

Simple ROI is another gross indicator that can be used to set priorities for capital investments. Here again, the effect of useful equipment life is not considered, so this method should not be used for determining the profitability of the proposed equipment:

$$\text{ROI} = \frac{\text{annual cost savings}}{\text{total capital investment}}$$

The ROI method that considers the effect of useful equipment life is

$$\text{ROI} = \frac{\text{annual savings} - \text{capital investment/useful equipment life}}{\text{capital investment}}$$

The discounted-cash-flow method of determining ROI indicates in a more realistic manner the equipment cost and return on investment by considering:

1. Savings and cost over equipment life period.
2. Net cash flow of the savings and depreciation.
3. Present worth of each year's cash flow. A factor is used to reduce the cash flow for each year to the amount of cash that would be required today to earn a desired rate of interest.
4. The effect of taxes on the rate of return.

The ROI is calculated as follows (Table 1-2):

1. Determine the cost savings for each year of the equipment useful life.
2. Deduct the estimated percentage for taxes for each year of equipment life.
3. Add depreciation for each year of the depreciation period.
4. Determine net cash flow, which is the algebraic total of items 1, 2, and 3 above.

TABLE 1-2   Example of Calculating ROI* by Cash-Flow Analysis

Factors								Amounts
Total capital investment from annual operating cost								$30,800
Equipment life								5 years
Depreciation straight line								5 years, 20%/year
Savings per year								$22,490

	Cash flow					Trial 1 @ 45%		Trial 2 @ 50%	
Year	Cost savings	Taxes	Savings after taxes	Depreciation	Net cash flow	Factor	Present worth	Factor	Present worth
1	22,490	11,245	11,245	6,160	17,405	0.690	12,009.45	0.667	11,609.14
2	22,490	11,245	11,245	6,160	17,405	0.476	8,284.78	0.444	7,727.82
3	22,490	11,245	11,245	6,160	17,405	0.328	5,708.84	0.296	5,151.88
4	22,490	11,245	11,245	6,160	17,405	0.226	3,933.53	0.198	3,446.19
5	22,490	11,245	11,245	6,160	17,405	0.156	2,715.18	0.132	2,297.46
					78,715		32,651.78		30,232.49

* Interpolating

$$\frac{32,651.78 - 30,800}{32,651.78 - 30,232.49} \times 5 = \frac{1,851.78}{2,419.29} \times 5 = 3.83$$

Add $3.83\% + 45\% = 48.83\%$ return on investment

TABLE 1-3   Present-Worth Values

Years	6	8	10	12	15	20	25	30	35	40	45	50
					Interest, %							
1	0.943	0.926	0.909	0.893	0.870	0.833	0.800	0.769	0.741	0.714	0.690	0.667
2	0.890	0.857	0.826	0.797	0.756	0.694	0.640	0.592	0.549	0.510	0.476	0.444
3	0.840	0.794	0.751	0.712	0.658	0.579	0.512	0.455	0.406	0.364	0.328	0.296
4	0.792	0.735	0.683	0.636	0.572	0.482	0.410	0.350	0.301	0.260	0.226	0.198
5	0.747	0.681	0.621	0.568	0.497	0.402	0.328	0.269	0.223	0.186	0.156	0.132
6	0.705	0.630	0.564	0.507	0.432	0.335	0.262	0.207	0.165	0.133	0.108	0.088
7	0.665	0.583	0.513	0.452	0.376	0.279	0.210	0.159	0.122	0.095	0.074	0.058
8	0.627	0.540	0.466	0.404	0.327	0.323	0.168	0.123	0.091	0.068	0.051	0.039
9	0.592	0.500	0.424	0.361	0.284	0.194	0.134	0.094	0.067	0.048	0.035	0.026
10	0.558	0.463	0.386	0.322	0.247	0.162	0.107	0.072	0.050	0.035	0.024	0.017
11	0.527	0.429	0.350	0.288	0.215	0.135	0.086	0.056	0.037	0.025	0.017	0.012
12	0.497	0.397	0.319	0.257	0.187	0.112	0.069	0.043	0.027	0.018	0.012	0.008
13	0.469	0.368	0.290	0.229	0.162	0.094	0.055	0.033	0.020	0.013	0.008	0.005
14	0.442	0.340	0.263	0.205	0.141	0.078	0.044	0.025	0.015	0.009	0.006	0.003
15	0.417	0.315	0.239	0.183	0.123	0.065	0.035	0.020	0.011	0.006	0.004	0.002
16	0.394	0.292	0.218	0.163	0.107	0.054	0.028	0.015	0.008	0.005	0.003	0.002
17	0.371	0.270	0.198	0.146	0.093	0.045	0.022	0.012	0.006	0.003	0.002	0.001
18	0.350	0.250	0.180	0.130	0.081	0.038	0.018	0.009	0.004	0.002	0.001	0.001
19	0.330	0.232	0.164	0.116	0.070	0.031	0.014	0.007	0.003	0.002	0.001	0.000
20	0.312	0.214	0.149	0.104	0.061	0.026	0.012	0.005	0.002	0.001	0.001	0.000
	1.030	1.039	1.049	1.059	1.073	1.097	1.120	1.143	1.166	1.189	1.211	1.233

5. Consult present-worth value table (Table 1-3) and select an interest value for the first trial.

6. Multiply the net cash flow by the factor selected in step 5.

7. If the present-worth cash flow is higher than the capital investment, select the present-worth factor for the higher percentage; if lower, select present-worth factor for the lower percentage.

8. Continue the discounted-cash-flow trials until the total discounted cash flow equals the capital investment cost. Interpolation will generally be necessary to determine the exact percent of ROI.

9. The trial present-worth calculations that equal the net cash flow total are those that are used to determine the ROI.

REFERENCES AND BIBLIOGRAPHY

1. Sims, E. Ralph, Jr.: *Planning and Managing Material Flow,* Industrial Education Institute, Boston, 1968.

2. Apple, James M.: *Material Handling Systems Design,* Ronald, New York, 1971.

3. Muther, Richard, and Knut Haganas: *Systematic Handling Analysis,* Management & Industrial Research Publications, 1969.

4. Muther, Richard: *Systematic Layout Planning,* Industrial Education Institute, Boston, 1961.

5. Tompkins, J. A.: "Computer-Aided Plant Layout," *Modern Material Handling,* 7 part series, May–September 1978.

6. Merkle, W.: "Dock Planning Guide," *Material Handling Engineering,* August 1980.

7. Bolz, Harold A., et al. (ed.): *Materials Handling Handbook,* Wiley-Interscience, New York, 1958.

CHAPTER 8-2
CONTAINERIZATION

K. W. Tunnell Co., Inc.
King of Prussia, Pennsylvania

INTRODUCTION

One of the basic principles of materials handling is that materials should be converted wherever possible to unit loads to avoid manual handling. A unit load is defined as a standard container package containing one or more items that can be handled in a standard way. The *unit-load principle* suggests that the larger the load to be handled or moved, the lower the overall handling cost. To meet this objective, materials-handling systems must be designed to handle the materials-handling volume within the constraints imposed by load size as well as the material properties involved in the production or process cycle. The decisions regarding size, shape, and configuration of the unit load should also take into account compatibility.

Some *guidelines for the specification of unit load sizes* leading to the design of containerization methods and hardware to transport and store materials include:

1. Use the same pallet or container throughout the system, or at least standardize on a limited number of containers wherever possible.
2. Plan to use raw material or parts directly out of the original container.
3. Use stackable containers to permit stacking without racks.
4. Consider collapsible containers to save space and freight costs, if they are to be used also as returnable shipping containers.
5. Use nesting.
6. Be sure that the size selected fits efficiently into standard trailers and/or railcars if containers are to be used for shipping.
7. Design or select containers suitable for mechanical handling.
8. Plan containers to accommodate a wide range of products and parts.
9. Design containers to fit into building geometry.
10. Design containers that do not require special orientation to accomplish movement.
11. Use the lightest-weight material possible.
12. Consider the use of recyclable and reusable materials to reduce waste.
13. Use containers through which contents can be identified.
14. Keep the design simple and inexpensive.

CONTAINERIZATION HARDWARE

Containerization hardware can generally be grouped into five main categories:

- Pallets
- Containers
- Tote boxes and bins
- Dunnage
- Outer securement

Standard Pallets

Pallets are used mainly as supports, carrier surfaces, or storing structures for unit loads.

The most commonly used material is *wood,* and pallets are available in a number of different hardwood and softwood varieties (Table 2-1). The type of wood, like any other material that is specified, should depend on load capacity, load requirements, durability, and the handling and storage environment. In general, softwood pallets are lighter and suitable for shipping pallets, while hardwood pallets are stronger, have a longer life, and are less susceptible to the wear and tear associated with interplant movement. Local, indigenous woods should be specified wherever possible to minimize costs.

Principles of Pallet Construction

Nomenclature, Design, Style, and Size.   The principal pallet parts and the most commonly used construction features are indicated in Fig. 2-1. By convention, the length of the pallet is the first-stated dimension, the dimensions are always stated in inches, and the width is the dimension that is parallel to the top of the deck boards.

Types.   Wood pallets fall into three general groups:

1. *Expendable* (one-way pallets).   Cost is the major factor and the design and construction must meet the requirements for this purpose.
2. *Special-purpose.*   Design and construction must meet the special requirements for the product or material to be moved or stored.
3. *General-purpose.*   Uses standard design and features which enable the pallet to be used in a wide range of applications and also to be replaced and exchanged easily.

Pallet Configuration.   This is specified by a combination of design, style, and construction features. The National Wooden Pallet and Container Association has established the descriptions of each parameter.

Typical pallet configurations are shown in Fig. 2-2. Pallets are available in a wide range of sizes; however, the most popular size is the 48×40 in $(1.7 \times 1.4$ m) pallet which accounts for over 27 percent of all pallets produced.

There is movement within some industries, particularly the food and grocery industries, to standardize pallet sizes. It has been determined that size standardization, among other obvious benefits, could also increase the use of pallet pools or exchange programs, which would have cost advantages throughout the distribution cycle.

DESIGN.   The most common designs of wood pallets are:

1. *Two-way pallets.*   Permit the entry of forklift or hand pallet trucks from two sides only and in opposite directions.
2. *Four-way pallets.*   Permit entry on all four sides.
   a. *Notched stringer design.*   Has four-way entry *only* with forklift trucks, and two-way entry with hand pallet trucks
   b. *Block design.*   Has four-way entry with both forklift and hand pallet trucks.

TABLE 2-1   Strength Properties of Commercial Woods Employed for Pallets
(Figures shown are for 12 percent moisture content.)

Species	Static bending fiber stress at proportional limit, lb/in²*	Compression perpendicular to grain, lb/in²*	General properties
Group IV			
Oak, red	8,400	1,260	Heaviest hardwood species; greatest nail-holding power and beam strength; best shock-resisting capacity; greatest tendency to split at nails; difficult to dry
Oak, white	7,900	1,410	
Maple, sugar	9,500	1,810	
Beech	8,700	1,250	
Birch	10,100	1,250	
Hickory, true	10,900	2,310	
Ash, white	8,900	1,510	
Pecan	9,100	2,040	
Group III			
Ash, black	7,200	940	More inclined to split when nailed; greater nail-holding and shock-resisting power, beam strength, and easier to dry than group IV
Gum, black	7,300	1,150	
Maple, silver	6,200	910	
Gum, red	8,100	860	
Sycamore	6,400	860	
Tupelo	7,200	1,070	
Elm, white	7,600	850	
Group II			
Douglas fir	7,400	950	
Hemlock (W)	6,800	680	
Larch (Tamarack)	8,000	990	
N.C. pine	7,700	1,000	
Southern yellow pine (longleaf)	9,300	1,190	
Group I			
Aspen	5,600	460	Relatively free from splitting when nailed; moderate nail-holding power and shock-resisting capacity; lightweight, easy to work, holds shape well, and easy to dry
Cottonwood	5,700	470	
Redwood	6,900	860	
Spruce	6,700	710	
Sugar pine	5,700	590	
Ponderosa pine	6,300	740	
White fir	6,300	610	
White pine (N)	6,300	550	
White pine (W)	6,200	540	
Yellow poplar	6,100	580	

* Multiply by 6900 for newtons per square meter.

STYLE.   There are two styles of wood pallets, and they are (Fig. 2-2):

1. *Single-face pallet.*   Has only one deck as the top surface.

2. *Double-face pallet.*   Has both top and bottom decks and comes in two different designs, viz.:

   a. *Reversible.*   Has identical top and bottom decks, and goods may be stacked on either deck.

   b. *Nonreversible.*   Top and bottom decks have different configurations, and substitute goods may be stacked only on the top deck.

CONSTRUCTIONS.   Wood pallet constructions are as follows:

1. *Flush stringer.*   A pallet in which the outside stringers or blocks are flush with the ends of the deckboards.

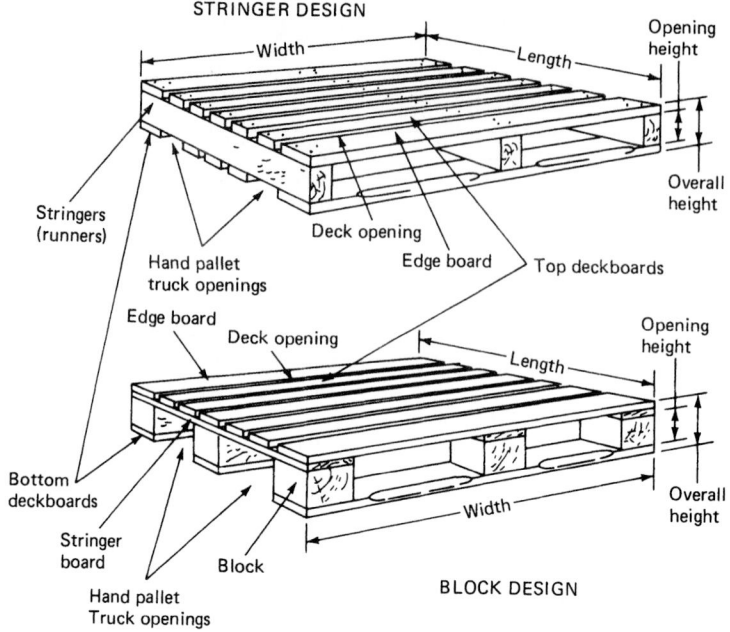

FIGURE 2-1 Principal parts of wooden pallets. (*National Wooden Pallet and Container Association.*)

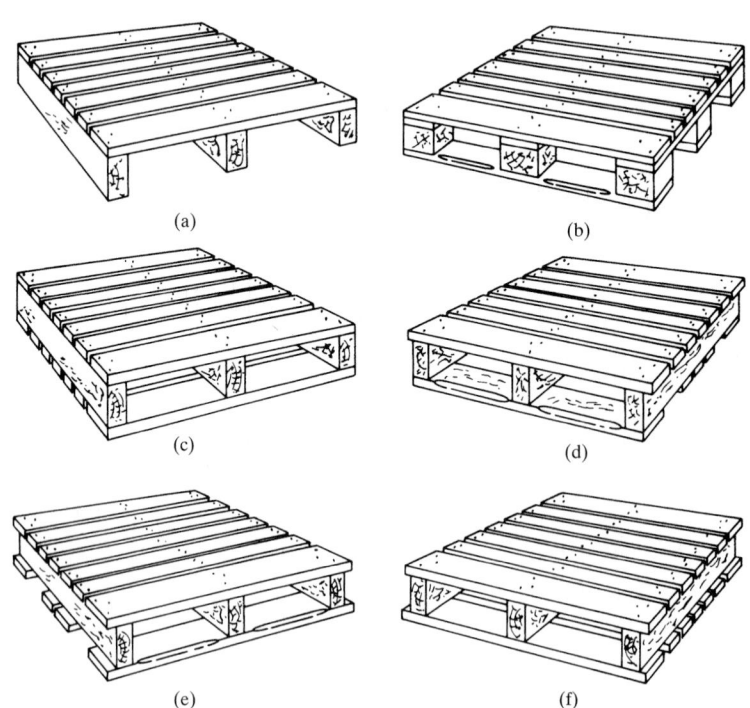

FIGURE 2-2 Typical pallet configurations. (*a*) Single-face; (*b*) double-face, reversible; (*c*) double-wing, double-face, nonreversible; (*d*) double-face, nonreversible; (*e*) single-wing, double-face, nonreversible; (*f*) double-wing, double-face, reversible. (*National Wooden Pallet Association.*)

2. *Single wing.* A pallet in which the outside stringers are set inboard of the top deck, while the stringers are flush with the ends of the bottom deckboards.

3. *Double wing.* A pallet in which the outside stringers are set inboard of both top and bottom deckboards to accommodate bar slings or other devices for handling pallets.

Maintenance and Repair. Procedures should also be established within the system to identify worn pallets that require repair or disposal. To accomplish this effectively, the acquisition date should be marked on the pallet and older pallets should be inspected periodically to detect wear. The following are guidelines for repair operations:

1. Never repair a pallet a second time.

2. Never repair more than three deckboards or one stringer on a given pallet. If the *average* replacement is more than 1½ boards per pallet, repair is uneconomical.

3. Productivity should average 100 repaired pallets per worker per 8-h shift for those on the repair line—forklift support and supervisory personnel excluded.

4. Cost of repair should not exceed half the price of a new, similar pallet.

Pallets for Use with Forklifts

Expendable Wood Pallets. These pallets are used to support a unit load for one-way and one-time use. Pallets of this type must be specified with the capacity to carry unit load but do not require the durability of reusable types. The single-face style (Fig. 2-2) is primarily used for this purpose. Plywood deck surfaces are frequently used for expendable pallets.

Metal Pallets. These pallets can be made of corrugated steel, expanded metal, steel wire, aluminum, and combinations of metal and wood. Metal pallets are more expensive than wood pallets and are used mainly for movement of materials inside the plant where additional strength and life is required.

Corrugated-Metal Pallet Bases. These pallets (Fig. 2-3) are often integrated into the design of corrugated-steel containers with a number of other features. This permits wide versatility in parts handling and storage in the plant. The style variations available are similar to those of their wood pallet counterparts to permit movement in both two-and four-way entry bases by forklift trucks and pallet hand trucks.

All-Steel, Single-Face Pallets. Supported on three runners, this type is designed to handle heavy loads and containers. Recessed side channels bound in flanges can be incorporated in the design to permit safe movement by hand. Their double-faced, reversible design eliminates sharp edges, and thus prevents damage to bagged materials.

One-Piece, Formed-Metal Pallets. These pallets have a built-in nesting feature that permits a number of empty pallets to be stored conveniently. They are useful where pallet storage space is scarce.

Wire-Mesh Pallets. These pallets use galvanized or painted steel or aluminum deck sections with formed, corrugated support structures and are used where durability and light weight are required. The wire-mesh pallet, like the corrugated-metal pallets, are often incorporated as bases in wire-mesh containers.

Corrugated Pallets. These pallets (Fig. 2-4) are useful for light unit loads that are less than 1500 lb (700 kg) and for stacked loads that are less than 1000 lb (450 kg) per pallet leg. If employees handle pallets or if employee injury is a problem, these lightweight pallets should be considered. The corrugated pallets have a low cost and can be recycled as corrugated. Because of their light weight, the pallets will also save money on shipping or airfreight charges.

Plastic Pallets. These pallets are more expensive than wood ones and in some cases are more expensive than metal ones. However, good or broken plastic pallets can be recycled. Sometimes, a broken pallet can also be repaired. Many manufacturers guarantee life of the pallet to be 5 to 10 times longer than an ordinary wood pallet. Food and pharmaceutical industries have been the traditional users of plastic pallets, since they require a high standard of cleanliness.

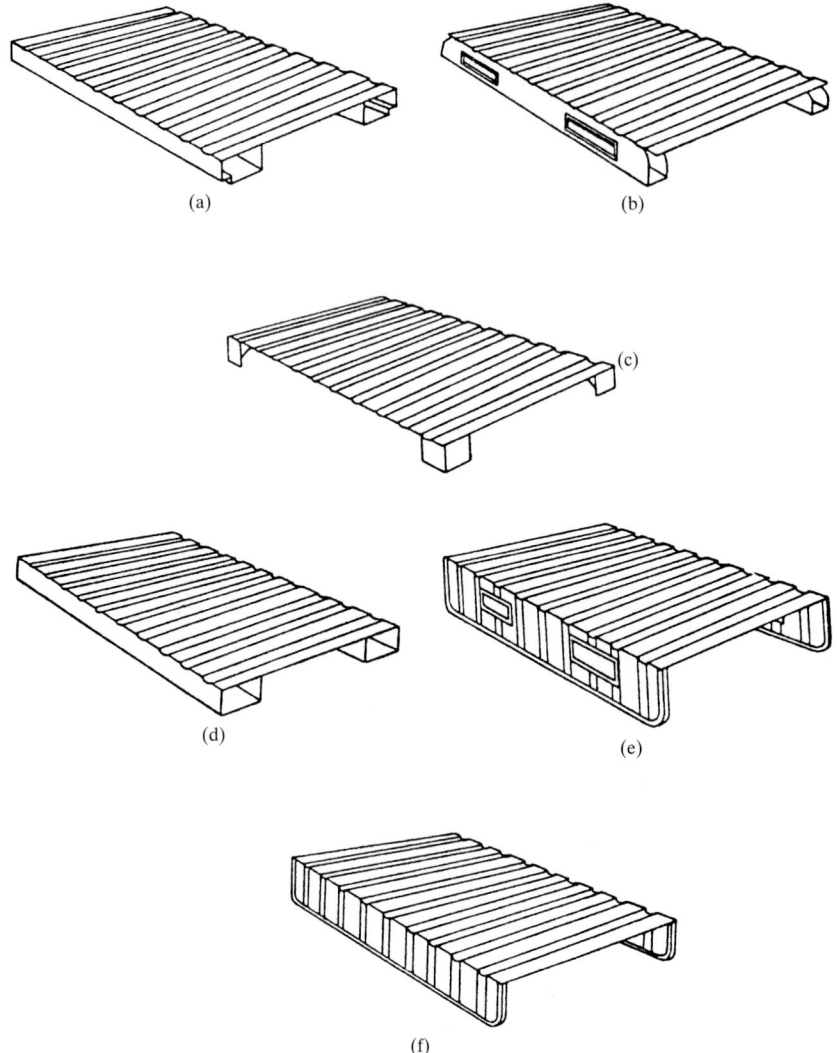

FIGURE 2-3 Corrugated-steel pallet container bases. (*a*) Two-way entry pallet style, (*b*) four-way entry pallet style, (*c*) box or angle-style pallet, (*d*) two-way box runner, (*e*) skid or pallet truck, (*f*) standard pallet with runners.

Other Types of Pallets.   In addition to using forklift trucks or hand-operated equipment for major movements in the plant, there are other handling requirements for movement of materials within and between manufacturing operations. Generally there is very little standardization in this area, since the carrier surfaces have to be specified to be compatible with equipment or product.

Slip-Sheet Systems.   Such systems enable a unit load to be handled and moved without being supported on a pallet type of platform. Slip sheets (Fig. 2-5) are made of heavy corrugated paperboard, plastic, or kraft fiber composition and function as the base surface for the unit load. Special equipment or *push-pull* forklift truck attachments are required to move and handle loads unitized by this method. The cost benefits of slip-sheet systems are obvious: in

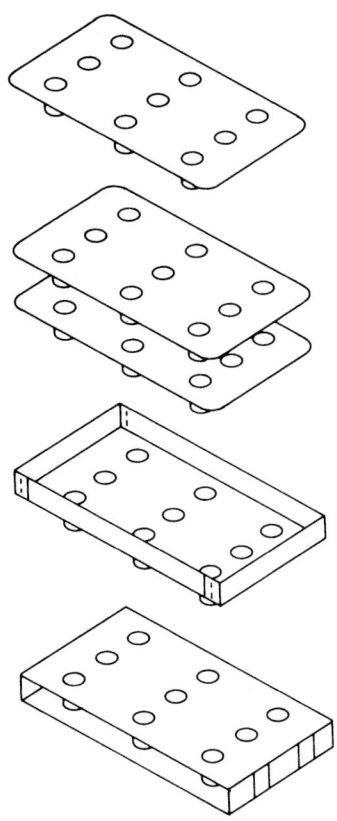

FIGURE 2-4 Cardboard expandable pallet. (*Memosha Corporation.*)

addition to lower initial cost, storage space requirements are $\frac{1}{100}$ of the cube required for empty pallets and shipping costs are less than for comparable loads using wood pallets.

Slave Pallets.   These are used for assembling unit loads before transfer to other containers, for moving odd-shaped loads on conveyors, for serving as accumulating and transfer platforms for automated computer-controlled storage and retrieval systems, and for supporting unit-load containers that are not designed for use on conveyors.

Slave pallets are normally plywood-sheet surfaces, but if interim storage is required in racks where the pallet-edge surfaces are supported by shelf angles, pallet specifications become more critical from the standpoint of supporting loads and safety. As a general rule, to achieve maximum strength and stiffness, face grain should be across supports. Design criteria include pallet size, total uniform load, permissible deflection, clear span, and uniform load in pounds per square foot (newtons per square meter). Selection of the proper grade and thickness of plywood can then be determined. Information regarding recommended maximum uniform loads and deflections is available from the American Plywood Association.

Air Pallets.   This type uses a bed of air to support a unit load and enables large loads to be moved and maneuvered. Air pallets or air-film equipment can be used to convey parts, rotate work stock, and move palletized loads in and out of buildings as well as trucks, railcars, and other conveyances.

Portable Stacking Racks.   These racks are used for storage of palletized loads that cannot be stacked on each other. Pallet stacking frames (Fig. 2-6) are used to confine and protect irregularly shaped, fragile, or nonuniform loads during in-process or temporary storage. The pallet itself is the base unit and rests on the frame of the pallet beneath it. The second kind of portable stacking rack (Fig. 2-7) consists of a base unit and removable post and end frames. Pallets are stored on the base units and the base units, when stacked, nest in the end frame.

Pallet Loading Patterns.   A pallet pattern is an arrangement of units on a pallet and ideally is the most effective way of loading a pallet with the least loss of cube. There are a number of ways to select the optimum pattern, ranging from trial and error to the use of computer models. No matter what technique is used, the following factors must be taken into consideration:

1. *Size of material.*   There may be several ways, one way, or no way to place a given size material onto a given pallet.

2. *Weight of material.*   In the case of very heavy material, fewer layers will be stacked on a pallet. To a certain extent the number of layers will depend on the strength of the containers, if any are used.

3. *Size of unit load.*   Taken as a whole, the length, width, and especially the height of the load must be considered.

4. *Loss of space within unit load.*   Some patterns have too many large gaps between units. This kind of piling is particularly bad when paper pallets are used because the weight should be distributed evenly and the units should brace each other.

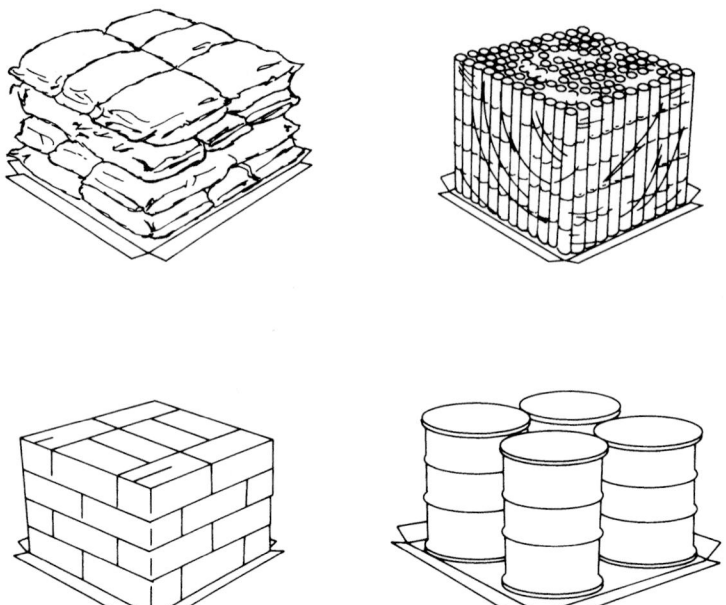

FIGURE 2-5   Typical uses of slip-sheet system. (*Little Giant Products.*)

5. *Compactness.*   Some patterns do not tie together well; they will not interlock.

6. *Methods of binding products in patterns.*   If the units of a load are glued together, one kind of pattern may be ideal; with strapping, another type may be the best; and if no fastening at all is used, some combination of stacking may be the most suitable method to interlock and hold the load together.

Some general rules that should be followed in establishing pallet patterns are:

1. Interlocking unit loads should be used when possible to make the most effective use of the cube and to provide load stability.

2. Overhang, where unit loads extend beyond the edge of a pallet, should be avoided or minimized to a point where container damage or load stability is not affected. The added

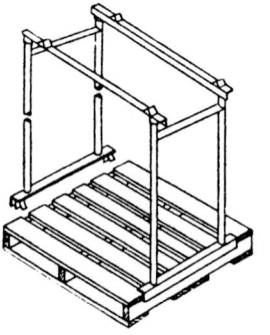

FIGURE 2-6   Pallet stacking frame using pallet as base unit.

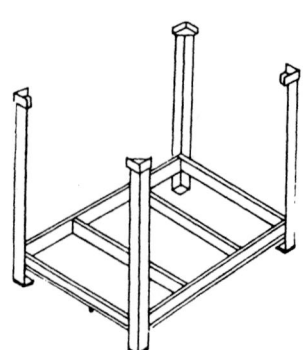

FIGURE 2-7   Pallet stacking frame with base unit.

dimensions caused by this condition should not exceed the width or length of the shipping conveyance or reduce the utilization of the conveyance.

3. Underhang, where unit loads do not fill the deck surface and where there are large voids, should be avoided.

4. Utilize the basic pallet patterns (Fig. 2-8) effectively. Use block patterns for containers of equal width and length. This type of pattern is the least stable and may require bonding and fastening if considerable movement is involved.

5. Brick, row, and pinwheel patterns are used for containers of unequal length or width. All three patterns result in the interlocking that stabilizes a load.

Pallet patterns have been developed empirically for materials that have rectangular dimensions. The U.S. Navy Research and Development Facility has developed such a pattern.[1]

Container capacities range from 500 to 6000 lb (230 to 2700 kg), and standard base sizes cover the range of sizes of wood pallets, including 40×48 in (1.4×1.7 m). The $44 \times 54 \times 40$ in ($1.6 \times 2 \times 1.4$ m) size is ideal for use when making shipments by rail or truck because the container dimensions are exact multiples of trailer and railcar dimensions and therefore can use the cube of these conveyances fully.

Metal Containers

Three types of metal containers are in general use: wire mesh, noncorrugated steel, and corrugated steel. Current development trends tend toward increasing versatility by incorporating features such as stacking and dumping capability and pallet-type bases to allow and facilitate movement.

Welded-Wire-Mesh Containers.   These containers (Fig. 2-9) are fabricated from welded wire for containment of materials. Additional structural sections are added for additional strength, and optional features can be included for specific uses and applications. The kinds of material and product that can be handled is limited only by size that would fall through the wire mesh and total container volume. Mesh openings from $\frac{1}{2} \times \frac{1}{2}$ in (1.3×1.3 cm) to 4×4 in (10×10 cm) are available to accommodate a wide range of product or material sizes.

Advantages that are generally cited in using this type of container are:

- Lightweight as compared with other metal containers
- Allows visibility of product for easy and quick identification
- Self-cleaning by shedding debris
- Material can sometimes be processed in the container in such processes as degreasing, cleaning, and air drying.

Wire-mesh container stacking is accomplished in two ways: (1) interlocking through the corner posts and (2) the arch (saddle) of the upper container rests on the rim of the container below.

Wrap-Around Collapsible Frame.   This forms the most basic type of wire-mesh container by using a standard pallet as a base.

Collapsible Container.   This type of container is constructed to permit the sides to fold down when not in use. The obvious advantage of this design, saving space, must be weighed against its shorter life and smaller payload capacity.

Rigid Wire Container.   This type is designed with additional vertical structural members that increase the strength of the containers, resulting in longer life and greater capacity than the collapsible types can provide. A heavy-duty rigid container has been developed to handle heavier loads in more strenuous environments. Additional horizontal bracing has been added to achieve the capability.

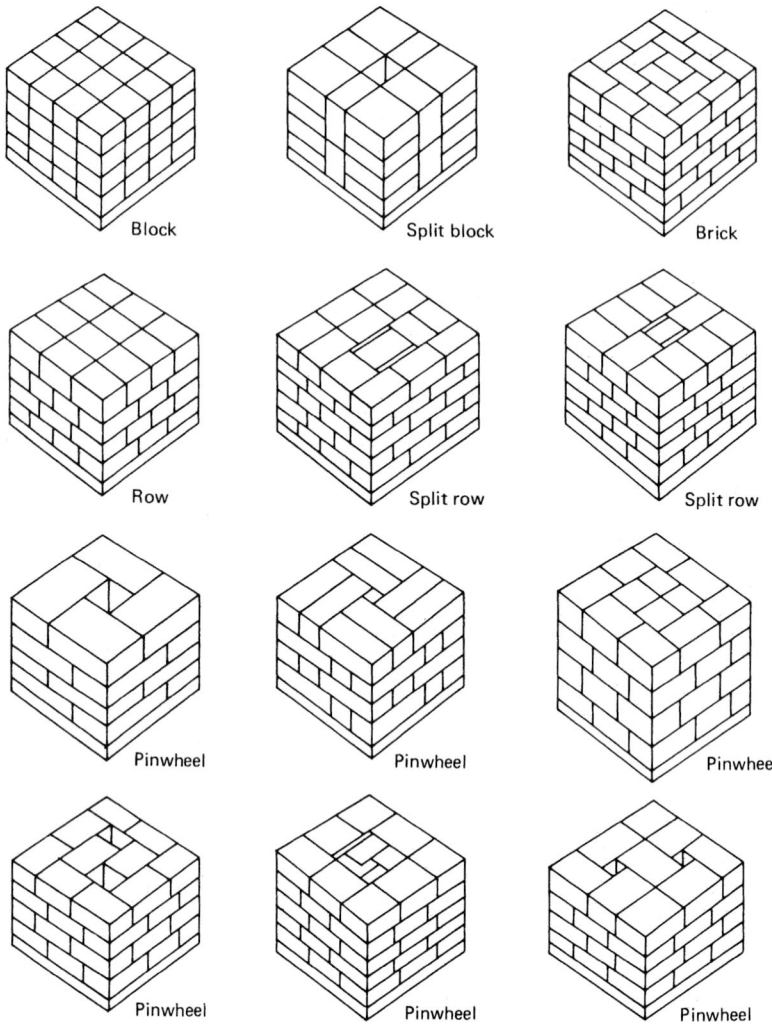

FIGURE 2-8 Typical pallet patterns. Paper or fiberboard binders are used between layers if necessary.

Collapsible Rigid Container. This is a heavy-duty version of the collapsible container. It is nearly equal in strength to the heavy-duty rigid type, but the higher original cost must be compared with savings on return freight costs.

Corrugated-Steel Containers. These are probably the strongest type of metal container available, since corrugation permits a longer surface of material to be used for a given size of a container than any other method of construction, and it is fabricated from hot-welded steels 0.105 to 0.179 in (2.7 to 4.6 mm) thick. This type of container has progressed from the one-type-only gondola bin to configurations that are almost virtually materials-handling systems in themselves. They can be considered as consisting of three basic *modules:* base, lifting and stacking aids, and container box, with options for specific applications.

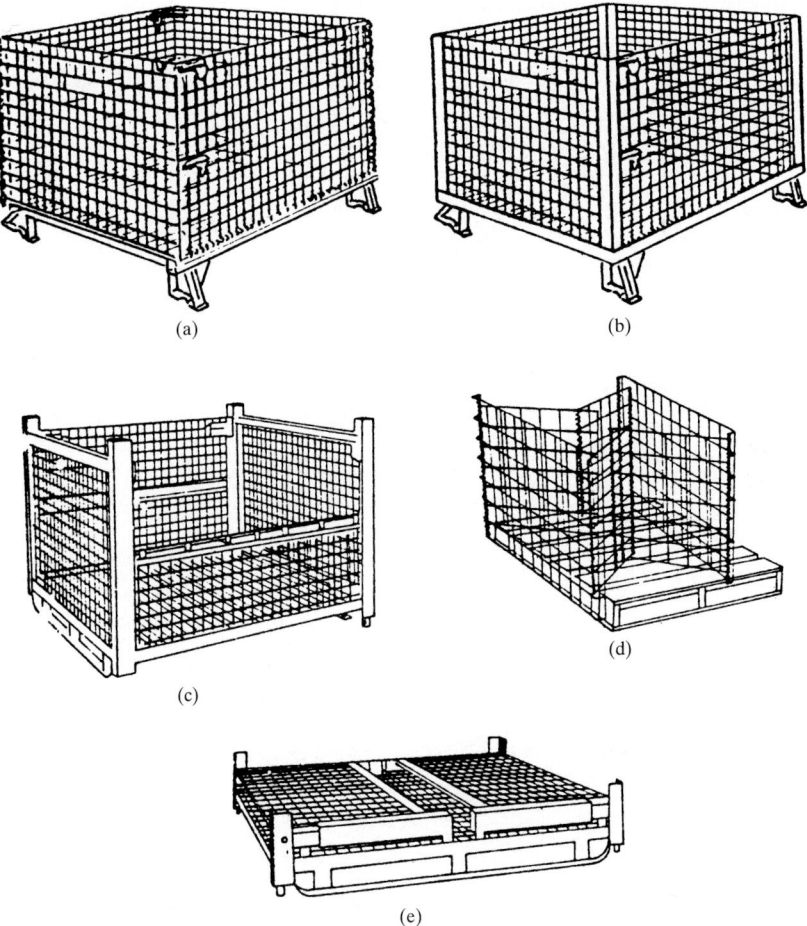

FIGURE 2-9 Kinds of welded-wire-mesh containers. (*a*) Collapsible wire container, (*b*) rigid wire container, (*c*) heavy-duty rigid, (*d*) wrap-around, (*e*) folded-down collapsible rigid.

Container Bases. Container bases are used to facilitate surface movement and can be essentially categorized as metal pallets since there are provisions for two- and four-way entry with forklift trucks and other materials handling equipment. The general features of these bases were covered in the pallet section of this chapter.

Container Sections. Container sections can include a number of options (Fig. 2-10) to provide hopper dumping or accessibility, drop-bottom dumping, and end gates. Air- or hydraulic-actuated equipment and tilt stands are used in conjunction with, and as means to extend the versatility of, containers in assembly or machining stations. Container sections come in a wide range of heights; the deeper containers are used for dumping applications, and the shallower sizes are more suitable for manual handling of parts.

Several lifting and stacking aids can be designed or are available as part of the container system. Overhead movement can be accomplished by the addition of overhead crane lugs, chain-sling lugs, and bar-lift or sling-lift notches in the base. Stacking is accommodated by corner stacking angles, self-aligning hairpin brackets, and stacking lugs.

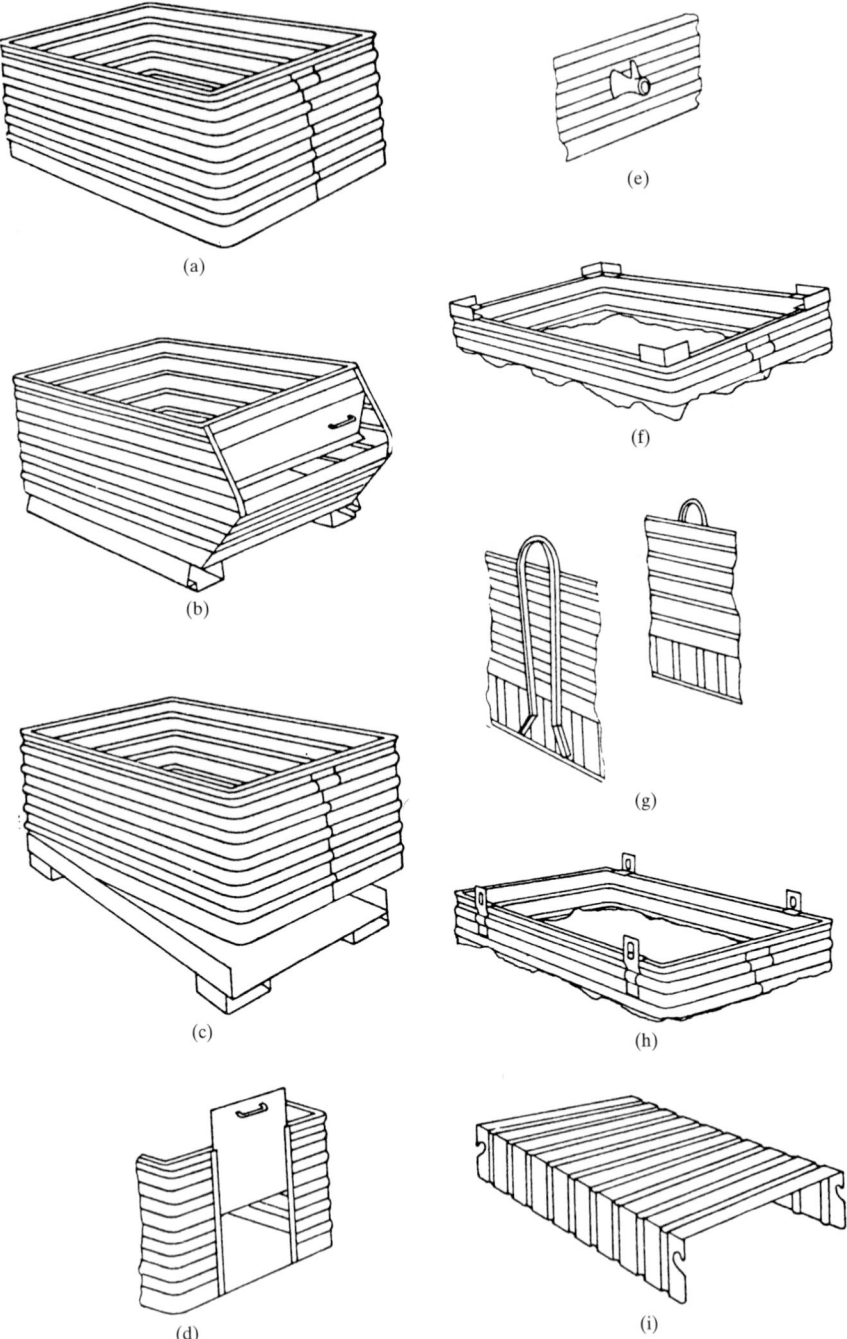

FIGURE 2-10 Corrugated-metal-container styles and lifting and stacking aids. (*a*) Basic corrugated box, (*b*) hopper-front pallet base container, (*c*) drop-bottom container, (*d*) end gate option, (*e*) overhead crane lugs, (*f*) corner-stacking lugs, (*g*) chain sling and stacking lugs, (*h*) bar lift, (*i*) sling lift notches.

Industry Specifications.   Specifications issued by the Industrial Metal Containers Product section of the Material Handling Institute specify the materials, design, construction, testing procedures, environmental considerations, utilization, and safety practices regarding the use of metal containers. The safety guidelines do not recommend the use of wire-mesh containers for applications where parts and material protrude or for dumping purposes. A load and capacity rating plate is used to indicate the load capacity of each container and the number of containers that can be safely stacked on top of each other.

Wood Containers

Wood containers are of three basic types.

Types

1. Bins with bases and closed sides and ends
2. Boxes with bases, closed sides and ends, and a top
3. Crates with open or slatted sides and ends

Wood containers with standard pallet bases are finding increasing use in applications where mechanized handling and storage are required for products ranging from solid materials of irregular shapes and sizes to granular materials. Pallet containers are now being used in the agricultural area, where fruits and vegetables are loaded into pallet containers when picked and then washed, transported, and placed in supermarkets in the same container.

The pallet container design may include collapsible sides, a feature which saves space when the container is not in use or when it is being returned empty.

Construction.   The four major types of end-panel and side-panel construction in wood containers are:

1. *Solid.*   Usually of plywood, this type of construction provides great strength as well as a smooth interior surface.
2. *Vertical-slat.*   Used for deep containers and requires more bracing than the solid or horizontal-slat construction to prevent rocking.

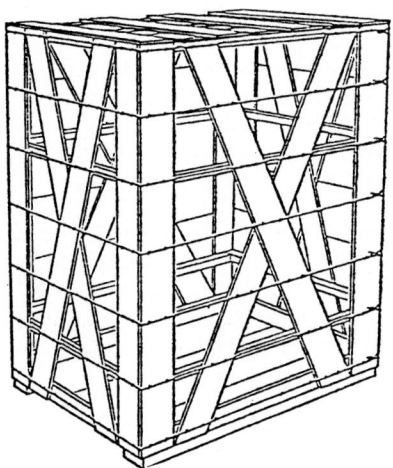

3. *Horizontal-slat.*   Used for shallower containers and requires less bracing than containers with vertical-slat construction.
4. *Wirebound.*   Provides the economy of lightweight construction with the added strength of being wire-bound (Fig. 2-11). The main advantages of this construction is a high-strength container with low tare weight.

Selection of Wood.   In the selection of the wood species to be used for wood containers, the following factors should be considered:

1. Intended usage and life requirements of the container
2. Pressure to be exerted on the bottom and sides by the goods
3. Permissible bulging of sides and edges

FIGURE 2-11   Typical wirebound container.

4. Degree of impact resistance required

5. Type of handling equipment used

6. Degree of weather and water resistance required for exposure to weather or cleaning operations

Corrugated-Cardboard Containers

Corrugated-cardboard containers offer a wide range of economical solutions for packaging or materials-handling problems. There are literally hundreds of unique designs of corrugated containers. Because of the relatively low cost, it is feasible to "tailor-make" a configuration that is an optimum design for a particular product and situation. This container may be one of, or a modification of, five common types.

Types

1. *Regular slotted container.* The most commonly used style. All flaps are of equal length, and other flaps meet when closed. Contents of the box are protected by one thickness of corrugation on the side and two thicknesses on top. If additional top and bottom protection is required, both outer top and bottom flaps can be designed to overlap.

2. *Telescope box.* A two-piece box designed so one part fits into the other.

3. *Five-panel folder.* A corrugated flat sheet, scored into five panels, which folds into a four-sided tube-type container that is closed by end flaps.

4. *One-piece folder or book fold.* Used for shipping books, catalogs, wearing apparel.

5. *Gaylord.* A corrugated container that has a base, generally consisting of two or more wood runners that allow the container to be moved by fork lift equipment.

Corrugated Material and Construction. The basic corrugated material is referred to as "double-face" or single-wall, consisting of outer facing, corrugated medium, and inner facing, joined by adhesive. Corrugated material is also available in single-face, double-wall, and triple-wall designs.

Types of Board. These include Fourdrinier kraft linerboard, the highest-quality and -cost material made from virgin pulpwood, and cylinder linerboard which is generally made from a combination of reclaimed fibers and virgin pulp. The weight of a linerboard required for the contents of a corrugated container is specified in the Uniform Freight Classification and Motor Truck Classification.

Corrugating Medium. Straw, reclaimed fibers, or woods can be used as a corrugating medium. The combination of corrugated-medium thickness, weight, and flute configuration determines the strength and moisture-lockout properties of the container. Corrugating media are specified by thickness and weight per 1000 ft^2 (MSF).

FLUTE CONFIGURATION. This specifies the number of corrugations per lineal foot. The three most common flutes used are:

1. *A flute.* The highest flute with the least number of corrugations (36 per linear foot, 0.1875-in high) (12 per centimeter, 4.2 mm). When used in an upright position, A flute has the best stacking strength and greater capacity to absorb shock in the direction of the thickness.

2. *B flute.* Has the greatest number of corrugations per foot with the lowest flute height and is stiffer and less shock-absorbent than A flutes, but it has greater crush resistance to loads placed in the direction of thickness.

3. *C flute.* A compromise between A and B flutes.

Methods of Fastening Joints. The accepted methods are taping, stitching, or gluing. Common carriers publish detailed regulations governing the method to be used in regard to content type, weight, and other factors.

Corrugated boards may be specially treated to provide additional properties to the container, such as a coating and lamination, to:

- Retard slippage
- Inhibit mold
- Retain temperature
- Increase water or moisture resistance

Tote Boxes and Bins

Tote boxes are used for unit loads of smaller parts that can be moved manually through the operation or can be stacked in a larger container to become part of a unit load. Tote boxes are available mainly in metal and plastic and are also fabricated from other materials such as wood, cardboard, fiberboard, and Plexiglas.

Plastic Tote Boxes.   Plastic tote boxes have many applications where small and light parts are handled and in environments where protection from corrosive chemicals or a high degree of cleanliness is required. Plastic containers are easily cleaned without harm or deterioration to the material. Molding capabilities permit desirable features to be incorporated as an integral part of the container, permitting a number of provisions for nesting and stacking. A typical tote box is shown in Fig. 2-12. There are three major types:

Straight-Nesting. This refers to tote boxes that can be nested when not used. This type requires the use of lids or covers if stacking is required but results in maximum product protection, since one box will not fall into another. The design of straight-nesting boxes is characterized by tapered sides which reduce cube utilization and should not be used for storing on shelves.

Straight Stacking. This method of stacking boxes is ideal, because of minimum tapered sides, for shelf storage and use as an inner container of maximum cube utilization. Since the sides and ends support the loads, greater weights can be stacked than when using the straight-nesting variety.

Combination of Stack and Nest. This feature is available in some boxes and can be altered by the orientation of boxes in relation to each other.

The most common plastic materials and their major properties are indicated in Table 2-2.

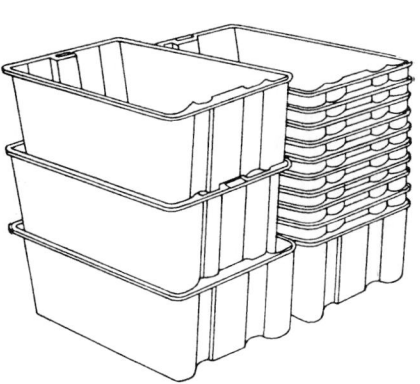

FIGURE 2-12   Typical tote boxes.

DUNNAGE AND OUTER SECUREMENT OF CONTAINERS AND UNIT LOADS

Dunnage

Dunnage refers to inner package containment methods or material that is used to protect the contents of a container from damage. This is done in one of two ways, either by preventing the movement of the contents or by providing a cushioning medium to absorb shocks.

Plastic and other petroleum-base materials are used for dunnage because of their light weight and low bulk density.

TABLE 2-2   Plastic Materials Used in Tote Boxes

Material	General properties
ABS (acrylonitrile-butadiene-styrene)	High impact absorption, good compressive strength; more expensive than other thermoplastics
High-density polyethylene	Good to excellent stiffness, excellent temperature range, −40 to 150°F (−71 to 51°C); commonly used for food applications with USDA and FDA approval
High-impact polypropylene	More durable than polyethylene, not as stiff; tendency to crack at temperatures below 0°F (−32°C)
High-impact polystyrene	Extremely stiff, excellent compressive load strength, good temperature range; tendency to crack easily under high impact; readily attacked by solvents and oils
FRP (fiberglass-reinforced polyester)	Exceptional compressive load strength; can be heat-, fire-, and wear-resistant

Dunnage Materials.   Polystyrene is used to cushion package contents in three general forms:

1. Loose foam strands are used to fill the airspace in the package and provide a cushioning barrier around the contents.
2. Polystyrene can be molded to the general form of the part in the container and actually becomes an inner case for the part.
3. Polystyrene is also used for corner forms to strengthen corrugated containers.

Bubblepack is two thin sheets of polyethylene with air entrapped within the "bubble" sections when laminated together. The contents of a container may be wrapped in bubblepack for protection during shipment or movement.

Corrugated board can be easily formed into many shapes to protect, support, and cushion products. The trend is to reduce the number of inserts by combining features into a single interior form, reducing the cost and inventory expense of packaging materials. Typical inner packings, portions, and sheets used for this purpose are shown in Fig. 2-13.

Outer Securements

Container closure can be achieved by sealing flaps with glue and tape, by stapling, and by strapping with plastic or steel bands.

The glue and tape sealing method lends itself to automation by use of case-sealing equipment which automatically dispenses glue or tape close to the flaps. Stapling can also be automated by passing containers through, under, and between staple heads.

Strapping.   Strapping can be used to secure not only containers but stand-alone unitized loads and palletized unit loads as well. There are two major strapping classifications: steel and plastic. Steel strapping is dimensionally stable under all but extreme conditions and plastic strapping is more resilient.

Common cold-rolled-steel strapping, the least stretchable of all steel strapping, is good for strapping lightweight packages or pallet loads that are not subject to high impact or shock. Heavy-duty steel strapping, both hot- and cold-rolled steel, absorbs high impacts without breaking; however, it stretches under great stress and requires staples to keep it in place.

Plastic strapping continues to stretch under tensioned loads and therefore should not be used where continuous loads are present. However, their resilience keeps them tight on a package or load that shrinks or settles.

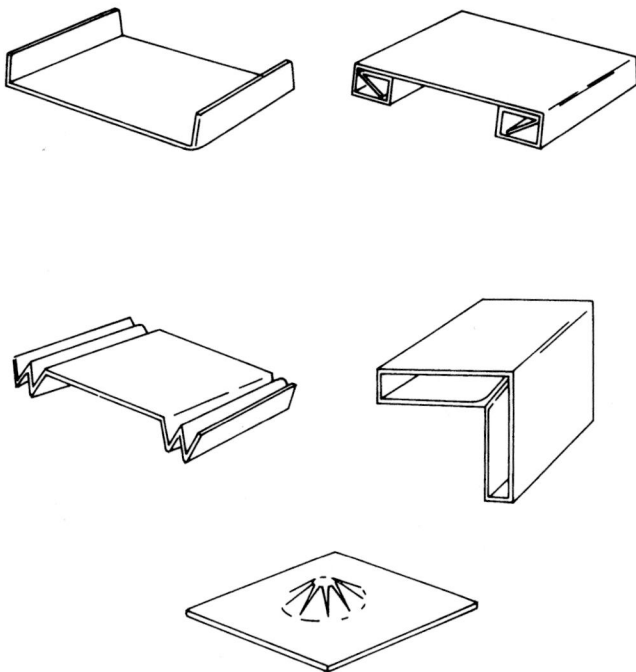

FIGURE 2-13 Typical inner packings, portions, and sheets.

Steel strapping may be applied by manually operated tensioning tools which notch or crimp steels to retain the strapping. Plastic strapping can also be applied both manually and automatically in the same manner as steel strapping. Friction-welding and heat-sealing systems are also available.

Stretch Wrap.   Stretch wrap is one method of confining unitized or pallet loads by wrapping a film of polyethylene material around the load. The stretch film is wound under light tension by rotating the load on a platform on horizontal- and spiral-type stretch film equipment. Horizontal-type equipment uses a full sheet wrap, while spiral-type equipment bands the load by dispensing several overlapping layers. Vertical wrapping equipment rotates the film around the load and is generally used when the load is not on a pallet.

Shrink Wrap.   Shrink wrap uses a polystyrene film that can be a bag or flat sheet that is put over or around the unit load and then placed in an oven. Bag design should be selected to achieve the desired protection required or to optimize the holding power for the load configuration. While in the oven, the film reaches a temperature of 240°F (116°C). During the cooling cycle, the film molecules try to return to their original compact orientation, shrinking the film tightly around the load.

Three types of ovens are used for this purpose, depending on the volume handled. Closet types can normally handle up to 20 loads per hour; bell-type ovens are for higher volume operations, up to 20 loads per hour; and tunnel or feedthrough ovens are generally specified for automated lines and handle more than 75 loads per hour.

In addition to securing products in a unit load, there are extra benefits in using shrink wrap (Fig. 2-14). Irregular, hard-to-pack loads (like those in order-picking warehouses) can be secured with shrink wrap. Products can be protected from damage caused by weather, dirt, or moisture. Clear film allows for easy viewing for identification and inventorying of product. Opaque film can be used to conceal or protect product from light.

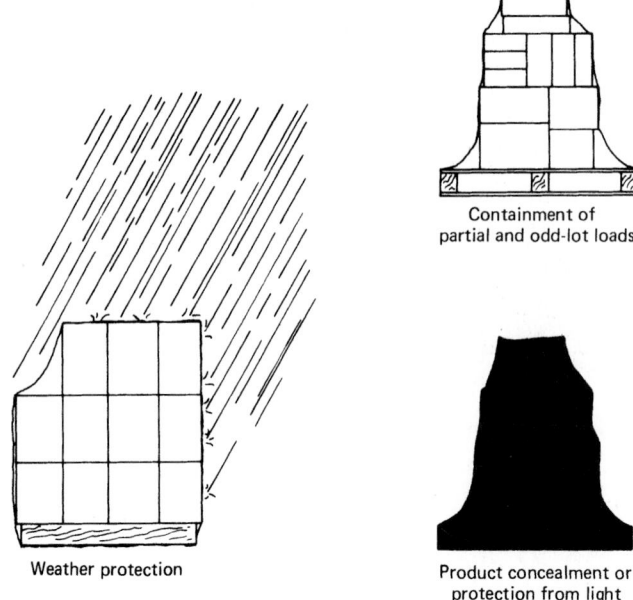

Containment of
partial and odd-lot loads

Weather protection

Product concealment or
protection from light

FIGURE 2-14   Other benefits from use of shrink wrap. (*Black Body Corp.*)

REFERENCES AND BIBLIOGRAPHY

1. "Storage and Materials Handling," Departments of the Army, Navy, Air Force, and U.S. Marine Corps, Washington, D.C., 1955.
2. "Unit Load Stretch Wrapping," *Modern Materials Handling,* October 1979.
3. Schumf, G., "Slip Sheets," *Material Handling Engineering,* July 1980.
4. "Pallets: Wood isn't the only Answer," *Material Handling Engineering,* November 1990.

CHAPTER 8-3
FIXED-PATH EQUIPMENT

K. W. Tunnell Co., Inc.
King of Prussia, Pennsylvania

INTRODUCTION

Conveyors, cranes, and hoists are generally considered fixed-path materials-handling equipment, since they often become a fixed part of the physical plant. Once in place, a considerable amount of time, disruption, and cost is needed to change the arrangement of the equipment. It is therefore very important to plan the installation of these pieces of equipment very carefully.

A complete materials-handling system can include a wide variety of fixed-path equipment for unit loads and bulk materials handling, as well as mobile handling equipment and storage racks. This further complicates the planning process, since the fixed-path equipment not only has to satisfy the requirements of the fixed-path handling but must also be compatible with the overall flow of the total handling system.

There are many considerations involved in planning fixed-path equipment installations; many of these considerations are unique to a specific type or class of equipment, but general areas that must be addressed in the planning and exploration stage are:

- *Flexibility of the system.* Must a wide range of unit-load sizes or bulk material be handled or conveyed?

- *State of materials to be handled.* Is it in a unit load or bulk form?

- *Weight, dimensions, and physical properties of the material being handled or moved.* Is it fragile, light, firm, or does it have other properties that require special attention?

- *Loading and unloading methods.* Is it handled manually or received from or delivered to other equipment such as lift trucks, palletizers, or packaging equipment?

- *Capacity of equipment.* Does the conveying speed match the speed or capacities of the equipment it is being interfaced with? Is there sufficient capacity or length to accumulate material when required?

- *Supporting-system requirements.* Is the material to be sorted, accumulated, weighed, or further processed while being handled or conveyed?

- *Environmental conditions.* Must provisions be made for dust, high or low temperature, high humidity, or other ambient conditions in the plant or outside?

- *Safety.* What special precautions must be taken to protect operating personnel or personnel working near the equipment? What provisions must be made to comply with regulatory requirements?

- *Maintenance.*
- *Facility restrictions.*   Are overhead heights or floor loading capacities adequate for supporting and accommodating equipment? Is there sufficient plant area? Will the fixed-path system impede access to equipment and the flow of personnel and other materials within the plant?
- *Horizontal or vertical distances to be covered.*   What hardware is required to negotiate inclines and declines throughout the system?
- *Power and energy requirements.*

There are many types and varieties of fixed-path equipment. Each of the major classifications of this type of equipment are discussed and described here, but no effort will be made to list all of the items that are contained in each classification. The classifications that are covered include:

- Conveyors and monorails
- Sorting, consolidating, and diverting devices
- Hoists and cranes
- Automatic guided vehicles
- Robots

CONVEYORS

Conveyors are gravity or power devices commonly used to move uniform loads continuously from point to point over fixed paths. The primary function of the conveyor is to move materials when the loads are uniform, and the routes do not vary. The movement rate and direction is usually fixed, although powered conveyors have the capability to alter the rate of speed The major types of conveyor and related devices are chutes and wheel and roller conveyors.

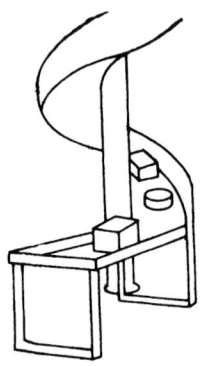

Chutes.   Chutes are the simplest fixed-path devices that use gravity to convey bulk or unit loads down declines. Straight and spiral types are available. The spiral chute (Fig. 3-1) is a continuous trough over which bulk materials or discrete objects are guided in a helical path.

Wheel and Roller Conveyors.   These depend on both gravity and power to move materials. Objects of various shapes can be handled by changing the cross section of the rolling surface or by aligning the objects in the conveyor framework. These conveyors are generally used to move materials horizontally.

FIGURE 3-1   Spiral chute.

Considerations for Chutes and Wheel and Roller Conveyors.   The following sections discuss points that must be considered in specifying and designing both of these classes of conveyors.

Load Characteristics.   These include maximum and minimum sizes of loads and the shapes and carrying surfaces of all units. The suitability of a load configuration to be handled on roller or wheel conveyor is important. Unsupported packages such as bags (Fig. 3-2) are not recommended for this type of equipment.

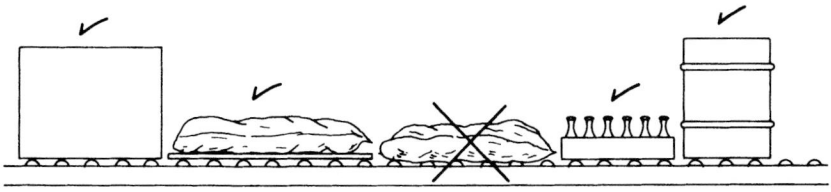

FIGURE 3-2   Can it be handled on a roller conveyor? (*Litton UHS.*)

Operating Conditions.   These include the size and weight of the conveying surfaces, environmental conditions, and loading and unloading methods. These considerations determine the type and capacity of frame, roller, or wheel material and sizes, and the type of bearings that should be used.

Roller or Wheel Spacing and Pattern.   This is determined by the size of the minimum package or unit load. (See Fig. 3-3.) To determine roller centers, divide the minimum load length by three. Wheel pattern should be specified to provide a minimum of five wheels under the package. Other guidelines include:

1. A minimum of three rollers under a hard bottom surface
2. A minimum of four rollers under a flexible bottom surface

Roller and wheel capacity is determined by dividing the weight of the heaviest load to be handled by the minimum number of rollers or wheels under the carrying surface of the load. If special requirements must be considered, such as drop, shock, or side loads, then a roller with a higher load rating will have to be considered.

Conveyor Width; Wheel and Roller Setting.   The width of conveyor is determined by the back-to-back frame dimension required to ensure sufficient clearance to carry the load

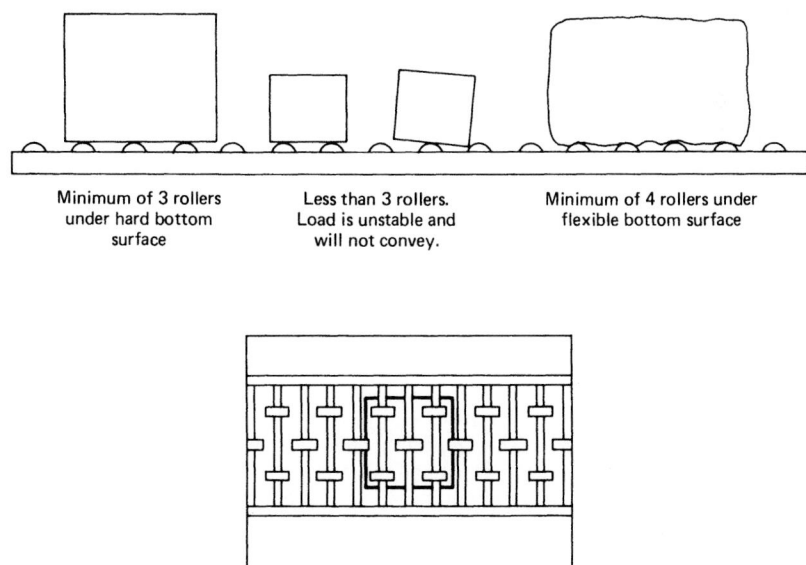

Minimum of 3 rollers under hard bottom surface

Less than 3 rollers. Load is unstable and will not convey.

Minimum of 4 rollers under flexible bottom surface

5-wheel minimum under package

FIGURE 3-3   Roller and wheel spacing guidelines. (*Litton UHS.*)

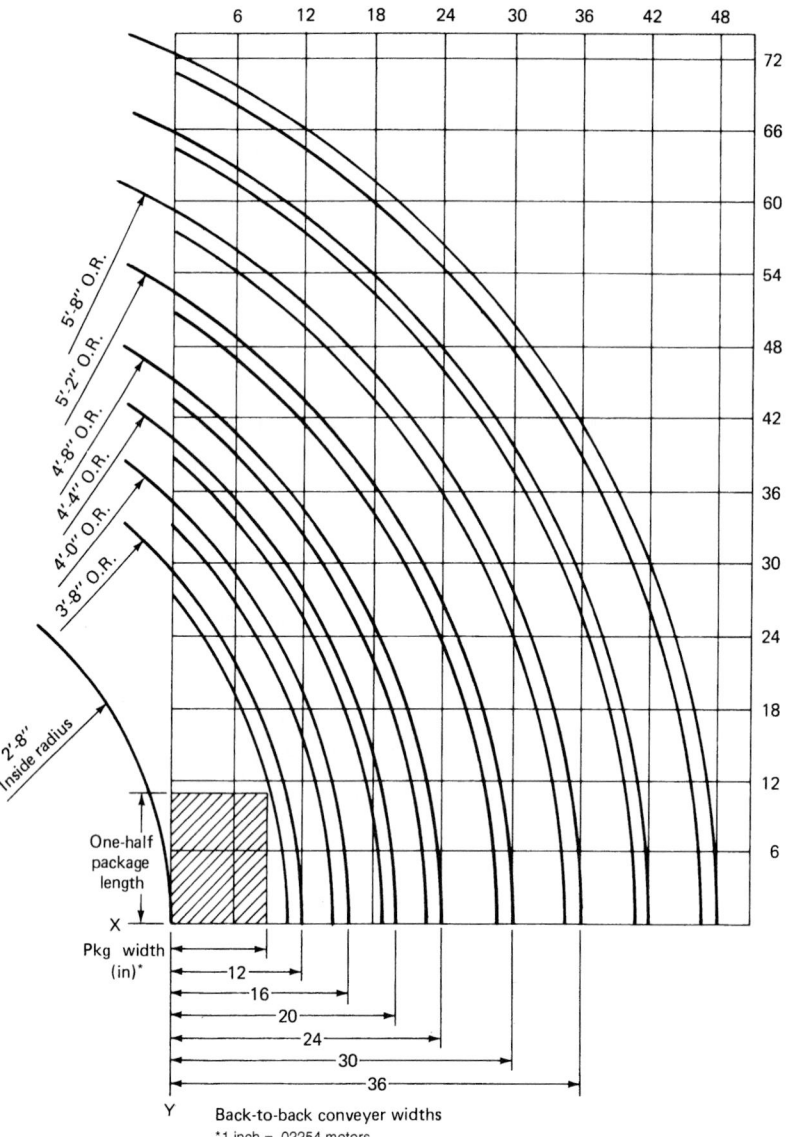

FIGURE 3-4   Curve-radius selection.

around a 90° curve. The minimum clearance is dependent on the roller setting. If rollers are set high, the conveyor can handle loads up to 1.25 times the width of the conveyor. If the rollers are set low, a minimum of 1 in (2.5 cm) between frame and load must be allowed on each side. Package skew should also be considered in determining this dimension. Specification of curve sections can be calculated graphically from the chart in Fig. 3-4. The design of curve sections depends on the size and shapes of loads. Tracking of packages is important, especially when there are a number of turns involved and the skewing effect becomes cumulative. This effect can be minimized by using tapered rollers (Fig. 3-5) or a double-roller differential section.

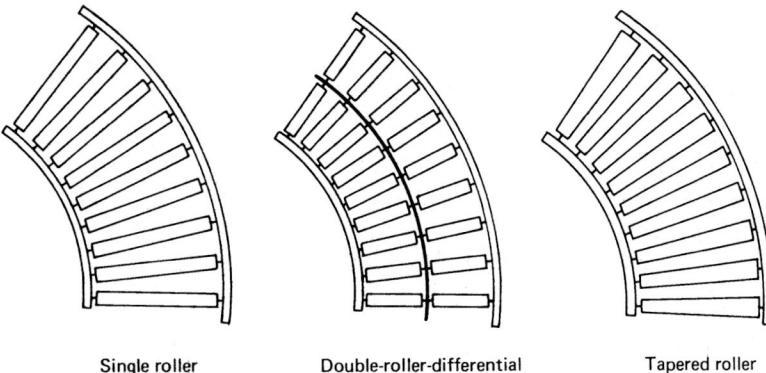

Single roller   Double-roller-differential   Tapered roller

FIGURE 3-5   Roller-conveyor curve sections. (*Litton UHS.*)

Bearing Selection.   This is dependent upon conveyor operating conditions. Plain ball bearings are used for indoor use where severe environmental conditions are not present. Dust-tight bearings, which are designed to run dry, are ideal in dusty atmospheres. Greased bearings require more force to turn and their use should be kept to a minimum on gravity-type conveyors.

Conveyor Pitch.   The pitch that is required cannot be easily determined because it is dependent on a combination of many factors such as:

- Weight and stability of unit load
- Smoothness of bottom of load
- Firmness of load surface
- Length of rollers
- Number of rollers under load
- Length of runs
- Types of bearings

The suggested pitch for a number of types of unit loads is shown in Table 3-1 and should be used as a general guide for determining pitch.

Conveyor Support and Frame Capacity.   Conveyor supports can be one of three types: permanent-floor, ceiling-hung, or portable. Supporting points (Fig. 3-6) should be located to handle the load equally. The design load is the weight of the conveyor section plus the maximum unit load for that section of the conveyor.

Special Considerations for Wheel Conveyors.   Wheel conveyors are used for light-duty applications and have several advantages over roller conveyors for lightweight unit loads. Gravity wheel conveyors consist of a series of wheels which can be one of many different styles and materials, mounted on common axles and supported between two frames. They are generally less expensive and lighter in weight, making them ideal for portable applications. Light unit loads travel better on wheel conveyors because less pitch is needed and less force is required to start the wheels in motion (see Table 3-1). Another advantage inherent in the use of multicontact conveying surfaces is that the wheels provide a turning action which enables the package to maintain its original position.

Frames that support the wheel axles are either steel or aluminum. Low weight and corrosion resistance are properties that make aluminum attractive, but steel should be used where conditions require the conveyor to be more rugged.

TYPES OF WHEELS.   There is a wide variety of both metal and plastic wheels now available, including:

TABLE 3-1 Suggested Pitch for Gravity Conveyor

Container being conveyed	Approx. cont. wt., lb	Gravity roller conv., plain and dust-tight bearings			Gravity roller conv., pressure-lubricated bearings			Pi gravity wheel conv. or live rail conv.		
		Pitch per ft, pitch per 10'0", and pitch per 90° curve								
		1"/ft	10'0"	90°	1"/ft	10'0"	90°	1"/ft	10'0"	90°
Cartons (fiber smooth bottom)	10	⅝	6¼	5				⅜	3¾	4
Cartons (fiber smooth bottom)	20	½	5	5				¼	2½	3½
Cartons (fiber smooth bottom)	45	⅜	3¾	3½	¾	7½	6	3/16	1⅞	3
Cartons (fiber smooth bottom)	100	¼	2½	3	⅝	6¼	5	¼–3/16		3
Fiber beverage carton empty	5							1½	15	10
Fiber beverage carton empty bottles	35	½	5	4–5	¾	7½	6	⅜	3¾	4
Fiber beverage carton filled bottles	45	⅜	3¾	3½	⅝	6¼	5	¼	2½	3½
Wood cases or boxes	5	⅝	6¼	5				⅜	3¾	5
Wood cases or boxes	10	⅜	3¾	4	¾	7½	6	¼	2½	5
Wood cases or boxes	25	¼	2½	4	⅝	6¼	5	¼	2½	4
Wood cases or boxes	50	3/16	1⅞	3	½	5	4	¼	2½	3½
Wood cases or boxes	100	3/16	1⅞	3	⅜	3¾	3½	⅛	1¼	2½
Steel drums	20	⅝	6¼	5½	¾	7½	6			
Steel drums*	55	7/16–½	4¼–5	5	⅝	6¼	5			
Steel drums	120	⅜	3¾	4	½	6	4½			
Steel drums	250	¼	2½	3	⅜	3¾	3½			
Steel drums*	550	¼–3/16	2½–1⅞	3	¼	2½	3			
Wood barrels	100	½	5	5	⅝	6¼	6			
Wood barrels	400	⅜	3¾	4	½	5	5			
Metal and fiberglass tote boxes	10	½	5	5				⅜	3¾	4
Metal and fiberglass tote boxes	25	⅜	3¾	4	¾	7½	6	¼	2½	3½
Metal and fiberglass tote boxes	50	¼	2½	3	⅝	6¼	5	3/16	1⅞	3
Milk cans empty	25	⅝	6¼	6	¾	7½	6½			
Milk cans full	105	⅜	3¾	4	½	5	5			
Milk crates empty	10	¾	7½	6	1	10	7½			
Milk crates empty bottles	45	½	5	5	⅝	6¼	5			
Milk crates full bottles	60	⅜	3¾	4	½	5	5			
Wood pallets smooth runner†	350	⅜	3¾		7/16	4¼				
Wood pallets smooth runner†	750	5/16	3⅛		⅜	3¾				
Wood pallets formica base	350	¼	2½		5/16	3½				
Wood pallets formica base†	750	⅛	1¼		3/16	2½				
Wood pallets pine plywood†	350	⅜	3¾		7/16	4¼				
Wood pallets pine plywood†	750	5/16	3⅛		⅜	3¾				
Wood beverage case empty	6	13/16	8⅜	6¾				¼	2½	3½
Wood beverage case empty bottles	30	½	5	5	¾	7½	6	⅛	1¼	2½
Wood beverage case full bottles	40	7/16	4¼	4	½	5	5	⅛	1¼	2½
Multiwall bags, firm	50							⅝	6¼	6
Multiwall bags, firm	100							½	5	5

* Varies with new or reconditioned drums.
† Depends on the way it is nailed and if banded or not. Bad nailing or banding will considerably increase the pitch and make a planned slope impractical.

- *Steel wheels with ball bearings.* The most rugged and commonly used wheels, these are used where long life is a requirement. Life potential of this wheel is 10 times that of aluminum. Steel wheels can be covered with *neoprene tires* and are used to reduce shock, prevent slippage, increase traction, prevent marring fragile surfaces, and reduce noise.

- *Aluminum wheels with steel or plastic ball bearings.* Used in applications where weight is a factor, particularly for portable conveyors. Plastic ball bearings should be used in corrosive atmospheres.

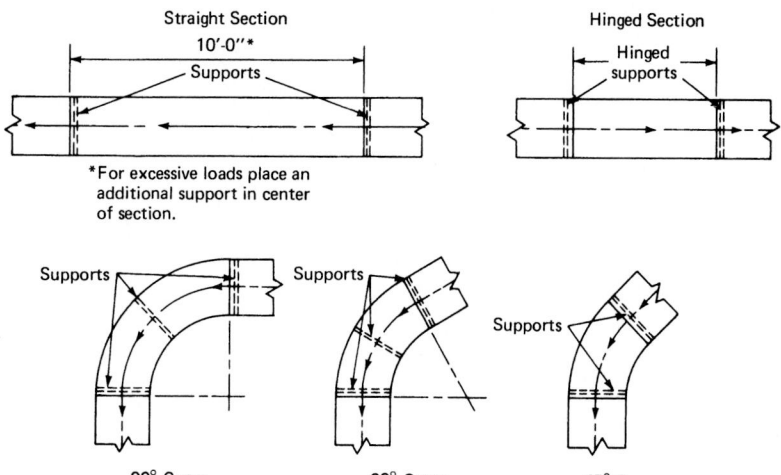

FIGURE 3-6 Suggested support locations.

- *Nylon wheels.* Used where resistance to salt, water, and chemicals is required, as well as in applications where conveyors are cleaned frequently. Nylon wheels also do not mar or mark containers.
- *Polypropylene plastic wheels.* Have many properties which make them ideal for a wide range of applications. This material is highly impervious to a wide range of corrosive materials and is temperature-resistant from 230 to −30°F (110 to −34°C). The wheels do not absorb moisture and can be steam-cleaned repeatedly.
- *Hysteretic wheels.* Metal wheels surrounded by a tire formed by elastomeric material, these are used for line storage of heavy loads. The purpose is to absorb the energy of the initial load impact and to control the movement of the load to a safe speed.

LUBRICATION. Metal wheels can be greased, oiled, or dry. Nylon and plastic wheels are always furnished dry. Oiled or dry bearings should be used where high temperatures can cause thinning and leakage of grease. Dry bearings are recommended where temperatures are below 0°F (−18°C).

Special Types of Wheel Conveyors. These have been designed for handling specific products or for special industries. Samples of these are shown in Fig. 3-7.

Powered Conveyors. These are designed for continuous control of products on level surfaces, through inclines and declines, and around curves. Many powered conveyors are equipped with a computerized control system to provide tracking and diagnostics. Basic considerations for powered conveyors are the same as for gravity conveyors. Powered roller and belt conveyors are the major powered types used to move unit loads.

Powered Roller Conveyors. These are used mainly to accumulate loads because power-drive disengagement can be accomplished very simply when the forward motion of the unit load is stopped. Generally, power-drive disengagement is triggered when the unit load meets an obstruction, creating an opposite reaction which causes the carrying roller bushing to move up an angular slot, thus relieving the pressure and contact between the drive belt and rollers.

Powered roller conveyors are either chain- or belt-driven. Chain-driven units are used in heavy-duty applications and where oil or contaminants would have an adverse effect on the belting. The belt-drive-powered trains are designed for accumulation where the belt-to-roller pressure is very light or for transportation sections where belt-to-roller pressure is increased by center takeup rollers and the use of high friction drive belts.

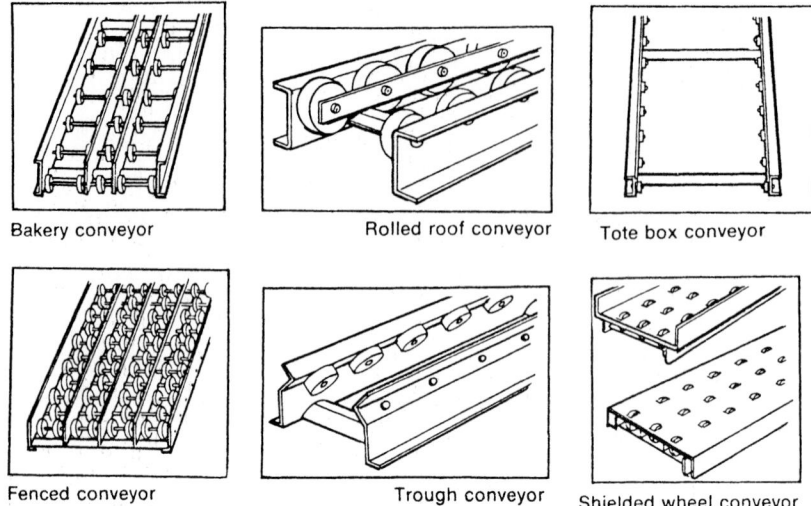

FIGURE 3-7   Special types of wheel conveyors.

Powered roller conveyors are not used for inclines greater than 5° since the contact force between the unit load and roller surface is not sufficient to overcome the gravity force due to a low coefficient of friction. This type of conveyor is not normally used over straight runs because of the higher cost as compared with belt conveyors.

Belt Conveyors.   Belt conveyors consist of an endless moving belt which carries materials within a supporting frame. The belt can be made from a variety of materials and may or may not be equipped with cleats or other grabbing devices. The belt may be supported by a solid-slider-type bed of wood or metal or by rollers.

Conveyor manufacturers suggest friction surface belts on inclines up to 13°, and rough-top rubber belts should be used for inclines up to 25°. In applications where a steeper incline is required, heavily textured, nubbed or cleated surface belts can be used. Also, special requirements for belt surface material should be considered in applications where chemical or oil resistance is needed or for mandated cleanliness requirements.

Belt Conveyor Parameters.   The parameters that must be defined before equipment is specified are belt speed, length, maximum load on belt at one time, tension loads, power requirements, and support and mounting hardware. Belt speed should be specified to be compatible with process equipment and other materials-handling hardware. Belt length should be adequate to accumulate the maximum expected product capacity. The maximum load on the belt at any one time can be calculated from the following formula:

$$P = \frac{K}{S \times 60 \text{ min}} \times C \text{ (ft)}$$

where P = maximum product weight
$\quad\quad\quad K$ = load per hour, lb
$\quad\quad\quad S$ = speed of belt, ft/min
$\quad\quad\quad C$ = center-to-center distance

For example, if

Load per hour in pounds = 10,000 lb
Speed of belt = 50 ft/min
Center-to-center distance = 36 ft

Then, the maximum product weight is

$$P = \frac{10,000}{50 \times 60} \times 36$$

$$= 1200 \text{ lb } (544 \text{ kg})$$

Considerations for Bulk-Materials Belt Conveyors.   These considerations are similar to those for all conveyors; however, the properties of the materials to be moved affect the parameters of and the specification of the conveyor. The use of belt conveyors for bulk materials is limited by the characteristics of materials, some of which are:

- Stickiness, which may prevent materials from completely discharging from the conveyor or interfering with the power-train components.
- Temperatures that exceed 150°F (71°C) would cause deterioration or damage to most belt materials.
- Chemical reactions of conveyed materials with belt material. Some oils, chemicals, fats, and acids can damage belts.
- Large lump size becomes a factor and generally requires the system to be oversized for the amount of weight being moved.

Weight and friction are the common factors that determine the amount of incline that is possible for unit-load and bulk-materials-handling belt conveyors. Bulk-materials belt conveyors must also include materials characteristics such as size consistency, shape of lumps, moisture content, angle of repose, and flowability. The maximum angle of incline for various bulk materials is shown in Table 3-2. The ideal combination of belt width and speed (Table 3-3) is determined by the characteristics of the materials handled.

TABLE 3-2   Maximum Angle of Incline

Material carried	Maximum angle of incline, deg*	Material carried	Maximum angle of incline, deg*
Alumina, dry, free-flowing, ⅛″ lumps	10 to 12	Grain	8–16
		Ore (see stone)	15–20
Beans, whole	8	Packages	15–25
Coal, anthracite	16	Pellets, depending on size, bed of material and concentricity (taconite, fertilizer, etc.)	5–15
Coal, bituminous, sized, lumps over 4 in	15		
Coal, bituminous, sized,† lumps 4 in and under	16	Rock (see stone)	15–20
Coal, bituminous, unsized†	18	Sand, very free-flowing¶	15
Coal, bituminous, fines, free-flowing‡	20	Sand, sluggish (moist)§	20
Coal, bituminous, fines, sluggish§	22	Sand, tempered foundry	24
Coke, sized	17	Stone, sized, lumps over 4 in	15
Coke, unsized	18	Stone, sized, lumps 4 in and under, over ⅜ in	16
Coke, fines and breeze	20	Stone, unsized, lumps over 4 in	16
Earth, free-flowing‡	20	Stone, unsized, lumps 4 in and under, over ⅜ in	18
Earth, sluggish§	22		
Gravel, sized, washed	12	Stone, fines ⅜ in and under	20
Gravel, sized, unwashed	15	Wood chips	27
Gravel, unsized	18		

* For ascending conveyors when uniformly loaded and with constant feed.
† See second footnote (†) to Table 3-3 for definitions of "sized" and "unsized" as used in Material Carried columns of Table 3-2.
‡ Angle of repose 30 to 45°.
§ Angle of repose greater than 45°.
¶ Very wet or very dry, with angle of repose less than 30°.

TABLE 3-3 Recommended Belt Speed as Determined by Material Handled

Material		Recommended belt speed, ft/min*†												
		Belt width, in†												
Characteristics§	Example	14	16	18	20	24	30	36	42	48	54	60	72	84
Maximum size lumps, sized or unsized														
Mildly abrasive	Coal, earth	300	300	400	400	450	500	550	600	600	650	650	650	650
Very abrasive, not sharp	Bank gravel	300	300	400	400	450	500	550	550	600	600	600	600	600
Very abrasive, sharp and jagged	Stone, ore	250	250	300	350	400	450	500	500	550	550	550	550	550
Half max. lumps, sized or unsized														
Mildly abrasive	Coal, earth	300	300	400	400	500	600	650	700	700	700	700	700	700
Very abrasive	Slag, coke, ore, stone, cullet	300	300	400	400	500	600	650	650	650	650	650	650	650
Flakes	Wood chips, bark, pulp	400	450	450	500	600	700	800	800	800	800	800	800	800
Granular ⅛″ to ½″ lumps	Grain, coal, cottonseed, sand	400	450	450	500	600	700	800	800	800	800	800	800	800
Fines														
Light, fluffy, dry, dusty	Soda ash, pulverized coal						220–250 ft/min							
Heavy	Cement, flue dust						250–300 ft/min							
Fragile, where degradation is harmful	Coke, coal										200–250 ft/min			
	Soap chips						150–200 ft/min							

* Normal for belts traveling horizontally on ball- or roller-bearing idlers. For picking belts, speed is usually 50 to 100 ft/min. Belts with discharge plows should not travel faster than 200 ft/min. For tripers, recommended speed is 300 to 400 ft/min. Trippers for higher-speed applications can be furnished. A speed of at least 300 ft/min should also be maintained for proper discharge when using 35 to 45° idlers, and also for materials tending to cling to belt.

† 1 in = .02254 m; 1 ft/min = .00508 m/s.

§ *Unsized* means a uniform mixture of material in which not more than 10 percent are lumps ranging from maximum size to ½ maximum size, at least 15 percent are fines or lumps smaller than ⅒ maximum, and the remaining 75 percent are lumps of any size smaller than ½ maximum. *Sized* means a uniform mixture in which not more than 20 percent are lumps ranging from maximum size to ½ maximum size, and the remaining 80 percent are lumps no larger than ½ maximum size and no smaller than ⅒ maximum size.

Metal-Belt Conveyors. Similar in design to standard belt conveyors, these differ in that their surface is a belt of woven or solid metal. The materials include carbon steel, galvanized steel, chromium stainless steel, and other metals or special alloys that are required for a specific application and environment. Wire belts are also available for use where processing temperatures vary from 320 to 2500°F (160 to 1416°C). Wire-belt conveyors are used primarily to move product or unit loads through processes that include liquid or chemical treatment, heat treatment, or kiln firing operations. Wire belts can be cleaned or sterilized while in motion. Mesh openings in the belt permit circulation of water, gases, heat, and cooling air. Typical uses for metal-belt conveyors include operations such as spray-washing glass containers, moving baked goods to ovens, conveying cathode-ray tubes through various processes, and moving hot forgings from automatic die casting equipment.

Tracking of a wire-mesh belt is a problem since the belt is formed by a number of different sections joined together and a wide range of temperatures used in processing operations causes expansion and contraction of the belt material. The conveyor specification must frequently include one of the following features to compensate for these conditions and assure straight belt tracking.

- Multitooth sprocket belt drive
- Belt aligners, consisting of pulleys or rollers mounted on the supporting frame

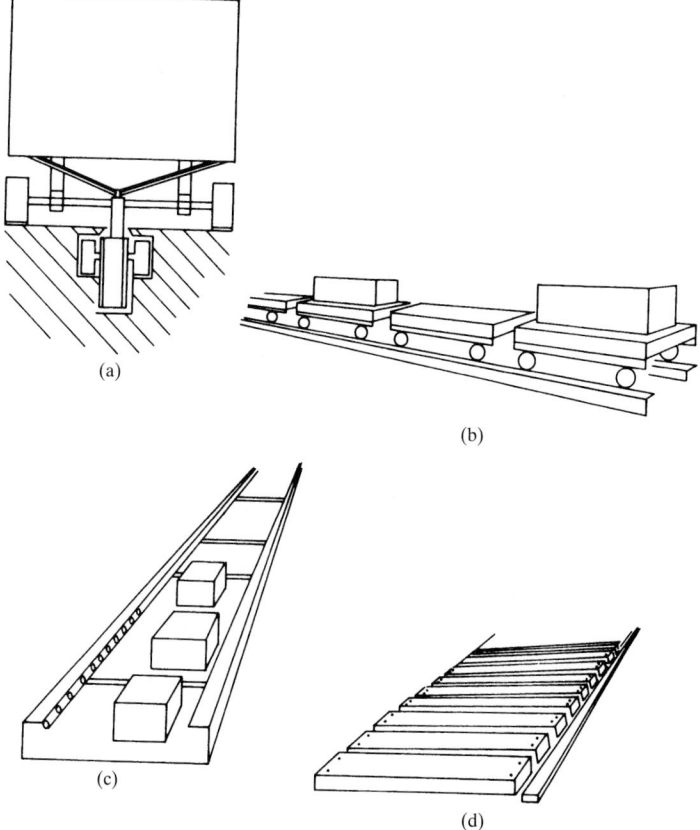

FIGURE 3-8 Types of conveyors. (*a*) In-floor towline, (*b*) trolley conveyor, (*c*) pusher bar conveyor, (*d*) slat conveyor.

- Self-tracking belt that has V-shaped wires on the underside that run through grooved driver drums

Surface Chain Conveyors.   Surface chain conveyors (Fig. 3-8) include sliding chain, pusher bar, slat, and tow types and car-type trolley conveyors.

Sliding Chain Conveyors.   These are the simplest type since they use the chain itself to convey packages down two sliding tracks. The conveyors are used to handle heavier loads than can belt conveyors, such as loaded pallets or unitized loads, but they have the same incline limitations as belt and powered-roller conveyors.

Pusher Bar Conveyors.   These are able to convey loads up steeper inclines (to 45°) because the load is pushed by a car connected to the chain drives and this arrangement moves the load along a metal bed or trough. Pusher bar conveyors are generally used for floor-to-floor movement in multistory warehouses or facilities.

Slat Conveyors.   These employ an endless chain to drive a conveyor surface of nonoverlapping, noninterlocking slats made of wood or metal. Slat conveyors can be used as moving work tables and to move heavy unit loads and are ideal for applications where the conveyor surface must be flush with a work station or with a floor surface. In the latter application, the installation will permit industrial trucks to cross over or be carried on the slat surface. Slat conveyors can be operated on inclines or declines, the angle of which is limited by the friction between slat surface and the load. Cleats may be added to support loads where steeper inclines are required.

Towline Conveyor. A towline conveyor uses an endless chain either supported from an overhead track or running in a track below the floor to tow trucks, dollies, or carts. The in-floor towline system is the type commonly found in warehouses. Existing building floors can be fit with towline by digging up the floor or mounting a rail on top, although it is preferable to install the system in the floor at the time the building is built. The recessed track allows the use of floor space for other equipment, but the track cannot easily be relocated once installed. It is truly versatile as it can be looped around storage areas, moved down aisles, and forked into spur sections for loading, unloading, and empty car storage. Switching onto spurs can be accomplished through the use of magnetic probes, radio-frequency signals, scanners, or mechanical switching. Carts and trucks used in this system can range from the ordinary pallet truck fitted with tow pins to engage with the chain drive to special carts or trucks.

Car-Type Trolley Conveyors. These employ an endless chain to pull a series of small cars or trolleys which carry the material to be moved. These often have fixtures to be used in assembly lines or contain molds for use in foundry processing operations.

Overhead Conveyors. Overhead conveyors include both trolley conveyors and power and free types of equipment. These conveyors are supported and function within a trolley track driven by a chain power drive to move parts or product. The path of the conveyor can be straight, inclined, declined, and around corners; it can make optimum use of building geometry and follow the general work flowpath within the limitations of building constraints and equipment design parameters. Conveyors can be supported independently or attached to existing beams and trusses, depending on the load factors involved.

In order to determine equipment design parameters, the following procedure should be followed.

1. From process flowcharts, determine all operations to be serviced by the conveyor.

2. Determine the path of the conveyor on a scaled plant layout (Fig. 3-9), showing all obstructions such as columns, walls, machinery, and work aisles.

3. Develop a vertical elevation view to determine incline and decline dimensions (Fig. 3-10). At this point a three-dimensional view could be prepared to give a multiplan view of the proposed installation.

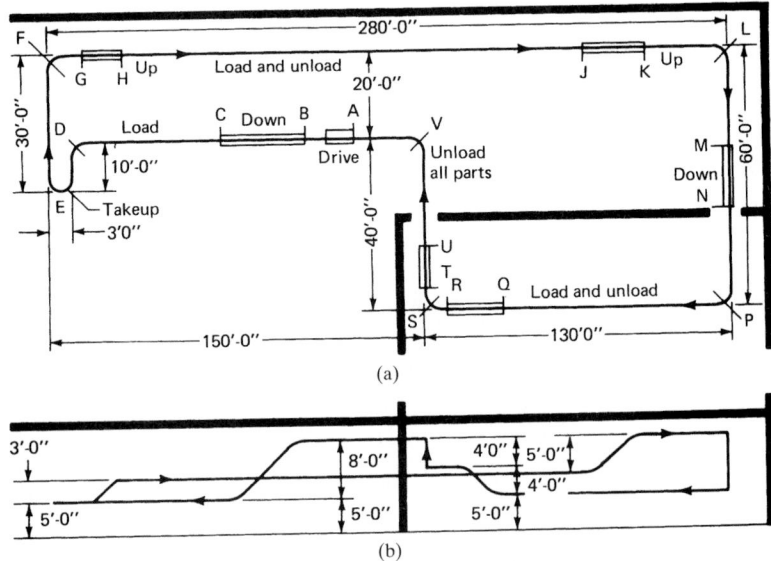

FIGURE 3-9 Plan and vertical elevation views of trolley conveyor system.

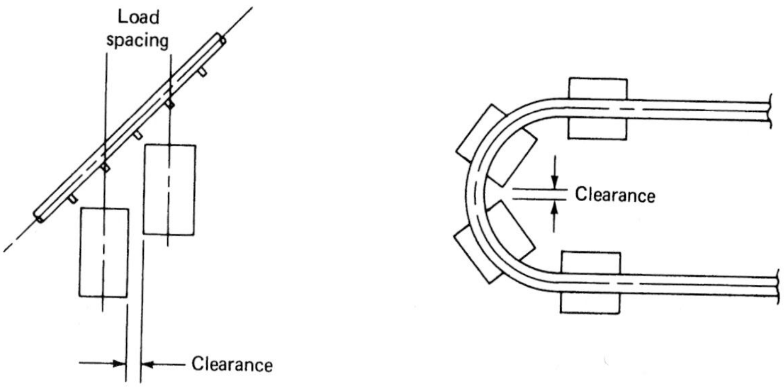

FIGURE 3-10 Load-spacing considerations for overhead conveyors.

4. Determine the movement rate, unit load size, spacing, and carrier design.
5. Modify turn radii to provide clearances that allow for desired clearance (Fig. 3-10) on turns.
6. Modify loading spacing to provide clearance on inclines and declines. As inclines and declines get steeper, load spacing has to be increased to provide a constant clearance or separation between loads. Table 3-4 shows the load spacing required for a given separation at various incline angles.
7. Redraw the conveyor path and vertical elevation views using new radii and incline information.
8. Compute the chain pull, which is the total weight of the chain, trolleys, and other components, as well as the weight of the carriers and load. For example, for a given system the tentative chain pull is calculated as follows:

TABLE 3-4 Load Clearance on Inclined Track for Overhead Conveyors

Load spacing, in	Incline angle, deg											
	5	10	15	20	25	30	35	40	45	50	55	60
	Horizontal centers, in*											
12	12	11⅞	11⅝	11¼	10⅞	10⅜	9⅞	9¼	8½	7¾	6⅞	6
16	15⅞	15¾	15½	15⅛	14½	13⅞	13⅛	12¼	11⅜	10⅜	9¼	8
18	18	17¾	17⅜	17	16⅜	15⅝	14¾	13⅞	12¾	11⅜	10⅜	9
24	24	23⅝	23¼	22⅝	21¾	20⅞	19¾	18⅜	17	15½	13¾	12
30	29⅞	29⅝	29	28¼	27¼	26	24⅝	23	21¼	19⅜	17¼	15
32	31⅞	31½	31	30⅛	29	27¾	26¼	24½	22⅝	20⅝	18⅜	16
36	35⅞	35½	34¾	33⅞	32⅝	31¼	29½	27⅝	25½	23⅛	20⅝	18
40	39⅞	39⅜	38⅜	37⅝	36¼	34⅝	32¾	30⅝	28¼	25¾	23	20
42	41⅞	41⅜	40⅜	39½	38⅛	36⅜	34⅜	32¼	29¾	27	24⅛	21
48	47⅞	47¼	46⅜	45⅛	43½	41⅝	39⅜	36¾	34	30⅞	27⅝	24
54	53⅞	53¼	52¼	50¾	49	46¾	44¼	41⅜	38¼	34¾	31	27
56	55⅞	55⅛	54⅛	52¾	50¾	48½	45⅞	42⅞	39⅝	36	32⅛	28
60	59¾	59⅛	58	56⅜	54⅜	52	49⅛	46	42½	38⅝	34½	30
64	63¾	63	61⅞	60⅛	58	55½	52½	49	45¼	41⅛	36¾	32
72	71¾	70⅞	69⅜	67¾	65¼	62⅜	59	55¼	51	46¼	41⅜	36
80	79¾	78⅞	77¼	75¼	72½	69⅜	65½	61⅜	56⅜	51½	45⅞	40

* 1 in = .02254 m.

$$\text{Total tentative chain pull} = 700 \times 60.0 \times 0.03 = 1260$$

where   700 = conveyor length, ft
          0.03 = coefficient of friction, %
          60.0 = 10.0 lb/ft (chain and trolleys) + 12.5 lb/ft (carriers) + 37.5 lb/ft (line load)

For this initial calculation, inclines and declines are assumed to be level sections if the number of declines balances out the number of inclines; however, for each additional incline, the weight has to be added to determine the total chain pull. If, in our example, a vertical incline that raises a load 8 ft is required, then the additional chain pull is

$$37.5 \text{ lb} \times 8\text{-ft lift} = 300 \text{ lb (136 kg)}$$

The total chain pull then becomes $1260 + 300$ lb $= 1560$ lb (707 kg).

9. Select tentative conveyor size based on trolley load and chain pull.

10. Select vertical curve radii.

11. Determine power requirements and drive locations. This requires a point-to-point calculation of chain pull around the complete path of the conveyor, which is shown in Fig. 3-9. The following three formulas are used to compute point-to-point chain pull.

   a. Pull for each straight horizontal run:

$$P_H = XWL$$

where $X = 0.02$ for standard ball-bearing trolleys
          W = total moving weight, lb/ft (empty or loaded, as the case may be)
          L = length of straight run, ft

   b. Pull for each traction wheel or roller turn:

$$P_T = YP$$

where $Y = 0.02$ for traction wheel or roller turn and P = pull at turn, lb.

   c. Pull for each vertical curve:

$$P_v = XWS + ZP + HW(1 + Z)$$

where $X = 0.02$ for standard ball-bearing trolleys
          W = total moving weight, lb/ft
          S = horizontal span of vertical curve, ft
          H = total change of level of conveyor, ft (plus, when conveyor is traveling up the curve; minus, when conveyor is traveling down the curve).
          $Z = 0.03$ for 30° incline; 0.045 for 45° incline; 0.06 for 60° incline; 0.09 for 90° incline
          P = pull at start of curve, lb

Drive horsepower may be calculated from the following formula:

$$\text{Drive hp} = \frac{\text{drive capacity (lb)} \times \text{maximum speed}}{33,000 \times 0.6}$$

12. Design conveyor supports and superstructures.

13. Design guards which are required by federal, state, and other codes under high trolley runs, particularly over aisles and work areas. Guard panels are normally made from woven or welded wire mesh with structural angles and channels to suit the size and weight of the material being handled.

   Power and Free Conveyors.   These consist of two separate trolley systems: one moves and is powered by a chain drive; the other has a track under the powered track that accommodates a free-moving trolley containing a carrier from which a load is suspended (Fig. 3-11). In

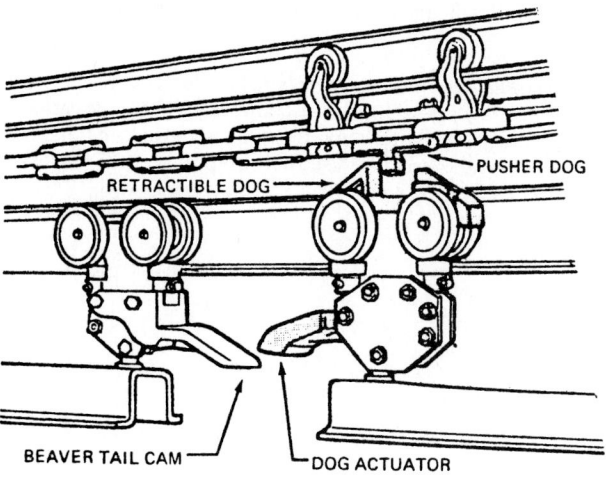

TRANSPORTATION MODE

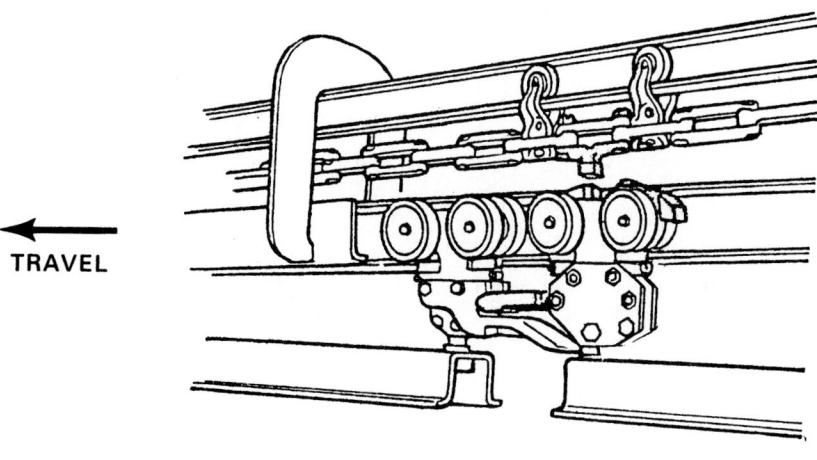

ACCUMULATED MODE

FIGURE 3-11 Power and free trolley.

the powered mode, the powered trolley is engaged with the free trolley through contact of a pusher dog on the powered system to a retractable dog on the free system. Disengagement is accomplished by contact with another load or by actuating the dog actuator. The system is extremely flexible since each carrier can be stopped or started without interrupting the system. This conveyor can be utilized in a process where operation times vary, or where units need to be accumulated into a batch before the next operation begins.

Two variations of the power and free conveyor, the inverted and side-by-side, have been developed recently to overcome some limitations of the original. To decrease the amount of vertical space needed for the two trolleys, a side-by-side system was created, where the powered trolley is located next to the load trolley. The inverted power and free conveyor mounts the tracks on the floor, with the free track above the powered track. This configuration permits work to be moved at assembly levels.

The same design criteria apply to power and free conveyors as to other chain-driven trolley systems.

Bulk-Materials Vertical Conveyors.   Bulk-materials vertical conveyors (Fig. 3-12) are generally used to lift bulk materials up to silos, hoppers, or other storage containers from which the material may be dispensed into a mixing, packing, truck-loading operation, or directly to a process. Some of the industries that use this equipment include glass, agricultural fertilizer, and powdered chemicals.

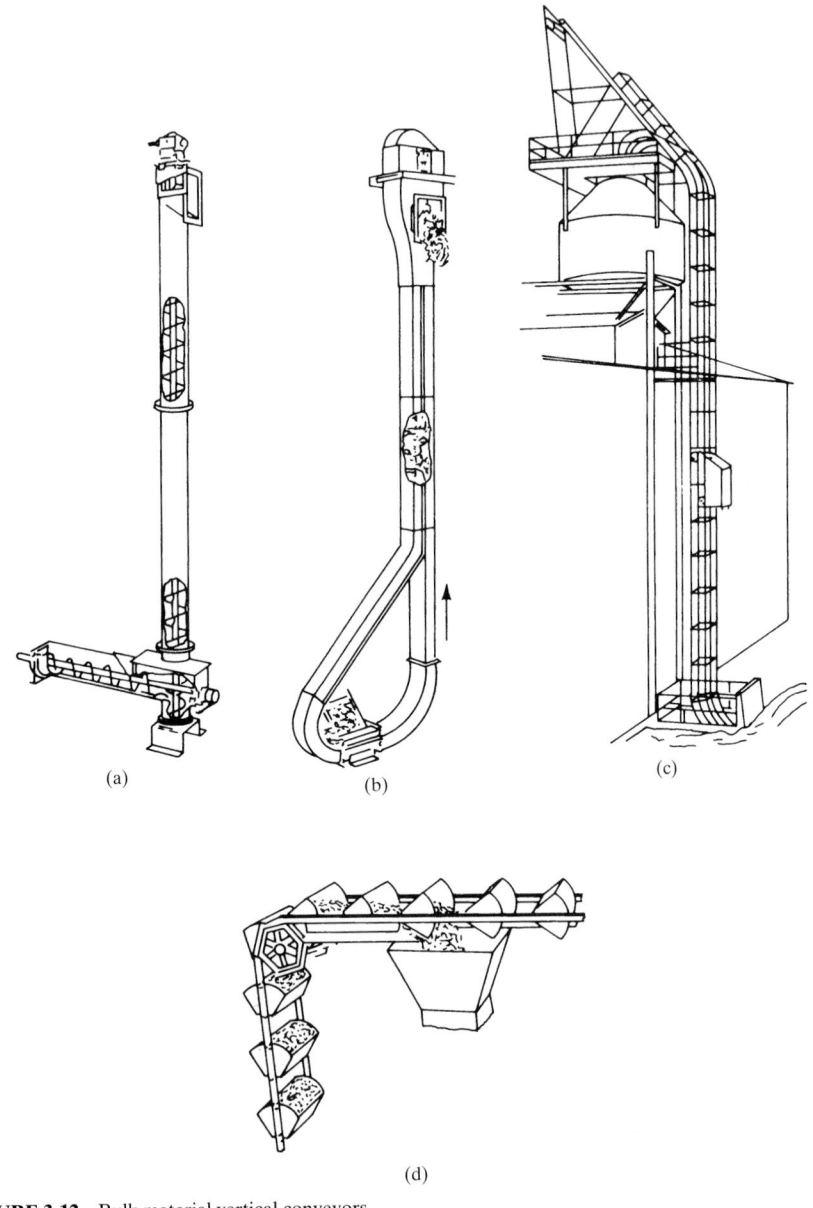

(a)   (b)   (c)

(d)

FIGURE 3-12   Bulk material vertical conveyors.

Skip Hoists.   These are used to lift bulk materials handled in batches to very high points. A bucket which carries the material moves vertically in guides and is raised and lowered by a hoist-operated cable.

Gravity Discharge Conveyor-Elevators.   These carry material in both horizontal and vertical paths. The buckets are rigidly mounted on two strands of chain running in tracks. Material is loaded into a bucket at the base of the equipment by feeding material into a lower trough, and discharge is effected when the bucket position changes in the horizontal run.

Bulk-Flos.   These lift material by the use of flights attached to a chain drive which is contained in a dust-tight casing. Bulk-Flos are self-feeding and -discharging and lend themselves to continuous bulk-material processes.

Rotor Lifts.   These are similar to screw conveyors but are mounted vertically to effect the lifting of bulk materials and are contained in a dust- and weatherproof casing. Screw feeders or conveyors are generally used to deliver material to rotor lifts.

Other Specialty Conveyors.   There are innumerable variations on standard conveying systems, some of which are unique to individual industries. Six common examples are described below.

Screw Conveyor.   This conveyor (Fig. 3-13) consists of a screw rotating in a stationary trough and the material moving along its length by rotation of the screw. This type of conveyor serves a dual purpose since it can also be used to perform processes such as blending and mixing of material while the material is being moved. The conveyor is generally enclosed

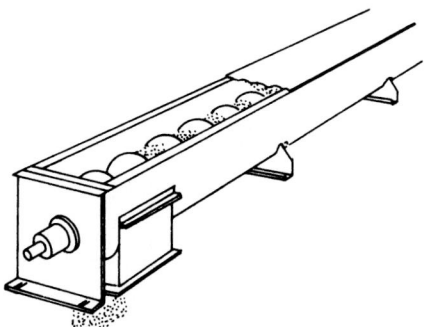

FIGURE 3-13   Screw conveyor.

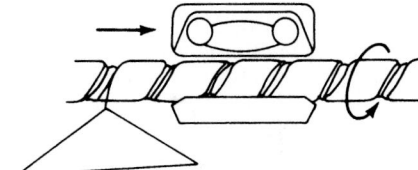

FIGURE 3-14   Spiral track conveyor.

to prevent dust or fumes from escaping and allow the conveyor to be cooled or heated. Loading or discharging can be located at any point along a conveyor.

Spiral Track Conveyors.   These conveyors (Fig. 3-14) consist of a continuous spiral track with a power drive which turns the track, moving anything which is hung on it. It has wide application in the garment industry. It is generally used for items weighing less than 10 lb (5 kg). Interlocking nylon wafers can permit turns to be made in any direction on a radius of 18 in (46 cm).

Oscillating and Vibrating Conveyors.   These use the natural frequency vibration of a trough to provide a conveying action to move material. Oscillating conveyors use a mechanically driven power train to move a trough carrying material against spring supports which provide a fast return and downward stroke, causing the trough to vibrate and convey the material. Vibrating conveyors utilize some form of magnetic pulsation to create this vibration motion. Wider variations of frequency are possible by simple control for vibrating conveyors, enabling speed changes compensating for material differences.

Application of both types of conveyors is growing in a number of different industries for uses such as: conveying light food products such as cereal in the food industry; moving, cooling, and breaking up lumps of casting sand in foundries; quenching and removal of glass cul-

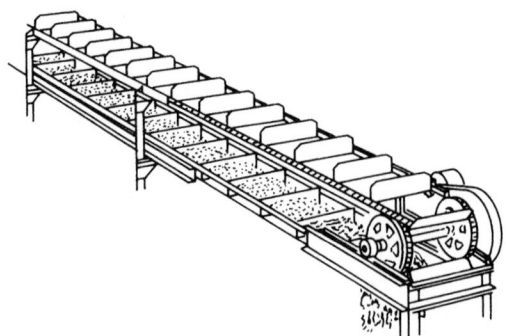

FIGURE 3-15 Flight conveyor.

let in water-filled troughs in the glass industry; removing ferrous from nonferrous materials in separation systems; and feeding small parts into automatic packaging or assembly equipment.

Flight Conveyors. These conveyors (Fig. 3-15) use scraper plates to push nonabrasive bulk material through a trough which can be horizontal or inclined.

Apron Conveyors. These conveyors use a series of interlocking apron pans supported in a stationary frame for conveying materials that are heavy, abrasive and lumpy, such as ore, stone, industrial refuse, and waste materials.

Pneumatic Tubes. These use a pressure or vacuum system to move materials or a container at relatively high speed. The major application is that of an internal mail carrier, although it can also be used to move certain types of high-volume fine particulate.

Monorails. A monorail is usually an overhead system on which carriers transport materials from one point to another on a track. Unlike trolley conveyors, each carrier is independent and the system can be powered or unpowered. A powered system, or automated electrified monorail (AEM), requires two rails like power and free, but each carrier is equipped with an electric motor that draws energy from an electrified rail. The monorail system can be designed with spurs, and carriers can travel forward or backward, eliminating the need for a closed loop. This equipment can also travel small vertical inclines without any assistance, and can be equipped with a drive chain to climb steeper slopes.

An AEM is suitable for use in most industries since monorail carriers can carry up to 10,000 lb (4545 kg) and travel up to 600 ft/min (3 m/s). For example, a transmission assembly plant uses monorails in all stages of assembly and testing, with assembly occurring directly on the carrier. In an AEM system, the carriers often have sensors or microprocessors on board to communicate to a central computer about its position, type of load, and even diagnostic data. Generally, monorails are given only the intelligence that is necessary so that factories beginning to automate can incorporate monorails into their system. As expansions are necessary, carrier and/or additional track can be added without disrupting the existing process.

SORTING, CONSOLIDATING, AND DIVERTING DEVICES

A materials-handling system must frequently have the ability at some point to identify, sort, and divert parts, products, or unit loads. Peripheral accessories and equipment do this, ranging from simple mechanical diverters to sophisticated optical recognition reading devices, which can actually read and identify alphanumeric characters and sort 20,000 items per hour and which are used mainly for check and mail handling. Whatever the complexity of the system, three basic elements must be considered: identification of the item to be sorted or consolidated, recognition of the item, and the command to activate the mechanisms to divert the item.

Simple Mechanical Sorting. Simple mechanical sorting utilizes inherent differences such as size, shape, weight, or other physical differences to identify or recognize items; it generally is

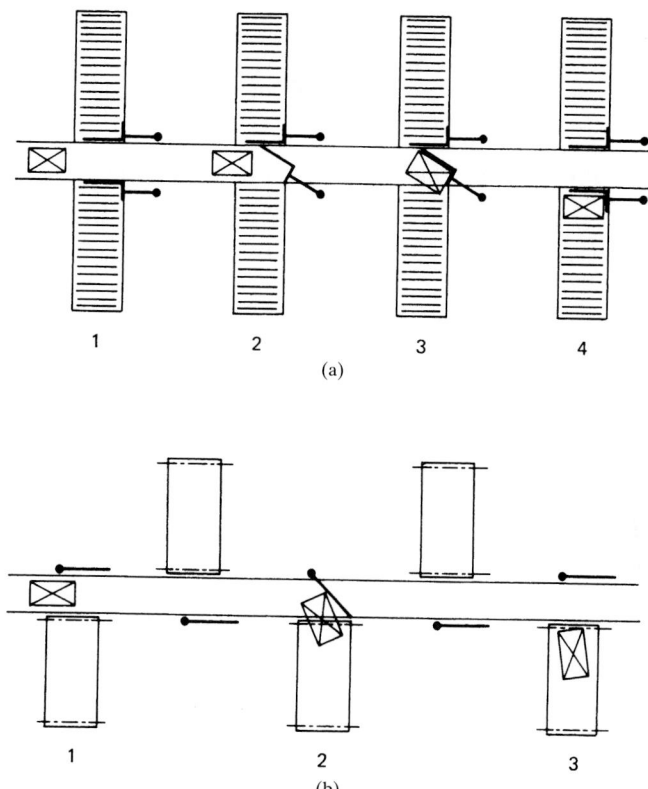

FIGURE 3-16 Diverting mechanisms.

contact sorting in which an item must make contact with a channel or feeler guides or discerns physical differences and contacts a cam or other simple mechanism to activate a diverter chute or other diverting device.

Diverting Mechanisms.   Diverting mechanisms can be grouped into devices that deflect, push off, drive off, or tilt; many variations are included within each group (Fig. 3-16).

Electromechanical Sorting.   Electromechanical sorting uses noncontacting identification devices that can sense both inherent differences and applied differences. These are identified on the load or package by a code that can be discriminated by a sensing or scanning device and that triggers a diverting mechanism.

    Photosensors.   These are the most commonly used sensing and scanning devices. A photoelectric control consists of a light source, photoreceiver, amplifier, and output. A beam of light from the light source activates the photosensitive elements of the photoreceiver which produces an electric signal, which drives a relay to activate the diverting mechanism. When used as a sensor, photoelectric controls can be used to:

- Sense the presence or absence of containers or products on a conveyor
- Detect over- and undersize products
- Sort products by size
- Count items

Photoelectric controls can also be arranged in an array or ganged in a manner that a code on a container can be read. Each sensor that goes into the scanning device will detect a specific mark or blank space from the code which when scanned produces binary information into a logic function of a controller. This in turn supplies a signal for the diverting mechanism. Typical codes are ladderlike in format, and this allows a scanning device to read the code vertically.

Automatic Identification.   Automatic identification refers to the ability to track materials in the factory through the use of semi- or fully automated technologies. Most common is bar code technology, which employs a scanner swept across the bar code and has been in use for 20 years. The bar code, which is a series of black bars of varying thickness and approximity, is used to identify the product. The human eye is not able to decipher the bar code, but a scanner can identify the product easily, since bar codes were designed for computers. Scanners can be hand-held wands, laser guns or a moving-beam laser scanner. A hand-held wand must touch the bar code whereas several inches may separate the laser gun and code. Moving-beam laser scanners are ideal for reading bar codes on items being transported on a conveyor. The scanner is mounted in a location where it can emit a beam searching for the barcode.

Optical character recognition (OCR) is an alphanumeric character set which can be read by a special scanner, and can be read by humans. However, OCR technology is less reliable and more costly than bar coding. A compromise between the two is placing a label next to the bar code. An emerging technology is radio-frequency identification devices (RFIDs), which use a read-only tag fastened to a unit load to emit radio signals. When the signals are received by the computer, the contents of the load are identified. Some companies are experimenting with installing RFIDs on the carrier of a trolley and bar codes on the unit load to integrate tracking of materials and conveyor systems.

Palletizers.   Palletizers receive individual packages, cases, or bags from a conveyor and automatically arrange them on a pallet in a predetermined pattern with the required number of tiers. Each tier need not have the same predetermined pattern. Generally, units to be stacked are received on a control belt at the entrance to the machine. At this point the unit will be counted and oriented depending on the patterns required. As each row is completed, a pusher moves the cases onto an apron. When the tier is completed, the apron is withdrawn, depositing the tier on the pallet or tier below. The operation is repeated until the pallet load is completed, when it is discharged and replaced with an empty pallet.

Large volumes of standard units are required, and it is estimated that palletizers become economical when approximately 900 units per hour require palletizing. The larger palletizers can handle in excess of 6000 cases per hour of certain products.

Depalletizers.   Depalletizers are highly specialized pieces of equipment which automatically depalletize cartons and cases. Automatic squaring mechanisms permit the handling of loose pallet loads. Depalletizers generally operate in the range of 3500 cases per hour and are seen primarily in beverage distribution.

HOISTS AND CRANES

Hoists and cranes are materials-handling equipment used to move varying loads intermittently within a fixed area. The loads vary in size and weight and are not uniform. Most of the materials movement is devoted to raising and lowering loads, although some units are so constructed as to permit them to travel laterally over a specific area. The types of hoists, cranes, and attachments are listed below.

Hand and Powered Hoists.   Hand and powered hoists (Fig. 3-17) are the most basic and economical lifting equipment which enables an operator to move a large load, up to 50 tons (45,360 kg), vertically by using some kind of mechanical advantage.

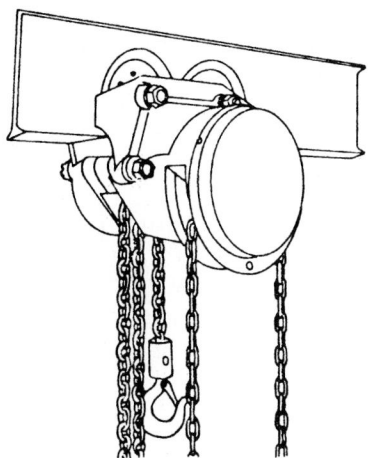

FIGURE 3-17   Hoist.

Jib Cranes.   Jib cranes (Fig. 3-18) consist of a hoist that is mounted on a boom track. The hoist mechanism can be moved laterally in the track and the boom can be turned in an arc limited by the building restrictions or the mounting arrangement of the boom. Jib cranes are classified into basic groups of bracket jib, cantilever jib, and pillar jib. Load capacities range from small manually operated cranes to loading towers that exceed 300 tons (272,160 kg).

Bridge Cranes.   Bridge cranes consist of a hoist mounted on a guider bridge which is supported by two trucks on each end and rides on runways supported by building members. Top-running bridges, where end trucks ride on top of runway tracks are able to support a total bridge and load weight of hundreds of tons, but underhung or bottom-running bridges, where the trucks are suspended from the lower flanges of the runway track, normally are used for loads less than 20 tons (18,144 kg). Bridge cranes can be operated manually or powered or in the cases of very large cranes can be operated by remote control (Fig. 3-18).

Gantry Cranes.   The gantry crane is very similar to a bridge crane except it is supported by self-contained vertical support members that travel in tracks on the floor surface and it is generally used where overhead runways are not feasible due to building restrictions. The gantry crane system also has the advantage of being usable in outdoor operations without the construction of an expensive supporting structure (Fig. 3-18).

Stacker Cranes.   The stacker crane consists of a rigid mast suspended from an overhead bridge that travels laterally. A platform or a set of forks moves up and down on slider bars to lift and lower loads. The stacker crane is most commonly used to place or retrieve loads to and from racks from both sides of an aisle. In automatic storage and retrieval systems, the stacker crane is computer-controlled. The computer has the rack location of each item stored in the memory and is able to command the load-carrying platform to a specific location for storage and retrieval of a load.

Lifters.   A lifter (Fig. 3-19) is an attachment suspended from the load hook of a hoist or crane that permits a load to be handled more easily or quickly than possible with a hook, and many load configurations cannot be handled with a hook. In many cases, lifters are designed for a specific application, but there are many standard types that are available for a wide range of applications. Lifters are categorized by the method in which the load is carried.
   Supporting Lifters.   These carry the load on the surface of the lifter, on bearing surfaces of cradles, or hooks and slings attached to lifters.
   Clamping Lifters.   These hold the load by surface friction or by squeezing load.
   Surface-Attaching Lifters.   These consist of both magnetic or vacuum types. Magnetic lifters can use either a permanent magnet that requires a strip-off device to release the load or an *on-off magnet* that can be activated by applying a voltage. Vacuum pads can be used to lift loads with nonporous and smooth surfaces and are commonly used to handle glass and aluminum.
   Manipulating Lifters.   These move the load through one or more axes for operations such as positioning or dumping.

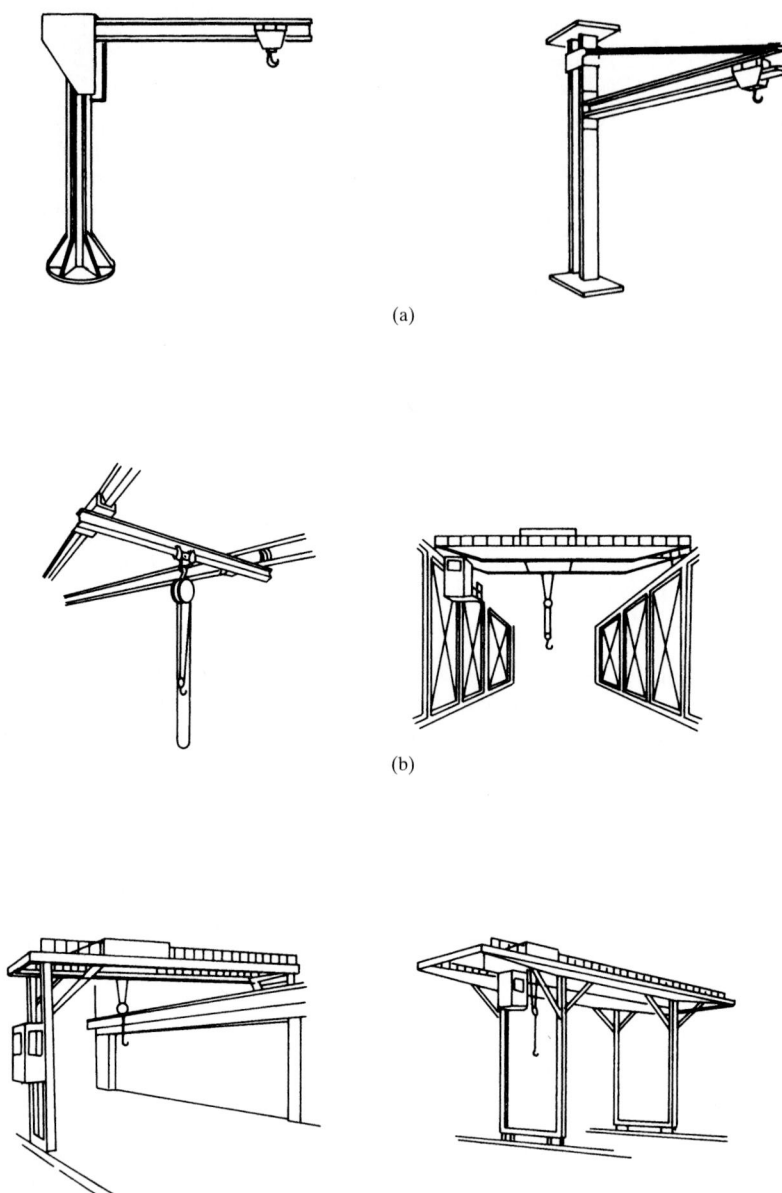

FIGURE 3-18   Types of cranes. (*a*) Jib crane, (*b*) bridge crane, (*c*) gantry crane.

AUTOMATIC GUIDED VEHICLES

Automatic guided vehicles move material over fixed paths but do not require the use of an operator or a mechanical drive train located below the floor surface or an overhead towline. They are useful when a variety of materials must be moved over long distances to and from a variety of fixed destinations. There are three identifiable types of vehicles: first, the driverless

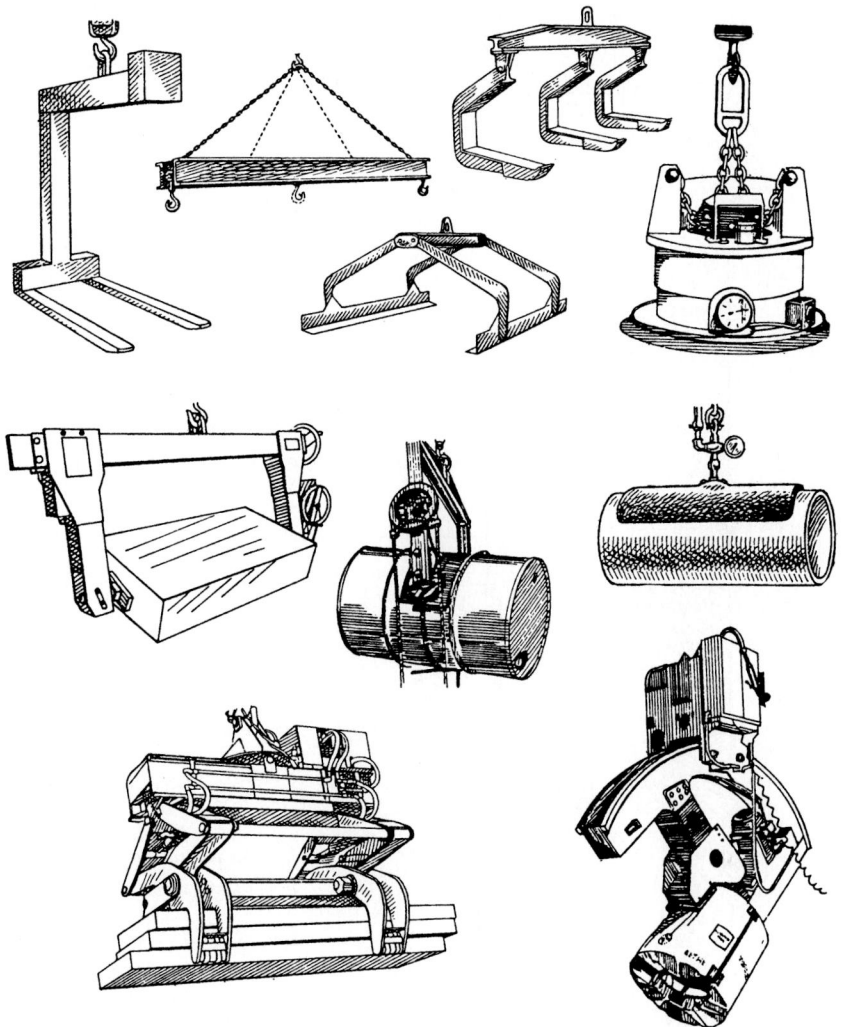

FIGURE 3-19 Types of lifters. (*Reproduced with permission from Material Handling Engineering Handbook and Directory, 1977/1978, published by Material Handling Engineering, Cleveland.*)

tractor (Fig. 3-20) which hauls trailers or cartloads of material; second, the individual unit-load or pallet mover (Fig. 3-21); and third, the multishelved self-contained vehicle. The last type is used primarily to move mail in office buildings or for food and supply deliveries in hospitals.

Guidance and Control Systems. Guidance and control systems are similar for all three systems. Two systems are used: optical, where the unit follows a line taped or painted on the floor surface; or magnetic, where a thin wire is set in a shallow channel sealed over in the floor. This latter system is less flexible and more costly to control but is not subject to obliteration or wear, which can be a problem in certain factory environments.

The driverless tractor, being unable to reverse on its own trailers, generally requires a closed-loop system. However, multiple-loop systems can be used. Unit-load movers are generally reversible and can operate on a spur.

The programming information which determines the paths and stops can be preset on the tractor programmer or can be controlled from a central dispatching point. These systems generally have the logic to allow the tractor to take the shortest route to the destination without traveling through the entire loop. Radio-control-transmitters are often used to reposition the train within a loading station, eliminating unnecessary walking in operations such as order picking or loading the train at the receiving dock.

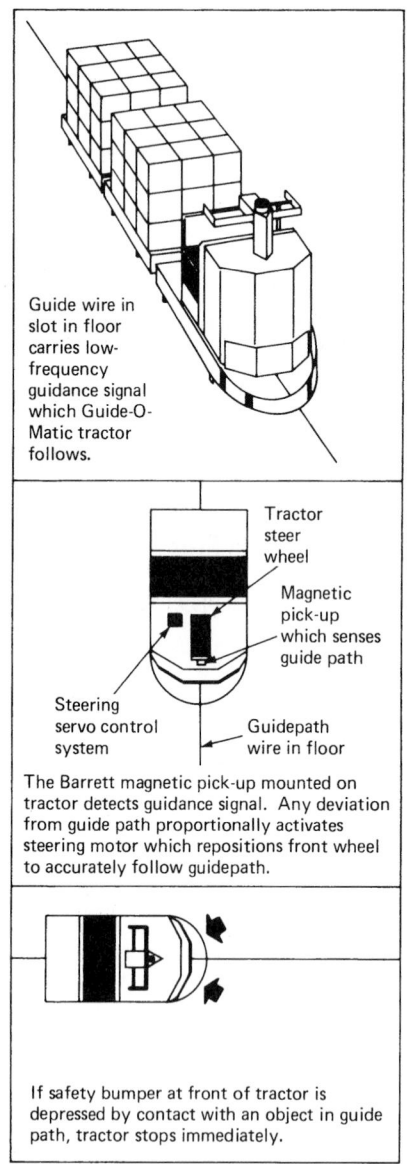

Guide wire in slot in floor carries low-frequency guidance signal which Guide-O-Matic tractor follows.

Tractor steer wheel

Magnetic pick-up which senses guide path

Steering servo control system

Guidepath wire in floor

The Barrett magnetic pick-up mounted on tractor detects guidance signal. Any deviation from guide path proportionally activates steering motor which repositions front wheel to accurately follow guidepath.

If safety bumper at front of tractor is depressed by contact with an object in guide path, tractor stops immediately.

FIGURE 3-20 Typical features of a driverless tractor system.

Loading and Unloading.   Although all vehicles can be loaded and unloaded with operator assistance, both tractors and unit-load movers can have automatic load and unload features. The tractor-trailer arrangement can have an automatic uncoupling option. More common are options whereby the trailers have rollers on the carrying surface and the loading-unloading stations where a pusher can be used to move the load. Similar systems can be used for unit-load movers, sometimes using powered roller systems. More common is the lifting device established in Fig. 3-21. This has particular potential in manufacturing operations where materials can be brought directly into the work station.

Routes are dependent on surface conditions. Cracked and broken slab can cause discontinuity in the tape or wire guides. Inclines and declines within a plant must be considered, in which case an acceleration or deceleration feature must be specified for the equipment. External routes linked with automatic door control, internal traffic lights, and automatic ramps to cover rail lines have been used. However, external use of this equipment is not widespread, and external surfaces must be prepared very carefully, especially in regions where snow and ice are involved.

Safety.   Driverless tractors are available with many more safety options than any other automatic conveying system and include such features as encounter detection, sonic detectors, and optical detectors, which will all shut the tractor down if an object is detected in the path. Additional safety devices include a strobe light, siren, and panic buttons which can override all other controls. Using warning signs and placing mirrors at corners and blind spots are good preventive measures and so is keeping the tractor speed below 5 mi/h.

ROBOTS

Robots are programmable machines capable of automatically moving individual parts or objects over precise paths in space.[1] A robot can also be programmable so that it is able to move parts

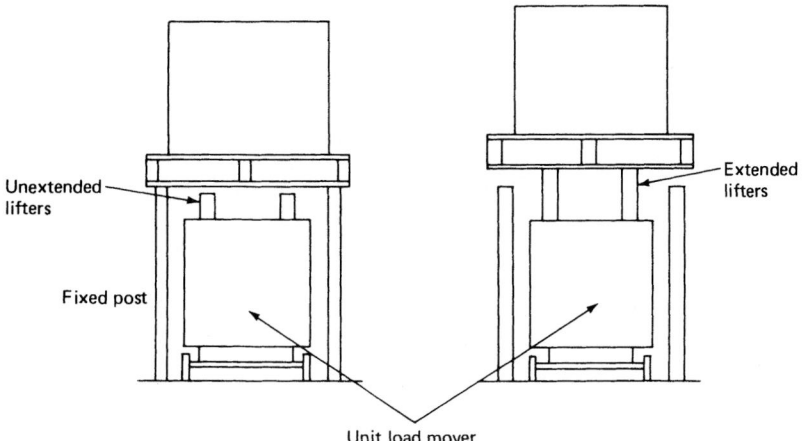

FIGURE 3-21   Individual unit load or pallet mover.

through different paths, capable of performing repetitive motions, able to duplicate the movements of the human arm by moving parts through four axes in space.

Applications.   Present applications related to materials handling include machine loading and unloading, conveyor transfer, and pallet loading. The most practical applications for materials handling will be those areas that require repetitious manual operations, particularly those involving the interface between workers and machines. Robots are also ideal for these types of operations in poor working environments, such as those where heat, cold, fumes, or radiation exposure is present. Painting and welding are typical major potential application areas.

Design Components.   Robots (Fig. 3-22) are available with a wide range of capabilities and in various design configurations. The major components include a manipulator which actually performs an operation and moves parts, a controller that stores data and directs the movements of the manipulator, and the energy source to power the robot.

A sophisticated robot with six axes of motion can perform many of the same movements as the shoulder, elbow, and wrist. Simpler, less expensive units with two degrees of freedom, called *put-and-place units,* are typically used for machine loading and should become widely used in the materials-handling field in the next decade.

Manipulator.   The handling of objects by the manipulator is facilitated by the use of tools that give the robot "hand" capability. The general categories for this purpose are either grippers or surface-lift devices.

MECHANICAL GRIPPERS.   These grippers (Fig. 3-23) are usually movable fingerlike levers paired to work in opposition to each other. They can be thought of as mechanical equivalents of the thumb and forefinger.

SURFACE-LIFT DEVICES.   These can include simple forklift attachments, vacuum pickups (Fig. 3-24), hooks, or magnetic devices.

CONTROLLER.   The controller initiates the motions of the manipulator through a sequence at the desired points and stops the motion when required. The controller can be programmed by adjustment of mechanical cams, stops, and limit switches on the simpler types of put-and-place robots. The more sophisticated robots can be "taught" a sequence of movements by an operator. In the teaching mode, the programmer manually moves the manipulator through the motions of the operation, and the coordinates of the path are stored in the controller memory.

Energy Sources.   Nonservo, or *pick-and-place* robots operate through activation of a hydraulic or pneumatic system and are the simplest, lowest-cost units. They have limited flex-

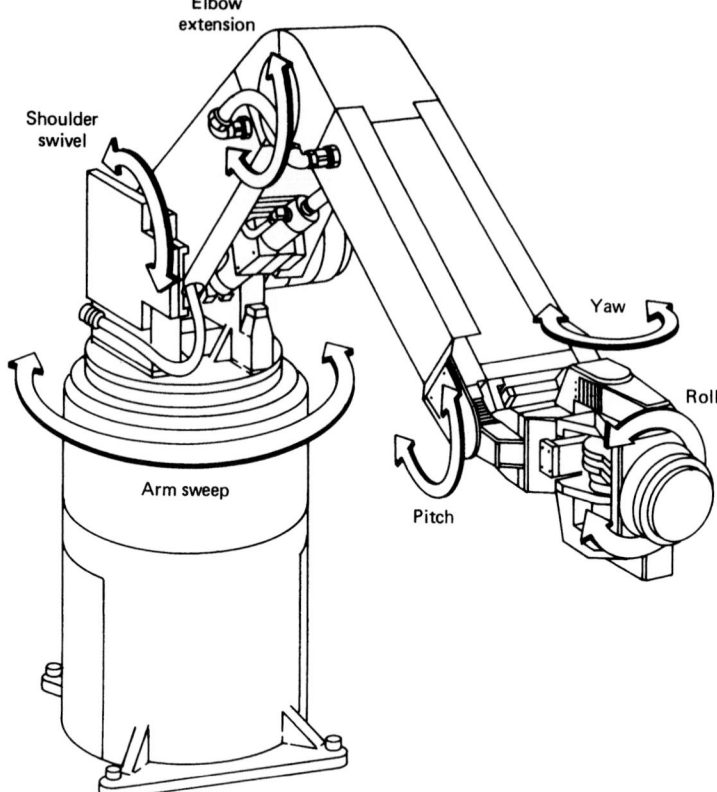

FIGURE 3-22 Robot with six axes of motion.

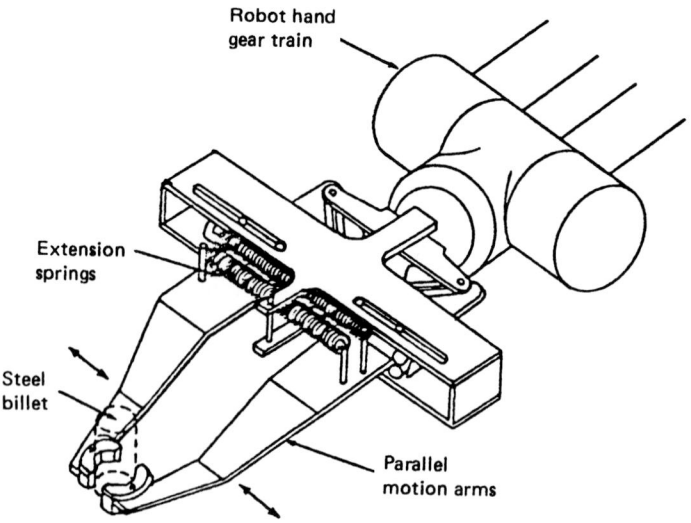

FIGURE 3-23 Robot grippers equipped with spring-loaded fingers.

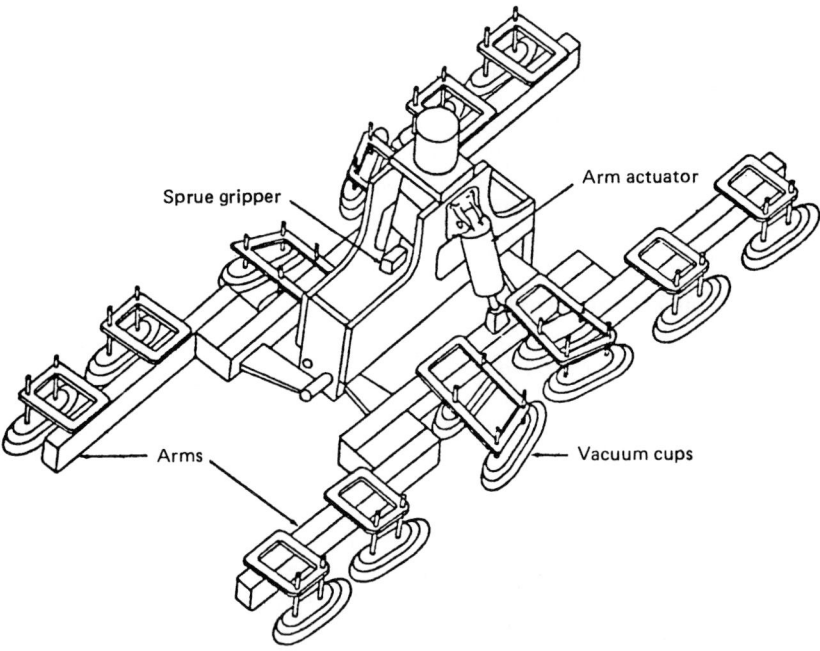

FIGURE 3-24   Vacuum pickup device for robot.

ibility in terms of program capability and positioning capability but are highly reliable. In the operation of this type of robot, as the sequence is indexed, the manipulator members move until the present limit of travel is reached. Since there are only two positions for each axis to assume, programming can be done by adjusting the end stops for each axis to establish the operation sequence.

Servo-type robots use servo motors or valves to move the manipulator members and can be further classified into either point-to-point or continuous-path types. *Point-to-point* servo robots are programmed or taught by feeding them manipulator-position data at discrete points and, in performing a task, they will internally select a path to that point. *Continuous-path* servo robots are programmed or taught to follow a precise path and are used for operations where movement is important, particularly in spray painting.

Future Developments.   *The technology of robots will be expanded in the future to include the capability to discriminate differences in objects by optical- or mechanical-sensing devices* which would send a feedback signal to the controller which will make a decision to initiate a movement command to the manipulator. Further future developments include speech recognition for robot programming and three-dimensional optical-sensing devices. Also, while robots now in operation are generally large, floor-mounted units, future robots will also include table-mounted units able to assist in small subassembly and final assembly operations.

Planning Considerations for the Use of Robots.   There are four points that must be considered when evaluating the feasibility of using a robot in materials handling. They are rate of handling, weight of the object, orientation of the object, and number of different items to be handled.

Rate of Handling.   Robots are not high-speed handling equipment. If the handling rate is greater than 15 items per minute, another approach should be considered.

Weight of Object.   The weight-handling capacity of robots is presently 500 to 2000 lb (227 to 907 kg), depending on the type of robot. The heavier the load, the lower the handling rate.

Orientation of the Object. Position of the object is important and should be consistent. A primary limitation of current robots is the precise orientation required of parts to be picked up by the robot and, hence, a feeding or positioning mechanism to the robot itself is often required.

Number of Items to be Handled. Setup time for product changes can be reduced by quick changeover grippers and automatic program selecting capability. In cases where dissimilar parts are handled in the same operation, a multipurpose gripper or "hand" should be used, along with a sensing device that can command the robot to switch to a preset program.

REFERENCES AND BIBLIOGRAPHY

1. Tanner, W. R.: *Industrial Robots,* Vols. 1 and 2, Society of Manufacturing Engineers, Dearborn, Mich., 1979.

2. *Automated Storage/Retrieval Systems Planning Guide,* Clark Handling Systems, 525 W. 26th St., Battle Creek, MI 49016

3. *Automated Storage/Retrieval Systems Justifications,* Clark Handling Systems 525 W. 26th St., Battle Creek, MI 49016.

4. Industrial Robots, *Modern Material Handling,* April 1980.

5. Salvendy, G.: *Handbook of Industrial Engineering,* Wiley, New York, 1992.

6. "Towline conveyors," *Material Handling Engineering,* February 1991.

7. "Power and free means flexibility," *Material Handling Engineering,* April 1992.

8. "How to evaluate and plan for warehouse automation," *Material Handling Engineering,* March 1992.

9. "Monorails deliver the goods," *Plant Engineering,* March 7, 1991.

10. "Automated electrified monorails," *Material Handling Engineering,* April 1990.

CHAPTER 8-4

MOBILE MATERIALS-HANDLING EQUIPMENT

K. W. Tunnell Co., Inc.
King of Prussia, Pennsylvania

INTRODUCTION

The group of equipment that is described as mobile materials-handling equipment is made up of machines that essentially depend on a self-contained power source for movement and are independent in their movement route. The equipment, being self-contained material movers, provides a flexible, relatively inexpensive transportation link between plant activities. This broadly classified group of equipment includes devices and equipment from the simplest two-wheeled hand truck to highly sophisticated movers controlled by computer-based systems.

Within the mobile materials-handling equipment group there is a wide array of general-purpose and specialized material movers. Basically, there are two broad categories of mobile equipment. The powered equipment depends on a built-in power source for its operation. The unpowered device relies on a detachable prime mover, either a piece of powered equipment, or in many cases, the equipment operator. The least complex equipment provides transportation between two points without positioning or lifting capabilities. Other units lift or roughly position the load being transported as well as move the material. The multiple-axis movers transport the load; they also have a position capability along two or more axes to accomplish loading and unloading.

Generically, mobile materials-handling equipment falls into five groups, each of which will be discussed in this chapter:

1. Floor trucks and operator-powered movers

2. Powered lift trucks

3. Burden carriers

4. Tractors and tractor trains

5. Mobile industrial cranes

APPLICATION CONSIDERATIONS

Equipment Utilization and Selection

From available records, it appears that mobile equipment often has a low level of utilization. Powered equipment is often employed well beyond its economic life, generating penalty costs in spare-parts inventories, maintenance, and productivity.* Five to seven years has been calculated to be the average economic life of a powered vehicle, provided proper maintenance has been performed. Keeping a lift truck beyond the optimal time increases maintenance costs by 30 to 40 percent. Proper operator training, which is required by the U.S. Occupational Safety and Health Administration (OSHA), can improve efficiency and reduce maintenance costs as well. By tracking costs and utilization, it is possible to reduce the size of the lift truck fleet. Often, two old lift trucks can be replaced with one newer model.

Other general considerations in establishing equipment requirements include:

- Unit-load condition and size and center of load
- Terrain, environment, and aisle width in the movement area
- Length, type, and frequency of moves
- Positioning requirements of load(s)
- Operating economies and maintenance
- Standardization of equipment
- Critical nature of operation(s) serviced

Factors in Wheel Selection and Use

Solid Wheels.   These are made in semi-steel, forged steel, or molded plastic, hard rubber, and composite materials. They should be limited to small diameters and low-speed movement and should not be used to transmit power. They have low resistance to roll, but a short life span when overloaded or subjected to rough floor conditions. They will cause load vibration because of a lack of cushioning.

Rubber-Cushioned Tired Wheels.   These consist of a metal wheel having a machined diameter onto which a rubber tire is pressed or molded. It has the lightest load-carrying capacity of those used on mobile equipment. Minimal power is required to move material, since rolling friction is minimized.

Oil-Resistant Tired Wheels.   The tires are made of special oil-resistant rubber compounds which will resist the degrading effects of oil on rubber.

High-Traction Tired Wheels.   The tires are made of rubber impregnated with abrasive or other materials to give additional traction on ice or in wet conditions.

Low-Power Tired Wheels.   The tires are fabricated from rubber compounds that offer minimum roll resistance and have lower power requirements, causing less drain on battery-operated equipment.

Nonmarking Tired Wheels.   The tires use a rubber compound filler other than carbon to avoid floor marking and contamination.

Conductive Tired Wheels.   The tires avoid the chance of static sparking in hazardous or explosive environments by maintaining vehicle-to-floor conductivity.

Laminated Tired Wheels.   The tires for these wheels are made up of sections of pneumatic tire carcasses threaded onto a steel band. Such tires are extremely tough, with a harsh ride. They are well suited to littered environments, such as scrap yards, and trash handling.

Polyurethane Tired Wheels.   Though more expensive than rubber, these wheels have a significantly higher load-carrying capacity and are less susceptible to cuts than most rubber

---

* "Use the Optimum Economic Life to Help Cut Costs," *Modern Materials Handling,* February 1991.

and rubber-compound wheels. Wheel hardness of polyurethane tires results in a harsher ride and increased plant floor damage.

Inflatable Tired Wheels.   These wheels have vulcanized, reinforced rubber tires similar to automotive tires. The tires are both tube and tubeless. They generally carry a lower load rating for their size than solid-tire wheels. Their use will provide greater load cushioning, higher speed capability, easier maintenance, and less floor damage.

Factors in Internal-Combustion-Engine Selection and Use

Internal Combustion Engines.   These are used in outdoor applications, in well-vented interiors, and in nonhazardous environments. They are generally powered by gas or liquid propane gas, although compressed natural gas (CNG) is a promising alternative. In anticipation of new government regulations, manufacturers are redesigning engines with reduced emissions and improved fuel efficiency.

Industrial Engine.   Typically, this heavier engine is designed to operate in a lower rpm range than an automobile engine. It can be expected to give about 10,000 h of useful life before overhaul. At an equivalent operating speed of 20 mi/h (32 km/h) in an automobile, this would equate to 200,000 mi (321,800 km).

Automotive Engine.   This is of lighter construction than the industrial engine and, because of the quantities in which it is produced, is of relatively lower cost. It generally operates most efficiently in a higher rpm range than the industrial engine and can be expected to give about 7000 h of useful life prior to overhaul. This life is equivalent to about 140,000 mi (225,260 km) of automobile travel. An advantage of this type of engine is the availability of replacement parts through automotive supply firms.

Air-Cooled Engine.   This is restricted to lighter-duty applications where weight, size, and initial cost are the prime concerns. The absence of a separate cooling system is a distinct advantage, although this engine's life expectancy is a relatively short 1500 to 2000 h of operation.

Diesel Engine.   Typically, this type is installed in large pieces of equipment where the additional size and cost is not significant. However, because of recent improvements in engine design, diesel engines are becoming more prominent in smaller trucks. This is largely due to the reduced need for periodic maintenance, greater fuel economy per hour of operation, and longer expected life—up to 20,000 h.

Compressed Natural Gas Engine.   This engine design is ideal for indoor use due to its low noise and low emissions. CNG is a low-cost fuel and the truck can run a full shift before requiring fuel. Other benefits include fewer oil changes and lower maintenance costs. This truck is suited for most types of use and can accommodate loads up to 6000 lb (2700 kg).

Factors in Battery-Powered-Vehicle Selection and Use

Battery-Electric Equipment.   This is mechanically simpler in design than engine-driven equipment. Typically, the high-torque dc electric-drive motor is coupled directly to the drive axle through a constant-mesh drive train. An electronic silicon-controlled rectifier (SCR) speed-control device regulates the motor's revolutions per minute through operator foot control. Direction is reversed electrically with a delay interlock to avoid reversing motor direction while in motion.

Storage Battery.   These must be replenished frequently either by recharging or by exchanging them for fully charged batteries. Batteries used in a given piece of equipment should provide ample power to operate effectively for an 8-h day as determined by their ampere-hour (Ah) rates. The Ah rating, to some degree, limits the effective operating range of battery-operated equipment and requires that routine schedules for replenishment are followed. Also, because of the weight of a large storage battery, equipment application is sometimes adversely limited.

Advantages of Battery Vehicles.   The advantages are low fume emission and heat contamination, quietness and cleanliness, and generally lower maintenance requirements.

Types of Batteries. The two primary types of batteries used are lead-acid and nickel-iron-alkaline. A lead-acid battery will provide 2.0 to 2.3 V per cell, while the nickel-iron-alkaline battery will provide 1.2 V per cell. Voltages used for modern battery-powered mobile equipment are 12, 24, 36, 48, and 72, with some higher voltages used in larger equipment.

Advantages. The advantages of the lead-acid battery are a lower initial cost, high ampere-hour capacity, and low resistance to self-discharge. The nickel-iron-alkaline battery is desirable because of its longer life expectancy, resistance to physical damage, noncorrosive electrolyte (KOH), and more rapid and less critical recharge rates.

Recharging Times. These are adjusted for different batteries by dividing the Ah rating of the battery by the 8-h Ah rating of the charger and multiplying by 8. For example, a battery having a 600-Ah rating and a 450-Ah charger will require

$$(600 \div 450) \times 8 = 10.64 \text{ h}$$

FLOOR TRUCKS AND OPERATOR-POWERED MOVERS

This type of equipment is the most fundamental materials-handling aid available. The basic simplicity permits easy adaptation for single-purpose application. Standard catalogs indicate the wide variety available, often designed for specific industries. However, custom design may be specified with very little, if any, cost penalty.

Generally, floor trucks are described as follows.

Two-Wheeled Hand Trucks. Two-wheeled hand trucks (Fig. 4-1) are essentially levers on two wheels. The axle connecting the wheels serves as the fulcrum of the lever and carries up to 80 percent of the total load moved. The two-wheeled cart is normally used for short nonrepetitive moves of smaller loads over smooth floors. Carts are generally 48 to 64 in (1.2 to 1.6 m) high, and are designed to carry a variety of materials in bags, barrels, bales, boxes, and bins. Typical accessories include height extension, stair climbers, safety brake, spread clamps, and straps.

Dollies. Dollies are smaller-wheeled platforms upon which a load is placed for short distance and intermittent moves. Typically, dollies are fitted with caster-type wheels and are either pulled or pushed by an operator.

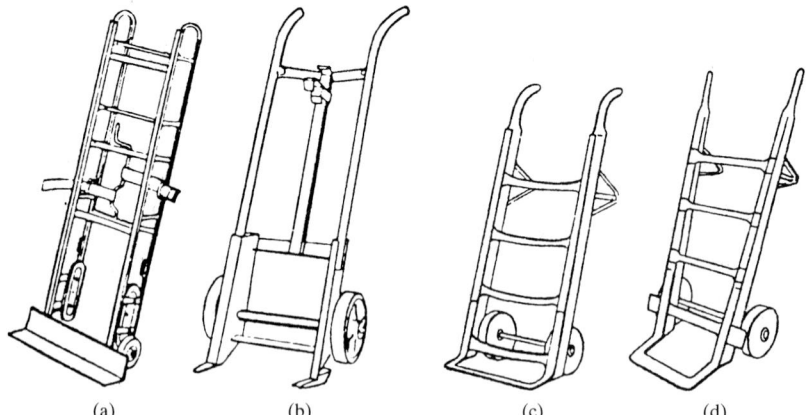

(a)　　　　(b)　　　　(c)　　　　(d)

FIGURE 4-1 Two-wheeled hand trucks. (*a*) Appliance type, (*b*) drum and barrel mover, (*c*) general type with Western handle, (*d*) general type with Eastern handle. (Reproduced with permission from *Material Handling Engineering Handbook and Directory, 1979–1980,* published by *Material Handling Engineering* magazine, Cleveland, Ohio.)

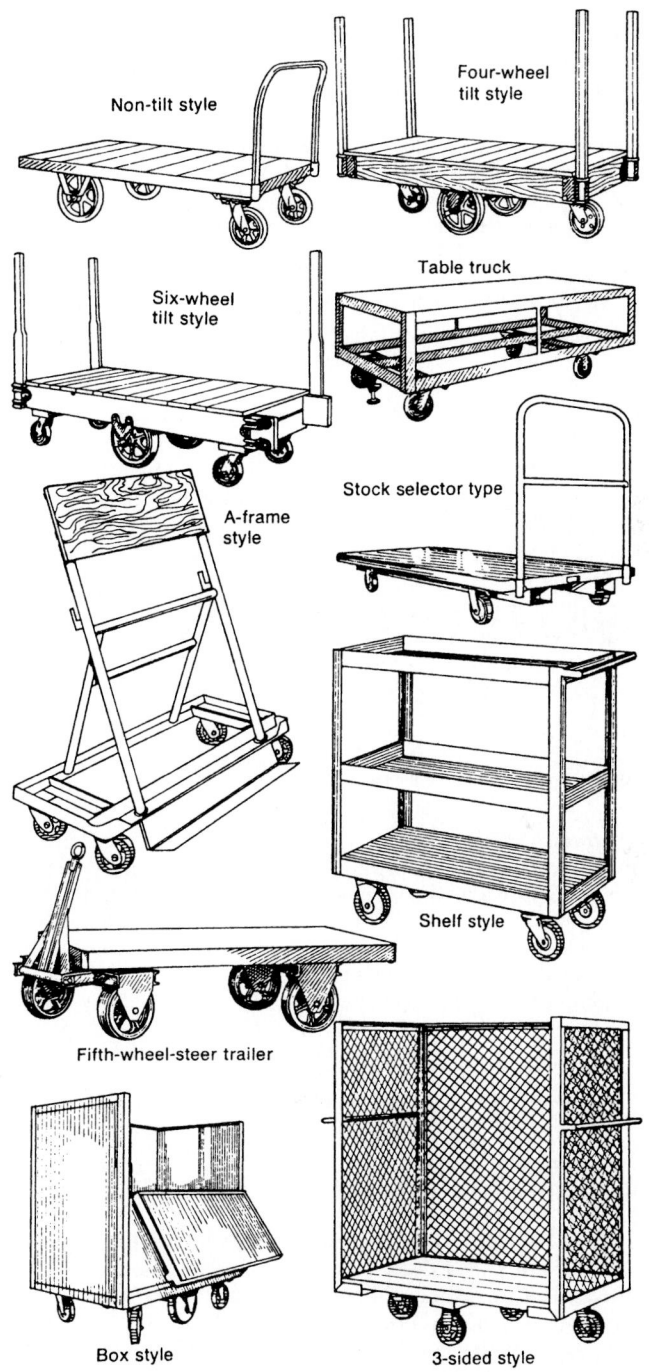

FIGURE 4-2 Factory trucks and wheel arrangement patterns. (Reproduced with permission from *Material Handling Engineering Handbook and Directory, 1979–1980,* published by *Material Handling Engineering* magazine, Cleveland, Ohio.)

Factory Trucks.   Factory trucks (Fig. 4-2) are wheeled platforms or containers either moved by an operator or towed by detachable power units. There is a wide variety of devices in this group and an even wider variety of uses for materials movement and as mobile storage.

The hand factory truck is hand-powered, guided by the direction of the moving force, and closely related to the dolly. Several wheel-arrangement patterns are available with tradeoffs between maneuverability and stability.

The towed factory truck is connected to the prime mover by a tow bar which provides the steering direction. Both two-wheel and four-wheel steering are available on towed factory trucks. Two-wheeled steering is generally the least expensive and most commonplace. Because of the steering geometry involved, each truck will follow a turn of shorter radius than the preceding vehicle. As several of these units are connected in trains, the continual tightening of turns requires more space for maneuvering.

The four-wheel-steered truck, with properly adjusted steering, is capable of following the same path as the vehicle in front of it. Where long trains are economically justified and desirable, the four-wheel-steered devices may be used to minimize commitment of valuable manufacturing space to aisles.

The Semilive Skid.   The semilive skid is a rectangular platform or box having two wheels on one end and two fixed supports on the other. The end having the fixed supports is also fitted with a heavy pickup pin to which a two-wheeled jack is attached. The jack and handle are used as the lifting device and tiller, allowing the skid to be maneuvered by the operator.

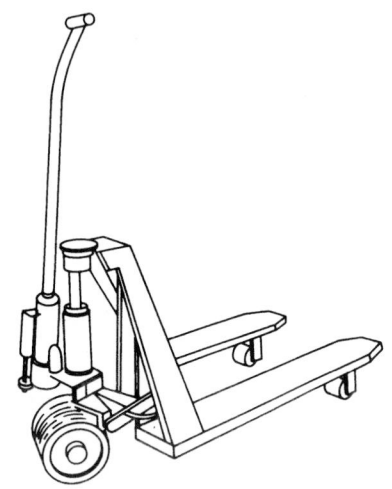

FIGURE 4-3   Hydraulic-lift truck.

Hydraulic-Lift Trucks.   Hydraulic-lift trucks (Fig. 4-3) are used for short distance moves at the workplace. They generally range in capacity from 2500 to 8000 lb (1130 to 3625 kg). These trucks require a minimum amount of maintenance, and can last for 20 years.[2] The trucks can be equipped with a jacklike manually operated hydraulic lift or pedal operated system to elevate a loaded pallet. Some units use an electrically driven hydraulic system to lift, often above the maximum 5 in of the manual system. These lift trucks generally use forks for lifting pallets or platforms for special containers and positioning heavy loads.

POWERED-LIFT TRUCKS

This equipment group represents what is probably the largest and most varied of equipment for materials handling. The powered-lift truck owes its popularity to its versatility, being able to easily pick up a unit load, transport it quickly in a variety of environments, and then position the load vertically at almost any point within the capability of the equipment. Depending on the volumes involved, they become less economical for moves over 300 ft (90 m) since rated speeds are generally between 5 and 10 mi/h (7 and 14 km/h). Powered lift trucks are usually fitted with lifting forks to carry a unit load, although a wide variety of special load-carrying attachments can be used in place of forks. Power for lift trucks is either by internal-combustion engine or battery electricity.

The various pieces of equipment in this group can be operated over a variety of terrains, depending upon the design and, specifically, the wheel and tire combination used. Load-carrying capacities from 1000 to over 40,000 lb (450 to 18,000 kg) are common. Large vehicles are available with capacities in excess of 100,000 lb (45,000 kg). The very large vehicles are generally used outside, particularly for the moving and stacking of shipping containers.

Establishing aisle widths and their relation to fork-truck selection are critical when significant storage areas are involved. Clearly, the narrower the aisles, the more rows of storage. Equipment manufacturers have been ingenious in designing specialty trucks to operate in narrow aisles. It should be noted that manufacturers specify equipment turning circles and, thus, aisles will require space to aid in fork-truck maneuverability. Specialty trucks designed to operate in narrow aisles permit better space utilization, but tend to trade off some aspect of performance, a factor to be considered in specifying specialty as opposed to general-purpose equipment.

Truck capacity is generally calculated as follows (see Fig. 4-4):

A = distance, in, from center of front axle to heel of fork

B = distance, in, from heel of fork to center of load

C = distance $(A + B)$ from center of front axle to center of load

D = length, in, of load on fork

W = weight of load, lb

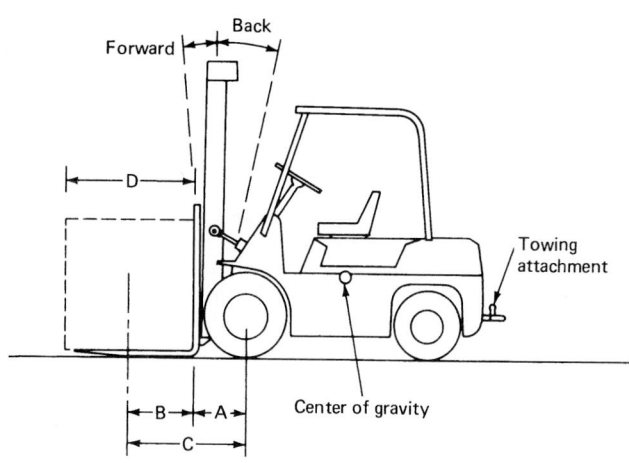

FIGURE 4-4   Rated truck capacity and counterbalanced truck.

1. *Inch · pound rating*

$$\text{Inch} \cdot \text{pound rating} = W \times C$$

2. *Maximum load length for given load*

$$C = \frac{\text{inch} \cdot \text{pound rating}}{W}$$

3. *Maximum load for given load length*

$$W = \frac{\text{inch} \cdot \text{pound rating}}{C}$$

A specific example is given to illustrate the actual calculations.

1. Truck is rated 3000 lb (W) at 20 in [3000-lb load which has a center 20 in (B) from heel of fork].
2. Distance from center of axle to heel of fork is 10 in (A).
3. Pallet load to be handled is 2000 lb:

$$C = A + B = 10 + 20 = 30 \text{ in}$$
$$\text{Inch-pound rating} = W \times C = 3000 \times 30 = 90,000 \text{ in} \cdot \text{lb}$$
$$C = \frac{\text{inch} \cdot \text{pound rating}}{W} = \frac{90,000}{2000} = 45 \text{ in}$$
$$B = C - A = 45 - 10 = 35 \text{ in}$$
$$D = 2 \times B = 2 \times 35 = 70 \text{ in allowable load length}$$

4. When selecting attachments, refer to the truck manufacturer to determine the amount of negative effect the attachment has on the truck's useful load-carrying capacity.

Aisle widths are generally established as follows:

A = aisle width
TR = turning radius of truck
L = load length
C = aisle clearance (total on both sides)
AX = distance from rear corner of load to centerline of axle:

$$A = TR + L + C + AX$$

The several varieties of powered-lift trucks are described below.

Counterbalanced Trucks. The counterbalanced trucks (Fig. 4-4) use their large, carefully positioned weight mass to offset (counterbalance) the moved load mass. These trucks are generally equipped with a tilting mast which will "tilt" the lifting mechanism rearward from the vertical lifting position and further counterbalance the load during movement. The load is positioned fully in front of the truck so that the truck structure does not interfere with adjacent stacks of material. This minimizes the aisle widths that are required.

Straddle Trucks. The straddle trucks (Fig. 4-5) differ from the counterbalanced type in that they do not depend on weight mass to counteract the weight of the load being handled. Instead, the straddle forklift positions the two main load-carrying wheels at or forward of the material load center. The truck is extremely stable as a result of this arrangement.

The straddle design is more compact and of lighter weight than the counterbalanced type. It is necessary, when negotiating loads into or out of racks, that either the straddle truck be equipped with an extending fork mechanism (pantograph) or the racks be positioned or constructed to allow the forward wheels of the truck to enter them.

Side-Loading Trucks. Side-loading trucks (Fig. 4-6) are a unique combination of a straddle-lift truck and a narrow-aisle truck. They are used where there are narrow aisles, where rapid transportation is called for, and where long narrow loads such as pipe and bar stock are handled. Side-loading trucks do not have to be turned to engage or place loads.

Nonrider Lift Trucks. Nonrider lift trucks (Fig. 4-7) are those where the operator walks along with the truck, directing the operation through a control unit attached to the truck. These units have basically the same features found in larger counterbalanced and straddle trucks. They are used for lifting and stacking light loads and moving these loads short distances.

Straddle Carriers. Straddle carriers (Fig. 4-8) are large-capacity, highly maneuverable, powered lift trucks. To load and unload, the vehicle is driven over the unit load(s). The actual loading and unloading is extremely fast, although precise positioning of loads requires other methods. Unit loads can be transported at rates approaching highway speeds.

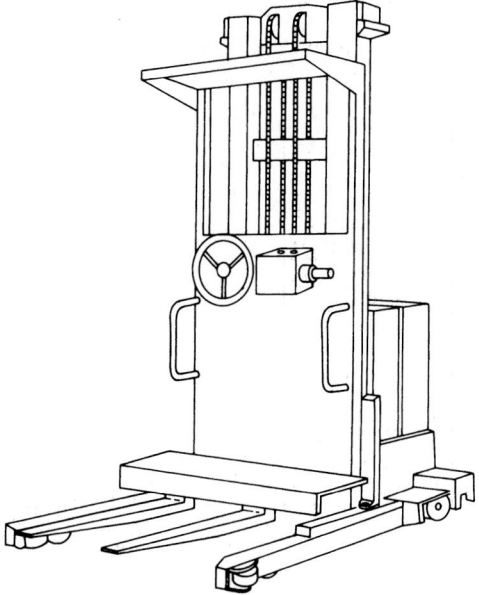

FIGURE 4-5   Straddle truck.

Order-Picker Trucks.   Order-picker trucks have an elevated platform forward of the mast from which the truck and the platform can be operated. Typically, the trucks are used for picking partial loads in narrow aisles to heights of 24 ft, allowing for significant labor and space saving.

Materials-Handling Attachments

The most widely used attachments are the forks themselves. They can be set at various widths and generally range between 30 and 60 in (80 and 160 cm) in length. The forks should be at least two-thirds the length of the maximum load to be lifted.

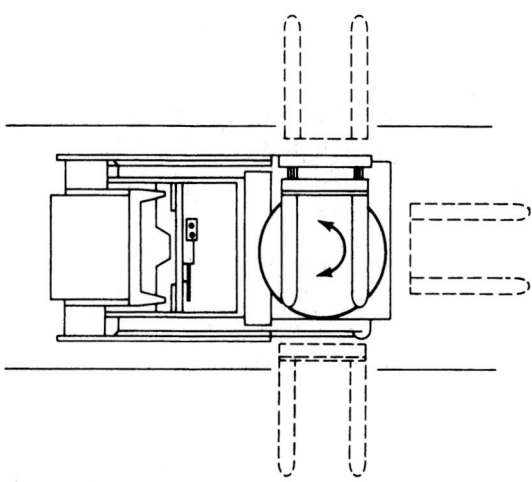

FIGURE 4-6   Side-loading truck.

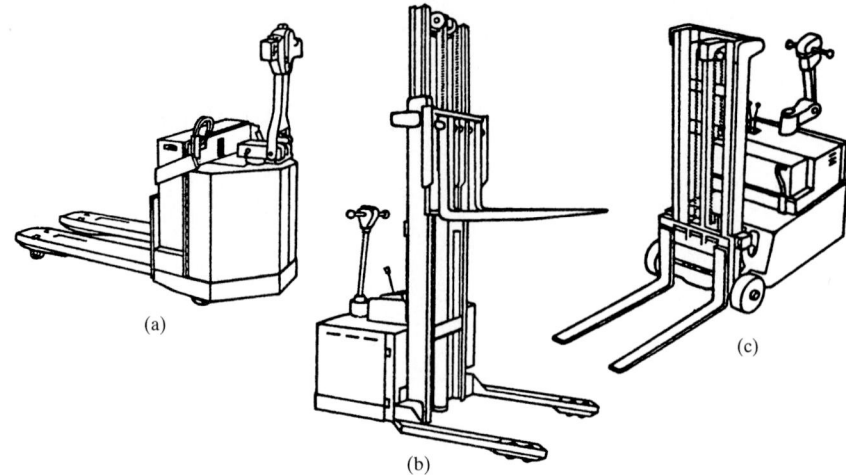

(a)

(b)

(c)

FIGURE 4-7 Nonrider lift trucks. (Reproduced with permission from *Material Handling Engineering Handbook and Directory, 1979–1980,* published by *Material Handling Engineering* magazine, Cleveland, Ohio.)

Standard two-stage uprights provide a lift height of approximately 18 ft (5.5 m), and three- and four-stage uprights provide heights to 20 ft (6 m). Certain specialty vehicles are designed to operate above 20 ft (6 m). The difference in fork height and total extended height is generally 4 ft (1.2 m), reflecting the height of the backrest. For low buildings, *free-lift* trucks should be specified. This feature permits the forks to be raised to lift loads to nearly half the total lift height without extending the uprights.

Frequently, a forklift truck will be fitted with an attachment or combination of attachments which allows the vehicle to perform special handling functions or simply allows it to operate more efficiently in a given situation. In some cases, these attachments replace the conventional forks for handling products which the forks cannot. In other instances, the attachments are used to augment the original fork function by giving the load-carrying forks additional motions.

When selecting attachments, it is always wise to consult with the truck manufacturer since attachments have a negative effect on a truck's useful load-carrying capability. When attachments are installed, the truck's information plate must be restamped, indicating the new effective truck capacity as required by OSHA 1910.178(4).

Attachments usually limit a forklift truck to a specialized function and, to some extent, limit its overall in-plant versatility. Some of the more simply designed attachments mount on the fork attachment rails and require only a few minutes to install or remove. The more complicated attachments, particularly those requiring hydraulic connections, should be considered as permanent conversions.

The following is a list and a brief description of some of the more common attachments (Fig. 4-9):

1. *Ram.* A single projection, mounted in place of the forks for carrying coiled materials which can be easily entered horizontally. Rams have a variety of lengths and diameters to handle a variety of products, from steel coils to rolled carpet.

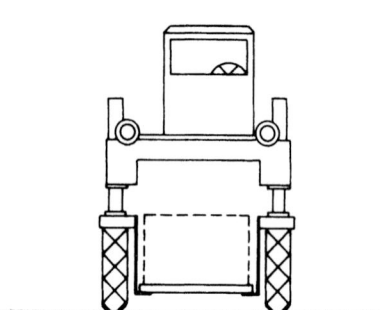

FIGURE 4-8 Straddle carrier.

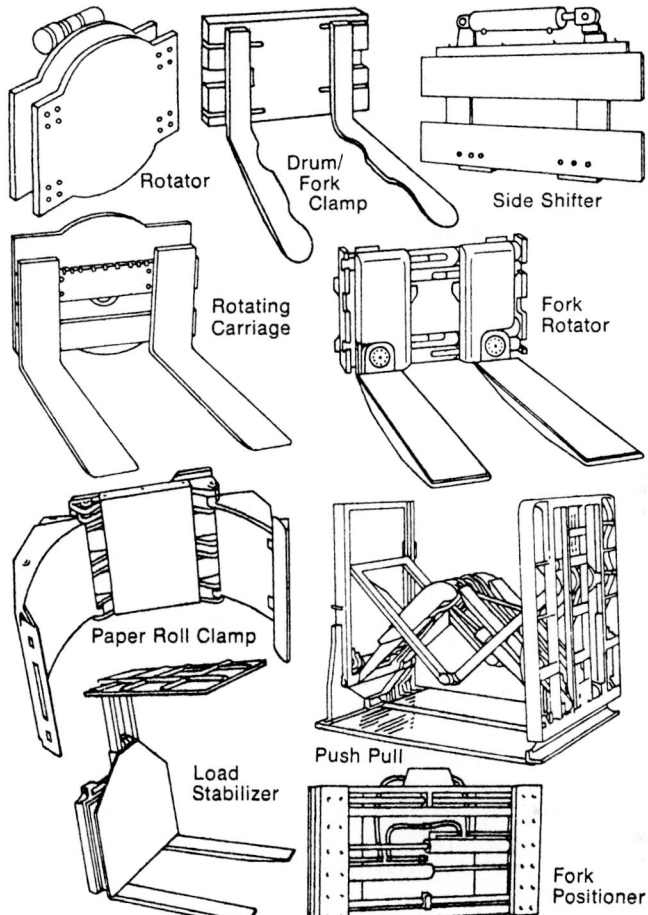

FIGURE 4-9 Common materials handling attachments. (Reproduced with permission from *Material Handling Engineering* 1979–1980, published by *Materials Handling Engineering* magazine, Cleveland, Ohio.)

2. *Barrel attachment.*   Used to grasp the top seam of a steel drum and transport it in the vertical position.

3. *Concrete-block fork.*   This and the similar brick fork are designed specifically for handling stacks of masonry products without pallets.

4. *Paper-roll clamp.*   Specifically designed to carefully grasp and transport rolled materials in the vertical position. It is frequently combined with a rotator which allows the roll to be carried horizontally in the case of loosely rolled or easily damaged materials.

5. *Push-pull.*   Uses a polished platen instead of forks to carry the load. Its purpose is to position loads in dense environments without the use of a pallet. In place of a pallet, a thin slip sheet is used under the load. This sheet is grasped by hydraulic clamps and pulled into the truck platen for loading and pushed off again into its next position.

6. *Bale clamp.*   Used to grasp and carry baled materials and depends on hydraulic pressure to grasp the bales from the sides.

7. *Scoop.* Used to handle loose or granular bulk material and consists of a metal bucket mounted in place of the fork, with a dumping capability usually provided. Tilting the bucket for loading and transport is accomplished by tilting the lift truck's mast forward and back.

8. *Squeeze clamp.* Used to grasp the sides of boxed products in a manner similar to the bale clamp, except that the grasping arms are smooth and deliver an even pressure to the carton to avoid damaging its contents. This device eliminates the need for pallets. It requires, however, additional side clearance on each side of the material moved to accommodate the clamps.

9. *Top-handling lift.* Used to handle folded cartons by hooking into the folded lip of the top carton. The most important advantage is that extremely high storage density can be accomplished since only minimum side clearances are required without the use of either pallets or slip sheets.

10. *Side shifter.* Used with almost any type of attachment as well as forks, the side shifter allows loads to be positioned accurately from right to left without relocating the truck. Its major function is to speed the positioning of loads and to minimize rack space between loads. The side shifter will also reduce wear on the truck itself by reducing repositioning.

11. *Adjustable forks.* Where a variety of pallet and load sizes are encountered, adjustable forks are used. While most fork arrangements are manually adjustable, the mechanically adjustable forks allow the operator to accomplish the operation while remaining in the driver's seat.

12. *Load stabilizers.* To assure that loosely arranged and unstable loads are firmly contained during transit, various load stabilizers are available. Such a device is essentially a vertical clamp which exerts a downward pressure on a load and thus holds it in position while it is being moved.

13. *Clamping forks.* Similar in design to the fork positioner, clamping forks can be used to pick up loads in a conventional manner or may be used to clamp loads between the forks. This device is quite commonly used with special notched forks for transporting drums.

14. *Rotator.* The use of a rotator allows a load to be rotated through 360 degrees, generally for dumping. The rotator is used with unit-load devices that fully enclose the forks and thus remain attached to the fork during rotation. They are also used with various clamping devices when rotation is required.

15. *Extended-reach forks.* Commonly used with straddle forklifts to enable the truck to reach a load in the racks while the forward wheels remain outside of the rack space. The attachment also allows racked materials to be reached when two-deep storage is used. The reaching mechanism consists of a hydraulically operated pantograph system between the truck mast and the forks.

BURDEN CARRIERS

In the manufacturing process where sufficient volumes are involved, conveyor systems are often used to move materials from point to point. When smaller volumes or several moves of varying density are involved, however, a fixed-platform device is often used. These fixed-platform vehicles depend on an auxiliary loading and unloading method and are not tied to a specific unit-load module. Such devices are called burden carriers.

Burden carriers come in a wide variety of sizes and shapes. They are available in two basic types (Fig. 4-10). One is the walkie (nonriding) type and the other is the riding type. Both are available with battery-electric and internal-combustion power sources. They are usually limited in load-carrying capacity. High loads are generally handled by other types of handling equipment.

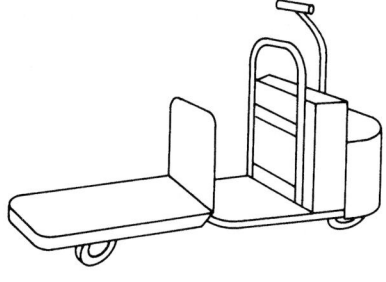

Walkie Burden Carrier. The walkie burden carrier is typically a three-point suspension hauler using battery-electric power, although some units are available that are powered by a small air-cooled engine. They are similar in design to the previously discussed walkie lift trucks, except that they have a fixed platform. Load ranges of 1000 to 3000 lb (450 to 1360 kg) are available and application is limited to non-contained loads. Loading is generally done by hand or, in the case of heavier loads, by hoists and cranes.

Rider Burden Carrier. The rider-type burden carrier is often tailored to a variety of special applications such as personnel carriers, fire trucks, and portable maintenance shops. In its simplest form, the truck provides a driver's seat and a flat load-carrying bed. In this configuration it serves most commonly as a miscellaneous hauler to deliver supplies and materials in-house for distances of more than 300 ft (90 m). The power source for the rider-type truck is fairly evenly divided between air-cooled gasoline engines and battery-electricity. Both three-point and four-point suspensions are common, with an operating suspension system being incorporated in many larger units, along with pneumatic tires. These vehicles are able to negotiate rougher terrains and may attain speeds of up to 20 mi/h (30 km/h).

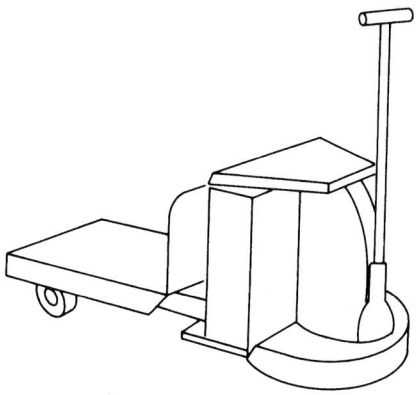

FIGURE 4-10 Types of burden carriers.

TRACTORS AND TRACTOR TRAINS

The term *tractor* (Fig. 4-11) refers to a detachable power source supplying locomotion to one or a group of load-bearing vehicles not having on-board power. The tractor is a steerable mover which is directed by an operator. They are generally classified according to their draw-bar pulling rating (DPR) into small, medium, and large sizes.

On all grades above 5 percent, the individual manufacturer should be consulted since a variety of other factors which must be considered vary with individual tractor designs. Minimum safety criteria for industrial tractors are covered in OSHA Standard Section 1910.178 (Powered Industrial Trucks) and should be referred to when equipment is being selected.

The main application for these vehicles is the movement of goods in volume over distances too long to be economically moved by fork trucks—approximately 300 ft (90 m). Since the tractor trains are not self-loading, a system of tractor loading stations and surplus tractors and trailers is required, involving constant hitching and unhitching of tractors and trailers. An alternative is to use a forklift as a tractor with the operator of the fork truck loading the trailers.

Apart from fork trucks, five types of tractors are used for most industrial applications.

Highway Tractors. Highway tractors are typically used in over-the-road applications and are relatively specialized to serve this purpose. They do, however, find application in large manufacturing complexes for the movement of materials between remote locations where warranted by the speed and density of materials flow. This type of tractor is also frequently used in factory shipping yards for the positioning of both loaded and unloaded semitrailers.

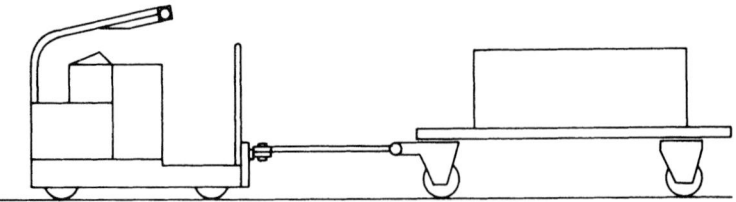

FIGURE 4-11   Tractor used in industrial applications.

Walkie Tractors.   Walkie tractors are the smaller variety of industrial tractors. These tractors are battery-electric with motive power, braking, and steering being provided by a single wheel or a close-coupled pair of wheels. The drive mechanism is tiller-controlled through hand controls, as in other walkie equipment, and dead-man controls are provided. Two other wheels are provided for stability at the rear of the unit. A variety of coupling devices are available for attaching the tractor to trailers and semilive skids.

Walkie-Rider Tractors.   The walkie-rider tractor is essentially a larger version of the walkie tractor. The major differences are that in a walkie-rider tractor a platform is provided for the operator to stand on during operation and two travel speeds are provided. A slow speed comparable to the operator's walking pace, on the order of 3 mi/h (5 km/h) and a higher speed of roughly 7 mi/h (11 km/h) is common in this type of equipment. Owing to higher operating speeds, these tractors have wider operating ranges. Because of the longer range of these tractors, larger-capacity batteries are used and, therefore, the units are heavier and larger than pure walkie tractors.

Rider Tractors.   Rider tractors are available in both stand-up and sit-down configurations. The stand-up variety is more compact and generally applicable to more congested situations. The sit-down tractor is generally larger and is used where higher speed and longer distances, up to ½ mi (0.8 km) or more, are encountered. Battery-electric and internal-combustion engines are used as power sources in both versions; however, battery-electric power is more prevalent in the stand-up models, and the internal-combustion engine is the frequent choice in sit-down tractors.

Specialty Tractors.   Specialty tractors are usually confined to very heavy load applications and are often built as an integral part of the load carrier itself. Two more common applications of these specialty tractors are large bulk-handling carriers for molten metals and granular materials and for spotting of railway cars.

MOBILE INDUSTRIAL CRANES

Mobile industrial cranes (Fig. 4-12) serve a variety of plant and production-related materials-handling functions. They are especially adaptable to loads of large or unusual size and where careful placement is required. In some applications, they are used only to position a given load, while in other applications they are used as both prime mover and positioner.

Mobile cranes differ from other plant hoisting equipment in that they operate independently of any supporting structure. The primary advantage of a crane is its ability to reach into places not normally accessible by other types of materials-handling equipment. With the exception of straddle cranes, the industrial crane depends on a boom for its reach and lift capability. It is the positioning of the boom that ultimately determines where a load will be placed and how large a load can be safely lifted.

The following text discusses the types of mobile cranes in use.

FIGURE 4-12   Mobile industrial crane.

Portable Hand-Powered Crane.   The portable hand-powered crane is similar in design to a small manual-lift truck, except that the load-carrying forks have been replaced by a boom and hook. This equipment is commonly used to move and position work pieces into and out of process equipment where volumes do not warrant a permanently installed hoisting system. It is also frequently found in maintenance and repair shops to assist in the disassembly and reassembly of in-plant equipment. Lifting is accomplished either through a hand winch and cable system or a manually operated hydraulic system. Typical lifting capacities are limited to 2000 lb (900 kg) or less.

Stevedore Crane.   The stevedore crane is a nonswinging crane which requires that the hook be positioned by maneuvering the entire vehicle. This limits its use to relatively unobstructed areas. The boom may be extended outward by the operator to reach the load and returned back to a position closer to the vehicle for transport. The crane is a relatively fast vehicle which is used to pick up a load and transport it to a final destination.

The front, load-carrying wheels are also the powered wheels, with steering being achieved by the trailing wheels. Both three- and four-point suspensions are used, and the crane is often used to tow factory trucks while also loading and unloading them. Typical load capacities range from 2 to 4 tons (1800 to 3600 kg).

Swing-Boom Crane.   The swing-boom crane is a larger-capacity crane than the stevedore crane and is used more for positioning loads than for transportation. The boom structure is constructed so that it can be rotated by the operator through 180°. Outriggers are provided for stability. They are usually powered by diesel or spark-ignition engines, with battery-electric power also being available.

Full Revolving Cranes.   Full revolving cranes are capable of swinging a load through a full 360° and are generally the largest of mobile cranes. Their use is normally one of positioning loads as opposed to transportation. This type of crane will often be mounted on a truck-type chassis for rapid movement between jobsites. Power is provided by diesel or spark-ignition engines through direct hydraulic torque converters.

Load-lifting capacities at the boom's most upright position can be as high as 100 tons (90,000 kg) with reaches in excess of 100 ft (30 m) possible. Power is provided by diesel or spark-ignition engines through direct hydraulic torque converters. Industrial applications are almost totally limited to construction activities and maintenance of large structures.

Straddle Crane.   The straddle crane has no boom but has a wheel-mounted framework on which are mounted two hoists. These hoists are capable of moving within the limits of the framework for precise load positioning. The straddle crane is related to the straddle carrier. It is a highly versatile crane, finding application as both positioner and mover of materials. In addition, its design is such that it is extremely stable and can move at relatively high speeds.

The framework consists of four vertical columns mounted above the vehicle's high flotation wheels, supporting two horizontal crane rails which carry the traveling hoists. Load-carrying capacity ranges from approximately 10 to 60 tons (9000 to 55,000 kg) per hoist for an aggregate capacity of approximately 20 to 120 tons (18,000 to 110,000 kg).

A variety of power systems are used, all of which are engine-driven. Hydraulic systems are those most commonly used for transport, hoisting, and positioning. However, one manufacturer employs an engine-driven electrical power plant to operate the crane's functions through electric motors.

The straddle crane is capable of operating in high-density areas and is highly maneuverable, since all four of its wheels can be turned and powered independently. Common applications are in steel storage yards, loading and handling of shipping containers, commercial concrete castings, truck and car loading, and boatyards. Special load-handling devices are easily adapted to this crane, increasing its versatility.

REFERENCES AND BIBLIOGRAPHY

1. "Better Maintenance Improves the Bottom Line," *Modern Materials Handling,* February 1991.
2. "Hand Pallet Trucks," *Material Handling Engineering,* July 1991.

CHAPTER 8-5

WAREHOUSING AND STORAGE

K. W. Tunnell Co., Inc.
King of Prussia, Pennsylvania

INTRODUCTION

In the overall materials-handling system, warehousing provides the facilities, equipment, personnel, and techniques required to receive, store, and ship raw materials, goods in process, and finished goods. Storage facilities, equipment, and techniques vary widely depending on the nature of the material to be handled. Characteristics of materials, such as size, weight, durability, shelf life, and order lot size, are factors in designing a warehousing system and in solving warehousing problems.

Economics is also of great importance in the design of warehousing systems. Storage and retrieval costs are incurred, but add no value to the product. Thus, the investment in storage and handling equipment and in floor space must be based on minimizing unit storage and handling costs.

Other factors to be considered in designing warehousing systems include control of inventory size and location, provisions for quality inspection, provisions for order picking and packing, staging for receiving and shipping, appropriate numbers of shipping and receiving docks, and maintenance of records.

WAREHOUSING ACTIVITIES

Warehousing activities vary according to material amounts and characteristics. However, the activities associated with warehousing generally include the following procedures:

1. Unload inbound vehicles.
2. Accumulate received material in a staging area.
3. Examine the quantity and quality and assign a storage location.
4. Transport the material to the storage area.
5. Place the material in the assigned storage location.
6. Retrieve the material from storage and place it in an order-picking line, if a picking line is used.

7. Fill orders, if applicable.

8. Sort and pack, if applicable.

9. Accumulate for shipping.

10. Load and check outbound vehicles.

WAREHOUSING ADMINISTRATIVE CONTROL

Associated with the physical handling and storage of materials is an administrative control system. The administrative control system provides for:

1. Acknowledging receipt of goods for accounting purposes

2. Verifying the quality and quantity of received goods

3. Updating the inventory records to reflect receipts

4. Locating all goods in storage

5. Updating the inventory records to reflect shipments

6. Notification to the accounting function of shipments for billing purposes

Many administrative control systems are computerized and/or automated. The cost-effectiveness of such systems over manual systems depends on such factors as:

1. The number of line items in storage

2. The number of customers served

3. The volume of goods shipped

Generally, computerization and automation are cost-effective for industries and distribution centers having many line items in storage, many customers, and a large volume of goods shipped. Distributors of grocery, health, and beauty-aid products often have computerized and automated systems.

TYPES OF MATERIALS

Materials to be stored may be broadly classified as bulk materials or packaged goods. Bulk materials such as fuels, chemicals, minerals, and grain are stored in specialized storage facilities and transported in pipes, screw conveyors, power shovels, etc. In the many industries which handle and store bulk goods, each accomplishes these tasks with very specialized equipment and techniques. This discussion will be limited to warehousing packaged goods. The reader should consult specific publications that apply to bulk materials-handling industries for particulars in bulk handling.

Within the packaged-goods classification, materials are subdivided into categories according to their state of completion in the manufacturing process. Categories include raw materials, goods in process, and finished goods.

Raw materials. These vary widely in characteristics, depending on the industry. A few examples are raw foods and ingredients for food processors, thousands of small parts for electronics assemblers, engines and motors for manufacturers of vehicles, and wood and finishes for furniture manufacturers. Raw materials are the goods on which the manufacturing process will operate to produce salable products. Indeed, the finished goods of one manufacturer often become the raw materials of another.

Goods in process. This refers to goods which have completed some but not all of the manufacturing process. Typically, a manufacturing process involves several operations utilizing different equipment, skills, and materials. Goods in process are stored while awaiting the next manufacturing operation. They are often stored along the manufacturing process rather than in the warehouse proper.

Finished goods. These goods are those which have completed the manufacturing process and are stored in inventory to fill customer orders. Finished goods may be further subdivided into reserve and order-picking stock. Customer orders are filled from order-picking stock while the picking stock is replenished from reserve stock.

The amount of raw materials, goods in process, and finished goods to be handled and stored varies considerably from industry to industry. Industries having large inventories of raw materials usually are converters of bulk materials such as paper and steel. Manufacturers of highly complex equipment such as computers and automobiles require a significant amount of raw-materials storage for parts as well.

Industries having significant needs for goods in process handling and storage are those whose manufacturing process is not automated. Machine-shop and electronic-assembly operations are examples.

Finished-goods handling and storage capacity are a function of manufacturing volume and product bulk. Industries having high-volume and high-bulk output generally require a considerable handling capacity for finished goods. The paper conversion and bottling industries are examples.

CONSIDERATIONS IN WAREHOUSE PLANNING

The objective of warehouse planning is to provide space and equipment to hold and preserve goods until they are used or shipped in the most cost-effective manner. The efficient accomplishment of warehousing activities listed in Chap. 8-1 is dependent on thorough planning. The following sections discuss these considerations as a guide to the warehouse planner.

Type and Number of Materials

The type and number of materials to be stored and handled form the basis for warehouse planning. The physical characteristics of the material, to a great extent, determine materials-storage and -handling methods. Physical factors include dimensions, weight, shape, and durability. As a first step in warehouse planning, all materials to be stored must be identified and their physical characteristics listed.

The quantity of each material item to be stored must be established. The planner may require assistance from sales management for finished-goods inventory levels and manufacturing management for establishing levels of raw materials and goods in process. In establishing inventory levels, seasonality, changes in product mix, and expected turnover rate become factors.

With the inventory level of each item of stored material established, a storage unit is selected. A storage unit is the least number of an item which is stored as one unit. Examples include a single crated refrigerator, a pallet containing 20 cases of canned goods, and a bundle of pipe. The storage unit is usually selected according to the physical characteristics of the material, the available handling and storage equipment, the quantity, and the manner in which the material is received or shipped.

A storage unit may be larger than a shipping unit or a manufacturing unit. In this case, order-picking facilities are provided for items used or shipped in lots smaller than a storage unit. The service level of storage in an order-picking operation must be established as well.

Factors affecting order-picking stock levels include minimum order quantity, volume, and the physical characteristics discussed earlier. Sheet-metal screws, for example, might be in 3-months supply, while cased canned goods might be in only 8-h supply.

Storage Equipment

Storage-equipment selection follows the establishment of the reserve and order-filling inventory storage units and levels.

In the case of selecting equipment for an existing building, the constraints of the building itself must be taken into consideration. Storage equipment must be compatible with floor loading capacity, clear height beneath sprinklers and structural steel, column spacing, and location of shipping and receiving docks, etc.

The characteristics of the storage unit, pallet, drum, bundle, etc., largely determine the type of storage equipment required. The inventory levels to be maintained determine the number of pieces of storage equipment. Materials characteristics and the volume of materials movement generally are deciding factors in selecting materials-handling equipment. Materials-handling equipment is discussed in Chaps. 8-3 and 8-4.

Storage equipment usually consists of general-purpose or specialty storage racks of varying height, depth, and load capacity. However, the warehouse floor may serve as all or part of the required equipment. Storage units such as pallets of cased canned goods, which have the rigidity and stability to support loads placed on top of them, are normally stored on the floor in stacks. Rolls of paper and coils of steel are frequently stacked on end. Storage units which have rigidity and are many in number lend themselves to floor-stacking techniques.

Heavy or bulky storage units which lack rigidity or which are few in number are generally better stored in storage racks. Storage units which are small, such as wristwatches or thumbtacks, are suitable for storage in shelving and bins. Containers used in conjunction with shelving or by themselves are discussed in Chap. 8-2.

Some types of available storage equipment are described below. Custom-designed special equipment is offered by many storage-equipment manufacturers.

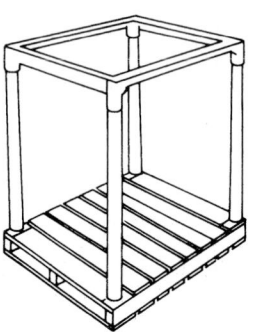

FIGURE 5-1 Pallet frame.

Pallet Frames. Pallet frames (Fig. 5-1) are useful where materials lack the rigidity or stability to be stacked on the floor and where there are a large number of storage units in inventory. The pallet frame attaches to the pallet and extends above the material. The frame acts as a structure on which another pallet is stacked. Pallets so stacked are often placed several stacks deep and thus conserve floor space as compared with pallet racks which require aisle access. The frames are removable for pallet loads not requiring support.

Pallet Racks. Pallet racks are the most commonly used storage aids and are available in many configurations adapted to particular materials characteristics and turnover rates. Pallet racks, for the purpose of this discussion, are classified into five groups.

One-Deep Pallet Racks. These are used when many items with small inventory quantities must be stored for ready accessibility. They may be configured to accommodate containers and other unit loads in addition to pallets. They are also used for order picking when it is most economical to pick directly from storage units.

One-deep pallet racks consist of vertical upright frames connected by horizontal crossbeams on which pallets and containers are placed one deep. Uprights are available in various heights and depths, and crossbeams are available in various lengths to accommodate most storage unit sizes. The load-carrying capacity for the upright and beam combinations is established by the manufacturers.

The normal storage height for this type of rack is from 20 to 24 ft (6 to 7 m) from the floor to the top of the top load. Lifting operations tend to be inefficient at greater heights because it becomes too difficult for the lift operator to accurately place the storage unit. Specialized equipment for heights greater than 24 ft (7 m) is available, however.

The horizontal crossbeams are adjustable so that the vertical height of the rack may be divided into as many storage levels as desired. The individual storage-opening height is tailored to suit the height of the storage unit. Clearance of 4 to 6 in (10 to 15 cm) from the top of the load to the bottom of the crossbeam above it is usually provided. In establishing the maximum height of the top load, the height of the fire-protection sprinklers must be considered. Most fire-protection codes and fire-insurance underwriters require a minimum clearance of 18 in (45 cm) between the top storage unit and the sprinklers. The warehouse planner should consult the local applicable fire code and the insurance underwriter.

The horizontal width of the storage opening is determined by two factors. These are the maximum weight and the maximum width of the loads to be stored in the opening. It should be noted that the load width may be larger than the pallet width because of load overhang. Normally, 4 in (10 cm) is provided horizontally between loads and between loads and uprights. Typically, two pallet loads are placed side by side in one opening. When the horizontal dimension of the opening has been determined, the rack manufacturer's catalog is consulted to select a compatible crossbeam length and weight capacity.

At this point in warehouse planning, the planner should calculate the floor load resulting from the fully loaded pallet rack. The floor loading will become a design parameter for new construction. In the case of an existing facility, the floor will be confirmed as adequate or the rack arrangement will be shown to be unfeasible.

The number of pallet racks required is determined by dividing the maximum number of storage units by the number of those units contained in one rack.

Two-Deep Pallet Racks.   These racks (Fig. 5-2) are similar in design to the one-deep pallet rack except that two pallets, one behind the other, are stored in each position. Two-deep racks are used when there is insufficient floor space to accommodate the required number of one-deep racks. Two one-deep racks are normally placed side by side and require aisle access from each side of the two-rack combination. The two-deep rack requires access from only one side but stores the same amount of material as the two one-deep racks placed side by side. The ratio of aisle to storage is thus reduced by using two-deep racks.

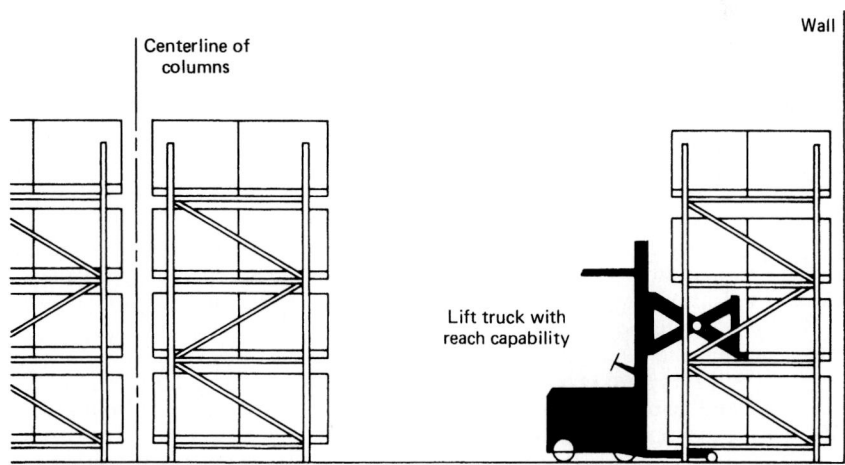

FIGURE 5-2   Two-deep pallet racks.

Two-deep racks have some costs associated with them, however. Lift equipment must be fitted with extended reach capability in order to position loads in the rear storage position. The efficiency of storing and retrieving the load in the rear storage position is less than with single-position loading and unloading. Two-deep racks are often more expensive than their two, one-deep, side-by-side counterparts. Storage units are sometimes damaged when positioned in or retrieved from the rear position.

The manner of selecting the height, depth, width, and number of two-deep racks is similar to that for one-deep racks.

Drive-In or Drive-Through Pallet Racks. These racks (Fig. 5-3) are designed to provide storage several pallets deep. The racks consist of vertical uprights which are braced across the top of the rack. Angle-iron ledges are welded or bolted to the insides of the uprights to support the pallets. This arrangement allows the lift vehicle to enter the rack to place or retrieve a pallet.

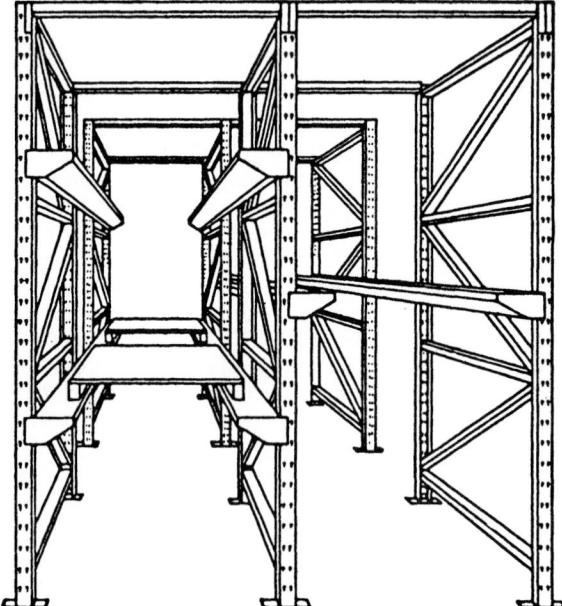

FIGURE 5-3 Drive-in or drive-through rack. (Reproduced with permission from *Material Handling Handbook and Directory, 1977/1978,* published by *Material Handling Engineering* magazine, Cleveland, Ohio.)

Drive-in or -through pallet racks are used where floor space is limited and where there are many storage units of a particular item to be accommodated. Palletized items shipped or delivered by the entire truckload would be candidates for storage in this type of rack. The total number of positions of storage in one storage aisle in the rack could be designed to contain one truckload.

There are several limitations of drive-in or -through racks. Pallets stored in the rear or middle of a storage aisle cannot be retrieved until those in front are removed. This feature limits first-in–first-out inventory control except by loading or unloading entire storage-aisle lots one at a time. When entire storage-aisle lots are so treated, empty pallet positions are created if less than the entire aisle is filled or emptied. Storage efficiency is thereby reduced.

The lift operator must move and lift the storage unit in very confined spaces. Damage to the goods as a result of close tolerances is more frequent in this rack than in others. It is also clear that the lift operator's efficiency is reduced by the requirement of driving into the rack in confined spaces.

Since the ledges that support the pallets are fixed, storage units of uniform dimensions are required. Storage units having overhang on the side of the pallet generally do not lend themselves to this type of storage. Finally, the lift vehicle may be no wider than the distance between the ledges. In selecting drive-in or -through racks, the planner should keep in mind that the usual maximum height is again 20 to 24 ft (6 to 7 m) and that drive-in racks usually are no more than six pallets deep. Due to their depth and the relative lack of bracing of their own, higher drive-in and -through racks generally require bracing to the building structure.

Gravity-Flow Racks.   These racks (Fig. 5-4) are constructed to contain several pallets in depth and to support the pallets on inclined roller conveyors. Pallets are loaded on the high side of the roller conveyor and removed from the low side. As a pallet is removed from storage, the pallets behind it roll down toward the retrieval opening.

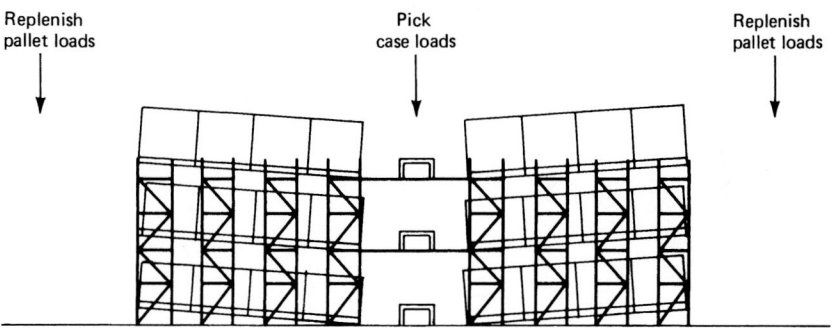

FIGURE 5-4   Gravity-flow racks.

Gravity-flow pallet racks and smaller versions for individual cartons and containers are commonly employed in order-picking operations. A continuous supply of an item is presented to the order picker without replenishment interference. Gravity-flow racks are also useful in maintaining first-in–first-out inventory control.

Gravity-flow pallet racks generally do not exceed six pallets in depth because of the high cost. However, the depth of the rack may be designed to contain a particular time period's supply. This configuration is appropriate when continuous replenishment is not employed.

The height of gravity-flow racks seldom exceeds 24 ft (7 m). The height of the rack is often limited to that conveniently reached by the order picker. In some cases two-level picking on the inside by personnel on foot is replenished by lift vehicles from the back side. See Fig. 5-4.

The height and width of storage or picking openings in a gravity-flow system are usually fixed with little or no adjustment conveniently possible. Instead, storage units are arranged to fit the gravity-flow configuration.

Gravity-flow racks may not be suited to very unstable storage units due to the shock of impact of movement and sudden stops on the inclined roller conveyor. Such difficulties are overcome by placing the unstable items in suitable containers.

Logic-Flow Racks.   These are, in principle, designed to accomplish the same functions as gravity-flow racks. Instead of gravity providing the motive force to move full storage units to the picking opening, a powered conveyor does so. In most applications the order picker operates the powered conveyor with start-stop control. This arrangement eliminates the shock of impact experienced in gravity conveyors. Unstable and very delicate storage units are handled and stored in this manner.

In general, due to its high cost, the logic-flow rack is employed only for very specific, small storage situations. For the most part, these systems are manufactured from custom designs.

Bins and Shelving.   Bins and shelving are widely used for the storage of goods in small lot sizes as raw materials, goods in process, and as finished goods, particularly in order-picking applications. They are available in many sizes, strengths, and degrees of closure. Indeed, pallet racks, previously discussed, may easily be converted to shelving.

In selecting shelf and bin storage, the planner determines for each storage item an appropriate shelf opening and depth or bin-drawer size. Shelves, bins, and drawers may be fitted with dividers to contain more than one item. The degree of protection from dust, light, theft, etc., determines the degree of closure required. Shelving and bin closures are available from totally open to totally enclosed and individually locked. Where many items require the same degree of protection, the shelving-bin system may be enclosed in a protective enclosure such as a clean room or refrigerated room.

Shelf, bin, and drawer arrangements can be obtained as separate units or in customized combinations. Customized combinations are more costly but may be justified in situations where stock may be advantageously stored in some picking order. Order-picking efficiency is maximized by reducing search and travel time on the part of the order picker.

Automatic Storage and Retrieval Systems. Automatic storage and retrieval systems (Fig. 5-5) are employed to achieve highly dense storage and very efficient placement and retrieval of materials. Many of the other activities listed under "Warehousing Activities" at the beginning of this chapter may also be mechanized and partially or fully automated as well.

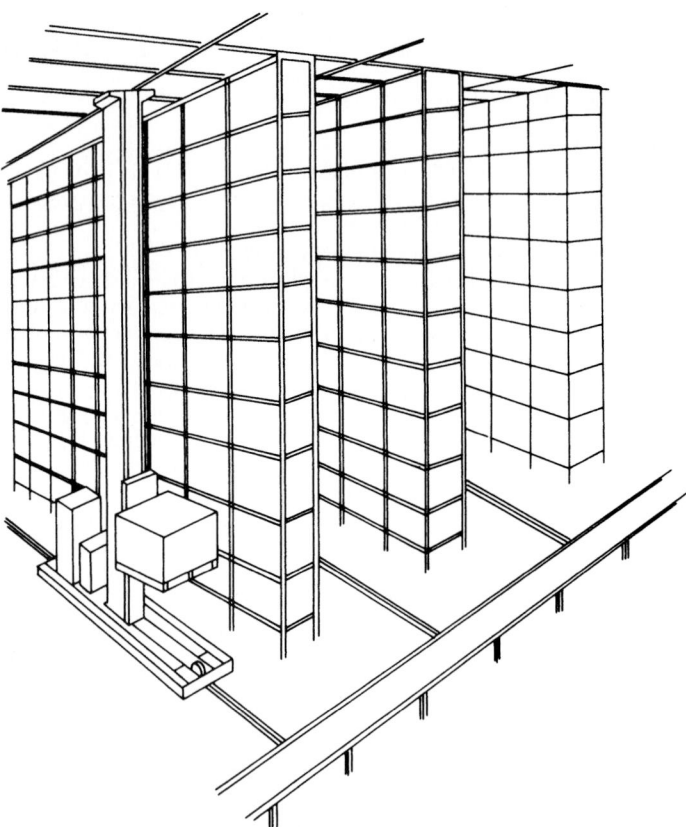

FIGURE 5-5 Automated storage and retrieval system.

The mechanization and automation of warehousing activities require a high capital investment and a very comprehensive feasibility study to justify the investment. The success of mechanized and automated warehousing also requires the *complete commitment by management* to support the planning, design, procurement, installation, and *especially* debugging. In the past, planning to start-up could take over three years, but now manufacturers of these systems are providing pre-engineered proven components such as controls and racks, to reduce excessive start-up times.

Mechanized and automated warehousing systems may be considered by the planner if some or all of the following conditions exist:

- Many varieties of items in storage
- High-volume storage items
- High turnover in general
- Highly seasonal storage items
- High cost of land and floor space
- High labor costs
- Need for rapid customer service
- Random storage desirable
- Storage units uniform in size

Automatic storage and retrieval systems, whether automated or not, achieve their high density by storing goods at greater heights than in conventional racks. *High cube* warehousing from 20 to 100 ft (6 to 30 m) is in use. At heights above 20 ft (6 m) the system may become the structure of the building to which walls and the roof are attached.

The materials-handling equipment, referred to as storage and retrieval (S/R) machines, can be stacker cranes, turret trucks or automatic guided vehicles. The S/R machine travels on rails between the storage units and is guided by rails at the top of the storage units. It can operate in aisles as wide as itself. For example, turret trucks can accommodate up to 3300 pounds (1500 kg) in aisles only 66 in (1.7 m) wide. Each aisle has a dedicated machine which services both sides of the aisle, although systems can be designed to allow machine to transfer to other aisles. To determine the feasibility of aisle transfer machines, one should consider planned system utilization and required response time of storage and retrievals.

In a semiautomatic system, there is an operator on the S/R machine. In this type of system, the S/R machine can have the operator travel with it horizontally and vertically or just horizontally. The operator will select the bay and level on a keyboard, and the machine will position itself to perform the operation. In a fully automatic system, the operator may control the movements of the S/R machines from the computer console located at the pick and deposit station of the system. There are also systems in which a computer system will issue the commands to the S/R machines.

Goods to be placed in storage are often delivered to the S/R machine by conveyor; likewise, outgoing goods are sent by conveyor. Often, the conveyor is centrally located at the pick and deposit station and can be semi- or fully automated.

The degree of mechanization and automatic control of warehousing varies from user to user and from manufacturer to manufacturer. The planner should consider engaging consultants and equipment manufacturers in the planning process. Most manufacturers provide planning guides to assist in identifying requirements. See Refs. 2 and 3, page 8-56, for more information. Prior to or during the identification of requirements for a mechanized-automated system, the planner should also determine requirements for a comparable conventional warehouse system. The capital investment and the operating cost of each system are than analyzed for economic justification.

Typically the automated system will require a higher initial capital investment but incur lower annual operating costs than a conventional system. The automated system would be economically justified if its payback period and return on investment are satisfactory to management. There also may be tax implications in choosing an automated storage and retrieval system. Where the racking structure supports the building walls and roof, the structure may be considered equipment. Equipment may be depreciated at a faster rate than buildings. Other factors influencing the decision to mechanize and automate include:

- Competitive advantage in servicing customers
- Reliability and the need for backup systems
- Degree to which the market will change
- Time to become operational
- Availability of capital

Storage and retrieval for small lots can be accomplished with mechanized and automated arrangements. Horizontal (Fig. 5-6) and vertical carousels are frequently used, and can achieve picking rates of 100 picks/h. A vertical carousel uses less floor space and resembles a horizontal carousel rotated onto one end. However, the vertical carousel requires an automated retrieval system, since it can reach heights of 35 ft (10.6 m). In either carousel system, bins of material are transported to a stationary order picker. The operator may select the picking face to be transported by an ON-OFF control panel in a semiautomatic configuration. Frequently, the picking list is prepared by computer in the order of storage to minimize moves. In automated systems, the computer automatically positions the next picking face as the order picker indicates completion of the last pick or that the item is out of stock. Robotic arms, guided by computer, may be used to perform the pick operations. Complete automation may also include provisions for automatic packing-list preparation, billing, and reordering.

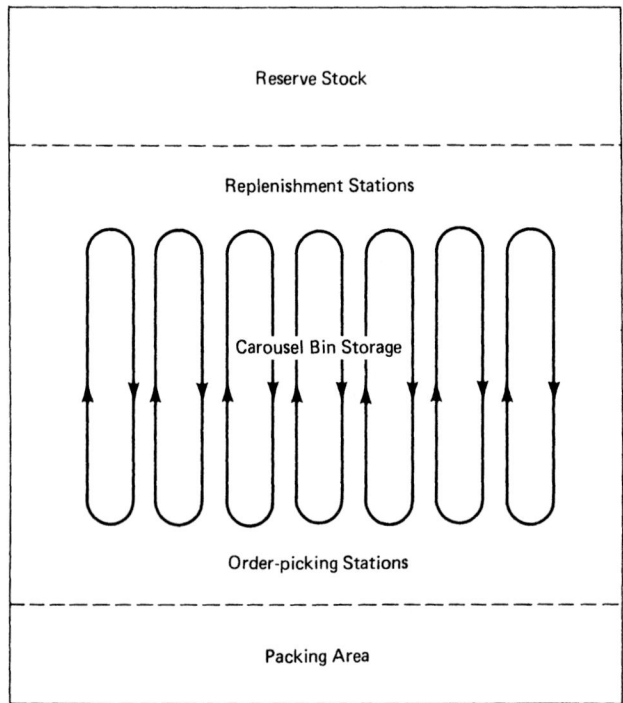

FIGURE 5-6 Schematic plan of automated bin storage.

Whether manual or mechanized, shelving and bin storage may be arranged in multilevels by the use of mezzanines. See Fig. 5-7. This configuration is appropriate when high bay space is available and high storage density is required. In general, high-volume and high-weight items are stored in lower levels, and lighter, slow-moving items in upper levels.

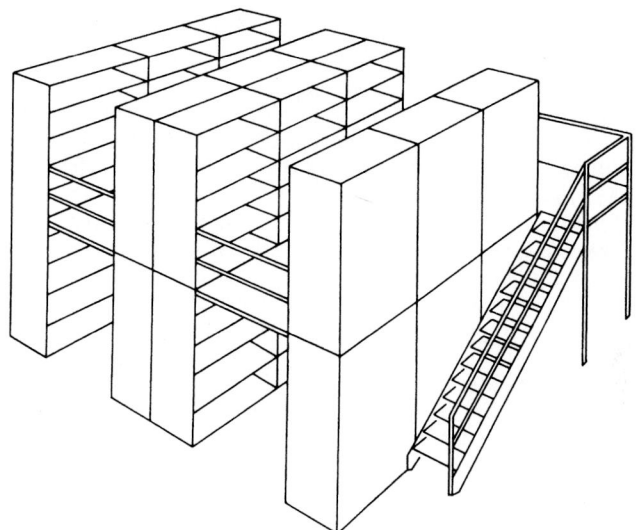

FIGURE 5-7   Multilevel shelving.

Shipping and Receiving Docks

Shipping and receiving docks are an important factor in warehouse planning because inefficient layouts may use too many lift trucks and personnel to achieve the necessary loading/unloading rates. Of prime importance is the number of docks and type of equipment needed. Recently, dock management software has been developed to track dock performance and interface with other software.

In warehousing situations involving very high inbound and outbound volume, the principles of queuing theory are applied to assess peak dock activity. The peak dock activity, using alternative numbers of docks, may then be simulated using computer methods to determine the best combination of receiving and shipping docks. Suppliers of dock equipment will often assist in the planning.

In practice, warehouses having moderate to low inbound-outbound traffic are analyzed from historic or expected data. The peak rate of deliveries and shipments is determined and expressed in vehicles per hour. The rate at which vehicles are loaded and unloaded is also determined and expressed in vehicles per hour per dock. Dividing the vehicle rate of arrival by the rate at which the vehicles are loaded or unloaded results in the number of docks required.

Example

$$\text{Peak rate of truck deliveries} = 10 \text{ trucks per hour}$$

$$\text{Rate at which trucks are unloaded} = 2 \text{ trucks per hour per dock}$$

$$\text{No. receiving docks required} = \frac{\text{rate of truck arrivals}}{\text{rate trucks are unloaded}} = \frac{10 \text{ trucks per hour}}{2 \text{ trucks per hour per dock}} = 5 \text{ docks}$$

The type of dock and the equipment provided at the dock are dependent upon the type of material to be handled, the need for specialized loading/unloading equipment, and the need for security or weather protection.

Types of Docks.   Types of docks to be considered include the following.

Indoor Docks.   These are designed to accommodate the delivery vehicle under the roof of the warehouse building. Accommodation for entire tractor-trailers, trailers only, small delivery trucks, and railcars are common. These arrangements are appropriate where there is need to contain heated or cooled air, where security is important, and where materials-handling systems such as bridge cranes load or unload the material.

Flush Docks.   These are constructed flush with the warehouse floor and with the outer wall of the building. This type of dock is generally built at a height above the outside grade level to accommodate the height of the vehicles to be serviced. Where the terrain is flat, ramps down to the docks are usually provided. This type of dock is normally provided with dock seals for weather protection. Also typical are dock leveler installations to accommodate minor differences in the heights of vehicle load beds.

Open Docks.   These are less expensive than those previously discussed. However, they offer the least protection from weather and pilferage. Open docks are appropriate in warmer climates when handling goods which are not weather-sensitive or pilferable. When installed, a canopy over the dock area is usually provided.

Sawtooth Docks.   These are arranged at an angle to the face of the building wall. This configuration is applicable where maneuvering room for shipping and delivery vehicles is limited. The sawtooth arrangement may be fully enclosed, covered, or open, as described above.

Dock Equipment.   This must accommodate the materials to be handled, the vehicle to be serviced, the loading and unloading equipment, and the need for weather and security protection. Some standard equipment includes the following.

Dock Doors.   These should be of the overhead type, counterbalanced for ease of operation. The doors should ride vertically along the wall of the building. Doors with tracks curving inward, such as a household garage door, could be damaged by materials-handling equipment. Doors are sized to accommodate the loaded materials-handling equipment passing through them and/or the size and configuration of the delivery-shipping vehicle. Options available for dock doors include the material from which the door is made, insulation, windows, and mechanized door-opening or -closing operators.

Dock Levelers and Dock Boards.   These provide a bridge between the delivery or shipping vehicle and the dock (Fig. 5-8). They also serve to accommodate differences in height between vehicles and the dock. Dock levelers are typically installed to be flush with the floor of the dock when retracted. Models which attach to the outside of the dock as a retrofit are also available. The levelers are activated or retracted by spring pressure or hydraulics. Dock boards are reinforced steel plates which are manually lifted into place to form the bridge.

Factors used in selecting the appropriate dock leveler or board include: the weight of the heaviest load and materials-handling vehicle combination to cross it, the distance which the unit must span for bridging, and the combined width of the load and materials-handling vehicle. Manufacturers of this equipment offer a wide variety of weight capacities and sizes.

Weather-Protection Equipment.   This equipment (Fig. 5-9) consists of devices to seal or cover the loading-dock area. Truck-dock seals used in conjunction with flush docks are popular. They have flexible construction and are often inflated. The arriving truck backs into the seal surrounding the door to effect the seal. Also available are hood-type seals which are mechanically activated. Made of flexible material, the hood extends out from the dock and conforms to the shape of the truck or railcar.

Other devices in common use are inside docks (discussed above) and canopies extending over the outside dock area for rain protection. Where high activity means that dock doors are seldom closed, weather curtains are indicated. The curtains consist of strips of clear flexible material covering the door opening. Materials-handling equipment can drive through the cur-

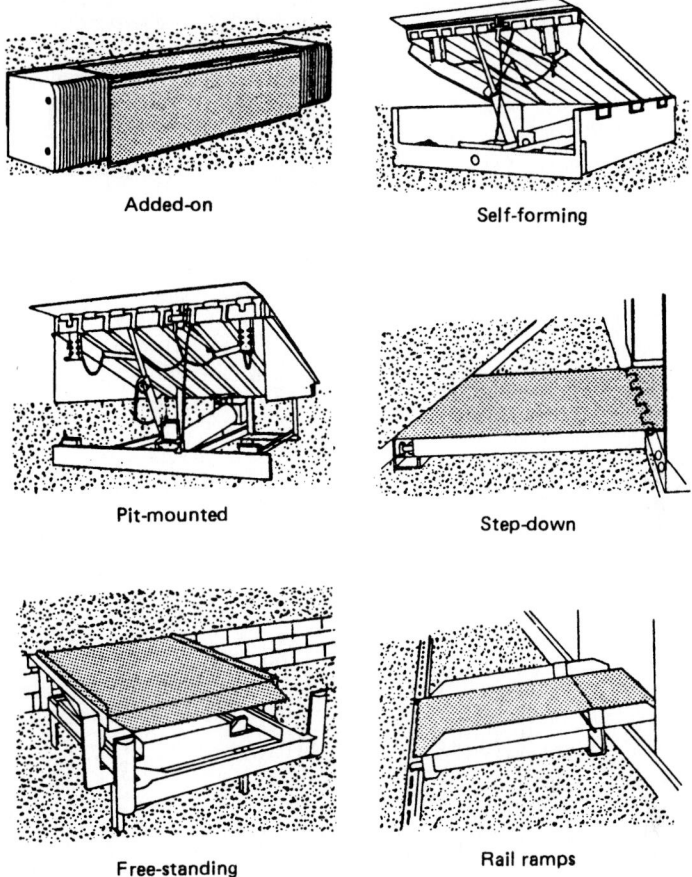

FIGURE 5-8 Types of dock levelers and dock boards. (Reproduced with permission from *Material Handling Engineering Handbook and Directory, 1977/1978,* published by *Material Handling Engineering* magazine, Cleveland, Ohio.)

tain. When there is no traffic through the curtain, the strips act, to some extent, to seal the door from weather.

Dock Lighting.   Dock lighting is required for nighttime operations. Floodlights are typical for lighting outside driveways, rails, and maneuvering areas to facilitate spotting delivery and shipping vehicles. Lighting for open docks is required to facilitate loading- and unloading-vehicle movement. When dock seals or hoods are used, lighting may be required for the inside of the truck or railcar. Portable or adjustable fixed lighting for these purposes is available. See Chap. 3-5, "Lighting."

Warehouse Layout

The warehouse layout is the final and perhaps the most important step in the planning process. Prior to undertaking the layout, the planner establishes the activities to be completed and the type and number of materials to be stored and handled, storage and handling equipment, and docks. (See "Warehousing Activities" at the beginning of this chapter.) The ware-

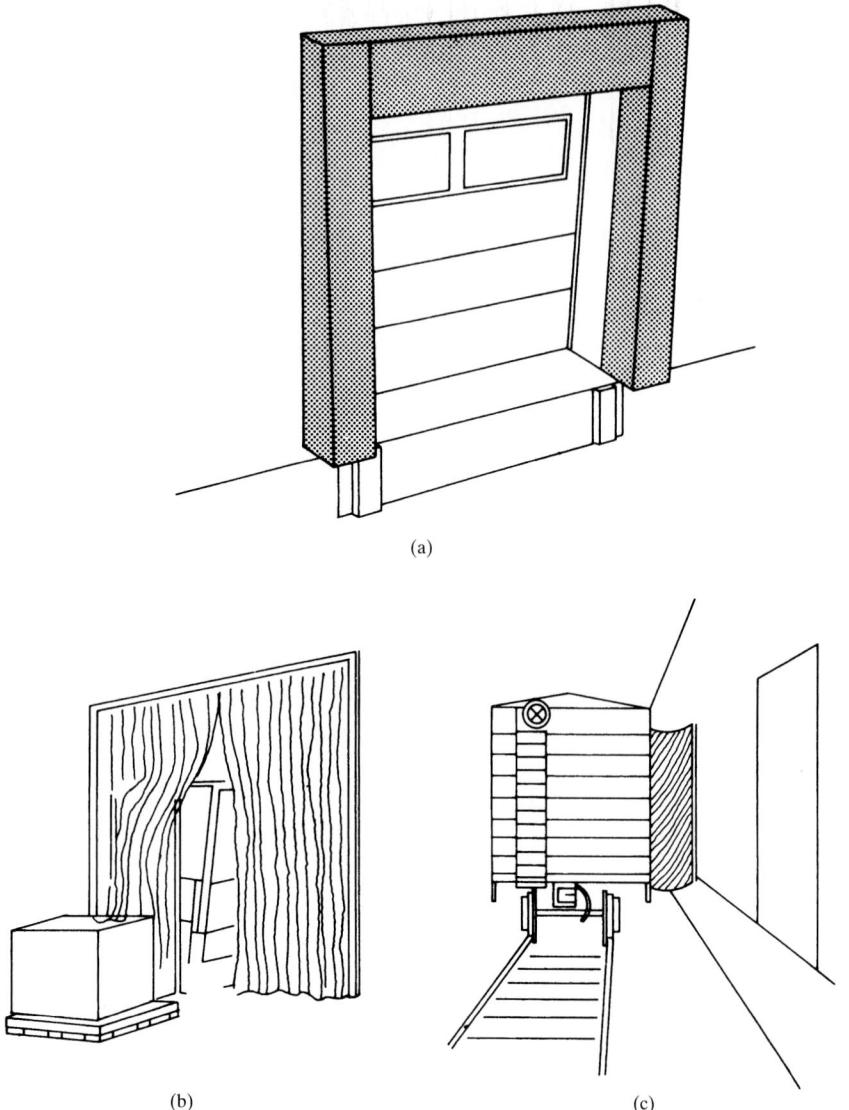

(a)

(b)   (c)

FIGURE 5-9 Types of dock weather protection.

house layout should be planned to provide the space and arrangement that makes the best use of

- Storage cubes
- Efficiency of the flow of materials from activity to activity
- Effective communications between activities

Because thousands of combinations of types, sizes, weights, and volumes of materials have been observed, specific warehouse layout characteristics cannot be described in this book. However, general principles for warehouse design are discussed below.

Location in Storage.   The location in storage (Fig. 5-10) of particular items is of importance. The following points should be considered.

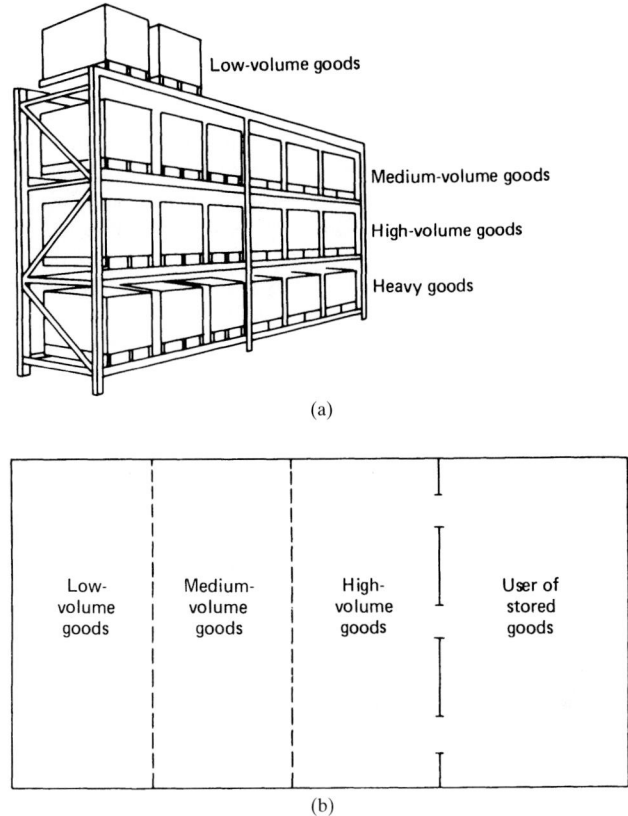

(a)

(b)

FIGURE 5-10   Location in storage according to volume.

- Items having a high turnover should be located near the user. The user may be a manufacturing operation, the shipping docks, or a quality-inspection area.
- Items having a high turnover should be stored and retrieved in the most convenient level vertically—slow movers high and fast movers low.
- Heavy and/or difficult-to-move items should be stored low.
- Where few items but large volumes of commodities are characteristic, individual loads of an item should be stored together in semidedicated areas.
- Where many items, but few of each, are encountered, random storage should be considered. A locator system, perhaps computerized, may be necessary.
- The nature of some storage items may require them to be stored in dedicated space. Some examples include hazardous materials, items of high value, and perishable goods.

Aisles

- Minimum aisle width is determined by the loaded maneuvering characteristics of materials-handling equipment. Determination of minimum aisle width is discussed in Chap. 8-4.

- Aisle width may be reduced by imposing one-way traffic.
- Aisles should open from the supplying area and open to the user area for maximum efficiency.
- Aisles should not be located next to walls as only one storage face is presented.

Storage Equipment Location and Arrangement

- The arrangement may be effected by column spacing in existing buildings or may determine the column spacing in new facilities. Normally, one-deep, two-deep, and drive-in racks, as well as shelving, are placed end on end, back-side along column lines. This arrangement eliminates column interference with aisles. See Fig. 5-2.
- One-deep, two-deep, and drive-in racks, as well as shelving, are most effectively placed back-to-back in open floor areas. This arrangement minimizes access aisle requirements. In the case of racks, space between them must be provided for pallet overhang. Frequently, the width of a line of columns provides this space.
- Storage racks, except gravity-flow and logic-flow, in addition to shelving, are efficiently placed along walls with openings for doors and fire-protection equipment. See Fig. 5-2.
- The height of the storage equipment is limited to that which provides no less than 18 in (45 cm) of clearance beneath fire-protection sprinklers. Local codes or fire underwriters may require a different clearance.

Docks

- Receiving and shipping docks are usually located to accommodate the flow of materials in the manufacturing process. The most common manufacturing flow patterns are straight-through and U-shaped. See Fig. 5-11.
- In the straight-through processes, raw materials are received and stored at the beginning of the manufacturing process. Finished goods appear at the end of the process and are stored and shipped from that location. Receiving and shipping areas which are so separated generally require more personnel and docks than an equivalent U-shaped arrangement.
- In U-shaped process flow, raw materials arrive at the same side of the building as that from which the finished goods are shipped. Shipping and receiving docks may be separated by no more than an imaginary line. This arrangement may offer economies in lower personnel requirements and in the number of docks since receiving and shipping personnel and equipment may be interchanged when necessary. The U-shaped process flow is also advantageous if high bay storage for both raw materials and finished goods is required.
- Spacing between docks is established to minimize interference between the docks during operations.
- Areas adjacent to docks for staging off-loaded material or material awaiting shipment are normally required.
- Provisions for enclosed space near docks may include administrative offices, personnel comfort facilities, and quality-inspection areas.

Building Characteristics

- Storage height may be limited not only by fire codes but also by local zoning restrictions.
- Building services such as piping and space heaters should be placed in aisles to avoid interfering with storage equipment and to be accessible for maintenance.
- Lighting is normally designed to aid materials-handling equipment operators and order-picking personnel in locating and identifying stored items. Architectural and engineering firms normally assist the planner in determining the number and location of lighting fixtures.

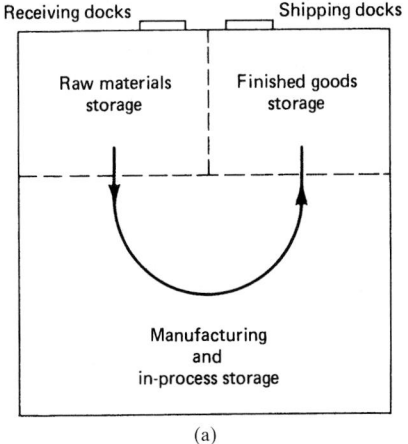

(a)

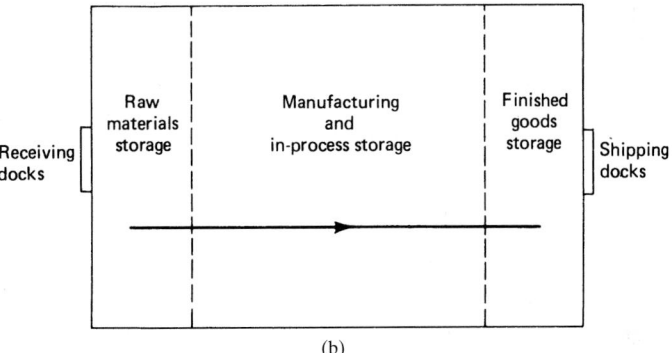

(b)

FIGURE 5-11   Materials flow patterns. (*a*) U-shaped materials flow, (*b*) straight-through materials flow.

- The type and number of units of fire-protection equipment are governed by fire code and fire underwriter requirements. Generally, the flammability and the amount of material stored determines the requirements.

- Floors may be enhanced to increase durability and housekeeping qualities. Coatings are available to increase surface hardness and wearability and to reduce dust. Typically, 3- to 4-in (8- to 10-cm) lines are painted on the floor to mark traffic and storage aisles.

SECTION 9

HYDRAULIC AND PNEUMATIC SYSTEMS

CHAPTER 9-1
HYDRAULIC SYSTEMS*

INTRODUCTION

A system comprises a group of devices forming a network. A hydraulic system involves the devices and networks that operate by the pressure of liquids, whereas a pneumatic system works with gases. The most predominant liquid in hydraulic systems is water, the second is oil. In pneumatic systems, air is the most common fluid with natural gas and steam also in frequent use. Water, oil, and/or air systems and components will be mainly discussed in these chapters.

A typical system includes a pressurizer source (a high elevation tank or a pump), a conveyance system (channels, pipes, valves, etc.), and a sink. Thus, in a fluid (liquid or gas) system, a fluid is conveyed from one point with a certain energy to another point. Because of the resistance in the system, some pressure energy is lost as heat energy in the network.

PRINCIPAL COMPONENTS OF FLUID SYSTEMS

Following is a list of the components most frequently used in fluid systems:

---

* Updated for this Second Edition by the Editor-in-Chief.

Accumulators

Actuators

Compressors, vacuum pumps, and blowers

Couplings, quick-connect, hydraulic

Couplings, quick-connect, pneumatic

Cylinders

Demineralizers

Dryers

Expansion joints

Filters, air-line

Filters, hydraulic

Fittings, tube and port, hydraulic

Fittings, tube and port, pneumatic

Fluids

Gauges, pressure and flow, hydraulic

Gauges, pressure and flow, pneumatic

Heat exchangers

Hose, hose fittings, and hose assemblies, hydraulic

Hose, hose fittings, and hose assemblies, pneumatic

Hydrostatic drives

Intensifiers

Interface devices

Joints, rotating and swivel, hydraulic and pneumatic

Logic devices, air

Lubricators

Manifolds

Measuring devices and meters

Motors, air rotary

Motors, electrohydraulic stepping

Motors, hydraulic rotary

Motors, low-speed–high-torque

Pipe

Pulsation dampers

Pumps

Reservoirs and accessories

Restrictive orifices

Seals, scrapers, backup rings, and boots

Shock absorbers

Steam traps

Strainers

Switches, flow

Switches, level

Switches, limit and proximity

Switches, pressure and temperature, hydraulic

Switches, pressure and temperature, pneumatic

Transducers, pressure

Tubing

Valves, directional control

Valves, electrohydraulic servo

Valves, flow control

Valves, pressure control

Valves, level control

Various materials are used in these components. It is important to be aware of their compatibility with fluids used in industry. Table 1-1 provides such data.

Some of the major components of fluid systems will be discussed here in detail. Consult other sections of this handbook as well.

PUMPS

A pump is the most essential component of a hydraulic system in the absence of another source of pressure. The most common other source of pressure is a reservoir kept at high elevation (or potential energy). However, water at high elevation automatically exerts a static pressure and does not require much more explanation. Since pumps have diverse characteristics according to their speed and size and require extended discussion for a thorough understanding, only the most essential details will be discussed here. The Hydraulic Institute[1] classification of pumps given in Fig. 1-1 is useful.

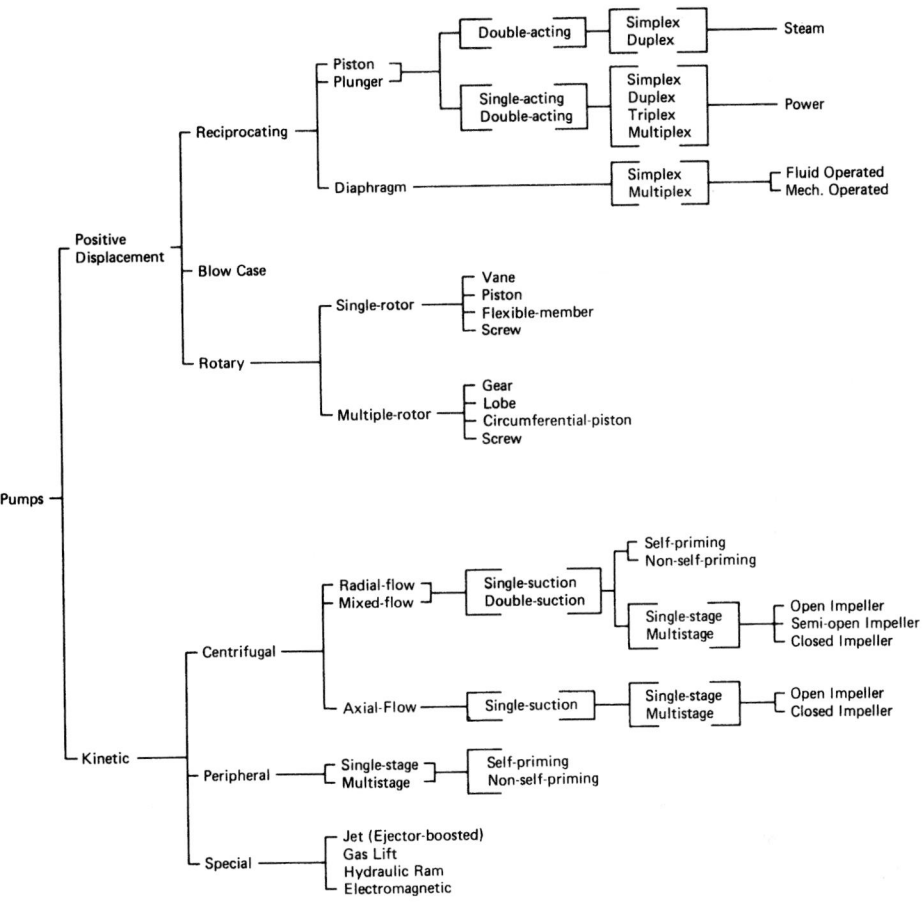

FIGURE 1-1 Classification of pumps.

Types of Pumps

Positive-Displacement-Type Pumps. These pumps (reciprocating plunger, rotary-gear, screw, piston, vane, etc.) create pressure by a direct-contact push to the liquid. They are employed generally for medium-pressure, low-flow applications, such as a metering pump to displace a known volume of fluid in a specified time. Large-size positive-displacement pumps usually become uneconomical because of space requirements.

Rotary-Gear Pumps. A rotary-gear pump, shown in Fig. 1-2, depends for its action on a pair of gears closely fitted in a housing. Fluid enters the tooth spaces usually on the inlet side and is carried along the casing to the outlet side.

Centrifugal Pumps. The pumps more commonly used in plant applications are of the centrifugal type, in which the rotary motion of the impeller imparts centrifugal force to the liquid, thereby raising the pressure. The selection of the impeller of a particular centrifugal pump (Fig. 1-3) is based upon the specific speed N_s as defined below:

$$N_s = \frac{N\sqrt{Q}}{H^{3/4}}$$

(1)

TABLE 1-1 Suitability of Various Metals and Alloys for Various Fluids*†

70°F = 21°C

Corrosive	Steel‡ C.I. D.I.	Brz.	316SS	CA-20	CD4MCu	Mon	Ni	H-B	H-C	Ti	Zi
Acetaldehyde, 70°F	B	A	A	A	A	A	A		A	A	A
Acetic acid, 70°F	X	A	A	A	A	B	B	A	A	A	A
Acetic acid, <50%, to boiling	X	B	A	A	B	B	B	C	A	A	A
Acetic acid, >50%, to boiling	X	X	B	A	C	B	B	X	A	A	A
Acetone, to boiling	A	A	A	A	A	A	A	A	A	A	A
Aluminum chloride, <10%, 70°F	X	B	C	B	C	B	C	A	A	B	A
Aluminum chloride, >10%, 70°F	X	X	C	B	C	C	X	A	B	B	A
Aluminum chloride, <10%, to boiling	X	X	X	C	X	X	X	A	X	X	A
Aluminum chloride, >10%, to boiling	X	X	X	X	X	X	X	A	X	X	A
Aluminum sulfate, 70°F	X	B	A	A	A	B	B	A	A	A	A
Aluminum sulfate, <10%, to boiling	X	B	B	A	B	X	X	A	B	C	B
Aluminum sulfate, >10%, to boiling	X	C	C	B	C	X	X	B	B	C	B
Ammonium chloride, 70°F	X	X	B	B	B	B	B		A	A	A
Ammonium chloride, <10%, to boiling	X	X	B	C	C	C	C	B	C	C	C
Ammonium chloride, >10%, to boiling	X	X	X	B	C	X	X		C	C	C
Ammonium fluosilicate, 70°F	X	X	C	B	C	X	X	X	C	X	X
Ammonium sulfate, <40%, to boiling	X	X	B	B	C	B	B	X	B	A	A
Arsenic acid, to 225°F	X	X	C	B	C	X	X		B	A	A
Barium chloride, 70°F, <30%	X	B	C	B	C	B	B	B	B	B	B
Barium chloride, <5%, to boiling	X	B	C	B	C	B	B	B	B	A	A
Barium chloride, >5%, to boiling	X	C	X	C	X	C	C	C	C	C	C
Barium hydroxide, 70°F	B	X	A	A	A	B	A	B	B	A	A
Barium nitrate, to boiling	C	X	B	B	B	B	B	B		B	B
Barium sulfide, 70°F	C	C	B	B	B	X	X			A	A
Benzoic acid	X	C	B	B	B	B	B	A	A	A	A
Boric acid, to boiling	X	C	B	B	B	C	C	A	A	A	B
Boron trichloride, 70°F, dry	B	B	B	B	B	B	B	B	B	A	B
Boron trifluoride, 70°F, 10%, dry	B	B	B	A	B	A	A		B		
Brine (acid), 70°F	X	X	X	X	X	X	X	B	B		
Bromine (dry), 70°F	X	X	X	B	X	X	C	B	B	B	X
Bromine (wet), 70°F	X	X	X	X	X	X	C	B	B	X	X
Calcium bisulfite, 70°F	X	X	B	B	B	X	X	A	B	A	A
Calcium bisulfite, to hot	X	X	C	B	C	X	X		C	A	A
Calcium chloride, 70°F	B	C	B	B	B	B	B	A	A	A	A
Calcium chloride, <5%, to boiling	C	C	B	B	C	A	A	A	A	B	C
Calcium chloride, >5%, to boiling	X	C	C	B	C	C	C	A	A	A	B
Calcium hydroxide, 70°F	B	B	B	B	B	B	B	A	A	A	A
Calcium hydroxide, <30%, to boiling	C	B	B	B	B	B	B	A	A	A	A
Calcium hydroxide, >30%, to boiling	X	X	C	C	C	C	C		B	A	A
Calcium hypochlorite, <2%, 70°F	X	X	X	C	X	X	X	A	A	A	A

Chemical											
Calcium hypochlorite, >2%, 70°F	B	A		X	X	X	C	X	X	B	X
Carbolic acid, 70°F (phenol)	A	A	B	A	A	A	B	C	B	C	C
Carbon bisulfide, 70°F		A	B	B	B	A	B	B	A	B	B
Carbonic acid, 70°F	A	A	A	B	B	A	B	B	B	B	B
Carbon tetrachloride, dry to boiling	A	A	B	A	C	B	A	X	B	C	B
Chloric acid, 70°F		A	B	A	A	A	B	C	C	B	X
Chlorinated water, 70°F			A	X	B	B	A	X	X	C	C
Chloroacetic acid, 70°F	A	B	A	A	X	C	X	X	X	X	X
Chlorosulfonic acid, 70°F	B	B	B	C	C	C	X	C	X	X	X
Chromic acid, <30%	X	X	A	A	A	A	C	C	X	B	B
Citric acid	A	A	A	A	A	A	A	B	X	A	A
Copper nitrate, to 175°F	A	B	B	B	X	X	X	X	X	B	C
Copper sulfate, to boiling	A	C	C	B	X	X	X	X	C	C	C
Cresylic acid		B	C	X	B	C	C	C	X	C	C
Cupric chloride	B	X	X	X	X	X	X	C	B	X	X
Cyanohydrin, 70°F		C	B	B	B	C	X	B		B	B
Dichloroethane		B	C	B	B	B	B	B	B	B	B
Diethylene glycol, 70°F	B	A	A	A	A	A	B	A	B	A	A
Dinitrochlorobenzene, 70°F, dry	A	A	A	A	A	A	A	A	A	A	A
Ethanolamine, 70°F	X	X	B	C	B	X	C	X		B	B
Ethers, 70°F	A	A	A	A	A	B	B	A	B	B	A
Ethyl alcohol, to boiling	A	A	B	A	B	B	A	A	A	A	A
Ethyl cellulose, 70°F	B	B	B	B	B	B	A	B	B	B	B
Ethyl chloride, 70°F	B	B	C	A	C	A	B	B	B	B	B
Ethyl mercaptan, 70°F			C	A	B	B	B	B	B	B	B
Ethyl sulfate, 70°F	B	B	B	A	B	B	B	B	B	B	B
Ethylene chlorohydrin, 70°F	B	B	B	A	B	B	B	C	B	A	A
Ethylene dichloride, 70°F	B	B	B	B	B	A	B	X	C	A	A
Ethylene glycol, 70°F	B	B	B	B	A	A	A	A	B	A	A
Ethylene oxide, 70°F	X	X	B	X	B	B	B	X	B	B	X
Ferric chloride, <5%, 70°F	X	X	X	X	X	X	X	C	X	A	A
Ferric chloride, >5%, 70°F	X	X	B	X	X	X	X	X	X	B	B
Ferric nitrate, 70°F	X	B	C	B	C	C	X	B		B	B
Ferric sulfate, 70°F	X	C	C	B	C	C	C	B	B	B	C
Ferrous sulfate, 70°F	C	C	B	A	B	B	A	C	A	B	A
Formaldehyde, to boiling	B	B	C	A	C	X	A	B	B	A	B
Formic acid, to 212°F	X	X	X	A	X	X	B	C	A	A	A
Freon, 70°F	A	A	A	A	A	A	A	A	A	A	A
Hydrochloric acid, <1%, 70°F	X	C	C	B	C	C	B	X	X	B	B
Hydrochloric acid, 1-20%, 70°F	X	X	X	X	X	X	X	X	X	X	X
Hydrochloric acid, >20%, 70°F	X	X	X	X	X	X	B	X	X	B	B
Hydrochloric acid, <½%, 175°F	X	C	C	C	X	X	B	C	B	B	C
Hydrochloric acid, ½-2%, 175°F	X	X	X	X	C	X	B	X	B	B	B
Hydrocyanic acid, 70°F	X	C	B	A	B	B	A	X	A	A	A
Hydrogen peroxide, <30% <150°F	C	B	B	C	B	C	C	B	B	B	B
Hydrofluoric acid, <20%, 70°F	X	C	X	X	X	X	X	B	X	B	B
Hydrofluoric acid, >20%, 70°F	X	X	X	X	X	X	X	C	X	X	X
Hydrofluoric acid, >20%, 50°F	C	C	X	C	X	C	C	C	O	C	C
Hydrofluoric acid, to boiling	X	O	X	X	X	X	X	C	C	X	X
Hydrofluosilicic acid, 70°F	X	X	C	B	C	X	C	X	X	B	B

TABLE 1-1 Suitability of Various Metals and Alloys for Various Fluids*† (Continued)

70°F = 21°C

Corrosive	Steel C.I. D.I.	Brz.	316SS	CA-20	CD4MCu	Mon	Ni	H-B	H-C	Ti	Zi
Lactic acid, <50%, 70°F	X	B	A	A	A	X	C	B	B	A	A
Lactic acid, >50%, 70°F	X	B	B	B	B	C	C	B	B	A	A
Lactic acid, <5%, to boiling	X	X	C	B	C	X	X	B	B	A	A
Lime slurries, 70°F	B	B	B	B	A	B	B	B	B	B	B
Magnesium chloride, 70°F	C	C	B	A	B	C	C	A	A	A	A
Magnesium chloride, <5%, to boiling	X	C	C	B	C	C	C	A	A	A	A
Magnesium chloride, >5%, to boiling	X	C	X	C	X	C	C	B	B	B	B
Magnesium hydroxide, 70°F	B	A	B	B	A	B	A	B	B	B	
Magnesium sulfate	C	C	B	B	B	B	B	C	C	B	B
Maleic acid	C	C	B	B	B	C	C	B	B	A	
Mercaptans	A	X	A	A	A	X	X				
Mercuric chloride, <2%, 70°F	X	X	X	X	X	X	X		B	A	A
Mercurous nitrate, 70°F	C	X	B	B	B	C	C		C		
Methyl alcohol, 70°F	A	A	A	A	A	A	A	A	A	A	A
Naphthalene sulfonic acid, 70°F	X	C	B	B	B	C	C	B	B		B
Naphthalenic acid, to hot	C	C	B	B	B	C	C	B	B		A
Nickel chloride, 70°F	X	X	C	B	C	C	X	A		B	B
Nickel sulfate	X	X	B	B	B	C	C		B	B	A
Nitric acid	X	X	B	B	B	X	X		B		B
Nitrobenzene, 70°F	A	C	A	A	A	B	B	B	B	B	B
Nitroethane, 70°F	A	A	A	A	A	A	A	A	A	A	A
Nitropropane, 70°F	A	A	A	A	A	A	A	A	A	A	A
Nitrous acid, 70°F	X	X	X	X	X	X	X				
Nitrous oxide, 70°F	C	C	C	C	C	X	X		C		
Oleic acid	C	C	B	B	B	C	C	C	C	C	C
Oleum, 70°F	B	X	B	B	B	X	X	B	B	B	
Oxalic acid	X	C	C	B	C	C	C	B	B	X	A
Palmitic acid	B	B	B	A	B	B	B	B			
Phenol (see carbolic acid)											
Phosgene, 70°F	C	C	B	B	B	C	C	B	B		
Phosphoric acid, <10%, 70°F	X	C	A	A	A	C	C	B	B	A	A
Phosphoric acid, >10–70%, 70°F	X	C	A	A	A	C	C	A	A	B	B
Phosphoric acid, <20%, 175°F	X	C	B	B	B	C	C	B	A	C	B
Phosphoric acid, >20%, 175°F <85%	X	C	C	B	C	C	C	A	A	A	C
Phosphoric acid, >10%, boil, <85%	C	C	X	C	C	B	C	B	C	C	C
Phthalic acid, 70°F	C	B	B	A	B	A	B	B	C	C	C
Phthalic anhydride, 70°F	B	C	A	A	A	A	A	A	A	B	A
Picric acid, 70°F	X	X	C	B	C	C	X		B	X	
Potassium carbonate	B	B	A	A	A	B	B	B	B		A
Potassium chlorate	B	C	A	A	A	C	C				
Potassium chloride, 70°F	C	C	B	B	B	B	B	B	B	A	A
Potassium cyanide, 70°F	B	X	B	B	B	C	C	B	B	A	A

Chemical											
Potassium dichromate	B	C	X	C	X	B	B	B	B	A	A
Potassium ferricyanide	C	B	B	B	B	B	B	B	B	A	A
Potassium ferrocyanide, 70°F	X	B	B	B	B	B	B	B	B	B	B
Potassium hydroxide, 70°F	C	C	C	B	A	C	A	A	B	B	A
Potassium hypochlorite	X	C	B	C	B	X	B	B	B	A	—
Potassium iodide, 70°F	C	B	B	B	B	B	B	B	B	B	B
Potassium permanganate	B	B	B	B	B	B	B	B	B	B	—
Potassium phosphate	C	B	B	C	B	B	C	B	B	B	B
Seawater, 70°F	C	B	B	B	A	A	A	A	A	A	A
Sodium bisulfate, 70°F	X	C	C	C	B	C	C	A	B	B	B
Sodium bromide, 70°F	B	B	B	B	B	B	B	B	B	B	A
Sodium carbonate	B	B	B	B	A	B	B	B	B	A	A
Sodium chloride, 70°F	C	B	B	B	B	B	B	A	B	B	B
Sodium cyanide	B	B	B	B	B	X	B	B	B	B	—
Sodium dichromate	B	X	B	B	B	B	B	B	B	B	B
Sodium ethylate	B	A	A	A	A	A	A	A	A	—	—
Sodium fluoride	C	B	B	B	B	B	B	C	C	B	B
Sodium hydroxide, 70°F	B	B	B	B	B	B	A	A	A	A	A
Sodium hypochlorite	C	C	C	C	C	X	X	B	B	A	B
Sodium lactate, 70°F	X	C	C	C	C	X	C	B	C	C	—
Stannic chloride, <5%, 70°F	C	X	X	X	B	C	C	B	B	A	A
Stannic chloride, >5%, 70°F	X	X	X	X	B	X	X	C	C	B	B
Sulfite liquors, to 175°F	X	C	B	B	B	C	B	B	A	A	A
Sulfur (molten)	B	A	A	A	C	C	C	A	A	—	—
Sulfur dioxide (spray), 70°F	C	B	B	B	B	C	B	B	B	C	A
Sulfuric acid, <2%, 70°F	X	B	B	B	A	C	A	A	A	A	A
Sulfuric acid, 2–40%, 70°F	X	C	B	B	B	C	A	A	A	B	C
Sulfuric acid, 40%, <90%, 70°F	X	X	C	C	C	X	A	A	A	C	C
Sulfuric acid, 93–98%, 70°F	B	B	B	B	B	X	B	B	B	B	B
Sulfuric acid, <10%, 175°F	X	C	C	X	C	X	C	C	C	X	C
Sulfuric acid, 10–60% & >80%, 175°F	X	X	B	X	B	X	C	B	B	X	C
Sulfuric acid, 60–80%, 175°F	X	X	B	X	B	X	C	B	B	X	C
Sulfuric acid, <¾%, boiling	X	C	X	B	C	X	C	B	A	X	C
Sulfuric acid, ¾–40%, boiling	X	X	X	C	C	X	X	C	C	X	X
Sulfuric acid, 40–65% & >85%, boil	X	X	X	X	X	X	X	X	X	X	X
Sulfuric acid, 65–85%, boiling	X	X	X	X	X	X	X	X	X	X	X
Sulfurous acid, 70°F	C	C	C	B	B	X	B	B	B	A	B
Titanium tetrachloride, 70°F	C	C	C	B	B	C	C	B	B	A	A
Trichlorethylene, to boiling	B	B	B	B	B	B	B	B	B	B	B
Urea, 70°F	C	C	C	B	B	C	C	C	C	A	B
Vinyl acetate	B	B	B	B	B	B	B	B	B	A	—
Vinyl chloride	B	C	B	B	B	B	B	B	C	A	—
Water, to boiling	A	A	A	A	A	A	A	A	A	A	A
Zinc chloride	C	B	B	B	B	B	B	B	B	A	A
Zinc cyanide, 70°F	X	B	B	B	B	B	B	B	B	B	B
Zinc sulfate	X	C	A	A	C	C	A	B	C	A	B

* *Source:* Goulds Pumps, Inc., Seneca Falls, N.Y.

† Ni, nickel, ASTM A 296 Gr. CZ-100; H-B, Hastelloy alloy-B, ASTM A 494; H-C, Hastelloy alloy-C, ASTM A 494; Ti, titanium unalloyed, ASTM B 367 Gr. C-1; Zi, zirconium.

‡ Code: A, fully satisfactory; B, useful resistance; C, limited use; X, unsuitable.

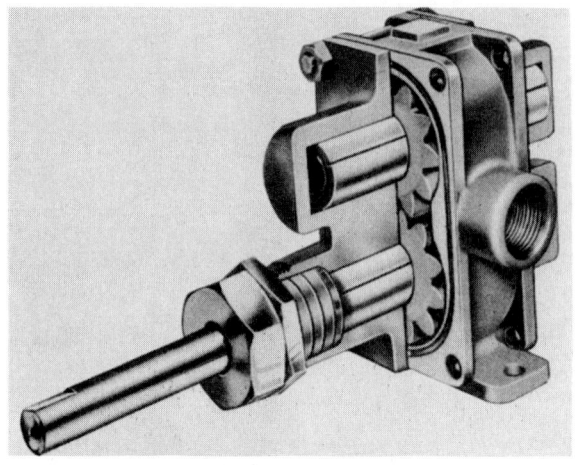

FIGURE 1-2 Rotary gear pump. (*ECO Pump Co.*)

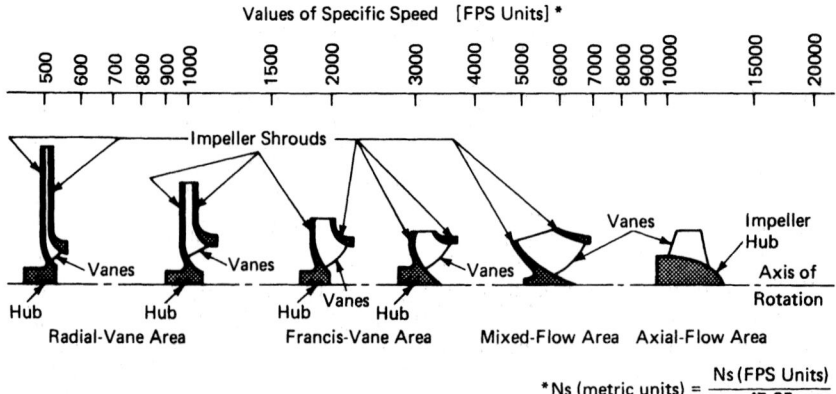

FIGURE 1-3 Selection of impeller design based on specific speed.

where N = pump rotation speed, r/min
 Q = nominal rate of flow to be pumped, gal/min (m³/s) (should be halved for double suction pump)
 H = total pressure head to be created by pump, ft (m)

In the specific speed range of 1000 to 6000 r/min double-suction impellers can also be used if axial thrust needs to be balanced.

Pump Terms

Total Dynamic Head.   The total dynamic head (TDH) of the pump needs to be determined. With reference to Fig. 1-4,

$$H = \text{TDH} = h_g^* + h_d + h_L \tag{2}$$

Also

$$H = h_{g,1} - h_{g,2} + \frac{V_2^2}{2g} - \frac{V_1^2}{2g} \tag{3}$$

where h_g^* = static suction head of the pump, ft (m)
 h_d = static delivery discharge head of the pump, ft (m)
 h_L = head losses in the piping, including entrance, friction, bends, fittings, exit, etc., ft (m)
 $h_{g,1}^*$ = pressure (converted to head) indicated by suction gauge (vacuum gauge), ft (m). The asterisk indicates + Ve if pump is higher than suction water surface and − Ve if pump is lower than suction water surface.
 $h_{g,2}$ = pressure (converted to head) indicated by discharge gauge, ft (m)
 H = total static head of the pump, ft (m)

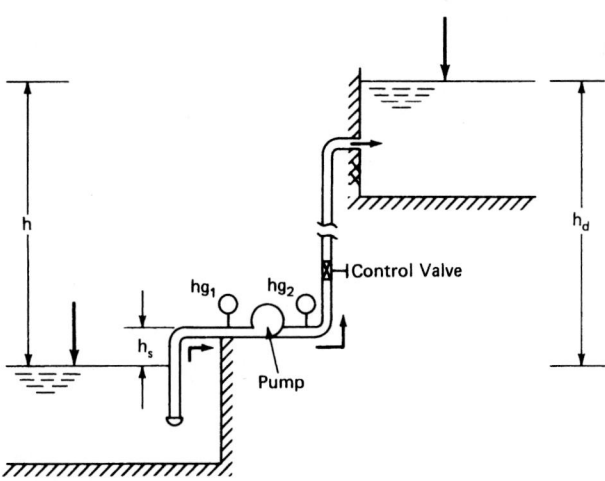

FIGURE 1-4   Definition sketch for pump heads.

Net Positive Suction Head.   The net positive suction head (NPSH) is another term that needs to be determined for the cavitation-free design and performance of a pump. It is the net absolute static pressure above the vapor pressure of the liquid in the pump:

$$\text{NPSH} = P_b - h_g^* - h_{f,s} - P_v \tag{4}$$

where P_b = barometric pressure (absolute), ft (m)
    P_v = vapor pressure of the liquid being pumped, ft (m)
    h_{fs} = head losses in suction line up to pump, ft (m)

The available NPSH (NPSHA) at a pump application (in a pump house) should be greater than the NPSH required (NPSHR) by the pump for an efficient (cavitation-free) operation. If NPSHA is less than NPSHR, it means that vapor is likely to form inside the pump. This vapor can accumulate and form bubbles which, when burst, can produce cavities (nonsmooth surfaces on impeller vanes).

Suction Specific Speed.   Here another term comes into the picture, the *suction specific speed S_s*:

$$S_g = \frac{N\sqrt{Q}}{(\text{NPSHR})^{3/4}} \tag{5}$$

The Hydraulic Institute[1] recommends S_s between 7480 and 10,690 r/min. See Eq. (1) for definitions of N and Q.

Data Specifications

A useful blank form for a specification sheet of pump data is given in Table 1-2. All data should be filled in and sent to vendors for further completion and bid preparation.

Pump Characteristic Curves.   Pump characteristic parameters that are a measure of the pump performance are discharge, head, horsepower, efficiency, and NPSH. These characteristics vary with the pump type, size, speed, etc. Some typical characteristics are shown in Fig. 1-5.

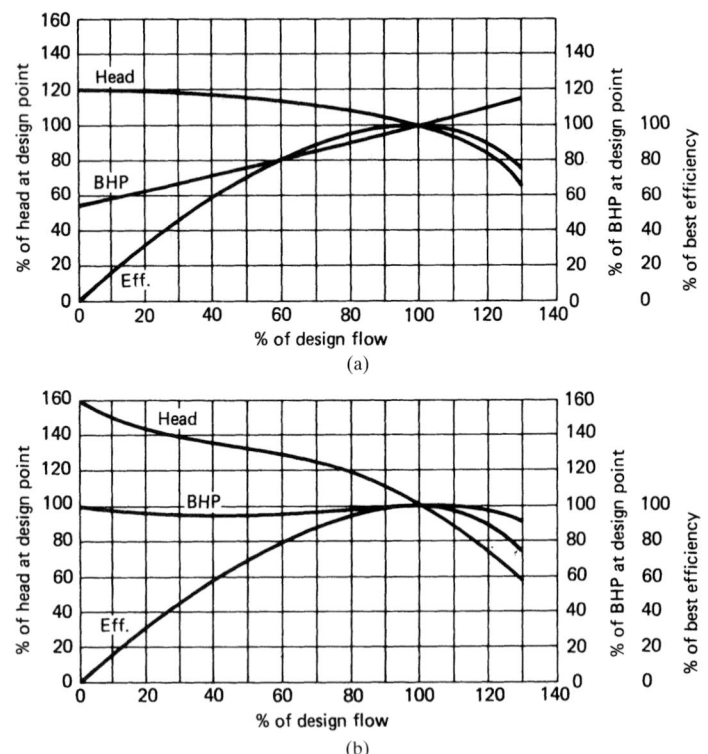

FIGURE 1-5 Pump characteristic curves: (*a*) radial-flow pump, (*b*) mixed-flow pump. (*Goulds Pumps, Inc.*)

TABLE 1-2 Centrifugal Pump Steam Turbine Specification Sheet

Client	Job no.
Plant location	Date
Inquiry no.	Equip. no.
Pump service	No. required

Operating Conditions	Specifications*	
Fluid pumped	Pump type	Cat. no.
	Stages	r/min
Pumping temp., °F	Suct. size, in.	Location
Spec. grav. @ P.T.	Noz. series	Flange facing
Visc. @ P.T., cP	Disch. size, in.	Location
Vap. press. @ P.T.	Noz. series	Flange facing
Solids % & comp.	Hydraulic hp	Efficiency, %
Suct. head, psia ft	bhp	Max. hp
Disch. head, psia ft	NPSH required by pump, ft fluid	
TDH, ft, normal Design	Pump materials & details*	
Pump cap., gal/min, normal Design	Case	Max. imp.
NPSH available, ft, fluid	Case Th'kn.	Corr. all.
Nonoverloading	Shaft	Dia. Keyway
Rotation (facing coupling end)	Shaft sleeves	Brinell
Motor by	Impeller	Type O.D.
hp V Ph. Freq.	Impeller wear ring	
Frame St. torque	Case wear ring	
Mfr. & type	Radial brg.	Mfg. no.
Enclosure Class Group	Thrust brg.	Mfg. no.
Turbine by	Packing	No. rings
Mfr. Model	Seal cage	Seal fluid
Type	Packing gland	
Rated hp	Mech. seal	Mfr.
Inlet steam, psia Temp., °F	Coupling	
Exh. steam, psia Temp., °F Quality	Base plate	
No. hr steam fl ¾ L ½ L	Drip (lip) (pan)	
Turbine performance curves, details, cuts, and	Wt. pump, lb.	
dimension sheets, etc., must be submitted by bidder	Wt. base plate, lb.	
Driver mounted by	Wt. driver, lb.	
Remarks	Total wt., lb.	
	Case design temp. °F	
	Case design press., psig	
	Case hydrostatic test, psig	
	Pump performance curves, details, cuts, dimension sheets, etc., must be submitted by bidder	

Bidder in proposal to complete these spaces and others				
left vacant. Successful bidder shall supply:				
Copies of certified dimension drawings				
Copies of performance curves for fluid pumped				
Copies of spare parts list				
Copies of operating instructions	No.	Date	Revision	Appr.

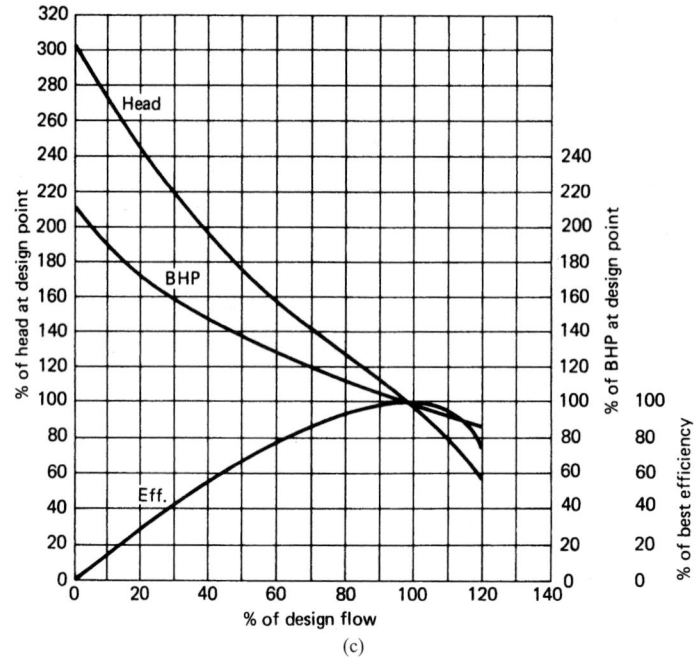

(c)

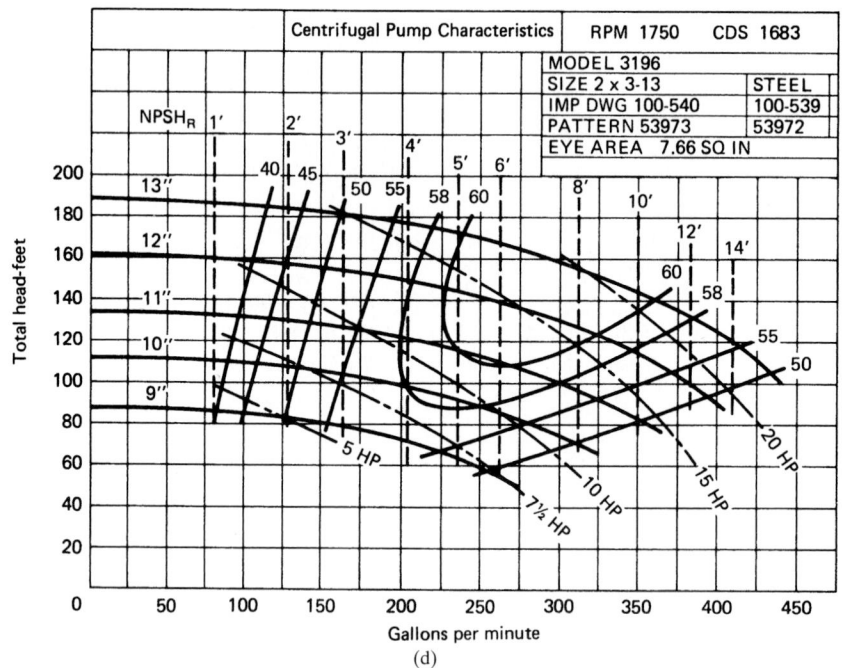

Gallons per minute

(d)

FIGURE 1-5 Pump characteristic curves: (*c*) axial-flow pump, (*d*) composite performance curve. (*Goulds Pumps, Inc.*)

The normal operating point of the pump should be selected somewhere on the sloping portion of the curve, not too close to shutoff or run-out conditions. The manufacturer usually recommends a pump that supplies within +10 percent of design flow or +5 percent of design TDH.

Figures 1-6 and 1-7 are typical curves developed by manufacturers to aid in pump selection.

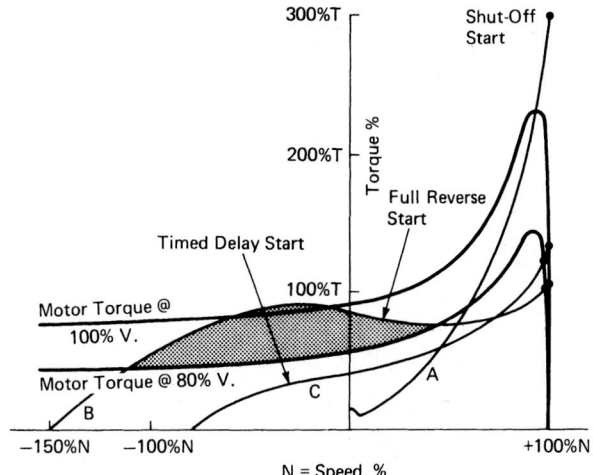

FIGURE 1-6   Start-up and shutdown of pumps. (*Allis-Chalmers.*)

Pump Construction and Maintenance.   Figures 1-8 and 1-9 show cross sections through some typical pumps. To control leakage, mechanical seals (discussed elsewhere in this book) serve best. The American National Standards Institute is often referred to for a proper design of pumps. ANSI B73.1 is a standard for horizontal centrifugal pumps.

Proper design of the pumphouse and pump-suction bays, inlet conditions, etc., is very important for proper performance of the pumps.[2]

Basic dimensions of the pumps required are first evolved on the basis of the Hydraulic Institute publication, "Standards for Centrifugal Pumps"; however, the final dimensions on the construction drawings have to be based on the pump manufacturers' recommendations, as their requirements are evolved on the basis of their own model tests. A matter of great importance is to determine the pump TDH and the NPSH which in turn reflect the overall dimensions of the suction intakes. Shape of the intake, depth, and clearances are among the important critical factors that affect the performance of large circulating-water pumps.

Hydraulic performance of a large-capacity pump is also affected by the formation of submerged or surface vortices in the sump area, which in practice are not visually observable because of the cover on the sump necessary to mount the pumping equipment and motors. Therefore, it is imperative to give careful consideration to the sump dimensions, preferably by the way of model experiments (discussed later). Moreover, the size of the pump house (including intake canal, cooling-tower basin for closed system, etc.) should be enough to store (or bypass) any transient quantities caused by sudden pump failures or operation of valves. Another important aspect of the pump house is to provide a device for measuring the actual flow and discharge pressure of each pump.

Preliminary dimensions of a pump house can be arrived at by using the guidelines given in Ref. 1 or a vendor's engineering data book.

Maintenance.   Basically, pump maintenance requires proper lubrication according to the manufacturer's recommendations. Stuffing boxes and packings must be inspected and maintained as necessary. If proper setup, operation, and maintenance are not performed, the defects shown in Table 1-3 will be evident.[3] They should be corrected as soon as discovered.

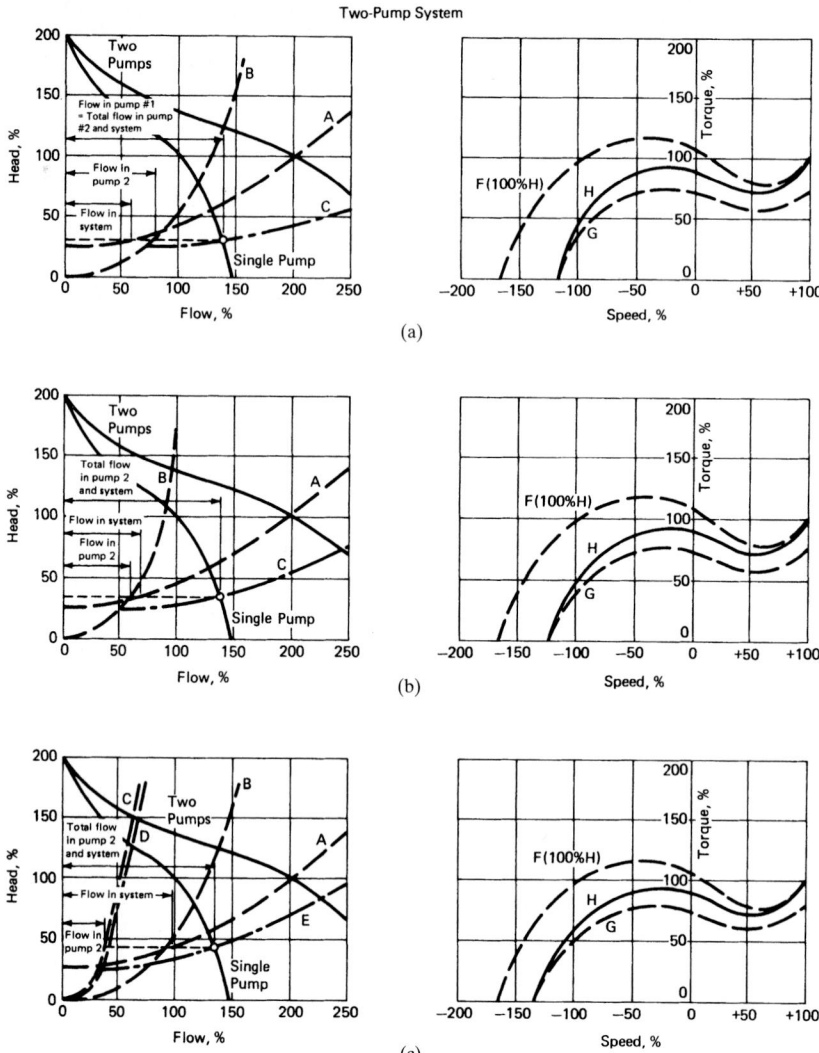

FIGURE 1-7 Starting large custom pumps against reverse flow. (*a*) Friction curves with pump characteristics are used to determine complete speed-torque curve. Pump 1 is operating and pump 2 is being started against reverse flow with valve open. (*b*) Starting at zero speed with valve open and reverse flow in pump, the speed-torque curve is identical. Because anti-reverse device prevents reverse rotation, maximum torque requirements are less. (*c*) Interlocking of valve operator and motor starter requires consideration of friction-head characteristic of the valve. The figure gives head vs. flow curves for single-pump operation and for two pumps in parallel operation, when both are running in the forward direction. The transient phase of starting is shown by dashed/dotted lines. The corresponding torque requirements are shown on the right. (*Allis-Chalmers.*)

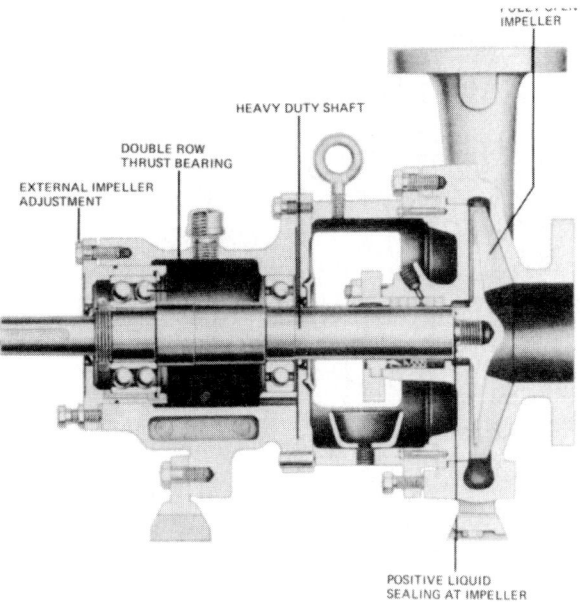

FIGURE 1-8   Cross-sectional view of a horizontal centrifugal pump.
(*Goulds Pumps, Inc.*)

VALVES

A valve is used to regulate the flow in a pipe. A hydraulic system may contain several valves, some of which may be just for full open-close positions, while other valves regulate the quantity of flow as desired. The latter are usually categorized as control valves. Control valves can be either manually or automatically operated depending upon the desired amount of flow, according to pressure, temperature, level, etc. (See Chap. 11-2, "Automatic Controls.") Instrumentation is usually provided in the system to measure and sense the quantities. In automatic operation of the valve, the sensors send signals directly to the air-electric or other operating mediums that supply force to the automatic-controlling mechanisms. The valves are available as flanged, screwed, or welded inlet-outlet ports. The standards normally referenced for valves are ANSI-B16.10 and ASME Boiler and Pressure Vessel Code VIII, III. See also Chap. 10-6, "Valves."

Valve Pressure Drop

A way to represent the pressure drop through the valves (especially for control valves) is called the *flow coefficient* C_v. It is defined as the number of gallons per minute of water which will pass through a given flow restriction with a pressure drop of 1 lb/in^2. (The actual fluid does not necessarily have to be water. There are formulas available for calculating C_v for other fluids also.)

The relationship between C_v and valve loss coefficient K (see Table 1-4) is easy to derive from definitions. For liquid service,

$$C_v = Q \sqrt{\frac{G_f}{\Delta P}} \tag{6}$$

$$\Delta P = K \frac{V^2}{2} \tag{6a}$$

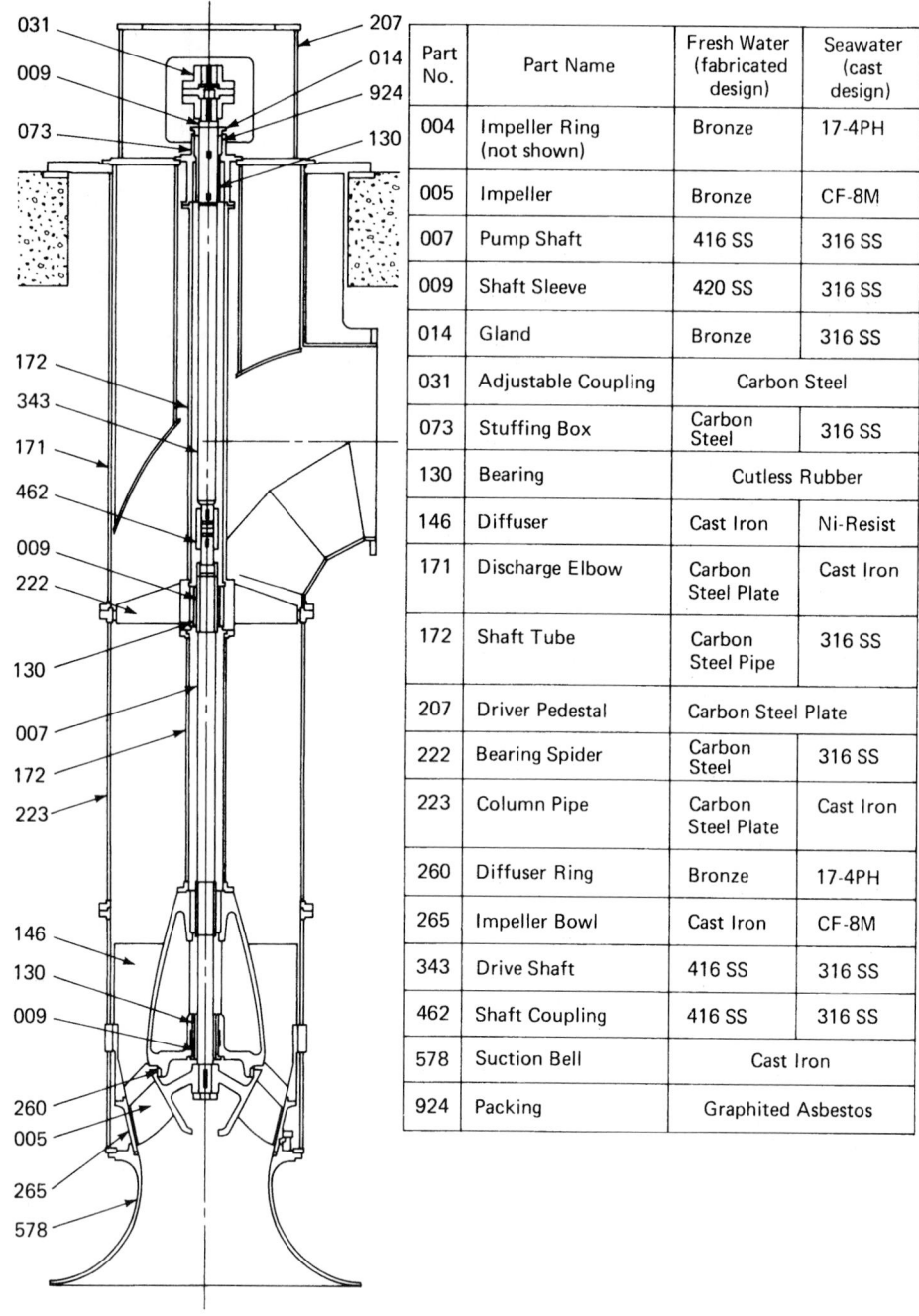

Part No.	Part Name	Fresh Water (fabricated design)	Seawater (cast design)
004	Impeller Ring (not shown)	Bronze	17-4PH
005	Impeller	Bronze	CF-8M
007	Pump Shaft	416 SS	316 SS
009	Shaft Sleeve	420 SS	316 SS
014	Gland	Bronze	316 SS
031	Adjustable Coupling	Carbon Steel	
073	Stuffing Box	Carbon Steel	316 SS
130	Bearing	Cutless Rubber	
146	Diffuser	Cast Iron	Ni-Resist
171	Discharge Elbow	Carbon Steel Plate	Cast Iron
172	Shaft Tube	Carbon Steel Pipe	316 SS
207	Driver Pedestal	Carbon Steel Plate	
222	Bearing Spider	Carbon Steel	316 SS
223	Column Pipe	Carbon Steel Plate	Cast Iron
260	Diffuser Ring	Bronze	17-4PH
265	Impeller Bowl	Cast Iron	CF-8M
343	Drive Shaft	416 SS	316 SS
462	Shaft Coupling	416 SS	316 SS
578	Suction Bell	Cast Iron	
924	Packing	Graphited Asbestos	

FIGURE 1-9   Vertical mixed-flow column pump. (*Allis-Chalmers.*)

where Q = liquid flow rate, gal/min = 448.8AV
       G_f = specific gravity of liquid, for water = 1
       ΔP = pressure drop at the valve for flow Q, lb/in^2
       V = flow velocity, ft/s

For critical and flashing flows, when the pressure drop cannot be obtained from Eq. (6a), the equation is

$$\Delta P = C_f^2 \, \Delta P_s \tag{7}$$

$$\Delta P_s = P_l - P_v \tag{8}$$

where C_f = critical flow factor = 0.6 to 0.9 depending upon valve type
       P_l = pressure upstream of the valve
       P_v = vapor pressure of liquid

For gas and vapor flow, the above formulas are modified to suit the flow units.[4] Chapter 10-6, "Valves," describes the more important valves in plant use.

OTHER COMPONENTS OF A SYSTEM

Besides pumps and valves, system piping must be considered. This includes associated fittings such as bends, reducers, branches, elbows, and T connections. (See Chap. 10-2.) Standard pipe dimensions, i.e., nominal diameter, inside diameter, thickness, etc., for various schedule pipes, are available from literature.[5,6] Table 1-5 gives the important dimensions and burst pressures for some of the sizes and classes. The velocity of flow in a pipe should normally range from 8 to 15 ft/s (2.44 to 4.57 m/s) in order to keep the pressure drop reasonably low for a given pump size and also to deliver an optimum amount of fluid.

Other components are often a part of hydraulic systems. These include heat exchangers, filters, strainers, demineralizers, spray nozzles, steam traps, expansion joints, restrictive orifices, and measuring devices (already discussed).

Graphic Symbols for Fluid Power Systems

According to the American National Standards Institute definition, fluid power systems are those that transmit and control power through the use of a pressurized fluid within an enclosed circuit. ANSI Y32.10 gives graphic symbols commonly used for drawing circuit diagrams of fluid power systems. They show connections, flow paths, and functions of components represented. Some of the important symbols are given here in Fig. 1-10.

Figure 1-11 is an illustration of a power system and its symbolic representation. This example illustrates a pump that transfers liquid from reservoir through a check valve and a four-way control valve to hydraulic cylinders, the other ends of which are connected to another open reservoir containing liquid.

A TYPICAL HYDRAULIC SYSTEM

In order to illustrate the use of hydraulic components, one hydraulic system will be discussed here in detail. It is the circulating-condenser, cooling-water system, one of the very important systems for a thermal power plant.[2] It is important because of the large quantity of water required which in turn necessitates large open channels, pipes, valves, etc., in the system.

TABLE 1-3 Causes and Symptoms of Malfunctions of Pumps

Causes	Symptoms									
	The pump fails to deliver liquid	Capacity is inadequate	Head is inadequate	The pump cuts out after starting	Power required by pump is too high	Excessive leakage of stuffing box	Packing must be renewed too frequently	The pump vibrates or is noisy	Bearings heat up	Pump runs heavily or seizes
Pump and suction line are not sufficiently primed with the liquid handled	•			•						
Excessive suction lift	•	•		•				•		
Insufficient margin between suction lift and vapor pressure	•	•		•				•		
Liquid contains gas	•	•		•						
Air pocket in suction line		•		•						
Air leak in suction line	•	•		•						
Air leaks into pump along stuffing box		•		•						
Foot valve too small		•								
Foot valve partly clogged		•						•		
Foot valve and suction line not fully submerged	•	•		•				•		
Connection of water seal on suction stuffing box blocked				•			•	•		
Lantern ring in stuffing box incorrectly fitted				•		•	•			
Speed too low	•	•	•							
Speed too high	•				•					
Incorrect direction of rotation	•	•	•		•					
Total manometric head of system greater than manometric head of the pump	•	•	•		•					
Total manometric head of system lower than manometric head of the pump					•					
Specific gravity of liquid handled not what it was originally supposed to be					•					•
Viscosity of liquid handled not what it was originally supposed to be		•	•		•					•

Pump operating at too low a capacity

Parallel connection unsuitable for the specific operating conditions

Line, impeller, or pump casing clogged

Pump set incorrectly aligned

Foundation not level

Pump shaft warped

A rotating part runs against a stationary part, e.g., impeller runs against wearing rings

Bearing(s) defective

Wearing rings worn

Impeller damaged

Pump shaft or shaft sleeve worn locally at the stuffing box

Stuffing box incorrectly packed

Type of packing used unsuitable for liquid handled

Impeller out of balance

Failure to apply water cooling when handling hot liquids

Clearance between pump shaft and bore of pump casing at the bottom of the stuffing box too great

Liquid for water seal contains impurities

Gland overtightened

Axial fit of complete pump shaft with impeller incorrect

Insufficient or excessive lubrication

Lubricant contains impurities

Bearings incorrectly fitted

TABLE 1-4   Typical Values of $K*$

45° bend	0.35 to 0.45
90° bend	0.50 to 0.75
Tees	1.50 to 2.00
Gate valves (full open)	about 0.25
Check valves (open)	about 3.0
Ball valve (open)	about 0.1
Butterfly valve (open)	about 1.0
Globe valve (open)	about 2.0
Plug valve (open)	about 0.5

* In the one-quarter-open position, a valve will have a K value several times that in the full-open position.

TABLE 1-5   Important Pipe Dimensions and Burst Pressures (U.S. Customary Units)

Nominal pipe size, in	Outside diameter of pipe, in	Schedule 40 (standard)		Schedule 80 (extra strong)		Schedule 160		Double (extra strong)	
		Inside diameter of pipe, in	Burst pressure, lb/in^2	Inside diameter of pipe, in	Burst pressure, lb/in^2	Inside diameter of pipe, in	Burst pressure, lb/in^2	Inside diameter of pipe, in	Burst pressure, lb/in^2
¼	0.540	0.364	16,000	0.302	22,000	—	—	—	—
⅜	0.675	0.493	13,500	0.423	19,000	—	—	—	—
½	0.840	0.622	13,200	0.546	17,500	0.466	21,000	0.252	35,000
¾	1.050	0.824	11,000	0.742	15,000	0.614	21,000	0.434	30,000
1	1.315	1.049	10,000	0.957	13,600	0.815	19,000	0.599	27,000
1¼	1.660	1.380	8,400	1.278	11,500	1.160	15,000	0.896	23,000
1½	1.900	1.610	7,600	1.500	10,500	1.338	14,800	1.100	21,000
2	2.375	2.067	6,500	1.939	9,100	1.689	14,500	1.503	19,000
2½	2.875	2.469	7,000	2.323	9,600	2.125	13,000	1.771	18,000

Hydraulics

A typical circulating-water system for a power plant is shown schematically in the plan view in Fig. 1-12. Large quantities of cooling water are withdrawn from a river by pumps provided in the intake canal. Trash racks and traveling screens are usually provided in the intake canal in order to keep the unwanted debris from entering the pumps and condensers. The discharge from the condensers can be thrown off-site into a large body of water (e.g., the ocean) for final heat dissipation. A weir is usually provided downstream of the condenser to avoid the impact on the condensers from the downstream water-level fluctuations (e.g., due to tides). In order to dissipate the extra energy available from the fall over the weir and to accommodate a hydraulic jump, a stilling basin is usually provided downstream of the weir. If there is another waterway (say river) to be crossed downstream before approaching the ocean, pipes can pass under that waterway. Finally, under modern environmental practice, the hot water cannot be discharged into the ocean too near the shore. Therefore, water is pumped from the discharge canal to give offshore final discharge submerged for good heat dissipation. Valves are provided in the piping to control flow. No further discussion of heat dissipation is required here because the purpose of this chapter is not just to understand one system, but how to engineer a fluid system in general. A comprehensive knowledge of circulating water systems, if required, can be obtained from Ref. 2.

The first step in design is to plot a developed view of the system to scale, with all the hydraulic components (mentioned previously) indicated at least schematically. All the horizontal and vertical distances to these components should be plotted and the piping drawn properly. *Developed view* indicates plotting in two dimensions only. If there is a third dimen-

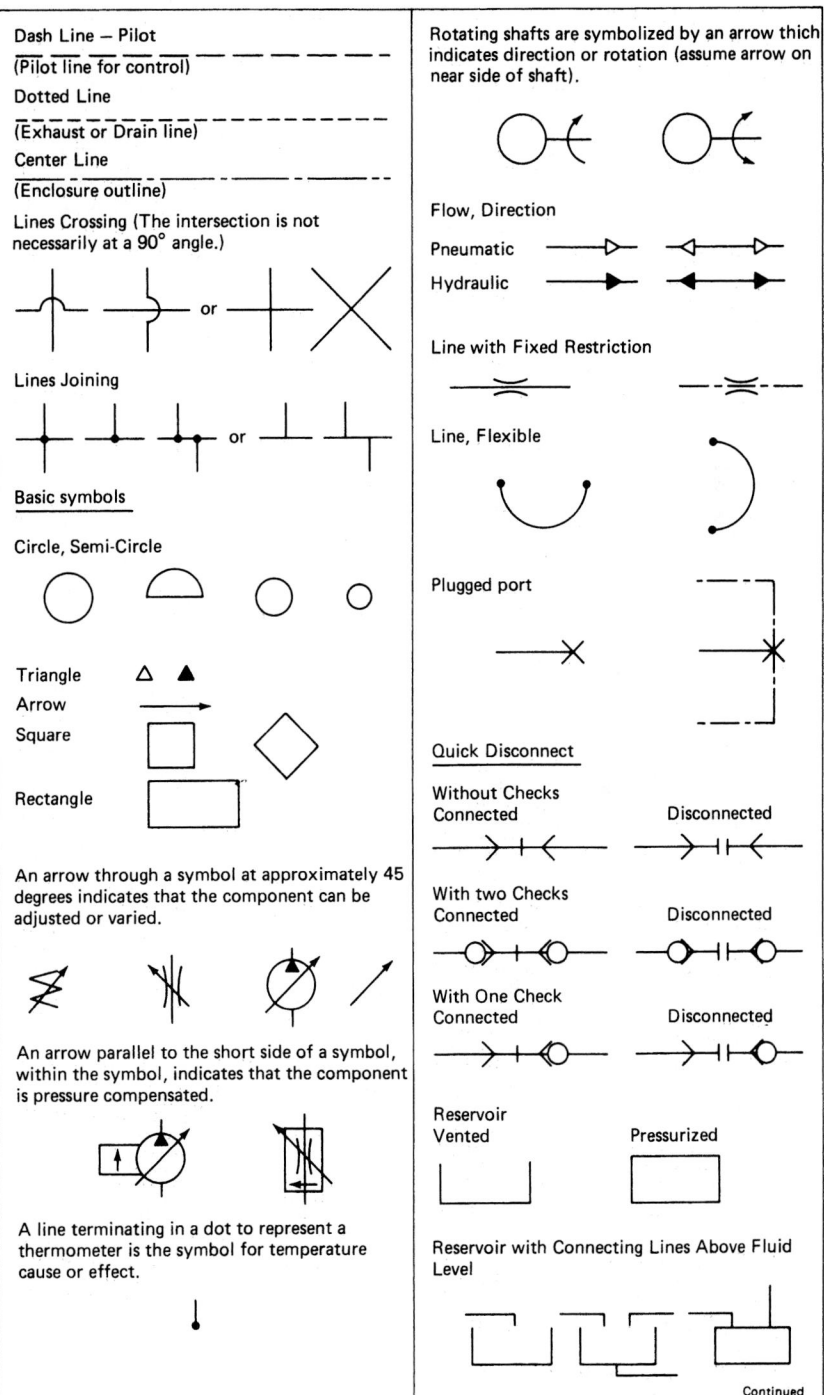

Dash Line — Pilot

(Pilot line for control)

Dotted Line

(Exhaust or Drain line)

Center Line

(Enclosure outline)

Lines Crossing (The intersection is not necessarily at a 90° angle.)

or

Lines Joining

or

Basic symbols

Circle, Semi-Circle

Triangle

Arrow

Square

Rectangle

An arrow through a symbol at approximately 45 degrees indicates that the component can be adjusted or varied.

An arrow parallel to the short side of a symbol, within the symbol, indicates that the component is pressure compensated.

A line terminating in a dot to represent a thermometer is the symbol for temperature cause or effect.

Rotating shafts are symbolized by an arrow thich indicates direction or rotation (assume arrow on near side of shaft).

Flow, Direction

Pneumatic

Hydraulic

Line with Fixed Restriction

Line, Flexible

Plugged port

Quick Disconnect

Without Checks
Connected   Disconnected

With two Checks
Connected   Disconnected

With One Check
Connected   Disconnected

Reservoir
Vented   Pressurized

Reservoir with Connecting Lines Above Fluid Level

Continued

FIGURE 1-10   Graphic symbols.

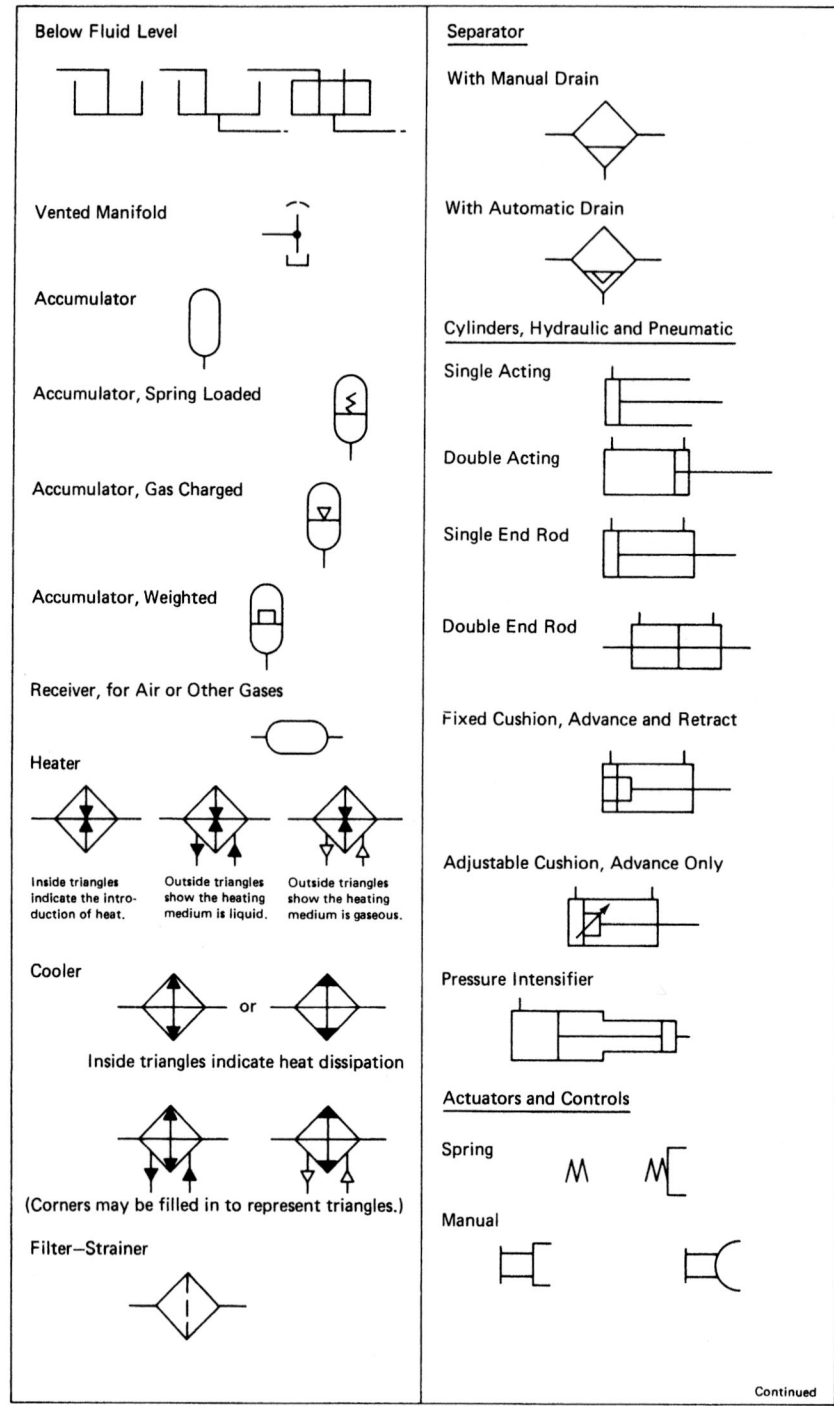

Below Fluid Level

Vented Manifold

Accumulator

Accumulator, Spring Loaded

Accumulator, Gas Charged

Accumulator, Weighted

Receiver, for Air or Other Gases

Heater

Inside triangles indicate the introduction of heat.

Outside triangles show the heating medium is liquid.

Outside triangles show the heating medium is gaseous.

Cooler

or

Inside triangles indicate heat dissipation

(Corners may be filled in to represent triangles.)

Filter—Strainer

Separator

With Manual Drain

With Automatic Drain

Cylinders, Hydraulic and Pneumatic

Single Acting

Double Acting

Single End Rod

Double End Rod

Fixed Cushion, Advance and Retract

Adjustable Cushion, Advance Only

Pressure Intensifier

Actuators and Controls

Spring

Manual

Continued

FIGURE 1-10 (*Continued*)

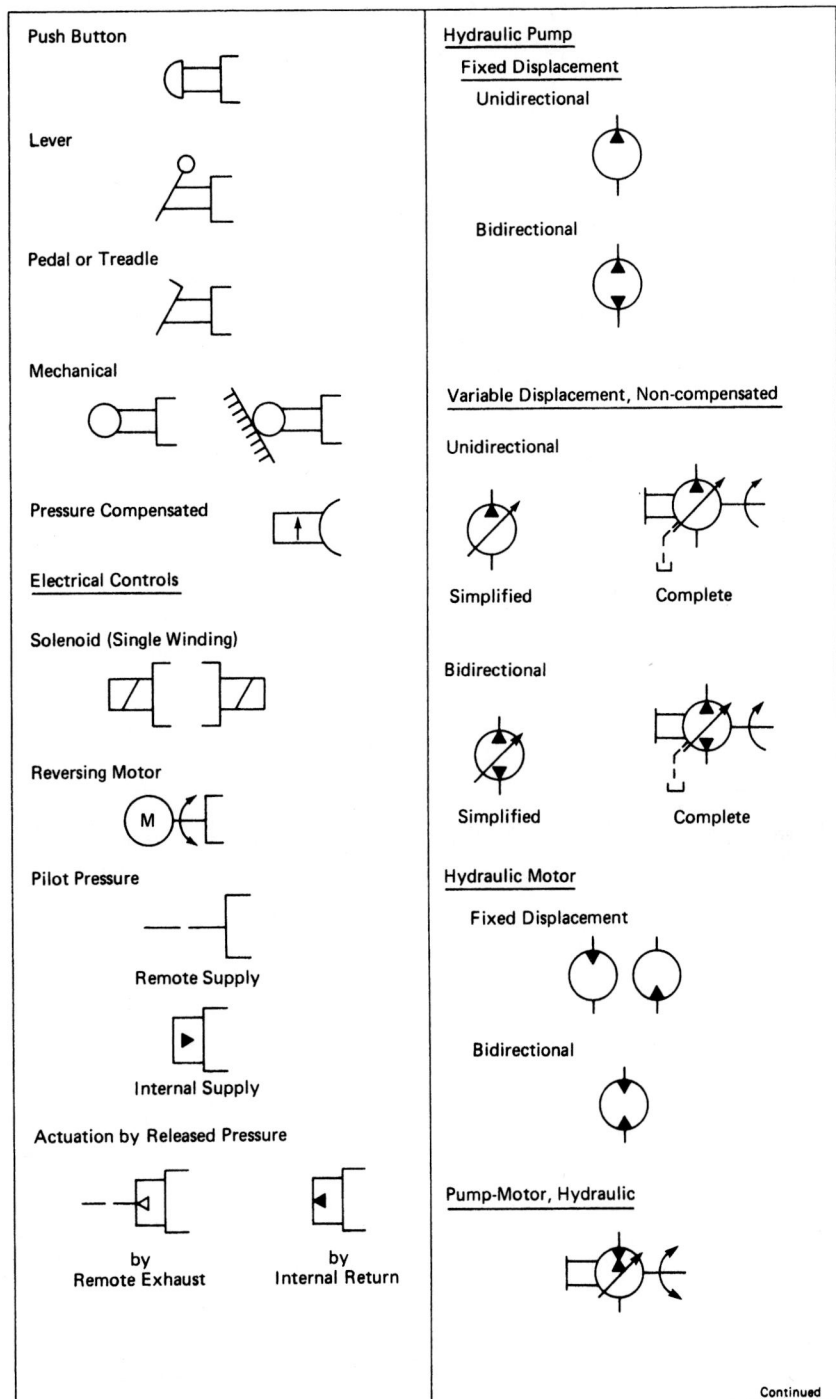

Push Button

Lever

Pedal or Treadle

Mechanical

Pressure Compensated

Electrical Controls

Solenoid (Single Winding)

Reversing Motor

Pilot Pressure

Remote Supply

Internal Supply

Actuation by Released Pressure

by
Remote Exhaust

by
Internal Return

Hydraulic Pump

Fixed Displacement

Unidirectional

Bidirectional

Variable Displacement, Non-compensated

Unidirectional

Simplified   Complete

Bidirectional

Simplified   Complete

Hydraulic Motor

Fixed Displacement

Bidirectional

Pump-Motor, Hydraulic

Continued

FIGURE 1-10   (*Continued*)

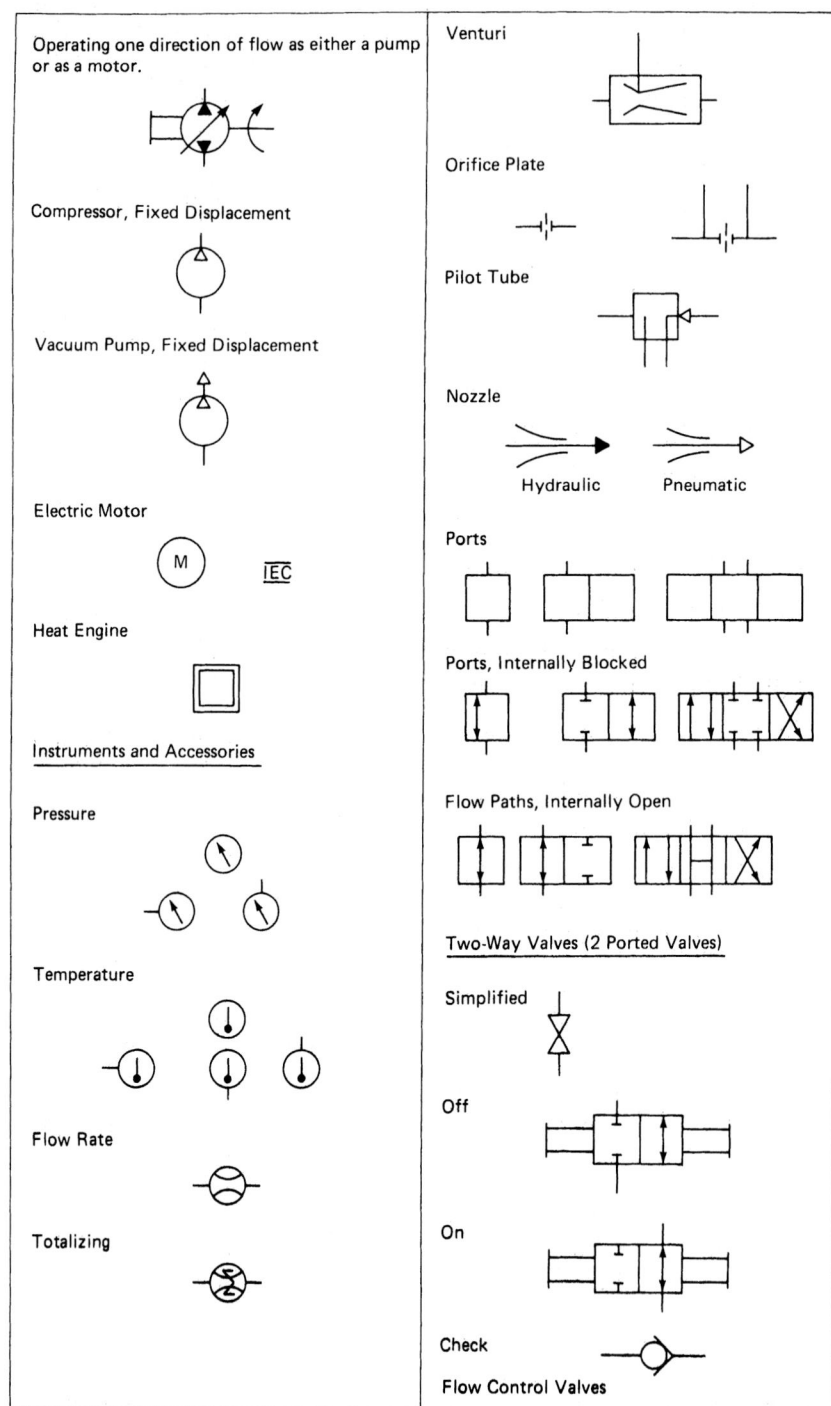

FIGURE 1-10 (*Continued*)

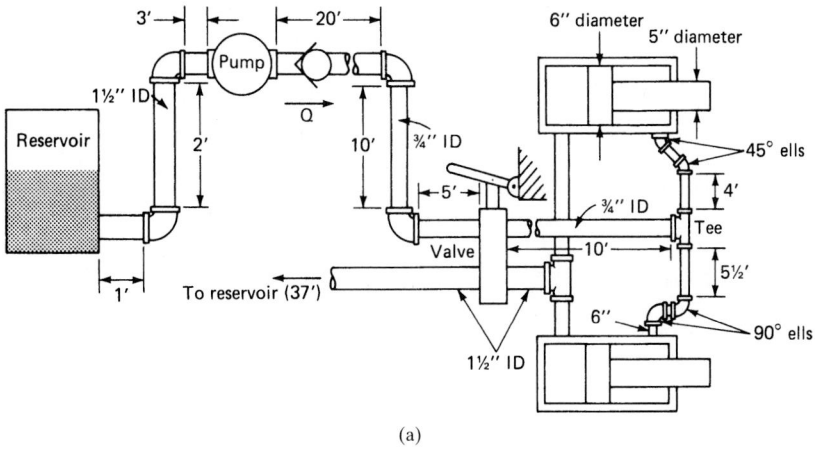

(a)

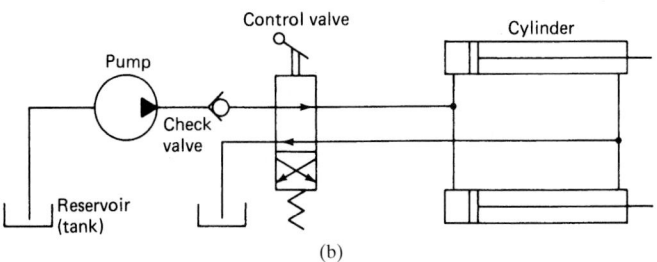

(b)

FIGURE 1-11   Illustration of power systems symbols.

sion, it should be rotated horizontally to bring it to the second dimension at the point where it occurs. Thus all the dimensions get accounted for. The vertical scale can be distorted (different from horizontal scale) in order to be able to see the elevations of each point clearly. All the components, transitions, bends, etc., should be properly accounted for.

For the circulating water system mentioned above, a developed picture is shown in Fig. 1-13, with some assumed dimensions. The next step is to plot a hydraulic gradient line for this system. In order to do this, all the head losses in the open channels, piping, and appurtenances have to be calculated and pump TDH established for the known flow rate, as mentioned in previous sections. In Fig. 1-13, the losses for valves, bends, etc., and the friction loss in the pipeline drop from the upstream end to the downstream end of the pipe as shown on the hydraulic gradient line.

The calculations of head losses in pipe fittings, valves, etc., and determination of pump TDH can best be accomplished by using a tabular form, e.g., Table 1-6. This keeps the number of computation sheets to a minimum, and the important factors are not omitted. It should be noted that the head-loss data for certain components, e.g., heat exchanger (condenser in this typical example), orifice plates, control valves, filters, etc., should be obtained from the catalogs of the manufacturers of specific components.

The TDH of the pump should be conservatively estimated so as not to fall short of pressure in the system, especially as the system gets older and scale deposits form, thereby increasing the pressure drops. If a little extra pressure is available from the pump in the beginning, the runout of the pump (excessive flow) can be controlled by throttling the flow at the

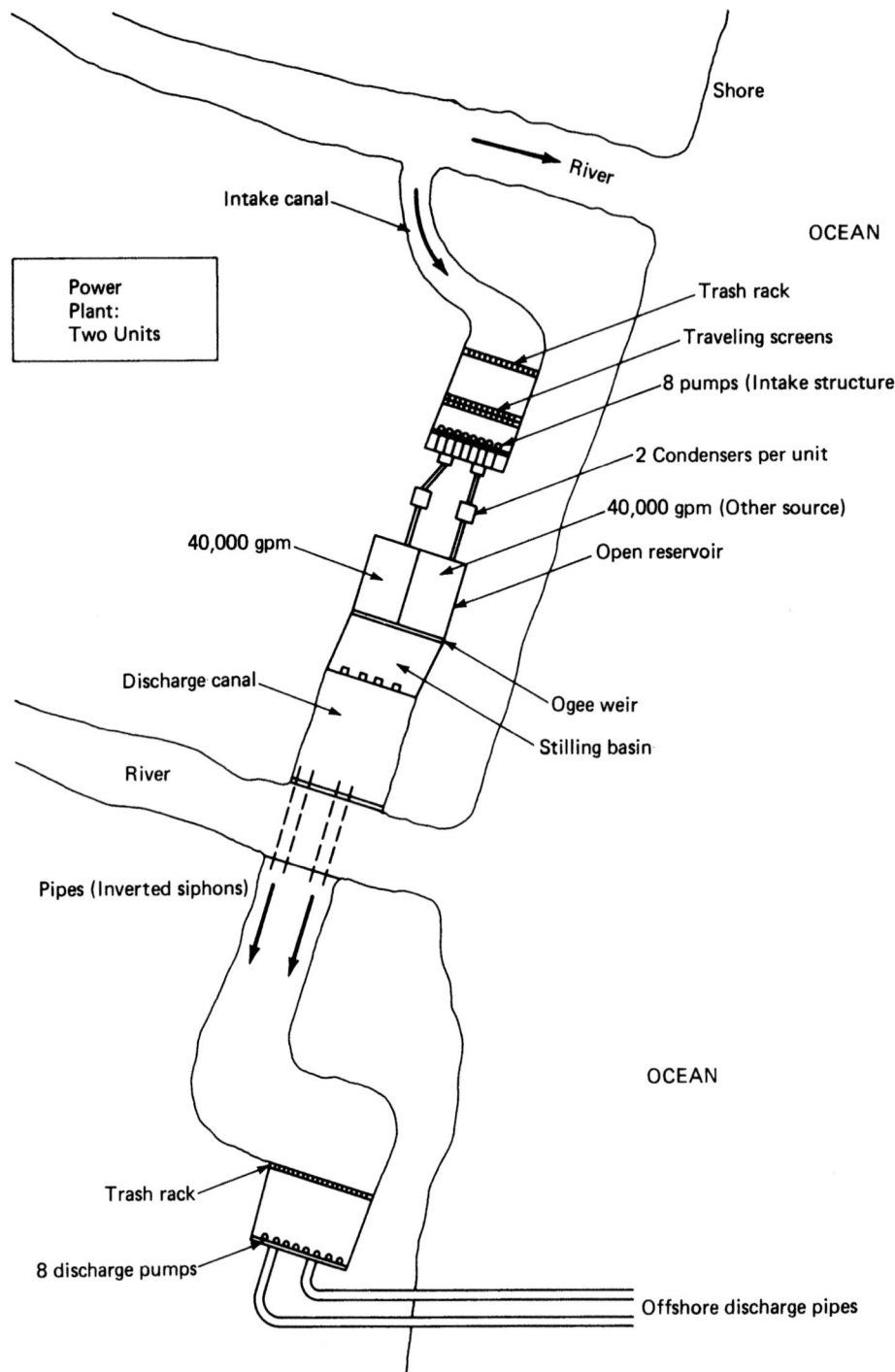

FIGURE 1-12 Cooling water system for a power plant.

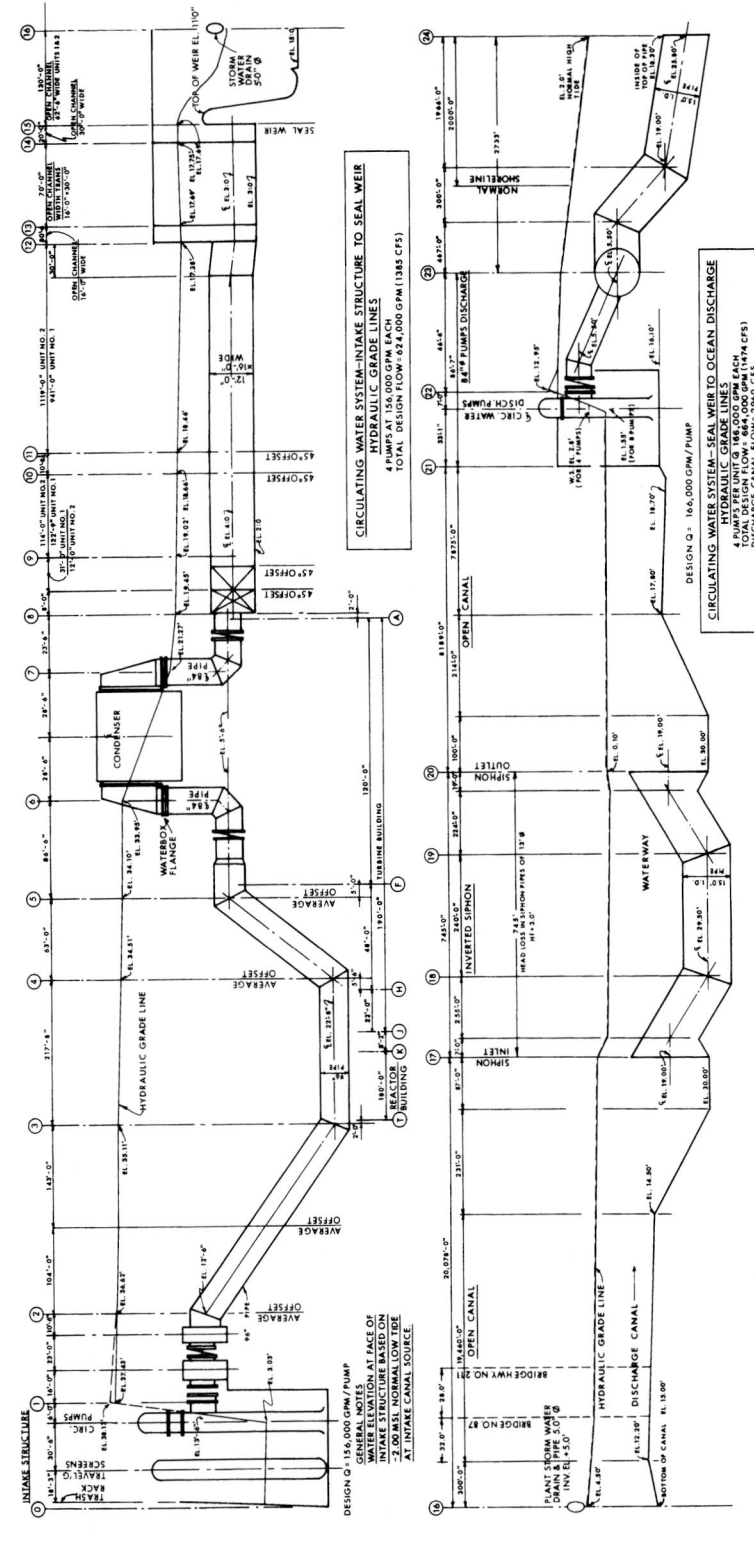

FIGURE 1-13 Hydraulic gradient of a circulating water system.

control valves in the system. Therefore, it is usually good to have some throttling-type valves in the system.

The TDH of the pump and performance of a system can be determined or verified in the field on the large-size systems because laboratory facilities are usually not large enough to handle full-scale flows. Field testing can be achieved by following one of the several measurement techniques outlined in a previous section. More sophisticated instrumentation and techniques are also available these days, such as annubar, current meter, etc., which are discussed in Ref. 7. More sophisticated flowmeters, e.g., magnetic-acoustic, are also available in the market.

Hydraulic transients and water-hammer aspects for varied system-pump-valve operations should be studied.

Process Instrumentation

The engineering of systems, such as the circulating water system discussed above, of course involves other aspects besides hydraulics. The most important, from a systems point of view, is to establish the various modes of operation and logic of the system components, e.g., pumps, control valves, etc. For this purpose, process instrumentation and control and logic diagrams are developed with reference to the system descriptions. More details on these are shown in Chap. 9-2, "Pneumatic Systems," but is applicable to both.

Other Aspects

Other important aspects include preparation of detailed technical specifications for the various types of equipment in the system. Besides the process aspects of the equipment, the materials and safety aspects should also be accounted for. A table of recommended materials and metals for various applications has already been discussed. It is recommended that the manufacture of the equipment should be closely monitored for quality assurance reasons and proper shop and field testing should be conducted *before* commercial operation.

Of course, maintenance of the systems and components is also a very important aspect. Only equipment properly inspected and maintained through lubrication and replacement of parts at periodic intervals will fulfill its life expectancy. Some checkpoints similar to those given in the discussion on pumps should be developed for all systems and components.

MODEL EXPERIMENTS

The science of hydraulic engineering depends on practical experience obtained from prototypes, or models. For the design of any hydraulic system, e.g., circulating water system, it is advisable to conduct model studies in order to determine the flow, pressure, and velocity distributions. In recent years, hydraulic-model studies have been conducted on the pump houses, channels, pipes, intake structures, diffusers, surrounding fluid fields, etc.

Intake, Discharge, and Pump House

Pump-house (and channels) hydraulics is unusual in that the flow pattern in the approach to the pump suction must be uniform, tranquil, and nonvortexing; it has a flow velocity of about 1 ft/s (0.305 m/s). Failing to conform to these criteria can result in inefficient performance of the system. Model studies on pump houses are conducted in order to ensure these criteria by providing enough length, width, transition, splitters, baffles, rounding of corners, etc., in the approach channel. Such model studies are usually conducted at a geometric scale of 1:8 to

TABLE 1-6 Pump Calculation Sheet (U.S. Customary Units)

Project _____ Design gal/min _____ Design TDH _____ Pump no. _____
Pump service _____ Date _____ Sch. & pipe matl. _____
Pump no. _____ Fluid pumped _____
Lb/h _____ Temp., max _____ Min _____ F
Normal gal/min _____ From _____ To _____ F
Design gal/min _____
Reference drawings _____

Viscosity @ min P.T. _____ cP(μ)
Spec. grav. @ min P.T. _____ (SG)
Kinematic viscosity _____ cS(z)
Vapor press. @ max P.T. _____ mmHg(VP)

	Suction line	Discharge line
Line no. & schedule		
Nom. line size, inches I.D. in; ft D/d — d		
Velocity, ft/s — V		
Frict. loss, ft fluid/100 ft — or f		
Reynolds number $V^2/2g$ — Re		
Lineal feet of pipe, or K\$		
Gate valves	@	@
Globe valves	@	@
Ells	@	@
Tees, thru branch	@	@
Tees, thru run	@	@
Ells 45° or other L	@	@
Butterfly/diaphragm	@	@
Check valves	@	@
Total equivalent length — EL		
Line frict. (F × EL/100)1.15 — $F_s^\dagger$ / $F_d^\dagger$		
Vessel pres. psig × 2.31/SG — $P_s^\dagger$ / $P_d^\dagger$		
Liquid elev. above pump, ft — h_s^* / h_d		
Tank contr. or enl. loss — h_c / h_e		
Alg. sum = suct. or disch. head — Hs / Hd		
Total dynamic head, Hd−Hs — TDH	_____ Ft(_____ " Suct. _____ " Disch.)
NPSH available:		
Abs pressure head — $P_s^\dagger + 34/SG$	−	+
Static head — h_s^*	+	+
Friction head — $h_e + F_s$	−	−
Vap. pres. head — $0.045 \times VP/SG$	−	−
Alg. sum = NPSH ft fluid		

$z = \mu/SG$
$h_c = V^2/128.8$
$h_e = V^2/64.4$

$$Re = \frac{3162 \times \text{gal/min} \times SG}{d \times \mu}$$

K\$ can be given in terms of f. K for pipe = fl/d.

*Minus for suction lift.
†Minus for pressure less than atmospheric. For elevations above sea level, decrease 34 by 1.1 ft for each 1000 ft of altitude above sea level.
Formulas:
$1\ \text{lb/in}^2 = (2.31/SG) = $ _____ ft. fluid
$V = 0.408\ \text{gal/min} \cdot d^2$

$$d = \sqrt{\frac{\text{gal/min}}{2.45v}}$$

1:15. Kinematic and dynamic similarities are achieved by further scaling according to the laws of Froude, Reynolds, etc. One important consideration is to see that supercritical flow and hydraulic jump (limiting the amount of flow and creating turbulence) do not exist in the approach channel. Sometimes flags or strings are attached at the bottom of the sump below the suction bell in order to see that all the flags are pointing radially and uniformly all around the bell. Lighted transparent (glass) window sections are provided at the important points, and dye injection tests are conducted in order to visualize the flow patterns.

Velocities are usually measured by miniature current meters, and pressures (or depth of water) are generally measured by piezometers. The pump bells are made geometrically similar, but the pumps themselves are usually not modeled in these tests. Instead, a siphon arrangement usually serves for the correct amount of simulated flow. The models for pumps and their internal hydraulics of vanes are generally tested by pump manufacturers only in order to determine their pump characteristics for the prototype.

A general question comes up, "Why it should be necessary to test a sump pump and not just utilize the existing experience or literature for design?" The answer is that most layouts and flow quantities are typical. If a pump house has been working efficiently for a long time and another similar one (geometrically and dynamically) is required, there is no need to test it. However, if a design is provided based on existing literature, e.g., Hydraulic Institute standards, usually the dimensions are very large and, therefore, result in expensive construction. Usually, a lot of construction quantities and costs can be saved by reducing the size of pump house to its optimum by a model test, the cost of which is usually only a fraction of the savings. Moreover, a design based on literature or experience may not guarantee a certain desirable flow pattern without conducting a test.

Hydrothermal Diffusion Problems

Another field in which extensive test work on models has been conducted recently is hydrothermal diffusion at the point of hot-water discharge into a natural body of water. The importance of this field has been increased due to the recent public concern for environmental protection. It is generally considered that hot-water discharge is harmful to ecological balance. Therefore, a careful study in the area of hot-water discharge should be conducted in order to determine the extent of potential harm and to reduce it to allowable limits. Physical model studies have proved useful to determine the isotherm patterns in the vicinity of discharges. However, there is a general concern that some of the hot water may be returning from the far field. This type of model study will need very large models and has been tried in some cases with only a limited success.

For the near field studies, physical models have generally been constructed to a scale of 1:80 to 1:130. The densimetric Froude number is generally used for similarity. This is also done for the bottom topography of the body of water. Most of the time, the purpose of testing the model is to determine what dimensions, shape, and size of discharge structure (diffuser with ports) will give the most efficient mixing in the least surface area resulting in maximum temperature isotherms. Temperature distributions in the surrounding area are measured by a series of thermostats. Data accumulation and processing is done side by side with the experiment by using computers. Several arrangements are tried, and the best ones are selected with their corresponding merits and demerits. Dye tests are also conducted to observe the flow patterns. It is important to model enough area around the diffuser. The temperature in the model room has to be properly controlled. The tidal effects, currents, and surface tension should be properly controlled or modeled.

Other Model Tests

Another field in which model studies are helpful is determining flow patterns (velocity distributions) near intake and discharge structures in order to determine biota intake and sedimentation-erosion quantities. Also, some model studies have been conducted for flow into and out of the individual intakes and diffuser ports, respectively. Some model studies have also been conducted to determine the hydrodynamic forces on immersed structures.

HYDRAULIC FORCE AND TORQUE

What we have discussed so far in hydraulic systems is largely related to what is involved in transmitting the fluid from one point to another. However, sometimes the purpose is not just to deliver a bulk quantity but also to deliver pressure to activate other components. The pressure is ultimately utilized either as a force or a torque.

Some simple uses of hydraulic pressure as a force become evident in applications such as a hydraulic press (which operates basically on Pascal's law, discussed previously), a hydraulic-brake system on an automobile, or a hydraulic crane for lifting objects. Some indirect uses, by passing through actuators and valves, become evident on applications such as the hydraulic milling machine, shaper or surface grinder, or lathe. For rotary action, hydraulic couplings and torque converters are used.

Pressure Accumulator

This is a device to accumulate or store liquid under pressure delivered by the pump when it is not required by the machine. The pressure can be later supplied to the machine when needed.

Various industrial presses require separate pumping units to furnish liquid at the desired pressure. Such pumps are known as *press pumps*. Normally, the pressure generated by these pumps ranges from 50 to 150 kg/cm^2 and is uniform throughout the supply period. However, the demand for liquid and its required pressure is variable. At some intervals the machine may not be doing any work at all, and to deal with such operating conditions an arrangement to receive and store the pressurized liquid being constantly supplied by the pump is necessary. The device must be able to deliver the liquid back to the machine on demand. In some cases it may be even desirable to retrieve the stored liquid at a pressure higher than that provided by the pump itself. All this is done by the pressure or hydraulic accumulator.

Hydraulic Accumulator.   The hydraulic accumulator (Fig. 1-14) consists of a cylinder and a plunger generally known as a *ram*. One side of the cylinder is connected to the press pump and the other to the hydraulic machine. Either the cylinder or the ram may be fixed. Generally the cylinder is fixed and the ram moves up and down to accommodate a variable quantity of liquid inside by the cylinder.

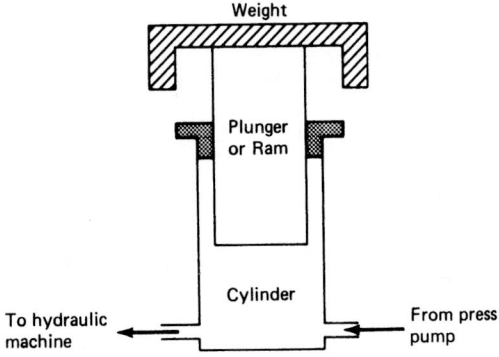

FIGURE 1-14 Hydraulic accumulator.

Accumulators may be dead-load or variable-load type. In the former, dead weights are employed to press the plunger in, while the latter employs steam pressure. The main advantage of the steam-pressure type is that the pressure may be varied at will, but it is handicapped in many applications by the need of a boiler to supply steam. However, it can be used on ships if steam is readily available.

The accumulator also serves the purpose of a pressure regulator. A suitable arrangement can be easily designed to switch on a pump motor after a predetermined travel of the ram.

Capacity of Accumulator. This is the maximum amount of energy stored by an accumulator. The storage capacity is equal to the potential energy of the lifted ram together with its weight.

Let d = diameter of ram
 s = stroke or lift of ram
 p = intensity of pressure of water supplied

The total moving weight or weight of the ram is

$$W = \frac{\pi}{4} \, d^2 p \tag{9}$$

The work done in lifting the ram, or capacity of the accumulator, is

$$Ws = \frac{\pi}{4} \, d^2 ps \tag{10}$$

The volume of the accumulator is $(\pi/4)d^2 s$, and

$$\text{Capacity of ram} = p \times \text{volume} \tag{11}$$

The capacity of the accumulator and that of the ram are same.

Pressure Intensifier

The pressure intensifier, sometimes known as *differential accumulator,* is a device to multiply the pressure supplied by the pump to suit the requirements of a high-pressure machine. Often a fluid pressure machine requires a high pressure at a particular stage in its operation. It can be easily provided by the intensifier.

Normally, a simple intensifier (refer Fig. 1-15) consists of two coaxial rams or pistons moving in cylinders as shown in Fig. 1-12. Low-pressure liquid is admitted to the ram or piston of large cross-sectional area, which then transmits force to a small ram or piston by a rod connecting the two. Since the piston on the left-hand side has a smaller cross-sectional area, the pressure of the liquid coming out will be high. The volume between the two pistons must be vented.

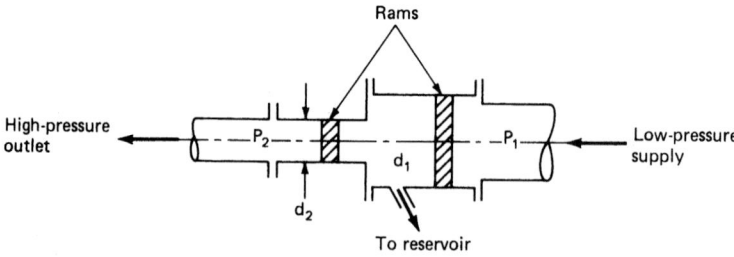

FIGURE 1-15 Pressure intensifier.

Let d_1 and d_2 be the diameters of the two rams and p_1 and p_2 the respective pressure of the liquid inside them. Then, if the ram moves slowly, forces

$$p_1 = p_2$$

or

$$p_1 \frac{\pi}{4} d_1^2 = p_2 \frac{\pi}{4} d_2^2$$

or

$$p_2 = p_1 \frac{d_1^2}{d_2^2} \tag{12}$$

Figure 1-16 shows a modified form of intensifier which consists of two coaxial rams inside a cylinder. The cylinder and the outer ram are fixed. A, B, and C are the valves provided for fixed cylinder, sliding ram, and fixed ram, respectively. To start with, the hollow sliding ram is filled with liquid; valves A and C are open. A liquid having a low pressure p_1 enters from the mains through A and forces the sliding ram upward, so that the liquid inside the sliding ram goes out through valve C at a greater pressure p_2. When the sliding ram has reached its top position, valve B opens while valves A and C close. The liquid, now trapped between the fixed cylinder and sliding ram, enters inside the hollow sliding ram which then comes back to its starting position. This completes one cycle of the intensifier. Sometimes, compressed air is supplied to the larger cylinder in place of low-pressure hydraulic supply, in which case the intensifier is known as a hydropneumatic accumulator or intensifier.

Steam can also be supplied to the larger cylinder in place of low-pressure hydraulic supply or compressed air. It is then called a *steam intensifier.*

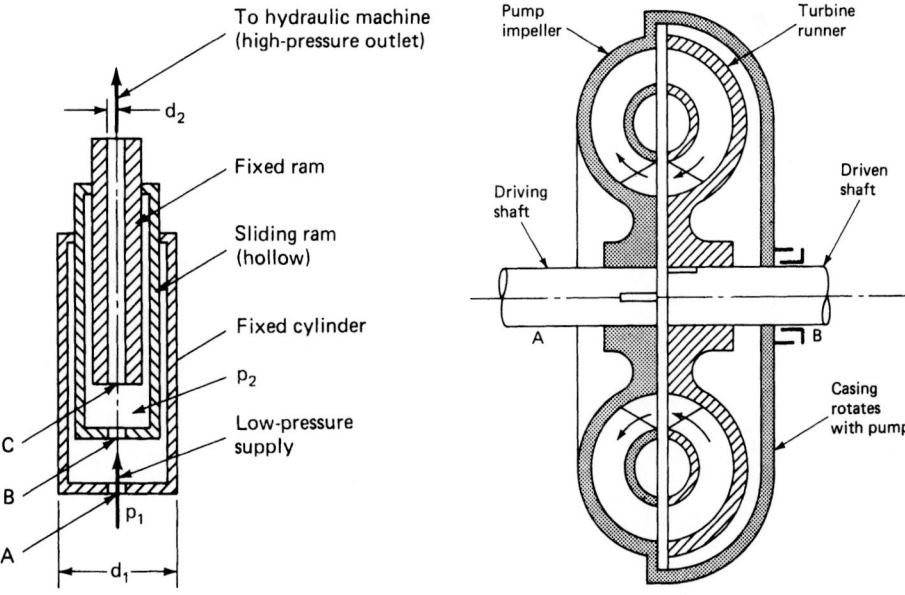

FIGURE 1-16 Modified form of intensifier.

FIGURE 1-17 Fluid or hydraulic coupling.

Fluid or Hydraulic Coupling

The fluid coupling consists of a radial pump impeller keyed to a driving shaft *A* (refer to Fig. 1-17) and a reaction (radial-type) turbine runner keyed to driven shaft *B*. There is no mechanical connection between the driving and driven shafts. The impeller and turbine runner together form a casing completely filled with oil, the fluid with which shafts *A* and *B* are to be coupled. The fluid is usually conventional lubricating oil. If the shaft *A* is made to revolve slowly, the oil, due to a forced vortex, will flow out from the impeller and will strike the turbine runner blades. After sufficient head has been built up by increasing the speed of *A*, the fluid will drive the turbine runner and thus set the shaft *B* in motion. When at full speed, the two shafts rotate at almost the same rate; in practice, owing to slip, the driven shaft speed is typically about 2 percent less. Thus, the efficiency of the typical coupling would be 98 percent. If both driver and follower were to rotate at the same speed, no circulation of oil could take place. It is the difference between centrifugal forces set up in the driver and the follower which causes oil circulation. The necessary reduction in the speed of the driven shaft thus maintains the continuous flow of oil from impeller to the turbine runner. The blades of impeller and runner are generally a straight radial type.

REFERENCES

References are listed at the end of Chap. 9-2.

CHAPTER 9-2
PNEUMATIC SYSTEMS*

INTRODUCTION

Pneumatic systems involve gases (usually compressed air, including negative gauge pressures for a vacuum system). The most important component of a pneumatic system, therefore, is a compressor (or blower, or fan). Other components include filters, aftercoolers, moisture separators, air tanks, air dryers, piping, valves, etc., the basic functions of which can be deduced just from their names. Some of these components have already been discussed as parts of hydraulic systems. A compressor usually supplies pressurized gas into a line. A pressure regulator is provided on every branch where gas is to be used at a specific pressure.

The fundamentals of airflow are similar to those of the flow of water. The methods of calculating the pressure drops in order to compute the pressure requirements of a compressor are similar to those with water, with a few minor exceptions due to the compressibility of air. First, the density, viscosity, etc., of air at the operating temperature must be considered.

Second, the flow computations with air are made in terms of cubic feet per minute. In dealing with equations for gases, absolute temperature and pressure are used. Absolute temperature is the temperature above absolute zero, which is equivalent to $-460°F$ ($-273°C$). When the Fahrenheit temperature is converted to absolute, it is sometimes referred to as degrees Rankine (°R), and °C converted to absolute is kelvins (K). Thus

$$T(K) = 273 + T(°C)$$

$$T(°R) = 460 + T(°F)$$

Similarly,

$$P \text{ absolute (lb/in}^2) = P \text{ gauge (lb/in}^2) + 14.7$$

$$P \text{ absolute (kg/m}^2) = P \text{ gauge (kg/m}^2) + 10,335$$

The pressure drop for flow through pipes is calculated usually to start with airflow conditions at 100 psig and 60°F. Then the pressure drop is converted to the actual flow temperature t and pressure p conditions by the following equation:

$$\frac{460 + t}{520} \frac{100 + 14.7}{p + 14.7} = \frac{\Delta p}{\Delta p_{100}} \qquad \text{(U.S. customary units)} \qquad (1)$$

where Δp_{100} = pressure drop for flow of air at 100 psi, 60°F, and Δp = pressure drop for actual air.

It should be kept in mind that this pressure drop is for a flow volume, actual cubic feet per minute (acfm), at p, t conditions. The corresponding standard cubic feet per minute (scfm) of air, that is, at 14.7 psia and 60°F, can be computed from the following equation:

$$\frac{520}{460 + t} \frac{14.7 + p}{14.7} = \frac{\text{scfm}}{\text{acfm}} \qquad \text{(general gas)} \qquad (2)$$

---

* Updated for this Second Edition by the Editor-in-Chief.

Reference 5 gives tables for specific numbers corresponding to the above equations, in order to simplify calculations.

Tables[5] are also available for computing the pressure drop at different flow rates. These tables are usually specific p and t values only, but one can easily proceed with calculating pressure drop Δp using the Harris formula:

$$p = \frac{cL}{R} \frac{Q^2}{D^5} \tag{3}$$

where c = a coefficient of pressure drop = $(0.1025/D^{0.33})$ (U.S. customary units)
L = length of pipe, ft
R = compression ratio = $(p + 14.7)/14.7$
Q = flow rate, ft³/s of free air
D = pipe diameter, in

FANS

In plant applications, fans are used for circulating air in rooms, as well as delivering air for plant systems.

Forward-curved-fan characteristics are given in Fig. 2-1. The horsepower curve is continuously increasing with flow rate. Such fans are used in low-pressure applications.[8]

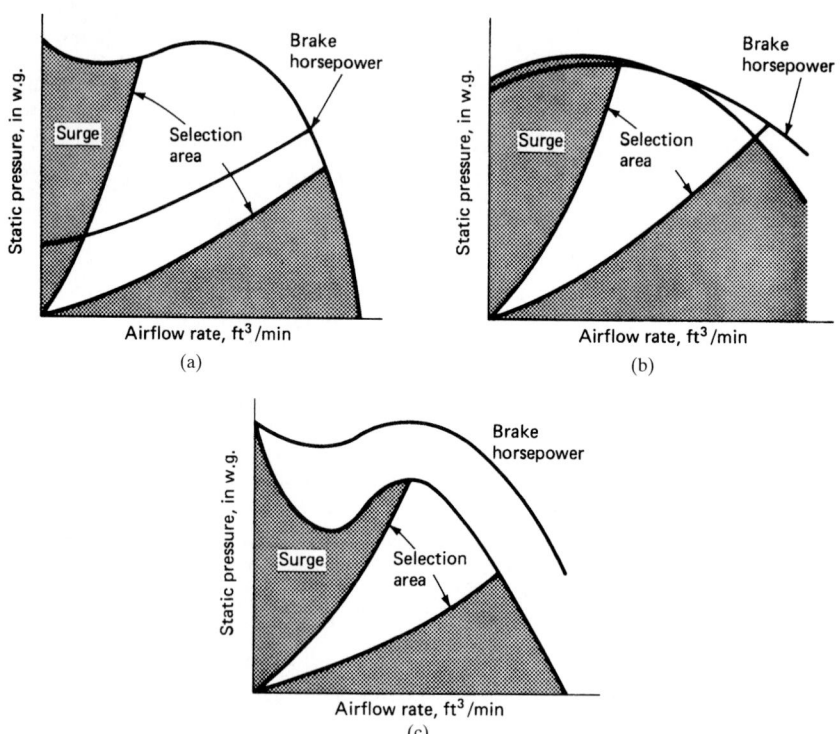

FIGURE 2-1 Fan characteristics: (*a*) forward-curved vanes, (*b*) backward-curved vanes, (*c*) axial vanes.

Backward-curved fans have a horsepower curve that rises slightly in the beginning and then drops. This is the type most commonly used in large air-handling systems.

Vane-axial fans that are mostly used in air-conditioning systems have a dip in the horsepower curve.

All types of fans mentioned above have an unstable surge zone in the low-flow zone, as the fan is started or stopped. This zone is considered unsuitable for normal fan operation. Similarly, a steep portion of the pressure curve toward the end, where pressure drops fast with a small change in flow, is unsuitable (and not very predictable) for normal operation. Therefore the system-demand curve should fall within the selection area. The best zone of selection on the curve is where there is a uniform gradual well-defined variation of pressure with flow (one pressure for one flow and not varying too fast).

Small fans usually have a bigger zone to modulate airflow but are usually less efficient.

COMPRESSORS

Compressors are just like pumps in basic construction as well as function. The basic function of a compressor is to pressurize gas just as a pump pressurizes liquid. Like pumps, compressors have positive displacement (reciprocating, rotary screw, sliding vane) as well as turbo types. Metal diaphragm compressors[9] are used for compressing gases where leakage to the environment could be hazardous or wasteful. Reciprocating compressors operate on the principle of a piston sliding in a cylinder. A turbocompressor is shown in Fig. 2-2.

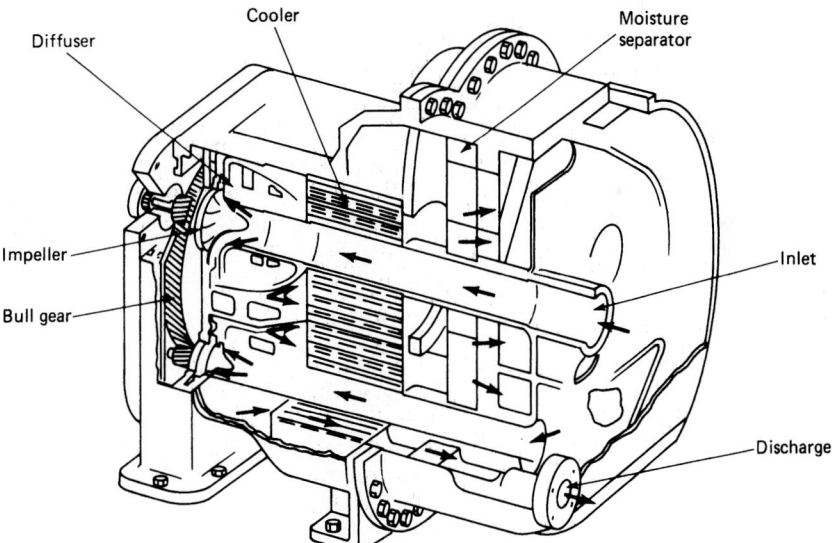

FIGURE 2-2   Centrifugal compressor. (*Ingersoll-Rand Corp.*)

The horsepower of a centrifugal compressor is given by the following equation:

$$\text{hp} = \begin{cases} \dfrac{WH_{\text{ad}}}{550\eta_{\text{ad}}} & \text{(U.S. customary units)} \\[3mm] \dfrac{WH_{\text{ad}}}{75\eta_{\text{ad}}} & \text{(SI units)} \end{cases} \qquad (4)$$

where W = weight of flow

η_{ad} = adiabatic efficiency of the compressible flow and all other efficiencies, including mechanical, disk friction, motor, etc.

H_{ad} = adiabatic head of the compressible flow including all the pressure losses in the system and the final pressure required for use

H_{ad} can also be calculated from the following equation:

$$H_{ad} = \frac{1545T_1}{\overline{m}\sigma} \ (R_c - 1) \tag{5}$$

where $\sigma = k_1/k$

k = coefficient of adiabatic expansion

   = 1.4 for air

$\overline{m}$ = molar weight

R_c = compression ratio = $\dfrac{\text{after compression abs. press.}}{\text{before compression abs. press.}}$

T_1 = absolute temperature at suction

There are two basic types of turbocompressors, axial and centrifugal. Input energy is of course provided by an engine or motor. In the axial compressor the air is forced to move parallel to the centerline of the propeller. Stationary vanes divert the flow to the succeeding row of rotating vanes.

Centrifugal compressors are more common. A high-speed impeller forces airflow in a radial direction inside the compressor, thereby causing a pressure rise. The air at the periphery is then ducted to the successive stages.

Pulseless, high volumetric flow rates with oil-free discharge are the basic attractions of centrifugal compressors. Typical performance charts of compressors are shown in Fig. 2-3, for backward-leaning vs. radial vanes. Notice the general loss of capacity and higher power requirements of the radial vanes. The heat is rejected by the compressor to the air (therefore, there are cooling water requirements). The horsepower required by the compressor for a certain scfm capacity and the number of stages are important parameters for a final selection.

More stages are often desirable. API Standards 617 and 618 are commonly used in connection with compressors.

TYPICAL PNEUMATIC SYSTEMS

A typical air-supply system diagram along with the primary controls and final uses is shown in Fig. 2-4. Free air is sucked through a filter into the compressor and discharged into a service air receiver (after passing through an aftercooler to remove the heat from the compressor and moisture separator). The air receiver is kept under pressure and also serves as a surge chamber. The relief valve protects against overpressures. From the receiver, the air can either be directly used or dried and chilled before use, as in instrument-air applications.

Another typical pneumatic system would include a vacuum pump (really a "negative" air compressor) to pump out air *from* a system as in applications to a condenser that functions best under vacuum, or in a negative-pressure air-vent system. The vacuum pumps function in a way similar to vacuum cleaners. One important component in such a system is a valve that shuts itself and the vacuum system upon sensing a particular water level in a container at the top of the water box of a condenser. The valve reopens and the vacuum system starts when air is again sensed inside the water box. There are other arrangements that require air to enter the system when a vacuum is sensed in order to avoid either pipe collapse or system cavitation due to vapor pressures forming inside. One such air and vacuum valve is shown in Fig. 2-5, with the corresponding performance graph shown in Fig. 2-6. Such a valve has a large ori-

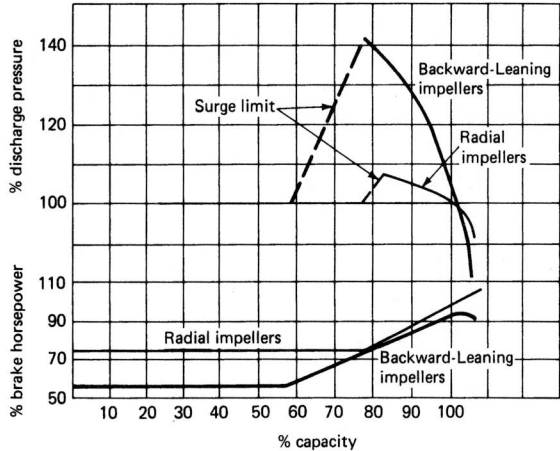

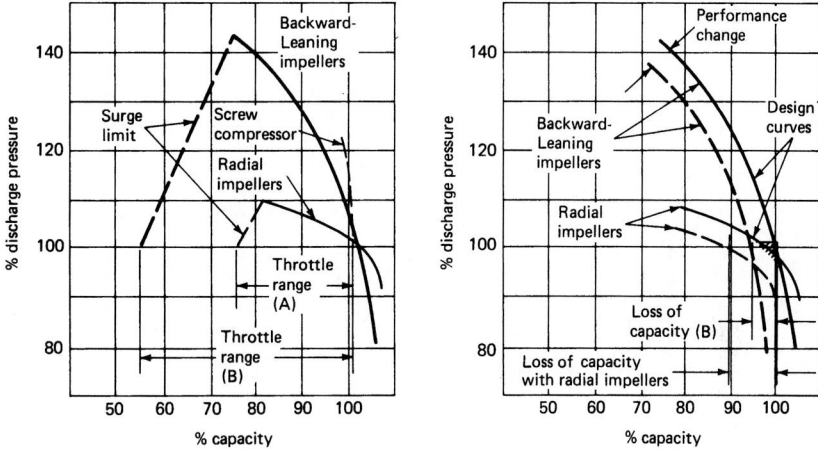

FIGURE 2-3 Typical performance curves of centrifugal compressors with backward-leaning impellers (A) vs. compressors with radial impellers (B). (*Ingersoll-Rand Corp.*)

fice through which a great amount of air escapes when the system is being filled with liquid. Once the system is filled, the fluid lifts the float in the valve, closes the orifice, and stays closed until the system is drained.

REFERENCES

1. "Standard for Centrifugal, Rotary & Reciprocating Pumps," Hydraulic Institute, Cleveland, Ohio, 13th ed., 1975.

2. Satija, K. S., and N. M. Shah: *On Circulating Water for Power Plants,* Proceedings Second World Congress, International Water Resources Association, India, 1975.

3. Lal, Jagdish: *Hydraulic Machines,* Metropolitan Book Company Pvt. Ltd., Delhi, India, 1975.

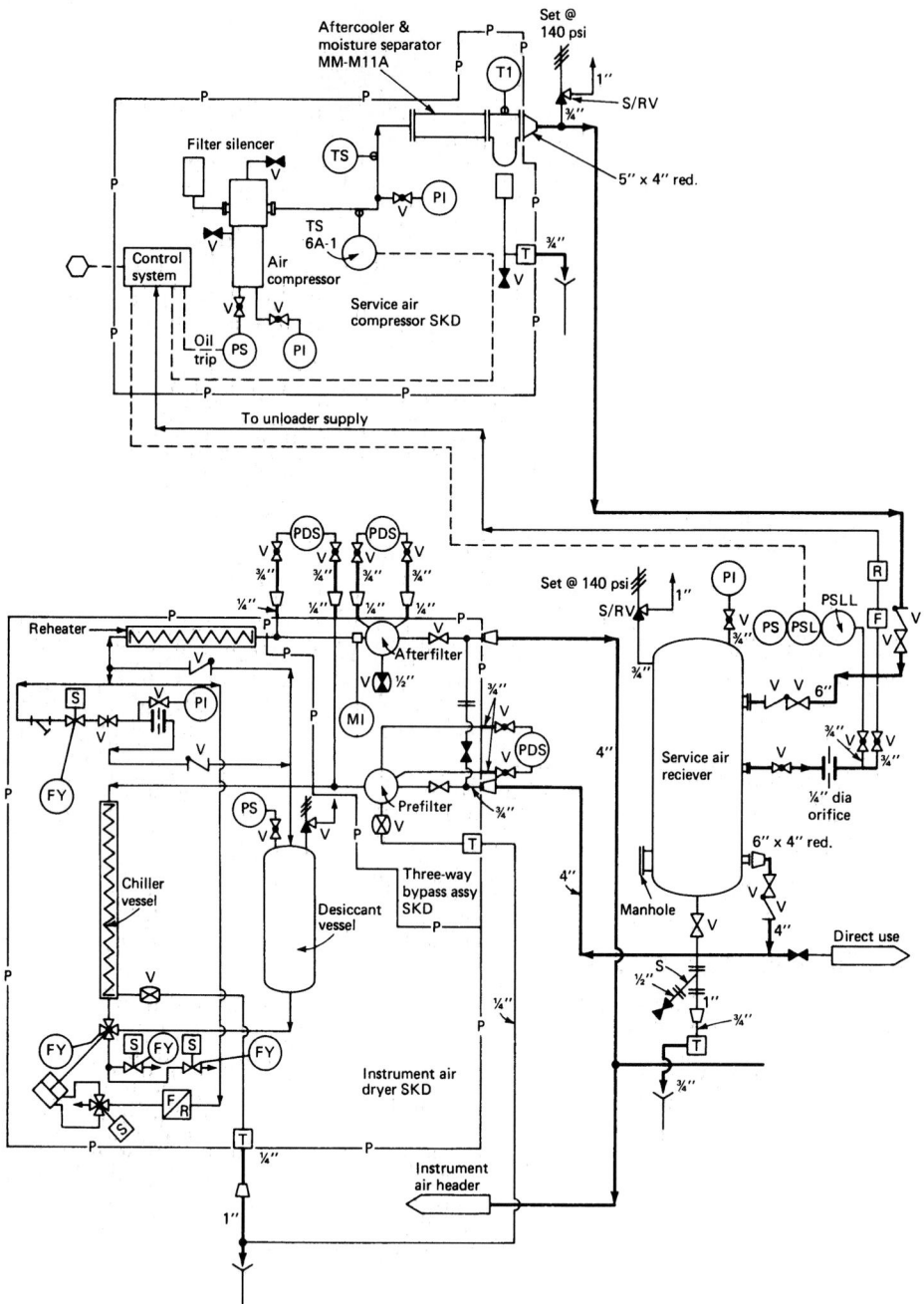

FIGURE 2-4 Typical pneumatic system. Key: PI = pressure indicator, T1 = temperature indicator, PS = pressure switch, TS = temperature switch, T = moisture trap, S/RV = safety/relief valve, V = valve, PDS = pressure differential switch, S = solenoid, FI = flow indicator, PSL = pressure switch low, PSLL = pressure switch low-low.

FIGURE 2-5   Air and vacuum valve. (*APCO Valve & Primer Corp.*)

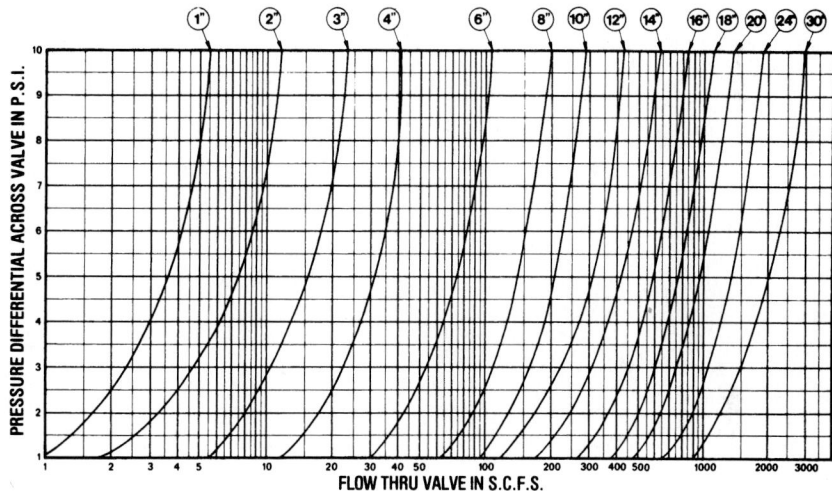

FIGURE 2-6   Performance graph for air and vacuum valve. (*APCO Valve & Primer Corp.*)

4. *Masoneilan Handbook for Control Valve Sizing,* 6th ed., Masoneilan International, Inc., Norwood, Mass., 1977.

5. *Flow of Fluids Through Valves, Fittings, and Pipe,* Crane Company, New York, 1976.

6. Wylie, E. B., and V. L. Streeter: *Hydraulic Transients,* McGraw-Hill, New York, 1969.

7. Satija, K. S.: "Prototype Testing of Circulating Water Systems," paper presented at the *ASCE Hydraulics Division Conference,* Seattle, Wash., 1975.

8. Patterson, N. R.: "Variable Air Volume Systems", *Plant Engineering,* February 7, 1980.

9. Lingston, E. H.: "Metal Diaphragm Compressors," *Plant Engineering,* April 19, 1979.

SECTION 10

PIPING AND VALVING

CHAPTER 10-1
PIPING SYSTEM DESIGN AND COMPONENTS

Walter J. Sperko, P.E.
President
Sperko Engineering Services, Inc.
Greensboro, North Carolina

Lawrence A. Loziuk, P.E.
Principal Engineer
Vectra Technologies, Inc.
Lincolnshire, Illinois

INTRODUCTION

The design of piping systems is straightforward. This chapter presents a simplified, step-by-step approach to designing, analyzing, and supporting piping systems.

Fundamental Considerations

Pipe has to be sufficiently large in diameter to carry the fluid being transported without excessive velocity, which can lead to erosion and excessive pumping cost. At the same time, the initial cost of the pipe and its installation should not be greater than it needs to be. Once the pipe has been sized and laid out, the primary concern in designing, analyzing, and supporting a piping system is to maintain the integrity of the pressure boundary. To do this, pipe has to be thick enough to withstand the internal pressure stress. Pipe also has to be supported in such a way that it is not subjected to excessive bending stress due to its deadweight and, at the same time, it has to be sufficiently free to expand and contract as it is heated and cooled. Since the design process is not precise, factors of safety have to be included in these calculations. Finally, pipe has to be able to withstand transient loading due to system operation.

Selection of an Appropriate Code

The piping system should be designed and built in accordance with one section of the American Society of Mechanical Engineers (ASME) B31 *Code for Pressure Piping*. This Code is over 75 years old, and it represents the cumulative experiences of many generations of engineers working in the piping industry. It specifies materials that have proven service histories; allowable stress levels for all materials (including factors of safety); fabrication and installation methods; and inspection, examination, and testing requirements. The Code can serve as the basis for agreement between the designer and the installer regarding the technical details of the installation work. Finally, the Code is a recognized industry standard which provides a basis for liability protection regarding the design and installation of the system. The various sections of the Code are:

ASME B31.1	*Power Piping*
ASME B31.3	*Chemical Process and Petroleum Refinery Piping*
ASME B31.4	*Liquid Transportation Systems for Hydrocarbons, Liquid Petroleum Gas, Anhydrous Ammonia and Alcohols*
ASME B31.5	*Refrigeration Piping*
ASME B31.8	*Gas Transmission and Distribution Piping Systems* (Governed by 49CFR192)
ASME B31.9	*Building Services Piping*
ASME B31.11	*Slurry Transportation Piping Systems*

Most process piping should be built to B31.3. Air lines up to 150 lb/in^2 (10 bar) and 200°F (93°C), steam up to 125 psig (8.5 bar), and liquids up to 300 psig (20 bar) and at temperatures from 0°F (−18°C) to 350°F (177°C) should be built to B31.9 for pipe sizes up to NPS 24 (DN 600) and up to one-half inch (12.5 cm) wall thickness when used as building services piping. When piping operating within these parameters is located in a refinery or chemical plant, it may be designed and installed as B31.3 Category D piping. Steam and water piping operating over these temperatures should be built to B31.1 when their design life is over 25 years; otherwise, such piping in process plants should be built to B31.3. Other nonflammable and nontoxic liquids and gases up to 300 psig (20 bar) and 250°F (121°C) should be built to B31.3 Category D. The applicable code section should be clearly indicated on the designer's drawings and specifications and on the contract with those performing the fabrication and installation of the piping system.

MATERIAL SELECTION AND ASSEMBLY METHODS

Piping system materials should be selected to be compatible with the fluid being handled. Generally, the material used should be based on successful use of that material for similar existing systems. The list of materials available for use is also limited to those materials listed in the ASME B31 code section selected for the work; this is not very limiting, however, since materials from cast iron to copper to nickel alloys to plastics are listed in the B31 code sections. The method of joining piping system components should be based on the nature of the fluid being handled, the service pressure and temperature, the installation and maintenance cost, and the overall service conditions. Smaller diameter systems handling steam or water of lower pressure and temperature are frequently joined by threading. Water and steam piping operating under 250°F (121°C) is also readily joined using "groove and shoulder" couplings. Flammable or other hazardous fluids are usually handled in pipe that is welded together. Welding procedures and the qualification of welders should be in accordance with the ASME Boiler and Pressure Vessel Code, Section IX, *Welding and Brazing Qualifications;* use of this code section is required when any section of the B31 *Code for Pressure Piping* is contractually specified.

PRELIMINARY PIPING SYSTEM LAYOUT

An initial isometric sketch of the piping system should be prepared. The length of pipe runs; the number and types of fittings and valves; and the location of pumps, pressure vessels, and storage tanks should be shown. Approximate dimensions and elevations should be shown. Provisions must be made to support the pipe at regular intervals. The pipe must be routed to avoid structures and equipment that may interfere with its expansion and contraction as it is heated and cooled. Sloping of the pipe to allow drainage of liquids should be included at the final stages of layout, including provisions to remove such liquids when appropriate. The location and adequacy of building structures or other provisions to support the pipe should be considered when routing the pipe.

PIPE SIZE DETERMINATION

The textbook formulas for determining the pressure drop of a fluid through a pipe were developed by Hazen-Williams, Darcy-Weisbach, Manning, Scobey, and others. These formulas relate the pressure drop through the pipe to the fluid viscosity, the smoothness of the pipe wall, the diameter of the pipe, the total length of piping and the fluid velocity. The pressure drop through the pipe due to flow is most sensitive to the velocity, since the pressure drop is a function of the square of the velocity. Other factors are roughly linear.

The simplest approach to determining the pressure drop through the system is to select a pipe size using the nomographs shown in Figs. 1-1 and 1-2, which show the flow velocity and the pressure drop per 100 ft (30 m) of pipe. These charts provide a rough but generally conservative pressure drop determination for a given set of flow conditions and pipe size. This determination is normally adequate for most applications. If a more accurate solution is required, refer to *Piping Engineering,* the source of these charts.

Maximum flow rates through pipe should be limited to the following:

12 ft/s (4 m/s) for liquids

15 ft/s (5 m/s) for air and other single-phase gases

150 ft/s (50 m/s) for low-pressure wet steam

200 ft/s (65 m/s) for steam over 25 lb/in^2 (2 bar).

300 ft/s (100 m/s) for steam over 25°F (15°C) superheat.

One may need to consider other factors in limiting the flow rate through the pipe, including noise, erosion, suspension of solids, and the requirements of connected equipment. Minimum flow rates of approximately one-half the maximum flow rates are recommended to ensure cost-effective sizing.

To extend the pressure drop determination from the basis of 100 ft (30 m) of pipe to the actual system, the total number of feet of straight pipe are added. The pressure loss through fittings can be calculated by using Fig. 1-3. This chart allows one to determine an equivalent length of straight pipe for each valve and each fitting in the piping system. This equivalent straight pipe length for each valve and each fitting is added to the total length of actual straight pipe. After the straight pipe plus equivalent straight pipe lengths have been added, the total is multiplied by the pressure drop per 100 ft (30.5 m) to determine the pressure drop for the system. Pressure differences due to static fluid head, pumps, and pressure inside tanks have to be added to determine the total system pressure balance. If the pressure drop is acceptable, the pipe is appropriately sized. If the pressure drop is too great, select a larger pipe size. If there is very little pressure drop, a smaller pipe size may be appropriate to reduce material and installation cost.

Determining the pipe size requires striking a balance between the cost of materials and installation and the cost of pumping energy. Usually, the selection of pipe that is one size larger than the minimum is a reasonable compromise.

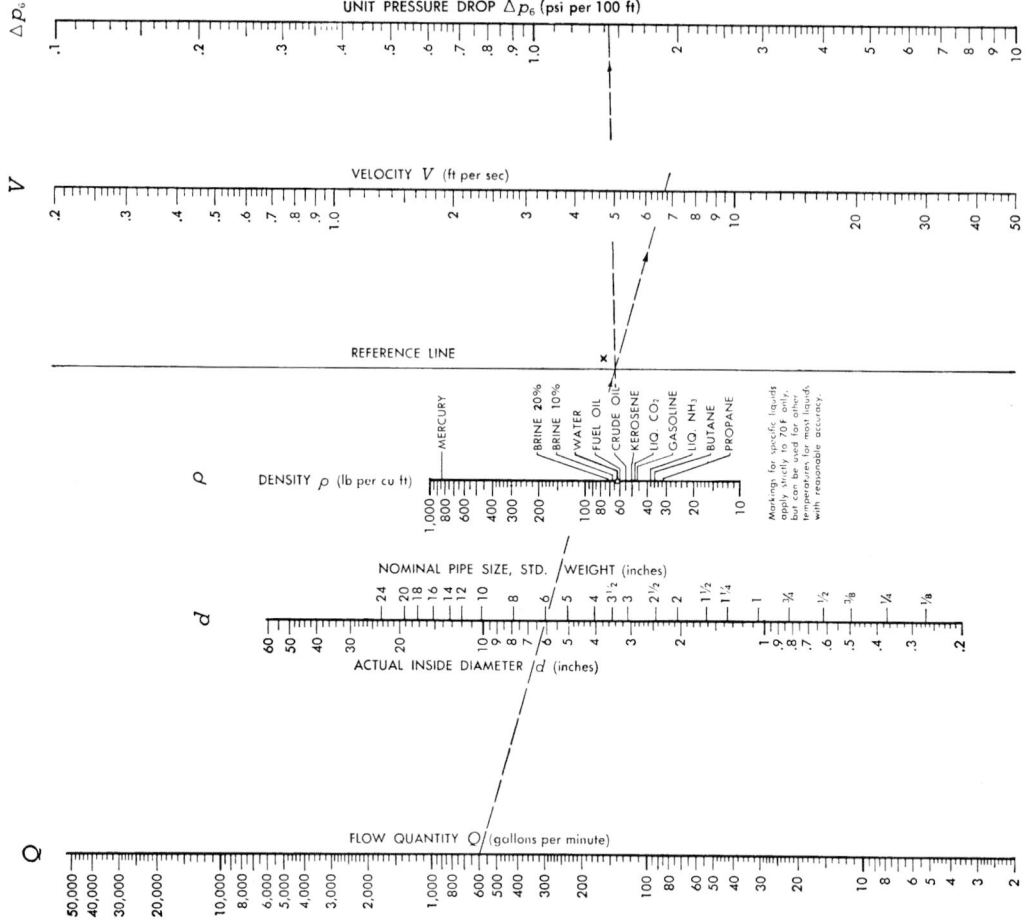

FIGURE 1-1 Rational solution (estimate) of pressure drop for liquids (turbulent flow). In the average problem, the flow quantity Q is known and either a pipe diameter d or a flow velocity V is assumed. With any two of the three quantities Q, d, and V known, obtain the third by locating the two known values on their respective scales and drawing a straight line through them; its intersection with the third scale gives the unknown quantity. This same line also will intersect the Reference Line. Draw a straight line through this intersection point and the point corresponding to the density of the fluid on the ρ-scale; its intersection with the Δp_6-scale gives the pressure drop (based on a friction coefficient of 0.006).

Example: A 6″ standard weight new steel line carries 600 gpm of water of 150°F temperature. What is the flow velocity and the pressure drop per 100 ft of line? *Quick estimate:* Connect "600 gpm" on Q-scale with "6-in." on right side of d-scale and extend line to V-scale; read velocity of 6.7 ft per sec. At the same time, intercept x with Reference Line is established. Connect this with mark "Water" on ρ-scale and extend line to Δp_6-scale; read pressure drop of 1.43 psi per 100 ft of pipe.

TYPES OF STRESSES AND FAILURE MODES

In designing piping or other pressure-containing devices, there are many loads to consider. The simplest classification system is to determine whether or not a particular type of load will cause gross plastic deformation and failure of the pressure boundary, i.e., catastrophic failure. Stresses that will cause catastrophic failure are referred to as primary stresses. Internal pressure and deadweight are loads that generate primary stresses. Other loads, such as bending of components due to thermal expansion, dissimilar coefficients of thermal expansion, and rapid

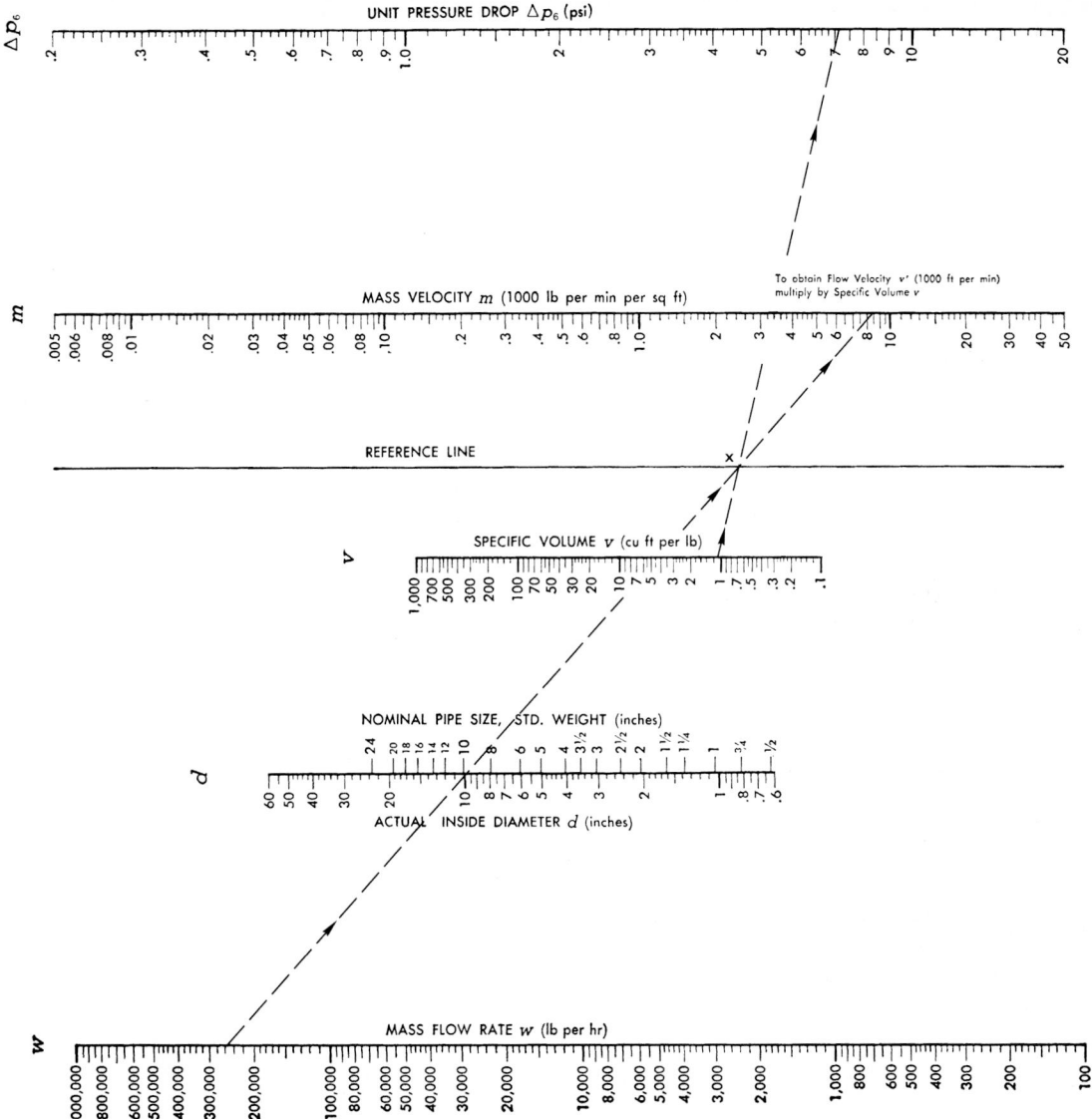

FIGURE 1-2 Rational solution (estimate) of pressure drop for gases and steam. In the average problem, the mass flow rate w is known and either a pipe diameter d or a flow velocity V' is assumed. The chart is based on the use of the mass velocity m, which is obtained by dividing the flow velocity V' by the specific volume v. With any two of the three quantities w, d, and m known, obtain the third by locating the two known values on their respective scales and drawing a straight line through them; its intersection with the third scale gives the unknown quantity. This same line also will intersect the Reference Line. Draw a straight line through this intersection point and the point corresponding to the specific volume of the fluid on the v-scale; its intersection with the Δp_6-scale gives the pressure drop (based on a friction coefficient of 0.006).

Example: For a steam flow of 250,000 lb per hr through a 10″ schedule 80 pipe at 635 psig and 850°F, determine velocity and pressure drop per 100 ft. *Quick estimate:* Connect "250,000" on w-scale with "9.56 in." on left side of d-scale and extend line to m-scale: read value of 8.3 × 1000 and convert into a flow velocity of 9550 ft per min by multiplying by the specific volume. Now connect intercept x with value of 1.15 on the v-scale and extend to the Δp_6-scale, and read a pressure drop of 7.20 psi per 100 ft thereon.

Procedure for solution of natural gas compressor station piping problem: (1) Multiply the volume flow rate (1000 cu ft per day) of standard gas (Sp. Gr. = 0.6) by 0.00188 and enter this value in w column mass flow rate (lb per hour). (2) Then follow general procedure described above; specific volume (cu ft per lb) is equal to 1 ÷ density (lb per cu ft). (3) For an approximate solution, multiply the Δp_6 value of unit pressure drop by $c = 0.6$. This value of c is based on pressure drop measurements at several compressor station installations with flows having Reynolds Numbers of the order of 10^6 and 10^7. (4) To add in the equivalent lengths of fittings follow the instructions and formula in Fig. 1-3 using $c = 0.6$.

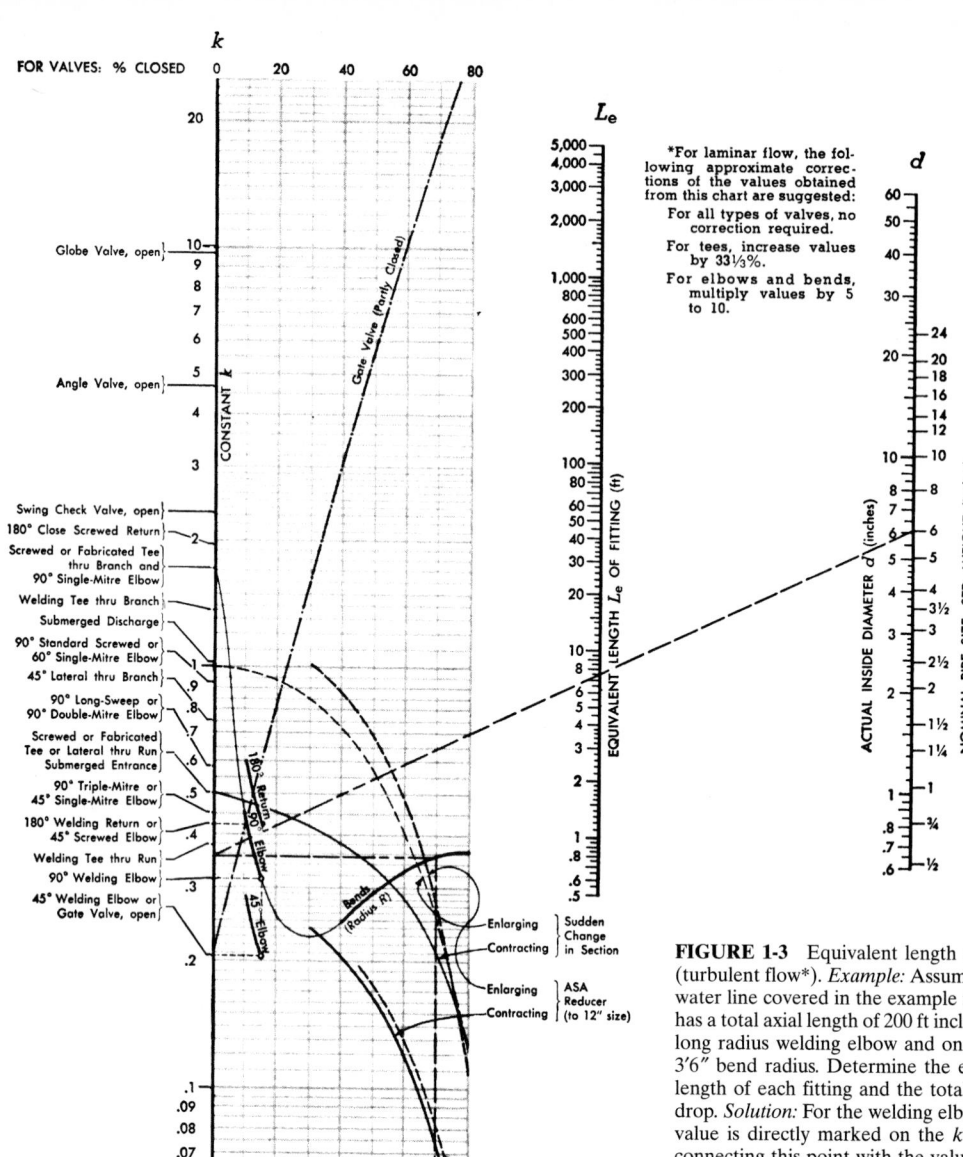

FIGURE 1-3 Equivalent length of fittings (turbulent flow*). *Example:* Assume that the water line covered in the example in Fig. 1-1 has a total axial length of 200 ft including one long radius welding elbow and one bend of 3′6″ bend radius. Determine the equivalent length of each fitting and the total pressure drop. *Solution:* For the welding elbow, the *k*-value is directly marked on the *k*-scale. By connecting this point with the value marked "6-in." on the *d*-scale, the equivalent length is directly read on the L_e-scale as 6.5 ft. To find L_e for the bend, enter the *R/d* scale at the bottom with the value 42/6 = 7, project up to curve marked "Bends" and across to *k*-scale. Connecting this point with value "6-in." on the *d*-scale, the equivalent length for the bend is found as 7.5 ft on the L_e-scale. The total pressure drop ΔP in the line is found as follows, utilizing the unit pressure drop Δp_6 and correction *c* evaluated in the example in Fig. 1-1:

$$\Delta P = \frac{\Delta p_6}{100}(cL + \Sigma L_e)$$

$$= \frac{1.43}{100}(0.70 \times 200 + 6.5 + 7.5)$$

$$= 0.0143 \times 154 = 2.20 \text{ psi}$$

*For laminar flow, the following approximate corrections of the values obtained from this chart are suggested:
For all types of valves, no correction required.
For tees, increase values by 33⅓%.
For elbows and bends, multiply values by 5 to 10.

changes in fluid temperature, are considered secondary stresses; these result in eventual failure due to fatigue cracking. Fatigue cracking typically results in leakage of the pipe before catastrophic failure occurs.

Primary Stresses Due to Pressure

After the pipe has been properly sized for flow, the next step is to provide sufficient material thickness in the pipe wall so that the stress in the pipe wall does not exceed the yield strength of the pipe material. There are two principal directions of stress that can cause failure of the pressure boundary: circumferential and axial. The stress due to pressure in the axial direction is approximately one-half of the stress due to pressure in the circumferential direction.

The B31 *Code for Pressure Piping* provides formulas for calculating the minimum pipe wall thickness due to circumferential stress. These formulas are of the form:

$$t = PD/(2SE + PY) + CA$$

where
t = the minimum wall thickness (See Table 1-1 for standard wall thicknesses).
P = the design pressure
D = the outside diameter of the pipe
S = the allowable stress per the applicable Code Section
E = the joint quality factor:

1.0 for seamless or 100% radiographed

0.90 for spot radiographed

0.85 for electric resistance welded

0.85 for arc welded from two sides

0.80 for arc welded from one side

0.60 for furnace butt welded.

CA = the corrosion allowance
Y = the neutral axis shift factor (See Table 1-2)

Materials are listed in the applicable B31 code section by ASTM specification, type, and grade. The specification, type, and grade of materials selected by the designer should be shown or referred to on the drawing so that the fabricator/installer uses the same materials for construction that the designer used in the design. Typical allowable stresses, based on ASME B31.1, are shown in Table 1-3. Since the allowable stresses vary between code sections, the allowable stresses given in the applicable code section for the specific material that is selected should be used for all formal calculations, rather than the typical values previously listed. These allowable stress limits provide a safety factor of 4 for temperatures of 650°F (343°C) and below. Under no circumstances should piping operating in the creep range (typically above 650°F [343°C] for steels) be permitted to operate continuously above the design temperature, since there is very little safety factor relative to over-temperature conditions when the design is controlled by creep.

Example. A 12-NPS (300-DN) seamless carbon steel pipe is to be used to carry steam at 900°F (482°C) and 900 lb/in² (6.2 MPa). The corrosion allowance is 0.0625 in (1.5 mm). What is the minimum permissible wall thickness?

$$t = PD/(2SE + PY) + CA$$

$$t = \frac{900\,(12.75)}{2(10{,}800)(1.0) + 900(0.4)} + 0.0625$$

$$t = 0.584 \text{ in minimum wall}$$

TABLE 1-1 Pipe Sizes and Generally Available Nominal Wall Thicknesses

		Conventional Units								
Nominal pipe size	Outside diameter (in)	Schedule or designation								
		5S	10S	Std	40	XS	80	120	160	XXS
⅛	0.405	0.035	0.049	0.068	0.068	0.095	0.095			
¼	0.540	0.049	0.065	0.088	0.088	0.119	0.119			
⅜	0.675	0.065	0.065	0.091	0.091	0.126	0.126			
½	0.840	0.065	0.083	0.109	0.109	0.147	0.147		0.187	0.294
¾	1.050	0.065	0.083	0.113	0.113	0.154	0.154		0.218	0.308
1	1.315	0.065	0.109	0.133	0.133	0.179	0.179		0.250	0.358
1¼	1.660	0.065	0.109	0.140	0.140	0.191	0.191		0.281	0.382
1½	1.900	0.065	0.109	0.145	0.145	0.200	0.200		0.281	0.400
2	2.375	0.065	0.109	0.154	0.154	0.218	0.218		0.344	0.436
2½	2.875	0.083	0.120	0.203	0.203	0.276	0.276		0.375	0.552
3	3.500	0.083	0.120	0.216	0.216	0.300	0.300		0.438	0.600
3½	4.000	0.083	0.120	0.226	0.226	0.318	0.318			0.636
4	4.500	0.083	0.120	0.237	0.237	0.337	0.337	0.438	0.531	0.674
5	5.563	0.109	0.134	0.258	0.258	0.375	0.375	0.500	0.625	0.750
6	6.625	0.109	0.134	0.280	0.280	0.432	0.432	0.562	0.719	0.864
8	8.625	0.109	0.148	0.322	0.322	0.500	0.500	0.594	0.906	0.875
10	10.75	0.134	0.165	0.365	0.365	0.500	0.594	0.719	1.125	1.000
12	12.75	0.156	0.165	0.375	0.406	0.500	0.688	0.844	1.312	1.000
14	14.00	0.156	0.250	0.375	0.438	0.500	0.750	1.094	1.406	
16	16.00	0.165	0.250	0.375	0.500	0.500	0.844	1.219	1.594	
18	18.00	0.165	0.188	0.375	0.562	0.500	0.938	1.375	1.781	
20	20.00	0.188	0.250	0.375	0.594	0.500	1.219	1.500	1.969	
24	24.00	0.218	0.250	0.375	0.688	0.500	1.219	1.812	2.344	
>24				0.375		0.500				

		SI Units								
Diameter number	Outside diameter (mm)	Schedule or designation								
		5S	10S	Std	40	XS	80	120	160	XXH
3	10.3	0.089	1.24	1.73	1.73	2.41	2.41			
6	13.7	1.24	1.65	2.24	2.24	3.02	3.02			
10	17.1	1.65	1.65	2.31	2.31	3.20	3.20			
15	21.3	1.65	2.11	2.77	2.77	3.73	3.73		4.87	7.47
20	26.7	1.65	2.11	2.87	2.87	3.91	3.91		5.56	7.82
25	33.4	1.65	2.77	3.38	3.38	4.55	4.55		6.35	6.35
30	42.2	1.65	2.77	3.56	3.56	4.85	4.85		6.35	9.70
40	48.3	1.65	2.77	3.68	3.68	5.08	5.08		7.14	10.15
50	60.3	1.65	2.77	3.91	3.91	5.54	5.54		8.74	11.07
65	73.0	2.11	3.05	5.16	5.16	7.01	7.01		9.53	14.02
80	88.9	2.11	3.05	5.49	5.49	7.62	7.62		11.13	15.24
90	101.6	2.11	3.05	5.74	5.74	8.08	8.08			16.15
100	114.3	2.11	3.05	6.02	6.02	8.56	8.56	11.13	13.49	17.12
125	141.3	2.77	3.40	6.55	6.55	9.53	9.53	12.70	15.88	19.05
150	168.3	2.77	3.40	7.11	7.11	10.97	10.97	14.27	18.26	21.95
200	219.1	2.77	3.76	8.18	8.18	12.70	12.70	18.26	23.10	22.23
250	273.0	3.04	3.96	9.27	9.27	12.70	15.09	21.44	28.58	25.40
300	323.8	3.96	3.96	9.53	10.31	12.70	17.48	25.40	33.23	25.40
350	355.6	3.96	6.35	9.53	11.13	12.70	19.05	25.40	35.71	
400	406.4	3.96	6.35	9.53	12.70	12.70	21.44	30.96	40.49	
450	457	3.96	6.35	9.53	14.27	12.70	23.83	34.93	45.24	
500	508	4.78	6.35	9.53	15.09	12.70	26.19	38.10	50.01	
600	601	5.54	6.35	9.53	17.48	12.70	30.96	46.02	59.54	
>600				9.53		12.70				

TABLE 1-2   Values for Temperature Coefficient Y for $D/t < 6$

Materials	Temperature, °F (°C)					
	<900(482)	950(510)	1000(538)	1050(566)	1100(593)	>1050(593)
Ferritic steel	0.4	0.5	0.7	0.7	0.7	0.7
Austenitic steel	0.4	0.4	0.4	0.4	0.5	0.7
Other ductile metals	0.4	0.4	0.4	0.4	0.4	0.4
Cast iron	0.0	—	—	—	—	—

For D/t greater than or equal to 6, use $Y = d/(d + D)$, where d is the inside diameter of the pipe.

TABLE 1-3   Typical Allowable Stresses (lb/in² and MPa) based on ASME B31.1

	lb/in²					
Material	Temperature, °F					
	to 650	700	800	900	1000	1100
Carbon steel	15,000	14,400	13,000	10,800	—	—
1¼% Cr/½% Mo	15,000	15,000	14,400	13,600	6,300	2,800
2¼% Cr/1% Mo	15,000	15,000	15,000	13,100	7,800	4,200
9%Cr/1%Mo/V	20,500	20,000	18,700	16,700	14,300	10,300
Type 304 Stainless	11,300	11,100	10,600	10,200	9,800	8,900
Type 316 Stainless	11,600	11,300	11,000	10,800	10,600	10,300

	MPa					
Material	Temperature, °C					
	to 343	371	427	482	538	593
Carbon steel	103.4	99.3	89.6	74.5	—	—
1¼% Cr/½% Mo	103.4	103.4	99.3	93.8	43.4	19.3
2¼% Cr/1% Mo	103.4	103.4	103.4	90.3	53.8	28.9
9%Cr/1%Mo/V	141.3	137.9	128.9	115.1	98.6	77.0
Type 304 Stainless	77.9	76.5	73.1	70.3	67.6	61.4
Type 316 Stainless	80.0	77.9	75.83	74.5	73.1	71.0

In metric units:

$$t = \frac{6.2(324)}{2(74.5)(1.0) + 6.2(0.4)} + 1.25$$

$$t = 15 \text{ mm}$$

Since the minimum permissible wall thickness of seamless pipe is 87.5 percent of the nominal wall thickness, the minimum wall thickness must be divided by 0.875 to obtain the minimum nominal wall thickness:

Nominal wall = 0.584/0.875 = 0.668 in (17 mm)

A review of Table 1-1 (showing sizes and wall thicknesses of pipe) indicates that the nominal wall thickness of 12-NPS (300-DN) schedule 80 pipe is 0.688 in (17.5 mm). Since this is greater than the calculated minimum nominal thickness, it is acceptable.

In addition to the circumferential stress, pressure causes an axial load on the pipe. This load is the pressure times the internal cross-section area of the pipe. The resulting stress is this value divided by the metal cross-section area of the pipe wall. This calculation reduces to approximately the following:

$$S = PD/4t$$

The variables are as defined above.

Example.   A 12-NPS (300-DN) seamless carbon steel pipe is to be used to carry steam at 900°F (482°C) and 1000 lb/in² (6.9 MPa). The corrosion allowance is 0.0625 in (1.5 mm). What is the axial stress if 12-NPS (300-DN) schedule 80 [0.688 in (17.5 mm)] pipe is used?

The under tolerance and the corrosion allowance must be deleted:

$$0.875(0.688) - 0.0625 = 0.540$$

$$S = \frac{1000\ (12.75)}{4(0.540)}$$

$$S = 5900\ \text{lb/in}^2$$

In metric units:

$$0.875\ (17.5) - 1.5 = 13.7\ \text{mm}$$

$$S = \frac{6.9\ (324)}{4\ (13.7)}$$

$$S = 40.8\ \text{MPa}$$

Since the axial pressure stress is approximately one-half of the circumferential stress, it practical to assume that the axial stress is one-half of the allowable stress when the actual wall thickness (less under tolerance and corrosion allowance) is close to the minimum wall thickness.

Pipe fittings, such as tees, elbows, caps, and reducers, are designed by the fitting manufacturer based on the schedule of the mating pipe. That is, if the designer has determined that 6-NPS (DN-150) Schedule 80 pipe is the correct size and wall thickness for the pipe, then he may specify Schedule 80 tees, elbows, and reducers without performing additional calculations. Manufacturers of these fittings have determined by proof testing that the thickness of metal in the fittings that they supply provides strength equal to or greater than that of the pipe to which the fitting is attached. See Tables 1-4, 1-5, 1-6, and 1-7 for typical dimensions of pipe fittings.

Socket welded and threaded fittings are covered by ANSI Standard B16.11. These fittings are matched to the schedule of pipe that fits in the socket based on the coupling's pressure class. A 3000 Class coupling is suitable for use with pipe up to Schedule 80, a 6000 Class coupling is suitable for use with pipe up to Schedule 160, and 9000 Class couplings are suitable for double-extra strong (XXS) pipe. The dimensions for socket welded fittings are shown in Table 1-8.

Pipe flanges are available as weld neck, slip-on, threaded, socket welded, lapped, and blind types. Flanges are selected based on the material from which the flange is made, the service temperature, and the service pressure. Based on these factors, the appropriate pressure class of flange is selected. Flange class ratings are given in ANSI B16.5; they start at the lowest rating of 150 Class and extend to 2500 Class. Tables 1-9 and 1-10 show the ratings for 600 and 900 Class flanges, respectively, and Table 1-11 shows the material classifications based on the specification of material from which the flange is made.

It should be noted that selection of the flange class is influenced by external forces and moments on the pipe due to weight, thermal expansion, and other loads. These loads may require selection of a higher class flange or a different material in order to prevent leakage in the presence of external loads across the flange. Although calculation of the forces due to these loads is not a code requirement, it should be done for good design since they can cause leakage. The external flange force and moment can be converted into an equivalent pressure P_{equiv} in lb/in² (MPa) using the following formula:

$$P_{equiv} = 16M/\pi\ G^3 + 4F/\pi\ G^2$$

where M = the bending moment at the flange, in-lb (N-m)
F = the axial force pulling the flanges apart, lb (N)
G = the average diameter of the gasket, in (m)

The equivalent pressure calculated above is added to the internal pressure; the class of flange is selected based on the combined pressures.

TABLE 1-4   Dimensions of Long Radius Elbows

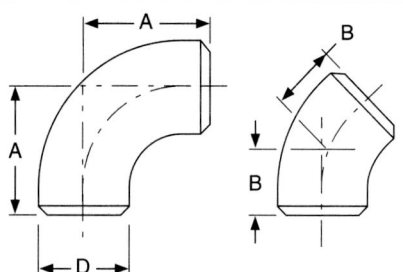

Nominal pipe size (NPS)	Outside diameter at bevel D	Center-to-end 90 deg. elbows A	Center-to-end 45 deg. elbows B
½	0.84	1.50	0.62
¾[1]	1.05	1.12	0.44
1	1.32	1.50	0.88
1¼	1.66	1.88	1.00
1½	1.90	2.25	1.12
2	2.38	3.00	1.38
2½	2.88	3.75	1.75
3	3.50	4.50	2.00
3½	4.00	5.25	2.25
4	4.50	6.00	2.50
5	5.56	7.50	3.12
6	6.62	9.00	3.75
8	8.62	12.00	5.00
10	10.75	15.00	6.25
12	12.75	18.00	7.50
14	14.00	21.00	8.75
16	16.00	24.00	10.00
18	18.00	27.00	11.25
20	20.00	30.00	12.50
22	22.00	33.00	13.50
24	24.00	36.00	15.00
26	26.00	39.00	16.00
28	28.00	42.00	17.25
30	30.00	45.00	18.50
32	32.00	48.00	19.75
34	34.00	51.00	21.00
36	36.00	54.00	22.25
38	38.00	57.00	23.62
40	40.00	60.00	24.88
42	42.00	63.00	26.00
44	44.00	66.00	27.38
46	46.00	69.00	28.62
48	48.00	72.00	29.88

Dimensions are in inches.

Note:
(1) *A* and *B* dimensions of 1.50 in and 0.75 in, respectively may be furnished for NPS ¾ at the manufacturer's option.

TABLE 1-5   Dimensions of Short Radius Elbows

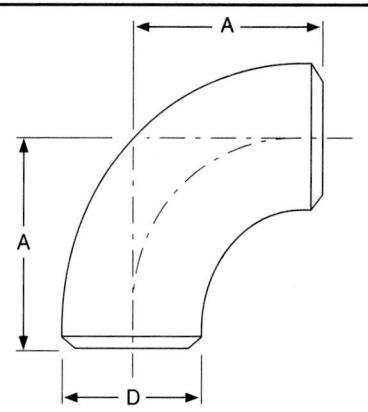

Nominal pipe size	Outside diameter at bevel D	Center-to-end A
1	1.32	1.00
1¼	1.66	1.25
1½	1.90	1.50
2	2.38	2.00
2½	2.88	2.50
3	3.50	3.00
3½	4.00	3.50
4	4.50	4.00
5	5.56	5.00
6	6.62	6.00
8	8.62	8.00
10	10.75	10.00
12	12.75	12.00
14	14.00	14.00
16	16.00	16.00
18	18.00	18.00
20	20.00	20.00
22	22.00	22.00
24	24.00	24.00

Dimensions are in inches.

TABLE 1-6 Dimensions of Straight Tees and Crosses

Nominal pipe size (NPS)	Outside diameter at bevel D	Center-to-end	
		Run C	Outlet[1,2] M
½	0.84	1.00	1.00
¾	1.05	1.12	1.12
1	1.32	1.50	1.50
1¼	1.66	1.88	1.88
1½	1.90	2.25	2.25
2	2.38	2.50	2.50
2½	2.88	3.00	3.00
3	3.50	3.38	3.38
3½	4.00	3.75	3.75
4	4.50	4.12	4.12
5	5.56	4.88	4.88
6	6.62	5.62	5.62
8	8.62	7.00	7.00
10	10.75	8.50	8.50
12	12.75	10.00	10.00
14	14.00	11.00	11.00
16	16.00	12.00	12.00
18	18.00	13.50	13.50
20	20.00	15.00	15.00
22	22.00	16.50	16.50
24	24.00	17.00	17.00
26	26.00	19.50	19.50
28	28.00	20.50	20.50
30	30.00	22.00	22.00
32	32.00	23.50	23.50
34	34.00	25.00	25.00
36	36.00	26.50	26.50
38	38.00	28.00	28.00
40	40.00	29.50	29.50
42	42.00	30.00	28.00
44	44.00	32.00	30.00
46	46.00	33.50	31.50
48	48.00	35.00	33.00

Dimensions are in inches.

Notes:
(1) Outlet dimension M for NPS 26 and larger is recommended but not required.
(2) Dimensions applicable to crosses NPS 24 and smaller.

TABLE 1-7 Dimensions of Caps

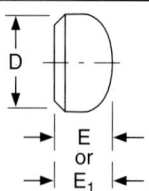

Nominal pipe size (NPS)	Outside diameter at bevel D	Length[1] E	Limiting wall thickness for length E	Length[2] E_1
½	0.84	1.00	0.18	1.00
¾	1.05	1.00	0.15	1.00
1	1.32	1.50	0.18	1.50
1¼	1.66	1.50	0.19	1.50
1½	1.90	1.50	0.20	1.50
2	2.38	1.50	0.22	1.75
2½	2.88	1.50	0.28	2.00
3	3.50	2.00	0.30	2.50
3½	4.00	2.50	0.32	3.00
4	4.50	2.50	0.34	3.00
5	5.56	3.00	0.38	3.50
6	6.62	3.50	0.43	4.00
8	8.62	4.00	0.50	5.00
10	10.75	5.00	0.50	6.00
12	12.75	6.00	0.50	7.00
14	14.00	6.50	0.50	7.50
16	16.00	7.00	0.50	8.00
18	18.00	8.00	0.50	9.00
20	20.00	9.00	0.50	10.00
22	22.00	10.00	0.50	10.00
24	24.00	10.50	0.50	12.00
26	26.00	10.50	—	—
28	28.00	10.50	—	—
30	30.00	10.50	—	—
32	32.00	10.50	—	—
34	34.00	10.50	—	—
36	36.00	10.50	—	—
38	38.00	12.00	—	—
40	40.00	12.00	—	—
42	42.00	12.00	—	—
44	44.00	13.50	—	—
46	46.00	13.50	—	—
48	48.00	13.50	—	—

Notes:
(1) Dimensions are in inches.
(2) The shape of these caps shall be ellipsoidal and shall conform to the shape requirements as given in the ASME Boiler and Pressure Vessel Code.

Example.   A 12-NPS (300-DN) seamless carbon steel pipe is to be used to carry steam at 600°F (316°C) and 1000 lb/in² (7.0 MPa). At a flange, there is a deadweight load of 14,000 lb (62.3 N) and a bending moment of 120,000 in-lbs (13,600 N-m). What is the correct class flange needed to guard against leakage? (The average diameter of the gasket is 14 in.)

$$P_{\text{equiv}} = \frac{16\,(120{,}000)}{\pi\,14^3} + \frac{4\,(14{,}000)}{\pi\,14^2} = 220 + 91 = 311 \text{ lb/in}^2 \text{ (2.1 MPa)}$$

The combined internal pressure plus equivalent pressure is 1000 + 311 = 1311 lb/in² (9.04 MPa). While the pressure rating charts of B16.5 (Tables 1-10 and 1-11) allow a Class 600 flange made from carbon or low alloy steel for a pressure of 1000 lb/in², a Class 600 flange is no longer acceptable when the external loads listed previously are considered. A Class 900 flange from any carbon or low alloy material group is required.

Primary Stresses Due to Deadweight and Bending

Longitudinal deadweight tensile stresses (i.e., those stresses that tend to pull the metal apart) occur only in vertical runs of pipe when the pipe is supported from the top and the weight of each piece of pipe supports the weight of all the pieces of pipe that hang below it. If pipe is not properly supported in vertical runs, the deadweight axial stress can become significant. This effect is easily minimized by supporting vertical runs at some midpoint along the vertical length, or from the bottom, such that the deadweight loads are kept low or compressive. However, there should be some lateral support at the top of any vertical pipe runs to provide column stability. This load is not a concern for pipe that runs vertically for short distances, since the stress caused by short vertical runs is low. Note that the longitudinal deadweight stress is a compressive stress (i.e., a stress that tends to push the metal together) for those portions of a vertical run that are supported at some lower point in the run. Very long vertical runs should be supported in several places to avoid excessive column loading, which can result in buckling.

The other load in the longitudinal direction results in bending stress. This occurs in horizontal pipe runs due to the weight of the pipe plus its contents hanging between supports. Pipe behaves as a simply supported beam of uniform load. Bending stress is different than the aforementioned axial pressure stresses, since it is not uniform around the pipe. At a support, bending stresses typically are tensile stresses at the top of the pipe compressive at the bottom of the pipe. Halfway between supports, however, the stresses are reversed, tensile at the bottom and compressive at the top. These stresses, although complex, are easily handled. ASME B31.1 provides a table of support spacing for various pipe sizes; when these spacings are used, the bending stress is limited to approximately 2300 lb/in² (15.8 MPa), which is relatively low. The recommended support spacings are shown in Table 1-12. Bending stresses can become high where there is a change in the direction of a run, such as at an elbow. In addition, bending stress can become quite high if there is a concentrated deadweight load, such as a valve or vertical pipe run, that is not separately supported. This effect can be overcome by supporting the concentrated deadweight loads first. Once this is done, the balance of the pipe can be supported using the support spacings suggested by the codes.

Rigid supports (i.e., rods and clamps) should be used to support the deadweight of the pipe wherever possible. If the pipe moves in the vertical direction due to thermal expansion, it is necessary to provide spring supports at the required intervals based on both load and deflection. Springs should also be used at equipment nozzles and locations where the movement of the pipe exceeds three-sixteenth in. (46 mm)

In addition to providing vertical support for deadweight, it is good practice to provide restraint in the horizontal plane to stabilize the pipe and prevent excessive horizontal movement in the event of earthquake, hydraulic transients, flow-induced vibration, or other external excitation. It is good practice to limit horizontal movement of piping by providing one horizontal restraint for approximately every five vertical supports.

TABLE 1-8   Steel Socket-Welding Fittings

90° elbow   Cross   Tee

Nom. pipe size	Socket bore dia.(2) B	Bore diameter of fittings(2) D Pressure class designation			Socket wall thickness(1) C Pressure class designation						Body wall G Pressure class designation		
		3000	6000	9000	3000 Ave.	3000 Min.	6000 Ave.	6000 Min.	9000 Ave.	9000 Min.	3000 Min.	6000 Min.	9000 Min.
⅛	0.430	0.299	0.189		0.125	0.125	0.156	0.135			0.095	0.124	
	0.420	0.239	0.126										
¼	0.565	0.394	0.280		0.149	0.130	0.181	0.158			0.119	0.145	
	0.555	0.334	0.220										
⅜	0.700	0.523	0.389		0.158	0.138	0.198	0.172			0.126	0.158	
	0.690	0.463	0.329										
½	0.865	0.652	0.494	0.282	0.184	0.161	0.235	0.204	0.368	0.322	0.147	0.188	0.294
	0.855	0.592	0.434	0.222									
¾	1.075	0.854	0.642	0.464	0.193	0.168	0.274	0.238	0.385	0.337	0.154	0.219	0.308
	1.065	0.794	0.582	0.404									
1	1.340	1.079	0.845	0.629	0.224	0.196	0.312	0.273	0.448	0.392	0.179	0.250	0.358
	1.330	1.019	0.785	0.569									
1¼	1.685	1.410	1.190	0.926	0.239	0.208	0.312	0.273	0.478	0.418	0.191	0.250	0.382
	1.675	1.350	1.130	0.866									
1½	1.925	1.640	1.368	1.130	0.250	0.218	0.351	0.307	0.500	0.438	0.200	0.281	0.400
	1.915	1.580	1.308	1.070									
2	2.416	2.097	1.717	1.533	0.273	0.238	0.430	0.374	0.545	0.477	0.218	0.344	0.436
	2.406	2.037	1.657	1.473									
2½	2.921	2.529			0.345	0.302					0.276		
	2.906	2.409											
3	3.550	3.128			0.375	0.327					0.300		
	3.535	3.008											
4	4.560	4.086			0.421	0.368					0.337		
	4.545	3.966											

Dimensions are in inches.
(1) Average of socket wall thickness around periphery shall be no less than listed values. The minimum values are permitted in localized areas.
(2) Upper and lower values for each size are the respective maximum and minimum dimensions.

Additional horizontal restraint is required when the pipe will be outdoors and exposed to the wind. Wind restraints should be designed based on the wind force per square foot times the area of pipe exposed to the wind. The restraints should be analyzed as simply supported pipe sections that are uniformly loaded.

The actual horizontal supports are usually tubular or box sections that are clamped to the pipe and anchored to fixed structural elements. Ball joints are used at the ends of the struts to permit free movement of the strut, and care must be taken that the arrangement of the struts does not cause binding with structures or equipment because of thermal growth of the pipe during operation. When piping must be restrained against dynamic events but still free to move due to thermal growth, snubbers or energy absorbers are used. These devices are available from the following organizations:

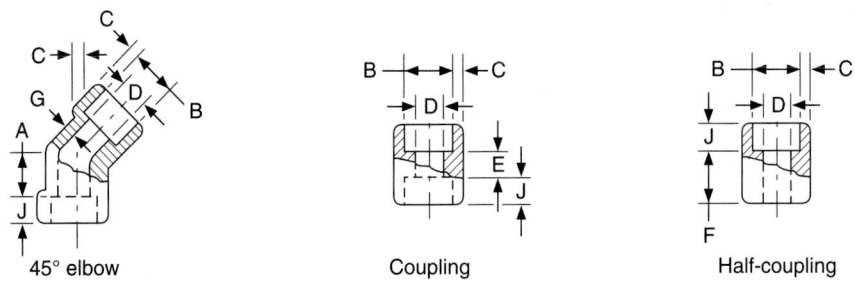

45° elbow   Coupling   Half-coupling

Center to bottom of socket—A

Depth of Socket J Min.	90° Elbows, tees, and crosses			45° Elbows			Laying lengths		Tolerances ±		
	Pressure Class Designation						Couplings	Half couplings			
	3000	6000	9000	3000	6000	9000	E	F	A	E	F
0.38	0.44	0.44		0.31	0.31		0.25	0.62	0.03	0.06	0.03
0.38	0.44	0.53		0.31	0.31		0.25	0.62	0.03	0.06	0.03
0.38	0.53	0.62		0.31	0.44		0.25	0.69	0.06	0.12	0.06
0.38	0.62	0.75	1.00	0.44	0.50	0.62	0.38	0.88	0.06	0.12	0.06
0.50	0.75	0.88	1.12	0.50	0.56	0.75	0.38	0.94	0.06	0.12	0.06
0.50	0.88	1.06	1.25	0.56	0.69	0.81	0.50	1.12	0.08	0.16	0.08
0.50	1.06	1.25	1.38	0.69	0.81	0.88	0.50	1.19	0.08	0.16	0.08
0.50	1.25	1.50	1.50	0.81	1.00	1.00	0.50	1.25	0.08	0.16	0.08
0.62	1.50	1.62	2.12	1.00	1.12	1.12	0.75	1.62	0.08	0.16	0.08
0.62	1.62			1.12			0.75	1.69	0.10	0.20	0.10
0.62	2.25			1.25			0.75	1.75	0.10	0.20	0.10
0.75	2.62			1.62			0.75	1.88	0.10	0.20	0.10

Device	*Manufacturer*
Hydraulic Snubber	Most pipe support manufacturers
Mechanical Snubber	Pacific Scientific, San Francisco, CA
	Anchor-Darling, Williamsport, PA
WEAR™ (Wire Energy Absorbing Rope) Restraint/Support	Vectra Technologies, Inc., Lincolnshire, IL

Primary Stresses Due to Nozzle Openings

It is common practice to use manufactured tees when a branch line has to be attached to a run pipe. Although it is a simple matter to specify tees, delivery of the required size in a timely

TABLE 1-9 Class 900 Pressure-Temperature Ratings

Pressures are in pounds per square inch, gage (psig)

Carbon steel groups: 1.1* = Norm., 1.2 = High, 1.4* = Low

Temp. °F	1.1* Norm.	1.2 High	1.4* Low	1.5 C-½Mo	1.7 ½Cr-½Mo Ni-Cr-Mo	1.9 1¼Cr-½Mo	1.10 2¼Cr-1Mo	1.13 5Cr-½Mo	1.14 9Cr-1Mo	2.1 Type 304	2.2 Type 316	2.3 Type 304L/316L	2.4 Type 321	2.5 Types 347/348	2.6 Type 309	2.7 Type 310
−20 to 100	2220	2250	1850	2085	2250	2250	2250	2250	2250	2160	2160	1800	2160	2160	2015	2015
200	2025	2250	1685	2035	2250	2135	2150	2250	2250	1800	1860	1520	1830	1910	1815	1815
300	1970	2185	1640	1955	2185	2020	2030	2185	2185	1585	1680	1360	1635	1765	1705	1705
400	1900	2115	1585	1920	2115	1975	1945	2115	2115	1410	1540	1240	1485	1665	1600	1600
500	1795	1995	1495	1865	1995	1925	1920		1995	1310	1435	1145	1375	1555	1510	1510
600	1640	1815	1370			1815	1815			1245	1355	1080	1310	1475	1435	1435
650	1610	1765	1345			1765	1765			1225	1330	1050	1280	1440	1395	1395
700	1600	1705	1345			1705	1705			1210	1295	1030	1260	1405	1370	1370
750	1510	1510	1325			1595	1595			1195	1270	1010	1245	1385	1340	1340
800	1235	1235	1110			1525	1525	1490	1525	1180	1245	985	1240	1370	1305	1305
850		805				1460	1460	1315	1460	1165	1215	965	1225	1330	1275	1275
900		515				1350	1350	1060	1350	1150	1180		1215	1295	1245	1245
950		310		845	1030	1130	1130	780	1110	1125	1160		1160	1160	1160	1160
1000		155		495	640	670	805	575	875	965	1090		1070	1090	1010	1050
1050					565	410	595	420	565	925	1080		1040	1080	875	1000
1100						290	340	310	340	770	965		905	965	670	875
1150						155	310	205	225	585	825		710	825	515	740
1200						105	165	135	155	465	620		545	515	390	620
1250										330	545		420	370	300	485
1300										245	410		320	280	235	360
1350										185	310		245	205	175	235
1400										145	225		185	155	135	165
1450										105	175		145	125	95	115
1500										70	125		115	105	70	70

* Do not use ASTM A181 Grade I or II material.

NOTES:
1. Ratings shown apply to other material groups where columns dividing lines are omitted.
2. Provisions of Section 2 apply to all ratings.

TABLE 1-10 Class 600 Pressure-Temperature Ratings

Pressures are in pounds per square inch, gage (psig)

Temp. °F	1.1* Norm.	1.2 High	1.4* Low	1.5 C-½Mo	1.7 ½Cr-½Mo Ni-Cr-Mo	1.9 1¼Cr-½Mo	1.10 2¼Cr-1Mo	1.13 5Cr-½Mo	1.14 9Cr-1Mo	2.1 Type 304	2.2 Type 316	2.3 Type 304L / Type 316L	2.4 Type 321	2.5 Types 347 348	2.6 Type 309	2.7 Type 310	Temperature °F
	Carbon steel	Carbon steel	Carbon steel														
−20 to 100	1480	1500	1235	1390	1500	1500	1500			1440	1440	1200	1440	1440		1345	100
200	1350	1500	1125	1360	1500	1425	1430			1200	1240	1015	1220	1270		1210	200
300	1315	1455	1095	1305	1455	1345	1355			1055	1120	910	1090	1175		1140	300
400	1270	1410	1060	1280	1410	1315	1295			940	1030	825	990	1110		1065	400
500	1200	1330	995	1245	1330	1285	1280	1330		875	955	765	915	1035		1010	500
600	1095	1210	915			1210			1330	830	905	720	875	985		955	600
650	1075	1175	895			1175				815	890	700	855	960		930	650
700	1065	1135	895			1135				805	865	685	840	935		910	700
750	1010	1010	885			1065				795	845	670	830	920		895	750
800	825	825	740			1015		995		790	830	660	825	910		870	800
850		535				975		880		780	810	645	815	890		850	850
900		205				900		705		770	790		810	865		830	900
950		105		560	685	755		520	740	750	775		775	775		775	950
1000				330	425	445	535	385	585	645	725		715	725	670	700	1000
1050					380	275	400	280	380	620	720		695	720	585	665	1050
1100						190	225	205	225	515	645		605	645	445	585	1100
1150						105	205	140	150	390	550		475	550	345	495	1150
1200						70	110	90	105	310	410		365	345	260	410	1200
1250										220	365		280	245	200	325	1250
1300										165	275		210	185	160	240	1300
1350										125	205		165	135	115	160	1350
1400										90	150		125	105	90	110	1400
1450										70	115		95	80	60	75	1450
1500										50	85		75	70	50	50	1500

* Do not use ASTM A181 Grade I or II material.

NOTES:
1. Ratings shown apply to other material groups where columns dividing lines are omitted.
2. Provisions of Section 2 apply to all ratings.

TABLE 1-11   Material Groupings for Flange Classes

Mat'l group	Materials (spec-grade)	Mat'l group	Materials (spec-grade)
1.1	A105, A181-II, A216-WCB, A515-70 A516-70 A350-LF2, A537-C1.1	2.1	A182-F304, A182-F304H A240-304, A351-CF8 A351-CF3
1.2	A203-B, A203-E, A216-WCC A350-LF3, A352-LC2, A352-LC3	2.2	A182-F316, A182-F316H, A240-316 A240-317, A351-CF8M A351-CF3M
1.4	A181-I, A515-60 A516-60 A350-LF1	2.3	A182-F304L, A240-304L A182-F316L, A240-316L
1.5	A182-F1, A204-A, A204-B, A217-WC1 A352-LC1	2.4	A182-F321, A240-321 A182-F321H, A240-321H
1.7	A204-C A182-F2, A217-WC4 A217-WC5	2.5	A182-F347, A240-347 A182-F347H, A240-347H A182-F348, A240-348 A182-F348H, A240-F348H
1.9	A182-F11, A182-F12, A387-11, C1.2 A217-WC6	2.6	A240-309S, A351-CH8, A351-CH20
1.10	A182-F22, A387-22, C1.2 A217-WC9	2.7	A182-F310, A240-310S A351-CK20
1.13	A182-F5a, A217-C5		
1.14	A182-F9, A217-C12		

TABLE 1-12   Recommended Vertical Support Spacing

Nominal pipe size	Maximum span between supports (ft)	
	Water service	Steam service
1	7	9
2	10	13
3	12	16
4	14	17
6	17	21
8	19	24
12	23	30
16	27	35
20	30	39
24	32	42

DN	Maximum span between supports (m)	
	Water service	Steam service
25	2.3	3.0
50	3.3	4.3
75	4.0	5.3
100	4.7	5.7
150	5.7	7.0
200	6.3	8.0
300	7.7	10.0
400	9.0	11.7
500	10.0	13.0
600	10.7	14.0

fashion can be a problem. In addition, the cost of tees plus the cost of making three welds to install a tee is frequently greater than the cost of cutting and welding one pipe to another. Typical fabricated branch connections are shown in Fig. 1-4.

The presence of a hole in a header pipe for the branch pipe increases the membrane stress around the hole. In order to compensate for the higher membrane stress, sufficient material must be present in the vicinity of the hole. B31 Code requires that sufficient extra metal be present near the hole to compensate. The Pipe Fabrication Institute (Springdale, PA) publishes worksheets that simplify calculation of the amount of required area in accordance with ASME B31.1 and B31.3. When the intrinsic reinforcement is not sufficient, a reinforcing pad or "saddle" must be used.

One simple observation about reinforcement of outlet openings is that if the header pipe wall minimum thickness is more than twice the calculated minimum wall thickness plus the corrosion allowance, the wall thickness in the header pipe itself is sufficient for 90° branch connections and additional reinforcement is not required. In addition, B31.9 provides graphs for both 45° and 90° branch connections showing permissible combinations of various sizes of carbon steel branch pipe and header that do not require reinforcement for pressures of 100, 200, 300, and 350 lb/in² (0.7, 1.4, 2.1, and 2.4 kPa).

Example. A 12-NPS (300-DN) seamless carbon steel pipe is to be used to carry steam at 300°F (150°C) and 100 lb/in² (0.69 kPa). The corrosion allowance is 0.0625 in (1.5 mm). The minimum permissible wall thickness is:

$$t_{min} = \frac{100\,(12.75)}{2(15,000)(1.0) + 100(0.4)} + 0.0625$$

$$t_{min} = 0.105 \text{ in minimum wall}$$

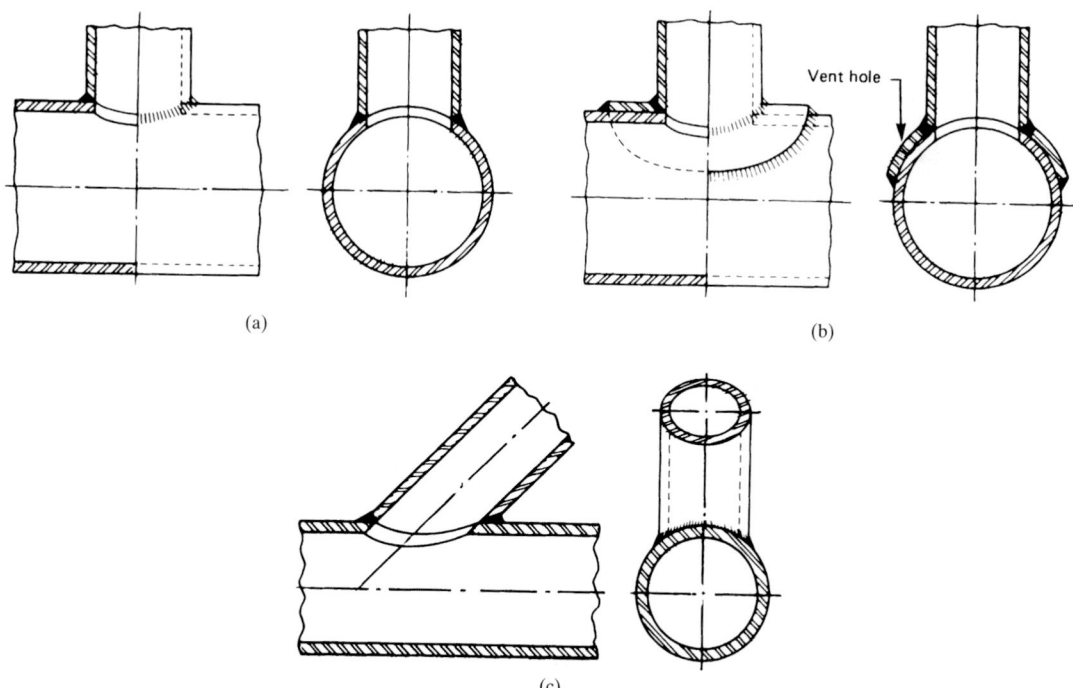

(a)

(b)

Vent hole

(c)

FIGURE 1-4 Typical fabricated branch connections. (*a*) Without added reinforcement; (*b*) with added reinforcement; (*c*) angular branch without added reinforcement.

In metric units:

$$t_{min} = \frac{0.69\,(324)}{2(103)(1.0) + 0.69(0.4)} + 1.5 = 2.55$$

If 12-NPS (300-DN) standard weight pipe ($t_{nom} = 0.375$ in [9.5 mm]) is used for the header, any branch outlet up to 12 NPS (300 DN) may be used without additional reinforcement, since:

$$2(t_{min} - CA) = 2(0.105 - 0.625) = 0.119 \text{ in} < 0.375 \times 0.875 - 0.625 = 0.266 \text{ in}$$

In metric units:

$$2(t_{min} - CA) = 2(2.55 - 1.5) = 3.02 \text{ mm} < 9.5 \times 0.875 - 1.5 = 6.83 \text{ mm}$$

Primary Stresses in Flat Plates Used for Closures

The best engineering practice to use when closing off the end of a pipe for testing or other purposes is to use a standard pipe fitting, such as a plug or pipe cap. Flat plates may be used as a permanent closure for the end of a pipe if the plate is a blind flange meeting the requirements of ASME B16.5, or the plate thickness t is calculated in accordance with the following:

$$t = d(CP/SE)^{1/2} + CA$$

where d = the outside diameter of the pipe
P = the design pressure
S = the allowable stress per the applicable code section
E = the joint quality factor = 1.0 unless the plate is welded
CA = the corrosion allowance
$C = 0.5t_m/T$, but not less than 0.3 (t_m = the calculated minimum wall thickness, T = the minimum pipe wall thickness for the size and schedule pipe being used)

Attachment of the end plate to the pipe is very important. Permissible and prohibited methods of attaching the plate to the pipe are shown in Fig. 1-5.

Expansion Joints, Flexible Couplings, and Vibration Isolation Devices

Bellows type expansion joints and rubber flexible connection devices are sometimes used to allow for pipe expansion or to isolate mechanical equipment and piping from each other. These devices are rated by their manufacturers for certain pressure and temperature conditions. It is important to recognize that there is a pressure force on such components that tends to stretch the component in its axial direction. This force is equal to the pressure inside the pipe times the internal area of the pipe. For example, for 8-NPS (200-DN) schedule 40 pipe operating at 300 lb/in^2 (2 MPa), the approximate axial load is:

$$300 \text{ lb/in}^2 \times 50 \text{ in}^2 = 1500 \text{ lb}$$

In metric units:

$$2 \text{ MPa} \times 3225 \text{ mm}^2 = 6672 \text{ N}$$

A more accurate value is obtained when the actual average inside diameter of the component is used in calculating the area.

A metal bellows will stretch longitudinally as a result of this force unless it is restrained by anchors on the pipe or by tie-rods across the bellows. Reinforced rubber isolators will also be subjected to this force, which will tend to pull the rubber out from between the flanges that hold the rubber in place, resulting in failure of the pressure boundary. In this case, the axial pressure force must to be transferred to a restraint or anchor that limits the motion of the pipe parallel to the isolator's axis while permitting lateral and vertical movement. This will allow the isolator to perform its job without being loaded excessively in the axial direction.

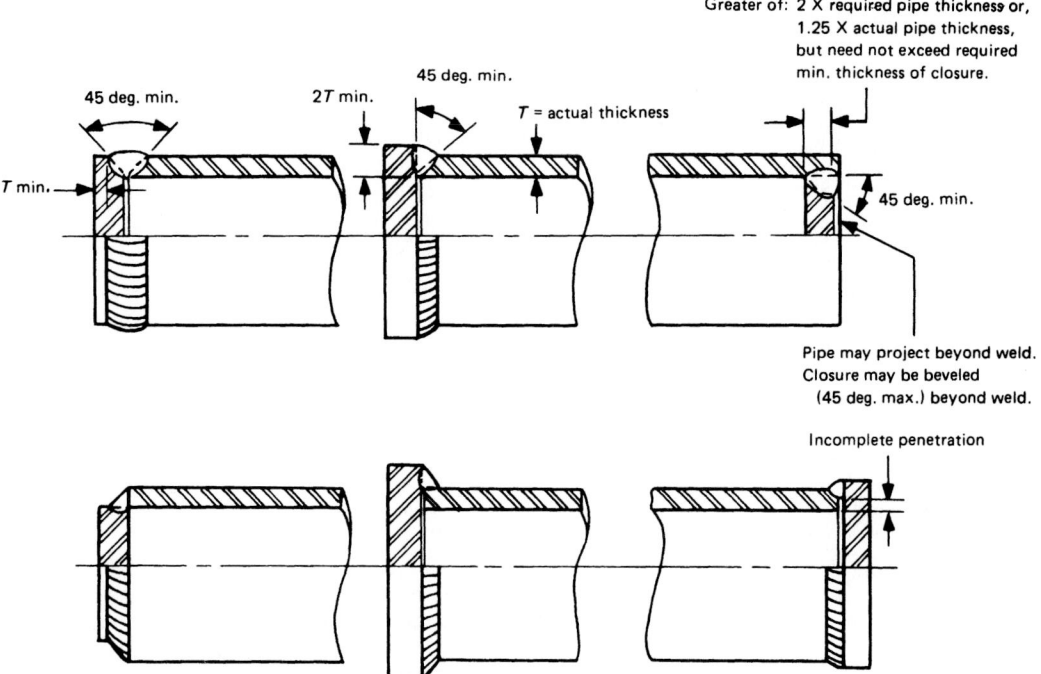

FIGURE 1-5 Acceptable and unacceptable welds for flat heads.

Secondary Stresses due to Thermal Expansion

When most metals are heated and cooled, they expand and contract. A rule of thumb for this change in dimension with temperature is that steel expands approximately 1 in (25 mm) per 100°F (38°C) temperature change per 100 ft (30.5 m) of pipe. 500 ft (167 m) of pipe that operates at 400°F (204°C) grows nearly 17 in (0.43 m) as it goes from ambient to service temperature. This change in length can move equipment, bend nozzles, cause support failure, and buckle pipe if the piping system is not properly designed. This is why most high-temperature piping has expansion loops or why it may appear to be routed in an inefficient manner.

When a length of pipe is connected to two pieces of equipment, the connection points are usually assumed to be rigid. When a simple two-legged piping system is heated, it expands as shown in Fig. 1-6.

When properly designed, the dimensional changes of the pipe caused by expansion are taken up by bending of the pipe. This results in bending moments throughout the system and at connections to the equipment. Since the displacement can be calculated, the resulting stress in the pipe also can be easily approximated at the connections and at highly stressed components such as elbows.

When a new or replacement piping system duplicates an existing piping system that has operated successfully for a given set of operating conditions, it is acceptable to duplicate that system without further analysis for thermal effects. It should be recognized that the support and restraint of an existing system are critical aspects of the design of the piping system, and that not only the routing, but also the support types, locations, and directions must be duplicated for systems to be similar.

Initial screening for thermal expansion can be performed using the following formula when the system is composed of all ductile metal (i.e., no cast iron), has no more than two anchors and no intermediate rigid restraints:

$$D_n \, Y/(L - U)^2 < 0.03 \text{ if in English units or 210 if in metric units}$$

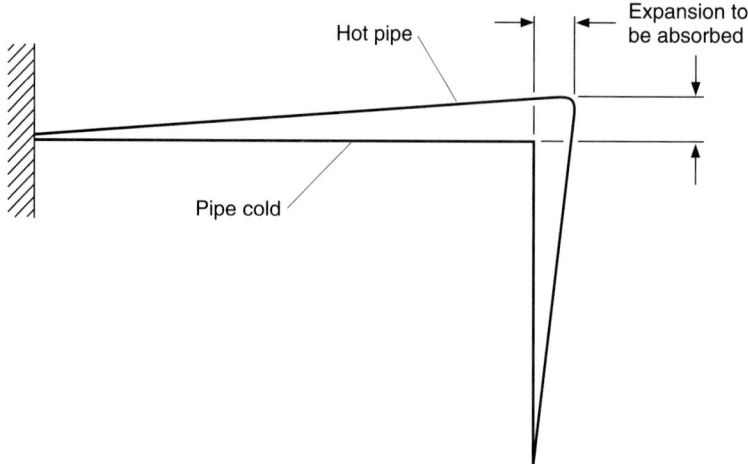

FIGURE 1-6   Generic thermal expansion.

where D_n = the nominal size of the larger pipe in the segment (in, mm)

Y = the result of the changes in length to be absorbed (ft, m). (Pipe may be oriented in more than one plane when using this formula. Any anchor movement resulting from temperature changes of the equipment to which the pipe is attached must be added to the pipe length change.)

L = the developed length of the pipe between anchors (ft, m)

U = the linear distance between anchors (ft, m)

This formula should not be used when the pipe size between anchors changes by more than one nominal size or if the pipe wall thickness varies more than 75 percent. This formula may not be conservative enough for nearly straight sawtooth segments or for unequal-leg U bends where $L/U > 2.5$.

Example.   Pipe that is 12-NPS (300-DN) standard weight runs between two points as shown in Fig. 1-7. The pipe operates at 400°F (205°C). Are the stresses due to thermal expansion acceptable?

The result of the deflections is:

$$Y = (1.65^2 + .83^2)^{1/2} = 1.85 \text{ in } (47 \text{ mm})$$

The developed length of pipe between the anchors $L = 50$ ft (16.7 m) + 25 ft (8.4 m) = 75 ft (25 m).
The distance between the anchor points $U = (50^2 + 25^2)^{1/2} = 55.1$ ft (18.4 m).
The pipe outside diameter is 12.75 in (324 mm).

$$D_n Y/(L - U)^2 < 0.03 \text{ if in English units or 210 if in metric units}$$

$$(12.75 \times 1.85)/(75 - 55.1)^2 = 0.059 \qquad \text{Not Acceptable!}$$

In metric units:

$$(324 \times 47)/(22.8 - 16.8)^2 = 423 \qquad \text{Not Acceptable!}$$

It is evident from the layout that the 25-ft (8-m) leg is too short to absorb the growth of the 50-ft (16-m) leg. If the developed length is increased along the 25-ft (8-m) direction, the divisor increases. Reroute the pipe as shown in Fig. 1-8.

Expansion due to the 50-ft (16-m) leg is absorbed by the longer developed length:

$$(12.75 \times 1.85)/(85 - 55.1)^2 = 0.026 \qquad \text{Acceptable!}$$

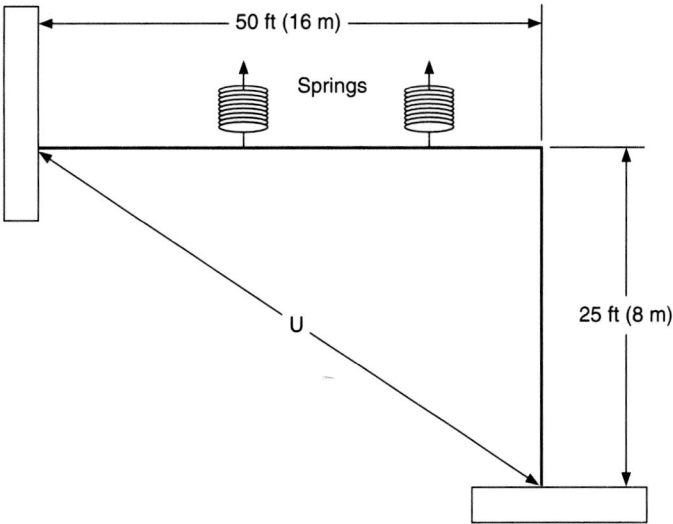

FIGURE 1-7 Simple model for thermal analysis.

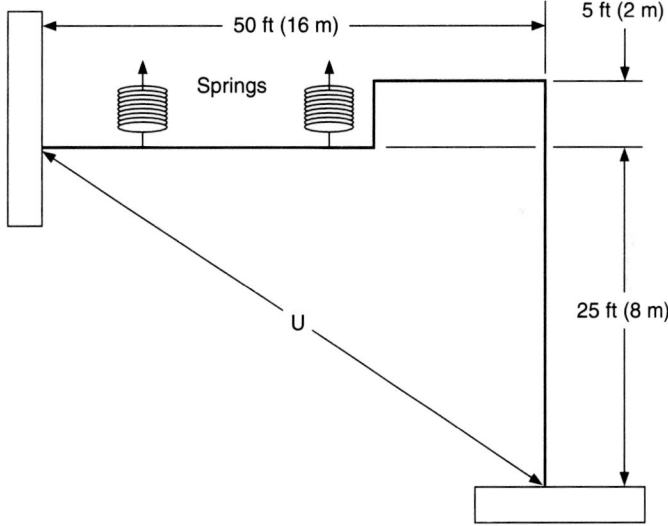

FIGURE 1-8 Simple model modified for thermal analysis.

In metric units:

$$(324 \times 47)/(28.3 - 18.4)^2 = 155 \qquad \text{Acceptable!}$$

A more sophisticated method of analysis is called the *fixed-fixed beam* or *guided cantilever* method. This method assumes that both ends of any straight length of pipe are anchored, and that the anchor moves due to the expansion of the leg that is perpendicular to the leg under consideration, resulting in bending the pipe (see Fig. 1-9). This allows one to calculate the stress σ in the pipe, the reaction forces *R,* and moments *M.*

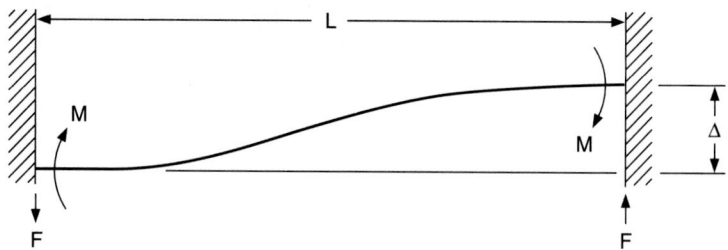

FIGURE 1-9 Fixed-fixed beam concept model.

The applicable equations are:

$$M = 6\ EI\Delta/L^2$$

$$R = 2\ M/L = 12\ EI\Delta/L^3$$

$$\sigma = MD/2L = 3E\Delta D/L^2$$

where E = Young's Modulus (30×10^6 lb/in^2, 200 GPa)
I = the moment of inertia of the pipe (in^4, mm^4)
M = the moment that results from the displacement of B (ft-lb, m-N)
σ = the bending stress developed in the pipe (lb/in^2, MPa)
D = the outside diameter (OD) of the pipe (in, mm)

Using the L-shaped configuration shown in Fig. 1-10, assume that joint B is fixed against rotation and allow expansion of leg BC to be absorbed by bending of leg AB:

$$\Delta_{L2} = \alpha \Delta T L_2\ (\alpha = \text{pipe coefficient of thermal expansion})$$

$$\sigma_{AB} = 3E\Delta_{L2}\ D/L_1^2$$

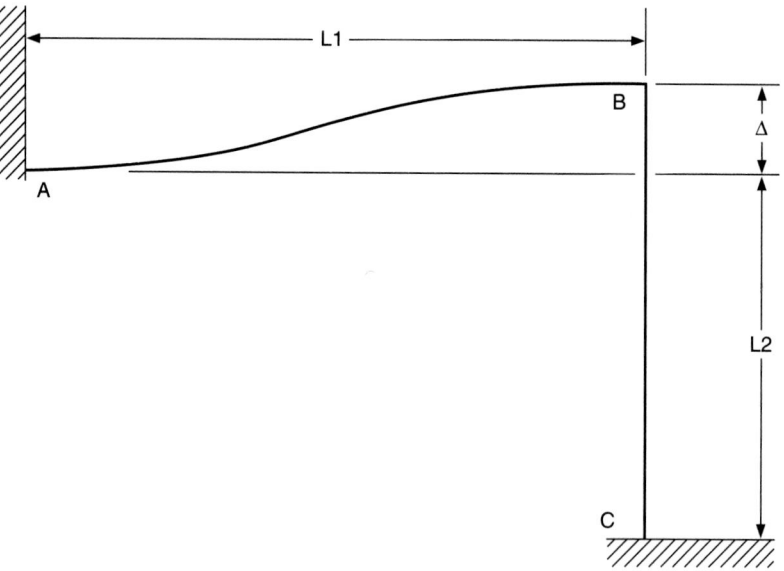

FIGURE 1-10 Fixed-fixed beam two-leg model—part 1.

Next, assume joint B fixed against rotation and allow expansion of leg AB to be absorbed by bending of leg BC, as shown in Fig. 1-11.

$$\Delta_{L1} = \alpha \Delta T L_1$$

$$\sigma_{BC} = 3E\Delta L1D/L_2^2$$

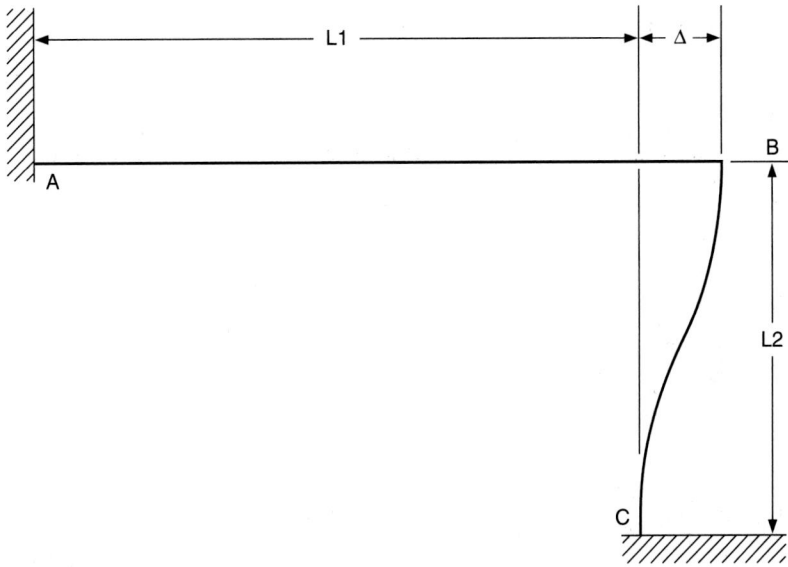

FIGURE 1-11   Fixed-fixed beam two-leg model—part 2.

Let the bending moment at B be the maximum of σ_{AB} and σ_{BC}. According to the B31 Code Sections, the expansion stress $S_E = iM/Z = is$, where Z is the section modulus of the connecting piping and i is the stress intensification factor (SIF) based on the values of the pipe radius r, the bend radius R_1, and nominal wall thickness of the fitting T calculated in accordance with Table 1-13. Calculation formulas for SIFs for other components than elbows are also shown in Table 1-13.

The allowable stress, S_a, is based on the allowable stress range permitted by B31.1:

$$S_a = f(1.25S_c + 0.25S_h) \ (\text{lb/in}^2, \text{MPa})$$

where S_c = the allowable stress of the pipe material when cold (lb/in², MPa)
   S_h = the allowable stress of the pipe material when hot (lb/in², MPa)
   f = a factor that reduces the allowable stress range as a function of the number of thermal cycles shown in Table 1-14

Rather than solving for the stress to see if the system design is acceptable, solve for the required length of pipe for a given deflection, pipe size, allowable stress range, and stress intensification before laying out the system. Solving for the length of pipe L required to absorb the deflection (Δ):

$$L = (3E\Delta D/\sigma)^{1/2}$$

Reducing this formula,

$$L = (\Delta iD \times 10^6/1.6S_a)^{1/2}$$

TABLE 1-13 Flexibility and Stress Intensification Factors

Description	Flexibility factor k	Stress intensification factor (never < 1.0) Out-of-plane i_o	In-plane i_i	Flexibility characteristic h	Sketch
Welding elbow or pipe bend	$\dfrac{1.65}{h}$	$\dfrac{0.75}{h^{2/3}}$	$\dfrac{0.9}{h^{2/3}}$	$\dfrac{\bar{T}\,R_1}{r_2^2}$	R_1 = Bend radius
Closely spaced miter bend $s < r_2$ $(1 + \tan\theta)$	$\dfrac{1.52}{h^{5/6}}$	$\dfrac{0.9}{h^{2/3}}$	$\dfrac{0.9}{h^{2/3}}$	$\dfrac{\cot\theta}{2}\ \dfrac{s\bar{T}}{r_2^2}$	$R_1 = \dfrac{s\cot\theta}{2}$
Single miter bend or widely spaced miter bend $s \ge r_2\,(1 + \tan\theta)$	$\dfrac{1.52}{h^{5/6}}$	$\dfrac{0.9}{h^{2/3}}$	$\dfrac{0.9}{h^{2/3}}$	$\dfrac{1 + \cot\theta}{2}\ \dfrac{\bar{T}}{r_2}$	$R_1 = \dfrac{r_2\,(1 + \cot\theta)}{2}$
Welding tee per ASME B16.9 with $r_x \ge \tfrac{1}{8}D_4\ T_c \ge 1.5\,\bar{T}$	1	$\dfrac{0.9}{h^{2/3}}$	$\tfrac{3}{4}\,i_e + \tfrac{1}{4}$	$4.4\,\dfrac{\bar{T}}{r_2}$	
Reinforced fabricated tee with pad or saddle	1	$\dfrac{0.9}{h^{2/3}}$	$\tfrac{3}{4}i_a + \tfrac{1}{4}$	$\dfrac{(\bar{T} + \tfrac{1}{2}\bar{T}_r)^{2.5}}{\bar{T}^{1.5}\,r_2}$	Pad Saddle
Unreinforced fabricated tee	1	$\dfrac{0.9}{h^{2/3}}$	$\tfrac{3}{4}i_o + \tfrac{1}{4}$	$\dfrac{\bar{T}}{r_2}$	

In metric units:

$$L = (0.62\ \Delta i D/S_a)^{1/2}$$

where L = the required length of pipe before the anchor or first rigid hanger (ft, m). (Note that long runs of pipe can be broken into L-shaped segments that can be analyzed individually. See the example problem.)

Δ = the change in distance to be absorbed perpendicular to the axis of the pipe section that is under consideration (in, mm)

i = the stress intensification factor

D = the outside diameter of the pipe (in, mm)

TABLE 1-14 Stress Range Reduction Factors

Number of cycles	Factor f
7,000 and less	1.0
Over 7,000 to 14,000	0.9
Over 14,000 to 22,000	0.8
Over 22,000 to 45,000	0.7
Over 45,000 to 100,000	0.6
Over 100,000 to 200,000	0.5
Over 200,000 to 700,000	0.4
Over 700,000 to 2,000,000	0.3

In most cases, the number of thermal cycles is less than 7,000.

This formula can be simplified even further when the allowable stress range divided by the stress intensification factor (S_a/i) is 10,000 lb/in^2 or greater. In these cases, the minimum distance to the first rigid hanger can be found using Table 1-15.

Example Using Fixed-Fixed Beam Approximation.   Analyze the piping system shown in Fig. 1-12.
   Given:

NPS-2 (DN-50) standard weight carbon steel pipe, 2.375 in (60.3 mm) OD

$t = 0.154$ in (5.54 mm)

Temperature range 70 to 300°F (20 to 149°C)

Coefficient of Expansion: 6.6×10^{-6} in/in/°F (12×10^{-6} mm/mm/°C)

Less than 7000 lifetime cycles

$$\Delta = \alpha(\Delta T)L = 6.6 \times 10^{-6}\,(300 - 70) \times L \times 12$$

$$\Delta = 0.01822L \ (L \text{ is in feet})$$

TABLE 1-15   Minimum Distance to First Rigid Hanger*

Deflection	Pipe size																	
	1	1¼	1½	2	2½	3	3½	4	5	6	8	10	12	14	16	18	20
¼	4.5	5.0	5.5	6.0	6.5	7.5	8.0	8.5	9.5	10	11.5	13	14	15	16	17	17.5
½	6.5	7.0	7.5	8.5	9.5	10.5	11	12	13	14.5	16.5	18.5	20	21	22.5	23.5	25
½	8.0	9.0	9.5	10.5	11.5	13	14	14.5	16	17.5	20	22.5	24.5	25.5	27.5	29	30.5
1	9.0	10	11	12	13.5	15	16	17	18.5	20.5	23	26	28	29.5	31.5	33.5	35.5
1¼	10	11.5	12	13.5	15	16.5	17.5	18.5	21	22.5	26	29	31.5	33	35.5	37.5	39.5
1½	11	12.5	13.5	15	16.5	18	19.5	20.5	23	25	28.5	32	34.5	36	38.5	41	43.5
1¾	12	13.5	14.5	16	17.5	19.5	21	22	24.5	27	30.5	34	37	39	42	44.5	47
2	13	14.5	15.5	17	19	21	22.5	23.5	26.5	29	33	36.5	40	42	44.5	47.5	50
2¼	13.5	15.5	16.5	18.5	20	22	23.5	25	28	30.5	35	39	42.5	44.5	47.5	50.5	53
2½	14.5	16	17	19.5	21	23.5	25	26.5	29.5	32	36.5	41	44.5	47	50	53	56
2¾	15	17	18	20	22	24.5	26	28	31	33.5	38.5	43	47	49	52.5	55.5	58.5
3	15.5	17.5	19	21	23	25.5	27.5	29	32.5	35	40	45	49	51	55	58	61
3½	17	19	20.5	23	25	27.5	29.5	31.5	35	38	43.5	48.5	53	55.5	59	63	66
4	18	20.5	22	24.5	27	29.5	31.5	33.5	37.5	40.5	46.5	52	56.5	59	63	67	70.5
4½	19	21.5	23	26	28.5	31.5	33.5	35.5	39.5	43	49.5	55	60	63	67	71	75
5	20.5	23	24.5	27	30	33	35.5	37.5	41.5	45.5	52	58	63	66	70.5	75	79
5½	21.5	24	25.5	28.5	31.5	34.5	37	39.5	43.5	47.5	54.5	61	66	69.5	74	78.5	83
6	22	25	26.5	30	33	36	38.5	41	45.5	50	57	63.5	69	72.5	77.5	82	86.5

$* L = \sqrt{\dfrac{\Delta \times \text{O.D. of pipe} \times 10^6}{1.6S}}$; $S = 10{,}000 \text{ lb/in}^2$

In metric units:

$$\Delta = \alpha(\Delta T)L = 12 \times 10^{-6}\,(149-19) \times L \times 1000$$

$$\Delta = 1.56L \;(L \text{ is in meters})$$

The stress range for carbon steel pipe (e.g., A106 Grade B) per B31.1 is

$$S_a = 1.0\,[1.25(15{,}000\ \text{lb/in}^2) + 0.25(15{,}000\ \text{lb/in}^2)] = 22{,}500\ \text{lb/in}^2$$

In metric units:

$$S_a = 1.0\,[1.25(103\ \text{kPa}) + 0.25(103\ \text{kPa})] = 155\ \text{MPa}$$

The stress intensification factor for a long-radius NPS-2 (DN-50) standard weight elbow is

$$i = 0.9/h^{2/3} = 0.9/[(0.154 \times 2)/1.110^2]^{2/3} = 2.25$$

In metric units:

$$i = 0.9/h^{2/3} = 0.9/[(5.54 \times 60.3)/28.2^2]^{2/3} = 2.25$$

For segment 1–3 in Fig. 1-13, $\Delta = 0.0182 \times 20$ ft $= 0.364$ in ($\Delta = 1.56 \times 6.13$ m $= 9.6$ mm) as shown in Fig. 1-13. Assume that locations 3 and 4 are fixed against rotation, while only leg 1–3

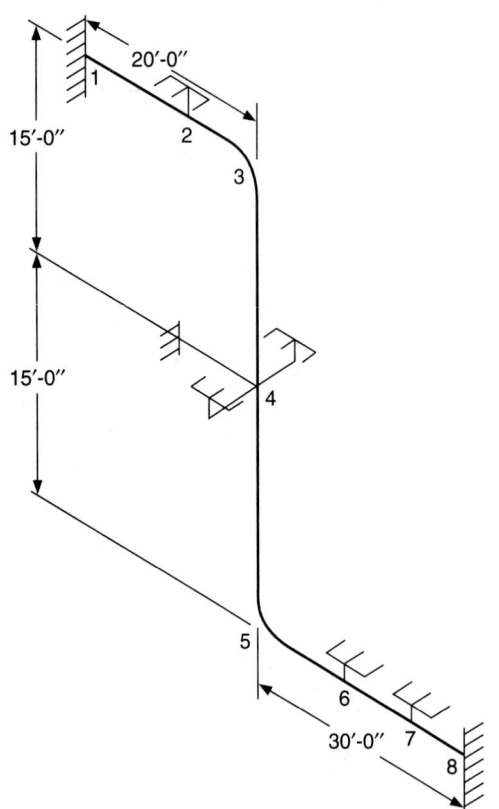

FIGURE 1-12 System for thermal analysis.

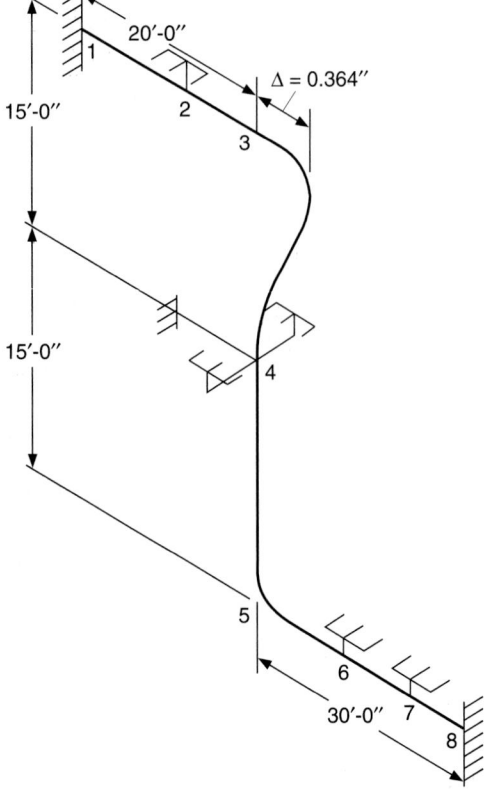

FIGURE 1-13 System for thermal analysis—leg 1–3.

expands. The thermal deflection is absorbed by leg 3–4. The minimum required distance from point 3 to the first rigid horizontal support along 3–4 is:

$$L = [\Delta\, iD\, 10^6/(1.6\, S_a)]^{1/2}$$

$$L = [0.364 \times 2.25 \times 2.375 \times 10^6/(1.6 \times 22{,}500)]^{1/2} = 7.35 \text{ ft}$$

In metric units:

$$L = (0.62\, \Delta iD/S_a)^{1/2}$$

$$L = (0.62 \times 9.6 \times 2.25 \times 60.3/155)^{1/2}$$

$$L = 2.28 \text{ m}$$

Since this is less than the 15-ft (4.6-m) distance from point 3 to point 4, this leg 3–4 is acceptable. For segments 3–4 and 5–4, $\Delta = 0.01822 \times 15$ ft $= 0.273$ in (6.93 mm), as shown in Fig. 1-14.

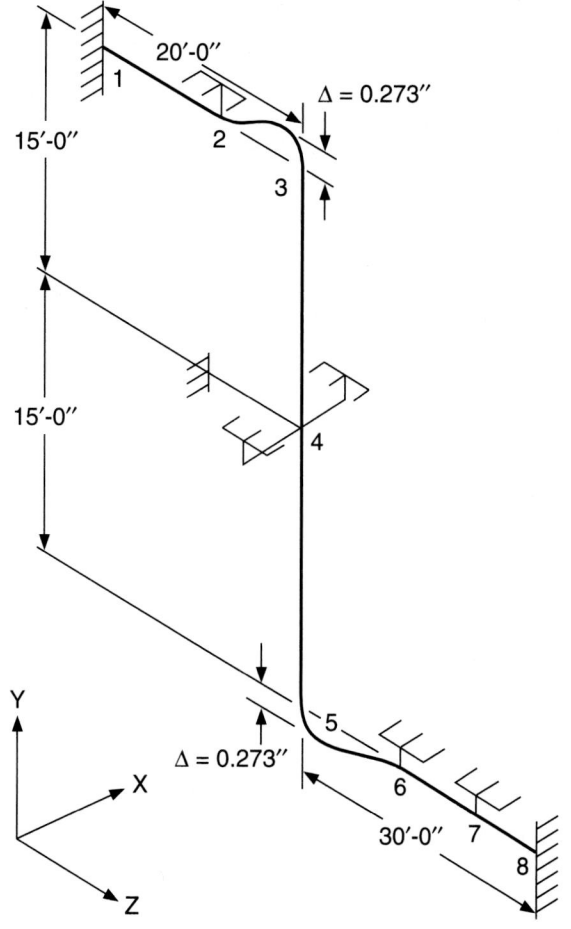

FIGURE 1-14   System for thermal analysis—legs 3–4 and 4–5.

Assume that locations 2, 3, 5, and 6 are fixed against rotation, while the thermal deflection is absorbed by legs 2–3 and 5–6. The minimum distance from points 3 and 5 to the first rigid support along 3–5 is:

$$L = [0.273 \times 2.25 \times 2.375 \times 10^6/(1.6 \times 22{,}500)]^{1/2} = 6.36 \text{ ft}$$

In metric units:

$$L = (0.62 \, \Delta \, iD/S_a)^{1/2}$$
$$L = (0.62 \times 7.1 \times 2.25 \times 60.3/155)^{1/2}$$
$$L = 1.96 \text{ m}$$

Locate rigid hangers 2 and 6 at least 6.25 ft (2 m) from points 3 and 5 to accommodate the growth in the vertical direction.

For segment 5–8, $\Delta = 0.01822 \times 30$ ft $= 0.547$ in (13.9 mm) as shown in Fig. 1-15. Assume that locations 4 and 5 are fixed against rotation, while only leg 5–8 expands. The thermal deflection is absorbed by leg 4–5. The minimum distance from point 5 to the first rigid support along 4–5 is:

$$L = [0.546 \times 2.25 \times 2.375 \times 10^6/(1.6 \times 22{,}500)]^{1/2}$$
$$L = 9.0 \text{ ft}$$

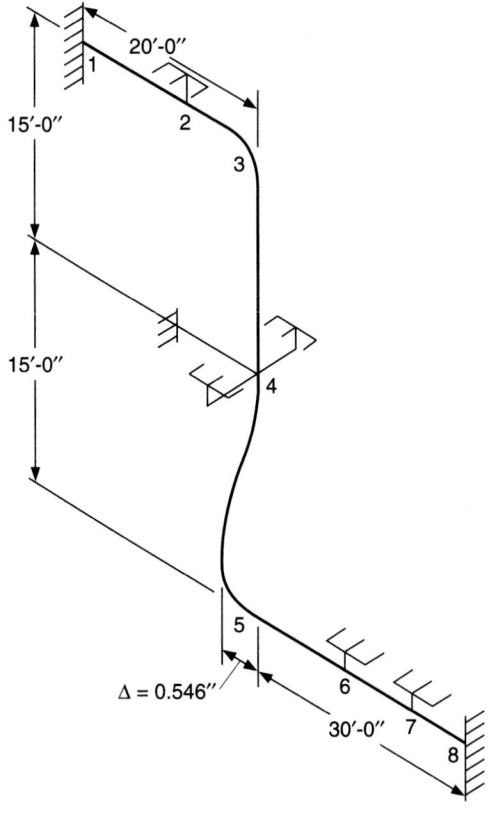

FIGURE 1-15   System for thermal analysis—leg 5–8.

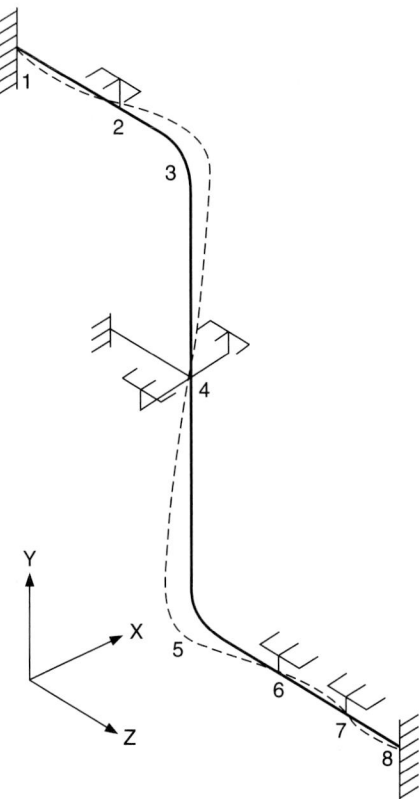

In metric units:

$$L = [0.62 \times 13.9 \times 2.25 \times 60.3/155]^{1/2}$$

$$L = 2.75 \text{ m}$$

Since this is less than the 15-ft (4.6-m) distance from point 5 to point 4, the design is acceptable. The final deflected shape is shown in Fig. 1-16.

PIPING SYSTEMS THAT OPERATE IN DIFFERENT MODES

When piping systems have branch runs that can be isolated using valves, different thermal modes of operation occur. Complete analysis of each thermal mode of operation may or may not be necessary, but each mode requires investigation, since the lengths of each leg change with different operating modes.

In the system shown in Fig. 1-17, all valves are open in mode 1 and all segments of the system are at the same temperature. In mode 2, however, one of the valves is closed, which lowers the temperature of the piping downstream from that valve. Since the upper two legs are no longer the same length, the stress condition is different in mode 2 than it was in mode 1, and analysis of the new mode should be performed. In this situation, the segment of pipe between the two upper leads must be long enough to absorb the local differential expansion. Modes 3 and 4 are examples of other operating modes.

FIGURE 1-16 System for thermal analysis—system displaced.

Obviously, other modes are possible. It is critical that all operating modes be considered, and not only those modes that the designer believes to be important. The full range of piping system deflections must be considered, especially in the design of support systems for piping.

COMPUTERIZED DESIGN AND ANALYSIS

In order to simplify stress analysis due to thermal expansion and other conditions including deadweight, concentrated loads, pressure design, and the like, various computer programs are available that will run on desktop personal computers. These programs are generally easy to use and highly graphic for model construction and display of results. Most will assist in designing supports and all contain large libraries of data that eliminate having to look up pipe sizes and schedules, weight per unit length, thermal expansion data, allowable stresses, and so on. Some suppliers of piping analysis software are listed here. Some software is available in less expensive limited run versions in addition to unlimited run versions.

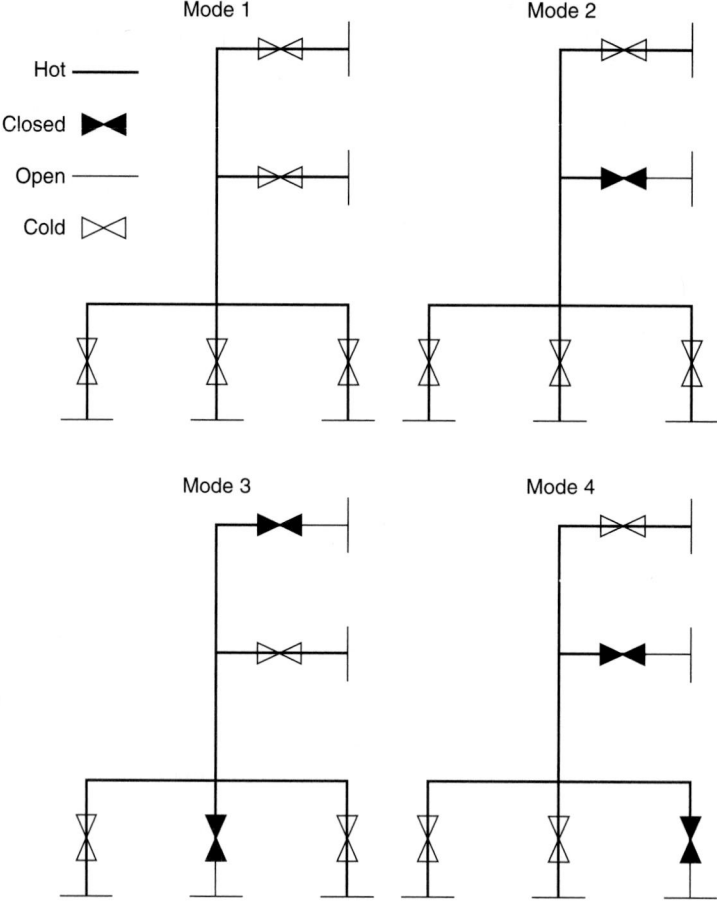

FIGURE 1-17   Modes of thermal operation.

List of suppliers of computer programs for analyzing of piping systems:

Program Name	Location
AutoPipe	Engineering Design Automation 1600 Riviera Ave, Walnut Creek, CA 94596 (Free fully functional demonstration diskette, limited to 20 nodes, is available) 510-993-2525
TriFlex	AAA Technologies 300 Rogerdale Rd Houston, TX 713-789-6200
Caesar II	Coade 12777 Jones Road, Suite 480 Houston, TX 77070 713-890-4566

PipePlus	Algor 150 Beta Drive Pittsburgh, PA 15238 412-967-2700
CAEPipe	SST Systems 21020 Homestead Road Cupertino, CA 95014 408-773-1171
SimFlex	Peng Engineering P.O. Box 801167 Houston, TX 77280-1167 713-462-7390

BIBLIOGRAPHY

Nayyar, M. L.: *Piping Handbook,* 6th ed., McGraw-Hill, New York, 1992.
Tube Turns, Inc.: *Piping Engineering,* 6th ed., Louisville, Ky., 1986.

CHAPTER 10-2
PLASTICS PIPING

Stanley A. Mruk

Executive Director, Plastics Pipe Institute
A Division of the Society of the Plastics Industry
Washington, D.C.

INTRODUCTION

Outstanding chemical resistance is a principal reason for the growing use of plastics piping in practically every phase of U.S. industry including the pharmaceutical, chemical, food, paper and pulp, electronics, oil and gas production, water and waste treatment, mining, power generation, steel production and metal-refining industries. With the general recognition of its other features (e.g., it is easy to work with, durable, and economically advantageous), plastics piping has also become widely accepted for a broad range of applications for other reasons than just its chemical inertness. Current major uses include water mains and services, gas distribution, storm and sanitary sewers, plumbing (drain, waste, and vent piping and hot- and cold-water piping), electrical conduit, power and communications ducts, chilled-water piping, and well casing.

    The diversity of plastic pipe—reflecting the many available materials, wall constructions, diameters, and techniques for joining—is so great and the attendant technology is evolving at such a rate that it is difficult to present in a concise reference all the pertinent information available. This chapter, therefore, offers only basic and general information. In applying plastic pipe, the reader is advised to ensure that all appropriate code requirements and government safety regulations are complied with. Sources and references for additional information are provided for this purpose at the end of the chapter.

DESCRIPTION, CLASSIFICATION, AND TYPICAL USES

"Plastic" pipe is as indefinite a term as "metal" pipe. As with metal products, plastic pipes are made from a variety of materials. Plastics used for pipe exhibit a wide range of properties and characteristics. The variabilities in properties of plastics are derived not only from the chemical composition of the basic synthetic resin, or polymer, but are also largely determined by the kind and amount of additives, the nature of reinforcement, and the process of manufacture. For example, it is possible to formulate mixtures of polyvinyl chloride (PVC) resins plus appropriate additives that range from a clear, soft, and pliable product (such as that used for laboratory tubing and upholstery) to a rigid and strong product (such as for pressure pipe). Another example is the construction of reinforced thermosetting resin pipe (RTRP) by using glass-fiber winding techniques that can adjust to the desired value the ratio of the circumferential (or hoop) strength to the axial strength.

Plastics are divided into two basic groups, thermosetting and thermoplastic, both of which are used in the manufacture of plastic pipe. Thermoplastics, as the name implies, soften upon the application of heat and reharden upon cooling: they can be formed and reformed repeatedly. This characteristic permits them to be easily extruded or molded into a wide variety of useful shapes, including pipe and fittings. Because thermoplastics are shaped, by a die or mold, while in a "molten" state their properties are essentially isotropic (i.e., independent of direction). In some processes and under some conditions, some anisotropy (i.e., direction dependence) may result.

Thermosetting plastics, on the other hand, form permanent shapes when cured by the application of heat or a "curing" chemical. Once shaped and cured during the manufacturing process, they cannot be reformed by heating. The excellent adhesion properties of thermosetting resins permits their utilization in composite structures by which strength and stiffness can be greatly enhanced through the use of reinforcements and fillers. The greater strength and higher temperature limits of these composite structures permit RTRP to handle fluids at temperatures and pressures beyond the limits for thermoplastic pipe. Piping systems now available are capable of operating at temperatures in excess of 300°F (148°C). All important commercial constructions of thermosetting pipe utilize some form of reinforcement and/or filler. By orienting the reinforcement, RTR pipes can be given directionally dependent properties.

Thermoplastic Pipe

Most thermoplastic pipes and fittings are made from materials containing no reinforcements, although fillers are occasionally used. Pipe is manufactured by the extrusion process, whereby molten material is continuously forced through a die that shapes the product. After being formed by the die, the soft pipe is simultaneously sized and hardened by cooling it with water. Fittings and valves are usually produced by the injection molding process, in which molten plastic is forced under pressure into a closed metal mold. After cooling, the mold is opened and the finished part is removed. Some items, especially larger-sized fittings for which there is insufficient demand to justify construction of injection-molding tooling, are fabricated from pipe sections, or sheets, by utilizing thermal or solvent cementing fusion techniques. To compensate for the lower strength, the fitting may either be made from a heavier wall stock or reinforced with a fiberglass-resin overwrap. The engineer designing a pressure-rated system should make sure that the pressure ratings of the selected fittings are adequate.

There is some thermoplastic pipe made of a cellular-core construction (for example, ASTM* F 628) in which the pipe wall consists of thin inner and outer solid skins sandwiching a high-density foam (Fig. 2-1). The primary benefit of such construction is improved ring and longitudinal (beam) stiffness in relation to the material used. Because the foam-wall structure results in some loss of strength, applications for cellularcore pipe are in nonpressure uses, such as for above- and below-ground drainage piping, which can take advantage of the more material-efficient ring and beam stiffness.

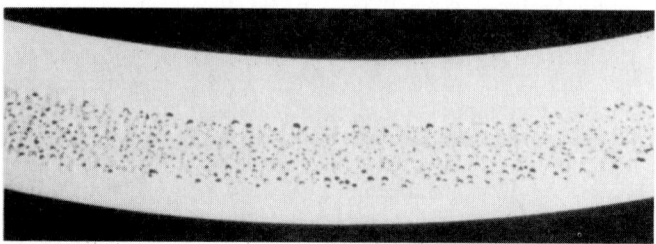

FIGURE 2-1 ABS cellular-core construction. (*Borg-Warner Chemicals.*)

For buried nonpressure applications, a composite pipe (ASTM D 2680) is produced that consists of two concentric tubes that are integrally braced with a truss webbing. The resultant openings between the concentric tubes are filled with a lightweight concrete. This construction increases both the ring and the beam stiffness. Composite pipe is used only for nonpressure buried applications such as sewerage and drainage.

Several other processes for improving the radial (i.e., ring) stiffness of thermoplastic pipe for buried applications have in common the formation of some type of rib reinforcement. A well-established technique is forming corrugations in the pipe wall. Corrugated polyethylene pipe (ASTM F 405) in sizes from 2 to 12 in (5 to 30 cm) is widely used for building foundations, land, highway, and agricultural drainage, and communications ducts. Ribbed pipe also is commercially made by the continuous spiral winding of the plastic over a mandrel of a specially shaped profile. Adjacent layers of this profile are fused to each other to form a cylinder that is smooth on the inside and has ribbed reinforcements on the outside (Fig. 2-2). The smooth inside diameter is preferable for many applications, such as sewerage, because it creates no flow disturbances. Pipes with ribbed construction are available in PVC and polyethylene (PE). PE pipes, which are made with hollow ribs to minimize material usage, are available in sizes from 18 to 120 in (45 cm to 3 m) in diameter.

The distinctive characteristics of the principal thermoplastic piping materials are discussed in the following pages.

Polyvinyl Chloride. Polyvinyl chloride (PVC) piping is made only from compounds containing no plasticizers and minimal quantities of other ingredients. To differentiate these materials from flexible, or plasticized PVCs (from which are made such items as upholstery, luggage, and laboratory tubing) they have been labeled rigid PVCs in the United States and unplasticized PVC (uPVC) in Europe. Rigid PVCs used in piping range from Type I to Type III, as identified by an older classification system that is still much in use. In this system, the type designations are supplemented by grade designations (e.g., Grade 1 or 2) which further define the material's properties. Type I materials, from which most pressure and nonpressure pipe is made, have been formulated to provide optimum strength as well as chemical and temperature resistance. Type II materials are those formulated with modifiers that improve impact strength but that also somewhat reduce, depending on modifier type and quantity, the

* American Society for Testing and Materials.

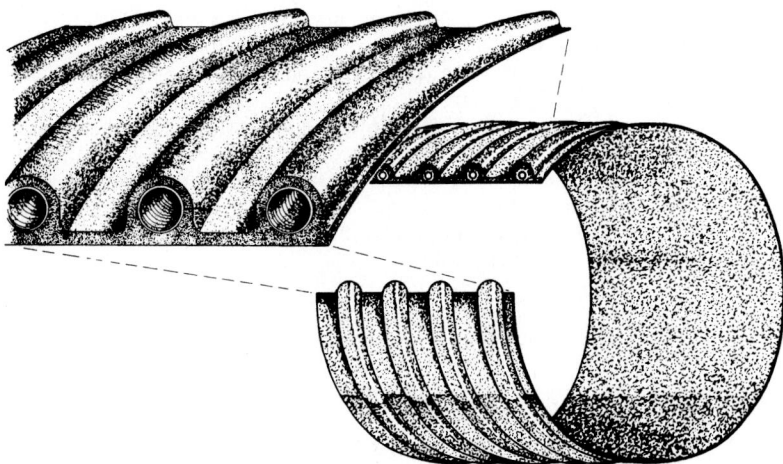

FIGURE 2-2   Typical profile of hollow ribbed polyethylene pipe. (*Chevron Chemical Co.*)

aforementioned properties of Type I materials. There is little call for Type II pipe, as the impact strength of the stronger Type I pipe is more than adequate for most uses. Type III materials contain some inert fillers which tend to increase stiffness concomitant with some lowering of both tensile and impact strength and chemical resistance. Some nonpressure PVC piping, such as that used for conduit, sewerage, and drainage, is made from Type III PVCs.

The currently used classification system for rigid PVC materials for piping and other applications is described in ASTM D 1784, "Standard Specification for Rigid Polyvinyl Chloride and Chlorinated Polyvinyl Chloride Compounds." This specification categorizes rigid PVC materials by numbered cells that designate value ranges for the following properties: impact resistance (toughness), tensile strength, modulus of elasticity (rigidity), deflection temperature (temperature resistance), and chemical resistance. The following table cross-references the designations of the principal PVC materials from the older to the newer classification system.

By cell classification system of ASTM D1784 minimum cell class	By older system	
	Type and grade	Designation
12454-B	Type I, Grade 1	PVC 11
12454-C	Type I, Grade 2	PVC 12
12433-D	Type II, Grade 1	PVC 21
13233	Type III, Grade 1	PVC 31

Because (as expanded in the discussion on properties) short-term properties of plastic materials are not a reliable predictor of long-term capabilities, those PVC materials that have been formulated for long-term pressure applications are also designated by their categorized maximum recommended hydrostatic design stress (RHDS) for water at 73.4°F (23°C) as determined from long-term pressure testing. The most commonly used designation system for PVC pressure-piping materials is based on the above older designation system with two added digits that identify, in hundreds of pounds per square inch, the maximum recommended design stress.* For example: PVC 1120 is a Type I, Grade 1 PVC (minimum cell class

---

* Since the maximum recommended design stress is for continuous water pressure at 73°F (23°C), it is up to the designer to determine the extent, if any, by which this stress should be reduced to account for any departure from these conditions and the need for a suitable margin of safety against other considerations. See the discussion on design.

12454-B) with a maximum recommended HDS of 2000 lb/in^2 (13.8 MPa) for water at 73.4°F (23°C); PVC 2110 is a Type 2, Grade 1 PVC (minimum cell class 14333-D) with an RHDS of 1000 lb/in^2 (6.9 MPa). Other PVC material designations available for pressure pipe are listed in Table 2-4. Most pressure-rated PVC pipe is made from PVC 1120 materials.

The combination of good long-term strength with higher stiffness explains why PVC has become the principal plastic pipe material for both pressure and nonpressure applications. Major uses include: water mains; water services; irrigation; drain, waste, and vent (DWV) pipes; sewerage and drainage; well casing; electric conduit; and power and communications ducts. A much broader range of fittings, valves, and appurtenances of all types is available in PVC than in any other plastic.

Chlorinated Polyvinyl Chloride.   As implied by its name, chlorinated polyvinyl chloride (CPVC) is a chemical modification of PVC. CPVC has properties very similar to PVC but the extra chlorine in its structure extends its temperature limitation by about 50°F (28°C), to nearly 200°F (93°C) for pressure uses and about 210°F (99°C) for nonpressure applications. ASTM D 1784, the rigid PVC materials specification, also covers CPVC which it classifies as Class 23477-B. By the older designation system, it is known as Type IV, Grade 1 PVC. CPVCs for pressure pipe are designated CPVC 4120 (i.e., Type IV, Grade 1 CPVC with a maximum recommended hydrostatic design stress of 2000 lb/in^2 (13.8 MPa) for water at 73.4°F [23°C]). At 180°F (82°C) the maximum recommended hydrostatic design stress* for CPVC is 500 lb/in^2 (3.4 MPa).

Principal applications for CPVC are for hot or cold water piping and for many industrial uses which take advantage of its higher temperature capabilities and superior chemical resistance.

Polyethylene.   Polyethylene (PE) is the best-known member of the polyolefin group—plastics that are formed by the polymerization of straight-chain hydrocarbons—known as olefins—that include ethylene, propylene, and butylene. Polyethylene plastics are tough and flexible even at subfreezing temperatures. They are generally formulated with only an antioxidant (for protection during processing) and some pigment (usually carbon black) or other agent designed to screen out ultraviolet radiation in sunlight which over long-term exposure could be damaging to the natural-color polymer.

ASTM D 1248, the PE molding and extrusion materials specification, classifies these materials into three types depending on the density of the natural resin. Type I consists of lower-density materials which are relatively soft and flexible and have low heat resistance. Type II PEs are of medium density, slightly harder, more rigid and more resistant to elevated temperatures; they also have better tensile strength. Type III materials show maximum hardness, rigidity, tensile strength, and resistance to the effects of increasing temperature. Pipe is made almost exclusively from Type II and Type III PEs. ASTM D 1248 also provides for grade designations to further classify PEs according to other physical characteristics. PE piping materials for pressure piping are classified by a designation system that combines the type and grade coding with that for the maximum RHDS* for water at 73.4°F (23°C). PEs utilized for pressure piping, and so designated, are listed in Table 2-4.

The more recently issued standard, ASTM D 3350, classifies PE piping materials according to broader physical property criteria, including long-term strength, and it is expected to become the primary PE piping material standard.

Outstanding toughness and relatively low flexural modulus, which permits coiling of smaller-diameter pipe, are large factors in PE's prominence in gas-distribution and water-service piping. Other features, such as heat fusibility, good abrasion resistance, and availability in large diameters [up to 120 in (3 m)], account for the use of PE piping for chemical transfer lines, slurry transport, sewage force mains, intake and outfall lines, power ducts, and renewal (by insertion into the old pipe) of deteriorated sewer, gas, water, and other pipes.

---

* Since the maximum recommended design stress is for continuous water pressure at 73°F (23°C), it is up to the designer to determine the extent, if any, by which this stress should be reduced to account for any departure from these conditions and the need for a suitable margin of safety against other considerations. See the discussion on design.

Cross-Linked Polyethylene (PEX).   PEX pipe and tubing is made from essentially the same materials and by the same extrusion process used to manufacture PE pipe. The difference is that during or directly after extrusion the polymer molecules are cross-linked to form a thermosetting material. The cross-linking may be effected by the addition of cross-linking compounds to the PE, or by subsequent electron or high-frequency radiation.

The primary benefit of cross-linking is the raising of PE's upper operating temperature limit. PEX can be used for pressure applications up to 200°F (93°C).

Principal applications for PEX and tubing are for under-floor heating systems, melting of ice and snow, and hot-cold water piping.

Polybutylene.   Polybutylene (PB) is a unique polyolefin. Its stiffness resembles that of low-density PE, yet its strength is higher than that of high-density PE. However, its most significant feature is that it retains its strength better with increasing temperature. Its upper temperature limit is higher than that for any PE: nearly 200°F (93°C) for pressure uses and somewhat higher for nonpressure applications.

PB piping materials are covered by ASTM D 2581. Materials for pressure applications are designated PB 2110; the last two digits signify a maximum recommended hydrostatic design stress* of 1000 lb/in² (6.9 MPa) for water at 73.4°F (23°C). At 180°F (83°C) this design stress is 500 lb/in² (3.4 MPa).

Major applications of PB pipe tend to take advantage of its improved temperature resistance and its toughness. They include hot or cold water piping and industrial uses such as hot effluent lines. Because of its excellent abrasion resistance, PB pipe is also used for slurry lines.

Polypropylene.   Polypropylene (PP) is a polyolefin similar in properties to Type III PE but is slightly lighter in weight, more rigid, and more temperature-resistant. PPs are classified by ASTM D 2146 into two types: Type I covers homopolymers that generally have the greatest rigidity and strength but offer only moderate impact resistance; Type II covers copolymers of propylene and ethylene, or other olefins, which are less rigid and strong but have much improved toughness, particularly at lower temperatures.

Although on the basis of its short-term properties PP shows better resistance to temperature, this material is inherently somewhat more sensitive to thermal aging than PE. To overcome this sensitivity, specially formulated grades containing appropriate heat-stabilizer systems have been developed. For pressure uses, the adequacy of long-term heat stability is evaluated by means of long-term pressure tests of the PP formulation, conducted at various higher temperatures. A PP material containing flame-retardant additives is available for drainage-piping applications.

Polypropylene piping is used for chemical waste and drainage and various other industrial uses that take advantage of excellent chemical resistance, good rigidity and strength, and higher-temperature operating limits. One feature that accounts for its use in laboratory and industrial drainage is its superior resistance to many organic solvents.

Acrylonitrile-Butadiene-Styrene.   Acrylonitrile-butadiene-styrene (ABS) is a family of materials formed from three different monomers (chemical building blocks), acrylonitrile, butadiene, and styrene. The proportions of the components and the way in which they are combined can be varied to produce a wide range of properties. Acrylonitrile contributes rigidity, strength, hardness, chemical resistance, and heat resistance; butadiene contributes toughness; and styrene contributes gloss, rigidity, and ease of processing.

ASTM D 1788 classifies ABS plastics into numbered cells that designate value ranges for each of three properties: impact strength (toughness), tensile stress at yield (strength), and deflection temperature under load. ABS pipe materials are categorized into types and grades in accordance with established minimum cell requirements for each type and grade. Like the other major thermoplastics, ABS materials for pressure pipe are designated by a coding that identifies both short-term properties and long-term strength. For example, ABS 1316 is a

---

* Since the maximum recommended design stress is for continuous water pressure at 73°F (23°C), it is up to the designer to determine the extent, if any, by which this stress should be reduced to account for any departure from these conditions and the need for a suitable margin of safety against other considerations. See the discussion on design.

Type I, Grade 3 (minimum cell classification 3-5-5 per D 1788) material with a maximum RHDS* of 1600 lb/in^2 (11.2 MPa) for water at 73.4°F (23°C). Other ABS pressure-pipe materials are listed in Table 3-4.

An advantageous combination of toughness with good strength and stiffness largely accounts for the most common uses for ABS piping, i.e., for drain, waste, and vent (DWV) applications as well as for sewers, well casings, and communications ducts. One especially tough formulation of ABS is utilized to manufacture piping for compressed-air service. Most other thermoplastic materials are not recommended for above-ground compressed-air service because, should they fail, the pipe failure mechanism would sometimes produce flying fragments which could be injurious.

Polyvinylidine Fluoride.   Polyvinylidine fluoride (PVDF) is a fluoroplastic, i.e., its chemical composition includes the element fluorine. Fluoroplastics are distinguished by their exceptional chemical and solvent resistance, excellent durability, and broad working-temperature range. To these features PVDF adds good strength and toughness and radiation resistance (which explains its use for conveying radioactive materials). The ASTM Specification covering PVDF molding and extrusion materials is D 3222. A standard for PVDF pressure piping is under development at ASTM. Standard recommended hydrostatic design stresses for PVDF have not yet been established, and an effort to develop these values is underway. Manufacturers of PVDF piping systems should be consulted for recommended design-stress values.

PVDF piping is utilized primarily for chemical processing and other industrial applications that are beyond the reach of the more common thermoplastics. These include the handling of active materials such as chlorine and bromine and piping materials that subject it to higher temperatures. Because of its immunity to radiation, PVDF piping is also used in reprocessing nuclear wastes.

Other Thermoplastics.   Some thermoplastics of lesser current commercial importance are either used for special reasons or were more popular some time ago. Among these is *chlorinated polyether,* a tough rigid material of outstanding chemical resistance and useful to about 220°F (104°C). PVDF has largely displaced it as a specialty material. *Cellulose acetate butyrate* (CAB) was extensively used in petroleum production for conveying saltwater and crude oil as well as for natural gas distribution. However, because of its relatively low strength and moderate resistance to temperature and chemicals, it has been largely displaced by other materials. Nylon, a tough, strong, and heat-resistant material that is also very resistant to aromatic and chlorinated solvents, has some special uses. One of these is for coiled small-diameter tubing for compressed-air service. Nylon insert (with barbs) fittings are also made for use with polyethylene pipe.

Polyacetal, a strong, hard plastic with relatively good temperature resistance, is being increasingly used for various hot- or cold-water plumbing components such as fittings, valves, and faucets.

Reinforced Thermosetting Resin Pipe

Reinforced thermosetting resin pipe (RTRP) is a composite largely consisting of a reinforcement imbedded in, or surrounded by, cured thermosetting resin. Included in its composition may be granular or platelet fillers, thixotropic agents, pigments, or dyes. The most frequently used reinforcement is fiberglass, in any one or a combination of the following forms: continuous filament, chopped fibers, and mats (Fig. 2-3). While reinforcements such as asbestos or other mineral fibers are sometimes used, fiberglass-reinforced pipe (FRP) is by far the most popular. One form of FRP, called reinforced plastic mortar pipe (RPMP), consists of a com-

---

* Since the maximum recommended design stress is for continuous water pressure at 73°F (23°C), it is up to the designer to determine the extent, if any, by which this stress should be reduced to account for any departure from these conditions and the need for a suitable margin of safety against other considerations. See the discussion on design.

posite of layers of thermosetting resin—sand aggregate mixtures that are sandwiched by layers of resin-fiberglass reinforcements. In another construction, the sand is replaced by glass microspheres. The high content of reinforcements in RTRP, which may run from 25 to 75 percent of the total pipe weight, and the specific design of the composite wall construction are the major determinants of the ultimate mechanical properties of the pipe. The resin, although also influencing these properties somewhat, is the binder that holds the composite structure together, and it supplies the basic source of temperature and chemical resistance. Glass fibers, as well as many other reinforcements, do not have high resistance to chemical attack. For enhanced chemical and/or abrasion resistance, RTRP construction may include a liner consisting of plastic (thermosetting or thermoplastic), ceramic, or other material. The outer surface of the pipe—especially that of the larger diameter sizes—may also be made "resin rich" to better resist weathering, handling, and spills. Reinforced thermosetting resin pipe is available in a variety of resins, wall constructions, and liners with diameters ranging from 1 in (2.5 cm) to more than 16 ft (5 m). Stock and specially fabricated fittings are readily available.

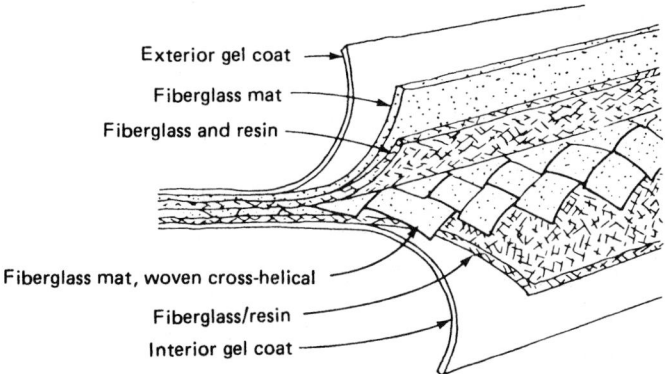

FIGURE 2-3   Fiberglass-reinforced pipe.

Filament Winding.   Pipe is produced by machine-winding, under controlled tension and in predetermined patterns, of glass reinforcement—which may consist of continuous-filament strands, woven roving, or roving tape—onto the outside of a mandrel. The reinforcement may be saturated with a liquid resin or pre-impregnated with partially cured resin. After the pipe has been formed and cured, the mandrel is removed. The dimension of the inside diameter is set by the mandrel; that of the outside diameter by the thickness of the wall.

A high glass content and a precise machine-controlled fiber orientation which permits control of the radio of circumferential to axial strength makes this pipe more economically suited for certain uses including higher-pressure applications. Since for a given pressure rating the axial strength of filament-wound pipe tends to be lower than that for pressure-molded pipe, it may have to be offset by more frequent support spacing. The use of automatic machines results in pipes of closer dimensional tolerance and in mechanical properties that are very consistent. To provide a stronger barrier against corrosion of the fiberglass filaments, a resin-rich liner, 0.02 to 0.1 in (0.5 to 2.5 mm) thick, is usually deposited on the inside of the pipe. In one process a thick, highly chemically resistant liner is produced by overwrapping a PVC, CPVC, or PVDF pipe (the only materials used at this time) with resins that can bond tightly to the thermoplastic.

The matched bell-and-spigot socket and the butt-and-strap methods are those primarily used to join filament-wound pipe.

Centrifugal Casting.   In this process, resin and reinforcements (such as chopped fibers) are applied to the inside of a rotating mold. After the pipe has cured by action of heat or a catalyst, it is removed from the mold. The outside diameter of the pipe is set by the mold dimensions: the inside diameter is determined by the amount of material introduced into the mold. This type of pipe is almost fully machine-made and it provides very consistent mechanical properties and the closest tolerances. Because its glass fiber content is lower than that of filament-wound pipe it offers generally better chemical resistance. For additional resistance it may be made with a corrosion-resistant liner. The strength properties of centrifugally cast pipe are less direction-dependent than those of filament-wound pipe. Fittings are normally of the socket type for bell and spigot joining. The joint may be overwrapped if added strength is desired.

The smaller-diameter fittings for RTRP are usually produced by a molding (compression or injection) process that is similar to that used with thermoplastics. Fittings may also be made by the filament-winding or contact-molding process whereby the part is first fabricated on a steel or fiberglass form, then cured and removed. Centrifugal casting is also sometimes employed. By all these procedures (except filament winding) random orientation of the reinforcement is obtained.

Resins Used for Piping

Brief descriptions of the more important resins used for piping are given in the following text.

Epoxies.   Epoxy resins are strong and have good resistance to solvents, salts, caustics, and dilute acids. Epoxies are cross-linked by curing agents which become an integral part of the polymer and affect the thermal, chemical, and physical properties of the polymer. For instance, the maximum service temperature of epoxy pressure pipe cured with anhydrides is 180°F (83°C), and it has little resistance to caustics; that cured with aromatic amines can be used at temperatures above 225°F (107°C), and it has good caustic resistance.

The major use of epoxy pipe is in oil fields where its resistance to corrosion and paraffin buildup makes it preferable to steel pipe for crude collection and saltwater injection lines. Other uses are in the chemical process industry, in heating and air conditioning, in food processing, for gasoline and solvents, and in mining applications (including abrasive slurry transport, communications ducts, and power conduits).

Polyesters.   Although typically not as strong as the epoxies, polyesters offer good resistance to mineral acids, bleaching solutions, and salts. The most commonly used polyester resins for pipe are isophthalic polyesters and bisphenol A fumarate polyesters. Isophthalics have poorer resistance to caustics and oxidizers. Bisphenol A fumarates have improved resistance to these materials and are widely used in paper mills for bleach lines.

Isophthalic resin pipe is used in waste-treatment and power plants in services where corrosive conditions are not severe. Maximum operating-temperature limits for pressure pipe vary, depending upon the specific material, but are generally below 200°F (93°C).

Vinyl Esters.   These resins include chemical features of both epoxies and polyesters. Vinyl ester resins offer better chemical resistance, somewhat higher temperature limits, and better solvent resistance than ordinary polyesters but generally do not compare to epoxies in these properties. Vinyl ester resins are preferred over polyesters because they are more chemical-resistant than the isophthalics and less brittle than the bisphenol A fumarates. Typical services are in fertilizer plants (acid lines), chlorine plants (chlorine-saturated brine lines), and paper mills (caustic and black-liquor lines).

Furans.   Furan resins offer very good chemical, solvent, and temperature resistance—up to about 300°F (150°C). Because they extend the limitations of the other resins, they are often selected for use in the processing industries in place of exotic metal piping.

Desirable Qualities of FRP Resins

The performance criteria that usually determine the choice of one or more FRP resins over another include chemical resistance, mechanical strength, heat resistance, and (for the manu-

TABLE 2-1   Qualitative Summary of FRP Resin Performance*

Resin	Chemical resistance			Other properties		
	Acids	Bases	Solvents	Processability	Strength	Heat resistance
Polyester resins	Fair–good	Poor	Fair	Good	Fair–good	Fair–good
Isophthalic acid based	—	O	+	+	+	—
Het acid based	—	O	+	+	+	+
BPA/fumarates	+	—	—	+	+	—
Vinyl ester terminated polyesters	—	—	—	+	+	+
Vinyl ester resins	Good	Fair–good	Fair–good	Good	V. good	Good–v. good
BPA/ECH epoxy derived						
$n = 0$	+	—	+	+	++	+
$n = 2$	+	+	—	+	++	—
Phenolic-Novolac epoxy derived	+	—	+	—	+	+
Epoxy resins	Fair	Good	V. good	Fair	V. good	Good–v. good
Aliphatic amine cured	—	—	+	—	+	+
Aromatic amine cured	—	+	++	—	++	++
Anhydride cured	—	O	+	+	+	+
Lewis acid cured	+	+	+	—	+	++
Furan resins	Fair	Good	V. good	Poor	Good	V. good
Furfuryl alcohol derived	—	+	++	O	+	++

* ++ = Very Good, + = Good, — = Fair, and O = Poor.
Source: Based on table from M. B. Launikitis, "Chemically Resistant FRP Resins," *Proceedings of 1977 Plastics Seminar,* National Association of Corrosion Engineers, Houston, Texas.

facturer) processability. A qualitative summary of FRP resin performance is presented in Table 2-1. For the final choice of the appropriate FRP resin(s) and liner combination for a given service (chemical environment, weathering exposure, abrasion resistance, etc.) more detailed information, including case history data, should be obtained.

PROPERTIES

Compared with other materials, pipes made of plastic have less strength and rigidity and are more temperature-sensitive. However, they offer these essential properties sufficiently to satisfy the performance requirements of most industrial piping applications. Moreover, they have good to excellent strength-to-weight ratios; are durable and easy to install and maintain; and have outstanding chemical resistance. The thermoplastics are lower than thermosets in strength, rigidity, and maximum operating temperature. However, their chemical resistance tends to be superior. Thermosets, in contrast, are capable of handling corrosive fluids at pressures and temperatures well beyond the service limits of most thermoplastic pipe.

Physical and Mechanical

Typical physical, mechanical, and thermal properties of the major thermoplastic piping materials are presented in Table 2-2. Those for thermosets are given in Table 2-3. The actual values for any pipe will vary according to the specific material(s) used and, in the case of composite products, such as the thermosets, will also depend on the specific wall construction.

Because the properties of plastics are influenced by duration of loading, temperature, and environment, data-sheet values for mechanical properties such as those presented in Tables

TABLE 2-2 Typical Physical Properties of Major Thermoplastic Piping Materials*[†]

	ASTM Test no.	ABS		PVC		CPVC	PE		PB	PP	PVDF
		I	II	I	II		II	III			
Specific gravity	D 792	1.04	1.08	1.40	1.36	1.54	0.94	0.95	0.92	0.92	1.76
Tensile strength, lb/in^2 ($\times 10^3$)	D 638	4.5	7.0	8.0	7.0	8.0	2.4	3.2	4.2	5.0	7.0
Tensile modulus, lb/in^2 ($\times 10^6$)	D 638	0.3	0.3	0.41	0.36	0.42	0.12	0.13	0.06	0.2	0.22
Impact strength, Izod, ft · lb/in notch	D 256	6	4	1	6	1.5	>10	>10	>10	2	3.8
Coeff. of linear expansion, in/(in)(°F)($\times 10^{-5}$)	D 696	5.5	6.0	3.0	5.0	3.5	9.0	9.0	7.2	4.3	7.0
Thermal conductivity, (Btu)(in)/(h)(ft^2)(°F)	C 177	1.35	1.35	1.1	1.3	1.0	2.9	3.2	1.5	1.2	1.5
Specific heat, Btu/(lb)(°F)	—		0.32	0.34	0.25	0.23	0.20	0.54	0.55	0.45	0.45	0.29
Approx operating limit[‡]											
°F, nonpressure	—	180	180	150	130	210	130	160	210	200	300
°F, pressure	—	160	160	140	120	200	120	140	200	150	280

* The properties of a piping material may vary from one commercial material to another. The pipe manufacturer should be consulted for specific properties.
[†] Consult Table 2-4 for values of long-term strength at 73°F.
[‡] Exact operating limit may vary from each particular commercial plastic material (consult manufacturer). Effects of environment should also be considered.

TABLE 2-3 Typical Physical Properties of Glass-Fiber-Reinforced Thermosetting Resin Pipe*[†]

Property at 75°F	Test no.	Polyester	Filament wound epoxy	Filament wound vinyl ester	Filament wound reinforced plastics mortar
Specific gravity	D 792	1.6	1.9	1.9	1.7 to 2.2
Tensile strength, lb/in^2 ($\times 10^3$)	D 2105				
Hoop direction		35	20 to 50	20 to 50	15 to 60
Axial direction		25	2 to 10	2 to 10	3 to 20
Tensile modulus, lb/in^2 ($\times 10^6$)	D 2105				
Hoop direction		1.4	1.5 to 4	1.5 to 4	1.4 to 3.6
Axial direction		1.4	0.8 to 2.0	0.8 to 2.0	0.8 to 1.8
Coeff. of linear expansion, in/(in)(°F)($\times 10^{-5}$)	D 696				
Hoop direction		1.3	0.5 to 0.7	0.5 to 0.8	1.0
Axial direction		1.3	1.0 to 1.8	1.0 to 1.8	1.5
Thermal conductivity, (Btu)(in)/(h)(ft^2)(°F)	C 177				
		0.9	1.5 to 4.2	1.5 to 4.2	1.3
Approximate temperature limit[‡]					
°F, nonpressure		240	300	250	200
°F, pressure		200	240	220	140

* The properties of a piping material may vary from one commercial material to another. The pipe manufacturer should be consulted for specific properties.
[†] Consult Table 2-4 for values of long-term strength at 73°F.
[‡] Exact operating limit may vary from each particular commercial plastic material (consult manufacturer). Effects of environment should also be considered.

2-2 and 2-3 are not satisfactory for design purposes. The stress-strain, and strain-stress, responses of plastics reflect their viscoelastic nature. The viscous, or fluidlike, component tends to damp or slow down the response between strain and stress. For example, if a load is continuously applied on a plastic material, it creates an instantaneous initial deformation that then increases at a decreasing rate. This further deformation response is known as *creep.* If the load is removed at any time, there is a partial immediate recovery of the deformation followed by a gradual creep recovery. If on the other hand the plastic is deformed (i.e., strained) to a given value that is then maintained, the initial load (stress) created by the deformation slowly decreases at a decreasing rate. This is known as the *stress-relaxation response.* The ratio of the actual values of stress to strain for a specific time under continuous stressing, or straining, is commonly referred to as the *effective creep modulus,* or the *effective stress-relaxation modulus.* In the case of thermoplastics this effective modulus is significantly influenced by time. For continuous loading of 20 years' duration, it can be from one-quarter to one-third the value of the short-term modulus. In the case of reinforced thermosets the viscous response is of lower order and the long-term effective modulus tends to be at least three-quarters of the short-term values. Most pipe manufacturers are prepared to provide values of effective moduli for specific materials and loading conditions.

The effective strength of plastics is influenced by time, temperature, and environment. For example, the breaking point for a thermoplastic material under short-term tensile testing is reached only after considerable material deformation has taken place, at least 10 percent, and in some cases over 100 percent (the ultimate elongation for reinforced thermosets is lower than for thermoplastics). Under long-term continuous loading material failure (or an unacceptable level of material damage) will occur at much lower deformations than in tensile testing. With thermoplastics the strain levels at failure can be as low as 3 percent, and with some reinforced thermosets they may be below 0.5 percent. Material damage, and not creep or excessive deformation, represents the durability limit for plastics subject to long-term loading. These durability limits, are time-, temperature-, and environment-dependent.

Durability under Continuous Loading.   To establish its longer-term hydrostatic strength, plastics pipe is tested in accordance with ASTM D 1598, "Time to Failure of Plastic Pipe Under Constant Internal Pressure." After obtaining a sufficient number of stress vs. time-to-fail points that must span a testing time from 10 to 10,000 h, the data are extrapolated to determine the estimated average 100,000 h strength. The extrapolating procedures are those of ASTM method D 2837, "Obtaining Hydrostatic Design Basis for Thermoplastic Materials," or procedure B of ASTM D 2992, "Obtaining Hydrostatic Design Basis for Reinforced Thermosetting Resin Pipe and Fittings." The extrapolated long-term hydrostatic strength (LTHS) so determined is then rounded off into the appropriate hydrostatic design basis (HDB). The HDBs are design-stress categories represented by a series of preferred numbers (i.e., 2000, 2500, 3150, 4000, 5000, etc.) that ascend in steps of 25 percent. The following relationship, known as the ISO (International Standards Organization) plastics pipe hoop stress equation, is used to relate the test pressure and pipe dimensions to the resultant circumferential stress in the pipe wall:

$$S = \frac{p}{2} \frac{D_m}{t} \qquad (1a)$$

where S = hoop stress, lb/in^2 (N/m^2)
p = internal hydraulic pressure, lb/in^2 (N/m^2)
D_m = mean pipe diameter, in (cm)
t = minimum pipe wall thickness, in (cm)

Once the HDB is established and then reduced to a hydrostatic design stress (HDS) by the application of an appropriate service (or design) factor, the same formula, rewritten as follows, may be used to compute the pipe pressure rating:

$$p = 2\text{HDS} \frac{t}{D_m} \qquad (1b)$$

where HDS = hydrostatic design stress, lb/in^2 (N/m^2)

= HDB × SF

SF = service factor

The selected service factor considers two general groups of conditions: The first encompasses the normal variations in material and pipe manufacture and the second those of the pipe's application and use (environment, hazards, life expectancy). The general practice has been to use service factors of not more than 0.5 for static water pressure at 73°F (23°C). Smaller factors are used for more demanding conditions.

The HDBs for static water pressure at 73°F (23°C) for the major thermoplastic pipe materials are presented in Table 2-4. As indicated by this table, the ASTM material designations for pressure thermoplastics code the material according to its short-term properties and its maximum RHDS. The RHDS is determined by applying a factor of 0.5 to the material's HDB for water at 73°F (23°C). Values of HDB for other environments and temperatures will be different, even for materials of the same ASTM designation. For example, not all PE 3408s will

TABLE 2-4 Hydrostatic Design Basis* (Strength Categories) for Thermoplastic Pipe Compounds Determined with Water at 73.4°F (23°C)

Material designation[†]	HDB lb/in^2 (MPa), 73.4°F (23°C)[‡]
PE 1404	800 (5.5)
PE 2406	1250 (8.6)
PE 3406	1250 (8.6)
PE 3408	1600 (11.2)
PEX 0006	1250 (8.6)
PVC 1120	4000 (27.6)
PVC 1220	4000 (27.6)
PVC 2116	3150 (21.7)
PVC 2120	4000 (27.6)
CPVC 4120	4000 (27.6)
ABS 1208	1600 (11.2)
ABS 1210	2000 (13.8)
ABS 1316	3150 (21.7)
ABS 2112	2500 (17.2)
PB 2110	2000 (13.8)
PFA 1008	1600 (11.2)
PVDF 2020	4000 (27.6)

* Per ASTM D 2837.

[†] The last two digits code the maximum recommended hydrostatic design stress (RHDS), expressed in hundreds of pounds per square inch. RHDS = HDB × 0.5, where 0.5 is the generally accepted maximum value for the design factor. Lower values than 0.5 may be justified by certain operating and safety considerations. The first two digits code the material according to short-term properties.

[‡] Since thermoplastics, even though of the same ASTM designation, may be affected differently by increasing temperature, HDBs at higher temperatures must be established for each specific commercial product. A number of such products have HDBs for temperatures as high as 180°F (82°C). Consult the most current Plastics Pipe Institute (1275 K Street NW, Suite 400, Washington, DC 20005) Technical Report TR-4 for latest listing of HDBs of commercial pipe compounds.

show the same long-term strength at 120°F (49°C). For other than the standard HDB rating conditions the pipe manufacturer should be consulted for data or recommendations on the specific pipe material.

In the case of thermosets, because of their composite construction, their HDB is determined not only by the properties of the materials used but also by the specific wall construction and manufacturing process. Typical HDBs for some machine-made RTRPs for water service at 73°F (23°C) are given in Table 2-5. The pipe manufacturer should be consulted for HDBs for the specific pipe construction under consideration.

Durability under Cyclic Loading. The higher shorter-term strength of plastics permits them to easily tolerate relatively infrequent short-lived excursions in pressure beyond those established for static pressure conditions. However, under repeated cyclic stressing, as in pressure surging, plastics tend to fatigue and their long-term strength is reduced. The fatigue sensitivity varies from plastic to plastic, and for each material it is dependent on various factors including the amplitude and the frequency of the cyclic stressing. The reduction in limiting strength of thermoplastics may range from slight to as much as one-half the value under static conditions. For services with only moderate and infrequent surging, as is the case in many water piping systems, selecting the pipe pressure rating solely on the basis of the maximum static pressure has been demonstrated to be effective. The American Water Works Association Standard for PVC Water Piping (AWWA C-900) establishes pipe pressure classes with a built-in consideration of cyclic pressure.

Reinforced thermosetting plastic pipes are somewhat more sensitive to fatigue than thermoplastic pipes. Accordingly, they are often pressure-rated for surge service on the basis of their HDB as determined by Procedure A of the aforementioned ASTM D 2992 from test data obtained in accordance with ASTM D 2143, "Test for Cyclic Pressure Strength of Reinforced Thermosetting Plastic Pipe." Typical HDB values for cyclic pressure service for certain RTRPs are also shown in Table 2-5.

Durability under Continuous Straining. Stress relaxation gradually reduces the initial stress level that is first generated when a plastic material is strained to a given level and then

TABLE 2-5 Hydrostatic Design Basis for Machine-Made Reinforced Thermosetting Resin Pipe

ASTM pipe specification*	Type	Classification per ASTM D 2310[†]			HDB, lb/in²[‡]	
		Grade	Class	Designation	Static	Cyclic
D 2517 (gas pressure pipe)	Filament-wound	Epoxy, glass-fiber-reinforced	No liner	RTRP-11AD	—	5000
				RTRP-11AW	16,000	—
D 2996	Filament-wound	Epoxy, glass-fiber-reinforced	No liner	RTRP-11AD	—	5000
				RTRP-11AW	16,000	—
	Filament-wound	Epoxy, glass-fiber-reinforced	Reinforced epoxy liner	RTRP-11FE	—	6300
				RTRP-11FD	—	5000
	Filament-wound	Polyester, glass-fiber-reinforced	Reinforced polyester liner	RTRP-12EC	—	4000
				RTRP-12ED	—	5000
				RTRP-12EU	12,500	—
	Filament-wound	Polyester, glass-fiber-reinforced	No liner	RTRP-12AD	—	5000
				RTRP-12AU	12,500	—
D 2997	Centrifugally cast	Polyester, glass-fiber-reinforced	Polyester liner	RTRP-22BT	10,000	—
				RTRP-22BU	12,500	—
	Centrifugally cast	Epoxy, glass-fiber-reinforced	Epoxy liner	RTRP-21CT	10,000	—
				RTRP-21CU	12,500	—

* See Table 2-8 for the abbreviated title of the pipe standard.
[†] "Standard Classification for Machine-Made Reinforced Thermosetting Resin Pipe," ASTM D 2310. (The first three symbols following RTRP designate type, grade, and class; the last symbol codes the HDB.)
[‡] Multiply by 6894 to convert to pascals.

maintained there. As a consequence of this reduction in stress, plastics can tolerate somewhat larger strains under constant-strain (i.e., stress-relaxation) conditions than the ultimate strain that ensues in a constant-load condition (under which there is no stress relaxation). At present there is no unanimously preferred method for establishing limiting strain values for conditions of stress relaxation. Appendix X2 to ASTM D 3262, "Standard Specification for Reinforced Plastic Mortar Sewer Pipe," includes a method, not officially part of the standard, by which one may evaluate the strain limits of the subject pipe in an acid environment. The strain limits for RTRPs tend to be significantly lower than those for thermoplastics piping. In fact, under conditions of continuous straining, limiting strain is not a design constraint for most thermoplastics. When dealing with situations such as in pipe bending or in deflection of pipe under earth loading (in which limiting strain is a possible consideration), recommended design values for maximum permissible strain should be obtained for the specific material and end-use conditions.

Durability under Cyclic Straining. Both ultimate strength and allowable strain may be reduced by fatigue. Guidance should be sought from the pipe manufacturer.

Other Mechanical Properties. In addition to the test for long-term strength, a number of special tests have also been established for evaluating other relevant properties of plastic pipe:

ASTM D 2444	"Impact Resistance of Thermoplastic Pipe and Fittings by Means of a Tup (Falling Weight)"
ASTM D 2105	"Longitudinal Tensile Properties of Reinforced Thermosetting Pipe and Tube"
ASTM D 2925	"Measuring Beam Deflection of Reinforced Thermosetting Pipe Under Full Bore Flow"
ASTM D 2412	"External Loading Properties of Plastic Pipe by Parallel-Plate Loading"
ASTM D 2924	"External Pressure Resistance of Reinforced Thermosetting Resin Pipe"

Flow Properties

Plastic pipes offer minimal resistance to fluid flow. Tests indicate that they may be characterized as hydraulically smooth conduits according to the well-established rational flow formulas. The Hazen-Williams equation, a frequently used engineering approximation formula, yields good correlations for water flow when a C_H factor of 150 to 155 is used. For calculating water flows in open channels, or nonfull flow in conduits, Manning's equation is often used. The Manning n factor for plastics for clean water is approximately 0.0085 to 0.0095. With sewerage, values of $n = 0.010$ to 0.012 are used since they provide margin for flow-disturbing influences such as sedimentation and slime growth.

Since plastics do not corrode, their original flows do not deteriorate with time. Plastics are also easier to clean than other materials.

Chemical Resistance

Plastics do not corrode in the sense that metals do. Being nonconductors they are immune to galvanic or electrochemical effects. If they are affected by an environment, it is generally through direct chemical attack, solvation, or strain corrosion. In addition to differences in chemical resistance due to the nature of the plastic and pipe wall construction, the extent of resistance may also depend on time and temperature of contact and, in some cases, on the presence of an externally applied stress.

In direct chemical attack, the molecules of either the polymer or the reinforcement are altered, and the alteration leads to a gradual deterioration of properties. Such attack can be brought about by strong oxidizing and reducing agents and by ultraviolet and other radiation. Thermoplastics as a group tend to be inherently more resistant than thermosets to chemical attack. Good protection against ultraviolet radiation (which might be required with the more ultraviolet-sensitive pipes that are to be used in continuous exposure to the weather) is afforded by incorporation into the formulation of a finely divided carbon black, titanium dioxide, or some other opaque pigment.

Solvation is the absorption of an organic solvent by the plastic. Its effect may range from a slight swelling and softening, with minor effects on properties, to a complete solution. The solvent cementing of ABS and PVC pipe is based on solvation. By the use of selective solvents that evaporate after their task is completed, solvent cementing makes it possible to create a monolithic joint that retains the properties of the base material. Thermosets, because of their cross-linked chemical structure, tend to have superior resistance to solvation.

In strain corrosion, damage will occur only under the combined action of strain (i.e., stress) and environment. In the case of thermoplastics this form of attack is called environmental stress cracking. The mechanism, although not fully understood, is essentially the development and ensuing slow growth and propagation of cracks by the combined action of stress and a sensitizing agent. Stress-cracking agents tend to be materials such as detergents and alcohols that have a surface-wetting tendency. Stress cracking may be controlled by selecting stress-crack-resistant grades of material or by creating designs that ensure that the stress, or strain, is below the threshold value necessary to set this mechanism in action.

In the case of thermosetting materials, the formation of crazes or microcracks exposes the glass fiber, or other reinforcement, to possible chemical attack. To protect against this, a tough resilient liner is used, and the stress, or strain, level is limited to established safe values which will preclude the formation of crazing under the specific exposure conditions.

Table 2-6 presents a broad guide to the chemical resistance of the major thermoplastic piping materials. Table 2-1 includes a general guide to FRP resin performance. Final selection of material and pipe wall construction for chemical or corrosive service should follow consultation with more detailed chemical-resistance information. Because ultimate resistance is affected by stress, time, and temperature, it may not be reliably predicted by shorter-term "soak" tests. Successful previews in similar service are the best guide. Lacking these, new applications would best be evaluated by actual service testing. An advantage of service testing is that it is sure to include some minor (but often overlooked) contaminant which could influence the final result.

In the case of RTRP piping, the liner is considered the first line of defense and therefore a critical factor in corrosive service selection. Special resin liners, which may be deposited in extra thicknesses, are available for extra protection. Pipes with thermoplastic liners are also available.

Inertness to Potable Water and Other Fluids

Nearly all of the base materials from which plastic pipes are made are inert to potable water. It is possible, however, that through the addition of ingredients such as stabilizers, catalysts, modifiers, and pigments, the final formulation may render a pipe inadequate for potable water in terms of its effect on the toxicological safety and the taste and odor quality of the water. To safeguard against this, most potable water piping standards require that the pipe be evaluated for this purpose by a laboratory recognized by the public health profession. A very commonly used laboratory is NSF International, Ann Arbor, Michigan. NSF evaluates, and lists as acceptable, those plastic pipes that satisfy the requirements of their standards for potable water service.

Because they do not contaminate fluids with metallic ions, plastic pipes are often utilized in the transport of pure materials, including de-ionized water. For food service there are pipes available that have been made from materials approved by the Food and Drug Administration.

TABLE 2-6 Thermoplastic Piping Materials: Chemical-Resistance Guide for Ambient Temperatures*

Attacking chemicals	ABS	PVC I	PVC II	CPVC	PE	PB	PP	PVDF
Inorganic compounds								
Acids, dilute	G	G	L	G	G	G	G	G
Acids, concentrated 80%	L	L	L	G	L	L	L	G
Acids, oxidizing	L	P	P	L	P	P	P	G
Alkalies, dilute	G	G	G	G	G	G	G	G
Alkalies, concentrated 80%	L	G	L	G	G	G	G	G
Gases, acid (HCl and HF), dry	L	L	L	L	G	G	G	G
Gases, acid (HCl and HF), wet	L	G	L	G	G	G	G	G
Gases, ammonia, dry	L	G	L	G	G	G	G	G
Gases, halogens, dry	L	L	L	L	L	L	P	G
Gases, sulfur gases, dry	P	G	L	G	G	L	P	G
Salts, acidic	G	G	G	G	G	G	G	G
Salts, basic	G	G	G	G	G	G	G	G
Salts, neutral	G	G	G	G	G	G	G	G
Salts, oxidizing	L	L	L	L	G	G	G	G
Organic compounds								
Acids	G	G	G	L	G	G	G	G
Acid anhydrides	L	L	L	P	L	L	L	L
Alcohols, glycols	L	G	L	G	L[†]	G	G	G
Esters, ethers, ketones	P	P	P	P	L	L	L	L
Hydrocarbons, aliphatic	L	L	L	G	L	L	L	G
Hydrocarbons, aromatic	P	P	P	L	P	P	P	G
Hydrocarbons, halogenated	L	L	L	L	P	P	P	L
Natural gas (fuel)	G	G	G	G	G	G	G	G
Mineral oil	G[†]	G	G	G	L[†]	G	G	G
Oils, animal and vegetable	G[†]	G	G	G	L[†]	G	G	G
Synthetic gas (fuel)	L	L	L	L	L	L	L	G

* G, good; P, poor; L, limited knowledge: determination requires precise knowledge of individual conditions.
[†] Stress-crack-resistant grade should be used.

COMMON METHODS FOR JOINING PLASTIC PIPES

Plastic pipe may be joined by a variety of methods (see Table 2-7), the choice of which is influenced in some cases by the properties of the basic material. For example: the polyolefins (PE, PB, and PP) may not be solvent-cemented; the vinyls (PVC and CPVC) and ABS heat-fuse with relative difficulty; and the thermosets may not be either heat-fused or solvent-cemented. Of the available choices, the one that is selected will depend upon pipe performance, installation, and maintenance requirements as well as availability of fitting and joining equipment. Heat fusion (of PE, PP, PB, and PVDF), solvent-cementing (of ABS, PVC, CPVC), and adhesive joining (of reinforced thermosetting resin pipe), all methods which produce monolithic joints, are preferred for applications requiring maximum strength and optimum chemical resistance (Fig. 2-4). Bell (sometimes referred to as socket) and spigot connections are utilized to join pipe by these three techniques. RTRP may also be joined by the butt-and-strap method

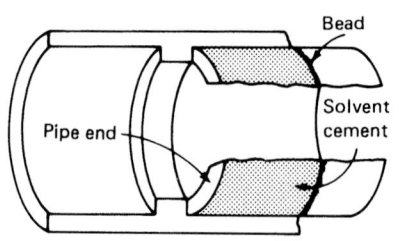

FIGURE 2-4 Threadless joint in PVC coupling (inside view).

TABLE 2-7   Techniques for Joining Plastic Pipe

Method of joining	Thermoplastic pipe							RTR pipe
	ABS	PVC	CPVC	PE	PP	PB	PVDF	
Adhesive	—	—	—	—	—	—	—	o
Solvent cements	o	o	o	—	—	—	—	—
Heat fusion	—	—	—	o	o	o	o	—
Threading*	o	o	o	o	o	—	o	o
Flanged connectors[†]	o	o	o	o	o	o	o	o
Grooved joints[‡]	o	o	o	o	o	—	o	o
Mechanical compression[§¶]	o	o	o	o	o	o	o	o
Elastomeric seal[¶]	o	o	o	o	o	o	o	o
Flaring	—	—	—	o	—	o	—	—
Insert	—	—	—	—	—	o	—	—

* Molded thread adapters are available for attachment on the pipe by another technique. Threads may not be cut in thermosetting pipe. Some thermosetting threaded connections may be adhesive-bonded for extra strength. For threading, the wall thickness of thermoplastic pipe should be not less than Schedule 80.

[†] Flanged adapters are applied on pipe by heat fusion, solvent-cementing, or threading.

[‡] Minimum wall thicknesses are prescribed depending on the pipe material.

[§] With thinner-walled pipe, stiffening inserts must be used.

[¶] Many designs of elastomeric seal and compression fittings provide no thrust restraint and therefore may be used only in situations, such as buried pipe, in which the pipe is restrained from pullout. Elastomeric seal and compression fittings are available in special designs that incorporate end restraint.

whereby two pieces of pipe are butted together and overlays of a laminate are then applied over the butted section and allowed to cure (Fig. 2-5). Larger-diameter polyolefin pipe is joined by the heat fusion of the pipe butt ends.

Flanged connections are often used in industrial applications, particularly when making transitions to other materials, such as when connecting to a metal valve or to a tank outlet, and when it is advantageous to provide for easy removal of a pipe section or other component from the system for cleaning, maintenance, or other purpose.

Threading is also used with plastic pipe. However, molded threads are preferred for thermoplastics and are required for most thermosetting pipe. Molded threaded adapters are available and may be applied by solvent-cementing or with adhesive, whichever is applicable. Threads may not be cut on most thermosetting pipe for they may damage the structural integrity of the pipe wall. Thermoplastic pipe may be threaded, provided its wall thickness is not less than a prescribed minimum, normally at least that of Schedule 80 pipe.

For installations not excluding the use of elastomeric sealants such as neoprene or red rubber, there are mechanical-compression as well as bell and spigot connectors which incorporate such sealants into their design. Much thermoplastic and thermosetting piping specifically made for buried water and sewer lines is available with integral elastomeric-seal bell and spigot connectors. Such connectors greatly facilitate pipe construction, partly because of the ease of making the

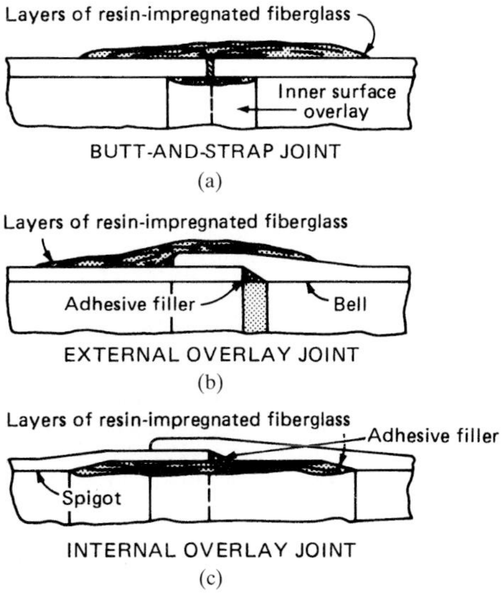

FIGURE 2-5   Butt and strap joints.

connection (a stab fit) and partly because the connection may be made under almost any weather or field condition.

Sometimes connectors utilizing grooved pipe are used with standard grooved-end systems such as Victaulic or Gustin-Bacon. With thermoplastic pipe of sufficient wall thickness, the grooves may be cut or rolled in some cases. Cutting is not permitted with thermosetting pipe. Grooved adapters are available for both thermoplastic and thermosetting pipes.

COMMERCIALLY AVAILABLE PRODUCTS

Plastics piping is manufactured in an imposing array of materials, constructions, diameters, wall thicknesses, lengths, and fitting types. The more important products are listed in Table 2-8 which also reports for each product the available size range and its important end uses. Whenever the product is covered by a major standard, the applicable document is identified. Because of the dynamic rate at which new plastic piping standards are currently being written (and older ones revised), the reader is advised to check with the major standards issuing organizations for the most current listing.*

Fittings for larger-diameter pipes are not listed in Table 3-8 because they are often custom-fabricated rather than available from stock. Also not listed in Table 3-8 are piping components such as valves and flanges. In diameters ranging from ⅜ to 4 in, valves made from PVC, CPVC, PP, and PVDF are available in a great variety of different styles including check, ball, diaphragm, globe, gate, and needle. They are available with socket (for solvent-cementing or heat-fusion joining), butt, flanged, or threaded ends. Valves are also available in "Tru" union style and with multiports. A number of models may be obtained with pneumatic or electric actuators for automatic valve positioning. In the ⅜- to 4-in (0.95- to 10-cm) sizes a large array of other piping components, such as strainers, expansion joints, roof and floor drains, and line tapping fittings, is also available. Many of these items may be obtained up through about 8-in (20-cm) diam. Larger-sized components are sometimes specially fabricated, or metallic products are used which are connected to the plastic pipe by means of flanges or some other suitable connector.

Standard and special design manholes and access holes are available in both thermoplastic and thermosetting materials for sweerage and drainage applications. ASTM D 3753, "Specification for Glass Fiber Reinforced Manholes," is, to date, the only adopted standard for such products.

PRODUCT STANDARDS, CODES, AND APPROVALS

Standards

The primary source of standards on plastics piping is the American Society for Testing and Materials (ASTM), 1916 Race Street, Philadelphia, PA 19103. (See Table 2-8.) There are a number of other organizations that alse develop such standards, generally on products related to their particular interest or activities. These include the following: American Water Works Association (AWWA), 6666 West Quincy Avenue, Denver, CO 80235, which issues standards for water distribution; the American Petroleum Institute (API), 300 Corrigan Tower Building, Dallas, TX 75201, on piping for oil and gas production; the National Electrical Manufacturers Association (NEMA), 2101 L Street, N.W., Washington, DC 20037, on conduit and

---

* The Plastics Pipe Institute, a Division of the Society of the Plastics Industry, 1275 K Street NW, Suite 400, Washington, DC 20005, regularly updates its TR-5, "Standards for Plastics Piping," which lists standards for thermoplastics piping that is issued by all major United States, Canadian, and international standards organizations.

ducting; the Underwriters Laboratories (UL), 333 Pfingston Road, Northbrook, IL 60062, on conduit and ducting. In addition, the federal government and some state agencies have also issued standards on plastic pipe, generally for projects in which they exercise regulatory or financial functions, or for purchases on their own behalf. Typical of these are the standards issued by the U.S. Department of Agriculture (USDA), the U.S. Department of Defense (DOD), the Federal Housing Administration (FHA), and the Gneneral Services Administration (GSA). Most of these documents parallel the basic requirements of ASTM and other listed standards.

The most frequently used dimensioning scheme for setting the outside diameter (OD) of plastic pipe is the traditional iron pipe size (IPS) system of commercial wrought steel pipe (ANSI B36.10). Most thermoplastic pipes are available with standard IPS outside diameters. Some PE and PB pipes which are designed to be joined with insert-type fittings are sized to the same inside diameters as Schedule 40 wrought steel pipe. In the case of thermoset pipes their outside diameters may be exactly, or approximately equal to the reference dimension depending on whether the pipe is sized from the outside in (as in centrifugally casting) or from the inside out (as when filament-winding over a mandrel). Other diameter systems that are utilized include:

- *Copper tubing size (CTS).*   Based on standard outside diameters of copper tubes, CTS pipe is used for water and gas services and for hot- or cold-water plumbing.
- *Cast-iron (CI) pipe size.*   PVC and RTR water-main piping is made to this outside-diameter basis as well as to the IPS system.
- *International Standards Organization (ISO) sizes.*   Some of the larger polyolefin pipes are made with these internationally set outside diameters.

Much pipe, especially in the larger sizes (for which compatibility with traditionally sized plastic piping components such as valves and fittings is not necessary), is made to fit into special diameter-sizing systems determined by the specific product standard or by the pipe manufacturer. Most of these systems have established diameter dimensions of such proportions that the resultant size of the inside bore is close to the pipe nominal diameter.

The wall thicknesses of most thermoplastic pipe of solid and homogeneous wall construction are defined in accordance with the standard dimension ratio (SDR) concept whereby the ratio of *average* outside diameter to *minimum* wall thickness is a constant value for each SDR pipe series over the entire range of pipe diameters. The standard diameter ratios that have been adopted by ASTM and other standard-writing organizations represent a series of preferred numbers that increase in steps of 25 percent, as follows: 11, 13.5, 17, 21, 26, 32.5, 41, etc. The advantage of establishing wall-thickness categories for thermoplastic pipe according to a constant ratio of diameter to wall thickness is evident from inspection of Eq. (1*b*): within each SDR category the pressure rating is the same for all pipe sizes. There is some pipe made to other than the established SDRs; for such pipe the actual diameter to wall-thickness ratio is simply referred to as the diameter ratio (DR).

Thermoplastic pipes specifically intended for industrial uses are often made to the IPS Schedule 40, 80, and 120 system which sets not only the outside diameter but also the wall thickness for each nominal size in each schedule. Since in a given pipe schedule the ratio of diameter to wall thickness tends to decrease with increasing diameter, so too does the pipe pressure rating. Schedule 80 wall thickness, or greater, is required whenever pipe is threaded. The pressure rating of thermoplastic threaded pipe is reduced to half that for unthreaded pipe.

The wall thicknesses of thermoset pipe are not defined in the same way as for thermoplastic pipe because key properties such as strength and stiffness depend not only on material but also on exact wall construction, which can vary not only among manufacturers but even with pipe diameter. The resultant pipe wall thickness will generally be set by the performance requirements of the pipe. Some standards set minimum values for wall thickness. Thermosetting pipe may not be field-threaded. If the pipe is to be joined by threading, it is available with factory-applied molded threads. Threaded adapters are also available.

TABLE 2-8 Principal Commercially Available Plastic Piping Products

Pipe material	Product standard*	Title (abbreviated) of standard or brief product description	Diameter range, in	Mains	Services	Drop pipe, wells	Well casing	Various: industrial, coml.	Distributing: cold only	Distributing: hot & cold	Collecting system	Building connections	Drainage	Drain, waste, & vent	Natural gas distribution	Corrosives and abrasives	Compressed gases†	Liquid fuels	Conduit (above ground)	Duct (below ground)
				Water supply and distribution							**Sewer and drain**					**Industrial**			**Duct**	
PVC, PE & PB	ASTM D 2513	Thermoplastic Gas Pressure Pipe & Fittings	½–24												X		X			
ABS, PVC & SR	ASTM F 480	Thermoplastic Water Well Casing	2–16				X													
ABS, PVC & PP	ASTM D 3311	DWV Plastic Fittings Patterns	1¼–6											X						
ABS & PVC	ASTM D 2680	ABS & PVC Composite Sewer Pipe	6–15								X	X								
ABS & PVC	ASTM F 409	ABS & PVC Accessible & Replaceable Tube and Fittings	3–12											X						
ABS	ASTM D 1527	ABS Plastic Pipe, Sch. 40 & 80	½–12	X	X	X		X	X			X				X	X			
	D 2282	ABS Plastic Pipe, SDR-PR	½–12	X	X	X		X	X			X				X	X			
	D 2468	ABS Plastic Pipe Fittings, socket, sch. 40	½–8		X	X		X	X			X				X	X			
	D 2661	ABS DWV Pipe and Fittings	1¼–6											X						
	D 2750	ABS Utility Conduit & Fittings	1–6									X	X							X
	D 2751	ABS Sewer Pipe and Fittings	1–6									X	X							
	F 628	ABS Foam Core DWV	1¼–6											X						
PVC	ASTM D1785	PVC Plastic Pipe, Sch. 40–80 & 120	½–24	X	X	X		X	X			X				X	X			
	D 2241	PVC Plastic Pipe, SDR-PR	½–36	X	X	X		X	X			X				X	X			
	D 2464	PVC Plastic Pipe Fittings, threaded sch. 80	½–6		X	X		X	X			X				X	X			
	D 2466	PVC Plastic Pipe Fittings, socket, sch. 40	½–8		X	X		X	X			X				X	X			
	D 2467	PVC Plastic Pipe Fittings, socket, Sch. 80	½–8		X	X		X	X			X				X	X			
	D 2665	PVC DWV Pipe & Fittings	1¼–6											X						

	D 2672	PVC Plastic Pipe, Bell End	⅛–8	X	X	X		X	X			X				X	X			
	D 2729	PVC Drain Pipe & Fittings	2–6										X							
	D 2740	PVC Plastic Tubing	½–1¼		X	X		X												
	D 2949	3-in PVC Thin Wall DWV Piping	3											X						
	D 3034	PVC Sewer Pipe & Fittings, type PSM	4–15								X	X	X							
	F 512	PVC Conduit for Buried Installation	2–6																	
	F 679	PVC Sewer Pipe & Fittings	18–36								X		X							
	F 758	PVC Underdrain Piping	4–8										X							
	F 789	PVC Sewer Pipe, Type 46	4–15								X	X	X							
	F 794	PVC Sewer Pipe, Ribbed Wall	4–48								X		X							
	F 891	PVC Pipe With a Cellular Core	1½–18								X	X	X	X						
	F 949	PVC Corrugated Pipe, Smooth I.D.	4–18								X	X	X							
	F 1336	PVC Sewer Gasketed Fittings	4–27								X		X							
	AWWA C900	PVC Pressure Pipe for Water	4–12	X				X												
	C 905	PVC Water Transmission Pipe	14–36	X				X												
	C 907	PVC Pressure Fittings	4–8	X				X												
	UL 514	Electrical Outlet Boxes & Fittings	½–6																X	
	651	Rigid Nonmetallic Conduit	½–6																X	
NEMA	TC-2	Electrical Plastic Tubing & Conduit	½–6																X	
	TC-3	PVC Fittings for Conduit & Tubing	½–6																X	
CPVC	ASTM D 2846	CPVC Hot Water Distribution Systems	⅜–2							X										
	F 437	CPVC Plastic Pipe Fitting, threaded, Sch. 80	¼–6					X		X						X	X	X		
	F 438	CPVC Plastic Pipe Fittings, socket, Sch. 40	¼–6					X		X						X	X	X		
	F 439	CPVC Plastic Pipe Fittings, socket, Sch. 80	¼–6					X		X						X	X	X		
	F 441	CPVC Plastic Pipe, Sch. 40 & 80	¼–12					X		X						X	X	X		
	F 442	CPVC Plastic Pipe, SDR-PR	¼–12					X		X						X	X	X		
	F 443	CPVC Bell End Pipe	⅛–8					X		X						X	X	X		

* Issuing agency identified in discussion on standards.

† Thermoplastic piping is not normally recommended for above-ground service because of safety considerations should the pipe fail. A special grade is available (see ABS piping).

TABLE 2-8 Principal Commercially Available Plastic Piping Products (*Continued*)

				End use — Water supply and distribution							End use — Sewer and drain				Natural gas distribution	Industrial			Duct	
Pipe material	Product standard*	Title (abbreviated) of standard or brief product description	Diameter range, in	Mains	Services	Drop pipe, wells	Well casing	Various: industrial, coml.	Distributing: cold only	Distributing: hot & cold	Collecting system	Building connections	Drainage	Drain, waste, & vent		Corrosives and abrasives	Compressed gases†	Liquid fuels	Conduit (above ground)	Duct (below ground)
PE	**ASTM**																			
	D 2104	PE Plastic Pipe, Sch. 40	½–6	X	X	X		X	X		X	X				X	X	X		
	D 2239	PE Plastic Pipe, SDR-PR	½–6	X	X	X		X	X		X	X				X	X	X		
	D 2447	PE Plastic Pipe, OD-based, Sch. 40 & 80	½–12	X	X	X		X	X		X	X				X	X	X		
	D 2609	Plastic Insert Fittings for PE Pipe	½–4	X	X	X		X									X			
	D 2683	PE Fittings, socket-fusion type for OD-based pipe	½–4	X	X	X		X	X		X	X				X	X	X		
	D 2737	PE Plastic Tubing	½–2		X	X		X	X								X	X		
	D 3035	PE Pipe, OD-Based, SDR-PR	½–24	X	X	X		X	X		X	X	X			X	X	X		
	D 3261	PE Fittings, Butt-fusion Type	½–10	X	X	X		X	X		X	X				X	X	X		
	F 405	PE Corrugated Tubing & Fittings	3–8										X							
	F 667	PE Corrugated Tubing & Fittings, Larger Diam.	8–24										X							
	F 714	PE Plastic Pipe, SDR-PR larger diam.	3–63	X				X			X	X	X			X	X	X		
	F 771	PE Irrigation Piping	½–6					X												
	F 810	PE Pipe for Drainage & Absorption Fields	3–6										X							
	F892	Corrugated PE Pipe with Smooth Interior	4								X		X							
	F 894	PE Profile Wall Pipe	18–120										X							
	F 1055	PE Fittings, Electrofusion Type	½–8												X					
	AWWA C901	PE Pipe, tubing & fittings for water	½–3		X															
	C 906	PE Water Transmission Pipe	4–63	X				X								X				
	API 5LE	PE Line Pipe	½–12					X	X							X	X	X		

Material	Standard	Description	Size range (in)
PB	ASTM-		
	D 2662	PB Plastic Pipe, SDR-PR	½–6
	D 2666	PB Plastic Tubing	½–2
	D 3000	PB Plastic Pipe, SDR-PR, OD-controlled	½–6
	D 3309	PB Plastic Hot-Water Distributing Systems	¼–2
	F 809	PB Plastic Pipe, SDR-PR, larger diam	3–42
	F 845	Plastic Insert Fittings for PB Tubing	⅜–¾
	AWWA C902	PB Pipe, tubing & fitting for water	½–3
PP	ASTM F412	PP Chemical Drainage Pipe & Fittings	1½–4
RTRP	ASTM		
	D 2517	RTR Pipe & Fittings for Gas	2–12
	D 2996	Filament Wound RTR Pipe	1–16
	D 2997	Centrifugally Cast RTR Pipe	1–14
	D 3262	Filament Wound RTR Pipe & Fittings	8–144
	D 3517	Filament Wound RTR Pressure Pipe	8–144
	D 3754	Filament Wound RTR Sewer & Industrial Pipe	8–144
	D 3840	RTR Fittings for Nonpressure	8–144
	D 4024	RTR Flanges	½–24
	F 1173	Epoxy Fiberglass Piping for Marine Applications	½–24
	AWWA C 950	Fiberglass Pipe for Water	1–144
	API 15 LR	Lower Pressure Fiberglass Pipe	2–12
	15 HR	Higher Pressure Fiberglass Pipe	1–8
	15 AR	Fiberglass Tubing	1–4½
	MIL-P-28584	Steam Condensate Lines, RTRP Filament Wound	2–6
	MIL-P-22245	Pipe and Pipe Fittings, glass-fiber-reinforced plastic	2–16

* Issuing agency identified in discussion on standards.

† Thermoplastic piping is not normally recommended for above-ground service because of safety considerations should the pipe fail. A special grade is available (see ABS piping).

Codes

The use of piping for plumbing, fire protection, and for the transport of hazardous materials may be subject to the provisions of a code and/or to those of local, state, federal, or other regulations. All the major model plumbing codes which have become adopted, or referenced, by state and local jurisdictions permit and prescribe to a varying but fairly extensive degree the use of plastics piping for hot-cold water lines; water services; drain, waste, and vents (DWV); sewerage; and drainage. Plastics piping is also covered by other codes, such as the following which are of interest to industrial users:

American National Standards Institute Codes

ANSI B31.3	Chemical Plant and Petroleum Refinery Piping
ANSI B31.8	Gas Transmission and Distribution Piping Systems
ANSI Z223.1	National Fuel Gas Code

Department of Transportation, Hazardous Materials Board, Office of Pipeline Safety Operations

Code of Federal Regulations (CFR), Title 49, Part 192, Transportation of Natural Gas and Other Gas by Pipeline: Minimum Federal Safety Standards

Code of Federal Regulations (CFR), Title 49, Part 195, Transportation of Liquids by Pipeline, Minimum Federal Safety Standards

The National Fire Protection Association (Quincy, Mass.) Model Codes

NFPA 30	Flammable and Combustible Liquids Code
NFPA 54	National Fuel Gas Code
NFPA 70	***National Electrical Code®****
NFPA 70A	Electrical Code for One and Two Family Dwellings
NFPA 34	Outdoor Piping

Approvals

Some standards and various jurisdictions and authorities require that before a pipe may be used for certain applications it first must be approved for that use by a recognized, or specifically designated, organization. Organizations with listing and approval programs for plastic pipe include the following:

- *For Potable Water*   NSF International, NSF Bldg., P.O. Box 1468, Ann Arbor, MI 48105; Canadian Standards Association, 178 Rexdale Boulevard, Rexdale, Ontario, Canada M9W 1R3
- *For Drain, Waste, and Vent*   NSF International and Canadian Standards Association (see above)
- International Association of Plumbing and Mechanical Officials, 5033 Alhambra Ave., Los Angeles, CA 90032
- *For Meat- and Food-Processing Plants*   U.S. Department of Agriculture, 14th and Independence S.W., Room 0717 South, Washington, DC 20250
- *For Underground Fire Protection Systems*   Underwriters Laboratories, Inc., 333 Pfingston Road, Northbrook, IL 60062; Factory Mutual Research Corporation, 1151 Boston-Providence Turnpike, P.O. Box 688, Norwood, MA 02062
- *For Underground Gasoline and Petroleum Lines*   Underwriters Laboratories Inc. (see above)

---

* ***National Electrical Code®*** is a Registered Trademark of The National Fire Protection Association, Quincy, MA 02269.

DESIGN AND INSTALLATION

Standard piping products offered for specific uses such as cold water; hot or cold water; drain, waste, and vent; sewerage; and drainage are largely predesigned. For example, CPVC and PB hot- or cold-water tubing systems made in accordance with their respective standards ASTM D 2846 and D 3309 are pressure-rated at 100 lb/in² (690 kPa) for water at 180°F (83°C). Design and installation recommendations are included in an appendix to these documents. Since most standards for products dedicated to a specific application contain design and installation recommendations, such documents should be consulted by designers and installers. The installation of plastic plumbing piping products is often regulated by the applicable plumbing code. More detailed information on design and installation may be obtained from most manufacturers and plastic pipe trade associations (see "Additional Information").

When design is conducted to meet special requirements of a given application, particular attention must be given to the effects of solvents and corrosives on piping properties. Temperature and unusual loadings (such as cyclic pressure and vibration) must also be considered. Most manufacturers of industrial piping products can provide performance data and design and installation recommendations for special as well as ordinary conditions. Various references that provide design and installation information are listed under "Additional Information."

Fundamentally, the principles of the design and installation of plastic piping are the same as those applying to steel piping. However, because of differences in their properties, certain aspects of the design and installation of plastics may require different emphasis and solutions. The following paragraphs briefly discuss these more important aspects. Detailed design and installation recommendations for each specific product should be followed.

Pressure Rating

Continuous Pressure. The pipe pressure rating should be based on the design stress [see Eq. (1b)] that is established by taking into account the anticipated effect of time, temperature, and environment on the pipe strength properties. It should be recognized that because of material and fabrication differences, plastic fittings and joints may have a pressure rating lower than that for the pipes. The design stress should include adequate margin for safety considerations. With this in mind it should be recognized that most thermoplastics, excepting those specially formulated for this purpose, are not suitable for conveying compressed gases in above-ground service. In the event of accidental pipe failure, the large potential energy stored in compressed gases could precipitate a catastrophic-type failure mechanism that sometimes produces dangerous flying debris. Thermosets and certain specially formulated thermoplastics resist such failure and are suitable for this application.

Vacuum or External Pressure. The service capabilities of thinner-walled pipes made of less rigid materials may be determined in some cases not by internal pressure but by vacuum conditions created by transients (surges) or by external hydrostatic pressure loading. The buckling resistance of plastic pipes may be estimated using Timoshenkos's classic elastic buckling equation including the following adaptation which gives consideration to the effect of pipe ovality:

$$P_c = \frac{2E}{1 - \mu^2} \left(\frac{t}{D_m} \right)^3 C \tag{2}$$

where P_c = collapsing pressure of unconstrained pipe, lb/in²
   E = effective modulus of elasticity of pipe material, lb/in²
   μ = Poisson ratio (approximately from 0.35 to 0.45 for thermoplastics for short-term loading)

t = pipe-wall thickness, in
D_m = pipe mean diameter, in
C = factor correcting for pipe ovality = $(r_o/r_i)^3$, where r_i is the major radius of curvature of the ovalized pipe, and r_o is the radius assuming no ovalization

For short-term loading conditions, the values of E and μ as obtained from short-term tensile tests yield reasonable correlations. For long-term loading, appropriate values as determined from long-term loading tests should be employed.

Cyclic Pressure.   The shock load or high-pressure surge created by sudden closure of valves could exceed the pressure capabilities of a pipe and, if the pipe is not properly anchored, could result in fitting failure by overstraining of joints. Excessive surging should be eliminated by control of the rate of valve closure or the installation of accumulators. All plastic pipe can tolerate some surging in excess of working pressure, and because of its greater flexibility and viscoelastic properties the pressures generated by surging are of lower order than those for metal piping and are more quickly damped. However, under frequent and continuous surging the long-term strength of plastic pipe tends to be reduced by fatigue. Under these conditions an appropriately lowered value of hydrostatic design stress should be used.

Considerations for Above-Ground Uses

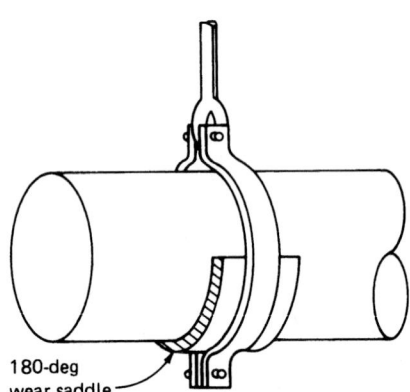

FIGURE 2-6 Wear-saddle prevents damage from standard hanger.

Supports, Anchors, and Guides. Most manufacturers supply information on support spacings. Typical recommendations are presented in Tables 2-9 and 2-10. Values are usually given for either single or continuous spans and for a given liquid specific gravity. A most important consideration is to ensure that the span distance between supports is based on the maximum system temperature. Depending on the piping material, pipe dimensions, and application, the support span may be dictated by the permissible deflection (generally about ½ in (1.3 cm) at midspan) or maximum allowable stress. The allowable stress should provide allowance for stresses generated by fluid pressure and by thermal and other loadings. Vertical pipe runs can be supported either in compression or tension. Long runs should be checked to ensure that the tensile or compressive load does not exceed the permissible design value. Standard strap, sling, clamp, clevis, and saddle supports providing at least 120° of contact are generally recommended (Fig. 2-6). Supports offering narrow or point contact should be avoided. Valves and other heavy piping components should be individually supported.

Anchors, which divide a pipe system into sections, must positively restrain the movement of pipe against all applied and developed forces, particularly dynamic loading. Anchors should generally be employed near changes of direction, when transitioning to another piping material or when there is a change in line size. In long, straight runs, anchor spacing is generally recommended at about 200 to 300 ft (60 to 90 m). Anchor spacing and location will also be determined by the selection of anchoring for the control of expansion and contraction.

When the pipe is restrained against expansion and contraction it should be guided to prevent buckling. The guides should encircle the pipe but be loose enough to allow it to move freely in its axial direction.

TABLE 2-9 Typical Recommended Maximum Support Spacing, in Feet, for Thermoplastic Pipe for Continuous Spans and for Uninsulated Lines Conveying Fluids of Specific Gravity up to 1.35

Pipe dimension		PVC			CPVC				PVDF				PP			
Nominal diam, in	Wall schedule	60°F	100°F	140°F	60°F	100°F	140°F	180°F	80°F	100°F	140°F	160°F	60°F	100°F	140°F	180°F
½	Schedule 40	4½	4	2½	5	4½	4	2½	3¾	3½	2	Continuous support recommended	1¾	1¾	1½	1¼
¾		5	4	2½	5½	5	4	2½	4	3¾	2½		2	2	1¾	1¾
1		5½	4½	2½	6	5½	4½	2½	4¼	4	2½		2	2	2	1¾
1¼		5½	5	3	6	5½	5	3	—	—	—		2½	2¼	2	2
1½		6	5	3	6½	6	5	3	4½	4¼	2½		2½	2½	2¼	2
2		6	5	3	6½	6	5	3	4½	4½	2¾		3	2¾	2½	2¼
3		7	6	3½	8	7	6	3½					3½	2¾	3	2¾
4		7½	6½	4	8½	7½	6½	4					4	3¾	3½	3
6		8½	7½	4½	9½	8½	7½	4½								
8		9	8	4½												
½	Schedule 80	5	4½	2½	5½	5	4½	2½	4½	4½	2½	Continuous support recommended	2	2	2	1½
¾		5½	4½	2½	6	5½	4½	2½	4½	4½	3		2½	2½	2¼	2
1		6	5	3	6½	6	5	3	5	4¾	3		2½	2½	2¼	2
1¼		—	—	—	—	—	—	—	—	—	—		3	2¾	2½	2½
1½		6½	5½	3½	7	6½	5½	3½	5½	5	3		3	3	2¾	2½
2		7	6	3½	7½	7	6	3½	5½	5¼	3		3½	3¼	3	2¾
3		8	7	4	9	8	7	4					4	4	3½	3½
4		9	7½	4½	10	9	7½	4½					4½	4½	4	3½
6		10	9	5	11	10	9	5								
8		11	9½	5½												

TABLE 2-10 Typical Recommended Maximum Support Spacing, in Feet, for Fiberglass-Reinforced Pipe for Temperatures up to 150°F (65°C) for Uninsulated Lines Conveying Fluids of up to 1.25 Specific Gravity

Nominal pipe size, in	Continuous span	Single span
1	7.5	6.3
1½	8.5	7.2
2	9.9	8.4
3	11.2	9.4
4	11.9	10.0
6	14.2	11.9
8	15.7	13.2
10	17.4	14.6
12	18.9	15.9

Control of Expansion and Contraction. Because of the inherent flexibility of plastic piping, it is generally possible to design a pipe system so that no expansion joints are necessary. Their use should be avoided where possible, since they are expensive, and they remove the ability of the pipe to carry longitudinal loads. Offsetting this load with anchors can be an added problem with larger pipes. Preferred techniques for dealing with expansion and contraction are: (1) anchoring and guide spacing, (2) changing direction (offset legs), and (3) using expansion loops.

Although plastics expand more than steel, their relatively low modulus of elasticity results in significantly lower end load for the same temperature change. The smaller thermal forces can generally be readily relieved by changes in direction. However, when using directional change to absorb thermal forces, neither the pipe nor any of its components should be subjected to a bending stress (or strain) in excess of that recommended by the manufacturer. The stress may be controlled by placement of anchors not closer than a calculated distance from the point of change of direction. The length of the legs of expansion loops should similarly be determined.

Oscillations and Vibrations. Because plastic pipe is so much more flexible than steel pipe, oscillations due to changes in velocity of fluid set up more easily and tend to be of greater amplitude. In long runs this is generally no problem but they could damage connected piping by subjecting it to excessive stresses or strains. The solution is to restrain the pipe by the use of anchors. High-amplitude vibrations from connected equipment, such as pumps, should be isolated from the piping by the use of flexible connectors.

Considerations for Below-Ground Uses

In terms of their underground performance all plastic pipes are classified as flexible, which signifies that when they are properly installed they are capable of developing sufficient diametrical deformation, without incurring material failure, to fully activate soil support forces. Soil-assisted flexible pipes can easily support earth loads that would crush stronger rigid pipes for which total load bearing ability is almost entirely dependent on their own strength. To activate soil support, flexible pipes must be embedded in soils that are stable and that have been properly placed and densified around the pipe. ASTM documents D 2321, "Underground Installation of Flexible Thermoplastic Sewer Pipe," and D 3839, "Underground Installation of Flexible Reinforced Thermosetting Pipe and Reinforced Plastic Mortar Pipe," present detailed recommendations on the proper installation of flexible plastic pipe designed for nonpressure uses. Nonpressure pipe, which is generally of thinner wall construction and not rounded by internal pressure, requires somewhat more care in installation than heavier-wall pressure pipe. Recommendations for installation of thermoplastic pressure pipe are given in ASTM D 2774, "Underground Installation of Thermoplastics Pressure Piping."

The basic principle of the installation of buried plastic piping is to embed it in a soil of such quality that the resultant ultimate pipe deflection is controlled to an acceptable value that is limited by either the pipe performance requirements or the pipe material capabilities. The former generally permits deflection up to about 10 percent (some engineers may set conservatively lower values) while the latter is determined by the maximum allowable stress, or strain, in the pipe wall for the given pipe material and construction. The pipe supplier can provide the limiting deflection values for a given pipe material and construction. These values may depend on the fluids being handled. With thermoplastic pipe of solid wall construction deflection will seldom be limited by material performance constraints.

The extent to which a flexible pipe will deflect when embedded in a given quality of soil may be estimated by a variety of methods. One of the better-known relationships, sometimes called the Iowa equation, was developed for flexible metal conduits at Iowa State University. A modification of this equation is

$$\frac{\Delta x}{D_i} = \frac{L_D K P}{EI/r^3 + 0.061\ E'}$$

where Δx = horizontal deflection of the pipe, in (For relatively small deflections, the change Δy in vertical diameter of a circular section deforming elliptically is equal to $1.10\ \Delta x$. As an approximation, it is often assumed $\Delta y = \Delta x$.)

D_i = pipe inside diameter prior to loading, in

L_D = deflection lag factor compensating for the time dependence of soil deformation, dimensionless

K = bedding constant which varies with the angle of bedding (i.e., bedding support), dimensionless (The bedding constant ranges from 0.110 for a point support on the bottom of a pipe to 0.083 for full support. For plastic pipe, the typical value is taken as 0.10.)

P = total vertical pressure acting on the pipe, lb/in^2

r = pipe radius, in

E = modulus of elasticity of pipe material, lb/in^2

I = moment of inertia of pipe wall per unit length, in^4/in (For round pipe $I = t_a^3/12$, in which t_a is the average wall thickness.)

E' = modulus of passive soil resistance, lb/in^2

As a result of extensive field investigations of the load vs. deflection characteristics of various flexible pipes the U.S. Bureau of Reclamation[*] has developed a series of soil reaction E' values for use in the Iowa equation under the assumption that $K = 0.1$ and $D_L = 1.0$. These E' values may be used to estimate a pipe's initial average deflection. To assist in estimating the initial maximum (i.e., acceptance) deflection as a consequence of both soil loading and installation factors, the Bureau of Reclamation has also reported the observed upper limits of deflection values. Both these limits, which primarily apply to pipes of lower ring stiffness, and the values of E' are shown in Table 2-11 as a function of the embedment materials recommended by D 2321.

In actual practice, it is seldom necessary to go through the Iowa equation calculation, for if the recommended installation practices in D 2321 are followed, initial installed deflections can quite readily be held to approximately 5 percent and less. Burial of the thinner-walled, more flexible pipes may also require consideration of the adequacy of the pipe's wall compressive strength as well as its buckling stability (Fig. 2-7).

Recommendations for the design and installation of buried plastic pipe may be obtained from pipe manufacturers, trade associations, or from the listed information given under "Additional Information."

---

[*] Amster K. Howard, "Modulus of Soil Reaction Values for Buried Flexible Pipe," *Journal of the Geotechnical Division of the American Society of Civil Engineers,* vol. 103, No GTI, January 1977, pp. 33–43.

TABLE 2-11   Bureau of Reclamation Values of E' for Iowa Formula for Initial Average Deflection of Flexible Pipe

Soil type for pipe embedment material per ASTM D 2321	Soil type description (United Classification System, ASTM D 2487)	E', lb/in² for degree of compaction of embedment (proctor density, %)*			
		Dumped	Slight (>85%)	Moderate (85–95%)	High (>95%)
I	Manufactured angular, granular materials (crushed stone or rock, broken coral, cinders, etc.)	1000 (+4%)	3000 (+4%)	3000 (+3%)	3000 (+2%)
II	Coarse-grained soils with little or no fines	N.R.†	1000 (+4%)	2000 (+3%)	3000 (+2%)
III	Coarse-grained soils with fines	N.R.	N.R.	100 (+3%)	2000 (+2%)
IV	Fine-grained soils	N.R.	N.R.	N.R.	N.R.
V	Organic soils (peats, mulches, clays, etc.)	N.R.	N.R.	N.R.	N.R.

* Values in parentheses give the approximate limit of deflection beyond the average deflection that is computed by using the given E' values. These limits are for pipe of relatively low stiffness. As pipe stiffness increases, the limit is narrowed.
† N.R. indicates use not recommended by ASTM D 2321.

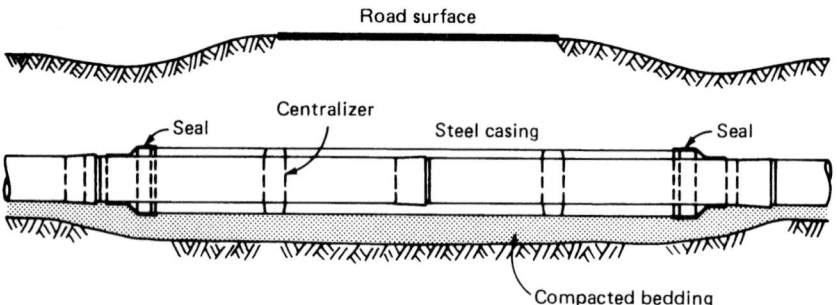

FIGURE 2-7   Steel casing protects pipe from concentrated loadings.

ADDITIONAL INFORMATION

The various plastic pipe trade associations issue reports, manuals, and lists of references on design and installation of their members' products. A list of current reports may be obtained by contacting each organization as follows:

- *Reinforced Thermosetting Piping*   Fiberglass Pipe Institute/Composites Institute, a Division of the Society of the Plastics Industry, 355 Lexington Avenue, New York, NY 10017; The Materials Technology Institute of the Chemical Process Industries, Inc., 12747 Olive St. Rd., Suite 203, St. Louis, MO 63141-6269
- *Thermoplastics Pipe (Industrial, Gas Distribution, Sewerage, Water, and General Uses)* The Plastics Pipe Institute, a Division of the Society of the Plastics Industry, Inc., 1275 K Street NW, Suite 400, Washington, DC 20005
- *Thermoplastics Pipe (Plumbing Applications)*   Plastics Pipe & Fittings Association, 999 North Main Street, Glen Ellyn, IL 60137
- *PVC Piping (Water Distribution, Sewerage, and Irrigation)*   Uni-Bell Plastics Pipe Association, 2655 Villa Creek Drive, Suite 164, Dallas, TX 75234

BIBLIOGRAPHY

The following references include useful information on plastics piping:

"PVC Pipe, Design and Installation," AWWA Manual No. M23, American Water Works Association, Denver, 1980.

"Standard for Reinforced Thermosetting Resin Pipe," AWWA C-950, American Water Works Association, Denver. (Appendix to standards includes much design and installation information.)

Britt, William F., Jr.: "Design Considerations for FRP Piping Systems," *Proceedings of the 1979 Conference on Managing Corrosion with Plastics,* National Association of Corrosion Engineers, Houston.

Cheremisinoff, Nicholas P., and N. Paul: *The Fiberglass-Reinforced Plastics Deskbook,* Ann Arbor Science, Ann Arbor, Michigan, 1978.

Cooney, J. L.: "Guidelines for the Inspection and Maintenance of FRP Equipment and Piping," *Proceedings of the 1979 Conference on Managing Corrosion with Plastics,* National Association of Corrosion Engineers, Houston.

Escher, G. A.: "Transition to FRP, Basic Guidelines for Piping Designers and Users," *Proceedings of the 1975 Conference on Managing Corrosion with Plastics,* National Association of Corrosion Engineers, Houston.

Escher, G. A., and W. B. MacDonald: "Chemical and Mechanical Properties of Butt and Strap Joints," *Proceedings of the 1975 Conference on Managing Corrosion with Plastics,* National Association of Corrosion Engineers, Houston.

Greenwood: "Buried FRP Pipe—Performance Through Proper Installation," *Proceedings of the 1975 Conference on Managing Corrosion with Plastics,* National Association of Corrosion Engineers, Houston.

Kutschke, C. T.: "Use of Plastic Pipe for Industrial Applications," *Proceedings of the 1975 Conference on Managing Corrosion with Plastics,* National Association of Corrosion Engineers, Houston.

Launikitis, M. B.: "Chemically Resistant FRP Resins," *Proceedings of the 1977 Conference on Managing Corrosion with Plastics,* National Association of Corrosion Engineers, Houston.

Mallison, John H.: *Chemical Plant Design with Reinforced Plastics,* McGraw-Hill, New York, 1969.

Mruk, Stanley: "Thermoplastics Piping: A Review," *Proceedings of the 1979 Conference on Managing Corrosion with Plastics,* National Association of Corrosion Engineers, Houston.

Petroff, Larry J., and Luckenbill, Michael: "Flexibility of the Design of Fiberglass Pipe," *Proceedings of the 1981 International Conference on Plastic Pipe,* American Society of Civil Engineers, New York.

Plastics Piping Manual, The Plastics Pipe Institute, 1275 K Street NW, Suite 400, Washington, DC 20005, 1976.

Rolston, Albert: "Fiberglass Composite and Fabrication," *Chemical Engineering,* January 28, 1980, pp. 96–110.

Rubens, A. C.: "Designing RTRP Systems Utilizing Published Engineering Data," *Proceedings of the 1979 Conference on Managing Corrosion with Plastics,* National Association of Corrosion Engineers, Houston.

Schrock, B. J.: "Thermosetting Resin Pipe," Preprint 3088, American Society of Civil Engineers, New York, 1977.

Proceedings of the International Conference on Underground Plastic Pipe, March 30–April 1, 1981, New Orleans, La., American Society of Civil Engineers, New York.

CHAPTER 10-3
ASBESTOS-CEMENT PIPE AND FITTINGS

Association of Asbestos Cement Pipe Producers
Arlington, Virginia

DESCRIPTION AND APPLICATIONS

Asbestos-cement (A/C) pipe, composed of an intimate mixture of portland cement and asbestos fiber, with or without silica, is completely inorganic and free from metallic substances. In the manufacturing process, these ingredients are combined, mixed with water, and formed as pipe on a rotating steel mandrel, creating a dense wall with a smooth interior surface. The pipe is cured in autoclave ovens for dimensional and chemical stability; during the curing time the silica reacts with the free lime, present in normally cured cement products, to form relatively insoluble calcium silicate compounds. These give A/C pipe added resistance to corrosive soils and fluids; as a nonconductor, it is immune to electrolysis.

The resulting A/C pipe is light in weight, resists corrosion, maintains good flow characteristics, and possesses high crush, flexural, and hydrostatic strength.

The most common applications for A/C pipe are for water mains, sewage force mains, and gravity sewer systems. Other uses for A/C pipe are storm drains, perforated under-drains, electric and telephone conduits, irrigation systems, air and vent ducts, and building sewers. Because of its high corrosion resistance to many chemicals and freedom from rust and metallic oxides, A/C pipe is also used in many industrial services and, on occasion, for overhead process piping services. In addition, pre-insulated pressure pipe utilizes an outer asbestos-cement casing to contain an inner insulated core capable of handling underground installations of chilled liquids and high-temperature water.

FITTINGS AND COUPLINGS

Standard asbestos-cement or plastic fittings such as elbows, tees, wyes, adapters, and couplings are available for most sewer-pipe sizes and for building sewer lines. Metal fittings other than the couplings are normally used for pressure-pipe connections. A/C pipe products are designed for quick compatibility with cast-iron and ductile-iron fittings and easy interfacing with accessories made of these materials.

The joining of one A/C pipe to another is achieved easily with a push-together coupling, consisting of an asbestos-cement sleeve with rubber rings as shown in Fig. 3-1. Compressing the rubber rings between the sleeve and the factory-machined pipe ends provides a tight seal that resists shock, vibration, and earth movement while compensating for the expansion and contraction of the pipe lengths. These joints, when used on pipe under pressure, withstand pressure equal to the rated pipe pressures with adequate safety factors. A coupling is pre-balled at the factory on one end of each standard section of A/C pipe.

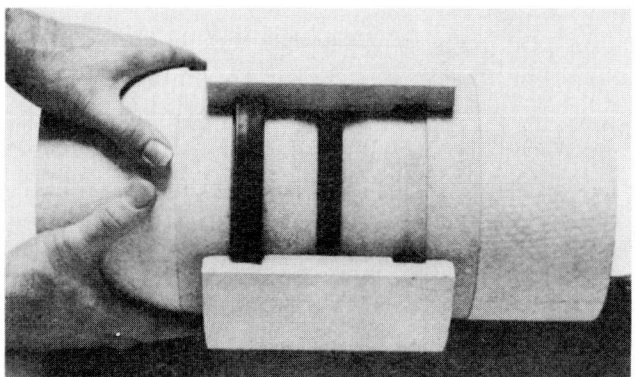

FIGURE 3-1   Asbestos-cement pipe coupling. *(CertainTeed Corporation.)*

AVAILABLE SIZES AND FORMS

Asbestos-cement pipe is manufactured in standard lengths of either 10 or 13 ft (3 or 4 m) and is also available in half, quarter, or eighth lengths.

Sewer Pipe

Gravity Sewer Systems.   A/C pipe is manufactured in five strength classifications which are designated as Classes 1500, 2400, 3300, 4000, and 5000. The class designation represents minimum crushing strength in pounds per linear foot of pipe, regardless of size. The pipe is manufactured with nominal inside diameters from 4 to 36 in (100 to 900 mm) and in some areas up to 42 in (1050 mm). Larger diameters and higher strength classifications may also be obtained on special order.

Sewage Force Mains.   A/C pipe is manufactured in three classes of operating pressures: 100, 150, and 200. The class designation represents the operating pressure in pounds per square inch. These three classes of pressure pipe, available in sizes from 4 to 16 in (100 to 400 mm), are capable of withstanding the crushing loads shown in Table 3-1.

Water Pipe

Distribution Systems.   For distribution systems which have relatively unpredictable flows and many appurtenances, A/C pressure pipe is available in sizes from 4 to 16 in (100 to 400

TABLE 3-1 Asbestos-Cement Pressure Pipe, Minimum Crushing Load

Nominal pipe size, in	lb per linear ft		
	Class 100	Class 150	Class 200
4	4,100	5,400	8,700
6	4,000	5,400	9,000
8	4,000	5,500	9,300
10	4,400	7,000	11,000
12	5,200	7,600	11,800
14	5,200	8,600	13,500
16	5,800	9,200	15,400

mm) for operating pressures of 100, 150, and 200 lb/in^2 designated as Classes 100, 150 and 200, respectively. The crushing strengths of these three classes which are also used for pressure sewer systems are given in Table 3-1.

Transmission Systems.   For transmission systems which have relatively steady flow and few appurtenances, A/C pipe is available in sizes from 18 to 42 in (450 to 1050 mm). The strength classifications of 30, 35, 40, 45, 50, 60, 70, 80, and 90 represent one-tenth of minimum allowable hydrostatic bursting strength in pounds per square inch for A/C transmission pipe. A/C transmission-piping systems are designed on the combined loading theory in which the design engineer takes into consideration and determines the operating and surge pressures, the earth and superimposed external loads, and safety factors. The relationship of design internal pressures and external loads for A/C transmission pipe is shown in Table 3-2.

INSTALLATION AND MAINTENANCE

Asbestos fibers with a tensile strength four to five times greater than that of steel provide significant reinforcement in A/C pipe products to withstand internal hydrostatic pressure, exter-

TABLE 3-2 Asbestos-Cement Transmission Pipe, Design Internal Pressure (P, lb/in^2), and Design External Loads (W, lb/linear ft)

Pipe size, in	Strength Classification								
	30 $P = 300$ W	35 $P = 350$ W	40 $P = 400$ W	45 $P = 450$ W	50 $P = 500$ W	60 $P = 600$ W	70 $P = 700$ W	80 $P = 800$ W	90 $P = 900$ W
18	2,500	3,000	4,000	5,000	6,500	8,500	11,000	14,000	18,000
20	2,500	3,500	4,500	5,500	7,100	9,500	12,000	15,000	20,000
21	2,500	3,500	4,500	5,800	7,300	9,700	12,500	16,000	21,000
24	2,800	3,800	5,000	6,200	8,100	11,000	15,000	19,000	24,000
27	3,500	4,200	5,500	7,000	8,800	12,500	16,500	20,500	27,000
30	3,500	4,500	6,000	7,500	9,700	13,500	18,000	22,500	30,000
33	3,500	5,000	6,500	8,000	10,500	14,500	19,500	24,500	33,000
36	4,000	5,000	7,000	9,000	11,200	16,000	21,000	26,000	36,000
39	4,200	5,300	7,500	9,700	12,000	17,200	22,500	28,000	39,000
42	4,300	5,700	8,000	10,500	13,000	18,500	24,000	30,000	42,000

Note: 1 lb/in^2 = 6.895 kilopascals.

nal loads, or combinations of these forces. Even so, good construction procedures applicable for any underground piping systems are equally appropriate for A/C piping systems. Recommended practices for receiving, storage and handling, joint assembly, installation, and inspection and testing are covered in detail in A/C pipe manufacturers' literature, in American Society of Testing and Materials (ASTM) and American Water Works Association (AWWA) standards, and in the plans and specifications of the piping-system's design engineer. Terminology commonly used in a trench installation of A/C pipe is shown in Fig. 3-2. Following are highlights on installation of A/C pipe from these standards and specifications.

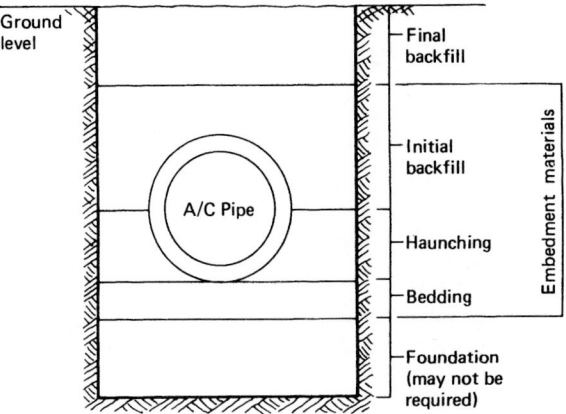

FIGURE 3-2   Trench cross section and terminology used in embedment and backfilling asbestos-cement pipe.

Receiving, Storage, and Handling

When receiving A/C pipe, each shipment should be inspected and inventoried. See Fig. 3-3. The pipe is inspected and carefully loaded at the factory using methods acceptable to the carrier whose responsibility it is to deliver the pipe in good condition. It is the responsibility of the receiver to ensure that there has been no loss or damage. Pipes should be stored, if possible, at the work site in the package units provided by the manufacturer. Rubber gaskets should be protected from oil and grease, direct sunlight, excessive exposure to heat, and elec-

FIGURE 3-3   Asbestos-cement pipe shipment. *(CertainTeed Corporation.)*

tric motors which produce ozone. At all times, A/C pipe should be handled with care to avoid damage. Whether moved by hand, skidways, hoists, forklifts, or other handling equipment, A/C pipe should not be thrown, dragged, or bumped.

Trench Excavation

As a general rule, do not open the trench too far ahead of laying the pipe. In preparation for pipe installation, place (string) pipe as near the trench as possible but leave adequate space to perform necessary excavating and other related functions. If the trench is open, place the pipe on the opposite side from the excavated earth. When necessary to prevent caving, trench excavation should be sheeted and braced or sloped in accordance with applicable laws and ordinances. The trench width at the ground surface should be ample to permit the pipe to be laid and the backfill to be placed and throughly compacted. The trench width at the top of the pipe should not be more than the outside diameter of the pipe barrel plus two ft (0.6 m). The trench should be kept free from water at all times. See Fig. 3-4.

Pipe should not be lowered into the trench until the pipe bed has been brought to correct grade. Any part of the trench bottom below grade should be backfilled with thoroughly compacted material. When an unstable subgrade condition is encountered, additional trench depth should be excavated and refilled with suitable, thoroughly compacted foundation material. All rocks, boulders, and large stones should be removed to provide a clearance of 6 to 9 in (150 to 225 mm) below and on all sides of pipe and fittings. When excavation is completed, a bed of sand, crushed stone, or earth that is free from rocks, frozen earth, or clods larger than 1 in (25.4 mm) should be placed and thoroughly compacted to properly regrade the trench bottom. A minimum clearance of 2 in (50 mm) below the coupling should be provided at each joint to permit proper joint assembly. The pipe should be provided continuous support between coupling holes.

FIGURE 3-4 Asbestos-cement pipe installation. *(CertainTeed Corporation.)*

Joint Assembly

Pipe and accessories should be lowered carefully into the trench by hand or with suitable equipment to avoid damaging the pipe and fittings or injuring the installers. Pipe ends, the coupling interior, and especially the exposed coupling groove and rubber gasket should be thoroughly cleaned prior to assembly. Joint assembly should be performed as recommended by the manufacturer. After alignment, insertion of the rubber gasket, and thorough lubrication of the pipe end as specified by the pipe manufacturer, the assembly of the joint is completed by a sliding action during which the lubricated pipe end slides under the rubber gasket located in the coupling groove and into the coupling to an automatic stop point. Each pipe joint is sealed with a coupling consisting of a sleeve and compressed rubber rings which keep the pipe ends separate, automatically providing for expansion, contraction, and joint flexibility. When pipelaying is not in progress, the open ends of installed pipe should be kept closed to prevent entrance of trench water, dirt, and other foreign matter into the pipeline.

Since 1986, special closure lengths and couplings have been available. This innovation has resulted in reduced installation time and elimination of cutting tools, reducing labor and equipment costs.

Pipe Embedment and Backfilling

All pipe embedment material should be selected carefully, free from organic debris. The embedment material and its placement and compaction are important considerations in assuring that the pipe will satisfactorily resist trench loading conditions during construction and after the pipeline is completely installed.

Pipe-loading carrying capability is also greatly influenced by the degree of soil compaction around the lower half of the pipe section to provide satisfactory haunching. The initial backfill material should be placed to a minimum depth of 1 ft (30 cm) over the top of the pipe. After placement and compaction of pipe-embedment materials, the final backfill, which is usually placed by machine, need not be as carefully selected as the initial material but should contain no large stones or rocks, frozen soil, or debris.

Maintenance

Pipeline projects should be tested upon completion of installation to assure functional water and sewer systems construction. Before testing, all parts of the pipeline must be backfilled and braced to prevent movement under pressure. Since asbestos-cement will absorb some water, the line must be filled with water for a minimum of 24 h before being subjected to a hydrostatic pressure test. Approved methods of testing asbestos-cement pressure pipe (pressure-strength test and leakage testing) and nonpressure sewer pipe (infiltration, exfiltration, or low-pressure air-loss tests) are described in specifications listed in Table 3-3.

TABLE 3-3 Specifications

	AWWA
C 400	Asbestos-Cement Distribution Pipe, 4 to 16 in
C 401	Selection of Asbestos-Cement Distribution Pipe, 4 to 16 in
C 402	Asbestos-Cement Transmission Pipe, 18 to 42 in
C 403	Selection of Asbestos-Cement Transmission and Feed Pipe, 18 to 42 in
C 603	Installation of Asbestos-Cement Pressure Pipe
	ASTM
C 296	Asbestos-Cement Pressure Pipe
C 668	Asbestos-Cement Transmission Pipe
C 428	Asbestos-Cement Nonpressure Sewer Pipe
C 663	Asbestos-Cement Storm Drain Pipe
C 508	Asbestos-Cement Underdrain Pipe
C 875	Asbestos-Cement Conduit
D 1869	Rubber Rings for Asbestos-Cement Pipe

Implementation of proper installation, inspection, and testing procedures should assure maintenance-free, long-term performance of buried asbestos-cement piping systems.

In turn, good work practices complement proper construction procedures. Airborne asbestos fiber has been identified as a possible health hazard. The asbestos fiber in asbestos-cement pipe are not free, but are encapsulated, or locked into, the cement binder. Based on the best scientific data available, the use of A/C pipe does not pose a health hazard by reason of ingestion of asbestos fibers. Experience has shown, however, that minimizing exposure to airborne dust is the only effective method of preventing asbestos-related diseases. In 1978, AWWA first published Manual No. 16, "Work Practices for Asbestos-Cement Pipe," which, based on results of field testing and study, recommended general guides to achieve safe and clean jobsite conditions when working with A/C pipe products. The manual will be updated in 1994 and includes current information as described above.

STANDARDS AND SPECIFICATIONS

Asbestos-cement pipe is specified by pipe diameter, class or strength, and type of joint. Codes and specifications applicable to A/C pipe are issued by a number of organizations including various federal agencies, fire protection associations, and national and regional plumbing associations. A/C pipe should conform, as appropriate, to the standard specifications (Table 3-3) published by the American Water Works Association (AWWA) and the American Society for Testing and Materials (ASTM).

BIBLIOGRAPHY

American Water Works Association: "Work Practices for Asbestos-Cement Pipe," AWWA No. M16, Denver, Colorado, to be published in 1994.

Capco: "Installation Guide for Asbestos Cement Distribution and Transmission Pipe," Birmingham, Alabama, 1992.

ACKNOWLEDGMENT

For the preparation of this chapter, the author has drawn on standards published by the American Water Works Association and the American Society for Testing and Materials, as well as on source material supplied by asbestos-cement pipe manufacturers.

CHAPTER 10-4
PIPE INSULATION

Michael R. Harrison
Vice President and General Manager
Manville Mechanical Specialty Insulations
Schuller International, Inc.
Denver, Colorado

Ricardo R. Gamboa
Manager, Engineering and Technical Services
Manville Mechanical Specialty Insulations
Schuller International, Inc.
Denver, Colorado

HEAT-TRANSFER FUNDAMENTALS

Heat energy is transferred from one location to another by three different mechanisms: *conduction, convection,* and *radiation.* In insulation design theory, the objective is to minimize the contribution of each mode in the most efficient and economical manner. As temperatures vary, the relative importance of each transfer mechanism also varies, making different insulation designs appropriate for various applications.

Conduction

Energy transfer by conduction is a result of atomic or molecular motion. As molecules become heated, their vibration increases and energy is transferred to surrounding molecules. Conduction occurs in all three forms of matter: gas, liquid, and solid. Within most insulation, solid conduction is minimized by using an open-pore structure and a minimum amount of solid material. Conduction within a gas is more difficult to control; to achieve much greater insulation efficiency, this mode must be limited. One method employs a vacuum, thus eliminating the gas from the system. This is very effective but costly, since the vacuum seal must be maintained in order to assure adequate performance. The second method of controlling gas conduction is to replace the air in the insulation by a heavier gas such as Freon®. Again, the seal must be maintained to avoid eventual air and moisture migration back into the cell structure.

Convection

Convective currents are established when a hot fluid (gas or liquid) rises from a heat source and is replaced by a cooler fluid, which in turn is heated and rises carrying the energy with it. In an insulation structure with many small cells, convection is minimized since the gas cannot freely pass through the structure. Most insulations are of sufficient density and formation to almost eliminate this mode within them, but convection plays a very important part in transferring energy from the insulated surface to the surrounding environment.

Radiation

As temperature increases, electromagnetic radiation gains in significance with regard to the total amount of energy transferred. Radiation occurs in a vacuum as well as in a gaseous environment, and its magnitude is dependent on the emittance of the radiating and receiving surfaces and the temperature difference between them. To control radiant flow, low-emittance surfaces are used in conjunction with absorbers and reflectors within the insulation itself. The mass density of the insulation is very important with a higher density reducing the level of radiation transfer.

There are obvious tradeoffs that must be made in controlling the various heat-transfer mechanisms. Figure 4-1 illustrates the contribution to total conductivity of each mechanism at three different temperatures. The most efficient insulation design, both thermally and economically, will vary depending on the application conditions. References 1 and 2 are basic texts on heat transfer for further study.

Heat Flow

The level of heat flow to or from a system is directly proportional to the difference between the system and ambient temperatures, and inversely proportional to the thermal resistance placed in the heat flow path:

$$\text{Heat flow} = \frac{\text{temperature difference}}{\text{resistance to heat flow}}$$

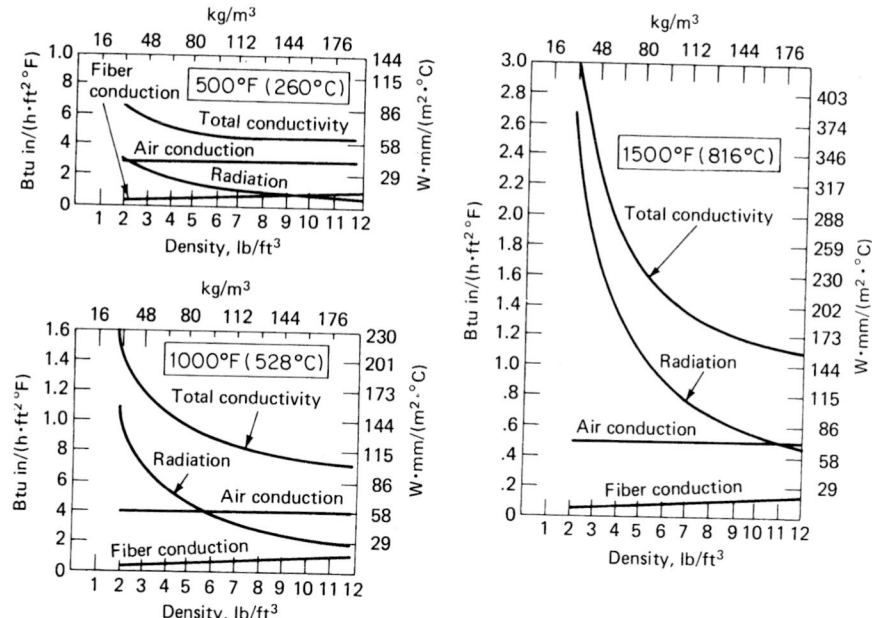

FIGURE 4-1   Contribution of each mode of heat transfer.[3]

In this light, the temperature difference is the forcing function; as long as there is a differential, energy will flow. No amount of thermal resistance can completely stop the heat transfer; it can only slow the rate at which it occurs.

Total thermal resistance is generally composed of two distinct types of resistances: insulation and surface. Insulation resistance for a homogeneous material is determined by dividing the insulation thickness tk by its thermal conductivity.

$$R_I = th/k$$

The thermal conductivity, or k value, is an experimentally measured property of homogeneous material indicating the time rate of steady state heat flow induced by an unit temperature gradient in a direction perpendicular to that unit area. k are expressed in in-lb units (Btu)(in)/(h)(ft$_2$)(°F) and in SI units (W/m · °C). In the case of nonhomogeneous thermal insulation, materials that exhibit thermal transmission by several modes of heat transfer (resulting in property variation with specimen thickness or surface emmitance), an apparent thermal conductivity is assigned.

The accurate measurement of thermal conductivity is very important since materials are often compared on this basis. The American Society for Testing and Materials (ASTM) has developed standardized test methods for measuring thermal conductivity. For pipe insulation, the standard test is C 335.[4]

Since thermal conductivity increases with temperature, it is important to use the k value at the insulation mean temperature rather than the value at either the operating temperature (too high) or the ambient temperature (too low).

The other type of thermal resistance is surface resistance:

$$R_s = 1/f$$

where f represents the surface film coefficient. Surface emittance, air velocity across the surface, and temperature difference all influence the value of R. Table 4-1 lists various R_s values for three common surface types, temperature differentials, and wind velocities. These values will be used in subsequent heat-transfer calculations.

TABLE 4-1 Values for Surface Resistance, R_s, (h)(ft²)(°F) and Btu (m² · °C/W)

A. Values for still air

$t_s - t_a$		Plain, fabric dull metal	Aluminum	Stainless steel
°F	°C	$\varepsilon = 0.95$	$\varepsilon = 0.2$	$\varepsilon = 0.4$
10	5	0.53 (0.093)	0.90 (0.158)	0.81 (0.142)
25	14	0.52 (0.091)	0.88 (0.155)	0.79 (0.139)
50	28	0.50 (0.088)	0.86 (0.151)	0.76 (0.133)
75	42	0.48 (0.084)	0.84 (0.147)	0.75 (0.132)
100	55	0.46 (0.081)	0.80 (0.140)	0.72 (0.126)

B. R_s Values with wind velocities

Wind velocity		Plain, fabric dull metal		Aluminum		Stainless steel	
mi/h	km/h	mi/h	km/h	mi/h	km/h	mi/h	km/h
5	8	0.35	0.06	0.41	0.07	0.40	0.07
10	16	0.30	0.05	0.35	0.06	0.34	0.06
20	32	0.24	0.04	0.28	0.05	0.27	0.05

* For heat-loss calculations, the effect of R_s is small compared with R_I, so the accuracy of R_s is not critical. For surface-temperature calculations, R_s is the controlling factor and is, therefore, quite critical. The values presented in Table 5-1 are commonly used values for piping and flat surfaces. More precise values based on surface emittance and wind velocity can be found in the referenced texts.
  Source: Schuller International, Inc., Ref. 5.

Since thermal resistances are additive, they are very convenient to work with in calculating heat transfer. From the basic definition,

$$Q = \frac{\Delta t}{R_I + R_s} = \frac{\Delta t}{tk/k + R_s} \tag{1}$$

becomes the basic equation for heat transfer through insulation. Use of this equation is illustrated later.

Insulation Effectiveness

Before leaving the fundamentals, the importance of insulation should be illustrated. Table 4-2 shows the amount of heat transfer from a bare surface at a given temperature differential. Essentially, these values are calculated from the fundamental heat-transfer equation, Eq. (1), with the insulation thickness being zero. Listed below are three different sets of operating conditions for an 8-in (20-cm) pipe. To show the effectiveness of insulation, heat losses are shown for the bare pipe and for the pipe with 1 in of fiberglass insulation applied, even though a greater thickness would normally be used.

Operating temp., °F	Ambient temp., °F	Bare heat loss Btu/(h)(ft)	Heat loss with 1 in fiberglass, Btu/(h)(ft)	Reduction in heat loss, %
200	80	617	70	88.7
350	80	1882	188	90.1
500	80	3998	353	91.2

TABLE 4-2 Heat Loss from Bare Surfaces*

Nominal pipe size, inches	Temperature difference, °F															
	50	100	150	200	250	300	350	400	450	500	550	600	700	800	900	1000
½	22	47	79	117	162	215	279	355	442	541	650	772	1047	1364	1723	2123
¾	27	59	99	147	203	269	349	444	552	677	812	965	1309	1705	2153	2654
1	34	75	124	183	254	336	437	555	691	846	1016	1207	1637	2133	2694	3320
1¼	42	94	157	232	321	425	552	702	873	1070	1285	1527	2071	2697	3406	4198
1½	49	107	179	265	367	487	632	804	1000	1225	1471	1748	2371	3088	3899	4806
2	61	134	224	332	459	608	790	1004	1249	1530	1837	2183	2961	3856	4870	6002
2½	74	162	271	401	556	736	956	1215	1512	1852	2224	2643	3584	4669	5896	7267
3	89	197	330	489	677	897	1164	1480	1841	2256	2708	3219	4365	5685	7180	8849
3½	102	225	377	558	773	1024	1329	1690	2102	2576	3092	3675	4984	6491	8198	10100
4	115	254	424	628	869	1152	1496	1901	2365	2898	3479	4135	5607	7304	9224	11370
4½	128	282	471	698	965	1280	1662	2113	2628	3220	3866	4595	6231	8116	10250	12630
5	142	313	524	776	1074	1424	1848	2350	2923	3582	4300	5111	6931	9027	11400	14050
6	169	373	624	924	1279	1696	2201	2799	3481	4266	5121	6086	8254	10750	13580	16730
7	195	430	719	1064	1473	1952	2534	3222	4007	4910	5894	7006	9501	12380	15630	19260
8	220	486	813	1203	1665	2207	2865	3643	4531	5552	6666	7922	10740	13990	17670	21780
9	246	542	907	1343	1859	2464	3198	4066	5057	6197	7440	8842	11990	15620	19720	24310
10	275	606	1014	1502	2078	2755	3576	4547	5655	6930	8320	9888	13410	17470	22060	27180
11	300	661	1106	1638	2267	3005	3901	4960	6169	7560	9076	10790	14630	19050	24060	29660
12	326	718	1202	1779	2463	3265	4238	5338	6701	8212	9859	11720	15890	20700	26140	32210
14	357	783	1319	1952	2703	3582	4650	5912	7354	9011	10820	12860	17440	22710	28680	35350
16	408	901	1508	2232	3090	4096	5317	6759	8407	10300	12370	14700	19940	25970	32790	40410
18	460	1015	1698	2514	3480	4012	5987	7612	9467	11600	13930	16550	22450	29240	36930	45510
20	510	1127	1885	2790	3862	5120	6646	8449	10510	12880	15460	18380	24920	32460	40990	50520
24	613	1353	2263	3350	4638	6148	7980	10150	12620	15460	18570	22060	29920	38970	49220	60660
30	766	1690	2827	4186	5795	7681	9971	12680	15770	19320	23200	27570	37390	48700	61500	75790
Flat	98	215	360	533	738	978	1270	1614	2008	2460	2954	3510	4760	6200	7830	9650

* Losses given in Btu per hour per linear foot of bare pipe at various temperature differences and Btu per hour per square foot for flat surfaces.
  Source: Reference 3.

PIPE INSULATION MATERIALS

Table 4-3 lists the principal insulations being used along with their important properties. To assure accurate information, current data sheets from the manufacturer should always be consulted before specifying a particular product. Table 4-3 also provides a brief description of each type of material and the benefits and drawbacks of each.

Calcium Silicate

Lime, silica, and reinforcing fibers are used as main raw materials in a chemical process to form rigid insulations. Since no organic binders are used, the products are noncombustible and maintain their physical integrity at very high temperatures. These materials are known for their exceptional durability and strength and are the high-quality standard in industrial plant environments where physical abuse is always a problem. Calcium silicate insulations are more expensive than fibrous materials but are more thermally efficient at higher temperatures.

Cellular Glass

This product is also rigid and completely inorganic, composed of millions of completely sealed glass cells. It is unique among insulation materials in that it is made up of totally closed cells and will not absorb any liquids or vapors. Although its thermal conductivity is higher than most of the other insulations, the product is widely used in pipe systems operating below ambient temperatures and buried applications where moisture is often a problem. Similarly, lines carrying flammable liquids often use cellular glass around valves and fittings to minimize the hazard of a saturated insulation. The product is load-bearing, but it is also brittle and must be protected when installed on pipes where vibrations are likely to occur. The material is subject to thermal shock at temperatures above 400°F (204°C).

Expanded Perlite

A naturally occurring material, perlite is expanded at high temperature to form a structure of tiny air cells within a vitrified product. Organic and/or inorganic binders are used in conjunction with reinforcing fibers to hold the perlite structure together. At temperatures below 300°F (167°C), these products have low moisture absorption, but this increases after exposure to elevated temperatures. The products are rigid and load bearing, but are more brittle and less thermally efficient than the calcium silicate materials.

Mineral Rock or Slag Wool

Formed from molten rock or slag, these products have a higher recommended temperature limit than fiberglass, but they utilize similar organic binders for structural integrity. The products are not load bearing and contain varying amounts of unfiberized material typically called shot. The greatest drawbacks of the mineral rock or slag wool materials is the short fiber length and shot content, which allow vibration and physical abuse to cause severe damage, particularly after the organic binder is oxidized at around 400 to 500°F (204 to 260°C). However, the products have a lower first cost than most of the rigid insulations.

TABLE 4-3 Properties of Various Industrial Pipe Insulation Materials

Insulation type	Temp. range, °F (°C)	Thermal conductivity (Btu)(in)/(h)/(ft²)/(°F) at T mean, °F (°C) (W·mm/m² · °C)			Compresive strength, lb/in² (kPa) at % deformation	Classification or flame-spread smoke developed*	Cell structure (permeability and moisture absorption*)
		75°F (42°C)	200°F (93°C)	500°F (260°C)			
Calcium silicate	1200 to 1500 (649 to 815)	(41.6) 0.37 (52)	(93.3) 0.41 (59)	(260) 0.53 (76)	100 to 250 @ 5% (689 to 1722)	Noncombustible	Open cell
Cellular glass	−450 to 900 (268 to 482)	0.38 (54)	0.45 (65)	0.72 (104)	100 @ 5% (689)	Noncombustible	Closed cell
Expanded perlite	1200 to 1500 (649 to 815)	—	0.46 (66)	0.63 (91)	90 @ 5% (620)	Noncombustible	Open cell
Mineral fiber	to 1900 (1038)	0.23 to 0.34 (33 to 49)	0.28 (40)	0.45 (65)	1 to 18 @ 10% (6.9 to 124)	Noncombustible to 25/50	Open cell
Glass fiber	to 850 (454)	0.23 (33)	0.30 (43)	0.62 (89)	.02 to 3.5 @ 10% (.13 to 24)	Noncombustible to 25/50	Open cell
Urethane foam	−100 to −450 to 225 (−73 to −268 to 107)	0.16 to 0.18 (23 to 26)	—	—	16 to 75 @ 10% (110 to 516)	25 to 75 140 to 400	95% closed cell
Isocyanurate foam	to 350 (177)	0.15 (22)	—	—	17 to 25 @ 10% (117 to 172)	25 55 to 100	93% closed cell
Phenolic foam	−40 to 250 (−40 to 121)	0.23 (33)	—	—	13 to 22 @ 10% (89 to 151)	25/50	Open cell
Elastomeric closed cell	−40 to 220 (−40 to 104)	0.25 to 0.27 (36 to 39)	—	—	40 @ 10% (275)	25 115 to 490 50 ≤ ¾" 50–100 > ¾"	Closed cell

* FHC from ASTM E 84 and UL 723 which indexes flame and smoke development to that generated by Red Oak which has 100/100 FHC.

Glass Fiber

Fiberglass pipe insulations are formed from molten glass and bonded with organic resins. The principal products for commercial piping systems are the one-piece molded insulations, which install rapidly by hinging open and then closing around the pipe. Flexible wraparound products are also available for large-diameter pipes and vessels. Fiberglass products are also available for large-diameter pipes and vessels. Fiberglass products are very thermally efficient and easy to work with.

The only question about their use is for applications above the binder oxidation temperature of 400 to 500°F (205 to 260°C). Most manufacturers rate their products above the binder temperature and are confident of their performance due to the long glass fiber matrix. However, there are certain applications that combine severe vibration with high temperature. In such cases, fiberglass products, like mineral wools, may tend to sag on the pipe and lose some of their thermal efficiency.

Foams

Four products in the general foam category are now being used primarily for cold service and plumbing applications. Polyurethane- and isocyanurate-foamed plastics offer the lowest thermal conductivity since the cells are filled with fluorocarbon blowing agents that are heavier than air. However, the products still need to be sealed to prevent the migration of air and water vapor back into the cells. There have been problems with urethane regarding both dimensional stability and fire safety; the isocyanurates were developed, in part, to deal with these problems. However, a surface burning characteristic of 25/50 FHC (fire hazard classification) is still being sought for these materials.

Phenolic foams have the required level of fire safety but do not offer thermal efficiencies much better from that of fiberglass. They are limited in temperature range, but their rigid structure allows them to be used without special pipe saddle-supports on small lines.

Elastomeric closed-cell materials are the fourth type and are used primarily in plumbing and refrigeration work. These products are both flexible and closed-cell, permitting rapid installation without an additional vapor retarder lagging for moderate design conditions. These materials have a surface burning characteristic of 25/50 FHC only for thicknesses ¾ in (1.9 cm) and below; this restricts their use in certain applications.

MATERIALS SELECTION AND APPLICATION

There are many factors involved in selecting the best insulation for specific application. First, the service requirements and locations must be analyzed to determine which products will, for example, meet the pipe temperature requirements and also be able to withstand the anticipated abuse. Also, special considerations such as fire protection, removability, and chemical resistance must all be reviewed in the selection process.

Finally, three insulation cost factors should be carefully analyzed. The *initial cost* of the material and installation is straightforward; competitive products can be readily compared. *Maintenance costs* are not as clear-cut and vary greatly from one material to another, with the nonrigid materials usually requiring more maintenance in industrial environments. The last cost element is that of the *heat lost* through the insulation system. If the same thickness is specified for several different materials, the product with the lowest thermal conductivity will provide the lowest lost-heat cost. Similarly, a material that requires less maintenance may well retain its original performance longer than a material that is easily damaged and degraded. All of these costs should be reviewed before choosing the lowest bid package, which only deals with initial costs.

The following paragraphs deal with insulation selection based on operating temperature, design considerations, and common industrial use.

Cryogenic

Cryogenic insulation systems (–455 to –150°F [–271 to 101°C]) are usually custom engineered due to the critical nature of such service. The two problems encountered are moisture migration and low insulation efficiency. Unequal vapor pressure serves to drive moisture to the cold pipe which results ultimately in ice formation and the subsequent deterioration of the insulation. Multiple vapor barriers are used to prevent this, and cellular glass adds additional security since it is totally closed cell. The system must also be thermally efficient so as to keep the outside surface temperature above the ambient dew point.

This may require outlandish thicknesses of conventional insulations, although the more efficient plastic foams are frequently used for this reason. The most severe applications employ vacuum products with multiple layers of reflective foil or vacuum cavities with powder fill.

Low-Temperature

Refrigeration, plumbing, and HVAC systems operate in the range of –150 to 212°F (–101 to 100°C). Cellular glass, fiberglass, and foam products are the most frequently used products. Vapor-barrier requirements are still important for all applications below ambient temperatures, but the level of protection needed becomes less as ambient conditions are approached. Applications above ambient require little special attention with the exception that the plastic foams begin to reach their temperature limits around 200°F (93°C).

Much of this temperature service is in residential and commercial buildings. A variety of fire codes are in force for insulation—ranging from a requirement for noncombustibility to allowing smoke development up to 400. Many codes call for a flame spread of 25 or less, and products that carry a composite 25/50 FHC are suitable for virtually all applications. In general, foam products and cellular glass are used for most of the below-freezing applications while fiberglass is the primary product used for chilled water and above-ambient temperature work. Also, premolded PVC fitting covers with fiberglass inserts are frequently used as a quick and efficient way of insulating the wide variety of fittings encountered.

Intermediate-Temperature

Almost all steam and hot-process piping systems operate in the temperature range of 212 to 1000°F (100 to 538°C). The products most frequently used are calcium silicate, fiberglass, mineral wool, and expanded perlite. Choices are usually based on thermal conductivity and resistance to physical abuse where applicable. Fiberglass products are the most thermally efficient at lower temperatures, with calcium silicate being the best at higher temperatures. *It is important to use the insulation mean temperature when comparing thermal conductivities* in order to make the proper comparison.

Fiberglass pipe insulations reach their temperature limits within this range, usually at 850°F (454°C). However, they all have organic binders (as do the mineral wools) that begin to oxidize from 400 to 500°F (204 to 260°C). This should be recognized when applying the products to piping above this temperature, but should not be used as an arbitrary cutoff point for fibrous products unless the service conditions are severe enough to warrant it. Vibration and physical abuse conditions should be analyzed for each particular application.

Fire safety is another concern, in this instance from the standpoint of fire protection rather than fire hazard. Figure 4-2 shows the results of fire tests run with three high-temperature materials. The water of hydration in the calcium silicate prolonged the time required for the steel pipe to reach an unacceptable temperature.

Valves and fittings are most often insulated with field-mitered sections of the standard pipe insulation or shop-fabricated fitting covers. There is limited usage of mesh-enclosed blankets which are laced around large valves. Also, cellular glass valve and flange covers are

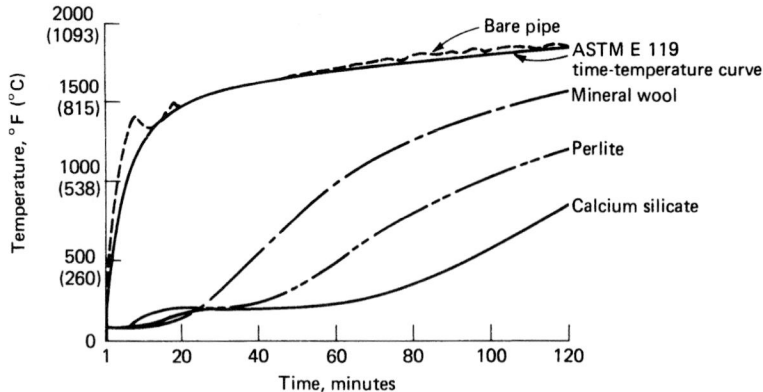

FIGURE 4-2   Fire-resistance test data for pipe insulation. *(Journal of Thermal Insulation[6])*

often used in conjunction with other insulations when the fluid being transported is volatile or has a low flash point.

Reviewing the entire range, fiberglass insulation is most often used in lower-temperature applications where physical abuse is not a problem because of its thermal efficiency and rapid installation. Calcium silicate is the standard type for higher-temperature work and in severe service. Expanded perlite provides the benefit of moisture resistance at lower temperatures, and mineral wool offers initial cost economies for higher-temperature work.

High-Temperature

Superheated steam, exhaust ducting, and some process operations are the few piping applications in the temperature range of 1000 to 1600°F (538 to 871°C). Again, calcium silicate, expanded perlite, and mineral wool are the usual materials employed. These products reach their temperature limits within this range, and higher temperature requirements are usually met by ceramic fiber blanket materials wrapped around the piping.

Installation Techniques and Specifications

The proper installation of pipe insulation is critical to the in-place performance of the product. Figure 4-3*a* illustrates installation methods for glass fiber pipe insulation with different jacket materials and pipe supports. Figure 4-3*b* illustrates insulation methods for a 90° elbow. References 7 and 8 provide detailed schematics and procedures for such work and should be consulted by plant maintenance workers involved in insulation application. Similarly, the proper selection of protective coatings and jackets will greatly influence the long-term product performance. These references, along with technical data from coating and jacketing manufacturers, provide appropriate information for proper selection.

INSULATION THICKNESS AND HEAT-LOSS CALCULATIONS

Terminology

The following symbols, definitions, and units will be used throughout the calculations.

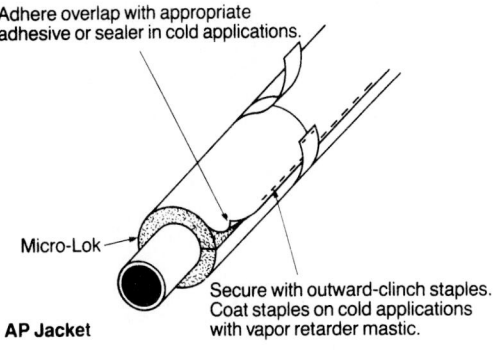

Adhere overlap with appropriate
adhesive or sealer in cold applications.

Micro-Lok

AP Jacket

Secure with outward-clinch staples.
Coat staples on cold applications
with vapor retarder mastic.

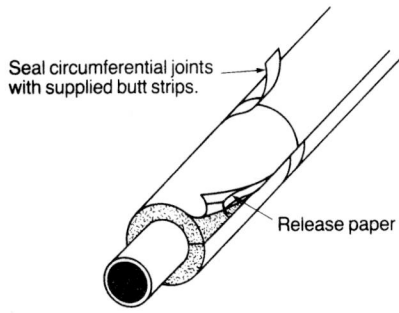

Seal circumferential joints
with supplied butt strips.

Release paper

AP-T Plus Jacket

Overlap jacket sufficiently to
provide weather resistance.

Aluminum jacket with
laminated moisture retarder.

Secure Micro-Lok with
wire or band.

Secure metal with metal bands at
butt joint overlaps and between joints.

Field-Applied Metal Jacket

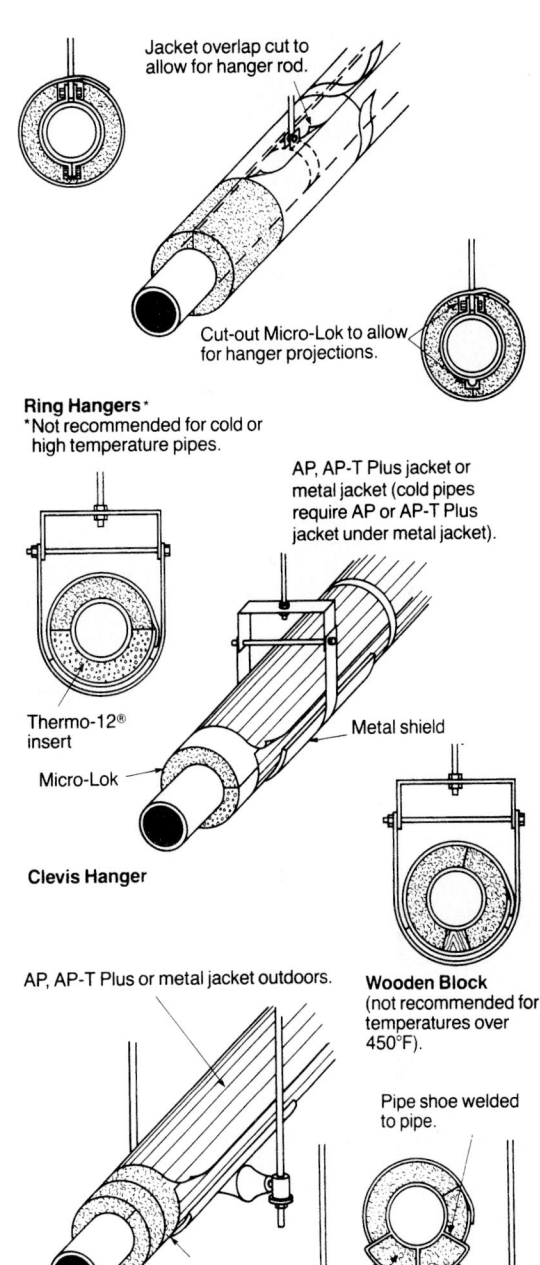

Jacket overlap cut to
allow for hanger rod.

Cut-out Micro-Lok to allow
for hanger projections.

Ring Hangers *
*Not recommended for cold or
 high temperature pipes.

AP, AP-T Plus jacket or
metal jacket (cold pipes
require AP or AP-T Plus
jacket under metal jacket).

Thermo-12®
insert

Micro-Lok

Metal shield

Clevis Hanger

AP, AP-T Plus or metal jacket outdoors.

Wooden Block
(not recommended for
temperatures over
450°F).

Pipe shoe welded
to pipe.

Pipe shoe
ends-seal
with mastic
or caulking.

Insulation inserted
inside pipe shoe.

FIGURE 4-3a   Installation methods.

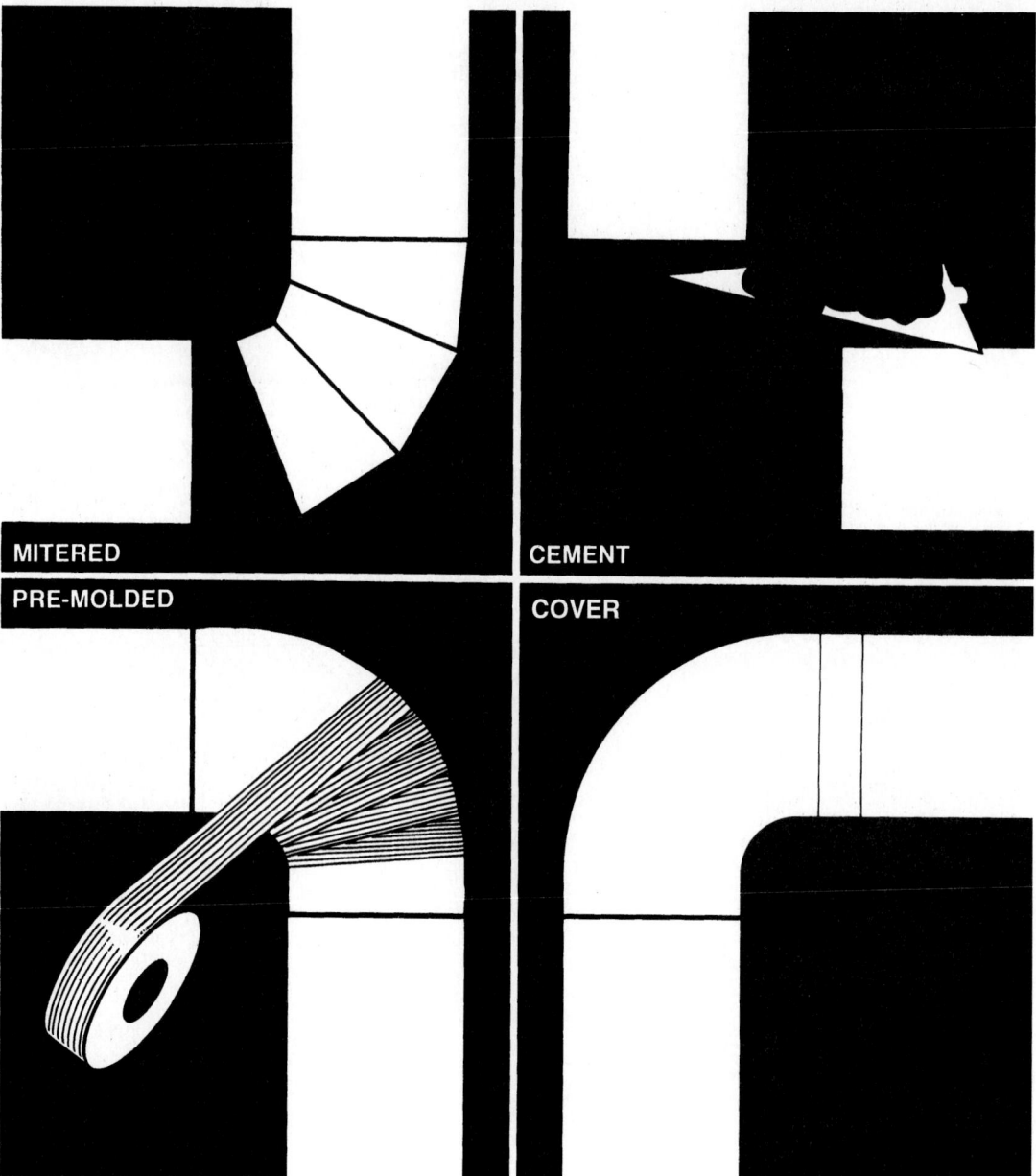

MITERED

CEMENT

PRE-MOLDED

COVER

FIGURE 4-3*b*   Insulating 90° elbows—four methods.

t_a = ambient temperature, °F (°C)

t_s = surface temperature of insulation next to ambient, °F (°C)

t_h = hot-surface temperature, normally the operating temperature (cold-surface temperature in cold applications), °F (°C)

k = thermal conductivity of insulation, always determined at the mean temperature, (Btu)(in)/(h)(ft^2)(°F) [W·mm/m^2 · °C]

$t_m = (t_h + t_s)/2$, mean temperature of insulation, °F (°C)

tk = thickness of insulation, in (mm)

r_1 = actual outer radius of steel pipe or tubing, in (mm)

$r_2 = r_1 + tk$, radius to outside of insulation on piping, in (mm)

$eq\ tk = r_2 \ln (r_2/r_1)$, equivalent thickness of insulation on a pipe, in (mm)

f = surface air film coefficient, Btu/(h)(ft^2)(°F) [W/m^2 · °C] $1/f$ = surface resistance, (h)(ft^2)(°F)/Btu [m^2 · °C/W]

$R_1 = tk/k$, thermal resistance of insulation, (h)(ft^2)(°F)/Btu [m^2 · °C/W]

Q_F = heat flux through a flat surface, Btu/(h)(ft^2) [W/m^2]

$Q_P = Q_F \times 2\Pi r_2/12$, heat flux through a pipe, Btu/(h)(ft) (For SI, Q_P and $Q_F \times 2\Pi r_2$, W/m)

Δ = difference by subtraction, unitless

RH = relative humidity, percent

DP = dew-point temperature, °F(°C)

SI Conversions from USCS Units

$$k_{\text{Eng}} \times 144.2279 = k_{SI}$$

$$R_{\text{Eng}} \times 0.17611 = R_{\text{SU}}$$

$$Q_{F,\ \text{Eng}} \times 3.155 = Q_{F,\ \text{SU}}$$

$$Q_{P,\ \text{Eng}} \times 0.962 = Q_{P,\ \text{SI}}$$

Specific SI units use kelvins rather than degrees Celsius, but in Δ calculations, there is no difference between the two. Degrees Celsius are used here for convenience.

Calculation Fundamentals

There are two concepts that must be understood before proceeding with the calculations. First in a system in steady-state equilibrium, the heat transfer through each portion of the system is the same. Specifically, the heat transfer through the insulation is equal to the heat transfer from the insulation surface to the surrounding air.

Since the heat loss is proportional to both the temperature difference and thermal resistance of any portion of the system, the following equations result:

$$Q = \frac{t_h - t_a}{R_1 + R_s} = \frac{t_h - t_s}{R_1} = \frac{t_s - t_a}{R_s} \qquad (2)$$

The second principle relates to the equivalent-thickness concept of pipe insulation. Since the outer insulation surface area is greater than the interior surface area, the heat flux "sees" a greater insulation thickness than the installed nominal thickness of the material. This equivalent thickness (*eq tk*) is used as the insulation thickness for the thermal calculation, but the nominal thickness is used for calculating the surface area per linear foot of insulated pipe. The equation for equivalent thickness is:

$$eq\ tk = r_2 \ln \frac{r_2}{r_1} \qquad (3)$$

where r_1 and r_2 represent the inner and outer radii of the insulation system, respectively. Figure 4-4 provides for easy conversion to equivalent thickness from any specific thickness and

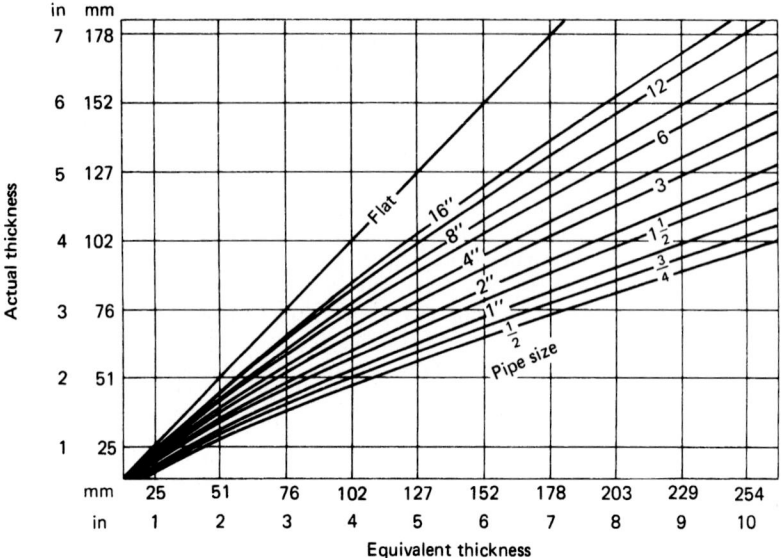

FIGURE 4-4   Equivalent thickness chart.[5]

pipe size. Some materials are manufactured in true even thicknesses, whereas most others follow the schedule in ASTM C 585. In any event, the proper determination of insulation resistance for pipe insulation is

$$R_I = \frac{eq\ tk}{k}$$

Figures 4-5 and 4-6 provide typical thermal conductivity values for sample calculations.

After the material is selected, an appropriate thickness of the material as well as the heat loss or gain with that thickness must be determined. The proper amount of insulation to use

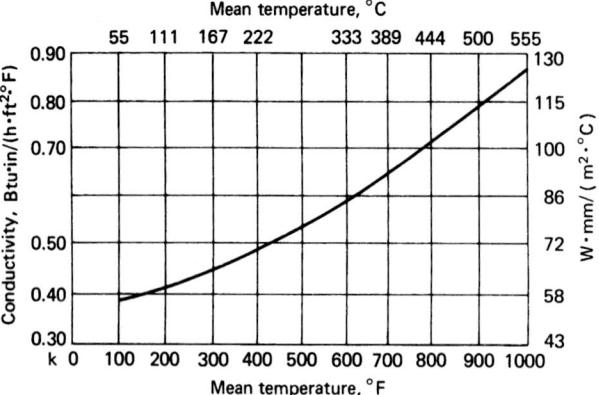

FIGURE 4-5   Thermal conductivity for typical calcium silicate pipe insulation.

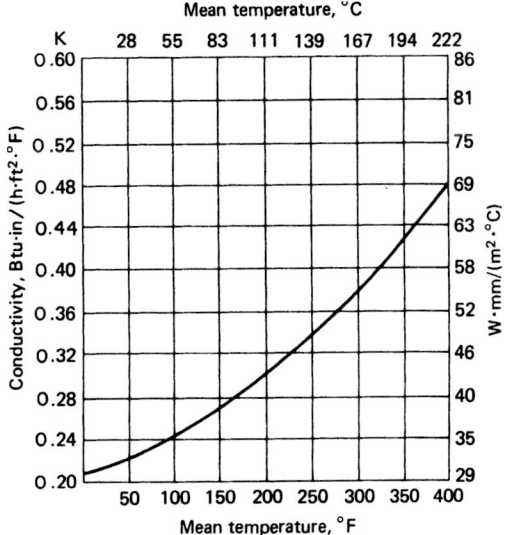

FIGURE 4-6 Thermal conductivity for typical fiberglass pipe insulation.

depends on the *thermal design objective* of the system: What is the insulation supposed to accomplish? There are five broad categories that encompass most insulation objectives:

1. Personnel protection
2. Condensation control
3. Process control
4. Economics
5. Energy and environment conservation

Personnel Protection

To protect workers from getting burned on hot piping, the insulation surface temperature should be within the safe touch range of 130 to 150°F; 140°F(60°C) is the temperature most often specified. Both ambient temperature and surface resistance R are important in this calculation.

As noted in Table 4-1, the R_s values for aluminum are greater than for full surfaces and will result in higher surface temperatures for the aluminum over the same thickness of insulation.

To calculate the thickness required to achieve a specific surface temperature, the basic heat-loss equation is manipulated as follows:

$$Q = \frac{t_h - t_s}{R_I} = \frac{t_s - t_a}{R_s}$$

$$R_I = R_s \frac{t_h - t_s}{t_s - t_a} \quad \text{and} \quad R_I = \frac{eq\ tk}{k}$$

$$\therefore eq\ tk = kR_s \frac{t_h - t_s}{t_s - t_a}$$

Example. An 8-in pipe is in operation at 700°F (371°C) ambient temperature with aluminum jacketing. Determine the thickness of calcium silicate required to keep the surfaces at 140°F (60°C).

Step 1.   Determine k at $T_m = (740 + 140)/2 = 420°F$:

$$k = 0.49 \ (\text{Btu})(\text{in})/(h)(Ft^2)(F) \ [71 \ W.mm/(m^2)(C)$$

from Fig. 4-4 for calcium silicate.

Step 2.   Determine R_s from Table 5-1 for aluminum:

$$t_s - t_a = 140 - 85 = 55°F$$

So, $R_s = 0.85 \ (h)(ft^2)(°F)/\text{Btu} \ [0.1497 \ (m^2)(°C)/W]$

Step 3.   Calculate

$$eq \ tk = (0.49)(0.85)(700 - 140)/(140 - 85)$$

$$= 4.24 \ \text{in}$$

In SI units $= (71)(0.1497)(371.11 - 60)/(60 - 29.44)$

$$= 10.8 \ \text{mm}$$

Step 4.   Determine from Fig. 4-4 that 4.24 in $eq \ tk$ on an 8-in pipe can be accomplished with 3.25-in (83-mm) insulation. Always rounding off to the next half-inch increment, the recommendation would be 3.5-in (89-mm) calcium silicate.

Condensation Control

On cold systems, the insulation thickness must be sufficient to keep the insulation surface above the dew point of the ambient air. Table 4-4 gives the dew point for various temperature and relative-humidity combinations. The calculation is the same as for personnel protection with the surface temperature taking on the value of the dew-point temperature.

$$eq \ tk = kR_s \frac{(t_h - DP)}{(DP - t_a)}$$

Example. A 4-in (10 cm) diam chilled water line is operating at 40°F (4.4°C) in an ambient temperature of 90°F (32.2°C) and 90 percent RH. Determine the amount of fiberglass pipe insulation with a kraft jacket required to prevent condensation.

Step 1.   The dew point from Table 4-4 for 90°F, 90 percent RH is DP = 87°F (30.6°C)

Step 2.   Determine k at $t_m = (40 + 87)/2 = 63.5°F$ (17.5°C); $k = 0.23$ from Fig. 4-6 for fiberglass

Step 3.   Determine R_s from Table 4-1 for fabric jacket and t_a − DP = 90 − 87 = 3°F (−16.1°C), $R_s = 0.54$

Step 4.   Calculate $eq \ tk = (0.23)(0.54) \ (40 - 87)/(87 - 90) = 1.95$ in (49.5 mm)

Step 5.   Actual thickness required from Fig. 4-4 for a 4-in (101-mm) pipe is 1.5 in (38.1 mm). It would not be unreasonable to specify 2-in (50.8-mm) thickness for this application since 1.5 in is borderline.

Table 4-5 gives the thickness of fiberglass pipe insulation required to prevent condensation for various operating temperatures and three different ambient conditions.

Process Control

There are many complex flow calculations required to determine the amount of insulation required to maintain process temperature or allow a specific temperature drop. The simple calculation below is for determining heat loss only and is basic to all the process control calculations. The heat loss from a pipe is

$$Q_p = Q_F \frac{2\pi r_2}{12} = \frac{t_h - t_a}{R_I + R_s} \frac{2\pi r_2}{12} \qquad \text{Btu/(h)(ft)} \qquad (4)$$

where

$$R_I = \frac{eq\ tk}{k}$$

In this calculation, a surface temperature t_s first must be estimated to arrive at a t_m and R_s. Then, when the t_s estimate is checked, the calculation can be redone with the new estimate if necessary.

Example. A 16-in diameter steam line operating at 850°F (454°C) in an 80°F (27°C) ambient temperature is insulated with 3.5 in (89 mm) of calcium silicate with an aluminum jacket. Determine the heat loss per linear foot and the surface temperature.

Step 1.   Assume $t_s = 140°F$, $t_m = \dfrac{850 + 140}{2} = 495°F$; k from Fig. 4-5 for calcium silicate is 0.53.

Step 2.   Determine R_s for aluminum from Table 4-1 for $t_s - t_a = 60°F$; $R_s = 0.85$.

Step 3.   Determine $eq\ tk$ from Fig. 4-4 for 3.5 in (9 cm) on a 16-in (40-cm) pipe, $eq\ tk = 4.2$ in:

$$R_I = \frac{eq\ tk}{k} = \frac{4.2}{0.53} = 7.92$$

Step 4.   Calculate heat loss per square foot:

$$Q_F = \frac{850 - 80}{7.92 + 0.85} = 87.8 \text{ Btu/(h)(ft}^2) \ [(227 \text{ W/m}^2)]$$

Step 5.   Check surface temperature assumption by

$$t_s = t_a + (R_s \times Q_F) = 80 + (0.85 \times 87.8)$$
$$= 155°F$$

This leads to a new $t_m = 502.5$, which is close enough to the assumed $t_m = 495$ that k will not change.

Step 6.   Calculate heat loss per linear foot:

$$Q_p = Q_F \frac{2\pi r_2}{12} = 87.8 \frac{2\pi(8 + 3.5)}{12}$$
$$= 529 \text{ Btu/(h)ft} \qquad (508 \text{ W/m})$$

Freeze Protection

Water lines must either be heat-traced or have a controlled flow to prevent freezing. These calculations can be performed for various combinations of water temperature, line length, and ambient conditions. Table 4-6 shows the number of hours until freezing occurs along with

TABLE 4-4 Dew-Point Temperature

Dry-bulb temp, °F	Percent relative humidity																		
	10	15	20	25	30	35	40	45	50	55	60	65	70	75	80	85	90	95	100
5	-35	-30	-25	-21	-17	-14	-12	-10	-8	-6	-5	-4	-2	-1	1	2	3	4	5
10	-31	-25	-20	-16	-13	-10	-7	-5	-3	-2	0	2	3	4	5	7	8	9	10
15	-28	-21	-16	-12	-8	-5	-3	-1	1	3	5	6	8	9	10	12	13	14	15
20	-24	-16	-11	-8	-4	-2	2	4	6	8	10	11	13	14	15	16	18	19	20
25	-20	-15	-8	-4	0	3	6	8	10	12	15	16	18	19	20	21	23	24	25
30	-15	-9	-3	2	5	8	11	13	15	17	20	22	23	24	25	27	28	29	30
35	-12	-5	1	5	9	12	15	18	20	22	24	26	27	28	30	32	33	34	35
40	-7	0	5	9	14	16	19	22	24	26	28	29	31	33	35	36	38	39	40
45	-4	3	9	13	17	20	23	25	28	30	32	34	36	38	39	41	43	44	45
50	-1	7	13	17	21	24	27	30	32	34	37	39	41	42	44	45	47	49	50
55	3	11	16	21	25	28	32	34	37	39	41	43	45	47	49	50	52	53	55
60	6	14	20	25	29	32	35	39	42	44	46	48	50	52	54	55	57	59	60
65	10	18	24	28	33	38	40	43	46	49	51	53	55	57	59	60	62	63	65
70	13	21	28	33	37	41	45	48	50	53	55	57	60	62	64	65	67	68	70
75	17	25	32	37	42	46	49	52	55	57	60	62	64	66	69	70	72	74	75
80	20	29	35	41	46	50	54	57	60	62	65	67	69	72	74	75	77	78	80
85	23	32	40	45	50	54	58	61	64	67	69	72	74	76	78	80	82	83	85
90	27	36	44	49	54	58	62	66	69	72	74	77	79	81	83	85	87	89	90
95	30	40	48	54	59	63	67	70	73	76	79	82	84	86	88	90	91	93	95
100	34	44	52	58	63	68	71	75	78	81	84	86	88	91	92	94	96	98	100
105	38	48	56	62	67	72	76	79	82	85	88	90	93	95	97	99	101	103	105
110	41	52	60	66	71	77	80	84	87	90	92	95	98	100	102	104	106	108	110
115	45	56	64	70	75	80	84	88	91	94	97	100	102	105	107	109	111	113	115
120	48	60	68	74	79	85	88	92	96	99	102	105	107	109	112	114	116	118	120
125	52	63	72	78	84	89	93	97	100	104	107	109	114	117	119	121	123	125

-15.0	-37.2	-34.4	-31.7	-29.4	-27.2	-25.6	-24.4	-23.3	-22.2	-21.1	-20.6	-20.0	-18.9	-18.3	-17.2	-16.7	-16.1	-15.6	-15.0
-12.2	-35.0	-31.7	-28.9	-26.7	-25.0	-23.3	-21.7	-20.6	-19.4	-18.9	-17.8	-17.2	-16.1	-15.6	-15.0	-13.9	-13.3	-12.8	-12.2
-9.4	-33.3	-29.4	-26.7	-24.4	-22.8	-20.6	-19.4	-17.8	-16.7	-15.6	-15.0	-14.4	-13.3	-12.8	-11.7	-11.1	-10.6	-10.0	-9.4
-6.7	-31.1	-26.7	-24.4	-22.2	-20.0	-18.3	-16.7	-15.0	-14.4	-13.3	-12.2	-11.7	-10.6	-10.0	-8.9	-7.8	-7.2	-6.7	-6.7
-3.9	-28.9	-23.9	-22.2	-20.0	-17.8	-16.1	-14.4	-12.2	-11.7	-10.6	-9.4	-8.9	-7.8	-7.2	-6.1	-5.0	-4.4	-3.9	-3.9
-1.1	-26.1	-22.8	-20.6	-18.9	-16.1	-13.3	-11.7	-9.4	-8.9	-7.8	-6.7	-6.1	-5.0	-4.4	-3.3	-2.2	-1.7	-1.1	-1.1
1.7	-24.4	-20.6	-19.4	-16.7	-14.4	-11.7	-10.0	-7.8	-6.7	-5.6	-4.4	-3.9	-2.8	-2.2	-1.1	0.0	0.6	1.1	1.7
4.4	-21.7	-17.8	-17.2	-15.0	-12.2	-10.6	-7.8	-6.7	-4.4	-3.3	-2.2	-1.7	-0.6	0.0	1.1	2.2	2.8	3.3	4.4
7.2	-20.0	-16.1	-15.6	-13.3	-11.7	-8.9	-6.7	-4.4	-3.9	-2.2	-1.1	-0.6	0.6	1.1	2.2	3.9	5.0	6.1	7.2
10.0	-18.3	-13.9	-12.8	-11.7	-9.4	-7.8	-5.0	-3.3	-2.2	-0.6	0.0	1.1	2.2	3.3	3.9	5.6	6.7	8.3	10.0
12.8	-16.1	-11.7	-10.6	-8.9	-6.7	-5.0	-3.3	-1.1	0.0	1.1	2.8	3.9	5.0	5.6	7.2	8.3	9.4	11.1	12.8
15.6	-14.4	-10.0	-8.9	-6.7	-4.4	-2.2	-0.6	1.1	2.8	3.9	5.0	6.1	7.2	8.3	9.4	11.1	12.8	13.9	15.6
18.3	-12.2	-7.8	-6.7	-4.4	-2.2	0.0	1.7	3.9	5.0	6.1	7.8	8.9	10.0	11.1	13.3	13.9	15.0	16.7	18.3
21.1	-10.6	-6.1	-4.4	-2.2	0.0	1.7	3.9	5.6	6.7	7.8	9.4	10.6	11.7	12.8	13.9	15.6	16.7	18.9	21.1
23.9	-8.3	-3.9	-2.2	0.0	1.7	3.9	6.1	7.8	8.9	10.0	11.1	12.8	13.9	15.0	16.1	17.8	19.4	20.6	23.9
26.7	-6.7	-2.2	0.0	2.8	3.9	6.1	8.3	10.0	11.1	12.8	13.9	15.0	16.1	17.2	18.3	20.0	21.7	23.3	26.7
29.4	-5.0	0.0	2.8	5.0	6.7	8.9	10.6	12.8	13.9	15.0	16.7	17.8	18.9	20.0	21.1	22.8	24.4	25.6	29.4
32.2	-2.8	1.7	5.0	7.2	8.9	11.1	12.8	15.0	16.1	17.2	18.9	20.0	21.1	22.2	23.3	25.0	26.7	28.3	32.2
35.0	-1.1	4.4	7.2	9.4	11.1	13.3	15.6	17.2	18.3	19.4	21.1	22.2	23.3	24.4	25.6	27.2	28.9	31.1	35.0
37.8	1.1	6.7	9.4	12.2	14.4	16.1	18.9	20.0	21.7	22.8	24.4	25.0	26.1	27.2	28.3	30.0	31.7	33.3	37.8
40.6	3.3	8.9	11.7	14.4	16.7	18.9	21.1	22.8	23.9	25.0	27.2	27.8	28.9	30.0	31.1	32.8	33.9	36.1	40.6
43.3	5.0	11.1	13.3	16.7	19.4	21.1	23.3	25.6	26.7	27.8	30.0	30.6	31.7	32.8	33.9	35.6	36.7	38.3	43.3
46.1	7.2	13.3	15.6	18.9	21.7	23.3	26.1	27.8	28.9	30.6	31.7	32.8	33.9	35.0	36.1	37.8	39.4	41.1	46.1
48.9	8.9	15.6	17.8	21.1	23.9	25.6	27.8	30.0	31.1	32.2	33.9	35.0	36.1	37.8	38.3	40.6	42.2	43.9	48.9
51.7	11.1	17.2	22.2	25.6	28.9	31.7	33.9	36.1	37.8	40.0	41.7	42.8	43.9	45.6	47.2	48.3	49.4	50.6	51.7

TABLE 4-5   Minimum Insulation Thickness of Fiberglass Pipe Insulation Needed to Prevent Condensation (Based on Still Air and AP Jacket)

Operating pipe temperature	80°F (26.6°C) & 90% RH			80°F (26.6°C) & 70% RH			80°F (26.6°C) & 50% RH		
		Thickness			Thickness			Thickness	
	Pipe size, in	in	mm	Pipe size, in	in	mm	Pipe size, in	in	mm
0–34°F (−18–1°C)	Up to 1	2	51						
	1¼ to 2	2½	63	Up to 8	1	25	Up to 8	½	13
	2½ to 8	3	76	9 to 30	1½	38	9 to 30	1	25
	9 to 30	3½	89						
35–49°F (1–9°C)	Up to 1½	1½	38						
	2 to 8	2	51	Up to 4	½	13	Up to 30	½	13
	9 to 30	3	76	4½ to 30	1	25			
50–70°F (10–21°C)	Up to 3	1½	38						
	3½ to 20	2	51	Up to 30	½	13	Up to 30	½	13
	21 to 30	2½	63						

Source: Schuller International, Inc., Ref. 5.

the gallons per minute flow required in a 100-ft (30.3-m) pipe run to prevent freezing. The calculations are based on fiberglass pipe insulation with $k = 0.23$, initial water temperature of 42°F (6°C), and an ambient air temperature of −10°F (−23°C). The flow rate for the 100-ft (30.3-m) length may be prorated for longer or shorter pipes.

Economics

With energy costs on the rise, insulating for economic reasons is becoming the standard for most insulation-thickness calculations. The first economic thickness equations were presented in a 1926 by L.B. McMillan[8]. Since then, many monographs and computer programs

TABLE 4-6   Freeze Protection Data, Hours to Freeze, and Flow Rate (gal/min) Required to Prevent Freezing*

Nominal pipe size IPS	Insulation thickness					
	1 in		2 in		3 in	
	Hours to freeze	Flow rate, gal/min per 100 ft	Hours to freeze	Flow rate, gal/min per 100 ft	Hours to freeze	Flow rate, gal/min per 100 ft
½	0.30	0.087	0.42	0.282	0.50	0.053
¾	0.47	0.098	0.66	0.070	0.79	0.058
1	0.66	0.113	0.96	0.078	1.16	0.065
1½	0.90	0.144	1.35	0.096	1.67	0.078
2	1.72	0.169	2.64	0.110	3.31	0.088
2½	2.13	0.195	3.33	0.124	4.24	0.098
3	2.81	0.228	4.50	0.142	5.80	0.110
4	3.95	0.279	6.49	0.170	8.49	0.130
5	5.21	0.332	8.69	0.199	11.54	0.150
6	6.48	0.386	10.98	0.228	14.71	0.170
7	7.66	0.437	13.14	0.255	17.75	0.189
8	8.89	0.487	15.37	0.282	20.89	0.207

* Based upon 42°F (6°C) initial water temperature and −10°F (−23°C) ambient temperature.
Source: Schuller International, Inc., Ref. 5.

have been developed to perform these complex calculations[10]. Discounted cash-flow techniques, fuel escalation, maintenance and installed insulation costs, and after-tax effects are all involved in the computations.

However, the economic thickness of insulation (ETI) concept is still quite simple. Economic thickness is defined as that thickness of insulation at which the cost of the next increment is just offset by the energy savings due to that increment over the life of the project (see Fig. 4-7.).

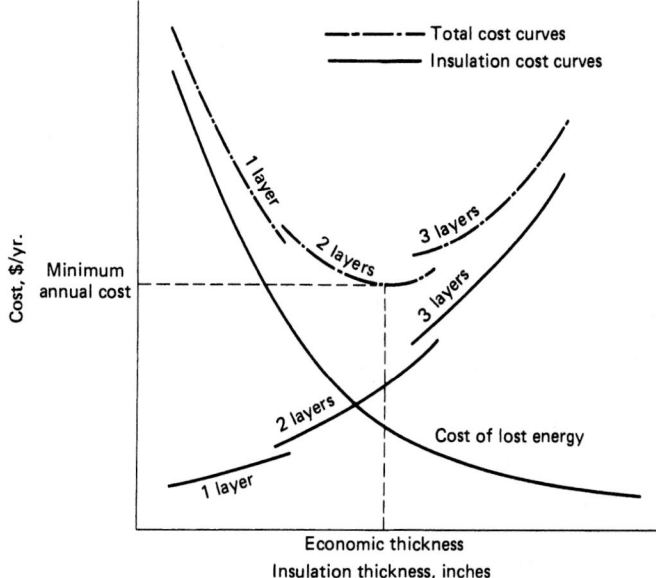

FIGURE 4-7   Economic thickness of insulation (ETI).

Energy and Environment Conservation

This era brings a new set of energy management challanges including a renewed focus on conservation measures and emisson reductions in the manufacturing sector. A national study completed in 1990 found that thermal insulation offers one of the most significant means to conserve energy and reduce CO_2 emissions. The study sponsored by the North American Insulation Manufacturers Association (NAIMA) and conducted by Dr. Harry L. Brown, Professor of Mechanical Engineering and Mechanics, Drexel University, found a potential reduction of 78 million tons of CO_2 emissions and equivalent fuel savings of up to 204 million barrels of oil a year by insulating bare pipe and equipment and upgrading existing insulation to the economic thickness of insulation (ETI). In order to determine the ETI insulation thickness, heat loss, surface temperature, annual payback energy cost, and annual savings, a computer program was developed with a published a set of tables. The computer program entitled "3E-Plus for Energy * Environment * Economics" incorporates the economic parameters required to calculate the ETI insulation thickness, fuel savings, and reduction of CO_2 emissions. (See Ref. 12.)

Values used in these calculations are:

Annual hours of operation	8760
Fuel cost	$2, $6, $10 per million Btu

Annual fuel inflation rate	5%
Interest rate or return on investment	10%
Effective income tax rate	30%
Physical plant depreciation period	15 years
New insulation depreciation period	15 years
Incremental equipment investment rate	2.00 $/million Btu/h
Percent of new insulation cost for annual insulation maintenance	5%
Percent of annual fuel bill for physical plant maintenance	5%
Ambient temperature	75°F
Emittance of outer jacketing (oxidized aluminum)	0.15
Wind speed	0 mi/h
Emittance of existing bare pipe surface	0.90
Reference thickness for payback calculations (bare pipe, no insulation)	0.0 in
Labor rate (means building construction cost data—1991)	$38.35

Below are the results calculated for a 6-in steam pipe operating at 450°F (232°C) using natural gas at $3.36 per MCF with a heating value of 1000 Btu per MCF. As seen by the results listed in Fig. 4-7, the 3E-Plus computer program is a powerful tool by which to begin conserving fuel and reducing emissions by including an insulation upgrade package in your energy management.

Economic thickness at 450°F	3 in
Heat loss	115 Btu/ft/h
Surface temperature	123°F
Payback	.4 of a year
Annual cost of owning insulation is	$8.41 ft/yr
Total annual savings	$89/ft/yr
CO_2 reduction	2131/lb/ln ft/yr
Total annual fuel savings for 1000 feet	$8900.00
Total CO_2 reduction	2,131,000 lb/yr

REFERENCES

1. McAdams, W. H.: *Heat Transmission,* McGraw-Hill, New York, 1954

2. Sparrow, E. M., and R. D. Cess: *Radiation Heat Transfer,* McGraw-Hill, New York, 1978.

3. Greebler, P.: "Thermal Properties and Applications of High Temperature Aircraft Insulation," American Rocket Society, 1954. Reprinted in *Jet Propulsion,* November-December 1954.

4. American Society for Testing Materials: *Annual Book of ASTM Standards,* Vol. 04.06, Thermal Insulation; Environmental Acoustics.

5. Schuller International, Inc., Mechanical Insulations Division. Technical and Product Data Sheets, Denver, CO.

6. Kanakia, M., W. Herrera, and F. Hutto, Jr.: "Fire Resistance Tests for Thermal Insulation," *Journal of Thermal Insulation,* Vol. 1, No. 4, Technomic Publishing Company, Westport, CT, April 1978.

7. *Commercial & Industrial Insulation Standards,* Midwest Insulation Contractors Association, Omaha, NE, 1979.

8. Malloy, J. F.: *Thermal Insulation,* Reinhold, New York, 1969.

9. ASTM, Vol. 04.06, Standard C 585 (see Ref. 4).

10. McMillan, L. B.: "Heat Transfer through Insulation in the Moderate and High Temperature Fields: A Statement of Existing Data," No. 2034, The American Society of Mechanical Engineers, New York, 1934.

11. *Economic Thickness of Industrial Insulation,* Conservation Paper No. 46, Federal Energy Administration, Washington, DC, 1976. Available from Superintendent of Documents, U.S. Government Printing Office, Washington, DC 20402, Stock #041-018-00115-8.

12. NAIMA "3E-Plus" Computer Program, 44 Canal Center Plaza, #310, Alexandria, VA 22314.

CHAPTER 10-5
INDUSTRIAL HOSE

Ron Wacker
Product Application Engineer
Gates Rubber Company
Denver, Colorado

INTRODUCTION

There are many varieties of industrial hose and associated couplings. Each type is designed to give a satisfactory and safe level of performance for particular applications where needed for flexible conveyance of liquids, gases, and certain solids in powder or granular form.

To obtain maximum service for any type of industrial hose, the user must: consider the application, select certified hose and coupling combinations assembled to the manufacturer's specifications, take reasonable care of the hose assembly, and observe all applicable safety regulations. Periodic inspection of the hose is vital! Even properly selected hose has a limited service life which is effected by many factors such as handling, use, storage, and the environment.

Even regular care, inspection, and maintenance would help very little to prolong the life of an industrial hose assembly *that was not originally selected to suit the application.* Hoses will soon fail regardless of the care given them in situations that are beyond the design of the hose.

For example: A hose with a natural rubber tube will fail in gasoline service. The tube stock swells, the hose loses its tensile strength and discolors the fluid. High pressures will burst a hose designed for low pressure; coupled assemblies will fail when low-pressure couplings are used on high-pressure hoses. A hose with a steel wire support helix is run over and permanently crushed by a forklift. But a hose with a plastic support helix is resilient or relatively crush-resistant and will often spring back open when the external force is removed and will be fully functional again. And a hose with a thin tube not resistant to abrasion will soon wear through when handling abrasive products.

So that safest and most reliable service can be obtained, the plant engineer needs to know a few basic things about industrial hose—such as the kinds of hose available, limitations and applications, care and maintenance. We look at these factors one by one.

TYPES OF INDUSTRIAL HOSE

Following are brief descriptions of, and recommendations for, the basic kinds of industrial hose.

Air Hose

Air hose is used for efficient handling of air and compressed air in low-pressure industrial applications. These hoses can be used for air tools, air drills, air and vapor ducts, agriculture, and paint spraying.

Water Hose

Water hoses are designed for transport of water (but not recommended for use as vibration dampers or in closed water systems). Applications include water suction, water discharge, cleanup, and general-purpose water usage.

Steam Hose

This is a very specialized hose used to convey wet saturated steam, dry saturated steam, and superheated steam. Alternating between water and steam is not recommended because it may cause "popcorning" or bursting of gas pockets, thus blowing holes in the inner tube of the hose.

Materials-Handling Hose

These are specially designed to handle a wide variety of bulk commodities. Applications include: beverage and food, sand suction, dredge sleeves, cement, plaster, vacuums, sand blasting, fish handling, grains and flour.

Acid and Chemical Hose

These hoses are designed to withstand the corrosive effects of caustic, acidic, oxidizing, or chlorinated liquids as well as toxic substances such as anhydrous ammonia. Particular caution should be taken with these applications due to the potential for extremely hazardous conditions.

Petroleum-Transfer Hose

This is manufactured particularly to handle fuel oil, liquid petroleum gases, hot asphalt, gasoline, and diesel fuel.

HOSE CONSTRUCTION

Industrial hose generally consists of three parts—tube, reinforcement, and cover—plus all the necessary cements. See Fig. 5-1.

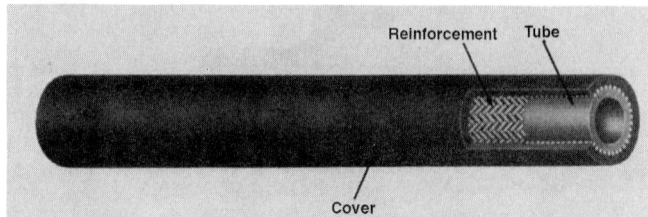

FIGURE 5-1 Reinforced-hose construction. *(Gates Rubber Company.)*

Tube

The *tube* is the inner layer and its function is to contain the substance being transported and evenly transmit forces, due to pressure, to the reinforcing element. Made of rubber or plastic, it is either extruded or made from sheet stock by spiraling or laminating this material onto the manufacturing mandrel.

Reinforcement

Outside the tube is the *reinforcement*. This is the material which provides the overall strength, pressure resistance, and sometimes the collapse resistance.

For some industrial hose applications, the service pressure is low enough that the strength of the tube stock is sufficient to meet the required service. This hose is called tubing, or non-reinforced, hose. All other hoses require some type of textile, plastic, or wire reinforcement. Common textile reinforcements are made of cotton, rayon, nylon, and polyester; and they may take the form of a yarn- or fabric-like material. Wire reinforcements vary as to size and composition of the material used to make the wire. Plastics are sometimes used in helical filament form to resist collapse from suction or external pressure. Identification of the hose usually relates to the method of reinforcement. For example, a hose with a braid reinforcement would be called a braided hose. Following are the principal forms of reinforcement.

- **Knit.** The knit reinforcement is applied around the tube by a knitting machine. A lock-stitch pattern provides greater resistance to diametrical hose growth. Knit hose is used in low-pressure ranges, seldom exceeding 100 to 120 lb/in^2 (680 to 816 kPa).

- **Braid.** Braided hose has the reinforcement—either yarn or wire—applied by using horizontal or vertical braiders. The terms vertical and horizontal refer to the axis of the hose as it is being braided. Hose with a braid reinforcement finds applications in many areas, including air, water, hydraulic, and steam. Braided hoses are generally more flexible than spiral-reinforced hose.

- **Spiral.** Spiral-reinforced hose has all the wire or textile strands in one layer laid parallel on the hose in one direction. At least two layers, or multiples of two layers, of reinforcement are normally required: with the layers spiraled in alternating directions to form a balanced construction. Additional layers of reinforcement may be applied to increase the service-pressure level, with a usual maximum of six layers. Typical applications of spiral hose range from low-pressure general-purpose to high-pressure hydraulic.

- **Wrapped.** The greatest variety of hoses are those in which woven reinforcement is wrapped onto the tube. These hoses range from ¼-in-ID (6.35 cm) air hose up to 36 to 48-in (91.4 to 121.9 cm) diam suction and discharge hose. Wrapped hoses have the reinforcement applied by either spiraling or laminating the material onto the tube. There can be less open space between spiral reinforcement strands than with braid and therefore more support of the tube. The sacrifice is often less flexibility than with a braided reinforcement construction.

Cover

The *cover* is usually a rubber or plastic layer placed over the reinforcement. It protects the reinforcement and serves to keep elements such as weather, abrasion, and chemicals from weakening it.

The application of a cover over the reinforcement is completed in much the same manner as the tube is fabricated. The cover may be applied using an extruder to form a seamless, cylindrical tube around the hose or by spiraling or laminating calendered cover material onto a mandrel-supported hose.

SELECTION OF INDUSTRIAL HOSE

The industrial hose purchaser should determine the following:

1. Inside diameter of hose required, which can be determined from the flow rate needed to transport the material
2. Length required
3. Material to be conveyed, including chemical makeup and temperature range
4. Suction and/or discharge rated working pressure
5. Hose ends or fittings required
6. External environment (temperature range, corrosive fluids, complete weather conditions)
7. External stresses (kinking, crushing, pulling, excessive bending)
8. Special customer requirements, government and safety regulations, special tests, and industry specifications such as SAE, U.L., MSHA, etc.

When analyzing the cost differences among industrial hoses to be selected for in-plant piping, several factors must be considered. Keep in mind that matching a hose to the application that it was designed to handle is a prerequisite to any cost evaluation.

First consider the method of construction. A vertical braided hose is the least expensive because it is built in long, continuous lengths and its reinforcement consists of yarn or wire. Vertical braided hoses have small inside diameters, up to 1½ in. The horizontal braided hose construction provides larger hose diameters and greater working pressures than the vertical braided construction. Reinforcements consist of one or more layers of braided fibers or wire. Horizontal braided-wire reinforcement is similar to the standard horizontal braided hose with the addition of a reinforcing wire spiralled between the fiber braid reinforcement. Wrapped and wire-reinforced hoses are the most expensive, primarily because they are individually hand-built. Wire spiraled onto the hose between multiple plies of wrapped fabrics also adds to the cost of making these hoses.

Realizing that the mass-produced vertical braided hose is less expensive than wrapped hose and that yarn reinforcement usually costs less than wire, the next cost factor to be considered is the stock type used to construct the tube and cover of the hose. Considerations of performance and cost must be balanced. Table 5-1 shows the elastomers most commonly used in industrial hose in order of relative cost, from top to bottom.

The general properties listed in Table 5-1 provide a reliable guideline. However, the user should always follow the manufacturer's recommendations as to the use of any particular rubber composition. This is especially true with respect to the resistance of the rubber composition to the materials it is exposed to, from within and without. Temperature can have a dramatic effect on chemical compatibility. A hose may carry a material quite safely at room temperature but begin to degrade or swell if exposed to the same material at higher temperatures.

Although the construction methods and materials used to make the hose provide a cost comparison, a true cost index must take into account certain variables. These include the dimensions of the hose, the quantity of materials used, and the changing price of many petroleum-based raw materials.

Table 5-2 is a selection of hose types most commonly found in industrial plants. The hoses are grouped by general application, description, and cost index.

TABLE 5-1   Characteristics of Hose Stock Types and Relative Cost Comparisons*

Common name	Usage in hose	Typical hose application	General properties
EPDM (Ethylene propylene diene)	Tube and cover	Steam (dry or wet), hot water, engine coolant, air (hot or cold), mild chemicals, and generally nonoily products	Excellent ozone, chemical, and aging characteristics; poor resistance to petroleum-based fluids
Natural rubber or synthetic (styrene-butadiene) rubber (SBR)	Tube and cover	Materials handling, water, air, chemicals, and generally nonoily products	Excellent abrasion and good low-temperature resistance; poor resistance to petroleum-based fluids
Buna-N	Tube	Fuel oils, diesel oils, aromatics, gasolines, and other petroleum products special applications	Excellent resistance to petroleum-based fluids; good physical properties; good resistance to heat and chemicals
Neoprene	Tube and cover	General-purpose air and water, saturated steam, materials handling, acid-chemical, and petroleum	Good to excellent abrasion, flame, petroleum, weathering, ozone, and heat resistance
Butyl	Tube and cover	Dry steam, engine coolant, hot air, chemicals, and generally nonoily products	Very good weathering resistance; low permeability to air; good physical properties
Hypalon	Tube and cover	Acid-chemical transfer	Excellent ozone, chemical, and aging resistance; good abrasion and heat resistance; fair resistance to petroleum-based fluids
Gatron	Tube	Acid-chemical transfer	Excellent general chemical, ozone, and weathering resistance; wide temperature flexibility range
FPM	Tube	Acid-chemical transfer	Excellent resistance to aromatic fluids and chlorinated hydrocarbons; outstanding heat resistance; excellent weathering resistance

* Chemical and physical properties are subject to a considerable amount of control through compounding. Characteristics given below for each stock type are therefore generalized to some degree. *These stocks are listed in order of relative costs*, with EPDM being the least expensive and FPM being the most expensive. Neoprene and Buna-N are in the same general cost range.

TABLE 5-2 Hose Types in Industrial Use

Application	Method of construction	Tube stock	Cover stock	Relative* cost index
General-purpose hose				
Low-pressure air or water	Spiral or vertical braided	EPDM	EPDM	1
High-pressure air or water (improved resistance to heat, oil, and abrasion)	Vertical braided	Buna-N	Neoprene	2
Petroleum-product transfer				
Aromatic fuels at full suction	Horizontal braided, wire reinforced	Buna-N	Neoprene	3
Butane-propane	Horizontal braided	Neoprene	Neoprene	4
Steam hose				
Saturated and superheated steam up to 250 lb/in² (1.72 MPa) and 450°F (232°C)	Wire braided (one or two layers)	EPDM	EPDM	5
Saturated steam up to 200 lb/in² (1.38 MPa) and 450°F (232°C)	Wire braided (one or two layers)	EPDM	EPDM	4
Materials-handling hose				
Bulk commodity, highly abrasion resistant	Wire reinforced	SBR	SBR	5
Food handling, primarily oils up to 150°F (65°C)	Wire reinforced	Food-grade neoprene	Neoprene	6
Dusty materials or abrasives in water suspension	Wire reinforced	Gum rubber (to absorb impact)	SBR	8
Acid-chemical transfer hose				
Strong, oxidizing solutions	Horizontal braided, wire reinforced	Hypalon	Neoprene	6
Highly aromatic fluids and chlorinated hydrocarbons	Horizontal braided, wire reinforced	FPM	Neoprene	12

* Using general-purpose hose as least expensive. Relative cost will vary, depending on size.

In applying any product, the more the plant engineer knows about the details of application, the better the product that can be selected to those needs. *This is particularly true with industrial hose because of the many variables involved.*

The process of selecting a hose usually involves one of two situations:

1. Making the optimum choice from several suitable selections for general application.

2. Making the one choice which satisfies all the requirements of a special application such as transferring anhydrous ammonia or LP gas.

In the first case, final selection is usually made on the basis of cost. In the second, it is usually a matter of satisfactorily meeting the most important or critical conditions *first* and then the conditions of lesser importance. Real cost takes into account the length of service life of the product.

SELECTION OF INDUSTRIAL COUPLINGS

In most hose catalogs, couplings are listed by name, and each is described as to construction, application, thread, and method of attaching it to the hose. Adapters and fittings are available for special applications. A complete up-to-date catalog should be obtained from the manufacturer before buying decisions are made.

Couplings can be grouped by a pressure rating of low, medium, or high. These terms have a general meaning as follows:

Low pressure   100 lb/in^2 (680. kPa) maximum

Medium pressure   315 lb/in^2 (2135 kPa) maximum

High pressure   800 lb/in^2 (5520 kPa) maximum

Coupling ratings apply only when the recommended clamps or bands are used. Care should be taken that the proper size of clamp is selected, since many clamps will fit only one size of hose or a narrow range of sizes. Some couplings are permanently attached to hose ends by crimping, swaging, or internal expansion. Always follow the manufacturer's recommendations for the methods that are available.

GENERAL APPLICATIONS

Five different coupling types can be used to handle approximately 90 percent of all hose applications found in industrial plants. The standard air-hose coupling or insert (Fig. 5-2) is a machine brass, low- or medium-pressure coupling for use on air hose.

The combination nipple (Fig. 5-3) is made of swaged steel pipe with scored or serrated shank and NPT (American Standard Taper Pipe Threads) threads on the male end. This nipple can be used with low- or medium-pressure water hose or materials handling hose.

Quick-connecting couplings (Fig. 5-4) are used primarily in medium-pressure applications where the hose is frequently connected and disconnected such as at tank farms, bulk-liquid storage receptacles, and tank trucks. The two parts of this coupling fit snugly together and are held in place by two cams on the female shank coupler which rotate against a groove in the male adapter.

For maximum safety when handling high-pressure air, water, or steam, special high-pressure couplings must be employed. These are interlocking couplings, with a ground joint seal or with a washer joint seal (Fig. 5-5).

A coupling especially recommended for use on air hose is the universal quick-acting coupling. Several types of heads are available, but all have the same size attaching heads regardless of the hose size (Figs. 5-6 to 5-9).

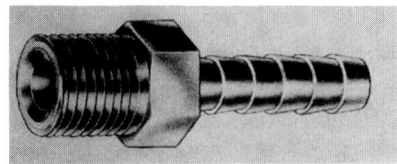

FIGURE 5-2   Air-hose coupling.

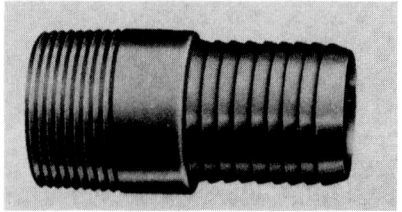

FIGURE 5-3   Combination nipple. *(Gates Rubber Company.)*

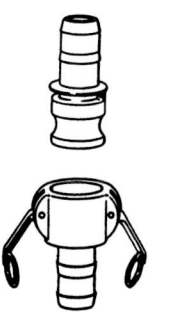

FIGURE 5-4 Quick-connecting coupling. *(Gates Rubber Company.)*

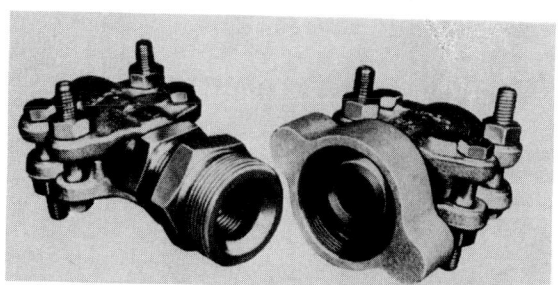

FIGURE 5-5 Interlocking coupling. *(Gates Rubber Company.)*

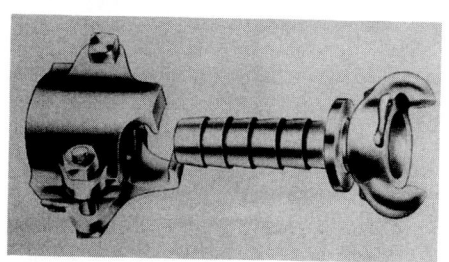

FIGURE 5-6 Quick-acting coupling, hose end (right), and clamp. *(Gates Rubber Company.)*

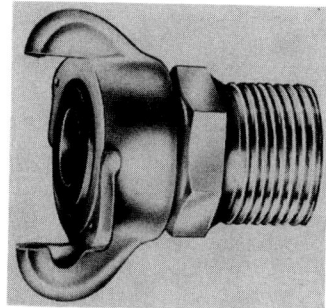

FIGURE 5-7 Quick-acting coupling, male end. *(Gates Rubber Company.)*

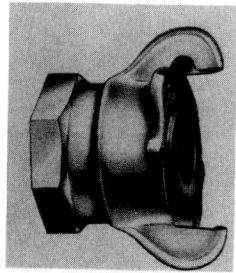

FIGURE 5-8 Quick-acting coupling, female end. *(Gates Rubber Company.)*

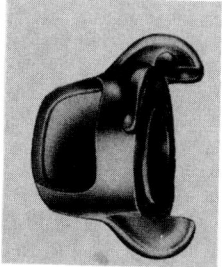

FIGURE 5-9 Quick-acting coupling, blank. *(Gates Rubber Company.)*

CRITICAL APPLICATIONS

For certain critical fluids, specific couplings are used, e.g., nonsparking for inflammable fluids. Below are guides to critical applications:

1. Use only the couplings recommended by the manufacturer for conveying:

   Steam

   LP gas

   Anhydrous ammonia

   Corrosive chemicals

   Petroleum products

2. For any high-temperature application, use only interlocking-type couplings.

3. For conveying flammable fluids, use couplings made of nonsparking materials, such as brass or aluminum.

4. For ground fueling of aircraft, use coupled assemblies only, as recommended by the supplier.

5. For food products use couplings made of materials approved by USDA and FDA, such as stainless steel.

Permanently swaged on or internally expanded couplings (Fig. 5-10) are often used on oil suction and discharge hoses, dredge hoses, or other material-handling hoses. Permanently crimped-on couplings (Fig. 5-11) may be specified for use on smaller diameter, general purpose hoses for air, water, etc. Built-in couplings (Fig. 5-12) also are often recommended for use with oil suction and discharge hoses, food grade hoses, and material-handling hoses.

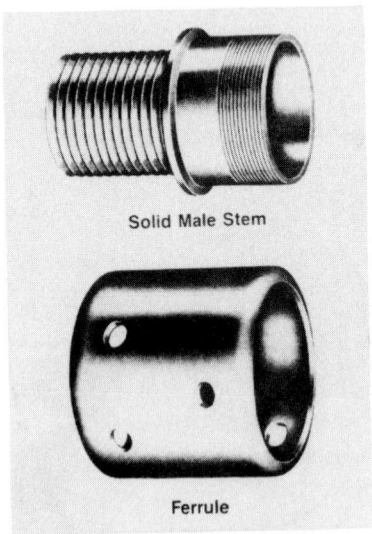

Solid Male Stem

Ferrule

FIGURE 5-10 Swage or internal expansion coupling. *(Gates Rubber Company.)*

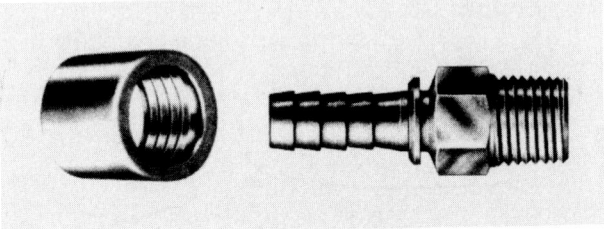

FIGURE 5-11 Permanent crimp-style couplings. *(Gates Rubber Company.)*

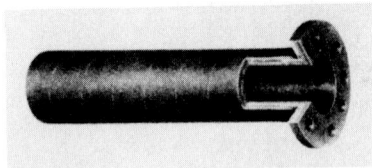

FIGURE 5-12 Permanent built-in couplings. *(Gates Rubber Company.)*

MAINTENANCE

Hose Care

Hose has definite service limitations and will certainly fail prematurely *if care is not taken to avoid exceeding these limitations.* General rules for caring for a hose are quite elementary but can be easily overlooked. They are especially important *because of the limited amount of maintenance or repair that can be made to extend the life of the hose assembly.*

Storage is important. If new hose is stored carefully, hose shelf life will be about 5 years before gradual deterioration begins. The hose should be stored in its original packing container or crate, out of direct sunlight. Avoid extremes of temperatures and exposure to ozone or direct heat. If the hose is shipped coiled, lay coils flat on the shelf; hose shipped straight should be stored straight.

Considerations for Hose Service

Environment.   The general rule is to avoid those conditions which will accelerate hose aging. If conditions are unusually severe, a hose designed for that application must be used.

First, avoid extreme heat or cold unless the hose has been designed and built to withstand such extremes. The typical industrial hose will give satisfactory life in a temperature range of 0 to 150°F (–18 to 65°C). At –20°F (–7°C) the hose will lose some flexibility. At –30 to –40°F (–14 to –40°C) normal hose may crack if flexed sharply. Special hoses are available that will be serviceable down to –60°F (–50°C).

The limitations at about 150°F (65°C) vary with the type of elastomer and service, so general rules cannot be given. Always follow the manufacturer's recommendations for hose to be used in high ambient temperatures. As temperature increases, the hose service life decreases. Temperatures below the lowest rating for the hose may result in cracks in the hose tube and cover during flexing.

In addition, exposure to high concentrations of ozone will cause hose covers to crack. This is not a problem with routine applications, but the cracking can be severe in high smog areas, or near electric generating machinery.

Finally, consider weathering. Hoses in continuous service outdoors should have weather-resistant covers and, in all cases, should not be continuously exposed to oil or corrosive chemicals.

External Abuse.   Do not over-bend the hose to the point of kinking. Always observe minimum-bend-radius recommendations. It is true that wire-reinforced hose may have greater rigidity, but it can be crushed or deformed by external weight or forces. Couplings and hose can also be damaged by too much end pull. A hard pull at any angle may kink the hose next to the coupling, especially in subzero temperatures. Never bend a hose at the coupling. Try to allow the hose to extend out from the coupling for a minimum distance of three times the outside diameter of the hose. Bend restrictors over the coupling and hose end may help keep hose from bending away from the coupling.

Large-diameter hoses [4-in (10-cm) ID and greater] have some special considerations. One problem may be overstressing the hose carcass. Handle heavy hoses with slings every 6 to 10 ft (2 to 3 m) and do not lift a long section from the middle with the ends hanging down.

Another concern—sometimes the hose cover is exposed to wear in one particular spot. In this case, the user should add a protective outside cover to avoid wearing through the cover and exposing the reinforcement.

Maintenance and Repair

Good maintenance programs including inspection, testing, and repair will ensure that maximum, safe service life is obtained from the hose and that damaged hose will be removed from service before it becomes a hazard.

All hoses should be inspected periodically. Hoses used in hazardous applications should be inspected at more frequent intervals. Basically, the user should be looking for evidence of stress or external abuse such as abrasion, cuts, and exposure to chemicals and oils. Obviously, the sources of these abuses should be corrected or eliminated.

The user should also look for evidence of failure that will necessitate taking the hose out of service or require recoupling or other repairs.

Inspection procedures for industrial hoses in nonhazardous applications are:

1. Lay hose out straight in a dry, lighted area.

2. Visually inspect hose for kinks, bulges, or soft spots in the cover, and excessive cover wear that exposes reinforcement. Evidence of this kind usually means the hose should be removed from service.

3. Inspect couplings for signs of slippage. Examine hose adjacent to couplings for breakage. If necessary, hose can be cut off behind the couplings and recoupled. Retighten bolted clamps if necessary.

4. Excessive amounts of oil or chemicals on the cover should be wiped off. Periodic or specialized inspection and testing are necessary for hoses used in hazardous applications. These hoses should be inspected at definite intervals following established procedures. The *Hose Handbook* and individual bulletins published by the Rubber Manufacturers Association outline daily inspection procedures for hoses used for hard-to-handle anhydrous ammonia, liquid petroleum gas, oil suction and discharge, and aviation ground fueling, as well as for motor-vehicle hose.

TABLE 5-3 OSHA Standards

Standards paragraph	Application
1910.106 Flammable and Combustible Liquids	General Transfer Curb pump, UL listed Flexible connectors, UL listed
1910.107 Spray Finishing Using Flammable and Combustible Materials	a. General, low, or medium pressure b. High pressure, airless, with static wire
1910.109 Explosives and Blasting Agents	As specified; special electrical properties
1910.110 Storage and Handling of LP Gas	As specified; UL listed
1910.111 Storage and Handling of Anhydrous Ammonia	Transfer service
1910.134 Respiratory Protection	Hoses for face masks
1910.158 Stand Pipe and Hose System for Fire Equipment	Various
1910.165a Sources of Standards	Fire extinguishers
1910.177 Indoor General Storage	Sprinkler systems
1910.243 Guarding of Portable Power Tools	Various air hoses
1910.1252 Welding, Cutting & Brazing	General welding and related

Hose Repair   Hoses can be recoupled to replace damaged couplings or to rejoin the ends of a failed section of hose that is cut out of the original length. The extent of recoupling or coupling repair that can be done depends on the type of couplings, the hose size, and, most importantly, the overall condition of the hose.

Hoses that have plain ends can be recoupled by cutting off the old coupling and applying a new one, provided the overall length is not too short. All braided hoses and some wrapped hoses up through 4-in (10-cm) ID have plain ends. Hoses having special ends or built-in couplings cannot normally be recoupled.

Large-diameter built-in nipples that have been worn thin by abrasives can be built up with plates. However, the rubber stock must be protected from any welding heat.

Beyond recoupling, there are very few ways in which a damaged or badly worn hose can be safely reclaimed. The hose manufacturer should be consulted for recommendations on how best to do this.

STANDARDS

Table 5-3 lists applicable OSHA standards and their applications.

BIBLIOGRAPHY

OSHA standards are contained in *Federal Register.* October 18, 1972, vol. 37, no. 22, part II.

Hose Handbook, Rubber Manufacturer's Association, 1901 Pennsylvania Ave., N.W., Washington, DC 20006.

"Industrial Hose Finder," No. 39995. The Gates Rubber Company, P. O. Box 5887, Denver, CO 80217.

CHAPTER 10-6
VALVES

Valve Manufacturers Association
Washington, D.C.

INTRODUCTION

A valve may be defined as a mechanical device by which the flow of liquid or gas may be started, stopped, or regulated by a movable part that opens, shuts, or partially obstructs one or more ports or passageways.

Plant engineers describe a valve as one of the most essential control instruments used in industry.

By the nature of their design and materials, valves can open and close, turn on and turn off, regulate, modulate, or isolate an extremely large array of liquids and gases, from the most basic to the most corrosive or toxic. They range in size from a fraction of an inch to 30 ft (9 m) in diameter. They can handle pressures ranging from vacuum to more than 20,000 lb/in^2 (140 MPa/m^2) and temperatures from the cryogenic region to 1500°F (815°C). Some applications require absolute sealing; in others leakage is not a factor.

CATEGORIES OF VALVES

Because of all these variables, there can be no universal valve; therefore, to meet the changing requirements of industry, innumerable designs and variations have evolved over the years as new materials have been developed. All these designs fall into nine major categories: gate valves, globe valves, ball valves, butterfly valves, pinch valves, diaphragm valves, plug valves, check valves, and relief valves.

These basic categories are described in the following paragraphs. It would be impossible to mention every feature of every valve manufactured, and we have not attempted to do this. Instead, a general overview of each type is presented in outline format, giving service recommendations, applications, advantages, disadvantages, and other information helpful to the reader. In many cases, a disadvantage inherent in a type of valve has been overcome or corrected by a particular manufacturer. Therefore, for specific applications, manufacturers' recommendations should be sought.

Gate Valves

A gate valve is a multiturn valve in which the port is closed by a flat-faced, vertical disk that slides at right angles over the seat (Fig. 6-1).

Recommended

- For fully open or fully closed, nonthrottling service
- For infrequent operation
- For minimum resistance to flow
- For minimum amounts of fluid trapped in line

Applications

- General service, oil, gas, air, slurries, heavy liquids, steam, noncondensing gases and liquids, corrosive liquids

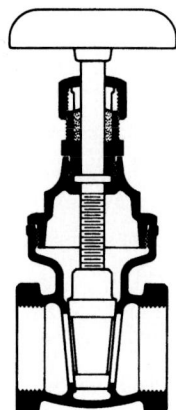

FIGURE 6-1   Gate valve.

Advantages

- High capacity
- Tight shutoff
- Low cost
- Simple design and operation
- Little resistance to flow

Disadvantages

- Poor flow control
- High operating force
- Cavitates at low pressure drop
- Must be kept in fully open or fully closed position
- Throttling position will erode seat and disk

Variations

- Solid wedge, flexible wedge, split wedge, double disk

Materials

- Body: bronze, cast iron, iron, forged steel, Monel, cast steel, stainless steel, PVC plastic
- Trim: various

Special Installation and Maintenance Instructions

- Lubricate on regular schedule
- Correct packing leaks immediately
- Always cool system when closing down a "hot" line and checking closed valves
- Never force valves closed with wrench or pry
- Open valves slowly to prevent hydraulic shock in line
- Close valves slowly to help flush trapped sediment and dirt

Ordering Specifications

- Type of end connections
- Type of wedge
- Type of seat
- Type of stem assembly
- Type of bonnet assembly
- Type of stem packing
- Pressure rating: operating and design
- Temperature rating: operating and design

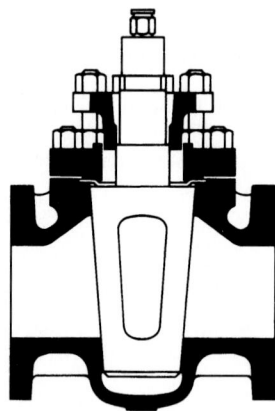

FIGURE 6-2   Plug valve.

Plug Valves

A plug valve is a quarter-turn valve that controls flow by means of a cylindrical or tapered plug with a hole through the center, which can be positioned from open to closed by a 90° turn (Fig. 6-2).

Recommended

- For fully open or fully closed service
- For frequent operation
- For low pressure drop across the valve
- For minimum resistance to flow
- For minimum amount of fluid trapped in line

Applications

- General service, slurries, liquids, vapors, gases, corrosives

Advantages

- High capacity
- Low cost
- Tight shutoff
- Quick operation

Disadvantages

- High torque for actuation
- Seat wear
- Cavitation at low pressure drop

Variations

- Lubricated, nonlubricated, multiport

Materials

- Iron, ductile iron, carbon steel, stainless steel, Alloy 20, Monel, nickel, Hastelloy, plastic-lined

Special Installation and Maintenance Instructions

- Allow space for operation of handle on wrench-operated valves
- For lubricated plug valves, lubricate before putting into service
- For lubricated plug valves, lubricate on regular schedule

Ordering Specifications

- Body material
- Plug material
- Temperature rating
- Pressure rating
- Port arrangement, if multiport valve
- Lubricant, if lubricated valve

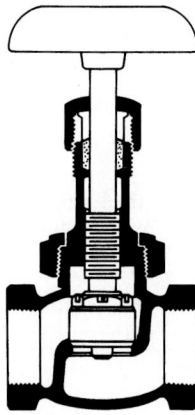

FIGURE 6-3   Globe valve.

Globe Valves

A globe valve is multiturn valve in which closure is achieved by means of a disk or plug that seals or stops the fluid on a seat generally parallel to the line flow (Fig. 6-3).

Recommended

- For throttling service or flow regulation
- For frequent operation
- For positive shutoff of gases or air
- Where some resistance to flow is acceptable

Applications

- General service, liquids, vapors, gases, corrosives, slurries

Advantages

- Efficient throttling with minimum wire drawing or disk or seat erosion
- Short disk travel and fewer turns to operate, saving time and wear on stem and bonnet
- Accurate flow control
- Available in multiports

Disadvantages

- High pressure drop
- Relatively high cost

Variations

- Standard, Y pattern, angle, three-way

Materials

- Body: bronze, all iron, cast iron, forged steel, Monel, cast steel, stainless steel, plastics
- Trim: various

Special Installation and Maintenance Instructions

- Install so pressure is under disk, except in high-temperature steam service
- Lubricate on strict schedule
- Flush foreign matter off seat by opening valve slightly
- Correct packing leaks immediately by tightening the packing nut

Ordering Specifications

- Type of end connection
- Type of disk
- Type of seat
- Type of stem assembly
- Type of stem seal
- Type of bonnet assembly
- Pressure rating
- Temperature rating

Ball Valves

A ball valve is a quarter-turn valve in which a drilled ball rotates between resilient seats, allowing straight-through flow in the open position and shutting off flow when the ball is rotated 90° and blocks the flow passage (Fig. 6-4).

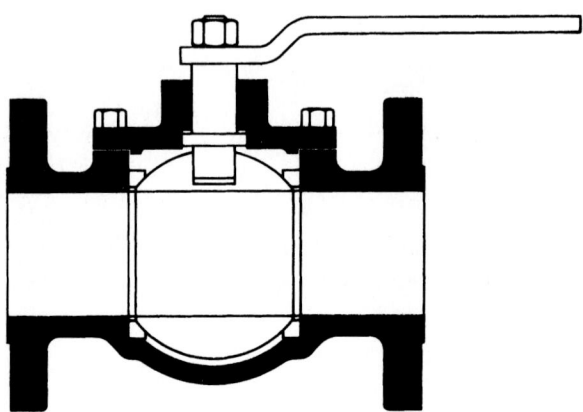

FIGURE 6-4   Ball valve.

Recommended

- For ON-OFF, nonthrottling service
- Where quick opening is required
- For moderate temperature requirements
- Where minimum resistance to flow is needed

Applications

- General service, high temperatures, slurries

Advantages

- Low cost
- High capacity
- Bidirectional shutoff
- Straight-through pattern
- Low leakage
- Self-cleaning
- Low maintenance
- No lubrication requirement
- Compact
- Tight sealing with low torque

Disadvantages

- Poor throttling characteristics
- High torque for actuation
- Susceptible to seal wear
- Prone to cavitation

Variations

- Top entry, split body or end entry, three-way, venturi, full-ported, reduced port

Materials

- Body: cast iron, ductile iron, bronze, brass, aluminum, carbon steels, stainless steels, titanium, tantalum, zirconium, and polypropylene and PVC plastics
- Seat: TFE, filled TFE, nylon, Buna-N, neoprene

Special Installation and Maintenance Instructions

- Allow sufficient space for operation of long handle

Ordering Specifications

- Operating temperature
- Type of port in ball
- Seat material
- Body material
- Operating pressure
- Full or reduced port
- Top entry or side entry

FIGURE 6-5   Butterfly valve.

Butterfly Valves

A butterfly valve is a quarter-turn valve that controls flow by means of a circular disk with its port axis at right angles to the direction of flow (Fig. 6-5).

Recommended

- For fully open or fully closed service
- For throttling service
- For frequent operation
- Where positive shutoff is required for gases or liquids
- Where minimum amount of fluid trapped in line is allowed
- For low pressure drop across valve

Applications

- General service, liquids, gases, slurries, liquids with suspended solids

Advantages

- Compact, lightweight, low-cost
- Low maintenance
- Minimum number of moving parts
- No pockets
- High capacity
- Straight-through flow
- Self-cleaning

Disadvantages

- High torque for actuation
- Limited pressure-drop capability
- Prone to cavitation

Variations

- Wafer, lug wafer, flanged, screwed, fully lined, high-performance

Materials

- Body: iron, ductile iron, carbon steels, forged steel, stainless steels, Alloy 20, bronze, Monel
- Disk: all metals, elastomer coatings such as TFE, Kynar, Buna-N, neoprene, Hypalon
- Seat: Buna-N, Viton, neoprene, rubber, butyl, polyurethane, Hypalon, Hycar, TFE

Special Installation and Maintenance Instructions

- May be operated by lever, handwheel, or chainwheel
- Allow sufficient space for operation of handle if lever-operated
- Valves should remain in closed position during all handling and installation operations

Ordering Specifications

- Type of body
- Type of seat
- Body material
- Disk material
- Seat material
- Type of actuation
- Operating pressure
- Operating temperature

FIGURE 6-6 Diaphragm valve.

Diaphragm Valves

A diaphragm valve is a multiturn valve that effects closure by means of a flexible diaphragm attached to a compressor. When the compressor is lowered by the valve stem, the diaphragm seals and cuts off flow (Fig. 6-6).

Recommended

- For fully open or fully closed service
- For throttling service
- For service with low operating pressures

Applications

- Corrosive fluids, sticky and/or viscous materials, fibrous slurries, sludges, foods, pharmaceuticals

Advantages

- Low cost
- No packing glands
- No possibility of stem leakage
- Immune to problems of clogging, corroding, or gumming of media

Disadvantages

- Diaphragm subject to wear
- High torque under live-line closure

Variations

- Weir type and straight-through type

Materials

- Metallic, solid plastic, lined—wide variety of each

Special Installation and Maintenance Instructions

- Lubricate on a regular schedule
- Do not use bars, wrenches, or cheaters to close

Ordering Specifications

- Body material
- Diaphragm material
- End connections
- Type of stem assembly
- Type of bonnet assembly
- Type of operation
- Operating pressure
- Operating temperature

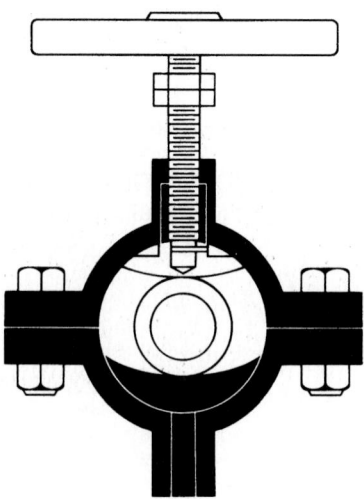

FIGURE 6-7   Pinch valve.

Pinch Valves

A pinch valve is a multiturn valve that effects closure by means of one or more flexible elements, such as diaphragms or rubber tubes, that can be pressed together to cut off flow (Fig. 6-7).

Recommended

- For ON-OFF service
- For throttling service
- For moderate temperatures
- Where pressure drop through valve is low
- For services requiring low maintenance

Applications

- Slurries, mining slurries, liquids with large amounts of suspended solids, systems that convey solids pneumatically, food service

Advantages

- Low cost
- Low maintenance
- No internal obstruction or pockets to cause clogging
- Simple design
- Noncorrosive and abrasion-resistant

Disadvantages

- Limited vacuum application
- Difficult to size

Variations

• Exposed sleeve or body, encased metallic sleeve or body

Materials

• Rubber, white rubber, Hypalon, polyurethane, neoprene, white neoprene, Buna-N, Buna-S, Viton-A, butyl rubber, silicone, TFE

Special Installation and Maintenance Instructions

• Large sizes may require supports above or below the line if pipe supports are inadequate

Ordering Specifications

• Operating pressure
• Operating temperature
• Sleeve material
• Exposed or encased sleeve

Check Valves and Relief Valves

Two categories of valves are specific-purpose rather than general-service valves. These are check valves and relief valves. Unlike the other types described in this section, they are self-actuated valves and operate without outside control, depending for their operation on flow direction or pressures within the piping system. Since both types are normally used in conjunction with flow-control valves, the choice of valve is often determined by the same conditions that determine the selection of the flow-control valve.

Check Valves. A check valve (Fig. 6-8) is designed to check reversal of flow. Fluid flow in the desired direction opens the valve; reversal of flow closes it. There are three basic styles of check valves: (1) swing check, (2) life check, and (3) butterfly check.

Swing Check Valve. A swing check valve has a hinged disk designed to open completely with line pressure and close when line pressure ceases and backflow begins. There are two designs: a Y pattern, which has an access opening in the body for easy regrinding of the disk without removing the valve from the line, and a straight-through pattern that has replaceable seat rings.

RECOMMENDED

• Where minimum resistance to flow is needed

• Where there is infrequent change of direction in the line

• For service in lines using gate valves

• For vertical lines having upward flow

APPLICATIONS

• For low-velocity liquid service

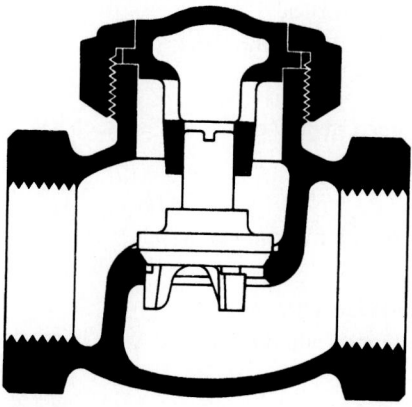

FIGURE 6-8   Check valve (lift type).

ADVANTAGES

- Unobstructed view
- Turbulence and pressure within valve are very low
- Y-pattern disk can be reground without removing valve from line

VARIATIONS

- Tilting-disk check valve

MATERIALS

- Body: bronze, all iron, cast iron, forged steel, Monel, cast steel, stainless steel, carbon steel
- Trim: various

SPECIAL INSTALLATION AND MAINTENANCE INSTRUCTIONS

- In vertical lines, pressure should always be under seat
- If valve fails to seal, check seating surfaces
- If seat is damaged or scored, regrind or replace
- Before reassembling, clean internal portions thoroughly

Lift Check Valve. A lift check valve is similar in design to a globe valve except that the disk is lifted by the forward line pressure and closed by gravity and backflow.

RECOMMENDED

- Where there are frequent changes of direction in the line
- For use with globe and angle valves
- For use where pressure drop across valve is not a problem

APPLICATIONS

- Steam, air, gas, water, and vapor lines with high flow velocities

ADVANTAGES

- Minimum travel of disk for fully open position
- Quick-acting

VARIATIONS

- Three body patterns: horizontal, angle, vertical
- Ball check, piston check, spring-loaded check, stop check

MATERIALS

- Body: bronze, all iron, cast iron, forged steel, Monel, stainless steel, PVC, Penton, impervious graphite, TFE-lined
- Trim: various

SPECIAL INSTALLATION AND MAINTENANCE INSTRUCTIONS

- Line pressure should be under seat
- Horizontal pattern should be installed in horizontal lines
- Vertical pattern is used for vertical pipes with flow upward, from beneath seat
- If backflow leaks, check disk and seat

Butterfly Check Valve. A butterfly check valve has a split disk hinged on a shaft in the center of the disk so that a flexible sealing member attached to the disk is at a 45° angle to the valve body when the valve is closed. The disk then has to move only a short distance away from the body toward the center of the valve to open fully.

RECOMMENDED

• Where minimum resistance to flow in the line is needed
• Where there is frequent change of direction in the line
• For use with butterfly, plug, ball, diaphragm, or pinch valves

APPLICATIONS

• For liquid or gas service

ADVANTAGES

• Body design lends itself to installation of various types of seat liners
• Less expensive for corrosion resistance
• Quiet operation
• Simplicity of design permits construction in large diameters
• May be installed in virtually any position

VARIATIONS

• Fully lined
• Soft-seated

MATERIALS

• Body: steel, stainless steel, titanium, aluminum, PVC, CPVC, polyethylene, polypropylene, cast iron, Monel, bronze
• Flexible sealing members: Buna-N, Viton, butyl rubber, TFE, neoprene, Hypalon, urethane, Nordel, Tygon, silicone

SPECIAL INSTALLATION AND MAINTENANCE INSTRUCTIONS

• On lined valves, liner should be protected from damage during handling
• Make sure valve is installed so that forward flow opens valve

Relief Valves.   A relief valve (Fig. 6-9) is a self-actuated valve designed to provide accurate automatic pressure regulation. The valve is used primarily for noncompressible fluid service and opens slowly as pressure increases, regulating the operating pressure.

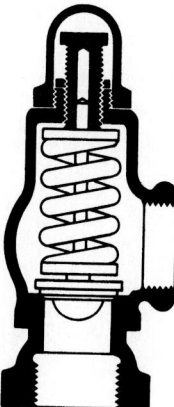

FIGURE 6-9   Relief valve.

Closely related to the relief valve is the safety valve, which opens quickly with a pop action to relieve excessive pressure caused by gases or compressible fluids.

Sizing is very important in relief valves and is determined by specific formulas.

Recommended

• In systems where a predetermined pressure range is required

Applications

• Hot water, steam, gases, vapor

Advantages

• Inexpensive
• No auxiliary power required for operation

Variations

- Safety, safety relief
- Diaphragm construction for valves used in corrosive service

Materials

- Body: cast iron, carbon steel, glass-TFE, bronze, brass, TFE-lined, stainless steel, Hastelloy, Monel
- Trim: various

Special Installation and Maintenance Instructions

- Should be installed in accordance with provisions of ASME Unfired Pressure Vessel Code
- Should be installed in readily accessible areas for inspection and maintenance

CODES AND STANDARDS

Various professional and industrial organizations have created codes and standards that are applicable to the design, selection, and use of industrial products. Certain of these standards are peculiar to specific industries, such as those set up by the American Water Works Association (AWWA), American Gas Association (AGA), American National Standards Institute (ANSI), American Society of Mechanical Engineers (ASME), and Manufacturers Standardization Society of the Valve and Fittings Industry (MSS). These are but a few of the existing organizations.

The valve specifier should be aware of those codes that apply to a specific industry and the application in question. For further information on the codes and standards available, these organizations may be contacted at the addresses listed below:

AWWA, 6666 W. Quincy Avenue, Denver, CO 80235
ANSI, 1430 Broadway, New York, NY 10018
AGA, 1515 Wilson Boulevard, Arlington, VA 22209
API, 1220 L St., NW, Washington, DC 20005
ASME, 345 East 47th Street, New York, NY 10017
MSS, 127 Park St., NE, Vienna, VA 22180

BIBLIOGRAPHY

Merrick, Ronald C.: *Valve Selection and Specification Guide,* Van Nostrand Reinhold, New York, 1991.
Ulanski, Wayne: *Valve and Actuator Technology,* McGraw-Hill, New York, 1991.
Zappe, R. W.: *Valve Selection Handbook,* Gulf Publishing Co. Book Division, Houston, 1987.

SECTION 11

INSTRUMENTATION AND AUTOMATIC CONTROLS

CHAPTER 11-1

INSTRUMENTATION

Ranjit S. Randhawa
The Foxboro Company
Foxboro, Massachusetts

TERMINOLOGY

Accuracy An ideal instrument would be one whose input-to-output relationship has a defined linear or nonlinear equation. Instruments, however, suffer from errors such as hysteresis, deadband, conformity, and repeatability. *Hysteresis* and *deadband* errors are illustrated in Fig. 1.1.

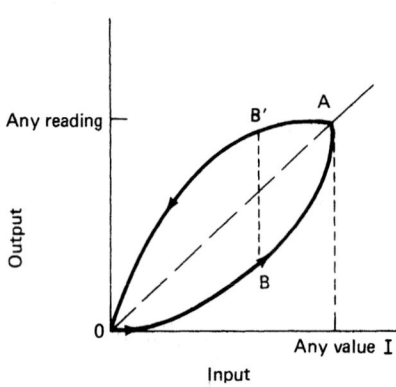

FIGURE 1-1 Hysteresis and deadband errors.

Hysteresis error Suppose, as input increases, the reading follows along curve *OBA*. If input returns to *O*, the reading may follow *AB′O*, a different path. The difference *BB′* at any input is the *hysteresis* error, a repeatable error due to energy absorption by the instrument element (typically a spring, diaphragm, or magnetic core).

Deadband error Suppose input increases from *O* to any value *I*, and the output reading does not change (due to friction, for example) until the input is at *I*, whereupon the output reading jumps to *A*. If the input reverses, returning to *O*, the output may remain at *A* until the input returns to *O*; then the output jumps to *O*. The value of *I* is the *dead band*, the amount by which the input changes for a change in output.

Conformity The maximum deviation of an instrument's actual calibration curve as compared to its specified characteristic curve is called its *conformity*. There are two methods by which a numerical value for conformity is derived. First is the terminal-based method whereby the calibration curve is forced to coincide at the end points with the specified characteristic curve. With the second method, the calibration curve is forced to concide only with the lower-range value of the characteristic curve of the instrument.

Repeatability The closeness of agreement among a number of consecutive measurements of the output for the same value of the input under the same operating conditions, i.e., approaching from the same direction for full-range traverses, is called repeatability. It is usually measured as nonrepeatability and expressed as repeatability in percent of span. It does *not* include hysteresis since input measurements are varied in only one direction. See Fig. 1-2.

Accuracy rating This is a number or quantity that defines a limit which errors will not exceed when a device is used under specified operating conditions. When operating conditions are not specified, reference conditions are assumed. For example, a primary flow device may lose accuracy at higher fluid temperatures. Unless specified otherwise, however, a reference or standard test temperature is assumed.

As a performance specification, accuracy (or reference accuracy) is assumed to mean the accuracy rating of the device when used at reference operating conditions. The units being used must be stated explicitly. Preferably, a ± sign should precede the number or quantity, but absence of a sign is taken to mean ±.

Accuracy rating can be expressed in a number of ways. The following examples are typical:

1. Accuracy rating expressed in terms of the *measured variable itself.* Typical expression: The accuracy rating for a certain temperature recorder-indicator is ±2°F or ±1°C.
2. Accuracy rating expressed in terms of *span.* Typical expression: The accuracy rating is ±0.5 percent of span. (This percentage is calculated using scale units such as degrees Fahrenheit, pounds per square inch gauge, etc.). With that accuracy rating, a pressure transmitter with a span of 200 psig (1400 kPa) would be inaccurate by ± 1 psig (6.89 kPa).
3. Accuracy rating expressed in percent of the *upper-range value.* Typical expression: The accuracy rating is ±0.5 percent of the upper-range value. (This percentage is calculated using scale units such as kilopascals, degrees Fahrenheit, etc.) Thus, a temperature recorder with an upper range of 50-mV thermocouple input would be inaccurate by ±2.5 mV.
4. Accuracy rating expressed in percent of *scale length.* Typical expression: The accuracy rating is ±0.5 percent of scale length. A manometer with a scale length of 20 in (0.5 m) would have an error of 0.1 in (±0.25 cm).

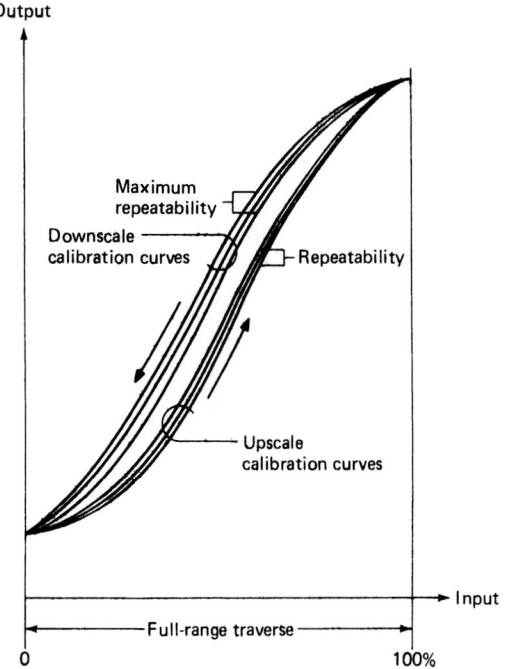

FIGURE 1-2   Repeatability.

5. Accuracy rating expressed in percent of *actual output reading.* Typical expression: The accuracy rating is ±1 percent of actual output reading. Thus, a manometer reading of 0.2 m with a ±1 percent reading error would have an error of ±0.2 cm *at that reading.*

Span   The algebraic difference between the upper and lower range values. For example:

1. Range 0 to 150°F—span 150°F
2. Range −20 to 200°F—span 220°F
3. Range 20 to 150°C—span 130°C

For multirange devices, this definition applies to the particular range that the device is set to measure.

Span adjustment   Means provided in an instrument to change the slope of the input-output curve. See Fig. 1-3.

Zero adjustment   Means provided in an instrument to produce a parallel shift of an input-output curve. See Fig. 1-3.

Elevated zero range   A range in which the zero value of the measured variable, measured signal, etc., is greater than the lower range value. The zero may be between the lower- and upper-range values, at the upper-range value, or above the upper-range value. Examples: range −20 to 200°F, −100 to −10°C. The terms *suppression, suppressed range,* or *suppressed span* are also frequently used to denote elevated zero range.

Suppressed zero range   A range in which the zero value of the measured variable is less than the lower range value. For example: 20 to 100 scale range. The terms *elevation, elevated range,* and *elevated span* are also used to denote suppressed zero range.

Reproducibility   The closeness of agreement among repeated measurements of the output for the same value of input made under the same operating conditions over a period of time, approaching from both directions. It is usually measured as a nonreproducibility and expressed as reproducibility in percent of span for a specified time interval.

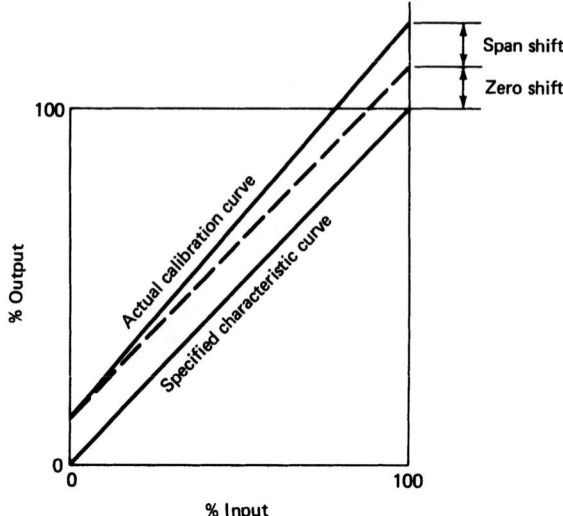

FIGURE 1-3   Accuracy rating span shift and zero shift.

INTRODUCTION

Measurement of physical phenomena is the basis of all technical activity. Obtaining, displaying, and conveying the quantitative facts of physical processes are the prime functions of instrumentation. This chapter presents the practical fundamentals of this technology.

LEVEL-MEASUREMENT METHODS

Level, as a process variable, is a common measurement both for control and indication. Various methods are used, and the selection of any one is based on many factors. Refer to Table 1.1.

Float Method

This is the simplest of level-measuring methods and makes use of a float which essentially follows the level in a closed or open vessel. The position of the float can be used to sense the level at a predetermined point by magnetically coupling the float to a mercury switch or miniature-type switch. This method is normally used for sensing high and/or low levels in a vessel. In large storage tanks, where a local indication or recording of the level is required, the float is coupled with a tape or cable which then, through a pulley mechanism, positions a local pointer for indication or applies a torque in a recorder. In both applications turbulence is kept to a minimum.

Displacement Method

The method employs a displacer which is located so that it is totally immersed when the level is at its predetermined maximum point (Fig. 1-4). The amount of force acting on the displacer is equal to the weight of the liquid displaced. The displacer weighs more than the maximum

TABLE 1-1 Level-Measurement Methods

Method	Type of liquid			Range	Relative cost	Output type
	Clean	Hard to handle	Solid			
Float	Good	Fair	—	75 mm–15 m (3 in–50 ft)	Low	Contact or tape
Displacement	Fair	Poor	—	150 mm–4 m (6 in–12 ft)	Med	Contact and/ or signal
Head (pressure)	Good	Excellent	—	50 mm on (2 in on)	Med	Signal
Differential pressure	Good	Excellent	—	130 mm on (5 in on)	Med	Signal
Air (gas) bubbler	Fair	Fair	—	250 mm–75 m (10 in–250 ft)	Low	Signal
Capacitance	Good	Fair	Good	Wide	Med	Signal
Conductivity	Fair	—	Poor	Point	Med	Contact
Thermal	Good	—	—	Point	Med	Contact
Radiation	Good	Excellent	Good	Wide	High	Signal
Weighing	Good	Excellent	Good	Wide	High	Signal
Ultrasonic	Good	Excellent	Good	Wide	High	Signal

amount of liquid it can displace and is normally cylindrical in shape so that the relationship of buoyancy to submersion is linear. The displacer is linked to a torque tube which twists linearly with the buoyance of the displacer.

The buoyant force can be determined by

$$F = V \frac{L_w}{L} D \tag{1}$$

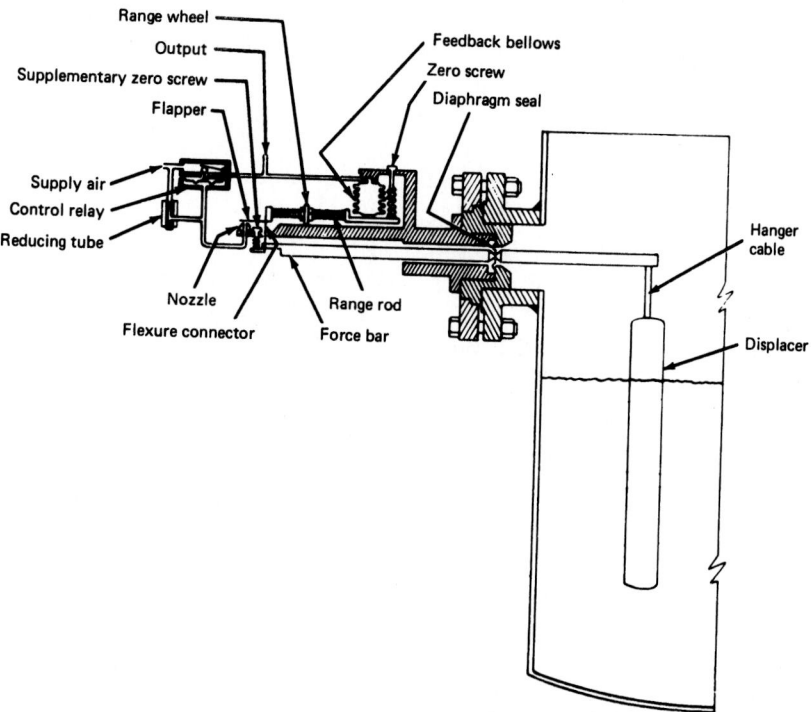

FIGURE 1-4 Schematic diagram of buoyancy transmitter with displacer.

where V = total displacer volume
L_w = working length of displacer
L = total length of displacer
D = density of fluid

The level measurement is independent of the pressure in the vessel but may be subject to problems where extreme turbulence is encountered. Special precautions have to be taken under these circumstances.

The same principle of measurement can be used for measuring density. Here the displacer is kept fully immersed; the buoyant force is then a function of the span of density to be measured. A further application of this type of measurement is the interface level between two liquids. The interface level is allowed to vary over the length of the displacer while it is fully immersed. The force now depends upon the difference in densities of the two liquids. Standard displacers are designed for a range of buoyancies from 1.47 lb (0.67 kg) to about 12 lb (5.45 kg), including the weight of the hanger assembly.

Head-Pressure Method

This is a useful means of measuring level when a pressure transmitter is used to convert the head pressure in an open tank to an equivalent level. The transmitter output can be used for remote indication or control. The difficulties in this type of measurement usually arise because most tanks are closed vessels that are also pressurized, thus causing variations in pressure to affect level measurements. Furthermore, temperature variations may cause density, too, to vary, which will then affect the level measurement. These problems limit the usefulness of this method for level measurements, but it is an excellent method for determining the density of liquids by keeping the level of the liquid constant in either a vessel with constant pressure or an open vessel with no pressure. An installation where pressure variations in the vessel can be taken into account will use a differential pressure measurement where the tank pressure is subtracted from the measured head. The differential pressure transmitter should be calibrated for a range of $H(G_2 - G_1)$, and its elevation is HG_1. Refer to Fig. 1-5.

Differential-Pressure Method

This is the most common method of measurement for both control and indication. Refer to Fig. 1-6.

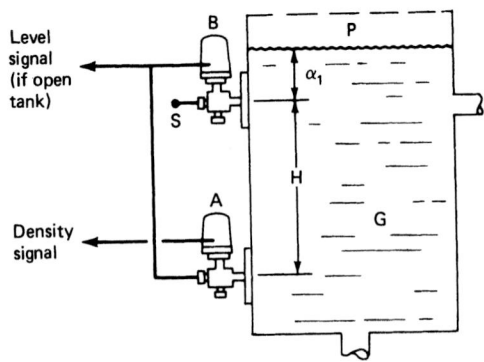

FIGURE 1-5 Differential pressure method of density measurement. *Key: A,* differential pressure transmitter; *B,* 1:1 repeater; *G,* specific gravity of liquid; *P,* pressure.

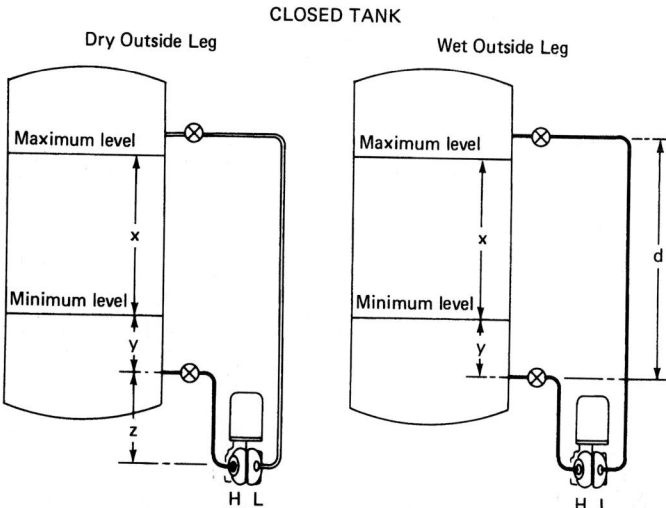

FIGURE 1-6   Differential-pressure level measurement. For dry outside leg, Span $= xG_L$ and Elevation $= yG_L + 'zG_S$; for wet outside leg, Span $= xG_L$ and Suppression $= dG_S - yG_L$. In both cases, G_L is the specific gravity of the liquid in the tank and G_S is the specific gravity of the liquid in the outside filled line. If the transmitter is at the level of the lower tank tap or if an air purge is used, $z = 0$.

A typical force-balance type of differential pressure (d/p) pneumatic transmitter (the d/p Cell*) is shown in Fig. 1-7. An electric transmitter would work essentially on the same principle (force-balance) except that the detection, output, and feedback-balancing force would be accomplished with electric components, e.g., a differential transformer and a feedback motor. The output is normally a current signal, the standard being 4 to 20 mA.

Air Bubbler Method

This is a common measuring method for large, open-storage vessels. The level is measured by determining the pressure required to force air or gas into the liquid at a point beneath the surface. Figures 1-8 to 1-10 indicate various types of installations. The bubble pipe can be of any material and is notched at the end, as shown in Fig. 1-11. This prevents large bubbles from forming.

Capacitance Method

The capacitance between two concentric cylinders is a direct function of the dielectric material between the two cylinders. Level measurements are accomplished by using a probe (one plate of the capacitor) and the tank, which acts as the second plate. As the level varies, the capacitance varies linearly, and this change in capacitance can be detected by using a bridge excited by a high-frequency oscillator. For nonconductive materials, an uninsulated probe can be used. Conductive materials require that the probe be coated with an insulator.

A number of possible errors can occur. For example, changes in the composition and in the temperature of a material will cause changes in its dielectric constant. The amount of water in

* d/p Cell is a trademark of The Foxboro Company, Foxboro, Massachusetts.

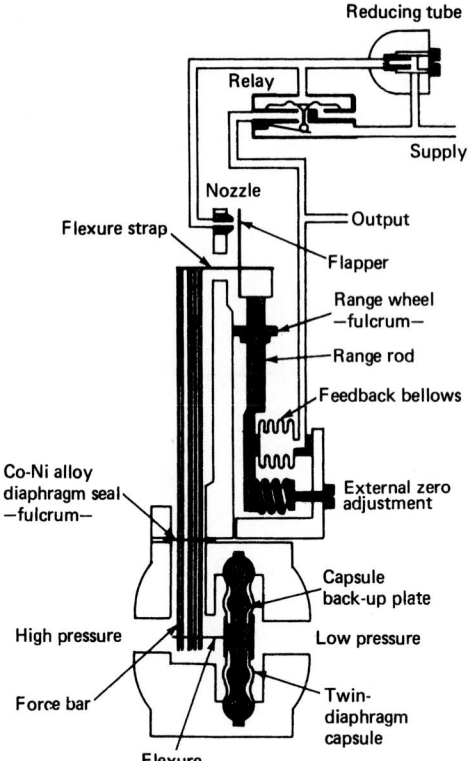

FIGURE 1-7 Differential-pressure transmitter. (*The Foxboro Company.*)

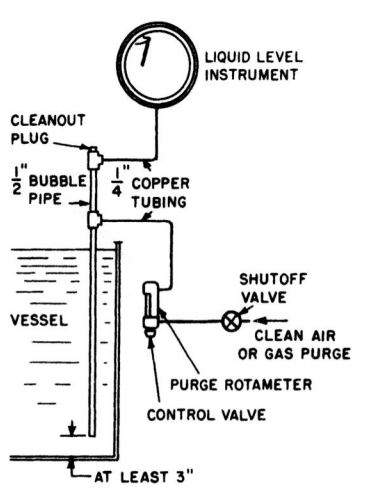

FIGURE 1-8 Using a bubble tube.

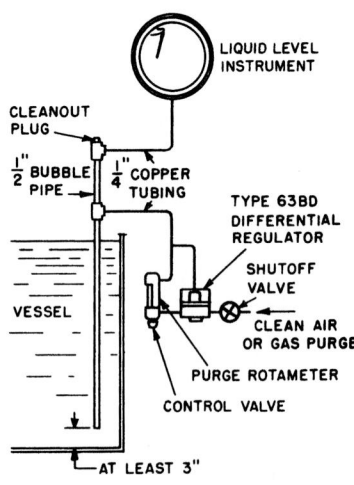

FIGURE 1-9 Using a bubble tube and differential-pressure regulator.

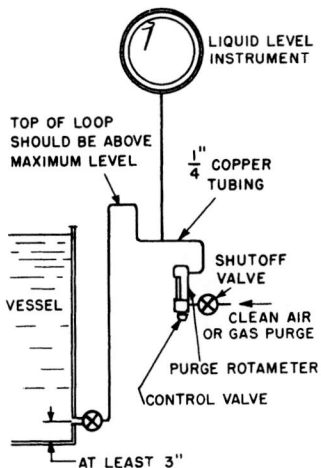

FIGURE 1-10 Purging directly into the side of a vessel.

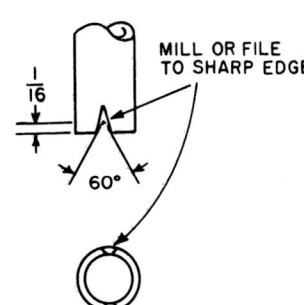

FIGURE 1-11 Detail of the notch in a bubble pipe.

a material has a profound effect on its dielectric constant. These changes will directly affect the level measurement. If the liquid tends to wet or adhere to the probe, then the level is measured only as far as the the probe is wetted, especially if the material is conductive. This is one of the serious drawbacks of this measuring method. The accuracy depends upon the differential capacitance, which is usually designed to be greater than 10 pF. The narrower this capacitive span, the more difficult the measurement.

Conductivity Method

This method is applicable for single-point measurement with a conductive process material. Two probes are used and placed such that an electric path is provided through the conductive material when both probes are covered. This is used to close the circuit of a relay, thereby providing a contact output for a certain level. Multipoint measurements can be made to provide point measurements for different levels. The method is inexpensive and the equipment fairly rugged, but it is not intrinsically safe unless special precautions are taken.

Thermal Element Method

The thermal element method is again used for point measurements and depends upon the fact the thermal conductivity of most process liquids is much higher than its associated vapor. When the thermal element comes in contact with liquid, the rate of heat transfer increases, causing its resistance to increase. This increased resistance is detected by an increased voltage drop which can then be used to activate a relay. The equipment used in this method is rugged and not affected by process changes, but the method is not intrinsically safe, and the heat input may cause changes in the quality of the measured product. This method, in general, has limited use in practice.

Radiation-Difference Method

This method is very useful in those applications in which the dangerous or extremely corrosive nature of the process fluid requires a noncontact type of measurement. The method depends upon the absorption of radiation by the process material. As the level of this material increases or decreases, the amount of radiation absorbed increases or decreases. This can then be determined by using a low-level detector, such as the Geiger-Müller tube. This method is applicable both for point measurement or a range of measurements. Safety considerations have to be kept in mind when considering installation, especially in terms of radiation exposure. The normal sources of radiation used are radium, cesium 13, and cobalt.

Weighing Method

This method, like radiation, is well suited for measuring process materials which do not allow contact-type measurement methods. Basically, the vessel weight is continuously measured by using either strain-gauge-type weigh cells or hydraulic pressure. Knowing the weight of the empty vessel, the weight of the process material in the vessel can be related to the depth of the material in the tank. Special precautions have to be taken to balance the vessel so that associated piping connected to the vessel does not affect the actual weight. The method has limited use in actual process control compared with some of the other methods, e.g., differential-pressure measurement using isolating seals for corrosive process materials.

Ultrasonic Method

This method uses an ultrasonic oscillator (20,000 Hz and higher) to excite a sensor. For point measurements, the signal is picked up by another sensor as long as a transmission path is available. When the level rises, the path is interrupted, thereby indicating the level. Another method is to allow the process material to damp the vibration of the sensor. This damping can be detected to provide a point measurement. Continuous measurements can be accomplished by using intermittent transmission and measuring electronically the time taken for the reflected signal to return to the sensor. This method is applicable to both liquids and solids; measurement of the level of solids in silos or storage bins has been the most popular application.

PRESSURE-MEASUREMENT INSTRUMENTS

Overview

Pressure is a fundamental process variable and its measurement can be used either directly for control or to infer other measurements, for example, level, flow, and temperature. There are many types of transducers that can be used. The most common are listed in Table 1-2.

The transducers can be linked to either a pneumatic or an electronic transmitter to develop a signal 3 to 15 psig (0.02 to 0.1 MPa) or 4 to 20 mA. The heart of the pneumatic

TABLE 1-2 Pressure-Measurement Elements*

Element	Local	Remote	Range	Contact with process	Relative cost	Accuracy, % of span
Bourdon tube	✓	✓	0–12,000 psig (0–83 MPa)	Yes*	Low	±0.25–5
Bellows		✓	0–3000 psig (0–20 MPa)	Yes*	Med	±0.5–1
Manometer	✓		0.05 in Hg–1 atm (3–100 kPa)	Yes	Low	0.1–1
Diaphragm	✓	✓	0.05 in Hg–1 atm (3–100 kPa)	Yes	Med	±0.5
Strain gauge		✓	1 atm on (0.1 MPa on)	No	High	±1
Dead weight	✓		1 atm on (0.1 MPa on)	No	High	High

* A chemical seal can be used for isolation.

transmitter is the flapper-nozzle assembly, including the pneumatic relay. The output from the relay is controlled by the back pressure developed in the nozzle which, in turn, is developed by the relationship of the flapper to the nozzle opening. Figures 1-12 and 1-13 indicate this relationship and a typical relay.

There are two arrangements for making use of the flapper-nozzle relationship. These arrangements lead to either *motion-balance* or *force-balance* instruments. Figures 1-14 and 1-15 indicate schematics of the two types. Force-balance instruments tend to be more widely used because of their ruggedness, high degree of insensitivity to vibration, and method of mounting.

Electronic transmitters generally tend to be of the force-balance type. Figure 1-16 indicates a typical layout of a differential transformer type.

The pressure applied to the bellows capsule is applied to the force bar through a flexure and is transmitted to the detector. The lever system moves the ferrite disk (part of the detector), causing a change in the output of the differential transformer. This change in output is sensed

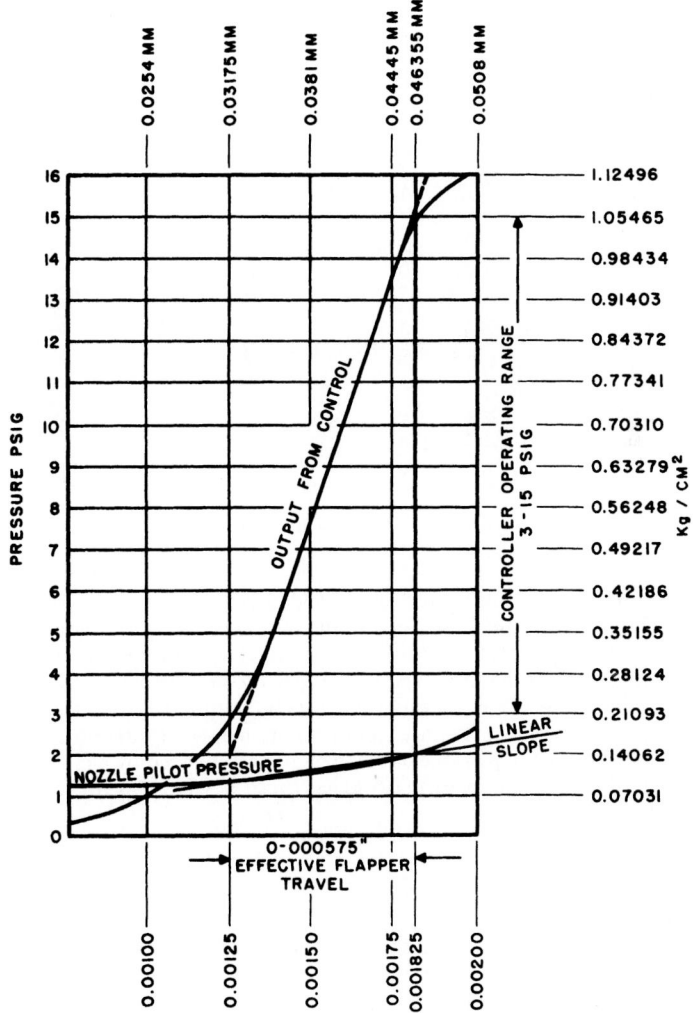

FIGURE 1-12 Curves for flapper-nozzle relation vs. operating pressure.

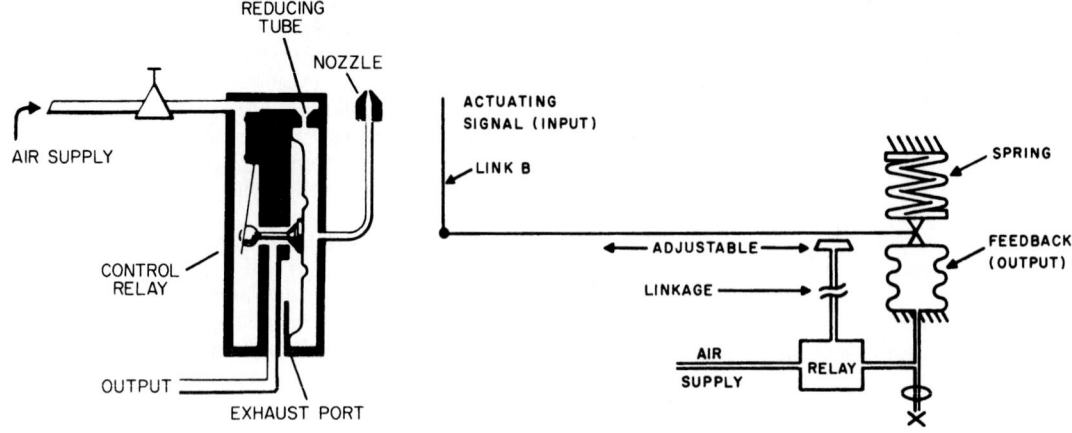

FIGURE 1-13 Pneumatic relay G.

FIGURE 1-14 Motion-balance schematic.

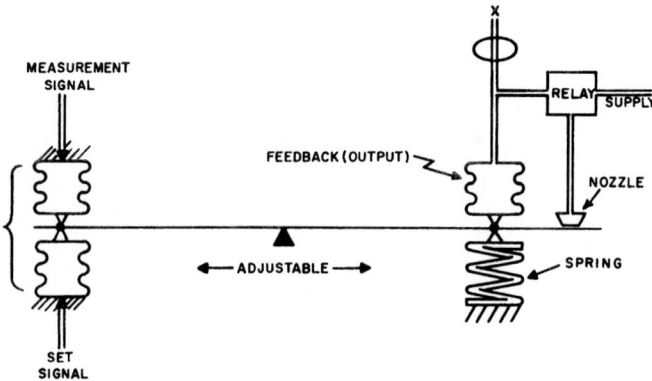

FIGURE 1-15 Force-balance schematic.

by the amplifier oscillator circuit, and its output is rectified to provide the transmission signal. The feedback coil, in series with the output signal, supplies the balancing feedback force.

There are other types of detectors that have also been used: the inductance type, where the movement of the ferrite piece changes the air gap, which then changes the inductance of an oscillator circuit and thereby changes its output; and the variable reluctance type, where the movement of an armature causes the inductance ratio between two coils to change. The two coils are part of a bridge circuit which is rebalanced by a feed-back amplifier, thereby changing the capacitance in the bridge. These devices can be considered to be motion-balance instruments.

Bourdon Tube

Simplest of the pressure-sensing elements, the Bourdon tube consists of a curved flattened tube with one end sealed and either connected to an indicator through linkage and gears or applied through a flexure mechanism to the force bar of a transmitter. The other end is connected to the process. Figure 1-17 shows a typical layout of an indicator. As pressure is applied, the tube tends to straighten, causing a small movement of the tip.

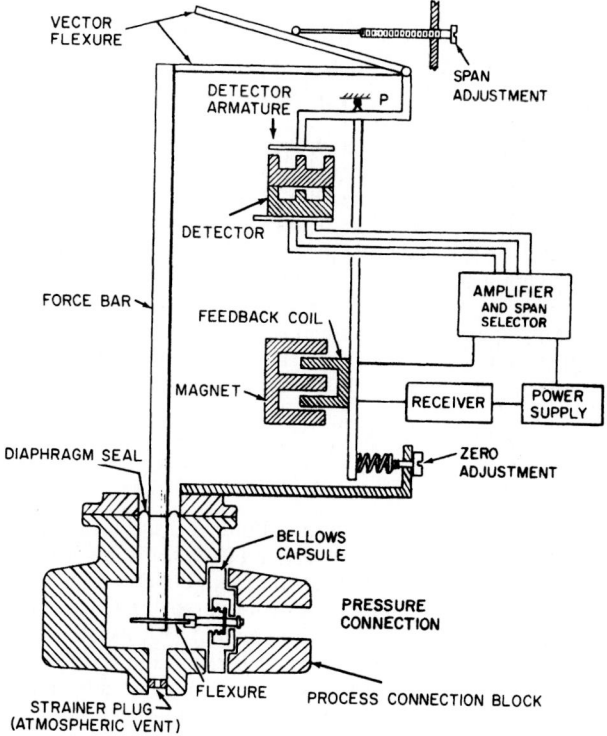

FIGURE 1-16   Differential transformer-type pressure transmitter.

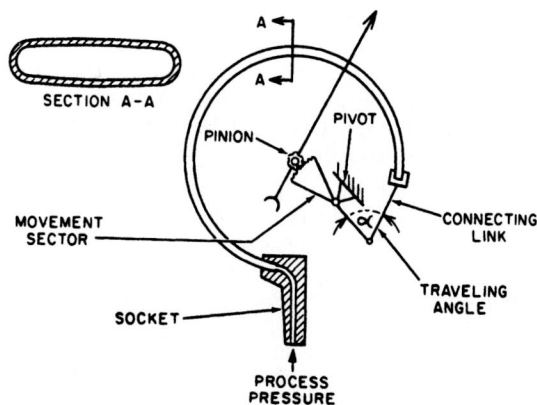

FIGURE 1-17   C Bourdon pressure element.

There are a number of other types of tube designs that have been developed. Figure 1-18 illustrates some of them.

The material of the tube can vary from bronze for some low-pressure ranges [up to 400 lb/in^2 (2.76 MPa)] to Ni-Span C* alloy which allows a C Bourdon tube to range up to 12,000 lb/in^2 (83 MPa). Absolute pressure measurements are limited to a maximum of 100 lb/in^2 (0.7 MPa).

In applications where the process fluid is extremely corrosive, it is normal to use pressure seals, connected directly or through capillary tubing. The system is solidly filled with a suitable liquid transmission medium. Process pressure is applied to the flexible member of the seal cavity in the measuring element, causing element movement in proportion to applied pressure. The spring rate of the flexible member must be less than that of the measuring element to allow full-range operation. A number of filling fluids have been used, the standard being DC-704, a silicone-base (Dow Corning Co.) product. This fluid has a low thermal coefficient of expansion with temperature limitation of 0 to 700°F (−18 to 370°C). The fluid must completely fill the system, as pockets of gas or air can cause large errors. There are many different types of seals available. Figure 1-19 indicates some of them.

Bellows

Refer to Fig. 1-20. Widely used both for measurement and control, bellows can be arranged as motion-balance or force-balance instruments. Figure 1-20 indicates the use of a bellows capsule for pressure measurement. Two-bellows systems are used when compensation is required, e.g., in absolute pressure measurement. One of the bellows is completely evacuated and acts in opposition to the measurement bellows. As atmospheric pressure varies, the evacuated bellows expands or contracts, thereby adding or subtracting from the measured absolute pressure. The size of the bellows can be varied for different pressure ranges from 0 to 7 lb/in^2 (0 to 50 kPa) to 0 to 2000 lb/in^2 (0 to 14 MPa).

Diaphragm

Refer to Fig. 1-21. The pressure-measuring element consists of a series of diaphragms which are connected together. Application of pressure causes the elements to expand, and the movement is then used for indication. These elements are typically used for low pressure applications of less than 5 lb/in^2 (1 kPa).

Figure 1-22 indicates a differential-pressure transmitter using a diaphragm capsule. The size of the capsule determines the range. Differential-pressure ranges from as low as 0 to 5 in H$_2$O (0 to 20 mm H$_2$O) to 0 to 850 in H$_2$O (0 to 330 cm H$_2$O) under static pressures up to 6000 lb/in^2 (41 MPa) are available.

Special Instruments

There are other types of pressure-measuring instruments that are available but have limited application in process industries. A manometer and a deadweight type are still quite popular, primarily for calibration of other pressure elements. The deadweight tester converts a known weight into a given liquid pressure which is then used in the calibration of an instrument.

---

* Ni-Span C is a trademark of Huntington Alloys, Inc., Huntington, West Virginia.

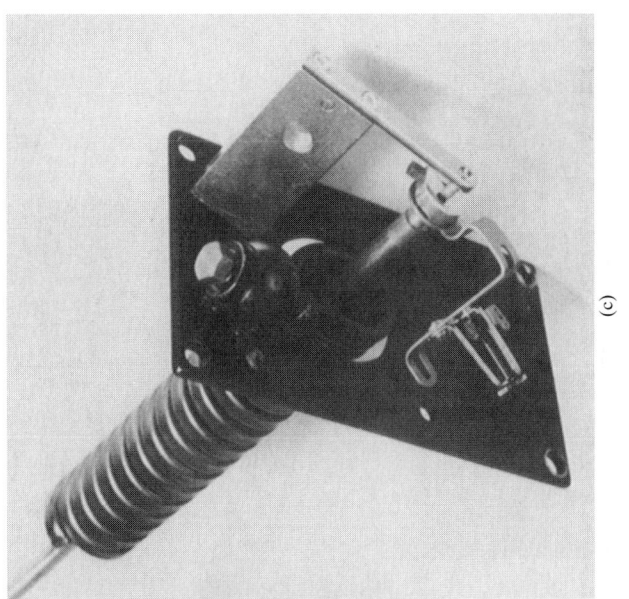

(c)

(b)

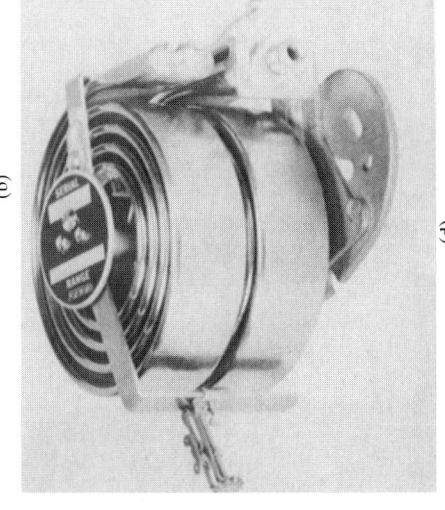

(d)

(a)

FIGURE 1-18 Bourdon-tube pressure elements. (*The Foxboro Company.*)

(a)

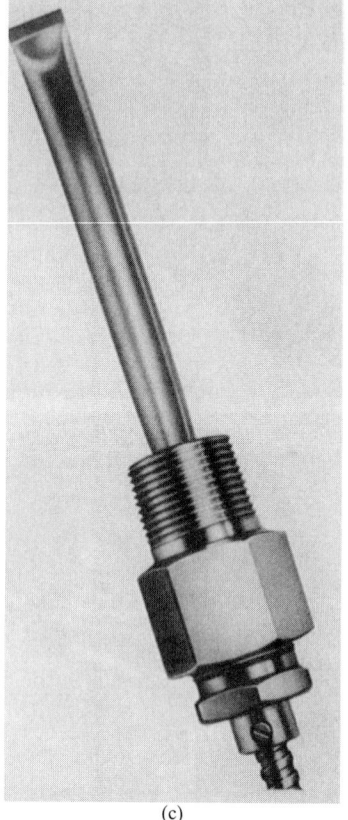

(c)

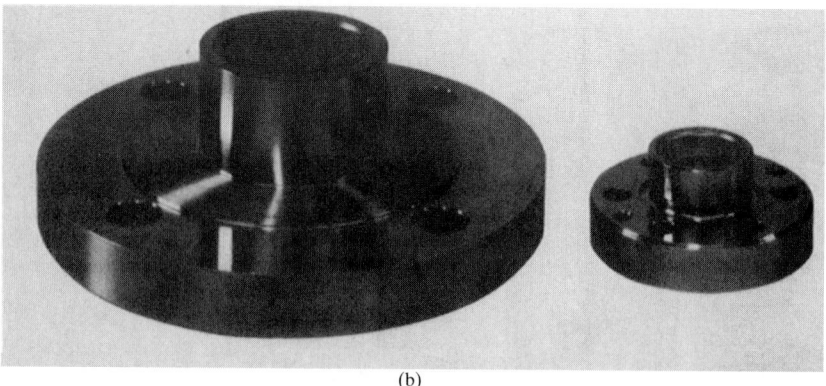

(b)

FIGURE 1-19   Pressure seals. (*The Foxboro Company.*)

(d)

(e)

FIGURE 1-19   (*Continued*)

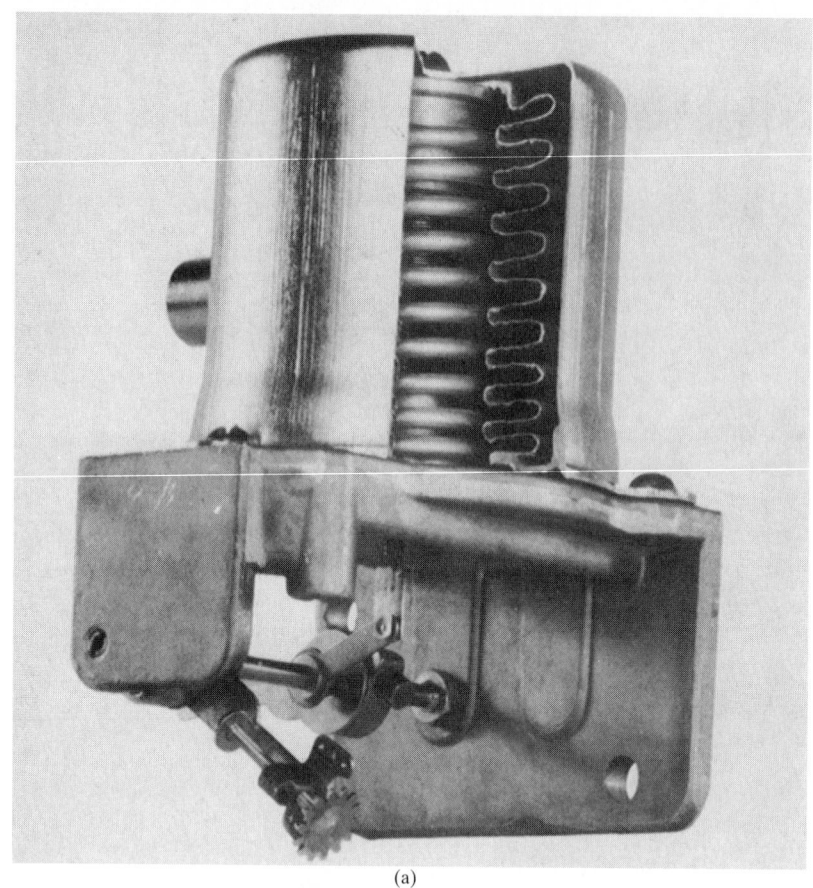

(a)

(b)

FIGURE 1-20   Bellows-type elements. (*The Foxboro Company.*)

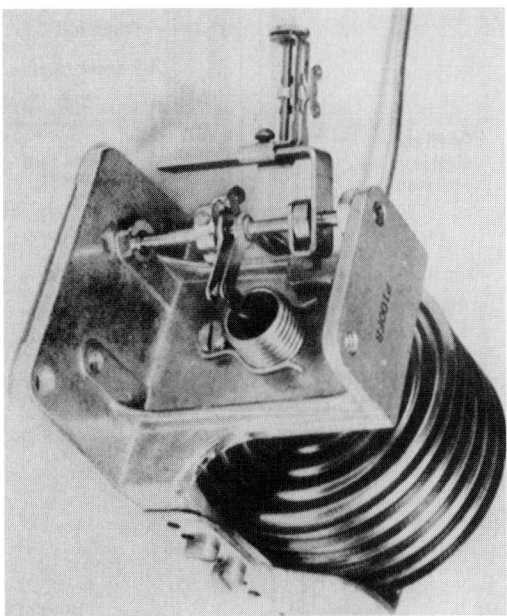

FIGURE 1-21 Diaphragm element. (*The Foxboro Company.*)

TEMPERATURE-MEASURING METHODS

Refer to Table 1-3 for the more common methods used for measuring temperature in an industrial process environment. Each of these is discussed in detail in the following text.

Filled Thermal Systems

The basis of measurement consists of a bulb connected by a capillary to a helical or C Bourdon tube element. The system is filled under pressure so that an increase in pressure causes a movement of the helical or Bourdon tube element. This movement can then be linked for local indication or through a transmitter for an electric or pneumatic signal.

Filled systems are classified by SAMA (Scientific Apparatus Makers Association) into four classes with subclassifications in each class.

Classes IA and IB. These are liquid-filled systems. Class IA refers to fully compensated systems while Class IB refers to case-compensated systems. Fully compensated refers to compensation of ambient temperature variation along the length of the connecting capillary tubing. It consists of (in addition to the normal measuring bulb) a connecting capillary and pressure element, with a second capillary tube and pressure element. The two capillary tubes are run together while the pressure elements are connected such that equal amounts of motion nullify each other. Thus ambient-temperature variation along the length of the capillary tubes and at the case produce equal movements of the pressure elements and hence cancel the effect on the output of the instrument. Class IB, *case compensation,* nullifies ambient temperature variations at the case in a similar fashion but may only use a bimetallic strip instead of a pressure element. These instruments are generally mounted very close to the bulb.

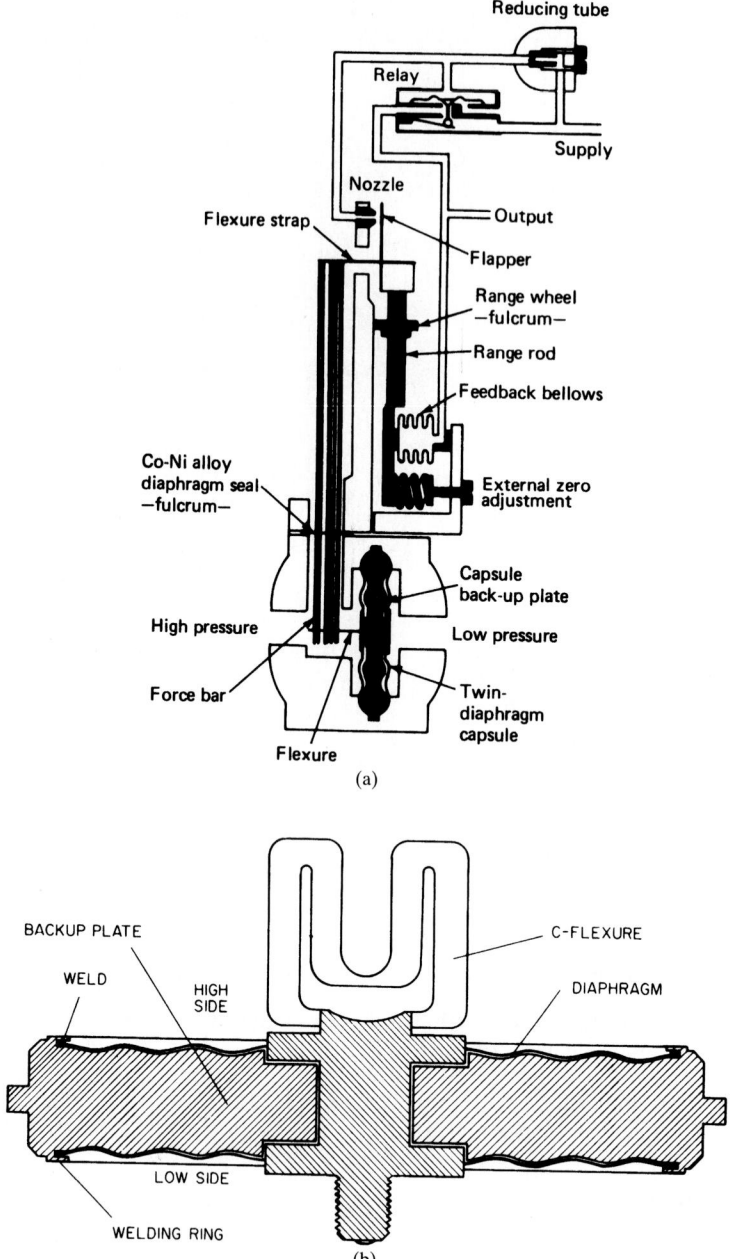

FIGURE 1-22 Diaphragm capsule for differential pressure measurement: (*a*) in situ in transmitter; (*b*) detailed structure.

TABLE 1-3 Temperature-Measuring Methods

	Local	Remote	Range, °F (°C)	Accuracy ±% span	Cost	Ease in replacement of components
Filled thermal system	✓	✓	−450 to 1400 (−260 to 760)	0.5 to 2	Low-med	Intermediate
Thermocouples		✓	−420 to 2000 (−250 to 1100)	0.3 to 1	Med	Easy
Resistance measurement		✓	−450 to 1625 (−260 to 900)	0.1 to 0.5	High	Difficult
Thermistors		✓	−200 to 500 (−130 to 260)	0.1	Med	Difficult
Bimetallic	✓		−80 to 800 (−60 to 420)	1 to 2	Low	Easy
Pyrometers	✓		High temperature	1 to 2	High	—
Paints	✓		100 to 2000 (40 to 1100)	—	Low	—

The initial pressure in this class of instruments is very high, making it a volumetric instrument, free of static errors from bulb position with respect to the instrument case. Furthermore, being volumetric devices, the amount of available volume for expansion is limited, also limiting the amount of available overrange.

These instruments can also be used for measuring temperature differences by using two bulbs with associated capillary tubing and pressure elements. The pressure elements are arranged in a manner similar to Class IA fully compensated systems. Ambient-temperature variations are minimized by running the capillary tubes as close to each other as possible. Temperature-difference spans greater than 36°F (20°C) are normally required.

Classes IIA, IIB, IIC, and IID. In these systems, the bulb, capillary tube, and pressure-measuring element are partially filled with a volatile fluid such that the vapor-liquid interface level occurs in the bulb. As the temperature rises, the vapor pressure increases and this increase can then be sensed via the pressure element. The system is stable and unaffected by ambient-temperature variations. They are the simplest to manufacture and therefore least expensive, both initially and in use.

The difference characterizing the four subclassifications is as follows: In a Class IIA system the capillary tube and the pressure element are filled with liquid while the bulb has both vapor and liquid. These systems are used when the bulb temperature is higher than the ambient temperature. Class IIB systems are the reverse of Class IIA, with the bulb used for temperatures less than the ambient temperature. In Class IIA systems, the effect of the liquid head in the capillary has to be considered if the bulb is installed above or below the instrument case. Class IIC systems are systems where the bulb temperature crosses the ambient temperature over its operating range. This causes the capillary to be filled with liquid or vapor, resulting in static head errors unless the bulb is mounted at the same level as the case. Class IIC instruments are normally used as local indicators. Class IID systems are like Class IIC systems, except that the capillary tube and the pressure element are filled with a non-volatile fluid, while the bulb contains liquid and vapor.

In all these classes the output is nonuniform and depends upon the vapor-pressure-vs.-temperature curve of the volatile fluid. Applications are geared such that normal operating temperatures are at the higher end of the scale where the scales are much wider, allowing greater readability.

Class III. These are gas-filled systems which are, like Class II systems, simple to construct, with wide applicable range limits. They are normally used with large bulbs which override the pressure variations in the capillary tube due to ambient-temperature changes. Gas pressure allows less power to be developed in the pressure-sensing element, making this class suited for wide temperature spans. The large bulbs are also well suited for average temperature measurements. Case compensation using a bimetallic strip is used in Class IIIB systems. Class IIIA systems use the normal parallel thermal system without a bulb.

Thermocouples

These sensors have in recent years achieved greater popularity with increasing use of electronic instruments. Basically, a thermocouple consists of two dissimilar metal wires, such as iron and constantan, joined to produce a thermal electromotive force (emf) when the junctions are at different temperatures. The measuring or hot junction is the end inserted in the medium where the temperature is to be measured. The reference or cold junction is the open end that is normally connected to the measuring-instrument terminals. The emf generated is a function of the difference in junction temperatures. Refer to Fig. 1-23.

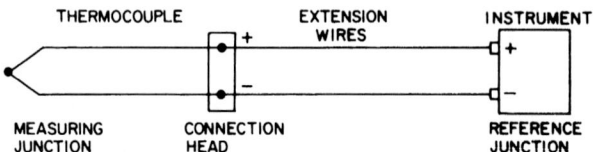

FIGURE 1-23 Thermocouple connection with extension wires.

The thermal emf developed by a thermocouple of two homogeneous metals is independent of the temperature gradient and distribution along the wires. Inhomogeneity in a thermocouple passing through a temperature gradient will produce undesirable emf's with resultant errors in temperature readings.

Introduction of intermediate metals into a thermocouple circuit will not affect the emf of the circuit, provided that the new junctions remain at the same temperature as the original junction. This fact is used in applying extension wires to cut costs, since some of the thermocouples are made of expensive metals. These extension wires must be made of materials having the same thermal emf characteristics as the thermocouple. If copper wires are used, temperature fluctuations at the reference junction (in this case the connection head) will introduce errors in proportion to the magnitude of the temperature changes. Use of proper extension wires moves the reference junction to the measuring instrument where temperature compensation can be applied. Figure 1-24 indicates the relationship of five standard thermocouples.

Table 1-4 highlights the different features of some standard thermocouples.

Figure 1-25 illustrates a simplified circuit of a Foxboro Series 33B transmitter. TC is a temperature-sensitive resistor which varies the bridge output as the actual reference-junction temperature varies from the design reference-junction temperature.

It should be noted that thermocouples are point-measuring devices. To get average temperature one should connect a number of thermocouples in parallel as shown in Fig. 1-26. Figure 1-27 shows the connection of two thermocouples for differential pressure measurement. The following points should be considered:

1. Swamping resistors are required to compensate for varying resistance of the thermocouple and extension wires.

2. In order to prevent ground loop currents the thermocouples must *not* be grounded.

3. The thermocouples and extension wires *must* be of the same type.

4. In differential measurement no reference-temperature compensation is required. Copper leads can be used between the connection box and the instrument.

Resistance Temperature Detectors

Based on the change of electric conductivity with temperature, the resistance temperature detector (RTD) consists of a coil of wire made of materials such as nickel and platinum. Spans

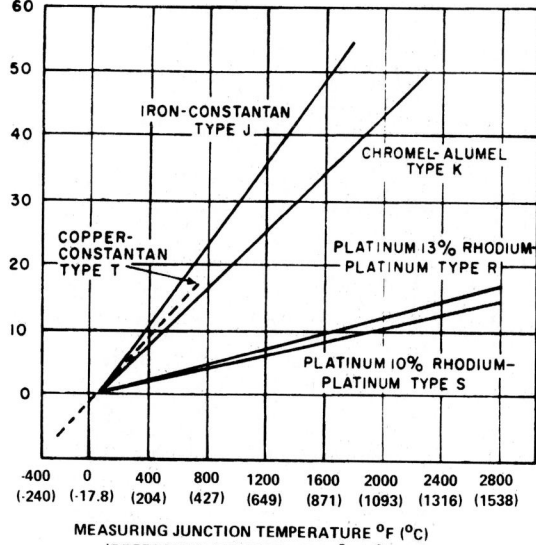

FIGURE 1-24 Thermocouple relationships.

as low as 5°F (3°C) can be achieved with a nickel RTD with a certified accuracy of 0.1°F (0.06°C). The sensor can be constructed with two, three, or four leads. For most industrial applications, two- or three-lead sensors are used in a Wheatstone bridge as shown in Fig. 1-28.

Differential temperature differences can also be measured by using two equal RTDs in adjacent sides of a Wheatstone bridge. The linearity of measurement is to an extent a function of the span of measurement. For wide-span instruments and extreme accuracy, nonlinear scales and charts are recommended. A certain amount of linearity can be achieved by connecting large-value equal resistors in series with the leads of the sensor.

TABLE 1-4 Thermocouple Comparison

ISA type	Positive wire	Negative wire	Recommended temp °F (°C)	Atmospheric conditions	Standard limits of error
T	Copper	Constantan	−450 to +750 (−270 to 400)	Oxidizing reducing	±2% of reading at low temperatures to ±¾% of reading at high temperatures
J	Iron	Constantan	0 to +1650 (−18 to +900)	Reducing	±¾% of reading at high temperatures
K	Chromel	Alumel	0 to 2300 (−18 to 1260)	Oxidizing or neutral	±¾% of reading at high temperatures
E	Chromel	Constantan	−300 to +1600 (−180 to 870)	Oxidizing	±¾% of reading at high temperatures
R,S	Platinum-rhodium	Platinum	0 to 2800 (−18 to 1530)	Oxidizing	0.5% of reading
B	Pt70-Rh30	Pt94-Rh6	0 to 3200 (−18 to 1760°C)	Inert or slow oxidizing	0.5% of reading

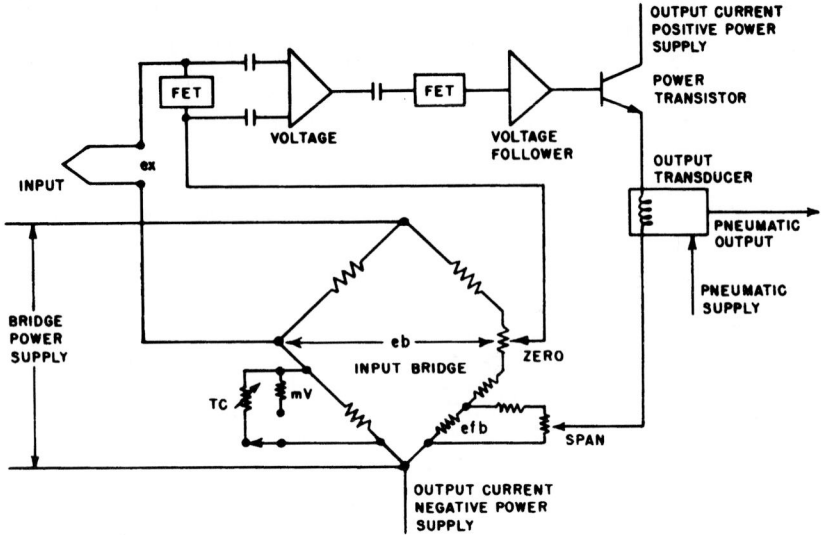

FIGURE 1-25 Simplified circuit diagram of Foxboro 33B series transmitter. (*The Foxboro Company.*)

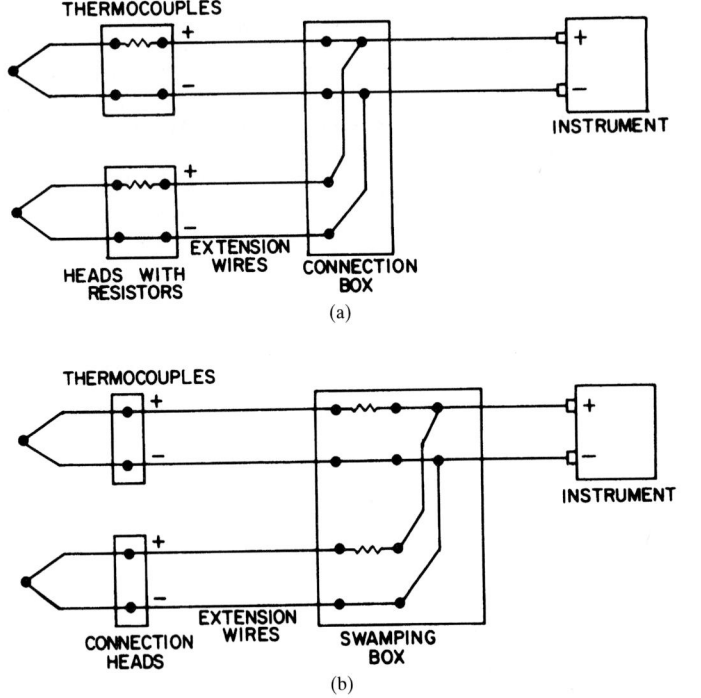

FIGURE 1-26 Average temperature circuits.

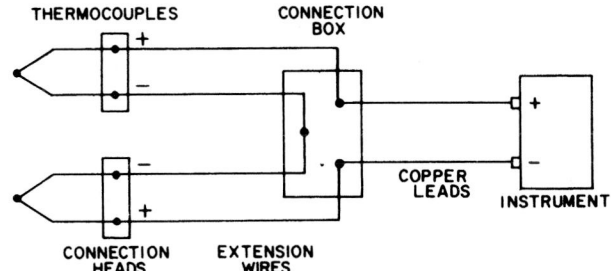

FIGURE 1-27   Differential temperature circuit. (*The Foxboro Company.*)

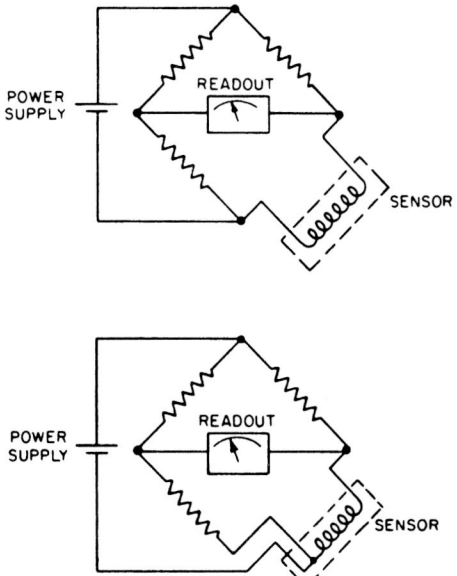

FIGURE 1-28   Two- and three-wire Wheatstone bridge.

Thermistors

These are metal oxide resistors having high temperature coefficients (usually negative), with resistance being a function of absolute temperature. They are used much like the RTDs. The large temperature coefficient makes them useful for very narrow-span temperature measurement. Self-heating is a problem to be considered when current flow through the sensor causes sensor temperature to be higher than ambient temperature.

Though not widely used in process environment, the application of thermistors in various types of electronic circuitry for temperature compensation has been widespread. The temperature-resistance characteristic curve tends to be fairly nonlinear, making interchangeability of sensors a problem.

Radiation Pyrometers

These instruments are a special class used in those applications where very high temperatures are to be measured and normal contact-type measurement is not possible. The basic principle is the use of an optical system to focus energy radiated to a detector. The system can be manual where this focused energy is compared with a calibrated optical filament, or automatic by using thermopiles or photomultiplier tubes. The accuracy depends on many factors, such as the emissivity of the source, reflections from other sources, and the line of sight. The temperature scale is nonlinear and the system tends to be expensive.

FLOW MEASUREMENT

The primary purpose of industrial control systems is to balance the material and energy flows in a process. Flow is the most common of the process variables. Accurage measurement and control are the two most important instrumentation functions. Table 1-5 lists some of the more common measurement methods and their characteristics.

TABLE 1-5 Flow Measurements*

Head type	Liquids	Viscous liquid	Slurry	Gas	Solids	Linear	Rangeability	Cost	% full-scale accuracy	Indirect totalizer	Pressure loss
1. Orifice plates	✓	L		✓		SR	4:1	Low	¼–2	✓	High
2. Rotameters	✓	L	L	✓		✓	10:1	Med	½–2	—	F
3. Venturi tubes, nozzles	✓	L	✓	✓		SR	4:1	High	¼–3	✓	Med
4. Pitot tubes	✓			✓		SR	3:1	Low	2–5	—	L
5. Elbow	✓	L	L	✓		SR	3:1	Low	5–10	—	No
6. Target meters	✓	L	L			SR	4:1	Med	½–2	✓	High
7. Weirs, flumes	✓	L	L			NL	100:1	Low	2–5	—	Med
Velocity type											
1. Magnetic	✓	✓	✓			✓	20:1	High	½–1	✓	No
2. Vortex	✓	L				✓	10:1	Med	½–2	✓	Med
Displacement											
1. Positive displacement	✓	L				✓	20:1	Med	¼–1	✓	Med
2. Turbine	✓	L	L	✓		✓	20:1	Med	¼–1	✓	Med
Mass flow											
1. Weight types					✓	✓	20:1	Med	½–3	—	—
2. Solids flowmeters					✓	✓	20:1	Med	½–3	—	—

* L, limited; NL, nonlinear; SR, square root; F, fixed.

Head-Type Devices

These are the most common types of measurement devices. Basically they depend upon a constriction in the fluid flow, thereby causing a pressure drop which can then be measured by a differential-pressure type of instrument.

Orifice Plates.   Figure 1-29 indicates the pressure profile for an orifice plate.

The *vena contracta* is the location where the downstream flow has the maximum velocity and the minimum cross-sectional area. Figure 1-30 indicates this location with respect to the diameter ratio of orifice opening to pipe inside diameter. Figure 1-31 illustrates the various types of orifice plates.

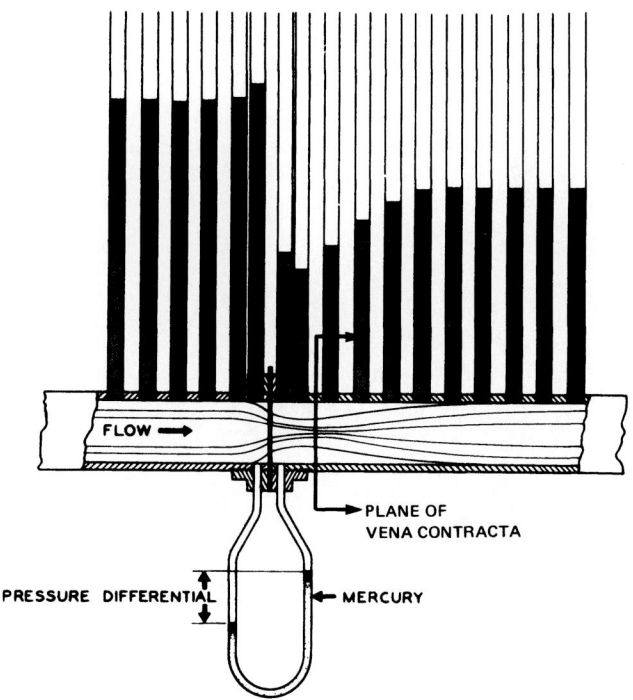

FIGURE 1-29   Pressure profile using an orifice plate.

The location of the orifice plate depends upon the type of taps used for the measurement of differential pressure. A certain section of straight pipe is required both upstream and downstream. Figure 1-32 is an example of the dimensions required using straightening vanes, which are devices that eliminate swirls, crosscurrents, and eddies set up by pipe fillings and valves in the upstream run.

Other types of primary elements that are used are shown in Fig. 1-33.

Figure 1-29 indicates that the pressure downstream of the primary element does not recover to its full value. Figure 1-34 indicates the permanent head loss as a percent of measured differential.

The following equations can be used for calculating flow rates for different services. Representative values for the *S* factor are given in Fig. 1-35.

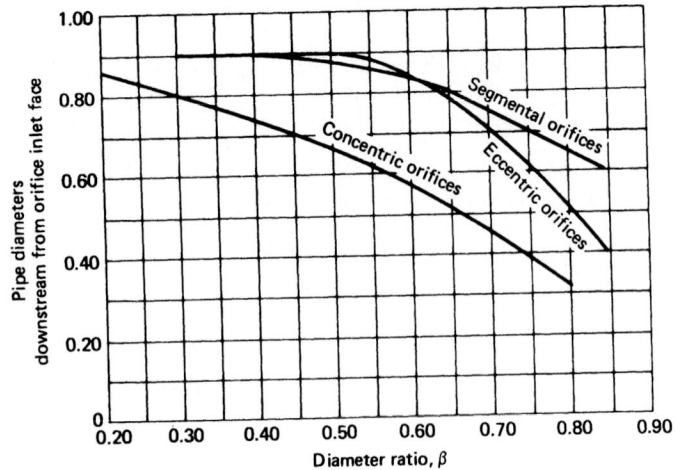

FIGURE 1-30 Location of the vena contracta.

FIGURE 1-31 Types of orifice plates.

Liquids:

$$\text{gal/min} = \frac{5.67SD^2\sqrt{h_w}}{G} \qquad \text{(to get L/min use 0.0066 instead of 5.67)}$$

Steam or other vapors:

$$\text{lb/h} = 359SD^2\sqrt{wh_w} \qquad \text{(to get kg/h use 0.01251 instead of 359)}$$

Gas:

$$\text{scfh} = 338.17SD^2F_gF_{tf}\sqrt{ph_w} \qquad \text{(to get Nm}^3\text{/h use 1 instead of 338.17)}$$

The standard condition is defined to be at 60°F (16°C) and 14.73 psia (760 mmHg), and the symbols in the equations are defined as follows:

S = flow coefficient (see Fig. 1-35)
G = specific gravity of the process fluid

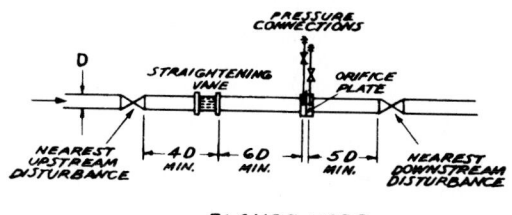

FLANGE TAPS

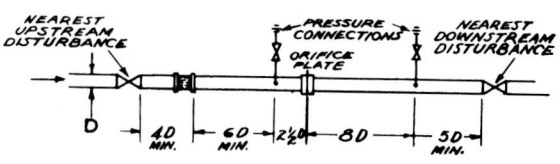

2 1/2 D AND 8 D TAPS

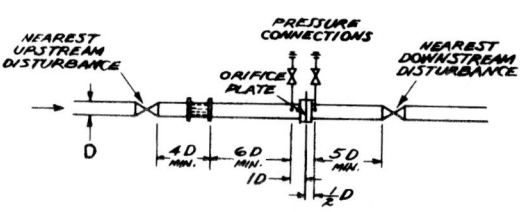

1 D AND 1/2 D TAPS

FIGURE 1-32   Liquid flow installation.

h_w = differential pressure, mm H_2O
w = steam or vapor density, lb/ft^3 (kg/m^3)
$F_g = \sqrt{1/G}$
F_{tf} = factor for flowing gas temperature, $\sqrt{520/(460 + °F)}$ or $\sqrt{228.7/(273.1 + °C)}$
    P = static pressure psia (kg/cm^2 abs) [either p_1 (upstream) or p_2 (downstream) since the differential h_w is ordinarily chosen to be less than 4 percent of p]

Target Flowmeter.   Another constriction-type device that has become popular recently is the target flowmeter. Figure 1-36 indicates a typical assembly with a pneumatic transmitter.

Steam- and water-flow measurements in outdoor installations are common applications. The complications of condensate pots, heat tracing, seal fluids, and antifreeze compounds to prevent freezing in cold weather are avoided.

The flow in volume or mass units is proportional to the square root of the force on the target.

Measurement accuracy of the head-type meters discussed so far depends on the Reynolds number R_D, which can be defined by

$$R_D = \rho \, \frac{VD}{\mu}$$

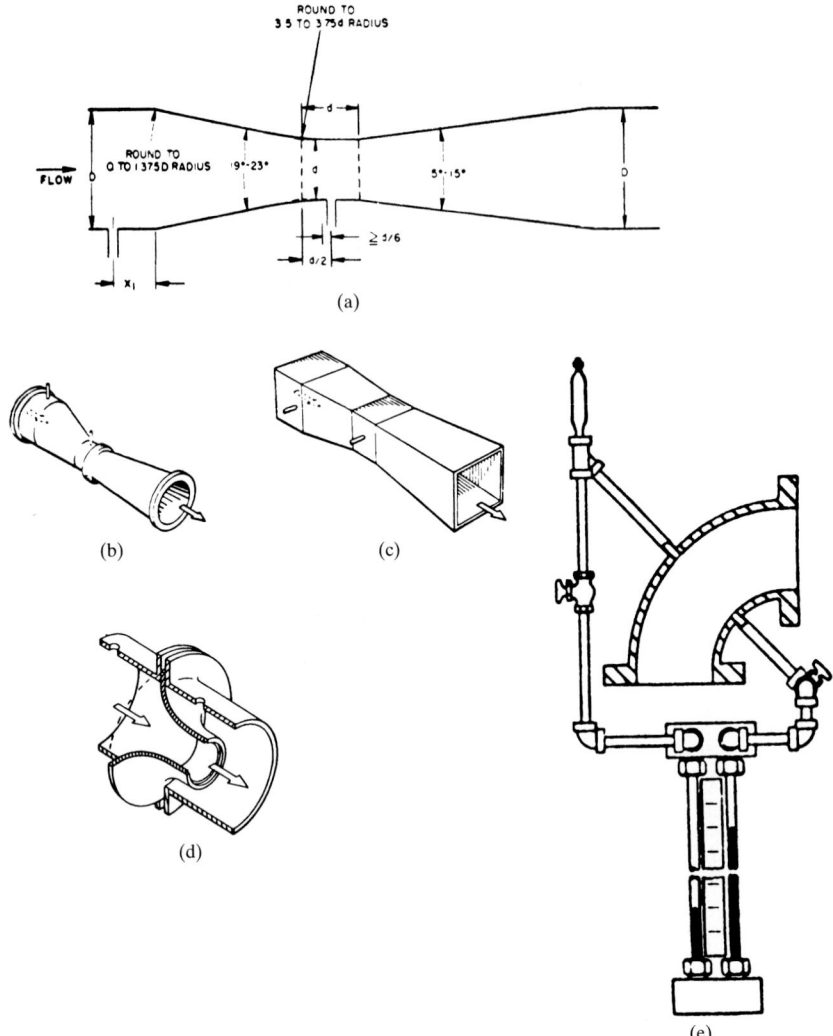

FIGURE 1-33 Flow nozzles, venturi tubes, and elbows. (*a*) The critical dimensions of the classical venturi tube. (*b*) An eccentric venturi tube. (*c*) A rectangular venturi tube. (*d*) Flow nozzle. (*e*) Elbow (used as primary device).

where ρ = density
         V = velocity
         D = pipe inside diameter (I.D.)
         μ = viscosity

The higher the Reynolds number, the flatter the velocity profile of the flow across the pipe inside diameter. If we define a flow coefficient K_a as a factor that when multiplied by the measured phenomena gives the required flow, then the plot of K_a vs. R_D for head-type meters is given in Fig. 1-37.

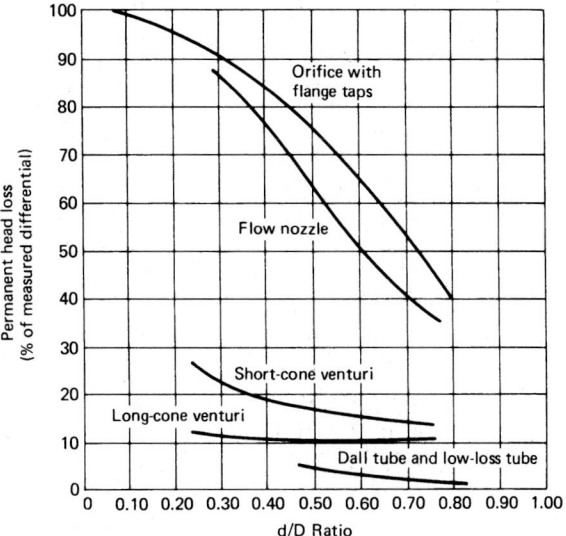

FIGURE 1-34 Permanent head loss for various devices.

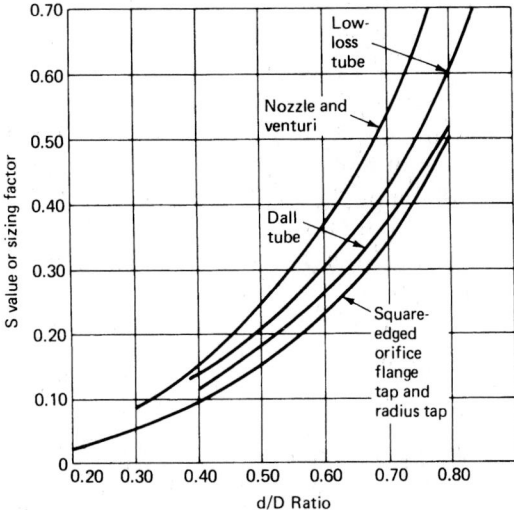

FIGURE 1-35 S values for various differential devices against beta ratios (d/D).

Weirs and Flumes. Open-channel measurements are important, especially in the waste- and water-treatment fields. Head H_a is developed by placing a weir in the flowpath as shown in Fig. 1-38. Aeration under the nappe is required for accurate flow measurement.

Formulas for different types of weirs are given below. For a V-notch weir (Fig. 1-39a),

$$\text{Flow} = Q_{cfs} = 2.48 \tan (\theta/2)\ H^{5/2} \qquad \text{ft}^3/\text{S}$$

For a rectangular weir (Fig. 1-39b),

$$Q_{cfs} = 3.33\ (L - 0.2H)\ H^{3/2}$$

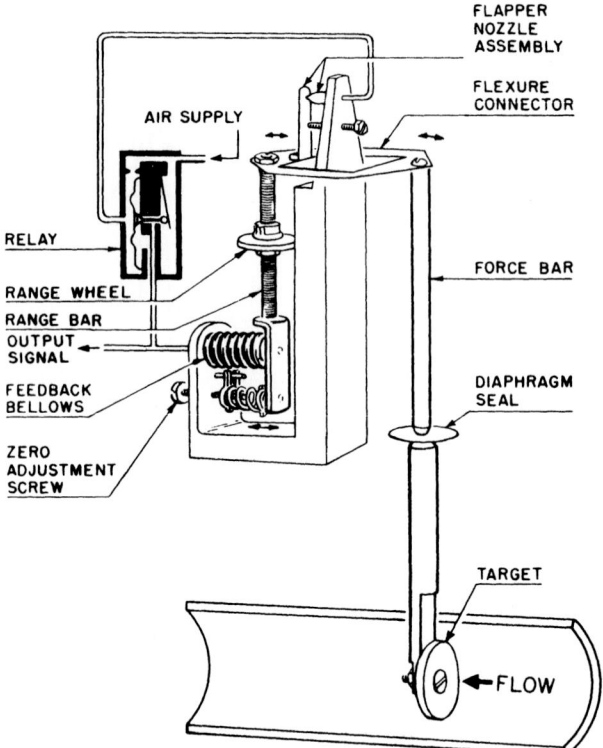

FIGURE 1-36 Target flowmeter. (*The Foxboro Company.*)

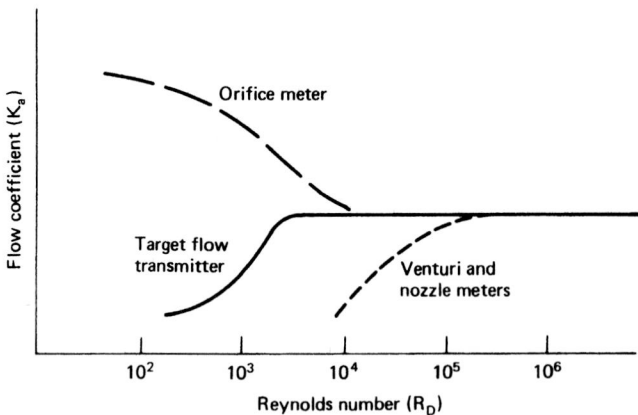

FIGURE 1-37 Typical flow-coefficient curves.

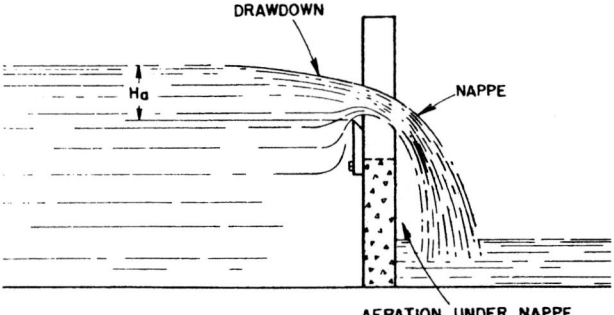

FIGURE 1-38   Aeration under nappe of weir.

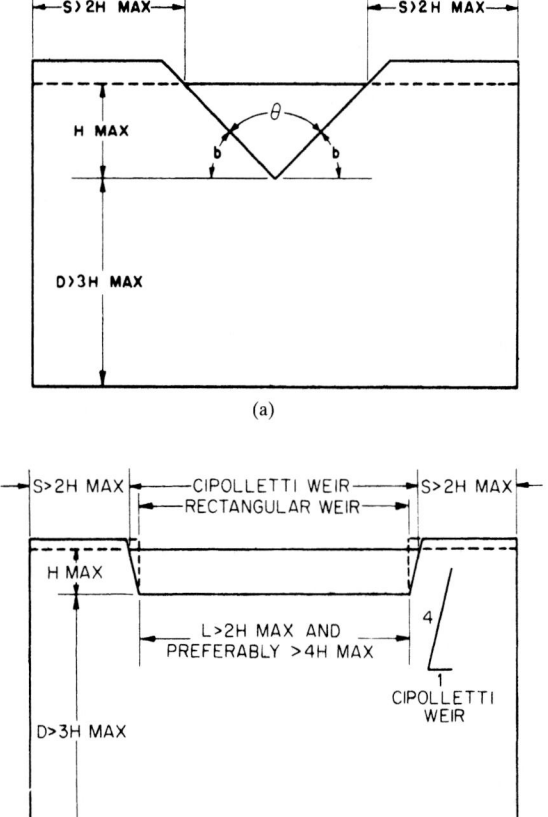

FIGURE 1-39   Weirs: (*a*) V-notch weir; (*b*) rectangular and Cipolletti weirs.

For a Cipolletti weir (Fig. 1.39b),

$$Q_{cfs} = 3.367LH^{3/2}$$

Figure 1-39 indicates L, H, and D, the typical dimensions for referenced weirs.

Flumes are low-head-loss measuring devices where a formed channel restriction changes static head to velocity head. Figure 1-40 illustrates the Parshall flume.

The three basic methods for measuring the head in a weir or flume are the float-and-cable, the in-flume float device, and the bubble tube.

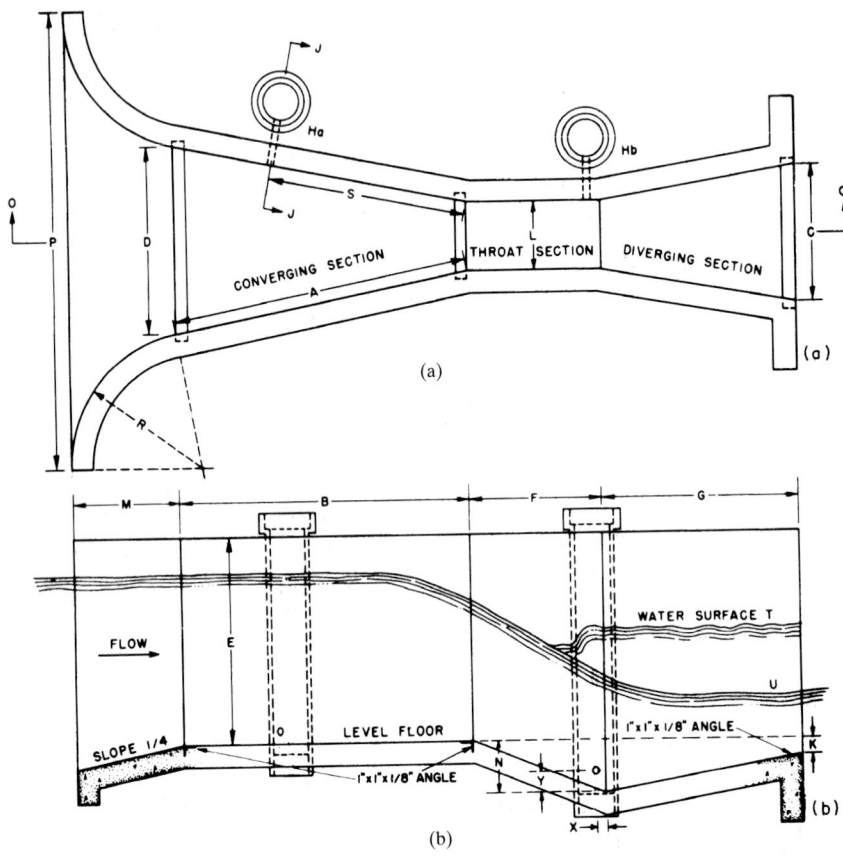

FIGURE 1-40 (a) Diagram and (b) dimensions of Parshall flume.

Rotameters. Our discussion so far has emphasized meters having a variable differential head and a constant restriction area. Rotameters, however, are devices using a constant differential and a variable restriction area. These instruments are typically used in measurement of small liquid or gas flows with local indication. Transmitter-type instruments for measuring large amounts of liquid flow (e.g., oil) are commercially available.

This device consists of a vertical tapered tube through which the flow passes in an upward direction. A float moves up until the upward force acting on the float is balanced by the downward gravitational force. If the tube is made out of glass, the position of the float is a direct and linear measurement of the flow. Transmitter-type instruments make use of a metallic tube in which the float is mechanically linked to the transmitter mechanism. Its accuracy is comparable to that of other head-type meters, with lower accuracy for indicating-type glass-tube meters. An advantage in transmitter-type instruments is the area available around the float for entrained fluid particles. The disadvantage is the mechanical linkage and its associated maintenance problems.

Velocity-Type Devices

The most common velocity device is the magnetic flowmeter. Its advantages are that no head loss occurs, it handles solids in suspension, no liquid connections are required, and an electronic output suitable for in-plant transmission is produced. Figure 1-41 shows a schematic drawing (a) and a cross section (b) of a typical instrument. Symbols used in Fig. 1-41 are listed:

E = generated voltage
C = meter constant
H = magnetic field
D = distance between conductors (pipe I.D.)
V = velocity of flow

The output is linear with velocity for a constant magnetic field. The instrument is fairly rugged and can measure wide ranges of flow. To minimize current flow in the measuring circuit, a high-input impedance amplifier is used, with special precautions for shielding the input circuit.

Another velocity meter of recent development is the vortex-shedding meter. Liquid flowing through the meter housing passes a specially shaped vortex element which causes vortices to form and shed (separate) from alternate sides of the element at a rate proportional to the flow rate of the liquid. These vortices create an alternating differential pressure which is sensed by a detector located at the "tail" of the vortex generator. An ac voltage signal is produced in the flowmeter with a frequency synchronous with the vortex-shedding frequency.

The meter offers accuracies on a par with turbine and positive displacement meters but has the advantage of requiring no moving parts in the liquid stream. Therefore, the problems arising from overspeeding the turbine with two-phase flows, or from damage when slugs of liquid impinge upon it, do not exist. The meter equation is

$$f = kQ$$

where f = frequency, pulses per minute
k = meter constant, pulses per unit volume
Q = flow rate

Figure 1-42 indicates the variation of k with respect to Reynolds number (signature curve) for a vortex flowmeter.

Displacement Meters

There are many configurations used for these types of meters. A rotor is placed in the flow-path and turns as a function of the force imparted to it by the flowing fluid. This motion can either be mechanically linked to a totalizer indicator or magnetically coupled so that each rotation produces a pulse. The meter output is linear with flow and is capable of being used over a wide range. The advantages of this meter lie in its accuracy and ruggedness in clean fluid application. The two disadvantages are the susceptibility of the rotor bearing to dirt and its limitation under high-velocity gas flows. These may occur due to flashing of the liquid under certain conditions of process operation. *Turbine meters* have to be designed such that pressure drop across the meter does not cause the flowing fluid to flash (Fig. 1-43a).

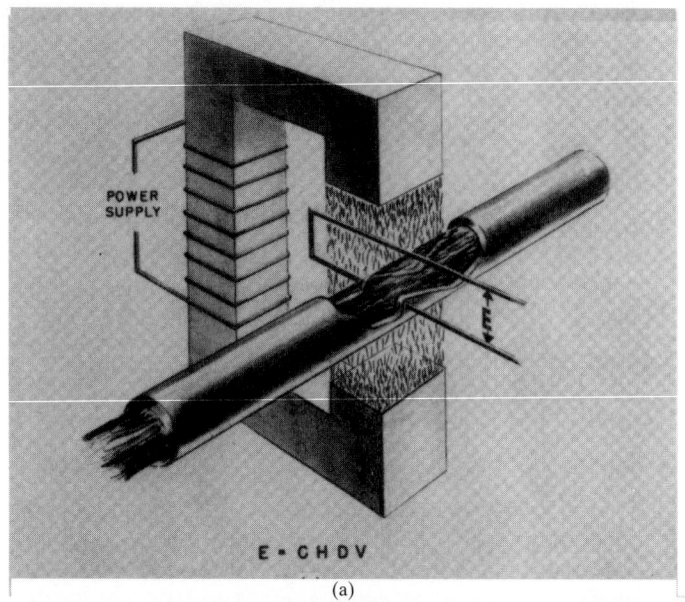

(a)

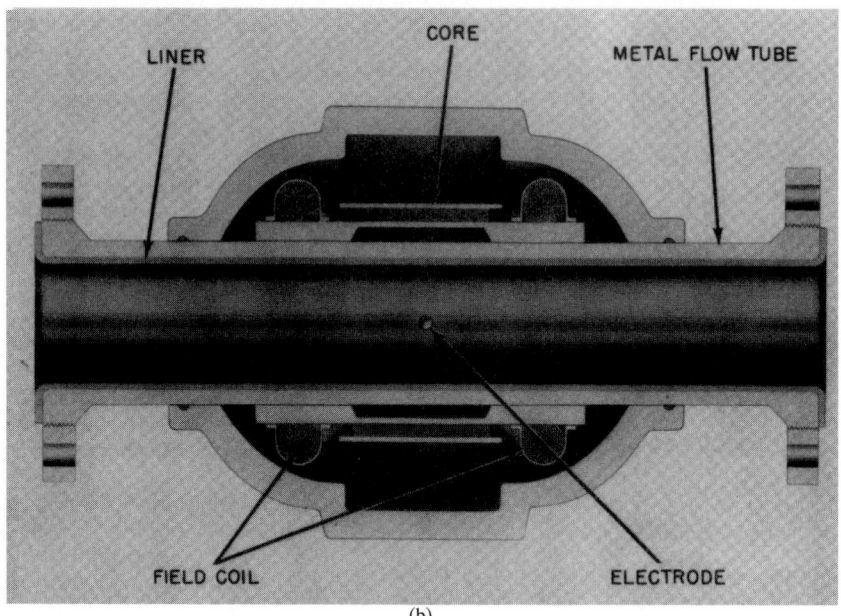

(b)

FIGURE 1-41 Magnetic flowmeter. (*a*) Schematic diagram. (*b*) Cross-sectional diagram. (*The Foxboro Company.*)

The meter accuracy is a function of viscosity, with the smaller-sized meters being affected more. Variation of k (equation similar to that for a vortex-shedding meter) is approximately ±3 percent for a 1-in (2.5-cm) meter while it is approximately ±0.75 percent for a 6-in (10.5-cm) meter. Figure 1-43*b* is a typical signature curve of a turbine meter showing the effect of viscosity.

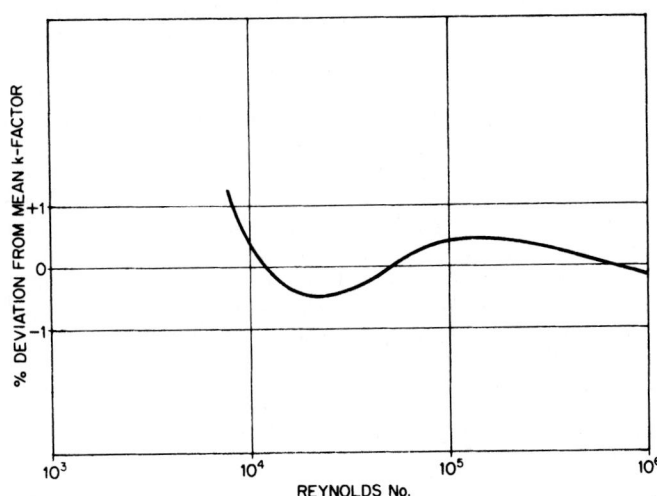

FIGURE 1-42   Typical signature curve of E83 vortex flowmeter.

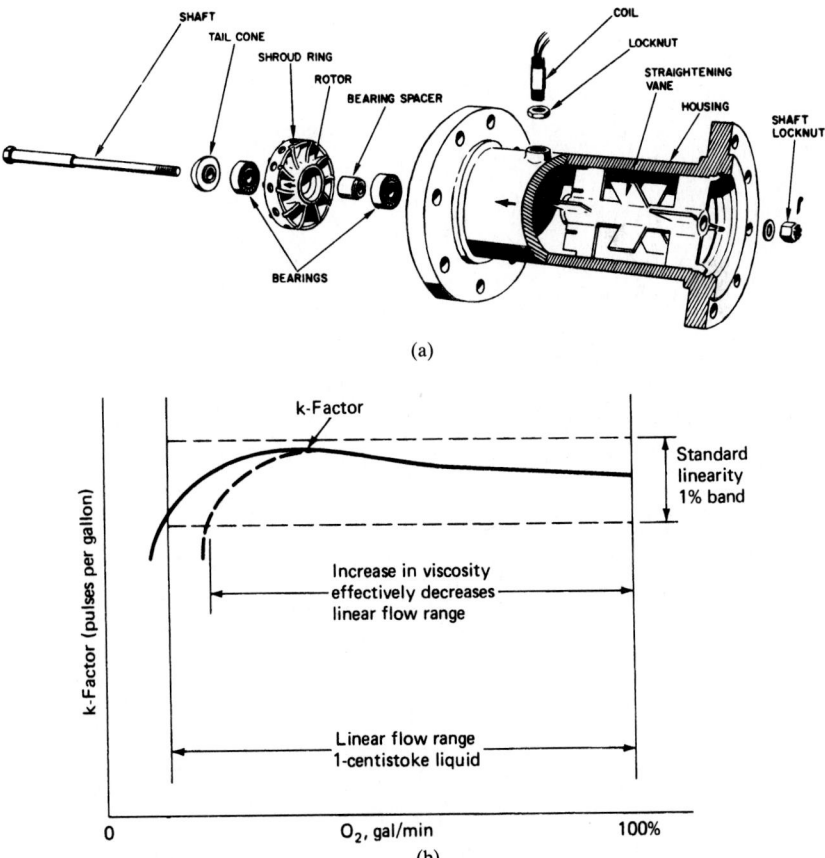

(a)

(b)

FIGURE 1-43   (*a*) Schematic of a turbine flowmeter. (*b*) A typical signature curve.

Mass Flowmeters

Mass flowmeters attract attention in two general applications. One is in processes that involve chemical reactions. Whether batch or continuous, chemical reactions are dependent on relative proportions of reactants and not on volume. Correct proportions of reactants minimize excess nonreacted materials, saving the cost of materials or further reprocessing. Chemical reactions include the burning of fuels. The second general application is in processes that manipulate materials that are bought/sold by weight and not by volume.

If volumetric flowmeters are used to determine mass flow, then it is necessary to measure and make corrections for variations in temperature, pressure, density, viscosity, and the like. This results in greater expense and the possibility of greater error.

The mass flowmeter, on the other hand, gives a direct measurement independent of others. It also has excellent accuracy and rangeability. Typical accuracy is $\pm$ 0.2 percent of flow reading or $\pm$ 0.02 percent of maximum flow rate, whichever is greater. As an example, say a meter has a maximum flow rate of 100 lb (45kg)/min. At the maximum flow rate the accuracy is $\pm$0.2 lb/min. From 100 to 10 lb (45 to 4.5 kg)/min the accuracy is $\pm$0.2 percent of the flow reading. For flow rates less than 10 lb (4.5 kg)/min the accuracy is $\pm$ 0.02 lb (0.9 kg)/min.

The Coriolis-type mass flow sensor has a sine wave voltage applied to an electromagnetic drive (or two) which produces an oscillating or vibrating motion (approximately 0.1 in [2.5 mm]) of the flow tube. The frequency of the sine wave is at the resonant frequency of the tube plus contents (approximately 70 to 100 Hz). The resulting motion is sensed by two

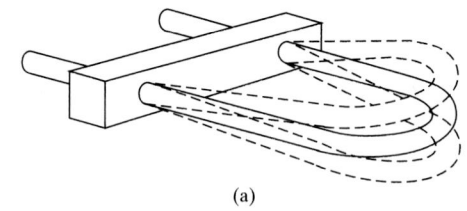

(a)

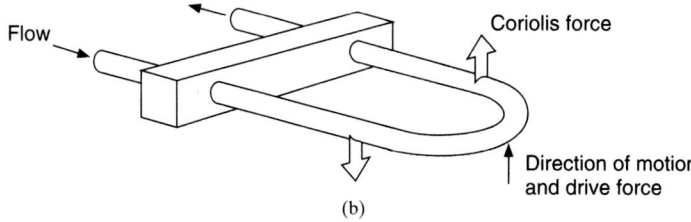

Flow

Coriolis force

Direction of motion and drive force

(b)

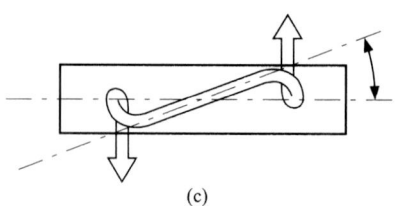

(c)

FIGURE 1-44 U tube mass flowmeter: (*a*) vibrating element; (*b*) drive and coriolis forces; and (*c*) angular twist.

electromagnetic devices which produce sine wave outputs. The output amplitudes are related to the mass flow. The frequency is related to the product density. The transmitter contains the electronic circuitry to look at the sensor outputs and extract the measurement of mass flow, density, and totalized flow. Additionally, a temperature sensor, used to compensate for temperature-caused errors in determining flow rate and density, may be available to indicate the product temperature. The transmitter may be a stand-alone device having pulse and/or milliampere outputs, or it may interface with a more sophisticated instrumentation system.

The reason the output amplitude changes with flow may be explained by the Coriolis effect. The vibration or motion of the flow tube is a slight angular rotation about a center point (similar to the motion of a spring diving board). When the flow moves away from the center, there is a resultant Coriolis force which opposes rotational motion. When the flow moves toward the center, there is a resultant Coriolis force which aids rotational motion. The resultant forces produce a greater motion (and sine wave output) in one sensor and a smaller motion in the other. With no flow the amplitudes are the same.

ANALYTICAL MEASUREMENTS

The successful operation of some complicated chemical processes is partially dependent upon analytical measurements and their use in process control. This discussion is limited to those measurements that can be made directly using a sensing electrode or other detectors. The accuracy and repeatability, to a certain extent, is a function of the "known" sample used for calibration. The application of the sensor is based to a great extent on the background chemistry of the process and, therefore, careful study of the alternatives is required before a particular choice can be made.

Chromatographs

These are general-purpose instruments used both for on-line process control and laboratory composition analysis. It would be difficult to run a modern chemical process without these instruments.

Components.   The three basic components of a chromatograph are (1) the sample injection mechanism, (2) the separation column, and (3) the detector. Figure 1-45 shows the basic operation. As long as conditions within the analyzer remain the same, the three components indicated will appear at the same instant of time as measured from the start of the analysis. The height of the peak identifies the percent of that component present in the stream. The chart record at the end of the cycle is called a chromatogram.

Analytical Conditions.   The four major conditions that the analysis depends upon are (1) sample size, (2) carrier-gas flow rate, (3) analyzer temperature, and (4) carrier-gas pressure. Sample size must remain constant because detectors "see" only the actual amount of a given component, not a percent of the whole sample. If a sample twice as large as an earlier sample were used, the detector would show twice as much of a given component, assuming the sample was taken from the same source. Therefore, to get a true percent analysis the sample size must remain constant.

Carrier-gas flow rate and carrier-gas pressure are interrelated. A more rapid carrier-gas flow rate will "carry" the sample and components through the column faster, causing the time of elution to be shorter. Analyzer temperature must be held constant, since a higher temperature will cause the column elution rate to increase.

Columns.   The column is used for separation on a time basis. It consists of a small-diameter tube made of type 316 stainless steel, varying in length from several inches (centimeters) to a few yards (meters). Three basic types of columns are used.

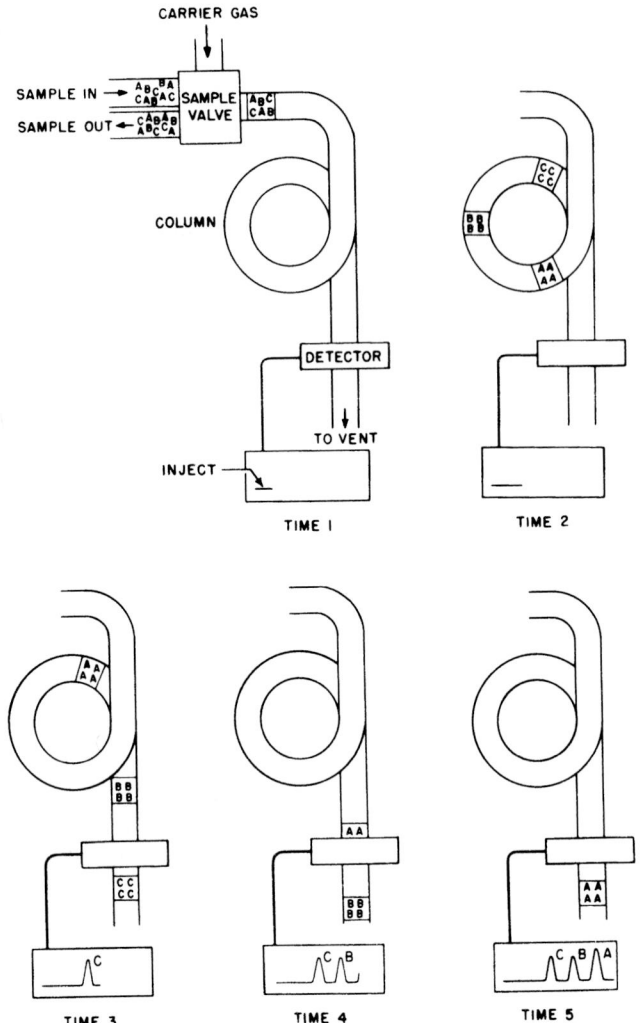

FIGURE 1-45 Chromatographic separation.

Partition Columns. The partition type uses a solid support, such as crushed firebrick coated with a high-boiling-point liquid (the liquid phase). Separation is achieved by the relative solubility of each component of the sample in the film of liquid (usually on oil) coating the support. A component of low solubility passes through the column much more quickly than one with high solubility. If the liquid phase had a high vapor pressure at the operating temperature, the flow of carrier gas would strip this liquid, leaving the column bare and thereby affecting the separating ability of the column. This phenomenon is known as *column bleed.*

Adsorption Columns. A second type of column is the adsorption column, where separation is based upon relative difference in adherence to an adsorbent material used to pack the column. These packing materials are surface-active solids such as charcoal, silica gel, and activated alumina. Components which adhere the least are eluted first.

Molecular Sieve. The third type of column includes Molecular Sieves, where the variation in molecular size of the components is used for the separation. The larger molecules are slowed down more than the smaller ones. These columns are most often used for hydrogen, oxygen, argon, nitrogen, carbon monoxide, and methane.

Backflushing.   Figure 1-46 shows a schematic diagram of a sample and a backflush valve. Backflushing is used to preserve the life of a column and/or decrease the total cycle time for the particular application.

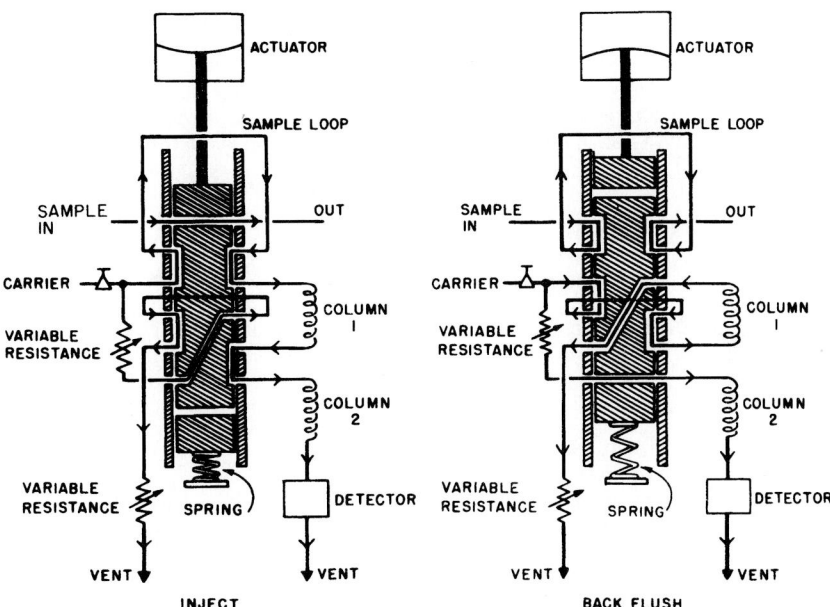

FIGURE 1-46   Schematic diagram of sample and back-flush valves.

Detectors.   There are many types of detectors that have been used. The thermal-conductivity type is based upon the difference in conductivity of the binary mixture flowing across the element. The flame-ionization type is based upon the ion current generated when the binary mixture of carrier gas and component is burned upon mixing with fuel, e.g., hydrogen. It does not work for inorganic compounds.

The gas-density type senses the change in density between the carrier gas and the binary mixture by using the change in differential density across an orifice or a "pneumatic" Wheatstone bridge.

The output of the detector is the chromatogram. Though this type of output is useful for laboratory-type analysis, a continuous-trend output is more useful for control. This is accomplished by incorporating extra circuitry to detect the peak for a given component and a memory circuit to hold this peak value between column cycles. The output can be a continuous signal which is used in the control loop.

Ion-Based Measurements

The most common of these is the measurement of pH. There are many applications for this measurement, with the field getting wider in scope. Some examples are:

1. Those chemical processes where the pH determines the reaction rate
2. Uniformity in product quality based upon maintaining correct pH valve

3. Neutralization of waste effluent for discharge into sewers and rivers (controlled by law)

4. Corrosion control in high-pressure boilers

The principle of measurement is based upon dissociation of chemical compounds into positively and negatively charged particles (known as cations and anions) in an aqueous solution. For a hypothetical chemical compound MA the chemical reaction may be written as

$$MA \rightleftharpoons M^+ + A^-$$

The amount of dissociation depends upon the compound and the temperature of the solution. At any fixed temperature, a fixed relationship exists between the ions and the undissociated compound. This relationship is based on the *activity* of the ions, a term which indicates the ability of an ion to take part in a reaction and is related to the *concentration* of the ions by

$$a = vc$$

where a = activity of the ion
  v = activity coefficient
  c = concentration of the ion

The dissociation is related to the activity of the ions by the dissociation constant k as follows:

$$k = \frac{[a_{M+}]\,[a_{A-}]}{a_{MA}}$$

where a_{M+}, a_{A-}, and a_{MA} are the activity of the positive and negative ions and the undissociated compound, respectively.

Therefore, if one could measure the activity of a particular ion, by knowing its activity coefficient the concentration of the particular ion in solution can be determined. If the ion of interest happens to be hydrogen [H^+], the measurement is known as pH, which is a short form for $1/a_{H+}$.

Recent research has been fruitful in developing sensors which can measure other types of ions, such as fluoride, silver, sulfide, chloride, and cyanide. Figure 1-47 shows a basic setup for measurement using two half-cells, one formed by the measuring electrode and the other by the reference electrode.

The potential generated by a measuring electrode is related to the ionic activity, and is expressed by the Nernst equation,

$$E = E^1 + \frac{2.3RT}{nF} \log \frac{a_1}{a_2}$$

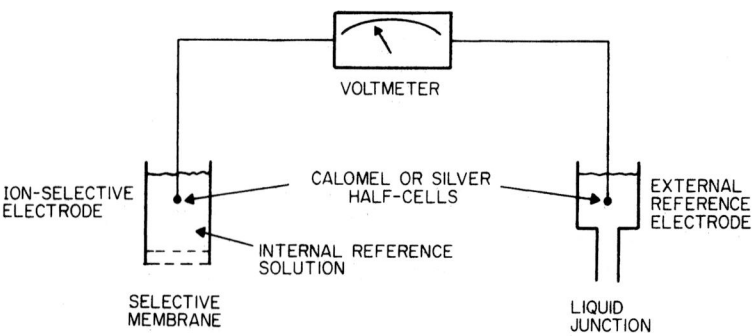

FIGURE 1-47   Basic arrangement for ion-selective measurement.

where E = electrode potential
E^1 = constant for a given electrode at a fixed temperature
R = gas law constant, 1.986 Btu/(lb)(mol)(°R) [1.986 cal/(g)(mol)(K)]
T = absolute temperature, K or °R
F = Faraday's constant, 96,490 C/g-ion
n = charge of an ion, including sign
a_1 = activity of measured ion in process solution
a_2 = activity of measured ion in the internal solution

If the internal solution is made up such that it has constant activity, the equation can be simplified to

$$E = E° + \frac{2.3RT}{nF} \log a_1$$

where $E°$ is the standard emf of the hydrogen cell.
For measurement of hydrogen activity the equation can be simplified to

$$E = 414.12 - [59.16 \text{ pH at } 77°F \ (25°C)] \qquad \text{in mV}$$

Since the simplified Nernst equation has a temperature term, errors can exist for pH measurements at any other point than pH = 7.0, which is the isopotential point for this ion measurement. Figure 1-48 indicates the errors that can be expected.

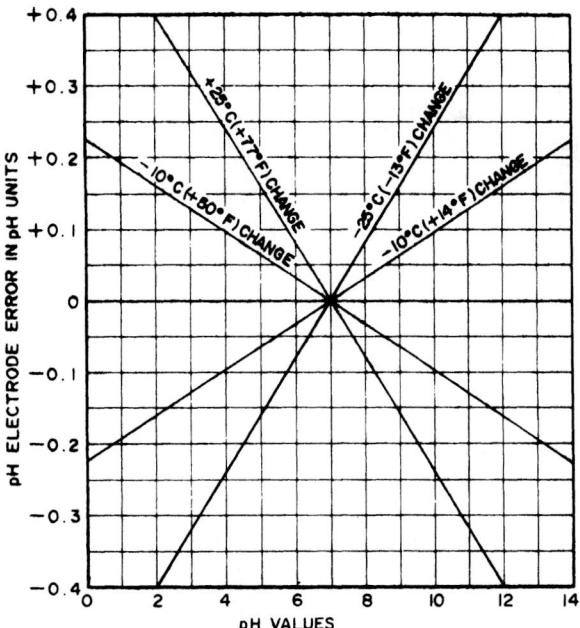

FIGURE 1-48 Graph of pH values at various solution temperatures vs. pH measurement errors due to temperature differences across the measurement electrode tip. No temperature error and no compensation required at pH 7.

Figure 1-49 shows the construction details of a glass pH measuring electrode with the internal solution buffered to have constant ph of 7.0. Figure 1-50 shows a flowing reference electrode with the ceramic tip acting as the liquid junction. The silver electrode with the silver chloride coating forms a silver-silver chloride half-cell in the reference electrode. To eliminate this potential in the overall measuring circuit (Figure 1-47), a similar half-cell is created in the measuring electrode, thereby having the meter read only the potential across the measuring electrode's ion-sensitive membrane. These electrodes can also come in the solid-state form, where the flow at the liquid junction is decreased to very small amounts.

It should be noted that the reference electrode does not create a measurement potential at the liquid junction since the flow of liquid prevents that. However, a small potential is still created by the ionic flow, and this may be compensated for in the measuring instrument. The measuring instrument must have a high input impedance to prevent current flows which can cause polarization problems in the electrodes. This high impedance requirement and millivolt measurement require special care in shielding of the measurement leads and grounding of the system.

While the Nernst equation was applied to the activity of specific ions, a more general form would be to consider it as follows:

$$E = E_0 + \frac{2.3RT}{nF} \, \log \frac{[a_{ox}]}{[a_{red}]}$$

where we consider the ratio of the activity of all the oxidized ions in solution to that of all the reduced ions. Oxidation here means the loss of an electron; reduction means a gain. The measuring electrode is a metallic plate (could be platinum), and the reference electrode is similar as for ion-selective measurement. E_0 is a constant which varies for differing types of reactions.

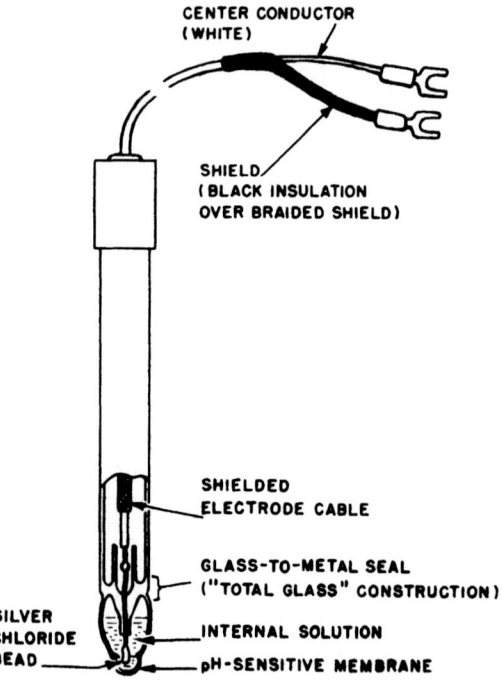

FIGURE 1-49 Construction of details of measuring electrode.

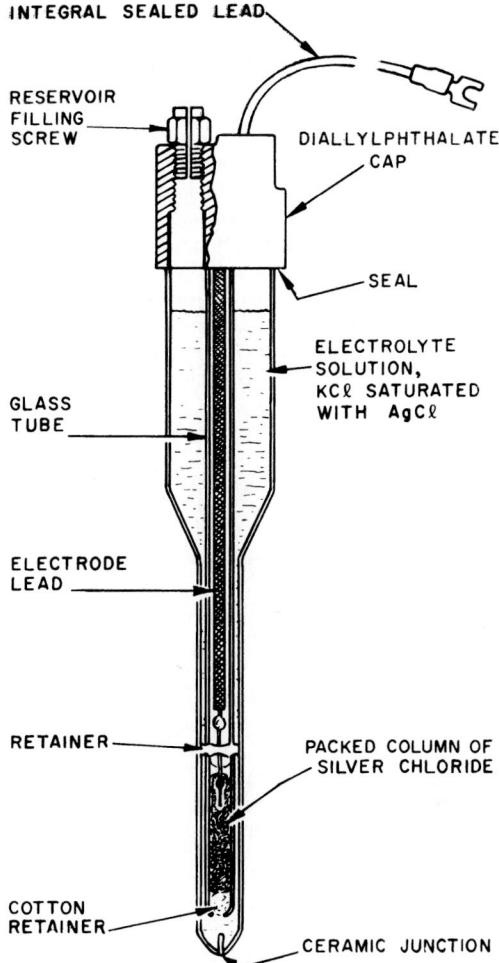

INTEGRAL SEALED LEAD

RESERVOIR
FILLING
SCREW

DIALLYLPHTHALATE
CAP

SEAL

GLASS
TUBE

ELECTROLYTE
SOLUTION,
KCℓ SATURATED
WITH AgCℓ

ELECTRODE
LEAD

RETAINER

PACKED COLUMN OF
SILVER CHLORIDE

COTTON
RETAINER

CERAMIC JUNCTION

FIGURE 1-50   Construction details of flowing reference electrode.

These types of measurements are called oxidation-reduction-potential (or redox) measurements and are used when an oxidation or reduction type of chemical reaction is taking place, e.g., oxidation of cyanide or reduction of chromate in effluent treatment. The installations tend to be unique and depend greatly upon the background chemistry.

Conductivity

Aqueous solutions are electrically conductive, the amount being a function of temperature and concentration of ions in solution. It is expressed as specific conductance or conductivity in siemens. The conductance between two electrodes can be given by

$$C = \frac{k}{(1/A)} \quad \text{or} \quad \frac{K}{F}$$

where F = cell factor in cm^{-1}, the ratio of the distance in cm between the two electrodes
A = area of the electrodes, cm^2
C = conductivity, normally given in microsiemens

The cell factor allows the spanning for the measuring instrument, which is basically a Wheatstone bridge. It should be noted that the measurement is non-ion-specific but is an indication of all ions present in solution. For calibration, known samples are used, thereby allowing the cell to be calibrated to read directly in concentration units.

The conductivity of a solution is a function of its temperature. Compensation can be provided if the solution's conductivity temperature curve is known. This limits the cell's application only to the solution for which the calibration was provided. When an electric current is passed through a solution, polarization can occur. One of the effects is electrolysis, whereby a gaseous layer can form on the electrode surface, thus increasing the relative resistance of the cell. For this reason, alternating currents are normally used.

Figure 1-51 illustrates the cell factor for various configurations of electrodes.

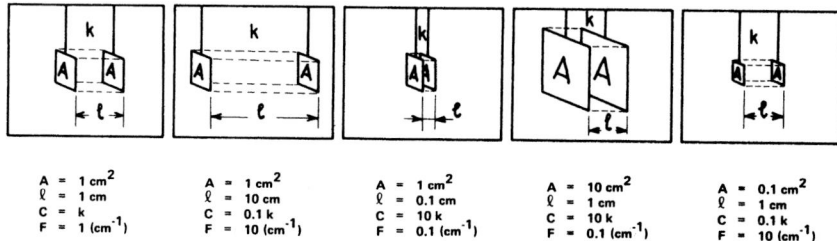

FIGURE 1-51   Electrode cell factors.

There are many applications where conductivity cells can provide a relatively inexpensive method for controlling processes like detecting impurities in boiler feedwater, concentration of black liquor, and other applications where the concentration of a known compound in solution has to be determined.

Oxygen and Dissolved Oxygen

These measurements have become increasingly important in the combustion and water-treatment fields. The most popular method for oxygen measurement is the electrochemical detector, which works in principle by using the Nernst equation. Figure 1-52 indicates a schematic drawing of the basic cell, with P_1 the partial pressure of oxygen in the reference gas and P_2 the partial pressure of oxygen in the measured gas. The equation is

$$E = E^\circ + \frac{2.3RT}{nF} \log \frac{P_1}{P_2}$$

and the resulting logarithmic output voltage is approximately 53 mV per decade change in oxygen content. The output decreases as the concentration (actually activity) of measured oxygen increases. The measurement is a percent measurement as related to all components in the sample gas, including water vapor. The probe can be installed on-line with no sample preparation system required.

There are many devices available for measuring dissolved oxygen (DO). In general, the construction requires two electrodes in an electrolyte enclosed by a permeable membrane. Depending upon the electrodes, a galvanic reaction or polarization takes place when a small voltage is applied to the electrodes. The dissolved oxygen diffuses through the membrane and

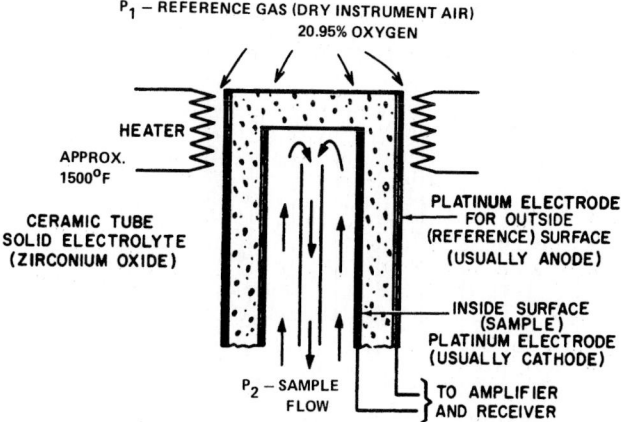

FIGURE 1-52   High-temperature electromechanical oxygen detector.

is dissolved in the electrolyte. An oxidation-reduction reaction causes a current flow which can then be measured as a percentage of the maximum amount that could be present at the existing temperature. Since temperature determines the saturation capability of the solution to dissolve oxygen, automatic compensation is usually required.

General

From a control-application viewpoint, all instruments based upon the Nernst equation have to take into account the nonlinear nature of the measurement. The logarithmic nature of the measurement requires special consideration of the rangeability requirements of the system. Figure 1-53 illustrates the nonlinear nature of the neutralization curve for strong acid or strong base solutions and the effect of buffering in the solution.

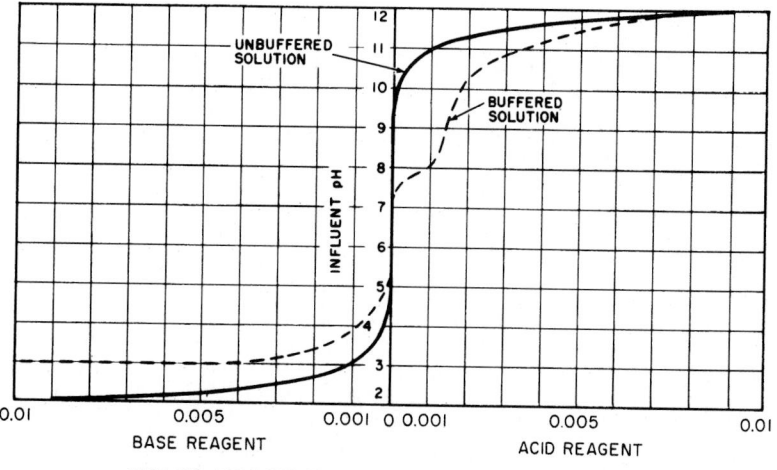

FIGURE 1-53   Typical neutralization curves for unbuffered solutions (strong acid or strong base) and buffered solutions.

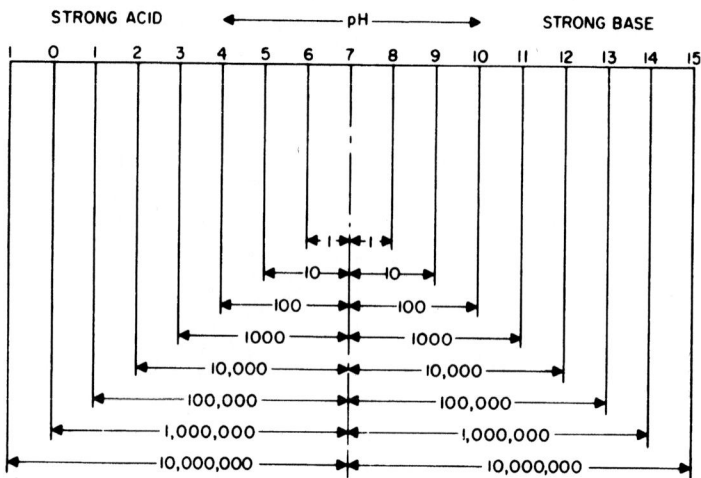

FIGURE 1-54 Graph of reagent demand. Reagent addition units are 10^{-6} mol/Li.

The rangeability requirements can be noted in Fig. 1-54. It can also be noted that while neutralization of an acid from pH 6.0 to 7.0 requires one unit of base, to go from pH 2.0 to 7.0 requires 10,000 units. Therefore, if the influent stream varies from pH 2.10 to 7.10, the control system must have a rangeability of 10,000:1.

CHAPTER 11-2
AUTOMATIC CONTROLS

Ranjit S. Randhawa
The Foxboro Company
Foxboro, Massachusetts

INTRODUCTION

Industrial processes are generally characterized by mass and energy flows. Application of automatic controls is concerned with the behavior of the process under dynamic or unsteady-state conditions where the accumulation of mass or energy cannot be tolerated. Hence the control problem is one in which the designer uses various engineering tools to match the supply against the demand over a period of time. The three terms, supply, demand, and time, can vary and depend to a great extent upon the type of processes considered. As processes get more and more complex and the availability of raw materials, including energy, becomes limited, the application of automatic control theory takes on greater significance.

Types of Controls

There are two basic types of control: open-loop and closed-loop.

Open-Loop Control. This is the simplest type of control that can be applied. It involves making an estimate of the amount of control action required based upon achieving a desired objective without regard to the actual conditions of the process. For example, a washing machine operates without regard to the actual condition of the clothes. The amount of detergent used and the settings on the machine are an estimate of the control action required in achieving the objective (clean clothes), they are not based on the actual state of our objective. This type of control is generally inadequate and is seldom encountered in industrial process work; however, this type of control cannot be completely ignored. With the advent of computers and their memory capability, control sequences based upon historical data may be considered in the future, especially for the kinds of processes where a measurement of the final objective may be difficult, if not impossible.

Closed-Loop Feedback. This is the most common type of control mechanism used. Any process in which the process variable under control is measurable allows the use of such control strategy. The importance of such a loop can be judged by the fact that most bio-socioeconomic processes incorporate some kind of closed-loop feedback mechanism, also known as a *servomechanism* (Fig. 2-1).

The controlled variable is the process variable which we are trying to maintain at some desired value (called the set point). Industrial processes are characterized by the many types of control variables that are encountered, e.g., temperatures, flows, and levels. The function of the transmitter is to quantify this variable in terms of signals, which could be pneumatic, electric, hydraulic, or just a mechanical output like the position of a lever. It should be remembered that not all these measurements are linear, i.e., the output signal is not necessarily linear with respect to the controlled variable or, even if it is linear, is not a direct reading of the controlled variable, e.g., the controlling flow based directly on the pressure drop ΔP across an orifice meter. In all these cases, linearization can be achieved, thereby making the transmitter output a direct indication of the controlled variable.

The manipulated variable is that which the controller varies in its efforts to maintain the controlled variable at set point. The controller output is a signal to, say, a valve actuator, causing the valve to move to a position which would depend upon the value of the signal, type of valve, and the process conditions under which it is operating. The valve positioner causes a fixed relationship between the controller signal and valve position. Even though this relationship could be linear, the relationship between valve position and flow-through is generally complex and nonlinear. The nonlinearities in measurement and in the control of the manipulated variable have a significant influence upon the performance of the control loop.

The feedback control loop operates in an environment where constant disturbances are taking place. These disturbances affect the controlled variable and could be due to changes in the manipulated variable other than those instituted by the controller; e.g., changes in mass or energy flows to the input of the process, or changes of the same variable on the output side of the process. Changes can also be initiated by the operator when changing the set point of the loop. The controller loop must therefore perform both as a regulator and as a servomecha-

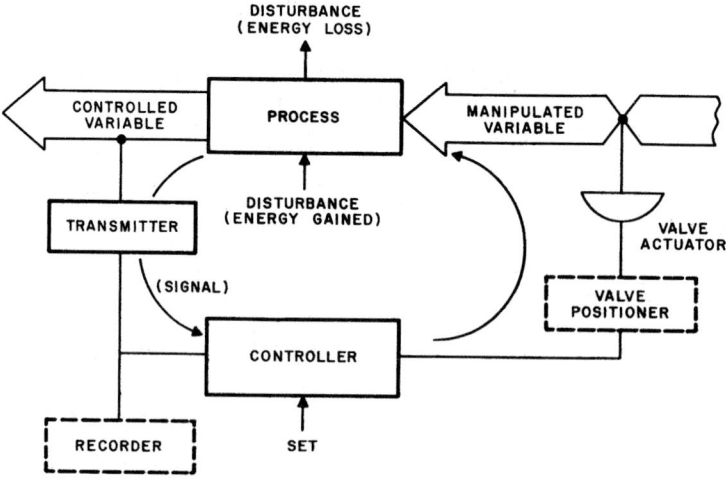

FIGURE 2-1 Closed-loop control. (*The Foxboro Company.*)

nism. The strategy used is straightforward and makes use of the error (the difference between set point and the measured controlled variable) to develop a control signal which will drive the error to zero and thereby achieve the objective. The performance of the loop can be judged as some integral function of error and time, the controller and its action then being set to minimize this function.

The existence of this error means a certain economic loss in the production process in terms of either the production of off-specification product, the use of excessive amounts of energy, or both. As these considerations become more and more important in the future, control loops will tend to get complex, and input disturbances will be measured and used in strategies called *feed-forward*. Here the measured inputs are used to compute the required positioning of the manipulated variable based upon some mathematical model of the process. The amount of correction required is then based on the variation of the inputs to the process. As the models tend to be simplified representations of the process, feed-forward strategies are not accurate over the entire operating range of the process. Feed-forward control strategies are normally used in conjunction with feedback, as shown in Fig. 2-2.

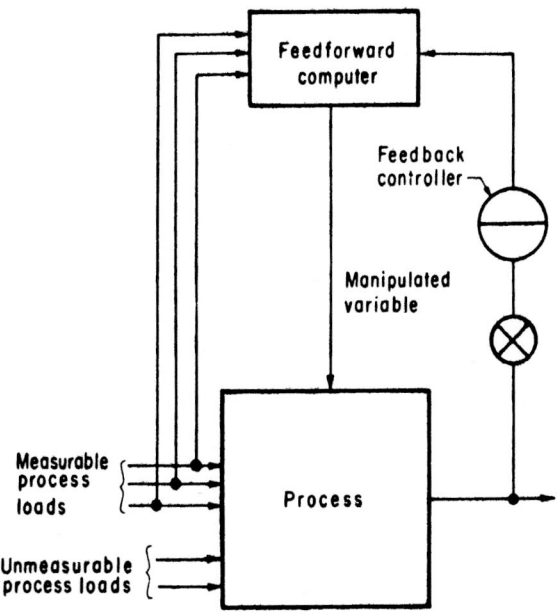

FIGURE 2-2   Feed-forward with feedback.

It should now be noted that the feedback controller does not have any direct control of the process but acts to take minor trim action on the feed-forward model. The major control function is accomplished by the feed-forward scheme. The limited action by the feedback controller allows a much more stable operation of the process, allowing set points to be set closer to the required specification values and also allowing increased throughput.

The time response of the entire control loop is made up of the sum of the responses of the primary element, the transmitter, all receivers in series with the controller, the controller, the final operator, and the process itself. There are two types of time elements which occur in industrial processes: first, dead time (or transportation lag) and, second, the resistance-capacitance (RC) time constant. To determine how much of each exists, a simple open-loop test can be performed as follows. With the loop in steady-state operation, the controller output is

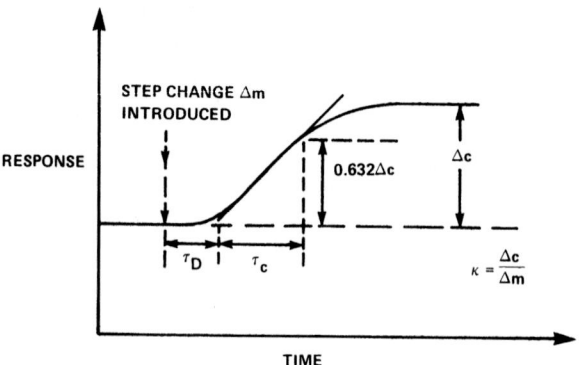

FIGURE 2-3 Open-loop response.

manually changed by a step amount. The response of the controlled variable is plotted as a function of time, as shown in Fig. 2-3.

The graphical construction is designed to approximate a process consisting of a dead time τ_D and a capacitance time τ_c. Most processes will have some combination of these two elements, with the control problem becoming easier as the ratio of τ_D/τ_c becomes smaller. While this example is a simple model of the process, more complex models are available which approximate the response curve more closely. These, however, become cumbersome for practical use. Time elements introduce a phase lag; i.e., the output is delayed with respect to the input. The phase lag varies as the frequency of the input signal and becomes larger as the frequency increases.

If a loop is to oscillate with a sustained cycle, the phase shift of an upset, after going through all the elements in the loop, must be exactly 360 degrees.

All feedback controllers contain an element called *negative feedback,* which introduces a phase shift of 180 degrees. The remainder of the control loop must create an additional 180 degrees for sustained oscillations to exist. The point at which this occurs is the natural period of the loop as long as the controller contributes no phase shift.

In addition to the phase shift in a loop, one must consider the gains of the various elements in a control loop. There are two types of gains, static and dynamic. Figure 2-3 introduces the static gain κ as the change in output divided by the change in input. Dynamic gain would be the same ratio but would be a function of the frequency of the input signal. The gain at any given frequency would be the product of the static and dynamic gains. A loop gain could then be defined as the product of the gains of the individual elements of a loop. It is a dimensionless number which is an indication of the stability of the loop. As the loop gain becomes greater than 1, the loop tends to oscillate with larger and larger amplitude, while a value less than 1 would cause a certain amount of damping of the amplitude of oscillation. Normal industry practice is to achieve a loop gain of 0.5, which is also called ¼ amplitude damping, where every amplitude is half the previous one. These criteria do not necessarily prevail in all industrial control loops, but they are typical. Particular process requirements may mandate other dynamic responses.

CONTROLLERS

The introduction to this chapter described a feedback loop. Figure 2-1 indicated the four basic elements, one of which is the controller. The actual hardware used could be pneumatic, electronic (analog or digital), and hydraulic. Any controller can be considered to be composed of two parts, as shown in Fig. 2-4.

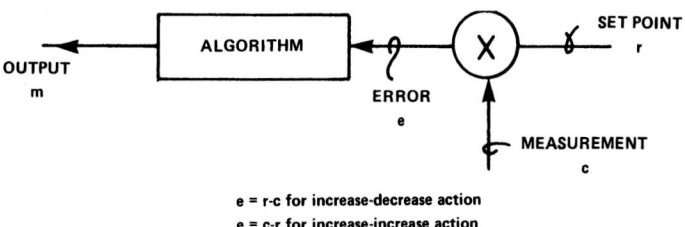

e = r-c for increase-decrease action

e = c-r for increase-increase action

FIGURE 2-4 Basic controller elements.

The error detector determines the magnitude and, more important, the direction of the error; the algorithm defines the specific action of any one particular type of controller. The type of error signal implemented defines the direction of the output as a function of the measurement. For example, if the measurement c exceeds the set point r, the error would be negative, which then causes the algorithm to decrease the output m. If an "air-to-open" type of valve had been used, the decrease in output would tend to close the valve, which would decrease the flow to the process and thereby decrease the measurement back toward the set point. There are occasions in which an "air-to-close" valve may have been used, in which case the action of the controller would have to be changed. This option to change the action of the controller is a normal feature of the controller.

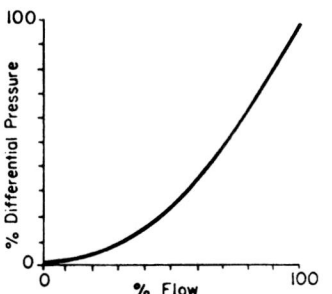

FIGURE 2-5 Flow measurement by differential pressure means.

While most control theory is based upon the linearity of the gain of various elements which make up a loop, practical design and operation must take into account the nonlinearities that occur due to variations in set point and/or variations in process load. For example, we have noted in Chapter 11-1, under "Flow Measurement," that the flow has a square-root relationship with the differential pressure measured. Figure 2-5 indicates this relationship.

The effect of this type of nonlinearity (it could occur in any of the four elements of a control loop) is normally to give good control at one set of operating conditions only. This could cause damaging results in those cases in which the controller had been set during low system gain because, at high system gain, the loop would tend toward oscillation. Elimination of these nonlinearities, by using special hardware or by selecting loop elements having equal and opposite characteristics, goes a long way in the overall stability of the loop, e.g., selecting a quick-opening valve whose characteristics would be opposite to a head-type flow measurement.

Selection of a controller is based to a great extent on the process characteristics and the precision needed to control it at an exact set point. The four basic control actions generally used are discussed in the text that follows.

Two-Position (ON-OFF)

This is the simplest of all control actions available. The output of the controller is at either 100 or 0 percent and could be either an analog signal or a contact actuation. The result in either case is that the final actuator is completely open or completely closed. The effect on the measured variable depends upon the type of process, specifically the capacity time constant. For a large-capacity process, the measured variable would change slowly to allow reasonable final actuator action. The measurement oscillations would be correspondingly small. Compare this to a process having very little capacity; the measured variable would tend to change very quickly, which would cause rapid actuator action, and this in turn would cause large and rapid oscillations in the measurement. Under these circumstances and where precise control is required, a throttling type of control action would be preferred.

There are three basic methods of achieving two-position control. Figure 2-6 illustrates the control action.

A thermostat for an electric heater is an example of an ON-OFF control system. Here, the controller operates continuously to control the temperature of the process. Another application is for safety shutdown of a process when safe operating conditions have been exceeded.

To avoid frequent cycling and maybe damaging results to the final actuator, a differential-gap controller is used. A band or gap exists around the control point. When the measured variable exceeds the upper boundary of the gap, the final actuator is closed and remains

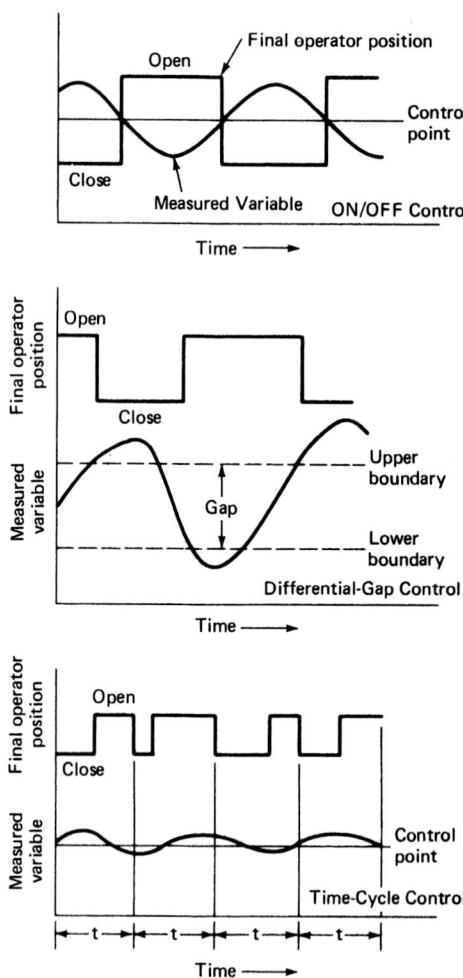

FIGURE 2-6 Two-position control.

closed until measurement drops below the lower boundary of the gap, at which point the final actuator opens. The control is not precise, but it does prevent excessive wear on the final actuator. In industry, this type of control is often found in noncritical-level control applications where the level could be anywhere between two limits.

In time-cycle control, a time base t is established. During this time period, the final operator is closed for a certain percentage of the time and open for the remainder. The ratio of closed time to open time is determined by the relationship between the measured variable and the control point.

A time-cycle controller is normally set up so that, when the measured variable equals the desired control point, the final operator will be open for half the time cycle and closed for the other half. As the measured variable drops below the control point, the final operator will remain open longer than it is closed. This type of control is often found on electrically operated heaters and on dry-solid control gates where a throttling gate position would cause buildup and clogging.

Proportional

To better understand this and the control actions described later, an open-loop response will be considered first. The open loop means that the controller is considered by itself with an artificially generated measurement signal. A change in input can be generated by changing either the set point or the measurement signal.

Figure 2-7 is a schematic diagram of a force-balance-type pneumatic proportional control; Fig. 2-8 is a schematic of an equivalent electronic controller using an operational amplifier.

The basic equation implemented is

$$m = (100/\%\text{PB})(r - c) + \text{bias}$$

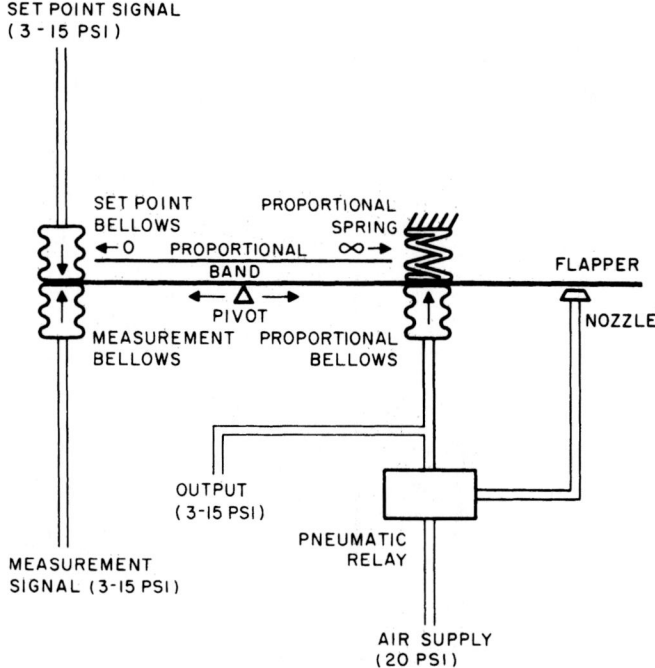

FIGURE 2-7 Pneumatic force-balance proportional controller.

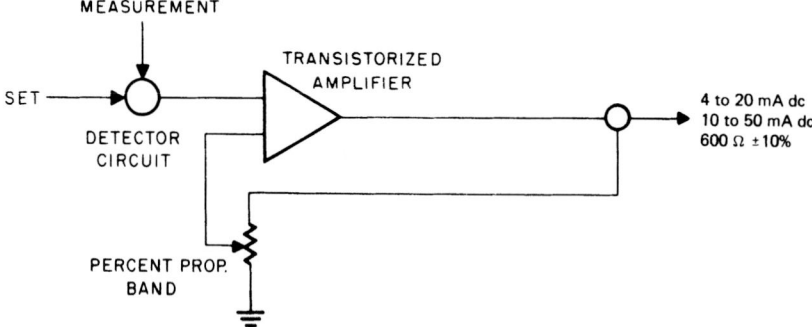

FIGURE 2-8 Electronic proportional controller.

where r = set point
             c = measurement
          %PB = proportional band, in percent

The factor 100/%PB is also termed the *gain* of the controller. The *bias* term allows the output to be approximately 50 percent of the signal range of the controller when measurement equals set point. This condition can occur only under one set of operating conditions, i.e., when the output from the controller positions the final actuator such that the manipulated process variable exactly matches the process requirements for the given load. For different operating conditions, the output from the controller is a function of the error (the difference between the set point and measurement) and the set proportional band (PB). Figure 2-9 shows the effect of PB on valve travel for various settings.

Line *A* indicates that for a PB of 100 percent, the measurement has to change from 0 to 100 percent of its span for a 0 to 100 percent throttling action. As the PB is decreased, lines *B, C,*

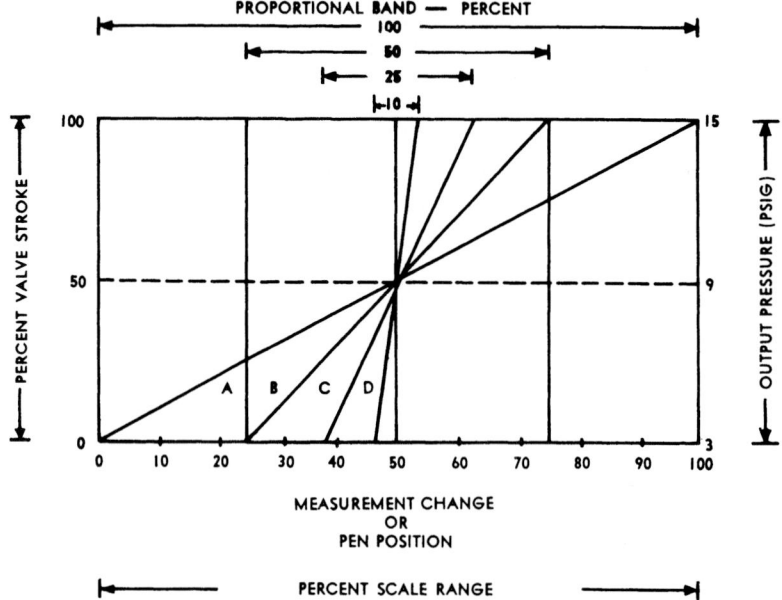

FIGURE 2-9 Proportional response to changes in proportional band (gain).

and *D* indicate that smaller changes in measurement allow full throttling action. When the PB is greater than 100 percent, the throttling action is reduced to less than 0 to 100 percent.

It should be noted that a limited type of proportional control—with correspondingly limited possibilities of application—can be handled by a transmitter. From the preceding discussion, it can be deduced that a pneumatic transmitter can perform as a 100 percent PB *controller* when connected directly to a pneumatic final actuator. Some tank-level controls are implemented this way, especially when strict level control is not required.

The controller algorithm indicates that, for an output other than 50 percent, an error must exist; the size of this error is dependent upon the PB (gain setting in the controller). There is nothing in the algorithm which would cause this error to be eliminated. This error is called the *offset,* and its size dependent upon the particular PB (gain) for a given set of conditions. Figure 2-10 illustrates the types of responses that can be achieved.

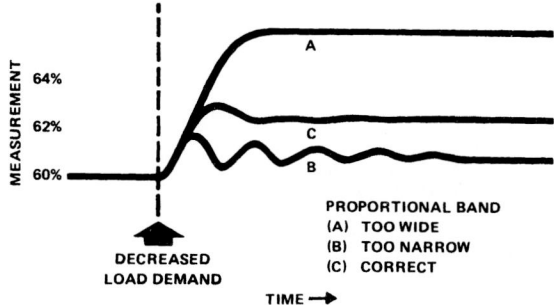

FIGURE 2-10   Proportional control response curves.

As the proportional band is decreased, the amount of offset decreases, but the response tends to become more oscillatory. This should be obvious when the loop gain is considered. As the PB is decreased, the controller gain increases, which causes the loop gain to increase thereby causing larger oscillations in the response. Large-capacity processes in general require narrow proportional bands, while processes having fast reaction times can accommodate wide proportional band settings only.

Proportional-Plus-Integral

These types of controllers are also known as *two-mode* controllers. In the discussion of proportional control, it was shown that the wide proportional bands required for some processes lead, in turn, to large offset errors. This is an intolerable condition in the majority of process applications. The application of the integral (also known as reset action) allows the final actuator-to-measurement relationship to change. This relationship changes when the measurement is not precisely at its set point. The effect is to cause the final actuator position to change in the direction, and at a predetermined rate, that will allow the measurement to equal the set point. Figures 2-11 and 2-12 are schematics of pneumatic and electronic proportional-plus-integral controllers.

The basic equation implemented in these controllers is

$$m = (100/\%\text{PB}) \, (e + 1\backslash R_T \, e \, dt)$$

where e = error $(r - c)$
R_T = the integral time constant

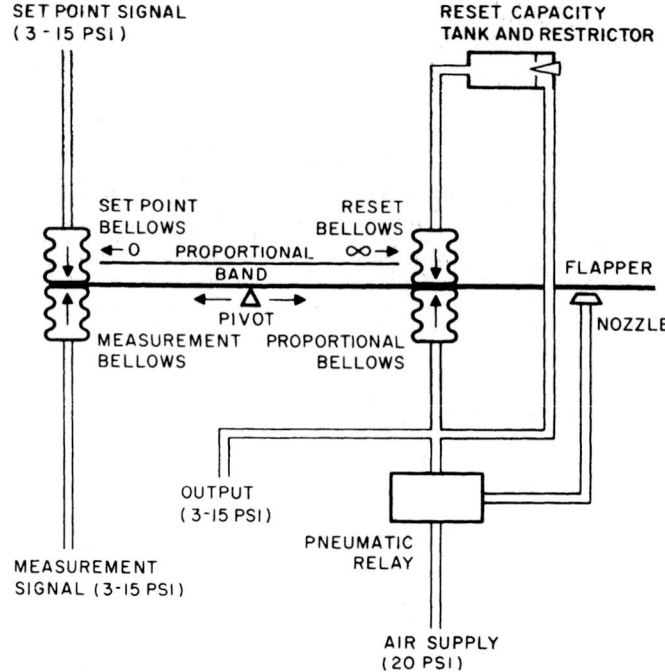

FIGURE 2-11   Pneumatic force-balance proportional-plus-integral controller.

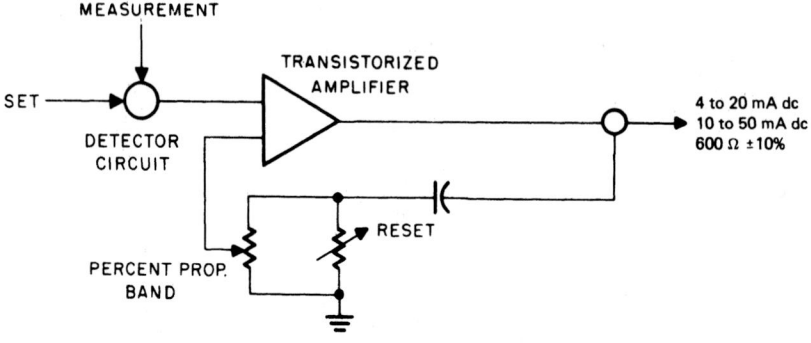

FIGURE 2-12   Electronic proportional-plus-integral controller.

We see from the above equation that the output of the controller is the sum of both the proportional action and the integral (reset) action. Figure 2-13 illustrates open-loop response of a proportional-plus-integral controller.

It should be noted that the integral action R_T can be defined as the time (in minutes) taken by the controller to change its output by an amount equal to the proportional action. This definition allows R_T to be calibrated in terms of minutes per repeat. An alternative way to set this calibration is the reciprocal of minutes per repeat, i.e., repeats per minute. Both these terms are equally popular among the various manufacturers. Though the introduction of integral action eliminates the offset error, it introduces a phase lag in the controller. The amount of gain is no longer the simple (100/%PB) term of the proportional controller, but the vector

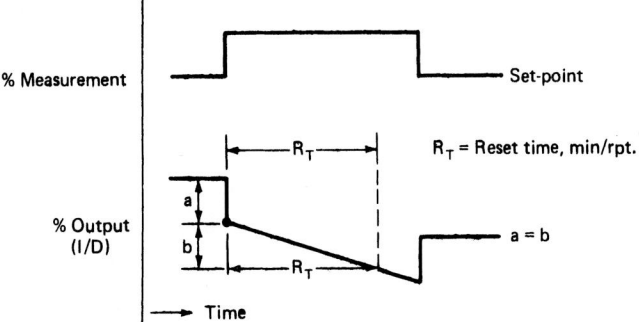

FIGURE 2-13   Open-loop response of proportional-plus-integral controller.

sum of the proportional part and integral part which gives a resultant larger than either. The phase lag introduced is the amount by which this resultant lags the proportional action. Two results can be deduced from this discussion. First, the addition of integral action for a given proportional action will cause the control-loop oscillations to increase, second, this oscillation will have a longer period than the original oscillations. Figure 2-14 shows response curves for a temperature loop where the integral is measured in minutes per repeat.

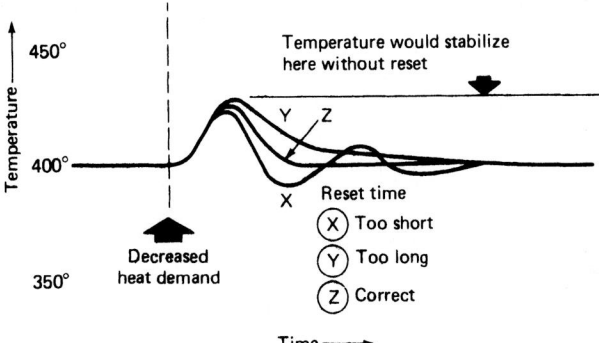

FIGURE 2-14   Proportional-plus-integral control response curves.

If the controller is unable to return the measurement to the set point, the integral action continues to increase or decrease the output until the saturation limit of the controller is reached. If at this time the measurement starts to change, the controller output does not change from its saturation limit until the measurement crosses the set point. If the system has any capacity, the measurement will overshoot the set point by an amount which depends upon the capacity and integral setting. This limitation is called *integral windup* and has to be seriously considered on discontinuous or batch-type processes. There are special batch-type controllers available which prevent the output of the controller from reaching saturation limits, thereby causing less or no overshoot in the measurement for the above conditions.

Proportional-Plus-Derivative

The addition of derivative action to the proportional controller can improve the response of the system, especially in those batch-type processes where integral windup can cause prob-

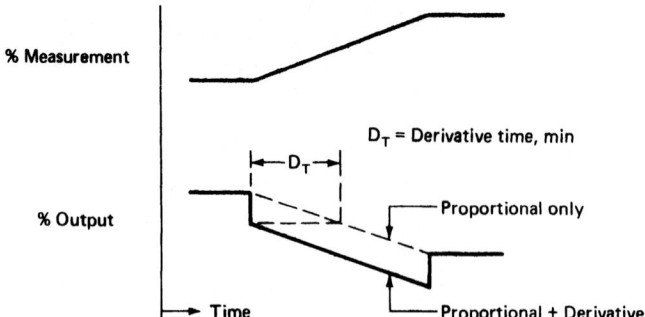

FIGURE 2-15 Open-loop response of proportional-plus-derivative controller.

lems. The amount of derivative action is proportional to the rate-of-change of the measurement. Figure 2-15 illustrates the open-loop response and defines the derivative time constant.

Since the derivative control is a function of the rate of change of measurement, introduction of this mode in applications where the measurement can change very rapidly, or if the measurement is noisy, can degrade the controllability of the loop. The most useful applications are those where the system has large capacities with little dead time.

Proportional-Plus-Integral-Plus-Derivative

This is also called the three-mode controller. The open-loop response indicates the sum of all three modes in its output. Figures 2-16 and 2-17 are schematics of a pneumatic and an electronic controller, respectively.

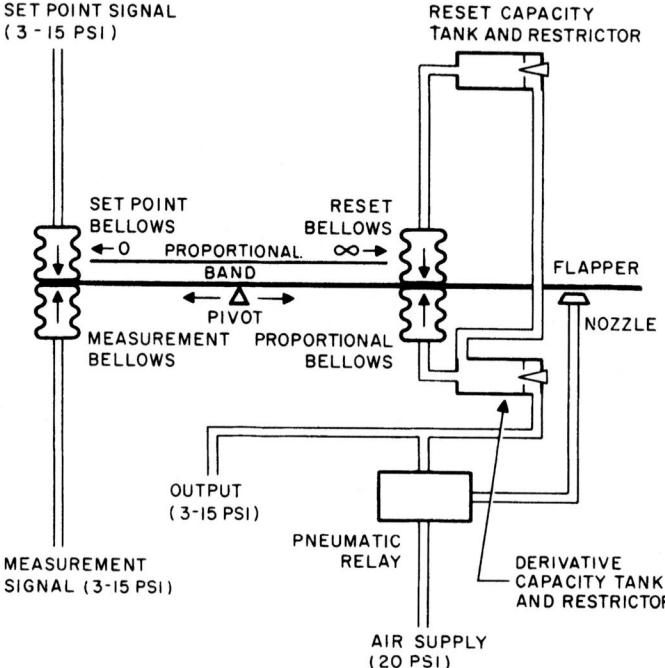

FIGURE 2-16 Pneumatic force-balance proportional-plus-integral-plus-derivative controller.

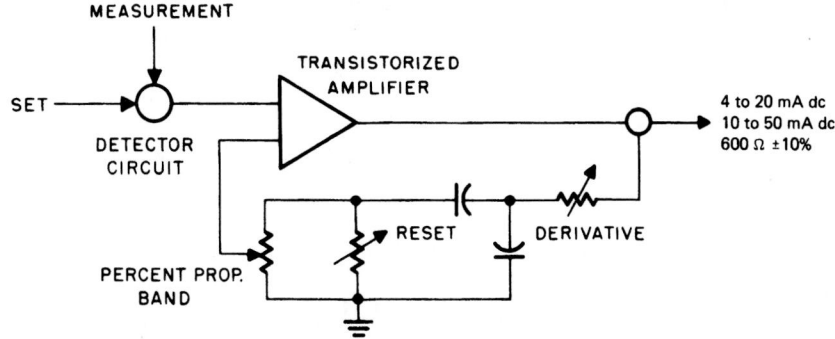

FIGURE 2-17   Electronic proportional-plus-integral-plus-derivative controller.

In our previous discussion, integral action was considered to cause an additional lag in the control loop. The derivative has an opposite effect, i.e., it causes a phase *lead* and is, therefore, sometimes also called *preact*. The total gain of the controller is the vector sum of the individual mode gains and the phase lag or lead introduced in the controller is the angle the resultant-gain vector makes with respect to the proportional-gain vector. If the resultant-gain vector has a phase lead, the resultant response of the system will have a period of oscillation smaller than the natural period. In general, if the integral time in minutes per repeat is made equal to the derivative time in minutes, the response is quite satisfactory. For large-capacity processes, the amount of derivative action may be increased.

Table 2-1 gives a brief summary of some standard process loops that are common in industrial process plants. Indicated are some major characteristics of the processes and the control systems.

Multivariable Control

The four common types of multivariable control loops are *ratio, cascade, feed-forward,* and *override.* The importance of these types of loops can be appreciated by considering that the response of any controlled variable in the industrial process environment will, in general, be a function of a number of other variables that could be either on the load side or on the input side of the unit. To account for these variables, multivariable control loops have to be considered.

Ratio.   Here the controlled variable is the ratio of two measured variables, where one of these is the controlled variable and the other is the "wild" variable. The wild variable is not necessarily uncontrolled, it could be a controlled variable of another loop. These systems need not be limited to two components but can have the wild variable set the ratio, through separate relays, to several controlled variables. An alternative to this method would be to set the ratio as a percentage of the required total flow, which itself is set by a master demand signal. The two types of systems are called *series* and *parallel,* respectively. The series approach has one basic advantage in having an inherent interlock between the wild variable and controlled variable.

There are a number of practical applications where these control schemes have been found useful. Examples are blending, control of air-to-fuel ratio in boilers, and ratioing of reactant flow in chemical processes. In steady-state operations, the system operates like an ordinary flow loop, i.e., dynamically quite fast. However, under changing loads, nonrecoverable errors can exist that can be removed in memory-type blending systems. Figure 2-18 indicates an example of the required setup.

These systems can be either analog or digital, and frequently employ pulse-type measuring instruments for precise measurement of total flow. It should be noted that a certain amount of downstream capacity is required so as to be able to eliminate the accumulated error.

TABLE 2-1 Summary of Common Loops

Variable	Process	Control System

Flow	Very fast
	Most lags are in the control system
	
	Nonlinear (square) measurement
	  common
	Noisy
		Proportional-plus-reset controllers
		Low gain, fast reset
		Derivative hurts
		Linear valves for differential pressure
		  measurement
		Equal percentage valves for linear measurement
		Valve is the major dynamic element

Pressure, liquid	Fast Most lags are in the control system Nonlinear (square) Noisy	Proportional-plus-reset controllers Gain near 1, fast reset rate Derivative of no value Linear valve
Pressure, gas	Single capacity No dead time Linear, no noise Simple process	Self-acting or high gain proportional controllers Reset seldom necessary Derivative unnecessary Valve characteristic relatively unimportant
Pressure vapor	Dynamics vary Dead time possible Slow compared to other pressure processes Linear, no noise	Three-response controllers Settings vary Equal percentage valves
Level	Single capacity (integrating) No dead time Linear Infrequent noise	Precise control: High gain or proportional-plus-reset controllers Averaging control: Low gain proportional plus reset or specialized controllers Valve characteristic unimportant
Temperature	Multiple-capacity system Dead time possible (especially in heat exchangers) Nonlinear No noise	Three-response controllers Settings vary, but gain usually above 1 Derivative of limited value if dead time is large Equal percentage valves Measurement dynamics are important
Composition	Dynamics vary Dead time usually present Usually linear Sometimes noisy due to poor mixing	Proportional-plus-reset controller Low gain, variable reset rate Derivative sometimes useful On-line analyzers fast, often noisy, pH nonlinear Sampling systems complicate both measurement and control, add dead time Linear valves

Cascade. In a single feedback loop, the output of the controller is directly used to manipulate the final actuator. Under these conditions, fluctuations on the input side of the manipulated variable will be noticed by the controller when the measurement changes. An example would be the header pressure change on a steam supply being used to control the outlet temperature from a heat exchanger. This after-the-fact control can be avoided by setting a secondary control loop which gets its set point from the primary controller. Figure 2-19 is a typical setup.

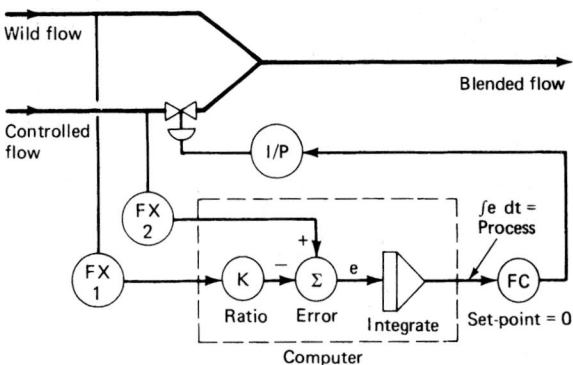

FIGURE 2-18   Memory-blending system controls accumulated flow ratio.

To properly apply these systems, the response of the secondary loop must be considerably faster than that of the primary loop. If this condition is not met, the resulting instability is the result of nearly simultaneous set-point and measurement changes in the secondary loop. It is for this reason that it is not recommended that a positioner be used on a final actuator in flow loops. The valve actuator contributes most of the capacity lag in a flow loop. With a positioner, this capacity lag exists in the secondary loop, with resultant instability of the entire flow loop.

A note of caution in actual operation of cascade loops is the integral windup that can occur in the primary controller, if the secondary controller were to be manual or if it were to fail. Special precautions have to be taken, and these could be either to interlock the stations or to use external integral feedback of the primary controller. The latter is the more useful method and is implemented by using the manipulated variable (steam flow in Fig. 2-19) as the external integral feedback signal.

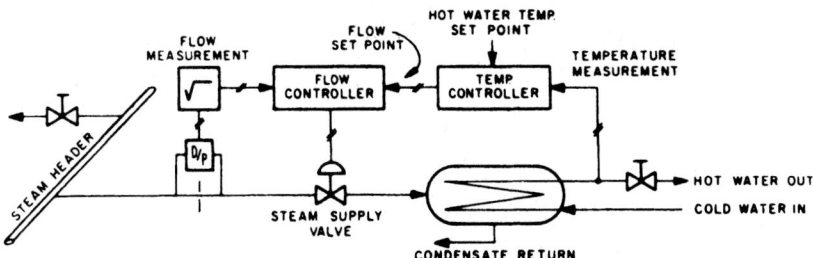

FIGURE 2-19   Cascade control of a heat exchanger.

Feed-Forward.   The introduction to this chapter included the basic strategy and philosophy of feed-forward control systems. With the availability of both analog and digital computation elements such as multipliers, adders, etc., it becomes relatively easy to physically put together the hardware to perform the feed-forward calculation. The difficulty arises in setting up the required process model based on energy- or mass-balance equations. These equations must also take into consideration the dynamics involved for each disturbance variable considered in the model. For example, in the previous discussion on cascade control of a heat exchanger, it is observed that the load disturbances due to changes in both the temperature of the incoming cold water and the amount of flow would affect the controlled variable (the outlet temperature).

A simple model based upon *energy in* equalling *energy out* could be set up with dynamic compensation for the rate of change of product coming in. This model could then be tuned for a given set of conditions by adjusting the value K as shown in Fig. 2-20.

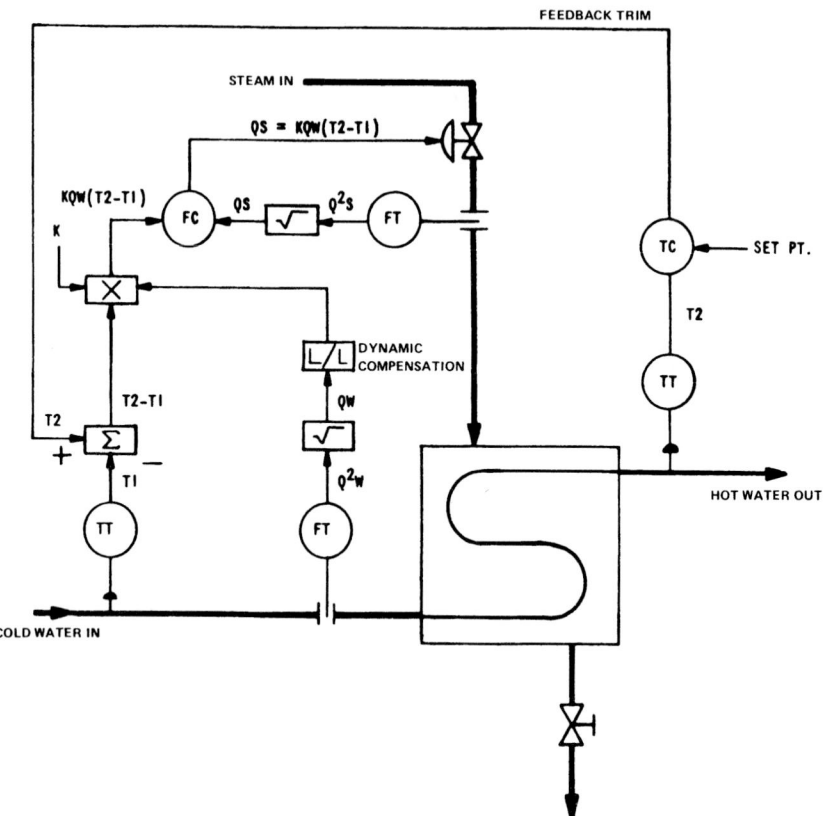

FIGURE 2-20 Feed-forward control with dynamic and feedback trim compensation.

If our process model had been perfect, a perfect control would have been possible. But this perfection is difficult to achieve, because of first the large number of variables that can affect the control variable and second the difficulty of achieving exact mathematical representation of the process. To take into account these inaccuracies, a feedback loop is normally used and is called the *feedback trim*. As the name suggests, the action of this loop is not to take over complete control of the manipulated variable but to adjust the feed-forward model for varying operating conditions. Since this action can be slow, the "tuning" constants of the feedback trim controller are normally set much wider than if it had been the main control mechanism.

There are numerous examples of the use of feed-forward control in varying industrial processes. The oldest practical application is the setting of feedwater flow via steam flow for the control of drum level in a boiler. There is a certain amount of inherent safety in most feed-forward control systems. For example, in drum-level control the loss of steam flow automatically shuts off the feedwater flow. This action is the opposite of what a feedback controller would do—open the feedwater actuator if drum level were below set point. This inherent safety feature was also described in our discussion of series-type valve-control systems, which can be considered to be feed-forward control systems. Distillation towers, evaporators, and waste-steam neutralization are some examples of processes where feed-forward systems have been successfully applied.

Override.   These systems are based on relays which allow the selection of the lowest or the highest input signals. The systems are used in the protection of equipment, in auctioneering, and in areas where redundant instrumentation has been used.

In the protection of equipment, it may be necessary to limit one variable to maintain safe operation. For example, a pump may have to be protected from both high discharge pressure and motor overload. If discharge pressure is the primary control, it will maintain control until an overload condition is detected. At that instant, the overload controller is selected for control by a low-select relay. Another example is the interlocking of fuel and air in boiler combustion control. Here, fuel is interlocked by air through a low-select relay, thereby preventing fuel flow from exceeding airflow; airflow is interlocked by fuel flow through a high-select relay, thereby preventing airflow from decreasing below fuel flow.

Auctioneering simply describes the selection of the highest or lowest of a set of signals. For example, if it is necessary to know the hottest spot in a reactor bed, a selection through a high-select relay for a number of inputs measuring temperature across the reactor bed could be used. In redundant instrumentation, the controls are set up to select a signal from a number of transmitters measuring the same variable. These are used in situations where loss of signal could produce an awkward control-system response.

Multiple-Loop Systems

Most industrial processes are composed of many individual control loops where one variable controls one manipulated variable or many input variables but still only one manipulated variable.

The first general problem is selection of the input variable that should control a selected manipulated variable. This is not obvious in some complex situations. However, a general rule is to select a manipulated variable having the greatest influence on the controlled variable. Other variables of interest would have to be taken into account by setting up cascaded systems or by operating them at fixed set points.

The second problem, the interaction between control loops, is a little more complex. An example of severe interaction is controlling both flow and pressure of gas in a pipe. For the smallest of upstream or downstream load upsets, the two control loops would interact because of the approximately equal natural period of oscillation of the two loops. The solutions are complex and use various decoupling circuits or detuning of controllers to prevent interaction. A physical solution is to structure the plant such that the dynamics of one variable could be changed by introducing capacity in one loop. In most cases the solutions are expensive and require a thorough knowledge of the process under consideration. The type of control hardware used also affects the problem. Although analog, pneumatic, and electronic components are available for most computing functions, a digital computer system provides the greatest ease and flexibility.

ELECTRONIC DIGITAL COMPUTERS

The present revolution in very large scale integrated (VLSI) circuit design is leading to a host of applications in the process-control field. These applications fall into three broad categories—smart measuring instruments, communications links, and controllers. These can be considered either in terms of dedicated application or shared application, where one controller can perform many functions on a time-shared basis.

Hardware

The foundation for these applications is the *microprocessor,* a basic building block that allows the application designer flexibility in configuring electronic circuitry to particular requirements. This flexibility is achieved because the microprocessor works somewhat similarly to a computer; it has a memory, an arithmetic and logic unit, a controller, and input-output circuitry. Refer to Fig. 2-21.

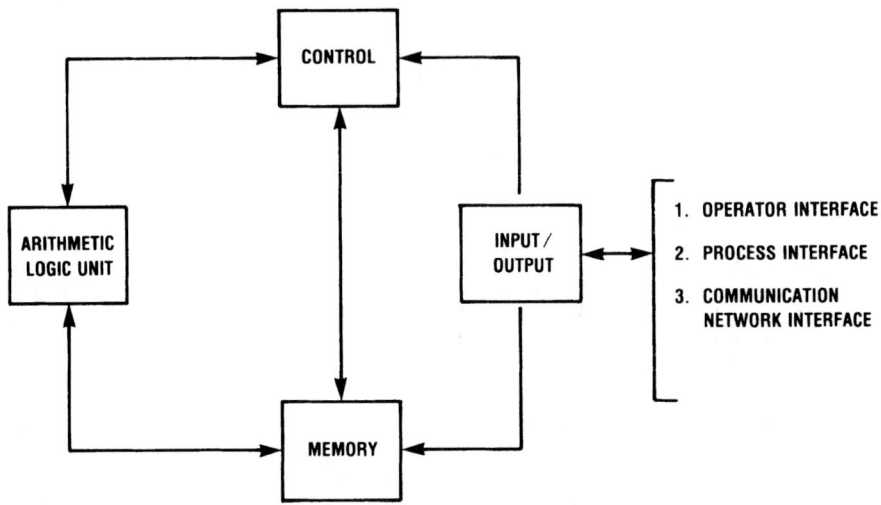

FIGURE 2-21 Basic processor.

The memory could be dedicated and part of the microprocessor or it could be external but under the processor's control. In either case, this fixed piece of memory (usually an ROM—read-only memory) contains words where the bit pattern for a particular set of words contains the requisite logic for the controller in the microprocessor to do a particular function. For example, this could be to read a word from the input and place it in the arithmetic logic unit (ALU). Another instruction could get another word from the input circuitry and also take it to the ALU. A third set of instructions could then add the two words together to give the required answer. Finally, one more instruction could take this answer and place it in the output circuitry. Given this basic instruction set, one could then develop the necessary logic for the microprocessor to accomplish the required functions.

This logic can now be implemented in two ways: The first is to design the microcode in such a manner that the microprocessor cycles through this code continuously, thereby dedicating the circuitry to performance of a predetermined function. The second is to define the microcode in such a manner that various sections of it could be used independently, and a particular function could then be externally selected. This external selection is accomplished by having an external memory (a RAM—random access memory) which contains words that, when decoded by the microprocessor, will point to the internal microcode instruction set that is required to be run. This allows the user to define requirements in a higher-level language for a given processor, rather than to work in terms of the machine-level microcode. Further, it now allows the processor to possibly do multiple tasks, where each task could be defined as a unique set of a higher-language code, basically a program. Thus, many programs could exist in the external memory and the processor would then run through each program, thereby performing many functions. The processor-memory combination looks basically like a regular computer, at least from the hardware description presented so far. It should be noted that there are many identifying characteristics of the various microprocessors now available. The first is word size, i.e., how many bits define a word? This could range from 4 bits to 16 bits. The 4-bit processors can be combined together to form larger word sizes. This is known as *bit slicing*. The size of the instruction set determines the power and flexibility in programming. Associated with the increased flexibility of the instruction set is the number of independently addressable (and therefore accessible) registers in the processors. This allows more complex programming. Another feature is the speed at which the microprocessor can perform the required function defined for each instruction in its higher-language repertoire.

In using a microprocessor as a computer, while considerations of the characteristics of the hardware are necessary, the major component that defines the uniqueness of each microprocessor is the operating system. In process control, the operating system complexity increases manyfold due to the real-time operation of the process. The operating system, also called the real-time executive, is a block of program logic that has five major functions to solve:

1. Scheduling the time of the processor among the many control programs
2. Managing the external main memory
3. Handling input and output for the various programs
4. Maintaining a data base for use by the tasks (programs) and also for reporting to management control
5. Allowing some mechanism whereby tasks can communicate with each other

As hardware costs of the microcomputer have steadily fallen, the software (executive programs) costs have taken on the major share in the overall cost of the computer installation. These needs lead to a large section of the main memory being taken by the real-time executive and up to 30 percent of the computer time. The rest of the memory space and processor time is available for actual application software.

These constraints are not necessarily a drawback. With the price of semiconductor memories falling rapidly, the expense of a large main memory is of minor consideration. Moreover, a limited memory space can be shared among many tasks or control loops, thus making even small microprocessor-based computers cost-effective compared with analog systems. With this price effectiveness is the increased reliability of the semiconductor components, allowing for an increased faith in the computer and thereby decreasing the requirements for backup. This backup could be either a duplicate computer or an analog system. In either case, the backup takes over control of the process on failure of the main system.

These computer-based systems are available in many sizes and varying capabilities. They can vary from being rather large and capable of controlling many hundreds of loops plus database management for report generation to being small dedicated units controlling a few loops. These smaller dedicated units can be linked together through a communication network, thereby leading into the beginning of application, i.e., distributed control. Each dedicated unit will perform its specialized function, which could be either measurement or control, or both. Normally, one large computer in the network would exist to act as the supervisor or master station.

In the application of computers for process control, some additional requirements have to be considered. Primary is the additional hardware required to multiplex a large number of inputs and outputs, which are analog in nature. A conversion process must be performed on these analog signals to present them in a digital word recognizable by the computer and then to convert the digital value back to an analog form useful to the final actuator. Refer to Fig. 2-22.

Software

The software, the second requirement, should be capable of operating in a real-time mode. For example, if one were to schedule a given control program to run every 5 s, the operating

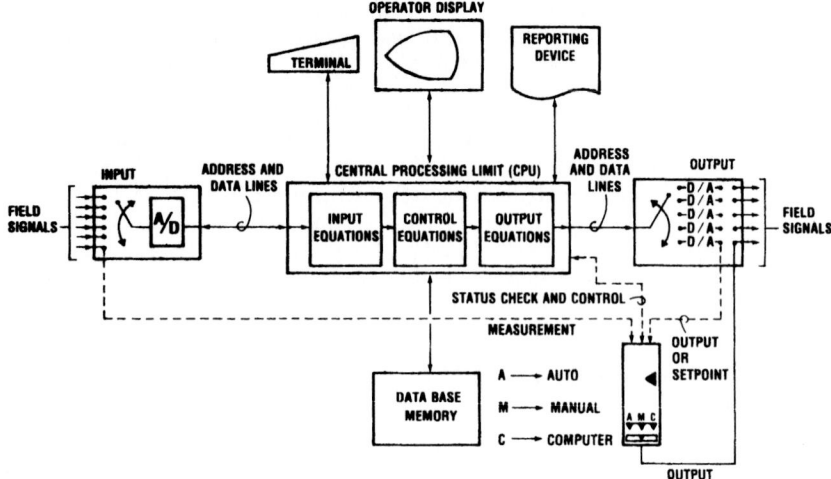

FIGURE 2-22 Basic elements of a computer for process control.

system would have to be smart enough to recognize the priority of this program with respect to others and ensure that this schedule is met. This priority positioning of the real-time programs allows many control loops to be set up, each working at a certain given scan cycle. This flexibility allows certain loops to be scheduled as a function of the process characteristics. Thus, a process which is inherently fast (as given by its natural period) should also have its control program scheduled fast. A general rule is to have this schedule 4 to 10 times faster than the natural period of the process. An additional feature that the application software should have is the easy configuration of the various control loops required by a particular plant. This feature distinguishes the use of a computer from an analog system. No physical wiring or tubing changes are necessary. Hence, it is possible to change the control configuration as plant conditions change or as more sophisticated control strategies are implemented. The number of control loops and the ease of configuration or modification are functions of a particular manufacturer's software package and should be considered in any evaluation.

Operator Interface

The third important point for process control computers is the *operator interface* with the process. It is necessary for the operator of the process to have a clear, up-to-date picture of the conditions in the plant. Conditions requiring immediate attention—various alarms, for example—should be clearly and immediately brought to the operator's attention. Next, the software should be able to recognize any action taken and update outputs to the plant. Graphic displays on CRTs (cathode-ray tubes) are now the most common method by which the operator interfaces with the plant. Three major factors have to be considered. First, the ease with which these displays can be created and if there are any limitations to the number of different displays a system allows. Second, the speed with which (1) various displays can be accessed by the operator and (2) the programs that update and read actions taken by the operator from a given display can be obtained. Third, the ease with which various levels of information can be accessed or changed. For example, one may want to go from a plant unit display to accessing a particular loop of the unit, to a particular section of the loop, to ultimately change some parameter value which could then reflect the alarm value. This could possibly affect the alarm limits, tuning constants, or some calibration or characterization curves. Again, levels of sophistication vary among manufacturers.

Loop Control

Control of loops on a sample basis affects the controllability of the loop. As the sample time is increased, the loop control degrades. This is related directly to the dollar cost of the operation. However, a decrease in sample rate increases the load on the computer which decreases its ability to do other computations. This can be related to the dollar cost of the computing effort. Figure 2-23 shows the relationship between the two costs.

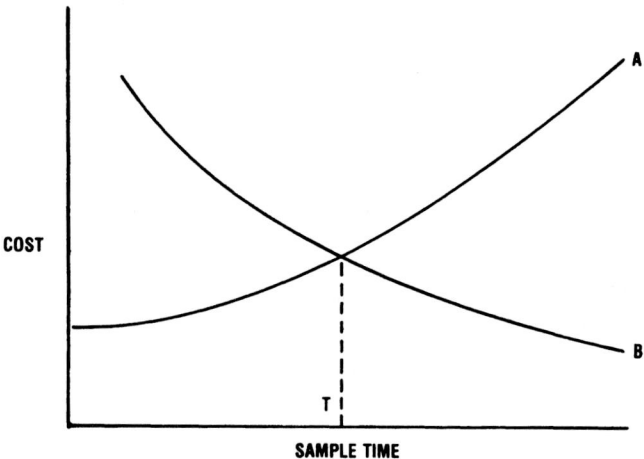

FIGURE 2-23   Sample rate costs.

Loop control is accomplished by basically solving equations for each loop. Normally there are three sections to these equations:

1. Input equation which reads the digital value from the input hardware (A/D), checks for validity, characterizes for some preset or calculated calibrations, and converts these into numbers meaningful to both the computer and the operator. They can be used to check for alarm limits and also can do some filtering of noisy measurement signals.

2. Control equation which basically gets its measurement from the input section, a setpoint value either from the operator or from some other program which may be calculating the required set point, and using the two basic values, calculating an output value for the final actuator.

3. Output value calculated could be checked for limit or alarm conditions, characterized for the final actuator and output hardware, and finally sent to the D/A converter and a sample-and-hold device which is required to retain the output value between sample times.

It should be appreciated that the inherent computational ability of the computer allows the use of complex control algorithms. This enhances the controllability of the plant. The control software should offer some standard algorithms (e.g., PID) and the capability for the user to create and use his or her own.

Backup

An important consideration in any computer application for continuous process control is safety. This involves computer backup. There are basically two options. One is to back up the main system with an identical system. The second is to have an analog backup for each loop. The analog backup would have the capability of either taking over full automatic control or being simply a manual backup in case of computer failure. This requires that the interface hardware recognize the computer failure status and transfer the analog loop to a predefined mode, auto or manual. On the other hand, the computer should be able to recognize the status of the backup station and any action the operator takes with it. Thus, when the operator does transfer to computer control, a smooth bumpless transfer should take place, again a function of the control software. The backup station need not be analog, but could be another computer (mostly dedicated), leading to the concept of distributed control and network hierarchies. Each of these dedicated computers is a particular plant unit control and a number of them are capable of talking to the main computer.

Whatever backup method is implemented, there are two basic methods of operating. First, the main computer does the full control with the backup simply tracking. This is called the DDC (direct digital control) mode. In the second, the main computer does not actually control the final actuator, but provides only a set point to the backup, which becomes the main controller. This is called SPC (supervisory control or set-point control). There are certain advantages in this mode. Failure of the supervisory computer does not affect the plant operation. The computation load decreases quite a bit since the dedicated controller provides the main control action. This decrease could be effectively utilized to run management reporting programs, build an historical data base, and institute both complex feed-forward control strategies and adaptive tuning techniques. In this mode of operation, the computer's advantage of computational power and its memory capability will be fully utilized.

Historical Data Base

The historical data base is the ability to store past plant operating data on a real-time basis, i.e., the data must relate to the actual time of plant operations to serve any useful purpose in either reporting for management control, for cost and efficiency calculations, or in using the data to plot or display trends of the various plant variables. Flexibility and memory size play an important part in the software that performs these functions. Flexibility in data-base development is the ability to add or delete variables to the data base. Furthermore, the data base should allow easy access for the reporting or trending software. When trying to determine the number of variables that can be used, one must take into account size considerations, how often the data collection is performed, and for how long a period the data are to be stored online for a given system. These factors have to be considered to determine the amount of online memory that is required. The reporting function may have three modes of operation: first, reports scheduled on a regular basis; second, reports called for on demand by operating personnel; and third, exception reports that are printed under given plant conditions.

Tuning Techniques

Feed-forward and adaptive tuning techniques lend themselves to easier treatment since complex equations and algorithms can easily be solved. The availability of memory allows past loop responses to be used to update terms of a given process model. These updated terms can be used to calculate tuning constants of a given control algorithm (for example, proportional gain, integral, and derivative of a PID control equation).

Whereas our discussion has been concentrated on the control of continuous loops, the use of a computer for logical operations can also be easily accomplished. For example, it can be used to control a batch process where very little continuous control may be needed but a large number of logical operations have to be performed. The computer inputs and outputs will be primarily digital (i.e., contacts) with some analog signals. The computer algorithms have to be set up to sequence through the required batch cycle while continuously monitoring the plant conditions and ensuring the completion of each batch cycle. Again, flexibility should be available to stop the sequence at any step, to continue the sequence, and to allow the operator manual sequencing of the process. Further, the operator should be allowed to change operations in a given sequence, for example, change the temperature ramp profile of a reactor or change the given product recipe. The software should also be able to perform relay-type logic, thus eliminating the need for hardware relay logic. Specialized computers specifically designed for these functions are called programmable logic controllers (PLC). These devices have a limited operating system which allows the running of one preprogrammed application program. Operator interface, if provided, is limited to some predefined function keys. The present trend is to make these devices more flexible, bringing them into the domain of minicomputers.

Because the technology is changing so rapidly now, the plant engineer should make a careful comparative study of available program controller units before making any key purchase decisions.

SECTION 12

NOISE AND VIBRATION CONTROL

CHAPTER 12-1

NOISE CONTROL

Eric W. Wood

Director, Environmental and Industrial Acoustics
Acentech Incorporated
Cambridge, Massachusetts

Douglas H. Sturz

Senior Acoustical Consultant
Acentech Incorporated
Cambridge, Massachusetts

INTRODUCTION

Noise produced inside industrial plants is most often controlled to provide a healthy, safe, and comfortable work environment. Controlling excessive workplace noise can reduce the occurrence of occupationally induced hearing loss among employees, reduce future payments associated with hearing loss compensation claims by employees, improve speech communication and the audibility of warning signals, improve productivity by reducing employee fatigue and discomfort, and help to enhance job satisfaction. Noise produced outside industrial plants is most often controlled to promote good neighborhood relations, to avoid degrading the local environment, and to meet local or state regulations. To be most effective, steps taken to control excessive noise must not cause problems that would impact on production, inspections, maintenance, or safety.

This chapter includes basic information about the measurement, evaluation, and control of noise at industrial plants. It does not provide "cookbook" solutions for controlling noise. Rather, engineering noise control information is based on the authors' experience gained from more than 20 years each of acoustical consulting practice.

Readers interested in specific or advanced noise control information are referred to the end of this chapter. Many texts, manuals, standards, and publications specializing in noise control that the authors have found to be useful over the years are listed.

OCCUPATIONAL NOISE EXPOSURE LIMITS

OSHA Safety and Health Standards (29 CFR 1910.95) provide maximum daily occupational-noise exposure limits that give both the level and the duration of the noise to which employees may be exposed while in the work place. This Standard allows 8-h exposures to a daily average noise level of up to 90 dBA. For shorter durations, the maximum limits are greater. A 4-h exposure is allowed to a daily average noise level of 95 dBA *or* a 2-h exposure is allowed to a daily average noise level of 100 dBA. Exposure to continuous noise levels as great as 115 dBA are permitted for 15 min or less per day. It is the employee's time-weighted average (TWA) exposure or noise dose received while at work that is subject to the basic OSHA noise limits. These noise exposure limits and the method to calculate TWA exposures are listed in Table 1-1. In addition, the Standard also limits exposure to impulsive or impact noise, for example, from a punch press, to be no greater than 140 dB peak sound pressure level.

TABLE 1-1 Permissible Noise Exposures*

Daily duration, h	Sound level, dBA
8	90
6	92
4	95
3	97
2	100
1.5	102
1	105
0.5	110
0.25 or less	115

* When the daily noise exposure is composed of two or more periods of noise exposure of different levels, their combined effect should be considered, rather than the individual effect of each. If the sum of the following fractions: $C_1/T_1, + C_2/T_2 + C_n/T_n$ exceeds unity, then the mixed exposure is considered to exceed the limit value. C_n indicates the total time of exposure at a specified noise level, and T_n indicates the total time of exposure permitted at that level.

OCCUPATIONAL HEARING CONSERVATION REQUIREMENTS

In addition to the Table 1-1 noise exposure limits, OSHA Safety and Health Standards provide the requirement that employers administer an effective hearing conservation program to protect employees that may receive 8-h TWA noise exposures exceeding 85 dBA (a noise dose exceeding 50 percent). The 8-h TWA of 85 dBA is considered the "action level" at which an effective hearing conservation program becomes mandatory. No requirements are imposed when 8-h TWA noise exposures are less than 85 dBA (a noise dose less than 50 percent). The Standard describes in detail the many elements that must be included in an effective hearing conservation program. Some of these elements are summarized below. Readers responsible for establishing or administering such programs are referred to the Standard itself and the many professionals that specialize in this field.

Feasible administrative, scheduling, or engineering controls should be utilized to reduce TWA noise exposures to within the limits of Table 1-1. Hearing protection must be provided and used to achieve the TWA noise exposure limits of Table 1-1 whenever administrative, scheduling, or engineering controls fail to do so.

In plant areas where 8-h TWA noise exposures might exceed 85 dBA, monitoring must be performed to document noise levels or noise exposures. The monitoring must be repeated as necessary to ensure that results are kept up to date. Records of the monitoring results must be maintained and monitoring instruments must be calibrated.

Notification is required for all employees likely to receive TWA noise exposures greater than 85 dBA.

In addition, observation of the measurements must be allowed by employees likely to receive TWA noise exposures greater than 85 dBA and audiometric testing must be made available to these employees.

Hearing protectors must be made available at no cost to employees likely to receive TWA noise exposures greater than 85 dBA. A suitable variety of hearing protectors that are comfortable, well maintained, and effective must be provided, along with training in the fitting, care, and use of the hearing protectors. Effective hearing protectors must be worn by employees with a TWA noise exposure exceeding 90 dBA, and by some employees with a TWA noise exposure greater than 85 dBA. Although not required by the Standard, it is suggested that employees be required to wear hearing protectors every time they enter noisy work areas and encouraged to purchase hearing protectors for use at home when shooting or operating noisy equipment. For hearing protectors to be effective they must fit well, be comfortable and well maintained, and, of course, be worn.

Earplugs and earmuffs are the two most common types of hearing protectors used in industrial plants. Earplugs are generally of the formable or premolded type. Formable plugs made of an expandable closed-cell foam material are commonly used at many plants and can be effective at reducing noise at the users ears when inserted properly. Premolded plugs made of soft silicone, rubber, or plastic can also be effective. Failure to achieve a correct and snug fit will limit the noise attenuation of any plug. Workers should be instructed in how to straighten the ear canal and insert the plug correctly. While such instruction may appear unnecessary, many workers may need several tries before achieving a fit snug enough to get the best possible noise attenuation.

Earmuffs are also commonly used in many industrial plants and can be effective at reducing exposure when worn properly. Earmuffs consist of two plastic cups with interior sound-absorptive foam and soft seals that cover the entire external ear. They are held in place with a headband or are sometimes attached to a hard hat. Again, workers should be provided instruction in the proper use of earmuffs. Eyeglasses or long hair can cause a gap at the muffs' seals and reduce the noise attenuation.

Several types of effective earmuffs and/or earplugs should be made available to employees. They should be selected based on the type of noise to be attenuated and the degree of noise attenuation needed. They should also be comfortable to wear and easy to use. It is important that plant management support and encourage their use whenever workers enter noisy areas. Hearing protectors only work when worn properly!

Hearing protector attenuation must be evaluated for effectiveness in the specific noise environment in which the protector will be used. Hearing protectors provided to employees must attenuate noise exposures to an 8-h TWA of 90 dBA or less. For employees with significant hearing loss, hearing protectors must be provided that attenuate noise exposures to an 8-h TWA of 85 dBA or less. Manufacturers of hearing protectors provide a noise reduction rating (NRR) for their protectors based on laboratory testing. The published NRR is often much greater than the actual noise attenuation that is achieved by typical employees in real-world industrial working environments. A conservative estimate of the actual real-world attenuation provided by hearing protectors in typical industrial work environments is approximately equal to one-half of the NRR reduced by 7 (0.5 [NRR-7]). For example, a hearing protector with a NRR of 39 could be expected to reliably reduce typical industrial noise exposures by about 16 dBA. In a plant work area where the noise level is 100 dBA, a hearing protector rated at 39 NRR would reduce the noise to about 84 dBA at the worker's ear. For some work environments the actual noise attenuation might be less. This illustrates the importance of purchasing high-quality and high-performance hearing protectors.

Training programs must be provided at least annually to employees with 8-h TWA noise exposures greater than 85 dBA. These programs must be up to date and must inform employees of at least the following: the effects of noise on hearing; the purpose of hearing protectors; the performance of the various types of hearing protectors; and instructions on selection, fitting, use, and care of the hearing protectors. Employees must also be informed of the purpose and procedures of the audiometric testing.

The OSHA Noise Standard must be made available to all affected employees and a copy of it must be posted in the work place.

Accurate records of all employee exposure measurements must be maintained for at least two years. It is suggested that the records be well organized and maintained for a longer period in case of future hearing-loss compensation claims. Records of all audiometric test results must be maintained for the duration of an employee's employment. Again, it is suggested that they be well organized and maintained for a longer period in case of hearing-loss compensation claims. Copies of these records must be available to employees upon their request.

The Standard also includes many appendices providing detailed information on the required audiometric testing of employees, including computations, measurements, calibrations, recording keeping, and qualifications. People responsible for administering hearing conservation programs must be familiar with and understand the requirements contained in the appendices.

For a hearing conservation program to be effective, it must be well supported by plant management. Without management-level support and encouragement, the program is not likely to succeed at protecting employees hearing. The use of hearing aids is not a good answer to hearing loss, just as the use of wooden legs, mechanical hands, and false teeth is not a good answer to industrial accidents. The best answer is prevention—occupational hearing loss is preventable!

CONCEPTS AND VOCABULARY OF NOISE CONTROL

Sound   Noise is simply unwanted sound, which is a series of vibrations in the air. Human ears are sensitive to these vibrations; they sense them and pass them on to the brain to decipher. Acoustics—the branch of physics that deals with the production, transmission, and control of sound—has its own concepts and vocabulary. Several key terms and concepts needed by an engineer working in noise control are defined below.

Frequency   Frequency f is the number of oscillatory cycles a sound completes in one second. Units of frequency may be expressed in cycles per second (cps) or Hertz (Hz).

The audible frequency range extends from about 20 to 20,000 Hz for a young person with ideal hearing, but the frequency range for adults is frequently narrower due to aging and noise exposure effects. For engineering analysis purposes, the audible frequency range is often divided into a series of octave bands. Just as an octave on a piano keyboard, an octave in sound analysis represents the frequency interval between a given frequency and twice that frequency. For ease of use and to develop a consistent basis for communication, standard octave band widths have been defined and are built into measurement instrumentation. Each of the standard bands is identified by the frequency at the geometric mean of the frequencies at the extremes of the band. The center frequencies and approximate cutoff frequencies are listed in Table 1-2.

TABLE 1-2 Center and Approximate Frequency Limits for the Standard Set of Contiguous Octave Bands Covering the Audio Frequency Range

Lower band limit	Octave band center frequency	Upper band limit
11	16	22
22	31.5	44
44	63	88
88	125	177
177	250	355
355	500	710
710	1,000	1,420
1,420	2,000	2,840
2,840	4,000	5,680
5,680	8,000	11,360
11,360	16,000	22,720

Velocity of sound   Sound waves in air at normal temperatures and pressures (about 68°F [20°C] and 1 atmosphere pressure) travel at a velocity c that is approximately 1127 ft/s (344 m/s). The velocity of sound waves in air changes somewhat with temperature and pressure, but for most practical applications in plant engineering it can be considered a constant.

Wavelength   The distance that a sound wave travels in completing one cycle is the wavelength λ and can be calculated at any frequency by:

$$\lambda = \frac{c}{f}$$

Decibel   The decibel (dB) is a dimensionless unit for expressing the ratio of two numerical values on a logarithmic scale. It is convenient to use decibels in dealing with sound power, intensity, or pressure because of the tremendous range of values of these quantities that can be perceived by the ear. Audible intensities range from 10^{12} to 1 W/m^2.

Sound power and sound power level   Sound power describes the total acoustical energy emission of a sound source in watts (W). The sound power level (L_w or PWL) is the designation in decibels of the ratio of two sound powers expressed as follows:

$$L_w = 10 \log \frac{W}{W_r}, \text{ Customarily } L_w = 10 \log \frac{W}{10^{-12}} \text{ dB}$$

These terms can be applied to the entire frequency spectrum or to a narrow band width. These quantities can be thought of as being analogous to the total light energy emitted by a light bulb. They are independent of the environment and the distance from the source. The customary reference sound power W_r in use today and in this chapter is 10^{-12} W. Originally, 10^{-13} W was used as the standard reference sound power. When the reference sound power is 10^{-13}, the sound power level can be converted to a sound power level referenced to 10^{-12} by subtracting 10 dB. To avoid ambiguity, the reference sound power should always be stated with sound power level data.

Sound pressure and sound pressure level   Sound waves produce small changes in the density of air as they travel through it. These changes in the density cause pressure fluctuations around the ambient static pressure. The magnitude of the pressure fluctuations above and below the ambient pressure is the sound pressure p.

The unit approved by the International Standards Organization (ISO) for measuring sound pressure is the pascal (Pa), though the terms microbars (μbar), dynes per square centimeter (dyn/cm²), and newtons per square meter (N/m²) have all been used.

Conversion factors are

$$1 \text{ bar} = 10^5 \text{ Pa}$$
$$1 \text{ μbar} = 1 \text{ dyn/cm}^2$$
$$1 \text{ dyn/cm}^2 = 10^{-1} \text{ Pa}$$
$$1 \text{ N/m}^2 = 1 \text{ Pa}$$

The sound pressure level (L_p or SPL) is the designation in decibels of the ratio of the square of two sound pressures expressed as:

$$L_p = 10 \log \left(\frac{p}{p_r} \right)^2 \quad \text{or} \quad L_p = 10 \log \left(\frac{p}{2 \times 10^{-5}} \right)^2 \quad \text{dB}$$

The customary reference sound pressure p_r is 2×10^{-5} Pa and should be indicated with all data to avoid ambiguity. This reference sound pressure is set to be approximately equal to the threshold of hearing at 1000 Hz. So a sound pressure level of 0 dB at 1000 Hz corresponds to the approximate threshold of hearing.

The sound pressure level can be thought of as analogous to the light level in footcandles from a light bulb in a room. Just as the light level is a function of the distance from the bulb and the color of the walls of the room, so is the sound pressure level in a room a function of the distance from the source and the acoustical characteristics of the room. The distance from the source, and acoustical characteristics of the space in which the data were measured, or are to apply, should be stated with sound pressure level data.

Sound intensity and sound intensity level Sound intensity I is the sound power radiated in a specified direction through a unit area normal to the direction of propagation in units of W/m². The sound intensity level (IL) is the designation in decibels of the ratio of two intensities and is expressed by:

$$IL = 10 \log \left(\frac{I}{I_r} \right)$$

When indicating IL, it is customary to use a reference intensity of 10^{-12} W/m², which should be indicated to avoid ambiguity.

$$IL = 10 \log \frac{I}{10^{-12}} \quad \text{dB}$$

IL is a function of the distance from the source but, as typically used, does not take into account the environment. It is analogous to the amount of light energy from a light bulb that falls on your hand in a room at a particular distance from the bulb due to the direct emission from the bulb only and discounting any light energy that may fall on your hand due to reflections from the room surfaces. Sound intensities are more difficult to measure than sound pressures, and prior to recent developments in instrumentation this was not practically possible in the field. Even the latest instrumentation devices still measure pressures only (using two microphones instead of one), then internally calculate the associated intensities based on the phase relationship of the data from the two microphones. Measuring sound intensity can be useful in investigating a sound source in a reverberant space because associated with the magnitude is a direction of wave propagation. Sound pressure level measurements do not include information about the direction of sound propagation.

A-weighted sound level There are many single-number schemes for evaluating sounds according to people's response to how loud a noise is perceived to be. One of the simplest and most useful of these single-number schemes is the sound level in dBA. The "A" means that the frequency spectrum has been weighted by a specific electrical network in the sound-measuring equipment (or is done manually) before the single-number level is derived. It is simple to measure the A-weighted sound level and, fortunately, this single number often correlates with people's perceptions as well as or better than most other single-number noise ratings schemes. The frequency response of the A-weighting network in standard octave bands is shown in Table 1-3. To determine the A-weighted sound level from unweighted octave band levels, simply apply these factors to the levels in the various bands and add the weighted octave band levels as decibels.

TABLE 1-3 A-Scale Weighting Factors

Octave band center frequency, Hz	Approximate A-weighting relative response, dB
31.5	−39
63	−26
125	−16
250	−9
500	−3
1000	0
2000	+1
4000	+1
8000	−1

Table 1-4 shows some typical A-weighted sound levels in industrial environments.

TABLE 1-4 Typical A-Weighted Sound Levels in Industrial Plants, Near Various Equipment

Equipment	dBA
Synthetic spinning machine	95
Rock crusher	101
Letterpress	96
Hammer mill	96
Hand-held sand blaster	95
Plastic extruder	97
Candy wrapper	90
Fly shuttle loom	102
Can filling/seamer	98
Ring twister	94
Chipper	105
Wood chipper	109
Billet heater	102
Buffing machine	101
Punch press	102
Wire-drawing machine	96
Molding machine	98
Concrete-block machine	106

Addition of decibels Since decibels are logarithmic units, they are not added arithmetically. Decibels are added by converting them to power, intensity, or pressure; adding these quantities; and then converting them back to decibels. The mathematics involved may be somewhat complex for people not accustomed to working with logarithms so charts have been developed for convenience. See Fig. 1-1 for one example of such a chart. To add the sound levels of 80 dB and 74 dB that are produced individually by two separate sources, note that the difference between the two levels is 6 dB. Enter the chart in Fig. 1-1 at the 6 on the horizontal axis and draw a line straight up to the curve. From the intersection of the vertical line and the curve draw a horizontal line over to the vertical axis and read the decibel increment (1 dB) to be added to the higher of the two levels being added (80 dB). The total level is thus 81 dB. Similarly a 90 dB sound level added to another 90 dB sound level results in 93 dB.

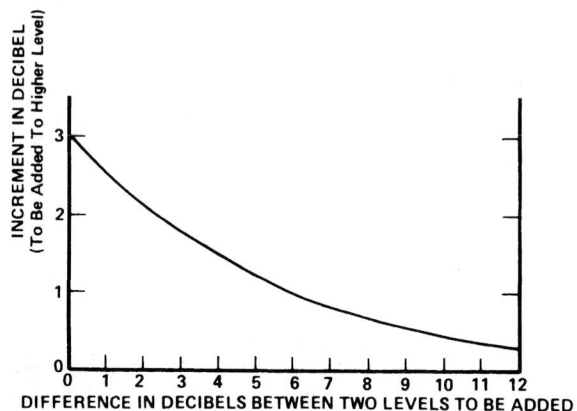

FIGURE 1-1   Chart for combining sound levels.

Sound propagation outdoors—the inverse square law   Under *free field* conditions—away from any nearby surfaces to reflect or disturb the sound field—sound radiates spherically away from a source. The acoustical energy is radiated to progressively larger spherical shells as it moves outward from the source. The acoustical energy per unit area (the intensity) is thus inversely proportional to the surface area of the spherical shell and this area is a function of the square of the radius of the shell. Hence, sound levels observed at any distance from a source are said to follow an inverse square relationship.

Two forms of the inverse square relationship that are useful for analyzing everyday acoustical problems are shown below in equation form. The first estimates of the sound pressure level at distances away from a source of known sound power level under free field conditions:

$$L_p = L_w + 10 \log \left(\frac{Q}{4\pi r^2} \right) + C \text{ dB}$$

where Q = the directivity of the source, which is equal to the inverse of the portion of a sphere to which the sound is radiated
C = 0 if r is expressed in m, and 10.5 if r is expressed in ft.

This relationship applied in reverse is also useful for estimating the sound power level of a source from sound pressure levels that are known at some distance from the source:

$$Lp_1 = Lp_0 - 10 \log(r_1^2/r_0^2) = Lp_0 - 20 \log(r_1/r_0)$$

This second equation allows calculation of the sound pressure level at one distance from a source, given the sound pressure level at some other known distance.

From both these equations, it can be seen that the sound pressure level in the free field falls off at the rate of 6 dB per doubling of distance from the source.

Absorption coefficient   The ability of a material to absorb or dissipate sound energy that is incident on its surface is of interest in assessing and treating acoustical problems. The sound absorption coefficient, α, indicates the percentage, in decimal form, of the incident sound that is absorbed (removed from the sound wave) through interaction with the surface. Sound absorption coefficients range from 0, for no absorption, to 1, for complete absorption. Some laboratory test data give absorption coefficients greater than 1, indicating that the surface absorbed more sound energy than was incident upon it. Clearly this cannot be; the data are the result of acoustical complexities and the standard laboratory test methodology. Absorption coefficients of materials are functions of frequency, the mounting condition of the material, and sometimes the angle of incidence of the sound upon the surface. Tables 1-5 and 1-6 show typical published data for random incidence sound. Note also that the percentage of sound that is reflected from a surface is $1 - \alpha$.

TABLE 1-5   Representative Sound Absorption Coefficients of General Building Materials and Furnishings*

Materials	Octave band coefficients					
	125	250	500	1000	2000	4000
Brick, unglazed	0.03	0.03	0.03	0.04	0.05	0.07
Brick, unglazed, painted	0.01	0.01	0.02	0.02	0.02	0.03
Carpet, heavy, on concrete	0.02	0.06	0.14	0.37	0.60	0.65
Same, on 40-oz hair felt or foam rubber	0.08	0.24	0.57	0.69	0.71	0.73
Same, with impermeable latex backing on 40-oz hair felt or foam rubber	0.08	0.27	0.39	0.34	0.48	0.63
Concrete block, coarse	0.36	0.44	0.31	0.29	0.39	0.25
Concrete block, painted	0.10	0.05	0.06	0.07	0.09	0.08
Fabrics						
Light velour, 10 oz/yd², hung straight, in contact with wall	0.03	0.04	0.11	0.17	0.24	0.35
Medium velour, 14 oz/yd², draped to half area	0.07	0.31	0.49	0.75	0.70	0.60
Heavy velour, 18 oz/yd², draped to half area	0.14	0.35	0.55	0.72	0.70	0.65
Floors						
Concrete or terrazzo	0.01	0.01	0.01	0.02	0.02	0.02
Linoleum, asphalt, rubber, or cork time on concrete	0.02	0.03	0.03	0.03	0.03	0.02
Wood	0.15	0.11	0.10	0.07	0.06	0.07
Wood parquet in asphalt on concrete	0.04	0.04	0.07	0.06	0.06	0.07
Glass						
Large panes of heavy plate glass	0.18	0.06	0.04	0.03	0.02	0.02
Ordinary window glass	0.35	0.25	0.18	0.12	0.07	0.04
Gypsum board, ½ in nailed to 2 × 4's 16-in o.c.	0.29	0.10	0.05	0.04	0.07	0.09
Marble or glazed tile	0.01	0.01	0.01	0.01	0.02	0.02
Openings						
Stage, depending on furnishings			0.25–0.75			
Deep balcony, upholstered seats			0.50–1.00			
Grills, ventilating			0.15–0.50			
Plaster, gypsum or lime, smooth finish on tile or brick	0.013	0.015	0.02	0.03	0.04	0.05
Plaster, gypsum or lime, rough finish on tile or brick	0.14	0.10	0.06	0.05	0.04	0.03
Same, with smooth finish	0.14	0.10	0.06	0.04	0.04	0.03
Plywood paneling, ⅜-in thick	0.28	0.22	0.17	0.09	0.10	0.11
Water surface, as in a swimming pool				0.02	0.02	0.02
Air, sabins per 1000 ft³ at 50% RH	0.01	0.01	0.01	.9	2.3	7.2

* Complete tables of coefficients of the various materials that normally constitute the interior finish of rooms may be found in the various books on architectural acoustics. The following short list will be useful in making simple calculations of the reverberation in rooms.

TABLE 1-6 Representative Sound Absorption Coefficients of Common Acoustic Materials

Materials*	Octave band coefficients					
	125	250	500	1000	2000	4000
Fibrous glass (typically 4 lb/ft³) on solid backing						
1-in thick	0.07	0.23	0.48	0.83	0.88	0.80
2-in thick	0.20	0.55	0.89	0.97	0.83	0.79
4-in thick	0.39	0.91	0.99	0.97	0.94	0.89
Polyurethane foam (open cell) on solid backing						
¼-in thick	0.05	0.07	0.10	0.20	0.45	0.81
½-in thick	0.05	0.12	0.25	0.57	0.89	0.98
1-in thick	0.14	0.30	0.63	0.91	0.98	0.91
2-in thick	0.35	0.51	0.82	0.98	0.97	0.95

* For specific grades, see manufacturer's data.

Room absorption   The total amount of sound absorption in a room can be determined by summing the products of the area of each type of surface material in a room times its absorption coefficient. Often this must be done separately for all frequency bands that are of interest. The term that is typically applied to this quantity for noise control purposes is the room constant R.* The units of R are designated Sabines and are in ft² or m². Take care to distinguish between English unit Sabines or metric unit Sabines when applying various formulas.

$$R = \sum S_1\alpha_1 + S_2\alpha_2 \ldots\ldots S_n\alpha_n \quad \text{m}^2 \text{ (ft}^2\text{)}$$

where S_1, S_2 and S_n are the areas of the individual materials.

Sound propagation indoors   The sound pressure level in a room due to a particular sound source can be estimated using the following relationship:

$$L_p = L_w + 10 \log \left(\frac{Q}{4\pi r^2} + \frac{4}{R} \right) + C \text{ dB}$$

where R is the room constant in units consistent with the units of r, and C is the appropriate conversion term for the units of r and R (0 dB if metric, 10.5 dB if English).

The first quantity within the parentheses is the direct sound field and is identical to the equation given previously for spherical spreading of sound in the free field. The second quantity within the parentheses is the reverberant sound field, which relates to how much sound absorption there is in the room and hence how much the sound is reflected within the room. The resulting total sound level is the decibel sum of the direct and reverberant sound levels. Note that the reverberant portion of the sound field is not a function of the distance from the source; it is essentially constant throughout the room. In typical rooms, the sound level due to a source diminishes at the rate of 6 dB per doubling of distance from the source until the direct field sound level equals the reverberant field sound level. Beyond this distance, the sound level remains essentially constant. Actually, in the transition region between the direct and reverberant fields the two levels add, resulting in a smooth transition between the regions. The relationship for the sound pressure level indoors is shown graphically in Figure 1-2.

---

* The room constant R is technically the sum of $S_n\alpha_n/1 - \alpha_n$, but for many practical applications and especially for rooms with relatively little sound absorption, R is closely approximated by the sum of the products of the surface area times its respective absorption coefficient.

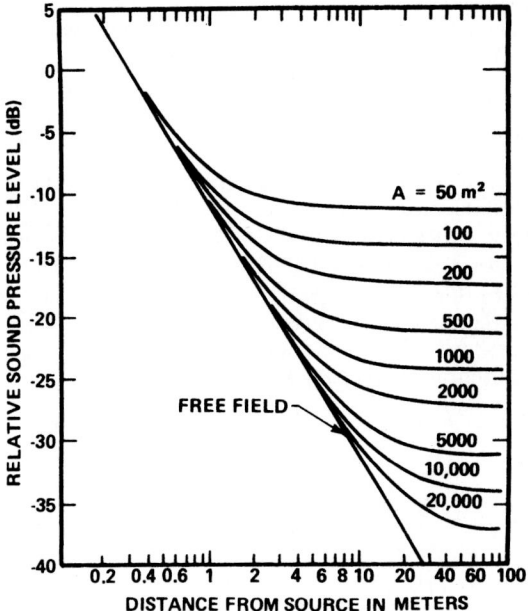

FIGURE 1-2 Drop-off of sound pressure level as a function
of distance from sound source.

Noise reduction by sound absorption   Sound that originates at a source in an enclosed factory space will spread until it reaches the surfaces, where it will either be absorbed or reflected. If the room surfaces are hard (reflective), sound will reverberate, intermittent sounds will be mixed together, and steady sounds will add up. The result may be a relatively noisy space. If room surfaces are soft (absorptive), the space will be less noisy, because the aforementioned effects will not occur. The noise level in the reverberant portion of the room, well away from any particular sound source, is a function of how much sound absorption is in the room. The relative noise reduction in the reverberant field that can be obtained through the introduction of sound absorption to the space can be estimated as follows:

$$NR = 10 \log \left(\frac{R_1}{R_0} \right) \quad \text{dB}$$

where R_0 is the original amount of sound absorption in the room and R_1 is the new amount of sound absorption.

For each doubling of the sound absorption in a room the reverberant field noise level is reduced by 3 dB.

Transmission coefficient   The ability of a material to block the transmission of sound is of interest in analyzing and treating acoustical problems and is given by the sound transmission coefficient τ, which is the fraction of incident sound energy that is transmitted through a barrier material. Thus:

$$\tau = \frac{W_2}{W_1}$$

where W_1 is the incident sound energy in watts and W_2 is the sound energy transmitted in watts.

Transmission loss   The sound transmission loss TL of a barrier material is defined as the ratio of the transmitted sound energy to the incident sound energy.

In decibel form, this ratio is expressed as:

$$TL = 10 \log \frac{W_1}{W_2} = 10 \log \frac{1}{\tau} \quad \text{dB}$$

To calculate in detail the sound transmission loss for even simple constructions is difficult. As a result, engineers usually rely on laboratory test data. The transmission loss of a particular material has to do with the material only and is only part of the equation to determine what noise level will occur on the opposite side of a barrier. See "Noise Reduction."

Mass law   For each doubling of the weight of a single-material construction, the average sound transmission loss increases by about 6 dB. Figure 1-3 shows a graphic presentation of the transmission loss of a single wall. The empirically determined curve (solid) is lower than the theoretical curve (dotted).

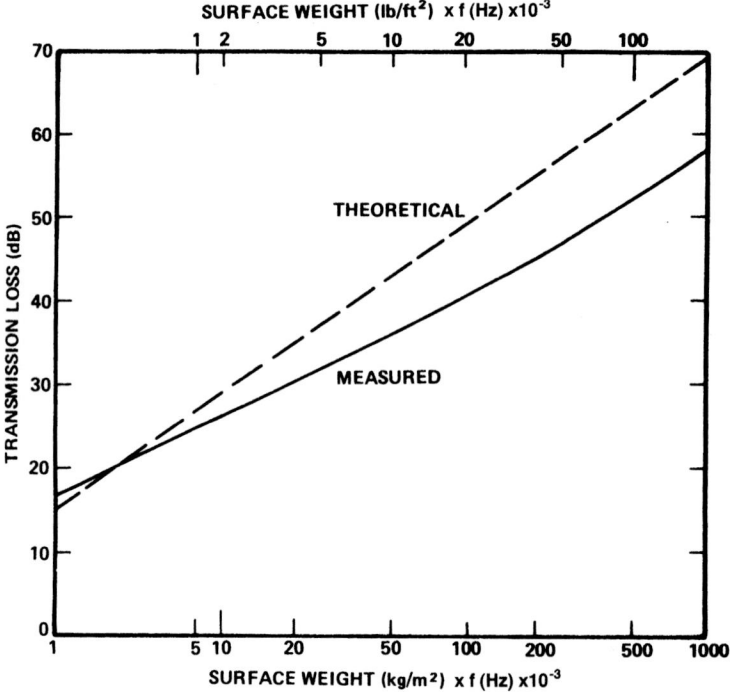

FIGURE 1-3   Average transmission loss of single homogeneous walls in the 100- to 3150-Hz frequency range.

Composite sound transmission loss   The composite sound transmission loss of a multielement barrier is estimated from the transmission coefficients for each part. The sound power transmitted by the elements with a common incident sound power is

$$W_{\text{trans}} = W_{\text{inc}} (\tau_1 S_1 + \tau_2 S_2) \quad \text{W}$$

where τ_1 and τ_2 are the transmission coefficients for the individual parts, and S_1 and S_2 are the areas of the individual parts in ft^2 (m^2).

The composite transmission loss becomes

$$TL = 10 \log \frac{S_1 + S_2}{\tau_1 S_1 + \tau_2 S_2} \quad \text{dB}$$

Noise Reduction   The difference in sound pressure levels between two rooms is called the noise reduction (*NR*). *NR* accounts for the total amount of energy being radiated through the common construction by way of the area term and the attenuating effect of sound absorption in the receiving room.

This noise reduction can be expressed as:

$$NR = TL - 10 \log \frac{S}{A_2} \quad \text{dB}$$

where S = area of common wall, ft^2 (m^2)
$\quad\quad\quad A_2$ = total sound absorption in the receiving room, ft^2 – sabin (m^2 – sabin)

HUMAN RESPONSE TO NOISE

Human response to noise is as varied as are people and the noises to which they respond. The noise of a mosquito or dripping sink may prevent one from sleeping, but the louder noise of surf at the beach or rain on the roof may induce sleep. The noise produced by operating machinery may be acceptable at a manufacturing plant, but intrusive and unacceptable at a nearby residential area. One person might hardly notice the noise produced by an ultrasonic welder and another person would find it to be unacceptable. Exposures to mid-frequency and high-frequency noise causes far more damage to hearing than exposure to low-frequency noise of the same level. Investigators have spent decades studying human response to noise and many books have been written on the subject. This section provides a brief overview of the subject.

The pressure oscillations of the sound in the air cause the eardrum and small bones of the middle ear to vibrate. These vibrations are transmitted to the fluid-filled cochlea, the inner ear's sensory organ. Sensory hair cells that line the cochlea translate these vibrations into nerve impulses that are transmitted to the brain where they are perceived and interpreted. Exposure to moderate levels of industrial noise may cause temporary hearing loss by over-stressing the sensitive hair cells in the cochlea. With time away from the noise, normal hearing typically returns. Long-term exposure to high levels of industrial noise destroys some of the sensory hair cells and causes permanent hearing loss because there are fewer functioning sensory cells. No treatment has yet been found to repair the cells and restore noise-induced hearing loss.

A faint sound level is in the range of 10 to 20 dB. A moderate sound level is about 50 to 60 dB, and a loud sound level is about 90 to 100 dB. Sound levels greater than about 130 dB often cause pain in the ear.

When the magnitude of a noise is increased (or decreased) by 10 dB, this is often perceived as a doubling (or halving) of the loudness. Changing the magnitude of a noise by 5 to 6 dB is generally considered significant, and is clearly noticeable. Changing the magnitude of a noise by less than 2 to 3 dB is often unnoticed.

The frequency of a noise is analogous to its tonal quality or pitch. The fundamental frequency of middle C on a piano keyboard, for example, is 262 Hz. A tuning fork produces sound at a single frequency, often called a discrete tone. Transformers produce sound at several discrete frequencies that are even multiples of line frequency. In the United States, transformer noise is concentrated at 120, 240, 360, 480, and 600 Hz. However, most sounds include a composite of many frequencies and are characterized as random or broadband. Rotating equipment such as fans and motors usually produce both broadband and discrete tonal noise.

The normal frequency range of human hearing extends from a low-frequency rumble at about 20 to 50 Hz up to a high frequency hiss at about 10,000 to 15,000 Hz, and sometimes higher for some people. People have different hearing sensitivity to different frequencies and generally hear best in the mid-frequency range that is common to human speech, about 500 to 4000 Hz.

The noise environment in most plants and communities varies from place to place and varies with time at any given location due to the composite of many noise sources. The noise environment may include intermittent high-noise single events and slowly varying background noises. The amplitude statistics of most noise environments are rather complex.

At any one location, a complete physical description of the noise environment might include its noise level at various frequencies as a function of time. It is common practice to simplify this multidimensional description by eliminating the frequency variable and measuring the A-weighted noise level, as observed on a standard sound level meter. The A-weighting filter emphasizes the mid-frequency components of the noise and demphasizes the low-frequency components in order to approximate the response and sensitivity of the human ear.

For certain applications, it is also common practice to further simplify this multidimensional description by eliminating the temporal variable and measuring the equivalent sound level (Leq) or OSHA sound level (Losha) time average sound level, as observed on standard dosimeters and modern sound level meters. Leq is often used in community noise analysis. It is also used during the analysis of employee noise exposures in many countries other than the United States. Losha is often used in employee noise exposure analysis in the United States.

The above simple measures are convenient and sufficient for many applications. However, a more sophisticated narrow-band frequency analysis is often necessary to evaluate fully a community's response to intruding noise from a plant. Narrow-band frequency analysis is almost always necessary during the engineering design or specification of noise control treatments.

Many acoustic rating scales and rating procedures have been developed by investigators interested in assessing people's reactions to intruding noise and evaluating adverse health effects from noise exposures. Several of the scales and procedures that are currently popular for assessing or evaluating plant noise are listed below.

Overall sound pressure level (Lp in dB)

A-weighted sound level or noise level (LA in dBA)

C-weighted sound level or noise level (Lc in dBC)

Energy equivalent sound level or noise level (Leq in dB)

OSHA equivalent sound level or noise level (Losha in dB)

Day-night sound level or noise level (Ldn in dB)

Speech interference level (SIL)

Noise criterion curves (NC)

Room criterion curves (RC)

Balanced noise criterion curves (NCB)

Definitions and uses of these acoustic rating scales and rating procedures can be found in acoustical references and textbooks.

MATERIALS SELECTION

The most commonly used materials for control of noise in industry are sound-absorbing and barrier materials for airborne sound, and vibration isolators and dampers for structureborne sound. Selection of materials is often affected by factors other than acoustics. Some factors are include:

- Vibration
- Corrosion
- Temperature
- Erosion by fluid flow
- Cost
- Appearance
- Structure
- Weight
- Clogging
- Restrictions on materials near food processing lines
- Requirements for materials not to be damaged by disinfecting
- Firebreak requirements on ducts, pipe runs, shafts
- Flame-spread rate limits
- Fire-endurance limits
- Restrictions on shedding of fibers in air by acoustically absorbing materials
- Elimination of uninspectable spaces in which vermin may hide
- Requirements for secure anchoring of heavy equipment
- Restrictions on hole sizes in machine guards (holes can reduce radiated noise of vibrating sheets)

CONTROL OF PLANT NOISE

Noise is controlled inside plants to provide a safe, healthful, and comfortable work environment. Noise is controlled outside plants to avoid degrading the neighborhood environment. Noise can be controlled directly at the *source*, such as a fan or transformer, where it is produced. Noise can also be controlled along the *paths* that it travels from the source to the receiver, for example, by the use of a barrier or a muffler. Noise can also be controlled at the *receiver*, for example, by earmuffs or earplugs, both of which were discussed earlier. This section addresses control of plant noise at the source and along propagation paths.

Some common methods used to control plant noise are barriers, enclosures, absorption, mufflers, lagging or wrapping, damping, isolation, equipment selection, and improved maintenance. An additional, newer method that is available to reduce plant noise is active noise control. Each of these methods are discussed subsequently. Further information about noise control techniques and costs is available from noise control hardware manufacturers and publications.

Mufflers

Mufflers, often called silencers or attenuators by their manufacturers, are located in pipes, ducts, and passageways used to convey gas, liquid, or solid materials to or from a machine, process, or area for the purpose of reducing the propagation of noise from the source to the receiver. Mufflers are commonly used at the intake and/or exhaust of engines, fans, and compressors and at the outlets of high-pressure gas vents.

The muffler must be designed, specified, and selected such that its dynamic acoustic insertion loss is adequate to meet the required noise attenuation design goal established for the specific application. In addition, noise that radiates from the outer shell of the muffler must be adequately controlled, which is sometimes accomplished by wrapping it with an acoustic lagging. To achieve high noise attenuation through a muffler usually requires that flexible connections be installed between the muffler and the noise source to reduce structureborne flanking and minimize shell-radiated noise. Also, noise caused by high-velocity gas flow at the muffler discharge (self-noise) must be adequately controlled for the specific application. Gas flow speed at the discharge should usually be low enough to achieve self-noise levels at least 10 dB less than the required design goal. Furthermore, the temperature of the gas within the muffler must be considered because the wavelength of sound increases as temperature increases and muffler performance varies with wavelength.

In harsh environments, mufflers must be designed and constructed to withstand erosion, corrosion, thermal stresses, and sometimes relatively high vibration caused by the noise source or turbulent gas flows. Mufflers installed in dirty air flows must be designed to avoid becoming clogged. In these applications, it is often necessary to specify and custom design open-cavity-type, nonclogging, tuned-dissipative mufflers. Mufflers installed in a fluid stream often must also be designed, constructed, and installed so as to avoid causing excessive pressure losses.

Dissipative mufflers, often in the form of parallel baffles used at the inlet and outlet of a noisy fan, provide noise attenuation through the use of a fibrous sound-absorptive material, such as glass-fiber insulation. Sound waves passing through the muffler enter the fibrous material and are absorbed or dissipated as movements of air molecules are converted to heat through friction effects. Dissipative mufflers are most often in the form of (1) a rectangular duct section containing absorptive parallel baffles or (2) a circular duct section containing absorptive material on the outer wall and/or an absorptive element ("bullet") on the duct center line. Figure 1-4 illustrates the approximate insertion loss achievable with 90-cm long mufflers designed with different spacing between the baffles and thickness of the baffles. Note that the insertion loss of these dissipative mufflers is greatest at mid-frequencies and least at low and high frequencies.

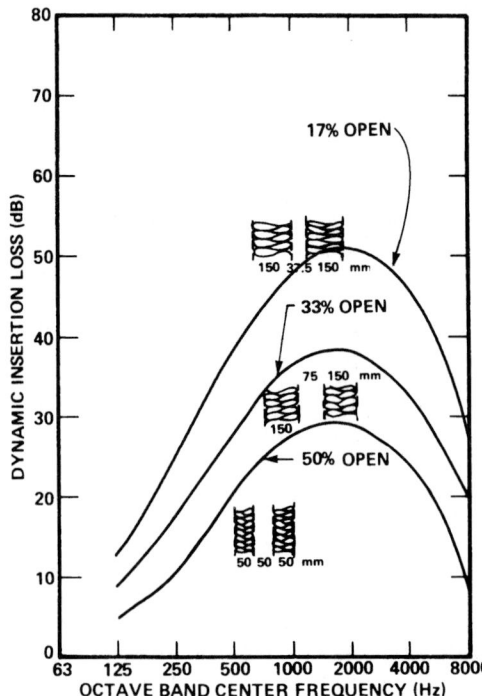

FIGURE 1-4 Acoustical performance of 90-cm (3-ft) long mufflers with different spacing and thickness of baffles.

The glass fiber material within dissipative mufflers must be protected with woven glass cloth and/or steel screen when exposed to high velocity gas flows. When used in wet environments or environments that need to be especially clean, the glass fiber material is often encapsulated in thin plastic bags to provide protection.

Reactive mufflers, such as those used at the outlet of reciprocating engines, provide noise attenuation through the use of one or more internal expansion chambers interconnected with perforated pipes. The expansion chambers serve to reflect acoustic energy in the gas stream back towards the source rather than along the pipe to the exit.

Reactive/dissipative mufflers include both reactive expansion chambers and dissipative insulation elements. They are commonly used when a large degree of noise attenuation is required at the exhaust of stationary reciprocating turbine engines and compressors. One advantage of reactive/dissipative mufflers used to control noise from large fans is that they can be designed to provide both broadband noise attenuation and additional attenuation of the tonal noise produced by the fan at its blade-passing frequency.

While not actually mufflers, diffusers formed with porous or sintered metal are sometimes installed at the outlets of small gas vents to reduce jet noise.

A wide variety of dissipative and reactive mufflers are available as predesigned catalogue items from many manufacturers. Simple dissipative and reactive mufflers will typically attenuate low-frequency noise by approximately 3 to 6 dB and mid-frequency noise by approximately 10 to 30 dB. Such mufflers are often well suited for common or simple noise control applications without special requirements. When significantly greater noise attenuation is needed, for complex installations or critical applications where low noise levels are required, and when low pressure loss is necessary, it is suggested that an experienced professional be consulted to advise in the design, specification, and selection of appropriate mufflers for the specific application.

Equipment Specification, Selection, Layout, Maintenance, and Operation

The specification, selection, layout, maintenance, and operation of plant equipment can influence plant noise levels and employee noise exposures. Each of these items is worth considering when evaluating noise control requirements and available options. For those companies that are moving office workers out onto the factory floor, these considerations are essential.

A wide variety of equipment is now available directly from manufacturers with noise levels reduced by as much as 5 to 15 dBA. Examples include compressors, motors, valves, transformers, cooling towers, and reciprocating and turbine engines. Entire manufacturing and assembly lines can be designed and installed to have reduced noise levels. To achieve this, a realistic understanding of the plant's noise-level/noise-exposure design goals and a well-written technical specification that defines the noise requirements are necessary. When purchasing replacement equipment, adding additional equipment, or designing a new plant, the specification of low-noise equipment is a worthwhile investment, yielding an improved work environment and less hearing loss among employees. In some cases, low-noise equipment also operates more efficiently than standard high-noise equipment.

It is obvious that equipment layout and spacing within a plant will affect both work-area noise levels and employee noise exposures. Sometimes logical adjustments to equipment layout during the design of a plant addition or new plant will yield an improved work environment without loss in production efficiencies. In some cases all that is needed is a fresh look at plant requirements rather than simply repeating previous layouts. Relocating equipment such as fans, pumps, engines, and metal shears away from conference rooms and office areas should be considered to avoid excessive intrusive noise. Questions should be asked when considering the layout of a new plant or plant addition: Is it necessary to locate several motor-pump sets so close together that maintenance workers inspecting or repairing one unit are exposed to excessive noise from the adjacent operating units? Can instrument panels and operator workstations be relocated somewhat farther away from particularly noisy equipment? Can a booth or shelter be incorporated into an employee workstation? Is it possible to locate workstations away from noisy equipment and noise-reflecting walls? Can very noisy operations, such as riveting, chipping, or metal grinding be located away from work areas that would otherwise be less noisy?

Well-maintained equipment tends to operate with less noise than does poorly maintained equipment. One obvious example is a small leak in the packing of a valve passing high-pressure steam and causing high noise levels nearby. Old engine exhaust mufflers and equipment enclosures are other examples. Loose guards and worn bearings are sometimes the source of unnecessary noise as are slipping belt drives and fans with distorted inflow conditions.

Equipment operation also affects noise. Most fans and some pumps produce higher noise levels when operated at low load rather than at full-rated load. For motor-driven units, variable-speed electronic drives are available that reverse this, resulting in less noise during low-load operation. Modifying the cutoff of high-pressure centrifugal fans may help to reduce the generation of tonal noise. Ventilation systems produce less noise when well balanced. It is well known that excessive noise is one result of metal cutting at incorrect speeds. Pump cavitation also causes excessive noise. Plant operation with open doors for additional ventilation during hot summer weather sometimes results in excessive community noise and poor public relations. Exercising emergency engine-generator sets during third shift, rather than during the daytime, can also result in poor community relations. The nighttime use (and occasional abuse) of outdoor paging systems, rather than radios or beepers, is sometimes the source of community noise complaints. The volume of indoor paging systems is sometimes set far higher than is necessary for adequate communication and contributes to employee noise exposures. All night idling of trucks, particularly refrigerated trucks, at warehouses has been the source of many community noise complaints. The noise caused by releasing high-pressure steam to atmosphere can be reduced significantly by the use of an operator-controlled valve with low noise trim.

Active Noise Control

Considerable research efforts are currently being undertaken to develop reliable and cost-effective means to actively (or electronically) control noise produced by equipment. Though not a new concept, modern theory and hardware for adaptive digital signal processing have recently made the commercial use of active noise control worth considering for various applications with special requirements.

One basic application of active noise control is the reduction of low-frequency tonal noise generated by fans in long ducts of relatively small cross section. An input microphone installed in the duct is used to generate a signal that is proportional to the unwanted noise. The signal is processed electronically and fed to a power amplifier that drives a loudspeaker mounted in the duct. The electrically generated sound from the loudspeaker is used to destructively interfere with and cancel a portion of the unwanted noise. In more complex applications, several microphones and loudspeakers must be employed. Most real-life applications include various physical conditions, such as temperature, flow velocity, and frequency, with temporal and spatially varying system characteristics. Adaptive active control systems that include one or more error-measuring microphones are being employed to improve noise attenuation performance in applications with varying system characteristics.

The use of active noise control should be considered when passive noise control methods are expensive, difficult, or impossible to install. The control of low-frequency noise in a duct is an example where passive noise control is at best difficult. In low-frequency applications where space is limited and no additional pressure is available, active noise control becomes even more attractive. However, it is important to recognize that the microphones, electronic circuits, and loudspeakers will require at least some ongoing maintenance, particularly when installed in hot or corrosive environments.

Active noise control has also been applied inside earmuffs and communication headsets to reduce noise exposure and improve speech intelligibility. Earmuffs and headsets with built-in active noise control elements are available for use in high-noise environments where conventional hearing protectors would not provide adequate noise attenuation.

For special applications requiring significant attenuation of low-, mid-, and high-frequency noise, it might be most practical to consider the use of both active and passive noise control methods. A passive noise control treatment, such as a small muffler or duct lining, can be installed to attenuate the mid- and high-frequency noise and active noise control might be employed to attenuate the low-frequency noise.

Additional information on active noise control and its applications can be found in sources listed at the end of this chapter.

Surface Damping

Machinery housings often consist of large areas of flexible metal plate; if they are set into vibration, such plate areas may become significant radiators of airborne noise. Vibration is caused by a forcing mechanism, such as internal oscillating, rotating, or reciprocating components, that may excite the machine's surfaces at their resonant (or natural ring) frequency. Application of damping (vibration-energy-absorbing) material to the surfaces will reduce the amplitude of vibration at the resonant frequency. Adding more material can stiffen and change the natural frequency so that it is no longer so easily excited.

Damping (viscoelastic) materials can be applied as either a free layer or a constrained layer. (See Figs. 1-5a and b.) The material can be troweled on, glued and baked on, or (for intermittent use) attached by a magnetic layer. Practical concerns regarding the specific material include ease of cleaning, toxicity, durability, and temperature-independent efficiency in the required frequency ranges. As a rule of thumb, for a damping material to be effective it must be at least as thick as the material to be damped.

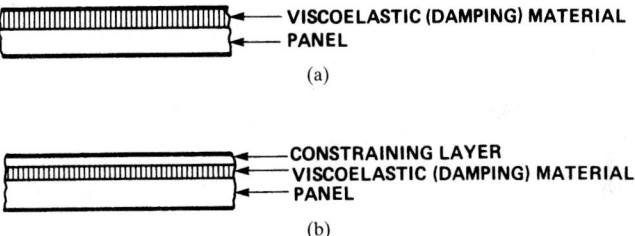

FIGURE 1-5   (a) Panel with free layer of viscoelastic (damping) material. (b) Panel with constrained layer of viscoelastic (damping) material.

Addition of Sound Absorptive Materials to a Room

One commonly used method for noise reduction in a room is to clad significant portions of the interior surfaces (usually the ceiling and walls) with highly sound-absorptive materials. Adding such materials to a room provides only minor noise reduction near the sources, but at greater distance, in the reverberant field, significant noise reduction may be achieved. If sound-absorptive material is added to a space that initially has little absorption in it, the reverberent-field noise reduction may be as high as 5 to 8 dB; however, in spaces that already have a modest level of absorption, the effect will be less. Reverberant-field noise reduction is approximately 3 dB per doubling of the amount of absorption in the room. For many spaces, a practical limit for noise reduction by adding absorptive material is about 5 dB. The first addition of absorption in a room provides the greatest reduction of noise and subsequent additions of absorption provide progressively less noise reduction (on a percentage basis). In some spaces, the cost of absorption to achieve the needed noise reduction may be higher than to other methods to reduce the noise.

Enclosures

Enclosures around noise sources or receiving personnel can provide effective noise reduction. They consist of materials with substantial sound transmission loss and are arranged to surround the noise source or receiver.

Equipment enclosures are structures that surround the noise source and thus contain the sound it generates. However, enclosures can cause a buildup of high-level acoustic energy within themselves. Enclosures, therefore, usually consist of a wall with surface weight chosen to provide the required attenuation and an inner lining of porous material to dissipate the buildup of acoustic energy. In some cases where complete enclosures are built, the machines inside may require placement on vibration-isolator devices that prevent the transmission of structureborne noise to the outer surfaces of the enclosure.

If there are gaps in the enclosure, sound can escape. The greater the percentage of open area in an enclosure, the smaller the reduction in radiated sound. Table 1-7 gives an indication of the effects of openings in otherwise well-designed enclosures.

TABLE 1-7   Noise Level Effects of Openings

Percentage of open area in enclosure	Maximum average noise reduction, dB
50	3
25	6
10	10
1	20

In a practical sense, enclosure designs often require some accommodation. For ease of maintenance, enclosures can be constructed to rise upward and away from the machinery by overhead cranes. Access openings can be provided by tunnels lined with acoustically absorbent material (in effect, mufflers). Access for controls can be designed with hinged covers that lift easily, or the controls can be relocated. Some enclosure panels can be lifted automatically at the correct point in the machine cycle to provide access. Ducts can be provided with small ventilating fans to produce a controlled cooling airstream and, if combined with filters, can allow a controlled environment for some operations.

Employees exposed to high-level noise from a number of sources can be protected by acoustic booths. These can range from small open-fronted telephone-booth-sized cabinets (into which the operator steps while observing the operation of a semiautomatic machine) to completely enclosed control consoles. In many cases, acoustic booths for personnel can provide an island of protection; an employee exposed to high-level noise during part of the workday can be protected well enough to reduce total exposure during normal working hours to less than the permissible exposure.

The design of worker enclosures requires suitable walls to produce the necessary sound reduction and also some internal sound absorption to prevent reverberant buildup of transmitted sound. The design and location of such booths require a careful review and measurement program of the acoustical situation.

Wrapping and Lagging

Noise-control wrappings (lagging) can be thought of as tight-fitting enclosures installed and supported directly on the surface of equipment such as ducts, pipes, valves, and machines to reduce noise radiation. For high-temperature noisy equipment, thermal insulation can often be adapted also to serve as effective noise-control wrapping. To serve both functions, the inner insulation layer must be both porous and resilient (e.g., a glass fiber blanket), so that it is both a good sound absorber and resilient enough to avoid transmitting vibration from the equipment surface to the outer noise barrier layer. The outer protective layer should be impervious, preferably limp, and isolated from the noise-radiating equipment surface. Most often the outer layer (jacket) is an aluminum or steel sheet metal, a mass-loaded silicone, or a vinyl material.

Noise-control wrappings can be thought of as a spring-mass isolation system, where the porous insulation forms the spring and the impervious jacket forms the mass. At frequencies equal to and below the system resonance, the noise attenuation (insertion loss) is zero or negative, sometimes providing an increase in low-frequency noise radiation. At higher frequencies, above about 200 Hz, noise attenuation increases with increasing frequency.

Noise attenuation of acoustical wrappings increases as (1) the surface weight of the impervious outer jacket is increased, (2) the stiffness per unit area of the porous insulation is reduced, (3) the thickness of the porous layer is increased, and (4) frequency is increased. Well-designed noise-control wrappings routinely provide mid- to high-frequency noise attenuations of 10 to 30 dB or more. To achieve substantial noise attenuation, it is essential that the outer jacket not contact the vibrating machine surface and that the insulation layer be resilient. Rigid or impervious thermal insulations such as calcium silicate, glass foam, and closed cell foams are generally not suited for noise-control applications.

Flexible blanket insulations have proven to provide substantial noise attenuation, be easy to remove and reinstall during equipment maintenance, and be cost effective in many applications requiring ready access to the equipment. Information about thermal-acoustic flexible blanket insulation is available from many manufacturers of industrial blanket insulation and in the sources listed at the end of this chapter.

Vibration Isolation

Large vibrating machinery housings or sections of framing may radiate large amounts of sound, even when the vibration is almost imperceptible. For noise control, the surfaces can be acoustically "isolated" from the vibrating drive mechanism by vibration isolation mounts, breaks, or pads installed between the vibrating source and the radiating surface. (See Chap. 12-2, "Vibration Control.")

Barriers

A barrier is a solid wall used to shield a receiver from the direct radiated sound of a machine. To be effective, it must be sufficiently massive to provide the required reduction in the sound transmitted through the barrier, and it must be sufficiently wide and high to prevent the sound defracted around the edges from becoming significant. Barriers should be placed close to either the source or the receiver for maximum effectiveness. A barrier positioned halfway between the source and the receiver will require the greatest dimensions to produce a given noise reduction.

Barriers can also be used to shield a group of workers not working on noisy machines from an area containing noisy machines. Of course, the effectiveness of such barriers can be significantly reduced by reflected sound, for example, from a ceiling or nearby sidewalls. Therefore, barriers may need to be combined with ceiling and possibly wall treatments to reduce the sound transmitted by alternative paths. Figure 1-6 shows the average mid-frequency noise reduction provided by a barrier. At low frequencies the reduction will be less and at high frequencies the reduction will be greater than shown in Fig. 1-6.

Barriers can be provided with acoustically absorptive material on the side facing the source to avoid a reflected buildup of sound near the machine. Without absorptive material, the barrier will tend to increase the noise level on the machine side of the barrier.

Simple small barriers can be located on some machinery to provide individual operator protection. In this case, a transparent material may allow visual monitoring. On small

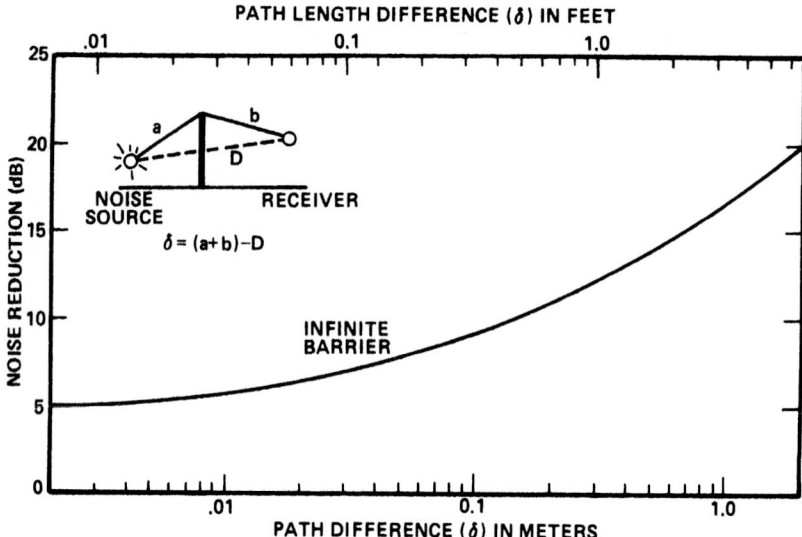

FIGURE 1-6   Average noise reduction of acoustical barrier of infinite length.

machines the controls may still be reached under or around the barrier. Such arrangements can also act as safety shields.

Although a barrier is designed to stop the sound from reaching a given receiver, the barrier does not necessarily have to impede the passage of materials and products. The use of overlapping entrances to produce a visual and acoustic blockage can allow easy access for forklift trucks and the locations of conveyors.

MEASUREMENT AND INSTRUMENTATION

Before a noise measurement program is started, its objective should be clearly understood. The objective could be to determine the approximate level of the noise during a short period of time or to find out whether the noise environment is hazardous to the health and welfare of the worker. The objective also might be to learn if the noise exceeds some locally adopted sound level limits. Depending on the purpose and the required accuracy, a wide range of instrumentation is available and the instruments may be used in a variety of ways. A basic program to assess noise throughout an entire plant may require many measurements. A noise-control investigation of a particular machine may require extensive, detailed information. Sometimes monitoring systems are set up to detect excessive levels.

The simplest instrument available to measure sound levels is a sound level meter. There are four different classifications of portable sound level meters:

1. Precision, used for laboratory work or other measurements requiring extreme accuracy
2. General purpose, used for most industrial applications requiring normal accuracy
3. Survey, used for rapid surveys to determine approximate levels, typically measures A-weighted levels only
4. Special purpose, used for special purposes such as impulse noise measurements

The precision and tolerances of indicating meters and weighting networks vary significantly for the various types of sound level meters.

A sound-level meter must be calibrated on a regular schedule if it is to provide meaningful data. Most equipment is battery operated; the batteries must be fresh and capable of supplying the instrument with sufficient power. A battery check is followed by a field calibrator check. The calibrator produces a pure tone at a known sound-pressure level, which will allow appropriate adjustments to the meter.

Sound-level meters measure noise only at a given point at the time of observation. If the noise being measured is constant in both space and time, meters will give an accurate representation of the situation. However, if the sound level changes with time and location (for instance, as an operator moves around), it will be necessary to record either the sound level manually using short time intervals (5 to 10 s) or the noise data for later analysis of the time history of the noise. The second approach is preferable when a worker's noise exposure is related to duty cycles or product flow. In this case, extrapolations can be made on the basis of total day production to determine the noise exposure of an employee over a full day.

In industry there are situations in which time pressure is great, more than one person must be monitored, and duty cycles are not easily definable. In such cases, audiodosimeters can be used to measure employees' noise exposure. Audiodosimeters, devices about the size of a cigarette pack, are worn by employees to record the noise exposure of the wearers wherever they go. The microphone can be fixed to the unit or detached from the unit and placed in the hearing zone of the wearer. Audiodosimeters are available with an internal circuit that integrates the sound level and time in accordance with various noise exposure regulations.

BIBLIOGRAPHY

Textbooks, Manuals and Guides

Listed following are textbooks, manuals, and guides containing technical information that are useful in the application of noise control treatments at industrial and commercial facilities.

American Society of Heating, Refrigeration, and Air-Conditioning Engineers, Inc: *1991 ASHRAE Handbook: Heating, Ventilating, and Air-conditioning Applications,* Inch Pound Ed., Chap. 42, Atlanta, GA, 1991.

Beranek, Leo L., and István Vér: *Noise and Vibration Control Engineering Principles and Applications,* John Wiley & Sons, New York, 1992.

Bies, David A., and Colin H. Hansen: *Engineering Noise Control Theory and Practice,* Unwin Hyman Ltd., London, 1988.

Edison Electric Institute: *Electric Power Plant Environmental Noise Guide:* Vols. I and II, 2nd ed., Washington, D.C., 1984.

Harris, Cyril M.: *Handbook of Acoustical Measurements and Noise Control,* 3rd ed., McGraw-Hill, New York, 1991.

Jensen, Paul, Charles R. Jokel, and Laymon N. Miller: *Industrial Noise Control Manual,* U.S. Department of Health, Education, and Welfare, NIOSH, Cincinnati, Ohio, 1978.

Kinsler, Lawrence E., Austin R. Frey, Alan B. Coppens, and James V. Sanders: *Fundamentals of Acoustics,* 3rd ed., John Wiley & Sons, New York, 1982.

Peterson, Arnold P. G.: *Handbook of Noise Measurements,* 9th ed., Gen Rad, Concord, 1980.

Suter, Alice H., and John R. Franks: *A Practical Guide to Effective Hearing Conservation Programs in the Workplace,* U.S. Department of Health and Human Services, U.S. Government Printing Office, Washington, D.C., 1990.

U.S. Department of Health, Education, and Welfare, NIOSH: *Compendium of Materials for Noise Control,* Cincinnati, Ohio, 1975

Vér, István, and Eric J.W. Wood: *Induced Draft Fan Noise Control Technical Report and Design Guide,* Empire State Electric Energy Research Corp., ESEERCO Report No. EO82-15, New York, 1984.

Journals

Numerous journals dealing with acoustics and noise control engineering are available throughout the world. Three published in the United States have been selected and are listed here.

Sound & Vibration
Acoustical Publications, Inc.
27101 East Oviatt Road
PO Box 40416
Bay Village, Ohio 44141
216-835-0101

Noise Control Engineering Journal
Institute of Noise Control Engineering
PO Box 3206 Arlington Branch
Poughkeepsie, New York 12603
914-462-4006

Journal of the Acoustical Society of America
Acoustical Society of America
500 Sunnyside Boulevard
Woodbury, NY 11797
516-349-7800

Noise Control Equipment Manufacturers

Sound & Vibration magazine (listed above) publishes an annual list of companies that produce and sell hardware for the control of noise and vibration.

Acoustic Instrumentation

Sound & Vibration magazine (listed above) publishes an annual list of companies that produce and sell instrumentation for the measurement of noise and vibration.

Noise Control Consultants

National Council of Acoustical Consultants, 66 Morris Avenue, Springfield, NJ 07081, (voice) 201-379-1100, (fax) 201-379-6507.

Professional Organizations

Professional organizations engaged in acoustics and noise control engineering are located in more than thirty countries. Two organizations in the United States are listed here.

Acoustical Society of America
500 Sunnyside Boulevard
Woodbury, NY 11797
516-349-7800

Institute of Noise Control Engineering
PO Box 3206 Arlington Branch
Poughkeepsie, New York 12603
914-462-4006

Standards

Standards dealing with acoustics and noise control engineering applicable to industrial plants have been prepared by and are available from the following organizations, most of which are located in the United States. Many excellent standards are available from similar organizations located in other countries.

Acoustical Society of America (ASA)

Air Conditioning and Refrigeration Institute (ARI)

Air Movement and Control Association (AMCA)

American Boiler Manufacturers Association (ABMA)

American Gear Manufacturers Association (AGMA)

American National Standards Institute (ANSI)

American Society of Heating, Refrigeration and Air-Conditioning Engineers (ASHRAE)

American Society for Testing and Materials (ASTM)

Compressed Air and Gas Institute (CAGI)

Cooling Tower Institute (CTI)

Diesel Engine Manufacturers Association (DEMA)

Industrial Silencer Manufacturers Association (ISMA)

Institute of Electrical and Electronic Engineers (IEEE)

International Electrotechnical Commission (IEC)

International Organization for Standardization (ISO)

National Electrical Manufacturers Association (NEMA)

National Fluid Power Association (NFPA)

Society of Automotive Engineers (SAE)

CHAPTER 12-2
VIBRATION CONTROL

Eric E. Ungar
Chief Consulting Engineer
BBN Systems & Technologies
Cambridge, Massachusetts

CHARACTERIZATION OF VIBRATIONS

Vibration refers to oscillatory (back and forth) motions of structures, mechanical systems, or components of these. A vibration generally is characterized by the displacement, velocity, or acceleration measured at one or more points on the item of interest in specific directions of interest (e.g., perpendicular to a floor or wall).

The time variation of a vibration sometimes appears approximately like the idealized curve shown in Fig. 2-1a, obtained from a sensor and displayed on an oscilloscope or chart recorder. Such a regular curve, which corresponds mathematically to a sine or cosine, is called *sinusoidal* or *simple harmonic.* Note that it deviates from zero (the middle position) equally in both directions; the maximum excursion from zero in *one* direction is called the *amplitude A,* the total excursion in *both* directions is called the *double amplitude 2A* (or sometimes the peak-to-peak value). Amplitudes may be given in units of displacement, velocity or acceleration, depending on how the vibration is measured.

The time interval *T* between successive peaks is called the *period* and usually is measured in seconds. The number of vibration cycles (i.e., the number of periods) that occur per second is called the *frequency f* and is generally measured in hertz (Hz), which is the internationally standardized name that has replaced cycles per second (cps).

In practice one rarely obtains a simple signal like that of Fig. 2-1a. One is more likely to obtain one that looks like Fig. 2-1b, which consists of a basic sinusoid like that of Fig. 2-1a, to which there are added one or more sinusoids with higher frequencies (shorter periods) and generally smaller amplitudes. Fig. 2-1b is said to represent a *multifrequency* or *complex* vibration. The component with the lowest frequency (greatest period) is called the *fundamental* component. Components that occur at frequencies that are integer multiples of that of the fundamental one are called *harmonics.*

Vibrations like those illustrated by Fig. 2-1c, which have no well-defined period or amplitude—i.e., where the signal essentially never repeats itself—are called *nonperiodic* or *irregular.*

A vibration that has essentially the same amplitude over an extended time period is called *steady,* whereas a vibration with time-varying amplitude is called *transient.* Figures 2-1a, b, and c illustrate steady vibrations, whereas Fig. 2-1d illustrates a typical decaying transient con-

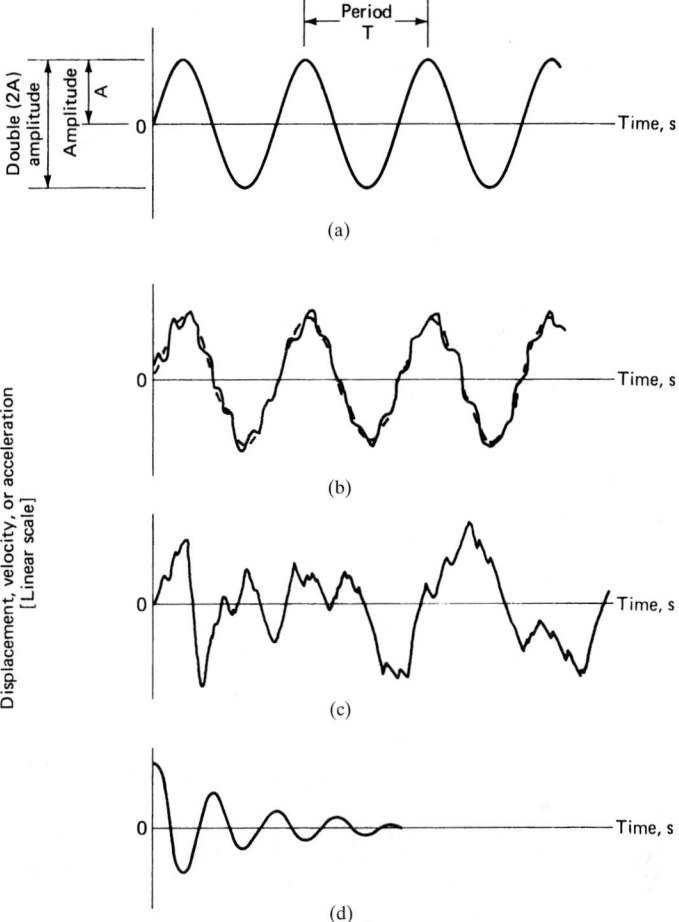

FIGURE 2-1   Typical vibration records: (*a*) steady sinusoidal or simple harmonic vibration; (*b*) steady multifrequency vibration; (*c*) irregular (nonperiodic) vibration; (*d*) decaying transient single-frequency vibration.

taining a single-frequency component; similar transients with multiple-frequency components or with irregular behavior may readily be visualized.

It is often useful to characterize a vibration in terms of a plot of amplitude vs frequency. Such a plot is called a *spectrum*. There are available a variety of instruments called *spectrum analyzers* that automatically provide amplitude-frequency displays for vibration signals fed into them.

Knowing the amplitude at a given frequency in terms of any one of the three motion quantities (displacement *d*, velocity *v*, acceleration *a*), one can calculate the amplitude in terms of the other two from:

$$a = 2\pi fv = (2\pi)^2 f^2 d$$

$$v = \frac{a}{2\pi f} = 2\pi fd \tag{1}$$

$$d = \frac{a}{(2\pi)^2 f^2} = \frac{v}{2\pi f}$$

where *a, v,* and *d* always contain the same length units and seconds and *f* is in hertz. For example, to *d* given in mils there corresponds *v* in mils/s and *a* in mils/s². For *v* = 10 ft/s and 20 Hz, $a = 2\pi(20)(10) = 1256$ ft/s² and also $d = 10/2\pi(20) = 0.080$ ft. Acceleration is often expressed in units of gravitational acceleration *g,* where $1g = 32.2$ ft/s² = 386 in/s² = 9.80 m/s².

Figure 2-2, which is based on Eq. (1), is a convenient chart for the approximate conversion between motion quantities.

CAUSES OF VIBRATIONS

Vibrations are always caused by unsteady forces, that is, by forces that may be oscillatory in magnitude or direction or by forces that are suddenly applied or released. These forces need not be due to mechanical causes; electromagnetic, aerodynamic or fluid-related forces also are often encountered in practice.

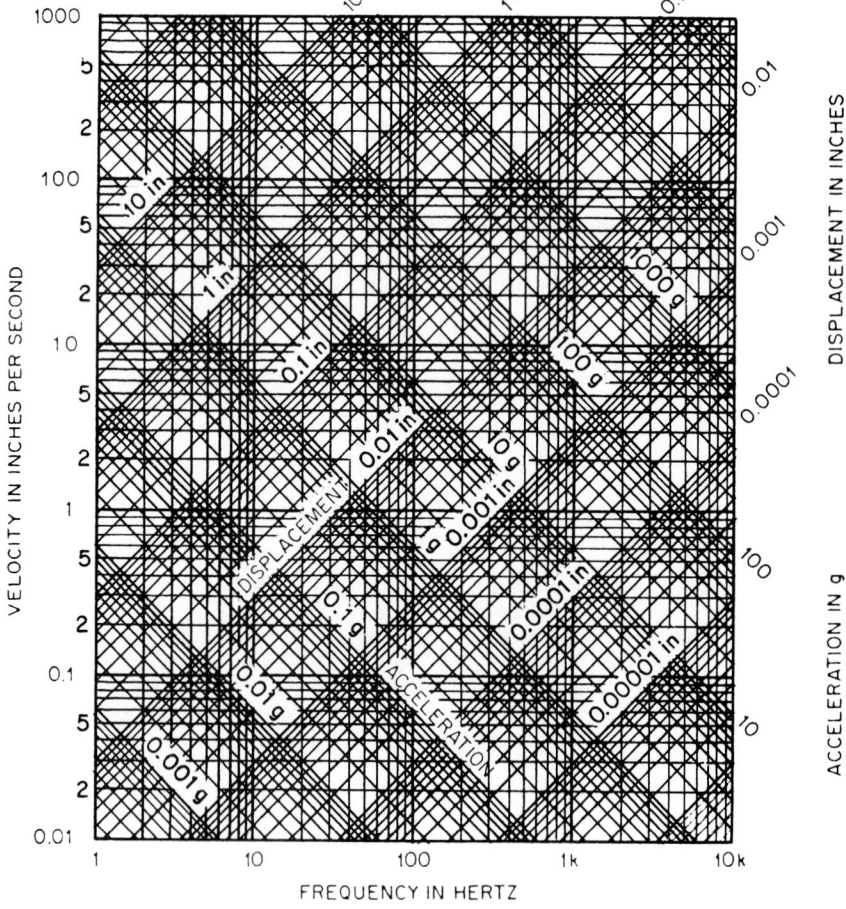

FIGURE 2-2 Chart for conversion between displacement, velocity, and acceleration. Reproduced with permission from *Handbook of Acoustical Measurements and Noise Control,* C. M. Harris (ed.), 3d ed., McGraw-Hill, New York, 1991.[1]

Unbalances in rotating machines produce net centrifugal forces that change direction in space as the machine rotates. For a machine with a horizontal shaft, such a force acts upward at one instant and downward a half-rotation later, thus producing a force that acts on the floor vertically at a frequency that corresponds to the *shaft rotation frequency* f_r (hertz) = $N/60$, where N denotes the shaft rotation speed in revolutions per minute. As such a machine comes up to speed, it produces transient vibrations that increase in frequency and amplitude until steady operating conditions are reached; when such a machine is turned off and coasts toward a stop, it produces decaying transient vibrations with ever-decreasing amplitude and frequency.

Reciprocating machines also produce unbalanced inertia forces which are transmitted to the machine housing and supports. The primary components of these forces occur at the crankshaft's rotational frequency and at the first few integer multiples of that frequency. These forces generate vibrations along the direction of piston travel, as well as perpendicular to that direction, in the plane of the crank, and also produce vibratory moments or couples; the relative magnitudes depend on the cylinder arrangement and the degree of dynamic balance.

Fans, blowers, and pumps tend to generate steady vibrations, due to both unbalances and repetitive fluid pulses. The latter occur primarily at the *blade passage frequency,* which is the frequency with which blades pass a fixed point. For a rotor with n blades, rotating at N r/min, the blade-passage frequency is given by f_b (hertz) $= nN/60$.

Turbulent flows of water or air in a duct, or flows from a blower or airjet impinging on a surface, typically produce irregular forces on the structural surfaces. Similarly, irregularly repeated impacts, e.g., due to footfalls produced by many people walking on a floor, tend to produce irregular vibrations.

Single impacts, such as are produced by a single operation of a punch press, generate force pulses that typically result in decaying transient vibrations. Repetitive impacts result in repetitive transients, but if these impacts are repeated so rapidly that the vibrations due to one impact do not decay much before the next impact occurs, then the vibrations tend to have more of a steady irregular character. For example, continuing impacts of materials against the bottoms and sides of a gravity chute tend to produce essentially nonperiodic (irregular) vibrations.

Rattling, slippage, and nonlinearities (deviations from proportionality between forces and displacements) associated with large excursions generally introduce higher-frequency components than those associated with the basic forces and motions.

EFFECTS OF VIBRATIONS: THE NEED FOR VIBRATION CONTROL

Excessive vibrations can have adverse effects on personnel, equipment, and structures. Vibrations can annoy people, can interfere with their ability to perform or concentrate on mental tasks, can make it difficult for them to carry out precise movements or to make accurate readings of instruments, and in extreme cases can lead to physical disabilities and injuries. Vibrating surfaces also act somewhat like loudspeaker membranes in that they radiate sound, which again may range from annoying to painful to injurious, depending on its intensity. Vibrations may also produce such secondary effects as rattling of windows or motion of lights, which also tend to be annoying or distracting.

Vibration of a machine may reduce the life of its components, particularly those that are most highly loaded. Oscillatory stresses induced in machine parts, supports, building structures, and also in connections (hold-down bolts, pipes, cables) tend to produce failures of these items due to structural fatigue. Machine tools subjected to excessive vibrations may produce poor finishes; some precision equipment (optical systems, microscopes, gauges, microassembly equipment) cannot be effectively used at all in the presence of significant vibrations.

The need for vibration control occurs wherever there exist adverse effects due to vibrations. The amount of reduction that is required depends on the existing vibration and on what level of vibration is acceptable; zero vibration is as much an impossibility as an immovable object or an irresistible force. For many items of sensitive equipment, the manufacturers indicate what vibrations should not be exceeded. (Some related general vibration criteria are given in references 2 and 3.) The vibration limits acceptable to people are available in handbooks.[4,5] In many other cases, unfortunately, no solid vibration criteria are available, so that one is forced to proceed by trial and error.

Control of vibration is a highly developed specialized branch of engineering, which has been the subject of numerous papers, many texts, and several handbooks. Many of these publications deal primarily with analysis or specialized problems and thus require study and interpretation before they can be put to practical use. References 6 and 7 are most directly applicable to plant engineering. Much related information may be found in Ref. 8.

DIAGNOSING A VIBRATION PROBLEM

It is usually convenient to consider any vibration problem in terms of: (1) the *source* of the undesirable vibrations, (2) the *receiver,* i.e., whatever is adversely affected by vibrations and requires protection, and (3) the *path* along which vibrations from the source reach the receiver. In practical situations, many sources often contribute to the vibrations experienced by a single receiver, and vibrations from a given source often reach a single receiver via several paths.

The most convincing approach for identifying the vibration source responsible for a given problem consists of turning off all possible sources, then turning them on one at a time while observing the resulting effects at the receiver of interest. Similarly, one can best identify the predominant paths by interrupting one at a time or by disabling all and then reestablishing one at a time. These procedures can only rarely be carried out in practice to their full extent, but they can often be carried out sufficiently to provide valuable partial, if not full, insight into the problem.

It is often useful to supplement the on-off procedures discussed in the foregoing paragraph by comparison of the vibration spectra measured on or near various sources with the spectrum measured at the receiver. If the receiver, for example, experiences adverse vibrations only at 50 and 80 Hz, then a source that generates vibrations at only 30 Hz cannot be responsible for these receiver vibrations; one would look for sources that produce vibrations near 50 and 80 Hz. Similarly, measurements made along the important contributing paths would reveal 50- and 80-Hz components, whereas these components would be present to a lesser extent along the less significant paths.

There are also available *correlation methods* for source and path identification. These methods, however, require specialized equipment and expertise.[8]

In dealing with any vibration problem, one must keep in mind the phenomenon called *resonance.* Any mechanical system or structure has a number of frequencies at which it can be set into vibration very easily; these are called *natural frequencies.* The lowest of these, called the *fundamental natural frequency,* is often most easily excited and of greatest importance. Resonance occurs if a system is subjected to a vibratory force or motion at one of its natural frequencies; large vibrations can then result *even with small inputs.* The natural frequencies of a system can be determined readily; if a system is deflected and released, or if it is struck, it will vibrate at one or more of its natural frequencies. For observation of the natural frequencies, however, it is usually necessary to have all relevant vibration sources turned off, so that the natural frequencies will not be masked by the excitation frequencies.

A *stroboscope* is often useful for diagnostic purposes. This consists of a light that is made to flash at precisely timed intervals. The light is aimed at a vibrating part and the flashing frequency is adjusted manually until the vibrating part appears to stand still; the frequency of the vibration can then be read from the instrument. Then, by changing the flashing frequency slightly, one can observe the vibration in apparent slow motion to see where the largest excursions occur.

VIBRATION CONTROL STRATEGY

It is generally best to control a vibration at its source, because this approach avoids problems at all potential receivers. However, in cases where only a limited number of receivers are of concern and where control at the source(s) is not feasible, control at the receiver(s) may be preferable. Reduction or elimination of vibrations at the source typically involves improving the dynamic balance of rotating or reciprocating equipment, substituting items with lesser vibrations for those with more (e.g., centrifugal pumps for reciprocating pumps), or changing operating speeds to eliminate resonance conditions. Reduction of the adverse effects of vibrations at the receiver generally involves substitution of less-vibration-sensitive items or processes, or adding stiffening or mass judiciously in order to eliminate resonances, if any are present.

Vibration *isolation* most often turns out to be the most cost-effective means for vibration control. Isolation involves insertion of soft flexible elements in the propagation path so as to reduce the transmitted forces and motions. Because of the multitude of paths that can begin at any source or terminate at any receiver, isolation is best accomplished near a source or receiver.

Some other vibration control methods that are useful only under certain specific circumstances are described at the end of this chapter.

Vibration Isolation at the Source

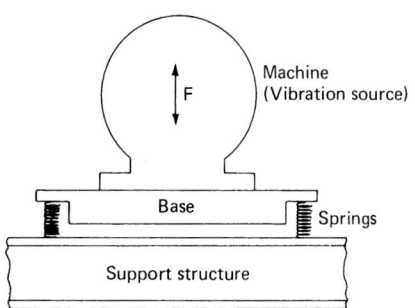

FIGURE 2-3 Conceptual sketch of isolation of vibration source.

Basic Principles. The basic concepts of vibration isolation can be understood with the aid of the schematic sketch of Fig. 2-3, which shows a machine that generates a vertical oscillatory force of amplitude F (e.g., due to an imbalance) rigidly attached to a base. This base, which may represent a machine housing or frame, a foundation, or inertia base, is mounted atop a supporting structure via a series of springs or other resilient elements generally called *isolators.*

The oscillatory force produces motion by accelerating the combined mass m of the machine and the base. This motion of the base produces oscillatory compression (and extension) of the springs (superposed on the static compression due to the weight they support), which in turn gives rise to oscillatory forces on the support.

If the force varies slowly, i.e., at low frequencies, then the inertia of the mass offers little opposition to the motion, and the force essentially acts directly to compress the springs. The machine-base mass here moves just enough for the total spring force to match the externally applied force, as it would if the force were applied statically, and thus the entire applied force is transmitted to the support structure. On the other hand, if the force F varies rapidly, i.e., at high frequencies, then the inertia of the mass opposes the motion to such an extent that the inertia's effect is much greater than that of the springs. The springs then compress and extend very little, and only the spring forces resulting from these small spring deflections are transmitted to the support structure.

The ratio of the amplitude F_s of the total force that the springs exert on the support (assumed rigid) to the amplitude F of the exciting force is called the *transmissibility T.* The transmissibility also is equal to the factor by which the force that acts on the support is reduced if the machine is supported on the given isolators instead of being fastened rigidly to the support structure. Very often this factor is at least approximately equal to the factor by which the vibratory motion of the support structure is reduced when the isolators are used in place of rigid connections. The *isolation efficiency E,* which is defined by $E = 1 - T$ indicates what fraction of the exciting force is prevented from acting on the support and approximately by what factor the motion of the support is reduced due to use of the springs or springlike elements. For example, if a given isolation system results in a transmissibility of 0.05, then its isolation efficiency is 0.95, indicating that the use of the isolators reduces the vibratory force on the support structure by 95 percent.

To produce a significant vibration reduction, the isolators must be soft enough to result in a transmissibility T of 0.1 or less. For soft isolators the total stiffness k (i.e., the sum of the stiffnesses of all isolators) is related to the total mass m of the machine and base by

$$k \approx mf^2 \, T/C_1 \tag{2}$$

where f represents the disturbing frequency in hertz and $C_1 = 10$ for k in units of lb/in and m in lb ($C_1 = 25$ for k in units of N/mm and m in kg). For springs that have a straight-line force/deflection curve (of which the slope corresponds to the stiffness k), the spring stiffness is directed related to the *static deflection s* that the springs experience as they support the mass m statically, so that

$$s = C_2 \frac{m}{k} = \frac{C_3}{f^2 T} \tag{3}$$

For s in in, m in lb, and k in lb/in: $C_2 = 1$ and $C_3 \approx 10$; for s in mm, m in kg, and k in N/mm: $C_2 = 9.8$ and $C_3 \approx 250$. For a given frequency f, spring stiffness k, and supported mass m, the transmissibility T and isolation efficiency E may be calculated from

$$T = 1 - E = C_1 k/mf^2 = C_3/sf^2 \tag{4}$$

Here the amplitude of the vibration of the machine and base is inversely proportional to the total mass m.

Practical Considerations. As evident from the foregoing expression, the lowest disturbing frequency f corresponds to the greatest vibration transmission. Therefore, an isolation system must be designed for the lowest disturbing frequency of concern.

In general, the vibration transmission can be reduced in two ways: (1) by using softer resilient elements (reducing the total stiffness k and thus increasing the static deflections) or (2) by increasing the supported mass m. It should be noted that the use of softer springs (beyond those needed to achieve a transmissibility of 0.1) leads to greater static deflection and reduced vibration transmission, but has little effect on the vibratory motion of the machine and base. If the supported mass is increased (e.g., by the addition of a heavy "inertia" base) and the total spring stiffness is not changed, then there results greater static deflection, reduced vibration transmission, and a reduction in the vibratory motion of the machine. In practice, where springs or other isolators often are selected to carry as much load as they can support safely, the addition of mass requires that more and/or stiffer isolators be used, so that the total spring stiffness is increased approximately by the same factor as the mass; in this case the static deflection and vibration transmission essentially remain unchanged, but the vibratory motion of the mass is reduced.

It is important to note that useful isolation can be achieved only if the resilient elements (springs) are *considerably softer* than the supporting structure, i.e., only if the resilient elements deflect considerably more under a given load than does the support structure. Otherwise, the support structure provides the predominant resilience and the springs merely serve to transmit the forces to the support essentially without attenuating them.

Figure 2-4 is a convenient chart for estimating the major isolation system parameters needed in order to achieve a desired vibration reduction or transmissibility. The dashed line in the figure illustrates the case where there exists a disturbing frequency of 3000 cpm (corresponding to 50 Hz), at which it is desired to reduce the vibration by 99.9 percent, i.e., to 0.01

times its original value. The chart shows that here a value for k/m of about 2.5 (lb/in)/lb is needed; thus, for a 2000-lb mass, a total stiffness of $2.5 \times 2000 = 5000$ lb/in is required. (Of course, a lesser stiffness would provide better isolation than that prescribed, whereas a greater stiffness would result in poorer isolation.) One may also read from the chart that to $k/m = 2.5$ (lb/in)/lb there corresponds a static deflection of about 0.4 in and a resonance frequency of about 300 cpm or 5 Hz.

Selection of an isolation system must account for the fact that an excitation frequency f that is produced by a machine usually varies with the machine's rotational speed. As a machine is brought up to speed or slowed to a stop, a speed at which the exciting frequency matches the natural frequency of the machine on its resilient supports may be encountered. This speed may be estimated from

$$N \text{ (cpm)} = C_4/\sqrt{s} = C_5/\sqrt{k/m} \tag{5}$$

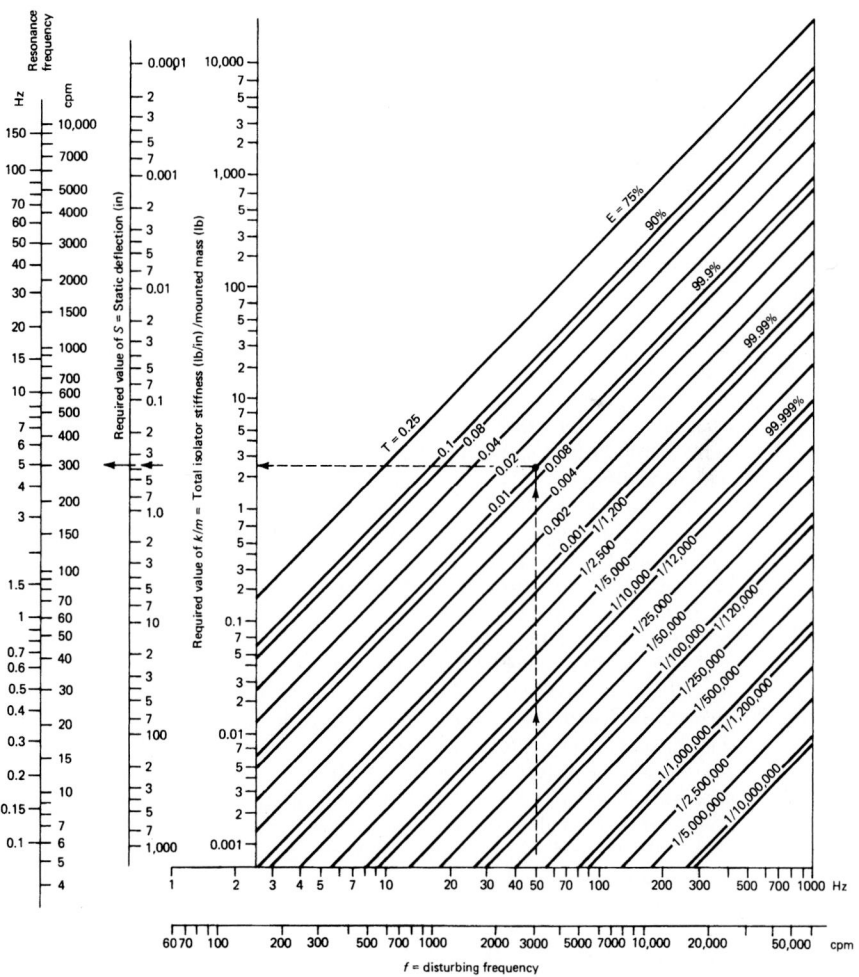

FIGURE 2-4   Chart for estimation of isolation-system requirements. (1 in = 25.4 mm; 1 [lb/in]/lb = 0.386 [N/mm]/kg.)

where $C_4 = C_5 = 188$ for s in in, k in lb/in, and m in lb ($C_4 = 945$ and $C_5 = 302$ for s in mm, k in N/mm, and m in kg). At this speed, intense vibrations may occur. Their magnitude depends on how fast the machine passes through this resonance speed and on the damping characteristics of the isolation system. If the machine accelerates or decelerates rapidly, vibrations do not have time to buildup. For machines that accelerate or decelerate slowly, the magnitude of the vibration produced at resonance is inversely proportional to the damping in the system.

Damping refers to a spring's or a structure's capability for dissipating oscillatory energy; a bell or a steel spring rings (i.e., vibrates) for a long time after it is struck; that is, it takes a relatively long time to dissipate the vibratory energy imparted to it. On the other hand, a rubber or cork rod vibrates only briefly after an impact; it dissipates vibratory energy rapidly and thus is highly damped. For machines that accelerate or coast down slowly, isolation elements of highly damped materials (e.g., rubber or cork) should be used, or energy-dissipation devices (e.g., friction pads or dashpots) should be added in parallel with the resilient members. In some cases, the incorporation of snubbers in the isolation systems may suffice to limit the excursions of the base as the machine passes through resonance. Such snubbers may, for example, be in the form of rubber cones that are mounted so that the base bumps against them when its excursion exceeds a given amount. Snubbers are incorporated in many commercial isolator assemblies.

If slow acceleration or coast-down is no problem, then the type of isolator material and the isolator configuration essentially make no difference; the only parameter that counts is the total stiffness k under the expected load conditions and operating frequencies. For many resilient elements, particularly metal springs, the stiffness is practically independent of frequency and also of load within the design load range. Whenever vibrations in more than one direction (e.g., in the horizontal, as well as the vertical direction) are of concern, however, the proper resilience for isolation in all directions must be provided. In this case, appropriately selected and aligned springs, specially configured rubber pads, or suitably chosen commercial isolators should be employed.

Because of the beneficial effect of increased mass of the machine base, it usually is desirable to mount several machines on the same base. In this way, the vibration transmitted from each machine is attenuated by the mass of the base and also by the masses of the other machines. If such a common base is to be effective, it must not have any resonances of its own at or near the operating speeds of all machines mounted on it; ideally, its fundamental resonance should occur above all operating frequencies. This implies that such bases should be as stiff as possible.

Attention must also be given to avoidance of excessive rocking vibrations of isolated bases. For this purpose it is usually useful to employ wide bases, so that the springs act with large moment arms. It is also beneficial, particularly for bases supporting several items, to have the springs distributed so that they "pick up" the loads locally, e.g., so as to have stiffer or more closely spaced springs near the heavier items and less stiff or more widely spaced springs near the lighter items.

In practice one usually needs to make provisions to avoid the transmission of vibrations via paths that bypass the isolated base. For this purpose it usually is desirable to provide flexible sections of piping, electrical conduit, cable, and ducts between the isolated machines and the unisolated surroundings. (Appropriate devices especially designed for vibration isolation are commercially available; devices such as loops and bellows that are primarily designed to accomodate thermal expansion rarely are adequate for vibration isolation.) Similarly, hold-down bolts through isolators, and similar arrangements that in effect serve as vibration "short-circuit" paths around the isolators, must be removed or themselves isolated, e.g., with soft rubber sleeves and washers.

Isolation of Vibration-Sensitive Items

Basic Principles.   The fundamental concepts pertaining to isolation of items to be protected from vibrations may be visualized with the aid of the schematic sketch of Fig. 2-5. This shows

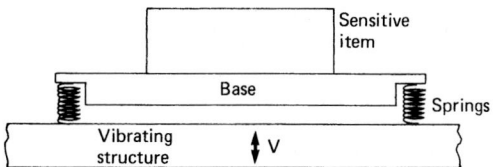

FIGURE 2-5   Conceptual sketch of isolation of a sensitive item.

a vibration-sensitive item attached to a base, which is fastened to a vibrating structure (e.g., a floor of a building housing vibration sources) via resilient elements, represented in the sketch by springs. In reality, the base may consist of a machine frame or foundation, an inertia block, or a floated (isolated) slab or floor.

If the sensitive item is attached to the vibrating structure directly, without springs, then it vibrates with the same amplitude as the vibrating structure. The same is true if the attachment springs are stiff. However, if the springs are soft, then the oscillatory deflection of the vibrating structure leads to only relatively small forces acting on the base; the inertia of the mass of the base resists acceleration and thus keeps the resulting motion small. This inertia effect is more pronounced for larger accelerations, i.e., higher frequencies, and therefore better isolation is obtained at higher disturbance frequencies, all other things being equal.

The ratio of the amplitude of the motion V_I (displacement, velocity, or acceleration) of the sensitive item to that of the vibrating structure, V (measured in terms of the same quantity as is V_I), is called the *motion transmissibility* T_v, or just *transmissibility*.* This transmissibility also is equal to the factor by which the amplitude of the vibratory motion of the sensitive item is reduced if it is supported on the given isolators instead of being fastened rigidly to the vibrating structure.[†]

The *isolation efficiency*[‡] E_v is defined by $E_v = 1 - T_v$ and thus indicates what fraction of the motion of the vibrating structure is kept from the sensitive item. For example, if $T_v = 0.01$, then the isolation efficiency is 99 percent; the sensitive item vibrates only 1 percent as much as it would if it were rigidly attached to the vibrating structure.

Equations (2) to (5) and the discussions accompanying them also apply if T and E are replaced by T_v and E_v and if m is taken to represent the mass of the isolated item and its base.

Practical Considerations.   Because the lowest disturbing frequency f corresponds to the greatest transmissibility T_v, an isolation system must be designed with respect to the lowest disturbing frequency of interest.

Figure 2-4 is a convenient chart for estimating the major isolation system parameters needed in order to achieve a desired vibration reduction or transmissibility. The dashed line in the figure illustrates the approach for a case where there exists a disturbing frequency of 3000 cpm (corresponding to 50 Hz) at which frequency it is desired to reduce the vibration by 99.9 percent, i.e., to 0.01 of its original value. The chart shows that here a value of k/m of about 2.5 (lb/in)/lb is needed; thus, for a 2000-lb mass, a total stiffness of $2.5 \times 2000 = 5000$ lb/in is required. (Of course, a lesser stiffness would provide better isolation than that prescribed, whereas a greater stiffness would result in poorer isolation.) One may also read from the chart that to $k/m = 2.5$ (lb/in)/lb there corresponds a static deflection of about 0.4 in and a resonance frequency of about 300 cpm or 5 Hz. Improvement in the isolation (reduction in the

---

* It is somewhat unfortunate that the same word, "transmissibility," is used to refer to the force transmissibility T associated with source isolation as is used to refer to the motion transmissibility T_v associated with receiver (sensitive-item) isolation. However, because T and T_v obey the same relation, this usage tends to cause little confusion.

[†] This equality holds only if the motion of the vibrating structure is unaffected by the magnitude of the reaction forces that act on that structure.

[‡] Again, "isolation efficiency" is common usage, although *motion isolation efficiency* is more appropriate.

transmissibility) can be obtained by (1) using softer springs and/or (2) increasing the mass of the base. Reducing the spring stiffness by a given factor has the same effect on reducing the motion of the isolated item as increasing the combined mass of the item and its base by the same factor. Use of softer springs is usually less difficult and less costly than obtaining significantly increased base mass; thus, use of softer springs is generally preferable. However, softer springs are subject to greater static deflection and also tend to permit the isolated item to vibrate or to rock more due to motions of its own parts (e.g., of pistons, slides, spindles). In order to minimize this rocking and secondary vibration, it is often useful to balance the isolated items and to distribute the springs so as to oppose the dynamic loads directly (by placing more or stiffer springs where the greater loads act and having the spring force axes aligned with the direction of the loads).

In practice, isolators often are loaded to their full capacity. In such a case, an increase in the mass supported by the isolators requires that more and/or higher capacity (and therefore stiffer) isolators be used, which results in the static deflection and transmissibility remaining essentially unchanged. A mass increase then has practically no effect on the transmitted vibrations, but it does reduce the vibration of the isolated item due to the aforementioned motions of its own parts.

In all cases, in order to be able to provide useful isolation, the resilient elements (springs) must be more flexible than the vibrating structure to which they are attached and the base supporting the sensitive item. That is, for a given force applied at the center of gravity of the isolated item, the resilient elements must deflect more than either one of the structures to which they are attached. The base of the sensitive item, in addition to being as heavy as possible, should be as stiff as possible.

It often is advantageous to have several sensitive items mounted on the same base; then the total mass of all items and the base act together to assist in the isolation of each item. In this case it is important that the base be as rigid as possible, so that all masses are well interconnected dynamically. In selecting items to be mounted on a common base, it must be kept in mind that items rigidly fastened to the same base can transmit vibrations and rocking motions to each other; thus it is generally inadvisable to mount extremely sensitive items together with items that may cause dynamic disturbances.

Any connections between the isolated item or its base and the vibrating structure must be less stiff than the resilient (spring) elements if these connections are not to transmit more vibration than the springs. Thus, care must be taken to use flexible bellows, tubing, hoses, conduits, cables, etc., with coils and loops where appropriate, to reduce the vibration transmission via these connections.

Some Specialized Control Techniques

Two-Stage Isolation.[7]   In the cases illustrated by Figs. 2-3 and 2-5, a rigid connection is implied between the base and the equipment it supports. If resilient connections (e.g., rubber pads or springs) are used instead, then there are two stages of isolation: one below the base and one above it. Two-stage isolation systems can provide increased isolation at high frequencies, but they introduce additional system resonances at which there may occur large motions and dynamic forces. The greater the included mass (e.g., that of the doubly isolated base), the greater is the vibration reduction at high frequencies and the lower is the frequency at which the benefit of the included mass comes into play. Careful isolation-system design is important to avoid these potential adverse effects.

Detuning and Structural Damping.   The large vibrations that occur if any system or structure vibrates at a resonance may best be reduced by *detuning*—changing the excitation or the system so as to avoid operation at resonance. If such changes cannot be made—either for operating reasons or because a system is subject to multifrequency excitation or because it may have a multitude of resonances at closely spaced frequencies—then increasing the damping constitutes essentially the only means for obtaining useful vibration reductions.

For thin metal panels, increased damping can usually be obtained most conveniently by means of layers of viscoelastic (tacky, rubbery) damping material that may be sprayed, troweled, or glued onto the metal panels. A variety of such materials is commercially available, and suppliers of these materials have experience and data pertaining to desirable material thicknesses.

For thick plates of metal or concrete, or for beams, it is often useful to employ a viscoelastic damping material as the middle layer of a sandwich configuration, with the outer layers consisting of the structural material. Careful design of such damped sandwich configurations, based on well-known but somewhat intricate specialized procedures, is required if these are to work properly.

In cases where large structures vibrate severely, it is sometimes useful to fasten boxes filled with sand or some other granular material at the locations where the greatest motions occur. Agitation of grains—and their "rattling" against each other and against the sides of the box—extracts energy from the vibration, thus reducing it.

Vibration Absorbers.[8] Vibration absorbers, often also called *dynamic absorbers* or *dampers,* are useful primarily where a fixed-frequency vibration is of concern. Such an absorber consists of a mass that is attached to a vibrating system via a spring, with the mass and spring values chosen so that the resonance frequency of this absorber system coincides with the frequency of concern. When this mass-spring system is attached to the base or housing of the vibrating machine or to the vibrating structure, it acts to reduce the vibratory motion of the item to which it is attached. The motion of the added mass is opposite to that of the structure to which it is attached; thus, the mass makes the spring push down on the vibrating structure when the latter moves upward, and vice versa.

For a vibrating component or structure with an attached absorber, the product of the absorber mass and its excursion amplitude is equal to the product of the mass of the component and its excursion. Thus, absorbers with small masses need to operate at large excursions; trading off between absorber masses and excursions is part of the design process.

REFERENCES

1. Harris, C. M. (ed.): *Handbook of Acoustical Measurements and Noise Control,* 3d ed. McGraw-Hill, New York, 1991.

2. Ungar, E. E., D. H. Sturz, and H. A. Amick: "Vibration Control Design of High Technology Facilities." Sound and Vibration *24,* 20–27, July, 1990.

3. House, M. H., and R. Randell: "Some measurements of acceptable levels of vibration in scientific, medical, and ophthalmic microscopes," *Vibration Control in Optics and Metrology,* Society of Photo-Optical Instrumentation Engineers, Vol. 732, pp. 74–80, 1987.

4. von Gierke, H. E., and W. D. Ward: "Criteria for Noise and Vibration Exposure." Chap. 26 of Ref. 1.

5. Griffin, M. J.: *Handbook of Human Vibration,* Academic Press, London, 1990.

6. Ungar, E. E., and D. H. Sturz: "Vibration Control Techniques," Chap. 28 of Ref. 1.

7. Beranek, L. L., and I. L. Ver: *Noise and Vibration Control Engineering,* John Wiley & Sons, New York, 1992.

8. Harris, C. M., and C. E. Crede (eds.): *Shock and Vibration Handbook,* 3d ed. McGraw-Hill, New York, 1988.

SECTION 13

POLLUTION CONTROL AND WASTE DISPOSAL

CHAPTER 13-1
AIR POLLUTION CONTROL

Richard B. Ruch, Jr.
Vice President
Roy F. Weston, Inc.
West Chester, Pennsylvania

REGULATORY REQUIREMENTS

Although considerable federal and state legislation concerning air quality was developed during the 1960s, the primary statutory framework now in place was established by the Clean Air Act (CAA) of 1970. This legislation was amended in 1974 to incorporate a program to ensure attainment of the ambient air quality standards for certain pollutants and emission or performance standards for certain industrial sources. In 1977 Congress enacted additional revisions, including the Prevention of Significant Deterioration (PSD) and nonattainment requirements applicable to new or modified sources locating in pollutant attainment or nonattainment areas, respectively.

Reauthorization of the CAA was due in 1983; however, it was November 1990, after many years of intensive and acrimonious debate by Congress, before the statue was amended again. The CAA amendments of 1990 are extensive and will double the annual costs to industry in order to achieve compliance over the next 10 years or more. The major components of the preamendment clean air program are set forth below:

Pre-1990 Regulations and Standards

National Ambient Air Quality Standards. The National Ambient Air Quality Standards (NAAQS) define the quality of air which must be achieved to prevent adverse effects. The primary air quality standards specify levels of pollution which cannot be exceeded without threatening adverse effects on human health. The secondary air quality standards set limits not to be exceeded without adverse effects on public welfare, including property, vegetation, and the like. For certain pollutants, both short- and long-term standards have been established. For each criteria pollutant there is a set of these standards, each with its own regulatory program to limit atmospheric concentration levels at or below the levels set by its standards. The secondary standards are identical to these primary standards, except for sulfur dioxide (for which there is a 3-h, short-term secondary standard of 1300 µg/m³). Refer to Table 1-1. Whenever air pollution exceeds the standard (i.e., nonattainment areas), the thrust of the program is to mandate efforts to reduce air emissions to improve air quality.

State Implementation Plan.   The State Implementation Plan (SIP) provides a scheme under which the National Air Quality Standards are expected to be achieved and maintained. These plans, which must be approved by federal EPA, provide comprehensive programs by each state to reduce pollution through a variety of specific abatement measures, some of which are delineated in facility-specific compliance programs. Once approved by EPA, these state-specific or facility-specific requirements become federally enforceable limitations. When deficiencies in the SIPs are apparent, modifications can be made, using specific legal procedures set forth by EPA, but the process of issuing or modifying a SIP can be complicated and time consuming.

Air Quality Control Regions.   The Air Quality Control Region (AQCR) is a basic delineation of each state into appropriate geographical airsheds. Within AQCR, a state must define the attainment status for each pollutant. There are 247 AQCRs in the United States in which air quality is defined by ambient-air monitoring data, estimates made from mathematical dispersion analyses, or both. Each AQCR has its own program and schedule specified in the SIPs (some AQCRs are interstate), which have been developed to achieve and/or maintain acceptable air quality.

New Source Performance Standards.   The New Source Performance Standards (NSPS) are an indirect way of limiting emissions from certain new or modified sources and improving air quality. These standards now cover more than 60 basic industrial and process categories. A new plant is subject to the NSPS only if these standards are proposed by the EPA for a certain service category before the plant is under construction. Thus, before proceeding with a new plant, a company should determine which categories are covered by the NSPS. Industries affected by the NSPS are shown in Table 1-2. Industrial categories scheduled for NSPS development are listed in Table 1-3.

TABLE 1-1   National Primary and Secondary Ambient Air Quality Standards

Pollutant	Type of standard	Averaging time	Compliance frequency parameter	Concentration µg/m³	ppm
Sulfur oxides (as sulfur dioxide)	Primary and secondary	24 h	Annual maximum*	365	0.14
		1 yr	Arithmetic mean	80	0.03
		3 h	Annual maximum*	1,300	0.5
Particulate matter of 10 µm or less (PM$_{10}$)	Primary and secondary	24 h	Annual maximum	150	—
		24 h	Annual arithmetic mean	50	—
Carbon monoxide	Primary and secondary	1 h	Annual maximum*	40,000	35
		8 h	Annual maximum*	10,000	9
Ozone	Primary and secondary	1 h	Annual maximum*	235	0.12
Nitrogen dioxide	Primary and secondary	1 yr	Arithmetic mean	100	0.05
Lead	Primary and secondary	3 mon	Arithmetic mean	1.5	—

* No more than one expected exceedance per year.

TABLE 1-2   Typical Categories for Federal New Source Performance Standards*

Subpart	Category 40 CFR 60	Proposed	Promulgated	Revised
D	Fossil-Fuel-Fired Steam Generators—8/71–9/78	8/17/71	12/23/71	2/14/89
Da	Electric Utility Steam Generating Units—9/78	9/19/78	6/11/79	2/14/89
Db	Industrial Boilers (greater than 100 MMBtu)	6/19/84	11/25/86	12/16/87
E	Incinerators	8/17/71	12/23/71	2/14/89
Ea	Municipal Waste Combustors	8/12/91	—	—
F	Portland Cement Plants	8/17/71	12/23/71	2/14/89
G	Nitric Acid Plants	8/17/71	12/23/71	2/14/89
J	Petroleum Refineries	6/11/73	3/8/74	8/17/89
K	Storage Vessels for Petroleum Liquids—6/11/73–5/19/78	6/11/73	3/8/74	4/8/87
L	Secondary Lead Smelters	6/11/73	3/8/74	2/14/89
Na	Secondary Emissions from BOP Steel Facilities	1/20/83	1/02/86	2/14/89
O	Sewage Treatment Plants	6/11/73	3/8/74	2/14/89
P	Primary Copper Smelters	10/16/74	1/15/76	2/14/89
V	Phosphate Fert. Indus.: Diammonium Phosphate Plants	10/22/74	8/5/75	2/14/89
Z	Ferroalloy Production Facilities	10/21/74	5/4/76	2/14/90
AAa	Steel Plants: Electric Arc Furnaces—8/7/83	8/7/83	10/31/84	5/17/89
BB	Kraft Pulp Mills	9/24/76	2/23/78	2/14/90
DD	Grain Elevators	1/13/77	8/3/78	2/14/89
GG	Stationary Gas Turbines	10/3/77	9/10/79	6/27/89
HH	Lime Manufacturing PLants	5/3/77	4/26/84	2/14/89
KK	Lead-Acid Battery Manufacturing Plants	1/14/80	4/16/82	2/14/89
LL	Metallic Mineral Processing Plants	8/24/82	2/21/84	2/14/89
MM	Light-Duty Truck Surface Coating Operations	10/5/79	12/24/80	12/13/90
NN	Phosphate Rock Plants	9/21/79	4/16/82	5/17/89
PP	Ammonium Sulfate Manufacture	2/4/80	11/12/80	2/14/89
RR	Pressure Sensitive Tape/Label Surface Coating Operations	12/30/80	10/18/83	12/13/90
VV	Equipment Leaks of VOC/Synthetic Organic Chemicals Manufacture	1/5/81	10/18/83	12/13/90
XX	Bulk Gasoline Terminals	12/17/80	8/18/83	2/14/89
DDD	VOC Emissions from the Polymer Mfg. Industry	9/30/87	—	—
FFF	Coating of Flex Vinyl and Urethane	1/18/83	6/29/84	8/17/84
GGG	Equipment Leaks of VOCs in Petroleum Refineries	1/4/83	5/30/84	—
III	VOC Emissions from SOCMI Air Oxidation Unit Processes	10/21/83	6/29/90	—
LLL	Onshore Natural Gas Processing—SO₂	1/20/84	10/01/85	2/14/89
NNN	VOC Emissions from SOCMI Distillation Operations	12/30/83	6/29/90	—
PPP	Wool Fiberglass Insulation	2/7/84	2/25/85	2/14/89
QQQ	VOC Emissions from Petroleum Refinery Wastewater Systems	5/4/87	11/23/88	—
RRR	VOC Emissions from SOCMI Reactor Processes	6/29/90	—	—
TTT	Plastic Parts for Business Machines Coating	1/1/86	1/29/88	10/30/89

* For complete list, consult Environmental Protection Agency, Washington, D.C.

PSD/New Source Review.   A special feature of the clean air program, largely added by the 1977 amendments, applies to new or modified facilities that cause a significant increase in air emissions. The two primary features of this review process pertain to new or modified facilities located in areas where a significantly emitted pollutant is either in attainment or not in attainment of the applicable ambient air quality standard. For those areas in attainment of the standard, the proposed industrial project must avoid a significant deterioration of the air quality by complying with the Prevention of Significant Deterioration (PSD) requirements. In nonattainment areas, the project will be subject to New Source Review (NSR) nonattainment requirements designed to achieve a net improvement of the air quality. It is important to note that PSD and nonattainment requirements are applied separately to each regulated pollutant. Thus, a new plant to be located in an area classified as nonattainment for ozone and attainment for particulates and sulfur dioxide could be required to comply with both the PSD

TABLE 1-3   Industrial Categories for Which New Source Performance Standards Are to Be Developed

Stationary fuel combustion
   Stationary internal combustion engines

Metallurgical processes
   By-product coke ovens
   Foundries: gray iron
   Foundries: steel
   Secondary aluminum
   Secondary copper
   Secondary zinc
   Uranium refining

Mineral products
   Brick and related clay products
   Castable refractories
   Ceramic clay
   Fiberglass
   Gypsum
   Nonmetallic mineral processing
   Perlite
   Sintering: clay and fly ash

Polymers and resins
   ABS-SAN resins
   Acrylic resins
   Phenolic resins
   Polyester resins
   Polyethylene
   Polypropylene
   Polystyrene
   Urea-melamine resins

Food and agricultural
   Alfalfa dehydrating
   Ammonium nitrate fertilizer
   Animal feed defluorination
   Starch
   Urea (for fertilizer and polymers)
   Vegetable oil

Waste disposal
   Hazardous waste transfer, storage, and disposal
      facilities
   Medical waste incinerators

Basic chemical manufacture
   Synthetic organic chemical manufacturing
   Borax and boric acid
   Hydrofluoric acid
   Phosphoric acid: thermal process
   Potash
   Sodium carbonate

Chemical products manufacture
   Ammonia
   Carbon black
   Charcoal
   Detergent
   Explosives
   Fuel conversion
   Printing ink
   Synthetic fibers
   Synthetic rubber
   Varnish

Evaporative loss sources
   Industrial surface coating: autos
   Industrial surface coating: fabric
   Industrial surface coating: paper

Petroleum industry
   Crude oil and natural gas production
   Gasoline additives
   Petroleum refinery
   Transportation and marketing

Wood processing
   Chemical wood pulping: acid sulfite
   Chemical wood pulping: neutral sulfite (NSSC)
   Plywood manufacture

Consumer products
   Textile processing

increment and the nonattainment offset requirements. The principal requirements of each program are presented below.

Prevention of Significant Deterioration.   EPA's regulations for the Prevention of Significant Deterioration (PSD) of air quality in clean air areas represent one of the most complicated parts of the entire Clean Air Act. Their basic purpose is to prevent unlimited industrial growth from degrading air quality in those areas where the ambient air quality standards are being met and thus to assure preservation of cleaner air. The system designed to achieve that goal includes technology standards to assure that any new major facility or modification incorporates the Best Available Control Technology (BACT), an incremental system to prevent any single project from having undue impacts on air quality, and an intricate scheme of procedural and technical requirements to assure compliance with the technological and incremental limitations. In brief, the system works as follows:

- *BACT (Best Available Control Technology)*.   All new plants and modifications subject to PSD must install BACT. What constitutes BACT is determined on a case-by-case basis. Over the past few years, EPA has instituted a "top-down" system of BACT determination under which the applicant first identifies the state-of-the-art control technology which could possibly be used and then places the burden on the applicant to justify any variations from such controls by demonstrating that they cannot be used with respect to the actual proposed facility based upon technological, environmental, energy, or cost considerations. EPA has established a BACT clearinghouse for each source category; however, it is the responsibility of the applicant to define, support, and defend the selected BACT.

- *Increments of Air Quality.*   Even after satisfying the BACT controls, the applicant will not be permitted to proceed unless the remaining emissions can be accommodated within an available "increment" of air quality. The incremental limitations rest first upon an *area classification system* under which all areas in the country meeting air quality standards are classified as either Class I (to be kept in especially pristine condition) or Class II (where normal industrial growth is to be permitted). Whichever area is involved, emissions from the new facility or modification must not cause a projected degradation in pre-existing air quality beyond the amount of the allowable increment. The idea is that in areas which today are much cleaner than required to satisfy the ambient air quality standards, the air cannot be degraded so that it just barely satisfies the air quality standards. In fact, in Class I areas, virtually no degradation will be allowed. It should be noted that these increments have been established for sulfur dioxide, nitrogen dioxide, and particulates. Air quality modeling analysis must be conducted to demonstrate compliance with applicable PSD increments and NAAQS. Depending on the geographical and topographical features as well as the existing sources in the vicinity of the proposed facility, the modeling analysis can be extremely complicated and costly. A modeling protocol is typically required by regulatory authorities before any refined or detailed analysis is conducted.

- *Preconstruction Approval.*   Plants and modifications subject to PSD review cannot begin construction until a permit has been issued. To complete PSD review in areas where the air quality baseline has not been established, an applicant generally must present *extensive monitoring data to establish the baseline* against which the increment will be calculated. Both meteorological and air quality monitoring may be required for a period ranging from 4 to 12 months. These preconstruction requirements may delay any permit submission by a total of 7 to 18 months. A typical schedule of activities for a PSD-affected facility is shown in Figure 1-1.

  Plants subject to PSD review include plants within 28 specified industrial categories (See Table 1-2) if potential emissions of any regulated pollutant exceed 100 tons per year and plants in other industrial categories if potential emissions would exceed 250 tons. These plants are defined as "major sources" under the PSD program. Modifications to major sources that would result in a "significant net emissions increase" of any regulated pollutant also are subject to PSD review requirements (see Table 1-4). The significance levels vary for many of the regulated pollutants, but for sulfur dioxide, nitrogen oxides, and volatile organic compounds, an increase of 40 tons per year is deemed significant.

New Source Review.   In areas classified as nonattainment for any regulated pollutant, a different set of special rules restricts the construction of new sources. The basic thrust of these New Source Review (NSR) rules is to require that such new sources install state-of-the-art control technology and also provide supplemental reductions in emissions from neighboring sources to more than offset whatever new emissions would result from the new source even after best controls are utilized. The principal requirements are as follows:

- *LAER—Lowest Achievable Emission Rate.*   This requirement deliberately imposes a *technology-forcing standard of control.* The 1977 amendments specified that it must reflect (1) the most stringent emission limitation contained in any State Implementation Plan (unless the applicant can demonstrate that such limitations are not achievable) or (2) the most stringent emission limitation achieved in practice within the industrial category, whichever is more stringent. In no event can LAER be less stringent than any applicable

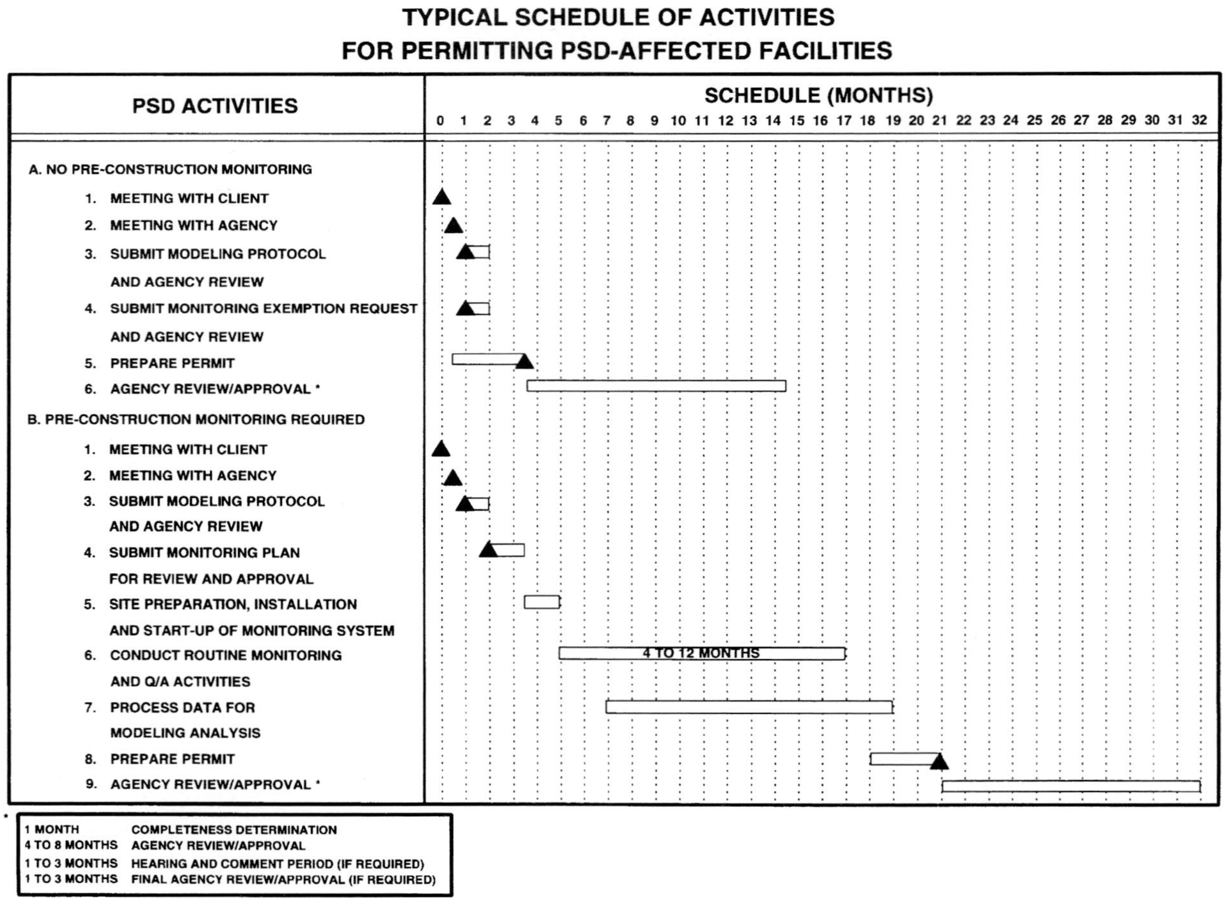

TYPICAL SCHEDULE OF ACTIVITIES
FOR PERMITTING PSD-AFFECTED FACILITIES

FIGURE 1-1 Typical schedule of activities for permitting PSD-affected facilities.

TABLE 1-4 Significant Net Emissions Increase

Pollutant	Increase, ton/yr
CO	100
NO_x (as NO_2)	40
SO_2	40
Particulate matter	25
Ozone	40 of volatile organic compounds
Lead	0.6
Asbestos	0.007
Beryllium	0.0004
Mercury	0.1
Vinyl chloride	1
Fluorides	3
Sulfuric acid mist	7
Hydrogen sulfide	10
Total reduced sulfur	10
Reduced sulfur compounds	10
Other CAA pollutants	> 0

new source performance standard. Often it is comparable to the BACT standard, but in many cases it can be more stringent. Specific applications of this standard must be determined on a case-by-case basis.

- *Emission Offsets.*   The key feature of offsets is that they must comprise legally enforceable reductions in emissions from other sources above and beyond those which would otherwise be required. These can be derived from installation of advanced controls producing extra reductions in emissions from existing sources or from the shutdown of such sources. Under the 1977 amendments, offsets can be traded on the market and, subject to certain limitations, can be "banked" for future use. Offsets must be measured against prior actual emissions and must be sufficient to cover potential emissions from the new source. They must also produce a "net air quality benefit" in the vicinity of the new source.

- *Other Requirements.*   All other plants in the state owned by the same company must be in compliance with applicable regulations, and the state's SIP must also be carried out.

- *Sources Covered.*   Any new plant with potential emissions of 100 tons per year or more of particulates, SO_2, NO_x, VOCs, or CO is subject to the requirements of the 1977 amendments. Modifications to these major sources are subject to review if they result in significant increases, as with the PSD program. Under the 1990 amendments, these levels are being lowered for the more seriously polluted ozone, CO, and PM-10 nonattainment areas.

The most significant impact of these nonattainment requirements has been the restrictive effect of limitations on the availability of offsets. In earlier years, offsets could be more readily found, but as the regulatory requirements have become more stringent, especially in the more serious nonattainment areas, it has become increasingly difficult to find potential reductions in current emissions beyond those already demanded by regulatory controls.

Because of the procedural delays and difficulties of complying with PSD or nonattainment regulations, companies have sought to avoid these requirements by designing projects that cause little or no net increase in emissions. Federally enforceable permit conditions have been developed and approved by the permitting authority as a means of avoiding these requirements. A set of internal "netting" rules governing the assessment of net emissions increases has also allowed certain projects to avoid the NSR process entirely.

Post-1990 Regulations and Standards

The CAA amendments of 1990 will have a major impact on virtually every industrial and many commercial operations throughout the country. These are significant onerous requirements which will affect the economic viability of some existing facilities and the design and scheduled operation of new or modified facilities. Fortunately, the requirements of some provisions of the Act will be implemented over a 10-year period. Unfortunately, the economic burden to industry over this period may represent an incremental cost increase on a national basis of 20 to 30 billion dollars per year.

The primary provisions of the Act are summarized below:

- *Nonattainment.* Title I of the Act established a new classification of nonattainment areas for each pollutant and includes deadlines and mandates degrees of emission reductions required to achieve attainment, based on the severity of present pollution levels.

- *Mobile Sources.* As part of the ozone and carbon monoxide nonattainment programs, Title II directs further tightening of emission standards applicable to motor vehicles. The Title II provision also establishes new requirements for petroleum companies to produce alternative fuels for motor vehicles and for the automotive industry to design and manufacture vehicles that are capable of using such alternative fuels, intended for sale to fleet operations in designated areas.

- *Air Toxics.* Title III establishes requirements to limit routine emissions of hazardous air pollutants and measures to prevent accidental releases of extremely hazardous substances.

- *Acid Rain.* Title IV provisions establish a new set of requirements, primarily on coal-fired power plants, designed to cut emissions of sulfur dioxide in half and to reduce emissions of nitrogen oxides. The amendments also provide market-driven mechanisms to facilitate achievement with the acid rain requirements.

- *Operating Permit Program.* Title V stipulates that each state develop and implement a comprehensive new operating permit program for all significant air emission sources. The program must require rigorous monitoring, reporting, and compliance certification, as well as annual permit fees.

- *Stratospheric Ozone.* Title VI establishes new requirements to restrict emissions of chloroflorocarbons as a major step toward addressing problems of stratospheric ozone depletion and global warming.

- *Enforcement.* Title VII greatly strengthens enforcement authorities, particularly by adding new criminal sanctions. Unlike the other provisions of the Act, the new enforcement requirements were effective the day the Act was signed into law.

The three areas of primary concern to industry are the nonattainment, air toxics, and permit provisions of the amended Act. The major requirements and planning considerations associated with each of these provisions are discussed in the remainder of this section. It is important to note that development and implementation of the regulations for some of these provisions has been delayed by the EPA and various states. As a result, it is incumbent upon each company to track the status and schedule of new regulations, including penalties for noncompliance, and appropriately comment on proposed rules as they are developed.

Nonattainment Requirements. Currently, there are roughly 100 areas of nonattainment for ozone, over 40 for carbon monoxide, and 70 for particulate matter. Also, there are a number of areas not in compliance with sulfur dioxide standards. Thus, existing or proposed new or modified industrial facilities located in or near these areas will be subject to a variety of new requirements designed to limit existing and future emissions of these nonattainment pollutants. For certain existing sources, Reasonably Available Control Technology (RACT) requirements will be imposed. The construction of a new or modified source may require the installation of Lowest Achievable Emission Rate (LAER) technology and emission offsets.

RACT. The CAA amendments of 1990 have expanded the type and number of existing sources that will be subject to the RACT requirements. Previously, the requirement was generally applicable to major emission sources (i.e., with a potential to emit of 100 tons per year) of volatile organic compounds (VOCs) located in ozone nonattainment areas. Up to this point, the ozone nonattainment problem was addressed almost exclusively through the control of VOCs. The amended Act extends applications of this basic RACT requirement to oxides of nitrogen (NO_x), with RACT now being applied to smaller sources in more seriously polluted areas. NO_x in the presence of VOCs and sunlight can contribute to the formation of ground-level ozone. Existing major sources subject to the new RACT requirement are shown in Table 1-5. It is important to note that any existing source located in an 11-state area extending from the Washington metropolitan area to Maine, with the potential to emit 50 TPY of VOCs and 100 TPY of NO_x, will also be defined as a major source and subject to RACT requirements. This area has been established by the CAA amendments and is known as the Northeast Ozone Transport Region.

TABLE 1-5 Existing Source RACT Applicability Requirements for Each Ozone Nonattainment Area Category

Category of nonattainment area	Size of VOC or NO_x sources affected
Extreme	10
Severe	25
Serious	50
Moderate and marginal	100

Ozone attainment stated and classification must be identified. Size is defined as the potential to emit of VOC or NO_x in tons per year.

A determination of the practices or procedures required to satisfy RACT regulations can or should be made on a case-by-case review of the circumstances at each individual facility. However, EPA has adopted the mechanism of issuing Control Technology Guidelines (CTGs) to provide a generic definition of RACT for specified industrial categories. Although this procedure has provoked criticism of EPA, it has in effect required states to apply the CTG requirements as though they have regulatory effect. EPA has issued 29 CTGs to date, with another dozen underway. CTGs have been developed and issued only for VOC source categories. Since RACT must be defined, approved, and installed for applicable sources by May 31, 1995, EPA guidance may not be available for NO_x emission sources. As a result, categorical limits and/or presumptive requirements may be established by various states for NO_x-related combustion sources.

For sources potentially subject to these regulations, it will be important to quantify VOC and/or NO_x emissions over a range of operating conditions. It may be possible to accept permit conditions to limit emissions if the source is not defined as a major source and thus not subject to the RACT requirements. In any event, it will be important to review the specific regulations and discuss the requirements with regulatory authorities prior to preparing any RACT determination. It is most likely that RACT determinations will vary from state to state, especially for NO_x emission sources.

LAER. One of the most significant impacts of the nonattainment requirements affecting American industry will be the construction of new or modification of existing facilities. When any increase in emissions of a major source above the minimum amounts would result from an expansion or modernization project or certain other changes, the project will be subject to New Source Review requirements. These requirements under the amended Act have expanded and complicated the permitting process. The principal requirements are: (1) a construction permit must be obtained, (2) technology standards reflecting LAER must be satisfied, and (3) offsets representing emission reductions from other sources must be provided.

The definition of *source applicability* or what constitutes a *major source* is the primary concern. The amended Act reduces the present definition (100 tons per year) to lower levels in certain ozone, CO, and PM-10 nonattainment areas. This will expand the reach of New Source Review to cover smaller sources. In addition, new or modified NO_x emission sources in ozone nonattainment areas will be subject to the same threshold levels and new source review requirements as VOCs emission sources. The amendments make no change in the LAER technology requirements. However, the amendments do tighten the offset requirements by increasing the ratio offsets needed in areas with higher ozone levels. The revised major source definition and offset ratios are presented in Table 1-6.

TABLE 1-6   Major Source Definitions and Offset Ratios in Ozone
Nonattainment Areas

Category	Size of major source	Ratios offset
Marginal	100 TPY	1.1:1
Moderate	100 TPY*	1.15:1
Serious	50 TPY*	1.2:1
Severe	25 TPY*	1.3:1
Extreme	10 TPY	1.5:1

TPY = tons per year.
* States have the option of choosing a major source definition of 5 TPY (and accepting other conditions) in order to avoid complying with requirement that emissions be reduced 15% over the first six years. See §182(b)(1)(A)(ii).

The enhanced new source review requirements as well as the expanded regulations will have a dramatic effect on new source construction and availability of emission offsets. Existing sources will apply RACT to control NO_x and/or VOC emissions. Unless an existing source "over-controls" either VOC and/or NO_x emissions beyond RACT-related requirements or a source is permanently shut down, emission credits or offsets may not become available. Thus, any existing source should be hording any internally created emission credits. These internally derived emission reduction credits may represent the only offsets available within certain geographic areas, especially for NO_x sources. However, the geographic area may expand considerably for existing sources or sources proposed in the Northeast Ozone Transport Region. With EPA's approval, it is the intent for states located in the region to allow intrastate emission trading and the establishment of a regional emission "bank." This approach would significantly improve the likelihood for industrial growth because of an expanded geographic area and the opportunity to trade emission offsets on a regional basis.

One final aspect peculiar to new or modified major sources pertains to NO_x emissions. NO_x emission sources in certain ozone nonattainment areas can be subject to both PSD and LAER requirements. For example, an existing major source (i.e., greater than 100 TPY of one of the 28 PSD source categories) located in a severe nonattainment area intends to install an NO_x emission source with the potential to emit of 50 TPY. The source would be required to apply LAER (i.e., more stringent than BACT) and obtain offsets at a 1.3-to-1 ratio. However, a modeling analysis may be required to demonstrate that the PSD increment and/or the applicable ambient air quality standard will not be exceeded. The applicant needs to be aware of these unusual and unique situations which must be considered in developing an overall permitting strategy.

Air Toxics

ROUTINE RELEASE CONDITIONS.   The 1990 amendments include a substantially revised program to regulate HAPs. Hazardous air pollutants are defined as 189 substances that may cause health and environmental effects at low concentrations and are not regulated as criteria pollutants.

The 1990 amendments define a major HAP source as any stationary source or group of stationary sources located within a contiguous area under common ownership that emits or has the potential to emit, considering controls, 10 tons or more per year of any single HAP or 25 tons or more per year of any combination of HAPs. Even seemingly minor facilities may be considered major sources of HAP emissions under these extremely stringent definitions. It should be noted that the EPA Administrator has the discretionary power to establish lower quantity threshold values for highly toxic or carcinogenic compounds. The triggering levels for these substances could be considerably less than 10 tons per year.

The first step in determining the impact of the new air toxics programs is to simply compare the results of the emission inventory to the 10- and 25-ton thresholds. For certain operations, secondary by-products may be chemically created and exist in the effluent discharge stream. If they are triggered for any one or more of the 189 HAPs, the following provisions need then to be evaluated in detail.

The new HAP emissions control program requires the installation of state-of-the-art pollution control technology on the vast majority of emission sources. However, process modifications or product substitution may represent an acceptable alternative approach.

The HAP provisions regulate emissions in a two-step process:

1. Promulgation of emissions limits reflecting Maximum Achievable Control Technologies (MACT) for 174 categories of industrial sources potentially emitting HAPs over 10 years

2. Residual risk determination to control categories of sources whose emissions still present health risks even after the application of MACT

In step 1, the EPA is mandated to develop a technology-based (MACT) regulatory framework to regulate source categories and limit HAP emissions by source categories over the next 10 years. HAP emissions will be reduced by setting limits on specific industrial emission sources. The EPA has identified and will issue regulations for 174 categories of industrial sources that emit substantial quantities of HAPs. Emissions allowances reflecting MACT will be established for each regulated source category. These allowances will be used ultimately to set source-specific limits in facility operating permits. The entire process will be similar to that for NPDES permits in which effluent guidelines are used to set facility-specific limits.

For new major sources, the HAP emission standards must be at least as stringent as the controls achieved in practice by the best controlled stationary source in the same category, and may be still more stringent when feasible. In essence, for new stationary sources the HAP standards will be equivalent to BACT requirements.

For existing major sources, HAP emission standards may be less stringent than the standards for new stationary sources in the same category, but may not permit less control than that achieved by the best performing controls.

As described above, step 1 in the HAP program is setting the technology-based control standards for HAP emissions sources. Step 2 is determining whether more stringent limits are required to protect public health and the environment with an "ample margin of safety" after setting the control standards. The issue of residual risk and its measurement and control will be studied by the government over the next few years. The EPA will then establish a second tier of emission standards for pollutants that present a cancer risk that is greater than one-in-a-million, even when complying with the emission limits established by this program. Thus, HAP emissions sources may become subject to a second phase of increasingly stringent regulation. It is important to note that some states may retain their existing air toxic regulations. These regulations may be in the form of ambient air concentration level guidelines. Thus, after the application of MACT, a source may be required to demonstrate compliance with a state's more stringent health-rated standard.

ACCIDENTAL RELEASE CONDITIONS. The 1990 amendments include requirements for preventing and minimizing the consequences of accidental releases of hazardous substances. Part of the law required the Occupational Safety and Health Administration (OSHA) to promulgate a chemical process safety management standard to protect workers from hazards associated with accidental releases of extremely hazardous chemicals in the workplace. The final standard, called the Process Hazard Safety Standard, was published in the *Federal Register* on February 24, 1992.

The 1990 amendments also required the EPA to promulgate the final form of the accidental release prevention regulations by November 15, 1993, for preventing and minimizing, if necessary, the consequences of accidental air releases from stationary facilities. The proposed risk management planning regulations were issued on October 20, 1993. Whereas the OSHA standard protects the worker form accidental releases, the EPA regulations protect the community and the environment, covering the off-site effects of accidental releases as well as on-site prevention and response. The accidental release program will be developed in close coordination with the existing OSHA process safety management standard in order to minimize any unnecessary duplication of certain requirements.

The EPA's accidental release prevention regulations require certain facilities handling more than a threshold amount of Extremely Hazardous Substances (EHSs) to develop detailed and integrated accidental release prevention and risk management plans, in most cases far beyond what has previously been expected of industry. The EPA's initial proposed list of 162 EHSs was published in the January 19, 1993, *Federal Register.*

Operating Permit Program Requirements. The 1990 amendments established a massive new operating permit program to be administered by state agencies. The EPA's formal requirements regarding permit programs were promulgated as 40 CFR Part 70 on July 21, 1992. The new operating permit program will be administered by state and local permitting authorities and will require nearly all sources of even minor amounts of air emissions to apply for and obtain operating permits. As shown in Table 1-7, the new operating permit program is substantially different than present operating permit requirements.

TABLE 1-7 Comparison of Pre- and Post-1990 Operating Permits

Pre-1990	Post-1990
Compliance required with nonspecific state regulations	Permit lists stack-by-stack allowable emissions
Emission monitoring rarely required	Continuous compliance monitoring
Annual emission reports (not compliance)	Semiannual emission reporting; annual compliance certification
	Five-year maximum term
	Significant permit fees

Existing major sources as well as newly constructed sources will require permits. Even those facilities and operations previously grandfathered from permit requirements will now be required to obtain permits. After the permit program is in full force, a facility will not be able to operate without both a permit and meeting the requirements stated in the permit.

The operating permit program is generally modeled after the NPDES program under the Clean Water Act. Under the 1990 amendments, operating permits will become the "centerpiece for compliance"—the new operating permits are intended to contain all of a facility's requirements for compliance with all air quality regulations in one enforceable document. A typical operating permit for a facility will be many pages in length and will require the collection and maintenance of reams of emissions data for each source or source grouping. Furthermore, industrial facilities will be required to pay permit fees as a condition of the permit. The new operating permits will be vastly different from existing operating permits.

Initially, all major sources of air pollution will be required to obtain an operating permit. The definition of "major" varies depending upon the regulatory program and geographic location of the facility. Using the emission inventory data developed as part of the compliance review, Table 1-8 provides a summary of the types of sources required to apply for operating permits.

TABLE 1-8 Operating Permit Program Applicability

Source type	Major source threshold (potential to emit)
Hazardous air pollutant	10 tpy* any single HAP or 25 tpy aggregate HAP emissions
VOC in an ozone nonattainment area	10–100 tpy VOC emissions
VOC in Northeast Transport Region	50 tpy VOC emissions
NO$_x$ in an ozone nonattainment area	10–100 tpy NO$_x$ emissions
CO in a serious nonattainment area	50 tpy
Particulate matter (PM-10 nonattainment area)	50–70 tpy
All others	100 tpy any emissions
Sources subject to NSPS, NESHAP, PSD/NSR and acid rain regulations	No threshold quantity

* tpy = tons per year.

When an industrial operation is subject to the permit program as a major source for any one pollutant, all potential emissions of every regulated pollutant at the facility must be addressed in the permit application. The following section outlines the minimum operating permit program elements.

At a minimum, state agencies must include certain specific elements in their operating permit programs for approval by the EPA: requirements for permit applications, emission monitoring, compliance certification reporting, permit fee authority, personnel, funding, and authority to issue and process permits.

By regulation, facilities are required to submit permit applications by November 1995 at the latest. In most cases, states will require permit application submittal before November 1994. To submit a timely and complete permit application, it is essential that facilities begin to prepare the information as early as possible. With dozens to hundreds of individual emissions units in a large industrial facility, accurate and well-documented information is essential. Unless a company negotiates its permits properly, after these emission limitations have been established much of the operating flexibility of the past may be gone.

The permit application should include:

- Potential emission of each regulated pollutant from a company's facilities
- Emission limits on a pollutant-by-pollutant basis for both hourly and annual emissions
- Acceptable emissions limits
- Potential emission rates in tons per year and in compliance terms (e.g., pounds per gallon, pounds per million Btu)

It is possible that the permit will cap both annual and short-term emissions for certain sources or grouping of sources. The permit application must cite and describe the regulatory requirements applicable to the facility. Requirements expected to become applicable during the term of a permit must also be identified in the application.

Permits will become the principal mechanism for detailing the specific requirements applicable to individual sources. It will be extremely important to negotiate a permit that will allow substantial operating flexibility. Otherwise, the time required to modify air permits may seriously impede product development and facility planning processes.

If a facility is out of compliance at the time that the permit application is submitted, a schedule for compliance, including enforceable milestones, will be required. This compliance plan would then become an enforceable part of the facility permit.

The new operating permit program establishes procedures for several classes of changes at industrial facilities (Table 1-9). In the past, many of these changes required no EPA involvement. In the future, however, almost any change in methods of operation will require EPA approval. Changes at sources are classified as (1) administrative permit amendments, (2) minor permit modifications, or (3) significant permit modifications.

TABLE 1-9 Minor versus Significant Permit Modifications

Minor modifications	Significant modifications
Small emissions increases	Not a minor modification or an administrative change; typically a Title I modification
Insignificant monitoring changes	Significant monitoring changes
Facility can make change before modification is reviewed if state regulations accept EPA guidance	Full review process before facility can make change
No shield	State may allow a shield

The new air permits will summarize existing restrictions applicable to an operation. A permit change is not required to authorize a change in practice that is otherwise legal under the state's rules and regulations. Any change in practices or procedures that is not prohibited by the permit and is otherwise legal may be made without a permit modification. Permit modifications, particularly significant ones subject to EPA involvement, could take from many months to more than a year for approvals. Preparation of complete permit applications and their timely submittal are critical items in responding to the amendments' permitting requirements. The permit application and permit eventually crafted by the agencies based on the application will define a company's operations for many years to come. Applications require careful consideration of each item required in the permit application, as well as consideration of the potential for future process modifications or production increases, to ensure that the operating permit provides sufficient flexibility to allow the facility to run within a range of likely emissions and to avoid very lengthy permit modifications.

EMISSIONS SURVEY

The initial step in defining the emissions levels and determining the BACT or LAER technology (for a modification or a proposed new facility) or RACT or MACT requirements (to control atmospheric emissions from an existing plant) is an emissions survey. All applicable pollutant sources and quantities of emissions must be identified. The results of this survey will provide management with a representative and comprehensive overview and with sufficient detail with which to formulate abatement plans and design programs in order to file the permit application. The basic steps in a typical survey include:

- Cataloging emission sources
- Quantifying emissions
- Preparing a source identification file

Cataloging Emission Sources

General Plant Information.   The first step in such cataloging activities is to develop general plant information. This information is required to provide a general background and overview of the proposed or existing plant and/or its modifications and define applicable regulatory requirements. The following data should be provided:

- A schematic block flow diagram of the process(es) for the plant showing the flow of raw materials into and out of the process(es), and the design/operation of the air pollution control equipment. This diagram should identify sources of all potentially regulated pollutants, both process and fugitive emissions, which could be released into the atmosphere. Potential secondary or transformation by-product pollutants may need to be considered.

- A materials balance across the process(es) and across the air pollution control equipment.
- Airflows, either shown on a schematic block flow diagram for the process(es) and the control equipment, or provided separately.
- Dimensional information of the plant buildings showing the length, width, and height of all structures, *present* and *proposed.*
- Details of existing and proposed stack(s): height, diameter, exit gas flow, and temperature.
- Details of the design characteristics of the air pollution control equipment.
- Details on the potential release of fugitive emissions from existing or proposed new operations.
- A facility plot plan, including all fenced-off areas, identifying all sources, buildings, and plant property lines.

Process Flowsheets.   The second step is to prepare process flowsheets in sufficient detail to indicate the flow of all raw materials, additives, by-products, and waste streams. The flowsheet should identify all points of feed input, and all points at which atmospheric, liquid, and solid wastes are discharged. The engineer or supervisor responsible for each process should verify that the flowsheets identify all sources. Many plants have numerous sources, which must be identified correctly for tracking purposes.

Survey Data Sheets.   Analysis of process flowsheets can be further verified by review of prior permit applications, process blueprints, photographs, and inspection manuals. With the aid of these and any other resources available, the emissions surveyor can then develop checklists in the form of survey data sheets that will be used in the plant tour to ensure complete and efficient gathering of pertinent data. These survey data sheets will pertain chiefly to process and feed data, and control equipment and emissions data. In addition, the survey form should identify the permit status (i.e., grandfathered, exempt, regulated, or not permitted) and the expiration dates of permits for each stack and/or vent. Figure 1-2 shows an example of a process survey data sheet, representing presurvey evaluation of a fuel-fired combustion source. Such an example can be modified to apply to most types of emission sources now in operation. The process survey data sheet should include the following:

- Detailed information on operating conditions for the process as designed
- Identification of normal and maximum throughput or processing rates during continuous, batch, or intermittent operation, with frequency of emission discharges for each
- Description of raw materials, products, and wastes
- Values for normal operating temperature, equipment performance ratings, flows, pressures, and similar data that are routinely monitored and/or recorded

Control Equipment Survey Information.   The information given in a control equipment survey sheet is outlined in Tables 1-10 to 1-14. Table 1-10 shows information for a general survey evaluation form, while Tables 1-11 to 1-14 outline data requirements for control methods for particulates and acid gases.

Identical information and data must be developed and evaluated for any new or modified facility in order to select the control system that represents BACT or LAER technology.

Tour of Plant Facilities.   The fourth step is a tour of the plant facilities. The tour should include discussions with the process engineer or supervisor in order to ensure identification of all sources, verify the process and control-equipment flowsheets, and account for any equipment modifications already made. Sufficient data should be gathered to allow computation of material balances in order to have a basis for quantifying each emission source.

The plant tour starts at the files. There the survey will gather design specifications for each process and control device. Correspondence may also yield pertinent information relating to operation and maintenance of process and control equipment, current status of compliance,

POWER PLANT SURVEY FORM

Type of Heat Exchanger   Primary   Standby

        Coal-fired   ☐   ☐
        Oil-fired   ☐   ☐
        Gas-fired   ☐   ☐
        If multiple-fired, check appropriate boxes

Rated Input Capacity_____Btu/hr
Maximum Operating Rate_____Btu/hr
Rated Steam Output _____lb/hr___(a)_____Btu/lb steam
Maximum Steam Output _____lb/hr___(a)_____Btu/lb steam
Furnace Volume   width___ft x depth___ft x height ___ ft = _____ cu ft
Operating Schedule_____ hr/day___day/wk ___wk/yr

Coal Firing

    Type of Firing   ☐ Grate   Type _____
                ☐ Spreader stoker
                ☐ Pulverized coal   ☐ Dry bottom   ☐ Wet bottom
                ☐ Cyclone

    Fly Ash Reinjection   ☐ Yes   ☐ No

    Soot Blowing

        ☐ Continuous
        ☐ Intermittent

        Time Interval Between Blowing_____minutes

        Duration_____minutes

    Outside Coal Storage   ☐ Yes   ☐ No

        Maximum Amount Stored Outside_____tons

FIGURE 1-2 Sample presurvey data sheet for fossil-fuel-fired steam generators.

comments of control agencies, public complaints, and the like. This kind of background information can enhance the understanding needed for a meaningful on-site inspection of each process and control device. If the particular (existing) emission source requires an air permit, most of the pertinent information on the operating and emission characteristics are contained in the permit. Under the new operating permit program, permits must be renewed every five years.

Each air containment source generally has a duct that vents from the process to an outside chimney or stack. The exhaust gas is moved by a fan or, in some instances where heat is applied, by natural draft. For each operation, the ducting should be followed from the process to the point of entry to the atmosphere. In some instances, the exhaust gas stream is difficult

TABLE 1-10   General Control Equipment Data

A. At maximum continuous production rate (MCPR)
   1. Inlet and outlet absolute cubic feet per minute (ACFM).*
   2. Inlet and outlet gas temperatures.
   3. a. Inlet and outlet percent of H_2O.
      b. Dew point.
   4. Inlet pollutant levels for
      a. TSP, lb/h, gr/scf[†], etc., also provide particulate size distribution.
      b. SO_2, lb/h, gr/scf, etc.
      c. NO_x, lb/h, gr/scf, etc.
      d. HC, lb/h, gr/scf, etc.
      e. CO, lb/h, gr/scf, etc.
   5. Expected and guaranteed efficiencies for each of the above pollutants.
   6. Expected and guaranteed pollutant levels at outlet for each of the above pollutants.
   7. If available, make, model, and type of control system(s).
   8. Explain basis for ACFM and °F selection for design. *Caution:* These may be different from data used in dispersion modeling.
   9. Material balance across control equipment.
   10. Block flow diagram of control equipment.
   11. Inlet particulate size distribution.
B. For system(s) which may have a lower efficiency at normal operating rates as compared to MCPR, provide all data outlined above at normal operating rate.

* Actual cubic feet per minute.
[†] Standard cubic feet.
Note: If available, provide specification sheets. Provide drawings of internals.

TABLE 1-11   Multiclone and Cyclone Data

   1. Number of tubes for multiclones (multiple cyclones).
   2. Length of tubes.
   3. Fractional size efficiency vs. *P* curves.
   4. Diameter of tubes for multiclone or diameter of cyclone.
   5. Pressure drop, in H_2O column.
   6. Particulate size distribution into cyclone and/or multiclone.
   7. Grain loading (gr/dscf)* at inlet and/or outlet.
   8. ACFM at °F.
   9. Design efficiency.
   10. Disposal and handling of dry, collected dust.
   11. Preventive maintenance program.

   * Dry standard cubic feet.

to follow. The introduction of makeup air, splitting of gas streams, and ducting of several operations to a common stack complicate the overall exhaust system structure and require careful tracing to ensure that exhaust-gas paths are properly defined. Placement of fans and control devices must be noted along with the height and location of each stack. Air-conditioning, heating, and makeup vents must not be mistaken for process stacks. After defining all process sources, the surveyor should check the roof to identify any unaccounted emission points. Finally, potential sources of fugitive emissions should be confirmed.

Quantifying Emissions

All of the data obtained thus far from the process flowsheets, process survey forms, control equipment survey forms, stack survey forms, photographs, correspondence, discussions, and

TABLE 1-12 Data for Scrubber for SO_2 and/or Other Pollutants

1. Design inlet and outlet volume flows, temperatures, percent moisture, and SO_2 loadings.
2. Type of scrubber. Wet or dry. If wet, operational mode.
3. Is reheat necessary? Describe.
4. Percentage of exhaust gases? Describe.
5. Any prequench section? Describe.
6. Type of demister.
7. Type of internal construction.
8. Minimum number of isolatable modules.
9. Minimum liquid-to-gas ratio.
10. Minimum-maximum pH of scrubbing liquor.
11. Maximum gas face velocity.
12. Minimum ratio of reagent to SO_2 and chemical composition solution.
13. Pressure drop, in H_2O column.
14. Is any bypass to be provided?
15. Outline any measures to be taken to produce more uniform SO_2 loading to the scrubber (e.g., precleaning, coal blending, etc.).
16. Design efficiency for PM and/or SO_2 and/or other pollutants.
17. Redundancy of control equipment.
18. Parameters for packed-bed scrubbers.
    a. Type of packing
    b. Packing size and/or shape
    c. Packing height
19. Parameters for spray scrubbers:
    a. Number of nozzles
    b. Nozzle droplet size
    c. Nozzle design and/or shape
    d. Nozzle pressure psig
20. Materials of construction.
21. Disposal of sludge or wet dust.
22. Effluent to streams from sludge pond.
23. Percolation from sludge ponds to aquifers.
24. Preventive maintenance program.

TABLE 1-13 Fabric Filter or Baghouse Data

1. Type of filter media.
    a. Chemical composition
    b. Woven cloth or felt
    c. Porosity of new cloth
    d. Weight of cloth in ounces per square yard
    e. Napped or nonnapped fibers in woven bags
    f. Life of bags
2. Air-to-cloth ratio.
3. Cleaning mechanism.
4. Number of compartments. Can one compartment be shut down for maintenance while rest of the baghouse continues operation? How is overall collection efficiency affected?
5. How is damage from gas dew point circumvented? What is dew point?
6. Overall collection efficiency.
7. Materials of construction.
8. Disposal of collected materials.
9. Preventive maintenance program.

TABLE 1-14 Electrostatic Precipitator (ESP) Data

---

1. Collection area, square feet per 1000 ACFM.
2. Number of fields.
3. Number of compartments. Can one compartment be shut down for maintenance while rest of ESP continues operation? How is the overall collection efficiency affected during maintenance?
4. Gas velocity through ESP, feet per second.
5. Description of gas conditioning techniques.
6. Design of charging area: weighed wires, rigid frames, etc.
7. Temperature of operation.
8. Resistivity of fly ash or particulate matter at temperature of operation.
9. Inlet gas details: How is turbulence minimized? Any aerodynamic gas flow studies?
10. Rapping or cleaning details: provisions to minimize reentrainment when cleaning.
11. Design efficiency for preventive maintenance.
12. Design of collecting rappers to prevent bridging, plugging, or improper operation.
13. Materials of construction.
14. Disposal of collected materials.
15. Preventive maintenance program.

---

the plant tour can now be organized to develop an emission survey plan. This plan must indicate the quantity of emissions estimated from each source, with possible variations due to season, time of day, feed materials, and similar variables. The emissions characterization should identify all important parameters affecting control of the pollutants and possible sampling techniques. These data will be used to review the compliance status for each source. These programs will describe the plans that will be implemented by the company to achieve or maintain compliance and should contain the following increments of progress or milestones:

- Date of submittal of the final compliance plan or permit to the appropriate air pollution control agency
- Date of issuance of an approved compliance plan or permit
- Date by which contracts for emission control systems or process modifications will be awarded, or date by which orders will be issued for purchase of component parts to accomplish emission control or process modification
- Date of initiation of on-site construction or installation of emission control equipment or process change
- Date by which on-site construction or installation of emission control equipment or process modification is to be completed
- Date by which final compliance or full operation is to be achieved

Figure 1-1 presents an example of the activities that must be completed before compliance can be achieved. Depending on the nature of the emission source and the complexity and size of the modifications required, the time requirements for compliance can range from a few months to several years.

Quantification techniques can then be applied in order to develop and utilize the emission survey information. Mass balances usually can be established around each process, particularly when the throughput rates and the composition of raw materials are known. The materials balance will indicate the extent of solid, liquid, and gaseous wastes.

A review of applicable air pollution control regulations will provide the basis for the mass balance. The control regulations state what pollutants are regulated and define each pollutant. The definition of each pollutant determines the conditions under which the pollutant is sampled and its chemical and physical makeup. For instance, because water vapor is not considered an air pollutant, it is not necessary to accurately account for it in the mass balance. Emissions of SO_2 or organic substances are usually regulated and must be estimated in the materials balance.

A materials balance for gaseous pollutants can be determined by analysis of raw materials, fuels, and products to give the gaseous pollutant potential of many of the compounds liberated during a combustion or chemical process. Knowledge of fuel composition is especially useful in estimating emissions, since many gaseous compounds in the fuel become airborne after combustion (e.g., sulfur in fuel-oil exhausts as sulfur dioxide). Other constituents, such as ash and volatile matter, directly affect the quantity of particulate emissions. Stack sampling tests may be the only acceptable way to quantify emissions of certain pollutants (e.g., VOCs and HAPs).

In reviewing a permit application, the regulatory authorities typically use an EPA publication titled, "A Compilation of Emission Factors" (AP-42), in order to estimate the potential uncontrolled and controlled emissions of a particular pollutant. This document and all its supplements should be obtained by the plant engineer and used as reference material.

Preparing a Source Identification File

A source identification file provides a means of standardizing data for the emission survey. For each pollutant source, a standard identification form gives a description of the process, a summary of emission data, the current compliance status, and the proposed actions, if any are intended. A basic source identification form is shown in Fig. 1-3. Some sources involve several emission points with more than one pollutant at each point.

The source identification file should be indexed to provide easy access by any concerned party. The index should list all sources and identify the emission point for each source. Assignment of a number for each emission point will facilitate an alphanumeric search for emission points in the source identification file.

EMISSION CONTROL METHODS

Emission control alternatives might be broadly grouped under the categories of (1) process or raw material changes that reduce the quantity of pollutant, (2) changes that eliminate production of a particularly undesirable pollutant, and (3) collection and removal of the pollutant from the gas stream. Current designs employ some combination of these alternatives, with interaction between the alternatives. For example, using a scrubber to selectively remove a pollutant may lower an exhaust-gas temperature, which could significantly reduce the thermal buoyancy of the effective plume rise, thereby necessitating the requirement for plume reheat and/or increase in stack height. Disposal of an undesirable liquid or removal of solid waste from a gas stream may be a greater problem than abatement of gaseous pollutants. Clearly, there must be a compromise. The control system must be evaluated with regard to capital and operating costs, level of control, by-product generation, reliability, and other practical considerations.

The most important process parameters for selection of control equipment are the following:

Flue gas characteristics

- Total flue gas flow rate
- Flue gas temperature
- Control efficiency required
- Composition of emissions
- Corrosiveness of flue gas over operating range
- Moisture content
- Stack pressure

Emission Point No. _____

Emission Point Name _____

Date of Record _____

Source Name _____

Description of Source _____

Type of Permit _____

Date of Permit _____

Applicable Regulation(s) _____

Particulate Emissions _____ units _____

Allowable Emissions _____ units _____

Method of Determination _____

Gaseous Emissions _____

    type _____ units _____

Allowable Emissions _____ units _____

Method of Determination _____

Compliance Status _____

Date Contract Awarded _____

Date Construction Began _____

Monitoring _____

    ambient _____

    stack _____

FIGURE 1-3 Source identification form.

Process or site characteristics (field survey)

- Reuse or recycling of collected emissions
- Availability of space
- Availability of additional electrical power
- Availability of water
- Availability of wastewater treatment facilities
- Frequency of start-up and shutdown

Controlling Particulate and Sulfur Dioxide Emissions

Traditional and nontraditional air pollution control systems that primarily limit particulate and sulfur dioxide SO_x emissions are discussed in this subsection. Some of the devices described here can be used in series or alone to reduce particulate and acid gas emissions to acceptable levels.

Mechanical Collectors.   The most familiar and widely used mechanical collector is the cyclone separator (Fig. 1-4). Gas enters tangentially at the top of a cylindrical shell and is forced downward in a spiral of decreasing diameter in a conical section. Particles are centrifugally thrust outward and forced to spiral downward to the bottom, which is closed by an air lock. Since gas cannot escape at the bottom, it is forced to turn and travel, still whirling, back up the center of the vortex and exit at the top. Particles are discharged from the bottom through the air lock.

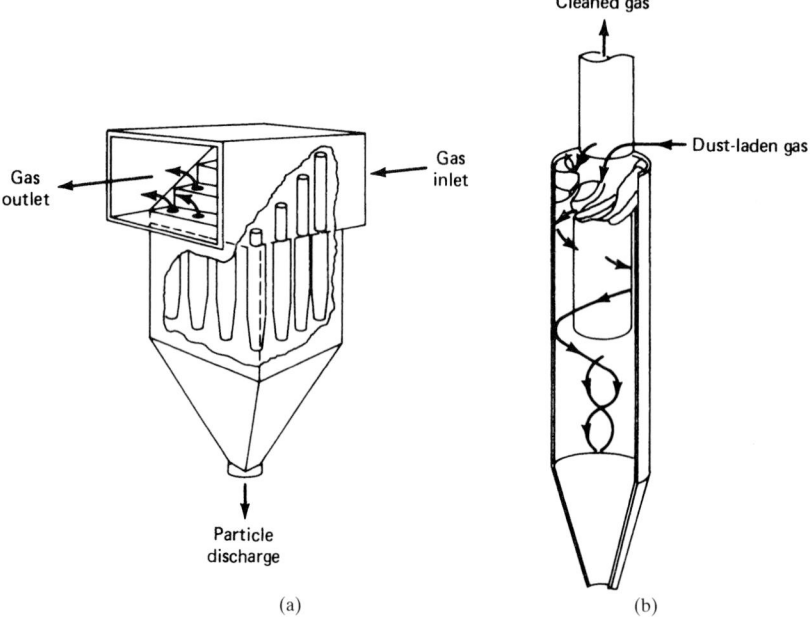

FIGURE 1-4   Mechanical collector-cyclone.

The tighter the spiral in which gas must flow, the greater the centrifugal force acting on a particle of given mass, and thus the more efficient the cyclone can be. Top diameters of cyclones range from more than 120 in (3 m) to as small as 24 in (60 cm), and capabilities reach 85 percent efficiency with particles as small as 10 μm at pressure drops from 0.5- to 3-in (13- to 77-mm) water gauge.

Cyclones alone are seldom adequate for pollution control, except where the load consists almost entirely of coarse particles, as in woodworking shops, or where particle density is unusually high. Cyclones are often used when there is a special reason to separate and collect reusable coarse particles from useless fines (in fluid-bed catalyst regenerators, for example, through which the fines pass for subsequent separation by more efficient means). Cyclones are sometimes applied where gas cooling is necessary (for example, where the cyclone is followed by a fabric filter, the cyclone scalps the coarse fractions of the dust load and at the same time provides cooling).

Scrubbers. Scrubbers are collectors capable of separating solid or liquid particles from a gas stream. They are also used to separate a chemically reactive or soluble gas constituent from other gas constituents in a flue gas stream. The most common use for gas separation involves its use in *flue gas desulfurization* (FGD).

In the simplest application of scrubbing, liquid is sprayed in at the top of a column, and collision for particulate wetting or capture occurs as drops fall through a rising gas stream. Pressure drop is low, and application is limited to situations where 50 percent efficiency or less is acceptable and the percentage of particles smaller than 10 μm is low, or where coarse particles are to be scalped ahead of a precipitator or a more efficient scrubber. A spray column is often used primarily for quenching hot gas, with coarse particulate removal a useful but incidental effect.

Centrifugal Scrubbers. In a centrifugal scrubber, column design and directed sprays cause droplets and gas to mix in a rising vortex such that centrifugal force increases the momentum of collisions between particles and drops. Thus, smaller particles can be captured, and efficiencies as high as 90 percent can be achieved with particles as small as 5 μm, at pressure drops from 2- to 6-in (50- to 150-mm) water gauge.

Packed Scrubbers. A column may be fitted with impingement plates, wetted mesh, or fibrous packing, or packed with saddles, rings, or other solid shapes. In such scrubbers, typically at a 1- to 10-in (25- to 250-mm) water-gauge pressure drop, efficiencies can reach 95 percent with particles as small as 5 μm. Packed beds designed for gas absorption, however, are subject to fouling if the gas stream contains a significant fraction of solid particulates. In designs that use sprays to wash the packing, or that are packed with small spheres agitated by the gas flow, the fouling problem is reduced. In some systems, a moist chemical-foam packing is used which drains slowly from the scrubber along with captured particulates and is then replaced.

Venturi Scrubbers. A venturi tube operating on the eductor or ejector principle, with scrubbing liquid as the motive fluid, can collect particles as small as submicrometer size with efficiencies as high as 95 percent, if grain loading is low. Gas-pressure drop is not needed for power input, and there can even be a gain in gas pressure across such a scrubber. The disadvantages are the requirement for substantial scrubbing-liquid flow at high pressure and the scrubber's inability to remove large particles because the induced gas-stream velocity is low.

Scrubbing a particulate- and acid-containing gas stream by bringing it into contact with a liquid is an effective means of removing both the dust and the acids. The collected particles, along with any acids (in either a "raw" or neutralized form), are disposed of in a wet form and present their own set of disposal problems. This is one of the major drawbacks to wet scrubbing and a reason that dry scrubbing systems are gaining wide acceptance.

When treating an acid-gas stream, an alkali compound (caustic soda, lime) is added to the scrubber water. The water is brought into contact with the gas stream through dispersed droplets (spray tower), contraction of the gas stream (venturi), or counter-current flow (collision). This violent contact removes the particles and acids from the gas stream, but wet scrubbing is very dependent on size and concentration (for gases) at a potentially high energy cost. In general, the greater the degree of acid gas or the amount of particulate removal required (or the smaller the particle to be removed), the more energy must be expended to reach this goal. This energy usage is found in both the pumps to move the scrubbing liquor and the fan power to move the gas.

Semidry Scrubbers. Semidry scrubbing systems start with a wet scrubbing medium (usually a lime slurry or a soda ash solution) and produce a dry waste product. The central device of a semidry scrubbing system is the spray dryer similar to equipment that has been used for years in industry to manufacture everything from powdered coffee and milk to paint pigments and detergents.

In a semidry scrubbing system, the solution or slurry is dispersed by nozzles or rotary atomization systems into a fine cloud of droplets. These droplets are brought into contact with a hot gas stream (and herein lies a disadvantage to semidry scrubbing systems) that proceeds to evaporate the water in the droplets. As the water evaporates, the acids in the gas stream react with the alkali material in the drying droplets and neutralize them, forming a fine powder. Most of this powder is removed from the bottom of the spray dryer while the remainder is entrained in the gas stream and carried out to either a fabric filter or an electrostatic precipitator.

The necessity for a secondary emissions control device is another disadvantage of semidry scrubbing systems and usually will result in a cost about 5 to 10 percent higher than wet scrubbing systems. Two major advantages of the semidry scrubbing system are its relative simplicity to operate and the relative ease (compared to wet scrubbing systems) of the disposal of the dry waste product.

Another advantage of the semidry scrubbing systems is that, combined with a fabric filter, there is almost complete (95 percent for SO_2, 90 to 95 percent for HCl) removal of acid gases, particulates, metals, and, when used with activated carbon injection, dioxins and furans.

Dry Injection Systems.   Dry injection systems are effective in removing acids from gas streams. In operation, this method is very similar to the semidry scrubbing system in that a dry powder (usually lime or soda ash) is injected into a gas stream. In some applications this powder injection may be enhanced by a separate fine water spray to humidify the gas stream.

The acids will react with the injected powder and, again like the semidry systems, be removed from the gas stream (along with other particles) in either an electrostatic precipitator or a fabric filter. Two great advantages of the dry injection system are the simplicity of its operation and, depending upon the layout and length of ductwork, its ease of retrofit into a manufacturing facility with an existing particulate control device.

One major disadvantage of the dry injection system is that without the aid of gas-liquid-solid mass transfer, as in the wet or semidry scrubbing systems, a much higher stoichiometry of alkali is required for an equivalent removal.

Fabric Filters.   Fabric filters collect solid particles by passing gas through cloth bags that most particles cannot penetrate. As the layer of collected material builds on the fabric, the pressure differential required for continued gas flow increases; consequently, the accumulated dust must be removed at frequent intervals. Fabric used to form the filter elements can range from nylon to wool to Teflon™-coated fiberglass, shaped into cylindrical bags or envelopes with a roughly elliptical cross section.

Fabric filters are capable of 99+ percent collection efficiency with particles as small as submicrometer size. High efficiency is attained with moderate pressure drops, typically in the range from 2- to 4-in (50- to 100-mm) water gauge. Power input is thus comparable to that of multitube mechanical collectors, while the capability to collect fine particles is much greater. Operating costs including maintenance are somewhat higher, however, because some moving parts are involved and bags must be replaced periodically. Unlike wet scrubbers, the performance of fabric filters is relatively unaffected by variations in gas-flow rate. Fabric filters are sometimes preceded by mechanical dust collectors or settling chambers in the baghouse when excessive grain loading or abrasive, coarse particles, or both, are involved.

At certain times during operation, the pressure drop will increase to the point that necessitates removal of the particles from the fabric. Depending upon the filter system design, the cleaning process is accomplished by either shaking the bags, sending a pulse of compressed air into the filter bag, or sending a stream of clean gas in a reverse direction through the filter compartment.

As effective as fabric filters are, there are some drawbacks to their use. Excessive pressure drops may occur as the fabric becomes plugged with small particles or from water droplets in the gas stream; ripping or pinholing of the fabric will reduce its effectiveness; and retrofit of filters may be difficult depending upon the layout of the process and the facility.

Electrostatic Precipitators.   Electrostatic precipitators are extremely efficient air pollution control devices which can remove more than 99 percent of the particles in a gas stream

(Fig. 1-5). This high efficiency is possible because, unlike other pollution control devices, the precipitator applies the collecting force only to the particles to be collected, not to the entire gas stream. Thus, an extremely low, energy-saving power input (about 200 W/1000 ft^3/min [0.5 m^3/s]) is required.

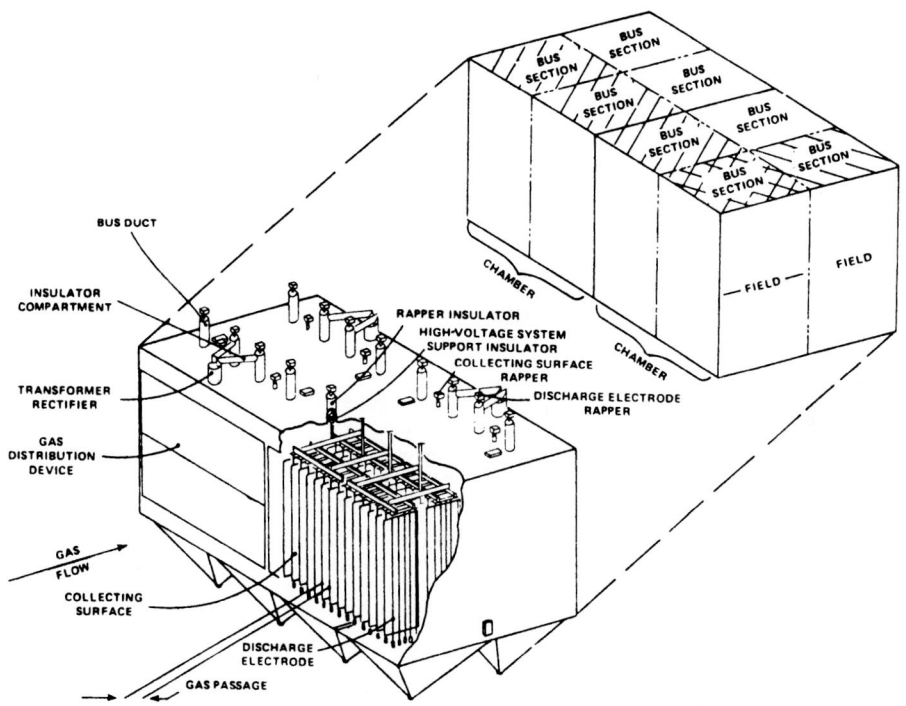

FIGURE 1-5 Electrostatic precipitator.

   In operation, a voltage source creates a negatively charged area, usually by means of wires suspended in the gas-flow path. On either side of this charged area are grounded collecting plates. The high potential difference between these plates and the discharge wires creates a powerful electric field. As the polluted gas passes through this field, particles suspended in the gas become electrically charged and are drawn out of the gas flow by the collecting plates. They adhere to these plates until removed for disposal. Removal is accomplished mechanically by periodic vibration, rapping, or rinsing. The gas stream, now substantially free of particulate pollution, continues to flow for release to the atmosphere.

   Since its collection mechanism depends upon charging the particles in the gas stream, an electrostatic precipitator will be strongly affected by the characteristics of both the particle and the gas stream in which it is contained. Particles with too high a conductivity (low resistivity) will bleed their charge either before being collected or will be released back into the gas stream after impacting with the collecting electrodes.

   Conversely, particles with very low conductivity (high resistivity) will not be easily charged and may require a very large precipitator to achieve an adequate collection efficiency. In specifying a precipitator, the user should have either a qualified testing company or a reputable vendor perform resistivity and particle size distribution measurements on the gas stream to be controlled to develop the needed design data. If this testing is not possible, then a qualified consultant or company experienced in precipitator design should be used.

Controlling VOC Emissions

The air pollution control equipment marketplace offers many competing technologies for controlling emissions of volatile organic compounds (VOC). It is important to note that over half of the HAPs are considered VOCs. Thus, controlling VOCs will limit HAP emissions. If any technology was economically and technically superior under all conditions, it would be the only one on the market. In fact, each technology used to control VOCs is superior under some set of conditions.

The reasons for choosing one control technology over another are situation specific. Some general guidelines to VOC-control technologies and the situations where they may be appropriate are presented in this subsection. Table 1-15 summarizes the control technologies and their applications.

TABLE 1-15   Control Technologies for VOCs

Air streams with a high VOC content (>500ppm)
- Refrigerated vapor condenser
- Solvent Vapor Adsorption
- Flare

Air streams with a moderate VOC content (about 100 to 500 ppm)
- Thermal incinerator
- Catalytic incinerator
- Regenerative (ceramic) incinerator
- Regenerative carbon adsorber

Air streams with low VOC content (< 100 ppm)
- Once-through carbon adsorption
- Carbon adsorber-incinerator systems
- Reducing process air flow rates

High VOC Air Streams.   Air streams with a high VOC content are defined here as those containing several hundred parts per million (ppm) and greater.

Refrigerated Vapor Condenser.   This removes VOCs from a gas stream by condensation at very low temperatures, typically around −112°F (−80°C). As an example, refrigerated condensation is used to remove gasoline from air displaced by fuel transfer operations. It is most applicable to gas streams with flow rates less than 1000 scfm and VOC concentrations of at least several hundred ppm.

Many hydrocarbons have significant vapor pressures even at −112°F (−80°C). This limits the attainable recovery. For example, the vapor pressure of toluene at −112°F (−80°C) is 0.052 millimeters of mercury or 69 ppmv at atmospheric pressure. If the initial toluene concentration is 1000 ppmv, at least 90 percent removal is attainable. If the initial toluene concentration is 100 ppmv, recovery can be no better than 30 percent.

Everything passing through the system is cooled to −112°F (−80°C)—VOC, air, inert gas, and water vapor. Water is converted to ice, which could plug the system. Therefore, high humidity must be avoided. Refrigeration requirements are a large part of the cost of operating the system, and refrigerating low VOC concentrations has less efficient recovery and higher operating costs. This restricts refrigerated condensation to relatively high VOC concentrations at relatively low flow rate conditions.

Solvent Vapor Adsorption.   VOC-containing air passes through a nonvolatile solvent which adsorbs most of the VOC. VOCs are stripped from the loaded solvent with heat and a partial vacuum and are recovered by condensation. Recovered VOCs can be recycled, which can offset some or all of the costs of operating the system. The VOC concentration must be at least 100 ppmv. Skid-mounted package units might be used for fuel transfer and can handle up to 1000 scfm. Larger custom units can handle several thousand scfm and might be used for controlling chlorinated hydrocarbon emissions from degreasers.

Flares.   Flares are considered an acceptable device for emission control. Instances where there is both a sustained high gas flow and a high VOC concentration are rare since the losses would be economically unacceptable. A flare would be effective for controlling intermittent short-term high flow rate or high concentration surges.

The flare has the advantages of relatively low capital cost, minimal operating cost, and the ability to deal with VOC surges. VOC control to 95 to 98 percent can be assumed. In addition, flares are a combustion source and will result in emissions of oxides of nitrogen (NO_x) and carbon monoxide (CO).

Moderate VOC Concentration.   Air streams with a moderate VOC concentration are defined here as ranging from 100 to 500 ppmv.

Thermal Incinerators.   VOC-containing air is heated in a combustion chamber to a temperature of 1400° to 1800°F (760° to 982°C). A supplemental fuel is always required and natural gas is the usual choice. A temperature of (780°C) is adequate for most VOCs and will assure more than 99 percent destruction. The heat content of the VOC usually does not contribute significantly to the fuel requirements.

Heat exchangers can be added into the incinerator to use the stack gas to preheat the incoming VOC stream. Up to 65 percent heat recovery is attainable. The heat exchanger reduces the fuel at the expense of a higher capital cost. The incinerator may need to be made of more expensive metals if chlorides are present.

The thermal incinerator is a simple and effective system. The disadvantage is the cost of the supplemental fuel and increase in emissions of combustion-related gases (i.e., NO_x and CO). Fuel cost is less of a concern for low air flow rates and where operation is not continuous. For example, a 2000 scfm incinerator would require about 3.5×10^6 Btu per hour. For a one-shift, five-days-per-week operation, the incinerator would operate about 2200 h a year (allowing for warm-up), creating an annual fuel requirement of about 7700×10^6 Btu. Depending on natural gas prices, a $100,000 heat exchanger might not be justifiable. For the same air stream and a three-shift operation, a heat exchanger probably would be a good investment.

For a 20,000 scfm air stream, fuel requirements would be about 35 million Btu per h. A thermal incinerator should certainly have a heat exchanger, so other VOC control methods should be considered.

Catalytic Incinerator.   VOC combustion takes place on a catalyst surface at about 800°F (427°C). Fuel costs are lower than for a thermal incinerator because it takes less fuel to heat air to 800°F (427°C) than to 1435°F (780°C). Also, the heat value of the VOC may contribute significantly to the fuel requirements.

Capital costs of thermal and catalytic incinerators are about the same. The cost of the catalyst is a significant part of the cost of a catalytic incinerator. But this is offset because a catalytic incinerator can be made of less expensive materials due to the lower combustion temperature. The lower fuel cost means that catalytic incineration can be evaluated as an alternative to thermal incineration at air flow rates above a few thousand scfm. A catalytic incinerator will typically achieve greater than 98 percent destruction of VOCs. This is very acceptable for controlling VOCs from coating and printing operations.

Replacing the catalyst is expensive, so catalytic incinerators should not be used when the catalyst could be contaminated. Burning chloride-containing VOCs produces HCL, which can attack the catalyst. Sulfur-containing VOCs can also attack some catalysts. Air streams that contain suspended particulate or produce particulate on combustion can cause the catalyst to be coated and rendered inert. If there is a VOC surge in the air stream, the VOC's fuel value could cause an exothermic reaction, raising the combustion temperature above the design limit and rendering the catalyst inert ("burning" the catalyst). This could result from a drying oven being loaded with freshly coated surfaces, thus producing an initial rapid evaporation of the VOCs.

Regenerative (Ceramic) Incinerators.   The regenerative incinerator has a ceramic heat exchanger. Heat from burning the VOCs is transferred to the ceramic exchanger. This heat then is used to heat the incoming VOC stream. The system has dual exchangers with one exchanger being heated while the other is giving up its heat. The incinerator achieves 98 to 99 percent destruction of VOCs at a combustion temperature of about 1400°F (760°C) with a thermal efficiency of up to 95 percent. The regenerative incinerator has the highest thermal efficiency of any incinerator, and therefore the lowest fuel cost. It is very effective in treating high volume air streams containing a VOC concentration up to a few hundred ppm.

The units typically range from 5000 to 100,000 scfm and weigh several tons. The size and weight restricts the location of the incinerator. The recuperative incinerator should be considered when air flow rates are several thousand scfm.

Regenerative Carbon Adsorption.   VOC-containing air passes through a bed of activated carbon. The VOCs are adsorbed into the carbon. When the bed is sufficiently loaded, VOCs are stripped from the bed using low-pressure steam followed by air drying. Steam and VOCs are recovered by condensation. For continuous operation, there are two or three carbon beds with one bed being regenerated while the other beds are loading. Regenerative carbon adsorption requires on-site steam and compressed air.

Carbon adsorption works very well for water-insoluble organic compounds that are liquid at room temperature. Process economics benefit if the recovered VOCs can be recycled. A single-stage unit can achieve up to 99 percent control. Carbon adsorption is usable for VOC concentrations between ten and several hundred ppm.

Carbon adsorption is less effective for:

- Organic compounds that are gases or very low boiling liquids at ambient temperatures
- Air streams above 100°F (38°C)
- Air streams above 50 percent relative humidity

Under these conditions, VOCs are not tightly held on carbon, and control efficiencies can be unsatisfactorily low. Ketones can undergo exothermic polymerization on the carbon surface, coating the carbon with a solid polymer that is not removable by steam stripping and so rendering the carbon nonadsorptive. The heat buildup can cause the carbon bed to ignite. If the VOCs are water soluble, they are dissolved in the condensed steam and the condensate requires treatment prior to discharge. Using an alternative VOC control method is usually preferable to treating the VOCs in the condensate.

Low VOC Concentration.   Air streams with a low VOC concentration are those below 100 ppm.

Once-Through Carbon Adsorption.   This differs from regenerative carbon adsorption in that activated carbon is in canisters furnished by the carbon supplier. VOC-containing air passes through the canisters. Instead of regenerating the carbon, spent canisters are exchanged by the supplier for fresh canisters.

Advantages are: minimal capital investment; steam and compressed air are not required, which makes canisters suitable for field sites; minimal labor and attention are required; and effective VOC loading is better in the low ppm concentration range.

Activated carbon will load 0.3 lb of typical VOCs per lb of carbon at 100 ppm and 0.15 lb per lb of carbon at 5 ppm. Steam stripping will leave 0.2 and 0.13 lb of VOCs on the carbon, respectively. So, for regenerative carbon the working margin is 0.1 lb of VOC per lb of carbon at 100 ppm (0.3 – 0.2) and 0.02 lb of VOC per lb of carbon at 5 ppm (0.15 – 0.13). Hence at 5 ppm, once-through carbon can load 0.15 lb of VOC per lb of carbon compared with 0.02 lb for regenerative systems.

The carbon canisters lack instrumentation and controls, so the carbon could become overloaded unless it is carefully monitored. Fluctuating or less-than-design air flow rates could cause the carbon to form channels reducing the effective capacity of the canister.

The VOC control cost is high for nonregenerative carbon. At a loading of 0.15 lb of VOC per lb of carbon and a carbon cost of $2.40 per lb, the VOC control cost for carbon alone is

$32,000 per ton ($2.40/0.15 × 2000). Any VOC control strategy is expensive for 5-ppm streams.

Carbon Adsorber-Incinerator Systems. A combination of a carbon adsorber and an incinerator can be used to control a high-volume, low-VOC content stream. For example, suppose it is necessary to control a 100,000-scfm stream having a 30-ppm VOC content and that incineration is the appropriate control method. Whatever mode of incineration was used, the fuel cost would be very high. However, the fuel cost could be greatly reduced by first passing the air stream through a carbon adsorber, followed by stripping the adsorber with warm air (say [121°C]), and then routing that air stream to the incinerator. The air stream out of the carbon adsorber could be 10,000 scfm with a VOC content of 300 ppm. In a catalytic incinerator, little or no supplemental fuel would be required. Capital costs for two control systems would be higher than for a single system, and two control systems would have more chance of being out of commission, but they would significantly reduce a very high fuel cost.

Reducing Process Air Flow Rates. Regulatory agencies now look at making VOC controls more feasible by reducing process air flow rates. For example, suppose a coating operation has five stations, each with an air flow rate of 20,000 scfm and a VOC content of 80 ppm. The combined air flow rate is 100,000 scfm and the VOC content is still 80 ppm. VOC controls would be very expensive. However, if the air flow from the five stations was put in series (the air from Station 1 goes to Station 2, which goes to Station 3, etc.), then the air flow rate is 20,000 scfm with a VOC content of 400 ppm. If the lower flammability level of this VOC is 1.6 percent or 16,000 ppm, the VOC content is still well below 25 percent of the LEL and may be economically controllable. When VOC controls are required, it may be technically and economically preferable to reduce the process air flow rate rather than buying a larger and more expensive control system.

Controlling NO$_x$ Emissions

Nitrogen oxides (NO$_x$) are products of all conventional combustion processes. Nitric oxide (NO) is the predominant form of NO$_x$ emitted by such sources with lesser amounts of nitrogen dioxide (NO$_2$) and nitrous oxide (N$_2$O). The NO can further oxidize in the atmosphere to NO$_2$. The generation of NO$_x$ from fuel combustion is a result of two formation mechanisms. Fuel NO$_x$ is formed by the reaction of nitrogen chemically bound in the fuel and oxygen in the combustion air at high temperature in the combustion zone. Thermal NO$_x$ is produced by the reaction of the molecular nitrogen and oxygen contained in the combustion air at high temperature in the combustion zone. The main factors influencing the NO$_x$ reaction are combustion temperature, residence time within the combustion zone, amount of fuel-bound nitrogen, and oxygen levels present in the combustion zone.

For some combustion sources, RACT, BACT, and LAER have and will require add-on controls or combustion modifications to limit NO$_x$ emissions. These add-on control technologies are relatively new and can represent high capital and maintenance costs, especially for industrial boilers and heaters. The low-cost combustion modification techniques involve burner modifications with total capital cost under $50,000 per boiler.

Combustion Modification Techniques

Burners Out of Service (BOOS). On multiple-burner units, simply taking one or more burners out of service lowers the potential flame temperature (PFT) through several mechanisms. These include increasing gas flow to any particular remaining burner and reducing the flame temperature by reducing the flame-to-flame radiant exchange.

BOOS cost little to implement. This technique often is most effective in reducing NO$_x$ for burners at middle to upper elevations in a boiler.

Boiler Derating. Boiler derating can be an acceptable procedure for industrial boilers under certain conditions. For example, steam demand may decrease when certain processes are phased out or replaced by a more energy-efficient process; or a plant's energy use can be reduced through efficiency planning. In such cases, the boilers may be derated to fire at lower loads.

Derating can be as simple as reducing the firing rate. Or a facility may be permanently derated, for regulatory reasons, to take advantage of a higher NO_x limit for a lower-rated boiler. Even permanent derating can be accomplished inexpensively, for example, by installing a permanent restriction, such as an orifice plate, in the fuel line. If a boiler derating is impossible, often the burners themselves can be modified to reduce NO_x concentrations.

Burner-System Modification. BSM is a relatively underused and low-cost strategy that can produce marked NO_x reductions. It can be used on ring and spud burners, the two main types. BSM may also consist of modifications to the air registers surrounding the burner. These modifications may require a level of expertise not usually found in the boiler house. However, many industrial facilities possess a machine shop and fabrication capabilities. In such a case, the costs of BSM can be reduced by performing the work in-house under the guidance of a qualified combustion consultant.

Oxygen and Combustible Trim. Installation of oxygen or combustible trim controls increases boiler efficiency and reduces NO_x by limiting the amount of influent air admitted to the boiler. Systems costing less than \$10,000 are available to monitor and automatically trim O_2 or combustibles to the desired levels. O_2 is usually reduced to about 3 percent. Combustible trim reduces combustible concentration to a target level, e.g., 200 ppmvd in the furnace. Combustibles are usually reduced to lower their levels at the stack outlet due to their subsequent oxidation in the boiler. An alternative type of trim—the deliberate generation of combustibles—forces oxygen concentration to its minimum possible concentration, thereby reducing PFT. However, combustibles must not exceed certain levels because boiler corrosion can be accelerated by attendant flame impingement and a reducing atmosphere, or, in the case of unstable flames, by an alternating reducing and oxidizing atmosphere.

Steam Injection (SI) and Water Injection (WI). SI and WI are commonly applied to gas turbines to limit NO_x emissions. SI reduces the PFT by diluting oxygen near the burner front and directly removing heat from the burner flame. WI functions in a similar way, but removes even more heat from the burner flame due to its heat of vaporization. Both SI and WI lower boiler thermal efficiency—typically by no more than 1 or 2 percent. Most industrial boilers can turbine these losses, through utility units cannot. SI or WI may be the lowest cost option for reducing NO_x to less than 40 ppmvd, if simple combustion modifications are not successful.

Staged Combustions (SC). This technique deliberately partitions the air (air staging) or fuel (fuel staging) to create an initial, fuel-rich zone followed by an air-rich one to complete the combustion. SC uses a volume of air that is equal to or slightly greater than that for conventional combustion; however, the PFT is reduced because initial oxygen concentrations are reduced. SC is usually done in two separate sections of the boiler, and requires a large furnace volume. SC is sometimes adaptable to smaller boilers. Some low-NO_x burners stage combustion over short lengths to reduce NO_x.

The term *staging* means allowing fuel and air to react in multiple zones, or stages, rather than all at once. Compared with conventional combustion, SC tends to limit large excesses of temperature and oxygen, producing lower NO_x. This can be accomplished over small distances along the burner itself if the fuel, air, or both, are injected at multiple locations along the burner.

Alternate Fuels. This term refers to fuels other than natural gas and fuel oil. If a boiler cannot meet mandated NO_x levels with its existing fuel, a switch to an alternate fuel may prove worthwhile. Capital costs for implementing alternate fuels range widely. For example, a facility containing equipment that can handle both fuel oil and natural gas can switch between fuels with minimal costs. However, if using an alternate fuel requires new handling and storage equipment, costs may exceed \$50,000 per boiler.

Flue-Gas Recirculation (FGR). In this technique, a portion of the flue gas is withdrawn from the boiler stack and introduced with the combustion air. The oxygen availability is reduced, thus reducing the PFT and NO_x. Most applications recirculate roughly 20 percent of the flue gas to achieve less than 40 ppmvd NO_x. However, excessive FGR can produce unsafe, unstable flames and result in an increase in CO emissions.

Low-NO$_x$ Burners (LNB). These reduce NO$_x$ by replacing high-NO$_x$-producing burners. Most, but not all, LNBs are spud-type burners specifically designed to produce flames with lower PFT. This is usually done with bluff bodies and gas ports that induce recirculation zones and reduce local oxygen concentrations close to the burner. Bluff bodies also increase flame stability, which is more critically needed when local oxygen concentrations are deliberately reduced. LNB is nearly always combined with FGR.

Postcombustion Techniques

Selective Catalytic Reduction (SCR). In the SCR process, NO$_x$ is reduced to N$_2$ and H$_2$O by ammonia (NH$_3$) within a temperature range of approximately 540 to 840°F in the presence of a catalyst, usually a base metal. The lower end of the operating temperature range is feasible when the acid gas impurity level is relatively low. NH$_3$ has been used as an acceptable reducing agent for NO$_x$ in combustion gases because it selectively reacts with NO$_x$, while other reducing agents such as H$_2$, CO, and CH$_4$ also readily react with O$_2$ in the gases. In a typical configuration, flue gas from the combustion source is passed through a reactor which contains the catalyst bed. Parallel flow catalyst beds may be used in which the combustion exhaust gas flows through channels rather than pores to minimize blinding of the catalyst by particulate matter. Ammonia in vapor phase is injected into the flue gas downstream of the other control equipment that may be required for the particular combustion process (for removal of pollutants such as particulate matter and sulfur dioxide). The ammonia is normally injected at a 1-to-1 molar ratio based upon the NO$_x$ concentration in the flue gas. Major capital equipment for SCR consists of the reactor and catalyst, ammonia storage tanks, and an ammonia injection system using either compressed air or steam as a carrier gas. Because of the toxic characteristics of NH$_3$, appropriate storage and handling safety features must be provided if anhydrous NH$_3$ is used. NO$_x$ removal efficiencies approaching 90 percent have been reported when using SCR systems for boiler and gas-turbine applications.

Selective noncatalytic reduction (SNCR) involves ammonia, either anhydrous or in solution with water, or urea injection without a catalyst. Major SNCR systems commercially available are: the Exxon Thermal DeNO$_x$ ammonia (anhydrous or aqueous) injection system, Nalco Fuel Tech NO$_x$OUT urea injection system and the Noell (formerly Emcotek) two-stage DeNO$_x$ (urea or aqueous ammonia) injection system.

Exxon Thermal DeNO$_x$. Exxon Thermal DeNO$_x$ ammonia injection, like SCR, uses the NO$_x$/ammonia reaction to convert NO$_x$ to molecular nitrogen. However, without catalyst use or supplemental hydrogen injection, NO$_x$ reduction reaction temperatures must be tightly controlled between 1600 and 2200°F (871 and 1204°C) (between 1600 and 1800°F (871 and 981°C) for optimum efficiency). Below 1600°F (871°C), and without hydrogen also being injected, ammonia will not fully react, resulting in what is called ammonia breakthrough or slip. If the temperature rises above 1800°F (981°C), a competing reaction begins to predominate:

$$NH_3 + \tfrac{5}{4} O_2 \rightarrow NO + \tfrac{3}{2} H_2O$$

As indicated above, this reaction increases NO emissions. Therefore, the region within the boiler where ammonia is injected must be carefully selected to ensure that the optimum reduction reaction temperature will be maintained.

For this noncatalytic NO$_x$ reducing process, ammonia must be injected at a 2:1 molar ratio (based upon the flue gas NO$_x$ concentration). Therefore, there is some "slip" of ammonia that does not react completely and can potentially cause odors. Also, fine particulate emissions that create a visible plume can be formed from the reaction of ammonia and hydrogen chloride (a solid fuel combustion by-product) downwind of the stack. It is, therefore, important to keep the NO$_x$ injection rate to the minimum necessary.

Noell Staged DeNO$_x$ Injection System. The staged DeNO$_x$ system, developed and patented by Noell, Inc., utilizes successive stages of postcombustion chemical injection. Bulk granular urea is mixed with water or aqueous ammonia is injected in four injection "windows" around the boiler. The process is similar to the Exxon process described previously.

The main difference is that by "staging" the injection points of the urea or aqueous ammonia, greater reduction of NO_x missions are achieved. The staging is particularly effective in larger boilers where wide fluctuations in temperature are common. The staging allows for strategic placement of the injected points in areas of higher temperature. Since the boilers are relatively small compared to utility boilers, staging will not significantly alter NO_x control efficiency.

BIBLIOGRAPHY*

1. EPA: "Compilation of BACT/LAER Determinations—Revised," EPA 450/2-80-70, May 1980.
2. EPA: "Compilation of Emission Factors," AP-42 and Supplements, Research Triangle Park, North Carolina, April 1981.
3. EPA, OAQPS: "Ambient Monitoring Guidelines for Prevention of Significant Deterioration (PDS)," EPA 450/4-80-012, November 1980.
4. EPA, OAQPS: *Guidelines for Air Quality Maintenance Planning and Analysis,* vol. 10, "Procedures for Evaluating Air Quality Impact of Near Stationary Sources," EPA-450/4-77-001, Research Triangle Park, North Carolina, October 1977.
5. EPA, OAQPS: "Guideline on Air Quality Models," EPA-450/2-78-027, Research Triangle Park, NC, April 1978.
6. EPA, OAQPS, Region III: "Guidelines for Determining BACT," Philadelphia, December 1978.
7. EPA, Region III: "Permit Application Kit, Prevention of Significant Air Quality Deterioration," Air Programs Branch, Philadelphia, November 1978.
8. EPA, Technology Transfer: "Industrial Guide for Air Pollution Control," Contract 68-01-4147, by PED Co. Environmental, Inc., June 1978.
9. EPA: *Control Techniques for Particulate Emissions from Stationary Sources,* vol. 1, EPA 450/3-81/005a Research Triangle Park, NC, 1982.
10. EPA: *Handbook-Control Technologies for Hazardous Air Pollutants* EPA 625/6-86/014 Center for Environmental Research Information, 1986.
11. *Federal Register,* 1977 Clean Air Act, PSD, SIP Requirements, Part 52, June 19, 1978.
12. *Federal Register,* 40 CFR Parts 51 and 52, September 5, 1979.
13. *Federal Register,* 40 CFR Parts 51 and 52, February 5, 1980.
14. Quarles, J., Jr.: "Federal Regulation of New Industrial Plants," P.O. Box 998, Ben Franklin Station, Washington, DC 20044, January 1979.
15. Rymarz, T. M., and D. H. Klipstein: "Removing Particulates from Gases," *Chemical Engineering Deskbook,* vol. 82, no. 21, October 6, 1975, pp. 113–120.
16. Corbitt, R. A.: *Standard Handbook of Environmental Engineering,* McGraw-Hill, New York, 1990.

*Due to the proliferation of new regulations and technology, the reader is urged to research the latest publications, government and private.

CHAPTER 13-2
LIQUID-WASTE DISPOSAL*

William M. Throop, P.E.
Envirex Inc.
Waukesha, Wisconsin

GLOSSARY

Alkalinity Ability to neutralize acids—determined by the water's content of carbonates, bicarbonates, hydroxides, and borates, silicates, and phosphates, if present. Expressed in milligrams per liter of calcium carbonate ($CaCo_3$).

BOD_5 (biochemical oxygen demand) A measure of oxygen metabolized, in milligrams per liter, in five days by microorganisms that consume biodegradable organics in wastewater under aerobic (with air) conditions.

COD (chemical oxygen demand) The amount of oxygen, in milligrams per liter, needed to oxidize both organic and oxidizable inorganic compounds.

Effluent The liquid end product discharging from a process.

Floating matter Matter that passes through a 2000-μm sieve and separates by flotation in an hour.

Settleable solids Solids larger than 0.01 mm in diameter settling in two hours under quiescence.

---

*Updated for this Second Edition by the Editor-in-Chief.

Suspended solids   Small filterable particles of solid pollutants in wastewater. The examination of suspended solids and the BOD_5 test constitute the two main determinations for water quality.

Total solids   All dissolved, suspended, and settleable solids contained in a liquid.

Turbidity   The amount of suspended matter in wastewater; quantity obtained by measuring its light-scattering ability.

DESCRIPTION OF THE PROBLEM

The passage of the Federal Water Pollution Control Act as amended in 1977 under Public Law 92-217 forced the plant engineer to become familiar with its many ramifications. Among the provisions of this act that are of direct interest to industry is the establishment of water quality standards typified by Table 2-1, column A, for maintaining aquatic life.[1] These restrictions are enforced by the requirement that a permit be issued before discharges are permitted under the National Pollutant Discharge Elimination System (NPDES). Every holder of a NPDES permit is required to comply with monitoring sampling, recording, and reporting requirements.

In 1987, further amendments were incorporated into the Water Quality Act (WQA). These amendments were aimed principally to improve water quality in areas that lacked compliance with minimum national discharge standards. This is an ongoing, active regulatory area; the reader is urged to check the latest regulations before proceeding with plant modifications.

Many local ordinances have pretreatment requirements limiting high effluent concentrations of wastes and toxic materials which might adversely affect treatment processes of publicly owned treatment works (POTW). A typical list of effluent limitations is shown in Table 2-1, column B.[2] When discharging to POTWs, industry is expected to pay its proportionate share of capital cost of the POTWs collection and treatment equipment. These user fees are usually based on a multiplier of BOD_5, suspended solids, and liquid volume, and vary with each municipality.

For specific pollutants, effluent guidelines for specific industrial categories are published in the *Code of Federal Regulations* (40 CFR 401).

Different effluent levels are allowable depending on the following:

1. Industrial subcategory
2. Control technology required (e.g., best available technology economically achievable)
3. Existing or new source (new sources are more severely regulated than existing sources)
4. Where the effluents are discharged (effluent levels discharged into POTWs are different from direct discharges into navigable water)

For details pertaining to emissions by specific industry, the *Code of Federal Regulations* should be consulted. Because the promulgation of effluent guidelines is an ongoing process, the EPA should be contacted for the latest information.

All pollutants are classified as either conventional, toxic, or nonconventional. Conventional pollutants include BOD_5, TSS (total suspended solids), and pH. There are 129 priority pollutants that appear on the toxics list in the *Federal Register* 43(164)4108 (February 1978). Nonconventional pollutants are those that are neither toxic nor conventional, such as nitrogen, oil, and grease. Best conventional pollutant control technology will be required for conventional pollutants by July 1, 1984. Best available technology economically achievable will be required for toxic and nonconventional pollutants by the same date.

TABLE 2-1 Maximum Discharge Limits

Constituent	A Direct discharge or recycle, mg/L	B* To POTW
Ammonia nitrogen (as N)	1.5	—
Arsenic (total)	1.0	—
Barium (total)	5.0	—
Boron (total)	1.0	1.0
Cadmium (total)	0.05	2.0
Chromium (total)	—	25.0
Chromium (total hexavalent)	0.05	10.0
Chromium (total trivalent)	1.0	—
Copper (total)	0.02	3.0
Cyanide (total)	0.025	@150°F & pH 4.5 = 2.0
Fluoride (total)	1.4	—
Iron (total)	1.0	50.0
Iron (dissolved)	0.5	—
Lead (total)	0.1	0.5
Manganese (total)	1.0	—
Mercury (total)	0.0005	0.0005
Nickel (total)	1.0	10.0
Fats, oils, and greases (FOG)	15.0	100.0 total
pH	5.0–10.0	4.5–10.0
Phenols	0.1	—
Phosphorus (as P)	1.0	—
Selenium (total)	1.0	—
Silver	0.005	—
Sulfate	500.0	—
Temperature	—	150°F (65°C)
Zinc (total)	1.0	—
Total dissolved solids	1000.0	No limit

* Units are milligrams per liter unless otherwise specified.

PLANT SURVEY

The accurate measurement of flow volume and pollutants in the waste flow are essential in assessing any wastewater problem, and in designing a wastewater treatment system. Limitations on effluent (see Table 2-1) make it imperative to analyze flows and impurities quickly, accurately, and at reasonable cost.

The best approach is to make a comprehensive wastewater survey that will (1) determine the quantity of wastewater discharge, (2) locate the major sources of waste within the plant, (3) determine wastewater composition, (4) explore in-plant or process changes to minimize the waste problem, (5) establish the basis for wastewater treatment, and (6) evaluate effect of wastes on the receiving stream.

Composition of wastewater varies with the amount of impurities initially present in water and the chemical analysis of any pollutants that are added. While domestic sewage has a fairly uniform composition, industrial wastes have an almost infinite variety of characteristics, as shown in Table 2-2. Wastewaters should be analyzed for at least BOD_5, COD, color, total solids (suspended and dissolved), pH, and turbidity. Other impurities of interest will vary with the source and type of wastewater.

TABLE 2-2 Typical Process Discharge Volumes, BOD_5, and Suspended Solids for Industrial Wastewater Before Treatment

	Unit processed	Discharge per unit		BOD_5, mg/L	Suspended solids, mg/L
		Gallons	Liters		
Aluminum & copper	lb (kg)	12–13	45–50	N/A	300–500
Automotive	Car	10800	40900	190	215
Beverage, malt	bbl (L)	330	1250	390–1800	70–100
Canning					
Fruit	Case	20–40	75–150	300–1600	200–500
Vegetable	Case	50–100	190–380	700–2000	300–2000
Coal washing	ton (tonne)	125	138	N/A	2000–3000
Cooking	ton (tonne)	1500–2800	1650–3090	50–200	90
Dairy, milk	gal (L)	4–12	15–45	1800	560–4000
Electrical	kWh (kJ)	80	110	N/A	50–2000
Laundry					
Commercial wash	ton (tonne)	8600	36000	600–1860	400–2200
Industrial	ton (tonne)	5000	20000	650–1300	4900–8600
Manufacturing, gen. fabr.	ton (tonne)	700	3000	50–1500	200–15000
Meat packing					
Cattle	Animal	400–2000	1515–7575	400–900	400–800
Chicken	Bird	8–9	30–34	150–2400	100–1500
Hogs	Animal	300–600	1136–2273	1000	650
Office building	Person	30–45	114–170	117	176
Paint, latex	gal (L)	3	11	2000–3000	15000–60000
Paper making	lb. (kg)	65	108	200–800	500–1200
Pharmaceutical	—	—	—	600–2500	500–1000
Phenolic resins	ton (tonne)	75000	313000	11500	40
Railway maintenance	Locomotive	3000	11360	500–800	200–600
Refining	bbl crude	770	2900	100–500	300–700
Rubber, synthetic	Car tire	500	1890	25–1600	60–2200
Steel					
Cold-rolled	lb (kg)	9	15	150	100–300
Hot-rolled	lb (kg)	18	30	80	500–2000
Tanning, hide	lb (kg)	8–12	30–45	900	6000
Textiles					
Synthetic	lb (kg)	12–25	45–95	1500–6000	500
Wool	lb (kg)	70	265	900	100
Vegetable oil	gal (L)	22	83	3050	900

Concentration of pollutants must be correlated with average, minimum, and maximum flows encountered. The analysis program must also take effluent water quality standards into account (see Table 2-1) and the BOD_5 reduction required to meet them. Any toxic impurities in the wastewater that adversely affect water quality must be determined.

Sampling and Flow Measurement

The starting point in any wastewater survey is an effective program of sampling and flow measurement. To be useful, a sample of wastewater must accurately represent the source from which it is taken and be large enough to run all the laboratory tests required. This means the method of sampling must be tailored to the type and kind of wastewater flow. A close check of each waste source will reveal whether flow is continuous or intermittent and any wide swings in flow rate.

It is also important to know if the concentration of pollutants changes drastically or is fairly constant. The presence of oil or excessive suspended solids may also cause problems.

An integral part of this program is the need to obtain flow information on various in-plant streams as well as the plant outfalls. Wastewater flows are measured for the following reasons:

1. To determine the quantity of water being discharged, as well as variations in the flow rate
2. To determine the number of pounds of constituents being discharged on the basis of the analytical data and the determined flow rate
3. To evaluate segregation possibilities
4. To determine the effect of the wastewater discharge on the receiving stream, if applicable

Measuring Rate of Flow.   Rates of flow can be approximated by the methods discussed in the following paragraphs.

Water Meters on Influent Lines.   Water consumption in the plant should be determined during a wastewater survey to check on wastewater-flow measurements and to compute a water balance for the plant. Meters can also be installed at particular water-using operations to obtain flow data.

Container and Stopwatch.   The time required to obtain a given volume of water in a container is measured. Volume can be determined either by weight added or by a calibrated collection container. The weight of water added is divided by 8.34 lb/gal to determine the number of gallons collected. The flow is then determined by the formula

$$\frac{\text{Gal in container} \times 60}{\text{Time, s, to fill container}} = \frac{\text{gal/min}}{15.85} = \text{L s}^{-1}$$

If the container fills in less than 10 s, the accuracy of this method is questionable.

Weirs.   A weir acts like a dam or obstruction, with the water flowing through the notch, which is usually rectangular or V-shaped.

To ensure accurate weir measurements:

1. The weir crest must be sharp or at least square-edged. Steel is the best construction material, but tempered wood is also used.
2. The weir must be ventilated. There must be air on the underside of the falling water.
3. Leaks around the weir plate must be sealed.
4. The weir must be exactly level.
5. Weirs should be kept clean.
6. The head on the weir should be measured at a distance of 2.5 times the head upstream from the weir.
7. The channel upstream from the weir should be straight, level, and free from disturbing influences. A stilling box may be used to quiet the water flow.
8. The weir should be sized after the flow is estimated by other methods. The head on any weir should be greater than 3 in (7.6 cm) but not more than 2 ft (61 cm).

The flow over V-notched (triangular) weirs and rectangular weirs can be taken from the nomographs shown in Fig. 2-1.

Parshall Flume.   A Parshall flume (Fig. 2-2) can be used to measure flows in open channels at or near ground surface. This device is valuable when it is not possible to dam the water. It is also advisable for a permanent installation because it is self-cleaning.

Flow under submerged conditions can be calculated from readings taken at gauges. If the water surface downstream from the flume is high enough to retard the rate of discharge, submerged flow exists. When there is no backwater effect, water passing through the throat and diverging section assumes a level which corresponds to the floor of the channel. This pattern demonstrates free flow.

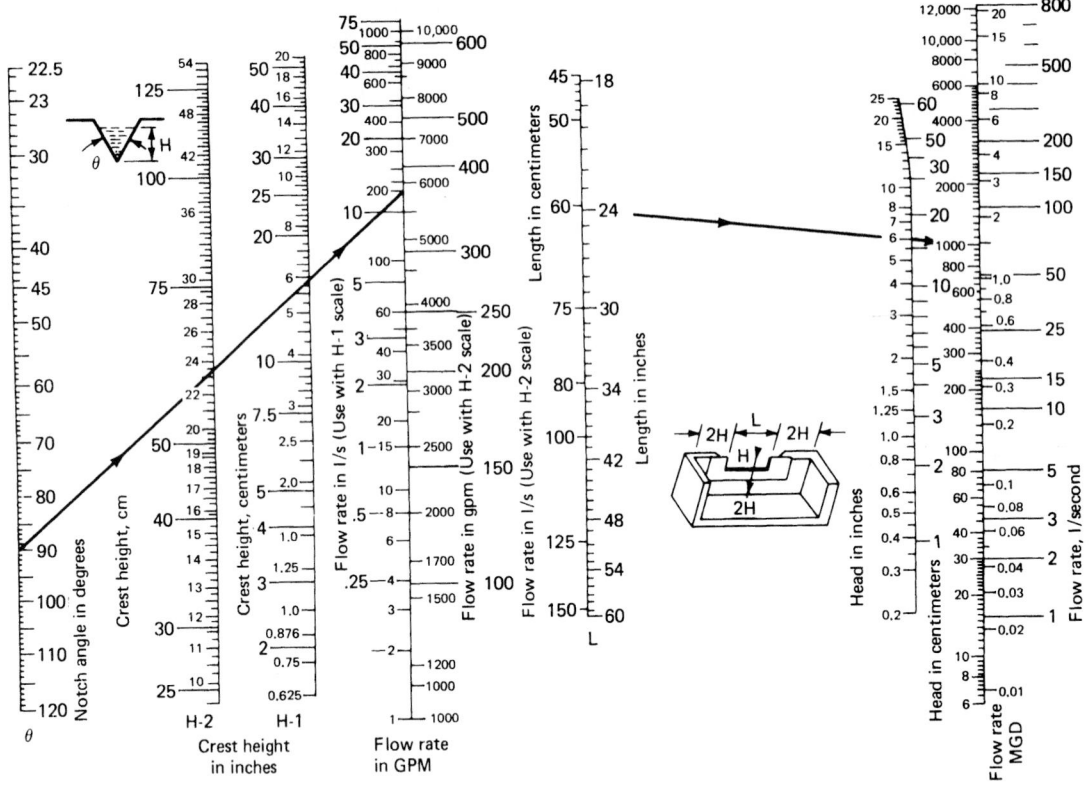

Flow for V-notch (triangular) weirs

Flow for rectangular weirs

FIGURE 2-1   Nomographs for measuring flow over weirs.

The flow of a free discharge from a Parshall flume is calculated by

$$Q = 4WH_an$$

where Q = flow, ft^3/s
W = throat width, ft
H_a = head of water above level floor, ft
n = $1.522\ W^{0.026}$

or in metric units

$$Q = 8.52 \times 10^3 (11.4 \log W) H_a (1.57 + 0.09 \log W)$$

where Q = flow, m^3/h
W = throat width, m
H_a = head of water above level floor, m

Flow under submerged conditions can be calculated from readings taken at gauges, one located at a point two-thirds the length of the converging section measured back from the crest of the flume H_a and one located near the downstream end of the throat section H_b. Degree of submergence is given by the ratio H_b/H_a.

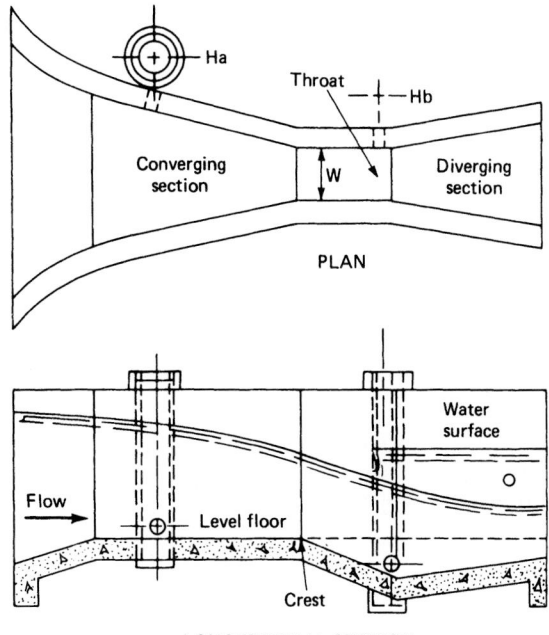

FIGURE 2-2 Parshall flume.

Sample Collection and Analysis.   Wastewaters are sampled and analyzed to identify those pollutants that require treatment and to select the proper treatment process.

   Collecting Samples.   Since a wastewater's characteristics can vary considerably, composite samples are collected to obtain a truer representation of the waste. Small samples are collected at frequent intervals during the sampling period. They are mixed together to form the composite sample.

   Compositing Samples.   Depending on plant operation, 8-, 16-, or 24-h composites can be collected. Daily sampling for 3 days generally constitutes a sampling program. Samples can be composited on the basis of the following criteria.

   Flow. The amount of sample collected at any time during the sampling period is proportional to the flow of wastewater at that time.

   Time. The same amount of sample is collected at every interval during the sampling period regardless of variations in wastewater flows.

   Sample Size.   The sample size collected at any one time should be at least 200 mL. Composite samples can be collected either manually or with automatic samplers. Automatic, battery-operated samplers are available for collecting composite samples on the basis of flow or time.

   Amount of sample to be collected depends upon the laboratory tests to be run. The amount of sample required for each test to be performed should be determined before the sampling program is begun to ensure that sufficient sample is collected.

   Analytical Determinations.   Determinations that may be conducted on a wastewater sample are:

pH	Copper
Alkalinity or acidity	Nickel
Total hardness	Zinc

Chloride	Chromium, hexavalent
Sulfate	Chromium, total
Suspended solids	Iron
Volatile suspended solids	Manganese
Settleable solids	Solvent soluble (oil)
Total nitrogen	Phenol
Ammonia nitrogen	Biochemical oxygen demand (BOD_5)
Total phosphate	Chemical oxygen demand (COD)
Total solids	Total organic carbon (TOC)
Volatile total solids	Cyanide

Standard methods are available for conducting these determinations. Phases involved in a full pollution control program are:

I. Definition of the problem and development of an action plan (survey or feasibility study)
II. Detailed engineering
III. Construction and start-up

An outline of the steps involved in each of these phases is shown in Table 2-3.

TREATMENT

The necessity of effective industrial wastewater treatment must be considered an integral part of the manufacturing process, and the cost of treatment must be charged against the product.

The method of treatment depends on economic considerations and the degree of treatment required. The best alternative system for pollutant removal must be selected on the basis of a case-by-case study of efficiency and actual costs. It must be recognized that a complete system may involve several unit components and that pretreatment is required before tertiary treatment.

Figure 2-3 illustrates various treatment units combined to form a treatment system. Figure 2-4 shows the various treatment processes classified according to type, and illustrates how they can be combined to give the desired effluent quality.

Primary Treatment

The physical removal or combined chemical coagulation and physical removal of solids from wastewater is classified as primary treatment, especially if these processes are followed by biological treatment. Gravity or flotation units are used to remove suspended or coagulated colloidal material. Solids thus concentrated can be treated more economically by disposal, incineration, or biological degradation.

Oily waters are usually treated separately to remove the oil prior to mixing them with other waste streams. Chemicals can be used to enhance gravity separation of oil when emulsions are present.

Figure 2-5 presents a general guide for the design of a gravity separator based on parameters set forth by the American Petroleum Institute. It is desirable to have a minimum depth of 5 ft (1.5 m), a maximum horizontal flow-through velocity not exceeding 3 ft³/min (0.015 L/s), and a minimum length-to-width ratio of 3:1 with a depth-to-width ratio of 0.3 to 0.5

Alkaline or acidic waste streams must be neutralized before secondary treatment or discharge.

TABLE 2-3 Pollution Control Program

I. Survey or feasibility study
   A. Fact finding:
      1. Develop a plant water balance for average and peak operating conditions.
      2. Inventory all industrial processes using water.
      3. Determine characteristics of the receiving waterway both upstream and downstream from plant's discharge.
      4. Determine chemical characteristics of waste streams.
      5. Study all operations using water and producing wastes.
      6. Determine local requirements with respect to pollution.
   B. Analyze data to determine:
      1. Sources of offending contaminants.
      2. Feasibility of segregating contaminated wastes requiring treatment from dilute wastes which would be acceptable without treatment.
      3. Availability of "natural" dilution waters, that is, waters employed for useful purposes but not contaminated.
      4. Quality of effluent required for compliance with discharge standards.
      5. Whether treatment is necessary.
   C. Exploit in-plant and/or process changes to minimize the problems by:
      1. Reducing wastes or waste volume at sources.
      2. Exploring the possibilities for reuse of process materials without treatment.
      3. Investigating recovery of valuable process materials.
      4. Reexamining the degrees of treatment required to meet standards.
      5. Reevaluating to decide whether treatment is necessary.
   D. Detailed report on the engineering survey:
      1. Recommend a preliminary course of action.
      2. Advise management whether a waste-treatment plant is necessary.
      3. Describe the general type of plant required.
      4. Provide preliminary estimate of construction cost.
      5. Prepare preliminary estimate of operating costs.
II. Detailed engineering
   A. Process design and evaluation:
      1. Assign liaison and engineering personnel as required.
      2. Evaluate bench scale or pilot plant data.
      3. Translate the total evaluated data into process flow diagrams and functional specifications for the treatment plant.
      4. Prepare plot plan showing layout on plant site.
      5. Assemble an engineering report for review and approval.
      6. Obtain preliminary approval of regulatory agency.
   B. Definitive engineering:
      1. Prepare detailed engineering flow diagrams which form the basis of final plant design.
      2. Obtain approval of overall plant design.
      3. Complete the definitive design.
      4. Obtain final approval and permit of regulatory agency.
III. Construction and start-up
   A. Procurement and scheduling:
      1. Prepare complete equipment specifications, bills of material, and preliminary timetable.
      2. Prepare item delivery and installation schedule.
      3. Use critical-path scheduling when warranted.
      4. Coordinate and inspect all phases of the work performed by fabricators.
   B. Facilities erection and testing:
      1. Plan, supervise, and coordinate erection of the complete wastewater-treatment plant.
      2. Conduct unit tests, after assembly, to assure proper functioning of all related facilities.
      3. Inspect, adjust, and calibrate instruments and controls to conform to high accuracy standards, with engineers performing the work.

TABLE 2-3 Pollution Control Program (*Continued*)

C. Operator training:
    1. Prepare detailed operating manuals for all unit operations in the plant.
    2. Assemble vendors' manuals for use by plant personnel in maintaining, repairing, and replacing mechanical, instrument, and electric equipment parts.
    3. Assist with training of operating crews while construction work is in the final stages.
D. Start-up of treatment facilities:
    1. Initiate a control testing program.
       a. Operational
       b. Quality of effluent
    2. Initiate an efficiency testing program.
    3. Establish conditions for operations.
    4. Initiate a development program.
    5. Establish record-keeping procedures.
E. Supervise operation.

Secondary Treatment

Secondary treatment is used to reduce soluble organic pollutants that are degradable to certain levels of organic materials remaining (the degradation products). If the effluent quality required is higher than that which can be obtained by biological treatment, tertiary processes are needed to remove the degradable with the undegradable fractions.

Commonly used secondary-treatment processes include the completely mixed activated-sludge process, extended aeration, aerobic and aerated lagoons, trickling filters, and anaerobic and facultative waste stabilization ponds.

Table 2-4 is indicative of removal efficiencies for unit treatment processes.

EQUIPMENT

Various unit items of equipment are combined to provide the degree of treatment required.

TABLE 2-4 Treatment-Process Removal Efficiencies

		Removal efficiency, %			
Treatment method	BOD$_5$	Suspended solids	Total dissolved solids	Fats, oils, & greases	Alkalinity
Screening	0–5	5–20	0	0	0
Sedimentation	5–15	15–6	0	5–15	0
Chemical precipitation	25–60	30–90	0–50	10–40	80–95
Dissolved-air flotation	10–30	70–85	10–20	80–95	10–20
Trickling filter	40–85	80–90	0–30	10–20	10–25
Nonaerated lagoon	30–70	30–70	30–80	0–40	10–20
Aerated lagoon	50–80	50–90	0–40	5–15	10–20
Activated-sludge	70–90	85–95	0–40	0–15	15–30
Filtration	80–85	30–70	10–60	0–10	10–20
Activated carbon	95–99	95–99	10	N/A	85–90
Ion-exchange	N/A	N/A	95–99	N/A	99
Reverse osmosis	N/A	N/A	99	N/A	99

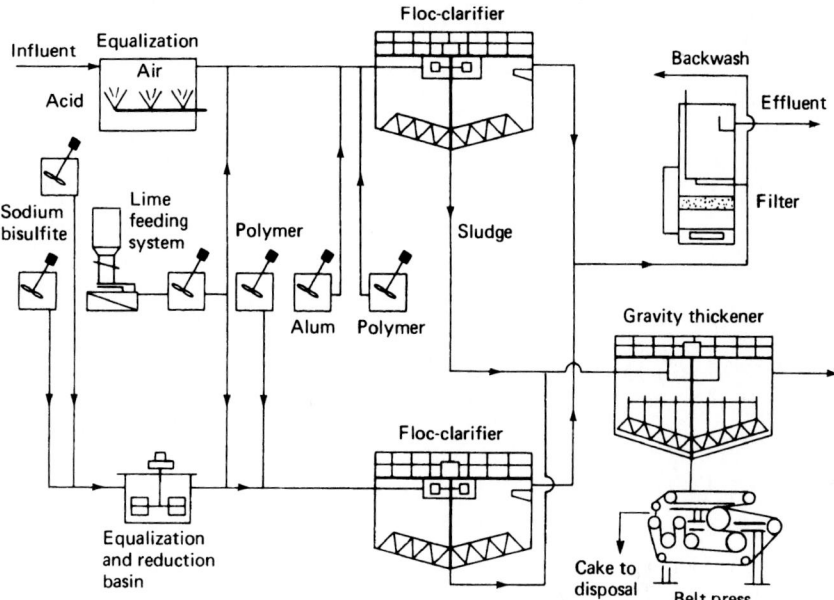

FIGURE 2-3   General manufacturing wastewater treatment.

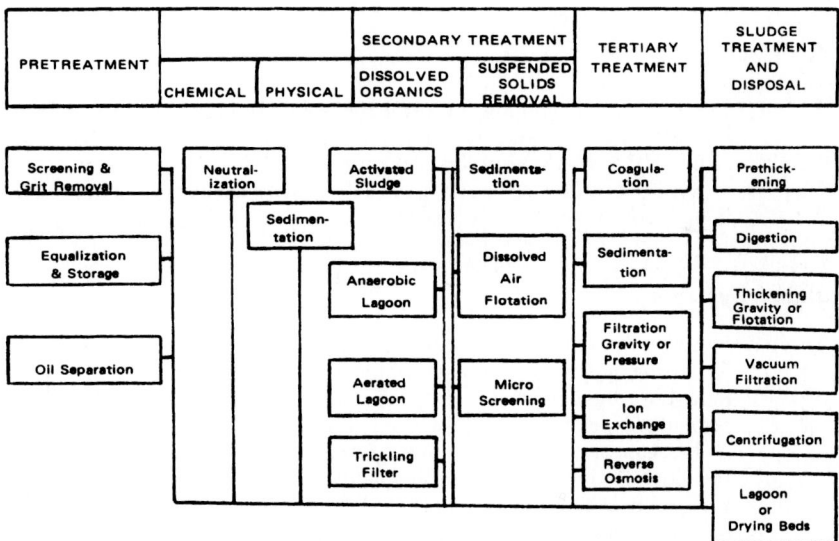

FIGURE 2-4   Alternatives for wastewater pollutant removal processes and how they may be combined in treatment programs.

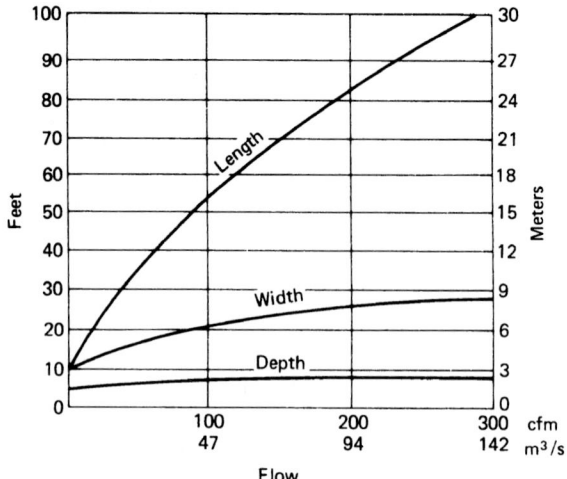

FIGURE 2-5 Design of gravity separator.

Bar Screens

A mechanically cleaned bar screen, like the one shown in Fig. 2-6, is the simplest tool for removing debris or suspended matter which could damage equipment or disrupt the treatment process. All solids with larger than ¾- to 2-in (2- to 5-cm) bar rack openings are trapped on the upstream side and removed by moving rakes.

Clarifiers

Clarifiers used for removal of settleable solids and readily floating oils and greases are either rectangular or circular basins (Figs. 2-7 and 2-8). Clarifiers are sized on the basis of settling rate (area) and detention time (volume).

Typical overflow rates vary from 250 to 1400 gal/(day)(ft^2) [10 to 50 m^3/(day)(m^2)]. Detention time is in the range of 1 to 4 h.

Flocculation Systems

Flocculation is the agglomeration of finely divided suspended matter and floc caused by gently stirring or agitating the wastewater. The resulting increase in particle size increases the settling rate and improves suspended solids removal by providing more efficient contact between suspended solids, dissolved impurities, and chemical coagulants.

Mechanical flocculation uses paddles slowly rotating on a horizontal or vertical axis (Fig. 2-9). Peripheral speed at the paddle tip is about 1 ft/s. Various other mechanical devices are used to achieve the same result. An air flocculation system has diffusers along one side of the basin near the bottom to produce a gentle rollover action perpendicular to flow.

The size of the required basin is determined by the detention time, which is normally in the range of 20 to 30 min at rated flow. In some cases involving industrial wastes, detention may be reduced to as little as 10 min.

Combined Equipment

Many clarifier designs, such as the solids contact unit (Fig. 2-10), combine mixing, flocculation, and coagulation in one basin. This may have economic advantages and may produce bet-

FIGURE 2-6 Mechanically cleaned bar screen. (*Envirex.*)

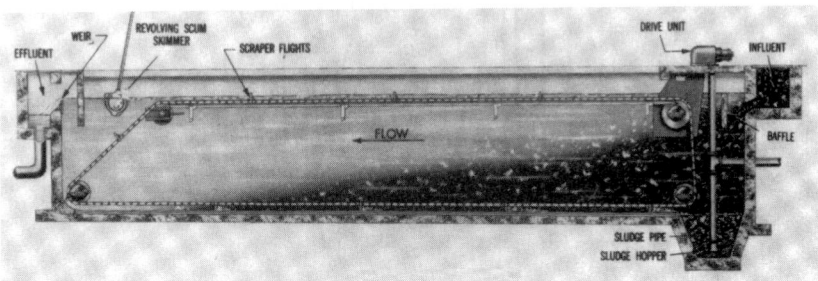

FIGURE 2-7 Clarifier for a rectangular basin. (*Envirex.*)

ter-quality effluent with shorter overall detention time than the approach using separate treatment units.

Flotation Systems

Flotation is sedimentation in reverse to remove floatable materials and solids with a specific gravity so close to that of water that they settle very slowly or not at all. The principle of air flotation is based on the fact that when the pressure on a liquid is reduced, dissolved gases are released as extremely fine bubbles. These bubbles attach themselves to any suspended matter present and rapidly float them to the surface, where they concentrate and can be removed by skimming.

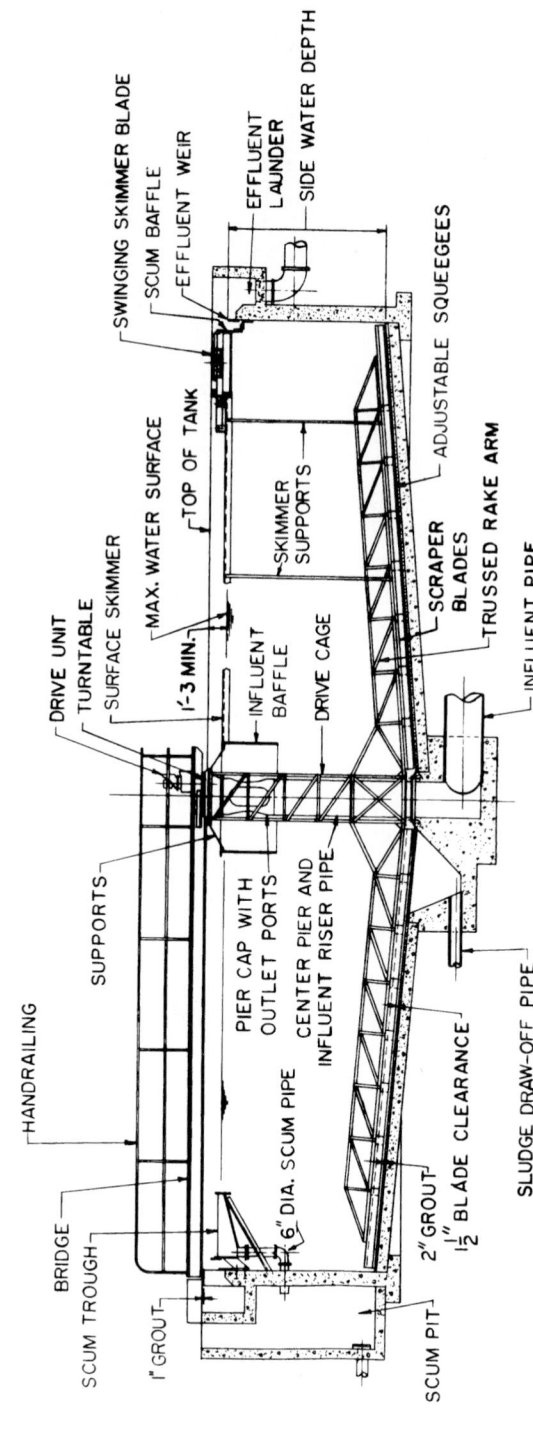

FIGURE 2-8 Clarifier for a circular basin.

HANDRAILING

BRIDGE

SCUM TROUGH

1" GROUT

SCUM PIT

SUPPORTS

DRIVE UNIT

TURNTABLE

SURFACE SKIMMER

INFLUENT BAFFLE

DRIVE CAGE

PIER CAP WITH OUTLET PORTS

CENTER PIER AND INFLUENT RISER PIPE

6" DIA. SCUM PIPE

2" GROUT

1½" BLADE CLEARANCE

SWINGING SKIMMER BLADE

SCUM BAFFLE

EFFLUENT WEIR

EFFLUENT LAUNDER

SIDE WATER DEPTH

MAX. WATER SURFACE

TOP OF TANK

1'-3 MIN.

ADJUSTABLE SQUEEGEES

SKIMMER SUPPORTS

SCRAPER BLADES

TRUSSED RAKE ARM

INFLUENT PIPE

SLUDGE DRAW-OFF PIPE

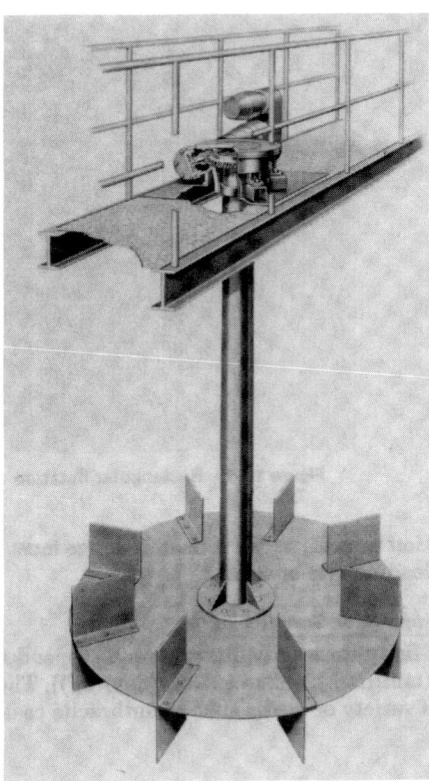

FIGURE 2-9 Mechanical flocculation device. (*Envirex.*)

Pressure-flotation units dissolve air in the water under pressure and then release it to the atmosphere in the flotation tank.

Flotation equipment may be circular or rectangular.

Recycle Pressurization. The rectangular unit in Fig. 2-11 illustrates the use of recycle pressurization. Air is injected into the effluent recycle stream before it discharges into the inlet compartment of the flotation unit. There it is mixed with the incoming raw waste and releases the required air for flotation. The amount of effluent recycled varies from 25 to 50 percent of the forward flow. This approach has advantages when the raw waste is highly variable in composition or contains large amounts of solids.

Flotation units are normally designed for a feed-flow detention period of 15 min and an overflow rate of 1.5 to 4.0 gal/(min)(ft^2) [760 to 2025 L/(day)(m^2)]. Increased detention time is needed if floated sludge must be thickened since surface area is based on the loading rate of solids.

High-Rate Gravity Filters. High-rate gravity filters remove suspended solids and operate in the range of 5 to 10 gal/(min)(ft^2) [2532 to 5063 L/(day)(m^2)]. They may be vertical or horizontal and filled with a variety of media such as anthracite coal, sand, and gravel.

FIGURE 2-10 Solids contact clarifier. (*Envirex.*)

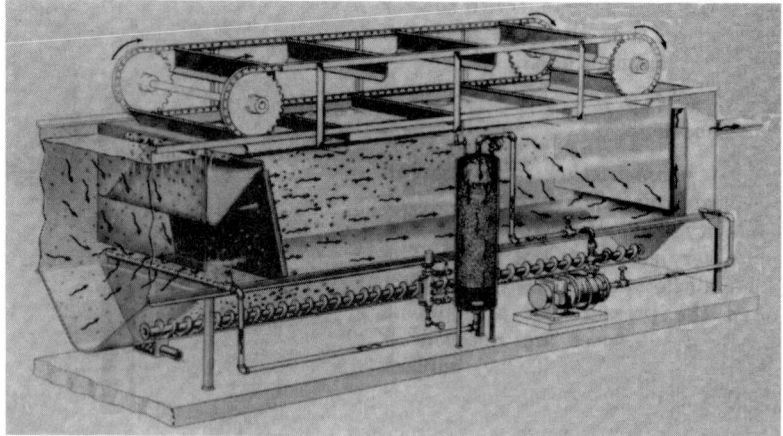

FIGURE 2-11 Rectangular flotation unit with recycle pressurization. (*Envirex.*)

PRODUCT RECOVERY

In many cases, industrial wastes contain valuable products such as high-value metals, acids, and other substances which can be used for manufacturing by-products, and these, when recovered, will yield high economic returns. Also obtainable are solvents, recovered with activated-carbon adsorption used for removal and recycling of solvents contained in the waste as vapors; these solvents include hydrocarbons, esters, alcohols, freons, ketones, and chlorinated or fluorinated organic compounds.

In the plating industry, rinse waters contain many of the following contaminants, usually in intolerable amounts: hexavalent chromium; sodium cyanide; complex cyanides of the heavy metals, such as cadmium, copper, zinc, and sometimes silver and gold; soluble nickel salts, strong mineral acids, and strong alkalis. Of these, the most toxic are the hexavalent chromium and cyanide ions.

Batch Treatment Method

There are several basic methods of treating such rinse waters for disposal or recovery of products. The oldest is the batch treatment method whereby the rinse waters are collected for treatment and disposal. The destruction of toxic chemicals is accomplished by oxidation of the cyanides and reduction of chomium. Chlorine (Cl_2) is used to destroy cyanides (CN^-), and the chlorinated rinse water is pumped into a reduction tank containing sulfuric acid and a reducing agent such as ferrous sulfate ($FeSO_4$), sodium bisulfite ($NaHSO_4$), or sulfur dioxide (SO_2). Chromium is reduced from its hexavalent state (Cr^{6+}) to the trivalent state (Cr^{3+}) and precipitated as a hydroxide, along with other metal hydroxides, by the addition of lime. The clear water from the clarifier is then ready for discharge into a sewer, and the sludge can be vacuum-filtered or disposed of in an acceptable manner.

Continuous-Flow Method

Another treatment of rinse water is the continuous-flow method. To be effective, this requires good instrumentation to monitor the flow and deliver the proper amount of reactant.

Ion Exchange

When the volume of chromic acid and sodium or potassium cyanide used is great enough, the recovery of the cyanides and chromic acid by ion exchange and evaporation has obvious economic advantages.

An integrated system for ion-exchange treatment of cyanide and chromium wastes has been found to be suitable for a plating operation that is split up into several parts. The system involves countercurrent rinsing, and the basic advantage of this system is that the toxic contaminants are destroyed before they can enter the rinse water, rather than having to be removed later.

Ion exchange plays an important part in chemical reclamation. The rinse waters are kept separate in the following categories:

1. Hard chrome rinse waters
2. Cyanide rinse waters containing silver, gold, or any other valuable metal
3. Miscellaneous wastes such as alkaline cleaners and acids

The hard chrome rinse waters are passed through a cation exchange and a strong-base anion exchanger. The contaminating metals such as copper, nickel, and trivalent chromium are exchanged on the cation exchanger, while the hexavalent chromium is exchanged on the anion exchanger. Upon exhaustion of the system, the cation exchanger is regenerated with an acid and the anion exchanger regenerated with caustic soda.

The regenerant effluent from the cation exchanger can be discharged to a collection chamber for neutralization. The regenerant effluent from the anion exchanger will contain sodium chromate and some caustic soda. This material can then be converted to chromic acid by passing it back through the cation exchanger so that the two exchangers may be alternated between service and conversion.

Table 2-5 shows recovery value of by-products from plating wastes.

An ion-exchange demineralization unit with a cation-anion mixed bed results in an effluent of less than 1 mg/L of total dissolved solids at a cost of roughly 5 cents per 1000 gal of waste treated. Membrane reverse-osmosis units can be used, but at substantially increased costs of five times or more than ion exchange.

Closed-Loop System

In the area of metal fabrication, parts are frequently washed or rinsed to clean away oils and other wastes. With a little care, improved wash operations cut downtime, reduce energy requirements, and cut soap costs. This is accomplished by a closed-loop washwater treatment system.

A typical closed-loop system (Fig. 2-12) is best described as a continuous-batch oil separator. It has dual compartments holding caustic wash solution, each equipped with an oil roll

TABLE 2-5 Economic Value of By-Product Recovery

Process	By-product	Concentration, mg/L	1980 value, $/1000 gal
Rinse water	Copper	100–500	0.85–4.26
	Nickel	150–900	1.14–9.94
	Zinc	70–350	0.57–3.40
	Cadmium	50–250	1.70–8.50
	Chromium	400–2000	4.50–21.30
	Tin	100–600	1.14–6.80
Aluminum, bright dip	Phosphoric acid	10%	630

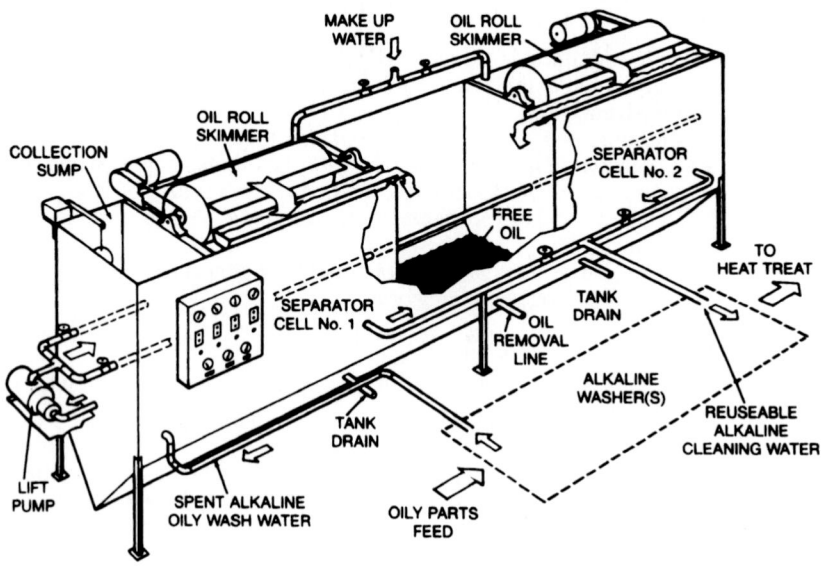

FIGURE 2-12 Alkaline wash system.

skimmer and separated by a waste tank. Piping leads from each compartment to a series of washers and back to a pump. Automated valves control flow from the pump to one of the two compartments.

One compartment continuously supplies caustic solution to a group of washers as the other stands for 24 h, allowing heavy materials to settle as oils float to the surface. Then, surface oils containing less than 0.1 percent water are skimmed off and drained into a waste tank; these may then be sold to an oil reclamation firm. While one wash solution in the first compartment undergoes treatment, the clean solution in the other compartment is circulated through the washers.

Treatment of Spent Coolants

Spent coolants can be treated for recovery of oil by acidification and centrifugation or by heat treatment at 223°F (106°C) for 22 h.

In the heat-treatment process, three distinct layers develop after there is water loss of approximately 12 percent through evaporation. The top layer consists of reusable oil, amounting to approximately 24 percent of the original scum volume; the middle layer, containing approximately 16 percent of the scum, is called the *rag layer* and consists of flocculated particulate matter; the bottom layer contains approximately 48 percent of the total scum and appears as relatively clear water. This bottom water layer is returned to the spent-coolant holding tanks for retreatment, and the rag, or intermediate, layer is combined with the swarfing dust and other heavy solids for removal by haulage.

A portion of the recovered oil can be used as the fuel for heating the floated scum, thereby making the system self-sustaining. The balance can be reprocessed for reuse as coolant. A simple product balance would show that for every 100 L of coolant treated, from 0.3 L to as much as 5 L of reusable oil can be recovered. A minimum flow of about 30,000 L of coolant per day might be selected as an economic break-even point.

At this minimum flow, taking, on an average, 3 L of recoverable oil for each 100 L of feed, 750 L per day of coolant would be recovered. Of this, approximately 50 L would be required to heat the scum to 223°F (106°C) for the 22-h break period, leaving a net total of 700 L of recovered oil.

Cost recovery can vary, depending upon the type of coolant used. Caution should be exercised when this system is used where plated parts are machined, as there is the hazard of cyanide buildup in the oil after prolonged usage.

Water Recovery

Recycled water may ultimately be the major valuable product because of increasing water-supply costs, increasing water-treatment costs, and mounting charges for using municipal wastewater facilities. The recovery of product fines, usable water, and thermal energy are important methods of reducing overall waste-disposal costs and should be seriously considered in every case.

Frequently, waste streams can be eliminated or reduced by process modifications or improvements. A notable example of this is the use of save-rinse and spray-rinse tanks in plating lines. This measure brings about a substantial reduction in waste volume and frequently a net reduction in metal dragout.

Segregation of waste streams is a necessity at times, not from the product-recovery point of view, but from the operational point of view. An example of this is segregation of acidic metal rinses from cyanide streams to avoid the production of toxic hydrogen cyanide (HCN) and thus eliminate potential safety hazards.

The prime requirement of waste treatment, by-product recovery, and water reuse is that the principal product or products of the plant be satisfactory to the consumer, and the secondary requirement is that the operation of the plants be efficient and economical.

By-Product Recovery and Use

The urgent problems facing industries are how to recover by-products from the waste materials inherent in every industrial operation and what to do with the by-products. Confronted with the growing dangers of pollution, the anticipation of government regulation, and the loss of valuable materials through unprofitable waste-disposal methods, industries are forced to develop sophisticated refining methods for processing chemical and industrial by-products and even to develop markets for by-products.

Industry is becoming increasingly aware of the necessity for pollution abatement and product recovery, not only because of its effect upon the general welfare of the public, but also because of its own dependence upon rivers and streams for suitable water for manufacturing processes. Industries are also increasingly aware of the fact that the benefits accruing from pollution abatement through product recovery may be quite significant.

SOURCE CONTROL AND WATER REUSE AND RECYCLING

The plant layout and arrangement of process and manufacturing sequences must be considered with regard to wastewater pollution control. This means undertaking a complete engineering survey of water use to develop an accurate water balance for peak and average operating conditions. In effect, what is needed is a complete inventory of all plant operations that use water and produce wastes.

With these data in hand, a fresh look should be taken at plant and process operations to see if any changes can be made that will reduce the amount of water used or decrease the flow of wastewater produced. A simple process adjustment is often all that is required to lower the concentration of pollutants. Perhaps there are valuable chemicals that can be recovered; or there may be alternative approach that might change the nature of the waste to make it easier to handle. Sometimes, segregating a contaminated process water from the rest of the waste discharge can reduce the size of the wastewater-treatment system.

The survey will uncover applications for water that can be recycled for repeated reuse. Some wastewater, now discharged to the sewer, may be well suited for cooling or boiler feed. The economics of using cooling towers to replace once-through cooling systems should be reconsidered. In some cases it may even pay to switch to air-cooled heat exchangers.

Machinery or operations having a common waste product can be connected to a centralized system of contaminant collection and treatment. With early involvement, the plant engineer can anticipate potential pollution problems and advise preventive measures. Where possible, the plant engineer should strive to prevent pollution at the source, thus minimizing the need to incorporate pollution control facilities. Typical methods of preventing pollution at the source include:

1. Substituting process materials
2. Modifying manufacturing procedures
3. Changing production equipment
4. Recycling process water

Examples of materials substitution are the use of chlorinated solvents of less toxicity for carbon tetrachloride and using a paint with reduced lead or zinc content.

Cascading or countercurrent water-use systems (where an operation that requires relatively low quality water uses wastewater from another operation) or recycling systems (where water is treated and returned to the same operation) can greatly reduce intake water requirements.

The quantities listed in column B, Table 2-1, should be considered the maximum pollutant values for reuse of process water.

REFERENCES AND BIBLIOGRAPHY

1. "Environmental Register," Illinois Environmental Protection Agency, Springfield, Ill., March 12, 1979.
2. "Industrial Waste Ordinance," Metropolitan Sanitary District of Greater Chicago, Chicago, Ill., January 19, 1978.

Beslievre, Edmund, and Schwartz, Max: *The Treatment of Industrial Wastes,* Industrial Water Engineering Bookshelf, Darien, Conn., 1978.

Corbitt, E. A.: *Standard Handbook of Environmental Engineering,* McGraw-Hill, New York, 1990.

Eckenfelder, W. Wesley, Jr.: *Industrial Water Pollution Control,* McGraw-Hill, New York, 1988.

EPA–RCRA Orientation Manual, EPA/530-SW-86-001, Washington, DC, 1986.

Freeman, H. M.: *Standard Handbook of Hazardous Waste Treatment and Disposal,* McGraw-Hill, New York, 1989.

Lund, Herbert F.: *Industrial Pollution Control Handbook,* McGraw-Hill, New York, 1971.

Nemerow, Nelson L.: *Theories and Practices of Industrial Waste Treatment,* Addison-Wesley, Reading, Mass., 1963.

CHAPTER 13-3
SOLID-WASTE DISPOSAL*

Charles Albert Johnson, Ph.D.
Technical Director
National Solid Wastes Management Association
Washington, D.C.

INTRODUCTION

One of the most significant factors in the successful operation of any industrial plant is the proper disposal of solid waste.

Obviously, such waste can be simply hauled away as generated by an outside contractor, or by plant personnel, to an appropriate disposal site. This chapter, however, discusses the alternative: employing an in-plant system to reduce the volume and weight of solid waste as generated so as to reduce haulage costs. However, hazardous material must be disposed of (usually without treatment) by specialists; this subject is discussed in the last portion of this chapter.

SYSTEM DESIGN

Due to large variations in the types of waste found in an industrial plant, each refuse-handling system should be custom-designed to fit the needs of each plant. The key to a successful design is understanding current operations—that of the plant engineer as well as the operations of the outside solid-waste managers (refuse collectors, equipment distributors, and manufacturers) servicing the plant. With this combination of knowledge, the most economical and efficient waste-handling system for a plant can be designed.

First, five essential factors must be analyzed:

1. The volume of waste produced
2. Its composition and characteristics
3. Special handling requirements
4. Location and other physical constraints
5. Requirements for safety and security

---

*Updated for this Second Edition by the Editor-in-Chief.

DISPOSAL METHODS

Having evaluated the five criteria, the plant engineer must determine the best method of disposal to be used. Two common methods employed in many industrial plants are (1) *compaction* and (2) *incineration.*

Compaction

Compaction is the method whereby a large volume of solid waste is reduced (squeezed) under high pressure, minimizing both container space and the number of times the container must be emptied. This reduces collection costs and permits a safe, clean method of handling in-plant refuse. The installation of an efficient compaction system, including chutes, conveyors, and large refuse-compactor containers, can reduce in-plant trash-handling costs by as much as 90 percent. Also, with an appropriate installation, "rear-door" pilfering can be practically eliminated.

Purchasers often want to specify *compaction ratio* or the density that can be produced by a compactor. Most manufacturers decline to guarantee specific compaction performance because it depends upon both the specific machine employed and the material being compacted. Typically, however, compactors will reduce the volume of wastes by factors ranging from 2 to 5.

Stationary Compactors. If stationary compaction is chosen, several factors must be considered. The parameters of stationary compactors include charging-chamber volume, pressure of the packer ram, cycle time, penetration of the packing ram into the compaction container, and compactor base size.

To assist purchasers of stationary compactors, the Waste Equipment Manufacturers Institute (WEMI) of the National Solid Wastes Management Association has developed a standardized method of rating compactors. Periodically WEMI publishes a book of standardized ratings for the equipment sold by its members.

Figure 3-1 shows a sketch of the most widely used style of stationary compactor, the horizontal detachable unit. Ratings are also provided for compactors with pivoting rams and self-contained compactors in which the compaction ram is integrally mounted within a refuse container.

Charging Chamber Volume. This must be large enough to accommodate, without any difficulty, the largest piece of refuse generated by the user.

Additional considerations must be taken into account when determining charging-chamber size. For example, the industrial plant may utilize in-plant trash carts of a specific size, so the charging chamber should be able to receive the entire contents of a full trash cart or a full container load. In many instances, this could mean that the charging area should be substantially greater than the largest single piece of refuse generated at the location.

Physical Dimensions of the Compactor. It may seem obvious that a compactor machine must fit properly into the space where it is intended to operate. However, errors made in this area are common, and utmost care is advised in planning. Conversely, a number of installation possibilities exist which may enable the utilization of a machine which, at first glance, would not appear to fit into the available space.

As a general rule, the placing of a stationary compactor should be calculated not only on the basis of the actual operating machine, but must include: (1) space for access to the charging chamber, (2) space for the container for the compacted wastes, and (3) space required for the pickup vehicle to maneuver, pull away the full container, replace an empty one, and then haul the full box away. Finally, sufficient room must be provided at the loading area to accommodate trash carts, containers, or even a conveyor chute leading to the hopper.

Dock space may be saved and plant security increased by installing the machine through the wall so that the charging area and the working mechanism remain inside the building, but

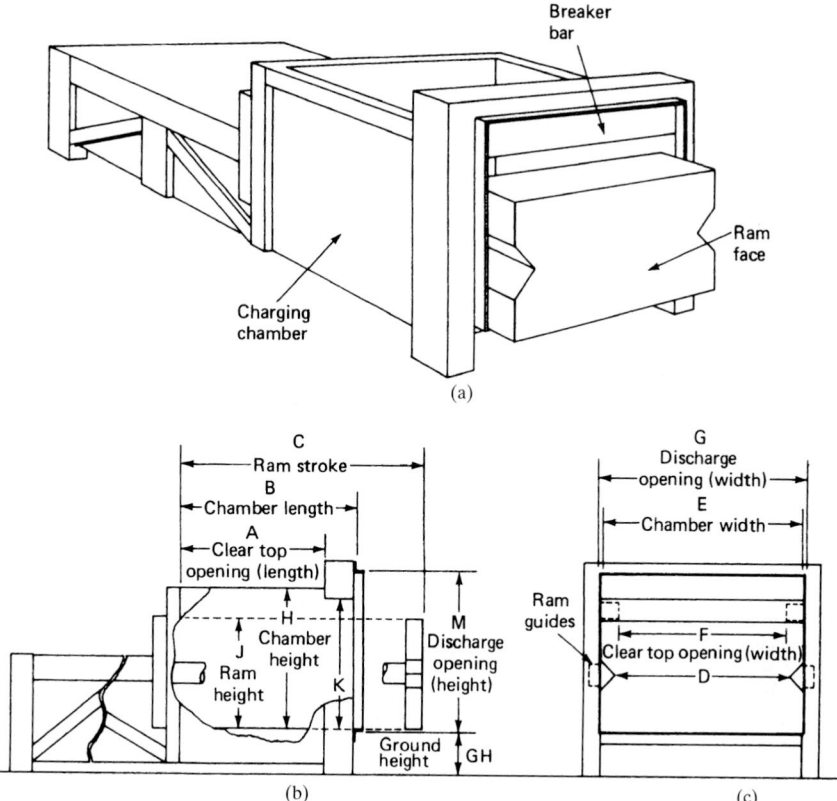

FIGURE 3-1 Horizontal commercial-industrial stationary compactor.

the container is attached to the machine through an opening in the wall. Also, chutes from upper floors may run to the charging area, decreasing internal transportation costs and reducing the need for additional dock space.

Cycle Time. Cycle time is an important parameter of a container specification. It refers to the time required for a fully retracted ram face to pack the refuse from the charging box into the container and return to its original fully retracted position ready for another load of refuse.

Cycle times run from as short as 20 s to more than 1 min. Short cycle times are important if the application under consideration requires the capability of accepting refuse very quickly. A purchaser should carefully consider whether a compactor with a short cycle time is needed. Often compactors built with a rapid cycle utilize a small-diameter hydraulic cylinder which consequently exerts a relatively low force on the ram face, thereby sacrificing compaction pressure and material density.

Pressure of the Ram Face. A third important parameter of a stationary-compactor specification is the pressure of the ram face. Pressure, in pounds per square inch, is more important than total force in determining compaction density.

The ram pressure is the total force exerted on the ram, divided by the area of the ram. For a hydraulically operated compactor, the total ram force is the product of the hydraulic pressure and the hydraulic cylinder area.

For example, a compactor with a ram face measuring 30×60 in (0.8×1.6 m) has an area of 1800 in^2 (1.3 m^2). If it is acted upon by a 5-in (12-cm) diameter hydraulic cylinder with a fluid pressure of 2000 lb/ft (14×10^6 N/m^2), the total ram force will be 39,200 lb (175,000 N), and the pressure exerted by the ram will be 21.7 lb/in^2 (140,000 N/m^2).

Most compactors have both a normal and maximum pressure rating. The higher pressure is used when finally packing out a container to make it easy to detach the container and ensure that the waste remains within it.

Penetration of the Ram into the Container.   The penetration of the ram face into the container is an important factor in the operation of a compactor. Essentially, it represents the position of the forward ram stroke available for final compaction of the refuse load into the container. As the container begins to fill up with compacted waste, there is a tendency for the portion of refuse closest to the ram to fall back into the charging area. This is of most concern when the container is detached because waste falling from the container will litter the environment. The further a ram penetrates into the compaction container, the easier it is to load and detach a container cleanly.

Base Size.   Compactor specifications are summarized as a single parameter, the base size. This is defined as the volume of waste theoretically moved through the compactor in a single stroke. Purchasers commonly use the base size as the primary specification, adding the parameters, listed above as necessary. Table 3-1 gives typical uses of compactors of various base sizes.

TABLE 3-1   Typical Compactor Applications

Use	Base size	
	yd^3	m^3
High-rise apartment building	Up to 1	0.8
Commercial establishment	1 to 4	0.8 to 3
Industrial plants	1.5 to 7	1.2 to 5.5
Transfer stations	7 to 12	5.5 to 9

Rated stationary compactors manufactured by members of the WEMI carry the NSWMA Rating Seal. This seal assures performance conforming to established standards, certified by a registered professional engineer. Table 3-2 gives a hypothetical sample listing of rated compactors.

In addition to obtaining a compactor, the plant engineer will have to specify a container, which is usually provided by the refuse hauler. Before purchasing any equipment, compactor or container, the engineer should always consult the hauler to determine what type, size, and weight of containers can be handled. Some points to watch for are:

1. The container must be able to withstand the pressure of the waste without damage or distortion.

2. Roll-off and drop-off hoists, which are used to remove containers, have weight limits. The hoist will not be able to lift containers which exceed these limits.

3. State highway laws limit the amount of weight which can be carried on each chassis.

4. The length of the container affects the compaction ratio. The larger the container, generally the less the compaction.

There is no single formula for use in selecting a compactor for a plant. However, careful consideration of the tangible and intangible factors that have been outlined here will aid in avoiding costly mistakes.

TABLE 3-2 NSWMA Commercial-Industrial Stationary Compactor Ratings

Manufacturer: Hypothetical Manufacturing, Inc.   Date: August 1977

Model number	NSWMA base size, yd³	Clear top opening length (L) width (W), in	Chamber length, in	Ram stroke, in	Ram penetration, in	Force rating normal (N) maximum (M), (ram lb/in² per force, lb)	System pressures normal (N) maximum (M)	Ram face, in	Volume displacement rate, yd³/h	Rated motor size, hp	Cycle time, s	Discharge opening width (W) height (H), in	Ground height, in	Base unit weight, lb
A	0.38	$L = 24.0$ $W = 34.5$	24.5	30.0	5.5	$N = 25.3/18200$ $M = 27.8/20000$	$N = 1450$ $M = 1600$	$W = 36.0$ $H = 20.0$	39	1	35	$W = 37.0$ $H = 24.5$	15.5	1800
B	1.06	$L = 36.0$ $W = 51.5$	39.0	50.0	11.0	$N = 28.5/36200$ $M = 30.8/39100$	$N = 1850$ $M = 2000$	$W = 53.0$ $H = 24.0$	106	10	36	$W = 53.5$ $H = 32.5$	16.0	4000
C	1.60	$L = 40.0$ $W = 58.5$	41.0	55.0	14.0	$N = 21.6/38800$ $M = 24.3/43700$	$N = 2000$ $M = 2250$	$W = 60.0$ $H = 30.0$	144	10	40	$W = 61.0$ $H = 37.5$	15.5	5100
D	1.91	$L = 48.0$ $W = 58.5$	49.0	65.0	16.0	$N = 24.3/43700$ $M = 27.6/49600$	$N = 2250$ $M = 2550$	$W = 60.0$ $H = 30.0$	146	10	47	$W = 61.0$ $H = 37.5$	15.5	5900
E	3.43	$L = 84.5$ $W = 58.0$	89.0	110.0	21.0	$N = 55.8/100400$ $M = 61.4/110500$	$N = 2000$ $M = 2200$	$W = 60.0$ $H = 30.0$	225	20	55	$W = 61.5$ $H = 37.5$	16.5	13000

© 1977 National Solid Wastes Management Association.

Note: The National Solid Wastes Management Association presents this technical information on commercial-industrial stationary compaction equipment to assist users in the selection of equipment. The National Solid Wastes Management Association does not present these data as a warranty for equipment performance. The ratings represent data supplied by manufacturers that have been computed according to the NSWMA criteria and certified for accuracy by a registered professional engineer, selected by the manufacturer.

In-Plant Incineration

An alternative method of disposal is *incineration.* Although incinerators are more expensive to build and install than stationary compactors, their use can provide additional savings in refuse hauling costs. Energy recovery in the form of steam may also be considered as a source of additional savings.

When one is considering an incinerator, one should evaluate the following factors:

1. Any limitations imposed by air pollution emission limits in the area of the plant.
2. The physical constraints imposed by the dimensions of the plant.
3. The appropriateness in quantity and composition of the solid waste generated within the plant: a sufficiently high fired Btu value.
4. Fuel requirements. Most incinerators require supplementary fuel, either gas or oil, to control air pollution. Fuel costs can be high, and fuel availability may become uncertain. However, energy recovery can offset some of the costs.
5. By-product disposal: Adequate methods of disposal must be provided to handle the by-products of the incinerated waste.

Controlled-air incinerators (Fig. 3-2), the most frequently used incinerators today, were first commercially available in the United States in the early 1960s, but they were not really accepted until the late 1960s and early 1970s. This acceptance was mostly due to the increasing demands for high performance as measured by very low particulate emissions and a very high reduction ratio.

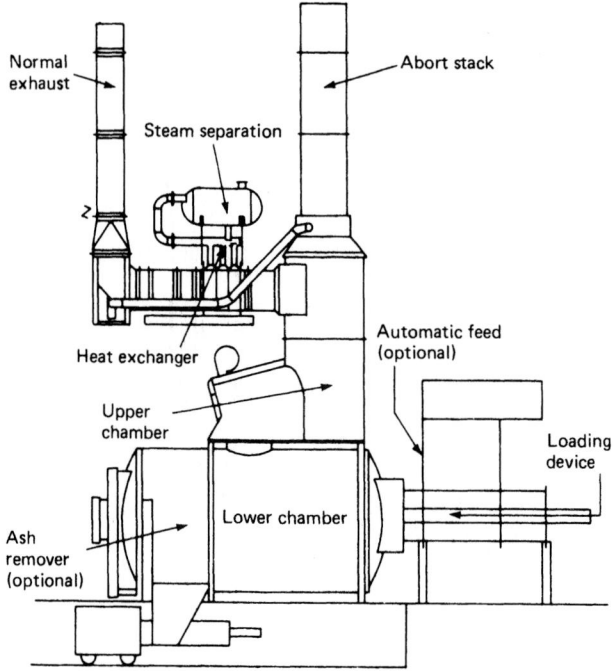

FIGURE 3-2 Controlled-air incinerator. (*Adapted with permission from the* American City & County Magazine.)

Most controlled-air incinerators employ two chambers. These chambers are designated lower, or primary, and upper, or secondary. Performance of the antipollution functions of the system depends on controlling the conditions within these two chambers. The lower chamber is required to operate at low interior gas velocities and under controlled temperature conditions. This is done by limiting the air introduced into the primary chamber to less than the amount required for complete combustion (hence, the system is sometimes called "starved-air" incineration). This gives the lower chamber the operating characteristics of a partial oxidation system.

The heat released in the lower chamber is controlled by limiting the introduction of combustion air to an amount which will give partial oxidation of the waste in the chamber. The heat is sufficient to sustain the partial oxidation reactions. The gases from the lower chamber pass into the upper chamber through a turbulent zone, where additional air is added and ignition takes place to complete the oxidation reactions. The noncombustible portion of the waste and the carbonaceous residue from the reactions remain in the lower chamber. The noncombustibles are rendered sterile by the relatively high temperature while the carbonaceous material is further oxidized by the incoming air. The result is a high-quality sterile ash.

The gas velocity in the lower chamber is influenced by several factors. The gas which evolves from the chamber is a result of the interaction of the air, the auxiliary fuel, and the oxidation and volatilization products from the waste. The quantity of gas from the waste can vary substantially depending on chamber conditions of the waste and could therefore alter the gas velocity in the lower chamber significantly. The airflow controls of the upper and lower chambers are integrated in order to minimize cycling and provide a uniform flow of gases. This is important for controlling pollution performance and especially so for an efficient energy-recovery system.

When volatilization proceeds at an excessive rate as a result of the high temperatures, two distinct adverse effects ensue. First, the velocity in the lower chamber will exceed the design velocity, and particles which are too large to be oxidized properly will be carried into the upper chamber. Second, the gases will flow to the upper chamber at a rate which exceeds the capacity of the chamber and can result in excessive particulate emissions or smoking.

The function of the upper chamber is to complete the oxidation reactions of the combustible products as they are received from the lower chamber. In order to accomplish this, conditions in the chamber must be controlled within a rather narrow band, from inputs which vary rather widely. The control system is designed to maintain the required conditions by modulating both air and fuel to the system. This in effect controls the air input, auxiliary fuel input, and gas flow from the lower chamber.

The gases pass from the lower chamber into the upper chamber through a turbulent mixing region in a controlled manner. Additional air is introduced into the system and the gases are ignited, again under controlled conditions. The gas temperature at this point is somewhat higher than in the lower chamber, and the atmosphere is oxidizing (more than sufficient air for complete combustion). Temperatures in the upper chamber are limited to less than 2500°F (1400°C) in order to minimize production of nitrogen oxides and in the interest of equipment durability. On the lower-temperature side, it is recommended that at least 1800°F (1000°C) be maintained in order to stabilize an adequate reaction rate to complete the combustion process. The desired operating temperature point is adjustable but is factory preset for maximum performance. The primary means of controlling the temperature in the upper chamber is to control the quantity of combustion air. Air quantity is decreased when the temperature drops below the set point and increased when the temperature rises above the set point.

If heat is to be recovered, the gas temperature at the inlet to the heat exchanger is not allowed to exceed 1800°F (1000°C). This is done to protect the heat exchanger and is an addition to the normal safety controls. An over-temperature condition will automatically drive the hot-gas flow to the abort stack.

Compared with compaction, incineration is a more costly and more complex way of disposing of waste; however, the energy-recovery potential may in the long run prove to be a decisive factor for incineration in many plants.

REGULATIONS

Transportation, treatment, storage, and disposal of hazardous waste are regulated under the Resource Conservation and Recovery Act (RCRA), enacted in 1976 and amended in 1984 (usually referred to as the Solid Waste Disposal Act).

The Hazardous Materials Transportation Act was enacted in 1974. In 1990 it was amended to incorporate tighter regulations on transportation of hazardous materials on highways, railways, and waterways. Authority to determine what is a hazardous material rests with the U.S. Dept. of Transportation.

To arrange for disposal of hazardous wastes, a plant engineer should contact a waste service company *that is fully permitted to transport and dispose of those wastes*. The company should provide a written statement certifying where the wastes are to be taken and how they are to be treated or disposed of. The disposal facilities should be inspected and the actual waste disposition verified.

The hazardous-waste generator will be requested to initiate a manifest for shipments of hazardous wastes going off-site for disposal and will also be required to designate where the wastes are to be taken.

This is an ongoing, active regulatory area; the reader is urged to check the latest regulations before proceeding with plant modifications.

BIBLIOGRAPHY

Corbitt, Robert A.: *Standard Handbook of Environmental Engineering,* McGraw-Hill, New York, 1990.
EPA-RCRA Orientation Manual, EPA/530-SW-86-001, Washington, DC, 1986.
Freeman, H.M.: *Standard Handbook of Hazardous Waste Treatment,* McGraw-Hill, New York, 1989.
Lindgren, G.F.: *Guide to Managing Industrial Hazardous Waste,* Butterworth Publishers, 1983.

SECTION 14

PLANT SAFETY AND SANITATION

CHAPTER 14-1
SAFETY IN PLANT OPERATIONS

Eric M. Bergtraun, CPE
Manager of Plant Maintenance and In-House Construction
National Semiconductor Corporation
Santa Clara, California

INTRODUCTION

In any plant operation it is important that management provides a positive attitude toward safety awareness that protects employees and the assets of the corporation. It is the plant engineer's responsibility to safeguard the facility in order to avoid accidents that can cause injuries and losses. This can best be done by administering safety programs that assure success.

Keeping the workplace safe and avoiding accidents that can cause injuries, damage to facilities, and work interruptions is a principal task and responsibility of the plant engineer and all facility professionals. The cost of accidents has reached such dimensions that companies cannot afford to neglect safety programs and accident prevention. Surveys have shown that at least 80 percent of all industrial accidents are the result of *unsafe acts* rather than unsafe conditions.

The basic ingredients of a good and successful safety program are:

1. Displaying management leadership and commitment to safety
2. Establishing safety responsibility of upper management and first-line supervision. Assigning responsibilities for safe procedures
3. Forming safety management committees and teams with documented responsibilities to hold regular safety meetings, complete with agendas, minutes, and action plans
4. Forming an in-house emergency response team (ERT)
5. Performing regular safety and housekeeping inspections with follow-up procedures
6. Maintaining a safe working environment
7. Initiating on-site traffic and parking regulations and establishing fire lanes
8. Initiating fire protection training
9. Conducting training programs
10. Enforcing wearing of personal protective clothes and equipment

11. Establishing a hazard communication system
12. Publishing a disaster emergency plan and recovery plan
13. Establishing an effective record keeping system
14. Preparing for medical emergencies and ensuring medical follow-up
15. Initiating safety instructions for new and transferred employees as part of new employee indoctrinations

LEGAL ASPECTS OF SAFETY

In the early part of this century the legal aspects of industrial safety were limited by laws that developed around just compensation to injured parties in connection with many workers' compensation acts. Slowly these actions helped to establish accident investigation procedures and hazard regulations.

Since then the legal aspects of safety have changed a lot. The Congress of the United States has made on-the-job safety a national purpose. The Occupational Safety and Health Act (OSHA) of 1970 recognizes the right of every individual to safe and healthful working conditions. It has always been the plant engineer's duty to protect lives on the job, work being done, and the property involved from damage and harm. When the Williams-Steiger OSH Act became law on April 28, 1971 it was passed "to assure as far as possible every working man and woman in the Nation safe and healthful working condition and to preserve our national resources...." Hardly anybody can take issue with the intent of OSHA. The achievement of the ultimate goals depends, to a large extent, on how well we discharge our responsibilities and how well management, labor, and government agencies cooperate.

Although the law *says* that workers shall comply with company regulations and safety procedures, there is no provision for enforcing compliance. In other words, it is entirely up to the company to make sure that the workers comply. There is a strong implication that if the workers do not comply, the company is at fault—a failure in training, motivation, supervision, or the like. A critical part of work motivation is the day-to-day maintenance and reinforcement of the training message. In most companies, this is accomplished by a combination of good supervision and the company's general safety program. If your top management does not make a strong corporate commitment to safety, and if safety is not a top priority objective at every management level, your efforts to motivate your handling people will have three strikes against them to start. This cannot be too strongly emphasized. In other words, successful motivation of the workers is more than training, supervision, and continual repetition of the message. *To work, motivation must include the psychological effect of the entire safety program.*

If safety is presented as an integral part of the job that basically involves employee responsibility that will be used to assess employee achievement, and that will lead to eventual advancement, then safety and consideration of safety will help to motivate the worker on the job. If you are not willing to place this kind of emphasis on safety, then safety considerations have little chance of success in becoming part of the worker's motivational structure.

The greatest safety problems is apathy—indifference toward safety. One of the reasons for this is found in the definition of the word *accident:* "an unsuspected or unplanned occurrence." This is merely rationalization to avoid guilt. *Every accident can be predicted and avoided.*

Every job has two parts:

- What we do (work)
- How we do it—safely or unsafely

Supervisors are responsible to see that every worker is adequate on the job. Physically, mentally, and emotionally inadequate employees are accident-prone. Personal hazards are lack of knowledge, conflict of motives, and physical and mental factors. No matter what their jobs, employees want much more from management than just a weekly pay check. Since supervisors are in the front line of management, workers expect such support from them.

The OSHA Safety and Health Standards are available from the Superintendent of Documents, Washington, DC 20402. This document is a *must* for plant engineers, managers, and supervisors.

Other laws applicable to industrial plants are:

1. Environmental Protection Agency

   Atomic Energy Act
   Clean Air Act
   Clean Water Act
   Energy Supply and Environmental Coordination Act
   Endangered Species Act
   Fish and Wildlife Coordination Act
   Marine, Protection, Research and Sanctuaries Act
   National Environment Policy Act
   Safe Drinking Water Act
   Toxic Substances Control Act
   Water Pollution Control Act

2. Solid Waste Disposal Act

3. Department of Transportation

   Hazardous Material Transportation Act
   Ports and Waterways Safety Act
   Transportation Safety Act

4. Resource Conservation and Recovery Act

5. Federal Insecticide, Fungicide, and Rodenticide Act

6. Consumer Product Safety Commission

   Consumer Product Safety Act
   Federal Hazardous Substances Act
   Poison Prevention Packaging Act

7. Mine Safety and Health Act

8. Emergency Planning and Community Right-to-Know Act

These are only the most important laws which plant engineers should be familiar with. The adoption of specific federal legislation has also led to an increase in the number of civil suits. The violation of a federal standard may become prima facie evidence of negligence. Such cases have been very costly.

SETTING UP A SAFETY PROGRAM

The first step in setting up a safety program, say instructors of the National Safety Council, is to make policy crystal clear to every worker in the plant. Put it in writing where all can see it: "We have a safety policy. It will be enforced. Everyone who wants to work here must abide by it!"

Once this policy has been established by upper management, the plant engineer with the help of other safety officials in a company can take the following steps to organize a safety program:

1. Publish and post a letter, signed by the chief executive officer, stating that abiding by the company safety rules is a requirement of employment. At the same time, the publishing and posting of safety rules and a code of safe practices should start.

2. Hang up safety posters and warning signs. Another effective method is the use and upkeep of a poster showing the number of days since the last injury accident occurred. Such posters are usually available from insurance companies.

3. In the departments and especially in hallways, post maps which show emergency evacuation routes. Study the layout of the parking lot and look into traffic safety as well as the establishment and control of fire lanes and emergency vehicle access to all buildings.

4. Take the lead in starting safety committee meetings in your maintenance organization. The format of these meetings, complete with agendas, minutes, and follow-up procedures, should become an example for others in the company.

5. Install safety suggestion boxes. This will help to get employees involved in participating with good ideas. In some companies this method of getting employees involved has also been adapted to their electronic mail.

6. Form an emergency response team. Such a team must be extensively trained to take charge of all kinds of emergencies including: power failures, floods, gas leaks, rainwater leaks, fires, medical emergencies, and many more. Once employees get used to this immediately available group of dedicated company specialists who can take care of smaller problems instantly and can get things under control when larger problems arise until the fire department arrives, they will depend heavily on the ERT and will appreciate that the company has put such a vehicle in action for their safety.

7. Organize fire prevention training. Your insurance carrier can provide invaluable help in this area. Larger companies have a contracted fire sprinkler company which not only installs the system but can make periodic inspections. Besides this company there are service companies that install supervisory systems that provide alarms for water flows, fire pump problems, pressure drops, and tampering with riser valves. These companies should be contracted for periodic checks of the entire system to make sure that everything works properly in case of need to put out fires. Similar attention should be given to the many portable fire extinguishers which should be available throughout a facility. Besides periodic checks there is always the need to make sure that these extinguishers are installed properly and are the right design for the application. Information on all of this is available from the National Fire Protection Association in the publication NFPA 10, *Portable Fire Extinguishers*. As part of the fire prevention training you should arrange fire drills, during which as many workers as possible should get hands-on training of how to use the extinguishers. The fire department is an excellent source to help with this training.

8. List the personal protection equipment that is required for the factory workers. List any special protection equipment that is needed for the handlers of chemicals, gases, and toxic materials and for special operations involving lasers, confined space entry, radiation, forklift operation, hazardous energy control (lockout/tagout), welding, cutting, and many more. Once such lists have been made available, the next step is to insist that supervisors enforce the use of all personal protection equipment.

9. Establish fall protection training. New OSHA fall protection standards are now in full effect. Anyone exposed to falls of over 4 ft is subject to this regulation. In facilities with heavy maintenance, construction, and rearrangements, all workers need to be trained in this. Suppliers of fall arrest and restraint equipment are available to give special demonstrations and training.

10. Establish a hazard communication system. Federal and state agencies are enforcing the new hazard communication standards which include setting up an inventory and assessment of chemicals used in the workplace. Labeling discipline must be enforced and an inventory of material safety data sheets (MSDSs) must be readily available. Workers must learn how to read, use, and understand these MSDSs. Companies are required to make the information available to their workers, and they must train them to recognize the hazards and how to best protect themselves.

WORKING WITH CONTRACTORS

When the plant engineer retains a contractor or a subcontractor, it is very important to understand the legal and working relationship between owner and contractor. In larger companies the purchasing department, as well as risk and loss or insurance departments, work together with legal advisors to make sure that all understand their responsibilities. Once the contracts and purchase orders are signed, it is the plant engineer's responsibility to represent the owner while the work is performed. During construction, safety and fire prevention, in the form of a complete loss control, is the combined responsibility of the plant engineer, job supervisors, and the job management of each contractor. Their combined prime consideration must always be the safety of their workers and prevention of even minor accidents and the loss of material and property. Safety and fire prevention on any job requires the control of people, machinery, equipment, material, and production. Accidents have damaging effects on construction operation, worker efficiency, and the overall profit-and-loss picture of both contractors and their customers. Even the smallest accidents interrupt construction, increase costs, disturb schedules, and interrupt production of contractors and customers. Next to personal injury accidents, major losses are caused by fires, collapse incidents, and floods caused by broken pipes and sprinkler heads.

MOCK OSHA INSPECTIONS

We can learn a lot from how OSHA trains its inspectors and what is emphasized in an OSHA inspection. Some of the training of OSHA inspectors follows a program known by the acronym RAP: *recognition* of potential hazards, *avoidance* of these hazards, and *prevention* of accidents. OSHA inspectors stress the word *apparent* and base their reports and findings on observable conditions and facts.

Once a safety program is in place it is of great importance that the plant engineer gives the entire facility a thorough mock OSHA inspection. Organize a team of your staff and supervisors and inspect the facility in the same manner that an OSHA inspector would do it. The same holds true for a fire marshall, code enforcing, or insurance inspection. Such inspections usually provide lots of surprises and will initiate long lists of corrective action when they are first started. Once the inspections are done on a regular basis, these findings will rapidly decrease and your facility will be a safer place to work in. Just pretend that you are an OSHA inspector and inspect the facility the way he or she would. The more common items that inspectors look for are:

- Proof that your company operates a good safety program:
  Folder with organized sections of the company's safety program
  Management's directives to employees to abide by all safety rules
  Company's safety rules and code of safety practices
  Safety committee organization, meeting agendas, and minutes
  Safety training records
  Records of periodic safety inspections, citations, and follow-up records
- Inspection of the facility:
  Open fire lanes around all buildings
  Properly maintained driveways, access roads, and parking lots, without chuck holes
  Emergency doors that are not blocked

All emergency lighting and exit lights in working condition

No accumulated rubbish and tripping hazards

No structural unsafe openings: floors, windows, stairways, roof access, shafts, sumps, pits, and tanks

- Machinery and equipment:

Proper clearance around machinery

Machine guards in place

Machinery in safe working condition

Warning signs for automatically starting machinery

No signs of dripping oil, chemicals, or water

Proper tools used to operate and adjust machinery

- Tools:

All tools cared for properly

Periodic inspections and repairs made and records available

Tools checked for electric grounding before being issued

Special care taken in the use of ladders and scaffolding

Special fire safety used for fluids in hydraulic-powered (hand) tools

Checklists that show leased tools and equipment comply with OSHA

- Safe working procedures:

All workers wearing and using personal protective clothing and safety equipment

Use of lockouts when working on machinery

Provision that oiling of machine parts can be done without removing guards

Provision in place that the operator of equipment and tools can perform the work without having to reach over, through, or under dangerous equipment; cannot start machinery accidentally; cannot be endangered while operating front, back, or either side of machinery; cannot be pushed, shoved, or struck by passing vehicles; can hear audible signals when used

Presence of starting, stopping, and lockout devices within reach of operator; operator not wearing any loose clothing or jewelry

All machinery and equipment in safe operating condition

- Material handling:

All areas properly illuminated

All storage racks properly installed with seismic safeguards in place

Powered materials handling equipment in safe operating condition

Toxic and hazardous material properly stored, handled, and transported in accordance with all safety regulations

Cylinders stored and secured properly

Wheel chocks and restraint devices available, operating properly, and in use

- Fire protection:

Automatic fire sprinkler system in proper working condition; maintenance and inspection records kept

Fire alarm system operational and testing records available

Portable fire extinguishers provided and locations identified, accessible, and inspected

Fire doors in good working condition, automatic closers working and not disabled

All fire exits marked and not blocked

Fire extinguisher training and evacuation drills held periodically and records kept

- Electrical:

No unapproved extension cords or temporary wiring in use

All outlet and junction boxes covered

All circuits and receptacles properly grounded

Electrical panels unlocked and available for emergency switching; index of circuits available and showing what breaker controls what

Switches locked in the ON position, without holes, marked and clean

Motors and controls clean, free of oil, grease, and dust

- Housekeeping and maintenance:

All work areas maintained in a clean, orderly, and safe manner

Floors not slippery, tiles not chipped, and no obstructions

Waste material stored and cared for properly

Restrooms and changerooms clean and orderly

Exhaust systems adequate and in good operating condition

Welding and paint areas clean and well-ventilated; maintenance records kept

The above list of items in a mock OSHA inspection is so basic that every plant engineer should know these as obvious things that must always be in good order. *Yet nearly every OSHA, fire, or safety inspection uncovers these basic items during inspections and causes the facilities to receive bad ratings, fines, and strict warnings.* Plant engineers and facility and safety officials do not perform enough thorough inspections of their own and allow outside inspectors to find these items, to their own embarrassment.

ACCIDENT REPORTING AND INVESTIGATING

Investigations and research show that for every industrial injury that requires medical attention, there are 75 smaller incidents and injuries that occur without inquiries and investigations. A good and proven way to keep accidents to a minimum is to insist that any incident, accident, and injury requires reporting. The magnitude of the report and inquiry should increase with the amount of work interruption, first-aid need, and material loss. Report forms are available from insurance companies. These forms should have enough space for a full explanation of the incident or injury and must have space for explanation of how it could have been avoided and what steps will be taken to prevent it from happening in the future. This reporting will give supervisors and managers a chance to see how many small losses occur and how they can be avoided in the future. Too often managers measure their safety performance by the number of hours and days of lost-time accidents. It is more important to prevent accidents from happening than to react after they have happened. Companies should initiate hazard and loss control as a very important management tool. It is an accepted estimate that for every single dollar of direct loss there are $3 to $10 of indirect losses. Indirect losses are downtime, investigation cost, cleanup and repair, productivity decline, sales losses, etc.

SAFETY DURING CONSTRUCTION AND ALTERATIONS

Safeguarding of workers and equipment during a construction and alteration project is the responsibility of the plant engineer, project managers, and work supervisors. While some of these responsibilities will be handled by outside contractors, the plant engineer and facility professionals share in this responsibility.

"Safety first" is part of any project management and cannot be separated from any other function of the project engineer. It has been established that nearly 90 percent of all industrial accidents are the result of unsafe acts rather than unsafe conditions. Hence, lowering the accident rate is directly related to how well workers are trained and how they are supervised in their daily effort.

Early planning is the most important step to make any construction project successful and safe. The following checklist is a reminder of the items that project engineers should watch for closely:

- Scheduling work with safety in mind

  Has work been planned so that not too many trades will be required to work in a small area at the same time?

  Will safety equipment be available for the workers to use?

  Have supervisors/foremen and workers been instructed in accordance with the Safe Practices and Operations Code which is part of the Construction Safety Orders adopted by the Division of Industrial Safety of each state?

- Use of building material, machinery, and testing labs

  Will only new, undamaged material be used, as well as specially approved material and equipment [Underwriters Laboratories (UL) labeled, for example], when needed?

  Will only material and equipment specified by the architect/engineer be used?

  Are inspections and overhauls planned for, whenever machinery and equipment is relocated?

  Will all high-voltage wiring and equipment be properly tested before use?

  Will piping and tanks be properly checked for leaks?

  Have underground tanks and piping been designed with double containment?

  Has work been planned so that no fire-resistance rating will be voided by improper storing or handling of material and equipment?

  Have arrangements been made for independent testing: soil (including compaction), concrete hardness and curing, structural-steel welds, noise levels, etc.?

- Handling materials

  Has proper material-handling equipment been provided (e.g., cranes, hoists, elevators, trucks, etc.)?

  Is adequate space available for loading, unloading, and storing materials?

  Have arrangements been made for securely stacking and storing materials?

  Have good housekeeping practices been set up to eliminate tripping, fire, and pest hazards? (Work surfaces must be kept dry—not slippery.)

  Have plans been made for separate storage of materials with greater-than-ordinary combustibility, with special precaution taken against fire hazard?

  Have special areas, enclosures, clearances, and precautions been taken for storage of chemicals, explosives, highly flammable material, pressure cylinders, etc?

  Are "No Smoking" signs posted conspicuously at storage areas?

  Have special arrangements been made for proper storage and daily disposals of any combustible waste material?

  In areas where sprinkler systems have been provided, have they been inspected for proper operation?

- Tools and equipment

  Have adequate tools and equipment been provided for each part of the job?

  Have arrangements been made for proper care to be given to all tools and equipment?

  Will all tools be checked before issue?

  Will periodic inspections of tools be made on the jobsite while they are in use?

  Will only OSHA-approved electrical extension cords, plug caps, and receptacles be used?

  Have adequate guards been provided for exposed gears, sprockets, pulleys and flywheels, belt and chain drives, set screws, etc. of any power transmission equipment?

  Is adequate lighting and exhaust provided where needed?

  Is protective clothing and eye and ear protection available where needed?

  Will special care be taken in the use of ladders and scaffolds?

  Will special fire-safety precautions be used for fluids in hydraulic-powered hand tools?

  Will all leased equipment be checked to see that it complies with OSHA standards?

  Have arrangements been made to ensure that all hazardous shipments meet Department of Transportation regulations?

  Did workers get *confined-entry procedure* training before working in areas that are difficult to enter and leave due to tight openings and restricted space availability, and that present serious hazards to the workers?

SAFETY TRAINING

In order to start, set up, and maintain the safety program, extensive safety training has to be used to assure success.

Everybody who works in a company needs some kind of safety training. It all must start with those employees who are primarily responsible to administer the safety program: safety professionals, facility management, production supervisors, engineers, purchasing, security people, etc. Once they are thoroughly trained, we expect of them to use the safety knowledge which they have gained to train every worker and employee in their company. These trainers have to get the best training available in order to become good safety instructors.

Initial training should be performed by professional safety trainers. Training courses and books are available from many sources:

The National Safety Council

OSHA

National Fire Protection Association

State and local code-enforcing agencies

Insurance carriers

Engineering and professional societies

Equipment manufacturers

Chemical and process gas suppliers

One of the very best books available for intensive study and practical application of safety training is the *National Safety Council Supervisors' Safety Manual,* 7th ed.

OSHA has now mandated employee safety training and this has also been adopted by occupational safety plans of states as well as by insurance companies and local code enforcing agencies. Employers have to provide:

Employee safety training and educational programs
Pertinent information about safety on the job
Proper working conditions and precautions
Information of all hazards that employees are exposed to on the job
Emergency treatment exposure

In order to accomplish this training it is important for companies to include the following main parts:

Training of supervisors
Orientation of new and transferred employees
How to design and use safety operating procedures
Use of protective equipment
Training for specific job hazards
Training to control harmful environmental hazards
Training to understand and reduce ergonomic problems
Safeguarding machinery
Training how to properly use tools
Training in material handling and storage
Electric safety
Fire prevention safety
First-aid training and CPR
Training how to write and investigate accident reports
Training how to conduct safety inspections and correction follow-up

SAFETY CONTESTS

Facility workers, like other employees, are very competitive and love contests as a training tool. In case you want to try a contest in your facility, here are the details:

Participants

Four "football" teams selected to provide equal number of participants.

Purpose

To provide safety attitude and performance by providing the incentive of winning a contest.

Object

The first team to score a touchdown or that gains the most "yardage" by the end of the 3 months wins the contest. In the event of a tie in "yardage," the team with the fewest safety deficiencies noted during inspections will be declared a winner.

Rules

1. All teams start on the "20-yard" line.
2. Teams advance 5 "yards" for every week without a lost time accident.
3. Additional yardage can be accrued for each week for the following:
    a. Safety inspections of a shop or assigned common area with no deficiencies noted—5 yards
    b. Safety inspections of three job sites with no deficiencies noted—5 yards
    c. "Significant" safety suggestion—5 yards
4. Penalties will be assessed for the following:
    a. Observing a member of the team in any work location not wearing the proper protective equipment—5 yards
    b. More than 5 deficiencies noted in the weekly inspection of single shop or common area or total for multiple work sites (this penalty will be rescinded if the deficiencies are corrected within 24 h)—5 yards
    c. Arguing with safety referee—5 yards
    d. Written safety violation is issued to any member of the team—10 yards
5. A maximum of 10 extra yards (above the base of 5, for no-time-loss accidents) can be added each week per team.
6. A maximum of 15 yards can be lost each week per team.
7. Members of the Safety Department are the referees for the contest. Their decision in any dispute is final.
8. Safety will perform an unannounced inspection of the shops/common areas/job sites for each team on a weekly basis.
9. Safety will review the accident records for each team every week.
10. A scoreboard showing the progress of each team will be posted. Safety will update the board every Tuesday afternoon.
11. The prize will be a barbeque for all members of the winning team, plus a drawing for two tickets to a Forty-niners' football game.
12. The winning team will select a most valuable player. This person should be the team member who contributed most toward the winning of the contest. The most valuable player will choose an official team jacket.

CHAPTER 14-2

FIRE PROTECTION AND PREVENTION

Casey C. Grant
Chief Systems and Applications Engineer
National Fire Protection Association
Quincy, Massachusetts

GLOSSARY

Boiling point   The temperature at which the liquid boils when under normal atmospheric pressure (14.7 psia). The boiling point increases as pressure increases and is dependent on the total pressure.

Combustible   A material or structure that can burn is considered combustible. Combustible is a relative term; many materials that will burn under one set of conditions will not burn under others, e.g., structural steel is noncombustible, but fine steel wool is combustible. The term *combustible* does not usually indicate ease of ignition, burning intensity, or rate of burning, except when modified, as in *highly combustible interior finish*.

Fire prevention   Measures directed toward avoiding the inception of fire.

Fire load   The amount of combustibles present in a given situation, usually expressed in terms of weight of combustible material per unit area. This measure is employed frequently to calculate the degree of fire resistance required to withstand a fire or to judge the rate of application and quantity of extinguishing agent needed to control or extinguish a fire.

Fire point   The lowest temperature of a liquid in an open container at which vapors are evolved fast enough to support continuous combustion.

Fire resistance   A relative term, used with a numerical rating or modifying adjective to indicate the extent to which a material or structure resists the effect of fire, e.g., "fire resistance of 2 hours."

Fire-resistive   Pertains to properties or designs that resist the effects of any fire to which a material or structure may be expected to be subjected. *Fire-resistive materials* or assemblies of materials are noncombustible, but noncombustible materials are not necessarily fire-resistive; *fire-resistive* implies a higher degree of fire resistance than *noncombustible*. *Fire-resistive construction* is defined in terms of specified fire resistance as measured by the standard time-temperature curve.

Fire-retardant   Usually denotes a substantially lower degree of fire resistance than fire-resistive and is often used to refer to materials or structures which are combustible in whole or in part, but have been subjected to treatments of have surface coverings to prevent or retard ignition or the spread of fire under the conditions for which they are designed.

Flame-resistant   A term that may be used more or less interchangeably with flame-retardant.

Flame-retardant   Materials, usually decorative, which due to chemical treatment or inherent properties, do not ignite readily or propagate flaming under small to moderate exposure.

Flammable   A combustible material that ignites very easily, burns intensely, or has a rapid rate of flame spread. Flammable is used in a general sense without reference to specific limits of ignition temperature, rate of burning, or other property. *Flammable* and *inflammable* are identical in meaning. Flammable is used in preference to inflammable.

Flammable limits   The extreme concentration limits of a combustible in an oxidant through which a flame will continue to propagate at the specified temperature and pressure. For example, hydrogen-air mixtures will propagate flame between 4.0 and 75 percent by volume of hydrogen at 21°C and atmospheric pressure. The smaller value is the lower (lean) limit, and the larger value is the upper (rich) limit of flammability. For liquid fuels in equilibrium with their vapors in air, a minimum temperature exists for each fuel above which sufficient vapor is released to form a flammable vapor-air mixture. There is also a maximum temperature above which the vapor concentration is too high to propagate flame. These minimum and maximum temperatures are referred to respectively as the lower and upper *flash points* in air. The flash-point temperatures for a combustible liquid vary directly with environmental pressure.

Flashover   The phenomenon of a developing fire (or radiant heat source) producing radiant energy at wall and ceiling surfaces within a compartment. The radiant feedback from those surfaces heats the contents of the fire area so that all the combustibles in the space become heated to their ignition temperature.

Flash point   The lowest temperature at which the vapor pressure of a liquid will produce a flammable mixture and resultant flame. The flame will not continue to burn at this temperature if the source of ignition is removed.

Glowing combustion and flame   Combustion is the process of exothermic, self-catalyzed reaction involving either a condensed-phase or a gas-phased fuel, or both. The process is usually (but not necessarily) associated with oxidation of a fuel by atmospheric oxygen. Condensed-phase combustion is usually referred to as *glowing combustion,* while gas-phase combustion is referred to as a *flame.*

Ignition temperature (autoignition temperature, autogenous ignition temperature)   The minimum temperature to which a substance in air must be heated in order to initiate, or cause, self-sustained combustion independently of the heating or heated element. The ignition temperature of a combustible solid is influenced by rate of airflow, rate of heating, and size and shape of the solid.

Latent heat   Heat is absorbed by a substance when converted from a solid to a liquid and from a liquid to a gas. Conversely, heat is released during conversion of a gas to a liquid, or a liquid to a solid. Latent heat is the quantity of heat absorbed or given off by a substance in passing between liquid and gaseous phases (latent heat of vaporization) or between solid and liquid phases (latent heat of fusion). The high heat of vaporization of water is a reason for the effectiveness of water as an extinguishing agent.

Noncombustible   Not combustible.

Nonflammable   Not flammable.

Specific heat   The heat, or thermal capacity, of a substance is the number of calories required to raise 1 gram of a particular substance 1°C. The specific heats of various substances vary over a considerable range; for all common substances, except water, they are less than unity. Specific-heat figures are significant in fire protection as they indicate the relative quantity of heat needed to raise the temperature to a point of danger, or the quantity of heat that must be removed to cool a hot substance to a safe temperature.

Vapor density   The weight of a volume of pure gas compared with the weight of an equal volume of dry air at the same temperature and pressure. A figure less than 1 indicates that a gas is lighter than air, and a figure greater than 1 indicates that a gas is heavier than air. If a flammable gas with a vapor density greater than 1 escapes from its container, it may travel at a low level to a source of ignition.

Vapor pressure   Because molecules of a liquid are always in motion (with the amount of motion depending on the temperature of the liquid), the molecules are continuously escaping from the free surface of the liquid to the space above. Some molecules remain in space while others, due to random motion, collide with the liquid. If the liquid is in an open container, molecules (collectively called *vapor*) escape from the surface, and the liquid is said to evaporate. If, on the other hand, the liquid is in a closed container, the motion of the escaping molecules is confined to the vapor space above the surface of the liquid. As an increasing number strike and reenter the liquid, a point of equilibrium is eventually reached with the rate of escape of molecules from the liquid equals the rate of return to the liquid. The pressure exerted by the escaping vapor at the point of equilibrium is called *vapor pressure.* Vapor pressure is measured in millimeters of mercury (mm), or torr.

INTRODUCTION

Fire protection is an area in which most plant engineers can make a significant contribution to plant operations. At many facilities, the chief engineer may also serve as the *fire marshal* or *fire chief.* Even at larger plants, where there is a full-time safety or fire-protection engineer responsible for plant protection and loss prevention, the plant engineer should be familiar with the fire problem, fire-prevention methods, and fire protection systems.

Fires in private industry have a great potential for significant economic and financial loss to both the industrial plant and the community. Recovery from an industrial fire includes not only replacement of equipment and facilities at higher costs, but also temporary and permanent lost business income, loss of skilled employees during the time the plant is closed, loss of profits on damaged finished goods, and extra expenses to restore operations. Many plants destroyed by fire do not reopen, contributing to local unemployment and disrupting the lives of employees.

This chapter is intended to give the plant engineer a basic understanding of fire protection and prevention, to provide some basic information about fire, and to identify other resources for the incorporation of fire safety in every aspect of plant operations.

In addition to the National Fire Protection Association (NFPA) in Quincy, Mass., and the Federal Emergency Management Agency (FEMA) in Washington, D.C., the following fire protection services are also available in most cities in the United States: the Society of Fire Protection Engineers (SFPE), fire protection consultants, equipment manufacturers, testing laboratories, companies specializing in special-hazard protection and control, fire investigation firms, and organizations that perform fire-protection equipment testing, installation, and servicing. There are also state and regional training facilities, and the resources of municipal fire departments should not be overlooked.

This chapter does not attempt to discuss management programs which may have significant impact on plant fire protection. Information regarding risk management, personnel training, plant fire brigades, plant emergency organization, and fire-prevention programs must be obtained from other sources.

THE NATURE OF FIRE

A simple method of visualizing what fire is and how burning takes place is to use a four-sided object, a tetrahedron. Each surface of the tetrahedron is used to represent one of the conditions necessary for fire to occur (see Fig. 2-1).

The four components of this simple fire model are fuel, heat, oxidant, and the chemical chain reaction. While this model does not provide a complete scientific description of fire, it is sufficient for explaining most fire-protection concepts. In chemical terminology, the *fuel*

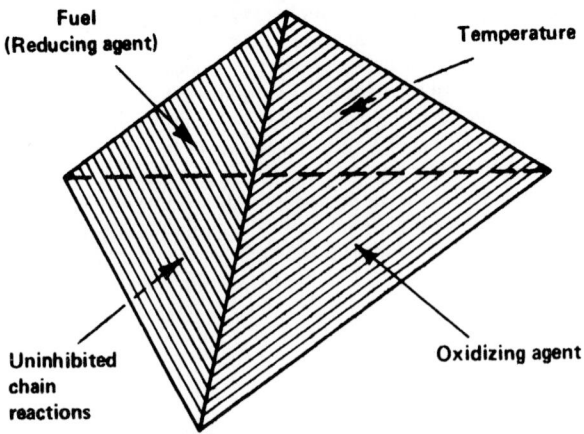

FIGURE 2-1   Tetrahedron fire model. (*From R. Tuve,* Principles of Fire Protection Chemistry, *NFPA, Quincy, Mass., 1976.*)

component may also be referred to as a *reducing agent*. During the fire reaction the reducing agent looses electrons. The *heat* component includes both the heat which causes the fire and the heat emitted by the fire which causes it to be self-sustaining. The *oxidant* required for fire is most often provided by the oxygen in the ambient air, approximately 21 percent. Although oxygen is the most common oxidizing agent and is usually necessary for fire to occur, there are some chemicals that release oxygen and some that can burn in an oxygen-free atmosphere.

Vapor State of Fuel

Before a fuel can be burned it must be in a vapor state. Therefore, flammable gases are most easily ignited. Even solids and liquids, such as wood and gasoline, must be vaporized before they will burn. The decomposition of matter due to heat which generates flammable vapors is called *pyrolysis.*

The initial vaporization of the fuel may be caused by heat from a source of ignition such as a chemical reaction, electric energy, or mechanical heat energy. Ambient heat may also be sufficient to vaporize fuels which are normally liquids.

Once sufficient vaporization has occurred, the combustible vapors can be ignited by an open flame of spark or, at a sufficiently high temperature, the vapor and oxygen mixture will ignite spontaneously.

After ignition of the vaporized fuel has occurred, the heat generated by the fire will cause further vaporization of the fuel and the intensity of the fire will increase. This process is known as *radiation feedback.*

Heat Transfer

The heat that causes the fuel to ignite and the heat generated by the resulting fire can be transmitted by one or all of the following three methods:

- *Conduction.* Heat transferred by direct contact from one body to another.
- *Radiation.* Energy travel through space or materials as waves.
- *Convection.* Heat transferred by a circulating medium, either a gas or a liquid.

Products of Combustion

There are four categories of products of combustion: (1) fire gases, (2) flame, (3) heat, and (4) smoke. All of these products are produced in varying degrees by each fire. The material or materials that are involved in the fire and the resulting chemical reactions produced by the fire determine the products of combustion.

Fire Gases.   The primary cause of loss of life in fires is the inhalation of heated, toxic, and oxygen-deficient gases and smoke. The amount and kind of fire gases present during and after a fire vary widely with the chemical composition of the material burning, the amount of available oxygen, and the temperature. The effect of toxic gases and smoke on people will depend on the time of exposure, the concentration of gases in air, and the physical condition of the individual.

There are usually several gases present during a fire. Those that are commonly considered lethal are carbon monoxide, carbon dioxide, hydrogen sulfide, sulfur dioxide, ammonia, hydrogen cyanide, hydrogen chloride, nitrogen dioxide, acrolein, and phosgene.

Flame.   The burning of materials in a normal oxygen-rich atmosphere is generally accompanied by flame. For this reason, flame is considered a distinct product of combustion. Burns can be caused by direct contact with flames or heat radiated from flames. Flame is rarely separated from the burning materials by an appreciable distance.

Heat.   Heat is the combustion product most responsible for fire spread. Exposure to heat from a fire will affect persons in proportion to the length of exposure and the temperature of the heat. The dangers of exposure to heat from fire range from minor injury to death. Exposure to heated air increases the heart rate and causes dehydration, exhaustion, blockage of the respiratory tract, and burns. Fire fighters should not enter atmospheres exceeding 120°F (48°C) to 130°F (54°C) without special protective clothing and masks. The maximum survivable breathing level of heat from fire in a dry atmosphere for a short period has been estimated at 300°F (148°C). Any moisture present in the air greatly increases the danger and sharply reduces the time of survival.

Smoke.   Smoke is matter consisting of very fine solid particles and condensed vapor. Fire gases from common combustibles (such as wood) contain water vapor, carbon dioxide, and carbon monoxide. Under the usual conditions of insufficient oxygen for complete combustion, methane, methanol, formaldehyde, and formic and acetic acids are also present. These gases are usually evolved from the combustible with sufficient velocity to carry droplets of flammable tars which appear as smoke. Particles of carbon develop from the decomposition of these tars; they are also present in the fire gases from the burning of petroleum products, particularly from the heavier oils and distillates.

Modes of Combustion

The combustion process may occur in two modes, *flaming* (including explosion) and *flameless* (including glow and deep-seated glowing embers). The flaming mode is characterized by relatively high burning rates. Intense and high levels of heat are usually associated with the flaming mode.

The flaming and flameless modes are not mutually exclusive; combustion may involve one or both modes. Often combustion may occur in the flaming mode and gradually make a transition to the flammable mode. At one point in this process both modes occur simultaneously.

Fire Control

Fire prevention and fire extinguishment can be described in terms of the fire model previously discussed. Fire prevention is generally a matter of keeping heat and fuel separated; or, in some processes, keeping heated fuel from combining with oxygen.

Fire extinguishment can be summarized by four methods:

1. Removal or dilution of air or oxygen to a point where combustion ceases.
2. Removal of fuel to a point where there is nothing remaining to oxidize.
3. Cooling of the fuel to point where combustible vapors are no longer evolved or where activation energy is lowered to the extent that no activated atoms or free radicals are produced.
4. Interruption of the flame chemistry of the chain reaction of combustion by injection of compounds capable of quenching free-radical products.

Removal of Oxygen.   The amount of dilution of oxygen necessary to stop the combustion varies greatly with the kind of material that is burning. Ordinary hydrocarbon gases and vapors will not burn when the oxygen level is below 15 percent. Acetylene will continue to burn unless the oxygen concentration is lowered, but will continue to glow on the surface even if the oxygen level is as low as 4 to 5 percent.

A fire in a closed space can extinguish itself by consuming the oxygen. However, incomplete combustion, which takes place when the oxygen is consumed, usually results in considerable generation of flammable gases.

A commonly used method of putting a fire out by removing or diluting the oxygen is by flooding the entire fire area with carbon dioxide or with some other inert gas.

Fuel Removal.   Fuel removal can be accomplished in a variety of ways. One of the most common examples is the practice of building a firebreak across the path of an advancing forest fire.

Fires in large coal or wood pulp piles can usually be controlled only by moving the pile of the fire zone. Fires in large oil storage tanks have been controlled by pumping the oil out of the burning tank into an empty tank. If a gas line is ruptured and the gas ignited, shutting off the supply of gas is the only way to stop the fire.

If it is not practical to remove the fuel, extinguishment can be accomplished by shutting off the fuel vapors or by covering the burning or glowing fuel. The use of fire-fighting foams and dry powder extinguishers are effective procedures for covering or coating a fire.

Cooling.   For most common combustibles such as wood, paper, and cloth, the simplest and most effective means of removing the heat of a fire is through the application of water. Water application can be varied and will depend on the fire.

Applying water to the burning fuel cools the fuel until the rate of release of combustible vapors and gases is reduced and ultimately stopped. Heat developed by a fire is carried away by radiation, conduction, and convection. This helps reduce the amount of heat and makes the use of water more effective. Only a relatively small proportion of the heat evolved needs to be cooled by the water in order to extinguish the fire.

Effective use of water cannot be accomplished if the water cannot reach the burning fuel directly. For this reason, areas where fire fighters cannot readily reach the fire with water streams, such as high-rise buildings and high-piled storage areas, must be provided with automatic sprinklers or other automatic fire-protection system.

Interruption of Chemical Reaction.   Extinguishment by cooling, by oxygen dilution, and by fuel removal, is applicable to all classes of flaming and glowing fires. Extinguishment by chemical flame inhibition applies to the flaming mode only.

In the fourth method of extinguishment, the action occurs only during contact of the chemical agents with activated groups or with atoms being produced by the combustion process. In a sense this could be seen as a temporary extinguishment process, operating only when the agent particles are present in the flame. If activation energy continues to exist after withdrawal of the flame-inhibiting agent, the flame reaction will re-establish and will continue.

Summary

Combustion occurs under the following conditions:

1. An oxidizing agent, a combustible material, and an ignition source are essential for combustion
2. The combustible material must be heated to its ignition temperature before it will burn
3. Combustion will continue until:
   a. The combustible material is consumed or removed.
   b. The oxidizing agent concentration is lowered to below the concentration necessary to support combustion.
   c. The combustible material is cooled below its ignition temperature.
   d. Flames are chemically inhibited.

THE PLANT FIRE PROBLEM: CAUSES AND PREVENTION

In general, the cause of most plant fires is the exposure of a fuel to a source of heat. Where the fuel, such as accumulations of trash or debris, is not necessary plant operation, fires can be prevented by removal of the fuel. Where the exposed fuel, such as raw materials or finished products, is essential, the source of heat must be protected or controlled.

Some of the most common sources of heat and fuel that cause plant fires are heating and cooking equipment, smoking, electric equipment, burning, flammable liquids, open flames and sparks, incendiary (arson), spontaneous ignition, gas fires, and explosions. These sources of heat are summarized below.

Heating and Cooking Equipment

Defective or Overheated Equipment.   This includes improperly maintained or operated furnaces, smoke pipes, vents, portable and stationary heaters, industrial commercial furnaces, and incinerators.

Chimneys and Flues.   Fire can arise from ignition of accumulated soot or inadequate separation from combustible material.

Hot Ashes and Coals.   These can cause problems when improper disposal or disposal in combustible containers or with combustible debris occurs.

Improper Location.   This can mean installation too close to combustible or accumulation of combustibles near an appliance.

Electric Equipment

Wiring and Distribution Equipment.   These include short-circuit faults, arcs, and sparks from damaged, defective, or improperly installed components.

Motors and Appliances.   These include careless use, improper installation, and poor maintenance.

Flammable Liquids

Storage and Handling.   These hazards include careless spills, leaking fuel, and overturned tanks.

Inadequate Safeguards.   Fires can be started by improper storage containers or facilities, improper electrical equipment near open processes, or improper bonding and grounding of transfer processes.

Open Flames and Sparks

Trash and Rubbish.   Burning trash and rubbish can furnish the fuel for accidental ignition; careless burning ignites other material.

Sparks and Embers.   Problems include ignition of roof coverings by sparks from chimneys, incinerators, rubbish fires, locomotives, etc.

Welding and Cutting.   Hazards include ignition of combustibles by the arc or flame itself, heat conduction through the metals being welded or cut, molten slag and metal from the cut, and sparks.

Friction, Sparks from Machinery.   Friction heat or sparks resulting from impact between two hard surfaces are a hazard.

Thawing Pipes.   Open-flame devices are a hazard when used in the dangerous practice of thawing pipes.

Other Open Flames.   These include ignition sources such as candles, locomotive sparks, incinerator sparks, and chimney sparks.

Lightning.   This includes building fires caused by the effects of lightning.

Exposure.   Exposure fires are those originating in places other than buildings, but which ignite buildings.

Incendiary, Suspicious.   These are fires that are known to be or thought to have been set, fires set to defraud insurance companies, fires set by mentally disturbed persons, and fires set by malicious persons.

Spontaneous Ignition.   This means fires resulting from the uncontrolled spontaneous heating of materials.

Gas Fires and Explosions.   These are fires and explosions that involve gas that has escaped from piping, storage tanks, equipment, or appliances and fires caused by misuse of faulty operation of gas appliances.

Smoking.   The use of smoking materials in flammable or explosive atmospheres, or discarding smoking materials in combustible debris.

PLANT FIRE HAZARDS

Fire hazards in industrial and manufacturing plants are a mix of exotic hazards specific to particular industries and common hazards analogous to those found in any other type of property—electrical systems, heating, smoking, common appliances and tools, even cooking and children playing with fire. Table 2-1 provides an overview of the leading causes in industrial and manufacturing fires. Note that the special industrial hazards lead the list but that collectively, the more common hazards account for the majority of fires, deaths, and injuries. (Because of the effect of individual fires involving very large losses, the majority of property damage in the period indicated occurred in fires started by hazards special to industrial occupancies.)

Many texts and handbooks exist to address the methods for preventing, mitigating, and controlling fires involving each of the many special industrial hazards. These references are listed in the last section of this chapter.

TABLE 2-1   Industrial and Manufacturing Facility Structure Fires, by Cause of Fire

Annual average of 1986–90 structure fires reported to U.S. fire departments

Cause of fire	Fires	Civilian deaths	Civilian injuries	Direct loss, millions
Other equipment	7,870	20	361	$440.51
(Furnace, oven or kiln)	(1,100)	(1)	(32)	($12.91)
(Working or shaping machine)	(900)	(0)	(34)	($9.49)
(Unclassified process equipment)	(680)	(12)	(40)	($317.30)
(Separate motor or generator)	(480)	(0)	(16)	($10.58)
(Heat treating equipment)	(440)	(0)	(15)	($11.01)
(Unclassified special equipment)	(420)	(0)	(21)	($6.28)
Open flame	3,290	4	125	$46.73
(Torch)	(1,860)	(3)	(94)	($31.69)
(Open fire)	(400)	(0)	(3)	($2.57)
Electrical distribution system	2,520	2	80	$68.33
(Fixed wiring)	(800)	(0)	(15)	($27.60)
(Fuses, circuit breakers or related panels)	(370)	(1)	(29)	($10.82)
Natural causes	1,780	10	97	$36.46
(Spontaneous ignition)	(680)	(9)	(55)	($23.33)
Heating equipment	1,760	0	47	$73.80
(Fixed space heater)	(420)	(0)	(7)	($6.81)
Incendiary or suspicious causes	1,740	2	22	$87.94
Appliances, tools or air conditioning	1,250	2	46	$16.76
(Clothes dryer)	(470)	(0)	(13)	($5.82)
Exposure (to other hostile fire)	830	0	7	$18.50
Other heat source	810	3	21	$13.76
Smoking material (i.e., lighted tobacco product)	690	2	25	$29.18
Cooking equipment	670	1	19	$10.95
Child playing	140	0	4	$0.74
Total	23,350	47	854	$843.66

Note: Sums may not equal totals because of rounding error. Fires are expressed to the nearest ten and direct property damage to the nearest ten thousand dollars. Losses have not been adjusted for inflation. Second-level causes are shown if they accounted for at least 1.5% of reported fires.

Source: NFPA, Quincy, Mass.

Tables 2-2 and 2-3 provide overviews of the same industrial and manufacturing fires described in Table 2-1, but in terms of the use and composition, respectively, of the items first ignited in the fire. Note the implied importance of housekeeping, as dust, fiber, lint, and trash are among the most common items ignited.

Table 2-4 provides a final overview of the same fires in terms of the areas where fire originated. While the leading areas are all work areas special to industrial and manufacturing operations, note the high ranking for many concealed spaces and service facilities and for exterior surfaces and areas of the building.

In all these tables, the statistics are NFPA estimates from two data bases on structure fires reported to U.S. local fire departments. Only direct losses are reported, so such indirect losses as business interruption losses are not reflected.

FIRE HAZARDS OF MATERIALS

Virtually all matter can be changed by exposure to sufficient quantities of energy. Energy in the form of heat was previously discussed. The heat energy which causes or is produced by a fire usually causes undesired changes to the material involved. The relative fire risks and products of burning of different types of materials are presented in this section.

Wood

When in contact with sufficient heat, all wood or wood-based products will ignite, the time of ignition depending on the ignition source and the length of exposure.

Wood or wood-based products can be treated with fire-retardant chemicals. When so treated, the flammability of wood and wood-based products is reduced. The flammability of these products can also be reduced when they are used in combination with other materials, such as insulation.

Wood is made up primarily of carbon, hydrogen, and oxygen. Live wood cells retain considerable moisture. When the wood is dead, air replaces most of the water in the cellular structure of wood. Some of the concerns associated with wood are further addressed in NFPA 664, *Woodworking and Woodprocessing Facilities*.

The fire behavior of wood and other combustible solids of the same size and shape varies greatly with the moisture content. Wet wood is harder to ignite and will not burn as fast as dry wood. The burning rate is also influenced by the moisture content in materials. See Table 2-5 for heat of combustion for various wood-based products composed with petroleum-based materials.

Even when exposed to a relatively high heat source for a prolonged period of time, ignition is generally difficult when the moisture content of wood (and similar fuels) is above 15 percent. Once ignition and resultant fire have begun, heat radiation and the rate of pyrolysis reduce the importance of the moisture factor.

Plastics

There are thousands of plastic product formulations that are produced in a variety of shapes and sizes, such as solid shapes, films and sheets, foams, molded forms, synthetic fibers, pellets, and powders. They are classified into 30 major groups of plastics and polymers. In addition, most finished products contain additives such as colorants, reinforcing agents, fillers, stabilizers, and lubricants. These additives vary the chemical nature of the product still more.

Most plastics are combustible, but the degree of combustibility varies widely because of the range of chemical compositions and combinations. As a result, it is virtually impossible to assign a fire hazard or flammability limit to any general plastic group. The only method of

TABLE 2-2 Industrial and Manufacturing Facility Structure Fires, by Form of Material First Ignited

Annual average of 1986–90 structure fires reported to U.S. fire departments

Form of material first ignited	Fires	Civilian deaths	Civilian injuries	Direct losses, millions
Unclassified item	2,260	3	99	$51.07
Dust, fiber, or lint	2,030	2	52	$15.09
Trash	1,940	1	29	$33.05
Electrical wire or cable insulation	1,590	1	50	$17.38
Structural member or framing	1,540	1	18	$40.45
Accelerant or other gas or liquid in or from pipe or container	950	14	155	$283.98
Agricultural product	870	0	10	$15.29
Exterior roof covering, surface or finish	670	0	10	$6.11
Exterior sidewall covering, surface or finish	630	0	3	$6.80
Fuel	610	1	42	$16.47
Chips	550	0	8	$5.35
Multiple items first ignited	510	3	50	$37.46
Box, carton, or bag	480	1	15	$14.78
Interior wall covering	470	0	10	$14.15
Thermal or acoustical insulation within concealed space	420	0	5	$10.69
Atomized or vaporized liquid	350	2	38	$4.48
Cooking materials	320	0	9	$2.13
Growing or living form, such as a plant	220	0	0	$1.70
Cleaning supplies	210	0	8	$3.28
Conveyor belt, drive belt, or V-belt	210	0	5	$2.41
Papers, including magazines, newspapers, and files	200	0	2	$2.20
Unclassified power transfer equipment or fuel	200	0	5	$4.77
Basket or barrel	190	7	7	$10.07
Unclassified supplies or stock	190	0	10	$3.10
Floor covering, including tile, vinyl flooring, carpet, rug, wood flooring, and stairs	190	0	2	$3.19
Rolled materials	180	0	8	$1.58
Clothing, whether on or not on a person	180	1	10	$1.58
Ceiling covering	170	0	6	$3.44
Transformer	160	0	7	$3.81
Unclassified structural component or finish	160	0	1	$3.95
Unknown-type structural component or finish	140	0	1	$1.90
Linen, other than bedding	140	0	5	$1.45
Bale storage	130	0	3	$3.82
Packing or wrapping material	130	0	1	$6.55
Exterior trim or appurtenance, including doors, porches and platforms	120	0	2	$0.84
Cabinetry, including tables, desks, chests, dressers, bookcases, and filing cabinets	120	0	2	$4.13
Mattress, pillow, bedding or blanket	110	1	4	$0.60
Pallet or skid (not in use)	100	0	1	$3.46
Fabric, yard goods or other goods not made up	100	0	14	$1.44
Other known	930	3	46	$48.81
Unknown	2,680	6	101	$150.87
Total	23,350	47	854	$843.66

Note: Sums may not equal totals because of rounding error. Fires are expressed to the nearest ten and direct property damage to the nearest ten thousand dollars. Losses have not been adjusted for inflation.

Source: NFPA, Quincy, Mass.

TABLE 2-3   Industrial and Manufacturing Facility Structure Fires, by Form of Material First Ignited

Annual average of 1986–90 structure fires reported to U.S. fire departments

Type of material first ignited	Fires	Civilian deaths	Civilian injuries	Direct loss, millions
Sawn wood	3,140	1	31	$66.57
Paper, untreated and uncoated	1,350	0	21	$30.28
Wood shavings	1,330	1	19	$12.93
Unclassified type of material	1,140	0	32	$19.20
Grass, leaves, hay or straw	880	0	4	$13.59
Rubber	780	0	23	$9.85
Cotton or rayon or related fabric or finished goods	690	1	29	$4.64
Unknown-type plastic	630	0	36	$12.62
Unclassified plastic	600	0	28	$9.85
Class IIIB combustible liquid	600	2	34	$13.72
Adhesive, resin or tar	540	0	19	$5.22
Multiple types of material first ignited	530	0	22	$21.66
Cardboard	500	1	15	$14.00
Man-made fabric or fiber or related finished goods	480	0	15	$8.31
Applied paint or varnish	410	0	20	$8.19
Hardboard or plywood	400	0	9	$7.89
Polyvinyl	380	0	42	$6.50
Class II combustible liquid	350	1	16	$7.82
Unclassified wood or paper	350	0	3	$4.47
Grain or natural fiber	310	0	3	$3.74
Unknown-type flammable or combustible liquid	300	8	19	$11.49
Fiberboard	290	0	3	$1.75
Fat or grease (food)	280	0	11	$6.99
Unknown-type wood or paper	260	0	4	$4.19
Combustible metal	250	1	14	$3.11
Class IB flammable liquid	200	1	56	$9.00
Gasoline	200	1	11	$6.21
Natural gas	190	1	20	$36.35
Oily rags	190	0	2	$3.27
Grease (nonfood)	180	0	1	$1.34
Unclassified flammable or combustible liquid	180	2	16	$4.55
Asphalt treated material	180	0	6	$1.07
Food or starch (excluding fat and grease)	160	0	3	$1.56
Unclassified natural product	150	0	4	$1.11
Polyurethane	140	0	7	$3.83
Acetylene	130	0	6	$0.87
Class IC flammable liquid	120	0	18	$4.61
Class IA flammable liquid	120	9	34	$253.16
Unclassified material compounded with oil	120	0	3	$1.80
Unclassified fabric, textile or fur	120	0	2	$2.15
Polyester	120	0	5	$3.91
Other known	1,420	7	100	$30.31
Unknown	2,650	5	90	$170.00
Total	23,350	47	854	$843.66

Note: Sums may not equal totals because of rounding error. Fires are expressed to the nearest ten and direct property damage to the nearest ten thousand dollars. Losses have not been adjusted for inflation.

Source: NFPA, Quincy, Mass.

TABLE 2-4   Industrial and Manufacturing Facility Structure Fires, by Area of Origin

Annual average of 1986–90 structure fires reported to U.S. fire departments

Area of origin	Fires	Civilian deaths	Civilian injuries	Direct loss, millions
Process or manufacturing area	4,490	19	264	$381.36
Machinery room	2,070	1	94	$50.01
Product storage room or area	1,500	4	54	$44.18
Maintenance shop or area	1,270	2	58	$35.03
Duct	870	0	19	$4.48
Heating area	770	1	24	$40.30
Attic or ceiling/roof assembly or concealed space	730	0	6	$15.66
Exterior wall surface	710	0	4	$23.57
Exterior roof surface	600	0	5	$3.63
Trash area	560	0	10	$4.28
Tool room or supply storage area	530	0	16	$14.27
Unclassified area	470	0	11	$9.29
Unclassified structural area	460	0	7	$12.59
Unclassified storage area	420	2	5	$7.24
Unclassified service facility	390	8	30	$9.14
Wall assembly or concealed space	350	0	2	$4.85
Kitchen	340	1	6	$2.58
Switchgear area or transformer room	310	2	26	$8.34
Office	300	0	6	$11.72
Laboratory	290	1	50	$4.04
Lawn, field or open area	290	0	2	$2.44
Shipping, receiving or loading area	280	0	9	$16.39
Ceiling/floor assembly or concealed space	280	0	3	$8.40
Electronic equipment room	270	0	13	$7.51
Laundry room	250	0	3	$1.43
Conveyor	220	0	3	$1.45
Printing or photographic room	220	0	12	$6.01
Bathroom	200	0	4	$1.33
Unclassified function area	200	0	6	$6.46
Chimney	200	0	1	$1.47
Garage	160	0	2	$3.53
Area of origin not applicable	160	1	3	$1.80
Utility shaft	140	0	2	$0.95
Crawl space or substructure space	130	0	2	$1.30
Incinerator room or area	120	0	2	$0.35
Unclassified service facility	110	0	2	$0.73
Other known	1,190	0	41	$24.71
Unknown	1,520	2	47	$70.81
Total	23,350	47	854	$843.66

Note: Sums may not equal totals because of rounding error. Fires are expressed to the nearest ten and direct property damage to the nearest ten thousand dollars. Losses have not been adjusted for inflation.

Source: NFPA, Quincy, Mass.

TABLE 2-5 Heat of Combustion of Various Wood and Wood-Based Products and Comparative Substances

Substance	Heating value, Btu/lb
Wood sawdust (oak)	8,493*
Wood sawdust (pine)	9,676*
Wood shavings	8,248*
Wood bark (fir)	9,496*
Corrugated fiber carton	5,970*
Newspaper	7,883*
Wrapping paper	7,106*
Petroleum coke	15,800
Asphalt	17,158
Oil (cottonseed)	17,100
Oil (paraffin)	17,640

* Dry.

Source: Extracted from *Kent's Mechanical Engineers' Handbook,* 12th ed., H. B. Carmichael and J. K. Salisbury, eds., Wiley-Interscience, New York, 1950.

determining the fire hazard of a particular plastic is to fire test the plastic under exact end-use conditions. See Tables 2-6 and 2-7.

The chemical composition, the physical form, and the manner and arrangement in which plastics are stored greatly affect the degree of fire hazard that is present. Large quantities of smoke are usually generated when stored plastics are involved in fire, a condition made more or less difficult by the amount of ventilation present or available in a give storage area.

Thermoplastics, such as polyethylene and plasticized polyvinylchloride, and thermosets, such as polyesters, present challenging fire hazards. Plastics in foamed material form present the most severe hazard of all. In a fire, thermoplastics will melt and break down and behave and burn like flammable liquids. Automatic sprinkler systems with high sprinkler-discharge densities are necessary for adequate fire protection.

Dusts

When some combustible solids are ground or rubbed into minute particles, the particles tend to mix with the air in much the same way that vapor or gas mixes with the air. The finer the

TABLE 2-6 Small-Scale Test for Combustibility of Plastics

Test method	Sample size, in	Position of sample	Ignition source, flame, in	Time and limit of exposure, s	Value reported, in/min	Usual material application
ASTM D 635	⅛ × ½ × 5	Horizontal	1	2–30	Burning rate	Rigid plastic
ASTM D 568	0.05 × 1 × 18	Horizontal	1	15	Burning rate	Films
ASTM D 229	1/32 × ½ × 5	Horizontal	1	30	Burning time for 4 samples	Electrical insulation
ASTM D 1692	½ × 2 × 6	Horizontal	1	60	Burning rate	Foam
UL 94*	⅛ × ½ × 5	Horizontal	¾	30	Burning rate	
	⅛ × ½ × 5	Vertical	¾	2–10	Extinguishment time	Rigid plastics Rigid plastics
NFPA 701	2¾ × 10	Vertical	1½	12	Length of char	Films
UL 214	2¾ × 10	Vertical	1½	12	Length of char	Films

* UL stands for Underwriters Laboratories Inc.

Source: NFPA, Quincy, Mass.

TABLE 2-7   Medium- and Large-Scale Tests
for Combustibility of Plastics

Test for	Number
Surface burning of building materials	NFPA 255
	UL 723
	ASTM E 84
Fire tests of building construction and materials	NFPA 251
	UL 263
	ASTM E 119
Fire tests of roof coverings	NFPA 256
Radiant panel test for flame spread	ASTM E 162
Factory mutual calorimeter test	
UL and FM corner wall tests*	
Full-room burnouts—FM, UL	
Flame-retardant films	NFPA 701
	UL 214

* UL stands for Underwriters Laboratories Inc. FM stands for
Factory Mutual Systems.
   Source: NFPA, Quincy, Massachusetts.

dust particle, the more completely it will mix with the air and remain suspended in the air.
Although dust particles from all combustible solids do not result in potentially explosive dust
particles, a large number of combustible solids can yield explosive dust particles. See Table
2-8. A variety of NFPA standards deal directly with this subject. These include:

NFPA 61A, *Facilities Manufacturing and Handling Starch*

NFPA 61B, *Grain Elevators and Bulk Handling Facilities*

NFPA 61C, *Fire and Dust Explosions in Feed Mills*

NFPA 61D, *Milling of Agricultural Commodities for Human Consumption*

TABLE 2-8   Common Combustible Solid Dusts Generating Severe Explosions

Type of dust	Maximum explosion pressure		Maximum rate of pressure rise	
	psig	bar	psig/s	bar/s
Corn (processing)	95	6.55	6,000	413.7
Cornstarch	115	7.93	9,000	620.5
Potato starch	97	6.89	8,000	551.6
Sugar (processing)	91	6.27	5,000	344.7
Wheat starch	105	7.24	8,500	586.0
Ethyl cellulose plastic molding compound	102	7.03	6,000	413.7
Wood flour filler	110	7.58	5,500	379.2
Natural resin	87	6.0	10,000	689.5
Aluminum	100	6.9	10,000	689.5
Magnesium (powder)	94	6.48	10,000	689.5
Silicon (powder)	106	7.31	10,000	689.5
Titanium (powder)	80	5.52	10,000	689.5
Aluminum magnesium alloy (powder)	90	6.20	10,000	689.5

Source: Extracted from U.S. Bureau of Mines Investigations and Reports, nos. 5753, RI 5971, RI 6561.

NFPA 650, *Pneumatic Conveying systems for Handling Combustible Materials*

NFPA 654, *Dust Explosions in Chemical Dye, Pharmaceutical and Plastics Industry*

NFPA 655, *Prevention of Sulfur Fires and Explosions*

Metals

Nearly all metals will burn in air under certain conditions. See Table 2-9. Some oxidize rapidly in the presence of air or moisture, generating sufficient heat to reach their ignition temperatures. Others oxidize so slowly that heat generated during oxidation is dissipated before they become hot enough to ignite. Certain metals, notably magnesium, titanium, sodium, potassium, calcium, lithium, hafnium, zirconium, zinc, thorium, uranium, and plutonium, are referred to as combustible metals because of the ease of ignition of thin sections, fine particles, or molten metal. The same metals in massive solid form are comparatively difficult to ignite.

Hot, burning metals may react violently with the extinguishants used on fires involving ordinary combustibles or flammable liquids. A few metals, such as uranium, thorium, and plutonium, emit ionizing radiations that can complicate fire fighting and introduce a contamination problem.

Temperatures in burning metals are generally much higher than the temperature in burning flammable liquids. Some hot metals can continue burning in nitrogen, carbon dioxide, or steam atmospheres in which ordinary combustibles or flammable liquids would be incapable of burning. NFPA standards that specifically address metals include:

NFPA 65, *Processing and Finishing of Aluminum*

NFPA 480, *Processing, Handling, and Storage of Magnesium*

TABLE 2-9   Melting, Boiling, and Ignition Temperature of Pure Metals in Solid Form

	Temperature					
	Melting point		Boiling point		Solid metal ignition	
Pure metal	°F	°C	°F	°C	°F	°C
Aluminum	1220	660	4445	2452	1832*‡	555*‡
Barium	1337	725	2084	1140	347*	175*
Calcium	1548	842	2625	1440	1300	704
Hafnium	4032	2223	9750	5399	—	—
Iron	2795	1535	5432	3000	1706*	930*
Lithium	367	186	2437	1336	356	180
Magnesium	1202	650	2030	1110	1153	623
Plutonium	1184	640	6000	3315	1112	600
Potassium	144	62	1400	760	156*†	69†*
Sodium	208	98	1616	880	239‡	115‡
Strontium	1425	774	2102	1150	1328*	720*
Thorium	3353	1845	8132	4500	932*	500*
Titanium	3140	1727	5900	3260	2900	1593
Uranium	2070	1132	6900	3815	6900*§	3815*§
Zinc	786	419	1665	907	1652*	900*
Zirconium	3326	1830	6470	3577	2552*	1400*

* Ignition in oxygen.
† Spontaneous ignition in moist air.
‡ Above indicated temperature.
§ Below indicated temperature.

Source: From Arthur E. Cote, ed., Fire Protection Handbook, NFPA, Quincy, Mass., 1991.

NFPA 481, *Processing, Handling, and Storage of Titanium Production*

NFPA 482, *Processing, Handling and Storage of Zirconium Production*

NFPA 651, *Manufacture of Aluminum or Magnesium Powder*

Flammable and Combustible Liquids

The improper storage, handling, and use of flammable and combustible liquids has been the cause of many deaths, injuries, and disastrous fires. Various NFPA standards provide detailed requirements on this subject, including:

NFPA 30, *Flammable and Combustible Liquids Code*

NFPA 30A, *Automotive and Marine Service Station Code*

NFPA 30B, *Manufacture and Storage of Aerosol Products*

NFPA 31, *Installation of Oil Burning Equipment*

NFPA 321, *Classification of Flammable and Combustible Liquids*

NFPA 395, *Farm Storage of Flammable and Combustible Liquids*

It is the vapor from the evaporation of a flammable or combustible liquid when exposed to air or under the influence of heat, rather than the liquid itself, which burns or explodes when mixed with air in certain proportion in the presence of some source of ignition. There is a flammable range below which the vapor mixture is too lean to burn or explode, or above which the vapor mixture is too rich to burn or explode. (see Table 2-10.)

For gasoline, one of the most common and widely used flammable liquid, the flammable range is 1.4 and 7.6 percent by volume. When the vapor-air mixture is near either the lower flammable limit (LFL) or upper flammable limit (UFL), the explosion is less intense than when the mixture is in the intermediate range. The violence of the explosion depends on the concentration of the vapor as well as the quantity of vapor-air mixture and the type of container. Thus, it is important in controlling the fire hazard, to store a flammable liquid in the

TABLE 2-10   Flash Points and Flammable Limits of Some Common Liquids and Gases

Liquid (or gas at ordinary temps.)	Flash point		Flammable limits, percent by volume
	°F	°C	
Acetylene	(Gas)		2.5–81.0*
Benzene	12	–11	1.3–7.1
Ether (ethyl ether)	–49	–45	1.9–36.0
Fuel oil			
Domestic, no. 2	100 (min.)	38	None at ordinary temperatures
Heavy, no. 5	130 (min.)	54	None at ordinary temperatures
Gasoline (high test)	–36	–38	1.4–7.4
Hydrogen	(Gas)		4.07–75.0
Jet fuel (A & A-1)	110 to 150	43 to 65	None at ordinary temperatures
Kerosene (Fuel oil, No. 1)	100 (min.)	38	0.7–5.0
LPG (propane-butane)	(Gas)		1.9–9.5
Lacquer solvent (butyl acet.)	72	22	1.7–7.6
Methane (natural gas)	(Gas)		5.0–15.0
Methyl alcohol	52	11	6.7–36.0
Turpentine	95	35	0.8–(undetermined)
Varsol (standard solv.)	110	43	0.7–5.0
Vegetable oil (cooking, peanut)	540	282	Ignition temperature = 833°F

Source: NFPA, Quincy, Mass.

proper type of closed container and minimize the exposure to air. When exposed to heat from a fire, a tank or other container may rupture with dangerous results if properly designed vents are not provided or if the exposed tank or container is not cooled by hose streams. The principal fire and explosion prevention measures under such circumstances are: (1) exclusion of sources of ignition, (2) exclusion of air, (3) keeping the liquid in a closed container, (4) ventilation to prevent the accumulation of vapor in the flammable range, and (5) use of an atmosphere of inert gas instead of air.

The following system of classifying liquids is generally recognized:

Flammable Liquids.   Flammable liquids are any liquid having a flash point below 100°F (38°C) and a boiling point below 100°F (38°C) and having a vapor pressure not exceeding 2068.6 mmHg at 100°F (38°C). Class I liquids include those having flash points below 100°F (38°C) and may be subdivided as follows:

Class IA includes those having flash points below 73°F (23°C) and a boiling point below 100°F (38°C).

Class IB includes those having flash points below 73°F (23°C) and a boiling point at or above 100°F (38°C).

Class IC includes those having flash points at or above 73°F (23°C) and below 100°F (38°C).

Combustible Liquids.   Liquids with a flash point at or above 100°F (38°C) are referred to as combustible liquids. They are:

Class II liquids include those having flash points at or above 100°F (38°C) and below 140°F (60°C).

Class IIIA liquids include those having flash points at or above 140°F (60°C) and below 200°F (93°C).

Class IIIB liquids include those having flash points at or above 200°F (93°C).

Some typical liquids would be classed as follows:

Denatured alcohol	Class IB
Fuel oil	Class II
Gasoline	Class IB
Kerosene	Class II
Peanut oil	Class IIIB
Turpentine	Class IC
Paraffin wax	Class IIIB

Proper storage and handling of flammable and combustible liquids are necessary to prevent fire or explosion. Ventilation to prevent accumulations of flammable vapors is of primary importance because there is the possibility of breaks or leaks in the storage and handling in a closed system. It is important to eliminate possible sources of ignition in an area where flammable liquids are stored, handled, or used.

Ventilation of an area where flammable liquids are manufactured or used can be accomplished by natural or mechanical means. Wherever possible, equipment such as compressors, stills, and pumps should be located in a spacious, open area. Most flammable liquids produce heavier-than-air vapors that flow along the ground or floor and settle in depressions. These can travel long distances and be ignited and flash back from a point remote from the origin of the vapors. NFPA 30, *Flammable and Combustible Liquids Code,* is the accepted national standard for fire protection of such liquids.

NFPA standards specify the construction, installation, spacing, venting, and diking of aboveground and underground storage tanks, container storage in buildings, loading and unloading practices, safeguards for dispensing the liquids, and standards for transporting the liquids in trucks, ships, or pipelines (Tables 2-11 and 2-12).

TABLE 2-11 Storage Limitations for Inside Storage Rooms

Fire protection* provided	Fire resistance, h	Maximum size, ft^2	Allowable loading, gal/ft^2 floor area
Yes	2	500	10
No	2	500	4
Yes	1	150	5
No	1	150	2

* Fire-protection system of sprinkler, water spray, carbon dioxide, dry chemical, halon, or other acceptable type of system.

Source: NFPA, Quincy, Mass.

TABLE 2-12 Storage Limitations for Warehouses or Storage Buildings

Class liquid	Storage level	Protected storage* maximum per pile height		Unprotected storage maximum per pile height	
		gal	ft	gal	ft
IA	Ground and upper floors	2,750	3	660	3
	Basement	(50)	(1)	(12)	(1)
		Not permitted		Not permitted	
IB	Ground and upper floors	5,500	6	1,375	3
	Basement	(100)	(2)	(25)	(1)
		Not permitted		Not permitted	
IC	Ground and upper floors	16,500	6	4,125	3
	Basement	(300)	(2)	(75)	(1)
		Not permitted		Not permitted	
II	Ground and upper floors	16,500	9	4,125	9
	Basement	(300)	(3)	(75)	(3)
		5,500	9	Not permitted	
		(100)	(3)		
Combustible	Ground and upper floors	55,000	15	13,750	12
	Basement	(1,000)	(5)	(250)	(4)
		8,250	9	Not permitted	
		(150)	(3)		

* A sprinkler or equivalent fire-protection system installed in accordance with the applicable NFPA Standard. (Numbers in parentheses indicate corresponding number of 55-gal drums.) *Note 1:* When two or more classes of materials are stored in a single pile, the maximum gallonage permitted in that pile is the smallest of the two or more separate maximum gallonages. *Note 2:* Aisles are provided so that no container is more than 12 ft from an aisle. Main aisles shall be at least 8 ft wide and side aisles at least 4 ft wide. *Note 3:* Each pile is separated from each other pile by at least 4 ft. When stored on suitably protected racks or when the storage is suitably protected, containers may be piled up but no closer than 3 ft to the nearest beam, chord, girder, or other obstructions. Good practice is to maintain 3 ft clearance below sprinkler deflectors or discharge orifices or other overhead fire protection systems.

Source: NFPA, Quincy, Massachusetts.

Gases

There are many kinds of materials that exist in the form of gas. In general, gases are thought of and described when the substance exists in a gaseous state at normal temperature and pressure 70°F (21°C) and 114.7 psia (101,430 N/m^2). NFPA standards that provide detailed information on this subject include:

NFPA 43C, *Gaseous Oxidizing Materials*

NFPA 50, *Bulk Oxygen Systems at Consumer Sites*

NFPA 50A, *Gaseous Hydrogen Systems at Consumer Sites*

NFPA 50B, *Liquefied Hydrogen Systems at Consumer Sites*

NFPA 51, *Oxygen-Fuel Gas Systems, Welding and Cutting*

NFPA 51A, *Acetylene Cylinder Charging Plants*

NFPA 54, *National Fuel Gas Code*

NFPA 58, *Storage and Handling of Liquefied Petroleum Gases*

Classification by Chemical Properties.   Gases can be broadly classified according to chemical properties, physical properties, or usage. Classification by chemical properties helps to define the hazards of gases to people and in fires.

Flammable Gases.   Any gas that will burn in the normal concentrations of oxygen in the air is a flammable gas. Like flammable liquid vapors, the burning of this gas in air is in a range of gas-air mixture (the flammable range). See Table 2-13.

Nonflammable Gases.   Nonflammable gases will not burn in air or in any concentration of oxygen. A number of nonflammable gases, however, will support combustion. Such gases are often referred to as *oxidizers* or *oxidizing gases*. A common oxidizer is oxygen or oxygen in a mixture with other gases.

Nonflammable gases that will not support combustion are usually called *inert gases*. Common inert gases are nitrogen, carbon dioxide, and sulfur dioxide.

Toxic Gases.   Toxic gases endanger life when inhaled. Gases such as chlorine, hydrogen sulfide, sulfur dioxide, ammonia, and carbon monoxide are poisonous or irritating when inhaled.

Reactive Gases.   Reactive gases react with other materials or within themselves by a reaction other than burning. When exposed to heat and shock, some reactive gases rearrange themselves chemically. Such gases can produce hazardous quantities of heat or reaction products. Fluorine is a highly reactive gas. At normal temperatures and pressures it will react with most organic and inorganic substances, often fast enough to result in flaming. Other examples of reactive gases are acetylene and vinyl chloride.

Classification by Physical Properties.   Gases can also be classified by their physical properties. They can be compressed, liquefied, or cryogenic.

Compressed Gases.   A compressed gas is at normal temperature inside a gas container and exists solely in the gaseous state under pressure; common compressed gases are hydrogen, oxygen, acetylene, and ethylene.

Liquefied Gases.   Liquefied gases can be liquefied relatively easily and stored at ordinary temperatures at relatively high pressure. Liquefied gas exists in both liquid and gaseous states; at storage pressure, both the liquid and gas in the liquefied-gas container are in equilibrium and will remain so as long as any liquid remains in the container. Liquefied gas is more concentrated than compressed gas.

Cryogenic Gases.   Cryogenic gases are stored in a completely liquid state. They must be maintained in their containers as low-temperature liquids at relatively low pressure. Cryogenic gases must be stored in special containers that allow the gas from the liquid to escape in order to prevent a pressure buildup caused by the production of the gaseous state within the container, which would result in container failure.

TABLE 2-13   Combustion Properties of Common Flammable Gases

Gas	Btu/ft³ (gross)	mJ/m³ (gross)	Limits of flammability, % by volume in air		Specific gravity (air = 1.0)	Air needed to burn 1 ft³ of gas, ft³	Air needed to burn 1 m³ of gas, m³	Ignition temperature	
			Lower	Upper				°F	°C
Natural gas									
High inert type (*Note 1*)	958–1051	35.7–39.2	4.5	14.0	0.660–0.708	9.2	9.2		
High methane type (*Note 2*)	1008–1071	37.6–39.9	4.7	15.0	.590–.614	10.2	10.2	900–1170	482–632
High Btu type (*Note 3*)	1071–1124	39.9–41.9	4.7	14.5	.620–.719	9.4	9.4	—	—
Blast furnace gas	81–111	3.0–4.1	33.2	71.3	1.04–1.00	0.8	0.8	—	—
Coke oven gas	575	21.4	4.4	34.0	.38	4.7	4.7	—	—
Propane (commercial)	2516	93.7	2.15	9.6	1.52	24.0	24.0	920–1120	493–604
Butane (commercial)	3300	122.9	1.9	8.5	2.0	31.0	31.0	900–1000	482–538
Sewage gas	670	24.9	6.0	17.0	0.79	6.5	6.5	—	—
Acetylene	1499	208.1	2.5	81.0	0.91	11.9	11.9	581	305
Hydrogen	325	12.1	4.0	75.0	0.07	2.4	2.4	932	500
Anhydrous ammonia	386	14.4	16.0	25.0	0.60	8.3	8.3	1204	651
Carbon monoxide	314	11.7	12.5	74.0	0.97	2.4	2.4	1128	609
Ethylene	1600	59.6	2.7	36.0	0.98	14.3	14.3	914	490
Methylacetylene, pro-padiene, stabilized (*Note 4*)	2450	91.3	3.4	10.8	1.48	—	—	850	454

Note 1: Typical composition CH_4 71.9–83.2%; N_2 6.3–16.20%.
Note 2: Typical composition CH_4 87.6–95.7%; N_2 0.1–2.39%.
Note 3: Typical composition CH_4 85.0–90.1%; N_2 1.2–7.5%.
Note 4: MAPPd gas.
Source: From Arthur E. Cote, ed., *Fire Protection Handbook,* NFPA, Quincy, Mass., 1991.

Classification by Usage.   An understanding of gases as they are classified by usage is important to those involved in fire protection because the terms of these classifications are used in codes, standards, and general industrial and medical terminology (Table 2-13).

Fuel Gases.   These gases are customarily used for burning with air to produce heat which in turn is used as a source of heat (comfort and process), power, or light. The principal and most widely used fuel gases are natural gas and the liquefied petroleum gases, butane and propane.

Industrial Gases.   These are classified by chemical properties customarily used in industrial processes, for welding and cutting, heat treating, chemical processing, refrigeration, water treatment, etc.

Medicinal Gases.   These are for medical purposes such as anesthesia and respiratory therapy. Cyclopropane, oxygen, and nitrous oxide gases are common medical gases.

Corrosive Chemicals

Corrosive chemicals are usually strong oxidizing agents that can increase fire hazards. Caustics, which are classified as water- and air-reactive chemicals, are also corrosive. Two types of corrosive chemicals that deserve consideration are inorganic acids and halogens.

Concentrated aqueous inorganic acids are not in themselves combustible; however, in addition to their corrosive and destructive effect on living tissue, their chief fire hazard results from the possibility of their mixing with combustible materials or other chemicals, resulting in fire or explosion. Almost all corrosive chemicals are strong oxidizing agents.

Halogens are salt-producing chemicals that are very active. They are noncombustible but will support combustion; presence of halogens causes turpentine, phosphorus, and finely divided metals to ignite spontaneously. The fumes are poisonous and corrosive.

Storage of corrosive chemicals should be provided with two considerations in mind: (1) protection against the damaging effect of corrosive chemicals on living tissue and (2) guarding against any fire and explosion hazard that might be associated with the corrosive chemical.

Inorganic Acids. These should be stored in cool, well-ventilated areas that are not exposed to the sun or other chemical and waste materials; they should be protected from freezing temperatures. Water in spray form is the recommended procedure for fighting fires in inorganic acid storage areas; in fires involving perchloric acid, extra care should be taken, since this may mix with other organic materials and result in an explosion.

Halogens. Fluorine and chlorine should be stored in special containers; fluorine may be safely stored in nickel or Monel cylinders. Impurities or moisture in the cylinder may cause an explosive reaction; chlorine, a serious inhalation hazard, should be stored in areas where ventilation is a prime consideration. Where chlorine leakage is suspected, use a self-contained breathing apparatus; fluorine requires protection of the self-contained breathing apparatus and special protective clothing.

Very often, corrosive vapors are a by-product of an industrial or chemical process. Ducts must be used to carry these vapors safely from the area. The type of duct used is determined by the vapor. Heavier-gauge metal may be sufficient, although a protective coating or special lining may be required in the ducts. Stainless steel, asbestos cement, and plastic linings have been used with success, depending on the corrosive vapor.

Radioactive Materials

The main concern in fire protection of radioactive materials is to prevent the release (or control the release) of these materials during fire extinguishment. Although fire protection operations are similar to those used when nonradioactive materials are involved, fire involving buildings or areas containing radioactive materials presents two additional considerations: (1) the presence of harmful radioactive materials might necessitate changing normal fire-fighting procedures and (2) because of the presence of radioactive matter, delay in salvage and resumption of normal operations may occur. NFPA standards that address radioactive materials include:

NFPA 801, *Facilities Handling Radioactive Materials*

NFPA 802, *Nuclear Research Reactors*

NFPA 803, *Light Water Nuclear Power Plants*

DESIGN AND CONSTRUCTION FOR FIRE SAFETY

Fire-safety objectives must be determined before a facility is designed. The architectural design and the building methods and materials used for a structure will often determine how a fire will be confined or will spread. At times, code compliance is not sufficient to meet the level of risk acceptable to a particular organization.

Fire-safety design decisions are necessary in at least three objective areas: life safety, property protection, and continuity of operations. A fourth objective area that is gaining prominence in recent years is the protection of the environment, such as would be considered for a hazard like large outdoor used-rubber-tire storage yards. Building codes, fire codes, and, increasingly, systems-analysis techniques are used by fire protection engineers to determine the level of protection to meet design objectives.

Building and Site Planning for Fire Safety

Two categories of decisions should be made in the design process to provide effective fire-safe design: interior building functions and exterior site planning. Building fire defenses, active and passive, should be designed so that the building assists in the suppression of fire while providing for safety of occupants.

Fire-Safety Planning for Buildings.   Interior layout, circulation patters, finish material, and building services are all important fire-safety considerations in building design. Building design also has a significant influence on the efficiency of fire-department operations.

Fire-fighting accessibility to building's interior includes access to the building itself as well as access to the interior of the building. Spaces in which fire-fighting access and operations are restricted because of architectural, engineering, or functional requirements should be provided with effective protection. A complete automatic sprinkler system is often the best solution, providing both life safety and property protection.

Ventilation is of vital importance in removing smoke, gases, and heat. Appropriate skylights, roof hatches, emergency escape exits, and similar devices should be provided when the building is constructed. NFPA has several design documents that address smoke control and ventilation.

Ventilation of building spaces performs the following important functions:

1. Protection of life by removing or diverting gases and smoke to allow for egress.
2. Control of the spread/direction of fire by setting up air currents that limit fire movement.
3. Provision of a release for unburned, combustible gases before they acquire a flammable mixture, thus avoiding a backdraft explosion and reducing burning temperatures.

NFPA 204, *Smoke and Heat Venting Guide,* recommends automatic smoke venting of large industrial buildings. NFPA 92A (*Smoke Control Systems*) and 92B (*Smoke Management Systems in Malls, Atria, and Large Areas*) present design methods for smoke control systems in other types of buildings.

In large-area buildings, curtain boards are an important element, unless vented areas are subdivided by means of walls or partitions. The function of curtain boards is to delay and limit the horizontal spread of heat by providing the horizontal confinement needed to obtain the desired *stack* action. The depth of such curtain boards largely determines the height of the stack, which affects the capacity of the vent. If an area is protected by automatic sprinklers, curtain boards have added values: confinement of heat to speed up operation of sprinklers over the fire and obstructed lateral spread of heat to minimize the operation of an excessive number of sprinklers. See Fig. 2-2.

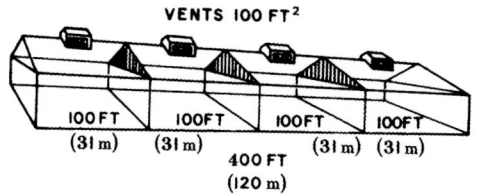

FIGURE 2-2   Curtain boards and roof vents. (*From Fire Protection Handbook, 14th ed., G. P. McKinnon, ed., NFPA, Quincy, Mass., 1976.*)

Fire-Safety Planning for Sites.   Proper building design for fire protection should include a number of factors outside the building itself. The site on which the building is located will influence the design. Among the more significant features are traffic and transportation conditions, fire department accessibility, and fire water supply. Inadequately sized water mains and poor spacing of hydrants have contributed to the loss of many buildings.

Is the building truly accessible to fire apparatus? Ideal accessibility occurs where a building can be approached from all sides by fire-department apparatus; congested areas, topography, or buildings and structures located appreciable distances away from the street can cause difficulty and prevent effective use of fire apparatus. Inadequate attention to site details can place the building in an unnecessarily vulnerable position; if fire defenses are compromised by preventing adequate fire-department access, the building itself must make up the difference in more complete internal protection.

Are the water mains adequate, and are the hydrants properly located? The number, location, and spacing of hydrants and the size of the water mains are vital considerations; consult local standards and insurance requirements.

The Built Environment

Interior finish is defined as those materials that make up the exposed interior surface of wall, ceiling, and floor constructions. The common interior-finish materials are wood, plywood, plaster, wallboards, acoustical tile, insulating and decorative finishes, plastics, and various wall coverings.

Some building codes, and NFPA 101, *Life Safety Code,* include floor coverings under their definition of interior finishes that vary according to occupancy type.

Fire Tests

It is possible to estimate the damage that fire can cause to a building by studying: (1) the amount and kind of combustible materials in the building and (2) the way they are distributed throughout the building. These two factors help to indicate the rate of combustion, the duration of the fire, and the degree of difficulty in extinguishing the fire.

The effects of fire on the components of a building (such as the columns, floors, walls, partitions, and ceiling or roof assemblies) are tested against both time and temperature. Results of the tests, specific to the construction configuration, are recorded in hours or minutes and indicate the duration of fire resistance.

Ratings for flame spread of interior finish materials have been established with the use of the 25-ft (7.6-m) tunnel developed by A. J. Steiner at Underwriters Laboratories Inc. and defined in NFPA 255, *Surface Burning Characteristics of Building Materials.* These ratings are used in NFPA 101, *Life Safety Code,* and in other codes to indicate the area in which finishes of varying flame spread characteristics may be used (See Table 2-14). The classifications used in NFPA 101, *Life Safety Code,* are:

Class	Flame-spread range
A	0–25
B	26–75
C	76–200

The higher the flame spread, the greater the hazard. Exit stairway enclosures typically require Class A interior finishes.

Materials are measured on a relative scale with inorganic-reinforced cement board rated 0 and red oak flooring rated at approximately 100. Some highly combustible wallboards received ratings as high as 1500.

TABLE 2-14 Summary of Life Safety Code Requirements for Interior Finish

Occupancy	Exits	Access to exits	Other spaces
Assembly—new*			
Class A or B	A	A or B	A or B
Class C	A	A or B	A, B, or C
Assembly—existing*			
Class A or B	A	A or B	A or B
Class C	A	A or B	A, B, or C
Educational—new*	A	A or B	A or B
			C on low partitions**
Educational—existing*	A	A or B	A, B, or C
Day-care centers—new	A	A	A or B
	I or II	I or II	
Day-care centers—existing	A or B	A or B	A or B
Group day-care homes—new	A or B	A or B	A, B, or C
Group day-care homes—existing	A or B	A, B, or C	A, B, or C
Family day-care homes	A or B	A, B, or C	A, B, or C
Health care—new (A.S. mandatory)	A or B	A or B	A
		C lower portion of	C in small individual
		corridor wall**	rooms**
Health care—existing	A or B	A or B	A or B
Detention and correctional—new	A*	A*	A, B, or C
	I	I	
Detention and correctional—existing	A or B*	A or B*	A, B, or C
	I or II	I or II	
Residential, hotels, and dormitories—new	A	A or B	A, B, or C
	I or II	I or II	
Residential, hotels, and dormitories—existing	A or B	A or B	A, B, or C
	I or II†	I or II†	
Residential, apartment buildings—new	A	A or B	A, B, or C
	I or II**	I or II**	
Residential, apartment buildings—existing	A or B	A or B	A, B, or C
	I or II†	I or II†	
Residential, board and care‡	See *Life Safety Code,* Chaps. 22 and 23		
Residential, 1- and 2-family, lodging or rooming houses	A, B, or C	A, B, or C	A, B, or C
Mercantile—new*	A or B	A or B	A or B
Mercantile—existing Class A or B*	A or B	A or B	Ceilings—A or B
			Existing on walls
			—A, B, or C
Mercantile—existing Class C*	A, B, or C	A, B, or C	A, B, or C
Office—new	A or B	A or B	A, B, or C
	I or II	I or II	
Office—existing	A or B	A or B	A, B, or C
Industrial	A or B	A, B, or C	A, B, or C
Storage	A or B	A, B, or C	A, B, or C
Unusual structures	A or B	A, B, or C	A, B, or C

* Interior wall and ceiling finish in corridors, exits, and any space not separated from the corridors and exits by a partition capable or retarding the passage of smoke shall meet this interior finish classification.

** Refer to the *Life Safety Code* for details.

A.S. = automatic sprinklers

N.R. = not regulated

† Previous installed floor coverings may be continued in use, subject to the approval of the authority having jurisdiction.

‡ See Chap. 21 of NFPA 101.

Notes:

Class A interior wall and ceiling finish—flame spread 0–25, smoke developed 0–450.

Class B interior wall and ceiling finish—flame spread 26–75, smoke developed 0–450.

Class C interior wall and ceiling finish—flame spread 76–200, smoke developed 0–450.

Class I Interior Floor Finish—minimum 0.45 W/cm^2.

Class II Interior Floor Finish—minimum 0.22 W/cm^3.

Automatic Sprinklers—where a complete standard system of automatic sprinklers is installed, interior finish with flame spread rating not over Class C may be used in any location where Class B is normally specified and with rating of Class B in any location where Class A is normally specified; similarly, Class II interior floor finish may be used in any location where Class I is normally specified and no critical radiant flux rating is required where Class II is normally specified.

Exposed portions of structural members complying with the requirements for heavy timber construction may be permitted.

Source: From Arthur E. Cote, ed., *Fire Protection Handbook*, NFPA, Quincy, Mass., 1991.

One of the best sources of information showing the wide variety of building assemblies and giving the fire-resistance ratings of beams, columns, floors, walls, and partitions is the Underwriters Laboratories Inc. *Fire Resistance Directory,* published annually.

Confinement of Smoke and Fire

Design criteria for plant facilities are generally based on estimated fire severity (see Table 2-15). Specific industrial-hazard fire-severity data may be obtained from insurance organizations (see Table 2-16 and Fig. 2-3).

TABLE 2-15   Estimated Fire Severity for Offices and Light Commercial Occupancies

Combustible content, total, including finish, floor and trim, lb/ft^2	Heat potential assumed Btu/ft^2*	Equivalent fire severity, approximately equivalent to that of test under standard curve for the following periods
5	40,000	30 min
10	80,000	1 h
15	120,000	1½ h
20	160,000	2 h
30	240,000	3 h
40	320,000	4½ h
50	380,000	7 h
60	432,000	8 h
70	500,000	9 h

* Heat of combustion of contents taken at 8000 Btu/lb up to 40 lb/ft^2; 7600 Btu/lb for 50 lb, and 7200 Btu for 60 lb and more to allow for relatively greater proportion of paper. The weights contemplated by the tables are those of ordinary combustible materials, such as wood, paper, or textiles.

Source: From Gordon P. McKinnon, ed., *Fire Protection Handbook,* NFPA, Quincy, Mass., 1976. Data applying to fire-resistive buildings with combustible furniture and shelving.

Fire doors are the most widely used and accepted means of protecting vertical and horizontal openings. Suitability of fire doors is determined by nationally recognized testing laboratories; doors that have not been tested cannot be relied on for effective protection. Doors are tested with the frame, hardware, wired-glass panels, and other accessories necessary to complete the installation to simulate expected installed exposure.

Most building codes reference NFPA 80, *Standard for Fire Doors and Fire Windows.* This standard establishes the minimum rating for the most commonly encountered types of openings in walls stated in hours. With regard to fire doors, the following is a description of various types:

Composite doors.   Typically flush design and consisting of a manufactured core material with chemically impregnated wood-edge banding and untreated wood-face veneers, or laminated plastic faces, or surrounded by and encased in steel.

Hollow-metal doors.   Typically flush and paneled design consisting of metal covered with steel of 24 gauge or lighter.

Sheet-metal doors.   Typically formed no. 22 gauge or lighter steel and of the corrugated, flush, and paneled designs.

Rolling steel doors.   These are of the interlocking steel slat design or plate steel construction.

Tin-clad doors.   Typically of two- or three-ply wood-core construction, covered with no. 30 gauge galvanized steel or terneplate (maximum size 14 by 20 in) or no. 24 gauge galvanized steel sheets not more than 48 in wide.

TABLE 2-16   Fire Severity Expected by Occupancy

(See Fig. 2-3)

Temperature curve A (slight)
  Well-arranged office, metal furniture, noncombustible building
  Welding areas containing slight combustibles
  Noncombustible power house
  Noncombustible buildings, slight amount of combustible occupancy
Temperature curve B (moderate)
  Cotton and waste-paper storage (baled) and well-arranged, noncombustible building
  Paper-making processes, noncombustible building
  Noncombustible institutional buildings with combustible occupancy
Temperature curve C (moderately severe)
  Well-arranged combustible storage, e.g., wooden patterns, noncombustible buildings
  Machine shop having noncombustible floors
Temperature curve D (severe)
  Manufacturing areas, combustible products, noncombustible building
  Congested combustible storage areas, noncombustible building
Temperature curve E (standard fire exposure—severe)
  Flammable liquids
  Woodworking areas
  Office, combustible furniture and buildings
  Paper working, printing, etc.
  Furniture manufacturing and finishing
  Machine shop having combustible floors

Source: NFPA, Quincy, Mass.

Curtain-type doors.   Typically consisting of interlocking steel blades or a continuous formed-spring-steel curtain in a steel frame.

The suitability of fire door is based on the fire barrier resistance rating stated in time necessary life safety or property protection requirements.

NFPA 80, *Fire Doors and Fire Windows,* lists requirements for the installation of doors, windows, and shutters, and also specifies how the opening should be constructed and how the door or window should be mounted, equipped, and operated.

FIRE-DETECTION AND -ALARM SYSTEMS

There are several general systems and many devices which can be effectively used to detect fire and transmit a warning. This section briefly describes this equipment. Details of this subject are addressed by NFPA 72, *National Fire Alarm Code.*

Heat Detectors

Heat-detection devices are categorized in two ways: (1) those that respond when the detection element reaches a predetermined temperature (fixed-temperature types), and (2) those that respond to an increase in heat at a rate greater than some predetermined value (rate-of-rise types). Some devices combine both principles. The same principles apply whether the devices are of the spot-pattern type, in which the thermally sensitive element is a unit, or the line-pattern type, in which the element is continuous along a line or a circuit.

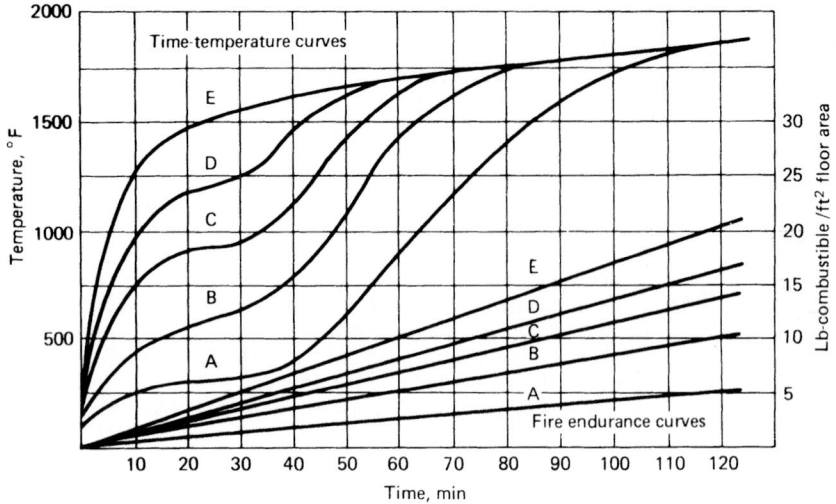

FIGURE 2-3 Possible classification of building contents for fire severity and duration. The straight lines indicate the length of fire endurance based on amounts of combustibles involved. The curved lines indicate the severity expected for the various occupancies (see Table 2-16). There is no direct relationship between the straight and curved lines, but, for example, 10 lb of combustibles per square foot will produce a 90-min fire in a C occupancy, and a fire severity following the time-temperature curve C might be expected. (*From R. Tuve,* Principles of Fire Protection Chemistry, *NFPA, Quincy, Mass., 1976.*)

Fixed-Temperature Detectors.   Thermostats are one of the most widely used fixed-temperature heat detectors in signaling systems.

Bimetallic Thermostats.   The common form of thermostat is the bimetallic type that utilizes the different coefficients of expansion of two metals under heat to cause a movement resulting in closing of electrical contacts (see Fig. 2-4).

Snap-Action Disk Thermostats.   A metal disk goes from concave to convex when the temperature rating of the thermostat is reached. One special advantage of these thermostats is that when the temperature goes down, they are restored to their original condition.

Line Thermostats.   The *thermostat cable* is a line type of thermostat. The cable is made up of two metals separated from each other by a heat-sensitive covering applied directly to the wires. When the rated temperature is reached, the covering melts and the two wires come in contact to initiate an alarm. The section of wire affected must be replaced after operation.

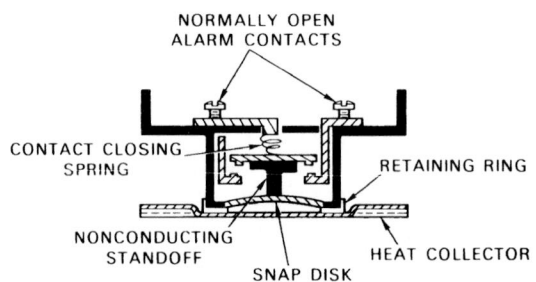

FIGURE 2-4 Spot-type, fixed-temperature snap-disk detector.

Other Types.   Other forms of fixed-temperature heat detectors are the *fusible link,* occasionally employed to restrain operation of an electrical switch until the point of fusion is reached, and the *quartzoid bulb thermostat,* which depends on removal of the restriction by breaking the bulb. Both of these units require replacement after operation.

Rate-of-Rise Detectors.   Fire detectors that operate on the rate-of-rise principle function when the rate of temperature increase exceeds a predetermined rate. Detectors of this type combine two functioning elements, one of which initiates an alarm on a rapid rise of temperature, while the other acts to delay or prevent an alarm on a slow temperature rise. Advantages of rate-of-rise devices are: (1) they can be set to operate more rapidly under most conditions than can fixed-point devices; (2) they are effective across a wide range of ambient temperatures; (3) they recycle rapidly and are usually readily available for continued service; (4) they tolerate slow increases in ambient temperature without giving an alarm. The disadvantages of rate-of-rise detectors for some applications are their susceptibility to false alarms where there is a rapidly increasing temperature and their possible failure to respond to a fire that propagates very slowly.

Pneumatic-tube detectors operate on the rate-of-rise principle. When the temperature increases at a certain rate, the air in the tube expands and causes a diaphragm to move and close a circuit, thus causing an alarm. The device will not cause an alarm if the temperature rise is slow.

Combined Rate-of-Rise and Fixed-Temperature Detectors.   Thermostats have been developed to take advantage of the rate-of-rise feature to sense a fast-developing fire; the fixed-temperature part takes care of a fire whose growth is slow. The typical form of the rate-of-rise thermostat is a vented air chamber that heats up in a flexible diaphragm carrying electric contacts (see Fig. 2-5). Heat outside the chamber causes air within the chamber to expand. When such expansion exceeds the capacity of the vent to relieve pressure, the diaphragm is flexed, thus closing the electric contacts. Slow changes in ambient temperature near the chamber allow it to "breathe" through its vent, and the diaphragm is not moved sufficiently to cause an alarm.

Rate-Compensation (Anticipation and Differentiation) Devices.   These provide an assured actuation at some predetermined maximum temperature and compensate for changes in rates of temperature rise (see Fig. 2-6). This essentially compensates for any expected thermal lag that would temporarily delay detector operation.

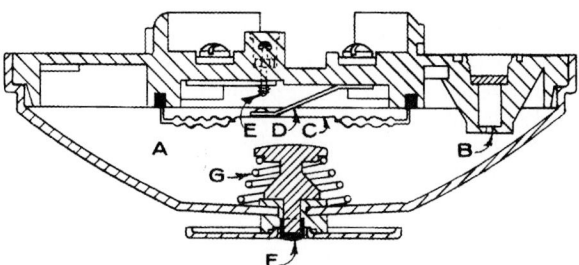

FIGURE 2-5   A spot-type combination rate-of-rise, fixed-temperature device. The air in chamber A expands more rapidly than it can escape from vent B. This causes pressure to close electrical contact D between diagram C and insulated screw E. Fixed-temperature operation occurs when fusible alloy F melts releasing spring G which depresses the diaphragm, closing the contact points.

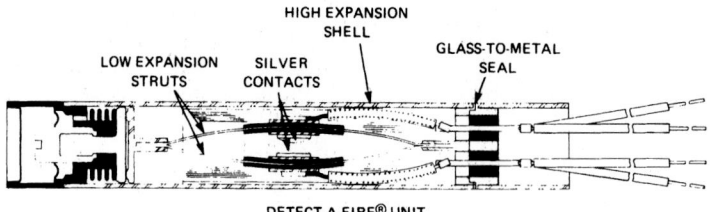

FIGURE 2-6   Rate-compensation heat detector. (*From* Fire Protection Handbook, *14th ed., G. P. McKinnon, ed., NFPA, Quincy, Mass., 1976.*)

Smoke Detectors

There are four types of smoke detectors: (1) photoelectric, (2) beam-type, (3) ionization, and (4) sampling detectors.

Photoelectric Detectors.   These detectors operate on a beam of light. The smoke either obscures a beam of light directly, or enters a refraction chamber where the smoke reflects the light into the photocell. The change in electric current resulting from either partial obscuring of a photoelectric beam by smoke particles, or the scattering of light onto a photosensitive device, causes an alarm sound when the smoke reaches a sufficient density. (See Fig. 2-7*a* and *b*, respectively.)

Beam-Type Detectors.   These employ a light beam that is carried between elements at extreme ends or sides of the protected area and crosses the area to be protected. The beam is projected into a photosensing cell. Smoke between the light source and the receiving photocell reduces the light that reaches the cell, activating the alarm. (See Fig. 2-8.)

Ionization Detectors.   These detectors consist of one or more ionization chambers and the necessary related amplification circuits. The ionization detector has as a sensing element, the ionization chamber, in which air is made electrically conductive (ionized) by a minute source of radioactive material. A voltage applied across the ionization chamber causes a very small electric current to flow as the ions travel to the electrode of opposite polarity. When smoke particles enter the chamber, they attach themselves to the ions and cause a reduction in mobility and thus a reduction in current flow. The reduced current flow increases the voltage on the electrodes which, when reaching a predetermined level, results in an alarm. (See Fig. 2-9.)

Sampling Detectors.   These consist of tubing distributed from the detector unit into the area(s) to be protected. An air pump draws air from the protected area back to the detector. A high-intensity strobe, laser particle counter, or cloud-chamber smoke detector may be used as a sampling detector. The air pump draws a sample of air into a chamber for a highly sensitive analysis. These types of detectors are increasing in popularity.

Flame Detectors

There are four basic types of flame detectors: (1) infrared, (2) ultraviolet, (3) photoelectric, and (4) flame flicker.

Infrared and Ultraviolet.   These detectors have sensing elements responsive to radiant energy outside the range of human vision.

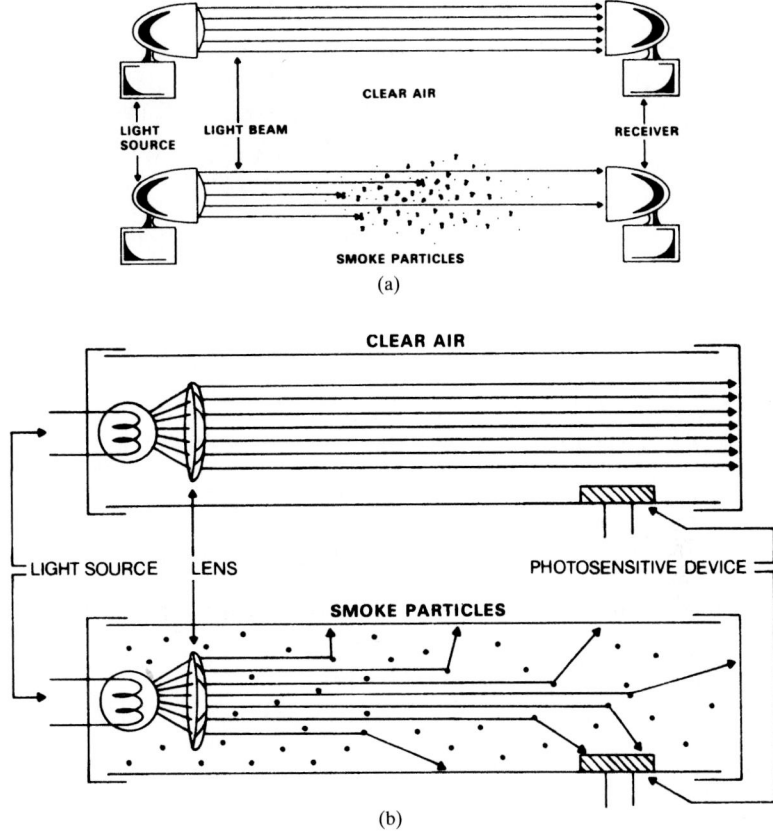

FIGURE 2-7 Principle of operation for (*a*) a photoelectric obscuration smoke detector and (*b*) a photoelectric scattering smoke detector.

Photoelectric.   This type employs a photocell that either changes its electric conductivity or produces an electric potential when it is exposed to radiant energy.

Flame Flicker.   This is a photoelectric type of detector that includes means to prevent response to visible light unless the observed light is modulated at a frequency characteristic of the flicker of a flame.

Gas Detectors

Various detection devices will monitor the amount of flammable gases or vapors in an area. Portable gas detectors are used to detect the presence of combustible gas or vapor in basements, sewers, manholes, etc. Other devices will analyze the air samples brought into the device from various points. Gas and vapor testing equipment is valuable for preventing fires and explosions in petroleum and chemical plants and in industries where combustible vapors may be generated.

Fire-detection devices are usually installed in systems which combine manually activated fire-alarm stations and audible and visual warning devices. They may also be connected to fire-suppression systems in some hazardous areas.

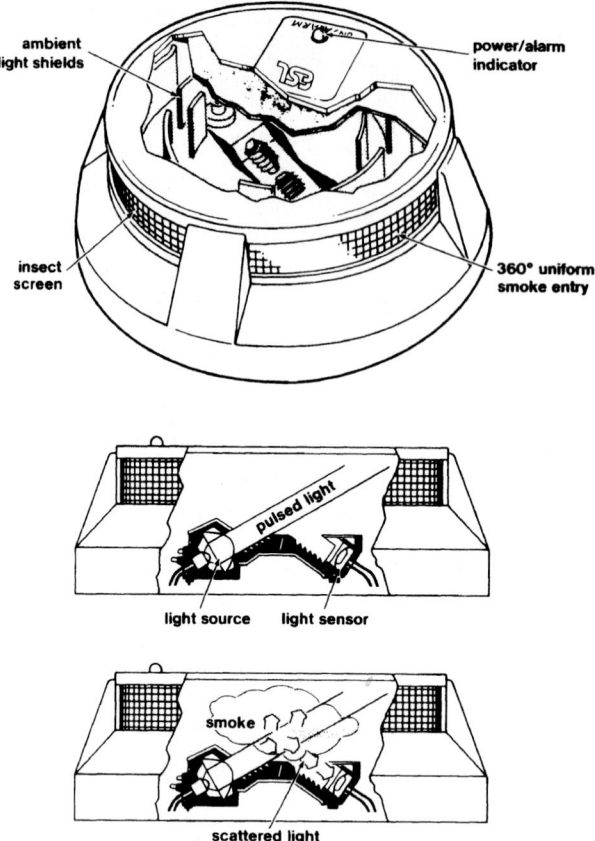

FIGURE 2-8   Cross-sectional view of a photoelectric light-scattering smoke detector. (*Electro Signal Lab., Inc.*)

Protective Signaling Systems

The detection and alarm systems in a plant building should be connected to a constantly supervised monitoring system. The most common systems are described in this section.

Local Systems.   These systems produce a signal manually or automatically at the protective premises for an alarm of fire and for required supervisory services, including supervision of a security guard's rounds, supervision of sprinkler water-flow alarm service and of sprinkler systems, etc. Local systems are used for the protection of property and for the protection of life by indicating the necessity for evacuation of the building.

Proprietary Systems.   Proprietary systems are used for individual properties where the system is under constant supervision by competent and experienced personnel in a central supervisory station at the property protected. Such systems are usually found in large industrial plants; signals are received at a central supervisory station where experienced operators are on duty at all times. The central supervisory station is under the control of the owner or occupant of the protected property and is usually on or near that property.

Remote-Station Systems.   These are usually used to protect premises on which there is frequently no one present. The signal is received at fire-alarm headquarters or at the office of a

IONIZATION DETECTOR

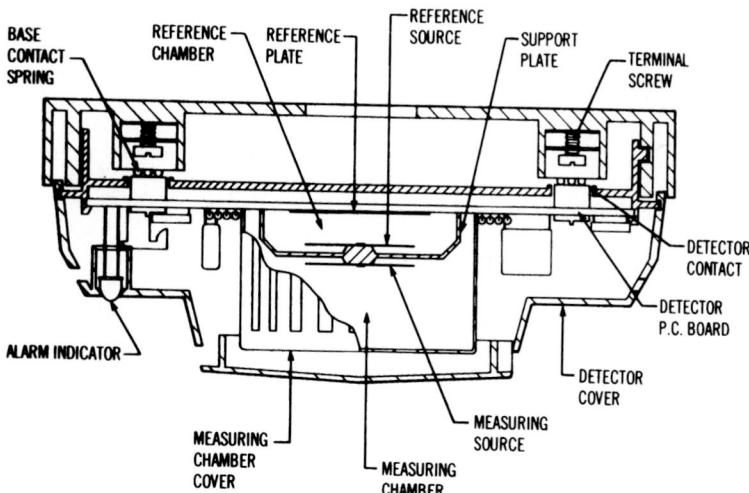

FIGURE 2-9   Cross-sectional view of an ionization smoke detector. (*Pyrotronics, Inc.*)

communications agency, usually located at a distance from the protected property. Signals are transmitted and received on privately owned equipment; the agency receiving the signals may be a municipal fire department or a communications agency capable of receiving the signals and acting upon them.

Auxiliary Systems.   This type connects devices in the protected plant with the municipal fire-alarm system. Alarms are received at fire-alarm headquarters on the same equipment and by the same alerting methods as alarms transmitted from municipal street boxes. Signals are recorded at a municipal fire department; connecting facilities between the protected property and the fire department are part of the municipal fire-alarm system. Devices in the protected plant are customarily owned and maintained by the property owner. Equipment that connects the devices to the city's circuits is owned and maintained by the municipality, or leased by it, as part of the municipal alarm system and limited to alarm service only.

Central Station Systems.   Central station systems are operated by firms whose principal business is the furnishing and maintaining of supervised signaling service. The central station services properties subscribing to the service; alarm and signaling devices on the subscribers' property are connected to the central station where operators are on hand to receive the signal and take the appropriate action. Central station operators retransmit alarms to the fire department.

Standards for the installation and maintenance of fire detection and alarm equipment are listed in the last section of this chapter.

WATER-BASED FIRE-PROTECTION SYSTEMS

This section describes systems which suppress or control fires.

Water Supply

The most common type of fire-protection systems rely on water. Therefore it is essential that adequate supplies of water be provided and maintained. NFPA 24, *Installation of Private Fire Service Mains and their Appurtances,* provides requirements for on-site water supply systems.

The plant water-supply system or nearby public water supply will usually be the primary source used by the plant fire brigade or public fire department. Water must be provided with flows and pressure that are sufficient for supplying automatic sprinkler systems and fire hoses, in addition to normal plant requirements. When the public water supply is inadequate for plant protection, supplemental private supplies are necessary.

Pipe Networks.   The minimum recommended pipe size for underground fire protection pipings is 6 in (15 cm). It is desirable to loop the pipes in a grid pattern (Fig. 2-10) and minimize the friction loss wherever possible. Various pipe materials are available including steel, cast iron, and plastic for use underground. The selection of size and type of pipe should be based on the expected flows, soil conditions, and other similar factors.

Fire Hydrants.   Fire hydrants are provided on public mains to allow the fire department to draw water with mobile pumpers to supply sprinkler and standpipe systems, as well as hose streams. Fire hydrants are provided on private mains to allow the fire brigade or fire department to supply hose streams, and to support sprinkler and standpipe systems with mobile pumpers.

Hydrants are available as wet-barrel (California, see Fig. 2-11) and dry-barrel (base valve, see Fig. 2-12) types. Dry-barrel hydrants are necessary where there is any chance of freezing.

Hydrants on plant pipe networks are normally located every 250 ft (76 m) and about 40 ft (12 m) from the buildings protected. They must be protected from damage by vehicles or machinery.

The available water flow for fire suppression is determined by flow testing the hydrant system. The water flow available at 20 psig (138 kPa) is determined, since this is the minimum pressure that usually must be maintained to satisfy water regulatory rules.

Valves in pipelines supplying fire-protection water are generally required to be indicating valves. These include underground gate valves with indicator post, underground butterfly valves with indicator post, and outside screw and yoke (OS&Y) gate valves.

Closed valves have been the primary cause of sprinkler systems' failing to control fires.

Fire Pumps.   Fire pumps are essentially the same as typical water-supply pumps. Additional considerations for fire pumps are outlined in NFPA 20, *Installation of Centrifugal Fire Pumps.* Factors that should be considered with fire pumps include:

- Use of equipment listed for fire pumps
- Use of approved accessories
- Adequate capacity to meet fire-flow demands
- Selection of fire pump driver based on reliability, adequacy, economy, and safety of power source
- Automatic operation
- Safe location for uninterrupted service
- Weekly and annual testing
- Maintenance

Sprinkler Systems

A sprinkler system, for fire-protection purposes, is an integrated system of underground and overhead piping designed in accordance with fire-protection engineering standards. The

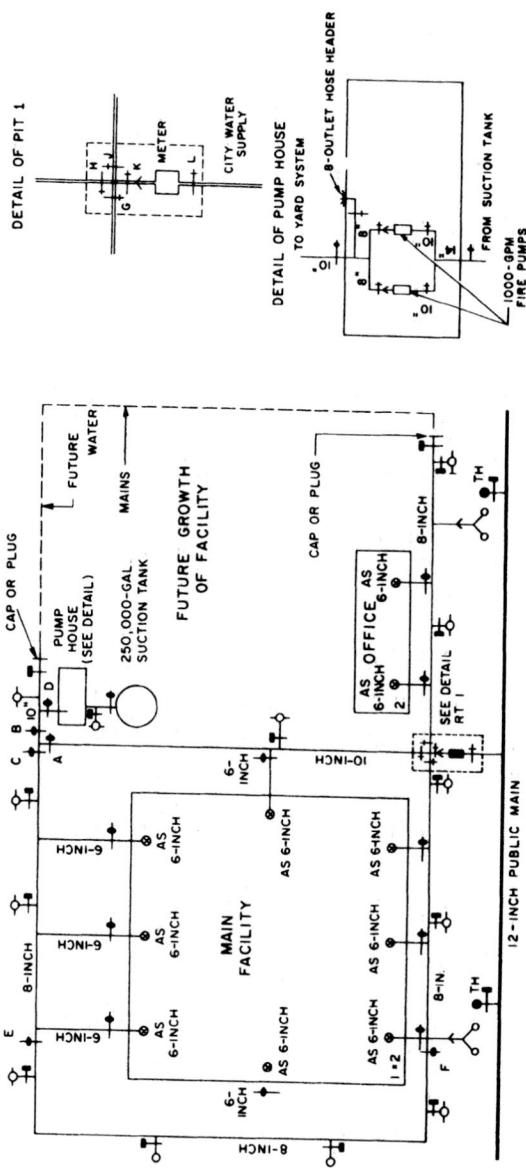

FIGURE 2-10 Water-pipe network. *(From Arthur E. Cote, ed., Fire Protection Handbook, NFPA, Quincy, Mass., 1991.)*

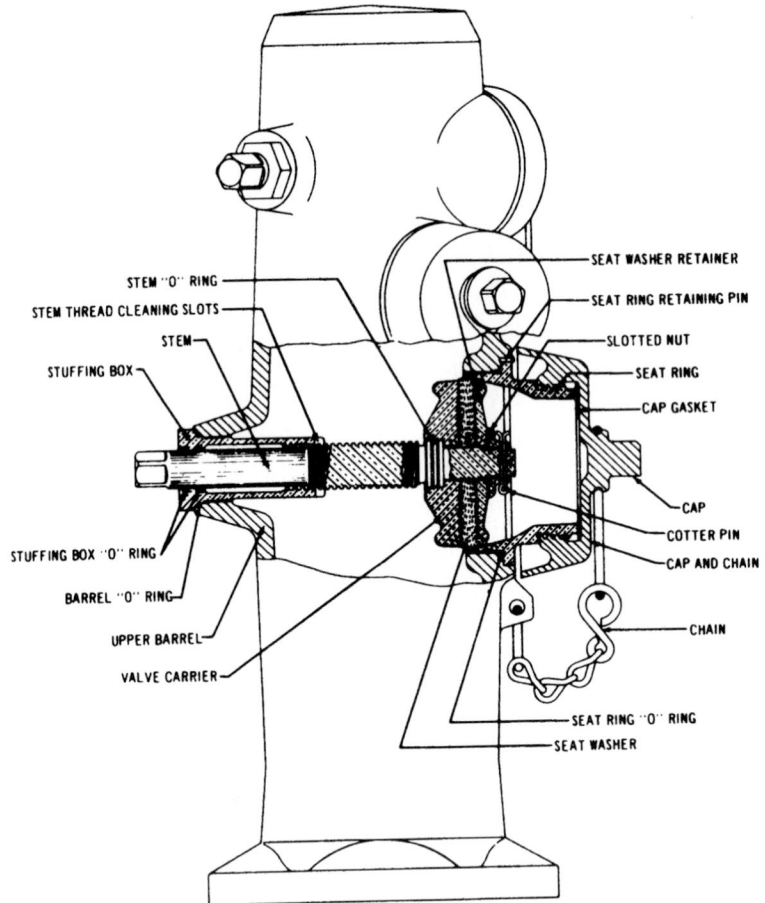

STEM "O" RING
STEM THREAD CLEANING SLOTS
STEM
STUFFING BOX

SEAT WASHER RETAINER
SEAT RING RETAINING PIN
SLOTTED NUT
SEAT RING
CAP GASKET

STUFFING BOX "O" RING
BARREL "O" RING
UPPER BARREL
VALVE CARRIER

CAP
COTTER PIN
CAP AND CHAIN

CHAIN

SEAT RING "O" RING
SEAT WASHER

FIGURE 2-11   Wet-barrel hydrant. (*Mueller Co.; from Arthur E. Cote, ed.,* Fire Protection Handbook, *NFPA, Quincy, Mass., 1991.*)

installation includes one or more water supplies. The portion of the sprinkler system above-ground is a network of specially sized or hydraulically designed piping installed in a building, structure, or area, generally overhead, and to which sprinklers are connected in a systematic pattern. The valve controlling each system riser is located in the system riser or its supply piping. Each sprinkler system riser includes a device for actuating an alarm when the system is in operation. The system is usually activated by heat from a fire and discharges water over the fire area. Further information on this subject is included in NFPA 13, *Installation of Sprinkler Systems.*

Wet-Pipe Systems.   This type of system contains water under pressure at all times; water will be discharged immediately on operation of an automatic sprinkler. Water flowing from the wet-pipe sprinkler system actuates an alarm valve that gives off a signal. Figure 2-13 illustrates the total concept of the wet-pipe automatic sprinkler system.

The essential features of wet-pipe sprinkler systems, which represent about 80 percent of sprinkler installations, include provisions for water supplies, piping, and location and spacing of sprinklers. This system is generally used wherever there is no danger that the water in the pipes will freeze and wherever there are no special conditions requiring one of the other

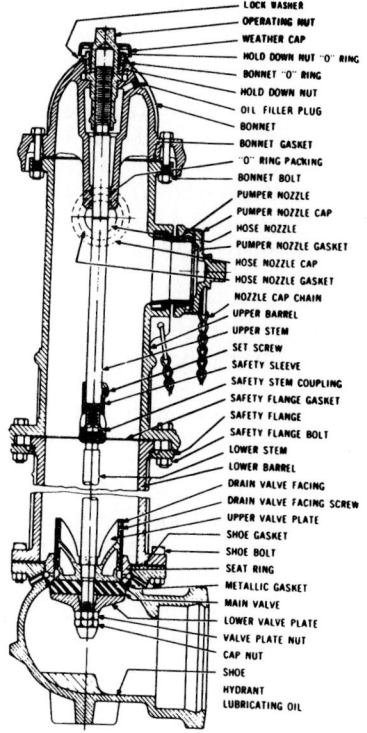

LOCK WASHER
OPERATING NUT
WEATHER CAP
HOLD DOWN NUT "O" RING
BONNET "O" RING
HOLD DOWN NUT
OIL FILLER PLUG
BONNET
BONNET GASKET
"O" RING PACKING
BONNET BOLT
PUMPER NOZZLE
PUMPER NOZZLE CAP
HOSE NOZZLE
PUMPER NOZZLE GASKET
HOSE NOZZLE CAP
HOSE NOZZLE GASKET
NOZZLE CAP CHAIN
UPPER BARREL
UPPER STEM
SET SCREW
SAFETY SLEEVE
SAFETY STEM COUPLING
SAFETY FLANGE GASKET
SAFETY FLANGE
SAFETY FLANGE BOLT
LOWER STEM
LOWER BARREL
DRAIN VALVE FACING
DRAIN VALVE FACING SCREW
UPPER VALVE PLATE
SHOE GASKET
SHOE BOLT
SEAT RING
METALLIC GASKET
MAIN VALVE
LOWER VALVE PLATE
VALVE PLATE NUT
CAP NUT
SHOE
HYDRANT
LUBRICATING OIL

FIGURE 2-12 Dry-barrel hydrant. (*Mueller Co.;* *from Arthur E. Cote, ed.,* Fire Protection Handbook, *NFPA, Quincy, Mass., 1991.*)

systems. Inspection of the wet-pipe sprinkler system at regular intervals is essential, and quarterly inspection of all water-control valves and water flow alarms is recommended.

Where subject to temperatures below 40°F (5°C), a wet-pipe system cannot be used. There are two recognized methods of maintaining automatic sprinkler protection in such locations: (1) through the use of systems where water enters the sprinkler piping only after operation of a control valve (dry-pipe, preaction, etc.) and (2) by the use of antifreeze solution in a portion of the wet-pipe system.

Dry-Pipe Systems. In locations where the building temperature cannot be maintained at 40°F (5°C), or higher a dry-pipe system is usually provided. In dry-pipe systems, the sprinkler piping contains air or nitrogen under pressure instead of water, and admission of the water into the system is controlled by a dry-pipe valve. When a sprinkler is opened by heat from a fire, the air pressure is reduced, the dry-pipe valve is opened by water pressure, and water travels to and flows out of any opened sprinklers.

Preaction Systems. Systems in which the air in the piping may or may not be under

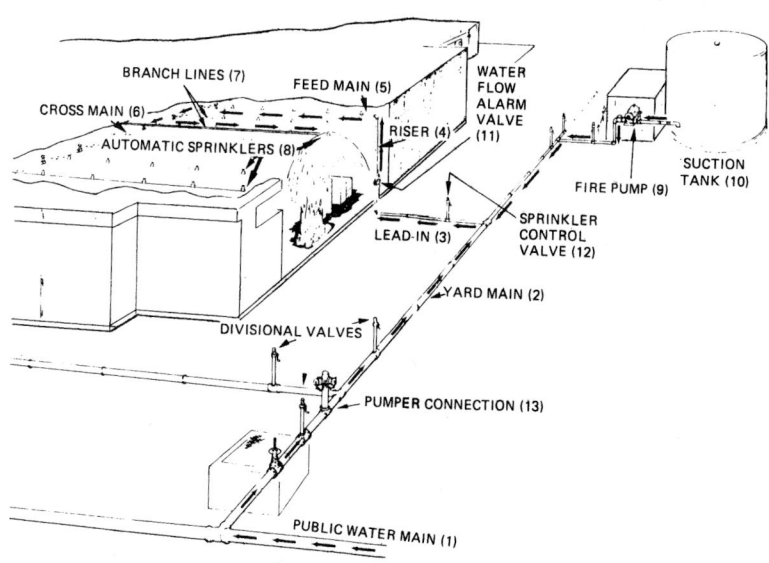

BRANCH LINES (7)
FEED MAIN (5)
WATER FLOW ALARM VALVE (11)
CROSS MAIN (6)
AUTOMATIC SPRINKLERS (8)
RISER (4)
SUCTION TANK (10)
FIRE PUMP (9)
LEAD-IN (3)
SPRINKLER CONTROL VALVE (12)
YARD MAIN (2)
DIVISIONAL VALVES
PUMPER CONNECTION (13)
PUBLIC WATER MAIN (1)

FIGURE 2-13 A typical sprinkler installation. (*From Arthur E. Cote, ed.,* Fire Protection Handbook, *NFPA, Quincy, Mass., 1991.*)

pressure are called *preaction systems*. These systems are designed primarily to protect properties where the danger of water damage from broken sprinklers or piping could be serious. (*Note:* Although inadvertent water discharging from a sprinkler system is extremely rare, this option is still viable.) The water supply valve is actuated independently of the opening of the sprinklers by an automatic fire-detection system; the valve is opened sooner than with the dry-pipe system, and the alarm is given when the valve is opened.

The preaction system has several advantages over a dry-pipe system. The valve is opened sooner because the detection system will usually respond to the fire prior to operation of the first sprinkler. Sprinkler piping is normally dry; thus, preaction systems are not subject to freezing and can be used when a dry-pipe system is required.

Deluge Systems. Deluge systems are reserved for use in some types of extra-hazard occupancies. All sprinklers are open at all times so that when the water comes on, the entire area is deluged with water; when heat from a fire actuates the fire-detecting device, water flows to and is discharged from all sprinklers on the piping system, thus "deluging" the protected areas. These systems are often used in airplane hangers and in areas where flammable liquids are handled or stored. Often, these systems use a foam solution, allowing faster control of the fire.

By using heat detection devices operating on the rate-of-rise or fixed-temperature principle, or other devices such as ultraviolet or infrared detectors designed for individual hazards, it is possible to apply water to a fire more quickly than with systems in which operation depends on opening of sprinklers only as the fire spreads.

Sprinklers

Sprinklers are designed with temperature ratings ranging from 135°F (57°C) to as high as 650°F (343°C). Ratings of 165°F (74°C) are usual for use in buildings that are maintained at normal, constant temperatures.

The location and spacing of sprinklers depends on the degree of hazard and type of construction. NFPA 13, *Installation of Sprinkler Systems,* provides detailed design and installation requirements. Table 2-17 provides a summary of spacing requirements for sprinkler installation.

Standpipes

The four generally recognized standpipe system concepts are described below. The design and installation of these systems is based upon NFPA 14, *Installation of Standpipe and Hose Systems.* See Table 2-18.

1. A wet-standpipe system, having supply valve open and water pressure maintained at all times. This is the most desirable type of system.

2. A dry-standpipe system arranged to admit water to the system through manual operation of approved remote-control devices located at each hose station. The water-supply control mechanism introduces an inherent reliability factor that must be considered.

3. A dry-standpipe system in an unheated building. The system should be arranged to admit water automatically by means of a dry-pipe valve or other approved device. The depletion of system air at the time of use introduces a delay in the application of water to the fire and increases the level of competency required to control the pressurized hose and nozzle assembly during the charging period.

4. A dry-standpipe system having no permanent water supply. This type is usually reserved for use in low-risk buildings. This type of system might also be used in buildings under construction, where allowed in lieu of the wet standpipe in unheated areas.

TABLE 2-17   Summary of Spacing Rules

	Light hazard	Ordinary hazard	Extra hazard[5]	High-piled storage[6]	Large-drop sprinklers[7]	Early suppression fast-response sprinklers[7,8]
Unobstructed construction[1]	225[2]	130	100	100	130	100
Noncombustible obstructed construction	225[2]	130	100	100	130	100
Combustible obstructed construction	168[3,4]	130	100	100	100	N/A

Note 1: Wood truss construction as defined in NFPA 13 is classified as obstructed construction for the purpose of determining sprinkler protection areas.
Note 2: For light hazard occupancies, the protection area per sprinkler for pipe schedule systems shall not exceed 200 ft² per sprinkler.
Note 3: For light combustible framing members spaced less than 3 ft on center, maximum spacing is 130 ft².
Note 4: For heavy combustible framing members spaced 3 ft or more on center, maximum spacing is 225 ft².
Note 5: For extra-hazard occupancies:
    1. The protection area per sprinkler for pipe schedule systems shall not exceed 90 ft².
    2. The protection area per sprinkler for hydraulically designed systems with densities below 0.25 gal/min·ft² may exceed 100 ft², but shall not exceed 130 sq ft².
Note 6: For high-piled storage occupancies:
    1. The protection area per sprinkler may exceed 100 sq ft but shall not exceed 130 sq ft for systems hydraulically designed in accordance with NFPA 231 and 231C for densities below 0.25 gal/min·ft².
    2. Where protection areas are specifically indicated in the design criteria of other portions of this standard or other NFPA standards, those protection areas shall be used.
    3. For protection involving large-drop sprinklers use the large-drop sprinkler column in the table.
Note 7: For large-drop and ESFR sprinklers, the minimum spacing is 80 ft² per sprinkler.
Note 8: For special sprinkler protection areas, see 4-3.2 of NFPA 13.
N/A denotes data not available in current standard.
Source: From NFPA 13, *Standard for the Installation of Sprinkler Systems,* Quincy, Mass., 1991.

TABLE 2-18   Summary of Types of Standpipe

Type	Intended use	Size hose and distribution	Minimum size pipe	Minimum water supply
Class I	Heavy streams Fire department	2½-in connections All portions of each story or section within 30 ft of nozzle with 100 ft of hose	4 in up to 100 ft 6 in above 100 ft	500 gal/min first standpipe 250 gal/min each additional (2500 gal/min maximum)
	Trained personnel			
	Advanced stages of fire		(275 ft maximum unless pressure regulated)	30-min duration
Class II	Small streams	1½-in connections (distribution same as class I)	2 in up to 50 ft	65 psi at top outlet with 500 gal/min flow 100 gal/min per building
	Building occupants Incipient fire		2½ in above 50 ft	30-min duration
Class III	Both of above	Same as class I with added 1½-in outlets or 1½-in adapters and 1½-in hose.	Same as class I	65 lb/in² at top outlet with 100 gal/min flowing Same as class I

Source: From NFPA 14, *Standard for the Installation of Standpipe and Hose Systems,* Quincy, Mass., 1993.

Water-Spray Fixed Systems

Water-spray fixed systems are generally used to protect flammable liquid and gas storage vessels; piping and equipment; electrical equipment such as transformers, oil switches, and rotating electrical machinery; and openings in firewalls and floors through which conveyors pass. The type of water spray required for any particular hazard depends, of course, on the nature of the hazard and the purpose for which the protection is provided.

NFPA 15, *Water Spray Fixed Systems for Fire Protection,* calls for nozzles, piping, valves, pressure gauges, and detection systems to be of an approved type. The spray nozzles generally used in these systems are open, and the pipes, especially outdoor ones that are subject to freezing temperatures, are usually dry.

Foam Extinguishing Systems

Foam extinguishing systems have been used extensively for many years, especially in the petrochemical industry, for the extinguishment of flammable liquid fires. The principal kinds of foam are chemical and mechanical (determined by how they are generated), though chemical foams are generally considered obsolete. These classes are further subdivided. NFPA standards that address this subject include:

NFPA 11, *Low Expansion Foam Extinguishing Systems*

NFPA 11A, *Medium and High Expansion Foam Extinguishing Systems*

NFPA 16, *Foam-Water Sprinkler and Spray Systems Systems*

NFPA 16A, *Closed Head Foam-Water Sprinkler Systems*

Special compatible foam concentrates result in the generation of a foam that does not break down as readily as ordinary foam when mixed with dry chemical extinguishing agent. Other special foams are available for application on fires in alcohols, esters, ketones, and ethers (called *water-soluble* or *polar liquids*). This concentrate produces a foam that does not deteriorate like ordinary foam when in contact with water-miscible solvents.

Inspection, Testing, and Maintenance

NFPA 25, *Inspection, Testing and Maintenance of Water Based Fire Protection Systems,* provides requirements and procedures for ensuring that the systems discussed in the section will perform as intended. The standard provides requirements for proper inspection, test, and maintenance procedures for sprinkler, standpipe and underground supply systems, as well as fire pumps, water storage tanks, spray systems and foam-water sprinkler systems. Other chapters address record retention provisions, valve inspection procedures and system impairment procedures.

NFPA 25 states the frequency of a procedure at the particular element (inspect, test, or maintain) and the method by which the procedure is carried out at that element. For purposes of NFPA 25, inspection is a visual examination, testing is a physical check of the component, and maintenance is work performed on a component to keep it operable.

SPECIAL AGENT SUPPRESSION SYSTEMS

Carbon Dioxide Systems

Carbon dioxide is a noncombustible gas that has been effectively used to extinguish certain types of fires. It acts to dilute the oxygen in the fire area to a point where it will no longer support combustion (Table 2-19). Because carbon dioxide is stored under pressure, it can readily be ejected from its storage container. Carbon dioxide is inert and will not conduct electricity. It can be used safely on energized electric equipment fires without causing damage to the equipment. NFPA 12, *Carbon Dioxide Extinguishing Systems,* provides details on these types of systems.

TABLE 2-19   Minimum Carbon Dioxide Concentrations for Extinguishment

Material	Theoretical min. CO_2 concentration, %	Minimum design CO_2 concentration, %
Acetylene	55	66
Acetone	27*	34
Aviation gas grades 115/145	30	36
Benzol, benzene	31	37
Butadiene	34	41
Butane	28	34
Butane—I	31	37
Carbon disulfide	60	72
Carbon monoxide	53	64
Coal gas or natural gas	31*	37
Cyclopropane	31	37
Diethyl ether	33	40
Dimethyl ether	33	40
Dowtherm	38*	46
Ethane	33	40
Ethyl alcohol	36	43
Ethyl ether	38*	46
Ethylene	41	49
Ethylene dichloride	21	34
Ethylene oxide	44	53
Gasoline	28	34
Hexane	29	35
Higher paraffin hydrocarbons $C_mH_{2m} + 2m - 5$	28	34
Hydrogen	62	75
Hydrogen sulfide	30	36
Isobutane	30*	36
Isobutylene	26	34
Isobutyl formate	26	34
JP-4	30	36
Kerosene	28	34
Methane	25	34
Methyl acetate	29	35
Methyl alcohol	33	40
Methyl butene—I	32	36
Methyl ethyl ketone	32	40
Methyl formate	32	39
Pentane	29	35
Propane	30	36
Propylene	30	36
Quench, lubricating oils	28	34

Note: The theoretical minimum extinguishing concentrations in air for the above materials were obtained from a compilation of Bureau of Mines limits of flammability of gases and vapors (Bulletins 503 and 627). Those marked with * were calculated from accepted residual oxygen values.

Source: From Arthur E. Cote, ed., *Fire Protection Handbook,* NFPA, Quincy, Mass., 1991.

Because carbon dioxide does little or no damage to equipment or materials with which it comes in contact, it is very useful for protection of rooms with contents of high value and contents subject to water damage. Typical of such occupancies are rooms housing live electric equipment. Carbon dioxide is also widely used for extinguishing flammable liquid fires.

Halogenated Extinguishing Systems

A halon is a hydrocarbon (hydrogen and carbon) in which some of the hydrogen atoms have been replaced by such elements as bromine, chlorine, or fluorine, or by combinations of these (see Table 2-20). A number of halons are toxic, thus making them undesirable for general use; two of them, halon 1301 and halon 1211, have acceptable levels of toxicity and excellent flame extinguishment properties.

Halon 1211 and halon 1301 are the only two agents recognized by the NFPA Technical Committee on Halogenated Fire Extinguishing Agent Systems. The two standards handled by this Committee are NFPA 12A, *Halon 1301 Fire Extinguishing Systems,* and NFPA 12B, *Halon 1211 Fire Extinguishing Systems.* Both halon 1211 and 1301 are widely used for protection of electric equipment (both are nonconductors of electricity), airplane engines, and computer rooms. As both of these halons rapidly vaporize, they leave little corrosive or abrasive residue to clean up and do not interfere as much with visibility during fire fighting as foam or carbon dioxide. Halon 1211 is used in portable fire extinguishers and halon 1301 is used in total flooding systems.

Today, fire-protection halons are subject to international restrictions imposed by the Montreal Protocol on Substances that Deplete the Stratospheric Ozone Layer. Consequently, production of these fire protection agents has been phased out as of January 1, 1994. New halon replacements are now available. See NFPA 2001, *Clean Agent Fire Extinguishing Systems.*

Dry-Chemical Extinguishing Systems

Dry-chemical extinguishing agents consist of finely divided powders that effectively extinguish a fire when applied to the fire by portable extinguishers, hose lines, or fixed systems. The original dry powder was sodium bicarbonate (ordinary baking soda). Potassium bicarbonate and other chemical powders, with additives to make the powders free flowing and more moisture resistant, are now also in use. Dry chemical has been found to be an effective extinguishing agent for fires in flammable liquids and in certain types of ordinary combustibles and electric equipment, depending on the type of dry chemical used. Detailed installation requirements are included in NFPA 17, *Dry Chemical Extinguishing Systems,* and NFPA 17A, *Wet Chemical Extinguishing Systems.*

Dry-chemical extinguishing systems are used to protect flammable-liquid storage rooms, dip tanks, kitchen range hoods, deep-fat fryers, and similar hazardous areas and appliances. Because dry chemical is nonconductive, these systems are useful in the protection of oil-filled transformers and circuit breakers. Dry-chemical systems are not recommended for telephone-switchboard or computer protection. Dry chemicals are also widely used in portable fire extinguishers.

Combustible-Metal Extinguishing Systems

A number of metals and metal powders found in industrial situations and in transport will burn. Some metals burn when heated to high temperatures by friction or exposure to external heat. Others burn from contact with moisture or in reaction with other materials. These metals and metal powders require special extinguishing agents and special fire-fighting techniques. Some result in explosions and very high temperatures, and some react violently with water. Still others give off toxic fumes when burning.

TABLE 2-20 Some Physical Properties of the Common Halogenated Fire-Extinguishing Agents

Agent	Chemical formula	Halon no.	Type of agent	Approx. boiling point, °F†	Approx. freezing point, °F†	Specific gravity of liquid at 68°F† (water = 1)	Approx. critical temp., °F†	Estimated pressure, psig‡ At 130°F†	Estimated pressure, psig‡ At critical temp.	Latent heat of vaporization, cal/g water = 540 cal/g CO_2 = 138 cal/g
Carbon tetrachloride	CCl_4	104	Liquid	170	-8	1.595				46
Methyl bromide	CH_3Br	1001	Liquid	40	-135	1.73				62
Bromochloromethane	CH_2BrCl	1011	Liquid	151	-124	1.93				
Dibromodifluoromethane	CF_2Br_2	1202	Liquid	76	-223	2.28	389	23	585	29
Bromochlorodifluoromethane	CF_2BrCl	1211	Liquefied gas*	25	-257	1.83	309	75	580	32
Bromotrifluoromethane	CF_3Br	1301	Liquefied gas	-72	-270	1.57	153	435	560	28
Dibromotetrafluoroethane	$C_2F_4Br_2$	2402	Liquid	117	-167	2.17		3.8		25

* May be kept as a liquid at reduced temperatures.
† 5/9 (°F −32) = °C.
‡ 1 psig = 6.895 kPa.

Source: From Arthur E. Cote, ed., *Fire Protection Handbook*, NFPA, Quincy, Mass., 1991.

Some combustible metal extinguishing agents' success in handling metal fires has led to the terms *approved extinguishing powder* and *dry powder*. Such terms have been accepted in describing extinguishing agents for metal fires, and should not be confused with the name *dry chemical,* which normally applies to an agent suitable for use on flammable-liquid and live electric equipment fires. Graphite powder, talc, and sand have all been used to smother metal fires.

PORTABLE FIRE EXTINGUISHERS

Portable fire extinguishers are required in most plants by local, state, and federal regulations and insurance companies. Where there are trained personnel available to use the proper extinguisher on a small incipient fire, extinguishers may prove useful in preventing a larger, more devastating fire.

The limitations of extinguishers, personal exposure to fire and smoke, capacity range, selectivity, and availability necessitate that training be provided if they are expected to be effective. Use of extinguishers should be simultaneous with notification of the fire brigade or department.

Types of Portable Fire Extinguishers

The kind and number of extinguishers needed for particular types of fires are specified in NFPA 10, *Portable Fire Extinguishers.* The most common types of extinguishers in use are the pressurized water, carbon dioxide, and multipurpose dry chemical. Other extinguishers commonly used are water pump tanks, halon 1211, and combustible-metal-type dry powder.

Application of Portable Fire Extinguishers

NFPA 10, *Portable Fire Extinguishers,* classifies fires in four ways:

Class A. Fires involving ordinary combustible materials (wood, cloth, paper, rubber and many plastics) (Table 2-21).

Class B. Fires involving flammable or combustible liquids, flammable gases, greases, and similar materials (Table 2-22).

Class C. Fires involving live electric equipment where safety to the operator requires the use of electrically nonconductive extinguishing agents. (*Note:* When electric equipment is de-energized, the use of Class A or B extinguishers may be used.)

TABLE 2-21 Fire Extinguisher Size and Placement for Class A Hazards

	Light-(low) hazard occupancy	Ordinary-(moderate) hazard occupancy	Extra-(high) hazard occupancy
Minimum rated single extinguisher	2-A	2-A	4-A*
Maximum floor area per unit of A	3000 ft^2	1500 ft^2	1000 ft^2
Maximum floor area for extinguisher	11,250 ft^{2†}	11,250 ft^{2†}	11,250 ft^{2†}
Maximum travel distance to extinguisher	75 ft	75 ft	75 ft

* Two 2½-gal (9.46-L) water-type extinguishers can be used to fulfill the requirements of one 4-A rated extinguisher.
† See Appendix E-3.3 of NFPA 10, *Portable Fire Extinguishers.* For SI units: 1 ft = 0.305 m; 1 ft^2 = 0.929 m^2.
Source: From Arthur E. Cote, ed., *Fire Protection Handbook,* NFPA, Quincy, Mass., 1991.

TABLE 2-22   Fire Extinguisher Size and Placement for Class B Hazard Excluding Protection of Deep Layer Flammable Liquid Tanks

Type of hazard	Basic minimum extinguisher rating	Maximum travel distance to extinguishers, ft (m)
Low	5-B	30 (9)
	10-B	50 (15)
Moderate	10-B	30 (9)
	20-B	50 (15)
High	40-B	30 (9)
	80-B	50 (15)

Source: From Arthur E. Cote, ed., *Fire Protection Handbook,* NFPA, Quincy, Mass., 1991.

Class D.   Fires involving certain combustible metals (such as magnesium, titanium, zirconium, sodium, and potassium) requiring a heat-absorbing extinguishing medium not reactive with the burning metals.

Figures 2-14 and 2-15 illustrate fire extinguishing agents, classifications, and symbols.

ORDINARY

A

COMBUSTIBLES

1. Extinguishers suitable for "Class A" fires should be identified by a triangle containing the letter "A." If colored, the triangle shall be colored green.*

FLAMMABLE

B

LIQUIDS

2. Extinguishers suitable for "Class B" fires should be identified by a square containing the letter "B." If colored, the square shall be colored red.*

ELECTRICAL

C

EQUIPMENT

3. Extinguishers suitable for "Class C" fires should be identified by a circle containing the letter "C." If colored, the circle shall be colored blue.*

COMBUSTIBLE

METALS

4. Extinguishers suitable for fires involving metals should be identified by a five-pointed star containing the letter "D." If colored, the star shall be colored yellow.*

FIGURE 2-14   Fire extinguisher identification.* Recommended colors per PMS (Pantone Matching System): green—*Basic Green,* red—*192 Red,* blue—*Process Blue,* yellow—*Basic Yellow.* (*From NFPA 10,* Standard for Portable Fire Extinguishers, *Quincy, Mass., 1990*).

CODES AND STANDARDS

Model Building Codes

Currently, there are three "model" building codes available in the United States. Each of these three model codes utilizes NFPA standards as the basis for the technical details of its fire-prevention and fire-control measures. These three codes are: (1) the *Uniform Fire Code,* published by the International Conference of Building Officials in cooperation with the Western Fire Chiefs Association; (2) the *BOCA Basic Fire Prevention Code,* published by the Building Officials and Code Administrators International, Inc.; and (3) the *Southern Standard Fire Prevention Code* of the Southern Building Code Congress. When a code commission or building official is revising an outdated building code, one of the primary referenced documents is one of these model building codes along with NFPA 101, *Life Safety Code.*

Fire Safety Standards-Making Organizations

American National Standards Institute (ANSI).   ANSI sets public requirements for national standards and develops and

Typical Pictorial Extinguisher Marking Labels

*NOTE: Recommended colors, per PMS (Pantone Matching System):
(BLUE–*299*)
(RED–*Warm Red*)

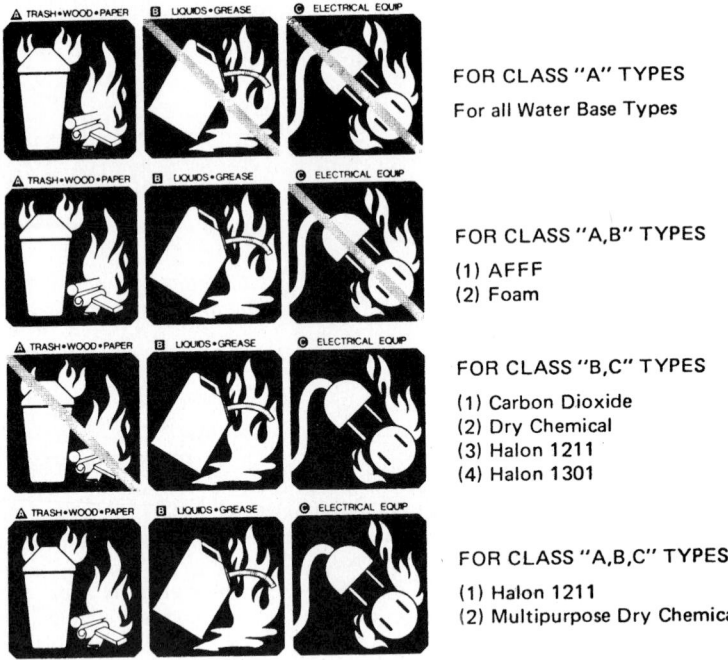

FOR CLASS "A" TYPES

For all Water Base Types

FOR CLASS "A,B" TYPES

(1) AFFF
(2) Foam

FOR CLASS "B,C" TYPES

(1) Carbon Dioxide
(2) Dry Chemical
(3) Halon 1211
(4) Halon 1301

FOR CLASS "A,B,C" TYPES

(1) Halon 1211
(2) Multipurpose Dry Chemical

Color Separation Identification (picture symbol objects are white; background borders are white)

BLUE * — background for "YES" symbols
BLACK — background for symbols with slash mark ("NO")
RED * — slash mark for black background symbols

FIGURE 2-15 Fire extinguisher symbols. (*From NFPA 10,* Standard for Portable Fire Extinguishers, *Quincy, Mass., 1990.*)

publishes them on a wide range of subjects. In order to achieve uniformity in voluntary and mandatory state and federal standards, it coordinates voluntary standardization activities of concerned organizations.

ANSI standards cover a variety of products, materials, and equipment that is used both in highly specialized fields and in nearly all other areas of modern life. ANSI publishes standards on ceramic tiles, chemical process equipment, home appliances, electronics equipment, motion picture film and equipment, acids, refractory materials, oil burners, office machines and supplies, hospital supplies, and combustion engines.

American Society for Testing and Materials (ASTM).   ASTM develops and publishes standards on finished products and on materials used in manufacturing and construction. Because some products and materials are used only within certain companies, industries, and government agencies, not all ASTM standards are developed by the full-consensus system. However, standards that deal with commodities used by the general public are developed by a full-consensus procedure, wherein all interested parties are fairly represented in the committee writing the standard. The standard committee is made up of anyone technically qualified or knowledgeable in the area of the committee's scope.

National Fire Protection Association (NFPA).   Approximately 275 various NFPA codes and standards encompass the entire scope of fire prevention, fire protection, fire fighting, and fire hazards, ranging from the ***National Electrical Code,**** believed to be the most widely adopted set of safety requirements in the world, to codes or standards of specific limited areas.

Once a code or standard has been adopted by the NFPA, it becomes available for adoption by any organization or jurisdiction having enforcement authority. A number of NFPA standards are widely used and commonly referenced in fire legislation.

Fire Testing and Research Laboratories.   There are many laboratories in the United States capable of performing, in varying degrees, fire tests of materials and/or equipment; many of these same laboratories, as well as other laboratories, have facilities for conducting fire-related research work. Generally, these laboratories can be classified into three categories: (1) private and industrial laboratories, (2) university laboratories, and (3) government laboratories. In the United States there are approximately 65 private and industrial laboratories that perform a wide range of fire tests. Space does not permit that each be described in detail. However, there are two, Underwriters Laboratories Inc. (UL) and Factory Mutual Laboratory Facilities (FM), whose work warrants particular emphasis.

Annually UL publishes lists of manufacturers whose products, when tested, have proved acceptable under appropriate standards which are subjected to one of the follow-up services provided by the laboratories as a counter-check. The work *listed* appears on UL labels attached to these products as authorized evidence that these products have been found to be in compliance with the laboratories' requirements.

Factory Mutual maintains testing facilities in Norwood, Mass., and also conducts large-scale applied research in its 1-acre, 60-ft-high FM test center in West Gloucester, R.I. Factory Mutual laboratory facilities are available on a contract basis through Factory Mutual Research.

More than 40 American colleges and universities are equipped with laboratories for fire testing and research. In addition to the colleges and universities that serve primarily as institutions for fire science training and education, there are others, both private and state-supported, whose engineering, physics, or science departments engage in such activities.

Several departments of the federal government—Agriculture, Air Force, Army, Commerce, Navy, and Transportation—as well as independent agencies also have research laboratories located throughout the country. These facilities are a direct result of an increasing national interest in fire safety as well as other safety- and health-related issues.

Insurance Organizations.   Many important groups perform varied fire protection and inspection services on behalf of the insurance industry and its insureds. For example, the Association of Mill and Elevator Mutual Insurance Companies serves the mill and elevator industry's needs; the American Institute of Marine Underwriters is organized to serve marine underwriters and to promote, advance, and protect their interests.

There are five large insurance organizations, however, that serve a wide range of casualty and property insurers and contribute to fire protection in many ways. They are: (1) American Insurance Association, (2) American Mutual Insurance Alliance, (3) Factory Mutual System, (4) Industrial Risk Insurers, and (5) Insurance Services Office.

---

* ***National Electrical Code*** is a Registered Trademark of the National Fire Protection Association, Quincy, MA 02269.

BIBLIOGRAPHY

Bryan, John L.: *Automatic Sprinkler and Standpipe Systems,* NFPA, Quincy, Mass., 1976.

Bryan, John L.: *Fire Supression and Detection Systems,* Glencoe Press, Beverly Hills, 1974.

Bugbee, Percy: *Principles of Fire Protection,* NFPA, Quincy, Mass., 1978.

Cote, Arthur E., ed.: *Fire Protection Handbook,* 17th ed., NFPA, Quincy, Mass., 1991.

Cote, Arthur E., ed.: *Industrial Fire Hazards Handbook,* 3d ed., NFPA, Quincy, Mass., 1990.

Factory Mutual: *The Handbook of Property Conservation,* Factory Mutual System, Norwood, Mass.

Factory Mutual: *Loss Prevention Data Books,* Factory Mutual System, Norwood, Mass.

Factory Mutual: *Property Conservation Workbook,* Factory Mutual System, Norwood, Mass., 1979.

Kimball, Warren Y.: *Fire Department Terminology,* NFPA, Quincy, Mass., 1979.

Magison, Ernest C.: *Electrical Instruments in Hazardous Locations,* 3d ed., Instrument Society of America, Triangle Park, N.C., 1978.

NFPA: *Guide to OSHA Fire Protection Regulations,* NFPA, Quincy, Mass.

NFPA: *Industrial Fire Brigades,* NFPA, Quincy, Mass., 1978.

NFPA: *Introduction to Fire Protection,* NFPA, Quincy, Mass., 1982.

NFPA: *National Fire Codes,* NFPA, Quincy, Mass., annual.

Planer, Robert G.: *Fire Loss Control, A Management Guide,* Marcel Dekker, New York, 1979.

Roytman, M. Ya.: *Principles of Fire Safety Standards for Building Construction,* Amerind, New Delhi, India, 1975.

Tuck, Charles A., ed.: *NFPA Inspection Manual,* NFPA, Quincy, Mass., 1976.

Tuve, Richard C.: *Principles of Fire Protection Chemistry,* NFPA, Quincy, Mass., 1976.

U.S. Department of Labor: *General Industry Standards,* part 1910, title 29, Code of Federal Regulations, Occupational Safety and Health Administration.

Williams, C. A., Jr., and Heins, R. M.: *Risk Management and Insurance,* McGraw-Hill, New York, 1976.

Zajic, J. E., and Himmelmann, W. A., *Highly Hazardous Materials Spills and Emergency Planning,* Marcel Dekker, New York, 1978.

CHAPTER 14-3

ELECTRICAL HAZARD PROTECTION AND PREVENTION

Robert L. Smith, Jr.
George W. Walsh
General Electric Company
Schenectady, New York

GLOSSARY

Basic impulse insulation level (BIL)   A reference level expressed in impulse crest of a standard 1.2×50-μs wave. The withstand of apparatus insulation, as demonstrated by suitable tests, shall be equal to or greater than the basic impulse insulation level.

Chopped wave   An impulse voltage wave that is suddenly reduced substantially to zero value by the sparkover of an air gap.

Crest value of a wave   The maximum value (voltage or current) attained by a wave.

Discharge current   The surge current that flows through an arrester.

Discharge voltage   The voltage that appears across the terminals of an arrester during the passage of discharge current.

Full wave   An impulse voltage wave that rises to crest value and then decays in a normal manner without modification by the sparkover of an air gap or similar occurrence (contrast with "chopped wave").

Impulse   A surge of unidirectional polarity.

Resistance to grounding (earth)   Resistance of the soil from the shield wire ground (down) lead and/or arrester ground lead to infinite earth—the subsurface point or plane of zero earth potential sought by lightning current.

Surge   A transient variation in the current or potential at a point in a circuit.

Surge arrester   A protective device for limiting surge voltages on equipment by discharging a surge current. It prevents continued flow of follow current and is capable of repeating these functions.

Switching surge (slow-front)   Impulse of front time of 30 to 2000 μs, generally, with time to half-crest on the tail appreciably longer than twice the time to crest.

Traveling wave   The resulting wave when the electric variation in a circuit takes the form of energy translation along a conductor, such energy being always equally divided between current and potential forms.

Voltage rating of an arrester   The highest permissible rms alternating voltage that may be present between the line and ground terminals of the arrester while it is performing its operating duty cycle prescribed by standards. Nameplate voltage.

Wave   The variation of current and/or voltage in an electric circuit with respect to time or distance.

Wave front   That part of a surge or impulse which occurs prior to reaching the crest value.

Wave shape   The variation of voltage or current of an impulse with time. For test purposes it is expressed as a combination of two numbers. The first, an index of wave-front steepness, is the time in microseconds from a virtual zero to the instant at which the crest value is reached. The second, an index of duration, is the time in microseconds from the virtual zero to the instant at which one-half of the crest value is reached on the wave tail. Examples are 1.2×50 and 8×20 waves.

Wave tail   That part between the crest value and the end of an impulse.

OVERLOAD AND FAULT PROTECTION

Medium- and low-voltage systems require both *overload* and *fault* protection. An overload is circuit operation in excess of its capability for a time long enough to cause damage or dangerous overheating. A fault is either a short circuit or an open circuit. A bolted short circuit is a solid connection between two phase conductors, a phase conductor and ground, or all three phase conductors. Protective devices activated by overloads or faults include fuses which melt as well as relays and direct-acting trip devices which open circuit breakers, open contactors, or sound alarms.

Overload Protection

Overloads may cause damaging elevated temperatures to persist for extended periods of time. Resistance temperature detectors are overload-protective devices which sense temperature directly. They are sometimes used to protect the most vulnerable parts of major equipment. Other overload-protective devices measure current in a circuit element and operate after a specific overcurrent persists for a time inversely related to current magnitude. Some current-detecting devices are ambient-compensated to make the protection sensitive to total hot-spot temperature. Since current unbalances resulting from unbalanced voltages cause rotating machine overheating, some protective devices sense current unbalance; others sense voltage unbalance. See Table 3-1 for a list of common overload-protective devices.

Fault Protection

Short-Circuit Fault Protection.   Short-circuit currents of large magnitude flow when circuit insulation suddenly fails. These currents usually are much greater than normal load or over-

TABLE 3-1 Overload Protective Devices

Device	Device function number	Measured quantity	Sensor	Usual application
Fuse		Current	Fusible element	Low- or medium-voltage circuits
Direct-acting trip device		Current	Trip device sensor	Low-voltage circuits
Thermal overcurrent relay	49	Current	Relay element	Low-voltage motor controller size 4 and smaller
			Current transformer	Low-voltage motor controller size 5 and larger
			Current transformer	Medium-voltage motor controller or circuit breaker
Time-delay magnetic or solid-state overcurrent relay	51	Current	Current transformer	Medium-voltage circuits
Temperature relay	49	Temperature	Resistance temperature detectors	Motors 1500 hp (1120 kW) and over
				Transformers over 10 MVA
Combination solid-state relay	49	Current and temperature	Current transformers and resistance temperature detector	Motors 1500 hp (1120 kW) and over
Solid-state or magnetic voltage balance relay	60	Voltages	Potential transformers	Motor buses
Solid-state or magnetic current balance relay	46	Currents	Current transformers	Motors 1500 hp (1120 kW) and larger

load currents. Sudden failure of insulation results from either gradual deterioration or sudden overvoltage. Short-circuit current flow usually damages adjacent circuit components or equipment by arcing, explosive heating, or fire. Under short-circuit conditions, currents much greater than load currents flow in all circuit components between the source and the fault. A system short-circuit study can be conducted to reveal the magnitudes of short-circuit current throughout a system for important fault locations and can guide selection of system components rated for the calculated duties.

Short-circuit protective devices such as fuses, overcurrent trip devices, or relays operate in durations that can be preset or preselected depending on the magnitude of fault current. Series overcurrent devices between a source and a fault all experience the same short-circuit current, changed in magnitude only by the presence of transformers. This fact can be used to provide a completely selective protective device system in which the system device closest to the point of fault operates first and other series devices operate later. When several devices exist between the point of fault and the source, device characteristics other than progressively longer times are appropriate, because delays to attain complete time interval selectivity tend to get too long for source end devices.

If more than one source supplies a system, each source circuit breaker usually requires directional as well as nondirectional relays for best continuity of service. See Refs. 8 and 9 for description of this type of relaying.

Important system components require rapid removal of a short circuit in order to minimize fault damage. Differential relaying accomplishes this without compromising system selectivity.

Differential relaying compares the currents entering and leaving a circuit element and operates if the difference exceeds the setting or sensitivity of the relay. This relaying requires separate current transformers for both the incoming and outgoing conductors to a circuit element in order to obtain the proper sensitivity and accuracy. A special exception for motor circuits uses three current transformers, one for *both ends* of *each* motor phase winding.

Fault pressure relays provide excellent protection for internal transformer tank faults by detecting the sudden change in internal tank pressure which accompanies the initial insulation breakdown when a fault occurs. These completely selective relays usually are applied to main stepdown liquid-filled transformers. They can also be applied to smaller liquid-filled transformers.

Occasionally, distance relays instead of overcurrent relays are used to provide selective operation for large industrial systems. These relays measure the impedance from the relay to some system location. They operate only for faults within the protected zone.

Providing a reasonably selective system with appropriate system component protection involves compromises between overcurrent selectivity and protection. A system coordination study performed by a qualified power-system protection engineer incorporates the appropriate compromises to assure optimum system selectivity and protection. See Table 3-2 for a list of common short-circuit fault-protective devices.

Open-Circuit Fault Protection.   An open-circuit fault condition results from the opening of any or all phase conductors at any point between the source and the load. Single-phase or three-phase undervoltage devices or relays easily detect this condition instantaneously on systems with no motors or generators connected. Protective devices consist of instantaneous or time-delay circuit-breaker undervoltage trip devices, instantaneous undervoltage relays with or without a timer, or time-delay undervoltage relays. These devices may be connected directly to a circuit or connected through potential transformers. They may operate to open a source or feeder circuit breaker, initiate an automatic throwover to an alternative source, or start an automatic sequence to energize the system from a standby generator.

Local generation can maintain both voltage and frequency at normal system values after a system disconnection, provided the generation is not overloaded. Overloading causes both of these quantities to decay.

Motors connected to an electric system maintain the system voltage for some short time after the source system is disconnected. The length of time this voltage is maintained and its frequency depend on motor size, the amount of connected motor load, and motor plus load inertia.

Out-of-phase reclosing may ensue if power is lost for systems without local generation or if the loss overloads local generation and system voltage decay is not rapid enough to cause undervoltage relays to operate and disconnect the local system from the source before the source is automatically reclosed. This can result in extensive motor and associated equipment damage. To mitigate this possible event, various arrangements of sensitive reverse power, under- or overfrequency, or synchronizing check relays are available.

Over-undervoltage relays connected to a single line-to-ground potential transformer detect line-to-ground faults on an incoming line that is disconnected from a grounded system at the source end. Such relays also can detect the return of normal voltage to a de-energized source and initiate automatic reclosing of the incoming-line circuit breaker.

Selection of appropriate relay settings for other than overcurrent relays is an important part of any system coordination study. Such selection may depend on the results of load flow, load shedding, or stability studies. The selection of the type of study necessary is at the discretion of the power-system protection engineer.

Figure 3-1 shows a typical industrial plant one-line diagram. Device function numbers identify the protective devices included. Figure 3-2 compares the time-current characteristics of some protective devices. It is of utmost importance to identify each device represented by manufacturer and model number or other manufacturer's nomenclature when making a coordination study for selecting device settings.

Additional discussion of fault protection will be found in Sec. 3, Chap. 1, "Power Distribution Systems."

TABLE 3-2   Short-Circuit Fault Protective Devices

Device	Device function number	Measured quantity	Detection devices	Usual application
Fuse		Current	Fuse element	Low- or medium-voltage circuits
Direct-acting trip device		Current	Trip device sensor	Low-voltage circuits
Overcurrent relay		Current	Current transformer	Medium-voltage circuits:
	50/51			Feeder-phase-time and instantaneous
	50/51N			Feeder residual ground time and instantaneous
	50GS			Feeder-ground sensor, instantaneous
	51GS			Feeder-ground sensor, time
	51N			Incoming or tie-residual ground, time
	51G			Neutral ground, time
	51			Incoming or tie phase, time
Differential relay		Current	Current transformer	Medium-voltage circuits:
	87T			Transformer over 10 MVA
	87T-G			Transformers, resistance grounded, overcurrent 10 MVA
	87M			Motors 1500 hp (1120 kW) and over
	87B			Buses with 750 MVA or over, short circuit
	87L			Lines, ties to subbuses
	87G			Generators, any rating
Fault pressure relay	63FP	Pressure	Tank-mounted relay	Medium-voltage liquid-filled transformers over 10 MVA
Directional over-current relays	67 67N	Current and voltage	Current and potential transformers	Medium-voltage sources connected to a common bus
Distance relays	21	Current and voltage	Current and potential transformers	Large industrial medium- or high-voltage circuits

POWER MANAGEMENT SYSTEMS FOR INTEGRATED PROTECTION, METERING, AND EVENT RECORDING*

Power management for electrical distribution systems has taken major steps forward, paced by new cost-effective alternatives in software, communications, and component devices. A primary characteristic of new component devices is the combination of traditional functions such as overcurrent protection, metering, and voltage and phase protection in a single device.

Overcurrent protection can be ordered with specific attributes such as LT, ST, inverse, or very inverse or can be ordered so the user can configure these in the field. This convenience

---

* by David J. West, General Electric Co.

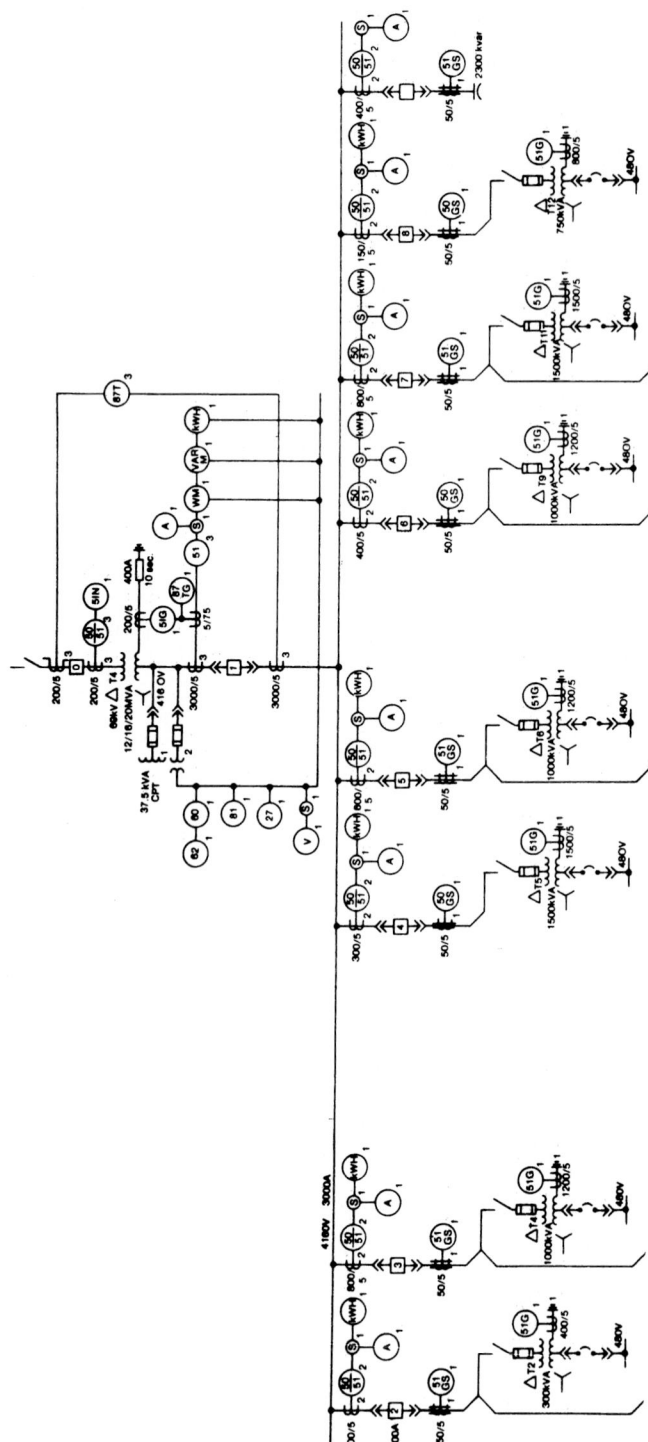

FIGURE 3-1 Typical industrial-plant one-line diagram. (*From Industrial Power Systems Magazine, General Electric Co., Schenectady, N.Y., March 1980, pp. 8–9.*)

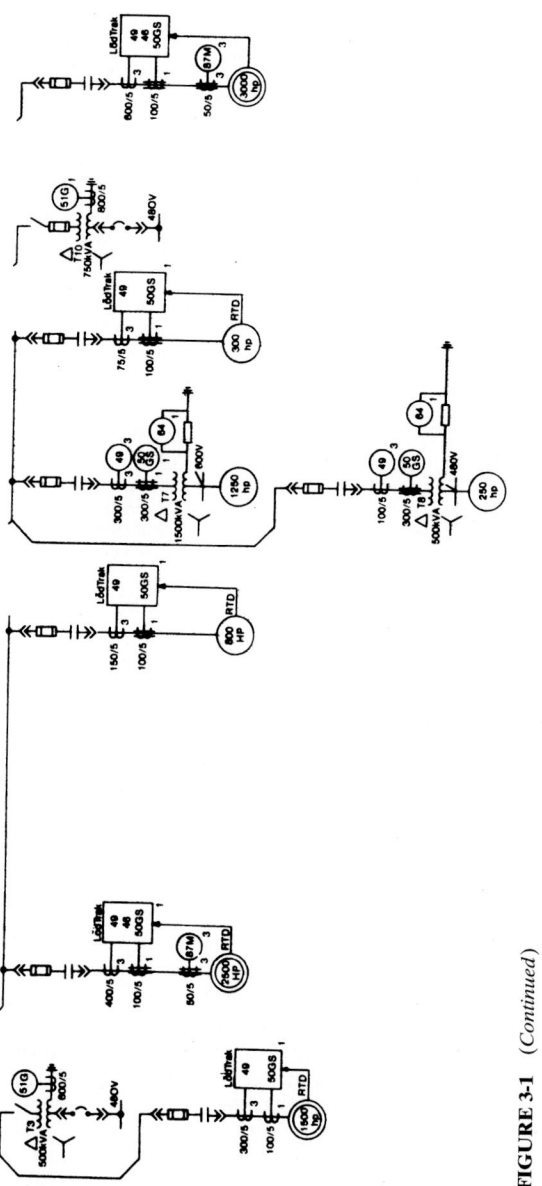

FIGURE 3-1 (*Continued*)

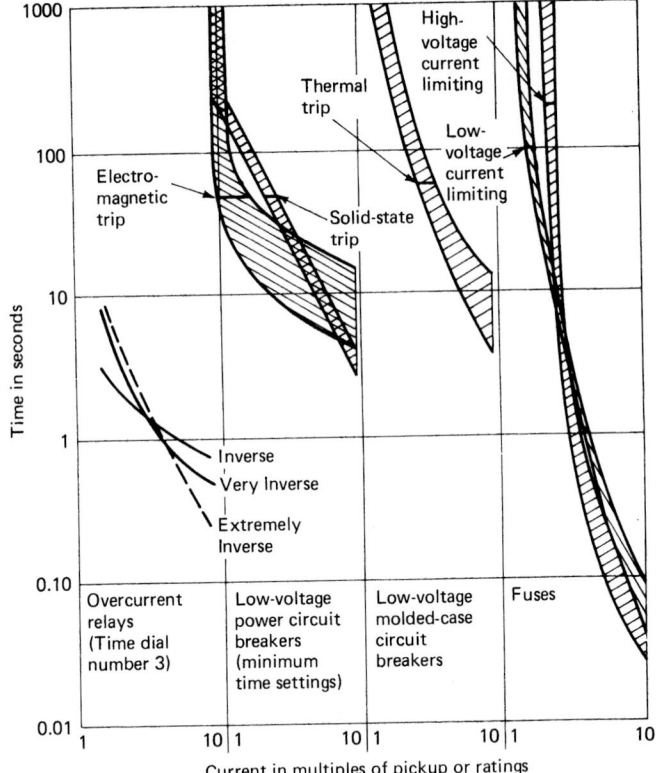

FIGURE 3-2   Operating time-current characteristics of four most commonly used power-system protective devices; note that plots have been developed by plotting on log-log paper on a common time basis. The more common relays normally applied on high-voltage systems operate considerably faster than the low-voltage devices with which selectivity is desired. (*Reproduced with permission from* Plant Engineering *Magazine, February 7, 1974, p. 87.*)

allows the device settings to be defined later in the design cycle and allows greater flexibility in the future. Protection against loss of phase or phase unbalance is often provided by a combination of voltage- and current-based definite-time relays.

The addition of communication capability to metering and protection is the key to productivity gains offered by power management. The ability to quickly identify sequences of events for system disturbances significantly reduces outage times. Better systems not only report change of breaker status, but also report the type (overload or short circuit) and magnitude of fault and time of occurrence. Industrial power management systems can expect $\frac{1}{100}$-s resolution on time stamps in event logs. The same data are useful in postfault engineering analysis.

Metered data communicated electronically allow a reduction of time needed for routine data collection such as monthly meter readings. Special study cases can be quickly set up and trended to help operations identify overloads and load shifts or optimize energy consumption relative to time of use utility billing rates.

Third-generation host computer programs make the tracking and analysis of power system events and metered data an easy-to-learn and easy-to-do activity. Programs exist that will run on multitasking, multiuser minicomputers and even on simple desktop personal computers.

SURGE-VOLTAGE PROTECTION OF ELECTRIC-POWER-SYSTEM EQUIPMENT

Apparatus-Insulation Capability

Surge protection is intended to avoid surge stresses beyond the fairly well standardized surge capabilities of power-system-apparatus insulation. Apparatus-insulation capability and surge-arrester protective ability are both established by tests with various elevated voltage and/or current waveshapes.

Tables 3-3 to 3-6 list surge capabilities of basic power-system equipment and ac rotating machines. Impulse withstand of open-wire lines varies somewhat in specific value, depending upon construction, maintenance, weather, etc., but is generally considered well above that of associated transformers. An open-wire 13.8-kV distribution circuit, for example, is typically considered to have a 400-kV BIL. While cables do not have assigned BILs (basic impulse insulation levels), they too have impulse capability significantly higher than associated liquid-filled transformers.

TABLE 3-3   Impulse Test Levels for Liquid-Filled Transformers*

Insulation class and nominal bushing rating, kV	Windings				Bushing withstand voltages		
	High-pot. tests, kV	Chopped wave		BIL full wave (1.2×50), kV	60-cycle 1-min dry, kV (rms)	60-cycle 10-s, kV (rms)	BIL full wave (1.2×50), kV (crest)
		Minimum time to flashover					
		kV	μs				
1.2	10	54(36)	1.5(1)	45(30)	15(10)	13(6)	45(30)
2.5	15	69(54)	1.5(1.25)	60(45)	21(15)	20(13)	60(45)
5.0	19	88(69)	1.6(1.5)	75(60)	27(21)	24(20)	75(60)
8.7	26	110(88)	1.8(1.6)	95(75)	35(27)	30(24)	95(75)
15.0	34	130(110)	2.0(1.8)	110(95)	50(35)	45(30)	110(95)
25.0	50	175	3.0	150	70	70(60)	150
34.5	70	230	3.0	200	95	95	200
46.0	95	290	3.0	250	120	120	250
69.0	140	400	3.0	350	175	175	350
92.0	185	520	3.0	450	225	190	450
115.0	230	630	3.0	550	280	230	550
138.0	275	750	3.0	650	335	275	650
161.0	325	865	3.0	750	385	315	750

* Values in parentheses are for distribution transformers, instrument transformers, constant-current transformers, step- and induction-voltage regulators, and cable potheads for distribution cables. Data taken from industry standards.

TABLE 3-4   Impulse Test Levels for Power Circuit Breakers, Switchgear Assemblies, and Metal-Enclosed Buses

Voltage rating, kV	BIL full wave (1.2×50), kV, crest	Voltage rating, kV	BIL full wave (1.2×50), kV, crest	Voltage rating, kV	BIL full wave (1.2×50), kV, crest
2.4	45	23	150	115	550
4.6	60	34.5	200	138	650
7.2	75*	46	250	161	750
13.8	95	69	350	230	900
14.4	110	92	450	345	1300

* 95 kV for metal-clad switchgear with power circuit breakers.

TABLE 3-5   Impulse Test Levels for Dry-Type Transformers*

Nominal equipment voltage		High pot. test, kV (rms)	Standard BIL (1.2 × 50), kV, crest
Delta or ungrounded wye	Grounded wye		
120–1,200		4	10
	1,200/693	4	10
2,520		10	20
	4,360/2,520	10	20
4,160–7,200		12	30
	8,720/5,040	10	30
8,320		19	45
12,000–13,800		31	60
	13,800/7,970	10	60
18,000		34	95
	22,860/13,200	10	95
2,300		37	110
	24,940/14,400	10	110
27,600		40	125
	34,500/19,920	10	125
34,500		50	150

* Data from Ref. 11, ANSI C57.12.01, "General Requirements for Dry-Type Distribution and Power Transformers."

TABLE 3-6   AC Rotating Impulse Levels

Motors			Generators		
Voltage rating, kV	High pot. test, kV (rms)	Impulse capability,* kV, crest	Voltage rating, kV	High pot. test, kV (rms)	Impulse capability,* kV, crest
2.3	5.6	9.9	2.4	5.8	10.2
4.0	9.0	15.9	4.16	9.3	16.5
6.6	14.2	25.1	6.9	14.8	26.2
13.2	27.4	48.4	13.8	28.6	50.6

* Equivalent BIL, commonly accepted values. Not standardized.

Surge-Protection Techniques

Electric-power-system components are protected against lightning and switching-produced surges by *interception* and *diversion* of the surges to ground. Shielding via overhead static wire and by conducting structures is used to greatly reduce the probability of significant lightning penetration of the system. Surge arresters are applied between line and ground at selected locations to divert surges from important and sensitive power-system and utilization equipment. Additionally, surge capacitors are sometimes applied at the terminals of motors and generators to reduce the surge voltage gradient. See Fig. 3-3.

Shielding

Lightning exposure to plant power systems is principally through outdoor supply substations and associated overhead lines. Effectively shielded installations are desirable. These are described in standards[13] as having shielding against direct strokes for the station and for all connected lines, at least for ½ mi from the station (line end protection).

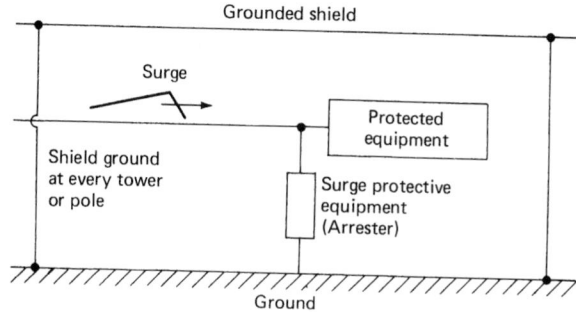

FIGURE 3-3   Schematic diagram of basic lightning-protection philosophy. Grounded shield intercepts a very large percentage of direct
strokes. Surges that appear on incoming circuits are diverted to
ground by surge arresters located at or near terminals of equipment
to be protected.

Shielding of outdoor substation areas is usually provided by masts, or equivalent, which are designed to form a protective zone (not likely to be entered by lightning) within which all vulnerable parts will lie. With a single mast the protective zone is usually considered to be a cone having its apex at the top of the mast and whose sides make an angle with the vertical of 30 to 45°. With two or more masts the protective zone of each is increased somewhat in the area between them. With the usual spacings between masts, this shielding angle may increase to 60°. See Fig. 3-4.

Incoming line shielding is provided by overhead ground wire(s) which should be grounded at each pole or tower, through as low a ground resistance as it is practicable to obtain, and should be connected to the ground bus at the substation. Low ground resistance is particularly important for the ground connection at the first few poles or towers adjacent to the substation. Locating the shield wire(s) with respect to the power lines entails several considerations, as noted in Fig. 3-5. Practical shielding of overhead lines cannot be perfect, and a finite (but usually very low) probability of associated lightning-related outages must be accepted. Analysis procedures and associated databases have been developed to predict shielding performance for a given shielding configuration and vice versa. Such analysis can be practically done only by those practiced in lightning protection of overhead lines.

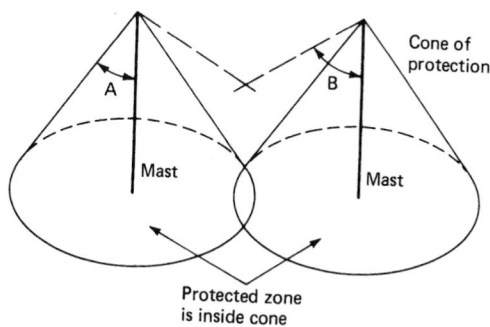

FIGURE 3-4   Shielding by masts. Protected zone with single mast is cone as illustrated with angle *A* of 30° to 45°. Cone
of protection between masts extends up to 60°, angle *B*.

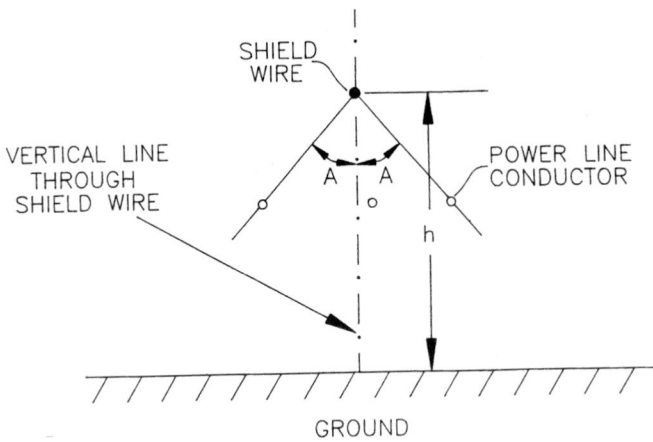

FIGURE 3-5 Illustration of horizontal array of the three-phase power conductors with single shield wire. The effectiveness of the shielding depends upon the height h of the shield wire, the shielding angle A, the resistance to ground of the shield wire, and the terrain over which the line is built—to name a few factors. Shielding practices, which vary widely, may be further affected by the frequency of lightning in the area and the cost of the associated line outages.

Proper connection to earth is vital to the satisfactory performance of shielding and surge arresters. Resistance to ground should not exceed 1 Ω for large substations and generating stations, and 5 ohms for small substations and industrial plants. The *National Electric Code*[5] sets maximum resistance to ground at 25 Ω and requires arrester ground lead size not less than No. 6 AWG.* In noneffectively shielded substations and lines, which are subject to much higher surge exposure, it is important that the lowest practical ground resistance be obtained to minimize voltage gradients caused by surge current discharge to ground and to enhance overall surge-protective performance.

Surge Arresters

Valve-type arresters are used for surge protection of plant power systems. The principal active (valve) element in these arresters is a nonlinear resister that exhibits low resistance under high surge voltage and that diverts the surge current to ground at a safe level in its protective function. At power system operating voltages, these arresters exhibit very high resistance to avoid excessive continuous losses. There are many old-technology arresters in service that utilize silicon-carbide valve elements. Current-technology arresters utilize metal-oxide valve elements that are superior; these arresters represent all new installations.

Arrester Protective Characteristics. Three classes of arresters are recognized by standards[12] for medium-voltage and high-voltage systems—station class, intermediate class, and distribution class. Low-voltage-system (below 1000 V) arresters are classified as secondary arresters. Arrester manufacturers list arrester-surge-protective performance characteristics by arrester class. These performance characteristics are based on surge-voltage and surge-current test waveshapes also specified by standards. See Fig. 3-6. The two surge-voltage tests most fre-

---

* *National Electrical Code*® is a Registered Trademark of the National Fire Protection Association, Quincy, MA 02269.

quently used for such listing are the front-of-wave sparkover and the 1.2×50-μs wave test. Equivalent front-of-wave test data are also listed for the nongapped zinc oxide arresters. The standardized 8×20-μs current wave is the basis for listing arrester-discharge-voltage levels. See Tables 3-8 to 3-10. As such, the listed characteristics usually provide the *maximum* surge voltage permitted (between arrester terminals) at the arrester location for the specified surge current duties.

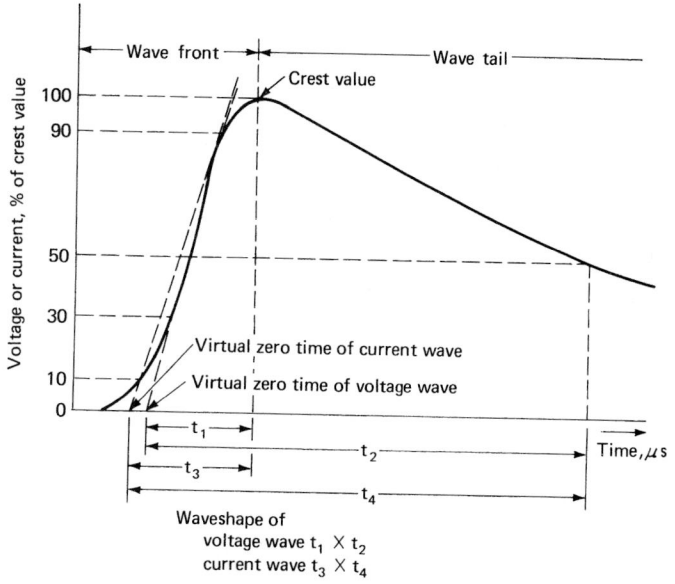

FIGURE 3-6 Wave geometry used to designate waveshape for purposes of standardizing surge-arrester protective characteristics and specifying insulation surge capability.

Application of Arresters.   The application of arresters depends upon three basic selections: (1) selection of arrester rating, (2) selection of arrester class, and (3) selection of arrester location. Check the adequacy of protection of the resulting application.

Selection of Arresting Rating.   Surge arresters should be selected with the *minimum* ratings that will have a satisfactory service life on the system. This will provide the greatest practical margin of protection for the protected equipment insulation and at the lowest cost.

Although protective margins are increased by reducing arrester ratings, there is a practical limit to such reduction because arresters are rated in relation to their ability to withstand continuous power-frequency voltage. Arrester survivability also depends upon its capability to withstand temporary power-frequency overvoltage (TOV).

Tables 3-7, 3-8, and 3-9 list maximum continuous operating voltage capability (MCOV). Since arresters are virtually always connected line to ground, the selected arrester ratings must have MCOV capabilities which equal or exceed the *maximum line-to-ground operating voltage* of the system.

A number of circumstances can produce arrester TOV. The condition of single line to ground on a three-phase system establishes the minimum arrester TOV which must be

TABLE 3-7 Surge-Protective Characteristics of Station-Class Arresters with Metal-Oxide Valve Elements*

Arrester rating, kV rms	Maximum continuous operating voltage, (MCOV) capability, kV rms	Front-of-wave (FOW) protective level, kV crest	Maximum discharge voltage (kV crest) at indicated impulse current for an 8/20 μs current wave							Maximum switching surge protective level, kV, crest at indicated current	
			1.5 kA	3.0 kA	5.0 kA	10 kA	15 kA	20 kA	40 kA	kV	kA
2.7	2.2	7.8	5.9	6.2	6.5	6.9	7.4	7.8	8.9	5.4	0.5
3.0	2.55	9.1	6.9	7.2	7.5	8.0	8.6	9.0	10.3	6.3	0.5
4.5	3.7	13.0	9.9	10.3	10.8	11.5	12.3	12.9	14.8	9.0	0.5
5.1	4.2	14.8	11.2	11.8	12.3	13.1	14.0	14.7	16.9	10.3	0.5
6.0	5.1	17.9	13.6	14.2	14.8	15.8	16.9	17.7	20.3	12.4	0.5
7.5	6.1	21.4	16.2	17.0	17.7	18.9	20.2	21.2	24.3	14.8	0.5
8.5	6.9	24.2	18.4	19.2	20.0	21.4	22.9	24.0	27.5	16.8	0.5
9.0	7.65	26.6	20.2	21.1	22.0	23.5	25.1	26.4	30.2	18.4	0.5
10	8.4	29.3	22.2	23.3	24.2	25.9	27.7	29.1	33.3	20.3	0.5
12	10.2	35.5	26.9	28.2	29.4	31.4	33.5	35.2	40.4	24.6	0.5
15	12.7	44.2	33.5	35.1	36.6	39.1	41.8	43.9	50.3	30.6	0.5
18	15.3	53.3	40.4	42.3	44.1	47.1	50.3	52.8	60.6	36.8	0.5
21	17.0	59.1	44.8	46.9	48.9	52.3	55.8	58.7	67.2	40.9	0.5
24	19.5	67.8	51.4	53.8	56.1	60.0	64.1	67.3	77.1	46.9	0.5
27	22.0	76.5	58.0	60.8	63.3	67.7	72.3	75.9	87.0	52.9	0.5
30	24.4	84.9	64.3	67.4	70.3	75.1	80.2	84.2	96.5	58.7	0.5
36	29.0	101	76.4	80.0	83.4	89.2	95.2	100	115	69.7	0.5
39	31.5	110	83.0	86.9	90.6	96.9	104	109	125	75.8	0.5
45	36.5	128	96.8	102	106	113	121	127	146	88.3	0.5
48	39	136	103	108	113	120	128	135	155	93.8	0.5
54	44	144	111	116	120	127	135	141	159	102	0.5
60	49	160	124	129	134	141	150	157	177	113	0.5
66	53	175	136	142	147	155	165	172	194	124	0.5
72	58	191	148	154	160	169	179	188	212	136	0.5
90	73	239	185	193	200	211	224	234	264	169	0.5
96	78	255	197	206	213	225	239	250	282	181	0.5
108	87	287	222	232	240	254	270	282	318	204	0.5
120	98	321	249	259	269	284	301	315	355	235	1.0
132	107	353	273	285	295	312	331	346	390	258	1.0
144	117	382	296	309	320	338	359	375	423	280	1.0
168	136	446	345	360	373	394	418	437	493	326	1.0
172	140	457	353	369	382	404	429	448	505	334	1.0
180	146	477	369	385	399	422	448	468	528	349	1.0
192	156	509	394	411	426	450	477	499	563	372	1.0
228	185	604	467	487	505	534	566	592	668	442	1.0
240	194	635	491	513	531	562	596	623	703	465	1.0

* Courtesy General Electric Co.

TABLE 3-8 Surge-Protective Characteristics of Intermediate-Class Arresters with Metal-Oxide Valve Elements*

Arrester rating, kV rms	Maximum continuous operating voltage capability (L-G), kV rms	Maximum equivalent front-of-wave protective level, kV crest	Maximum discharge voltage (kV crest) at indicated impulse current using an 8×20 μs current wave					Maximum switching surge protective level, kV crest†
			1.5 kA	3.0 kA	5 kA	10 kA	20 kA	
2.7	2.2	7.7	6.2	6.5	6.8	7.4	8.3	5.6
3.0	2.55	8.8	7.1	7.5	7.8	8.5	9.6	6.4
4.5	3.70	12.8	10.3	10.8	11.3	12.3	13.8	9.3
5.1	4.2	14.5	11.6	12.2	12.8	13.9	15.7	10.5
6.0	5.10	17.5	14.1	14.8	15.5	16.8	19.0	12.7
7.5	6.10	21.0	16.9	17.8	18.6	20.2	22.7	15.3
8.5	6.9	23.8	19.1	20.1	21.0	22.8	25.7	17.2
9.0	7.65	26.1	21.0	22.1	23.1	25.0	28.2	19.0
10	8.4	28.6	23.0	24.2	25.3	27.4	30.9	20.8
12	10.2	34.7	27.9	29.3	30.7	33.3	37.5	25.2
15	12.7	43.3	34.8	36.6	38.3	41.5	46.8	31.4
18	15.3	52.1	41.9	44.0	46.1	49.9	56.3	37.8
21	17.0	57.9	46.5	48.9	51.2	55.4	62.6	42.0
24	19.5	66.5	53.4	56.1	58.8	63.7	71.8	48.2
27	22.0	74.9	60.2	63.3	66.3	71.8	81.0	54.4
30	24.4	83.1	66.7	70.2	73.5	79.6	89.8	60.3
36	29.0	98.8	79.3	83.4	87.4	94.6	107	71.7
39	31.5	108	86.1	90.6	94.9	103	116	77.8
45	36.5	125	99.8	105	110	119	135	90.2
48	39.0	134	107	113	118	128	144	96.7
54	44.0	151	121	127	133	144	163	109
60	49.0	168	135	142	148	160	181	122
72	58.0	198	159	167	175	190	214	144
90	73.0	251	202	212	222	241	271	182
96	78.0	267	214	225	236	256	289	194
108	88.0	301	242	254	266	288	325	218
120	98.0	335	269	283	296	321	362	243

* Courtesy General Electric Co.
† At 500-amp switching surge current.

TABLE 3-9   Surge-Protective Characteristics of Distribution-Class Arresters with Metal-Oxide Valve Elements*

Arrester rating, kV rms	MCOV kV rms	Maximum equivalent front-of-wave protective level, 0.5 μs kV crest	Maximum discharge voltage, kV crest, at indicated impulse current using an 8 × 20 current wave			
			1.5 kA	5 kA	10 kA	20 kA
3	2.55	13.5	9.7	10.9	12.0	13.7
6	5.10	25.2	18.2	20.5	22.5	25.7
9	7.65	35.3	25.5	28.7	31.5	35.9
10	8.40	39.2	28.3	31.9	35.0	40.0
12	10.20	46.0	33.1	37.4	41.0	46.7
15	12.70	56.0	40.4	45.6	50.0	57.0
18	15.30	67.2	48.5	54.7	60.0	68.5
21	17.00	78.4	56.6	63.9	70.0	79.8
27	22.00	100.8	72.7	82.1	90.0	102.5

* Courtesy General Electric Co.

accommodated. It is the arresters on the two unfaulted phases/lines that experience this very significant TOV. Such TOV relates to the manner in which the system is grounded. Guides to selection of arrester ratings therefore reflect the role of system grounding to provide for arrester TOV duties associated with ground faults. Also, of course, such guides reflect the role of the system nominal voltage. See Table 3-10. Arresters are acutely sensitive to the time duration of the overvoltage and Table 3-10 is based on a relayed system which affects immediate clearing of ground faults and therefore greatly reduces arrester exposure. Nonrelayed system applications wherein ground faults are permitted to remain for an extended time (beyond a few seconds) should be referred to the arrester vendor or a specialist.

TABLE 3-10   Voltage Ratings of Arresters Usually Selected for Three-Phase Systems*

Nominal system voltage, kV	Voltage rating of arrester, kV	
	System ungrounded or resistance-grounded	System solidly grounded
0.120/0.208Y	0.65	0.175
0.240	0.65	0.65
0.480	0.65	0.65
0.600	0.65	0.65
2.4	3 (2.7)	3 (2.7)
4.16	4.5	3 (4.5)
4.8	6.0 (5.1)	4.5 (5.1)
6.9	7.5	6.0
12.47	15, 12	10, 9
13.8	15	12, 10
23	24	24, 21, 18
34.5	39, 36	30, 27
46	48	39
69	72	60, 54
115	120	90, 96, 108
138	144	108, 120
161		120, 132, 144
230		172, 180, 192

* Based on maximum operating voltage of 1.05 times nominal and immediate (within a few seconds) clearing of ground faults.

Standards contain various aids to determine arrester TOV versus mode of system grounding. However, the vast majority of plant medium-voltage systems are resistance-grounded or ungrounded and as such require arrester ratings that are at least equal to the system nominal voltage. See Table 3-10. The singular exception is the application of 12-kV–rated arresters on 12.47-kV nominal ungrounded or resistance-grounded systems. Solid system grounding permits the use of lower rated arresters (approximately 75 to 80 percent) compared to arresters for resistance-grounded and ungrounded systems, but the limited number of arrester ratings available often does not permit the benefit of this advantage particularly at the lower voltages. Multigrounded (four-wire) distribution systems and most high-voltage systems (69 kV and above) may safely use lower rated arresters. Those systems require individual study to ensure the most economical, secure arrester rating selection.

Selection of Arrester Class.   In order of cost, protective efficiency, and durability, the three classes of arresters are: (1) station class, (2) intermediate class, and (3) distribution class. As a general guide to arrester-class usage vs. equipment size, the following may be considered typical practice:

Station class. Component protection of 7.5 MVA and above substations and large or essential rotating machines

Intermediate class. Component protection of 1 to 20 MVA substations, overhead lines, and rotating machines

Distribution class. Distribution-class apparatus, dry-type transformers, and small rotating machines

These classes overlap considerably. There is a tendency to use higher-class arresters at higher voltages. Limitations on the available range of ratings of distribution-class and intermediate-class arresters eliminate them as a choice in higher-voltage applications.

While actual lightning-protective practices may necessarily vary from one type of installation to the next, all installations are either effectively shielded or noneffectively shielded. There are different degrees of jeopardy for each of these two basic categories, and the degree may vary with a change in system arrangement or operating mode.

Excessive arrester discharge currents in noneffectively shielded installations are a prime cause of arrester failure, and inadvertent loss of protection may occur when arrester discharge voltages exceed anticipated levels. In effectively shielded systems, arrester discharge currents are unlikely to exceed 5000 A as a conservative maximum, but 20,000 A is a conservative maximum for noneffectively shielded systems. This encourages use of station-class and intermediate-class arresters in noneffectively shielded installations.

Location of Arresters.   The ideal location for surge arresters, from the standpoint of protection, is directly at the terminals of equipment to be protected. Usually, low-BIL apparatus (certain dry-type transformers and rotating machines) requires surge-protective devices in direct shunt with associated insulation. Otherwise practical circumstances dictate often that arresters be remote, requiring that one set of arresters protect more than one piece of apparatus.

For remote arresters it is necessary to estimate the depreciation in protection caused by separation distances between the arresters and the protected equipment. These determinations require the use of traveling wave mechanics by a practiced surge protection engineer. The following are *general guides* for locating arresters relating to typical components and their arrangements.

EFFECTIVELY SHIELDED SUBSTATIONS.   Arresters are required on each overhead line as it enters the substation, for protection of disconnect switches, buses, etc. Separation distances of 75 to 200 ft (23 to 61 m) and sometimes more, between arresters and full-BIL equipment can be tolerated at 23 kV and above. At 15 kV and below, practice usually avoids appreciable separation distance. Usually arresters are applied at transformer incoming line terminals.

NONEFFECTIVELY SHIELDED SUBSTATIONS.   Arresters should be applied at or very close to terminals of transformers and breakers. A minimum separation distance between arresters and overcurrent protection equipment is permissible.

METAL-CLAD SWITCHGEAR.   Metal-clad switchgear installed in substations (as above) should be protected in the same fashion as transformers. In effectively shielded substations where continuous metallic-sheathed cable (or equivalent) intervenes between the switchgear and exposed line, an arrester at the junction of line and cable suffices if it is station class, intermediate class, or special distribution class. When exposure is through a power transformer protected on the exposed side, generally arresters are not necessary at the switchgear.

DRY-TYPE TRANSFORMERS.   Full-BIL dry-type transformers should be protected as described above for full-BIL equipment. Reduced-BIL dry-type transformers (with BILs below comparably rated liquid-filled distribution transformers) require arresters at their terminals when connected directly to overhead lines. When exposure is through continuous metallic-sheathed cable (or equivalent), a line-cable junction arrester may or may not protect the low-BIL dry-type transformer. In such cases, a distribution-class arrester at the transformer terminals will suffice. If exposure is through another transformer, usually arresters are not required at the dry-type transformer.

CABLE.   Cable should be surge-protected the same as full-BIL transformers.

AERIAL CABLE.   Arresters are required at junctions of open-wire line and aerial cable. Messenger and sheath should be grounded through a low value of ground resistance at every pole. Aerial cable should be considered the same as open-wire line for protection of terminal equipment.

Surge Protective Margins.   Standards application guides recommend that apparatus surge-withstand capability (as in Tables 3-3, 3-4, 3-5, and 3-6) exceed surge arrester protective levels (as in Tables 3-7, 3-8, and 3-9) by 20 percent for the most important surge categories. Specifically, apparatus BIL (1.2×50 μs wave) should exceed the arrester maximum discharge voltage—for an 8×20-μs current wave protective level, by 20 percent. Similarly the transformer chopped wave withstand capability (as in Table 3-3) should exceed the arrester FOW (front-of-wave) protective level by 20 percent.

Rotating-Machine Protection

Medium-voltage (2.3- to 13.8-kV) rotating machines require: (1) a strictly effectively shielded environment, (2) arresters at the terminals of the machine, (3) surge capacitors at the terminals of the machine, and (4) strict adherence to good grounding practices. The surge capacitors are used to reduce the voltage gradient of surges that may be damaging to machine turn insulation. Such capacitors should be connected in the closest possible shunt relation to the machine line-to-ground insulation. Table 3-11 lists commonly available surge-protective capacitors. Note surge-protective capacitors are rated on a line-to-line (rms) voltage basis with associated designated capacitance per pole (terminal to case).

Switching events within the distribution system (e.g., motor switching, fault inception, fault removal, insulation flashover, capacitor switching, etc.) present surge exposure possibilities to motors and generators. In practice, a high percentage of machines above 4 kV have arresters and surge capacitors. At least half of the 4-kV motor installations are so protected, while at

TABLE 3-11   Ratings and Sizes of Surge-Protective Capacitors

Voltage rating, rms, V, L-L	Maximum voltage, rms, V, L-L	Poles per unit	μF per pole
0–650	715	3	1.0
2,400	2,640	3	0.5
4,160	4,576	3	0.5
6,900	7,590	1	0.5
13,800	15,180	1	0.25
24,000	26,400	1	0.125

2.3 kV only a minority are so protected. Low-voltage motors and generators (below 1000 V) seldom have such surge protection, except in exposed pumping applications.

REFERENCES AND BIBLIOGRAPHY

Standards (Use Latest Issue)

1. ANSI C42.100-(year), "IEEE Standard Dictionary of Electrical and Electronics Terms."

IEEE Recommended Practices

2. IEEE 141-(year), "IEEE Recommended Practice for Electric Power Distribution for Industrial Plants."
3. IEEE 142-(year), "IEEE Recommended Practice for Grounding of Industrial and Commercial Power Systems."
4. IEEE 242-(year), "IEEE Recommended Practice for Protection and Coordination of Industrial and Commercial Power Systems."
5. NFPA 70-(year), *National Electrical Code.*®
6. NFPA 70E-(year), "Electrical Safety Requirements for Employee Workplaces."
7. NFPA 70B-(year), "Recommended Practice for Electric Equipment Maintenance."

ANSI Standards for Equipment

8. ANSI C19 Series, "Package Control Equipment."
9. ANSI C37.2-1994, "Switchgear."
10. ANSI C51:1-1994, "Safety Standards for Construction and Guide for Selectors, Installation and Use of Electric Motors and Generators."
11. ANSI C57 Series, "Transformers, Regulators, Reactors."
12. IEEE Std 28-1994; also ANSI C62.1-1994, "Surge Arresters for Alternating-Current Power Circuits."
13. ANSI C62.2-1994, "Guide for Application of Valve Type Lightning Arresters for Alternating-Current Systems."

Books

14. Beeman, D. L. (ed.): *Industrial Power Systems Handbook,* McGraw-Hill, New York, 1955.
15. *Electrical Transmission and Distribution Reference Book,* Westinghouse Electric Corp., Pittsburgh, 1950.
16. *Applied Protective Relaying,* Westinghouse Electric Corp., Pittsburgh, 1976.
17. Smeaton, R. W. (ed.): *Switchgear and Control Handbook,* 2d ed., McGraw-Hill, New York, 1987.

CHAPTER 14-4
SECURITY EQUIPMENT

Anthony C. Fague
Director, Engineering
ADT Security Systems, Inc.
Morris Plains, New Jersey

INTRODUCTION

The term security may be defined as *the protection of life and property.* Two of the basic hazards are fire (see Chap. 14-2) and intrusion. Intrusion hazards, which will be covered in this chapter, consist of intruders who enter a premises to steal physical property or secret information or commit sabotage or vandalism.

The purpose of intrusion security is to deter the entry of potential criminals or vandals, to detect intruders, and to alert a guard force as promptly as possible. A basic premise of good security is protection in depth—the provision of more than one line of defense to discourage incursions, to slow the advance of knowledgeable intruders, and to provide secondary defenses in case of penetration beyond the first line.

Security is much more than an alarm system, and must include:

1. A complete plan, attitude, and purpose by the persons involved in securing life and property
2. Physical security
3. Detection and reporting methods
4. Signal transmission
5. Signal handling
6. Continuing review of quality, value, and changing conditions, with the intent to amend and upgrade as necessary

TYPES OF SYSTEMS

The alarm industry recognizes four types of alarm systems:

1. *Local alarm.* A system which produces an audible and/or visible signal at the protected premises only as a result of an alarm condition or fault (capability degradation).

2. *Direct connect (or headquarters).* A system in which signals are transmitted to police or fire headquarters is sometimes combined with a local alarm system.

3. *Central station.* A system in which signals of various types are transmitted to an independent monitoring center where trained personnel are present 24 h a day to supervise the status of protected premises and take appropriate action upon the receipt of signals. The central station is generally considered to be the preferred form of protection because of this constant supervision.

4. *Proprietary.* This system is similar to the central station system, except that the monitoring center is staffed and maintained by the owner of the protected properties.

In practice, fire protection and intrusion detection systems are closely related, and the equipment and services needed for both types of systems are usually provided by the same equipment manufacturers, installers, and service companies.

In many large plants, proprietary fire and burglary alarm systems are integrated with other building automation systems. Air conditioning, heating, energy management, closed-circuit television, access control, and communications, together with the protection services, are controlled from a central computer that has been programmed to initiate the proper actions and responses needed under a wide variety of operating and emergency conditions.

Companies that have many plant locations or branch offices often use the same interplant communication network for voice, data, video, and security signal transmissions.

SECURITY PLANNING

The planning of a plant security system requires some technical skills, and the use of an independent consultant or a security service company representative is recommended. Consultation should begin before the plans for a new building are completed, since there are aspects of architecture and design which affect security.

With the aid of an expert, a security system can be designed to deal with these sometimes conflicting factors:

1. *Likelihood of attack.* A precious metals refinery is more likely to be attacked than a junk storage area. Burglars prefer readily portable articles of high value. Local crime statistics should also be considered.

2. *Police response.* A large, well-equipped police force which can respond within a few minutes contributes to lowering the security risk. Plants located in remote or rural settings often are at greater risk.

3. *Building construction.* A new masonry structure is more resistant to attack than an old wooden building.

4. *Insurance.* The security expert can assist in the selection of equipment and techniques for both security and fire-alarm systems that will meet the requirements of Underwriters Laboratories, Inc., Factory Mutual, and the National Fire Protection Association. This is often a condition of the plant insurer or can lead to insurance premium reductions.

5. *False-alarm minimization.* These include a variety of technical considerations leading to systems that reliably detect and transmit alarm signals with a minimum of nuisance alarms and other trouble conditions, and assure compliance with any local codes and ordinances.

PHYSICAL SECURITY

Physical security is passive in nature as opposed to the active methods used for the detection and reporting of intruders. It is often the first line of defense and can be seen in the form of fences, walls, and moats. It includes visual definition of boundary lines as psychological barriers, for example, low fences, a line of shrubs, well-kept lawns, and a change of walkway materials, such as from concrete to brick.

National statistics indicate that crime against property averages 90 percent of all reported crime and that, in the majority of all burglary cases, entry was gained through doors or windows. In spite of this knowledge, there is a consistent use of inferior, low-security hardware, locks, and other materials.

In some localities in the United States, there are codes and ordinances which set forth standards for door frames, doors, door locks, windows, window locks, elevators, and other openings, such as skylights, hatchways, air ducts, vents, and transoms. In the absence of local standards, or the presence of outdated codes, reference should be made to the Law Enforcement Assistance Administration, National Institute of Law Enforcement and Criminal Justice Standards (NILECJ; see "Information Sources").

Physical security is dependent on good housekeeping. The best security equipment and alarm systems lose effectiveness when doors are not locked at night.

DETECTION AND REPORTING METHODS

Outdoor Perimeter Protection

The protection of an outdoor perimeter is the first line of defense in a protection-in-depth security plan. It can start with a masonry wall or a fence constructed of wood. A widely used construction is chain-link fence, 6 or more feet in height, and topped with an outward slanting barbed-wire or razor-ribbon coil section to discourage fence climbers. While difficult to climb for the inexperienced, such a barrier is susceptible to attack with wire cutters, or by jacking up from the bottom. Thus, it may be necessary to add a patrolling guard, with or without dogs.

An alternative to the expense of a guard force is the use of an electronic barrier consisting of fence-mounted transducers to detect and annunciate the mechanical vibrations caused by attempts to climb or cut the fence. However, these transducers also detect vibrations due to other causes (severe weather, animals, passersby, etc.) and should be used only in conjunction with other measures taken to reduce these nuisance alarms.

Another form of electronic barrier comprises a series of posts strung with a number of wires in telephone line style. This type of fence presents no physical barrier to an intruder, but the electromagnetic field set up by the current flowing through the wires is disturbed by the intruder. This field disturbance is detected electronically and annunciated at a guard station. Once again, field disturbances can occur due to many other causes (birds, animals, etc.), so this type of barrier should also be used only in conjunction with physical barriers to reduce the possibility of nuisance alarms.

In an effort to reduce the costs of installing and maintaining a long line of posts and wires, projected energy beams are sometimes used. Beams of infrared light or microwave energy are projected from a transmitter to a receiver and, when interrupted by the passage of an intruder, an alarm is annunciated at the guard station. (See Fig. 4-1.) This type of system is best adapted to flat terrain where the beam length can be relatively long. The transmitters and receivers can be shrouded in a way such that an intruder cannot detect the location of the beam. By spacing and positioning the beams properly, and requiring two or more beams to be interrupted simultaneously to create an alarm condition, several possible causes of nuisance alarms (birds and animals) can be eliminated.

All these types of electronic intrusion barriers require constant maintenance to control the growth of vegetation which may be the source of nuisance alarms. Erosion of the earth under the barrier must also be controlled to prevent access paths.

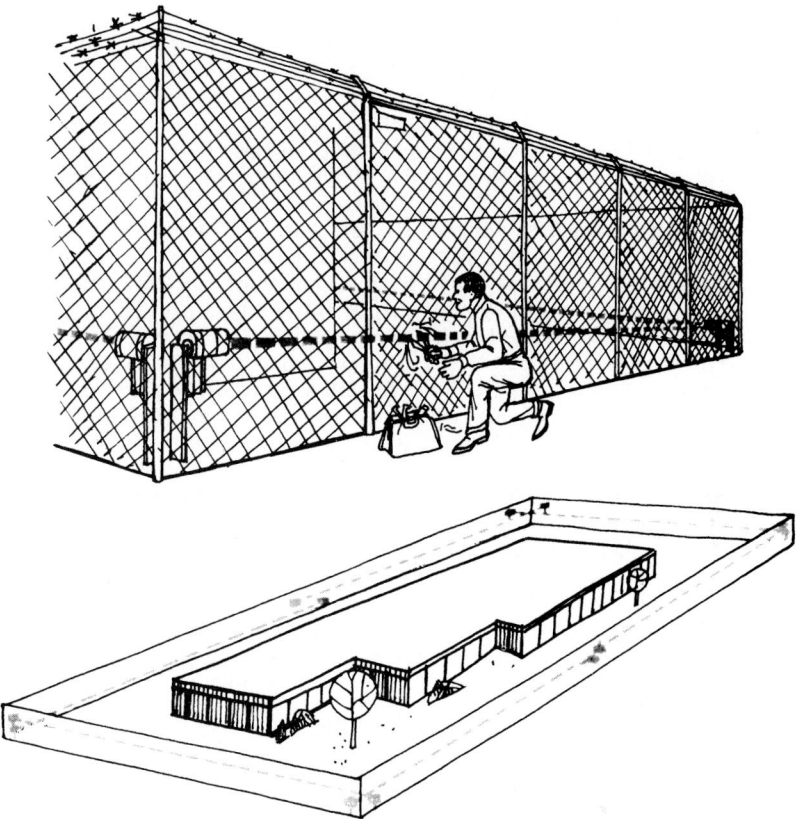

FIGURE 4-1 Use of light beams to protect a restricted area.

Seismic sensors are sometimes used to detect intruders where no physical barrier is desired. However, these sensors are very vulnerable to nuisance alarms (vibrations due to heavy vehicles, animals, and other sources of shock or vibration, either nearby or at some distance) and are not recommended unless used in combination with some other form of detection.

Television cameras can be used in combination with any of these perimeter intrusion detection systems to verify alarm conditions. Using closed-circuit television (CCTV), a single guard can monitor the entire perimeter from inside a guard house. *Motion detection* capability can be added to the CCTV system to cause an alarm condition when motion occurs in a particular segment of the field of view. This allows the guard to attend to other duties without concern about missing an event on the video monitor. With the addition of video recorders, pictures of the field of view can be captured before, during, and after the potential alarm event. For these reasons, CCTV is recommended as a backup to, and often a substitute for, other forms of perimeter intrusion detection.

Portal Protection

Outdoor perimeter fences as well as building entrances must have portals that are guarded in such a manner that authorized persons may be admitted and others excluded. This may be done by means of a guard who provides other services as well, such as directing visitors.

The cost of guard service may be reduced by an electric lock on the door with a voice intercom, as is commonly provided in apartment house lobbies. Where voice identification is not sufficient, a closed-circuit television system will permit visual inspection before admission. A single guard or receptionist at a central location can monitor many portals.

The simplest means of admission control is to provide authorized persons with a key to the door. Push button locks minimize the problems of lost and stolen keys, since it is easier and cheaper to change the combination when necessary than to provide a new lock and set of keys.

Card access systems avoid the problems associated with metallic keys and provide other advantages. In its simplest form, the card access system is the equivalent of a metallic door key. When a photograph plus other information is applied to the card, it becomes an identification card that can be presented to building guards when needed. With a computer-based system, additional sophistication is possible. Zoned systems may be established in which many persons may be allowed to enter one area, and smaller subsets of that population granted access to several other limited access areas in the same premises or group of buildings. Certain people may be granted access to one or more areas only during business hours, while others may have access at all times. Cleaners and other service people may be granted access only to those areas, and at such times as are appropriate for their function. Alarm signals will be generated when a wrong card is presented, and a record of who entered what door at what time can be kept.

Recent advances in image-reading technology have produced systems that can scan a television picture of the person seeking access and store the image in computer memory along with data about when and where the person was granted access.

Access control systems can be used as time and attendance recording systems or to limit the number of people in an area or a building at any time. They can also be used to ensure the evacuation of premises and account for all inhabitants in case of fire or a bomb threat.

Building Perimeter Protection

A great majority of burglary attacks are made on doors and windows. The burglar alarm contact is the basic device used for protecting these openings. It consists of two components—a miniature relay and a magnet. One is mounted on the movable part of the door or window, and the other is attached to the door jam or window frame. When the two are separated, as when the door or window is opened, the magnetic field is broken and the relay activates, causing an alarm signal to be transmitted. These devices are available in many different shapes and sizes to accommodate different types of doors and windows, and are still the most reliable and effective means of perimeter protection.

Window glass has traditionally been protected by applying a current-carrying foil strip around the margin of the glass. When the glass is broken, the foil is ruptured, initiating an alarm signal. The foil is coated with lacquer to protect it from damage, but still requires regular maintenance to prevent degradation and subsequent nuisance alarms.

Electronic glass-break detectors of several types can also be used to protect windows. These devices consist of a transducer applied directly to the glass or to the window frame, or a microphone placed near the window. They are designed to respond to the specific sound frequencies produced when glass is broken. However, they are still less reliable than contacts and foil or motion detectors, described below.

Another form of protection for windows and other openings is the burglar alarm screen, consisting of a small-diameter, current-carrying wire imbedded in a frame of wooden dowels. To pass such a barrier, the intruder must break at least some of the dowels (and the embedded wire) and so activate the alarm signal.

Since it is also possible to effect entry by penetration of the walls, floors and ceilings, such surfaces can be protected by pads of wire, mesh, or foil mounted on building material panels attached to the surface to be protected. Figure 4-2 illustrates these as well as other devices described next.

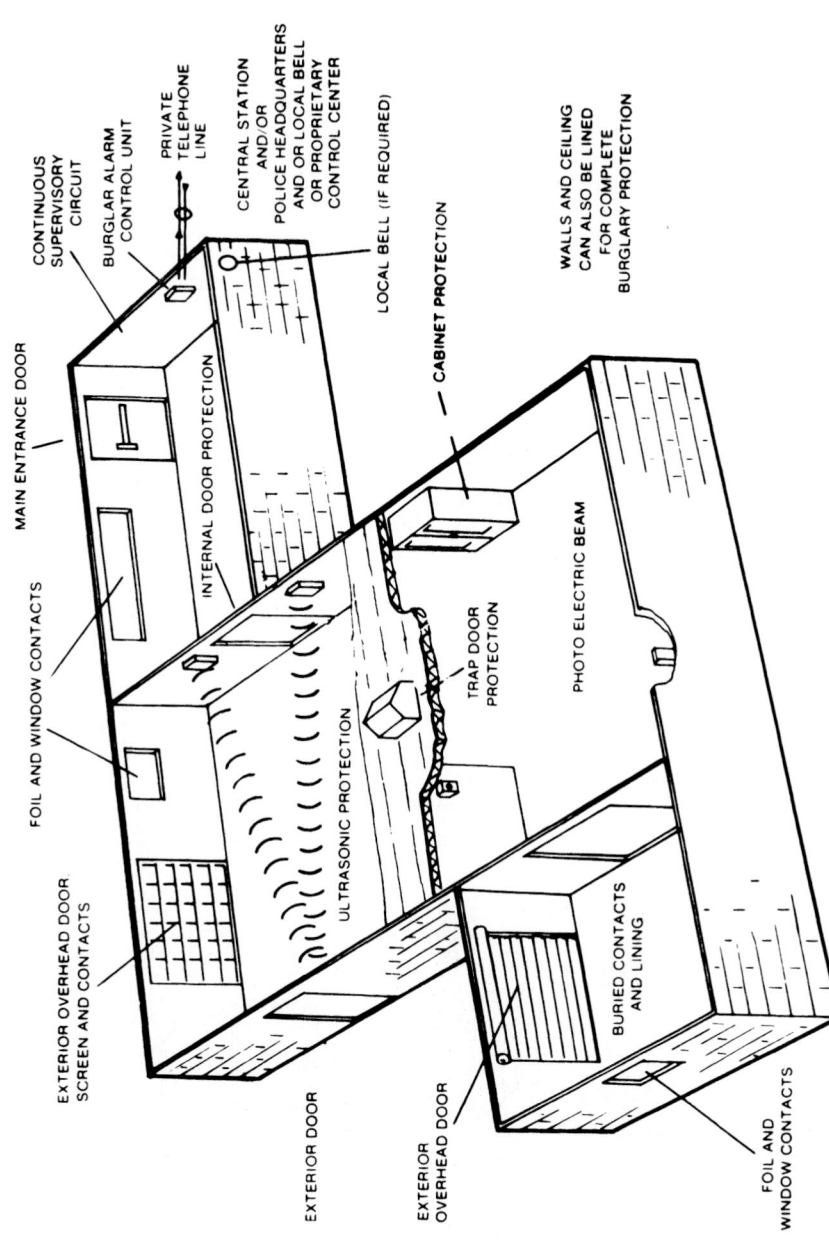

CONTINUOUS SUPERVISORY CIRCUIT

BURGLAR ALARM CONTROL UNIT

PRIVATE TELEPHONE LINE

CENTRAL STATION AND/OR POLICE HEADQUARTERS AND OR LOCAL BELL OR PROPRIETARY CONTROL CENTER

LOCAL BELL (IF REQUIRED)

CABINET PROTECTION

WALLS AND CEILING CAN ALSO BE LINED FOR COMPLETE BURGLARY PROTECTION

MAIN ENTRANCE DOOR

FOIL AND WINDOW CONTACTS

INTERNAL DOOR PROTECTION

EXTERIOR OVERHEAD DOOR SCREEN AND CONTACTS

ULTRASONIC PROTECTION

TRAP DOOR PROTECTION

PHOTO ELECTRIC BEAM

EXTERIOR DOOR

EXTERIOR OVERHEAD DOOR

BURIED CONTACTS AND LINING

FOIL AND WINDOW CONTACTS

FIGURE 4-2 Typical perimeter and interior protection plan. (*American District Telegraph Co.*)

Interior Protection

In accordance with the principle of protection in depth, traps are employed to detect the intruder who has penetrated the perimeter. A simple and effective trap is the pressure mat hidden under the carpet which produces an alarm signal when stepped on by the intruder. The floor trap is a trip-wire device in which the wire need not be broken; its displacement alone will initiate the alarm signal. An infrared photoelectric beam can be used as the electronic equivalent of a trip wire—when the intruder breaks the invisible beam, an alarm signal is generated.

Safes and file cabinets may be protected by contacts to give warning of their being opened, but it is better to have an alarm occur *prior to opening*. For this purpose, capacitance alarm systems, which produce an electric field around the protected object, will give an alarm signal when the intruder approaches—before he or she touches the object.

Cabinets can also be lined with foil or wire mesh to protect the contents. Penetration of the cabinet, as in the case of the burglar alarm screen, initiates an alarm signal.

Space Protection

About 1950, the concept of space protection was introduced in the form of the ultrasonic motion detector. The space to be protected is flooded with sound energy in the ultrasonic range, and the motion of the intruder causes a Doppler shift in the frequencies of the signals detected at the receiver which is employed to actuate the alarm signal. See Fig. 4-3. Nuisance alarms can be caused by air turbulence. Motion detectors based on the same Doppler shift principle, but using microwave energy, are immune to the air turbulence problem. See

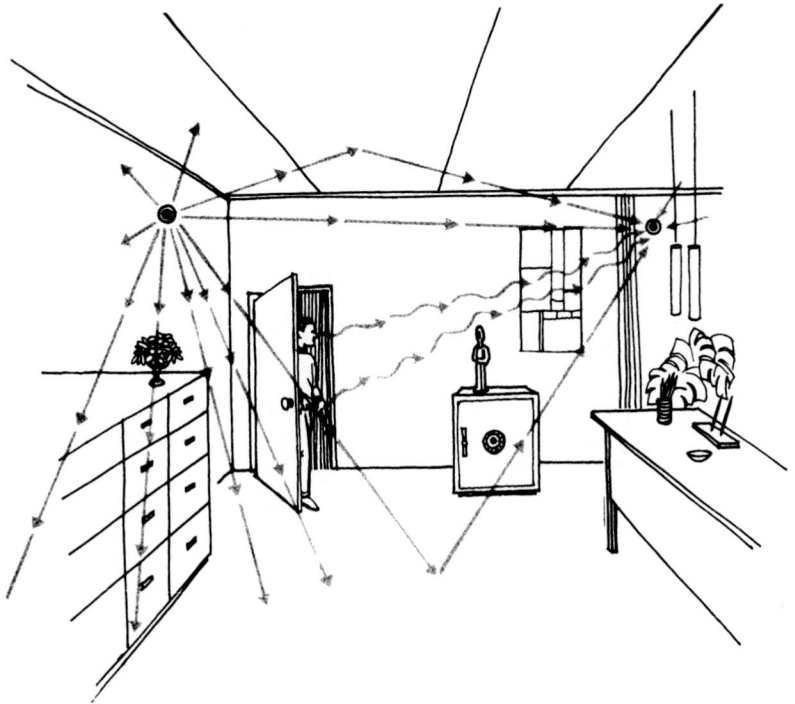

FIGURE 4-3   Diagram shows how system utilizes Doppler effect, a scientific phenomenon that causes sound waves to change tone when hitting a moving surface. The change triggers an alarm.

Fig. 4-4. However, microwave energy is difficult to contain, and often these detectors activate on motion sensed outside the building. Passive infrared detectors sense the difference in heat being emitted from an intruder's body against the heat of a cooler background. But heated air, sunlight, or other heat sources can cause nuisance alarms.

Since all of these motion detectors are susceptible to nuisance alarms from at least one source, but each nuisance source is different, redundant detectors were developed. These devices combine two sensor technologies in one detector (microwave and infrared is the most popular combination) and will not initiate an alarm signal until both sensors activate. This reduces the number of nuisance alarms without appreciably affecting detection capabilities. Another approach, currently used with passive infrared sensors, is to divide the detector's field of view into segments, and require a signal from more than one segment before initiating an alarm signal. With the introduction of small microprocessor devices in sensors, the detection logic has become more sophisticated and immune to nuisance alarms.

Designated areas may be kept under constant surveillance by means of closed-circuit television cameras and microphones which relay images and sounds to a central monitoring point. Movable television cameras that rotate 360° or travel up and down a ceiling-mounted

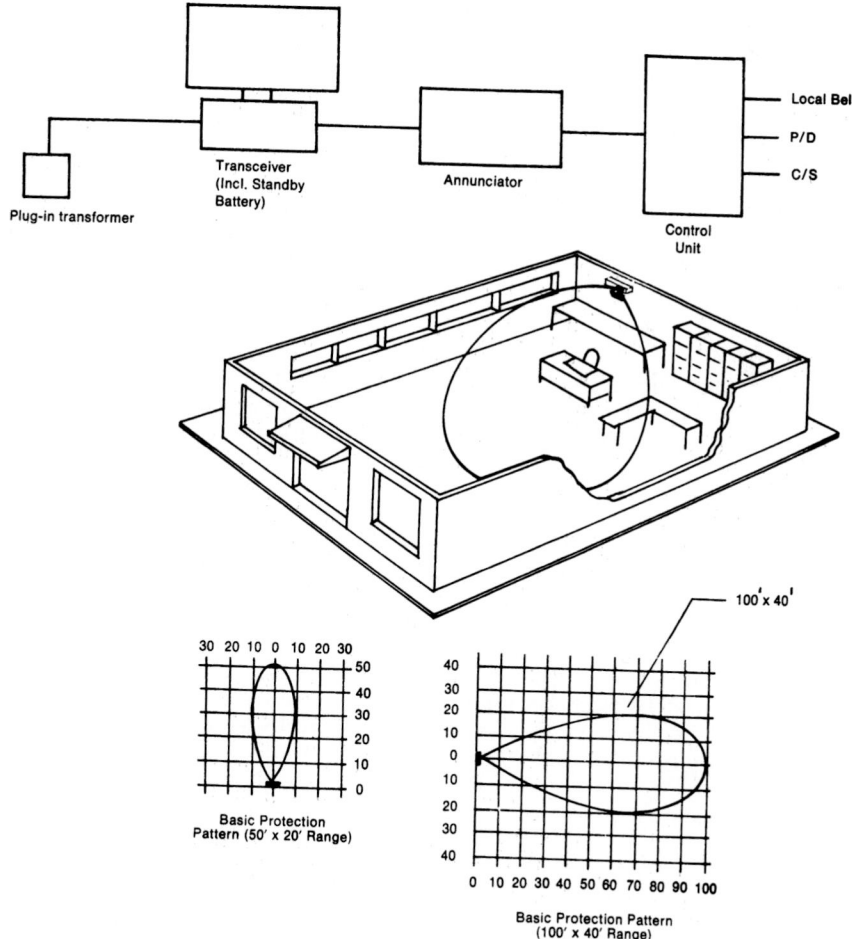

FIGURE 4-4   Typical protection patterns with microwave beams.

track can be used to cover a large area that would otherwise require multiple cameras. These cameras can operate behind one-way vision shrouds to conceal their presence.

Vaults, like those used for safe deposit, furs, and narcotics are often protected by alarm systems responsive to the sounds created during an attack which range from the single high-intensity burst of a dynamite blast to the low-level noise produced by scraping away of mortar with a pointed tool, such as a screwdriver. Two basic types of systems are used: one is responsive to airborne sounds and the other to sounds transmitted through the structure of the vault.

Attacks conducted with oxyacetylene torches or burning bars are detected by heat and smoke detectors.

Night depositories can be protected by lead-sheathed, current-carrying cables embedded in the concrete during construction. Rupture of the cable during the course of an attack results in an alarm.

Holdup Alarms

It is often advisable to provide a holdup alarm system for payroll departments or other high-risk areas so that assistance may be summoned rapidly during or after a raid. This system could also actuate television or film cameras. The initiating devices are concealed hand- or foot-operated switches and short-range radio transmitters which are carried on the belt or in a pocket.

There are also a variety of cash-drawer devices intended to permit the surreptitious initiation of a signal. Examples are pressure pads which can be pressed by the cashier when removing money from the drawer and a money clip which is a switch whose contacts are held apart by one or more pieces of paper currency whose withdrawal allows the contacts to close and actuate a silent alarm.

SIGNAL TRANSMISSION

On Premises

There are several ways in which alarm signals are transmitted from detectors to a local control unit. Hard-wired systems require a pair of wires to be run from each detector to the control. Other systems employ a multiplex transmission scheme, with a single trunk cable installed throughout the premises, and branch wiring to the individual detectors. This has the advantage of reducing the amount of wire that must be installed. Some multiplex systems provide power to the sensors from the control unit over a separate pair of wires in the trunk cable. Systems with radio-frequency (rf) transmitters at each sensor sending signals to a central receiver are sometimes used in very large facilities to save the cost of wire installation.

All of these local transmission systems provide continual supervision of the sensors by way of monitoring the presence of a specific voltage on the line or interrogate/response polling. This ensures that the signal transmission paths are clear and functioning at all times.

In addition to monitoring the integrity of the local transmission system, the control unit provides a means for users to arm/disarm the security system and determine the current status of all sensors. The control unit also provides a means for communicating alarm signals off premises.

Off Premises

Traditional central station service employs two basic means of off-premises transmission. *Direct wire service* uses a dedicated telephone connection from each subscriber to an individual readout device at the central station and is the equivalent of a private-wire telephone connection. *Circuit burglar alarm service* connects a number of subscribers to a common circuit, as in party-line telephone service, and the individuals are identified at the central station by coded signals. The McCulloh circuit arrangement is usually employed to permit continued operation when faults appear on the line.

Both of these traditional services are provided by dc circuits which have distance limitations, and are being made obsolete by the telephone companies, which are eliminating metallic circuits as they convert to digital networks at a rapid pace. Since about 1960, ac multiplex transmission networks, dedicated to alarm signaling, have been available to overcome the distance limitations of dc circuits. Interrogate/respond polling techniques enhance the reliability and security of this service.

Where high security risks are involved, some form of line security should be provided to detect and prevent attempts to compromise the telephone lines. The messages being transmitted are often encrypted to provide the highest level of security.

The most popular form of alarm signal transmission in use today is the automatic telephone dialer, also referred to as a digital communicator. This device dials the central station telephone number when it receives an alarm message, and delivers the message over the public switched telephone network. Early versions of this device used tape-recorded messages and lacked the ability to detect a connection with the central station before sending a message. Both of these shortcomings have been eliminated in the digital communicators now being used, which are also capable of sending frequent test signals to assure an open communication channel. To provide additional assurance of getting signals through, digital communicators are sometimes used as a backup for other forms of transmission.

Derived channel transmission is a service offered by telephone companies since the early 1980s. It utilizes the public switched network, but provides some of the security and reliability of dedicated networks at a lower cost. It is currently available only in certain geographic areas.

Other transmission forms include dedicated radio over privately maintained radio networks and cellular radio over the public cellular network. Both of these methods are generally used as backups for digital communicators, but can be used alone where no other transmission facilities exist.

SIGNAL MONITORING

Most signal monitoring centers today are automated to some degree. Computers are used to receive alarm signals, process messages, retrieve data on the premises from which the alarm was received, and provide the appropriate emergency response for each premises.

As the power of computers increases, and costs decrease, it is possible for monitoring center operators to handle many more signals simultaneously and assure that the appropriate responses are made for each situation.

These signal receiving and processing capabilities can also be used to provide records and reports that can pinpoint security problems very quickly. For example, alarm messages not only identify the type of alarm (burglary, fire, etc.) and the premises from which it was sent, but can also identify the specific sensor generating the alarm. This allows for quicker response to the source of the emergency signal. But it also allows identifying and tracking nuisance alarms from a particular sensor so that corrective action can be taken. This level of detailed data analysis is possible only with computers.

REVIEW AND UPGRADING

Security is a never-ending procedure because it must be *constantly reviewed and upgraded* to allow for changes in the physical structure of the protected premises as well as their content and the environment. In addition, continual consideration must be given to the replacement of aging equipment with new technology that offers superior performance.

INFORMATION SOURCES

National Institute of Law Enforcement and Criminal Justice, NILECJ-STD-0306.00, May 1976, "Physical Security of Door Assemblies and Components," National Institute of Law Enforcement and Criminal Justice, Law Enforcement Assistance Administration, U.S. Department of Justice.

NILECJ-STD-0316.00, March, 1979, "Physical Security of Window Units", National Institute of Law Enforcement and Criminal Justice, Law Enforcement Assistance Administration, U.S. Department of Justice.

Security World Publishing Company, P.O. Box 272, Culver City, CA 90230, and Butterworth-Heinemann, 80 Montvale Ave., Stoneham, MA 02180, specialize in books and periodicals relating to security.

Underwriters Laboratories, Inc., 333 Pfingsten Road, Northbrook, IL 60062-2096, tests security and fire equipment and lists equipment that meets its standards of performance.

CHAPTER 14-5

TOXIC SUBSTANCES AND RADIATION HAZARDS

Jaswant Singh
Senior Vice President
Clayton Environmental Consultants, Inc.
Cypress, California

GLOSSARY

Aerosols Liquid droplets or solid particles dispersed in air that are of fine enough particle size (0.01 to 100 µm) to remain so dispersed for a period of time.

Alveoli Tiny air sacs of the lungs, formed by a dilation at the end of a bronchiole; through the thin walls of the alveoli, the blood takes in oxygen and gives up its carbon dioxide through respiration.

Anthrax A highly virulent bacterial infection picked up from infected animals and animal products.

Aplastic anemia A condition in which the bone marrow fails to produce an adequate number of red blood corpuscles.

Asbestos A hydrated magnesium silicate in fibrous form.

Asbestosis   A disease of the lungs caused by the inhalation of fine airborne asbestos fibers.

Asphyxia   Suffocation from lack of oxygen. *Chemical asphyxia* is produced by a substance, such as carbon monoxide, that combines with hemoglobin to reduce the blood's capacity to transport oxygen. *Simple asphyxia* is the result of exposure to a substance, such as carbon dioxide, that displaces oxygen.

Bronchi   The two main branches of the trachea that go into the right and left lung.

Bronchiole   The smallest of the many tubes that carry air into and out of the lungs.

Byssinosis   Disease occurring to those who experience prolonged exposure to heavy air concentrations of cotton dust.

Carcinoma   Malignant tumors derived from epithelial tissues, that is, the outer skin, the membranes lining the body cavities, and certain glands.

Cesium 137   An isotope of the element cesium having an atomic mass number of 137. One of the important fission products.

Chloracne   A disease caused by chlorinated polyphenyls and nephthalenes acting on sebaceous glands and the liver.

Chronic bronchitis   An inflammation of the bronchial tubes lasting a long period of time or occurring frequently.

Cilia   Tiny hairlike "whips" in the bronchi and other respiratory passages that aid in the removal of dust trapped on these moist surfaces.

Conjunctivitis   Inflammation of the delicate mucous membrane (conjunctiva) that lines the eyelids and covers the front of the eyeball.

Contact dermatitis   Dermatitis caused by a primary irritant.

Cristobalite   A crystalline form of free silica. Quartz in refractory bricks and amorphous silica in diatomaceous earth are altered to cristobalite when exposed to high temperatures (calcined).

Curie   A measure of the activity, or the rate, at which a radioactive material throws off particles. The radioactivity of one gram of radium is a curie. One curie corresponds to 37 billion disintegrations per second or 37 becquerels. The becquerel (abbreviated Bq) is the SI unit that supersedes the curie (abbreviated Ci).

Cutie-pie   A portable instrument equipped with a direct-reading meter used to determine the level of radiation in an area.

Cyclone   As used in industrial-hygiene monitoring, a particle-size selector whose operation is based on imparting sufficient tangential velocities to relatively larger (heavier) particles sufficient to cause impaction on the walls of a conical chamber, while permitting smaller (respirable) particles to remain entrained in the air system.

Diatomaceous earth   A soft, gritty, amorphous silica composed of small aquatic plants. Used in filtration and decolorization of liquids. Calcined and flux-calcined diatomaceous earth contains appreciable amounts of cristobalite.

Dose   The total amount of a substance taken into the body by all routes of exposure during some recognized time period.

Dyspnea   Shortness of breath, difficult or labored breathing.

Edema   A swelling of body tissues as a result of being waterlogged with fluid.

Electromagnetic radiation   The propagation of varying electric and magnetic fields through space at the speed of light, exhibiting the characteristics of wave motion.

Emphysema   A lung disease, in which the walls of the alveoli have been stretched too thin and broken down; frequently accompanied by impairment of the heart action.

Epidemiology   The science of correlating incidence and distribution of disease with causative factors or agents.

Etiology   The study or knowledge of the causes of disease.

Fibrosis   A growth of fibrous tissue in an organ in excess of that naturally present. A condition marked by increase of interstitial fibrous tissue.

Forced vital capacity (FVC)   The maximum volume of air that can be expelled with maximum effort after a full inspiration.

Free crystalline silica   Silicon dioxide with the SiO_2 molecule oriented in a fixed tetrahedral (crystalline) pattern, the most prevalent forms being quartz, cristobalite, and tridymite.

Hemoglobin   The red coloring matter of the blood which carries the oxygen.

Ionizing radiation   Refers to (1) electrically charged or neutral particles or (2) electromagnetic radiation which will interact with gases, liquids, or solids to produce ions.

Industrial hygiene   The science of recognizing, evaluating, and controlling environmental stresses arising in or from the workplace.

Inertial impaction   The forceful impingement on, or striking of, a particle on a surface with resulting adherence.

LD_{50}   Abbreviation of lethal dose 50, the dose which is required to produce death in 50 percent of the exposed species. Death is usually reckoned as occurring within the first 30 days.

Leukemia   A blood disease distinguished by overproduction of white blood cells. It may result from overexposure to radiation or it may generate spontaneously.

Lymph   A clear, colorless fluid which circulates through the vessels of the lymphatic system.

Maser   Microwave amplification by stimulated emission of radiation.

Metastasis   Spread of malignancy from the site of primary cancer to secondary sites due to transfer through the lymphatic or blood system.

mg/m^3   Milligrams of substance per cubic meter of air, a common unit of exposure concentration.

Milliroentgen   One one-thousandth of a roentgen. A roentgen is a unit of radioactive dose.

mppcf   Millions of particles per cubic foot of air, a common unit of exposure concentration for mineral dusts.

Narcosis   Stupor or unconsciousness produced by chemical substances.

Necrosis   Destruction of body tissue.

Papilloma   A small growth or tumor of the skin or mucous membrane.

Phagocyte   A cell in the body that characteristically engulfs foreign material and consumes debris and foreign bodies, bacteria, and other cells.

Pharynx   A part of the alimentary canal located between the mouth and the esophagus.

Pneumoconiosis   A disease of the lungs caused by irritation of dusts and other particles.

Pulmonary function tests   Measurement of ventilatory capacity of the lung by a series of tests, such as forced expiratory volume (FEV) and forced vital capacity (FVC).

Quartz   The most prevalent, naturally occurring form of free silica, the basic raw material for the industrial and sand industry.

Rad   Standard unit of radioactive dose. It supersedes the roentgen.

Radioactivity   Emission of energy in the form of alpha, beta, or gamma radiation from the nucleus of an atom.

Radiologist   A specialist in the diagnostic and therapeutic use of x-rays and other forms of ionizing radiant energy.

Respirable   Capable of penetrating into the lower respiratory tract, generally regarded as requiring a particle size of 10 μm or less.

Respirable mass   That portion of total suspended particulate matter capable of penetrating into the lower respiratory tract.

Roentgen A unit of radioactive dose or exposure (abbreviated R). A roentgen is that amount of x- or gamma radiation that will produce one electrostatic unit of charge, of either sign, in one cubic centimeter of dry air at standard temperature and pressure. It is equivalent to 2.58×10^{-4} C/kg in air.

Roentgenogram The shadow picture formed on a sensitized film or plate by x-rays passing through a body.

Sensitizer A chemical that, at first exposure, may or may not cause irritation. After extended or repeated exposure, some individuals develop an allergic type of skin irritation called sensitization dermatitis.

Siderosis Lung disease resulting from inhalation of iron oxide.

Silicosis A lung disease resulting from fibrosis of the lungs due to inhalation of silica dust.

Spirometry The measurement of air movement in or out of the lungs with the use of a spirometer.

Synergism Combined action of substances whose total effect is greater than the sum of their separate effects.

Talc A hydrous magnesium silicate used in ceramics, cosmetics, paint, pharmaceuticals, and soap.

TLV Threshold-limit value. An exposure level under which most people can work consistently for 8 hour/day, day after day, with no harmful effects. A table of these values and accompanying precautions is published annually by the American Conference of Governmental Industrial Hygienists (ACGIH); TLV is a registered trademark of ACGIH.

Time-weighted average concentration A calculated average obtained by dividing the sum of products of concentration times time for all activities by the total time of exposure.

Trachea The cartilaginous and membranous tube (windpipe) by which air passes to and from the lung.

Tridymite A vitreous, colorless form of free silica formed when quartz is heated to 870°C (1598°F). A form of crystalline silica rarely found in naturally occurring deposits.

X-ray diffraction Since all crystals act as three-dimensional gratings for x-rays, the pattern of diffracted rays is characteristic for each crystalline material. This method is of particular value in determining the presence or absence of crystalline silica in industrial dusts.

INTRODUCTION

Workplace safety and health are critical issues confronting employers today. Increasingly stringent right-to-know laws about environmental hazards and tightening of the permissible exposure limits (PELs) to toxic substances have intensified the need for employers to evaluate and control employee exposures to environmental stress in the workplace. These regulations have also heightened employee awareness of workplace hazards and have resulted in lawsuits against employers.

Exposure to an ever-increasing number of new chemicals in the workplace poses a continual challenge for the employer today. Moreover, the regulatory standards are continually being expanded and updated and, in most cases, result in lower and more stringent permissible exposure limits.

As an example, in one swift action January 1989, the U.S. Occupational Safety and Health Administration (OSHA) lowered 212 PELs and set new PELs for 164 substances not previously regulated by OSHA. The enormity of this step can be appreciated when one realizes that prior to January 1989, and during its 19 years of existence, OSHA issued only 24 such standards. The remaining 400-plus chemicals published in OSHA's original 1910.1000 regulation (the Z tables) were adopted from the 1968 American Conference of Governmental

Industrial Hygienists (ACGIH) threshold limit values (TLVs), and had remained unchanged since 1970.

Enactment of occupational health standards by OSHA has forced many plant engineers to become involved in the evaluation and control of industrial hygiene problems not only in existing facilities, but in the design of new facilities as well. For example, industrial hygiene considerations play a dominant role when considering ventilation systems (local and general), makeup air, enclosure and/or isolation of processes using toxic chemicals, handling and storage of toxic materials, and cleanup of exhaust emissions. Adequate disposal of toxic or hazardous wastes is also important to prevent environmental contamination and exposure of workers handling them. Plant engineers, therefore, need to be aware of toxic chemical and radiation hazards and how to effectively deal with them.

Industrial hygiene is defined by the American Industrial Hygiene Association (AIHA) as "that science and art devoted to the recognition, evaluation, and control of those environmental factors or stresses, arising in or from the workplace, that may cause sickness, impaired health, and well-being, or significant discomfort and inefficiency." An industrial hygienist is someone trained in "engineering, chemistry, physics, or medicine or related biological sciences (augmented by) special studies and training in all of the above cognate sciences" to practice industrial hygiene as defined above. A fully staffed industrial-health team also includes, at minimum, an *industrial physician,* an *industrial toxicologist,* a *analytical chemist,* and an *environmental* or *process engineer.*

TOXIC SUBSTANCES

Identifying Hazards: The Workplace Survey

Identifying potential health hazards requires knowledge of processes and the materials used. For example, it is safe to assume that petrochemical workers will probably be exposed to one or more of a variety of organic vapors, that sandblasters risk overexposure to respirable dusts (crystalline silica, etc.), and that radiation is a potential hazard affecting workers in nuclear power plants.

In many other situations, the presence of a hazard may only be suspected, as when employee complaints of disease symptoms fall into an identifiable pattern or when strange odors are detected in the workplace. These cases call for a more rigorous exploratory survey, to both identify the hazard and measure its extent.

Whether the identity of the contaminant is known or not, a workplace survey should be conducted that includes an inventory of the chemicals and the processes in the work area or entire plant, the chemicals used in these processes, the raw materials, by-products, etc. Generally, a comprehensive investigation requires the services of an experienced professional, such as a certified industrial hygienist. When the nature of the contaminant is indeterminate, the industrial hygienist should work with an industrial physician and a process engineer.

Many times in an investigation, visibility is a positive indicator of a hazard. The absence of visibility of dusts and fumes, however, does not mean that there are not dangerous levels of contaminants present, since many contaminants constitute a hazard at levels much too low to be visible.

In the same way, the investigator uses the sense of smell to pinpoint certain contaminants. For example, it is possible to distinguish between the haylike odor of phosgene and the fishlike odor of trimethylamine. Here again, however, certain precautions must be observed. For example, although hydrogen sulfide has a very distinct rotten-egg-like odor, it can also dull the sense of smell after prolonged exposure, and thus effectively mask heavy concentrations of other substances.

Tables 5-1 and 5-2 provide examples of typical occupational exposure to particulates and gaseous toxic agents.

TABLE 5-1   Examples of Occupational Exposure to Particulate Toxic Agents

Contaminant	Physical state	Occupation
Asbestos	Dust, fiber	Fireproofers, insulation strippers, asbestos-cement workers, auto-garage mechanics, construction workers, shipbuilding and repair workers, gasket manufacturing workers, rubber compounders, vinyl-tile workers, maintenance workers, and asbestos abatement workers
Silica	Dust	Abrasive blast cleaners, pottery makers, glass makers, cement workers, coal miners, construction workers, enamellers, foundry workers, smelters
Lead	Dust, fume	Babitters, glassmakers, foundry workers, pottery makers, printers, paint manufacturers and sprayers, can and dye makers, and lead abatement workers
Chromic acid	Mist	Electroplaters, picklers, colored glass, ink, and refractory makers
Arsenic	Dust, fume, or gas (arsine)	Copper smelters, brass manufacturing workers, ceramic and glass makers, insecticide manufacturing workers, electroplaters
Beryllium	Dust, fume	Beryllium metal and alloy manufacturing workers, alloy machinists, glass and neon tube makers, rocket fuel manufacturing workers
Coal-tar pitch volatiles	Dust, fume	Metallurgical operations workers, metal casters, petroleum refinery workers, coking operations workers

TABLE 5-2   Examples of Occupational Exposure to Gaseous Toxic Agents

Contaminant	Physical state	Occupation
Carbon monoxide	Gas	Cokers, smelters, metal caster, forklift drivers, garage operators, heat treaters, coal conversion workers, pottery makers
Nitrogen oxides	Gas	Welders, electroplaters, forklift drivers, fertilizer manufacturing workers, explosive manufacturers, dye workers
Fluorocarbons	Gas or vapor	Food processors, storage workers
Sulfur dioxide	Gas	Brewers, copper smelters, ore roasters, petroleum refiners, glassmakers, powerplant operators, paper makers
Benzene	Vapor	Petroleum refiners, coke oven workers, organic chemical manufacturing workers, gasoline station attendants, ink makers, insecticide makers, lithographers, paint makers, rubber makers
Toluene	Vapor	Core makers (foundry operation), polyurethane foam makers and users, spray painters, ship welders

Work and Process Inventory

The first step is to obtain descriptions of job functions within the facility. This information may be provided by the personnel department and/or manufacturing staff, and should include the following:

- Nature of the job
- Description of the process
- Work duration
- Nature of potential exposure (if known)

This information allows the investigator to group various workers according to similarity of exposure to chemical and physical stresses. This grouping is essential later in selecting representative workers who may need to be sampled for exposure levels.

Chemical Inventory

The investigator conducting the industrial hygiene survey should be knowledgeable about the chemicals that are used in the plant. In preparing a chemical inventory (preferably with the help of the purchasing department), all processes using chemicals are taken into consideration, including waste treatment, boiler operations, air conditioning, and any other pertinent sources including those involving raw materials, intermediate products, finished products, and cleaning compounds.

A major problem in recognizing chemical hazards arises from the variety of chemical formulations from different suppliers and manufacturers. Industry uses a large variety of materials sold under various trade names. Obtaining sufficient or accurate information on the composition of each product is often difficult. Obtaining *material-safety data sheets* (MSDSs) from the supplier is helpful in this regard. Updating of the MSDSs is recommended, using various relevant publications and fact sheets, including the hygiene guides prepared by the American Industrial Hygiene Association and the chemical-safety data sheets supplied by organizations such as the Chemical Manufacturers Association.

Consideration must also be given to toxic materials that may be present as impurities in relatively safe materials—diatomaceous earth, for example, which is supposedly 100 percent amorphous silica and thus generally considered a safe material. Diatomaceous earth has extensive applications, including use as a filtering aid and as a filler in cosmetics, detergents, and other household products. However, certain varieties of diatomaceous earth used as filtration aids have been found to contain significant quantities of crystalline silica, a widely recognized occupational health hazard.

Moreover, certain materials that apparently exist at subtoxic levels in the workplace can substantially appreciate in toxicity by undergoing chemical reaction within the body. For example, a metabolic reaction occurs in the case of benzidine dyes. The carcinogenic nature of benzidine has been recognized for many years, but benzidine-based dyes have been considered relatively safe on the assumption that they contain very little free or unreacted benzidine Studies of analyses of urine samples collected from workers exposed to these dyes, however, indicate that metabolization of benzidine dye results in significantly elevated benzidine levels within the body.

Routes of Entry

Contaminants enter the body principally in three ways:

- Inhalation (through the respiratory tract)
- Skin absorption (through the skin)
- Ingestion (through the digestive tract)

Inhalation is by far the most common access for airborne contaminants to the body because of the continuous need to oxygenate the tissue cells and because of intimate contact with the body's circulatory system.

The effect of exposure to toxic agents is usually classified as acute or chronic.

Acute Exposure.   Acute exposure is characterized by exposure to high concentrations of the toxic material over a short period. The exposure occurs quickly and can result in immediate damage to the body. For example, inhaling high concentrations of carbon monoxide gas or carbon tetrachloride vapors will produce acute poisoning.

Chronic Exposure.   Chronic exposure occurs when there is continuous absorption of small amounts of contaminants over a long period. Each dose, taken independently, would have little toxic effect, but the quantity accumulated over a number of years can result in serious damage. Chronic poisoning can also be produced by exposure to small amounts of harmful material that produces irreversible damage to tissues and organs so that the injury rather than the poison accumulates. An example of such a chronic effect is silicosis, a disease produced by inhaling crystalline silica dust over a period of years.

Nature of Contaminants

Airborne contaminants can be present as liquids or solids, as gaseous material in the form of a true gas or vapor, or in combination of both gaseous and particulate matter. Most often, airborne contaminants are classified according to physical state and physiological effect on the human body. Knowledge of these classifications is necessary for proper evaluation of the work environment. One must also consider the route of entry and action of the contaminant.

Physiological Classification of Toxic Effects

Irritants.   Irritants cause inflammation of the moist mucous surfaces of the body. Irritants are corrosive, but inflammation of tissues may result from concentrations well below those needed to produce corrosion. Examples of irritant materials include aldehydes, alkaline and acid mists, and ammonia. Materials that affect both the upper respiratory tract and lung tissues are chlorine and ozone. Irritants that affect primarily the terminal respiratory passages are nitrogen dioxide and phosgene.

Asphyxiants.   Asphyxiants deprive the tissues of oxygen. They are generally divided into two classes—simple and chemical.

Simple Asphyxiants.   These are physiologically inert gases that deprive the tissue of oxygen by diluting the available atmospheric oxygen. Examples include nitrogen, carbon dioxide, hydrogen, helium, and aliphatic hydrocarbons such as methane.

Chemical Asphyxiants.   These prevent either oxygen transport in blood or normal oxygenation of the tissues. Chemical asphyxiants are active far below the level required for damage from simple asphyxiants. Examples include carbon monoxide, hydrogen cyanide, and nitrobenzene.

Primary Anesthetics.   Anesthetics depress the central nervous system, particularly the brain. Examples include ethylene and ethyl ether.

Systemic Poisons.   Systemic poisons cause injury to particular organs or body systems. The halogenated hydrocarbons (such as carbon tetrachloride) can damage the liver and kidneys, whereas benzene, aniline, and phenol may cause damage to the blood-forming system. Examples of materials classified as neurotoxic agents include carbon disulfide, methyl alcohol, tetraethyl lead, and organic phosphorus insecticides. Examples of metallic systemic poisons include cadmium, lead, manganese, and mercury.

Carcinogens in the Workplace

Concern about occupational carcinogens has increased with the promulgation of the OSHA hazard communication standard and the various state worker right-to-know laws. Management concerns have also heightened because of the potential for huge financial liabilities resulting from cancer-related litigation. Educating management and workers about actual or perceived carcinogenic risks is a delicate and difficult task for the industrial hygienist and the personnel/labor relations manager.

OSHA and ACGIH prepare the most commonly used workplace carcinogen lists. OSHA-regulated carcinogens are included in Table 5-3. The ACGIH publishes an annual list of threshold limit values (TLVs), including a list of human and suspect (i.e., animal) carcinogens. ACGIH TLVs and criteria are used extensively in the United States and many other countries.

Chemical carcinogens can cause tumors in mammalian species. Carcinogens may induce a tumor type not usually observed, or induce an increased incidence of a tumor type normally seen, or induce such tumors at an earlier time than would otherwise be expected. In some instances, the worker's initial stages of exposure to the carcinogen and the tumor appearance are separated by a latent period of 20 to 30 years. Examples of chemical carcinogens include benzo(a)pyrene, beta-naphthylamine, vinyl chloride, and chromates.

Reproductive Hazards in the Workplace

Exposure to chemicals that affect the reproductive systems are an increasing concern among employees. California's Proposition 65 underscores these concerns shown by regulatory agencies regarding exposure of workers and the community to teratogens and other chemicals that display reproductive toxicity. In health-care facilities, exposure to anesthesia gases of hospital

TABLE 5-3   Individual Chemical Substance Standards

29 CFR 1910	Chemical name	Exposure limits		
		TWA	Ceiling	Action level
1000	Air contaminants			
1001	Asbestos	0.2 fibers/cm^3	1.0 fibers/cm^3	0.1 fibers/cm^3
1002	Coal tar pitch volatiles	0.2 mg/m^3		
1003	4-nitrobiphenyl	*		
1004	α-naphthylamine	*		
1005	Reserved			
1006	Methyl chloromethyl ether	*		
1007	3, 3'-dichlorobenzidine (and its salts)	*		
1008	bis-chloromethyl ether	*		
1009	β-naphthylamine	*		
1010	Benzidine	*		
1011	4-aminodiphenyl	*		
1012	Ethyleneimine	*		
1013	β-propiolactone	*		
1014	2-acetylaminofluorene	*		
1015	4-dimethylaminoazobenzene	*		
1016	N-nitrosodimethylamine	*		
1017	Vinyl chloride	1 ppm	5 ppm/15 min	0.5 ppm
1018	Inorganic arsenic	10 μg/m^3		5 μg/m^3
1025	Lead	50 μg/m^3		30 μg/m^3
1028	Benzene	1 ppm	5 ppm/15 min	0.5 ppm
1029	Coke oven emissions	150 μg/m^3		
1043	Cotton dust	200 μg/m^3 (yarn manufacturer)		100 μg/m^3
		500 μg/m^3 (textile mill wastehouse)		250 μg/m^3
		750 μg/m^3 (slashing and weaving)		375 μg/m^3
1044	1,2-Dibromo-3-chloropropane	1 ppb		
1045	Acrylonitrile	2 ppm	10 ppm/15 min	1 ppm
1047	Ethylene oxide	1 ppm	5 ppm/15 min	0.5 ppm
1048	Formaldehyde	1 ppm	2 ppm/15 min	0.5 ppm

* These carcinogen standards require that these chemicals be handled only in completely enclosed systems with exposures reduced to the lowest feasible level.

employees, anaesthetist nurses, and physicians, in particular, has long been a concern among occupational health specialists.

Exposure to chemicals that are known or suspected to cause reproductive abnormalities is also causing an employee relations/discrimination dilemma for employers. Companies that have instituted policies of not assigning women employees of child-bearing age in work areas where teratogenic and other reproductive toxicants are in use now face potential discrimination charges. In fact, there have been several cases of litigation by female employees challenging such policies. The March 20, 1991 U.S. Supreme Court decision on discriminatory fetal protection policies will require employers to reassess health risks and potential liabilities associated with exposure to chemicals with reproductive hazard potential. The emerging professional and legal view is that "reproductive health can no longer be separated from general occupational health" and that "workers should not have to choose between having a safe workplace and having a family."

Particulate Size

Airborne particulate matter varies in size from less than 0.01 to more that 25 μm (one micrometer equals approximately 1/25,000 inch). These particles are invisible to the naked eye.

Nonrespirable particulates consist of particles that are either too large to escape the respiratory tract's defenses before they can reach the lungs or that are too small to be retained in the lungs even if they get that far. Nonrespirable particulates present other types of health problems. Toxic fumes and nonrespirable dusts that are inhaled or ingested (or, less commonly, that come into contact with the skin) may be eventually absorbed into the bloodstream and cause systemic poisoning. Other nonrespirable dusts, inert "nuisance" substances like limestone and gypsum, can severely irritate the upper respiratory tract, endangering health as well as causing great discomfort.

Particulates that are small enough to find their way into the lungs and remain there, including dusts fine enough to be classified as *respirable dusts,* can produce serious chronic conditions such as the group of diseases known as *pneumoconiosis*—lung diseases like coal miners' black lung disease and silicosis.

In view of the above, the measurement of dust exposure in many cases needs to be limited to that fraction of inhaled particles small enough to be deposited in alveolar spaces. Thus, a size-selective air-sampling method is required to separate the respirable fraction from the coarser material that is deposited in the upper respiratory tract. The size selector most commonly used in respirable dust sampling has the following characteristics:

Aerodynamic diameter, μm (unit density sphere)	% passing size selector
2.0	90
2.5	75
3.5	50
5.0	25
10.0	0

Measurement of Worker Exposure

A variety of techniques are used in measuring exposure of workers to toxic chemicals. Techniques used for measuring particulates differ somewhat from those used to measure gases and vapors.

Sampling to determine worker exposure to particulates is most often done by filtration using a battery-operated pump that draws air through a filter, usually 37 mm in diameter and made of paper, fiberglass, or synthetic materials such as mixed cellulose-ester, polyvinyl chloride, or polycarbonate. An impinger is recommended in sampling for some particulates. The solution within the impinger can also collect gases and vapors and, in fact, impingers are used more for this purpose than for sampling for particulates.

Time-Weighted Average Exposure

Threshold-limit values usually refer to time-weighted concentrations for a 7- or 8-h workday and 40-h workweek, although recent efforts of National Institute for Occupational Safety and Health (NIOSH) and OSHA have been aimed at defining permissible exposure limits for up to 10-h workdays.

Short-term exposures to concentrations above the threshold limit are permitted provided that they are compensated for by equivalent excursions below the limit during the workday. For example, if the permissible exposure limit is 10, a worker could be permitted to work in concentrations as high as 15 for 4 h, provided that the remainder of this 8-h shift did not result in exposure to concentrations above 5, thus yielding an average 8-h weighted concentration of 10.

Stated mathematically, the time-weighted average concentration, based on an 8-h shift, is defined as

$$\text{TWA} = \frac{1}{8} \sum_{i=1}^{N} \bar{C}_i t_i$$

where $\bar{C}$ is the average concentration of the contaminant at location i, N is the total number of work locations, Σ refers to the summation of the products of concentration $\bar{C}$ in percent, and t is the time in house spent at location i. Expressed otherwise,

$$\text{TWA} = \frac{(\text{exposure time})(\text{con. } A) + (\text{exposure time})(\text{con. } B) + \cdots}{\text{total work time per shift}}$$

Obviously, this approach requires reliance on personal-breathing-zone sampling or detailed job analyses for all classifications studied, and a comprehensive program of sampling sufficient to establish average airborne concentrations at all work sites.

Who to Sample

Sampling programs are based on statistical considerations, as it may be impractical and is often unnecessary to sample every worker's exposure. Thus, various statistical approaches have been devised to determine the minimum number of workers to be sampled to achieve adequate representation. A simple approach recommended by NIOSH is summarized as follows:

Number of employees exposed	Minimum number of employees whose individual exposures shall be determined
1–20	50% of the total number of exposed employees
21–100	10 plus 25% of the excess over 20 exposed employees
Over 100	30 plus 5% of the excess over 100 exposed employees

Indoor Air Quality

Over the past 40 years, significant changes have occurred in the construction and operation of buildings. Some of these changes have led to the generation of new classes of air contaminants. During the past 10 years, particularly in office buildings, the presence of indoor air pollutants has been associated with reports of new maladies known as *sick-building syndrome* and *building-related illness.*

> *Sick-building syndrome.*   Many occupants complain of headache, fatigue, eye, nose, and throat irritation, as well as dry skin. Complaints are more intense in the afternoon. Relief is experienced shortly after occupants leave the building.
>
> *Building-related illness.*   One or more occupants develop a clinically diagnosed disease that may be related to the occupant's presence in the building. Examples include humidifier fever, asthma, hypersensitivity pneumonitis, Legionnaires' disease, and Pontiac fever.

Employee health may be adversely affected by indoor air contaminants including environmental tobacco smoke, volatile organic compounds, bioeffluents, microbial allergens, and Legionella (a bacterium). Some of these contaminants can cause discomfort; eye, nose, and throat irritation; humidifier fever; and hypersensitivity pneumonitis. Legionella can cause Legionnaires' disease and Pontiac fever. Some contaminants may be carcinogenic.

The action of building owners and office managers is important in preventing sick-building syndrome and building-related illness. Indoor air quality problems can be mitigated by such practices as purchasing of finishing materials with minimum volatile organic emissions and insisting on careful maintenance of the building's heating, ventilating, and air-conditioning (HVAC) system. See Sec. 5, "Heating, Ventilating, and Air Conditioning."

An essential aspect of solving most indoor air pollution problems is a thorough understanding of how the HVAC system moves air through the building. Whether or not a consultant is needed to solve an indoor air quality problem depends on the expertise of the facilities engineering and environmental health staff. A considerable amount of literature is available for the guidance of in-house activities. Some aspects of an indoor air quality evaluation, such as ventilation assessment and sampling for volatile organic compounds and microorganisms, often require the services of a consultant.

Occupational Safety and Health Standards

Measured results are compared to OSHA health standards or other widely accepted standards such as the American Conference of Governmental Industrial Hygienists threshold-limit values.

Federal Standards (29 CFR 1910 subpart Z).   The first compilation of health and safety standards promulgated by OSHA was based on the existing federal and national consensus standards.

Table 5-3 lists the standards in Sec. 1910.1001 through 1910.1046 of Title 29, Chap. XVII, Sect. 1910.1000 (available through OSHA as Publication 2206). These standards are detailed sets of regulations for individual substances. In addition to setting exposure limits, they require exposure monitoring and medical surveillance of exposed employees. OSHA plans to promulgate many more complete standards.

Private Organizations.   The first influential American organization in the field of occupational safety was the American Conference of Governmental Industrial Hygienists. The ACGIH publishes each year its revised and updated list of occupational exposure limits, commonly referred to as the TLVs. This listing is more extensive than the OSHA listing of air contaminants in CFR 29 1910.1000. It should be noted that the term TLV is a registered trademark of the ACGIH and should not be used to refer to OSHA permissible exposure limits. Another organization involved in the promulgation of such standards, although its concerns extend into several other areas, is the American National Standards

Institute (ANSI). Two prominent organizations in the occupational health field are the American Board of Industrial Hygiene (ABIH) and the American Industrial Hygiene Association (AIHA), both established in the 1950s; among the services they provide are the certification of industrial hygienists and accreditation of laboratories that analyze workplace samples.

Control Strategy—Reducing or Eliminating Hazards.
A strategy for reducing or eliminating workplace hazards can include either or both of two approaches: engineering and/or administrative controls.

Engineering controls. Some examples are substituting relatively safe chemicals for more toxic ones, altering a process in such a way as to reduce worker exposure to contaminants, changing or upgrading ventilation systems, and isolating or enclosing contaminated areas.

Administrative controls. An example is adjusting work schedules so that workers receive only a fraction of their present exposure to contaminants.

As an example of an engineering control, if asbestos is used as insulation, it may be possible to replace it with fiberglass or calcium silicate, materials which do not present the same degree of hazard. Here again, however, it should never be assumed that such a substitution completely eliminates the hazard. The hazardous potential for fiberglass is not completely known, for example, while certain varieties of calcium silicate, generally regarded as a relatively safe substance, have been found to contain measurable amounts of asbestos fibers and/or free crystalline silica, another hazardous material.

A control strategy must take into account work *practices,* which can be a major factor in workplace exposure. Poor work practices result from lack of awareness of the potential hazards of a toxic material. For example, in one paint factory, workers were observed dusting off their clothes with a compressed-air line, starting from the shoes and proceeding upward. The raw material in the plant's primary process included, among other substances, lead chromate. Sampling measurements in the plant indicated that worker exposures to lead and hexavalent chromium (both highly toxic materials) were not excessive under normal working conditions. It was determined that *this dusting off procedure with compressed air, however, exposed the workers to higher concentrations of lead and chromium during a 2- to 4-min period than they were exposed to during the remainder of the day* when handling these materials frequently. Vacuuming of dusty clothing (rather than blowing the dust off) could easily prevent this exposure. In such cases, employee-awareness programs can be highly effective in preventing work practices that result in unnecessary exposure.

The evaluation of existing and planned engineering controls is a major goal of an effective industrial-hygiene program. OSHA considers engineering controls to be the primary and most effective means of reducing or eliminating exposure to toxic substances in the workplace. The extent of engineering controls needed can be better determined after sampling measurements have been taken, other aspects such as work practices and housekeeping have been evaluated, and corrective actions have been instituted. Examples of poor engineering controls are all too plentiful.

Exposure Surveillance Programs

A comprehensive ongoing occupational health or industrial hygiene program includes a monitoring program for surveillance of worker health in addition to determining compliance with the applicable regulatory standards. The *surveillance program* consists not only of ongoing sampling of worker exposure to airborne concentrations of chemicals but also monitoring for exposure to such physical agents as noise, radiation, and heat stress. The frequency of sampling will depend on the levels of various contaminants, the toxicity of the material, and the specific requirements under the applicable codes.

Biological monitoring of worker exposure to chemical hazards through analysis of samples of blood, urine, expired air, etc., is required in those cases where measurement of airborne concentration alone is not a reliable indicator of exposure hazard. In some instances, the metabolite (chemical produced within the body) of a toxic substance rather than the substance itself may be measured in the biological fluids.

Medical surveillance of exposed workers is also a necessary tool for protection against toxic exposures. Pre-employment and periodic medical examinations can reveal the presence of toxic effects at an early stage, when a cure is often possible. Medical examinations should include specific organ functions to detect changes relative to the specific contaminants to which the worker is exposed.

RADIATION HAZARDS

Radiation is energy which is emitted, transmitted, or absorbed in wave or energetic particle form. The electromagnetic (EM) waves consist of electric and magnetic forces. When these forces are disturbed, EM radiation results. Figure 5-1 is an arrangement of known EM radiations according to their frequency and/or wavelength. It includes microwave, infrared, visible,

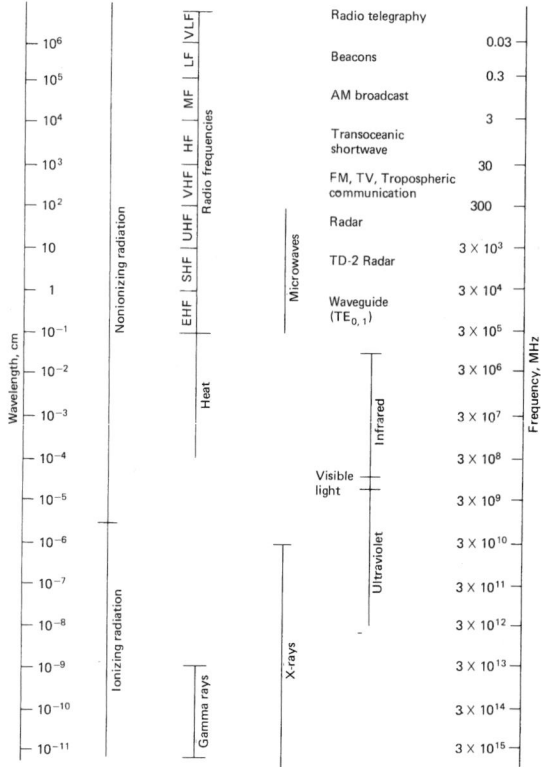

FIGURE 5-1   Electromagnetic spectrum.

TABLE 5-4   Example of Occupational Exposure to Ionizing and Nonionizing Radiation

Type of radiation	Occupation
Ionizing (radioactive isotopes, x-rays)	Nuclear powerplant workers, food preservers, electron microscopists, biologists, food sterilizers, high-voltage repairmen, ceramic workers, drug makers
Ultraviolet	Meat curers, movie projectionists, pipeline workers, paint curers, nurses, bacteriologists, dentists, food preservers, lithographers, laboratory workers, welders, textile inspectors, plastic curers, printers
Infrared	Bakers, electricians, furnace workers, glassblowers, heat treaters, solderers, welders, firemen, steel workers
Microwave radio-frequency	Automotive workers, paper product workers, plastic heat-sealing workers, rubber-product workers, textile workers, tobacco workers, electronics workers, advertising sign workers
Laser	Medical technicians, surgeons, aerospace workers, semiconductor workers

and ultraviolet radiation. The range of biological effects of exposure within the electromagnetic spectrum is, therefore, extremely broad and diverse.

Radiation is generally divided into two categories: *ionizing* and *nonionizing*. Ionizing radiation includes x-rays, alpha particles, and beta, gamma, and neutron rays. Nonionizing radiation includes ultraviolet, visible, infrared, microwave, and radio-frequency. Laser radiations fall into most of these bands. Examples of occupational exposure to ionizing and nonionizing radiation are shown in Table 5-4.

Ionizing Radiation

Of the types of ionizing radiation, alpha particles are the least penetrating—paper and skin will ordinarily stop alpha particles.

Beta radiation has considerably more penetrating power than alpha particles. X-rays and gamma rays both have very good penetrating power and require the use of heavy shielding material (lead). Neutrons are very penetrating and require shielding with materials of higher hydrogen atom content rather than the use of mass alone.

Alpha emitters are an internal hazard because they do not have the ionizing ability to travel very long distances. One must take precaution against breathing or ingesting the alpha emitters. Beta emitters are also generally considered an internal hazard.

Regulations Regarding Ionizing Radiation.   Jobs involving exposure to ionizing radiation fall under the provisions of Nuclear Regulatory Commission (NRC) standards (10 CFR Part 20). OSHA standards (Sec. 1910.96) on ionization radiation apply in cases where employees may not be protected under the NRC standards.

Table 5-5 summarizes the most frequent types of radiation encountered in health physics surveys and the type of detection most commonly used.

TABLE 5-5   Types of Detectors Used for Various Types of Radiation

Type of detector	Type of radiation
Proportional or scintillation counter	Alpha
Geiger-Mueller tube or proportional counter	Beta
Ionization chamber	X and gamma
Proportional counter	Neutron

A photographic film badge can be used for determining beta and gamma doses. Such film badges give a sufficiently quantitative indication of the integrated weekly doses of individuals. These should be recorded along with other records of radiation levels.

Nonionizing Radiation

Ultraviolet Radiation.   The major source of ultraviolet radiation is the sun. Common constructed sources are mercury discharge lamps, welding and plasma torches, xenon discharge lamps, and lasers. The symptoms of overexposure to ultraviolet radiation are those characteristic of a severe sunburn.

Currently, there are no OSHA standards for exposure to ultraviolet radiation. OSHA Sec. 1910.97 concerning nonionizing radiation includes exposure levels and warning signs. However, this is an advisory and not a mandatory standard.

NIOSH has a recommended standard for occupational exposure to ultraviolet radiation. The American Conference of Governmental Industrial Hygienists has developed threshold-limit values for ultraviolet radiation in the spectral region between 180 and 400 nm and represent conditions under which it is believed that nearly all workers may be repeatedly exposed without adverse effect. The ACGIH urges caution in the use of the threshold values in that these values should be used as guides in the control of exposure to ultraviolet sources and should not be regarded as a fine line between safe and dangerous levels.

Infrared Radiation.   Infrared radiation (ir) can be associated with the heat given off by all bodies that radiate heat and covers wavelengths from 0.75 μm to about 1 mm. Infrared rays are mostly absorbed by the skin and burn the skin in the same way the sun does. Like ultraviolet radiation, infrared radiation is invisible. Although infrared radiation may not be felt, over the years it can cause permanent eye damage. Water can be used as a barrier, as it can absorb most ir waves. Regular clothing protects the skin against ir, but goggles should be worn when there is a potential for overexposure.

Except for thermal burns (below wavelengths of 1.5 μm,), infrared radiation is insignificant as a health hazard. However, when highly intense and compacted sources of radiant energy are being used, as with lasers, injury can occur in fractions of a second, before pain is evident.

Microwave Radiation.   There has been a great deal of exposure to microwaves among people in the armed forces because microwave radiation is used for radar. With the advent of microwave ovens, however, this type of radiation is now encountered in the home. Microwaves have wavelengths of 3 m to 3 mm and their effect is related to power intensity and time of exposure as well as to the wavelength. Their ability to heat the body allows them to be used for medical treatment. This ability, however, can also be a hazard to the overexposed, unprotected worker. Microwaves penetrate deeply into the body and cause body temperature to rise; if the body temperature rises high enough, the person can go into a coma and die.

Before personnel are assigned to work in or about radar equipment, they should be given a complete physical including eye and blood examinations. Workers should be instructed never to look directly at a radar beam and should be given physicals periodically and whenever exposure is indicated. Most microwave measuring devices are based on (1) bolometry, (2) colorimetry, (3) voltage and resistance changes in detectors, or (4) radiation pressure on a reflecting surface. The bolometry method is one of the most widely used in commercially available power meters.

One troublesome fact in the measurement of microwave radiation is that the near field (reactive field) of many sources may produce unpredictable radioactive patterns. Energy density rather than power density may be a more appropriate means of expressing hazard potential in the near field.

Radio-Frequency Radiation.   Radio-frequency (rf) electromagnetic radiation obeys the general laws of electromagnetic radiation and is characterized by the following basic parameters: frequency f in hertz (1 Hz = 1 cycle per second), propagation time T, wavelength λ in meters, and velocity c, which in free space under normal conditions is equal to the velocity of light, i.e., 300,000 km/s. These quantities are interrelated according to the formula

$$\lambda = c\mathrm{T}$$

Radio-frequency radiation covers wavelengths from 300 m to 1 mm. For measurement, either electric or magnetic field strength meters or power meters are used.

In power meters, the rf energy causes a change of temperature-sensitive element which is monitored by a bridge circuit and meter calibrated in units of $\mu W/m^2$ or mW/m^2.

All effects of rf radiation may be classified as either thermal or nonthermal, leading to heat stress or disturbance of the nervous system, respectively.

Nonionizing Radiation Instruments

Ultraviolet and Infrared Radiation Monitoring Devices.   A variety of instruments are commonly used to measure ultraviolet and infrared radiation. They are classified according to the type of detector used, which is generally one of two types: thermal detectors or photoelectric detectors. Thermal detectors are those in which the absorbed radiation is degraded to heat and subsequently converted to an electric signal by changing the electric resistance of a filament. Photoelectric detectors are based on the principle that the absorbed photons eject electrons from a material. Most of these instruments are precalibrated by the manufacturer, but should be routinely checked prior to field use.

Microwave Monitoring Devices.   Most microwave radiation detectors consist of the following components: a test antenna, an attenuator, a bolometer or thermistor, and a power meter. These detectors are usually in the form of a single integrated unit. The test antenna is specific to certain wavelengths and, therefore, interchangeable. These units must be calibrated at frequencies throughout the band to ensure accuracy.

Laser Monitoring Devices.   A wide variety of laser radiation detectors are commercially available to fulfill the diversified needs resulting from different wavelengths, pulse durations, and power and energy densities of various laser instruments. Laser radiation detectors are generally based on either of two basic principles—photon or thermal detection.

Lasers

Laser technology has increased rapidly since its inception in 1960. Presently it involves virtually every scientific field in one way or another.

Laser is an acronym for light amplification by stimulated emission of radiation. A laser is a source of coherent energy which may appear in the near or far infrared, long or short ultraviolet, or visible regions. The properties of lasers are similar to those of other devices for various regions of the electromagnetic spectrum, except that the laser normally achieves great power densities. A laser beam does not rapidly diverge since a laser operates at specific frequencies in the electromagnetic spectrum. It travels in one direction in a straight line.

There are four types of lasers, classified by generating medium:

* Solid-state (the ruby crystal is the most common)
* Gaseous-state (the helium-neon is the most common)

- Semiconductor or junction
- Liquid-state, using organic dyes as a medium

Some lasers operate continuously while others operate in pulses, sometimes as short as 10^{-11} s. Output levels range from milliwatts to kilowatts for continuous operation and up to gigawatts in pulse operations.

The two main areas of potential health effects from laser radiation are the eye and the skin. Associated electrical, chemical, and explosive hazards are also possible. Knowledge of and continued interest in laser safety are necessary in developing applications of lasers.

Ocular Hazards.   Protective eyewear should be worn whenever hazardous conditions may result from operation of a laser product. Laser radiation in the infrared region is highly absorbed at the surface of the cornea and could induce opacities in the cornea and destruction of the protective epithelial layer. In the ultraviolet region, exposure may result in extreme discomfort, but a moderate exposure is not thought to produce permanent damage. In the region of the spectrum from 320 to 1500 nm (the visible range is normally 380 to 760 nm), eye hazards are confined primarily to the retina and choroid. The most critical area for vision is the fovea. Thus, safety guidelines for laser radiation are designed to protect against foveal area damage. There is an often-undetected hazard from diffused laser radiation in the visible region due to the ability of the eye to focus such radiation to a very small spot on the retina. If the laser beam is incident upon a diffuse surface, the illuminated diffuse surface can serve as a secondary extended source. In this case, the retinal power density is unaltered regardless of viewing angel and how far away the surface is from the viewer.

Skin Hazards.   The effects of laser radiation on the skin may vary from mild reddening (erythema), to blistering and charring, depending on the amount of energy absorbed, the wavelengths of the radiation, skin pigmentation, individual sensitivity, and duration of exposure.

Electrical and Explosion Hazards.   Live parts of circuits and components with peak open-circuit potentials over 42.5 V are considered hazardous, unless limited to less than 0.5 mA circuit components of combustible materials. For example, transformers are potential fire hazards unless individual noncombustible enclosures are provided.

In the event of a tube or lamp failure, components such as electrolytic capacitors may explode if subjected to voltages higher than their ratings. A misdirected laser beam, in this case, could steam the coolant of a high output laser system to trigger an explosion.

Chemical Hazards.   OSHA currently has no occupational health standards for laser products. Threshold limits established by the American Conference of Governmental Industrial Hygienists are the recommended values to use. All laser products should meet specifications of the **National Electrical Code**® (NFPA 70-1981),* Arts. 300 and 400. Adherence to control procedures required under this standard should eliminate any significant probability of detrimental health effects from laser product operations. Therefore, an extensive, medical surveillance protocol for laser operators is not required under this standard.

BIBLIOGRAPHY

American Industrial Hygiene Association Journal, 66 South Miller Road, Akron, OH 44313.
American Journal of Public Health, American Public Health Association, 1015 Eighteenth St. NW, Washington, DC 20036.

---

* **National Electrical Code**® is a trademark of the National Fire Protection Association, Quincy, MA 02269.

Archives of Environmental Health, American Medical Association, 535 N. Dearborn St., Chicago, IL 60610.

Cember, H.: *Introduction to Health Physics,* Pergamon, New York, 1969.

Clarke, A. M.: *Ocular Hazards from Lasers and Other Optical Sources,* CRC Press, Boca Raton, Fla., 1970.

Clayton, F. E., and G. D Clayton (eds.): *Patty's Industrial Hygiene and Toxicology: General Principles,* vol. I, 3d ed., 1978; *Toxicology,* vol. IIA, 3d ed.; Wiley-Interscience, New York, 1981.

Cleary, S. F.: *The Biological Effects of Microwave and Radiofrequency Radiations,* CRC Press, Boca Raton, Fla., 1970.

Code of Federal Regulations: 29 Part 1910, U.S. Government Printing Office, Washington, D.C., 1991.

Cralley, L. J., and L. V. Cralley (eds.): *Patty's Industrial Hygiene and Toxicology: Theory and Rationale of Industrial Hygiene Practice,* vol. III, Wiley-Interscience, New York, 1979.

Cralley, L. V. and L. J. Cralley (eds.): *Industrial Hygiene Aspects of Plant Operations,* vol. I, 1982, and vol. II, 1983, Macmillian Publishing Co., Inc., New York.

Morey, Philip R., and Jaswant Singh: *Patty's Industrial Hygiene and Toxicology: General Principles,* vol. I, Part A, 4th ed., Wiley-Interscience, New York, 1991.

OSHA Final Rule, *Air Contaminants, Permissible Exposure Limits:* Title 29 Code of Federal Regulations Part 1910.1000, Federal Register, January 19, 1990.

Threshold Limit Value and Biological Exposure Indices for 1991–1992: American Converence of Governmental Industrial Hygienists, Cincinnati, Ohio, 1991–1992.

CHAPTER 14-6
SANITATION CONTROL AND HOUSEKEEPING

Robert L. Bays
Technical Support Director
Huntington Laboratories, Inc.
Huntington, Indiana

GLOSSARY

Acid   A compound that gives a pH below 7. Most soils including oils, greases, and waxes are acids.

Alkali   A compound that gives a pH between 7 and 14. Hard-water films, carbonates, potash, and phosphates are alkaline.

Deodorize   Destroying, masking, or modifying foul and unpleasant odors. May be accomplished by killing bacteria that make foul odors.

Detergent   Any product that cleans. Usually a synthetic detergent but may be a soap or even an abrasive material.

Disinfectant   Product used on hard inanimate surfaces which destroys microorganisms but not necessarily spores. Also called germicide.

Finish   A protective coating used as a top coat.

Germicide   See Disinfectant.

Hard floors   Concrete, terrazzo, ceramic, quarry, slate, etc.

Polymer   See Finish.

Resilient floors   Vinyl, vinyl asbestos, asphalt, rubber, linoleum, etc.

Sanitary   Relating to health or to the preservation of or restoration of health and hygiene.

Sanitation   Use of sanitary measures to clean and maintain a building.

Sanitize   Reduce bacterial counts to safe levels as determined by health requirements.

Sealer   A product used to prevent excessive absorption of finish coats into porous surfaces. An undercoat.

INTRODUCTION

Proper housekeeping procedures play an important role in the total plant operation. Custodial employees work with a variety of chemicals, equipment, and procedures. They work in a building that has taken considerable money to construct, and improper chemicals and procedures can shorten the normal life of the building. In a relatively few years, the owners will have *spent more money on housekeeping and maintenance than the initial cost of the building and its furnishings.* Custodians should be well-trained to perform their tasks. Table 6-1 gives average cleaning times for various duties so that an estimate of efficiency can be determined. In addition to maintaining the appearance and prolonging the life of the building, good housekeeping provides immeasurable safety, hygienic, and sanitary benefits.

Safety is a key reason for good custodial procedures. The Occupational Safety and Health Administration of the U.S. Department of Labor states in its Standards and Interpretations, 1910.22(a) Housekeeping:

> (1) All places of employment, passageways, storerooms, and service rooms shall be kept clean and orderly and in a sanitary condition.
> (2) The floor of every workroom shall be maintained in a clean, and so far as possible, a dry condition. Where wet processes are used, drainage shall be maintained, and false floors, platforms, mats, or other dry standing places should be provided where practicable.
> (3) To facilitate cleaning, every floor, working place, and passageway shall be kept free from protruding nails, splinters, holes, or loose boards.

Other benefits from the results of a well-trained custodial work force are:

1. A clean, sanitary environment contributes to the health of all the personnel.
2. Training improves the morale and mental attitude of each worker.
3. Each worker can have a feeling of pride in a job well done.
4. A well-maintained building is easier to keep in shape, thus saving time and money.
5. A well-maintained building and a crew of employees that enjoy their work contribute to goodwill and public relations.
6. The life of the various parts of the building and the building itself can be greatly extended by proper housekeeping procedures.

TABLE 6-1   Cleaning Operation Time Estimate*

Calculating cleaning times is a complex and frequently frustrating business. All cleaning times are estimates. There is no absolute time standard—nor can there be one. Two workers with the same tools, instructions, and area will clean at a different pace. A worker who must trek to the basement of a building to empty dirty cleaning solution will not clean as productively as a worker with convenient custodial closets and sinks on every floor.

When calculating cleaning times there are many other variables to consider. These include: age of the building, design of the building, climate, season, outside soil, placement of custodial closets, type of floors and walls, custodial training, day vs. night cleaning shifts, vandalism factor, etc.

To achieve a cleaning time standard there must be a set of uniform conditions. For example, each custodian must:

- Have sufficient materials, supplies and equipment to perform the work
- Be sufficiently trained to perform the task with the materials and supplies available
- Demonstrate the ability to perform the standard using the available supplies and materials
- Be aware of a cleaning time expectation
- Be regularly evaluated to provide for ongoing adherence to cleaning time standards.

General cleaning		
Dusting surfaces: dust with duster	150 ft^2	0.90 min
Dusting surfaces: dust with treated cloth	150 ft^2	1.80 min
Dusting surfaces: damp wipe with trigger sprayer and cloth	150 ft^2	2.88 min
Dusting surfaces: dust with hand-held duster vacuum	150 ft^2	1.35 min
Dusting surfaces: dust with tank/canister vacuum	150 ft^2	2.25 min
Dusting surfaces: dust with backpack vacuum	150 ft^2	1.62 min
Furniture, upholstered: vacuum with hand-held duster vacuum	25 ft^2	2.10 min
Furniture, upholstered: vacuum with tank/canister vacuum	25 ft^2	2.55 min
Furniture, upholstered: vacuum with backpack vacuum	25 ft^2	2.10 min
Glass door and hardware: clean using trigger sprayer and cloth (2 sides)	1 item	3.00 min
Glass panel/partition: clean using trigger sprayer and cloth	30 ft^2	3.42 min
Handrails/banister: damp-wipe with trigger sprayer and cloth	48 ft^2	0.86 min
Mats, walk-off: vacuum with upright vacuum	36 ft^2	1.08 min
Mats, walk-off: vacuum with tank/canister vacuum	36 ft^2	1.08 min
Mats, walk-off: vacuum with backpack vacuum	35 ft^2	0.95 min
Seating, upholstered: vacuum with hand-held duster vacuum	1000 ft^2	84.00 min
Seating, upholstered: vacuum with tank/canister vacuum	1000 ft^2	102.00 min
Seating, upholstered: vacuum with backpack vacuum	1000 ft^2	87.00 min
Telephone, desk: sanitize using trigger sprayer and cloth/cleaner–disinfectant	1 item	0.67 min
Telephone, wall: sanitize using trigger sprayer and cloth/cleaner–disinfectant	1 item	1.00 min
Trash removal		
Trash removal: empty trash/ash trays/pencil sharpener and wipe clean	2 items	1.00 min
Trash removal: empty trash/ash trays/pencil sharpener, wipe clean and reline basket	2 items	1.50 min
Trash pickup: pick up loose debris with lobby pan and porter broom/scrape up gum	1000 ft^2	18.00 min
Clean and polish		
Furniture, hard surface: clean/polish with trigger sprayer/chemical and cloth	100 ft^2	8.40 min
Stainless steel: clean/polish with trigger sprayer/chemical and cloth	10 ft^2	1.20 min
Wood paneling: clean/polish with trigger sprayer/chemical and cloth	100 ft^2	12.00 min
Restroom service		
Restroom pickup service: trash/replace supplies/touch-up, as needed	9 fixtures	9.02 min
Restroom service: trash/clean, disinfect/fixtures/wipe mirrors/replace supplies/sweep floor	9 fixtures	27.00 min

TABLE 6-1   Cleaning Operation Time Estimate* (*Continued*)

Restroom service (*continued*)		
Restroom service: trash/clean, disinfect fixtures/wipe mirrors/replace supplies/dust mop floor	9 fixtures	21.60 min
Restroom service: trash/clean, disinfect fixtures/wipe mirrors/replace supplies/wet-mop floor	9 fixtures	44.98 min

Carpet care		
Protect from soiling using pump sprayer and soil protection chemical	1000 ft^2	10.20 min
Spot-remove by testing, applying spot remover and blotting	1 spot	4.00 min
Bonnet clean with immersion method using 17-in rotary floor machine	1000 ft^2	69.60 min
Bonnet clean with immersion method using 20-in rotary floor machine	1000 ft^2	60.00 min
Bonnet clean with immersion method using 24-in rotary floor machine	1000 ft^2	50.40 min
Bonnet-clean with spray-on method using 17-in rotary floor machine	1000 ft^2	54.00 min
Bonnet-clean with spray-on method using 20-in rotary floor machine	1000 ft^2	44.40 min
Bonnet-clean with spray-on method using 24-in rotary floor machine	1000 ft^2	34.80 min
Dry-clean, pretreat carpet with prespray chemical and pump tank sprayer	1000 ft^2	10.20 min
Dry-clean, spread dry cleaning compound	1000 ft^2	13.20 min
Dry-clean, agitate dry compound with 12-in revolving-brushes machine	1000 ft^2	34.80 min
Dry-clean, agitate dry compound with 24-in revolving-brushes machine	1000 ft^2	25.20 min
Dry-clean, vacuum up dry compound with 12-in upright vacuum	1000 ft^2	34.80 min
Dry-clean, vacuum up dry compound with 14-in twin-motor upright	1000 ft^2	31.00 min
Dry-clean, vacuum up dry compound with 16-in upright vacuum	1000 ft^2	30.00 min
Dry-clean, vacuum up dry compound with 18-in twin-motor upright	1000 ft^2	25.00 min
Dry-foam-clean using 12-in machine that requires separate foam pickup	1000 ft^2	34.80 min
Dry-foam-clean using 14-in machine that requires separate foam pickup	1000 ft^2	30.00 min
Dry-foam-clean using 18-in machine that requires separate foam pickup	1000 ft^2	25.20 min
Dry-foam-clean using 28-in machine that requires separate foam pickup	1000 ft^2	19.80 min
Dry-foam-clean using one-pass 13-in machine with simultaneous foam pickup	1000 ft^2	33.00 min
Dry-foam-clean using one-pass 24-in machine with simultaneous foam pickup	1000 ft^2	22.80 min
Extraction-clean using portable machine with hose and 12-in suction head	1000 ft^2	120.00 min
Extraction-clean using portable machine with hose and 16-in suction head	1000 ft^2	110.00 min
Extraction-clean using portable machine with hose and 12-in agitator power head	1000 ft^2	64.80 min
Extraction-clean using portable machine with hose and 16-in agitator power head	1000 ft^2	60.00 min
Extraction-clean using portable machine with hose and 17-in turbo rotating power head	1000 ft^2	15.00 min
Extraction-clean using 12-in self-contained, self-propelled machine	1000 ft^2	55.00 min
Extraction-clean using 16-in self-contained, self-propelled machine	1000 ft^2	29.00 min
Extraction-clean using 21-in self-contained, self-propelled machine	1000 ft^2	15.00 min
Rotary-shampoo with 175-r/min 17-in rotary floor machine	1000 ft^2	60.00 min
Rotary-shampoo with 175-r/min 20-in rotary floor machine	1000 ft^2	55.20 min
Rotary-shampoo with 350-r/min 17-in rotary floor machine	1000 ft^2	49.80 min
Rotary-shampoo with 350-r/min 20-in rotary floor machine	1000 ft^2	45.00 min
Rinse and extract shampoo using portable extractor with hose and 12-in suction head	1000 ft^2	60.00 min
Rinse and extract shampoo using portable extractor with hose and 16-in suction head	1000 ft^2	55.20 min
Scrub using one-pass machine with 12-in twin cylindrical brushes and wet pickup	1000 ft^2	27.00 min
Scrub using one-pass machine with 24-in twin cylindrical brushes and wet pickup	1000 ft^2	15.00 min
Vacuum with 12-in upright vacuum	1000 ft^2	22.80 min
Vacuum with 14-in upright vacuum	1000 ft^2	21.00 min
Vacuum with 14-in twin motor upright	1000 ft^2	17.00 min
Vacuum with 16-in upright vacuum	1000 ft^2	19.20 min
Vacuum with 18-in upright vacuum	1000 ft^2	17.40 min
Vacuum with 18-in twin motor upright	1000 ft^2	15.00 min

TABLE 6-1   Cleaning Operation Time Estimate* (*Continued*)

Carpet care (*continued*)		
Vacuum with 20-in upright vacuum	1000 ft²	15.60 min
Vacuum with 22-in upright vacuum	1000 ft²	13.80 min
Vacuum with 24-in upright vacuum	1000 ft²	12.00 min
Vacuum with 26-in large-area push-type vacuum	1000 ft²	10.80 min
Vacuum with 28-in large-area push-type vacuum	1000 ft²	7.50 min
Vacuum with 30-in large-area push-type vacuum	1000 ft²	6.00 min
Vacuum with 32-in large-area push-type vacuum	1000 ft²	4.00 min
Vacuum with 34-in battery-powered vacuum	1000 ft²	6.50 min
Vacuum with backpack vacuum and 12-in orifice carpet tool	1000 ft²	21.60 min
Vacuum with backpack vacuum and 14-in orifice carpet tool	1000 ft²	19.80 min
Vacuum with backpack vacuum and 16-in orifice carpet tool	1000 ft²	18.00 min
Vacuum with backpack vacuum and 18-in orifice carpet tool	1000 ft²	16.20 min
Vacuum with backpack vacuum and 20-in orifice carpet tool	1000 ft²	14.40 min
Vacuum with backpack vacuum and 22-in orifice carpet tool	1000 ft²	12.60 min
Vacuum with backpack vacuum and 24-in orifice carpet tool	1000 ft²	10.80 min
Vacuum with scrap-trap-type vacuum with 12-in carpet tool	1000 ft²	12.00 min
Vacuum with scrap-trap-type vacuum with 16-in carpet tool	1000 ft²	11.00 min
Vacuum with tank-type/canister vacuum and 12-in orifice carpet tool	1000 ft²	24.00 min
Vacuum with tank-type/canister vacuum and 14-in orifice carpet tool	1000 ft²	22.20 min
Vacuum with tank-type/canister vacuum and 16-in orifice carpet tool	1000 ft²	20.40 min
Vacuum with tank-type/canister vacuum and 18-in orifice carpet tool	1000 ft²	18.60 min
Vacuum with tank-type/canister vacuum and 20-in orifice carpet tool	1000 ft²	16.80 min
Vacuum with tank-type/canister vacuum and 22-in orifice carpet tool	1000 ft²	15.00 min
Vacuum with tank-type/canister vacuum and 24-in orifice carpet tool	1000 ft²	13.20 min
Wet pickup with tank-type wet vacuum and 12-in orifice pickup tool	1000 ft²	30.00 min
Wet pickup with tank-type wet vacuum and 14-in orifice pickup tool	1000 ft²	28.20 min
Wet pickup with tank-type wet vacuum and 16-in orifice pickup tool	1000 ft²	26.40 min
Wet pickup with tank-type wet vacuum and 18-in orifice pickup tool	1000 ft²	24.60 min
Wet pickup with tank-type wet vacuum and 20-in orifice pickup tool	1000 ft²	22.80 min
Wet pickup with tank-type wet vacuum and 22-in orifice pickup tool	1000 ft²	21.00 min
Wet pickup with tank-type wet vacuum and 24-in orifice pickup tool	1000 ft²	19.20 min
Hard-floor care		
Apply floor finish using mop	1000 ft²	36.00 min
Apply floor finish using lambswool applicator	1000 ft²	30.00 min
Apply floor finish using gravity-feed applicator	1000 ft²	24.00 min
Apply floor seal using mop	1000 ft²	36.00 min
Apply floor seal using lambswool applicator	1000 ft²	30.00 min
Apply floor seal using gravity-feed applicator	1000 ft²	24.00 min
Clean baseboards with manual swivel cleaning tool and handle	100 linear ft	6.60 min
Clean baseboards with automatic rotary vertical brush machine	100 linear ft	3.00 min
Damp-mop with 12-oz mop head using single bucket and wringer	1000 ft²	16.80 min
Damp-mop with 12-oz mop head using double bucket and wringer	1000 ft²	15.60 min
Damp-mop with 16-oz mop head using single bucket and wringer	1000 ft²	14.40 min
Damp-mop with 16-oz mop head using double bucket and wringer	1000 ft²	13.20 min
Damp-mop with 24-oz mop head using single bucket and wringer	1000 ft²	12.00 min
Damp-mop with 24-oz mop head using double bucket and wringer	1000 ft²	10.80 min
Damp-mop with 32-oz mop head using single bucket and wringer	1000 ft²	9.60 min
Damp-mop with 32-oz mop head using double bucket and wringer	1000 ft²	8.40 min
Damp-mop with 18-in flat mop using single bucket and wringer	150 ft²	2.52 min
Dry-buff/polish with 175-r/min 12-in rotary floor machine	1000 ft²	40.20 min
Dry-buff/polish with 175-r/min 14-in rotary floor machine	1000 ft²	34.80 min
Dry-buff/polish with 175-r/min 17-in rotary floor machine	1000 ft²	30.00 min

TABLE 6-1   Cleaning Operation Time Estimate* (*Continued*)

Hard-floor care (*continued*)		
Dry-buff/polish with 175-r/min 20-in rotary floor machine	1000 ft^2	25.20 min
Dry-buff/polish with 175-r/min 24-in rotary floor machine	1000 ft^2	19.80 min
Dry-buff/polish with 350-r/min 17-in rotary floor machine	1000 ft^2	19.80 min
Dry-buff/polish with 350-r/min 20-in rotary floor machine	1000 ft^2	15.00 min
Dry-buff/polish with 350-r/min 24-in rotary floor machine	1000 ft^2	10.20 min
Dry-buff/polish with 1000+ r/min 17-in rotary floor machine	1000 ft^2	7.20 min
Dry-buff/polish with 1000+ r/min 20-in rotary floor machine	1000 ft^2	6.60 min
Dry-buff/polish with 1000+ r/min 24-in rotary floor machine	1000 ft^2	5.40 min
Dry-buff/polish with 1000+ r/min 27-in rotary floor machine	1000 ft^2	4.80 min
Dry-burnish with 2000+ r/min 17-in rotary floor machine	1000 ft^2	6.60 min
Dry-burnish with 2000+ r/min 20-in rotary floor machine	1000 ft^2	6.00 min
Dry-burnish with 2000+ r/min 24-in rotary floor machine	1000 ft^2	4.80 min
Dry-burnish with 2000+ r/min 27-in rotary floor machine	1000 ft^2	4.20 min
Dust-mop with 12-in mop using dust treatment chemical	1000 ft^2	13.20 min
Dust-mop with 18-in mop using dust treatment chemical	1000 ft^2	9.00 min
Dust-mop with 24-in mop using dust treatment chemical	1000 ft^2	7.20 min
Dust-mop with 30-in mop using dust treatment chemical	1000 ft^2	6.00 min
Dust-mop with 36-in mop using dust treatment chemical	1000 ft^2	4.80 min
Dust-mop with 42-in mop using dust treatment chemical	1000 ft^2	3.60 min
Dust-mop with 48-in mop using dust treatment chemical	1000 ft^2	2.40 min
Dust-mop with 60-in mop using dust treatment chemical	1000 ft^2	1.80 min
Dust-mop with 72-in mop using dust treatment chemical	1000 ft^2	1.20 min
Scrub with 175-r/min 12-in floor machine that requires separate wet pickup	1000 ft^2	48.00 min
Scrub with 175-r/min 14-in floor machine that requires separate wet pickup	1000 ft^2	40.20 min
Scrub with 175-r/min 17-in floor machine that requires separate wet pickup	1000 ft^2	31.20 min
Scrub with 175-r/min 20-in floor machine that requires separate wet pickup	1000 ft^2	27.00 min
Scrub with 175-r/min 24-in floor machine that requires separate wet pickup	1000 ft^2	23.40 min
Scrub with 350-r/min 17-in floor machine that requires separate wet pickup	1000 ft^2	19.80 min
Scrub with 350-r/min 20-in floor machine that requires separate wet pickup	1000 ft^2	16.80 min
Scrub with 350-r/min 24-in floor machine that requires separate wet pickup	1000 ft^2	13.20 min
Scrub using one-pass machine with 12-in twin cylindrical brushes and wet pickup	1000 ft^2	12.00 min
Scrub using one-pass machine with 24-in twin cylindrical brushes and wet pickup	1000 ft^2	6.00 min
Scrub with 17-in automatic scrubber that includes wet pickup	1000 ft^2	9.00 min
Scrub with 21-in automatic scrubber that includes wet pickup	1000 ft^2	7.80 min
Scrub with 24-in automatic scrubber that includes wet pickup	1000 ft^2	6.00 min
Scrub with 27-in automatic scrubber that includes wet pickup	1000 ft^2	5.40 min
Scrub with 32-in automatic scrubber that includes wet pickup	1000 ft^2	4.20 min
Scrub with 36-in automatic scrubber that includes wet pickup	1000 ft^2	3.00 min
Spray-buff with 175-r/min 12-in rotary floor machine and finish restorer	1000 ft^2	45.00 min
Spray-buff with 175-r/min 14-in rotary floor machine and finish restorer	1000 ft^2	40.20 min
Spray-buff with 175-r/min 17-in rotary floor machine and finish restorer	1000 ft^2	34.80 min
Spray-buff with 175-r/min 20-in rotary floor machine and finish restorer	1000 ft^2	30.00 min
Spray-buff with 175-r/min 24-in rotary floor machine and finish restorer	1000 ft^2	25.20 min
Spray-buff with 350-r/min 17-in rotary floor machine and finish restorer	1000 ft^2	25.20 min
Spray-buff with 350-r/min 20-in rotary floor machine and finish restorer	1000 ft^2	19.80 min
Spray-buff with 350-r/min 24-in rotary floor machine and finish restorer	1000 ft^2	15.00 min
Spray-buff with 1000+ r/min 17-in rotary floor machine and finish restorer	1000 ft^2	8.40 min
Spray-buff with 1000+ r/min 20-in rotary floor machine and finish restorer	1000 ft^2	7.80 min
Spray-buff with 1000+ r/min 24-in rotary floor machine and finish restorer	1000 ft^2	6.60 min
Spray-buff with 1000+ r/min 27-in rotary floor machine and finish restorer	1000 ft^2	6.00 min
Spray-buff with 2000+ r/min 17-in rotary floor machine and finish restorer	1000 ft^2	7.80 min
Spray-buff with 2000+ r/min 20-in rotary floor machine and finish restorer	1000 ft^2	7.20 min
Spray-buff with 2000+ r/min 24-in rotary floor machine and finish restorer	1000 ft^2	6.00 min
Spray-buff with 2000+ r/min 27-in rotary floor machine and finish restorer	1000 ft^2	5.40 min

TABLE 6-1   Cleaning Operation Time Estimate* (*Continued*)

Hard-floor care (*continued*)		
Strip with 175-r/min 17-in rotary floor machine that requires separate wet pickup	1000 ft²	79.80 min
Strip with 175-r/min 20-in rotary floor machine that requires separate wet pickup	1000 ft²	75.00 min
Strip with 350-r/min 17-in rotary floor machine that requires separate wet pickup	1000 ft²	52.80 min
Strip with 350-r/min 20-in rotary floor machine that requires separate wet pickup	1000 ft²	45.00 min
Strip with mop-on chemical that requires separate wet pickup	1000 ft²	18.00 min
Sweep with 8-in corn/synthetic broom	1000 ft²	25.20 min
Sweep with 12-in push broom	1000 ft²	15.00 min
Sweep with 16-in push broom	1000 ft²	12.00 min
Sweep with 18-in push broom	1000 ft²	10.80 min
Sweep with 24-in push broom	1000 ft²	8.40 min
Sweep with 30-in push broom	1000 ft²	6.00 min
Sweep with 36-in push broom	1000 ft²	4.80 min
Sweep with 42-in push broom	1000 ft²	3.60 min
Sweep with 48-in push broom	1000 ft²	2.40 min
Sweep with 24-in push sweeper machine	1000 ft²	6.00 min
Sweep with 30-in push sweeper machine	1000 ft²	5.40 min
Sweep with 36-in rider power sweeper machine	1000 ft²	3.00 min
Sweep with 42-in rider power sweeper machine	1000 ft²	1.80 min
Sweep with 60-in rider power sweeper machine	1000 ft²	0.60 min
Wet pickup with tank-type wet vacuum and 12-in orifice pickup tool	1000 ft²	27.00 min
Wet pickup with tank-type wet vacuum and 14-in orifice pickup tool	1000 ft²	25.20 min
Wet pickup with tank-type wet vacuum and 16-in orifice pickup tool	1000 ft²	23.40 min
Wet pickup with tank-type wet vacuum and 18-in orifice pickup tool	1000 ft²	21.60 min
Wet pickup with tank-type wet vacuum and 20-in orifice pickup tool	1000 ft²	19.80 min
Wet pickup with tank-type wet vacuum and 22-in orifice pickup tool	1000 ft²	18.00 min
Wet pickup with tank-type wet vacuum and 24-in orifice pickup tool	1000 ft²	16.20 min
Wet-mop and rinse with 12-oz mop using single bucket and wringer	1000 ft²	45.00 min
Wet-mop and rinse with 12-oz mop using double bucket and wringer	1000 ft²	42.00 min
Wet-mop and rinse with 16-oz mop using single bucket and wringer	1000 ft²	34.80 min
Wet-mop and rinse with 16-oz mop using double bucket and wringer	1000 ft²	31.80 min
Wet-mop and rinse with 24-oz mop using single bucket and wringer	1000 ft²	23.40 min
Wet-mop and rinse with 24-oz mop using double bucket and wringer	1000 ft²	20.40 min
Wet-mop and rinse with 32-oz mop using single bucket and wringer	1000 ft²	18.00 min
Wet-mop and rinse with 32-oz mop using double bucket and wringer	1000 ft²	15.00 min

Stairways and landings		
Sweep with push broom	150 ft²	4.50 min
Dust-mop using dust treatment chemical	150 ft²	3.60 min
Damp-mop with mop bucket and wringer	150 ft²	5.40 min
Vacuum with tank/canister vacuum	150 ft²	4.50 min
Vacuum with backpack vacuum	150 ft²	3.15 min
Vacuum with upright vacuum	150 ft²	5.85 min

Overhead services		
Ceiling acoustical: clean with spray-on chemical and extension handle	1000 ft²	84.00 min
Ceiling: wash manually with sponge using ladder and bucket	1000 ft²	168.00 min
Light fixture diffusers: remove and clean in ultrasonic dip and return	4 items	12.00 min
Light fixtures: damp wipe with trigger sprayer and cloth using ladder	1 item	3.00 min
Overhead surfaces: damp-wipe with trigger sprayer and cloth using ladder	150 ft²	9.90 min
Overhead surfaces: dust with backpack vacuum using ladder	150 ft²	16.20 min
Overhead surfaces: dust with duster and extension handle	150 ft²	0.90 min
Overhead surfaces: dust with tank/canister vacuum using ladder	150 ft²	17.10 min
Overhead surfaces: dust with hand-held duster vacuum using ladder	150 ft²	12.60 min
Vents: damp-wipe with trigger sprayer and cloth using ladder	1 item	0.50 min

TABLE 6-1   Cleaning Operation Time Estimate* (*Continued*)

Miscellaneous services		
Cubical curtain: remove and replace with clean curtain	1 item	3.00 min
Furniture, upholstered: shampoo with portable machine	25 ft²	12.45 min
Garbage/trash cans: wash with pressure washer	1 item	2.00 min
Garbage/trash cans: wash with special can mounting sprayer system	1 item	1.00 min
Light bulbs/tubes: replace using ladder	1 item	3.00 min
Mats, fatigue: wash with pressure washer	36 ft²	3.02 min
Mats, walk-off: wash with pressure washer	36 ft²	3.02 min
Wall/partition, fabric: vacuum with backpack vacuum and 12-in-orifice tool	120 ft²	3.24 min
Wall/partition, fabric: vacuum with tank/canister vacuum and 12-in-orifice tool	120 ft²	3.96 min
Walls: wash manually with wall mop, extension handle, bucket and wringer	120 ft²	23.98 min
Walls: wash manually with sponge, bucket and wringer using ladder	120 ft²	36.00 min
Walls: wash with wall washing machine using ladder	120 ft²	12.02 min

Windows		
Exterior: wash with brush, squeegee, and bucket	100 ft²	10.02 min
Exterior: wash with high-rise extension tools	100 ft²	13.20 min
Exterior: wash with trigger sprayer and cloth	100 ft²	11.40 min
Interior and exterior: wash with trigger sprayer and cloth	200 ft²	22.80 min
Interior: wash with brush, squeegee, and bucket	100 ft²	10.02 min
Interior: wash with trigger sprayer and cloth	100 ft²	11.40 min
Multiple pane: wash with trigger sprayer and cloth	1 pane	0.07 min

Walkways and steps		
Sweep with 8-in corn/synthetic broom	300 ft²	7.56 min
Sweep with 12-in push broom	300 ft²	4.50 min
Sweep with 16-in push broom	300 ft²	3.60 min
Sweep with 18-in push broom	300 ft²	3.24 min
Sweep with 24-in push broom	300 ft²	2.52 min
Sweep with 30-in push broom	300 ft²	1.80 min

* Reprinted with permission from International Sanitary Supply Association. These cleaning time estimates represent average cleaning times. Layout, obstacles, maintenance level desired, environmental conditions, etc., will affect cleaning time.

TRAINING TIPS

Some key tips to use in training are:

1. The longer a soil, stain, or coating is allowed to remain on the surface, the harder it will be to remove.
2. Quality products made by reputable manufacturers are usually best in the long run.
3. Chemicals should be measured and applied properly when required.
4. Two thin coats of a finish are better than one thick coat.
5. Always follow directions on labels or given in training, for safety as well as effectiveness.
6. Do not depend upon perfumed products to cover up odors. Clean thoroughly and kill germs with disinfectants or sanitizers and there will not be putrefaction odors.
7. Surfaces vary considerably and aging often changes them.
8. Use products and procedures that will do the best job and that are made for that particular surface.
9. Clean and maintain equipment in proper working order.

10. Learn how to use equipment to the best advantage.

11. Use products with the best blend of properties to do the job intended.

12. Read supplier directions, literature, trade books, and magazines for generating ideas and becoming aware of new products.

13. Talk with fellow custodians about common problems and situations.

14. Attend local, regional, or state training programs where possible.

15. Practice cooperating with other departments, and they will cooperate with you.

PLANT DESIGN

The actual design of the plant can play a key role in contributing to simpler maintenance. Too often, those responsible for maintaining the building are never consulted during the early planning of the building design. If given a chance, many experienced custodians can provide some good ideas in planning or rearranging plant areas. Following are some basic suggestions:

1. Custodial service closets should be provided on every floor and be centrally located to save walking time.

2. The closet should have sufficient shelving, floor space, a floor-level sink, hard surface floors and wall racks for mops and brooms, and other facilities that fit the needs.

3. Keys for doors, cabinets, machines, etc., should be planned and organized to make locking and unlocking by the custodians quick and easy as well as secure.

4. Access through one room, closet, or office to another should not be permitted.

5. Restrooms should be planned to make use and cleaning easy. (Wall-hung fixtures, placement of fixtures for sequential use, glazed walls, ceramic floors, and floor drains are good choices.)

6. Kick plates and push plates can help the appearance and cleanability of the custodial closet, restroom, and other doors.

7. Wall and furniture surfaces should be easily washable.

8. Entrance mats should be either recessed or integrated so that tracked-in soils are reduced.

9. Light-colored carpeting should not be laid where soiling will show quickly.

10. OSHA states in Standards and Interpretations 1910.22(b) aisles and passageways:

    (1) Where mechanical handling equipment is used, sufficient safe clearances shall be allowed for aisles, at loading docks, through doorways and wherever turns or passage must be made. Aisles and passageways shall be kept clear and in good repair, with no obstruction across or in aisles that could create a hazard.
    (2) Permanent aisles and passageways shall be appropriately marked.

EQUIPMENT

Cleaning equipment may vary somewhat according to type of surfaces, size of area, and other factors. Though it is tempting to order large versions of all equipment to apparently save time in covering large surface areas, there are many occasions when the larger equipment version will be too clumsy, heavy, and hard to adapt to the inevitable smaller areas. When it is impractical to own a variety of sizes to fit every need, consider a compromise size. Many units have attachments to broaden their usage in various areas; they may combine two or more functions and may be of the rider type. Details and demonstrations should always be obtained from equipment suppliers prior to commitment. All equipment should be cleaned after each use and kept in working order. Standardization of purchases can make training easier, requires stocking of fewer replacement parts, and makes possible larger quantity discounts. Following are some of the basic items:

1. Rotary *floor machines* for use in scrubbing, stripping, scouring, and polishing resilient and hard-surface floors as well as shampooing carpets. A 20-in model is most efficient.

2. Wet or dry *vacuums* are available in a number of different varieties. They may use a wand or squeegee, be lightweight backpack models, be extra quiet, contain filters, and be of various sizes or suction powers. Sweeper versions may be of the rider type.

3. *Automatic scrubber vacuums* to scrub soils and pick up the scrub solution.

4. Pressure sprayers for fast and effective cleaning.

5. Wall-washing equipment with many variations.

6. *Carpet extractors* for cleaning and rinsing on location.

7. *Compactors* for trash disposal.

8. Mops, buckets, wringers, carts, pads, sprayers, brushes, dispensers, and many other miscellaneous items.

CHEMICALS

Understanding some of the basic properties of the products used for cleaning, sanitation, and/or disinfecting should become one of the most important goals of maintenance personnel. Each product will perform certain tasks if used properly but have the potential to harm surfaces or personnel if improperly applied. Use only where and in the manner recommended. Observe the cautions on labels to preclude dangerous situations. Use the mildest abrasive, coupled with the mildest chemical possible, to complete the task and protect the surface.

A cleaning product may be either all-purpose for a variety of tasks or highly specialized. Mild *alkaline cleaners* will remove oily, greasy soils from any surface not harmed by water alone. Special alkaline cleaners are recommended for specific tasks such as stripping of floor coatings, window washing, carpet cleaning, wall washing, etc. Strong alkaline cleaners and degreasers are for heavy industrial soil buildups. *Acid cleaners* remove lime and hard-water deposits or rust stains from hard surfaces such as toilet bowls, metals, ceramics, and concrete. *Solvents* are generally used solely for spot removers in housekeeping.

Abrasive or mechanical action of some sort is usually necessary for the best cleaning procedures. Scouring powders, abrasive hand pads, abrasive floor pads, brushes, pressure sprayers, and simple "elbow grease" rubbing are supplements to the chemicals.

Germicides combined in certain cleaners can help control harmful microorganisms and unpleasant odors. This results in a healthful as well as a pleasant environment.

Floor coatings are of two types, sealer and finish. Sealers are generally designed for porous surfaces to smooth them out and make them easier to maintain. Concrete and terrazzo sealers stop dusting and may be used to provide a good base for a finish. Wood sealers bring out the natural beauty of wood, prevent penetration of stains, and provide gloss, nonslip, and other desirable properties. Resilient-tile sealers are mainly for porous tile and provide a good base for a finish. Note that some products may perform both as a sealer and finish.

Finishes generally are water-based and easily removed with a detergent stripping solution. The first finishes were made of natural waxes that required much dry buffing to retain a smooth, glossy appearance. The relatively recent chemical revolution has brought about many new coatings. Table 6-2 outlines specific solutions to floor finish problems.

TABLE 6-2 Solving Floor Finish Problems*

Problems

Black marking	Conspicuous formation of traffic lanes	Detergent resistance (poor)	Dirt pickup	Discoloration	Dullness in side aisles	Excessive foaming of polish or seal	Floor will not come clean during stripping	Gloss (poor initial)	Mop marks in finish	Gloss does not last	Pad marks in finish	Polish not leveling well	Polish not adhering to floor	Powdering or dusting	Scratching
■		■	■	■	■		■	■			■	■	■		
							■				■				
■	■			■			■								
					■										
			■								■	■	■		
		■		■			■	■			■	■	■		
		■	■	■			■		■		■	■	■		
			■					■	■						■
							■		■	■					
		■	■	■	■		■	■	■		■	■	■		
	■	■	■												
			■	■											■
			■	■											■
			■	■											■
							■		■		■				
		■					■		■		■	■	■		
■							■					■	■		
		■	■	■			■								
						■									
	■			■				■							
			■	■											
		■	■	■	■			■							
										■				■	
	■														
		■		■								■			
		■		■				■							
			■	■						■					
■	■	■	■	■				■							
		■		■	■		■		■			■	■	■	
			■			■									

* Most floor finishes are quality formulations, yet many outside factors can cause the finest products to do a poor job. This chart explains some of the problems and their solutions.

Source: Huntington Laboratories Inc., Huntington, Indiana.

Problems

The solutions	Scuffing excessively	Slipperiness	Streaked appearance	Tackiness	Uneven or dull film	Unpleasant odor	Water resistance (poor)	Whitening of polish film
Do not pour used polish or seal back into container	■		■	■	■	■	■	
Buff clean dry floor before applying polish or seal				■				
Use seal				■				
Do not use mop wringer								
Remove all previous coatings or factory finish	■			■				
Use floor neutralizer after stripping	■		■				■	
Check for product freezing damage	■		■	■	■	■		
Use fine or medium scrubbing pads rather than coarse			■	■				
Allow adequate drying time between coats				■	■			
Use clean equipment and applicator	■		■		■	■	■	
Remove excess wax buildup on surface	■							
Remove dust and loose soil more frequently								
Make sure adequate walkoff mats are available								■
Use automatic scrubber daily								
Check for proper ventilation			■	■				
Check for and remove soap or oil film from floor	■	■	■	■			■	■
Unstable plasticizer in tile—allow curing time	■		■					
Clean equipment properly after use			■		■			
Use stronger stripper and/or allow more dwell time	■							
Areas not being buffed often enough—check schedule		■	■					
Areas not being cleaned properly—check schedule							■	■
Mix cleaner according to directions								
Use a less aggressive buffing pad					■			
Feather new coats into old at edge of traffic lane							■	
Check for use of metal drum pump in polish—use plastic pump		■		■		■		
Check for foreign materials being used	■			■		■	■	■
Check for the use of too strong a cleaner	■			■				
Check for over use of polish		■	■		■			
Make sure you are recoating and using restorer as recommended	■		■				■	
Rinse floor thoroughly after stripping, deep scrubbing and cleaning				■				
Floor may not be properly stripped—restrip					■			

UNDERSTANDING OSHA'S RIGHT-TO-KNOW LAW

The original right-to-know law was passed by Congress in 1970. The law said that chemical manufacturers and importers must determine the physical and health hazards of each product they make or import. Then they must pass the information about these hazards on to users through material safety data sheets and container labels. As of May 23, 1988 employers in the nonmanufacturing sector were included and must be in compliance with provisions of the OSHA standards.

Most chemicals in use have been diluted. They are not nearly so dangerous as the concentrate form when they are put to use by the user employee. There are notable exceptions, and there is the possibility of dangerous situations occurring because of lack of knowledge or carelessness. A serious emphasis on communication and training will help people to know and then reduce the risk by sensible handling of the chemicals.

What Does the OSHA Standard Require?

Three particular groups are mentioned by the OSHA standard: chemical manufacturers, distributors, and importers. They are required to evaluate each of their chemicals for possible physical and health hazards and then communicate the information from the research on each chemical by material safety data sheets and product labels. Employers who use chemicals in their business are required to: develop a written hazard communication program, inform employees about hazardous chemicals at the time of initial assignment, and, whenever a new hazard is introduced to the area, maintain a list of hazardous chemicals used and an available file of material safety data sheets (MSDSs) for reference when needed. They are also required to conduct employee training that includes at least:

1. Methods and observations that may be used to detect the presence of a hazardous chemical in the work area.
2. Recognition of the physical and health hazards of chemicals in the work area.
3. Measures employees can take to protect themselves from these hazards.
4. Details of the hazard communication program developed by the employer—including an explanation of the labeling system and material safety data sheets.
5. Documentation of the training program and those in attendance.

It stands to reason that if hazardous chemical precautions are going to function, the employee must read labels and follow the directions and information presented and know where the MSDSs are filed and refer to them if an unusual situation requires it.

What Is a Hazardous Chemical?

Hazardous chemical means any chemical which is a physical hazard or a health hazard. The warning required relative to a hazardous chemical could be words, pictures, symbols, or combination of these appearing on a label or other appropriate form of warning which convey the hazards of the chemical in the container.

What Is on a Label?

Labels are the direct link in communication from the chemical source to the employee who will use the product. Seldom will it be necessary for the employee to refer to the MSDS. Although regulation requires ready access to the MSDS, it would be only an emergency situaation where such reference would be helpful. All the important, practical information is on the label.

Labeling problems sometimes occur when large containers of product are shipped and transfer is made into smaller unlabeled containers. If it is important to transfer products, labels with complete information are available for easy application to the new container. Even dispensers with silk-screened information are available for product when appropriate.

Labels provide the information needed for safe use of the chemical. They must include:

1. Identification of product
2. Active ingredients
3. Use information
4. Physical hazards
5. Health hazards
6. First-aid information
7. Storing and handling instructions
8. Basic protective clothing, equipment, and procedures that are recommended when working with this chemical
9. Name and address of the manufacturer

The labels must also:

1. Not be removed or defaced
2. Identify the material that may be hazardous
3. Warn of hazards in a consistent language:
   a. *Caution* is the least hazardous and indicates slight irritation from eye and skin contact with the concentrated chemical product.
   b. *Warning* is the next most hazardous and indicates moderate eye and skin irritation from the concentrated chemical.
   c. *Danger* is the most hazardous and indicates severe eye and skin irritation potential from the concentrated product.

Material Safety Data Sheets

The material safety data sheets (Fig. 6-1) must be available and are required from chemical manufacturers and importers for each hazardous chemical they produce or import. Employers in the manufacturing sector are required to have a material safety data sheet for each hazardous chemical which they use. Employers in the nonmanufacturing sector were required to be in compliance with the provisions for communication on hazardous materials by May 23, 1988.

The material on the MSDS will not be as helpful to the employee using the chemical as the product label. Nevertheless, the MSDS must be on file and accessible. In time of need for information not included on the label, the MSDS should be available for referral. The MSDS will:

1. Identify the source of the chemical
2. List the hazardous components
3. Give physical and chemical characteristics
4. Warn about possible physical hazards
5. Note the stability or possible reactivity of the product
6. List possible health hazards
7. Give precautions for safe handling
8. Suggest control measures and protective equipment and what to do in an emergency

Huntington.

MATERIAL SAFETY
DATA SHEET

MSDS DATE __10/01/91__
PRODUCT NO. __102915__

CUSTOMER
SEE
REVERSE
SIDE

DATE __12/25/91__

CUSTOMER NO. _____   INVOICE NO. _____

SECTION I - IDENTITY

MANUFACTURER'S NAME	EMERGENCY TELEPHONE NO.	ADDRESS (Number, Street, City, State and Zip Code)
Huntington Laboratories, Inc.	219/356-8100	970 East Tipton Street, Huntington, Indiana 46750

CHEMICAL NAME AND SYNONYMS	TRADE NAME AND SYNONYMS
N/A	BLUE BLAZES

CHEMICAL FAMILY	FORMULA
DETERGENT	N/A

SECTION II - HAZARDOUS INGREDIENTS

CAS NO.	PRINCIPAL HAZARDOUS COMPONENTS	%	ACGIH TLV	OSHA PEL
141-43-5	MONOETHANOLAMINE	1-10	3 PPM	3 PPM
	OTHER INGREDIENTS > OR = 3%:			
7732-18-5	WATER			

SECTION III PHYSICAL DATA

APPEARANCE AND ODOR	BLUE LIQUID, CLEAN AND FRESH ODOR	pH VALUE	10.2-11.2

SPECIFIC GRAVITY (H₂O=1)	PERCENT, VOLATILE BY VOLUME (%)	REACTIVITY IN WATER	EVAPORATION RATE
0.99	>99	NONE	(WATER = 1) 1

BOILING POINT (°F.)	SOLUBILITY IN WATER	VAPOR DENSITY (AIR=1)	VAPOR PRESSURE (mm Hg.)
212	100%	<1	17.5

SECTION IV - FIRE AND EXPLOSION DATA

FLASH POINT METHOD USED	FLAMMABLE LIMITS UPPER	LOWER	AUTO-IGNITION TEMP.	SPECIAL FIRE FIGHTING PROCEDURES
NONE, TCC	N/A	N/A	UNK	NONE

CONT:

EXTINGUISHING MEDIA   AS FOR SURROUNDING FIRE.

UNUSUAL FIRE AND EXPLOSION HAZARDS   NONE

SECTION V - PHYSICAL HAZARDS

STABILITY	UNSTABLE	STABLE	X	CONDITIONS TO AVOID	NONE

INCOMPATABILITY (MATERIALS TO AVOID)   STRONG ACIDS, OXIDIZERS

HAZARDOUS DECOMPOSITION PRODUCTS THERMAL DECOMPOSITION MAY YIELD OXIDES OF CARBON AND NITROGEN.

HAZARDOUS POLYMERIZATION	MAY OCCUR	WILL NOT OCCUR	X	CONDITIONS TO AVOID	NONE

SECTION VI - HEALTH HAZARD DATA

THRESHOLD LIMIT VALUE	SEE SEC II	EFFECTS OF OVEREXPOSURE	1. INHALATION	NO ADVERSE REACTION EXPECTED.

2. EYES CAUSES IRRITATION.

3. SKIN MAY CAUSE IRRITATION.

4. INGESTION MAY BE HARMFUL.

CHEMICAL LISTED AS CARCINOGEN OR POTENTIAL CARCINOGEN	• NATIONAL TOXICOLOGY PROGRAM	YES	NO	I.A.R.C. MONOGRAPHS	YES	NO	OSHA	YES	NO
			X			X			X

EMERGENCY AND FIRST AID PROCEDURES   1. INHALATION MOVE TO FRESH AIR.

2. EYES IMMEDIATELY FLUSH EYES WITH PLENTY OF WATER FOR AT LEAST 15 MINUTES. CALL A PHYSICIAN.

3. SKIN FLUSH SKIN WITH PLENTY OF WATER. REMOVE CONTAMINATED CLOTHING AND WASH BEFORE REUSE. CALL A PHYSICIAN IF IRRITATION PERSISTS.

4. INGESTION GIVE VICTIM A GLASS OF WATER. CALL A PHYSICIAN. NEVER GIVE ANYTHING BY MOUTH TO AN UNCONSCIOUS PERSON.

SECTION VII - SPILL OR LEAK PROCEDURES

STEPS TO BE TAKEN IN CASE MATERIAL IS RELEASED OR SPILLED	WASTE DISPOSAL METHOD
CONTAIN SPILL. DO NOT CONTAMINATE FOOD, FEED, OR WATER.	DISPOSE OF IN ACCORDANCE WITH ALL LOCAL, STATE, AND FEDERAL REGULATIONS.

SECTION VIII - SPECIAL PROTECTION INFORMATION

RESPIRATORY PROTECTION (SPECIFY TYPE)	NONE REQUIRED.	VENTILATION	LOCAL EXHAUST	MECH	SPECIAL	OTHER
				X		

PROTECTIVE GLOVES	RUBBER	EYE PROTECTION	SAFETY GLASSES	OTHER	NONE

SECTION IX - SPECIAL PRECAUTIONS

PRECAUTION TO BE TAKEN IN HANDLING AND STORING AVOID PRODUCT CONTACT WITH EYES, SKIN, AND CLOTHING. WASH THOROUGHLY AFTER HANDLING.

OTHER PRECAUTIONS KEEP OUT OF REACH OF CHILDREN.

FIGURE 6-1 Sample material safety data sheet.

Note that MSDSs: are required, must be accessible to the worker, and give all the information you need to work safety with the chemical.

It is essential to follow through in maintaining safety in the work place. A key element to safety and well-being in the work place is the employee. Reading the label does not ensure safety. Doing what it says will. The law means that employees have a right to know about chemical hazards where they work. But hazard communication can protect only if they:

1. Read labels and, when appropriate, material safety data sheets
2. Know where to find information about their chemicals
3. Follow warnings and instructions
4. Use the correct protective clothing and equipment when handling hazardous substances
5. Learn emergency procedures
6. Practice sensible, safe work habits

Our concern for hazards in the work place can, to a great extent, be minimized if we conform to the following simple rules:

1. Use common sense
2. Read the label
3. Follow the directions
4. Be considerate of others

Your Right to Know—A Summary

Chemical manufacturers and importers are required to:

- Evaluate products and determine whether there are any health hazards associated with using them.
- Communicate their findings by providing labels and material safety data sheets for each product they manufacture or import.

Employers are required to:

- Establish a written hazard communication program explaining how workers will be informed about hazards and how to handle them. The written program should be available for workers to read or review at all times.
- Label products appropriately.
- Obtain and keep available material safety data sheets for all products with physical or health hazards. These documents should be kept in a place where both workers and leadership can easily refer to them.
- Train employees to identify and deal with hazardous materials and make them aware of any new hazards introduced into the work area.

Employees should:

- Read labels, follow directions, and be knowledgeable about MSDS.
- Identify any hazardous materials and obtain the proper equipment to work with them safely.
- Use proper techniques to perform tasks and be familiar with appropriate emergency procedures.
- If they have questions, ask their supervisor.

The Hazard Communication Standard says you have a right to know about chemical hazards where you work, but remember, hazard communication can protect you only if you:

- Read labels and follow the directions.
- Know where to find information about your chemicals.
- Follow instructions and respect warnings.
- Use proper protective clothing and equipment when handling hazardous substances.
- Know what to do in an emergency.
- Use common sense and work safely.

OSHA COMPLIANCE

Understanding and Complying with OSHA's *Occupational Exposure to Bloodborne Pathogens: Final Rule*

Industries where workers are in contact with or handle blood and other potentially infectious materials *will* be affected by OSHA's *Occupational Exposure to Bloodborne Pathogens: Final Rule* (29 CFR 1910.1030). Over 500,000 establishments and 5,000,000 workers are estimated to be governed by this rule. OSHA has calculated that *occupational exposures* are responsible for 5800 to 6600 cases of hepatitis B (HBV) every year and believes that the majority of these cases can be avoided by following this standard. Compliance with this standard is estimated to prevent approximately 8800 occupational and nonoccupational cases of HBV infections per year. These cases could result in an estimated 190 deaths.

What Is the Final Rule?   On December 6, 1991 OSHA published its final rule on *occupational exposure* to bloodborne pathogens. This standard marks the end of a four-year rule-making process and produced the first comprehensive and specific OSHA standard to deal with HBV, AIDS, (HIV), and other bloodborne pathogens.

The standard specifies universal precautions, engineering and work practice controls, personal protective equipment, and housekeeping, combined with HBV vaccinations/post-exposure follow-up, hazard communication labels/signs, record keeping and training, to reduce *occupational exposure* for all employees exposed to blood and potentially infectious materials. Meeting these requirements is *not optional* to employers or employees: *it is now required by law.*

Who Is Affected?   Since there is no population free from the risk of HIV or HBV infection, *any employee* who has *occupational exposure* to blood or other potentially infectious material will be included in this standard. *Twenty-four industries* were identified for the regulatory impact and flexibility analysis, but the scope of this standard is in *no way limited* to employees in those job classifications.

States with state plans are required to adopt standards (within six months after the publication of the final standard) at least as effective as federal OSHA standards. The 23 states and 2 territories with state plans are: Alaska, Arizona, California, Connecticut, Hawaii, Indiana, Iowa, Kentucky, Maryland, Michigan, Minnesota, Nevada, New Mexico, New York, North Carolina, Oregon, Puerto Rico, South Carolina, Tennessee, Utah, Vermont, Virginia, the Virgin Islands, Washington, and Wyoming. In Connecticut and New York, the plans cover only state and local employees. Until the state plan is promulgated, interim protection is provided by the federal OSHA standard.

In states with *no* state plan, the public employees are not covered by the federal OSHA standard. Although state, county, and municipal employees are *not* covered by the federal OSHA standard, OSHA has urged these states to extend the protection of their requirements to public employees who have exposure to blood and other infectious materials. OSHA will refer complaints or inquiries to the state public health agency having jurisdiction over these health care facilities.

Exposure Control Plan.   The exposure control plan is a pivotal provision of the bloodborne standard. It requires the employer to identify the employees who will receive the training, protective equipment, vaccinations, and other provisions of the standard. The employer must identify the positions and task procedures where *occupational exposure* to blood and other potentially infectious materials can occur.

Methods of Compliance.   Methods of compliance shows the employer how to protect employees from the hazards of bloodborne pathogens and comply with the standard through universal precautions, engineering and work practice controls, personal protection equipment, housekeeping, and the handling of regulatory waste.

Vaccinations/Postexposure and Follow-Up

Hepatitis B vaccinations, postexposure evaluations, and follow-up are required by the employer for all employees who have occupational exposure or an exposure incident. This is to ensure that *all* employees are protected from infection. It also makes sure the employee receives appropriate medical follow-up after *each* exposure incident.

Hazard Communication.   Hazard communication requires that employees receive warning through labels, signs, and training in order to eliminate or minimize their exposure to bloodborne pathogens. Warning labels are to be fluorescent orange or orange-red with lettering or symbols in contrasting color and include the *biohazard* legend.

Record Keeping

The records must be kept for *each* employee covered by the Occupational Exposure of Bloodborne Pathogens Standard. Training records, medical evaluations and treatment are important to the employer in determining vaccination status and follow-up involving exposure.

Availability of Records.   The employer shall ensure that all records required to be maintained shall be made available on request to the assistant secretary of labor for Occupational Safety and Health Administration, the director of the National Institute for Occupational Safety and Health, U.S. Department of Health and Human Services, or designated representatives for copying and examination.

Compliance

It is *not* the responsibility of either the federal OSHA department of the state OSHA department to individually *notify public or private employers/employees of this standard.* Notification of the standard is done via press releases and publication in the *Federal Register.* Ignorance of the law is no excuse for not being in compliance.

BIBLIOGRAPHY

Edwards, J. K. P.: *Floors and Their Maintenance,* Butterworths, London, 1972.
Federal Register, vol. 52, no. 163, Monday, Aug. 24, 1987, Rules and Regulations.

Federal Register, vol. 56, no. 235, Friday, Dec. 6, 1991, Rules and Regulations.

Feldman, Edwin B.: *Building Design for Maintainability,* McGraw-Hill, New York, 1975.

Feldman, Edwin B.: *Housekeeping Handbook for Institutions, Business and Industry,* Frederick Fell Publishers, New York, 1978.

General Industry Standards and Interpretations, U.S. Department of Labor, Occupational Safety and Health Administration, 1977.

Meyers, Earl M.: "Standardized Housekeeping Program Improves Utilization of Manpower and Materials," *Maintenance Engineering,* October 1972.

Ruhlin, Robert R.: "Work Control: A Sure Way to Improve Building Maintenance," *Buildings,* February 1974.

Sack, Thomas F.: *A Complete Guide to Building and Plant Maintenance,* Prentice-Hall, Englewood Cliffs, N.J., 1971.

Sipes, Sherrill F., Jr.: "Plan to Manage Your Maintenance Program," *Buildings,* May 1971.

"292 Cleaning Times," International Sanitary Supply Association Inc. (ISSA), Lincolnwood, Ill.

SECTION 15

ENERGY CONSERVATION

James L. Davis
Consulting Engineer
San Rafael, California

INTRODUCTION

Companies today can increase profitability and productivity and achieve competitive advantage through effective energy management programs. Some of the best of these are simple and inexpensive to implement. In one company, an inexpensive awareness program was initiated to inform all employees of the dollar cost of failure to turn off lights and other equipment. The company saw an immediate decrease in lighting energy of 50 percent and a decrease in energy for major equipment of 86 percent, an overall saving of over $300,000 per year with no investment in equipment.

The key to success is *commitment from all levels of the organization,* from the CEO and top executives to plant managers and engineers to workers in the field. It is common for a facility to allocate 3 to 10 percent of its annual energy budget to administration of an energy management program.

The effort to conserve energy must never be allowed to interfere with production or to cause discomfort or inconvenience to workers. If it does, the program will be doomed to failure.

ORGANIZATION FOR ENERGY MANAGEMENT

The first step in organizing an energy management program is to develop a clear statement of the organization's policy about energy efficiency, waste, and the lengths to which the company is willing to go to promote efficiency and control waste. This will form the basis for a plan of action.

In order for the effort to be effective, energy management must be given the same importance and accountability as management of any other cost or profit center. Responsibility for execution of the energy management plan must be clearly assigned, preferably not as an auxiliary duty to someone who is already occupied with other work. If the responsible person does not have the technical knowledge needed, arrangements should be made to obtain the services of a qualified consultant. Management should set the goals, but the responsibility for results should rest at the lowest level possible.

To provide a good chance for success, top management must allocate adequate resources and ensure that energy information is distributed to all parts of the organization. This information should include:

- The amount of energy used by individual departments or functional areas
- The cost of that energy
- The importance of energy to job viability
- What energy conservation can mean to operations
- The relationship between production rates and energy use
- The benefits, such as greater comfort, to be gained by support of energy management programs

In addition, company management should provide necessary support to achieve results and monitor cost effectiveness of the program.

If possible, support of energy management efforts should be made part of each supervisor's job description and a point in performance evaluation. If the supervisors understand that top management considers energy management an important subject, they will motivate employee interest and cooperation.

DEVELOPMENT OF AN ENERGY PLAN

Once the policy and resources are in place, a plan must be developed to implement the policy. The plan must contain measurable goals for conservation and/or cost reduction. These goals must be based on a thorough understanding of the facility's energy costs. To achieve the necessary understanding of current and historical energy costs, the company should establish a system of energy accounting.

Energy Accounting

A system for energy accounting should do the following:

- Collect a database of past energy usage and cost.
- Establish a base year for comparison.
- Standardize data as much as possible. (To address the consistent expression of energy consumption parameters, use ASHRAE Standard 105-1984, *Standard Methods of Measuring and Expressing Building Energy Performance.*)
- Establish a use per square foot, per occupant, or per unit of production or a sales basis.
- Adjust for degree-day differences.
- Account for changes in occupancy.
- Adopt energy accounting procedures for future use.

It is sometimes useful to show the energy use of various functional areas in the form of a pie chart as shown in Fig. 1-1. The energy might be expressed in terms of Btus or Dollars, or both.

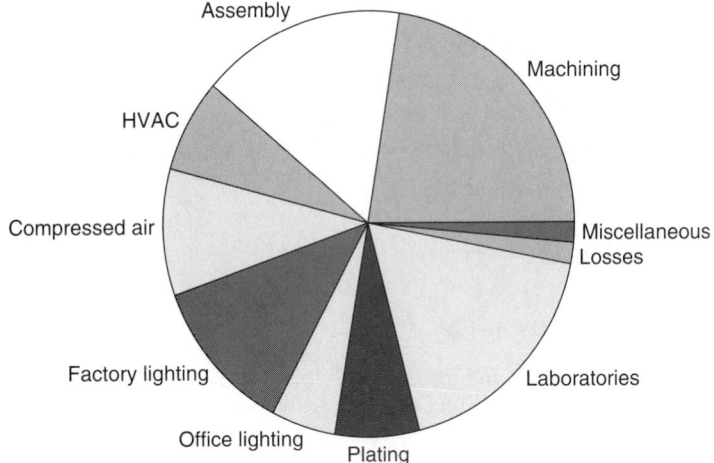

FIGURE 1-1   Typical distribution of energy use for an industrial facility.

Multiple Energy Sources

Consider the characteristics of the various sources for energy available at each facility, including:

- Dependability of supply
- Transportation
- Cost and pricing formulas
- Other costs of use (pollution controls, ash disposal, etc.)
- Quantity used (energy units and dollars)

Rate Structures

Study the utility rate structures that apply to each facility. Work with utility personnel to ensure that the most effective methods of metering and billing are used in each case. Be sure to evaluate the peak demand and time-of-use charges applied by most utilities.

Energy Audits

All facilities and functional areas should be subject to thorough energy audits to aid in understanding energy use patterns. The audits should consider general building information, historical energy consumption data, and energy systems data.

To the extent that it is feasible, energy systems should be surveyed from the end use back to the source. This approach will give the best understanding of the systems and their opportunities for energy savings.

Energy Conservation Opportunities (ECOs)

To take advantage of ECOs, company personnel should:

- Identify applicable opportunities
- Generate as many ideas as possible
- Use brainstorming techniques
- Evaluate each opportunity, considering:
    Rate of return (e.g., simple payback, life cycle costing)
    Total savings possible (direct cost and cost avoidance)
    Initial cost
    Possible side benefits (e.g., safety, comfort, improved productivity)
    Possible increased costs
    Risk of failure
- Prioritize ECOs in terms of the results expected and resources required

Existing Conservation Measures

Survey conservation measures that have already been implemented and determine their initial effectiveness. Target these measures for follow-up evaluation to assure that they are still functioning properly and make repairs or adjustments if needed.

Management Report

Assemble a list of recommended measures and make a report to management estimating the benefits to be achieved and the resources required, particularly management involvement, manpower, and capital.

Capital may be available from many sources. The combination of funding sources to be used will materially affect the program, but such decisions are generally made by upper management. Some common sources of funds include:

- Operating profits or new investment
- Loans
- Restructured budget priorities
- Energy cost savings and utility rebates
- Shared savings plans with outside firms

Schedule

Develop a priority schedule for implementation of conservation measures that have been approved by management.

IMPLEMENTATION OF PLAN

The key to a successful energy management program, obviously, is effective and organized implementation, which should do the following:

- Accomplish conservation measures.
- Maintain conservation measures once they are operational.
- Reevaluate the program periodically in view of changing needs in the facility and current economic trends.

- Provide sufficient instrumentation and metering to allow the energy manager to track the performance of conservation measures. At a minimum, he or she should be able to measure the energy consumption of each facility or functional area on a periodic basis.

- Establish on-going accounting in the energy system to continue documentation of results and to indicate additional opportunities.

- Continue energy awareness communication to all levels of the organization.

CONSERVATION MEASURES AND STRATEGIES

The number of measures and strategies available is extremely large. A thorough discussion of them is well beyond the scope of this chapter. Consequently, you will not become an expert on the subject from this chapter alone, but you will be introduced to a number of approaches to better energy efficiency.

As mentioned earlier, many energy conservation strategies are extremely simple, such as reminding people to turn off the lights when they leave the room, or installing occupancy sensors or time clocks to do it for them. Others might include manually or mechanically changing the set points for heating and cooling in response to changes in occupancy or outside temperature, or using time clocks to turn the systems off completely when the facility is not in use. Equipment and processes should be checked to see that they are turned off when not needed.

Steam Systems

Steam systems are subject to losses from boiler combustion inefficiency, which can be helped by keeping the burner unit in proper adjustment. Modern boiler controls that control not only combustion parameters but blowdown and, in some cases, fuel conditioning can improve overall boiler efficiency. Setback controls that reduce boiler operating temperature as outdoor temperature increases can reduce fuel consumption. The steam distribution system can be a source of losses from leakage and inadequate insulation. Another prevalent source of steam system losses is outmoded or poorly maintained steam traps. While it is not a simple project, tremendous savings in distribution losses are possible by rearranging the steam piping system. For example, a part of the facility that requires long piping runs might be given an independent boiler disconnected from the central system, thereby reducing losses.

Ventilation

Where significant amounts of air must be exhausted from the facility, keep in mind that such air is already conditioned to indoor temperature. Air-to-air heat exchangers can allow the makeup air to be preheated or cooled by the exhaust stream, thus reducing the load on the heating or cooling equipment. Processes, machinery, and operations should be audited to minimize the amount of heat or cooling they add to the building and to assure that excessive ventilation is not being used. (See Chap. 5-1, Heating and Ventilating.)

HVAC

HVAC systems provide many opportunities for energy conservation, such as:

- Changing operating temperatures with demand
- Turning equipment off when not needed
- Using outside air for heating or cooling (when the situation permits)

- Using the cooling tower as an evaporative cooler to cool circulating water without running the chiller
- Using variable speed fans and pumps to reduce energy consumption during periods of low demand
- Cycling fans and chillers OFF for a percentage of the time (which will reduce energy consumption with no noticeable effect on building comfort when the load is less than peak [most of the time])
- Using waste heat or cold from processes (e.g., to heat or cool air for the building directly or to operate absorption chillers)
- Replacing chiller capacity with modern two-stage evaporative cooling equipment (which can, in many areas, produce energy reductions for cooling of up to 75 percent)

All of these measures assume that the system makes efficient use of energy. If not, thought should be given to conversion of the whole system to a more efficient type. These conversions frequently pay for themselves quickly in energy savings.

Building Shell

The building shell should be examined for opportunities to insulate walls, roof, and floor adequately for the climate and convert windows and doors to low thermal conduction types. Eliminate infiltration of outside air, particularly around windows and doors; all air should come in through the ventilation system. Provide shading for windows to control solar heat gains.

Lighting*

Since lighting represents 35 to 50 percent of the energy consumption of most buildings, the impact of energy conservation efforts in this area can be substantial, affecting not only energy charges but also demand charges. Most of the energy fed into the lighting system ends up as heat in the space. Therefore, energy conserved in lighting also benefits air conditioning costs by reducing heat load. Today it is possible to practice energy conservation by using more efficient light sources while maintaining safety, security, and employee morale. See Fig. 1-2.

Following is a list of lamps currently available and descriptions of their efficiency:

- Incandescent lamps are one of the least efficient light sources available, producing about 24 lumens of light for each watt of electricity they consume. They have the lowest first cost and are easiest to install. They should be replaced with more efficient lamps wherever possible.
- Tungsten halogen lamps are not much more efficient at 25 lumens per watt and their first cost makes them even less desirable than incandescents.
- Mercury vapor lamps with 63 lumens per watt are a substantial improvement, but still not high enough to be recommended.
- High-efficiency fluorescent lamps with electronic ballasts can deliver up to 100 lumens per watt. This makes them a good choice for many applications.
- Metal halide and high-pressure sodium lamps deliver 125 to 140 lumens per watt and are increasing in popularity for many applications.
- Low-pressure sodium lamps currently deliver about the highest efficiency available with a peak of 200 lumens per watt. They should always be considered when designing a lighting installation.

---

* See also Chap. 3-5.

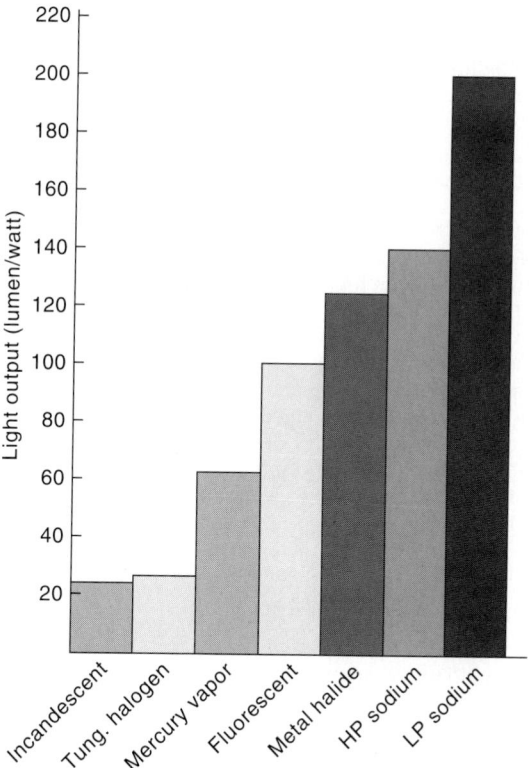

FIGURE 1-2   Energy efficiencies for various light sources.

Unfortunately, the selection of lighting equipment for an application is not as simple as just choosing the one with the highest energy efficiency. Factors such as color rendition, flicker, start-up time, sizes available, aesthetics, glare, lamp life, first cost, and so on are often important in lighting choices. The best lighting choices are those that provide the optimal compromise among the many criteria.

Almost as important as the efficiency of the lighting equipment is the operating schedule for the lighting. If lighting is being operated when it is not needed, for example, in an empty conference room, additional control strategies should be considered to correct this.

Load Shifting

In the case of electrical energy, the cost is usually made up of two components: the charge for the amount of energy consumed (including the charge imposed by the utility for the peak load [the highest load metered]) and the time of day when the energy is used. The overall cost of energy can be lowered by using strategies that even out the load by limiting demand peaks, for example, by turning off nonessential equipment to prevent the building load from rising above some predetermined level (load shedding). To lower peak demands, it is sometimes practical to install a generator in the facility to provide part of the necessary power at times of high use (peak shaving). Consider performing some operations at times when the time-of-use charges do not apply, usually late at night.

A system that uses both of these approaches is called thermal storage, which involves the manufacture of ice or chilled brine at night (when the time-of.use charges do not apply) to use for air conditioning the next day. This reduces the amount of energy used by the chillers when the building load is the highest and, thus, minimizes peak load charges.

Computerized Energy Management

As can be seen from the previous paragraphs, energy management involves the monitoring and control of a large number of system parameters. These can become difficult tasks if they are attempted manually. A much better approach is to establish a computerized monitoring system for the entire facility, which would also use the collected information to manipulate system parameters to optimize energy utilization. Care must be taken that the system not be allowed to impair occupant comfort, safety, or productivity.

A computerized energy management system provides energy cost savings through optimization techniques and reduced usage. It can also increase staff efficiency through centralized monitoring and control of energy use. The economic payback of such systems comes from the lowered energy costs and increased staff efficiency and productivity.

Most of these systems allow simple integration of all types of equipment and services under the control of one central system. Some typical system features include:

- Electric load shedding, smoothing, and cycling
- Optimized equipment start and stop
- Building precooling
- Zone temperature night setback
- Outside air control
- Hot and chilled water temperature optimization
- Weather data collection
- System trending
- Monitoring of energy consumption

Consult your local utility for recommendations relevant to your plant.

THE MAINTENANCE FUNCTION: BASIC EQUIPMENT AND SUPPLIES

SECTION 16

MAINTENANCE AND REPAIR TECHNOLOGY

CHAPTER 16-1
WELDING, CUTTING, BRAZING, AND SOLDERING

Howard B. Cary
Senior Advisor, Welding Technology
Hobart Bros. Co.
Troy, Ohio

GLOSSARY*

Alternating current An electric current that reverses its direction at regularly recurring intervals.

Ammeter An instrument for measuring electric current in amperes by an indicator activated by the movement of a coil in a magnetic field or by the longitudinal expansion of a wire carrying the current.

Arc blow The deflection of an electric arc from its normal path because of magnetic forces.

Arc length The distance between the tip of the electrode and the weld puddle.

Arc voltage The voltage across the welding arc.

As-welded The condition of weld metal, welded joints, and weldments after welding, but prior to any subsequent thermal, mechanical, or chemical treatments.

Backing A material (base metal, weld metal, copper, carbon, ceramic, or granular material) or device placed at the root of a weld joint for the purpose of supporting molten weld metal.

Backstep sequence A longitudinal sequence in which weld passes are made in the direction opposite to the progress of welding.

Base metal (material) The metal (material) to be welded, brazed, soldered, or cut.

Bevel angle The angle formed between the prepared edge of a member and a plane perpendicular to the surface of the member.

Braze welding A welding process variation in which a filler metal, having a liquidus above 840°F (450°C) and below the solidus of the base metal, is used. Unlike brazing, in braze welding the filler metal is not distributed in the joint by capillary action.

Brazing A group of welding processes that produces coalescence of materials by heating them to the brazing temperature in the presence of a filler metal having a liquidus above 840°F (450°C) and below the solidus of the base metal. The filler metal is distributed between the closely fitted faying surfaces of the joint by capillary action.

Cast iron A wide variety of iron-base materials containing carbon 1.7 to 4.5 percent; silicon, 0.5 to 3 percent; manganese, 0.2 to 1.3 percent; phosphorus, 0.8 percent max.; sulfur, 0.2 percent max.; molybdenum, nickel, chromium, and copper can be added to produce alloyed cast irons.

Consumable insert Preplaced filler metal that is completely fused into the joint root and becomes part of the weld.

Crack A fracture-type discontinuity characterized by a sharp tip and high ratio of length and width to opening displacement.

---

* Based on American Welding Society definitions.

Crater   A depression at the termination of a weld bead.

Cylinder   A portable container used for transportation and storage of a compressed gas.

Deflect   A discontinuity or discontinuities that by nature or accumulated effect (for example total crack length) render a part or product unable to meet minimum applicable acceptance standards or specifications. This term designates rejectability.

Depth of fusion   The distance that fusion extends into the base metal or previous pass from the surface melted during welding.

Direct-current electrode negative (DCEN)   The arrangement of direct-current arc welding leads in which the workpiece is the positive pole and the electrode is the negative pole of the welding arc.

Direct-current electrode positive (DCEP)   The arrangement of direct-current arc welding leads in which the workpiece is the negative pole and the electrode is the positive pole of the welding arc.

Discontinuity   An interruption of the typical structure of a weldment, such as lack of homogeneity in the mechanical, metallurgical, or physical characteristics of the material or weldment. *A discontinuity is not necessarily a defect.*

Duty cycle   The percentage of time during an arbitrary test period, usually 10 min, during which a power supply can be operated at its rated output without overheating.

Electrode (arc welding)   A component of the welding circuit through which current is conducted and that terminates at the arc, molten conductive slag, or base metal.

Face reinforcement   Weld reinforcement at the side of the joint from which welding was done.

Filler metal   The metal to be added in making a welded, brazed, or soldered joint.

Flux   Material used to prevent, dissolve, or facilitate removal of oxides and other undesirable surface substances.

Globular transfer (arc welding)   The transfer of molten metal in large drops from a consumable electrode across the arc.

Groove   An opening or channel in the surface of a part or between two components which provides space to contain a weld.

Groove radius   The radius used to form the shape of a J- or U-groove weld joint.

Groove weld   A weld made in the groove between the workpieces. The standard types of groove welds are shown in the next section.

Hard facing   A surfacing variation in which surfacing metal is deposited to reduce wear.

Heat-affected zone   That portion of the base metal which has not been melted, but whose mechanical properties or microstructure have been altered by the heat of welding, brazing, soldering, or cutting.

Inert gas   A gas that normally does not combine chemically with materials.

Interpass temperature   In a multipass weld, the temperature of the weld area between weld passes.

Kerf   The width of the cut produced during a cutting process.

Joint penetration   The depth a weld extends from its face into a joint, exclusive of reinforcement.

Liquidus   The lowest temperature at which a metal or an alloy is completely liquid.

Manifold   A multiple header for interconnection of gas or fluid sources with distribution points.

Melting range   The temperature range between solidus and liquidus.

Melting rate   The weight or length of electrode melted in a unit of time.

Open-circuit voltage   The voltage between the output terminals of the welding machine when no current is flowing in the welding circuit.

Overlap   The protrusion of weld metal beyond the weld toe or weld root.

Pass   A single longitudinal progression of a welding operation along a joint of weld deposit. The result of a pass is a weld bead.

Peening   The mechanical working of metals using impact blows.

Penetration   The distance the fusion zone extends below the surface of the part(s) being welded.

Pool   That portion of a weld that is molten at the place the heat is applied.

Porosity   Cavity-type discontinuities formed by gas entrapment during solidification.

Postheating   The application of heat to an assembly after welding, brazing, soldering, thermal spraying, or thermal cutting.

Preheating   The application of heat to the base metal immediately before welding, brazing, soldering, thermal spraying, or cutting.

Procedure qualification   The demonstration that welds made by a specific procedure can meet prescribed standards.

Size of weld   *Groove weld:* The joint penetration (depth of chamfering plus the root penetration when specified). *Fillet weld:* For equal fillet welds, the leg length of the largest isosceles right triangle which can be inscribed within the fillet-weld cross section. For unequal fillet welds, the leg lengths of the largest right triangle which can be inscribed within the fillet-weld cross section.

Soldering   A group of welding processes that produces coalescence of materials by heating them to the soldering temperature and by using a filler metal having a liquidus not exceeding 840°F (450°C) and below the solidus of the base metals. The filler metal is distributed between the closely fitted faying surfaces of the joint by capillary action.

Solidus   The highest temperature at which a metal or alloy is completely solid.

Spatter   The metal particles expelled during fusion welding that do not form a part of the weld.

Spray transfer   Metal transfer in which molten metal from a consumable electrode is propelled axially across the arc in small droplets.

Stress-relief heat treatment   Uniform heating of a structure or a portion thereof to a sufficient temperature to relieve the major portion of the residual stresses, followed by uniform cooling.

Track weld   A weld made to hold parts of a weldment in proper alignment until the final welds are made.

Tensile strength   The greatest longitudinal stress (measured in pounds per square inch) a substance can bear without tearing apart.

Throat of a fillet weld   *Theoretical throat:* The distance from the beginning of the joint root perpendicular to the hypotenuse of the largest right triangle that can be inscribed within the cross section of a fillet weld. This dimension is based on the assumption that the root opening is equal to zero. *Actual throat:* The shortest distance between the weld root and the face of a fillet weld. *Effective throat:* The minimum distance minus any convexity between the weld root and the face of a fillet weld.

Tungsten electrode   A nonfiller metal electrode used in arc welding or cutting, made principally of tungsten.

Underbead crack   A crack in the heat-affected zone generally not extending to the surface of the base metal.

Undercut   A groove melted into the base metal adjacent to the weld toe or weld root and left unfilled by weld metal.

Weaving   A technique of depositing weld metal in which the electrode is oscillated.

Weld   A localized coalescence of metals or nonmetals produced either by heating the materials to the welding temperature, with or without the application of pressure, or by the application of pressure alone and with or without the use of filler metal.

Welder   One who performs a manual or semiautomatic welding operation.

Welder certification   Certification in writing that a welder has produced welds meeting prescribed standards.

Welder performance qualification   The demonstration of a welder's ability to produce welds meeting prescribed standards.

Welding procedure   The detailed methods and practices involved in the production of a weldment.

Weld pass   A single progression of welding along a joint. The result of a pass is a weld bead or layer.

Weld pool   The localized volume of molten metal in a weld prior to its solidification as weld metal.

Wire feed speed   The rate of speed at which wire is consumed in arc welding.

BASIC PRINCIPLES

Welding is the most economical and efficient way to permanently join metal. It is the only way of joining two or more pieces of metal to make them act as a single piece. Welding can be used to join almost all the commercial metals. However, some metals are more difficult to weld

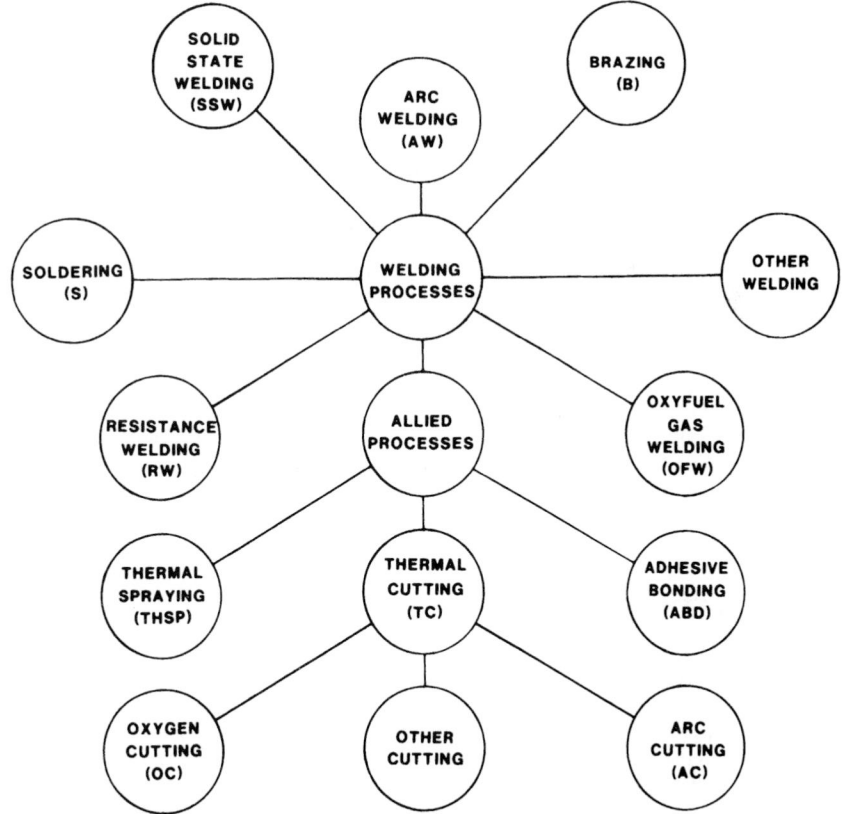

FIGURE 1-1   American Welding Society master chart of welding and allied processes.

than others. There are more than 100 different welding processes and process variations which include brazing, soldering, and thermal cutting. These are broken into seven groups of welding processes and six groups of allied processes, as shown by the master chart of welding and allied processes, Fig. 1-1.

Many of the processes can be applied in different ways; i.e., they may be applied as manual, semiautomatic, mechanized, automatic, or automatic with adaptive control processes. Manual process applications require a high degree of skill, while automatic welding requires a minimum amount of welding skill. This is important with respect to training and qualification of personnel.

There are certain fundamentals which must be grasped to properly understand welding. Some of the most important are as follows:

The *weld joint* relates to the junction arrangement of the members to be joined. There are five basic types of joints, similar to those used by other crafts. They are the butt joint, the corner joint, the edge joint, the lap joint, and the T joint. They are sometimes used in combination.

Another basic concept relates to the *type of weld.* See Fig. 1-2. The weld is the localized coalescence of metal at the specific junction of the parts. The many different types of welds are best described by the shape they show in cross section. Most popular are the *fillet* welds, followed by the *groove* weld. There are seven basic types of groove welds: square groove, bevel groove, V groove, J groove, U groove, flare V, and flare bevel. Many of these can be used in combination as double-groove welds. In order to completely describe a weld joint, the weld and the joint should both be defined (a "single V-welded butt joint," for example). See Fig. 1-3.

Some welds use *filler metals.* In the resistance-welding processes, filler materials are not used. In the arc-welding processes filler metals are usually used. When filler metal is used, it must be properly specified in order to produce a weld joint of the specified strength.

The various *welding positions* (see Fig. 1-4) are particularly important when the welder's skill is involved. There are four basic positions: flat, horizontal, overhead, and vertical. These positions are rather obvious, but specific definitions are used. In identifying welding procedures, the position of the weld is highly important.

Another important factor is the *type of process:* electric or some other. The arc-welding processes are all electrically related, as are the resistance-welding processes. For gas welding, heat is obtained by chemical reactions of one type or another. In other cases, pressure is used, and it can be applied in various ways. In general, it is best to refer to the master chart of processes and then to the specific process that is to be employed.

Each process has its specific advantages and rationale for use. Many of them also have specific shortcomings and cannot be used effectively in certain applications.

The safety and health of welders must always be considered. Welding is no more dangerous than other industrial occupations, provided that the recommended safety precautions are followed. These precautions are given here and also appear on labels of filler metals and fluxes and on equipment for making welds.

This chapter describes the more popular welding processes in sufficient detail so that they can be properly understood and effectively applied. Included also are a description of various processes, a discussion of safety and health aspects, and guides to selecting filler material for welding various metals.

WELDING SAFETY AND HEALTH

Welding is no more hazardous than any other metalworking occupation, provided that proper precautionary measures are followed. This requires continuous awareness of possibilities of danger and habitual safety precaution by the welders. They have an obligation to learn safe practices, to obey safety rules and regulations, and to work in a safe manner. It is the responsibility of supervisors to enforce safety rules and regulations. The two most important regulations concerning the subject are the American National Standard Z49.1, *Safety in Welding and Cutting,* available from the American Welding Society (AWS), and the Occupational

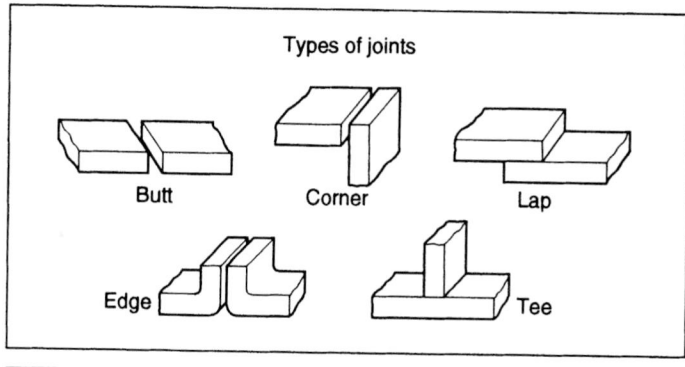

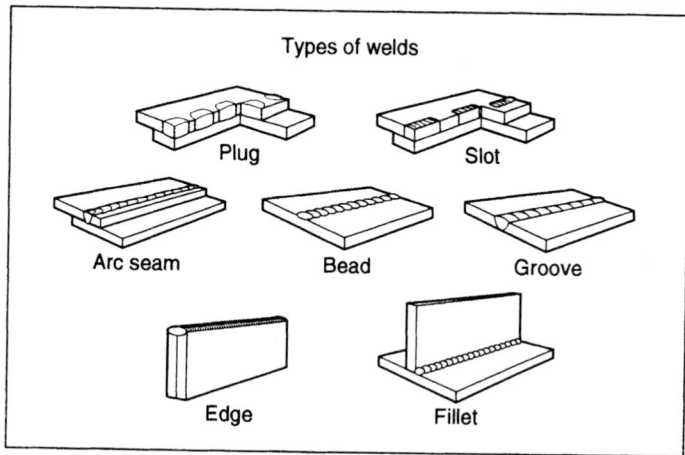

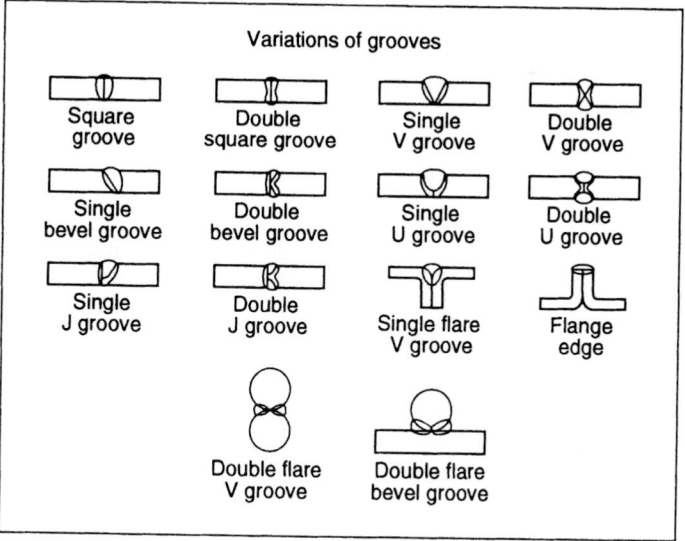

FIGURE 1-2 Types of welds, joints, and grooves.

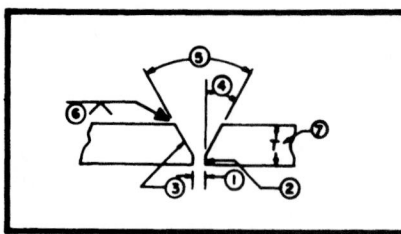 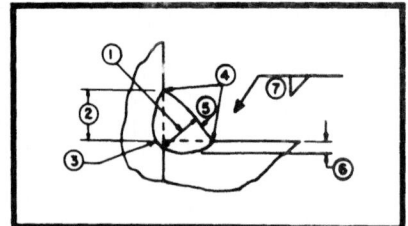

1. ROOT OPENING (RO): The separation between the members to be joined at the root of the joint.
2. ROOT FACE (RF): Groove face adjacent to the root of the joint.
3. GROOVE FACE: The surface of a member included in the groove.
4. BEVEL ANGLE (A): The angle formed between the prepared edge of a member and a plane perpendicular to the surface of the member.
5. GROOVE ANGLE (A): The total included angle of the groove between parts to be joined by a groove weld.
6. SIZE OF WELD(S): The joint penetration (depth of chamfering plus root penetration when specified).
7. PLATE THICKNESS (T): Thickness of plate welded.

1. THROAT OF A FILLET WELD: The shortest distance from the root of the fillet weld to its face.
2. LEG OF A FILLET WELD: The distance from the root of the joint to the toe of the fillet weld.
3. ROOT OF WELD: Deepest point of useful penetration in a fillet weld.
4. TOE OF A WELD: The junction between the face of a weld and the base metal.
5. FACE OF WELD: The exposed surface of a weld on the side from which the welding was done.
6. DEPTH OF FUSION: The distance that fusion extends into the base metal.
7. SIZE OF WELD(S): Leg length of the fillet.

FIGURE 1-3   Common terms applied to a weld. (*American Welding Society.*)

Safety and Health Administration (OSHA) Safety and Health Standard 22CFR1910, available from the U.S. Department of Labor.

General Safety Rules

To protect yourself and others, read and understand these rules.

1. Electric shock
   a. Electric shock can kill.
   b. Do not touch live electric parts.
   c. Make sure that the welding equipment is properly installed, the case is grounded, and the equipment is in good working condition.
   d. Avoid welding in a wet or damp area. If this is unavoidable, wear rubber boots and stand on a dry, insulated platform. Stay dry.
   e. Always use insulated electrode holders. When it is not in use, hang the holder on brackets provided. Never place it under your arm.
   f. Make sure that all electric connections are tight, clean, dry, and insulated.
   g. Never attempt to repair electric equipment inside the welding machine or inside control panels, etc.
   h. Make sure that power cables are insulated. Make sure that welding cables are insulated. Do not wrap cables around your body.
   i. Do not use cables with frayed, cracked, or bare spots in the insulation. If there is a splice in the welding cable, make sure it is tight and insulated.
2. Arc radiation
   a. Arc rays can injure eyes and burn skin.
   b. Protect your eyes from the rays of the arc. Wear a head shield with the proper filter shade when welding or cutting. See lens shade selector chart, Table 1-1.
   c. Be sure protective equipment is in good condition. Wear safety glasses in the work area at all times.

Welding positions

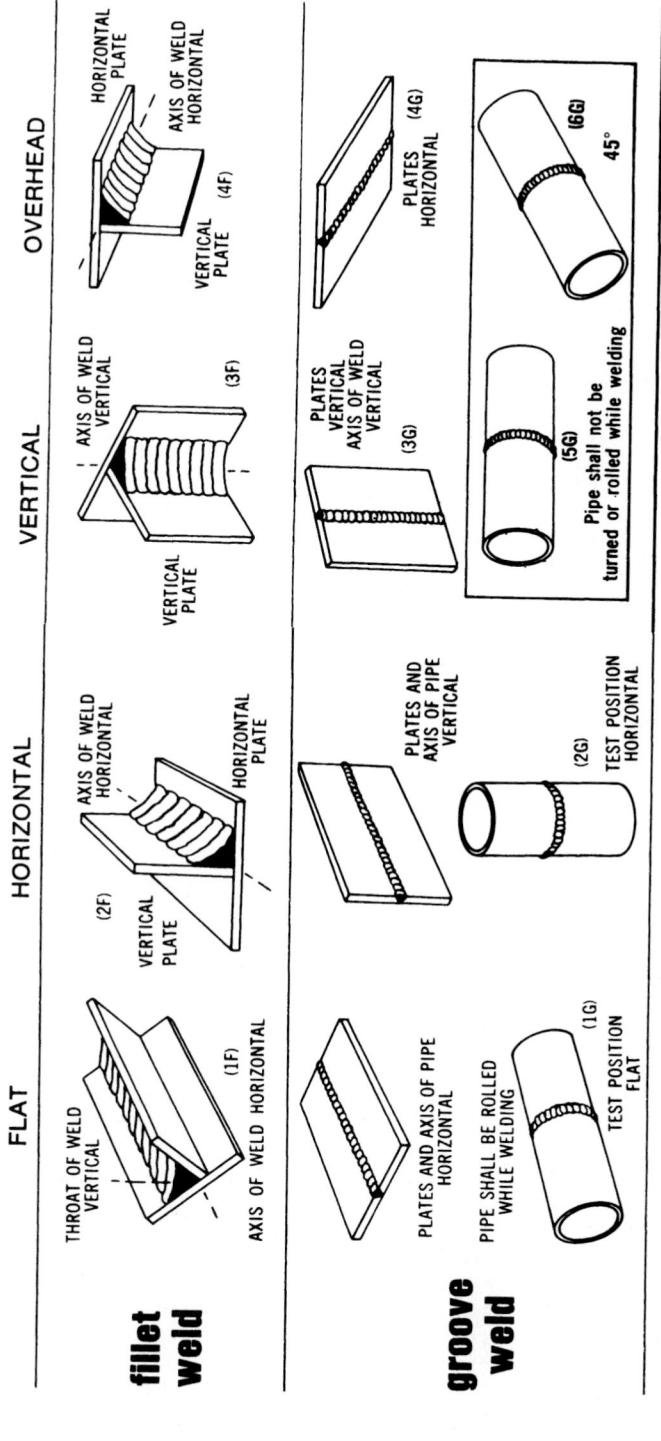

FIGURE 1-4 Welding positions. (*American Welding Society.*)

TABLE 1-1   Lens Shade Selector for Goggles
or Helmet

Operation	Shade number
Soldering	2
Torch bazing	3 or 4
Oxygen cutting	
Up to 1 in (25 mm)	3 or 4
1 to 6 in (25 to 150 mm)	4 or 5
6 in (150 mm) and over	6 or 8
Gas welding	
Up to ⅛ in (3 mm)	4 or 5
⅛ to ½ in (3 to 13 mm)	5 or 6
½ in (13 mm) and over	6 or 8
Shielded metal arc welding (stick)	
1/16-, 3/32-, ⅛-, 5/32-in (1.6-, 2.3-, 3-, 5-mm) electrodes	10
Nonferrous metal welding:	
Gas tungsten arc welding	
Gas metal arc welding	11
1/16-, 3/32-, ⅛-, 5/32-in (1.6-, 2.3-, 3-, 5-mm) electrodes	
Plasma arc welding	
Ferrous metal welding:	
Gas tungsten arc welding	
Gas metal arc welding	12
1/16-, 3/32-, ⅛-, 5/32-in (1.6-, 2.3-, 3-, 5-mm) electrodes	
Plasma arc welding	
Shielded metal arc welding (stick)	
3/16-, 7/32-, ¼-in (4-, 5.5-, 6-mm) electrodes	12
5/16-, ⅜-in (8-, 9-mm) electrodes	14

Source: The chart is based on ANSI Standard Z49.1, *Safety in Welding and Cutting,* published by the American Welding Society.

    d. Wear protective clothing suitable for the welding work being done. Wear leather gloves and aprons with sleeves for heavy-duty welding. Protective clothing should shield the skin from arc rays.
    e. Do not weld near degreasing operations. Arc rays may turn vapors into dangerous fumes.
    f. Protect others from arc rays or flash with protective screens or barriers painted with nonreflecting plant.
  3. Air contamination
    a. Fumes and gases can be dangerous to your health.
    b. Keep your head out of the fumes. Do not get too close to the arc.
    c. Use enough ventilation and/or exhaust at the arc to keep fumes and gases from your breathing zone. Use natural drafts or fans to keep fumes away from your face.
    d. Use mechanical exhaust when welding lead, cadmium, chromium, manganese, beryllium, bronze, zinc, or galvanized steel.
    e. Do not weld in confined spaces without extra precautions.
    f. Do not weld on plated materials or material covered with vinyl or heavy paint without mechanical exhaust. The coatings can release toxic fumes or gases.
    g. Read and obey the warning label that appears on all containers of welding materials.
  4. Fire and explosion
    a. Arc welding and flame cutting involve high-temperature arcs and open flames which can create fires.
    b. Keep your work area neat, clean, dry, and free of hazards.
    c. Have fire-fighting equipment ready for immediate use and know how to use it.

   d. Do not weld near flammable, volatile, or explosive liquids or gases. Remove all potential fire hazards from welding area.

   e. Do not weld on or near fuel tanks of engine-driven equipment.

   f. Do not weld on containers such as drums, barrels, or tanks that may have held combustibles or hazardous materials without taking extra special precautions. See the AWS bulletin "Safe Practices for Welding and Cutting Containers That Have Held Combustibles."

   g. Do not weld on sealed containers or compartments without providing vents and taking extra precautions.

5. Compressed gases

   a. Handle all compressed-gas cylinders with extreme care. Keep cylinder caps on when cylinder is not in use.

   b. Make sure that all gas cylinders are secured to the wall or other structural support. Protect them from mechanical shocks.

   c. *Never* strike an arc on a compressed-gas cylinder. A gas cylinder should *not* be a part of an electric circuit.

   d. When compressed-gas cylinders are empty, close the valve and mark the cylinder "EMPTY."

   e. Store compressed-gas cylinders in a safe place with good ventilation. Acetylene cylinders and other fuel-gas cylinders should be stored separately from oxygen cylinders. Avoid excessive heat.

   f. Acetylene cylinders should be stored and used in the vertical position.

6. Cleaning and chipping welds and other hazards

   a. Wear protective chipping goggles when chipping weld slag. Chip away from your face.

   b. When you are grinding or using power tools, you should wear safety glasses with side shields under the welding helmet.

   c. Dispose of electrode stubs in containers; stubs on the floor are a safety hazard.

   d. When working above ground, make sure that scaffolds, ladders, or work surfaces are substantial and solid.

   e. When welding in high places without railings, use a safety belt or lifeline.

   f. When working in noisy areas or using noisy processes, wear ear protection.

   g. When working in confined areas take special precautions because of fire and explosion problems with fuels. Guard against inert gas or fume buildup from welding. Provide lookouts and special ventilation.

ARC WELDING AND CUTTING PROCESSES

Shielded-Metal Arc Welding

Process.   Shielded-metal arc welding (SMAW), also known as *stick welding* or *manual metal arc welding,* shown by Fig. 1-5, is one of the most popular welding process in use today. It is an electrical arc welding process which fuses the parts to be welded by heating them with an arc between a covered consumable metal electrode and the work. Shielding is obtained from the decomposition of the electrode covering. This process became very popular in the early 1930s when different electrode coatings were developed. SMAW is normally manually applied and can be used for welding thin and thick steels and some nonferrous metals, in all positions. The process requires a relatively high degree of welder skill. The diagram of the SMAW process in Fig. 1-6 shows the covered electrode, the core wire, the arc, the shielding atmosphere, the weld, and the solidified slag. Deposited metal is obtained from the end of the electrode, which melts and crosses the arc.

Application.   This manually controlled process welds all ferrous metals ranging in thickness from 18 gauge [0.048 in (1.2 mm)] to the maximum encountered. When material thicknesses are over ¼ in (6.2 mm), a bevel edge preparation is used and a multipass welding technique is

FIGURE 1-5 Application of shielded-metal arc welding. (*Hobart Brothers Company.*)

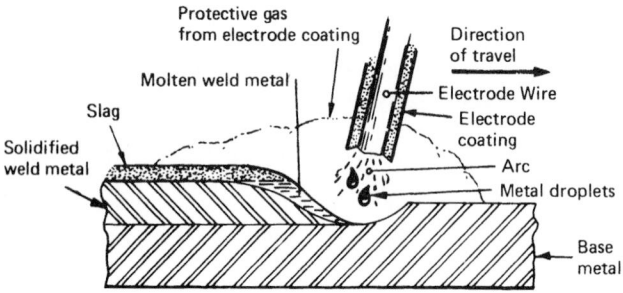

FIGURE 1-6 Process diagram for shielded-metal arc welding.

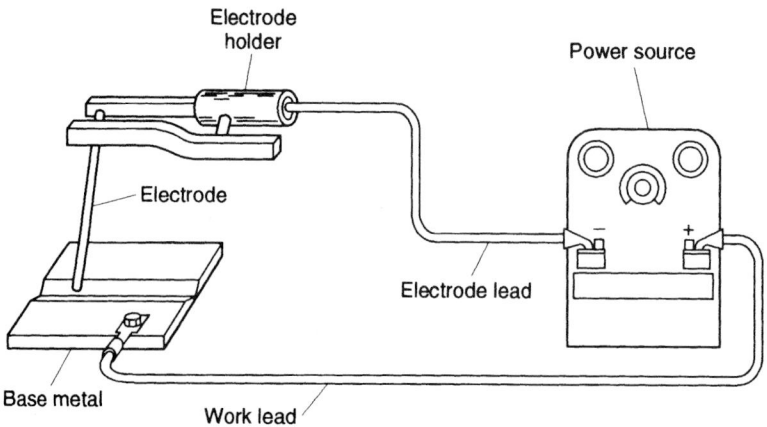

FIGURE 1-7 Equipment for shielded-metal arc welding.

employed. The process allows for all-position welding. The arc is under the control of, and is visible to, the welder. Slag removal is required.

Equipment.   The major parts needed for the SMAW process are:

- The welding machine (power source)
- The covered electrode
- Electrode holder
- Welding leads or cables to complete the welding circuit

These are shown in Fig. 1-7.

Welding Machine.   The welding machine (power source) must provide electric power of the proper current and voltage sufficient to maintain a stable welding arc. The SMAW process can use either alternating or direct current, the direct current being of either polarity. Straight polarity is with the electrode negative; reverse polarity is with the electrode positive.

There are many different types of welding machines. The least expensive, lightest, and smallest welding machine is the alternating-current (ac) transformer type. It provides alternating welding current at the arc. It is usually a single-control type of machine having one knob, which is used to vary the current output. Other types have plug-in connectors or tap switches for this purpose. Transformer machines range from the smallest hobby type up to heavy industrial machines for automatic welding. AC power sources are usually single-phase machines.

The rectifier-type welding machine converts ac power to dc power and provides direct current at the arc. This type of machine usually has a single control knob; however, range switches are sometimes used. These machines come in various sizes. They normally operate on three-phase primary power.

Another power source is the ac-dc transformer-rectifier type that is especially designed to allow either ac or dc welding. A selector switch allows either alternating current or direct current of either polarity.

Another type of power source for welding is the electric generator. This type of machine can provide either ac or dc welding current. The generator is usually powered by an air-cooled or liquid-cooled internal-combustion engine fueled by either gasoline or diesel. It is usually used for in-the-field welding.

Electrode Holder.   The electrode holder, which is held by the welder, is used to grip the electrode and carry the welding current to it. Electrically insulated holders should be used. They come in different types: the pincer type and the twist-collet type. They also come in different sizes rated according to the maximum current that can be used. Holders having larger current ratings are heavier and will accommodate larger cables and bigger electrodes. Personal preference of the welder has much to do with the selection of electrode holders.

Welding Leads.   The welding cables and connectors provide the electric circuit necessary to transmit power from the welding machines to the arc. The *electrode lead* forms one side of the circuit and runs from the electrode holder to the electrode terminal of the power source. The *work lead* (erroneously called *ground lead*) is the other side of the circuit and runs from the work clamp to the work terminal of the welding machine. Welding cables are made of strands of copper wire; aluminum, however, is sometimes used. The cable is covered by a sheath of tough insulating material to protect it and avoid short circuits. The cable size is based on the welding current to be used. Cable sizes range from AWG No. 6 to AWG No. 4/0, which is the largest and is used for heavy-duty applications. The leads should be no longer than is required for the work to be done.

Covered Electrodes.   Covered electrodes come in various diameters from $\frac{1}{16}$ to $\frac{1}{4}$ in (1.6 to 6.4 mm), and their length is normally 14 or 18 in (36 or 46 cm). The electrodes are available for welding different types and strengths of metals. The composition of the core wire and the composition of the electrode coating determines its use. Electrodes are designed to match most common metals and also to deposit hard metal surfaces.

The covering on the electrode is designed to provide:

1. Gas to shield the arc from the atmosphere, obtained by the decomposition of the ingredients in the coating

2. Deoxidizers for purifying the deposited weld metal

3. Slag formers to protect the deposited weld metal from the atmosphere

4. Ionizing elements to make the electrode operate more smoothly, especially on alternating current

5. Alloying elements to provide deposited metal matched to the base metal

6. Iron powder to improve the productivity of the electrode

Covered electrodes are specified by the American Welding Society Specification A5.1, "Carbon Steel Covered Arc Welding Electrodes," and A5.5, "Low Alloy Steel Covered Electrodes," as well as others for the different available electrodes.

Gas Tungsten Arc Welding

Process. Gas tungsten arc welding (GTAW), also known as *TIG welding* and *argon arc welding,* is used to weld nonferrous and special metals. It is illustrated in Fig. 1-8. It is an electric arc welding process which fuses the parts to be welded by heating them with an arc between a nonconsumable tungsten electrode and the work. Filler metal may or may not be used. Atmosphere shielding is obtained from an inert gas or inert gas mixture. The process is normally applied manually and is capable of welding special steels and nonferrous metals in all positions. The process is commonly used to weld thin metals and for the root-pass welding on tubing and pipe. It requires a relatively high degree of welder skill and produces excellent quality welds.

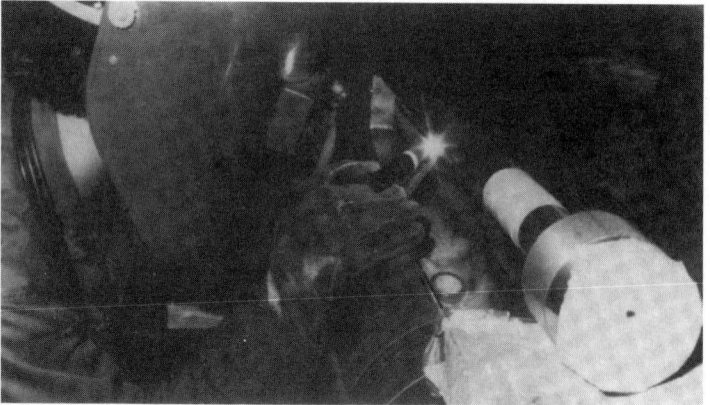

FIGURE 1-8 Application of gas tungsten arc welding. (*Hobart Brothers Company.*)

GTAW was developed by the aircraft industry in the early 1940s to join hard-to-weld metals, particularly magnesium, aluminum, and stainless steels. Figure 1-9 is a diagram of the GTAW process. The tungsten electrode is fastened in a torch which also has a nozzle for directing the shielding gas around the arc area. The arc is between the tungsten electrode and the work. Filler metal in the form of a rod or wire when used, is usually fed manually, although it can be fed automatically.

Application. The outstanding features of the GTAW process are:

1. It can produce high-quality welds on almost all metals and alloys

2. Little or no postweld cleaning is required

3. The arc and weld pool are clearly visible to the welder

4. There is no filler metal crossing the arc, hence little or no weld spatter

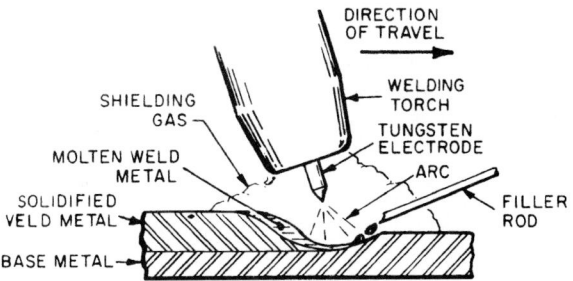

FIGURE 1-9   Process diagram for gas tungsten arc welding.

5. Welding is possible in all positions

6. There is no production of slag which might be trapped in the weld

GTAW is used for welding aluminum, magnesium, stainless steel, bronze, silver, copper and copper alloys, nickel and nickel alloys, cast iron, and steel. It will weld a wide range of metal thicknesses but is most economical on thinner gauges. Argon is usually used as the shielding gas, although helium or argon-helium mixtures are sometimes used.

Equipment.   The major components required for GTAW are shown in Fig. 1-10. These items are:

- The welding machine or power source
- The GTAW torch, including the tungsten electrode
- The shielding gas and controls
- The welding cables
- The filler rod, when required

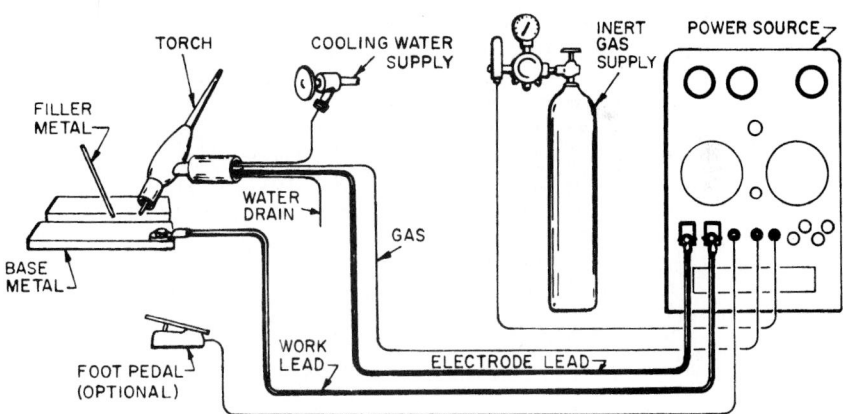

FIGURE 1-10   Equipment for gas tungsten arc welding.

There are several optional accessories available including a remote-controlled foot rheostat which permits the welder to control current while welding; others are arc timers and controllers or programmers, high-frequency units, water circulators, etc.

Welding Machine.   A specially designed welding machine or power source is normally used for GTAW. Power sources for GTAW have drooping characteristics. Both alternating and direct current are used. A transformer/rectifier-type is usually employed. The power source usually contains a high-frequency generator which is used to aid arc starting for welding with direct current and is used continuously for welding with alternating current. The selection of alternating or direct current depends on the material being welded. AC is recommended for welding aluminum and magnesium. DC is recommended for welding stainless steels, carbon steels, copper and its alloys, nickel and its alloys, and precious metals.

Most machines for GTAW include solenoid valves for controlling the shielding gas and cooling water, when used. The high-frequency spark gap oscillator is also included in the welding machine, as well as the special connectors for attaching the welding torch and cable assembly to the machine. The welding machine may also include meters and programmers. Some machines provide pulsed current capability.

Welding machines designed for GTAW can also be used for SMAW and several other processes.

Welding Torch. The GTAW torch holds the tungsten electrode and directs the shielding gas and welding power to the arc. Torches come in different sizes and current capacitors. The larger sizes are usually water-cooled. The torches come equipped with a cable assembly which directs the shielding gas, welding-power current, and cooling water (when used) from the machine to the torch.

Tungsten Electrodes. The electrodes used with the GTAW process are made of tungsten or tungsten alloys. Tungsten has the highest melting point of any metal (6170°F or 3405°C) and is considered nonconsumable. When properly used, the electrode does not touch the molten weld pool. If the tungsten electrode accidentally touches the weld pool, it becomes contaminated and must be cleaned immediately. If it is not cleaned, an erratic arc will result. Electrodes are available in alloys as well as pure tungsten. Pure tungsten is the least expensive; however, alloys containing 1 or 2 percent thoriated tungsten are quite popular. This type of electrode is somewhat more expensive but is recommended for welding specific metals. Another alloy is the zirconiated tungsten which is often used for x-ray–quality work. The different tungstens are identified by AWS Specification A5.12, "Specifications for Tungsten Arc Welding Electrodes," and are color-coded for ease of recognition. Tungsten electrodes come in diameters ranging from 0.020 in (0.5 mm) up through ¼ in (6 mm). The electrode surfaces come in either a ground finish or a cleaned finish. The lengths of tungsten rods are normally 3 to 6 in (7.5 to 15 cm).

Shielding Gas. An inert shielding gas must be used. Argon is the most popular; however, helium is used in certain applications, and in some cases a mixture of argon and helium is used. Argon is more easily obtainable and is less expensive than helium. Also it is heavier than helium and provides better shielding at lower flow rates. The arc produced with helium for shielding is considered hotter and is used for obtaining deeper penetration. Helium is also used for welding in the overhead position. Helium is usually used at a higher flow rate than argon.

Filler Metal. Though filler metal may or may not be used, it is normally used except when welding very thin material. The filler metal is normally not a part of the electrical circuit. The composition of the filler metal should match that of the base metal. Filler metals may not be available in every alloy; therefore, filler-metal charts show the recommended type for use on different metals. The size of the filler-metal rod depends on the thickness of the base metal and the welding current. Filler metal is usually added manually to the weld pool, but automatic feed is sometimes used. For surfacing to obtain higher deposition rates, power may be connected to the filler rod. AWS specifications provide composition information about filler wires available.

Gas Metal Arc Welding

Process. The gas metal arc welding process (GMAW) is an arc-welding process which fuses the parts to be welded by heating them with an arc between a continuous, consumable solid wire electrode and the work. Shielding is obtained from an externally supplied gas or gas mixture. The process is normally applied semiautomatically; however, it can be applied by machine or by automatic equipment. The process can be used to weld thin and fairly thick metals, both steel and nonferrous. It is also used for surfacing. The arc is visible to the welder, and it can be used in all positions. A lesser degree of welding skill is required; however, the equipment is more complex than that used for SMAW.

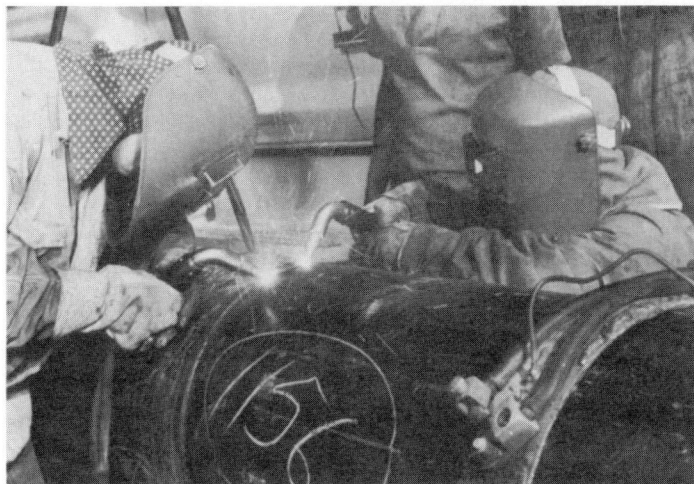

FIGURE 1-11   Application of gas metal arc welding. (*Hobart Brothers Company.*)

This process, shown in Fig. 1-11, was developed in the early 1950s.

This process, sometimes called *MIG welding* (standing for metal inert-gas welding), CO_2 *welding,* etc. is one of the more popular welding processes. The electrode is melted by the heat of the arc, and the melted metal is transferred across the arc to become the deposited weld metal.

The GMAW process is shown in Fig. 1-12, which shows the electrode wire, the nozzle of the welding gun or torch, the shielding-gas envelope, and the arc between the end of the electrode and the base metal.

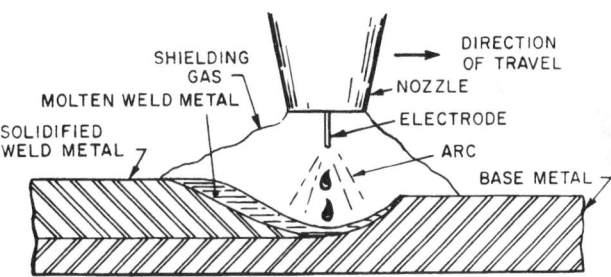

FIGURE 1-12   Process diagram for gas metal arc welding.

There are a number of variations of the GMAW process. These depend on the type of shielding gas which relates to the type of metal transfer across the arc as follows:

- MIG welding using inert-gas shielding on nonferrous metals
- Short-circuiting transfer (small wire or short-circuiting arc), normally using CO_2 gas or CO_2 gas mixtures and small-diameter electrode wire, allows welding in all positions and on thin metals
- CO_2 welding using CO_2 shielding gas and larger electrode wires is restricted to steels
- Spray arc welding, which uses the argon-oxygen shielding gas normally restricted to steels
- Pulsed arc welding which provides pulsed metal transfer and uses a special power source

Application.   The outstanding features of GMAW are:

1. High-quality welds on most metals
2. Minimum postweld cleaning
3. The arc and weld pool are visible to the welder
4. Welding is possible in all positions depending on electrode size
5. Relatively high-speed welding
6. Little or no slag produced
7. It is considered a "low-hydrogen" welding process

Variations of the process offer special advantages. The short-circuiting arc (small wire) will weld most steels in the thinner gauges. CO_2 welding allows for high-speed travel on steel. The spray arc variation produces high-speed welds with minimum spatter and cleanup, and the MIG process welds the nonferrous metals at a much higher rate of speed than the GTAW process. Pulsed welding is used on some hard-to-weld metals.

Equipment.   Major components required for GMAW are shown in Fig. 1-13. These are:

- The welding machine or power source
- The electrode wire-feed system and control
- The welding gun and cable assembly (for semiautomatic welding) or welding torch (for automatic welding)
- The shielding gas supply and controls
- The consumable electrode

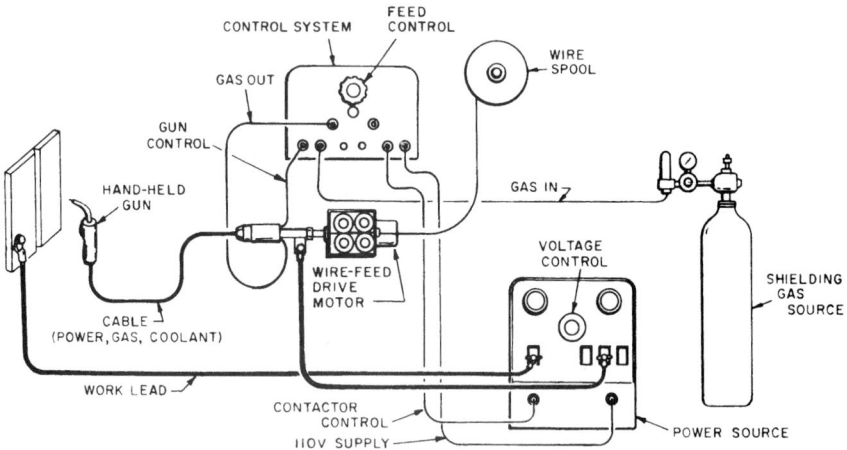

FIGURE 1-13   Equipment for gas metal arc welding.

Welding Machine.   The power source for GMAW is normally a constant-voltage (CV) or constant-potential (CP) type. Its characteristic output volt-ampere curve is essentially flat with a small droop. The output voltage is approximately the same though the welding current changes. The output voltage is adjusted at the power source, which is normally a transformer-rectifier welding machine. A CV or CP power source does not have a welding-current control and is not used for shielded-metal arc welding. The welding-current output is determined by the electric load on the machine which depends on the electrode wire-feed speed. DC electrode positive current is normally used. Machines for this process are available from 75 A up to as high as 1000 A and should be rated at 80 to 100 percent duty cycle. They should include a contactor and meters and should provide 115-V ac power for the electrode wire feeder. A conventional or constant current welding machine can be used; however, a more complex controlled wire feeder is required.

Wire Feeder. The wire-feed system must be matched to the power supply. The CV system of welding relies on the relationship between the electrode wire burn-off rate and the welding current. This relationship is fairly constant for a given electrode wire size, composition, and shielding atmosphere. At a given wire-feed speed rate, the welding machine will supply the proper amount of current to maintain a steady arc. Thus the wire-feed speed control adjusts the welding current. The CV welding system is a self-regulating system and is recommended when small-diameter electrode wires are used. A miniaturized wire feeder built into the welding gun is popular for welding with small-diameter aluminum wire. The wire-feed system and controls are essentially the same for semiautomatic, mechanized, or automatic welding.

Welding Gun. The welding gun and cable assembly are used to carry the electrode wire, the welding current, and the shielding gas to the welding arc. For higher-current applications, water-cooled guns are used and the water is also carried through the cable assembly. There are two general types of welding guns, the pistol-grip and curved-head (gooseneck). The gooseneck type is more popular for small-diameter electrode wire. The pistol-grip type is usually used for welding with larger electrode wires and for welding with nonferrous electrodes. Guns used for heavy-duty work at high currents and guns using inert gas for shielding at medium to high currents are water-cooled. For mechanized or automatic welding, a welding torch is used. The automatic torches are either air- or water-cooled, depending on the welding application, as mentioned above. For CO_2 welding, a side-delivery gas nozzle is often used with automatic torches. The wire guides in all guns and torches must match the size of the electrode wire being used.

Shielding Gas. The shielding gas displaces the air around the arc to prevent contamination by the oxygen and nitrogen of the atmosphere. The gaseous shielding envelope must efficiently shield the arc in order to obtain high-quality weld metal. Various shielding gases can be used, depending on the process variation and the base metal being welded. Carbon dioxide is the least expensive and is very popular. Mixtures of CO_2 and argon and mixtures of argon and oxygen are also used. Shielding gas must be specified *welding grade*. This means the gas has a high purity and low moisture content indicated by its dew-point temperature. The type of gas for shielding and the flow rate are given by welding procedure tables for welding various metals with different process variations. The gas-flow rates depend on the type of gas, metal being welded, welding position, etc. When welding outside or when air currents disturb the gas shield, higher gas-flow rates are necessary. For high flow of CO_2 gas, two or more cylinders are manifolded together to avoid freezing of the CO_2 pressure regulators.

Electrode. The composition of the electrode for GMAW must be selected to match the metal being welded, the variation of the process, and the shielding atmosphere. The diameter or size of the electrode depends on the variation of the process and the welding position. All electrode wires are normally solid and bare except for a thin, protective coating on carbon steel wires. The welding procedure tables indicate the proper electrode wire, type, and size for welding different metals. Electrode wires are available in a wide variety of diameters, spools, coils, and reels and are specified by AWS specifications.

Flux-Cored Arc Welding

Process. The flux-cored arc welding process (FCAW), also known as FabCO, Dualshield, Fabshield, self-shield, Innershield, etc., is an arc welding process which fuses the parts to be welded by heating them with an arc between a continuous flux-filled electrode wire and the work. Shielding is obtained from gas generated by the decomposition of the minerals inside the tubular wire; however, additional shielding may be obtained from an externally supplied gas or gas mixture. The process, usually applied semiautomatically, is shown in Fig. 1-14. It also can be applied by mechanized or automatic equipment. It is normally used for welding medium-thick steels and stainless steel and for surfacing. It is normally not used for welding nonferrous metals. Small-diameter electrodes allow all position welding. With larger-size electrodes, the welder is restricted to the flat and horizontal positions. The arc is visible to the welder, and the skill level required is similar to that for GMAW.

FIGURE 1-14   Application of flux-cored arc welding. (*Hobart Brothers Company.*)

The process diagram shown in Fig. 1-15 shows the two variations, with the optional items for the externally gas-shielded variation indicated by the dotted lines. The flux-cored electrode wire and the arc between it and the base metal are shown. The process normally produces a slag covering which must be removed after welding. The externally gas-shielded variation was the original process and employed CO_2 for external shielding. The self-shielding variation generates sufficient shielding gas from the decomposition of the ingredients in the core of the electrode wire. The gas shield prevents the atmospheric oxygen and nitrogen from reaching the arc area. This process was developed in the mid-1950s and became popular in the 1960s.

Application.   The two variations of the process provide slightly different welding features. With external shielding gas, the features of the process are (1) extremely smooth, sound, high-quality welds; (2) deep penetration; and (3) good properties for x-ray–quality welds.

The gasless or self-shielding variation offers the following features: (1) elimination of gas supply, controls, and gas nozzle; (2) moderate penetration; and (3) ability to weld in drafts or breezes.

Both variations have the following features: (1) high deposition rates, (2) visibility of the arc to the welder, (3) all-position welding based on the size of the electrode, and (4) similarity of the weld-joint design to those used for the other arc welding processes. Both variations are normally restricted to the welding of carbon and stainless steels and for overlaying. The external gas-shielded version can be used for welding many low-alloy steels.

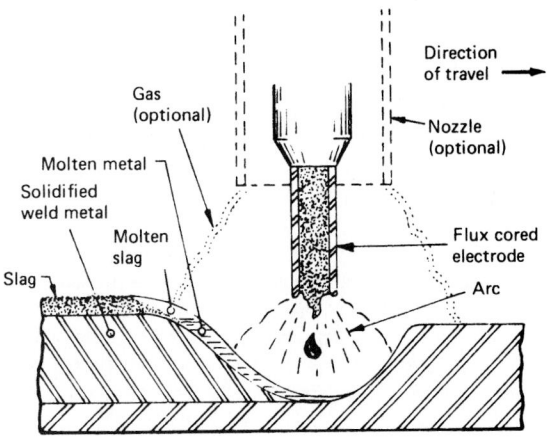

FIGURE 1-15   Process diagram for flux-cored arc welding.

Equipment.   The major components required for the FCAW process are shown in Fig. 1-16. Equipment is generally similar to that used for GMAW and is common for both variations except for the gas shielding supply. The items involved are:

- The welding machine or power source
- The wire-feed drive system and control
- The welding gun and cable assembly for semiautomatic welding or a welding torch for automatic welding
- The flux-cored electrode wire

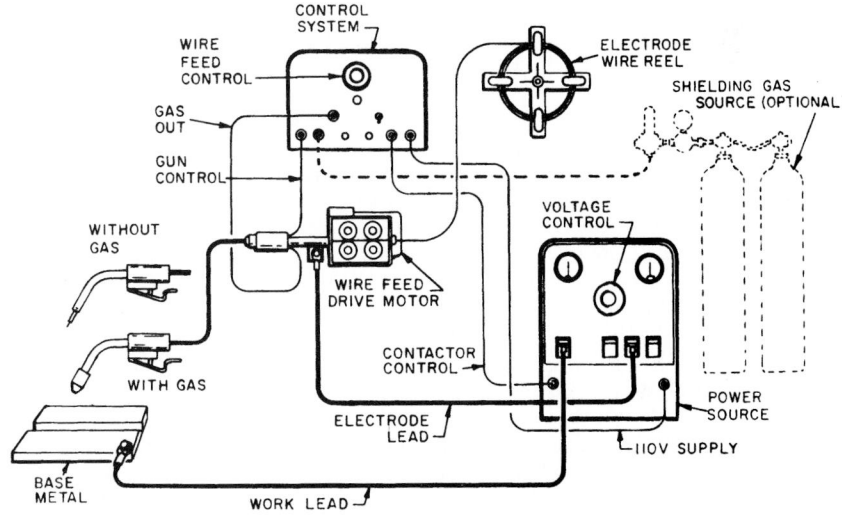

FIGURE 1-16   Equipment for flux-cored arc welding.

The external gas-shielded version requires the external shielding gas supply, flow meter–regulator, gas valves and control, and the gas nozzle on the gun. The self-shielding type uses a lightweight gun; however, such guns often will include smoke-exhaust nozzles.

Welding Machine. The welding machine or power source for flux-cored arc welding is normally a CV or CP type. These types of welding machines have an output characteristic volt-ampere curve that is essentially flat with a minimum droop. The output voltage for the welding machine is adjusted by a control on the welding power source which is normally a transformer-rectifier machine. CV-type power sources do not have a current control and, therefore, cannot be used for welding with the SMAW process. The welding-current output is determined by the electric load on the power source. This is dependent on the electrode wire-feed speed rate. DC electrode positive is normally used for externally gas-shielded electrodes. Self-shielding electrodes normally use dc with the electrode negative. AC is normally not used. Power sources are available for FCAW ranging from 150 to 1000 A and should be rated at 80 to 100 percent duty cycle. They should include a contactor and meters, and should provide 115-V ac power for the electrode wire feeder. A conventional, or constant-current, welding machine can be used; however, a more complex controlled wire feeder is required.

Wire Feeder. The wire-feeding mechanism feeds the flux-cored electrode wire automatically from a coil or spool through the cable assembly and welding gun into the arc. The wire-feed system must match the type of power supply used. The CV-type power supply is normally used; therefore, a constant-speed wire-feed system with adjustable speed is used. The wire-feed speed rate controls the welding current. The CV welding system is a self-regulating system. Voltage-sensing wire-feed systems can be used when matched to a drooping-characteristic-type power source, but they are not too popular for FCAW. Basically the same type of wire feeder that is used for GMAW can be used for FCAW. The drive rolls, either two or four, must match the size and type electrode wire.

Welding Gun. The welding gun is used to deliver the electrode wire, the current, and the shielding gas (when used) to the arc area. Guns with shielding gas nozzles are water-cooled for high-current, heavy-duty cycle welding. Water cooling is not used for the gasless variation welding gun. Both pistol-grip and gooseneck guns are available. Sometimes, with the gasless variation, a special insulated extension nozzle, which adds to the electrical stickout, is added to the gun to provide higher deposition rates.

Shielding Gas (External Gas-Shielded Variation). The shielding gas displaces the air around the arc area, preventing contamination by oxygen and nitrogen of the atmosphere. CO_2 is normally used as the shielding gas for steel; however, for stainless steel and certain alloy steels, a gas mixture is used. The composition of the shielding gas must be related to the electrode wire and base metal. Gas-flow rates depend on the type of gas being used, the metal being welded, welding position, welding current, etc. Procedure tables provide this information.

Electrode Wire. The electrode wire employed must be selected to match the composition and mechanical properties of the base metal. The selection must also be based on whether it is to be used with external shielding gas or not. Procedure tables indicate the type of electrode wire to be used. Various diameters are available for different applications. Electrode wires are packaged on spools, coils, and in payoff-type packs. The American Welding Society classifies flux-cored electrodes according to the strength level, properties, and deposited weld metal composition.

Submerged Arc Welding

Process. Submerged arc welding (SAW), also known as *welding under powder* or *hidden-arc welding*, is an arc-welding process which fuses the parts to be welded by heating them with an arc or arcs between a bare electrode or electrodes and the work. The arc is shielded by a blanket of granular flux on the work. The process is normally applied by mechanized or automatic equipment but may use semiautomatic equipment on a limited basis. It is used to weld medium to thick steels in the flat or horizontal position. Manual welding skill is not required; however, a technical understanding of the equipment and the welding procedure is necessary. SAW, shown in Fig. 1-17, was developed in 1930. It has become extremely popular for heavy plate welding because it produces high-quality weld metal at a minimum cost. Figure 1-18 shows the base metal, the consumable electrode wire, the granular flux covering, the slag cover, the arc area, and the molten metal. SAW is normally used for welding steels and surfacing steels and is not normally used for welding nonferrous metals.

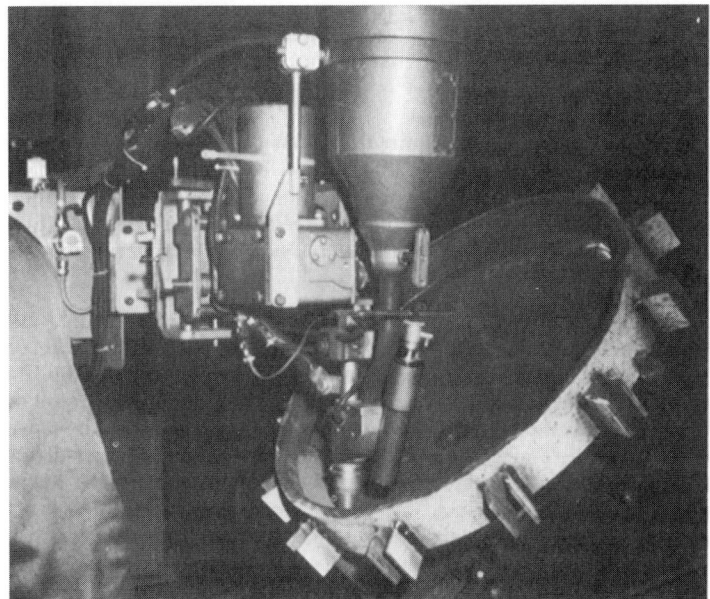

FIGURE 1-17   Application of submerged arc welding. (*Hobart Brothers Company.*)

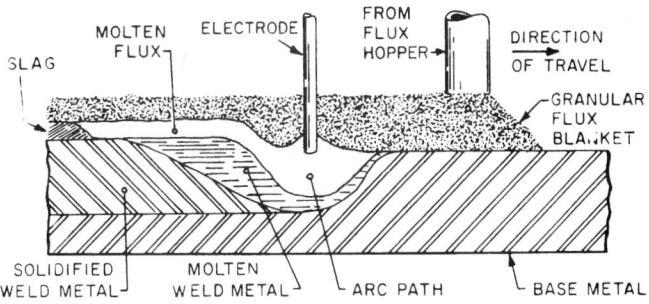

FIGURE 1-18   Process diagram for submerged arc welding.

Application.   The outstanding features of the SAW process are:

1. High metal deposition rates
2. High welding travel speed
3. Deep penetration

4. Good x-ray quality

5. Smooth weld appearance

6. Easily removed slag covering

7. A wide range of weldable metal thicknesses

The arc is not visible to the welder. The automatic or machine methods of application are most commonly used. The semiautomatic application method is less popular. SAW is used to weld low- and medium-carbon steels, low-alloy high-strength steels, quenched and tempered steels, and many stainless steels. It is also for hard-surfacing and buildup work. Metal thicknesses ranging from 16 gauge to ½ in (13 mm) are welded with no edge preparation. With edge preparation and multiple-pass welding, the maximum thickness welded is practically unlimited. SAW is restricted to the flat and horizontal positions.

Equipment. The major equipment components required for SAW are shown in Fig. 1-19. These are:

• The welding machine or power source

• The wire-feeding mechanism and control

• The welding torch for automatic welding or the welding gun and cable assembly for semi-automatic welding

• The flux hopper and flux feeding mechanism

• The travel mechanism and controller for automatic welding

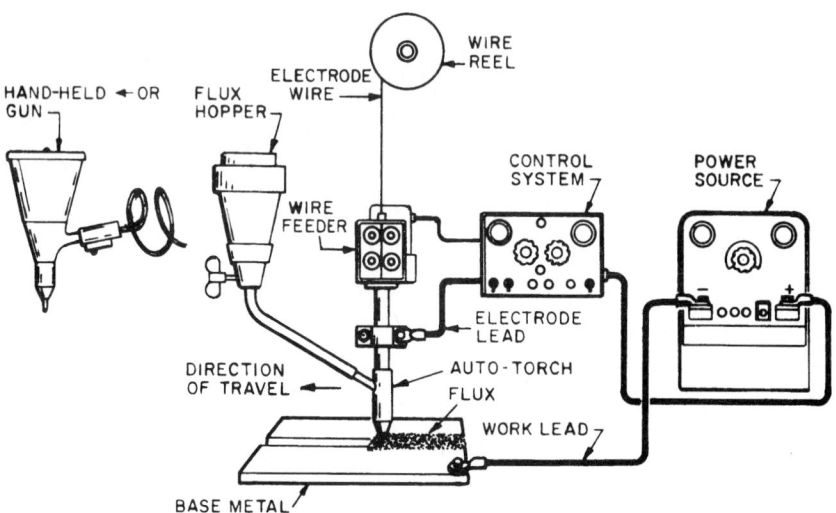

FIGURE 1-19 Equipment for submerged arc welding.

A flux recovery system is usually included in an automatic installation.

Welding Machine. The welding machine or power source for SAW can be either an ac or dc power source. It must be rated at a 100 percent duty cycle, since welding operations are continuous and the length of time in operation will normally exceed the 10-min base period used for rating duty cycle. For dc SAW, the CV-type or CC-type power source can be used. The CV type is more common for small-diameter electrode wires, usually ⅛ in (3 mm) and smaller in diameter. The CC type is more commonly used for larger-diameter electrode wires, usually ⁵⁄₃₂ in (4 mm) and larger. The wire feeder must be matched to the type of power source used. When alternating current is employed, the machine is a constant-current (CC) type. Welding machines for SAW range in size from 200 to 1000 A. In some cases two or more electrode wires are employed in the same arc pool, and in some cases one electrode may be on direct current and the other on alternating current.

Wire Feeder.   The wire-feeding mechanism and its associated control feed the electrode wire into the welding arc. When a CC or drooping-type power source is employed, a voltage-sensing wire-feeder must be used. This type of wire feeder maintains a specific arc voltage and feeds the electrode wire at the proper rate to maintain this value. If a CV or flat-characteristic power source is used, the constant-speed wire feeder and control should be employed. In this case, the wire feeder feeds the electrode wire at a constant but adjustable rate in order to draw the prescribed welding current from the power source. The arc voltage is adjusted by changing the output voltage of the power source. The control system initiates the arc, provides the proper electrode wire-feed speed and, in automatic operation, performs other necessary functions such as start and stop of motion or travel.

Welding Torch or Gun.   For automatic welding, the torch directs the electrode wire into the arc and transfers the welding current to the wire as it leaves the torch. The torch is usually attached to the electrode wire-feeder and travel mechanism. A flux hopper is usually attached to or is adjacent to the torch. For semiautomatic operations, a welding gun and cable assembly are used to transmit the electrode wire and the welding current to the arc and to provide the flux at the welding zone. A small flux hopper may be attached to the gun, and it dispenses flux over the weld area in accordance with the manipulation of the gun. In another system, the flux is fed through a conduit to the gun from a hopper and dispensed at the welding zone. Semiautomatic guns usually have a trigger switch for initiating the arc. For automatic welding, a flux recovery system is usually attached to the travel mechanism.

Welding Flux.   The SAW flux is a granular, fusible material which is poured over the arc area. This flux performs the same functions as the covering on a coated electrode. It protects the arc and molten metal from atmospheric contamination, acting as a scavenger to clean and purify the weld metal. Additionally, it may be used to add alloy elements to the deposited weld metal. A portion of the flux is melted by the heat of the welding arc. The molten flux then cools and solidifies, forming a slag on the surface of the weld. The portion of the flux which is not melted can be recovered and reused. There are different grades and types of submerged arc flux, and it is important to select the proper flux-wire combination to match the chemistry and properties of the metal being welded. AWS Specification 5.17 provides the information necessary to match the properties of the metal being welded.

Electrode.   The electrode wires used for SAW are usually solid and bare except for a thin protective coating on the surface, usually copper. The electrode contains deoxidizers which help clean and scavenge the weld metal to produce a quality weld. Alloying elements may also be included in the composition of the electrode. The electrode composition and the type of flux must be matched to the requirements of the base metal in order to provide a quality weld. This is covered by AWS Specification 5.17. Electrode wires are available in diameter sizes of ¹⁄₁₆, ⁵⁄₆₄, ³⁄₃₂, ⅛, ³⁄₁₆, ⁷⁄₃₂, and ¼ in (1.6, 2, 2.4, 3, 4.8, 5.6, and 6.2 mm). Wire is usually available in coils ranging from 25 to 1000 lb (11 to 450 kg).

Plasma Arc Welding

Process.   Plasma arc welding (PAW) is an electric arc welding process which fuses the parts to be welded by heating them with a constricted arc between the electrode and the work (transferred-arc mode). Shielding is obtained from the hot ionized gases issuing from the torch orifice. Auxiliary inert shielding gas or a mixture of inert gases supplements the plasma gas system. Filler metal may or may not be used. *Plasma,* the fourth state of matter, is defined as a gas which has been heated to a high enough temperature to become ionized. When it is ionized, the gas, or plasma, becomes electrically conductive.

The process, shown in Fig. 1-20, is commonly applied manually but may be applied as a mechanized or fully automated process. It can be used to weld almost all metals and can be used in all positions. It is normally used on thinner materials. For manual application the process requires a fairly high degree of welder skill. Mechanization applications require a through knowledge of the equipment. There are two ways of using the PAW process. One is known as the *melt-in* technique and the other, the *keyhole* technique. The melt-in technique is very similar to gas tungsten arc welding. The keyhole technique actually makes a hole which is then filled as welding progresses. Process details in the keyhole mode are shown in Fig. 1-21.

FIGURE 1-20   Application of plasma arc welding. (*Hobart Brothers Company.*)

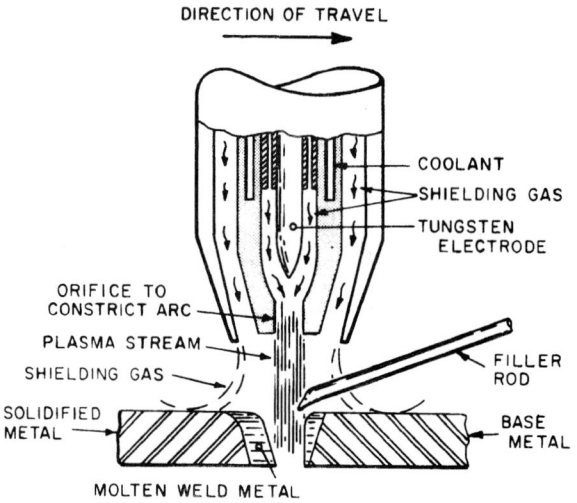

FIGURE 1-21   Process diagram for plasma arc welding.

Application. PAW is similar to GTAW. The major difference in that the arc in PAW between the electrode and the work is constricted and forced to go through a small hole or orifice in the torch. A gas is also forced, through the orifice; this creates the plasma. The temperature of the plasma is considerably higher than the temperature of the gas tungsten arc. The process diagram (Fig. 1-21) shows the tungsten electrode inside the torch and the plasma extending through the torch orifice to the work. The plasma fed through the orifice is ionized and has a columnar form rather than the flare common with GTAW. The ionized gas, or plasma, travels at extremely high speeds and has a force action on the base material, which is important when using the keyhole technique.

One of the advantages of PAW over GTAW is the columnar structure of the plasma which reduces the effect of changes in torch-to-work distance. The high-velocity, high-temperature plasma causes deep penetration in the base metal and allows full penetration of keyhole, single-pass, butt-welding joints. The welds produced have unusually deep penetration with a relatively narrow bead width. The plasma process will weld all the metals that are welded with the GTAW process.

Equipment. The major components required for PAW are shown in Fig. 1-22. They include:

- A welding machine or power source
- A special plasma arc console which contains the control system
- The plasma welding torch
- The source of plasma and shielding gas
- Filler metal when required

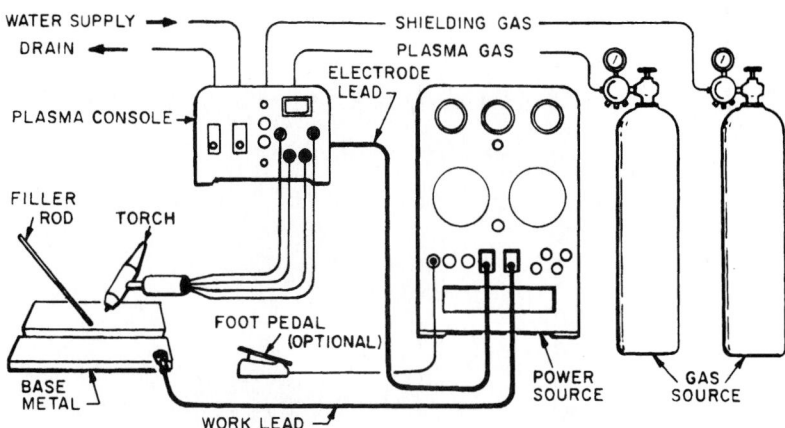

FIGURE 1-22 Equipment for plasma arc welding.

Welding Machine. The power source for PAW is the CC type with a drooping output characteristic. A GTAW power source is normally used for plasma welding since it includes a contactor, remote current control, and provisions for shielding gas and cooling water. For more complex weldments, programmed current control including upslope and downslope and pulsing is used.

Plasma Console. This unit contains a high-frequency arc starter, a nontransferred pilot-arc current supply, torch protection devices, flow meters, and other meters. It may be included in the power supply. It may also include the water control system and protective interlocks to protect the plasma arc torch.

Plasma Torch.   The torch contains a tungsten electrode (Usually 2 percent thoriated type) and a nozzle having a constricting orifice. Since the arc is enclosed within the torch, all plasma torches are water-cooled. The torches are either manual or machine type, with the smaller sizes restricted to the manual applications. Different sizes are available, depending on the current level to be employed.

Shielding Gas Plasma Gas.   Inert gas, often argon, is normally used as the plasma gas. In addition, argon, helium, or a mixture of the two is used as an auxiliary gas to shield the arc and arc area from the atmosphere. Argon is more commonly used because it is less expensive and easier to obtain. It also provides for better shielding because it is heavier than air.

Filler Metal.   Filler metal may or may not be used. It is not used on very thin metals but is normally used for normal sheet-metal thickness and heavier material. The composition of the filler metal should match that of the base metal. Welding procedure charts will show the recommended filler material used for different base metals. The size of the filler metal (filler rod diameter) depends on the thickness of the base metal and the welding current. Filler metal is usually added to the pool manually, but automatic feed can be used.

Stud Arc Welding

Process.   Stud arc welding (SW) is a special-purpose arc-welding process used to attach studs to base metal. Partial shielding is obtained by a ceramic ferrule surrounding the stud. It is a machine-welding process using a special gun that holds the stud and makes the weld. The process is normally used on steels in the flat and horizontal positions. A relatively low degree of welding skill is required. There are several variations.

The SW process, shown in Fig. 1-23, was developed in the mid-1930s to satisfy the need to attach brackets, cover plates, etc. to steel plate, particularly in the shipbuilding industry. It became popular for securing wood decking to steel plate, for attaching pipe hangers, etc.

FIGURE 1-23   Application of stud welding. (*Ohio Edison Co.*)

The operation of the SW process is shown in Fig. 1-24. This operation is as follows:

1. A stud gun holds the stud in contact with the workpiece. The welding operator pulls the gun trigger, which causes the welding current to flow through the circuit to the stud, which is the electrode, to the work surface.

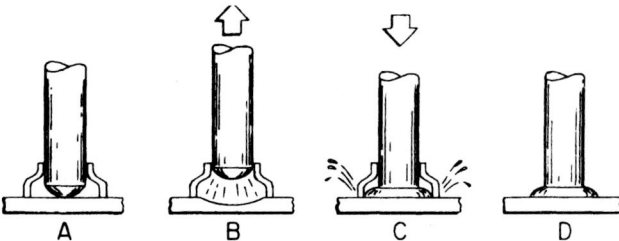

FIGURE 1-24 Process diagram for stud welding.

2. The welding current activates the solenoid within the gun, which draws the stud away from the work surface and establishes an arc. The heat of the arc melts the surface of the workpiece and the end of the stud. The arc time period is controlled by a timer built into the controller.

3. When the welding current is automatically shut off, the gun solenoid releases its pull on the stud and spring action plunges the stud into the molten pool of the workpiece.

4. The molten stud end and the molten pool on the work surface solidify, and the stud weld is completed. The ferrule is broken off and discarded.

The process is either a machine application or an automatic application, with machine application being the more popular. For automatic application, the studs are fed automatically into the gun. Welding can be done in all positions; however, flat and horizontal positions are those most commonly used.

Application.   SW is widely used for attaching studs and other similar devices to plate or structural members. Studs are normally threaded, round fasteners; however, rectangular devices, hooks, pins, brackets, and other configurations can be stud-welded. A popular application is the attachment of shear connectors to structural steelwork. Shear connectors are round, usually with a head welded to the upper flange of beams over which concrete is poured, most commonly for bridges and decking. Another popular application is the use of studs for attaching wood decking over steel decking on ships, particularly aircraft carriers. SW is used for welding studs used to attach pipe hangers, electric boxes, and other miscellaneous items in ship construction. It is also widely used for attaching insulation to the inside of steel structures. Other uses include attaching and holding insulation to pipe surfaces, attaching studs to hold inspection plates, etc. It is normally used for steels and stainless steels, but variations of the process can be used on nonferrous metals.

Equipment.   The major components for SW are shown in Fig. 1-25. These include:

- The welding machine or power source
- The stud gun
- THe control unit
- The studs
- The disposable ferrules

Welding Machine.   The welding machine or power source is a dc power source which can be a transformer-rectifier or a generator, engine-driven. A conventional CC or drooping-characteristic-type power source is required. The welding current is dictated by the size or diameter of the stud. The electrode, or the stud, is the negative pole (straight polarity). Amperage required for smaller studs in the $\frac{5}{16}$-in-diameter (8-mm) size ranges from 200 to 500 A. With larger size studs, the amperage can be as high as 2300 A. For high current requirements, two or more power sources are connected in parallel. Welding machines for SW should have high overload capacity and a relatively high open-circuit voltage of 95 to 100 V.

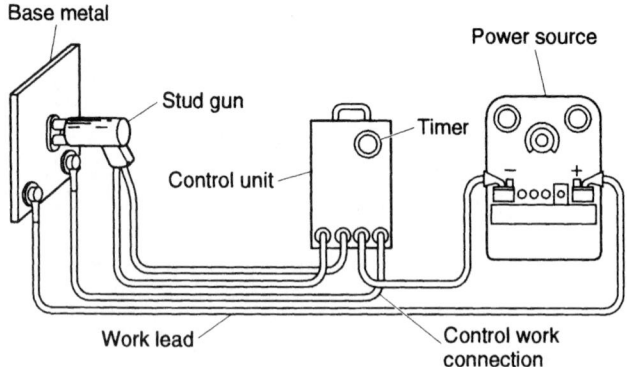

FIGURE 1-25 Equipment for stud welding.

Stud Gun. The stud gun holds the stud and has a trigger switch which starts the control sequence. It also includes the solenoid that provides the withdrawal or lift action to establish the arc. A spring mechanism within the gun applies the pressure required to plunge or push the stud into the pool of the workpiece. The gun should be properly adjusted to accommodate the size of the stud that is being used and to provide the correct arc length during the arc period. The stud gun is normally hand-held and must be held perpendicular to the work. The welding current passes through the stud gun to provide power for the solenoid. The process can be automated. The stud gun must match, or be of the same make as, the controller.

Control Unit. The control unit consists of a welding-current contactor, a timing device, and the necessary interconnections. Some control units regulate the speed at which the stud is pushed into the molten base metal; this kind of regulation tends to eliminate spatter and provide more control over the weld shape and quality. The control unit must be of the same type or make as the stud gun. The control unit and power source may be combined in the same case.

Studs. Steel studs range in diameter from ⅛ to 1 in (3 to 25 mm) and vary in length; they can be threaded or plain. There are many types, as shown in Fig. 1-26. Studs produced by different manufacturers contain somewhat different fluxing devices on the end of the stud. In most cases, the arcing end contains a portion of welding flux or some material for shielding the arc area. The fluxes protect the weld and the arc from atmospheric contamination and contain scavengers which purify the melted metal. Essential stud welding data are shown in Table 1-2.

TABLE 1-2 Stud Welding Data

Stud diameter, in	Current, A DCEP	Welding specifications			
		Voltage, V	Time, s	Lift, in	Plunge, in
³⁄₁₆	300	30	7	¹⁄₁₆	⅛
¼	400	30	10	¹⁄₁₆	⅛
⁵⁄₁₆	500	30	15	¹⁄₁₆	⅛
⅜	600	28	20	¹⁄₁₆	⅛
⁷⁄₁₆	700	28	25	¹⁄₁₆	⅛
½	900	28	30	³⁄₃₂	⁵⁄₃₂
⅝	1150	28	40	³⁄₃₂	⁵⁄₃₂
¾	1600	26	50	⅛	³⁄₁₆
⅞	1800	24	60	⅛	³⁄₁₆
1	2000	24	70	⅛	³⁄₁₆

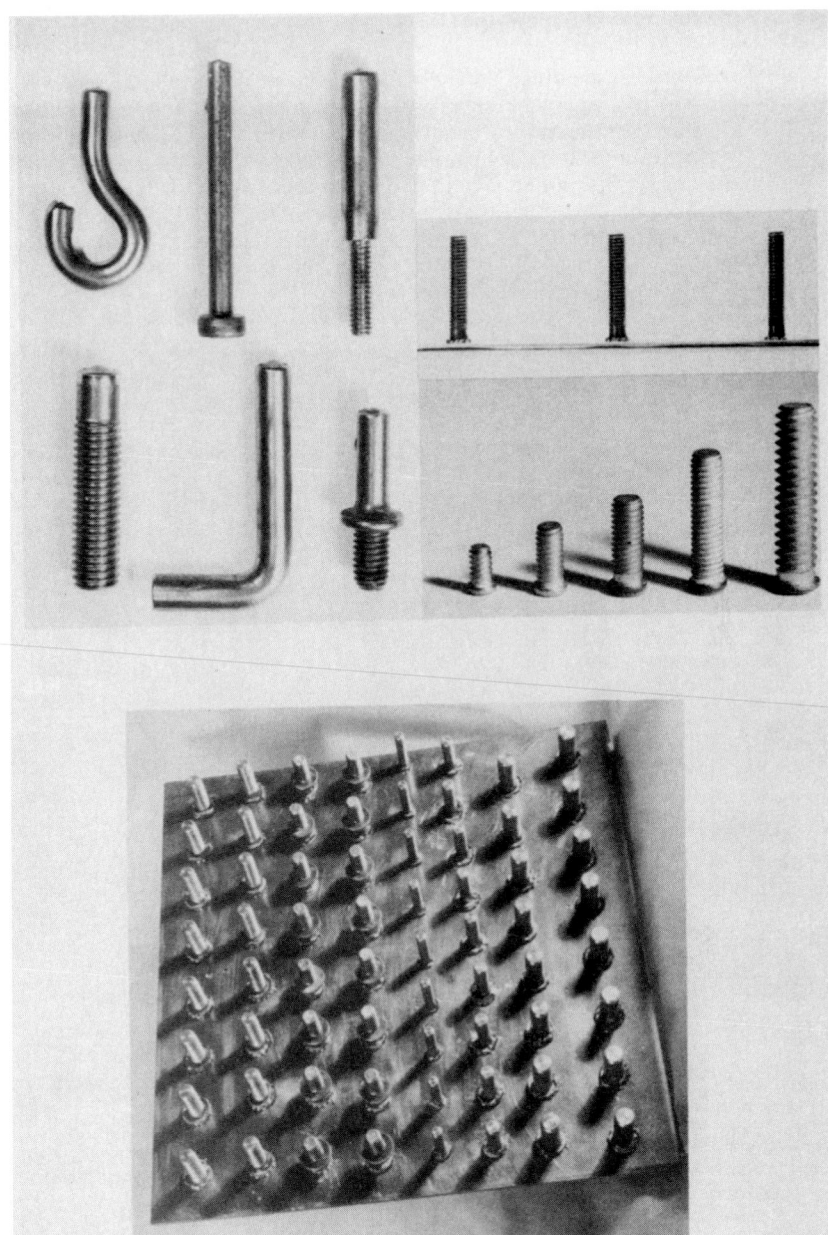

FIGURE 1-26 SW types of studs.

Ferrules.   A ferrule is used with each stud. Ferrules are made of a ceramic material and are broken off and discarded after each weld is made. They shield the arc area, protect the welding operator, and eliminate the need for a welding helmet. The ferrule concentrates the heat during welding and confines the molten metal to the weld area. It helps prevent oxidation of the molten metal during the arcing cycle, but it must fit the studs being used. There is no common specification for studs or ferrules, which are manufactured by stud-welding companies.

Air Carbon Arc Cutting and Gouging

Process.   The air carbon arc (CAC-A) cutting and gouging process is also known as *arc air cutting*. It is an arc-cutting process in which metals to be cut are melted by the heat of a carbon arc and the molten metal is removed by a blast of air. It is shown in Fig. 1-27. A high-velocity air jet traveling parallel to the electrode hits the molten puddle just behind the arc and blows the molten metal out of the puddle. It is usually a manually controlled operation and can be used in all positions. It can also be applied automatically. The process normally creates considerable noise, and ear protection is required. A special electrode holder includes the air-jet opening. The other features of the process are similar to carbon arc welding. Figure 1-28 shows the details of the process.

FIGURE 1-27   Application of air-carbon arc cutting. (*Hobart Brothers Company.*)

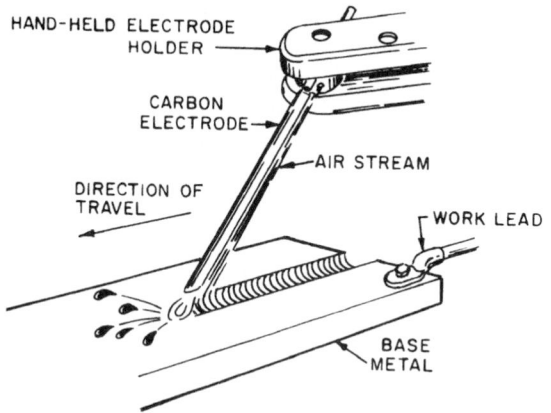

FIGURE 1-28   Process diagram for air-carbon arc cutting.

Application.   The air carbon arc cutting and gouging process is used to cut metal, gouge out defective metal, remove old or inferior welds, back-gouge roots of welds, and prepare grooves for welding. The cutting process is used where slightly ragged edges are not objectionable. It is normally used on steels but can be used on other metals. It is popular for preparing scrap metal for remelting. The surface of some metals deteriorates when cut or gouged by this process. The area of the cut is relatively small since the molten metal is quickly removed. The surrounding area does not reach high temperatures, thus reducing the tendency toward warpage and cracking. In some cases the surface must be ground to provide quality weld-joint preparation.

Equipment.   Equipment for cutting and gouging is the same as for carbon arc welding and for SMAW, with the exception of the special electrode holder and the required compressed-air supply. The necessary equipment is shown in Fig. 1-29. This consists of:

- The welding machine or power source
- The special electrode holder or torch and cables
- A carbon electrode
- The compressed air supply

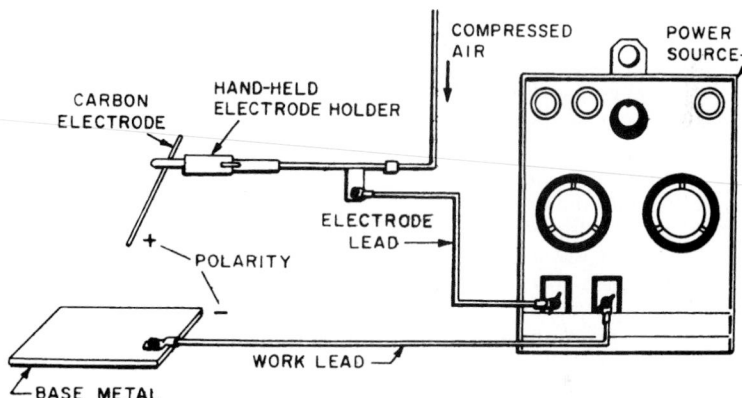

FIGURE 1-29   Equipment for air-carbon arc cutting.

Welding Machine.   The welding machine or power source is normally a CC drooping-characteristic type, either a transformer-rectifier or generator. CV machines with flat characteristics may be used, but precautions must be taken to operate them within their rated output. Specially designed heavy-duty machines are used for CAC-A cutting or gouging with large electrodes. Machines of this type are available with a capacity up to 1000 A. The ac power source CC types can be used for special applications; however, ac-type carbon electrodes are required.

Electrode Holder.   The electrode holder or torch is of a special design which includes the air-jet stream nozzle and the valve. In addition, it must clamp the carbon electrode tightly. Electrode holders come in several sizes, depending on the size of the carbon electrode to be used. Larger holders may be water-cooled. The cable assembly includes the compressed-air hose which is connected to the compressed-air supply.

Electrodes.   Electrodes used for cutting and gouging can be of pure carbon or the graphite type. Electrodes are also available with a copper coating which tends to make the electrodes last longer. Electrodes erode away rapidly during heavy-duty cutting. Electrode diameters may be $\frac{3}{16}$, $\frac{1}{4}$, $\frac{5}{16}$, $\frac{3}{8}$, $\frac{1}{2}$, or $\frac{5}{8}$ in (4.7, 6, 7.8, 9.3, 12, or 15.6 mm). Larger sizes are also available.

Air Supply.   A supply of dry compressed air is required. The air pressure is not critical and ranges from 80 to 100 lb/in.^{2} (551 to 690 kPa). It is normally obtained from shop lines or from an air compressor.

Arc Cutting, Including Plasma Arc Cutting

The electric arc, a highly concentrated energy source, is useful for cutting metals. The arc alone does not produce good-quality cuts, but, when assisted by a jet of oxygen or air, or by plasma, the quality of the cut is greatly improved. There are several arc-welding processes which can also be used for cutting: the plasma arc, the carbon arc, the arc between covered electrodes and the work, and a system that uses a special, hollow, covered electrode whereby oxygen can be introduced inside the electrode to produce a quality cut.

The principle of cutting with an arc is to melt metal. This is done by increasing the heat input faster than heat is extracted from the arc area. On thin materials, the molten metal will fall away by gravity, and a rather crude cut will result. In emergency situations, the arc alone can be used. This is not recommended for industrial applications.

For carbon arc cutting, a single carbon electrode is used with a dc power source using the electrode on the negative pole. The carbon should be sharpened to a long taper approximately half its diameter at the end. It should be gripped close to the arc end to avoid overheating. Position the material to be cut so that it projects over a table edge with a container to catch the molten metal. The arc is struck on the edge of the plate, with a fairly long arc maintained until a puddle is melted at the edge. The arc should then be shortened; this will help force the molten puddle to fall away from the material. A sawing-type motion can be used to help remove the metal from the material being cut. The "icicles" which tend to form on the bottom of the cut can be removed by the arc. Holes may be pierced in steel plates up to ⅜-in (9.8-mm) thick by striking the arc and holding it in one spot until a large puddle is formed. Feed the electrode downward and force it through the plate as the metal becomes molten.

Cutting with the shielded-metal electrode can be accomplished in much the same way as the carbon-arc cutting described above. A smaller-size electrode is used, usually ⅛, ⁵⁄₃₂, or ³⁄₁₆ in (3, 3.8, or 4.5 mm) in diameter, but the welding machine must have sufficient capacity for the size of the electrode selected. The E6011 type is recommended. The coating on the electrode provides a little more arc force than is available with the carbon arc. If electrodes are quickly dipped in water prior to use for cutting, they tend to provide more of a cut before they are consumed in the arc. The shielded-metal and carbon-arc cuts are extremely rough and are normally used only for emergency situations when the proper cutting equipment may not be available.

Oxygen arc cutting is a proprietary method using covered electrodes having a hollow core. A special electrode holder is required. This electrode allows oxygen to pass through the hole in the center of the electrode. A valve on the electrode holder allows the oxygen to be started or stopped. In this process, the arc is struck in the normal way and, as soon as the metal becomes molten, the oxygen is turned on; this provides a jet that oxidizes the molten metal and carries it away. This process is extremely useful for cutting materials such as cast iron, high-chromium stainless steels, and other hard-to-cut substances.

Plasma Arc Cutting.   The plasma arc cutting process (PAC) has become very popular in the last few years. Plasma arc cutting is very similar to plasma arc welding. It uses a *plasma,* which is the fourth state of matter, defined as a gas which has been heated to a high enough temperature to become ionized. When it is ionized, the gas or plasma becomes electrically conductive.

Plasma arc cutting is applied either manually or as a mechanized or fully automated process. It is normally applied manually for thinner materials and is used fully automated for cutting thicker materials and for shape cutting.

The keyhole technique, which actually makes a hole, is used for plasma cutting. The arc in plasma arc cutting, between the electrode and the work, is constricted and forced through a small hole or orifice in the torch. A gas is also forced through this orifice which creates the plasma. The temperature of the plasma is considerably higher than the temperature of the gas tungsten arc. The ionized gas or plasma travels at extremely high speeds and has a force action on the base material which creates the keyhole. The plasma cutting process will cut all commercial metals.

Equipment.   The major components required for PAC are the same as shown for PAW in Fig. 1-22. The power source for PAC is the CC type with a drooping output characteristic. It includes a contactor, since high open-circuit voltages are used. It also includes a controller which operates contactors and solenoid valves for plasma gas and cooling water.

The plasma console includes a high-frequency arc starter, torch protection devices, flow meters, and electric meters. It may also include water-controlled systems and protective interlocks to protect the torch. It may be included in the power-supply case.

The plasma torch contains an electrode which for mechanized welding is usually a tungsten electrode, but for manual cutting contains an electrode made of hafnium. All plasma torches are water-cooled and they come in different sizes, depending on the current level employed. Plasma gas need not be inert. The plasma gas for cutting can be nitrogen or even air. The type of gas used depends on the materials being cut, the expected life of the electrode in the torch, and the quality of the cut.

For mechanized cutting, complex-shape-cutting machines very similar to those used for oxygen cutting are used. These may be operated by controllers which are computer guided or driven by special tracing devices.

Manual plasma arc cutting is shown by Fig. 1-30. Figure 1-31 shows the schedule of plasma cutting parameters on different materials.

GAS WELDING AND CUTTING

Oxyacetylene Welding

The oxyacetylene welding (OAW) process—sometimes called *gas welding, oxyfuel gas welding,* or *torch welding*—is an oxyfuel gas process used to fuse the parts to be welded by heating with a gas flame or flames obtained from the combustion of acetylene with oxygen. The process, shown in Fig. 1-32, may be used with or without filler metal added to fill gaps or grooves. It can be used on thin- to medium-thickness metals of many types. It is most commonly used on ferrous metals and can be used in all positions. It is applied as a manual process and requires a relatively high degree of skill on the part of the welder.

Oxyacetylene welding is the oldest of the modern welding processes. It came into popularity in the late 1800s and is widely used for repair and maintenance, overlaying, sheet-metal welding, and small-diameter-pipe welding.

The oxyacetylene welding process is diagrammed in Fig. 1-33. The oxyacetylene flame is extremely hot, approaching 6300°F (3200°C). This hot flame melts the surface of the materials to be joined so that they flow together to produce a weld. Filler material in the form of a rod is added to fill gaps or grooves. The mixing of the oxygen and fuel gas takes place in the welding torch, and the flame is initiated by means of a spark lighter. The atmosphere provided by the burning of the gases shields the molten metal from the atmosphere.

Process.   The oxygen and acetylene flow through the hoses from the supply source or from individual cylinders to the welding torch, where they are mixed and burned to produce the flame at the torch tip. The reaction for this is

$$2C_2H_2 + O_2 = 2CO + H_2 + \text{heat}$$

This is the primary reaction that occurs in the inner cone of the flame adjacent to the welding tip. The secondary reaction is

$$2CO + H_2 + 1.5O_2 = 2CO_2 + H_2O + \text{heat}$$

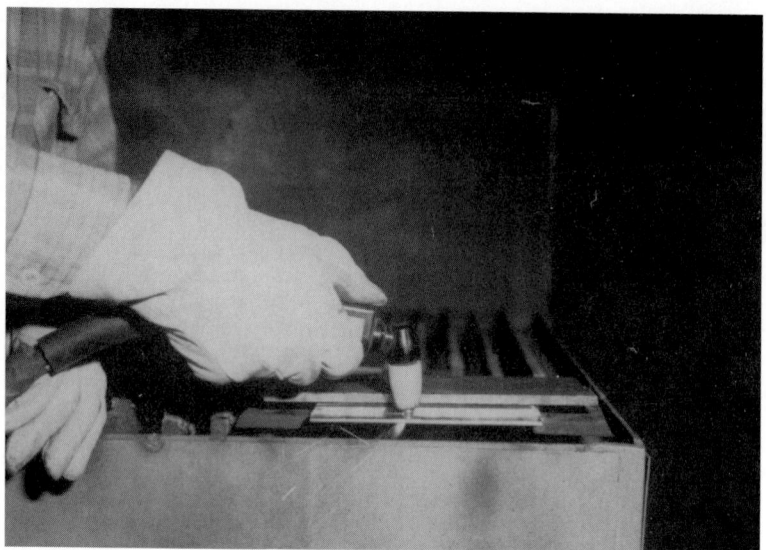

FIGURE 1-30   Manual plasma arc cutting.

Material/ Thickness	⅛ in (3.2 mm)	¼ in (6.4 mm)	½ in (12.8 mm)	¾ in (1.9 mm)	1 in (25.4 mm)
Stainless steel	100	60	24	20	10
Aluminum	125	90	34	25	12
Carbon steel	75	45	24	Not recommended	

FIGURE 1-31   Plasma arc cutting speeds vs. material type and thickness.

FIGURE 1-32   Application of oxyacetylene welding. (*Hobart Brothers Company.*)

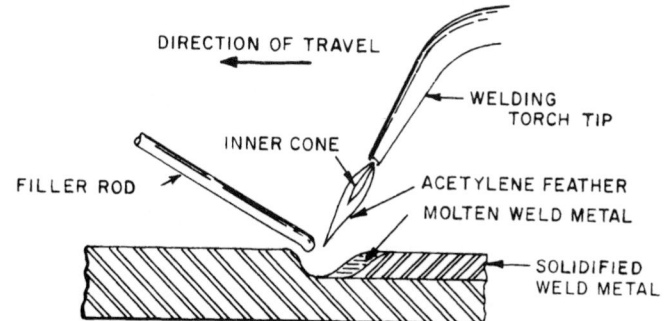

FIGURE 1-33   Process diagram for oxyacetylene welding.

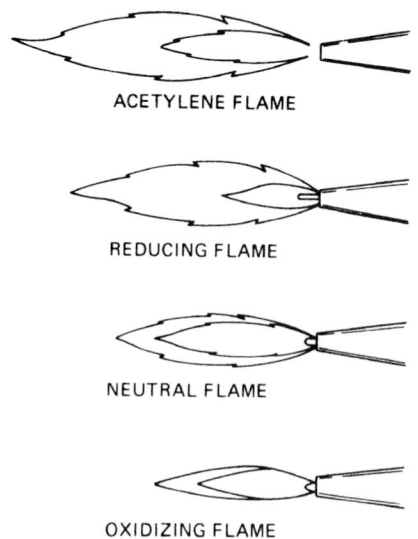

ACETYLENE FLAME

REDUCING FLAME

NEUTRAL FLAME

OXIDIZING FLAME

FIGURE 1-34   Flame types for oxyacetylene welding.

This occurs in the outer portion of the flame, and the extra oxygen is obtained from the atmosphere. Note that CO_2 and water vapor result from the secondary reactions. The CO_2 shields the molten metal from the atmosphere.

In the combustion of oxygen and acetylene, the gases are mixed in the torch in about equal volumes, but the remaining oxygen is obtained from the atmosphere. When the proportions of oxygen and acetylene from the cylinders are the same, the flame is referred to as a *neutral flame,* shown in Fig. 1-34. The exact torch adjustment is such that the inner cone is defined, with no feather of acetylene appearing in the flame. This type of flame is used mostly for welding, brazing, and heating.

When slightly more acetylene is applied to the neutral flame, a visible feather is seen extending from the inner cone. This is known as a *reducing flame.* It has excess acetylene and is used for welding alloy steels, aluminum, and cast iron and for certain surfacing applications. It is slightly cooler than the neutral flame.

When additional oxygen is supplied, the inner cone becomes darker and shorter and the entire flame is smaller and hotter. This flame is called an *oxidizing flame* because of the excess oxygen. An oxidizing flame is normally not used for welding but is used for oxygen flame cutting.

Application.   The oxyacetylene welding process has advantages:

1. The equipment is very portable
2. It is highly versatile
3. The weld pool is visible to the welder
4. Welding is possible in all positions
5. The equipment is relatively inexpensive
6. The same basic equipment can be used for welding, heating, torch brazing, and oxygen flame cutting

The main disadvantage of oxyacetylene welding is the fact it is relatively slow and expensive to use because of the prices of the gases.

Oxyacetylene welding is most useful for joining thin [up to ¼ in (6.2 mm)] steel, copper, and copper alloys, and it can be used for welding aluminum and other nonferrous alloys. It can also be used for overlaying, for surfacing, for wear resistance, etc. as well as for heating metals for bending, straightening, etc. Its industrial applications include maintenance and repair, auto body repair, welding small-diameter piping, brazing, and light manufacturing.

Equipment. Equipment for oxyacetylene welding includes, as shown in Fig. 1-35:

- The welding torch and tips
- The hose for transporting the gas from the supply to the torch
- Regulators for oxygen and acetylene (normally attached to cylinders or to the supply-pipe system)
- A cylinder or supply of oxygen
- A cylinder or supply of acetylene

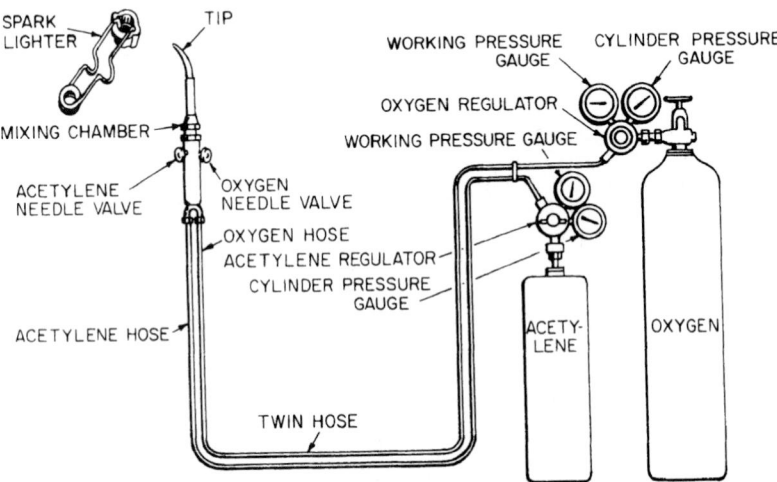

FIGURE 1-35 Equipment for oxyacetylene welding.

In addition, a spark lighter, torch, and cylinder wrench are required. Often a cylinder cart for transporting the cylinders and apparatus is used.

Welding Torch. The welding torch, sometimes called a *blowpipe,* is the major piece of equipment for the process. It performs the function of mixing acetylene with oxygen to produce the required type of flame, which is then directed manually as desired. The torch consists of a handle, or body, which contains the hose connections for oxygen and acetylene and the oxygen and acetylene valves (sometimes called *needle valves*) for regulating gas flow into the torch and a mixing chamber. A medium-pressure oxyacetylene torch is shown in Fig. 1-36. Different sizes of tips can be attached to the torch. These are identified by manufacturers' numbers which indicate the size of the hole or orifice in the end of the tip. There is no standard system for identifying tip sizes, and each manufacturer has its own system; however, in every case the system relates to a drill size which identifies the diameter of the hole.

Gases. The gases used for oxyacetylene welding are oxygen and acetylene. Acetylene produces the highest-temperature flame and is considered the all-purpose fuel for this process. Acetylene is colorless but it has an easily detected odor somewhat like the odor of onions. When the torch is used for heating, brazing, or soldering, other fuel gases may be used,

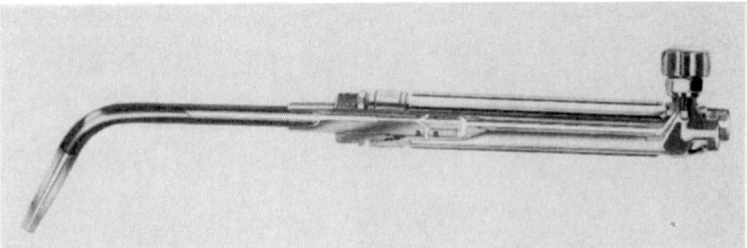

FIGURE 1-36 Medium-pressure torch for oxyacetylene welding. (*Smith Torch Company.*)

such as natural gas, propane, and proprietary fuel gases. Different tips and mixers are needed when other gases are used.

Regulators.   The pressure of the gas used for oxyacetylene welding is relatively low; however, the pressure of the gas in the supply system or in individual cylinders is relatively high. Therefore, a *gas regulator* is used to reduce the pressure from the high pressure to the correct working pressure which should not exceed 15 lb/in^2 (103 kPa) for the torch. This is a complex unit, made of needle valves, springs, and diaphragms, for precisely producing the lower pressure used by the torch. Figure 1-37 shows a gas regulator. The regulators for oxygen and acetylene are different and *cannot be interchanged.* Oxygen connections have right-hand threads and acetylene and other fuel gas connections have left-hand threads. A gas regulator will keep the gas pressure constant and has gauges showing the pressure going to the torch and sometimes has gauges showing the pressure of the supply. Two-stage regulators are normally used with cylinders, and single-stage regulators are normally used for supply lines.

FIGURE 1-37 Gas regulator for oxyacetylene welding. (*Hobart Brothers Company.*)

Gas Cylinders.   Oxygen and acetylene are both supplied in individual cylinders. A pair of cylinders used for oxyacetylene welding is shown in Fig. 1-38. Oxygen cylinders are made of a high-strength steel and contain oxygen at a very high pressure: up to 24,000 lb/in^2 (165 MPa) *CAUTION: Cylinders must be treated carefully and inspected periodically. Mistreating cylinders can damage them and may cause them to explode, creating a very dangerous situation.*

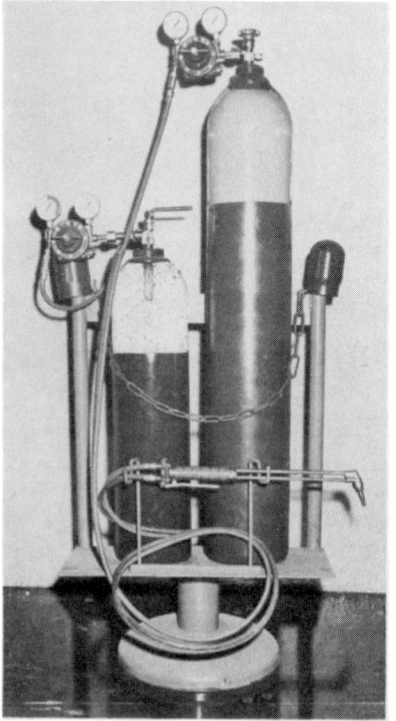

FIGURE 1-38 Gas cylinders for oxyacetylene welding. (*Hobart Brothers Company.*)

Acetylene is stored at a relatively low pressure. Acetylene cannot be stored safely over 15 lb/in² (103 kPa). It is dissolved in liquid acetone which is contained by a filler material in the cylinder. An acetylene cylinder will have a working pressure of 250 lb/in² (1724 kPa); however, most of the acetylene is dissolved in the acetone, which keeps it stable and eliminates the danger from high-pressure free acetylene. Acetylene cylinders should always be kept away from high heat and should be treated with the respect due *any* gas cylinder. There is no uniform national color code for gas cylinders. Each company supplying gases has its own color code. However, there is standardization of threads on the fittings of the cylinders; remember, oxygen cylinders have right-hand threads and acetylene cylinders have left-hand threads.

Cylinder Carts. For portable installations, cylinder carts are usually employed. This allows the cylinders to be attached to a structure even though it is portable. It allows the storage of the hoses and torch and is useful for maintenance applications.

Safety Precautions. The safety precautions for oxyacetylene and gas welding are somewhat special for the process. It is important to follow these safety directions when you are using oxyacetylene welding equipment.

Oxy-Fuel Gas Cutting

Process. The oxy-fuel gas cutting (OFC) process, also known as *oxygen cutting, gas cutting, burning,* and so on, is a thermal process used to sever metals by heating the metal with a flame to an elevated temperature and then using pure oxygen to oxidize the metal and produce the cut. Different fuel gases can be used, including acetylene, natural gas, propane, and a variety of proprietary or tradename fuel gases. The process shown in Fig. 1-39 can be applied manually or by machine. It can be used to cut ferrous materials in sections varying from thin to thick, and it can be used in all positions. Manual OFC requires a fairly high degree of skill to produce quality cuts.

Details of the process are diagrammed in Fig. 1-40. This diagram shows the torch and cutting tip, the preheating flames to bring the

FIGURE 1-39 Application of oxy-fuel gas cutting. (*Hobart Brothers Company.*)

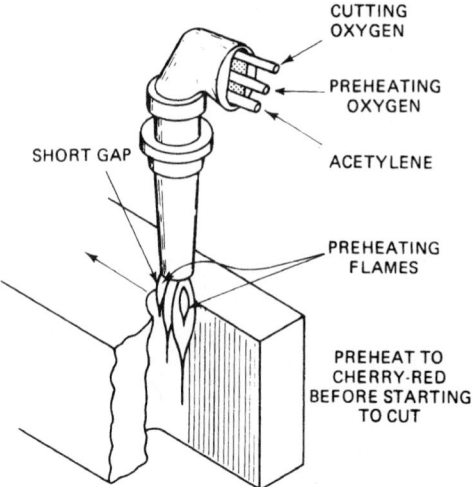

FIGURE 1-40   Process diagram for oxy-fuel gas cutting.

metal up to the kindling temperature, and the oxygen jet supplied to oxidize, or burn, metal away to produce the cut.

Application.   The cutting process:

1. Is very portable
2. Is versatile
3. Allows cutting in all positions
4. Uses relatively inexpensive equipment
5. Can be used to cut steels

The disadvantages of the process are:

1. It cannot be used to cut nonferrous materials
2. The cut surfaces are not as smooth as mechanically cut surfaces

It is widely used throughout industry as a manual process. It is also widely used as a machine-cutting or automatic-cutting process with special torch controls and programmers for cutting shapes. When it is used as an automatic process, extremely smooth surfaces can be obtained.

Equipment.   Oxy-fuel gas welding equipment includes:

• The cutting torch and tips
• Oxygen and fuel gas hoses
• Regulators for oxygen and fuel gas or acetylene
• A supply of oxygen and fuel gas from cylinders or a piping system

The manual equipment is essentially the same as used for oxyacetylene welding. For automatic applications, complex motion devices and controllers are required.

   The Cutting Torch.   The cutting torch can be a combination cutting and welding torch or a torch especially designed for cutting only. The gases are mixed within the torch, and needle valves control the quantity of each gas flowing into the mixing chamber. A lever-type valve controls the oxygen flow for cutting. Various sizes and types of tips are used with the cutting torch for specific applications of cutting, gouging, beveling, etc. The cutting tips are sized by the oxygen orifice size in the cutting tip. There is no standard cutting-size designation, and each company has its own system; however, each tip size relates to the standard drill size for the cutting orifice. In this way they can be related to the thickness of metal to be cut. Preheat flames are arranged around the central cutting orifice and are sufficient to bring the metal to the kindling temperature prior to cutting. Fig. 1-41 shows the flame cutting torch.

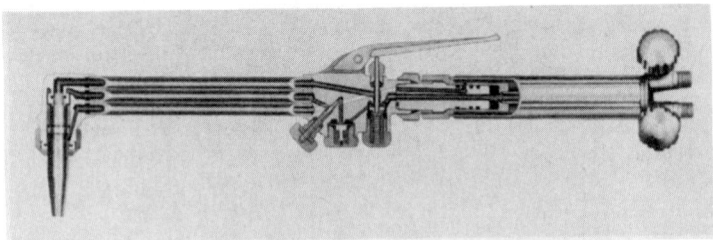

FIGURE 1-41 Cutting assembly with welding torch body. (*Smith Torch Company.*)

The rest of the equipment is the same as that used in the oxyacetylene welding process.

Gases. The gas used for oxygen cutting is normally pure oxygen, while the fuel gas is always a hydrocarbon gas, often acetylene. Other fuel gases used are natural gas, propane, and a variety of proprietary liquid-petroleum-base or propane-base gases. The selection of fuel gas is extremely complex. The fuel gas is used for the preheating flame that brings the material to be cut up to its kindling temperature. The basic cutting process using oxygen is not affected by the choice of preheat fuel gas. The type of fuel gas relates primarily to the time period required to bring the material up to the kindling temperature.

Safety Precautions. Safety precautions for oxygen–fuel gas cutting are extremely important because it is widely used in maintenance and construction work. The normal precautions involving gases under pressure should be observed. Additional precautions relate to the cutting of vessels and containers that may be sealed and/or may have contained combustible materials. This should not be done without taking extra-special precautions. Another problem relating to oxygen cutting is the fact that hot metal from the cut will travel many, many feet and will retain sufficient heat to set combustible materials on fire. Metallic or noncombustible material should be used to backstop the hot metal being ejected from the cut. Cutting should never be attempted in confined areas without first testing the atmosphere and providing a fire watch or observers to continually watch the cutter while it is in operation.

Machine or Automatic Cutting. Mechanized cutting has become very popular in the manufacturing industry. Figure 1-42 shows typical automatic cutting equipment. Multiple torches can be used. The controller can be a simple contour-following device, electric-eye tracing system, or computer-controlled system. The selection of automatic equipment depends on the size and thickness of the material being cut, the production quantity requirements, and the control systems that are to be utilized.

BRAZING AND SOLDERING

The primary difference between brazing and soldering is the arbitrary temperature of 840°F (450°C). Both are a group of processes which join materials by heating them to a suitable temperature; both use a filler metal which is distributed between closely fitted surfaces of the

FIGURE 1-42   Automatic cutting equipment.

joint by capillary attraction. Solder, the filler metal used in soldering, has a melting temperature below 840°F (450°C). In brazing, the filler metal has a melting temperature above 840°F
(450°C). Both solder and brazing alloy have a composition somewhat different from that of
the base metal. Also, for both soldering and brazing, a fluxing material is normally used.

There is one other term that should be mentioned: *braze welding.* It refers to a process that
is similar to, but different from, brazing in that capillary attraction is not used to distribute the
filler metal. Braze welding is used quite often to join cast-iron sections.

Heating

The method of heating the materials to be joined is the method usually used to differentiate
between the different soldering and brazing processes. The same methods of heating can be
used for both soldering and brazing. A gas torch is one of the most common methods of both
brazing and soldering. Dipping the materials in flux or molten filler metal is another method
of heating. Another method of heating the parts is by means of a furnace. Heat can be applied
by induction or infrared radiation. Generating heat by means of the resistance of the parts to
current flow is also used, but introducing heat by means of an iron is a method used only for
soldering. Other heating methods are less popular.

Torch brazing is the method discussed here for applying heat to the parts to be joined. In
torch brazing or soldering, heat can be applied by using different fuel gases and oxygen or air
combinations.

The torch for melting high-temperature brazing alloys is the same as that used for oxy-fuel
gas welding, whereas the torch for soldering uses a fuel-gas–air system. Different torches or
tips are used for the different fuel gas and oxygen or air combinations. In each case, however,
the use of the torch and its manipulation are essentially the same. The basic principle is to provide uniform heating of the parts being joined. Proper fluxing and proper fit of the parts are
essential to allow capillary attraction to pull the molten filler metal into the joint.

Joints

Both brazed and soldered joints require close fit of the parts to be joined. This is necessary to provide the capillary attraction to pull the alloy filler metal into the joint and to provide sufficient area of filler metal to ensure a sufficiently strong joint. The lap-type joint is most commonly used, since it provides for sufficient faying surfaces to attract the filler material. Butt-type joints are rarely used for soldering or brazing. One of the most common types of joints is the socket joint used for pipe and tubing.

Fluxes

Flux is almost always used in torch brazing. The flux helps maintain cleanliness of the faying surfaces so that the filler metal will adhere properly. The joints should be properly cleaned before applying flux because cleaning the surface *is not* the function of the flux. It does, however, help by combining with, dissolving, or inhibiting the formation of chemical compounds which would interfere with the quality of the joint. The flux also protects the surface during the heating operation. The type of flux to be used is chosen on the basis of the process function and metal to be joined. The flux and the filler metal must also be matched. The AWS *Brazing Manual* provides information concerning fluxes and matching them to the base metal and filler metal. The American Welding Society provides a specification for brazing fluxes, A5.31. AWS Specification A5.8 covers filler metals for brazing, and ASTM Specification B 32 provides the composition and uses of solders. The AWS *Soldering Manual* provides complete information concerning this process. The particular alloy or type of filler metal to be used depends on the process and the metals being joined.

Summary

Quality brazes or soldered joints can be made by following the basic principles of cleanliness, fluxing, joint detail, and matching the proper flux and filler metal alloy.

OTHER WELDING PROCESSES

The previous sections provided information concerning arc-welding processes and some of the other welding and cutting processes most commonly used by plant engineers. However, there are many other welding processes used in manufacturing that should be mentioned.

The American Welding Society's master chart for welding and allied processes (Fig. 1-1) shows seven families of welding processes, two families of allied processes (thermal spraying and adhesive bonding), and three families of thermal cutting processes. Previously we have described arc welding, brazing, soldering, oxy-fuel gas welding, oxygen cutting, and arc cutting. Some other important processes are now briefly described.

Resistance Welding

Resistance welding is a group of welding processes that produce joints of metal by means of heat obtained from resistance and pressure. The resistance is that of the work to the electric current in a circuit of which the work is a part, and the pressure is applied externally. Spot welding is the most popular of the resistance-welding processes. Spot welding is accomplished with a machine which uses electrodes to carry the current to and through the joint being welded. The electrodes also apply the pressure which is necessary to force the parts together after the current has heated the metal to the welding temperature. Resistance welding is extremely fast, and filler metal is normally not required. It is very popular for welding automobile bodies and for making household appliances. Other resistance-welding processes are projection welding, seam welding, flash welding, and high-frequency resistance welding, with many variations of each. Most metals can be resistance-welded. Special precautions are required, however, for certain metals.

Solid-State Welding

The solid-state family of welding processes includes friction welding, cold welding, ultrasonic welding, explosion welding, among others. These processes are not widely used for maintenance and repair.

Friction Welding. In friction welding, the weld is produced by heat obtained from a mechanical sliding motion between rubbing surfaces. The process usually involves rotating one part against another to generate frictional heat at the junction. When a suitably high temperature has been reached, rotational motion ceases and pressure is applied to create the weld. Equipment is similar to a lathe; it is extremely fast, and no filler metal is required. It can be used to weld dissimilar metals together. It is restricted primarily to mass-production industries and is used to weld plastics.

Cold Welding. Cold welding is a solid-state process where pressure at room temperature is used to produce the weld. The metals are substantially deformed, and extremely high pressures are required on extremely clean interfacing surfaces. This process is restricted to thinner materials, and it is often used for welding nonferrous materials such as aluminum and copper. It is also used to weld aluminum to copper.

Explosion Welding. Explosion welding is also a solid-state process. In this case the weld is obtained by high-velocity movement toward each other of the parts to be joined. The movement is caused by an explosion. The interface between the parts welded shows a sawtooth-type configuration. Heat is instantly produced from the shock wave associated with impact. This process is often used to weld dissimilar parts together and is used for overlaying or cladding materials.

Ultrasonic Welding. Ultrasonic welding is another of the solid-state processes. It produces the joint by local application of high-frequency energy to the parts being welded, while they are held together under pressure. Welding occurs when the electrode, which couples the energy to the work, is vibrating at ultrasonic frequencies. This, plus pressure, creates the weld. Ultrasonic welding is restricted to thinner materials and is quite often used in the packaging industries. It is also used for welding plastics.

Electron-Beam Welding

Electron-beam (EB) welding is one of the most important non-arc welding processes. In EB welding, the heat for welding is obtained from a concentrated beam of high-velocity electrons impinging upon the surface of the work. Pressure is not used, but filler metal is sometimes added.

EB welding is normally done in a vacuum chamber. The work and work-moving devices, as well as the electron beam, are contained in the chamber. The electron beam is generated by an electron gun and is similar to that in an x-ray tube. The work is taken to the machine and must fit within the chamber. Evacuation of the chamber was a major part of the operation. Recently, however, specially designed chambers which allow continuous entrance and exit of parts have been used in mass-production industries. A lower vacuum in the chamber is sometimes used. EB welding in the atmosphere is also possible. However it is restricted to operating close to the electron gun, which must be in a vacuum chamber. The capital cost for EB welding is quite high, and this type of welding, therefore, is restricted to specialty materials and special applications. It is also used for cutting, but is not too popular in that application.

Laser-Beam Welding

Laser-beam welding is very similar to electron-beam welding except that the heat is obtained from a concentrated coherent light beam impinging on the surface of the work; a vacuum chamber is not required. However, the generation of a laser beam is extremely complex and expensive and the electrical efficiency of the process is relatively low. This process is quite new, and additional developments are expected. The laser beam is used for cutting as well as for welding and will cut nonmetals as well as metals. There are more applications for laser cutting than for laser welding. *However, developments in this field are accelerating and the reader is urged to investigate the state of the art when considering the various alternatives for any application.*

Thermite Welding

One of the older welding processes still in use is *thermite welding.* In this process, the weld is produced by heating the parts to be joined with superheated liquid metal obtained from a chemical reaction between a metal oxide and aluminum. The filler metal is obtained from the superheated liquid metal. The heat is obtained from an exothermic reaction between iron oxide and aluminum. This reaction occurs immediately above the weld, and when it has gone to completion, the superheated liquid flows into the weld area and is retained by a mold. The process is used for joining rails, reinforcing bars, and other similar items.

QUALITY CONTROL AND INSPECTION METHODS

The quality of welds can be determined by nondestructive testing methods. Welds made in most commercial metals will normally equal the strength of the base metal. This depends on the proper selection of the process and procedure including the filler metal. Welds in metals having special properties due to heat treatment or working may not equal the strength of the base metal, since the heat of making the weld will deteriorate these special properties adjacent to the weld. For these types of metals special precautions are required. For all other welds, however, the quality of the weld can be determined and controlled. Adherence to procedures that are known to produce quality welds is necessary. After the weld has been made, it can be inspected by a number of nondestructive evaluation techniques. The most popular is visual inspection. Visual testing (VT) is used by welders, supervisors, and inspectors to look for potential defects such as undersized welds that can be checked by gauges, rough or irregular surfaces, surface cracks, surface porosity, and undercuts. In addition, weld quality can be determined by at least four other evaluation techniques.

Visual Inspection

Visual welding inspection is the most widely used and most valuable welding inspection technique. Particularly for noncritical welding production, it is the most effective. It requires less time than any other inspection method and is also the least expensive. In addition to being a weldment inspection technique, it provides a review of the welding procedures and qualification records and thus is also a preventive tool. The inspector is able to watch and require procedure conformity during weldment production.

Visual inspection throughout the production of a weldment can catch errors in each step and find items which might develop, errors such as using faulty materials or procedures. Repairs are less expensive when made on an incompleted piece of work. The inspector can verify the basic materials, the joint preparation, the process equipment, and welding technique long before the weldment is completed. This early correction of the weld problems is particularly important on highly critical weldments.

Inspection can find errors in weld preparation, dimensions, alignment, fit-up, cleanliness, welding procedure, finish, and marking. They can detect scabs, seams, scale, laminations, roughness, spatter, craters, surface porosity, undercuts, overlaps, cracks, and inadequate penetration. They can check for many of these at once and can note several defects simultaneously.

For any other welding inspection technique, the inspector needs to be able to interpret different types of indicators. With visual inspection they must know welding more thoroughly and be able to inspect all areas of the weldment production. The success depends on the alertness, eyesight, welding knowledge and subjective judgment of the inspector.

Visual inspection is unreliable on subsurface problems, and suspicion of subsurface flaws results primarily from the inspector's judgment of the welder's actual work. Tiny flaws can be overlooked very easily and can be covered by peening and hammering when slag is removed.

Because of the absence of elaborate equipment, and the simplicity and low cost of visual inspection, it may be relied on too heavily when used entirely by itself rather than in conjunction with subsurface inspection methods.

Equipment.   A pocket magnifier, a flashlight, a borescope, a viewing mirror, a weld gauge, a scale and tape measure, a straightedge, a T square, and weld standards are all needed for visual inspection.

Other Methods of Nondestructive Testing (NDT)

Nondestructive testing (NDT) techniques are often used to supplement visual inspection. Many of these techniques provide a permanent record of defects and most have the capability of detecting subsurface flaws. Exception of this is penetrant examination. This technique is a highly sensitive method for detecting minute discontinuities which are open to the surface. It is used on all commercial metals and on plastics and ceramics.

In penetrant testing (PT), a liquid penetrant is applied to the surface of the parts to be inspected. It seeps into any surface opening and becomes visible after an absorbent material is applied. This results in a blotting action which draws the penetrant from any surface opening and makes an indication that is larger than the actual defect. Equipment is relatively inexpensive and uses pressurized cans for the chemicals employed.

Magnetic testing (MT) is widely used and will detect cracks, porosity, seams, inclusions, lack of fusion, and other discontinuities in ferromagnetic materials below the surface. This method involves the establishment of a magnetic field in the part being inspected. Applying magnetic particles to the surface and examining the surface for accumulation of particles is an indication of a defect. Electric power is required; however, equipment can be portable, although stationary units are not normally portable. Dry powder or liquid detection material is used.

Radiographic testing (RT), another nondestructive examination method, uses x-rays or gamma radiation to examine the interior of welds. Radiographic examination gives a permanent film record of defects, which are relatively easy to interpret. X-rays generated by electron bombardment of tungsten and gamma rays emitted by radioactive elements penetrate materials. The radiation intensity is modified by the passage through the material. The amount of energy absorbed by a material depends on the thickness and density. A film is produced which shows different densities that can be easily related to defects and provides a permanent record. Gamma radiation equipment is quite portable but x-ray equipment is less so.

Ultrasonic testing (UT) is another popular examination technique. It is a nondestructive method which employs mechanical vibrations similar to audible sound waves but of a higher frequency. A beam of ultrasonic energy is directed into the workpiece being examined. The beam travels through the material with only a small loss except when it is intercepted and reflected by a discontinuity or a change in material. Ultrasonic examination will find subsurface as well as surface discontinuities. A cathode-ray tube is used to display the indication. The vibrations are transmitted into the test piece through a coupling from a transducer, which is used to send the ultrasonic energy and to receive the reflected energy. A permanent record can be made of this technique. It is extremely sensitive and is becoming more widely used.

Table 1-3 is a guide to welding quality control nondestructive techniques.

WELDING CODES AND QUALIFICATIONS OF WELDERS

Before a welder can begin work on any product covered by a welding code or specification, he or she must become certified under the code that applies. Many different codes are in use, and it is exceedingly important that the specific code is referred to when taking qualification tests. The following types of products are covered by codes: pressure vessels and pressure piping, highway and railway bridges, the steel framework of public buildings, tanks and containers that will hold flammable or explosive materials, cross-country pipelines, aircraft, ordnance material, ships, and boats. A qualified welding procedure is required, and written permission is necessary before repairing or modifying any of these products.

Certification is obtained differently under the different codes. Certification under one code may not necessarily qualify a welder to weld under a different code. In most cases certification for one employer will not allow the welder to work for another employer. The American Welding Society is also qualifying and certifying welders under different codes and standards. If the welder uses a different process or if the welding procedure is altered drastically, recertification is required. In most codes, if the welder is continually employed, welding recertification is not required, provided the work performed meets the quality requirement. An exception is the military aircraft code, which requires requalification periodically.

Qualification tests may be given by responsible manufacturers, contractors, or testing agencies. On pressure vessels the welding procedure must be qualified before the welders can be qualified. To become qualified, the welder must make specified welds using the selected process, base metal, thickness, electrode type, position, and joint design. Standard test specimens must be made under the observation of a qualified person. In government specifications a government inspector must witness the making of welding specimens. Specimens must be properly identified and tested.

The most common test is the guided bend test. In some cases x-ray examinations, fracture tests or other tests are employed. Satisfactory completion of the tests, provided that they meet acceptability standards, will qualify the welder for specific types of welding. The welding that will be allowed depends on the particular code. In general, the code indicates the range of thicknesses which may be welded, the positions which may be employed and the alloys which may be welded.

Qualification of welders is an extremely technical subject and cannot be adequately covered here. The actual code must be obtained and studied prior to taking any test.

The two most important codes are:

Structural Welding Code, AWS D1.1

"Welding Qualifications," Sec. IX of the *ASME Boiler and Pressure Vessel Code*

These codes can be obtained from the sponsoring association. If the product is covered by casualty insurance, consult your insurance representative.

TABLE 1-3 Guide to Welding Quality Control (NDT) Techniques

Technique	Equipment	Defects detected	Advantages	Disadvantages	Other considerations
Visual, VT	Pocket magnifier, welding viewer, flashlight, weld gauge, mirror	Weld preparation, fit-up; cleanliness, roughness, spatter, undercuts, overlaps, inadequate penetration and size; welding procedures	Easy to use; fast, inexpensive, usable at all stages of production	For surface conditions only; dependent on subjective opinion of inspector	Most universally used inspection technique
Magnetic particle, MT	Iron powder, wet, dry, or fluorescent; commercial power source; black light for the fluorescent type	Surface and near-surface discontinuities, cracks, etc.; subsurface porosity and slag on light materials	Indicates discontinuities not visible to the naked eye; useful in checking edges prior to welding, also, repairs; no size restriction	Used on magnetic materials only; surface roughness may distort magnetic field	Testing should be from two perpendicular directions to catch discontinuities which may be parallel to one set of magnetic lines
Liquid penetrant, PT	Fluorescent or visible commercial penetrating liquids and developers; black light for the fluorescent type	Defects open to the surface only	Very small, tight, surface imperfections show up. Easy to apply and to interpret; inexpensive; use on either magnetic or nonmagnetic materials	Somewhat time-consuming in the various steps of the processes	Often used on root pass of highly critical pipe welds; if material improperly cleaned, some indications may be misleading
Radiographic, RT	X-ray or gamma-ray equipment; film-processing equipment; film-viewing equipment; penetrometers	Most internal discontinuities and flaws; limited by direction of discontinuity	Provides permanent record; indicates both surface and internal flaws; applicable on all materials	Usually not suitable for fillet-weld inspection; film exposure and processing critical; slow and expensive	Most popular technique for subsurface inspection; required by many codes and specifications
Ultrasonic, UT	Commercial ultrasonic units and probes; reference and comparison patterns	Can locate all flaws located by other methods with the addition of other exceptionally small flaws	Extremely sensitive; use restricted to only very complex weldments; can be used on all materials	Time-consuming; demands highly developed interpretation skill; permanent record not normally obtained	For irregularly shaped parts, immersion testing often used; required by some codes

WELDING SYMBOLS

Welding symbols are the method of communicating welding sizes and weld designs from the engineer or designer to the shop set-up operator and welder. It is a graphical method developed and established by the American Welding Society and widely used in North America. It has become a national standard and is broadly adopted by many countries throughout the world. More complete information concerning welding symbols is covered in the latest edition of the AWS publication *Standard Symbols for Welding, Brazing, and Nondestructive Examination,* AWS A2.4. Welding symbols must be used and understood by the designer, engineer, and drafter, and placed on all weldment drawings. The symbols must also be well known by the set-up operator, the welder, welding supervisors, and welding inspectors so that the instructions from the designer are properly followed in manufacturing the weldment in the shop. Training programs for teaching welding symbols are available. They are widely used and should always be used for weldments in that they greatly reduce notes and superfluous information on drawings.

The basic information concerning welding symbols is shown in Fig. 1-43. For more information on this important subject, consult the AWS publication.

POWER SOURCES (MACHINES) FOR ARC WELDING

Many different types and sizes of arc welding machines are commercially available. It is important to select the machine most suited for the particular work to be done. The following describes the different types of machines available, and enables you to select the one most ideally suited for your work.

There are two basic categories of power sources, the conventional, or *constant-current* (CC) variable-voltage, welding machine with the drooping volt ampere curve, and the *constant-voltage* (CV), or constant-potential (CP), or modified constant-voltage machine with the fairly flat characteristic curve. The CC machine can be used for manual welding and, under some conditions, for automatic welding. The CV machine is used *only* for continuous-electrode-wire arc-welding processes operated automatically or semiautomatically. These types of machines are best understood by comparing their respective volt-ampere characteristic output curves. This type of curve is obtained by loading the welding machine with variable resistance and plotting the voltage at the electrode and work terminals against the ampere output. Fig. 1-44 shows two characteristic curves.

Conventional or Constant-Current (CC) Welding Machines

The conventional or constant-current welding machine is used for manual covered (stick) electrode arc welding or SMAW, the gas tungsten (TIG) process or GTAW, carbon arc welding (CAW), arc gouging, and stud welding (SW). It can be used for automatic welding with larger-sized electrode wire, but only with a *voltage sensing* wire feeder.

The constant-current welder produces a volt-ampere output curve, as shown by curves in Fig. 1-44.

A brief study of the curve will reveal that a machine of this type produces maximum output voltage with no load (zero current), and, as the load increases, the output voltage decreases. Under welding conditions the output voltage is between 20 to 40 V. The open-circuit voltage is between 60 and 85 V. Constant-current machines are available that produce either ac or dc welding power or both ac and dc.

On the constant-current welding machine, when welding is done with covered electrodes, the arc voltage is partially controlled by the welder and has a direct relationship to the arc length. As the arc length is increased (a long arc), the arc voltage increases. If the arc length is decreased (a short arc), the arc voltage decreases. The output curve shows that when the arc voltage increases (long arc), the welding current decreases, or when the arc voltage decreases (short arc), the welding current increases. Thus, without changing the machine setting, the welder can vary the current in the arc or "welding heat" a limited amount by lengthening or shortening the arc.

Constant-current machines are designed for ac or dc welding power and can be rotating (generators) or static (transformers or transformer/rectifier) machines.

Generator Welding Machines

The generator welding machine driven by an electric motor is becoming less popular. It has been replaced by less expensive machines such as the transformer, transformer/rectifier, the inverter, etc. However, for field work the engine-driven generator is still very popular. The generator is powered by an internal combustion engine fueled by gasoline, diesel, or liquefied petroleum (LP) gas. Engine-driven welders are powered by either water- or liquid-cooled engines, and many provide auxiliary power for emergency lighting, power tools, etc. These machines are usually of the constant-current type with drooping volt-ampere characteristic. This type of machine can be used for automatic welding in the field. In this case, voltage-sensing-type controls for the wire feeder are required. This type of system is not used for small-diameter electrode wire automatic welding.

Transformer Welding Machines

The transformer-type welding machine is the least expensive, lightest, and smallest of the different types. It produces alternating current for welding. The transformer takes power directly from the utility line, transforms it to the power required for welding and, by means of various magnetic circuits, inductors, etc., provides the volt-ampere characteristics proper for welding. The welding current output of a transformer may be adjusted in many different ways. The simplest method is to use a tapped secondary coil on the transformer. This is a popular method employed by many of the limited-input small welding transformers. The leads to the electrode holder and the work are connected to plugs, which may be inserted in sockets on the front of the machine in various locations to provide the required welding current. On some machines, a tap switch is employed instead of the plug-in arrangement.

On industrial transformer welding machines, a continuous output current control is usually provided. This can be mechanical or electrical control. The mechanical method involves moving the core of the transformer or moving the position of the coils within the transformer. The more advanced method of adjusting current output is by means of electrical circuits. In this method the core of the transformer or reactor is saturated by an auxiliary electric circuit which controls the amount of current delivered to the output terminals. By adjusting a small knob, it is possible to provide continuous current adjustment from the minimum to maximum of the output.

The transformer machine has some limitations. The power required is supplied by a single-phase system. This may create an unbalance of the power supply lines, which is objectionable to most utility power companies. In addition, transformers have a rather low-power-factor demand unless they are equipped with power-factor-correcting capacitors. The addition of capacitors corrects the power factor under load and produces a reasonable power factor which is not objectionable to electric power companies.

Transformer welding machines have the lowest initial cost, are the least expensive to operate, and require less space. In addition, alternating current welding power supplied by transformers reduces arc blow, which can be troublesome on many welding applications.

Transformer/Rectifier Welding Machines

Some types of electrodes operate best with dc power. A method of supplying dc to the arc is by adding a rectifier, an electrical device which changes ac into dc. Rectifier welding machines use three-phase power input, which overcomes the line unbalance mentioned before.

AMERICAN WELDING SOCIETY

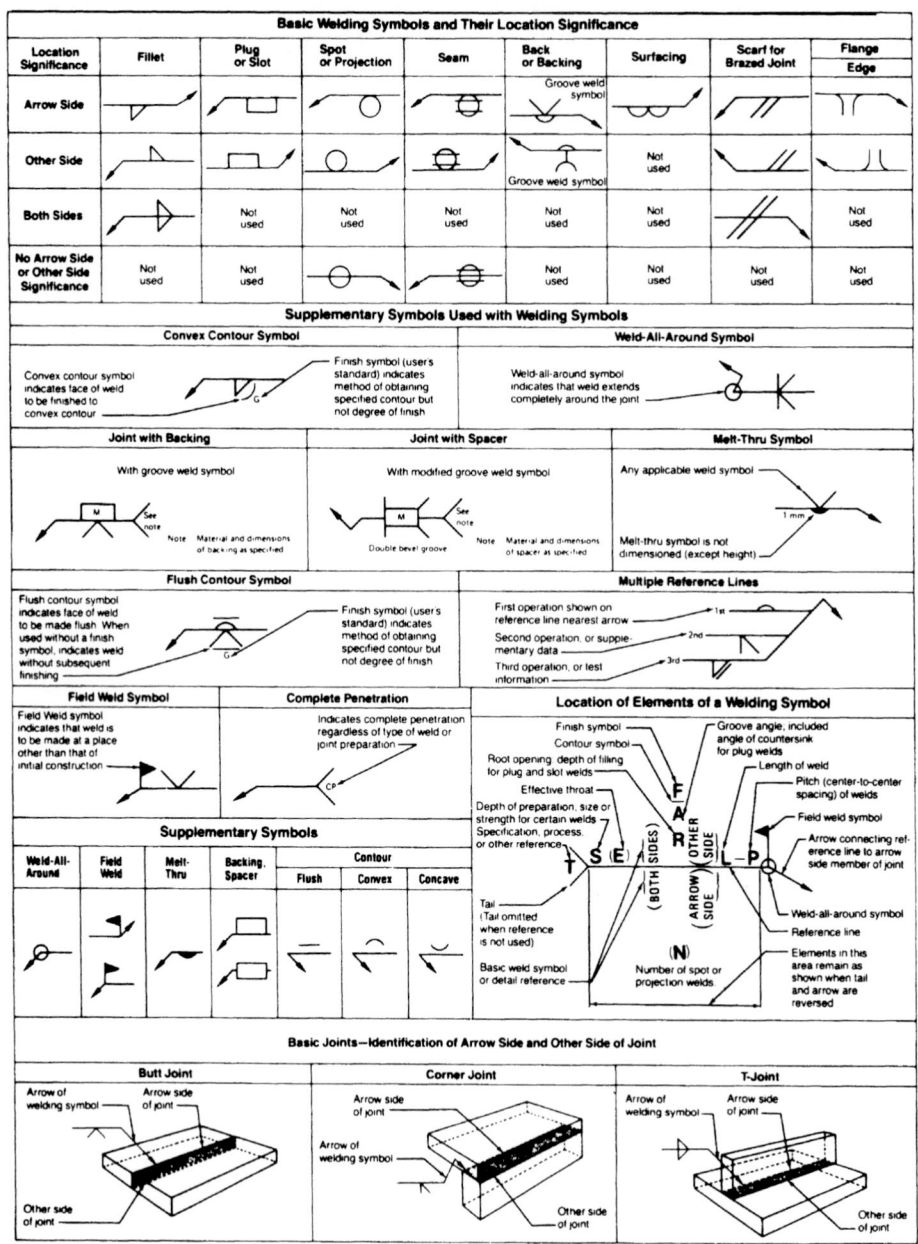

FIGURE 1-43 American Welding Society standard welding symbols.

STANDARD WELDING SYMBOLS

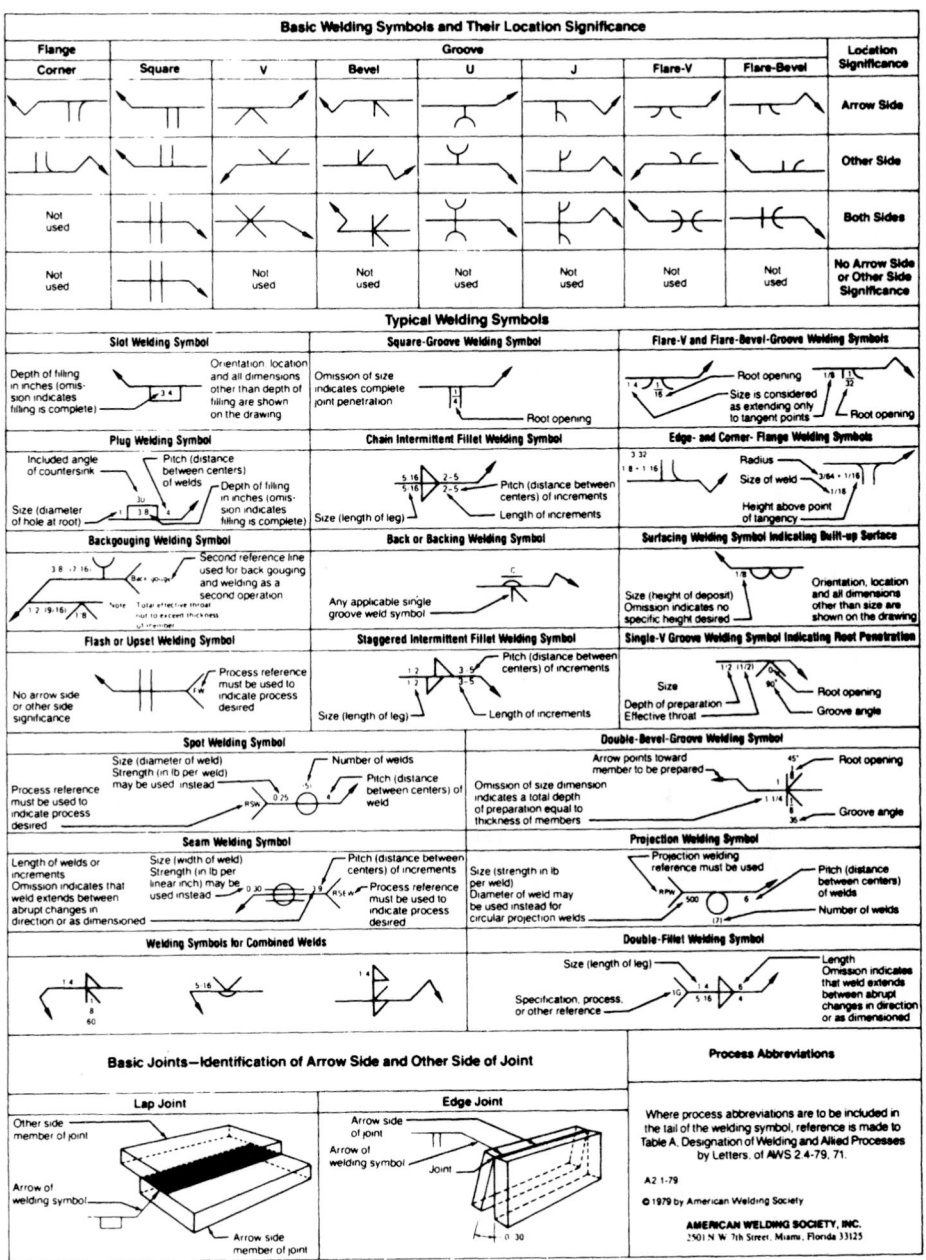

FIGURE 1-43 *(Continued)*

AMERICAN WELDING SOCIETY ◇ STANDARD WELDING SYMBOLS

Basic Welding Symbols and Their Location Significance

	Square	V	Bevel	U (Groove)	J (Groove)	Flare-V	Flare-bevel
						Not used	Not used
						Not used	Not used
						Not used	Not used
	Not used	Not used	Not used	Not used	Not used		

Supplementary Symbols

Weld-all-Around	Field Weld	Melt-thru

Contour		
Flush	Convex	Concave

Designation of Welding and Allied Processes by Letters

GMAW P .... gas metal arc welding—pulsed arc
GMAW S .... gas metal arc welding— short circuiting arc
GTAC .... gas tungsten arc cutting
GTAW .... gas tungsten arc welding
GTAW P .... gas tungsten arc welding—pulsed arc
HFRW .... high frequency resistance welding
HPW .... hot pressure welding

IB .... induction brazing
INS .... iron soldering
IRB .... infrared brazing
IRS .... infrared soldering
IS .... induction soldering
IW .... induction welding
LBC .... laser beam cutting
LBW .... laser beam welding

LOC .... oxygen lance cutting
MAC .... metal arc cutting
OAW .... oxyacetylene welding
OC .... oxygen cutting
OFC .... oxyfuel gas cutting
OFC-A .... oxyacetylene cutting
OFC-H .... oxyhydrogen cutting
OFC-N .... oxynatural gas cutting

OFC-P .... oxypropane cutting
OFW .... oxyfuel gas welding
OHW .... oxyhydrogen welding
PAC .... plasma arc cutting
PAW .... plasma arc welding
PEW .... percussion welding
PGW .... pressure gas welding
POC .... metal powder cutting

PSP .... plasma spraying
RB .... resistance brazing
RPW .... projection welding
RS .... resistance soldering
RSEW .... resistance seam welding
RSW .... resistance spot welding
ROW .... roll welding
RW .... resistance welding

S .... soldering
SAW .... submerged arc welding
SAW-S .... series submerged arc welding
SMAC .... shielded metal arc cutting
SMAW .... shielded metal arc welding
SSW .... solid state welding
SW .... stud arc welding
TB .... torch brazing

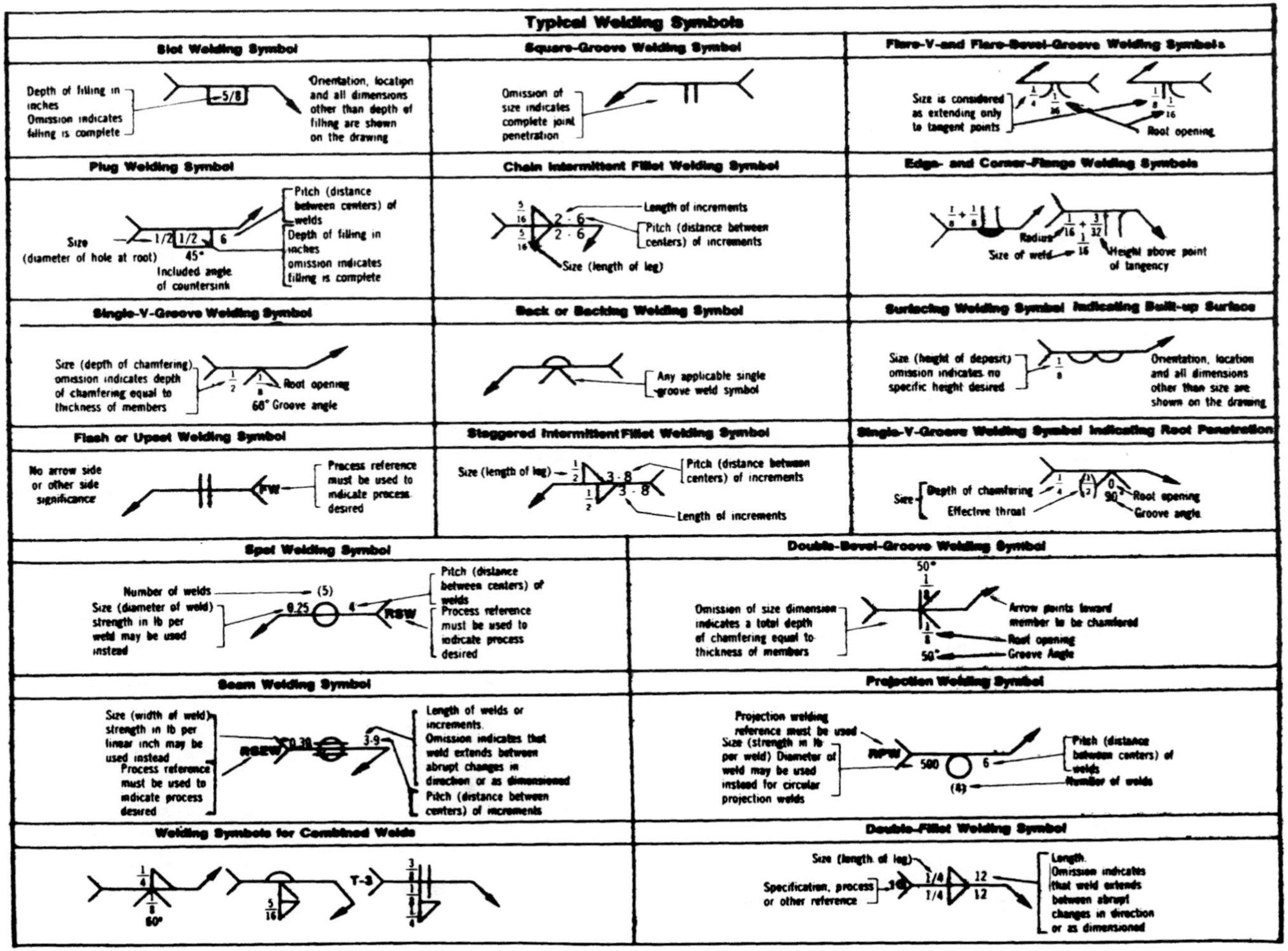

FIGURE 1-43 *(Continued)*

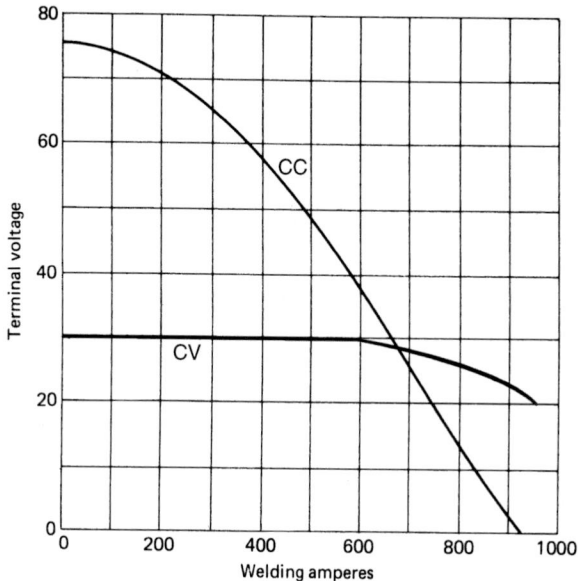

FIGURE 1-44 Voltage-current characteristic curve.

In this type of machine, the transformers feed into a rectifier bridge which then produces dc for the arc. In other cases, where both ac and dc may be required, a single-phase ac transformer is connected to the rectifier. By means of a switch the welder can select either ac or dc straight- or reverse-polarity current for the welding requirement. In some types of ac-dc machines, a high-frequency oscillator, plus water and gas control valves, is installed. This then makes the machine suited for gas tungsten arc welding as well as for manual coated-electrode welding.

Transformer/rectifier welding machines are available in different sizes and for single-phase or three-phase power supply. They may also be arranged for different primary voltages from the power line. The transformer/rectifier unit is more efficient electrically than the generator and provides quite operation.

Constant-Voltage (CV) Welding Machines

A constant-voltage power source, sometimes called *constant-potential,* or *modified constant-voltage* power source, is a welding machine that provides a nominally constant voltage over a range of current. The characteristic curve of this type of machine is shown by the CV volt-ampere curve of Fig. 1-44. This type of machine is used for semiautomatic or automatic arc welding with small continuously fed electrode wire. These machines are designed to produce only dc.

In continuous-wire welding, the burn-off rate of a specific size and type of electrode wire is proportional to the welding current. As the welding current increases, the amount of wire burned off increases proportionally. This is graphically shown by Fig. 1-45 which shows burn-off rate vs. current chart. Thus, it can be seen that if wire were fed into an arc at a specific rate it would automatically draw a proportionate amount of current from a constant-voltage power source. The constant-voltage machine provides the amount of current required from it by the load imposed on it. The wire is fed into the arc by means of a constant- but adjustable-speed feed motor. The system is inherently self-regulating. Thus, if the electrode wire were fed in faster, the current would increase. If it were fed in slower, the current would decrease automatically. The current output of the welding machine is thus set by the speed of the wire feed motor. The voltage at the arc is regulated by an output control on the power source. Only two controls maintain the proper welding current and voltage when the constant-voltage system is used.

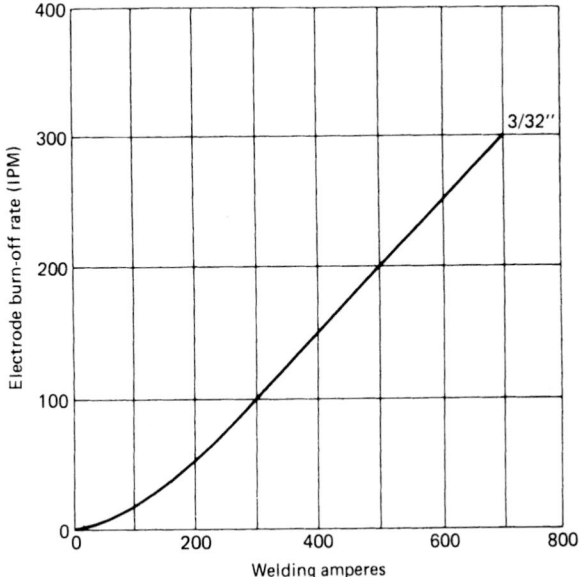

FIGURE 1-45   Chart showing burn-off rate vs. current.

The characteristic curves of constant-voltage machines have a slight inherent droop. This droop can be increased, or made steeper, by various methods. Many machines have different taps, or controls, for varying the slope of the characteristic curve. It is important to select the slope most appropriate to the process variation and the type of work being welded. Constant-voltage machines can be either the generator or transformer/rectifier type.

Combination CV-CC Welding Machines

The most flexible type of welding machine is a combination type that can provide direct-current welding power with either a drooping or flat output characteristic volt-ampere curve by using different terminals and/or changing a switch. This type of welding machine allows the welder to use any of the arc welding processes.

Specialty Welding Machines

Special welding machines are now becoming available for specific applications such as low-current TIG welding, plasma welding, programmable controlled machines, and lightweight machines. Most of these new machines use inverter technology, which is a method of changing the frequency of the incoming power to a high frequency, then transforming it to dc, controlling it, and finally rectifying it for use at the arc. These machines can be very small, particularly the low-current machines. Most such machines include programmers, arc starters, and solenoid valves for gas and water control, and are designed for specific applications. This technology is changing rapidly and it is suggested that you contact your welding supplier for more details.

Specifying a Welding Machine

Selection of the welding machine is based on:

1. The process or processes to be used
2. The amount of current required for the work
3. The power available to the job site
4. Convenience and economic factors

The previous information about each of the arc welding processes indicates the type of machine required. The size of the machine is based on the welding current and duty cycle required. Welding current, duty cycle, and voltage are determined by analyzing the welding job and considering weld joints, weld sizes, etc. and by consulting welding procedure tables. The incoming power available must also be considered. Finally, the job situation, personal preference, and economic considerations narrow the field to the final selection. The local welding equipment supplier should be consulted to help make your selection.

To order a welding machine properly, the following data should be given:

1. Manufacturer's type designation or catalog number
2. Manufacturer's identification or model number
3. Rated load voltage
4. Rated load amperes (current)
5. Duty cycle
6. Voltage of power supply (incoming)
7. Frequency of power supply (incoming)
8. Number of phases of power supply (incoming)

Welding Machine Duty Cycle

Duty cycle is defined as the ratio of arc time to total time. For a welding machine, a 10-min time period is used. Thus, for a 60 percent duty cycle machine, the rated welding load would be applied continuously for 6 min and would be off for 4 min. Most industrial-type constant-current (drooping) machines are rated at 60 percent duty cycle. Most constant-voltage (flat) machines used for automatic welding are rated at 100 percent duty cycle.

Figure 1-46 represents the ratio of the square of the rated current to the square of the load current multiplied by the rated duty cycle. Rather than work out the formula, use this chart. Draw a line parallel to the sloping lines through the intersection of the subject machine's rated current output and rated duty cycle. For example, a question might arise whether a 400-A, 60 percent duty cycle machine could be used for a fully automatic requirement of 300 A for a 10-min welding job. Line *A* shows this to be possible. It shows that the machine can be used at slightly over 300 A at a 100 percent duty cycle. Conversely, there may be a need to draw more than the rated current from a welding machine, but for a short period. Line *B*, for example, shows that the 200-A, 60 percent rated machine can be used at 250 A, provided the duty cycle does not exceed 40 percent (or 4 min out of each 10 min).

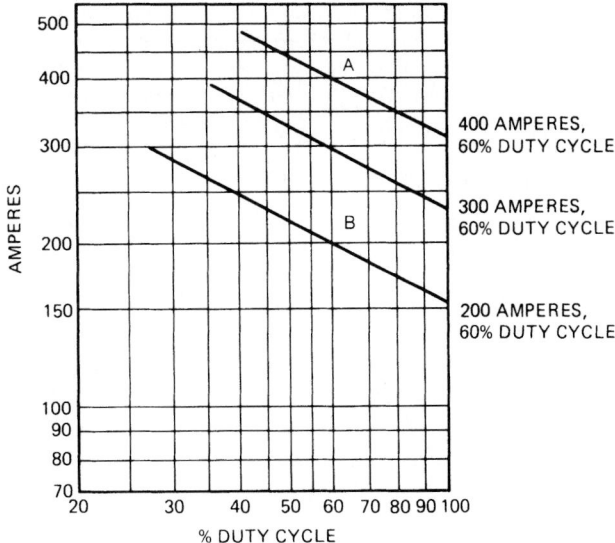

FIGURE 1-46   Percent of working time vs. welding current.

Use this chart to compare various machines. Relate all machines to the same duty cycle for a true comparison.

WELDING CABLE SELECTION

The size and length of welding leads, welding cable, and work cable have a definite influence on the cost of welding. As the length of the leads is increased, their diameter should be increased in order to avoid excessive voltage drop between the machine and the electrode and, particularly, to avoid wasted power as a result of the cables heating excessively.

To determine the power lost in the welding leads, measure the voltage at the welding machine terminals. Then measure the voltage at the arc (meter connected between electrode holder and the work). Also measure the welding current. The voltage loss in the leads equals the difference between the voltage at the terminals and at the holder. Multiply this by the welding current and the result is the power lost:

$$[V \text{ (at terminal)} - V \text{ (at holder)}] \times \text{welding current} = \text{power lost}$$

Example:

$$(35 - 32) \times 250 = 750 \text{ W lost}$$

Recommended Cable Sizes for Leads of Various Lengths

Table 1-4 shows cable sizes recommended for different lengths of leads. The footage shown includes the complete welding circuit—welding lead and work lead combined. For example, the 60-ft (1.8-m) column refers to two 30-ft (0.9-m) leads.

TABLE 1-4 Copper Welding Cable Size (AWG) Guide

Weld type	Weld current, A	Length of cable circuit, ft (m)*—cable size					
		60 (1.8)	100 (3)	150 (4.5)	200 (6.9)	300 (9)	400 (12)
Manual (low duty cycle)	100	4	4	4	2	1	1/0
	150	2	2	2	1	2/0	3/0
	200	2	2	1	1/0	3/0	4/0
	250	2	2	1/0	2/0		
	300	1	1	2/0	3/0		
	350	1/0	1/0	3/0	4/0		
	400	1/0	1/0	3/0			
	450	2/0	2/0	4/0			
	500	2/0	2/0	4/0			
Automatic (high duty cycle)	400	4/0	4/0				
	800	4/0 (2)	4/0 (2)				
	1200	4/0 (3)	4/0 (3)				
	1600	4/0 (4)	4/0 (4)				

* Length of cable circuit equals total of electrode and work cables.

DC Voltage Drop per 100 ft (30 m) of Leads

Table 1-5 shows the voltage drop that will occur in a given length of cable of a given size when welding with a given current value.

When a cable is overheated, its life is shortened. These figures assume all connections to be tight and that electrode holder and ground connection are in good condition.

For higher amperage than given in the table, divide the load *equally* across two input cables of sufficient size to carry half the load.

To determine proper power cable wire size, consult the welding machine nameplate or data sheet for amperage drawn at input line voltage. Data based on **National Electrical Code**®* for welding equipment, Sec. 630.

WELDING DIFFERENT METALS

In order to produce a quality weld it is necessary to know the composition or analysis of each piece of metal that is to be welded. Once the properties or specifications are known, the proper filler metal can be selected so that the deposited weld metal will meet or exceed the mechanical properties and have approximately the same composition and physical properties.

The composition or analysis of the base metal, or parts to be welded, must be known in order to determine their physical and mechanical properties. This can be determined if the composition, specifications, or trade name of the material is known. The filler metal to be used can then be selected. The deposited weld metal should overmatch the mechanical properties of the base material. This can be done by selecting filler metals in accordance with the following information.

The exact selection procedure for filler metals varies according to the welding process that will be used and on the classification of metal that is to be welded.

---

* **National Electrical Code**® is a Registered Trademark of the National Fire Protection Association, Inc., Quincy, MA 02269.

TABLE 1-5   DC Voltage Drop per 100 ft (3 m) of Leads*

Welding current, A	Cable size (AWG)					
	2	1	1/0	2/0	3/0	4/0
50	1.0	0.7	0.5	0.4	0.3	0.3
75	1.3	1.0	0.8	0.7	0.5	0.4
100	1.8	1.4	1.2	0.9	0.7	0.6
125	2.3	1.7	1.4	1.1	1.0	0.7
150	2.8	2.1	1.7	1.4	1.1	0.9
175	3.3	2.6	2.0	1.7	1.3	1.0
200	3.7	3.0	2.4	2.0	1.5	1.2
250	4.7	3.6	3.0	2.4	1.8	1.5
300		4.4	3.4	2.8	2.2	1.7
350			4.0	3.2	2.5	2.0
400			4.6	3.7	2.9	2.3
450				4.2	3.2	2.6
500				4.7	3.6	2.8
550					3.9	3.1
600					4.3	3.4
650						3.7
700						4.0

* Figures in this table are for three-conductor cable. For four-conductor cable, reduce the ampere rating of each wire size by 20%.

Shielded Metal Arc Welding

The shielded metal arc welding process is commonly used for welding carbon steels, low-alloy steels, and stainless steels, and for surfacing. It is normally not used for welding aluminum, magnesium, titanium, and other hard-to-weld metals. The gas-shielded processes are used for welding the nickel alloys, copper alloys, high-strength steels, tool steels, and similar material.

The following guidelines are to be used for selecting covered electrodes for welding carbon and low-alloy steels. These are related to the American Welding Society Filler Metal Specifications A5.1 "Carbon Steel Covered Arc Welding Electrodes" and A5.5 "Low Alloy Steel Covered Arc Welding Electrodes." The classification for these types of electrodes is shown below. The prefix letter E designates an electrode. The first two or three digits indicate tensile strength and other mechanical properties. The third (or fourth) digit indicates the welding position that can be used and the last digit indicates usability of the electrode. These data are shown in Table 1-6.

The suffix letter, when used after the four- or five-digit classification, designates the composition of the deposit weld metal. This is normally used for the low-alloy, high-strength type electrode and does not apply to the 60XX classification. The suffix letters and the nominal composition are shown in Table 1-7.

For exact data the filler metal specification should be consulted.

The operational factors relating to covered electrodes are as follows:

1. *Welding position.*   Electrodes are designed to be used in specific positions. The third (or fourth) digit of the electrode classification indicates the welding position that can be used. Match the electrode to the welding position that will be encountered.

2. *Welding current.*   Some electrodes are designed to operate best with dc, others on ac. Some will operate on either ac or dc. The last digit indicates the welding current usability. Select the electrode to match the type of power source that will be used.

3. *Thickness and shape of base metal.*   Weldments may include thick and heavy material of complicated design. The electrode selected should have maximum ductility to avoid weld cracking. Select the low-hydrogen types, EXX15, 16, 18, or 28.

TABLE 1-6 AWS Classification System for Covered Mild and Low-Alloy Steel Electrodes

A. Prefix: E designates an electrode
B. First two or three digits: mechanical properties

Classification	Minimum tensile strength, lb/in^2 (MPa)	Minimum yield strength, lb/in^2 (MPa)	Minimum elongation, %
E60XX	62,000 (427)	50,000 (345)	22
E70XX	70,000 (483)	57,000 (393)	22
E80XX	80,000 (552)	67,000 (462)	19
E90XX	90,000 (621)	77,000 (531)	17
E100XX	100,000 (690)	87,000 (600)	16
E110XX*	110,000 (758)	97,000 (669)	15
E120XX*	120,000 (827)	107,000 (738)	14

C. Third (or fourth) digit: applicable welding positions
   EXX1X: flat, horizontal, vertical, and overhead
   EXX2X: flat and horizontal fillet
D. Last digit: electrode usability

Classification	Current[†]	Arc	Penetration	Covering slag	Iron powder, %[‡]
EXX10	DCEP	Digging	Deep	Cellulose-sodium	0–10
EXX11	AC, DCEP	Digging	Deep	Cellulose-potassium	0
EXX12	AC, DCEN	Medium	Medium	Rutile-sodium	0–10
EXX13	AC, DCEN, dcep	Soft	Light	Rutile-potassium	0–10
EXX14	AC, DCEN, dcep	Soft	Light	Rutile-iron powder	25–40
EXX15	DCEP	Medium	Medium	Low-hydrogen–sodium	0
EXX16	AC, DCEP	Medium	Medium	Low-hydrogen–potassium	0
EXX18	AC, DCEP	Medium	Medium	Low-hydrogen-iron powder	25–40
EXX20 and EXX22 (single pass)	AC, DCEN, dcep	Medium	Medium	Iron oxide-sodium	0
EXX24	AC, DCEN, dcep	Soft	Light	Rutile–iron powder	50
EXX27	AC, DCEN, dcep	Medium	Medium	Iron oxide–iron powder	50
EXX28	AC, DCEP	Medium	Medium	Low-hydrogen–iron powder	50
EXX48 (vertical down)	AC, DCEP	Medium	Medium	Low-hydrogen–iron powder	25–50

* Low-hydrogen-type coating only.
† DCEP = electrode positive—reverse polarity; DCEN = electrode negative—standard polarity.
‡ Iron powder percentage based on weight of the covering.

4. *Weld design and fit-up.* Welding electrodes are designed with a digging, medium, soft, or light penetrating arc. The last digit of the classification indicates this usability factor. Deep penetrating electrodes with a digging arc should be used when edges are not beveled or fit-up is tight. At the other extreme, light penetrating electrodes with a soft arc are required when welding on thin material or when root openings are too wide.

5. *Service conditions and specifications.* Weldments subjected to severe service conditions such as low temperature, high temperature, and shock loading need special consideration. Select the electrode to match the base metal properties including not only composition

TABLE 1-7   Chemical Composition of Deposited Weld Metal

Suffix	C	Mn	Si	Ni	Cr	Mo	V
			Weld metal composition, %*				
A1	0.12	0.60 or 1.00†	0.40 or 0.80†			0.40–0.65	
B1	0.12	0.90	0.60 or 0.80†		0.40–0.65	0.40–0.65	
B2L	0.05	0.90	1.00		1.00–1.50	0.40–0.65	
B2	0.12	0.90	0.60 or 0.80†		1.00–1.50	0.40–0.65	
B3L	0.05	0.90	1.00		2.00–2.50	0.90–1.20	
B3	0.12	0.90	0.60 or 0.80†		2.00–2.50	0.90–1.20	
B4L	0.05	0.90	1.00		1.75–2.25	0.40–0.65	
B5	0.07						
‡	0.15	0.40–0.70	0.30–0.60		0.40–0.60	1.00–1.25	0.05
C1	0.12	1.20	0.60 or 0.80†	2.00–2.75			
C2	0.12	1.20	0.60 or 0.80†	3.00–3.75			
C3	0.12	0.40–1.25	0.80	0.80–1.10	0.15	0.35	0.05
D1	0.12	1.25–1.75	0.60 or 0.80†			0.25–0.45	
D2	0.15	1.65–2.00	0.60 or 0.80†			0.25–0.45	
‡							0.10 min.
G		1.00 min.	0.80 min.	0.50 min.	0.30 min.	0.20 min.	
M	0.10	0.60–2.25†	0.60 or 0.80†	1.40–2.50	0.15–1.50†	0.25–0.55†	0.05

* Compositions are maximum unless otherwise indicated.
† Amount depends on electrode classification.
‡ A suffix is not applied to E60XX classification.

and ductility but also toughness. This is indicated by the toughness requirement of the specification. Low-hydrogen electrodes are required.

6. *Production efficiencies/job conditions.*   Certain electrodes are designed for high deposition rates but may be used only under certain position requirements. Where they can be used, select the high-iron powder types, the EXX24, 27, or 28 types. Other conditions may require some experimentation to determine the best electrode for the job, allowing for the most efficient production.

Carbon steel and low alloy steel electrodes may be classed into four general groups:

F-1   High-deposition group   E6020, E7024, E6027, E6028

F-2   Mild-penetrating group   E6012, E6013, E7014

F-3   Deep-penetrating group   E6010, E6011

F-4   Low-hydrogen group   E6015, E7016, E7018, E6028

Electrodes in the same grouping operate and are run in the same general manner.

GENERAL RECOMMENDATIONS FOR PREHEATING AND ELECTRODE SELECTION

1. No welding should be done when the ambient temperature is below 0°F (–18°C). When the base metal temperature is below 32°F (0°C), preheat the base metal to at least 70°F (22°C) and maintain this minimum temperature during welding. Light sections require only local preheating, but heavy sections require general preheating. For structures, the American Welding Society specifies that the preheat be maintained on all the surface of the plate within 3 in (76 mm) of the point of welding.

2. Electrodes that are not of the low-hydrogen type can be used to weld thinner sections of mild carbon steel when proper preheat temperatures are maintained. Low-hydrogen electrodes are recommended for thicker sections of the steel and for low-alloy steel in all thickness ranges. When low-hydrogen electrodes are used, they must be thoroughly dry. They may be kept dry by storing in a heated box and removed immediately prior to using.

3. Any preheating indicated should be done prior to any tack welding as well as prior to the principal welding, and the temperature should be maintained as a minimum interpass temperature as welding proceeds.

4. When low-alloy steels are welded to lower-strength grades, select electrodes to match the strength of the lower-strength steel, but use welding practice suitable for the higher-strength steel.

Constructional Steels

A36	Structural steel
A131	Structural steel for ships
A201	Carbon-silicon steel plates of intermediate tensile ranges for fusion-welded boilers and other pressure vessels
A212	High-tensile-strength carbon-silicon plates for boilers and other pressure vessels
A242	(Weldable grade) high-strength low-alloy structural steel
A283	Low- and intermediate-tensile-strength carbon steel plates of structural quality
A441	high-strength low-alloy manganese vanadium steel

Use low-hydrogen electrodes only. For high-restraint weldments of thick steel, use 400°F (205°C) to 500°F (260°C) maximum preheat. It is important to keep heat input low to obtain fast cooling. Do not weave electrode more than 2½ times electrode diameter. Multipass welding employing the stringer bead technique should be used. Allow beads to cool below 200°F (95 to 121°C) before making additional passes.

Use E11018 electrodes and E12018 in cases of high restraint. When postweld stress-relief heat treatment is applied to steel weldments, the weld metal should not contain added vanadium. Stress relief temperature is 1100°F (594°C). Fillet welds may be made with E9018 or E10018. For joints where the weld metal is expected to provide yield and tensile strengths equal to that of the base metal, electrodes of the E11018 series are ordinarily employed.

Abrasion-Resistant Steels (320 BHN to 400 BHN)

The same procedures as outlined for the constructional steels should be followed using techniques ordinarily employed on hardenable alloy steels. Weld metal with the lowest permissible strength often is selected to assure adequate ductility and toughness in the weld deposits. Where the hardness or toughness of a welded zone appears unsuited for service conditions, a postweld tempering may be done. However, the temperature should be limited to 800°F (426°C) to avoid lowering the overall hardness of the treated plate.

Stainless Steels

In order to properly select the electrode for welding stainless steels, or, more correctly, corrosion-resisting steels, it is necessary to know and understand the numbering system used. The numbering system established by the American Iron and Steel Institute (AISI) is based on the composition of the stainless steel, (i.e. type 308, type 312, etc.). These are three-digit numbers which classify the steel according to its metallurgical structure. Stainless steels are sometimes known and identified according to their principle alloying element, such as 18/8, 25/20, etc.

TABLE 1-8 Electrode Selection for Welding Stainless Steels

AISI No.	Carbon	Manganese	Silicon	Chromium	Nickel	Other elements	Hobart electrode no.
	Carbon	Manganese	Silicon	Chromium	Nickel	Other elements	Hobart electrode no.
Austenitic							
201	0.15 max.	5.5–7.5	1.0	16.0–18.0	3.5–5.5	N_2 0.25 max.	308
202	0.15 max.	7.5–10	1.0	17.0–19.0	4.0–6.0	N_2 0.25 max.	308
301	0.15 max.	2.0	1.0	16.0–18.0	6.0–8.0		308
302	0.15 max.	2.0	1.0	17.0–19.0	8.0–10.0		308
302B	0.15 max.	2.0	2.0–3.0	17.0–19.0	8.0–10.0		308
303	0.15 max.	2.0	1.0	17.0–19.0	8.0–10.0	S 0.15 min.	308DC
303Se	0.15 max.	2.0	1.0	17.0–19.0	8.0–10.0	Se 0.15 min.	308DC
304	0.08 max.	2.0	1.0	18.0–20.0	8.0–12.0		308
304L	0.03 max.	2.0	1.0	18.0–20.0	8.0–12.0		308L
305	0.12 max.	2.0	1.0	17.0–19.0	10.0–13.0		308
308	0.08 max.	2.0	1.0	19.0–21.0	10.0–12.0		308
309	0.20 max.	2.0	1.0	22.0–24.0	12.0–15.0		309
309S	0.08 max.	2.0	1.0	22.0–24.0	12.0–15.0		309
310	0.25 max.	2.0	1.50	24.0–26.0	19.0–22.0		310
310S	0.08 max.	2.0	1.50	24.0–26.0	19.0–22.0		310
314	0.25 max.	2.0	1.5–3.0	23.0–26.0	19.0–22.0		310DC
316	0.08 max.	2.0	1.0	16.0–18.0	10.0–14.0	Mo 2.0/3.0	316
316L	0.03 max.	2.0	1.0	16.0–18.0	10.0–14.0	Mo 2.0/3.0	316L
317	0.08 max.	2.0	1.0	18.0–20.0	11.0–15.0	Mo 3.0/4.0	317
321	0.08 max.	2.0	1.0	17.0–19.0	9.0–12.0	Ti 5 × C min.	347
347	0.08 max.	2.0	1.0	17.0–19.0	9.0–13.0	Cb + Ta 10 C min.	347
348	0.08 max.	2.0	1.0	17.0–19.0	9.0–13.0	Ta 0.10 max.	347
Martensitic							
403	0.15 max.	1.0	0.5	11.5–13.0			410
410	0.15 max.	1.0	1.0	11.5–13.5			410
414	0.15 max.	1.0	1.0	11.5–13.5	1.25–2.5		410
416	0.15 max.	1.25	1.0	12.0–14.0		S 0.15 min.	410DC
416Se	0.15 max.	1.25	1.0	12.0–14.0		Se 0.15 min.	410DC
420	Over 0.15	1.0	1.0	12.0–14.0			410
431	0.20 max.	1.0	1.0	15.0–17.0	1.25–2.5		430
440A	0.60–0.75	1.0	1.0	16.0–18.0		Mo 0.75 max.	
440B	0.75–0.95	1.0	1.0	16.0–18.0		Mo 0.75 max.	
440C	0.95–1.2	1.0	1.0	16.0–18.0		Mo 0.75 max.	
Ferritic							
405	0.08 max.	1.0	1.0	11.5–14.5		Al 0.1/0.3	410
430	0.12 max.	1.0	1.0	14.0–18.0			430
430F	0.12 max.	1.25	1.0	14.0–18.0		S 0.15 min.	430DC
430FSe	0.12 max.	1.25	1.0	14.0–18.0		Se 0.15 min.	430DC
446	0.20 max.	1.50	1.0	23.0–27.0		N 0.25 max.	309

TABLE 1-9 Guide to the Choice of Filler Metal for Aluminum

In the table below, the first two filler-metal columns (43, 355, 356 and 214, A214, B214, F214) fall under the heading **Casting alloys**.

Base metal	Casting alloys: 43, 355, 356	Casting alloys: 214, A214, B214, F214	6061, 6062, 6063, 6151	5456	5454	5154, 5254 (1)	5086, 5356	5083	5052, 5652 (1)	5005, 5050	3004, CLAD 3004	1100, 3003, CLAD 3003	1060
A 1060	ER4043	ER4043	ER4043	ER5356 (3), (5)	ER4043	ER4043	ER5356 (3), (5)	ER5356 (3), (5)	ER4043	ER1100 (3)	ER4043	ER1100 (3)	ER1260
B 1100, 3003, CLAD 3003	ER4043	ER4043 (5)	ER4043 (5)	ER5356 (3), (5)	ER4043 (5)	ER4043 (5)	ER5356 (3), (5)	ER5356 (3), (5)	ER4043 (5)	ER4043 (5)	ER4043 (5)	ER1100 (3)	
C 3004, CLAD 3004	ER4043	ER4043 (5)	ER4043 (2)	ER5356 (5)	ER5356 (3), (5); ER4043	ER5356 (5)	ER5356 (5)	ER5356 (5)	ER5356 (3), (5); ER4043 (5)	ER4043 (5)	ER4043 (4), (5)		
D 5005, 5050	ER4043	ER4043 (5)	ER4043 (2)	ER5356 (5)	ER5356 (5)	ER5356 (3), (5)	ER5356 (5)	ER5356 (5)	ER5356 (5)	ER4043 (4), (5)			
E 5052, 5652 (1)	ER5356 (5)	ER5356 (2)	ER4043 (2), (3)	ER5356 (5)	ER5356 (2), (3)	ER5356 (5)	ER5356 (5)	ER5356 (5)	ER5652 (2), (3)				
F 5083	ER5356 (3), (5)	ER5356 (2)	ER5356 (5)	ER5183 (5), (6)	ER5356 (5)	ER5356 (5)	ER5356 (5)	ER5183 (5), (6)					
G 5086, 5356	ER5356 (3), (5)	ER5356 (5)	ER5356 (5)	ER5356 (5)	ER5356 (5)	ER5356 (5)	ER5356 (5)						
H 5154, 5254 (1)	ER5356 (3), (5)	ER5356 (5)	ER5356 (5)	ER5356 (5)	ER5356 (5)	ER5254 (2)							
I 5454	ER5356 (3), (5)	ER5356 (2)	ER5356 (2), (3)	ER5356 (5)	ER5554 (5)								
J 5456	ER5356 (3), (5)	ER5356 (2), (3)	ER5356 (5)	ER5556 (5), (6)									
K 6061, 6062, 6063, 6151	ER5356 (2)	ER5356 (5)	ER4043 (2), (3)										
L 214, A214, B214, F214	ER4043 (5)	ER5356 (2)											
M 43, 355, 356	ER4043 (4)												

Source: American Weld Society.

(1) Base-metal alloys 5652 and 5254 are used for welding both alloys for low-temperature service (150F and below). ER5652 filler metal is used for welding 5652 for high-temperature service (150F and above).

(2) ER5154, ER5254, ER5183, ER5356, ER5556, and ER5554 may be used. In some cases, they provide: (1) improved color match after anodizing treatment, (2) highest weld ductility, and (3) higher weld strength. ER5554 is suitable for elevated temperature service.

(3) ER4043 may be used for some applications.

(4) Filler metal with the same analysis as the base metal is sometimes used.

(5) ER5356, ER5183, or ER5556 may be used.

(6) ER5356 is the third choice.

Iron is the main element of all stainless steels; however, to make it corrosion-resistant, chromium must be present in the amount of 11.5 percent or more. The addition of chromium to iron provides a fine film of chromium oxide which forms on the surface and acts as a barrier to further oxidation, rust, or corrosion. The addition of nickel in the proper ratio results in a stainless-steel series referred to as *chrome nickel* types. They all contain a percentage of nickel and are nonmagnetic. The addition of nickel increases the corrosion resistance, ductility, electrical resistance, impact properties, and fatigue resistance.

There are three basic classes of stainless steel which are grouped according to their metallurgical microstructure. They are known as the austenitic, martensitic, and ferritic types. The properties of these three classes of stainless steel differ and require different welding electrodes and procedures.

Electrodes for welding stainless steels are identified by the American Iron and Steel Institute (AISI) three-digit number following the prefix letter E and followed by the usability classification, normally 15 or 16. The usability classification can also be followed by a letter such as L indicating *low carbon*. All stainless-steel electrodes have a low-hydrogen-type coating. The EXXX-15 designation indicates a line coating which is normally used with direct current. The EXXX-16 type uses titanium base coating and can be used with ac or dc. The type 16 is a smoother-running electrode, however, the type 15 may be the best for out-of-position welding. The mechanical properties are not specified for stainless-steel electrodes, since the deposit weld metal will be nearly identical to the base metal and will have physical properties normal for the composition of the metal deposit. Table 1-8 gives the proper electrode for welding the different types of stainless steel.

Nonferrous Metals

The gas-shielded arc welding processes are more popular for welding nonferrous metals. When using these processes, select a welding electrode having a composition similar to the metal being welded. Unfortunately, electrodes are not available in every conceivable composition, and, therefore, charts showing recommended electrodes for different types of metals are available. A guide for the choice of filler metals for welding aluminum is shown in Table 1-9. This chart can be used for either gas metal-arc welding or gas tungsten-arc welding. Similar charts are available for welding magnesium, however, for welding nickel base of copper base electrodes the manufacturer of the base metal or manufacturers of nonferrous electrodes should be consulted.

CHAPTER 16-2

METAL RESURFACING BY THERMAL SPRAYING

M. R. Dorfman
E. Novinski
Senior Staff Engineers
Metco/Perkin Elmer
Westbury, New York

GLOSSARY

Abrasive   A hard material such as sand, aluminum oxide, steel grit, or silicon carbide used to clean and roughen a surface.

Base metal   The part or substrate to be resurfaced.

Blasting   The process in which an abrasive material is propelled, usually by air pressure, onto a surface to effect both cleaning and roughening.

Coating   The spray material which is applied to the base metal.

Deposition rate   The amount of material which adheres to the base metal per unit of time.

Bond or bond strength   A measure of how well a sprayed coating has adhered to the base metal.

HVOF   High-velocity oxy-fuel process.

Thermal spraying   A group of processes which involve the melting and accelerating of an atomized spray of particles onto a surface forming a solid coating.

INTRODUCTION

The application of a coating by the thermal spray process is an established industrial method for resurfacing metal parts. The process is characterized by the simultaneous melting and transporting of the spray material, usually a metal or ceramic, onto the surface of the part to be coated. The spray material is propelled in the form of fine molten droplets which, on striking the part, solidify and adhere by a mechanical and metallurgical interaction. Each applied layer of spray material bonds tenaciously to the previously deposited layer. The process is continued until the desired coating thickness is achieved.

Thermal spraying can be used to apply a coating to machine element or structural parts to satisfy any one of the following broad requirements:

- To repair worn areas on parts damaged in service
- To restore dimensions to mismachined parts
- To increase the service life of a part by optimizing the surface physical properties

In addition to satisfying any one of these broad requirements, thermal spraying can be a cost-effective repair procedure when compared to the high cost of replacing worn or misma-chined parts and the economic losses incurred as a result of machine downtime.

The primary advantages of thermal spraying over other methods of metal resurfacing are the wide range of chemically different materials which can be sprayed, the high coating depo-sition rate which allows thick coatings to be applied economically, and the portability of the spray equipment.

PHYSICAL PROPERTIES OF COATINGS

Thermally sprayed coatings are composed of individual particles of the spray material alloyed and mechanically interlocked together to form a solid coating. In general, there is only limited metallurgical bonding between the coating and the base metal. The coating adheres primarily by a mechanical anchoring mechanism. To ensure adequate bonding of the coating, the base metal must be free from oil or dirt contamination and should be roughened by machining or blasting.

Sprayed coatings are harder and more wear-resistant than cast or wrought alloys of the same material. The increased properties are due to fine oxides and a combination of work hardening and rapid quenching of the spray particles on impact with the base metal. Rapid quenching causes hard metastable phases to form.

Some degree of porosity is present in all sprayed coatings and results from the presence of air gaps between the spray particles. Typically, thermally sprayed coatings are 80 to 99 percent as dense as cast or wrought alloys of the same material. In applications where the coating is used as a bearing surface, the porosity helps to retain lubricating oil and gives the coating a degree of self-lubricity. In corrosion applications where it is necessary to protect the base metal, the coating should be sealed with an epoxy or phenolic to close off the pores.

The surface texture or roughness of thermal sprayed coatings is coarser than cast or wrought surfaces, and a subsequent finishing operation such as sanding, machining, or grind-ing is often required before the resurfaced part can be placed into service. Thermally sprayed coatings are generally not as machinable as wrought or cast alloys of the same chemistry due to the presence of oxides in the coating. Because tool wear is greater, sprayed coatings should be machined with the most abrasion-resistant carbide cutting tools available.

MATERIAL SELECTION

The first step in the selection of a thermally sprayed coating for a specific in-plant application is to define the coating function. For example, if a badly worn shaft is to be repaired by thermal spraying, then the desired coating function is increased wear resistance. Table 2-1 lists the most common coating functions encountered, one or two typical application areas, and the appropri-ate thermal spray materials which satisfy each coating function. It should be noted that, for each coating function, a number of spray materials are indicated. In order to pinpoint the best mate-rial for the application, secondary considerations such as equipment available, coating thickness required, material availability, and final method of finishing should be evaluated.

TABLE 2-1 Coating Material Selection by Function

Coating function	Application	Material selection
Adhesive wear	Bearings Impeller shafts Piston rings	Babbitt Aluminum bronze Cast iron–molybdenum Molybdenum-based self-fluxing alloy Alumina-titania
Abrasive wear	Couplings Cutting blades	Tungsten carbide Chromium carbide Aluminum oxide Chromium oxide Self-fluxing alloys
High-temperature oxidation	Exhaust mufflers Annealing pans	Aluminum Nickel-chromium Aluminum alloy
Atmospheric water and saltwater	Exposed steel structure	Alumina Zinc
Restoration of dimension	Mismachined parts and castings	Carbon steels Stainless steels Nickel alloys Aluminum
Clearance control	Compressor housings	Aluminum-graphite Nickel-graphite Aluminum-polyester
Thermal barrier	Blades, vanes, burner cans	Yttria-zirconia
Electrical conductivity	Grand connectors	Copper
Electrical resistivity	Insulation for heater tubes	Aluminum oxide

PROCESS DESCRIPTION

Thermal spraying consists of six basic processes: wire flame spraying, powder flame spraying, arc wire spraying, plasma arc spraying, detonation, and high-velocity oxy-fuel methods. Figure 2-1 compares the spray patterns for a wire flame gun and a high-velocity oxy-fuel gun. An illustration as to the type of microstructure observed with this process is seen in Fig. 2-2. Of these processes, the HVOF and the detonation process give coating microstructure densities closest to wrought materials.

Both wire and powder flame spraying utilize the heat generated by the combustion of an oxygen fuel flame (typically oxyacetylene, oxypropane, or oxyhydrogen) to melt the spray material. (Figs. 2-3 and 2-4). A wire flame spray gun pulls the wire into the combustion flame by means of either a self-contained, variable-speed, air-driven turbine or an electric motor. A high-pressure stream of air both constricts the combustion flame and atomizes the molten tip of the wire, forming a spray of metal. A powder flame spray gun operates by feeding a fine powder into the combustion flame by a combination of suction and gravity. The powder is both melted and propelled by the combustion flame.

Both arc wire spraying and plasma arc spraying utilize an electric arc rather than a combustion flame to melt the spray material (Figs. 2-5 and 2-6). Arc wire spraying is becoming increasingly important because it yields lower operating costs and higher deposition rates than wire flame spraying. Plasma spraying is utilized in the gas turbine industry where optimum thermal-barrier ceramics and wear-resistant coatings are desired.

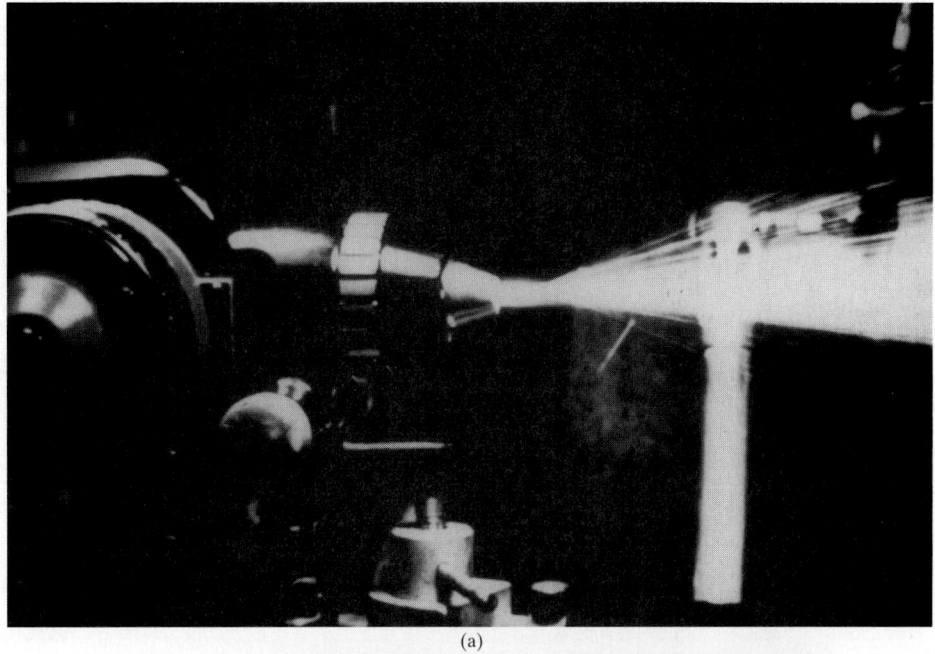

(a)

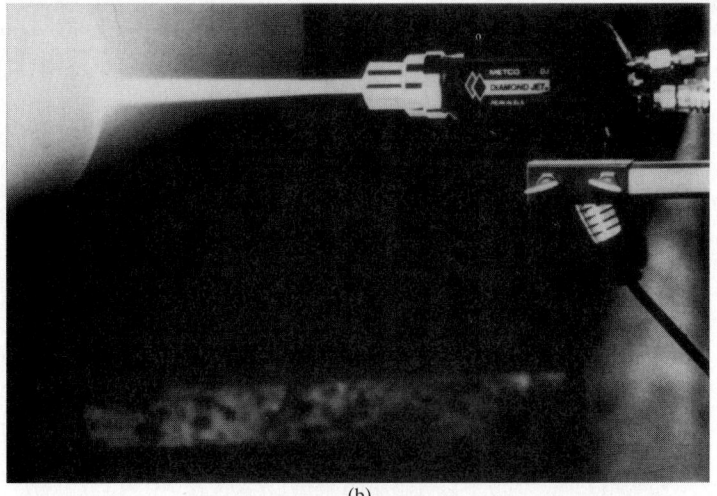

(b)

FIGURE 2-1   Photomicrograph of typical spray pattern of (*a*) combustion wire process and (*b*) high-velocity oxy-fuel process.

Alternative high-velocity technologies used to deposit optimum wear-resistant tungsten carbide and chromium carbide coatings are the oxy-fuel detonation process and the HVOF process. The detonation process operates by exploding metered amounts of an oxygen-fuel gas mixture in a gun-like barrel into which powdered material is injected. A spark device ignites the gas mixture in a sequence of several times per second. The spray material is heated

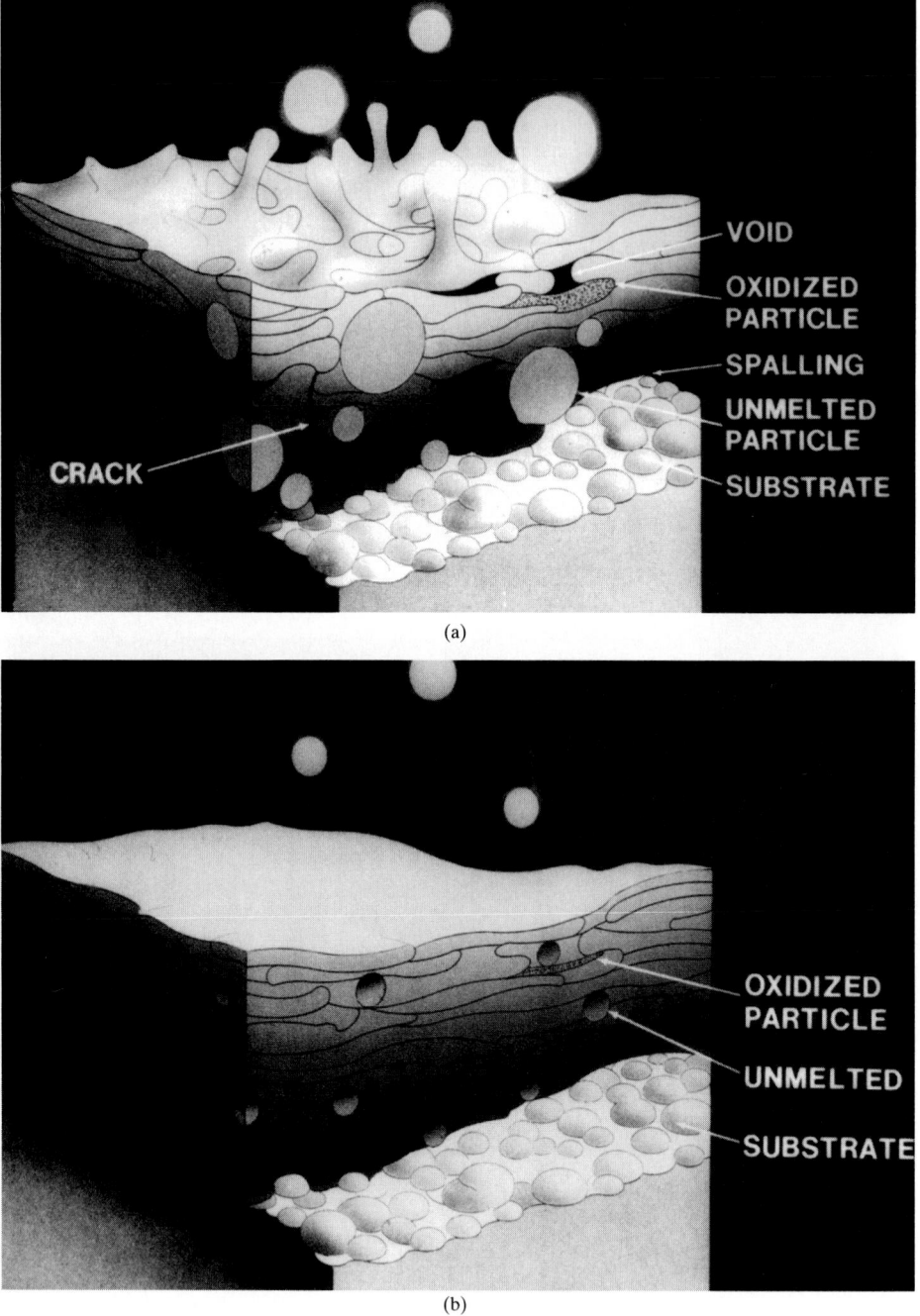

FIGURE 2-2   Cross sections of coatings made by (*a*) traditional combustion wire process and (*b*) high-velocity oxy-fuel process.

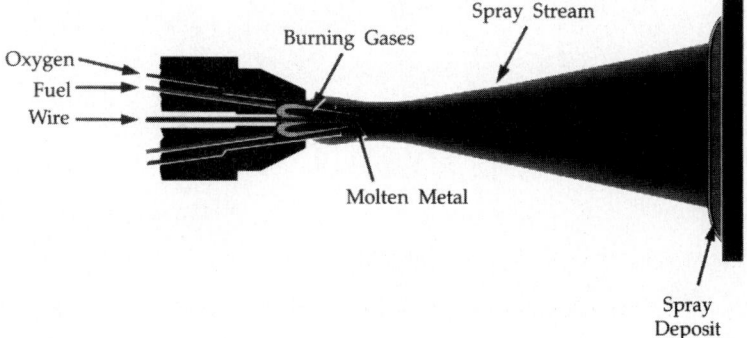

FIGURE 2-3 Wire flame process.

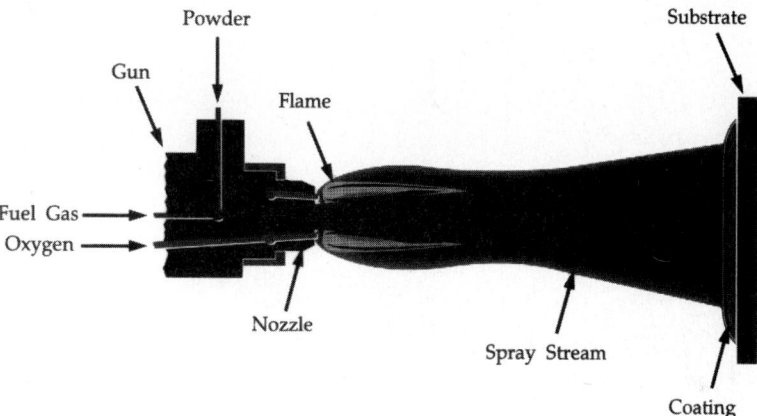

FIGURE 2-4 Powder flame process.

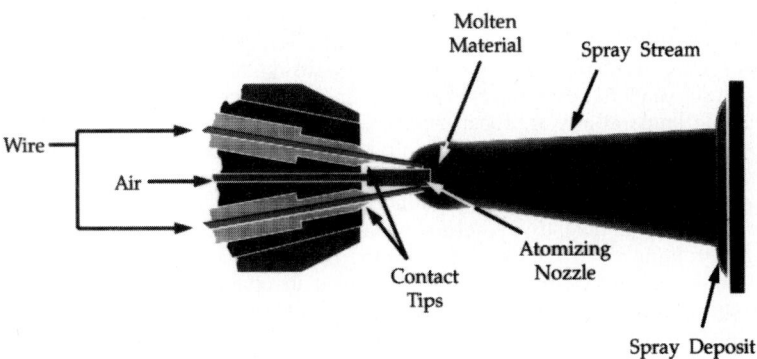

FIGURE 2-5 Electric arc gun.

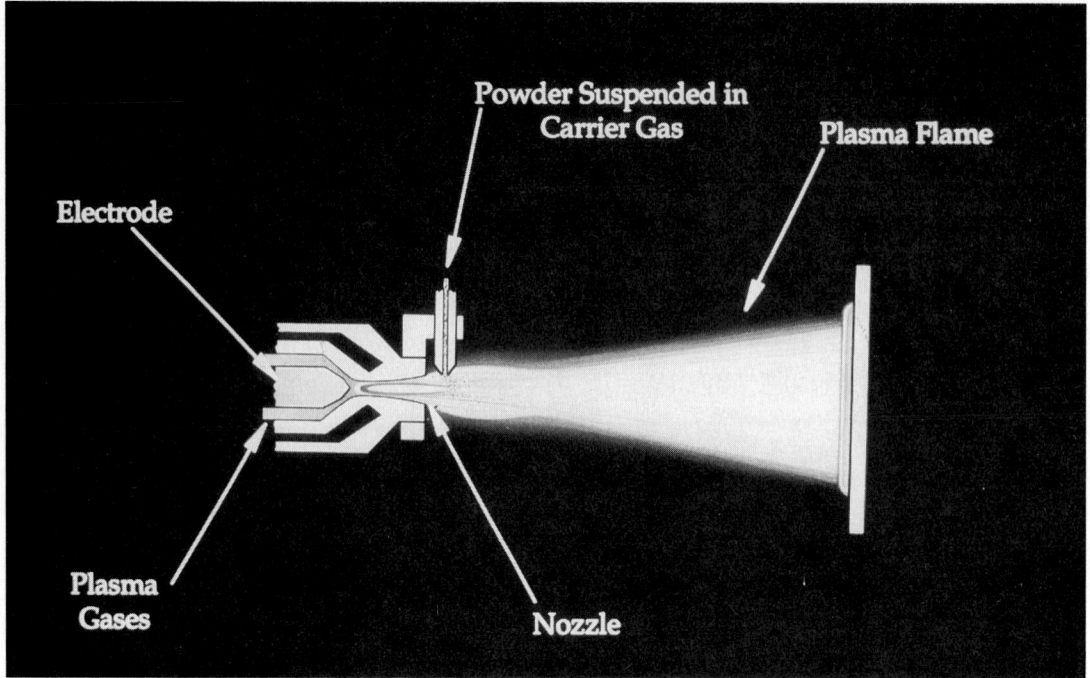

FIGURE 2-6 Plasma flame spray gun.

and transported down the barrel by the expansion of the exploding gases. The process produces a dense coating similar to that of the HVOF method. The process is, however, restricted to laboratory work and simple part geometries because of the large equipment size and required process controls.

The HVOF process represents the state of the art for thermal sprayed metallic coatings. HVOF uses extremely high kinetic energy and controlled thermal energy output to produce very low porosity coatings that exhibit high bond strength, fine as-sprayed surface finish, and low residual stresses.

The process operates with an oxygen-fuel mixture consisting of either propylene, propane, or hydrogen fuel gas depending on coating requirements. Fuel gases flow through a siphon system where they are thoroughly mixed with oxygen (Fig. 2-7). In one design, the mixed gases are ejected from the gun nozzle and are ignited. The high-velocity gases produce a unique characteristic of multiple-shock diamond patterns which are visible in the flame. Combustion temperatures approach 5000°F (2800°C) and form a circular flame configuration. Powder is injected into the flame axially to provide uniform heating and powder particles are accelerated by the high-velocity gases. The velocity typically approaches 4500 ft/s (1370 m/s). The low residual coating stress produced by the HVOF process allows significantly greater thicknesses than the plasma method while providing lower porosity, lower oxide content, and higher coating adhesion. Coatings with the HVOF process also show major improvements in machinability compared to other methods and coating porosity has closely approached wrought materials as verified by recent gas-permeability testing. The equipment necessary for manual spraying is seen in Fig. 2-8. Systems are available with closed-loop computer control and robotics capability, as with the plasma process. A comparison of a number of major thermal spray processes is seen in Table 2-2.

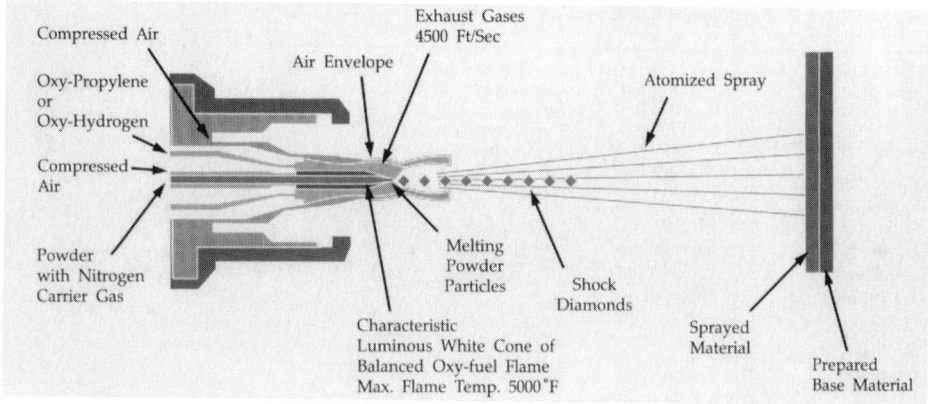

FIGURE 2-7   Schematic cross-section of high velocity oxy-fuel (HVOF) gun.

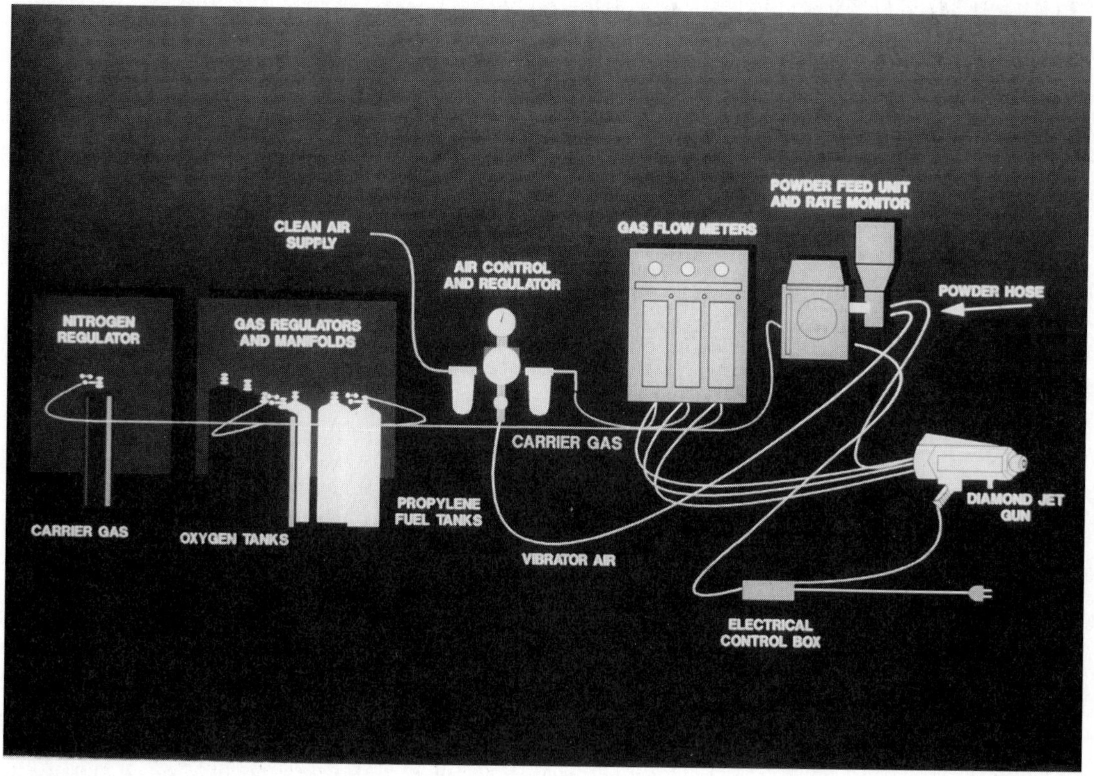

FIGURE 2-8   Manual HVOF spray system.

TABLE 2-2 Comparison of Major Thermal Spray Coating Processes

Property or characteristic	Coating type	Wire flame spray	Powder flame spray	Electric arc	Plasma spray	High-velocity oxy-fuel (HVOF)
Bond strength, MPa (10^3 psi)	Ferrous metals	14 (2)	28 (4)	41 (6)	34+ (5+)	62 (9)
	Nonferrous metals	21 (3)	21 (3)	41+ (6+)	34+ (5+)	70 (10.2)
	Self-fluxing alloys		69+ (10+)*			62 (9)†
	Ceramics		14–34 (2–5)		21+ (3+)	
	Carbides		34–48 (5–7)		55–69 (8–10)	83+ (12+)
Density, % of equivalent wrought material	Ferrous metals	90	90	90	95	98+
	Nonferrous metals	90	90	90	95	98+
	Self-fluxing alloys		100*			100*
	Ceramics		95		95+	
	Carbides		90		95+	98+
Hardness	Ferrous metals	84 RB–35 RC	80 RB–35 RC	95 RB–40 RC	80 RB–40 RC	90 RB–50 RC
	Nonferrous metals	95 RH–40 RC	30 RH–20 RC	40 RH–80 RB	40 RH–40 RC	100 RH–55 RC
	Self-fluxing alloys		30–60 RC			50–60 RC
	Ceramics		50–65 RC		50–70 RC	
	Carbides		50–60 RC		50–60 RC	55–65 RC
Permeability	Ferrous metals	Medium	Medium	High	Low	Negligible
	Nonferrous metals	Medium	Medium	High	Low	Negligible
	Self-fluxing alloys		None*			None*
	Ceramics		Medium		Low	
	Carbides		Low		Low	Negligible
Coating thickness limitation, mm (in)	Ferrous metals	1.25–2.5 (0.05–0.1)	1.25–2.5 (0.05–0.1)	1.25–2.5 (0.05–0.1)	1.25–2.5 (0.05–0.1)	1.25–2.5 (0.05–0.1)
	Nonferrous metals	1.25–5 (0.05–0.2)	1.25–5 (0.05–0.2)	1.25–5 (0.05–0.2)	1.25–5 (0.05–0.2)	2.5–5 (0.1–0.2)
	Self-fluxing alloys		0.4–2.5 (0.015–0.1)			1.25 (0.05)
	Ceramics		0.4 (0.015)		0.4 (0.015) max.	
	Carbides		0.4 (0.015)		0.4 (0.015) max.	0.6 (0.025)

* Fused coating.
† Unfused coating.

SAFETY

Thermal spraying will generate airborne dust and metal fumes to varying degrees, depending on the material being sprayed. Therefore, always provide adequate ventilation in the spray area to ensure operator safety. In cases where sufficient ventilation is not possible, spray operators should be equipped with dust masks or auxiliary ventilation equipment such as an exhaust hood or exhaust booth.

Every thermal spray process produces an intense bright light generated by either an electric arc or combustion flame. Eye protection as provided by dark glasses or an approved welding helmet is required.

In cases where the spray material is known to be toxic or suspected of containing potentially toxic elements, the recommendations of the thermal spray equipment manufacturer should be followed.

BIBLIOGRAPHY

Ballard, W. E.: *Metal Spraying and the Spray Depositions of Ceramics and Plastics,* 4th ed., Charles Griffin, London, 1963.

Burns, R. M., and W. W. Bradley: *Protective Coatings for Metals,* 3d ed., Reinhold, New York, 1967.

Ehrhardt, R. A., and A. Mendizza: "Sprayed Metal Coatings" in *Metal Handbook,* 1948 ed., American Society for Metals, Metals Park, Ohio, 1948.

Herman, H.: "Advances in Thermal Spray Technology," *Advanced Materials and Processes,* vol. 137, no. 4, April 1990.

Ingham, H. S., and A. P. Shepart: *METCO Flame Spray Handbook,* vols. I and II, METCO Inc., New York, 1964.

Kulkarni, K. M., "Overview of Hardfacing Materials and Processes," International Powder Metallurgy Conference, Toronto, 17–22 June 1984.

"Thermal Spray Terms and Their Definitions," Booklet AWS C2 9-70, American Welding Society, New York, 1970.

CHAPTER 16-3
STRUCTURAL ADHESIVES

JoAnn DeMarco
Senior Development Scientist
Loctite Corporation
Newington, Connecticut

James Murratti
Director of Product Management
Loctite Corporation
Newington, Connecticut

GLOSSARY*

Adherend A body which is held to another body by an adhesive.

Adhesive, contact An adhesive that is apparently dry to the touch and which will adhere to itself instantaneously on contact.

Adhesive, heat-setting An adhesive that requires a temperature above 87°F (31°C) to set it.

Adhesive, pressure-sensitive A viscoelastic material which in solvent-free form remains permanently tacky. Such material will adhere instantaneously to most solid surfaces with the application of very slight pressure.

---

* Reprinted with permission from the *Annual Book of ASTM Standards,* Part 22. Copyright American Society for Testing and Materials, 1916 Race St., Philadelphia, PA 19103.

Adhesive, room-temperature setting   An adhesive that sets in the temperature range of 68° to 86°F (20° to 30°C).

Bond strength   The unit load, applied in tension, compression, flexure, peel, impact, cleavage, or shear, required to break an adhesive assembly with failure occurring in or near the plane of the bond.

Catalyst   A substance that markedly speeds up the cure of an adhesive when added in minor quantity compared with the amounts of the primary reactants.

Creep   The dimensional change with time of a material under load, following the initial instantaneous elastic or rapid deformation.

Cure   To change the physical properties of an adhesive by chemical reaction.

Failure, adhesive   Rupture of an adhesive bond such that the separation appears to be at the adhesive-adherend interface.

Failure, cohesive   Rupture of an adhesive bond such that the separation appears to be within the adhesive.

Fillet   Adhesive which fills the corner or angle where two adherends are joined.

Flow   Movement of adhesive during the bonding process, before the adhesive is set.

Hardener   A reacting substance or mixture that promotes or controls the curing reaction.

Joint, lap   Joint made by overlapping and bonding two adherends.

Polymerization   A chemical reaction whereby monomer molecules link together to form larger ones.

Post cure   To expose an adhesive to additional cure (usually heat), following initial cure.

Primer   A coating applied to a surface, prior to the adhesive, to improve the bond performance.

Storage life   Time during which adhesive can be stored and still be suitable for use (also called *shelf life*).

Structural adhesive   Adhesive used for transferring required loads between adherends exposed to service environments typical for the structure involved.

Surface preparation   Physical and/or chemical preparation of an adherend to make it suitable for adhesive bonding.

Thermoplastic   A material that will repeatedly soften when heated and harden when cooled.

Thermoset   A material that will undergo or has undergone a chemical reaction by the action of heat, catalyst, etc., leading to a relatively infusible state.

Time, assembly   The time interval between the spreading of the adhesive on the adherend and the application of pressure or heat, or both, to the assembly.

Working life   The period of time during which an adhesive, after mixing with catalyst, solvent, or other compounding ingredients, remains suitable for use.

INTRODUCTION

Joining of materials with adhesives offers significant benefits over mechanical methods of uniting two materials. An adhesive distributes a load over an area rather than concentrating it at a point, resulting in a more even distribution of stresses. An adhesive-bonded joint is therefore more resistant to flex and vibration stresses than, for example, a riveted joint. An adhesive forms a seal as well as a bond. This eliminates corrosion which often occurs in a mechanically fastened joint. An adhesive joins irregularly shaped surfaces more easily than does a mechanical fastener. Other benefits include negligible weight addition and virtually no change to part dimensions or geometry. Limitations include the time in which strength must be achieved, the need for some type of surface preparation, and the need for eventual disassembly.

The variety of adhesives available in the marketplace has increased greatly in the past few years. Selection of the proper adhesive to do a job successfully can be a challenging experience. In addition to technical requirements, time and cost are often important considerations. Choice of an adhesive should start with answering questions about the parts to be bonded. Proper choice of an adhesive is based on knowledge of suitability of the adhesive for the particular substrates to be bonded, appropriate surface preparation, curing the adhesive correctly, and matching the strength and durability characteristics of the adhesive to its intended use. This chapter will address the requirements needed for successful selection and use of adhesives.

DESCRIPTION AND USES OF COMMON TYPES OF ADHESIVES*

Emulsion Adhesives

This group of adhesives, commonly known as *white glues,* is based on a wide variety of polymeric materials dispersed in an aqueous phase. A general requirement for use is that at least one of the substrates to be bonded be permeable to allow water to escape from the adhesive. These adhesives find wide use in bonding wood, paper, fabrics, leather, and other porous substrates. While resistance to moisture is generally good, solvent resistance is low.

Contact Cements

Contact cements consist of elastomers dissolved in a solvent or dispersed in water. Solvent-based contact cements are very hazardous to use on a job site. The solvents are either flammable or consist of chlorinated materials. Water-based cements require high pressure for successful use, therefore are often not practical. Contact cements find widest use in making laminates.

Hot-Melt Adhesives

Hot-melt adhesives are based on thermoplastic polymers (polyethylene, polyamide) and copolymers (ethylene-vinyl acetate). They are usually applied with electric glue guns. They have rather sharp melting points, therefore one must work fast with them because they set up quickly on cooling a few degrees. While they adhere to a wide variety of surfaces, they are best-suited to spot applications rather than large areas because of their rapid solidification properties.

Cyanoacrylates

Cyanoacrylates, also called *instant adhesives,* are one-part adhesives that cure very rapidly when confined between closely fitting surfaces. Minute amounts of moisture present on virtually any surface act as a catalyst for the cure. They are usable on a very wide variety of surfaces including metals and plastics. Because they are thermoplastics, environmental resistance is limited.

---

* See also Table 3-1.

TABLE 3-1 Common Adhesive Types

Adhesive	Advantages	Limitations
Cyanoacrylates	Rapid cure Single component Work on many surfaces High tensile strength Indefinite pot life Easy dispensing	High price Limited gap curing Poor durability Low solvent resistance Poor temperature resistance Bond skin
Anaerobics	Moderate price High strength Rapid cure Good solvent resistance Variable viscosities No mixing Indefinite pot life Easy dispensing Easy automation	Moderate gap curing Not for plastic or rubber Air prevents curing 300–400°F (150–205°C) limit Need clean surfaces
Acrylics	Moderate price Good gap cure Good impact, peel, shear Medium/fast cure Work on dirty surfaces Adhere to many surfaces	Cure more slowly than anaerobics Hot strength under 300°F (150°C) Primer required
Urethanes	Moderate price Tough, flexible Adheres to many materials Flexible at low temperatures	Two-part or oven cure Sensitive to moisture Short pot life Low heat resistance
Silicones	Moderate price Good gap filling Good for glass Flexible High temperature resistance Good water resistance	Low strength Limited solvent resistance Very flexible Slow curing Needs moisture to cure Hard to clean

Epoxies	Low price
	Good gap fill
	High strength
	Good temperature/solvent
	  resistance
	Bond to many surfaces
		Measuring and mixing
		  needed
		Short pot life
		Fixture and cure time
		  may be slow
		Heat may be needed
		  for cure

Hot melts	Low price Good gap fill Fast setting Versatile formulas Adhere to polyolefins	Must be applied hot Low heat resistance Messy, stringy

Solvent cement	Low price
	Many types
	Easily applied
	Moderate clamping needed
	Long shelf life
		Poor gap fill
		Slow drying
		Poor temperature
		  resistance
		Attack plastics
		Flammable or toxic
		  solvents
		Poor solvent resistance

Anaerobic Adhesives

Anaerobic adhesives are one-part materials that cure when confined in a joint that excludes oxygen. Long used for thread locking and sealing (originally known as *chemical lock washers*), they are available in many strength variations and viscosities. True structural anaerobic adhesives are also available. A surface activator is generally needed with the structural adhesives. Anaerobic adhesives generate high strengths and, being thermosets in the cured state, exhibit excellent temperature and environmental durability. They perform best on clean metal surfaces. They cure rapidly and at room temperature.

Acrylic Adhesives

Also called *tough acrylic adhesives,* these adhesives require a surface activator to initiate the cure mechanism. They are versatile materials in that they adhere to a wide variety of surfaces. While older-technology products are flammable, many nonflammable versions are available today. Strength and durability are good. Rapid room-temperature cure is a feature of these adhesives.

Epoxy Adhesives

Epoxies are probably the most widely used structural adhesives, having originated several decades ago. They are usable on many types of surfaces, and generate high-strength bonds. Originally rigid materials, flexibility has been designed into newer versions. This improves their impact resistance and peel strength. Epoxies are available as one- or two-part systems. The one-part systems usually have to be stored at low temperatures, even frozen. Two-part epoxies are by far the more popular. While measuring and mixing may not be convenient, these adhesives cure at room temperature and may be formulated to set rapidly. As a general rule, the higher the cure temperature, the greater the durability, but room-temperature-cured epoxies often exhibit very good durability.

Silicones

Silicones are one-part adhesives that cure on exposure to atmospheric moisture to form thermoset elastomers. While they are compatible with a variety of surfaces, they generate only modest strengths. They are excellent sealants, exhibiting high moisture and temperature resistance.

Pressure-Sensitive Adhesives

The formulation and use of pressure-sensitive adhesives is very similar to contact adhesives, except that no solvent is involved. These are typically film adhesives, and can be two-side-coated. They are useful where instant fixture is required, and some versions have good durability; however, they are thermoplastic in nature.

Polyurethane Adhesives

Polyurethane adhesives are either two-part systems or require a heat cure. Because of their handling properties, they are best suited for use in a production environment. They are good for joining dissimilar materials and maintain flexibility at very low temperatures. They are very flexible at room temperature, therefore do not exhibit high strengths.

Phenolic and Polyimide Adhesives

While these two types of adhesives are chemically different, they have major characteristics in common. Both are difficult to process and require high temperatures often accompanied by pressure to cure. The resulting bonds are extremely high strength and very temperature and solvent resistant. They have little practical use outside a controlled production environment.

JOINT DESIGN

Most adhesives are strong in tension or shear strength but very weak in cleavage and/or peel strength (see Fig. 3-1). Cleavage and peel forces should be eliminated from adhesive joints to the greatest extent possible. Good joint design should also allow for the maximum possible bond area and mechanical locking as well as adhesive bonding. The simple lap joint of Fig. 3-2 can be improved in many ways: by increasing the thickness of each adherend or by making a type of double-lap shear joint. Both joints reduce the peel and cleavage forces at the edge of the bond joint caused by the eccentricity of the adherends. Other typical bonded joints are shown in Fig. 3-2. Figure 3-3 shows both good and bad ways to bond flexible adherends.

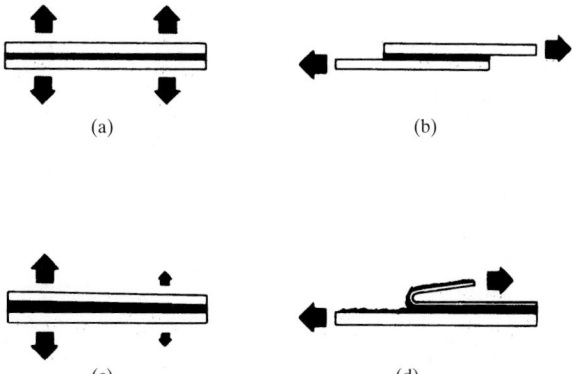

(a)   (b)

(c)   (d)

FIGURE 3-1   Stresses on bonded joints.

The following axioms may be of help in the design of bonded joints:

1. The failing load of lap joints increases as the width of the joint increases. A 1-in-wide joint has twice the strength of a half-inch joint.

2. The failing load of lap joints does not increase proportionately with length or area. A 2-in-long joint is not twice as strong as a 1-in joint. A 4-in-long joint may not take an appreciably greater load than a 2-in-long joint.

3. Although typically a stronger adhesive may produce a stronger joint, a higher-elongation adhesive with lower strength can produce a stronger joint.

4. The stiffness of the adherends and adhesive influences the failure load of a joint. In general, the stiffer the adherend with respect to the adhesive, the less the failing load of the joint is influenced by joint geometry.

5. The adhesive layer thickness is not a strong influence on the strength of the joint. More important is a uniform and void-free adhesive layer.

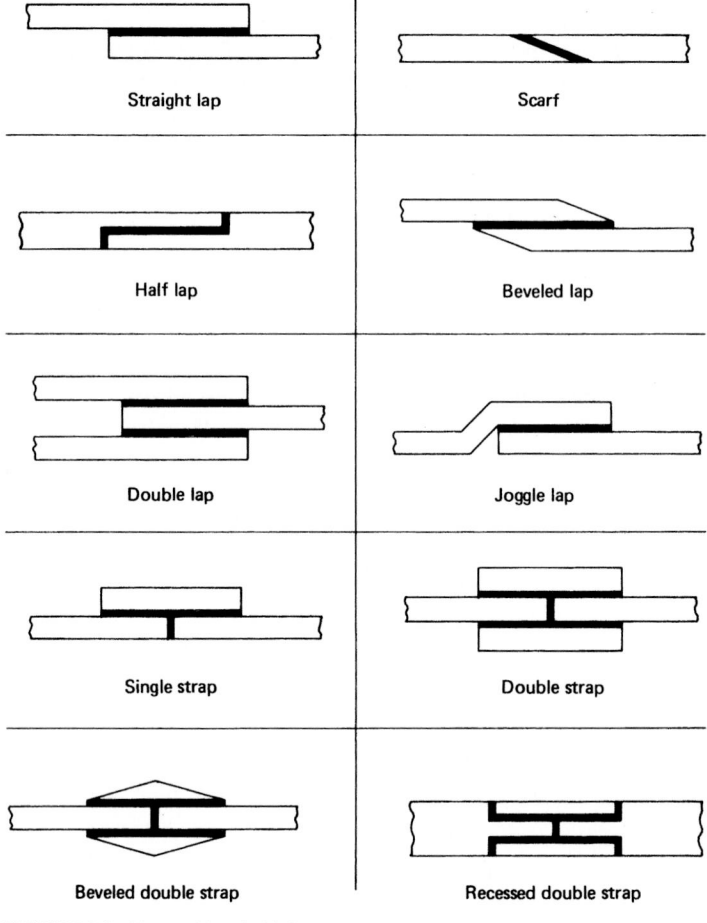

FIGURE 3-2 Types of bonded joints.

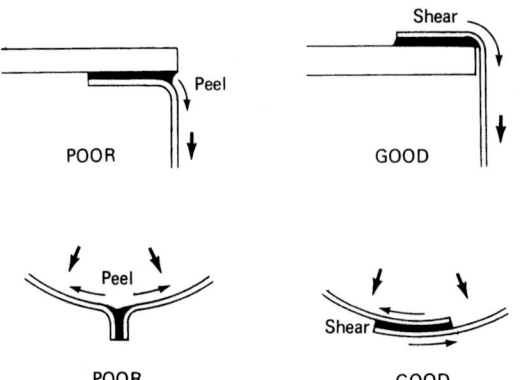

FIGURE 3-3 Joints for flexible adherends.

6. The higher the E_t of the adherend, the stronger the joint. A 0.040-in (1-mm) sheet-steel lap joint is stronger than a 0.040-in (1-mm) sheet-aluminum joint. A 0.094-in (2.4-mm) sheet-aluminum lap joint is stronger than a 0.040-in (1-mm) sheet-aluminum lap joint.

PREPARATION FOR BONDING

Surface Preparation

Surface preparation is the most critical step in the adhesive-bonding process. Unless a satisfactory surface preparation is accomplished, the bond will fail adhesively and unpredictably at the adherend-primer interface. With proper surface preparation, bonds can be made that will ensure that any failure is cohesive in nature, thus realizing the predicted strength of the adhesive and primer combination. Proper surface preparation is a key factor not only in the initial strength of a bonded joint but, even more importantly, in its long-term environmental resistance.

Surface preparation methods must, as a minimum, remove oil, grease, and any coating whose bond strength to the adherend is apt to be less than that of the adhesive bond. Simple abrasion and/or solvent wiping are used for some metallic and plastic adherends. However, on most metals these simple surface preparations are usually not sufficient to obtain good adhesion or long-term environmental resistance. For metals, usually the preferred surface treatment is one that chemically removes priming or bonding or, for aluminum, builds up of a controlled oxide layer. ANSI/ASTM D2093[5] and ANSI/ASTM D 2651-90 contain detailed recommended methods for preparation of various plastic and metal surfaces. (See Tables 3-2, 3-3, and 3-4.)

TABLE 3-2   Physical Treatments

Plastic adherend (Group I)	Cleaning procedure
Cellulose acetate, cellulose acetate butyrate, cellulose nitrate, methylstyrene, polycarbonate, polystyrene, vinyl chloride, polymethylmethacrylate, cellulose propionate, ethylcellulose, acrylonitrile butadiene styrene (ABS)	Wipe with methanol, sand, wipe with a clean dry cloth, then repeat methanol wipe.
Epoxy, polyester, phenolic, urea-formaldehyde, diallyl phthalate, melamine, nylon, and polyurethane	Wipe with acetone, sand, wipe with a clean dry cloth, then repeat acetone wipe.

TABLE 3-3   Chemical Treatments

Plastic adherend (Group II)	Cleaning procedure
Polyolefins (low and high density polyethylene, polypropylene, irradiated polyethylene), chlorinated polyether, polyformaldehyde	Wipe with acetone and treat with sulfuric acid-dichromate solution. Polyolefins should be treated for at least 1 h at temperature. Chlorinated polyether should be treated for 5 min at $160 \pm 5°F$ $(71 \pm 3°C)$. Polyformaldehyde may be treated up to 10 s at room temperature.
Trifluoromonochloroethylene, tetrafluoroethylene	Wipe with acetone and treat with sodium naphthalene complex for 15 min at room temperature.

TABLE 3-4 Surface Treatments for Metals*

Material	Procedure
Aluminum	(1) Phosphoric acid anodizing in accordance with Practice D3933. (2) FPL (Forest Products Lab) etch: degrease, hot alkaline cleaner, hot sulfuric acid–sodium dichromate etch, rinse, and dry.
Carbon steel and stainless steel	Degrease, followed by mechanical abrasion-vapor blasting, sand blasting, etc.
Titanium, magnesium, copper	Require chemical treatment.

* Abstracted from ANSI/ASTM D2651 (Ref. 5).

Durability

In selecting an adhesive for a particular application, one of the most important considerations is the environment or surroundings to which the adhesive joint will be subjected. Of course, the force acting on the joint is of prime consideration, and the adhesive joint must be capable of carrying the maximum expected load (without excessive creep) and amount of fatigue or cyclic stresses. Cyclic stresses, particularly slow ones, are much more damaging to an adhesive joint than a steady stress. The adhesive selected for a particular application must be able to resist these loads and stresses not only initially but also after exposure to the most severe environmental factors to be encountered during the life of the adhesive joint. Heat and humidity are usually the most damaging environmental factors for most bonded joints. Thermal-expansion stresses created between dissimilar materials having widely different coefficients of thermal expansion, e.g., a plastic-to-metal bond joint, require low-modulus (nonbrittle) adhesives for best performance. Other deleterious factors are solvents and ultraviolet or other energy. Always choose an adhesive that is resistant to these factors; do not plan on coating the adhesive joint with some "protective" coating which can possibly crack or eventually become permeable to solvents or moisture.

Primers

For many adhesives, a primer is not merely desirable but absolutely essential in order to obtain maximum bond strength and environmental durability. Usually, the adhesive manufacturer recommends a compatible adhesive primer. The primer performs several functions. The primer, being less viscous than the adhesive, wets the adhered surface and adheres to it better than does the adhesive. Corrosion-resistant primers used particularly with epoxies and aluminum adherends contain chromates that leach out and protect the adherend from corrosion. Corrosion-inhibited adhesive primers (CIAPs) are essential to environmentally durable aluminum bonding.

ENVIRONMENTAL HEALTH AND SAFETY

The impending impact of both the Clean Air Act of 1990 and the Montreal Protocol will dramatically reduce and then eventually eliminate from the workplace over the next several years the use of chlorofluorocarbons (CFCs), 1, 1, 1 trichloroethane (methyl chloroform), and all halogenated solvents.

As this movement to ban environmentally hazardous solvents gains momentum in the coming years, *the systems approach to bonding will require a new dimension.* Environmental engineering will likely become an integral part of the design-for-manufacturing equation, where application engineering, assembly engineering, manufacturing engineering, and maintenance engineering are considered concurrently to review the environmental impact of the adhesive system used.

REFERENCES AND SOURCES OF INFORMATION

1. *Adhesives Desk-Top Data Bank,* 3d ed., The International Plastics Selector, Inc., San Diego, 1980–1981.
2. Thrall, E. W., and R. W. Shannon: *Adhesive Bonding of Aluminum Alloys for Aircraft,* Marcel Dekker, New York, 1982.
3. *Adhesives Red Book, Directory of the Adhesives Industry,* Communication Channels, Inc., Atlanta, 1982.
4. *Adhesives in Modern Manufacturing,* Society of Manufacturing Engineers (SME), Dearborn, Mich., 1970.
5. *ASTM Annual Book of Standards,* part 22, American Society for Testing and Materials, 1982.
6. ARP 1524, "Aerospace Recommended Practice, Surface Preparation and Priming of Aluminum Alloy Parts for High Durability Structural Bonding, Phosphoric Acid Anodizing," 1978.
7. ARP 1575, "Aerospace Recommended Practice, Surface Preparation and Priming of Aluminum Alloy Parts for High Durability Structural Adhesive Bonding, Hand Applied Phosphoric Acid Anodizing," 1979.
8. D.A.T.A. Digest, *Adhesives, Sealants and Primers,* Edition 5, D.A.T.A. Business Publishing, San Diego, 1989.

CHAPTER 16-4
DIAGNOSTIC INSTRUMENTATION

R. Lane Swensen
Technical Writer
Bently Nevada Corporation
Minden, Nevada

INTRODUCTION

Plant management, engineering, and maintenance personnel continually deal with a variety of demands, such as those for increasingly sophisticated machinery, decreasing maintenance budgets, increasing machine availability, and improving productivity and profit. Effective techniques for monitoring and maintaining machinery include reliance on instrumentation. Reliable machinery monitoring and diagnostic systems, provided with the correct measurement input signals, are widely recognized for their value.

The signals acquired from an industrial machine are a direct indication of machinery health. When considering machinery monitoring and diagnostics, *safety, quality, timeliness,* and *cost* factors must be considered with respect to each piece of machinery. More specifically, major objectives include:

- Increasing plant *safety* by minimizing the occurrence of hazardous or catastrophic conditions.
- Improving product *quality* by minimizing process variances caused by improperly operating machinery.
- Maximizing plant *timeliness* or availability by servicing only those machines that require it and having more efficient plant turnarounds.
- Reducing plant operating *costs* by minimizing unplanned shutdowns and by making more efficient use of maintenance resources.

It is important to know the facts about industrial machinery monitoring and diagnostics. The key is one's familiarity with the various types of measurements, transducer characteristics, and applications.

MONITORING SYSTEMS

Industrial machinery maintenance has evolved over the years. Originally, it involved the practice of *breakdown maintenance,* with maintenance being performed only after a breakdown occurred. From there, maintenance began to be regularly performed through *preventive maintenance* whether or not it was needed. The current trend, that of *predictive maintenance,* involves using modern machinery instrumentation to monitor developing fault conditions. Once a fault is identified, personnel can then use existing or additional instrumentation to diagnose the fault. If the fault is diagnosed as being real, then plans can be made for maintenance. *The objective is to identify the fault in its earliest stage before any damage can occur.* Early problem identification leads to better and more informed maintenance decisions. Predictive maintenance involves servicing only those machines that require it, when they require it. Time and money are not wasted.

Predictive maintenance is broken down further into two categories: continuous monitoring (machinery protection) and periodic monitoring (machinery information). Continuous monitoring uses permanently installed continuous-monitoring systems to provide protection on critical machines. Periodic monitoring uses either permanently installed (on-line periodic monitoring) or portable (manual periodic monitoring) instrumentation to collect machinery operating condition data at set time intervals.

Continuous Monitoring

Continuous monitoring typically utilizes permanently installed transducers whose signals are input to a rack of monitors. These monitors provide continuous information and protection for the machines. The term *protection* means that the continuous monitoring system can shut down a machine without requiring human interaction. Each transducer in the system has its own dedicated monitoring circuitry, alarm set points, and relay outputs.

Continuous monitoring is more expensive than periodic monitoring, as data collection and machinery protection are provided at all times (Fig. 4-1). Continuous monitoring is best suited for applications involving machines labeled critical in terms of process or cost. High-speed rotating and reciprocating machinery, such as turbine generators and reciprocating compressors, typically require continuous monitoring.

On-Line Periodic Monitoring

On-line periodic monitoring is the latest development in the field of machinery monitoring instrumentation. It uses a computer-based system that continuously and sequentially collects condition data from permanently installed transducers located in the machinery. Unlike continuous monitoring, on-line periodic monitoring does not provide machinery protection, since

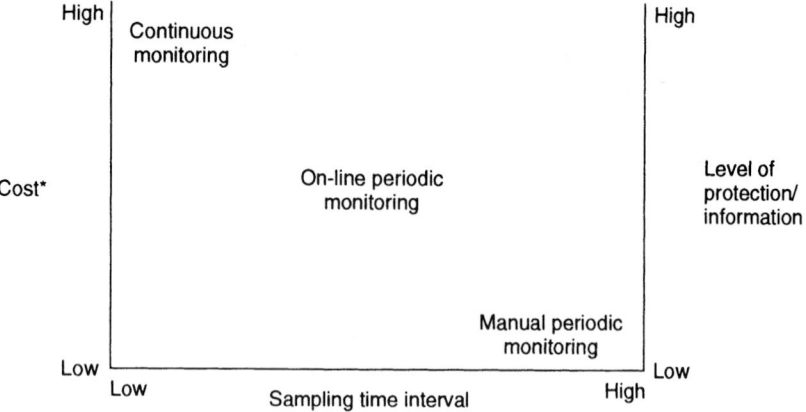

FIGURE 4-1   Machinery monitoring system comparison chart.

the system's signal processing circuitry is shared between all points in the system. At any given time, data are collected at only one point in the system. Because of this, it should be applied only to essential or general-purpose machinery. It is commonly referred to as a *scanning system.*

An on-line periodic monitoring system cannot shut down a machine on its own; shutdown must be initiated by human interaction. The on-line periodic system provides the maintenance professional with the data collection and diagnostic capabilities needed to make informed maintenance decisions. Since this on-line system uses permanently installed instrumentation, updated information is immediately available without the need to manually gather data.

On-line periodic monitoring falls between continuous monitoring and manual periodic monitoring in terms of protection, sampling time, and cost (Fig. 4-1). It is typically applied in those situations involving essential or general-purpose machinery located in hazardous areas, remote locations, or difficult-to-reach places.

Manual Periodic Monitoring

With manual periodic monitoring, a computer is typically used to download route information to portable equipment. Maintenance personnel then follow the route information, manually collecting the data which are later uploaded to the computer for analysis. This process is repeated at certain time intervals, typically every 2 to 6 weeks, based on the size and layout of the plant and the availability of trained personnel.

While manual periodic monitoring typically involves a smaller initial investment, it does not provide a high level of machinery protection or timely collection of data and involves recurring labor costs (Fig. 4-1). Manual periodic monitoring should be used only with general-purpose machinery in which fault conditions occur during extended periods of time. It should not be used for high-speed, critical machinery in which failures can occur quickly once a fault condition is exhibited.

An ideal predictive maintenance program will typically involve all three levels of machinery monitoring. Continuous monitoring would be applied to the critical machines. On-line periodic monitoring would be applied to the essential or general-purpose machinery located in concentrated, hazardous, remote, or difficult-to-reach areas. Finally, manual periodic monitoring would be applied to those general-purpose machines not covered by the on-line periodic monitoring system.

Computerized Communication

Often, the data from a monitoring system are integrated into the database of a process computer, digital/distributed control system, or programmable logic controller. This enhances data manipulation and enables the user to monitor the rate of change of significant parameters, compare one measured variable with others on the same machine, and perform other tasks. Computers are also excellent for routine data storage, trending, alarm sequencing, and data comparison in a machine-upset condition.

TRANSDUCER SELECTION

Because each transducer must be suited to a particular machine application, *proper selection is critical.* By carefully choosing the correct transducer for an installation, the designer ensures that all hardware and software products used in the system can measure and reduce accurate data.

Transducer selection is influenced by several factors. The most important is mechanical, addressing machinery characteristics under both normal and malfunction operating conditions. The optimum transducer is one which produces a maximum change in output signal as a result of a minimum change in machine condition; it is therefore best-suited for both machinery monitoring and malfunction diagnosis.

Proximity Probe Transducer Systems

Proximity probe transducer systems are required for machines with journal (fluid film) bearings. This displacement measuring device indicates the dynamic motion of the shaft relative to the bearing. The peak-to-peak relative displacement measurement can be directly related to internal clearances within the machine (bearings and seals).

In addition to measuring shaft vibration, the proximity probe average (dc) signal represents the average radial position of the shaft within the bearing. This is a definite advantage of the proximity probe measurement, since certain machine malfunction mechanisms cause a significant change in shaft average position either before, or instead of, a change in shaft vibration.

For machines with journal bearings, two probes should be installed per bearing, mounted radially at 90° (*x-y*). Even for asymmetrical bearing designs, there is no symmetry to shaft relative motion, considering all types of machine malfunction mechanisms. The *x-y* arrangement is also necessary to accurately determine the average radial shaft position within the bearing clearance.

Seismic Sensors

Velocity sensors or accelerometers are typically used on general-purpose machines with rolling-element bearings. These seismic transducers are installed on the bearing housing and, in general, reflect the shaft-transmitted energy in the form of absolute vibration (relative to free space).

The choice of whether to use a velocity or acceleration sensor is a function of several factors. One consideration is the vibration frequency range of interest. Velocity transducers are generally suited for lower-frequency measurements because they give a higher signal output at low frequencies. When appropriate, fans, pumps, and compressors with rolling-element bearings running at low to medium speeds should use a velocity transducer as the primary seismic vibration sensor. In contrast, the accelerometer has a good signal-to-noise ratio at high frequencies. The upper frequency range of most accelerometers far exceeds that of most velocity transducers. Other selection factors include physical installation requirements, temperature limits, long-term environmental and mechanical reliability, and cost.

Accelerometers are also used to supplement proximity probe measurements for some fluid-film-bearing machine types which exhibit distinctive high-frequency vibration. Examples include vibration from gear mesh, vane or blade passing, blade resonance, and fluidic disturbances such as cavitation. In most cases, the vibration frequency is not beyond the range of the proximity probes, but the vibration displacement can be so small at high frequencies that the signal may be lost in the overall measurement. Accelerometers, on the other hand, emphasize higher-frequency vibrations.

Mode Identification Probes

Machinery monitoring and problem diagnosis can be further improved by the addition of proximity probes used as mode identification (MI) probes which help to accurately identify synchronous mode shapes. Lateral mode shape information is extremely valuable for balancing rotating machinery and identifying faults such as shaft cracks, bearing failures, and rotor to stator rubs. However, lateral mode shape information and the location of rotor nodal points (zero motion) along the machine train are typically not provided by equipment manufacturers. Without this information, proximity probes may inadvertently be positioned at nodal points. If a probe is located at a nodal point, it observes little or no shaft motion and therefore cannot provide meaningful information. Casing-mounted transducers cannot be substituted for the MI probes since they do not observe shaft motion directly.

To ensure that valid information is available for machinery monitoring and diagnostics, at least one MI probe should be installed at each end of the machine or at each radial bearing, at the same angular location as one of the x-y probes installed at the nearest bearing. As a general rule, its axial location should be a minimum of two shaft diameters away from the nearest set of x-y probes. Expanding the single MI probe to an x-y pair and installing additional MI probe sets along the shaft will provide even more valuable information for diagnostic and baseline purposes.

Rolling-Element-Bearing Proximity Systems

A high-sensitivity proximity probe transducer system is recommended for monitoring machines with rolling-element bearings. With a rolling-element bearing, there is virtually no clearance between the shaft and bearing, making a shaft relative measurement inappropriate under normal conditions. Shaft vibration is transmitted directly to the bearing and must be absorbed by the bearing support structure.

The high-sensitivity proximity probe is installed through the bearing housing to directly observe the bearing outer ring. Because this transducer is closer to the origin of vibration than traditional bearing-housing-mounted seismic transducers, it is more sensitive to changes in bearing condition and is the best choice for machines with rolling-element bearings.

The Keyphasor® Transducer

The Keyphasor® transducer system provides a once-per-shaft-turn voltage pulse resulting from a keyway, slot, or projection on the shaft. While proximity probes should be installed as permanent transducers, an optical transducer measuring a change in reflectivity can be used temporarily. This type of system is used for shaft rotative speed measurement and is essential as a phase reference transducer for complete machinery diagnosis.

Torque Measurement

Identifying machine performance at varying operating loads and speeds allows machinery to run at maximum efficiency. Measuring torque helps identify when machine performance is degrading. The torque measurement can compare actual machine operation to its design criteria and identify the rotating system's dynamic torque characteristics. Machine performance can then be checked for compliance to specifications under steady-state and transient conditions at test stands, manufacturing shops, and on-site, after machine installation.

By mounting on and around the existing machine coupling or spool piece, the torque sensor provides an indication of how efficient machinery is operating by continuously monitoring the actual torque and power being supplied by the prime mover. The torque sensor should measure dynamic and steady-state torque with high accuracy and repeatability and should be well-suited for industrial environments.

Other Transducers

Other types of measurements are typically employed on large rotating machinery. Extended-range proximity probes are used as differential expansion transducers. Linear variable differential transformers (LVDTs) are installed to make casing expansion measurements. LVDTs or rotary potentiometers are used for measuring inlet steam valve (assembly) position. Resistance temperature detectors (RTDs) are used to measure bearing or lube oil temperatures. In all cases, the correct transducer must be used with each installation for the remaining system components to measure and reduce accurate data.

DATA DOCUMENTATION AND DIAGNOSTICS

The use of on-line computer systems for data collection, documentation and machinery diagnostics has become increasingly common. On-line data collection and monitoring systems can rapidly provide essential information on the mechanical condition of machinery in easy-to-interpret formats. Automatic capture and storage of data, which might otherwise be lost, can drastically reduce the need to call plant engineers, technicians, and maintenance personnel. Stored data can be reviewed and analyzed when convenient or sent on disk to be reviewed by consultants.

Most portable diagnostic instrumentation currently available also has the ability to capture and store data. Multiple channels of information can be sampled simultaneously and subsequently downloaded to a computer for analysis. Hard-copy documentation is then available from a variety of output devices including graphics/laser printers or plotters. Most digital oscilloscopes and signal analyzers also have memory and hard-copy output capability. Although tape recorders remain a valuable tool for capturing and reproducing vibration data, their use has been significantly reduced due to the storage and processing capabilities of current portable diagnostic instrumentation.

Static and Dynamic Data

There are two fundamental types of data: static and dynamic. For analysis purposes, static data should include trending of:

- Overall (direct) vibration amplitude
- DC probe gap voltage (if applicable)
- Amplitude and phase angle for $1\times$, $2\times$ and $n\times$ vibration vectors

- Shaft rotative speed
- Process variable values (temperature, pressure, etc.)

Dynamic waveform data is used to produce:

- Orbit and time base presentations
- Frequency spectra
- Amplitude and phase values for user specified orders of the rotative speed component (1×, 2×, n×, etc.)

Machines of the same make and model may exhibit varying degrees of behavioral similarity. However, all machinery will demonstrate some unique operating characteristics. Machine response can be significantly affected by a variety of parameters, including bearing and seal clearances, alignment, support stiffness, and thermal/load effects. Vibration characteristics of a machine can and will be greatly affected by process changes and other factors external to a machine train. A comparison of changes in machine dynamic behavior and process-related variables can provide valuable insight on operational conditions.

Steady-State and Transient Data Formats

There are two basic data formats, each of which can include static and dynamic information. Steady-state data are captured under constant operating conditions (speed, load, etc.). Transient data are captured under changing operating conditions, typically shaft rotational speed. Certain plot types may apply to both steady-state as well as transient data formats. Listed below are the basic formats necessary to evaluate machine condition and selected examples.

Steady State

- *Acceptance region.*   A specific type of trend display in a polar format. A selected vibration vector is plotted as a function of time. The *acceptance region* is a defined boundary (amplitude and phase) representing the normal state of machine operating conditions.
- *Orbit/time base.*   Primarily used for orthogonal (*x-y*) shaft-observing proximity displacement transducers. The orbit display is the dynamic path of the shaft centerline within the bearing clearance; the time base display shows the two waveform signals that are used to produce the orbit (Fig. 4-2). A Keyphasor® mark provides vibration phase information on both the orbit and time base waveforms.
- *Amplitude/phase vs. time (APHT).*   Overall vibration or a specific vibration vector (1×, 2×, etc.) in terms of amplitude and phase. The overall vibration value and vector amplitude and phase are plotted in a rectangular coordinate system. Amplitude and phase data are plotted independently as a function of time.
- *Spectrum.*   The frequency content of a vibration signal (Fig. 4-3). This format is typically displayed with amplitude on the vertical axis and frequency on the horizontal axis. Frequency can be scaled in hertz, cycles per minute, or orders of shaft running speed (1×, 2×, etc.).
- *Waterfall.*   A series of spectra taken at defined time intervals. The display is in a rectangular coordinate system in terms of amplitude and frequency. Time and amplitude are displayed on independent vertical axes.

Transient

- *Orbit/time base.*   Primarily used for orthogonal (*x-y*) shaft-observing proximity displacement transducers. The orbit display is the dynamic path of the shaft centerline within the bearing clearance; the time base display shows the two waveform signals that are used to produce the orbit (Fig. 4-2). A Keyphasor mark provides vibration phase information on both the orbit and time base waveforms.

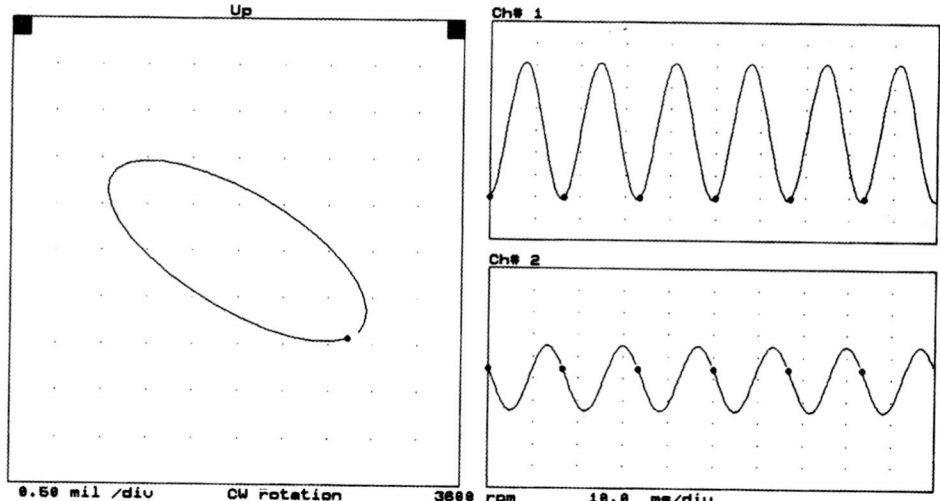

FIGURE 4-2   Orbit/time base plot.

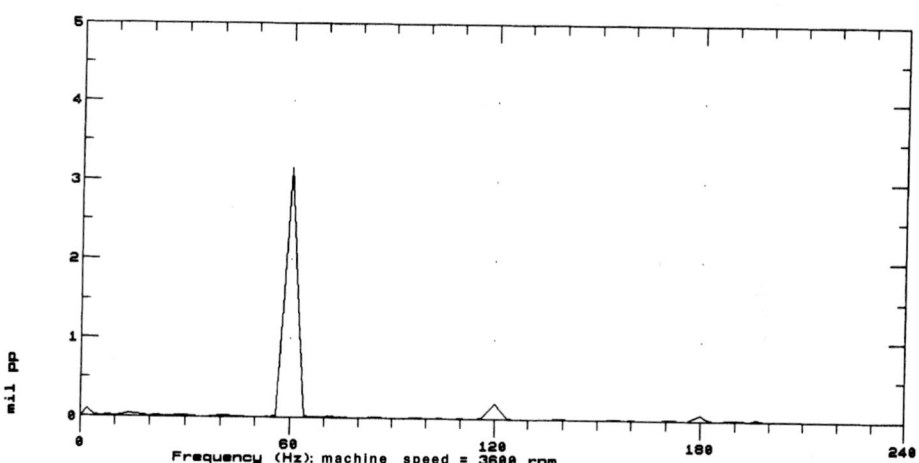

FIGURE 4-3   Spectrum plot.

- *Polar.*   A polar graph of a specific vibration vector (1×, 2×, etc.) in terms of amplitude and phase (Fig. 4-4). The vector amplitude and phase is plotted at defined shaft rotative speed intervals during a start-up or coast-down.

- *Bode.*   Overall vibration and/or a specific vibration vector (1×, 2×, etc.) in terms of amplitude and phase (Fig. 4-5). The overall vibration value and vector amplitude and phase are plotted at defined shaft rotative speed intervals during a start-up or coastdown. The display is in a rectangular coordinate system with amplitude and phase plotted independently as a function of shaft rotative speed.

- *Cascade.*   A series of spectra taken at defined shaft rotative speed intervals during a start-up or coastdown (Fig. 4-6). The display is in a rectangular coordinate system in terms of

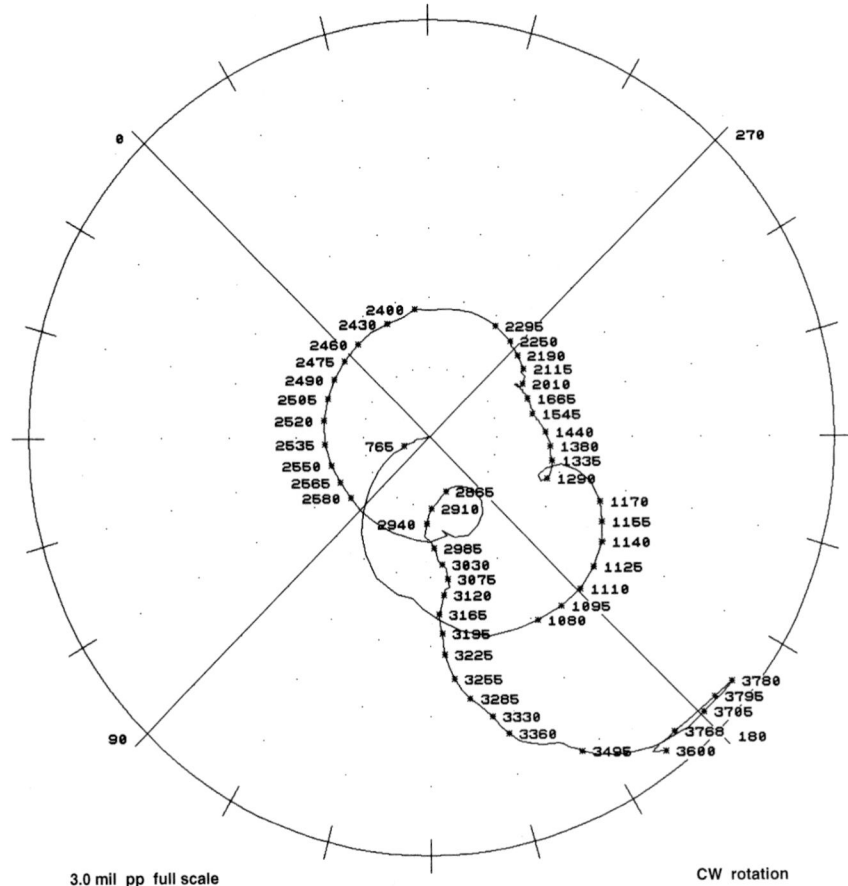

3.0 mil pp full scale   CW rotation

FIGURE 4-4 Polar plot.

amplitude and frequency. Shaft rotative speed and amplitude are displayed on independent vertical axes.

- *Shaft centerline.*   Represents the average position of the shaft with respect to the radial bearing clearance (Fig. 4-7) and is used for orthogonal (*x-y*) shaft-observing proximity displacement transducers. The plot is derived from probe gap voltage data from the two proximity probes.

Shaft Crack Analysis

Shaft crack problems represent a significant safety and loss hazard, particularly in the power generation industry. Implementation of an effective shaft crack detection program can prove highly beneficial in applications involving medium to large turbogenerator sets, reactor coolant pumps used in nuclear power plants, and other critical machinery. Permanent monitoring systems and computerized systems can be used together to measure, process, and present the information needed for early shaft crack detection.

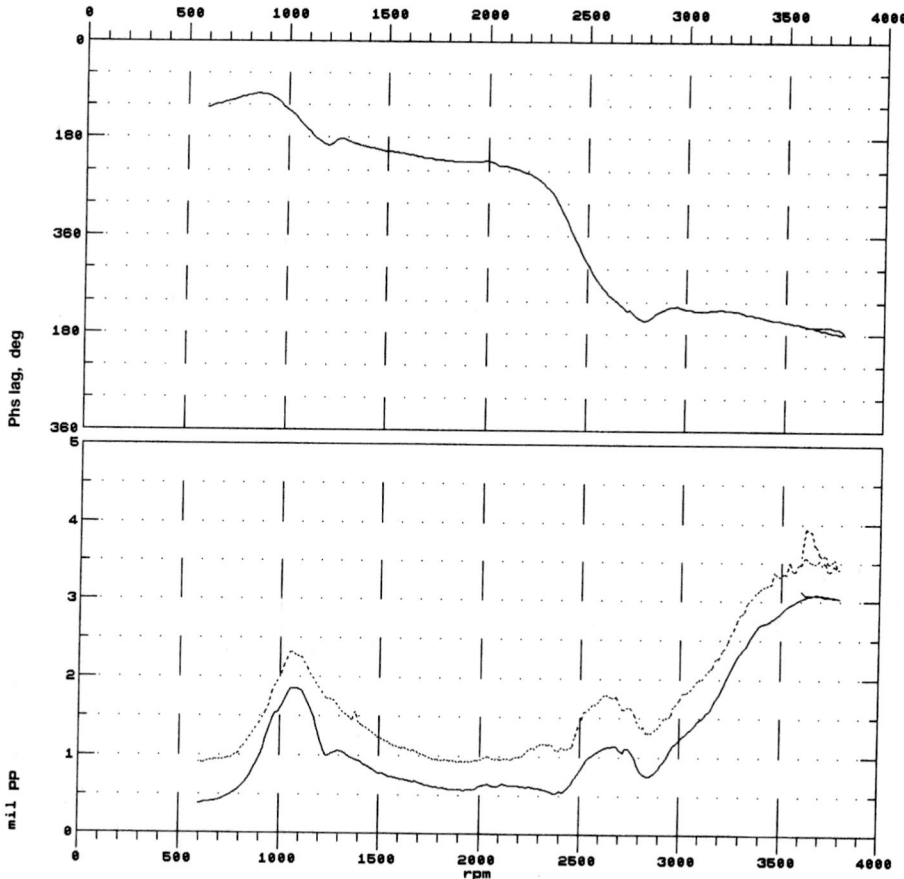

FIGURE 4-5 Bode plot.

REAL-TIME INSTRUMENTATION FOR DATA REVIEW AND DOCUMENTATION

Oscilloscope

The oscilloscope is a fundamental vibration analysis instrument, capable of clearly displaying the raw, composite signal from vibration transducers in time base or orbit formats. For shaft x-y relative displacement probes, time base and orbit presentations allow the evaluation of the true shape of the shaft's dynamic motion within its bearing clearance.

The average shaft centerline position, about which the shaft orbits, can also be assessed by using the dc portion of a proximity probe signal. This allows the dc gap voltage associated with displacement transducers to be offset so that the relatively small dc voltage changes associated with shaft centerline position movement within its bearing can be studied with increased resolution.

A Keyphasor signal can be used to trigger the oscilloscope, providing a reference point from which to make phase angle measurements. This is achieved by connecting the Keyphasor pulse to the z-axis input. This input superimposes the Keyphasor signal on the time base and orbit traces, producing the bright/blank (or blank/bright) Keyphasor mark.

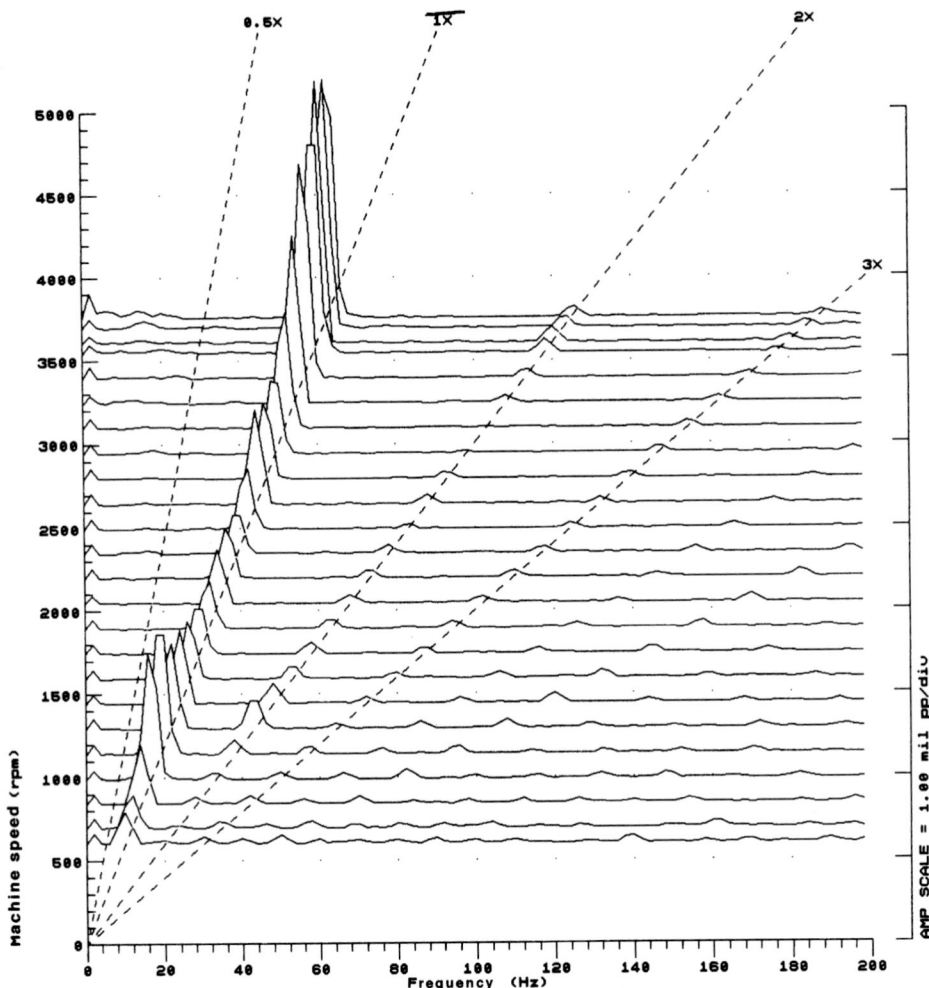

FIGURE 4-6   Cascade plot.

The oscilloscope can also be used in parallel with other diagnostic and recording equipment to provide an instantaneous presentation of the machine's dynamic behavior during a start-up or shutdown. When a machine event takes place, the oscilloscope instantly responds to changing conditions.

Spectrum Analyzers

These instruments consist of many bandpass filters. Vibration amplitudes at specific frequencies are continuously displayed, with any changes in the spectrum content being identified while the machine is running. Since many common machine malfunctions produce unique vibration frequencies, the spectrum display may be used to indicate the presence of these malfunctions and the relative magnitudes of each. Spectrum analysis involves the comparison of vibration spectra taken at different points on a machine or the comparison of spectra taken at the same measurement location at different points in time.

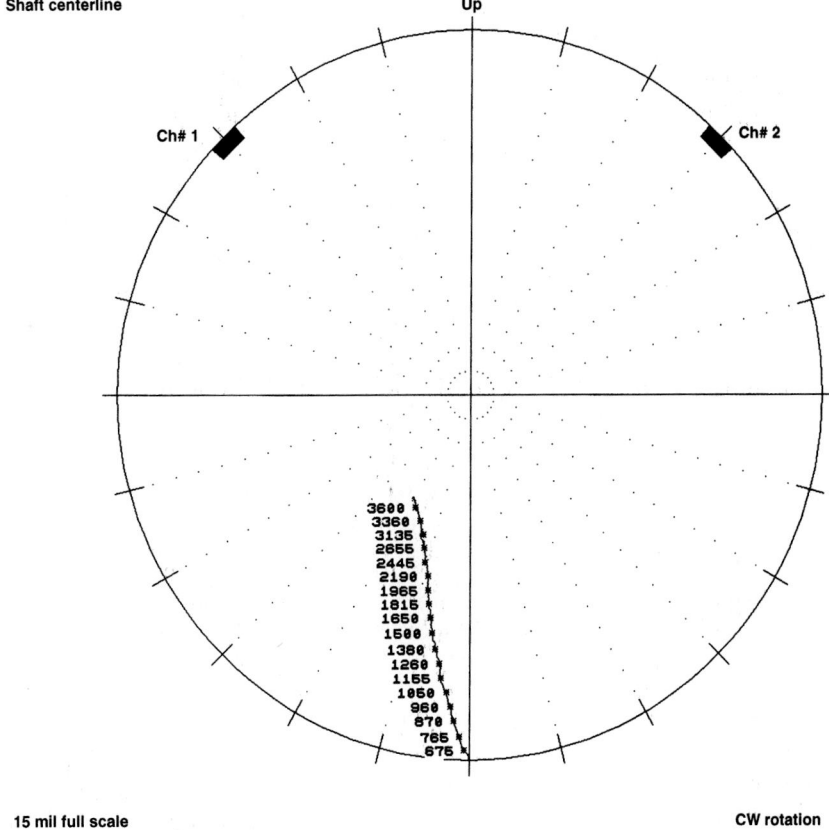

FIGURE 4-7 Shaft centerline plot.

Multifunction Instruments

Symptom-to-malfunction analysis is not always straightforward. Diagnostic instrumentation must provide meaningful information if it is to allow proper malfunction diagnosis. Only by utilizing all of the information available can proper diagnostic methods be effective. Without complete information, it is possible to either miss the presence of a malfunction or to improperly diagnose it.

Diagnostic instruments are available for permanent, on-line applications as well as portable, field applications. These units typically have processing and storage capabilities for multiple channels of steady-state and/or transient machinery condition information which is then transferred to a personal computer for more extensive trending and diagnostics.

EXPERT SYSTEMS

An expert system is a software program that, by simulating the thought processes of experts, assists the machinery specialist with decision making. This assistance is provided through comprehensive computer screen displays and hard-copy engineering reports.

With an expert system, data are received directly from the on-line computerized monitoring and diagnostic system. The user then inputs the machine configuration, transducer locations, etc. and the expert system will read the actual machine vibration data.

Machinery specialist and new engineer training is one of the best advantages of a quality expert system. With the inclusion of tutorial text, explanations are given to illustrate how a particular decision was reached. Once a machine audit is completed, the user can review information to see how the analysis was made.

Information Extraction

An expert system should be capable of correlating diagnostic knowledge with specific information, including:

- *Vibration magnitude.*   Indicates the severity of a machine problem and the urgency of any corrective action required. The presence of excessive vibration is the primary indicator of a malfunction.
- *Vibration frequency.*   Classifies the nature of the machine fault. Specific vibration frequencies are significantly related to specific machine malfunction conditions.
- *Vibration form or shape.*   Further classifies machine malfunctions. The orbit form indicates the shape of the dynamic path of the shaft centerline during a vibration cycle. Different conclusions can be drawn from a highly elliptical orbit versus a circular orbit. A description of the shape of the vibration must include orbit precession, the direction of shaft centerline movement relative to the direction of rotation. Precession can be either forward (in the same direction as shaft rotation) or reverse.
- *Amplitude and phase angle.*   Describes the response of the rotor to the forcing function. This information is collected from bearings across the machine train, permitting the application of techniques to define the source location of a malfunction.
- *Radial position.*   The position of shaft centerline within the bearing characterizes the effective dynamic stiffness of the rotor/bearing system, thus revealing the margin of system stability.
- *Process variable information.*   When used in conjunction with vibration data, this information allows correlation of the observed vibration behavior with the current operational mode of the machine. Typical process variables include load, flow rates, pressures, and temperatures.

MONITORING RECIPROCATING COMPRESSORS

While reciprocating compressors are initially less expensive than centrifugal compressors per horsepower (watt), maintenance costs per horsepower (watt) are greater than those for centrifugal compressors. This is due to the large number of moving parts subject to wear. Valves and rider bands are at the top of the list of high-maintenance items on these machines.

Modern machinery information systems are available for effective predictive maintenance on reciprocating compressors, eliminating the need for costly, and perhaps unnecessary, machine shutdowns associated with preventive maintenance. Valve temperature, rider band wear, and frame vibration allow an accurate assessment of reciprocating compressor condition.

Leaking valves can be detected by measuring valve cover plate temperatures. When a valve is leaking, the same gas is recompressed over and over, increasing the temperature. Temperature monitors can accurately compare the temperatures of similar valves in the same cylinder; as a result, even subtle changes in temperature can be detected.

Rider bands are made of a plastic expendable material and are used on horizontal reciprocating compressors to support the piston in the cylinder and prevent metal-to-metal contact. While rider bands are designed to last several years, actual wear is a function of operating conditions, gas type, and amount of particulate in the gas steam. To prevent the piston from contacting the cylinder, rider band wear is measured electronically by observing the piston rod with a proximity probe. To eliminate the effects of dynamic piston motion, a reading is taken once per crankshaft revolution. The resulting rider band wear trend indicates the approximate remaining life of the band without shutting down the machine.

Reciprocating compressors tend to exhibit higher normal levels of vibration than centrifugal machines; however, even small changes in vibration can indicate an impending problem. Changes in a reciprocating compressor's frame vibration can indicate loose internal parts. Seismic transducers mounted horizontally on the machine case can be connected to a permanent monitoring system.

Reciprocating compressor main bearings can be monitored in the same manner as centrifugal compressors with x-y proximity probes at each bearing, indicating both radial vibration and shaft position. Changes in bearing vibration, along with bearing metal temperatures, provide an early warning of a reciprocating compressor failure.

CONCLUSION

Technical data and specification sheets for machinery analysis instrumentation and products are available from a variety of manufacturers. Most manufacturers also publish technical articles describing the specific uses of these products. Articles regarding machinery malfunction diagnosis are periodically published in industrial trade journals.

Reliable machinery monitoring and diagnostic systems, provided with the correct measurement input signals, can supply valuable information concerning industrial machinery health. Analysis using state-of-the-art data collection and diagnostic instrumentation must be combined with sound engineering judgment and a thorough understanding of machinery behavior in order to effectively meet *safety, quality, timeliness,* and *cost* demands.

SECTION 17

LUBRICANTS AND LUBRICATION SYSTEMS

CHAPTER 17-1
LUBRICANTS: GENERAL THEORY AND PRACTICE*

GENERAL THEORY

Functions of Lubricants

Lubricants perform a variety of functions. The primary, and most obvious, function is to reduce friction and wear in moving machinery. In addition, lubricants can

- Protect metal surfaces against rust and corrosion
- Control temperature and act as heat-transfer agents
- Flush out dirt and wear-debris contaminants
- Transmit hydraulic power
- Absorb or damp shocks
- Form seals

Because reducing friction is such an important function of lubricants, it is necessary to understand how they perform.

Friction. Friction is the resistance to motion between two bodies in intimate contact. Two types of friction can be identified: solid (or dry) friction and fluid friction.

---

*Updated for this Second Edition by George Arbocus, Elf Lubricants, Linden, N.J.

Solid Friction. Solid friction occurs when there is physical contact between two solid bodies moving relative to each other. The type of motion divides solid friction into two categories, sliding and rolling friction.

SLIDING FRICTION. This is the resistance to movement as one body slides over another. Solid surfaces which appear smooth to the eye will in fact consist of many peaks and valleys. The resistance to motion is due primarily to the interlocking of these asperities. Under conditions of extreme pressure, the heat generated by sliding friction can result in welding of the points of contact.

ROLLING FRICTION. This is the resistance to motion as one solid body rolls over another. It is caused primarily by the deformation of the rolling elements and support surfaces under load. For a given load, rolling friction is significantly less than sliding friction.

Fluid Friction. Fluid friction occurs when two solid bodies in relative motion are completely separated by a fluid. It is caused by the resistance to motion between the molecules in the fluid. For a given load, fluid friction usually is significantly less than sold friction. The film thickness, relative to the height of the surface asperities, distinguishes three types of lubrication:

- Full or thick-film lubrication
- Mixed-film lubrication
- Boundary lubrication

FULL OR THICK-FILM LUBRICATION. This exists when the lubricant film between two surfaces is of sufficient thickness to completely separate the asperities in the two surfaces. In this case, true fluid friction exists between the moving surfaces and no metal-to-metal contact will occur (Fig. 1-1*a*).

MIXED-FILM LUBRICATION. This exists when the lubricant film between the two surfaces is of sufficient thickness to separate most of the surface asperities but some metal-to-metal contact may occur (Fig. 1-1*b*).

BOUNDARY LUBRICATION. This exists when the film thickness is equal to the asperity heights and extensive metal-to-metal contact occurs (Fig. 1-1*c*).

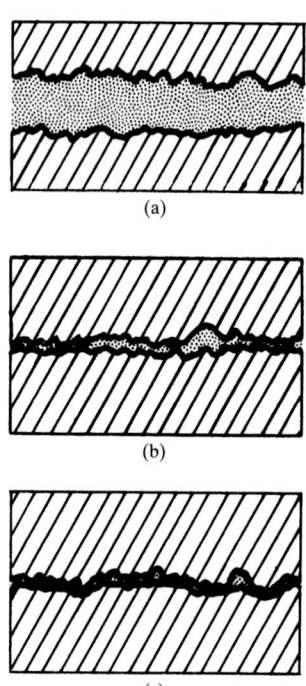

(a)

(b)

(c)

FIGURE 1-1 (*a*) Full-film lubrication. (*b*) Mixed-film lubrication. (*c*) Boundary lubrication.

Formation of the Lubricant Film

The lubricant film may be formed and maintained in one of two ways:

- Hydrostatically
- Hydrodynamically

Hydrostatic Lubrication. Hydrostatic lubrication occurs when the film is formed by pumping the lubricant under pressure between the bearing surfaces. The surfaces may or may not be moving with respect to each other. The hydrostatic pressure acts to completely separate the surfaces, and full-film lubrication is established.

Hydrodynamic Lubrication. Hydrodynamic lubrication depends on motion between the two solid surfaces to generate and maintain the lubricating film. In a plain bearing that is not rotating, the shaft will rest on the bottom of the bearing and will tend to squeeze any lubricant out from between the surfaces. When the shaft begins to rotate, a very thin film of lubricant will tend to adhere to the shaft surface and will be drawn between the shaft and the bearing. A self-acting film that will ultimately separate the load-bearing surfaces is established. A lubricant film generated in this manner is called a hydrodynamic film.

The thickness of the hydrodynamic oil film developed in a properly designed plain bearing is dependent on the oil viscosity, the bearing load, speed, metallurgy, and quality of the bearing surfaces. The dimensionless bearing parameter ZN/P conveniently describes the combined effect of viscosity Z, speed N, and load P.

The thickness of the hydrodynamic film and the amount of friction developed in the bearing can be predicted by means of the bearing parameter ZN/P. Plotting the bearing coefficient of friction vs the bearing parameter for a particular bearing and lubricant gives a characteristic curve similar to the one in Fig. 1-2. Experience has shown that the thickness of the lubricant film developed in a bearing can be determined by estimating where on the curve a bearing is operating (see Fig. 1-2).

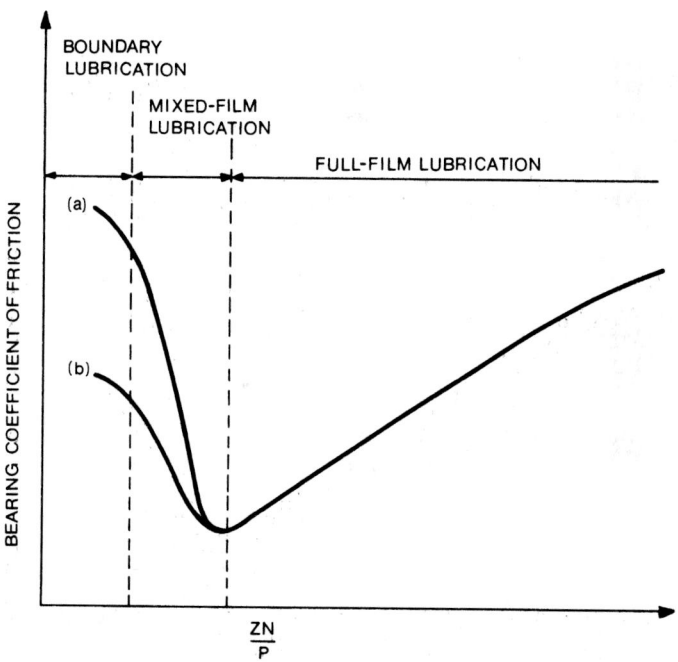

FIGURE 1-2   Typical ZN/P vs coefficient of friction curve.

Changes in the quality of the bearing's metallurgy or surface finish, or the lubricant's "oiliness" or film strength, will cause shifts in coefficient of friction under boundary or mixed-film lubrication conditions. For example, when holding everything else constant, adding an oiliness additive to the lubricant will shift the bearing performance curve from curve a to curve b. As this indicates, it is possible to reduce the amount of friction generated in a particular bearing under boundary or mixed-film lubrication conditions through the use of certain additives.

TYPES OF LUBRICANTS

There are three major categories of lubricants:

- Fluid Lubricants
- Greases (semisolid lubricants)
- Solid Lubricants

Each lubricant has its own physical properties that affect its performance in different applications. A knowledge of the various types of lubricants on the market today and a basic understanding of their advantages and limitations is most helpful in the selection of the best lubricant for a particular application.

Fluid Lubricants

Fluid lubricants are the most widely used. The most common are petroleum oils, synthetic fluids, and animal or vegetable oils. Many other fluids can fulfill a lubrication function under special conditions when the use of oils may be precluded.

Petroleum or Mineral Oils.   Petroleum or mineral oils refined from petroleum crude have good characteristics and are low in cost, giving them wide acceptance as lubricants.

Synthetic Fluids.   Synthetic fluids include all man-made fluids used for lubricating purposes. Included in this category are synthesized hydrocarbons, esters, silicones, polyglycols, and phosphate esters. These are discussed in more detail in Chap. 17-2.

Animal and Vegetable Oils.   Animal and vegetable oils, as the terms indicate, are oils made from either animal fat or vegetables. They are used primarily where food contact is likely to occur and the lubricant must be edible. Their main disadvantage is that most of them tend to deteriorate rapidly in the presence of heat.

In the past, oils made from animal fats, such as sperm whale oil and lard oil, were frequently used for their "oiliness" properties. Today, however, these are frequently being replaced with synthesized fatty oils which perform the same function.

Greases

Greases are fluid lubricants with dispersed thickeners to give them a solid or semisolid consistency. The fluid content of a grease performs the actual lubricating function. The thickener acts to hold the lubricant in place, to prevent leakage, and to block the entrance of contaminants.

Many types of thickeners are used in the manufacture of modern greases. Each type imparts certain properties to the finished product. Table 1-1 describes some of the typical properties and applications of greases manufactured with certain common thickeners.

Solid Thickeners

Solid lubricants, such as graphite, molybdenum disulfide (moly) and PTFE (polytetrafluoroethylene), are not only used by themselves but are also frequently added to oils and greases to improve their performance under boundary lubrication conditions. Chapter 17-3 discusses these in more detail.

TABLE 1-1 Grease Application Guide

Thickeners Properties	Lithium	Lithium complex	Calcium	Calcium complex	Aluminum complex	Sodium	Polyurea	Clay
Dropping point, °F	350–375	500+	200–225	500+	500+	325–350	550	None
Average max usable temp, °F	275	300	175	325	300	250	350	275
High temperature characteristics	Good	Good	Poor	Good	Good	Fair-good	Excellent	Good
Thermal stability	Good	Good	Poor	Good	Good	Fair-good	Excellent	Good
Low temperature characteristics	Good	Good	Fair	Fair-good	Fair-good	Fair	Good	Good
Pumpability	Excellent	Excellent	Fair-good	Fair	Fair-good	Poor	Good-excellent	Good
Mechanical stability	Excellent	Excellent	Good	Fair-good	Excellent	Poor	Excellent	Good
Oil separation	Good	Excellent	Poor	Excellent	Good	Fair-good	Excellent	Excellent
Water resistance	Good	Excellent	Excellent	Good	Excellent	Poor	Excellent	Good
Texture	Smooth & buttery	Smooth & buttery	Smooth & buttery	Smooth & buttery	Smooth & buttery	Buttery to fibrous	Smooth & buttery	Smooth & buttery
Rust protection	Fair to good	Good	Poor	Excellent	Good	Excellent	Excellent	Poor
Oxidation stability	Fair to good	Good	Poor	Good	Good	Poor	Excellent	Good
Other properties				Good inherent EP properties		Good adhesive and cohesive properties		
Applications	Multipurpose All applications except extra high temperatures	Multipurpose Many uses	Where water is dominant factor Wet, moderately low temperature conditions Plain and roller bearings, water pumps, slides	High temperatures Corrosive conditions Do not use in centralized lubrication systems	Multipurpose Moderately high temperatures	Antifriction and plain bearings Electric motors, fans Must be used in dry conditions	Multipurpose High temperatures Antifriction and plain bearings Electric motors, fans, Wet conditions Corrosive conditions	Multipurpose High temperatures

IMPORTANT LUBRICANT CHARACTERISTICS

Various physical and chemical properties of lubricants are measured and used to determine a lubricant's suitability for different applications.

Oil Properties

Viscosity.   Of the various lubricant properties and specifications, viscosity (also referred to as the "body" or "weight") normally is considered the most important. It is a measure of the force required to overcome fluid friction and allow an oil to flow.

Industry uses several different systems to express the viscosity of an oil. Figure 1-3 gives a comparison of some of the most common. Lubricant specifications usually express viscosity in Saybolt Universal (SUS or SSU) at 100 and 210°F (37.8 and 98.9°C) and/or in centistokes (cSt) at 40 and 100°C (104 and 212°F). Viscosity expressed in centistokes is called the kinematic viscosity.

With the general move toward metrication and the establishment of the International Organization for Standardization (ISO) viscosity grade identification system, the centistoke has become the preferred unit of measure. The ISO viscosity grade system contains 18 grades covering a viscosity range from 2 to 1500 cSt at 40°C. Each grade is approximately 50 percent more viscous than the previous.

Laboratories determine oil viscosity experimentally using a viscometer (Fig. 1-4). The viscometer measures an oil's kinematic viscosity by the time (in seconds) it takes a specified volume of lubricant to pass through a capillary of a specified size, at a specified temperature. The kinematic viscosity is then derived by calculations based on constants for the viscometer and the time it took the sample to pass through the instrument.

Viscosity Index.   The viscosity index (VI) is an empirical measure of an oil's change in viscosity with temperature. The greater the value of the viscosity index, the less the oil viscosity will change with temperature. Originally ranging from 0 to 100, viscosity indexes greater than 100 are now achieved with certain synthetic oils or through the use of additives. The higher the number, the smaller the relative change in viscosity with temperature.

Oxidation Stability.   Oxidation stability defines a lubricant's ability to resist breakdown at elevated temperatures. Products of oxidation include carbonaceous deposits, sludge, varnish, resins, and corrosive and noncorrosive acids. Oxidation usually brings with it an increase in the viscosity and acidity of the lubricant.

The rate of oxidation is dependent on the chemical composition of the oil, the ambient temperature, the amount of surface area exposed to air, the length of time the lubricant has been in service, and the presence of contaminants which can act as catalysts to the oxidation reaction.

Depending on the intended end use of the oil, oxidation stability will be measured or expressed in different ways. All of the oxidation stability tests are based on placing a sample of oil under conditions that will greatly increase the rate of oxidation. Buildups of reaction products are then measured. The American Society for Testing and Materials (ASTM) D-943 test is the most widely used. Conducted under prescribed conditions, it measures the time (in hours) for the acidity of a sample of oil to increase a specified amount. The more stable the oil, the longer it will take for the change in acidity to occur.

Used-oil analysis to determine if the oil is suitable for further service is based on a comparison between the used oil and the new oil. Increases in viscosity, acidity, and development of insoluble contaminants are usually indicators that oxidation has occurred.

Thermal Stability.   Thermal stability is a measure of an oil's ability to resist chemical change due to temperature. Since oxygen is present in most lubricant applications, the term *thermal stability* is frequently used in reference to the oxidation resistance of an oil.

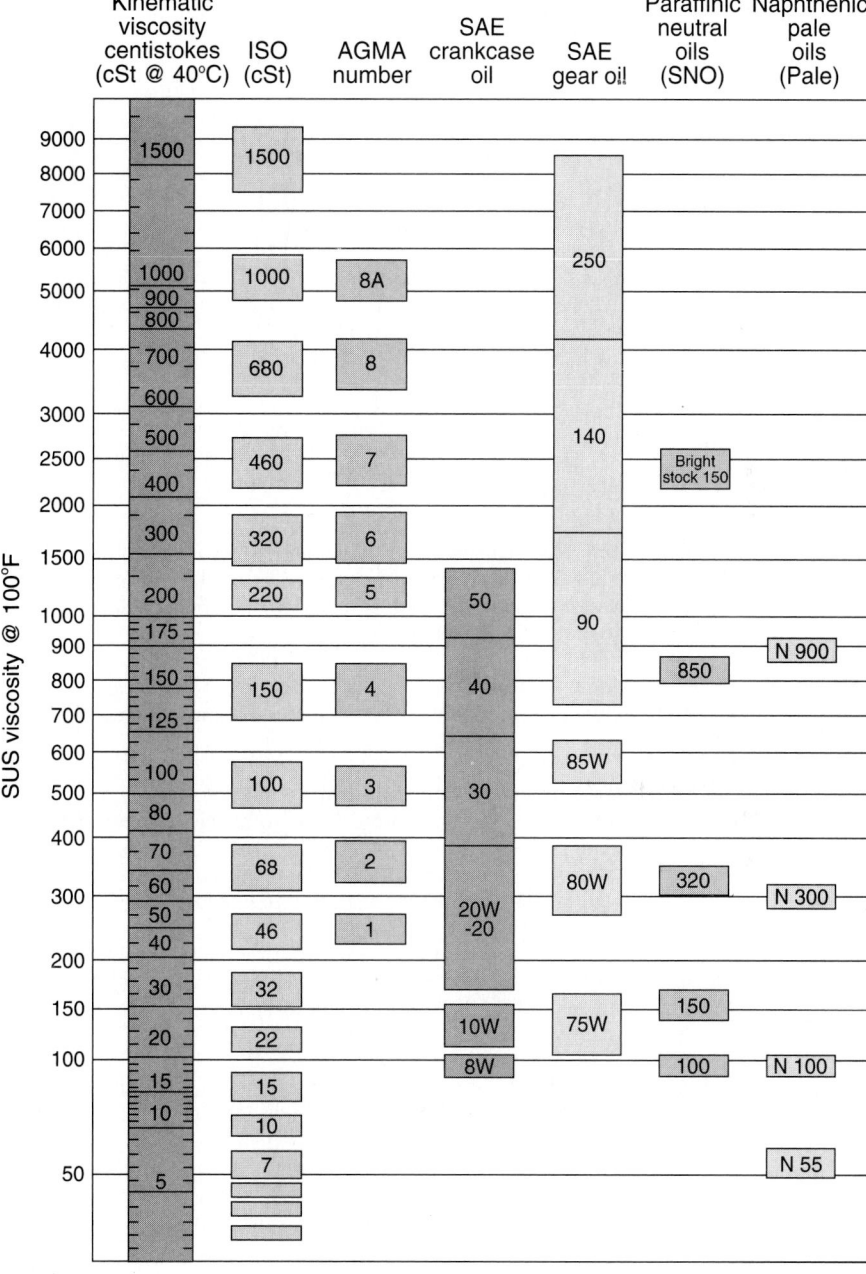

FIGURE 1-3   Base oil and finished product viscosity grade comparisons. (*Texaco Lubricants Company.*)

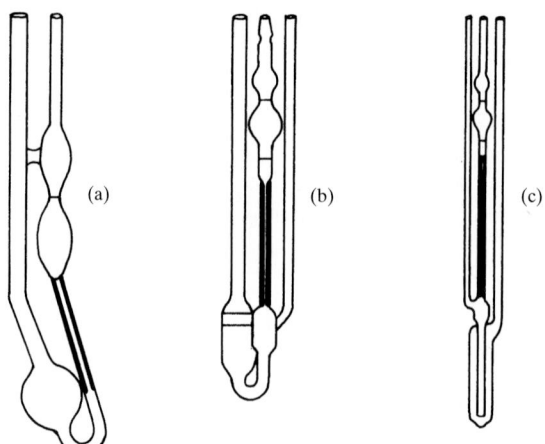

FIGURE 1-4   Capillary tube viscosimeters used to measure kinematic viscosity: (*a*) modified Ostwald, (*b*) Ubbelohde, (*c*) Fitz Simmons. (*Gulf Oil Corporation.*)

Chemical Stability.   Chemical stability defines an oil's ability to resist chemical change. Usually it, too, is used to refer to the oxidation stability of an oil. Chemical stability, other than resistance to oxidation, sometimes can refer to an oil's inertness in the presence of various metal and outside contaminants.

Carbon Residue.   The carbon-forming tendencies of an oil can be determined with a test in which the weight percent of the carbon residue of a sample is measured after evaporation and pyrolysis.

Neutralization Number.   The neutralization number (neut. no.) is a measure of the acidity or alkalinity of an oil. Usually reported as the total acid number (TAN) or total base number (TBN) it is expressed as the equivalent milligrams of potassium hydroxide required to neutralize the acidic or basic content of a 1-g sample of oil. Increases in the TAN or decreases in the TBN are usually indicators that oxidation has occurred.

Lubricity.   Lubricity is the term used to describe an oil's "oiliness" or "slipperiness." If two oils of the same viscosity are used in the same applications and one causes greater reduction in friction and wear than the other, it is said to have better lubricity than the first. This is strictly a descriptive term.

Saponification Number.   The saponification number (SAP no.) is an indicator of the amount of fatty material present in an oil. The SAP no. will vary from 0, for an oil containing no fatty material, to 200, for 100 percent fatty material.

Demulsibility.   Demulsibility is the term used to describe an oil's ability to shed water. The better the oil's demulsibility, the more rapidly the oil will separate from water after the two have been mixed together.

API Gravity.   API gravity is a relative measure of the unit weight of a petroleum product. It is related to the specific gravity in the following manner:

$$\text{API gravity @ 60°F} = \frac{141.5}{\text{specific gravity @ 60°F}} - 131.5$$

Pour Point.   Pour point is the lowest temperature at which an oil will flow in a certain test procedure. It is usually not advisable to use an oil at temperatures lower than 15°F (8°C) above its pour point.

Flash Point.   Flash point is the oil temperature at which vapors from the oil ignite when an open flame is passed over a test sample.

Fire Point.   Fire Point is the oil temperature at which vapors from the oil will ignite without benefit of an outside flame.

Grease Properties

Penetration.   Penetration is an indicator of a grease's relative hardness or softness and not a criterion of quality. Measured on a penetrometer at 77°F (25°C), it is the depth of penetration (in tenths of millimeters) into the grease of a standard 150-g cone. The softer the grease, the greater the penetration number will be.

If the penetration test is performed on an "undisturbed" sample, the results are reported as unworked penetration. If the sample has been subjected to extrusion by a reciprocating perforated piston for a number of strokes (most commonly 60 strokes) prior to the penetration test, the results are reported as worked penetration. It is desirable to have as little difference between the worked and the unworked penetration as possible.

NLGI Consistency Numbers.   The National Lubricating Grease Institute (NLGI) has developed a number system ranging from 000 (triple zero) to 6 to identify various grease consistencies. This system is used by most of industry. Table 1-2 gives the NLGI numbers, their corresponding worked penetration ranges, and their descriptions (their corresponding consistencies). Most multipurpose greases are of either a no. 1 or 2 consistency.

TABLE 1-2   NLGI Classification of Greases

NLGI consistency grade	Worked penetration ASTM D-217-60T	Description
000	445–475	Very fluid
00	400–430	Fluid
0	355–385	Semifluid
1	310–340	Very soft
2	265–295	Soft
3	220–250	Semistiff
4	175–205	Stiff
5	130–160	Very stiff
6	85–115	Hard

Dropping Point.   Dropping point is the temperature at which a grease liquifies and will flow. Generally it is not advisable to use a grease at temperatures higher than 50°F (28°C) below its dropping point.

Soap.   The thickener used to manufacture greases can be called "soap." Many greases use metallic soaps as thickeners. Table 1-1 shows a comparison of some of the key properties of greases manufactured with different soaps and their typical applications.

ADDITIVES USED IN LUBRICATING OILS

It is possible, through the use of chemical additives, to improve a lubricant's natural ability to protect metal surfaces, resist chemical changes, and drop out contaminants.

Since industrial lubricating oils are frequently described by the additives they contain, it is helpful to understand the functions of the major types of additives. Following are general definitions of some of the most common, listed in alphabetical order:

Antifoam agents. Promote the rapid breakup of foam bubbles and release of entrapped air.

Antiseptic agents or bactericides. Prevent the growth of microorganisms and bacteria. These are found primarily in water-soluble coolants.

Antiwear agents. Decrease the coefficient of friction and reduce wear under boundary or mixed-film lubrication conditions.

Demulsifiers. Assist the natural ability of an oil to separate rapidly from water. These agents can be helpful in preventing rust since they help to keep water out of the oil and thus away from the metal surfaces.

Detergent-dispersant agents. Reduce the formation of varnish and sludge and act as cleaning agents. They are most commonly found in engine oils.

Emulsifiers. Permit the mixing of oil and water to form stable emulsions. They are used primarily in the manufacture of water-soluble oils.

Extreme-pressure agents. Protect against metal-to-metal contact and welding after the oil film has been ruptured by high or sliding velocities. The majority of the extreme-pressure oils on the market today are of the sulfur-phosphorus type and are noncorrosive to most metals including brass. This was not true of some of the earlier formulations, and many misconceptions still exist in this regard.

"Oiliness" or fatty compounds. Improve the lubricity or slipperiness of an oil. Friction is reduced by formation of an adsorbed film.

Oxidation inhibitors. Prevent or retard the oxidation of a lubricant thereby reducing the formation of deposits and acids.

Pour-point depressants. Lower the pour point of paraffinic or mixed base petroleum oils.

Rust and corrosion inhibitors. Improve an oil's ability to protect metal surfaces from rust and corrosion.

Tackiness agents. Improve the adhesive qualities of an oil.

Viscosity index improves. Increase the viscosity index of an oil by increasing an oil's viscosity at high temperatures. These additives are most widely used in motor oils to create multigrade oils.

LUBRICANT SELECTION

Proper lubricant selection depends upon the system needs and cost considerations. The final choice depends on the equipment design, operating conditions, method of application as well as health, safety, and environmental considerations. Whenever possible, these recommendations should be followed. In addition, most reputable oil suppliers keep in close contact with major equipment builders and are available to consult with users on lubricant selection. In addition, many PC software programs have recently become available that guide the user in making intelligent selections for specific equipment.

The recommendations included in this chapter are based on standard practices and are intended solely as guidelines.

General Selection Guidelines

The design of the equipment and the expected operating conditions will determine which functions the lubricant is expected to perform and will dictate the type of lubricant and additives that will be best suited.

The oil of proper viscosity for an application is a function of speed, load, and ambient temperature. Conditions of high loads and slow speeds will require a high-viscosity oil. Similarly, a low viscosity oil is best suited to conditions of low loads and high speeds. Ideally, one would like to select the oil of lowest possible viscosity that is capable of maintaining a lubricant film between the moving surfaces. Selection of a higher-viscosity oil than is needed can result in power losses and temperature buildups due to the higher internal fluid friction of the lubricant.

The effect of operating temperatures on the selection of the lubricant should not be overlooked. Since oil viscosity decreases as temperatures increase, it is necessary to select high-viscosity fluids for high temperature applications and lower-viscosity fluids for low temperature applications in order to ensure adequate lubricant film thickness and minimal fluid friction. Fluids with high-viscosity indexes (high VI) should be used for applications where wide temperature ranges are anticipated.

Operating Limits of Petroleum Oils

As a result of additive technology, a suitable petroleum-based lubricating oil can be found for most applications. Exceptions can exist where fire-resistant fluids are required or extreme temperature conditions exist. There are a variety of fire resistant fluids available which may replace petroleum oils in hazardous situations. These include:

- Water/glycol base
- Oil in water emulsions
- High water base (95/5)
- Phosphate esters
- Polyol esters

The water-containing fluids are suitable where operating temperatures do not exceed 140°F. It is important that the hydraulic system or other application be suitable for the prospective fluid. System components like seals, paints, plastics, pump pressures, etc., must be compatible and acceptable to the candidate fluid. It is recommended that the manufacturer of the equipment be consulted before final selection is made.

Synthetic lubricants should be considered under three types of extreme temperature conditions:

- Excessively high temperatures
- Excessively low temperatures
- Wide temperature variations

Petroleum oils will adequately withstand very high temperatures for only very short periods of time. Problems will occur when the oil is subjected to high temperatures for extended periods of time. The rate of oxidation of petroleum oils subjected to constant temperatures above 115°F (45°C) will approximately double for every 15 to 20°F (8 to 10°C) rise in temperature. Temperatures above 200°F (95°C) will almost always result in excessive sludge and deposit formation and should be avoided. In circulating systems, the reservoir should always be cool enough to comfortably hold a hand on it. The oxidation rate is usually negligible at temperatures below 115°F (45°C).

Petroleum oils should not be used at temperatures less than 10 to 15°F (5 to 8°C) above their pour point. For applications subjected to large temperature variations only high-viscosity index fluids should be used. The viscosity index should be high enough to ensure that the oil viscosity remains within the recommended limits at both the high and low temperature extremes to which the equipment is subjected.

Plain-Bearing Lubrication

Plain bearings, also called journal or sleeve bearings, comprise one of the simplest machine components. The type of motion between the bearing and the shaft is pure sliding.

In plain bearings, the lubricant must reduce sliding friction, carry away any heat generated in the bearing, prevent rust and corrosion, and serve as a seal to prevent the entry of foreign material.

Barring any unusual operating conditions, plain bearings will operate satisfactorily with a good rust- and oxidation-inhibited lubricant of the correct viscosity. Special operating conditions may require the use of oils containing other additives. Antiwear and extreme pressure oils may be desirable for plain bearings operating intermittently or under very high loads.

Most plain bearings are designed to operate under full-film hydrodynamic lubrication. Referring to Fig. 1-2, and assuming the bearing load and oil viscosity to be constant, the lubricant film development would be expected to follow the ZN/P curve as the shaft speed increases. If oil of the proper viscosity is selected for the load and speed conditions, full-film hydrodynamic lubrication will prevail during continuous operation.

Numerous mathematical models of plain-bearing lubrication have been used in attempts to select best oil viscosity. In the past these models were complicated and expensive to use. Today, however, several PC software programs exist that can do these calculations rapidly and accurately. Table 1-3 offers a general guide for viscosity selection for plain bearings subjected to average loading.

TABLE 1-3   Oil Viscosity Selection for Plain Bearings

ft/min	m/min	cSt	SUS
Below 100	30	150–325	600–1500
100–500	30–150	46–150	300–600
500–1000	150–300	22–68	150–300
1000–2500	300–800	15–32	75–150
over 2500	800	5–15	40–75

Speed factor = FPM
FPM = RPM × shaft diam (ft) × 3.14

Plain bearings may be grease lubricated if contact surface operating speed does not exceed approximately 30 ft/min (9m/min). At higher speeds, excessive temperature buildup and grease breakdown will occur.

In general, relatively soft greases are used for centralized systems and harder greases for compression cups and open journals. Each application should be considered on its own merits, taking into consideration the operating conditions. Temperature and water contamination require particular attention.

Plain bearings are frequently grooved (Fig. 1-5) to improve the distribution and flow of the lubricant. Normally, two important rules should be followed when grooving a plain bearing:

• Grooves should not extend into the load-carrying area of the bearing because this would increase unit pressure.

• Groove edges should be rounded to prevent scraping the lubricant off the journal.

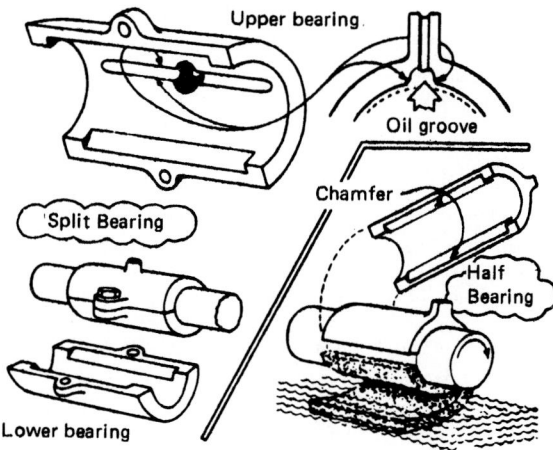

FIGURE 1-5   Oil groove. (*Association of Iron and Steel Engineers; reprinted with permission from* The Lubrication Engineers Manual, *copyright 1971.*)

Antifriction-Bearing Lubrication

Antifriction or rolling element bearings use balls or rollers to substitute rolling friction for sliding friction. This type of bearing has closer tolerances than do plain bearings and is used where precision, high speeds, and heavy loads are encountered.

In antifriction bearings a lubricant facilitates easy rolling, reduces the friction generated between the rolling elements and the cages or retainers, prevents rust and corrosion, and serves as a seal to prevent the entry of foreign material.

High-quality rust- and oxidation-inhibited (R & O) oils are generally recommended, especially where high-temperature conditions may oxidize the oil and so lead to the formation of deposits which could interfere with the free action of the rolling elements. Extreme pressure and antiwear additives may also be desirable under conditions of heavy or high shock loads.

Because of its better cooling ability, oil is generally preferred to grease if the bearing is enclosed in an oil-sealed housing. Table 1-4 gives general guidelines to the proper viscosity selection of oils for antifriction bearings.

Most antifriction bearings are grease lubricated because of simple seal and housing designs, protection from dirt and water, and requires infrequent attention.

The selection of the proper type and grade of grease depends on the operating conditions and the method of application. Generally, soft greases (i.e., NLGI no. 1 consistency) with low base oil viscosity are preferred for use at low temperatures and in central systems. Harder greases (i.e., NLGI no. 2 consistency) with low base oil viscosity perform better at high speeds.

Care should be taken not to over-grease antifriction bearings because this can lead to excessive temperature buildup. Generally the bearing housing should be one-third to one-half filled.

Many PC software programs exist today that can aid in the selection of lubricants in the initial design and failure analysis.

Gear Lubrication

The motion between gear teeth as they go through mesh is a combination of sliding and rolling. The type of gear, the operating load, speed, temperatures, method of application of the lubricant, and metallurgy of the gears are all important considerations in the selection of a lubricant.

TABLE 1-4   Oil Viscosity Selection for Antifriction Bearings

Speed factor bearing bore, mm × r/min	Operating temperatures		Viscosity	
	°F	°C	ISO viscosity grade	SUS at 100°F
Up to 75,000	−40–32	−40–0	15–32	70–150
	32–150	0–65	32–100	150–800
	150–200	65–93	100–220	800–1200
	200–250	93–21	220–680	1100–3000
75,000–200,000	−40–32	−40–0	7–22	50–100
	32–150	0–65	22–68	100–300
	150–200	65–93	68–100	300–800
	200–250	95–121	150–320	700–2100
200,000–400,000	−40–32	−40–0	7–15	50–70
	32–150	0–65	15–46	70–200
	150–200	65–93	32–68	150–300
	200–250	93–121	68–150	400–900
Above 400,000	−40–32	−40–0	5–10	40–80
	32–150	0–65	10–32	80–150
	150–200	65–93	22–46	100–200
	200–250	93–121	68–100	300–800

Industrial gearing may either be enclosed, in which case the gears and the bearings which support them are operated off the same lubricant system; or open, in which case the bearings are lubricated separately from the gears themselves.

Due to the high sliding forces encountered in enclosed worm and hypoid gears, lubricant selection for these should be considered separately from lubrication of other types of enclosed gears.

As with all equipment, the first rule in selecting a gear lubricant is to follow the manufacturer's recommendation, if at all possible. In general, one of the following types of oils is used:

Rust- and Oxidation-Inhibited Oil.   R & O oils are good quality petroleum-base oils containing rust and oxidation inhibitors. These oils provide satisfactory protection for most lightly to moderately loaded enclosed gears.

Extreme-Pressure Oils.   EP oils are usually high-quality petroleum-based oils containing extreme-pressure additives. These products are especially helpful when high-load conditions exist and are a must in the lubrication of enclosed hypoid gears.

Compounded Oils.   These are usually petroleum-based oils containing 3 to 5 percent fatty or synthetic fatty oils (usually animal fat or acidless tallow). They are usually used for worm-gear lubrication where the fatty content helps reduce the friction generated under high-sliding conditions.

Heavy Open-Gear Compounds.   These are very-heavy-bodied tarlike substances designed to stick to the metal surfaces. Some are so thick they must be heated or diluted with a solvent to soften them for application. These products are used in cases where the lubricant application is intermittent.

A large number of gear lubrication models and viscosity selection guides exist. In the United States, the most widely used selection method employs the American Gear Manufacturers Association (AGMA) standards. Under its specifications for enclosed industrial gear drives the AGMA has defined lubricant numbers which designate viscosity grades for gear oils. Table 1-3 identifies the AGMA viscosity numbers with their corresponding ISO viscosity grades.

As a rule, low speeds and high pressures require high-viscosity oils. Intermediate speeds and pressures require medium-viscosity oils, and high speeds and low pressures require low-viscosity oils. Table 1-5 gives some very broad guidelines for viscosity and type of lubricant for industrial gearing.

TABLE 1-5   Oil Selection for Enclosed Gear Drives

Service	ISO viscosity grade	Oil type
Helical, herringbone, straight-bevel, spiral-bevel, and spur-gear drives		
Operating at normal speeds and loads	220	EP or R & O
Operating at normal speeds and high loads	220	EP
Operating at high speeds (above 3800 r/min)	68	EP or R & O
Warm-gear drives	480	Compounded or EP
Hypoid-gear drives		
Normal speeds (1200–2000 r/min)	220	EP
High speeds (above 2000 r/min)	180	EP
Low speeds (below 1200 r/min)	480	EP

Open gears operate under conditions of boundary lubrication. The lubricant can be applied by hand or via drip-feed cups, mechanical force-feed lubricators, or sprays.

Heavy-bodied oils with good adhesive and film-strength properties are required because centrifugal forces tend to throw the lubricant off the gear teeth.

Several PC software programs exist to aid in lubricant selection to reduce wear, scuffing, and pitting of gear teeth surfaces.

Compressor Lubrication

The compressor model and type, the loading, the gas being compressed, and other environmental conditions dictate the type and viscosity of the oil to be used. Most compressors are lubricated with petroleum oils; however, there has been considerable interest in synthetic lubricants for compressor lubrication in recent years.

Compressing gases other than air creates problems which require special lubrication consideration because of possible chemical reactions between the gas being compressed and the lubricant. Since no two cases are alike, it is recommended that the compressor manufacturer and lubricant supplier be consulted for recommendations for a particular operation.

Oils for use in compressors should have the following characteristics:

Good Stability.   A good compressor oil must have high oxidation stability to minimize the formation of gum and carbon deposits. Such deposits can cause valve sticking. This can lead to very-high-temperature conditions, compressor malfunction, and fire or explosion.

Good Demulsibility.   A good compressor oil must be able to shed water readily to prevent formation of emulsions which could interfere with proper lubrication.

Anticorrosion and Antirust Properties.   A compressor lubricant must protect the valves, pistons, rings, and bearings against rust and corrosion. This is especially important in a humid atmosphere or in compressors that operate intermittently.

Good Antiwear Properties.   Good compressor oils must form and maintain a strong lubricant film at relatively high temperatures; therefore, good antiwear properties are required.

Nonfoaming Properties.   This requirement is especially important in crankcases where air-oil mixtures could impair good lubrication.

Low Pour Point.   This property is necessary for low-temperature start-up. Usually it is a factor only in portable air compressors that will frequently be used outdoors.

Proper Viscosity.   The operator's manual should be consulted for the manufacturer's viscosity recommendations for the prevailing operating temperatures and conditions.

SPECIFICATIONS AND STANDARDS

"Lubrication of Industrial Enclosed Gear Drives," AGMA Standard 250.04, American Gear Manufacturers Association, Arlington, VA, September, 1981.

"Lubrication of Industrial Open Gearing," AGMA Standard 251.02, American Gear Manufacturers Association, Arlington, VA, September 1981.

Annual Book of ASTM Standards, Vols. 05.1, 05.02, and 05.03, American Society for Testing and Materials, Philadelphia, 1992.

Factory Mutual System—(1992 Approval Guide), Factory Mutual Engineering & Research.

Compressed Air and Gas Institute, Cleveland, Ohio.

BIBLIOGRAPHY

Actis Institute: Computer Software Programs, ASME, 1993.

Billett, Michael: *Industrial Lubrication: A Practical Handbook for Lubrication and Production Engineers,* Pergamon, Oxford, England, 1979.

Blau, P.J. (ed.): *ASM Handbook Vol. 18: Friction, Lubrication and Wear Technology,* ASM International, 1992.

Booser, E.R. (ed.): *CRC Handbook of Lubrication: Applications and Maintenance,* Vol. 1., CRC Press, 1983.

Booser, E.R. (ed.): *CRC Handbook of Lubrication: Theory and Design,* Vol. 2., CRC Press, 1983.

Brewer, Allen F.: *Effective Lubrication,* Robert E. Krieger, Huntington, NY, 1974.

Ellis, E.G.: *Fundamentals of Lubrication,* 2d ed., Scientific Publications, Broseley, England, 1970.

Fuller, Dudley D.: *Theory and Practice of Lubrication for Engineers,* 2d ed., Wiley, New York, 1984.

Neale, M.J. (ed.): *Tribology Handbook,* Wiley, New York, 1973.

O'Connor, J.J., and J. Boyd (eds.): *Standard Handbook of Lubrication Engineers,* McGraw-Hill, New York, 1968.

Shigley, Joseph E.: *Mechanical Engineering Design,* 2d ed., McGraw-Hill, New York, 1972.

Szeri, A.Z. (ed.) *Tribology: Friction, Lubrication, and Wear,* McGraw-Hill, 1980.

Winer, W., and Peterson, M. (ed): *Wear Control Handbook,* Research Committee on Tribology, ASME, 1980.

CHAPTER 17-2
SYNTHETIC LUBRICANTS

John H. Marino
President
Mining and Industrial Lubricants Consultants, Inc.
Overland Park, Kansas

DEFINITION AND CLASSIFICATION

Synthetic lubricants, or synlubes, are made by blending chemically synthesized base fluids with the proper lubricant additives. For some applications the synthesized base fluids are used neat, without additives. Synthesized base fluids are formed by combining low-molecular-weight components via chemical reactions into higher molecular weight compounds. Thus each base fluid's molecular structure is planned and controlled and its properties are predictable. Synthetic base fluids do not occur in nature, as does the crude petroleum oil from which conventional mineral-oil-base stocks are derived by refining processes. Only by *super-refining,* could petroleum-base stocks be obtained with properties comparable to those of synthesized base fluids. Yet most synthetic base fluids come from petroleum via synthesis using components derived from petroleum hydrocarbons.

Principal reasons for the increasing uses of synlubes are their abilities to:

- Lubricate where conventional lubricants will not
- Comply with certain specifications or regulations such as military, OSHA, safety, pollution
- Provide enhanced cost effectiveness, including energy savings

The *distinguishing feature* of all synthetics is superiority in one or more respects to the mineral oils. Advantageous characteristics of the most widely used synlubes, in varying degrees, are:

- Low-temperature fluidity
- High-temperature oxidation stability and fire resistance (high flash, fire, and autoignition points)
- Low volatility in relation to viscosity
- High viscosity index (less change of viscosity with temperature)

Some synthetics are chemically inert; some are fire-resistant or nonflammable.

Thus synlubes are high-performance, problem-solving lubricants that provide operating benefits such as: (1) less frequent lubrication ("sealed for life" in some machines); (2) less maintenance; (3) higher productivity; (4) lower parts rejection (due to more uniform tolerances and quality); (5) longer machine life; (6) reduced fire hazard; (7) greater resistance to acids, bases, and solvents; (8) more economical metalworking-oil or coolant applications; and (9) easier reclamation or disposal.

Although synthetic base fluids make possible these benefits, *proper compounding* of base fluids with performance additives is essential to achieving finished synlubes with the desired advantages. Getting one's money's worth from a more-expensive, high-quality synlube is best assured by buying specification-grade, approved synlubes from reputable suppliers *who know how to maximize the advantages of each base fluid's properties,* which include (1) *rheology,* or flow characteristics; (2) *volatility;* (3) *stability:* thermal, oxidative, hydrolytic, chemical; (4) *additives' compatibility* and *response;* and (5) *effects on elastomers, paint, and other softwear.*

The *classification* of synthetic base fluids was proposed by an ad hoc ASTM committee and subsequently adopted by SAE in Standard J 357a and by RCCC, as follows:

1. *Synthetic Hydrocarbons*

   Alkylated aromatics (dialkylbenzenes, DAB) and cycloaliphatics
   Polyalphaolefins (PAO)
   Polybatenes

2. *Organic Esters*

   Dibasic acid esters (diesters)
   Polyol esters
   Polyesters

3. *Other*

   Halogenated hydrocarbons
   Phosphate esters
   Polyglycols (polalkylene glycols, PAG)
   Polyphenyl ethers
   Silicate esters
   Silicones

4. *Blends* Synthetic base stock may be mixtures of the above which are compatible.

By specific omission from this classification, other compounds and mixtures such as the following are *not classified* as synthetic lubricants: (1) molybdenum disulfide (MoS_2), graphite, and other solids; (2) plastics (PE, PTFE, nylon, et al.); (3) inert and liquefied gases; (4) liquid metals (as Na, K); (5) exotic natural products (as jojoba oil); and (6) surfactant-chemical-concentrate, high-water-content, or "water-additive" coolants and other metalworking fluids (which are nevertheless called "synthetic" by some people in the metalworking industry).

Unless a lubricant consists of at least 90 percent synthetic base fluid, it should not be designated a synlube; rather it should be labeled "partial synthetic," "fortified synthetic," "semisynthetic," or some similar term.

PROPERTIES AND USES OF SYNTHETIC LUBRICANTS

The most widely used industrial synlube classes are: (1) polyalphaolefins, (2) organic esters, (3) phosphate esters, (4) polyalkylene glycols, and (5) silicones. Their operating-temperature ranges are shown in Fig. 2-1, their performance vs mineral oil, in Table 2-1. Most are supplied in several viscosity grades and can be formulated with proper additives to make industrial lubricants—circulating oils, gear and bearing lubes, and greases and other functional fluids for use with gears, traction drives, compressors, pumps, turbines, calenders, motors, hydraulic systems, valves, instrumentation, and other machinery and equipment, including metalworking applications (see Table 2-2). Many companies compound such lubricants from their own or from purchased synthetic base fluids and additives. Viscosity grades range from 1.5 cSt at 212°F (100°C) to firm greases.

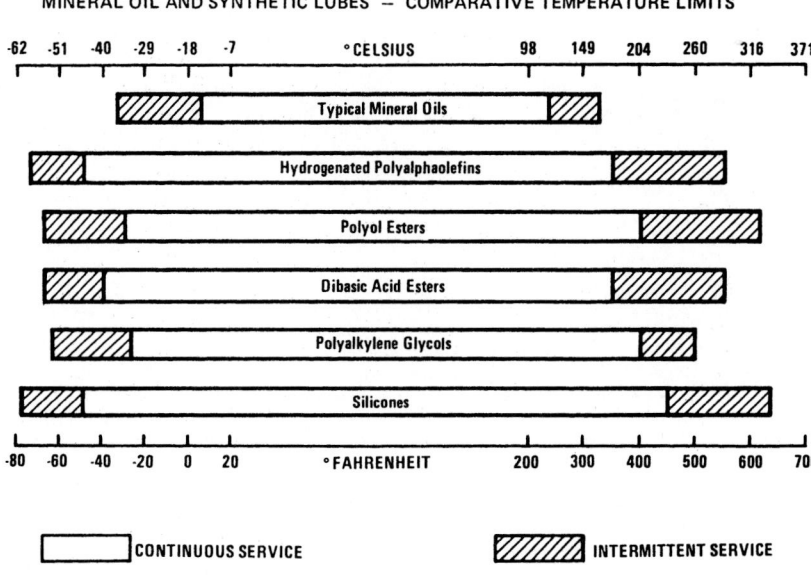

FIGURE 2-1 Mineral oil and synlubes—comparative temperature limits.

Polyalphaolefins

Polyalphaolefins (PAO), or olefin alpha oligomers, are derived from linear alphaolefins which are made from ethylene, a basic building block from petroleum or natural gas liquids. Manufacturers are Bray, Ethyl/Cooper, Gulf, Lubrizol, Mobil, Emery, and Uniroyal. Shell, Conoco, Texaco, Arco, and others are potential manufacturers.

The largest volume use for PAO is in crankcase oils for internal combustion engines—gasoline, diesel, and natural gas. Principal industrial PAO lubricants are for gears, calenders, textile machinery, conveyors, gas turbines, hydraulic systems, instrumentation, rotary-screw and reciprocating compressors, pumps, equipment, and many grease applications—particularly in harsh environments (chlorine, HCl, and hot process gases). PAO products serve well as lubricants and sealant fluids for rotary mechanical seals of chemical process pumps and agitated kettles. The longer functional life of a PAO grease in a high-speed ball-bearing test is shown in Fig. 2-2. Food-grade synlubes, compounded from FDA-approved PAO white oils, also are available.

Because PAO lubes are compatible with mineral oils and with existing systems designed for mineral oil products, they can be used in such systems without changing seals, hoses, or materials of pumps and other equipment. PAOs are often incorporated into organic ester lubes to assure seal compatibility.

TABLE 2-1 Relative Performance of Synlubes vs. Mineral Oil*

| | | Synthetics | | | | | | |
| | | Synthesized hydrocarbons | | Organic esters | | | | |
Properties	Mineral oil	Polyalpha-olefin (PAO)	Dialkylated (C$_{12}$) benzene (DAB)	Dibasic	Hindered polyol	Polyalkylene glycol (PAG)	Phosphate ester	Silicone fluid
Viscosity-temperature properties (VI)	F	G	F	VG	G	G	P	E
Low-temperature fluidity, low pour point	P	G	G	G	G	G	F	G
High-temperature oxidation resistance with inhibitors	F	VG	G	G	E	F	F	G
Compatibility with mineral oils	E	E	E	G	F	P	F	P
Low volatility	F	E	G	E	E	G	G	G
Effect on most paints and finishes	N	N	N	S	M	M	C	S
Stability in presence of water (hydrolytic stability	E	E	E	F	F	VG	F	G
Antirust properties, with inhibitor	E	E	E	F	F	G	F	G
Additive solubility	E	G	E	G	G	F	G	P
Elastomer swelling tendency—buna rubber	L	N	L	M	H	L	H	L

* Letter signifies performance level: P = poor, F = fair, G = good, VG = very good, E = excellent, M = moderate, H = high, C = considerable, N = none or nil, S = slight, L = light.

TABLE 2-2 Principal Uses of Synthetic Lubricants*

	Int. comb. engines	Gears and bearings	Greases	Compressors turbines[†]	Hydraulic fluids[†]	Water emulsions
Polyalphaolefins	E	E	E	VG	E	F
Organic esters	G	VG	VG	VG	VG	P
Polyalkylene glycols	—	VG	G	G	E(FR)	E
Phosphate esters	—	—	—	VG(FR)	E(FR)	—
Silicones	—	VG	E	E	E	—
Mineral oils	VG	VG	VG	VG	VG	F

* Letter signifies performance level: P = poor, F = fair, G = good, VG = very good, E = excellent.
[†] FR = Fire-resistant.

Organic Esters

Diesters. Diester, or dibasic acid ester, base fluids are made by reacting short-chain C$_{8-13}$ oxo alcohols with dibasic acids, such as adipic and phthalic (from petroleum), azelaic (from tallow), and dimer acids (from tall oil). Diesters are a subclass of polyesters, which include tri- and tetra-esters. More than 50 United States companies have the capacity for manufacturing at least 2×10^8 gal/year of these and many other diesters, primarily for plasticizers for PVC (vinyl) products. Manufacturers specializing in lubricant-grade diesters are Emery, Exxon, Hatco, Inolex, Mobil, Röhm and Haas, Tenneco, and Witco.

Diester lubricants are used mainly in oil-flooded air and natural-gas compressors. Their polar nature, due to the carbonyl group in their chemical structure, facilitates additive accep-

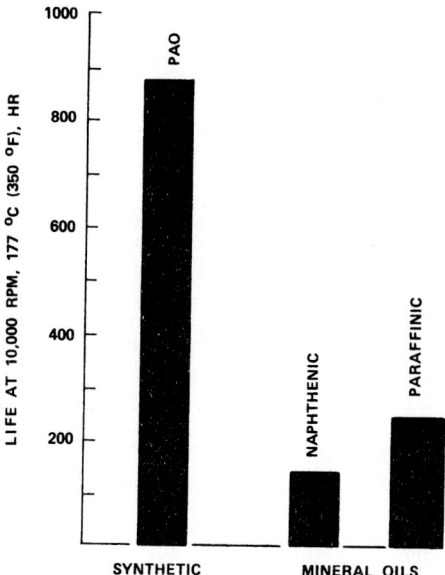

FIGURE 2-2 Functional-life ball-bearing test for grease, Federal Standard 791, No. 333.

tance and provides solvation properties that help maintain clean intake and exhaust valves, thereby extending lubricant drain periods and improving ignition safety. Several makers of reciprocating compressors specify diester lubricants for some models. Diester lubricants are used in oven chain lubricants, in some gas-turbine engine oils, and as greases in certain low-temperature applications.

Polyol Esters. Polyol, or neopentyl, esters are formed by combining, linear short-chain (C_{5-10}) fatty acids with polyols, usually pentaerythritol (PE) or trimethylolpropane (TMP). Such "hindered esters" exhibit very high thermal stability, inherently higher than diesters. Emery, Hatco, Hercules, Witco/ Humko, Mobil, and Stauffer are the current manufacturers of lubricant-grade polyol esters.

Polyol esters are chiefly used in military and commercial jet aircraft and in surface gas-turbine engines supplied by the jet-engine makers (Pratt & Whitney—TP & M, Detroit Diesel-Allison, GE aircraft-type models). Excellent gear oils, greases, and other industrial lubricants can be formulated from polyol ester fluids. However, their use in industry has been constrained by comparably performing, but lower-cost, diester and PAO lubricants. Polyol esters are sometimes combined with PAO to enhance solubility of certain additives and to optimize elastomer seal swell characteristics.

Polyalkylene Glycols. Polyalkylene glycols (PAG or polyglycols) are synthesized by combining ethylene oxide and propylene oxide under a variety of processing conditions. Consequently PAGs are available in the widest range of viscosities and hydrophobic/hydrophilic balances of any synthetic functional fluid (Table 2-3). The fluids are noncarbonizing and possess high viscosity indices. A limiting characteristic is their incompatibility with mineral oils and several conventional lubricant additives. Union Carbide is the dominant supplier. BASF, Dow, Olin, and Texaco also supply many PAG grades.

A large use for PAG is in metalworking fluids, e.g., coolants. The different degrees of water solubility of the different grades enable metal heat-treating quenchants to be selected for the desired rate of heat removal. Other large-volume applications of compounded PAG include

TABLE 2-3 Polyalkylene Glycol Fluids

Viscosity, cSt				Pour point			Flash—C.O.C.		Auto-ignition	
212°F (100°C)	100°F (38°C)	0°F (−18°C)	Viscosity index	°F	°C	Sp. gr. 20/20°C	°F	°C	°F	°C
2.75	11.7	270	83	−70	−57	0.960	325	163	410	210
6.80	35.3	1,400	169	−50	−46	0.983	460	238	572	300
18.5	112	7,100	196	−30	−34	0.997	505	263	671	335
53	365	31,000	219	−10	−23	1.002	515	268	752	400
165	1,100	71,000	281	−20	−29	1.063	545	285	779	415
255	1,970	—	282	40	4.4	1.094	490	254	797	425
2,600	19,400	—	414	40	4.4	1.097	620	327	833	445

heat-transfer oils, fire-resistant hydraulic fluids, rubber and textile processing aids, and gas compressor lubricants. PAG lubricants are unsuitable for air and refrigeration compressors. There are some gear lubricant and grease applications.

Phosphate Esters

Phosphate esters derive from the reaction of phosphorus oxychloride with cresylic acids, synthetic alkyl phenols, or certain alcohols. FMC Houghton, Monsanto, and Stauffer are the largest suppliers, with IMC (Sobin/Montrose) expanding its position.

Fire resistance is unquestionably the most notable property of inorganic phosphate esters. Where combustibility is a hazard, OSHA, Factory Mutual, and other standards increasingly require phosphate ester lubricants. Low volatility and chemical stability are other advantageous properties, but their incompatibility with mineral oil systems is often a disadvantage. Phosphate esters craze and soften certain plastics, coatings, neoprene and nitrile elastomers, and pipe-joint compounds.

Hydraulic fluids and compressor lubricants are the principal uses. Some greases also are used where safety from fire or from very high temperatures is important.

Silicones

Silicones are the reaction products of silicon (from sand or quartz) and different halo-carbons, such as alkyl or aryl chlorides. Fluorosilicones are also available. Dow Corning is the major supplier. GE, Union Carbide, and Stauffer's SWS affiliate are becoming more active.

Chemical inertness is the major advantage of silicones. Low flammability and self-extinguishing properties make silicones desirable for many uses. Widespread applicability is limited by their incompatibility with mineral oils and certain additives.

Many specialty applications exist for silicones: moisture-proof seals and lubricants for ignition and electronic equipment and greases for valves and swivel joints exposed to chlorine gas and strong oxidizing or corrosive chemicals. Silicones are used as hydraulic fluids and compressor lubricants. Silicone brake fluids are being used in new systems designed to benefit from their unique properties.

Other Synlubes

Alkylated Aromatics. Alkylated aromatics (dialkylbenzenes, or DAB) were originally co-products of the manufacture of linear alkylbenzene (LAB) "soft" detergent alkylate. Conoco is the major manufacturer. DAB is compounded into low-temperature engine oils, gear lubricants, hydraulic fluid, and grease. Chevron recovers some bottoms from their dodecylbenzene (DDB) "hard" detergent alkylate plant. This highly branched-chain DAB is the base for a high-quality refrigerator-compressor oil and a dielectric fluid.

Cycloaliphatics. Cycloaliphatics are obtained by dimerizing and then hydrogenating the by-product α-methyl styrene from synthetic phenol plants. Monsanto is the only manufacturer today, but Sun also has the technology.

The unique property of these synthesized hydrocarbons is their high traction coefficient. Lubricants compounded from such fluids become shear-resistant semisolids at the high momentary contact pressure in adjustable-speed traction drives. This enables power to be transmitted from one smooth-rolling element to another—without gears, chains, belts, etc. The driving member drives the driven member with essentially no slipping (see Fig. 2-3).

Applications for traction drives include wire-drawing machines, injection molders, filament-payout stands, boring machines, press-roll drives, spring coilers, and gun mills.

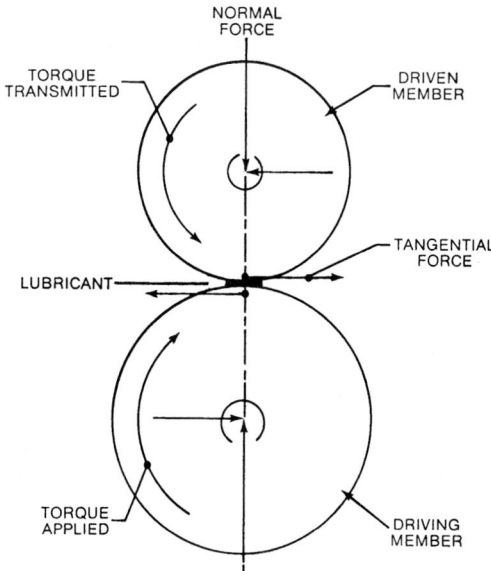

FIGURE 2-3   Traction coefficient = tangential force/normal force.

Polybutenes.   Polybutenes are oligomers of C_4 olefins, principally isobutene. Amoco, Chevron, and Cosden sell some of what they produce, but Exxon and Lubrizol use most of their output as intermediates for lubricant additives.

Polybutenes combine lubricity with complete burn-off at relatively mild elevated temperatures [600°F (315°C)]. Thus no deposits or stains are left on the hot surfaces. Because of these properties, polybutenes are used in rolling and wire drawing of nonferrous metals. They are also used as lubricants for compressors of nonoxidizing gases, including ethylene and propylene compressors in polyethylene and polypropylene plants.

Halogenated Hydrocarbons.   Halogenated hydrocarbons are primarily classified as (1) chlorofluorocarbons, made by Halocarbon, and (2) perfluorinated polyethers, made by duPont and Montedison, and purified further by Bray (distilled fractions).

The extremely inert chlorofluorocarbons are essentially fireproof. They are used in liquid, grease, and plastic form in oxygen plants and in vacuum pumps in gaseous diffusion plants separating isotopes of uranium hexafluoride, an extremely reactive compound. Also they lubricate diaphragm compressors of radioactive gases in nuclear power plants and serve as special fire-resistant hydraulic fluids and suppressants. Because of their high cost, systems to recover the fluid from the gases are generally installed.

Perfluorinated polyethers combine nonflammability with good lubricity. They perform well at temperature extremes and in contact with gases such as oxygen, ozone, fluorine, BF_3, UF_6, etc. Other industrial lubricant applications include furnaces, ovens, chains, rollers, conveyors, and plastic film orienters.

Polyphenyl Ethers.   Polyphenyl ethers are best characterized as bis(pheno-oxyphenoxy) benzene, made by Monsanto. This compound possesses extraordinary resistance to degradation by heat, oxygen, radiation, hydrolysis, and chemical attack. It is particularly effective in lubricating electric contacts, especially noble metals. The oil also is used as a very-high-temperature bearing lubricant, in critical heat-transfer systems and in cases where radiation resistance is important.

Silicate Esters. Silicate esters are made from silica sand and phenols or polyols by Chevron, Monsanto, Olin, and Union Carbide. The principal applications are in fire-resistant hydraulic fluids, dielectric coolants, and heat-transfer mediums. Excess moisture causes hydrolysis of silicate esters.

New Developmental Synthetic Functional Fluids. New developmental synthetic functional fluids include perfluorinated triazine and other *s*-triazines, perfluoro alkylated ethers and substituted polyphenyl ethers, as well as heterocyclic derivatives.

SELECTING THE RIGHT SYNLUBE

Some original equipment makers (OEMs) and operating agencies specify certain synthetic lubricants. In other instances, the OEMs or agencies provide a list of approved synlubes or a list of the types and properties of synlubes that have been found satisfactory. In an increasing number of situations, use of the proper synlube will markedly improve operations and result in lower overall costs. Two examples (Tables 2-4 and 2-5) illustrate simple cost-benefits analyses. They show that synlubes, when properly employed in certain applications, are well worth their higher prices.

TABLE 2-4 Cost Benefits* of Synthetic Lubricant: Reciprocating Sodium Hydroxide Metering Pump, Teflon-Impregnated Asbestos Packing

Per year	Packing only (no lubrication)	Packing with fluorosilicone grease
Packing changes	12	1
Labor costs (for changes)	600	60
Packing costs	60	7
Grease cost	—	100
Total maintenance costs	$672	$168

Benefits: • $504 annual savings • Less production downtime (worth $$$)

   * In 1993 dollars.

TABLE 2-5 Annual Costs (in 1993 Dollars) for 20 Reactor Drives

	Mineral oil	PAO synlube
Lube price, $/gal	3	12
Lube, changes	Monthly	4 months*
Requirements, gal	(600)	(200)
Cost,	1500	2400
Labor, 1 h/change/drive at $30/h	8400	2800
Average repair costs		
Labor at $20/h/repair	3600	1200
Materials at $100/repair,	1,200	400
Lost productivity	?	—
Reduced equipment service	?	—
Total tangible costs	14,700	6812
Savings	—	7888

   * Lube change and failure rate is ⅓ of that with mineral oil.

The high costs of new equipment, parts, and labor necessitate keeping machines running better and longer. Such increased efficiency and extended life can be obtained by the judicious use of synthetic lubricants. As costs soar and downtime becomes more expensive, the economics will swing more and more in favor of longer-life, maintenance-saving synlubes—even though their price may be higher than mineral oil's. Where safety is the overriding consideration, cost of the safer synlube will of course remain secondary.

There is no perfect synlube for all applications. Tradeoffs always exist. For some uses mixed-base synlubes are best. Each synthetic has its own individual characteristics. The most appropriate synlube must be carefully selected on the basis of characteristics most suited for the specific conditions and equipment. Endorsements and recommendations of equipment builders and of synlube suppliers should be considered seriously. Only proven products from reliable suppliers should be used. It is wise to review experiences of others in similar situations before trying a new synlube. Synlube papers published by technical associations usually contain worthwhile information. Brochures and bulletins of synlube suppliers, of course, present much detailed data. More and more independent lubricant suppliers are expanding their lines of synlubes, and are increasingly able to provide high-performance products supported by competent technical service.

BIBLIOGRAPHY

Campen, M.: "PAO-based Lubricants in Power Transmission Applications," *6th Annual Conference on Power Transmission,* Chicago, November 1979.

Green, R. L., and F. L. Langenfeld: "Lubricants for Traction Drives," *Machine Design,* May 2, 1974.

Gunderson, R. W., and A. W. Hart: *Synthetic Lubricants,* Reinhold, New York, 1962.

Manley, L. W.: "New Developments in Synthetic Lubricants," *World Petroleum Congress,* Bucharest, September 1979.

Mueller, E. R.: "Polyalkylene Glycol Fluids and Lubricants," *ASLE Seminar on Synthetic Lubes,* Pittsburgh, February 10, 1977.

O'Connor, J. J., and J. Boyd: *Standard Handbook of Lubrication Engineering,* McGraw-Hill, New York, 1968, chap. 11, "Synthetic Liquid Lubricants."

Reid, H. F.: *A New Report on Ester Lubricants,* Hatco Chemical Co., Fords, N.J., June 1977.

Smith, R. E.: "Silicone Lubricants for the Chemical Processing Industry," *30th Annual Meeting ASLE,* Atlanta, May 5–8, 1975.

Wolfe, G. F., Cohen, M., and V. T. Dimitroff: "Ten Years Experience with Fire Resistant Fluids in Steam Turbine Electrohydraulic Controls," *24th Annual ASLE Meeting,* Philadelphia, May 5–9, 1969.

Suppliers' technical bulletins and brochures.

SUPPLIER SOURCES OF ADDITIONAL INFORMATION

BASF Wyandotte Corporation, Parsippany, NJ
Bray Oil Company, Irvine, CA
Chevron USA, San Francisco, CA
Conoco Oil Company, Houston, TX
Dow Corning Corporation, Midland, MI
Emery Industries Incorporated, Cincinnati, OH
Ethyl/Edwin Cooper, St. Louis, MO
Exxon USA, Houston, TX
FMC Corporation, Chicago, IL
General Electric Company, Waterford, NY
Gulf Oil Company, Houston, TX

Gulf Oil Chemicals Company, Houston, TX
Hatco Chemical Corporation, Fords, NJ
Hercules, Incorporated, Wilmington, DE
Humko Sheffield Chemical Company, Memphis, TN
Mobil Corporation, New York, NY
Monsanto Company, St. Louis, MO
Olin Corporation, Stamford, CT
Stauffer Chemical, Westport, CT
Tenneco Chemicals, Incorporated, Piscataway, NJ
Union Carbide Corporation, New York, NY
Uniroyal Chemical, Naugatuck, CT
Witco, Fairfax, VA

TECHNICAL SOCIETIES

ASME—American Society of Mechanical Engineers.
NLGI—National Lubricating Grease Institute.
STLE—Society of Tribologists & Lubricating Engineers (formerly ASLE—American Society of Lubricating Engineers).

CHAPTER 17-3
SOLID LUBRICANTS*

INTRODUCTION

Solid lubricants are selected solid materials with friction-reducing, low-shear properties. Typical of these materials are graphite, MoS_2 (molybdenum disulfide), PTFE (polytetrafluoroethylene), and mica. They may be used as powders in their natural form, or dispersed in fluids (oils, water) and greases; or they may be added to binders, as pigments to paint, and used as *dry-film* bonded lubricants.

USES

There are many exotic uses for solid lubricants in aerospace, electronics, and instrumentation industries, and machine designers should consider their use wherever conventional lubrication is impracticable. However, solid lubricants play an important role in the practice of industrial "preventive maintenance" as an antiwear, load-bearing component in plant lubricants. Their major benefits are: longer service life of machinery, extended lubrication intervals, and the ability to function in environments hostile to conventional lubricants. They are also used extensively by equipment manufacturers in "lubricated-for-life" components; they are the basis for the 30,000-mile chassis lubrication interval in automobiles.

All machined surfaces, even the ground and polished ones, can be defined in terms of surface roughness, or the dimensions of microscopic high spots called *asperities*. Between the rubbing surfaces of bearings, the lowest coefficient of friction is achieved by maintaining separation of these surfaces by a full *fluid film* (hydrodynamic lubrication). As the oil-film thickness decreases with higher loads, shock loading, or diminishing surface speeds, asperities on opposing surfaces come into contact in *mixed-film* lubrication with a resultant increase in friction.

With increasing severity, a much higher coefficient of friction is experienced during *boundary* lubrication when asperity contact is sufficient to cause microscopic welding and shearing between the two rubbing surfaces. Under the pressures and heat of contact, the solid lubricants may or may not react with the metal substrates, but they do interpose themselves as a barrier coating in which shearing may take place more easily and with less friction than if the bearing metals were shearing in pure contact. As the wear phenomenon is related to the shearing of contacting asperities, wear also may be reduced by the interposing of a solid lubricant barrier.

---

*Updated for this Second Edition by the Editor-in-Chief.

FORMS AND APPLICATIONS

The useful forms in which solid lubricants are prepared include powders, pastes (compounds), bonded coatings, greases, and dispersions. Powders, burnished into rubbing metal surfaces, have a limited wear endurance and offer virtually no protection from the atmosphere. Pastes are heavy concentrates (up to 65 percent) of solid lubricants in a fluid or grease base; they offer longer, but limited, service life and may include corrosion protection. Bonded coatings may be applied by spray or brush (like paint), by plasma techniques, or by an impingement process if tolerances are critical.

Greases used in antifriction bearings usually contain less than 3 to 5 percent solids, and their particle size is closely monitored, especially for precision and high-speed bearings. Heavy-duty and special-purpose greases may contain up to 25 percent solids. Finished lubricating oils may contain dispersed solid lubricants for improved load-carrying and antiwear characteristics; concentrated dispersions in oil are available as lubricating-oil additives.

The carrier fluids in pastes, greases, and dispersions are not always petroleum-base, but may be water-base or any number of synthetic fluids including glycols, esters, synthetic hydrocarbons, or silicones. Most solid lubricants can tolerate hazardous environments better than most carrier fluids can; thus the carrier is usually selected on the basis of the expected environment. For example: some solids, primarily graphite and MoS_2, are excellent oven-bearing and high-temperature chain lubricants in their powdered form; certain petroleum, glycol, and ester fluids, selected for their favorable volatility are used as media to carry the solids into the rubbing areas to reduce friction and wear even after the fluid has evaporated.

Rubbing metal surfaces are most subject to high friction and wear when they are new or resurfaced, and their ultimate condition and service life depend upon whether they succeed or fail in "running in," or seating properly. Early destruction of contacting asperities or their orderly distortion will determine the true load-bearing area. The less destructive the run-in, the lower will be the magnitude of instantaneous loading. Thus among the most common industrial applications are *wear-in, press-fit,* and *threaded connections.* An expansion on industrial uses appears in Table 3-1.

In addition to the aforementioned materials, hundreds of solid lubricants have been described in technical literature. Those described include metallic oxides and sulfides, soft metals, calcium fluoride, zinc pyrophosphate, talc, and vermiculite. The low-shear characteristics of solid lubricants may be the result of crystal structure, interstitial matter, bond strength, or chemical interaction of the surface and the solid. The effectiveness of solid lubricants stems from the almost fail-proof film which they form on moving surfaces, usually beyond the yield strength of the metal asperities. The mechanism of solid lubrication is not dependent on any single property of the lubricant; it is an interdependence of the surface, the solid lubricant composition, the geometry of the particles and the metal surface, and the nature of the processes that occur on or near the bearing surfaces.

CHARACTERISTICS

Solid lubricants composed of two or more materials often combine their most favorable characteristics to provide synergistic lubricating properties that are superior to any single lubricating solid. A brief review of the characteristics of the most commonly used solids can give insight into the lubrication mechanism of solids alone or in combination. The most widely used inorganic and metal base materials are graphite and MoS_2; the most widely used film-forming plastic is PTFE.

Inorganic Lubricants

Graphite and MoS_2 differ in composition, general properties, and type of chemical bonding, but they do have in common their layer-lattice structure. Their characteristic crystal structures are layers of sheets within which the atoms are tightly packed and strongly bonded; but

TABLE 3-1   Some Industrial Uses of Solid Lubricants

Industrial application	Product form
Wear-in—protection against galling and seizure of newly machined surfaces at start-up and early running-in; examples: gears, slides and ways, cams, valve sleeves, splines, bearings	Preassembly: powder, paste, bonded coating Initial fill: finished oil dispersion or concentrate
Press-fit—to reduce pressure required, prevent galling, seizure, and possible misalignment; at times clearances are negative; examples: antifriction bearings, splines, keyed shafts, sleeves	Preassembly: powder, paste
Threaded connections, fasteners—to reduce torque loss due to friction, galling, and seizure; promotes optimum uniformity in the tension of assembly bolts and facilitates nondestructive disassembly	Preassembly: pastes (thread compounds), bonded coatings
Life-of-part prelubrication—where maintenance lubrication is impossible, or improbable; examples: enclosed mechanisms, hinges, locks, linkages, instruments, appliances	Preassembly: powder, paste, bonded coating
Lubrication of machine in operation—applied by all conventional systems: drop-feed, circulation, reservoir, air mist; grease gun, automatic grease dispensing systems; for heavy-duty installations and/or extending lubrication intervals and machine service life	Ongoing plant lubrication: finished lubricating oils and greases containing dispersions of solid lubricants
Antiwear, load-bearing additive in lubricants—to fortify conventional lubricating oils and greases used in plant lubrication, initial fills for wear-in, and in units experiencing progressive wear rates	Pastes added to greases, and concentrated dispersions added to oils
Additive to metalworking fluids—to reduce friction, lengthen life, and reduce metal pickup on punching and forming dies and all types of cutting tools	Concentrated dispersions added to metalworking fluids and pastes added to compounds
Reduce fretting (friction oxidation)—to protect against fretting corrosion of metal surfaces under static loads (vibrating) as on bearings, bearing housings, splines, and various press-fit components	Preassembly: pastes and bonded coatings
Antiwear, load-bearing additive in self-lubricated components—to extend life of parts and reduce friction and distortion when blended into rubber, plastics, elastomers, and sintered metals	Powder is added as a component in the raw material for the fabrication of bushings, O-rings, etc.
Dry-film lubrication—for use in dusty atmospheres to minimize the adherence of abrasive particles to metal surfaces of open gears, bearings, cams, and slides	Bonded coatings, pastes, greases
High-temperature applications—oven conveyor chains and bearings, kiln-car wheelbearings, mechanical devices operating at temperatures above the capability of fluids	Dispersions in fluids and greases designed to volatilize leaving mainly the solid lubes; some bonded coatings
Equipment exposed to destructive environments—acids, alkali, solvents, detergent, steam, etc. For load-carrying, antiwear characteristics	Greases, constructed from materials also resistant to the environment

these sheets (laminae) are separated by relatively large distances and held together by weak residual forces. In graphite, a crystalline form of carbon, the distances of atoms within the sheets is 1.4×10^{-8} cm, but between sheets it is as much as 3.4×10^{-8} cm. When under shear, there are strong forces within the graphite sheets, but the forces holding the sheets together are much weaker, allowing them to slip over one another.

A theoretical explanation for the lubricity of molybdenum disulfide is similarly found in its molecular structure. Each lamina of this compound is composed of a layer of molybdenum atoms with a layer of sulfur atoms on each side. The sulfur and molybdenum layers bond tightly but the adjacent laminae interface at their layers of sulfur atoms which form weak bonds between the laminae. The weak sulfur bonds between the laminae form the slippage planes of low shear resistance as between the carbon layers in graphite. Both graphite and MoS_2 display an affinity for metal substrates, and under high loads both have been found to alloy with ferrous metal, forming even greater bonds at the surface.

Under heavy forces (loads) perpendicular to bearing surfaces, these laminae are compressed and oriented parallel to the bearing surfaces and have the strength to resist rupture. The low friction reflects the low resistance of the laminae sliding on one another. Cohesive forces within graphite and MoS_2 are sufficient to allow for self-healing of interruptions in the solid lubricant film.

Plastics

Of the plastic materials used as solid lubricants, PTFE has the greatest affinity for metal surfaces, the lowest internal shear resistance, and the greatest ability to be self-healing. As no plastics have a tight molecular structure or laminar nature, they are unable to take the heavy loads carried by graphite or MoS_2. At loads up to 25,000 lb/in^2 (1760 kg/cm^2) however, PTFE has the lowest coefficient of friction of all solid lubricants.

Common Characteristics

A primary characteristic of these three leading solid lubricants is their ability to lubricate as dry powders. Almost all other solid lubricants require some addition of fluid or grease to lubricate for any period without noise and increasing friction. Nor do other solids have the excellent film-forming and self-healing characteristics of these three which often form the base to which other solids are added. Some of the following are the characteristics which are sought by the use or addition of other solids: particle geometry suited to antiseize or wear-in of coarse surfaces, improved protection against fretting wear, improved bulk-film load-carrying capability, and the thickening of some fluids for greases. Some white solid lubricants, e.g., zinc sulfide, are used alone where a white or colorless lubricant is required for appearance. Solids, even though not laminar, still become interposed between rubbing surfaces when dispersed in fluids or greases.

It is again the superior properties of graphite, MoS_2, and PTFE that allow for their use in very adverse environments. In high-temperature operations graphite is commonly used to 800°F (425°C) and intermittently to 1200°F (650°C). In vacuum at high temperature, or in high vacuum, graphite loses a water-vapor layer which is found naturally adsorbed at the surfaces of the laminae and is felt to be largely responsible for the weak attraction or bond between them. Loss of the water vapor results in a significant increase in friction and a tendency toward abrasion. On the other hand, MoS_2 has a lower coefficient of friction in the absence of water vapor and it can withstand very high vacuum, but it is not as resistant to oxidation as is graphite. MoS_2 performs well up to 650°F (345°C). Above this temperature, in air, its oxidation rate increases until at 750°F (400°C) it oxidizes quite rapidly. PTFE will perform well in vacuum and at temperatures up to 600°F (315°C) at which it begins to decompose.

Solvents and chemicals provide some of the environments most destructive to conventional lubricants. Again, the leaders are the most impervious of all solid lubricants, being virtually unaffected by direct contact. Graphite and PTFE are nearly indestructable by any chemicals, and MoS_2 is relatively unaffected except by hot strong oxidizing acids like aqua regia and chromic acid. At times, the removal of MoS_2 from metal surfaces requires strong caustic cleaners and abrasive action. Special solvent-, chemical-, and detergent-resistant greases containing solid lubricants require also the careful selection of fluid carriers and thickeners.

SUMMARY

There is a need for a solid lubricant wherever a hydrodynamic oil film cannot be sustained. Whether the film becomes insufficient because of high pressure or shock loading, elevated temperatures, or exposure to solvents and chemicals or is depleted by the extension of lubrication cycles, solid lubricants can extend service life by inhibiting asperity welding (wear), galling, and the ultimate seizure of bearing metals. All bearings are in boundary lubricating conditions during stop-start operations since full fluid-film lubrication requires motion to propagate.

BIBLIOGRAPHY

Acheson, E. G.: U.S. Patent 813,426, February 5, 1907.

ASLE* Proceedings, International Conference on Solid Lubrication, Chicago, 1971.

ASLE* Proceedings, 2nd International Conference on Solid Lubrication, Chicago, 1978.

Basics of Design Engineering, 1993 volume (published annually), Penton Publishing Co, Cleveland, OH.

Bowden, F. P., and D. Tabor: *The Friction and Lubrication of Solids,* Oxford, New York, 1950.

Braithwaite, E. R.: *Solid Lubricants and Surfaces,* Pergamon, New York, 1964.

Braithwaite, E. R.: *Lubrication and Lubricants,* Elsevier, New York, 1967.

Campbell, M.E.: *Solid Lubricants, A Survey,* NASA SP-5059 (01), 1972.

Deoine, N. J., E. R. Tourson, J. P. Cerini, and R. J. McCartney: "Solids and Solid Lubrication," *Lubrication Engineering,* January 1965.

E. Hall: U.S. Patent 2,700,623, April 26, 1950, and U.S. Patent 2,703,768, April 21, 1954.

McCabe, J. T.: "Molybdenum Disulfide—Its Role in Lubrication," reprint of a paper presented at International Industrial Lubrication Exhibition, New Hall, Westminster, London, March 8–11, 1965.

Neale, M. J. (ed.): *Tribology Handbook,* Wiley, New York, 1973.

Notes on Solid Lubricants, Seminar Proceedings at Rensselaer Polytechnic Institute, 1966.

Solid Lubricants, NTIS/PS 75/715, 78/0816, 78/0817, 78/0818, 78/0819, NTIS Bulletins, U.S. Dept. of Commerce, Washington, D.C.

Stock, A. J.: "Graphite, Molybdenum Disulfide and PTFE—A Comparison" *Lubrication Engineering,* August 1963.

Ubbelohde, Q. R., and F. A. Lewis: *Graphite and its Crystal Compounds,* Oxford/Clarendon, 1960.

Waite, J. R. and W. D. Janssens: "Use of Inorganic Solids in Lubricating Oils," Presented at ASLE Annual Meeting, Cleveland, Ohio, May 6–9, 1968.

Youse, E. L., NLGI Spokesperson: *Characteristics and Selection of Graphite as a Lubricant,* January 1962, Kansas City, Mo.

* Note: ASLE (American Society of Lubricating Engineers) has been superceded by STLE (Society of Tribologists and Lubricating Engineers).

CHAPTER 17-4
LUBRICATION SYSTEMS

George Arbocus

Elf Lubricants
Linden, New Jersey

INTRODUCTION

An effective lubrication system is any system or device which dispenses the correct lubricant, at the correct point, in the correct amount, at the correct time. Systems may vary from hand oiling to a complicated centralized system. Escalating costs and the development of high-speed precision machinery are necessitating changes in plant lubrication practices.

ALL-LOST SYSTEMS

All-lost or once-through lubrication (Fig. 4-1) systems are those in which the lubricant is used only once. Manual all-lost systems such as hand oiling, individual grease fittings, wick lubricators, oil cups, and drop-feed oilers are rapidly becoming a part of history. These systems are inexpensive to install but require close attention on the part of the operator to ensure that each point is relubricated on a regular basis for adequate lubrication.

The most common all-lost systems in use today are automatic. Mist systems and mechanical force-feed lubricators are common examples. The reason for their popularity is their ability to lubricate more than one point on a machine from a central reservoir and to automatically dispense the lubricant in metered amounts at the point of application.

Mist systems rely on compressed air to atomize the oil into fine droplets and deliver it through pipes to the point of application. Frequently used to lubricate bearings and gears, the air passing over the part assists the oil in carrying off heat and preventing the entry of dirt.

Mechanical force-feed lubricators were originally designed to deliver oil to cylinders but are no longer limited to that application. They consist of small pumping units mounted on a common shaft which take oil from a reservoir through pipes to the point of application. The driving mechanism may be an electric motor or some moving part of the machine being lubricated. Each pumping unit may be set to deliver the precise amount of oil which is required at a particular application point. Both the mist system and the mechanical force-feed lubricator require little maintenance beyond ensuring that no lines are plugged.

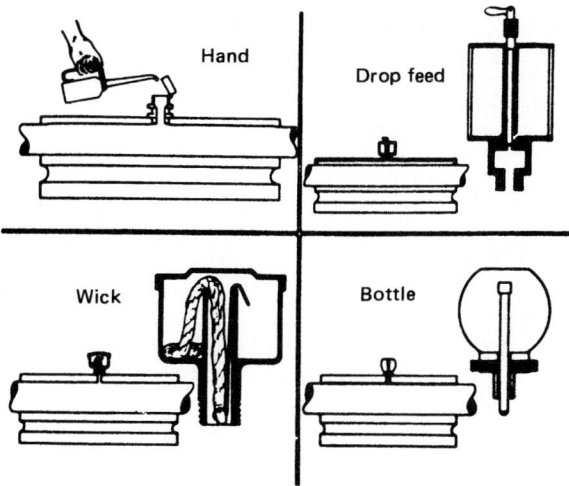

FIGURE 4-1 Once-through oiling. (*AISE; reprinted with permission from* The Lubrication Engineers Manual, *copyright 1971.*)

OIL-RESERVOIR SYSTEMS

Unlike all-lost systems, oil-reservoir or self-contained systems reuse the same oil over and over again. These methods depend on a common housing containing the oil and the parts to be lubricated (Fig. 4-2).

Gears and cylinders lubricated by these methods usually depend on the splashing action of one or more moving parts dipping into the pool of oil at the bottom of the housing.

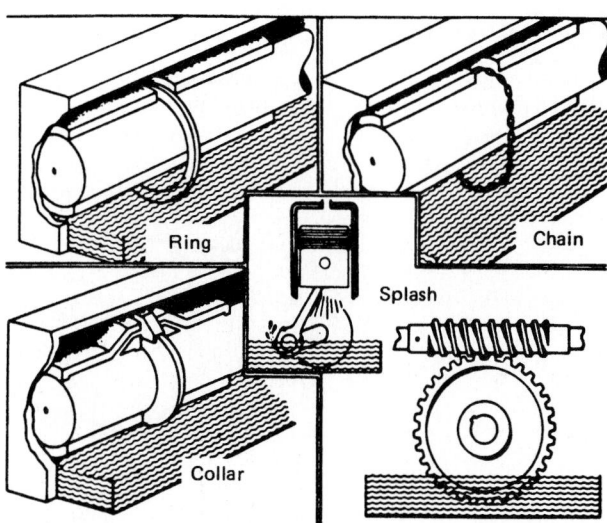

FIGURE 4-2 Oil reservoirs. (*AISE; reprinted with permission from* The Lubrication Engineers Manual, *copyright 1971.*)

Bearings lubricated by self-contained systems may be splash-lubricated or rely on a ring, chain, or collar to dip into the oil and carry the oil to the top of the journal. Collar bearings are used at higher speeds than rings or chains since the latter will tend to slip excessively at high speeds, precluding adequate lubrication.

To ensure adequate lubrication it is important that the oil be maintained at the proper level. Insufficient oil could result in a lack of lubrication, while overfilling can cause foaming and temperature buildups due to excessive churning.

CENTRALIZED SYSTEMS

Like oil-reservoir systems, centralized systems use the oil over and over again. They can range from a simple reservoir, pump, and return-line setup to complex systems with electronic controls, servo valves, heat exchangers, and filters.

Depending on the complexity of the system, costs vary greatly. The cost-effectiveness of centralized systems depends heavily on the length of time the fluid can remain in circulation before it needs to be changed.

To ensure maximum fluid life, oil-reservoir temperatures should be controlled as well as the amount of contaminants in the oil. If petroleum oils are used, reservoir temperatures should be maintained between 110 and 130°F (43 and 54°C) for optimum fluid life. Synthetics can be operated at somewhat higher temperatures. Reservoir temperatures can be controlled through the use of heat exchangers and proper reservoir design.

The oil reservoir should be large enough to allow the oil to rest for a minimum of 15 min before being recirculated. It should be baffled to ensure that returning oil is not immediately pumped back into circulation. This rest time in the reservoir allows the oil to drop out contaminants and dissipate the heat and air it has picked up while in circulation.

The oil-reservoir's fluid level is also very important to the trouble-free operation of circulating systems. If the suction line is not completely submerged in oil at all times, pump cavitation could result. Also, it is important that the return line be submerged in the oil to reduce air entrainment and thus prevent foaming problems which could occur if the returning oil is allowed to splash into the reservoir. Figure 4-3 is an example of a properly designed reservoir.

Monitoring and Warning Devices

A properly designed centralized or automatic lubrication system can provide effective equipment lubrication with very little human intervention. The main drawback is the risk of catas-

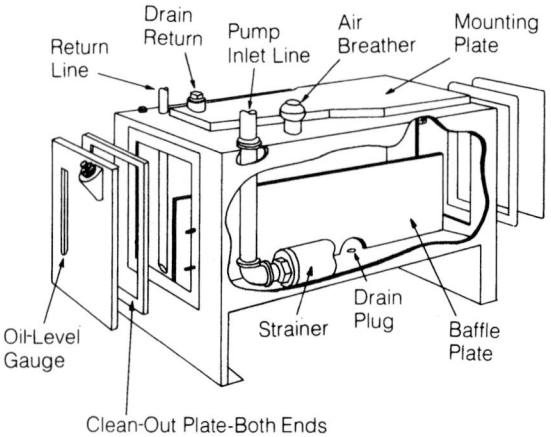

FIGURE 4-3 Typical circulating system reservoir.

trophic equipment failure which may result when a malfunction occurs. To prevent this, monitoring and warning devices are installed to alert operators to lubrication malfunctions. These may be bells, sirens, flashing lights, automatic equipment shut-down, or telltale indicators. All of these can be effective if maintained in proper operating condition.

CRITERIA FOR SELECTING A LUBRICATION SYSTEM OR DEVICE

A lubrication system should be selected with one purpose in mind: *to get the proper quantity of the correct lubricant where and when it is needed.* Before purchasing or installing a new lubrication system it is recommended that the application be studied to aid in the selection of the most economical and effective system for a particular application. Factors to be considered include:

Equipment considerations

- The components to be lubricated
- The lubricant to be applied
- The lubrication-point accessibility
- The number of lubrication points the system is expected to service

Operation condition considerations

- Equipment speeds
- Operating temperatures
- Expected relubrication intervals

Economic and plant practice considerations

- Plant's past experience with various types of lubrication systems
- Available capital
- Staff available to maintain and monitor systems
- Downtime costs of the equipment
- Environmental impact

Oil companies, equipment builders, and lubricant-dispensing-equipment suppliers are available to assist in the design and selection of lubrication systems. A list of some manufacturers of lubricant-dispensing equipment follows:

Alemite Division, Stewart-Warner Corp., Chicago, IL.

Bijur Lubricating Corp., Bennington, VT.

Farval Division, Fluid Control Division, Eaton Corp., Cleveland, OH.

Lincoln, A Pentair Company, St. Louis, MO.

Madison-Kipp Corp., Madison, WI.

C.A. Norgren Co., Littleton, CO.

Oil-Rite Corp., Manitowoc, WI.

Trabon Lubriquip, Cleveland, OH.

BIBLIOGRAPHY

Alemite Division, Stewart-Warner Corp.: *Oil Mist Application Engineering Manual,* 1991.

Bailey, Charles A., and Joseph S. Aarons (eds.): *The Lubrication Engineers Manual,* Association of Iron and Steel Engineers (AISE), Pittsburgh, 1971.

Brewer, Allen F.: *Basic Lubrication Practice,* Reinhold, New York, 1955.

Brewer, Allen F.: *Effective Lubrication,* Robert E. Krieger, Huntington, NY, 1974.

SECTION 18

CORROSION AND DETERIORATION OF MATERIALS

CHAPTER 18-1
CAUSES AND CONTROL OF DETERIORATION

Jose L. Villalobos
President
V & A Consulting Engineers
Oakland, California

INTRODUCTION

Over time, all materials deteriorate. It is the *rate of deterioration* that is important in the operation and maintenance of facilities. Facilities are designed with a specific design life. The rate of deterioration of the facility must be considered in estimating the life of the facility. Experience has shown that various materials will deteriorate at varying rates. The rate of deterioration is a dynamic function affected by environment, as well as type and length of service.

In the current regulatory climate, materials used for repair or maintenance of facilities must be evaluated in terms of their effects on both worker safety and the environment. By its nature, the deterioration process releases materials into the environment. Many existing facilities contain hazardous materials such as lead-based paints and asbestos. A project safety work plan must be written before any work involving these materials is undertaken. Also, material safety data sheets for all materials used in a repair must be read and precautions taken by the user to insure a safe work environment.

Current plant engineering practice requires that facilities be monitored on a regular basis. This is imperative to maintain the useful life of a facility as designed and to extend the useful life of the facility if conditions change.

The total performance of a facility refers to the ability of both internal and external materials to fulfill their intended function over the useful life of the facility. As a general rule, the external components of a facility are subject to a harsher environment than internal components. For this reason, and because of recent experience with failures of new building materials, considerable care must be exercised when using new materials.

Atmospheric data that indicate the level of severity of the site in terms of deterioration or corrosion potential are generally available for a planned or existing facility. Data such as amount of rainfall; relative humidity; and levels of carbon dioxide, carbon monoxide, sulfur dioxide, sulfur trioxide, and nitrous oxide will greatly assist in the evaluation of the deterioration potential of a site. Some of the chemical components listed above can combine with moisture to form carbonic, sulfurous, sulfuric, or nitric acids. All of these acids will deteriorate the various facility components at varying rates.

Primarily due to new zoning requirements and design trends, various combinations of materials are being used in new residential, commercial, and industrial facilities. Concrete, paving brick, terrazzo, slate, bluestone, granite, glass, aluminum, copper, and plastics are being used in new construction and in repair of existing facilities.

This chapter will focus on the following materials, which are being used in the construction and repair of facilities today:

- Concrete
- Masonry
- Metals
- Wood
- Plastics

The primary factors that effect the deterioration of the materials listed are atmospheric exposure, exposure to water and, to a lesser extent, exposure to soils.

Atmospheric exposure can result in corrosion, chemical attack, and deterioration of all five listed materials. Also, depending on location, ultraviolet light can have a negative impact on certain plastics. Various studies have shown that when the relative humidity rises over approximately 50 percent, corrosion rates for metals accelerate significantly.* Acid fog has been seen to cause localized pH as low as 2 in certain parts of the country. Many materials can become severely deteriorated by this type of exposure.

Water is considered to be the universal solvent. Given the right set of circumstances, water will over time dissolve or cause the deterioration of concrete, masonry, metals, wood, and plastic.

The single largest cause of failure of materials in facilities due to water-related damage is infiltration of water, which can be caused by events such as the failure of roof systems. The parapet is a common source of water infiltration caused by lack of proper flashing details, poor mortar joints, or failure of sealants. Differential expansion of a roof membrane can lead to splitting of the membrane, resulting in water infiltration. If improperly designed, vertical walls of a facility are also subject to the intrusion of water. High winds and rain also can cause water to infiltrate the facility and result in deterioration and corrosion of materials. Failure of glazing systems is another source of water infiltration.

---

* ASTM "Atmospheric Factors Affecting the Corrosion of Engineering Metals," STP 646, 1978.

If moisture is present, then corrosion of metals can result. To protect metals from corrosion, most uses of metal in facility construction today call for protective coatings specifically designed for the intended exposure. A very significant part of the design process is proper material selection. Certain metals perform their desired function quite well in certain environments, while others may fail in a matter of weeks. For example, 304 stainless steel is an excellent material for commercial kitchens because it does not corrode under the conditions generally found in this application. However, if 304 stainless is buried in a saline soil with a very low oxygen content, it will corrode. Most metals are subject to atmospheric exposure, and require some form of protective coating. If a metal is going to be immersed in water or some other liquid, it must be protected by a suitable coating system and possibly, depending upon the specific requirements, protected by cathodic protection. Cathodic protection is an electrical means of controlling corrosion of metals and is discussed later in this chapter.

Exposure to soil can have a negative impact on materials, depending on the chemical constituents of the soil. Some soils contain in excess of 2500 parts per million (ppm) of chlorides. These types of soils will cause significant corrosion of metals and reinforcing steel in concrete. If a soil groundwater has over 10,000 ppm of sulfate, then concrete in contact with this type of soil will be severely damaged. High sulfate-containing soils are found in the southwestern United States. For new facilities, it is imperative that the soils at a proposed site be tested prior to design to allow the design engineer the opportunity to factor in the required protective measures for the specific facility.

CONCRETE

Causes for the Deterioration of Concrete

The visual symptoms of concrete deterioration are cracking, spalling, and disintegration. Each is visible and may occur individually or in combination. The American Concrete Institute* has identified six primary factors that positively affect the durability of concrete structures; these are:

1. Design of the structure to minimize exposure to moisture
2. Low water/cement ratio
3. Use of appropriate air entrainment
4. Quality of materials such as aggregates and mix water
5. Adequate curing before first freezing cycle
6. Special attention to construction practices

Deterioration generally results from the nonapplication of the above listed items. Some of the more common forms of concrete deterioration are discussed in the following paragraphs.

Incomplete Design Details. Deterioration can often be traced to incomplete design details of joints between various concrete members; poorly sealed joints; inadequate drainage at foundations, horizontal surfaces (such as roofs and tops of walls), and incorrectly placed or incomplete weep holes; incompatibility of materials (such as aluminum in direct contact with concrete); use of chloride-containing admixtures (which can cause corrosion of the reinforcing steel); neglect of the cold-flow factor (in the deformation on concrete under stress); and incomplete provision for expansion joints, control joints, and contraction joints. During design *the designer must factor in the movement of water through concrete.* No matter how dense the concrete mix, unless there is a water or vapor barrier, moisture will migrate through

---

* ACI 201.2R-92.

concrete. For example, if high levels of chloride are present in the soils and ground water around a concrete basement wall and no protection was provided for the concrete in the form of a water or moisture barrier, then eventually the chloride will migrate through the concrete until it comes into contact with the reinforcing steel. Once this happens, corrosion will begin, with the resultant spalling of the concrete.

Concrete is suitable for use in environments where the pH is greater than 5.5. If concrete is to be used and the environment has a pH of less than 5.5, then a coating or lining is required. Coatings must also be considered where chloride concentrations exceed 300 ppm in the soil or groundwater. Similarly, Type V cement is required where sulfate concentrations in the groundwater exceed 1500 ppm. Cathodic protection must be considered for concrete cylinder pipe where the soil resistivity is less than 2000 ohm-cm and the chloride content of the soil or ground water is greater than 300 ppm or the sulfate concentration is greater than 1000 ppm. Where prestressed concrete pipe is being considered, extreme care must be exercised in the protection of this type of pipe. Recent findings indicate that this type of pipe is subject to corrosion-related failures due to corrosion of the prestressing wire.

Concrete is typically a durable material in underground service. It is rarely affected by electrolytic corrosion as metals are. Unless the pH of the soil, groundwater, or process stream is less than 5.5, the chloride concentration is 300 ppm or more, or the sulfate concentration is greater than 1000 ppm, concrete is suitable for use in soil exposures. (For example, the San Diego, California, area may contain significant concentrations of chlorides and sulfates that are detrimental to concrete and reinforcing steel.) Attack on concrete and steel is likely when soils are acidic. When the pH of the soil is at or below 5.5, barrier coatings are required to protect the concrete surface. In areas of high sulfate concentrations in the groundwater (greater than 1500 ppm), modification of water/cement ratio, use of Type V cements (sulfate resistant), and barrier coatings must be considered for all buried concrete.

Concrete structures can be attacked by biologically formed sulfuric acid, which may occur in sewer pipelines. This acid formation is greatest where hydrogen sulfide is readily available and where aerobic conditions and moisture are present to oxidize the sulfides to sulfuric acid. These conditions exist where biological slimes are present on the pipe walls and aerobic conditions and moisture exist above the wastewater flow.

Construction Operations. The primary construction activity that can impact the degradation of concrete is improper placing of the concrete resulting in the segregation of materials followed by use before improper curing has occurred. Segregation can be minimized by using proper water/cement ratios. Proper compaction and vibration is mandatory.

Drying Shrinkage. Proper design should control damage caused by drying and shrinkage. Some of the factors that go into proper design are appropriate water/cement ratios, correct vibration, adequate reinforcement, and effective curing-membrane selection.

Temperature Stress. Variations in the atmospheric and internal temperatures can cause enough stress in concrete to cause cracking. Variations in temperature and the coefficient of expansion for concrete must be considered during design. This is particularly important during the curing of the concrete.

Moisture Absorption. Premature spalling can be caused by moisture absorption. The use of appropriate sealers and air entrainment can minimize this type of disintegration.

Corrosion of Reinforcing Steel. Corrosion of reinforcement can be attributed to two situations. First, certain types of cements, sands, aggregates, and water can cause corrosion of reinforcing steel. Also, additives containing high levels of chlorides can cause corrosion. Second, if a reinforced concrete structure is exposed to chloride-containing water, soil corrosion of the reinforcing steel may result. The use of deicing salts has caused a great deal of deterioration of bridge decks and parking garages because salt water is highly corrosive to concrete. Acids formed by various sources, such as pollution and acid rain, can attack concrete and result in corrosion of reinforcing steel. Good housekeeping can avoid some exposures of bare concrete to high chlorides. Spillage of salts from water-softening units on bare concrete can cause severe corrosion of reinforcing steel.

Wear.   Erosion or abrasion are common factors that affect concrete, particularly in high traffic areas. Hydraulic structures, such as dams, are subject to cavitation erosion because of rapidly moving water. Flow velocities in excess of 10 f/s (3m/s) should be avoided.

Impact.   Floors in industrial facilities are particularly subject to damage by heavy live loading. Heavy reinforcement and high strength concrete are the usual methods for improving resistance to live-loading conditions.

Weathering.   All concrete exposed to the atmosphere is subject to attack from the elements, including ultraviolet light and chemicals found in the atmosphere.

Carbonation.   When concrete is exposed to carbon dioxide, a reaction producing carbonates takes place, which causes shrinkage of the concrete and cracking. Carbon dioxide may be introduced through the atmosphere or in liquids carrying carbon dioxide. The highest rates of carbonation in atmospheric exposures occur when the relative humidity is between 25 and 75 percent. Ground water with high levels of carbon dioxide will also cause deterioration of concrete.

Exposure to Water.   Concrete designed for immersion in water or other liquids must be protected. Recent observations at water and wastewater treatment facilities point to the need for protection of bare concrete. Certain types of water will leach components of concrete, leaving the aggregate behind. Eventually, enough of the cement material binding the aggregate together is removed to cause the concrete to fail. There are many products that can be used to provide a barrier between concrete and water in new and existing reinforced-concrete facilities.

Exposure to Soil.   Soils with groundwater containing more than 1500 ppm of sulfate will cause deterioration of concrete. Once the concrete is damaged, the reinforcing steel is exposed and corrosion of the reinforcing steel can progress once the corrosion-inhibitive properties of the concrete are no longer present. Soils containing high levels of chloride can cause significant corrosion of reinforced concrete. When the chloride migrates through the concrete wall and comes in contact with the reinforcing steel, corrosion is initiated. Recently, floor slabs of homes built on soils with very high chloride levels have been experiencing corrosion failures, approximately 10 to 15 yrs after construction.

Diagnosing Durability Problems

Deterioration of concrete may result from chemical attack, corrosion of the reinforcing steel, structural movement, and wear and tear. Various methods are available to identify possible causes for deterioration of concrete:

1. Review the original design to ensure that proper selection of materials has been completed. This should be completed by someone familiar with the original design intent.
2. Review the original mix design and the use of additives in the concrete. Also, look into the construction methods and records to determine if anything during construction could have caused the problem.
3. List the various exposures of the concrete and the seasonal variations that may exist. If the concrete is exposed to saline water, then the water quality should be investigated to determine actual exposures. Atmospheric properties of the project site should be documented. If a chemical that is part of the local atmosphere can have a negative impact on concrete,

it may be part of the cause of the deterioration. One important factor to keep in mind is that a chemical present in a small amount may cause significant deterioration of concrete, if the concrete is already under stress. The stress or loading of a concrete member is very important in making an assessment of the possible deterioration levels that can be expected at a facility.

4. List the types of failures and their possible causes. Conditions such as spalling, cracking, and corrosion of the reinforcing steel will assist in determining the cause of the concrete deterioration:

   - If the concrete is spalling, check for variation in temperature, chemical attack, corrosion of the reinforcing steel, and incomplete design details.
   - If the concrete is disintegrating, check for chemical attack, erosion, and general weathering.

Once the source and cause of the deterioration have been identified, corrective action can be taken. There are several accepted procedures and methods for repairing cracks in concrete structures, spalled concrete floors, and pavements. Table 1-1 outlines several types of materials for such repairs. The materials described also can be used for repair of masonry members.

Repairing Cracks

It has often been said that concrete is destined to crack. The purpose of proper design and the objective of the design engineer are to minimize cracking without the expectation of eliminating it. When cracking does develop, it is important to determine the basic causes, as well as its extent, before deciding on the method of repair.

The surface of concrete will often exhibit shrinkage cracks—these are not necessarily defects, but they are aesthetically undesirable. They are usually attributed to the use of a high-slump concrete that contains excessive water. Cracking occurs when excess moisture leaves the concrete too soon—before the concrete has sufficient tensile strength. Such cracks can be minimized by using a sheet membrane or curing compounds. Although this type of cracking may not necessarily lead to problems and it may often be ignored, applying a sealer based on a synthetic-rubber compound to protect the concrete from further damage is prudent.

Cracks can be described as active or dormant. An active crack will open and close with changes in temperature and with cyclic movement of the structure. Dormant cracks may not go through such movement, but they can still leak, collect dirt, interfere with traffic, etc. A structural crack usually can be attributed to inadequate structural design, insufficient strength (material composition), or poorly designed joints. If joints are not provided in concrete slabs, the concrete will create its own joints by cracking, and these cracks will continue to develop until the concrete member comes to equilibrium.

Active cracks may be sealed with an elastomeric sealant. Dormant cracks may be sealed with a fluid epoxy sealer that can be pumped into the crack or allowed to flow in by gravity. An epoxy sealer of 100 percent solid content will seal the crack without shrinkage and will join the crack faces to re-form a monolithic structure. This seal will be strong enough to resist further cracking. However, should stress still occur, cracking will take place somewhere else in the structure.

Horizontal cracks may be filled by simply pouring in a liquid epoxy sealer until it overflows, indicating that the crack has been filled.

Vertical cracks may be filled with a liquid epoxy sealer. First, the face of the crack is sealed with a fast-setting epoxy compound, which is allowed to cure thoroughly. Small holes are then drilled into the crack through the epoxy seal, and nipples are installed in these holes and bonded with the same fast-setting epoxy. Low-viscosity epoxy sealer is then injected into the lowest nipple. Pressure is maintained until liquid begins to seep out of the next higher nipple. These two nipples are then plugged and the same procedure is resumed with the third nipple. This operation is continued until the entire crack is filled. After the sealer has cured, the nipples may be cut off flush with the concrete surface.

TABLE 1-1 Latex and Epoxy Adhesives and Bonding Agents for Concrete

	Latices			Epoxies				
				Epoxy-polysulfide binder only	Binder with sand	Epoxy-polyamide		Epoxy-coal tar binder only
	Acrylic	Polyvinyl-acetate (nonre-emulsifiable)	Butadiene-styrene			Binder only	Binder with sand	
Appearance	Milky white	Milky white	Milky white	Light straw to amber	Light straw to amber	Light straw to amber	Light straw to amber	Black
Solids content, %	45	55	48	100	100	95 to 100	95 to 100	100
Reference specifications	MIL-B-19235	MIL-B-19235	MIL-B-19235	MMM B-350A; AASHTO M-200	MMM G-650A; AASHTO M-200	AASHTO M-200	AASHTO M-200	AASHTO M-200
Chemical resistance								
Acids	Fair	Fair	Fair	Excellent	Excellent	Excellent	Excellent	Excellent
Alkalis	Very good	Very good	Very good	Excellent	Excellent	Excellent	Excellent	Excellent
Salts	Very good	Very good	Very good	Excellent	Excellent	Excellent	Excellent	Excellent
Solvents	Fair to good	Fair to good	Fair to good	Excellent	Excellent	Excellent	Excellent	Excellent
Compressive strength, lb/in² (2-in cubes; ASTM C 109)	3200 to 4100	3400 to 3600	3300 to 4000	8000 to 10,000	12,000 to 15,000	6000 8000	10,000 to 13,000	3000 to 4000
Tensile strength, lb/in² (1-in briquettes; ASTM C 190)	580 to 615	340 to 450	450 to 580	—	—	—	—	—
Tensile strength, lb/in² (ASTM D 638)	—	—	—	3000 to 3500	—	—	3500 to 4000	400 to 800
Tensile elongation, % (ASTM D 368)	—	—	—	2.5 to 15	—	6 to 25	—	35 to 40
Flexural strength, lb/in² (bar; ASTM C 348)	950 to 1400	1000 to 1250	1250 to 1650	—	—	—	—	—
Compressive double-shear strength, lb/in² (MMM G-650A)	—	—	—	900 to 1000	700 to 1000	400 to 500	500 to 650	300 to 400
Application notes	Suitable for indoor and outdoor exposure on concrete, steel, wood, thin section toppings; shotcrete, plaster bond within 45 to 60 min; not suitable for extreme chemical exposure — Not for use with air entrainers	Not for conditions of high hydrostatic head — Can be used with accelerators, retarders, and water-reducing agents, but not with air entrainers	Not for constant water immersion — Not for use with air entrainers or accelerators	Suitable for filling cracks in concrete to bond both sides of crack into an integral member; preparation of epoxy mortars by adding sand — For maximum chemical and physical properties; highest cost; not for use on surfaces treated with rubber or resin-curing membranes, dirty surfaces, weak concrete, or bituminous surfaces	Suitable for bonding hardened concrete and other materials to hardened concrete; setting dowels; bonding plastic concrete to hardened concrete; bonding skid-resistant materials to hardened concrete	Suitable for filling cracks in concrete to bond both sides of crack into an integral member; preparation of epoxy mortars by adding sand — For maximum chemical and physical properties; not for use on surfaces treated with rubber or resin-curing membranes, dirty surfaces, weak concrete, or bituminous surfaces	Suitable for bonding hardened concrete and other materials to hardened concrete; setting dowels; bonding plastic concrete to hardened concrete; bonding skid-resistant materials to hardened concrete	Suitable for preparation of epoxy mortars by adding sand; bonding skid-resistant materials to hardened concrete; membrane between asphalt and concrete — For resistance to grease, oil, gasoline, and traffic; use on bituminous concrete; lower cost applications of nonskid membranes; not to be used for bonding new wet concrete to old or where black color will be undesirable

The tensile strength of a cracked concrete member may also be restored by stitching. U-shaped iron rods known as *stitching dogs* are inserted in drilled holes to transfer stress across the crack. Holes are drilled on both sides of a structural crack, far enough away not to cause additional breaks but not in parallel position, which would produce a plane of weakness. The legs of the stitching dogs are designed to be long enough to provide adequate pull strength. After the legs of the stitching dogs are inserted into the holes, the holes may be grouted with a nonshrinking grout. The crack itself should be sealed with an elastomeric or an epoxy sealer to prevent water from entering.

The elastomeric sealants should be based on polysulfide or urethane rubbers (preferably a two-component formulation in traffic grade) and comply with Federal Specification TT-S-00227E. The epoxy sealers may be epoxy-polysulfides (complying with Corps of Engineers Specification MMM B-350A) or epoxy-polyamides (complying with Specification M-200-65 of the American Association of State Highway and Transportation Officials). The epoxy compounds are described in Table 1-1.

In crack repair, certain procedures are detrimental to the successful repair of the crack:

- Filling cracks with new mortar will result in further cracking.
- Placing a topping over a crack to seal it, unless the topping is elastomeric, will inevitably result in the crack passing through the topping itself.
- Repairing a crack without relieving the restraints that caused it will cause cracking elsewhere.
- Repairing a crack with exposed reinforcing that has begun to corrode should not be done until the steel has been cleaned and protected with a rust-inhibitive paint.
- Burying a joint that has been repaired prevents frequent inspection to determine whether further failure has occurred.

Repairing Surfaces of Pavement and Slabs

A spalled concrete surface is the beginning of continued disintegration of the concrete. If the cost of replacement is at all comparable with the cost of repair, replacement is recommended. Replacement is also recommended when changing the level of the final surface is impractical. Otherwise, the concrete can be resurfaced with new concrete, epoxy topping, latex mortar, or iron topping.

Resurface with New Concrete.   When there is no problem in changing the level of the surface, it may be resurfaced with new concrete. It is always recommended that new concrete be laid with a bonding agent. The old surface should be prepared by removing all loose material and contaminants.

A simple bonding can be made by scrubbing a neat cement slurry (a mixture of straight portland cement and water) into the surface. The new concrete may then be placed with the expectation of a good bond.

Concrete placement should follow recommended practice. The concrete mix should have a water/cement ratio of 0.50 or less and a slump of 3 to 4 in (8 to 10 cm). It is also recommended that reinforcement be embedded in the middle of the topping slab, rather than allowed to lie at the bottom of the slab.

Finishing procedures will depend on the required surface: use a wood float finish for a regular surface and steel troweling for a hard, smooth, sealed finish. The slab should be cured by covering it with sheet materials or liquid-curing membranes. Concrete overlays of this type should be at least 2½- to 3-in (6.5- to 8-cm) thick.

A more positive bond may be achieved by using an epoxy bonding agent, either a filled epoxy-polysulfide or an epoxy-polyamide bonding agent (see Table 1-1). The epoxy bonding agent may be a proprietary formulation or one meeting the specification of a governmental agency. The bonding agent must be thoroughly mixed and applied by brush, broom, or spray. Do not apply more bonding agent than can be covered with new concrete while the bonding agent is still tacky. If the film of bonding agent has set, apply fresh epoxy adhesive before applying new concrete.

Shearing of the new concrete course from the base slab at the bond line is unlikely if the bonding-agent film is still tacky when the topping is placed. However, should a crack develop in the base slab, there is a definite possibility that this crack will transfer through the epoxy bonding-agent glue line and through the new wearing course.

New urethane bonding agents, which are often used between slab waterproofing membranes, can inhibit crack transfer from the base slab to the topping. The urethane membrane is also a two-component system that is applied in the same way as an epoxy bonding agent. Being elastomeric, the urethane membrane can absorb more of the stresses that are set up as the concrete overlay cures and contracts. It is also flexible enough to stretch and bridge cracks that develop in the substrate as well as in the wearing course, thereby preventing transfer of cracks.

A relatively inexpensive bonding agent that may be used to ensure a positive bond of a new concrete overlay is a latex-reinforced cement slurry grout. Portland cement and sand (in a ratio of 1:3 by volume) are combined with a gauging liquid that is a mixture of equal volumes of water and an acrylic or polyvinyl acetate latex emulsion, as described in the table. This emulsion must be nonre-emulsifiable. The gauging liquid, based on the latex blend, is added to the cement-sand powder until a creamy paste is developed. This paste is scrubbed into the surface of the base slab, covering the surface thoroughly. New concrete is then placed on this bond line, which is approximately $\frac{1}{16}$-in thick.

It is recommended that the latex slurry not be applied too far ahead of the placement of the concrete.

The latex bonding agent should not be used by itself because too much could be absorbed by a porous substrate, leaving a minimal thickness in the glue line. It may also dry too quickly to form an effective bond by the time new concrete is applied. It is best used in the form of a slurry grout.

Resurface with an Epoxy Topping. When the level of the surface must be kept close to the original elevation and a chemically resistant and tougher wearing surface must be provided, an epoxy topping may be the answer. After the base slab has been thoroughly cleaned by sandblasting, grinding, or acid etching, it is rinsed and allowed to dry. The epoxy mortar is supplied as a three-package proprietary system consisting of a base epoxy resin, a catalyst, and a measured quantity of dry, salt-free sand. The ingredients are mixed together to form a mortar which is applied to a thickness ranging from $\frac{1}{8}$ to $\frac{3}{8}$ in (3–10 mm), screeded, and troweled smooth. Most systems also include a primer, based on an epoxy system, to be applied before the epoxy mortar. There are many products available to complete this type of repair. Input from local vendors is recommended.

Resurface with a Latex Mortar. Although less resistant to chemicals than epoxies, latex mortar toppings also allow resurfacing without significantly changing surface elevation. The mortar may be made by blending 1 part (by volume) portland cement with 3 parts mason's sand. Latex is then added at the rate of 10 percent solids based on the cement content. Enough water is added to make a trowellable mixture. A typical formulation would be:

Portland cement (Type I)	1 bag [94 lb (43 kg)]
Mason's sand	3 bags [300 lb (135 kg)]
Latex emulsion (50 percent solids)	2 gal (11 liters)
Water	4–5 gal (15–19 liters)

Before the latex mortar is applied, a latex cement slurry should be applied as a bonding agent. The slurry may have the same latex as that used in the mortar topping. Latex mortar is best spread and leveled with a wood float rather than a steel trowel, because the latex tends to rise to the surface and cause a drag on the steel trowel.

After the latex mortar is finished, a sealer should be applied. The sealer, which functions as a curing membrane and protects the latex mortar against contamination from grease, oil, and deicing salts, may be based on a chlorinated rubber, a butadiene styrene rubber, or a methyl methacrylate resin. This type of sealer may be applied to all new concrete.

Resurface with an Iron Topping. Areas subject to very heavy traffic, particularly to steel-wheeled vehicles, require an extra-durable surface such as that produced by an iron topping. It is usually applied in thicknesses of 1 in (25 mm). Specially graded iron particles are substituted for a major percentage of the sand aggregate in a mortar or concrete mix. This topping may be bonded to a substrate, using a neat cement slurry, a latex cement slurry, or a urethane or epoxy bonding agent. This iron topping is usually available in a ready mixed form or can be blended at the jobsite following the recommendations of the supplier of the iron particles.

Repairing Disintegrated Concrete Members

Methods and materials for repairing columns, beams, piers, and precast concrete panels will generally be similar to those used in repairing concrete pavements. However, because such concrete members are either load bearing or an integral part of a structure, it is not always possible to remove and replace them. Therefore, repairs must be made to the existing structure using the best means available.

Before any repair or replacement of concrete sections is attempted, steel that is exposed by spalled or disintegrated concrete must be treated to prevent further corrosion, which may have been the initial cause of the disintegration. Rusty steel is best cleaned by sandblasting—a process that will also prepare the concrete surface by removing disintegrated and loose material. The steel should be treated with a rust-inhibitive chemical or coating, which may be a zinc-rich primer or another quality metal primer, and allowed to dry before new concrete is placed.

If the disintegration is deep, it may be necessary to use jackets or forms to hold the fresh concrete in place until it hardens. A bonding agent is recommended to ensure proper adhesion of the new concrete to the base substrate. A latex-cement slurry is the simplest and most economical bonding agent. However, for maximum adhesion, an epoxy bonding agent is recommended. This epoxy compound, painted on the reinforcing steel as well as on the surrounding concrete before placing the concrete, will also serve as a rust-inhibitive primer. A urethane bonding agent may not be suitable since this repair work is not on a deck over occupied areas requiring waterproofing properties.

Repair concrete should have a low water/cement ratio and a low slump. It should also be consolidated in the forms by direct vibration or by vibrating the form. After the concrete has been set for the minimum period of time, the forms may be removed and a liquid sealer may be applied. The sealer will continue to assist in the cure of the concrete and will protect the concrete against weathering.

If the disintegration is shallow, it may be possible to use a latex-fortified or an epoxy mortar to patch the area. The mixtures of latex and cement and sand described under "Repairing Surfaces of Pavement and Slabs" may be used. An epoxy mortar may also be used, but it may not blend readily with the surrounding concrete in color or appearance.

Proper preparation of the surface and proper priming are still necessary. If latex mortar is used, a sealer should be applied. It is not necessary to apply a sealer to an epoxy mortar since this compound is dense and resistant enough to require no additional protection.

Shotcrete or gunned mortar can be used on spalled areas by an experienced contractor who has the necessary equipment. The mortar or cement plaster is usually formulated to a 1:4.5 ratio of cement to sand, although richer 1:3 mixtures are often used. If, as in some cases, the shotcrete does not have the necessary adhesive qualities, a bonding agent (a latex-cement slurry or an epoxy compound) is used as a prime coat. Shotcrete applied in very thin layers may have to be reinforced with a latex emulsion admixture. When the necessary equipment can be obtained, this application can be made by plant maintenance people. Care should be taken in the application of shotcrete on vertical walls and ceilings. Equipment that produces vibration may cause the shotcrete to spall before it cures.

*MASONRY**

Masonry structures, like all plant structures, are susceptible to deterioration caused by natural weathering and deleterious effects of the industrial environment. Steps can be taken to modify the rate of attack when the basic principles involved in weathering deterioration are understood.

Brick Masonry Construction

Although bricks may be made of many materials, the term *brick masonry* is normally applied only to that type of construction employing comparatively small units of burned clay or shale. Ordinary brick is economical, and, when hard burned and laid in good mortar, it is one of the most durable construction materials available for buildings.

Clay is produced naturally by the weathering of rocks. Shale, produced in much the same way but with compression and perhaps heating, is denser than clay and more difficult to mine. Various brick colors and textures result from different chemical compositions and methods of firing.

Clay is ground, mixed with water, and molded into bricks by several methods: (1) stiff-mud process in which stiff, plastic clay is pushed through a die and cut into desired lengths, (2) soft-mud process in which clay is pressed into forms, and (3) dry process in which relatively dry clay is put into molds and compressed at pressures from 550 to 1500 lb/in^2.

After some drying, green bricks are fired in large kilns. The total firing process takes between 75 and 100 h. The brick must be gradually brought to the vitrification point (the temperature at which clays begin to fuse) and then must be gradually cooled.

Common brick, also known as hard or kiln-run, is made from ordinary clay or shale and is fired in the usual manner. Overburned bricks, called "clinkers," are unusually hard and durable.

A standard brick is 8-in long, 2¼-in deep, and 3¾- to 3⅞-in wide and weighs approximately 4½ lb. It should be rough enough to assure good bonding with mortar and should not absorb more than 10 to 15 percent of its weight in water during a 24-h soaking.

Types of Brick.   Common bricks are often classified according to their position in the kiln, as follows:

Arch and *clinker bricks* are close to the fire in the kiln and are overburned and extremely hard and durable. They are often irregular in shape and size.

Red, well-burned, and *straight-hard* are well-burned, hard, and durable bricks. Stretcher bricks come from these classifications and are selected for uniformity of hardness, size, and durability.

Rough-hard bricks are in the clinker class.

Soft and *salmon* bricks are farthest from the fire in the kiln and are underburned, soft, and less durable.

Special kinds of brick include the following:

Face brick is made from specially selected materials to control color, texture, hardness, uniformity, and strength. It is used in veneering and exterior tiers, chimneys, etc.

Pressed brick is made by the dry process and has regular smooth faces, sharp edges, and perfectly square corners. This type is generally used as face brick.

Glazed brick has the front surface glazed in white or other colors. It is used in dairies, hospitals, and other buildings where cleanliness and ease of cleaning are important.

Fire-brick is made from a special type of fire clay to resist high temperatures.

Imitation brick is usually made from portland cement and sand rather than from clay. It is not burned, but has qualities similar to good mortar.

---

* This material is adapted with permission from *Plant Engineering,* November 10, 1977, pp. 203–207.

Mortar. Mortar serves several functions in brick construction. It holds bricks together, compensates for brick irregularities, and distributes load or pressure among the units.

Properties of mortar depend, to a large extent, on the type and quantity of sand used. Good mortar is made from sharp, clean, and well-screened sand. When sand is too fine, the mortar has less "give" and water works out of it, making it stiff and difficult to trowel. It may also set before the bricks can be placed. Too much sand robs the mortar of its cohesive consistency and makes it difficult to work with.

Mortar may be classified into five general types, on the basis of composition: straight lime, straight cement, cement lime, masonry cement, or lime pozzolan.

Natural cement is an important constituent of masonry cement because of its gradual strength-gaining properties, high plasticity, excellent water retention, and good adherence to aggregates. Combining natural cement with portland cement, which has early-strength properties, provides a hydraulic cement ideally suited for masonry mortar. Cement-lime mortars are usually classified in accordance with the ratios of cement, lime, and sand, by volume, in Table 1-2.

Causes of Deterioration of Brick Masonry. Repeated natural destructive forces, mild though they may be, break down hard rock into clay. These same forces act on clay bricks, fired tile, and fired terra cotta to cause deterioration. Natural stones and the binding mortars of masonry construction are similarly affected. In addition, airborne chemicals in industrial atmospheres and pollutants from internal-combustion engines contribute greatly to rapid soiling and chemical destruction of these binding materials and masonry units.

Frost Damage. One of the more destructive agents of weathering is frost. Water expands 9 percent as it freezes. Under certain conditions, such expansion may produce stresses that disrupt the bricks and cause spalling.

To take up water, a brick must be porous. There are two measures of water absorption: one obtained after soaking the brick for 24 h in cold water and another, larger one obtained after boiling the brick for 5 h. The difference between the two values represents the so-called sealed pores (pores that are not accessible to water under normal conditions, such as wetting by rain). If all open pores are filled with water, the unfilled sealed pores provide space into which water can expand on freezing with little or no development of stress.

Efflorescence. Pitting and spalling of clay products and natural stones is associated with efflorescence, a phenomenon in which salts percolate through the member and crystallize on the surface of a brick, stone, or mortar joint. These salts may be the sulfates of calcium, magnesium, sodium, potassium, and, in some cases, iron. Soluble salts may be present in the clay, or they may be formed by the firing process (oxidation of pyrites, or reaction of sulfurous fuel gases with carbonates in the clay).

Other sources of soluble salts are portland cement and hydraulic lime mortars, which contain soluble sulfates and carbonates of sodium and potassium; mortar containing magnesium

TABLE 1-2 Cement Lime Mortars for Masonry Construction

Mortar	Use	Proportions* Portland cement	Hydrated lime	Damp, loose sand[†]	Minimum compressive strength, lb/in²	(k bar)
Type M	Maximum compressive strength	1	¼	2⅛–3¾	2500	17.3
Type S	Maximum bond	1	½	3⅜–4½	1800	12.4
Type N	General purpose	1	1	4½–5	750	51.8
Type O	Non-load-bearing interior construction	1	2	6¾–9	350	24.1

* Parts by volume.
[†] Sand quantity is 2¼ to 3 times combined volume of cement and lime.

lime, which can produce destructive magnesium sulfate; and gypsum plaster or dry wall. Salts may also be drawn by capillary action from the ground soil and limestone or concrete copings.

For efflorescence to occur, salts must be present, water must be available to take them into solution, and a drying surface on which evaporation can proceed to deposit crystals at the surface must exist. Water is always available and drying is periodic. The potential for efflorescence can be reduced by specifying well-fired brick that, generally, contains less soluble salts, or by specifying special-quality brick formulated with minimum soluble salts. The place where efflorescence appears is no indication of its source because solutions of salts may migrate considerable distances. Efflorescence on a particular surface merely indicates that it provided a convenient drying area. When a very dense impermeable mortar touches a more permeable brick, efflorescent salts will often appear on the brick, although the salts may have migrated from the mortar.

Glazed brick veneers do not always eliminate efflorescence. Although the glazing is impermeable to water entry from the exterior, moisture can still move slowly from the interior of the building toward the exterior face. Salts transferred to the exterior glazing create enough pressure to produce shaling of the glazed face. This phenomenon is common, especially when the brick has been inadequately fired. The result is unattractive, and the brick is exposed to further degradation.

Dimensional Changes.   Expansion or contraction of building units may not in itself be harmful. However, the continuation of differential movements of dissimilar materials may give rise to difficulties. Live-load changes and foundation settlement can cause whole buildings to move. Building joints must be properly designed and located to accommodate these movements. Lime-sand mortar, used in older structures, is able to accommodate large movements without distress. Modern, higher-strength cement mortars, on the other hand, are less flexible and may shrink excessively on setting to cause cracking.

The movement of moisture in porous building materials can cause expansion and contraction. Expansion generally takes place with wetting; shrinkage occurs with drying. Water taken up by new brick when it is laid in fresh mortar causes the unit to expand Meanwhile, the mortar is shrinking. Such action can be minimized by wetting kiln-fresh bricks before they are used, avoiding excessively rigid mortars, and providing adequate joints. Reinforced concrete frames may also lead to failure of brick cladding when there is vertical shrinkage of the frame and when no movement joints are provided.

Steel columns clad with brick, common in structures built two decades or more ago, also can cause brick failure. As water enters this cladding, through either the brick or the mortar, the steel column rusts. Expansion of the rust pushes the brick cladding away from the column.

Mortar Deterioration.   Mortar may decay from the formation of calcium sulfo-aluminate (which causes expansion and loss of mortar strength) and by the attack of pollutants in the atmosphere. Portland cement contains tricalcium aluminate, which reacts with sulfates in solution to form calcium sulfo-aluminate. Exhaust gases from automobiles contain sulfur dioxide, sulfur trioxide, and nitrous oxides. These oxides react with moisture in the atmosphere to form sulfurous acid, sulfuric acid, and nitric acid, which are the attacking agents. As attack continues over the years, the mortar joints may crack, the surface of the joint may spall off, and the mortar may become softer and more crumbly.

Sulfate-resistant cements used in mortar will inhibit this disintegration.

Repointing Mortar Joints

Repointing, or tuckpointing, is the process of removing deteriorated mortar from masonry joints and replacing it with new mortar to correct some perceptible problem, such as falling mortar, loose bricks, or damp walls. All contributing factors to the problem should be thoroughly investigated and corrected before repointing because the great amount of hand work and special materials required make repointing expensive and time consuming. Matching bricks may have to be obtained or specially made. Existing mortar may have to be analyzed before a repointing mortar can be formulated to match its color, texture, and physical properties.

It is a common error to assume that hardness or high strength is a measure of durability. A mortar that is stronger and harder than the masonry units will not "give," causing stress concentrations in the masonry units. These stresses are usually relieved by cracking and spalling. Mortar should contain as much sand as possible (consistent with workability) to help reduce shrinkage while drying. It should have good cohesive and adhesive qualities, be easy to handle on the pointing tool, and have good water retention (to resist rapid loss of water through absorption by the brick). It should not be sticky.

There is some controversy as to whether high-lime mortar is preferable to portland cement mortar for tuck pointing. High-lime mortar is suggested for use on old buildings because it is soft and porous, has low volume change, and is slightly soluble in water.

A slight amount of high-lime mortar will dissolve in rain and precipitate in small cracks; during drying, these small cracks and voids will seal. A small amount of white portland cement will accelerate setting of this normally slow-setting mortar. Even if the building was originally constructed with cement mortar, high-lime mortar may be recommended to reduce shrinkage and potential stresses at the edges of the masonry.

Mortar Mixes. The mixes outlined in Table 1-3 provide a starting point for developing a visually and physically acceptable mortar.

TABLE 1-3 Trial Mortar Mixes for Repointing Masonry

Mortar	Portland cement	Hydrated lime	Sand	Acrylic latex (50% solids)
Formula A	¼ bag	1 bag	3 ft³	—
Formula B	1 bag	1–1½ bags	5–6½ ft³	—
Formula C	1 bag	—	3 ft³	2 gal

Sometimes, small amounts (5 to 10 percent) of finely divided iron are added to the repointing mixes to provide slight expansion rather than normal shrinkage. Too much iron may produce excessive expansion and may cause iron-rust stain. Repointing mortars can be further modified by adding (1) water-reducing agents to keep water content or water-cement ratio low, (2) waterproofing admixtures such as stearate soaps to minimize the absorption of water, (3) air-entraining agents to increase resistance to freeze-thaw weathering in areas of extreme exposure, and (4) mineral oxide colors to blend the mortar color with the brick.

Requirements for Mortar Materials. Materials used in preparing pointing mortars should comply with the following specifications and requirements:

Lime "Standard Specification for Hydrated Lime for Masonry Purposes (ASTM C 207)," Type S; Federal Specification SS-L-351B.

Cement. "Standard Specification for Portland Cement (ASTM C 150)," Type I or II; Federal Specification SS-C-192G(3). The cement should not have more than 0.60 percent alkali (sodium oxide), or not more than 0.15 percent water-soluble alkali by weight.

Sand. "Standard Specification for Aggregate for Masonry Mortar (ASTM C 144)," Federal Specification SS-A-281B(1), paragraph 3.1.

Water. Potable water free from acids, alkalis, and organic materials.

Execution of the Work. Generally, old mortar should be cut out to a depth of ¾ to 1 in (2–2.5 cm) to ensure an adequate bond between old and new mortar and to prevent popouts. For joints that are less than ⅜-in (1-cm) wide, cutting back ½ in (1.3 cm) is usually sufficient. Using power tools is risky, unless they are handled by a skilled mason, because bricks can be easily damaged by such equipment. The use of hand chisels is still the best procedure.

Dry mortar ingredients should be mixed first. They should be prehydrated with only enough water to make a damp, stiff mortar to help prevent drying shrinkage. After an hour or two, the mortar is mixed with additional water to provide trowelability.

The joints should be thoroughly cleaned and moistened before the mortar is placed. A chemical bonding agent may be used; however, care must be exercised in painting it into the joint so that it is not smeared on the brick face. Mortar must not be placed before the bonding agent has set.

The mortar is best placed in ¼-in (6-mm) layers and then packed until the void is filled. When the final layer of mortar is thumbprint hard, the joint should be tooled to the desired shape with the correct size of pointing tool. If old bricks have worn, rounded corners, the final mortar surface should be slightly recessed to avoid leaving uneven joints that may be damaged easily.

The small amount of excess mortar left on the wall from a careful repointing job can be removed with a bristle brush before it hardens. Hardened mortar can be removed with a wooden paddle or chisel. Care should be exercised in using any chemicals, especially acids.

Grouting techniques can be used to repoint joints that show only minor defects such as very shallow deterioration, hairline cracks, or slight loss of adhesion to the brick. One method, often referred to as a bagging operation, can be used on glazed brick. A grouting mortar such as formula C in Table 1-3 is mixed to the consistency of a creamy paste and brushed onto the wall surface. After a short period (15 to 30 min, depending on temperature and degree of set) burlap bags or rags are used to bag or wipe the grout from the surface of the nonabsorptive glazed brick; grout is left only in the mortar joint. After an entire section is done, the area may be washed to remove any grout remaining on the glazed brick faces.

Another method involves the same bagging or grouting operation, but it may be done on unglazed or any standard face brick. This method involves masking each brick with tape cut to the same dimensions as the brick. The same type of latex grout is applied by brush over a wider area. The masking tape is removed after the grout sets, leaving neat, clean, and sharp mortar joints. This method is commonly called mask and grout.

Some mortar joints, especially very narrow ones, may be sealed with an elastomeric sealant applied by a caulking gun. Cracked bricks may also be repaired by widening the crack and sealing it with an elastomeric sealant.

Cleaning Plant Buildings

There are a number of valid reasons for cleaning building exteriors. Before building units are repaired or replaced, the original colors and textures of these units must be known so they can be properly matched. And, when new materials are installed, uniform appearance and weathering of the entire structure are desirable.

Preventive maintenance is an often-overlooked reason for cleaning. Dirt provides a much greater surface area than clean building materials; and, the more surface area that is exposed to atmospheric pollutants, the greater are the possibilities for destructive chemical reactions to be started. Dirty areas remain wet longer, resulting in more severe freeze-thaw cycling. And wet, dirty areas can support microorganisms that can cause disintegration, dissolution, and staining.

Selecting an appropriate cleaning method can be challenging, because dirt composition is so complex. Dirt is a surface deposit of finely divided solids held together by various organic materials. The solids are primarily carbon soot, siliceous dust, and inorganic sulfates. The organic binders consist largely of hydrocarbons from incomplete combustion products of various fuels. A combination of adsorption and electrostatic attractive forces hold the dirt to the masonry. Other adherent factors include efflorescent salts, leached cementitious materials, and recrystalized carbonates.

Acidic cleaners can be very damaging, particularly to marble and limestone, and alkaline cleaners can also be harmful. It is recommended that cleaners be tested on small areas to determine their effectiveness and reaction to the substrates.

One of the most versatile techniques for cleaning building exteriors is water washing. Although it requires minimal expenditure for materials and equipment, it can be time consuming, particularly if hand scrubbing is involved. There are three types of water-washing procedures: low pressure, high pressure, and steam cleaning.

The low-pressure wash is carried out over an extended period. The prolonged spraying loosens heavy dirt deposits; then, moderate pressure [200 to 600 lb/in² (1380 to 4140 bars)] can be used to flush away loosened dirt.

High-pressure water cleaning involves equipment capable of supplying water to a special high-pressure gun that jets the water at pressures of 1000 to 1800 lb/in² [6.9 to 12.4 kb]. The gun can deliver up to 1700 gal of water per hour. A special nozzle can aerate the water, thereby minimizing physical damage to the masonry.

Steam cleaning involves the use of low-pressure (10 to 30 lb/in² [6.90 to 2100 kb]), large-diameter (½ in [12 mm]) nozzles; steam is generated from a flash boiler. The equipment is relatively more expensive and presents some safety hazards to the operators. It is also possible to add detergents or surfactants to the water in the flash boiler. Adequate dirt removal requires an average working time of 1 min/ft² (9 min/m²).

Chemical cleaners can be acidic (low pH) or alkaline (high pH). Both types are used with surfactants (1 to 2 percent) to promote detergency and wetting. Acidic cleaners are often based on hydrofluoric acid or phosphoric acid in concentrations of less than 5 percent in water. Alkaline cleaners are often based on sodium hydroxide, ammonium hydroxide, or ammonia. Sometimes, all purpose cleaners, such as ammonium bifluoride, are used.

Abrasive blasting, both dry and wet processes, are effective on all substrates, but they require experienced mechanics to minimize damage to surfaces. Pressures used are usually between 20 and 110 lb/in² (140 and 760 bars), and working distances are from 3 to 12 in (7.6 to 30 cm). The abrasives are usually silica sand, but crushed slags and coal wastes are often used. The mesh sizes are very fine, either 0 or 00. Round particles are less abrasive and damaging than crushed grains.

Cleaning may precede or follow replacement of masonry units and repointing, depending on conditions. Cleaning before repair helps reveal original colors and textures and prepares substrates for receiving new mortars and bonding agents. Cleaning after repairs helps remove any excess droppings, splashings, or other accidental contamination. Whether done before or after, cleaning is a very important aspect of masonry and concrete restoration.

Sealing the Surface

A final step in the entire restoration process involves sealing all porous surfaces on the exterior facade. This procedure waterproofs the masonry to minimize the ingress of water, protects against attack by pollutants and other chemicals, minimizes the collection of dirt, and protects against graffiti damage.

One of the best sealers is a methyl methacrylate in organic solvent, containing 15 to 20 percent solids and, preferably, having a matte finish. The sealer may be applied in one or two coats, depending on the porosity of the substrate, by brush, spray, or roller. The sealer is water white, will not yellow or embrittle, and may be effective for 5 to 10 years or longer.

Silicone compounds are not particularly recommended, primarily because they are effective only for relatively short periods and are water-repellent rather than waterproofing.

METALS

Principles of Corrosion Control

When people first began mining ores and reducing iron from its natural state, they reversed a fundamental process of nature. This process is the breakdown and blending of all unnatural materials into a neutral state. Iron is not natural or stable in its refined state and, as occurs with many materials, it tends to return to its natural state. The primary destructive forces that try to return steel, iron, and other materials to their natural states are known collectively as corrosion.

Corrosion damage is responsible for a greater loss in material and economic investment than any other factor in our modern society. Billions of dollars are spent annually replacing or repairing plant equipment and structures damaged by corrosion. Although minor maintenance of equipment and structures will always be necessary, material and economic losses can be minimized by reducing corrosion activity. Some of the methods that may be used to reduce corrosion include materials selection, proper design, coatings, corrosion monitoring, chemical treatment, and cathodic protection.

Corrosion deterioration can have a serious impact on a variety of facilities and equipment. The types of facilities and structures may include industrial plants, water and wastewater plants, pipelines, tanks, and the like. Hazards due to leakage, such as chemical spills, may occur. Volatile liquids such as fuel are more likely to ignite and explode when leaks have developed in the storage facility. Corrosion damage may also cause system downtime for facilities such as water-treatment plants, liquid-storage tanks, pipelines, metal-cased water wells, bridges, drydock structures, and many others. Funds allocated for capital improvements or new equipment may have to be diverted to rebuild existing structures and utilities damaged by corrosion.

Department of Transportation (DOT) regulations prescribe minimum requirements for the protection of metallic pipelines from internal, external, and atmospheric corrosion. These regulations are divided into the following three parts:

1. New construction
2. Existing pipelines and tanks
3. Monitoring of corrosion control and record keeping

These regulations and the need to ensure continued operation of facilities, structures, and pipelines make it necessary to establish a continuing corrosion-control program. Corrosion control can be accomplished by selection of appropriate materials, design practices, coatings, and proactive corrosion-control systems, such as cathodic protection. The program must be planned and budgeted to meet the requirements for new and existing construction and to establish continual monitoring of corrosion protection with the requisite records.

Even though the bulk of facilities and structures that are part of the U.S. infrastructure are currently not governed by DOT regulations, consideration of corrosion and corrosion-control measures should be incorporated into all facilities and structures during the planning, design, construction, and postconstruction phases. By taking this level of care in the planning and implementation of projects, regardless of their specific purpose or location, the long-term cost of the project will be greatly reduced. For example, a pipeline or plant facility that is well planned and has a corrosion control system that is maintained can last well over 50 years without any major leaks, material failures, or need for repair. Whereas, without corrosion-control measures, the pipeline or plant facility may only last 7 to 10 years before it must be repaired or replaced.

Corrosion protection systems should not be forgotten or ignored after they are installed. A comprehensive maintenance policy should be implemented to ensure that proper operation of the system is preserved. The policy should include regular testing, inspection, and record keeping.

In summary, the following key features should be incorporated into any project involving a facility or structure:

1. Planning to eliminate potential corrosion cells
2. Designing to eliminate corrosion cells which may include:
   a. Modifying the environment to eliminate the potential corrosion cell
   b. Selecting materials that are inert or corrosion resistant for the planned service

  c. Coating the structure or facility with a suitable coating system
  d. Providing a cathodic protection system for metal-based facilities or structures
  e. Providing a plan to operate and maintain the corrosion system after construction

Causes of Corrosion

Corrosion is defined as the deterioration of a material by chemical or electrochemical action as a result of a reaction with the environment into which it is placed. Chemical attack of a metal is the simple dissolution of a metal as it reacts to a particular chemical. Electrochemical attack requires four components, an electrolyte, an anode, a cathode, and a metallic connection between the anode and cathode (see Fig. 1-1).

One of the most important factors is the rate of corrosion. In certain cases the rate of corrosion is not critical to the operation of a facility and in other cases it can be a very critical factor. The factors that tend to accelerate corrosion rates are:

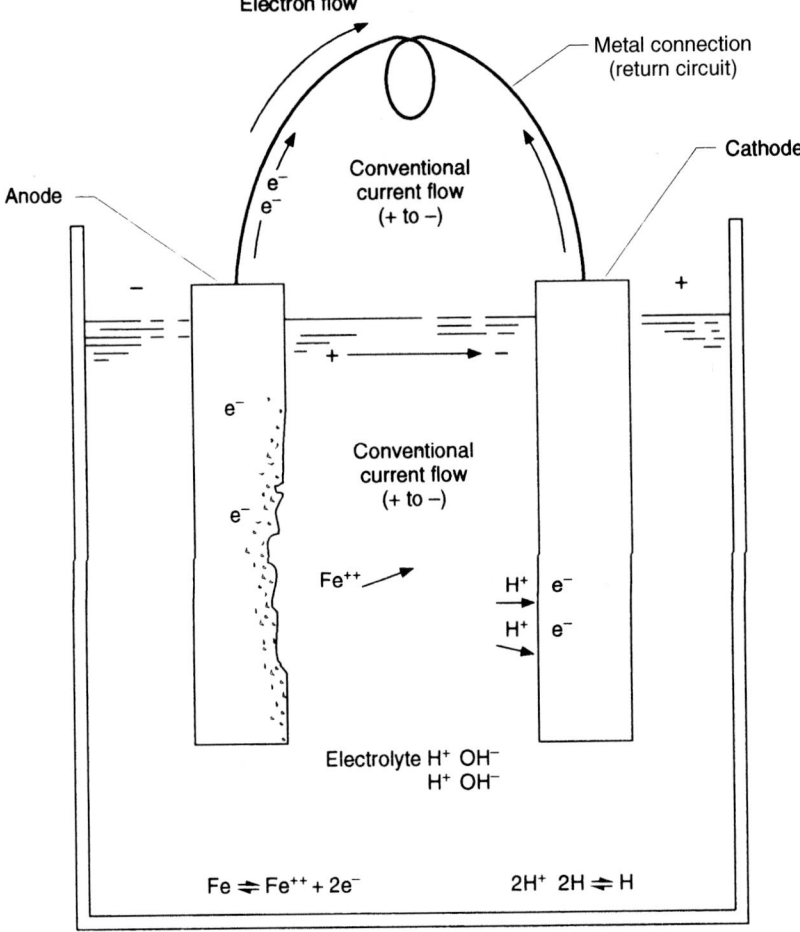

FIGURE 1-1 Four essential elements of the basic corrosion cell are electrolyte, anode, cathode, and return circuit.

1. Temperature
2. Low or high pH of environment
3. High mechanical stress
4. Soils high in concentrations of aggressive chemicals
5. Metallic connections between dissimilar metals
6. Small anodic (corroding) areas in contact with large cathodic (protected) areas

The deterioration of metals, commonly referred to as corrosion, is a critical factor affecting the useful life of metals in facilities. Most importantly, the rate of corrosion affects how long a particular metal component will function in its intended use. Some metals corrode at a very slow rate, which makes them good candidates for certain applications. For example, aluminum has been found to be an excellent material for hatch covers in atmospheric exposures. On the other hand, the use of 304 stainless steel for pipe hangers in piers over salt water has resulted in failures within a year. The application, the environment, and the intended service are critical to proper material selection.

Atmospheric Exposure

Facilities and structures exposed to the atmosphere are subject to corrosion primarily from the chemical contaminants of the local atmosphere. For example, a galvanized metal roof will last 30 to 50 years in a rural environment but only 5 to 10 years in a heavily polluted, industrial environment. If structures and facilities are near the ocean, the impact of corrosion due primarily to the chlorides in the atmosphere will be significant if no protective measures are taken. For atmospheric corrosion to occur there must be a metallic substrate, moisture, and a chemical agent.

Submerged Exposure

Facilities and structures exposed to immersion in service are subject to corrosion due to exposure to a liquid (electrolyte). The most common example of this type of corrosion cell is an anchor bolt attached to the wall of a concrete tank which is holding water or some other electrolyte. The anchor bolts are usually tied to the reinforcing steel in the concrete wall of the tank. In this situation all of the conditions for a corrosion cell exist as well as several factors that affect the rate of corrosion. They are:

1. The anchor bolt is a small anode tied to a very large cathode (all of the reinforcing steel in the tank walls).
2. The anchor bolt is usually under stress.
3. There is a metallic path between the anodic and cathodic sites.
4. There is a large potential difference between the anchor bolt and the reinforcing steel in the tank.
5. There is an electrolyte present to facilitate the corrosion process.

In summary, for submerged exposures, most metals require some form of protection from corrosion. The key factors that affect the corrosion rate in this type of exposure are:

- The properties of the electrolyte (for example, seawater is more corrosive than fresh water)
- The type of immersed material (for example, monel is more resistant than mild steel when immersed in water)

Corrosion control measures for immersion-type applications include:

- Material selection
- Coating systems
- Cathodic protection

Buried Exposure

In the case of buried exposure, facilities and structures are subject to corrosion primarily due to the interaction between the facility or structure and the soil environment. The properties of the soil are therefore very important when planning a pipeline or other buried facility or structure. Based on the experience of corrosion engineers, it appears that soil resistivity is the one soil property that is the best indicator of corrosion potential for buried metal-based structures and facilities. The lower the soil resistivity, the greater is the tendency for corrosion. Another key factor in buried exposure is the amount of chloride present in the soil. Levels of 500 ppm or more in a soil will cause corrosion of metal-based systems.

The presence of ground water and the properties of that ground water will greatly affect the corrosivity of a soil. The more brackish the ground water the more corrosive it will be to metal-based systems.

The various corrosion-control measures listed previously cannot all be used in buried exposures. From a practical point of view there is not much that can be done to modify the environment to make it less corrosive, and material selection options are often limited by engineering requirements. Although clean, uniform, well-draining backfill materials will reduce corrosion activity, chemicals present in the soil will tend to leach into the backfill due to movement of water through the soil.

Other types of corrosion cells can be caused by manmade conditions. Three manmade corrosion cells—dissimilar metals, damaged coating, and stray current—are illustrated in Fig. 1-2.

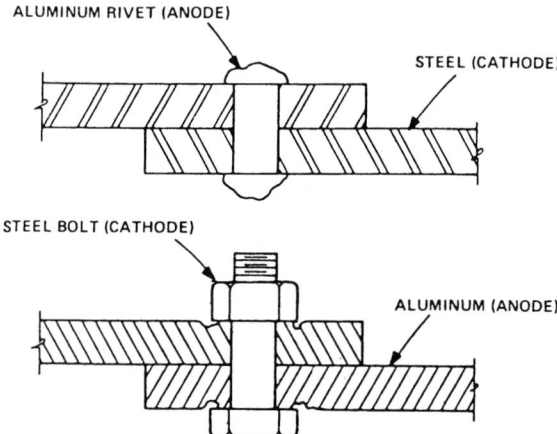

FIGURE 1-2 In a galvanic couple of aluminum and steel, anodic aluminum corrodes while cathodic steel is relatively unaffected. It is important that fasteners be compatible with building materials.

When two dissimilar metals are connected together and buried or submerged, an electrolytic corrosion reaction will occur. This is due to the difference in electrical potential between the two metals. This difference in potential produces a driving force, causing corrosion activity on the least noble of the metals.

Galvanic series of metals and alloys in seawater are listed in Fig. 1-3. These values are typical values which are observed in the field.

If an anode and a cathode are placed in a jar containing a salt or acid electrolyte, and connected together by a piece of copper wire as shown in Fig. 1-1, an electric current will flow through the wire. Except for differences in the details and materials of construction, this cell is the same as a flashlight battery.

The current through the metal connection flows from the cathode to the anode. The current flows from the anode into the electrolyte. This current flows through the electrolyte and is picked up at the cathode. The electrical circuit is then completed by current flow through the metallic connection between the anode and the cathode.

If the cell is permitted to operate long enough, the anode will deteriorate, but the cathode will not. This is because anode ions are going into solution in the electrolyte, forming an oxide or similar compounds. This process releases hydrogen ions from the solution which migrate to the cathode and deposit electrons on it. If the anode were steel with a copper cathode, the steel would corrode and provide protection to the copper. This is the basic mechanism of a corrosion cell.

Material Selection

In selecting materials for use at a plant or other facility, two main factors must be considered. The materials must perform the desired function in a safe and economical manner and operate satisfactorily over the design life of the facility. As corrosion-caused deterioration of materials is a likely mode of failure for buried or submerged components, it is important to select materials able to withstand the environment in which they will function. The following discussion will focus on the implications of corrosion on material selection for a variety of environments.

Corrosion of metals can occur in a number of situations. Corrosion activity may be initiated at internal or external structure surfaces. External surfaces may be buried, submerged, exposed to the atmosphere, or some combination of the above. Corrosion of internal surfaces may be due to the environment created by storage or flow of process streams.

Another corrosion mechanism, galvanic corrosion, is possible when two dissimilar metals such as copper and steel are connected together, whether buried or submerged. An electrolytic corrosion reaction will occur due to the difference in electrical potential between the two metals in contact with each other. This difference in potential produces a driving force, causing corrosion activity on the less noble of the two metals. Such galvanic couples must be avoided or isolated so that the possibility of corrosion damage is minimized.

As discussed previously, some soil environments and ground waters can be corrosive to buried metal structures. Resistivity measurements, which can be made both in the field and in the laboratory, indicate how corrosion currents will flow through soils or ground waters. High concentrations of chlorides and sulfates contribute to a reduction in resistivity and an increase in the corrosion activity of a material. In the presence of oxygen, chloride ions can be extremely corrosive to steel. Similarly, high levels of sulfates can cause a reduction in soil or groundwater resistivity and corrosion of steel and concrete.

Surfaces exposed to fluids include the interiors of pipelines, tanks and other basins. For example, metals in contact with wastewater streams are subject to corrosion, particularly when exposed in splash zones and where the surface is subject to exposure to hydrogen sulfide and its by-products.

Atmospheric exposures can include a variety of pollutants as well as airborne salts and locations in which structures may be exposed to direct salt spray. Atmospheric exposure may, therefore, be severe. The combination of wet/dry cycling in the presence of chlorides found in salt spray creates the potential for significant corrosion activity on all exposed metal surfaces. In addition to marine exposures, plant processes and sanitary sewers are likely to generate airborne substances such as hydrogen sulfide which also is deleterious to metallic and concrete structures.

The following describes the performance that can be expected from various materials.

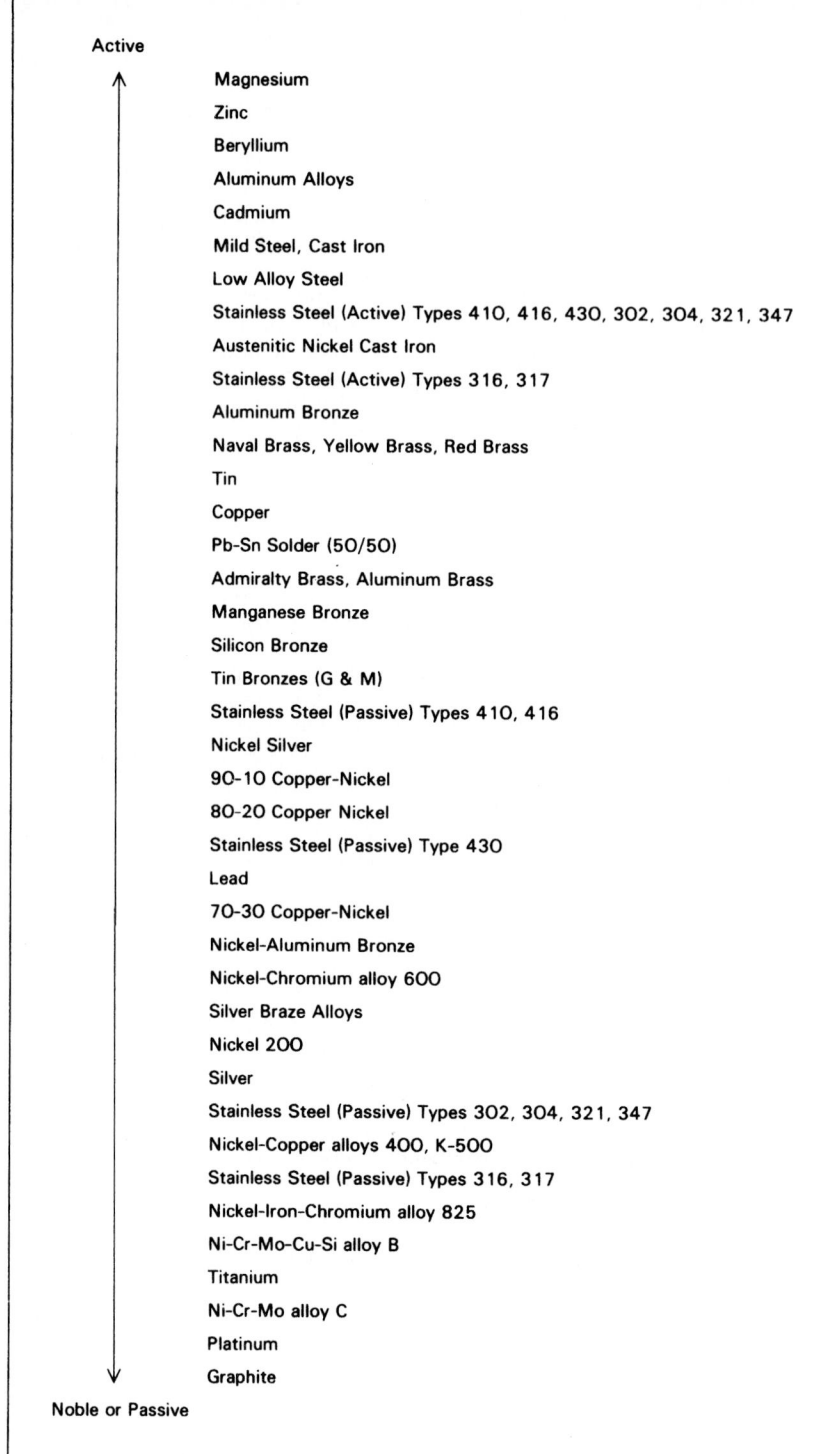

FIGURE 1-3 Galvanic series of metals and alloys in seawater. Metals and alloys are listed in the order of their corrosion potential in seawater. When two metals are coupled, those close together in the list are less susceptible to galvanic corrosion than those widely separated in list.

Steel

Coatings must be considered for all applications of steel. Cathodic protection should be considered for steel pipe where soil or groundwater resistivity is less than 10,000 ohm-cm, and where steel will be in contact with process streams. Cathodic protection of steel is strongly recommended where resistivity is less than 5000 ohm-cm. For all exposures, steel should be electrically isolated from dissimilar metals to prevent the formation of unfavorable galvanic corrosion cells. In areas where abrasive materials are likely to damage coatings, cathodic protection by impressed current or galvanic anodes may be desirable.

Low resistivities and high chloride concentrations in the soil may lead to corrosion of buried steel pipelines or structures. Cathodic protection should be considered for all buried steel pipelines or structures. Where cathodic protection is not provided, corrosion monitoring equipment should be incorporated into the design to allow the operating staff to monitor the condition of the pipelines or structures. Nonwelded joints should be bonded for electrical continuity. In addition, coatings should also be considered. Coatings may be used alone or in conjunction with cathodic protection. Recommendations for coating systems are discussed later.

Bare or galvanized steel is subject to corrosion when exposed to aggressive fluids. Corrosion is most severe in the splash zone where readily available oxygen hastens the corrosion process. Submerged steel should be coated with a material suitable for use in the anticipated exposure. Where there are concerns regarding the corrosion of steel in contact with process streams, cathodic protection should be provided for steel structures considered to be in a corrosive exposure. This type of corrosion control should be incorporated along with suitable coatings.

Corrosion of steel structures at facilities generally occurs as a result of exposure to atmospheric chlorides (near marine environments), chlorine process streams, hydrogen sulfide, or other air pollutants. Steel structures of particular concern should be coated. Even in those areas where temperatures are maintained above the dew point and sulfide concentrations are expected to be relatively low, steel should receive a protective coating.

Hydrogen sulfide attacks steel rapidly and it can be assumed that bare or galvanized steel will not endure in outdoor ambient conditions where hydrogen sulfide is present. The use of galvanized or bare steel should therefore be limited. Steel structural materials or piping exposed to the atmosphere should be coated with suitable coatings, as discussed in Chap. 18-2, for nearly all exposures.

Aluminum

Aluminum is suitable for atmospheric exposure. It may not be used in direct contact with concrete; there must be physical isolation, generally by coating the aluminum or placing it in PVC cast in the concrete.

Aluminum is not recommended for use when in contact with soil or process streams with high or low pH. In very broad terms, dry, sandy, and well-aerated soils are not corrosive to aluminum. However, as moisture and dissolved salts increase, the soil becomes more aggressive to aluminum. Where levels of chlorides, sulfates, or pH are high, contact with the soil may be detrimental to buried aluminum. Its use, therefore, is not generally recommended for underground applications.

Aluminum has excellent resistance to atmospheric sulfides and other pollutants. Its resistance to atmospheric corrosion is due to a tightly adherent oxide film, and destruction of this film by either mechanical or chemical means exposes a very reactive surface. If the protective oxide film is disturbed, the presence of salts, including chlorides, can cause rapid pitting of aluminum. Further, electrical coupling to iron, stainless steel, or copper will accelerate this deterioration.

Because aluminum is an electrically active metal (standard potential of −1.66 v versus standard hydrogen electrode), its use in water is limited. If coupled to any of the common engineering alloys (steel, iron, stainless steel, and copper and its alloys), aluminum will become the anode and galvanically corrode. For this reason, aluminum must be electrically isolated from dissimilar materials.

Severe pitting of aluminum can occur where iron or copper ions are in a solution in contact with aluminum, creating a galvanic couple in which aluminum is attacked at localized areas. Chloride ions can also lead to pitting in aluminum. This is most likely to occur in crevices and where stagnant water collects. The introduction of chemicals like ferric chloride or chlorine into process streams would cause severe degradation to aluminum, leading to rapid failure.

When exposed to fluids, aluminum is stable only in a small band of pH values from 4 to 8.5. Because it is an amphoteric material, it is attacked by both acids and bases. Contact with solutions with pH greater than 8.5 or less than 4 will cause corrosion of the aluminum. For example, aluminum handrails to be installed in concrete (pH 12 to 13) should be placed in plastic shields cast into the concrete, and a sealant should be placed between the plastic shield and the aluminum. Under these conditions, aluminum will provide acceptable performance.

Alloys typically used include 5052 and 6061, but expect that most alloys will show similar atmospheric corrosion characteristics. The aluminum-copper precipitation hardening grades (2000 series) would generally show somewhat greater corrosion, and the pure aluminum and al-clad varieties (1000 series) would exhibit somewhat less corrosion. Aluminum is not recommended in areas where spillage of chlorine, sodium hydroxide, or other strong acids or bases may occur. Anodized aluminum has shown excellent performance in certain applications. Although it would most likely be dinged and abraded in uses like handrails, anodized aluminum can be used in a number of other areas, such as electrical switchgear enclosures.

Copper and Brass

Consideration must be given to coating and cathodic protection of copper and brass used in contact with soil. Care must be taken to prevent direct electrical connection of piping operated at different temperatures. Copper and brass must not be used in contact with process streams containing chlorine in excess of 2 ppm or in environments with pH less than 5.5.

Copper and brass typically perform quite well in underground applications where the pH is neutral to alkaline and the concentration of aggressive ions, such as chlorides and sulfates, is low. They are often used for potable water lines and fittings. Copper is a corrosion-resistant material that is not dependent on the formation of an oxide or other surface film to be protected from corrosion. Because it is cathodic to iron and aluminum, it will hasten their corrosion when coupled to them. Isolation of copper from most materials commonly used in plant construction is therefore required in buried service. Because copper is an excellent electrical conductor, and maintains a low resistivity interface with the soil, bare copper cable is often used for grounding systems. Unfortunately, this can lead to galvanic corrosion of steel and iron, as described previously, and also to very high current requirements for cathodic protection systems. Various solutions have been proposed, such as grounding cells, which are essentially dielectric until large potential differences (ground faults) occur. When ground faults do occur, the cell short circuits and dissipates the charge.

Copper is subject to changes in corrosion resistance with changes in temperature, so electrolytic corrosion can occur in hot and cold water lines buried in a common trench. To prevent this, the two lines should be isolated from each other at points of electrical contact. This can be accomplished with the use of insulating-type couplings. However, where high concentrations of chlorides (300 ppm or more) and sulfates (1000 ppm or more) and low pH values (5.5 or less) are found, copper or brass piping should not be used without a tape wrap coating and cathodic protection. Furthermore, when copper or brass is used in an aggressive environment, it should be electrically isolated from other structures. If copper piping is used for connection of copper service lines to plastic mains, this should be accomplished by using brass tapping saddles.

Although copper and brass typically have good corrosion resistance in aqueous solutions, they may be subject to corrosion in plant environments, depending upon the process stream. The presence of sulfides and ammonia compounds in wastewater can lead to dissolution of cuprous compounds. Further, if copper is coupled to a less noble metal like steel or aluminum, galvanic corrosion of the less noble metal may result. Because copper is a fairly soft material, it is also subject to erosion. This type of corrosion is accelerated by high fluid velocities, high temperatures, and abrasive particulate matter.

Copper and brass should not be used in any process flow stream that will allow exposure of the metal to solutions carrying chlorine (2 ppm or more). This is especially critical in reclaimed water systems, since chlorine can cause severe corrosion of copper and brass. Brasses containing over 15 percent zinc may suffer dezincification. This form of corrosion is especially prevalent in stagnant, acidic solutions.

Although copper and brass typically have excellent atmospheric corrosion resistance, they are actively attacked by hydrogen sulfide. Due to the probability of the presence of hydrogen sulfide in the atmosphere at a wastewater treatment plant and the possible implications in the operation of electrical systems, copper, brass, and bronze should not be used without protective coatings. Since it is impossible in many cases to eliminate the use of cuprous alloys, particularly in electrical systems such as switches and fuses, extreme care should be taken to prevent rapid deterioration. One means to reduce corrosion in electrical applications is to use well-sealed junction boxes (typically NEMA 4X). These boxes should be constructed of either stainless steel or a noncorroding, nonmetallic material (e.g., glass reinforced plastic, polycarbonate, or polyester), and completely sealed. Conduit entrances should be sealed tightly to the boxes and conduits should be internally sealed to prevent transmission of corrosive gases between boxes. Vapor corrosion inhibitors may also be required in certain applications. Further protection can be afforded by the use of spray- or dip-type corrosion-inhibiting coatings. A limited number of these products have been tested, and have in some cases yielded better results than the vapor-phase corrosion inhibitors.

Stainless Steel

Coating and cathodic protection should be considered for stainless steel in soil and water. Stainless steel may be used in most atmospheric exposures and may also be used as hardware for connection to steel. Stainless steel should not be used for complex structures with overlapping bolted connections in soil or fluid exposures. Bolted connections of this type in soil or fluid exposures can experience very rapid crevice corrosion.

In soil, stainless steel is fairly resistant to uniform corrosion, which occurs over the entire surface; however, it may be subject to pitting corrosion. Stainless steel is most often used in situations where contamination of the material carried in the pipe is the prime concern. However, as pitting of the buried structures might occur, where soil conditions surrounding the pipe vary, it would be prudent to install stainless steel pipe with a uniform, well-installed backfill where differential oxygen corrosion cells will not occur. Coatings and cathodic protection of buried pipelines in corrosive soils should be considered. In noncorrosive soils, coatings for stainless steel are recommended.

Stainless steel is typically resistant to corrosion in flowing waters. Of the various types of stainless steel, the austenitic grades (300 series) have shown the best performance. In stagnant waters, however, pitting of stainless steel may occur. Oxidizing metal salts such as ferric chloride may also attack stainless steel. Types 304 and 316 alloys are more resistant to chlorine, hypochlorous acid (HOCl), and hypochlorite ions than other alloys that might be used in the process streams. Stainless alloys are also resistant to hydrogen sulfide and other organic materials likely to be found in plant or wastewater environments.

Cathodic protection of stainless steel is an option for preventing pitting. Although stainless steel is essentially immune to uniform corrosion, pitting has been encountered in many aqueous environments and can be prevented by the use of cathodic protection. By electrically coupling stainless steel to a large immersed structure made of steel, zinc, or other metal that is more anodic to stainless steel, pitting can be reduced or eliminated. It should be recognized, however, that where galvanic couples exist, stainless steel will increase the magnitude of corrosion deterioration of the structure to which it is bonded. It is therefore recommended that electrical contact be eliminated where the anode/cathode ratio is not favorable, i.e., small anode to large cathode.

Stainless steel has been used with much success in both outdoor and indoor applications. Of the various types of stainless steel, the austenitic grades (typically 302, 304, and 316) generally have the best corrosion resistance. Of the three alloys listed above, 316, although more expensive than the others, is the most resistant to pitting.

The austenitic alloys are resistant to hydrogen sulfide, chlorides, and moisture. There are also advantages to using stainless steel in combination with other metals. This is true where the more anodic material has a much larger surface area than the cathodic material. For example, galvanic corrosion has not been a problem where stainless steel fasteners are used to hold down aluminum deck plates. This is because the amount of stainless steel (cathodic material) used to hold down the aluminum (anodic material) is quite small when comparisons of surface area ratios are made. Overall, stainless steel has been demonstrated to provide excellent corrosion resistance in severe atmospheric environments.

Zinc

Although zinc can be used in the form of rolled sheet and strip, its widest use in building is for protective plating. When exposed to weather, zinc on the surface of galvanized steel develops a passive film that protects the underlying zinc and, thus, the steel. When the surface is scratched or scored, the anodic zinc corrodes, protecting the cathodic steel from attack.

Zinc can be applied to metal surfaces with hot-dip galvanizing, electrolytic processes, metal spraying, sherardizing, and zinc-rich paints. Hot-dip galvanizing provides excellent coverage and bonding leaving a film 3- to 5- (75- to 125-µm) mil thick. The interface is actually a zinc-iron alloy. Electrolytic processes provide a thin coating up to 1-mil (25-µm) thick. Metal spraying provides a 4- to 20-mil (100- to 500-µm) thick zinc film. Sherardizing, the heating of small components in a container of zinc dust, produces films of 0.5- to 1.5-mils (12- to 36-µm) thick. The dry film of zinc-rich paint should be at least 90 percent zinc to provide adequate galvanic protection to a steel substrate.

Atmospheric exposure gives the zinc surface a coating of zinc carbonate that reacts with sulfurous and sulfuric acids in the atmosphere to form zinc sulfate, which is water-soluble and can be washed off by rain.

Zinc sheeting is susceptible to attack from condensation on its underside. Proper ventilation of roof spaces and use of vapor barriers and suitable underlays can minimize such conditions. Zinc surfaces should be designed to allow rapid drying.

Local air pollution should be considered when designing zinc roofs, and proper fasteners should be specified. Zinc should be prevented from contacting copper and the chlorides and sulfates in concrete and mortar. Acids from certain timbers and some wood preservatives can also attack zinc. Bituminous coatings are recommended for protection.

Weathered galvanized members can be painted after being properly cleaned. Freshly galvanized members can also be painted. The Zinc Institute now recommends solvent cleaning or detergent washing, rather than acid etching, before painting. Suitable primers include zinc dust, zinc oxide primers, vinyl wash primers, and latex emulsion primers.

WOOD AND PLASTIC*

Wood and plastic building materials resist many of the natural and industrial environmental factors that affect concrete, masonry, and metals. However, wood and plastic are susceptible to other types of attack—fungi and insects can destroy wood, and ultraviolet light and temperature can affect some plastics.

Wood

When exposed to the elements, wood is affected by water and light. Pollutants have little effect on wood except to dirty it. It has good resistance to chemical corrosion, and its thermal expansion is slight.

---

* This material adapted with permission from *Plant Engineering*, February 16, 1978, pp. 149–152.

Wood normally contains 12 to 18 percent water, but it can absorb moisture and swell up to 5 percent. Ultraviolet light can cause chemical and color change (accelerated by the extraction of water-soluble materials). The stresses set up by fluctuating moisture content and ultraviolet light cause splitting and checking (defects in the wood surface that allow more water to enter to produce gross dimensional changes). Weathering effects of moisture and sunlight can be reduced by applying a film-forming or penetrating finish.

Biological Attack.   Wood is subject to decay caused by certain types of fungi. In extreme cases, such as in tropical climates, unprotected timber may be destroyed in a few months. Keeping wood adequately dry (less than 20 percent moisture) minimizes fungal damage. Structural timber should be protected from the weather by a well-ventilated shelter, and wood members should not be framed close to the ground.

Deprivation of air causes fungi to become dormant and, finally, die. Encasement in concrete or heavy bituminous coatings can shut off the air supply; ordinary painting will not. Embedment of timbers in soil can also shut off access to air, but it can cause other problems.

Temperatures between 50 and 90°F are optimum for the growth of fungi. They become dormant at temperatures over 110°F and near 32°F, but can reactivate when temperatures moderate.

Protection against fungal decay can be provided by various chemical treatments.

In wood exposed to marine atmospheres, attack by marine borers may lead to destruction. Aggressive organisms such as teredo or shipworms, various mollusks, and wood lice attack wood by burrowing or boring and gnawing.

Their terrestrial counterparts—termites, beetles, caterpillars, bees, and ants—eat the wood. Such attack reduces the strength of the timbers and weakens and ultimately destroys the structure.

Termites are one of the most destructive organisms to timber. They are found in almost all areas of the country, with greater concentrations in warmer and more humid regions. Their diet is based on cellulose. There are wood-dwelling and earth-dwelling types. Visible symptoms of termite attack are subtle and difficult to recognize.

Protection of most wood against termites is provided by chemical treatments or by poisoning the ground with chemicals such as copper sulfate, sodium fluosilicate, borax, paradichlorobenzene, and various commercial poisons.

Chemical Preservatives.   A number of species of wood have natural decay resistance. The heartwood of several species native to North America—especially redwood, cedar, cypress, and juniper—has good decay resistance; however, the sapwood of substantially all common species has poor resistance. Regardless of the species, chemical protection of woods is recommended. The preservative treatment makes the wood poisonous to fungi, insects, and marine borers. There are three classes of preservatives: waterborne, oilborne, and creosote.

Waterborne Salts.   Waterborne salts for wood preservation include zinc chloride, chromated zinc chloride, copperized chromated zinc chloride, zinc meta arsenite, chromated zinc arsenate, chromated copper arsenate, ammoniacal copper arsenite, acid copper chromate, and fluor chrome arsenate phenol. These chemicals leave little odor and have little effect on the appearance of the wood, which may also be painted. The zinc chloride salts, at high penetrations, also provide fire retardance. Wood should be reseasoned before use because this type of chemical treatment injects a large amount of water into the wood.

Oilborne Preservatives.   These include penta (pentachlorophenol) and copper naphthenate. Penta does not change the color of the wood, but copper naphthenate gives wood a green shade. Paintability after treatment depends on the type of oil or solvent used as a vehicle.

Creosote.   Creosote is excellent for preventing decay, especially in exterior use or in contact with water. Its advantages include relative insolubility in water (giving it a high degree of permanence), good penetration, good availability, and low cost; in addition, it causes little dimensional change in the wood. Disadvantages include its potential fire hazard; a distinctive, sometimes unpleasant odor that can affect foods; volatile vapors that can affect plant life; black color; and staining of adjacent woods or porous materials. Treated wood cannot be painted, and on hot days it may sweat and become wet and tacky.

Treatment Processes.   Methods for treating timber with chemicals include pressure, coating, dipping and steeping, thermal, and diffusion.

Pressure Process.   These processes produce relatively deep penetration of the preservative into the wood. Although various processes differ in detail, the basic principle of all is the same—wood is placed in a pressure vessel that is filled with preservative. Pressurization then drives preservative into the wood to meet penetration and retention specifications.

Coating.   Coating by brush or spray may be done at the site. At least two, preferably three, applications are made; each coat is applied after the previous one has been absorbed. Brush and spray treatments are generally used only when more effective treatments are not practical.

Dipping and Steeping.   This involves immersing the wooden member in the preservative liquid. From a few minutes to as long as several days of immersion may be required. It provides greater penetration of the preservative than brush and spray treatments, but it generally less effective than pressure processes.

Thermal Treatment.   Thermal treatment, or hot and cold dipping, is similar to dipping, except the member is first heated in the preservative in an open tank and is then submerged in cold preservative. This procedure provides deeper penetration of preservative than dipping and steeping.

Diffusion Processes.   Diffusion processes can be used while the timber is in place. Water-soluble preservatives, carried in bandages or pastes or in retaining rings applied to the member, diffuse into the water present in the wood.

All of these methods should meet the standards and specifications of the American Wood-Preservers' Association (AWPA); see Tables 1-4 to 1-6. Any use of treated wood should be checked for conformance to current environmental regulations.

TABLE 1-4   Selected AWPA Standards for Preservatives

Standard numbers	Preservative	Symbol	Trade names[†]
P1 or P13	Coal tar creosote	—	—
P2 or P12	Creosote-coal tar solution	—	—
P5	Acid copper chromate	ACC	Celcure*
	Ammoniacal copper arsenite	ACA	Chemonite*
	Chromated copper arsenate	CCA	Type A: Greensalt* Langwood*
			Type B: Boliden* CCA Koppers CCA-B[a] Osmose K-33*
			Type C: Chrom-Ar-Cu(CAC)* Osmose K-33C* Wolman* CCA Wolmanac* CCA
	Chromated zinc chloride	CZC	—
	Fluor chromate arsenate phenol	FCAP	Osmosalts* (Osmosar*) Tanalith* Wolman* FCAP Wolman* FMP
P8 and P9	Pentachlorophenol	Penta	—

* Reg. U.S. Pat. Off.
† *Source:* American Wood-Preservers' Association.
[a] Koppers is now known as Kop-coat.

Repairing Termite-Damaged Wood.   Wood that has been weakened or damaged by termite attack may be repaired without removing the wooden member from the structure. The procedure is similar to pressure-grouting cracks in concrete. For termite-damaged wood, a form

TABLE 1-5 Selected AWPA Standards for Pressure-Treatment Processes

AWPA* standard	Product
C1	All timber products (general)
C2	Lumber, timber, bridge ties, and mine ties
C3	Piles
C4	Poles
C9	Plywood
C11	Wood blocks for floors and platforms
C14	Wood for highway construction
C18	Piles and timbers for marine construction
C23	Round poles and posts used in building construction
C29	Lumber to be used for the harvesting, storage, and transportation of foodstuffs

* American Wood-Preservers' Association.

TABLE 1-6 Preservatives and Minimum Retentions for Various Wood Products[a]

Product and service condition	AWPA product[b] standard	Recommended minimum net retention, lb/ft[3c]						
		Waterborne preservatives[d]					Oilborne[d,e]	
		CCA	ACA	ACC	CZC	FCAP	Penta[f]	Creosote
LUMBER and TIMBER								
Above ground	C2	0.23	0.23	0.25	0.46	0.22	0.40	8
Soil or water contact								
Nonstructural	C2	0.40	0.40	0.50	NR	NR	0.50	10
Structural	C14	0.60	0.60	NR	NR	NR	NR	12
In salt water	C14	2.5	2.5	NR	NR	NR	NR	25
PLYWOOD								
Above ground	C9	0.23	0.23	0.25	0.46	0.22	0.40	8
Soil or water contact	C9	0.40	0.40	0.50	NR	NR	0.50	10
PILING								
Soil or fresh water	C3	0.80	0.80	NR	NR	NR	0.60	12
In salt water								
Severe borer hazard (Limnoria)	C18	2.5 & 1.5[g]	2.5 & 1.5[g]	NR	NR	NR	NR	NR
Moderate borer hazard (Pholads)	C18	NR	NR	NR	NR	NR	NR	20
Dual treatment (Limnoria and pholads)								
First treatment	C18	1.0	1.0	NR	NR	NR	NR	—
Second treatment	C18	—	—	NR	NR	NR	NR	20
POLES								
Utility in normal service	C4	0.60	0.60	NR	NR	NR	0.38	7.5
Utility in severe decay & termite areas	C4	0.60	0.60	NR	NR	NR	0.45	9.0
Building poles (structural)	C23	0.60	0.60	NR	NR	NR	0.45	9.0
POSTS								
Fence								
Round, half-round, quarter-round	C14	0.40	0.40	0.50	NR	NR	0.40	8
Sawn four sides	C14	0.50	0.50	0.62	NR	NR	0.50	10
Guardrail and sign								
Round	C14	0.50	0.50	NR	NR	NR	0.50	10
Sawn four sides	C14	0.60	0.60	NR	NR	NR	0.60	12

[a] Key to symbols: ACA, ammoniacal copper arsenate; ACC, Acid copper chromate; CCA, chromated copper arsenate; CZC, chromated zinc chloride; FCAP, Fluor chrome arsenate phenol; NR, not recommended; Penta, pentachlorophenol.

[b] See Table 1-5.

[c] Minimum net retentions conforming to AWPA standards for softwood lumber and plywood. Retentions for piles, poles, and posts are for southern pine. AWPA Standard C1 applies to all processes.

[d] See Table 1-4.

[e] Creosote, creosote-coal tar solution, and oilborne penta are not recommended for applications that require clean, paintable, or odor-free wood.

[f] Penta can be applied in liquid petroleum gas or light solvents to provide a clean, paintable surface

[g] Two assay zones: 0 to 0.5 in and 0.5 to 2.0 in.

sleeve must be built around the damaged wooden member; then, a low-viscosity epoxy-resin compound is injected until all voids have been filled. The form sleeve may be treated with oil or wax to prevent the epoxy resin from sticking to the form. After the epoxy resin has hardened, the wood member's structural strength may be even greater than originally. If, as so often happens, the termite damage is inside the wooden member and the outside shell is intact, the epoxy-resin sealer may be invisible. However, should it be exposed, its light amber color may blend with the wood's color.

Sometimes, epoxy-resin compounds used for repairing wood may be manufactured with protective chemicals such as pentachlorophenol to help prevent further attack by termites. Termites cannot damage the epoxy compound. These special epoxy-resin compounds are generally available in boat yards or marinas, where they are widely used to repair wood damaged by rot or marine borers.

Plastics

Use of reinforced plastics in all construction is growing by millions of pounds yearly. These materials are finding extensive use in ceiling and floor systems, piping, skylights, translucent panels, structural shapes, grating, etc.

Plastics are usually strong, durable, lightweight, and resilient; they are easy to manufacture and install and have low maintenance costs. Color can be built in over a wide range, enhancing their use for exterior decoration.

Plastics, a term used for synthetic or modified natural polymers, are classified into two major groups: thermoplastics, which can be softened by heat and lend themselves readily to molding, and thermosetting plastics, which do not soften under heat once they are cured. Plastics used for exterior applications in the construction industry can be formulated to almost any set of properties, including light stability, rigidity, opacity, water absorption, and abrasion and fire resistance.

Weathering of plastics involves ultraviolet radiation, infrared radiation, water, temperature, microorganisms, industrial gases, and stresses from wind and snow loadings. Some plastics discolor after weathering, but discoloration can usually be minimized by selecting materials containing ultraviolet absorbers. Certain pigments can also increase stability for exterior exposure.

Thermoplastic polymers should not be used in areas where high temperatures are present to cause distortion. Distortion temperatures of commercial plastic materials should be a guide in this respect. Low temperatures can cause embrittlement. Oxidation can cause changes in the molecular structure of a plastic similar to those in paint films. In most cases, plastics are reasonably resistant to industrial pollution and microorganisms, but they will discolor as dirt collects. However, frequent simple washings can maintain plastics adequately.

The most important generic types of plastics for exterior application include polyvinyl chloride, glass-reinforced polyester, acrylics, phenolics, and amino resins.

Polyvinyl Chloride (PVC). One of the most extensively used plastics in construction, PVC is often used for roofing panels, gutters and downspouts, pipes, cladding, wall and floor coverings, and window frames. PVC film has also been used extensively on metal sheeting as a protective and decorative finish. Heavy use is made of PVC in hidden items, such as water stops, vapor barriers, and waterproofing membranes.

PVC is a thermoplastic material with a wide range of properties determined by stabilizers, plasticizers, ultraviolet absorbers, lubricants, and other additives. For fire-resistant properties, antimony trioxide is often used. Methods of manufacture include extrusion, injection molding, blow molding, and calendering.

When properly formulated and fabricated under controlled conditions, a PVC product can have a life of 20 to 30 years. Certainly, a PVC waterstop, buried in a concrete foundation wall, must last for the life of the structure.

Translucent or transparent PVC sheet does not weather as well as the opaque form because stabilizers and ultraviolet absorbers affect light-transfer properties.

If weathering causes color change or differential fading, the PVC member can be painted after proper preparation of the surface by washing and light sanding.

Glass-Reinforced Polyester.   Laminates of glass-reinforced polyester find wide use in automobile bodies, aircraft, boats, swimming pools, tanks, prefabricated housing systems, curtain walls, and lightweight building panels.

Polyesters are thermosetting resins produced by the reaction of mixtures of glycols and dibasic acids. The compound is comparable to an alkyd resin used in paints. However, it is further modified by dissolving it in styrene, and it is cured into a thermosetting plastic by the addition of catalysts and accelerators. The plastic can be modified with additives similar to those used in the PVC compounds.

The polyester resin, by itself, is not strong enough for industrial use, so it must be reinforced with glass fibers. A laminate is manufactured by spreading the catalyzed polyester resin onto a form or mold. While it is still uncured, woven glass cloth, swirled mat, or chopped strands are laid up into the film. Then, more coats of catalyzed polyester and glass fibers are added until the necessary number of layers is installed. The final coat of polyester is normally heavy enough to cover the glass fibers thoroughly. The last layer of resin will be exposed to weathering and can have color and all the necessary additives built in.

The polyester resin may be modified with methyl methacrylate resins for better clarity and transparency. Recent developments involve the use of acrylates or polyvinyl fluoride as surface coatings bonded to the laminate for longer gloss retention. The product is cured at ambient temperatures, although heat will accelerate the cure and ensure a more satisfactory laminate. The same procedures are also followed in producing epoxy-resin laminates, although these are not as widely used in the construction industry.

A glass-reinforced polyester laminate may fail if the surface resin is not thick enough to cover the glass strands, or if weathering wears away the surface color. Change of color, fading, and loss of gloss may also develop. Good maintenance depends on regular and thorough washing to remove dirt. When the surface must be refurbished, steel wool may be used to remove dirt and loose resin and fibers. A surface layer of polyester resin or an acrylic sealer may be applied. Frequent washing to remove dirt is usually the best method of maintenance.

Acrylics.   Methyl methacrylate is the basic monomer for acrylic resins, materials that found their first extensive uses in cockpit covers of airplanes. Today, methyl methacrylate and its modifications are used in making window panes, fascia panels, skylights, sunshades, bath and shower enclosures, roof lights, etc. These thermoplastic materials are water-white and have almost the same light transmission properties as glass. They have good impact resistance, can be easily formed and machined, are easy to handle and install, and possess outstanding weathering resistance and durability. However, acrylics have low abrasion resistance and a very high coefficient of thermal expansion.

Periodic cleaning and washing of acrylic members is recommended as the best method of maintenance. However, they are easily scratched. Polishing with a soft rouge can remove scratches without affecting transparency. Colored acrylic members may be produced, and there is little or no fading or change in color. Painting is seldom required.

Phenolics and Amino Resins.   Reacting aldehydes with phenol and amino compounds (such as urea and melamine) can produce thermosetting plastics with good chemical resistance. One of the first synthetic resins of this type was Bakelite, a phenolic resin. This group of plastics is used in making laminates, usually with reinforcement, for curtain wall paneling, wall linings, corrugated roofing, etc. Melamine formaldehyde is used in making the laminate known as Formica. These plastics, particularly the phenolics, can change color and weathering and develop very fine crazing patterns with aging. Painting can restore surface appearance and color after proper washing and light sanding. Frequent washing is recommended for maintenance.

Other plastics are used in plant structures, although less extensively. Among these are the acrylonitrile butadiene styrene (ABS) resins, the polyvinyl fluoride resins, the polycarbonate resins, and the polyurethanes. The epoxy resins have been used extensively in structural applications (such as flooring) and adhesives. Specialized applications include use in chemically resistant coatings and in plasters for exposed aggregate wall finishes.

As research and development proceed, improved formulations of available plastics and completely new resins will find their way into plant structures.

BIBLIOGRAPHY

American Concrete Institute:

201.2R-92	Guide to Durable Concrete
212.3R	Chemical Admixtures for Concrete
222R	Corrosion of Metals in Concrete
224R	Controlling Cracking in Concrete Structures
503R	Use of Epoxy Compounds with Concrete
503.2	Standard Specification for Bonding Plastic Concrete to Hardened Concrete with a Multi-Component Epoxy Adhesive
506R	Guide to Shotcrete

ASTM:

C 881	Specification for Epoxy-Resin-Base Bonding System for Concrete
C 1059	Specification for Latex Agents for Bonding Fresh to Hardened Concrete

GLOSSARY OF CORROSION-RELATED TERMS

Active   The negative direction of electrode potential. Also used to describe a metal that is corroding without significant influence of reaction product.

Aeration cell   An electrolytic cell whose electromotive force is due to electrodes of the same material located in different concentrations of dissolved air.

Anion   A negatively charged ion of an electrolyte that migrates toward the anode under the influence of a potential gradient.

Anode   The electrode of an electrolytic cell at which oxidation occurs.

Cathode   The electrode of an electrolytic cell at which reduction occurs.

Cathodic protection   A means of applying an external electric current to reduce corrosion virtually to zero. A metal surface can be maintained in a corrosive environment without deterioration as long as the cathodic protection system provides the external current. Cathodic protection can be galvanic, such as that on galvanized pipe, or it can be impressed current, such as that usually found on large potable water tanks and pipelines.

Cation   A positively charged ion of an electrolyte that migrates toward the cathode under the influence of a potential gradient.

Corrosion cell   Electrochemical system consisting of an anode and cathode immersed in an electrolyte. The anode and a cathode may be separate metals or dissimilar areas on the same metal.

Corrosion   The deterioration of material, usually a metal, by reaction with its environment.

Corrosion fatigue   Damage to a metal from a combination of corrosion and fatigue (cyclic stresses).

Corrosion potential   The potential of a corroding surface in an electrolyte relative to the reference electrode. Also called rest potential, open-circuit potential, freely corroding potential.

Bimetallic corrosion or **couple**   See Galvanic corrosion.

Electrode potential   The potential of an electrode measured against a reference electrode.

Electrolysis   The chemical change in an electrolyte resulting from the passage of electricity.

Electrolyte   A chemical substance or mixture, usually liquid, containing ions which migrate in an electric field.

Electromotive force series (EMF Series)   A list of elements arranged according to their standard electrode potentials, the sign being positive for elements whose potentials are cathodic to hydrogen and negative for those anodic to hydrogen.

Environment   The surroundings or conditions (physical, chemical, or mechanical) in which a material exists.

Erosion   Deterioration of a surface by abrasive action of moving fluids.

Erosion corrosion   Combined effects of erosion and corrosion on a metal surface.

Galvanic corrosion   Corrosion associated with the current resulting from the electrical coupling of dissimilar electrodes in an electrolyte.

Galvanic series   A list of alloys arranged according to their corrosion potentials in a given environment.

General corrosion   A form of deterioration that is distributed more or less uniformly over a surface.

Holiday   Any discontinuity or bare spot in a coated surface.

Ion   An electrically charged atom or group of atoms.

Local cell   Galvanic cell produced by differences in the composition of the metal or electrolyte.

Noble metal   A metal or alloy such as silver, gold, or platinum having high resistance to corrosion or oxidation.

Open-circuit potential   See Corrosion potential.

Oxidation   Loss of electrons by a constituent of a chemical reaction.

Passivation   A reduction of the anodic reaction rate of an electrode involved in corrosion.

Passive   Metal corroding under the control of a surface reaction product.

Patina   A green coating that slowly forms on copper and copper alloys exposed to the atmosphere. A patina contains mainly copper sulfates, carbonates, and chlorides.

Pits   Localized corrosion of a metal surface, confined to a small area, which takes the form of cavities.

Potential   The reversible work required to move a unit charge from the electrode surface through the solution to the reference electrode.

Reduction   Gain of electrons by a constituent of a chemical reaction.

Reference electrode   A reversible electrode used for measuring the potentials of other electrodes.

Rust   A reddish brown corrosion product of iron and ferrous alloys. It is primarily hydrated ferric oxide.

Sacrificial protection   Reduction of corrosion of a metal in an electrolyte by galvanically coupling it to a more anodic metal. A form of cathodic protection.

Tuberculation   The formation of localized corrosion products scattered over the surface in the form of knoblike mounds (tubercules).

Tubercules   See Tuberculation.

Voids A term generally applied to paints to describe holidays, holes, and skips in the film. Also used to describe shrinkage in castings or welds.

Working electrode cell The test or specimen electrode in an electrochemical cell.

Sources of Glossary Terms

1. NACE, *Materials Protection,* Vol. 7, No. 10, pp. 68–71 (1968).
2. NACE, *Materials Protection,* Vol. 4, No. 1, pp. 73–80 (1965).
3. NACE, Standard MR-01-75 (1978 Revision).
4. NACE, H.H. Uhlig, *Corrosion Handbook,* Wiley (1948).
5. ASM, *Metals Handbook,* Vol. 1, 8th Edition (1961).

CHAPTER 18-2
PAINTS AND PROTECTIVE COATINGS

P. Richard Hergenrother
Richard R. Roesler
Miles Inc.
Pittsburgh, Pennsylvania

BASICS OF PROTECTIVE COATINGS

The Corrosion Process

A detailed discussion of corrosion and other surface deterioration can be found in Chap. 18-1.

Steel, the material of choice for many construction projects, is susceptible to corrosion. A clear understanding of the corrosion process is essential to understand the steps to inhibit corrosion with protective coatings.

Oxygen combines with iron—the major element in steel—to form rust. This electrochemical process returns the iron metal to the state in which it existed in nature—iron oxide. The most common form of iron oxide or iron ore found in nature is hematite (Fe_2O_3), equivalent to what we call *rust*. Iron in iron ore is separated from the oxide to yield usable forms of iron, steel, and various other alloys through rigorous electrochemical reduction processes. Because iron has a strong affinity for oxygen it is necessary to deal with its ever present tendency to form the more electrochemically stable iron oxides.

The process of combining iron and oxygen, called *oxidation,* is accompanied by the production of a measurable quantity of electrical current, which is why this is called an electrochemical reaction. For the reaction to proceed, an anode, a cathode, and an electrolyte must be present. This is termed a *corrosion cell.* In a corrosion cell the anode is the negative electrode where corrosion occurs (oxidation), the cathode is the positive electrode, and the electrolyte is the medium through which an electrical current flows.

The surface of steel is not homogeneously pure. If it were, there would be no corrosion cells present. Because steel has inconsistencies in the alloy and possibly even impurities in the metal and because the surface of the steel may be contaminated with dirt, steel itself consists of many tiny corrosion cells. The anode of each of these cells will begin to oxidize. As the corrosion products build up they cause an increasing resistance to the electrochemical reaction. Eventually the cell neutralizes itself and the corrosion stops. However, the rust becomes cathodic in comparison to the metal surface. Since the metal surface is now anodic, a new corrosion cell has formed and the anode regions begin to rust. The process of the old corrosion cells becoming inactive and of new cells being formed continues until all of the iron has been converted to its oxide.

Coating in Corrosion Control

Corrosion can be interrupted by eliminating any of the reactants in the process. A simplified description of the rusting process is the reaction of iron with oxygen. Actually, this reaction is very slow at room temperature unless a catalyst is present. The catalyzed process requires the presence of water and maybe acids or salts. If a barrier is put onto the iron which prevents oxygen and/or water from coming in contact with steel, the corrosion process can be very much delayed. Steel is not the only surface that can be protected by such barriers. Other alloys and metals such as stainless steel, brass, and aluminum and other materials such as concrete, wood, paper, and plastic also can be protected from the environment with coatings. Protective coatings that serve as barriers are undoubtedly engineers' principal means to protect their structures.

A coating may be defined as a material which is applied to a surface as a fluid and forms, by chemical and/or physical processes, a solid continuous film bonded to the surface.

COMPOSITION OF COATINGS

Most coatings are made up of four principal parts: pigments, nonvolatile vehicles (resins or binders), volatile vehicles (organic solvents, water, or the combination of both), and additives (specialty chemicals that make the coating function). All of the components of a coating interact to accomplish the purpose for which the coating was designed.

Volatile vehicles are used to reduce the viscosity of the paint, which permits easy application of the coating. This viscosity reduction enables the applied coating to flow out and adequately wet the surface to allow for adhesion of the film. Once the paint is applied and flows out, the volatile vehicle should evaporate from the film causing it to "dry." The coating may simply physically dry, as is the case with lacquers and dispersions; or the coating may polymerize as with an air oxidative coating or a chemically curing coating. In either case the dry, and perhaps cured, film isolates the surface from the elements.

An excellent reference which discusses each paint ingredient in detail is available from the Federation of Paint Societies.[1]

Pigments

Pigments are included in coatings to perform any of the following functions:

- Add color
- Adjust the flow properties of wet coatings
- Resist light, heat, moisture, and chemicals
- Inhibit corrosion
- Reflect light for opacity or hiding
- Contribute to mechanical strength

Pigments whose prime function is to contribute opacity to coatings are called *hiding* or *prime* pigments. The *principal* white hiding pigment is titanium dioxide. There are hundreds of colored hiding pigments which, when used alone or in combination with other pigments, give coatings their variety of colors. Hiding pigments can be very expensive. In order to make the paint less costly, nonhiding or extender pigments are used.

Pigments are used to adjust the viscosity and thixotropy (flow properties) of the paint in order to obtain paint that won't sag at high film builds. Using pigments with low oil absorption can decrease the amount of solvents in the paints.

Pigments used to reduce or prevent corrosion of a coated surface are called *inhibitive* pigments. The use of inhibitive pigments in modern industrial coatings brings to the war against corrosion all of the principles of corrosion control, including cathodic protection, passivation of the coated surface, and the creation of barrier films.

Pigments help protect the resin in the film from the degradation of solar radiation. Hiding pigments do the best job of protecting the resin from the harmful portion of solar radiation by blocking its penetration into a film. Pigments in the film inhibit penetration of corrosive elements, thus protecting the substrate. Pigments also can add mechanical reinforcement to a film, adding strength, flexibility, and abrasion resistance.

Binders

The binder or resin portion of the coating is the "glue" that holds the coating together and on to the substrate. The physical properties of the coating are mainly derived from the physical properties of the solid resin, but pigments and additives can affect the final properties. Coatings are generally named after the type of resin used as the coating binder, probably because they strongly contribute to the performance properties of the film. Traditionally binders were derived from natural sources such as vegetable oils, petroleum and coal tar distillates and bottoms, and mined organic materials. Some of the more familiar ones are tung and linseed oils, asphalt, pitch, and gilsonite. Many natural binders have been replaced with synthetically produced resins because of economy and consistent performance properties. The properties of the natural oils and petroleum products vary somewhat depending on the conditions during which the materials were produced, e.g., weather, soil, mines, and wells. The properties of synthetic resins, on the other hand, can fall within a very narrow set of specifications.

Resin binders change from liquid to solid state by several different drying or curing mechanisms:

1. Lacquer, dispersion, and latex paints dry through evaporation of solvent and/or water.
2. Vegetable oil and alkyd paints harden through oxidative cure.

3. Two-component chemically reactive paints harden through chemical cure; that is, two components are mixed prior to application and polymerize on the substrate. Examples are epoxy and polyurethane.

4. One-component chemically reactive paints harden through the reaction of a resin which has an active chemical group with atmospheric moisture releasing a new chemical group that causes the resin to crosslink.

The simplest drying mechanism is evaporation of the volatile vehicle. Solvent-borne lacquers generally have very high solvent contents because very hard resins needed for good film properties require a lot of solvent to reduce the paint viscosity to application consistency. Vinyl and chlorinated rubber coatings are examples of resins relying on solvent evaporation. These coatings have excellent moisture permeation and acid and base resistance, but because they are not crosslinked they have poor solvent resistance and soften at elevated temperatures.

Another type of a paint that dries through simple evaporation of the volatile vehicle is waterborne paint. Here a major portion of the volatile vehicle is water, which acts to lower the viscosity of the paint. Water-borne resin technology can deliver useful performance, but there are some shortcomings with this approach. First, waterborne coatings may use a considerable amount of organic solvents to coalesce the polymer particles and stabilize the dispersion. Sometimes waterborne coatings use as much solvent as do high-solid, solventborne coatings. Secondly, the resin dispersions generally contain wetting and dispersing agents, which remain in the film after the volatile vehicle leaves. These agents are water sensitive and increase the moisture permeability of these coatings when compared to the solventborne counterparts. Finally, film coalescence depends on an optimum rate of evaporation of the water and coalescing solvent. If the temperature or humidity is high, the solvent may evaporate before resin coalescence is complete, leaving a porous film. Acrylic and vinyl latices and polyurethane dispersions are examples of this technology.

Coatings based on natural oils or alkyd binders modified with drying oils develop their film properties principally through oxidative curing. Atmospheric oxygen creates active cross-linking sites on vegetable oils or the drying oil portion of the synthetic resin. These sites connect to form a three-dimensional chemically-bonded network. Linseed, alkyd, and epoxy ester binders are examples of systems that cure by a combination of solvent evaporation and oxidation.

Two-component chemically reactive paint is manufactured and sold in two separate containers. The two multifunctional reactive resinous materials are mixed together just prior to use. The two resins immediately begin to react together to form a polymeric matrix. During polymerization the paint viscosity will increase. This means that the paint has a specific use life before the paint will gel. The starting materials are generally lower in molecular weight than other paint types, which means that less solvent is needed to reduce viscosities for application. Because this type of coating exhibits excellent chemical and physical properties it is generally termed a high performance coating. Polyurethanes and epoxies use this type of curing mechanism.

One-component chemically reactive paint utilizes polyisocyanate chemistry. The isocyanate group reacts with atmospheric moisture to yield an amine group. The amine reacts very rapidly with additional isocyanate to form a urea crosslink. This paint offers the ease of use of other one-can technologies with the performance of a two-component paint. Manufacture is difficult because of the need to scrupulously dry all raw materials.

Solvents

A solvent is used to dissolve the resins and additives in order to reduce the viscosity of the mixture to provide application consistency and allow the paint to flow out properly. In every case, it is designed to evaporate from the film during or after application.

Solvents are also used in waterborne dispersions and latices. Paints made from dispersions or latices are similar to lacquers in that the volatile vehicle evaporates after application of the coating and the coating is formed through a physically drying mechanism.

Dispersions and latices consist of high molecular weight, usually hard resins that are dispersed in a water medium. At some point in either the manufacture of the resin or the paint, solvents are added to soften the resin. During the drying of the paint film, the water evaporates. The dispersion or latex particles come into contact and flow together to form a continuous film. Finally, the solvent evaporates from the film. This process, called coalescence, would not take place without the solvent because resins that are hard enough to produce tough films are too hard to coalesce without the solvent. Waterborne coatings are gaining interest by specifiers because they are perceived as being environmentally friendly. Although many waterborne coatings do have low levels of solvent, *some waterborne paints contain solvents in amounts equivalent to those in high-solid, solventborne coatings.*

Coatings suppliers select the type of solvent suitable for each type of coating formulation. The choice of solvents is made based on the optimum paint viscosity and evaporation rate that result in proper paint flow and thus the intended appearance and adhesion. Coating applicators may need to add solvents during application to control viscosity over the various temperature ranges encountered in the field.

The wrong choice of solvents can jeopardize an application. If the chosen solvent evaporates too fast, bubbles caused by the vapor pressure of the solvent may appear in the surface. If the coating is spray-applied the solvent may "flash out" of the spray mist before it reaches the surface, and the spray may become too dry for the paint particles to flow together. This latter effect is called *dry spray.* A solvent that is too slow to evaporate may remain in the film too long, causing sags and runs and resulting in a film that is soft and has other altered performance properties.

The applicator must also take care not to add thinning solvent beyond that recommended by the manufacturer, because the paint viscosity may be so low so that the wet films will sag and run. Over-thinned paint that is applied at too low a film build may result in films that are too thin and have no hiding power. Overthinned paint applied in thicknesses high enough to achieve hiding may run or sag.

Solvent Content.   Environmental concerns are forcing raw material suppliers and paint producers to lower the solvent content of the products they supply in order to reduce the amount of volatile organic compounds (VOCs) released into the atmosphere.

Early paint formulas used naturally occurring or synthetic binder resins with a relatively high molecular weight in order to achieve desired performance. This meant that a large proportion of the paint had to be solvent in order to reduce the viscosity of the coating to a consistency that could be easily applied.

It has been found that when certain types of solvents (such as xylol or straight chain ketones) evaporate, they can react with the atmosphere to form pollutants. Over the last few decades, efforts have been made by government agencies to control the type and amount of solvents used in paint manufacture.

Newer synthetic technology has enabled paint formulators to use low molecular weight, two-component technology to achieve desired performance properties. In general, low molecular weight resins require less solvent to achieve application viscosity in paints. The two-component coatings build molecular weight after application and can achieve the same paint properties as the old, low-solid/resin-based paints. Polyurethane and epoxy technology have been very successful with these techniques.

Another approach to reducing solvent emissions is to switch from lacquer-type coatings to waterborne dispersions. As noted previously, some waterborne paints contain as much solvent as high-solid, solventborne coatings.

With the advent of high-solid, low-solvent technology, the paint applicator must exercise greater skill to achieve the desired dry film thickness. Because there is less solvent in the coating, there is less shrinkage as the wet film dries. The painter must remain inside a narrower wet film range, both maximum and minimum thickness, to achieve the same quality of work as when solvent content was higher.

Additives

Additives make up only a small proportion of any paint. Yet without these chemicals the paint could not deliver all of its potential performance.

Paint additives are used to aid pigment grinding, stabilize resin and pigment dispersions, break foams, aid flow, prevent film surface defects, catalyze chemical reactions, prevent oxidation, enhance adhesion, provide slip and abrasion resistance to the film surface, prevent corrosion, improve weathering resistance, enhance color retention, etc.

These additives can be inexpensive or the most expensive component on a per pound basis of any ingredient. In these days of cost competition, it is not unusual for a paint manufacturer to cut costs by leaving out one of these vital ingredients. *Sometimes the effects may not be known until years after the paint application.* For example, in a high performance polyurethane topcoat, it is usual practice to add antioxidants and UV absorbers to enhance the weathering resistance. If these additives are left out of the formulation to lower cost, instead of the 5 to 10 years of gloss and color retention, only one to two years might be expected. It is imperative that expected paint performance as well as paint cost be listed in the job specification.

SURFACE PREPARATION

Clean Surfaces and Performance

No matter how carefully a coating is formulated and manufactured, how sound the research on which it was based, or how sophisticated the technology, the coating will fail prematurely in service if the surface to which it was applied is inadequately prepared. No coating can form a strong bond to a surface if there is contamination under the coating that is weakly bound to the substrate. Peeling coatings, dirt, rust, mill scale, oil, wax, moisture, and other foreign materials provide a poor foundation to hold a coating, sometimes even when the contamination is present in such small quantities as to be invisible to the eye. The eventual result will be loss of adhesion. *Proper surface preparation is vital to maximize the service life of a coating.*

Surface preparation must be considered as an integral part of the coating specification. The specification must include not only the generic description of the paint used for each coat of paint, but the surface preparation and the kind and number of the individual coats of paint and their film thicknesses. *Specifications must be written for coating systems that include these items as well as the expected performance properties of the entire system over the life of the protected piece.*

Steel

Steel is one of the most widely used structural materials in industrial plants. Due to its penchant to corrode, steel is nearly always protected with a coating. This section of the chapter deals with surface preparation as a portion of the painting specification.

New steel used as a construction item is the easiest to protect from corrosion because it probably has not been contaminated with salts that act as electrolytes for the corrosion cells. When salts are not present it is easier to achieve the degree of surface preparation needed to protect steel. Older steel (and especially corroded steel) may have soluble salts imbedded in corroded pits and intergranular surfaces. Even though the salts may be of a soluble type, they are difficult to remove even with the most rigorous cleaning procedures. They tend to shorten the service life of coatings systems when compared to the life of the same systems on new steel.

Mill scale is a hard, smooth, blue-black layer of iron oxide (Fe_2O_3) that forms on steel during the hot rolling process. Mill scale is very inert. When intact, it forms a very efficient barrier to protect steel from corrosion. Unfortunately it has a different coefficient of expansion than steel and is very brittle. Because of this, it cracks and chips. The remaining mill scale then becomes cathodic with respect to steel, forming very efficient corrosion cells. The result is that *mill scale must be removed before painting.*

Red rust, a form of mixed iron oxides, is a surface contaminant familiar to everyone. It varies in color from light red to dark brown and may be loose and powdery or hard and granular. Red rust provides a weak foundation for paint, contributes to the formation of corrosion cells, and contributes to the destruction of coatings.

Before proceeding with cleaning, the surface must be inspected for corrosion imperfections and corrected as follows:

1. Rough welds and sharp edges must be ground smooth.

2. Corners must be rounded.

3. Weld splatter must be knocked off.

4. Seams joined with a skip weld must be rewelded to form a continuous, smooth bead.

5. Rivets and bolts must be set firm and tight, and caulked if they are angled or not flush.

6. Crevices and pits should be caulked.

Welding should be done *before* cleaning; caulking should be done *after* cleaning.

The degree and type of surface preparation chosen is based upon the type of structure, economy, environmental regulations, primer, and service life expected. In general, the service life of a coating system increases as the degree of surface preparation increases. The cost of surface preparation also increases as the degree of surface cleanliness is increased. Environmental concerns are becoming more important. When old paint contains lead or chromate pigments, the debris from the old paint as well as the blasting media must be isolated and collected, the disposed of in a hazardous waste facility. Local ordinances may be in effect simply to restrict the amount of nuisance dust emitted during blast cleaning.

Specifications.   Specifications and pictorial standards for surface preparation have been published by the Steel Structures Paint Council and are considered to be the supreme reference for the maintenance engineer. The complete specification for the above procedures may be found in Vol. 2, "Systems and Specifications," of the *Steel Structures Painting Manual.*[2] Pictorial standards for these procedures are also available from this group. Following is a brief description of the specifications.

Solvent Cleaning, SSPC-SP 1, describes a method for removing all visible oil, grease, soil, drawing and cutting compounds, and other soluble contaminants from surfaces.

It is intended that solvent cleaning be used prior to any of the other surface preparation methods for the removal of rust, mill scale or paint. If this is not done, contaminants such as oil or salt on the surface of rust or paint could be driven into the substrate and then be difficult if not impossible to remove.

Hand Tool Cleaning, SSPC-SP 2, describes a method for preparing surfaces by the use of nonpower tools. Before hand-tool cleaning, remove all visible oil, grease and soluble welding residues, and salts by the method outlined in SSPC-SP 1. Hand-tool cleaning is intended to remove all loose mill scale, rust, paint, and other detrimental foreign matter. It is not intended that adherent mill scale, rust, and paint be removed by this process. Materials are considered adherent if they cannot be lifted with a dull putty knife. Examples of hand tools are a wire brush and sandpaper.

Power Tool Cleaning, SSPC-SP 3, describes a method of preparing steel surfaces by the use of power-assisted hand tools. Before power-tool cleaning, remove all visible oil, grease and soluble welding residue, and salts by the method outlined in SSPC-SP 1. Power-tool cleaning is intended to remove all loose mill scale, rust, paint, and other foreign matter. It is not intended that adherent mill scale, rust, and paint be removed by this process. Materials are considered adherent if they cannot be lifted with a dull putty knife. Examples of power tools are a rotary abrader and an electric sander.

White-Metal Blast Cleaning Specification, SSPC-SP 5, describes a method of cleaning surfaces by the use of abrasives. Before white-metal cleaning remove all visible oil, grease and soluble welding residue, and salts by the method outlined in SSPC SP-1. When white-metal cleaned surfaces are viewed without magnification they should be completely free of all visible oil, grease, dirt, dust, mill scale, rust, paint, oxides, corrosion products, and other foreign matter. Blast media can be metal shot or mineral grit.

Commercial Blast Cleaning, SSPC-SP 6, describes a method for cleaning surfaces by the use of abrasives. Before blast cleaning, visible deposits of oil or grease should be removed by the method outlined in SSPC-SP 1. When commercial blast cleaned surfaces are viewed without magnification, they should be free of all visible oil, grease, dirt, dust, mill scale, rust, paint oxides, corrosion products, and other foreign matter, except for staining, as described in section 2.2 of that specification.

Brush-Off Blast Cleaning, SSPC-SP 7, describes a method of cleaning surfaces by the use of abrasives. Before blast cleaning, visible deposits of oil or grease should be removed by the method outlined in SSPC-SP 1. When brush-off cleaned surfaces are viewed without magnification they should be free of all visible oil, grease, dirt, dust, loose mill scale, loose rust, and loose paint. Tightly adherent mill scale rust and paint may remain on the surfaces. Materials are considered tightly adherent if they cannot be lifted with a dull putty knife.

Pickling, SSPC-SP 8, describes a method of cleaning steel surfaces by means of chemical action, electrolysis, or both. Before pickling, visible deposits of oil or grease should be removed by the method outlined in SSPC-SP 1. When pickled surfaces are viewed without magnification they should be free of visible mill scale or rust.

Near-White Metal Blast Cleaning, SSPC-SP 10, describes a method of cleaning surfaces by use of abrasives. Before blast cleaning, visible deposits of oil or grease should be removed by the method outlined in SSPC-SP 1. When near-white cleaned surfaces are viewed without magnification they should be free of visible oil, grease, dirt, dust, mill scale, rust, paint, oxides, corrosion products, and other foreign matter, except for staining as described in section 2.2 of that specification.

Power Tool Cleaning, SSPC-SP 11, describes a method of cleaning surfaces to bare metal and retaining or producing a surface profile with the use of power tools. This method differs from SSPC-SP 3 (Power Tool Cleaning) in that SSPC-SP 3 requires only the removal of loosely adherent material and does not require the production or retention of a surface profile. Before power-tool cleaning, visible deposits of oil or grease should be removed by the method outlined in SSPC-SP 1. When SSPC-SP 11 power-tool-cleaned surfaces are viewed without magnification, they shall be free of all oil, grease, dirt, dust, mill scale, rust paint, oxide and corrosion products, and other foreign matter. Slight residues of rust and paint may be left in the lower portion of pits if the original surface is pitted.

Other Substrates

In addition to steel there are other surfaces that must be coated for aesthetic, safety, or corrosion-inhibition purposes. These surfaces also must be prepared properly for coating.

Cast iron is a porous material that is likely to absorb moisture or other liquids with which it comes in contact. These liquids must be removed prior to surface preparation and painting. The absorbed fluids can be driven from the pores of the cast iron by placing the piece in an oven at 300°F (149°C) for 8 to 12 h or by heating the piece with torches until that temperature is reached. The requirements of the paint system control the degree of blast cleaning.

Zinc surfaces (galvanized or metal sprayed) should first receive a surface cleaning according to SSPC-SP 1 (Solvent Cleaning). The surface should then be etched with materials like mild phosphoric acid or ammonium hydroxide to give a rough surface profile suitable for the specified coating. If zinc is allowed to weather naturally, zinc oxide will provide a tooth suitable for many coatings.

Alkyd- or ester-based coatings must not be applied directly to zinc surfaces. Zinc oxide is an amphoteric material that is capable of acting as either as an acid or base. The zinc oxide can destroy the integrity of an ester/alkyd coating by saponifying the ester link, producing a zinc soap. The result can be deterioration of film properties and loss of adhesion of the coating to the zinc surface.

Copper and Brass should be sand blasted according to SSPC-SP 7 (Brush-Off Blast Cleaning) in order to remove corrosion products and provide a surface profile.

Concrete should be coated for protection from chemical attack and/or the physical damage of spalling. There are several factors to consider when preparing concrete to receive a coating.

- *Laitance* is a thin layer of fine particle on the surface of fresh concrete caused by the upward migration of water during the mixing and finishing process. Because this layer has poor adherence to the main body of concrete, it must be removed before coating. This can be accomplished by sand blasting or acid etching.

- *Efflorescence* is the deposition of salts on the concrete surface caused by moisture release during curing or moisture migration through the concrete as it ages. These alkaline deposits act much like concrete laitance and must be removed by acid etching.

- *Form oil* is applied to concrete forms as a release agent prior to pouring cement to ensure easy removal of the forms after the cement sets. Some form oils are transferred to the concrete surface as a contaminant and must be removed by detergent and water washing before acid etching or sand blasting.

- *Concrete hardeners* are sometimes used to modify the strength and permeability of concrete. They tend to migrate to the surface and cannot be acid etched. They must be removed before sandblasting.

The surface of the concrete is usually treated to guarantee adhesion of the coating system. Either physical abrading or chemical cleaning methods are used. Physical abrading can be done with, for example, sandpaper or a powder abrading machine. Chemical cleaning can be done with any number of chemicals such as trisodium phosphate or muriatic (hydrochloric) acid. After treatment, the surface must be dry and free from grit.

USE OF PROTECTIVE COATINGS

Systems Concept

It is not unusual for a specifying engineer to select a coating system based on cost, availability, color, or trust of the paint supplier. The engineer is surprised when the coating fails to meet (unstated) expectations. *A specifier should go through a logical process to design a system.*

Before a specifying a system, the engineer must:

1. Consider the performance of previously used systems
2. Define the environment where the system will be
3. Determine the degree of surface preparation based on physical or economic limitations
4. Define the life expectancy of the coating
5. Determine the required performance characteristics
6. Choose the appropriate system

Studying previously used systems, in the form of case histories, can be the easiest way to determine if an appropriate system is being proposed. If a system has been protecting a structure satisfactorily, there may be no need to change it. Maintenance repainting may then be as simple as adding another coat of paint. If complete rehabilitation is desired, the solution would be to repaint with the same system. On the other hand, if the current system had poor performance, the maintenance engineer should inquire into better performing systems.

The environment in which the structure sits is a major factor in the choice of a coating system. A specifier must define the environment in terms of corrosiveness, immersion service, solvent and chemical exposure, abrasion, and perhaps exposure to heat, humidity, and sunlight.

Corrosiveness is often defined as the amount of steel lost in a given environment. A panel of hot-rolled, sandblasted ASTM A-36 steel may lose greater than 4 mils of steel when exposed to a hot and humid marine atmosphere or less than 1 mil of steel in a benign environment. One way to quantify corrosiveness is shown in the following table.

Environment	Metal loss of A-36, sandblasted, hot-rolled steel
Mild	0–1 mil
Moderate	1–2 mils
Corrosive	2–4 mils
Severely corrosive	>4 mils

A system designed for immersion or chemical exposure may be different than one designed for simple atmospheric exposure. The specifier must define the media to which the structure is exposed, for example, whether the reagents be fresh or salt water, acidic or alkaline, organic or inorganic, etc.

A specifying engineer must consider whether the coating system will be for a structure in a highly abrasive environment, for example, wind-blown sand or snow; in a high heat environment, for example, a chimney; or in an high sunlight environment, for example, Florida or Arizona. *No one system is suitable for all situations and compromises must be made.*

Surface preparation can easily be the most expensive part of a maintenance painting system. The degree and type of surface preparation are generally mandated by the environment of the system, the longevity expected from the coating system, the type of prime coating used, and the amount of money available. In general, more aggressive environments require more surface preparation, coating systems with longer service life require better surface preparation, and zinc-rich coatings require better surface preparation than do barrier-type primers.

Surface preparation is costly because it is labor intensive and time consuming. An additional cost is the collection and/or containment of spent abrasive. When the removed paint and spent abrasive are considered hazardous waste, disposing of them from the job site in accordance with local, state, and federal regulations is a costly operation.

There may be structures, for example, operating factories, for which sandblasting is not permitted. The specifying engineer must then find alternative methods to remove the old paint.[1]

The service life of each generic type of coating system is different. Usually, the coating system with the longest service life reduces the cost for corrosion prevention even when the initial cost is more expensive. It makes sense to use the highest degree of surface preparation along with the system calculated to have the longest service life only if the unit to be protected is expected to be in existence throughout the anticipated coating life. If a unit is to be phased out or if it is subject to mechanical damage, a specifier may choose a less expensive method of surface preparation and paint system. Under these circumstances a system whose strength is ease of repair may be chosen over one with exceptional longevity.

The performance characteristics desired by the specifier must be quantifiable. These can then be compared to the performance of commercially available coating systems. The coating manufacturers are the best source of information on the performance of their paints in specific environments. Technical groups such as the National Association of Corrosion Engineers and the Steel Structures Painting Council are dedicated to helping coating specifiers write specifications.

It is difficult to thoroughly discuss all the characteristics of the many coating types that are available. Table 2-1 summarizes the comparative performance of several generic resin types for selected coating properties. These performance properties are averages of many different types of available paints. Specific product literature should be consulted before selecting a

TABLE 2-1 Comparative Performance Properties

Resin	Application	Solvent resistance	Chemical resistance	Weathering resistance	Corrosion resistance	Life cycle cost	Abrasion/ erosion	Hardness	Immersion service
Epoxy	4	5	4–5	1	5	3	4	4–5	5
Epoxy ester	4	3	2–3	1	4	2–3	3	3–4	2
Epoxy coal tar	4	3–4	4	1	5	4–5	4	4–5	5
Alkyd	5	1	1	2–3	2–3	2	2	2–3	1
Acrylic latex	4	2	2–3	3–4	3	2–3	2	2–3	1
Polyurethane									
aliphatic	4	3–5	3–5	4–5	4–5	4–5	5	4–5	1
aromatic	4	4–5	5	2–3	5	4–5	5	4–5	2–4
Silicone	4	3	5	5	4	3–4	2	2	3
Siliconized alkyd	5	1	1	3–4	2–3	3	2	2	1
Bituminous	3	1	3	1	5	5	1	1	1
Chlorinated rubber	2	1	4	1	4	2	2	2	5
Vinyl	2	1	5	2	4	3	2	2	5

1—indicates poor performance or not recommended
5—indicates excellent performance or strongly recommended

paint. More detailed tables of these and other performance properties are available from the Federation of Paint Societies.

The nine different categories of comparison are defined as follows:

1. *Application* is a measure of the degree of skill required to apply that type of coating. A coating receiving a high score would be easy to apply.
2. *Solvent resistance* is a measure of how resistant a coating is to a wide range of solvents. Resistance to specific solvents should always be tested. For example, bituminous coatings, if coal-tar derived, have excellent resistance to aliphatic hydrocarbons and poor resistance to aromatic hydrocarbons, while asphalt coatings have poor solvent resistance to either class.
3. *Chemical resistance* is a measure of how resistant a coating is to acids and bases.
4. *Weathering resistance* is a measure of gloss and color retention when exposed to sunlight.
5. *Corrosion resistance* is a measure of the effectiveness of a coating to protect a substrate from the corrosion process.
6. *Life cycle cost* is an indicator of the cost effectiveness of a coating. It is determined by considering the cost and the life expectancy of the paint.
7. *Abrasion/erosion* measures the resistance to the effects of wind-driven rain, ice, and dirt, or scuffing.
8. *Hardness* lists higher scores for harder films.
9. *Immersion service* indicates the effectiveness of a coating to perform in total water immersion.

ECONOMICS

Cost of Materials

The choice of coating type is, most often, an economic decision. Unfortunately, when done properly, it is not an easy task. Coatings decisions all too often are based on the cost per gallon or liter of paint as supplied. Instead, the cost of the solids portion of the paint should be considered. For example, a paint at $15/gal (1993 dollars) with only 50 percent solids is really more expensive than a paint which costs $20/gal and has 75 percent solids. This is because the real cost must be based on the amount of surface that can be covered. In the example the second paint will cover 50 percent more surface at only 33 percent more cost.

Life Cycle Cost

The paint raw material cost is only a small portion of the cost attributed to corrosion prevention through coating. A specifier must look at the cost of protection throughout the life of the coating cycle, including inspection, surface preparation, the paint, application labor, containment and disposal. Paint costs can vary between 5 and 15 percent of the total cost. Since more expensive coatings systems usually last longer, they lead to lower lifetime costs than do low-cost coatings that do not last as long.

Inspection

Inspection is a major factor in achieving a successful paint job. The inspector assists the engineer in writing the specification, acts as arbitrator with the contractor, oversees surface preparation and paint application, and overall, acts as the quality-control expert. After the job, the inspector can act as troubleshooter for failing systems. To obtain planned economics and realize the maximum potential of a coating system, it is essential that the system be installed exactly as designed. The employment of a qualified inspector is a means of increasing the probability of a successful application. Though inspection is an additional expense incurred by the structure owner, it should be viewed as purchasing an insurance policy.

Application.   Inspection of the application process begins with the paint. The inspector must be able to sample the materials delivered to the site so that sufficient testing can be conducted to determine that the coatings are the ones specified. Records must be kept of the code and batch numbers of the paints and where they were applied. Paints should be inspected for skinning, thickening, gassing, gelling, and excessive settling. The paint must be mixed and thinned according to the manufacturer's instructions. Attention must be given to two-component materials to insure that both components are used and stirred together in the appropriate ratio. The inspectors have the responsibility to make certain that those two-component paints, which require an induction time after mixing but before use, and which have a limited use life, are used correctly.

Application equipment must be in good repair to ensure that it meets the requirements of the coating being applied.

The application of all coatings must be closely followed by an inspection to make sure the equipment and the paint are behaving as expected and that the coatings are being applied at the wet and dry film thickness required by the specification. A prong-type wet-film-thickness gauge is an inexpensive tool that should be used continuously by both the applicator and the inspector.

Weather conditions are another important factor affecting the success of a coating application. In general, coatings should not be applied when metal temperatures are below 40°F (4°C) (or are expected to fall below 40°F (4°C) before curing) or above 120°F (49°C) and should be applied when the temperature is at least 5°F (3°C) above the dew point. Some two-component materials such as epoxies may have tighter temperature controls while one- and two-component polyurethanes may not be as restrictive. In all cases the manufacturer's instructions should be followed.

Dry Film Appearance.   The dry film also should be inspected for failure to dry or cure and for poor intercoat adhesion, peeling, blistering, pinholing, fish-eyeing, sagging, or blushing. Defects in each coat should be repaired before the application of the next coat. Each coat must have its dry film thickness measured. Thin coats can be easily repaired by applying more of the subsequent coat to bring the film thickness up to requirements. Too heavy of a film may waste paint or cause sags and runs. If the cohesive strength of a coating with excessive thickness is poor, the paint in the defective layer may have to be removed and reapplied before proceeding with the project. Dry film measurements must be made by a standard procedures such as SSPC PA-2, Measurement of Dry Film Thickness With Magnetic Gauges.

While the absence of pinholes is important for all coatings, it is extremely important for coatings to be placed in immersion service. Coatings for these applications should be tested for pinholes after drying with suitable instruments such as the Tinker Razor Holiday Detector.

Surface Preparation

Before the cleaning operation begins, all parties concerned with a particular job must agree on the definition of the specified surface preparation. If agreement is reached before the job starts it can save much time and trouble for all parties later. The Steel Structures Painting Council has written surface preparation specifications and Visual Standards[3] that will help this process. It is also recommended that the ability of the contractor be demonstrated prior to beginning the project. It is highly recommended that the painting contractor prepare a 4-ft^2 (0.1-m^2) test patch demonstrating the surface preparation. This also provides a good check on the ability of the contractor to achieve the desired profile. The test panel can also be used to make sure the specified prime coating is appropriate for the surface being painted.

Transfer Rates

Another factor that must be considered is the amount of material lost during the application process. For example, application by brush will result in a 4 to 8 percent loss; by roller, 4 to 8 percent; by conventional spray, 20 to 40 percent; or by airless spray, 10 to 20 percent. In addition, the amount of loss will vary with the size and shape of the surface being coated and the environmental conditions. For example, under adverse conditions of high wind and small surfaces, spray loss can be as high as 50 percent or more.

Estimating Paint Requirements

When the amount of surface to be painted is known, the amount of paint to order can be calculated by taking into account the surface area, the solids of the paint, the dry-film thickness, and the application loss.

Application

Application of paint not only involves the methods and equipment but also other factors, such as maximum and minimum temperatures and humidities during application and curing, minimum surface preparation, maximum and minimum recoat schedules, paint mixing, and thinning instructions. This material is generally covered in the coating manufacturer's literature. To prevent problems, this literature must be read and understood before the project begins not only by the applicator, but also by the owner and the inspector.

HEALTH AND SAFETY

Painting structural steel is a hazardous occupation. It involves climbing on and painting structures not normally designed for foot traffic. There is always a risk of falling from the structure or into operating equipment. Sandblasters and painters must use approved safety equipment and procedures to protect themselves and others on the job. OSHA is the key reference for equipment use and operating practices.

Sandblasters and painters are, by the nature of their work, exposed to high concentrations of dust, heavy metals, silicates, solvents, resins, and pigments. The health risks of exposure to many of these materials are well known, but the risks of contact with other materials may not yet be known. Workers should use respiratory- and skin-protective equipment that meets all local, state, and federal laws. This should be done to protect themselves from known and yet-to-be discovered health risks as well as to protect the structure owners from future liabilities.

Sandblasting and painting can also expose the environment to contamination from dust, heavy metals (from the blasting operation) and solvents, resins, and pigments (from painting). All local, state, and federal laws governing air and water contamination must be strictly followed to protect the environment and the applicator. This also will protect the facility owner from legal action due to contaminating the environment.

APPLICATION EQUIPMENT

Conventional Air Spray

Conventional air-spray equipment consists of a paint pot, air and fluid hose, a conventional spray gun, and air supply. The pressure pot may be used to hold the paint and should be equipped with a double regulator, to regulate both the fluid and atomizing air pressure. The pressure pot should be equipped with an agitator to maintain a uniform paint consistency during application. All parts of the equipment should be tightly connected to prevent leaks.

In conventional air spraying, paint is sucked into the spray gun by air passing over the paint siphon tube. This process can be assisted by placing the paint in a pressurized pot that pushes the paint up the tube. The paint is atomized just after the paint leaves the nozzle by jets of air directed at the paint. The output of paint flowing from the nozzle is relatively low, but the degree of atomization is very good. The capability of the applicator to control paint thickness and appearance is very good.

Conventional spray application, properly performed, produces the best-looking paint job, but produces overspray that wastes material and can contaminate adjacent structures.

Airless Spray

Airless spray equipment is made up of a paint reservoir, a hydraulic pump, high pressure fluid hose, an airless spray gun and a source to drive the hydraulic pump, usually an air motor. Extreme care must be taken to keep all fittings on the high pressure side of the hydraulic pump tight. No one should touch a leak coming from the high pressure side or the spray tip because paint can be injected into the skin.

In airless spraying, paint is pumped mechanically from the paint reservoir through a high pressure hose to an airless spray gun. The paint exits the airless spray gun through a small orifice at high pressure and velocity. It is pumped at such a high pressure and velocity that it atomizes as it leaves the spray tip when it is exposed to the much lower atmospheric pressure. Atomization is not nearly as fine as with conventional spray, but, if required, the use of air atomization with a special air-assisted, airless spray gun improves the atomization somewhat. The volume of paint moved by airless spray is much greater than with conventional spray, making the airless spray technique more appropriate for painting very large surfaces, such as large steel girders or tanks. The possibility of creating stray spray mist is still present but less of a problem than with conventional spray. Airless spray can be used to apply coatings with fairly high viscosities and can be used to apply higher film builds per coat.

Plural-Component.   Airless spray equipment can be designed to mix multiple-component materials at the spray tip. This is very convenient for mixing multiple-component paints based on chemically curing resins, especially if they have a very fast reaction speed, and so, a short use life. In this case the airless spray equipment requires two pumps and two paint reservoirs. Since multiple-component paint must be mixed in a very specific ratio, depending on the type of paint, the pumps must be capable of maintaining a highly precise feed rate. The paint is either mixed just prior to exiting the spray gun by the use of static mixers or just after exiting by the use of impingement mixing.

Brush and Roller

Brushes and rollers must be selected according to their compatibility with the coating to be applied. Brush and roller applications of maintenance paint are generally applied when the area to be coated is small, when the risk of stray spray mist contaminating adjacent structures is very high, or, in some circumstances, when the accessibility of the structure mandates manual application of paint. Brush and roller applications are slower than spray and therefore are more costly.

RESOURCE INFORMATION

This chapter has given a general overview of corrosion control through the use of coatings. More detailed information on the corrosion process and the many other disciplines mentioned in this chapter, such as surface area estimation, surface preparation, inspection techniques, and systems and coating technology, are published by professional societies.

The Steel Structures Painting Manual is published by the Steel Structures Painting Council, a technical society dedicated to providing documents for the maintenance-coating professional to use in order to help provide the kind of coating system desired. Information on the electrochemical corrosion process, selections of coatings and their systems, and the estimation of surface area from the weight of steel used in construction, can be found in Vol. 1, "Good Painting Practice."[3] Detailed specifications on surface preparation, coatings systems, and coatings can be found Vol. 2, "Systems and Specifications."[2]

A second source for information on corrosion inhibition through coatings is the National Association of Corrosion Engineers. Although metallurgy and design are the disciplnes of specialization for this group, the NACE committee T6, Protective Coatings and Linings, has published the *Coatings and Linings Handbook* and *Corrosion Control by Organic Coatings.*[4]

The Federated Society of Coatings Technologies has printed a series of brochures that describe the features and benefits of resins used to produce coatings.[1] These brochures give detailed information on expected performance properties of specific coating types. They are written for the coatings formulating chemist, but easily understood by others. This series also explains how one can calculate the theoretical spreading rate of coatings based on their solids content. This series also discusses topics such as corrosion, paint raw materials, and the physics and chemistry of paint film formation.

The Manual of Steel Construction (ADS), 9th Ed., published for the American Institute of Steel Construction is a valuable reference for the calculation of surface area of different geometric shapes.[5] It contains a section labeled "Properties of Geometric Sections." This section gives the mathematical formulas for calculating the surface areas cylinders, spheres, trapezoids, and others. Estimation of surface area is important when calculating the amount of paint required for coverage.

Your coatings supplier is in fact the best source of information available for coatings technology. The supplier will have detailed information on the performance and safe use of the product. Explain your requirements in terms of coating performance for the system you want in order to achieve the cost performance you expect.

REFERENCES

1. *Federation Series on Coating Technology,* edited by The Federation of Society of Paint Technology, Philadelphia, PA (1964–1993).

2. *Steel Structures Painting Manual,* Vol. 2, "Systems and Specifications" Steel Structures Painting Council, Pittsburgh, PA (1989).

3. *Steel Structures Painting Manual,* Vol. 1, "Good Painting Practice," Steel Structures Painting Council, Pittsburgh, PA (1989).

4. *Corrosion Control by Organic Coatings,* National Association of Corrosion Engineers, Houston, TX (1981).

5. *The Manual of Steel Construction,* (ADS) 9th Ed. 1990 American Institute of Steel Construction, Chicago, IL (1990).

INDEX

1

ABOUT THE EDITOR-IN-CHIEF

Robert C. Rosaler, P.E., is an engineering and management consultant with more than 40 years of experience as an engineering executive in both large and small corporations. He is the creator and co-editor of McGraw-Hill's *Handbook of HVAC Design,* as well as editor-in-chief of the First Edition of McGraw-Hill's *Standard Handbook of Plant Engineering,* winner of the American Publishers Award as Outstanding Engineering Book of 1982.